FROM THE EDITORS of OLD CARS PUBLICATIONS

standard catalog of
AMERICAN CARS
1976–1986

by James M. Flammang

SECOND EDITION

COPYRIGHT MCMLXXXIX BY KRAUSE PUBLICATIONS, INC.

cop. 1

Published by Krause Publications, Inc.
700 E. State St.
Iola, WI 54990
Telephone: 715-445-2214

INTERNATIONAL STANDARD BOOK NUMBER: 0-87341-133-1
LIBRARY of CONGRESS CATALOG NUMBER: 88-081627
Printed in the United States of America

CATALOG STAFF

PUBLISHER:	John A. Gunnell
EDITOR:	James T. Lenzke
PHOTO RESEARCH:	Kenneth Buttolph
DATA PROCESSING:	Bruce Denny
COVER DESIGN:	Paul Tofte
BOOKS MANAGER:	Pat Klug

FORWARD

The concept behind Krause Publication's "Standard Catalogs" is to compile massive amounts of information about motor vehicles and present it in a standard format which the enthusiast, collector or professional dealer can use to answer common questions.

Those questions include: What year, make and model is the vehicle? What did it sell for new? How rare is it? What's special about it? Some answers are provided by photos, others by the fact-filled text.

In this catalog, a well-known automotive historian has gathered facts about major American built cars manufactured between the 1976 and 1986 model years. The format he used to guide his research includes descriptive data; information about standard equipment; vehicle identification code interpretations; tables giving model codes, body type descriptions, original retail price, shipping weight and available production totals; engine specifications; technical information; and historical facts.

Alternative cars of interest to collectors are covered either in the same standard format or with photos and captions. No estimates of current values are included, since many of these cars still have normal "blue book" prices that change regularly several times a year.

No claim is made about the catalogs being history textbooks or encyclopedias. They are not repair manuals. They are collecting guides which are larger in size, wider in scope and more deluxe in format than similar books.

The long-range goal of Krause Publications is to make all of these catalogs as near perfect as possible. We've been told that they have provided nearly 100,000 automobile and truck enthusiasts with hours of enjoyable reading. This one should be particularly helpful to car buffs searching for future collectibles, as well as people seeking to purchase good used cars.

Other catalogs currently available are: *The Standard Catalog of American Cars 1805-1942; The Standard Catalog of American Cars 1946-1975; The Standard Catalog of Light-Duty American Trucks 1896-1986.* For ordering information and current prices write: **Krause Publications/Old Cars Weekly, 700 E. State St., Iola, WI 54990.**

CONTENTS

ACKNOWLEDGEMENTS

No work of this magnitude could be completed without the help and cooperation of many individuals. In addition to Chester L. Krause, John Gunnell and the staff at Krause Publications, the author wishes to thank the following people and organizations for going out of their way to provide information and assistance; Diane Richmond and the staff of the Science/Technology Department of the Chicago Public Library; David R. Crippen (Ford Archives); Kay Ward and Ed Lechtzin (Chevrolet); Karla Rosenbusch and Ron Papa (Chrysler); the staff of the Transportation Library at Northwestern University; Lawrence Gustin (Buick); Helen Earley Jones (Oldsmobile); and Sheri Quick (Pontiac).

Special thanks go to Linda Giglio and James Wren of the Motor Vehicle Manufacturers Association; and to Ronald Grantz at the National Automotive History Collection, in the Detroit Public Library.

Without the assistance and encouragement of three people, in particular, this catalog could never have been completed. Terry and Sally Boyce not only provided information and advice, but offered the hospitality of their home during research visits to the Detroit area. Marianne Flammang delivered an invaluable combination of support, suggestions and research assistance.

PHOTO CREDITS

The majority of photos found in this book are publicity photos issued by auto-makers when the cars were new. For such photos, the codes appearing after each caption indicate the source from which the copy of the photo was obtained. In some cases the prints came directly from the manufacturers. In other cases, they were obtained from automotive photo dealers, archives and museums, publications or private photo collections.

Where such photos were not available, artwork from advertisements and brochures or photos of private cars are shown. In these cases, the codes appearing after the caption indicate the person or collection from which the artwork was borrowed for reproduction in this catalog or the photographer or the owner of the vehicle.

Copies of the photos/artwork used are not available from Krause Publications, as all originals have been returned to the various contributors. For standard sources of such material check advertisements in *Old Cars Weekly*.

AA .... Applegate & Applegate
AMC .... American Motors
B .... Buick
C .... Cadillac
CC .... Chrysler Corporation
CH .... Chevrolet
CK .... Tom and Cheryl Kell
CM .... Chrysler Motors
CP .... Crestline Publishing Co.
D .... Dodge
F .... Ford
IMSC .... Indianapolis Motor Speedway Corp.
JG .... Jesse Gunnell
L .... Lincoln
M .... Mercury
OCW .... Old Cars Weekly

ABOUT THE AUTHOR

James M. Flammang is a full-time freelance writer/editor specializing in automobiles, computers and electronics. He has written extensively about automotive history and technology, the social impact of the motor car and repair/restoration techniques. He also writes regularly about the purchase and ownership of each class of vehicle: new, secondhand and collectible. His automotive articles have appeared not only in *Old Cars Weekly* and other collector car publications, but also in periodicals as diverse as *American Heritage* and *Consumer's Research*. Two of his books were published by Tab Books and he is a frequent contributor to Consumer Guide publications.

Jim's interest in transportation dates back to childhood and encompasses just about everything that moves and carries passengers or cargo: not only cars and trucks, but also trains, buses and ships. No single era or vehicle type commands his full attention. He appreciates just about every form of automobile from primitive turn-of-the-century European and American carriages to contemporary high-tech front-drives; from low-budget minicars to glamorous luxury models; from humdrum family vehicles to exotic sports cars. Favorites include the 1937 Cord, 1941-1948 Lincoln-Continental, XK-120 Jaguar, Studebaker GT Hawk, 1948-1954 Hudsons, early Oldsmobile 88s, Volvos and Renaults of the '50s and '60s, Citroens of any vintage, Skodas, early Nash Ramblers and Metropolitans, Camaros and Firebirds, Tuckers, Chrysler Cordobas, Ford Taurus, Buick Regals, Cadillac Sevilles and — believe it or not — many, many more.

INTRODUCTION

The *Standard Catalog of American Cars 1976-1986* is the fourth in a four-volume library of information on collectible vehicles. Taken together, they provide the automobile and light-duty truck collector, enthusiast or hobbyist with a comprehensive guide to facts about thousands of vehicles built from the early days of motoring to recent years.

Long before 1976, the total number of major manufacturers had fallen to just the Big Three (Ford, Chrysler and General Motors), along with American Motors Corp. (AMC).

In addition to information on the dozens of makes produced by these four companies, the "alternative cars" section of this catalog includes data on automobiles made by low-volume and specialty manufacturers. Coverage ranges from an Alfa Romeo kit car to the Zimmer, a luxury market neo-Classic.

For all major makes and some alternative cars, the data compiled includes a physical description; list of equipment; original specifications; technical data; production/sales figures and historical footnotes. Over 1,000 photos are used to illustrate the appearance of different models. Each model year is presented in the same standardized format. This allows for easy comparisons between years, makes and models.

The *Standard Catalog of American Cars 1976-1986* provides all students of the recent American-built automobile, from the novice hobbyist to the advanced collector, with a thorough and easy-to-use reference guide. Also included are many details that will help the practicing historian or professional car restorer.

Some observers have suggested that cars of the 1976-1986 era are inappropriate for restoration and of little interest to collectors. They say this not only because the cars are of recent vintage, but because this period was not the finest decade, overall, for production of memorable automobiles. It is true that many cars of this era were humdrum and repetitive in design, lackluster in performance, easy to forget and difficult to tell apart.

When seeking one factor that differentiated models of the late-'70s from another, windows come to mind. Rear side windows. After the true pillarless hardtop faded away, just about every manufacturer switched to some form of opera window on the sail panel and often to more than one on each side of the car. Some were big, others tiny. Most were placed there more for decoration than visibility. Several bizarre examples of styling that almost outdid the tailfinned '50s in excess will be seen in these pages.

In the 1980s, it was grilles the stylists overdosed on. Just as manufacturers once competed to see who could offer the most chrome up front, now they turned away from bright grilles to blacked-out versions. Black, it seemed, was sporty, modern, sensible. Chrome suggested the past.

But, always remember that just a few years back, similar criticisms were made of '50s and '60s models, which later attracted considerable collector attention. Amid the boxy econocars of the '80s and over-sized late '70s remnants of the big-car era, there really are quite a few notable vehicles. The catalog text points out some of them and careful attention will lead you to others.

A Chevette Scooter or base Omni may not set many hearts to pounding, but how about a Pontiac Can Am or Mustang SVO? How about one of the last 400 cid engines; or one of the sporty mid-'80s models that appeared as part of the rebirth of high-performance?

In addition to models of interest, quite a few special option packages can turn a relatively ordinary vehicle into something special. And (best of all in this time of astronomical prices for earlier collector vehicles) most of the models covered in this book are affordable and likely to remain well within the pocketbook range of the ordinary motorist for some time yet.

Not everyone realizes it, but the 1976-1986 period was an era of change. The elephantine-size bodies (and engines) that remained in 1976 faded away within a year or two, replaced by more modest body dimensions and smaller displacement engines. Efficiency was in. Brute force was out. In addition to year-to-year revisions, running changes (made during the model year) became rampant. Moreover, many announcements of upcoming changes didn't materialize or appeared later than predicted or changed form by the time they finally arrived.

Thus, it was a decade of contradiction, too, if not misinformation. Reports in the trade and popular press sometimes made it sound like a new model was moments away from delivery. Yet, it might not really appear for months or in the next model year or ever. In the computer industry (where premature announcements are almost the norm) this phenomenon is called "vaporware."

Similarly, specifications were often announced near the beginning of each model year. These were duly picked by the press, neatly positioned in charts published by auto-makers (as well as outside publishers) and then revised by the time the first car of the model year actually hit the road. Perhaps they were even changed again, a month or six months later.

It's not uncommon to check four different "authoritative" sources and find three different figures for 1976-1986 engine horsepower or body length. Auto-makers and their agencies, in fact, employ people whose job it is to keep track of the immense number of changes. Discrepancies are hardly rare on equipment lists, either. Standard features announced before a car arrived on the market didn't always come true on intro day.

All of this makes the job of the automotive historian a tedious, confusing one. It's no easy matter to determine which facts and figures really were "true" and totally accurate and which were wishful thinking, hopeful guesses or temporary realities.

The first half of this period was also a time of immense differences between 49-state (federal) cars and those destined for California or government designated high-altitude county sales. Some amounted to a slight change in specifications, while in many cases, California regulations required a completely different engine. Specifications in this catalog normally apply to 49-state models; California versions are mentioned only to clarify the availability of certain engines or equipment.

As far as possible, this catalog reflects factory prices and specifications that were in effect on or near a model's introduction date. Mid-year changes and introductions are usually included only where significant. Since heavy (even double-digit) inflation marked much of this period, prices sometimes rose sharply as a new model year began, then a few more times *during* the model year.

Most information in this catalog has been obtained from factory and trade publications. Supplementary data comes from a wide variety of popular publications. The author and your editor welcome corrections. Please be sure your information is correct, however, and that it applies to models produced early in the model year. Contact the author or editors in care of: Krause Publications, 700 East State St., Iola, WI 54990. Every effort will be made to include improvements or corrections in future editions of this catalog.

James M. Flammang
Chicago, Illinois
August 24, 1988

HOW TO USE THIS CATALOG

1979 CORVETTE

APPEARANCE AND EQUIPMENT: Word descriptions identify cars by styling features, trim and (to a lesser extent) interior appointments. Most standard equipment lists begin with the lowest-priced model, then enumerate items added by upgrade models and option packages. Most lists reflect equipment available at model introductions.

I.D. DATA: Information is given about the Vehicle Identification Number (VIN) found on the dashboard. VIN codes show model or series, body style, engine size, model year and place built. Beginning in 1981, a standardized 17 symbol VIN is used. Earlier VINs are shorter. Locations of other coded information on the body and/or engine block may be supplied. Deciphering those codes is beyond the scope of this catalog.

SPECIFICATIONS CHART: The first column gives series or model numbers. The second gives body style numbers revealing body type and trim. Not all cars use two separate numbers. Some sources combine the two. Column three tells number of doors, body style and passenger capacity ('4-dr Sed-6P' means four-door sedan, six-passenger). Passenger capacity is normally the maximum. Cars with bucket seats hold fewer. Column four gives suggested retail price of the car when new, on or near its introduction date, not including freight or other charges. Column five gives the original shipping weight. The sixth column provides model year production totals or refers to notes below the chart. In cases where the same car came with different engines, a slash is used to separate factory prices and shipping weights for each version. Unless noted, the amount on the left of the slash is for the smallest, least expensive engine. The amount on the right is for the least costly engine with additional cylinders. 'N/A' means data not available.

ENGINE DATA: Engines are normally listed in size order with smallest displacement first. A 'base' engine is the basic one offered in each model at the lowest price. 'Optional' describes all alternate engines, including those that have a price listed in the specifications chart. (Cars that came with either a six or V-8, for instance, list the six as 'base' and V-8 'optional'). Introductory specifications are used, where possible.

CHASSIS DATA: Major dimensions (wheelbase, overall length, height, width and front/rear tread) are given for each model, along with standard tire size. Dimensions sometimes varied and could change during a model year.

TECHNICAL DATA: This section indicates transmissions standard on each model, usually including gear ratios; the standard final drive axle ratio (which may differ by engine or transmission); steering and brake system type; front and rear suspension description; body construction; and fuel tank capacity.

OPTIONAL EQUIPMENT LISTS: Most listings begin with drivetrain options (engines, transmissions, steering/suspension and mechanical components) applying to all models. Convenience/appearance items are listed separately for each model, except where several related models are combined into a single listing. Option packages are listed first, followed by individual items in categories: comfort/convenience, lighting/mirrors, entertainment, interior, then wheels/tires. Contents of some option packages are listed prior to the price; others are described in the Appearance/Equipment text. Prices are suggested retail, usually effective early in the model year. ('N/A' indicates prices are unavailable.) Most items are Regular Production Options (RPO), rather than limited-production (LPO), special-order or dealer-installed equipment. Many options were available only on certain series or body types or in conjunction with other items. Space does not permit including every detail.

HISTORY: This block lists introduction dates, total sales and production amounts for the model year and calendar year. Production totals supplied by auto-makers do not always coincide with those from other sources. Some reflect shipments from the factories rather than actual production or define the model year a different way.

HISTORICAL FOOTNOTES: In addition to notes on the rise and fall of sales and production, this block includes significant statistics, performance milestones, major personnel changes, important dates and places and facts that add flavor to this segment of America's automotive heritage.

SERIES Z — V-8 — "The Corvette evolution continues," declared this year's catalog. Not much of that evolution was visible, however, after the prior year's massive restyle. Under the hood, the base engine got the dual-snorkel air intake introduced in 1978 for the optional L82 V-8. That added 10 horsepower. The L82 V-8 had a higher-lift cam, special heads with larger valves and higher compression, impact-extruded pistons, forged steel crankshaft, and finned aluminum rocker covers. The "Y" pipe exhaust system had new open-flow mufflers, while the automatic transmission got a higher numerical (3.55:1) rear axle ratio. All Corvettes now had the highback bucket seats introduced on the 1978 limited-edition Indy Pace Car. A high pivot point let the seat backrest fold flat on the passenger side, level with the luggage area floor. An AM/FM radio was now standard. Of ten body colors, only one (dark green metallic) was new this year. The others were Classic white, black and silver, plus Corvette dark or light blue, yellow, light beige, red, and dark brown. Interiors came in black, red, light beige, dark blue, dark brown, oyster, or dark green. Corvettes had black roof panel and window moldings. Bolt-on front and rear spoilers (also from the Pace Car) became available. Buyers who didn't want the full Gymkhana suspension could now order heavy-duty shocks alone. Standard equipment included the L48 V-8 with four-barrel carb, either automatic transmission or four-speed manual gearbox (close-ratio version available), power four-wheel disc brakes, and limited-slip differential. Other standards: tinted glass; front stabilizer bar; concealed wipers/washers; day/night inside mirror; wide outside mirror; anti-theft alarm system; four-spoke sport steering wheel; electric clock; trip odometer; heater/defroster; bumper guards; and luggage security shade. Tires were P225/70R15 steel-belted radial blackwalls on 15 x 8 in. wheels. Corvettes had four- wheel independent suspension. Bucket seats came with cloth/leather or all-leather trim. The aircraft-type console held a 7000 R.P.M. tachometer, voltmeter, oil pressure, temp and fuel gauges. Seat inserts could have either leather or cloth trim.

I.D. DATA: Coding of the 13-symbol Vehicle Identification Number (VIN) was similar to 1978. Engine codes changed to '8' base L48 and '4' optional L82. Model year code changed to '9' for 1979. Serial numbers began with 400001.

CORVETTE

Model Number	Body/Style Number	Body Type & Seating	Factory Price	Shipping Weight	Production Total
1Y	Z87	2-dr. Spt Cpe-2P	10220	3372	53,807

ENGINE DATA: BASE V-8: 90-degree, overhead valve V-8. Cast iron block and head. Displacement: 350 cu. in. (5.7 liters). Bore & stroke: 4.00 x 3.48 in. Compression ratio: 8.2:1. Brake horsepower: 195 at 4000 R.P.M. Torque: 285 lbs.-ft. at 3200 R.P.M. Five main bearings. Hydraulic valve lifters. Carburetor: 4Bbl. RPO Code: L48. VIN Code: 8. OPTIONAL V-8: Same as above, except C.R.: 8.9:1. B.H.P.: 225 at 5200 R.P.M. Torque: 270 lbs.-ft. at 3600 R.P.M. RPO Code: L82. VIN Code: 4.

CHASSIS DATA: Wheelbase: 98.0 in. Overall length: 185.2 in. Height: 48.0 in. Width: 69.0 in. Front Tread: 58.7 in. Rear Tread: 59.5 in. Wheel Size: 15 x 8 in. Standard Tires: P225/70R15 SBR. Optional Tires: P225/60R15.

TECHNICAL: Transmission: Four-speed manual transmission (floor shift) standard. Gear ratios: (1st) 2.85:1; (2nd) 2.02:1; (3rd) 1.35:1; (4th) 1.00:1; (Rev) 2.85:1. Close-ratio four-speed manual trans. optional: (1st) 2.43:1; (2nd) 1.61:1; (3rd) 1.23:1; (4th) 1.00:1; (Rev) 2.35:1. Three-speed automatic optional: (1st) 2.52:1; (2nd) 1.52:1; (3rd) 1.00:1; (Rev) 1.93:1. Standard final drive ratio: 3.36:1 w/4spd, 3.55:1 w/auto. Steering: Recirculating ball. Front Suspension: Control arms, coil springs and stabilizer bar.

Rear Suspension: Independent, with single transverse leaf spring and lateral struts. Brakes: Four-wheel disc (11.75 in. disc dia). Ignition: Electronic. Body construction: Fiberglass, on separate frame. Fuel tank: 24 gal.

CORVETTE OPTIONS: L82 350 cu. in., 4Bbl. V-8 engine ($565). Close-ratio four- speed manual transmission (NC). Turbo Hydra-matic (NC). Highway axle ratio ($19). Gymkhana suspension ($49). H.D. shock absorbers ($33). Heavy-duty battery ($21). Trailer towing equipment inc. H.D. radiator and Gymkhana suspension ($98). California emissions system (N/A). High-altitude emissions (N/A). Four season air cond. ($635). Rear defogger, electric ($102). Cruise-master speed control ($113). Tilt/telescopic leather-wrapped steering wheel ($190). Power windows ($141). Power windows and door locks ($272). Convenience group ($94). Sport mirrors, left remote ($45). AM/FM stereo radio ($90); with 8track or cassette player ($228-$234). AM/FM stereo radio w/CB and power antenna ($439). Dual rear speakers ($52). Power antenna ($52). Removable glass roof panels ($365). Aluminum wheels ($380). P225/70R15 SBR WL tires ($54). P225/60R15 Aramid-belted radial WL tires ($226).

HISTORY: Introduced: Sept. 25, 1978. Model year production: 53,807 (Chevrolet initially reported a total of 49,901 units.) Calendar year production: 48,568. Calendar year sales by U.S. dealers: 38,631. Model year sales by U.S. dealers: 39,816.

Historical Footnotes: For what it's worth, 7,949 Corvettes this year were painted in Classic White, while 6,960 carried silver paint. Only 4,385 Corvettes had the MM4 four-speed manual gearbox, while 4,062 ran with the close-ratio M21 version.

BODY STYLES

Body style designations describe the shape and character of an automobile. In earlier years automakers exhibited great imagination in coining words to name their products. This led to names that were not totally accurate. Many of those **'car words'** were taken from other fields: mythology, carriage building, architecture, railroading, and so on. Therefore, there was no 'correct' automotive meaning other than that brought about through actual use. Inconsistences have persisted into the recent period, though some of the imaginative terms of past eras have faded away. One manufacturer's 'sedan' might resemble another's 'coupe.' Some automakers have persisted in describing a model by a word different from common usage, such as Ford's label for Mustang as a 'sedan.' Following the demise of the true pillarless hardtop (two- and four-door) in the mid-1970s, various manufacturers continued to use the term 'hardtop' to describe their offerings, even though a 'B' pillar was part of the newer car's structure and the front door glass may not always have been frameless. Some took on the description 'pillared hardtop' or 'thin pillar hardtop' to define what observers might otherwise consider, essentially, a sedan. Descriptions in this catalog generally follow the manufacturers' choice of words, except when they conflict strongly with accepted usage.

One specific example of inconsistency is worth noting: the description of many hatchback models as 'three-door' and 'five-door,' even though that extra 'door' is not an entryway for people. While the 1976-1986 domestic era offered no real phaetons or roadsters in the earlier senses of the words, those designations continue to turn up now and then, too.

TWO-DOOR (CLUB) COUPE: The Club Coupe designation seems to come from club car, describing the lounge (or parlor car) in a railroad train. The early postwar club coupe combined a shorter-than-sedan body structure with the convenience of a full back seat, unlike the single-seat business coupe. That name has been used less frequently in the 1976-86 period, as most notchback two-door models (with trunk rather than hatch) have been referred to as just 'coupes.' Moreover, the distinction between two-door coupes and two-door sedans has grown fuzzy.

TWO-DOOR SEDAN: The term sedan originally described a conveyance seen only in movies today: a wheelless vehicle for one person, borne on poles by two men, one ahead and one behind. Automakers pirated the word and applied it to cars with a permanent top, seating four to seven (including driver) in a single compartment. The two-door sedan of recent times has sometimes been called a pillared coupe, or plain coupe, depending on the manufacturer's whim. On the other hand, some cars commonly referred to as coupes carry the sedan designation on factory documents.

TWO-DOOR (THREE-DOOR) HATCHBACK COUPE: Originally a small opening in the deck of a sailing ship, the term 'hatch' was later applied to airplane doors and to passenger cars with rear liftgates. Various models appeared in the early 1950s, but weather-tightness was a problem. The concept emerged again in the early 1970s, when fuel economy factors began to signal the trend toward compact cars. Technology had remedied the sealing difficulties. By the 1980s, most manufacturers produced one or more hatchback models, though the question of whether to call them 'two-door' or 'three-door' never was resolved. Their main common feature was the lack of a separate trunk. 'Liftback' coupes may have had a different rear-end shape, but the two terms often described essentially the same vehicle.

TWO-DOOR FASTBACK: By definition, a fastback is any automobile with a long, moderately curving, downward slope to the rear of the roof. This body style relates to an interest in streamlining and aerodynamics and has gone in and out of fashion at various times. Some (Mustangs for one) have grown quite popular. Others have tended to turn customers off. Certain fastbacks are, technically, two-door sedans or pillared coupes. Four-door fastbacks have also been produced. Many of these (such as Buick's late 1970s four-door Century sedan) lacked sales appeal. Fastbacks may or may not have a rear-opening hatch.

TWO-DOOR HARDTOP: The term hardtop, as used for postwar cars up to the mid-1970s, describes an automobile styled to resemble a convertible, but with a rigid metal (or fiberglass) top. In a production sense, this body style evolved after World War II, first called 'hardtop convertible.' Other generic names have included sports coupe, hardtop coupe or pillarless coupe. In the face of proposed rollover standards, nearly all automakers turned away from the pillarless design to a pillared version by 1976-77.

COLONNADE HARDTOP: In architecture, the term colonnade describes a series of columns, set at regular intervals, usually supporting an entablature, roof or series of arches. To meet Federal rollover standards in 1974 (standards that never emerged), General Motors introduced two- and four-door pillared body types with arch-like quarter windows and sandwich type roof construction. They looked like a cross between true hardtops and miniature limousines. Both styles proved popular (especially the coupe with louvered coach windows and canopy top) and the term colonnade was applied. As their 'true' hardtops disappeared, other manufacturers produced similar bodies with a variety of quarter-window shapes and sizes. These were known by such terms as hardtop coupe, pillared hardtop or opera-window coupe.

FORMAL HARDTOP: The hardtop roofline was a long-lasting fashion hit of the postwar car era. The word 'formal' can be applied to things that are stiffly conservative and follow the established rule. The limousine, being the popular choice of conservative buyers who belonged to the Establishment, was looked upon as a formal motorcar. So when designers combined the lines of these two body styles, the result was the Formal Hardtop. This style has been marketed with two or four doors, canopy and vinyl roofs (full or partial) and conventional or opera-type windows, under various trade names. The distinction between a formal hardtop and plain pillared-hardtop coupe (see above) hasn't always followed a strict rule.

CONVERTIBLE: To Depression-era buyers, a convertible was a car with a fixed-position windshield and folding top that, when raised, displayed the lines of a coupe. Buyers in the postwar period expected a convertible to have roll-up windows, too. Yet the definition of the word includes no such qualifications. It states only that such a car should have a lowerable or removable top. American convertibles became extinct by 1976, except for Cadillac's Eldorado, then in its final season. In 1982, though, Chrysler brought out a LeBaron ragtop; Dodge a 400; and several other companies followed it a year or two later.

ROADSTER: This term derives from equestrian vocabulary where it was applied to a horse used for riding on the roads. Old dictionaries define the roadster as an open-type car designed for use on *ordinary* roads, with a single seat for two persons and, often, a rumbleseat as well. Hobbyists associate folding windshields and side curtains (rather than roll-up windows) with roadsters, although such qualifications stem from usage, not definition of term. Most recent roadsters are either sports cars, small alternative-type vehicles or replicas of early models.

RUNABOUT: By definition, a runabout is the equivalent of a roadster. The term was used by carriage makers and has been applied in the past to light, open cars on which a top is unavailable or totally an add-on option. None of this explains its use by Ford on certain Pinto models. Other than this inaccurate usage, recent runabouts are found mainly in the alternative vehicle field, including certain electric-powered models.

FOUR-DOOR SEDAN: If you took the wheels off a car, mounted it on poles and hired two weightlifters (one in front and one in back) to carry you around in it, you'd have a true sedan. Since this idea isn't very practical, it's better to use the term for an automobile with a permanent top (affixed by solid pillars) that seats four or more persons, including the driver, on two full-width seats.

FOUR-DOOR HARDTOP: This is a four door car styled to resemble a convertible, but having a rigid top of metal or fiberglass. Buick introduced a totally pillarless design in 1955. A year later most automakers offered equivalent bodies. Four-door hardtops have also been labeled sports sedans and hardtop sedans. By 1976, potential rollover standards and waning popularity had taken their toll. Only a few makes still produced a four-door hardtop and those disappeared soon thereafter.

FOUR-DOOR PILLARED HARDTOP: Once the 'true' four-door hardtop began to fade away, manufacturers needed another name for their luxury four-doors. Many were styled to look almost like the former pillarless models, with thin or unobtrusive pillars between the doors. Some, in fact, were called 'thin-pillar hardtops.' The distinction between certain pillared hardtops and ordinary (presumably humdrum) sedans occasionally grew hazy.

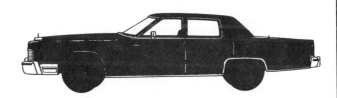

FOUR-DOOR (FIVE-DOOR) HATCHBACK: Essentially unknown among domestic models in the mid-1970s, the four-door hatchback became a popular model as cars grew smaller and front-wheel-drive versions appeared. Styling was similar to the orignal two-door hatchback, except for — obviously — two more doors. Luggage was carried in the back of the car itself, loaded through the hatch opening, not in a separate trunk.

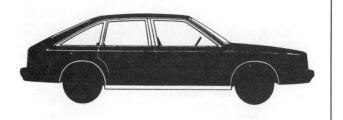

LIMOUSINE: This word's literal meaning is 'a cloak.' In France, Limousine means any passenger vehicle. An early dictionary defined limousine as an auto with a permanently enclosed compartment for 3-5, with a roof projecting over a front driver's seat. However, modern dictionaries drop the separate compartment idea and refer to limousines as large luxury autos, often chauffeur-driven. Some have a movable division window between the driver and passenger compartments, but that isn't a requirement.

TWO-DOOR STATION WAGON: Originally defined as a car with an enclosed wooden body of paneled design (with several rows of folding or removable seats behind the driver), the station wagon became a different and much more popular type of vehicle in the postwar years. A recent dictionary states that such models have a larger interior than sedans of the line and seats that can be readily lifted out, or folded down, to facilitate light trucking. In addition, there's usually a tailgate, but no separate luggage compartment. The two-door wagon often has sliding or flip-out rear side windows.

FOUR-DOOR STATION WAGON: Since functionality and adaptability are advantages of station wagons, four-door versions have traditionally been sales leaders. At least they were until cars began to grow smaller. This style usually has lowerable windows in all four doors and fixed rear side glass. The term 'suburban' was almost synonymous with station wagon at one time, but is now more commonly applied to light trucks with similar styling. Station wagons have had many trade names, such as Country Squire (Ford) and Sport Suburban (Plymouth). Quite a few have retained simulated wood paneling, keeping alive the wagon's origin as a wood-bodied vehicle.

LIFTBACK STATION WAGON: Small cars came in station wagon form too. The idea was the same as bigger versions, but the conventional tailgate was replaced by a single lift-up hatch. For obvious reasons, compact and subcompact wagons had only two seats instead of the three that had been available in many full-size models.

ABBREVIATIONS

Adj. .... Adjustable
A/C .... Air conditioning
AM, FM, AM/FM .... Radio types
Amp .... Ampere (or amplifier, for radio)
Approx. .... Approximately
Auto. .... Automatic
Base .... Base (usually lowest-priced) model
Bbl. .... Barrel (carburetor): 2Bbl.
B.H.P. .... Brake horsepower
Bonn. .... Bonneville (Pontiac)
Brghm .... Brougham (Cadillac and others)
BSW .... Black sidewall (tire)
Capr. .... Caprice (Chevrolet) ....
Carb .... Carburetor
Cass. .... Cassette (tape player)
Cat. .... Catalina (Pontiac)
Cav .... Cavalier (Chevrolet)
CB .... Citizens Band (radio)
Celeb .... Celebrity (Chevrolet)
CEO .... Chief Executive Officer
CFI .... Cross Fire (fuel) Injection
Chgr .... Charger (Dodge)
Chvt .... Chevette (Chevrolet)
C.I.D. .... Cubic inch displacement
Cit. .... Citation (Chevrolet)
Col .... Colonnade (coupe body style, esp. GM)
Col. .... Column (shift)
Con. .... Concord (AMC)
Cont. .... Continental (Lincoln)
Conv. .... Convertible
Cord. .... Cordoba (Chrysler)
Cpe .... Coupe (body style)
C.R. .... Compression ratio
Crown Vic .... Crown Victoria (Ford)
Crsr .... Cruiser
Cu. In. .... Cubic inch (displacement)
Cust. .... Custom
Cyl. .... Cylinder
Del .... Deluxe
DeV .... DeVille (Cadillac)
DFRS .... Dual facing rear seats
Dia. .... Diameter
Diplo .... Diplomat (Dodge)
Disp. .... Displacement
Dr. .... Door (2-dr.)
Ea. .... Each
EFI .... Electronic fuel injection
"Eight" .... Eight-cylinder engine
8-tr. .... Eight-track (tape player)
Eldo .... Eldorado (Cadillac)
EPA .... Environmental Protection Agency
Equip. .... Equipment
Est Wag .... Estate wagon
Exc. .... Except
F .... Forward (3F - 3 forward speeds)
Fml .... Formal
"Four" .... Four-cylinder engine
4WD .... Four-wheel drive
4-dr. .... Four-door
4-spd .... Four-speed (transmission)
4V .... Four-barrel carburetor
Ft. .... Foot/feet

F.W. .... Fleetwood (Cadillac)
FWD .... Front wheel drive
G. Am .... Grand Am (Pontiac)
G. Marq. .... Grand Marquis (Mercury)
G.P. .... Grand Prix (Pontiac)
Gal. .... Gallon
GBR .... Glass-belted radial (tire)
GM .... General Motors (Corporation)
Grem. .... Gremlin (AMC)
GT .... Gran Turismo
GTO .... Gran Turismo Omologato
Hatch or H.B. .... Hatchback (body style)
H.D. .... Heavy-duty
HEI .... High Energy ignition
H.O. .... High-output
H.P. .... Horsepower
Hr. .... Hour
HT .... Hardtop (body style)
Hwy. .... Highway
I .... Inline
I.D. .... Identification
Imp. .... Imperial (Chrysler) or Impala (Chevrolet)
In. .... Inches
Incl .... Included or including
Int. .... Interior
Lan .... Landau (coupe body style)
Lb. or Lbs. .... Pound(s)
Lbs.-Ft. .... Pound-feet (torque)
LeB .... LeBaron (Chrysler)
LeM .... LeMans (Pontiac)
LH .... Left hand
Lift .... Liftback (body style)
Limo .... Limousine
LPO .... Limited production option
Ltd. .... Limited
Mag. .... Magnum (Dodge) or wheel style
Mat. .... Matador (AMC)
Max. .... Maximum
MFI .... Multi-port fuel injection
MK .... Mark (Lincoln)
M.M. .... Millimeters
Monte .... Monte Carlo (Chevrolet)
MPG .... Miles per gallon
MPH .... Miles per hour
N/A .... Not available (or not applicable)
NC .... No charge
Newpt .... Newport (Chrysler)
N.H.P. .... Net horsepower
No. .... Number
Notch or N.B. .... Notchback
N.Y. .... New Yorker (Chrysler)
OHC .... Overhead cam (engine)
OHV .... Overhead valve (engine)
OPEC .... Organiz. of Petroleum Exporting Countries
Opt. .... Optional
OWL .... Outline white letter (tire)
Oz. .... Ounce
P .... Passenger (e.g., 4P)
Paris. .... Parisienne (Pontiac)
PFI .... Port fuel injection
Phnx .... Phoenix (Pontiac)
Pkg. .... Package (e.g., option pkg.)

Pres.	President	Sta Wag	Station wagon
Prod.	Production	Std.	Standard
Pwr	Power	Supr.	Supreme (Oldsmobile)
R	Reverse	Tach	Tachometer
RBL	Raised black letter (tire)	Tax.	Taxable (horsepower)
Reg.	Regular	TBI	Throttle body (fuel) injection
Remote	Remote control	T-Bird	Thunderbird (Ford)
Req.	Requires	T&C	Town & Country (Chrysler)
Rev	Reverse (gear)	T.C.	Town Car (Lincoln)
RH	Right-hand drive	Temp	Temperature
Riv	Riviera (Buick)	THM	Turbo Hydra-matic (transmission)
Roch.	Rochester (carburetor)	3S	Three-seat
R.P.M.	Revolutions per minute	Toro	Toronado (Oldsmobile)
RPO	Regular producton option	Trans.	Transmission
RV	Recreation vehicle	2-dr.	Two-door
RWL	Raised white letter (tire)	2V	Two-barrel (carburetor)
SAE	Society of Automotive Engineers	2WD	Two-wheel drive
SBR	Steel-belted radial (tire)	U.S.A.	United States of America
SE or S.E.	Special edition	V	Venturi (carburetor)
Sed	Sedan	V-6, V-8	Vee-type engine
SeV	Seville (Cadillac)	Vic	Victoria
SFI	Sequential fuel injection	VIN	Vehicle Identification Number
"Six"	Six-cylinder engine	V.P.	Vice-president
Spd	Speed	w/	With
Spec.	Special	w/o	Without
Spt	Sport	Wag	Wagon
Sq. In.	Square inch	W.B.	Wheelbase
SS	Super sport	WLT	White-lettered tire
St. R.	St. Regis (Dodge)	WSW	White sidewall (tire)

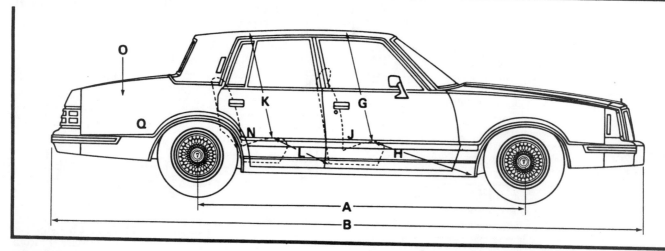

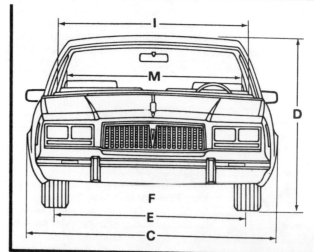

DIMENSIONS

Exterior:
- A Wheelbase
- B Overall length
- C Width
- D Overall height
- E Tread, front
- F Tread, rear

Interior—front:
- G Headroom
- H Legroom
- I Shoulder room
- J Hip room

Interior—rear:
- K Headroom
- L Legroom
- M Shoulder room
- N Hip room
- O Trunk capacity (liters/cu. ft.)
- P Cargo index volume (liters/cu. ft.)
- Q Fuel tank capacity (liters/gallons)

Best known through the 1950s and '60s for its compact economy cars, Wisconsin-based American Motors Corp., by 1976 appeared to be ready to abandon its largest models. The full-sized Ambassador disappeared after 1974. It was a victim of the U.S. gasoline crisis. So did the sporty Javelin coupe, leaving Matador as the largest AMC model. In 1970, the Gremlin—known for its "sawed-off" rear-end look—had arrived as the first domestic-built subcompact, just as Rambler had pioneered the compact trend two decades earlier. Another 1970 arrival was the compact Hornet, soon to become one of AMC's best sellers. Of even greater ultimate importance that year, however, was AMC's acquisition of Kaiser-Jeep's Toledo plant. Ordinary passenger cars did not always fare well through the 1970s and early '80s, but the company stayed afloat largely as a result of four-wheel-drive Jeep production (as chronicled in the *Standard Catalog of American Light Duty Trucks*).

Gremlin wasn't the only curious looking AMC model. At the Chicago Auto Show in 1975, the hatchback Pacer appeared, wearing an unusually large amount of glass and a passenger door larger than its mate, among other design features. Promoted as the "first wide small car," Pacer was designed from the ground up as a receptacle for a new front-drive Wankel (rotary) engine expected from GM. When that engine failed to materialize, Pacer had to turn to conventional powerplants, including the familiar AMC inline six and, later, a V-8. It was one of the first American cars with rack-and-pinion steering.

1976 Gremlin X liftback coupe (AMC)

Not much changed for 1976. Matadors could get a choice of 360 cu. in. V-8s under the hood, and a stylish Barcelona package for the coupe. Gremlin offered a pair of packages to enhance its appeal: a sporty 'X' appearance option, and a more curious "Levi's" trim package. That one put simulated blue denim (actually nylon) and fake "buttons" on the seats and interior panels, and attracted quite a lot of attention. Though popular at first, Pacer sales flagged this year. People didn't seem so interested in smaller cars as the gas crunch eased.

Only Gremlin got any noticeable restyling for 1977—along with a new four-cylinder powerplant, supplied by Volkswagen. Pacer added a station wagon to the original

hatchback sedan. The AMX name, abandoned a couple of years earlier, appeared again on a limited-edition Hornet model with front air dam, blackout grille, back-window louvers, and body graphics. Styling touches of that sort soon would become common on sporty models from just about every domestic manufacturer. High-performance 360 cu. in. V-8s were no longer offered under Matador hoods, and the 401 V-8 wasn't even available to police agencies, as it had been before. Following a $46 million loss in fiscal year 1976, AMC switched to black ink on the 1977 ledger book—but as a result of strong Jeep sales, not conventional passenger cars. Even price cuts and rebates didn't help. Other companies were planning compact models, and imports gained strength each year, but AMC couldn't seem to take hold of a major niche of the market. The agreement to purchase engines from VW/Audi was something new, and foretold the European connection that would eventually "save" AMC (temporarily) in the 1980s.

AMC took a stronger stab at the youth market in 1978, making AMX a separate model—again heavy on black accents— instead of a Hornet option. Hornet, in fact, was gone, replaced by a new and posher (but similar) Concord. Even Gremlin turned a bit toward performance with a new GT option package that used fiberglass body components. Pacers now came with a 304 cu. in. V-8 as well as two six-cylinder choices. Matador again offered a Barcelona package for the coupe, but this would be the mid-size's final season. Corporate net earnings reached their highest peak since 1973, but again due to Jeep popularity. Negotiations with Renault were already underway. They culminated in an agreement whereby AMC would distribute the French-built Le Car (and Renault might do likewise with Jeeps). More important for the future was the announcement that the two corporations planned a joint-venture passenger car to be built in the U.S. In another agreement, AMC contracted to buy "Iron Duke" four-cylinder engines from Pontiac.

Gremlin bit the dust in 1979, replaced by a more stylish (but not dramatically different) Spirit subcompact. The performance-minded AMX switched to the shorter Spirit platform. AMC profits reached a record level as Renault ought an interest in the company for $200 million. Plans were made to begin assembly of Renault-designed cars in Kenosha as early as the 1982 model year—a target date that proved slightly premature.

V-8 engines disappeared for good the next year, as Pacer and AMX entered their final years. Eagle was the big news: the first major four-wheel-drive passenger car produced in America in modern times. Riding a Concord platform, the Eagle sat three inches higher off the ground to allow for the 4WD structure. It was also the first 4WD model to be built in volume with independent front suspension, and gave AMC something to offer that no other domestic automaker had. Unfortunately, not enough customers seemed to care. In December 1980, AMC stockholders agreed to give Renault a 46 percent share of the company.

For 1981, AMC's selection shrunk to only three models: Spirit, Concord and Eagle, with Pontiac's 151 cu. in. four-cylinder engine under their hoods. The 4WD Eagle was now offered on two platforms: the original Concord size,

and an SX/4 coupe (and Kammback wagon) on the smaller Spirit chassis. Both Eagles sported dark Krayton lower body treatments. Sales slipped over 8 percent, but AMC's market share hung almost steady.

Neither the compact Concord nor subcompact Spirit was doing well as 1982 began, and their days were numbered. Spirit's new five-speed overdrive manual gearbox didn't help. Switchable two/four wheel drive was standard on Eagles, which attracted a moderate—but hardly overwhelming— following. The company's market share sunk below 2 percent, but late in the model year, production of the new Renault Alliance began in Kenosha. Early Alliance sales even helped AMC to recapture fourth place in domestic sales for the first time since 1978, beating out Volkswagen of America. Late in September, production of Spirits and the smaller Eagles moved to Canada, while big Eagles continued to be built in Wisconsin.

1984 AMC Eagle four-door sedan (JG)

Only Eagles retained the Pontiac four-cylinder base engine for 1983. All final Spirits and Concords carried sixes. The new subcompact Alliance, designed in France, was revised to suit American tastes. That included electronic controls, Bendix fuel injection, and power steering and brakes. The 1.4-liter powerplants came from France. New Alliance notwithstanding, AMC managed to lose over $146 million in 1983, nearly as disastrous a figure as the 1982 loss. Early Alliances sold well, but the

good news didn't last, especially as mechanical problems became evident.

A Renault-styled hatchback Encore joined the notchback Alliance for 1984, as Spirit and Concord departed. Only the big 4WD Eagle remained, powered by an AMC-built four or six. Eagle sales had looked promising at first, but sagged badly. For a change, AMC enjoyed a bit of profit this year, and could be forgiven a taste of optimism in what would prove to be a temporary respite.

The Renault-based models got bigger engine choice for 1985, as a convertible Alliance arrived — the first AMC soft-top since the '68 Rambler Rebel. Eagle added "shift-on-the-fly" 4WD but dropped the four-cylinder engine. The modest profit for 1984 indeed proved to be temporary, as AMC lost over $125 million this time around. Low-rate financing was tried for the first time, but couldn't attract enough customers. Production was slashed several times, with workers laid off. The UAW agreed to a pay cut only after AMC threatened to cease production entirely.

Jose Dedeurwaerder, AMC's president, predicted that "the worst is over," and the loss of $91 million in 1986 wasn't as bad as previous totals. But the company's share of sales dwindled to just 1 percent, even after low-rate financing of "zero" was offered. Even American Honda earned a bigger share. Eagle sales slipped below 10,000, amid AMC's insistence that the tough 4WD would remain in production in Canada—and despite rising interest in 4WD models. Chrysler's agreement to build its M-body cars at AMC's Kenosha facility helped pave the way for the Chrysler takeover (for $1 billion) a year later, in August 1987. Only a few months after that, Chrysler drew fire from workers and residents of Kenosha when it announced imminent closing of the plant— after allegedly promising to give it another five years.

Collector interest in 1976-86 AMC models has been, to say the least, modest. But a few examples are worth noting, for curiosity value if nothing else. Gremlin 'X' is one possibility. So is the revived AMX. The last Matadors, specially with Barcelona trim, may be worth a glance. Not everyone loved Eagles when they were new, but as the pioneer of modern 4WD, they might draw modest attention one day. The SX/4 coupe, in particular, is rather attractive. AMC cars may not be exciting, but at least they're inexpensive.

1976 AMC

Following the introduction of the Pacer in mid-1975, changes for the 1976 AMC model year were modest. Speedometers now reached only 90 mph. Some models had a new lockable, padded console. After January 1, brakes were enlarged to meet Federal standards. Six-cylinder engines had reshaped carburetor air passages, a new thermostat, and an electric choke on some models. Since the full-size Ambassador had been dropped for 1975, AMC stressed economy. Three-fourths of the company's vehicles rated over 20 MPG in EPA highway mileage estimates. Engines carried electronic ignition. "Safe-Command" features on all models included: energy-absorbing bumpers and steering column; front head restraints; 4-way hazard warnings; lane-changer turn signals; backup and marker lights; padded sun visors and instrument panel; double-safety brake system with warning light. All models were painted in "Luster-Guard" acrylic baked enamel. Standard body colors were Black; Sienna or Alpine Orange; Seaspray Green; Sand Tan; Firecracker Red; Brilliant Blue; Sunshine Yellow; plus Nautical Blue, Medium Blue, Dark Cocoa, Autumn Red, Evergreen, Burnished Bronze, Silver Frost or Limefire metallic.

1976 Gremlin X liftback coupe (AMC)

GREMLIN — SERIES 40 — SIX/V-8 — Introduced with considerable sales success during 1970 as the first American-made subcompact, the sawed-off Gremlin entered 1976 wearing a new grille. A horizontal crossbar stood between (and surrounded) round amber parking lights. Originally created by chopping 17 inches width from the Hornet design, it remained the only domestic subcompact without a four-cylinder engine. Standard engine was a 232 cubic-inch six with three-speed column shift; a 258 six and 304 V-8 were optional. More distinctive than most small cars, with a design not universally loved, Gremlin gained refinements through its early years but few major changes in its single two-door body style. From the 'B' pillar forward, it's essentially a Hornet, but with a flat hatchback that almost looks like a real hatch. Standard equipment included 6.45 x 14 blackwall tires, foam-cushioned seats, front ashtray, folding rear seat, Weather Eye heater/defroster, two-speed electric wipers/washers, dome light, rear lift window, front sway bar (V-8 only), rear bumper guards, front bumper nerfing strips, a 50-amp battery, and aluminum hubcaps. The sporty 'X' package, available only on Custom models, added a full-length body stripe with 'X' decal, painted lower back panel, engine-turned finish instrument cluster overlay, glove box decal, D70 x 14 tires on slot-style wheels, and a "Space Saver" spare tire. Available again was the unique "Levi's" trim package, with sporty bucket seats, stowage/litter pouches and door trim in simulated blue denim (actually spun nylon) complete with "buttons;" plus blue headlining and sun visors, and "Levi's" front fender decals. Rally stripes continued their unusual "hockey stick" design.

1976 Pacer X liftback coupe (AMC)

PACER — SERIES 60 — SIX — Great expectations greeted the wide, glassy "bubble" Pacer when it appeared as a mid-1975 model. Riding a 100 in. wheelbase, it stood 77 in. wide, billed as "the first wide small car." *Business Week* called it the "hottest car of 1975." Unique features included a passenger door nearly 4 inches wider than that of the driver. A surprisingly roomy four-passenger interior belies the car's compact 170 in. length. The entire rear section tied into the massive B-pillar structure, cutting both length and weight. Aerodynamic styling helped improve fuel economy. A short, sharply-sloped hood and enormous glass area give impressive visibility. But that hood was actually the result of having designed the car for a front-drive Wankel rotary engine, which never materialized from GM. Pacer was one of the first American cars to offer rack and pinion steering. Major change for 1976 was the availability of an optional 258 cu. in. six, with one- or two-barrel carburetor, in addition to the economy 232 six. Air conditioning was a most desirable extra, due to the large glass area. Twin

gas-filled cylinders assisted opening of the large rear lift window. 'X' package included vinyl bucket seats with manual floor shift, woodgrain dash overlay, sports steering wheel, extra-quiet insulation, 'X' ornamentation, color-keyed body side scuff moldings, bumper nerfing strips, front sway bar, and D78 x 14 blackwall tires. The luxurious D/L package consisted of basketry fabric interior, padded steering wheel, carpeted cargo area, woodgrain-overlay dash, wheel covers, color-keyed scuff moldings, bright license molding, nerfing strips, front sway bar, and special emblems. D/L models could also have Hyde Park fabric seat trim. Standard equipment included three-speed column shift; 6.95 x 14 tires; foam-cushioned bench seat; body side scuff molding; Weather Eye heater/defroster; concealed two-speed wipers/washers; dome light; 50-amp battery; aluminum hub caps; ashtray and lighter. Body colors were identical to other models, but not including Black, Sienna/Alpine Orange, Dark Cocoa, Limefire, or Nautical Blue. Alpine White, Golden Jade metallic, Aztec Copper metallic, Brandywine metallic, and Marine Aqua colors were unique to Pacer.

1976 Hornet DL sedan (AMC)

HORNET — SERIES 01 — SIX/V-8 — Introduced in 1970 at a cost of $40 million, the compact Hornet, new from the ground up, became one of AMC's best sellers. As in 1975, the Hornet lineup consisted of four models: a two-door hatchback (added for 1973), two- and four-door sedans, and a four-door Sportabout wagon. Appearance changed little this year, apart from thin rubber strips placed at lower bumper ends. Hornet nameplates sat behind the front side market lamps, and on the right rear panel. A 232 cu. in. six with three-speed column shift was standard; 258 six and 304 V-8 optional. Three option packages were available. Sportabouts and hatchbacks could have a "Touring Interior" with individual reclining seats in tan vinyl; matching headliner, visors and door pull straps; sports steering wheel; woodgrain dash overlay; and carpeted lower door panels. The sporty 'X' package, also for Sportabouts and hatchbacks, consisted of full-length rally striping, slot wheels with D70 x 14 blackwall tires, 'X' ornamentation on dash and lower back panel, plus black grille accents. Sedans with the luxury D/L package had reclining front seats and trim in tan "Kasmir Knit" fabric; D/L Sportabouts came with "Potomac Stripe" fabric (or vinyl) plus woodgrain body paneling, custom wheel covers, roof rack, and air deflector. Standard Hornet equipment included rear bumper guards, front bumper nerfing strips, Weather Eye heater/defroster, locking glove box, color-keyed carpeting and mats, two-speed wipers/washers, front sway bar (V-8s), 50-amp battery, aluminum hubcaps, 6.95 x 14 blackwalls, and aluminum hubcaps. Hatchbacks and Sportabouts had a fold-down rear seat and rear lift window.

1976 Matador Barcelona Brougham coupe (AMC)

MATADOR (COUPE) — SERIES 10 — SIX/V-8 — Starting in 1975, the stylish mid-size Matador coupe stood apart from the four-door sedan and wagon, with a different wheelbase and series number. For 1976 the coupe gained a new full-width, two-section grille that extended out to the fender tips, below the huge headlamp openings. Amber parking lights were rectangular. The Brougham package included individual reclining seats in "Hunter's Plaid" fabric, custom door trim panels, woodgrain dash overlay, full carpeting, wheel discs, hood paint stripes, bumper nerfing strips, rocker moldings, roll-down quarter windows, full-length body side scuff moldings, wheel lip and grille moldings. Going a step further, a new Barcelona luxury package (only on the Brougham) added plush, crumpled-look velvety upholstery in tan or black Knap knit to the reclining front seats, plus special wheel covers and medallions. Barcelona buyers also got color-keyed cut pile carpeting, door pull straps and headlining, plus (with tan interior) tan grille, headlamp bezel and rear license accents. Distinctive red/yellow side striping, a unique hood ornament, hood and deck nameplates, and fender and glove box medallions identified the Barcelona. Base engine was the 258 cu. in. six, with three V-8 options: a 304, 360 with 2Bbl. carburetor, and 360 with 4Bbl. and dual exhausts. Standard equipment was similar to Matador sedan, including front disc brakes.

MATADOR (SEDAN AND WAGON) — SERIES 80 — SIX/V-8 — AMC's intermediate model, little changed from 1975 when it gained a new hood, grille and bumpers, came in standard and Brougham trim. The grille has full-width horizontal blades, plus eight bright vertical divider bars along the protruding center section. Nameplates are behind the front wheel openings, just below the front of the three-quarter length belt moldings. Base engine was the 258 cu. in. six in sedans, a 304 V-8 in wagons (and all California Matadors). Two 360 cu. in. V-8s were optional. Only 20 Matadors held a 401 V-8, available only to law enforcement agencies. Standard equipment included a three-speed column shift transmission (automatic on wagons), foam-cushioned seats, color-keyed carpeting, front and rear ashtrays (front lighter), extra-quiet insulation

package, Weather Eye heater/defroster, day/night mirror, two-speed wipers/washers, dome light, dual-swing wagon tailgate, front sway bar, bumper guards (front only on wagon), plus manual front disc brakes on sedan (power discs on wagon). Sedans wore standard E78 x 14 blackwall tires (F78 x 14 with V-8); wagons H78 x 14. The Brougham package gave individual reclining seats in Custom Hyde Park fabric (Sof-Touch vinyl in wagons), woodgrain dash overlay, full carpeting, wheel covers, 'Brougham' script on 'C' pillars, roof rack and tailgate air deflector (wagon), hood paint stripes, a back panel overlay (sedan), and rocker panel moldings (except two-tone or woodgrain-panel wagon).

I.D. DATA: The 13-symbol Vehicle Identification Number (VIN) was embossed on a metal plate riveted to the top left surface of the instrument panel, visible through the windshield. The first letter (A) indicated the manufacturer, American Motors. The second digit denoted the model year ('6' 1976). Third came a letter identifying transmission type: 'S' three-speed manual, column shift; 'O' three-speed column shift with overdrive; 'E' three-speed floor shift; 'D' three-speed floor shift with overdrive; 'A' column-shift automatic; 'C' floor-shift automatic. The fourth digit denoted the car line (series): '0' Hornet; '1' Matador coupe; '4' Gremlin; '6' Pacer; '8' Matador sedan/wagon. Fifth digit identified body style: '3' two-door hatchback; '5' four-door sedan; '6' two-door sedan; '8' four-door station wagon. Digit six showed the model/group (body class): '3' Gremlin standard; '5' Gremlin Custom; '7' Pacer/Hornet/Matador; 'P' Police. The seventh letter indicated engine type: 'E' 232-6 1Bbl.; 'A' 258-6 1Bbl.; 'C' 258-6 2Bbl.; 'H' 304 V-8 2Bbl.; 'N' 360 V-8 2Bbl.; 'P' 360 V-8 4Bbl.; 'Z' 401 V-8 4Bbl. (police only). Digits 8 through 13 made up the sequential serial number, starting with 100,001 for vehicles made at Kenosha, Wisconsin and 700,001 for those manufactured at Brampton, Ontario.

Note: Digits 4-6 are identical to the model number. A safety sticker attached to edge of left front door shows the month and year built, plus the VIN. A unit body identification plate riveted to the edge of the left front door displays the body number, model number, trim number, paint code number, and build sequence number. A six-symbol Build Code was engraved on a machined surface of the cylinder block of six-cylinder engines, between cylinders 2 and 3; or stamped on a metal tag attached to right bank valve cover on V-8 engines. The first digit indicates model year; second and third digits, the month of manufacture (1 January). The fourth letter indicates engine type, and is identical to the seventh letter of the VIN. Digits five and six denote the day of manufacture. V-8 engines also have cubic-inch displacement cast into the side of the block, between the second and third freeze plugs, usually under the motor mount.

GREMLIN SERIES 40

Series Number	Body/Style Number	Body Type & Seating	Factory Price	Shipping Weight	Production Total
40	7646-3	2-dr Sed-4P	2889/3051	2771/3020	Note 1
40	7646-5	2-dr Cust Sed-4P	2998/3160	2774/3023	Note 1

Note 1: Total model year production, 52,941 Gremlins (only 826 with V-8 engine).

PACER SERIES 60

60	7666-7	2-dr Sed-4P	3499	3114	117,244

HORNET SERIES 01

01	7603-7	2-dr Hatch-5P	3199/3344	2920/3169	Note 2
01	7605-7	4-dr Sed-6P	3199/3344	2971/3220	Note 2
01	7606-7	2-dr Sed-6P	3199/3344	2909/3158	Note 2
01	7608-7	4-dr Sta Wag-6P	3549/3694	3040/3289	29,763

Note 2: Total model year production, Hornet sedans and hatchbacks, 41,814 units (41,025 with six-cylinder engine, 789 with V-8). Of the 29,763 Sportabout wagons, 26,787 had a six, 2976 a V-8 engine.

MATADOR (COUPE) SERIES 10

10	7616-7	2-dr Cpe-6P	3621/3725	3562/3811	Note 3

MATADOR (SEDAN AND WAGON) SERIES 80

80	7685-7	4-dr Sed-6P	3627/3731	3589/3838	Note 3
80	7688-7	4-dr Sta Wag-6P	-- /4373	-- /4015	11,049

Note 3: Model year production of coupe and sedan totaled 30,464 units (4993 sixes and 25,471 V-8s).

FACTORY PRICE AND WEIGHT NOTE: Figure before the slash is for six-cylinder engine, after slash for V-8 engine.

ENGINES: BASE SIX (Gremlin, Hornet, Pacer): Inline. OHV. Six-cylinder. Cast iron block. Displacement: 232 cu. in. (3.8 liters). Bore & stroke: 3.75 x 3.50 in. Compression ratio: 8.0:1. Brake horsepower: 90 (SAE net) at 3050 R.P.M. Torque: 170 lbs.-ft. at 2000 R.P.M. Seven main bearings. Hydraulic valve lifters. Carburetor: 1Bbl. Carter YF. BASE SIX (Matador coupe/sedan); OPTIONAL (Gremlin, Hornet, Pacer): Inline. OHV. Six-cylinder. Cast iron block. Displacement: 258 cu. in. (4.2 liters). Bore & stroke: 3.75 x 3.90 in. Compression ratio: 8.0:1. Brake horsepower: 95 at 3050 R.P.M. Torque: 180 lbs.-ft. at 2100 R.P.M. (Matador, 2000 R.P.M.). Seven main bearings. Hydraulic valve lifters. Carburetor: 1Bbl. Carter YF. OPTIONAL SIX (Pacer only): Same as 258 cu. in. six above, but with Carter BBD 2Bbl. carburetor. Horsepower: 120 at 3400 R.P.M. Torque: 200 lbs.-ft. at 2000 R.P.M. BASE V-8 (Matador station wagon); OPTIONAL (Gremlin, Hornet, other Matadors): 90-degree, overhead valve V-8. Cast iron block. Displacement: 304 cu. in. (5.0 liters). Bore & stroke: 3.75 x 3.44 in. Compression ratio: 8.4:1. Brake horsepower: 120 at 3200 R.P.M. Torque: 220 lbs.-ft. at 2200 R.P.M. Five main bearings. Hydraulic valve lifters. Carburetor: 2Bbl. Motorcraft 2100. OPTIONAL V-8 (Matador): 90-degree, overhead valve V-8. Cast iron block. Displacement: 360 cu. in. (5.9 liters). Bore & stroke: 4.08 x 3.44 in. Compression ratio: 8.25:1. Brake horsepower: 140 at 3200 R.P.M. Torque: 260 lbs.-ft. at 1600 R.P.M. Five main bearings. Hydraulic valve lifters. Carburetor: 2Bbl. Motorcraft 2100. OPTIONAL HIGH-PERFORMANCE V-8 (Matador): Same as 360 cu. in. V-8 above, but with 4Bbl. Motorcraft 4350 carburetor and dual exhausts. Horsepower: 180 at 3600 R.P.M. Torque: 280 lbs.-ft. at 2800 R.P.M. POLICE V-8 (Matador): 90-degree, overhead valve V-8. Cast iron block. Displacement: 401 cu. in. Bore & stroke: 4.165 x 3.68 in. Compression ratio: 8.25:1. Brake horsepower: 215 at 4200 R.P.M. Torque: 320 lbs.-ft. at 2800 R.P.M. Five main bearings. Hydraulic valve lifters.

CHASSIS DATA: Wheelbase: (Gremlin) 96 in.; (Pacer) 100 in.; (Hornet) 108 in.; (Matador coupe) 114 in.; (Matador sedan/wagon) 118 in. Overall length: (Gremlin) 169.4 in.; (Pacer) 170 in.; (Hornet) 186 in.; (Matador coupe) 209.4 in.; (Matador sedan) 216 in.; (Matador wagon) 215.5 in. Height: (Gremlin) 52.3 in.; (Pacer) 52.7 in.; (Hornet) 52.2 in. except 4-dr sedan, 51.7 in.; (Matador coupe) 51.8 in.; (Matador sedan) 54.7 in.; (Matador wagon) 56.8 in. Front Tread: (Gremlin/Hornet) 57.5 in.; (Pacer) 61.2 in.; (Matador coupe) 59.7 in.; (Matador) 59.8 in. Rear Tread: (Gremlin/Hornet) 57.1 in.; (Pacer) 60.2 in.; (Matador) 60.0 in. Standard Tires: (Gremlin six) 6.45 x 14; (Gremlin V-8, Pacer, Hornet) 6.95 x 14; (Hornet V-8 sedan or wagon) D78 x 14; (Matador coupe/sedan, six) E78 x 14; (Matador coupe/sedan, V-8) F78 x 14; (Matador wagon) FR78 x 14 steel radial, or H78 x 14.

TECHNICAL: Three-speed manual transmission was standard: floor shift on Gremlin and Hornet hatchbacks, column shift on other models. Overdrive standard on Pacer with 258 cu. in. six (2Bbl.); optional with other Pacers and Gremlin/Hornet six. Manual transmission gear ratios: (1st) 2.99:1; (2nd) 1.75:1; (3rd) 1.00:1; (Rev) 3.17:1. Torque-Command three- speed automatic transmission optional on all models; column or floor shift selector. Standard axle ratio: (Gremlin) 2.73:1 except 304 V-8 with three-speed manual, 3.15:1 and 304 V-8 with automatic, 2.87:1; (Pacer) 2.73:1 except automatic shift and all with 258 six and 2Bbl. carb, 3.08:1; (Hornet) 2.73:1 except 304 V-8 with automatic, 2.87:1, and hatchback with floor shift, 3.15:1; (Matador) 2.87:1 except base six with manual shift, 3.54:1, and base six with automatic, 3.15:1. Hotchkiss drive. Steering: (Pacer) rack and pinion; (others) recirculating ball. Suspension: independent front coil springs (Pacer springs mounted between the two control arms); semi-elliptic rear leaf springs except (Matador) coil springs. Brakes: drum; front discs optional (standard on Matador). Breakerless Inductive Discharge electronic ignition. Fuel tank: (Gremlin/Matador wagon) 21 gal.; (Pacer/Hornet) 22 gal.; (Matador coupe/sedan) 24.5 gal. Uses unleaded fuel only.

DRIVETRAIN OPTIONS: 258 cu. in. six-cylinder engine, 1Bbl carb: Gremlin/Pacer/Hornet ($69); 258 cu. in. six, 2Bbl.: Pacer ($99); Pacer with air conditioning ($69). 304 cu. in. V-8, 2Bbl.: Gremlin ($162); Hornet ($145); Matador ($104) but standard on wagon. 360 cu. in. V-8, 2Bbl.: Matador sedan/coupe ($150); wagon ($46). 360 cu. in. V-8, 4Bbl., dual exhausts: Matador sedan/coupe ($266); wagon ($162). Three-speed floor shift: Pacer with bucket or individual reclining seats ($21). Three-speed column shift with overdrive: Pacer, Hornet Sportabout with 232 six ($157). Three-speed floor shift with overdrive: Grem. or Hornet hatchback six ($157); Torque-Command automatic transmission, column shift: Grem./Hornet six, Pacer ($252); Grem. V-8 ($281); Hornet V-8 ($262); Matador six ($261); Mat. 304 cu. in. V-8 ($268); Mat. 360 V-8 ($281); Mat. wagon ($13). Torque-Command with floor shift lever: Grem. six, Pacer with bucket or reclining seats, and Hornet hatchback/Sportabout six ($273); Grem., Hornet hatchback/Sportabout V-8 ($283); Matador coupe with 304 V-8 and bucket seats ($330); Mat. coupe with 360 V-8 ($343). Optional axle ratio: Grem./Pacer/Hornet ($13); Mat. ($14). Twin Grip differential: Grem./Hornet ($49); Pacer ($49); Mat. ($53). Heavy-duty engine cooling system: Matador coupe ($18); others ($25); but standard with air conditioning. Heavy-duty suspension: Grem./Hornet ($27) including front sway bar for six-cylinder; Pacer/Matador ($32) with front sway bar on Pacer, rear on Matador. Front sway bar: Pacer ($18) but included with 'X' package. Rear sway bar: Matador ($16). 70-amp battery: Grem./Pacer/ Hornet ($15); Mat. ($16). California emission system ($50). Trailer towing package: Matador V-8 ($116); with air conditioning ($91). Highway cruising package (cruise control and 2.53:1 axle ratio with six, 2.87:1 with V-8): Gremlin with auto. trans. ($59).

GREMLIN/HORNET/MATADOR CONVENIENCE/APPEARANCE OPTIONS: 'X' package: Gremlin ($189); Hornet ($179). Hornet sedan D/L package with "Kasmir Knit" fabric ($169). Sportabout D/L package with "Potomac Stripe" fabric ($350); with vinyl ($309); with touring interior ($214). Touring interior in "Sof-Touch" vinyl: Hornet hatchback/Sportabout ($169). Brougham package: Matador sedan ($179); Matador wagon ($199); Matador coupe ($249). Barcelona package: Matador coupe with Brougham package only ($149). "Levi's" custom fabric trim package: Gremlin ($89). Opera windows and padded vinyl roof package: Matador coupe ($524). Interior appointment package (parcel shelf, glove box lock, lighter): Grem. ($21). Interior decor package (appointment pkg., carpeted cargo area, extra-quiet insulation): Grem. ($49). Decor package (wheel covers and moldings): Grem./Hornet ($45); Grem. 'X' ($13); Hornet 'X' or D/L ($14); Mat. coupe without Brougham pkg. ($59). Extra Quiet insulation package: Grem. ($32); Hornet ($31). Protection group: Grem./Hornet ($59); Mat. coupe ($69), or ($20) with Brougham package; Mat. sedan/wagon ($21). Convenience group (dome/reading light, electric clock, stowage containers, dual horns): Grem./Hornet ($49); Matador ($52). Visibility group (remote control left mirror, visor mirror, 12" day/night mirror, deluxe wipers): Grem./Hornet ($45); Matador ($49). Remote control right mirror: Matador ($27), available with visibility group only. Power steering: Grem./Hornet ($125); Matador coupe ($136); Mat. sedan/wagon ($137). Power front disc brakes: Grem./Hornet ($84); Mat. ($60). Manual front disc brakes: Grem./Hornet ($50). Cruise control: Grem./Hornet ($69); Mat. ($72). All Season air conditioning: Grem./Hornet ($425); Mat. ($473). Air conditioning package (incl. tinted glass and power steering): Grem./Hornet ($579). AM radio: Grem./Hornet ($75); Matador ($76). AM/FM/Stereo four-speaker radio ($199). Rear speaker for AM radio: Grem./Hornet ($20); Mat. ($21). 8-track tape player and AM/FM/Stereo radio: Matador ($299). Power windows: Matador Brougham sedan/wagon ($138). Power side and tailgate windows: Matador Brougham wagon ($179). Power tailgate window: Matador Brougham wagon ($41). Console: Grem./Hornet hatchback ($25). Hidden compartment: Grem. ($20); Hornet hatchback ($41). Individual fabric reclining seats: Hornet ($104); Matador Brougham wagon ($31); no charge on Matador Brougham coupe. Individual vinyl reclining seats: Hornet sedan ($84); Sportabout ($63); Matador Brougham coupe/sedan ($31). Bucket seats: Hornet hatchback ($49); Matador coupe ($96) but no charge with Brougham pkg. Fabric cushion trim, bench seat: Grem. ($29); no charge on Hornet sedan/hatchback, Matador. Vinyl cushion trim, bucket seats: Grem. ($49); Hornet sedan/hatchback ($21); no charge on Sportabout. Vinyl cushion trim, bench seat: Matador coupe ($31). Third seat: Matador wagon ($127). Carpeted cargo area: Grem. Custom ($15). Deluxe wipers: Grem./Hornet ($26); Mat. ($28). Rear defogger: Grem., Hornet hatchback/Sportabout ($63); Matador coupe/sedan ($73). Rear defogger, blower- type: Hornet sedan ($41). Light group: Grem. ($26); Hornet ($30); Matador ($29). Fuel economy gauge: Grem./Hornet ($26); Mat. ($28); but no charge with convenience group. Custom steering wheel: Grem. ($15). Sports steering wheel (3-spoke): Gremlin ($35); Grem. Custom, Hornet ($20); Mat. ($21). Leather-wrapped steering wheel: Gremlin ($49); Grem. Custom, Hornet ($34); Hornet hatchback/Sportabout with touring interior ($14); Matador ($35). Tilt steering wheel: Grem./Hornet ($52); Mat. ($54). Tinted glass: Grem. ($44); Hornet ($47); Matador ($51). Tinted windshield: Hornet ($36); Matador sedan/wagon ($42). Two-tone paint: Hornet except Sportabout ($36); Matador ($42) except wagon ($79). Special color combinations ($21) except Matador ($22). Vinyl roof: Grem. ($74); Hornet ($93); Mat. coupe/sedan ($105). Rally side stripes: Grem. ($39); Matador coupe except Barcelona ($41). Woodgrain panels: Hornet Sportabout ($99); included with Sportabout D/L pkg.; Matador wagon ($118). Roof rack: Grem. ($53); Sportabout ($75); Matador wagon ($62). Locking gas cap ($6). Tailgate air deflector: Gremlin ($22); Matador wagon ($24). Inside hood release: Grem./Hornet ($14). Front bumper guards: Grem./Hornet ($15); Engine block heater: Grem./Hornet ($17); Mat. ($18). Wheel covers (set of 4): Gremlin ($32); Hornet ($31); Matador ($34). Custom wheel covers: Mat. ($55), or ($22) with Brougham pkg. Styled wheels with trim rings for D-size tires: Grem./Hornet ($121); with Gremlin Custom 'X' or Hornet hatch/Sportabout 'X' pkg. ($56); Sportabout D/L ($68); Matador ($127), but ($93) with Brougham or Decor pkg. Aluminum styled wheels for D-size tires: Grem./Hornet ($210); Gremlin Custom 'X' or Hornet hatch/Sportabout 'X' pkg. ($145); Sportabout D/L pkg. ($157); Matador ($221), but ($187) with Brougham or Decor pkg. Space-Saver spare tire: Gremlin or Sportabout with regular wheels ($16); no charge with special wheels/tires. Tires: 6.45 x 14 whitewall: Gremlin ($36). 6.95 x 14: Grem. V-8 ($16). 6.95 x 14 whitewall: Grem. V-8 ($52); Hornet ($36); D78 x 14: Hornet ($16). D78 x 14 whitewall: Grem. with styled wheels ($68); Hornet ($52). D70 x 14 with white letters: Grem. Custom 'X', Hornet 'X' ($48). DR78 x 14 steel radial: Grem. ($140); Hornet ($124); Grem. Custom 'X' or Hornet 'X' ($66). DR78 x 14 whitewall: Grem. ($176); Hornet ($160); Grem. Custom 'X' or Hornet 'X' ($102). DR70 x 14 radial with white letters: Grem. ($212); Hornet ($196); Grem. Custom 'X' or Hornet 'X' ($139).

E78 x 14 whitewall: Mat. ($38). E78 x 14 MSR: Matador V-8 coupe ($20). F78 x 14 whitewall: Matador ($58). F78 x 14 MSR: Mat. sedan with V-8 ($20). FR78 x 14 steel radial: Matador ($134). FR78 x 14 whitewall: Matador ($172). H78 x 14 whitewall: Matador wagon ($38). HR78 x 14: Matador ($154); wagon ($114). HR78 x 14 whitewall: Matador ($192); wagon ($152).

PACER CONVENIENCE/APPEARANCE OPTIONS: 'X' package ($339). D/L package ($199); not available with 'X' package. Rally package: front console, leather-wrapped steering wheel, tachometer, electric clocks, gauges ($139). Decor package: wheel covers and exterior moldings ($89; with D/L ($57). Extra Quiet insulation package ($35). Protection group: floor mats, rocker panel moldings, scuff panel extensions ($37). Convenience group: dome/reading light, electric clock, stowage containers, dual horns ($49); with Rally package ($34). Visibility group: remote left mirror, visor mirror, 12 in. day/night mirror, deluxe wipers ($55). Rear visibility package: rear wiper/washer, defogger ($99). Power steering ($125). Power front disc brakes ($84). Manual front disc brakes ($50). Cruise control ($69). All Season air conditioning ($425). AM radio ($75). AM/FM/Stereo radio ($199). Rear speaker ($20). 8-track tape player and AM/FM/Stereo radio ($299). Console ($25). Hidden compartment ($31). Individual reclining seats, D/L package: "Basketry" fabric ($63); "Hyde Park" fabric ($84). Bucket seats ($84). "Sof-Touch" vinyl ($99); with D/L ($70). Vinyl bench cushion trim ($21). Deluxe wipers ($26). Rear defogger ($63). Rear wiper/washer ($52). Light group ($28). Fuel economy light ($18). Sports steering wheel ($20). Leather-wrapped steering wheel ($34); with 'X' package ($14). Tilt steering wheel ($52). Tinted glass ($52). Door vent windows ($30). Two-tone color ($52). Special color combinations ($21). Vinyl roof ($105). Roof rack ($52). Locking gas cap ($6). Bumper guards and nerfing strips ($53); with D/L or 'X' ($34). Engine block heater ($17). Wheel covers: set of 4 ($32). Styled wheels with trim rings for D-size tires: ($121); with 'X' package ($56); with D/L or Decor pkg. ($89). Aluminum styled wheels for D-size tires: ($210); with 'X' ($145); with D/L or Decor pkg. ($178). Tires: 6.95 x 14 whitewall ($36); D78 x 14 ($16); D78 x 14 WSW ($52); DR78 x 14 steel radial ($124); DR78 x 14 WSW ($160); DR70 x 14 radial with white letters ($196). Tires with 'X' package: D78 x 14 whitewall ($36); DR78 x 14 steel radial ($108); DR78 x 14 WSW ($145); DR70 x 14 radial with white letters ($181).

HISTORY: All 1976 AMC models debuted September 24, 1975. Model year production totaled 283,275 (242,164 sixes and 41,111 V-8s). That came to 3.5 percent of the industry total, down from 3.74 percent the previous year and a healthy 5.3 percent in 1973. Calendar year production amounted to 213,606 units, well below the 323,704 total for 1975. Production halted on June 25, 1976. Calendar year sales came to 247,640, down markedly from the previous year's 322,272. Hornets sold the best, while Matadors declined the most.

Historical Footnotes: While other U.S. automakers recovered from the disastrous sales slump of 1975, AMC fell short of optimistic expectations. Pacer sales, in particular, slackened after an early surge, largely the result of a weakening market for small cars. Production rose from an initial 480 Pacers per day to 800 by late 1975; but a few months later, dealers were glutted. "We were too aggressive," admitted AMC president William V. Luneberg, due to early enthusiasm. Production was slashed, and 2700 workers laid off. As the model year opened, AMC announced the acquisition of a new plant at Richmond, Indiana to build a two-liter four-cylinder engine, whose design and tooling had been purchased from Audi for $60 million.

1977 AMC

AMC entered the 1977 model year with the same four models as before, ranging from the subcompact Gremlin to the mid-size Matador. Only the Gremlin received significant restyling, plus a new four-cylinder engine later in the model year. All six-cylinder engines now had a "quench-head" design. Reshaped combustion chambers brought the compressed mixture closer to the spark plug. More models had a catalytic converter or Air Guard system for emission control. Coolant overflow systems were more common. Most sixes had a two-barrel carburetor. Front disc brakes became standard. Manual transmissions were fully synchronized, but the column shifter was gone; both standard three-speed and optional four-speed gearboxes had floor shifters. Standard AMC colors were Classic Black, Alpine White, Sand Tan, Firecracker Red, Brilliant Blue, Powder Blue, Sunshine Yellow, Lime Green, Tawny Orange and Sun Orange; plus nine metallics: Brandywine, Silver Frost, Misty Jade, Mocha Brown, Autumn Red, Midnight Blue, Loden Green, Golden Ginger, and Captain Blue. Vinyl roofs came in six "Bravado Grain" colors.

1977 Gremlin X liftback coupe (AMC)

GREMLIN — SERIES 40 — FOUR/SIX — Gremlin entered the 1977 model year wearing a new grille, bumper and front end sheet metal, enlarged taillights, plus a bigger all-glass rear lift window—the first body restyle since the subcompact's 1970 debut. Though 4 inches shorter than before, with increased rear glass area, Gremlin's basic (and distinctive) appearance was essentially unchanged. The length loss came from reducing the car's front overhang, while horizontal amber markers stood at the forward end of the new slanted, four-row eggcrate grille. Rectangular parking lights were inset within the front fenders. The 'Gremlin' nameplate no longer stood on the front of the hood bulge. But the biggest change didn't come until February 1977, when the four-cylinder 121 cu. in. engine, recently acquired from Volkswagen, was offered under Gremlin hoods. Rated 80 horsepower, the VW/Audi four had a belt-driven overhead cam, aluminum cross-flow head, and aluminum intake manifold. The 232 cu. in. six remained standard, but the V-8 was gone, enhancing Gremlin's image (and gas mileage ranking) in the economy car sweepstakes. Also appearing this year was a new Borg-Warner four-speed manual transmission with floor shifter. Industry sources show that 17.6

percent of Gremlins carried a four-speed. Foam-cushioned seats were upholstered in Rallye perforated vinyl. Standard equipment now included front disc brakes and three-speed floor shift, plus Weather Eye heater/defroster, front ashtray and lighter, locking glove box, two-speed wiper/washers, dome light, color-keyed carpeting, body paint stripes, folding rear seat, rear bumper guards, and bright moldings for drip rails, wheel lips and rocker panels. Standard tires again were 6.95 x 14 blackwalls. Gremlin's sporty 'X' package used a new striping treatment, flowing at the rear in a slight curve rather than the familiar "hockey stick" shape. That package included bucket seats trimmed in Hot-Scotch plaid fabric, sports steering wheel, instrument panel overlay, 'X' decals on body stripes and glove box door, a lower back panel stripe decal, D70 x 14 tires on slot-styled wheels, and extra-quiet insulation. The unique "Levi's" trim package was available again this year.

1977 Pacer D/L station wagon (AMC)

PACER — SERIES 60 — SIX — Biggest news for the year-and-a-half old Pacer was the addition of a station wagon to the existing hatchback sedan. Adding cargo space to the already roomy design, it was meant to challenge Chrysler's new compact wagons. Overly optimistic production plans had to be cut back, however, since domestic small cars weren't selling well. With rear seat folded, the wide wagon—just 4 in. longer than the sedan—held 47.8 cu. ft. of cargo. Styling was identical to the hatchback sedan from the doors forward, but wagons had vertically-oriented three-section taillamps, unlike the sedan's horizontal units. The wagon's wide lift-up hatch reached down nearly to the bumper, for easy loading. Large side windows included "flipper" vents for improved ventilation. Despite its short wheelbase, the wide (77 in.) Pacer ranked as a compact. Standard engine was again the 232 cu. in. six, with a 258 option. Foam-cushioned bench seats were trimmed in Rallye Perforated vinyl on wagons, in Basketry Print fabric on hatchback sedans. Standard equipment included a three-speed floor shift, front disc brakes, 6.95 x 14 blackwall tires (D78 x 14 on the wagon), heater/defroster, two-speed wiper/washers, dome light, ashtray and lighter, built-in assist on the rear hatch, color-keyed carpeting, folding second seat, and body side scuff moldings. Wagons had a locking stowage compartment in the rear quarter panel. Pacer's 'X' package included perforated vinyl sedan bucket seats, woodgrain dash overlay, sports steering wheel, custom door trim with vinyl inserts and door pull straps, upper door moldings, DR78 x 14 tires on slot-styled wheels, plus high level ventilation and extra-quiet insulation packages. The D/L package contained individual reclining seats, custom door panels with assist straps, woodgrain dash overlay, custom steering wheel, light group, day/night mirror, high level ventilation, wheel lip and rocker panel moldings, rear wheelhouse pads, bumper nerfing strips, extra-quiet insulation, and D78 x 14 whitewalls on styled wheels. D/L wagon bodies had woodgrain side/rear overlays.

1977 Hornet DL sedan (AMC)

HORNET AND AMX — SERIES 01 — SIX/V-8 — For its final year, the Hornet line was highlighted by a limited edition AMX hatchback package, bringing back a nameplate that many remembered for sporty performance a few years earlier. In addition to 'AMX' graphics between door and rear wheelhouse, and at rear, the package included a front air dam, color-coordinated bumpers, blacked-out grille, body-color rear window louvers, Euro-style brushed aluminum larga roof band, twin flat black mirrors, floor console, gauges (including tachometer), soft-feel steering wheel, and brushed aluminum instrument panel overlay. Flared fenders topped DR78 x 14 tires. Base Hornet engine remained the 232 six coupled to three-speed floor shift, with a 258 six or 304 V-8 optional. Sixes could get the new four-speed manual shift. AMX hatchbacks required the 258 with four-speed, or V-8 with automatic. Standard Hornet equipment included rear bumper guards, corner nerfing strips on front bumpers, color-keyed carpeting and mats, Weather Eye heater/defroster, locking glove box, and two-speed wiper/washers. Hornet V-8 sedans and wagons wore standard D78 x 14 tires; other models, 6.95 x 14 blackwalls. All trim packages and options were upgraded. Such luxuries as vinyl bucket seats, sports steering wheel and a carpeted cargo area were standard on hatchback Hornets. Foam-cushioned bench seats were trimmed in Veracruz fabric on sedans, Rallye perforated vinyl on wagons. Both 'X' and D/L packages were offered again. D/L models now included reclining front seats in Veracruz fabric on sedans (Rallye perforated vinyl on wagons) plus dual horns, light group, woodgrain dash overlay, 12 in. day/night mirror, D78 x 14 whitewalls, and dual body side stripes (sedans) or woodgrain body panel overlays (wagons).

1977 Matador coupe (AMC)

MATADOR (COUPE) — SERIES 10 — SIX/V-8 — Unchanged externally, the new Matadors contained interior packages that had formerly been offered only in the luxury Brougham model (which was dropped this year). Engine choices remained as in 1976, but the high-performance 360 cu. in. V-8 was gone, as was the police 401. Standard equipment now included a 258 cu. in. six, Torque Command automatic transmission, power steering and front disc brakes, individual reclining seats in Brampton Plaid fabric, heater/defroster, color-keyed carpeting, front/rear ashtrays, front lighter, extra-quiet insulation, two-speed wiper/washers, light group, protective bodyside scuff moldings, wheel covers, bumper guards, front sway bar, day/night mirror, and custom steering wheel. F78 x 14 blackwalls were standard. The luxury Barcelona package added tan Nap Knit fabric seats, color-keyed door trim panel panels and headlining, tan grille surround and headlight bezels, tan license plate depression and wheel covers, plus a special hood ornament, insignias and nameplates.

1977 Matador sedan (AMC)

MATADOR (SEDAN AND WAGON) — SERIES 80 — SIX/V-8 — As in 1976, the coupe was officially a different series than the Matador sedan and wagon. Base engine remained a 258 cu. in. six with one-barrel carb, with 304 or 360 cu. in. V-8 optional. (The 304 V-8 was standard in wagons and California Matadors.) Standard equipment was similar to the coupe, but wagons wore H78 x 14 blackwalls and their seats were covered in Crush-Grain vinyl.

I.D. DATA: As before. the 13-symbol Vehicle Identification Number (VIN) was embossed on a metal plate riveted to the upper left surface of the instrument panel. Coding was the same as 1976, with the following changes. Model year code (second symbol) changed to '7' for 1977. Codes 'D', 'O' and 'S' for column- shift manual and overdrive transmissions (third symbol) were dropped; code 'M' for four-speed floor shift was added. Two digits were now used for model/group (sixth symbol): '5' Gremlin; '7' Pacer/Hornet/Matador. Engine letters (seventh symbol) changed to: 'G' 121-4 2Bbl.; 'E' 232-6 1Bbl.; 'A' 258-6 1Bbl.; 'B' 258-6 2Bbl.; 'H' 304-8 2Bbl.; 'N' 360-8 2Bbl. In addition to month and year built, plus the VIN, the safety sticker attached to left front door now showed a safety compliance statement and consumer information (vehicle class, acceleration/passing figures, tire reserve load, and stopping distance). A federal emission control information label in the engine compartment identified the engine type and gave basic tune-up specs. The unit body identification plate was the same as 1976.

GREMLIN SERIES 40 (SIX-CYLINDER)

Series Number	Body/Style Number	Body Type & Seating	Factory Price	Shipping Weight	Production Total
40	7746-5	2-dr Sed-4P	2995	2811	Note 1
40	7746-7	2-dr Cust Sed-4P	3248	2824	Note 1

GREMLIN SERIES 40 (FOUR-CYLINDER)

40	7746-4	2-dr Sed-4P	3248	2564	7558

Note 1: Total model year production, 46,171 Gremlins (38,613 six- cylinder).

PACER SERIES 60

60	7766-7	2-dr Sed-4P	3649	3156	20,265
60	7768-7	2-dr Sta Wag-4P	3799	3202	37,999

HORNET SERIES 01

01	7703-7	2-dr Hatch-5P	3499/3662	3012/3245	11,545
01	7705-7	4-dr Sed-6P	3449/3613	3035/3268	31,331
01	7706-7	2-dr Sed-6P	3399/3563	2971/3204	6076
01	7708-7	4-dr Sta Wag-6P	3699/3863	3100/3333	28,891

Note 2: Total model year production, 77,843 Hornets (73,752 with six- cylinder engine, 4091 with V-8).

MATADOR (COUPE) SERIES 10

10	7716-7	2-dr Cpe-5P	4499/4619	3704/3872	6825

MATADOR (SEDAN AND WAGON) SERIES 80

80	7785-7	4-dr Sed-6P	4549/4669	3713/3876	12,944
80	7788-7	4-dr Sta Wag-6P	-- /4899	-- /4104	11,078

Note 3: Model year production of Matador coupe and sedan totaled 19,769 units (2447 sixes and 17,322 V-8s).

FACTORY PRICE NOTE: Figure before the slash in Hornet and Matador price columns is for six-cylinder engine, after slash for V-8 engine.

ENGINES: BASE FOUR (Gremlin): Inline. Overhead cam. Four-cylinder. Cast iron block; cast aluminum alloy head. Displacement: 121 cu. in. (2.0 liters). Bore & stroke: 3.41 x 3.32 in. Compression ratio: 8.1:1. Brake horsepower: 80 at 5000 R.P.M. Torque: 105 lbs.-ft. at 2800 R.P.M. Five main bearings. Solid valve lifters. Carburetor: 2Bbl. Holley 5210. **BASE SIX (Gremlin, Hornet, Pacer):** Inline. OHV. Six-cylinder. Cast iron block. Displacement: 232 cu. in. (3.8 liters). Bore & stroke: 3.75 x 3.50 in. Compression ratio: 8.0:1. Brake horsepower: 88 at 3400 R.P.M. Torque: 164 lbs.-ft. at 1600 R.P.M. Taxable H.P.: 33.75. Seven main bearings. Hydraulic valve lifters. Carburetor: 1Bbl. Carter YF. **BASE SIX (Matador coupe/sedan):** Inline. OHV. Six-cylinder. Cast iron block. Displacement: 258 cu. in. (4.2 liters). Bore & stroke: 3.75 x 3.90 in. Compression ratio: 8.0:1. Brake horsepower: 98 at 3200 R.P.M. Torque: 193 lbs.-ft. at 1600 R.P.M. Seven main bearings. Hydraulic valve lifters. Carburetor: 1Bbl. Carter YF. **OPTIONAL SIX (Gremlin, Hornet, Pacer):** Same as 258 cu. in. six above, but with Carter BBD 2Bbl. carburetor. Horsepower: 114 at 3600 R.P.M. Torque: 192 lbs.-ft. at 2000 R.P.M. **BASE V-8 (Matador station wagon):** 90-degree, overhead valve V-8. Cast iron block. Displacement: 304 cu. in. (5.0 liters). Bore & stroke: 3.75 x 3.44 in. Compression ratio: 8.4:1. Brake horsepower: 121 at 3450 R.P.M. (Matador, 126 at 3600). Torque: 219 lbs.-ft. at 2000 R.P.M. Taxable H.P.: 45. Five main bearings. Hydraulic valve lifters. Carburetor: 2Bbl. Motorcraft 2100. **OPTIONAL V-8 (Matador):** 90-degree, overhead valve V-8. Cast iron block. Displacement: 360 cu. in. (5.9 liters). Bore & stroke: 4.08 x 3.44 in. Compression ratio: 8.25:1. Brake horsepower: 129 at 3700 R.P.M. Torque: 245 lbs.-ft. at 1600 R.P.M. Taxable H.P.: 53.3. Five main bearings. Hydraulic valve lifters. Carburetor: 2Bbl. Motorcraft 2100.

CHASSIS DATA: Wheelbase: (Gremlin) 96 in.; (Pacer) 100 in.; (Hornet) 108 in.; (Matador coupe) 114 in.; (Matador sedan/wagon) 118 in. Overall length: (Gremlin) 166.4 in.; (Pacer sedan) 170 in.; (Pacer wagon) 174 in.; (Hornet) 186 in.; (Matador coupe) 209.4 in.; (Matador sedan) 216 in.; (Matador wagon) 215.5 in. Height: (Gremlin) 52.3 in.; (Pacer sedan) 52.7 in.; (Pacer wagon) 53.0 in.; (Hornet) 52.2 in. except 4-dr sedan, 52.7 in.; (Matador coupe) 51.8 in.; (Matador sedan) 54.7 in.; (Matador wagon) 56.8 in. Front Tread: (Gremlin/Hornet) 57.5 in.; (Pacer) 61.2 in.; (Matador coupe) 59.7 in.; (Matador sedan) 59.8 in. Rear Tread: (Gremlin/Hornet) 57.1 in.; (Pacer) 60.2 in.; (Matador) 60.0 in. Standard Tires: (Gremlin) 6.45 x 14; (Pacer sedan, Hornet) 6.95 x 14; (Pacer wagon; Hornet V-8 sedan/wagon) D78 x 14; (Matador coupe/sedan) F78 x 14; (Matador wagon) H78 x 14.

TECHNICAL: Three-speed, fully synchronized manual floor-shift transmission was standard on all except Matadors, which had standard automatic transmission. Four-speed floor shift optional. Three-speed manual gear ratios: (1st) 2.99:1; (2nd) 1.75:1; (Rev) 3.17:1. Four-speed ratios: (1st) 3.50:1; (2nd) 2.21:1; (3rd) 1.42:1; (Rev) 3.39:1. Torque-Command three-speed automatic transmission optional on Gremlin, Hornet and Pacer; column or floor shift selector. Three-element torque converter. Automatic gear ratios: (Low) 2.45:1; (Intermediate) 1.45:1; (High) 1.00:1; (Rev) 2.20:1. Standard axle ratios: (Gremlin/Pacer/Hornet six) 2.73:1; 2.53:1 and 3.08:1 optional. (Hornet V-8) 2.87:1; 3.15:1 optional. (Matador six) 3.15:1 (Matador V-8) 2.87:1; 3.15:1 and 3.54:1 available. Steering: (Pacer) rack and pinion; (others) recirculating ball. Suspension: independent front coil springs (Pacer springs mounted between the two control arms); semi-elliptic rear leaf springs except (Matador) coil springs. Brakes: front discs; rear drum. Breakerless Inductive Discharge electronic ignition. Fuel tank: (Gremlin and Matador wagon) 21 gal.; (Pacer/Hornet) 22 gal.; (Matador coupe/sedan) 24.5 gal. Uses unleaded fuel only.

DRIVETRAIN OPTIONS: 258 cu. in. six-cylinder engine, 2Bbl. carb: Gremlin/Pacer/Hornet ($79). 304 cu. in. V-8, 2Bbl.: Hornet ($164); Matador ($179) but standard on wagon. 360 cu. in. V-8, 2Bbl.: Matador sedan/coupe ($179); wagon ($59). Four- speed manual floor shift: Gremlin, Pacer, Hornet hatchback ($105). Torque-Command automatic transmission, column shift: Gremlin, Hornet except hatchback ($267). Torque-Command with floor shift lever: Gremlin, Pacer, Hornet hatchback/Sportabout ($289); Matador coupe with V-8 and bucket seats ($66). Twin Grip differential: Grem./Hornet/Pacer ($52); Matador ($56). Heavy-duty engine cooling system: Gremlin ($49); others ($27); but standard with air conditioning. Maximum cooling system: Matador V-8 ($45); Mat. V-8 with air ($18). Auxiliary automatic transmission oil cooler: Matador ($32). Heavy-duty suspension: Grem./Hornet ($29); Pacer/Matador ($34) with front sway bar on Pacer, rear on Matador. Front sway bar: Grem./Hornet/Pacer ($17) but included with radial tires. Rear sway bar: Matador ($17). Air-adjustable shock absorbers: Matador ($45); with H.D. suspension ($41). 70-amp battery: Grem./Pacer/Hornet ($32); Mat. ($18). California emission system ($53). High altitude package ($15). Gremlin performance package: 258 engine, four-speed, sports steering wheel, heavy-duty suspension ($259); with floor-shift automatic ($443). Pacer performance package: same as Gremlin but including tach, clock and gauges ($349); with floor-shift automatic ($533). Hornet hatchback performance package: 258 engine, four-speed, soft-feel steering wheel, heavy-duty suspension ($239); with floor- shift automatic transmission ($423).

1977 AMX/Hornet coupe (AMC)

GREMLIN/HORNET/MATADOR CONVENIENCE/APPEARANCE OPTIONS: AMX package: Hornet hatchback ($799). 'X' package: Gremlin ($299); Hornet hatchback/wagon ($199). Hornet D/L package: sedan ($299); wagon ($399). Barcelona package: Matador coupe ($158). "Levi's" custom fabric trim package: Gremlin ($99); Gremlin 'X' ($50); Hornet hatchback ($49). Extra- Quiet insulation package: Grem./Hornet ($34); included with Gremlin 'X' pkg. Protection group: Grem./Hornet ($62). Interior decor/convenience group (vanity mirror, dome/reading light, clock, stowage containers, rubber mats): Gremlin ($65); Hornet ($71); Matador ($86). Visibility group (remote control left mirror, manual right mirror, day/night mirror, deluxe wipers): Grem./Hornet ($67). Visibility group (dual remote mirrors, deluxe wipers): Matador ($76). Deluxe visibility group (adds rear defogger): Gremlin, Hornet hatch/wagon ($134); Hornet sedan ($111); Mat. coupe ($154). Remote control left mirror: Grem./Hornet ($15); Matador ($16). Power steering: Grem./Hornet ($133). Power front disc brakes: Grem./Hornet ($60). Cruise control: Hornet ($60); Matador ($77). All Season air conditioning: Grem./Hornet ($451). Air conditioning package (incl. tinted glass and power steering): Grem./Hornet ($619); Matador ($557). AM radio: Grem./Hornet ($80); Matador ($81). AM/FM/Stereo four-speaker radio ($211). Rear speaker for AM radio ($21-22). Eight-track tape player and AM/FM/Stereo radio: Matador ($317). Power windows: Matador sedan/wagon ($146). Power side and tailgate windows: Matador wagon ($190). Power tailgate window: Matador wagon ($44); standard in three- seat. Console: Gremlin/Hornet hatchback ($27). Hidden compartment: Hornet hatchback ($44). Individual reclining seats: Hornet sedan/wagon ($67). Bucket seats: Matador coupe ($102). Custom vinyl door panel/bucket seat trim: Gremlin ($49); NC with bench seats or 'X' pkg. Third seat: Matador wagon ($135). Rear defogger: Gremlin, Hornet hatch/wagon ($67); Matador coupe/sedan ($78). Rear defogger, blower-type: Hornet sedan ($44). Dual horns: Grem./Hornet ($11). Light group: Grem. ($28); Hornet ($33). Sports steering wheel: Grem./Hornet hatchback ($21); Matador ($22). Soft-feel sports steering wheel: Gremlin, Hornet sedan/wagon ($36); Hornet hatchback or with 'X' pkg. ($11); Mat. ($37). Tilt steering wheel: Hornet sedan/wagon ($55); Matador ($57). Tinted glass: Gremlin ($47); Hornet ($50); Matador ($55). Two-tone paint: Hornet except Sportabout ($38); Matador ($45) except wagon ($84). Special color combinations ($23). Vinyl roof: Hornet ($99); Mat. coupe/sedan ($111). Rally side stripes: Gremlin ($41); Matador coupe ($43). Woodgrain paneling: Hornet Sportabout except 'X' ($105); incl. w/Sportabout D/L pkg.; Matador wagon ($125). Roof rack: Matador wagon ($66). Roof rack and air deflector: Hornet wagon ($80). Tailgate air deflector: Matador wagon ($25). Inside hood release: Gremlin ($15); Hornet ($25). Front bumper guards: Grem./Hornet ($16). Bumper nerfing strips: Matador coupe ($25). Door edge guards: Matador ($10). Engine block heater ($18-19). Wheel covers (set of 4): Gremlin, Hornet sedan/wagon ($34). Custom wheel covers: Gremlin, Hornet sedan/wagon ($56); Hornet hatchback, Matador ($22). Styled wheels with trim rings for D-size tires: Gremlin, Hornet sedan/wagon ($128); Hornet hatchback ($94); with 'X' or D/L pkg. ($63). Aluminum styled wheels for D-size tires: Gremlin, Hornet sedan/wagon ($223); Hornet hatchback ($189); with 'X' or D/L ($158). Aluminum styled wheels: Matador ($198). Space- Saver spare tire: Gremlin or Sportabout with regular wheels ($17); no charge with special wheels/tires. Tires: 6.45 x 14 whitewall: Gremlin ($38). 6.95 x 14: Grem. ($17). 6.95 x 14 whitewall: Gremlin ($55); Hornet ($38). D78 x 14: Grem. ($34); Hornet ($17). D78 x 14 WSW: Grem. ($72); Hornet ($55); incl. with Hornet D/L. D70 x 14 with white letters: Gremlin, Hornet hatchback/wagon 'X' ($51). DR78 x 14 steel radial: Gremlin ($148); Hornet ($131); with Hornet D/L ($76); with 'X' pkg. ($71). DR78 x 14 whitewall: Gremlin ($186); Hornet ($169); with Hornet sedan/wagon D/L ($114); with 'X' ($109). DR78 x 14 white-letter radial: Hornet ($208); with D/L ($153). DR70 x 14 radial with white letters: Gremlin ($225); Gremlin or Hornet hatch/wagon with 'X' ($148). F78 x 14 whitewall: Matador coupe/sedan ($40). FR78 x 14 WSW steel radial: Matador ($160). H78 x 14 WSW: Matador wagon ($40). HR78 x 14 WSW steel radial: Matador ($182); wagon ($160).

PACER CONVENIENCE/APPEARANCE OPTIONS: 'X' package: sedan ($379). D/L package: sedan ($349); wagon ($379). Decor package: body moldings ($77); included with D/L pkg. Extra-Quiet insulation package ($37); incl. with 'X' and D/L pkgs. Interior decor/convenience group: lighted vanity mirror, dome/reading light, clock, stowage containers, rubber mats ($82). Visibility group: remote left mirror, right mirror, day/night mirror, deluxe wipers ($67). Deluxe visibility group: same, plus rear defogger ($134). Power steering ($133). Power disc brakes ($60). Cruise control ($73). All Season air conditioning ($451). AM radio ($80). AM/FM/Stereo four-speaker radio ($211). Rear speaker ($20). 8-track tape player and AM/FM/Stereo radio ($317). Console ($27). Hidden compartment:sedan ($33). Individual reclining seats ($69); included with D/L pkg. Vinyl bucket seats ($69); standard with 'X' pkg.; no charge with D/L. "Levi's" custom fabric trim ($99); with 'X' or D/L ($30). Rear defogger with tinted glass ($67). Rear wiper/washer ($56). Light group ($30). Sports steering wheel ($21); incl. with 'X' pkg. Soft-feel sports steering wheel ($36); with 'X' pkg. ($15). Tilt steering wheel ($55). Tinted glass ($20). Door vent windows ($32). Two-tone color: sedan ($55). Special color combinations ($23). Vinyl roof ($111). Roof rack ($56). Bumper guards and nerfing strips ($56). Bumper nerfing strips (#24); incl. with D/L pkg. Bumper guards ($32). Engine block heater ($18). Wheel covers: set of 4 ($34). Styled wheels for D-size tires: ($128); with sedan 'X' pkg. ($63); incl. in D/L pkg. Aluminum styled wheels for D-size tires: ($223); with 'X' sedan ($158); with D/L wagon ($95). Tires: 6.95 x 14 whitewall, sedan ($38); D78 x 14, sedan ($17); D78 x 14 whitewall: sedan ($55); wagon ($38); no charge with D/L. DR78 x 14 radial: sedan ($131); wagon ($114); with D/L ($76). DR78 x 14 whitewall radial: sedan ($169); wagon ($152); with D/L ($114). DR70 x 14 radial with white letters: sedan ($208); wagon ($191); with D/L ($153). Tires with sedan 'X' package: DR78 x 14 whitewall steel radial ($38); DR70 x 14 white-letter radial ($77).

HISTORY: All 1977 AMC models were introduced October 5, 1976. Model year production: 213,125 (173,076 sixes, 32,491 V-8s and 7,558 Gremlin fours); production in U.S. only, 182,005. For calendar year 1977, U.S. production amounted to 156,994 units. Calendar year sales: 184,361 (2.0 percent of the industry total), down from 247,640 the year before. Model year sales (worldwide) amounted to 246,640, a 23 percent drop from 1976. The 1977 models began production at Kenosha on August 2.

Historical Footnotes: Although the Jeep business remained strong (and profitable), boosting AMC's fiscal status, passenger cars weren't selling as the 1977 model year ended. After a $46.3 million loss in fiscal 1976, the company ended 1977 in the black to the tune of almost $8.3 million, with $2.2 billion in sales. AMC raised prices almost 5 percent (average) for 1977 and experienced inventory troubles, as dealers had too many '77 models on hand. This led to price cuts and rebates at the end of 1976, in an attempt to sell off the bloated stocks of Gremlins and Pacers. The intensive marketing campaign, which included such extras as free air conditioning, didn't help enough. The restyled Gremlin slipped 12 percent, Pacer sales slid 23 percent, while the Matador, nearing its last days, fell 37 percent. The production line closed periodically, for a week at a time. AMC was feeling pressured to strengthen its role as a producer of small cars, as other automakers had been introducing compact models—and many more were to come in the next few years. Although the Gremlin had been the first domestic vehicle to go head-to-head against the imports, neither it nor other AMC models were now selling well as the downsizing era began. Analysts remained puzzled as to the reason. Though common in Europe, the agreement to purchase completed four-cylinder engines from VW/Audi was new to the U.S. Those engines were delivered intact to AMC's new plant at Richmond, Indiana for hot testing. As of January 1977, there were 1690 AMC dealer franchises. AMC's Buyer Protection Plan II now included a 24-month/24,000-mile engine/drivetrain warranty. Management received an ample shakeup. AMC president and CEO William V. Luneberg retired in May 1977, succeeded by Gerald C. Meyers. R.D. Chapin, Jr. remained as chairman, but turned over much of the responsibility to Meyers and his team.

1978 AMC

Three of the four 1977 models carried over into the 1978 model year. The Hornet name disappeared, replaced by a similar Concord compact. Instead of an option package for the Hornet, the AMX became a full-fledged model. This would be the final year for both the subcompact Gremlin and mid-size Matador. The Solid State Ignition (SSI) system introduced on some 1977 Canadian models was now standard. A new antimony battery never needed extra water. An AM/FM/stereo radio with Citizens Band and four speakers joined the option list (except on Gremlins). So did a digital clock. Standard colors were Classic Black, Alpine White, Powder Blue, Captain Blue metallic, Midnight Blue metallic, Sunshine Yellow, Sand Tan, Golden Ginger metallic, Mocha Brown metallic, Sun Orange, Khaki, British Bronze metallic, Loden green metallic, Quick Silver metallic, Firecracker Red, Autumn Red metallic, and Claret metallic.

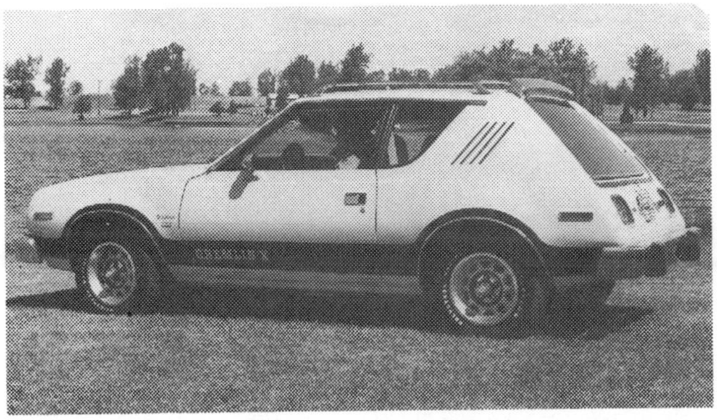

1978 Gremlin X "Levi's" liftback coupe (AMC)

GREMLIN — SERIES 40 — FOUR/SIX — Following its 1977 restyle, Gremlin turned to interior refinements for the '78 model year. These included color-keyed carpeting, a custom steering wheel, and a new instrument panel with standard AM radio. Engineering improvements cut down on engine noise and exhaust manifold rattles. Thirteen colors were available on Gremlins. Air conditioning was available with the four-cylinder engine. Custom Gremlins now sported standard whitewall B78 x 14 tires with wheel covers, plus scuff moldings. Standard equipment also included a 232 cu. in. six-cylinder engine (or 2.0-liter four) with electronic ignition, three-speed floor shift, manual front disc brakes, heater/defroster, vinyl seat upholstery, rear bumper guards, body paint stripes, locking glove box, and rocker panel moldings. Custom models also had wheel lip moldings and a parcel shelf, plus vinyl bucket seats up front; base Gremlins had bench seats front and rear. Six- cylinder Customs could come equipped with four-speed manual floor shift. Gremlin's 'X' package, offered only on Custom models, included bucket seats and interior trim in "Levi's" fabric; sport steering wheel; lower body decal stripes with contrasting pinstripes and "GREMLIN X" insignia on front door portion; "Levi's" decal; brushed aluminum instrument panel overlays; extra-quiet insulation; decals on back panel and 'C' pillar; black wiper arms, 'B' pillars and side window frames. A front sway bar and DR78 x 14 blackwall radial tires on slot styled 14 x 6 in. wheels completed the 'X' package. Early in 1978, a performance-oriented Gremlin GT hit the market, wearing fiberglass body components. Actually a $649 option package, the GT's external features included a body- colored front air dam with striping, front and rear fender flares matched to body color, black side stripes with color- keyed pinstriping, color-keyed front/rear bumper guards and nerfing strips, black grille insert, black mirrors (left one remote-controlled), hood striping, black door and quarter- window frames, and black wiper arms. GT Gremlins rode DR70 x 14 white-letter radials on spoke-style wheels with trim rings, and had a front sway bar. Bucket seats were soft-feel vinyl, with "Levi's" upholstery optional. Motoring nicctioc also included a sports steering wheel, gauge package, brushed aluminum instrument panel overlay, extra-quiet insulation package, and day/night mirror.

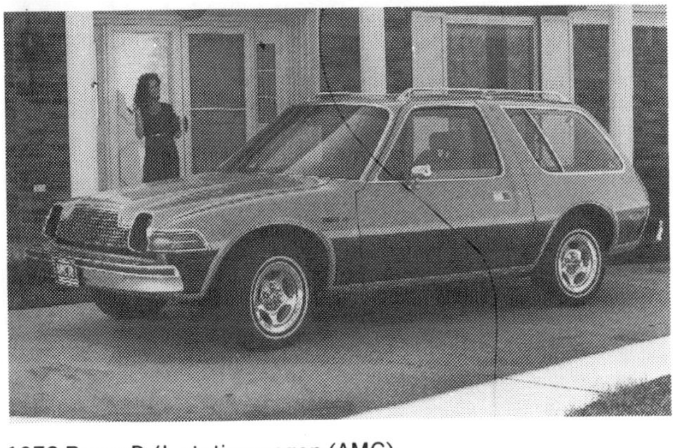

1978 Pacer D/L station wagon (AMC)

PACER — SERIES 60 — SIX/V-8 — Performance-minded Pacer buyers could now choose an optional 304 cu. in. V-8 rather than the 232 or 258 six. Again offered in hatchback sedan and wagon body styles, the panoramic Pacer also gained a new hood and grille, a longer station wagon liftgate, plus improved seat and leg room up front. The new, upward-bulging eggcrate grille, dominated by horizontal bars, had two lower rows extending full-width between the headlights; two narrower upper bars protruded

up into the hood area. Huge parking lights wrapped around, from headlights well into fender sides. Some of that new front-end restyling was done to squeeze in the V-8 engine. Various items that had formerly been optional now became standard, including individual reclining front seats, rear armrests, a day/night rear-view mirror, electric clock, custom steering wheel, woodgrain instrument panel, and color-keyed wheel covers. Also standard were a light group, cigarette lighter, extra-quiet insulation package, dual horns, inside hood release, locking glove box, rocker panel and wheel lip moldings, hood and fender moldings, heater/defroster, carpeting, and bumper nerfing strips. Base engine was the 232 six with three-speed floor shift and D78 x 14 whitewall tires. As before, Pacers featured rack-and-pinion steering and an isolated suspension design, plus an oversized passenger door. Fifteen body colors were offered, including new Quick Silver, Khaki, British Bronze, and Claret. Pacer's Sport package, available on the hatchback sedan with 258 six or 304 V-8, included soft-feel vinyl bucket seats, a sports steering wheel, DR78 x 14 blackwall tires on slot style wheels with trim rings, and two-tone paint on lower body sides. The 'X' package was dropped.

1978 Concord D/L coupe (AMC)

CONCORD — SERIES 01 — FOUR/SIX/V-8 — For 1978, the compact Hornet was reworked to become a luxurious Concord, with the same 108 in. wheelbase and four body styles: two- and four-door sedan, hatchback, or station wagon. The hatchback coupe was a particularly attractive design, with huge cargo space. Sporty too, with an optional 'X' package. Styling features included rectangular headlamps and bezels, a bright six-section crosshatch grille with clear squarish parking lights behind the outer sections, and tri-color horizontal taillamps. All Concords had front disc brakes, front sway bar, inside hood release, rocker panel moldings, hood ornament, and full wheel covers. Walnut-vinyl inserts accented instrument panels. Base Concords ran with a 232 cu. in. six and three-speed floor shift. Automatic shift and a 304 V-8 were optional, plus a four-cylinder engine (formerly on Gremlins alone) early in 1978. Sedans had Velveteen fabric bench seats in five colors; hatchbacks, soft-feel vinyl buckets. Standard equipment also included a heater/defroster, color-keyed carpeting, padded door trim panels, lighter, rear bumper guards, dual bodyside pinstripes, color-keyed scuff moldings, locking glove box, and C78 x 14 blackwall tires. Wagons carried a space-saver spare tire and held a locking hidden compartment. Hatchbacks had a sports steering wheel and flipper-type rear vent windows; four-doors, roll-down rear windows. Concord's Sport package, available on all models with 258 six or 304 V-8, included soft-feel vinyl bucket seats, with individual reclining seats (vinyl or velveteen crush fabric) optional in sedans and wagons. It also included a sport steering wheel, slot-style wheels with DR78 x 14 blackwall steel-belted radials, brushed aluminum instrument panel overlays, wide rocker panel moldings, lower bodyside tape stripe, and extra-quiet insulation. For luxury, Concord offered the D/L package on all but the hatchback. It featured individual reclining seats in velveteen crush fabric (soft-feel vinyl in wagons) plus map pockets in custom door trim panels, woodgrain instrumnent panel overlays, light group, dual horns, hood pinstripes, parcel shelf, digital clock, wide rocker moldings, bumper nerfing strips front and rear, extra-quiet insulation, day/night mirror, and D78 x 14 whitewalls with color-keyed wheel covers. D/L sedans had a landau vinyl roof and color-keyed scuff moldings, plus trunk carpeting and spare tire cover; two-doors, opera windows with silver accents. D/L wagons came with woodgrain side overlays (which could be deleted) and cargo floor skid strips. A Touring Wagon package added unique door trim panels in beige with orange/brown accents, leather-wrapped steering wheel, and wide brown/orange scuff moldings.

1978 Hornet/AMX coupe (AMC)

AMX HATCHBACK — SERIES 01 — SIX/V-8 — Reviving a name associated with performance a few years earlier, AMC tried once again to capture a slice of the youth/performance market with a new AMX, first introduced as a Hornet option in 1977. Built on the Concord platform, with an all new, slightly wedge-shaped front, AMX came with a load of appealing features, heavy on black. They included black fender flares front and rear, rear window louvers, an 'AMX' decal just to the rear of the doors, front air dam, painted bumpers with guards and nerfing strips, black scuff moldings,

dual flat black mirrors (the left one remote-controlled), color-coordinated slot wheels—plus a blacked-out grille with round signal lights and 'AMX' emblem in the center. Inside, drivers found a floor console, rally gauges with tachometer, map pockets in custom door trim panels, brushed aluminum instrument panel overlays, a black soft-feel sport steering wheel, day/night mirror, package tray, special graphics, and inside hood release. Soft-feel vinyl bucket seats came in black, blue or beige, with "Levi's" trim package optional. A brushed aluminum roof band with special insignia helped make the AMX easy to spot. Five colors were offered: Alpine White, Firecracker Red, Sunshine Yellow, Quick Silver Metallic, and Classic Black. That black AMX (a $49 option) had unique gold rally striping on the roof band, front doors and fenders, plus gold stripe on black slot-styled wheels and black windshield reveal moldings. The optional decal package with Classic Black body included gold/orange decals (black/orange with other body colors). A 258 cu. in. six with four-speed floor shift was standard. Automatic shift was required for the optional 304 cu. in. V-8. Standard AMX equipment also included front disc brakes, front sway bar, and DR78 x 14 blackwall steel-belted radial tires.

1978 Matador Barcelona Brougham coupe (AMC)

MATADOR (COUPE) — SERIES 10 — SIX/V-8 — For their final year, Matador coupes changed little in outside appearance but added some luxury features. The list includes power steering, power front disc brakes, automatic transmission, coolant recovery system, electric clock, dual horns, and a 12 in. day/night mirror. Individual reclining seats were upholstered in velveteen crush fabric. The light group consisted of a glove box light, engine compartment light, courtesy lights, and ashtray light. Matadors also had extra-quiet insulation, front/rear bumper guards, and a front sway bar. The coupe's Barcelona package added individual reclining seats in velveteen crush fabric with woven accent strips, plus custom door trim panels, a unique headliner, 24-oz. carpeting, headlight bezels painted in accent color, black trunk carpet, a rear sway bar, body-colored front/rear bumpers, bumper nerfing strips, landau padded vinyl roof, opera quarter windows with accents, and dual remote-control mirrors painted in body color. Barcelona medallions stood on fenders and glove box door. Two-tone combinations included Golden Ginger metallic on Sand Tan, or Autumn Red metallic on Claret. Standard engine was a 258 cu. in. six, with 360 V-8 optional.

1978 Matador station wagon (AMC)

MATADOR (SEDAN AND WAGON) — SERIES 80 — SIX/V-8 — Like the coupe, Matador sedans and wagons changed little outside, but added the new luxury items. Station wagon seats were upholstered in crush grain vinyl. Sedans came with a 258 cu. in. six, but wagons carried the 304 V-8 as standard equipment. Both had three-speed automatic transmission and door vent windows. Standard equipment was the same as the coupe, except for the coolant recovery system. Matadors came in 13 body colors, including new Quick Silver and Claret metallics, plus seven vinyl roof colors. The Barcelona package, formerly a coupe option only, was now available on sedans.

I.D. DATA: The 13-symbol Vehicle Identification Number (VIN), as before, was embossed on a metal plate riveted to the upper corner of the instrument panel, behind the left wiper pivot and 'A' pillar, visible through the windshield. Coding was the same as 1976-77. Symbol one ('A') indicated American Motors Corp. Model year (second symbol) changed to '8' for 1978. The third symbol was a letter for transmission type: 'A' column-shift automatic; 'C' floor-shift automatic; 'E' three-speed floor shift; 'M' four-speed floor shift. Digits indicating series (fourth symbol) were now: '0' Concord/AMX; '1' Matador coupe; '4' Gremlin; '6' Pacer; and '8' Matador sedan/wagon. The body-type digit (symbol five) changed to: '3' two-door hatchback; '5' four-door sedan; '6' two-door sedan or hatchback; '8' station wagon. Symbol six indicated model/group: '4' Gremlin four-cylinder; '5' base Gremlin; '7' Pacer, Concord, Matador or Gremlin Custom; '9' AMX. Symbol seven showed engine type: 'A' 258-6 1Bbl.; 'C' 258-6 2Bbl.; 'E' 232-6 1Bbl.; 'G' 2.0-liter four 2Bbl.; 'H' 304 V-8 2Bbl.; 'N' 360 V-8 2 Bbl. The final six digits were the sequential serial number: 100,001 to 699,999 for Kenosha manufacture; 700,001-999,999 for Brampton, Ontario. A non-removable Federal emission control information label in the engine compartment identified the engine family and gave basic tune-up specs. A non-removable safety sticker affixed to the edge of the left front door showed month and year built, the VIN, and a safety compliance statement, as well as consumer information (vehicle class, acceleration/passing figures, tire reserve load, and stopping distance). A unit body identification plate riveted to the edge of the left front door showed: vehicle Body Number (K Kenosha, followed by a six-digit sequence number); the five-digit Model Number (model year, body, and standard appointment group); a four-digit Trim Number; Paint Code Number; and a Build Sequence Number preceded by a letter showing the production line at which the car was manufactured.

GREMLIN SERIES 40 (SIX-CYLINDER)

Series Number	Body/Style Number	Body Type & Seating	Factory Price	Shipping Weight	Production Total
40	7846-5	2-dr Sed-4P	3539	2834	Note 1
40	7846-7	2-dr Cust Sed-4P	3789	2822	Note 1

GREMLIN SERIES 40 (FOUR-CYLINDER)

40	7846-4	2-dr Cust Sed-4P	3789	2556	6349

Note 1: Total model year production, 22,104 Gremlins (15,755 six- cylinder).

PACER SERIES 60

60	7866-7	2-dr Sed-4P	4048/4298	3197/3430	7411
60	7868-7	2-dr Sta Wag-4P	4193/4443	3245/3478	13,820

Note 2: Of the 21,231 Pacers produced during the model year, 2514 had a V-8 engine.

CONCORD SERIES 01

01	7803-7	2-dr Hatch-4P	3849/4099	3051/3284	2572
01	7806-7	2-dr Sed-5P	3749/3999	3029/3262	50,482
01	7805-7	4-dr Sed-5P	3849/4099	3099/3332	42,126
01	7808-7	4-dr Sta Wag-5P	4049/4299	3133/3366	23,573

Note 2: Total model year Concord production, 121,293 units (110,972 with six-cylinder engine, 6541 with V-8, and 3780 with a four).

AMX SERIES 01

01	7803-9	2-dr Hatch-4P	4649/4899	3159/3381	2540

MATADOR (COUPE) SERIES 10

10	7816-7	2-dr Cpe-5P	4799/4989	3709/3916	2006

MATADOR (SEDAN AND WAGON) SERIES 80

80	7885-7	4-dr Sed-6P	4849/5039	3718/3921	4824
80	7888-7	4-dr Sta Wag-6P	-- /5299	-- /4146	3746

Note 3: Of the total model year production of 10,576 during the model year, only 23 came with a six-cylinder engine.

FACTORY PRICE AND WEIGHT NOTE: Figure before the slash in price columns (except Gremlin) is for six-cylinder engine, after slash for V-8 engine.

ENGINES: BASE FOUR (Gremlin): Same as 1977; see 1977 specifications. BASE SIX (Gremlin, Pacer, Concord): Inline. OHV. Six-cylinder. Cast iron block. Displacement: 232 cu. in. (3.8 liters). Bore & stroke: 3.75 x 3.50 in. Compression ratio: 8.0:1. Brake horsepower: 90 at 3400 R.P.M. Torque: 168 lbs.-ft. at 1600 R.P.M. Taxable H.P.: 33.75. Seven main bearings. Hydraulic valve lifters. Carburetor: 1Bbl. Carter YF. BASE SIX (AMX, Matador sedan/coupe); OPTIONAL (Gremlin, Pacer, Concord): Inline. OHV. Six-cylinder. Cast iron block. Displacement: 258 cu. in. (4.2 liters). Bore & stroke: 3.75 x 3.90 in. Compression ratio: 8.0:1. Brake horsepower: 120 at 3600 R.P.M. Torque: 201 lbs.-ft. at 1800 R.P.M. Seven main bearings. Taxable H.P.: 33.75. Hydraulic valve lifters. Carburetor: 2Bbl. Carter BBD. BASE SIX (California models): Same as 258 cu. in. six above, but with Carter YF 7235 1Bbl. carburetor. Horsepower: 100 at 3400 R.P.M. Torque: 200 lbs.-ft. at 1600 R.P.M. OPTIONAL V-8 (Pacer, Concord, AMX): 90-degree, overhead valve V-8. Cast iron block. Displacement: 304 cu. in. (5.0 liters). Bore & stroke: 3.75 x 3.44 in. Compression ratio: 8.4:1. Brake horsepower: 130 at 3200 R.P.M. Torque: 238 lbs.-ft. at 2000 R.P.M. Taxable H.P.: 45. Five main bearings. Hydraulic valve lifters. Carburetor: 2Bbl. Motorcraft 2100. BASE V-8 (Matador wagon); OPTIONAL (Matador coupe/sedan): 90-degree, overhead valve V-8. Cast iron block. Displacement: 360 cu. in. (5.9 liters). Bore & stroke: 4.08 x 3.44 in. Compression ratio: 8.25:1. Brake horsepower: 140 at 3350 R.P.M. Torque: 278 lbs.-ft. at 2000 R.P.M. Taxable H.P.: 53.3. Five main bearings. Hydraulic valve lifters. Carburetor: 2Bbl. Motorcraft 2100.

CHASSIS DATA: Wheelbase: (Gremlin) 96 in.; (Pacer) 100 in.; (Concord/AMX) 108 in.; (Matador coupe) 114 in.; (Mat. sed/wagon) 118 in. Overall length: (Gremlin) 166.6 in.; (Pacer sedan) 172 in.; (Pacer wagon) 177 in.; (Concord) 183.6 in.; (AMX) 186 in.; (Matador coupe) 209.9in.; (Matador sedan) 218.3 in.; (Matador wagon) 219.3 in. Height: (Gremlin) 51.5 in.; (Pacer sedan) 52.8 in.; (Pacer wagon) 53.2 in.; (Concord) 51.3-51.7 in.; (AMX) 52.2 in.; (Matador coupe) 51.6 in.; (Matador sedan) 53.9 in.; (Matador wagon) 56 in. Front Tread: (Gremlin/Concord) 57.5 in.; (Pacer) 61.4 in.; (Concord) 57.6 in.; (Matador) 59.6 in. Rear Tread: (Gremlin/Hornet) 57.1 in.; (Pacer) 60 in.; (Concord) 57.1- 57.5 in. (Matador) 60.6 in. Standard Tires: (Gremlin) B78 x 14 whitewall; (Pacer) D78 x 14; (Concord) C78 x 14 except with D/L package, D78 x 14; (AMX) DR78 x 14; (Matador coupe/sedan) F78 x 14; (Matador wagon) H78 x 14.

TECHNICAL: Three-speed manual floor-shift transmission was standard on Gremlin base six, Concords and Pacers. Four-speed floor- shift was standard on Gremlin Custom six, Gremlin four, and AMX. Matadors came with Torque Command three-speed column- shift automatic; optional on others. Automatic shift gear ratios: (1st) 2.45:1; (2nd) 1.45:1; (Rev) 2.20:1. Steering: (Pacer) rack and pinion; (others) recirculating ball. Suspension: independent front coil springs (Pacer springs mounted between the two control arms); semi- elliptic rear leaf springs except (Matador) coil springs. Brakes: front discs; rear drums. Fuel tank: (Gremlin) 21 gal. exc. four-cylinder, 13 gal.; (Pacer) 20 gal.; (Concord/AMX) 22 gal.

DRIVETRAIN OPTIONS: 258 cu. in. six-cylinder engine: Gremlin/Pacer/Concord ($120). 304 cu. in. V-8, 2Bbl.: Pacer/Concord/AMX ($233). 360 cu. in. V-8, 2Bbl.: Matador sedan/coupe ($190). Four- speed manual floor shift: Gremlin/Pacer/Concord ($111). Torque-Command automatic transmission, column shift: Gremlin ($270); Pacer/Concord ($296). Torque-Command with floor shift lever: Gremlin ($294); Pacer/Concord/AMX ($320); Matador coupe with V-8 and bucket seats ($70). Twin Grip differential ($55-$59). Heavy-duty engine cooling system ($29-$37) but standard with air conditioning. Maximum cooling system: Matador V-8 ($48); Matador V-8 with air ($19). Auxiliary automatic transmission oil cooler: Matador ($34). Heavy-duty suspension ($31-$36); incl. front sway bar on Gremlin/Pacer, rear on Matador. Front sway bar: Gremlin/Pacer ($18) but incl. with radial tires. Rear sway bar: Matador ($18). Air-adjustable shock absorbers: Matador ($44-$48). H.D. 70-amp battery ($17-$19). California emission system ($74). High altitude package ($23).

GREMLIN/CONCORD/MATADOR CONVENIENCE/APPEARANCE OPTIONS: 'X' package: Gremlin ($249). GT package: Gremlin ($649). Concord D/L package ($200). Concord Sport package: hatch ($289); sed/wag ($379). Barcelona package: Matador coupe ($849); Matador sedan ($699). "Levi's" trim package: AMX ($49). 'AMX' decal pkg. (black/orange decal on hood and liftgate): AMX ($49). Extra Quiet insulation package: Gremlin/Concord/AMX ($45); included with Concord Sport and D/L pkg. Protection group: Gremlin ($42); Concord ($27). Interior decor/convenience group: Gremlin ($69); Concord ($79); Concord D/L ($54); AMX/Matador ($59). Gauge package: Gremlin Cust. six ($75); Concord ($99). Visibility group (remote control left mirror, manual right mirror, day/night mirror, intermittent wipers): Gremlin/Concord ($71). Visibility group (dual remote mirrors, deluxe wipers): Matador ($81). Remote control left mirror ($16- $17). Intermittent wipers ($30-$32). Power steering ($141-$147). Power front disc brakes ($64). Cruise control ($99); N/A on Gremlin four. Air conditioning system: Grem./Conc./AMX ($478). Air conditioning package (incl. tinted glass and power steering): Gremlin ($669); Conc./AMX ($679); Matador ($590). AM radio ($80-$81). AM/FM/Stereo four-speaker radio: Gremlin ($144); others ($224). AM/CB Radio: Gremlin ($119); others ($199) AM/FM/CB Radio ($299); N/A on Gremlin. Rear speaker for AM radio ($22-23). Tape player and AM/FM/Stereo radio: Matador ($336). Digital clock: Gremlin/Concord ($25). Tachometer: Gremlin four ($49). Power windows: Matador sedan/wagon ($155). Power side and tailgate windows: Matador wagon ($202). Power tailgate window: Mat. wagon ($47); standard in three-seat. Console: Gremlin/Concord ($29). Hidden compartment: Concord hatch/AMX ($31). Individual reclining seats: Matador (NC). Vinyl bucket seats: Gremlin ($49); Concord ($69); Concord D/L and Matador coupe (NC). Third seat: Matador wagon ($143). Stowage/litter containers ($10). Rear defroster ($81-$88). Dual horns: Gremlin/Concord ($12). Light group: Concord/AMX ($30). Sports steering wheel: Gremlin Cust./Concord/Matador ($20). Soft-feel sports steering wheel: Gremlin Cust., Conc. sed/wag, Matador ($31); Gremlin 'X', Concord hatch or Sport pkg. ($11). Tilt steering wheel: Concord ($64); Matador ($67). Tinted glass ($52-$64). Two-tone paint: Concord D/L ($75); Matador ($48). Delete two-tone: Matador Barcelona sedan (deduct $100). Special color combinations ($24) except AMX Classic Black ($49). Vinyl roof: Concord ($105); Matador ($118). Rally side stripes: Gremlin ($43); Mat. coupe ($46). Woodgrain wagon paneling: Concord ($75); Matador ($133). Delete woodgrain from Concord D/L wagon (deduct $75). Roof rack: Gremlin ($59); Matador wagon ($84). Roof rack and air deflector: Concord wagon ($85). Tailgate air deflector: Gremlin (24); Matador ($27). Inside hood release: Gremlin ($16). Front bumper guards: Gremlin/Concord ($19). Bumper nerfing strips: Concord ($34). Side scuff molding: base Gremlin ($29). Protective innercoating ($95) except Matador ($106). Door edge guards: Matador ($11). Locking gas cap ($7). Engine block heater ($19-$20). Wheel covers (set of 4): Gremlin ($36). Custom wheel covers ($23); Styled wheels for D-size tires ($136) except AMX, 'X' or Sport pkg. ($71). Aluminum styled wheels ($236) except AMX, 'X' or Sport pkg. ($171). Space-Saver spare tire: Gremlin or Concord with regular wheels ($18); no charge with special wheels/tires. Tires: B78 x 14 whitewall: Gremlin (NC). D78 x 14: Grem. (NC); Conc. ($18). D78 x 14 whitewall: Grem. ($36); Conc. ($63). DR78 x 14 SBR: Gremlin ($112); Concord ($139); with Conc. D/L ($76); Gremlin Cust. 'X' (NC). DR78 x 14 white SBR: Gremlin ($157); Concord ($184); Conc. D/L ($121); AMX, Conc. Sport, Gremlin 'X' ($45). DR78 x 14 white-letter SBR: Gremlin Cust. ($172); Concord ($199); Conc. D/L ($136); AMX, Sport, 'X' pkg. ($60);. DR78 x 14 white GBR: Gremlin ($36); Concord ($159); Concord Sport ($165); Conc. D/L ($96). F78 x 14 whitewall: Matador coupe/sedan ($48). FR78 x 14 white SBR: Matador ($175). H78 x 14 whitewall: Matador wagon ($48). HR78 x 14 white SBR: Matador ($198); wagon ($175).

PACER CONVENIENCE/APPEARANCE OPTIONS: Sport package ($165); N/A on wagon or w/232 engine. Interior decor/convenience group ($59). Visibility group: remote left mirror, right mirror, intermittent wipers ($61). Left remote mirror ($16). Gauge package ($99). Intermittent wipers ($30). Power steering ($147). Power disc brakes ($64). Cruise control ($99). Air conditioning ($478). Air conditioning pkg.: tinted glass and power steering ($679). AM radio ($80). AM/FM/Stereo four-speaker radio ($224). AM/CB Radio ($199). AM/FM/CB Radio ($299). Rear speaker ($22). Tape player and AM/FM/Stereo radio ($336). Console ($29). Hidden compartment:hatch ($35). Individual reclining seats: velveteen crush or reflection print fabric, or soft- feel vinyl (NC). Vinyl bucket seats (NC). Stowage/litter compartment ($10). Rear defroster ($81). Rear wiper/washer ($59). Sports steering wheel ($20); incl. with Sport pkg. Soft-feel sports steering wheel ($31); with Sport pkg. ($11). Tilt steering wheel ($64). Tinted glass ($58). Door vent windows ($34). Two-tone color: hatch ($84). Special color combinations ($24). Woodgrain wagon paneling ($111). Protective inner coating ($95). Vinyl roof ($118). Roof rack ($59). Bumper guards ($38). Locking gas cap ($7). Custom wheel covers ($23). Styled wheels ($136); with Sport hatch pkg. ($71). Aluminum styled wheels ($236); with Sport hatch ($171). Tires: DR78 x 14 SBR ($76). DR78 x 14 white SBR ($121). DR78 x 14 white-letter SBR ($136). DR78 x 14 white GBR ($96). E78 x 14 whitewall ($18). ER78 x 14 SBR ($94). ER78 x 14 white SBR ($139). ER78 x 14 white-letter SBR ($154). Tires with Sport hatchback package: DR78 x 14 white SBR ($45); DR78 x 14 white-letter SBR ($60); ER78 x 14 ($18); ER78 x 14 white ($63); ER78 x 14 white-letter ($78).

HISTORY: Introduced: September 9, 1977 except the new Concord, in October; modified Gremlins and Concords debuted later. Model year production: (U.S.) 137,860, for 1.55 percent of the industry total; North American production for U.S. market, 175,204 units (10,129 four-cylinder, 145,467 six- cylinder and 19,608 V-8). Calendar year production: (U.S.) 164,351, led by Concord with 108,414 cars manufactured. Calendar year sales by U.S. dealers: 170,739 (1.8 percent of industry total).

Historical Footnotes: AMC's fiscal picture improved again during the 1978 model year, with net earnings at their highest point since 1973. Much of the company's strength, however, continued to stem from its Jeep subsidiary. Except for the new Concord, North American production slipped substantially in every division. Gremlin prices were cut in November 1977. Promise for the future came in the form of negotiations with Regie Nationale des Usines Renault, the French firm that produced the Renault. The arrangement reached between the two companies in January 1979 would permit AMC to distribute the Renault Le Car, and perhaps allow Renault to distribute AMC Jeep vehicles. Far more significant, though, was the announcement that AMC planned to produce a joint- venture Renault vehicle in the United States. Gerald C. Meyers took over as the new chairman and CEO at AMC, while W. Paul Tippett stepped into his former role as president and chief operating officer. James L. Tolley moved from PR director at Chevrolet to vice-president of public relations at AMC. Passenger car operations were consolidated at Kenosha during the year. The Milwaukee body plant turned to stamping, while the Brampton, Ontario facility converted to Jeep production. Four-cylinder engines had first been purchased intact from Volkswagenwerk. During 1977, AMC initiated a plan to assemble the engines itself, on an assembly line bought from VW. But as the 1978 model year began, AMC contracted instead to purchase "Iron Duke" fours from Pontiac.

1979 AMC

American Motors left the mid-size market by abandoning the Matador, which had been selling poorly. Meanwhile, the Gremlin was replaced by a similar, but more stylish, subcompact, the new Spirit; and the performance-oriented AMX moved to the shorter

Spirit chassis. Spirit, Concord and Pacer base models included as standard equipment a high-pressure compact spare tire, manual front disc brakes, inside hood release, lighted ashtray, full wheel covers, rear bumper guards, custom steering wheel, and color-keyed 12-oz. carpeting. A new, upscale trimlevel was added: the Limited. This signaled AMC's move away from austerity and toward a touch of luxury, even in economy cars. Standard colors for all models (except AMX) were Olympic White, Classic Black, Quick Silver metallic, Cumberland Green metallic, Wedgewood Blue, Starboard Blue metallic, Khaki, British Bronze metallic, Saxon Yellow, Morocco Buff, Alpaca Brown metallic, Sable Brown metallic, Firecracker Red, Russet metallic, and Bordeaux metallic. Torque Command transmissions (supplied by Chrysler) with V-8 engines received a lockup torque converter. Over two-thirds of AMC passenger cars had air conditioning.

1979 Spirit Limited liftback coupe (AMC)

SPIRIT — SERIES 40 — FOUR/SIX — Gremlin's more luxurious replacement kept the same engine choices and basic design as its subcompact predecessor, but with much larger rear side windows on the two-door sedan. New quad rectangular headlamps flanked a clean four-row, horizontally ribbed grille with center medallion. Clear, wide parking lights sat below the headlights. Horizontal amber reflectors were mounted at the forward end of the front fenders, 'Spirit' emblems at their rear. Slightly rounded rectangular taillamps held inset backup lights. Aluminum bumpers had black end caps. Joining that familiar sedan was a good-looking two-door Liftback coupe. Front styling was similar, but the rear end held extra-wide four-section taillamps that stretched from the license plate to the outer edge of the panel. The liftback's big pop-up hatch sloped much more sharply than the sedan's back end. Basic engine was the Volkswagen/Audi 121 cu. in. four-cylinder, with 232 and 258 cu. in. sixes optional. Liftbacks could also have a 304 V-8. A four-speed floor shift transmission was standard; floor or column shift automatics optional. A three-speed manual shift was available with the 232 six, at reduced price. Base Spirit standard equipment included blackwall C78 x 14 tires, vinyl bucket seats, four-spoke steering wheel, lighter, locking glove box, folding rear seat, spare tire cover, dual paint stripes, plus moldings for wheel lip, drip rail, hood front edge, windshield surround and rocker panels. Liftbacks included a front sway bar to improve handling. The DL model added custom bucket seats in Caberfae Corduroy fabric or Sport Vinyl, walnut burl woodgrain instrument panel overlay, woodgrain steering wheel, day/night mirror, digital clock, extra-quiet insulation, dual horns, courtesy lights, package shelf, folding split rear seatback, front/rear bumper guards, and whitewall tires with color-keyed styled wheel covers. For more luxury, Spirit's Limited included leather bucket seats, an AM radio, power door locks, power steering, power liftback release, dual remote mirrors, light and visibility groups, convenience and protection groups, tilt steering wheel, full-length console with center armrest, 18- oz. carpeting, and P195/75R14 glass-belted whitewalls. DL and Limited liftbacks could also have the sporty GT package, which included a black full-length console, black leather-wrapped steering wheel, black instrument panel with woodgrain overlay, woodgrain door panel accents, tachometer, black bumpers with nerfing strips and guards, twin black remote mirrors, black exterior trim moldings, black grille insert and headlight bezels, and black rear venturi area. GT models carried P195/75R14 steel-belted radials on spoke style wheels; V-8s with manual shift even had a Performance Tuned exhaust sound. 'GT' emblems were placed below the 'Spirit' badges on front fenders. For handling to match the sharp looks, a GT Rally Tuned Suspension Package added a tuned front sway bar, rear sway bar, heavy-duty adjustable Gabriel "Strider" shocks, tuned strut rod bushings and rear spring iso-clamp pads, Hi-Control rear leaf springs, unique steering gears, and heavy-duty brakes.

1979 Hornet/AMX coupe (AMC)

AMX — SERIES 40 — SIX/V-8 — AMX liftbacks entered the 1979 model year sitting on a short (96 in.) Spirit wheelbase, rather than the previous Concord platform. "Expect to be noticed," the factory declared. To make sure, every AMX had front/rear black bumpers with guards and nerfing strips, a front air dam and rear deck spoiler

with accent stripes, front/rear fender flares, a new rectangular blackout grille with center 'AMX' emblem, twin remote mirrors, and Turbocast II aluminum wheels with white- letter ER60 x 14 radial tires. Eye-catching graphics included 'AMX' decals on doors and quarters, plus a huge flame decal on the hood. Quad headlamps sat over clear rectangular signal/parking lights. Inside, drivers sat in Sport Vinyl or Caberfae Corduroy bucket seats, gripped a leather-wrapped steering wheel, watched a full gauge array with brushed aluminum instrument panel overlays, and enjoyed a center console with four-speed floor shift. Standard engine was the 258 cu. in. six (304 V-8 optional) with four-speed floor shift. A Rally Tuned suspension system helped handling, while V-8s with manual shift included a performance-tuned exhaust sound. That suspension included Gabriel "Strider" shocks, front sway bar, heavy-duty rear sway bar, and Hi-Control rear leaf springs. AMX colors were Olympic White, Classic Black, Wedgewood Blue, Saxon Yellow, Morocco Buff, and Firecracker Red.

1979 Pacer Limited liftback coupe (AMC)

PACER — SERIES 60 — SIX/V-8 — Except for an upright hood ornament above the upward- bulging grille, changes to the Pacer hatchback sedan and wagon consisted mainly of a larger (258 cu. in.) base engine and the addition of a Limited upgrade to the basic DL model. Standard DL equipment included individual reclining seats in Caberfae Corduroy or Sport Vinyl, windsplit molding, front/rear bumper guards, folding rear seat back, extra-quiet insulation, day/night inside mirror, electric clock, dual horns, courtesy lights, two-speed wiper/washers, custom steering wheel with woodgrain overlays, and woodgrain-overlay instrument panel. DL models had color-keyed wheel covers, P195/75R14 whitewall glass-belted radials, front sway bar, and color-keyed wide scuff moldings. Bucket seats upholstered in Caberfae Corduory fabric were also offered on DL Pacers. Beyond those features, the Limited included power steering, front windows and door locks, an AM radio, leather reclining seats with beige corduroy accents, woodgrain tilt steering wheel, dual remote-control mirrors, visibility and convenience groups, light and protection groups, folding center armrest, 18-oz. color-keyed carpeting, and color-keyed styled wheel covers. In addition to the standard colors, Pacers were available with Misty Beige clearcoat and in six two-tone combinations. Four-speed manual shift was standard (with floor lever); column- or floor-shift automatic optional. Once again, a 304 cu. in. V-8 was available, which required power steering and brakes. According to industry sources, only 184 Pacers had a sunroof; 347 had vinyl tops.

1979 Concord coupe (AMC)

CONCORD — SERIES 01 — FOUR/SIX/V-8 — Front-end styling changed appreciably on the compact, luxurious Concord, with wide clear parking/signal lights setting below quad rectangular headlamps. The restyled formal grille was considerably taller, with seven vertical bars. Bright aluminum bumpers had black end caps and guards. Standard engine remained the 232 cu. in. six, but a 258 six, 304 V-8 and 121 four were all optional. Four-speed manual floor shift was standard; column-shift automatic transmission optional. Concords now came in three trim levels: base, DL, and Limited (no Limited for the hatchback body). Base Concords were equipped with a front sway bar, lighted ashtray, sport vinyl notched bench seat (Striped Knit fabric available with automatic transmission), color-keyed 12- oz. carpeting, full wheel covers, dual bodyside pinstripes, hood ornament, and moldings for drip rail, wheel lip, hood front edge, and windshield surround. Tires were D78 x 14 blackwalls. DL versions had individual reclining seats in Velveteen Crush fabric or Sport Vinyl, as well as a day/night mirror, digital clock, extra-quiet insulation, dual horns, courtesy lights, under-hood light, walnut burl woodgrain instrument panel overlay, custom steering wheel with woodgrain overlays, custom headliner and sunvisors, package shelf, front/rear bumper guards, color-keyed wheel covers, and whitewall tires. DL sedans and hatchbacks also sported a landau vinyl roof; wagons had woodgrain bodyside overlays. Genuine leather individual reclining seats with beige corduroy accents came on the plush Limiteds, as did an AM radio, power door locks, twin remote mirrors, adjustable tilt woodgrain steering wheel, light group, visibility group, convenience and protection groups, styled wheel covers, 18-oz. carpeting, and P195/75R14 whitewall glass-belted radials (except hatchbacks).

I.D. DATA: The 13-symbol Vehicle Identification Number (VIN) again was embossed on a metal plate riveted to the top left surface of the instrument panel, visible through the windshield. Coding was the same as 1976-78. Model year code (symbol two) changed to '9' for 1979. Series code (symbol four) now included: '0' Concord; '4' Spirit/AMX; '6' Pacer. The model/group code (symbol six) now included: '0' base model; '5' DL; '7' Limited; and '9' AMX.

SPIRIT SERIES 40

Series Number	Body/Style Number	Body Type & Seating	Price Four/Six	Shipping Weight	Production Total
40	7943-7	2-dr Lift-4P	3999/4049	2545/2762	Note 1
40	7946-7	2-dr Sed-4P	3899/3949	2489/2706	Note 1

SPIRIT DL

40	7943-7	2-dr Lift-4P	4199/4249	2635/2852	Note 1
40	7946-7	2-dr Sed-4P	4099/4149	2579/2796	Note 1

SPIRIT LIMITED

40	7943-7	2-dr Lift-4P	5199/5249	2732/2949	Note 1
40	7946-7	2-dr Sed-4P	5099/5149	2676/2893	Note 1

AMX SERIES 40

Series Number	Body/Style Number	Body Type & Seating	Price Six/V-8	Shipping Weight	Production Total
40	7943-9	2-dr Lift-4P	5899/6149	2899/3092	3657

Note 1: Total Spirit/AMX model year production, 52,714 cars (16,237 four-cylinder, 36,241 six-cylinder, 3893 V-8).

PACER DL SERIES 60

60	7966-7	2-dr Hatch-4P	4699/5177	3133/3360	2863
60	7968-7	2-dr Sta Wag-4P	4849/5327	3170/3397	7352

PACER LIMITED

60	7966-7	2-dr Hatch-4P	5699/6177	3218/3445	Note 2
60	7968-7	2-dr Sta Wag-4P	5849/6327	3255/3482	Note 2

Note 2: Production totals above include both DL and Limited models. Of the 10,215 Pacers made during the model year, 1014 carried a V-8 engine.

CONCORD SERIES 01

01	7903-7	2-dr Hatch-4P	4149/4399	2888/3095	2331
01	7906-7	2-dr Sed-5P	4049/4299	2873/3080	40,110
01	7905-7	4-dr Sed-5P	4149/4399	2939/3146	40,134
01	7908-7	4-dr Sta Wag-5P	4349/4599	2977/3184	20,278

CONCORD DL

01	7903-7	2-dr Hatch-4P	4448/4698	3003/3210	Note 3
01	7906-7	2-dr Sed-5P	4348/4598	2982/3189	Note 3
01	7905-7	4-dr Sed-5P	4448/4698	3040/3247	Note 3
01	7908-7	4-dr Sta Wag-5P	4648/4898	3072/3279	Note 3

CONCORD LIMITED

01	7906-7	2-dr Sed-5P	5348/5598	3090/3297	Note 3
01	7905-7	4-dr Sed-5P	5448/5698	3146/3253	Note 3
01	7908-7	4-dr Sta Wag-5P	5648/5898	3177/3384	Note 3

Note 3: Production totals shown include base, DL and Limited models. Total Concord model year production, 102,853 (6355 four-cylinder, 91,842 six-cylinder and 4656 V-8). Note 4: Four-cylinder engine was offered on Concords at six-cylinder price.

FACTORY PRICE AND WEIGHT NOTE: Figure before the slash is for six- cylinder engine, after slash for V-8 engine; except Spirit, which is four-cylinder and six-cylinder.

ENGINES: BASE FOUR (Spirit); OPTIONAL (Concord hatchback/sedan): Inline. Overhead cam. Four-cylinder. Cast iron block; cast aluminum alloy head. Displacement: 121 cu. in. (2.0 liters). Bore & stroke: 3.41 x 3.32 in. Compression ratio: 8.2:1. Brake horsepower: 80 at 5000 R.P.M. Torque: 105 lbs.-ft. at 2800 R.P.M. Five main bearings. Solid valve lifters. Carburetor: 2Bbl. Holley 5210. BASE SIX (Concord); OPTIONAL (Spirit): Inline. OHV. Six-cylinder. Cast iron block. Displacement: 232 cu. in. (3.8 liters). Bore & stroke: 3.75 x 3.50 in. Compression ratio: 8.0:1. Brake horsepower: 90 at 3400 R.P.M. Torque: 168 lbs.-ft. at 1600 R.P.M. Seven main bearings. Hydraulic valve lifters. Carburetor: 1Bbl. Carter YF. BASE SIX (AMX, Pacer); OPTIONAL (Spirit, Concord): Inline. OHV. Six-cylinder. Cast iron block. Displacement: 258 cu. in. (4.2 liters). Bore & stroke: 3.75 x 3.90 in. Compression ratio: 8.3:1. Brake horsepower: 110 at 3200 R.P.M. Torque: 210 lbs.-ft. at 1800 R.P.M. Seven main bearings. Hydraulic valve lifters. Carburetor: 2Bbl. Carter BBD. OPTIONAL SIX (California models): Same as 258 cu. in. six above, but with 1Bbl. Carter YF carburetor. Horsepower: 100 at 3400 R.P.M. Torque: 200 lbs.-ft. at 1600 R.P.M. Compression Ratio: 8.1:1. OPTIONAL V-8 (Spirit Liftback, AMX, Pacer, Concord): 90-degree, overhead valve V-8. Cast iron block. Displacement: 304 cu. in. (5.0 liters). Bore & stroke: 3.75 x 3.44 in. Compression ratio: 8.4:1. Brake horsepower: 125 at 3200 R.P.M. Torque: 220 lbs.-ft. at 2400 R.P.M. Five main bearings. Hydraulic valve lifters. Carburetor: 2Bbl. Motorcraft 2100.

CHASSIS DATA: Wheelbase: (Spirit/AMX) 96 in.; (Pacer) 100 in.; (Concord) 108 in. Overall length: (Spirit/AMX liftback) 168.5 in.; (Spirit sedan) 166.8 in.; (Pacer hatchback) 172.7 in.; (Pacer wagon) 177.7 in.; (Concord) 186 in. Height: (Spirit/AMX) 51.6 in.; (Pacer hatch) 52.8 in.; (Pacer wagon) 53.1 in.; (Concord) 51.1-51.6 in. Front Tread: (Spirit/AMX) 58.1 in.; (Pacer) 61.2 in.; (Concord) 57.6 in. Rear Tread: (Spirit/AMX/Concord) 57.5 in.; (Pacer) 60.0 in. Standard Tires: (Spirit) C78 x 14; (AMX) ER60 x 14 Flexten belted radial OWL; (Pacer) P195/75R14 GBR. (Concord) D78 x 14 except Limited, P195/75R14 GBR.

TECHNICAL: Four-speed manual transmission with floor shift was standard. Three-speed available on Spirit. Column-shift automatic available on Spirit/Concord/Pacer. Floor-shift automatic available on Spirit/AMX/Pacer. Three-speed manual shift gear ratios: (1st) 2.99:1; (2nd) 1.75:1; (3rd) 1.00:1; (Rev) 3.17:1. Four-speed gear ratios: (1st) 3.98:1; (2nd) 2.14:1; (3rd) 1.42:1; (4th) 1.00:1; (Rev) 3.99:1. Standard axle ratio: (Spirit four) 3.08:1 with four-speed, 3.31:1 with automatic; (Spirit six) 2.53:1 except 232 with three-speed, 2.73:1; (Spirit/AMX V-8) 2.87:1 except 2.56:1 with automatic, w/o Twin-Grip differential; (AMX six) 2.53:1; (Pacer six) 2.53:1; (Concord four) 3.31:1 w/four-speed, 3.58:1 w/automatic; (Concord six) 2.53:1 except wagon w/automatic, 2.73:1; (Pacer/Concord V-8) 2.56:1 exc. 2.87:1 w/Twin-Grip. Steering: (Pacer) rack and pinion; (others) recirculating ball. Suspension: independent front coil springs; semi- elliptic rear leaf springs. Brakes: front disc, rear drum. Fuel tank: (Spirit four sedan) 13 gal.; (Spirit/AMX/Pacer) 21 gal.; (Concord) 22 gal.

DRIVETRAIN OPTIONS: 232 cu. in. six-cylinder engine: Spirit ($50). 258 cu. in. six-cylinder engine: Spirit/Concord ($130). 304 cu. in. V-8 ($250); N/A in Spirit sedan. Three-speed manual floor shift: Spirit with 232 six (deduct $50). Torque- Command automatic transmission, column shift: Spirit six ($296); Pacer/Concord ($323). Torque-Command with floor shift: Spirit ($321); Pacer ($348); AMX ($296). Twin Grip differential ($63). Heavy-duty engine cooling system: Pacer ($31); Concord/AMC ($39) but standard with air conditioning. Maximum cooling system: Concord V-8 ($59); Concord V-8 with air ($20). Auxiliary automatic transmission oil cooler: Pacer/Concord V-8 ($36). Handling package (unique front sway bar, rear sway bar): Concord six ($30). Air shock absorbers, rear: Concord ($98). Heavy-duty shock absorbers: Pacer/Concord ($14). H.D. 70-amp battery ($18); N/A on Spirit; 56-amp with Pacer V-8. Cold climate group (H.D. battery and alternator, engine block heater): Pacer/Concord/AMX ($96); with air cond. or rear defroster ($38). California emission system ($78).

SPIRIT/CONCORD/AMX CONVENIENCE/APPEARANCE OPTIONS: Spirit liftback GT package ($469); with Limited ($200-$469). Spirit liftback GT rally tuned suspension package ($99). Extra Quiet insulation package: Concord ($48). Protection group: Concord ($87); Conc. DL ($21); AMX ($27). Convenience group incl. headlight-on buzzer, intermittent wipers, dual vanity mirrors ($75). Gauge package (incl. parcel shelf): Spirit six/V-8 ($104); Spirit GT ($52). Visibility group (remote control left/right mirrors, day/night mirror): Spirit/Concord ($62); DL models ($50); std. on Spirit GT. Remote control left mirror: Spirit/Concord ($17). Power steering ($152-$158); std. on Ltd. models. Power front disc brakes ($70). Cruise control ($104). Air conditioning system: Spirit V-8/Concord/AMX ($513). Air conditioning package (incl. tinted glass and power steering): Spirit/Concord/AMX ($722-$731); N/A on Concord Ltd. AM radio ($84); std. on Concord Ltd. AM/FM/Stereo four-speaker radio: Concord/AMX ($236); Concord Ltd. exc. hatch. ($152). AM/FM/CB Radio ($314) exc. Ltd. ($230). Rear speaker for AM radio ($24). Digital clock: Spirit/Concord ($40) but std. on Ltd. Tachometer: Spirit/Concord ($52); std. with Spirit GT pkg. Power door locks: Spirit/AMX ($72); std. on Ltd. Power liftback release: Spirit ($30); std. on Ltd. Caberfae corduroy fabric bucket seats: AMX (NC). Bench seat: Spirit sedan (NC). Bucket seats: Spirit (NC). Console: Spirit ($75); std. w/GT. Hidden compartment: Concord hatch ($33). Rear defroster ($89). Dual horns: Spirit/Concord ($13); std. on DL and Ltd. Light group: Spirit ($45); Spirit DL, AMX ($35); Concord ($49); Concord DL ($39); std. on Ltd models. Leather-wrapped sport steering wheel: Concord ($49) exc. Ltd. ($20). Woodgrain steering wheel: Concord DL ($29); std. on Ltd. Tilt steering wheel ($72); std. on Ltd. models. Tinted glass ($57-$60). Two- tone paint: Spirit lift ($65); Concord DL and Ltd. ($100). Special color combinations: ($26) exc. AMX. Pop-up moon roof ($178). Rally side stripes: Spirit ($46). Delete woodgrain from Concord DL wagon (deduct $75). Roof rack: Spirit sed. ($62); Concord wagon ($90). Tailgate air deflector: Spirit sed. ($26). Front bumper guards: Concord ($21); std. on DL and Ltd. Side scuff molding: AMX ($31). Protective inner coating ($100) exc. Spirit. Locking gas cap ($8) exc. Spirit. Styled wheel covers: Concord ($35); N/A on Ltd. Color-keyed wheel covers: Concord DL exc. wgn. ($45); std. on Ltd. Spoke style 14 x 6 in. wheels with trim rings: Concord ($145); Concord Ltd. exc. hatch. ($100). Turbine forged aluminum wheels: Concord ($300); Concord Ltd. except hatch. ($255). Tires: C78 x 14 whitewall: base Spirit ($48). D78 x 14: base Spirit ($19); D78 x 14 whitewall: Spirit ($67); Spirit DL ($19); Conc. ($48). P195/75R14 GBR: Spirit ($120); Spirit DL ($72); Concord ($101); Conc. DL ($53). P195/75R14 white GBR: Spirit ($168); Spirit DL ($120); Concord ($149); Conc. DL ($101). P195/75R14 SBR: Spirit ($168); Spirit DL ($120); Spirit Ltd. (NC); Concord ($149); Conc. DL ($101); Conc. Ltd. sed/wgn (NC). P195/75R14 white SBR: Spirit ($216); Spirit DL (168); Spirit Ltd. (48); Concord ($197); Conc. DL ($149); Concord Ltd. sed/wgn ($48). DR70 x 14 Flexten radial: Spirit ($238); Spirit DL ($190); Spirit Ltd. ($70); Concord ($219); Conc. DL ($171); Conc. Ltd. ($70). DR70 x 14 OWL Flexten radial: Spirit ($302); Spirit DL ($254); Spirit Ltd. ($134); Concord ($283); Conc. DL ($235); Conc. Ltd. ($134).

PACER CONVENIENCE/APPEARANCE OPTIONS: Convenience group: headlight-on buzzer, intermittent wipers, dual lighted vanity mirrors ($75); std. on Ltd. Visibility group: remote left and right mirrors ($50); std. on Ltd. Left remote mirror ($17). Gauge package ($129); N/A w/Ltd. or center armrest. Power steering ($158); std. on Ltd. Power disc brakes ($70). Cruise control ($104). Air conditioning ($513). Air conditioning pkg. with tinted glass and power steering ($734); N/A w/Ltd. AM radio ($84); std. w/Ltd. AM/FM/Stereo four-speaker radio ($236); w/Ltd. ($152). AM/FM/CB Stereo Radio ($314); w/Ltd. ($230). Rear speaker ($24). Tape player and AM/FM/Stereo radio ($353); w/Ltd. ($269). Center armrest ($49); std. on Ltd. Hidden compartment: hatch ($37). Caberfae corduroy bucket seats (NC). Power door locks ($72). Power window and door locks ($194). Light group ($39); std. on Ltd. Rear defroster ($89). Rear wiper/washer ($62). Leather-wrapped sport steering wheel ($49); w/Ltd. ($20). Woodgrain steering wheel ($29); incl. w/Ltd. Tilt steering wheel ($72); std. w/Ltd. Tinted glass ($63). Door vent windows ($36). Two-tone color: black rocker panels deleted ($65). Special color combinations ($26); N/A w/two- tone or Ltd. Misty beige clearcoat: Ltd. ($60). Woodgrain wagon paneling ($117). Protective inner coating ($100). Pop-up moon roof: hatch ($178). Vinyl roof: hatch ($124). Roof rack ($62). Locking gas cap ($8). Styled wheel covers ($35); N/A on Ltd. Spoke style 14 x 6 in. wheels ($145); w/Ltd. ($100). Turbine forged aluminum 14 x 6 in. wheels ($300); w/Ltd. ($255). Tires: P195/75R14 black SBR (NC). P195/75R14 white SBR ($48).

HISTORY: Introduced: September 19, 1978. Model year production (U.S.): 169,439 (1.8 percent of the industry total). Calendar year production: 184,636 cars, including 88,581 Concords. Calendar year sales by U.S. dealers: 162,057 (1.9 percent of industry total). Concords sold the best (85,432), Pacers the worst (8168).

Historical Footnotes: Record-breaking profits highlighted AMC's year, along with a strengthened tie to Renault, the French-owned automaker. Renault paid $200 million for an interest in AMC, carrying forward the agreement that had begun the previous year. Plans were made to begin assembling Renault autos at Kenosha for the 1982 model year, with Renault supplying the engines and transmissions. Meanwhile, Pacer sales continued to slip, due in part to marginal fuel economy, but mainly to the fact that its curious design never quite caught on. This was true even though Pacer had been, according to *Automotive Industries* magazine, "widely acclaimed as a daring innovation in design." Perhaps too daring for popular tastes. As Renault became AMC's major stockholder, the company looked forward to major changes in the coming years. A three- year corrosion warranty debuted in May 1979.

1980 AMC

Major news for the 1980 model year was the appearance of the Eagle. Based on the Concord chassis, it was the first major four-wheel-drive passenger car produced in the U.S. in modern times. Otherwise, the lineup remained the same as in 1979, though this would be the final year for both Pacer and AMX. The V-8 engine was gone for good. All models had front disc brakes, standard four-speed floor shift, a high-pressure compact spare tire, inside hood release, dome light, cigar lighter, front stabilizer bar (except Spirit sedan), high level ventilation, and a parking brake warning light. To improve corrosion resistance, rust-prone regions used more galvanized materials and special coatings. One-side galvanized steel went inside hoods, deck lids, and door panels. Front fenders were plastic-lined, while petroleum wax coatings went on door panel bottoms, fender bottoms, and rear seam areas. Four-cylinder engines used a Delco High Energy Ignition system. Standard colors for all models were Cardinal Red, Cameo Blue, Navy Blue, Saxon Yellow, Cameo Tan, Medium Brown metallic, Classic Black, and Olympic White. All models except the AMX could also be obtained in Russet, Bordeaux, Medium Blue, Dark Brown, Quick Silver or Smoke Gray metallic. One noteworthy new option: a leather-wrapped steering wheel, offered on all models. Premium sound systems could include a cassette tape player.

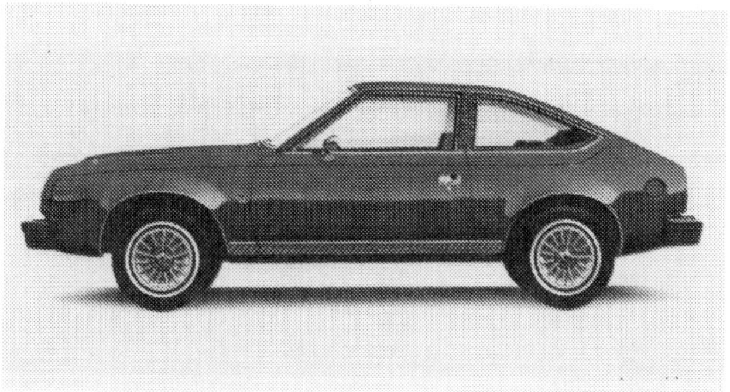

1980 Spirit liftback coupe (JG)

SPIRIT — SERIES 40 — FOUR/SIX — For its second year, Spirit continued with little change except for a new beltline molding on DL sedans, extending just below the front fender nameplates. The original 121 cu. in. four departed, so base Spirits were now powered by a 2.5- liter (151 cu. in.) four from Pontiac, with four-speed manual floor shift, and rode C78 x 14 whitewalls. A 258 six remained optional, but the V-8 was dropped. Standard equipment included manual front disc brakes, full wheel covers, dual paint stripes, energy-absorbing bumpers, custom steering wheel, lighted ashtray, locking glove box, Sport vinyl bench seats (buckets in liftback), anodized aluminum bumpers with black end caps, and quad rectangular headlamps. In addition to the colors above, Spirits were available in Caramel. Spirit buyers could step up to a DL and get reclining bucket seats up front and split folding seat in back, with Caberfae Corduroy or Sport vinyl upholstery; an AM radio and day/night mirror; digital clock; luxury woodgrain steering wheel; woodgrain instrument panel overlay; premium cloth headliner and visors; parcel shelf; full-styled wheel covers; front/rear bumper guards; dual horns; extra-quiet insulation; plus blackout rocker panels and wide lower body side moldings. Topping the line was the Spirit Limited, with reclining leather bucket seats and split folding rear seat, power steering, woodgrain-accent door panels, 18-oz. carpeting, console with center armrest, tilt steering wheel, power door locks and liftback release, bumper nerfing strips, protection and convenience groups, visibility group with dual remote mirrors, lights-on buzzer, and P195/75R14 whitewall glass-belted radials with wire wheel covers. Performance fans could again get a Spirit GT liftback with tachometer and sport steering wheel inside, black bumpers and rear venturi area, blackout grille and headlight bezels, blackout moldings, black left remote mirror, dual pinstripes, and spoke styled wheels with P195/75R14 fiberglass-belted radial tires. Six-cylinder GT models with manual shift also included deep-tone exhaust. The GT package was available on base and DL Spirits. Once again, a Rally-tuned suspension package was offered for six- cylinder GT models.

AMX — SERIES 40 — SIX — The 'AMX' badge on the grille moved from the corner to the center for 1980, but other changes for the sporty performance AMC model were minor in its final outing. Base engine was the 258 cu. in. six with four-speed manual shift. Standard gear included a GT Rally-tuned suspension system, tachometer, black left remote mirror, sports steering wheel, deep-tone exhaust (with manual shift), dual note horns, and extra-quiet insulation. An 'AMX' nameplate was on the glove box door, as well as on the grille, rear spoiler, and entry doors. Spoke style wheels held DR70 x 14 white-letter tires. As before, black accents set the tone for AMX. It had black bumpers, guards and nerfing strips; front/rear fender flares with accent stripes; front air dam; grille insert and headlight bezels; door, quarter window and rear window surround moldings; and windshield wiper arms. The color-keyed rear spoiler had accent stripes. A floor-shift automatic transmission was optional. An AMX custom interior package included reclining bucket seats in Sport vinyl or Caberfae corduroy.

PACER — SERIES 60 — SIX — Striking and innovative when it first appeared in 1975, Pacer sales never met expectations; so it was dropped after 1980. As before, the top two rows of the four-row grille bulged up into the hood area. Subdued blackout vertical grille elements were dominated by the horizontal bars. Pacer was the only AMC model that never received quad headlamps. DL Pacers came equipped with individual reclining seats in Sport vinyl, woodgrain-accent door trim panels, woodgrain instrument panel overlays, custom steering wheel with woodgrain accents, 12-oz. color-keyed full carpeting, rear seat armrests and ashtray, day/night mirror, clock, courtesy lights, key warning buzzer, locking glove box, extra-quiet insulation, and dual note horns. Tires were P195/75R14 fiberglass-belted radial whitewalls with styled wheel covers. Pacers also had front and rear bumper guards, a squarish hood ornament, wide color-keyed bodyside scuff moldings, and wide rocker panel moldings. Upgrading to a Limited brought Chelsea leather reclining seats, a folding vinyl center armrest, woodgrain tilt steering wheel, and 18-oz. carpeting. Limiteds also had power steering, power windows and door locks, dual remote mirrors, an AM radio, dome/map light, glove box and under-hood lights, intermittent wipers, and lighted passenger visor mirror. In addition to the standard colors, Pacers were offered in Caramel and Misty Beige Clearcoat.

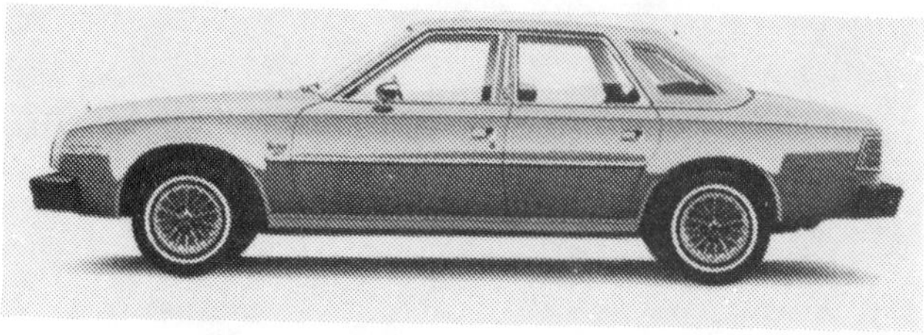

1980 Concord D/L sedan (JG)

CONCORD — SERIES 01 — FOUR/SIX — AMC's compact gained a new horizontal-bar grille for 1980, with quad rectangular headlamps and big full-width, wrap-around taillamps. 'Concord' badges sat at the side of the grille, as well as the trailing edge of the front fenders and the trunk lid. Only the front-fender amber reflectors remained. New, distinctive opera windows on DL Concords added both elegance and visibility for rear passengers. A four- cylinder 151 cu. in. Pontiac engine was now standard, with the 258 six optional. In addition to the basic body colors, Concords came in Dark Green metallic. Added to the option list: six-way power seats, automatic-leveling air shocks, power windows, and power deck lid release. Wagons could now have a rear window wiper/washer. Base Concords rode D78 x 14 blackwall tires with full wheel covers. Standard equipment included anodized aluminum bumpers with black end caps, dual bodyside pinstripes, narrow wheel lip and rocker panel moldings, bench seats in Stripe Knit fabric or Sport vinyl, front/rear ashtrays, hood ornament, narrow black side scuff moldings, and 12-oz. full carpeting. DL Concords added a day/night mirror, digital clock, courtesy light, dual note horns, extra-quiet insulation, front/rear bumper guards, individual reclining seats in Sport vinyl, full woodgrain instrument panel overlay, woodgrain-accented steering wheel, trunk carpeting, wide wheel lip and rocker panel moldings, 'B' pillar crests, and whitewall tires. Four-door DL sedans had rear opera windows and full vinyl roof, while two-doors featured a landau roof with stylish half-covered opera windows. Concord Limited sedans and wagons offered power steering, power door locks, tilt steering wheel, AM radio, dual remote mirrors, dome/map light, under-hood and trunk lights, lighted visor mirror, lights-on buzzer, intermittent wipers, woodgrain steering wheel, and bumper nerf strips. Their individual reclining seats were upholstered in either Chelsea leather or St. Lauren deep plush fabric. Limited tires were P195/7514 fiberglass-belted whitewall radials with wire wheel covers.

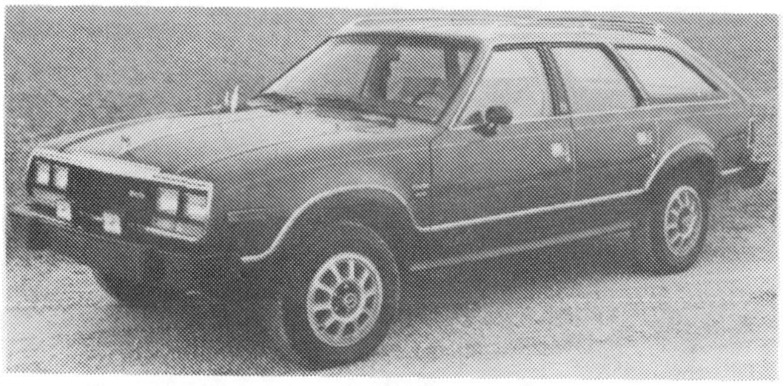

1980 American Eagle station wagon (JG)

EAGLE — SERIES 30 — SIX — Eagles arrived to the tune of a jingle, called "The Eagle Has Landed On All Fours." The Concord-based 4WD specialty vehicle was intended to combine the traction and handling of a truck with the comforts and conveniences of a luxurious passenger auto. Measuring 109.3 in., its wheelbase was an inch longer than Concord's. The Eagle also sat three inches higher off the ground, making it easy to spot from a distance. Tires were 15-inch size. Three bodies were offered: two- and four-door sedans and a four-door wagon. Grilles had seven narrow horizontal bars and an 'Eagle" badge in the upper corner, plus an 'AMC' emblem on the wide upper bar (at the opposite end). 'AMC' and 'Eagle' nameplates stodd on the deck lid; '4 Wheel Drive' (or 'Automatic 4WD') on rear quarter panels. Distinctive opera windows were half-concealed, as on Concords. Hood ornaments were made up of twin rectangles. Eagles soon became noticed not only for their increased height and ground clearance, but for their accent-colored lower body treatment. That darker area stretched the full body length, over wide fender flares, set apart by a bright molding. Both the lower rocker sill strips and 3 in. fender flares (front and rear) were made of Krayton, a durable injection-molded plastic that was also used for bumper ends. Eagle's special bumpers had to match truck standards. A stone/gravel deflector formed the lower section of the front- end panel. AMC's Eagle was the first volume-produced 4WD with independent front suspension, allowing a lower center of gravity, smooth ride, and improved stability. The advanced 4WD system could interpret road conditions, automatically distributing power to the wheels (front or rear) that needed help most. A viscous coupling with 43 plates in the transfer case provided the necessary slippage, while it also absorbed vibration in the driveline. Standard equipment for the four-wheel-drive Eagle included a 258 cu. in. six with two-barrel carburetor and Torque Command automatic transmission, plus power disc brakes, power steering, inside hood release, dual horns, front/rear bumper guards, electric clock, lighter, heavy-duty cooling system, and wheel opening moldings. Four-doors wore a full vinyl roof; two-doors a landau vinyl roof. Eagles rode P195/75R15B whitewall glass-belted radials with argent styled wheel covers. Body colors were the same as Concord's. Eagle's Limited added power windows, a parcel shelf, upgraded carpeting, premium door trim, a luxury woodgrain steering wheel, visibility group, and individual reclining seats. Eagle's Sport package, available for all but the four- door sedan, included low-gloss black Krayton flares and rocker panels; black bumpers with nerfing strips; black taillamp treatment, grille insert, windshield/liftgate moldings, and remote-control twin mirrors; halogen headlamps and foglamps (except Limited), and blackwall all-weather Goodyear Tiempo steel-belted radials. Sport models wore a '4x4' silver decal on the lower door.

I.D. DATA: As in 1976-79, the 13-symbol VIN was embossed on a metal plate riveted to the top left surface of the instrument panel, visible through the windshield. Coding was the same as before. The model year code (symbol two) changed to '0' for 1980. Under series (symbol four) a '3' code was added for the Eagle. Only two engine codes (seventh symbol) were used: 'B' 151-4; 'C' 258-6.

SPIRIT SERIES 40

Series Number	Body/Style Number	Body Type & Seating	Factory Price	Shipping Weight	Production Total
40	8043-0	2-dr Lift-4P	4293/4422	2556/2758	Note 1
40	8046-0	2-dr Sed-4P	4193/4322	2512/2714	Note 1

SPIRIT DL

40	8043-5	2-dr Lift-4P	4592/4721	2656/2854	Note 1
40	8046-5	2-dr Sed-4P	4492/4621	2611/2813	Note 1

SPIRIT LIMITED

40	8043-7	2-dr Lift-4P	5091/5220	2675/2877	Note 1
40	8046-7	2-dr Sed-4P	4991/5120	2630/2832	Note 1

Note 1: Total production for the model year, 71,032 Spirits (37,799 four-cylinder and 33,233 six-cylinder). Model year sales: 55,392.

AMX SERIES 40

40	8043-9	2-dr Lift-4P	5653	2901	N/A

PACER DL SERIES 60

60	8066-5	2-dr Hatch-4P	5407	3147	405
60	8068-5	2-dr Sta Wag-4P	5558	3195	1341

PACER LIMITED

60	8066-7	2-dr Hatch-4P	6031	3172	Note 2
60	8068-7	2-dr Sta Wag-4P	6182	3220	Note 2

Note 2: Production totals for Pacer DL also include Limited.

CONCORD SERIES 01

01	8006-0	2-dr Sed-5P	4753/4882	2646/2844	27,845
01	8005-0	4-dr Sed-5P	4878/5007	2712/2910	35,198
01	8008-0	4-dr Sta Wag-5P	5078/5207	2741/2939	17,413

CONCORD DL

01	8006-5	2-dr Sed-5P	5052/5181	2764/2962	Note 3
01	8005-5	4-dr Sed-5P	5177/5306	2834/3032	Note 3
01	8008-5	4-dr Sta Wag-5P	5377/5506	2855/3053	Note 3

CONCORD LIMITED

01	8006-7	2-dr Sed-5P	5551/5680	2789/2987	Note 3
01	8005-7	4-dr Sed-5P	5676/5805	2859/3057	Note 3
01	8008-7	4-dr Sta Wag-5P	5876/6005	2886/3084	Note 3

Note 3: Production totals under base model include DL and Limited. Total model year production, 80,456 Concords (9949 four-cylinder, 70,507 six-cylinder). Model year sales: 70,336.

EAGLE SERIES 30

30	8036-5	2-dr Sed-5P	6999	3382	10,616
30	8035-5	4-dr Sed-5P	7249	3450	9956
30	8038-5	4-dr Sta Wag-5P	7549	3470	25,807

EAGLE LIMITED

30	8036-7	2-dr Sed-5P	7396	3397	Note 4
30	8035-7	4-dr Sed-5P	7646	3465	Note 4
30	8038-7	4-dr Sta Wag-5P	7946	3491	Note 4

Note 4: Production totals shown under base Eagle include Limited. Model year Eagle sales: 34,041.

FACTORY PRICE AND WEIGHT NOTE: Figure before the slash in Spirit and Concord prices is for four-cylinder engine, after slash for six- cylinder.

ENGINES: BASE FOUR (Spirit, Concord): Inline. OHV. Four-cylinder. Cast iron block and head. Displacement: 151 cu. in. (2.5 liters). Bore & stroke: 4.0 x 3.0 in. Compression ratio: 8.2:1. Brake horsepower: 82 at 4000 R.P.M. Torque: 128 lbs.-ft. at 2400 R.P.M. Five main bearings. Hydraulic valve lifters. Carburetor: 2Bbl. Rochester 2SE. Manufactured by Pontiac. BASE SIX (AMX, Pacer, Eagle); OPTIONAL (Spirit, Concord): Inline. OHV. Six-cylinder. Cast iron block. Displacement: 258 cu. in. (4.2 liters). Bore & stroke: 3.75 x 3.9 in. Compression ratio: 8.3:1. Brake horsepower: 110 at 3200 R.P.M. Torque: 210 lbs.-ft. at 1800 R.P.M. Seven main bearings. Hydraulic valve lifters. Carburetor: 2bbl. Carter BBD.

CHASSIS DATA: Wheelbase: (Spirit/AMX) 96 in.; (Pacer) 100 in.; (Concord) 108 in.; (Eagle) 109.3 in. Overall length: (Spirit/AMX) 167 in.; (Pacer hatchback) 173.9 in.; (Pacer wagon) 178.8 in.; (Concord) 185 in.; (Eagle) 184 in. Height: (Spirit/AMX) 51.5 in.; (Pacer hatchback) 52.7 in.; (Pacer wagon) 53.1 in.; (Concord) 51.3-52.6 in.; (Eagle) 55-55.8 in. Front Tread: (Spirit/AMX) 58.1 in.; (Pacer) 61.2 in.; (Concord) 57.6 in.; (Eagle) 59.6 in. Rear Tread: (Spirit/AMX) 57.0 in.; (Pacer) 60.0 in.; (Concord) 57.1 in.; (Eagle) 57.6 in. Standard Tires: (Spirit) C78 x 14; (AMX) DR70 x 14; (Pacer) P195/75R14; (Concord) D78 x 14; (Eagle) P195/75R15.

TECHNICAL: Four-speed floor-shift manual transmission standard; three- speed Torque Command automatic transmission optional (floor or column shift) on all models except Eagle, which had standard automatic shift. Manual shift gear ratios: Four-cylinder (1st) 3.50:1; (2nd) 2.21:1; (3rd) 1.43:1; (4th) 1.00:1; (Rev) 3.39:1. Six-cylinder (1st) 4.07:1; (2nd) 2.57:1; (3rd) 1.66:1; (4th) 1.00:1; (Rev) 3.95:1. Standard axle ratios: (Spirit/Concord four, Eagle) 3.08:1; (other models) 2.53:1. Steering: recirculating ball. Suspension: independent front coil springs; semi-elliptic rear leaf springs. Brakes: front discs, rear drum. Fuel tank: (Spirit/AMX/Pacer) 21 gal.; (Concord) 22 gal.

DRIVETRAIN OPTIONS: 258 cu. in. six-cylinder engine: Spirit/Concord ($129). Torque-Command automatic transmission, column shift: Spirit ($305); Pacer/Concord ($333). Torque-Command with floor shift: Spirit/AMX ($331); Pacer ($359). Optional 3.54:1 axle ratio: Eagle ($19). Twin Grip differential ($65); N/A Eagle. Heavy-duty engine cooling system (H.D. radiator, viscous fan): Spirit/Concord six ($41) but std. w/air conditioning. H.D. cooling system (H.D. radiator, seven-blade flex fan/shroud: Pacer ($37). Extra-duty suspension package (rear sway bar, H.D. shocks/springs): Eagle ($65). Handling package (unique front sway bar, rear sway bar): Sppirit/Concord six exc. GT ($31). Front sway bar: Spirit six sed. ($20). Front suspension skid plate: Eagle ($65). Automatic load-leveling (air shocks): Concord six, Eagle ($145). Air shock absorbers, rear: Spirit ($52). Heavy-duty shock absorbers: Pacer/Concord ($15). H.D. battery ($19). Cold climate group: H.D. battery and alternator, engine block heater ($107); with air cond. or rear defroster ($47). California emission system ($250). Trailer towing package 'A' (to 2000 lbs.): Concord/Eagle ($85).

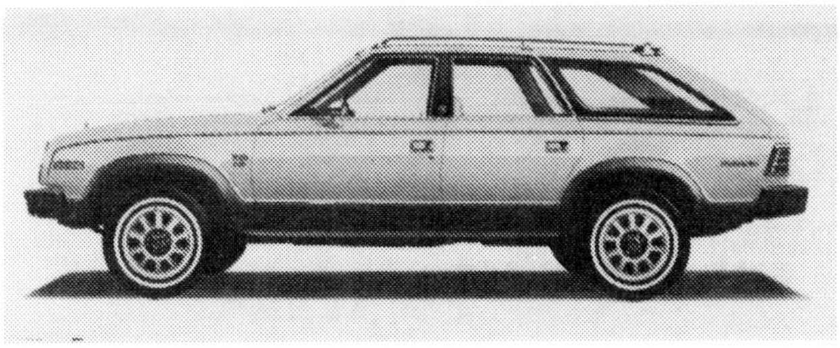

1980 American Eagle station wagon (JG)

SPIRIT/CONCORD/AMX/EAGLE CONVENIENCE/APPEARANCE OPTIONS: Spirit liftback GT package: base/DL ($249). Spirit liftback GT rally tuned suspension package ($109). AMX custom interior package (reclining vinyl bucket seats, custom door panels, split rear seat, day/night mirror, courtesy lights, parcel shelf): AMX w/vinyl trim ($149); w/fabric trim ($179). Eagle Sport package: base 2-dr./wag. ($299). Extra-quiet insulation package: base Spirit/Concord ($50); Conc. DL wag. ($19). Protection group (stainless door edge guards, front bumpers guards and nerf strips, front mats): Spirit ($111); Spirit DL ($67); Spirit GT, AMX ($31). Protection group w/front and rear guards and mats: Concord ($114); Concord DL ($70). Eagle protection group (stainless door edge guards, front/rear bumper nerf strips, front/rear mats): Eagle ($70) exc. w/Sport pkg. ($34). Convenience group incl. headlight-on buzzer, intermittent wipers, vanity mirror ($63). Gauge package (clock, tach, oil, amp, vacuum): Spirit six ($129) exc. DL/Ltd. ($77); AMX GT ($75); N/A base Spirit. Visibility group (remote control left/right mirrors, day/night mirror): Spirit/Concord/AMX ($64); DL or GT ($52). Eagle visibility group (remote left/right mirrors) ($52). Remote control left mirror ($18); N/A AMX. Pop-up moon roof: Spirit/AMX/Concord ($195). Power steering ($164). Power front disc brakes ($74). Cruise control ($108). Air conditioning system ($529). Air conditioning package (incl. tinted glass and power steering): Spirit/AMX ($752); Concord ($758). Halogen headlamps ($20). Fog lamps (dealer-installed): Eagle ($69). Light group ($37- $53). AMX hood decal ($60). AM radio ($89). AM/FM/stereo radio ($219) exc. Spirit DL/Ltd. ($130). AM/FM/stereo radio w/cassette ($335) exc. Spirit DL/Ltd. ($246). AM/FM/CB stereo radio ($475) exc. Spirit DL/Ltd. ($386). Premium sound system ($95). Digital clock: Spirit/Concord ($52). Tachometer: Spirit/Concord/Eagle ($54); std. with Spirit GT pkg. Power door locks: Spirit, AMX, Concord/Eagle 2-dr. DL/Ltd. ($75); Concord/Eagle 4-dr. DL/Ltd. ($108); N/A base Spirit. Power door/window locks: Concord DL, base Eagle ($199-$289). Power liftback release: Spirit ($32). Power decklid release: Eagle/Concord sed wag. ($32). Power six-way driver's seat: Concord DL/Ltd. ($149). Power driver/pass. seat: Concord DL/Ltd. ($249). Caberfae corduroy fabric bucket seats: Spirit DL ($29). Vinyl bench seat: Spirit sedan (NC); Concord w/striped knit fabric ($29). Vinyl reclining seats: Concord DL (NC). Rochelle velour stripe fabric reclining seats: Concord DL ($29). Leather reclining seats: Concord Ltd. (NC). Silver knit fabric reclining seats: Concord/Eagle Ltd. (deduct $100). Plaid fabric seats: Eagle ($29); N/A Ltd. Console: Spirit/AMX ($78). Rear defroster ($93). Rear wiper/washer: Eagle wag. ($79). Dual horns: Spirit/Concord ($14); std. on DL and Ltd. Leather-wrapped sport steering wheel: Spirit/Conc./Eagle ($51); Spirit DL/Ltd./GT, Concord Ltd., AMX ($21). Woodgrain steering wheel: Concord DL, Eagle ($30). Parcel shelf ($22). Tilt steering wheel ($75-$78). Tinted glass ($59-$65). Two-tone paint: Spirit GT ($84); Concord D/L and Ltd. ($103). Special color combinations: ($30) exc. AMX, Eagle Ltd. Rally side stripes: Spirit ($65). Delete woodgrain from Concord DL/Ltd. or Eagle wagon (deduct $75). Roof rack: Spirit sed. ($64); Concord/Eagle wagon ($93). Tailgate air deflector: Spirit sed. ($27). Front/rear bumper guards: Spirit/Concord ($44). Side scuff molding: Spirit ($32). Locking gas cap ($9). Styled wheel covers: Spirit/AMX/Concord ($35); N/A on Ltd. Spoke style 14 x 6 in. wheels with trim rings: Spirit/Concord ($150) exc. DL ($115); Ltd. ($15). Turbine forged aluminum wheels: Spirit/Concord ($310) exc. DL ($275); Ltd. ($175); Spirit GT ($160). Turbocast II aluminum 14 x 7 in. wheels: Spirit ($350) exc. DL ($315); Ltd. ($215); GT, AMX ($200). Wire wheel covers: Spirit/Concord ($135) exc. DL ($100). Spirit/Concord/AMX Tires: D78 x 14: Spirit (NC). D78 x 14 whitewall: Spirit ($23); Concord ($49). P195/75R14 GBR: Spirit ($75); Concord ($101); Concord DL/Ltd. ($52). P195/75R14 white GBR: Spirit ($124); Spirit GT ($50); Concord ($150); Concord DL/Ltd. ($101). P195/75R14 SBR: Spirit ($125); Spirit GT ($130); Concord ($151); Concord DL/Ltd. ($102). P195/75R14 white SBR: Spirit ($174); Spirit GT ($195); Concord ($200); Concord DL/Ltd. ($151). DR70 x 14 Flexten radial: Spirit ($205); Concord ($231); Concord DL/Ltd. ($182). DR70 x 14 OWL Flexten radial: Spirit ($270); Concord ($296); Concord DL/Ltd. ($247). ER60 x 14 OWL Flexten radial: AMX w/Turbocast II wheels ($53). Eagle Tires: P195/75R15 SBR Tiempo ($42). P195/75R15 white SBR Tiempo ($91) exc. Sport ($49).

PACER CONVENIENCE/APPEARANCE OPTIONS: Convenience group incl. headlight-on buzzer, intermittent wipers, right lighted vanity mirror ($63). Visibility group: remote left and right mirrors ($52). Protection group: front/rear bumper nerf strips, door edge guards, front/rear floor mats ($70). Left remote mirror ($18). Power steering ($164). Power front disc brakes ($74). Cruise control ($108). Air conditioning ($529). Air conditioning pkg. with tinted glass and power steering ($761). AM radio ($89). AM/FM/stereo four-speaker radio ($219). AM/FM/stereo radio w/8-track ($335). AM/FM/CB stereo radio ($475). Center armrest ($51); std. on Ltd. Rochelle velour stripe fabric seats: DL ($29). Vinyl sport seat trim: DL (NC). Power door locks ($75). Power window/door locks ($199). Light group ($43). Rear defroster ($93). Rear wiper/washer ($79). Leather-wrapped sport steering wheel ($31); w/Ltd. ($21). Woodgrain steering wheel ($30). Tilt steering wheel ($78). Tinted glass ($68). Door vent windows ($50). Two-tone color: black rocker panels deleted ($67). Special color combinations ($30); N/A w/two-tone or Ltd. Misty beige clearcoat: Ltd. ($90). Woodgrain wagon paneling ($121). Pop-up moon roof: hatch ($195). Roof rack ($78). Locking gas cap ($9). Wire wheel covers ($100). Spoke style 14 x 6 in. wheels ($115); w/Ltd. ($15). Turbine forged aluminum 14 x 6 in. wheels ($275); w/Ltd. ($175). Tires: P195/75R14 white SBR ($49).

HISTORY: Introduced: (Eagle) September 27, 1979; (others) October 11. Model year production (U.S.): 199,613, which was 2.9 percent of the industry total. Calendar year production (U.S.): 164,728 cars. Model year sales by U.S. dealers: 163,502. Calendar year sales: 149,438 (2.3 percent of total).

Historical Footnotes: For rating purposes, the new Eagle was declared a "four-wheel-drive automobile" rather than a passenger car. Thus, its so-so gas mileage didn't count in AMC's corporate average fuel economy (CAFE) rating, because it was classed as a light truck. And for meeting safety standards, Eagle ranked as a multi-purpose vehicle. The new Eagles were assembled in the same Kenosha production line as passenger cars, however. Early in the model year (December 1979), AMC announced that the slow-selling Pacer would be dropped to allow for increased Eagle production at the Kenosha facility. Eagle sold well, though not to AMC's 50,000-unit expectations. Eagle's 4WD had been developed by FF Developments in Britain, but made by Chrysler's New Process Gear Division. Four-wheel-drive passenger cars weren't entirely new. Britain's limited-production Jensen Interceptor had used 4WD in the 1960s. But as the '80s decade began, Subaru's version, introduced in 1975 in wagon form, was Eagle's sole competition for the all-wheel fancier's dollars. During 1980 contract talks, AMC became the second domestic auto company (after Chrysler) to accept a member of the United Auto Workers union on its board. After record-breaking profits in the previous year, AMC ended the 1980 period with a loss of $155.7 million. Yet continued strong Jeep sales (with increased outlets worldwide) and a cash inflow from Renault, plus plans to market several French-built models in the U.S., helped keep AMC's prospects on the bright side. AMC's rustout warranty was extended to five years.

Innovations: Four-wheel-drive passenger car. New microprocessor-controlled feedback carburetor system deveoped.

1981 AMC

With the Pacer gone, AMC's lineup dwindled to just three models. But the four-wheel-drive Eagle, which appeared the year before on a modified Concord platform, added a Spirit-based version for 1981. All models came with a standard 151 cu. in. four-cylinder engine. The optional 258 cu. in. six was redesigned using aluminum and other lightweight materials, cutting 90 pounds from its previous heft. Camshaft alterations reduced its valve overlap, allowing slower, smoother idling and more low-speed torque. Three-speed automatic transmissions now included a lockup torque converter. Galvanized steel (one-sided) outer body panels provided improved rust protection and AMC continued its five-year no- rust-through warranty, introduced the previous year. Upper deck panels were now two-sided galvanized steel. Standard 1981 colors were Classic Black, Olympic White, Cameo Tan, Montana Blue, Moonlight Blue, Autumn Gold, Oriental Red, and Beige; plus 13 metallics (Quick Silver, Medium Blue, Medium or Dark Brown, Copper Brown, Chestnut Brown, Vintage Red, Deep Maroon, Steel Gray, Blue, Silver, Sherwood Green, and Dark Green).

1981 Spirit D/L liftback coupe (AMC)

SPIRIT — SERIES 40 — FOUR/SIX — Styling changes on the subcompact Spirit included a new crossbar-style grille with emblem on lower corner, rally stripes, altered wheel covers, and a new selection of body colors. Power windows and radio antenna were optional for the first time. Spirits were now equipped with P185/75R14 blackwall glass-belted radial tires and had wheel covers, front disc brakes, a lighted front ashtray and lighter, carpeting, vinyl bucket front seats, vinyl spare tire cover, and rear bumper guards. In addition to whitewalls and an AM radio, DL models offered extra-quiet insulation, dual horns, custom door panels with map pockets, a luxury woodgrain steering wheel, day/night inside mirror, electric clock, front bumper guards, styled wheel covers, and a carpeted spare tire cover. A GT package with full instrumentation was available again this year.

1981 Concord-Griffith AM-TC convertible (JG)

CONCORD — SERIES 01 — FOUR/SIX — For improved rust protection, all exterior Concord body panels were now galvanized steel. Glass-belted P195/75R14 blackwall radial tires with wheel covers were standard; steel- belted tires and wire wheel covers optional. The restyled grille used three vertical bars to accent the five horizontal bars. Opera windows were restyled. New colors and fabrics were offered. Base engine was the 151 cu. in. four with four-speed manual floor shift. Standard equipment included a stowaway spare tire, front and rear armrests, lighter, carpeting, bench seats, folding rear wagon seat, rear bumper guards, and moldings for drip rail, wheel lip, hood front edge, windshield and rear window surrounds, rocker panels, and bodyside scuff area. An optional retractable cargo area cover could hide luggage in Concord wagons. A vinyl landau roof highlighted Concord's DL sedans. DL models also had stainless steel wheel covers, individual reclining seats, a custom steering wheel, day/night mirror, cargo area skid strips, electric clock, trunk carpeting, front bumper guards, striping, dual horns, woodgrain wagon side panels, extra sound insulation, and whitewall tires. Two-doors featured opera quarter windows. The luxurious Limited added visibility and light groups as well as a luxury woodgrain steering wheel and styled wheel covers, plus premium seat and door trim.

1981 American Eagle SX/4 liftback coupe (AMC)

EAGLE SX/4 AND KAMMBACK — SERIES 50 — FOUR/SIX — Since the original 4WD Eagle showed promise, AMC added a shrunken version for 1981, based on the Spirit chassis. Billed as "the sports car that doesn't always need a road," the SX/4 two-door hatchback had a sporty look, but hardly qualified as a sports car. Also in the lineup was a Kammback wagon, derived from the Spirit/Gremlin sedan design. Both rode a 97.2 in. wheelbase but carried 15 in. tires, which gave 3 in. more ground clearance than the Spirits. Front-end styling focused on a new 8x3 checkerboard-style grille, like the senior Eagles. An 'Eagle' nameplate was up front, as well as at the usual front fender locations. An 'AMC' badge sat atop the grille. 'SX/4' decals were on lower front doors, part of the wide accent-colored Krayton plastic body striping that ran from front to back, over the fender flares. A bright molding separated the two body colors. '4WD' emblems stood on quarter panels. Subcompact Eagles came with a 2.5-liter (151 cu. in.) four-cylinder engine, four-speed floor shift and transfer case, the same as their bigger brothers. Three-speed automatic shift was optional, as was the 258 cu. in. six. The smaller Eagles rode well enough to rate with ordinary passenger cars— far more smoothly than the typical off-road vehicle—and performed with reasonable liveliness and impressive gas mileage. Eagles had power front disc brakes, power steering, front sway bar, high energy ignition, 42-amp alternator, 55-380 (cold crank rating) battery, quad rectangular headlamps, 21- gallon fuel tank, and compact spare tire. Standard equipment also included P195/75R15 blackwall glass belted radial tires with wheel covers, vinyl bucket seats and fold-down rear bench seat, two-speed wipers, carpeting, locking glove box, front armrests, lighted front ashtray, lighter, coat hooks, inside hood release, dome light, body pinstripes, spare tire cover, and front/rear bumper nerf strips. The DL upgrade added custom vinyl reclining bucket seats up front and a split vinyl rear seat, Alpine cloth custom headliner and visors, woodgrain instrument panel overlay, woodgrain horn cover on a custom steering wheel, day/night mirror, and digital clock. It also featured left/right remote- control chrome mirrors, chrome side marker lights, dual horns, extra-quiet insulation, and P195/75R15 whitewall glass-belted radials with argent styled wheel covers. DL liftbacks had blackout window frames, belt moldings, and door/quarter frame moldings. Off-road enthusiasts could elect an optional Sport package that included a floor shift console, parcel shelf, and vinyl sport steering wheel inside. Outside, they featured a 'Sport' nameplate plus low-gloss black Krayton flares and rocker panels; black bumpers with guards and nerf strips; black grille insert, moldings, taillamp treatment, and left/right remote sport mirrors. Sport models rode P195/75R15 blackwall steel-belted radial Goodyear Arriva tires with styled wheel covers, and carried halogen headlamps and foglamps.

EAGLE — SERIES 30 — FOUR/SIX — Eagle's new checkerboard grille, with an 8x3 pattern, differed considerably from its Concord cousin. Like their new smaller companions, the big Eagles were noteworthy for their dark Krayton lower body treatment. With standard four-speed manual shift, Eagle rated 22 MPG in the EPA fuel economy rankings. Outside body panels were now one-side galvanized steel for added rust protection. Standard equipment was the same as the smaller Eagle 50, but with individual vinyl reclining front seats, dual horns, the extra-quiet insulation package, whitewall P195/75R15 glass-belted radials and argent styled wheel covers. Eagle 30s also had front/rear armrests with woodgrain overlay, cargo area skid strips, day/night mirror, digital clock, Alpine cloth headliner and visors, locking cargo compartment, woodgrain steering wheel and instrument panel overlays, and front/rear bumper nerf strips. Two-door sedans sported a landau roof design; four-doors, a full vinyl roof. Wagon rear seats folded down. The Eagle 30 Limited added leather reclining seats, 18- oz. carpeting, luxury woodgrain steering wheel, and a parcel shelf. The Sport package, highlighted by a '4x4' silver decal on the lower door and a 'Sport' nameplate, contained a leather-wrapped sport steering wheel; low-gloss black flares and rocker panels; plus black bumpers/guards, nerf strips, hood molding, taillamp treatment, grille insert, headlamp bezels, door frames, moldings, and remote-control dual sport mirrors. Also halogen headlamps and foglamps, and P195/75R15 blackwall steel-belted Arriva radial tires.

I.D. DATA: A new 17-symbol Vehicle Identification Number (VIN) was embossed on a metal plate riveted to the upper left surface of the instrument panel, visible through the windshield. It began with a digit indicating country of manufacture: '1' U.S.; '2' Canada. The second symbol identified the manufacturer: 'A' AMC; 'C' American Motors (Canada). Third symbol showed vehicle type: 'M' passenger car; 'C' multi-purpose vehicle (Eagle); 'E' export. Symbol four denoted engine type. The fifth symbol identified transmission (and transfer case) type: 'M' four-speed manual floor shift; 'G' four-speed with full-time 4WD; 'W' five-speed floor shift; 'N' five-speed with 4WD; 'A' column-shift automatic; 'C' floor-shift automatic; and 'K'

floor-shift automatic with 4WD. The next two digits identified the line and body type: '05' Concord four-door; '06' Concord two-door; '08' Concord wagon; '35' Eagle four-door sedan; '36' Eagle two-door sedan; '38' Eagle four-door wagon; '43' Spirit two-door Liftback; '46' Spirit two-door sedan; '53' Eagle SX/4 two-door Liftback; '56' Eagle (Kammback) two-door sedan. The eighth symbol identified trim level: '0' base model; '5' DL; '7' Limited. Next came a check digit to mathematically determine validity of a car's VIN. Symbol ten was a letter indicating model year: 'B' 1981. Symbol eleven showed manufacturing plant: 'K' Kenosha; 'B' Brampton, Ontario. Finally came a six-digit sequence number. An engine Build Code was stamped on a machined surface of the block of six-cylinder engines, between cylinders two and three; and at the rear of the engine, near the flywheel, on 151 cu. in. fours. The fourth symbol of that code was identical to the engine code of the VIN. Symbol one is year ('1' 1981); symbols 2-3, the month built (01-12); symbols 5-6, the day of the month. The VIN is also on the Federal Safety Label attached to the edge of the left door, above the door lock; or on the bottomline of a metal plate attached to upper left corner of firewall, under the hood. A Unit Body/Trim Plate on left door edge shows Body Number, Model Number, Trim Number, Paint Code, and Build Sequence Number.

SPIRIT SERIES 40

Series Number	Body/Style Number	Body Type & Seating	Factory Price	Shipping Weight	Production Total
40	8143-0	2-dr Lift-4P	5190/5326	2587/2716	42,252
40	8146-0	2-dr Sed-4P	5090/5226	2542/2671	2367

SPIRIT DL

40	8143-5	2-dr Lift-4P	5589/5725	2673/2802	Note 1
40	8146-5	2-dr Sed-4P	5489/5625	2627/2756	Note 1

Note 1: Production totals include base and DL models. Total model year production, 44,599 Spirits (26,075 four-cylinder and 18,524 six- cylinder). Model year sales: 38,334.

CONCORD SERIES 01

01	8106-0	2-dr Sed-5P	5819/5955	2672/2798	15,496
01	8105-0	4-dr Sed-5P	5944/6080	2738/2864	24,403
01	8108-0	4-dr Sta Wag-5P	6144/6280	2768/2894	15,198

CONCORD DL

01	8106-5	2-dr Sed-5P	6218/6354	2767/2893	Note 2
01	8105-5	4-dr Sed-5P	6343/6479	2837/2963	Note 2
01	8108-5	4-dr Sta Wag-5P	6543/6679	2852/2978	Note 2

1981 Concord Limited coupe (AMC)

CONCORD LIMITED

01	8106-7	2-dr Sed-5P	6665/6801	2789/2915	Note 2
01	8105-7	4-dr Sed-5P	6790/6926	2859/2985	Note 2
01	8108-7	4-dr Sta Wag-5P	6990/7126	2880/3006	Note 2

Note 2: Production totals shown for base Concord include DL and Limited models. Total model year production, 55,097 Concords (7067 four-cylinder and 48,030 six-cylinder). Model year sales: 63,732.

1981 American Eagle-Griffith convertible (JG)

EAGLE SERIES 50

50	8153-0	2-dr SX/4 Lift-4P	6717/6853	2967/3123	17,340
50	8156-0	2-dr Kamm Sed-4P	5995/6131	2919/3015	5603

EAGLE DL SERIES 50

50	8153-5	2-dr SX/4 Lift-4P	7119/7255	3040/3196	Note 3
50	8156-5	2-dr Kamm Sed-4P	6515/6651	2990/3146	Note 3

Note 3: Production totals includes both base and DL models.

EAGLE SERIES 30

30	8136-5	2-dr Sed-5P	7847/7983	3104/3260	2378
30	8135-5	4-dr Sed-5P	8097/8233	3172/3328	1737
30	8138-5	4-dr Sta Wag-5P	8397/8533	3184/3340	10,371

EAGLE LIMITED

30	8136-7	2-dr Sed-5P	8244/8380	3114/3270	Note 4
30	8135-7	4-dr Sed-5P	8494/8630	3180/3336	Note 4
30	8138-7	4-dr Sta Wag-5P	8794/8930	3198/3354	Note 4

Note 4: Production totals shown under base Eagle include Limited. Total model year production, 37,429 Eagles (11,344 four-cylinder and 26,085 six-cylinder). Model year sales: 42,904.

FACTORY PRICE AND WEIGHT NOTE: Figure before the slash is for four- cylinder engine, after slash for six-cylinder.

ENGINES: BASE FOUR (all models): Inline. OHV. Four-cylinder. Cast iron block and head. Displacement: 151 cu. in. (2.5 liters). Bore & stroke: 4.0 x 3.0 in. Compression ratio: 8.24:1. Brake horsepower: 82 at 3800 R.P.M. Torque: 125 lbs.-ft. at 2600 R.P.M. Five main bearings. Hydraulic valve lifters. Carburetor: 2Bbl. Rochester 2SE. OPTIONAL SIX (all models): Same as 1980 specifications (258 cu. in. inline OHV).

CHASSIS DATA: Wheelbase: (Spirit) 96 in.; (Concord) 108 in.; (Eagle 50) 97.2 in.; (Eagle 30) 109.3 in. Overall length: (Spirit) 167 in.; (Concord) 185 in.; (Eagle 50 SX/4) 164.6 in.; (Eagle 50 Kammback) 164.4 in.; (Eagle 30) 184 in. Height: (Spirit) 51.5 in.; (Concord) 51.3-51.5 in.; (Eagle 50) 55.3-55.5 in.; (Eagle 30) 55.0-55.8 in. Width: (Spirit) 72 in.; (Concord) 71 in.; (Eagle) 73 in. w/flares. Front Tread: (Spirit) 58.1 in.; (Concord) 57.6 in.; (Eagle) 59.6 in. Rear Tread: (Spirit) 57 in.; (Concord) 57.1 in.; (Eagle) 57.6 in. Standard Tires: (Spirit) P185/75R14 BSW GBR; (Concord) P195/75R14 BSW GBR; (Eagle) P195/75R15 BSW BGR.

TECHNICAL: Four-speed manual floor shift standard. Gear ratios: (1st) 4.07:1; (2nd) 2.39:1; (3rd) 1.49:1; (4th) 1.00:1; (Rev) 3.95:1. Torque Command three-speed automatic transmission optional; lockup torque converter. Standard axle ratio: (Spirit/Conc. four) 3.08:1; (Spirit/Conc. six) 2.37:1; (Eagle four) 3.54:1; (Eagle six) 2.73:1. Steering: recirculating ball. Suspension: independent front coil springs; semi-elliptic rear leaf springs. Clutch dia.: 9.12 in. Brakes: front discs, rear drums; (Spirit) 10.3 in. disc; (Concord) 10.8 in. disc; (Eagle) 11 in. disc. Electronic ignition.

1981 Concord-Griffith AM-TC convertible (JG)

SPIRIT/CONCORD/EAGLE DRIVETRAIN OPTIONS: 258 cid six-cylinder engine ($136). Column-shift automatic transmission: Spirit/Concord ($350). Floor-shift automatic transmission: Spirit/Eagle ($350). Optional 3.08:1 axle ratio: Eagle 30 six with automatic ($20). Twin Grip differential: Spirit/Concord ($69). Heavy-duty engine cooling system (H.D. radiator, viscous fan/shroud, coolant recovery system): Spirit/Concord six ($61) but std. w/air cond.; Eagle four ($51). Maximum cooling system (H.D. radiator and viscous fan): Eagle ($62). Handling package (unique front sway bar, rear sway bar): Spirit, Concord six ($42); N/A w/Spirit GT. H.D. shock absorbers: Spirit/Concord ($16); N/A with Spirit GT rally tuned pkg. Automatic load leveling (air shocks): Concord/Eagle ($153). Extra duty suspension pkg. (rear sway bar and H.D. shocks/springs): Eagle 50 ($37); Eagle 30 ($69). Extra heavy-duty suspension (H.D. springs, shocks, control arms/bushings): Concord ($59). Front suspension skid plate: Eagle ($69). Trailer towing package 'A' (to 2000 lbs.): Concord/Eagle 30 ($90). Trailer towing package 'B' (to 3500 lbs.): Eagle 30 ($195). H.D. (56/450 cold crank) battery ($20). 80-amp battery: Concord/Eagle ($32). H.D. alternator ($63). Cold climate group incl. H.D. battery/alternator, engine block heater ($113); w/air cond. or rear defroster: Spirit/Concord ($50). California emission system ($50).

CONVENIENCE/APPEARANCE OPTIONS: Spirit liftback GT package ($372); DL ($272). Spirit liftback GT rally-tuned suspension package ($119). Eagle Sport package: Eagle 30 2-dr./wag. ($314); Eagle 50 lift. ($472); Eagle 50 DL lift. ($367). Extra-quiet insulation package ($53). Protection group (stainless door edge guards, front/rear bumper guards and nerfing strips, front/rear floor mats): Concord ($120); DL/Ltd. ($71-$74); Spirit GT ($33). Eagle protection group incl. stainless door edge guards, front/rear bumper guards, front/rear floor mats ($79-$82); w/Sport pkg. ($33-$36). Convenience group: headlight-on buzzer, intermittent wipers, right lighted vanity mirror ($67). Gauge package (clock, tach, oil, amp or volt, vacuum): Spirit, Eagle 50 ($136); Spirit GT/DL ($79-$81); Eagle 30 or DL ($81). Pop- up sun roof w/tinted glass ($246). Rear spoiler: Spirit GT, Eagle Sport lift. ($99). Light group ($46-$56). Left remote control mirror ($19) exc. GT; N/A on Eagle 30. Left/right remote chrome mirrors ($56) exc. Spirit GT/DL; std. on Concord DL/Ltd.; N/A Eagle 30. Left/right sport mirrors: Spirit, Eagle 50 ($56); Eagle 50 DL (NC). Left/right electric remote chrome mirrors: Spirit/Concord ($132); Concord DL and Eagle 30 ($76-$77). Day/night mirror ($13); std. on DL/Ltd. Power steering: Spirit/Concord ($173). Power front disc brakes: Spirit/Concord ($80). Electronic

cruise control ($132). Air conditioning system ($531-$585). Air conditioning package incl. tinted glass and power steering: Spirit ($774); Concord ($833). Halogen headlamps ($40). Foglamps (dealer-installed): Eagle ($73). Dual horns: Spirit/Concord ($15). AM radio ($92). AM/FM/CB stereo four-speaker radio ($456) exc. Spirit DL ($364). AM/FM/stereo four-speaker radio ($192) exc. Spirit DL ($100). AM/FM/cassette stereo radio ($356) exc. Spirit DL ($264). Premium audio system incl. power amplifier, four hi-fi speakers, fader ($100). Power antenna ($53). Power door locks: Spirit DL, Concord DL/Ltd. 2-dr. sed. ($90); Concord DL/Ltd. and Eagle 30 4-dr./wag. ($130-$131). Power windows and door locks: Spirit DL, Concord DL, Concord DL/Ltd. 2-dr. sed. ($231); Concord DL/Ltd. and Eagle 30 4- dr./wag. ($330). Power liftback release: Spirit/Eagle 50 ($34). Power decklid release: Concord/Eagle 30 sed. ($34). Power six-way driver seat: Concord DL/Ltd., Eagle 30 ($157). Power six-way driver/pass. seat: Concord DL/Ltd., Eagle 30 ($262). Center console w/armrest: Spirit ($82). Floor shift console: Eagle ($52). Parcel shelf ($24). Bench seat (striped knit fabric): Concord ($48). H.D. seat frame assembly for bench seat: Concord ($31). H.D. vinyl seat trim: Concord ($60); N/A w/DL or four-speed. Coventry Check seat fabric, reclining bucket seats: Spirit DL, Eagle 50 ($31). Velour stripe fabric on reclining seats: Concord DL, Eagle 30 ($58). Durham plaid fabric or Rochelle sculptured velour on reclining seats: Eagle 30 ($58). Cargo area cover: Concord/Eagle wag. ($62). Digital clock ($55); std. on DL/Ltd. Rear wiper/washer ($99). Rear defroster ($102-$107). Vinyl sport steering wheel: Spirit/Eagle 50 ($34). Woodgrain steering wheel: Spirit/Concord DL, Eagle 30 ($32). Leather- wrapped sport steering wheel ($54) exc. GT/Ltd., Eagle 50 Sport ($20-$34). Tilt steering wheel: Spirit ($79); Eagle ($82). Tinted glass ($70-$75). Two-tone paint (w/o pinstripes): Spirit, Concord DL/Ltd. ($109). Special color combinations ($32). Rally side stripes: Spirit ($79). Woodgrain paneling: Eagle wag. ($128). Woodgrain from Concord DL/Ltd. wag. (deduct $75). Side scuff moldings ($44). Roof rack: Spirit sed., Eagle 50 ($74); Concord/Eagle 30 wag. ($98). Locking gas cap ($10). Tailgate air deflector: Spirit/Eagle 50 sed. ($29). Front/rear bumper guards ($47). Styled wheel covers (argent): Spirit ($37) exc. GT; Concord ($74); Concord DL ($37); Eagle ($48). Custom wheel covers: Concord ($37); std. on DL. Wire wheel covers: Spirit/Concord ($142); DL ($105); N/A on GT. Spoke style 14 x 6 in. wheels w/trim rings: Spirit/Concord ($158) exc. DL ($121); Concord Ltd. ($16). Turbocast II aluminum 14 x 7 in. wheels ($368) exc. DL ($331-$345); Spirit GT ($210); Concord Ltd. ($226). Aluminum 15 x 6 in. wheels: Eagle ($310-$335). Spirit/Concord Tires: P185/75R14/B white GBR: Spirit ($52). P195/75R14/B black GBR: Spirit ($25) exc. DL (NC). P195/75R14/B white GBR: Spirit ($76); Spirit DL ($25); Concord ($52). P195/75R14/B white SBR Arriva: Spirit ($129); Spirit DL ($77); Concord ($104); Conc. DL/Ltd. ($53). P195/70R14/B RWL polysteel radial: Spirit ($229); Spirit DL ($178); Concord ($205); Conc. DL/Ltd. ($154). Eagle Tires: P195/75R15 white GBR: Eagle 50 ($52). P195/75R15 black SBR Arriva ($52-$53). P195/75R15 white SBR Arriva: Eagle 30 ($96); Eagle DL ($96); Eagle Sport ($52). P215/65R15 OWL SBR Eagle GT: Eagle 30 ($245); Eagle Sport ($201). P215/75R15 OWL SBR Eagle GT: Eagle 50 ($254); Eagle DL ($245).

HISTORY: Introduced: September 25, 1980. Model year production: 137,125 (44,486 fours and 92,639 sixes), which came to 2.1 percent of the industry total. Calendar year production (U.S.): 109,319. Model year sales by U.S. dealers: 145,206 (including 236 leftover Pacers). Calendar year sales: 136,682 cars. Concords sold the best, followed by Eagles, then Spirits.

Historical Footnotes: Strengthening its tie with the French automaker, AMC marketed as a "captive import" the new Renault 18i. On December 16, 1980, AMC stockholders approved the arrangement that would give Renault a 46 percent share of the corporation. Three more Renault officers joined the AMC board, making a total of five. Skyrocketing interest rates received part of the blame for sluggish sales of AMC domestic cars, which slipped 8.2 percent from 1980. Still, the company's market share was down only slightly. Operation resumed at AMC's Milwaukee plant in August 1981, after a nine-month closure. One of the two Kenosha production lines shut down to retool for manufacturing the planned Renault/AMC joint-venture front-wheel-drive subcompact model. Eagle sales edged out those of the 4WD Subaru, but that flash of popular wasn't destined to last long.

1982 AMC

Both the compact Concord and subcompact Spirit had slipped further down in sales volume, but returned for another try in 1982, along with both Eagle 4WD versions. Styling changed little from 1981. The foremost technical change was the availability of a T5 five-speed overdrive manual transmission from Warner Gear, which boosted fuel economy ratings. Its overdrive fifth gear (0.76:1 or 0.86:1) was in the rear housing of the transmission. Four-speed manual and three-speed automatic transmissions were redesigned; as before, the automatics came from Chrysler. Lower final drive ratios on all models were intended to improve economy. Sixes with automatic received wider-ratio gearboxes. The optional 258 cu. in. six-cylinder engine gained a serpentine accessory drive system for added fuel savings. One belt powered the alternator, water pump, air pump, and power steering pump. GM cars using Pontiac's "Iron Duke" four gained fuel injection this year, but AMC's version stuck to carburetion. Front disc brakes gained low-drag calipers. New body colors were added: Topaz Gold metallic, Sea Blue metallic, Deep Night Blue, Slate Blue metallic, Jamaican Beige, Mist Silver metallic, and Sun Yellow. Carryover metallic colors were Deep Maroon, Vintage Red, Copper Brown, Sherwood Green, and Dark Brown; plus Oriental Red, Olympic White, and Classic Black.

1982 Spirit liftback coupe (JG)

SPIRIT — SERIES 40 — FOUR/SIX — Spirits looked the same outside, but could be purchased with the new five-speed overdrive transmission—the first domestic subcompact to offer that option. Once again, base and DL trim were available, along with the sporty GT package. Base powertrain was the 2.5-liter (151 cu. in.) four-cylinder "Iron Duke" engine from Pontiac, with four-speed floor shift, manual front disc brakes, and P185/75R14 black glass-belted radial tires. Standard equipment also included two-speed wiper/washers, front sway bar, compact spare tire, lighter, color-keyed carpeting, inside hood release, locking glove box, dome light, vinyl bucket front seats, fold-down rear bench seat, energy-absorbing bumpers, side pinstriping, and wheel covers. DL Spirits rode P185/75R14 whitewall glass-belted radials on argent styled wheel covers and added reclining vinyl bucket seats, a premium split rear seat, Alpine fabric headliner and visors, AM radio, woodgrain dash overlay, day/night mirror, extra-quiet insulation package, dual horns, and a digital clock. Black rocker panel moldings, chrome side marker lights, a chrome remote-control left mirror and front/rear bumper guards also marked the DL. Liftback buyers could choose a Spirit GT package, which included spoke-style 14 x 6 in. wheels with P185/75R14 blackwall glass-belted radial tires; tachometer; sport steering wheel; left-hand remote sport mirror; black body trim moldings at windshield and rear window surround, belt, drip, and 'B' pillar; black grille insert, headlight bezels, bumpers with nerfing strips and rear venturi; and 'GT' nameplates.

1982 Concord sedan (JG)

CONCORD — SERIES 01 — FOUR/SIX — Base Concords again were powered by a 151 cu. in. four with four-speed floor shift and had manual disc brakes, bench seats, a front sway bar, P195/75R14 blackwall glass-belted radial tires with wheel covers, and a compact high-pressure spare tire. They also had the option of a five-speed overdrive floor shift, which produced a 37 MPG EPA highway rating with the four. A reworked, wider-ratio automatic transmission also helped mileage, when coupled to the optional 258 six with a lower final axle ratio. External appearance was unchanged. Standard equipment also included two-speed wiper/washers, dome light, lighter, carpeting, a hood ornament, dual body pinstripes, and black scuff moldings on body sides. Concord DL models added invidivial vinyl reclining seats, molded fiberglass headliner and visors (Alpine fabric), a day/night inside mirror, dual rear ashtrays, digital electronic clock, woodgrain instrument panel overlay, dual horns, extra-quiet insulation, bumper guards front and rear, a remote-control left mirror, and custom wheel covers with whitewall tires. As before, DL two-doors carried opera windows and a landau vinyl roof, while four-doors had a full vinyl roof and wagons sported woodgrain side panels. Moving another step up, the Limited added leather reclining seats, heavy carpeting (18- ounce in passenger area), a luxury woodgrain steering wheel, parcel shelf, chrome right-hand remote-control mirror, and wire wheel covers with its whitewall tires.

EAGLE — SERIES 50 — FOUR/SIX — "Select Drive" let motorists switch easily between two- wheel-drive and full-time 4WD on the short-wheelbase, Spirit-based Eagle. That was formerly an option. Although the 151 cu. in. four still served as base engine, with four-speed floor shift, Eagles could also get the new five-speed manual or three-speed automatic, along with the 258 cu. in. six-cylinder powerplant. All Eagles included power steering and brakes, and a front sway bar, and rode 15-in. tires with wheel covers. P195/75R15 blackwall glass-belted radials were standard, with a compact spare tire. Eagles also came with color-keyed carpeting, custom vinyl bucket front seats (fold-down rear bench seat), front/rear bumper nerfing strips, inside hood release, dome light, locking glove box, wheelwell and rocker panel moldings, and body pinstriping. Lower door sections were painted in accent color. Eagle DL models added reclining bucket seats up front, a split rear seat, woodgrain dash overlay, day/night mirror, digital clock, Alpine fabric headliner/visors, remote-control left mirror (chrome), extra- quiet insulation, twin horns, and argent styled wheel covers with whitewall tires. Appearing again on the SX/4 Liftback option list was an Eagle Sport package, including low-gloss black Krayton rocker panels and flares; black bumpers with guards and nerf strips; colored inserts in lower body side moldings; black grille insert, windshield, headlamp bezels, liftgate, drip/belt moldings, and taillamp treatment; a black remote-control left sport mirror; plus halogen headlamps and foglamps. Inside, Sport models had a floor shift console, parcel shelf, and vinyl sport steering wheel. They wore P195/75R15 blackwall steel-belted Arriva radial tires with styled wheel covers.

1982 American Eagle station wagon (JG)

EAGLE — SERIES 30 — FOUR/SIX — Concord-based Eagle sedans and wagons also had switch- selected 2WD/4WD, with optional five-speed overdrive transmission. The 151 cu. in. four with four-speed floor shift remained standard; 258 six optional (with automatic). Base- model big Eagles were a bit more luxurious than their smaller brothers, fitted with standard equipment that required a model upgrade in the 50 Series. The list included individual reclining front seats, extra-quiet insulation, dual horns, day/night mirror, lighter, Alpine fabric headliner/visors, digital clock, vinyl door trim, left remote chrome mirror, and woodgrain dash overlay. Two-doors featured opera quarter windows with landau roof, four-doors a full vinyl roof, and wagons held a fold-down rear seat. Standard Eagles rode P195/75R15 whitewall glass-belted radials with argent styled wheel covers. Eagle Limiteds contained leather reclining seats and heavy carpeting, plus a woodgrain steering wheel, parcel shelf, 'Limited' nameplate on front fender, and twin remote- control mirrors. The Sport package included a leather-wrapped steering wheel; black bumpers and guards; black headlamp bezels, grille insert, windshield/liftgate modlings, door frames, 'B' pillars and remote left sport mirror; low-gloss black rocker panels and flares; halogen headlamps and foglamps; colored inserts in lower bodyside moldings, hood molding and nerf strip; a '4x4' silver decal on lower door; and steel-belted blackwall radial tires. The Sport package was available only on base Eagle two-door sedans and wagons. Two trailer towing packages were available, for light or medium loads.

I.D. DATA: The 17-symbol VIN, visible through the windshield, used the same coding as in 1981.

SPIRIT SERIES 40

Series Number	Body/Style Number	Body Type & Seating	Factory Price	Shipping Weight	Production Total
40	8243-0	2-dr Lift-4P	5576/5726	2588/2687	20,063
40	8246-0	2-dr Sed-4P	5476/5626	2538/2637	119

SPIRIT DL

40	8243-5	2-dr Lift-4P	5959/6109	2666/2765	Note 1
40	8246-5	2-dr Sed-4P	5859/6009	2614/2713	Note 1

Note 1: Production totals shown under base Spirit include DL models. Total model year production, 20,182 Spirits (9290 four-cylinder and 10,892 six-cylinder). Model year sales: 18,161.

CONCORD SERIES 01

01	8206-0	2-dr Sed-5P	5954/6104	2693/2773	6132
01	8205-0	4-dr Sed-5P	6254/6404	2752/2842	25,572
01	8208-0	4-dr Sta Wag-5P	7013/7163	2786/2876	12,106

CONCORD DL

01	8206-5	2-dr Sed-5P	6716/6866	2768/2858	Note 2
01	8205-5	4-dr Sed-5P	6761/6911	2841/2931	Note 2
01	8208-5	4-dr Sta Wag-5P	7462/7612	2940/3030	Note 2

CONCORD LIMITED

01	8206-7	2-dr Sed-5P	7213/7363	2790/2880	Note 2
01	8205-7	4-dr Sed-5P	7258/7408	2862/2952	Note 2
01	8208-7	4-dr Sta Wag-5P	7959/8109	2892/2982	Note 2

Note 2: Production totals under base Concord include DL and Limited. Total model year production, 33,693 Concords (2038 four-cylinder and 31,655 six-cylinder) including Canadian output for U.S. market. Model year sales: 36,505.

EAGLE SX/4 SERIES 50

50	8253-0	2-dr SX/4 Lift-4P	7451/7601	2972/3100	10,445
50	8256-0	2-dr Kamm Sed-4P	6799/6949	2933/3061	520

EAGLE 50 DL

50	8253-5	2-dr SX/4 Lift-4P	7903/8053	3041/3169	Note 3
50	8256-5	2-dr Kamm Sed-4P	7369/7519	3000/3128	Note 3

Note 3: Production totals shown under base Eagle 50 include DL models. Of the 10,965 Eagle 50s manufactured, 3529 had four-cylinder engine.

EAGLE SERIES 30

30	8236-5	2-dr Sed-5P	8719/8869	3107/3235	1968
30	8235-5	4-dr Sed-5P	8869/9019	3172/3300	4091
30	8238-5	4-dr Sta Wag-5P	9566/9716	3199/3327	20,899

EAGLE 30 LIMITED

30	8236-7	2-dr Sed-5P	9166/9316	3115/3243	Note 4
30	8235-7	4-dr Sed-5P	9316/9466	3180/3308	Note 4
30	8238-7	4-dr Sta Wag-5P	10013/10163	3213/3341	Note 4

Note 4: Production totals shown under base Eagle 30 include Eagle Limited. They include Canadian output for U.S. market. Only 6056 Eagle 30 sedans and two wagons were made in U.S. Model year Eagle sales: 37,797.

FACTORY PRICE AND WEIGHT NOTE: Figure before the slash is for four- cylinder engine, after slash for six-cylinder.

ENGINES: BASE FOUR (all models): Inline. OHV. Four-cylinder. Cast iron block and head. Displacement: 151 cu. in. (2.5 liters). Bore & stroke: 4.0 x 3.0 in. Compression ratio: 8.2:1. Brake horsepower: 82 at 3800 R.P.M. Torque: 125 lbs.-ft. at 2600 R.P.M. Five main bearings. Hydraulic valve lifters. Carburetor: 2Bbl. Rochester 2SE. exc. E2SE with automatic transmission. OPTIONAL SIX (all models): Inline. OHV. Six-cylinder. Cast iron block and head. Displacement: 258 cu. in. (4.2 liters). Bore & stroke: 3.75 x 3.90 in. Compression ratio: 8.6:1. Brake horsepower: 110 at 3000 R.P.M. Torque: 205 lbs.-ft. at 1800 R.P.M. Seven main bearings. Hydraulic valve lifters. Carburetor: Carter BBD 2Bbl.

CHASSIS DATA: Wheelbase: (Spirit) 96 in.; (Concord) 108 in.; (Eagle 50) 97.2 in.; (Eagle 30) 109.3 in. Overall length: (Spirit) 167 in.; (Concord) 185 in.; (Eagle 50) 164.5 in. but 166.5 in. w/bumper guards; (Eagle 30) 184 in. but 186.3 in. w/guards. Height: (Spirit) 51.5 in.; (Concord) 51.3-51.5 in.; (Eagle 50) 55.4 in.; (Eagle 30) 55.0-55.8 in. Front Tread: (Spirit) 58.1 in.; (Concord) 57.6 in.; (Eagle) 59.6 in.; Rear Tread: (Spirit) 57.0 in.; (Concord) 57.1 in.; (Eagle) 57.6 in.; Standard Tires: (Spirit) P185/75R14 GBR; (Concord) P195/75R14 GBR; (Eagle) P195/75R15 GBR.

TECHNICAL: Four-speed manual floor shift standard; five-speed overdrive transmission optional; three-speed automatic optional. Eagles: "Select Drive" 4WD with transfer case. Four-speed manual gear ratios: (1st) 4.03:1; (2nd) 2.37:1; (3rd) 1.50:1; (4th) 1.00:1; (Rev) 3.78:1. Five-speed gear ratios: same as four- speed with additional fifth gear (0.86:1 for four-cylinder, 0.76:1 for sixes). Standard axle ratio: (four-cylinder engine) 3.08:1; (Spirit/Concord six) 2.35:1 exc. w/auto. trans. 2.21:1; (Concord) 2.21:1; (Eagle 50 six) 2.35:1; (Eagle 30 six) 2.73:1 exc. w/auto. 2.35:1. Steering: recirculating ball. Suspension: independent front with coil springs, upper/lower control arms, anti-roll bar; semi-elliptic rear leaf springs with "live" (rigid) rear axle. Brakes: front disc, rear drum; (Spirit/Concord) 10.8 in. disc, 9 in. drum; exc. Conc. wagon, 10 in. drums; (Eagle) 11 in. discs, 10 in. drums. Electronic ignition. Fuel tank: (Spirit/Eagle 50) 21 gal.; (Concord/Eagle 30) 22 gal.

DRIVETRAIN OPTIONS: 258 cid six-cylinder engine ($150). Five-speed floor shift with overdrive ($199). Column-shift automatic transmission: Spirit/Concord ($411). Floor-shift automatic transmission: Spirit/Eagle ($411). Optional axle ratios: Concord six (2.73:1) or Eagle 30 six (3.08:1) with automatic and trailer towing pkg. ($21). Twin Grip differential: Spirit/Concord ($75-$79). Heavy-duty engine cooling system (H.D. radiator, viscous fan, coolant recovery system): Spirit six, Concord ($75) but std. w/Concord air cond.; Eagle ($65). Maximum cooling system: Eagle ($68). Handling package: Spirit/Concord ($46). H.D. shock absorbers: Spirit/Concord ($17); N/A with Spirit GT rally tuned pkg. or load-leveling. Automatic load leveling: Concord six ($163). Extra duty suspension package: Eagle 30 ($75). Extra duty suspension pkg. incl. rear sway bar and H.D. shocks: Eagle 50 ($40). Front suspension skid plate: Eagle ($75). Trailer towing package 'A': Concord/Eagle 30 ($101). Trailer towing package 'B': Eagle 50 six ($215). H.D. battery ($25). Cold climate group incl. H.D. battery and engine block heater ($56). California emission system ($50).

CONVENIENCE/APPEARANCE OPTIONS: Spirit GT package: on DL liftback ($399). Spirit GT rally tuned suspension package: liftback ($129). Eagle Sport package: Eagle 30 2-dr./wag. ($333); Eagle 50 lift. ($499); Eagle 50 DL lift. ($394). Extra-quiet insulation package: Spirit/Concord/Eagle 50 ($59); std. on Concord DL/Ltd., Eagle DL. Protection group (stainless door edge guards, bumper guards and nerfing strips, front mats): Spirit/Concord ($128); DL/Ltd. ($78); Spirit GT ($42). Eagle protection group incl. stainless door edge guards, bumper guards, floor mats ($92); w/Sport pkg. ($42). Convenience group (headlight-on buzzer, intermittent wipers, lighted vanity mirror) ($71). Gauge package (clock, tach, oil, amp or volt, vacuum): Spirit, Eagle 50 ($147); Spirit GT/DL, Eagle 30 or DL ($88). Pop-up sun roof: sedans, Eagle 50 ($279). Rear spoiler: Spirit GT, Eagle 50 Sport lift. ($101). Light group ($59). Left remote control mirror ($30) exc. GT; std. on DL models; N/A on Eagle 30. Right remote mirror (chrome): DL models, Eagle 30 ($31). Left/right remote chrome mirrors ($61) exc. Spirit GT/DL; std. on Concord Ltd.; N/A Eagle 30. Right remote sport mirror (black): Spirit GT lift., Eagle Sport ($31). Left/right electric remote chrome mirrors ($142) exc. DL and Eagle 30 ($112); Eagle 30/Concord Ltd. ($81). Day/night mirror ($14); std. on DL/Ltd.; N/A Eagle 30. Power steering: Spirit/Concord ($199). Power front disc brakes ($99). Electronic cruise control ($159). Air conditioning ($609-$679). Air conditioning package incl. tinted glass and power steering: Spirit/Concord ($890-$973). Halogen headlamps ($41). Halogen foglamps: Eagle ($79). Dual horns ($16) exc. Eagle 30; std. on DL/Ltd. AM radio ($99). AM/FM/CB stereo four-speaker radio ($456) exc. Spirit DL ($357). AM/FM/Stereo four-speaker radio ($208) exc. Spirit DL ($109). AM/FM/cassette stereo radio ($356) exc. Spirit DL ($257). Electronically tuned AM/FM/cassette stereo radio w/power amplifier and four coax speakers ($499); Spirit DL ($400). Premium audio system incl. power amplifier, 4 hi-fi speakers, fader ($115). Power antenna ($56). Power door locks: Spirit DL, Concord DL/Ltd. 2-dr. sed., Eagle DL ($106); Concord DL/Ltd. and Eagle 30 4-dr./wag. ($152). Power door locks and windows: Spirit DL, Concord DL/Ltd. 2-dr. sed., Eagle DL ($275); Concord DL/Ltd. and Eagle 30 4-dr./wag. ($391). Power liftback release: Spirit/Eagle 50 ($37) but incl. w/rear spoiler. Power decklid release: Concord/Eagle sed. ($37). Power six-way driver's seat: Concord DL/Ltd., Eagle 30 ($171). Power six-way driver/pass. seat: Concord DL/Ltd., Eagle 30 ($281). Center console w/armrest: Spirit ($89). Floor shift console: Eagle ($56). Parcel shelf ($26). Coventry Check fabric reclining bucket seats: Spirit/Eagle 50 ($32). Individual reclining seats (Castilian sculptured fabric): Concord DL, Eagle 30 ($59). Individual reclining seats (Durham plaid fabric): Eagle 30 ($59). Cargo area cover: Concord/Eagle wag. ($68). Digital clock ($59); std. on DL/Ltd.; N/A Eagle 30. Rear wiper/washer ($119). Rear defroster ($125). Vinyl sport steering wheel: Spirit/Eagle 50 ($39) but std. w/GT. Woodgrain steering wheel: DL models, Eagle 30 ($35). Leather-wrapped sport steering wheel ($58) exc. GT/Ltd., Eagle 50 Sport ($19-$23). Tilt steering wheel ($99). Tinted glass ($82-$95). Two-tone accent color: Spirit exc. GT, Concord DL/Ltd. ($119); Special color combinations ($33). Rally stripes: Spirit ($85). Woodgrain paneling: Eagle 30 wag. ($139). Delete woodgrain from Concord DL/Ltd. wag. (deduct $75). Scuff moldings ($47). Roof rack: Spirit sed./Eagle 50 ($85); Concord/Eagle 30 wag. ($105). Locking gas cap ($10). Tailgate air deflector: Spirit sed., Eagle kammback ($32). Bumper guards ($50) but std. w/DL, GT, Ltd., Eagle Sport pkg. Styled wheel covers (argent): Spirit ($40) exc. GT; std. on Spirit DL; Concord ($84); Concord DL ($43); Eagle 50 ($52). Custom wheel covers: Concord ($41); std. on DL. Wire wheel covers ($155); Spirit DL exc. GT ($115); Concord DL ($114). Spoke style 14 x 6 in. wheels w/trim rings ($172) exc. DL ($131-$132); Concord Ltd. ($17). Turbocast II aluminum 14 x 7 in. wheels ($398) exc. DL ($357-$358); Spirit GT ($226); Concord Ltd. ($243). Sport aluminum 15 x 6 in. wheels: Eagle ($335-$387). Spirit/Concord Tires: P185/75R14 white GBR: Spirit ($66). P185/75R black GBR: Spirit GT sed. (NC). P195/75R14 black GBR: Spirit ($40). P195/75R14 white GBR: Spirit ($108); Spirit DL ($40); Concord ($66). P195/75R14 white SBR Arriva: Spirit ($177); Spirit DL ($111); Concord ($137); Concord DL/Ltd. ($71); P205/70R14 RWL polysteel radial: Spirit ($252); Spirit DL ($186); Concord ($227); Concord DL/Ltd. ($161). Eagle Tires: P195/75R15 white GBR: Eagle 50 ($60). P195/75R15 black SBR Arriva: Eagle 30 ($25); Eagle 50 ($85); Eagle DL ($25). P195/75R15 white SBR Arriva: Eagle 30 ($85); Eagle 30 Sport ($60); Eagle 50 ($145); Eagle DL ($85); Eagle Sport ($60). P215/65R15 OWL SBR Eagle GT: Eagle 30 ($200); Eagle 30 Sport ($175); Eagle 50 ($260); Eagle DL ($200); Eagle Sport ($175).

HISTORY: Introduced: September 24, 1981. Model year production (U.S.): 70,898 (1.4 percent of industry total). Of that number, 14,972 were four-cylinder, 55,926 six-cylinder. Calendar year production (U.S.): 109,746 (including new Alliances for 1983). Model year sales by U.S. dealers: 99,300 (including 6837 new Alliances), for a market share of 1.8 percent. Calendar year sales: 112,433 (2.0 percent share of industry sales).

Historical Footnotes: On June 15, 1982, production of the new Renault-designed, front-drive Alliance finally began at the Kenosha, Wisconsin plant. Its acceptance in the marketplace could signal whether AMC's passenger car operation would continue to survive. The Alliance would not debut until September, as a 1983 model. Even including its captive import Renault models (Fuego, 18i and LeCar), AMC's market share declined to well under 2 percent for the '82 model year. Sales of the 4WD Eagle dipped too, though not nearly so badly as the other models in the lineup. Only the Renault connection, it seemed, had a reasonable chance of rescuing the ailing company. With the assistance of early Alliance sales in the fall, AMC managed to beat Volkswagen of America to recapture fourth place in the domestic rankings, for the first time since 1978. In October, the company announced a reduction in the white-collar work force, relying on attrition and early retirement as well as layoffs. An unusual 1982 agreement with the UAW allowed AMC to invest up to $2,000 from workers' paychecks in new product programs, to be repaid starting in 1985 with 10 percent interest. W. Paul Tippett Jr. was installed as chairman and CEO, replacing Gerald C. Meyers, who resigned in January 1982. In late September, all Spirit and Eagle SX/4 production moved to the plant at Brampton, Ontario. Big Eagles continued to be made in Kenosha. Concords were built at both factories.

Innovations: Switchable two/four wheel drive. Built-in computer in electronic fuel feedback carburetion system to assist mechanics with swift diagnosis.

1983 AMC

Both Spirit and Concord prepared for their final outings, but American Motors entered the 1983 model year with a Small French Hope: the front-drive Alliance. Mixing driver conveniences with technological sophistication, the AMC/Renault joint-venture soon would be the only two-wheel-drive offering from AMC. The venerable 258 cu. in. six gained a fuel feedback system with oxygen (knock) sensor, along with a healthy jump up to 9.2:1 compression. Gearing changed slightly to achieve better performance, in response to 1982 alterations that boosted mileage.

1983 Renault Alliance sedan (AMC)

(Renault) ALLIANCE — SERIES 90 — FOUR — Drivetrains for the new subcompact Alliance came from France, but cars were assembled in Wisconsin. A fuel-injected version of the 1.4-liter four-cylinder engine, as used on the imported Le Car, provided the power through a four-speed overdrive manual shift. Alliances featured rack-and-pinion steering and front drive, with fully independent (front and rear) suspension. A five-speed manual transmission was optional; also a three-speed automatic. Two- and four-door notchback sedans were offered, with standard power front disc brakes. Quad rectangular headlamps flanked a horizontal-bar grille with center emblem. Parking lights were below the bumpers. An 'Alliance' emblem sat ahead of the front doors, as on other AMC models. MacPherson struts and coil springs made up the front suspension design, which included front (and rear) stabilizer bars. Alliances rode 155/80GR13 blackwall glass-belted radials with semi-styled wheels and hub covers. Body features included moldings for roof drip rail, rear window, rocker panels, body sides, and windshield surrounds. Inside were vinyl bucket seats (non-reclining), a console with lighter, fabric-covered headliner, a trip odometer, electric wipers with pulse action, and soft-feel steering wheel. Trunks were carpeted; hoods released from inside the car. A microcomputer monitored engine functions, sending signals to a dashboard indicator. The pedestal front seats rocked on curved tracks, adding to leg room for rear passengers. One unusual option: an infra-red door locking/unlocking device, similar to a remote-controlled garage door opener. Another: a "Systems Sentry" that warns (via lights) of low fluid levels and brake pad wear. Three upgrades were available. The L Alliance added dual accent pinstripes, a bright grille and hub covers, day/night mirror, and blacked-out rocker panels. It also carried moldings for beltline, bumper inserts and taillamps. DL models included deluxe six-way cloth bucket rocker/recliner seats, door panels with "hockey stick" armrests, a soft-hub steering wheel, extra-quiet insulation, tinted glass, dual rear ashtrays, tachometer, color-keyed remote left mirror, dual- note horn, and digital clock. The five-speed transmission was standard on DL models, which wore 175/70SR13 blackwalls with metric white trim rings. Topping the line was the Limited, with textured fabric bucket rocker/recliner seats and luxury door panels. Extras included a rear center armrest, light group, bright wheel lip moldings, luxury wheel covers, visibility group, and halogen headlamps. Alliance body colors were: Almond Beige; Olympic White; Deep Night Blue; Jade Mist; Sebring Red; and Sterling, Garnet, Cinnamon, Amberglow or Diamond Blue metallic clearcoat. Later in the model year an MT edition appeared, painted in special charcoal gray metallic clearcoat with 'MT' decals and a black rear panel. Additional gear included a decklid luggage rack, right-hand remote mirror, bright instrument panel molding, bodyside and hood pinstriping, painted aluminum wheels, and leather-wrapped steering wheel. Inside the MT were Limited fabric rocker/recliner seats and a six-speaker, electronic-tuning stereo radio.

SPIRIT — SERIES 40 — SIX — Not much changed on the body of the Spirit in its final year, but it gained bigger tires (P195/75R14 whitewalls), styled wheel covers, and a pushbutton AM radio as standard DL fittings. The sedan was gone; only the liftback remained. Rather than the previous four, AMC's 258 cu. in. six-cylinder engine (now with knock sensor) became the sole powerplant. Four-speed manual floor shift was standard; five-speed overdrive or automatic (column or floor shift) optional. Mixing the standard goodies from the previous base and DL models, this year's Spirit came with vinyl reclining bucket seats, lighted ashtray (and lighter), front armrest, locking glove

box, dome light, day/night mirror, digital clock, bumper guards, remote left mirror, styled wheel covers, a front sway bar, and extra-quiet insulation package. Formerly an option package, the Spirit GT became a separate model this year. Performance extras included a handling package, gauge package with tachometer, and P195/75R14 SBR Arriva tires on Turbocast II aluminum wheels. Among its other goodies: a leather-wrapped sport steering wheel, black bumpers with guards and nerfing strips, black pinstripes, fog lamps, black moldings and dual remote-control sport mirrors, and center console with armrest. GT Spirits had no clock or radio as standard equipment.

1983 Concord sedan (JG)

CONCORD — SERIES 01 — SIX — Like the Spirit, the Concord carried a standard 258 cu. in. six for 1983, abandoning the four-cylinder. That engine now had a new fuel feedback system and knock sensor for added efficiency. Only the twin four-door models remained: sedan and station wagon, in base or DL or trim (plus a Limited wagon). DL sedans sported a full vinyl roof and opera windows. The enlarged standard equipment list included a front sway bar, front and rear ashtrays, lighter, coat hooks, color-keyed carpeting, Alpine fabric headliner and sun visors, energy- absorbing front/rear bumpers, a hood ornament, drip rail and windshield moldings, wide rocker panel moldings, and scuff belt moldings. DL and Limited equipment was similar to 1982. The 'Concord' nameplate was on the upper corner of the grille, as well as on front fenders.

EAGLE — SERIES 50 — FOUR/SIX — Only the four-wheel-drive Eagles kept the old 151 cubic- inch (Pontiac) four-cylinder engine as base powerplant, with an optional 258 six. And only the Liftback SX/4 model remained, with body graphics to prove it. Base models included a padded horn bar; DL versions a custom woodgrain steering wheel. Otherwise, equipment remained similar to the previous year. A Sport package was offered again, with halogen headlamps and fog lamps (the latter mounted above the front bumper). The package included a 'Sport' nameplate and red or silver inserts in lower bodyside moldings. Other details were the same as the 1982 Sport package, with a heavy emphasis on black accents. Shorter (3.54:1) gearing with the four-cylinder engine boosted performance.

1983 American Eagle station wagon (JG)

EAGLE — SERIES 30 — FOUR/SIX — Senior Eagles lost several models this year: the two-door sedan, and the Limited four-door. Standard engine was the familiar 151 four with four-speed manual shift; 258 six optional, along with five-speed overdrive gearbox or floor- shift automatic. At mid-year, a new AMC-built four, measuring 150 cu. in., replaced the Pontiac 151. Base Eagles were well equipped, including armrests, Alpine fabric headliner/visors, digital clock, trunk and cargo area carpeting, day/night rearview mirror, dome light, locking glove compartment, a custom woodgrain steering wheel, woodgrain instrument panel, bumper nerf strips, wheel opening and rocker panel moldings, and chrome remote-control left mirror. Reclining front seats were upholstered in deluxe grain vinyl. Wagons had a fold-down rear bench seat and flip-up tailgate, plus a retractable cargo area cover. Sedans included a full vinyl roof. Whitewall P195/75R15 B glass-belted radials came with full wheel covers. Accenting Eagle bodies were molding on the drip rail, beltline, backlight, and windshield. All Eagles had power steering and brakes. The Limited wagon held Chelsea leather reclining seats and other extras similar to the 1982 version: 18-oz. carpeting, woodgrain steering wheel, parcel shelf, and a second remote-control mirror. The Sport package was offered again, but only on the station wagon. Its contgents were the same as in 1982, with red or silver inserts in the lower bodyside moldings, a silver '4x4'decal on the lower door, and P195/75R15 blackwall Arriva steel-belted radials.

I.D. DATA: The 17-symbol VIN, embossed on a metal plate on the top surface of the instrument panel, used the same coding as in 1981-82; see previous section for details. The model year code changed to 'D' for 1983. Engine codes for the 151 cu. in. four were on a pad at the right side of the block, below the cylinder head. Six-cylinder codes were on a pad between cylinders two and three. Alliance's 17-symbol VIN was similar. The first three symbols ('1AM') indicated U.S., AMC, and passenger car. The fourth symbol showed fuel injection type: 'D' Bendix TBI; 'E' Bosch multi-point. Symbol five shows transmission type: 'M' four-speed manual; 'W' five-speed; 'C' automatic. Digits 6-7 indicate body style: '95' four-door sedan; '95' two-door sedan. Digit eight shows trim level: '0' base model; '3' L; '6' DL; '8' Limited. Ninth is a check digit; tenth, the model year code ('D' 1983). In eleventh position, 'K' Kenosha manufacture. Finally comes a six-digit sequence number.

ALLIANCE (BASE) SERIES 90

Series Number	Body/Style Number	Body Type & Seating	Factory Price	Shipping Weight	Production Total
90	8396-0	2-dr Sed-5P	5595	1945	Note 1

ALLIANCE L

90	8396-3	2-dr Sed-5P	6020	1945	55,556
90	8395-3	4-dr Sed-5P	6270	1980	86,649

ALLIANCE DL

90	8396-6	2-dr Sed-5P	6655	1945	Note 1
90	8395-6	4-dr Sed-5P	6905	1980	Note 1

ALLIANCE LIMITED

90	8395-8	4-dr Sed-5P	7470	1980	Note 1

ALLIANCE MT

90	8396-6	2-dr Sed-5P	7450	N/A	Note 1
90	8395-6	4-dr Sed-5P	7700	N/A	Note 1

Note 1: Production totals shown under Alliance L include base, DL and Limited models. Model year sales: 124,687 Alliances.

SPIRIT DL SERIES 40

40	8343-5	2-dr Lift-4P	5995	2732	Note 2

SPIRIT GT SERIES 40

40	8343-9	2-dr Lift-4P	6495	2756	Note 2

Note 2: Total model year production, 3491. Model year sales: 6487.

CONCORD (BASE) SERIES 01

01	8305-0	4-dr Sed-5P	6724	2820	4433
01	8308-0	4-dr Sta Wag-5P	7449	2864	867

CONCORD DL

01	8305-5	4-dr Sed-5P	6995	2900	Note 3
01	8308-5	4-dr Sta Wag-5P	7730	2938	Note 3

CONCORD LIMITED

01	8308-7	4-dr Sta Wag-5P	8117	2990	Note 3

Note 3: Production totals shown under base Concord include DL and Limited models. Model year sales: 16,576 Concords.

EAGLE SX/4 SERIES 50

50	8353-0	2-dr Lift-4P	7697/7852	2956/3084	2259

EAGLE SX/4 DL

50	8353-5	2-dr Lift-4P	8164/8319	3025/3153	Note 4

Note 4: Production total includes SX/4 base and DL models.

EAGLE SERIES 30

30	8335-5	4-dr Sed-5P	9162/9317	3181/3309	3093
30	8338-5	4-dr Sta Wag-5P	9882/10037	3201/3329	12,378

EAGLE 30 LIMITED

30	8338-7	4-dr Sta Wag-5P	10343/10498	3215/3343	Note 5

Note 5: Station wagon production total shown includes base and Limited models. Total Eagle model year production, 17,730 (only 464 of them with four-cylinder engine). Model year sales: 31,604.

1983 Alliance coupe (JG)

EAGLE FACTORY PRICE AND WEIGHT NOTE: Figure before the slash is for four-cylinder engine, after slash for six-cylinder.

ENGINES: BASE FOUR (Eagle): Inline. OHV. Four-cylinder. Cast iron block and head. Displacement: 151 cu. in. (2.5 liters). Bore & stroke: 4.0 x 3.0 in. Compression ratio: 8.2:1. Brake horsepower: 84 at 4000 R.P.M. Torque: 125 lbs.-ft. at 2600 R.P.M. Five main bearings. Hydraulic valve lifters. Carburetor: 2Bbl. Rochester 2SE. **REPLACEMENT FOUR** (Eagle): Inline. OHV. Four-cylinder. Cast iron block. Displacement: 150 cu. in. (2.46 liters). Bore & stroke: 3.88 x 3.19 in. Compression ratio: 9.2:1. Brake horsepower: N/A. Torque: 132 lbs.-ft. at 3200 R.P.M. Five main bearings. Hydraulic valve lifters. Carburetor: 1Bbl. electronic feedback Carter YFA. **BASE SIX** (Spirit, Concord); **OPTIONAL** (Eagle): Inline. OHV. Six-cylinder. Cast iron block and head. Displacement: 258 cu. in. (4.2 liters). Bore & stroke: 3.75 x 3.90 in. Compression ratio: 9.2:1. Brake horsepower: 110 at 3200 R.P.M. Torque: 210 lbs.-ft. at 1800 R.P.M. Seven main bearings. Hydraulic valve lifters. Carburetor: 2Bbl. Carter BBD. **BASE FOUR** (Alliance): Inline. OHV. Four-cylinder. Cast iron block; aluminum head. Transverse mounted. Displacement: 85.2 cu. in. (1.4 liters). Bore & stroke: 2.99 x 3.03 in. Compression ratio: 8.8:1. Brake horsepower: 56 at 4200 R.P.M. Torque: 75 lbs.-ft. at 2500 R.P.M. Five main bearings. Solid valve lifters. Single-point Bendix (throttle-body) fuel injection.

CHASSIS DATA: Wheelbase: (Alliance) 97.8 in.; (Spirit) 96 in.; (Concord) 108 in.; (Eagle 50) 97.2 in.; (Eagle 30) 109.3 in. Overall length: (Alliance) 163.8 in.; (Spirit) 167.2 in.; (Concord) 185 in.; (Eagle 50 SX/4) 164.6 in.; (Eagle 30) 183.2 in. Height: (Alliance) 54.5 in.; (Eagle 30 wagon) 55 in.; (Spirit) 51.5 in.; (Concord) 51-51.6 in.; (Eagle SX/4) 55 in.; (Eagle 30) 55.4 in. Width: (Alliance) 65.0 in.; (Spirit) 71.9 in.; (Concord) 71 in.; (Eagle SX/4) 73 in.; (Eagle 30) 72.3 in. Front Tread: (Alliance) 55.2 in.; (Spirit/Concord) 57.6 in.; (Eagle) 59.6 in. Rear Tread: (Alliance) 54.9 in.; (Spirit/Concord) 57.1 in.; (Eagle) 57.6 in. Standard Tires: (Alliance) 155/80GR13 GBR; (Spirit/Concord) P195/75R14 GBR; (Eagle) P195/75R15 GBR.

TECHNICAL: Transmission: four-speed manual floor shift standard, five-speed manual and automatic optional. Alliance transaxle: four-speed; five-speed and automatic optional. Manual transmission gear ratios (Alliance four-speed); (1st) 3.73:1; (2nd) 2.06:1; (3rd) 1.27:1; (4th) 0.90:1. (Alliance five-speed): (1st) 3.73:1; (2nd) 2.06:1; (3rd) 1.27:1; (4th) 0.90:1; (5th) 0.73:1. Spirit/Concord/Eagle (Borg-Warner T4) manual shift gear ratios: (1st) 4.03:1; (2nd) 2.37:1; (3rd) 1.50:1; (4th) 1.00:1; (Rev) 3.76:1. Borg-Warner T5 five-speed: same but 0.86:1 (four-cyl.) or 0.76:1 (six-cyl.) top gear. Standard axle ratio: (Alliance) 3.56:1 w/automatic, 3.29:1 w/4-spd., 3.87:1 w/5-spd.; (Spirit) 2.35:1; (Concord) 2.35:1 except 5-spd., 2.73:1; (Eagle four) 3.54:1; (Eagle SX/4 six) 2.35:1; (Eagle 50 six) 2.73:1 exc. w/auto., 2.35:1. Drive: (Alliance) front; (others) rear. Clutch dia.: (Alliance) 7.1 in.; (others) 9.1 in. exc. six-cylinder, 9.5 in. Transverse-mounted engine (Alliance). Steering: (Alliance) rack and pinion; (others) recirculating ball. Suspension: (Spirit/Concord/Eagle) independent front coil springs with anti-roll bar, semi-elliptic rear leaf springs; (Alliance) fully independent—MacPherson strut front, twin transverse torsion bar rear, anti-roll bars. Brakes: front disc, rear drum; (Alliance) 9.4 in. disc, 8 in. drum; (Spirit/Concord) 10.8 in. disc, 9x2 in. drum; (Concord wagon) 10x1.75 in. drum; (Eagle) 11 in. disc, 10x1.75 in. drum. . Electronic ignition. Unibody construction. Fuel tank: (Alliance) 12.5 gal.; (Spirit, SX/4) 21 gal.; (Concord/Eagle) 22 gal.

1983 Spirit D/L liftback coupe (JG)

SPIRIT/CONCORD/EAGLE DRIVETRAIN OPTIONS: 258 cid six-cylinder engine: Eagle ($155). Five-speed floor shift with overdrive: Spirit/Concord ($125). Five-speed floor shift with overdrive and Select Drive: Eagle $219. Column-shift automatic transmission: Spirit/Concord ($423). Floor-shift automatic transmission: Spirit ($423); Eagle ($437). Optional axle ratios: Concord/Eagle six (2.73:1), or Eagle 30 six (3.08:1) with automatic and trailer towing pkg. ($30). Twin Grip differential: Spirit/Concord ($82). Heavy-duty engine cooling system (H.D. radiator, viscous fan/shroud, coolant recovery system): Spirit/Concord ($77) but std. w/air cond. H.D. engine cooling (H.D. radiator, viscous fan): Eagle four ($67). Maximum cooling system: Eagle six ($70). Handling package (unique front sway bar; rear sway bar): Spirit/ Concord ($48). Automatic load leveling (air shocks): Concord/Eagle 30 ($169). Extra duty suspension pkg. (special front sway bar, rear sway bar and H.D. shocks): Eagle SX/4 ($65); also incl. H.D. springs, Eagle 30 ($77). Front suspension skid plate: Eagle ($77). Trailer towing package 'A' (to 2000 lbs.): Concord/Eagle 30 ($104). Trailer towing package 'B' (to 3500 lbs.): Eagle 30 ($222). H.D. battery ($26). Cold climate group incl. H.D. battery and engine block heater ($58). California emission system ($65).

SPIRIT/CONCORD/EAGLE CONVENIENCE/APPEARANCE OPTIONS: Eagle Sport package: Eagle SX/4 ($516); Eagle 30 DL ($407); Eagle 30 wag. ($344). Extra-quiet insulation package: Concord/Eagle SX/4 ($61); std. on Concord DL/Ltd. Protection group (stainless door edge guards, bumper guards and nerfing strips, front mats): Spirit ($30-$40). Protection group w/o nerfing strips: Concord ($132); Concord DL/Ltd. ($81). Eagle protection group (stainless door edge guards, bumper guards, floor mats:Eagle 30 ($75); w/Sport pkg. ($23). Eagle protection group with front mats only: SX/4 ($72); w/Sport pkg. ($20). Convenience group: headlight-on buzzer, intermittent wipers, right lighted vanity mirror ($73). Gauge package (clock, tach, oil, amp or volt, vacuum): Eagle SX/4 ($152); Spirit, Eagle 30, SX/4 DL ($91). Pop-up sun roof ($295). Rear spoiler (incl. power liftback release): Spirit, Eagle SX/4 ($104). Light group ($61). Left remote control mirror: Concord, Eagle SX/4 ($32); std. on DL models. Right remote mirror (chrome): DL models, Eagle 30 ($32). Left/right remote chrome mirrors: Concord, Eagle SX/4 exc. Sport/DL ($64). Right remote sport mirror (black): Eagle 30 Sport wag. or SX/4 Sport ($32). Left/right electric remote chrome mirrors: SX/4 ($147); DL models ($115-$116); Ltd. wagons ($83). Day/night mirror: Concord, SX/4 ($15). Power steering: Spirit/Concord ($212). Power front disc brakes: Spirit/Concord ($100). Electronic cruise control ($170). Air conditioning system ($670-$725). Halogen headlamps ($20). Halogen foglamps: Eagle ($82). Dual horns: Concord, SX/4 ($17).; std. on DL/Ltd. AM radio ($82- $83). AM/FM/CB stereo four-speaker radio ($471) exc. Spirit DL. AM/FM/Stereo four-speaker radio ($389). AM/FM/Stereo four-speaker radio ($199) exc. Spirit DL ($117). AM/FM/cassette stereo radio ($329) exc. Spirit DL ($247). Electronically tuned AM/FM/cassette stereo radio w/power amplifier and four coax speakers ($499); Spirit DL ($417). Power door locks: Spirit, SX/4 DL ($120); Concord DL/Ltd. and Eagle 30 ($170). Power windows and door locks: Spirit, SX/4 DL

19

($300); Concord DL/Ltd. and Eagle 30 ($425). Power liftback release: Eagle SX/4 ($40); incl. w/rear spoiler. Power decklid release: Concord/Eagle sed. ($40). Power six-way driver's seat: Concord DL/Ltd., Eagle 30 ($189). Power six-way driver/pass. seat: Concord DL/Ltd., Eagle 30 ($302). Center console w/armrest: Spirit DL ($92). Floor shift console: Eagle ($65). Parcel shelf ($27). Coventry Check fabric bucket seat trim: Spirit/Eagle SX/4 ($39). Castilian sculptured fabric seat trim: Concord DL, Eagle 30 ($67). Durham plaid fabric seat trim: Eagle 30 ($67). Digital clock: Concord, SX/4 ($61); std. on DL/Ltd. Rear wiper/washer ($124). Rear defroster ($135). Vinyl sport steering wheel: Spirit DL, Eagle SX/4 ($40). Woodgrain steering wheel: DL models, Eagle 30 ($36). Leather-wrapped sport steering wheel ($60) exc. Concord Ltd. Wag. and Eagle 30 Ltd. ($24); SX/4 Sport ($20); N/A Spirit DL. Tilt steering wheel ($106). Tinted glass ($95-$105). Two-tone accent color: Spirit exc. GT, Concord DL/Ltd. ($135); Special color combinations ($49). Rally stripes: Spirit DL ($88). Woodgrain paneling: Eagle 30 wag. ($144). Delete woodgrain from Concord DL/Ltd. wag. (deduct $75). Scuff moldings ($55). Roof rack: Concord/Eagle 30 wag. ($115). Locking gas cap ($10). Bumper guards:Concord/Eagle ($52) but std. w/DL, Ltd., Eagle Sport pkg. Styled wheel covers (argent): Concord ($87); Concord DL ($45); Eagle SX/4 ($54); N/A Concord Ltd. Custom wheel covers: Concord ($42); std. on DL. Wire wheel covers: Spirit DL ($119); Concord ($160). Spoke style 14 x 6 in. wheels w/trim rings: Spirit/Concord DL ($136); Concord ($178); Concord Ltd. Wag. ($18). Turbocast II aluminum 14 x 7 in. wheels: Spirit DL ($370); Concord ($411); Concord DL/Ltd. Wag. ($251). Sport aluminum 15 x 6 in. wheels: Eagle ($346-$400).

Spirit/Concord Tires: P195/75R14 B white GBR: Spirit DL (NC). P195/75R14 B black SBR Arriva: Spirit GT (NC). P195/75R14 B white SBR Arriva: Spirit DL, Concord DL/Ltd. ($73); Concord ($142). P205/70R14 B RWL polysteel radial: Spirit/Concord DL/Ltd. ($192); Spirit GT ($188); Concord ($281).

Eagle Tires: P195/75R15 B white GBR: SX/4 ($69). P195/75R15 B black SBR Arriva: Eagle 30, SX/4 DL ($20); SX/4 ($73). P195/75R15 B white SBR Arriva: SX/4 ($142); Eagle 30, SX/4 DL ($73); Sport ($69). P215/65R15 B OWL SBR Eagle GT: SX/4 ($269); Eagle 30, SX/4 DL ($200); Eagle Sport ($196).

ALLIANCE OPTIONS: Five-speed manual transmission, floor shift, w/overdrive: L ($95). Floor-shift automatic tranmission ($420) exc. DL/MT/Ltd. ($325). H.D. battery ($25). Cold climate group ($36-$79). H.D. cooling ($67). Systems Sentry (monitors for low oil, coolant, brake fluid, disc wear, washer/power steering fluid, transaxle oil) ($125). Extra-quiet insulation package: L ($62). Protection group incl. door edge guards, carpeted mats, locking gas cap ($52); N/A base. Visibility group (dual remote mirrors, lighted visor mirror, intermittent wipers: L ($160); DL ($129); MT ($97). Light group ($46). Halogen headlamps: L/DL/MT ($20). Tachometer: L ($82). Power steering ($199). Speed control ($170); N/A base. Air conditioning ($630). Power windows ($300-$350). Intermittent wipers: L/DL/MT ($50). Keyless entry system ($95). Power door locks ($120-$170) exc. base model. Rear defroster ($130). Tinted glass ($90). AM radio exc. MT ($82). AM/FM radio exc. MT ($135). AM/FM stereo radio: L/DL/Ltd. ($199). Electronic- tuning AM/FM stereo four-speaker radio w/cassette: L/DL/Ltd. ($465). Speaker for left I.P. ($28). Vinyl reclining bucket seats: base/L ($65). Vinyl rocker/reclining buckets: DL (NC). Cloth bucket seats: L ($30). Cloth reclining bucket seats: L ($95). Leather rocker/reclining bucket seats: Ltd./MT ($413). Two-tone paint: L/DL/Ltd. ($160). Metallic accent paint: DL/Ltd. (NC); L ($62). Black leather-wrapped sport steering wheel: L/DL/Ltd. ($60). Luxury wheel covers: L ($88); DL ($36). Wheel trim rings: L ($52). Aluminum wheels: L/DL/Ltd. ($249-$337). Tires: 155/80GR13 white GBR: base/L ($61). 175/70SR13 SBR: L ($72). 175/70SR13 white SBR: L ($132); DL/Ltd. ($60). Spare tire (to replace polyspare): L/DL/MT/Ltd. ($35).

HISTORY: Introduced: September 22, 1982. Model year production (U.S.): 168,726, which amounted to nearly 3 percent of the industry total—more than double the 1982 percentage. Of that number, 142,669 were four-cylinder, 25,057 six-cylinder. Calendar year production (U.S.): 201,993 (including new Encores for 1984). Eagle production of 6979 units was dwarfed by the 152,581 Alliances made during 1983. But 23,012 Eagles were built in Canada. Model year sales by U.S. dealers: 183,005 (including 3651 new Encores). Calendar year sales: 193,251 for a 2.8 percent market share, up substantially from the 1.9 percent in 1982.

Historical Footnotes: Designed by Renault in France, but manufactured in Kenosha, Wisconsin, the subcompact front-drive Alliance set the stage for other joint ventures betweeen American and foreign companies. Promoted as combining "advanced European technology with American expertise," Alliance attempted to lure buyers from both the domestic and import ranks. Its design evolved from the Renault 9, acclaimed "Car of the Year" by the European press in 1982. Tooling had begun in August 1981. Some $200 million was spent on development and production, over a 2 1/2-year period. Ample changes were made to adapt the car for American tastes, including the addition of American-designed power steering and brake systems, Bendix fuel injection, and electronic controls. Meanwhile, the Spirit and Concord quietly disappeared as AMC focused on its joint- venture and the 4WD Eagle. AMC registered a loss of $146.7 million for the year, nearly as bad as 1982, though the final quarter showed a modest profit—perhaps pointing toward a better year ahead. In July, AMC sold its defense subsidiary, AM General Corp.: next month, its lawn tractor operation, Wheel Horse Products. Corporate headquarters in Southfield, Michigan was sold too, then leased back—all in an attempt to raise cash for product development. Production of a new 150 cu. in., four-cylinder engine began in February 1983, installed on Eagles starting at mid-year.

1984 AMC

The slimmed-down AMC lineup, reduced to a single Eagle model and the Kenosha-built French subcompact, had one major addition for 1984. A hatchback Encore, with three or five doors, joined the original twin front-drive Alliance sedans.

Note: By this time, many automakers (including AMC) had begun to count the rear hatch of their small cars as a door; thus, a three-door hatchback has only two "real" doors; and a five-door has only four doors suitable for people to enter. Listings in this catalog follow the numbering used by the manufacturer.

(Renault) ENCORE — SERIES 90 — FOUR — Built on the same 97.8 in. wheelbase as the Alliance, the sportier Encore hatchback stood 3 in. shorter in overall length. It was AMC's attempt to attract youthful buyers, now that the Spirits and GTs were gone. Encores used the same 1.4- liter four-cylinder engine as the Alliance, with a standard four-speed (overdrive) manual transmission; five-speed optional. Three- and five-door versions were offered (see note above). Each had a stubby rear end with distinctive backlight and taillamp structure. Encore's emblem sat on the side of the grille, while Alliance's was at the center. Base Encores were nicely fitted inside with carpeting, fabric-covered headliner molding and visors, a day/night rearview mirror, lighter, inside hood release, console with stowage box, plus vinyl bucket front seats and 60/40 fold-down rear seat. Externally, they featured quad rectangular halogen headlamps and a horizontal-bar style black grille with bright molding, with blackout rocker panels and liftgate. Encores also had pulse wiper/washers, front and rear stabilizer bars, flip-out rear windows, power brakes, and P155/80GR13 glass-belted radials on semi-styled wheels with black hubcaps. Stored in back was a polyspare tire. The engine had electronic ignition and fuel injection. Suspension was fully independent, with MacPherson struts. Rack-and-pinion steering helped handling. Three upgrades were offered. S models held an AM radio, with dual accent pinstripes, cargo area cover, bright grille and wheel covers; the five-door had roll-down rear windows. LS Encores moved up to 175/70SR13 steel-belted radial tires (blackwall) with luxury sport wheel covers, plus a five-speed overdrive transmission. Other LS luxuries included tinted glass, digital clock, extra-quiet insulation, dual-note horn, oil level gauge, tachometer, "hockey stick" armrests, and rocker/recliner bucket seats in deluxe striped fabric. A chime warned of key left in ignition, headlamps-on, and seatbelts unbuckled. A black rear spoiler and left remote mirror completed the LS package. Sporty GS Encores added light and visibility groups and Westchester fabric rocker/recliner buckedt seats, plus black luxury sport wheel covers, black accent stripes, black sport steering wheels, and pinstripes along hood, bodyside and tailgate. Five-door Encores came only in S or LS versions. A Diamond Edition Encore, added later, featured gold bumper inserts and gold aluminum wheels, plus special pinstriping on hood and bodysides. Painted Olympic White or Classic Black, the Diamond Encore's wing seats were upholstered in honey fabric, while its dash held an electronic-tuning AM/FM/stereo radio with cassette player.

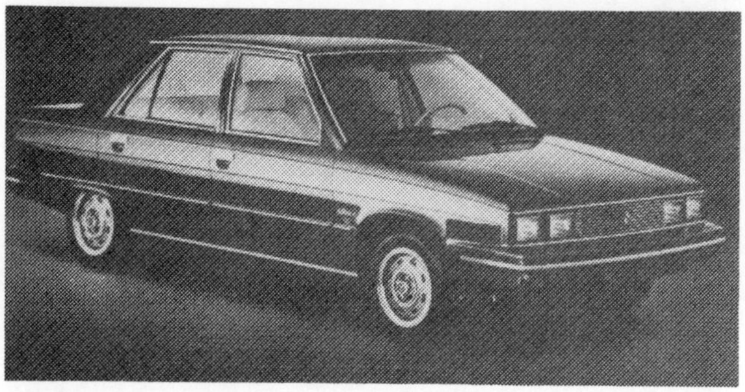

1984 Alliance sedan (JG)

(Renault) ALLIANCE — SERIES 90 — FOUR — After a strong start in the marketplace, Alliance changed little for its second year—though its price rose in several jumps. External niceties included blackout rocker panels and a black grille (with bright surround). Inside, a day/night mirror became standard on the base model, which wore P155/80GR13 blackwall tires. L models added dual accent pinstripes, bright grille and hub covers, and childproof rear door locks. DL rocker/recliner seats now held Lucerne fabric upholstery, while DL dashes contained low-fuel and oil level gauges. Calais fabric upholstery went on Limited rocker/recliner seats, which also offered hood pinstripes, a blackout lower back panel, and bright decklid luggage rack. Otherwise, standard equipment for each trim level was about the same as in 1983. Three colors were added and radio operation was improved. A second windshield washer outlet was added. Alliance's Diamond Edition was equipped like that of the Encore hatchback.

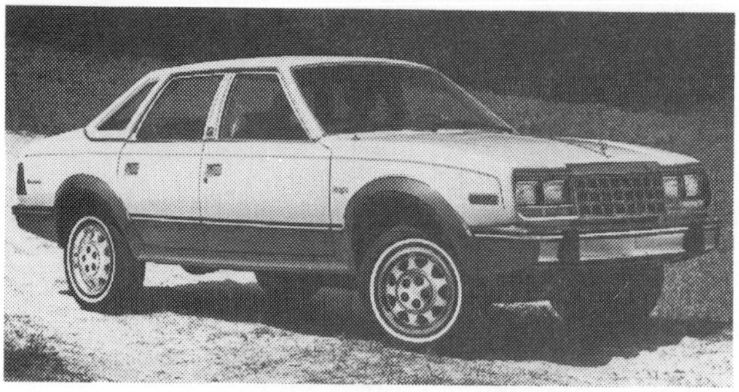

1984 Eagle four-door sedan (AMC)

EAGLE — SERIES 30 — FOUR/SIX — Only the larger Eagle survived into 1984, in four-door sedan and wagon form, powered by the new AMC-manufactured four-cylinder engine. The new 150 cu. in. (2.46 liter) four, introduced during the 1983 model run, featured a single-barrel electronic feedback carburetor. Also standard on Jeeps, it replaced the GM-built 151 cu. in. four, which had powered Spirits and Concords as well as Eagles. The standard four- speed manual transmission now included an upshift indicator light to warn drivers when a gear change was wise. As before, the 258 cu. in. six-cylinder engine was optional. The "live" rear axle suspension consisted of computer-selected springs and telescoping shock absorbers. Front suspension included full coil springs and stabilizer bar. Standard equipment was similar to the 1983 Eagle 30, including the familiar Krayton protective treatment on lower bodysides, argent styled wheel covers, dual pinstripes, dual horns, and a lockable wagon cargo compartment. Moldings highlighted drip and quarter windows areas, plus the belt surround. Power brakes and steering were standard; so was a hood ornament. Taillamps were large wraparound style. Leather reclining seats served as the main attraction on the Limited wagon. Eagle's Sport package, on base station wagons only, consisted of a leather-wrapped sport steering wheel, low-gloss black rocker panels and fender flares, black bumpers with guards and nerf strips, red or silver inserts in lower bodyside and hood moldings, black taillamp treatment, black windshield/liftgate moldings, black 'B' pillars and door frames, a left-side remote-controlled black sport mirror, and halogen headlamps. Halogen fog lamps sat above the front bumper. Sport tires were blackwall P195/75R15 steel-belted Arriva radials. A silver '4x4' decal highlighted the lower door, as did the 'Sport' nameplate.

I.D. DATA: Eagle's 17-symbol Vehicle Identification Number (VIN) was embossed on a metal plate riveted to the top left surface of the instrument panel, visible through the windshield. Coding was the same as 1981-83; see 1981 for breakdown details. Engine codes (symbol four) for 1984 were: 'C' 258-6; 'U' 150-4. Model year code (symbol ten) changed to 'E' for 1984. Alliance/Encore's 17-symbol VIN was also similar to 1983 coding, but with additions for the new Encore. Symbols 6-7 (body style) were now: '93' three-door liftback; '99' five-door liftback; '95' four-door sedan; '96' two-door sedan. Symbol eight (trim level) included: '0' base model; '3' Alliance L or Encore S; '6' Alliance DL or Encore LS; '8' Limited; '9' Alliance GT or Encore GS. Model year code (symbol ten) changed to 'E' for 1984.

ENCORE (BASE) SERIES 90

Series Number	Body/Style Number	Body Type & Seating	Factory Price	Shipping Weight	Production Total
90	8493-0	3-dr Lift-5P	5755	1974	Note 1

ENCORE S

Series Number	Body/Style Number	Body Type & Seating	Factory Price	Shipping Weight	Production Total
90	8493-3	3-dr Lift-5P	6365	1985	55,343
90	8499-3	5-dr Lift-5P	6615	2008	32,266

ENCORE LS

90	8493-6	3-dr Lift-5P	6995	2033	Note 1
90	8499-6	5-dr Lift-5P	7195	2059	Note 1

ENCORE GS

90	8493-9	3-dr Lift-5P	7547	2043	Note 1

ENCORE DIAMOND EDITION

90	8493-6	3-dr Lift-5P	7570	N/A	N/A
90	8499-6	5-dr Lift-5P	7770	N/A	N/A

Note 1: Production totals under S series include base, LS and GS Encore models. Model year sales: 72 076 Encores.

ALLIANCE (BASE) SERIES 90

90	8496-0	2-dr Sed-5P	5959	1934	Note 2

ALLIANCE L

90	8496-3	2-dr Sed-5P	6465	1936	50,978
90	8495-3	4-dr Sed-5P	6715	1964	70,037

ALLIANCE DL

90	8496-6	2-dr Sed-5P	7065	1975	Note 2
90	8495-6	4-dr Sed-5P	7365	2002	Note 2

ALLIANCE LIMITED

90	8495-8	4-dr Sed-5P	8027	2019	Note 2

ALLIANCE DIAMOND EDITION

90	8496-6	2-dr Sed-5P	7715	N/A	N/A
90	8495-6	4-dr Sed-5P	8015	N/A	N/A

Note 2: Production totals under L series include base, DL and Limited Alliance models. Model year sales: 105,340.

EAGLE SERIES 30

30	8435-5	4-dr Sed-5P	9495/9666	3189/3307	4241
30	8438-5	4-dr Sta Wag-5P	10225/10396	3220/3338	21,294

EAGLE LIMITED SERIES 30

30	8438-7	4-dr Sta Wag-5P	10695/10866	3236/3354	Note 3

Note 3: Production total shown for Eagle wagon includes base and Limited models. Of the 25.535 Eagles manufactured in the model year, only 184 had four-cylinder engine. Model year sales: 23,137.

FACTORY PRICE AND WEIGHT NOTE: Figure before the slash in Eagle listings is for four-cylinder engine. after slash for six-cylinder.

ENGINES: BASE FOUR (Alliance/Encore): Inline. OHV. Four-cylinder. Cast iron block; aluminum head. Transverse mounted. Displacement: 85.2 cu. in. (1.4 liters). Bore & stroke: 2.99 x 3.03 in. Compression ratio: 9.0:1. Brake horsepower: 56 at 4200 R.P.M. Torque: 75 lbs.-ft. at 2500 R.P.M. Five main bearings. Solid valve lifters. Single-point Bendix (throttle-body) fuel injection. BASE FOUR (Eagle): Inline. OHV. Four-cylinder. Cast iron block. Displacement: 150 cu. in. (2.46 liters). Bore & stroke: 3.88 x 3.19 in. Compression ratio: 9.2:1. Brake horsepower: N/A. Torque: 132 lbs.-ft. at 3200 R.P.M. Five main bearings. Hydraulic valve lifters. Carburetor: 1Bbl. electronic feedback Carter YFA. OPTIONAL SIX (Eagle): Same as 1983 specifications (258 cu. in. inline OHV).

CHASSIS DATA: Wheelbase: (Encore/Alliance) 97.8 in.; (Eagle) 109.3 in. Overall length: (Encore) 160.6 in.; (Alliance) 163.8 in.; (Eagle) 180.9 in. Height: (Encore/Alliance) 54.5 in.; (Eagle) 54.4 in. Width: (Alliance/Encore) 65 in.; (Eagle) 72.3 in. Front Tread: (Encore/Alliance) 55.2 in.; (Eagle) 59.6 in. Rear Tread: (Encore/Alliance) 52.8 in.; (Eagle) 57.6 in. Standard Tires: (Encore/Alliance) P155/80GR13 GBR; (Eagle) P195/75R15 GBR.

TECHNICAL: Transmission: four-speed manual standard; five-speed manual and three-speed automatic optional. Floor shift lever. Eagle 4WD: selectable 2/4 wheel. Alliance manual transmission gear ratios: (1st) 3.73:1; (2nd) 2.06:1; (3rd) 1.27:1; (4th) 0.90:1; (5th) 0.73:1; (Rev) 3.54:1. Eagle manual gear ratios: (1st) 4.03:1; (2nd) 2.37:1; (3rd) 1.50:1; (4th) 1.00:1; (5th) 0.86:1 exc. 0.76:1 w/six cyl. engine; (Rev) 3.54:1. Clutch dia.: (Alliance/Encore) 7.14 in.; (Eagle four) 9.1 in.; (Eagle six) 10.3 in. Standard axle ratio: (Alliance/Encore) 3.29:1 w/4-spd.; 3.87:1 w/5-spd.; 3.27:1 w/automatic; (Eagle four) 3.54:1; (Eagle six) 2.73:1 except w/towing pkg., 3.08:1. Steering: (Alliance/Encore) rack and pinion; (Eagle) power-assisted recirculating ball. Suspension: (Alliance/Encore) fully independent: front, MacPherson struts w/lower control arms, coil springs, anti-roll bar; rear, transverse semi-torsion bar, swinging longitudinal trailing arms, anti-roll bar; (Eagle) independent front coil springs with anti-roll bar; semi-elliptic rear leaf springs. Brakes: front disc, rear drum; (Alliance) 9.4 in. discs, 8 in. drums; (Eagle) 11 in. discs, 10 in. drums. Electronic ignition. Fuel tank: (Alliance/Encore) 12.5 gal.; (Eagle) 22 gal.

EAGLE DRIVETRAIN OPTIONS: 258 cid six-cylinder engine ($171). Five-speed floor shift with overdrive and select drive ($227). Floor-shift automatic transmission: six ($452). Optional axle ratios (2.73:1 or 3.08:1): Eagle six ($31). H.D. engine cooling (H.D. radiator, viscous fan): Eagle four ($69). Maximum cooling system: Eagle six ($72). Automatic load leveling (air shocks): six ($175). Extra duty suspension pkg. (special front sway bar, rear sway bar, H.D. shocks and springs ($80). Front suspension skid plate ($80). Trailer towing package 'A' to 2000 lbs. ($108). Trailer towing package 'B' to 3500 lbs. ($230). H.D. battery ($27). Cold climate group incl. H.D. battery and engine block heater ($60). California emission system ($78).

EAGLE CONVENIENCE/APPEARANCE OPTIONS: Eagle Sport package ($356). Protection group (stainless door edge guards, bumper guards, floor mats) ($78); w/Sport pkg. ($24). Convenience group (headlight-on buzzer, intermittent wipers, right lighted vanity mirror) ($76). Gauge package (clock, tach, oil, volt, vacuum) ($94). Light group ($63). Right remote mirror: black or chrome ($33). Left/right remote chrome mirrors ($119); Ltd. wag. ($86); N/A w/Sport pkg. Electronic cruise control ($176). Air conditioning system ($750). Halogen headlamps ($15). Halogen foglamps ($85). AM radio ($86). AM/FM/Stereo four-speaker radio ($206). AM/FM/cassette stereo radio ($340). Electronically tuned AM/FM/cassette stereo radio w/power amplifier and four coax speakers ($516). Power door locks ($176). Power windows and door locks ($440). Power decklid release ($41). Power six-way driver's seat ($196). Power six-way driver/pass. seat ($313). Floor shift console ($67). Parcel shelf ($28). Fabric seat trim ($69). Rear wiper/washer: wagon ($128). Rear defroster ($140). Woodgrain steering wheel ($37) N/A w/Sport pkg. Leather-wrapped sport steering wheel ($62) exc. Ltd. Wag. ($25). Tilt steering wheel ($110). Tinted glass ($109). Woodgrain paneling: wag. ($119). Black scuff moldings ($57). Roof rack: wag. ($119). Locking gas cap ($10). Bumper guards ($54). Sport aluminum 15 x 6 in. wheels ($358). Tires: P195/75R15 B black SBR Arriva ($21). P195/75R15 B white SBR Arriva ($76); Sport wag. ($72). P215/65R15 B OWL SBR Eagle GT ($207); Sport wag. ($203).

ALLIANCE/ENCORE OPTIONS: Five-speed manual transmission, floor shift, w/overdrive: Alliance L, Encore S ($97). Three-speed floor-shift automatic tranmission ($435) exc. Alliance DL/Ltd., Encore LS/GS ($338). H.D. battery ($27). H.D. engine cooling ($69); std. w/air cond. Cold climate group (H.D. battery/alternator, engine coolant heater) ($38-$81). Systems Sentry (monitors for low oil, coolant, brake fluid, disc wear, washer/power steering fluid, transaxle oil) ($128); N/A base models. Extra-quiet insulation package: L/S ($64). Rear black spoiler: Encore base/S ($72). Protection group (door edge guards, front/rear carpeted mats, locking gas cap) ($53); N/A base models.. Visibility group (dual remote mirrors, lighted visor mirror, intermittent wipers): L/S ($164); DL/LS ($133). Light group ($47); N/A base models. Fog lamps ($77). Tachometer: L/S ($84). Power steering ($215). Cruise control ($174); N/A base. Air conditioning ($653). Intermittent wipers ($51). Keyless entry system ($97); N/A base. Power door locks ($123-$174). Power windows and door locks ($308-$359). Power liftgate lock release: Encore S/LS ($31). Digital clock ($58); N/A base. Rear wiper/washer: Encore ($120). Rear defroster ($133). Tinted glass ($92). AM radio: base models ($84). AM/FM radio: base models ($147); others ($63). AM/FM four-speaker stereo radio ($120); N/A base. Electronic-tuning AM/FM stereo four-speaker radio w/cassette ($427); N/A base. Vinyl reclining bucket seats: base/L/S ($67). Vinyl rocker/reclining bucket seats: LS/DL (NC). Cloth bucket seats: L/S ($75). Cloth reclining bucket seats: L/S ($142). Luxury cloth rocker/reclining bucket seats: Ltd. ($299). Leather rocker/reclining bucket seats: DL/LS ($349); GS/Ltd. ($299). Metallic paint: L/S ($150). Leather steering wheel: base/L/S ($53) Decklid luggage rack: Alliance L/DL ($108). Luxury wheel covers: Alliance L ($90); DL ($37). Wheel trim rings: base/L/S ($53). Aluminum wheels: Alliance L ($345); Ltd./LS/GS ($255). Tires: P155/80GR13 white GBR: base/L/S ($63). P175/70SR13 SBR: base/L/S ($74). P175/70SR13 white SBR: base/L/S ($135); others ($61). Conventional spare tire: Alliance exc. base ($36).

HISTORY: Introduced: September 25, 1983. Model year production: 234,159 (208,808 four-cylinder and 25,351 Eagle six-cylinder). U.S. production totaled 208.624 cars, which amounted to more than 2.5 percent of the industry total. Calendar year production (U.S.): 192,196 Encores and Alliance made in Kenosha, Wisconsin; (Canada) 22,982 Eagles. Model year sales by U.S. dealers: 201,275 (including 336 leftover Concords and 386 Spirits). Calendar year sales: 190,255, for a 2.4 percent share of the market.

Historical Footnotes: When Eagle was introduced for 1980, its only competitor for the 4WD market was Subaru. Four years later, Toyota had introduced its Tercel 4WD, while Audi brought out its costly versions. Yet AMC continued to push the Eagle, which remained the only domestic-built 4WD model, despite sagging sales and rumors that it would abandon production and sell the Brampton, Ontario plant to Chrysler. As Renault/Jeep Sport vice-president R.C. Lunn insisted, the Eagle "brought a whole new dimension of functional improvement to highway driving while still retaining the off-road capabilities...many consumers coming from the two-wheel-drive segments were buying the vehicles for the security they offered for on-highway driving." (That Sport group had recently been created to promote AMC's sporty image.) For the time being, at least, Eagle remained the only domestically-built 4WD passenger auto. Still, Eagle sales had declined to little more than half their 1981 level. A glance at sales figures demonstrated that the company's financial survival had to rely on the Renault front-drives. Renault now owned over 46 percent of AMC stock. The corporation showed a modest profit ($15.5 million) for the year, after a disastrous loss of $146.7 million for 1983. Even though Alliance sold strongly from the start, beating predictions by 31 percent, AMC had to halt production at Kenosha during 1984, to reduce its inventory. Encore/Alliance prices were cut late in 1984, following order price rises. Renault gradually abandoned its imported Le Car, to focus on the U.S.-built Encore. Although W. Paul Tippett Jr. remained AMC chairman, president Jose Dedeurwaerder was named CEO. Roy D. Chapin, Jr. went into retirement.

1985 AMC

Renault-designed AMC models gained a new engine choice for 1985: a 1.7-liter overhead-cam four, in addition to the previous 1.4-liter OHV. Alliance also gained a new convertible body style. New to the option list: Keyless Entry, which used infrared waves to lock and unlock the car doors remotely.

(Renault) ENCORE — SERIES 90 — FOUR — The new 1.7-liter engine and five-speed transmission went into all Encore GS models. Others kept the 1.4-liter four and four-speed as standard, but could get the bigger engine as an option. All Encores had power disc brakes and halogen headlamps. Base Encores came with a black grille, color-keyed bumpers, carpeting, lighter, console with stowage box, cloth headliner, front courtesy lights, left-hand black remote- control mirror, day/night inside mirror, pulse wiper/washers, front/rear stabilizer bars, trip odometer, and vinyl bucket seats. Black semi-styled wheels held standard P155/80GR13 glass-belted radial tires. S Encores added an AM radio, bright grille, 60/40 split rear seat, dual pinstripes, removable carpeted cargo cover, plus moldings for bumper insert, lower liftgate and windshield surround. Stepping up a notch, the LS offered five- speed manual overdrive transmission, digital clock, rear ashtray, dual note horn, extra-quiet insulation, tachometer, black rear spoiler, bright belt moldings, and cloth-covered rocker/reclining seats. Tires were P175/70SR13 steel- belted, with sport wheel covers. This year's sporty Encore GS featured a black front air dam, black grille, light and visibility groups, black belt moldings, black sport steering wheel, and black pinstripes on the hood, liftgate and bodysides. Aluminum wheels added to looks, a power liftgate release brought convenience, while a handling package helped performance and fog lamps added a practical touch.

1985 Alliance D/L convertible (JG)

(Renault) ALLIANCE — SERIES 90 — FOUR — AMC's biggest news was the addition of a convertible to the Alliance lineup—the first AMC ragtop since the Rebel, back in 1968. Built entirely at the Kenosha, Wisconsin plant, on the same assembly line as other Alliance/Encore models, the convertible adopted the new 1.7-liter Renault engine as standard powerplant, with five-speed manual overdrive transmission. AMC president Jose Dedeurwaerder expected that it would "enhance the image that young, new-value buyers already have of the Alliance and Encore." With a $10,295 (minimum) base price tag, it was promoted as the "lowest- priced domestic convertible" on the market. Three-speed automatic shift was optional, as on all models. Base and L sedans retained the smaller 1.4-liter four, but all DL Alliances also had the 1.7 four as standard. Convertibles came in two trim levels and six colors: white, beige and red, plus Mica Red, Light Blue, and Gold metallic clearcoat. Folding tops were white or almond color. Interior trim was blue or almond. DL convertibles could also have honey or garnet, in vinyl or cloth. The less-costly L ragtop included a black grille and front air dam, tinted glass, heavy-duty battery, twin ashtrays, locking lighted glove box, extra-quiet insulation, dual black remote-controlled mirrors, black bumper insert moldings, roll-down quarter windows, and bright wheel trim rings. Five-speed manual transmission was standard. The power- operated top had a black inner liner and zip-out rear window. Color-keyed top boots used hidden fasteners. DL convertibles came with standard AM/FM stereo radio, digital clock, dual note horn, cloth rocker/recliner bucket seats, power steering, leather-wrapped steering wheel, door storage bins, luxury wheel covers, and a tachometer. Both had black trim moldings and color-keyed sunvisors. Base Alliance equipment was similar to the Encore liftback's, but included blackout rocker panels with bright moldings. L sedans had a bright grille and bumper insert moldings, plus an AM radio and dual accent pinstripes. DL Alliance sedans were similar to Encore's LS, with full luggage compartment trim, color-keyed mirror, bright decklid and quarter window moldings, door storage bins, and bright wheel trim rings. They rode steel-belted P175/70SR13 radial tires. Stepping all the way up to the Limited brought buyers a rear center armrest, blackout lower back panel, light and visibility groups, decklid luggage rack, wheel lip moldings, hood pinstripes, intermittent wipers, plus luxury cloth rocker/recliner bucket seats. Entertainment options stretched to a six-speaker electronically-tuned stereo radio with cassette player.

1985 American Eagle station wagon (JG)

EAGLE — SERIES 30 — SIX — Eagles no longer had to be stationary to switch from two- wheel drive to four-wheel drive (and back again). "Shift-on-the-fly" capability let drivers change between the two while the car was moving. Only the 258 cu. in. six-cylinder engine was offered this year, with standard five-speed overdrive manual transmission. Alternator capacity jumped up to 56 amps (from 42). Hoods lost their former ornament, but added a scoop effect along the top surface. Full-face radios with four speakers became standard. Other base equipment was similar to that of 1984. Eagle's Limited added a right remote chrome mirror, parcel shelf, woodgrain steering wheel and leather reclining seats, plus a new extra this year: wire wheel covers. The Sport package was similar to 1984, with dual mirrors. Two new body colors, Medium Blue and Dark Blue metallic, joined Garnet, Silver, Autumn Brown, Almond, and Mocha Dark Brown, for a total of seven choices. Interiors came in garnet, honey or almond, plus—this year—blue.

I.D. DATA: Eagle's 17-symbol Vehicle Identification Number (VIN) was again embossed on a metal plate riveted to the top left surface of the instrument panel, visible through the windshield. Coding was the same as in 1981-84. Alliance/Encore also used a 17-symbol VIN, with coding the same as in 1984. Model year code (symbol ten) changed to 'F' for 1985. Engine codes were now: 'D' 1.4-liter four; 'E' California 1.4L four; 'A' 1.7-liter four; and 'C' 258 cu. in. six. The two-digit identified for body style (symbols 6-7) now included '97' convertible.

ENCORE (BASE) SERIES 90

Series Number	Body/Style Number	Body Type & Seating	Factory Price	Shipping Weight	Production Total
90	8593-0	3-dr Lift-5P	5895	1946	Note 1

ENCORE S

90	8593-3	3-dr Lift-5P	6360	1953	38,623
90	8599-3	5-dr Lift-5P	6610	2007	19,902

ENCORE LS

90	8593-6	3-dr Lift-5P	7060	1997	Note 1
90	8599-6	5-dr Lift-5P	7310	2055	Note 1

ENCORE GS

90	8593-9	3-dr Lift-5P	7560	2046	Note 1

Note 1: Production totals under S series include base, LS and GS Encore models. Model year sales: 46,923 Encores.

ALLIANCE (BASE) SERIES 90

90	8596-0	2-dr Sed-5P	5995	1922	Note 2

ALLIANCE L

90	8596-3	2-dr Sed-5P	6400	1929	33,617
90	8595-3	4-dr Sed-5P	6650	1964	50,906
90	8597-3	2-dr Conv.-4P	10295	2153	7141

ALLIANCE DL

90	8596-6	2-dr Sed-5P	7000	1962	Note 2
90	8595-6	4-dr Sed-5P	7250	2001	Note 2
90	8597-6	2-dr Conv.-4P	11295	2190	Note 2

ALLIANCE LIMITED

90	8595-8	4-dr Sed-5P	7750	2190	Note 2

Note 2: Production totals under L series include base, DL and Limited Alliance models. Model year sales: 75,208 Alliances. Note 3: Add $103 for 1.7-liter four-cylinder engine (except Encore GS, Alliance convertible and Alliance Limited, which had it as standard equipment).

EAGLE SERIES 30

30	8535-5	4-dr Sed-5P	10457	3306	2655
30	8538-5	4-dr Sta Wag-5P	11217	3337	13,535

EAGLE LIMITED

30	8538-7	4-dr Sta Wag-5P	11893	3368	Note 3

Note 3: Production total shown for Eagle wagon includes base and Limited models. All Eagles had six-cylinder engine. Model year sales: 15,362 Eagles.

ENGINES: BASE FOUR (Alliance/Encore): Inline. OHV. Four-cylinder. Cast iron block; aluminum head. Transverse mounted. Displacement: 85.2 cu. in. (1.4 liters). Bore & stroke: 2.99 x 3.03 in. Compression ratio: 9.0:1. Brake horsepower: 56 at 4200 R.P.M. Torque: 75 lbs.-ft. at 2500 R.P.M. Five main bearings. Solid valve lifters. Single-point Bendix (throttle-body) fuel injection. OPTIONAL FOUR (Alliance/Encore): Inline. Overhead cam. Four-cylinder. Cast iron block. Displacement: 105 cu. in. (1.7 liters). Bore & stroke: 3.19 x 3.29 in. Compression ratio: 9.5:1. Brake horsepower: 77.5 at 5000 R.P.M. Torque: 96 lbs.-ft. at 3000 R.P.M. Five main bearings. Throttle-body fuel injection (Bendix). BASE SIX (Eagle): Inline. OHV. Six-cylinder. Cast iron block. Displacement: 258 cu. in. (4.2 liters). Bore & stroke: 3.75 x 3.90 in. Compression ratio: 9.2:1. Brake horsepower: 110 at 3200 R.P.M. Torque: 210 lbs.-ft. at 1800 R.P.M. Seven main bearings. Hydraulic valve lifters. Carburetor: 2Bbl.

CHASSIS DATA: Wheelbase: (Encore/Alliance) 97.8 in.; (Eagle) 109.3 in. Overall length: (Encore) 160.6 in.; (Alliance) 163.8 in.; (Eagle) 180.9 in. Height: (Encore/Alliance) 54.5 in. exc. conv., 53.1 in.; (Eagle) 54.4 in. Width: (Encore/Alliance) 65.0 in.; (Eagle) 72.3 in. Front Tread: (Encore/Alliance) 55.2 in.; (Eagle) 59.6 in. Rear Tread: (Encore) 52.8 in.; (Eagle) 57.6 in. Standard Tires: (Encore/Alliance) P155/80GR13 GBR; (Eagle) P195/75R15 GBR.

TECHNICAL: Transmission: (Alliance/Encore) four-speed overdrive manual shift standard; five-speed manual and three-speed automatic optional; (Eagle) five-speed overdrive manual shift standard; three-speed automatic optional. Floor shift lever. Alliance/Encore manual transmission gear ratios: (1st) 3.73:1; (2nd) 2.05:1; (3rd) 1.32:1; (4th) 0.97:1; (5th) 0.79:1; (Rev) 3.56:1. Eagle manual transmission gear ratios: (1st) 4.03:1; (2nd) 2.73:1; (3rd) 1.50:1; (4th) 1.00:1; (Rev) 3.76:1. Clutch dia.: (Alliance/Encore) 7.1 in.; (Eagle) 10.3 in. Standard axle ratio: (Alliance/Encore) 3.29:1 except 3.56:1 w/5-spd. transmission; (Eagle) 2.73:1. Steering: (Alliance/Encore) rack and pinion; (Eagle) recirculating ball. Suspension: (Alliance/Encore) fully independent with MacPherson front struts and stabilizer bar, trailing rear arms with transverse torsion bars and stabilizer bar; (Eagle) independent front coil springs, semi-elliptic rear leaf springs Brakes: (Alliance/Encore) 9.4 in. front discs, 8 in. rear drums; (Eagle) 11 in. front discs, 10 in. rear drums. Electronic ignition. Fuel tank: (Alliance/Encore) 12.5 gal.; (Eagle) 22 gal.

EAGLE DRIVETRAIN OPTIONS: Three-speed floor-shift automatic transmission ($366). Optional 2.73:1 or 3.08:1 axle ratio ($32). H.D. engine cooling ($75). Automatic load leveling ($182). Extra-duty suspension pkg. ($83). Front suspension skid plate ($83). Trailer towing package 'A' to 2000 lbs. ($112). Trailer towing package 'B' to 3500 lbs. ($239). H.D. battery ($28). Cold climate group ($62). California emission system ($81).

EAGLE CONVENIENCE/APPEARANCE OPTIONS: Eagle Sport package: base wagon ($416). Protection group: bumper guards, floot mats and door edge guards ($81); w/Sport pkg. ($25). Convenience group: headlight-on buzzer, intermittent wipers, lighted vanity mirror ($79). Gauge package ($98). Light group ($66). Right remote mirror (black or chrome): base ($34). Left/right remote chrome mirrors ($90- $124). Cruise control ($183). Air conditioning system ($781). Halogen headlamps ($16). Halogen foglamps ($88). AM radio ($94). AM/FM/stereo radio ($235). Electronically-tuned AM/FM/cassette stereo radio ($432). Electronically-tuned AM/FM stereo radio w/cassette and Dolby sound ($537). Power door locks ($183). Power windows and door locks ($458). Keyless entry system ($101). Power decklid release: sed. ($43). Power six-way driver's seat ($204). Power six-way driver/pass. seat ($326). Console ($70). Parcel shelf ($29). Cloth reclining seats: base ($72). Rear wiper/washer: wagon ($133). Rear defroster ($146). Woodgrain steering wheel ($39). Leather- wrapped sport steering wheel ($65) exc. Ltd. ($26). Tilt steering wheel ($115). Tinted glass ($113). Woodgrain paneling: wag. ($155). Special color combinations ($53). Black scuff moldings ($59). Roof rack: wag. ($124). Bumper guards ($56). Sport aluminum 15 x 6 in. wheels ($373) exc. Ltd. ($217). Wire wheel covers ($156). Tires: P195/75R15 B black SBR Arriva ($22). P195/75R15 B white SBR Arriva ($75-$79). P215/65R15 B OWL SBR Eagle GT ($211-$215).

ALLIANCE/ENCORE OPTIONS: 1.7-liter four-cylinder engine ($103). Five-speed manual transmission, floor shift, w/overdrive: Alliance L, Encore S ($100). Three-speed floor-shift automatic tranmission ($448) exc. Alliance L conv., DL/Ltd., Enc. LS/GS ($348); N/A base Encore. Handling package: S/LS 3-dr. ($31). H.D. battery ($28). H.D. cooling ($71). Cold climate group ($62-$83). Systems Sentry: monitors for low oil, coolant, brake fluid, disc wear, washer/power steering fluid, transaxle oil ($132); N/A base models. Extra-quiet insulation package: L/S ($66). Rear spoiler: Encore base/S ($74). Sunshine package (sunroof, aluminum wheels and leather-wrapped steering wheel): DL/LS ($359). Pop-up sunroof ($324). Protection group ($55). Visibility group (dual remote mirrors, lighted visor mirror, intermittent wipers): L/S ($169); DL/LS ($137). Light group ($48). Fog lamps ($79). Tachometer: L/S ($87). Power steering ($221). Cruise control ($179); N/A base. Air conditioning ($673). Intermittent wipers ($53). Keyless entry system ($100). Power door locks ($127-$179) Power door/window locks ($318-$370). Power liftback release: S/LS ($32). Rear defroster ($137). Rear wiper/washer: Encore ($124) exc. GS ($70). Tinted glass ($95). AM radio: base models ($91). AM/FM radio: base models ($160); others ($69). AM/FM stereo radio ($144); N/A base. Electronic-tuning AM/FM stereo four-speaker radio w/cassette ($335) exc. DL conv. ($191); N/A base. Electronic-tuning AM/FM stereo radio w/cassette and Dolby ($440) exc. DL conv. ($296). Digital clock: L/S ($60). Vinyl reclining bucket seats: L, S, base Alliance ($69). Vinyl rocker/reclining buckets: DL/LS (NC). Cloth bucket seats: L/S ($77). Cloth reclining bucket seats: L/S ($146). Leather rocker/reclining bucket seats: LS/DL ($359); GS/Ltd. ($308). Door storage bins: L/S ($21). Metallic paint ($155) incl. clearcoat. Leather-wrapped sport steering wheel ($64); N/A base. Decklid luggage rack: Alliance L/DL ($111). Luxury sport wheel covers ($93) exc. L conv., DL ($38). Wheel trim rings ($55). Aluminum wheels ($216-$309). Tires: P155/80GR13 white GBR ($65). P175/70SR13 SBR ($76). P175/70SR13 white SBR ($63- $139). P185/60R14 SBR RBL: base/S/L ($155); others ($79). Spare tire (to replace polyspare): Alliance ($37).

HISTORY: Introduced: October 1, 1984. Model year production (U.S.): 150,189 Encores and Alliances made in Kenosha, which came to 1.9 percent of the industry total; (Canada) 16,190 Eagles. Calendar year production (U.S.): 111,138 Encores and Alliances; (Canada) 11,311 Eagles. Model year sales by U.S. dealers: 137,493. Calendar year sales: 123,449, for a 1.6 percent market share.

Historical Footnotes: Sales dropped sharply for the model year, as consumers turned toward bigger cars—partly a result of moderate, stable gasoline prices. First-year mechanical problems also turned some prospective buyers away from AMC's French-designed duo, especially as they rose in price. After a modest profit ($15.5 million) in the previous year, AMC posted a $125.3 million loss for fiscal 1985. Alliance/Encore prices were cut in December 1984. Then, in February 1985, AMC cut the financing rate to 8.5 percent—the first domestic company to offer such incentives, which soon became almost normal. AMC helped pioneer extended warranties, too, with new 5-year/50,000-mile coverage on the powertrain, plus 5 years for rust-through. The new Alliance convertible was a joint project of AMC and American Sun Roof corporation. On a special subassembly line at Kenosha, metal tops and 'B' and 'C' pillars were sliced off two-door sedans. Then, a series of reinforcing operations strengthened the cut-down bodies before they returned to the line for paint and trim. Eagle, meanwhile, continued its downhill slide that had begun in 1981—the only year AMC beat out Subaru in 4WD passenger car sales. Unlike most 4WD imports, which were efficient front-drive designs with transfer mechanisms in their transaxles, Eagle was essentially a rear-drive vehicle with front-drive axle and transfer case hooked on. In short, a clumsy mechanism in an aged body, its design reaching back to 1969. Production fell to just 85 Eagles per day at the Brampton, Ontario factory. Just after New Year's, AMC cut production at Kenosha, laying off 600 workers. Another slash came in February, with more to follow by the start of 1986 model production in July. The June labor contract cut AMC workers' wages to a level on a par with those at GM and Ford; the agreement was accepted only after AMC took steps to close down the Kenosha plant.

Innovations: "Shift-on-the-fly" four-wheel-drive. Convertible body style.

1986 AMC

All models added the high-mounted stop light required by law, and ashtrays left the standard equipment lists. Additions included gas-charged shock absorbers, a restyled instrument cluster, and larger-diameter stabilizer bars. New to the option lineup: a four-position tilt steering wheel.

ENCORE — SERIES 90 — FOUR — Base model Encores left the lineup, so S was the lowest- priced liftback. One new model was added: the top-level Electronic, whose instrument cluster held an array of hi-tech doodads. It included both digital and analog speedometers; a trip computer; tachometer; fuel gauge; oil level, temperature and pressure lights; plus a bar graph display that monitored engine functions. Elsewhere in the lineup, about the most thrilling change was an increase in alternator output from 50 to 60 amps. Only S and LS Encores were offered in five-door liftback form; the GS and Electronic were three-door (actually two passenger doors) only. The 1.4-liter four-cylinder engine was standard, 1.7-liter optional. Entry-level (S) Encores now sported black bumpers, cargo area carpeting, clearcoat paint, and an AM radio. Back seats were 60/40 split fold-down type. In addition to fancy instrumentation, Encore Electronics had cloth bucket seats, a color-keyed steering wheel, bright wheel trim rings, and a five-speed overdrive transmission. LS models lost their dual note horns, but added twin pinstripes. The top-level GS now featured dual exhausts and a soft-feel steering wheel, as well as the extras offered in 1985.

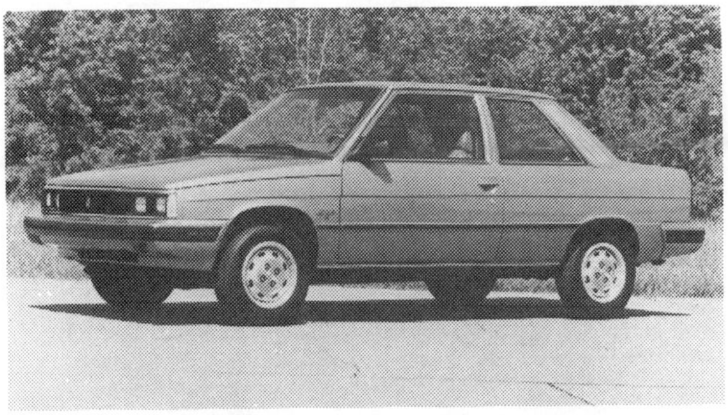

1986 Alliance L coupe (AMC)

ALLIANCE — SERIES 90 — FOUR — The luxurious Limited Alliance left the lineup for 1986. A revised L and DL grille used dark horizontal bars over five vertical bars, with center emblem. Extended taillamps were new, headlamps smaller, interior altered. A new base four-door sedan joined the 1985 two-door. Convertibles again carried the larger 1.7-liter four, which was optional on other Alliances. Base Alliances added black bumpers and clearcoat paint to their standard equipment list. L Alliances now included a color-keyed steering wheel and bumpers, plus bright grille and Sebring Red body paint. Except for semi-styled bright wheels, black belt molding and bright rocker panel and windshield moldings, the L convertible equipment was the same as in 1985. DL convertibles gained metallic paint and black bodyside scuff moldings with bright inserts, dual pinstripes, and a black soft-feel steering wheel. DL sedans lost their dual note horns, but added dual accent pinstripes.

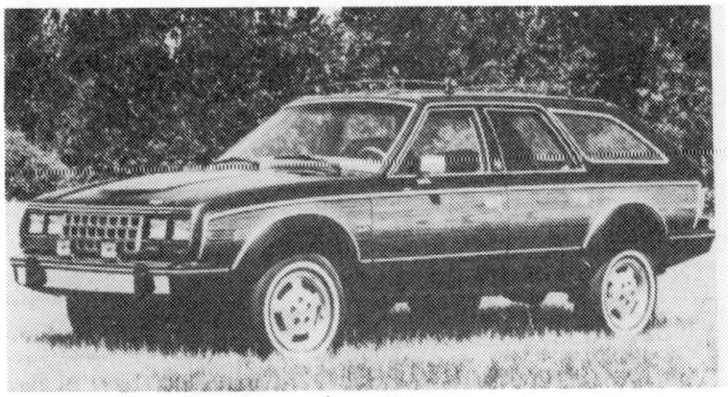

1986 American Eagle station wagon (JG)

EAGLE — SERIES 30 — SIX — Once again, Eagle was powered by the 258 six with five- speed overdrive transmission. A modest price increase was its only real change from 1985. Base models now had tinted glass (formerly an option) but lost a few minor items, including twin armrests and ashtrays. Extras on the Limited were the same as in 1985. The Sport package for base Eagle wagons was also the same as 1985, but included only the left-hand remote mirror.

I.D. DATA: Eagle's 17-symbol Vehicle Identification Number (VIN) was embossed on a metal plate riveted to the top left surface of the instrument panel, visible through the windshield. See coding details in 1981 listing. Model year (symbol ten) changed to 'G' for 1986. Alliance/Encore's VIN used the same coding as 1984-85. Model year code (tenth digit) changed to 'G' for 1986. The code for the Limited ('8' in the eighth digit position) was no longer used.

ENCORE S SERIES 90

Series Number	Body/Style Number	Body Type & Seating	Factory Price	Shipping Weight	Production Total
90	8693-3	3-dr Lift-5P	6710	1970	12,239
90	8699-3	5-dr Lift-5P	6960	2003	6870

ENCORE LS

90	8693-6	3-dr Lift-5P	7310	1974	Note 1
90	8699-6	5-dr Lift-5P	7560	2007	Note 1

ENCORE ELECTRONIC

90	8693-4	3-dr Lift-5P	7498	1974	Note 1

ENCORE GS

90	8693-9	3-dr Lift-5P	7968	1977	Note 1

Note 1: Production totals under S series include LS, Electronic and GS Encore models. Model year sales: 17,671 Encores.

ALLIANCE (BASE) SERIES 90

90	8696-0	2-dr Sed-5P	5999	1923	Note 2
90	8695-0	4-dr Sed-5P	6199	1957	Note 2

ALLIANCE L

90	8696-3	2-dr Sed-5P	6510	1928	23,204
90	8695-3	4-dr Sed-5P	6760	1962	42,891
90	8697-3	2-dr Conv.-4P	10557	2222	2015

1986 Alliance DL sedan (AMC)

ALLIANCE DL

90	8696-6	2-dr Sed-5P	7110	1935	Note 2
90	8695-6	4-dr Sed-5P	7360	1969	Note 2
90	8697-6	2-dr Conv.-4P	11557	2228	Note 2

Note 2: Production totals under L series include base and DL Alliance models. Model year sales: 55,603. Note 3: Prices shown are for 1.4-liter engine. Add $264 for 1.7-liter four-cylinder engine (except Alliance convertible, which had it as standard equipment).

EAGLE SERIES 30

30	8635-5	4-dr Sed-5P	10719	3307	1274
30	8638-5	4-dr Sta Wag-5P	11489	3341	6943

EAGLE LIMITED SERIES 30

30	8638-7	4-dr Sta Wag-5P	12179	3372	Note 4

Note 4: Production total shown for Eagle wagon includes base and Limited models. All Eagles had six-cylinder engine. Model year sales: 9020 Eagles.

ENGINES: BASE FOUR (Alliance/Encore): Inline. OHV. Four-cylinder. Cast iron block; aluminum head. Transverse mounted. Displacement: 85.2 cu. in. (1.4 liters). Bore & stroke: 2.99 x 3.03 in. Compression ratio: 9.0:1. Brake horsepower: 56 at 4200 R.P.M. Torque: 75 lbs.-ft. at 2500 R.P.M. Five main bearings. Solid valve lifters. Single-point Bendix (throttle-body) fuel injection. BASE FOUR (Alliance convertible, Encore Electronic/GS); OPTIONAL (other Alliance/Encore): Inline. Overhead cam. Four-cylinder. Cast iron block. Displacement: 105 cu. in. (1.7 liters). Bore & stroke: 3.19 x 3.29 in. Compression ratio: 9.5:1. Brake horsepower: 77.5 at 5000 R.P.M. Torque: 96 lbs.-ft. at 3000 R.P.M. Five main bearings. Bendix throttle-body fuel injection. BASE SIX (Eagle): Same specifications as 1985.

CHASSIS DATA: Wheelbase: (Encore/Alliance) 97.8 in.; (Eagle) 109.3 in. Overall length: (Encore) 160.6 in.; (Alliance) 163.8 in.; (Eagle) 180.9 in. Height: (Encore/Alliance) 54.5 in. exc. conv., 53.1 in.; (Eagle) 54.4 in. Width: (Encore/Alliance) 65.0 in.; (Eagle) 72.3 in. Front Tread: (Encore/Alliance) 55.2 in.; (Eagle) 59.6 in. Rear Tread: (Encore) 52.8 in.; (Eagle) 57.6 in. Standard Tires: (Encore/Alliance) P155/80GR13 GBR; (Eagle) P195/75R15 GBR.

TECHNICAL: Transmission: (Alliance/Encore) four-speed overdrive manual shift standard; five-speed manual and three-speed automatic optional; (Eagle) five-speed overdrive manual shift standard; three-speed automatic optional. Floor shift lever. Standard axle ratio: (Alliance/Encore) 3.29:1 except 3.56:1 w/5-spd. transmission; (Eagle) 2.73:1. Steering: (Alliance/Encore) rack and pinion; (Eagle) recirculating ball. Suspension: (Alliance/Encore) fully independent with MacPherson front struts and stabilizer bar, trailing rear arms with transverse torsion bars and stabilizer bar; (Eagle) independent front coil springs, semi-elliptic rear leaf springs Brakes: (Alliance/Encore) 9.4 in. front discs, 8 in. rear drums; (Eagle) 11 in. front discs, 10 in. rear drums. Electronic ignition. Fuel tank: (Alliance/Encore) 12.5 gal.; (Eagle) 22 gal.

EAGLE DRIVETRAIN OPTIONS: Three-speed floor-shift automatic transmission ($379). Optional 2.73:1 axle ratio ($33). H.D. engine cooling ($78). Automatic load leveling ($188). Extra-duty suspension pkg. ($86). Front suspension skid plate ($86). Trailer towing package 'A' to 2000 lbs. ($116). Trailer towing package 'B' to 3500 lbs. ($247). H.D. battery ($32). Cold climate group ($64). California emissions pkg. ($84).

EAGLE CONVENIENCE/APPEARANCE OPTIONS: Eagle Sport package: base model ($431). Protection group: front/rear bumper guards, front/rear mats, stainless steel door edge guards ($84); wagon w/Sport pkg. ($26). Convenience group: headlight-on buzzer, intermittent wipers, lighted vanity mirror ($82). Gauge package ($101). Light group ($68). Right remote mirror (black or chrome) ($35). Left/right remote chrome mirrors ($128) exc. Ltd. ($93). Cruise control ($189). Air conditioning system ($795). Halogen headlamps ($17). Halogen foglamps ($91). AM/FM radio ($186). Electronic-tuning AM/FM/Stereo radio ($243). Electronic-tuning AM/FM/cassette stereo radio ($189). Power door locks ($189). Power windows and door locks ($474). Keyless entry system ($105). Power decklid release: sedan ($45). Power six-way driver's seat ($211). Power six-way driver/pass. seat ($337). Floor shift console ($72). Parcel shelf ($30). Cloth seat upholstery: base ($75). Rear wiper/washer: wagon ($138). Rear defroster ($151). Woodgrain steering wheel: base ($40). Leather-wrapped sport steering wheel ($67) exc. Ltd. ($27). Tilt steering wheel ($119). Woodgrain paneling: wag. ($160). Black scuff moldings ($61). Roof rack: wag. ($128). Bumper guards ($58). Sport aluminum 15 x 6 in. wheels ($386) exc. Ltd. ($225). Wire wheel covers ($161). Tires: P195/75R15 B black SBR Arriva ($23). P195/75R15 B white SBR Arriva ($78-$82). P215/65R15 B OWL SBR Eagle GT ($218-$223).

ALLIANCE/ENCORE OPTIONS: 1.7-liter four-cylinder engine: Alliance L/DL, Encore S/LS ($164). Five-speed manual transmission, floor shift, w/overdrive: L/S ($100). Three-speed floor-shift automatic transmission ($469) exc. Alliance DL/conv., Encore LS/GS/Elect. ($369). Handling package: Encore 3-dr. exc. GS ($32). Cold climate group ($85) exc. ($64) w/air cond. H.D. engine cooling ($73). H.D. alternator and engine cooling ($107). H.D. battery ($29). Extra-quiet insulation package: L/S/Elect. ($68). Sunshine package (sunroof, soft-feel steering wheel and 14 in. aluminum wheels): DL exc. conv. ($407); L/S ($541); LS ($368). Pop-up sunroof ($332). Rear spoiler: Electronic/S ($76). Protection group: door edge guards and carpeted floor mats ($56). Visibility group (dual remote mirrors, intermittent wipers): L/S/Electronic ($173); DL/LS ($140); N/A conv. Light group ($65). Fog lamps ($81). Tachometer: L/S ($89). Power steering ($227). Cruise control ($183); N/A Alliance base. Air conditioning ($685). Digital clock: L/S/Elect. ($62). Keyless entry system ($103); N/A Alliance base/conv. . Power door locks ($130-$183). Power windows and door locks: conv. ($326). Power liftgate lock release: Encore ($40). Rear wiper/washer: Encore ($127). Rear defroster ($140). Tinted glass ($99). AM radio: base Alliance ($93). AM/FM radio ($71) exc. base Alliance ($164). Electronic-tuning AM/FM stereo radio ($192). Electronic-tuning AM/FM stereo radio w/cassette ($357) exc. DL conv. ($165); N/A Alliance base. Electronic-tuning AM/FM stereo radio w/cassette and (Dolby) Jensen Accusound ($614) exc. DL conv. ($422); N/A Alliance base. Vinyl reclining bucket seats: base/L Alliance, Encore S/Elect. ($71). Cloth bucket seats: base/L Alliance, Encore S ($79). Cloth reclining bucket seats: L/S ($150); Elect. ($71). Cloth rocker/reclining wing back seats: DL ($105); N/A conv. Sebring Red paint: Alliance ($50). Metallic paint ($159); DL conv. (NC). Black soft-feel sport steering wheel ($66). Tilt steering wheel: L/DL, Encore ($115). Decklid luggage rack: Alliance DL ($114). Luxury sport wheel covers ($39) exc. base/L Alliance, Encore S ($95); N/A GS. Wheel trim rings: base/L Alliance, S ($56). Aluminum wheels ($221-$316). Tires: P155/80GR13 white GBR ($67). P175/70SR13 SBR ($78). P175/70SR13 white SBR ($65-$143). P185/60R14 SBR RBL: DL/LS ($81); L/S/Elect. ($159); w/Sunshine pkg. (NC). Spare tire (to replace polyspare): L/DL sed. ($65).

HISTORY: Introduced: October 1, 1985. Model year production (U.S.): 64,873, down to only 0.8 percent of the industry total; (Total) 95,436, including 8217 Eagles. Calendar year production (U.S.): 49,435 Encores and Alliances made at Kenosha. Model year sales by U.S. dealers: 82,294. Calendar year sales: 72,849, for a market share of only 0.9 percent.

Historical Footnotes: AMC president Jose Dedeurwaerder believed "the worst is over" after rough times early in the model year. But corporate fortunes and prospects continued to decline, registering a $91.3 million loss for 1986. Model year sales dropped to only 1 percent of the domestic market, from 1.6 the year before. Struggling to stay alive, the company even slashed financing rates all the way down to zero interest (on two-year loans, that is). But both American Honda and Volkswagen of America beat AMC in sales, and Nissan came close. By year's end, the Encore was dropped, replaced by a hatchback Alliance. Eagle sales fell below the 10,000 mark, though AMC insisted the tired old 4WD would stay in production in Canada a while longer. The irony is that Eagle's failure came at a time when interest in 4WD passenger cars was rising. On the positive side, Chrysler Corp. agreed to build its M-body cars at AMC's Kenosha plant, which helped pave the way for the Chrysler takeover a year later. Joseph E. Cappy became AMC president and CEO; Pierre Semerena (from Renault) was named chairman. Jose Dedeurwaerder combined duties of AMC vice-chairman with those of executive V.P. of Renault worldwide sales and marketing. Rumors flurried over the next year, until the Chrysler deal was finally concluded.

Periodic flirtations with performance aside, Buick's reputation still relied most on its long history as a well-equipped, if slightly stodgy, family car. Not ordinarily a trend-setter, Buick regularly produced the kinds of reliable cars that millions of moderately well-off families wanted. By the mid-1970s, the sprightly GS and GSX editions had become memories. So had Buick ragtops, the last of which (a LeSabre) came off the line not long before the '76 model year began. Two years earlier, the pillarless two-door hardtop had given way to a "Colonnade" coupe design with large quarter windows. Those windows got smaller in subsequent years, but the "true" two-door hardtop was gone (though four-door pillarless hardtops hung on a bit longer).

1978 Electra Park Avenue Landau Coupe (B)

Century and Regal got their trimming-down for 1978. Buick displayed renewed interest in performance with the arrival of an optional turbocharged V-6 under Regal and LeSabre Sport Coupe hoods. In the other direction, the 231 cu. in. V-6 had its bore slimmed to become a 196, ready for the lighter-weight Century/Regal. Century coupes and sedans displayed a new "aeroback" profile that wouldn't attract as many customers as hoped for in the next couple of years. Among the more collectible Buicks is Riviera's silver/black 75th anniversary ('LXXV') model, of which 1,400 were produced.

Riviera not only shrunk in size for 1979; it switched to front-wheel drive, sharing mechanical components with Eldorado and Toronado. Named *Motor Trend* Car of the Year, the revised Riv was considered more closely related to the original '63 than to the boattail 1970s version. A sporty new S Type Riviera carried a turbo V-6. Century also added a Turbo Coupe package.

1976 Regal Landau Coupe (B)

For 1975, the Skylark badge had returned on a compact Buick, and the Monza-based Skyhawk subcompact coupe arrived. Those two entered 1976 with little change, joining the mid-size Century and Regal, full-size LeSabre/Electra duo, and upscale Riviera--powered by a giant 455 cu. in., 205 horsepower V-8. Skylark was the only domestic V-6 powered compact, LeSabre the only V-6 full-size, both carrying Buick's own 231 cu. in. engine. Skyhawks could have a new Borg-Warner five-speed gearbox—a choice not common at this time. Century coupes sported a fastback roofline, and a Hurst twin-panel Hatch Roof made the option list. The fabled "ventiports" (portholes) that had made their initial appearance in 1949 still stood on full-size Buick fenders, albeit in different form. After two years of decline, Buick sales zoomed upward by over 52 percent, approaching the model-year record set in 1973. A Buick paced Indy for the second year in a row: this time a turbocharged Century, which prompted issuance of replica models with the pace car colors.

Both bodies and engines shrunk for 1977, in the first wave of Buick downsizing. This time the victims were LeSabre, Electra and Riviera (the latter temporarily becoming a variant of LeSabre). A 403 cu. in. V-8 took over the 455's spot as biggest Buick engine. Three different 350 cu. in. V-8s (including Chevrolet's) were available, and made standard on the shrunken Electra and Riviera. Those non-Buick engines soon would cause a lot of trouble for GM, as certain customers felt themselves cheated. Record-setting sales ended the year, though, led by popularity of the downsized full-size models.

1979 LeSabre Sport Coupe (B)

First of the 1980 Buicks was the Skylark version of the new, but ill-fated X-car. Century continued its aero-style fastback coupe, but sedans switched to notchback bodies. That helped Century sales streak skyward. An aero restyle hit LeSabre/Electra. The 403 cu. in. V-8 disappeared, but Buicks might now have an enlarged (252 cu. in.) version of the familiar 231 V-6, a lightweight 265 V-8, or the troublesome Oldsmobile-built diesel V-8. Buick had installed its first V-8 back in 1953, but now produced no V-8 engines at all. Collectors might look for a limited-edition Regal Somerset, with tan/blue body and wire wheel covers, offered this year only. Skyhawk's Road Hawk option might also be tempting, and reasonably priced. This was the last year for Skyhawk, until it returned in front-drive form for 1982.

Regal took its turn at an aero restyle for 1981. All rear-drives now had a lockup converter clutch in their automatic transmissions. The sportiest Riviera was now called T Type, a designation that would find its way onto a whole line of sporty Buicks a few years later. Regal continued as Buick's best seller (and paced the Indy 500).

Either a four or V-6 powered the new '82 front-drive Skyhawk, while Century got an aerodynamic, wedge-shaped body. Regal, long offered only in coupe form, added a sedan and wagon. Turbocharged engines had lost popularity, and production fell to a small fraction of their former level. LeSabre's F/E limited-edition might be of modest interest, but Riviera's new convertible would probably attract more collector attention. So too might the revived Riv T Type, which now carried improved turbo power.

1983 Regal T Type coupe (AA)

All models except LeSabre/Electra came in T Type form for 1983. Only 1,750 Riv convertibles were built (and one paced Indy). Rarer yet is the 'XX Anniversary Edition' Riviera, painted two-tone beige with true wire wheels. Model year sales rose nicely, giving Buick a new record and a fourth-place ranking.

Late in the 1984 model year came what many view as the most wanted Buick of the era: the dramatic all-black turbo-powered Regal Grand National. Even while they were still in production, boosting Buick's image among younger motorists, some brought in startling amounts at auction. Car dealers who've managed to get their hands on one have sometimes put astronomical price tags on their windshields—or even implied that the car wasn't for sale at any price. Desirable, yes, but Grand Nationals aren't exactly Duesenbergs, so prices are likely to stabilize. On a more modest level, Century offered an Olympia Limited sedan to mark the Olympic Games. A turbocharged four became available under Skyhawk T Type hoods.

Front-drive moved all the way up the scale for 1985, reaching the Electra. A new Somerset Regal emerged as replacement for the Skylark X-car. Skylark actually sold fairly well through its 1980-85 lifespan, suffering less from the adverse publicity that its Citation cousin had endured as a result of recalls and lawsuits. Diesel engines finally left the lineup. Troublesome when new, they aren't likely to be much better under a collectible Buick's hood.

If Regal Grand Nationals were (and are) in strong demand, imagine the interest in LeSabre's version for 1986. Buick reports that only 117 of the special-edition coupes were built, receiving little publicity. Nearly as desirable, though, might be the performance-oriented, black-bodied Century Gran Sport. Just over a thousand of those came off the line. Turbochargers under Regal Grand National hoods added an intercooler this year, and 5,512 were produced. Anti-lock braking became a Buick option for the first time in 1986, and an all-new, V-6 powered front-drive LeSabre appeared. So did a revised Riviera, which no longer came in convertible form.

Turbocharged, all-black Buicks the most desirable? What happened to Buick's family-car image? It's been there all along, of course, and some of the luxury paint/trim options might be worth a close look today. Still, it's hard to resist the sight of a Grand National rolling by.

1976 BUICK

"Buick ownership," it was claimed, "is the knowledge that you have entered the House of Quality." And Buick for the Bicentennial year, according to the theme of the full- line catalog, was "Dedicated to the Free Spirit in just about everyone." No new models entered the lineup this year, but the Apollo name was dropped and replaced by Skylark. Convertibles were gone, the last LeSabre ragtop having been produced in July 1975. Depending on the Buick model ordered, though, air and sun fans could choose from four special roofs this year: an Astroroof, with sliding shade and heavily-tinted glass; electric sunroof; Hurst hatch roof; and on Skyhawk, a fixed- glass version with roof band. Rectangular headlamps that had been introduced previously on some models now appeared on Century, Regal and LeSabre. Buick's 231 cu. in. V-6, standard in Skyhawk, Skylark, Century and Regal Coupe, was the only V-6 designed and built in America. Its pistons, rings, wrist pins, rod bearings, timing gear and other parts were identical to those on the 350 V-8. But it weighed 200 pounds less and delivered a slightly better EPA rating than the inline six of 1975, due to improved fuel distribution. New carburetor calibrations for 1976 helped boost its performance. The V-6 could also squeeze into tighter engine compartments than an inline--a fact that would become more important as models were ownsized. High-Energy Ignition, used on all engines, sent 35 percent more voltage to spark plugs and eliminated the old points and condenser. All Buicks needed unleaded fuel, carried a catalytic converter, and required less routine maintenance than predecessors of a few years earlier. The new "Freedom Battery," standard on Skyhawk and available on others, required no maintenance or addition of water, and had a built-in "state of charge" indicator. The Quadrajet carburetor was redesigned. Spark advance increased on the 350 and 455 cu. in. V-8 engines. A new camshaft on the 350 V-8 gave more power at low engine speeds. Riviera, LeSabre and Electra had a lower (2.56:1) rear axle ratio for improved economy. The familiar three-speed column shift remained standard on several economy-model Buicks (but not available in California). Three different Turbo Hydra-matic versions were offered. Computers were used to determine the optimum spring rates for each model, to give best height control, ride, and maneuvering characteristics. Front disc brakes were standard on all Buicks. Most models now have rubber protective strips on bumpers. All had Full-Flo ventilation and full-foam, contour-molded seats. Spray-on corrosion protection was used, along with galvanized metal and drainage panels, to improve rust-resistance. Bodies were coated with primer, sealer, and multiple applications of high-gloss acrylic lacquer. In keeping with the Bicentennial, standard Buick body colors for '76 were: Judicial Black (code A), Liberty White (C), Pewter Gray (D), Potomac Blue (G), Continental Blue (H), Concord Green (J), Constitution Green (L), Mount Vernon Cream (M), Buckskin Tan (Q), Musket Brown (R), Boston Red (V), and Independence Red (W). The list of special colors included Congressional Cream (P) and Revere Red (X), neither of which was available on Skyhawk or Skylark; plus Colonial Yellow (N) and Firecracker Orange (U) for Skyhawk/Skylark and offered at extra cost on other models. Buick's standard safety features included seat belts with pushbutton buckles; seat/shoulder belts in front (with reminder light and buzzer); energy-absorbing steering column, padded instrument panel and front seatback tops; passenger guard door locks; safety door latches and hinges; soft, low-profile window control knobs; smooth contoured door and window regulator handles; lane-change feature in turn signal control; vinyl-edged wide-view inside mirror; dual master cylinder brake system with warning light; and dual- action safety latches (on front-opening hoods). Buick also announced an optional Air Cushion Restraint System for LeSabre, Electra and Riviera.

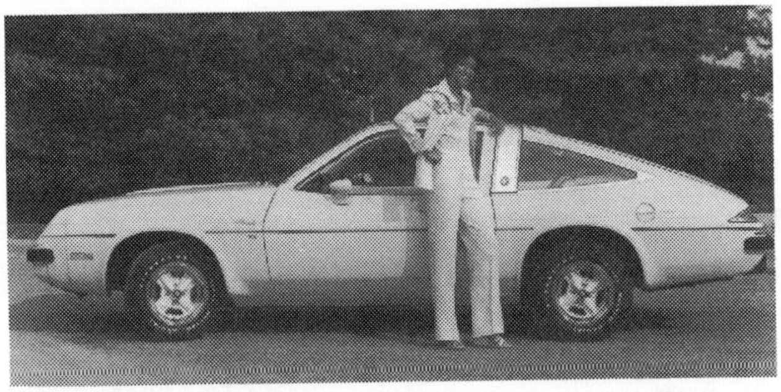

1976 Skyhawk hatchback coupe (B)

SKYHAWK — SERIES 4H — V-6 — Buick's variant of the subcompact H-body Chevrolet Monza, descended from the Vega and directly related to Olds Starfire, was called the "smallest Buick in 60 years." As part of the attempt to capture the emerging youth market, it was also dubbed "The Free Spirit Hawk." In addition to the standard hatchback coupe, a low-budget 'S' version had been introduced halfway through the 1975 model year and continued for '76. New to the option list this year was a wide brushed aluminum band that wrapped over the roof, embossed with a Skyhawk emblem, coupled with a heavily-tinted (smoke-colored) glass Astroroof. Performance fans could also order their Skyhawk with a new Borg-Warner five-speed manual gearbox (overdrive top gear), instead of the standard fully synchronized four-speed. Three-speed Turbo Hydra-matic was also available. Sole powerplant was a V-6 engine with two- barrel carburetor that combined economy and spirited power. With the five-speed, Skyhawk turned in an impressive 30 MPG highway rating in economy tests. Skyhawk's rakish hatchback body had a "slippery, aerodynamic look" with fastback roofline and bulging hood. That hood sloped down in the middle toward the grille, but bulged upward to meet the headlamp housings. The front end carried quad rectangular headlamps. 'BUICK' letters stood above the upper corner of the minimalist rectangular grille, with a single dark horizontal bar across its small opening. Energy-absorbing bumpers had protective strips, plus front and rear guards. Large amber park/turn lamps sat below the front bumper. 'Skyhawk' and 'V6' emblems were on front fenders, ahead of the door. White, gold or black accent stripes were standard; so were side-window reveal moldings. Inside were high-backed, full-foam bucket seats in a 2 2 seating arrangement (cloth/vinyl or vinyl upholstery), a center console, small "comfortably-angled" steering wheel, European-style handbrake, and floor gearshift lever. Large, bold, easy-to- read instruments included a circular 7000-rpm tachometer and KM/H-MPH speedometer, ammeter, and electric clock. In the trunk sat a stowaway spare tire. Skyhawk offered almost 28 cubic feet of storage with the rear seatback folded down. Skyhawk used unibody construction. Its radial-tuned suspension included computer-selected springs, front and rear stabilizer bars (except 'S' model), plus special suspension geometry and radial tires. Front disc brakes had vented rotors to dissipate heat for fade-resistant braking. Each pad had a brake lining wear sensor that emitted an audible squeak when replacement was needed. An oil pressure switch connected to the fuel pump shut off the fuel supply whenever oil pressure fell below the normal operating limit.

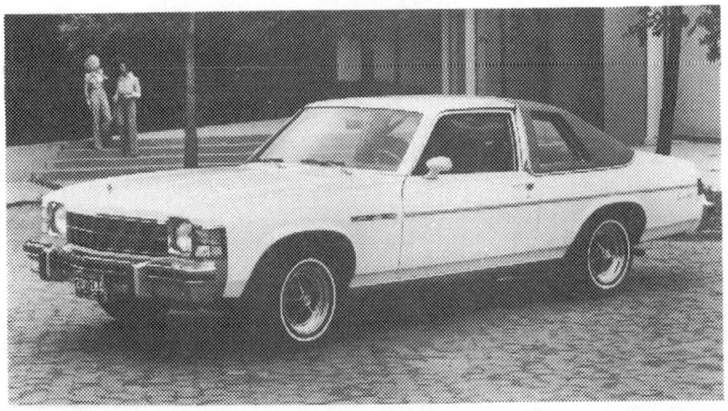

1976 Skylark landau coupe (B)

SKYLARK — SERIES 4X — V-6/V-8 — Buick's European-inspired compact sedan—the only American compact powered by a V-6—came in seven models, from low-priced 'S' to sporty S/R. Body styles included a coupe, hatchback and four-door sedan. The new horizontal-design grille was made up of thin horizontal and vertical strips forming wide segments, with a 'BUICK' badge in the lower corner. It was divided into upper and lower sections by a wider horizontal bar, with widest bar across the top. Twin round headlamps in square housings were flanked by stacked outboard park/signal lamps that wrapped around the front fenders, with amber reflectors at the rear of each unit. Skylark interiors also were new, while a thickly-padded Landau top with small side windows, accented by a brushed aluminum band, was optional. Other options included a Fuel Usage Light, Cruise-Master speed control, power windows, electric door locks, automatic trunk release, and tilt steering wheel. Skylark carried a standard 3.8-liter V-6 with High- Energy Ignition, plus front disc brakes, computer-selected springs, hefty front stabilizer bar, and large full-foam seats. That V-6 weighed 200 pounds less than the optional 350 V-8 (two- or four-barrel carburetor). The base V-8 option, though, was an economical 260 cu. in. (4.3-liter) version. A fully synchronized three-speed manual column shift was standard on V-6 powered Skylarks (except in California). The .73:1 rear axle ratio offered excellent economy. Semi-unit construction had Skylark's engine and front suspension mounted on a separate sub-frame that helped isolate vibration and road shock. Hatchbacks carried a stowaway spare tire and had 28 cubic feet of storage space. Skylark 'S' came with a vinyl bench seat; standard Skylark offered a choice of vinyl or cloth bench seats; while the S/R carried special thick, ribbed velour cloth and vinyl bucket seats (reclining on the passenger side). Roof drip moldings were standard on Skylark and S/R. The S/R instrument panel had large black dials. Its turn signal lever doubled as a headlight dimmer switch, as on European touring cars. S/R also had a rallye steering wheel; large sports console with gearshift lever and stowage bins; carpeted door trim with map pocket and reflector; stand-up hood ornament; plus radial-tuned suspension.

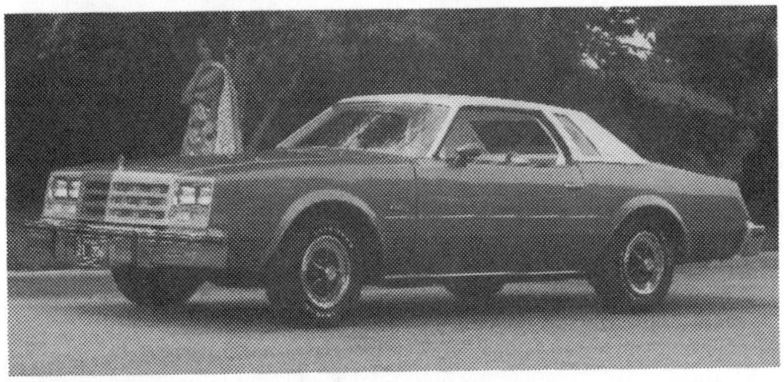

1976 Century Custom colonnade coupe (B)

CENTURY — SERIES 4A — V-6/V-8 — Buick's A-bodied Century models didn't all look alike for 1976. GM-designed rectangular headlamps were new, but two-door coupes also got new lower body sheetmetal, a fastback roofline, flared wheel openings, and a canted aerodynamic nosepiece containing a new grille with many vertical bars. The new "formal" bodies eliminated the prior "sculptured" look that had been introduced in 1973. The coupe grille was a curious six-slot design (three large horizontal crosshatched sections on each side), set in body-colored framing. Quad rectangular headlamps stood atop quad rectangular clear park/turn lamps, with 'BUICK' emblem above the grille's upper corner. A hood ornament was standard. The 'Century' emblem sat at the trailing edge of front fenders. Small side lenses were at the front edge of front fenders, and rear of rear fenders. The Custom Coupe had the same formal roofline as Regal, but with the new, aerodynamic front end. Four-door sedans retained their old basic bodies, but front ends changed to hold their new vertically-stacked headlamps. Sedans had the formal Regal-style grille with 'BUICK' badge at the side, vertically-stacked headlamps, and clear vertical park/signal lamps. The Regal, which was considered a part of the Century series (see below) also had the formal-look grille. All told, the nine-model Century/Regal lineup included four different rooflines. Sedan and station wagon wheelbases were 4 in. longer than coupes. Century was described as "a leaner, smaller breed of Buick....a custom-tailored road car that rivals even the most opulent Buicks." It was the only domestic mid-size powered by a V-6. Century Special was the economy version. Custom Wagons, offering over 85 cubic feet of cargo space, came with two or three seats, standard variable-ratio power steering, power front disc brakes, Turbo Hydra-matic, and a 350 cu. in. (5.7- liter) V-8 with four-barrel carburetor. Other models had a standard 231 cu. in. (3.8-liter) V-6, with V-8 optional (except in Special). A three-speed manual transmission with column shift was standard on V-6 coupes and sedans. All models except the Special had protective bumper strips. Wagons had a "Tailgate Ajar" warning light. Base Century and Special models offered a choice of cloth or vinyl bench seat. Century Custom could have cloth or vinyl notchback seating; wagons, vinyl notchback seats. Like full-size Buicks, Century was built on a full- perimeter frame. The radial-tuned suspension used computer- selected springs, front stabilizer bar and special suspension geometry. Power front disc brakes were standard on Custom sedan and wagon; power steering on all. Disc brake pads emitted an audible squeak to warn that replacement was needed. Options included an all-metal electric sunroof, Landau vinyl roof, Cruise-Master speed control, power windows, six- way power seats, tilt steering wheel, electric door locks, automatic trunk release, and low-speed-delay wipers that could be set to operate periodically. A Hurst Hatch Roof with twin removable smoked (gray tinted) glass panels was offered on the Custom (and Regal) coupe only. Buyers could choose from two air conditioners: Climate-Control that cooled and dehumidified, or Custom-Aire (semi-automatic). There were also two economy options: a Fuel Usage Gauge that showed whether you were driving economically, and a Speed Alert that warned when you exceeded a preset speed.

1976 Regal Landau Coupe (B)

CENTURY) REGAL — SERIES 4A — V-6/V-8 — Regal was considered the "high-line Century" rather than a truly separate model, but with its own styling touches. Those included a formal roofline and classic vertical crosshatch grille with 'Regal' script at the side. Like their parent Century, Regal coupes had new lower body sheet metal and flared wheel openings, plus a new formal-look grille. They also had horizontally-placed rectangular headlamps with outboard vertical amber side lenses. Regal sedans looked different, with quad stacked rectangular headlamps flanking thin vertical clear park/signal lamps that sat between headlamps and grille. Regal's crest stood at the trailing edge of front fenders; the 'Regal' script just behind opera windows on the coupe. Inside, seats were upholstered in velour, and the simulated woodgrain instrument panel held deep-set dials. Except in California, the Regal sedan came with a standard 350 cu. in. (5.7-liter) V-8, while coupes had a standard 231 cu. in. (3.8-liter) V-6. Regal sedans had Turbo Hydra-matic as standard equipment, but V-6 coupes came with three-speed manual (column) shift. Coupes could be ordered with 350 V-8 and automatic transmission. Power steering was standard. Regal's S/R package included reclining front bucket seats upholstered in ribbed velour; a large center console with gearshift lever; rallye steering wheel; headlamp dimmer in the turn signal lever; and GM-spec steel-belted radial whitewall tires.

1976 LeSabre Custom hardtop coupe (B)

LESABRE — SERIES 4B — V-8 — LeSabre for '76 received the quad rectangular headlamps that had gone on Electra in 1975, set above clear horizontal quad park/signal lamps. The new classic-look horizontal crosshatch grille had Buick letters set into the wide upper crossbar. Clear horizontal cornering lamps (optional) at front of front fenders accompanied smaller amber lenses. Trailing ends of rear fenders displayed 'LeSabre' script. LeSabres had large three-hole horizontal "ventiport" trim strips on the upper portion of front fenders, just ahead of the door--descendants of the old Buick portholes. Front and rear bumpers carried protective strips. In a last-minute addition to the model year lineup, LeSabre added a base V-6 version—the only full-sized, six- passenger car in the world with a V-6 engine. LeSabre Custom models came with standard 350 cu. in. (5.7-liter) V-8, power steering, power front disc brakes, and Turbo Hydra-matic. Gas mileage of the optional 455 cu. in. V-8 engine improved to an 18 MPG rating. Teflon inside coatings improved shock absorber operation. Ample space for six was offered with either cloth/vinyl or vinyl notchback seats. Among the many options were low- speed-delay windshield wipers, a positive-traction differential, and firm suspension package.

1976 Electra Limited hardtop sedan (B)

ELECTRA — SERIES 4C — V-8 — Buick's posh full-size Electra 225 and Electra Limited came in coupe or hardtop sedan form. Electra's new grille had a heavy upper bar inset with large Buick block letters, 17 vertical bars with crosshatch pattern inside each section, and 'Electra' script at the side. Unlike the 1975 version, this grille didn't extend below the headlamps. Quad rectangular headlamps sat atop four clear park/signal lights, with clear cornering lamps (optional) at front of front fenders.

Horizontal "ventiport" trim strips were on upper section of front fenders, ahead of the door. They had four "holes" (actually gouge-like depressions) to distinguish Electras from the LeSabre's three. Rear fender bottoms held a small reflector lens, below the long bodyside trim molding. Front and rear bumpers had protective strips. Standard equipment included Turbo Hydra-matic, power steering, and power front disc brakes, along with power windows and a digital clock. Four-link rear suspension gave a smooth, quiet ride, improved by Teflon-coated shock absorbers. A vapor return system reduced the chance of vapor lock. An altitude compensator in the Turbo Hydra-matic provided smooth shifting in various elevation. The EPA highway rating of the 455 cu. in. (7.5-liter) V-8 engine improved by 3 MPG. Increased economy came as a result of improved carburetion, new crankshaft design, increased spark advance, better axle ratio, and reduced weight. Buyers had a choice of new full-foam seat designs: cloth bench or notchback seats (or vinyl notchback in Electra 225 sedan); cloth or vinyl notchback in the Electra 225 coupe. Limited models had cloth 60/40 notchback seating (two-way power) with a fold-down center armrest. Limiteds also had wide rocker appearance moldings, and the Limited sedan included a dome reading lamp. Top-of-the-line was the Park Avenue edition of the Electra Limited hardtop sedan. That package included a formal "halo" vinyl roof, thick cut-pile carpeting, and velour upholstery that even reached the executive center console and ceiling. Two Landau tops were available: traditional, or a new type with smaller opera windows and thickly-padded vinyl with French seams on the back portion. An optional Astroroof was available on the coupe. Drivers could enjoy a glass-topped driving compartment, roll the sunshade to closed position, or retract the glass for open-air driving. Coupes could also have an electric sunroof. Other options: variable-delay wipers, and an automatic door locking system that worked when the gear selector was put into and out of Park position. Optional Automatic Climate Control incorporated both heater and air conditioner.

ESTATE WAGON — SERIES 4BR — V-8 — Full-size station wagons came with two or three seats and 106 cubic foot cargo area. Standard powertrain was the 455 cu. in. (7.5-liter) V-8 engine and Turbo Hydra-matic transmission, plus variable-ratio power steering, power front disc brakes, and computer-selected front coil and rear leaf springs. Estates had vinyl bench seating, a hidden storage compartment, inside hood release, and a power tailgate window. The clever glide-away tailgate's lower section would glide away under the floor, while the window receded up into the roof area. Three-seat models had a forward-facing third seat and divided second seat. Front and rear bumpers had protective strips. Estate Wagon's simulated woodgrain instrument panel, steering wheel, carpeting and available notchback seat were identical to LeSabre.

1976 Riviera S/R coupe (B)

RIVIERA — SERIES 4E — V-8 — As it had since the first version came off the line for 1963, Riviera combined luxury with road car capabilities. As the catalog proclaimed, the personal-luxury coupe blended "performance, elegance and romance." This year it had new seat designs and interior trim, plus a more efficient engine, transmission and axle ratio combination. Riviera's 455 cu. in. (7.5-liter) V-8 offered improved gas mileage this year. Standard equipment included variable- ratio power steering and power front disc brakes; six-position tilt steering wheel; two-way power seats; electric windows; cut-pile carpeting; front bumper guards; front and rear bumper protective strips; computer-selected coil springs at all four wheels; Teflon-coated shock absorbers; JR78 steel-belted radial tires; and a digital clock. Wraparound three-section (clear/amber/clear) park/turn lamps flanked quad rectangular headlamps. Separate B-U-I-C-K letters stood above the horizontal crosshatch grille, with 'Riviera' script at the side. Similar 'Riviera' script on the lower section of front fenders, to rear of wheel openings. A new two-tone color scheme was actually a vinyl applique bonded to bodysides. Silver plus a choice of four colors were available: dark red, dark blue, black, or dark gray. Options included a three-in-one Astroroof with heavily tinted glass and rollaway sunshade that permitted closed, open-air, or glass-topped motoring; Automatic Climate- Control; and an electric sunroof that came with or without a vinyl top. The popular Landau top returned for 1976.

I.D. DATA: The 13-symbol Vehicle Identification Number (VIN) was located on the upper left surface of the instrument panel, visible through the windshield. The first digit is '4', indicating the Buick division. The second symbol is a letter indicating series: 'S' Skyhawk; 'T' Skyhawk S; 'B' Skylark; 'C' Skylark S/R; 'W' Skylark S; 'D' Century; 'E' Century Special; 'H' Century Custom; 'J' Regal; 'K' Century Custom wagon; 'N' LeSabre; 'P' LeSabre Custom; 'R' Estate Wagon; 'V' Electra 225; 'X' Electra Limited; 'Z' Riviera. Next come two digits that denote body type: '07' Skyhawk hatchback coupe; '17' Skylark 2-dr. hatchback coupe; '27' Skylark 2-dr. thin-pillar coupe; '37' Century 2-dr. Colonnade coupe or Electra HT coupe; '57' Century/Regal 2-dr. Colonnade coupe or LeSabre HT coupe; '87' Riviera 2-dr. HT coupe; '29' 4-dr. Colonnade sedan; '39' 4-dr. HT sedan; '69' 4-dr. thin-pillar sedan; '35' 4-dr. 2-seat wagon; '45' 4-dr. 3-seat wagon. The fifth symbol is a letter indicating engine code: 'C' V6-231 2Bbl.; 'Y' V8-301 2Bbl.; 'U' V8-305 2Bbl.; 'H' V8-350 2Bbl.; 'L' V8-350 4Bbl. (LM1); 'R' V8-350 4Bbl. (L34); 'P' V8-350 4Bbl. (L77); 'K' V8-403 4Bbl. (L80). The sixth symbol denotes model year ('6' 1976). Next is a plant code: '2' Ste. Therese, Quebec (Canada); 'K' Leeds, Missouri; 'L' Van Nuys, Calif.; 'T' Tarrytown, NY; 'G' Framingham, Mass.; 'H' Flint, Mich.; 'Z' Fremont, Calif.; 'C' Southgate, Calif.; 'X' Fairfax, Kansas; 'E' Linden, New Jersey. The final six digits are the sequential serial number, which began with 100001 except for Skyhawks (700001 up); LeSabres, Estate Wagons, Electras and Rivieras built at Flint (400001 up). Engine numbers were stamped on the front of the block. A body number plate on the shroud identified model year, car division, series, style, body assembly plant, body number, trim combination, modular seat code, paint code, and date built code.

SKYHAWK (V-6)

Series Number	Body/Style Number	Body Type & Seating	Factory Price	Shipping Weight	Production Total
4H	T07	2-dr 'S' Hatch-4P	3903	2857	Note 1
4H	S07	2-dr. Hatch-4P	4216	2889	Note 1

Note 1: Total model year production (U.S.), 15,769 Skyhawks.

SKYLARK 'S' (V-6/V-8)

4X	W27	2-dr. Coupe-6P	3435/3470	3316/3515	Note 2

28

SKYLARK (V-6/V-8)

4X	B27	2-dr Coupe-6P	3549/3584	3327/3526	Note 2
4X	B17	2-dr Hatch-6P	3687/3722	3396/3591	6,703
4X	B69	4-dr Sedan-6P	3609/3644	3283/3484	48,157

Note 2: Total U.S. model year production, 51,260 Skylark base and 'S' coupes. Of the total 106,120 Skylarks produced, 87,881 had a V-6 engine, 18,239 a V-8.

SKYLARK S/R (V-6/V-8)

4X	C27	2-dr Coupe-5P	4281/4316	3319/3502	3,880
4X	C17	2-dr Hatch-5P	4398/4433	3338/3522	1,248
4X	C69	4-dr Sedan-5P	4324/4359	3312/3499	3,243

Note 3: Of the total 8371 S/R Skylarks produced for the model year, 4,818 had a V-6 engine and 3,553 a V-8. Prices shown are for the 260 cu. in. V-8; the 350 V-8 with 2Bbl. carburetor cost $50 more.

CENTURY SPECIAL (V-6)

4A	E37	2-dr Col cpe-6P	3935	3508	Note 4

CENTURY (V-6/V-8)

4A	D37	2-dr Col cpe-6P	4070/4155	3652/3844	Note 4
4A	D29	4-dr Col sed-6P	4105/4190	3741/3933	33,632

Note 4: Total Century and Century Special coupe production, 59,448. Of the 93,080 Century and Special models built, 66,440 had a V-6 engine and 26,640 a V-8.

CENTURY CUSTOM (V-6/V-8)

4A	H57	2-dr Col cpe-6P	4346/4431	3609/3801	34,036
4A	H29	4-dr Col sed-6P	4424/4509	3721/3913	19,728
4A	K35	4-dr Sta Wag-6P	-- /4987	-- /4363	Note 5
4A	K45	4-dr Sta Wag-8P	-- /5099	-- /4413	Note 5

Note 5: Total Century Custom wagon production, 16,625. Of the 70,389 Century Custom models built, 21,832 had a V-6 engine and 48,557 a V-8.

REGAL (V-6/V-8)

4A	J57	2-dr Col cpe-6P	4465/4910	3710/3902	124,498
4A	J29	4-dr Col sed-6P	-- /4825	-- /4104	17,118

Note 6: Total model year production, 141,616 Regals (31,907 with V-6 engine and 109,709 V-8).

LESABRE (V-6)

4B	N57	2-dr HT Cpe-6P	4815	4129	3,861
4B	N69	4-dr Sedan-6P	4747	4170	4,315
4B	N39	4-dr HT Sed-6P	4871	4056	2,312

LESABRE CUSTOM (V-8)

4B	P57	2-dr HT Cpe-6P	5114	4275	45,669
4B	P69	4-dr Sedan-6P	5046	4328	34,841
4B	P39	4-dr HT Sed-6P	5166	4386	46,109

ESTATE WAGON (V-8)

4B	R35	4-dr Sta Wag-6P	5591	5013	5,990
4B	R45	4-dr Sta Wag-8P	5731	5139	14,384

ELECTRA 225 (V-8)

4C	V37	2-dr Coupe-6P	6367	4502	18,442
4C	V39	4-dr HT Sed-6P	6527	4641	26,655

ELECTRA LIMITED (V-8)

4C	X37	2-dr Coupe-6P	6689	4521	28,395
4C	X39	4-dr HT Sed-6P	6852	4709	51,067

RIVIERA (V-8)

4E	Z87	2-dr Coupe-6P	6798	4531	20,082

FACTORY PRICE AND WEIGHT NOTE: Figure before the slash is for V-6 engine, after slash for V-8.

ENGINES: BASE EQUIPMENT V-6 (Skyhawk, Skylark, Century, Regal coupe, LeSabre): 90-degree, overhead-valve V-6. Cast iron alloy block and head. Displacement: 231 cu. in. (3.8 liters). Bore & stroke: 3.8 x 3.4 in. Compression ratio: 8.0:1. Brake horsepower: 105 at 3400 R.P.M. Torque: 185 lbs.-ft. at 2000 R.P.M. Four main bearings. Hydraulic valve lifters. Carburetor: 2Bbl. Rochester 2GC. VIN Code: C. OPTIONAL V-8 (Skylark): 90-degree overhead-valve V-8. Cast iron alloy block and head. Displacement: 260 cu. in. (4.3 liters). Bore & stroke: 3.50 x 3.385 in. Compression ratio: 8.5:1. Brake horsepower: 110 at 3400 R.P.M. Torque: 210 lbs.-ft. at 1600 R.P.M. Five main bearings. Hydraulic valve lifters. Carburetor: 2Bbl. Rochester. Built by Oldsmobile. VIN Code: F. BASE V-8 (Regal sedan); OPTIONAL (Skylark, Century/Custom, Regal cpe): 90-degree, overhead valve V-8. Cast iron alloy block and head. Displacement: 350 cu. in. (5.7 liters). Bore & stroke: 3.80 x 3.85 in. Compression ratio: 8.0:1. Brake horsepower: 140 at 3200 R.P.M. Torque: 280 lbs.-ft. at 1600 R.P.M. Five main bearings. Hydraulic valve lifters. Carburetor: 2Bbl. Roch. 2GC. VIN Code: H. BASE V-8 (Century wagon, LeSabre Custom); OPTIONAL (Skylark, Century/Custom, Regal): 90-degree, overhead valve V-8. Cast iron alloy block and head. Displacement: 350 cu. in. (5.7 liters). Bore & stroke: 3.80 x 3.85 in. Compression ratio: 8.0:1. Brake horsepower: 155 at 3400 R.P.M. Torque: 280 lbs.-ft. at 1800 R.P.M. Five main bearings. Hydraulic valve lifters. Carburetor: 4Bbl. Roch. M4MC. VIN Code: J. BASE V-8 (Electra, Estate Wagon, Riviera); OPTIONAL (LeSabre Custom): 90-degree, overhead valve V-8. Cast iron alloy block and head. Displacement: 455 cu. in. (7.5 liters). Bore & stroke: 4.3125 x 3.9 in. Compression ratio: 7.9:1. Brake horsepower: 205 at 3800 R.P.M. Torque: 345 lbs.-ft. at 2000 R.P.M. Five main bearings. Hydraulic valve lifters. Carburetor: 4Bbl. Roch. M4MC. VIN Code: T.

CHASSIS DATA: Wheelbase: (Skyhawk) 97.0 in.; (Skylark) 111.0 in.; (Century/Regal cpe) 112.0 in.; (Century/Regal sed/wag) 116.0 in.; (LeSabre) 124.0 in.; (Electra/Estate) 127.0 in.; (Riviera) 122.0 in. Overall length:- (Skyhawk) 179.3 in.; (Skylark) 200.3 in.; (Century/Regal cpe) 209.7 in.; (Century/Regal sed) 213.5 in.; (Century wag) 218.2 in.; LeSabre) 226.8 in.; (Electra) 233.3 in.; (Estate Wagon) 231.8 in.; (Riv) 218.6 in. Height:- (Skyhawk) 50.1 in.; (Skylark 2-dr.) 52.1 in.; (Skylark 4-dr.) 53.1 in.; (Century/Regal cpe) 52.6-52.8 in.; (Century/Regal sed) 53.6 in.; (Century wag) 55.3 in.; (LeSabre cpe) 53.2 in.; (LeSabre HT sed) 53.3 in.; (LeSabre 4-dr. sed) 54.0 in.; (Electra cpe) 54.0 in.; (Electra sed) 54.5 in.; (Estate 2S wag) 57.8 in.; (Estate 3S wag) 57.0 in.; (Riv) 53.0 in. Width:- (Skyhawk) 65.4 in.; (Skylark) 72.7 in.; (Century/Regal cpe) 77.0 in.; (Century/Regal sed/wag) 79.0 in.; (LeSabre/Electra/Estate/ Riv) 79.9 in. Front Tread:- (Skyhawk) 54.7 in.; (Skylark) 59.1 in.; (Century/Regal) 61.5 in.; (LeSabre/Electra/Estate/Riv) 63.4 in. Rear Tread:- (Skyhawk) 53.6 in.; (Skylark) 59.7 in.; (Century/Regal) 60.7 in.; (LeSabre/Electra/Estate/Riv) 64.0 in. Standard Tires:- (Skyhawk) BR78 x 13 SBR; (Skyawk 'S') B78 x 13; (Skylark) E78 x 14; (Skylark S/R) FR78 x 14 SBR WSW; (Century/Regal cpe) GR78 x 15 SBR; (Century Special cpe) FR78 x 15; (Century/Regal sed) FR78 x 15 SBR; (Century wagon) HR78 x 15; (LeSabre) HR78 x 15 SBR; (LeSabre w/455 V-8) JR78 x 15 SBR; (Electra/Riviera) JR78 x 15 SBR; (Estate) LR78 x 15 SBR.

TECHNICAL: Transmission:- Three-speed, fully synchronized manual gearbox (column shift) standard on Skylark, Century, and Regal cpe with V-6; Turbo Hydra-matic optional. Four-speed, fully synchronized floor shift standard on Skyhawk; five-speed optional. Turbo-Hydra-matic (three-speed) standard on Regal sedan, LeSabre, Electra, Estate and Riviera; also on other models with V-8 and Century sold in California. Three-speed manual transmission gear ratios: (1st) 3.11:1; (2nd) 1.84:1; (3rd) 1.00:1; (Rev) 3.22:1. Four-speed gear ratios: (1st) 3.11:1; (2nd) 2.20:1; (3rd) 1.47:1; (4th) 1.00:1; (Rev) 3.11:1. Five-speed gear ratios: (1st) 3.10:1; (2nd) 1.89:1; (3rd) 1.27:1; (4th) 1.00:1; (5th) 0.84:1; (Rev) 3.06:1. Automatic transmission gear ratios: (1st) 2.52:1; (2nd) 1.52:1; (3rd) 1.00:1; (Rev) 1.93:1 or 2.08:1. Standard axle ratio:- (Skyhawk) 2.56:1; (Skylark) 2.73:1; (Century/Regal) 3.08:1; (LeSabre/Electra/Riviera) 2.56:1. Hypoid bevel final drive. Steering:- recirculating ball; variable-ratio power steering standard on Century/Regal, LeSabre, Electra, Estate and Riviera. Suspension:- (Skyhawk) unequal-length front control arms w/anti-sway bar, rigid rear axle w/torque arm, Panhard rod and anti-sway bar; (Skylark) semi-elliptic rear leaf springs; (others) front/rear coil springs, independent front w/trailing links and anti-roll bar (exc. Special). Brakes:- front disc, rear drum; power brakes standard on LeSabre/Electra/Rivier plus Century Custom sedan/wagon and Regal sedan. Body construction:- (Skyhawk) unitized; (Skylark) separate front frame unit cushion-mounted to unitized body; (others) separate body and perimeter box frame. Fuel tank:- (Skyhawk) 18.5 gal.; (Skylark) 21 gal.; (Century/Regal/Estate) 22 gal.; (LeSabre/Electra/Riv) 26 gal. High-Energy electronic ignition (HEI) on all engines. Unleaded fuel only.

DRIVETRAIN OPTIONS: Engines:- 260 cu. in. V-8, 2Bbl.: Skylark ($35). 350 cu. in. V-8, 2Bbl.: Skylark, Century/Custom, Regal cpe ($85). 350 cu. in. V-8, 4Bbl.: Skylark, Century, Custom, Regal cpe ($140); Regal sed ($55). 455 cu. in. V-8, 4Bbl.: LeSabre Cust ($159). Transmission/Differential:- Five-speed manual floor shift: Skyhawk ($244). Turbo Hydra-matic.: Skyhawk ($244); Skylark, Century cpe/sed, Regal cpe ($262). Positive traction differential ($48-$54). Power Accessories:- Power brakes: Skyhawk ($55); Skylark/Century ($58) exc. Cust sed/wag. Power steering: Skyhawk ($120); Skylark ($136). Suspension:- H5 handling pkg.: Skyhawk 'S' ($104-$124). Firm ride/handling pkg. ($17-$21) exc. Skyhawk. Rallye ride/handling pkg.: Skylark ($39); Century, except Special wagon, Regal, Riviera ($34). Automatic level control: Century/Regal ($92); LeSabre/Electra/Riviera ($93). Other: Trailer towing flasher/harness: ($16-$27) except Skyhawk. Heavy-duty 80-amp alternator: Century/Regal/LeSabre/Electra/Riviera ($35-$39). Heavy-duty Energizer battery ($15-$17) except Electra, Riviera. Freedom battery ($28-$29) except Skyhawk/Electra. Heavy-duty cooling ($25-$52) except Skyhawk. Engine block heater ($12) except Skyhawk. Heavy-duty air cleaner ($11) except Skyhawk/Skylark. Chrome air cleaner: Riviera ($17). California emission system ($50).

SKYHAWK CONVENIENCE/APPEARANCE OPTIONS: Option Groups:- Shadow light Astroroof w/roof crown molding ($550). Appearance group: 'S' ($63). Convenience group ($20). Comfort/Convenience:- Air cond. ($424). Rear defogger, electric ($66). Soft Ray tinted glass ($44). Tinted windshield ($37). Rallye steering wheel: 'S' ($35). Tilt steering wheel ($48). Electric clock: 'S' ($16); clock and tach ($59). Right sport mirror ($12). Remote-control left sport mirror: 'S' ($15). Entertainment:- AM radio ($71). AM/FM radio ($134). AM/FM stereo radio ($219). Rear speaker ($19). Windshield antenna ($21). Exterior Trim:- Door edge guards ($8). Roof crown molding ($150). Protective bodyside moldings ($24-$39). Interior Trim/Upholstery:- Full-length console: 'S' ($73). Adjustable driver's seatback ($17). Front/rear floor mats ($14). Custom seatbelts ($13). Wheels:- Custom sport wheels ($74-$84). Deluxe wheel covers ($39); for radial tires only. Wheel trim rings ($33). Tires:- B78 x 13 WSW: 'S' ($26- $32). BR78 x 13 SBR blackwall: 'S' ($82-$103). BR78 x 13 SBR whitewall ($26-$135). BR70 x 13 SBR WLT ($35-$148).

SKYLARK CONVENIENCE/APPEARANCE OPTIONS: Option Packages:- Accessory pkg.: 'S' ($11). Convenience group ($29). Appearance group (wheel opening and roof drip moldings): 'S' ($31). Comfort/Convenience:- Air cond. ($452). Cruise Master ($73). Rear defogger, blower-type ($43). Power windows ($99-$140). Electric door locks ($62-$89). Rallye steering wheel ($35); std. on S/R. Tilt steering wheel ($52). Soft Ray tinted glass ($46). Dual horns ($7). Electric clock ($18). Headlamps-on indicator ($7). Fuel usage indicator ($16). Electric trunk release ($17). Three-speed wipers w/delay ($28). Remote-control left mirror ($14). Sport mirrors: left remote, right manual ($26); both remote ($40). Entertainment:- AM radio ($75). AM/FM radio ($137). AM/FM stereo radio ($233). AM radio and stereo tape player ($209). AM/FM stereo radio w/tape ($337). Rear speaker ($20). Windshield antenna ($22). Exterior Trim:- Custom vinyl roof ($91-$96). Landau top: cpe ($150-$155). Two-tone paint ($35). Special exterior paint ($107). Swing-out rear quarter vent window: two-doors ($48). Protective bodyside moldings ($37). Rocker panel moldings ($15). Wide rocker appearance group ($32). Decklid molding ($7). Custom door and window frame moldings ($23-$29). Door edge guards ($8-$12). Bodyside accent stripe ($23). Bumper guards, front ($17); front/rear ($34). Bumper strips, front/rear ($29). Interior Trim/Upholstery:- Full-length console ($71). Vinyl bucket seats: base ($79). Custom trim bench seats/cushion interior: base ($138). Custom seatbelts ($13-$15). Carpet savers ($8). Carpet savers and mats ($14). Carpeted door trim w/map pocket and reflector ($35); std. on S/R. Wheels:- Styled wheels ($77- $89). Chrome-plated wheels ($103-$122). Deluxe wheel covers ($31); for radial tires only. Deluxe wire wheel covers ($111); for radials only. Tires:- E78 x 14 whitewall ($26-$33) exc. S/R. ER78 x 14 SBR blackwall ($69-$86) exc. S/R. ER78 x 4 SBR whitewall ($95-$119) exc. S/R. FR78 x 14 SBR WLT ($119-$149) exc. S/R ($24-$30).

CENTURY/REGAL CONVENIENCE/APPEARANCE OPTIONS: Option Packages:- Regal S/R Coupe pkg. ($379). Sunroof: cpe ($370). Hurst hatch roof: Century Custom, Regal cpe ($550). Convenience group ($5-$29). Comfort/Convenience:- Air cond. ($476). Custom Aire semi-automatic air cond. ($513). Cruise Master ($73). Rear defogger: electric ($77); blower-type ($43). Soft Ray tinted glass ($50). Tinted windshield ($40). Six-way power seat ($124). Custom steering wheel ($18). Rallye steering wheel ($35). Tilt steering ($52). Power windows ($99-$140). Electric door locks ($62-$89). Electric trunk release ($17). Remote-control tailgate lock: Century wag ($20). Electric clock ($20). Headlamps-on indicator ($7). Instrument gauges and clock ($42) exc. wag. Fuel usage gauge ($25). Speed alert ($14). Dome reading lamp ($15). Three- speed wiper with delay ($28). Mirrors:- Remote control mirror ($14). Sport mirrors: left remote ($26). Lighted visor vanity mirror ($39). Entertainment:- AM radio ($79). AM/FM radio ($142). AM/FM stereo radio ($233). AM radio w/stereo tape player ($213). AM/FM stereo radio w/tape ($337). Rear speaker ($20). Front/rear speakers ($41). Windshield antenna ($22); incl. w/radios. Exterior Trim:- Landau vinyl top: Century Cust, Regal cpe ($110); Century/Spec. ($144). Custom vinyl top: Century cpe, Regal ($106). Short custom vinyl top: Century, Special cpe ($79). Custom vinyl top w/hood ornament: Century, Custom sed ($111). Swing-out rear quarter vent windows: Century 2S wag ($48). Two-tone paint ($30-$40). Special color paint ($125). Bumper guards, front/rear ($35); rear, Century wag ($17). Bumper strips: Century Special ($28). Protective bodyside and front fender moldings ($26). Lower bodyside molding and fender moldings ($34). Door edge guards ($8-$12). Wheel opening moldings: Century/Spec. ($18). Bodyside accent stripe ($49). Woodgrain applique: Century wag ($146). Luggage rack: Century wag ($71). Air deflector: Century wag ($24). Interior Trim/Upholstery:- Full-length console ($71). Custom notchback seat trim: Century, Special ($125-$151). Custom vinyl notchback seat trim: Century Cust cpe, Regal cpe ($99); cloth ($129). Custom vinyl 60/40 seat trim: Century Cust, Regal cpe ($185); cloth ($215). Custom reclining seat trim: Century Cust cpe ($226). Custom trim vinyl bucket seats: Century, Spec. ($132-$158). Vinyl bucket seats: Century Cust, Regal ($8). Custom seatbelts ($13-$20). Front/rear carpeting: Century Spec. ($23). Load floor mat: Century wag ($22). Carpet savers ($9); w/mats ($16). Litter pocket ($6). Wheels:- Chrome-plated wheels ($106-$149); N/A wagon. Styled wheels ($58-$89); N/A wag. Deluxe wire wheel covers: Century ($123); Regal ($91). Styled wheel covers: Century ($85); Regal ($53). Deluxe wheel covers: Century ($32). Super deluxe wheel covers: Regal ($62). Tires:- FR78 x 15 SBR WSW: Century ($28-$40). GR78 x 15 SBR BSW: Century/Cust sed ($20-$25); with V-8 (NC). GR78 x 15 SBR WSW $30-$62) exc. Century Special. White-letter tires ($22-$89) exc. Special. Space-saver spare tire (NC). Conventional spare tire: Century Spec. (NC).

LESABRE/ELECTRA/ESTATE WAGON/RIVIERA CONVENIENCE/APPEARANCE OPTIONS: Option Packages: Electra Limited Park Avenue pkg. ($419); w/deluxe console ($525). Riviera S/R pkg. ($276). Accessory group: LeSabre, Estate ($57-$72). Electric sunroof: Electra/Riviera cpe ($725). Astroroof: Electra/Riv cpe ($891). Comfort/Convenience:- Air cond. ($512). Automatic climate control air cond.: Electra/Riv ($594). Custom Aire air cond.: LeSabre/Estate ($549). Cruise Master ($79). Rear defogger, electric ($78); blower-type ($43). Soft Ray tinted glass ($64). Tinted windshield: LeSabre/Est ($41). Power windows: LeSabre/Est ($159). Electric door locks ($90). Power tailgate door: Estate ($52). Automatic door locks: Electra/Riv ($93-$120). Six-way power driver's seat ($98- $126) exc. base LeSabre. Six-way power bench seat ($126) exc. Electra Ltd. Dual six-way power seats ($220-$247) exc. base LeSabre. Custom steering wheel: LeSabre/Est ($16). Tilt steering wheel ($53); std. on Riv. Tilt/telescoping steering column ($95) exc. Riv ($42). Map light: Electra 225, Riv ($10). Low fuel indicator ($11). Fuel usage gauge ($25). Speed alert and trip odometer ($19). Electric trunk release ($17). Three-speed wipers w/delay ($28). Lighting, Horns and -Mirrors:- Cornering lamps ($40). Front light monitors: LeSabre/Est ($23). Front/rear monitors: Electra/Riv ($51). Door courtesy/warning lights: 2-dr ($30); 4-dr ($47). Headlamps-on indicator ($7). Dome/reading lamp ($15). Four- note horn ($17). Remote left mirror: LeSabre/Est ($14). Remote right mirror ($29). Dual remote sport mirrors ($36- $50). Remote left mirror w/thermometer ($19-$33). Lighted visor vanity mirror ($40). Entertainment:- AM radio ($92). AM/FM radio ($153). AM/FM stereo radio w/four speakers ($236). AM radio and stereo tape player ($228). AM/FM stereo radio and tape ($341). Rear speaker ($20). Front/rear speakers ($41); non-stereo radio req'd. Windshield antenna ($22); incl. w/radios. Power antenna ($40). Exterior Trim:- Landau top: Electra cpe ($549). Landau custom vinyl top: LeSabre/Electra cpe ($140-$159); Riviera ($399). Landau custom vinyl top w/roof crown molding: Riv ($499). Custom vinyl top: Electra Ltd sed ($62); heavy-padded ($399). Custom vinyl top and molding ($139-$150). Custom vinyl top w/halo molding: Electra cpe ($163). Two-tone paint ($35-$60); special Riviera two-tone ($135). Special color paint ($125). Protective bodyside moldings ($37-$52). Custom wide bodyside moldings: Electra ($72). Door edge guards ($8-$12). Wide rocker panel moldings: LeSabre Cust, Estate, Electra 225 ($32) Wide rocker moldings group: base LeSabre ($93); Estate ($77). Belt reveal molding: LeSabre, Estate ($30). Custom molding: base LeSabre ($61); Estate ($46). Custom door window frame molding: base LeSabre ($30). Bodyside accent stripes $33). Coach stripes: Electra ($52). Woodgrain applique: Estate ($193). Tailgate molding: Estate ($18). Bumper guards, front/rear ($37) exc. Riv; front, Riviera ($18). Front bumper reinforcement ($7-$14) exc. Riv. Luggage rack: Estate ($94). Locking luggage locker: Est ($14). Interior Trim/Upholstery:- Full-length console: Riv ($72). Custom notchback seat trim: Estate ($208); 60/40 ($295). Custom cloth notchback 60/40 seat trim: Riviera ($123); vinyl ($97); vinyl 40/40 seat ($97). Leather upholstery: Electra Ltd ($320). Leather upholstery group: Riv ($417). Custom seatbelts: LeSabre/Est ($17-$20). Carpet savers ($10); w/mats ($17). Litter container ($6). Deluxe trunk trim: LeSabre ($40). Load floor area carpet: Estate ($61). Wheels and Tires:- Chrome-plated wheels: LeSabre/Estate/Electra ($117-$151). Deluxe wheel covers: base LeSabre ($32). Super deluxe wheel covers: Riv ($40). Styled wheel covers ($32-$86). Deluxe wire wheel covers ($70-$124). Whitewall tires ($41-$47). Wide whitewalls: Electra/Riv ($60).

HISTORY: Introduced: September 25, 1975. Model year production (U.S.): 737,467 (238,298 sixes and 499,169 V-8s) for a 9.1 percent share of the industry total. Calendar year production (U.S.): 817,669. Calendar year sales by U.S. dealers: 738,385 for an 8.6 percent market share, up from 518,032 in 1975. Model year sales by U.S. dealers: 706,249 (plus 25,007 imported Opels), up from only 463,132 in 1975.

Historical Footnotes: Since the economy was rising, Buick forecast a 40 percent jump in sales for the Bicentennial model year. Year- end results exceeded even that optimistic prediction, with sales up 52.5 percent to 706,249. That total, in fact, almost reached the model-year record set in 1973—good news after two years of slippage. Calendar year production rose by 56 percent. Best sellers were the mid-size Century and compact Skylark, both up over 74 percent in sales. For 1976, Skylark production moved from Ste. Therese, Quebec, to Southgate, California. Skyhawk assembly continued in Canada. On the import front, a Japanese-built Opel Isuzu was introduced in mid-year. Sales amounted to less than half those of the former German-built Opel T-car, a result of dwindling import sales and a decline in the number of dealers carrying the car. Big cars, on the other hand, continued to sell strongly--a surprise to the industry. For the second year in a row, a Buick paced the Indianapolis 500 race. This year's pace car was a Century with turbocharged, highly modified 231 V-6. The turbo came from Rajay Industries, and the engine produced triple the normal horsepower. It was the first V 6 vehicle ever to handle the pace car duties. A total of 1,290 Century models wearing the pace car colors (orange, black and gray) and appropriate emblems were produced for the market.

1977 BUICK

This year saw a total restyle for the B- and C-bodied LeSabre, Electra and Riviera. All were downsized significantly, measuring closer to mid-size dimensions—but the trimmed-down designs didn't lose their traditional spacious comfort. LeSabre and Riviera coupes offered over 2-1/2 in. more rear leg room than in 1976, as well as increased head room. Trunk space also grew on some models. Most downsized GM cars, in fact, were 1-1/2 in. taller than before. Smaller Buick models had mainly cosmetic changes. The full-line catalog continued the previous year's theme, "dedicated to the Free Spirit in just about everyone." Buick called the slimmed-down designs "trim, functional, contemporary," adding that "Suspensions are taut. Handling and maneuverability, crisp and responsive." Heralding the move to smaller engines, the mighty 455 V-8 left the lineup, replaced by a 403 cu. in. (6.6-liter) V-8 as the biggest powerplant for full-size Buicks. New 301 and 305 cu. in. V-8 engines were offered as options on Skylark and LeSabre. The familiar 350 cu. in. (5.7-liter) four-barrel V-8, available on LeSabre, replaced the old 455 as standard equipment on the Electra, Riviera and Estate Wagon. Actually, three different 350 V-8s with four-barrel carburetor were offered, with two different bore/stroke dimensions, including one built by Chevrolet—a move that eventually led to serious criticism and lawsuits. The V-6 engine got redesigned cylinder heads with tapered-seat spark plugs, plus an added heat crossover hole in the head to speed warmups. Also new for 1977: an electric choke and back pressure exhaust gas recirculator. Diagnostic connections on full-size Buicks now allowed a mechanic to easily check the ignition switch, coil, starter and other critical areas by hooking up a diagnostic tester. All full-size Buicks had four-wheel coil-spring suspension, forward-mounted steering gear linkage, unequal- length front control arms, and four-link rear suspension. Corrosion protection was improved on big Buicks, including more use of galvanized steel and rust-resistant materials. Metric dimensions saw increased use. All Buicks could have a new Citizens Band radio option, including a CB transceiver built into the AM/FM stereo system. Full-size Buicks could have an all-metal electric sunroof, or the three-in-one Astroroof. Most Skylark, Century, Regal and LeSabre models could have the Highway Economy Package, including a specially-tuned V-6 engine with vacuum spark regulator, specially-calibrated Turbo Hydra- matic, lower (2.56:1) rear axle ratio, and a switch that shut off the air-conditioner compressor when the gas pedal was pushed to the floor. Various models could be ordered with special ride/handling suspension packages that included front and rear stabilizer bars, firmer springs, and stiffer shock-absorber valving. LeSabre Sport Coupe and Riviera carried this suspension as standard, along with quick-ratio power steering. Standard body colors for all 1977 models were: black; white; silver, light blue, dark blue or medium green metallic; light buckskin; buckskin, brown, firethorn or orange metallic. Dark blue gr. metallic, red and cream gold were offered as standard on all except Skyhawk and Skylark. Dark aqua metallic, bright yellow and bright red came only on Skyhawk and Skylark. Rivieras could also have blue, amber or red firemist.

SKYHAWK — SERIES 4H — V-6 — For its third model year, the subcompact Skyhawk got a new, completely different checkerboard grille: simply two rows of eight holes each, across the body-colored grille panel. Otherwise, there was little change in appearance. Built on an H-Special body, Skyhawk was a more luxurious, perhaps even sportier version of Chevrolet's Monza. Once again, the swept-back design came in standard or 'S' hatchback form. Large, easy-to-read instruments included an 7000-R.P.M. tachometer, ammeter, and electric clock. Though similar, the 'S' edition lacked such extras as the tach and clock. As before, Skyhawk was powered by a 231 cu. in. (3.8- liter) V-6 with standard four-speed manual shift. Five-speed overdrive gearbox and automatic transmisison were optional. The standard edition had front and rear stabilizer bars; the 'S' had front only. High-back bucket seats were upholstered in cloth or vinyl. The 'S' version also lacked the white, gold or black accent stripes. Skyhawks had side window reveal moldings, front and rear bumper guards, and bumper protection strips, plus a set-and-close door locking system. Options included a sliding glass sunroof, or fixed Astroroof with targa-type aluminum accent band that stretched over the car's roof.

SKYLARK — SERIES 4X — V-6/V-8 — Buick's compact derivative of the old Chevrolet Nova (also related to Olds Omega) again came in seven models: low-priced 'S', European-inspired S/R (Sports/Rallye), and standard Skylark. Coupe, hatchback and sedan bodies were again available. The 'S' coupe lacked some details, such as a cigarette lighter, roof and wheel-opening moldings, and inside day/night mirror. Though similar to before, the front end was changed. The new Skylark grille was composed entirely of vertical bars, peaked at the nose, with a wide horizontal bar across the top. Dual round headlamps were again flanked by clear park/signal lamps that wrapped around the fender into amber lenses. As in 1976, Skylark's three-hole "ventiport" fender trim piece sat just ahead of the wide bodyside molding that extended all the way to the tip of the rear quarter panels. A new instrument panel held large round gauges. Standard engine was the 231 cu. in. (3.8-liter) V-6, with two 5.0-liter V-8s available: 301 and 305 cu. in. Also optional was a 350 V-8 with four-barrel. All models had High- Energy ignition, front disc brakes, and front stabilizer bar. Skylark's S/R had standard Turbo Hydra-matic and full-length sports shifting console; others, three-speed manual (column shift). S/R also had a stand-up hood ornament, roof drip moldings, special cloth bucket seats with reclining right seatback, map pockets in doors, Rallye steering wheel, and console storage bins. Skylark's suspension consisted of wide- span front lower control arms with coil springs, and multiple-leaf rear springs. A new Acoustical Package to cut road noise consisted of special insulation in roof, floor and dashboard, as well as inside and under the doors, and between cowl and fenders. Also optional: a thickly-padded Landau top with small side windows, accented by brushed-aluminum band; and a V-6 Highway Economy Package.

CENTURY — SERIES 4A — V-6/V-8 — Century's body, lowered for 1976, received a new grille and header molding this year. As in 1976, coupes displayed a different front-end treatment, with canted-back grille, than the sedans. Century and Century Special coupe rooflines swept back and framed a large rear quarter window. The Custom coupe had a formal roofline like Regal's, plus the Regal rectangular opera windows. Century sedan's front-end looked similar to the Regal sedan, while coupes repeated the 1976 design, with crosshatching behind six large grille slots framed by body-colored segments. The model lineup included three coupes, two sedans, and a two- or three-seat wagon. Sedans and wagons were 4 in. longer in wheelbase than coupes. Station wagons had a 350 cu. in. (5.7-liter) V-8; other models, a 231 cu. in. V-6 or optional V-8. For 1977, the V-6 engine lost some weight. Power steering was standard. So were power brakes on the Custom Sedan and wagons. Three-speed manual (column) shift remained standard, except for wagons which had Turbo Hydra-matic. All models had front and rear ashtrays, and a wide-view day/night inside mirror. All except Special had front and rear bumper protection strips. Wipers had "mist control" that gave a single pass when you touched the switch. Custom coupes could have a Hurst hatch roof that consisted of twin rectangular panels of tinted glass, which could be removed and stored in the trunk (in a special "Hatch Hutch" case). Two air conditioners were optional: Climate Control or Custom-Aire. Joining the option list: the V-6 Highway Economy Package, consisting of specially tuned engine, specially calibrated Turbo Hydra-matic, 2.56:1 axle ratio, and wide-open-throttle air-conditioning shutoff.

1977 Regal Landau Coupe (B)

REGAL — SERIES 4AJ — V-6/V-8 — Regal's coupe and sedan, like Century, received a new grille and header molding. A look more formal than Century came from the vertical, squarish grille and squared-off roofline with a small, formal opera window in the rear pillar. The coupe's grille was new but not drastically different from 1976 version. Its small vertical segments separated into six sections by two horizontal strips and a narrow vertical bar. Quad headlamps and park/signal lamps were also similar to the prior model. A 'V6' emblem sat at the front of front fenders. Regal's sedan again had its own front-end design featuring vertically stacked rectangular headlamps and vertical signal lamps, plus a mildly revised grille divided into four sections by dominant single horizontal and vertical bars. The subdued vertical strips sat farther apart, separating the grille into five segments on each side. 'Regal' script was at the lower corner. Instruments were recessed in simulated woodgrain paneling, with two large dials directly ahead of the driver. Power front disc brakes were standard. Turbo Hydra-matic was standard on sedan; three-speed manual shift on coupe. Options included the Hurst hatch roof (like Century Custom coupe), plus Highway Economy Package with specially calibrated V-6 engine. Regal's S/R package included reclining bucket seats with new black velour fabric; large center console with aircraft-grip shift lever; rallye steering wheel; headlamp dimmer in the turn-signal lever; and whitewall steel-belted radial tires.

1977 LeSabre Custom sedan (B)

LESABRE — SERIES 4B — V-6/V-8 — Downsized LeSabre was 10 in. shorter, 2.7 in. narrower, and 665 pounds lighter than before, described as "the American full-size car redefined." Wheelbase dropped from 123.4 to 115.9 in., while trunk space actually grew: from 16.8 cu. ft. in 1976 to 21.2 in the "shrunken" version. Inside, head and leg room managed to grow as well. Aluminum reinforced bumpers cut 135 pounds from the car's weight, while a smaller frame saved 90 pounds. A 231 cu. in. V-6 was now standard. New styling included rear-canted headlamp bezels that sloped rearward from the upright grille, full-framed doors, and a pillared roof design. The airy four-door hardtop and thin-pillared variant were gone for good, replaced by sensible pillars and frames. The squared-off roof was designed to give maximum rear seat headroom. LeSabre's B-body was related to Chevrolet Caprice and Pontiac Bonneville/Parisienne, closer yet to Olds Delta 88, which received similar downsizing this year. Wraparound red/amber taillamps also served as side marker lights. Seven vertical bars divided the crosshatch grille into eight sections, slightly pointed at the front. Quad rectangular headlamps were directly above clear park/signal lamps; cornering lenses at the tip of front fenders. Farther back on the fender was the familiar three-hole "ventiport" LeSabre emblem. At the back of the rear fenders, a 'LeSabre' badge sat ahead of the wraparound taillamps. Bodyside moldings extended between front and rear wheel openings, but no farther onto the fenders. LeSabre was now powered by the 231 cu. in. (3.8-liter) V-6 or a choice of three optional V-8 engines: familiar 350 cu. in. (5.7-liter) four-barrel, new 403 cu. in. (6.6-liter) four-barrel, or new 301 cu. in. (5.0-liter) with two-barrel carburetor. Five models were offered this year: LeSabre and LeSabre Custom coupe or sedan, plus a new European-inspired LeSabre Sport Coupe. That one had a standard 301 cu. in. (5.0-liter) V-8, thin white-stripe radial tires, special steering linkage and suspension with higher-rate springs, Rallye steering wheel, chrome wheels, amber lights and, in Buick's words, "functional, downright mean-looking black accents." That meant black vertical grille bars; black anodized window frame, windshield and rear window moldings; wide black louvered rocker moldings; and wide black pillar appliques. Styling touches also included a stand-up tri-shield hood ornament, plus 'LeSabre Sport Coupe' nameplates on body and dash. Coupes had new inertia front seatback locks. Instrument panels were new, a maintenance-free Freedom battery and iagnostic connectors standard. Also standard: rear door (or rear quarter) armrests, Full-Flo ventilation, plus bumper protection strips front and rear. Crushed velour or vinyl bench seats were standard on base LeSabre models; notchback seats on Custom and Sport Coupe. The turn signal lever doubled as a dimmer switch. An optional Highway Economy Package, intended for cruising rather than urban stop-and-go, included a specially-tuned V-6, specially calibrated automatic transmission, 2.56:1 axle ratio, and larger (24.5- gallon) gas tank.

ESTATE WAGON — SERIES 4BR — V-8 — The basic Estate Wagon's front-end appearance was just like LeSabre, but a Limited package transformed the wagon to Electra's front-end styling. Limited equipment included custom 60/40 notchback seats, power windows, power door and tailgate locks, tilt steering wheel, custom seat/shoulder belts, sunshade map light, quartz crystal clock (dial or digital), acoustic package, stand-up hood ornament, and woodgrain vinyl applique. The package also contained wheel opening, wide rocker panel, lower front fender and rear quarter,

window frame scalp, and belt reveal moldings; plus bumper guards, luggage rack and air deflector, remote-control left mirror, and chrome-plated wheels. Base and Limited editions were available with either two or three seats; 60/40 notchback seating (cloth or vinyl) standard on Limited, vinyl bench seats on base models. Tiny lamps at the dashboard underside "floodlit" the instrument dials for night visibility. Standard equipment included a Freedom battery, power steering and brakes, 350 cu. in. (5.7-liter) V-8 with four-barrel carburetor, and Turbo Hydra-matic. Estate Wagons also had diagnostic connectors, lockable storage compartments, and rocker panel moldings. The 403 cu. in. (6.6-liter) V-8 was optional. So were five different sound systems. The standard three-way tailgate could fold down or swing open like a door, with power window up or down. Cargo area measured 87 cubic feet.

1977 Electra Limited sedan (B)

ELECTRA — SERIES 4C — V-8 — Like the LeSabre, Electra lost 10 in. in overall length in its downsizing, but remained similar in form to the previous 225 model. Fender lines were the same as in 1976, but with a more blunt front end and shorter overhangs, both front and rear. Buick called the fresh silhouette "lean, aerodynamic....a car of today, the future, instead of a tribute to the past." Electra's C-body was similar to Olds Ninety-Eight, slightly longer than LeSabre and riding the same platform as Cadillac DeVille. Turning diameter was 4 ft. tighter than in 1976. Models included a 225 coupe and sedan, Limited coupe and sedan, and top-line Park Avenue option package for the Limited sedan. All seated six with ease. Buyers now began with a standard 350 cu. in. (5.7-liter) engine, or could opt for the 403 cu. in. (6.6-liter) V-8. The big old 7.5-liter powerplant was gone. Power steering and brakes, Turbo Hydra-matic, diagnostic connectors, and Freedom battery were standard. New interior styling featured improved rear-seat access on coupes, a result of new inertia front seatback locks. The new crosshatch grille was divided into eight sections by two horizontal bars and three vertical bars. Quad rectangular headlamps sat atop clear quad rectangular park/signal lamps; amber lenses at front of fenders, just above the bumper. Electra's four-port trim piece was prominent at upper rear of front fenders, as in prior models. The 'Electra' nameplate stood at the back of the rear fenders, just below the long, slim bodyside molding. Wide taillamps were divided into upper and lower sections by a horizontal trim strip. Electras had bumper protective strips front and rear. Limiteds sported wide rocker panel moldings. The new instrument panel's controls and gauges set in brushed aluminum. Six sound systems were optional, including a digital-readout stereo radio that showed station frequency, time, date, and elapsed travel time. The Park Avenue package included a thickly-padded vinyl roof with coach lamps. Tiny lamps at the dashboard underside "floodlit" the instrument dials for night visibility. Cloth or vinyl notchback seats were standard on the 225; custom cloth or vinyl 60/40 notchback seating on Limited models; 50/50 cloth seats on the Park Avenue.

1977 Riviera coupe (BMD)

RIVIERA — SERIES 4BZ — V-8 — Buick's front-drive personal-luxury coupe received a total restyle, losing 5 in. of length and some 700 pounds. A new suspension was installed to improve roadholding and handling, while optional four-wheel disc brakes promised superior stopping power. Up front was a new vertical-bar grille. Body design included a pillared roof and full-frame door glass. Until a new downsized version emerged for 1979, Riviera was actually related to the B-body LeSabre. Its space-efficient six-passenger interior was more spacious and comfortable than before, with increased rear head/leg room. Trunk capacity grew too. Like its forerunners, the reduced Riviera was aimed at the buyer who would "like to surround him-self with quality. With things that are undeniably special." Riviera's "demeanor is that of a sporty road car," Buick insisted; "Its interior rivals the most opulent luxury cars." The new upright, formal appearing, vertical-bar grille-- a bit reminiscent of Rolls-Royce--curved outward at the base in a style that would soon become markedly Buick. Quad rectangular headlamps sat over quad clear park/signal lamps. Optional cornering lamps used a combination of clear, rectangular horizontal lens and smaller amber lens at the orward segment of each front fender. Standard fittings included a no-maintenance Freedom battery; lights for front ashtray, under-dash courtesy, glove compartment, trunk, and instrument flood; front and rear bumper protective strips; depressed-park windshield wipers; remote-control sport mirror on left side; custom wire wheel covers; and Rallye steering wheel. The new standard suspension included large-diameter front and rear anti-sway bars, plus special springs and shocks. New this year were inertia front seatback locks and a restyled instrument panel. Tiny lamps at the dashboard underside "floodlight" the instrument dials for night visibility. Buyers could have either the 350 cu. in. (5.7-liter) engine or new 403 cu. in. (6.6-liter) V-8. Standard 50/50 notchback seat with twin armrests were upholstered in plush velour cloth or vinyl. Custom wire wheel covers were standard. Options included a leather-covered steering wheel and CB transceiver. Lighted coach lamps came with the Landau vinyl top.

I.D. DATA: The 13-symbol Vehicle Identification Number (VIN) was located on the upper left surface of the instrument panel, visible through the windshield. The first digit is '4', indicating the Buick division. The second symbol is a letter indicating series: 'S' Skyhawk; 'T' Skyhawk S; 'B' Skylark; 'C' Skylark S/R; 'W' Skylark S; 'D' Century; 'E' Century Special; 'H' Century Custom; 'J' Regal; 'K' Century Custom wagon; 'F' LeSabre Sport Coupe; 'N' LeSabre; 'P' LeSabre Custom; 'R' Estate Wagon; 'Z' Riviera; 'V' Electra 225; 'X' Electra Limited. Next come two digits that denote body type: '07' Skyhawk hatchback coupe; '17' Skylark 2-dr. hatchback coupe; '27' Skylark 2-dr. coupe; '69' 4-dr. sedan; '29' 4-dr. Colonnade sedan; '37' Century/Regal 2-dr. Colonnade coupe or full- size 2-dr. coupe; '57' 2-dr. Colonnade coupe; '35' 4-dr. 2-seat wagon. The fifth symbol is a letter indicating engine code: 'C' V6-231 2Bbl.; 'Y' V8-301 2Bbl.; 'U' V8-305 2Bbl.; 'H' V8-350 2Bbl.; 'L' V8-350 4Bbl. (LM1); 'R' V8-350 4Bbl. (L34); 'J' V8-350 4Bbl. (L77); 'K' V8-403 4Bbl. (L80). The sixth symbol denotes model year ('7' 1977). Next is a plant code: '2' Ste. Therese (Canada); 'K' Leeds, MO; 'L' Van Nuys, CA; 'T' Tarrytown, NY; 'B' Baltimore, MD; 'G' Framingham, MA; 'H' Flint, MI; 'Z' Fremont, CA; 'C' Southgate, CA; 'X' Fairfax, KS; 'E' Linden, NJ. The final six digits are the sequential serial number, which began with 100001 except for Skyhawks (700001 up); LeSabres, Estate Wagons, Electras and Rivieras built at Flint (400001 up). Engine numbers were stamped on the front right of the block, except for L34 350 cu. in. V-8 and 403 cu. in. V-8, which were stamped on the front of the left side of the block. A body number plate on the shroud identified model year, car division, series, style, body assembly plant, body number, trim combination, modular seat code, paint code, and date built code.

SKYHAWK (V-6)

Series Number	Body/Style Number	Body Type & Seating	Factory Price	Shipping Weight	Production Total
4H	T07	2-dr 'S' Hatch-4P	3981	2805	Note 1
4H	S07	2-dr. Hatch-4P	4294	2817	Note 1

Note 1: Total model year production, 24,044 Skyhawks (built in Canada).

SKYLARK 'S' (V-6/V-8)

4X	W27	2-dr Coupe-6P	3642/3717	3258/3315	Note 2

SKYLARK (V-6/V-8)

4X	B27	2-dr Coupe-6P	3765/3830	3257/3314	49,858
4X	B17	2-dr Hatch-6P	3941/4006	3379/3436	5,316
4X	B69	4-dr Sedan-6P	3825/3890	3296/3353	48,121

SKYLARK S/R (V-6/V-8)

4X	C27	2-dr Coupe-5P	4527/4592	3277/3384	5,023
4X	C17	2-dr Hatch-5P	4695/4760	3304/3411	1,154
4X	C69	4-dr Sedan-5P	4587/4652	3271/3378	4,000

Note 2: Skylark 'S' is included in production total for base Skylark coupe. Of the 103,295 Skylarks built, 22,098 had a V-8 engine; of the total 10,177 Skylark S/R models, 5,040 had a V-8.

CENTURY SPECIAL (V-6)

4A	E37	2-dr Coupe-6P	4170	3590	Note 3

CENTURY (V-6/V-8)

4A	D37	2-dr Coupe-6P	4303/4470	3520/3643	52,864
4A	D29	4-dr Sedan-6P	4363/4530	3692/3815	29,065

Note 3: Century Special production is included in base Century coupe total. Of the 81,629 Century models built, 25,797 had a V-8 engine.

CENTURY CUSTOM (V-6/V-8)

4A	H57	2-dr Coupe-6P	4627/4794	3549/3672	20,834
4A	H29	4-dr Sedan-6P	4687/4854	3688/3811	13,645
4A	K35	4-dr Sta Wag-6P	-- /5218	-- /4260	19,282
4A	(AQ4)	4-dr Sta Wag-8P	-- /5371	-- / N/A	Note 4

Note 4: Three-seat wagon was an option package; production total included in K35 figure. Of the 53,761 Century Custom models built, only 12,142 had a V-6 engine.

REGAL (V-6/V-8)

4A	J57	2-dr Coupe-6P	4712/4915	3550/3673	174,560
4A	J29	4-dr Sedan-6P	-- /5243	-- /3928	17,946

Note 5: Only 36,125 Regal coupes carried a V-6 engine.

LESABRE (V-6/V-8)

4B	N37	2-dr Coupe-6P	5032/5142	3466/3578	8,455
4B	N69	4-dr Sedan-6P	5092/5202	3504/3616	19,827

LESABRE CUSTOM (V-6/V-8)

4B	F37	2-dr Spt Cpe-6P	-- /5818	-- /3634	Note 6
4B	P37	2-dr Coupe-6P	5321/5431	3474/3586	Note 6
4B	P69	4-dr Sedan-6P	5381/5491	3516/3628	103,855

Note 6: Total production, 58,589 Custom coupes (including Sport Coupe). Of all LeSabres built, just 19,744 were V-6 powered.

ESTATE WAGON (V-8)

4B	R35	4-dr Sta Wag-6P	5902	4015	25,075
4B	(AQ4)	4-dr Sta Wag-8P	6078	N/A	Note 7

Note 7: Three-seat Estate Wagon was an option package; production total is included in two-seat figure. Limited version was also an option package.

ELECTRA 225 (V-8)

4C	V37	2-dr Coupe-6P	6672	3761	15,762
4C	V69	4-dr Sedan-6P	6865	3814	25,633

ELECTRA LIMITED (V-8)

4C	X37	2-dr Coupe-6P	7032	3785	37,871
4C	X69	4-dr Sedan-6P	7225	3839	82,361

Note 8: Electra Park Avenue was a trim option, not a separate model.

RIVIERA (V-8)

4E	Z37	2-dr Coupe-6P	7357	3784	26,138

FACTORY PRICE AND WEIGHT NOTE: Figures before the slash are for V-6 engine, after the slash for V-8.

ENGINES: BUICK BASE EQUIPMENT V-6 (Skyhawk, Skylark, Century/Regal coupe, Century/Custom sedan, LeSabre): 90-degree, overhead-valve V-6. Cast iron alloy block and head. Displacement: 231 cu. in. (3.8 liters). Bore & stroke: 3.8 x 3.4 in. Compression ratio: 8.0:1. Brake horsepower: 105 at 3200 R.P.M. Torque: 185 lbs.-ft. at 2000 R.P.M. Four main bearings. Hydraulic valve lifters. Carburetor: 2Bbl. Rochester 2GC. VIN Code: C. BASE V-8 (Skylark, LeSabre Sport Coupe); OPTIONAL (other LeSabres): 90-degree overhead-valve V-8. Cast iron alloy block and head. Displacement: 301 cu. in. (5.0 liters). Bore & stroke: 4.0 x 3.0 in. Compression ratio: 8.2:1. Brake horsepower: 135 at 4000 R.P.M. Torque: 245 lbs.-ft. at 2000 R.P.M. Five main bearings. Hydraulic valve lifters. Carburetor: 2Bbl. Rochester M2MC. Built by Pontiac. VIN Code: Y. Ordering Code: L27. ALTERNATE 305 V-8; OPTIONAL (Skylark, Century wagon): 90-degree overhead-valve V-8. Cast iron alloy block and head. Displacement: 305 cu. in. (5.0 liters). Bore & stroke: 3.736 x 3.48 in. Compression ratio: 8.5:1. Brake horsepower: 145 at 3800 R.P.M. Torque: 245 lbs.-ft. at 2400 R.P.M. Five main earings. Hydraulic valve lifters. Carburetor: 2Bbl. Roch. 2GC. VIN Code: U. BASE V-8 (Regal sedan); OPTIONAL (Century/Custom cpe/sed, Regal cpe): 90-degree, overhead valve V-8. Cast iron alloy block and head. Displacement: 350 cu. in. (5.7 liters). Bore & stroke: 3.80 x 3.85 in. Compression ratio: 8.1:1. Brake horsepower: 140 at 3200 R.P.M. Torque: 280 lbs.-ft. at 1400 R.P.M. Five main bearings. Hydraulic valve lifters. Carburetor: 2Bbl. Roch. 2GC. VIN Code: H. Ordering Code: L32. BASE V-8 (Century wagon, Electra, Estate, Riviera); OPTIONAL (Skylark, Century/Regal cpe/sed, LeSabre): 90-degree, overhead valve V-8. Cast iron alloy block and head. Displacement: 350 cu. in. (5.7 liters). Bore & stroke: 3.80 x 3.85 in. Compression ratio: 8.0:1. Brake horsepower: 155 at 3400 R.P.M. Torque: 275 lbs.-ft. at 1800 R.P.M. Five main bearings. Hydraulic valve lifters. Carburetor: 4Bbl. Rochester M4MC. VIN Code: J. ALTERNATE 350-4 V-8; OPTIONAL (Skylark, Century/Custom cpe/sed, Regal, LeSabre): 90-degree, overhead valve V-8. Cast iron alloy block and head. Displacement: 350 cu. in. (5.7 liters). Bore & stroke: 4.057 x 3.385 in. Compression ratio: 7.9:1. Brake horsepower: 170 at 3800 R.P.M. Torque: 275 lbs.-ft. at 2000 R.P.M. Five main bearings. Hydraulic valve lifters. Carburetor: 4Bbl. Roch. M4MC. Built by Oldsmobile. VIN Code: R. Ordering Code: L34. Not available in California. ALTERNATE 350-4 V-8 (Chevrolet-built): 90-degree, overhead valve V-8. Cast iron alloy block and head. Displacement: 350 cu. in. (5.7 liters). Bore & stroke: 4.00 x 3.48 in. Compression ratio: 8.5:1. Brake horsepower: 170 at 3800 R.P.M. Torque: 270 lbs.-ft. at 2400 R.P.M. Five main bearings. Hydraulic valve lifters. Carburetor: 4Bbl. Roch. M4MC. VIN Code: L. Ordering Code: LM1. OPTIONAL V-8 (Century wagon, LeSabre, Electra, Estate Wagon, Riviera): 90-degree, overhead valve V-8. Cast iron alloy block and head. Displacement: 403 cu. in. (6.6 liters). Bore & stroke: 4.351 x 3.385 in. Compression ratio: 8.5:1. Brake horsepower: 185 at 3600 R.P.M. Torque: 320 lbs.-ft. at 2200 R.P.M. Five main bearings. Hydraulic valve lifters. Carburetor: 4Bbl. Roch. M4MC. Built by Oldsmobile. VIN Code: K. Ordering Code: L80.

CHASSIS DATA: Wheelbase: (Skyhawk) 97.0 in.; (Skylark) 111.0 in.; (Century/Regal cpe) 112.0 in.; (Century/Regal sed/wag) 116.0 in.; (LeSabre/Estate/Riviera) 115.9 in; (Electra) 118.9 in. Overall length:- (Skyhawk) 179.3 in.; (Skylark) 200.2 in.; (Century/Regal cpe) 209.8 in.; (Century/Regal sedan) 213.6 in.; (Century wagon) 218.3 in.; (LeSabre/Riv) 218.2 in.; (Electra) 222.1 in.; (Estate) 216.7 in.. Height:- (Skyhawk) 50.1 in.; (Skylark 2-dr.) 52.2 in.; (Skylark 4-dr.) 53.1 in.; (Century/Regal cpe) 52.7 in.; (Century/Regal sed) 53.6 in.; (Century wag) 55.3 in.; (LeSabre cpe) 54.6 in.; (LeSabre sed) 55.3 in.; (Electra cpe) 54.8 in.; (Electra sed) 55.7 in.; (Estate) 57.0 in.; (Riviera) 54.6 in. Width:- (Skyhawk) 65.4 in.; (Skylark) 72.7 in.; (Century/Regal cpe) 76.5 in.; (Century/Regal sed/wag) 79.0 in.; (LeSabre/Electra/Estate/ Riviera) 77.2 in. Front Tread:- (Skyhawk) 54.7 in.; (Skylark) 59.1 in.; (Century/Regal) 61.5 in.; (LeSabre/Electra/Riviera) 61.8 in.; (Estate) 62.2 in. Rear Tread:- (Skyhawk) 53.6 in.; (Skylark) 59.7 in.; (Estate) 64.1 in.; (others) 60.7 in. Standard Tires:- (Skyhawk) BR78 x 13 SBR; (Skyawk 'S') B78 x 13; (Skylark) E78 x 14; (Skylark S/R) ER78 x 14 SBR WSW; (Century/Regal cpe) FR78 x 15 SBR exc. V-6, GBR; (Century/Regal sed) FR78 x 15 SBR; (Century wagon) HR78 x 15 SBR; (LeSabre) FR78 x 15 GBR; (Electra/Riviera) GR78 x 15; (Estate) HR78 x 15 SBR.

TECHNICAL: Transmission:- Three-speed, fully synchronized manual gearbox (column shift) standard on Skylark, Century cpe/sed, and Regal cpe; Turbo Hydra-matic optional. Four-speed, fully synchronized floor shift standard on Skyhawk; five-speed and automatic optional. Turbo Hydra-matic standard on Skylark S/R, Regal sedan, LeSabre, Electra, Estate and Riviera. Three-speed manual transmission gear ratios: (1st) 3.11:1; (2nd) 1.84:1; (3rd) 1.00:1; (Rev) 3.22:1. Four-speed gear ratios: (1st) 3.11:1; (2nd) 2.20:1; (3rd) 1.47:1; (4th) 1.00:1; (Rev) 3.11:1. Five-speed gear ratios: (1st) 3.40:1; (2nd) 2.08:1; (3rd) 1.39:1; (4th) 1.00:1; (5th) 0.80:1; (Rev) 3.36:1. Automatic trans. gear ratios: (1st) 2.52:1; (2nd) 1.52:1; (3rd) 1.00:1; (Rev) 2.08:1. Skyhawk auto. trans. gear ratios: (1st) 2.74:1; (2nd) 1.57:1; (3rd) 1.00:1; (Rev) 2.07:1. Standard axle ratio:- (Skyhawk) 2.56:1; (Skylark) 3.08:1 w/manual, 2.56:1 w/automatic, 2.41:1 w/V-8; (Century/Regal) 3.08:1 w/manual, 2.73:1 w/automatic, 2.41:1 w/350 V-8; (Century wagon) 2.73:1; (LeSabre V-6) 2.73:1; (LeSabre V-8) 2.41:1; (Electra/Riviera) 2.41:1; (Estate) 2.73:1 exc. 2.56:1 w/403 V-8. Steering:- recirculating ball; variable-ratio power steering standard on Century/Regal, LeSabre, Electra, Estate and Riviera. Suspension and Body Construction:- same as 1976. Brakes:- front disc, rear drum; power brakes standard on LeSabre/Electra/Riviera plus Century Custom sedan/wagon and Regal. Four-wheel power disc brakes optional on Riviera. High-Energy electronic ignition (HEI) on all engines. Unleaded fuel only.

DRIVETRAIN OPTIONS: Engines:- 301 cu. in. V-8, 2Bbl.: Skylark ($65); LeSabre ($110). 350 cu. in. V-8, 2Bbl.: Century/Cust, Regal cpe ($167). 350 cu. in. V-8, 4Bbl.: Skylark ($155); Century/Cust, Regal cpe ($222); Regal sed ($55); LeSabre ($200); LeSabre spt cpe ($90). 403 cu. in. V-8, 4Bbl.: LeSabre ($287); LeSabre spt cpe ($177); Century wag, Estate/Electra/Riviera ($65). V-6 economy pkg.: Skylark, 'S' ($302); Skylark S/R, LeSabre ($25). Transmission/Differential:- Five-speed manual floor shift: Skyhawk ($248). Turbo Hydra-matic trans.: Skyhawk ($248); Skylark, Century cpe/sed, Regal cpe ($282); Optional rear axle ratio: Century/Regal 3.08:1 or 3.23:1 (NC); LeSabre/Electra/Riviera 3.08:1 (NC); LeSabre 3.23:1 (NC). Positive traction differential ($51-$58). Power accessories: Power brakes, Skyhawk ($58); Skylark/Century ($61). Four-wheel disc brakes: Riviera ($186). Power steering: Skyhawk ($130); Skylark ($147). Suspension: WH5 handling package: Skyhawk ($11-$133). F40 Firm Ride handling package: Skylark ($22); Century/Regal/LeSabre/Electra/Riviera ($18). FE2 Rallye ride/handling package: Skylark ($42); Century, except Special wagon, Regal ($36); Riviera ($18). Automatic level control: Century/Regal/LeSabre/Electra/Riviera ($102). Other: Trailer towing flasher/harness ($20-32) except Skyhawk. Heavy-duty 80-amp alternator: Century/Regal/LeSabre/Electra/Riviera ($37-42). Heavy-duty Energizer battery ($16-$18). Freedom battery: Century/Regal ($30). Heavy-duty cooling ($27-$55) except Skyhawk. Heavy-duty radiator: Skylark ($19); Engine block heater ($13) except Skyhawk. High altitude emission system ($22). California emission system ($70-71).

SKYHAWK CONVENIENCE/APPEARANCE OPTIONS: Option Packages:- Free Spirit Skyhawk pkg. ($148). Appearance group: 'S' ($67). Convenience group ($21). Shadow light Astroroof w/roof crown molding ($591). Manual glass sunroof ($210). Comfort/Convenience:- Air cond. ($442). Rear defogger, electric ($71). Soft Ray tinted glass ($48). Tinted windshield ($40). Rallye steering wheel: 'S' ($37). Tilt steering ($50). Electric clock: 'S' ($18); clock and tach ($63). Right sport mirror ($13). Remote left sport mirror: 'S' ($16). Entertainment:- AM radio ($71). AM/FM radio ($134). AM/FM stereo radio ($219). AM radio and tape player ($197). AM/FM stereo radio and tape ($316). Rear speaker for non- stereo radios ($20). Radio accommodation pkg. ($22). Exterior Trim:- Door edge guards ($9). Roof crown molding ($162). Protective bodyside moldings ($25-$40). Hawk accent stripe ($33). Interior Trim/Upholstery:- Full-length console: 'S' ($77). Adjustable driver's seatback ($18). Front/rear mats ($15). Custom seatbelts ($14). Wheels:- Custom sport wheels $79-$90). Deluxe wheel covers ($42). Wheel trim rings ($35). Tires:- B78 x 13 WSW: 'S' ($30-$38). BR78 x 13 SBR blackwall: 'S' ($82-$103). BR78 x 13 SBR whitewall ($38-$141). White- letter tires ($51-$168). Conventional spare tire (NC).

SKYLARK CONVENIENCE/APPEARANCE OPTIONS: Option Packages:- Accessory pkg. (day/night mirror, lighter): 'S' ($12). Acoustic insulation pkg. ($24-$36). Convenience group ($29-$31). Appearance group: 'S' ($33). Comfort/Convenience:- Air cond. ($478). Cruise Master ($80). Three-speed wipers w/delay ($30). Rear defogger, blower-type ($48). Power windows ($108-$151). Electric door locks ($68- $96). Rallye steering wheel ($37) exc. S/R. Tilt steering ($57). Soft Ray tinted glass ($50). Tinted windshield ($42). Dual horns ($7). Electric clock ($21). Headlamps-on indicator ($7). Electric trunk release ($21). Remote-control mirror ($15). Sport mirrors: left remote, right manual ($28). Entertainment:- AM radio ($75). AM/FM radio ($137). AM/FM stereo radio ($233). AM radio and tape player ($337). CB Transceiver ($195). Rear speaker ($21). Exterior Trim:- Custom vinyl roof: S/R ($93). Custom vinyl roof w/hood ornament: base, 'S' ($98). Landau top ($162-$167). Two-tone paint ($42). Special exterior paint ($116). Swing-out rear quarter vent window: two-doors ($51). Protective bodyside moldings ($38). Rocker panel moldings ($16). Wide rocker appearance group ($34). Decklid molding ($8). Custom door and window rame moldings ($25-$31). Door edge guards ($9-$13). Bodyside accent stripes ($25). Bumper guards, front ($19); front/rear ($38). Bumper strips, front/rear ($29). Interior Trim/Upholstery:- Full-length console ($75). Vinyl bucket seats: base Skylark ($84). Custom trim bench seats/interior: base ($151). Custom seatbelts ($14-$16). Front carpet savers ($9). Carpet savers and handy mats ($15). Carpeted door trim with map pocket and reflector: Skylark ($37). Wheels:- Styled wheels ($82-$94). Chrome-plated wheels ($112-$132). Deluxe wheel covers ($33). Styled wheel covers ($91). Deluxe wire wheel covers ($121). Tires:- E78 x 14 WSW ($31-$39) exc. S/R. ER78 x 14 SBR BSW ($69-$86) exc. S/R. ER78 x 14 SBR WSW ($100-$125) exc. S/R. FR78 x 14 SBR WLT ($29-$156). Stowaway spare tire ($17); S/R cpe (NC).

CENTURY/REGAL CONVENIENCE/APPEARANCE OPTIONS: Option Packages:- Regal S/R Coupe pkg. ($432-$499). Electric sunroof: cpe ($394). Hurst hatch roof: Century Cust, Regal cpe ($587). Convenience group ($16-$31). Comfort/Convenience:- Air cond. ($499). Custom Aire ($538). Cruise Master ($80). Rear defogger: electric ($82); blower-type ($48). Soft Ray tinted glass ($54). Tinted windshield ($43). Six-way power driver's seat ($137). Custom steering wheel ($17). Rallye steering wheel ($37). Tilt steering ($57). Power windows ($108-$151). Electric door locks ($68-$96). Electric trunk release ($21). Remote-control tailgate lock: Century wag $21). Electric clock ($21). Headlamps-on indicator ($7). Instrument gauges and electric clock ($45) exc. wag. Fuel usage gauge ($27). Speed alert ($15). Dome reading lamp ($16). Three-speed wiper with delay ($30). Lighting and Mirrors:- Remote control mirror ($15). Sport mirrors: left remote ($28). Lighted visor vanity mirror ($42). Trunk light: Century Cust, Regal cpe ($5). Entertainment:- AM radio ($79). AM/FM radio ($142). AM/FM stereo radio ($233). AM radio w/stereo tape player ($213). AM/FM stereo radio w/tape ($337). AM/FM stereo radio and CB ($453). CB Transceiver ($195). Rear speaker ($21). Front/rear speakers ($44). Exterior Trim:- Landau vinyl top: Century Cust, Regal cpe ($120); Century/Spec. ($156). Custom vinyl top: Century cpe, Regal ($111). Custom vinyl top w/hood ornament: Century/Cust cpe ($116). Swing-out rear quarter vent windows: Century wag ($51). Two-tone paint ($42) exc. wagon. Special color paint ($134). Bumper guards, front/rear ($38); rear, Century wag ($19). Bumper strips: Century Special ($30). Protective bodyside moldings ($27). Lower bodyside molding ($36). Door edge guards ($9-$13). Wheel opening moldings: Century, Special ($19). Bodyside accent stripes ($45). Woodgrain vinyl applique: Century wag ($185). Luggage rack: Century wag ($76). Air deflector: Century wag ($26). Interior Trim/Upholstery:- Full-length console ($75). Custom notchback seat trim: Century/Spec. ($136-$163). Custom vinyl notchback seat trim: Century Cust cpe, Regal ($108); cloth ($140). Custom vinyl 60/40 seat trim: Century Cust, Regal cpe ($199); loth ($231). Custom reclining seat trim: Century Cust cpe ($244). Custom vinyl bucket seats: Century/Spec. cpe ($143- $168). Custom seatbelts ($14-$18). Third seat: Century wag ($152). Front/rear carpeting: Century Special ($25). Load floor area carpet: Century wag ($24). Front carpet savers ($10). Carpet savers and handy mats ($17). Litter pocket ($7). Wheels:- Chrome-plated wheels ($114-$161). Styled wheels ($68-$94). Deluxe wire wheel covers: Century ($133); Regal ($99). Styled wheel covers: Century ($91); Regal ($57). Deluxe wheel covers: Century ($34). Moire wheel covers: Century ($102); Regal ($68). Tires:- FR78 x 15 GBR WSW ($33- $41) exc. Regal sed. FR78 x 15 SBR BSW ($36-$45) exc. Regal sed. FR78 x 15 SBR WSW ($69-$86) exc. Regal sed. GR78 x 15 SBR: Century/Cust, Regal cpe ($54-$67); with V-8 (NC). GR70 x 15 SBR WLT: Century/Cust, Regal cpe ($109-$136); with V-8 ($55-$69). GR78 x 15 SBR WSW: Century/Cust, Regal cpe ($88- $110); with V-8 ($34-$43). HR78 x 15 SBR WSW: Century wag ($47). Stowaway spare tire (NC). Conventional spare: Century Spec. (NC).

LESABRE/ELECTRA/ESTATE WAGON/RIVIERA CONVENIENCE/APPEARANCE OPTIONS: Option Packages: Estate Wagon Limited pkg. ($1442). Exterior molding pkg.: LeSabre/Estate/Electra 225 ($47-$152). Accessory group: LeSabre ($46-$84). Electric sunroof ($734). Astroroof ($898). Comfort/Convenience:- Air cond. ($539). Automatic climate control air cond.: Electra/Riv ($621). Custom Aire air cond.: LeSabre, Estate ($578). Cruise Master ($84). Rear defogger, electric ($83). Tinted glass ($69). Tinted windshield: LeSabre, Est ($44). Power windows: LeSabre, Est ($114-$171). Electric door locks ($70-$98). Automatic electric door locks: Electra/Riv ($124-$151). Nine- way power driver's seat ($109-$139). Six-way power seat: LeSabre, Electra 225 ($139). Six-way power passenger seat ($246-$276) exc. base LeSabre. Power passenger seatback recliner ($104); N/A on base LeSabre sedan. Custom steering wheel: LeSabre/Estate ($17). Leather steering wheel: Riviera ($36). Tilt steering ($58). Tilt/telescoping steering column ($44-$104) exc. LeSabre spt cpe. Digital clock (NC). Low fuel indicator ($12). Fuel usage light ($27). Speed alert and trip odometer ($20). Remote electric tailgate lock: Estate ($30). Electric trunk release ($21). Three-speed intermittent wipers ($30). Lighting, Horns and Mirrors:- Cornering lamps ($44). Front light monitors: LeSabre/Estate ($25). Front/rear monitors: Electra/Riv ($55). Door courtesy/warning lights ($32-$50). Rear courtesy lamps: Estate ($13). Headlamps-on indicator ($7). Dome reading lamp: LeSabre/Estate/Electra 225 ($16). Sunshade map light: Electra 225 ($11). Four-note horn ($18). Remote left mirror: LeSabre, Est ($15). Remote right mirror ($26-$31) exc. Riv. Remote right sport mirror: Riv ($19). Dual remote sport mirrors ($33-$53) exc. Riv. Remote left mirror w/thermometer ($20-$35) exc. Riv. Lighted visor vanity mirror ($43). Entertainment:- AM radio ($92). AM/FM radio ($153). AM/FM stereo radio w/four speakers ($236-$341). AM radio and stereo tape player ($228). AM/FM stereo radio and tape player ($341). AM/FM stereo radio and CB ($459). CB Transceiver ($197). Rear speaker ($21); front/rear ($44). Power antenna ($42). Exterior Trim:- Landau vinyl top: LeSabre ($146-$164). Custom padded landau vinyl top: Electra/Riv ($196). Padded landau vinyl top ($186-$417). Long vinyl top: base LeSabre, Electra ($135-$155). Two-tone paint: LeSabre/Electra ($51-$60); Riv ($185). Special color paint ($135) exc. Riviera Firemist ($152). Protective bodyside moldings ($38-$53). Hood ornament: base LeSabre, Estate ($22). Door edge guards ($9-$13). Wheel opening moldings: base LeSabre, Estate ($24). Bodyside accent stripes ($46). Woodgrain vinyl applique: Estate ($198). Bumper guards, front/rear ($38); front, Estate ($19). Luggage rack w/air deflector: Estate ($127). Interior Trim/Upholstery:- Custom notchback seat trim: Estate ($224); 60/40 ($318). Electra Park Ave. sedan seating ($385). Notchback 60/40 seating: LeSabre Cust/Spt Cpe, Electra 225 ($97). Third seat: Estate ($175). Custom seatbelts: LeSabre, Estate ($18-$21). Front carpet savers ($11-$12). Carpet savers and handy mats: ($18- $22). Litter pocket ($7) exc. Electra Ltd. Deluxe trunk trim: LeSabre ($43). Trunk carpeting: Electra/Riv ($53). Wheels:- Chrome-plated wheels: LeSabre/Estate/Electra ($116-$163); Riv ($51-$64). Styled wheels ($58-$92) exc. Riv. Deluxe wire wheels ($101-$135) exc. Riv. Custom wire wheels: Riviera (NC). Deluxe wheel covers: base LeSabre ($34). Super deluxe wheel covers: LeSabre/Electra ($24-$58). Moire wheel covers ($68-$102) exc. Riv. Tires:- FR78 x 15 SBR: LeSabre ($36-$45). FR78 x 15 SBR WSW: LeSabre ($33-$86). GR78 x 15 SBR WSW ($34- $43). GR78 x 15 SBR WSW ($47-$125). GR70 x 15 SBR WLT: LeSabre ($55-$136); LeSabre spt cpe ($7); Riviera ($55-$69). Stowaway spare tire (NC).

HISTORY: Introduced: September 30, 1976. Model year production (U.S.): 845,234, for 9.3 percent of the industry total. North American production for the U.S. market was 869,277 (234,520 V-6 and 634,757 V-8). Calendar year production (U.S.): 801,202. Model year sales by U.S. dealers: 773,313 (including 28,114 imported Opels). Calendar year sales (U.S.): 746,394 for an 8.2 percent market share.

Historical Footnotes: Sales set a record for the second year in a row, beating the 1955 mark by nearly 35,000 cars. Full-size Buick models accounted for a healthy 44 percent of sales, with each big Buick showing an impressive sales increase for the model year. Model year production gained 15 percent over 1976. Skylark production returned to Canada for 1977—but back again to Lordstown, Ohio in mid-year. An assembly line was added at Flint to build the popular V-6, which was also installed on other GM cars.

1978 BUICK

Following up on the 1977 slimming down of big Buicks, 1978 saw a trimming of the mid-size Century and Regal. Buick's full-line catalog featured many photos and descriptions of old Buicks, with a nod to the Buick Club of America. The catalog also admitted that Buicks were "equipped with GM-built engines produced by various divisions." That simple fact gained considerable publicity, as some buyers of a Buick or Olds that contained a "lesser" Chevrolet or Pontiac under the hood felt they'd been cheated. Five Buick series now offered the V-6 as standard equipment. For 1978, the V-6 added an "even-firing" feature. To improve smoothness, cylinder firing was changed from alternating 90- and 180-degree intervals of crankshaft rotation to even 120-degree intervals. Buick claimed that the revised V-6 idled like a V-8. A new smaller V-6, displacing just 196 cu. in. (3.2-liters), was available in the mid-size Century and Regal. This was essentially the 231 V-6 with bore reduced from 3.8 to 3.5 in. Four V-8 choices were offered: 301 cu. in. (4.9-liter), 305 (5.0-liter), 350 (5.7-liter) and 403 (6.6-liter) displacments. Of far greater interest to performance fansthen and nowwas the new turbocharged V-6. Turbocharging wasn't a new idea, of course, having been used in the 1960s Corvair Spyder and Olds F85. But in line with its advertising slogan ("A little science. A little magic."), Buick was now pioneering the turbocharging of a small engine for a family car. The turbo arrived in both Regal and LeSabre Sport Coupes, with either two- or four-barrel carburetor. This engine was a production version of the 3.8-liter V-6 used in the Indianapolis 500 Pace Car of 1976. It was a demand-type turbocharger that didn't affect power output at normal highway speeds, but only when the accelerator was pressed. Horsepower was 150 with two-barrel, 165 with four-barrel, as opposed to the normal 105. Buick's goal: to achieve performance that matched a 350 V-8, but without losing the fuel economy of six cylinders. Turbo Buicks came with a specially calibrated automatic transmission and special rear axle ratio. Buick also introduced a new electronic spark control system on the turbo V-6 for 1978, a first in the industry. It monitored detonation (knocking) level in the engine and retarded spark to control detonation during turbo boost. To ensure reliability, each turbocharged Buick got a two-mile road testa sensible practice that had virtually disappeared years before. Body colors available on all models were: white, silver metallic, black, medium blue metallic, light green metallic, tan, saffron metallic, dark gold metallic, brown metallic, and red metallic. Colors available only on Skyhawk/Skylark colors were bright blue metallic, dark green metallic, yellow, and bright red. Special Century/Regal, LeSabre, Estate Wagon, Electra and Riviera colors were: light blue, dark blue metallic, medium green metallic, and dark red metallic. For extra cost, Riviera buyers could have any of three Firemist metallic colors: blue, amber or red. Designers' accent colors this year were: gray accent (used with silver); or gold accent (used with tan). All Buicks had diagnostic connectors that enabled a mechanic to hook up a diagnostic test instrument to check operation of the ignition switch, coil, starter and other critical circuitry, much faster than traditional methods. All full-size Buicks (except Estate Wagon) might have a sunroof or Astroroof; cornering lights activated by the turn signal lever; or tri-color front light monitors. Other options included a new theft-deterrent system that included electric door, trunk and hood locks to trigger audible and visual alarms in the event of tampering, plus an outside mirror with built-in thermometer. Electra and Riviera could have a new frequency-synthesized radio with AM/FM stereo, 8-track tape, digital clock, and pushbutton scanner that automatically located and locked onto strong signals in remote areas. Also on their option list: an AM/FM stereo radio with built-in 40-channel CB transceiver and a Triband power antenna that disappeared into the car fender.

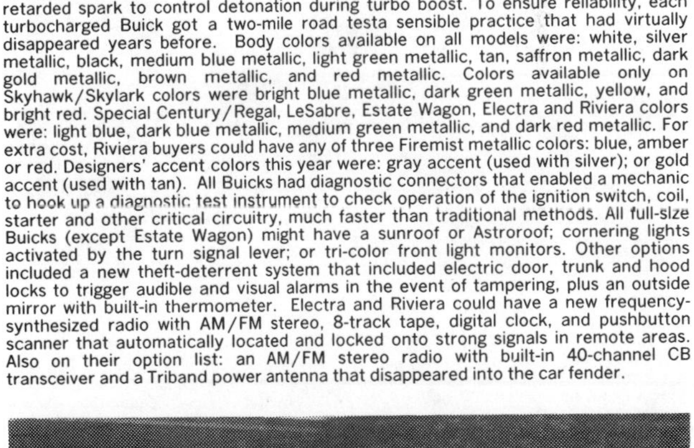

1978 Skyhawk hatchback coupe (B)

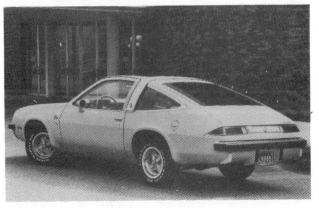

SKYHAWK — SERIES 4H — V-6 — Still riding a 97 in. wheelbase in one hatchback coupe body style, the subcompact Skyhawk returned for another season powered by the even-firing 231 cu. in. (3.8-liter) V-6. Standard gearbox was a four-speed manual floor shift, with automatic or five-speed overdrive manual available. Some California Skyhawks had a new Phase II three-way catalyst system that used an oxygen sensor to adjust the air/fuel mixture. Styling touches included rectangular headlamps, a domed hood, and louvered roof pillars. Interior trim was new this year. Low-cost 'S' Skyhawks wore standard rattan vinyl upholstery. Upper models could have vinyl or sporty hobnail velour and knit fabrics. Large gauges, including a voltmeter, were recessed in a simulated wood instrument panel. The 'S' model had a new two-spoke steering wheel. On the option list, both fixed-glass Astroroof (with Targa-type aluminum band) and manual sliding-glass sunroofs were offered, as was a Hawk accent stripe package. All Skyhawks had a cigarette lighter, heater/defroster, carpeting, front/rear bumper guards with protective strips, and front stabilizer bar. The base (S07) Skyhawk added a remote-controlled left-hand sport mirror, bodyside stripes (white, black or gold), wheel opening moldings, and steel-belted radial tires.

1978 Skylark Custom Landau Coupe (B)

SKYLARK — SERIES 4X — V-6/V-8 — A Custom Skylark replaced the former S/R version as the luxury edition. Standard and Custom Skylarks came in coupe, sedan and hatchback form, while the low-budget 'S' was again available only as a coupe. Powerplant choices were the standard 231 cu. in. (3.8-liter) "even-firing" V-6, or two optional V-8s. Standard transmission (except in California and high-altitude areas) was the three-speed manual shift. Apart from a similarly-shaped but restyled grille that added a pair of horizontal divider bands to the vertical-bar pattern, Skylark's styling changes were modest for 1978. The wraparound parking/signal lamps were divided into three sections rather than two. Taillamps were split into two horizontal sections instead of three, with full-height backup lamps at the inner ends. Interior trim was new. The Sport Package on base and Custom models included black paint accents on the front grille and around the headlamps, back window and side window frames. The package also featured ER78 x 14 blackwall steel-belted radials, a ride/handling suspension, black sport mirrors, and choice of four body colors: silver, dark gold, yellow, and bright red. All Skylarks except 'S' had front/rear ashtrays plus wheel opening and roof drip moldings. The Custom added a stand-up hood ornament, custom rocker panel moldings, and deluxe wheel covers.

1978 Century Sport Coupe (B)

CENTURY — SERIES 4A — V-6/V-8 — A redesigned and reduced mid-size "new generation" Century (and related Regal) emerged for 1978 about 10 inches shorter than before, and some 600 pounds lighter for improved gas mileage. The new and distinctive "aeroback" sedan, with "gracefully" sloping back end, measured 18 in. shorter and 7 in. narrower than its notchback predecessor. Yet passenger space stayed just about the same as in 1977. To keep inside space ample, designers reduced the Century and Regal bodyside curvature and pushed out the front support pillars. Instrument panels were moved closer to the windshield to add leg room. Coupe wheelbases were cut 4 in., and sedans and wagons by 8 in. The shorter 108 in. wheelbase reduced the car's turning radius. Both coupes and sedans displayed a completely new side appearance: an aerodynamic, fastback "European look." The rear roof pillar and deck lid were on the same plane. Coupes and sedans came in three series: Special, Custom, and Limited (with same lavish interior as Regal's Limited). The Century Sport Coupe came equipped with Designers' wheels and P205/70R14 steel-belted radial tires, special paint treatment and striping, body-color bumpers, and ride/handling package. The new, wide-spaced grille had a horizontal-slat pattern separated by two horizontal bars and a vertical center bar, plus six subdued vertical bars, with 'BUICK' badge at the side. Quad headlamps were replaced by single rectangular headlamps this year, with wraparound park/signal lamps. Wraparound taillamps were divided into three horizontal sections, with clear backup lights at the inner ends of the lower segments. The new wider grille, coupled with single-headlamp front end, made the car look broader, though it was actually 7 in. narrower than before. Century was closely related to Oldsmobile's Cutlass Salon and Cutlass Supreme. The new, "even-firing" 196 cu. in. (3.2-liter) V-6 with three-speed manual shift was standard, except in California and high-altitude areas which demanded the 3.8-liter V-6 and automatic shift. A 305 cu. in. (5.0-liter) V-8 was optional. So was a floor-mounted four-speed manual gearshift, with larger 231 cu. in. V-6 engine. All models carried a maintenance-free Delco Freedom battery. In addition to more extensive corrosion-resistant treatment, the front fender wells were made of corrosion-resistant plastic. Station wagons came in three forms: Special, Custom, and a Sport Wagon option that included Designers' Accent paint, Designers' Sport wheels,

Rallye suspension similar to Sport Coupe, body-color bumpers, and wide-oval (P205/70R14) steel-belted radial tires. Wagons in California and high-altitude areas required V-8 power rather than the standard 231 cu. in. V-6. A newly-designed fold-down rear deck and lift-up window made loading easier. Also, locking storage compartments were added behind the rear wheelhousings. The six-window sedans and wagons had fixed (not roll-down) windows in the back doors, and swing-out rear vent windows. All Century models now had a turn signal lever that doubled as a headlight dimmer, windshield wipers with single-wipe mist control, space-saving compact (temporary) spare tire, and coin holder in the glove box. Power-operated sunroof and Astroroof options were offered on coupes. Designers' Accent schemes used contrasting shades of similar colors to create a distinctive appearance, offered on all models except the Century Sport Coupe. Electronic leveling was another option. New standard compact spare tires, rated for 60 psi pressure, were meant for temporary use only.

1978 Regal Turbo Sport Coupe (B)

REGAL — SERIES 4A — V-6/V-8 — Regal became a separate Buick line this year, rather than a Century variant. The new version was 14 in. shorter than the '77 model, trimmed-down all around. Wheelbase cut from 112 to 108 in. permitted a smaller turning diameter. An entirely different, more formal look marked the restyled Regal. Gone were the skinny angled opera windows, replaced by upright rear windows that separated from the front windows by a bright vertical pillar. The new, slightly sloped grille, comprised of many vertical bars, angled outward at the base. Large single rectangular headlamps were recessed and flanked by wraparound park/signal lamps. As on Century, the instrument panel was moved closer to the windshield to add front knee/leg room. Gauges and warning lights set in a rectangular cluster, with radio, heater and air conditioner controls in a separate module. Notchback 55/45 seats (standard in Limited) were covered by crushed woven fabric, with standard folding center armrest. Door pull straps were standard. New thin-shell front seats allowed more leg room in back. Roof pillars were moved outward to add broad room. Only the coupe body was offered, in three levels: base Regal, Regal Sport Coupe, and Regal Limited. Base and Limited models carried a new 196 cu. in. (3.2-liter) V-6 (except in California and high-altitude areas, where a 231 cu. in. V-6 was required). Standard equipment included a compact spare tire (except with positive-traction differential), Freedom battery, P195/75R14 tires, cigarette lighter, front/rear ashtrays, wide-view day/night mirror, bin-type glove box with coin holder, front and rear bumper protective strips, and deluxe wheel covers. Electronic leveling was optional. Regal's hot personal-luxury Sport Coupe came with a new 231 cu. in. (3.8-liter) turbocharged V-6 as standard. Along with LeSabre, these were the only two standard turbocharged production cars made in America. (Worldwide, only Porsche and Saab offered turbos at this time.) Buick's chief engineer Lloyd E. Reuss called Regal "the performance car of the future," since its blower cut in only when needed. Standard Sport Coupe equipment included automatic transmission, Rallye ride/handling suspension with front and rear stabilizer bars, firmer springs and shocks, distinctive domed hood with 'Turbo 3.8 Litre' insignia on the sides of the "bubble" dome, power brakes, and P205/70R145 radial tires. A dash light showed turbo "boost."

1978 LeSabre Sport Coupe (B)

LESABRE — SERIES 4B — V-6/V-8 — Design changes were fairly modest this year, after prior downsizing. LeSabre's grille was shaped like the 1977 version but was now wider-spaced, with a dominant vertical bar at the forward peak, plus two horizontal bars dividing the grille into six segments. Grille framing bars reached all the way outward, below the headlamps, to wrap around fenders. Interior trim was new; electronic leveling optional. Standard equipment included automatic transmission, power steering and brakes, heater/defroster, intermittent wipers, inside hood release, and front/rear protective bumper strips. LeSabre's Sport Coupe, similar to the Regal version, carried the new turbocharged 231 cu. in. V-6 engine and handling suspension. That engine replaced the 305 cu. in. V-8 in the 1977 LeSabre Sport Coupe. Instead of LeSabre's customary three-hole emblem on the front fenders, the Sport Coupe had a distinctive 'Turbo 3.8 Litre' badge at the forward end. Other distinctive touches included matte black trim around the windows and in the grille. Wide GR70 x 15 radial tires rode 7 in. chrome wheels. Other LeSabres came with a standard 231 cu. in. V-6 or optional V-8.

ESTATE WAGON — SERIES 4BR — V-8 — Though related most closely to LeSabre, the Estate Wagon wore an Electra grille and front-end look. Its three-way tailgate could fold down or swing open, with power window up or down. The three-seat version carried up to eight passengers, or 87 cubic feet of cargo with rear seat folded down. Estate Wagon Limited option included 55/45 notchback front seating, power windows, tilt steering wheel, luggage rack with air deflector, electric door locks, remote tailgate lock, remote-control left mirror, bumper guards, map light, dial clock, exterior molding package, woodgrain vinyl applique, acoustic package, special ornamentation, and chrome-plated road wheels.

1978 Electra Park Avenue Landau Coupe (B)

ELECTRA — SERIES 4C — V-8 — Electra's restyled checkerboard grille was similar to 1977 version, but with only a single horizontal bar across the center. Wide wraparound taillamps were new, but otherwise the big Buick's design didn't change much. Coupe and sedan were offered in 225, Limited, or Park Avenue form. With vertical roofline and side-mounted coach lights, the elegant Park Avenue took on a more formal appearance. The Park Avenue coupe was new this year. Upholstery choices ranged from textured vinyl to buttoned-and-tufted crushed velour. Standard powerplant was again the 350 cu. in. (5.7- liter) V-8 with four-barrel carburetor, as well as automatic transmission, power steering and brakes, and the customary coil springs all around. Also standard: power windows and driver's seat, wipers with mist control, quartz clock (dial or digital), and remote-control outside mirror. Limited and Park Avenue Electras added wide rocker appearance moldings.

1978 Riviera coupe (B)

RIVIERA — SERIES 4BZ — V-8 — Riviera retained its new downsized look from 1977 with few significant changes, other than modest revisions in grille and taillamps. Spoked-look road wheels were intended to remind observers of its "classic-car orientation." Optional was a new electrically-driven height control system, with sensor mounted on car frame. Powerplants included the standard 350 cu. in. V-8 with four-barrel carburetor, or an optional 403 cu. in. V-8. Standard equipment included power steering, padded three- spoke steering wheel, and power front disc brakes (four-wheel discs optional). Rich velour 50/50 seats with dual front armrests, padded Rallye steering wheel, cut-pile carpeting, and custom wire wheel covers were standard. Chrome wire wheels were optional. The padded Landau roof option included coach lamps on the roof pillars. Most interesting to collectors and enthusiasts would be the 75th anniversary Riviera, commemorating the founding of the Buick company. Introduced at the Chicago Auto Show in February 1978, only 1,400 of the LXXV Rivieras were built. Two-tone bodies were silver on the bottom, black on top. Hood, trunk lid and vinyl top were also black. 'LXXV Buick' nameplates were on front fenders and trunk lid. Inside was gray leather upholstery and dark brushed silver trim plates on the dash, plus a sport steering wheel with brushed silver accent.

I.D. DATA: The 13-symbol Vehicle Identification Number (VIN) was again on the upper left surface of the instrument panel, visible through the windshield. Coding was similar to 1977, with the first digit ('4') indicating the Buick division. The second symbol is a letter indicating series: 'S' Skyhawk; 'T' Skyhawk; 'B' Skylark; 'C' Skylark Custom; 'W' Skylark S; 'E' Century Special; 'H' Century Custom; 'G' Century Sport Coupe; 'L' Century Ltd.; 'J' Regal; 'K' Regal Sport Coupe; 'M' Regal Ltd.; 'F' LeSabre Custom Sport Coupe; 'N' LeSabre; 'P' LeSabre Custom; 'R' Estate Wagon; 'V' Electra 225; 'X' Electra Limited; 'U' Electra Park Ave.; 'Z' Riviera. Next comes two digits that denote body type: '07' Skyhawk hatchback coupe; '17' Skylark hatchback coupe; '27' Skylark 2-dr. coupe; '69' 4-dr. sedan; '09' aero 4-dr. sedan; '37' LeSabre/Electra 2-dr. coupe; '47' Regal 2-dr. coupe; '87' aero 2-dr. coupe; '35' 4-dr. wagon. The fifth symbol is a letter indicating engine code: 'C' V6-196 2Bbl.; 'A' V6-231 2Bbl. (LD5); '2' V6-231 2Bbl. (LC6); 'G' V6-231 2Bbl. (LC5); '3' V6-231 4Bbl. (LC5); 'Y' V8-301 2Bbl.; 'U' V8-305 2Bbl.; 'H' V8-305 4Bbl.; 'L' V8-350 4Bbl. (LM1); 'R' V8-350 4Bbl. (L34); 'X' V8-350 4Bbl. (L77); 'K' V8-403 4Bbl. (L80). The sixth symbol denotes model year ('8' 1978). Next is a plant code: 'U' Lordstown, OH; 'W' Willow Run, MI; 'T' Tarrytown, NY; 'G' Framingham, MA; 'H' Flint, MI; 'Z' Fremont, CA; 'C' Southgate, CA; 'X' Fairfax, KS; 'E' Linden, NJ. The final six digits are the sequential serial number, which began with 100001 except for Skyhawks built at Lordstown and LeSabre/Electra models built at Flint, which started at 400001. Engine numbers were stamped on the front right of the block, except for L34 350 cu. in. V-8 and 403 cu. in. V-8, which were stamped on the front of the left side of the block. A body number plate on the shroud identified model year, car division, series, style, body assembly plant, body number, trim combination, modular seat code, paint code, and date built code.

SKYHAWK (V-6)

Series Number	Body/Style Number	Body Type & Seating	Factory Price	Shipping Weight	Production Total
4H	T07	2-dr 'S' Hatch-4P	4103	2678	Note 1
4H	S07	2-dr. Hatch-4P	4367	2707	Note 1

Note 1: Total production for the model year, 24,589 Skyhawks.

SKYLARK 'S' (V-6/V-8)

4X	W27	2-dr Coupe-6P	3872/4022	3201/3369	9,050

SKYLARK (V-6/V-8)

4X	B27	2-dr Coupe-6P	3999/4149	3203/3371	33,037
4X	B17	2-dr Hatch-6P	4181/4331	3313/3481	2,642
4X	B69	4-dr Sedan-6P	4074/4224	3234/3402	40,951

SKYLARK CUSTOM (V-6/V-8)

4X	C27	2-dr Coupe-5P	4242/4392	3186/3354	12,740
4X	C17	2-dr Hatch-5P	4424/4574	3285/3453	1,277
4X	C69	4-dr Sedan-6P	4317/4467	3219/3387	14,523

Note 2: Of the 114,220 Skylarks built, 17,116 carried a V-8 engine (only 287 'S' Skylarks had a V-8).

CENTURY SPECIAL (V-6/V-8)

4A	E87	2-dr Coupe-6P	4389/4599	3003/3149	10,818
4A	E09	4-dr Sedan-6P	4486/4696	3014/3160	12,533
4A	E35	4-dr Sta Wag-6P	4976/5126	3148/3314	9,586

CENTURY CUSTOM (V-6/V-8)

4A	H87	2-dr Coupe-6P	4633/4843	3011/3157	12,434
4A	H09	4-dr Sedan-6P	4733/4943	3038/3184	18,361
4A	H35	4-dr Sta Wag-6P	5276/5426	3181/3349	24,014

CENTURY SPORT (V-6/V-8)

4A	G87	2-dr Coupe-6P	5019/5228	3051/3197	Note 3

CENTURY LIMITED (V-6/V-8)

4A	L87	2-dr Coupe-6P	4991/5201	3048/3294	Note 3
4A	L09	4-dr Sedan-6P	5091/5301	3075/3221	Note 3

Note 3: Production of Century Sport and Limited models is included in figures above.

REGAL (V-6/V-8)

4A	J47	2-dr Coupe-6P	4852/5042	2992/3138	236,652

REGAL SPORT (V-6)

4A	K47	2-dr Coupe-6P	5853	3153	Note 4

REGAL LIMITED (V-6/V-8)

4A	M47	2-dr Coupe-6P	5233/5423	3041/3187	Note 4

Note 4: Production total listed under base Regal includes Sport and Limited models.

LESABRE (V-6/V-8)

4B	N37	2-dr Coupe-6P	5384/5582	3446/3613	8,265
4B	N69	4-dr Sedan-6P	5459/5657	3439/3606	23,354

LESABRE CUSTOM (V-6/V-8)

4B	P37	2-dr Coupe-6P	5657/5855	3413/3580	53,675
4B	P69	4-dr Sedan-6P	5757/5955	3450/3617	86,638

LESABRE SPORT (V-6)

4B	F37	2-dr Coupe-6P	6213	3559	Note 5

Note 5: Production of LeSabre Sport Coupe is included in standard LeSabre coupe total. Only 29,408 LeSabres came with a V-6.

ESTATE WAGON (V-8)

4B	R35	4-dr Sta Wag-6P	6301	4063	25,964

ELECTRA 225 (V-8)

4C	V37	2-dr Coupe-6P	7144	3682	8,259
4C	V69	4-dr Sedan-6P	7319	3730	14,590

ELECTRA LIMITED (V-8)

4C	X37	2-dr Coupe-6P	7526	3710	33,365
4C	X69	4-dr Sedan-6P	7701	3757	65,335

ELECTRA PARK AVENUE (V-8)

4C	U37	2-dr Coupe-6P	7837	3730	Note 6
4C	U69	4-dr Sedan-6P	8088	3777	Note 6

Note 6: Production totals listed under Electra Limited include the Park Avenue model. Total Limited production, 63,977.

RIVIERA (V-8)

4E	Z37	2-dr Coupe-6P	8082	3701	20,535

Note 7: Riviera had a hefty price increase during the model year, reaching $9224.

FACTORY PRICE AND WEIGHT NOTE: Figure before the slash is for V-6 engine, after the slash for smallest (lowest-priced) V-8 engine available.

ENGINES: BASE V-6 (Century, Regal): 90-degree, overhead-valve V-6. Cast iron alloy block and head. Displacement: 196 cu. in. (3.2 liters). Bore & stroke: 3.5 x 3.4 in. Compression ratio: 8.0:1. Brake horsepower: 90 at 3600 R.P.M. (95 at 3800 w/automatic). Torque: 165 lbs.-ft. at 2000 R.P.M. (155 at 2000 w/automatic). Four main bearings. Hydraulic valve lifters. Carburetor: 2Bbl. Rochester 2GE. VIN Code: C. Sales Code: LC9. BASE V-6 (Skyhawk, Skylark, Century wagon, LeSabre); OPTIONAL (Century sed/cpe, Regal): 90-degree, overhead-valve V-6. Cast iron alloy block and head. Displacement: 231 cu. in. (3.8 liters). Bore & stroke: 3.8 x 3.4 in. Compression ratio: 8.0:1. Brake horsepower: 105 at 3400 R.P.M. Torque: 185 lbs.-ft. at 2000 R.P.M. Four main bearings. Hydraulic valve lifters. Carburetor: 2Bbl. Rochester 2GE. VIN Code: A. Sales Code: LD5. Note: Alternate LC6 version had VIN code 2. TURBOCHARGED V-6 (Regal and LeSabre Sport Coupes): Same as 231 V-6 above, except as follows: Brake horsepower: 150 at 3800 R.P.M. Torque: 245 lbs.-ft. at 2400 R.P.M. VIN Code: G. Sales Code: LC5. TURBOCHARGED FOUR-BARREL V-6; OPTIONAL (Regal and LeSabre Sport Coupes): Same as turbocharged V-6 above, but with M4ME carburetor. Brake horsepower: 165 at 4000 R.P.M. Torque: 285 lbs.-ft. at 2800 R.P.M. VIN Code: 3. Sales Code: LC8. OPTIONAL V-8 (LeSabre) 90-degree overhead-valve V-8. Cast iron alloy block and head. Displacement: 301 cu. in. (4.9 liters). Bore & stroke: 4.0 x 3.0 in. Compression ratio: 8.2:1. Brake horsepower: 140 at 3600 R.P.M. Torque: 235 lbs.-ft. at 2000 R.P.M. Five main bearings. Hydraulic valve lifters. Carburetor: 2Bbl. Rochester M2MC. Built by Pontiac. VIN Code: Y. Sales Code: L27. OPTIONAL V-8 (Skylark, Century, Regal, LeSabre): 90-degree overhead-valve V-8. Cast iron alloy block and head. Displacement: 305 cu. in. (5.0 liters). Bore & stroke: 3.736 x 3.48 in. Compression ratio: 8.5:1. Brake horsepower: 145 at 3800 R.P.M. Torque: 245 lbs.-ft. at 2400 R.P.M. Five main bearings. Hydraulic valve lifters. Carburetor: 2Bbl. Rochester 2GC. Built by Chevrolet. VIN Code: U. Sales Code: LG3. OPTIONAL V-8 (Century/Regal): 90-degree, overhead valve V-8. Cast iron alloy block and head. Displacement: 305 cu. in. (5.0 liters). Bore & stroke: 3.736 x 3.48 in. Compression ratio: 8.5:1. Brake horsepower: 160 at 4000 R.P.M. Torque: 285 lbs.-ft. at 2400 R.P.M. Five main bearings. Hydraulic valve lifters. Carburetor: 4Bbl. Rochester 4GC. VIN Code: H. Sales Code: LG4. BASE V-8 (Electra, Estate, Riviera); OPTIONAL (Skylark, LeSabre): 90-degree, overhead valve V-8. Cast iron alloy block and head. Displacement: 350 cu. in. (5.7 liters). Bore & stroke: 3.80 x 3.85 in. Compression ratio: 8.0:1. Brake horsepower: 155 at 3400 R.P.M. Torque: 280 lbs.-ft. at 1800 R.P.M. Five main bearings. Hydraulic valve lifters. Carburetor: 4Bbl. Rochester M4MC. VIN Code: X. Sales Code: L77. ALTERNATE 350-4 V-8 (LeSabre, Electra, Estate, Riviera): 90-degree, overhead valve V-8. Cast iron alloy block and head. Displacement: 350 cu. in. (5.7 liters). Bore & stroke: 4.057 x 3.385 in. Compression ratio: 8.0:1. Brake horsepower: 170 at 3800 R.P.M. Torque: 275 lbs.-ft. at 2000 R.P.M. Five main bearings. Hydraulic valve lifters. Carburetor: 4Bbl. Rochester M4MC. VIN Code: R. Ordering Code: L34. OPTIONAL V-8 (Skylark, Century wagon): 90-degree, overhead valve V-8. Cast iron alloy block and head. Displacement: 350 cu. in. (5.7 liters). Bore & stroke: 4.00 x 3.48 in. Compression ratio: 8.2:1. Brake horsepower: 170 at 3800 R.P.M. Torque: 275 lbs.-ft. at 2000 R.P.M. Five main bearings. Hydraulic valve lifters. Carburetor: 4Bbl. Rochester M4MC. Chevrolet-built. VIN Code: L. Ordering Code: LM1. OPTIONAL V-8 (LeSabre, Electra, Estate, Riviera): 90-degree, overhead valve V-8. Cast iron alloy block and head. Displacement: 403 cu. in. (6.6 liters). Bore & stroke: 4.351 x 3.385 in. Compression ratio: 8.0:1. Brake horsepower: 185 at 3600 R.P.M. Torque: 320 lbs.-ft. at 2000 R.P.M. Five main bearings. Hydraulic valve lifters. Carburetor: 4Bbl. Rochester M4MC. Built by Oldsmobile. VIN Code: K. Ordering Code: L80.

CHASSIS DATA: Wheelbase: (Skyhawk) 97.0 in.; (Skylark) 111.0 in.; (Century/Regal) 108.1 in.; (LeSabre/Estate/Riviera) 115.9 in.; (Electra) 118.9 in. Overall length: (Skyhawk) 179.3 in.; (Skylark) 200.2 in.; (Century) 196.0 in.; (Regal) 200.0 in.; (LeSabre/Riviera) 218.2 in.; (Electra) 222.1 in.; (Estate Wagon) 216.7 in. Height: (Skyhawk) 50.2 in.; (Skylark 2-dr.) 52.2 in.; (Skylark 4-dr.) 53.1 in.; (Century cpe) 54.1 in.; (Century sed) 55.0 in.; (Century wagon) 55.7 in.; (Regal) 53.4 in.; (LeSabre/Electra/Riviera cpe) 55.0 in.; (LeSabre sed) 55.7 in.; (Electra sed) 55.9 in.; (Estate) 56.5 in. Width: (Skyhawk) 65.4 in.; (Skylark) 72.7 in.; (Century/Regal) 70.1 in.; (LeSabre/Electra/Riviera) 77.2 in.; (Estate) 79.9 in. Front Tread: (Skyhawk) 54.7 in.; (Skylark) 59.1 in.; (Century/Regal) 58.5 in.; (LeSabre/Electra/Riviera) 61.8 in.; (Estate) 62.2 in. Rear Tread: (Skyhawk) 53.6 in.; (Skylark) 59.7 in.; (Century/Regal) 57.8 in.; (LeSabre/Electra/Riviera) 60.7 in.; (Estate) 64.0 in. Standard Tires: (Skyhawk) BR78 x 13 SBR; (Skyhawk 'S') B78 x 13; (Skylark) E78 x 14; (Skylark Custom) ER78 x 14 SBR; (Century cpe/sed) P185/75R14 SBR; (Century wag/Regal) P195/75R14 SBR; (Century/Regal Spt Cpe) P205/70R14 SBR; (LeSabre) FR78 x 15 GBR; (LeSabre Spt Cpe) GR70 x 15 SBR: (Electra/Riviera) GR78 x 15; (Estate) HR78 x 15 SBR.

TECHNICAL: Transmission: Three-speed, fully synchronized manual gearbox (column shift) standard on Skylark, Century cpe/sed, and Regal cpe; Turbo-Hydra-Matic optional. Four-speed manual gearbox available on Century/Regal. Four-speed, fully synchronized floor shift standard on Skyhawk; five-speed and automatic optional. Turbo-Hydra-Matic standard on Regal sedan, LeSabre, Electra, Estate and Riviera. Three-speed manual transmission gear ratios: (1st) 3.50:1; (2nd) 1.81:1 or 1.90:1; (3rd) 1.00:1; (Rev) 3.62:1. Four-speed gear ratios: (1st) 3.50:1; (2nd) 2.48:1; (3rd) 1.66:1; (4th) 1.00:1; (Rev) 3.50:1. Five-speed gear ratios: (1st) 3.40:1; (2nd) 2.08:1; (3rd) 1.39:1; (4th) 1.00:1; (5th) 0.80:1; (Rev) 3.36:1. Automatic transmission gear ratios: (1st) 2.52:1; (2nd) 1.52:1; (3rd) 1.00:1; (Rev) 1.93:1. Standard axle ratios: (Skyhawk) 2.93:1 w/manual, 2.56:1 w/automatic; (Skylark) 3.08:1 w/manual, 2.56:1 w/automatic, 2.41:1 w/V-8; (Century/Regal) 2.93:1 w/manual, 2.56:1 w/automatic and 196 V-6, 2.73:1 w/231 V-6, 2.29:1 w/305 V-8; (Century wagon) 2.73:1 exc. 2.41:1 w/305 V-8; (Regal Sport Coupe) 2.73:1; (LeSabre V-6) 2.73:1; (LeSabre V-8) 2.41:1; LeSabre V-6 Sport Coupe) 2.58:1; (LeSabre V-8 Sport Coupe) 3.08:1; (Electra/Riviera) 2.41:1; (Estate) 2.73:1 exc. 2.56:1 w/403 V-8. Other axle ratios were standard in California and for high-altitude operation. Hypoid bevel final drive. Steering: recirculating ball; power assist standard on Century/Regal, LeSabre, Electra, Estate and Riviera. Suspension: front/rear coil springs, independent front except Skylark, semi-elliptic rear leaf springs. Front wishbones with lower trailing links and anti-roll bar; rigid rear axle with lower trailing radius arms, upper torque arms and transverse linkage bar. Brakes: front disc, rear drum; power brakes standard on LeSabre/Electra/Riviera plus Century wagon and Regal Sport Coupe. Four-wheel power disc brakes optional on Riviera. Body construction: (Skyhawk) unitized; (Skylark) separate front frame unit cushion-mounted to unitized body; (others) separate body and perimiter box frame. High-Energy electronic ignition (HEI) on all engines. Fuel tank: (Skyhawk) 18.5 gal.; (Skylark/LeSabre) 21 gal.; (Century/Regal) 18.1 gal.; (Electra/Estate/Riv) 22.5 gal. Unleaded fuel only.

DRIVETRAIN OPTIONS: Engines: 231 cu. in. V-6, 2Bbl.: Century cpe/sed, Regal ($40). Turbocharged 231 cu. in. V-6, 4Bbl.: Regal/LeSabre spt cpe ($50). 301 cu. in. V-8, 2Bbl.: LeSabre ($198). 305 cu. in. V-8, 2Bbl.: Skylark ($150); Century ($150-$210); Regal ($190); LeSabre ($198). 305 cu. in. V-8, 4Bbl.: Skylark ($265); Century ($200-$260); Regal ($240). 350 cu. in. V-8, 4Bbl.: Century wagon ($265); LeSabre ($313). 403 cu. in. V-8, 4Bbl.: LeSabre ($403). Transmission/Differential: Four-speed manual floor shift: Century cpe/sed, Regal w/231 2Bbl. V-6 ($125). Five-speed manual floor shift: Skyhawk ($175). Automatic trans.: Skyhawk ($270); Skylark, Century cpe/sed, Regal ($307). Optional rear axle ratio: Skyhawk 2.93:1 (NC); Skylark 3.08:1 or 3.23:1 (NC); Century/Regal 2.73:1 or 3.23:1 (NC); LeSabre/Electra/Riv 2.73:1, 3.08:1 or 3.23:1 (NC). Positive traction differential: Skyhawk ($56); Skylark/Century/Regal ($60); LeSabre/Electra/Riviera ($64). Power Accessories: Power brakes: Skyhawk ($66); Skylark, Century cpe/sed, Regal ($69). Four-wheel disc brakes: Riviera ($199). Power steering: Skyhawk ($134); Skylark/Century/Regal ($152). Suspension: WH5 handling pkg.: Skyhawk ($101-$122). F40 Firm ride/handling pkg.: Skylark ($24); Century/Regal/LeSabre/Electra/Riv ($20). FE2 Rallye ride/handling pkg.: Skylark ($46); Century exc. wag and spt cpe, Regal ($36); Riv ($20). Automatic level control: Century/Regal/LeSabre/Electra/Riv ($116). Other: Trailer towing flasher/harness: Skylark ($21-$34) exc. Skyhawk. Heavy-duty 80-amp alternator: LeSabre/Electra/Riv ($44). H.D. battery ($17-$20). H.D. cooling: Skylark/Electra/LeSabre/Riv ($29-$56). H.D. radiator: Skylark ($21); Engine block heater ($14) exc. Skyhawk. H.D. engine/transmission cooling: Century/Regal ($29-$56). High altitude emission system ($33). California emission system ($75).

SKYHAWK CONVENIENCE/APPEARANCE OPTIONS: Option Packages: Appearance group: 'S' ($73). Convenience group ($23). Shadow light Astroroof w/roof crown molding ($615). Manual glass sunroof ($215). Comfort/Convenience: Air cond. ($470). Rear defogger, electric ($79). Soft Ray tinted glass ($54). Tinted windshield ($42). Rally steering wheel: 'S' ($41). Tilt steering ($62). Electric clock ($19); w/tach ($69). Right sport mirror ($13). Remote left sport mirror ($18). Entertainment: AM radio ($74). AM/FM radio ($139). AM/FM stereo radio ($222). AM radio and 8-track player ($216). AM/FM stereo radio and 8-track ($320). Rear speaker ($23). Windshield antenna ($25); incl. w/radios. Exterior Trim: Door edge guards ($11). Roof crown molding ($176). Protective bodyside moldings ($28-$44). Hawk accent stripe ($36). Interior Trim/Upholstery: Full-length console ($77). Adjustable driver's seatback ($19). Front/rear mats ($18). Custom seatbelts ($16). Wheels: Custom sport wheels ($97). Deluxe wheel covers ($42). Wheel trim rings ($38). Tires: B78 x 13 WSW: 'S' ($35-$43). BR78 x 13 SBR BSW: 'S' ($84-$105). BR78 x 13 SBR WSW ($35-$148). BR70 x 13 SBR WLT ($64-$184). Conventional spare tire (NC).

SKYLARK CONVENIENCE/APPEARANCE OPTIONS: Option Packages: Sport Coupe or Sport Sedan pkg.: FE2 Rallye ride/handling suspension, ER78 x 14 SBR tires, black styling accents, sport mirrors ($182-$200); N/A on hatchback. Accessory pkg. (day/night mirror, lighter): 'S' ($14). Acoustic pkg. ($27-$40). Convenience group ($31-$34). Comfort/Convenience: Air cond. ($508). Cruise Master ($90). Two-speed wipers w/delay ($32). Rear defogger, blower-type ($51). Power windows ($118-$164). Electric door locks ($74- $103). Rallye steering wheel ($41). Tilt steering wheel ($69). Soft Ray tinted glass ($56). Tinted windshield ($44). Dual horns ($10). Electric clock ($22). Headlamps-on indicator ($10). Electric trunk release ($22). Remote left mirror ($16). Sport mirrors: left remote, right manual ($32). Entertainment: AM radio ($79). AM/FM radio ($149). AM/FM stereo radio ($236). AM radio and 8-track player ($279). AM/FM stereo radio and 8-track or cassette player ($341). Rear speaker ($23). Windshield antenna ($26); incl. w/radios. Exterior Trim: Landau vinyl top ($179-$184). Full vinyl top ($97-$102). Two-tone paint ($46). Special paint ($126). Swing-out rear quarter vent window: two-doors ($54). Protective bodyside moldings ($42). Roof drip and wheel opening moldings: 'S' ($36). Rocker panel moldings ($17); std. on Custom. Wide rocker appearance group ($43). Decklid molding ($9). Custom door and window frame moldings ($27- $34). Door edge guards ($11-$18). Bodyside stripes ($33). Bumper guards, front/rear ($40); front only ($20). Bumper strips, front/rear ($33). Interior Trim/Upholstery: Full- length console ($80). Vinyl bucket seats: base ($89). Cloth bucket seats: Custom ($109). Custom seatbelts ($16-$18). Front carpet savers ($9). Carpet savers and mats ($18). Carpeted door trim w/map pocket and reflector: base ($41). Wheels: Styled wheels ($22-$92). Chrome-plated wheels ($112- $130). Deluxe wheel covers ($38). Styled wheel covers ($63- $101). Deluxe wire wheel covers ($112-$150). Tires: E78 x 14 WSW ($35-$44). ER78 x 14 SBR BSW ($74-$92). ER78 x 14 SBR WSW ($35-$136). FR78 x 14 SBR WLT ($64-$171). Stowaway spare tire ($17).

CENTURY/REGAL CONVENIENCE/APPEARANCE OPTIONS: Option Packages: Century Custom Sport Wagon pkg. ($430). Electric sunroof: cpe ($499). Silver electric Astroroof: cpe ($699). Hatch roof: coupe ($625). Exterior molding pkg.: Century Spec., Regal ($9-$141). Convenience group: Century Spec. ($6-$44); Regal ($6-$18). Comfort/Convenience: Air cond. ($544). Automatic climate control air cond. ($626). Cruise Master ($90). Rear defogger, electric ($92). Tinted glass ($62). Tinted windshield ($45). Six-way power driver's seat ($151). Manual seatback recliner ($59); N/A Century Spec. sed/wag. Custom steering wheel: Century ($10) exc. Ltd. Rallye steering wheel: Century ($41) exc. Ltd.; Regal ($31). Sport steering wheel: Regal spt cpe ($31). Tilt steering ($69). Power windows ($124-$172). Electric door locks ($80-$112). Electric trunk release ($22). Remote tailgate lock: Century wag ($23). Electric clock, dial-type ($22). Digital clock ($49). Headlamps-on indicator ($10). Trip odometer ($12). Instrument gauges: temp and voltmeter ($26). Fuel usage light and instrument gauges ($55). Dome reading lamp ($18). Two-speed wiper with delay ($32). Lighting and Mirrors: Front light monitors ($28). Remote left mirror ($16). Remote right mirror ($28-$33). Sport mirrors: left remote ($27-$32). Dual remote sport mirrors ($52-$57). Lighted right visor vanity mirror ($45). Entertainment: AM radio ($83). AM/FM radio ($154). AM/FM stereo radio ($236); w/digital readout ($392). AM radio w/8-track ($233). AM/FM stereo radio w/8-track or cassette ($341-$351); w/CB ($571). Rear speaker: each ($24). Windshield antenna ($26); incl. w/radios. Automatic power antenna ($45-$71). Triband power antenna ($83-$109). Exterior Trim: Landau vinyl top: Regal ($140-$155); heavy-padded ($168-$216). Long vinyl top ($116). Designers' accent paint ($155-$206). Solid special color paint ($146). Bumper guards, front/rear ($40). Protective bodyside moldings ($33). Rocker panel moldings: Century Spec. ($17). Door edge guards ($11-$18). Wheel opening moldings: Century Spec. wag ($21). Bodyside stripes ($72-$93). Woodgrain vinyl applique: Century wag ($235-$256). Luggage rack: Century wag ($85). Air deflector: Century wag ($29). Interior Trim/Upholstery: Full-length console ($90). Bucket seats: Century Custom/spt cpe, Regal ($40). 55/45 seating: Century Custom/spt cpe, Regal ($98). Custom seatbelts ($16- $20). Load floor area carpet: Century Spec. wag ($49). Front carpet savers ($10); w/mats ($18). Front/rear carpet savers with inserts ($42); front ($23). Litter pocket ($8). Trunk trim covering ($30). Lockable storage compartment: Century wag ($35-$40). Wheels: Chrome-plated wheels: Century exc. Spt ($159); Regal ($141). Designers' sport wheels: Century exc. Spt ($117); Regal ($99). Deluxe wheel covers: Century exc. Spt ($38). Styled wheel covers: Century exc. Spt ($101); Regal ($63). Designers' wheel covers: Century exc. Spt ($65); Regal ($27). Wire wheel covers: Century exc. Spt ($150); Regal ($112). Tires: P185/75R14 GBR WSW: Century V-6 cpe/sed ($37). P195/75R14 GBR BSW: Century cpe/sed ($20). P195/75R14 GBR WSW ($39-$59). P195/75R14 SBR BSW: Century ($39-$59). P195/75R14 SBR WSW: Century ($78-$97). P205/70R14 SBR wide- oval BSW: Regal ($30). P205/70R14 SBR WSW: Century Spt, Regal ($42-$72). P205/70R14 SBR WLT ($54-$143).

LESABRE/ELECTRA/ESTATE WAGON/RIVIERA CONVENIENCE/APPEARANCE OPTIONS: Option Packages: Riviera Anniversary pkg.: black/silver Designers' Accent paint, gray 50/50 leather seats, carpeting and seatbelts ($586). Estate Wagon Limited pkg. ($1568). Estate Wagon convenience group ($12-$62). Exterior molding pkg.: LeSabre/Estate/Electra 225 ($37-$167). Convenience group: LeSabre ($19-$92). Power sunroof ($695-$778). Sliding Astroroof ($895-$978). Comfort/Convenience: Air cond. ($581). Automatic climate control air cond. ($669). Cruise Master ($95). Rear defogger, electric ($94). Soft Ray tinted glass ($76). Tinted windshield: LeSabre/Est ($46). Power windows: LeSabre/Est ($130-$190). Electric door locks ($82-$114). Automatic door locks: Electra/Riviera ($139-$167). Six-way power driver's seat ($120-$151). Dual power seats ($271- $302); N/A on base LeSabre. Electric seatback recliner, passenger ($113); N/A on base LeSabre sedan. Custom steering wheel: base LeSabre ($10). Rally steering wheel: LeSabre ($31-$41). Tilt steering ($70). Tilt/telescoping steering column ($46-$126). Digital clock (NC). Low fuel indicator ($10). Fuel usage light ($16); N/A spt cpe. Speed alert and trip odometer ($22). Remote electric tailgate lock: Estate ($32). Electric trunk release ($22). Theft deterrent system ($130); N/A on Estate. Three-speed wiper w/delay ($32). Lighting, Horns and Mirrors: Front cornering monitors: LeSabre/Est ($28). Front/rear monitors: Electra/Riviera ($60). Door courtesy/warning lights ($35-$55). Rear courtesy lamps: Est ($15). Headlamps-on indicator ($10). Dome reading lamp: LeSabre/Estate/Electra 225 ($18). Sunshade map light: Electra 225 ($12). Four-note horn ($22). Remote left mirror: LeSabre/Est ($16). Remote right mirror ($28-$33) exc. Riv. Remote right sport mirror: Riviera ($33). Dual remote sport mirrors ($36-$57) exc. Riv. Remote left mirror w/thermometer ($21-$37) exc. Riv. Lighted visor vanity mirror ($46). Entertainment: AM radio ($96); N/A on Riv. AM/FM radio ($165); N/A on Riv. AM/FM stereo radio ($239). AM/FM stereo w/digital readout: LeSabre/Est ($342-$ 392). AM radio and 8- track ($250); N/A on Riv. AM/FM stereo radio and 8-track or cassette player ($345-$355) exc. Riv ($106-$116). AM/FM stereo radio and CB ($577) exc. Riv ($338). Signal-seeking AM/FM stereo with 8-track: Electra ($514); Riv ($275). Rear speaker ($24) exc. Riv. Windshield antenna ($26) exc. Riv. Automatic power antenna ($45-$71). Triband power antenna ($83-$109). Exterior Trim: Landau vinyl top: LeSabre ($151). Heavy-padded landau vinyl top ($194-$405). Long vinyl top: LeSabre, Electra sed ($142-$161). Long, heavy-padded vinyl top: Electra/Riviera ($196). Two-tone paint: LeSabre ($56). Designers' accent paint: LeSabre/Riviera ($175-$201). Solid special color paint ($147) exc. Riviera Firemist ($165). Protective bodyside moldings ($42-$65). Hood ornament and windsplit: LeSabre/Est ($24). Door edge guards ($11-$18). Window frame scalp molding: LeSabre/Est ($33). Wheel opening moldings: LeSabre/Est ($26). Bodyside stripes ($50). Woodgrain vinyl applique: Estate ($235). Bumper guards, front/rear ($40); front, Estate ($20). Luggage rack w/air deflector: Estate ($135). Interior Trim/Upholstery: Third seat: Estate ($186). Custom seatbelts: LeSabre/Est ($20-$23). Front carpet savers ($11) exc. Riv. Carpet savers and handy mats ($21) exc. Riv. Front/rear carpet savers w/inserts: Riviera ($42); front ($23). Trunk carpeting/covering ($46- $58). Wheels: Chrome-plated wheels ($62-$161). Deluxe wheel covers: LeSabre ($38). Custom wheel covers ($28-$66) exc. Riv. Styled wheel covers ($65) exc. Riv. Moire wheel covers ($75-$113) exc. Riv. Deluxe wire wheel covers ($112-$150) exc. Riv. Custom red wire wheel covers: Riv (NC). Tires: FR78 x 15 GBR WSW: LeSabre ($37-$46). FR78 x 15 SBR: LeSabre ($39- $48). FR78 x 15 SBR WSW: LeSabre ($37-$46). GR78 x 15 SBR WSW ($39-$121). GR78 x 15 SBR wide WSW: LeSabre ($51-$136).

HISTORY: Introduced: October 6, 1977 (Regal Sport Coupe, August 1977). Model year production (U.S.): 803,187, for 9.0 percent of the industry total. Calendar year production (U.S.): 810,350. Model year sales by U.S. dealers: 795,316 (including 18,801 imported Opels). Calendar year sales (U.S.): 781,364 for an 8.4 percent market share.

Historical Footnotes: Buick now looked toward the youth market for potential customers. Said J.D. Duffy Jr., the new general sales manager, in *Ward's Auto World*: "We can't live on traditional Buick buyers. They're getting older every year." A record 776,515 domestic Buicks sold through U.S. dealers, more than 30,000 over the 1977 mark. Though impressive, the figure fell short of early forecasts. Defying predictions, Skyhawk and Skylark sales rose (as did the imported Opel), while mid- and full-size Buicks didn't reach expected levels. Trimmed-down Regals grew popular, but buyers didn't take so kindly to the new fastback Century sedan styling. And Riviera sales weakened when prospective buyers heard about the new front-drive version expected for 1979. Part of the loss in full-size sales, in fact, came because production at the Linden, New Jersey plant was halted early to allow for changeover to the new E-body Riviera. This helped cause model year production to fall somewhat for the year. As part of the 75th anniversary festivities, an open house at Flint in Junecoupled to a gathering of the Buick Club of Americadrew 36,000 visitors. Over 600 early Buicks paraded through town. Late in 1978, Donald H. McPherson became the new general manager of Buick division.

1979 BUICK

Riviera was downsized for 1979 and switched to front- wheel drive, while LeSabre and Electra were carried over except for trim changes. The free-breathing 90-degree V-6 engine, in 3.2- and 3.8-liter displacements, got a new carburetor, intake manifold, exhaust manifold, and camshaft this year. It also received an improved two-barrel carburetor (Dual Jet 210).

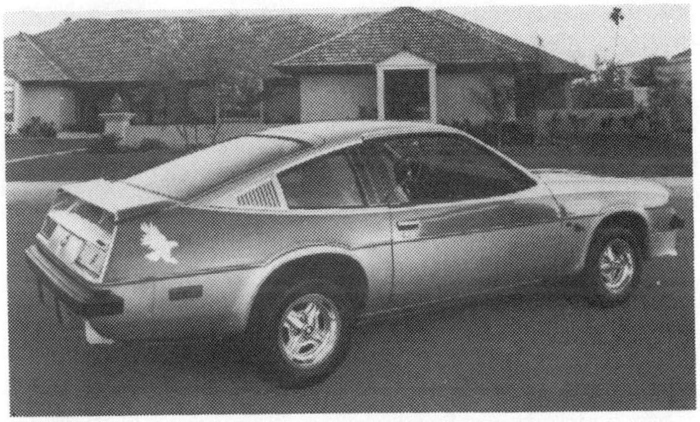

1979 Skyhawk "Road Hawk" hatchback coupe (B)

SKYHAWK — SERIES 4H — V-6 — All Skyhawks got a new hood and front-end treatment with single rectangular headlamps, meant to enhance the car's sporty image. The new body-color grille was comprised of many small openings, wider than they were high, split into 12 sections by five wider vertical bars and a single horizontal bar. A Hawk insignia sat above the grille, in the center. Buick block letters were off to the side, above the grille. Rounded-corner housings held Skyhawk's headlamps, with wide parking/signal lamps below the front bumper. The freshly styled hood had twin creases that tapered inward toward the front. Vertical louvers tapered back to the rear, from the quarter windows. Sport mirrors were standard. Sole powerplant remained the 231 cu. in. (3.8-liter) V-6, with the same choice of three transmissions as before: standard four-speed floor shift, five-speed overdrive, or automatic. Base Skyhawks (S07) had an AM radio, full-length console, sport steering wheel, twin sport mirrors (left remote-controlled), bodyside accent stripes, and bumper guards. The fewer-frills 'S' edition was again available, with rattan vinyl interior. Two special packages were offered this year, both stressing the "hawk" theme with air dam, spoiler, and hawk decal. The top level, limited-edition Road Hawk option included a Rallye ride-and-handling package with larger stabilizer bars and blackwall BR70 x 13 steel-belted radial tires. The package included 'Road Hawk' markings, Oyster White vinyl bucket seats with hawk emblem, altered interior trim, new steering wheel, black windshield wipers, black window reveal moldings and grille, plus a front air dam and sporty decklid spoiler integrated into the rear quarter panel. Body color was light silver above the beltline, darker silver below. Road Hawks also included fast-ratio power steering (when power steering was ordered). Skyhawk's "Designers' Accent Edition" came with a bright red or yellow exterior, flat black accent along and below the beltline, hawk decal on the hood, rear spoiler, deluxe wheel covers, and sporty-tone exhaust system.

SKYLARK — SERIES 4X — V-6/V-8 — Skylark entered 1979 with a totally redesigned front end, including new grille. The grille's crosshatch pattern split into four sections, peaked at the front. Single round headlamps combined with wraparound two-section park/signal lamps. Buick still promoted Skylark's tall "greenhouse" with its "generous glass." Fenders again sported triple-ventiport trim strips. Two-door, four-door and hatchback bodies were offered, in base or Custom trim. Custom Skylarks included a stand-up hood ornament, rocker panel moldings, carpeted door trim, map pockets, plus a visor vanity mirror and lights for underhood, glove box, trunk and ashtray. The low-budget Skylark 'S' lacked a day/night mirror, lighter, roof drip and wheel opening moldings. The new, improved, highly efficient "free breathing" 231 cu. in. (3.8-liter) 2Bbl. V-6 was standard, with smoother airflow adding 10 horsepower over the 1978 version. Standard powertrain was again the three-speed manual shift, with automatic transmission optional. Two V-8s were available. The Sport package (for coupe or sedan) included black paint accents on grille, around headlamps, windshield, back windows and side-window frames; plus ER78 x 14 steel-belted tires, ride/handling suspension and black sport mirrors. It came in four body colors: silver, dark gold, yellow, or bright red. Sport models could also have black painted wide rocker treatment and black protective side moldings. New individual options included sporty interiors, an AM/FM stereo radio with cassette player, and a wider range of colors and paint combinations that included a Designers' Accent treatment with darker accent color on the side body panels.

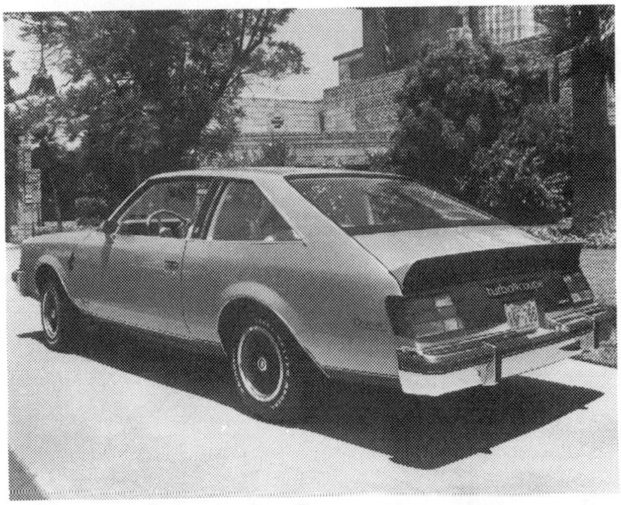

1979 Century Turbo coupe (B)

CENTURY — SERIES 4A — V-6/V-8 — Century continued its fastback styling, introduced for 1978, with a reworked front end. A new crosshatch grille had three rows of rectangular "holes." Three-section parking/signal lamps stood outboard of single headlamps, while tri-section taillamps wrapped around the rear fenders. Four models made up the lineup: coupe, sedan, sport coupe, and station wagon. Engine choices were revised slightly. Base engine was again the even-firing 196 cu. in. (3.2-liter) V-6; but 3.8 V-6 in California, and on wagons. Normal and turbocharged 3.8 V-6s were available. So was a 301 cu. in. (4.9-liter) V-8. California models had an electronic fuel control system. A new Turbo Coupe package was described as an enthusiast's car, powered by the free-breathing turbocharged 231 cu. in. (3.8-liter) V-6. The performance package included automatic transmission, power brakes and dual exhausts, plus a sport steering wheel, turbo hood ornament, 'Turbo Coupe' trunk decal in big and bold billboard letters on rear deck panels, and a turbo hood blister with 'Turbo 3.8 Litre' badge. In short, you couldn't help but think a turbo engine might lurk under the hood. It also included a front air dam and rear spoiler, flat black paint trim, and turbine-design polycast wheels with 7 in. rims. Many of the Turbo Coupe features were first seen on Buick's 1976 Indy 500 Pace Car, including the four-barrel turbocharged V-6, an improved-flow cylinder head, dual exhausts, front air dam, and rear spoiler. Turbo Coupes were offered in white, silver, medium blue, dark gold, and red. Century's basic Sport Coupe included flat black trim in the grille and around headlamps and moldings; black wipers; plus a hawk decal high on front fenders, ahead of the door. The package also featured Designers' Sport wheels, wide steel-belted tires, Rallye ride/handling suspension, fast- ratio power steering (optional), and a rear spoiler. Custom and Special sedans and wagons were also available, plus a Sport Wagon option with Rallye suspension, large (P205/70R14) tires on Designers' Sport wheels, hawk decal, sport mirrors, air deflector, and special paint with black accents on grille, headlamp trim, wipers, moldings and pillars. Sport Wagons had wide rocker panels and wheel opening moldings. All wagons had a split tailgate: the glass portion lifted up like a hatch, while the bottom section folded down. Limited sedans carried the same plush interior as the Regal Limited coupe, including crushed velour 55/45 seats, plus wide rocker panel and belt reveal moldings and a custom steering wheel. All three option packages were offered in a choice of five body colors. New options included different interior fabrics, reclining driver's seat, sport steering wheel, and visor vanity mirrors.

1979 Regal Limited Landau Coupe (B)

REGAL — SERIES 4A — V-6/V-8 — Regal had been set apart from the Century line for the first time in 1978. This year, the formal roofline and full-cut wheel openings were unchanged. Subdued horizontal bars were added to the basic Regal's strong vertical-patterned grille, which again sloped outward at the base. Taillamps were newly designed. So was the instrument panel. Cornering lamps were made available on all Regal models. Single rectangular headlamps were flanked by clear vertical park/signal lamps. The Buick name was inset in the top bar of the grille; 'Regal' script stood near the lower corner. Ahead of the door was an emblem denoting engine size in litres. Standard engine was the 196 cu. in. (3.2-liter) V-6, except in California. Options included the larger 231 V-6, or 301 and 305 V-8s. Standard transmission was three-speed manual (except in California, where automatic was required). California cars added a new C-4 (Computer Controlled Catalytic Converter) system to control emissions, which included an electronically-controlled carburetor and three-way catalytic converter. As noted on its fender insignia, Regal's Sport Coupe had the turbo 231 V-6 under the hood. Also standard was a Rallye ride/handling suspension with front/rear stabilizer bars; firmer springs and shocks; fast-ratio power steering; P205/70R14 tires; and turbo boost gauge on the dash. A special Sport Coupe Decor Package included blackout trim around windshield, on rocker moldings, wipers, door pillars, around taillamps and license plate molding; plus a blacked-out grille, twin sport mirrors, and Designers' Accent paint treatment on hood, top and deck lid. Four Turbine wheels, too. Regal interiors carried handy door-pull assist straps. A simulated woodgrain instrument panel with large instruments in squares sat far forward to allow extra leg room. Regal Limited added wide chrome rocker panel moldings plus 'Limited' insignia below the 'Regal' script on the roof pillar. Inside were soft velour 55/45 notchback seats, plus crushed velour door inserts and rear-seat side trim. New Regal options included cornering lamps, turbine-styled wheels, and visor vanity mirrors. Also available: a silver-tinted Astroroof, metal sunroof or Hatch roof; plus three vinyl top styles.

1979 LeSabre Sport Coupe (B)

LESABRE — SERIES 4B — V-6/V-8 — LeSabre's new grille had thin vertical elements separated into three sections by two horizontal bars. Quad rectangular headlamps sat over separate park/signal lamps. Buick block letters were atop the upper grille corner. Rear fenders held the LeSabre nameplates. Restyled taillamps split into two wide sections by a horizontal bar, with clear backup lamps toward the center and amber lenses wrapping around the rear quarter panels. Inside was plenty of space for six passengers. Under the hood, a standard 231 cu. in. (3.8-liter) V-6 or choice of optional V-8 engines. Standard were power steering and brakes. The new top-line LeSabre Limited coupe and sedan, replacing the former Custom model, had a special molding package. LeSabre Sport Coupe continued the turbocharged V-6 powerplant introduced for 1978, with four-barrel and automatic transmission. Grille, windows and moldings sported flat black trim, and wheels were chrome-plated. The special handling package included large front and rear stabilizer bars, firm springs and shocks, plus quick-ratio power steering and wide oval tires. Eight different sound systems were available to please audio fans. A four-page brochure announced LeSabre's Palm Beach limited edition, which featured Designers' Accent paint treatment with yellow beige accent color on door-handle inserts, center pillar applique (with logo), lower bodyside and fender moldings, grille bar sides, wheel covers, and bumper rub strips. Inside were 55/45 seats trimmed in yellow beige Palm Beach cloth; woodgrain door, dash and steering wheel appliques; and Palm Beach logo on the dash. Judging by its brochure picture, the Palm Beach with gold bodyside striping was a curious and colorful beast, reminiscent of some of the pastel cars of the Fifties.

ESTATE WAGON — SERIES 4BR — V-8 — Buick's full-size station wagon front end looked similar to LeSabre. As before, it seated up to eight with optional third seat. Cargo area amounted to 88.6 cubic feet with rear seat folded down. This year, Estate fender trim strips carried only three "ventiports" instead of the previous four. The Limited option package included a special grille, power windows, tilt steering column, 55/45 notchback seats, luggage rack with air deflector, chrome wheels, and simulated woodgrain vinyl applique. Two engine choices were offered: 350 or 403 cu. in. V-8s, both with automatic transmission.

1979 Electra Park Avenue sedan (B)

ELECTRA — SERIES 4C — V-8 — The posh full-size Buick got a new front end look this year with new quad rectangular headlamps, plus new vertical-style wraparound taillamps and new body colors. The new grille ran the entire car width, encompassing the headlamps. Its tiny crosshatch pattern was divided into a dozen sections by two horizontal and five vertical bars, slightly peaked at the front. Quad rectangular headlamps stood above horizontal park/signal lamps. The slanted headlamp bezels that had become an integral part of the Buick "look" were there again for 1979. Electra still displayed the four-section "ventiport" trim strip on squared-off front fenders—a vestige of the portholes famed on Buicks through the 1950s. Full-width wraparound taillamps were accented by the Electra crest. One bright bodyside molding sat low, not far above the rocker panels. In addition to the 14 standard Buick colors, there were three new Firemist colors (gold, gray and saffron) available on Electras. Inside was new simulated butterfly woodgrain trim on the instrument panel. A bank of lighted indicators atop the dashboard showed if high beams were on and gave information on engine operation, seat belts and parking brake position. Base engine was the 350 cu. in. (5.7-liter) V-8 with 4Bbl. carburetor; optional, the 403 (6.6-liter) V-8, which wouldn't be around much longer. Electra 225 and Limited models were offered again, plus the plush Park Avenue. That Park Avenue edition included elegantly buttoned-and-tucked velvet upholstery with an armrest for each 50/50 seat—a total of seven armrests in the car. Two velvet pockets were sewn into the back of the front seat. High-intensity reading lamps illuminated from the headliner. Outside were unique new coach lamps, using electroluminiscent panels that had no bulbs to burn out. Options included a lighted vanity mirror on the underside of the driver's sun visor, and a selection of five wheel cover styles.

1979 Riviera S Type Turbo coupe (B)

RIVIERA — SERIES 4BZ — V-6/V-8 — In Buick's words, the all-new Riviera was meant to be "a statement of what we think is to come, rather than simply a well-turned expression of what is already here." Freshly downsized, the new fifth-generation Riv was re-engineered to front-drive, sharing mechanical details with Cadillac Eldorado and Oldsmobile Toronado, and reclassified as a (spacious) four-passenger. Once again, it sported full-cut wheel openings and sweeping quarter panels. Underneath was a new fully independent suspension (front and rear), using front torsion bars and rear leaf springs, to improve the ride and handling. It included a standard rear stabilizer bar. Construction remained the separate body-and-frame design. Riv's raked-back front end and squared-off roofline suggested luxury. But this edition was almost a foot shorter overall than the 1978 Riviera, and 2 inches shorter in wheelbase. The grille was made up of vertical bars that sloped outward slightly, divided into eight sections by slightly wider bars. 'Riviera' script was at the side of the grille. Quad headlamps sat above clear parking/signal lamps. Another 'Riviera' script stood just ahead of the door, not far above the rocker panel molding. Two models were now available: luxury and sport. Standard Rivieras were powered by the 350 cu. in. (5.7-liter) V-8, but the sporty new S Type carried a special version of the turbocharged 231 cu. in. (3.8-liter) V-6 with four-barrel carburetor. This was the only turbo V-6 front-drive car made in the U.S. Actually, either Riviera model could be ordered with the other engine as an option. Though hardly a lightweight, the turbocharged Riv could hit 60 MPH in about 12 seconds, while returning fairly thrifty gas mileage on the road. Riviera's lengthy standard equipment list included a Delco AM/FM stereo radio with power antenna, six-way power driver's seat, power windows, power brakes and steering, automatic transmission, digital clock, air conditioning, Soft-Ray tinted glass, side-window defrosters, cornering lights, and automatic level control. Four-wheel disc brakes were again available; front discs standard. A wide variety of fabrics and leather upholstery was available. Standard setup was 45/55 seating with velour or vinyl and a folding center armrest. S Type had new bucket seats in vinyl or cloth, with leather available. Riviera also had maintenance-free wheel bearings, front and rear. The S Type's instrument panel was trimmed in brushed black, while its chassis held ride/handling extras. Standard equipment included firmer-rate front torsion bars and rear springs; firmer shock absorbers; larger-diameter stabilizer bars (front and rear); fast-ratio power steering; bucket seats and center storage console; plus a sport steering wheel with T-shaped center section and padded rim. Outside, the S Type had flat black trim around windows, and on grille and rocker panels; streamlined sport mirrors; amber front parking lights; and Designers' Sport wheel covers. New electronically-tuned (ETR) radios were available, with digital readout and signal seeking. Other notable (if not new) options: padded Landau top with coach lamps in roof pillars; electric sunroof; and glass Astroroof. A new digital speedometer and fuel gauge—part of the optional computer-controlled Trip Monitor—was offered later in the model year. Touch the right buttons and you could learn estimated time of arrival, how far you could travel on remaining fuel, and miles remaining to destination. Plus digital readouts of engine temperature, R.P.M. and voltage; current time, average speed and elapsed trip time; and a trip odometer. This option was a harbinger of things to come in digital equipment; but the standard Riviera dash still carried a conventional speedometer and fuel gauge.

I.D. DATA: The 13-symbol Vehicle Identification Number (VIN) was again on the upper left surface of the instrument panel, visible through the windshield. Coding was similar to 1978; see that listing for details. One series was added ('Y' Riviera S Type), and LeSabre (code 'P') was now called Limited rather than Custom. Engine coding (symbol five) was as follows: 'C' V6-196 2Bbl. (LD5); 'A' V6-231 2Bbl. (LD5); '2' V6-231 2Bbl. (LC6); '3' Turbo V6-231 4Bbl. (LC8); 'Y' V8-301 2Bbl. (L27); 'W' V8-301 4Bbl. (L37); 'G' V8-305 2Bbl. (LG3); 'H' V8-305 4Bbl. (LG4); 'L' V8-350 4Bbl. (LM1); 'R' V8-350 4Bbl. (L34); 'X' V8-350 4Bbl. (L77); 'K' V8-403 4Bbl. (L80). The sixth symbol (model year) changed to '9' for 1979. The code for the Lordstown plant changed to '7'.

1979 Skyhawk "Designer Accent Edition" hatchback coupe (B)

SKYHAWK (V-6)

Series Number	Body/Style Number	Body Type & Seating	Factory Price	Shipping Weight	Production Total
4H	T07	2-dr 'S' Hatch-4P	4380	2724	4,766
4H	S07	2-dr. Hatch-4P	4598	2740	18,373

SKYLARK 'S' (V-6/V-8)

4X	W27	2-dr Coupe-6P	4082/4277	3105/3224	1,605

BASE SKYLARK (V-6/V-8)

4X	B27	2-dr Coupe-6P	4208/4403	3114/3233	8,596
4X	B17	2-dr Hatch-6P	4357/4552	3195/3314	608
4X	B69	4-dr Sedan-6P	4308/4503	3158/3277	10,849

SKYLARK CUSTOM (V-6/V-8)

4X	C27	2-dr Coupe-5P	4462/4657	3123/3242	3,546
4X	C69	4-dr Sedan-6P	4562/4757	3176/3295	3,822

Note 1: Of the 20,053 base Skylarks built, 2,963 had a V-8; of the 7,368 Skylark Customs, 2,497 had a V-8.

CENTURY SPECIAL (V-6/V-8)

4A	E87	2-dr Coupe-6P	4599/4855	3038/3142	3,152
4A	E09	4-dr Sedan-6P	4699/4955	3053/3157	7,364
4A	E35	4-dr Sta Wag-6P	5247/5442	3158/3286	10,413

CENTURY CUSTOM (V-6/V-8)

4A	H87	2-dr Coupe-6P	4843/5099	3051/3155	2,474
4A	H09	4-dr Sedan-6P	4968/5224	3071/3175	6,987
4A	H35	4-dr Sta Wag-6P	5561/5756	3194/3322	21,100

CENTURY SPORT (V-6/V-8)

4A	G87	2-dr Coupe-6P	5151/5386	3047/3151	1,653

CENTURY LIMITED (V-6/V-8)

4A	L09	4-dr Sedan-6P	5336/5592	3104/3208	2,694

Note 2: Of the total 20,929 Century Specials built, 5,053 had a V-8 engine; of the 30,561 Century Customs, 16,110 were V-8 powered.

REGAL (V-6/V-8)

4A	J47	2-dr Coupe-6P	5080/5315	3029/3133	157,228

REGAL SPORT COUPE (TURBO V-6)

4A	K47	2-dr Coupe-6P	6223	3190	21,389

REGAL LIMITED (V-6/V-8)

4A	M47	2-dr Coupe-6P	5477/5712	3071/3175	94,748

LESABRE (V-6/V-8)

4B	N37	2-dr Coupe-6P	5680/5926	3428/3556	7,542
4B	N69	4-dr Sedan-6P	5780/6026	3459/3587	25,431

LESABRE LIMITED (V-6/V-8)

4B	P37	2-dr Coupe-6P	6124/6370	3454/3582	38,290
4B	P69	4-dr Sedan-6P	6249/6495	3503/3631	75,939

LESABRE SPORT COUPE (TURBO V-6)

4B	F37	2-dr Coupe-6P	6621	3545	3,582

Note 3: Only 14,851 base and Limited LeSabres had a V-6 engine.

ESTATE WAGON (V-8)

4B	R35	4-dr Sta Wag-6P	6714	4021	21,312

ELECTRA 225 V-8

4C	V37	2-dr Coupe-6P	7581	3767	5,358
4C	V69	4-dr Sedan-6P	7756	3831	11,055

ELECTRA LIMITED V-8

4C	X37	2-dr Coupe-6P	7981	3789	28,878
4C	X69	4-dr Sedan-6P	8156	3853	76,340

ELECTRA PARK AVENUE V-8

4C	U37	2-dr Coupe-6P	8423	3794	Note 4
4C	U69	4-dr Sedan-6P	8598	3860	Note 4

Note 4: Production totals listed under Electra Limited include Park Avenue models. A total of 61,096 Limiteds and 44,122 Park Avenue versions were produced. Note 5: Electra had massive price increases during the model year, of more than $1100. By mid-year, the base 225 coupe sold for $8703 and the Park Avenue sedan for $9959.

RIVIERA (V-8)

4E	Z57	2-dr Coupe-4P	10112	3759	37,881

RIVIERA S TYPE TURBO (V-6)

4E	Y57	2-dr Coupe-4P	10388	3774	14,300

Note 6: Total Riviera production includes 2,067 standard models with optional turbo V-6 engine, while S Type production includes 5,900 with a non-turbo V-8, which was offered with a price credit.

FACTORY PRICE AND WEIGHT NOTE: Figure before the slash is for V-6 engine, after the slash for smallest (lowest-priced) V-8 engine available.

ENGINES: BASE V-6 (Century, Regal): 90-degree, overhead-valve V-6. Cast iron alloy block and head. Displacement: 196 cu. in. (3.2 liters). Bore & stroke: 3.5 x 3.4 in. Compression ratio: 8.0:1. Brake horsepower: 105 at 4000 R.P.M. Torque: 160 lbs.-ft. at 2000 R.P.M. Four main bearings. Hydraulic valve lifters. Carburetor: 2Bbl. Rochester M2ME. VIN Code: C. Sales Code: LC9. BASE V-6 (Skyhawk, Skylark, Century wagon, LeSabre); OPTIONAL (Century sed/cpe, Regal): 90-degree, overhead-valve V-6. Cast iron alloy block and head. Displacement: 231 cu. in. (3.8 liters). Bore & stroke: 3.8 x 3.4 in. Compression ratio: 8.0:1. Brake horsepower: 115 at 3800 R.P.M. Torque: 190 lbs.-ft. at 2000 R.P.M. Four main bearings. Hydraulic valve lifters. Carburetor: 2Bbl. Rochester M2ME. VIN Code: A. Sales Code: LD5. Note: Alternate LC6 version (VIN code 2) with Computer Controlled Catalytic Converter (C4) and E2ME carburetor was used on California Century and Regal models. TURBOCHARGED V-6 (Regal and LeSabre Sport Coupes, Riviera S); OPTIONAL (Century, Riviera): Same as 231 V-6 above, but with M4ME four-barrel carburetor. Brake horsepower: 170 at 4000 R.P.M. (Century, 175 at 4000; Riviera, 185 at 4200). Torque: 265 lbs.-ft. at 2800 R.P.M. (Century, 275 at 2600; Riviera, 280 at 2400). VIN Code: 3. Sales Code: LC8. OPTIONAL V-8 (Century, Regal, LeSabre) 90-degree overhead-valve V-8. Cast iron alloy block and head. Displacement: 301 cu. in. (4.9 liters). Bore & stroke: 4.0 x 3.0 in. Compression ratio: 8.1:1. Brake horsepower: 140 at 3600 R.P.M. Torque: 235 lbs.-ft. at 2000 R.P.M. Five main bearings. Hydraulic valve lifters. Carburetor: 2Bbl. Roch. M2MC. Built by Pontiac. VIN Code: Y. Sales Code: L27. OPTIONAL V-8 (Century, Regal): As above but with M4MC 4Bbl. carburetor. Brake horsepower: 150 at 4000 R.P.M. Torque: 240 lbs.-ft. at 2000 R.P.M. VIN Code: W. Sales Code: L37. OPTIONAL V-8 (Skylark): 90-degree overhead-valve V-8. Displacement: 305 cu. in. (5.0 liters). Bore & stroke: 3.736 x 3.48 in. Compression ratio: 8.4:1. Brake horsepower: 130 at 3200 R.P.M. Torque: 245 lbs.-ft. at 2000 R.P.M. Five main bearings. Hydraulic valve lifters. Carburetor: 2Bbl. Rochester M2MC. Built by Chevrolet. VIN Code: U. Sales Code: LG3. OPTIONAL V-8 (Century/Regal in California and for high-altitude operation): 90-degree, overhead valve V-8. Cast iron alloy block and head. Displacement: 305 cu. in. (5.0 liters). Bore & stroke: 3.736 x 3.48 in. Compression ratio: 8.4:1. Brake horsepower: 115 at 4000 R.P.M. Torque: 225 lbs.-ft. at 2400 R.P.M. Five main bearings. Hydraulic valve lifters. Carburetor: 4Bbl. Rochester M4MC. VIN Code: H. Sales Code: LG4. BASE V-8 (Electra, Estate); OPTIONAL (LeSabre): 90-degree, overhead valve V-8. Cast iron alloy block and head. Displacement: 350 cu. in. (5.7 liters). Bore & stroke: 3.80 x 3.85 in. Compression ratio: 8.0:1. Brake horsepower: 155 at 3400 R.P.M. Torque: 280 lbs.-ft. at 1800 R.P.M. Five main bearings. Hydraulic valve lifters. Carburetor: 4Bbl. Rochester M4MC. VIN Code: X. Sales Code: L77. ALTERNATE 350-4 V-8 (Estate in California, Riviera); OPTIONAL (Calif./high-altitude LeSabre/Electra; Riviera S): 90-degree, overhead valve V-8. Cast iron alloy block and head. Displacement: 350 cu. in. (5.7 liters). Bore & stroke: 4.057 x 3.385 in. Compression ratio: 8.0:1. Brake horsepower: 160 at 3800 R.P.M. Torque: 270 lbs.-ft. at 2000 R.P.M. Five main bearings. Hydraulic valve lifters. Carburetor: 4Bbl. Rochester M4MC. Built by Oldsmobile. VIN Code: R. Ordering Code: L34. OPTIONAL V-8 (Skylark, Century wagon): 90-degree, overhead

valve V-8. Cast iron alloy block and head. Displacement: 350 cu. in. (5.7 liters). Bore & stroke: 4.00 x 3.48 in. Compression ratio: 8.2:1. Brake horsepower: 165 at 3800 R.P.M. Torque: 260 lbs.-ft. at 2400 R.P.M. Five main bearings. Hydraulic valve lifters. Carburetor: 4Bbl. Rochester M4MC. Chevrolet-built. VIN Code: L. Ordering Code: LM1. OPTIONAL V-8 (Electra): 90-degree, overhead valve V-8. Cast iron alloy block and head. Displacement: 403 cu. in. (6.6 liters). Bore & stroke: 4.351 x 3.385 in. Compression ratio: 8.0:1. Brake horsepower: 175 at 3600 R.P.M. Torque: 310 lbs.-ft. at 2000 R.P.M. Five main bearings. Hydraulic valve lifters. Carburetor: 4Bbl. Roch. M4MC. Built by Oldsmobile. VIN Code: K. Ordering Code: L80.

CHASSIS DATA: Wheelbase: (Skyhawk) 97.0 in.; (Skylark) 111.0 in.; (Century/Regal) 108.1 in.; (LeSabre/Estate) 115.9 in.; (Electra) 118.9 in.; (Riviera) 114.0 in. Overall length: (Skyhawk) 179.3 in.; (Skylark) 200.2 in.; (Century) 196.0 in.; (Regal) 200.0 in.; (LeSabre) 218.2 in.; (Electra) 222.1 in.; (Estate) 216.7 in.; (Riv) 206.6 in. Height: (Skyhawk) 50.2 in.; (Skylark 2-dr.) 52.2 in.; (Skylark 4-dr.) 53.1 in.; (Century cpe) 54.1 in.; (Century sed) 55.0 in.; (Century wagon) 55.7 in.; (Regal) 53.4 in.; (LeSabre/Electra cpe) 55.0 in.; (LeSabre sed) 55.7 in.; (Electra sed) 55.9 in.; (Estate) 56.5 in.; (Riv) 54.3 in. Width: (Skyhawk) 65.4 in.; (Skylark) 72.7 in.; (Century/Regal cpe) 76.5 in.; (Century/Regal) 72.2 in.; (LeSabre/Electra) 77.2 in.; (Estate) 79.9 in.; (Riv) 70.4 in. Front Tread: (Skyhawk) 54.7 in.; (Skylark) 59.1 in.; (Century/Regal) 58.5 in.; (LeSabre/Electra) 61.8 in.; (Estate) 62.2 in.; (Riv) 59.3 in. Rear Tread: (Skyhawk) 53.6 in.; (Skylark) 59.7 in.; (Century/Regal) 57.8 in.; (LeSabre/Electra) 60.7 in.; (Estate) 64.0 in.; (Riv) 60.0 in. Standard Tires: (Skyhawk) BR78 x 13; (Skyhawk 'S') B78 x 13; (Skylark) E78 x 14; (Century cpe/sed) P185/75R14 GBR; (Century wag/Regal) P195/75R14 GBR; (Century/Regal Spt Cpe) P205/70R14 SBR; (LeSabre) FR78 x 15 GBR; (LeSabre Spt Cpe) GR70 x 15 SBR: (Electra) GR78 x 15; (Estate) HR78 x 15 SBR.

TECHNICAL: Transmission: Three-speed, fully synchronized manual gearbox standard on Skylark (column), Century cpe/sed (floor), and Regal cpe (floor); Turbo Hydra-matic optional. Four-speed manual gearbox available on Century/Regal. Four-speed, fully synchronized floor shift standard on Skyhawk; five-speed and automatic optional. Turbo-Hydra-Matic standard on Regal sedan, LeSabre, Electra, Estate and Riviera. Three-speed manual trans. gear ratios: (1st) 3.50:1; (2nd) 1.81:1; (3rd) 1.00:1; (Rev) 3.62:1. Four-speed gear ratios: (1st) 3.50:1; (2nd) 2.48:1; (3rd) 1.66:1; (4th) 1.00:1; (Rev) 3.50:1. Five- speed gear ratios: (1st) 3.40:1; (2nd) 2.08:1; (3rd) 1.39:1; (4th) 1.00:1; (5th) 0.80:1; (Rev) 3.36:1. Automatic trans. gear ratios: (1st) 2.52:1; (2nd) 1.52:1; (3rd) 1.00:1; (Rev) 1.93:1. Electra automatic: (1st) 2.48:1; (2nd) 1.48:1; (3rd) 1.00:1; (Rev) 2.08:1. Century V-8/Riviera automatic: (1st) 2.74:1; (2nd) 1.57:1; (3rd) 1.00:1; (Rev) 2.07:1 (Riviera 2.57:1). Standard axle ratios: (Skyhawk) 2.93:1; (Skylark V-6) 3.08:1; (Skylark V-8) 2.41:1; (Century V6196) 2.93:1; (Century V6231, V8350) 2.73:1; (Century V8301) 2.29:1; (Century V8305) 2.41:1; (Century Turbo cpe) 3.08:1; (Regal) 2.93:1 exc. V-8, 2.29:1; (Regal Sport Coupe) 2.41:1; (LeSabre V-6) 2.73:1; (LeSabre V8301) 2.29:1; (LeSabre V-8) 2.41:1; (LeSabre V-6 Sport Coupe) 2.73:1; (Electra/Riviera) 2.41:1; (Riviera turbo) 2.93:1; (Estate) 2.73:1 exc. V8403, 2.41:1. Steering: recirculating ball; power assist standard on Century/Regal, LeSabre, Electra, Estate and Riviera. Suspension: (Riviera) front wishbones, longitudinal torsion bars and anti-roll bar; independent rear with swinging longitudinal trailing arms, transverse linkage bar and automatic leveling; front-wheel drive. (others) same as 1977- 78. Brakes: front disc, rear drum; power brakes standard on LeSabre/Electra/Riviera plus Century wagon and Regal Sport Coupe. Four-wheel power disc brakes optional on Riviera. Body construction: (Skyhawk) unitized; (Skylark) separate front frame unit cushion-mounted to unitized body; (others) separate body and frame. Fuel tank: (Skyhawk) 18.5 gal.; (Skylark) 21 gal.; (Century/Regal) 18.1 gal.; (LeSabre/Electra) 25.3 gal.; (Estate) 22.5 gal.; (Riv) 20 gal. Unleaded fuel only. High-Energy electronic ignition (HEI) on all engines.

DRIVETRAIN OPTIONS: Engines: 231 cu. in. V-6, 2Bbl.: Century cpe/sed, Regal ($40); Turbocharged 231 cu. in. V-6, 4Bbl.: Century cpe/sed ($470); Riv ($110). 301 cu. in. V-8, 2Bbl.: Century/Regal ($195-$256); LeSabre ($246). 301 cu. in. V-8, 4Bbl.: Century/Regal ($255-$316); 305 cu. in. V-8, 2Bbl.: Skylark ($195); 305 cu. in. V-8, 4Bbl.: Century/Regal ($255-$316). 350 cu. in. V-8, 4Bbl.: Skylark ($320); Century wagon ($320); LeSabre ($371); Riviera S (credit $110). 403 cu. in. V-8, 4Bbl.: Electra/Estate ($70). Transmission/Differential: Four- speed manual floor shift: Century cpe/sed, Regal with 231 V-6 ($135); Five-speed manual floor shift: Skyhawk ($175); Automatic trans.: Skyhawk ($295); Skylark, Century cpe/sed, Regal ($335); Optional rear axle ratio: Skylark 2.9:1, 3.08:1 or 3.23:1 (NC). Limited slip differential ($60-$68) exc. Riviera. Power Accessories: Power brakes: Skyhawk ($71); Skylark/Century/Regal ($76). Four-wheel disc brakes: LeSabre spt cpe, Riv ($205). Power steering: Skyhawk ($146); Skylark/Century/Regal ($163). Suspension: F40 Firm ride/handling pkg.: all exc. Skyhawk ($21). FE2 Rallye ride/handling pkg.: Century/Regal ($38). FE2 Rallye ride/handling pkg. incl. rear stabilizer bar: Skylark ($48), included in Sport package. Automatic level control: Century/Regal/LeSabre/Electra ($121). Other: Trailer towing flasher/harness package: Skylark/Century/Regal/LeSabre?Electra ($22-$35). Heavy-duty alternator, 80-ampere: LeSabre/Electra/Riviera V-8 ($43-$46). Heavy-duty battery ($18-21). Heavy-duty cooling: Skyhawk/Skylark ($30-$58). Heavy-duty radiator: Skylark V-8 ($22). Engine block heater ($15). Heavy-duty engine/transmission cooling: Century/Regal/LeSabre/Electra/Riviera ($30-$58). High altitude emission system ($35). California emission system ($83-$150).

SKYHAWK CONVENIENCE/APPEARANCE OPTIONS: Option Packages: Road Hawk pkg. (BR70 x 13 SBR wide-oval blackwall tires, specific suspension, blackout molding (N/A). Appearance group (wheel opening moldings and bodyside stripe): 'S' ($57). Acoustic pkg. ($25). Convenience group: day/night mirror, underhood light, glove box light, headlamp- on indicator ($24). Shadow light Astroroof ($641). Vista Vent roof ($180). Comfort/Convenience: Air cond. ($496). Rear defogger, electric ($87). Tinted glass ($60). Tinted windshield ($50). Tilt steering ($68). Instrument gauges, electric clock and tach ($73). Electric clock ($21). Visor vanity mirrors, pair ($10). Entertainment: AM/FM radio ($74). AM/FM stereo radio ($148). AM radio and 8-track player ($157). AM/FM stereo radio and 8-track ($250). Rear speaker ($23). Exterior Trim: Door edge guard moldings ($12). Roof crown moldings ($183). Protective bodyside moldings ($10- $45). Designer's accent paint ($175). Interior Trim/Upholstery: Adjustable driver's seatback ($20). Front/rear mats ($21). Custom seatbelts ($18). Wheels and Tires: Custom sport wheels ($58). Styled aluminum wheels ($230). B78 x 13 WSW ($36-$45) BR78 x 13 SBR BSW ($89-$111). BR78 x 13 SBR WSW ($36-$158). BR70 x 13 SBR wide-oval WLT ($49-$194). Conventional spare tire (NC).

SKYLARK CONVENIENCE/APPEARANCE OPTIONS: Option Packages: Sport Coupe or Sport Sedan pkg.: FE2 Rallye ride/handling suspension, ER78 x 14 SBR tires, sport mirrors ($202-$221); N/A on Skylark 'S'. Accessory pkg. (day/night mirror, lighter): 'S' ($15). Acoustic pkg. ($28-$42). Convenience group ($32-$43). Comfort/Convenience: Air cond. ($529). Cruise Master ($103). Two-speed wipers w/low-speed delay ($38). Rear defogger, blower-type ($55). Power windows ($126-$178). Electric door locks ($80-$111). Sport steering wheel ($42). Tilt steering ($75). Tinted glass ($64). Tinted windshield ($50). Dual horns ($10). Electric clock ($24). Headlamps-on indicator ($11). Remote-control left mirror ($18). Sport mirrors: left remote, right manual ($45). Electric trunk release ($24). Entertainment: AM radio ($82). AM/FM radio ($158). AM/FM stereo radio ($236). AM radio and 8-track player ($244). AM/FM stereo radio and 8-track or cassette ($345). Rear speaker ($25). Windshield antenna ($29); incl. w/radios. Exterior Trim: Landau vinyl top ($190- $195). Long vinyl top ($99-$104). Two-tone painted top ($48). Designers' accent paint ($161). Swing-out rear quarter vent window: two-doors ($59). Protective bodyside moldings ($43). Roof drip and wheel opening moldings: 'S' ($38). Rocker panel moldings ($18); std. on Custom. Wide rocker appearance group ($45). Decklid molding ($10). Custom door and window frame moldings ($28-$35). Door edge guards ($13-$21). Bodyside stripes ($34). Bumper guards, front/rear ($45). Bumper strips, front/rear ($37). Interior Trim/Upholstery: Full- length console ($80). Vinyl bucket trim: base Skylark ($90). Custom seatbelts ($19-$21). Front carpet savers ($15). Carpet savers and handy mats ($25). Carpeted door trim with map pocket and reflector: base ($43). Wheels: Styled wheels ($80- $99). Chrome-plated wheels ($120-$139). Deluxe wheel covers ($42). Custom wire wheel covers ($118-$160). Tires: E78 x 14 WSW ($37-$46). ER78 x 14 SBR BSW ($78-$97). ER78 x 14 SBR WSW ($37-$143). FR78 x 14 SBR WLT ($67-$180). Stowaway spare tire ($19).

CENTURY/REGAL CONVENIENCE/APPEARANCE OPTIONS: Option Packages and Groups: Regal Sport Coupe Decor ($473). Century Special Sport Wagon pkg. ($473). Century Turbo Coupe pkg.: special suspension, sporty exhaust, turbine wheels, decklid identification ($40). Electric sunroof: coupe ($529). Silver electric Astroroof: coupe ($729). Hurst hatch roof: Regal ($655). Exterior molding pkg. ($10-$147). Convenience group ($6-$58). Comfort/Convenience: Air cond. ($562). Automatic air cond. ($653). Cruise Master ($103). Rear defogger, electric ($99). Tinted glass ($70). Tinted windshield ($50). Six-way power driver's seat ($163). Manual seatback recliner ($62). Custom steering wheel: Century ($10). Sport steering wheel ($32-$42). Tilt steering ($75). Power windows ($132-$187). Electric door locks ($86-$120). Electric trunk release ($24). Remote tailgate lock: Century wag ($25). Electric dial clock ($24). Digital clock ($55). Headlamps-on indicator ($11). Trip odometer ($13). Instrument gauges ($27). Fuel usage light and instrument gauges ($57). Dome reading lamp ($19). Windshield wiper w/delay ($38). Lighting and Mirrors: Cornering lamps: Regal ($49). Front light monitors ($29). Remote left mirror ($18); right ($34- $39). Sport mirrors: left remote ($40-$45). Dual remote sport mirrors ($25-$70). Visor vanity mirrors, pair ($10). Lighted right visor vanity mirror ($46). Entertainment: AM radio ($86). AM/FM radio ($163). AM/FM stereo radio ($236). AM radio w/8-track ($248); w/digital readout ($402); w/CB ($574). AM/FM stereo radio w/8-track or cassette ($345-$351). Rear speaker ($25). Windshield antenna ($29); incl. with radios. Automatic antenna ($47-$76). Triband power antenna ($86-$115). Exterior Trim: Landau vinyl top: Regal ($146- $162); heavy-padded ($178-$228). Long vinyl top ($116). Designers' accent paint ($161-$213). Solid special color paint ($152). Bumper guards, front/rear ($45). Protective bodyside moldings ($48). Rocker panel moldings: Century Special ($18). Door edge guards ($13-$21). Belt reveal moldings ($34). Wheel opening moldings: Century Spec. wag ($22). Bodyside stripes ($34). Woodgrain vinyl applique: Century wag ($267-$289). Luggage rack: Century wag ($90). Air deflector: Century wag ($30). Interior Trim/Upholstery: Full- length console ($90). Bucket seats: Century Custom, Regal ($45); Century sport ($181). 55/45 seating: Century Custom, Regal ($102); Century spt ($238). Limited 55/45 seating: Regal spt cpe ($272). Notchback seating: Century spt ($136). Custom seatbelts ($19-$22). Load floor carpet area: Century Spec. wag ($51). Front carpet savers ($15-$25). Carpet savers and mats ($25). Front/rear carpet savers with inserts ($45). Litter pocket ($9). Trunk trim covering ($31). Loackable storage compartment: Century wag ($37-$42). Wheels: Chrome-plated wheels ($44-$169). Designer's sport wheels ($106-$125). Deluxe wheel covers: Century exc. spt ($42). Designer's wheel covers: Century exc. spt ($70); Regal ($28). Custom wire wheel covers: Century exc. spt ($160); Regal ($118). Tires: P185/75R14 GBR WSW: Century cpe/sed ($39). P195/75R14 GBR BSW: Century cpe/sed ($21). P195/75R14 GBR WSW ($40-$61). P195/75R14 SBR BSW: Century ($41-$61). P195/75R14 SBR WSW: Century ($81-$101). P205/70R14 SBR wide-oval BSW: Regal ($32). P205/70R14 SBR WSW: Century spt, Regal ($44- $76). P205/70R14 SBR WLT ($56-$149).

LESABRE/ELECTRA/ESTATE WAGON CONVENIENCE/APPEARANCE OPTIONS: Option Packages: LeSabre coupe Sport pkg.: cloth front bucket seats, remote sport mirror ($160); w/ full-length console ($254). Estate Wagon convenience group ($13-$68). Estate Wagon Limited pkg.: 55/45 front seating, tilt steering, custom belts, power windows, electric door locks, remote tailgate lock, remote left mirror, chromed wheels, luggage rack, bumper guards, map light, dial clock, exterior molding pkg., woodgrain vinyl applique, acoustic pkg., special ornamentation ($1853). Exterior molding pkg. ($53-$173). Convenience group: LeSabre ($19-$99). Electric sunroof ($725- $798). Sliding Astroroof ($925-$998). Comfort/Convenience: Air cond. ($605). Automatic air cond. ($688). Cruise Master ($108). Rear defogger, electric ($101). Tinted glass ($84). Tinted windshield: LeSabre, Estate ($51). Power windows: LeSabre, Estate ($138-$205). Electric door locks ($88-$122). Automatic door locks: Electra ($146-$175). Six-way power driver's seat ($135-$166). Dual power seats ($301-$332); N/A on base models. Manual seatback recliner, one side: LeSabre base or sport cpe ($62). Electric seatback recliner, one side ($118); N/A on base LeSabre sedan. Custom steering wheel: base LeSabre ($10). Sport steering wheel: LeSabre ($32-$42). Tilt steering ($77). Tilt/telescoping steering column ($44- $131). Digital clock: LeSabre, Estate (NC w/convenience group). Low fuel indicator ($17). Fuel usage light ($30). Speed alert and trip odometer ($23). Remote electric tailgate lock: Est ($34). Electric trunk release ($25). Electric fuel cap lock ($36). Theft deterrent system ($135); N/A on Estate. Three-speed wiper w/low-speed delay ($39). Lighting, Horns and Mirrors: Cornering lamps ($49). Front light monitors: LeSabre/Est ($29). Front/rear monitors: Electra ($62). Door courtesy/warning light ($36-$57). Rear courtesy lamps: Estate ($16). Headlamps-on indicator ($11). Dome reading lamp ($19). Sunshade map light: Electra 225 ($13). Four-note horn ($23). Remote left mirror: LeSabre/Est ($19). Remote right mirror ($34-$39). Dual remote sport mirrors ($49-$65). Dual electric remote mirrors: Electra ($97). Remote left mirror w/thermometer ($21-$38). Dual electric mirrors w/left thermometer: Electra ($118). Visor vanity mirrors, pair ($10). Lighted visor vanity mirror ($47). Entertainment: AM radio ($99); N/A on Electra. AM/FM radio ($174). AM/FM stereo radio ($239); w/CB ($581). AM/FM stereo radio w/digital readout: LeSabre, Estate ($347-$402). AM radio and 8-track ($265). AM/FM stereo radio and 8-track or cassette player ($349-$355). AM/FM stereo with 8-track and CB: Electra ($691). Signal-seeking AM/FM stereo radio with CB: Electra ($789); w/CB and 8-track ($899). Signal-seeking AM/FM stereo radio w/digital readout: Electra ($447); w/8-track ($557). Rear speaker ($26). Windshield antenna ($29); incl. w/radios. Automatic power antenna ($48-$77). Triband power antenna ($87-$116). Exterior Trim: Landau vinyl top: LeSabre ($155). Heavy-padded landau vinyl top: Electra ($200). Long vinyl top ($145-$164). Long, heavy-padded vinyl top: Electra ($206). Two-tone painted top: LeSabre ($58). Designers' accent paint: LeSabre, Estate ($182-$240). Solid special color paint ($153) exc. Firemist on Electra ($172). Protective bodyside moldings: LeSabre/Est ($43). Color-coordinated bodyside moldings: Electra ($66). Hood ornament and windsplit: LeSabre/Est ($25). Door edge guards ($14-$21). Window frame scalp molding: LeSabre/Est ($34). Wheel opening moldings: LeSabre/Est ($27). Belt reveal molding: LeSabre spt cpe ($34). Bodyside stripes ($52); N/A on Estate. Woodgrain vinyl applique: Estate ($293). Bumper guards, front/rear ($45). Luggage rack w/air deflector: Est ($140). Interior Trim/Upholstery: Custom seat trim: notchback, LeSabre spt cpe or Estate ($404); 55/45 ($506); 55/45, LeSabre Ltd or Electra ($102). Third seat: Estate ($194). Custom seatbelts: LeSabre/Est ($22-$25). Full-length console: LeSabre cpe w/sport pkg. ($94). Front carpet savers ($15-$25). Front/rear carpet savers w/inserts ($45). Litter pocket ($9). Trunk carpeting/covering ($48-$60). Wheels: Deluxe wheel covers: LeSabre ($42). Custom wheel covers ($29-$71). Wire wheel covers ($87-$161). Chrome-plated wheels ($120-$171). Wire spoke wheels ($473-$625). Stowaway spare tire (N/C).

RIVIERA CONVENIENCE/APPEARANCE OPTIONS: Roof Options: Electric sunroof ($798). Electric Astroroof ($998). Comfort/Convenience: Automatic air cond. ($88). Cruise Master ($108). Rear defogger, electric ($101). Automatic door locks ($58). Six-way power seat, passenger ($166). Electric seatback recliner, one side ($118). Manual seatback recliner, one side: S ($62). Sport steering wheel ($32). Tilt steering ($77). Tilt/telescope steering wheel ($121). Electric fuel cap lock ($36). Electric trunk releease ($25). Electric trunk lock ($60). Low fuel indicator, V-8 ($17). Fuel usage light, V-8 ($30). Lighting, Horns and Mirrors: Coach lamps ($85); incl. w/vinyl top. Front/rear light monitors ($62). Courtesy/reading lamp ($42). Lighted door lock and interior light control ($57). Headlamps-on indicator ($11). Four-note horn ($23). Remote left mirror w/thermometer ($21). Dual electric remote mirrors ($58); w/left thermometer ($79). Lighted visor vanity mirrors, each ($47). Entertainment: AM/FM stereo w/8-track or cassette player ($110-$116). AM/FM stereo radio w/CB ($294); w/CB and 8-track ($404). Signal-seeking AM/FM stereo radio w/digital readout ($182); w/8-track ($292). Signal-seeking AM/CB/FM stereo radio w/digital clock ($524); w/8-track and clock ($634). Triband power antenna ($39). Exterior Trim:

Heavy- padded landau top ($285). Long vinyl top ($285). Designers' accent paint ($193). Solid color special paint ($153) exc. Firemist ($172). Rear bumper guards ($22). Protective bodyside moldings ($59). Door edge guards ($14). Bodyside stripes ($52). Interior Trim/Upholstery: 45/55 notchback front seat, leather/vinyl ($350). Leather/vinyl bucket seats: S ($350). Front/rear carpet savers w/inserts ($57). Trunk mat ($12).

HISTORY: Introduced: September 28, 1978. Model year production (U.S.): 727,275. Calendar year production (U.S.): 787,123. Model year sales by U.S. dealers: 754,619 (including 17,564 imported Opels). Calendar year sales (U.S.): 714,508 which, though down significantly, still gave Buick an increased market share of 8.6 percent.

Historical Footnotes: Buick expected to emphasize the mid-size Century lineup with the new Turbo Coupe, but buyers still liked the look of Regal better. Most models rose in price during the model year, but none so dramatically as Electra, which shot upward by over a thousand dollars. Many observers felt that the all- new Riviera, built in Linden, New Jersey, was more a descendant of the 1963 original than the 1970s boattail version. *Motor Trend* named it "Car of the Year," the first Buick granted that title since the 1962 Special with its V-6 powerplant.

1980 BUICK

First arrival for the 1980 model year was the new Skylark, continuing the old name but on an all-new front- wheel drive chassis, cousin to the soon-to-be-notorious Chevrolet Citation X-car. All the X-bodies debuted in April. Century kept the aero-style fastback coupe a little longer, but sedans took on a fresh notchback appearance for 1980. Full-size LeSabres and Electras were restyled with aerodynamics in mind. New higher-pressure tires offered less rolling resistance. Riviera, Electra and LeSabre now had match-mounted tires/wheels. Some automatic transmissions contained a torque converter clutch to reduce slippage loss. Buick fielded three new engines: a larger 252 cu. in. (4.1-liter) version of the familiar Buick 3.8-liter V-6; a lightweight 265 cu. in. (4.3-liter) 2Bbl. V-8 option for Century and Regal, intended as a middle ground between the 3.8 V-6 and 4.9 V-8; and a 5.7-liter diesel V-8 produced by Oldsmobile. Standard on Electras, the 4.1 had a larger bore than the 3.8, siamesed (no water jacket between the bores) to allow for the larger pistons. It had a new aluminum intake manifold, steel head gaskets (rather than composition), intake manifold gaskets with smaller exhaust gas crossover holes, and revised engine mounts. The new diesel, available in Electras and Estates (later on LeSabre), differed a bit from the 5.7 diesel previously offered by other GM divisions. Its new fuel nozzle didn't require a return system to the fuel tank. For the first time, a V-6 was offered in every Buick series. The big 403 (6.6-liter) V-8 was finally gone. So were the small 3.2-liter V-6, and the 301 (4.9-liter) 2Bbl. V-8. Joining the option list was Twilight Sentinel, an automatic headlight control that would turn Electra or Riviera lights on when it grew dark, then off again as daylight emerged. The system, formerly available on Cadillacs, also kept headlights on for three minutes after you shut the engine off. Also new: tungsten-halogen high-beam headlamps that produced an intense white beam, standard on Regal/LeSabre Sport Coupes and Riviera S Type, optional elsewhere in the lineup. Electronic Touch Climate Control on Electra and LeSabre used a row of touch surfaces on a smooth panel in place of the usual protruding knobs and switches. Stereo entertainment stretched all the way up to a new six-speaker Concert Sound System available in the Electra Park Avenue sedan. Buick's Theft Deterrent System included door and trunk locks, plus a starter interrupt system to prevent the engine from firing.

1980 Skyhawk "Road Hawk" hatchback coupe (AA)

SKYHAWK — SERIES 4H — V-6 — For its final year in this form, Skyhawk received only modest interior changes. In addition to standard and 'S' models, the sporty "Road Hawk" was offered again. That package included Oyster White bucket seats with hawk accents; flat black wipers, grille, headlamp trim and molding; plus a rear spoiler and special suspension. The body featured silver/gray accent paint and striping. The Designers' Accent Edition, also available again this year, included a hawk decal, rear spoiler and special paint. Buick's subcompact was dropped early in the model year, to permit increased production of other H-Special bodied GM models. The name would return to an all-new model for 1982. Skyhawk's standard equipment included a maintenance-free battery, AM radio, front/rear bumper guards, protective bumper strips, deluxe wheel covers, carpeting, cigarette lighter, full-length console, high-energy ignition, day/night inside mirror, outside sport mirrors (left remote), vinyl bucket seats, sport steering wheel, rear stabilizer bar, space-saver spare tire, and four-speed floor shift. The 'S' Skyhawk lacked wheel opening moldings and bodyside stripes.

SKYLARK — SERIES 4X — FOUR/V-6 — To tumultous fanfare and glowing reviews, the new front-wheel drive Skylark, far different from its predecessor of that name, arrived in spring 1979 as an early 1980 model. Weighing much less (700-800 pounds) than prior Skylarks, it was part of the X-body family that also included Chevrolet Citation, Oldsmobile Omega, and Pontiac Phoenix. Fuel- efficient, with a roomy interior, transverse-mounted engine (four or V-6) and standard door and window frame moldings, the new Skylark came in standard and Limited or Sport trim. A compact spare tire replaced the old full-size version. The suspension used coil springs all around. The new Skylark was 19 inches shorter than its forerunner, and far more expensive (by some $1500). It carried five passengers (six with squeezing) and was

1980 Skylark Sport Coupe (AA)

powered by a standard "Iron Duke" 2.5-liter four-cylinder engine from Pontiac, or optional Chevrolet-built 2.8-liter V-6. The base Skylark and Limited had a slightly peaked checkerboard grille, single rectangular recessed headlamps, and vertical parking/signal lamps at the outer edge of the front-end. A Skylark nameplate was at the forward end of the front fenders; Buick lettering on the trunk lid. On the roof pillar was a round emblem. Skylark's standard AM radio could be deleted for credit. Other standard equipment included a four-speed manual transmission with floor shift lever, compact spare tire, glass-belted radial tires, rack-and- pinion steering, step-on parking brake, locking glove compartment, cigarette lighter, and cloth or vinyl notchback seating. The Limited had tan upholstery in brushed woven fabric, plus carpeted lower door panels and under-dash courtesy lamps. Other Limited extras were gas-assisted hood struts, acoustical insulation, stand-up hood ornament and windsplit molding, wheel opening moldings, wide rocker moldings that extended to front fenders and rear quarters, and deluxe wheel covers. Skylark's Sport Coupe and Sport Sedan options had an entirely different three-row, six-section blackout grille, with body-colored horizontal separators. They also had black body moldings, bright wheel opening moldings, bumper strips front and rear, smoked taillamp lenses, sport steering wheel, Designers' Sport road wheels, and amber parking/signal lamps up front. Sport Skylarks also carried a heftier Rallye suspension, larger rear stabilizer bar, black dash treatment with full instruments including a voltmeter, and P205/70R13 blackwall steel-belted radials. For extra accent, they could have wide lower body stripes with a hawk decal. One pleasant option: a flip-open glass sunroof. Before long, all the X-cars would be plagued by a long list of safety recalls and mechanical problems, which resulted in one of the worst reputations among modern American automobiles. Chevrolet's Citation got the worst publicity of the bunch, but the troubles affected all of the 980-85 X-bodied models, even though the most serious recalls applied only to the early editions.

1980 Century Sport Turbo Aerodynamic Coupe (AA)

CENTURY — SERIES 4A — V-6/V-8 After two years in slantback form, a new notchback sedan roofline replaced the fastback shape on two-door Century models. These new, dramatically styled sedans had a more formal appearance than before, resembling both Skylark and Regal. Styling features included wraparound taillamps, an angular-look decklid, and sloping fenders. A horizontal grille and new signal lamps emphasized the car's angular appearance. The four-row, eight-column crosshatch grille had a tiny crosshatch pattern within each segment. Vertical rectangular parking/signal lights sat between the single recessed rectangular headlamps and the grille, with amber lenses around the fender corners. Century coupes retained the fastback design for one final attempt at luring buyers. Custom and Special designations were dropped, with their equivalents now called, simply, Century. Thus, Century came in two trim levels: base and Limited. Optional models included a Turbo coupe and Sport coupe. This year saw a larger standard engine: the 231 cu. in. (3.8-liter) V-6. Options included new 4.3-liter and 4.9-liter V-8s (5.0-liter in California), plus the turbocharged V-6. Power brakes became standard this year. Century included a dome light; Limited added lights for front ashtray, under- dash courtesy, and glove compartment. Seats were upholstered in supple vinyl or plush, crushed-knit cloth; 55/45 type in the Limited sedan. Standard Century equipment included three-speed manual transmission, fiberglass-belted radial tires, compact spare tire, wide-view day/night mirror, protective bumper strips, and stand-up hood ornament. The Limited also offered wheel opening moldings and bodyside stripes. On the station wagon front, Century fielded standard and Estate (formerly Custom) Wagons, plus a Sport Wagon option. Each sat six, or held 71.8 cubic feet of cargo with second seat folded down. The Sport Wagon package contained black headlamp and grille trim, wipers, window reveal moldings, center pillar, wide rocker treatment, wheel opening moldings, air deflector, and sport mirrors; plus a hawk decal, Rallye suspension, and P205/70R14 steel-belted radial tires on Designers' Sport wheels. Sport Coupe and Turbo Coupe options had a black treatment on grille, headlamp bezels, windshield wiper arms, pillars, moldings, decklid panel, and instrument panel trim; plus twin sport mirrors and a functional rear spoiler. A hawk decal was on the front fender, just ahead of the door. Black- trimmed instrument panel, too. They also had the ride-and- handling Rallye package with firmer springs and shocks, plus larger-diameter stabilizer bars, Designers' Sport wheels, and P205/70R14 steel-belted radials. The Turbo version included a special bulged hood with 'Turbo 3.8 Litre' nameplate, Turbo Coupe identification on body side and deck lid, turbine wheels, and exhaust system with what Buick described as a "rather authoritative voice." Styled aluminum wheels were available for the first time on the Sport versions.

1980 Regal Sport Turbo Coupe (AA)

REGAL — SERIES 4A — V-6/V-8 — Regal's new look included wider taillamps and quad rectangular headlamps. It came in Limited and Sport Coupe trim, as well as standard Regal. New taillamps split by horizontal lines, stretching from license plate to decklid edge, gave a wider look to the back end. A restyled grille had an undivided, tight checkerboard pattern that angled outward at the base in the Buick style. Park/signal lamps set in the base of the front bumper. Regal Limited had special wide chrome rocker panel moldings, as well as standard crushed velour cloth upholstery. The Sport Coupe, still powered by a turbocharged 231 cu. in. (3.8-liter) V-6 engine, could have an optional Designers' Accent paint treatment, blacked-out grille and headlamp trim, plus sport mirrors and turbine wheels. New tungsten-halogen high beams that produced intense white light were standard on Sport Coupe, optional on other Regals. "Once in a while," declared the brochure describing the Regal Somerset limited edition, "you have an opportunity to buy a first edition....So owning one will be a rare treat." Owning one today might be similarly pleasing. The two-tone body came only in Somerset Tan and Dark Blue Designers' Accent. The dark blue swept back over the hood and onto the top of the roof. The package (offered for the Limited coupe) included wire wheel covers, sleek sport mirrors, and special Somerset identification on front fenders. Inside, the tan and dark blue motif continued with special Somerset design plush knit velour 55/45 seat upholstery and dark blue carpeting. A color-keyed umbrella fit in a pouch on the back of the front seat. Brushed aluminum trim highlighted the instrument panel and doors. There was a roof-mounted passenger assist strap, plus Somerset identification on the glove box door. Regal's base powerplant was the 231 cu. in. (3.8-liter) two-barrel, with other engine possibilities the new 265 (4.3- liter) two-barrel V-8, or 301 (4.9-liter) four-barrel. Power brakes and steering were standard. So were steel-belted radial tires, compact spare tire, day/night inside mirror, twin chrome outside mirrors, wipers with mist feature, an underhood light, and cigarette lighter. Regals had bumper guards and protective strips front and rear, a stand-up hood ornament, windshield and back window reveal moldings, and wheel opening moldings. Regal Limited added wide rocker moldings (extending to front fenders and rear quarter panels), belt reveal moldings, and bright pillar moldings.

1980 LeSabre Limited coupe (AA)

LESABRE — SERIES 4B — V-6/V-8 — New sheet metal arrived on both LeSabre and Electra to produce a lower, longer front end appearance. The reshaped rear end was higher, with a sharper forward thrust to the decklid. A rear deck spoiler treatment, sloping hood, and reduced front-end radius improved the car's aerodynamics, cutting air drag by a claimed 14 percent. New recessed quad rectangular headlamps, set in bezels with a vertical dividing wall, highlighted the angular look. A new checkerboard grille had large holes in four rows, and the bottom row extended outward all the way to fender edges. At the side of the grille was a Buick badge. Parking/signal lamps were now set into the bumper. The familiar LeSabre "ventiport" fender trim, descended from old Buick portholes, faded away with the new restyle. LeSabres now rode on high-pressure, low-rolling- resistance tires. Match-mounted tires and wheels, plus new shock absorbers, improved ride quality. Powerplant was again the standard 3.8-liter V-6, but a new and bigger 252 cu. in. (4.1-liter) V-6 was also offered (except in California). LeSabre could also have Oldsmobile's 350 cu. in. diesel V-8. The dashboard included a blacked-out panel that showed information on headlight beam, engine conditions, brake warning, and a seat belt reminder. A new side-frame jack was standard; wheel covers were new. Optional: a theft-deterrent system with starter interrupt. LeSabre's Sport Coupe featured a blacked-out grille, black window and side moldings, plus chrome wheels. Also a ride/handling package with large stabilizer bars, firm springs and shock valving, and fast-ratio power steering. Sport Coupes were again powered by the turbocharged 231 cu. in. V-6 with four-barrel carburetor. The dash had a vacuum boost light. Standard equipment included bucket seats, full-length console, tungsten-halogen headlamps, sport mirrors and sport steering wheel. Four-wheel disc brakes were optional. Standard LeSabre equipment included wheel opening and roof drip scale moldings, bumper protective strips and guards, rear end panel molding, notchback seating (cloth or vinyl), and a compact spare tire. To the basic list, LeSabre Limited added such styling touches as deluxe wheel covers, rocker panel moldings and black pillar applique.

ESTATE WAGON — SERIES 4B — V-8 — Not much was new in the Estate Wagon arena, as was usually the case. The LeSabre Estate seated six, with a third seat available, and had 86.8 cubic foot cargo volume. Standard powerplant was a 4.9-liter (301 cu. in.) gasoline V-8 this year (except in California); but the familiar 350 (5.7-liter) V-8 was available too. Electra's new Estate Wagon differed little and had the same engine choices. For the extra price, Electra buyers got standard air conditioning, tilt steering column, digital clock, remote-control left outside mirror, 55/45 notchback seating (cloth or vinyl), power windows, and chrome wheels. All Estates had mist wipers, dual outside mirrors, front and rear bumper guards with protective strips, power brakes and steering, and automatic transmission.

1980 Electra Estate Wagon (AA)

ELECTRA — SERIES 4C — V-6/V-8 — Sporting a new vertical-style grille, sloping fenders and higher decklid, Electra presented a streamlined appearance--and lost over 200 pounds of curb weight. Standard engine, except in California, was the new 252 cu. in. (4.1- liter) V-6, with 350 (5.7-liter) V-8 optional. For the first time, a diesel was also available. The new grille was divided into sections by nine vertical bars, tapering outward at the base, with Buick badge at the side. Quad rectangular headlamps sat in recessed housings. Park/signal lamps were inset in the bumper bottom. Electra's hood had a slight downward rake. The Electra 225 designation was dropped, replaced by Limited and Park Avenue series (those were formerly models rather than series). An Electra Estate Wagon was added (see above). Suspensions now used Pliacell-R- shock absorbers, and a new compact spare tire rested in the trunk. Park Avenue coupe and sedan instrument panels and coach lamps used new electro-luminescent lighting. Park Avenue also had a new standard padded-vinyl roof, plus knit velour fabric upholstery with a draped, sheared look (leather available). Both Limited and Park Avenue had new higher- pressure tires that offered less rolling resistance. New tungsten-halogen high-beam headlamps were available. So were 14 choices of entertainment systems, including a Concert Sound System for the Park Avenue with six speakers. Park Avenue also had exclusive Touch Climate Control with no levers, buttons or switches; just a smooth touch panel. Electra kept their four-section "ventiports," which formed part of the Park Avenue's wide full-length bodyside molding.

1980 Riviera coupe (AA)

RIVIERA — SERIES 4E — V-6/V-8 — The downsized Riviera body that had been introduced for 1979 received modest refinements this year, including revised body mounts. Rivs also got match-mounted tires and wheels, retuned shock absorbers, restyled mirrors that fit snugly against the car body for an integrated look, and a selection of new interior fabrics. Options included Twilight Sentinel, which gave automatic control of outside lights, controlled by a sensor atop the dashboard. As before, Riviera was front-drive, with fully independent suspension and 350 cu. in. (5.7-liter) V-8 engine. Pliacell-R- shock absorbers were new, as was an optional theft-deterrent system with starter interrupt system. Also optional: a digital Trip Monitor that displayed a selection of travel and engine functions. Riviera standard equipment included automatic transmission, power front disc brakes, cornering lights, six- way power driver's seat, power steering, digital clock, automatic level control, air conditioning, electric door locks, remote-controlled outside mirrors, and Delco AM/FM stereo radio with power antenna. One of the new interior colors, brown, was a Riviera exclusive. Four-wheel disc brakes were again available. Riviera's S Type had been chosen 1979 Car of the Year by *Motor Trend.* New flat black, styled outside mirrors complemented its flat black trim around windows, grille and rocker panels. Powerplant remained the turbocharged 231 cu. in. V-6 with four-barrel carb. Bucket seats were velour upholstered with ribbed inserts; the instrument panel was black-accented.

I.D. DATA: For one more year, a 13-symbol Vehicle Identification Number (VIN) was on the upper left surface of the instrument panel, visible through the windshield. Coding was similar to 1979, with the first digit ('4') indicating the Buick division. The next letter indicates series: 'S' Skyhawk; 'T' Skyhawk S; 'B' Skylark; 'C' Skylark Limited; 'E' Century wagon; 'H' Century cpe/sed and Estate wagon; 'G' Century Sport Coupe; 'L' Century Ltd.; 'J' Regal; 'K' Regal Sport Coupe; 'M' Regal Ltd.; 'F' LeSabre Sport Coupe; 'N' LeSabre; 'P' LeSabre Limited; 'R' LeSabre Estate; 'I' Electra Estate; 'X' Electra Limited; 'W' Electra Park Ave.; 'Z' Riviera; 'Y' Riviera S Type. The next two digits denote body type: '07' Skyhawk hatchback coupe; '09' aero 4-dr. sedan; '37' Skylark/LeSabre/Electra 2-dr. coupe; '47' Regal 2-dr. coupe; '57' Riviera 2-dr. coupe; '87' aero 2-dr. coupe; '69' 4-dr. sedan; '35' 4-dr. wagon. The fifth symbol indicated engine code: '5' 4-151 2Bbl.; '7' V6-173 2Bbl.; 'A' V6-231 2Bbl.; '3' Turbo V6-231 4Bbl.; 'S' V8-265 2Bbl.; 'W' V8-301 4Bbl.; 'H' V8-305 4Bbl.; 'R' V8-350 4Bbl. (L34); 'X' V8-350 4Bbl. (L77). The sixth symbol denotes model year ('A' 1980). Next is a plant code: '7' Lordstown, OH; 'W' Willow Run, MI; '6' Oklahoma City, OK; 'G' Framingham, MA; 'H' Flint, MI; 'Z' Fremont, CA; 'X' Fairfax, KS; 'E' Linden, NJ. The final six digits are the sequential serial number, which began with 100001, except 400001 for Skyhawks and for LeSabre/Electra/Estate models built at Flint. Engine numbers were stamped on the front right of the block, except for L34 and LF9 350 cu. in. V-8s, which were stamped on the front of the left side of the block; LD5, LC8 and LC6 V-6s, on left rear of block; Skylark V-6, on rear (or front) of right rocker cover; and Skylark four, on pad at left front below cylinder head. The body number plate on the shroud was the same as before.

42

SKYHAWK (V-6)

Series Number	Body/Style Number	Body Type & Seating	Factory Price	Shipping Weight	Production Total
4H	T07	2-dr 'S' Hatch-4P	4993	2754	Note 1
4H	S07	2-dr. Hatch-4P	5211	2754	Note 1

Note 1: Total production for the model year, 8,322 Skyhawks.

SKYLARK (FOUR/V-6)

4X	B37	2-dr Coupe-5P	5160/5385	2410/2449	55,114
4X	B69	4-dr Sedan-5P	5306/5531	2438/2477	80,940

SKYLARK LIMITED (FOUR/V-6)

4X	C37	2-dr Coupe-5P	5579/5804	2438/2477	42,652
4X	C69	4-dr Sedan-5P	5726/5951	2478/2517	86,948

SKYLARK SPORT (FOUR/V-6)

4X	D37	2-dr Coupe-5P	5774/5999	2443/2482	Note 2
4X	D69	4-dr Sedan-5P	5920/6145	2471/2510	Note 2

Note 2: Production of Skylark Sport models is included in Limited totals above. Total Limited production: 100,396.

CENTURY (V-6/V-8)

4A	H87	2-dr Aero Cpe-6P	5546/5751	3086/3190	1,074
4A	H69	4-dr Sedan-6P	5646/5851	3106/3210	129,740
4A	E35	4-dr Sta Wag-6P	5922/6102	3236/3364	6,493
4A	H35	4-dr Est Wag-6P	6220/6400	3247/3375	11,122

CENTURY SPORT (V-6/V-8)

4A	G87	2-dr Aero Cpe-6P	6063/6243	3150/3254	Note 3

CENTURY LIMITED (V-6/V-8)

4A	L69	4-dr Sedan-6P	6132/6337	3150/3254	Note 3

Note 3: Production figures shown for Century include Sport and Limited models.

REGAL (V-6/V-8)

4A	J47	2-dr Coupe-6P	6305/6485	3115/3243	Note 4

REGAL SPORT COUPE (TURBO V-6)

4A	K47	2-dr Coupe-6P	6952	3194	Note 4

REGAL LIMITED (V-6/V-8)

4A	M47	2-dr Coupe-6P	6724/6904	3142/3370	Note 4

Note 4: Total model year production, 214,735 Regals. Note 5: Prices shown after slash for Century/Regal V-8 are for the smaller (265 cu. in.) version; larger V-8 cost $115 more.

LESABRE (V-6/V-8)

4B	N37	2-dr Coupe-6P	6674/6971	3320/3440	8,342
4B	N69	4-dr Sedan-6P	6769/7064	3369/3497	23,873

LESABRE LIMITED (V-6/V-8)

4B	P37	2-dr Coupe-6P	6929/7224	3327/3455	20,561
4B	P69	4-dr Sedan-6P	7071/7366	3375/3503	37,676

LESABRE SPORT (TURBO V-6)

4B	F37	2-dr Coupe-6P	7782	3430	Note 6

Note 6: Production of Sport Turbo Coupe is included in totals for standard LeSabre coupe.

LESABRE ESTATE WAGON (V-8)

4B	R35	4-dr Sta Wag-6P	7673	3898	9,318
4B	(AQ4)	4-dr 3S Wag-8P	7866	3928	Note 7

Note 7: Three-seat Estate Wagon was actually an option package (AQ4); production of all Estate Wagons is included in above figure.

ELECTRA LIMITED (V-6/V-8)

4C	X37	2-dr Coupe-6P	9132/9467	3571/3756	14,058
4C	X69	4-dr Sedan-6P	9287/9622	3578/3763	54,422

ELECTRA PARK AVENUE (V-6/V-8)

4C	W37	2-dr Coupe-6P	10244/10579	3600/3785	Note 8
4C	W69	4-dr Sedan-6P	10383/10718	3607/3792	Note 8

Note 8: Production figures shown for Electra Limited include Park Avenue.

ELECTRA ESTATE WAGON (V-8)

4C	V35	4-dr Sta Wag-6P	10513	4105	N/A
4C	(AQ4)	4-dr 3S Wag-8P	10706	4135	N/A

RIVIERA (V-8)

4E	Z57	2-dr Coupe-4P	11492	3741	41,404

RIVIERA S TYPE TURBO (V-6)

4E	Y57	2-dr Coupe-4P	11823	3633	7,217

FACTORY PRICE AND WEIGHT NOTE: Figure before the slash is for V-6 engine, after the slash for smallest (lowest-priced) V-8 engine available. For Skylark, figure before the slash is for four-cylinder engine, after the slash for V-6.

ENGINES: BASE FOUR (Skylark): Inline, ohv, four-cylinder. Cast iron block and head. Displacement: 151 cu. in. (2.5 liters). Bore & stroke: 4.0 x 3.0 in. Compression ratio: 8.2:1. Brake horsepower: 90 at 4000 R.P.M. Torque: 134 lbs.-ft. at 2400 R.P.M. Five main bearings. Hydraulic valve lifters. Carburetor: 2Bbl. Rochester 2SE (Varajet II). VIN Code: 5. Sales Code: LW9. OPTIONAL V-6 (Skylark): 60-degree, overhead-valve V-6. Cast iron alloy block and head. Displacement: 173 cu. in. (2.8 liters). Bore & stroke: 3.5 x 3.0 in. Compression ratio: 8.5:1. Brake horsepower: 115 at 4800 R.P.M. Torque: 145 lbs.-ft. at 2400 R.P.M. Four main bearings. Hydraulic valve lifters. Carburetor: 2Bbl. Rochester 2SE. VIN Code: 7. Sales Code: LE2. BASE V-6 (Skyhawk, Century, Regal, LeSabre): 90-degree, overhead-valve V-6. Cast iron alloy block and head. Displacement: 231 cu. in. (3.8 liters). Bore & stroke: 3.8 x 3.4 in. Compression ratio: 8.0:1. Brake horsepower: 110 at 3800 R.P.M. Torque: 190 lbs.-ft. at 1600 R.P.M. Four main bearings. Hydraulic valve lifters. Carburetor: 2Bbl. Rochester M2ME. Even-firing. VIN Code: A. Sales Code: LD5. TURBOCHARGED V-6 (Regal and LeSabre Sport Coupes, Riviera S); OPTIONAL (Century, Riviera): Same as 231 V-6 above, but with M4ME four-barrel carburetor. Brake horsepower: 170 at 4000 R.P.M. Torque: 265 lbs.-ft. at 2400 R.P.M. VIN Code: 3. Sales Code: LC8. BASE V-6 (Electra); OPTIONAL (LeSabre): 90-degree, overhead-valve V-6. Cast iron alloy block and head. Displacement: 252 cu. in. (4.1 liters). Bore & stroke: 3.965 x 3.4 in. Compression ratio: 8.0:1. Brake horsepower: 125 at 4000 R.P.M. Torque: 205 lbs.-ft. at 2000 R.P.M. Four main bearings. Hydraulic valve lifters. Carburetor: 4Bbl. Rochester M4ME. VIN Code: 4. Sales Code: LC4. OPTIONAL V-8 (Century/Regal): 90-degree, overhead-valve V-8. Cast iron alloy block and head. Displacement: 265 cu. in. (4.3 liters). Bore & stroke: 3.75 x 3.00 in. Compression ratio: 8.0:1. Brake horsepower: 120 at 3600 R.P.M. Torque: 210 lbs.-ft. at 1800 R.P.M. Four main bearings. Hydraulic valve lifters. Carburetor: 2Bbl. Rochester M2ME. VIN Code: S. BASE V-8 (Estate); OPTIONAL (Century, Regal, LeSabre): 90-degree overhead-valve V-8. Cast iron alloy block and head. Displacement: 301 cu. in. (4.9 liters). Bore & stroke: 4.0 x .00 in. Compression ratio: 8.2:1. Brake horsepower: 140 at 4000 R.P.M. Torque: 240 lbs.-ft. at 1800 R.P.M. Five main bearings. Hydraulic valve lifters. Carburetor: 4Bbl. Rochester M4ME. Built by Pontiac. VIN Code: W. Sales Code: L37. OPTIONAL V-8 (Century/Regal): 90-degree, overhead valve V-8. Cast iron alloy block and head. Displacement: 305 cu. in. (5.0 liters). Bore & stroke: 3.736 x 3.48 in. Compression ratio: 8.6:1. Brake horsepower: 155 at 4000 R.P.M. Torque: 240 lbs.-ft. at 1600 R.P.M. Five main bearings. Hydraulic valve lifters. Carburetor: 4Bbl. Rochester M4MC. VIN Code: H. Sales Code: LG4. BASE V-8 (Riviera); OPTIONAL (LeSabre, Estate, Electra, Riviera S): 90-degree, overhead valve V-8. Cast iron alloy block and head. Displacement: 350 cu. in. (5.7 liters). Bore & stroke: 3.80 x 3.85 in. Compression ratio: 8.0:1. Brake horsepower: 155 at 3400 R.P.M. Torque: 280 lbs.-ft. at 1600 R.P.M. Five main bearings. Hydraulic valve lifters. Carburetor: 4Bbl. Rochester M4MC. VIN Code: X. Sales Code: L77. ALTERNATE 350-4 V-8: 90-degree, overhead valve V-8. Cast iron alloy block and head. Displacement: 350 cu. in. (5.7 liters). Bore & stroke: 4.057 x 3.385 in. Compression ratio: 8.3:1. Brake horsepower: 60 at 3600 R.P.M. Torque: 270 lbs.-ft. at 1600 R.P.M. Five main bearings. Hydraulic valve lifters. Carburetor: 4Bbl. Rochester M4MC. Built by Oldsmobile. VIN Code: R. Sales Code: L34. OPTIONAL DIESEL V-8 (Electra, Estate): 90-degree, overhead valve V-8. Cast iron alloy block and head. Displacement: 350 cu. in. (5.7 liters). Bore & stroke: 4.057 x 3.385 in. Compression ratio: 22.5:1. Brake horsepower: 105 at 3200 R.P.M. Torque: 205 lbs.-ft. at 1600 R.P.M. Five main bearings. Hydraulic valve lifters. Fuel injection. Oldsmobile-built. VIN Code: N. Sales Code: LF9.

CHASSIS DATA: Wheelbase:- (Skyhawk) 97.0 in.; (Skylark) 104.9 in.; (Century/Regal) 108.1 in.; (LeSabre) 116.0 in.; (Estate) 115.9 in.; (Electra) 118.9 in.; (Riviera) 114.0 in. Overall length:- (Skyhawk) 179.3 in.; (Skylark) 181.9 in.; (Century) 196.0 in.; (Regal) 200.3 in.; (LeSabre) 217.4 in.; (Electra) 220.9 in.; (Estate) 218.8 in.; (Riv) 206.6 in. Height:- (Skyhawk) 50.8 in.; (Skylark) 53.5 in.; (Century cpe) 54.6 in.; (Century sed/wag) 55.5 in.; (Regal) 54.6 in.; (LeSabre) 55.0 in.; (Electra cpe) 54.2 in.; (Electra sed) 55.6 in.; (Estate) 57.1 in.; (Riv) 54.3 in. Width:- (Skyhawk) 65.4 in.; (Skylark) 67.7 in.; (Century/Regal) 71.1 in.; (LeSabre/Electra) 78.0 in.; (Estate) 80.1 in.; (Riv) 72.7 in. Front Tread:- (Skyhawk) 54.7 in.; (Skylark) 58.5 in.; (Century/Regal) 58.5 in.; (LeSabre/Electra) 61.8 in.; (Estate) 62.2 in.; (Riv) 59.3 in. Rear Tread:- (Skyhawk) 53.6 in.; (Skylark) 57.0 in.; (Century/Regal) 57.8 in.; (LeSabre) 60.7 in.; (Electra) 61.0 in.; (Estate) 64.1 in.; (Riv) 60.0 in. Standard Tires:- (Skyhawk) BR78 x 13 SBR; (Skyhawk 'S') B78 x 13; (Skylark) P185/80R13 GBR; (Skylark Sport) P205/70R13 SBR; (Century cpe/sed) P185/75R14 GBR; (Century wag/Regal) P195/75R14; (Regal Spt Cpe) P205/70R14 SBR; (LeSabre) P205/75R15 SBR; (LeSabre Spt Cpe) P225/70R15 SBR: (Electra) P215/75R15 SBR; (Estate) P225/75R15 SBR; (Riviera) P205/75R15 SBR WSW; (Riviera S) GR70 x 15.

TECHNICAL: Transmission:- Three-speed, fully synchronized manual gearbox standard on Century cpe/sed; Turbo Hydra-matic optional. Four-speed, fully synchronized floor shift standard on Skyhawk/Skylark; automatic optional. Turbo Hydra-matic standard on Regal, LeSabre, Electra, Estate and Riviera. Three-speed manual transmission gear ratios: (1st) 3.50:1; (2nd) 1.81:1; (3rd) 1.00:1; (Rev) 3.62:1. Skyhawk four-speed gear ratios: (1st) 3.50:1; (2nd) 2.48:1; (3rd) 1.66:1; (4th) 1.00:1; (Rev) 3.50:1. Skylark four-speed gear ratios: (1st) 3.53:1; (2nd) 1.95:1; (3rd) 1.24:1; (4th) 0.81:1; (Rev) 3.42:1. Auto. trans. gear ratios: (1st) 2.52:1; (2nd) 1.52:1; (3rd) 1.00:1; (Rev) 1.93:1. Skylark automatic: (1st) 2.84:1; (2nd) 2.60:1; (3rd) 1.00:1; (Rev) 2.07:1. Automatic on Century V-8, Electra diesel and Riviera: (1st) 2.74:1; (2nd) 1.57:1; (3rd) 1.00:1; (Rev) 2.07:1. Standard axle ratio:- (Skyhawk) 2.93:1; (Skylark) 3.34:1; (Century/Regal V6-231) 3.08:1; (Century/Regal V8-265) 2.41:1; (Century/Regal V8-301) 2.14:1 or 2.41:1; (Century/Regal V8-305) 2.29:1 or 2.73:1; (Century/Regal/LeSabre turbo/spt cpe) 2.73:1 or 3.08:1; (Century wag) 2.29:1, 2.41:1, 2.56:1 or 2.73:1; (LeSabre V6-231) 2.73:1 or 3.23:1; (LeSabre V6-252) 2.93:1; (LeSabre V-8) 2.41:1 or 3.23:1; (Electra V-6) 2.93:1; (Electra V8-301) 2.56:1; (Electra V8-350) 2.41:1 or 3.23:1; (Electra diesel) 2.73:1; (Estate) 2.56:1, 2.73:1 or 3.08:1; (Riviera) 2.41:1 exc. turbo V-6, 2.93:1. Steering:- (Skylark) rack and pinion; others recirculating ball; power assist standard on Regal, LeSabre, Electra, Estate and Riviera. Suspension:- front/rear coil springs; (Skylark) MacPherson strut front suspension, trailing arm rear with track bar; (Riviera) same as 1979; (others) same as 1976-79. Brakes:- front disc, rear drum; power brakes standard on all except Skyhawk/Skylark. Four-wheel power disc brakes optional on Riviera. Body construction:- (Skyhawk, Skylark) unibody; (others) separate body and frame. Fuel tank: (Skyhawk) 18.5 gal.; (Skylark) 14 gal.; (Century/Regal) 18.2 gal.; (LeSabre/Electra) 25 gal.; (Riviera) 21 gal. Unleaded fuel only.

DRIVETRAIN OPTIONS: Engines:- 173 cu. in. (2.8-liter) V-6, 2Bbl.: Skylark ($225). Turbocharged 231 cu. in. V-6, 4Bbl.: Century cpe/sed ($500); Riviera ($160). 252 cu. in. (4.1-liter) V-6, 4Bbl.: LeSabre ($90). 265 cu. in. (4.3-liter) V-8, 2Bbl.: Century/Regal ($180-$205). 301 cu. in. (4.9-liter) V-8, 2Bbl.: LeSabre ($295). 301 cu. in. V-8, 4Bbl.: Century/Regal ($295-$320). 305 cu. in. V-8, 4Bbl.: Century/Regal ($295-$320). 350 cu. in. (5.7-liter) V-8, 4Bbl.: LeSabre ($425); Estate ($130); Electra ($335); Riviera S (credit $160). 350 cu. in. diesel V-8: Estate ($860); Electra ($930). Transmission/Differential:- Automatic trans., floor shift: Skyhawk ($320). Automatic trans., column shift: Skylark ($337); Century cpe/sed ($358). Optional rear axle ratio (NC). Limited slip differential: Skyhawk ($65); Century/Regal ($70); LeSabre/Electra ($74). Power Accessories:- Power brakes: Skyhawk/Skylark ($76). Four-wheel disc brakes: LeSabre spt cpe, Riv ($222). Power steering: Skyhawk ($158); Skylark ($164); Century ($174). Suspension:- F40 Firm ride/handling pkg.: all exc. Skyhawk ($21-$22). F41 Rallye ride/handling pkg.: Skylark ($129); incl. in Sport. FE2 Rallye ride/handling pkg.: Century/Regal ($41); Riv ($22). Automatic level control: Century/Regal/LeSabre/Electra ($145). Superlift rear shocks: Skylark ($55). Other:- Trailer towing flasher/harness ($24-$38) exc. Skyhawk. Heavy-duty alternator, 80-amp: LeSabre/Electra ($24-$61); 70-amp ($15- 52) exc. Skyhawk. H.D. battery ($19-$22); diesel ($44). H.D. cooling: Skyhawk/Skylark/Century/Regal ($32-$63). Engine block heater ($16). H.D. engine/transmission cooling: LeSabre/Electra/Riv ($32-$63). California emission system ($83-$250).

SKYHAWK CONVENIENCE/APPEARANCE OPTIONS: Option Packages:- Road Hawk pkg.: Oyster white vinyl bucket seats; black wipers, grille, headlamp trim, moldings, front air dam; body-color spoiler and sport mirrors; BR70 x 13 SBR wide-oval blackwall tires; special handling suspension; silver/gray paint ($696). Appearance group (wheel opening moldings and bodyside stripes): 'S' ($62). Acoustic insulation pkg. ($27). Convenience group: underhood light, glove box light, headlamp-on indicator ($22). Shadow light Astroroof ($693). Vista Vent roof ($193). Comfort/Convenience:- Air cond. ($531). Rear defogger, electric ($95). Tinted glass ($65). Tinted windshield ($54). Tilt steering ($73). Instrument gauges, electric clock and tach ($79). Electric clock ($23). Front/rear mats ($23). Tungsten-halogen high-beam headlamps ($27). Visor vanity mirrors, pair ($11). Entertainment:- AM/FM radio ($64). AM/FM stereo radio ($101). AM/FM radio and cassette player ($188). AM/FM stereo radio and 8-track ($176). Rear speaker for non- stereo radios ($18). Delete AM radio ($52 credit). Exterior Trim:- Bodyside stripes (NC). Door edge guards ($13). Roof crown moldings ($198). Protective bodyside moldings ($32- $49). Designer's accent paint ($189). Interior Trim/Upholstery:- Adjustable driver's seatback ($21). Custom seatbelts ($19). Wheels and Tires:- Custom sport wheels ($63). Styled aluminum wheels ($249). B78 x 13 WSW ($42-$52). BR78 x 13 SBR BSW ($104-$129). BR78 x 13 SBR WSW ($41-$181). BR70 x 13 SBR wide-oval WLT ($57-$226). Conventional spare tire (NC).

SKYLARK CONVENIENCE/APPEARANCE OPTIONS: Option Packages:- Acoustic pkg. ($43). Lamp group: underhood, glove box, ashtray, courtesy, trunk, headlamps-on ($41-$50). Vista Vent flip-open glass sunroof ($240). Comfort/Convenience:- Air cond. ($564). Cruise Master ($105). Two-speed w/delay ($39). Rear defogger, electric ($101). Power windows ($133-$189). Electric door locks ($87-$123). Six-way power driver's seat ($165). Manual seatback recliner: each ($42). Sport steering wheel ($42). Tilt steering ($75). Tinted glass ($70). Dual horns ($11). Electric clock ($25). Digital clock ($56). Trip odometer ($13). Gauge pkg. incl. trip odometer ($40). Electric trunk release ($25). Lights and Mirrors:- Tungsten-halogen high-beam headlamps ($27). Headlamps-on indicator ($11). Dome reading light ($19). Door courtesy/warning light ($39-$62). Sunshade map light ($13). Remote left mirror ($18); sport-type ($28). Sport mirrors: left remote, right manual ($43); dual ($28-$71). Visor vanity mirrors ($11). Lighted passenger visor mirror ($39). Entertainment:- AM radio delete ($52 credit). AM/FM radio ($64). AM/FM stereo radio ($101); w/8-track or cassette player ($176-$188). AM/FM stereo and CB radio ($413); w/8- track or cassette ($479-$491). Rear speaker ($18); pair, for non-stereo radio ($28). Power antenna ($48); triband ($88). Exterior Trim:- Landau vinyl top ($175). Long vinyl top ($116). Designers' accent paint ($174). Protective bodyside moldings ($43). Belt reveal moldings ($25). Wide rocker panel group ($54). Door edge guards ($13-$20). Hood ornament and windsplit ($25). Pillar applique molding ($22). Wheel opening moldings ($22). Bodyside stripes ($40). Bumper guards, front/rear ($32). Bumper strips, front/rear ($40). Roof rack ($87). Interior Trim/Upholstery:- Full-length console ($80). Bucket seats ($48). Notchback bench seat: Spt ($146). Color- keyed seatbelts ($23). Front carpet savers ($15). Carpet savers and mats ($25). Trunk trim carpeting ($31). Wheels:- Designers' sport wheels ($82-$101); incl. on Spt. Chrome- plated wheels ($40-$141). Deluxe wheel covers ($43). Custom wire wheel covers ($151-$194). Sport wheel covers ($11-$54). Tires:- P185/80R13 GBR ($45). P185/80R13 SBR ($49). P185/80R13 SBR WSW ($93). P205/70R13 SBR WSW ($51). P205/70R13 SBR WLT ($66).

CENTURY/REGAL CONVENIENCE/APPEARANCE OPTIONS: Option Packages:- Regal Somerset pkg.: blue/tan interior trim, umbrella pouch, roof assist strap, decor pkg., custom belts, brushed aluminum instrument panel, sport mirrors, wire wheel covers ($695). Regal Sport Coupe Decor pkg.: designers' accent paint, turbine wheels, sport mirrors and steering wheel, black paint accents ($511). Century Sport Wagon pkg. ($511). Century Turbo Coupe pkg.: special suspension and exhaust, 3.08:1 axle, turbine wheels ($43). Electric sunroof: cpe ($561). Silver electric sliding Astroroof: cpe ($773). Hatch roof: Regal cpe ($695). Exterior molding pkg. ($64- $178). Convenience group ($18-$67). Comfort/Convenience:- Air cond. ($601). Automatic air cond. ($700). Cruise control ($112). Rear defogger, electric ($107). Tinted glass ($75). Tinted windshield ($54). Six-way power driver's seat ($175); both ($350). Manual seatback recliner ($67). Custom steering wheel: Century ($11). Sport steering wheel ($35-$46). Tilt steering ($81). Power windows ($143-$202). Electric door locks ($93-$132). Electric trunk release ($26). Remote tailgate lock: wag ($27). Electric clock ($26). Digital clock ($59). Headlamps-on indicator ($12). Trip odometer ($14). Instrument gauges: temp, volt, trip odometer ($29-$43). Two- speed wiper w/delay ($41). Lighting and Mirrors:- Cornering lamps: Regal ($53). Tungsten-halogen high-beams ($27). Coach lamps ($92). Front light monitors ($31). Dome reading lamp $20). Door/courtesy/warning lights: Ltd sed ($39-$62). Underhood light ($5). Remote left mirror ($19); right ($37- $42). Sport mirrors: left remote ($44-$49). Dual remote sport mirrors ($27-$76). Visor vanity mirrors, pair ($11). Lighted right visor vanity mirror ($50). Entertainment:- AM radio ($97). AM/FM radio ($153). AM/FM stereo radio ($192); w/8- track or cassette ($272-$285). AM/FM stereo radio and CB ($525). Rear speaker ($20); pair ($30). Automatic power antenna ($51-$80). Triband power antenna ($93-$122). Exterior Trim:- Landau vinyl top: Regal ($158-$175). Heavy-padded landau vinyl top: Regal ($188-$238). Long vinyl top ($124). Long padded vinyl top: Century sed ($207). Designers' accent paint ($174-$230). Solid special color paint ($165). Bumper guards, front: Century ($25). Protective bodyside moldings ($52). Rocker panel moldings: Century ($19). Door edge guards ($14-$22). Belt reveal moldings ($37). Wheel opening moldings: Century ($24). Body accent stripes ($37). Woodgrain vinyl applique: Century wag ($292-$316). Luggage rack: wag ($98). Air deflector: wag ($32). Tailgate hinge cover ($13). Interior Trim/Upholstery:- Full-length console ($96). Bucket seats: cpe/wag ($38-$197). 55/45 bench seating: cpe/wag ($112-$159). Limited 55/45 seating: Regal spt cpe ($294). Notchback seating: Century spt ($147). Custom seatbelts ($20- $24). Load floor carpet area: Century wag ($55). Front carpet savers ($16). Carpet savers and mats ($27). Front carpet savers w/inserts ($27); rear ($49). Litter pocket ($10). Trunk trim covering ($33). Lockable storage compartment: wag $40-$45). Wheels:- Chrome-plated wheels ($48-$183). Designers' sport wheels ($116-$135). Styled aluminum wheels ($152-$335). Turbine wheels: Regal spt cpe ($116). Deluxe wheel covers: Century exc. spt ($45). Designers' wheel covers: Century exc. spt ($76); Regal ($31). Wire wheel covers: Century exc. spt ($208); Regal ($48-$164). Tires:- P185/75R14 GBR WSW: Century cpe/sed ($45). P195/75R14 GBR BSW: Century six cpe/sed ($25); V-8 (NC). P195/75R14 GBR WSW ($46-$171). P195/75R14 SBR BSW: Century ($46-$73). P195/75R14 SBR WSW: Century ($95-$119); Regal ($46). P205/70R14 SBR wide-oval BSW: Regal ($37). P205/70R14 SBR WSW: Century spt, Regal ($51-$88). P205/70R14 SBR WLT ($66-$176).

LESABRE/ELECTRA/ESTATE WAGON CONVENIENCE/APPEARANCE OPTIONS: Option packages: LeSabre coupe Sport package: front bucket seats, dual remote sport mirrors ($106-$126). Exterior molding pkg.: LeSabre ($95-$114). Lamp/indicator group: LeSabre ($48-$66). Sliding Astroroof: LeSabre ($981); Electra ($1058). Accessory group (color-coordinated seatbelts, left remote mirror, rocker panel moldings, trip odometer, visor mirrors): LeSabre ($35-$95). Accessory group (trip odometer; headlamps-on, low fuel and washer fluid indicators): Electra ($25-$55). Comfort/Convenience:- Air cond.: LeSabre ($647). Automatic air cond.: LeSabre ($738); Electra ($91). Touch climate control air cond.: LeSabre ($834); Electra ($187). Cruise control ($118). Rear defogger, electric ($109). Tinted glass ($90). Tinted windshield: LeSabre/Est ($55). Power windows: LeSabre/Est ($149-$221). Electric door locks ($95-$135). Automatic door locks: Electra ($158-$189). Six-way power driver's seat ($148-$179); passenger ($179). Manual seatback recliner, one side: LeSabre cpe ($67). Electric seatback recliner, each side ($128). Sport steering wheel: LeSabre ($35). Tilt steering ($83). Tilt/telescoping steering column ($121-$131). Dial clock: LeSabre ($60). Remote tailgate lock: LeSabre Est ($37). Electric trunk release ($27). Electric trunk lock: Electra ($65). Electric fuel cap lock ($39). Theft deterrent system ($146); N/A on Estate. Three-speed wiper w/delay ($42). Lighting, Horns and Mirrors:- Tungsten- halogen high-beam headlamps ($27). Cornering lamps ($53). Twilight Sentinel: Electra ($51). Front light monitors: LeSabre/Est ($31). Front/rear monitors: Electra ($67). Door courtesy/warning lights ($39-$62). Lighted door lock and interior ($62). Four-note horn ($25). Remote left mirror: LeSabre/Est ($20). Remote right mirror ($22-$42). Dual remote sport mirrors ($36-$76). Remote electric right mirror: Park Ave. ($54-$74). Dual electric remote mirrors ($85-$125). Remote left mirror w/thermometer ($33-$53). Remote electric left mirror w/thermoter: Park Ave. ($33). Dual electric mirrors w/left thermometer ($118-$158). Lighted visor vanity mirror, each ($40-$51). Entertainment:- AM radio: LeSabre ($99). AM/FM radio: LeSabre ($156). AM/FM stereo radio ($195); w/8-track or cassette player ($276-$289) exc. Park Ave. ($81-$94). Full-feature AM/FM stereo radio: Electra $208-$403); w/8-track or cassette ($289-$497). AM/FM stereo radio and CB: LeSabre ($533); Electra ($338-$533). AM/FM stereo with 8-track and CB: LeSabre ($603); Electra ($408- $603). Signal-seeking AM/FM stereo radio with CB: Electra ($521-$716); w/CB and 8-track or cassette ($635-$856). Signal-seeking AM/FM stereo radio w/digital readout: Electra ($185-$380); w/8-track ($298-$493); w/cassette ($325-$520). Rear speaker: LeSabre ($21); dual ($31). Windshield antenna ($29); incl. w/radios. Automatic power antenna ($52-$81). Tri-band power antenna ($94-$123); w/CB (NC). Delete radio: Park Ave. ($164 credit). Exterior Trim:- Heavy-padded landau vinyl top: LeSabre, Electra Ltd cpe ($213). Long vinyl top ($155-$174). Long, heavy-padded vinyl top: Electra Ltd ($216). Designers' accent paint: LeSabre ($197). Solid special color paint: LeSabre ($166) exc. Firemist on Electra ($186). Protective bodyside moldings: LeSabre/Est ($47). Color-coordinated bodyside moldings: Electra Ltd ($72). Door edge guards ($15-$22). Belt reveal molding: LeSabre spt cpe ($37). Bodyside accent stripes ($56); N/A on Estate. Luggage rack w/air deflector: LeSabre Estate ($152). Interior Trim/Upholstery:- Custom seat trim: notchback, LeSabre spt cpe ($152 credit); 55/45, LeSabre spt cpe ($40 credit); 55/45, LeSabre ($112). Limited notchback seating: LeSabre spt cpe ($8). Limited 55/45 seating: LeSabre spt cpe ($120); LeSabre Ltd ($112). Leather/vinyl 50/50 seating: Park Ave. ($466). Third seat: Estate ($193). Full-length console: LeSabre cpe w/spt pkg. ($102). Front carpet savers ($27). Front/rear carpet savers w/inserts ($49). Carpet savers and mats ($27). Litter pocket: LeSabre ($10). Trunk trim carpet ($52-$65). heels:- Chrome-plated wheels ($154-$188). Custom wheel covers: Electra ($31). Wire wheel covers ($130-$164). Tires:- P205/75R15 SBR WSW: LeSabre ($50). P215/75R15 SBR BSW: LeSabre ($31). P215/75R15 SBR WSW: LeSabre ($84); Electra ($53). P225/70R15 SBR WSW: LeSabre spt cpe ($56). P225/70R25 SBR WLT: LeSabre spt cpe ($72). P225/75R15 SBR WSW: Estate ($56); Electra ($87).

RIVIERA CONVENIENCE/APPEARANCE OPTIONS: Roof Options:- Electric sunroof ($848). Electric sliding Astroroof ($1058). Comfort/Convenience:- Trip monitor ($859). Automatic air cond. ($95). Cruise Master ($118). Rear defogger, electric ($109). Automatic door locks ($69). Six- way power seat, passenger ($179). Electric seatback recliner, one side ($128). Manual seatback recliner, one side: S ($67). Sport steering wheel ($35). Tilt steering ($83). Tilt/telescope steering wheel ($131). Electric fuel cap lock ($39). Electric trunk release ($27). Electric trunk lock ($65). Low fuel indicator ($18). Fuel usage light, V-8 ($32). Windshield washer fluid indicator ($11). Three-speed wipers w/delay ($42). Theft deterrent system ($146). Lighting, Horns and Mirrors:- Tungsten-halogen high beams ($27). Coach lamps ($92); incl. w/vinyl top. Front/rear light monitors ($67). Twilight Sentinel ($51). Courtesy/reading lamps ($45). Lighted door locks and interior light control ($62). Four- note horn ($25). Dual electric remote mirrors ($63). Lighted visor vanity mirrors, each ($51). Entertainment:- AM/FM stereo w/8-track or cassette tape player ($81-$94). AM/FM stereo radio w/CB ($290); w/CB and 8-track ($360). Full-feature AM/FM stereo radio ($208); w/8-track or cassette ($289-$302). Signal-seeking AM/FM stereo radio w/digital readout ($185); w/8-track or cassette ($298-$325). Signal-seeking AM/CB/FM stereo radio w/digital clock ($461); w/8-track or cassette ($587-$661). Triband power antenna ($42); w/CB radio (NC). Delete radio ($164 credit). Exterior Trim:- Heavy-padded landau top ($298). Long vinyl top w/coach lamps ($305). Designers' accent paint ($209). Solid color special Firemist paint ($186). Protective bodyside moldings ($64). Door edge guards ($15). Bodyside stripes ($56). Interior Trim/Upholstery:- 45/55 notchback front seat, leather/vinyl ($360). Leather/vinyl bucket seats: S ($360). Front/rear carpet savers w/inserts ($62). Trunk trim carpet ($27). Trunk mat ($13). Wheels and Tires:- Chrome-plated wheels ($130). Wire wheel covers ($166). GR70 x 15 SBR WSW tires ($33). P205/75R15 SBR WSW tires: S ($33 credit).

HISTORY: Introduced: October 11, 1979 (Skylark, April 19, 1979). Model year production (U.S.): 854,011 (including early '80 Skylarks). Calendar year production (U.S.): 783,575. Model year sales by U.S. dealers: 700,083 (including just 950 imported Opels). Calendar year sales (U.S.): 720,368, which gave Buick a healthy 11.0 percent share of the market.

Historical Footnotes: Although other automakers endured weak sales for the 1980 model year, Buick did comparatively well, ending the year in third place among the GM quintet. Sales that totaled 7 percent less than 1979 still proved better than the average industry loss of 22 percent. Part of the reason may have been an upsurge of interest in the new notchback Century four-door, which proved much more popular than its Aeroback predecessor. Century sales zoomed upward by 137 percent, and the aero coupe was abandoned in February 1980. Regal continued as Buick's best seller, even though sales fell by 28 percent. Full-size Buick sales dropped by similar levels. Skyhawk never had attracted many buyers, and was dropped from the lineup in December 1979. The last imported Opels were also sold during 1980. As of April 1980, Buick no longer manufactured a V-8 engine, thus ending a long series of popular V-8s that began in 1953. The Olds-built diesel V-8 offered beginning this year on Buicks created plenty of trouble, and eventually resulted in lawsuits against GM (and settlements) because of its mechanical problems. Rather than an all-new design, it was simply a modification of the standard gasoline-powered 350 cu. in. V-8 that had been popular in the 1970s, and couldn't withstand the pressures of diesel operation. Diesel popularity was short-lived, in any case, and it would be dropped after 1985. Skylarks were first built at Buick's Willow Run (Michigan) plant. Overall development of the GM X-car quartet had cost $1.5 billion. Initially priced at $4769 and up, Skylark endured a series of incresaes during its first half- season and beyond. Though priced higher than the Chevrolet, Olds and Pontiac versions, Skylark enjoyed strong demand.

1981 BUICK

One model was missing from the 1981 Buick lineup: the subcompact Skyhawk. The name would return the following year on an all-new model. Meanwhile, fuel economy was the focus for 1981. That included widened availability of the Olds-built 5.7-liter diesel V-8. Most Buicks had Computer Command Control, which responded to sensors around the engine and exhaust system to keep gas mileage up while meeting federal emissions regulations. All Buicks (and other GM vehicles) carried a new "Freedom II" maintenance-free battery, whose label included more test ratings and service information. Century, Regal and Skylark wore new high-pressure tires, introduced on 1980 B-bodies. All '81 Buicks had low rolling resistance radial tires, introduced a year earlier on Skylark, LeSabre and Electra. All tires except Skylark's were now match-mounted. Self-sealing tires were now available on most Buicks. A new "fluidic" windshield washer system sprayed two fans of fluid, but had no moving parts. Buick's turbocharged V-6 got changes for cold-engine driveability this year, including an aluminum intake manifold, thermal vacuum choke valve, and Early Fuel Evaporation system to help vaporize the air/fuel mixture. New "low-drag" brake calipers arrived on Skylark, LeSabre and Electra models, with a special piston seal to pull brake pads away from the rotor. B- and C-bodied models had new quick-takeup master cylinders with a large-bore third piston for faster initial flow of brake fluid. This was especially useful for the new calipers. Cruise-Master speed controls had a new resume-speed feature. Century, Regal, LeSabre and Electra with V-6 engines could have trailer-towing packages capable of hauling a 4000-pound load. The Turbo Hydra-matic 200-4R transmission, offered on full-size models with 5.0-liter V-8, had a new overdrive fourth-speed range to improve highway gas mileage, coupled to a higher axle ratio. It came on Electras and LeSabre Estate Wagons, and was available in LeSabre coupes and sedans. The new transmission was also standard in C-body GM cars with 4.1-liter V-6 engine. Its overdrive (0.67:1) fourth gear engaged at about 45 MPH. The converter clutch added to the standard automatic transmission on some 1980 models was now included on all rear-drive Buicks.

1981 Skylark Limited sedan (AA)

SKYLARK — SERIES 4X — FOUR/V-6 — Apart from a new grille and taillamps, Skylark didn't change much for 1981. The new grille, made up of vertical bars, offered a rather formal look not unlike the 1980 Electra. Buick block letters were inset across the bar at top of grille. Vertical rectangular signal lamps sat outboard of single rectangular headlamps. Skylark's nameplate was at the forward end of fenders. Revised full-width wraparound taillamps split into two horizontal segments, eliminating the amber turn signal lenses. Inside was new cloth upholstery. Limited models had new woven velour cloth. The standard Delco AM radio came with a new fixed-mast antenna to improve fringe-area reception. A center console with storage bin was added, and the instrument panel now had black-face gauges (as did full-size Buicks). Controls for turn signals, dimmer, wiper/washer (and optional cruise control with resume) were now on the multifunction stalk lever. Four-speed manual transmission remained standard, with automatic available. Base powerplant was again the transverse-mounted Pontiac 2.5-liter four-cylinder engine, or optional Chevrolet 2.8-liter V-6. Both engines had Computer Command Control. Rear suspension isolating/damping improved ride feel. Skylark also added higher-pressure tires with low resistance. Buick's mist wiper system continued. Skylark's Sport coupe and sedan had a new sport steering wheel to join the black-accented interior and body. Again, its grille was totally different from other Skylarks: a black-accented six-slot design. Sport models also had amber park/signal lamps, smoked taillamp lenses, bumper strips, Rallye suspension, and P205/70R13 steel-belted radial tires. Optional Sport lower body stripes included a Hawk decal. Electro-luminescent coach lamps were optional on the Limited.

1981 Century Limited sedan (AA)

CENTURY — SERIES 4A — V-6/V-8 — The Aeroback two-door was finally dropped, leaving only a notchback four-door to replace the prior fastback of 1978-80 (a design that wasn't universally loved). Century was described in the full-line catalog as Buick's "little limousine" for its "elegant, even formal, styling." It did indeed display a formal notchback roofline. The restyled grille contained a tiny checkerboard pattern in five rows, separated by a single vertical divider. Vertical rectangular parking lights sat between the grille and the single recessed rectangular headlamps. Amber lenses were at fender tips. Designers' Accent paint combinations were available. At the rear were new wraparound taillamps: red upper lenses, amber below. Just ahead of the taillamps was 'Century' lettering, with a 'BUICK' badge on the decklid. Base engine remained the 231 cu. in. (3.8-liter) V-6, with a 265 cu. in. V-8 the sole option. Century was the last Buick to carry a three-speed manual transmission (on the base model). All Century Limited had standard automatic transmission with converter clutch. All Century models had standard power steering and brakes. Two station wagons were offered: base and Estate Wagon. A fixed mast antenna improved radio reception range and interference level. A new side-lift frame jack replaced the former bumper jack. Interiors had new fabrics. Century Limited had new soft knit velour upholstery in 55/45 seating. Low-rolling-resistance tires were standard; new self-sealing tires were available. Optional wraparound moldings ran the full length of the car. Also optional: electro-luminiscent coach lamps, and a theft-deterrent system with starter interrupt.

1981 Regal coupe (AA)

REGAL — SERIES 4A — V-6/V-8 — After three years of life as a downsized coupe, Regal got a serious aerodynamic restyle for 1981, including a raked front end and taller back end, with spoiler-type cutoff. A new grille and downward-sloping hood helped to reduce Regal's drag coefficient by 18 percent over the 1980 model. The new vertical-bar grille angled outward sharply from a point near the top. Buick block letters were inset in the upper horizontal bar, with 'Regal' script at the lower corner. Bumper tips flush with fender edges added to the clean look. Wide horizontal turn/parking lamps were built into the bumper. At the rear sat full-width, squarish wraparound taillamps. A new rear deck was topped by an "aerodynamically correct" wedge-styled spoiler lip. Flush-set front and rear bumpers enhanced the smooth aero look. Regal Limited had a full-length, wide rocker panel molding that extended ahead of the front wheels and back of the rears for an unbroken front-to-back line. A new blue crest for '81, in stylized contemporary design, appeared on the hood, new wheel covers, and optional cornering lamps. In addition to solid colors or Designers' Accent schemes, Regals were available with a Decor Package in four colors, each with a silver lower section. The package also included sport mirrors, turbine wheels, and a sport steering wheel. The standard 231 cu. in. (3.8-liter) V-6 engine came with automatic transmission that carried a converter clutch. Options above the standard V-6 were a turbo edition and a 4.3-liter V-8. New standards included low-rolling-resistance tires and a new, lighter battery. Regal had a redesigned fiber-reinforced plastic wheelhouse panel that incorporated a battery tray, plus a new side-lift frame jack. An electronically-tuned radio with Extended Range speakers was offered for the first time on Regals. Self-sealing tires were available. Regal's Sport Coupe was easy to spot. A bulge at rear of hood displayed a 'Turbo 3.8 Litre' chrome emblem at its side. Sport Coupes kept their fast-ratio power steering, sport mirrors and other goodies, but added a new Gran Touring suspension for handling equivalent to LeSabre and Riviera T Type. That suspension (also available on other Century and LeSabre models) was intended to deliver a tempting combination of road feel and smooth ride. The two-tone Decor Package included a black-trimmed grille, headlamps and taillamps; wide bright center rocker molding; turbine-style wheels; sport steering wheel; and choice of four body colors over a silver lower section. Limited interiors used new soft knit velour fabric, even on the upper doors. New fur-like carpeting extended to lower door sections. Limiteds also had the option of new 45/45 seating, or standard 55/45 with fold-down center armrest.

1981 LeSabre coupe (AA)

LESABRE — SERIES 4B — V-6/V-8 — Restyled for 1980, the base and Limited LeSabres enjoyed some detail changes in their second year. The rectangular grille, though similar to 1980 version, gained an extra row of holes and a more refined look. Color-coordinated, protective bodyside moldings were now standard. Taillamps were also modified to all-red design. Base engine remained the 231 cu. in. (3.8-liter) V-6. Both the 252 cu. in. (4.1-liter) V-6 and 5.0-liter V-8 now came with new overdrive automatic transmission; the larger diesel V-8 kept the prior three-speed automatic. All gas engines had Computer Command Control. LeSabres had bumper guards and protective strips, cut-pile carpeting, mist wipers, compact spare tire and a side-frame jack, as well as power brakes and steering. Interiors sported woven velour fabrics. Black dial faces for easier reading were set off by woodgrain vinyl trim. Optional Cruise-Master speed control had a new resume-speed feature. Also optional: an illuminated entry system for nighttime convenience, newly-styled aluminum wheels with exposed chrome lug nuts, electro-luminescent coach lamps (for Limited), and automatic door locks. An option package for the new T Type included bucket seats, console, sport steering wheel, custom seatbelts, sport mirrors, black accented pillar, and Gran Touring suspension.

ESTATE WAGON — SERIES 4B/C — V-8 — Estate Wagons came in two versions: LeSabre and Electra. Dimensions were identical, with 87.9 cubic foot cargo area; but the lower-priced edition sported LeSabre's front end. Both carried the 307 cu. in. (5.0-liter) V-8 engine with overdrive automatic transmission, or optional 5.7-liter diesel. Standard equipment included whitewall steel-belted tires, air conditioning, power windows, power steering and brakes, tilt steering column, electric door locks, load floor carpeting, two-way tailgate, and roof rack with air deflector. A wide selection of interiors included five all-cloth front-seat colors on the 55/45 notchback seats, plus two vinyl trim possibilities, and two choices of cloth up front and vinyl in back. Estates sported new colonial oak exterior vinyl woodgrain trim. A dozen Delco radio choices were available.

1981 Electra Estate Wagon (AA)

ELECTRA — SERIES 4C — V-6/V-8 — Electra received few exterior changes except for its grille, which got a different paint treatment to set Electra apart from other Buick series. The basic Electra grille, a bold rectangular design, contained six separate crosshatch sections. Park Avenue's grille relied on vertical strips alone within each section, for a formal look. The new grille was created to blend with the downward-sloping hood, and with Park Avenue's brushed-finish bodyside molding. Fender "ventiports" disappeared from the Limited but remained on the Park Avenue, incorporated into the bodyside molding. Thus, Park Avenue was the only Buick left with vestigial portholes. The standard 252 cu. in. (4.1-liter) V-6 and optional 5.0-liter V-8 were coupled to a new overdrive automatic transmission, with a fourth gear that engaged at about 45 MPH. Diesel V-8 Electras retained the old automatic. Gas engines had Computer Command Control. Low-rolling-resistance whitewall tires were standard; self-sealing tires were offered. Match-mounted tires were offered. Electro-luminescent coach lamps, formerly only on the Park Avenue, were now offered on the Limited. Park Avenue's standard padded halo top revealed a sliver of body color above the windows. Park Avenue models had fur-like carpet as well as velour or leather seats. Aluminum wheels were newly styled. Electra also had new standard color-coordinated, protective bodyside moldings. As always, Electra carried plenty of standard equipment, including air conditioning, power brakes and steering, single-wipe feature on the windshield wipers, remote-controlled left outside mirror, digital clock, dome reading lamp, and lights for front ashtray, trunk, underdash and glove compartment. Park Avenue added wide rocker appearance moldings, an electric left mirror, and Delco AM/FM stereo radio.

1981 Riviera coupe (AA)

RIVIERA — SERIES 4E — V-6/V-8 — Buick's full-line catalog stressed the claim that some experts had declared Riviera to be on the "leading edge of Detroit technology" by combining "Interesting weight-saving materials and engineering approaches...in a way that's synergistic: the sum becomes greater than its parts." New touches this year included a revised, bolder, more distinctly detailed grille and gray bumper protective strips. The grille consisted of tiny crosshatch elements, split into eight sections by narrow vertical bars, with a 'Riviera' script at the side. Horizontal parking and signal lamps sat directly beneath the quad rectangular headlamps. The oval stand-up hood ornament carried an 'R' insignia. Rivieras rode new low-rolling-resistance radial tires, except for the T Type which carried GR70 x 15 tires. Self-sealing tires were offered as options. A new "fluidic" windshield washer used no moving parts to spray droplets in a fan pattern. Standard equipment included air conditioning, automatic transmission, six-way power driver's seat, quartz clock, electric door locks, and Delco AM/FM radio with power antenna. New shocks and chassis tuning allowed higher tire pressures while retaining smooth ride. Two new engines were offered: the base 252 cu. in. (4.1-liter) V-6 plus an optional 350 diesel V-8. That diesel, offered through 1985, would eventually cause more trouble than pleasure to both its owners and the company. T Type was the new designation for the sporty Riviera, replacing the S Type of 1980. Special touches included black accents and black side mirrors, plus the familiar amber turn signal lamps. The Gran Touring suspension was intended to give quicker steering and increased road feedback, without a harsh ride. Standard T Type engine continued to be the 231 cu. in. (3.8-liter) turbocharged V-6; but the 4.1-liter V-6 or 5.0-liter V-8 could also be ordered, as well as the diesel. The T Type's instrument panel was now simulated woodgrain. Seats were new, in cloth or leather. A new 45/45 seating arrangement up front featured a fold-down center armrest on the driver's side. Cloth bucket seats and a storage console were standard on the T Type. New option for stereo fans: a Concert Sound six-speaker system. Electronic climate control was also available.

46

I.D. DATA: All Buicks had a new 17-symbol Vehicle Identification Number (VIN), stamped on a metal tag attached to the upper left surface of the cowl, visible through the windshield. The number begins with a '1' to indicate the manufacturing country (U.S.A.), followed by 'G' for General Motors and '4' for Buick Division. The next letter indicates restraint system. The fifth symbol is a letter denoting series: 'B' Skylark; 'C' Skylark Limited; 'D' Skylark Sport; 'E' Century; 'H' Century Estate Wagon; 'L' Century Limited; 'J' Regal; 'K' Regal Sport Coupe; 'M' Regal Limited; 'N' LeSabre; 'P' LeSabre Limited; 'R' LeSabre Estate Wagon; 'V' Electra Estate Wagon; 'X' Electra Limited; 'W' Electra Park Avenue; 'Y' Riviera T Type; 'Z' Riviera. Digits six and seven indicate body type: '37' 2-dr. coupe; '47' 2-dr. coupe; '57' 2-dr. notchback coupe; '35' 4-dr. wagon; '69' 4-dr. sedan. Next is the engine code: '5' L4-151 2Bbl.; 'X' V6-173 2Bbl.; 'A' V6-231 2Bbl.; '3' V6-231 Turbo; '4' V6-252 4Bbl.; 'S' V8-265 2Bbl.; 'Y' V8-307 4Bbl.; 'N' V8-350 diesel. Symbol nine is a check digit ('8'). Symbol ten denotes model year ('B' 1981). Symbol eleven is the plant code: 'W' Willow Run, MI; '6' Oklahoma City, OK; 'G' Framingham, MA; 'H' Flint, MI; 'Z' Fremont, CA; 'K' Leeds, MO; 'X' Fairfax, KS; 'E' Linden, NJ. The final six digits are the sequential serial number, starting with 100001 except for full-size models built in Flint and Linden, which begin with 400001. A Body Style Identification Plate on the upper horizontal surface of the shroud showed the model year, series, style number, body number, body assembly plant, trim number, paint code, modular seat code, and roof option. Skylarks had their body plate on the front tie bar just behind right headlamp. The five-symbol series and body style number was identical to the combination of series and model number shown in the tables below. Example: 4XB37 indicates a Skylark two-door coupe ('4' indicates Buick; 'X' the X-body; 'B' for base Skylark; and '37' for coupe body style).

SKYLARK (FOUR/V-6)

Series Number	Body/Style Number	Body Type & Seating	Factory Price	Shipping Weight	Production Total
4X	B37	2-dr Coupe-5P	6405/6530	2424/2481	46,515
4X	B69	4-dr Sedan-5P	6551/6676	2453/2510	104,091

SKYLARK LIMITED (FOUR/V-6)

| 4X | C37 | 2-dr Coupe-5P | 6860/6985 | 2453/2510 | 30,080 |
| 4X | C69 | 4-dr Sedan-5P | 7007/7132 | 2484/2541 | 81,642 |

SKYLARK SPORT (FOUR/V-6)

| 4X | D37 | 2-dr Coupe-5P | 7040/7165 | 2453/2520 | Note 1 |
| 4X | D69 | 4-dr Sedan-5P | 7186/7311 | 2484/2541 | Note 1 |

Note 1: Production totals shown for Skylark include Sport models.

CENTURY (V-6/V-8)

| 4A | H69 | 4-dr Sedan-6P | 7094/7170 | 3179/3269 | 127,119 |
| 4A | E35 | 4-dr Sta Wag-6P | 7391/7441 | 3269/3384 | 5,489 |

CENTURY LIMITED (V-6/V-8)

| 4A | L69 | 4-dr Sedan-6P | 7999/8075 | 3191/3306 | Note 2 |

CENTURY ESTATE WAGON (V-6/V-8)

| 4A | H35 | 4-dr Sta Wag-6P | 7735/7785 | 3311/3426 | 11,659 |

Note 2: Century sedan production figure included Limited model. Century models had a significant price increase during the model year. The base sedan reached $7924, though rises for other models were less dramatic.

REGAL (V-6/V-8)

| 4A | J47 | 2-dr Coupe-6P | 7555/7605 | 3188/3303 | Note 3 |

REGAL SPORT COUPE (TURBO V-6)

| 4A | K47 | 2-dr Coupe-6P | 8528 | 3261 | Note 3 |

Note 3: Total Regal coupe production for the model year, 123,848.

REGAL LIMITED (V-6/V-8)

| 4A | M47 | 2-dr Coupe-6P | 8024/8074 | 3224/3339 | 116,352 |

LESABRE (V-6/V-8)

| 4B | N37 | 2-dr Coupe-6P | 7715/7715 | 3464/3623 | 4,909 |
| 4B | N69 | 4-dr Sedan-6P | 7805/7805 | 3493/3652 | 19,166 |

LESABRE LIMITED (V-6/V-8)

| 4B | P37 | 2-dr Coupe-6P | 7966/7966 | 3482/3641 | 14,862 |
| 4B | P69 | 4-dr Sedan-6P | 8101/8101 | 3515/3674 | 39,006 |

Note 4: A V-8 engine cost $203 extra on LeSabres; but no charge for the Computer Command version. Like other Buicks, LeSabres rose in price during the model year. The base V-6 coupe reached $8187. LeSabre Estate wagon rose even higher, reaching $9926.

LESABRE ESTATE WAGON (V-8)

| 4B | R35 | 4-dr Sta Wag-6P | 8722 | 4002 | 4,934 |

ELECTRA LIMITED (V-6/V-8)

4C	X37	2-dr Coupe-6P	10237/10237	3656/3817	10,151
4C	X69	4-dr Sedan-6P	10368/10368	3722/3883	58,832

ELECTRA PARK AVENUE (V-6/V-8)

4C	W37	2-dr Coupe-6P	11267/11267	3728/3889	Note 5
4C	W69	4-dr Sedan-6P	11396/11396	3788/3949	Note 5

Note 5: Production figures for Electra Limited also include Park Avenue models. Total model year production of Limited, 27,826; Park Avenue, 41,157. Only 13,922 Electras carried a V-6 engine. Prices for Electras rose $728 to $962 during the model year, while the Electra Estate Wagon reached $12.092.

ELECTRA ESTATE WAGON (V-8)

4C	V35	4-dr Sta Wag-6P	11291	4174	6,334

RIVIERA (V-6/V-8)

4E	Z57	2-dr Coupe-5P	12147/12147	3563/3724	Note 6

RIVIERA T TYPE TURBO (V-6)

4E	Y57	2-dr Coupe-5P	13091	3651	Note 6

Note 6: Total Riviera production, 52,007 (11,793 with V-6). For the model year, 3,990 turbocharged V-6 engines were produced.

FACTORY PRICE AND WEIGHT NOTE: Figure before the slash is for V-6 engine, after the slash for smallest (lowest-priced) V-8 engine available. For Skylark, figure before the slash is for four-cylinder engine, after the slash for V-6.

ENGINES: BASE FOUR (Skylark): Inline, ohv four-cylinder. Cast iron block and head. Displacement: 151 cu. in. (2.5 liters). Bore & stroke: 4.0 x 3.0 in. Compression ratio: 8.2:1. Brake horsepower: 84 at 3600 R.P.M. Torque: 125 lbs.-ft. at 2400 R.P.M. Five main bearings. Hydraulic valve lifters. Carburetor: 2Bbl. Rochester. Built by Pontiac. VIN Code: 5. Sales Code: LW9. OPTIONAL V-6 (Skylark): 60-degree, overhead-valve V-6. Cast iron block and head. Displacement: 173 cu. in. (2.8 liters). Bore & stroke: 3.5 x 3.0 in. Compression ratio: 8.5:1. Brake horsepower: 110 at 4800 R.P.M. Torque: 145 lbs.-ft. at 2400 R.P.M. Four main bearings. Hydraulic valve lifters. Carburetor: 2Bbl. Roch. 2SE. Built by Chevrolet. VIN Code: X. Sales Code: LE2. BASE V-6 (Century, Regal, LeSabre): 90-degree, overhead-valve V-6. Cast iron block and head. Displacement: 231 cu. in. (3.8 liters). Bore & stroke: 3.8 x 3.4 in. Compression ratio: 8.0:1. Brake horsepower: 110 at 3800 R.P.M. Torque: 190 lbs.-ft. at 1600 R.P.M. Four main bearings. Hydraulic valve lifters. Carburetor: 2Bbl. Rochester M2ME. VIN Code: A. Sales Code: LD5. TURBOCHARGED V-6 (Regal Sport Coupe, Riviera T Type); OPTIONAL (Riviera): Same as 231 V-6 above, but with E4ME four-barrel carburetor. Brake horsepower: 170 at 4000 R.P.M. (Riviera, 180 H.P.) Torque: 275 lbs.-ft. at 2400 R.P.M. (Riviera, 270 lbs.-ft.) VIN Code: 3. Sales Code: LC8. BASE V-6 (Electra, Riviera); OPTIONAL (LeSabre, Riviera T Type): 90-degree, overhead-valve V-6. Cast iron block and head. Displacement: 252 cu. in. (4.1 liters). Bore & stroke: 3.965 x 3.4 in. Compression ratio: 8.0:1. Brake horsepower: 125 at 4000 R.P.M. Torque: 205 lbs.-ft. at 2000 R.P.M. Four main bearings. Hydraulic valve lifters. Carburetor: 4Bbl. Rochester E4ME. VIN Code: 4. Sales Code: LC4. OPTIONAL V-8 (Century/Regal): 90-degree, overhead-valve V-8. Cast iron block and head. Displacement: 265 cu. in. (4.3 liters). Bore & stroke: 3.75 x 3.00 in. Compression ratio: 8.0:1. Brake horsepower: 119 at 4000 R.P.M. Torque: 203 lbs.-ft. at 2000 R.P.M. Five main bearings. Hydraulic valve lifters. Carburetor: 2Bbl. Roch. M2ME. Built by Pontiac. VIN Code: S. Sales Code: LS5. BASE V-8 (Estate); OPTIONAL (LeSabre, Electra, Riviera): 90-degree, overhead valve V-8. Cast iron block and head. Displacement: 307 cu. in. (5.0 liters). Bore & stroke: 3.80 x 3.385 in. Compression ratio: 8.0:1. Brake horsepower: 140 at 3600 R.P.M. Torque: 240 lbs.-ft. at 1600 R.P.M. Five main bearings. Hydraulic valve lifters. Carburetor: 4Bbl. Roch. M4MC. Built by Oldsmobile. VIN Code: Y. Sales Code: LV2. OPTIONAL DIESEL V-8 (Century, LeSabre, Electra, Estate, Riviera): 90-degree, overhead valve V-8. Cast iron block and head. Displacement: 350 cu. in. (5.7 liters). Bore & stroke: 4.057 x 3.385 in. Compression ratio: 22.5:1. Brake horsepower: 105 at 3200 R.P.M. Torque: 200 lbs.-ft. at 1600 R.P.M. Five main bearings. Hydraulic valve lifters. Fuel injection. Oldsmobile-built. VIN Code: N. Sales Code: LF9.

CHASSIS DATA: Wheelbase: (Skylark) 104.9 in.; (Century/Regal) 108.1 in.; (LeSabre/Estate) 115.9 in.; (Electra) 118.9 in.; (Riviera) 114.0 in. Overall length:- (Skylark) 181.1 in.; (Century) 196.0 in.; (Regal) 200.6 in.; (LeSabre) 218.4 in.; (Electra) 221.2 in.; (Estate Wagon) 220.5 in.; (Riviera) 206.6 in. Height:- (Skylark) 53.5 in.; (Century cpe/sed) 55.5 in.; (Century wag) 55.7 in.; (Regal) 54.1 in.; (LeSabre/Electra) 55.0 in.; (Estate) 57.1 in.; (Riviera) 54.3 in. Width:- (Skylark cpe) 69.1 in.; (Skylark sed) 68.9 in.; (Century/Regal) 71.5 in.; (Century wag) 71.2 in.; (LeSabre/Electra) 75.9 in.; (Estate) 79.3 in.; (Riviera) 71.5 in. Front Tread:- (Skylark) 58.7 in.; (Century/Regal) 58.5 in.; (LeSabre/Electra) 61.8 in.; (Estate) 62.2 in.; (Riviera) 59.3 in. Rear Tread:- (Skylark) 56.9 in.; (Century/Regal) 57.8 in.; (LeSabre/Electra) 60.7 in.; (Estate) 64.0 in.; (Riviera) 60.0 in. Standard Tires:- (Skylark) P185/80R13 GBR; (Skylark Sport) P205/70R13 SBR; (Century sed) P185/75R14 GBR; (Century wag) P195/75R14 GBR; (Regal) P195/75R14 SBR; (Regal Spt Cpe) P205/70R14 SBR; (LeSabre) P205/75R15 SBR; (Electra) P215/75R15 SBR WSW; (Estate) P225/75R15 SBR; (Riviera) P205/75R15 SBR WSW; (Riviera T) GR70 x 15 SBR WSW.

TECHNICAL: Transmission:- Three-speed, fully synchronized manual gearbox standard on Century; Turbo Hydra-matic optional. Four-speed, fully synchronized floor shift standard on Skylark; automatic optional. Turbo Hydra-matic standard on all other models. Century three-speed manual transmission gear ratios: (1st) 3.50:1; (2nd) 1.81:1; (3rd) 1.00:1; (Rev) 3.62:1. Skylark four-speed gear ratios: (1st) 3.53:1; (2nd) 1.95:1; (3rd) 1.24:1; (4th) 0.81:1; (Rev) 3.42:1. Automatic trans. gear ratios: (1st) 2.52:1; (2nd) 1.52:1; (3rd) 1.00:1; (Rev) 1.93:1. Skylark automatic gear ratios: (1st) 2.84:1; (2nd) 1.60:1; (3rd) 1.00:1; (Rev) 2.07:1. Riviera auto. gear ratios: (1st) 2.74:1; (2nd) 1.57:1; (3rd) 1.00:1; (Rev) 2.07:1. Overdrive automatic gear ratios: (1st) 2.74:1; (2nd) 1.57:1; (3rd) 1.00:1; (4th) 0.67:1; (Rev) 2.07:1. Standard axle ratio:- (Skylark) 3.32:1; (Century/Regal V-6) 3.08:1; (Century V-8) 2.41:1; (Regal V-8) 2.29:1; (Century wagon) 2.73:1; (Regal Sport Coupe) 2.73:1 or 3.08:1; (LeSabre) 2.41:1, 2.73:1, or 3.23:1; (Electra) 3.08:1 or 3.23:1; (Electra diesel) 2.41:1; (Riviera) 2.93:1 or 2.41:1. Other axle ratios were standard in California. Final drive: (Skylark) spiral bevel; (others) hypoid bevel. Steering:- (Skylark) rack and pinion; (others) recirculating ball; power assist standard on all except Skylark. Suspension:- same as 1980. Brakes:- front disc, rear drum; power brakes standard on all except Skylark. Four-wheel power disc brakes optional on Riviera. Body construction:- (Skylark) unitized; (others) separate body and frame. Fuel tank:- (Skylark) 14 gal.; (Century/Regal) 18.2 gal.; (LeSabre/Electra) 25 gal.; (Riv) 23 gal. Unleaded fuel only.

DRIVETRAIN OPTIONS: Engines:- 173 cu. in. (2.8-liter) V-6, 2Bbl.: Skylark ($125) Turbocharged 231 cu. in. (3.8-liter) V-6, 4Bbl.: Riviera ($750). 252 cu. in. (4.1-liter) V-6, 4Bbl.: LeSabre ($238); Riviera T Type ($750 credit). 265 cu. in. (4.3-liter) V-8: Century/Regal ($50-$76). 307 cu. in. (5.0-liter) V-8, 4Bbl.: LeSabre cpe/sed ($203) but (NC) with computer command control; Electra cpe/sed, Riviera (NC); Riviera T ($750 credit). 350 cu. in. (5.7-liter) diesel V-8: Century ($695- $721); LeSabre/Riviera ($695); Electra/Estate ($542). Transmission/Differential:- Three-speed automatic trans.: Skylark ($349); LeSabre cpe/sed with 4.1 or 5.0-liter ($153 credit). Optional rear axle ratio: Century/Regal/LeSabre/ Electra (NC). Limited slip differential: Century/Regal/ LeSabre/Electra ($69). Suspension, Steering and Brakes:- F40 Firm ride/handling pkg. ($21-$22). FE2 Gran Touring suspension: Century/Regal/LeSabre ($40); Riviera ($21). F41 Rallye ride/handling suspension incl. P205/70R13 SBR tires: Skylark ($134). Superlift rear shock absorbers: Skylark ($57). Automatic level control: Century/Regal/LeSabre/Electra ($142). Power steering: Skylark ($27). Power brakes: Skylark ($79). Four-wheel disc brakes: Riv ($215). Other:- Trailer towing flasher/harness ($23-$40). Trailer towing pkg.: Century/Regal ($148-$226); LeSabre ($434); Electra exc. wag ($141). H.D. alternator, 85-amp ($27-$75). H.D. battery ($21- $22) exc. diesel ($42). H.D. cooling: Skylark ($34-$63). Engine block heater ($16). Diesel fuel heater ($42). Heavy- duty engine/transmission cooling ($32-$61) exc. Skylark. California emission system ($46); diesel ($82).

SKYLARK CONVENIENCE/APPEARANCE OPTIONS: Option Packages:- Acoustic pkg. ($45). Flip-open Vista Vent glass sunroof ($246). Lamp group ($43-$52). Comfort/Convenience:- Air cond. ($385). Cruise Master w/resume ($132). Rear defogger, electric ($107). Power windows ($140- $195). Electric door locks ($93-$132). Six-way power driver's seat ($173). Manual seatback recliners, passenger ($43); both ($87). Sport steering wheel ($43); N/A on Sport. Tilt steering ($81). Tinted glass ($75). Instrument gauges incl. trip odometer ($42). Trip odometer ($14). Electric dial clock ($23). Digital clock ($55). Electric trunk release ($27). Two-speed wipers w/low-speed delay ($41). Lights, Horns and Mirrors:- Tungsten-halogen high beams ($27). Coach lamps: Ltd ($90). Headlamps-on indicator ($12). Dome reading light ($20). Dual horns ($12). Remote-control left mirror ($19); N/A on sport. Sport mirrors: left remote, right manual ($47). Dual remote sport mirrors ($28-$75). Visor vanity mirror, passenger ($12). Lighted visor vanity mirror, either side ($41). Entertainment:- AM/FM radio ($64). AM/FM stereo radio ($100); w/8-track or cassette player ($174-$186). AM/FM stereo radio with CB ($398); with CB and 8-track or cassette ($463-$475). Graphic equalizer ($146). Dual rear speakers $23-$28). Windshield antenna ($10). Power antenna ($47). Triband power antenna ($77). Delete AM radio ($51 credit). Exterior Trim:- Landau vinyl top: cpe ($173). Long vinyl top ($115). Designers' accent paint ($182); N/A on Sport. Protective bodyside moldings ($44). Wide rocker panel moldings ($56). Belt reveal moldings ($27). Wheel opening moldings ($25). Door edge guards ($13-$21). Pillar applique: sed exc. Spt ($23). Hood ornament and windsplit ($27); N/A on Sport. Bodyside or Sport stripes ($42). Bumper guards, front/rear ($34). Bumper strips, front/rear ($42). Interior Trim/Upholstery:- Full-length console ($86). Bucket seats, base ($48); limited cloth/vinyl ($48-$227); limited leather/vinyl ($308-$485). Notchback bench seating: Sport ($177). Color-keyed seatbelts ($24). Front carpet savers ($15). Carpet savers and mats ($25). Trunk trim carpeting ($33). Wheels:- Chrome-plated wheels ($21-$148). Designers' sport wheels ($107-$127). Sport wheel covers ($11-$56). Deluxe wheel covers ($45). Locking wire wheel covers ($157- $202). Tires:- P185/80R13 GBR WSW ($51); N/A on Sport. P185/80R13 SBR BSW ($47); N/A on Spt. P185/80R13 SBR wide WSW ($105); N/A on Spt. P205/70R13 SBR WSW ($58). P205/70R13 SBR WLT ($75). Self-sealing tires ($99).

CENTURY/REGAL CONVENIENCE/APPEARANCE OPTIONS: Option Packages:- Regal Limited Somerset II pkg.: designers' paint (dark sandstone and camel), turbine wheels with camel accents, doeskin 55/45 seats with dark brown buttons/laces ($459). Regal Turbo performance pkg.: dual exhausts and 3.08:1 axle ratio ($75). Regal Sport Coupe Decor pkg. ($427). Regal Coupe Decor pkg. ($385). Sliding electric Astroroof: Regal ($773). Electric sunroof: Regal ($561). Hatch roof: Regal ($695). Convenience group ($12-$78). Exterior molding pkg. ($94-$175). Comfort/Convenience:- Air cond. ($585); automatic ($677). Cruise Master with resume ($132). Rear defogger, electric ($107). Tinted glass ($75). Tinted windshield ($53). Six-way power seat, each side ($173). Manual passenger seatback recliner ($66). Custom steering wheel ($11). Sport steering wheel ($35-$46). Tilt steering ($81). Power windows ($140-$195). Electric door locks ($93- $132). Automatic door locks ($154-$183). Electric trunk release ($27). Remote electric tailgate lock: wag ($29). Electric dial clock ($23). Digital clock ($55). Headlamps-on indicator ($12). Trip odometer ($14). Instrument gauges: temp, voltage, trip odometer ($42). Two-speed wiper w/delay ($41). Theft deterrent system ($142). Lighting and Mirrors:- Tungsten-halogen high-beam headlamps ($27). Cornering lamps: Regal ($52). Coach lamps: Ltd ($90). Front lamp monitors ($31). Door courtesy/warning lights: Ltd ($38-$60). Dome reading lamp ($20). Underhood light ($5). Remote left mirror ($19); right ($35-$41). Dual sport mirrors, left remote ($41- $47). Dual remote sport mirrors ($28-$75). Visor vanity mirrors ($11). Lighted visor vanity mirror ($49). Entertainment:- AM radio ($90). AM/FM radio ($142). AM/FM stereo radio ($178); w/8-track or cassette ($252-$264). Signal-seeking AM/FM stereo radio ($379-$402). Electronic- tuning AM/FM stereo radio w/8-track or cassette ($483-$555). AM/FM stereo radio with CB ($487). Dual rear speakers ($23- $28). Fixed-mast antenna: w/radio ($10). Windshield antenna ($27); incl. w/radio. Automatic power antenna ($47-$74). Triband power antenna ($86-$113). Exterior Trim:- Landau vinyl top: Regal ($146). Heavy-padded landau vinyl top: Regal ($186). Long vinyl top ($115). Long padded vinyl top: Century ($192). Designers' accent paint ($130-$202). Solid special color paint ($162). Protective bodyside moldings ($48). Wraparound bodyside moldings: Century, Ltd ($62-$96). Rocker panel moldings: Century sed ($19). Wheel opening moldings: Century ($25). Door edge guards ($13-$21). Belt reveal moldings: Regal spt cpe w/decor pkg. ($36). Bodyside stripes ($36). Front bumper guards: Century ($24). Woodgrain vinyl applique: wag ($286-$311). Luggage rack: wag ($96). Air deflector: wag ($32). Tailgate follower board: wag ($13). Interior Trim/Upholstery:- Full-length console ($95). Non- shifting console: Regal ($69). Bucket seats ($72). Bench seat: Century sed ($144 credit). 55/45 seating: cloth bench ($134); leather/vinyl, Regal Ltd ($324). Limited 55/45 cloth seating: Regal spt cpe ($358); leather/vinyl ($682). 45/45 seating, Regal Ltd: cloth (NC); leather/vinyl ($324). Limited 45/45 Spt Cpe seating: cloth ($358); leather/vinyl ($682). Custom seat/shoulder belts ($23). Front carpet savers ($15). Carpet savers and mats ($25). Front/rear carpet savers with inserts ($45). Trunk trim covering ($44). Lockable storage compartment: wag ($45). Load floor carpet: wag ($54). Wheels:- Chrome-plated wheels ($47-$180). Styled aluminum wheels ($197-$329). Turbine wheels ($114-$158). Locking wire wheel covers: Century ($205); Regal ($47-$161). Deluxe wheel covers: Century ($45). Tires:- P185/75R14 GBR WSW: Century V-6 ($48). P195/75R14 GBR: Century V-6 ($26). P195/75R14 SBR BSW: Century ($53-$78). P195/75R14 GBR WSW: Century ($49-$76). P195/75R14 SBR WSW: Century ($101-$126); Regal ($49). P205/70R14 SBR wide-oval BSW: Regal ($39). P205/70R14 SBR whitewall: Regal ($54-$94). P205/70R14 SBR WLT: Century ($162-$187); Regal ($70-$109). Self-sealing tires ($99).

LESABRE/ELECTRA/ESTATE WAGON CONVENIENCE/APPEARANCE OPTIONS: Option Packages: LeSabre T Type pkg.: bucket seats, console, sport mirrors, sport steering wheel, Gran Touring suspension ($271-$295). LeSabre Coupe Sport pkg.: front bucket seats, remote sport mirrors ($103-$122). Accessory group: LeSabre ($24-$43); Electra ($30-$77). Lamp/indicator group: LeSabre ($47-$64). Comfort/Convenience:- Sliding electric Astroroof ($981-$995). Air cond.: LeSabre ($625). Automatic air cond.: LeSabre ($708); Electra ($83). Air cond. with touch-climate control: LeSabre ($796); Electra ($171). Cruise Master w/resume: LeSabre ($135). Rear defogger, electric ($107). Tinted glass ($107). Power windows: LeSabre ($143-$211). Electric door locks ($93-$132). Automatic door locks ($154-$183). Six-way power seat, driver's or passenger's ($146- $173); both ($319-$346). Electric seatback recliner, one side ($124). Manual seatback recliner, one side: LeSabre ($65). Sport steering wheel: LeSabre ($34). Tilt steering ($81). Tilt/telescoping steering column ($119-$128). Dial clock: LeSabre ($55). Trip

odometer: LeSabre ($14). Remote electric tailgate lock: LeSabre Estate ($43). Electric trunk lock: Electra ($63). Electric trunk release ($27). Electric fuel cap lock ($38). Theft deterrent system ($142); N/A on Estate. Three-speed wiper w/delay ($41). Lighting, Horns and Mirrors:- Tungsten-halogen high-beam headlamps ($27). Twilight Sentinel headlamp control: Electra ($50). Cornering lamps ($51). Coach lamps: Electra Ltd ($90). Light monitors, front: LeSabre, Electra Estate ($31); front/rear, Electra ($65). Door courtesy/warning lamps ($38-$60). Lighted door lock and interior light control ($60). Four-note horn ($24). Remote left mirror: LeSabre ($19). Remote right mirror: LeSabre ($40); Electra Ltd ($21-$40). Remote electric right mirror: Park Ave. ($52-$72). Dual remote sport mirrors: LeSabre ($56- $75); Electra Ltd, Estate ($37-$55). Dual electric remote mirrors: LeSabre ($102-$121); Electra Ltd, Estate ($83-$102). Remote left mirror w/thermometer: LeSabre ($32-$52); Electra Ltd, Estate ($19-$32). Electric left mirror w/thermometer: Electra Park Ave. ($32). Dual electric mirrors w/left thermometer: LeSabre ($134-$153); Electra ($115-$134). Visor vanity mirrors: LeSabre ($11). Lighted visor vanity mirror, driver or passenger ($115-$153). Entertainment:- AM radio: LeSabre ($90). AM/FM radio: LeSabre ($142). AM/FM stereo radio: LeSabre, Electra Ltd/Estate ($178). AM/FM stereo radio and 8-track or cassette player: LeSabre ($252-$264); Electra ($74-$264). Full-feature AM/FM stereo radio: LeSabre ($369); Electra ($346-$369); Park Ave. cpe ($191). Full-feature AM/FM stereo radio w/ 8-track or cassette: LeSabre ($420-$455); Electra ($265-$455). Signal-seeking AM/FM stereo radio: LeSabre ($379-$402); Electra ($170-$348). Signal-seeking radio and 8-track or cassette: LeSabre ($483-$555); Electra ($273-$500). AM/FM stereo radio with CB: LeSabre ($488). Signal-seeking AM/FM stereo radio with CB and 8-track or cassette player: Electra ($581-$783). Delete AM/FM stereo radio: Park Ave. ($150 credit). Concert Sound speaker system: Electra exc. wag ($91); ETR or full-feature radio req'd. Dual rear speakers ($23-$28) when ordered with radio. Windshield antenna ($27); incl. w/radio. Automatic power antenna ($48- $75). Triband power antenna ($86-$113); w/CB radio (NC). Exterior Trim:- Exterior molding pkg.: LeSabre ($92). Landau vinyl top: LeSabre, Electra Ltd cpe ($195). Long vinyl top: LeSabre, Electra Ltd sed ($142-$159). Heavy-padded long vinyl top: Electra Ltd sedan ($198). Designers' accent paint: LeSabre ($191). Special single-color paint: ($161); Firemist, Electra ($180). Protective bodyside moldings: Estate ($48). Wide rocker panel moldings: Electra Ltd/Estate ($56). Door edge guards ($14-$21). Bodyside stripes ($54). Woodgrain vinyl applique: LeSabre Estate ($279). Roof rack: LeSabre Estate ($139). Interior Trim/Upholstery:- Full console: LeSabre cpe ($100). 55/45 seating: LeSabre ($108). Leather/vinyl 50/50 seating: Electra ($452). Custom seatbelts: LeSabre ($23). Third seat: Estate ($108). Front carpet savers: Electra ($25). Carpet savers and handy mats ($25). Front/rear carpet savers w/inserts ($45). Trunk trim carpet ($51-$63). Trunk mat ($13). Wheels:- Chrome-plated wheels ($152-$182). Styled aluminum wheels ($253-$283). Custom wheel covers: Electra Ltd ($30). Custom locking wire wheel covers ($129-$159). Tires:- P205/75R15 SBR WSW: LeSabre ($53). P215/75R15 SBR WSW: LeSabre ($88). P225/75R15 SBR wide WSW: Electra ($36). P225/70R15 SBR wide WSW: LeSabre cpe ($139). Self-sealing tires ($99-$122).

RIVIERA CONVENIENCE/APPEARANCE OPTIONS: Comfort/Convenience:- Electric sliding Astroroof ($995). Electric sunroof ($848). Automatic touch climate control air cond. ($175). Cruise control w/resume ($135). Rear defogger, electric ($107). Automatic electric door locks ($62). Six-way power seat, passenger ($173). Electric seatback recliner, one side ($124). Sport steering wheel ($34). Tilt steering ($81). Tilt/telescope steering wheel ($128). Electric fuel cap lock $38). Electric trunk releease ($27). Electric trunk lock ($63). Low fuel indicator ($17). Fuel usage light ($31). Trip monitor ($833). Three-speed wipers w/delay ($41). Windshield washer fluid indicator ($11). Theft deterrent system ($142). Lighting, Horns and Mirrors:- Tungsten-halogen high-beam headlamps ($27). Twilight Sentinel ($50). Coach lamps ($90); incl. w/vinyl top. Front/rear light monitors ($65). Rear quarter courtesy/reading lamp ($43). Lighted door lock and interior light control ($60). Four-note horn ($24). Dual electric remote mirrors ($61). Lighted visor vanity mirrors, each ($50). Entertainment:- Full-feature AM/FM stereo radio ($190); w/8-track or cassette ($264-$276). AM/FM stereo radio w/8-track or cassette tape player ($74-$86); with CB and 8- track or cassette ($537-$561). Signal-seeking AM/FM stereo radio ($169); w/8-track ($273); w/cassette ($322). Delete radio ($150 credit). Rear speakers ($23). Concert Sound system ($91); N/A with base radio. Triband power antenna ($42). Exterior Trim:- Heavy-padded landau vinyl top w/coach lamps ($273). Designers' accent paint ($202). Special color Firemist paint ($180). Protective bodyside moldings ($59). Door edge guards ($14). Bodyside stripes ($54). Interior Trim/Upholstery:- 45/55 leather/vinyl front seat ($349). Storage console ($67). Front/rear carpet savers w/inserts ($55). Trunk trim carpeting ($27). Trunk mat ($13). Wheels and Tires:- Chrome-plated wheels ($126). Custom locking wire wheel covers ($161). GR70 x 15 SBR whitewalls ($33). Self- sealing tires ($122).

HISTORY: Introduced: September 25, 1980. Model year production (U.S.): 856,996 for a 12.8 percent share of the industry total. That number included 138,058 four-cylinder Buicks, 521,837 sixes, and 197,101 V-8s--quite a drop from the days when the V-8 was king among Buick buyers. Calendar year production (U.S.): 839,960. Model year sales by U.S. dealers: 756,186 (led by Regal and Skylark). Calendar year sales (U.S.): 722,617 for a market slice of 11.6 percent.

Historical Footnotes: Buick assembled its 23 millionth car in 1981 and enjoyed a good sales year as well, beating the 1980 mark by over 56,000 cars. Such good performance came as a surprise, as other U.S. automakers endured a slump. Skylark sales rose by over 25 percent, but Regal hung on as Buick's best seller. Sales of full-size Buicks dwindled. For the fifth time, a Buick served as pace car for the Indy 500. This time it was a Regal with special 4.1-liter V-6 engine, developed by Buick along with Baker Engineering. The souped-up 4.1 produced 281 horsepower, compared with 125 for the stock version used in full-size Buicks (not yet in Regals). The same car also paced the July 4 Pike's Peak hill climb.

1982 BUICK

After a year's absence, the Skylark name returned--but on an all-new front-wheel drive subcompact Buick. The new version debuted in March 1982 as a mid-year entry. Also new was a front-drive (and shrunken) Century, no longer closely related to the rear-drive Regal. Two new gas engines were offered: a high-output 2.8- liter V-6 for Skylarks (delivering 20 percent more horsepower), and a 181 cu. in. (3.0-liter) V-6 for Century, with shorter stroke than the 3.8 version from which it evolved. Flat-top pistons boosted the new 3.0's compression ratio to 8.45:1. It developed just as much horsepower as the 3.8, but at higher engine speed. The high-output 2.8 also gained compression, from standard 8.0:1 in the base version to 8.94:1 in the high-output variant, as a result of larger intake and exhaust valves and increased valve duration and lift. A new diesel 4.3-liter V-6 became available during the model year. On existing powerplants, the biggest news was fuel injection added to the Skylark (and new Century) four. Turbo performance in the Regal Sport Coupe and Riviera T Type got a boost for 1982. The turbocharged V-6 gained a low- restriction dual exhaust sytem as standard on the Regal Sport Coupe, along with upgraded electronics and a larger (five-quart) oil-pan capacity. Turbo response time was reduced, and incoming air was warmed in an exhaust-heated plenum chamber. Oldsmobile's big (5.7-liter) diesel V-8 was now available on Regal, LeSabre, Electra, Riviera, and Estate Wagons. More models added the overdrive automatic transmission that had been offered on selected 1981 Buicks. Producing a claimed 10-20 percent economy boost, overdrive was standard in Electra and Riviera, optional under LeSabre hoods. Pliacell-R- shock absorbers, formerly used only on big Buicks, were added to the rear of all 1982 models. They used a sealed fluid chamber and special gas rather than air. "Memory Seat" was offered as an option on Electra and Riviera, returning automatically to either of two selected positions at the touch of a button. 1982 Buick body colors were light gray, black and white, plus a selection of metallics: silver, dark gray Firemist, charcoal, light sandstone, medium sandstone, dark brown Firemist, medium blue, dark blue, light or dark jadestone, light or dark redwood, and red Firemist. Not all colors were available in all models.

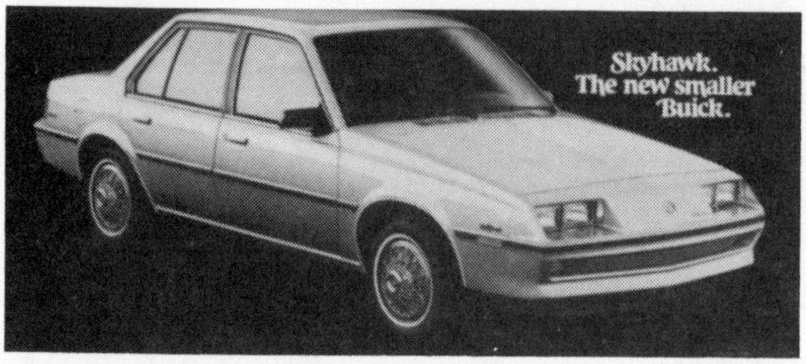

1982 Skyhawk Limited sedan (JG)

SKYHAWK — SERIES 4J — FOUR — Styled along Century lines on GM's J-car platform, the new Skyhawk rode a front-wheel drive chassis. According to Buick, it displayed the "aerodynamic wedge shape of the fuel- efficient future." The fresh subcompact debuted at the Chicago Auto Show in Feburary 1982. The contemporary five- passenger design featured a low hood and high rear deck to reduce drag, along with a unified front end and grille and integrated headlamp system. Backup lights sat in a black panel between the wraparound taillamps. Deluxe wheel covers carried the Buick tri-shield emblem. Buyers could eventually choose from three transverse-mounted engines. First came the base 112 cu. in. (1.8-liter) OHV four. Late arrivals were a fuel-injected 1.8-liter overhead-cam four from GM of Brazil, and a 121 cu. in. (2.0- liter) carbureted four. The 88-horsepower base engine had a cross-flow cylinder head design with intake valves on one side, exhaust on the other. GM's computer command control module controlled spark timing, and it used a fast-burn combustion chamber. The 2.0 engine was essentially the same, but with longer stroke, developing two more horsepower. Skyhawk's chassis now had MacPherson independent front suspension and semi-independent crank arm rear suspension, plus rack-and-pinion steering and Pliacell-R- rear shock bsorbers. Skyhawk came in Custom or Limited trim level, on coupe and sedan bodies. Limiteds carried standard soft knit velour upholstery, while Customs could have a woven cloth or vinyl interior. Coupes had swing-out rear quarter windows; sedans, roll-down rear windows. Coupes also had a standard "easy entry" passenger door. Standard Skyhawk equipment included a Delco 2000 series AM radio (which could be deleted), full console, reclining bucket seats, front and rear ashtrays, roof-mounted assist handles, Freedom II battery, two-speed wiper/washer, cigarette lighter, power brakes, power rack-and-pinion steering, side-window front defoggers, compact spare tire, front stabilizer bar, and black left-hand mirror. The Limited added a front-seat armrest, gauge package, trip odometer, custom steering wheel, and acoustic insulation package. Skyhawk options included electronic-tuning radios, six-way power driver's seat, remote trunk release, Vista-Vent flip- open removable glass sunroof, and styled aluminum wheels. A four-speed (overdrive) manual gearbox was standard, but five- speed became available later in the model year.

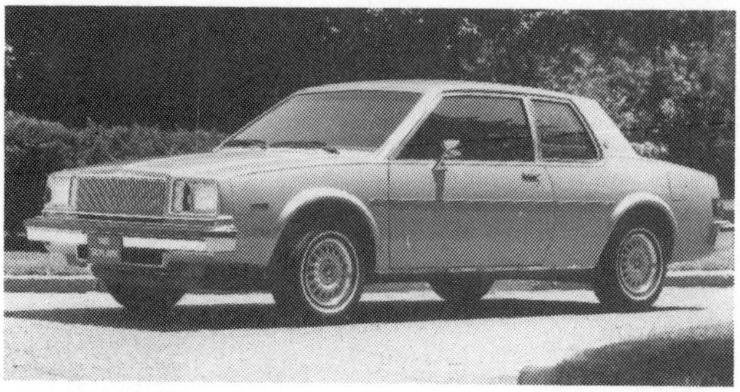

1982 Skylark coupe (AA)

SKYLARK — SERIES 4X — FOUR/V-6 — Six models made the Skylark lineup: coupe and sedan in base, Limited or Sport trim. Not much changed except for minor revisions in grille and front-end sheetmetal. Skylark now had a "fluidic" windshield washer with single spray nozzle, plus new Pliacell-R- shock absorbers in back. Major changes came under the hood and in the suspension. The base 151 cu. in. (2.5-liter) four switched from a carburetor to single-point electronic fuel injection, intended to improve cold-weather operation as well as gas mileage, and eliminate engine run-on. Two optional engines were offered: a standard 173 cu. in. (2.8-liter) V-6, or a high-output 2.8 V-6 with 20 percent more horsepower. That one had revised carburetion, larger valves, and an altered camshaft. Higher axle ratio boosted Skylark performance with the potent V-6 even more. Four-speed manual shift (floor lever) remained standard; automatic available. A refined interior replaced the vinyl bolsters with cloth fabric on Skylark and Sport notchback front seats. Limited and Sport again offered optional leather. There was a new steering wheel. Special lighting in glove box, under dash, in ashtray and elsewhere that was formerly optional now became standard. A Graphic Equalizer was now available with cassette tape players, offering tone control in five bands. Optional speakers delivered better frequency response. For the first time, Limiteds could have back-seat reading lamps. Also optional: the Vista-Vent flip-open glass sunroof.

CENTURY — SERIES 4A — FOUR/V-6 — Introduced after the model year began, Century underwent a total restyle for a contemporary, wedge-shaped aerodynamic appearance. Bumpers and outside mirrors integrated into the basic body form added to the slick, even "slippery" look. With a transverse-mounted four-cylinder engine under the hood and a front-drive chassis, the new Century hardly seemed related to the old rear-drive that wore that name for so many years. Gas and diesel V-6 engines were available, but it was still a much different car. The modern version had MacPherson strut independent front suspension, plus trailing axle rear suspension with

1982 Century Limited sedan (B)

Pliacell-R- shocks. Though almost 8 inches shorter than before, it retained similar interior dimensions and trunk capacity. An integrated grille with center crest had two bright horizontal bars and a single vertical bar. Half of the lower segment extended all the way outward and around the fender tips, below the wraparound lights. Wide wraparound taillamps were split into two sections by a body-color strip. A Century script badge was at the back of the rear quarter panels, and n engine identifier at the forward end of front fenders. The rear roof pillar held a crest. Grille, front end and hood were said to "flow in an unbroken line past the windshield and side windows." Those windows were flush-mounted to cut wind resistance, giving the new Century the lowest drag coefficient of any Buick. Standard engine was the 151 cu. in. (2.5-liter) four; optional, either a new 181 cu. in. (3.0-liter) V-6 or 4.3- liter diesel V-6. Standard three-speed automatic transmission included a converter clutch for added efficiency. Power rack- and-pinion steering was standard; so were power brakes and deluxe wheel covers. Custom and Limited models were offered. A new Delco AM2000 radio was standard. So were wide belt reveal moldings, color-coordinated bodyside moldings, front/rear bumper guards, wheel opening moldings, black rocker panels, front and side-window defoggers, black outside mirrors, cigarette lighter, and maintenance-free battery. Limiteds also carried dual horns, a stand-up hood ornament, 45/45 pillow seats (soft velour cloth or vinyl) with armrest, a custom steering wheel, and wide lower bodyside moldings. Rocker switches and thumbwheels controlled lights and other functions at the instrument panel.

1982 Regal Sport Turbo coupe (AA)

REGAL — SERIES 4G — V-6/V-8 — After several years of success in coupe form as a top Buick seller, Regal added a four-door sedan and Estate Wagon. Now that Century had turned to front-drive, Regal remained alone as a rear-drive mid-size. Regal's formal-look grille, made up of narrow vertical bars split into eight sections and angled outward at the base, went on both coupes and new models. Both the grille and taillamp displayed Regal identification. The new sedan offered dual outside mirrors plus color-coordinated bodyside moldings, with seating for six. The Regal Estate Wagon could carry up to 71.8 cubic feet of cargo with rear seat folded down. Standard fittings included deluxe wheel covers and whitewall tires, plus bodyside moldings and bumper guards. Standard engine was the familiar 231 cu. in. (3.8-liter) V-6, hooked to automatic transmission. All but the Regal Sport Coupe could have a 252 (4.1-liter) V-6, or choice of a V-6 or V-8 diesel. Coil spring suspensions used Pliacell-R- shock absorbers at the rear. Regal's Limited could be ordered with 45/45 front seating in a choice of two-tone combinations: sandstone and brown, or gray and black charcoal. Limiteds also sported a new deluxe steering wheel. The optional resume-speed cruise control now included a tiny memory light. Other new options: Delco electronically-tuned AM/FM stereo radio with tape player; quartz analog clock; rear-seat reading lamps; Twilight Sentinel headlamp control; and Electronic Touch Climate Control air conditioning (offered on other Buicks since 1980). A trailering package was available for the 3.8 engine. Regal Limiteds could also have electro-luminescent coach lamps, automatic door locks, and Gran Touring suspension. The turbocharged Regal coupe continued, with improved performance. The Sport Coupe featured a special hood, black accents, styled aluminum wheels, and Gran Touring suspension. Axle ratio switched to 3.08:1, and the turbo 3.8-liter V-6 now included a low-restriction dual exhaust system.

1982 LeSabre Custom coupe (AA)

LESABRE — SERIES 4B — V-6/V-8 — Still (relatively) full-size and rear-drive, the six-passenger LeSabre entered 1982 with a new grille and more trim, including convenience lights and new color on the woodgrain-trimmed instrument panel. The vertical-slat grille was divided into three rows and four columns, with Buick badge on the side of the center row. Quad headlamps were deeply recessed; parking/signal lamps set into the bumper. Taillamps were wide, but not full-width. The former base LeSabre was now called LeSabre Custom. Buyers could take the standard 231 cu. in. (3.8-liter) V-6 engine for economy, or elect a 252 cu. in. (4.1-liter) V-6 for power. Other options: a 5.0-liter gas V-8 and 5.7 diesel V-8. The 4.1 V-6 had the same electronic idle speed control as the smaller version, plus electronic spark control that adjusted the spark timing when it sensed that the engine was just about to begin knocking. More carpeting was on the floor up front. Standard equipment included whitewalls, wheel opening moldings, deluxe wheel covers, and color-coordinated bodyside moldings. LeSabres also had power brakes and steering, a maintenance- free battery, front/rear bumper guards and protective strips, a compact spare tire, instrument panel courtesy lights, and lights for dome, glove compartment, trunk, front ashtray and ngine compartment. The Limited carried the new woodgrain color on doors as well as dash, and also included tinted glass. New options: sail panel reading lights and programmable headlamps. Arriving later in the model year was a limited-edition LeSabre F/E ("formal edition"), offered in two-tone blue and gray. The body was blue all across the top and down to the beltline molding on doors, rear quarter and front fender. Below that point, it was solid gray. Inside were gray cloth seats in a dark blue interior. F/E had light gray bodyside moldings, special 'F/E' exterior identification, a Park Avenue type steering wheel, custom locking wire wheel covers, whitewall steel-belted radials, and remote sport mirrors.

ESTATE WAGON — SERIES 4B/C — V-8 — Estate Wagons available in LeSabre and Electra dress (plus the new Regal described above). LeSabre and Electra offered the same 87.9 cubic foot cargo area and powerteams: standard 5.0-liter gas V-8 or 5.7 diesel V-8, with automatic overdrive transmission. Electra included a standard power tailgate window with remote-controlled tailgate lock plus electric door locks, power windows, chrome-plated road wheels, and woodgrain vinyl applique.

1982 Electra Park Avenue sedan (AA)

ELECTRA — SERIES 4C — V-6/V-8 — Not much changed in the look of Electra, with its formal-style grille. Limited and Park Avenue editions were offered, in coupe or sedan form. New convenience features included optional electronic memory seats and standard Soft- Ray tinted glass. Automatic four-speed overdrive transmission, introduced the prior year, was refined. Electras's ample equipment list included standard right and left mirrors, whitewall tires, bumper guards and protective strips, digital clock, instrument panel floodlighting, two- way power driver's seat, power windows, and air conditioning. Base engine was the 252 cu. in. (4.1-liter) V-6; optional, a 307 cu. in. (5.0-liter) gasoline V-8 or the Oldsmobile 5.7- liter diesel V-8. Park Avenue again incorporated the traditional ventiport design into a bodyside molding, rather than separate as in past years. That model also featured wide, bright chrome rocker moldings and a padded halo vinyl top, plus standard Delco AM/FM stereo radio. Other Park Avenue extras: a six- way power driver's seat, remote-control trunk release, door courtesy and warning lights, and dome reading lamp. The Concert Sound Speaker introduced two years earlier was available again. The optional "Memory Seat" returned to either of two preferred positions automatically.

1982 Riviera coupe (AA)

RIVIERA — SERIES 4E — V/6-V-8 — Though the basic Riviera was basically a carryover for 1982, the biggest news came in mid-year with the arrival of the limited-production convertible--the first ragtop Buick since 1975. It came in Firemist red or white with white convertible top, red leather seats, four-wheel disc brakes, and locking wire wheel covers. According to the one-page flyer, only 500 Limited Edition convertibles were planned for the year. Buick wasn't the first domestic automaker to return to the ragtop fold in the 1980s, but its arrival was a welcome sign for open-air fans. The conversion was done by American Sunroof Corp. to Buick specifications, and sold with a Buick warranty. Riviera's T Type also reappeared later in the model year, after a six-month absence from the lineup. Now it carried the new-generation turbo V-6, four-wheel power disc brakes, tungsten-halogen high-beam headlamps, Gran Touring suspension, and special aluminum wheels. T Type's exterior was gray Firemist with custom blacked-out grille, twin styled remote mirrors, amber turn signal lamps, and matching gray interior with cloth bucket seats. New insignias on front fenders and deck lid highlighted the turbo V-6. Axle ratio changed to 3.36:1. Base engine remained the 252 cu. in. (4.1-liter) -6 with 4Bbl. carburetor. Options included the 305 cu. in. (5.0-liter) gas V-8 and 350 cu. in. (5.7-liter) diesel V-8. Additional standard

equipment included overdrive automatic transmission and resume-speed cruise control. The optional Gran Touring suspension offered quicker steering feel and increased road feedback. Also on Riviera's standard equipment list were cornering lights, automatic level control, power brakes and steering, and automatic overdrive transmission. A new deluxe steering wheel had a padded center. Bumpers had black protective strips. On the steering column, a new multi-function lever commanded turn signal, headlamps, wiper/washer, and resume- speed cruise control. The standard electronically-tuned AM/FM stereo radio with automatic power antenna could be deleted for credit.

I.D. DATA: All Buicks again had a 17-symbol Vehicle Identification Number (VIN), introduced in 1981, stamped on a metal tag attached to the upper left surface of the cowl, visible through the windshield. The number begins with a '1' to indicate U.S.A., followed by 'G' for General Motors and '4' for Buick Division. The next letter indicates restraint system. The fifth symbol shows series: 'S' Skyhawk; 'T' Skyhawk Limited; 'B' Skylark; 'C' Skylark Limited; 'D' Skylark Sport; 'H' Century Custom; 'L' Century Limited; 'J' Regal; 'K' Regal Sport Coupe; 'M' Regal Limited; 'N' LeSabre; 'P' LeSabre Limited; 'R' LeSabre Estate Wagon; 'V' Electra Estate Wagon; 'X' Electra Limited; 'W' Electra Park Avenue; 'Y' Riviera T Type; 'Z' Riviera. Digits six and seven indicate body type: '27' 2-dr. coupe; '37' 2-dr. coupe; '47' Regal 2-dr. coupe; '57' Riviera 2-dr. coupe; '67' 2-dr. convertible coupe; '35' 4-dr. wagon; '19' Century 4-dr. sedan; '69' 4-dr. sedan. Next is the engine code: 'G' L4-112 2Bbl.; 'O' L4-112 TBI; 'B' L4-151 TBI; 'R' L4-151 2Bbl.; 'X' V6-173 2Bbl.; 'Z' H.O. V6-173 2Bbl.; 'E' V6-181 2Bbl.; 'A' V6-231 2Bbl.; '3' V6-231 Turbo; '4' V6-252 4Bbl.; 'V' V6-263 diesel; 'Y' V8-307 4Bbl.; 'N' V8-350 diesel. Symbol nine is a check digit ('8'). Symbol ten denotes model year ('C' 982). Symbol eleven is the plant code. The final six digits are the sequential serial number. An additional identifying number can be found on the engine, showing codes for GM division, model year, assembly plant, and vehicle sequence number. A body number plate shows model year, car division, series, style, body assembly plant, body number, trim combination, modular seat code, paint code, and date build code.

SKYHAWK CUSTOM (FOUR)

Series Number	Body/Style Number	Body Type & Seating	Factory Price	Shipping Weight	Production Total
4J	S27	2-dr Coupe-5P	7297	2327	25,378
4J	S69	4-dr Sedan-5P	7489	2385	22,540

SKYHAWK LIMITED (FOUR)

4J	T27	2-dr Coupe-5P	7739	2349	Note 1
4J	T69	4-dr Sedan-5P	7931	2411	Note 1

Note 1: Production totals listed under Skyhawk Custom also include Limited models. A total of 32,027 Customs and 15,891 Limiteds were produced for the model year.

SKYLARK (FOUR/V-6)

4X	B37	2-dr Coupe-5P	7477/7602	2462/2519	21,017
4X	B69	4-dr Sedan-5P	7647/7772	2493/2550	65,541

SKYLARK LIMITED (FOUR/V-6)

4X	C37	2-dr Coupe-5P	7917/8042	2489/2546	13,712
4X	C69	4-dr Sedan-5P	8079/8204	2519/2576	44,290

SKYLARK SPORT (FOUR/V-6)

4X	D37	2-dr Coupe-5P	8048/8173	2494/2551	Note 2
4X	D69	4-dr Sedan-5P	8219/8344	2524/2581	Note 2

Note 2: Production figures listed under base Skylark also include equivalent Sport models. Total production for the model year came to 85,263 base Skylarks, 1,295 Skylark Sports, and 58,002 Limiteds.

CENTURY CUSTOM (FOUR/V-6)

4A	H27	2-dr Coupe-5P	8980/9105	2603/2684	19,715
4A	H19	4-dr Sedan-5P	9141/9266	2631/2712	83,250

CENTURY LIMITED (FOUR/V-6)

4A	L27	2-dr Coupe-5P	9417/9542	2614/2695	Note 3
4A	L19	4-dr Sedan-5P	9581/9706	2643/2724	Note 3

Note 3: Production figures for Century Custom coupe and sedan also include Century Limited models. Total production for the model year amounted to 45,036 Customs and 57,929 Limiteds.

REGAL (V-6)

4G	J47	2-dr Coupe-6P	8712	3152	134,237
4G	J69	4-dr Sedan-6P	8862	3167	74,428
4G	J35	4-dr Sta Wag-6P	9058	3317	14,732

REGAL LIMITED (V-6)

4G	M47	2-dr Coupe-6P	9266	3192	Note 4
4G	M69	4-dr Sedan-6P	9364	3205	Note 4

Note 4: Coupe/sedan production figures listed under base Regal also include Regal Limited. A total of 105,812 base Regals and 102,850 Regal Limiteds were made; only 8,276 of those had a V-8 engine.

REGAL SPORT COUPE (TURBO V-6)

4G	K47	2-dr Coupe-6P	9738	3225	2,022

LESABRE CUSTOM (V-6/V-8)

4B	N37	2-dr Coupe-6P	8774/9016	3474/3656	5,165
4B	N69	4-dr Sedan-6P	8876/9118	3503/3685	23,220

LESABRE LIMITED (V-6/V-8)

4B	P37	2-dr Coupe-6P	9177/9419	3492/3674	16,062
4B	P69	4-dr Sedan-6P	9331/9573	3625/3707	47,224

LESABRE ESTATE WAGON (V-8)

4B	R35	4-dr Sta Wag-6P	10668	4171	7,149

ELECTRA LIMITED (V-6/V-8)

4C	X37	2-dr Coupe-6P	11713/11713	3657/3836	8,449
4C	X69	4-dr Sedan-6P	11884/11884	3717/3896	59,601

ELECTRA PARK AVENUE (V-6/V-8)

4C	W37	2-dr Coupe-6P	13408/13408	3734/3913	Note 5
4C	W69	4-dr Sedan-6P	13559/13559	3798/3977	Note 5

Note 5: Production figures listed under Electra Limited also include Park Avenue coupes and sedans. A total of 22,709 Limited and 45,346 Park Avenue editions were produced, 9,748 with a V-6 engine.

ELECTRA ESTATE WAGON (V-8)

4C	V35	4-dr Sta Wag-6P	12911	4175	8,182

RIVIERA (V-6/V-8)

4E	Z57	2-dr Coupe-5P	14272/14272	3600/3760	42,823
4E	Z67	2-dr Conv-5P	23994/24064	N/A	1,248

RIVIERA T TYPE (TURBO V-6)

4E	Y57	2-dr Coupe-5P	14940	N/A	Note 6

Note 6: T Type production is included in basic Riviera figure.

FACTORY PRICE AND WEIGHT NOTE: Figure before the slash is for four- cylinder engine, after the slash for V-6. For full-size models, figure before the slash is for V-6 engine, after slash for V-8.

ENGINES: BASE FOUR (Skyhawk): Inline, overhead-valve four-cylinder. Cast iron block and head. Displacement: 112 cu. in. (1.8 liters). Bore & stroke: 3.50 x 2.91 in. Compression ratio: 9.0:1. Brake horsepower: 88 at 5100 R.P.M. Torque: 100 lbs.-ft. at 2800 R.P.M. Five main bearings. Hydraulic valve lifters. Carburetor: 2Bbl. Rochester E2SE. VIN Code: G. OPTIONAL FOUR (Skyhawk): Inline, overhead-cam four-cylinder. Cast iron block and head. Displacement: 112 cu. in. (1.8 liters). Bore & stroke: 3.33 x 3.12 in. Compression ratio: 9.0:1. Brake horsepower: 80 at 5200 R.P.M. Torque: 115 lbs.-ft. at 2800 R.P.M. Five main bearings. Hydraulic valve lifters. Throttle-body fuel injection. VIN Code: O. OPTIONAL FOUR (Skyhawk): Inline, overhead-cam four-cylinder. Cast iron block and head. Displacement: 121 cu. in. (2.0 liters). Bore & stroke: 3.50 x 3.14 in. Compression ratio: 9.0:1. Brake horsepower: 90 at 5100 R.P.M. Torque: 111 lbs.-ft. at 2700 R.P.M. Five main bearings. Hydraulic valve lifters. Carburetor: 2Bbl. Rochester E2SE. VIN Code: B. BASE FOUR (Skylark, Century): Inline, overhead-valve four-cylinder. Cast iron block and head. Displacement: 151 cu. in. (2.5 liters). Bore & stroke: 4.0 x 3.0 in. Compression ratio: 8.2:1. Brake horsepower: 90 at 4000 R.P.M. Torque: 134 lbs.-ft. at 2400 R.P.M. Five main bearings. Hydraulic valve lifters. Throttle-body fuel injection. Built by Pontiac. VIN Code: R. Sales Code: LW9. OPTIONAL V-6 (Skylark): 60-degree, overhead-valve V-6. Cast iron block and head. Displacement: 173 cu. in. (2.8 liters). Bore & stroke: 3.5 x 3.0 in. Compression ratio: 8.4:1. Brake horsepower: 112 at 5100 R.P.M. Torque: 148 lbs.-ft. at 2400 R.P.M. Four main bearings. Hydraulic valve lifters. Carburetor: 2Bbl. Rochester E2SE. Built by Chevrolet. VIN Code: X. Sales Code: LE2. HIGH-OUTPUT 173 V-6; OPTIONAL (Skylark): Same as 173 above, in. V-6 above except as follows: Compression ratio: 8.9:1. Brake horsepower: 135 at 5400 R.P.M. Torque: 142 lbs.-ft. at 2400 R.P.M. VIN Code: Z. OPTIONAL V-6 (Century): 90-degree, overhead-valve V-6. Cast iron block and head. Displacement: 181 cu. in. (3.0 liters). Bore & stroke: 3.8 x 2.66 in. Compression ratio: 8.45:1. Brake horsepower: 110 at 800 R.P.M. Torque: 145 lbs.-ft. at 2600 R.P.M. Four main bearings. Hydraulic valve lifters. Carburetor: 2Bbl. Rochester E2ME. VIN Code: E. BASE V-6 (Regal, LeSabre): 90-degree, overhead-valve V-6. Cast iron alloy block and head. Displacement: 231 cu. in. (3.8 liters). Bore & stroke: 3.8 x 3.4 in. Compression ratio: 8.0:1. Brake horsepower: 110 at 3800 R.P.M. Torque: 190 lbs.-ft. at 1600 R.P.M. Four main bearings. Hydraulic valve lifters. Carburetor: 2Bbl. Rochester M2ME. VIN Code: A. Sales Code: LD5. TURBOCHARGED V-6 (Regal Sport Coupe, Riviera T Type): Same as 231 V-6 above, but with E4ME four-barrel carburetor. Brake horsepower: 170 at 3800 R.P.M. (Riviera, 180 at 4000); Torque: 275 lbs.-ft. at 2600 R.P.M. (Riviera, 280 at 2400). VIN Code: 3. Sales Code: LC8. BASE V-6 (Electra, Riviera); OPTIONAL (Regal, LeSabre): 90-degree, overhead-valve V-6. Cast iron block and head. Displacement: 252 cu. in. (4.1 liters). Bore & stroke: 3.965 x 3.4 in. Compression ratio: 8.0:1. Brake horsepower: 125 at 4000 R.P.M. Torque: 205 lbs.-ft. at 2000 R.P.M. Four main bearings. Hydraulic valve lifters. Carburetor: 4Bbl. Rochester. VIN Code: 4. Sales Code: LC4. DIESEL V-6 (Century, Regal cpe/sed): 90-degree, overhead-valve V-6. Cast iron block and head. Displacement: 262.5 cu. in. (4.3 liters). Bore & stroke: 4.057 x 3.385 in. Compression ratio: 21.6:1. Brake horsepower: 85 at 3600 R.P.M. Torque: 165 lbs.-ft. at 1600 R.P.M. Four main bearings. Hydraulic valve lifters. Fuel injection. VIN Code: V. BASE V-8 (Estate); OPTIONAL (LeSabre, Electra, Riviera): 90-degree, overhead valve V-8. Cast iron block and head. Displacement: 307 cu. in. (5.0 liters). Bore & stroke: 3.80 x 3.385 in. Compression ratio: 8.0:1. Brake horsepower: 140 at 3600 R.P.M. Torque: 240 lbs.-ft. at 1600 R.P.M. Five main bearings. Hydraulic valve lifters. Carburetor: 4Bbl. Roch. M4MC. Built by Oldsmobile. VIN Code: Y. Sales Code: LV2. OPTIONAL DIESEL V-8 (Regal, LeSabre, Electra, Estate, Riviera): 90-degree, overhead valve V-8. Cast iron block and head. Displacement: 350 cu. in. (5.7 liters). Bore & stroke: 4.057 x 3.385 in. Compression ratio: 21.6:1. Brake horsepower: 105 at 3200 R.P.M. Torque: 200 lbs.-ft. at 1600 R.P.M. Five main bearings. Hydraulic valve lifters. Fuel injection. Oldsmobile-built. VIN Code: N. Sales Code: LF9.

CHASSIS DATA: Wheelbase: (Skyhawk) 101.2 in.; (Skylark/Century) 104.9 in.; (Regal) 108.1 in.; (LeSabre/Estate) 115.9 in.; (Electra) 118.9 in.; (Riviera) 114.0 in. Overall length:- (Skyhawk) 175.3 in.; (Skylark) 181.1 in.; (Century) 189.1 in.; (Regal cpe) 200.6 in.; (Regal sed) 196.0 in.; (Regal wag) 196.7 in.; (LeSabre) 218.4 in.; (Electra) 221.3 in.; (Estate Wagon) 220.5 in.; (Riviera) 206.6 in. Height:- (Skyhawk) 54.0 in.; (Skylark) 53.7 in.; (Century) 53.6 in.; (Regal cpe) 54.5 in.; (Regal sed) 55.4 in.; (Regal wag) 56.5 in.; (LeSabre) 56.0- 56.7 in.; (Electra) 56.8-56.9 in.; (Estate) 59.1-59.4 in.; (Riviera) 54.3 in. Width:- (Skyhawk) 62.0 in.; (Skylark) 69.1 in.; (Century) 66.8 in.; (Regal cpe) 71.6 in.; (Regal sed) 71.1 in.; (Regal wag) 71.2 in.; (LeSabre) 78.0 in.; (Electra cpe) 76.2 in.; (Estate) 79.3 in.; (Riviera) 72.8 in. Front Tread:- (Skyhawk) 55.4 in.; (Skylark/Century) 58.7 in.; (Regal) 58.5 in.; (LeSabre/Electra) 61.8 in.; (Estate) 62.2 in.; (Riviera) 59.3 in. Rear Tread:- (Skyhawk) 55.2 in.; (Skylark/Century) 57.0 in.; (Regal) 57.7 in.; (LeSabre/Electra) 60.7 in.; (Estate) 64.0 in.; (Riviera) 60.0 in. Standard Tires:- (Skyhawk) (Skylark/Century) P185/80R13 GBR; (Skylark Sport) P205/70R13 SBR; (Regal) P195/75R14 SBR WSW; (Regal Spt Cpe) P205/70R14 SBR; (LeSabre) P205/75R15 SBR WSW; (Electra) P215/75R15 SBR WSW; (Estate) P225/75R15 SBR WSW; (Riviera) P205/75R15 SBR WSW.

TECHNICAL: Transmission:- Four-speed, fully synchronized floor shift standard on Skyhawk/Skylark; automatic optional. Turbo Hydra- matic standard on all other models. Skyhawk four-speed gear ratios: (1st) 3.53:1; (2nd) 1.95:1; (3rd) 1.24:1; (4th) 0.81:1; (Rev) 3.42:1. Four-speed gear ratios: (1st) 3.53:1; (2nd) 1.95:1; (3rd) 1.24:1; (4th) 0.73:1; (Rev) 3.92:1. Skylark/Century auto. trans. gear ratios: (1st) 2.84:1; (2nd) 1.60:1; (3rd) 1.00:1; (Rev) 2.07:1. Three-speed auto. trans. gear ratios: (1st) 2.52:1; (2nd) 1.52:1; (3rd) 1.00:1; (Rev) 1.94:1. Four-speed automatic gear ratios: (1st) 2.74:1; (2nd) 1.57:1; (3rd) 1.00:1; (4th) 0.67:1; (Rev) 2.07:1. Steering:- (Skyhawk/Skylark/Century) rack and pinion; (others) recirculating ball; power assist standard on all except Skyhawk. Suspension:- front/rear coil springs; (Skyhawk/Skylark/Century) MacPherson strut front suspension; trailing axle rear; front/rear stabilizer bars. (Riviera) fully independent suspension with front torsion bar, front/rear stabilizers. Brakes:- power front disc, rear drum. Four-wheel power disc brakes available on Riviera. Body construction:- (Skyhawk/Skylark/Century) unitized; (others) separate body and frame. Wheel size:- (Skyhawk/Century) 13 x 5.5 in.; (Regal) 14 x 6 in.; (LeSabre/Riviera) 15 x 6 in.; (Estate) 15 x 7 in.

DRIVETRAIN OPTIONS: Engines:- 112 cu. in. (1.8-liter) EFI four: Skyhawk ($75). 121 cu. in. (2.0-liter) four, 2Bbl.: Skyhawk ($50). 173 cu. in. (2.8-liter) V-6, 2Bbl.: Skylark ($125); High-output 173 cu. in. (2.8-liter) V-6, 2Bbl.: Skylark ($250); 181 cu. in. (3.0-liter) V-6, 2Bbl.: Century ($125); 252 cu. in. (4.1- liter) V-6, 4Bbl.: Regal ($95); LeSabre exc. wag ($267) incl. overdrive automatic transmission. 263 cu. in. (4.3-liter) diesel V-6: Century ($859); Regal exc. spt cpe or wag ($874); 307 cu. in. (5.0-liter) V-8, 4Bbl.: LeSabre cpe/sed ($242) incl. overdrive automatic trans.; Electra cpe/sed (NC); Riviera (NC). 350 cu. in. (5.7-liter) diesel V-8: Regal exc. spt cpe ($924); LeSabre/Riviera ($924); LeSabre Estate, Electra ($752). Transmission/Differential:- Five-speed manual trans.: Skyhawk ($196). Three-speed auto. trans.: Skyhawk ($370); Skylark ($396); LeSabre cpe/sed with 4.1 or 5.0-liter ($172 credit); Optional rear axle ratio: Century 2.97:1 (NC); Regal 3.23:1 (NC); Regal cpe/sed 3.08:1 (NC); LeSabre 3.08:1 or 3.23:1 (NC). Limited slip differential: Regal/LeSabre/Electra ($80). Suspension, Steering and Brakes:- F40 Firm ride/handling pkg. ($27) exc. Skyhawk. F41 Gran Touring suspension: Skyhawk ($158); Century four, Riviera ($27); Regal exc. wag, LeSabre ($49). F41 Rallye ride/handling suspension incl. P205/70R13 SBR tires: Skylark ($206). Superlift rear shock absorbers: Skylark ($68). Automatic level control: Century/Regal/LeSabre/Electra ($165). Power steering: Skyhawk ($180). Four-wheel disc brakes: Riviera ($235). Other:- Trailer towing flasher/harness ($28-$43) exc. Skyhawk. Trailer towing pkg.: Regal exc. spt cpe ($182); LeSabre exc. wagon ($459); Electra exc. wagon ($167). Heavy-duty alternator, 85-amp ($32-$85). H.D.: ($22- $50). H.D. radiator: Skyhawk ($37-$67). H.D.: Skylark/Century ($38-$73); Engine block heater ($17-$18). H.D. engine/transmission cooling: Regal/LeSabre/Electra/Riviera ($38-$73). California emission system: Skyhawk ($46); Skylark ($65); Century ($65-$205). Diesel cold climate pkg. delete: Regal/LeSabre/Electra/Riviera ($99 credit).

SKYHAWK CONVENIENCE/APPEARANCE OPTIONS: Option Packages:- Vista Vent flip-open sunroof ($261). Acoustic pkg. ($36). Instrument gauge pkg.: temp, oil pressure, volts, trip odometer ($60). Gauges and tachometer ($78-$138). Comfort/Convenience:- Air cond. ($625). Rear defogger, electric ($115). Cruise control w/resume ($145- $155). Power windows ($152-$216). Power door locks ($99- $142). Six-way power driver's seat ($183). Tinted glass ($82). Tinted windshield ($57). Sport steering wheel ($45). Tilt steering ($88). Trip odometer ($15). Electric trunk release ($29). Two-speed wipers w/delay ($44). Lights, Horns and Mirrors:- Halogen high-beam headlamps ($29). Headlamps-on indicator ($15). Dome reading lamp ($21). Rear seat reading lamps ($30). Styled left remote mirror ($21). Dual styled mirrors: left remote ($51). Dual electric styled mirrors ($130). Visor vanity mirror, passenger ($7). Lighted visor vanity mirror, either side ($45). Entertainment:- AM radio w/digital clock ($55). AM/FM radio ($119). AM/FM stereo radio ($155); w/digital clock and 8-track tape player ($234); w/cassette ($272). Electronic-tuning AM/FM stereo radio ($385); w/8-track ($464); w/cassette ($497). AM radio delete ($56 credit). Power antenna ($50). Dual rear speakers ($25- $30). Exterior Trim:- Door edge guards ($14-$22). Bodyside stripes ($40). Designers' accent paint ($195). Decklid luggage rack ($98). Interior Trim/Upholstery:- Front carpet savers ($20); rear ($15). Trunk trim ($33). Wheels and Tires:- Styled aluminum wheels ($229). Styled wheel covers ($38). Custom locking wire wheel covers ($165). P175/80R13 GBR WSW ($55). P195/70R13 SBR BSW ($133). P195/70R13 SBR WSW ($55- $188). P195/70R13 SBR WLT ($72-$205). P195/70R13 SBR wide WSW ($55-$188). Self-sealing tires ($94).

SKYLARK CONVENIENCE/APPEARANCE OPTIONS: Option Packages:- Acoustic pkg. ($60). Flip-open Vista Vent glass sunroof ($275). Comfort/Convenience:- Air cond. ($675). Cruise Master w/resume ($155-$165). Rear defogger, electric ($125). Power windows ($165-$235). Electric door locks ($106- 152). Six-way power driver's seat ($197). Manual seatback recliners, passenger ($50); both ($100). Sport steering wheel ($50); N/A on Sport. Tilt steering ($95). Tinted glass ($88). Instrument gauges incl. trip odometer ($48). Trip odometer ($16). Electric dial clock ($30). Digital clock ($60). Electric trunk release ($32). Two-speed wipers w/delay ($47). Lights, Horns and Mirrors:- Coach lamps: Ltd ($102). Headlamps-on indicator ($16). Dome reading light ($24). Rear seat reading lamp: Ltd ($30). Dual horns ($15). Remote- control left mirror ($24); N/A on sport. Sport mirrors: left remote, right manual ($55); dual remote ($31-$86). Visor vanity mirror, passenger ($8). Lighted visor vanity mirror, either side ($50). Entertainment:- AM/FM radio ($75). AM/FM stereo radio ($106); w/8-track or cassette player ($192- $193). AM/FM stereo radio with CB ($419); with CB and 8-track or cassette ($494-$495). Graphic equalizer ($150). Rear speakers ($25-$30). Power antenna ($55). Triband power antenna ($100). Delete AM radio ($56 credit). Exterior Trim:- Landau vinyl top: cpe ($195). Long vinyl top ($140). Designers' accent paint ($210); N/A on Sport. Protective bodyside moldings ($47). Wide rocker panel moldings ($65). Belt reveal molding ($35). Wheel opening moldings ($28). Door edge guards ($15-$25). Pillar applique moldings: sed exc. Spt ($27). Hood ornament and windsplit ($32); N/A on Spt. Bodyside or Sport stripes ($48). Bumper guards, front/rear ($45). Bumper strips, front/rear ($49). Interior -Trim/Upholstery:- Full-length console ($100). 45/45 seating, cloth or vinyl ($57-$252). Leather/vinyl 45/45 limited seating ($358-$553). Notchback bench seating: Spt ($195). Front carpet savers ($16); rear ($11). Carpet savers w/inserts: front ($25); rear ($20). Trunk trim carpeting ($35). Wheels:- Chrome-plated wheels ($155-$175). Sport wheel covers ($20). Locking wire wheel covers ($165-$185). Tires:- P185/80R13 GBR WSW ($58); N/A on Sport. P185/80R13 SBR BSW ($64); N/A on Sport. P185/80R13 SBR wide whitewall ($122); N/A on Sport. P205/70R13 SBR WSW ($66). P205/70R13 SBR WLT ($88). Self-sealing GBR whitewall tires ($106).

CENTURY/REGAL CONVENIENCE/APPEARANCE OPTIONS: Option Packages:- Regal Sport Coupe Decor pkg.: designers' accent paint, wide rocker moldings, sport steering wheel, black paint treatment ($125). Regal Coupe Decor pkg. w/turbine wheels ($428). Sliding electric Astroroof: Regal cpe ($885). Flip-open Vista Vent glass sunroof: Century ($275). Hatch roof: Regal cpe ($790). Comfort/Convenience:- Air cond. ($675). Automatic touch climate control air cond.: Regal ($825). Cruise Master w/resume ($155). Rear defogger, electric ($125). Tinted glass ($88). Tinted windshield: Regal ($65). Six-way power seat, each side ($197); both ($394); passenger's side N/A on Century. Manual passenger seatback recliner ($50-$75); both seats, Century only ($100). Sport steering wheel ($40). Tilt steering ($95). Power windows ($165-$235). Electric door locks ($106-$152). Automatic door locks ($180-$215). Electric trunk release ($32). Remote electric tailgate lock: Regal wag ($38). Electric dial clock ($30). Digital clock ($60). Headlamps-on indicator ($16). Trip odometer: Regal ($16). Instrument gauges: temp, voltage, trip odometer ($48). Windshield wiper w/low-speed delay ($47). Theft deterrent system ($159). Lighting and Mirrors:- Tungsten-halogen high-beam headlamps ($10). Twilight Sentinel headlamp control ($57). Cornering lamps: Regal ($57). Coach lamps: Ltd ($102). Front lamp monitors ($37). Door courtesy/warning lights: Ltd ($44-$70). Rear seat reading light: Regal ($30). Dome reading lamps ($24). Remote left mirror ($24). Remote right mirror: Regal exc. spt cpe ($48). Dual mirrors, left remote ($48-$55). Dual electric remote mirrors: Century ($137). Dual remote sport mirrors: Regal ($31-$79). Visor vanity mirror ($8). Lighted visor vanity mirror ($58); driver's N/A on Regal. Dual horns: Century ($15). Entertainment:- AM radio: Regal ($99). AM/FM radio ($82-$153). AM/FM stereo radio ($118-$184). AM/FM stereo radio w/digital clock: Century ($178); w/8-track or cassette player ($277-$282). AM/FM stereo radio w/8-track or cassette: Regal ($270-$271). Electronic-tuning AM/FM stereo radio ($377-$402); w/8-track or cassette ($481-$555). AM/FM radio with CB: Regal ($497). CB radio: Century ($263). Dual rear speakers ($25-$30). Fixed-mast antenna: Regal ($39); w/radio $12). Automatic power antenna ($55-$90). Triband power antenna ($100-$135). Exterior Trim:- Landau vinyl top: cpe ($166). Heavy-padded landau vinyl top: Regal cpe ($220). Long vinyl top ($140). Long padded vinyl top: Regal sed ($220). Designers' accent paint ($195-$235). Solid special color paint ($200). Exterior molding pkg.: Regal exc. Ltd ($110). Protective bodyside moldings: Century, Regal spt cpe ($47- $51). Wraparound bodyside moldings: Regal sed ($104). Lower bodyside moldings: Century ($65). Hood ornament and windplit: Century ($32); std. on Ltd. Door edge guards ($15-$25). Belt reveal moldings: Regal spt cpe w/decor pkg. ($40). Bodyside stripe ($42). Woodgrain vinyl applique: Regal wag ($330). Roof rack: Regal wag ($115). Air deflector: Regal wag ($37). Interior Trim/Upholstery:- Full-length console ($100). Non- shifting console ($82). Bucket seats: Regal ($56). 55/45 seating: Regal ($133). Limited 55/45 seating: Regal spt cpe ($385). 45/45 seating: Century Cust ($133); Regal Ltd (NC). Front carpet savers ($16); rear ($11). Front carpet savers with inserts ($25); rear ($20). Litter pocket ($9). Trunk trim covering ($47). Lockable storage compartment: Regal wag ($55). Wheels:- Chrome-plated wheels ($40-$175); Regal spt cpe ($110 credit). Styled aluminum wheels: Regal exc. spt cpe ($150-$285). Turbine wheels: Regal exc. spt cpe ($135). Locking wire wheel covers: Century ($185); Regal ($50-$185); Regal spt cpe ($100 credit). Tires:- P185/80R13 GBR WSW: Century four ($58). P185/80R13 SBR BSW: Century four ($64). P185/80R13 SBR WSW: Century four ($122). P185/75R14 GBR and SBR: Century V-6 ($37-$159). P195/75R14 SBR BSW: Regal exc. spt cpe (NC). P205/70R13 SBR BSW: Century four w/F41 suspension ($179). P205/70R13 SBR WSW: Century four w/F41 suspension ($245). P205/70R13 SBR WLT: Century four w/F41 ($267). P205/70R14 SBR wide-oval BSW: Regal (N/A). P205/70R14 SBR WSW: Regal spt cpe ($66). P205/70R14 SBR WLT: Regal ($84- $88). Self-sealing tires ($106).

LESABRE/ELECTRA/ESTATE WAGON CONVENIENCE/APPEARANCE OPTIONS: Comfort/Convenience:- Sliding electric Astroroof ($1125). Air cond.: LeSabre ($695). Air cond. w/touch-climate control: LeSabre ($845); LeSabre Est, Electra ($150). Cruise Master with resume ($155); std. on Park Ave. Rear defogger, electric ($125). Tinted glass: LeSabre Cust ($102). Power windows: LeSabre ($165-$240). Electric door locks ($106-$152). Automatic door locks ($63-$215). Six-way power seat, driver's or passenger's ($167-$197); both ($364-$394). Memory driver's power seat: Electra ($178-$345). Electric seatback recliner, one side ($139). Sport steering wheel: LeSabre ($40). Tilt steering: LeSabre, Electra Ltd ($95). Tilt/telescoping steering column ($55-$150). Dial clock: LeSabre ($60). Digital clock: LeSabre, Estate (NC w/convenience group). Lamp and indicator group: LeSabre ($52-$70). Trip odometer: LeSabre ($16). Remote tailgate lock: LeSabre Estate ($49). Electric trunk lock: Electra Ltd ($72). Electric trunk release ($32). Electric fuel cap lock ($44). Theft deterrent system ($159); N/A on Estate. Two-speed wiper w/delay ($47). Accessory group (trip odometer, dome reading lamp, headlamps- on indicator, low fuel indicator, washer fluid indicator): Electra ($28-$86). Lighting, Horns and Mirrors:- Tungsten- halogen high-beam headlamps ($10). Twilight Sentinel ($57). Cornering lamps ($57). Coach lamps: LeSabre/Electra Ltd ($102). Light monitors, front: LeSabre, Electra Est ($37); front/rear, Electra ($74). Door courtesy/warning lamps ($44- $70). Rear seat reading lamp: LeSabre Ltd, Electra ($30). Lighted door lock and interior light control ($72). Four-note horn ($28). Remote left mirror: LeSabre ($24). Remote right mirror: LeSabre ($48); Electra Ltd, Est ($24). Remote electric right mirror: Electra Park Ave. ($57). Dual remote sport mirrors: LeSabre ($85); Electra Ltd, Estate ($38). Dual electric remote mirrors: LeSabre ($137); Electra Ltd, Estate ($90). Remote left mirror w/thermometer: LeSabre ($62); Electra Ltd, Estate ($38). Electric left mirror w/thermometer: Electra Park Ave. ($39). Dual electric mirrors w/left thermometer: LeSabre ($170), Electra Ltd, Estate ($123). Lighted visor vanity mirror, driver or passenger ($58). Entertainment:- AM radio: LeSabre ($99). AM/FM radio: LeSabre ($153). AM/FM stereo radio: LeSabre, Electra Ltd/Estate ($184). AM/FM stereo radio and 8-track or cassette player ($86-$271). Electronic-tuning AM/FM stereo radio: LeSabre ($377-$402); Electra ($170-$348). Electronic-tuning AM/FM stereo radio and 8-track or cassette ($273-$555). AM/FM stereo radio with CB ($314-$498). Electronic-tuning radio with CB and 8-track or cassette ($585-$841). Delete AM/FM stereo radio: Electra Park Ave. (credit $153). Concert Sound speaker system: Electra exc. wagon ($95); ETR radio req'd. Dual rear speakers ($25-$30) when ordered with radio. Automatic power antenna ($55-$90). Tri-band power antenna ($100-$135). Exterior Trim:- Exterior molding pkg.: LeSabre ($110). Landau vinyl top: LeSabre, Electra Ltd cpe ($225). Long vinyl top: LeSabre, Electra Ltd sed ($165-$180). Heavy-padded long vinyl top: Electra Ltd sedan ($225). Designers' accent paint: LeSabre ($215). Special single-color paint: ($200); Firemist, Electra exc. Est ($210). Protective bodyside moldings: Est ($51). Color-coordinated bodyside moldings: LeSabre Est ($51). Wide rocker panel moldings: Electra Ltd/Estate ($65). Door edge guards ($15-$25). Belt reveal molding: LeSabre ($40). Bodyside stripes ($63). Woodgrain vinyl applique: LeSabre Est ($320). Roof rack: LeSabre Est ($140). Interior Trim/Upholstery:- 55/45 seating: LeSabre ($125). Leather-vinyl 50/50 seating: Park Ave. ($525). Third seat: Estate ($215). Front carpet savers ($16); rear ($11). Front carpet savers w/inserts ($25); rear ($20). Trunk carpeting trim ($53-$65). Trunk mat ($13). Wheels:- Chrome-plated wheels ($180-$215). Styled aluminum wheels ($40-$255). Custom wheel covers: Electra Ltd ($35). Locking wire wheel covers ($150-$185); Electra Estate ($30 credit). Tires:- P215/75R15 SBR wide WSW: LeSabre cpe/sed ($39). P225/75R15 SBR wide WSW: LeSabre ($106); Electra ($39). Self- sealing tires ($106-$131).

RIVIERA CONVENIENCE/APPEARANCE OPTIONS: Comfort/Convenience:- Electric sliding Astroroof ($1125). Automatic touch climate control air cond. ($150). Rear defogger, electric ($125). Automatic electric door locks ($74). Six-way power seat, passenger ($197). Two-position memory power driver's seat ($178). Electric seatback recliner, one side ($139). Sport steering wheel ($40). Tilt steering ($95). Tilt/telescope steering wheel ($150). Electric fuel cap lock ($44). Electric trunk releease ($32). Electric trunk lock ($72). Low fuel indicator ($18). Fuel usage light, gas engine ($35). Two-wpeed wipers w/delay ($47). Windshield washer fluid indicator ($12). Theft deterrent system ($159). Lighting, Horns and Mirrors:- Tungsten-halogen high-beam headlamps ($10). Twilight Sentinel ($57). Coach lamps ($102); incl. w/vinyl top. Front/rear light monitors ($74). Rear quarter courtesy/reading lamp ($48). Lighted door lock and interior light control ($72). Four-note horn ($28). Dual

electric remote mirrors ($65). Lighted visor vanity mirrors, each ($58). Entertainment:- Full-feature electronic-tuning AM/FM stereo radio ($90). Electronic-tuning AM/FM stereo radio w/8-track or cassette tape player ($193-$242); w/CB and 8-track or cassette ($455- $479). Delete radio ($230 credit). Rear speakers ($25-$30). Concert Sound system ($95); N/A with base radio. Triband power antenna ($45). Exterior Trim:- Heavy-padded landau vinyl top w/coach lamps ($305). Designers' accent paint ($235). Special color Firemist paint ($210). Protective bodyside moldings ($61). Door edge guards ($15). Bodyside stripes ($63). Interior Trim/Upholstery:- 45/55 leather/vinyl front seat ($405). Front carpet savers w/inserts ($35); rear ($20). Trunk trim carpeting ($30). Trunk mat ($15). Wheels and Tires:- Chrome-plated wheels ($145). Custom locking wire wheel covers ($185). P225/70R15 SBR BSW: conv/T ($40). P225/70R15 SBR WSW: conv/T ($106). GR70 x 15 SBR WSW ($85). Self-sealing tires ($131).

HISTORY: Introduced: September 24, 1981 except Skylark, December 12, 1981; Century, November 30, 1981; and Century, March 4, 1982; and Riviera convertible, mid-April 1982. Skyhawk and Riviera convertible debuted at the Chicago Auto Show on Feb. 25, 1982. Model year production (U.S.): 739,984 for a 14.3 percent share of the industry total. That number included 157,668 four-cylinder Buicks, 409,857 sixes, and 172,463 V-8s. The total also included 35,062 diesel engines and 2,551 turbos. Calendar year production (U.S.): 751,338. Model year sales by U.S. dealers: 694,742. Calendar year sales (U.S.): 723,011 for a market share of 12.6 percent.

Historical Footnotes: A series of mid-year introductions drew customers' attention to Buick offerings. Several Buick plants turned to employee involvement programs in an attempt to cut absenteeism and improve quality. Officials at one plant reported an impressive improvement in both areas. Turbo V-6 production fell sharply, from 25,500 in the 1979 model year to just 3,990 in 1981, in response to sluggish demand for turbocharged engines. In February 1982, a limited-edition Grand National Regal ran at Daytona. A forerunner of one of the most sought-after 1980s Buicks, it sported silver-gray and charcoal-gray paint with red accent stripes, a T-top roof, blackout grille and trim, air dam and rear spoiler. Grand National's powerplant was the 4.1-liter V-6 with four-barrel carb.

1983 BUICK

Buick now offered four front-drive car lines, stretching from the subcompact Skyhawk to the big Riviera. The company's full-line color catalog focused on small town America this year, including small tales and lore on locales to which one might travel by Buick. Sporty T Types, with performance packages that included sport trim, special wheels and bucket seats, were offered on every line except LeSabre and Electra. Though different, they shared a family resemblance. All except Regal's featured blacked-out sections for a striking visual appearance. And all but Regal and Riviera had charcoal accents on the car's lower body. Regal's version, powered by the 180-horsepower turbo 3.8-liter V-6, was recorded as delivering 0-50 MPH acceleration time of 7.6 seconds. Riviera used the same turbo V-6, while Skyhawk T Type's 1.8-liter engine produced 84 horsepower at 5200 R.P.M. Each T Type carried a Gran Touring suspension except for Skylark, which had a Sport suspension. On all but Riviera, quick-ratio power steering replaced the standard version. The "T" in T Type, incidentally, didn't stand for anything in particular. An electrically-heated grid in the 3.8-liter V-6 now preheated the fuel/air mixture for better response with a cold engine. On 3.0- and 3.8-liter V-6 engines, the Exhaust Gas Recirculation system was refined to regulate both timing and rate of exhaust gas flow back into the air/fuel mixture. Turbocharged engines had a new piezo sensor in the Electronic Spark Control system, plus computer-controlled EGR. Optional on some models was a new digital readout instrument cluster, which displayed numbers for miles-per-hour, trip odometer, and fuel level in English or metric form. Instead of the previous buzzer, a new electronic tone warned that seatbelts were not buckled or the key remained in the ignition. Riviera coupes could get ultimate sound with the new Delco GM/Bose Music System that delivered 50 watts of audio output per stereo channel.

1983 Skyhawk Limited wagon (AA)

SKYHAWK — SERIES 4J — FOUR — Buick's front-drive, J-bodied subcompact looked about the same as in 1982. Eight new body colors and two carryover colors were offered. Skylark Limited had standard deluxe full wheel covers and wide rocker moldings. Both Custom and Limited had a wide wraparound bodyside molding that gave the impression of running all around the car. Standard engine this year was a fuel-injected 2.0-liter four, hooked to four-speed manual gearbox and low (4.10:1) final drive (transaxle). That engine was essentially a stroked variant of the carbureted 1.8-liter four that served as base engine the year before. Powertrain options included a fuel-injected 1.8-liter overhead-cam engine and five-speed manual shift, or three-speed automatic transmission with either engine. The 1.8 used a crossflow aluminum cylinder head, with intake and exhaust ports on opposite sides. Skyhawk offered a new station wagon for 1983, in both Custom and Limited trim--the first Buick front-drive wagons. Cargo volume was 64.5 cubic feet, with split-folding rear seat. Engine and transmission choices were the same as other Skyhawks, except the 1.8-liter engine wasn't available with air conditioning. Limited wagons had front armrests and reclining driver and passenger seats. The new subcompact T Type was "rather authoritative looking," according to Buick's catalog. Smallest of the T Types, it was powered by the overhead-cam 1.8-liter four, producing 84 horsepower, coupled to the five-speed manual overdrive gearbox. Axle ratio of 3.83:1 helped standing-start

performance. So did the engine's claimed quick throttle response and strong low-end torque. When hitting the gas hard, the air conditioner compressor shut off automatically so it wouldn't drain away needed power. T Types had the usual blacked-out grille--though in Skyhawk's case, even the standard grille was barely visible, consisting of a set of wide body-colored strips set below the headlamps and skinny minimal bumper. Other black accents were found on the T Type's headlamp housings, door handles, locks, and twin outside mirrors (the left one remote-controlled). Park/signal lamps had amber lenses, and foglamps were included. Lower bodies displayed charcoal accents. A Gran Touring suspension helped handling, while styled aluminum wheels held P195/70R13 blackwall tires. Skyhawk T's dash carried a voltmeter, oil pressure and temperature gauges, resettable trip odometer, and electronic tachometer. Skyhawks had standard reclining bucket seats. Both Limited and T Type had easy-entry front passenger seats. Limiteds used the same luxurious fabric as in Electras. T Types held charcoal cloth bucket seats with adjustable headrests.

1983 Century T Type sedan (AA)

SKYLARK — SERIES 4X — FOUR/V-6 — Buick continued to downplay Skylark's economy image, promoting it more as a car that "looks and feels like a Buick," which just happened to be compact in size. Styling was essentially unchanged this year, except for a new aerodynamically-designed lip above new taillamps. The left- hand mirror was also restyled. Five new interior colors were offered, plus new cloth trim on the Limited. Custom Skylarks had a new seat design with adjustable headrests. Skylark's chassis continued in the same form: MacPherson struts up front, trailing axle coil springs in the rear, with standard power rack-and-pinion steering and low-drag power front disc brakes. All Skylarks carried a new Delco Freedom II Plus battery. Base engine remained the Pontiac 2.5-liter four with electronic fuel injection; optional, two forms of Chevrolet's 2.8-liter V-6. One new Skylark appeared, however: the T Type, wearing a blacked-out grille as well as black accents at headlamp housings, door handles and locks, taillamp bezels, and styled outside mirror. Four body colors were offered (white, silver, dark red, or light sand gray), each with special charcoal lower accent paint that reached almost halfway up the doors. Taillamp lenses were smoked, parking/signal lenses amber, and 14 in. wheels of aggressive-looking styled aluminum held blackwall P215/60R14 steel-belted radials (the widest tires of any Buick T Type). Under the T's hood was the high-output (135 horsepower) 2.8-liter V-6 with specially tuned exhaust, manual four-speed gearbox, and 3.65:1 final drive ratio. Sport suspension consisted of stiffer rate springs and shocks, a stiffer front stabilizer bar, and a rear stabilizer bar. On the dash, T Types included a voltmeter and temperature gauge. Front and rear bumper rub strips and a front passenger assist strap were included, and the left-hand mirror was remote-controlled.

1983 Skylark T Type coupe (AA)

CENTURY — SERIES 4A — FOUR/V-6 — Buick's A-bodied five-passenger front-drive model, introduced for 1982, offered the lowest drag coefficient in the lineup. Appearance was similar to before, but Skyhawks could have ten new body colors and five new interior colors. Bodies had Plastisol-R- protection in critical spots. A new electronic tone reminded drivers to fasten seat belts and remove the ignition key. The Delco 2000 AM radio included dual front speakers. A digital readout instrument cluster was also offered. Buyers could choose from the standard 2.5- liter four-cylinder engine, a 3.0-liter gasoline V-6, or 4.3- liter diesel V-6. An on-board computer added EGR monitoring to the gas V-6. Century had standard automatic transmission, power steering and brakes. At mid-year came a new overdrive automatic transmission. Limited models had integrated bumpers and a bright wide lower molding. Joining the Custom and Limited models this year was a new T Type Century sedan and coupe. Styling touches included subtle black accents on grille and moldings, around headlamps and on taillamp bezels, plus twin black mirrors (left-hand remote controlled), antenna and door handles. The 'Buick' badge went to the lower corner of the grille rather than the side, and front fenders held 'Century T Type' nameplates. Painted silver over charcoal, T Types also had special bumper detailing plus black accent stripes on the body, and rode 14 in. styled aluminum wheels with P195/75R14 blackwall steel- belted radial tires. Their Gran Touring suspension included high-rate springs, revalved shocks, and front/rear stabilizer bars. The 110-horsepower 3.0-liter V-6 drove an automatic transmission and 2.97:1 final drive ratio. A leather-covered sport steering wheel, full-length storage console and 45/45 front seats filled out the T Type goodie list. Lear Siegler cloth bucket seats with leather trim were optional.

1983 Regal T Type coupe (AA)

REGAL — SERIES 4G — V-6 — Rear-drive Regals, little changed since their 1978 restyle, came with two personalities. Coupes were billed as having an "aerodynamic, sleek look" while sedans offered "crisp, limousine-like styling." All Regals had a new grille, with Buick block letters in the center of the upper horizontal bar. Strong vertical bars angled outward from a point above the halfway mark. Regal's script sat at the side of the grille. Wide parking/signal lamps were inset in the bumper. Quad rectangular headlamps were deeply recessed. Standard wheel covers got a restyle this year, and Regals came in a revised selection of body (four new choices) and interior colors. Regal's Estate Wagon was also powered by the 3.8-liter V-6 with automatic. Customers could choose a base Regal, Limited, or sporty turbo T Type. Limiteds could be ordered with leather- and vinyl-trimmed seats and cloth-trimmed doors. Standard engine was again the 231 cu. in. (3.8-liter) V-6, with automatic transmission. Larger V-6s (4.1-liter gas or 4.3-liter diesel) and a diesel V-8 were optional. A "discreet" tone told of unbuckled seatbelt, with the option of a chime that warned headlamps were still turned on. T Type coupes were easily identifiable by the bulge at the rear of the hood, as well T Type identification. They wore wide-oval P205/70R14 steel-belted radials on distinctively styled aluminum wheels. Under the hood, the turbocharged 3.8-liter V-6 fed into low-restriction dual exhausts for a "gutty exhaust growl," feeding power to a four-speed automatic overdrive transmission (with torque-converter clutching) and 3.42:1 performance axle ratio. T Type's handling was assisted by the Gran Touring suspension and fast-ratio power steering. At the dash, gauges showed turbo boost and engine temperature. A T Type Decor Package added Designers' Accent paint, blacked-out grille, black headlamp and taillamp trim, black wiper arms and blades, bright center rocker panel moldings, and a sport steering wheel. Regal T could have a hood ornament that said 'Turbo 3.8 Litre' below the Buick tri-shield emblem--words that also appeared on the hood bulge.

1983 LeSabre Limited sedan (AA)

LESABRE — SERIES 4B — V-6/V-8 — Once again, the 231 cu. in. (3.8-liter) V-6 was standard on LeSabre. This year, it received an electric preheater grid below the carburetor to warm up the fuel/air mixture when the engine was cold. On the powerplant option list: a 4.1-liter V-6 and 5.0-liter V-8, as well as the 5.7 diesel V-8. Automatic transmission was standard with all engines, and included overdrive (0.67:1 gearing) when coupled to any engine other than the base V-6. Converter clutches in third gear and overdrive, which engaged and disengaged at preset speeds, helped to eliminate slippage within the transmission. Of the dozen body colors, all but one was new for 1983. Designers' Accent paint treatments were also available, and interior colors were new. Custom seats were covered with rich velour, Limited seats with knit fabric. Electric seatback recliners were optional. A multi-function control lever handled turn signals, high/low beams, and wiper/washer. All LeSabres had front and rear armrests, and a woodtone dash. LeSabre Custom included standard whitewall tires, deluxe wheel covers, bumper guards and protective strips, cigarette lighter, left-hand outside mirror, compact spare tire, and color-coordinated bodyside moldings. Limiteds added such extras as a headlamps-on indicator/chime, tinted glass, simulated woodgrain door trim, 55/45 notchback seats, and custom steering wheel.

ESTATE WAGON — SERIES 4B/C — V-8 — As before, both Electra and LeSabre Estate wagons were offered (as well as a Regal version). Electra's was the most luxurious, with standard roof rack and air deflector, vinyl woodgrain trim, 55/45 seating up front with two-way power driver's seat, remote-control left-hand mirror, electric door and tailgate locks, power windows, and digital clock. The standard 307 cu. in. (5.0-liter) V-8 engine came with four-speed overdrive automatic transmission, and could be held in third-gear range when hauling a heavy load. LeSabre Estate Wagons offered the same cargo capacity but a little less luxury. They included a power tailgate window, two-way tailgate with 'ajar' indicator, air conditioning, Soft-Ray tinted glass, and the same standard V-8 engine. A diesel V-8 was also offered.

ELECTRA — SERIES 4C — V-6/V-8 — Apart from a dozen new body colors, the full-size Buick line didn't change much this year, either mechanically or in appearance. Measuring over 221 inches, it was still the longest regular production car made in America. A combination of slim bodyside moldings and wide rocker panel moldings accentuated Electra's long, formal lines. The upscale Park Avenue again displayed brushed aluminum bodyside moldings that contained the familiar ventiport identity

1983 Electra Park Avenue sedan (AA)

badge. A padded halo vinyl top was standard again, revealing a bit of body color at the edges. Wide rocker panel moldings continued onto front and rear fenders. Soft-Ray tinted glass was standard. Electras also included a headlamps-on indicator, digital clock, bumper guards and protective strips, 25-gallon fuel tank, compact spare tire, and power windows. In addition to wide color-keyed protective bodyside moldings, both models carried moldings for back and side window reveal, roof drip, window frame scalp, belt reveal, windshield, and wheel openings. Park Avenue added resume-speed Cruise Control and a tilt steering column, plus AM/FM stereo radio, six-way power driver's seat, electric door locks, and power remote left-hand mirror. Standard powertrain was the 252 cu. in. (4.1-liter V-6) and automatic transmission with overdrive (including torque converter clutch). Options included a 5.0-liter gas V-8 or the big diesel V-8, which offered excellent mileage but proved troublesome to many owners.

1983 Riviera convertible (AA)

RIVIERA — SERIES 4E — V-6/V-8 — To mark Riviera's 20th birthday, Buick produced 502 copies of a "XX Anniversary Edition." To the normally ample list of Riviera equipment was added a tempting selection of extras, including true wire wheels. The body was painted two-tone beige, with Anniversary grille and front-end panel. Bumper strips, front and rear, were brown with gold inserts. Rocker, belt and roof drip moldings were dark brown. Fender, decklid and grille emblems were plated in 24 carat gold. Special identification appeared on hood and wheel centers. The medium beech Anniversary interior featured English walnut wood veneer trim plates and 26-ounce wool-like carpeting. Suede inserts highlighted the glove leather seat upholstery. There was also a leather-wrapped wood steering wheel, wood horn cap, leather upper door trim, 140 MPH speedometer, and gold-plated Anniversary identification. Also standard: a rear window defogger, Gran Touring suspension and dual electric mirrors, plus Uniroyal goldwall stripe steel-belted radial tires. Even the trunk trim was distinctive. Standard engine was the 4.1-liter V-6, with 5.0-liter V-8 optional. Apart from that special edition there were three "ordinary" Rivieras: a basic but luxurious Coupe, sporty T Type, and recently-introduced convertible. Riviera's T Type had a blacked-out grille (with fewer vertical bars), amber park/signal lenses, tungsten-halogen high/low beam headlamps, accent stripes on the body, sport steering wheel, and special T Type identification inside and out. Styled aluminum wheels held self-sealing, all-season whitewall radial tires. Under the hood once again was the turbocharged 3.8-liter V-6, coupled to overdrive automatic transmission and 3.36:I final drive axle ratio. T Type's Gran Touring suspension blended higher-rate springs with recalibrated shock absorbers and special front/rear stabilizer bars. T Types were available in any Riviera color except light green and light brown. The hood ornament carried the letter 'R'. As usual, all Rivieras were loaded with power assists and conveniences, including air conditioning and an electronically-tuned Delco 2000 AM/FM stereo radio (which could be deleted for credit). Stereo buffs could go all the way up to a premium Delco GM/Bose Music System, acoustically tailored to the Riviera interior, with 50-watt power output. Interiors had new door pull straps, and the range of colors included a tan that was a Riviera exclusive. Standard equipment included a six-way power seat. A new optional digital instrument panel cluster showed miles-per-hour, remaining fuel, and a trip mileage in either English or metric values. Trailer towing equipment was available for loads up to 3,000 pounds. Convertibles were produced in somewhat limited number (only 1,750 this year) in choice of white or Firemist red with white top and contrasting bodyside stripes. Interiors were upholstered in soft red Sierra grain leather and vinyl. Four-wheel disc brakes were standard. Convertibles also had custom locking wire wheel covers and heavy-duty suspension. Standard Riviera powerplant was the 4.1-liter V-6 with overdrive automatic transmission, with option of a 5.0-liter gas V-8 or 5.7-liter diesel V-8. Convertibles could not have the diesel.

I.D. DATA: Buicks again had a 17-symbol Vehicle Identification Number (VIN), introduced in 1981, stamped on a metal tag attached to the upper left surface of the cowl, visible through the windshield. The number begins with '1' to indicate U.S.A., followed by 'G' for General Motors and '4' for Buick Division. The next letter indicates restraint system. Symbol five denotes series: 'S' Skyhawk; 'T' Skyhawk Limited; 'E' Skyhawk T Type; 'B' Skylark Custom; 'C' Skylark Limited; 'D' Skylark T Type; 'H' Century Custom; 'L' Century Limited; 'G' Century T Type; 'J' Regal; 'K' Regal T Type; 'M' Regal Limited; 'N' LeSabre Custom; 'P' LeSabre Limited; 'R' LeSabre Estate Wagon; 'V' Electra Estate Wagon; 'X' Electra Limited; 'W' Electra Park Avenue; 'Y' Riviera T Type; 'Z' Riviera. Digits six and seven indicate body type: '27' 2-dr. coupe; '37' Skylark 2-dr. coupe; '47' Regal 2-dr. coupe; '57' Electra 2-dr. coupe; '35' 4-dr. wagon; '19' 4-dr. sedan; '69' 4-dr. sedan. Next is the engine code: 'O' L4-112 TBI; 'P' L4-121 TBI; 'R' L4-151 TBI; 'X' V6-173 2Bbl.; 'Z' H.O. V6-173 2Bbl.; 'E'

V6-181 2Bbl.; 'A' V6-231 2Bbl.; '8' V6-231 Turbo; '4' V6-252 4Bbl.; 'V' V6-263 diesel; 'Y' V8-307 4Bbl.; 'N' V8-350 diesel. Symbol nine is a check digit. Symbol ten denotes model year ('D' 1983). Symbol eleven is the plant code. The final six digits are the sequential serial number. An additional identifying number can be found on the engine, showing codes for GM division, model year, assembly plant, and vehicle sequence number. A body number plate shows model year, car division, series, style, body assembly plant, body number, trim combination, modular seat code, paint code, and date build code.

SKYHAWK CUSTOM (FOUR)

Series Number	Body/Style Number	Body Type & Seating	Factory Price	Shipping Weight	Production Total
4J	S27	2-dr Coupe-5P	6958	2316	27,557
4J	S69	4-dr Sedan-5P	7166	2369	19,847
4J	S35	4-dr Sta Wag-5P	7492	2439	10,653

SKYHAWK LIMITED (FOUR)

4J	T27	2-dr Coupe-5P	7457	2333	Note 1
4J	T69	4-dr Sedan-5P	7649	2411	Note 1
4J	T35	4-dr Sta Wag-5P	7934	2462	Note 1

Note 1: Production figures listed under Skyhawk Custom also include equivalent Skyhawk Limited models. For the model year, a total of 45,105 Customs and 12,952 Limiteds were manufactured.

SKYHAWK T TYPE (FOUR)

4J	E27	2-dr Coupe-5P	7961	2336	5,095

SKYLARK CUSTOM (FOUR/V-6)

4X	B37	2-dr Coupe-5P	7548/7698	2462/2523	11,671
4X	B69	4-dr Sedan-5P	7718/7868	2493/2554	51,950

SKYLARK LIMITED (FOUR/V-6)

4X	C37	2-dr Coupe-5P	7988/8138	2489/2550	7,863
4X	C69	4-dr Sedan-5P	8150/8300	2519/2580	30,674

SKYLARK T TYPE (V-6)

4X	D37	2-dr Coupe-5P	9337	2608	2,489

CENTURY CUSTOM (FOUR/V-6)

4A	H27	2-dr Coupe-5P	8841/8991	2614/2719	13,483
4A	H19	4-dr Sedan-5P	9002/9152	2662/2767	114,443

CENTURY LIMITED (FOUR/V-6)

4A	L27	2-dr Coupe-5P	9261/9411	2632/2737	Note 2
4A	L19	4-dr Sedan-5P	9425/9575	2675/2780	Note 2

CENTURY T TYPE (V-6)

4A	G27	2-dr Coupe-5P	10017	2749	Note 2
4A	G19	4-dr Sedan-5P	10178	2801	Note 2

Note 2: Production figures listed under Century Custom also include Limited and T Type models. Total production for the model year came to 50,296 Customs, 73,030 Limiteds, and 4,600 Century T Types.

REGAL (V-6)

4G	J47	2-dr Coupe-6P	9100	3123	147,935
4G	J69	4-dr Sedan-6P	9279	3139	61,285
4G	J35	4-dr Sta Wag-6P	9550	3289	15,287

REGAL LIMITED (V-6)

4G	M47	2-dr Coupe-6P	9722	3164	Note 3
4G	M69	4-dr Sedan-6P	9856	3177	Note 3

Note 3: Production figures listed under base Regal coupe and sedan also include Regal Limited models. Total coupe/sedan production was 108,458 base Regals and 100,762 Limiteds. Only 4,340 Regals had the optional diesel V-8 engine.

REGAL T TYPE (V-6)

4G	K47	2-dr Coupe-6P	10366	3194	3,732

LESABRE CUSTOM (V-6/V-8)

4B	N37	2-dr Coupe-6P	9292/9517	3459/3631	6,974
4B	N69	4-dr Sedan-6P	9394/9619	3488/3660	31,196

LESABRE LIMITED (V-6/V-8)

4B	P37	2-dr Coupe-6P	9836/10061	3494/3666	22,029
4B	P69	4-dr Sedan-6P	9990/10215	3527/3699	66,547

LESABRE ESTATE WAGON (V-8)

4B	R35	4-dr Sta Wag-6P	11187	4105	9,306

ELECTRA LIMITED (V-6/V-8)

4C	X37	2-dr Coupe-6P	12415/12490	3644/3823	8,885
4C	X69	4-dr Sedan-6P	12586/12661	3704/3883	79,700

ELECTRA PARK AVENUE (V-6/V-8)

4C	W37	2-dr Coupe-6P	14094/14169	3716/3895	Note 4
4C	W69	4-dr Sedan-6P	14245/14320	3781/3960	Note 4

Note 4: Production figures listed under Electra Limited also include equivalent Park Avenue models. All told, 24,542 Limiteds and 64,043 Park Avenue Electras were built, only 4,878 with V-8 engine.

ELECTRA ESTATE WAGON (V-8)

4C	V35	4-dr Sta Wag-6P	13638	4175	9,581

RIVIERA (V-6/V-8)

4E	Z57	2-dr Coupe-5P	15238/15313	3609/3769	47,153
4E	Z67	2-dr Conv-5P	24960/24960	3795/3955	1,750

Note 5: Only 128 Riviera convertibles and 2,993 standard coupes had a V-6 engine.

RIVIERA T TYPE (V-6)

4E	Y57	2-dr Coupe-5P	15906	3593	1,331

FACTORY PRICE AND WEIGHT NOTE: Figure before the slash is for four-cylinder engine, after the slash for V-6. For full-size models, figure before the slash is for V-6 engine, after the slash for V-8.

BUICK ENGINES: BASE FOUR (Skyhawk): Inline, overhead valve four-cylinder. Cast iron cylinder block and head. Displacement: 121 cu. in. (2.0 liters). Bore & stroke: 3.50 x 3.14 in. Compression ratio: 9.0:1. Brake horsepower: 90 at 5100 R.P.M. Torque: 111 lbs.-ft. at 2700 R.P.M. Five main bearings. Hydraulic valve lifters. Throttle-body fuel injection. VIN Code: P. OPTIONAL FOUR (Skyhawk): Inline, overhead-cam four-cylinder. Cast iron block and head. Displacement: 112 cu. in. (1.8 liters). Bore & stroke: 3.34 x 3.13 in. Compression ratio: 9.0:1. Brake horsepower: 84 at 5200 R.P.M. Torque: 102 lbs.-ft. at 2800 R.P.M. Five main bearings. Hydraulic valve lifters. Throttle-body fuel injection. VIN Code: O. BASE FOUR (Skylark, Century): Inline, overhead-valve four-cylinder. Cast iron block and head. Displacement: 151 cu. in (2.5 liters). Bore & stroke: 4.0 x 3.0 in. Compression ratio: 8.2:1. Brake horsepower: 90 at 4000 R.P.M. Torque: 134 lbs.-ft. at 2400 R.P.M. Five main bearings. Hydraulic valve lifters. Throttle-body fuel injection. Built by Pontiac. VIN Code: R. OPTIONAL V-6 (Skylark): 60-degree, overhead-valve-V-6. Cast iron alloy block and head. Displacement: 173 cu. in. (2.8 liters). Bore & stroke: 3.5 x 3.0 in. Compression ratio 8.4:1. Brake horsepower: 112 at 5100 R.P.M. Torque: 148 lbs.-ft. at 2400 R.P.M. Four main bearings. Hydraulic valve lifters. Carburetor: 2Bbl. Rochester E2SE. Built by Chevrolet. VIN Code: X. HIGH-OUTPUT 173 V-6 (Skylark T Type) OPTIONAL (Skylark): Same as 173 cu. in V-6 above except as follows: Compression ratio: 8.94:1. Brake horsepower: 135 at 5400 R.P.M. Torque: 145 lbs.-ft. at 2400 R.P.M. VIN Code: Z. OPTIONAL V-6 (Century): 90-degree, overhead-valve-V-6. Cast iron block and head. Displacement: 181 cu. in. (3.0 liters). Bore & stroke: 3.8 x 2.66 in. Compression ratio: 8.45:1. Brake horsepower 110 at 4800 R.P.M. Torque: 145 lbs-ft. at 2600 R.P.M. Four main bearings. Hydraulic valve lifters. Carburetor: 2Bbl. Rochester E2ME. VIN Code: E. BASE V-6 (Regal, LeSabre): 90-degree, overhead-valve V-6. Cast iron alloy block and head. Displacement: 231 cu. in. (3.8 liters). Bore & stroke: 3.8 x 3.4 in. Compression ratio: 8.0:1. Brake horsepower: 110 at 800 R.P.M. Torque: 190 lbs.-ft. at 1600 R.P.M. Four main bearings. Hydraulic valve lifters. Carburetor: 2Bbl. Rochester. VIN Code: A. TURBOCHARGED V-6 (Regal T Type, Riviera T Type): Same as 231 V-6 above, but with E4ME four-barrel carburetor. Brake horsepower: 180 at 4000 R.P.M. Torque: 280 lbs.-ft. at 2400 R.P.M. (Riviera, 290 lbs.-ft.) VIN Code: 8. BASE V-6 (Electra, Riviera); OPTIONAL (Regal, LeSabre); 90-degree, overhead-valve V-6. Cast iron alloy block and head. Displacement: 252 cu. in. (4.1 liters). Bore & stroke: 3.965 x 3.4 in. Compression ratio: 8.0:1. Brake horsepower: 125 at 4000 R.P.M. Torque: 205 lbs.-ft. at 2000 R.P.M. Four main bearings. Hydraulic valve lifters. Carburetor: 4Bbl. Rochester, VIN Code: 4. DIESEL V-6; OPTIONAL (Century, Regal); 90-degree, overhead-valve V-6. Cast iron block; cast iron or aluminum head. Displacement: 262.5 cu. in (4.3 liters). Bore & stroke: 4.057 x 3.385 in. Compression ratio: 21.6:1. Brake horsepower: 85 at 3600 R.P.M. Torque: 165 lbs.-ft. at 1600 R.P.M. Four main bearings. Hydraulic valve lifters. Fuel injection. VIN Code: V. BASE V-8 (Estate); OPTIONAL (LeSabre, Electra, Riviera): 90-degree, overhead valve V-8. Cast iron block and head. Displacement: 307 cu. in. (5.0 liters). Bore & stroke: 3.80 x 3.385 in. Compression ratio: 8.0:1. Brake horsepower: 140 at 3600 R.P.M. Torque: 240 lbs-ft. at 1600 R.P.M. Five main bearings. Hydraulic valve lifters. Carburetor: 4Bbl. Rochester. Built by Oldsmobile. VIN Code: Y. OPTIONAL DIESEL V-8 (Regal, LeSabre, Electra, Estate, Riviera); 90-degree, overhead valve V-8. Cast iron block and head. Displacement: 350 cu. in. (5.7 liters). Bore & stroke: 4.057 x 3.385 in. Compression ratio: 21.6:1. Brake horsepower: 105 at 3200 R.P.M. Torque: 200 lbs-ft. at 1600 R.P.M. Five main bearings. Hydraulic valve lifters. Fuel injection. Oldsmobile-built. VIN Code: N.

CHASSIS DATA: Wheelbase: (Skyhawk) 101.2 in.; (Skylark/Century) 104.9 in.; (Regal) 108.1 in.; (LeSabre/Estate) 115.9 in.; (Electra) 118.9 in.; (Riviera) 114.0 in. Overall length:- (Skyhawk) 175.3 in.; (Skyhawk wag) 177.1 in.; (Skylark) 181.0 in.; (Century) 189.1 in.; (Regal cpe) 200.6 in.; (Regal sed) 196.0 in.; (Regal wag) 196.7 in.; (LeSabre) 218.4 in.; (Electra) 221.3 in.; (Estate Wagon) 220.5 in.; (Riviera) 206.6 in. Height:- (Skyhawk) 54.0 in.; (Skylark/Century) 53.6 in.; (Regal cpe) 54.5 in.; (Regal sed) 55.4 in.; (Regal wag) 57.1 in.; (LeSabre) 56.0 in.; (Electra cpe) 56.8 in.; (LeSabre/Electra sed) 56.7-56.9 in.; (Estate) 59.1 in.; (Riv) 54.3 in. Width:- (Skyhawk) 62.0 in.; (Skyhawk wag) 65.0 in.; (Skylark) 69.1 in.; (Century) 66.8 in.; (Regal cpe) 71.6 in.; (Regal sed/wag) 71.1-71.2 in.; (LeSabre) 78.0 in.; (Electra) 76.2 in.; (Estate) 79.3 in.; (Riv) 72.8 in. Front Tread:- (Skyhawk) 55.4 in.; (Skylark/Century) 58.7 in.; (Regal) 58.5 in.; (LeSabre/ Electra) 61.8 in.; (Estate) 62.2 in.; (Riviera) 59.3 in. Rear

Tread:- (Skyhawk) 55.2 in.; (Skylark/Century) 57.0 in.; (Regal) 57.7 in.; (LeSabre/Electra) 60.7 in.; (Estate) 64.0 in.; (Riviera) 60.0 in. Standard Tires:- (Skyhawk) P175/80R13 GBR; (Skylark/Century) P185/80R13 GBR; (Skylark T Type) P205/70R13 SBR; (Regal) P195/75R14 SBR WSW; (Regal T Type) P205/70R14 SBR; (LeSabre) P205/75R15 SBR WSW; (Electra) P215/75R15 SBR WSW; (Estate) P225/75R15 SBR WSW; (Riviera) P205/75R15 SBR WSW.

TECHNICAL: Transmission:- Four-speed, fully synchronized floor shift standard on Skyhawk/Skylark; automatic optional (standard on all other models). Five-speed standard on Skyhawk T Type. Four-speed gear ratios: (1st) 3.53:1; (2nd) 1.95:1; (3rd) 1.24:1; (4th) 0.81:1 or 0.73:1; (Rev) 3.42:1. Five-speed gear ratios: (1st) 3.91:1; (2nd) 2.15:1; (3rd) 1.45:1; (4th) 1.03:1; (5th) 0.74:1; (Rev) 3.50:1. Three-speed auto. trans. gear ratios: (1st) 2.74:1; (2nd) 1.57:1; (3rd) 1.00:1; (Rev) 1.93:1 or 2.07:1. Skyhawk/Skylark/Century auto. trans. gear ratios: (1st) 2.84:1; (2nd) 1.60:1; (3rd) 1.00:1; (Rev) 2.07:1. Four-speed overdrive automatic gear ratios: (1st) 2.74:1; (2nd) 1.57:1; (3rd) 1.00:1; (4th) 0.67:1; (Rev) 2.07:1. T Type Final Drive Ratios:- (Skyhawk) 3.83:1; (Skylark) 3.65:1; (Century) 2.97:1; (Regal) 3.42:1; (Riviera) 3.36:1. Steering:- Same as 1982. Suspension:- Same as 1982. Brakes:- Same as 1982. Body construction:- Same as 1982. Wheel size:- (Skyhawk/Century) 13 x 5.5 in.; (Regal) 14 x 6 in.; (LeSabre/Riviera) 15 x 6 in.; (Estate) 15 x 7 in. Fuel tank:- (Skyhawk) 13.6 gal.; (Skylark) 15.1 gal.; (Century) 15.7 gal.; (Regal) 18.1 gal.; (LeSabre/Electra) 25.0 gal.; (Estate) 22.0 gal.; (Riviera) 21.1 gal. Unleaded fuel only.

DRIVETRAIN OPTIONS: Engines:- 112 cu. in. (1.8-liter) EFI four: Skyhawk ($50). 173 cu. in. (2.8-liter) V-6, 2Bbl.: Skylark ($150). High-output 173 cu. in. (2.8-liter) V-6, 2Bbl.: Skylark ($300); std. on T Type. 181 cu. in. (3.0-liter) V-6, 2Bbl.: Century ($150). 252 cu. in. (4.1-liter) V-6, 4Bbl.: Regal ($150; LeSabre exc. wagon ($150). 263 cu. in. (4.3-liter) diesel V-6: Century Cust/Ltd ($599); Regal exc. T Type or wag ($599). 307 cu. in. (5.0-liter) V-8, 4Bbl.: LeSabre cpe/sed ($225); Electra cpe/sed, Riviera ($75). 350 cu. in. (5.7-liter) diesel V-8: Regal/LeSabre/Estate/Electra/Riviera ($799). Transmission/Differential:- Five-speed manual trans.: Skyhawk ($75). Automatic trans.: Skyhawk ($395); Skyhawk T Type ($320); Skylark ($425). Automatic overdrive trans.: LeSabre cpe/sed ($175); std. automatic on LeSabre (NC). Optional rear axle ratio: Regal exc. T Type 2.73:1 or 3.23:1 (NC); Regal, Ltd 3.08:1 (NC); LeSabre 2.73:1, 3.08:1 or 3.23:1 (NC); Electra 3.08:1 or 3.23:1 (NC). Limited slip differential: Regal/LeSabre/Electra ($95). Suspension, Steering and Brakes:- F40 Firm ride/handling pkg.: Skylark/Century Cust/Ltd ($27); Regal exc. T Type ($27); LeSabre/Electra ($27). F41 Gran Touring suspension: Skyhawk ($196); Century Cust/Ltd ($27); Regal/Ltd, LeSabre ($49); Riviera ($27). F41 Gran Touring ride/handling suspension incl. P205/70R13 SBR WSW tires: Skylark Cust/Ltd ($272). Superlift rear shock absorbers: Skylark Cust/Ltd ($68). Automatic level control: Century/Regal/LeSabre/Electra ($175). Power steering: Skyhawk ($199). Four-wheel disc brakes: Riviera ($235); std. on conv. Other:- Trailer towing pkg.: LeSabre exc. wag ($127). Heavy- duty alternator, 85-amp ($35-$85). H.D. battery: ($25); w/diesel ($50). H.D. radiator: Skyhawk ($40-$70). H.D. cooling: Skylark ($40-$70); Cold climate pkg.: Regal exc. T (NC). Engine block heater ($18). H.D. engine/transmission cooling: Century/Regal/LeSabre/Electra ($40-$70). High altitude emission pkg. (NC) except w/diesel cold climate pkg. delete ($49). California emission system ($75) exc. diesel ($215). Diesel cold climate pkg. delete ($99 credit).

SKYHAWK CONVENIENCE/APPEARANCE OPTIONS: Option Packages:- Vista Vent flip-open removable glass sunroof ($295). Acoustic pkg. ($36). Instrument gauge pkg.: temp, oil pressure, volts, trip odometer: Cust ($60). Gauges and tach: Cust ($138); Ltd ($78). Comfort/Convenience:- Air cond. ($625). Touch climate control air cond. ($775). Rear defogger, electric ($125). Cruise Master w/resume ($170). Power windows ($180-$255). Electric door locks ($120-$170). Six-way power driver's seat ($210). Easy-entry passenger seat adjuster: Cust cpe ($16). Tinted glass ($90). Sport steering wheel ($50). Tilt steering ($99). Trip odometer: Cust ($15). Electric clock ($35). Electric trunk release ($40). Remote tailgate lock: wag ($35). Tailgate wiper/washer: wag ($120). Two-speed wipers w/delay ($49). Lights, Horns and Mirrors:- Tungsten-halogen headlamps ($22). Headlamps-on indicator ($15). Dome reading lamp ($30). Dual horns: Cust cpe/sed ($15). Left remote mirror ($21). Dual mirrors: left remote ($51). Dual electric remote mirrors ($137); T Type ($86). Visor vanity mirror, passenger ($7). Lighted visor vanity mirror, either side ($45). Entertainment:- Basic electronic- tuning AM/FM stereo radio ($138); w/clock ($177); w/cassette ($277). Electronic-tuning AM/FM stereo radio ($302); w/cassette and graphic equalizer ($505). Radio delete ($56 credit). Power antenna ($60). Dual rear speakers ($25-$30). Exterior Trim:- Door edge guards ($15-$25). Rocker panel moldings: Cust cpe/sed ($26). Bodyside stripes ($42). Designers' accent paint ($195). Decklid luggage rack ($105). Roof rack: wag ($105). Interior Trim/Upholstery:- Suede bucket seats: Ltd cpe/sed ($295). Front carpet savers ($17); rear ($12). Front carpet savers w/inserts ($18); rear ($15). Deluxe trunk trim ($33). Wheels and Tires:- Styled aluminum wheels ($229). Styled wheel covers w/trim rings ($38). Custom locking wire wheel covers ($165). P175/80R13 GBR WSW ($54). P195/70R13 SBR BSW ($169). P195/70R13 SBR WSW ($62-$231). P195/70R13 SBR WLT ($84-$253). P195/70R13 SBR wide WSW ($62- $231). Self-sealing tires ($106).

SKYLARK/CENTURY CONVENIENCE/APPEARANCE OPTIONS: Option Packages: Acoustic pkg.: Skylark Cust ($60). Flip-open Vista Vent glass sunroof ($295). Standard option delete (rocker panel moldings and front armrest): Century Cust ($67 credit). Comfort/Convenience:- Air cond. ($725). Cruise Master w/resume ($170). Rear defogger, electric ($135). Power windows: cpe ($180); Skylark sed ($255). Electric door locks ($120-$170). Six-way power driver's seat ($210). Manual seatback recliners, passenger: Cust/Ltd ($45); both ($90). Sport steering wheel ($50). Tilt steering ($105). Tinted glass ($105). Instrument gauges incl. trip odometer ($48). Trip odometer: Skylark Cust/Ltd ($16). Digital electronic instrument cluster: Century ($299). Dial clock ($35). Electric trunk release ($40). Two-speed wipers w/delay ($49). Theft deterrent system: Century ($159). Lights, Horns and Mirrors:- Tungsten-halogen headlamps: Century ($22). Twilight Sentinel: Century ($57). Front light monitors: Century ($37). Coach lamps: Ltd ($102-$129). Headlamps-on indicator ($16). Door courtesy/warning light: Century Ltd ($44). Dome reading light ($24). Rear seat reading lamp: Skylark Ltd, Century ($30). Remote left mirror: Cust/Ltd ($24). Sport mirrors (left remote): Cust/Ltd ($59). Dual electric remote mirrors: Cust/Ltd ($137); T Type ($78). Visor vanity mirror, passenger ($7). Lighted visor vanity mirror, passenger: Skylark ($50); either side, Century ($58). Entertainment:- Same as Skyhawk above). Exterior Trim:- Landau vinyl top: Cust/Ltd cpe ($181-$215). Long vinyl top: Cust/Ltd ($155). Designers' accent paint: Cust/Ltd ($205-$210). Special solid color paint: Century Cust/Ltd ($200). Protective bodyside moldings ($55). Lower wide bodyside moldings: Century Cust ($65). Wide rocker panel/rear quarter moldings: Skylark Cust ($65). Belt reveal moldings: Skylark Cust, T ($40). Wheel opening moldings: Skylark Cust ($30). Door edge guards ($15-$25). Pillar applique moldings: Skylark Cust sed ($27). Hood ornament and windsplit: Cust ($22-$32). Bodyside stripe: Cust/Ltd ($42). Bumper guards, front/rear: Skylark ($45). Bumper strips, front/rear: Skylark Cust ($49). Front license plate mounting: Skylark (NC). Interior Trim/Upholstery:- Full-length console: Skylark ($100); Century ($57). Full-length operating console: Century ($75); T Type ($18). Bucket seats: Skylark ($95). Lear Siegler bucket seats: Century T Type ($600). 45/45 seating: cloth, Century Cust ($158); leather, Century Ltd ($295). Front carpet savers ($17); rear ($12). Carpet savers w/inserts: front ($25); rear ($20). Trunk trim ($35-$47). heels:- Styled aluminum wheels: Century Cust/Ltd ($195). Chrome-plated wheels: Skylark Cust/Ltd ($175). Locking wire wheel covers: Cust/Ltd ($185). Skylark Tires:- P185/80R13 GBR WSW: Cust/Ltd ($58). P185/80R13 SBR WSW: Cust/Ltd ($123). P205/70R13 SBR WSW: Cust/Ltd ($255). P215/60R14 SBR WLT: T Type ($92). Self-sealing tires: Cust/Ltd ($106). Century Cust/Ltd Tires:- P185/75R14 GBR WSW ($58). P185/75R14 SBR BSW $64). P185/75R14 SBR WSW ($122). P195/75R14 SBR BSW ($95). P195/75R14 SBR WSW ($157). Self-sealing tires ($106).

REGAL CONVENIENCE/APPEARANCE OPTIONS: Option Packages:- Regal T Type Decor pkg.: designers' accent paint, wide rocker molding, black paint treatment, sport steering wheel ($365). Sliding electric Astroroof: cpe ($895). Hatch roof: cpe ($825). Standard option delete: Regal sedan w/o narrow rocker moldings, bright steering wheel bezel, passenger mirror, underhood light, bodyside moldings, brushed deck lid molding, wheel opening and window reveal moldings; with P185/75R14 GBR WSW tires ($278 credit). Comfort/Convenience:- Air cond. ($725); climate control ($875). Cruise Master w/resume ($170). Rear defogger, electric ($135). Tinted glass ($105). Tinted windshield ($80). Six-way power seat, each side ($210); both ($420). Manual passenger seatback recliner ($75). Sport steering wheel ($50). Tilt steering ($105). Power windows ($180-$255). Electric door locks ($120-$170). Electric trunk release ($40). Remote electric tailgate lock: wag ($40). Electric clock ($35). Headlamps-on indicator ($16). Trip odometer ($16) exc. T. Instrument gauges: temp, voltage, trip odometer ($48). Two-speed wiper w/low-speed delay ($49). Theft deterrent system ($159); N/A on wag. Lighting and Mirrors:- Tungsten-halogen headlamps ($22). Twilight Sentinel headlamp control ($57). Cornering lamps ($57). Coach lamps: Ltd ($102). Door courtesy/warning lights: Ltd ($44-$70). Rear seat reading light ($30). Dome reading lamps ($24). Remote left mirror ($24) exc. T Type; right ($42). Dual sport mirrors, left remote ($51). Dual remote sport mirrors ($81); T ($30). Visor vanity mirror, passenger ($7). Lighted visor vanity mirror, passenger ($58). Entertainment:- AM radio ($112). AM/FM stereo radio ($198); w/cassette ($298). Electronic-tuning AM/FM stereo radio ($402); w/cassette ($555). Dual rear speakers ($25-$30). Automatic power antenna ($95); w/radio ($60). Exterior Trim:- Landau vinyl top: cpe ($181). Heavy-padded landau vinyl top: cpe ($240). Long vinyl top: sed ($155). Long padded vinyl top: sed ($240). Designers' accent paint ($200-$235). Solid special color paint ($200). Exterior molding pkg. ($110); std. on Ltd. Protective bodyside moldings: T Type ($55). Wraparound bodyside moldings: Ltd sedan ($104). Hood ornament and windsplit: Century ($22); std. on Ltd. Door edge guards ($15-$25). Belt reveal moldings: T Type w/decor pkg. ($40). Bodyside stripe ($42). Woodgrain vinyl applique: wag ($355). Roof rack: wag ($125). Air deflector: wag ($37). Interior Trim/Upholstery:- Full-length console ($82) exc. wag; operating console for bucket seats (NC). Bucket seats: cpe/sed ($195). 55/45 seating ($133). Limited 55/45 seating: T Type ($385). Limited 45/45 leather/vinyl seating: T ($680). Leather/vinyl 45/45 seating: Ltd ($295). Front carpet savers $17); rear ($12). Front carpet savers w/inserts ($25); rear ($20). Trunk trim covering ($47). Lockable storage compartment: wag ($55). Wheels:- Chrome-plated wheels ($195); T Type ($90 credit). Styled aluminum wheels ($285); std. on T. Locking wire wheel covers ($185); T ($100 credit). Body- color wheels ($85) exc. T. Tires:- P205/70R14 SBR WSW ($62-$66). P205/70R14 SBR WLT ($88). Self-sealing tires ($106) exc. T Type.

LESABRE/ELECTRA/ESTATE WAGON CONVENIENCE/APPEARANCE OPTIONS: Comfort/Convenience:- Sliding electric Astroroof: silver, gray or gold ($1195). Air cond.: LeSabre ($725). Air cond. w/touch-climate control ($875); LeSabre Estate, Electra ($150). Cruise Master w/resume ($170); std. on Park Ave. Rear defogger, electric ($135). Tinted glass: LeSabre Cust ($105). Power windows: LeSabre ($180-$255). Electric door locks ($120-$170). Automatic door locks ($200-$250); exc. Park Ave. ($80). Six-way power seat, driver's or passenger's ($180- $210); both ($390-$420). Memory driver's seat: Electra Ltd ($358); Park Ave. ($178). Electric seatback recliner, one side ($139). Sport steering wheel: LeSabre ($50). Tilt steering: LeSabre, Electra Ltd ($105). Tilt/telescoping steering column ($160) exc. Electra Park Ave./Estate ($55). Dial clock: LeSabre ($60). Trip odometer: LeSabre ($16). Remote tailgate lock: LeSabre Est ($50). Electric trunk lock: Electra ($80). Electric trunk release ($40). Electric fuel cap lock ($44) exc. wag. Theft deterrent system ($159); N/A on Estate. Two-speed wiper w/delay ($49). Accessory group (trip odometer, dome reading lamp, low fuel indicator, washer fluid indicator): Electra ($30-$70). Lighting, Horns and Mirrors:- Tungsten-halogen high-beam headlamps ($22). Twilight Sentinel ($57). Cornering lamps ($57). Coach lamps: LeSabre/Electra Ltd ($102). Light monitors, front: LeSabre, Electra Est ($37); front/rear, Electra ($74). Lamp and indicator group: LeSabre ($38-$70). Door courtesy/warning lamps ($44-$70). Lighted door lock and interior light control ($72). Four-note horn ($28). Remote left mirror: LeSabre ($24). Remote right mirror: LeSabre ($48); Electra Ltd, Est ($24). Remote electric right mirror: Electra Park Ave. ($57). Dual remote sport mirrors: LeSabre ($88); Electra Ltd, Est ($40). Dual electric remote mirrors: LeSabre ($137); Electra Ltd, Est ($89). Remote left mirror w/thermometer: LeSabre ($62); Electra Ltd, Est ($38). Electric left mirror w/thermometer: Park Ave. ($38). Dual electric mirrors w/left thermometer: LeSabre ($175); Electra Ltd, Est ($127). Lighted visor vanity mirror, driver or passenger ($58). Entertainment:- AM radio: LeSabre ($112). AM/FM stereo radio: LeSabre, Electra Ltd/Estate ($198); w/8- track or cassette ($298) exc. Park Ave. ($100). AM/FM stereo radio with CB: Estate ($473). Electronic-tuning AM/FM stereo radio: LeSabre ($377-$402); Electra ($165-$363). Electronic- tuning radio and 8-track or cassette ($491-$555) exc. Park Ave. ($319). Electronic-tuning radio with CB and cassette player: Estate ($766-$805). Delete AM/FM stereo radio: Electra Park Ave. ($153 credit). Concert Sound speaker system: Electra exc. wag ($95); ETR radio req'd. Dual rear speakers ($25-$30). Automatic power antenna ($95); w/radio ($60). Triband power antenna: Estate ($140); w/radio ($105). Exterior Trim:- Exterior molding pkg. (wide rocker panel, front/rear fender lower and belt reveal moldings): LeSabre ($110). Landau vinyl top: LeSabre, Electra Ltd cpe ($240). Long vinyl top: LeSabre, Electra Ltd sed ($180-$185). Heavy- padded long vinyl top: Electra Ltd sed ($240). Designers' accent paint: LeSabre ($215) exc. Estate. Special single- color paint: ($200); Firemist, Electra exc. Estate ($210). Protective bodyside moldings: Est ($55). Wide rocker panel moldings: Electra Ltd/Est ($65). Door edge guards ($15-$25). Belt reveal molding: LeSabre ($40). Bodyside stripes ($42). Woodgrain vinyl applique: LeSabre Est ($345). Roof rack w/air deflector: LeSabre Est ($150). Interior Trim/Upholstery:- 55/45 seating: LeSabre Custom/Est ($125). Leather/vinyl 50/50 seating: Park Ave. ($525). Third seat: Estate ($215). Front carpet savers ($17); rear ($12). Front carpet savers w/inserts ($25); rear ($20). Trunk carpeting trim ($53-$65). Trunk mat ($14). Wheels:- Chrome-plated wheels ($180-$215). Styled aluminum wheels ($220-$255) exc. Electra Est ($40). Custom wheel covers: Electra Ltd ($35). Locking wire wheel covers ($150-$185); Electra Est ($30 credit). Tires:- P215/75R15 SBR wide whitewall: LeSabre cpe/sed ($38). P225/75R15 SBR wide whitewall: Electra cpe/sed ($39). Self- sealing tires ($132).

RIVIERA CONVENIENCE/APPEARANCE OPTIONS: Comfort/Convenience:- Electric sliding Astroroof: silver, gray or gold ($210). Automatic touch climate-control air cond. ($150). Digital electronic instrument cluster ($238). Six-way power seat, passenger ($210). Two-position memory driver's seat ($178). Electric seatback recliner, one side ($139). Sport steering wheel ($40) exc. T Type. Tilt/telescope steering wheel ($55) exc. T Type. Electric fuel cap lock ($44). Electric trunk release ($40); lock ($80). Low fuel indicator ($16). Two-speed wipers w/delay ($49). Windshield washer fluid indicator ($16). Theft deterrent system ($159). Lighting, Horns and Mirrors:- Tungsten-halogen high-beam headlamps ($22); std. on T Type. Twilight Sentinel headlamp control ($57). Coach lamps ($102); incl. w/vinyl top. Front/rear light monitors: T Type ($74). Rear quarter courtesy/reading lamp ($48). Lighted door lock and interior light control ($72). Four-note horn ($28). Dual electric remote mirrors ($65). Lighted visor vanity mirrors, each ($58). Entertainment:- Full-feature electronic-tuning AM/FM stereo radio ($125); w/8-track tape player ($278). Basic electronic-tuning AM/FM stereo radio w/cassette player ($100). Electronic-tuning AM/FM stereo radio with cassette and graphic equalizer ($328); w/cassette, Dolby and Bose speaker system ($895) exc. conv. CB radio ($220). Delete radio ($230 credit). Rear speakers for base radio ($25). Concert Sound system ($95) exc. conv. Triband power antenna ($45); incl. w/CB. Exterior Trim:- Heavy-padded landau vinyl top w/coach lamps ($325). Designers' accent paint ($235). Special color Firemist paint ($210); std. on conv. Color- coordinated protective bodyside moldings ($55). Door edge guards ($15). Bodyside stripe ($42). Interior Trim/Upholstery:- 45/45 leather/vinyl front seat ($405) exc. conv. Front carpet savers w/inserts ($35); rear ($20). Trunk trim carpeting ($30). Trunk mat ($15). Wheels and Tires:- Chrome-plated wheels ($145); on conv. ($40 credit). Custom locking wire wheel covers ($185). P225/70R15 SBR wide oval tires: BSW or WSW (NC).

1984 BUICK

As in the industry generally, high-tech engines got the emphasis for 1984, along with modern electronics and aero styling. T Types were now offered on five Buick models, which gained a performance boost. Two new 3.8-liter V-6s were introduced: one with multi-port fuel injection (optional on Century), the other with sequential fuel injection (standard on Regal/Riviera T Types). With multi-port injection (MFI), a computer analyzed air/fuel requirements and sent a charge to all six cylinders during each engine revolution. Sequential injection gave each cylinder a precisely-metered charge, just before firing, for best performance all the way from idle to full load. Both V-6 versions had been developed at Buick Special Products Engineering. An acceleration/deceleration feature on the new electronic cruise control allowed speed change in 1 MPH increments by touching a button on the lever. Cellular phones were offered for the first time, factory-approved but installed by dealers. 1984 Buick body colors were: beige, light sand gray, bright red, white and black, plus a selection of metallics: light brown, brown, light green, green, light blue, blue, red Firemist, red, dark red, sand gray Firemist, gold Firemist, and silver. Firemists cost extra.

1984 Skyhawk T Type coupe (B)

SKYHAWK — SERIES 4J — FOUR — New front-end panels with bigger cooling slots went on all Skyhawks this year, along with new bumper rub strips and modified turn signal lamps. The aerodynamic design used a low hood and high deck for wedge-shaped profile. Skyhawk came in Custom and Limited trim as well as the sporty T Type, which expanded its color selection to include silver, light maple and white bodies, with charcoal accents. Newly optional: an electronic radio with five-band graphic equalizer and four speakers. All Skyhawks had an AM radio and power brakes. T Types turned to P195/70R13 tires on styled aluminum wheels and had dual mirrors (left remote-controlled), Gran Touring suspension, and a sport steering wheel. Apart from the T Type, the Chevrolet-built 121 cu. in. (2.0-liter) four remained standard, with four-speed gearbox; a 1.8 four from Brazil was again optional. Shortly after production began, a turbocharged version of the 1.8-liter overhead-cam four became available (at extra cost) on the Skyhawk T Type, with multi-port fuel injection. Horsepower shot up to 150; torque to 150 lb.-ft. Included with that turbo engine was a Level III suspension system, with 205/60 series Eagle GT tires on 14 in. forged aluminum wheels. Standard T type powerplant remained the normally-aspirated 1.8 four, with five-speed manual gearbox. Turbos ame with four-speed manual. All three engines could have three-speed automatic transmission instead.

SKYLARK — SERIES 4X — FOUR/V-6 — Aside from a distinctive new (notably Buick) grille, the X-bodied Buick didn't change much for '84. One new option on either coupe or sedan: a decklid luggage rack. Electronic cruise control was also available. T Type coupes now had an electronic LED tachometer. As before, the 151 cu. in. (2.5-liter) four was standard; a 173 cu. in. (2.8-liter) V-6 optional, with a more powerful version standard in the T Type and optional on other models. Overdrive automatic transmissions were now available in the similar-size A-cars, but not in X models. Standard equipment included an AM radio, power steering, four-speed manual gearbox, notchback bench seat with adjustable headrests, roof drip and window moldings, glovebox lock, cigarette lighter, compact spare, and P185/80R13 steel-belted radial tires. Skylark Limited also came with belt reveal and wheel-opening moldings, a hood ornament, wide rocker panel and rear quarter moldings, protective bumper rub strips, and a pillar applique on sedans. T Types added a tachometer, gauges, halogen headlamps, Rallye ride/handling suspension, specially styled sport aluminum wheels with P215/60R14 steel-belted radials, black sport mirrors, and a sport steering wheel. The sporty Skylarks also had a blacked-out grille; black anodized aluminum bumpers; smoked taillamp lenses; and styled black mirrors. T bodies came in silver, light maple or white, with charcoal accent.

1984 Skylark T Type coupe (B)

1984 Century Estate Wagon (B)

CENTURY — SERIES 4A — FOUR/V-6 — All Century models displayed a new grille, headlamp bezels, bumper rub strips and standard wheel covers, along with new graphics at front and rear. Coupes and sedans added a new rear end and taillamps, plus a modified back bumper. A new new three-passenger front seat gave the Custom space for six. Century offered two new wagons for 1984: Custom and Estate, each with a unique one-piece top-hinged tailgate. Both had a split-folding back seat and separate lift-up rear window with available washer/wiper. They replaced the old Regal rear-drive wagon, which dropped out this season. Carrying six passengers in normal trim, they could have a rear-facing third seat that held two more. Wagons could hold over 74 cubic feet of cargo. Century Customs came with a standard AM radio, power brakes and steering, three-speed automatic transmission, bumper guards and rub strips, dual horns, locking glove box, side-window defogger, storage console, and full carpeting. The Limited added 55/45 cloth seating, a hood ornament, and wide lower bodyside moldings. Among other sporty extras, T Types included dual exhausts, temp/volt gauges, a blacked-out grille, styled black mirrors, black moldings, charcoal lower accent paint and striping, Gran Touring suspension, cloth bucket seats, and styled aluminum wheels. T Type dashes carried a new ribbon-type LED tachometer, and could be equipped with a special Lear Siegler bucket interior. Base Century engine remained the 2.5-liter four with throttle-body fuel injection, rated 90 horsepower. Options included a carbureted 3.0-liter V-6 and a diesel V-6. Most notable, though, was the fuel-injected 231 cu. in. (3.8-liter) V-6, standard in T Type and optional elsewhere, available with four-speed overdrive automatic transmission. On the special-edition roster, to complement Buick's role as official car and sponsor of the games of the 23rd Olympiad in Los Angeles, there was a Century Olympia Limited sedan. Offered in white with "subtly classic" U.S. Olympic identification on front fender, decklid and hood ornament, the sedan was accented with gold body stripe and gold aluminum wheels. It had a decklid luggage rack, and the headrest on the tan cloth interior was embroidered with the official U.S. Olympic logo in dark brown.

1984 Regal coupe (JG)

REGAL — SERIES 4G — V-6 — Continuing for another season in rear-drive form, Regal dropped its station wagon this year. The diesel V-8 also disappeared, but a 4.3-liter V-6 diesel remained as an option. Regals showed a new grille and front end design, along with new graphics and taillamps, and a modified instrument panel. Coupes added new headlamp bezels and park/signal lamps. Joining the option list: a digital instrument cluster similar to Riviera's, with flourescent displays that showed speed, distance and fuel level. Standard equipment included dual mirrors and horns,

automatic transmission, power brakes and steering, bumper guards and rub strips, and whitewall P195/75R14 steel-belted tires. T Type tires were P215/65R15 blackwalls, on styled aluminum wheels. Limiteds carried a 55/45 notchback seat, along with wide rocker panel and rear quarter moldings. All engines except the base 231 cu. in. (3.8-liter) V-6 could have four-speed overdrive automatic transmission (standard in T Type) for $175 more. Regal's high-performance T Type had the new 3.8-liter V-6 with turbocharger and sequential port fuel injection, which produced 200 horsepower and 300 pound-feet of torque. Distributorless ignition on the turbo used three computer- controlled ignition coils to send current to the spark plugs. T Types came with a 3.42:1 performance axle ratio, overdrive utomatic transmission, Gran Touring suspension, leather- wrapped steering wheel, turbo boost gauge, trip odometer, tachometer, and air conditioning. Buick's display of turbo technology at auto shows during 1984 was highlighted later in the model year by emergence of the '84 Regal Grand National, "produced in limited numbers for those who demand a high level of performance." Its purpose: to give much of the feeling of a NASCAR race car. Though officially on the option list, carrying a relatively moderate $1282 price tag, not too many Regal customers managed to get their hands on the Grand National package. Grand Nationals carried the turbo 3.8 engine, P215/60R blackwalls, sport steering wheel, tachometer and boost gauge, and 94-amp Delcotron. Distinctive bodies came only in black, with black bumpers, rub strips and guards; black front air dam and decklid spoiler; black headlamp bezels; turbo aluminum wheels with black paint; and Grand National identification on front fender. A Lear Siegler interior held front seats embroidered with the Grand National logo. Though officially on the option list, carrying a relatively modest $1282 price tag, not many Grand National packages found their way onto T Type Regals in 1984.

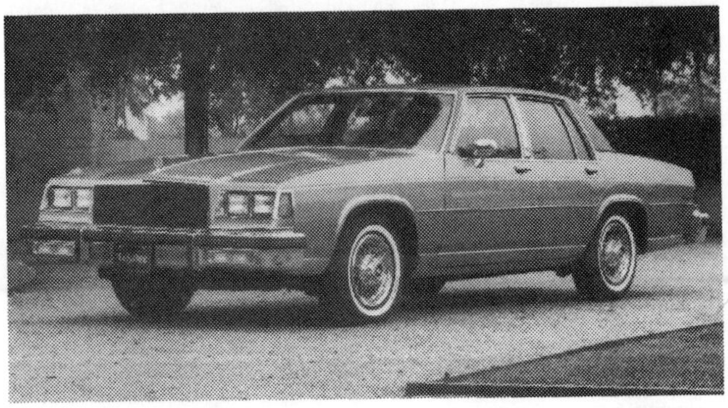

1984 LeSabre Custom sedan (B)

LESABRE — SERIES 4B — V-6/V-8 — Not much of substance changed this year on the rear- drive LeSabre, but a different grille and front-end panel gave a fresh look. Rear-end styling was also reworked, including new taillamps. New standard equipment included remote left (manual right) mirrors on all models and a redesigned steering wheel. Optional automatic touch climate control system was revised to give more precise temperature settings and control of fan speed. Standard under the hood was the familiar 231 cu. in. (3.8-liter) V-6, with 4.1-liter V-6 or 5.0-liter V-8 optional. So was the 5.7-liter diesel V-8, but not in California where it couldn't meet emissions standards. All LeSabres had color-keyed bodyside moldings, front and rear protective bumper strips, and bumper guards. Standard equipment also included dual horns, deluxe wheel covers, cut-pile carpeting, three-speed automatic transmission, power steering and brakes. LeSabre Limited added a two-way adjustable power driver's seat, headlamps-on indicator and warning chime, tinted glass, custom steering wheel, and woodgrain door trim. Limited instrument panels offered electro-luminiscent floodlighting. LeSabre Custom had standard notchback seats in cloth velour with woven fabric trim; Limited cloth seats were in 55/45 arrangement.

ELECTRA ESTATE WAGON — SERIES 4D — V-8 — For '84 the LeSabre Estate Wagon was dropped, so Electra's became the last remaining Buick full-size wagon. Base engine was again the 307 cu. in. (5.0-liter) V-8, with only the 350 diesel V-8 optional. Standard 55/45 notchback seating had two-way power for the driver's side. In back, buyers could have the same cloth-covered seating as in front, or easy-to-clean vinyl. Standard equipment also included a tilt steering column, digital clock, electric door locks, power windows, remote tailgate lock, air conditioning, Soft Ray tinted glass, door edge guards, light oak woodgrain vinyl applique, and a luggage rack.

ELECTRA — SERIES 4D — V-6/V-8 — Since a totally new front-drive Electra was expected soon (and arrived in the spring as an early '85), the old rear- drive carried on unchanged. The new compact Electra was scheduled to arrive earlier, but mechanical and assembly difficulties held back its debut. When it finally appeared, it cut sharply into sales of its larger predecessor--even though the rear-drive had earned some popularity lately. Base engine was the 252 cu. in. (4.1-liter) V-6, with 5.0-liter gas V-8 and 5.7 diesel available. Electra Limited carried standard equipment similar to LeSabre, including a remote-controlled left outside mirror, along with 55/45 cloth notchback seating, air conditioning, digital clock, power windows, and P215/75R1 whitewalls. Park Avenue buyers got 50/50 seats (power on driver's side), a t steering wheel, power door locks, electronic-tuning stereo radio, reading light, remc trunk release, and power remote left mirror.

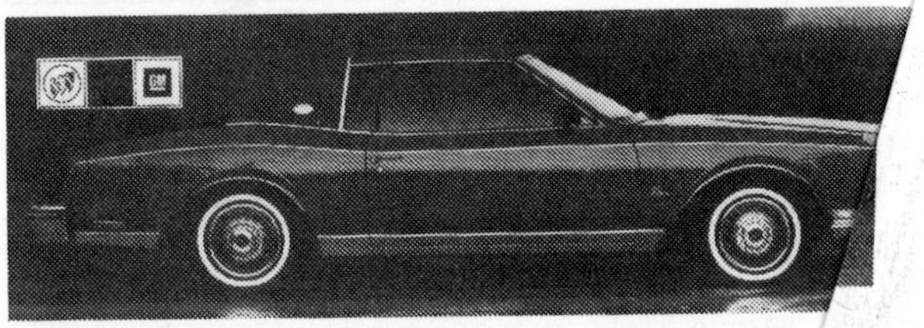

1984 Riviera coupe (JG)

RIVIERA — SERIES 4E — V-6/V-8 — Accompanying the new turbo boost .31 cu. in. (3.8- liter) V-6 engine on Riviera's T Type for '84 were a new stand black gauge and LED tachometer, leather- wrapped sport steering wheel, plus mirrors, and new accent stripes. All Rivs got a new grille and fronnch seat modified taillamp styling. Coupes (including T Type) now carried a up front. that held three people, while the convertible kept its bucke the glass Convertible tops held a new cloth headliner, while an electric defodified by back window was optional. As before, the convertible was sp. (4.1-liter) American Sunroof Corporation. Standard Riv powertrain was the carbureted four-barrel V-6 with four-speed overdrive automatic; or optiona

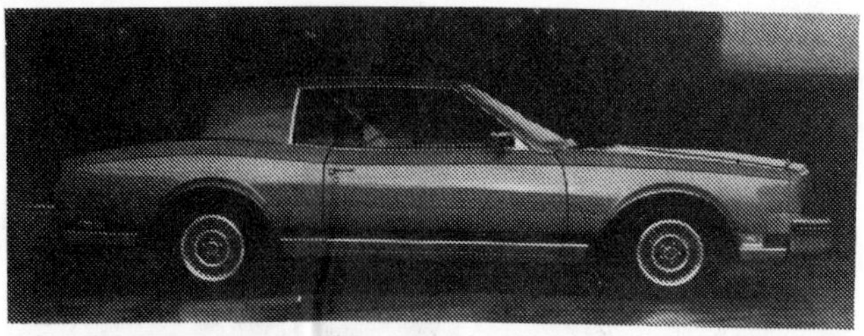

1984 Riviera T Type coupe (JG)

V-8. GM's 5.7-liter diesel V-8 was now offered as a Riviera option for the first time (except in California). Base Rivs had whitewall tires, power brakes and steering, a notchback 55/45 front seat, power windows, tinted glass, an AM/FM eletronically-tuned stereo with automatic power antenna and clock, electric door locks, power six-way driver's seat, cruise control, automatic level control, air conditioning, and P205/75R15 steel-belted radial tires. Tungsten-halogen headlamps, styled aluminum wheels, blacked- out grille and Gran Touring suspension were T Type standards. Riviera convertibles had Firemist paint and four-wheel disc brakes, plus custom locking wire wheel covers and trunk carpeting. On the option list (except for convertibles): a high-end Deco/Bose music system.

I.D. DATA: Buicks agair had a 17-symbol Vehicle Identification Number (VIN), stamped on a metal tag aached to the upper left surface of the cowl, visible through the windshield. Coding as similar to 1983. LeSabre Estate (series code 'R') was dropped, and the code or Electra Park Ave. changed from 'W' to 'U'. Two engine codes were added: ' turbo L4-110 MFI and '3' V6-231 MFI. The code for turbocharged V6-231 ow with SFI) changed to '9'. Model year symbol changed to 'E' for 1984. Symbol elen (plant code) was as follows: 'W' Willow Run, MI; '6' Oklahoma City, OK; ' Flint, MI; 'K' Leeds, MO; 'X' Fairfax, KS; 'E' Linden, NJ; and 'D' Doraville. The fir six digits are the sequential serial number, starting with 400001 except for LeSabr built in Flint, which began with 800001.

SKYHAWK CUST (FOUR)

Series Number	Bo/Style Nber	Body Type & Seating	Factory Price	Shipping Weight	Production Total
4J	S	2-dr Coupe-5P	7133	2316	74,760
4J		4-dr Sedan-5P	7345	2369	45,648
4J	5	4-dr Sta Wag-5P	7677	2439	13,668

SKYHAW MITED (FOUR)

4J	T27	2-dr Coupe-5P	7641	2356	Note 1
4J	T69	4-dr Sedan-5P	7837	2404	Note 1
4J	T35	4-dr Sta Wag-5P	8127	2469	Note 1

Not Skyhawk Custom production figures also include equivalent Limited models. Co sedan production came to 97,962 Customs and 22,446 Limiteds.

S AWK T TYPE (FOUR)

	E27	2-dr Coupe-5P	8152	2332	11,317

YLARK CUSTOM (FOUR/V-6)

X	B37	2-dr Coupe-5P	7545/7795	2458/2519	12,377
4X	B69	4-dr Sedan-5P	7707/7957	2489/2550	56,495

SKYLARK LIMITED (FOUR/V-6)

4X	C37	2-dr Coupe-5P	8119/8369	2484/2545	7,621
4X	C69	4-dr Sedan-5P	8283/8533	2515/2576	33,795

SKYLARK T TYPE (V-6)

4X	D37	2-dr Coupe-5P	9557	2606	923

CENTURY CUSTOM (FOUR/V-6)

4A	H27	2-dr Coupe-6P	9110/9360	2609/2714	15,429
4A	H19	4-dr Sedan-6P	9274/9524	2658/2763	178,454
4A	H35	4-dr Sta Wag-6P	9660/9910	2825/2930	25,975

CENTURY LIMITED (FOUR/V-6)

4A	L27	2-dr Coupe-6P	9562/9812	2631/2736	Note 2
4A	L19	4-dr Sedan-6P	9729/9979	2679/2784	Note 2
4A	L35	4-dr Sta Wag-6P	10087/10337	2843/2948	Note 2

CENTURY T TYPE (V-6)

4A	G27	2-dr Coupe-5P	10510	2775	Note 2
4A	G19	4-dr Sedan-5P	10674	2823	Note 2

Note 2: Production figures listed under Century Custom include totals for Century Limited and T Type models. In all, 71,160 Customs, 119,246 Limiteds and 3,477 Century T Types were manufactured.

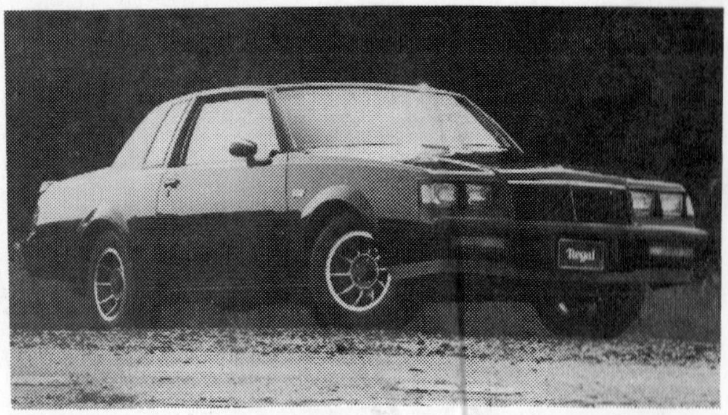

1984 Regal Grand National coupe (B)

REGAL (V-6)

4G	J47	2-dr Coupe-6P	9487	3079	160,638
4G	J69	4-dr Sedan-6P	9671	3125	58,715

REGAL LIMITED (V-6)

4G	M47	2-dr Coupe-6P	10125	3106	Note 3
4G	M69	4-dr Sedan-6P	10263	3125	Note 3

Note 3: Base Regal production totals also include Limited mo s. Total model year production, 106,306 base Regals and 113,047 Limiteds.

REGAL T TYPE (V-6)

4G	K47	2-dr Coupe-6P	12118	249	5,401

LESABRE CUSTOM (V-6/V-8)

4B	N37	2-dr Coupe-6P	9984/10534	3472/36	3,890
4B	N69	4-dr Sedan-6P	10129/10679	3484/36	36,072

LESABRE LIMITED (V-6/V-8)

4B	P37	2-dr Coupe-6P	10780/11330	3497/3688	8,332
4B	P69	4-dr Sedan-6P	10940/11490	3530/3721	,418

ELECTRA LIMITED (V-6/V-8)

4D	R37	2-dr Coupe-6P	13155/13380	3656/3835	5
4D	R69	4-dr Sedan-6P	13332/13557	3716/3895	5

ELECTRA PARK AVENUE (V-6/V-8)

4D	U37	2-dr Coupe-6P	14888/15113	3700/3879	Note
4D	U69	4-dr Sedan-6P	15044/15269	3766/3945	Note

Note 4: Park Avenue production totals are included in Electra Limited figures.

ELECTRA ESTATE WAGON (V-8)

4B	V35	4-dr Sta Wag-6P	14483	4160	17,563

RIVIERA (V-6/V-8)

4E	Z57	2-dr Coupe-5P	15967/16192	3574/3748	56,210
4E	Z67	2-dr Conv-5P	25832/26057	3680/3854	500

Note 5: Only 1,424 standard Riviera coupes and 58 convertibles had a V-6 engine this year.

RIVIERA T TYPE (V-6)

4E	Y57	2-dr Coupe-5P	17050	3660	1,153

FACTORY PRICE AND WEIGHT NOTE: Figure before the slash is for four-cylinder engine, after the slash for V-6. For full-size models, figure before slash is for V-6 engine, after slash for V-8.

ENGINES: BASE FOUR-CYLINDER (Skyhawk): Inline, overhead-valve four-cylinder. Cast iron block and head. Displacement; 121 cu. in. (2.0 liters). Bore & stroke: 3.50 x 3.15 in. Compression ratio: 9.3:1. Brake horsepower: 86 at 4900 R.P.M. Torque: 100 lbs.- ft. at 3000 R.P.M. Five main bearings. Hydraulic valve lifters. Throttle-body fuel injection. VIN Code: P. OPTIONAL FOUR (Skyhawk); STANDARD (Skyhawk T Type): Inline, overhead-cam four-cylinder. Cast iron block; aluminum cylinder head. Displacement: 110 cu. in. (1.8 liters). Bore & stroke: 3.34 x 3.13 in. Compression ratio: 9.0:1. Brake horsepower: 84 at 5200 R.P.M. Torque: 102 lbs.-ft. at 2800 R.P.M. Five main bearings. Hydraulic valve lifters. Throttle- body fuel injection. VIN Code: O. TURBOCHARGED FOUR (Skyhawk T Type): Same as 1.8-liter OHC four above, except-- Compression ratio: 8.0:1. Brake H.P.: 150 at 5600 R.P.M. Torque: 150 lbs.-ft. at 2800 R.P.M. Multi-point fuel injection. VIN Code: J. BASE FOUR (Skylark, Century): Inline, overhead-valve four-cylinder. Cast iron block and head. Displacement: 151 cu. in. (2.5 liters), Bore & stroke: 4.0 x 3.0 in. Compression ratio: 9.0:1. Brake horsepower: 92 at 4400 R.P.M. Torque: 132 lbs-ft. at 2800 R.P.M. Five main bearings. Hydraulic valve lifters. Throttle-body fuel injection. Built by Pontiac. VIN Code: R. OPTIONAL V-6 (Skylark): 60-degree, overhead-valve V-6. Cast iron block and head. Displacement: 173 cu. in. (2.8 liters). Bore & stroke: 3.50 x 2.99 in. Compression: 8.4:1. Brake horsepower: 112 at 5100 R.P.M. Torque: 148 lbs.-ft. at 2400 R.P.M. Four main bearings. Hydraulic valve lifters. Carburetor: 2Bbl. Rochester. Built by Chevrolet, VIN Code: X. HIGH-OUTPUT V-6; (Skylark T Type); OPTIONAL (Skylark); STANDARD (Skylark T): Same as 173 cu. in V-6 above except as follows: Compression ratio: 8.94:1. Brake horsepower: 135 at 5400 R.P.M. Torque: 145 lbs.-ft. at 2400 R.P.M. VIN Code: Z. OPTIONAL V-6 (Century); 90-degree, overhead-valve V-6. Cast iron block and head. Displacement: 181 cu. in (3.0 liters). Bore & stroke: 3.8 x 2.66 in. Compression ratio: 8.45:1. Brake horsepower: 110 at 4800 R.P.M. Torque: 145 lbs.-ft. at 2600 R.P.M. Four main bearings. Hydraulic valve lifters. Carburetor: 2Bbl. Rochester E2SE. VIN Code: E. BASE V-6 (Regal, LeSabre): 90-degree, overhead-valve V-6. Cast iron alloy block and head. Displacement: 231 cu. in. (3.8 liters). Bore & stroke: 3.8 x 3.4 in. Compression ratio: 8.0:1. Brake horsepower: 110 at 3800 R.P.M. Torque: 190 lbs-ft. at 1600 R.P.M. Four main bearings. Hydraulic valve lifters. Carburetor: 2Bbl. Rochester 2ME, VIN Code A. Base V-6 (Century T Type); OPTIONAL (Century): Same as 231 V-6 above, but with multi-point fuel injection. Compression ratio: 8.0:1. Brake H.P.: 125 at 4400 R.P.M. Torque: 195 lbs.-ft. at 2000 R.P.M. VIN Code: 3. TURBOCHARGED V-6 (Regal T Type); Same as 231 V-6 above, with turbocharger; switched from four-barrel carburetor to sequential fuel injection. Brake H.P.: 200 at 4000 R.P.M. Torque: 300 lbs.-ft. at 2400 R.P.M. TURBOCHARGED V-6 (Riviera T Type): Same as turbo 231 V-6 above, with sequential fuel injection. Brake H.P.: 190 at 4000 R.P.M. VIN Code: 9. BASE V-6 (Electra, Riviera); OPTIONAL (Regal, LeSabre); 90-degree, overhead-valve V-6. Cast iron alloy block and head. Displacement: 252 cu. in (4.1 liters). Bore & stroke: 3.965 x 3.4 in. Compression ratio: 8.0:1. Brake horsepower: 125 at 4000 R.P.M. Torque: 205 lbs.-ft. at 2000 R.P.M. Four main bearings. Hydraulic valve lifters. Carburetor: 4Bbl. Rochester. VIN Code: 4. DIESEL V-6; OPTIONAL (Century, Regal): 90-degree, overhead-valve V-6. Cast iron block; cast iron or aluminum head. Displacement: 262.5 cu. in. (4.3 liters). Bore & stroke: 4.057 x 3.385 in. Compression ratio: 21.6:1. Brake horsepower: 85 at 3600 R.P.M. Torque: 165 lbs-ft. at 1600 R.P.M. Four main bearings. Hydraulic valve lifters. Fuel injection. VIN Code: V. BASE V-8 (Estate); OPTIONAL (LeSabre, Electra, Riviera): 90-degree, overhead valve V-8. Cast iron block and head. Displacement: 307 cu. in. (5.0 liters). Bore & stroke: 3.80 x 3.385 in. Compression ratio: 8.0:1. Brake horsepower: 140 at 3600 R.P.M. Torque: 240 lbs.-ft. at 1600 R.P.M. Five main bearings. Hydraulic valve lifters. Carburetor: 4Bbl. Rochester M4ME. Built by Oldsmobile. VIN Code: Y. OPTIONAL DIESEL V-8 (LeSabre, Estate, Riviera): 90-degree, overhead valve V-8. Cast iron block and head. Displacement: 350 cu. in (5.7 liters). Bore & stroke: 4.057 x 3.385 in. Compression ratio: 21.6:1. Brake horsepower: 105 at 3200 R.P.M. Torque: 200 lbs-ft. at 1600 R.P.M. Five main bearings. Hydraulic valve lifters. Fuel injection. Oldsmobile-built. VIN Code: N.

CHASSIS DATA: Wheelbase: (Skyhawk) 101.2 in.; (Skylark/Century) 104.9 in.; (Regal) 108.1 in.; (LeSabre/Estate) 115.9 in.; (Electra) 118.9 in.; (Riviera) 114.0 in. Overall length:- (Skyhawk cpe) 171.3 in.; (Skyhawk wag) 173.3 in.; (Skylark) 181.1 in.; (Century) 189.1 in.; (Century wag) 190.9 in.; (Regal cpe) 200.6 in.; (Regal sed) 196.0 in.; (LeSabre) 218.4 in.; (Electra/Estate) 221.3 in.; (Riviera) 206.6 in. Height:- (Skyhawk) 53.4-53.6 in.; (Skylark/Century) 53.6 in.; (Century wag) 54.1 in.; (Regal cpe) 54.6 in.; (Regal sed) 55.5 in.; (LeSabre/Electra cpe) 56.0 in.; (LeSabre/Electra sed) 56.7-56.9 in.; (Estate) 59.1 in.; (Riv) 54.3 in. Width:- (Skyhawk) 65.0 in.; (Skylark) 69.1 in.; (Century) 66.8 in.; (Century wag) 69.4 in.; (Regal cpe) 71.6 in.; (Regal sed) 71.1 in.; (LeSabre) 78.0 in.; (Electra/Estate) 76.2 in.; (Riv) 72.8 in. Front Tread:- (Skyhawk) 55.3 in.; (Skylark/Century) 58.7 in.; (Regal) 58.5 in.; (LeSabre/Electra/Est) 61.8 in.; (Riv) 59.3 in. Rear Tread:- (Skyhawk) 55.1 in.; (Skylark) 57.0 in.; (Century) 56.7 in.; (Regal) 57.7-57.8 in.; (LeSabre/Electra/Est) 60.7 in.; (Riviera) 60.0 in. Standard Tires:- (Skyhawk) P175/80R13 GBR; (Skylark/Century) P185/80R13 GBR; (Skylark T Type) P205/70R13 SBR; (Regal) P195/75R14 SBR WSW; (Regal T Type) P205/70R14 SBR; (LeSabre) P205/75R15 SBR WSW; (Electra) P215/75R15 SBR WSW; (Estate) P225/75R15 SBR WSW; (Riviera) P205/75R15 SBR WSW.

TECHNICAL: Transmission:- Four-speed, fully synchronized floor shift standard on Skyhawk/Skylark; automatic optional (standard on all other models). Five-speed standard on Skyhawk T Type. Four-speed gear ratios: (1st) 3.53:1; (2nd) 1.95:1; (3rd) 1.24:1; (4th) 0.81:1 or 0.73:1; (Rev) 3.42:1. Skylark H.O. four-speed: (1st) 3.31:1; (2nd) 1.95:1; (3rd) 1.24:1; (4th) 0.81:1; (Rev) 3.42:1. Five-speed gear ratios: (1st) 3.91:1; (2nd) 2.15:1; (3rd) 1.45:1; (4th) 1.03:1; (5th) 0.74:1; (Rev) 3.50:1. Three-speed auto. trans. gear ratios: (1st) 2.74:1; (2nd) 1.57:1; (3rd) 1.00:1; (Rev) 2.07:1. Skyhawk/Skylark auto. trans. gear ratios: (1st) 2.84:1; (2nd) 1.60:1; (3rd) 1.00:1; (Rev) 2.07:1. Four-speed overdrive automatic gear ratios: (1st) 2.74:1; (2nd) 1.57:1; (3rd) 1.00:1; (4th) 0.67:1; (Rev) 2.07:1. Century four-speed automatic: (1st) 2.92:1; (2nd) 1.57:1; (3rd) 1.00:1; (4th) 0.70:1; (Rev) 2.38:1. Standard axle ratio:- (Skyhawk) 2.84:1 or 3.06:1 w/4- spd, 3.45:1 w/5-spd, 3.18:1 w/auto.; (Skyhawk turbo) 3.65:1 w/4-spd, 3.33:1 w/auto.; (Skylark) 3.32:1 or 3.65:1 w/4-spd, 2.39:1 or 2.53:1 w/auto., 3.23:1 w/H.O. V-6 and auto.; (Century) 2.39:1 or 2.53:1 w/3-spd, 2.84:1 or 3.06:1 w/4-spd; (Century wag) 2.84:1, 2.97:1 or 3.06:1; (Regal) 2.41:1 w/3-spd, 3.08:1 w/4-spd exc. diesel 2.93:1; (Regal T Type) 3.42:1; (LeSabre/Electra) 2.73:1 w/3-spd; 2.73:1, 2.93:1 or 3.23:1 w/4-spd; (Riviera) 2.73:1, 2.93:1 or 3.36:1; (Riv turbo) .36:1. Steering:- (Skyhawk/Skylark/Century) rack and pinion; (others) recirculating ball; power assist standard on all except Skyhawk. Suspension:- front/rear coil springs. (Skyhawk) MacPherson strut front; semi-independent beam rear axle w/trailing arms; stabilizer bar on T Type. (Skylark/Century) MacPherson strut front suspension; beam twist rear axle w/trailing arms and Panhard rod; front/rear stabilizer bars. (Riviera) fully independent suspension with front torsion bars, semi-trailing arms at rear, front/rear stabilizers and automatic level control. (Rear-drive models) front stabilizer bar; rear stabilizer bar on T Type; rigid four-link rear axle. Brakes:- power front disc, rear drum. Four-wheel power disc brakes available on Riviera (std. on conv.). Body construction:- (Skyhawk/Skylark/Century) unitized; (others) separate body and frame. Fuel tank:- (Skyhawk) 13.6 gal.; (Skylark 2-dr) 14.6 gal.; (Skylark 4-dr) 15.1 gal.; (Century) 15.7 gal.; (Regal) 18.1 gal.; (LeSabre/Electra) 26.0 gal.; (Estate) 22.0 gal.; (Riviera) 21.1 gal. Unleaded fuel only.

RIVETRAIN OPTIONS: Engines:- 110 cu. in. (1.8-liter) EFI four: Skyhawk ($50). rbocharged 110 cu. in. (1.8-liter) MFI four: Skyhawk T Type ($800). 173 cu. in. 8-liter) V-6, 2Bbl.: Skylark ($250). High-output 173 cu. in. (2.8-liter) V-6, 2Bbl.: lark ($400); std. on T Type. 181 cu. in. (3.0-liter) V-6, 2Bbl.: Century ($250). bocharged 231 cu. in. (3.8-liter) V-6: Riviera conv. ($900). 252 cu. in. (4.1-liter) 4Bbl.: Regal/LeSabre ($225). 263 cu. in. (4.3-liter) diesel V-6: Century/Regal /Ltd ($599). 307 cu. in. (5.0-liter) V-8, 4Bbl.: LeSabre ($375); Electra cpe/sed, a ($225). 350 cu. in. (5.7-liter) diesel V-8: LeSabre/Estate/Riviera ($799). mission/Differential:- Four-speed manual trans.: Skyhawk T ($75 credit). eed manual trans.: Skyhawk ($75). Automatic trans.: Skyhawk ($395); k T Type ($320); Skylark ($425). Automatic overdrive trans.: Century (N/A); eSabre ($175). Optional rear axle ratio: Skyhawk 3.43:1 (NC); Skylark 2.84:1 1; Century 2.84:1 or 2.97:1; Regal/LeSabre/Electra 3.08:1 or 3.23:1 (NC). slip differential: Regal/LeSabre/Electra ($95). Suspension, Steering and (F40 Firm ride/handling pkg. ($27). F41 Gran Touring suspension: Skyhawk Skylark ($207); Century Cust/Ltd cpe/sed, LeSabre, Riviera ($27); Au LeSabre ($49). Superlift rear shock absorbers: Skylark Cust/Ltd ($68). Sk level control: Century/Regal/LeSabre/Electra ($175). Power steering: Le 204). Four-wheel disc brakes: Riviera ($235). Other:- Trailer towing pkg.: ($3 28). Heavy-duty alternator: Skyhawk/Regal/LeSabre/Electra 85-amp Cen); 94-amp ($35 or $85) exc. Skylark; Skylark 99-amp ($35 or $85); ($40 108-amp ($40). H.D. battery: ($26); diesel ($52). H.D. radiator: Skyhawk engin D. cooling: Skylark ($40- $70); Engine block heater ($18). H.D. Califo ission cooling: Century/Regal/LeSabre/Electra/Riviera ($40-$70). ion system ($99).

SKYHAWK CONVENIENCE/APPEARANCE OPTIONS: Option Packages:- Vista Vent flip-open removable glass sunroof ($300). Instrument gauge pkg.: temp, oil pressure, volts, trip odometer: Cust ($60). Gauges and tach: Cust ($138); Ltd ($78). Acoustic pkg. ($36); std. on Ltd. Comfort/Convenience:- Air cond. ($630). Touch climate control air cond. ($780). Rear defogger, electric ($130). Electronic cruise control w/resume ($175). Power windows ($185-$260). Electric door locks ($125-$175). Six-way power driver's seat ($215). Easy- entry passenger seat adjuster: Cust cpe ($16). Tinted glass ($95). Sport steering wheel: Cust/Ltd ($50). Leather-wrapped steering wheel: T Type ($40). Tilt steering ($104). Trip odometer: Cust ($15). Electric clock ($35). Electric trunk release ($40). Remote tailgate lock: wag ($40). Tailgate wiper/washer: wag ($120). Two-speed wipers w/delay ($50). Lights, Horns and Mirrors:- Tungsten-halogen headlamps ($22). Headlamps-on indicator ($15). Dome reading lamp ($30). Dual horns: Cust cpe/sed ($15). Left remote mirror: Cust/Ltd ($22). Dual mirrors: left remote ($53). Dual electric remote mirrors ($139); T ($86). Visor vanity mirror, passenger ($7). Lighted visor vanity mirror, either side ($45). Entertainment:- Basic electronic-tuning AM/FM stereo radio ($138); w/clock ($177); w/cassette ($277). Electronic-tuning AM/FM stereo radio ($302); w/cassette and graphic equalizer ($505). Radio delete ($56 credit). Power antenna ($60). Dual rear speakers ($25-$30); incl. w/radios. Exterior Trim:- Door edge guards ($15-$25). Rocker panel moldings: Cust cpe/sed ($26). Bodyside stripes ($42). Designers' accent paint ($195). Decklid luggage rack ($100). Roof rack: wag ($105). Interior Trim/Upholstery:- Suede bucket seats: Ltd cpe/sed ($295). Front carpet savers ($17); rear ($12). Front carpet savers w/inserts ($18); rear ($15). Deluxe trunk trim ($33). Security cover: wag ($69). Wheels and Tires:- Styled aluminum wheels ($229). Styled wheel covers w/trim rings ($38). Locking wire wheel covers ($170). P175/80R13 GBR WSW ($54). P195/70R13 SBR BSW ($169). P195/70R13 SBR WSW or wide WSW ($62-$231). P195/70R13 SBR WLT ($84-$253). P205/60R14 SBR WLT: T Type ($94-$182). Self-sealing tires ($106).

SKYLARK/CENTURY CONVENIENCE/APPEARANCE OPTIONS: Option Packages:- Century Olympia Sedan pkg. (white body w/gold bodyside stripe, gold-accented aluminum wheels, decklid luggage rack, brown cloth seats with Olympic logo on headrests): Ltd sed ($406). Acoustic pkg.: Skylark Cust ($60). Flip-open Vista Vent glass sunroof ($300). Lamp group: Skylark Cust ($32-$42). Comfort/Convenience:- Air cond. ($730). Cruise control ($175). Rear defogger, electric ($135- $140). Power windows ($185-$260). Electric door locks ($125- $175). Six-way power driver's seat ($215). Manual seatback recliners, passenger ($45); both ($90). Sport steering wheel ($50). Leather-wrapped steering wheel: Skylark T ($40). Tilt steering ($110). Tinted glass ($110). Instrument gauges incl. trip odometer ($48). Tachometer: Skylark Cust/Ltd ($78). Trip odometer: Skylark Cust/Ltd ($16). Digital electronic instrument cluster: Century ($205-$299). Dial clock ($35). Electric trunk release ($40). Remote tailgate lock: Century wag ($40). Tailgate washer/wiper: Century wag ($120). Two-speed wipers with delay ($49-$50). Theft deterrent system: Century ($159). Lights, Horns and Mirrors:- Tungsten-halogen headlamps: Skylark Cust ($10); Century ($22). Twilight Sentinel: Century ($57). Front light monitors: Century ($37). Coach lamps: Ltd ($102-$129). Headlamps-on indicator ($16). Door courtesy/warning light: Century Ltd wag ($44). Dome reading light ($24). Rear seat reading lamp: Skylark Ltd, Century Cust ($30). Dual horns: Skylark Cust ($15). Remote- control left mirror: Cust/Ltd ($25). Sport mirrors (left remote, right manual): Cust/Ltd ($61). Dual electric remote mirrors: Cust/Ltd ($139); T Type ($78). Visor vanity mirror, passenger ($7). Lighted visor vanity mirror, passenger: Skylark ($58); either side, Century ($58). Entertainment:- Same as Skyhawk (above). Exterior Trim:- Landau vinyl top for Cust/Ltd cpe: Skylark ($220); Century ($186). Long vinyl top: Cust/Ltd ($160). Designers' accent paint: Cust/Ltd ($205- $210). Special solid color paint: Century Cust/Ltd ($200). Protective bodyside moldings ($55); color-coordinated on Century. Lower wide bodyside moldings: Century Cust ($65). Rocker panel moldings: Skylark Cust ($26). Wide rocker panel/rear quarter moldings: Skylark Cust ($91). Belt reveal molding: Skylark Cust, T Type ($40). Wheel opening moldings: Skylark Cust ($30). Door edge guards ($15-$25). Pillar applique moldings: Skylark Cust sed ($27). Hood ornament and windsplit: Cust ($22-$32). Bodyside stripe: Cust/Ltd ($45). Bumper guards, front/rear: Skylark ($45). Bumper strips, front/rear: Skylark Cust ($49). Front license plate mounting: Skylark (NC). Decklid luggage rack: Century ($100). Roof rack: Century wag ($105). Swing-out rear quarter vent windows: Century wag ($75). Woodgrain vinyl applique: Century wag ($350). Tailgate air deflector: Century wag ($37). Interior Trim/Upholstery:- Full-length console: Century ($57). Full-length operating console: Century ($80); T Type ($23). Bucket seats: Skylark Cust ($140); Skylark Ltd ($95); Century Cust ($97). 55/45 cloth seat trim: Century Cust ($133). Notchback bench seating w/armrest, cloth or vinyl: Skylark Cust ($45). Lear Siegler bucket seats: Century T type ($600). 45/45 seating: cloth, Century Ltd/Estate (NC); leather/vinyl ($295). Third seat: Century wag ($215). Front carpet savers ($17); rear ($12). Carpet savers w/inserts: front ($25); rear ($20). Trunk trim ($25-$47). Wheels:- Styled aluminum wheels: Century ($195); std. on T Type. Chrome-plated wheels: Skylark Cust/Ltd ($175). Locking wire wheel covers: Cust/Ltd ($175- $190). Skylark Tires:- P185/80R13 SBR WSW: Cust/Ltd ($58). P205/70R13 SBR WSW: Cust/Ltd ($180). P215/60R14 SBR WLT: T Type ($92). Self-sealing tires: Cust/Ltd ($106). Century Tires:- P185/75R14 SBR WSW: Cust/Ltd ($58). P195/75R14 SBR BSW: Cust/Ltd ($31). P195/75R14 SBR WSW: Cust/Ltd ($93). P195/70R14 SBR WLT: T Type ($84). P215/60R14 SBR BSW: T ($123). P215/60R14 SBR WLT: T ($215). Self-sealing tires: Cust/Ltd ($106).

REGAL CONVENIENCE/APPEARANCE OPTIONS: Option Packages:- Regal Grand National pkg. (black bumpers, lamps, moldings, spoilers, special interior trim w/console, special alum. wheels: T Type ($1282). Regal T Type Designer pkg.: designers' accent paint and rear spoiler ($403). Sliding electric silver Astroroof: cpe ($895). Hatch roof: cpe ($825). Comfort/Convenience:- Air cond. ($730); std. T Type. Touch climate control air cond. ($880); T Type ($150). Electronic cruise control w/resume ($175). Rear defogger, electric ($140). Tinted glass ($110). Tinted windshield ($90). Six-way power seat, each side ($215). Manual passenger seatback recliner ($75). Sport steering wheel ($50). Tilt steering ($110). Power windows ($185-$260). Electric door locks ($125-$175). Headlamps-on indicator ($16). Trip odometer ($16) exc. T Type. Electronic instrumentation ($299) exc. T Type ($173). Two-speed wiper w/low-speed delay ($50). Theft deterrent system ($159). Lighting and Mirrors:- Tungsten-halogen headlamps ($22). Twilight Sentinel ($57). Cornering lamps ($57). Coach lamps: Ltd ($102). Door courtesy/warning lights: Ltd ($44-$70). Rear seat reading light ($30). Dome reading lamp ($24). Remote left mirror ($25) exc. T Type. Dual sport mirrors, left remote ($53) exc. T. Dual remote sport mirrors ($83); T ($30). Visor vanity mirror, passenger ($7). Lighted visor vanity mirror, passenger ($58). Entertainment:- AM radio ($112). AM/FM stereo radio ($238). Electronic-tuning AM/FM stereo radio ($402); w/cassette and graphic equalizer ($605). Concert sound speaker system ($95). Dual rear speakers ($25-$30); incl. w/stereo radio. Automatic power antenna ($95); w/radio ($60). Exterior Trim:- Landau vinyl top: cpe ($186) exc. T Type; heavily-padded ($245). Long vinyl top: sed ($160); padded ($245). Designers' accent paint ($200-$205). Solid special color paint ($200). Exterior molding pkg.: wide rocker panel and belt reveal ($110); std. on Ltd. Protective bodyside moldings: T Type ($55); choice of six colors. Wraparound bodyside moldings: sed ($104). Door edge guards ($15-$25). Bodyside stripe ($42); choice of nine colors. Interior Trim/Upholstery:- Full-length console ($82). Bucket seats ($195) exc. Ltd. Lear Siegler bucket seats: T Type ($600). 55/45 seating ($133) exc. Ltd. 45/45 leather/vinyl seating: Ltd ($295). Front carpet savers ($17); rear ($12). Front carpet savers w/inserts ($25); rear ($20). Wheels:- Chrome- plated wheels ($195) T Type ($90 credit). Styled aluminum wheels ($285); std. T Type. Locking wire wheel covers ($190) exc. T. Body-color wheels ($85) exc. T. Tires:- P205/70R14 SBR WSW ($62) exc. T Type. P215/65R15 SBR WLT : T Type ($92). Self-sealing tires ($106) exc. T.

LESABRE/ELECTRA/ESTATE WAGON CONVENIENCE/APPEARANCE OPTIONS: Comfort/Convenience:- Sliding electric Astroroof: silver, gray or gold ($1195). Air cond.: LeSabre ($730). Air cond. w/touch-climate control: LeSabre ($880); Electra ($150). Cruise control w/resume ($175); std. Park Ave. Rear defogger, electric ($140). Tinted glass: LeSabre Cust ($110). Power windows: LeSabre ($185-$260). Electric door locks ($125- $175). Automatic door locks ($205-$255); exc. Park Ave. ($80). Six-way power seat, driver's or passenger's ($185- $215); both ($400-$430). Memory driver's seat: Electra Ltd ($363); Park Ave. ($178). Electric seatback recliner, either side ($139). Manual passenger seatback recliner: LeSabre/Estate ($75). Tilt steering: LeSabre, Electra Ltd ($110). Tilt/telescoping steering column: Electra Ltd ($165); Park Ave. ($55). Dial clock: LeSabre ($60). Digital clock: LeSabre Ltd ($60). Trip odometer ($16). Electric trunk lock: Electra ($80). Electric trunk release ($40). Electric fuel cap lock: Electra ($44) exc. wag. Theft deterrent system ($159); N/A on Estate. Two-speed wiper w/delay ($49-$50). Accessory group (trip odometer, dome reading lamp, low fuel indicator, washer fluid indicator): Electra ($46-$70). Lighting, Horns and Mirrors:- Tungsten-halogen high-beam headlamps ($22). Twilight Sentinel ($60). Cornering lamps ($60). Coach lamps: LeSabre/Electra Ltd ($102). Light monitors, front: LeSabre/Est ($37); front/rear, Electra $74). Lamp and indicator group ($38-$70). Door courtesy/warning lamps ($44-$70). Lighted door lock and interior light control ($75). Four-note horn ($28). Remote right mirror: LeSabre ($49); Electra ($25) exc. Park Ave. Remote electric right mirror: Park Ave. ($58). Dual electric remote mirrors ($91) exc. Park Ave. Dual electric mirrors w/left thermometer: Electra Ltd ($129). Lighted visor vanity mirror, driver or passenger ($58). Entertainment:- AM radio: LeSabre ($112). AM/FM stereo radio: Electra ($198); std. on Park Ave. Basic ETR AM/FM stereo radio: LeSabre/Estate ($238); w/clock ($277) but. std. on Park Ave.; w/cassette ($338-$402) exc. Park Ave. ($125). Electronic-tuning AM/FM stereo radio ($338-$402) exc. Park Ave. ($125). Electronic-tuning AM/FM stereo radio w/cassette and equalizer ($541- $605) exc. Park Ave. ($328). CB radio: Estate ($275). Delete AM/FM stereo radio: Park Ave. ($230 credit). Concert Sound speaker system: Electra exc. wagon ($95); ETR radio req'd. Dual rear speakers ($25-$30). Automatic power antenna ($95); w/radio ($60). Triband power antenna ($140); w/radio ($105). Exterior Trim:- Exterior molding pkg. (wide rocker panel, front/rear fender lower and belt reveal moldings): LeSabre ($110). Landau vinyl top: LeSabre, Electra Ltd cpe ($245). Long vinyl top: LeSabre, Electra Ltd sed ($185-$190). Heavy- padded long vinyl top: Electra Ltd sedan ($245). Designers' accent paint: LeSabre ($215). Special single-color paint: ($200); Firemist, Electra exc. Estate ($210). Protective bodyside moldings: Estate ($55). Wide rocker panel moldings: Electra Ltd/Est ($65). Door edge guards ($15-$25). Belt reveal molding: LeSabre ($40). Bodyside stripes ($42-$45); choice of nine colors. Interior Trim/Upholstery:- 55/45 seating: LeSabre Custom ($133). Leather/vinyl 50/50 seating: Park Ave. ($525). Third seat: Estate ($220). Front carpet savers ($17); rear ($12). Front carpet savers w/inserts ($25); rear ($20). Trunk carpeting trim ($53-$65). Trunk mat ($15). Wheels:- Chrome-plated wheels ($180-$215) exc. Estate ($40 credit). Styled aluminum wheels ($220-$255). Custom wheel covers: Electra Ltd ($35). Locking wire wheel covers ($155-$190) exc. Estate ($65 credit). Tires:- P215/75R15 SBR wide WSW: LeSabre ($38). P225/75R15 SBR wide WSW: Electra cpe/sed ($39). Self-sealing tires ($107-$132).

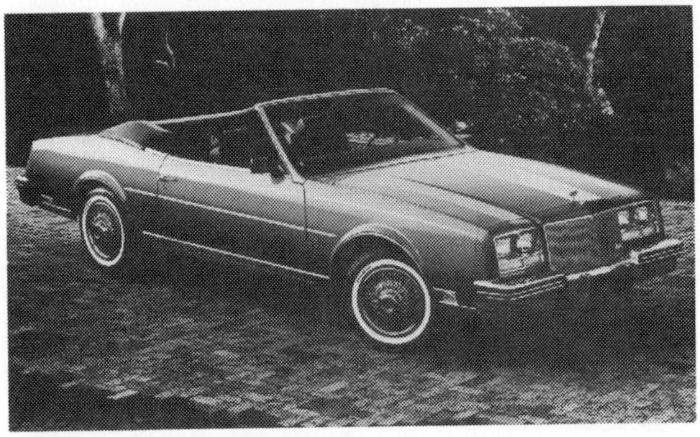

1984 Riviera convertible (B)

RIVIERA CONVENIENCE/APPEARANCE OPTIONS: Comfort/Convenience:- Electric sliding Astroroof: silver, gray or gold ($1195). Touch climate control air cond. ($150). Electric rear defogger ($140). Digital electronic instrument cluster ($238). Six-way power seat, passenger ($215). Two- position memory driver's seat ($178). Electric seatback recliner, either side ($139). Automatic door locks ($80). Leather-wrapped steering wheel ($96); std. on T Type. Tilt/telescope steering wheel ($55) exc. T Type. Electric fuel cap lock ($44). Electric trunk release ($40); lock ($80). Low fuel indicator ($16). Two-speed wipers w/delay ($49). Windshield washer fluid indicator ($16). Theft deterrent system ($159). Lighting, Horns and Mirrors:- Tungsten-halogen high-beam headlamps ($22); std. on T Type. Twilight Sentinel ($60). Coach lamps ($102); incl. w/vinyl top. Front/rear light monitors: T Type ($77). Rear quarter courtesy/reading lamp ($50). Lighted door lock and interior light control ($75). Four-note horn ($28). Dual electric remote mirrors ($66). Lighted visor vanity mirrors, each ($58). Entertainment:- Full-feature electronic-tuning AM/FM stereo radio ($125). Basic electronic-tuning AM/FM stereo radio w/cassette tape player ($125). Electronic-tuning AM/FM stereo radio with cassette and equalizer ($328); w/cassette, Dolby and Bose speaker system ($895) exc. conv. CB radio ($215). Delete radio ($230 credit). Rear speakers for base radio ($25). Concert Sound system ($95) exc. conv. Triband power antenna ($45); incl. w/CB radio. Exterior Trim:- Heavy- padded landau vinyl top w/coach lamps: base ($330). Designers' accent paint: base ($235). Special color Firemist paint ($210); std. on conv. Color-coordinated protective bodyside moldings ($55); choice of eight colors but only white and dark red on conv. Door edge guards ($15). Bodyside striping ($45). Interior Trim/Upholstery:- 45/45 leather/vinyl front seat ($487); std. on conv. 45/45 leather/suede seating w/storage console ($537) exc. conv. Front carpet savers w/inserts ($35); rear ($20). Trunk trim carpeting ($30); std. on conv. Trunk mat ($15). Wheels and Tires:- Chrome-plated wheels ($145); exc. conv. ($45 credit). Styled aluminum wheels: conv. w/turbo V-6 ($65). Locking wire wheel covers ($190); std. on conv. P225/70R15 SBR wide oval tires: BSW or WSW (NC).

HISTORY: Introduced: October 2, 1983. Model year production (U.S.): 987,980. The yearly total included 229,934 four-cylinder Buicks and 258,422 V-8s, demonstrating that the venerable V-8 was still hanging on. Of the total production, 4,428 Buicks had a diesel engine and 15,556 a turbo. Calendar year production (U.S.): 987,833. Model year sales by U.S. dealers: 906,626 (not including front-drive Electras built during the 1984 model year). Calendar year sales (U.S.): 941,611 for a market share of 11.8 percent. When Canadian totals were added in, calendar year sales topped a million for the first time in Buick history.

Historical Footnotes: Century became Buick's best seller this year, nudging aside the Regal which had held that title since Century sedan/wagon and Regal coupe merged under the Regal banner in 1982. Skylark sales, like those of the other GM X-cars, were slipping as a result of the lengthy recall list—including a well-publicized and inconclusive recall for replacement of rear brake linings—even though those problems mainly affected 1980-81 models. Regardless, Skylark now sold almost as well as Chevrolet's Citation, which was the X-car that suffered most from bad publicity. To boost Skyhawk sales, dealers were encouraged to offer the subcompacts with extras that might appeal to young, sporty-minded buyers: electronic radios, aluminum wheels, tachometers, luggage racks and the like. LeSabre and Electra gained renewed

popularity in 1982-83, with an impressive sales rise this year. Riviera was especially Popular among doctors, merchants and executives. As part of the preliminaries for the summer Olympics in Los Angeles, the cross-country torch passed through Flint in May, carried for a time by several Buick employees. A fleet of Rivieras and other Buick vehicles, modified for low- speed endurance running, accompanied torch-bearers on their way to L.A. For off-road racing, Buick added a Stage I piston and Stage II intake manifold to the long list of heavy-duty 4.1- liter V-6 components available at dealers. Several Buick- powered vehicles had proven successful on race courses, including a record set at Bonneville this year. Bobby Allison had also driven a Regal to win the 1983 NASCAR driver's prize. At more mundane levels, a portable Diagnostic Data Analyzer could hook the electronic control module of any 1981-84 Buick into the dealer's diagnostic display--or to the computer at Flint. From there, an engineer could even alter the faraway engine's speed for evaluating problems. Buick's objective, according to retiring general manager Lloyd Reuss, was to be "Best in Class" and rank No. 3 in sales. General Motors was divided into small-car and large- car groups in January 1984, with Buick falling into the latter category. Robert C. Stempel was named head of the B-O-C (Buick-Oldsmobile-Cadillac) group, while Donald E. Hackworth took over as GM vice-president and Buick's general manager.

1985 BUICK

This year marked both the beginning and end of several eras. The last rear-drive Electra had been built in April 1984, replaced by a totally different front-drive version. Though the name was the same, the contemporary Electra stood far apart from its traditional full-size predecessors. Regal's dramatic black Grand National coupe, though marketed in modest numbers, was altering Buick's image among youthful motorists. Diesels went under Buick hoods for the last time this year. The final X-bodied Skylark was produced, ending Buick's connection with that sad episode in GM history. Rear- drive days were numbered. This would be LeSabre's final season in that form, but the name reappeared on an Estate Wagon for 1985, after a year's absence. A new name joined the Buick lineup: Somerset Regal.

1985 Skyhawk Custom coupe (B)

SKYHAWK — SERIES 4J — FOUR — After setting a sales record in 1984, Buick's J-car subcompact entered 1985 with no significant change beyond new body colors and interior trim. The lineup continued as before: Custom and Limited versions of coupe and sedan, plus a station wagon. The T Type also continued, powered by a normally-aspirated or turbocharged 1.8-liter overhead-cam four that came from GM of Brazil. Turbos added a boost gauge on the dash this year, and produced 150 horsepower as opposed to only 84 with the non-turbo 1.8 engine. That much power in a lightweight brought 0-60 acceleration times down to less than 9 seconds. All-season (fourth-generation) radials were now standard on all Skyhawks. Chevrolet and Olds offered a 2.8-liter V-6 on their versions of the J-body, but Buick stuck with the fours. Standard powertrain was again the Chevrolet-made 121 cu. in. (2.0-liter) four with four-speed manual gearbox and 3.65:1 final drive ratio (three-speed automatic available). Non-turbo T Types had a five-speed gearbox; turbos the four- speed. T Types had a blacked-out grille and headlamp housings, black door handles and locks, and blackout side mirrors. Upper bodies came in silver, red or white; lower body was charcoal. Styled aluminum wheels held P195/70R13 blackwall radial tires; fatter 60-series tires were available, either blackwall or white-lettered. T Types had a leather-wrapped sport steering wheel, reclining bucket seats, foglamps, Gran Touring suspension, and full instruments. Powerplant was the 1.8-liter fuel-injected overhead-cam four. The optional turbo 1.8 with multi-port fuel injection rated 150 horsepower. On the Buick proving grounds, the turbo version reached 60 MPH in 8.5 seconds.

SKYLARK — SERIES 4X — FOUR/V-6 — Only the four-door sedan remained in Skylark's final year. The new Somerset Regal would offer buyers a coupe without the taint of the X-car's unpleasant recall and reliability history. Skylarks received a new grille that pushed outward near the base, new wide taillamps split into upper/lower sections, and altered interior trim. Vertical rectangular parking lights sat between grille and single headlamps. Accentuating the revised rear-end look was a new center applique, and the license plate moved from the trunk lid to the bumper. The standard 2.5-liter four-cylinder engine, now dubbed "Tech-4," gained new roller bearings. The 2.8-liter carbureted V-6 was again optional, but a new addition this year was a high-output version with port fuel injection. That 2.8 used injectors mounted on a fuel rail, a design from Bosch that fed fuel from a high-pressure electric pump in the gas tank. It also had a cast aluminum intake manifold. All engines had new hydraulic engine mounts to cut vibration.

1985 Skylark Limited sedan (B)

1985 Century Limited sedan (B)

CENTURY — SERIES 4A — FOUR/V-6 — Once again, Century offered coupe, sedan and station wagon models, in Custom or Limited trim, along with the performance T Type. All showed a new grille and hood ornament this year, along with a new selection of body colors. Front ends held quad headlamps; rear ends, full-width taillamps. Sedans had a narrow window behind the rear door. European-look T Types now carried the advanced 3.8-liter V-6 with multi-port fuel injection, which had become available late in the 1984 model year. That engine was also offered on other Century models. Base engine, however, remained the 2.5-liter four with throttle-body fuel injection. This year, it gained roller valve lifters. Buyers could also choose a Chevrolet-built 2.8-liter V-6, Buick's own 3.0-liter V-6, or the 4.3-liter diesel V-6. The 2.8 was offered in case Buick couldn't meet production demands of its own 3.0 V-6. Many buyers chose a gas V-6 over the low-powered 2.5 base engine. Century Customs came with three-speed automatic transmission, power brakes and steering, AM radio, notchback seating (cloth or vinyl), dual horns, bumper guards and protective strips, side-window defoggers, full carpeting, and P185/75R14 tires. Limiteds didn't add too much beyond wide lower bodyside moldings, a hood ornament and wind split moldings. In addition to the 3.8-liter engine and dual exhausts, T Types included four-speed overdrive automatic transmission, a left-hand remote-control mirror, blacked-out grille, temp/volt gauges, cloth bucket seats, Gran Touring suspension, leather-wrapped sport steering wheel, and styled aluminum road wheels with P195/70R14 tires. The F41 Gran Touring suspension, with firmer springs, recalibrated shocks and hefty stabilizer bars, was also available on other coupes and sedans.

1985 Somerset Regal coupe (B)

SOMERSET REGAL — SERIES 4N — FOUR/V-6 — Buick's totally new, formally styled personal-luxury sport coupe, meant to replace the X-bodied Skylark, targeted the affluent "yuppies" and baby boomers who might otherwise buy upscale imports. Oldsmobile's Calais and Pontiac's Grand Am were its close N-body front-drive relatives. Base engine was a "Tech-4" 2.5-liter four-cylinder with throttle-body fuel injection, plus new roller bearings. Standard transaxle was a five-speed manual, but three-speed automatic was optional. The optional 181 cu. in. (3.0-liter) V-6 engine with multi-port fuel injection, putting out 125 horsepower as in the same-size (lower-powered) V-6 in Buick's Century. Styled in a dramatic wedge shape, the compact coupe was accentuated by a sloping nose and raked-back windshield, plus a high roofline, large quarter windows, and vertical rear window. Somerset had body-colored bumpers with rub strips, a standard electronic-tuning AM radio, cloth or vinyl bucket seats, tachometer, trip odometer, tinted glass, full-length console, and a digital clock. The Limited added chrome bumpers, front/rear armrests, dual horns, woodgrain instrument panel, wheel opening moldings, and narrow rocker panel

moldings. Options included body-color side moldings. Somersets had standard electronic digital instrumentation, including a multi-gage which gave, at driver's command, readouts for voltage, oil pressure, engine temperature, and R.P.M. Radio controls were atop a pod remote from the radio itself. The right front seat slid forward when its seatback was tipped forward, for easy entry into the back. Controls sat in pods at each side of the steering column, and instruments were electronic. Somersets could be ordered with a high-mounted brake light (which would be required on '86 models). Somerset's chassis used a MacPherson strut front suspension, and at the rear a special trailing axle suspension patterned after the type used in the sporty Skyhawk.

1985 Regal T Type Grand National coupe (B)

REGAL — SERIES 4G — V-6 — Only the Regal coupe remained this year, as the four-door sedan left the lineup. In addition to base and Limited trim levels, buyers had a choice of two performance editions: the familiar T Type and a dramatic step-up Grand National. Regal's forward-slanted front end carried a new slanted grille. Wheel covers were restyled, new body colors were offered, and interiors came in an altered selection of colors. T Types had a new power brake system, with boost provided by an electric pump rather than the power steering pump. A carbureted 231 cu. in. (3.8-liter) V-6 was standard, with three-speed automatic transmission. A diesel V-6 was optional. Both performance Regals came with a turbocharged version of the 3.8, with sequential port fuel injection and four-speed overdrive automatic transmission. Base Regal equipment included bumper guards and protective strips, power brakes and steering, AM radio, cigarette lighter, dual horns, dual chrome mirrors, color-keyed bodyside moldings, notchback seats (cloth or vinyl), and P195/75R14 steel-belted radial whitewalls. Regal Limited added an exterior molding package and 55/45 notchback seating. T Types included air conditioning, a performance axle ratio, temp and turbo boost gauges, 94-amp alternator, leather-wrapped steering wheel, tachometer, trip odometer, and 15 in. styled aluminum wheels with wide 65-series tires. Grand National (actually a $675 T Type option package) was offered again for 1985 with its aggressive all-black exterior (even the windshield wipers), special black aluminum wheels, firm-ride Gran Touring suspension, and new two-tone cloth bucket seats. Grand Nationals carried a 200-horsepower turbo 3.8-liter V-6 with sequential fuel injection. On the test track it had hit 60 MPH in 8 seconds. Equipment also included black bumpers, rub strips and guards; black front air dam and decklid spoiler; and Grand National identification on body and instrument panel.

1985 LeSabre Limited Collector Edition sedan (B)

LESABRE — SERIES 4B — V-6/V-8 — For its final year as a rear-drive Buick, LeSabre received a new grille and a few new colors (inside and out), but few other changes. The new grille was made up of thin vertical bars and stood more vertically than the sloped-back quad-headlamp section. Coupes and sedans again came in Custom or Limited dress, but to make the final season the Limited was called a Collector's Edition. Standard engine remained the 231 cu. in. (3.8-liter) V-6, but buyers could also choose the familiar four-barrel 307 (5.0-liter) V-8, or the diesel V-8. Standard Custom equipment included an AM radio, power brakes and steering, three-speed automatic transmission (four-speed overdrive required with V-8 engines), woodtone dash applique, dual horns, compact spare tire, bumper guards and protective strips, and front armrest. LeSabre's Collector's Edition had plush velour upholstery on loose pillow seats. It also had a standard six-way power driver's seat, seatbelt and ignition key warning chime, headlamps-on indicator and chime, and Soft Ray tinted glass, plus wide rocker panel moldings and accent strips. Doors carried woodgrain trim; bodies showed special identification and hood ornament. Buyers even received a booklet on Buick history and special set of keys.

ESTATE WAGON — SERIES 4B/C — V-8 — LeSabre's Estate Wagon returned to the fold for 1985, after a year's absence. As usual, Electra's version was the posher of the pair. Even though the new Electra coupe and sedan were shrunken in size with front-drive, the wagons hung on with rear-drive. Two- and three-seat versions were offered. LeSabre included air conditioning, tinted glass, dual horns, AM radio, power steering and brakes, heavy-duty suspension, styled aluminum wheels, and narrow rocker panel moldings among its many standard items. Electra's wagon added front/rear armrests, a digital clock, AM/FM seek/scan stereo ratio, woodgrain vinyl applique, remote electric tailgate lock, power windows all around, and a roof luggage rack.

1985 Electra Estate Wagon (B)

ELECTRA — SERIES 4C — V-6 — An entirely new Electra debuted in early spring 1984, along with the similarly downsized Cadillac DeVille/Fleetwood and Oldsmobile Ninety-Eight. Dramatic cuts in exterior size and weight did not affect interior dimensions much (except for narrower width and smaller trunk volume), though Electra's six-passenger capacity tightened somewhat. The modern Electra weighed 600-900 pounds less than before, measured 2 feet shorter and 4 in. narrower, and rode a 110.8 in. wheelbase (8 in. shorter than in 1984). Electra's hood now opened from the rear. The new edition turned to contemporary front-wheel drive with a transverse-mounted engine: standard 181 cu. in. (3.0-liter) V-6, optional 231 cu. in. (3.8-liter) V-6 with multi-port fuel injection, or the 4.3-liter diesel. A coupe and four-door sedan came in base or plush Park Avenue form, or the enthusiast's T Type.

1985 Electra sedan (B)

The 3.8 V-6 was standard on both Park Avenue and T. (The very existence of a "sporty" T Type carrying the renowned Electra nameplate startled a good many traditional buyers.) Though far smaller than before, Electra hardly lacked poshness. Standard equipment on base Electras included four-speed overdrive automatic transmission, electronic climate and level controls, six-way power driver's seat, AM/FM stereo radio with seek/scan electronic tuning, power windows, side window defoggers, remote fuel filler door release, courtesy lights, headlamps-on reminder, trip odometer, velour upholstery, and P205/75R14 all-season radials. Stepping up to Park Avenue brought buyers the bigger (3.8-liter) V-6 along with power door locks, tilt steering, power decklid release, rear reading lamps, cruise control, wide bodyside moldings, accent paint striping, and luxury upholstery in cloth or leather.

1985 Riviera convertible (B)

RIVIERA — SERIES 4E — V-6/V-8 — Since a dramatically different Riviera was expected for 1986, not much changed this year for the coupe, T Type or convertible. Late in the 1984 model year, the 5.0-liter V-8 had become the standard Riv powerplant, and that continued in 1985. The coupe could also have a 5.7-liter diesel

for one more year, but T Types kept the 231 cu. in. (3.8-liter) turbocharged V-6 with sequential port fuel injection. Joining the option list was a cellular telephone--a factory-approved dealer option rather than a factory installation. A hundred or so test Rivieras carried a new optional Graphic Control Center, which had originally been planned as a regular production option. Drivers could select radio, climate control and trip functions by simply touching appropriate portions of the video screen. The convertible's hefty price tag kept sales down to a modest level, and this would be its final season. A limited-edition Riviera for 1985 featured genuine wood in the form a burled walnut veneer on dash and door panels, wood/leather steering wheel, and beige leather/suede interior trim.

I.D. DATA: All Buicks again had a 17-symbol Vehicle Identification Number (VIN), stamped on a metal tag attached to the upper left surface of the cowl, visible through the windshield. Coding was similar to 1984, starting with '1' to indicate the manufacturing country (U.S.A.), followed by 'G' for General Motors and '4' for Buick Division. The next letter indicates restraint system. Symbol five denotes series: 'S' Skyhawk Custom; 'T' Skyhawk Ltd.; 'E' Skyhawk T Type; 'B' Skylark Custom; 'C' Skylark Ltd.; 'J' Somerset Regal; 'M' Somerset Regal Ltd.; 'H' Century Custom; 'L' Century Ltd.; 'G' Century T Type (or Estate); 'J' Regal; 'K' Regal T Type; 'M' Regal Ltd.; 'N' LeSabre Custom; 'P' LeSabre Ltd.; 'R' LeSabre Estate Wagon; 'X' Electra; 'W' Electra Park Ave.; 'F' Electra T Type; 'V' Electra Estate Wagon; 'Z' Riviera; 'Y' Riviera T Type. Digits six and seven indicate body type: '27' 2-dr. coupe; '37' LeSabre 2-dr. coupe; '47' Regal 2-dr. coupe; '57' Riviera 2-dr. coupe; '11' Electra 2-dr. sedan; '19' Electra 4-dr. sedan; '35' 4-dr. wagon; '67' 2-dr. convertible coupe. Next symbol is the engine code: 'O' L4-110 TBI; 'J' turbo L4-110 MFI; 'P' L4-121 TBI; 'U' L4-151 TBI; 'R' L4-151 TBI; 'X' V6-173 2Bbl.; 'W' V6-173 MFI; 'E' V6-181 2Bbl.; 'L' V6-181 MFI; 'A' V6-231 2Bbl.; '3' V6-231 MFI; '9' turbo V6-231 SFI; 'T' diesel V6-263; 'Y' V8-307 4Bbl.; 'N' diesel V8-350. Symbol nine is a check digit. Symbol ten denotes model year ('F' 1985). Symbol eleven is the plant code: 'M' Lansing, MI; 'T' Tarrytown, NY; 'D' Doraville, GA; 'W' Willow Run, MI; '6' Oklahoma City, OK; 'H' Flint, MI; 'K' Leeds, MO; 'X' Fairfax, KS; 'E' Linden, NJ; '1' Wentzville, MO; '2' St. Therese, Quebec. The final six digits are the sequential serial number, starting with 400001. An additional identifying number may be found on the engine. A body number plate on upper shroud or radiator support assembly reveals model year, car division, series, style, body assembly plant, body number, trim combination, modular seat code, paint code, and date build code.

SKYHAWK CUSTOM (FOUR)

Series Number	Body/Style Number	Body Type & Seating	Factory Price	Shipping Weight	Production Total
4J	S27	2-dr Coupe-5P	7365	2276	44,804
4J	S69	4-dr Sedan-5P	7581	2325	27,906
4J	S35	4-dr Sta Wag-5P	7919	2401	5,285

SKYHAWK LIMITED (FOUR)

4J	T27	2-dr Coupe-5P	7883	2312	Note 1
4J	T69	4-dr Sedan-5P	8083	2429	Note 1
4J	T35	4-dr Sta Wag-5P	8379	2356	Note 1

Note 1: Skyhawk Custom production totals include equivalent Skyhawk Limited models. For the model year, 63,148 Custom and 9,562 Limited coupes and sedans were built.

SKYHAWK T TYPE (FOUR)

4J	E27	2-dr Coupe-5P	8437	2295	4,521

SKYLARK CUSTOM (FOUR/V-6)

4X	B69	4-dr Sedan-5P	7707/7967	2478/2539	65,667

SKYLARK LIMITED (FOUR/V-6)

4X	C69	4-dr Sedan-5P	8283/8543	2515/2576	27,490

CENTURY CUSTOM (FOUR/V-6)

4A	H27	2-dr Coupe-6P	9377/9637	2609/2714	13,043
4A	H19	4-dr Sedan-6P	9545/9805	2658/2763	215,928
4A	H35	4-dr Sta Wag-6P	9941/10201	2825/2930	28,221

CENTURY LIMITED (FOUR/V-6)

4A	L27	2-dr Coupe-6P	9841/10101	2632/2737	Note 2
4A	L19	4-dr Sedan-6P	10012/10272	2681/2786	Note 2
4A	L35	4-dr Sta Wag-6P	10379/10639	2845/2950	Note 2

CENTURY T TYPE (V-6)

4A	G27	2-dr Coupe-5P	11249	2802	Note 2
4A	G19	4-dr Sedan-5P	11418	2850	Note 2

Note 2: Century Custom production totals include equivalent Century Limited and T Type models. Total model year production came to 99,751 Customs, 125,177 Limiteds and 4,043 Century T Type coupes and sedans.

SOMERSET REGAL (FOUR/V-6)

4N	J27	2-dr Coupe-5P	8857/9417	2472/2523	48,470

SOMERSET REGAL LIMITED (FOUR/V-6)

4N	M27	2-dr Coupe-5P	9466/10026	2478/2529	37,601

REGAL (V-6)

4G	J47	2-dr Coupe-6P	9928	3066	60,597

REGAL LIMITED (V-6)

4G	M47	2-dr Coupe-6P	10585	3107	59,780

REGAL T TYPE (V-6)

4G	K47	2-dr Coupe-6P	12640	3256	4,169

Note 3: Regal T Type total includes 2,102 Grand Nationals.

LESABRE CUSTOM (V-6/V-8)

4B	N37	2-dr Coupe-6P	10453/11018	3438/3629	5,156
4B	N69	4-dr Sedan-6P	10603/10568	3447/3638	32,091

LESABRE LIMITED COLLECTOR'S EDITION (V-6/V-8)

4B	P37	2-dr Coupe-6P	11751/12316	3462/3653	22,211
4B	P69	4-dr Sedan-6P	11916/12481	3495/3686	84,432

LESABRE ESTATE WAGON (V-8)

4B	R35	4-dr Sta Wag-6P	12704	4085	5,597

ELECTRA (V-6)

4C	X11	2-dr Coupe-6P	14149	3114	5,852
4C	X69	4-dr Sedan-6P	14331	3158	131,011

1985 Electra Park Avenue sedan (B)

ELECTRA PARK AVENUE (V-6)

4C	W11	2-dr Coupe-6P	16080	3144	Note 4
4C	W69	4-dr Sedan-6P	16240	3190	Note 4

ELECTRA T TYPE (V-6)

4C	F11	2-dr Coupe-5P	15386	3138	Note 4
4C	F69	4-dr Sedan-5P	15568	3183	Note 4

Note 4: Production figures for base Electra coupe and sedan include totals for Park Avenue and T Type models. Total T Type production, 4,644.

ELECTRA ESTATE WAGON (V-8)

4C	V35	4-dr Sta Wag-6P	15323	4148	7,769

RIVIERA (V-6/V-8)

4E	Z57	2-dr Coupe-5P	-- /16710	-- /3748	63,836
4E	Z67	2-dr Conv-5P	27457/26797	3700/3873	400

Note 5: Only 49 Riviera convertibles had a turbo V-6 engine installed.

RIVIERA T TYPE (V-6)

4E	Y57	2-dr Coupe-5P	17654	3564	1,069

FACTORY PRICE AND WEIGHT NOTE: Figure before the slash is for four-cylinder engine, after the slash for V-6. For LeSabre and Riviera, figure before slash is for V-6 engine, after slash for V-8. **FACTORY PRICE NOTE:** Buick announced several price increases during the model run, including some for optional engines.

ENGINES: BASE FOUR (Skyhawk): Inline, ohv, four-cylinder. Cast iron block and head. Displacement: 121 cu. in. (2.0 liters). Bore & stroke: 3.50x3.15. Compression ratio: 9.3:1. Brake horsepower: 86 at 4900 R.P.M. Torque: 100 lbs.-ft. at 3000 R.P.M. Five main bearings. Hydraulic valve lifters. Throttle-body fuel injection. VIN Code: P. OPTIONAL FOUR (Skyhawk); STANDARD (Skyhawk T Type): Inline, overhead-cam four-cylinder. Cast iron block; aluminum cylinder head. Displacement: 110 cu. in. (1.8 liters). Bore & stroke: 3.34 x 3.13 in. Compression ratio: 8.8:1. Brake horsepower: 84 at 5200 R.P.M. Torque: 102 lbs.-ft. at 2800 R.P.M. Five main bearings. Hydraulic valve lifters. Throttle- body fuel injection. VIN Code: O. TURBOCHARGED FOUR (Skyhawk T Type): Same as 1.8-liter OHC four above, except--Compression ratio: 8.0:1. Brake H.P.: 150 at 5600 R.P.M. Torque: 150 lbs.-ft. at 2800 R.P.M. Multi-point fuel injection. VIN Code: J. BASE FOUR (Skylark, Century, Somerset Regal): Inline, overhead-valve four-cylinder. Cast iron block and head. Displacement: 151 cu. in. (2.5 liters). Bore & stroke: .0 x 3.0 in. Compression ratio: 9.0:1. Brake horsepower: 92 at 4400 R.P.M. Torque: 134 lbs.-ft. at 2800 R.P.M. Five main bearings. Hydraulic valve lifters. Throttle-body fuel injection. Built by Pontiac. VIN Code: R. OPTIONAL V-6 (Skylark, Century): 60-degree, overhead-valve V-6. Cast iron block and head. Displacement: 173 cu. in. (2.8 liters). Bore & stroke: 3.50 x 2.99 in. Compression ratio: 8.5:1. Brake horsepower: 112 at 4800 R.P.M. Torque: 145 lbs.-ft. at 2100 R.P.M. Four main bearings. Hydraulic valve lifters. Carburetor: 2Bbl. Built by Chevrolet. VIN Code: X. HIGH-OUTPUT V-6; OPTIONAL (Skylark): Same as 173 cu. in. V-6 above except--Compression ratio: 8.9:1. Brake horsepower: 125 at 5400 R.P.M. Torque: 165 lbs.- ft. at 3600 R.P.M. VIN Code: W. BASE V-6 (Electra); OPTIONAL (Century): 90-degree, overhead-valve V-6. Cast iron block and head. Displacement: 181 cu. in. (3.0 liters). Bore & stroke: 3.8 x 2.66 in. Compression ratio: 8.45:1. Brake horsepower: 110 at 3600 R.P.M. Torque: 145 lbs.-ft. at 2600 R.P.M. Four main bearings. Hydraulic valve lifters. Carb.: 2Bbl. VIN Code: E. OPTIONAL V-6 (Somerset Regal): Same as 181 cu. in. V-6 above, with multi-point fuel injection. C.R.: 9.0:1. B.H.P.: 125 at 4900 R.P.M. Torque: 150 lbs.-ft. at 2400 R.P.M. VIN Code: L. BASE V-6 (Regal, LeSabre): 90-degree, overhead-valve V-6. Cast iron alloy block and head. Displacement: 231 cu. in. (3.8 liters). Bore & stroke: 3.8 x 3.4 in. Compression ratio: 8.0:1. Brake horsepower: 110 at 3800 R.P.M. Torque: 190 lbs.-ft. at 1600 R.P.M. Four main bearings. Hydraulic valve lifters. Carb.: 2Bbl. VIN Code: A. BASE V-6 (Century T Type, Electra T/Park Ave.); OPTIONAL (Century, Electra): Same as 231 V-6 above, but with multi-point fuel injection. Brake H.P.: 125 at 4400 R.P.M. Torque: 195 lbs.-ft. at 2000 R.P.M. VIN Code: 3. TURBOCHARGED V-6 (Regal/Riviera T Type): Same as 231 V-6 above, but with turbocharger and sequential fuel injection. Brake horsepower: 200 at 4000 R.P.M. (Riviera, 190 H.P.). Torque: 300 lbs.-ft. at 2400 R.P.M. VIN Code: 9. DIESEL V-6; OPTIONAL (Century, Regal, Electra): 90-degree, overhead-valve V-6. Cast iron block. Displacement: 262.5 cu. in. (4.3 liters). Bore & stroke: 4.057 x 3.385 in. Compression ratio: 21.6:1. Brake horsepower: 85 at 3600 R.P.M. Torque: 165 lbs.-ft. at 1600 R.P.M. Four main bearings. Hydraulic valve lifters. Fuel injection. VIN Code: V or T. BASE V-8 (Estate, Riviera); OPTIONAL (LeSabre): 90-degree, overhead valve V-8. Cast iron block and head. Displacement: 307 cu. in. (5.0 liters). Bore & stroke: 3.80 x 3.385 in. Compression ratio: 8.0:1. Brake horsepower: 140 at 3200 R.P.M. (LeSabre, 140 at 3600). Torque: 255 lbs.-ft. at 2000 R.P.M. (LeSabre, 240 at 1600). Five main bearings. Hydraulic valve lifters. Carburetor: 4Bbl. Built by Oldsmobile. VIN Code: Y or H. OPTIONAL DIESEL V-8 (LeSabre, Estate, Riviera): 90-degree, overhead valve V-8. Cast iron block and head. Displacement: 350 cu. in. (5.7 liters). Bore & stroke: 4.057 x 3.385 in. Compression ratio: 21.6:1. Brake horsepower: 105 at 3200 R.P.M. Torque: 200 lbs-ft. at 1600 R.P.M. Five main bearings. Hydraulic valve lifters. Fuel injection. Oldsmobile-built. VIN Code: N.

CHASSIS DATA: Wheelbase: (Skyhawk) 101.2 in.; (Skylark) 104.9 in.; (Somerset Regal) 103.4 in.; (Century) 104.8 in.; (Century wag) 104.9 in.; (Regal) 108.1 in.; (LeSabre/Estate) 115.9 in.; (Electra) 110.8 in.; (Riviera) 114.0 in. Overall length:- (Skyhawk cpe) 175.3 in.; (Skyhawk sed/wag) 177.3 in.; (Skylark) 181.1 in.; (Somerset Regal) 180.0 in.; (Century) 189.1 in.; (Century wag) 190.9 in.; (Regal) 200.6 in.; (LeSabre) 218.4 in.; (Electra) 197.0 in.; (Estate) 221.3 in.; (Riviera) 206.6 in. Height:- (Skyhawk) 54.0 in.; (Skyhawk wag) 54.4 in.; (Skylark/Century) 53.6-53.7 in. (Century wag) 54.2 in.; (Somerset Regal) 52.1 in.; (Regal) 54.6 in.; (LeSabre cpe) 56.0 in.; (LeSabre sed) 56.7 in.; (Estate) 59.3 in.; (Electra/Riv) 54.3 in. Width:- (Skyhawk) 65.0 in.; (Skylark) 69.1 in.; (Somerset Regal/Century) 67.7 in.; (Regal) 71.6 in.; (LeSabre) 78.0 in.; (Estate) 79.3 in.; (Electra) 72.4 in.; (Riv) 72.8 in. Front Tread:- (Skyhawk) 55.3 in.; (Skylark/Century) 58.7 in.; (Somerset Regal) 55.5 in.; (Regal) 58.5 in.; (LeSabre) 61.8 in.; (Electra) 60.3 in.; (Estate) 62.2 in.; (Riv) 59.3 in. Rear Tread:- (Skyhawk) 55.1 in.; (Skylark) 57.0 in.; (Somerset Regal) 55.2 in.; (Century) 56.7 in.; (Regal) 57.7 in.; (LeSabre) 60.7 in.; (Electra) 59.8 in.; (Estate) 64.0 in.; (Riviera) 60.0 in. Standard Tires:- (Skyhawk) P175/80R13 SBR; (Skyhawk T Type) P195/70R13 SBR; (Skylark/Somerset Regal) P185/80R13 SBR; (Century) P185/75R14 SBR; (Century T Type) P195/70R14 SBR; (Regal) P195/75R14 SBR WSW; (Regal T Type) P215/65R15 SBR; (LeSabre) P205/75R15 SBR WSW; (Electra) P205/75R14 SBR BSW; (Estate) P225/75R15 SBR WSW; (Riviera) P205/75R15 SBR WSW.

TECHNICAL: Transmission:- Four-speed, fully synchronized floor shift standard on Skyhawk/Skylark. Five-speed manual standard on Somerset Regal, available on Skyhawk. Four-speed overdrive automatic standard on Electra/Riviera, available on Century/Regal/LeSabre; three-speed automatic on other models. Four-speed gear ratios: (1st) 3.53:1; (2nd) 1.95:1; (3rd) 1.24:1; (4th) 0.81:1 or 0.73:1; (Rev) 3.42:1. Skylark V-6 four-speed: (1st) 3.51:1; (2nd) 1.95:1; (3rd) 1.24:1; (4th) 0.90:1; (Rev) 3.42:1. Skyhawk five-speed gear ratios: (1st) 3.91:1; (2nd) 2.15:1; (3rd) 1.45:1; (4th) 1.03:1; (5th) 0.74:1; (Rev) 3.50:1. Somerset Regal five-speed: (1st) 3.73:1; (2nd) 2.04:1; (3rd) 1.45:1; (4th) 1.03:1; (5th) 0.74:1; (Rev) 3.50:1. Three-speed auto. trans. gear ratios: (1st) 2.74:1; (2nd) 1.57:1; (3rd) 1.00:1; (Rev) 2.07:1. Skyhawk/Skylark auto. trans. gear ratios: (1st) 2.84:1; (2nd) 1.60:1; (3rd) 1.00:1; (Rev) 2.07:1. Four-speed overdrive automatic gear ratios: (1st) 2.74:1; (2nd) 1.57:1; (3rd) 1.00:1; (4th) 0.67:1; (Rev) 2.07:1. Century/Electra four-speed automatic: 1st) 2.92:1; (2nd) 1.57:1; (3rd) 1.00:1; (4th) 0.70:1; (Rev) 2.38:1. Standard axle ratio:- (Skyhawk) 3.65:1 w/4-spd, 3.45:1 w/5-spd, 3.18:1 w/auto.; (Skyhawk turbo) 4.10:1 w/4-spd, 3.33:1 w/auto.; (Skylark) 3.32:1 or 3.65:1 w/4-spd, 2.39:1 or 2.53:1 w/auto., 2.84:1 w/H.O. V-6 and auto.; (Somerset Regal): 3.35:1 w/5-speed, 2.84:1 w/auto.; (Century) 2.84:1 or 2.97:1 w/3-spd, 2.84:1 or 3.06:1 w/4-spd; 2.39:1 w/diesel. (Regal) 2.41:1; (Regal T Type) 3.42:1; (LeSabre) 2.73:1 exc. diesel, 2.93:1; (Electra) 3.08:1 exc. V6-231, 2.84:1; (Riviera) 2.73:1; (Riv diesel); (Riv turbo) 3.15:1. Steering:- (Skyhawk/Skylark/Century/Somerset Regal) rack and pinion; (others) recirculating ball; power assist standard on all except Skyhawk. Suspension:- front/rear coil springs. (Skyhawk/Somerset Regal) MacPherson strut front w/stabilizer; semi-independent beam rear axle w/trailing arms; rear stabilizer bar optional, std. on T Type. (Skylark/Century) MacPherson strut front suspension; beam twist rear axle w/trailing arms and Panhard rod; front/rear stabilizer bars. (Electra) MacPherson front struts, barrel springs and stabilizer bar; rear struts w/stabilizer bar and electronic level control. (Riviera) fully independent suspension with front torsion bars, semi-trailing arms at rear, front/rear stabilizers and automatic level control. (Rear-drive models) front stabilizer bar; rear stabilizer bar on T Type; rigid four-link rear axle. Brakes:- power front disc, rear drum. Four-wheel power disc brakes available on Riviera (std. on conv.). Body construction:- (front-drive models) unitized; (others) separate body and frame. Fuel tank:- (Skyhawk/Somerset Regal) 13.6 gal.; (Skylark) 15.1 gal.; (Century) 15.7 gal.; (Regal) 18.1 gal.; (LeSabre) 25.0 gal.; (Electra) 18.0 gal.; (Estate) 22.0 gal.; (Riviera) 21.1 gal.

DRIVETRAIN OPTIONS: Engines:- 110 cu. in. (1.8-liter) EFI four: Skyhawk Cust/Ltd ($50). Turbocharged 110 cu. in. (1.8-liter) MFI four: Skyhawk T Type ($800). 173 cu. in. (2.8-liter) V-6, 2Bbl.: Skylark ($260); Century (N/A). High-output 173 cu. in. (2.8-liter) V-6, 2Bbl.: Skylark ($435). 181 cu. in. (3.0-liter) V-6, 2Bbl.: Century ($260); Somerset ($560). 231 cu. in. (3.8- liter) V-6, MFI.: Century ($520); std. T Type; early base Electra ($260). Turbocharged 231 cu. in. (3.8-liter) V-6, SFI: Riviera ($660); std. on T Type. 263 cu. in. (4.3-liter) diesel V-6: Century/Regal/Electra ($359) exc. T Type; Park Ave. ($99). 307 cu. in. (5.0-liter) V-8, 4Bbl.: LeSabre ($390). 350 cu. in. (5.7-liter) diesel V-8: Regal ($589); LeSabre ($489); Estate/Electra/Riviera ($99) exc. T Type or conv. Transmission/Differential:- Four-speed manual trans.: Skyhawk T Type ($75 credit). Five-speed manual trans.: Skyhawk Cust/Ltd ($75). Auto. trans.: Skyhawk/Skylark/ Somerset ($425); Skyhawk T Type ($350). Automatic overdrive trans.: Century Cust/Ltd/Est, LeSabre ($175); Regal (N/A). Optional rear axle ratio: Skyhawk 3.43:1; Skylark; Century 2.84:1 or 2.97:1; Regal; LeSabre; base Electra 3.33:1; Estate; Riviera 3.15:1 (all NC). Limited slip differential: Regal/LeSabre/Est ($95). Suspension, Steering and Brakes:- F40 Firm ride/handling pkg. ($27). F41 Gran Touring suspension: Skyhawk/Skylark/Somerset ($27); Century Cust/Ltd cpe/sed $27); Regal/LeSabre ($49); Electra/Riviera ($27). Special G.T. suspension: Skyhawk T Type (NC). Electronic control suspension: Electra (N/A); std. T Type. Superlift rear shock absorbers: Skylark ($68). Automatic level control: Century/Regal/LeSabre/Estate ($175). Power steering: Skyhawk ($215). Four-wheel disc brakes: Riviera ($235). Other:- Heavy- duty alternator: Skyhawk/Regal/LeSabre/Electra 85-amp ($35 or $85); 94-amp ($35 or $85); Century/Somerset/Electra 108-amp ($25-$40). Heavy-duty battery ($26); diesel ($52). Power reserve Freedom battery: Electra ($145) Heavy-duty radiator: Skyhawk ($40-$70). Heavy-duty cooling: Skylark ($40-$70). Engine block heater ($18). Heavy-duty engine/transmission cooling: Century/Regal/LeSabre/Electra/Riviera ($40-$70). High altitude emission package (NC). California emission system ($99).

SKYHAWK CONVENIENCE/APPEARANCE OPTIONS: Option Packages:- Decor pkg.: T Type ($195). Vista Vent flip- open removable glass sunroof ($310). Instrument gauge pkg.: temp, oil pressure, volts, trip odometer: Cust ($60). Gauges and tach: Cust ($138); Ltd ($78). Acoustic pkg. ($36); std. on Ltd. Comfort/Convenience:- Air cond. ($645); touch climate control ($795). Rear defogger, electric ($135). Cruise control w/resume ($175). Power windows ($195-$270). Electric door locks ($130-$180). Six-way power driver's seat ($225). Easy-entry passenger seat adjuster: Cust cpe ($16). Tinted glass ($25). Sport steering wheel: Cust/Ltd ($50). Leather- wrapped steering wheel: T Type ($40). Tilt steering ($115). Trip odometer: Cust ($15). Electric trunk or tailgate release ($40). Tailgate wiper/washer: wag ($125). Two-speed wipers w/delay ($50). Lights, Horns and Mirrors:- Tungsten-halogen headlamps ($18). Headlamps-on indicator ($15). Front seat reading light ($30). Dual horns: Cust cpe/sed ($15). Left remote black mirror: Cust/Ltd ($22). Dual black mirrors: left remote ($53). Dual black electric remote mirrors ($139); T Type ($86). Visor vanity mirror, passenger ($7). Lighted visor vanity mirror, either side ($45). Entertainment:- Electronic-tuning AM/FM stereo radio ($138); w/clock ($177). Seek/scan AM/FM stereo ET radio w/clock ($222); w/cassette ($344). Seek/scan AM stereo/FM ET stereo radio w/clock ($242); w/cassette and equalizer ($494). Radio delete ($56 credit). Automatic power antenna ($65). Dual rear speakers ($25). Exterior Trim:- Door edge guard moldings ($15-$25). Wide rocker moldings: Cust cpe/sed ($26). Bodyside stripes ($45). Designers' accent paint ($195). Decklid luggage rack ($100). Roof rack: wag ($105). Interior Trim/Upholstery:- Front console armrest: T Type ($45). Front carpet mats ($17); rear ($12). Front carpet mats w/inserts ($18); rear ($15). Front/rear fiber floor mats: T Type ($65). Deluxe trunk trim ($33). Security cover: wag ($69). Wheels and Tires:- Styled aluminum wheels ($229); std. T Type. Styled wheel covers w/trim rings ($38); N/A T Type. Locking wire wheel covers ($180); N/A T Type. P175/80R13 SBR WSW ($54). P195/70R13 SBR BSW ($104). P195/70R13 SBR WSW ($166). P195/70R13 SBR WLT ($188); T Type ($84). P205/60R14 SBR BSW: T Type ($94). P205/60R14 SBR WLT: T Type ($182). Self-sealing tires ($115).

SKYLARK/CENTURY CONVENIENCE/APPEARANCE OPTIONS: Comfort/Convenience:- Flip-open Vista Vent glass sunroof ($300). Acoustic pkg.: Skylark Cust ($60). Lamp group: Skylark Cust ($42). Air cond. ($730). Elect. cruise control ($175). Rear defogger, electric ($140). Power windows ($185- $260). Electric door locks ($125-$175). Six-way power driver's seat ($215). Manual seatback recliners, passenger ($45); both ($90). Sport steering wheel ($50). Tilt steering ($110). Tinted glass ($110). Instrument gauges incl. trip odometer ($48); w/tachometer, Century ($126). Tachometer: Skylark ($78). Trip odometer: Skylark ($16). Digital electronic instrument cluster: Century ($225); T Type ($131). Dial clock ($35). Electric trunk release ($40). Remote tailgate lock: Century wag ($40). Tailgate washer/wiper: Century wag ($120). Two-speed wipers w/delay ($50). Theft deterrent system: Century ($159). Lights, Horns and Mirrors:- Tungsten-halogen headlamps: Skylark Cust ($10); Century ($22). Twilight Sentinel: Century ($57). Front light monitors: Century ($37). Coach lamps: Ltd ($102-$129). Center-mounted high stoplight: Century ($25). Headlamps-on indicator ($16). Door courtesy/warning light: Century Ltd/wag ($44). Front seat reading lamp ($24). Rear seat reading lamp: Skylark Ltd, Century Cust/Ltd ($30). Dual horns: Skylark Cust ($15). Remote-control color-keyed left mirror: Cust/Ltd/Est ($25). Sport mirrors (left remote, right manual): Cust/Ltd/Est ($61). Dual electric remote mirrors ($139) exc. Century T Type ($78). Visor vanity mirror, passenger ($7). Lighted visor vanity mirror, passenger: Skylark ($50); either side, Century ($58). Entertainment:- Same as Skyhawk (above). Exterior Trim:- Landau vinyl top: Century Cust/Ltd cpe ($186); heavily-padded ($623). Long vinyl top: Cust/Ltd ($160). Designers' accent paint ($205-$210); N/A T Type. Special solid color paint: Century ($200) exc. T Type. Protective bodyside moldings ($55); color-coordinated on Century. Lower wide bodyside moldings: Century Cust ($65). Rocker panel moldings: Skylark Cust ($26). Wide rocker panel/rear quarter moldings: Skylark Cust ($91). Belt reveal molding: Skylark Cust ($40). Wheel opening moldings: Skylark Cust ($30). Door edge guards ($15-$25). Pillar applique moldings: Skylark Cust ($27). Hood ornament and windsplit: Skylark Cust ($32). Windsplit molding: Century Cust ($22). Bodyside stripe: Cust/Ltd/Est ($45). Bumper guards, front/rear: Skylark ($45). Bumper strips, front/rear: Skylark Cust ($49). Decklid luggage rack: Century ($100). Roof rack: Century wag ($105). Cargo area vent windows: Century wag ($75). Woodgrain vinyl applique: Century wag ($350). Tailgate air deflector: Century wag ($37). Front license bracket (NC). Interior Trim/Upholstery:- Front center armrest: Skylark Cust ($45). Full-length console: Century ($57). Full-length operating console: Skylark ($105); Century ($80); T Type ($23). Bench seat: Skylark Cust ($55 credit). Cloth bucket seats: Skylark Cust ($140); Ltd ($95); Century Cust ($97). 55/45 notchback cloth seating: Century Cust ($133). Lear Siegler bucket seats: Century T Type ($600). Cloth 45/45 seating: Century Ltd/Est (NC). Leather/vinyl 45/45 seating: Century Ltd ($295); T ($425). Third seat: Century wag ($215). Locking storage compartment: Century wag ($44). Front carpet mats ($17); rear ($12). Carpet mats w/inserts: front ($25); rear ($20). Trunk trim ($25-$47). Wheels:- Styled aluminum wheels: Century ($195); std. on T Type. Chrome wheels: Skylark ($175). Locking wire wheel covers ($190) exc. T Type. Skylark Tires:- P185/80R13 SBR WSW ($58). P205/70R13 SBR WSW ($180). Self-sealing tires ($105). Century Tires:- P185/75R14 SBR WSW: Cust/Ltd/Est ($58). P195/75R14 SBR BSW: Cust/Ltd/Est ($30). P195/75R14 SBR WSW: Cust/Ltd/Est ($92). P195/70R14 SBR WLT: T Type ($84). P215/60R14 SBR BSW: T ($122). P215/60R14 SBR WLT: T ($214). Self-sealing tires ($105).

SOMERSET REGAL CONVENIENCE/APPEARANCE OPTIONS: Comfort/Convenience:- Vista Vent flip-open removable glass sunroof ($310-$329). Air cond. ($645). Electronic cruise control ($175). Rear defogger, electric ($135). Six-way power driver's seat ($225). Sport steering wheel ($50) exc. Ltd. Tilt steering ($115). Power windows ($195). Electric door locks ($130); automatic ($220). Electric trunk release ($40). Two-speed wipers w/delay ($50). Lights and Mirrors:- Center high-mounted stoplight ($25). Front door courtesy/warning light: Ltd ($44). Front-rear seat reading/courtesy lights ($40-$54). Dual mirrors, left remote ($53); std. on Ltd. Dual electric remote mirrors ($86-$139). Lighted right visor vanity mirror ($38). Entertainment:- Seek/scan AM/FM stereo radio w/clock ($157); w/cassette and equalizer ($424); w/Delco GM/Bose music system and Dolby ($995). Cassette player ($142). Concert sound speakers ($100-$125). Dual extended-range speakers ($25). Automatic power antenna ($65). Exterior Trim:- Designers' accent paint ($195). Bodyside stripes ($45). Rocker panel moldings ($26); std. Ltd. Wide rocker panel moldings ($50-$76). Color-keyed protective bodyside moldings ($45). Wheel opening moldings ($30); std. Ltd. Decklid luggage rack ($100). Door edge guards ($15). Interior Trim/Upholstery:-

Leather bucket seats: Ltd ($275). Floor mats w/inserts: front ($18); rear ($15). Wheels and Tires:- Styled aluminum wheels ($229). P185/80R13 SBR WSW ($58). P205/70R13 SBR BSW ($114). P205/70R13 SBR WSW ($180). P205/70R13 SBR WLT ($202). Self-sealing tires ($115).

REGAL CONVENIENCE/APPEARANCE OPTIONS: Option Packages:- Regal Grand National pkg.: black exterior, front air dam, decklid spoiler, rub strips/guards, Gran Touring suspension, front bucket seats, aluminum wheels ($675). Regal T Type Designer pkg.: black/dark gray designers' accent paint and rear spoiler ($403). Base Regal exterior molding pkg.: wide rocker panel and belt reveal moldings ($110). Sliding electric silver Astroroof ($895). Hatch roof ($825). Comfort/Convenience:- Air cond. ($730); std. T Type. Touch climate control air cond. ($880); T Type ($150). Cruise control w/resume ($175). Rear defogger, electric ($140). Tinted glass ($110). Tinted windshield ($90). Six-way power seat, each side ($215). Manual passenger seatback recliner ($75). Sport steering wheel ($50); N/A T Type. Tilt steering ($110). Power windows ($185). Electric door locks ($125). Electric trunk release ($40). Digital electronic instrument cluster ($299); T Type ($173). Headlamps-on indicator ($16). Trip odometer ($16) exc. T. Two-speed wiper w/delay ($50). Theft deterrent system ($159). Lighting and Mirrors:- Tungsten-halogen headlamps ($22). Twilight Sentinel ($57). Cornering lamps ($57); N/A T Type. Coach lamps: Ltd ($102). Door courtesy/warning lights: Ltd $44). Front seat reading light ($24); rear ($30). Dual sport mirrors, left remote ($53); std. T Type. Dual remote sport mirrors ($83); T Type ($30). Dual chrome mirrors, left remote ($25); N/A T Type. Visor vanity mirror, passenger ($7); lighted ($58). Entertainment:- Same as Skyhawk (above) plus: Concert sound speakers ($95). Exterior Trim:- Landau vinyl top ($186) exc. T Type; heavily-padded ($245). Designers' accent paint ($205); N/A T Type. Solid special color paint ($200). Black protective bodyside moldings: T Type ($55). Door edge guards ($15). Bodyside stripe ($45). Interior Trim/Upholstery:- Storage console: Ltd ($82). Bucket seats ($195) exc. Ltd. Lear Siegler bucket seats: T Type ($600). 55/45 seating ($133) exc. Ltd. 45/45 leather/vinyl seating: Ltd ($295); T Type ($595). Front carpet mats ($17); rear ($12). Front carpet mats w/inserts ($25); rear ($20). Trunk trim ($44). Wheels:- Chrome-plated wheels ($195); N/A T Type. Styled aluminum wheels ($285); std. T Type. Locking wire wheel covers ($190) exc. T. Color-keyed wheels ($85) exc. T. Tires:- P205/70R14 SBR WSW ($62) exc. T Type. P215/65R15 SBR WLT: T Type ($92). Self-sealing tires ($105) exc. T.

LESABRE/ELECTRA/ESTATE WAGON CONVENIENCE/APPEARANCE OPTIONS: Comfort/Convenience:- Sliding electric Astroroof ($1195). Air cond.: LeSabre ($730); Est ($150). Air cond. with touch- climate control: LeSabre ($880); Electra ($165). Cruise control w/resume ($175); std. on Park Ave. Rear defogger, electric ($140). Tinted glass: LeSabre Custom ($110). Power windows: LeSabre ($185-$260). Keyless entry system: Electra ($185). Electric door locks ($125-$175). Automatic door locks ($205-$255) exc. Electra Est/Park Ave. ($80). Six-way power passenger seat ($215); driver's: LeSabre Cust, Est ($185- $215). Memory driver's seat: Electra ($178). Two-way power driver's seat: LeSabre Est ($60). Electric seatback recliner, either side ($139) exc. Electra Est passenger ($220). Manual passenger seatback recliner: LeSabre, Estate ($75). Tilt steering ($110); std. Park Ave. Tilt/telescoping steering column: Electra ($165); Park Ave. ($55). Dial clock: LeSabre Cust ($60). Digital clock: LeSabre Ltd ($60). Accessory group (low fuel indicator, trip odometer, reading lights, washer fluid indicator): Electra Est ($54-$86). Trip odometer: LeSabre ($16). Remote tailgate lock: LeSabre Estate ($50). Electric trunk lock: Electra ($80). Electric trunk release ($40). Theft deterrent system ($159); N/A on Estate. Two- speed wiper w/delay ($50); std. Park Ave. Lighting, Horns and Mirrors:- Tungsten-halogen headlamps ($22). Twilight Sentinel ($60). Cornering lamps: LeSabre, Electra Cust ($60). Coach lamps: LeSabre Ltd ($102). Light monitors, front: LeSabre ($37); front/rear, Electra ($77). Lamp and indicator group: LeSabre ($38-$70). Door courtesy/warning lamps ($44-$70). Lighted door lock and interior light control ($75). Four-note horn ($28). Dual remote chrome mirrors: LeSabre ($49). Dual electric remote mirrors ($91); std. Park Ave. Dual electric remote mirrors, left heated: Electra ($126); Park Ave. ($35). Lighted visor vanity mirror, driver or passenger ($58). Entertainment:- LeSabre--same selection as Skyhawk (above). Electra as follows--Seek/scan electronic-tuning AM stereo/FM stereo radio w/clock ($20); w/cassette and equalizer ($272). Seek/scan AM/FM stereo radio w/cassette ($122); w/cassette, Dolby and Delco GM/Bose music system ($895) but N/A on Estate. Delete radio ($275 credit). Concert Sound system ($95). CB radio: Estate ($275). Automatic power antenna: LeSabre/Electra/Est ($60). Triband power antenna: LeSabre, Est ($105). Exterior Trim:- Exterior molding pkg. (wide rocker panel, front/rear fender lower and belt reveal moldings): LeSabre ($110). Landau padded vinyl top: LeSabre cpe ($245). Long vinyl top: LeSabre ($185). Heavy-padded long vinyl top: Electra sed ($245). Designers' accent paint: LeSabre ($215). Special single-color paint: ($200); Firemist, Electra ($200). Protective bodyside moldings: Est ($55). Wide rocker panel moldings: Electra Est ($65). Door edge guards ($15-$25). Belt reveal molding: LeSabre Cust/Est ($40). Bodyside stripes ($45); std. Ltd/Park Ave. Rear air deflector: Est ($40). Woodgrain vinyl applique: LeSabre Estate ($345); delete from Electra Est ($320 credit). Luggage rack: LeSabre Estate ($150). Front license bracket (NC). Interior Trim/Upholstery:- Cloth 55/45 seating: LeSabre Cust. ($133). Leather/vinyl 50/50 seating: LeSabre Ltd ($525). Leather/vinyl 55/45 seating: Park Ave. ($425). Leather/vinyl 45/45 seating: Electra T Type ($175). Third seat: Estate ($220). Front carpet mats: LeSabre ($17); rear ($12). Front carpet mats w/inserts ($25); rear ($20). Trunk carpeting/trim ($53). Trunk mat ($15). Wheels:- Chrome-plated wheels: LeSabre ($215); Estate ($40 credit). Styled aluminum wheels ($220-$255); Electra T Type (N/A). Locking wire wheel covers ($155-$190) exc. Estate ($65 credit). Tires:- P215/75R15 SBR WSW: LeSabre ($42). P205/75R14 SBR WSW: Electra ($66); BSW, Park Ave. ($66 credit). Self- sealing tires ($105-$130).

RIVIERA CONVENIENCE/APPEARANCE OPTIONS: Comfort/Convenience:- Electric sliding Astroroof: silver, gray or gold ($1195). Touch climate control air cond. ($150). Electric rear defogger ($140). Digital electronic instrument cluster ($238); T Type ($160). Six-way power seat, passenger ($215). Two-position memory power driver's seat ($178). Electric seatback recliner, either side ($139). Automatic door locks ($80). Leather-wrapped steering wheel ($96);std. on T Type. Tilt/telescope steering wheel ($55) exc. T Type. Electric trunk release ($40); pulldown ($80). Low fuel indicator ($16). Two-speed wipers w/delay ($50). Windshield washer fluid indicator ($16). Theft deterrent system ($159). Lighting, Horns and Mirrors:- Tungsten-halogen high/low beam headlamps ($22); std. on T Type. Twilight Sentinel ($60). Coach lamps: base ($102); incl. w/vinyl top. Front/rear light monitors ($77) exc. conv. Rear reading lamps ($50) exc. conv. Lighted door lock and interior light control ($75). Four-note horn ($28). Automatic day/night mirror ($80). Dual electric remote mirrors ($66). Lighted visor vanity mirrors, each ($58); N/A conv. Entertainment:- Seek/scan electronic-tuning AM stereo/FM stereo radio w/clock ($20); w/cassette and equalizer ($272). Seek/scan AM/FM stereo radio w/cassette ($122); w/cassette, Dolby and Delco GM/Bose music system ($895). CB radio ($215). Delete radio ($275 credit). Concert Sound system ($95). Triband power antenna ($45); incl. w/CB radio. Exterior Trim:- Heavy-padded landau vinyl top w/coach lamps: base ($330). Designers' accent paint: base ($235). Special color Firemist paint ($210); std. on conv. Color- keyed protective bodyside moldings ($55). Door edge guards ($15). Bodyside stripe: base ($45). Interior Trim/Upholstery:- 45/45 leather/vinyl front seat ($487); std. on conv. Front floor mats w/inserts ($35); rear ($20). Trunk trim carpeting ($30); std. on conv. Trunk mat ($15); N/A conv. Wheels and Tires:- Chrome-plated wheels: base ($145); conv. ($45 credit). Styled aluminum wheels: conv. w/turbo V-6 ($65). Locking wire wheel covers: base ($190). Credit given for BSW tires on conv.; and for P225/70R15 SBR non-self-sealing on base and conv. P225/70R15 SBR WSW: T Type ($48); BSW ($26 credit).

HISTORY: General introduction was October 2, 1984; but Electras had been introduced on April 5, 1984 and the Skyhawk didn't appear until November 8, 1984. Model year production (U.S.): 1,002,906 (including early '85 Electras); that was the first time Buick passed the one million barrier. The total included 271,423 four-cylinder Buicks, 515,995 sixes, and 215,488 V-8s. Only 1,178 diesels and 6,137 turbos were installed this year. Calendar year production (U.S.): 1,001,461 (first time for breaking the million mark). Model year sales by U.S. dealers: 915,336, which amounted to 10.9 percent of the industry total. Calendar year sales (U.S.): 845,579 for a market share of 10.3 percent.

Historical Footnotes: The last rear-drive Electra had come off the line on April 25, 1984, a month after its rear-drive replacement emerged. It was the last of over 2.6 million old-style Electras, and would be joined by LeSabre for 1986. Clearly, front-drive and aero styling was the wave of the future, and Buick hoped to attract a new breed of buyer. Both the new Electra and the coming front-drive LeSabre were developed by the C/H Product Team ('C' for C-bodies, 'H' for the H-bodied LeSabre). Part of Buick's youth-oriented promotion for the Regal Grand National included a TV commercial with a song called "Bad to the Bone," performed by the Destroyers. Quite a change from the advertising aimed at gray-flannel-suited executives in the 1950s, or even the performance promotions during the muscle-car era. Looking farther back in history, the Classic Car Club announced acceptance of all 1931-42 Series 90 Buicks into classic status. Even a few custom- bodied Series 80 models might be deemed worthy on an individual basis.

1986 BUICK

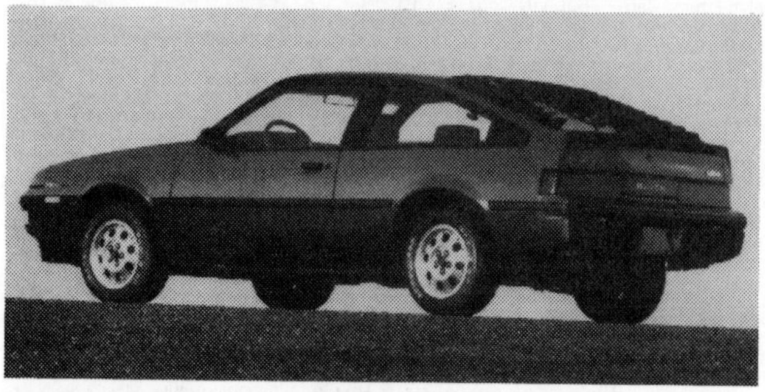

1986 Skyhawk T Type hatchback coupe (B)

Eleven new models joined Buick's list for '86, making a total of 39 (including a couple of special editions). Every line except Skylark and LeSabre fielded a T Type version. New choices included the Skyhawk Sport and T Type hatchback; Skylark Custom and Limited sedan; and Somerset T Type coupe. Most notable, though, were the all-new V-6 front-drive LeSabre (Custom and Limited coupe/sedan) and Riviera coupe and T Type. Leaving the lineup this year were Electra's T Type coupe and the Riviera convertible. On the 3.0-liter V-6 with multi-port fuel injection, introduced for 1985, a single belt drove all accessories. It also got a redesigned water pump, hardened valve seats, new air cleaner and inlet. A redesigned combustion chamber allowed more efficient combustion. This engine was 50 pounds lighter (and 5.5 inches narrower) than the carbureted 3.0 from which it evolved. Two versions of the 3.8-liter V-6 were offered: with or without roller valve lifters. A revised intake manifold improved breathing and gave more hood clearance. Spark plugs were placed in the center of the combustion chamber for added efficiency. Turbocharged 3.8s got a new intercooler between the compressor and intake manifold, to supply a denser air/fuel charge and boost horsepower output. New leading/trailing rear drum brakes on LeSabres were said to improve braking consistency and automatic adjustment. Hinged taillamps on Electra, LeSabre and Riviera allowed easier servicing of bulbs and lenses. More galvanized steel panels for rust protection were used on 1986 Buicks than on any previous models. LeSabre became the first to offer double-sided galvanized sheet metal on both sides of hood and fenders. Going a giant step further, the whole Riviera body (except the roof) would now be double-side, hot-dipped galvanized. Riviera's new Graphic Control Center, similar to the preliminary version introduced in 1984, drew considerable attention at the Chicago Auto Show. Also standard on Riviera was the Retained Accessory Power feature, which kept certain components operating after the ignition was shut off: radio, electric windows, wipers, fuel door, decklid, and glove compartment release. Most noteworthy among the new options was the anti-lock braking system (ABS), developed jointly with the West German firm of Alfred Teves GmbH, now offered on Electra. Sensors at each wheel could determine when a wheel was about to lock and relax braking pressure as needed, to prevent skidding on slippery surfaces. Pressure might be applied and released as many as 15 times per second, helping the driver to remain in control and stop in the shortest possible distance.

SKYHAWK — SERIES 4J — FOUR — Buick gained a full line of subcompact models with the mid-year addition of a new Sport/Hatch and T Type hatchback. Both hatchbacks and Limited/T Type coupes had a new front-end design that featured concealed tungsten-halogen headlamps behind electrically-operated doors. They also had smoked glass taillamps. Otherwise, styling was similar to prior models. As before, the wide body-colored grille sat low on the front end, below the narrow protective strip. The sharply slanted nose held a center crest. Wide taillamps wrapped slightly around the side. In all, the modern Skyhawk offered clean, wedge-shape styling with an "aggressive" profile, highlighted by flush-mounted glass, integrated bumpers, and styled mirrors. All Skyhawks were available in white, silver metallic, black, or red. All except the T Type could have bodies in metallic light blue, bright blue, dark red, gray, dark blue, light brown, or brown; or in regular cream beige. T Types could have gray metallic as the lower accent color. Hatchbacks featured a blackout treatment, and a rear spoiler was optional. Custom and Limited Skyhawks had new standard wheel covers, while hatchbacks came with turbine-design wheel covers. Hatchbacks could have an optional rectactable security cover to keep valuables out of sight. Base engine remained the fuel-injected 2.0-liter four with four-speed manual gearbox. Five-speed (overdrive) manual and three-speed automatic transmissions were available. So was a 1.8-liter powerplant. Skyhawk's T Type was powered by the 1.8-liter four with overhead camshaft, either normally aspirated or (at extra cost) turbocharged. Turbos produced 150 horsepower and had multi-port fuel injection. That version delivered a claimed 0-60 MPH test time of under 9 seconds. They came with a four- speed gearbox rather than the usual five. T Types also had cloth front bucket seats with console, gauges (including tachometer), sport steering wheel with T Type insignia, Gran Touring suspension, aluminum wheels, a front passenger assist strap, black antenna, foglamps, amber park/signal lamps, black door handles and locks, plus black moldings and mirrors. For looks without added performance, a low-cost SCS Coupe package came with the regular 2.0-liter engine and four-speed, riding P175/80R13 all-season blackwalls. The extras: custom cloth bucket seats and door panels, three-tone interior trim, custom steering wheel, black moldings, and styled steel wheels.

1986 Skylark Limited sedan (B)

SKYLARK — SERIES 4N — FOUR/V-6 — Now that the X-bodied Skylark was gone, Buick offered a four-door replacement to match the Somerset coupe. Even through the bad publicity about X-cars, Buick's version had sold well and the company didn't want to lose the power of the Skylark name, which began with the limited-edition convertible way back in 1953. The new five-passenger sedan came in Custom and Limited trim, with rakish windshield, flush-mounted glass, and rounded rear body corners. Front-end styling was just like Somerset's. The grille was comprised of tight vertical bars, flowing smoothly down from the sloping hood. Parking/signal lamps were inset low, below the bumper protective strip that wrapped around fender tips. The required high-mount stop lamp was placed on the rear shelf, flush with the back window. Bumpers were body-colored on the Custom, bright on the Limited. Standard body colors were white and tan, plus 10 metallics: silver, dark gray, black, light brown, brown, flame red, light blue, medium blue, light sage, and dark sage. Both Skylark and Somerset carried a new 'S' logo. Inside, brushed aluminum trim panels contained standard electronic digital instruments with vacuum-fluorescent displays that offered metric readings at the touch of a button. Readouts included voltage, engine speed, coolant temperature, oil pressure, and a trip odometer. Soft-touch, low-travel controls for lights, wiper/washers and other frequently-used functions were positioned on a pod near the steering wheel. Skylark's chassis layout consisted of a transverse-mounted engine, MacPherson struts, low-drag front disc brakes, and trailing-link rear suspension. Base engine was the 2.5-liter four, with electronic fuel injection and five-speed manual gearbox. Hydraulic clutch adjustment provided easier engagement and smooth shifting. A 3.0-liter V-6 was optional, with multi-port fuel injection and three-speed automatic transmission. The 125-horsepower V-6 had a high-efficiency combustion chamber and a gerotor oil pump.

1986 Buick Somerset T Type coupe (B)

SOMERSET — SERIES 4N — FOUR/V-6 — Introduced for 1985, the Somerset Regal coupe lost the "Regal" from its name this year. Now it served as a mate to the similar N-body Skylark sedan. One difference: Somerset now offered a T Type, while Skylark did not. Manual transmission Somersets had a new hydraulic clutch. All had a new brushed-finish instrument panel. The aerodynamically-styled, rounded wedge-look coupe came with a choice of four-cylinder or V-6 power and front-wheel drive, in Custom or Limited trim (or new T Type). Styling highlights included flush windshield and backlight glass. The smooth front end carried a grille with narrow vertical strips and Buick badge on the side, with wide parking/signal lamps down in the bumper below the rub strip. A Somerset script went at the forward end of the front fenders, above the amber lenses inset into the protective bumper strip. Somerset's chassis used MacPherson struts up front, with semi-independent coil spring suspension in the back. All Somersets had power rack-and-pinion steering, plus low-drag power front disc brakes. Limiteds carried new velour cloth upholstery. Reclining bucket seats were standard, with a front center armrest. Standard digital instruments included readouts for voltage, oil pressure, temperature, engine R.P.M. and trip odometer. Radio controls were housed in a pod separate from the radio, easy to reach. Standard powertrain was the 2.5-liter four-cylinder engine with electronic fuel injection, driving a close-ratio five-speed manual gearbox. Optional: an automatic transmission and 3.0-liter V-6 engine, with multi-port fuel injection. T Types carried the 3.0-liter V-6 with computer-controlled coil ignition. That meant no more distributor under the hood. A Gran Touring suspension (Level III) and low-profile P215/60R14 Eagle GT blackwall tires on new cast aluminum alloy wheels delivered a firmer ride than the standard Somerset. The minimally-trimmed body sported charcoal lower body accents all around the car, plus a new front air dam and blacked-out grille and trim items. The performance-oriented axle ratio was 3.18:1. Other T Type touches: gray instrument panel, console and door trim plates, leather-wrapped steering wheel, black pillar applique, wide charcoal rocker panel moldings, amber parking/signal lamp lenses, red/amber taillamps, gray protective bodyside moldings, and twin rear-view mirrors (the left one remote-controlled). T Type upper body colors were silver, black, white or red, all with dark gray lower accent. Tan and seven metallic finishes were offered on other Somersets: dark gray, light brown, brown, light blue, medium blue, light sage, and dark sage.

CENTURY — SERIES 4A — FOUR/V-6 — A distinctive new front-end look for Century focused on the slanted vertical-element grille that extended below the low-profile quad headlamps, all the way around the edges of front fenders. A horizontal/vertical

1986 Century Custom sedan (B)

crossbar pattern divided the grille into four sections, with Buick block letters off to the side, below the center. Parking/signal lamps were inset into the bumper protective strip, and amber wraparound cornering lenses stood outboard of the headlamps. A flush-mounted hood ornament completed the modern look. The T Type coupe was dropped this year, but the T sedan remained. Century's lineup also included Custom and Limited sedans and oupes, plus Custom or Estate Wagons. The contemporary Century was intended to compete with European sedans and coupes. Base powertrain was the 2.5-liter, 92-horsepower four with three-speed automatic transaxle. The formerly optional 3.0-liter V-6 was gone, replaced by a carbureted Chevrolet 2.8 V-6 (except in California). Also available: the 3.8-liter V-6, which gained 25 horsepower (now rated 150) by adding sequential port fuel injection and Computer Controlled Coil Ignition, along with low-friction roller valve lifters. T Type sedans ran with the 3.8-liter V-6, hooked to four-speed overdrive automatic. T Types also carried the Gran Touring suspension and low-profile (P215/60R14) steel-belted radial tires on cast aluminum wheels, and wore blackout trim. Instrument panels were gray, with LED tachometer, and the steering wheel was wrapped in leather. Blackout accents went on headlamp and taillamp bezels, radio antenna, door handles, moldings, grille, and accent stripes. Optional Lear Siegler bucket seats provided improved lateral and lumbar support. Wagons had standard side-window defoggers, split-folding rear seat, plus load area light and floor carpeting. Electronic cruise control and six-way power seats were optional this year. A Vista-Vent sunroof was available on all models. T Type body colors were gray, white, silver and black, with gray lower accent paint available. Other Century models came in cream beige or seven metallic shades: light brown, brown, light sage, light blue, dark blue, rosewood, or ark red. Vinyl tops came in white, black, light sage, dark red, dark gray, dark blue, or tan. Century's Gran Sport was described as "a car to be reckoned with," and as "the hottest Buick this side of a race course." Just 1,029 were produced. The Gran Sport package for the Custom coupe included the 3.8-liter V-6 SFI engine, tough suspension, tachometer, black/gray cloth reclining bucket seats with power-6 logo, console with shift lever boot, front/rear floor mats (GS insignia up front), seek/scan AM/FM stereo radio with cassette player and clock, temp/volt gauges, and black leather-wrapped sport steering wheel. The Gran Sport body had a front air dam and spoiler plus blackout grille, black moldings and headlamp bezels, and wide aero rocker panel moldings. Black front floor mats displayed a special Gran Sport insignia. Aluminum wheels with GS identification held P205/60R15 steel-belted radial Eagle GT tires. 'Buick' decals for door and spoiler were in the trunk, for installation by the dealer, and additional GS ornamentation was all over the car. To draw even more attention, the sporty exhaust emitted a "very authoritative growl," according to Buick. All told, a tempting selection of extras, but with a price tag approaching $4000.

1986 Regal T Type Turbo Coupe (B)

REGAL — SERIES 4G — V-6/V-8 — While most of Buick's lineup had switched to contemporary front-wheel drive, Regal hung on with rear-drive and little evident change. Under T Type turbo hoods, though, lay a major change: a new intercooler for the turbocharged 3.8-liter V-6. That fuel-injected engine now churned out 235 horsepower and 330 pound-feet of torque. The intercooler not only added power, but reduced the likelihood of detonation. Regal's T Type sported a blackout-trimmed grille, windows, wipers and headlamp bezels, plus a revised taillamp treatment with black moldings. It rode low-profile P215/65R15 tires on aluminum wheels, as opposed to the P195/75R14 whitewalls on regular Regals. The Gran Touring suspension included a rear stabilizer, larger-diameter front stabilizer bar, higher-rate springs and shocks. Performance rear axle ratio was 3.42:1. Engine identification appeared on the side of the hood bulge. T Types also had body-color sport mirrors, a trip odometer, turbo boost gauge, LED tachometer, leather-wrapped steering wheel, and air conditioning. An optional T Type Designers' Package added a front air dam, rear deck spoiler, and special black and dark gray accent paint on the body. Optional, firmer Lear Siegler bucket seats had an adjustable back. Regal's Grand National, the modern-day "muscle car," strode a lengthy step beyond the "ordinary" T Type. Its all-black body, complete with air dam and spoiler, held virtually no chrome or brightwork of any kind. Rolling on four stylish chrome-plated wheels, with handling provided by a firm, performance-tuned Gran Touring suspension, the driver enjoyed the comfort of gray cloth bucket seats. The turbocharged V-6 with intercooler and sequential port fuel injection was claimed to be "the most advanced high-performance engine offered in a Buick." Rated at more than twice the horsepower of the normally-aspirated version, it fed that power to a standard four-speed overdrive automatic transmission. Grand Nationals soon brought some hefty prices at auctions, a result of their striking and stark appearance and relatively low production figures. A total of 5,512 were produced this year. Customers could also choose a base or Limited Regal, and V-8 fanciers could order their Regals fitted with a 307 cu. in. (5.0-liter) engine, supplied by Oldsmobile. Standard powertrain was a carbureted 3.8-liter V-6, with three-speed automatic transmission. Optional: four-speed overdrive automatic. The diesel V-6 was gone. Regals were sold in an even dozen colors: white, black and cream beige, plus nine metallics: silver, gray, light brown, brown, light blue, dark blue, rosewood, dark red, and light sage (not available on T Types).

65

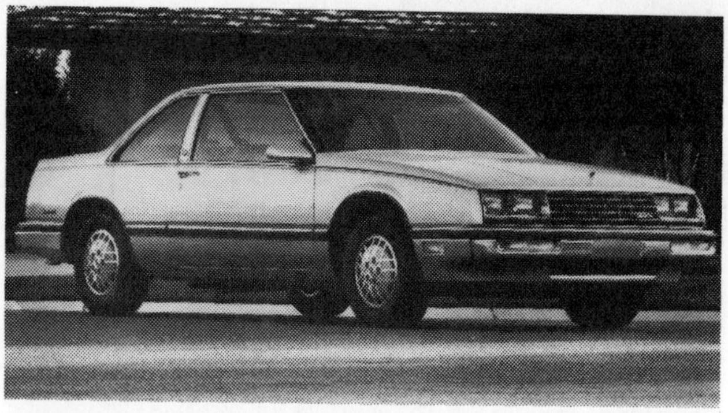

1986 LeSabre Limited coupe (B)

LESABRE — SERIES 4H — V-6 — Buick continued the trend toward aerodynamic design with a fully restyled LeSabre, still six-passenger but with a transverse-mounted engine and front-wheel drive. The new H-body version, sharing the same platform as Oldsmobile's Delta 88, was 400 pounds lighter and 22 inches shorter (on 5 in. shorter wheelbase), yet didn't lose much interior space. LeSabres came in fastback coupe or notchback sedan form, Custom or Limited trim, with front-hinged hood. The new grille had a wide five-row crosshatch pattern, with familiar Buick badge near the lower corner. As on earlier LeSabres, the bottom row of the grille extended outward to the outer tip of the fenders, below deeply recessed quad headlamps. Wide, clear parking/signal lamps were inset in the bumper, directly below the protective rub strip. Outside mirrors were sleek and modern looking. Bodyside moldings stretched the full length of the car, wrapping around into the front and back bumpers. Taillamps were hinged, with a slide-in license plate holder. LeSabre used new body/frame integral construction with a separate front frame to support the powertrain. The chassis used a modified MacPherson strut front suspension with barrel springs, and fully independent rear suspension with inboard coil springs. Standard engine (except in California) was a transverse- mounted 181 cu. in. (3.0-liter) V-6 with multi-port fuel injection, coupled to four-speed automatic transmission with overdrive top gear. Capable of 125 horsepower, the 3.0 had Computer Controlled Coil Ignition, Bosch injectors, a mass air flow sensor, high-output camshaft, plus cast aluminum intake manifold and rocker covers. Performance-minded buyers could choose the optional, proven 231 cu. in. (3.8-liter) V-6, with sequential port fuel injection and roller valve lifters, rated 150 horsepower. Power rack-and-pinion steering was standard. Tires were all-season P205/75R14 blackwalls. An optional "performance package" included the Gran Touring suspension, P215/65R15 Eagle GT tires, specific transmission calibration, faster steering response, and a leather-wrapped sport steering wheel. Custom models had notchback seats covered in velour cloth with woven fabric trim. Limiteds turned to plush, reclining loose-pillow velour seats in 55/45 arrangement. LeSabre's generous standard equipment list included air conditioning and tinted glass. Body colors were: white, black and tan; plus silver, dark gray, light brown, brown, dark teal, light blue, dark blue, flame red or dark red metallic. Sedan vinyl tops came in white, black, tan, dark red, dark gray, dark blue and dark teal. Electronic instrumentation was available. Ranking among the rarest of modern Buicks is the LeSabre Grand National. "We're looking for a few good drivers," proclaimed Buick's specialty brochure; drivers who are "serious about performance." Only 117 of the special-edition oupes were built. Powered by the turbocharged 3.8 V-6 with sequential fuel injection and roller lifters, and riding fat P215/65R15 Eagle GT tires on aluminum alloy wheels, Grand National's chassis carried a muscular, fully independent sport suspension. Bodies were finished in black or white, and the car was packed with extras including blackout moldings, a black 'B' pillar, ribbed quarter-window closeouts, leather- wrapped sport steering wheel, lay-down hood ornament, and dual-outlet exhaust. Grand National ornamentation was on front fenders; a power-6 logo on the front floor mats; interior upholstered in gray cloth.

ESTATE WAGON — SERIES 4B/C — V-8 As before, the old rear-drive Estate Wagons came in both LeSabre and Electra editions. Styling and capacity remained as in prior models. Sole powertrain was the old familiar 307 cu. in. (5.0-liter) V-8, producing 140 horsepower, with four- barrel carburetor and four-speed overdrive automatic transmission. Wagon colors were white, black and cream beige; plus metallic silver, gray, light brown, brown, light sage, light blue, dark blue, rosewood, or dark red.

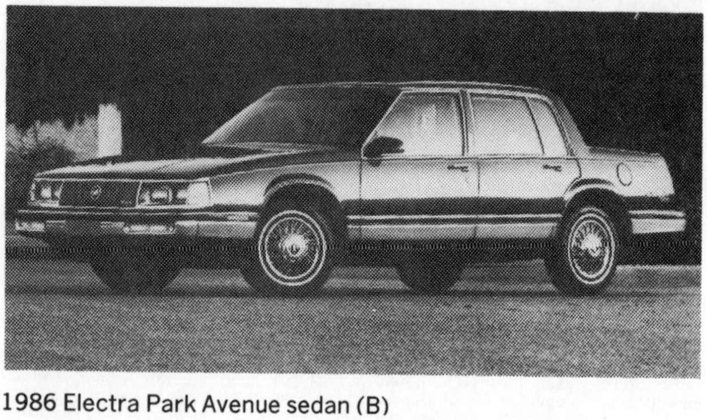

1986 Electra Park Avenue sedan (B)

ELECTRA — SERIES 4C — V-6 — Switched to front-drive a year earlier, Electra changed little for 1986. Coupe and sedan came in base or Park Avenue trim. The T coupe was abandoned, but the T sedan stayed in the lineup. The 3.0-liter V-6 offered in 1985 was no longer available. Sole powerplant was the 231 cu. in. (3.8-liter) V-6, producing 15 more horsepower with sequential fuel injection, driving a four-speed overdrive automatic transaxle. All Electras had power rack-and-pinion steering, a modified MacPherson strut front suspension with barrel springs, and independent rear suspension with automatic level control. Added to the option list was an anti-lock braking system (ABS) that sensed wheel speed and traction, adjusting pressure to prevent lockup during a quick stop or on slippery surfaces. Other new options: an electronic instrument cluster and automatic day/night rear view mirror. A Keyless Entry System option required that a five-number sequence be entered correctly on a little keyboard before the door would open. Electra's standard AM/FM stereo radio had seek-and-scan tuning. Other standard equipment included Soft-Ray tinted glass, an electric fuel filler door release, six-way power driver's seat, power windows, front-seat reading lamps, power windows, air conditioning, and the required high-mounted stop lamp. Park Avenue interiors featured rich velour upholstery in choice of five colors. Extra fittings included Electronic Cruise Control, tilt steering column, electric door locks, remote-control trunk lid, Soft-Ray back seat reading lamps, and lighted vanity mirror on the passenger's visor. Powered by the same 3.8 V-6, the T Type sedan carried a Gran Touring suspension and standard 15 in. aluminum wheels with P215/65R15 Goodyear Eagle GT tires. Also included were a leather-wrapped sport steering wheel, 45/45 seats in gray or red cloth, storage console, brushed gray instrument panel and door trim, front carpet savers with T Type logo, twin-outlet exhaust, and special taillamp treatment. T Types came in five body colors: silver, white, black, flame red, or dark gray. Other Electras could be in painted standard light or dark blue metallic, dark teal metallic, tan, or medium brown metallic. Dark brown, blue and red firemist metallic paint cost extra. Vinyl tops were offered in white, dark gray, black, dark blue, dark teal, beige, flame red, and red.

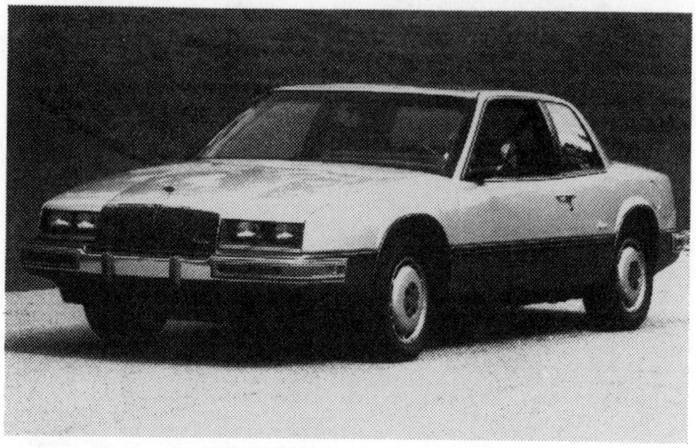

1986 Riviera T Type coupe (B)

RIVIERA — SERIES 4E — V-6 — In an attempt to lure both new and traditional Buick buyers, Riviera turned to a total restyle this year--the first since 1979. Still front-drive with fully independent suspension, Riv was otherwise all-new: over 19 inches shorter, with wheelbase cut by 6 inches (to 108). Curb weight shrunk to a mere 3,309 pounds, over 500 pounds less than before. Yet passenger space stayed close to previous dimensions. The modern version's silhouette was described as a "gentle wedge shape." Improved aerodynamically, it carried new high-intensity quad headlamps and wide taillamps. The sail panel area offered greater visibility. A new independent strut front suspension used barrel- type coil springs and a link-type control arm. Rear suspension was also a new design, using a transverse fiberglass leaf spring. Standard fittings included a front stabilizer bar, electronic level control, and four-wheel disc brakes. The new Riv was powered by the old favorite 231 cu. in. (3.8-liter) V-6, now producing 140 horsepower with sequential port fuel injection, a mass air flow sensor, and Computer Controlled Coil Ignition. Transmission was the four- speed automatic, with overdrive top gear. Rivieras contained from 7 to 10 microprocessors, depending on their option list. All of them worked with the exclusive Graphic Control Center (GCC), standard on all Rivieras. GCC, using a touch-sensitive cathode ray tube (video screen) in the center of the dash, served as the car's control center and information display. It replaced 91 controls that would otherwise be needed. When the ignition key was switched on, the display showed a summary page from the access areas: climate control, trip monitor, gauges, radio, and diagnostic data. Most of the time, no further effort was needed. But a touch of the screen at the appropriate spot pulled in further information. Certain electrical equipment could remain in use after the ignition was switched off. Standard equipment included electronic instrumentation and Electronic Touch Climate Control. Instrument panel, doors, glove box and pillars were cloth-covered. A console held controls for the glove box and deck lid release, fuel filler door, and cassette player. Also standard: side window defoggers (in doors), assist straps, sliding sun screen visor extensions, header console with dome and reading lamps, and electro-luminescent backlight control switches. A tool kit and new scissors jack fit under the trunk floor. Two new Riviera options: keyless entry and a heated outside driver's mirror. Riviera's new T Type included a Gran Touring (Level III) suspension, aluminum wheels with P215/60R15 Eagle GT blackwall tires, power comfort seats that even adjusted headrest height, reversible (leather/velour) front seat cushions and backs, leather-wrapped steering wheel and shift selector, plus gauges for washer fluid level, oil pressure, and external lamp monitors. T Types came in four two-tone body color combinations, with sporty graphics. Buick reported acceleration times of the T Type Riviera at 8.3 seconds to 50 MPH, or 11.3 seconds to 60.

I.D. DATA: Buicks continued the standardized 17-symbol Vehicle Identification Number (VIN), stamped on a metal tag attached to the upper left surface of the cowl, visible through the windshield. Coding was similar to 1985, starting with '1' to indicate U.S.A., followed by 'G' for General Motors, '4' for Buick Division, and a letter to indicate restraint system. Symbol five denotes series: 'S' Skyhawk; 'T' Skyhawk Ltd.; 'E' Skyhawk T Type; 'J' Skylark/Somerset Custom; 'M' Skylark/Somerset Ltd.; 'K' Somerset T Type; 'H' Century Custom; 'L' Century Ltd.; 'G' Century T Type; 'J' Regal; 'K' Regal T Type; 'M' Regal Ltd.; 'H' LeSabre; 'P' LeSabre Custom; 'R' LeSabre Ltd.; 'L' LeSabre T Type; 'X' Electra; 'W' Electra Park Ave.; 'F' Electra T Type; 'V' Electra Estate Wagon; 'Z' Riviera; 'Y' Riviera T Type. Digits six and seven indicate body type: '27' 2-dr. coupe; '37' LeSabre 2-dr. coupe; '47' Regal 2-dr. coupe; '57' Riviera 2-dr. coupe; '11' Electra 2-dr. sedan; '19' Electra 4-dr. sedan; '69' 4-dr. (4-window) sedan. '35' 4-dr. wagon. Next is the engine code: 'O' L4-110 TBI; 'J' turbo L4-110 MFI; 'P' L4-121 TBI; 'U' L4-151 TBI; 'R' L4-151 TBI; 'X' V6-173 2Bbl.; 'L' V6-181 MFI; 'A' V6-231 2Bbl.; '3' V6-231 SFI; 'B' V6-231 SFI; '7' turbo V6-231 SFI; 'T' diesel V6-263; 'Y' V8-307 4Bbl. Symbol nine is a check digit. Symbol ten denotes model year ('G' 1986). Symbol eleven is the plant code: 'M' Lansing, MI; 'T' Tarrytown, NY; 'D' Doraville, GA; '6' Oklahoma City, OK; 'H' Flint, MI; 'K' Leeds, MO; 'X' Fairfax, KS; '1' Wentzville, MO. The final six digits are the sequential serial number. An additional identifying number may be found on the engine. A body number plate on upper shroud or radiator support assembly reveals model year, car division, series, style, body assembly plant, body number, trim combination, modular seat code, paint code, and date build code.

SKYHAWK CUSTOM (FOUR)

Series Number	Body/Style Number	Body Type & Seating	Factory Price	Shipping Weight	Production Total
4J	S27	2-dr Coupe-5P	7844	2277	45,884
4J	S69	4-dr Sedan-5P	8073	2325	29,959
4J	S35	4-dr Sta Wag-5P	8426	2402	6,079

SKYHAWK LIMITED (FOUR)

4J	T27	2-dr Coupe-5P	8388	2314	Note 1
4J	T69	4-dr Sedan-5P	8598	2356	Note 1
4J	T35	4-dr Sta Wag-5P	8910	2429	Note 1

SKYHAWK SPORT (FOUR)

4J	S77	2-dr Hatch-5P	8184	2336	Note 2

SKYHAWK T TYPE (FOUR)

4J	E77	2-dr Hatch-5P	9414	2360	Note 2
4J	E27	2-dr Coupe-5P	8971	2301	Note 1

Note 1: Production figures listed under Skyhawk Custom coupe, sedan and station wagon include totals for Limited and T Type models. For the model year, 72,687 Custom, 6,584 Limited and 6,071 T Type coupes and sedans were built. Note 2: Total hatchback production, 9,499 units.

SKYLARK CUSTOM (FOUR/V-6)

4N	J69	4-dr Sedan-5P	9620/10230	2502/2611	Note 3

SKYLARK LIMITED (FOUR/V-6)

4N	M69	4-dr Sedan-5P	10290/10900	2519/2576	Note 3

Note 3: Total Skylark production, 62,235.

SOMERSET CUSTOM (FOUR/V-6)

4N	J27	2-dr Coupe-5P	9425/10035	2456/2561	Note 4
4N	M27	2-dr Coupe-5P	10095/10705	2473/2578	Note 4

SOMERSET T TYPE (V-6)

4N	K27	2-dr Coupe-5P	11390	2608	3,558

Note 4: Total Somerset production, 75,620. A total of 98,641 Skylark/Somerset Customs and 35,658 Limiteds were produced.

CENTURY CUSTOM (FOUR/V-6)

4A	H27	2-dr Coupe-6P	10052/10487	2616/2677	14,781
4A	H19	4-dr Sedan-6P	10228/10663	2663/2724	229,066
4A	H35	4-dr Sta Wag-6P	10648/11083	2828/2889	25,374

CENTURY LIMITED (FOUR/V-6)

4A	L27	2-dr Coupe-6P	10544/10979	2639/2700	Note 5
4A	L19	4-dr Sedan-6P	10729/11164	2685/2746	Note 5
4A	L35	4-dr Sta Wag-6P	11109/11544	2847/2908	Note 5

Note 5: Century Custom production totals include Limited models. Total model year coupe/sedan production, 116,862 Customs and 126,985 Limiteds. Coupe total includes 1,029 Gran Sport models.

CENTURY T TYPE (V-6)

4A	G19	4-dr Sedan-6P	12223	2863	5,286

REGAL (V-6/V-8)

4G	J47	2-dr Coupe-6P	10654/11194	3106/3345	39,734

REGAL LIMITED (V-6/V-8)

4G	M47	2-dr Coupe-6P	11347/11887	3132/3371	43,599

REGAL T TYPE (V-6)

4G	K47	2-dr Coupe-6P	13714	3285	7,896

Note 6: Regal production total includes 5,512 Grand Nationals.

LESABRE CUSTOM (V-6)

4H	P37	2-dr Coupe-6P	12511	3042	7,191
4H	P69	4-dr Sedan-6P	12511	3081	30,235

LESABRE LIMITED (V-6)

4H	R37	2-dr Coupe-6P	13633	3070	14,331
4H	R69	4-dr Sedan-6P	13633	3112	43,215

Note 7: Only 117 LeSabre Grand National coupes were built.

LESABRE ESTATE WAGON (V-8)

4B	R35	4-dr Sta Wag-6P	13622	4093	7,755

ELECTRA (V-6))

4C	X11	2-dr Coupe-6P	15396	3147	4,996
4C	X69	4-dr Sedan-6P	15588	3189	109,042

ELECTRA PARK AVENUE (V-6)

4C	W11	2-dr Coupe-6P	17158	3181	Note 8
4C	W69	4-dr Sedan-6P	17338	3223	Note 8

Note 8: Electra production figures include Park Avenue models. Total model year production, 23,017 base Electras and 91,021 Park Avenues.

ELECTRA T TYPE (V-6)

4C	F69	4-dr Sedan-6P	16826	3234	5,816

ELECTRA ESTATE WAGON (V-8)

4C	V35	4-dr Sta Wag-6P	16402	4172	10,371

RIVIERA (V-6)

4E	Z57	2-dr Coupe-5P	19831	3203	20,096

RIVIERA T TYPE (V-6)

4E	Y57	2-dr Coupe-5P	21577	3263	2,042

FACTORY PRICE AND WEIGHT NOTE: Figure before the slash is for four- cylinder engine, after the slash for V-6. For Regal, figure before the slash is for V-6 engine, after slash for V-8.

ENGINES: BASE FOUR (Skyhawk): Inline, overhead-valve four-cylinder. Cast iron block and head. Displacement: 121 cu. in. (2.0 liters). Bore & stroke: 3.50 x 3.15 in. Compression ratio: 9.0:1. Brake horsepower: 88 at 4800 R.P.M. Torque: 110 lbs.-ft. at 2400 R.P.M. Five main bearings. Hydraulic valve lifters. Throttle-body fuel injection. VIN Code: P. **OPTIONAL FOUR (Skyhawk); STANDARD (Skyhawk T Type):** Inline, overhead-cam four-cylinder. Cast iron block; aluminum cylinder head. Displacement: 110 cu. in. (1.8 liters). Bore & stroke: 3.34 x 3.13 in. Compression ratio: 8.8:1. Brake horsepower: 88 at 4800 R.P.M. Torque: 98 lbs.-ft. at 2800 R.P.M. Five main bearings. Hydraulic valve lifters. Throttle- body fuel injection. VIN Code: O. **TURBOCHARGED FOUR (Skyhawk):** Same as 1.8-liter OHC four above, except--Compression ratio: 8.0:1. Brake H.P.: 150 at 5600 R.P.M. Torque: 150 lbs.-ft. at 2800 R.P.M. Multi-point fuel injection. VIN Code: R. **BASE FOUR (Skylark, Century, Somerset):** Inline, overhead-valve four-cylinder. Cast iron block and head. Displacement: 151 cu. in. (2.5 liters). Bore & stroke: 4.0 x 3.0 in. Compression ratio: 9.0:1. Brake horsepower: 92 at 4400 R.P.M. Torque: 134 lbs.-ft. at 2800 R.P.M. Five main bearings. Hydraulic valve lifters. Throttle-body fuel injection. Built by Pontiac. VIN Code: R. **OPTIONAL V-6 (Century):** 60-degree, overhead-valve V-6. Cast iron block and head. Displacement: 173 cu. in. (2.8 liters). Bore & stroke: 3.50 x 2.99 in. Compression ratio: 8.5:1. Brake horsepower: 112 at 4800 R.P.M. Torque: 145 lbs.-ft. at 2100 R.P.M. Four main bearings. Hydraulic valve lifters. Carburetor: 2Bbl. Built by Chevrolet. VIN Code: X. **BASE V-6 (Somerset T Type, LeSabre); OPTIONAL (Somerset/Skylark):** 90-degree, overhead-valve V-6. Cast iron block and head. Displacement: 181 cu. in. (3.0 liters). Bore & stroke: 3.80 x 2.66 in. Compression ratio: 9.0:1. Brake horsepower: 125 at 4900 R.P.M. Torque: 150 lbs.-ft. at 2400 R.P.M. Four main bearings. Hydraulic valve lifters. Multi-point fuel injection. VIN Code: L. **BASE V-6 (Regal):** 90-degree, overhead-valve V-6. Cast iron alloy block and head. Displacement: 231 cu. in. (3.8 liters). Bore & stroke: 3.8 x 3.4 in. Compression ratio: 8.0:1. Brake horsepower: 110 at 3800 R.P.M. Torque: 190 lbs.-ft. at 1600 R.P.M. Four main bearings. Hydraulic valve lifters. Carb.: 2Bbl. VIN Code: A. **BASE V-6 (Century T Type); OPTIONAL (Century, LeSabre):** Same as 231 V-6 above, but with sequential fuel injection. Brake H.P.: 150 at 4400 R.P.M. Torque: 200 lbs.-ft. at 2000 R.P.M. VIN Code: 3. **BASE V-6 (Electra, Riviera):** Same as 231 V-6 above, with sequential fuel injection. Compression ratio: 8.5:1. Brake H.P.: 140 at 4400 R.P.M. Torque: 200 lbs.-ft. at 2000 R.P.M. VIN Code: B. **TURBOCHARGED V-6 (Regal T Type):** Same as 231 V-6 above, with turbocharger, intercooler and sequential fuel injection. Brake horsepower: 235 at 4400 R.P.M. Torque: 330 lbs.-ft. at 2800 R.P.M. VIN Code: 7. **BASE V-8 (Estate); OPTIONAL (Regal):** 90-degree, overhead valve V-8. Cast iron block and head. Displacement: 307 cu. in (5.0 liters). Bore & stroke: 3.80 x 3.385 in. Compression ratio: 8.0:1. Brake horsepower: 140 at 3200 R.P.M. Torque: 255 lbs.-ft. at 2000 R.P.M. Five main bearings. Hydraulic valve lifters. Carburetor: 4Bbl. Built by Oldsmobile. VIN Code: Y or H.

CHASSIS DATA: heelbase:- (Skyhawk) 101.2 in.; (Skylark/Somerset) 103.4 in.; (Century) 104.8 in.; (Century wag) 104.9 in.; (Regal) 108.1 in.; (Estate) 115.9 in.; (LeSabre/Electra) 110.8 in.; (Riviera) 108.0 in. Overall length:- (Skyhawk cpe) 175.3 in.; (Skyhawk sed/wag) 177.3 in.; (Skylark) 181.1 in.; (Somerset Regal) 180.0 in.; (Century) 189.1 in.; (Century wag) 190.9 in.; (Regal) 200.6 in.; (LeSabre) 196.4 in.; (Electra) 197.0 in.; (Estate) 221.3 in.; (Riviera) 187.8 in. Height:- (Skyhawk) 54.0 in.; (Skyhawk hatch) 51.9 in.; (Skyhawk wag) 54.4 in.; (Skylark) 52.2 in.; (Somerset) 52.1 in.; (Century cpe) 53.7 in.; (Century sed/wag) 54.2 in.; (LeSabre cpe) 54.7 in.; (LeSabre sed) 55.4 in.; (Estate) 59.3 in.; (Electra) 54.3 in.; (Riv) 53.5 in. Width:- (Skyhawk) 65.0 in.; (Skylark/Somerset) 66.6 in.; (Century) 69.4 in.; (Regal) 71.6 in.; (Estate) 79.3 in.; (LeSabre/Electra) 72.4 in.; (Riv) 71.3 in. Front Tread:- (Skyhawk cpe) 55.3 in.; (Skyhawk sed/wag) 55.4 in.; (Century) 58.7 in.; (Skylark/Somerset) 55.5 in.; (Regal) 58.5 in.; (LeSabre/Electra) 60.3 in.; (Estate) 62.2 in.; (Riv) 59.9 in. Rear Tread:- (Skyhawk) 55.1-55.2 in.; (Skylark/Somerset) 55.2 in.; (Century) 56.7 in.; (Regal) 57.7 in.; (LeSabre/Electra) 59.8 in.; (Estate) 64.0 in.; (Riviera) 59.9 in. Standard Tires:- (Skyhawk) P175/80R13 SBR; (Skyhawk T Type) P195/70R13 SBR; (Skylark/Somerset) P185/80R13 SBR; (Century) P185/75R14 SBR; (Somerset/Century T Type) P215/60R14 Eagle GT SBR; (Regal) P195/75R15 SBR WSW; (Regal T Type) P215/65R15 SBR; (LeSabre/Electra) P205/75R14 SBR WSW; (Electra T) P215/65R15 SBR Eagle GT; (Park Ave.) P205/75R14 SBR WSW; (Estate) P225/75R15 SBR WSW; (Riviera) P205/70R14 SBR WSW; (Riviera T) P215/60R15 Eagle GT SBR.

TECHNICAL: Transmission:- Four-speed, fully synchronized floor shift standard on Skyhawk. Five-speed manual standard on Skylark/Somerset, available on Skyhawk. Four-speed overdrive automatic standard on LeSabre/Electra/Estate/Riviera, available on Century/Regal, which have standard three-speed automatic. Three-speed auto. trans. gear ratios: (1st) 2.74:1; (2nd) 1.57:1; (3rd) 1.00:1; (Rev) 2.07:1. Skyhawk/Skylark/Somerset Century auto. trans. gear ratios: (1st) 2.84:1; (2nd) 1.60:1; (3rd) 1.00:1; (Rev) 2.07:1. Regal four-speed overdrive automatic gear ratios: (1st) 2.74:1; (2nd) 1.57:1; (3rd) 1.00:1; (4th) 0.67:1; (Rev) 2.07:1. Century/Electra four-speed automatic: (1st) 2.92:1; (2nd) 1.57:1; (3rd) 1.00:1; (4th) 0.70:1; (Rev) 2.38:1. Standard axle ratio:- (Skyhawk) 3.65:1 w/4-spd, 3.45:1 w/5-spd, 3.18:1 w/auto.; (Skyhawk turbo) 3.65:1 w/4-spd, 3.33:1 w/auto.; (Skylark/Somerset): 2.84:1; (Century) 2.84:1 w/3-spd, 2.84:1 or 3.06:1 w/4-spd. (Regal) 2.41:1 exc. w/V-8, 2.56:1; (Regal T Type) 3.41:1; (LeSabre) 2.73:1 or 3.06:1; (Electra/Riv) .84:1; (Estate) 2.73:1. Steering:- (Regal/Estate) recirculating ball; (others) rack and pinion; power assist standard on all except Skyhawk. Suspension:- (Skyhawk/Somerset/Skylark) MacPherson strut front w/stabilizer; semi-independent beam rear axle w/trailing arms; rear stabilizer bar optional, std. on T Type. (Century) MacPherson strut front suspension; beam twist rear axle w/trailing arms and Panhard rod; front/rear stabilizer bars. (Leabre/Electra) MacPherson front struts, barrel springs and stabilizer bar; fully independent rear suspension using struts w/stabilizer bar and electronic level control. (Riviera) four-wheel independent suspension with front struts, barrel springs, link control arms and stabilizer bar; transverse leaf rear springs w/control arms and electronic level control. (Regal/Estate) front/rear coil springs; stabilizer bars; rigid four-link rear axle. Brakes:- power front disc, rear drum. Four-wheel disc brakes on Riviera. Anti-lock braking system available on Electra. Body construction:- (front-drive models) unitized; (Regal/Estate) separate body and frame. Fuel tank:- (Skyhawk/Somerset/ Skylark) 13.6 gal.; (Century) 15.7 gal.; (Regal) 18.1 gal.; (LeSabre/Electra/Riv) 18.0 gal.; (Estate) 22.0 gal.

DRIVETRAIN OPTIONS: Engines:- 110 cu. in. (1.8-liter) EFI four: Skyhawk ($50); std. on T Type. Turbocharged 110 cu. in. (1.8-liter) EFI four: Skyhawk T Type ($800) incl. boost gauge, engine block heater and Shelby aluminum wheels. 173 cu. in. (2.8-liter) V-6, 2Bbl.: Century ($435). 181 cu. in. (3.0-liter) V-6, 2Bbl.: Skylark/Somerset ($610). 231 cu. in. (3.8-liter) V-6, SFI: Century ($695), std. on T Type; LeSabre ($370), std. w/Grand National pkg. 307 cu. in. (5.0-liter) V-8, 4Bbl.: Regal ($540). Transmission/Differential:- Four-speed manual trans.: Skyhawk T Type ($75 credit). Five-speed manual trans.: Skyhawk ($75); std. on T. Three-speed auto. trans.: Skyhawk ($465); Skyhawk T Type ($390); Skylark/Somerset ($465), std. on T Type. Four-speed automatic overdrive trans.: Century/Regal ($175); std. on T Type. Optional rear axle ratio: Skyhawk 3.19:1 or 3.43:1; Century 2.84:1; Regal; LeSabre 2.84:1; Electra 2.73:1 or 2.97:1 (all NC). Limited slip differential: Regal/Estate ($95). Suspension, Steering and Brakes:- F40 heavy-duty suspension ($27). F41 Gran Touring suspension ($27) exc. Regal ($49); N/A on Estate. Special G.T. suspension: Skyhawk T Type (NC). Automatic level control: Estate ($175). Power steering: Skyhawk ($215). Anti- lock brakes: Electra ($825). Other:- Heavy-duty alternator: 85, 94, 100, 108 and 120-amp ($20-$90). H.D. battery ($25- $26). H.D. radiator: Skyhawk ($40-$70); Century ($30). Engine block heater ($18). H.D. engine/trans. cooling: Century/Regal/LeSabre/Electra/Riviera ($40-$70). Trailer towing harness: Riviera ($30).

SKYHAWK CONVENIENCE/APPEARANCE OPTIONS: Option Packages:- Performance pkg.: GT suspension, aluminum wheels, P205/60R14 SBR BSW, leather-wrapped steering wheel ($574) exc. T type/wag. SCS pkg. (P185/70R13 SBR BSW, custom seats and door trim, custom steering wheel, black moldings): Cust cpe ($51). Vista Vent flip-open removable glass sunroof ($310). Acoustic pkg. ($36). Instrument gauge pkg.: temp, oil pressure, volts, trip odometer: Cust, Spt ($60). Instrument gauges and tachometer: Cust, Spt ($138); Ltd ($78). Comfort/Convenience:- Air cond. ($645). Rear defogger, electric ($135). Louvered rear window sun shield: hatch ($199). Cruise control w/resume ($175). Power windows ($195- $270). Power door locks ($130-$180). Six-way power driver's seat ($225). Easy-entry passenger seat adjuster: Cust cpe, Spt ($16). Tinted glass ($99). Sport steering wheel ($50). Leather-wrapped steering wheel: T Type ($40). Tilt steering ($115). Trip odometer: Cust, Spt ($15). Electric trunk release ($40). Remote tailgate release: wag ($40). Tailgate wiper/washer: wag, hatch ($125). Two-speed wipers w/delay ($50). Lights, Horns and Mirrors:- Tungsten-halogen headlamps ($25). Headlamps-on indicator ($15). Front seat reading lamp $30). Dual horns: Cust cpe/sed, Spt ($15). Left black remote mirror ($22) exc. T Type. Dual black mirrors: left remote ($53); std. T Type. Visor vanity mirror, passenger ($7). Lighted visor vanity mirror ($45). Entertainment:- Basic seek/scan electronic-tuning AM/FM stereo radio ($158); w/clock ($222); w/cassette ($344). Electronic-tuning AM/FM stereo radio ($242); w/cassette and graphic equalizer ($494). Radio delete ($56 credit). Power antenna ($65). Dual rear speakers ($25). Exterior Trim:- Rear spoiler: Sport ($70). Door edge guards ($15-$25). Wide chrome rocker panel moldings: Cust cpe/sed ($26). Black rocker panel moldings: Spt ($76). Black wheel opening moldings: Spt ($30). Bodyside stripes ($45). Sport stripes: Cust cpe ($95). Designers' accent paint ($195). Lower gray accent paint: T Type ($195). Decklid luggage rack ($100). Roof rack: wag ($105). Front license bracket (NC). Interior Trim/Upholstery:- Seat trim for SCS pkg.: Cust cpe ($291). Front armrest: Cust, T cpe ($45). Front/rear fiber floormats: Cust, T Type cpe ($66). Front carpet savers ($17); rear ($12). Front carpet savers w/inserts ($18); rear ($15). Deluxe trunk trim ($33). Rear compartment security cover ($69). Wheels and Tires:- Styled aluminum wheels ($229); std. T Type. Styled alum. wheels (14 in.): Sport ($259). Locking wire wheel covers ($180). Hubcaps and trim rings: Cust/Ltd ($38). P175/80R13 SBR WSW ($54). P195/70R13 SBR BSW ($104). P195/70R13 SBR WSW ($166). P195/70R13 SBR WLT ($188); T Type ($84). P205/60R14 SBR BSW: Spt ($198); T ($94). P205/60R14 SBR WLT: Spt ($286); T ($182).

SKYLARK/SOMERSET/CENTURY CONVENIENCE/APPEARANCE OPTIONS: Option Packages:- Century Gran Sport pkg.: 3.8-liter V-6, sporty exhaust, P205/60R15 SBR GT tires on alum. wheels, tach, black leather-wrapped steering wheel, AM/FM stereo w/cassette, air dam, spoiler, gauges, black trim, wide rocker moldings: Cust cpe ($3895). Skylark/Somerset performance pkg.: Gran Touring suspension, P215/60R14 BSW tires, alum. wheels, leather-wrapped steering wheel ($592). Flip-open Vista Vent removable glass sunroof ($310-$339). Skylark/Somerset value option pkg.: tilt steering, cruise control, electric door locks, delay wiper, wire wheel covers or alum. wheels ($200 credit from list price). Century value option pkg.: tilt, cruise, lighted vanity mirror, delay wiper and AM/FM ET radio ($200 credit). Comfort/Convenience:- Air cond. ($645); Century ($750). Cruise control ($175). Rear defogger, electric ($135-$145). Power windows: 2-dr. ($195); 4-dr. ($270). Electric door locks ($130-$180). Automatic door locks ($220-$270). Six-way power driver's seat ($225). Manual seatback recliner, passenger: Century ($45); both ($90). Sport steering wheel: Skylark/Somerset Cust, Century ($50). Tilt steering ($115). Tinted glass: Century ($115). Instrument gauges incl. trip odometer: Century ($48); w/tach $126). Trip odometer: Century ($16). Digital electronic instrument cluster: Century ($225); T Type ($131). Electric trunk release ($40-$45). Remote tailgate lock: Century wag ($40). Remote fuel filler door release: Skylark/Somerset Cust, T ($11). Two-speed wipers w/delay ($50). Rear wiper/washer: Century wag ($125). Low washer fluid indicator: Skylark/Somerset ($16). Theft deterrent system: Century ($159). Lights, Horns and Mirrors:- Tungsten-halogen headlamps: Century ($25). Twilight Sentinel: Century ($57). Coach lamps: Century Ltd ($129). Headlamps-on chime: Century ($16). Door courtesy/warning light: Ltd/wag ($44). Front/rear reading/courtesy lights: Skylark/Somerset ($40-$54). Rear seat reading lamp: Skylark/Somerset Ltd, Century ($30); front, Century ($24). Remote-control left mirror: Century Cust/Ltd ($25). Dual mirrors (left remote, right manual): Skylark/Somerset Cust ($53); Century ($61). Dual power remote mirrors: Cust, Century ($139); Ltd, T Type ($86). Dual black electric remote mirrors: Century ($139); T ($78). Visor vanity mirror, passenger: Century ($7). Lighted visor vanity mirror, passenger: Skylark/Somerset ($38); Century ($58). Entertainment:- Electronic-tuning seek/scan AM/FM stereo radio ($157); w/cassette and equalizer ($424-$494). Somerset/Skylark AM/FM stereo w/cassette and Delco-GM/Bose music system ($995). Century ET radio w/clock ($222-$242); w/cassette ($344). Cassette tape player: Somerset/Skylark ($142); stereo radio req'd. Concert sound six-speaker system $70-$125). Premium speakers: Century wag ($35-$60). Rear speakers ($25). Power antenna ($65). Delete radio ($56-$96 credit). Exterior Trim:- Landau vinyl top: Century cpe ($186); heavy-padded ($623). Long vinyl top: Century sed ($160). Designers' accent paint: Skylark/Somerset Cust/Ltd ($195); Century ($205). Charcoal lower accent: Century T ($205). Special solid color paint: Century Cust/Ltd/Estate ($200). Color-keyed bodyside moldings: Skylark/Somerset ($45); Century T ($55). Rocker panel moldings: Skylark/Somerset Cust ($26). Wide rocker panel/rear quarter moldings: Skylark/Somerset Cust ($76); Ltd ($50); Century Cust ($65). Wheel opening moldings: Skylark/Somerset Cust ($30). Windsplit molding: Century Cust ($22). Door edge guards ($15- $25). Bodyside stripes ($45). Woodgrain applique: Century wag ($350). Decklid luggage rack ($100). Tailgate air deflector: Century wag ($37). Roof rack: Century wag ($105). Swing-out rear quarter vent windows: Century wag ($75). Front license bracket (NC). Interior Trim/Upholstery:- Cloth 55/45 notchback seating: Century ($133). Cloth bucket seats: Century Cust ($97). Leather/vinyl 45/45 seats: Century Ltd ($295); T ($425). Cloth 45/45 seats: Century Ltd/Estate (NC). Full- length console: Century ($57). Operating console: Century ($85); T Type ($28). Leather/vinyl bucket seats: Skylark/Somerset Ltd ($275). Lear Siegler bucket seats: Somerset, Century T Type ($600). Front floor mats w/inserts: Skylark/Somerset ($18); rear ($15). Front mats: Century $17); rear ($12). Floor mats w/inserts: Century front ($25); rear ($20). Trunk trim: Century ($25-$47). Locking storage compartment: Century wag ($44). Wheels:- Cast aluminum wheels: Century ($199); std. on T. Styled aluminum wheels: Skylark/Somerset Cust/Ltd ($229). Locking wire wheel covers ($199). Skylark/Somerset All-Season Tires:- P185/80R13 SBR WSW ($58). P205/70R13 SBR BSW ($114). P205/70R13 SBR WSW ($180). P215/60R14 SBR WLT ($202). P215/60R14 SBR Eagle GT WLT: Somerset T ($92). Century All-Season Tires:- P185/75R14 SBR WSW ($58). P195/75R14 SBR BSW ($30). P195/75R14 SBR WSW ($92). P215/60R14 SBR WLT: T Type ($92).

REGAL CONVENIENCE/APPEARANCE OPTIONS: Option Packages:- Regal Grand National pkg. (black body, front/rear bumpers, front air dam, rub strips/guards; cloth bucket seats, operating console, spoiler, performance-tuned suspension, chromed wheels): T Type ($635). Regal T Type Designer pkg.: black front air dam, rear spoilers and special black/dark gray accent paint ($403). Sliding silver electric Astroroof ($925). Hatch roof ($850). Value option pkg.: 5.0- liter V-8, cruise control, lighted visor mirror, delay wiper, tilt steering, stereo radio w/cassette, automatic power antenna ($425 credit from list prices). Comfort/Convenience:- Air cond. ($750). Automatic touch climate control air cond. ($900); T ($150). Cruise control w/resume ($175). Rear defogger, electric ($145). Tinted glass ($115). Tinted windshield ($99). Six-way power driver's seat ($225). Manual passenger seatback recliner ($75). Digital electronic instrument cluster ($299); T Type ($173). Sport steering wheel ($50); N/A T Type. Tilt steering ($115). Power windows ($195). Electric door locks ($130). Electric trunk release ($40). Headlamps-on indicator ($16). Trip odometer ($16); std. T Type. Two-speed wiper w/delay ($50). Theft deterrent system ($159). Lighting and Mirrors:- Tungsten-halogen headlamps ($25). Twilight Sentinel ($57). Cornering lamps ($57) exc. T Type. Coach lamps: Ltd ($102). Door courtesy/warning lights: Ltd ($44). Rear seat reading light ($30); rear ($24). Dual sport mirrors, left remote ($53); std. T Type. Dual chrome mirrors, left remote ($25) exc. T. Dual remote color-keyed mirrors ($83); T ($30). Visor vanity mirror, passenger ($7). Lighted visor vanity mirror, passenger ($58). Entertainment:- Seek/scan electronic-tuning AM/FM stereo radio ($158); w/clock ($222); w/cassette ($344). Electronic-tuning AM/FM stereo radio ($242); w/cassette and equalizer ($494). Concert sound speakers ($95). Dual rear speakers ($25). Automatic power antenna ($65). Radio delete ($56 credit). Exterior Trim:- Landau vinyl top ($186) exc. T Type. Heavy-padded landau vinyl top ($245) exc. T Type. Designers' accent paint ($205). Solid special color paint ($200). Exterior molding pkg. (wide rocker panel and belt reveal moldings): base ($110). Black protective bodyside moldings: T Type ($55). Door edge guards ($15). Bodyside stripes ($45). Front license bracket (NC). Interior Trim/Upholstery:- Full-length console: Ltd/T ($82). Lear Siegler bucket seats: T Type ($600). Cloth bucket seats: base/T ($195). Cloth 55/45 seating ($133); std. on Ltd. Leather/vinyl 45/45 seating: Ltd ($295); T Type ($595). Front mats ($17); rear ($12). Front mats w/inserts ($25); rear ($20). Trunk trim covering ($47). Wheels:- Chrome-plated wheels ($195); N/A T Type. Cast aluminum wheels ($285); std. T Type. Color-keyed wheels ($85) exc. T Type. Locking wire wheel covers ($199); N/A T Type. All-Season Tires:- P205/70R14 SBR WSW ($62). P215/65R15 SBR WLT: T Type ($92).

LESABRE/ELECTRA/ESTATE WAGON CONVENIENCE & APPEARANCE OPTIONS: Option Packages: LeSabre Grand National pkg. (3.8-liter V-6, dual exhausts, white or black paint, 2.84:1 rear axle, P215/65R15 Eagle GT tires on alum. wheels, Gran Touring suspension, leather-wrapped sport steering wheel, front floor mats, side window and belt moldings, and quarter-window close-out): Cust cpe ($1237). LeSabre performance pkg.: G.T. suspension, 2.84:1 axle, P215/65R15 Eagle GT tires on alum. wheels, leather-wrapped steering wheel ($878); 3.8-liter engine incl. later. Electra performance pkg.: G.T. suspension, P215/65R15 tires on alum. wheels, leather-wrapped steering wheel ($508); Park Ave. ($407). Sliding electric Astroroof: Electra ($1230). Vista Vent flip-open sunroof: LeSabre ($310). Comfort/Convenience:- Air cond.: LeSabre ($150). Automatic air cond.: Electra ($165). Air cond. w/touch-climate control: Estate ($150). Cruise control ($175); std. on Park Ave. Rear defogger, electric ($145). Power windows: LeSabre ($195-$270). Power door locks ($130- $180). Automatic door locks: Electra ($220-$270); exc. Park Ave. ($90). Six-way power seat, passenger's: Electra ($225); either side, LeSabre ($225). Two-position memory driver's seat: Electra ($178). Power seatback recliner, one side: Electra ($145); passenger only, LeSabre Cust ($145); Ltd ($70). Manual seatback recliner, passenger: LeSabre Cust ($75). Sport steering wheel: LeSabre ($50). Tilt steering ($115); std. Park Ave. Tilt/telescoping steering column: Electra ($175) exc. Park Ave. ($60). Trip odometer: LeSabre ($16). Windshield washer fluid indicator ($16). Low fuel indicator ($16). Digital electronic instrumentation ($315). Keyless entry system: Electra ($185) exc. T Type. Electric trunk pulldown: Electra ($80). Electric trunk release ($40); std. on Park Ave.. Theft deterrent system: Electra ($159); N/A on Estate. Two-speed wiper w/delay ($50); std. on Park Ave. Lighting, Horns and Mirrors:- Lamp and indicator group: Estate ($70-$86). Tungsten-halogen headlamps ($25). Twilight Sentinel: Electra ($60). Cornering lamps ($60). Light monitors, front/rear: Electra ($77). Door courtesy/warning lamps ($44-$70). Lighted door lock and interior light control: Electra ($75). Four-note horn: Electra ($28). Dual chrome remote mirrors: Estate ($49). Dual electric remote mirrors: LeSabre ($91); Electra Ltd/T ($91). Dual electric remote mirrors (left heated): Electra ($126); Park Ave. ($35). Lighted visor vanity mirror ($58). Automatic day/night mirror: Electra ($80). Entertainment:- Seek/scan electronic- tuning AM/FM stereo radio w/clock: LeSabre ($222). AM/FM stereo ET seek/scan radio w/clock and casssette: LeSabre ($344); Electra ($122). AM stereo/FM stereo ET seek/scan radio w/clock: LeSabre ($242); Electra ($20). AM stereo/FM stereo radio w/cassette and equalizer: LeSabre ($494); Electra ($272). AM stereo/FM stereo ET radio w/Dolby cassette and Delco GM/Bose sound system: LeSabre ($1117); Electra ($895). Radio delete: LeSabre ($56 credit); Electra ($275 credit). Concert sound speakers ($70-$100). Power antenna: Electra ($65). Exterior Trim:- Exterior molding pkg. (wide rocker panel, rear fender lower and belt reveal moldings): LeSabre/Estate ($110). Landau vinyl top: LeSabre cpe ($185). Heavy-padded vinyl top: Electra ($245) exc. T Type. Special paint: Electra ($200) exc. Firemist ($210). Black lower bodyside moldings: LeSabre Cust ($55). Door edge guards ($15- $25). Bodyside stripes ($45). Woodgrain vinyl applique: LeSabre Estate ($345); delete from Electra Est ($320 credit). Roof rack w/air deflector: LeSabre Estate ($110). Rear air deflector: Est ($40). Decklid luggage rack ($100). Rear bumper guards: LeSabre ($24). Front license bracket (NC). -Interior Trim/Upholstery:- Cloth 55/45 seating: LeSabre Cust ($133). Leather/vinyl 55/45 seating: Park Ave. ($425). Leather/vinyl 45/45 seating: Electra T Type ($325). Third seat: Estate ($220). Front carpet mats w/inserts ($25); rear ($20). Trunk carpeting trim: Electra ($53). Trunk mat: Electra ($15). Wheels and Tires:- Chrome-plated wheels: Estate ($40 credit). Styled aluminum wheels ($220-$285). Custom locking wire wheel covers ($164-$199); Estate ($56 credit). P205/75R14 SBR WSW ($66). P215/65R15 SBR BSW: LeSabre ($100). Self-sealing tires ($140).

RIVIERA CONVENIENCE/APPEARANCE OPTIONS: Comfort/Convenience:- Performance pkg.: G.T. suspension, P215/60R15 tires on alum. wheels, leather-wrapped steering wheel ($454). Electric sliding Astroroof ($1230). Rear defogger, electric ($145). Keyless entry system ($185). Six- way power seat, passenger ($225). Electric seatback recliner, one side ($75). Leather-wrapped sport steering wheel ($96); std. T Type. Electric trunk pulldown ($80). Theft deterrent system ($159). Lighting, Horns and Mirrors:- Lamp and indicator group ($93). Twilight Sentinel ($60). Lighted door lock and interior light control ($75). Four-note horn ($28). Heated left mirror ($35). Lighted visor vanity mirrors, each ($58). Entertainment:- Electronic-tuning AM/FM stereo radio w/cassette and clock $342). Cassette player ($122); std. radio req'd. Electronic- tuning AM/FM stereo radio w/Dolby cassette tape player ($895). Concert Sound II speaker system ($70). Exterior Trim:- Designers' accent paint ($235). Special color Firemist paint ($210). Color-coordinated protective bodyside moldings ($55). Door edge guards ($15). Bodyside stripes ($45). Front license bracket (NC). Interior Trim/Upholstery:- Cloth bucket seats ($460). Leather/suede power reclining bucket seats ($487). Leather/suede bucket seats w/lumbar support ($947). Front mats w/inserts ($35); rear ($20). Trunk mat ($50). Wheels and Tires:- 14 in. aluminum wheels ($199); std. T Type. Locking wire wheel covers ($199) exc. T Type. P215/60R15 SBR WLT tires: w/performance pkg. ($70). P205/70R14 SBR BSW tires ($66 credit). Self-sealing tires ($140).

HISTORY: Buick's general introduction was October 3, 1985, but the new Somerset had debuted on August 28, 1985; and LeSabre and Riviera didn't emerge until November 14, 1985. Model year production (U.S.): 850,103 for a 10.7 percent share of the industry total. That number included 333,281 four-cylinder Buicks (up sharply from previous total), 442,699 with six cylinders, and only 74,124 V-8s—first time the V-8 total fell below 100,000. A total of 10,171 Buick engines were turbocharged this year. Calendar year production (U.S.): 775,966. Model year sales by U.S. dealers: 757,001 for a 9.4 percent share of the industry total. Calendar year sales (U.S.): 769,434 for a market share of 9.4 percent.

Historical Footnotes: Buick's sales slipped in 1986, down more than 17 percent — the lowest total since 1982. A V-6 shortage must have contributed to the slack figure. Century was the best seller by far. Starting in late September 1985, Riviera were built at the new plant in Hamtramck, Michigan. The downsized Rivieras didn't fare as well as expected, however, as big rear-drive cars began to enjoy a comeback. LeSabre production began on September 16, 1985 at the refurbished 1.5 million square-foot Buick City assembly plant in Flint, Michigan. Far fewer LeSabres than predicted were turned out. (Sales figures include the rear-drive B-body LeSabre station wagons.) The Buick City operation had a number of high-tech innovations. Instead of the usual receiving dock, 22 separate docking locations put incoming materials near the areas where they would be used. "Just-in-time" scheduling meant there was no provision for storage of inventory. Robots were to be used to unload engines, seats and transaxles. Nearly 200 robots were planned for use in body assembly. At the separate Dimensional Verification Center, a car could be placed on a huge granite block, then automatically measured to make sure all fixtures and tooling were sufficiently precise. Front-drive cars with V-6 engines—especially the 3.8- liter with sequential fuel injection—were gaining in popularity. So the Buick-Oldsmobile-Cadillac (BOC) Group boosted output at the Flint plant, and initiated V-6 production at the Lansing, Michigan facility as well. Some of the 2.8-liter V-6 engines were built in Mexico, while 1.8-liter Skyhawk fours came from Brazil. In a much different use of technology, new Consumer Information Centers were tested at shopping malls in Miami and suburban Dallas. They offered shoppers a variety of information on cars, driving, safety—and of course on the new Buicks. A futuristic Computerized Automotive Maintenance System could now let a dealer hook into a car's electronic control module to send data directly to Buick headquarters for analysis. At the design/evaluation stage, an OSCAR (On-Site Computer-Aided Research) system used sensors in a test car to send signals to a computer inside a nearby van.

From the beginning, Cadillac had been nearly synonymous with luxury. People spoke of countless products as "The Cadillac of (whatever)." Through the tailfinned postwar years, Cadillacs had been poshly (sometimes gaudily) appointed, gargantuan in size, powered by some of the biggest V-8s around. Owning one was viewed as a milepost, a demonstration that one had "arrived."

1976 Fleetwood Brougham pillared sedan (C)

As the 1976 model year began, signs were already appearing that change was imminent; that Cadillac's position might even be in jeopardy one day. For the moment, though, little had changed. Only Lincoln competed in the luxury market, as Chrysler had abandoned its Imperial. Beneath all full-size Cadillac hoods was the biggest V-8 of modern times: a 500 cu. in. behemoth, fully appropriate for the car's enormous length. On the other hand, during the '75 model year a much different kind of Caddy had emerged: the compact Seville, powered by a comparatively tiny, fuel-injected 350 V-8. Unlike the soft American ride and slushy handling typified by big Cadillacs, Seville delivered control more appropriate in a European sedan.

Amid massive publicity, the final front-drive Eldorado convertible came off the line in '76, selling for astounding sums to speculators before leveling off. The bottom-ranked Calais was in its final year, soon to leave only Fleetwood and DeVille to attract full-size coupe/sedan devotees. Luxury-minded customers had plenty to choose from, however, included three special editions: d'Elegance, Talisman and Cabriolet models. Yet this was the final season for the mammoth Seventy-Five limousine and nine-passenger sedan. Led by Seville's popularity, Cadillac set records for both sales and production.

In Cadillac's 75th anniversary year, the full-size models were downsized, losing almost half a ton each. Who would have believed it? Eldorado kept its former huge form a while longer, but all models (except Seville) now carried a new, smaller 425 cu. in. V-8 instead of the giant 500. Eldorado added another special edition, the Custom Biarritz, with padded Elk Grain cabriolet roof. The pillarless four- door hardtop was gone, as all sedans now had pillars and framed door glass. Downsizing didn't hurt, evidently, as sales and production scored gains once again.

1977 Seville sedan (C)

Not much happened for 1978, except for new DeVille Phaeton (coupe or sedan) and Seville Elegante special editions. Dunlop wire wheels were now available. Sevilles could be ordered with Oldsmobile's diesel V-8 engine. For the third year in a row, sales set a record.

Eldorado finally got its downsizing for 1979, along with a modest 350 cu. in. V-8 under the hood and independent rear suspension. Bigger Caddies kept the 425 V-8, and all models could get that Olds diesel. As usual, quite a selection of special editions was offered, some of which may appeal to later enthusiasts: Brougham and Seville d'Elegance, DeVille Custom Phaeton, Seville Elegante, and Eldorado Biarritz.

1980 Eldorado Biarritz coupe (AA)

While Brougham and DeVille got a moderate restyle for 1980, Seville changed drastically. Not everyone adored the new "bustleback" body and long hood, or the razor-edge contours reminiscent of 1950s Rolls-Royce bodies. The new Seville had front-wheel drive and, in a surprpising move, a standard diesel engine. Other Caddies turned to a 368 cu. in. V-8. A fuel-injected version was standard on Eldorado, available for Seville. Later in the year came more shocking powerplant news: a Buick-built V-6 under Cadillac hoods. Sales dropped sharply, and would do so again in 1981, but these were bad years for the industry as a whole.

A different kind of powerplant emerged for 1981, one that would bring Cadillac nothing but grief. The variable-displacement (V8-6-4) engine may have seemed like a good idea at the time, capitalizing on a rising interest in economy. But in real life it was trouble, and lasted only one year (though limousines kept it several years longer). The Buick V-6 continued as underhood alternate.

If the compact "international size" Seville had startled traditionalists back in 1975, what might they make of the latest Cadillac offering for 1982: the subcompact Cimarron? On the whole, not much. Cimarron never managed to catch on, perhaps because it was perceived as little more than a glorified (and costly) Cavalier.

1983 Cimarron sedan (AA)

Four-cylinder engines and manual gearboxes couldn't attract either former or new Cadillac buyers in significant numbers. A new aluminum-block 249 cu. in. HT-4100 V-8 replaced the troublesome V8-6-4 as standard engine in other models. Seville abandoned that standard diesel— another idea that never caught hold. Eldos added a special-edition Touring Coupe with special suspension and wide blackwall tires, in yet another shift away from the traditional. Sales rose for 1982, and again in 1983, which was a year without major change. Rear-drive Cadillacs, the biggest standard cars available, remained popular, and customers also seemed to like the HT-4100 engine a lot better than its predecessor. Cimarron introduced a d'Oro edition with black body and goldtone accents, which didn't exactly sparkle in the sales race.

Eldorado added a Biarritz convertible for 1984, as sales rose once again. This was the final season for the rear-drive DeVille, as front-drive versions were coming. The '85 Deville and Fleetwood were two feet shorter than their rear-drive forerunners, powered by a transverse-mounted V-6 or V-8. Even the Seventy-Five limos were front-drive, but Brougham carried on with rear-wheel drive, still finding quite a few customers. Cimarron could now have a V-6 engine (from Chevrolet).

Brand-new Eldorado and Seville bodies arrived for 1986, far more similar to each other than before. Sales of both fell sharply. No convertible was available, though Eldo could have a Biarritz option, Seville an Elegante. DeVille had an important new option: anti-lock braking. Touring Coupe and Sedan models came with a stiffer suspension to please performance-minded buyers. Diesel engines were gone completely. Limousines finally dropped the V8-6-4 engine. Fleetwood Brougham stuck around in rear-drive form, powered by a 5.0-liter V-8, enjoying a resurgence in sales. For the future, Cadillac was concentrating on its new Allante two-seater, due out in 1987.

The final '76 Eldorado convertibles weren't nearly so rare as promoters suggested, though collectors might still be interested since prices have fallen to more sensible levels. Naturally, the 1980s ragtops are also worth a look. So are many of the attractive special editions: d'Elegance, Elegante, Biarritz. Some models that attracted little interest when new find a future among enthusiasts later, but Cimarron isn't likely to be among them. The razor-edge Sevilles, on the other hand, seem to look more appealing with each passing year—especially since later Sevilles lost their unique styling touches. Two-tone Sevilles with their striking accent moldings and Elegante extras may well be worth considering.

1976 CADILLAC

Even though 1976 was a year of refinement rather than major body or engineering change at Cadillac, it signalled the end of several eras. GM's last convertible was in its final season. This would be the final year for the low-rung Calais (after a dozen years in the lineup), and for the traditional mammoth Cadillac. Full-size Cadillacs retained the same ample dimensions as in 1975, but the new international-size Seville (introduced in mid-year) was 27 in. shorter, 8 in. narrower and a thousand pounds lighter than a Sedan deVille. New grilles on all models carried on the traditional Cadillac crosshatch theme, though with a finer pattern than in 1975 (actually crosshatching within crosshatching). Cornering lamps on Calais, DeVille, Brougham, nine-passenger and limo got new horizontal chrome trim, while taillamps gained a new bold look. Standard wheel discs kept the three- dimensional Cadillac crest on the hub (except Eldorado). Cadillac's ten models came in four size categories: Family (Calais/DeVille), Personal (Eldorado), International (Seville), and Executive (Fleetwood Brougham and Seventy-Five). Full-size Caddies stretched as long in wheelbase as 133 inches and 233.7 in. overall (limos, 151.5 and 252.2 in. rspectively). They still carried a monstrous 500 cu. in. V-8. The smaller Seville, however, actually cost more than bigger Cadillacs. It was powered by a more reasonably sized 350 cu. in. V-8 with electronic fuel injection. (Fuel injection was optional in all models except the Fleetwood Seventy-Five.) Eight different color accent stripes were available, and seven convertible top colors for the Eldorado. Vinyl roofs now were integral padded Elk Grain material except on Seville and Seventy-Five, which had cross-grain padded vinyl. Interiors were essentially the same as in 1975 with rosewood grain trim, plus bright wreath/crest and script plaques. New trims for full-size models include sporty plaids, plush velours, knits, and 11 distinctive genuine leathers. Calais and DeVille coupes had a new vinyl roof, whose top molding served as continuation of the door 'belt' molding. All full-size Caddies except Eldorado included a Controlled (limited-slip) Differential for extra traction. All had lamp monitors atop each front fender to show status of front and rear lights. All could have optional illuminated entry and theft-deterrent systems. The new Freedom battery never needed water. All but Eldorado offered new-look turbine-vaned and wire wheel covers. A new option locked doors when the lever was shifted to "Drive." Cadillac also offered Track Master, a computerized skid-control system that automatically pumped the back brakes in an emergency situation to shorten stopping distance. Of special note on the option list was the Air Cushion Restraint System, announced for all models except Eldorado convertible and Fleetwood 75. This was a forerunner of the air bags that received so much publicity a few years later. Another option was the Astroroof, introduced in 1975, with sliding sunshade that permitted use as an electrically-operated sunroof or a transparent closed skylight. Both it and the "ordinary" sunroof panels could give safety along with an open-air feeling, now that the convertible was about to disappear. Three full-size special editions with new refinements were offered this year: d'Elegance, Talisman and Cabriolet. New options included a pushbutton Weather Band (exclusive to Cadillac) built into the AM/FM stereo signal-seeking radio; loose-pillow style seats for d'Elegance packages; plus power passenger and manual driver seatback recliners for 50/50 front seats. Of the 15 standard and six optional Firemist body colors, 13 were new this year. The list included: Cotillion White; Georgian Silver; Academy Gray; Sable Black; Innsbruck Blue; Commodore Blue; Dunbarton Green; Firethorn; Claret; Pueblo Beige; Kingswood Green; Calumet Cream; Phoenician Ivory; Brentwood Brown; and Chesterfield Brown. For extra cost, buyers could order any of six Firemist colors: Crystal Blue, Amberlite, Greenbrier, Galloway Green, Florentine Gold, or Emberglow. Vinyl roofs came in dark blue, silver blue, firethorn, mahogany, silver or dark brown metallic; or in basic white, black, dark blue-green, buckskin, or ivory. All Cadillacs had as standard: automatic climate control; bumper impact strips; digital clock; automatic glove box light; High Energy Ignition; inside hood release; lamp monitors; remote-control left-hand outside mirror; litter receptacle; automatic trunk light; map light; power six-way front-seat adjuster (not on Calais or 75 series); power front disc brakes (four-wheel on Eldorado); power door locks; power windows; power steering; AM/FM radio including power antenna; Soft Ray tinted glass; spare tire cover; tamper-resistant odometer; Turbo Hydra-matic transmission; washer fluid level indicator; and steel-belted whitewall tires.

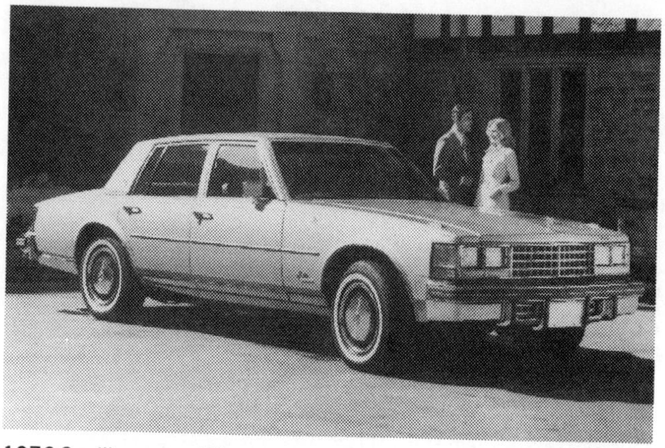

1976 Seville sedan (C)

SEVILLE — SERIES 6K — V-8 — Described as "among the most fully equipped cars in the world," Seville had debuted in May 1975 and changed little for its first complete model year. Marketed against Mercedes, the international-size, contemporary styled four- door sedan offered near-European ride/handling qualities, along with respectable fuel mileage. Seville could hit 60 MPH in 11 seconds or less, top 110 MPH, and cruise gently on the highway. The computer-designed chassis actually derived from Chevrolet's Nova, but Cadillac did an extensive reworking of the X-body, with exclusive body panels, and mounted a vinyl top. Seville's front end was unmistakably Cadillac. A horizontal crosshatch grille was arranged in three rows, divided into two sections by a vertical center bar. Quad rectangular headlamps sat above twin rectangular parking/signal lamps and alongside large wraparound cornering lamps. A Seville nameplate was fairly low on the front fender, behind the wheel opening. Up front: a stand-up wreath/crest hood ornament. Large wraparound taillamps (far different from full-size models) and full wheel openings complemented the formal profile. Body preparation included two primers, four finish coats, and an additional lacquer coat. New zincrometal was used in key areas to fight rust. All told, Seville was described as having an "uncluttered" look, less glitzy than other luxury cars had become. Measuring about two feet shorter than full-size domestic luxury cars, the new breed of Caddy sold well from the start. The standard 350 cu. in. V-8 (from Oldsmobile) with electronic fuel injection was mounted on a steel sub-frame connected to the body sheet metal through damping cushions, to isolate vibration. An impressive standard equipment list included air conditioning; variable-ratio power steering; power brakes, door locks and seat; courtesy lamps; electric trunk lock release; automatic level control; a fuel monitor; cornering lamps; signal-seeking AM/FM stereo radio with power antenna; tilt/telescoping steering wheel; and GR78 x 15-B steel-belted whitewall tires. Seville's dash held an upper "information band" with functional control panels to the river's left and right. 50/50 front seats were trimmed in seven Mansion Knit cloth colors, or optional genuine Sierra Grain leather in eight colors. A cross-grain padded vinyl roof was standard.

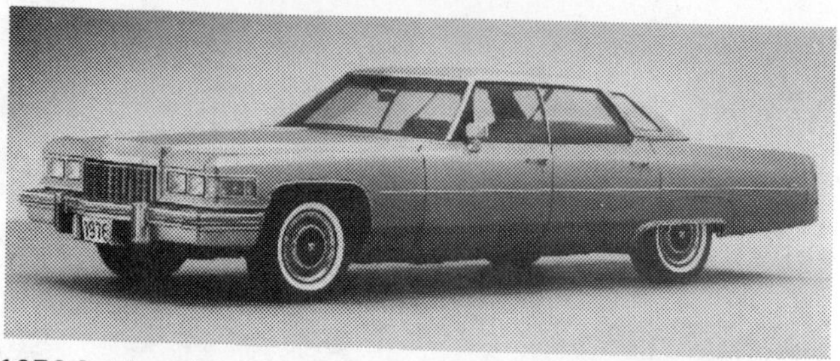

1976 Calais sedan (C)

CALAIS — SERIES 6C — V-8 — For its final outing, Calais displayed the same front-end look as the more expensive DeVille, with a Cadillac 'V' and crest at the hood front. Interiors could be Morgan Plaid in four possible color combinations, or expanded vinyl in antique light buckskin or black. Standard features included an AM/FM radio with automatic power antenna, automatic climate control, digital clock, tinted glass, lamp monitors, and power door locks. Sedans had small coach windows on the rear pillar; coupes much larger, squarish rear quarter windows. Rear fenders held script nameplates. Electronic fuel injection had become optional on the 500 cu. in. V-8 in March 1975, but the carbureted version continued as standard.

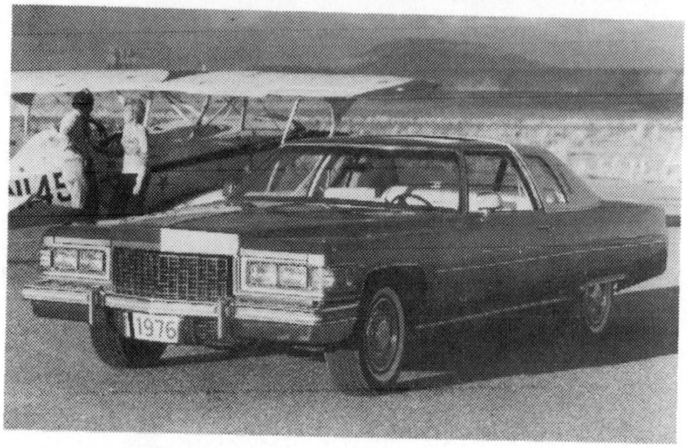

1976 Coupe deVille (C)

DEVILLE — SERIES 6C — V-8 — Coupe deVille, a name that had been around for over two decades, was advertised as "America's favorite luxury car." The mid-1970s edition had a vinyl cabriolet roof with chrome accent strip at the leading edge, and a squarish quarter window (considerably larger than most such windows at this time). Sedan deVille continued the pillarless hardtop that had been part of the GM tradition for years, but would soon be doomed to extinction. Sedans also featured narrow sail-shaped fixed windows in the roof quarter panels. DeVille's crosshatch grille was dominated by a framed set of vertical bars, peaking forward slightly at the center. An upper horizontal bar above the grille mesh held a Cadillac script at the side and swept down alongside the grille, then outward to wrap around the fenders just above the bumpers. Quad rectangular headlamps met wraparound cornering lamps. Set into traditional tall housings at rear fender tips were vertical inward- and outward-facing side lamps. Horizontal taillamps were below the deck lid; backup lamps in toward the license plate housing. Script nameplates were on rear quarter panels, just above the bodyside molding. New Magnan ribbed knit upholstery came in six colors; Merlin Plaid or Manhattan velour each in two. Eleven leather combinations were available. Distinctive simulated rosewood ppliques and laminates highlighted doors and dash. 50/50 seats had individual fold-down center armrests. The standard 500 cu. in. V-8 (whose days were numbered) could have either a four-barrel carburetor or fuel injection. The special-edition Coupe deVille d'Elegance now carried standard opera lamps behind the quarter windows, which were optional on other deVille coupes. D'Elegance hoods omitted the customary 'V' and crest, substituting a distinctive stand-up see-through ornament along the chrome windsplit. Styling highlights included dual accent stripes on front and sides of hood, door surfaces, and rear deck (in choice of eight colors). Interiors contained new loose-pillow style 50/50 seats in two-toned Magnan ribbed knit cloth (four colors). A 'DeVille d'Elegance' script was on the instrument panel and sail panels (coupe only). The package also included wide brushed-chrome lower door moldings, and bodyside moldings with colored vinyl inserts to match the vinyl roof color. Coupe deVille's Cabriolet roof option, with Elk Grain vinyl padded vinyl top, added for 1976 a decorative Cadillac crest on the sail panels. Also part of the package: a standup see-through hood ornament, chrome roof moldings, and French seam around the backlight. Cabriolet roofs had been available on Coupe deVille since 1974.

FLEETWOOD SIXTY SPECIAL BROUGHAM — SERIES 6C — V-8- For the last time, the luxurious Brougham would carry on the Sixty Special name, riding a lengthy 133 in. wheelbase-- three inches longer than a Sedan deVille. New 'Fleetwood' plaques replaced script on both Brougham and the longer- wheelbase Fleetwood Seventy-Fives (below). A stand-up "jewel- like" wreath-and-crest hood ornament was now standard on both. Basic styling was similar to DeVille, including the large chrome housings at rear fender tips that held inward- and outward-facing red lenses. The decklid held a wreath-and- crest emblem rather than Calais/DeVille's 'V' and crest. Modest Fleetwood nameplates on front fenders (behind the wheel openings, below the bodyside molding) and decklid corner were in block letters, colored to match the body. Brougham standards included a signal-seeking radio with power antenna, automatic level control, lamp monitors, six- way power seat, power windows and door locks, individual reading lights, and carpeted footrests. Standard Dual Comfort 60/40 front seats with fold-down center armrest could be upholstered in Minoa ribbed velour with leather bolsters (three colors) or smooth-finish Mansion (five colors). Sierra Grain

leather came in 11 trim combinations. Broughams could have premium wheel covers with Fleetwood wreath/crest and black centers. Two luxury option packages were offered again. Brougham's d'Elegance option changed for 1976 to include ontoured loose-pillow style seats trimmed in soft Mansion brushed-knit fabric (five colors available), with 50/50 Dual Comfort front seats, seatback pockets, extra-dense pile carpeting, 'Brougham d'Elegance' script on instrument panel, and wide brushed-chrome lower door moldings. The roof was thickly padded in Elk Grain vinyl with roller perimeter around the backlight, rich French seam, and bright chrome belt moldings. Also in the package: turbine-vaned wheel discs, opera lamps, and 'Brougham d'Elegance' script on the sail panels. The Fleetwood Talisman option package included 40/40 front seats with six-way power adjuster and power passenger recliner, trimmed in Medici crushed velour (black or dark blue); special interior trim; console with lighted compartment; stand-up wreath/crest hood ornament; padded Elk Grain vinyl roof; turbine-vaned wheel discs; and 'Fleetwood Talisman' identification on sail panels.

FLEETWOOD SEVENTY-FIVE LIMOUSINE — SERIES 6D — V-8 This would be the final year for the long Caddy limo and nine-passenger sedan (151.5 in. wheelbase and 252.3 in. overall), which weighed in at a whopping 5800 lbs. Their body style had first appeared for 1971. This year, like Fleetwood Brougham, they gained a new grille pattern plus revised cornering lamps with horizontal chrome trim. Base prices were 14,889 for the nine-passenger sedan and $15,239 for the eight-passenger limo. This model year, a total of 1,815 Fleetwood Seventy-Fives were built: 981 sedans and 834 limos. Fleetwood remained the only American-built vehicle that was designed and built strictly as a limousine. Big Fleetwoods had two separate automatic climate control systems. Interior choices were Medici crushed velour fabric in black or dark blue, or light gray Magnan Knit in light gray. Full-width folding seats held three extra passengers. Passengers could use the control panel to raise/lower windows, turn on reading lamps, operate radio, or (in limo) raise/lower the center partition. Fixed quarter windows behind the rear doors were larger than those on Sedan deVille. (Fleetwood Broughams had no such windows at all.) Electronic fuel injection was optional on the 500 cu. in. (8.2-liter) V-8 engine. A cross-grain padded vinyl roof was optional. Seventy-Five models had new graphite-treated rear brake linings, reinforced shoes, and Hydro-Boost power-brake booster. They also boasted four cigarette lighters rather than the usual two.

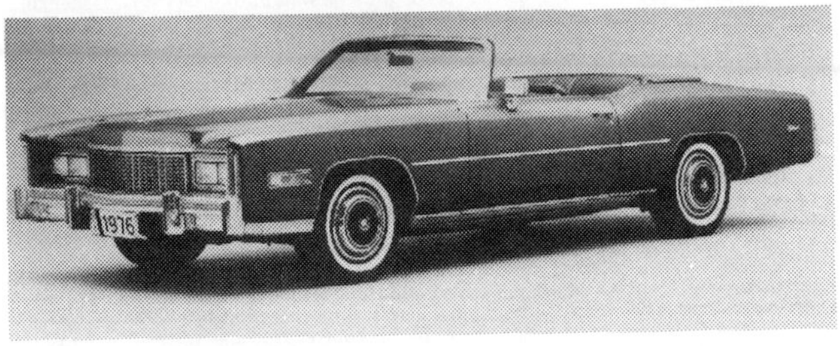

1976 Eldorado convertible (C)

ELDORADO — SERIES 6E — V-8 — Cadillac's personal-luxury coupe had lost its rear skirts in a major 1975 restyle. This year brought no drastic changes, but some styling refinements. The 'Cadillac' script signature was now on the hood (driver's side) rather than the grille itself. Though similar to the 1975 version, this year's crosshatch grille was dominated by vertical bars, peaked forward at the center. It also reached a bit higher than the quad rectangular headlamps. New amber-lensed parking lamps rested down in the bumper; horizontal amber-lensed cornering lamps sat back on front fenders. Massive vertical extensions of the outboard bumper protrusions stood at front fender tips. Eldorado script was on rear fenders and decklid. Wide, simple new taillamps were continuous red slots within wide bezel frames, below the decklid and above the bumper. Backup lights were on each side of the license plate. Additional red lenses, facing both side and rear, sat in the massive vertical chrome fender extensions. Distinctively- shaped opera windows sloped down and forward at the base, following the dip in the quarter panel. Other styling highlights included dual accent stripes next to upper and lower crease lines of the hood's beveled edges. Upper stripes ended at the hood's rear edge; lower stripes extended all the way to rear edge of door. The big 500 cu. in. V-8 powered Eldos once again, but in weakened, detuned state compared to prior years as a result of more rigorous emissions standards. Bendix electronic fuel injection, which had become optional in 1975, was available again; but the basic engine held a four-barrel carb. New wheel covers had a black center hub area with bright metal raised wreath-and-crest. Eldorado's simulated wood dash insert displayed a carved gunstock pattern. Four-wheel power disc brakes were standard, as was a padded vinyl "half" roof. A sunroof was optional. So was the Astroroof that debuted in 1975, with tinted panel for power sunroof, along with sunshade and metal slider. The front-drive Eldo's rear suspension included upper and lower control arms, helical-coil springs, and automatic level control. Up front were torsion bars. A chain drive connected the torque converter section to the gear portion of the automatic transmission. Interiors could be Mansion Knit fabric in any of four colors; Merlin Plaid in two; or 11 Sierra Grain leather possibilities. The Custom Cabriolet option had first appeared in 1972. That roof this year featured padded Elk Grain vinyl in choice of eleven colors with bright chrome molding, plus wreath/crest ornamentation on sail panels. A Custom Biarritz option arrived late in the model year. That one included thick padding on back roof area, a limousine-style backlight, opera lamps, chrome molding along fenderline, and Sierra Grain pillow-soft leather seats. The package came with or without an Astroroof or sunroof. Eldo held the dubious record of being the world's biggest car with front-wheel drive--delivering gas mileage to prove it. Back in '76, though, the coupe got far less attention than the convertible, simply because this was the final year for *any* GM ragtop. Though hardly rare with 14,000 copies rolling off the line, they gained considerable media coverage and the covetous attention of speculators hoping to profit mightily from the last of a long line of open-topped Caddies. Except for the final 200 all-white examples, Eldorado's convertible top came in white, black, dark blue, firethorn, dark blue-green, buckskin, or ivory color.

I.D. DATA: Cadillac's 13-symbol Vehicle Identification Number (VIN) was located on the forward edge of the windshield trim molding, visible through the windshield. The first digit is '6', indicating Cadillac division. The second symbol indicates series: 'B' Fleetwood Brougham; 'C' Calais; 'D' DeVille; 'F' Fleetwood 75; 'L' Eldorado; 'S' Seville; 'Z' commercial chassis. Symbols 3-4 show body type: '47' 2-dr. coupe; '49' 4-dr. hardtop sedan; '69' 4-dr. sedan; '23' 4-dr. sedan w/auxiliary seat; '33' 4- dr. limousine w/auxiliary seat and center partition window; '67' 2-dr. convertible; '90' commercial chassis. Symbol five is the engine code: 'R' V8-350 FI; 'S' V8-500 4Bbl. or FI. The sixth symbol indicates model year ('6' 1976). Symbol seven is for assembly plant: 'Q' Detroit, MI; 'E' Linden, NJ. The last six digits show the sequence in which the car was built: 100001 through 400000 for 'C' series made in Detroit and all Eldorados; 600001 through 690000 for 'C' models built in Linden. An engine unit number is on the block behind the left cylinder head; a nine-digit VIN derivative that shows model year, plant and sequence number is on the block behind the intake manifold. Engine number of 350 V-8 is stamped on the front left side of the block, below the head. A body identification plate on the top right surface of the shroud under the hood, near the cowl), reveals style number, trim number, body number, paint number, and date of assembly (month 01 through 12, week A through E) followed by codes for factory-installed options.

Series Number	Body/Style Number	Body Type & Seating	Factory Price	Shipping Weight	Production Total
SEVILLE					
6K	S69	4-dr Sedan-5P	12,479	4232	43,772
CALAIS					
6C	C47	2-dr Coupe-6P	8629	4989	4,500
6C	C49	4-dr HT Sed-6P	8825	5083	1,700
DEVILLE					
6C	D47	2-dr Coupe-6P	9067	5025	114,482
6C	D49	4-dr HT Sed-6P	9265	5127	67,677
FLEETWOOD BROUGHAM					
6C	B69	4-dr Sedan-6P	10,935	5213	24,500
FLEETWOOD SEVENTY-FIVE					
6D	F23	4-dr Sedan-9P	14,889	5746	981
6D	F33	4-dr Limo-8P	15,239	5889	834
6D	Z90	Commercial Chassis	N/A	N/A	1,509
ELDORADO					
6E	L47	2-dr Coupe-5P	10,586	5085	35,184
6E	L67	2-dr Conv-5P	11,049	5153	14,000

ENGINES: BASE V-8 (Seville): 90-degree, overhead valve V-8. Cast iron block and head. Displacement: 350 cu. in. (5.7 liters). Bore & stroke: 4.057 x 3.385 in. Compression ratio: 8.0:1. Brake horsepower: 180 at 4400 R.P.M. Torque: 275 lbs.-ft. at 2000 R.P.M. Five main bearings. Hydraulic valve lifters. Fuel injection (speed-density, port-injected). Built by Oldsmobile. VIN Code: R. BASE V-8 (all except Seville): 90-degree, overhead valve V-8. Cast iron block and head. Displacement: 500 cu. in. (8.2 liters). Bore & stroke: 4.300 x 4.304 in. Compression ratio: 8.5:1. Brake horsepower: 190 at 3600 R.P.M. Torque: 360 lbs.-ft. at 2000 R.P.M. Five main bearings. Hydraulic valve lifters. Carburetor: 4Bbl. Rochester M4ME. VIN Code: S. OPTIONAL FUEL-INJECTED V-8 (all except Seville): Same as 500 cu. in. V-8 above, except-- Horsepower: 215 at 3600 R.P.M. Torque: 400 lbs.-ft. at 2000 R.P.M.

CHASSIS DATA: Wheelbase: (Seville) 114.3 in.; (Calais/DeVille) 130.0 in.; (Fleetwood Brougham) 133.0 in.; (Fleetwood 75) 151.5 in.; (Eldorado) 126.3 in. Overall length:- (Seville) 204.0 in.; (Calais/DeV) 230.7 in.; (Brghm) 233.7 in.; (Fleetwood 75) 252.2 in.; (Eldorado) 224.1 in. Height:- (Seville) 54.7 in.; (Calais/DeV cpe) 53.8 in.; (Calais/DeV sed) 54.3 in.; (Brghm) 55.3 in.; (Fleetwood 75 sed) 56.8 in.; (Fleetwood 75 limo) 56.6 in.; (Eldo cpe) 54.1 in.; (Eldo conv.) 54.5 in. idth:- (Seville) 71.8 in.; (others) 79.8 in. Front Tread:- (Seville) 61.3 in.; (Eldo) 63.7 in.; (others) 63.3 in. Rear Tread:- (Seville) 59.0 in.; (Eldo) 63.6 in.; (others) 63.3 in. Standard Tires:- (Seville) GR78 x 15-B; (limo) LR78 x 15-D; (others) LR78 x 15-B. Wide whitewall except limo.

TECHNICAL: Transmission: Three-speed Turbo Hydra-matic standard on all models; column shift (400 series exc. Eldo, 425 series). Gear ratios: (1st) 2.48:1; (2nd) 1.48:1; (3rd) 1.00:1; (Rev) 2.07:1 or 2.09:1. Standard axle (final drive) ratio:- (Seville) 2.56:1; (limo) 3.15:1; (others) 2.73:1. Optional: (Seville) 3.08:1; (Eldo) 3.07:1; (others) 3.15:1. Hypoid rear axle exc. (Seville) Salisbury type. Steering:- variable ratio power assisted. Front suspension:- (Seville) unequal length upper/lower control arms, coil springs, stabilizer bar; (Eldo) upper/lower control arms, torsion bars; (others) upper/lower control arms, coil springs, rod-and-link stabilizer bar. Rear suspension:- (Seville) multiple leaf spring; (others) four-link drive, coil springs; automatic level control on all except Calais and DeVille. Body onstruction:- (full size) separate body and perimeter frame. Wheel size: (Seville) 15 x 6 JJ; (others) 15 x 6 JK. Brakes: front ventilated disc, rear drum exc. Eldorado, four-wheel disc; power booster on all. HEI electronic ignition. Fuel tank:- (Seville) 21 gal.; (others) 27.5 gal.

DRIVETRAIN OPTIONS: Fuel-injected V-8 engine ($647) exc. limo. Heavy-duty cooling system ($40). 80-amp alternator ($45). California emission equipment ($50). Limited slip differential ($61); N/A on Eldorado. Trailering pkg. ($85) exc. limo/Seville. Automatic level control: Calais/DeV ($92).

OPTION PACKAGES: Brougham d'Elegance ($885). Coupe deVille Cabriolet ($329); w/Astroroof ($1288); w/sunroof ($1104). DeVille d'Elegance ($650). Eldorado Cabriolet ($432); w/Astroroof ($1391); w/sunroof ($1207). Fleetwood Talisman: Brougham ($1813).

CONVENIENCE/APPEARANCE OPTIONS: Astroroof for full vinyl roof ($885) exc. limos. Astroroof (painted): Calais/DeV/Brghm/Eldo ($985). Sunroof for full vinyl roof ($701) exc. limo. Sunroof for painted roof ($800) exc. limo/SeV. Cruise control ($104). Controlled-cycle wipers ($28). Rear defogger, grid-type ($77) exc. limo. Six-way dual comfort power passenger seat: DeV/Brghm/Eldo ($131). Six-way power front lounge seat: Calais ($131); limo ($98). Power passenger 50/50 seat w/recliner: DeV/Brghm/Eldo ($221). Manual driver's 50/50 seatback recliner ($65) exc. Calais/limo. Power passenger seatback recliner: SeV ($90). Tilt/telescope steering wheel ($102). Automatic door locks $100). Illuminated entry system ($52). Fuel monitor ($26). Theft deterrent system ($114). Track master ($263) exc. SeV/Eldo. Remote trunk lock ($68) exc. SeV. Opera lamps: Calais/DeV cpe, Brghm, limo ($58). Twilight Sentinel ($47). Guidematic headlamp control ($54). Trumpet horn ($19) exc. SeV. Remote-control right mirror ($30). Thermometer on left mirror ($18) exc. SeV. Lighted vanity mirror, passenger ($44- $60). AM/FM stereo radio w/tape player: Calais/DeV/limo ($239); others ($93). Signal-seeking AM/FM stereo radio ($147). Signal-seeking AM/FM stereo radio w/weather band: Calais/DeV/limo ($209); others ($61). Signal-seeking AM/FM stereo radio w/rear control: limo ($275). Firemist paint ($146). Padded vinyl roof: Calais/DeV ($163); Eldo ($170); limo ($819). Hard boot (two-piece): conv. ($63). Accent stripes: Calais/DeV ($42). Door edge guards ($7-$11). License frame: each ($7). Expanded vinyl upholstery: Calais ($47). Dual comfort 50/50 front seat: DeV/Eldo ($185). Dual comfort 60/40 front seat: DeV ($123). Leather upholstery ($220-$235) exc. Calais/limo. Front shoulder belts: Eldo conv. ($36). Air cushion restraint system: Calais/DeV/Brghm/Eldo cpe (N/A). Carpeted rubber floor mats, front/rear ($38-$47) exc. limo, front ($26). Trunk mat ($10). Turbine-vaned wheel covers ($45); N/A on Eldorado. Wire wheel covers: ($167) exc. Eldo; on d'Elegance/Talisman ($122). Stowaway spare tire (NC) exc. limo.

HISTORY: Introduced: September 12, 1975 (in showrooms Sept.18). Model year production (U.S.): 309,139, which set a record. Calendar year production (U.S.): 312,845. Calendar year sales by U.S. dealers: 304,485 for a 3.5 percent share of the industry total, down from 267,049 (3.8 percent) in 1975. Model year sales by U.S. dealers: 299,579.

Historical Footnotes: This year beat the all-time record (set in 1973) for sales and production, with 309,139 Cadillacs built. Seville was the shining star of the sales rise. After a brief 1975 model run, production zoomed upward for full-year 1976. At $13,000, Seville was the most costly standard domestic production car built by the Big Four automakers. It also offered a foretaste of what was coming soon as GM downsized all its models. Most Cadillacs, including all Sevilles and Eldorados, were built in Detroit; but 42,570 vehicles emerged from the Linden, New Jersey plant. Full-size "standard" Cadillacs continued to sell well, defying the market conditions of the mid-1970s. Exactly 14,000 Eldorado convertibles were built in their final season (compared to just 8,950 in 1975). Cadillac promoted them as the "Last of a magnificent breed." The actual "last" American convertible was driven off the line at Cadillac's Clark Avenue plant in Detroit on April 21, 1976, by general manager Edward C. Kennard and manufacturing manager Bud Brawner. Passengers for this major media event included several production workers and Detroit mayor Coleman Young. Just 60 years before, the first Caddy to use the name "convertible" had appeared. For the past five years, Eldorado had been the only luxury American convertible; and for 1976, the sole survivor of the breed. Reasons cited for the loss of ragtop popularity included widespread use of air conditioners, high-speed cruising, sunroofs and vinyl roofs--even the improved audio qualities of stereo radio/tape systems, which couldn't be appreciated fully in an open vehicle. Actually, Cadillac produced 200 identical "final" convertibles, dubbed "Bicentennial Cadillacs" by Mr. Kennard. The one and only last example was kept for the company's collection. All 200 were white with white top, white wheel covers, and white leather upholstery with red piping, dash and carpeting. A dash plaque confirmed the fact that it was one of the last--at least until the ragtop mysteriously re- emerged once again in the early '80s. Speculation sent prices way up. Their original $11,049 sticker price meant little as some "collectors" quickly began to snap up open Eldos at prices approaching $20,000. But before too long, prices fell almost as swiftly. Convertibles never really disappeared. Within months, various conversion manufacturers were slicing metal roofs off Caddy coupes to create custom convertibles. But the next regular production ragtop would be Chrysler's LeBaron in 1982. In most recent years, over 2,000 Fleetwood commercial chassis had been produced annually, for conversion to hearses and ambulances. Most of those conversions were done by three companies: Superior, Miller-Meteor, or Hess & Eisenhardt. In addition, stretch limousines were built on Cadillac chassis by Moloney (in Illinois) and Wisco (in Michigan), among other specialty firms.

1977 CADILLAC

Cadillac's 75th anniversary year arrived with a shock to traditionalists, as full-size models endured an eye-opening downsizing. "You must drive it," the ads declared, "to see why we call it the next generation of the luxury car." The new C-bodied DeVille, Brougham and limousine were 8 to 12 in. shorter, 3-1/2 in. narrower, and an average of 950 pounds lighter than their massive predecessors. Still, many models managed to keep the same leg room in front and rear (or even more). Only Eldorado carried on in its mammoth form a while longer, and Seville had entered life in 1975 with contemporary dimensions. Even the commercial chassis shrunk, from 157.5 down to 144.5 inches in wheelbase, requiring funeral car and ambulance suppliers to create some new bodies. All models except Seville carried a new lighter, smaller 425 cu. in. (7.0- liter) V-8 engine. That powerplant emerged as the result of testing 110 experimental engines. The huge 500 V-8 was gone. Electronic fuel injection was optional in DeVille, Brougham and Eldorado. Standard Turbo Hydra-matic fed power to low-ratio drive axles. Four-wheel disc brakes were standard on Seville, Eldorado and Brougham. Astroroofs and sunroofs were again available. Carryover special editions included Coupe and Sedan DeVille d'Elegance and Brougham 'Elegance. One new special edition joined the lineup: the Eldorado Custom Biarritz. All sedans now had pillars and framed door glass. (The "true" four-door hardtop was gone for good.) With Calais departed, DeVille took over as the cheapest Caddy (base price under $10,000). Dash gauges could be pulled out from the front for servicing. All models had a new two-spoke steering wheel--but those were wide spokes. A new door design offered better hold-open qualities. Anti-corrosion treatment on all models included zinc-rich primers, hot melt sealers, wax coating, Plastisol-R-, and deadeners. Cadillac also expanded the use of Zincrometal-R- and bi-metal (stainless steel on aluminum), corrosion-resistant inner front fender panels, and elimination of areas that trapped dirt and water. Wheels and tires were now match-mounted for smoothest ride.

SEVILLE — SERIES 6K — V-8 — Seville had been the first production American car to offer a 350 cu. in. electronic-fuel-injected engine as standard, and it returned for 1977. Sensors fed engine data back to an on-board analog computer under the dash, which in turn signalled the eight injectors how to meter the fuel charge from the constant-supply fuel rail. Added this year were standard four-wheel power disc brakes, a retuned suspension system, and Butyl rubber body mounts. Other standard features included variable ratio power steering (16.4 to 13.8), front and rear stabilizer bars, 15 in. wide-whitewall steel-belted radial tires, and automatic level control. Seville entered the model year wearing a new vertical grille, rectangular quad headlamps, and new amber parking/signal lamps. A total of 21 body colors were offered (15 standard and six extra-cost Firemist), plus 16 color- coordinated Tuxedo Grain padded vinyl tops (including metallic colors). Painted metal tops were also available, but most customers chose vinyl. A new Scan button on the AM/FM signal-seeking stereo radio allowed sampling of each station for six seconds. Seville's front end was similar to full-size Cadillacs, but the grille used only three horizontal divider bars and many vertical bars, forming vertical "holes." That tight grille pattern was repeated between the license plate holder and bumper guards. Four amber-lensed parking/signal lamps sat below the quad rectangular headlamps, with large cornering lamps on fender sides. Cadillac's crest was on the rear pillar; a Seville nameplate on front fenders between door and wheels. Atop the hood was a stand-up wreath/crest ornament. On the option list: wire wheel covers. Standard upholstery was smooth Dover cloth in claret, black, light gray, dark blue, medium sage green, light yellow-gold, light buckskin, or medium saffron. Optional was Sierra Grain leather in ten colors (including white). Standard fittings included power windows and door locks; tilt/telescope steering wheel; individual rear reading lamps; automatic parking brake release; and a new seat/shoulder belt combination. A chime warned that seat belts weren't buckled. Concealed wipers worked with a Controlled Cycle system. Body finishing used extensive hand work. Large-diameter Pliacell-R- shock absorbers were the same as those on the Cadillac limo. Bolts were epoxy-encapsulated to prevent loosening.

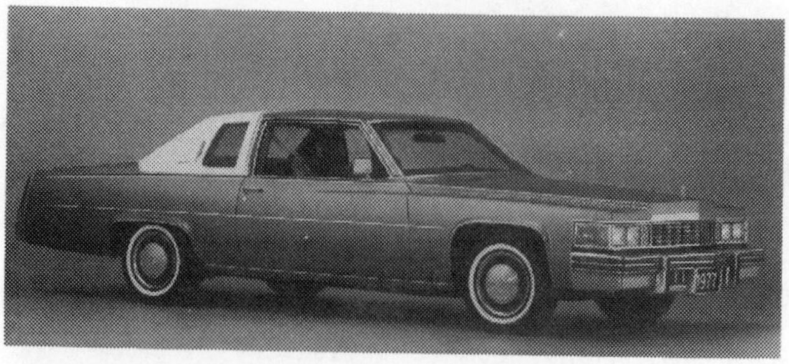

1977 Coupe deVille (C)

DEVILLE — SERIES 6C — V-8 — The new-generation Fleetwood/DeVille was, in Cadillac's words, "engineered from the ground up, to make more efficient use of space." That meant a new body, new chassis, new suspension, and new engine, in an integrated design. Trunk space grew larger. DeVilles gave more rear leg/headroom. Broughams (below) were just as spacious as before. DeVilles (and Fleetwoods) wore a new horizontal crosshatch grille with four horizontal and nine vertical divider bars, peaking forward at the center, topped by a 'Cadillac' script nameplate at the side of the wide upper bar. The grille pattern of wide holes was repeated down at the bumper, between the license plate and bumper guards. Small vertical parking/signal lamps just outside the grille, quad rectangular headlamps reaching all the way out to fender edges, and large cornering lenses at the side, were all the same height as the grille. That combination gave the whole front end a wide, uniform appearance that flowed into the bodysides. All that was topped off by a stand-up crest hood ornament. In sum, it carried on the traditional Cadillac look. Bodies had full rear wheel openings and vertical taillamps. New bumpers had dual rubber strip protective inserts. The new instrument panel had a "central control area" that allowed both driver and passenger to reach air conditioning, radio and accessory controls. Options included wire wheel discs, opera lamps, and accent stripes. Standard DeVille/Fleetwood equipment included wide- whitewall steel-belted radial tires, variable-ratio power steering (fixed ratio on limos), cornering lights, lamp monitors, power windows and door locks, Soft Ray tinted glass, three-speed wiper/washers, Freedom battery, digital clock, color-keyed litter container, six-way power driver's seat, center armrests, visor vanity mirror, and Turbo Hydra- matic transmission. Automatic climate control was redesigned so it operated only when necessary. Aberdeen cloth upholstery came in light yellow-gold, dark blue, medium saffron and claret. Ribbed Dynasty cloth came in six colors (including claret). Eleven other interior choices featured leather (including white). The standard AM/FM radio included an automatic power antenna. The DeVille d'Elegance special edition added pillow- style 50/50 Dual Comfort seats in Medici crushed velour cloth in claret, medium saffron, dark blue, or light buckskin color). Upper door pads, inserts in door pull straps and front seatback assist straps were also Medici cloth. Bodyside moldings held vinyl inserts that matched the body color. The Coupe deVille Cabriolet roof option came in 13 coordinated colors, with a Cadillac crest on the sail panel and bright roof moldings.

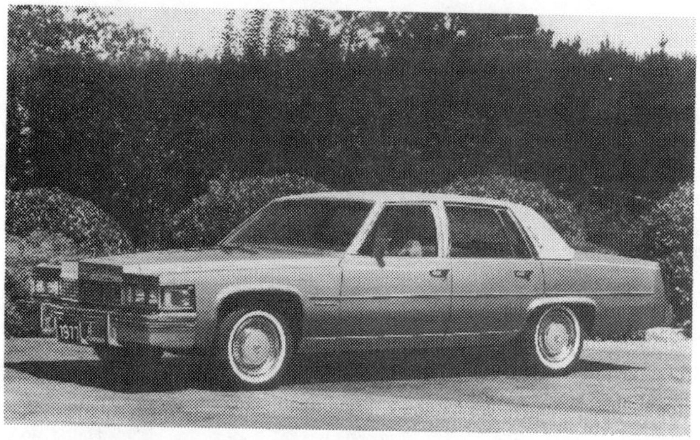

1977 Fleetwood Brougham pillared sedan (C)

FLEETWOOD BROUGHAM — SERIES 6C — V-8 — Billed as car "for very special people" (whatever that meant), the shrunken Brougham had a distinctively tapered center side pillar that leaned slightly backward, as well as a custom-trimmed small back window. Rocker panel moldings were wider, too. 'Fleetwood' block lettering appeared on the front fenders (just ahead of the door) and decklid. Otherwise, it looked much DeVille's sedan in the new downsized form. New engine was the 425 cu. in. (7.0-liter) V-8, and four-wheel disc brakes were standard. So was automatic level control. Wheelbase was now identical to DeVille (121.5 inches). Broughams displayed a distinctive roof treatment in Tuxedo Grain vinyl, with opera lamps, carpeted rear footrests, and one-piece wall-to-wall carpeting. New Florentine velour upholstery fabric came in medium saffron, light gray, dark blue, medium sage green, light yellow-gold, light buckskin or claret. Smooth-finish Dover fabric was offered in black, dark blue, light buckskin or claret. Standard 50/50 front seats had individual pull-down armrests and a six-way power adjustment for the driver (two-way for passenger). The AM/FM stereo radio included a signal-seeking scanner, and was available with 23-channel CB transceiver. Brougham d'Elegance came equipped with special contoured pillow-style seats trimmed in Florentine velour cloth (in light gray, dark blue, light buckskin, or claret). Upper door jambs and inserts in door pull straps and front seatback assist straps were also Florentine cloth. Also included were three roof-mounted assist straps, turbine-vaned wheel discs, 'd'Elegance' script on sail panel, and distinctive accent striping. Fleetwood Talisman was dropped.

FLEETWOOD LIMOUSINE — SERIES 6D — V-8 — Newly designed Fleetwood and Fleetwood Formal Limousines continued to serve as "flagships of the Cadillac fleet," but in sharply shrunken form. The contemporary edition was over a foot shorter and 900 pounds lighter. Large door openings allowed easy entry/exit. Automatic Climate Control could be operated from front or rear. A Dual Accessory Panel let passengers operate power windows and radio, or set temperature. Wheel covers could match any color. Both outside mirrors were remote-controlled. Upholstery choices included ark blue Florentine velour; light gray or black Dover cloth. Formal Limousines had black leather up front, plus a glass partition. Opera lamps were standard. Only 1,299 commercial chassis were turned out this year.

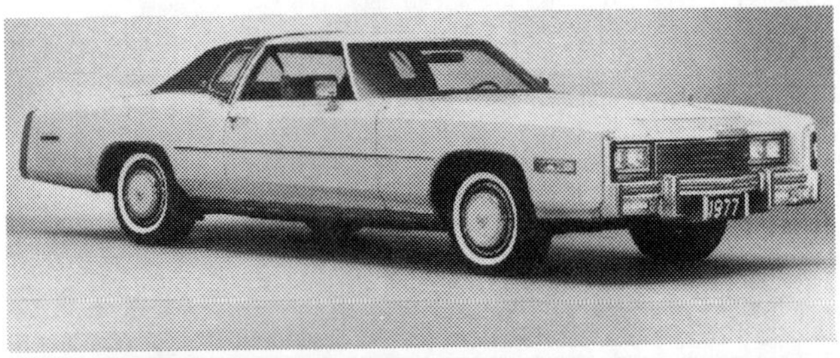

1977 Eldorado coupe (C)

ELDORADO — SERIES 6E — V-8 — Unlike the other full-size Caddies, Eldorado continued in its previous form (and elephantine size). A brushed chrome molding reached across the new coordinated horizontal-style grille and headlamps. This year's grille pattern featured more thin vertical bars than before and stood on a line with the headlamp tops. Individual 'Eldorado' block letters sat on the hood front, above the grille. Rear fenders held new rectangular side marker lamps, while new vertical taillamps formed into the bumper tips. Power four-wheel disc brakes had cooling fins. In the modified automatic climate control, the compressor ran only when needed. The $1760 Biarritz option (introduced during the 1976 model year) included a special fully-padded Elk Grain cabriolet roof, formal quarter and rear windows with French seams, and opera lamps. A matching vinyl insert accented the aluminum crossover roof molding. Stripes highlighted front fenders, doors and rear quarter panels. A script nameplate stood to the rear of quarter windows. Black-accented moldings ran from the hood front all the way back and around the roof. Sierra Grain leather covered contoured pillow seats.

I.D. DATA: All Cadillacs again had a 13-symbol Vehicle Identification Number (VIN) on the forward lower edge of the windshield frame, visible through the windshield. The first digit ('6') identifies the Cadillac Division. The second symbol denotes car line/series: 'S' Seville; 'D' DeVille; 'B' Fleetwood Brougham; 'F' Fleetwood limousine; 'L' Eldorado; 'Z' commercial chassis. Digits three and four indicate body type: '23' 4-dr. limousine w/auxiliary seat; '33' 4-dr. formal limousine with partition window; '47' 2-dr. coupe; '69' 4-dr. pillared sedan; '90' commercial chassis (number identifies name of body builder). Next comes the engine code: 'R' V8-350 EFI; 'S' V8-425 4Bbl.; 'T' V8-4250 EFI. Symbol six indicates model year ('7' 1977). Seventh is an assembly plant code: 'Q' Detroit; 'E' Linden, NJ. At the end is a six-digit sequence number, running from 100001 to 400000 for C-bodies and Eldos built in Detroit; from 450001 to 550000 for Sevilles from Detroit; and 600001 to 690000 for C-bodies built in Linden. A nine-digit derivative of the VIN appears on the engine. A Body Number Plate has codes for model year, model number, trim combination, body number (assembly plant and sequence built), paint color(s), and a number-letter code that shows the date built. That plate is mounted on the upper left cowl between hood rear seal and windshield except Eldorado, on left side of cowl next to hood rear bumper; and Seville, riveted to cowl above evaporator case.

SEVILLE

Series Number	Body/Style Number	Body Type & Seating	Factory Price	Shipping Weight	Production Total
6K	S69	4-dr Sedan-5P	13,359	4192	45,060

Note 1: In addition to amount shown, 1,152 Sevilles were built in Canada.

DEVILLE

6C	D47	2-dr Coupe-6P	9654	4186	138,750
6C	D69	4-dr Sedan-6P	9864	4222	95,421

FLEETWOOD BROUGHAM

6C	B69	4-dr Sedan-6P	11,546	4340	28,000

FLEETWOOD LIMOUSINE

6D	F23	4-dr Sedan-8P	18,193	4738	1,582
6D	F33	4-dr Fml Limo-7P	18,858	4806	1,032
6D	Z90	Commercial Chassis	N/A	N/A	1,299

ELDORADO

6E	L47	2-dr Coupe-6P	11,187	4955	47,344

ENGINES: BASE V-8 (Seville); 90-degree, overhead valve V-8. Cast iron block and head. Displacement: 350 cu. in. (5.7 liters). Bore & stroke: 4.057 x 3.385 in. Compression ratio: 8.0:1. Brake horsepower: 180 at 4400 R.P.M. Torque: 275 lbs.-ft. at 2000 R.P.M. Five main bearings. Hydraulic valve lifters. Electronic fuel injection (speed-density, port-type). Built by Oldsmobile. VIN Code: R. BASE V-8 (all except Seville): 90-degree, overhead valve V-8. Cast iron block and head. Displacement: 425 cu. in. (7.0 liters). Bore & stroke: 4.082 x 4.06 in. Compression ratio: 8.2:1. Brake horsepower: 180 at 4000 R.P.M. Torque: 320 lbs.-ft. at 2000 R.P.M. Five main bearings. Hydraulic valve lifters. Carburetor: 4Bbl. VIN Code: S. OPTIONAL V-8 (DeVille, Brougham, Eldorado): Same as 425 cu. in. V-8 above, but with electronic fuel-injection-- Horsepower: 195 at 3800 R.P.M. Torque: 320 lbs.- ft. at 2400 R.P.M. VIN Code: T.

CHASSIS DATA: Wheelbase: (Seville) 114.3 in.; (DeVille/Brougham) 121.5 in.; (Fleetwood limo) 144.5 in.; (Eldorado) 126.3 in. Overall length:- (Seville) 204.0 in.; (DeV/Brghm) 221.2 in.; (Fleetwood limo) 244.2 in.; (Eldo) 224.0 in. Height:- (Seville) 54.6 in.; (DeV cpe) 54.4 in.; (DeV sed) 55.3 in.; (Brghm) 56.7 in.; (Fleetwood limo) 56.9 in.; (Eldo) 54.2 in. idth:- (Seville) 71.8 in.; (Eldo) 79.8 in.; (others) 76.4 in. Front Tread:- (Seville) 61.3 in.; (Eldo) 63.7 in.; (others) 61.7 in. Rear Tread:- (Seville) 59.0 in.; (Eldo) 63.6 in.; (others) 60.7 in. Standard Tires:- (Seville/DeV) GR78 x 15-B SBR wide WSW; (Brghm) GR78 x 15-D SBR wide WSW; (Limo) HR78 x 15-D SBR wide WSW.

TECHNICAL: Transmission: Turbo Hydra-matic transmission standard on all models; column shift. Gear ratios: (1st) 2.48:1; (2nd) 1.48:1; (3rd) 1.00:1; (Rev) 2.07:1. Standard axle (final rive) ratio:- (Seville) 2.56:1, with 3.08:1 optional (std. at high altitude); (DeV/Brghm) 2.28:1, with 3.08:1 optional; (limo) 3.08:1. Hypoid rear axle except (Seville), Salisbury type. Steering:- variable-ratio, power assisted. Front suspension:- independent coil spring, link-type stabilizer exc. (Eldo) same as 1976. Rear suspension:- (Seville) Hotchkiss leaf spring, link-type stabilizer; (DeVille/Fleetwood) four-link drive, coil springs; (Eldo) same as 1976. Automatic level control (except DeVille). Body onstruction: (DeVille/Fleetwood) ladder type frame. Brakes:- front disc, rear drum except Brghm//Eldo/Seville, four-wheel disc. HEI electronic ignition. Fuel tank:- (Seville) 21 gal.; (DeV/Fleetwood) 24 gal.; (Eldo) 27.5 gal.

DRIVETRAIN OPTIONS: Fuel-injected V-8 engine: DeVille/Brougham/Eldo ($702). Heavy- duty cooling system ($43). 80-amp alternator ($47). California emission equipment ($70). Limited slip differential ($61); N/A on Eldorado. High altitude pkg. ($22). Trailering pkg.: SeV ($43); others ($90) exc. limo. Automatic level control: DeV ($100).

OPTION PACKAGES: Brougham d'Elegance ($885). Coupe deVille Cabriolet ($348); w/Astroroof ($1365); w/sunroof ($1169). DeVille d'Elegance ($650). Eldorado Cabriolet ($457); w/Astroroof ($1474); w/sunroof ($1278). Eldorado Custom Biarritz ($1760); w/Astroroof ($2777); w/sunroof ($2581).

CONVENIENCE/APPEARANCE OPTIONS: Astroroof for full vinyl roof ($938) exc. limos. Astroroof (painted): DeV/SeV/Eldo ($1043). Sunroof for full vinyl roof ($742) exc. limo. Sunroof (painted roof): DeV/SeV/Eldo ($846). Cruise control ($111). Controlled-cycle wipers ($30). Rear defogger, grid-type ($83). Six-way dual comfort power seat adjuster, passenger ($107-$138) exc. limo. Six-way power driver's seat adjuster: limo ($99). Power passenger 50/50 seat with six-way adjuster ($197-$248) exc. limo. Driver's 50/50 seat recliner ($110) exc. limo. Power passenger seatback recliner, notchback seat: DeV ($110). Tilt/telescope steering wheel ($109). Automatic door locks ($101). Illuminated entry system ($56). Fuel monitor ($28). Theft deterrent system ($123). Trunk lid release and power pull-down ($61-$73). Opera lamps: DeV ($60). Twilight Sentinel ($51). Guidematic headlamp control ($58). Trumpet horn ($20) exc. SeV. Remote-control right mirror ($32). Lighted thermometer on left mirror ($26). Lighted vanity mirror ($47). AM/FM stereo radio w/tape player: DeV/limo ($254); others ($100). AM/FM stereo radio w/digital display: DeV/limo ($254). AM/FM stereo radio w/CB: DeV/limo ($386); others ($230). Signal-seeking/scan AM/FM stereo radio ($156). Seek/scan AM/FM stereo radio w/rear control: limo ($326). Firemist paint ($153). Vinyl roof: DeV ($179); Eldo ($186). Bumper: DeV/Brghm/limo ($8). Accent stripes: DeV/Brghm ($45). Door edge guards ($8-$12). License frame: each ($7). Dual Comfort 50/50 front seats: DeV/Eldo ($187). Leather seats ($235-$252). Two-tone 50/50 dual comfort front seats: Eldo ($471). Twin floor mats ($13-$28) exc. Eldo. Floor mats, one- piece: Eldo front ($31); rear ($19). Trunk mat ($10). Turbine-vaned wheel covers ($49); N/A on Eldorado. Wire wheel covers: Brghm ($129); others ($176) exc. Eldo.

HISTORY: Introduced: September 23, 1976. Model year production (U.S.): 358,487 for a 3.9 percent share of the industry total. Calendar year production (U.S.): 369,254. Calendar year sales by U.S. dealers: 335,785 for a 3.7 percent market share. Model year sales by U.S. dealers: 328,129. Historical Footnotes: Cadillac executives didn't appreciate Ford's advertising claim that an LTD was now as good as a Cadillac. But the new smaller Caddies were selling well, at least at the beginning. Sales of 328,129 units scored 9.5 percent over the 1976 record. Model year production also beat the 1976 score, by 16 percent. Rumors early in the year suggested that Cadillacs might be "upsized" within a couple of years; but that didn't seem likely in view of the need to meet stricter Corporate Average Fuel Economy (CAFE) requirements. Now that the Fleetwood Seventy-Five was gone, conversion companies stepped up production of "stretch" limousines. Moloney Coachbuilders (in Illinois) offered a 40-inch stretch of Brougham for under $15,000 (plus the cost of the car, of course). Phaeton Coach Corp. of Dallas, and the California- based American Custom Coachworks, did similar work. The latter also created custom convertibles based on the Coupe deVille chassis, while an Ohio firm (Convertibles, Inc.) turned out ragtop Eldorado conversions.

1978 CADILLAC

Subtle exterior changes dominated the year, as wheelbases and dimensions were virtually identical to 1977. DeVille, Brougham, limo and Eldorado had a bolder horizontal crosshatch grille. All but Eldorado had new rear bumper ends with vertical taillamps and three-dimensional crest insignia. Most broughams, all California Cadillacs and the fuel- injected DeVille sedan sported aluminum hoods. After the start of production, Elk Grain vinyl tops would be used on all except Seville, which retained a padded Tuxedo Grain vinyl top. Passenger compartments had seven new interior colors and three new body cloths, including Random velour. Of the 21 body colors, 17 were new and all but two of those were exclusive to Cadillac. Signal-seeking AM/FM stereo radios were now standard on all Cadillacs. For the first time, chromed wire wheels from the British firm of Dunlop were offered as options on DeVille, Brougham and Seville models. New electronic level control (standard on all except DeVille) used a height sensor to signal a motor-driven compressor that automatically adjusted for changing loads. Transmissions had higher downshift speeds this year. DeVille and Brougham body mounts were retuned for a smoother, quieter ride. Four new special editions were offered: Seville Elegante, Phaeton Coupe (or Sedan) deVille, and revised Eldorado Custom Biarritz. An available diesel V-8 engine (built by Oldsmobile) for Seville was announced during the model year, at the Chicago Auto Show. So was a new electronic trip computer. All Cadillacs except Seville carried a standard 425 cu. in. V-8. Cadillac hardly tried to hide the boast that owning one had always "expressed success." As the full-line catalog modestly proclaimed, "calling something 'the Cadillac of its field' is one of the finest compliments you can pay a product."

SEVILLE — SERIES 6K — V-8 — At the rear, Seville displayed new bumper guards, an engraved chrome insignia on taillamps, and a painted accent stripe that extended across the decklid to give a wider, lower appearance. Lower bumper rub strips were body-colored. Seville's grille had vertical slots in four rows, with the pattern repeated in two openings on the bumper, alongside the license plate. Amber parking/signal lamps sat below the quad rectangular headlamps, with amber/clear cornering lamps on the fender sides. The Seville script was behind the front wheels; a Cadillac script at the back of rear fenders, just ahead of the angled wraparound taillamps, and on the upper grille bar (driver's side). Once again, the electronically fuel-injected 350 cu. in. V-8 engine was standard, with an on-board analog computer and new Electronic Spark Selection that altered spark advance to meet varying conditions. The intake manifold was lightweight aluminum. Oldsmobile's 350 cu. in. diesel V-8 became available in mid-year, first offered in seven major cities. Electronic load leveling was new this year. Standard equipment included a tilt/telescoping steering wheel, signal- seeking stereo radio, dual remote-control mirrors, fuel monitor system, power seat, power four-wheel disc brakes, controlled-cycle wipers, and many more luxuries. Sierra Grain leather

1978 Seville Elegante sedan (C)

1978 Fleetwood Brougham pillared sedan (C)

interiors came in ten colors. Dover cloth upholstery (seven colors) was standard. Buyers could choose either a matching metal roof or Tuxedo Grain padded vinyl top. Sevilles came in 15 standard body colors plus six Firemist options; the vinyl roof came in 16 colors including metallics. Options included real wire wheels as well as wire covers, plus opera lamps, a sunroof, 40-channel CB transceiver, plus electronically-tuned radios and tape player combinations. A new trip computer option offered 11 digital displays, including average speed and MPG, miles to destination, estimated arrival time, engine speed, coolant temp, and voltage. Seville Elegante was offered in two duo-tone body finishes: Platinum and Sable Black, or Western Saddle Firemist and Ruidoso Brown. Both had a painted metal top rather than vinyl. The second color began just above the beltline. Real wire wheels (not covers) had long-laced spokes. Full-length brushed chrome moldings had etched black grooving. An 'Elegante' script and crest were on the pillar behind the rear doors. Seats used perforated leather inserts (Antique Gray or Antique Medium Saddle) and soft, suede-like trim. Front seats were leather-wrapped to match. Front seats included storage pockets. A fold-down center armrest and console separated the driver and passenger. Compartments were provided for a telephone, tapes, and personal items. Only 5,000 or so Elegantes were built this year, but the special edition would remain for future seasons.

chromed wire wheels showed the Cadillac insignia on a hexagonal center hub. An electronic-tuning stereo radio with digital readout was available with 8-track tape player. The familiar Astroroof was available too. Brougham d'Elegance added contoured pillow-styled seats trimmed in Florentine velour (in five Antique colors), with velour trim in doors, pull straps and seatback assist straps. Medium Saddle leather was also available on the 50/50 Dual Comfort front seats. Plush pile carpeting reached up onto the lower doors, and covered front and rear floormats. A 'Brougham d'Elegance' insignia was on the glove box door; another outside. Also included: three above-door passenger assist grips, accent stripes, and available turbine-vaned wheel discs.

FLEETWOOD LIMOUSINE — SERIES 6D — V-8 — The twin posh "Flagships of the Cadillac fleet" carried styling alterations similar to the "lesser" Fleetwoods. New electronic leveling control was standard. Six-way power driver's seat controls were now in the door armrest. Standard limos sat eight. The seven-passenger Formal Limousine had a standard divided 45/45 front seat with black leather seating, plus a sliding glass partition. Both models had two additional fold-down seats. Florentine velour upholstery was offered in light gray, black, or dark blue. The Automatic Climate Control System could be operated by driver or passengers. A Dual Accessory Control Panel also let passengers operate the power windows--a logical decision, to be sure. A padded Elk Grain vinyl roof was standard. Not quite as many Formal limos were built as the standard variety. Chrome landau bars were available by special order. So were a full landau roof or cabriolet roof, both in padded Elk Grain vinyl. The landau option offered closed-in rear quarters and a smaller back window, as well as opera lamps.

1978 Coupe deVille (C)

DEVILLE — SERIES 6C — V-8 — Several styling refinements hit DeVille (and Fleetwood) for 1978. A new, bolder grille pattern in three-row checkerboard style was repeated to the left and right of the license plate below. The new pattern had fewer (and more square) holes than before. Cadillac's script was above the grille's header bar (mounted on the body), on the driver's side. A new solid-color wreath-and-crest ornament rode the hood. New, extra-slim vertical taillamps had thin backup lamps inset in the middle and built-in side marker lamps. Back bumpers were new. DeVille's padded vinyl roof had a custom-trimmed backlight. Rust-prevention measures included Zincrometal panels and bi-metal (stainless steel on aluminum) moldings, plus microencapsulated epoxy-coated screws in key areas. Underhood was the 425 cu. in. (7.0-liter) V-8 introduced the year before. Six-way power driver's seat controls were now in the door armrest. New interiors included seatback pockets. Standard on all models: an AM/FM Signal-Seeking stereo radio with scanner and disappearing antenna. Coupe and Sedan deVilles also had automatic climate control, power windows, and much more. Sunroof, wire wheel discs and 50/50 Dual Comfort seats were available. Nine interior color selections were offered in new Random velour or Hampton woven cloth. Up to a dozen Sierra Grain leather choices came with color-coordinated carpeting. Options included a custom-trimmed padded vinyl top, rear deck accent stripes, color-keyed bodyside moldings, chromed wire wheels, electronic leveling, and chrome accent moldings. Coupe deVille could have the Cabriolet roof package, including a chrome accent strip to highlight the Elk Grain vinyl top, Cadillac crests, and a French seam around the back windows--offered in 16 coordinated colors. A DeVille d'Elegance special edition featured pillow-style 50/50 Dual Comfort seats in new Random velour (antique dark green, light beige, light blue, or dark mulberry). Upper doors and front seatback assist straps wore matching Random velour. High-pile carpeting extended part way up the doors. The glove box door held a 'DeVille d'Elegance' insignia, as did the pillar behind back side windows. Hood, door and deck lid were striped. Side moldings held vinyl inserts that matched the body color. Other extras: opera lamps, three roof-mounted assist straps, and door pull handles. The d'Elegance trim package came in 21 body colors. Arriving later were Phaeton packages that featured a simulated convertible top (down to authentic-looking welts and stitching). Offered in Cotillion White, Platinum or Arizona Beige (with contrasting top colors), these were identified by 'Phaeton' nameplates on back fenders and wire wheels.

FLEETWOOD BROUGHAM — SERIES 6C — V-8 The most noticeable difference in appearance between Brougham and the less costly DeVille sedan lay in Brougham's distinctively tapered pillar design between front and rear doors. Brougham also stopped itself with four-wheel disc brakes. New this year were the restyled grille and back bumper, plus a weight-saving aluminum hood. Front seats now had seatback pockets. Brushed chrome moldings held new wreath-and-crest ornamentation. The Elk Grain vinyl roof held opera lamps just behind the back doors. Color-coordinated wheel discs repeated the body color in the center. Door-pull handles were new, and the door armrest held six-way power driver's seat controls. Brougham interiors held individual reading lamps. The Florentine velour interior was offered in mulberry, light gray, black, light blue, dark green, yellow, or light beige. Leather interiors came in 11 colors. Standard engine was the 425 cu. in. (7.0-liter) V-8. Oversized steel-belted radials ride match-mounted wheels. New standard equipment included electronic leveling control. Joining the option list were seven new interior colors, rear deck accent stripes, color-keyed bodyside moldings, and chrome accent moldings. Available

1978 Eldorado Biarritz coupe (C)

ELDORADO — SERIES 6E — V-8 — While waiting one more year for an all-new downsized body, Eldorado received no major change other than a revised crosshatch grille dominated by heavier horizontal bars. Also noteworthy on the outside was the padded Elk grain vinyl top. The four-row peaked checkerboard grille was flanked by quad rectangular headlamps. Amber parking lamps sat low on the bumper. The grille pattern was repeated between license plate and bumper guards, below the protruding protective strip. Massive chrome vertical bumper ends extended upward to form housings for auxiliary lamps, forming a huge bright extension of fender tips. Eldorado block letters stood above the upper grille bar, which tapered outward above the headlamps. Standard engine was the 425 cu. in. (7.0-liter) V-8, available with carburetor or fuel injection. Eldorados had four-wheel disc brakes, front-wheel drive, electronic level control, automatic climate control, power windows and door locks, cornering lights, six-way power seat, three-speed wipers, Freedom battery, and lamp monitors. What else? How about a trip odometer, wide-whitewall steel-belted radial tires, Soft Ray tinted glass, accent striping, remote control left-hand mirror, color-keyed litter container, vanity mirror, lighters, bumper impact strips, and a stowaway spare tire. Interiors might be Halifax knit in four colors, Random velour in choice of three, or a dozen Sierra Grain leather combinations. Dramatic two-tones were also available on Dual Comfort front seats, in three color combinations. Option included a 40-channel CB, 8-track tape player, Astroroof and sun roof. Eldorado Biarritz, which first appeared during the 1976 model year, now sported a convertible-like padded vinyl top, unique scripts, accent stripes, and distinctive chrome body moldings. Inside the Custom Biarritz were Sierra Grain leather contoured pillow-style seats in antique medium saddle, white, dark carmine, antique yellow, or antique light blue. The Cabriolet roof accented Eldo's distinctively-shaped quarter windows that tapered downward at the front, with a vinyl-insert molding across the fully padded Elk Grain vinyl top. Black-accented brushed stainless steel belt moldings stretched from rear to hood, terminating in a spearlike design at the front. Special stripes accented front fenders, doors and rear quarter panels. Biarritz came in five colors: Mediterranean Blue Firemist, Cotillion White, Carmine Red, Colonial Yellow, and Ruidoso Saddle. All had opera lamps, remote-control passenger-side mirror, and color-coordinated wheel discs. Customers also had the choice of a Custom Biarritz Classic, with two-tone paint scheme that not everyone found attractive.

I.D. DATA: Cadillac's 13-symbol Vehicle Identification Number (VIN) again was located on the forward edge of the windshield trim molding, visible through the windshield. Coding was similar to 1978. The model year code changed to '8' for 1978. Engine coding was now as follows: 'B' V8-350 EFI; 'S' V8-425 4Bbl.; 'T' V8-425 EFI; 'N' V8-350 diesel.

SEVILLE

Series Number	Body/Style Number	Body Type & Seating	Factory Price	Shipping Weight	Production Total
6K	S69	4-dr Sedan-5P	14,267	4179	56,985

DEVILLE

6C	D47	2-dr Coupe-6P	10,444	4163	117,750
6C	D69	4-dr Sedan-6P	10,668	4236	88,951

FLEETWOOD BROUGHAM

6C	B69	4-dr Sedan-6P	12,292	4314	36,800

FLEETWOOD LIMOUSINE

6D	F23	4-dr Sedan-8P	19,642	4772	848
6D	F33	4-dr Frml Limo-7P	20,363	4858	682
6D	Z90	Commercial Chassis	N/A	N/A	852

ELDORADO

6E	L47	2-dr Coupe-6P	11,921	4906	46,816

ENGINES: BASE V-8 (Seville): 90-degree, overhead valve V-8. Cast iron block and head. Displacement: 350 cu. in. (5.7 liters). Bore & stroke: 4.057 x 3.385 in. Compression ratio: 8.0:1. Brake horsepower: 170 at 4200 R.P.M. Torque: 270 lbs.-ft. at 2000 R.P.M. Five main bearings. Hydraulic valve lifters. Electronic fuel injection. Oldsmobile-built. VIN Code: B. BASE V-8 (All except Seville): 90-degree, overhead valve V-8. Cast iron block and head. Displacement: 425 cu. in. (7.0 liters). Bore & stroke: 4.082 x 4.06 in. Compression ratio: 8.2:1. Brake horsepower: 180 at 4000 R.P.M. Torque: 320 lbs.-ft. at 2000 R.P.M. Five main bearings. Hydraulic valve lifters. Carburetor: 4Bbl. VIN Code: S. OPTIONAL V-8 (DeVille, Brougham, Eldo): Same as 425 cu. in. V-8 above but with electronic fuel injection-- Horsepower: 195 at 3800 R.P.M. Torque: 320 lbs.- ft. at 2400 R.P.M. VIN Code: T. OPTIONAL DIESEL V-8: 90-degree, overhead valve V-8. Cast iron block and head. Displacement: 350 cu. in. (5.7 liters). Bore & stroke: 4.057 x 3.385 in. Compression ratio: 22.5:1. Brake horsepower: 120 at 3600 R.P.M. Torque: 220 lbs.-ft. at 1600 R.P.M. Five main bearings. Hydraulic valve lifters. Electronic fuel injection. Oldsmobile-built. VIN Code: N.

CHASSIS DATA: Dimensions same as 1977; see 1977 specifications. Standard Tires:- (Seville) GR78 x 15-B wide WSW; (DeVille) GR78 x 15-B wide WSW; (Brougham) HR78 x 15-B wide WSW; (Limo) HR78 x 15-D wide WSW; (Eldo) LR78 x 15-B.

TECHNICAL: Transmission: Turbo Hydra-matic transmission standard on all models; column shift. Gear ratios: (1st) 2.48:1; (2nd) 1.48:1; (3rd) 1.00:1; (Rev) 2.07:1. Standard axle ratio:- (Seville) 2.56:1 except high-alt. 3.08:1; (DeVille/Brougham) 2.28:1, with 3.08:1 available; (Limo) 3.08:1; (Eldo) 2.73:1 except high-alt. 3.07:1. Hypoid rear axle exc. (Seville) Salisbury type; (Eldo) spiral bevel. Steering/Suspension:- same as 1977. Brakes:- front disc, rear drum exc. Eldo/Seville/Brougham, four-wheel disc. HEI electronic ignition. Fuel tank:- (Seville) 21 gal.; (Eldo) 27 gal.; (others) 25.3 gal.

DRIVETRAIN OPTIONS: Fuel-injected V-8 engine: DeVille/Brougham/Seville ($744). Heavy-duty cooling system ($47). 80-amp alternator ($51). Engine block heater ($20). California emission equipment ($75). Limited slip differential ($67); N/A on Eldo. High altitude pkg. ($33). Electronic level control: DeV ($140). OPTION PACKAGES:- Brougham d'Elegance: cloth ($938); leather ($1270). DeVille Cabriolet ($369). DeVille Cabriolet w/Astroroof ($1450). DeVille Cabriolet w/sunroof ($1250). DeVille d'Elegance ($689). DeVille Custom Phaeton ($1929). Eldorado Cabriolet ($484). Eldorado Cabriolet w/Astroroof ($1565). Eldorado Cabriolet w/sunroof ($1365). Eldorado Custom Biarritz ($1865); w/Astroroof ($2946); w/sunroof ($2746). Eldorado Custom Biarritz Classic ($2466); w/Astroroof ($3547); w/sunroof ($3347). Seville Elegante ($2600); Elegante w/Astroroof ($3706); Elegante w/sunroof ($3506).

CONVENIENCE/APPEARANCE OPTIONS: Astroroof w/full vinyl roof ($995) exc. limos. Astroroof (painted): DeV/SeV/Eldo ($1106). Sunroof w/full vinyl roof ($795) exc. limo. Sunroof (painted roof): DeV/SeV/Eldo ($906). Cruise control ($122). Trip computer: Seville ($875). Controlled-cycle wipers ($32). Rear defogger, grid-type ($94). Six-way Dual Comfort power passenger seat adjuster ($118-$150). Power 50/50 seat recliner ($116). Power 50/50 passenger seat recliner ($210-$262). Power passenger seatback recliner, notchback seat: DeV ($116). Tilt/telescope steering wheel ($121). Automatic door locks ($114). Illuminated entry system ($59). Fuel monitor ($29). Theft deterrent system ($130). Trunk lid release and power pull-down ($80) exc. Seville. Trunk lid power pull-down: SeV ($67). Opera lamps: DeV/SeV ($63). Twilight Sentinel ($54). Guidematic headlamp control ($62). Trumpet horn ($21) exc. Seville. Remote- control right mirror ($34). Lighted thermometer on left mirror ($27). Lighted vanity mirror, passenger ($50). AM/FM stereo radio with digital display; ($106); w/tape player ($106); w/CB ($281); w/tape and CB ($427). Seek/scan AM/FM stereo radio with tape player and digital display: SeV/Brghm ($225). Seek/scan AM/FM stereo radio w/rear control: limo ($203). Firemist paint ($163). Padded vinyl roof: DeV/SeV ($215-$222). Front bumper reinforcement ($9) exc. Sev/Eldo. Chrome accent molding: DeV/Brghm ($85-$100). Accent stripes: DeV/Brghm ($53). Door edge guards ($11-$18). License frame: each ($9). Dual Comfort 50/50 front seats: DeV/Eldo ($198). Leather seating area ($295-$315); Eldo w/two-tone and 50/50 dual comfort front seats ($556). Carpeted rubber front floor mats ($31-$34); rear ($15-$21). Trunk mat ($12). Turbine-vaned wheel covers ($54); N/A on Eldo. Locking wire wheels ($541-$595). Locking wire wheel covers ($179-$233). Stowaway spare tire: limo (NC).

HISTORY: Introduced: September 29, 1977. Model year production (U.S.): 349,684 for a 3.9 percent share of the industry total and the second highest Cadillac total ever. Calendar year production (U.S.): 350,761. Calendar year sales by U.S. dealers: 350,813 for a 3.8 percent market share. Model year sales by U.S. dealers: 347,221.

Historical Footnotes: Record sales greeted Cadillac for the third year in a row. The model year total beat 1977's mark by 6 percent. The new Seville diesel (engine built by Oldsmobile) sold only about 2,800 copies, barely half the year's prediction. But it was introduced late in the model year. Sevilles in general hit a new production high. Eldorado did well also, as buyers snapped up the last of the vast Eldos before the 1979 downsizing. A three-month shutdown of the Linden, New Jersey plant, to tool up for the new E-body 1979 Eldorado, Toronado and Riviera models, contributed to a loss in calendar year production of DeVilles this year past. Cadillac asserted that the company "consistently leads all U.S. luxury car makes in repeat ownership. Once you own a Cadillac," they suggested, "it is difficult to accept anything less."

1979 CADILLAC

"For some," the 1979 catalog proclaimed, a Cadillac was "an integral part of the good life. For some...the fulfillment of a promise they made to themselves long ago." Could be, but apart from a daringly downsized E-body Eldorado, the year brought few stunning announcements. A new electronic-tuning AM/FM stereo radio with signal seeker and scanner included digital display of time and station frequencies. A new convex remote-control right mirror to increase the field of view was standard on Broughams and limos, optional on DeVilles. Lap seatbelts were the new "free-wheeling" style, and chimes now gently warned passengers to buckle up. A new dome light had dual spot map lamps. Seville and Eldorado could have an optional Trip Computer with digital display that showed average speed, miles yet to travel, engine speed, arrival time, and elapsed trip time. DeVilles, Fleetwood Broughams and limousines were powered by a 425 cu. in. (7.0-liter) V-8 with four-barrel carburetor. A fuel-injected version again was available. Oldsmobile's diesel V-8, first offered only on Seville and Eldorado, could go under DeVille/Brougham hoods by year's end. Options for the year included dual electric remote mirrors; an automatically-retracting radio antenna; plus -track and cassette tape players (with built-in 40-channel CB available).

1979 Seville Elegante pillared sedan (C)

SEVILLE — SERIES 6K — V-8 — Carried over with only modest trim changes, Sevilles got a retuned suspension to improve their ride, plus new body mounts. Nameplates moved from the upper right of the grille to the upper left, and that grille had a tighter pattern than before. The grille's pattern of vertical crosshatch slots was repeated in twin insets in the front bumper. Standard engine remained the 350 cu. in. (5.7-liter) V-8 with electronic fuel injection, now rated 170 horsepower. The diesel version introduced at mid-year was offered again. Sevilles destined for California received the three-way catalytic converter with closed-loop electronic controls, previously used only on other GM models. Bodies could have 14 standard colors, with seven Firemist colors available. Interiors came with new solid and striped Dante and Roma knit fabrics in six colors, or 11 shades of Sierra Grain leather. Either the Tuxedo Grain padded vinyl roof (in 17 colors, including metallics) or a plain metal top were offered at the same price. Options included the new digital trip computer and signal-seeking radios. Cadillac's catalog claimed that Seville had been chosen "one of the ten most beautifully designed production cars of the last 50 years." The special edition Elegante came in two-tone Slate Firemist and Sable Black, with accent striping and full- length side moldings with etched black grooving, plus a painted metal roof. Elegante was identified by a Cadillac wreath and crest as well as script nameplate. Standard were chrome-plated wire wheels with long-laced spokes. Seating areas and door panels had perforated leather inserts and suede-like vinyl trim, with leather-trimmed steering wheel. The Dual Comfort 40/40 seats had storage pockets and an integral fold-down center armrest. New for 1979 was plush fur-like Tangier carpeting. Elegante's price tag was $2735.

1979 deVille Special Edition Phaeton (C)

DEVILLE — SERIES 6C — V-8 — Appearance changes for DeVille/Fleetwood included restyled taillamps and a revised front-end look, plus new interior trim. This year's grille had many more horizontal and vertical bars in its simple crosshatch pattern, designed to accentuate the traditional Cadillac front end look. 'Cadillac' script returned this year to the wide upper grille bar (driver's side). A thin molding above the grille extended outward, over the headlamps, to wrap around each fender. Quad rectangular headlamps were outboard of twin vertical rectangular parking lamps. The crosshatch grille pattern repeated itself in twin rectangular openings in the bumper, on either side of the license plate, in familiar Cadillac style. Front fenders held large cornering lamps with clear and amber lenses. Seven new two-tone body color combinations were available for DeVille (and Fleetwood Brougham), with color-coordinated accent striping. New brushed chrome wheel covers showed the Cadillac crest on a black background. Also new: seatbelt chimes, a standard AM/FM stereo radio with digital display, dome light with dual spot map lamps, and optional electrically-controlled outside mirrors. Interiors were upholstered in Durand knit cloth (six colors) or genuine leather. Standard fittings included power door locks and windows, six-way power seat, and automatic climate control. The standard 425 cu. in. (7.0-liter) V-8 had new EGR riser tubes. A fuel-injected, 195-horsepower version was

optional. The Olds-built 350 cu. in. diesel V-8 became optional in mid-year. Special editions for 1979 included a Custom Phaeton Coupe and Custom Phaeton Sedan, both offering styling touches intended to remind observers of the "classic" convertibles. Features included brushed chrome moldings with flush-mounted opera lamps and the Cadillac crest; reduced-size quarter windows; a sporty convertible-like roof; 'Phaeton' script on each rear quarter panel; wire wheel discs; accent striping; 45/55 Dual Comfort front seats with leather seating; and leather-trimmed steering wheel. Phaeton editions came in three color combinations: Cotillion White with dark blue roof and white leather inside; Slate Firemist with black roof and antique slate gray leather upholstery; or Western Saddle Firemist with dark brown roof and antique saddle leather seating. Also on the option list was the DeVille d'Elegance, with new soft Venetian velour upholstery (in choice of four colors) on pillow-style 50/50 seats. It also had Tangier carpeting, special door pull handles, and 'DeVille d'Elegance' script on the glove box and exterior. Coupe d'Elegance had opera lamps; sedans had three roof-mounted assist straps. Both bodies had side moldings and accent stripes. Coupe deVille also came with a Cabriolet roof treatment, including chrome crossover roof molding, in 17 Elk Grain vinyl colors. A French seam surrounded the back window, and a Cadillac script and crest identified the Cabriolet model.

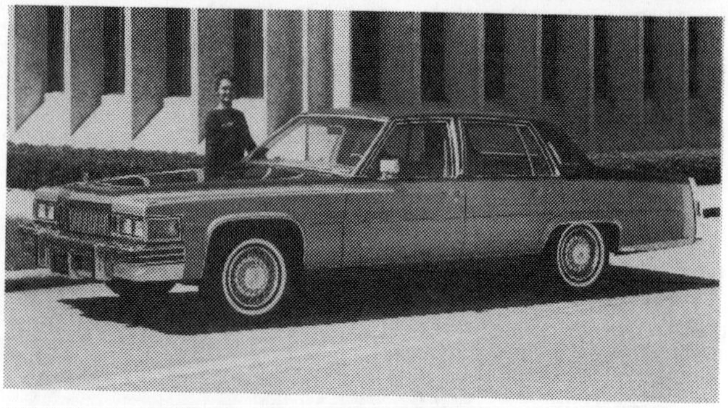

1979 Fleetwood Brougham d'Elegance pillared sedan (C)

FLEETWOOD BROUGHAM — SERIES 6C — V-8 – Brougham sedans had the same new front-end look and restyled taillamps as the less costly DeVille, and the same engine choices. New wheel covers of brushed chrome displayed the Cadillac wreath and crest on a dark red background. Dual comfort 45/55 front seats held three people. Upholstery was new slate gray Dante knit cloth. Genuine leather in 11 shades was also available. Tire pressure was raised to 32 psi, and engine recalibrated, to improve gas mileage. Brougham's suspension was retuned and body mounts were new. Inside were individual reading lamps and armrests. Broughams came with four-wheel disc brakes rather than DeVille's disc/drum combination. They also had a few distinctive styling touches to separate them from DeVilles. Pillars between front and rear doors tapered inward toward the beltline. Wide rocker panel moldings continued behind the rear wheels, stretching to the back bumper. Brougham d'Elegance carried new pillow-style seats in Dante and Roma knits, plus plush Tangier carpeting. Three roof-mounted assist straps, a choice of standard or turbine- vaned wheel covers, accent striping, and d'Elegance nameplate directly behind the rear side windows completed the package. Leather seating areas were also offered.

FLEETWOOD LIMOUSINE — SERIES 6D — V-8 - About 2,000 limos, offered in standard or Formal form, found buyers each year. Both had the same new crosshatch grille as Fleetwood Brougham, along with new simulated woodgrain interior, a lower profile, and revised two-spoke steering wheel. Fleetwood remained the only American-built chassis for use in "professional" cars used by funeral directors and for ambulances. The basic limo seated eight; the Formal edition, seven. Both were powered by the 425 cu. in. (7.0-liter) V-8, which had to haul over 4,800 pounds of car around. Standard interior was dark blue Dante cloth, but slate gray and black were available. Front compartment of the Formal limo was black, with black leather in seating areas, separated from the passenger compartment by a sliding glass partition. Interiors were also offered in slate gray and black. All limos included two fold-down auxiliary seats. There was a dual accessory control panel for climate control and windows, along with new optional rear seat controls for the radio. An optional 8-track tape player put controls in the back.

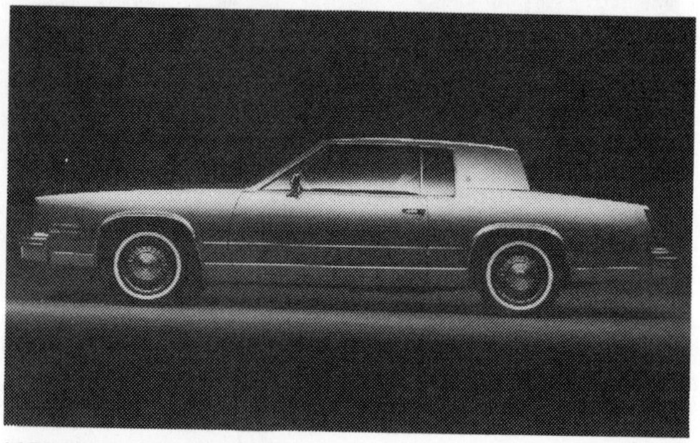

1979 Eldorado coupe (C)

ELDORADO — SERIES 6E — V-8 — Two years after other full-size Caddies were downsized, the personal-luxury coupe received similar treatment. Eldorado shrunk drastically in its new front-wheel drive form, down some 1,150 pounds in weight and 20 inches in overall length. Wheelbase was over a foot shorter at 114 inches, width narrower by more than 8 inches. Head and leg room managed to grow, though, in both front and rear seats. As before, Eldos included standard four-wheel disc brakes. But independent rear suspension was something new. The new space-efficient design also featured electronic level ontrol. Eldo's upright rectangular rear side windows also brought back the look of the recently-abandoned pillarless hardtop. Wide, squarish, closed-in rear quarters also helped give Eldo a distinctive appearance. Standard luxury touches included Twilight Sentinel headlamp control, automatic climate control, illuminated entry, and side window defoggers. New 50/45 Dual Comfort front seats came in 11 shades of leather, or pillow-style seating in new Dante knit cloth (six colors). The new instrument panel with driver-only controls on the left was simulated burl walnut. Steel-belted whitewall radial tires rode match-mounted wheels. A new flush-mounted windshield reduced wind noise. Standard dual outside mirrors were remote controlled (right mirror convex). New permanently-sealed wheel bearings never needed lubrication. Eldorado's boxy-looking crosshatch grille had rectangular openings and extended down into a cutaway portion of the bumper (not in two separate sections as on other full- size Cadillacs). Quad rectangular headlamps sat above horizontal park/signal lamps, with wide cornering lamps on the forward portion of the front fenders. An Eldorado script was on the trailing segment of the front fenders, as well as on the decklid. Narrow three-sided vertical taillamps were an Eldorado exclusive. Eldo still sported a familiar long hood and rather stubby trunk, and fender lines were similar to before. Lamp monitors and the instrument panel were restyled. Inside was a new Dual Comfort front seat with fold- down armrest and new seatback pockets, a new dome light with dual spot map lamps, plus a two-spoke steering wheel. New cast aluminum wheels were optional. So were wire wheel covers with locking device and electrically-controlled outside mirrors with lighted thermometer on driver's side. The optional Cabriolet roof was offered with or without padding. Base powerplant was now Seville's fuel-injected 350 cu. in. (5.7-liter) gasoline V-8. For the first time, the Olds- built 5.7-liter diesel V-8 was an Eldorado option. Eldorado Biarritz had a number of exclusive accents, including a Cabriolet roof treatment with new brushed stainless steel front roof cap and padded vinyl at the rear. The wide chrome crossover roof molding continued forward to the front fenders. Also in the package were new cast aluminum wheels, accent stripes, opera lamps, 'Biarritz' script, a tufted pillow-style interior in five shades of leather or in light blue Dante cloth, fur-like Tangier carpeting, individual rear seat reading lamps, and leather-trimmed steering wheel.

I.D. DATA: Cadillac's 13-symbol Vehicle Identification Number (VIN) was again on the upper left surface of the cowl, visible through the windshield. Coding was similar to 1977-78. The model year code changed to '9' for 1979. The body type code for Eldorado coupe changed to '57'. Assembly plant codes were: '9' Detroit; 'E' Linden, NJ (Eldorado only); and 'C' South Gate, CA (DeVille only). Sequence numbers began with 100001 at Detroit (except 450001 for Seville); 600001 at Linden; and 350001 at South Gate. Eldorado's body identification plate was on the top right side of the cowl. Diesel Seville body plates were on the top left side of the cowl.

SEVILLE

Series Number	Body/Style Number	Body Type & Seating	Factory Price	Shipping Weight	Production Total
6K	S69	4-dr Sedan-5P	15,646	4180	53,487

DEVILLE

6C	D47	2-dr Coupe-6P	11,139	4143	121,890
6C	D69	4-dr Sedan-6P	11,493	4212	93,211

FLEETWOOD BROUGHAM

6C	B69	4-dr Sedan-6P	13,446	4250	42,200

FLEETWOOD LIMOUSINE

6D	F23	4-dr Sedan-8P	20,987	4782	Note 1
6D	F33	4-dr Fml Limo-7P	21,735	4866	Note 1
6D	Z90	Commercial Chassis	N/A	N/A	864

Note 1: Total limousine production, 2,025.

ELDORADO

6E	L57	2-dr Coupe-4P	14,240	3792	67,436

ENGINES: BASE V-8 (Seville, Eldorado): 90-degree, overhead valve V-8. Cast iron block and head. Displacement: 350 cu. in. (5.7 liters). Bore & stroke: 4.057 x 3.385 in. Compression ratio: 8.0:1. Brake horsepower: 170 at 4200 R.P.M. Torque: 270 lbs.-ft. at 2000 R.P.M. Five main bearings. Hydraulic valve lifters. Electronic fuel injection. Oldsmobile-built. VIN Code: B. BASE V-8 (DeVille, Brougham, Fleetwood): 90-degree, overhead valve V-8. Cast iron block and head. Displacement: 425 cu. in. (7.0 liters). Bore & stroke: 4.082 x 4.06 in. Compression ratio: 8.2:1. Brake horsepower:180 at 4000 R.P.M. Torque: 320 lbs.-ft. at 2000 R.P.M. Five main bearings. Hydraulic valve lifters. Carburetor: 4Bbl. VIN Code: S. OPTIONAL V-8 (DeVille, Brougham): Same as 425 cu. in. V-8 above, with fuel injection-- Horsepower: 195 at 3800 R.P.M. Torque: 320 lbs.-ft. at 2400 R.P.M. VIN Code: T. OPTIONAL DIESEL V-8 (Seville, Eldorado, DeVille, Brougham): 90-degree, overhead valve V-8. Cast iron block and head. Displacement: 350 cu. in. (5.7 liters). Bore & stroke: 4.057 x 3.385 in. Compression ratio: 22.5:1. Brake horsepower: 125 at 3600 R.P.M. Torque: 225 lbs.-ft. at 1600 R.P.M. Five main bearings. Hydraulic valve lifters. Fuel injection. Oldsmobile-built. VIN Code: N.

CHASSIS DATA: Wheelbase: (Seville) 114.3 in.; (DeVille/Brougham) 121.5 in.; (Limo) 144.5 in.; (Eldorado) 113.9 in. Overall length:- (Seville/Eldo) 204.0 in.; (DeV/Brghm) 221.2 in.; (Limo) 244.2 in. Height:- (Seville) 54.6 in.; (DeV cpe) 54.4 in.; (DeV sed) 55.3 in.; (Brghm) 56.7 in.; (Limo) 56.9 in.; (Eldo) 54.2 in. idth:- (Seville) 71.8 in.; (Eldo) 71.4 in.; (others) 76.5 in. Front Tread:- (Seville) 61.3 in.; (Eldo) 59.3 in.; (others) 61.7 in. Rear Tread:- (Seville) 59.0 in.; (Eldo) 60.5 in.; (others) 60.7 in. Standard Tires:- (Seville) GR78 x 15-B SBR wide WSW; (Eldo) P205/75R15 SBR wide WSW; (DeV) GR78 x 15-B SBR wide WSW; (Brghm) HR78 x 15-B SBR wide WSW; (Limo) HR78 x 15-D SBR wide WSW.

TECHNICAL:- Transmission: Three-speed Turbo Hydra-matic transmission standard on all models; column shift. Eldorado/Seville gear ratios: (1st) 2.74:1; (2nd) 1.57:1; (3rd) 1.00:1; (Rev) 2.07:1. Other models: (1st) 2.48:1; (2nd) 1.48:1; (3rd) 1.00:1; (Rev) 2.07:1. Standard axle ratio:- (Seville) 2.24:1; (Eldo) 2.19:1; (DeV/Brghm) 2.28:1; (limo) 3.08:1. Steering:- recirculating ball. Front suspension:- (Eldo) independent transverse torsion bars, link stabilizer bar; (others) independent with ball joints and coil springs, stabilizer bar. Rear suspension:- (Eldo) independent trailing arm; (Seville) Hotchkiss 56 in. leaf springs, five leaves, link stabilizer; (others) four-link coil springs, link stabilizer. Electronic level control (except DeVille). Brakes:- front disc, rear drum except Brougham/Seville/Eldo, four-wheel disc. HEI electronic ignition. Fuel tank:- (Seville/Eldo) 19.6 gal.; (others) 25 gal.

DRIVETRAIN OPTIONS: 425 cu. in. V-8 FI engine: DeV/Fleetwood ($783). 5.7-liter diesel V-8 engine: Seville/Eldo ($287); DeV/Brghm, later in model year ($849). Heavy-duty cooling system ($49). 80 amp alternator ($54). Engine block heater ($21). California emission equipment ($83-$150). California fuel economy equipment: DeV/F.W. ($65). Limited slip differential ($70); N/A on Eldo. High altitude pkg. ($35). Electronic level control: DeV ($160). Trailering package ($49-$103).

OPTION PACKAGES: Brougham d'Elegance: cloth ($987); leather ($1344). DeVille Cabriolet ($384). DeVille Cabriolet w/Astroroof ($1522). DeVille Cabriolet w/sunroof ($1312). DeVille d'Elegance ($725). DeVille Custom Phaeton ($2029). Eldorado Cabriolet ($350). Eldorado Cabriolet w/Astrcroof ($1488). Eldorado Cabriolet w/sunroof ($1278). Eldorado Biarritz: leather seating ($2600); cloth ($2250). Eldorado Biarritz w/Astroroof: leather seating ($3738); cloth ($3388). Seville Elegante ($2735). Seville Elegante w/Astroroof ($3873). Seville Elegante w/sunroof ($3663).

CONVENIENCE/APPEARANCE OPTIONS: Astroroof (w/full vinyl roof): DeV/F.W./SeV ($998). Astroroof (painted): DeV/SeV/Eldo ($1163). Sunroof (full vinyl roof): DeV/F.W./SeV ($798). Sunroof (painted roof): DeV/SeV/Eldo ($953). Cruise control ($137). Controlled-cycle wipers: DeV/limo ($38). Rear defogger, grid-type ($101). Six-way Dual Comfort power passenger seat adjuster ($125-$160). Power driver's seat recliner ($122). Power passenger seat recliner with six-way adjuster ($221-$280). Power passenger seatback recliner, bench seat: DeV ($122). Tilt/telescope steering wheel ($130). Automatic door locks ($121). Illuminated entry system: DeV, limo ($62). Fuel monitor ($31). Trip computer: Seville ($920). Theft deterrent system ($137). Trunk lid release and power pull-down: DeV/limo ($85). Opera lamps: DeV/SeV ($66). Twilight Sentinel: DeV/limo ($56). Guidematic headlamp control ($91). Trumpet horn ($22). Remote-control right mirror: DeV ($40). Electric remote left mirror w/thermometer ($90). Lighted thermometer on left mirror ($28). Lighted vanity mirror, passenger ($52). Electronic- tuning seek/scan AM/FM stereo radio with 8-track tape player ($195); w/8-track and CB ($480); w/cassette ($225); w/CB ($380). Electronic-tuning seek/scan AM/FM stereo radio with 8-track player, rear control: limo ($398). Two-tone paint, partial Firemist ($361). Firemist paint ($171). Padded vinyl roof: DeV ($225). Front bumper reinforcement ($9). Chrome accent molding: DeV ($90-$105). Accent stripes: DeV/F.W. ($56). Door edge guards ($13-$20). License frame: each ($10). Dual comfort front seats: DeV ($208). Leather seating area ($330-$350). Carpeted rubber front floor mats ($33-$36); rear $16). Trunk mat ($13). Turbine-vaned wheel covers ($59); N/A on Eldo. Aluminum wheels ($350); N/A on Eldo. Locking wire wheels: DeV/SeV/F.W. ($569-$628). Locking wire wheel covers ($189-$292).

HISTORY: Introduced: September 28, 1978. Model year production (U.S.): 381,113 for a 4.1 percent share and a new record. Calendar year production (U.S.): 345,794. Calendar year sales by U.S. dealers: 314,034, which amounted to a 3.8 percent market share. Model year sales by U.S. dealers: 328,815.

Historical Footnotes: DeVilles this year were built at South Gate, California. The DeVille Phaeton's simulated convertible top was hardly likely to satisfy real ragtop fans who could afford the price of one of the re-manufactured versions. One such conversion by Hess & Eisenhardt, called "Le Cabriolet," was marketed through Cadillac dealers. Like other GM divisions, Cadillac had high expectations for diesel power, but that phenomenon was destined to evaporate in the next half-dozen years.

1980 CADILLAC

"Through the years," boasted the 1980 full-line catalog, "Cadillac has earned for itself an exclusive place...a solitary niche...in the pantheon of the world's truly fine automobiles." Readers were even reminded how Cadillac had twice won the DeWar trophy in the early years of the century, first for its use of interchangeable parts and, later, for pioneering the electric self-starter. This year brought a restyled Brougham and DeVille, with a more formal roofline that gave more space in back. Their new grille was supposed to boost aerodynamic efficiency too. Flush-mounted windshields on Eldorado and Seville added style and helped cut wind noise. Suspension refinements included low-friction ball joints and larger bushings, plus new low- rolling-resistance tires. New options: a three-channel garage door opener and heated outside mirrors. On the engine roster, the 368 cu. in. (6.0-liter) V-8 with four-barrel carburetor was standard on Fleetwood Brougham, DeVille and limousines. A digital fuel-injected version (with computerized self-diagnostic features) was standard on Eldorado, a no-cost option for Seville. The DFI V-8's memory turned on an "Engine Check" light to warn of malfunctions. Meantime, the engine's microprocessor could make substitutions that might allow the car to continue to run. An MPG Sentinel calculated continual, average and instantaneous miles-per-gallon readings at the touch of a button. Rounding out the lineup, Seville's standard 5.7-liter diesel V-8, manufactured by Oldsmobile, was also available under the hood of Eldorado, DeVille and Fleetwood Brougham. Late in the model year, a Buick 4.1-liter V-6 was added--the first such offering on a Cadillac, and the first engine other than a V-8 in six decades. Body colors for 1980 were: Cotillion White; Platinum; Sable Black; Steel Blue; Superior Blue; Twilight Blue; Canyon Rock; Princess Green; Blackwatch Green; Colonial Yellow; Flax; Sandstone; Columbian Brown; Bordeaux Red; Saxony Red; and Norfolk Gray. At extra cost, buyers could have any of five Firemist colors: Azure Blue, Desert Sand, Victoria Plum, Sheffield Gray, or Western Saddle. For rust protection, over 100 areas were specially treated. All lower body exterior panels were made from pre-coated metals. Each point of metal- to-metal contact contained either a gasket or bi-metal molding. All bodies were dipped in electrically charged primer to increase bonding adhesion.

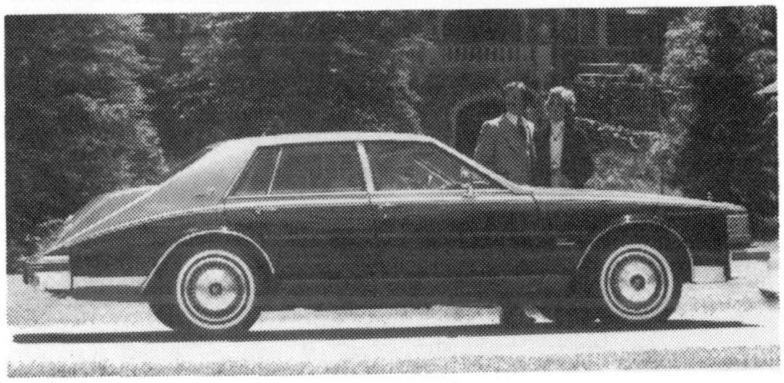

1980 Seville Elegante pillared sedan (AA)

SEVILLE — SERIES 6K — V-8 — Billed in the full-line catalog as "quite possibly the most distinctive car in the world today...and the most advanced," the all-new Seville was nothing if not dramatic. A total redesign gave buyers more interior space and trunk volume, along with the radical body shape. The side view was the most striking, even on the standard Seville with its straight bodyside molding. The humped deck lid began almost horizontal, but hit a distinctive horizontal crease before tapering down to wide taillamps. Small lenses were inset into the new one-piece, high-strength back bumper: two at the rear and two at the sides. The license plate sat in a deeply recessed housing. On the deck lid were Cadillac's wreath and crest, plus the Seville script. Both emblems were repeated on the back roof pillar. The Seville script was also on front fenders, just below the thin bodyside molding. Chrome rocker moldings were tall and strong. Designed by Wayne Cady, the bustleback body and long hood suggested more than a nodding acquaintance with the impressive old razor-edge styling used on Hooper and Vanden Plus Rolls-Royces in the 1950s. Not everyone loved Seville's bustleback shape, with sloping rear end and "boot" trunk, but it drew considerable attention. Wheelbase was 114 inches; length almost 205 inches; overall dimensions not much different than the 1979 edition. Running gear and front-drive chassis were shared with the other luxury E-body coupes: Eldorado, Buick Riviera, and Olds Toronado. But Seville hardly resembled its mechanical mates. Up front, the squared-off look was similar to earlier Sevilles. The front end was lower, and the car weighed 300 pounds less than before. The new yet traditional grille consisted of narrow vertical bars and a wide horizontal header bar with 'Cadillac' script at the side, plus a stand- up wreath and crest at the hood front. The windshield sat at a sharp angle. Rounded, flared wheel openings housed new all- weather radial tires on new cast aluminum wheels with brushed-chrome centers. Bodies came in a choice of 16 acrylic lacquer finishes with accent striping (plus two-tone treatments). Dual Comfort 50/45 front seats were offered in six shades of Heather cloth. Going beyond appearance, Seville was also described as an "electronic wonder." The new version was viewed as a "test" for other GM vehicles. Among other details, Seville was the first to offer a diesel as "standard" powerplant (except in California). The *optional* engine was a 6.0-liter gasoline V-8 with single-point fuel injection (heavy on digital electronics), which gave better cold-start performance and lower emissions. Front-wheel drive kept the floor flat, to add roominess. Sevilles had a new four-wheel independent suspension and disc brakes all around. All models had electronic level control, new electronic climate control, electrically-controlled outside mirrors (heated, with lighted thermometer), cruise control, and a rear defogger. Also standard: tungsten-halogen high-beam headlamps, Twilight Sentinel, side window defoggers, tilt/telescope steering wheel, Soft Ray tinted glass, a new high-pressure compact spare tire, cast aluminum wheels, illuminated entry system, new dual-spot map lamps/courtesy lights, and much more. Seek/scan radios were improved. Inside was an accessible center-console instrument display with digital MPG readouts. Stepping up a notch, an Elegante option made Seville's profile even sharper and more distinctive, as a sweeping French curve separated the two-tone upper and lower body colors. The full-length beltline molding swept downward aft of the back door, into the bustle-shaped back end, and the upper color tapered to a point at the base of the humped deck lid. Chrome-plated 'Elegante' script was on the sail panels. Also included was accent striping and a stand-up wreath/crest on the hood. Elegante came in three color combinations: Sable Black with Sheffield Gray Firemist, Sheffield Gray Firemist with Norfolk Gray, or Canyon Rock with Desert Sand Firemist. Other features were a leather-trimmed steering wheel, 40/40 Dual Comfort front seats, and leather-topped console with space for umbrella. Interiors were tailored in light beige or slate gray leather. The new simulated teak woodgrain instrument panel, with driver-only controls on the left, was said to have the look of Butterfly Walnut. Ads referred to "The Beauty of Being First" and dubbed Seville the car "that looks like no other car." William L. Mitchell, who retired as GM's design vice- president in 1977 but was responsible for Seville, insisted it was "destined to be tomorrow's style leader."

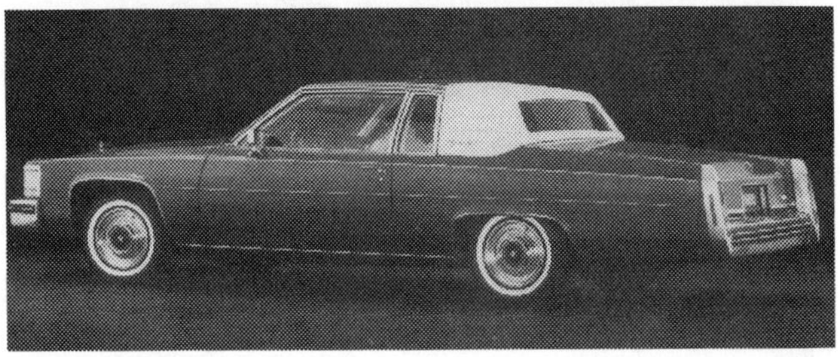

1980 Coupe deVille (AA)

DEVILLE — SERIES 6C — V-8 — Aerodynamic alterations gave DeVilles a more streamlined profile this year. The new, traditional-style "isolated" grille was made up of narrow vertical bars, peaked forward at the center. A Cadillac script was on the side of the heavy upper header. New flush-mount quad rectangular headlamps stood above new amber-lensed horizontal parking/signal lamps. Matching cornering lamps consisted of a large rectangular lens over a small horizontal one: one followed the line of the headlamps, the other wrapped around in line with the signal lamps. Wheel openings showed a squared-off, formal look. The rear roof pillar held a Cadillac 'V' and crest, plus script nameplate. New wheel covers displayed Cadillac's crest on a dark red background. DeVilles came in 21 body colors. Both DeVille and Brougham had a stiffer roof profile this year, with a sharpened crease line running the full length of the side. Decklids also had a higher profile, with beveled rear surface. The new roofline added two inches of legroom in the back seat. Base engine was the 368 cu. in. (6.0-liter) carbureted V-8, with 5.7-liter diesel available. Standard features included a convex remote-control right-hand mirror, simulated teak on instrument panel, and new dual-spot map lamps/courtesy lights. Durand knit cloth upholstery came in six colors, with Renaissance velour inserts. Leather seating areas came in ten colors. Options included heated side mirrors (available with rear defogger), Astroroof, self- sealing tires, six radio choices, and advanced theft- deterrent system. Coupe deVille was also offered with a dramatic Cabriolet roof that featured a chrome crossover roof molding. That came in 15 colors of Elk Grain vinyl, with French seam surrounding the back window. DeVille's D'Elegance had textured Venetian velour upholstery in any of four colors, plus Tampico carpeting, special door pull handles, and 'DeVille d'Elegance' script on the glove compartment. The body held accent stripes and another nameplate. Opera lamps were standard on the coupe, three roof-mounted assist straps on the sedan.

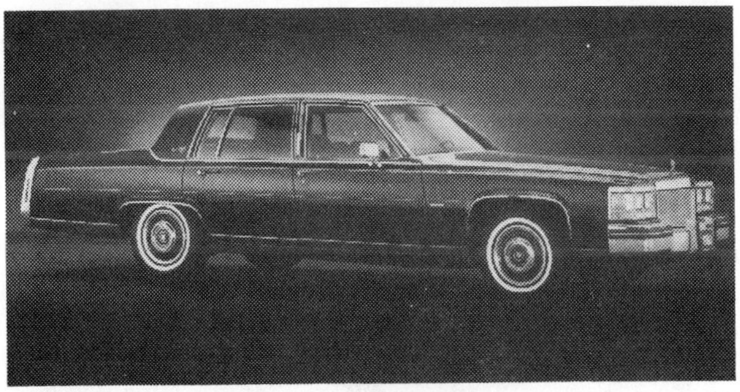

1980 Fleetwood Brougham pillared sedan (AA)

FLEETWOOD BROUGHAM — SERIES 6C — V-8 — Noticeable immediately on the "Cadillac of Cadillacs" was an exclusive new limousine-style, closed-in back window. Center pillars held new electro-luminiscent opera lamps, just above the beltline. New wheel covers with silver-colored vaned inserts contained the Cadillac wreath and crest on a dark red background. New body trim included a distinctive wide rocker molding that continued onto the rear quarter panels. The familiar tall chrome rear fender caps held integral marker lights, around the corner from the vertical taillamps. On the hood: a stand-up wreath and crest ornament. Brougham also had chrome belt moldings. Standard equipment included a Twilight Sentinel that turned headlamps on/off, illuminated entry system, six-way power Dual Comfort front seats, adjustable rear reading lamps, large door pull handles, and tilt/telescope steering wheel. Brougham interiors had new biscuit sculptured seats with bolsters, with embroidered Cadillac wreath on front and rear armrests. Upholstery was Heather knit with Raphael inserts, in slate gray, dark blue, dark green, saddle, light beige, or dark claret. Leather seating was optional in ten shades. At mid-year, a Brougham coupe joined the sedan. Its cabriolet-style roof contained a coach window, plus a chrome molding across the top. Opera lamps shined from each sail panel. Brougham d'Elegance emphasized the privacy window treatment, with the rear quarter panel wrapping around to the small, limo-like back window. Inside and on the sail panel was a d'Elegance script nameplate. Standard pillow-style 50/50 Dual Comfort seats combined Heather and Raphael knits. Leather was also available at higher cost.

FLEETWOOD LIMOUSINE — SERIES 6D — V-8 — Once again, the big Fleetwoods came in Limousine and Formal Limousine form, with dual accessory control panels. Interiors of the basic limo were upholstered in dark blue Heather cloth. Formal limos carried black leather upholstery up front, and either black or slate gray in back. All had two fold-down auxiliary seats. Opera lamps were now on the rear roof panels, behind the quarter windows. Deeply concave wheel covers had red inserts and Cadillac's wreath-and-crest.

ELDORADO — SERIES 6E — V-8 — Downsized the year before, Eldorado entered 1980 with few significant changes beyond a bolder crosshatch grille pattern, dominated by vertical bars. Its upper horizontal bar, with Cadillac script, peaked forward and upward. Quad rectangular headlamps sat above amber-lensed parking/signal lamps, with wide horizontal cornering lamps on the fenders. An Eldorado script was behind the front wheel openings, just above the bodyside molding. Wide rocker panel moldings stretched all the way front to rear. Atop the hood was a Cadillac wreath and crest. New two-tone paint schemes were offered. Multi-slot style wheel covers were standard. So was Heather knit-cloth pillow-type front upholstery, offered in six colors for the Dual Comfort 50/45 front seats (for two people). Customers could also select from 10 leather possibilities. The instrument panel featured simulated teak woodgrain. Eldorado enjoyed an improved EPA fuel mileage rating as a result of the 6.0-liter V-8 with electronic fuel injection. A new MPG Sentinel was available with the DFI engine, which also offered new on-board computer diagnostics. New Electronic Climate Control offered digital accuracy. An optional Cabriolet roof of textured Elk Grain vinyl came in 15 colors, including matching Firemist shades. The optional theft-deterrent system now disabled the starter motor. Eldorado Biarritz rode cast aluminum wheels and carried a number of unique styling accents, including an exclusive brushed stainless steel front roof section. The wide chrome molding crossing over that roof continued all the way to the front fenders. Biarritz script and opera lamps enhanced the rear roof pillars, and the model also featured accent stripes. Inside, the tufted pillow-sytle interior came in seven leather choices; or slate gray Heather knit fabric. The steering wheel was leather-trimmed. Biarritz carried a price tag of $18,003, compared to $15,509 for a base Eldo.

I.D. DATA: For the last time, Cadillacs had a 13-symbol Vehicle Identification Number (VIN) on the upper left surface of the cowl, visible through the windshield. Coding was similar to 1978-79. The code for model year changed to 'A' for 1980. Engine codes changed to the following: '8' V8-350 FI; '6' V8-368 4Bbl.; '9' V8-368 DFI; 'N' V8-350 diesel.

SEVILLE (DIESEL V-8)

Series Number	Body/Style Number	Body Type & Seating	Factory Price	Shipping Weight	Production Total
6K	S69	4-dr Sedan-5P	19,662	3911	39,344

DEVILLE

6C	D47	2-dr Coupe-6P	12,401	4048	55,490
6C	D69	4-dr Sedan-6P	12,770	4084	49,188

FLEETWOOD BROUGHAM

6C	B47	2-dr Coupe-6P	14,971	4025	2,300
6C	B69	4-dr Sedan-6P	14,927	4092	29,659

FLEETWOOD LIMOUSINE

6D	F23	4-dr Sedan-8P	22,586	4629	Note 1
6D	F33	4-dr Fml Limo-7P	23,388	4718	Note 1
6D	Z90	Commercial Chassis	N/A	N/A	750

Note 1: Total limousine production, 1,612.

ELDORADO

6E	L57	2-dr Coupe-4P	15,509	3806	52,683

PRICE NOTE: Cadillac announced a series of price rises during the model year. By summer, Seville cost $20,796; Deville coupe $13,115; Brougham sedan $15,816; Formal limo $24,714; and Eldorado $16,401.

ENGINES: BASE DIESEL V-8 (Seville); OPTIONAL (DeVille, Brougham, Eldorado): 90-degree, overhead valve V-8. Cast iron block and head. Displacement: 350 cu. in. (5.7 liters). Bore & stroke: 4.057 x 3.385 in. Compression ratio: 22.5:1. Brake horsepower: 105 at 3200 R.P.M. Torque: 205 lbs.-ft. at 1600 R.P.M. Five main bearings. Hydraulic valve lifters. Fuel injection. Oldsmobile-built. VIN Code: N. BASE V-8 (DeVille, Brougham, Fleetwood): 90-degree, overhead valve V-8. Cast iron block and head. Displacement: 368 cu. in. (6.0 liters). Bore & stroke: 3.80 x 4.06 in. Compression ratio: 8.2:1. Brake horsepower: 150 at 3800 R.P.M. Torque: 265 lbs.-ft. at 1600 R.P.M. Five main bearings. Hydraulic valve lifters. Carburetor: 4Bbl. VIN Code: 6. BASE V-8 (Eldorado); OPTIONAL (Seville): Same as 368 cu. in. V-8 above, but with digital fuel injection-- Horsepower: 145 at 3600 R.P.M. Torque: 270 lbs.- ft. at 2000

R.P.M. VIN Code: 9. BASE V-8 (Eldorado--California): 90-degree, overhead valve V-8. Cast iron block and head. Displacement: 350 cu. in. (5.7 liters). Bore & stroke: 4.057 x 3.385 in. Compression ratio: 8.0:1. Brake horsepower: 160 at 4400 R.P.M. Torque: 265 lbs.-ft. at 1600 R.P.M. Five main bearings. Hydraulic valve lifters. Fuel injection. VIN Code: 8.

CHASSIS DATA: Wheelbase: (Seville/Eldo) 114.0 in.; (DeVille/Brougham) 121.4 in.; (Limo) 144.5 in. Overall length:- (Seville) 204.8 in.; (DeV./Brghm) 221.0 in.; (Limo) 244.1 in.; (Eldo) 204.5 in. Height:- (Seville) 54.3 in.; (DeV cpe) 54.6 in.; (DeV sed) 55.6 in.; (Brghm) 56.7 in.; (Limo) 56.9 in.; (Eldo) 54.2 in. Width: (Seville) 71.4 in.; (Eldo) 71.5 in.; (others) 76.4 in. Front Tread:- (Seville/Eldo) 59.3 in.; (others) 61.7 in. Rear Tread:- (Seville/Eldo) 60.6 in.; (others) 60.7 in. Standard Tires:- (Seville) P205/75R15 SBR wide WSW; (DeV/Brghm) P215/75R15 SBR wide WSW; (Limo) HR78 x 15-D SBR wide WSW; (Eldo) P205/75R15 SBR wide WSW.

TECHNICAL: Transmission:- Turbo Hydra-matic transmission standard on all models: column shift. Gear ratios for DeVille/Brghm w/V8-368: (1st) 2.48:1; (2nd) 1.48:1; (3rd) 1.00:1; (Rev) 2.07:1. Other models: (1st) 2.74:1; (2nd) 1.57:1; (3rd) 1.00:1; (Rev) 2.07:1. Standard final drive ratio:- (Seville) 2.41:1; (DeV./Brghm) 2.28:1; (Eldo) 3.08:1; (Eldo) 2.19:1. Hypoid drive axle. Steering:- recirculating ball; power assisted. Front suspension:- (Seville/Eldo) independent torsion bars, link-type stabilizer bar; (others) coil springs and link-type stabilizer bar. Rear suspension:- (Seville/Eldo) independent trailing arm, coil springs, electronic level control; (others) four-link drive coil springs, electronic level control available (except limo). Brakes:- front disc, rear drum exc. Seville/Eldo, four-wheel disc. Fuel tank:- (Seville) 23 gal.; (others) 20.6 gal. exc. limos, 25 gal. (available on DeV/Brghm). Unleaded fuel only.

DRIVETRAIN OPTIONS: 6.0-liter FI V-8 engine: Seville ($266 credit). 5.7-liter diesel V-8 engine: Eldo ($266); DeV/Fleetwood ($924). Heavy- duty cooling system ($59). 100-amp alternator ($41-$59). Engine block heater ($43). California emission equipment ($83-$250). Limited slip differential ($86) exc. SeV/Eldo. Sport handling pkg.: SeV/Eldo ($95). Heavy-duty suspension: DeV/Brghm ($270). Electronic level control: DeV/Brghm ($169). Trailering package ($100-$118).

OPTION PACKAGES: Brougham d'Elegance: cloth ($1062); leather ($1525). Coupe DeVille Cabriolet ($350). DeVille d'Elegance ($1005). Eldorado Cabriolet ($363). Eldorado Biarritz: leather seating ($2937); cloth ($2494). Seville Elegante ($2934).

CONVENIENCE/APPEARANCE OPTIONS: Astroroof ($1058); N/A on limo. Cruise control ($147). Controlled-cycle wipers: DeV/limo ($43). Rear defogger, grid- type ($170). Six-way Dual Comfort power passenger seat adjuster: DeV ($395); Eldo ($171). Power driver's seat recliner ($130). Power passenger seatback recliner:Brghm ($71). Notchback passenger seatback recliner: DeV ($130). Tilt/telescope steering wheel ($142). Automatic door locks ($129). Illuminated entry system: DeV/limo ($67). Garage door opener ($125). Theft deterrent system ($153). Trunk lid release and power pull-down: DeV ($92). Opera lamps: DeV ($71). Twilight Sentinel: DeV/limo ($62). Guidematic headlamp control ($72). Front light monitor ($35). Trumpet horn ($26). Electric remote-control left mirror w/thermometer ($97). Lighted thermometer on left mirror ($30). Lighted vanity mirrors, pair ($112). Electronic-tuning seek/scan AM/FM stereo radio with 8-track tape player ($195); w/8-track and CB ($480); w/cassette ($225); w/CB ($380); w/cassette and CB ($510). Electronic-tuning seek/scan AM/FM stereo radio with 8-track player, rear control: limo ($398). Two-tone paint: DeV/Brghm ($293). Two-tone paint, partial Firemist: DeV/Brghm ($394). Firemist paint ($201). Padded vinyl roof: DeV ($240). Accent stripes: DeV ($61). Door edge guards ($16-$24). License frame: each ($11). Leather seating area ($435-$595). Carpeted rubber front floor mats ($35-$38); rear ($19). Trunk mat ($15). Turbine-vaned wheel covers: DeV ($63). Cast aluminum wheels: Eldo ($376); NC on diesel Seville. Locking wire wheels: DeV/Brghm ($755). Locking wire wheel covers ($262-$320); NC on Seville. Puncture-sealing tires ($105).

HISTORY: Introduced: October 11, 1979. Model year production (U.S.): 231,028 for a 3.4 percent share of the industry total. Calendar year production (U.S.): 203,992. Calendar year sales by U.S. dealers: 213,002 for a 3.2 percent market share. Model year sales by U.S. dealers: 238,999.

Historical Footnotes: This was not a top-notch year for Cadillac, as sales plummeted over 27 percent. Production fell even further for the model year, down 39.4 percent. The reason evidently was a declining eagerness for big cars, with rising interest in compact, fuel-efficient models. In an attempt to meet these changing attitudes, Cadillac had reduced the size of the standard gasoline engine from its prior 425 cu. in. displacement down to a mere 368 cu. in. (6.0 liters). Buick's V-6 became optional late in the year. But the division also speeded up production of the subcompact J-bodied Cimarron, originally intended for introduction in 1985. Cadillac had problems meeting emissions control standards of the California Air Resources Board, whose restrictions had long been considerably stricter than the rest of the country. The "standard" diesel on the new Seville wasn't offered in California. A new assembly plant for production of lightweight V-6 engines was announced at Livonia, Michigan. Convertible conversions continued to be turned out by (among others) Hess & Eisenhardt in Cincinnati, which claimed to be the largest producer of Cadillac ragtops. Their 1980 brochure displayed a Coupe deVille conversion.

1981 CADILLAC

Biggest news for 1981 was actually an '82 model: the new subcompact Cimarron, introduced in the spring. (More on that in the next section.) Second biggest was the new variable- displacement gasoline engine, developed by the Eaton Corporation and standard in all but Seville. Depending on driving conditions, the innovative V8-6-4 engine ran on four, six, or eight cylinders, switching back and forth as needed. The object, of course, was to conserve fuel in the wake of rising gasoline prices. A microprocessor determined which cylinders weren't necessary at the moment. Then it signaled a solenoid-actuated blocker plate, which shifted to permit the rocker arm to pivot at a different point than usual. Therefore, selected intake and exhaust valves would remain closed rather than operate normally. Valve lifters and pushrods traveled up-and-down in the normal manner, but unneeded valve pairs stood idle. When running on four, displacement grew back to eight as soon as you stepped on the gas to pass, demanding maximum power--an assurance to those who might wonder if a four-cylinder Cadillac powerplant was good enough. The system had been tested (and "proven") in over half a million miles of driving. Cadillac claimed that the "perceived sensation" during displacement changes was "slight," because no shifting was involved. Another feature: push a button and an MPG Sentinel showed the number of cylinders in operation; push again to see instantaneous miles-per-gallon. Though the principle was not new, having been experimented with during World War II, the new engine was hailed as a dramatic answer to the economy problem for large passenger cars. Expanded self-diagnostics now displayed 45 separate function codes for mechanics to investigate. Imaginative but complex, the V8-6-4 brought more trouble than ease to many owners and didn't last long in the overall lineup. On another level, Buick's 252 cu. in. (4.1-liter) V-6 engine, introduced late in the 1980 model year, continued for a full season as an economy option. Cadillacs now carried an on-board digital computer capable of making 300,000 decisions per second. It could even

provide continued operation of the car if critical sensors malfunctioned, making an instantaneous substitution—even turning to a built-in analog computer if the digital electronics collapsed. To improve emissions, the new Computer Command Control module used seven sensors to monitor exhaust, engine speed, manifold air pressure and coolant temperature, then adjust the air/fuel mixture. "Answering Today's Needs with Tomorrow's Technology" was the logical theme of the full-line catalog. Though technically impressive, 1981 was not a year of significant change beyond some new grilles and other cosmetic alterations. Oldsmobile's 350 cu. in. diesel V-8 was vailable in all six models: Fleetwood Brougham coupe and sedan, Coupe and Sedan deVille, Eldorado, and Seville. A new light went under the hood. Rust-prevention measures touched over 100 specially treated areas, including pre-coated metals. Overdrive automatic transmission was now available with the V-6 engine on Fleetwood Brougham and DeVille. A memory seat option returned the six-way power driver's seat to one of two selected positions.

1981 Fleetwood Brougham coupe (AA)

FLEETWOOD BROUGHAM — SERIES 6C — V-8 — Billed again as the "Cadillac of Cadillacs," Broughams came in coupe and sedan form with a grille and front-end look the same as DeVille. The coupe had an Elk Grain vinyl Cabriolet roof treatment with flush-look, small-size rear quarter windows and broad sail panels. Both coupe and sedan roofs had a chrome crossover roof molding at the front of the vinyl portion, stretching across the top and sides. Back windows were small (limousine-style). Options included an Astroroof and leather-trimmed steering wheel. A stand-up wreath-and-crest ornament adorned each hood. Standard wheel covers were vaned chrome with wreath-and-crest on a dark red background. Three powertrains were offered: standard fuel-injected V8-6-4, Buick V-6 with automatic overdrive transmission, or diesel V-8. Standard were the Twilight Sentinel that automatically turned headlamps on and off, illuminated entry, tilt/telescope steering wheel, six-way driver and passenger seats, and electro-luminescent opera lamps. Dual Comfort coupe front seats held three people; rear seats offered adjustable reading lamps. Standard interior upholstery was Heather knit with Raphael inserts, available in six colors. New door panels displayed an embroidered 'Fleetwood' script. Nine varieties of tucked leather in seating areas were also offered. Brougham d'Elegance had chrome wheel covers with body- colored vanes and wreath-and-crest on dark red background, plus d'Elegance script and accent striping on the body. Coupe interiors came in standard dark blue Heather and Raphael knit fabric; or optional Sierra Grain leather for tufted seating areas (dark claret, white, black, light slate gray, dark blue, light beige, doeskin, or light waxberry). Sedans had knit fabric in dark blue, dark claret, light slate gray or light beige; or leather in doeskin, light beige, light slate gray, dark blue, or dark claret.

FLEETWOOD LIMOUSINE — SERIES 6D - V-8 — Differing mainly in dimensions from DeVille and Fleetwood, carrying the new crosshatch grille, limos could not have the diesel engine option. Both standard and Formal Limousine models included a dual accessory panel so rear passengers could adjust the climate control and power windows. The formal edition held a sliding glass partition, with seating for seven. Standard limos held eight. Interiors came in dark blue Heather cloth, or black in the back. All carried two fold-down auxiliary seats.

1981 Seville Elegante sedan (AA)

SEVILLE — SERIES 6K — V-8 — Though basically unchanged for 1980, Seville got a few new touches including restyled (optional) wire wheel covers. Side accent moldings were now standard. An air dam below the front bumper was added, in an attempt to improve aerodynamic characteristics and gas mileage. Base engine was the Olds- built diesel V-8, now with roller cam followers on the valve lifters. That made Seville the only car around with a standard V-8 diesel. Also new: an improved water detection/removal system for the fuel tank. New component labeling procedures were supposed to prevent theft. Seville's long list of standard equipment included cast aluminum wheels, four-wheel disc brakes, cruise control, power windows and door locks, Soft Ray tinted glass, tilt/telescope steering wheel, lighted vanity mirrors, and illuminated entry system. Standard gear also included low- rolling-resistance tires, low-fuel warning, and improved windshield washers. New options: several radio and tape systems of advanced design, a memory system for the power driver's seat, and the modulated-displacement V8-6-4 engine that was standard in other Cadillacs. A Buick-built 252 cu. in. V-6 with four-barrel carburetor was also available this year. Both gasoline engines brought buyers a credit of several hundred dollars. Sevilles came in 13 high-gloss acrylic lacquer finishes, with accent striping and moldings. Optional were 13 two-tone combinations (such as Twilight Blue over Norfolk Gray) and 8 Firemist paints. Dual Comfort 45/45 seats were upholstered in Heather knit cloth; or 11 leather shades in tucked seating areas. Deep-pile Tiffany carpeting decorated the floor. Also standard: map lamps, assist straps, and an improved electronic-tuning AM/FM stereo radio. Hoods displayed a burnished wreath-and-crest ornament over the vertical-style grille with its large header bar, and engine compartments had a new light. Cast aluminum wheels were standard. One-piece bumpers had built-in guards. A Touring Suspension became optional during the 1981 model year. Seville Elegantes had been easy to spot with their bold "French Curve" molding separating two-tone body colors. This year, base Sevilles gained the full-length accent moldings that had formerly been an Elegante exclusive. The pricey Elegante package included tucked seating areas and steering wheel in Sierra Grain leather; 40/40 Dual Comfort seats; leather-topped console; Tampico carpeting; 'Elegante' script on glove box and body; cross-laced wire wheel covers; and chrome side moldings. Elegante came in four color combinations: Sheffield Gray Firemist over Sable Black (slate gray interior); Superior Blue Metallic over Twilight Blue (dark blue interior); Desert Sand Firemist over Briarwood Brown (light beige interior); or Mulberry Gray Firemist over Bordeaux Red (mulberry gray interior).

1981 Eldorado coupe (AA)

ELDORADO — SERIES 6E — V-8 — Up front, Eldo's new grille had a tiny crosshatch pattern below the wide, brushed-chrome finished, peaked upper bar. Quad rectangular headlamps sat above amber-lensed quad parking/signal lamps. Horizontal-style clear/amber cornering lamps sat a short distance back on the fenders. Like Seville, Eldorado also added a front air dam below the bumper. Wheel covers showed big red medallions. Inside, Eldos sported a new center console, woodgrain applique on door panels, and simulated teakwood dash trim. Standard equipment this year included low rolling-resistance tires, low-fuel warning, a new underhood light, and new windshield washers. Also standard: dual-spot map lamps/courtesy lights, seat belt chimes, lamp monitors, electric trunk release and power pull- down, compact spare tire, dual remote-control mirrors, six- way power driver's seat, electronic-tuning signal-seeking stereo radio, MPG Sentinel, Twilight Sentinel, accent stripes on bodysides and deck lid, and much more. As before, Eldos featured four-wheel independent suspension, four-wheel disc rakes, and electronic level control. On the option list was a Touring Suspension that included larger tires. New Dual Comfort 45/45 front seats held driver and passenger. Leather upholstery in tufted seating areas came in 10 hues including new doeskin, light waxberry, and dark jadestone. New standard Heather and Dundee fabric came in four colors. Door handles were new too. Standard engine was the new 368 cu. in. V8-6-4 with on- board computer diagnostics. Two options were offered: Buick's 4.1-liter V-6 with three-speed automatic transmission (four- speed overdrive with the V8-6-4), or the Oldsmobile diesel V-8. Major body components now carried labels conforming to vehicle identification numbers, in an attempt to prevent thefts. Eldorado Biarritz included tufted pillow-style seating and steering wheel in Sierra Grain leather, in any of five colors; Tampico carpeting; front console; individual rear reading lamps; opera lamps; accent stripes; and Biarritz script insignia. A brushed stainless steel roof section extended from the flush-mount windshield back to an Elk Grain vinyl cabriolet roof. A wide chrome molding crossed the roof, turning a square corner and extending forward to the front fenders. Biarritz came in 21 colors. New standard wire wheel covers had red center sections with the Cadillac wreath-and- crest medallion. The opera lamps were optional on other Eldos.

1981 Sedan deVille (AA)

DEVILLE — SERIES 6C — V-8 — Standard engine for DeVille and Fleetwood Brougham was the "modulated displacement" 368 cu. in. (6.0-liter) V8-6-4, with digital fuel injection. Optional: a 252 cu. in. (4.1- liter) V-6, provided by Buick. That V-6 had Computer Command Control and a knock sensor to adjust spark advance, as well as diagnostics. The Olds diesel V-8 was also offered. Externally, DeVilles and Fleetwoods carried a new forward-peaked grille with heavy wide upper header bar (Cadillac script again at the side) over an undivided tight crosshatch pattern. Quad headlamps sat above quad amber parking/signal lamps, with wraparound clear/amber cornering lights. Standard wheel covers displayed a Cadillac crest on dark red background. New standard Electronic Climate Control offered digital accuracy. Standard equipment also included a six-way power passenger seat, power windows, and low-fuel warning. New pillow-style seating came in rich Heather cloth (four colors); or leather in ribbed seating areas (ten colors). Sedan deVilles could have automatic lap-shoulder belt for driver and front passenger. Other options: a Heavy- Duty Ride package, wire wheel covers, and Elk Grain vinyl roof.

I.D. DATA: All Cadillacs had a new 17-symbol Vehicle Identification Number (VIN), stamped on a metal tag attached to the upper left surface of the cowl, visible through the windshield. The number begins with a '1' to indicate the manufacturing country (U.S.A.), followed by a 'G' for General Motors and a '6' for Cadillac Division. The next letter indicates restraint system: 'A' manual (standard); 'B' automatic. Symbol five is a letter denoting car line and series: 'S' Seville; 'B' Fleetwood Brougham; 'D' DeVille; 'F' Fleetwood limousine; 'Z' commercial chassis; 'L' Eldorado. Digits six and seven indicate body type: '47' 2- dr. coupe; '69' 4-dr. four-window sedan; '23' six-window, eight-passenger sedan w/auxiliary seat; '33' six-window formal limousine w/aux. seat and center partition; '90' commercial chassis (no body); '57' Eldorado coupe. Next comes an engine code: '4' V6-252 4Bbl.; 'N' V8-350 diesel; '6' V8-368 4Bbl.; '9' V8-368 DFI. The next symbol is a check digit. Symbol ten indicates model year ('B' for

1981). Symbol eleven denotes assembly plant: '9' Detroit; 'E' Linden, New Jersey (Seville/Eldo). The final six-digit production sequence number began with 100001 for Detroit-built models; 600001 (Eldo) or 680001 (Seville) for those built in New Jersey. An identification number for the V-6 engine was on the left rear of the block; on the V8-350, a code label was on top of the left valve cover and a unit number label atop the right valve cover. Other engines had a unit number on the block behind the left cylinder head, and a VIN derivative on the block behind the intake manifold. A body number plate on the upper horizontal surface of the shroud (except Seville, on front vertical shroud surface) showed model year, build date code, car division, series, style, body assembly plant, body number, trim combination, paint code, modular seat code, and roof option.

SEVILLE V-6/DIESEL V-8

Model Number	Body/Style Number	Body Type & Seating	Factory Price	Shipping Weight	Production Total
6K	S69	4-dr Sedan-5P	20598/21088	3688/4028	28,631

Seville Engine Note: Prices and weights shown are for optional gas V-6 and standard diesel V-8. A gas V-8 was also available.

DEVILLE (V-6/V8-6-4)

6C	D47	2-dr Coupe-6P	13285/13450	3801/4016	Note 1
6C	D69	4-dr Sedan-6P	13682/13847	3852/4067	Note 2

FLEETWOOD BROUGHAM (V-6/V8-6-4)

6C	B47	2-dr Coupe-6P	15777/15942	3854/4069	Note 1
6C	B69	4-dr Sedan-6P	16190/16355	3884/4115	Note 2

Note 1: Total two-door coupe production, 62,724. **Note 2:** Total DeVille/Fleetwood 4-door sedan production, 86,991.

FLEETWOOD LIMOUSINE (V8-6-4)

6D	F23	4-dr Sedan-8P	24464	4629	Note 3
6D	F33	4-dr Fml Limo-7P	25323	4717	Note 3
6D	Z90	Commercial Chassis	N/A	N/A	N/A

Note 3: Total limousine production, 1,200.

ELDORADO (V-6/V8-6-4)

6E	L57	2-dr Coupe-5P	17385/17550	3615/3822	60,643

FACTORY PRICE AND WEIGHT NOTE: Figures before the slash are for V-6 engine, after slash for variable-displacement gas V8-6-4. A diesel V-8 was also available on DeVille/Brougham/Eldorado. By late spring 1981, prices rose on all except Eldorado: Seville reached $23,000 for the diesel, Coupe deVille $14,345, Brougham sedan $17,420.

ENGINES: BASE DIESEL V-8 (Seville); OPTIONAL (DeVille, Brougham, Eldorado): 90-degree, overhead valve V-8. Cast iron block and head. Displacement: 350 cu. in. (5.7 liters). Bore & stroke: 4.057 x 3.385 in. Compression ratio: 22.5:1. Brake horsepower: 105 at 3200 R.P.M. Torque: 200 lbs.-ft. at 1600 R.P.M. Five main bearings. Hydraulic valve lifters. Fuel injection. Oldsmobile-built. VIN Code: N. OPTIONAL V-6 (all except limousines): 90-degree, overhead valve V-6. Cast iron block and head. Displacement: 252 cu. in. (4.1 liters). Bore & stroke: 3.965 x 3.40 in. Compression ratio: 8.0:1. Brake horsepower: 125 at 3800 R.P.M. Torque: 210 lbs.-ft. at 2000 R.P.M. Four main bearings. Hydraulic valve lifters. Carburetor: 4Bbl. Made by Buick. VIN Code: 4. OPTIONAL V-8: 90-degree, overhead valve variable-displacement. Cast iron block and head. Displacement: 368 cu. in. (6.0 liters). Bore & stroke: 3.80 x 4.06 in. Compression ratio: 8.2:1. Brake horsepower: 140 at 3800 R.P.M. Torque: 265 lbs.-ft. at 1400 R.P.M. Five main bearings. Hydraulic valve lifters. Digital fuel injection. VIN Code: 9. BASE V-8 (Commercial chassis only): Same specifications as 368 cu. in. engine above, but standard V-8 with four-barrel carburetor-- Brake H.P.: 150 at 3800 R.P.M. Torque: 265 lbs.-ft. at 1600 R.P.M. VIN Code: 6.

CHASSIS DATA: Wheelbase: (Seville/Eldo) 114.0 in.; (DeV/Brghm) 121.4 in.; (Limo) 144.5 in. Overall length:- (Seville/Eldo) 204.8 in.; (DeV/Brghm) 221.0 in.; (Limo) 244.1 in.; (Eldo) 204.5 in. Height:- (Seville/Eldo) 54.3 in.; (DeV/Brghm cpe) 54.6 in.; (DeV sed) 55.6 in.; (Brghm sed) 56.7 in.; (Limo) 56.9 in. Width: (Seville/Eldo) 71.5 in. max.; (others) 76.5 in. max. Front Tread:- (Seville/Eldo) 59.3 in.; (others) 61.7 in. Rear Tread:- (Seville/Eldo) 60.6 in.; (others) 60.7 in. Standard Tires:- (Seville/Eldo) P205/75R15 SBR wide WSW; (DeV/Brghm) P215/75R15 SBR wide WSW; (Limos) HR78 x 15-D.

TECHNICAL: Transmission: Turbo Hydra-matic transmission standard on all models; column shift. Gear ratios for DeV/Brghm/limo V8-368: (1st) 2.48:1; (2nd) 1.48:1; (3rd) 1.00:1; (Rev) 2.07:1. Other three-speed models: (1st) 2.74:1; (2nd) 1.57:1; (3rd) 1.00:1; (Rev) 2.07:1. Four-speed automatic in DeV/Brghm w/V-6: (1st) 2.74:1; (2nd) 1.57:1; (3rd) 1.00:1; (4th) 0.667:1; (Rev) 2.07:1. Standard final drive ratio:- (Seville/Eldo) 2.41:1 except w/V-6, 2.93:1; (DeV/Brghm) 2.41:1 except w/V-6, 3.23:1; (limos) 3.08:1. Steering:- recirculating ball (power assisted). Suspension:- same as 1980. Brakes:- front disc, rear drum exc. SeV/Eldo, four-wheel disc. Fuel tank:- (SeV/Eldo) 22.8 gal. w/diesel, 20.3 gal. w/V8-6-4, 21.1 gal. w/V-6; (DeV/Brghm) 24.6 gal. exc. diesel, 27 gal. and V-6, 25 gal.; (limos) 24.6 gal.

DRIVETRAIN OPTIONS: 4.1-liter gas V-6 engine ($165 credit); Seville ($490 credit). V8-6-4 gas engine: Seville ($325 credit). 5.7-liter diesel V-8 engine ($325-$351); N/A limo. California emission equipment ($46-$182). Engine block heater ($59). 100-amp alternator ($41). Heavy-duty cooling ($59). Limited slip differential: DeV/Brghm/limo ($86). Electronic level control: DeV/Brghm ($173). Heavy-duty ride package: DeV/Brghm sedan ($270). Touring suspension: Eldo/SeV ($95). Trailering pkg.: ($59-$100).

OPTION PACKAGES: Brougham d'Elegance: cloth seating ($1066); leather ($1536). DeVille d'Elegance ($1005). Coupe deVille Cabriolet ($363) Eldorado Biarritz ($2937). Eldorado Cabriolet ($363). Seville Elegante ($2734). Appearance value pkg.: DeV ($802).

CONVENIENCE/APPEARANCE OPTIONS: Astroroof ($1058); N/A on limo. Controlled-cycle wiper system: DeV/limo ($45). Rear defogger, grid-type ($134-$175). Automatic door locks ($129). Garage door opener ($125). Illuminated entry·system ($67). Digital instrument cluster: SeV/Eldo ($200). Dual Comfort front seats w/six-way power passenger seat adjuster: DeV ($395). Memory driver's seat ($169). Six-way power passenger seat: Eldo ($172). Power river's seat recliner ($130). Power passenger seat recliner: Brghm ($71). Power passenger seat recliner w/six-way power seat: Eldorado ($302). Notchback passenger seat recliner: DeV ($130). Leather-trimmed steering wheel ($79). Tilt/telescope steering wheel ($147). Power trunk lid release and pull-down: DeV/limo ($96). Theft deterrent system ($157). Twilight Sentinel: DeV/limo ($65). Guidematic headlamp control ($78). Opera lamps: DeV/Eldo ($72). Trumpet horn ($28). Thermometer on left mirror ($35). Electric remote mirrors w/thermometer on left: limo ($99). Twin lighted vanity mirrors ($116). Electronic-tuning seek/scan AM/FM stereo radio with 8-track tape player ($195); with 8-track and CB ($480); w/cassette ($281); w/cassette and CB ($547). Rear-control elect.-tuning radio with 8-track: limo ($398). Full padded vinyl roof: DeV ($240). Two-tone paint: Seville Firemist ($520); DeV/Eldo ($293); partial Firemist, DeV/Eldo ($394). Firemist paint ($208). Accent striping: DeV ($61). Door edge guards ($16- $24). License frames, each ($11). Front console: Eldo/SeV ($151). Leather seating area ($439-$595). Automatic lap/shoulder belts: DeV sed ($150). Carpeted rubber floor mats: front ($35-$38); rear ($20). Trunk mat ($16). Cast aluminum wheels: Eldo ($376); SeV (NC). Locking wire wheels: DeV/Brghm ($755). Turbine vaned wheel covers: DeV ($63). Locking wire wheel covers ($266-$328). Puncture-sealing tires ($106).

HISTORY: Introduced: September 25, 1980. Model year production: 253,591 (including 13,402 1982 Cimarrons built during the 1981 model year). The total included 30,440 cars with V-6 engine and 42,200 diesels. Calendar year production: 259,135. Calendar year sales by U.S. dealers: 230,665 for a 3.7 percent market share. Model year sales by U.S. dealers: 226,427 (including 8,790 Cimarrons built before September 1981).

Historical Footnotes: "Cadillac is class," the full-line catalog declared, echoing a theme that had been used for decades. "Class" seemed to take many forms by the 1980s. In addition to the customary funeral/ambulance adaptations and stretch limos from various manufacturers, two conversions came from Wisco Corporation (in Michigan): a Renaissance Coupe deVille and a Seville Caballero.

1982 CADILLAC

"Best of all...it's a Cadillac," declared the 1982 full- line catalog. Perhaps so, but long-time Caddy fans must have been startled by the company's latest offering: the four- cylinder Cimarron, with manual floor shift yet. Introduced several years earlier than originally planned, this drastically different breed of luxury was intended to give Cadillac a toehold in the rising market for smaller, fuel- efficient designs. On all except Cimarron, a new lightweight Cadillac 249 cu. in. (4.1-liter) HT 4100 V-8 engine with Digital Fuel Injection (DFI) became standard, coupled to overdrive automatic transmission. The Oldsmobile-built 5.7-liter diesel V-8 was also available. So was a Buick 4.1-liter V-6, offered as a credit option. A new Fuel Data Panel (standard with the HT 4100 engine) displayed instantaneous MPG, average MPG, estimated driving range, and amount of fuel used. Electronic Climate Control had a new outside temperature display, available by touching a button. New reminder chimes used different tone patterns to warn of unbuckled seatbelts, headlamps left on, or key in ignition. Body mounts, springs and shocks were revised to give a softer ride. All Cadillacs except Cimarron had standard cornering lamps, tungsten-halogen highbeam headlamps, power windows and oor locks, lamp monitors, twin remote-control mirrors, automatic power radio antenna, six-way power driver's seat, electronic-tuned AM/FM stereo radio with signal seeking/scanning, an underhood light, dual-spot map lamps/courtesy lights, steel-belted wide whitewall radial tires, and gas cap holder on fuel filler door, among their standard equipment. All except Seville with cloth interior had front seatback map pockets. New to the full-size option list was a remote-locking fuel filler door. The HT-4100 V-8 engine had an aluminum block for light weight and chrome-plated valve covers for looks. During manufacture, it received individually balanced components and automatic in-process gauging, and had to pass a 78-step "stress test" before installation. Features added to improve fuel economy included fast-burn compact combustion chambers, digital fuel injection, and bearings designed for low-drag lubricants. Standard with the HT-4100 engine was four-speed overdrive automatic transmission, helping to improve mileage further. EPA estimates reached 26 highway/17 city for Fleetwood DeVille models, 27 highway/18 city for Seville/Eldorado. A Fuel Data Panel computed average MPG on the road. On-board computer diagnostics warned of engine problems and helped the mechanic locate the trouble quickly. The digital fuel injection included automatic altitude compensation, determined by a microprocessor, plus constant idle speed. The HT-4100 replaced the troublesome V8-6-4 modular- isplacement engine, helping to boost both gas mileage and sales. That new engine was installed in some 90 percent of Sevilles, DeVilles and Eldorados. An HT-4100 nameplate went on front fenders of all models with that engine under the hood.

1982 Cimarron sedan (C)

CIMARRON — SERIES 6J — FOUR — After decades of success in manufacturing large luxury cars, Cadillac turned to a *small* luxury car in an attempt to rival BMW, Audi, Volvo, Saab, small Mercedes, and similar high-class imports. Cimarron came with a standard 112 cu. in. (1.8-liter) four-cylinder engine and four-speed overdrive manual shift with floor lever. Three-speed Turbo Hydra-matic was available. This was Cadillac's first four-cylinder engine since 1914, and the first manual shift since 1953. Most Cadillac buyers had never driven one without Hydra-matic in some form. Cimarron was billed as "a new kind of Cadillac for a new kind of Cadillac owner." The company first seemed a bit uncomfortable with its new addition, initially branding it Cimarron *by* Cadillac rather than a straight-out Caddy. Bodies carried a Cadillac emblem in the grille center, and on taillamps, but no script identification. Five people fit into the car's body-contoured leather seats with lumbar support, feet touching deep-pile Trianon carpeting. Even the trunk was carpeted. Dashes displayed a tachometer, oil pressure gauge and voltmeter. Nine hand-buffed body colors were offered, including four exclusive metallics (Superior Blue, Autumn Amber, Garnet, and Columbian Brown). Cimarron rode an exclusive Cadillac-tuned touring suspension with MacPherson struts up front and a semi-independent rear, plus front/rear stabilizer bars. Aircraft-type aluminum alloy wheels held match-mounted steel-belted radial tires. Sharing the same J-body as Chevrolet's Cavalier and the similarly derivative Pontiac J2000, Cimarron didn't quite manage a truly separate identity but offered a long list of standard features. Luxuries on every subcompact four-door sedan included air conditioning, twin power mirrors, leather-wrapped steering wheel, power rack-and-pinion steering, and AM/FM stereo radio. All this came at a cost, though: over $12,000 base price, which was far higher than its GM relatives, closer to the level of Eurosport sedans. Cimarron's front end carried a finely-meshed crosshatch horizontal chrome grille and quad rectangular tungsten- halogen headlamps. At the rear were horizontal taillamps. Four of the nine Cadillac body colors were intended solely for Cimarron, as were two of the five interior choices. Wheels displayed small slots, and the full-width back seat could hold three passengers. The initially short option list included a Vista Vent roof and vacuum-type cruise control.

1982 Seville Elegante sedan (AA)

SEVILLE — SERIES 6K — V-8 — "With styling imitated but never equalled, Seville is an American standard for the world." So claimed Cadillac in its full-line catalog for 1982. Little change was evident this year, but there was a new standard powerplant under the hood: the lightweight HT-4100 aluminum-block V-8. The idea of a standard diesel engine hadn't lasted long. Seville's chassis carried new shock absorbers and rear springs, along with the familiar four-wheel independent suspension and electronic level control. Optional wire wheel covers had a locking device; aluminum alloy wheels were available in black. Standard interiors used Heather cloth in a choice of five colors, or leather in stitched seating areas (eight colors). A full cabriolet roof became available in black, white or dark blue diamond-grain vinyl. That option gave Seville the look of a convertible sedan--at least from a distance. The available Touring suspension included P225/70R15 steel-belted radial tires, large-diameter front and rear stabilizer bars, altered power steering that gave more feedback, stiffer front torsion bar and rear spring rates, and increased shock absorber valving. Limited-edition Elegantes, with a package price of $3095, used a sweeping two-tone French curve to accent the burnished and bright full-length bodyside moldings. Sail panels carried the 'Elegante' script nameplate. Elegante also had accent striping and a stand-up wreath/crest hood ornament. It came in three two-tone color combinations, including Desert Dusk Firemist over Brownstone. Elegante interiors used tucked leather in seating areas, in three Sierra Grain colors. Steering wheels wore matching leather trim, and the console was leather-topped.

1982 Coupe deVille (AA)

DEVILLE — SERIES 6C — V-8 — Powered by the new HT 4100 Digital Fuel Injection V-8 with automatic overdrive transmission, DeVille's dash contained a new standard Fuel Data Panel to help determine the most fuel-efficient route. Pushbuttons could display outside temperature or average trip MPG, or amount of fuel used. This year's new grille was made up of thin vertical bars, sectioned by two horizontal bars. The wide upper horizontal header, finished in brushed chrome and running full width, held the customary Cadillac script. Quad rectangular headlamps stood directly above rectangular amber- lensed parking/signal lamps. Cornering lamps with clear and amber lenses wrapped around the fender sides. DeVilles displayed a wreath and crest stand-up hood ornament. Standard interiors used Heather knit cloth with matching Dundee ribbed cloth inserts, in five colors. Leather in the ribbed seating areas was

optional, in choice of eight shades. A Cabriolet roof with bright crossover roof molding was available for the Coupe deVille. DeVille d'Elegance had pillow-style seats in Venetian velour cloth, in four colors; plus opera lamps and accent striping. Sedan versions added three roof-mounted passenger assist straps. D'Elegance editions were identified by script on the roof sail panels.

1982 Fleetwood Brougham Coupe d'Elegance (AA)

FLEETWOOD BROUGHAM — SERIES 6D — V-8 — Priced nearly $3000 higher, Brougham coupes and sedans looked similar to their DeVille brothers from the front, with the same new three-row grille made up of narrow vertical bars. Standard equipment included a stand-up wreath and crest hood ornament, Twilight Sentinel, illuminated entry system, controlled-cycle wipers, tilt/telescope steering wheel, and six-way power seat for driver and passenger. Dual Comfort 55/45 front seats held three people and were trimmed in exclusive Fleetwood design, using Heather knit with Raphael cloth inserts. Eight colors of leather were also available. The coupe carried a distinctive Elk Grain vinyl Cabriolet roof with large quarter windows and electro-luminescent opera lamps. A chrome crossover molding highlighted its forward edge. Sedans had a small (limousine- style) back window and full Elk Grain vinyl roof, with Cadillac's wreath-and-crest insignia on the rear roof (sail) panels. A Brougham nameplate stood at the back of rear fenders. Color- keyed, vaned wheel covers were new. Optional: authentic wire wheels. Brougham d'Elegance offered tufted upholstery in cloth or leather, with 50/50 Dual Comfort seats, special trim and identifying scripts, and special wheel covers to match the body color.

FLEETWOOD LIMOUSINE — SERIES 6D — V8-6-4 — While the innovative (but flawed) variable-displacement V8-6-4 engine no longer powered other Cadillacs, it remained active under limousine hoods for several more years. Fleetwood's standard limo seated eight. For an extra thousand dollars or so, the Formal limo held seven, with a sliding glass partition between compartments. A second control panel let passengers adjust temperature and power windows. Heather cloth interior came in black or dark gray-blue. Front compartment of the Formal limo was black, with black leather in seating areas.

1982 Eldorado Biarritz coupe (AA)

ELDORADO — SERIES 6E — V-8 — While front-end appearance was similar to DeVille/Fleetwood, the personal-luxury Eldorado coupes were most noted for their side profile. That meant a somewhat stubby deck lid portion, upright rectangular quarter window, and bodyside molding that turned upward in a square corner just behind that quarter window. This year's vertical-style grille contained three narrow horizontal bars. Bumpers held new black rub strips with white centers, while revised taillamps displayed Cadillac's crest insignia. Eldo's full cabriolet roof option, appearing during the model year, offered the look (almost) of a convertible top. Base powerplant was the new HT-4100 DFI V-8 with overdrive automatic transmission. Buick's V-6 was also available. Eldos continued with four-wheel independent suspension and four-wheel disc brakes. Dual Comfort 45/50 seats held three people, with six-way power adjustment for the driver. Heather cloth upholstery with Dundee cloth inserts came in five colors; leather in eight trim colors. An optional Touring suspension (introduced the year before) included P225/70R15 steel-belted radial tires, large-diameter front and rear stabilizer bars, altered power steering that gave more feedback, stiffer front torsion bar and rear spring rates, and increased shock absorber valving. Eldorado's new Touring Coupe special-edition came with the touring suspension but added extra-wide blackwall tires on aluminum alloy wheels with exposed chrome lug nuts, reclining front bucket seats, a front console, cloisonne hood ornament, leather-wrapped steering wheel, plus red-over-black accent striping on a Sterling Silver metallic finish. Headlamp and taillamp bezels were body-colored. Wide ribbed rocker moldings were gray; wipers and window/windshield moldings black. Upholstery was gray leather, and a hood badge replaced the usual stand-up ornament. A Sable Black Touring Coupe arrived in mid-year, similar but wearing blacked-out reveal moldings and headlamp/taillamp bezels, black bumper rub strips, and aluminum wheels with center hubs. Eldorado Biarritz carried a brushed stainless steel roof cap, wire wheel covers, opera lamps, and 'Biarritz' script on the sail panels. Interiors used genuine leather in seating areas, in five colors, plus a leather-trimmed steering wheel, Tampico carpeting, and rear quarter reading lamps.

I.D. DATA: All Cadillacs again had a 17-symbol Vehicle Identification Number (VIN), stamped on a metal tag attached to the upper left surface of the cowl, visible through the windshield. Coding was similar to 1981. Model year code changed to 'C' for 1982. Code 'G' (Cimarron) was added to car line series. Engine coding was as follows: 'G' L4-112 2Bbl.; '4' V6-252 4Bbl.; '8' V8-250 DFI (HT4100); 'N' V8-350 diesel; '9' V8-6-4 368 DFI. Code 'C' for an assembly plant in South Gate, California was added.

CIMARRON (FOUR)

Model Number	Body/Style Number	Body Type & Seating	Factory Price	Shipping Weight	Production Total
6J	G69	4-dr Sedan-5P	12,181	2524	25,968

SEVILLE (V-6/V-8)

6K	S69	4-dr Sedan-6P	23269/23434	-- /3731	19,998

DEVILLE (V-6/V-8)

6C	D47	2-dr Coupe-6P	15084/15249	-- /3783	Note 1
6C	D69	4-dr Sedan-6P	15534/15699	-- /3839	Note 2

FLEETWOOD BROUGHAM (V-6/V-8)

6C	B47	2-dr Coupe-6P	17931/18096	-- /3825	Note 1
6C	B69	4-dr Sedan-6P	18402/18567	-- /3866	Note 2

Note 1: Total two-door coupe production, 50,130. Note 2: Total DeVille/Fleetwood four-door sedan production, 86,020.

FLEETWOOD LIMOUSINE (V8-6-4)

6D	F23	4-dr Sedan-8P	27961	4628	Note 3
6D	F33	4-dr Fml Limo-7P	28941	4718	Note 3
6D	Z90	Commercial Chassis	N/A	N/A	N/A

Note 3: Total limousine production, 1,450.

ELDORADO (V-6/V-8)

6E	L57	2-dr Coupe-6P	18551/18716	-- /3637	52,018

FACTORY PRICE AND WEIGHT NOTE: Figures before the slash are for V-6 engine, which was actually a $165 credit option; after slash for standard gasoline V-8. Diesel V-8 was also available.

ENGINES: BASE FOUR (Cimarron): Inline. OHV. Four-cylinder. Cast iron block and head. Displacement: 112 cu. in. (1.8 liters). Bore & stroke: 3.50 x 2.91 in. Compression ratio:9.0 :1. Brake horsepower: 88 at 5100 R.P.M. Torque: 100 lbs.-ft. at 2800 R.P.M. Five main bearings. Hydraulic valve lifters. Carburetor: 2Bbl. VIN Code: G. BASE V-8 (Seville, Eldorado, DeVille, Brougham): 90-degree, overhead valve V-8. Aluminum block w/cast iron liners; cast iron head. Displacement: 249 cu. in. (4.1 liters). Bore & stroke: 3.465 x 3.307 in. Compression ratio: 8.5:1. Brake horsepower: 125 at 4200 R.P.M. Torque: 190 lbs.- ft. at 2000 R.P.M. Five main bearings. Hydraulic valve lifters. Digital fuel injection. HT4100. VIN Code: 8. OPTIONAL V-6 (Seville, Eldorado, DeVille, Brougham): 90-degree, overhead-valve V-6. Cast iron block and head. Displacement: 252 cu. in. (4.1 liters). Bore & stroke: 3.9565 x 3.40 in. Compression ratio: 8.0:1. Brake horsepower: 125 at 4000 R.P.M. Torque: 205 lbs.-ft. at 2000 R.P.M. Four main bearings. Hydraulic valve lifters. Carburetor: 4Bbl. Made by Buick. VIN Code: 4. OPTIONAL DIESEL V-8 (Seville, Eldorado, DeVille, Brougham): 90-degree, overhead valve V-8. Cast iron block and head. Displacement: 350 cu. in. (5.7 liters). Bore & stroke: 4.057 x 3.345 in. Compression ratio: 21.6:1. Brake horsepower: 105 at 3200 R.P.M. Torque: 200 lbs.-ft. at 1600 R.P.M. Five main bearings. Hydraulic valve lifters. Fuel injection. Oldsmobile-built. VIN Code: N. BASE V8-6-4 VARIABLE DISPLACEMENT (Limousines only): 90-degree, overhead valve. Cast iron block and head. Displacement: 368 cu. in. (6.0 liters). Bore & stroke: 3.80 x 4.06 in. Compression ratio: 8.2:1. Brake horsepower: 140 at 3800 R.P.M. Torque: 200 lbs.-ft. at 1400 R.P.M. Five main bearings. Hydraulic valve lifters. Digital fuel injection. VIN Code: 9. BASE V-8 (Commercial chassis only): Similar to 368 cu. in. V8-6-4 above, but standard V-8 with 4Bbl. carburetor-- Brake H.P.: 150 at 3800 R.P.M. Torque: 265 lbs.-ft. at 1600 R.P.M.

CHASSIS DATA: Wheelbase: (Cimarron) 101.2 in.; (Seville/Eldo) 114.0 in.; (DeVille/Brghm) 121.4 in.; (Limo) 144.5 in. Overall length:- (Cimarron) 173.0 in.; (Seville) 204.8 in.; (DeVille/Brghm) 221.0 in.; (Limo) 244.0 in. Height:- (Cimarron) 52.0 in.; (Seville/Eldo) 54.3 in.; (DeVille/Brghm cpe) 54.6 in.; (DeVille sed) 55.6 in.; (Brghm sed) 56.7 in. Width:- (Cimarron) 66.3 in. max.; (Seville/Eldo) 71.5 in. max.; (others) 76.5 in. max. Front Tread:- (Cimarron) 55.4 in.; (Seville/Eldo) 59.3 in.; (others) 61.7 in. Rear Tread:- (Cimarron) 55.2 in.; (Seville) 60.0 in.; (Eldo) 60.6 in.; (others) 60.7 in. Standard Tires:- (Cimarron) P195/70R13 SBR; (Seville/Eldo) P205/75R15 SBR wide WSW; (DeVille/Brghm) P215/75R15 SBR wide WSW; (Limo) HR78 x 15-D wide WSW.

TECHNICAL: Transmission: Four-speed, floor shift manual transmission standard on Cimarron. Manual gear ratios: (1st) 3.53:1; (2nd) 1.95:1; (3rd) 1.24:1; (4th) 0.81:1; (Rev) 3.42:1. Turbo Hydra-matic (THM125C) optional on Cimarron w/floor selector: (1st) 2.84:1; (2nd) 1.60:1; (3rd) 1.00:1; (Rev) 2.07:1. Three-speed Turbo Hydra-matic (THM350C) standard on DeVille/Brghm diesel: (1st) 2.52:1; (2nd) 1.52:1; (3rd) 1.00:1; (Rev) 1.94:1. Turbo Hydra-matic (THM400) std. on limos: (1st) 2.48:1; (2nd) 1.48:1; (3rd) 1.00:1; (Rev) 2.07:1. Four-speed overdrive automatic standard on others (THM325-4L on Eldo/SeV, THM200-4R on DeVille/Brghm): (1st) 2.74:1; (2nd) 1.57:1; (3rd) 1.00:1; (4th) 0.667:1; (Rev) 2.07:1. All automatics except limo had torque converter clutch. Standard final drive ratio:- (Cimarron) 3.65:1 except w/auto. 3.18:1; (SeV/Eldo) 3.15:1 except diesel, 2.93:1; (DeV/Brghm) 3.42:1 except 2.93:1 w/diesel, 2.41:1 w/diesel and three-speed trans., 3.23:1 w/V-6; (Limos) 3.08:1. Steering:- (Cimarron) rack and pinion; (others) recirculating ball; power assist. Front suspension:- (Cimarron) MacPherson struts, anti-roll bar; (SeV/Eldo) torsion bar and link stabilizer bar; (others) coil springs and link stabilizer bar. Rear suspension:- (Cimarron) semi-independent trailing arm, coil springs, anti-roll bar; (SeV/Eldo) independent trailing arm, coil springs, electronic level control; (others) four-link, coil springs, elect. level control std. on limo and available on DeVille/Brghm. Brakes:- front disc, rear drum except SeV/Eldo, four-wheel disc. Fuel tank:- (Cimarron) 14.0 gal.; (SeV/Eldo) 20.3 gal. exc. 22.8 w/diesel, 21.1 w/V-6; (DeVille/Brghm) 24.5 gal. exc. 26 w/diesel; (Limos) 24.5 gal.

DRIVETRAIN OPTIONS: 4.1-liter V-6 engine ($165 credit). 5.7-liter diesel V-8 engine ($179-$351); N/A limo or Cimarron. California emission equipment: Cimarron ($46); others (N/A). Altitude emissions pkg.: diesel or 4.1 V-8 (NC). Engine block heater: limo ($26); Cimarron ($17). Heavy-duty battery: Cimarron ($22). 100-amp alternator ($48). H.D. radiator: Cimarron ($37). Three-speed auto. transmission: Cimarron ($370). Limited slip differential: DeV/Brghm/limo ($106). Electronic level control: DeV/Brghm ($198). Heavy-duty ride package: DeV/Brghm ($310). FE2 touring suspension: Eldo/SeV ($109).

OPTION PACKAGES: Brougham d'Elegance: cloth seating ($1195); leather ($1730). DeVille d'Elegance ($1115). DeVille Cabriolet ($398). Eldorado Biarritz ($3335). Eldorado Cabriolet ($398). Eldorado Touring Coupe ($1950). Seville Elegante ($3095).

SEVILLE/DEVILLE/FLEETWOOD BROUGHAM/LIMOUSINE/ELDORADO CONVENIENCE/APPEARANCE OPTIONS: Astroroof ($1195); N/A on limo. Electronic cruise control ($175). Controlled-cycle wiper system: DeV/limo ($53). Rear defogger w/heated outside mirrors ($150-$198). Automatic door locks ($145). Remote-locking fuel filler door ($56). Garage door opener ($140). Illuminated entry system ($76). Digital instrument cluster: SeV/Eldo ($229). Dual Comfort front seats w/six-way power passenger seat adjuster ($413). Memory driver's seat ($180). Six-way power passenger seat: Eldo/SeV ($197). Power driver's seat recliner ($150); passenger, DeV ($150). Power passenger seat recliner w/six-way power seat: Eldo ($347); SeV ($282). Leather-trimmed steering wheel rim ($95). Tilt/telescope steering wheel ($169). Power trunk lid release and pull-down: DeV/limo ($112). Theft deterrent system ($179). Twilight Sentinel: DeV/limo ($76). Guidematic headlamp control ($93). Opera lamps: DeV/Eldo ($85). Trumpet horn ($35) exc. Seville. Electric remote-control outside mirrors ($98). Electric remote mirrors w/thermometer on left: limo ($114). Twin lighted vanity mirrors ($136). Electronic- tuning seek/scan AM/FM stereo radio with 8-track tape player ($225); w/8-track and CB ($515); w/cassette and symphony sound system ($290). Elect.-tuning radio w/8-track and rear control: limo ($430). Triband antenna ($45). Fully padded vinyl roof: DeVille sed ($267). Two-tone paint: SeV ($590); DeV/Eldo ($335); partial Firemist, DeV/Eldo ($450). Firemist paint ($229). Accent striping: DeV ($74). Bodyside molding ($61). Door edge guards ($18-$27). License frame ($13). Leather seating area ($498-$680). Carpeted rubber floor mats: front ($41-$43); rear ($24). Trunk mat ($20). Aluminum wheels: Eldo ($429); SeV (NC). Locking wire wheels: DeV/Brghm ($860). Turbine vaned wheel covers: DeV ($75). Wire wheel covers ($298-$375). Puncture-sealing tires ($130-$175).

CIMARRON CONVENIENCE/APPEARANCE OPTIONS: Vista Vent w/rear tilt ($261). Cruise control, vacuum-type ($145-$155). Power windows ($216). Power door locks ($142). Power trunk release ($29). Tilt steering ($88). Six-way power driver's seat ($183); both seats ($366). Twin lighted vanity mirrors ($92). AM/FM stereo radio w/cassette ($153); w/cassette and CB ($560). Delete radio ($151 credit). Door edge guards ($22). License frame ($12). Decklid luggage rack ($98). Carpeted rubber floor mats: front ($38); rear ($22). Trunk mat ($18). Whitewall tires ($55).

HISTORY: Introduced: September 24, 1981 except Cimarron, May 21, 1981. Model year production: 235,584 (including early '82 Cimarrons). That total included 17,650 V-6 Cadillacs and 19,912 diesels. Only 1,017 Sevilles and 3,453 Eldorados had a V-6. Calendar year production: 246,602. Calendar year sales by U.S. dealers: 249,295 for a 4.3 percent share of the market. Model year sales by U.S. dealers: 237,032; also a 4.3 percent market share.

Historical Footnotes: In Cadillac's 80th anniversary year, it was the only GM division to show a sales rise, though not a gigantic one. A depressed economy typically affects luxury-car buyers the least. The new Cimarron, on the other hand, sold only one- third of the predicted output, and Seville also fell below expectations. Heavy dealer orders for the new models in September 1982 caused officials to add a second shift to the Livonia Engine Plant operation. Cadillac had considered selling the new HT-4100 4.1-liter engine to other GM divisions. As Cadillac's engine plant manager said: "There aren't many V-8s left, and ours is a highly efficient, light weight, high-quality powerplant." Until a lightweight V-6 engine could be developed, Cadillac planned to use Buick's 251 cu. in. (4.1-liter) V-6 in the new Cimarron, which was built in South Gate, California. But that would not happen. Cadillac's Corporate Average Fuel Economy (CAFE) rating zoomed up to 22.1 MPG this year, from only 18.7 in 1981, largely due to the improved efficiency of the new 4.1 V-8. In September 1982, Robert D. Burger replaced Edward C. Kennard as Cadillac's general manager.

1983 CADILLAC

Cadillac for 1983 heralded a new line of electronic- fuel-injected engines, eliminating the carburetor. The EFI lineup even included the 2.0-liter four that powered Cimarrons. Once again, the HT 4100 V-8 was Cadillac's standard engine (except on Cimarrons and limousines), now with 10 more horsepower. Automatic four-speed overdrive transmission was standard as well. The 5.7-liter diesel was available again. A new Freedom II battery gave better cold- cranking performance. The curious but undependable variable- displacement V8-6-4 engine was consigned only to limousine applications. Added to the Eldorado and Seville option lists was a Delco-GM/Bose Symphony Sound System with four amplifiers and speakers in separate enclosures, billed as the "industry's most advanced stereo." Sound was automatically balanced for all passengers, reflecting off the windows and interior. Acoustics were based on window location and shape, upholstery, carpeting, and position of driver and passengers. The system included an AM/FM stereo radio and integral cassette player with Dolby tape noise reduction and full-time loudness control. Tested with an "acoustically-sensitive" robot, the system was also offered on Buick Riviera and Olds Toronado.

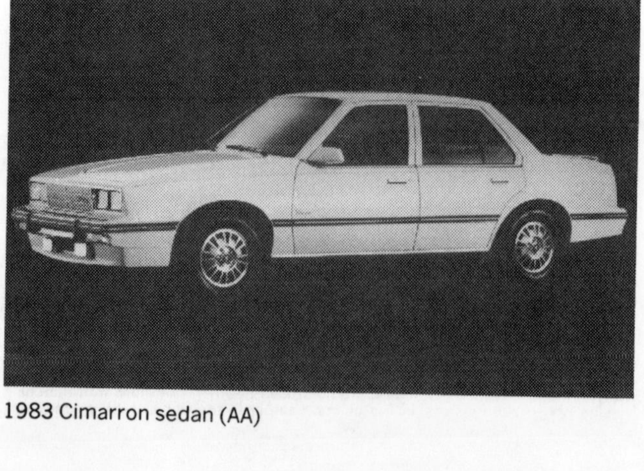

1983 Cimarron sedan (AA)

CIMARRON — SERIES 6J — FOUR — A newly fuel-injected 2.0-liter engine with five-speed gearbox promised better starting and gas mileage for Cadillac's smallest car. A new front end placed standard tungsten-halogen foglamps alongside the license plate, while a lower valance panel helped to separate Cimarron from its related (and much cheaper) J-body relatives. The grille had a finer mesh pattern than before, made up of thin vertical bars all the way across, divided into three sections by two subdued horizontal bars. Quad rectangular headlamps and amber parking/signal lamps were inset below the bumper rub strips. The hood medallion was new, and new aluminum alloy wheels contained bigger slots. Performance got a boost from the increased displacement and higher compression, along with the bigger engine's "swirl" intake ports and revised camshaft. That extra gear in the transmission didn't hurt either—especially since it delivered a higher first-gear ratio for quicker takeoffs, plus closer ratios overall for smoother shift transitions. Ratios in the optional three-speed automatic changed too. Cimarron's ample standard equipment list included air conditioning, tinted glass, P195/70R13 steel-belted radial tires on aluminum alloy wheels, controlled-cycle wipers, lighter, digital clock, electric rear and side window defrosters, tungsten-halogen high-beam headlamps, leather reclining bucket seats with lumbar support and adjustable headrests, and an AM/FM stereo radio with extended-range speakers. The dash held gauges for temp, oil pressure, voltage, trip odometer and tachometer. Bumpers contained guards, end caps and rub strips. Cimarrons had power rack- and-pinion steering with a leather-trimmed steering wheel. Drivers enjoyed dual electric remote mirrors, while the front passenger had a visor vanity mirror. In the trunk: a compact spare tire. Cimarron came in ten colors, accented by dual color painted stripes. Three were Cimarron exclusives: Antique Saddle, Midnight Sand Gray, and Garnet. Prices began at $12,215 this year.

1983 Seville Elegante sedan (AA)

SEVILLE — SERIES 6K — V-8 — With price tags starting at $21,440, Seville came well equipped with—among other niceties—reminder chimes, electronic climate control with outside temperature display, automatic truck locking (and release), side defoggers, rear reading lamps, overhead assist handles, and an automatic power antenna for the electronic-tuned radio. Also standard: an underhood light, lamp monitors, power windows and door locks, twin remote mirrors, cornering lamps, and four-wheel power disc brakes. Appearance changed little from 1982, except that this year's grille had a bit less vertical look and carried a Cadillac script. The front end held clear park/signal lamp lenses. Seville could be ordered with a full cabriolet roof that simulated a convertible top, available in black, dark blue, white, or dark briar brown. Inside was Heather cloth upholstery with matching Rocaille cloth inserts, in choice of four colors; or optional leather in nine shades. A new premium sound system was available, using Dolby tape noise reduction. The 4.1-liter aluminum-block V-8 received a horsepower and torque boost in its second year, to improve a power-loss problem. Third-gear acceleration rate was also revised. The 5.7-liter diesel included an engine block heater to improve cold-weather startups. Seville Elegante again came in two-tone with French curve side styling using chrome bodyside moldings, plus 'Elegante' script on the side panels and accent striping. Four two-tone combinations were offered. Sierra Grain tucked leather seating areas were color-coordinated to match the body color, and to complement the leather-trimmed steering wheel. The front console was leather-topped. Wire wheel covers were standard.

1983 Coupe deVille (AA)

DEVILLE — SERIES 6C — V-8 — Few changes were evident in the bodies of DeVille or Fleetwood coupe and sedan models, though underneath the exhaust system was modified. The refined new grille was similar to 1982 with narrow vertical bars separated into three rows, but Cadillac script moved from the upper horizontal bar to the side of the grille itself, leaving that upper bar bare. Distinctive taillamps carried on Cadillac's traditional style. On the hood was a stand-up hood ornament; on the decklid, Cadillac's 'V' and crest. Lengths reached as long as 221 inches, while prices began at $15,970. Horsepower rose by 10 on the HT 4100 Digital Fuel Injected 4.1-liter V-8. The miserly (if troublesome) 5.7- liter diesel was available on DeVille and Fleetwood Brougham models. Standard interior was Heather knit cloth with matching Dundee ribbed cloth inserts. Saddle leather was also available. DeVille d'Elegance offered pillow-style seating in Venetian velour, special trim, accent striping, and opera lamps. The Cabriolet version of Coupe deVille added an Elk Grain vinyl partial roof, in color to match the car body, with bright crossover roof molding.

FLEETWOOD BROUGHAM — SERIES 6C — V-8 — Offered in coupe and sedan form, Broughams displayed a front end similar to DeVille's, with stand-up wreath and crest hood ornament. Sedans featured a limousine-style rear window, while the coupe's standard Cabriolet vinyl roof featured "privacy-size" quarter windows (similar to DeVille's Cabriolet option). Standard equipment included illuminated entry, six-way power driver's and passenger's seat, plus a long list of Cadillac luxury touches. Dual Comfort 55/45 seats (for three people) came with standard Heather cloth upholstery, but leather in eight colors could be ordered. Brougham d'Elegance, offered with both coupe and sedan, featured Heather cloth upholstery in four colors or leather in six, plus special trim, deluxe carpeting and floor mats, and wheel covers that matched the body color. The package also included d'Elegance identifying script, both inside and outside the car.

FLEETWOOD LIMOUSINE — SERIES 6D — V-8-6-4 — Luxurious as ever, limousines saw no evident change this year. Sole powerplant was again the V8-6-4 variable-displacement engine, offered only in limos. Fleetwood remained the only domestic mass-produced limousine, though production was modest at only a thousand units. Seven or eight passengers rode in comfort and style, enjoying plentiful chrome and such extras as opera lamps.

1983 Cadillac Eldorado Touring Coupe (AA)

ELDORADO — SERIES 6E — V-8 — Like other Caddies, Eldorado saw no major changes in its body this year, though the automatic transmission and cruise control were recalibrated to boost performance. Standard engine was the HT 4100 4.1-liter V-8 with its complex (yet reliable) fuel injection system; optional, a 5.7-liter diesel. Prices began at $19,334 (suggested retail), which included plenty of standard equipment. The grille was similar to DeVille/Fleetwood, with Cadillac script at the driver's side in the center row. Front fender tips held no lights, so the quad rectangular headlamps and horizontal-style parking/signal lamps had a recessed look. Cornering lamps were in horizontal housings back on the front fenders. Heather cloth upholstery with Rocaille cloth inserts came in four colors; or buyers could choose from ten leather choices. Options included a digital instrument cluster with readouts for fuel level, speed and fuel range (English or metric). Eldorado's convertible had been gone for some time, but the optional full cabriolet roof simulated a convertible top, with canvas-look fabric, roof bows and welted seams. It came in black, dark blue, dark briar brown, and white. Eldos had a new optional premium sound system, as well as available aluminum wheels. Two special editions were offered again: the Touring Coupe and Biarritz. Touring Coupes had (no surprise) a touring suspension, large-diameter stabilizer bars, larger P225/70R15 steel-belted radial tires, and special cloisonné hood medallion. Only two body colors were available: Sonora Saddle Firemist (light brown) and Sable Black. Reclining saddle leather-faced front bucket seats offered lumbar and lateral support, and included a console. Eldo's Biarritz "dream machine" included a brushed stainless steel roof cap, wire wheel covers, opera lamps, and 'Biarritz' script on the sail panels. Tufted pillow-style seats came in Sierra Grain leather in six colors; so did the steering wheel.

I.D. DATA: All Cadillacs again had a 17-symbol Vehicle Identification Number (VIN), stamped on a metal tag attached to the upper left surface of the cowl, visible through the windshield. Coding was similar to 1981-82. Model year code changed to 'D' for 1983. Engine coding was as follows: 'P' L4-121 TBI; '8' V8-249 DFI; '9' V8-6-4 368 DFI; 'N' V8-350 diesel; '6' V8-368 4Bbl. See 1981-82 for further details.

CIMARRON FOUR)

Model Number	Body/Style Number	Body Type & Seating	Factory Price	Shipping Weight	Production Total
6J	G69	4-dr Sedan-5P	12,215	2639	19,194

SEVILLE (V-8)

6K	S69	4-dr Sedan-6P	21,440	3844	30,430

DEVILLE (V-8)

6C	D47	2-dr Coupe-6P	15,970	3935	Note 1
6C	D69	4-dr Sedan-6P	16,441	3993	Note 2

FLEETWOOD BROUGHAM (V-8)

6C	B47	2-dr Coupe-6P	18,688	3986	Note 1
6C	B69	4-dr Sedan-6P	19,182	4029	Note 2

Note 1: Total two-door coupe production, 65,670. Note 2: Total DeVille/Fleetwood four-door sedan production, 109,004.

FLEETWOOD LIMOUSINE (V8-6-4)

6D	F23	4-dr Sedan-8P	29,323	4765	Note 3
6D	F33	4-dr Fml Limo-7P	30,349	4852	Note 3
6D	Z90	Commercial Chassis	N/A	N/A	N/A

Note 3: Total limousine production, 1,000.

ELDORADO (V-8)

6E	L57	2-dr Coupe-6P	19,334	3748	67,416

ENGINES: BASE FOUR (Cimarron): Inline. OHV. Four-cylinder. Cast iron block and head. Displacement: 121 cu. in. (2.0 liters). Bore & stroke: 3.50 x 3.15 in. Compression ratio: 9.3:1. Brake horsepower: 88 at 4000 R.P.M. Torque: 110 lbs.-ft. at 2400 R.P.M. Five main bearings. Hydraulic valve lifters. Throttle-body fuel injection. VIN Code: P. BASE V-8 (Seville, DeVille, Brougham, Eldorado): 90-degree, overhead-valve V-8. Iron/aluminum alloy block; cast iron head. Displacement: 249 cu. in. (4.1 liters). Bore & stroke: 3.47 x 3.31 in. Compression ratio: 8.5:1. Brake horsepower: 135 at 4400 R.P.M. Torque: 200 lbs.-ft. at 2200 R.P.M. Five main bearings. Hydraulic valve lifters. Digital fuel injection. HT4100. VIN Code: 8. BASE V8-6-4 (Limousine): 90-degree, overhead valve variable-displacement. Cast iron block and head. Displacement: 368 cu. in. (6.0 liters). Bore & stroke: 3.80 x 4.06 in. Compression ratio: 8.2:1. Brake horsepower: 140 at 3800 R.P.M. Torque: 265 lbs.-ft. at 1400 R.P.M. Five main bearings. Hydraulic valve lifters. Digital fuel injection. VIN Code: 9. BASE V-8 (Commercial chassis only): Similar to 368 cu. in. V8-6-4 above, but standard V-8 with 4Bbl. carburetor. Brake H.P.: 150 at 3800 R.P.M. Torque: 265 lbs.-ft. at 1600 R.P.M. VIN Code: 6. OPTIONAL DIESEL V-8 (Seville, DeVille, Brougham, Eldorado): 90-degree, overhead valve V-8. Cast iron block and head. Displacement: 350 cu. in. (5.7 liters). Bore & stroke: 4.057 x 3.385 in. Compression ratio: 22.5:1. Brake horsepower: 105 at 3200 R.P.M. Torque: 200 lbs.-ft. at 1600 R.P.M. Five main bearings. Hydraulic valve lifters. Fuel injection. Oldsmobile-built. VIN Code: N.

CHASSIS DATA: Wheelbase: (Cimarron) 101.2 in.; (Seville/Eldo) 114.0 in.; (DeVille/Brougham) 121.4 in.; (Limousine) 144.5 in. Overall length:- (Cimarron) 173.1 in.; (Seville) 204.8 in.; (DeVille/Brougham) 221.0 in.; (Limousine) 244.3 in.; (Eldo) 204.5 in. Height:- (Cimarron) 52.0 in.; (Seville/Eldo) 54.3 in.; (DeVille/Brougham cpe) 54.6 in.; (DeV sed) 55.5 in.; (Brougham sed) 56.7 in. Width:- (Cimarron) 66.5 in.; (Seville/Eldo) 71.5 in. max.; (DeV/Brougham) 76.4 in. max.; (Limo) 75.3 in. Front Tread:- (Cimarron) 55.4 in.; (Seville/Eldo) 59.3 in.; (others) 61.7 in. Rear Tread:- Cimarron) 55.2 in.; (Seville/Eldo) 60.6 in.; (others) 60.7 in. Standard Tires:- (Cimarron) P195/70R13 SBR; (Seville/Eldo) P205/75R15 SBR wide WSW; (DeVille/Brougham) P215/75R15 SBR wide WSW; (Limousine) HR78 x 15-D SBR wide WSW.

TECHNICAL: Transmission: Five-speed manual transmission standard on Cimarron. Manual gear ratios: (1st) 3.92:1; (2nd) 2.15:1; (3rd) 1.33:1; (4th) 0.92:1; (5th) 0.74:1; (Rev) 3.50:1. Optional Cimarron three-speed Turbo Hydra-matic (THM125C) gear ratios: (1st) 2.84:1; (2nd) 1.80:1; (3rd) 1.00:1; (Rev) 2.07:1. Three-speed (THM400) automatic standard on limousine: (1st) 2.48:1; (2nd) 1.48:1; (3rd) 1.00:1; (Rev) 2.08:1. Four- speed overdrive automatic standard on all others: (1st) 2.74:1; (2nd) 1.57:1; (3rd) 1.00:1; (4th) 0.67:1; (Rev) 2.07:1. Standard final drive ratio:- (Cimarron) 3.83:1 w/5- spd, 3.18:1 w/auto; (SeV/Eldo) 3.15:1 except w/diesel 2.93:1; (DeVille/Brghm) 3.42:1 except w/diesel 2.93:1; (Limos) 3.08:1. Steering, Suspension and Brakes:- same as 1982. Fuel tank:- (Cimarron) 13.6 gal.; (SeV/Eldo) 20.3 gal. exc. w/diesel, 22.8 gal.; (DeVille/Brghm/limo) 24.5 gal. exc. w/diesel, 26 gal.

DRIVETRAIN OPTIONS: 5.7-liter diesel V-8 engine (NC); N/A limo or Cimarron. California emission equipment ($75) exc. diesel ($215). Engine block heater: limo ($27); Cimarron ($18). Heavy-duty battery: Cimarron ($25). 100-amp alternator ($50) exc. Cimarron. H.D. radiator: Cimarron ($40). Three-speed automatic trans.: Cimarron ($320). Electronic level control: DeV/Brghm ($203). Heavy-duty ride pkg.: DeV/Brghm ($319). FE2 touring suspension: Eldo/SeV ($115).

OPTION PACKAGES: Seville Elegante ($3879). Brougham d'Elegance: cloth seating ($1250); leather ($1800). DeVille d'Elegance ($1150). Cabriolet roof: DeV/Eldo cpe ($415). Full cabriolet roof: Eldo/Seville ($995). Eldorado Biarritz ($3395). Eldorado Touring Coupe ($1975).

SEVILLE/DEVILLE/FLEETWOOD BROUGHAM/LIMOUSINE/ELDORADO CONVENIENCE/APPEARANCE OPTIONS: Astroroof ($1225); N/A on limo. Electronic cruise control ($185). Controlled-cycle wiper system: DeV/limo ($60). Rear defogger w/heated outside mirrors ($160-$210). Automatic door locks ($157). Remote-locking fuel filler door ($59). Garage door opener ($140). Illuminated entry system ($76); std. on Brougham. Digital insrument cluster: SeV/Eldo ($238). Dual omfort front seats: DeV ($225). Memory driver's seat ($185) exc. limo. Six-way power passenger seat: DeV/Eldo/SeV ($210). Power driver's seat recliner ($155) exc. limo. Power passenger seat recliner: DeV ($155); Brghm ($90). Power passenger seat recliner w/six-way power seat: DeV/Eldo ($365); SeV ($300). Leather-trimmed steering wheel ($99). Tilt/telescope steering wheel ($179); std. on formal limo. Power trunk lid release and pull-down: DeV/limo ($120). Theft deterrent system ($185). Twilight Sentinel ($79). Guidematic headlamp control ($93). Opera lamps: DeV/Eldo ($88). Trumpet horn ($38) exc. SeV. Electric remote mirrors w/thermometer on left: limo ($99). Electric remote-control outside mirrors ($99) exc. limo. Twin lighted vanity mirrors ($140). Electronic-tuning seek/scan AM/FM stereo radio with 8-track or cassette tape player ($299); with cassette and CB ($577); w/cassette and Bose symphony sound system, Eldo/SeV ($895). Elect.-tuning radio w/8-track and rear control: limo ($475). Extended-range rear speakers ($25) w/std. radio. Triband antenna ($50). Full padded vinyl roof: DeVille sed ($280). Two-tone paint: SeV ($600); DeV/Eldo ($345); Firemist, DeV/Eldo ($465). Firemist paint ($235). Accent striping: DeV ($77). Bodyside molding: Eldo Touring cpe ($64). Door edge guards ($19-$29). License frames, each ($14) exc. Seville. Leather seating area ($515-$680). Carpeted rubber floor mats: front ($43-$45); rear ($25). Trunk mat ($21). Aluminum wheels: Eldo/SeV ($429). Locking wire wheels: DeV/Brghm ($860). Turbine vaned wheel covers: DeV ($77); Eldo/SeV ($389). Locking wire wheel covers ($310-$389) exc. limo. White-letter tires: Eldo touring cpe ($100). Puncture-sealing tires ($135-$180).

CIMARRON CONVENIENCE/APPEARANCE OPTIONS: Astroroof ($915). Vista Vent w/rear tilt ($295). Cruise control, vacuum-type ($170). Power windows ($255). Power door locks ($170). Power trunk release ($40). Garage door opener ($165); retainer ($25). Tilt steering wheel ($99). Six-way power driver's seat ($210); both seats ($420). Twilight Sentinel ($79). Twin lighted vanity mirrors ($95). AM/FM stereo radio with cassette ($203). Delete radio ($151 credit). Power antenna ($55). Door edge guards ($25). License frame ($12). Decklid luggage rack ($98). Carpeted rubber floor mats: front ($38); rear ($22). Trunk mat ($18). Whitewall tires ($55).

HISTORY: Introduced: September 23, 1982. Model year production: 292,714, which came to 5.1 percent of the industry total. That total included 5,223 diesels. Calendar year production: 309,811. Calendar year sales by U.S. dealers: 300,337. Model year sales by U.S. dealers: 290,138 for a 4.5 percent market share.

Historical Footnotes: Sales rose by over 22 percent for the 1983 model year, suggesting that Cadillac's appeal to luxury-minded buyers hadn't waned. Before taking over the Chevrolet division, Cadillac general manager Robert D. Burger told reporters that the company was "confident about the future of the luxury car business" since research by 1982 suggested a "long-term fundamental shift toward luxury cars...that hold their value." On the other hand, research also showed that Cadillac buyers were considerably older (median age about 60) than car buyers in general--a fact that could become a problem in future years. The popularity of the HT 4100 4.1-liter V-8 brought speculation that a transverse-mounted version would be planned for the 1984 Eldorado. That car's engine compartment would have to be widened, however, to accommodate the V-8. So the switch occurred only when Eldo got a new body for 1986. Rear-drive Cadillacs were the longest cars on the market, measuring 121 inches in wheelbase. Buyers still liked them. so they expected to remain in the lineup for a while longer.

1984 CADILLAC

This was more a year of waiting than one of major changes. All Cadillac engines were now fuel injected. All but Cimarron and Fleetwood limousines carried the HT 4100 cu. in. (4.1-liter V-8 with aluminum alloy block and digital fuel injection. This year, that 249 cu. in. engine gained a new exhaust system and catalytic converter, plus revised calibration settings, to meet high-altitude emissions standards. New features on DeVille, Fleetwood Brougham and limos included a goldtone horizontally-winged Cadillac crest ornament on front parking and turn signal lenses; new car- colored bodyside moldings; new goldtone vertically-winged Cadillac crest and goldtone accents on taillamp lenses; and new standard electronic level control. Diesel engine identification plaques were now on the left rear of the decklid. Faster-warming glow plugs went into the optional 5.7-liter diesel V-8, for improved cold-startups. A modified optional theft-deterrent system could detect any object on the driver's seat that weighed 40 pounds or more.

CIMARRON — SERIES 6J — FOUR — Cimarron's new crosshatch grille had a bolder look, but kept the Cadillac script at lower left corner. The new front end was evidently designed with a V-6 in mind--but that wouldn't be available just yet. The fuel-injected 2.0-liter four remained standard, with five-speed manual gearbox or optional three-speed automatic. Three new stripe insert colors (white, red, orange) were offered for bumper rub strips, end caps and bodyside moldings; plus gold for the Cimarron d'Oro. Foglamps introduced in 1983 continued as standard. A new rear-end lighting arrangement used horizontal upper red stop/taillamps, accented with flush-mounted winged Cadillac crest ornamentation. New amber turn signal lamps and more dominant white backup lamps were below the red tail/stop lamps. Interiors were now available in combinations of leather and cloth. Pushbutton heat/vent controls now had accent lights. A 24-position click-stop temperature control lever allowed more precise settings. Optional cruise control now included acceleration-/deceleration capability. Cimarron prices began at $12,614. The special edition Cimarron d'Oro, introduced during 1983, was available again with distinctive Sable Black body, highlighted by goldtone accents that replaced all the body chrome. D'Oro also sported black bumpers, headlamp bezels, rip rail and window reveal moldings, wheel opening and rocker panel moldings, and door handles. Goldtone touches included the grille; a lay-down 'Cadillac Cimarron' hood ornament; accent stripes on hood center, body beltline, bumper rub strips and bodyside moldings; "D'Oro" fender plaques; Cimarron trunk lid script; a '2.0-Liter Fuel Injection' plaque on the trunk lid; and winged Cadillac crest ornamentation on taillamps. Gold also tinted the steering wheel spokes and horn pad emblem. In an effort to attract younger motorists to the black/gold small Caddy, radio commercials played an upbeat jingle promoting the "Cimarron touch."

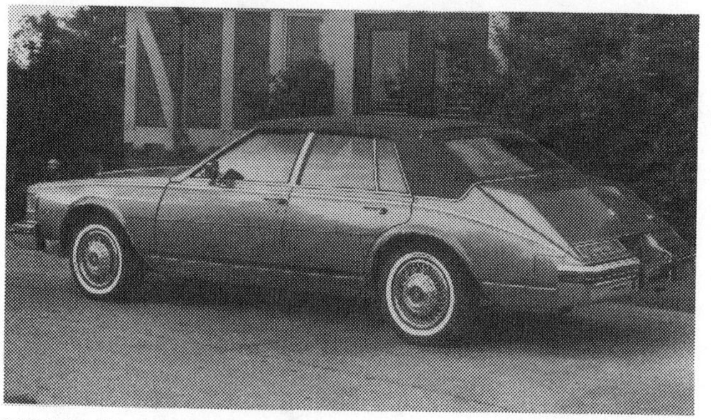

1984 Seville "Cabriolet" sedan (AA)

SEVILLE — SERIES 6K — V-8 — Restyled taillamps and new body-colored side moldings gave the bustleback front-drive Seville a slightly different look for 1984. Horizontal taillamps were modified to include a clear outer lens and red inner lens. This year's grille had fine vertical accents and a bright script Cadillac nameplate in the lower left corner. The traditional Cadillac stand-up wreath-and-crest hood ornament stood on a tapered hood center molding. Seville had new low-gloss black door trim bezels, instrument panel bezels and air conditioning outlets. New tufted multi-button cloth or leather/vinyl trim were the upholstery choices for base models. New options included luminum alloy wheels with center hubcaps and exposed chrome lug nuts. Sense-around Delco/Bose stereo was again available, and other sound systems were improved. Seville's lengthy standard equipment included rear reading lights, accent moldings, manual seatback recliner, overhead assist handles, door pull straps, four-wheel power disc brakes, air conditioning, power windows, bumper guards and rub strips, and P205/75R15 steel-belted radial whitewall tires. The limited-edition Elegante could now be ordered in a single color instead of two-tone. That $3879 package included a leather-trimmed steering wheel, leather 40/40 dual comfort front seats (six-way power adjustment with recliners), console, Tampico carpeting, chrome side moldings, wire wheel covers, and deluxe floor mats.

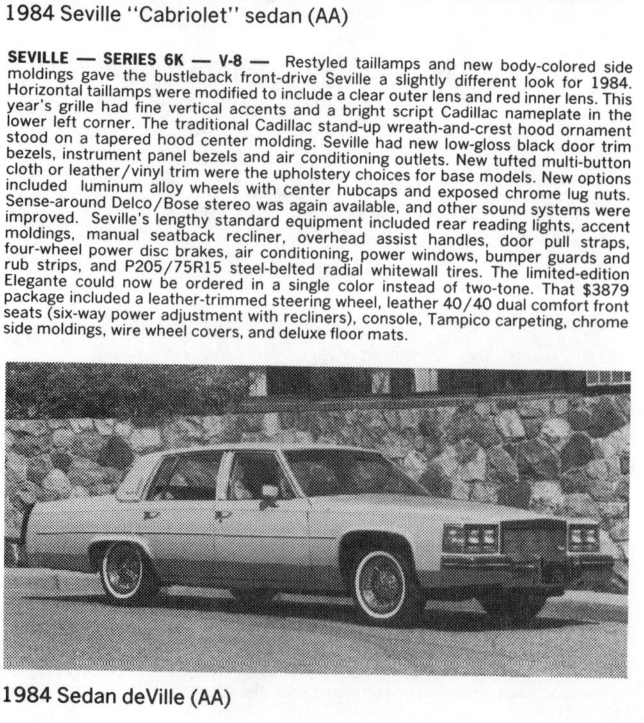

1984 Sedan deVille (AA)

DEVILLE — SERIES 6D — V-8 — New front-drive versions of DeVille and Fleetwood were anticipated, but delayed because of quality control questions; so for 1984 the rear-drive coupe and sedan carried on. Bodyside moldings were now color-keyed to the body finish. Taillamp lenses held goldtone Cadillac wing crests. All models now had electronic level control. The standard fuel-injected 249 cu. in. (4.1-liter) V-8 engine fed into a revised exhaust system with monolithic catalytic converter. Electronic controls were modified to meet stricter emissions standards in high-altitude regions. The diesel V-8 remained on the option list, except in California because of its emissions regulations. Standard equipment included power brakes and steering, whitewall steel-belted radials, electronic level control, automatic climate-control air conditioning, signal-seeking stereo radio with power antenna, cornering lights, and light monitors. All that plus power windows and six-way power seat, tinted glass, a remote- control left outside mirror, right visor mirror, automatic parking brake release, P215/75R15 tires and a stowaway spare. The front-wheel drive editions appeared during the '84 model year as early 1985s.

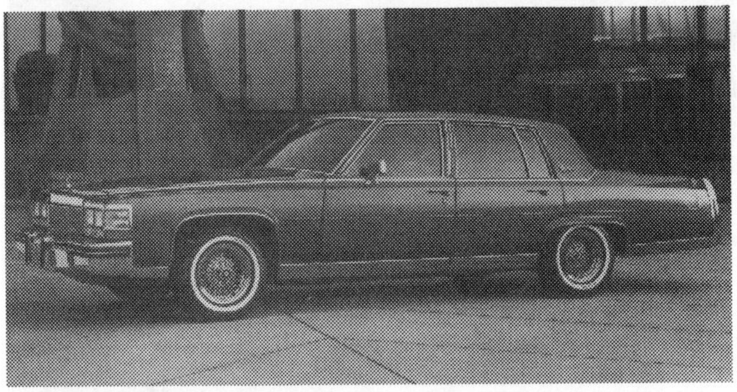

1984 Fleetwood Brougham Sedan d'Elegance (AA)

FLEETWOOD BROUGHAM — SERIES 6D — V-8 — Brougham sedans had a more closed-in back window plus bright belt and hood moldings, large rocker moldings, and wheel covers that were also used on limos. Electro- luminescent opera lamps were standard. The coupe had a stylish roof with custom cabriolet vinyl top enclosing a distinctive rear quarter window. Standard equipment was the same as DeVille coupe, but adding four-wheel power disc brakes, a remote-control right mirror, and 45/55 dual-comfort front seats.

FLEETWOOD LIMOUSINE — SERIES 6D — V-8 — Limousines carried the same standard equipment as DeVille, plus accent striping, opera lamps, and HR78 x 15-D tires. Only the formal limo had the six-way power seat. Fleetwood limos still used the variable-displacement 6.0- liter V8-6-4 engine.

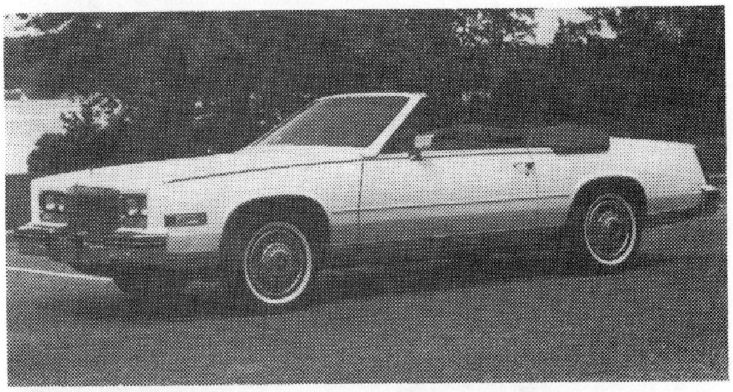

1984 Eldorado Biarritz convertible (AA)

ELDORADO — SERIES 6E — V-8 — For the first time since the famed '76 Eldorado ragtop, Cadillac offered a convertible: the new and posh Biarritz. Its rear side windows raised and lowered automatically with the power top, and it contained a glass back window. Convertible bodies came in three colors: Cotillion White, Hatteras Blue, and Autumn Maple Firemist. Each had a white diamond-grain vinyl top, glass rear window, and color- coordinated headliner. Reinforced frame rails and crossmember braces and a bolstered body structure added the necessary strength and rigidity. Convertibles had specific wide bright door and fender accent moldings; decklid accent striping; Biarritz script nameplate; and wire wheel covers. Also standard: special Biarritz multi-button tufted seat design and leather-wrapped steering wheel rim, plus Cadillac's theft deterrent system. The revived Biarritz convertible carried a hefty opening price tag: $31,286. That was nearly triple the cost of a '76 Eldo ragtop when it was new. Eldorado coupes started at a more modest $20,342. Eldorado's grille this year was vertically accented with a bright Cadillac script nameplate in the lower left corner. Rectangular headlamps sat above clear park/signal lamps. Appearance changes included new car-colored bodyside moldings plus new low-gloss black door trim bezels, instrument panel bezels, and air conditioning outlets. Base Eldos had a new leather seat trim design. Other additions: an improved theft- prevention system, new dashboard bezels, suspension refinements, improved stereo performance, and a new glow-plug system in the optional diesel V-8 engine. Coupes had a cabriolet vinyl top with glass rear window. brushed stainless steel roof cover, and opera lamps. Extended-range rear speakers became standard, except on the Delco/Bose sound system. The standard 4.1-liter V-8 engine added a new exhaust system, while the Oldsmobile diesel was not offered in convertibles (or in California). The Touring Coupe was again available, with a distinctive 'Eldorado Touring Coupe' cloisonne hood surface and sail panel ornaments. Also included: black-finished windshield window reveal moldings, quarter window channel moldings and wipers; plus body-colored headlamp and taillamp bezels and wheel opening moldings; large ribbed rocker panel moldings; and aluminum alloy wheels. Touring Coupes came only in Sable Black or Sonora Saddle Firemist.

I.D. DATA: All Cadillacs again had a 17-symbol Vehicle Identification Number (VIN), stamped on a metal tag attached to the upper left surface of the cowl, visible through the windshield. Some of the coding changed this year. The number begins with a '1' to indicate the manufacturing country (U.S.A.), followed by a 'G' for General Motors and a '6' for Cadillac Division. The next letter indicates restraint system: 'A' manual; 'B' automatic. Symbol five denotes car line and series: 'S' Seville; 'M' DeVille; 'W' Fleetwood Brougham; 'F' Fleetwood limousine; 'L' Eldorado. Digits six and seven indicate body type: '47' 2-dr. coupe; '69' 4-dr. sedan; '23' eight-passenger limousine; '33' formal limousine with center partition; '57' Eldorado coupe; '67' 2-dr. convertible coupe. Next comes the engine code: 'P' L4-121 TBI; '8' V8-250 FI; 'N' V8-350 diesel; '9' V8-6-4 368 FI. The next symbol is a check digit. Symbol ten indicates model year ('E' 1984). Symbol eleven denotes assembly plant. Last is a six-digit production sequence number. As before, engines carried an identifying number and bodies held a number plate.

CIMARRON (FOUR)

Model Number	Body/Style Number	Body Type & Seating	Factory Price	Shipping Weight	Production Total
6J	G69	4-dr Sedan-5P	12,614	2639	21,898

SEVILLE (V-8)

6K	S69	4-dr Sedan-6P	22,468	3844	39,997

DEVILLE (V-8)

6D	M47	2-dr Coupe-6P	17,140	3935	Note 1
6D	M69	4-dr Sedan-6P	17,625	3993	Note 2

FLEETWOOD BROUGHAM (V-8)

6D	W47	2-dr Coupe-6P	19,942	3986	Note 1
6D	W69	4-dr Sedan-6P	20,451	4029	Note 2

Note 1: Total two-door coupe production, 50,840. Note 2: Total DeVille/Fleetwood 4-door sedan production, 107,920.

6D	F23	4-dr Sedan-8P	30,454	4765	Note 3
6D	F33	4-dr Fml Limo-7P	31,512	4852	Note 3

Note 3: Total limousine production, 1,839.

ELDORADO (V-8)

6E	L57	2-dr Coupe-6P	20,342	3748	74,506
6E	L67	2-dr Conv-6P	31,286	N/A	3,300

ENGINES: BASE FOUR (Cimarron): Inline. OHV. Four-cylinder. Cast iron block and head. Displacement: 121 cu. in. (2.0 liters). Bore & stroke: 3.50 x 3.15 in. Compression ratio: 9.3:1. Brake horsepower: 88 at 4800 R.P.M. Torque: 110 lbs.-ft. at 2400 R.P.M. Five main bearings. Hydraulic valve lifters. Throttle-body fuel injection. VIN Code: P. BASE V-8 (Seville, DeVille, Brougham, Eldorado): 90-degree, overhead-valve V-8. Iron/aluminum alloy block; cast iron head. Displacement: 249 cu. in. (4.1 liters). Bore & stroke: 3.47 x 3.31 in. Compression ratio: 8.5:1. Brake horsepower: 135 at 4400 R.P.M. Torque: 200 lbs.-ft. at 2200 R.P.M. Five main bearings. Hydraulic valve lifters. Digital fuel injection (single-point, dual injectors). VIN Code: 8. 90-degree, overhead valve variable-displacement. Cast iron block and head. Displacement: 368 cu. in. (6.0 liters). Bore & stroke: 3.80 x 4.06 in. Compression ratio: 8.2:1. Brake horsepower: 140 at 3800 R.P.M. Torque: N/A. Five main bearings. Hydraulic valve lifters. Fuel injection. OPTIONAL DIESEL V-8 (Seville, DeVille, Brougham, Eldorado): 90-degree, overhead valve V-8. Cast iron block and head. Displacement: 350 cu. in. (5.7 liters). Bore & stroke: 4.05 x 3.38 in. Compression ratio: 22.7:1. Brake horsepower: 105 at 3200 R.P.M. Torque: 200 lbs.-ft. at 1600 R.P.M. Five main bearings. Hydraulic valve lifters. Fuel injection. Oldsmobile-built. VIN Code: N.

CHASSIS DATA: Wheelbase: (Cimarron) 101.2 in.; (Seville/Eldo) 114.0 in.; (DeVille/Brougham) 121.4 in.; (Limo) 144.5 in. Overall length:- (Cimarron) 173.1 in.; (Seville) 204.8 in.; (DeVille/Brougham) 221.0 in.; (Limo) 244.3 in.; (Eldo) 204.5 in. Height:- (Cimarron) 52.0 in.; (Seville/Eldo) 54.3 in.; (DeV/Brghm cpe) 54.6 in.; (DeV sed) 55.5 in.; (Brghm sed) 56.7 in.; (Limo) 56.9 in. Width:- (Cimarron) 66.5 in.; (Seville) 70.9 in.; (DeV/Brghm/limo) 75.3-76.4 in.; (Eldo) 70.6 in. Front Tread:- (Cimarron) 55.4 in.; (Seville/Eldo) 59.3 in.; (others) 61.7 in. Rear Tread:- (Cimarron) 55.2 in.; (Seville/Eldo) 60.6 in.; (others) 60.7 in. Standard Tires:- (Cimarron) P195/70R13; (Seville/Eldo) P205/75R15 SBR WSW; (DeV/Brghm) P215/75R15 SBR WSW; (Limo) HR78 x 15-D SBR WSW.

TECHNICAL: Transmission: Five-speed, floor shift manual transmission standard on Cimarron, Turbo Hydra-matic optional; gear ratios same as 1983. Three-speed automatic standard on limo; four- speed overdrive automatic on others; ratios same as 1983. Standard final drive ratio:- (Cimarron) 3.83:1 w/5-spd, 3.18:1 w/auto.; (SeV/Eldo) 3.15:1 exc. w/diesel, 2.93:1; (DeV/Brghm) 3.42:1 exc. w/diesel, 2.93:1. Steering:- (Cimarron) power rack and pinion; (others) power recirculating ball. Suspension and rakes:- same as 1983. Fuel tank:- (Cimarron) 13.6 gal.; (SeV/Eldo) 20.3 gal. exc. w/diesel, 22.8; (DeV/Brghm) 24.5 gal. exc. w/diesel, 26.0.

DRIVETRAIN OPTIONS: 5.7-liter diesel V 8 engine (NC); N/A limo or Cimarron. California emission equipment ($99). Engine block heater ($18-$45). Heavy-duty battery: Cimarron ($26); others ($40). 100-amp alternator ($50) exc. Cimarron. H.D. radiator: Cimarron ($40). Three-speed automatic transmission: Cimarron ($320). Limited slip differential: limo ($120). Heavy-duty ride package: DeV/Brghm ($319). FE2 touring suspension: Eldo/SeV ($115).

OPTION PACKAGES: Cimarron D'Oro ($350). Seville Elegante ($3879). Brougham d'Elegance: cloth seating ($1250); leather ($1800). DeVille d'Elegance ($1150). Cabriolet roof: DeV/Eldo cpe ($420). Full cabriolet roof: Eldo/SeV ($995). Eldorado Biarritz ($3395). Eldorado Touring Coupe ($1975).

DEVILLE/FLEETWOOD BROUGHAM/LIMOUSINE/ELDORADO/SEVILLE CONVENIENCE/APPEARANCE OPTIONS: Astroroof ($1225); N/A on limo. Electronic cruise control ($185). Controlled-cycle wiper system: DeV/limo ($60). Rear defogger w/heated outside mirrors ($165-$215). Automatic door locks ($162). Remote-locking fuel filler door ($59). Garage door opener ($140) exc. conv. Illuminated entry system ($76); std. on Brougham. Digital instrument cluster: SeV/Eldo $238). Dual comfort front seats: DeV ($225). Memory driver's seat ($205) exc. limo/conv. Six-way power passenger seat: DeV/Eldo/SeV ($215-$225). Power driver's seat recliner ($155) exc. limo. Power passenger seat recliner: DeV ($155); Brghm ($90). Power passenger seat recliner w/six-way power seat: DeV/Eldo/SeV ($315-$380). Leather-trimmed steering wheel ($99). Tilt/telescope steering wheel ($184); std. on formal limo. Power trunk lid release and pull-down: DeV/limo ($120). Theft deterrent system ($190). Twilight Sentinel ($79). Guidematic headlamp control ($93). Opera lamps: DeV/Eldo ($88). Trumpet horn ($38) exc. Seville. Electric remote mirrors w/thermometer on left: limo ($101). Electric remote- control outside mirrors ($101) exc. limo. Twin lighted vanity mirrors ($140). Electronic-tuning seek/scan AM/FM stereo radio with clock and cassette player ($299); with cassette and CB ($577) exc. Eldo/SeV;

w/cassette and Delco-GM/Bose sound system, Eldo/SeV ($895). CB radio: Eldo/SeV ($278). Rear-control ET radio w/cassette: limo ($475). Triband antenna ($50). Full padded vinyl roof: DeVille sed ($285). Two-tone paint: SeV ($600); DeV/Eldo ($345); Firemist, DeV/Eldo ($465). Firemist paint ($235). Accent striping: DeV ($77). Bodyside molding: Eldo Touring cpe ($64). Door edge guards ($19-$29). License frames, each ($14). Leather seating area ($515-$680). Carpeted rubber floor mats: front ($43- $45); rear ($25). Trunk mat ($21). Aluminum wheels: Eldo/SeV ($429). Locking wire wheels: DeV/Brghm ($860). Turbine vaned wheel covers: DeV ($77). Locking wire wheel covers ($315- $394) exc. limo. White-letter tires: Eldo touring cpe ($100). Puncture-sealing tires ($135-$180) exc. limo.

CIMARRON CONVENIENCE/APPEARANCE OPTIONS: Vista Vent w/rear tilt ($300). Electronic cruise control ($175). Power windows ($260). Power door locks ($175). Power trunk release ($40). Garage door opener ($165); retainer ($25). Tilt steering wheel ($104). Six-way power driver's seat ($215); both seats ($430). Twilight Sentinel ($79). Twin lighted vanity mirrors ($95). Seek/scan AM/FM stereo radio w/cassette ($203). Delete radio ($151 credit). Power antenna ($60). Door edge guards ($25). License frame ($12). Decklid luggage rack ($100). Cloth upholstery ($100 credit). Carpeted rubber floor mats: front ($38); rear ($22). Trunk mat ($18). Whitewall tires ($55).

HISTORY: Introduced: September 22, 1983. Model year production: 300,300 (not including early '85 DeVille/Fleetwoods). The total includes 2,465 diesels. Calendar year production: 328,534. Calendar year sales by U.S. dealers: 320,017 for a 4.0 percent market share. Model year sales by U.S. dealers: 327,587 (including 46,356 early '85 front-drives).

Historical Footnotes: Sales rose 13 percent for the model year, but Cadillac's market share declined. (Figures are a bit distorted because both front- and rear-drive DeVille/Fleetwood models were sold at the same time.) On the other hand, all the GM divisions experienced a drop in market share. Rising demand, though, kept plants working overtime during 1984. Cimarron continued as Cadillac's weakest seller, largely because it offered little more than the related J-car Chevrolet Cavalier gave for far fewer dollars. Best performers in terms of increased sales were the big Caddies: DeVille and Fleetwood Brougham. Research had shown, however, that over three-fourths of Cimarron buyers had never bought a Cadillac before; and that many of them had previously owned an import. Late in 1983, a modern new plant at Orion Township in Michigan had begun production of the new front-drive DeVille, to be introduced for 1985 after early production delays. Also late in 1983, Cadillac became part of the Buick-Cadillac-Oldsmobile group. In January 1984, John O. Grettenberger became Cadillac's new chief. Cadillac had offered the last American convertible in 1976, but wasn't the first to return with a ragtop in the '80s. Already on the market were Buick Riviera, Chevrolet Cavalier, Pontiac Sunbird, Chrysler LeBaron, Dodge 600, and Ford Mustang. Cadillac's version was, of course, the most costly of the lot for '84. The convertible was actually a conversion done by ASC Corporation in Lansing, Michigan, after the car was assembled in New Jersey. The work included reinforcing inner rockers, radiator support cross rods, and many body braces. Front and rear anti-roll bars and tougher suspension components were added along with the vinyl convertible top. All told, the convertible weighed 179 pounds more than the coupe from which it evolved.

1985 CADILLAC

Front-wheel drive now became the rule at Cadillac, as in nearly all other makes. Two grand old names, DeVille and Fleetwood, made the switch this year. All Cadillacs except the subcompact Cimarron (and carryover rear-drive Brougham) now carried a transverse-mounted, fuel-injected 4.1-liter V-8 engine with die-cast aluminum-block. Two safety improvements arrived this year: anti-lacerative windshield glass (with inner layer of two-part plastic) on Seville's Elegante, plus a high-mount stop lamp on all DeVilles and Fleetwoods. That stop lamp would become required on all cars for 1986.

CIMARRON — SERIES 6J — FOUR — Cadillac's compact received a major revision for 1985 but went on sale a little later than usual. Production of the 1984 models was extended into autumn 1985, to take advantage of the existing Corporate Average Fuel Economy standards, which were to grow more stringent for the coming year. An optional V-6 engine finally arrived for mid-year models, to deliver a much-needed performance boost. The new 173 cu. in. (2.8-liter) high-output V-6 with fuel injection was built by Chevrolet. Cimarron sales continued sluggish, but style and performance alterations were made to try to draw some younger customers. The restyled body also was intended to give Cimarron more of a Cadillac look. Prices began just under $13,000, well under other Caddies but a good deal higher than Chevrolet's Cavalier and the other J-bodied GM models. Stabilizer bars grew longer this year, and front springs became stiffer. Outside, Cimarron's front end grew by almost 5 inches. The new crosshatch grille reached out to black inner surfaces for headlamp bezels, which were positioned differently than before. Styled aluminum wheels were available for the first time, as an option. Standard transmission was a five-speed manual gearbox, with three- speed automatic or four-speed manual optional. Standard equipment included air conditioning, AM/FM stereo radio with power antenna, center armrests, overhead assist handles, power brakes and steering, bumper guards and rub strips, digital clock, power door locks, electric defoggers (rear and side window), halogen headlamps and foglamps, tinted glass, and electric remote mirrors. Inside were leather reclining bucket seats (driver's side six-way power adjustable), a leather-wrapped tilt steering wheel, tachometer, power windows, and power trunk release. All that and more) helped to justify Cimarron's hefty price tag. Cimarron D'Oro added fine-line gold accent stripes on beltline, hood center and rub strips; gold-accented grille and wheels; foglamp covers; lower bodyside accent moldings; saddle leather seats; plus gold-tinted hood ornament, steering wheel spokes and horn pad emblem. D'Oro bodies were either red or white, with plaques on front fender and dash.

1985 Seville Elegante sedan (C)

SEVILLE — SERIES 6K — V-8 — For its final season in this form, the front-drive Seville sedan changed little. Neither did its companion Eldorado, which used the same chassis layout. Standard engine, as before, was the fuel-injected 250 cu. in. (4.1-liter) V-8, with four-speed overdrive automatic transmission. Buyers could also choose a diesel V-8, but not many did. Seville's base price was $23,729. New to the option list: aluminum alloy wheels with a radial fin design and gray accents. Both spoked and non-spoke versions were available. Seville's Elegante had a new "Inner Shield" windshield with a two-section plastic layer intended to prevent cuts from splintered glass in an accident. Elegante's interior featured standard leather seats, color-coordinated with the car body. Late in the model year, a Commemorative Edition package was announced.

1985 Coupe deVille (C)

DEVILLE — SERIES 6C — V-8 — A dramatically different front-drive, C-body Coupe deVille (and Fleetwood sedan) hit the market late in March of 1984, as early '85 models. The Grand Old Caddies lost two feet in length and about 600 pounds. Their front-drive chassis layout was also used by Buick Electra and Oldsmobile Ninety-Eight. Though not exactly small, both were a far cry from the DeVilles and Fleetwoods of prior eras. Arriving in the fall was a new Fleetwood coupe, with formal cabriolet vinyl roof and opera lamps, as well as wire wheel covers. Both coupe and sedan carried a claimed six passengers. A transverse-mounted 249 cu. in. (4.1-liter) V-8 engine with throttle-body fuel injection was standard; 4.3-liter V-6 diesel a no-charge option. Cadillac's was the only transverse-mounted V-8 available in the world. Oldsmobile's diesel V-8 engine also was available. Inside the automatic transmission, the torque converter clutch was computer- controlled and operated by silicone fluid. All models included the Retained Power Accessory System, which permitted use of power windows and trunk release for 10 minutes after shutting off the engine. A third brake light was now mounted on the rear panel shelf. Standard equipment included four-speed overdrive automatic transmission, power steering and brakes, tungsten-halogen headlamps, body-colored protective side moldings, six-way power driver's seat, power windows and door locks, side window defogger, electronic climate control, a Delco 2000 AM/FM stereo radio with electronic tuning and seek/scan, remote-controlled outside mirrors, courtesy/reading lamps in the sail panel, and power decklid release. Tires were P205/75R14 all-season steel-belted radials.

1985 Fleetwood coupe (C)

FLEETWOOD — SERIES 6C — V-8 — Fleetwood coupes and sedans carried the same standard equipment as the DeVille duo, along with wire wheel covers, opera lamps, dual comfort front seats, and a limousine-style back window. Powertrains were the same as DeVille's. This was the final year for Fleetwood as a separate model. In 1986 it would become a DeVille option package. Fleetwood prices began at $21,495, which was more than $3000 higher than DeVille.

1985 Fleetwood 75 limousine (C)

FLEETWOOD SEVENTY-FIVE LIMOUSINE — SERIES 6C — V-8 — Like the Fleetwood sedan, the Seventy-Five limo switched to front-drive. The rear-drive version was dropped. To create the new limousine, a C-car platform (same as DeVille/Fleetwood) and coupe body were stretched almost two feet. Even so, the modern edition was more than two feet shorter than the old rear-drive, and weighed 1200 pounds less. Powertrain was the same as DeVille/Fleetwood: a transverse-mounted 4.1-liter V-8 and four-speed overdrive automatic. Rear control panels let passengers unlock the back doors, adjust climate, and control the stereo center. The basic limo still carried eight passengers, and a seven-passenger formal version appeared later in the model year. Fleetwood Seventy-Five limousines had power-operated mirrors, but other standard equipment similar to Fleetwood sedans. A matching formal Cabriolet vinyl roof was available. Aluminum alloy wheels were made standard on limos.

1985 Fleetwood Brougham sedan (C)

FLEETWOOD BROUGHAM — SERIES 6D — Brougham, the last surviving rear-drive Cadillac, changed little for 1985 and faced potential extinction in spite of increased sales. That didn't happen. The traditional rear-drive lingered on for several more years, even though all other Caddies (including limos) switched to front-drive and shrunken size. Vast inside and out, Broughams continued to attract traditional luxury-car buyers. The Brougham coupe was dropped from the lineup in mid-year. Sedans came with a standard full vinyl roof, while the Brougham coupe included a standard Cabriolet vinyl top with unique rear quarter window. Standard engine was the 4.1-liter V-8; diesel V-8 optional at no charge.

1985 Eldorado coupe (C)

ELDORADO — SERIES 6E — V-8 — Few changes were evident on the luxury front-drive personal coupe and convertible. The Biarritz convertible, introduced for 1984, could now get an optional electric defogger for its glass back window. New spoked aluminum alloy road wheels joined the option list. Standard engine remained the 4.1-liter V-8, with throttle-body fuel injection, hooked to four-speed overdrive automatic transmission. A big diesel V-8 also was available (at extra cost) in the coupe. Eldo's Biarritz coupe had a cabriolet vinyl roof with brushed steel cap, accent moldings, and opera lamps. Convertibles were similarly decked out. Touring Coupes had a stiffer suspension as well as blackout and body-color trim. Eldo coupes began at $21,355, but the convertible cost over $11,000 more. This would be the ragtop's final season, as Eldorado switched to a new body for 1986.

I.D. DATA: Cadillacs again had a 17-symbol Vehicle Identification Number (VIN), stamped on a metal tag attached to the upper left surface of the cowl, visible through the windshield. Coding changed to reflect the new front-drive models. The number begins with a '1' to indicate the manufacturing country (U.S.A.), followed by a 'G' for General Motors and a '6' for Cadillac Division. Symbol four is car line (GM body): 'J' Cimarron; 'K' Seville; 'C' DeVille/Fleetwood; 'D' Brougham; 'E' Eldorado. Symbol five indicates series: 'G' Cimarron; 'S' Seville; 'D' DeVille; 'B' Fleetwood; 'H' Fleetwood limousine; 'W' Fleetwood Brougham (rear-drive); 'L' Eldorado. Digits six and seven indicate body type: '47' 2-dr. coupe; '69' 4-dr. sedan; '23' eight-passenger limo; '33' formal limousine; '57' Eldorado coupe; 2-dr. convertible coupe. Next is engine code: 'P' L4-121 TBI; 'W' V6-173 FI; '8' V8-249 DFI; 'T' V6-262 diesel; 'N' V8-350 diesel. The next symbol is a check digit. Symbol ten indicates model year ('F' 1985). Next is a code for assembly plant: '9' Detroit; 'E' Linden, NJ; 'J' Janesville, WI. Finally comes a six-digit production sequence number, starting with 000001 for Detroit; 400001 for Janesville; 600001 for Linden (E-body); or 800001 for Linden (K-body). An identifying number is also on the engine, and a set of codes on a body number plate.

CIMARRON (FOUR)

Model Number	Body/Style Number	Body Type & Seating	Factory Price	Shipping Weight	Production Total
6J	G69	4-dr Sedan-5P	12962/13522	2630/ --	19,890

Price/Weight Note: Figure before the slash is for a four-cylinder engine, after the slash for the new Cimarron V-6.

SEVILLE (V-8)

6K	S69	4-dr Sedan-6P	23,729	3688	39,755

DEVILLE (FRONT-DRIVE V-8)

6C	D47	2-dr Coupe-6P	18,355	3330	Note 1
6C	D69	4-dr Sedan-6P	18,947	3327	Note 2

FLEETWOOD (FRONT-DRIVE V-8)

6C	B47	2-dr Coupe-6P	21,495	3267	Note 1
6C	B69	4-dr Sedan-6P	21,466	3364	Note 2

Note 1: Total two-door DeVille/Fleetwood production, 37,485. Note 2: Total DeVille/Fleetwood four-door production, 114,278. For the model year, 42,911 Fleetwoods and 108,852 DeVilles were produced. These figures do not include 45,330 DeVille/Fleetwoods produced as early 1985 models (9,390 two-doors and 35,940 four-doors).

FLEETWOOD LIMOUSINE (V-8)

6C	H23	4-dr Limo-8P	32,640	3543	Note 3
6C	H33	4-dr Fml Limo-7P	N/A	3642	Note 3

Note 3: Total limousine production was 405 units.

FLEETWOOD BROUGHAM (REAR-DRIVE V-8)

6D	W47	2-dr Coupe-6P	21,219	3873	8,336
6D	W69	4-dr Sedan-6P	21,835	3915	52,960

ELDORADO (V-8)

6E	L57	2-dr Coupe-6P	21,355	3623	74,101
6E	L67	2-dr Conv-6P	32,105	3804	2,300

Engine note: Diesel V-6 engines were available on DeVille/Fleetwood models; diesel V-8s on Seville, Fleetwood Brougham and Eldorado, with no extra charge.

ENGINES: BASE FOUR (Cimarron): Inline. OHV. Four-cylinder. Cast iron block and head. Displacement: 121 cu. in. (2.0 liters). Bore & stroke: 3.50 x 3.15 in. Compression ratio: 9.3:1. Brake horsepower: 88 at 4800 R.P.M. Torque: 110 lbs.-ft. at 2400 R.P.M. Five main bearings. Hydraulic valve lifters. TBI. OPTIONAL V-6 (Cimarron): 60-degree, overhead-valve V-6. Cast iron block and head. Displacement: 173 cu. in. (2.8 liters). Bore & stroke: 3.50 x 2.99 in. Compression ratio: 8.9:1. Brake horsepower: 125 at 4800 R.P.M. Torque: 155 lbs.-ft. at 3600 R.P.M. Four main bearings. Hydraulic valve lifters. Multi-point fuel injection. Chevrolet-built. BASE V-8 (Seville, Brougham, Eldorado): 90-degree, overhead valve V-8. Cast iron block and head. Displacement: 249 cu. in. (4.1 liters). Bore & stroke: 3.47 x 3.31 in. Compression ratio: 8.5:1. Brake horsepower: 135 at 4400 R.P.M. Torque: 200 lbs.-ft. at 2200 R.P.M. Five main bearings. Hydraulic valve lifters. Fuel injection. BASE V-8 (DeVille, Fleetwood, Limo): Same as 249 cu. in. V-8 above, but-- Brake H.P.: 125 at 4200 R.P.M. Torque: 190 lbs.-ft. at 2200 R.P.M. OPTIONAL DIESEL V-6 (DeVille, Fleetwood): 90-degree, overhead valve V-8. Cast iron block and head. Displacement: 262 cu. in. (4.3 liters). Bore & stroke: 4.06 x 3.39 in. Compression ratio: 21.6:1. Brake horsepower: 85 at 3600 R.P.M. Torque: 165 lbs.-ft. at 1600 R.P.M. Four main bearings. Hydraulic valve lifters. Fuel injection. OPTIONAL DIESEL V-8 (Seville, Brougham, Eldorado): 90-degree, overhead valve V-8. Cast iron block and head. Displacement: 350 cu. in. (5.7 liters). Bore & stroke: 4.06 x 3.39 in. Compression ratio: 22.7:1. Brake horsepower: 105 at 3200 R.P.M. Torque: 200 lbs.-ft. at 1600 R.P.M. Five main bearings. Hydraulic valve lifters. Fuel injection. Oldsmobile-built.

CHASSIS DATA: Wheelbase: (Cimarron) 101.2 in.; (Seville/Eldo) 114.0 in.; (DeVille/Fleetwood) 110.8 in.; (Brougham) 121.5 in. Overall length:- (Cimarron) 177.9 in.; (Seville) 204.8 in.; (DeV/Fleetwood) 195.0 in.; (Brghm) 221.0 in.; (Eldo) 204.5 in. Height:- (Cimarron) 52.0 in.; (Seville) 54.3 in.; (DeV/Fleetwood) 55.0 in.; (Brghm) 56.7 in.; (Eldo) 54.3 in.; (DeV/Fleetwood) 55.0 in.; (Brghm cpe) 54.6 in.; (Brghm sed) 56.7 in. Width:- (Cimarron) 65.1 in.; (Seville) 70.9 in.; (DeV/Fleetwood) 71.7 in.; (Brghm) 76.5 in.; (Eldo) 70.6 in. Front Tread:- (Cimarron) 55.4 in.; (Seville/Eldo) 59.3 in.; (DeV/Fleetwood) 60.3 in.; (Brghm) 61.7 in. Rear Tread:- (Cimarron) 55.2 in.; (Seville/Eldo) 59.8 in.; (DeV/Fleetwood) 59.8 in.; (Brghm) 60.7 in. Standard Tires:- (Cimarron) P195/70R13 SBR; (SeV/Eldo) P205/75R14 SBR WSW; (DeV/Fleetwood) P205/75R14 SBR WSW; (Brghm) P215/75R15 SBR WSW.

TECHNICAL: Transmission: Five-speed, floor shift manual transmission standard on Cimarron four: gear ratios: (1st) 3.92:1; (2nd) 2.15:1; (3rd) 1.33:1; (4th) 0.92:1; (5th) 0.74:1; (Rev) 3.50:1. Four-speed manual standard on Cimarron V-6: (1st) 3.31:1; (2nd) 1.95:1; (3rd) 1.95:1; (4th) 0.90:1; (Rev) 3.42:1. Cimarron three-speed Turbo Hydra-matic (THM125C) ratios: (1st) 2.84:1; (2nd) 1.60:1; (3rd) 1.00:1; (Rev) 2.07:1. Four-speed overdrive automatic (THM440-T4) standard on DeV/Fleetwood: (1st) 2.92:1; (2nd) 1.57:1; (3rd) 1.00:1; (4th) 0.67:1; (Rev) 2.38:1. Four-speed overdrive auto. std. on Eldo/SeV (THM325-4L) and Brougham (THM200-4R): (1st) 2.74:1; (2nd) 1.57:1; (3rd) 1.00:1; (4th) 0.67:1; (Rev) 2.07:1. Standard final drive ratio:- (Cimarron) 3.83:1 w/5- spd, 3.18:1 w/auto.; (SeV/Eldo) 3.15:1 exc. w/diesel, 2.93:1; (DeV/Fleetwood) 2.97:1 exc. w/diesel, 3.06:1; (Brghm) 3.42:1 exc. diesel, 2.93:1; (Limo) 2.97:1. Steering:- (Cimarron/DeV/F.W.) rack and pinion; (others) recirculating ball. Front suspension:- (Cimarron) Touring, w/MacPherson struts; (DeV/F.W.) MacPherson struts, lower control arms, coil springs and stabilizer bar; (SeV/Eldo) torsion bars, upper/lower control arms, stabilizer bar; (Brghm) upper/lower control arms, coil springs, stabilizer bar. Rear suspension:- (Cimarron) semi-independent, trailing arms, coil springs, stabilizer bar; (DeV/F.W.) independent struts, coil springs, stabilizer bar, electronic level control; (Eldo/SeV) independent with semi-trailing arms, coil springs, stabilizer bar and electronic level control; (Brghm) four-link rigid axle, coil springs, electronic level control. Brakes:- front disc, rear drum except Eldo/SeV, four-wheel discs. Disc dia.:- (Eldo/SeV) 10.4 in.; (DeV/F.W.) 10.25 in.; (Brghm) 11.7 in.; Drum dia.:- (DeV/F.W.) 8.9 in.; (Brghm) 11.0 in. Fuel tank:- (Cimarron) 13.6 gal.; (SeV/Eldo) 20.3 gal. exc.diesel, 22.8; (DeV/F.W.) 18.0 gal.; (Brghm) 24.5 gal.

DRIVETRAIN OPTIONS: 173 cu. in. (2.8-liter) V-6 engine: Cimarron ($560). 4.3-liter diesel V-6 engine: DeV/F.W. (NC). 5.7-liter diesel V-8 engine: Eldo/SeV/Brghm (NC). California emission equipment ($99). Engine block heater ($45) exc. Cimarron ($20). Heavy- duty battery: Cimarron ($26); others ($40). 100-amp alternator: Eldo/SeV/Brghm ($50). H.D. radiator: Cimarron ($45). Four-speed manual trans.: Cimarron ($350). Three-speed automatic trans.: Cimarron ($75 credit). Heavy-duty ride package: Brghm ($116). FE2 touring suspension: Eldo/SeV ($115). FE2 touring pkg. (alum. wheels, P215/65R15 Eagle GT tires, leather-wrapped steering wheel, revised suspension): DeV ($695); F.W. ($375). Delco/Bilstein suspension: Cimarron ($100); req'd w/V-6.

OPTION PACKAGES: Cimarron D'Oro ($975). Seville Elegante ($3879). Brougham or Fleetwood d'Elegance: cloth seating ($1250); leather ($1800). Cabriolet roof: DeV cpe ($498); Eldo ($420). Full cabriolet roof: Eldo/SeV ($995). Eldorado Biarritz ($3395). Eldorado Touring Coupe ($1975).

DEVILLE/FLEETWOOD/BROUGHAM/ELDORADO/SEVILLE CONVENIENCE/APPEARANCE OPTIONS: Astroroof ($1225); N/A on limo. Electronic cruise control $185). Controlled-cycle wiper system: DeV/F.W. ($60). Rear defogger w/heated outside mirrors ($165-$215). Automatic door locks ($162). Remote-locking fuel filler door ($59). Garage door opener ($140) exc. conv. Illuminated entry system ($76); std. on Brougham. Dual comfort 55/45 front seats: DeV ($235). Memory driver's seat ($205-$225) exc. limo/conv. Six-way power passenger seat ($225) exc. Brougham. Power driver's seatback recliner ($155) exc. Fleetwood ($90); N/A limo. Power passenger seatback recliner: DeV ($155); Brghm/ F.W. ($90). Power passenger seat recliner w/six-way power seat ($315-$380) exc. limo/Brghm. Leather-trimmed steering wheel ($99). Tilt/telescope steering wheel ($184). Power trunk lid release and pull-down: DeV/F.W. ($80-$120); release only, DeV/limo ($40). Theft deterrent system ($190). Twilight Sentinel ($79). Dimming Sentinel ($93-$128). Opera lamps: Eldo ($88). Trumpet horn ($38) exc. Seville. Electric remote- control outside mirrors ($101) exc. limo. Twin lighted vanity mirrors ($140). Automatic day/night mirror ($80). Electronic- tuning seek/scan AM/FM stereo radio w/cassette player ($299); w/cassette and Delco-GM/Bose sound system ($895) exc. Brghm. Electronic-tuning AM/FM stereo radio w/cassette and CB: Brghm ($577). CB radio ($278) exc. Brghm. Electronic-tuning radio with cassette and rear control: limo ($475). Triband antenna ($50). Two-tone paint: SeV ($600); Eldo ($345); partial Firemist, Eldo ($465). Firemist or Pearlmist paint ($235). Decklid and bodyside accent striping: DeV ($52). Bodyside molding: Eldo Touring cpe ($64). Door edge guards ($19-$29). License frames, each ($14). Front license bracket (NC) exc. DeVille. Leather seating area ($515-$680). Carpeted rubber floor mats: front ($43-$45); rear ($25). Trunk mat ($26). Aluminum wheels: Eldo/SeV/DeV ($429); F.W. ($114); std. on limo. Spoked aluminum alloy wheels: Eldo/SeV ($835); Biarritz/Elegante/conv. ($441). Locking wire wheels: Brghm ($860). Locking wire wheel covers ($315-$394) exc. Fleetwood. P225/70R15 white-letter tires: Eldo touring cpe ($100). Puncture-sealing tires ($135-$180) exc. limo. IMARRON CONVENIENCE/APPEARANCE OPTIONS: Vista Vent w/rear tilt ($310). Digital instrument cluster ($238). Garage door opener ($165); retainer ($25). Six-way power passenger seat ($225). Twilight Sentinel ($85). Twin lighted vanity mirrors ($95). Seek/scan AM/FM stereo radio w/cassette ($223). Delete radio ($151 credit). Lower bodyside accent moldings ($450). Door edge guards ($25). License frame, rear ($15). Decklid luggage rack ($130). Cloth upholstery ($100 credit). Carpeted rubber floor mats: front ($38); rear ($22). Trunk mat ($26). Aluminum wheels, 14 in. ($40). P195/70R13 SBR WSW tires ($55). P205/60R14 SBR Eagle GT ($94). P205/60R14 SBR OWL tires ($171).

HISTORY: Fleetwood and Deville were introduced April 5, 1984; Eldorado and Seville, October 2, 1984; Cimarron, November 8, 1984. Model year production: 394,840 (including 45,330 early '85 front-drive DeVille/Fleetwoods). That total included 11,968 V-6 engines and 1,088 diesels. Calendar year production: 322,765. Calendar year sales by U.S. dealers: 298,762 for a 3.6 percent market share. Model year sales by U.S. dealers: 310,942 (not including 46,356 front-drive DeVille/Fleetwoods sold as early 1985s).

Historical Footnotes: The delayed arrival of the new front-drive DeVille/Fleetwood was due to shortages of the Type 440 four- speed automatic transaxle, produced at GM's Hydra-matic Division. Production had been delayed for six months. For that reason, both rear-drive and front-drive DeVilles were offered to the public at the same time for a while during 1984. A strike at GM of Canada affected supplies to over 30 General Motors plants in the U.S., including Cadillac's.

1986 CADILLAC

All-new Eldorado and Seville models entered the lineup for 1986, loaded with a diagnostic system and electronic instruments. Anti-lock braking was a new option on Fleetwood and DeVille. All Cadillacs were now front-wheel drive except the big Brougham, which hung on for another year with a 5.0- liter V-8 under the hood. Luxury touches promoted in the full-line catalog ranged from golden ignition keys all the way to elegant option packages, to deliver "the feeling of uncompromising excellence." In keeping with that promise, diesel engines departed from the Cadillac option list, victims of lack of interest and an unimpressive reliability record. The HT 4100 V-8 added stainless steel exhaust manifolds. Door locks had new rocker switches. Floor consoles contained an ashtray that opened at a finger's touch. And to keep up with the times, a cellular telephone ("discreetly" positioned in fold-down armrest) joined the option list. To attract buyers who preferred good handling to a cushy ride, DeVilles could also get a Touring Coupe or Touring Sedan option with stiffer suspension and related extras. Over 40 body colors were available, including nine Firemist shades and two Pearlmist (black cherry or black emerald) that changed character according to the angle and intensity of sunlight striking the car's surface.

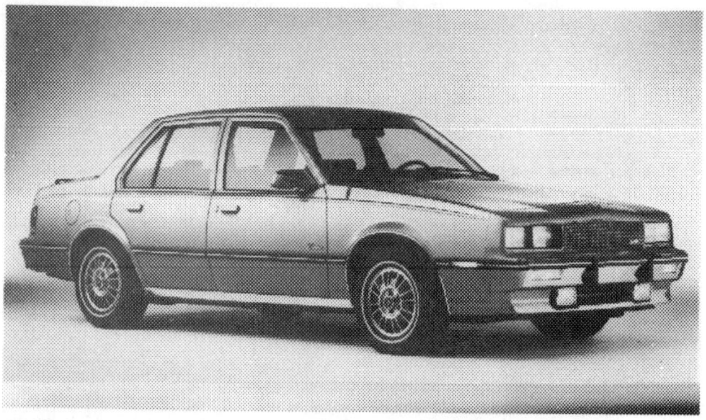

1986 Cimarron sedan (AA)

CIMARRON — SERIES 6J — FOUR/V-6 — Cimarron entered a new year sporting new wraparound taillamps at the restyled rear end, carrying a price tag that began above $13,000. Inside was new leather trim on the shift boot and knob (manual shift), at a redesigned console. A premium Delco-Bose sound system was now optional, and suspension components were revised. Cadillac's smallest had been extensively reworked as a mid-year 1985 entry with new front-end styling (more evidently Cadillac) and new optional electronic instrument cluster. Most important, though, was the V-6 option, giving the car a much-needed performance boost. That "second generation" 2.8-liter V-6 with multi-port fuel injection came from Chevrolet. Standard engine continued to be the 2.0-liter four with five-speed (Getrag-designed) manual gearbox. The 2.8 could have four-speed manual or three-speed automatic. Even with the V-6 available, Cimarron still wasn't selling strongly, enjoying only a modest increase for 1985. To improve handling there was an optional Delco/Bilstein suspension with gas-charged front struts and rear shocks, plus stiffer front spring rates and thicker front stabilizer bar. That suspension was required with the V-6 engine. An impressive standard equipment list included Sierra Grain leather seating areas, air conditioning, cruise control, leather-trimmed tilt steering wheel, aluminum alloy wheels, and plenty of power gadgetry from six-way driver's seat to windows to trunk lid release. The standard seek/scan AM/FM stereo radio included a power antenna. Cimarron used a fine-patterned crosshatch grille with 'Cadillac' script at the driver's side, plus recessed quad rectangular headlamps. Wide parking/signal lamps were inset below the bumper rub strips; foglamps below them, flanking the air dam. 'Cimarron' script appeared on front doors. Yellow beige "chamois" was a new Cimarron color. Twenty dual-color accent stripes were available. Also revised this year was the D'Oro version, whose distinctive front end featured aero composite halogen headlamps and wraparound side marker lights. Offered with a white or red body, the package included: gold custom fine line accent stripes on beltline, rub strips and hood center; gold-accented grille; foglamp covers; lower bodyside accent moldings; D'Oro plaques on front fenders and dash; gold- tinted lay-down hood ornament; and gold-tinted steering wheel spokes and horn pad emblem. P205/60R14 low-profile performance steel-belted radial tires rode on gold-accented 14 in. aluminum alloy wheels. D'Oro also had grooved, body- colored lower body accent moldings.

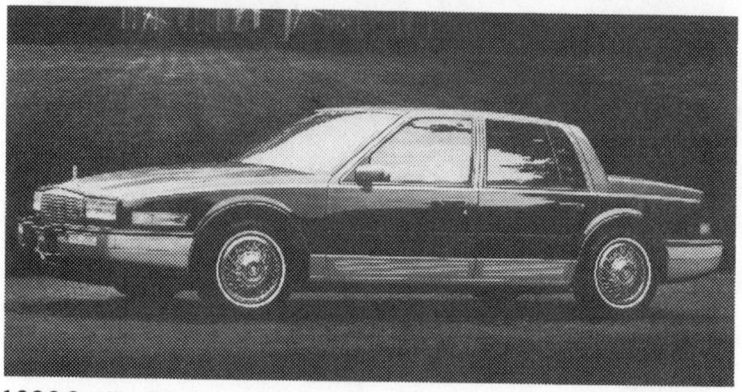

1986 Seville Elegante sedan (AA)

SEVILLE — SERIES 6K — V-8 — A brand new Seville rode the same new platform as Eldorado--17 inches shorter and 375 pounds lighter than before. Gone was the striking razor-edge styling of 1980-85, replaced by a body not much different from Eldorado's, or from other GM vehicles. Standard engine was the Cadillac 4.1- liter V-8, hooked to four-speed overdrive automatic transaxle. Seville's vertical grille had a fine-mesh crosshatch pattern. Clear rear lenses of the horizontal side marker lamps were angled to match wheel openings. Very wide, clear parking/signal lamps were inset into the bumper area. The Clearcoat finish had a new (standard) two-tone paint treatment. New front bucket seats were upholstered with Royal Prima cloth and Sierra Grain leather seating areas. The front console included a fold-down armrest and storage compartments, while American walnut highlighted the instrument panel, console and steering wheel. Optional: a cellular phone with removable handset in locking storage compartment, and hidden mike between the sun visors. A "driver information center" in the digital instrument cluster displayed electronic readouts of outside temperature, fuel economy and engine data, including a tachometer reading. Retained Accessory Power allowed many accessories to remain operative up to 10 minutes after shutting off the ignition (or until a door was opened). Standard equipment included reclining bucket seats, Twilight Sentinel heaedlamp control, cruise control, power trunk release, leather-trimmed tilt/telescope steering wheel, body- colored electric remote mirrors, an AM/FM stereo radio with seek/scan and digital display, power antenna, power four- wheel disc brakes, and aluminum alloy wheels. Seville's special-edition Elegante was offered again, carrying wire wheel covers and displaying a unique mid-tone paint scheme. The package included Tampico carpeting, deluxe floor mats, accent moldings, walnut appliques, front seatback pockets, dual power reclining front bucket seats with power lumber support, memory driver's seat and six-way power passenger seat. American walnut wood plates trimmed the doors. Elegante was upholstered in Mayfair cloth with Sierra Grain leather seating areas, with a package price tag of $3595 and up.

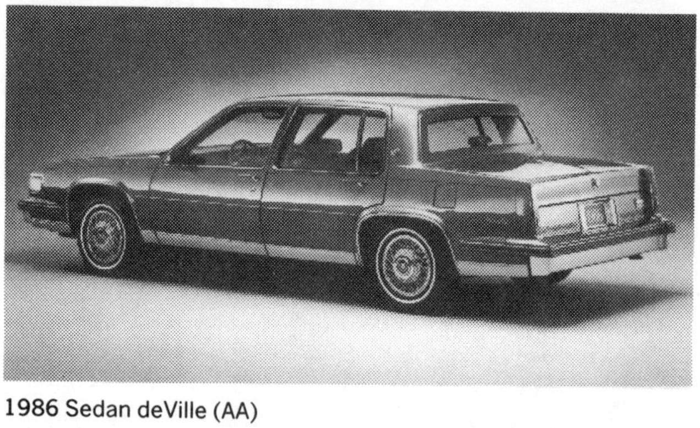

1986 Sedan deVille (AA)

DEVILLE — SERIES 6C — V-8 — Front-drive Caddies came in coupe and sedan form, with prices starting just under $20,000. Standard engine was the transverse-mounted Cadillac 4.1-liter V-8, with four-speed overdrive automatic. The six-passenger interior sported a new seat trim design, while a closed-in, limousine-style back window was standard. DeVille's grille used many thin vertical bars, along with three horizontal bars and a 'Cadillac' script at the lower corner. Wraparound cornering lamps contained a small amber lens and large clear lens. Wide rectangular parking lights were set into the bumper, below the protective gray rub strips. Coupe or Sedan DeVille script identification was at the back of the quarter panels. Wide, bright rocker moldings ran the length of the car. Coupe deVille's assist handles moved from front seatbacks to door lock pillars. Door panels and dash sported cherry woodgrain trim. Optional aluminum alloy wheels had new flush hubcaps. Anti-lock braking (ABS) was an important new option that would gradually find its way onto other models in the years ahead. Developed in accord with a German firm (Teves), ABS used sensors at each wheel to determine when one was about to lock. Then, the system would adjust hydraulic pressure to keep it from locking (and possibly skidding). ABS was also offered on Buick Electra and Olds Ninety-Eight this year. The 4.1-liter V-8 gained a little horsepower, while the 4.3-liter diesel departed. DeVille could have an optional touring package with handling components and "more aggressive, no-nonsense" look. It included gray rocker moldings and front air dam, rear spoiler, recessed foglamps,

body-color taillamp bezels, tighter steering ratio (18.4:1), improved spring rates, a solid front stabilizer bar (standard one was hollow), stronger front lower control arm bushings, a much thicker rear stabilizer bar (18 vs.12 MM), and 15 in. performance tires on aluminum alloy wheels. Gray bumper rub strips had silver accent stripes. Starting in February 1986, the touring package was upgraded to include bigger exhaust pipe diameter, higher shift point between first and second gear, and 5 more horsepower in the engine. The new ratings were 135 horsepower, and 205 pound-feet of torque at 2300 R.P.M. Available on either coupe or sedan, the Touring package also included color-keyed dual remote-control mirrors, leather- wrapped steering wheel, gray leather seats and interior trim--even removable quarter-window louvers (on coupe). A 'Touring Coupe' or 'Touring Sedan' signature went on back windows. Rather than the whole package, buyers could opt for the Touring Suspension alone: Goodyear Eagle GT blackwall tires on 15 in. aluminum alloy wheels, bigger rear stabilizer bar, tighter shock valving, higher spring/bushing rates, faster steering ratio, and leather-trimmed steering wheel. A newly optional cellular telephone had an overhead microphone, and could operate through the front stereo speakers.

FLEETWOOD — SERIES 6C — V-8 – Rather than a distinctly separate model, Fleetwood was actually an option package this year. A fine-grain formal cabriolet roof highlighted the closed-in rear window. The package consisted of reclining comfort seats with six-way power passenger adjustment, power trunk lid release, color- keyed power remote mirrors, a digital instrument panel, rear reading lamp, and accent striping on bodyside and decklid. Other styling extras: opera lamps, wire wheel covers, and Fleetwood identification. A Fleetwood d'Elegance option added walnut wood instrument panel and door trim plates along with deluxe carpeted floor mats, a leather-trimmed steering wheel, and d'Elegance identification.

FLEETWOOD SEVENTY-FIVE LIMOUSINE — SERIES 6C — V-8 — Traditionalists may have scoffed, but the modern front- drive, unibody Fleetwood limo still carried eight passengers in the style that appealed to "Seventy-Five" buyers a generation earlier. Under the hood was a transverse-mounted HT 4100 (4.1-liter) V-8 with digital fuel injection; at the chassis, independent four-wheel suspension. Interior trim was revised for '86, electronic instruments became standard, and passengers could take advantage of an optional cellular phone with overhead mike to keep busy hands free. Cherry grain replaced the former walnut woodgrain on instrument panel and door trim plates. Automatic door locking prevented the doors from opening with the limo in gear. Oddly, the stretched limos were created from coupes rather than sedans, with extra doors added in the process of stretching the wheelbase from the normal 110.8 inches to 134.4. Limos came in six body colors plus one Firemist shade and black cherry Pearlmist.

1986 Fleetwood Brougham Sedan d'Elegance (AA)

FLEETWOOD BROUGHAM — SERIES 6D — V-8 — Cadillac's traditional rear-drive sedan was now powered by Oldsmobile's 5.0-liter V-8 engine and four-speed overdrive automatic. Standard features included a limo-like closed-in back window and standard full-length vinyl roof, plus a long list of Cadillac equipment--all for a price that began at $21,265. The Brougham coupe was dropped soon before the model year began, and the sedan didn't appear until February 1986. So '85 models remained on sale through the end of the year. At 121.5 inches, Brougham's wheelbase was the longest of any production automobile other than the stretched (but limited- production) front-drive Fleetwood. Broughams came in a dozen standard colors plus five optional Firemist hues. Bright moldings ran from front fender tips, below the window line and back around the rear quarters. Broughams also carried large full-length rocker moldings and electro-luminescent opera lamps. Standard equipment included an illuminated entry system, electronic climate control with outside-temperature display, power windows and door locks, AM/FM stereo seek/scan radio with power antenna, full padded roof, and whitewall all-season tires. Luxury-minded buyers could again step up to a Brougham d'Elegance. That package consisted of 50/50 Dual Comfort seats (six-way power passenger seat) upholstered in tufted multi-button cloth or optional leather, a leather-trimmed steering wheel, power trunk release, rear reading lights, controlled-cycle wipers, Tampico carpeting, deluxe floor mats, three overhead assist handles, and turbine-vaned wheel covers.

1986 Eldorado Touring Coupe (AA)

ELDORADO — SERIES 6E — V-8 — A downsized E-body Eldo was designed, according to Cadillac, for "sporty elegance, and sheer driving pleasure." Buick Riviera and Olds Toronado rode the same chassis, but neither offered what Eldo had: a transverse-mounted V-8 under the hood. Like the similar Seville, the new Eldo was more than 16 in. shorter than its predecessor. On the down side, some of them now looked a little too much alike, lacking the special styling qualities that had set both apart in previous incarnations. Eldorado's side marker lamps were set into the bodyside moldings at front and rear, with 'Eldorado' script just ahead of the front wheel. A wreath- and-crest was on the wide rear pillar. At the rear were vertical

taillamps, with vertical rectangular backup lights alongside the license plate. Along with the altered body came the demise of the Eldo convertible (for the second time in a decade). To improve rust resistance, all body panels (except the roof) were two-sided galvanized metal. Flush composite headlamps held both high- and low-beam bulbs. The fully independent suspension used a fiberglass transverse single leaf spring in the back. A new digital instrument cluster included a tachometer and engine gauges in a "driver information center." Standard equipment included a floor shift lever for the four-speed overdrive automatic transaxle, leather-trimmed tilt/telescope steering wheel, four-wheel disc brakes, and front bucket seats with lumbar support. Also standard: cruise control, power windows and door locks, power trunk lid release, Twilight Sentinel, body-colored electric outside mirrors, seek/scan stereo radio with power antenna, aluminum alloy wheels, and electronic level control. Eldorado's Biarritz package included a formal cabriolet vinyl roof, opera lamps, wide bodyside accent moldings, two- tone paint, and wire wheel covers. Inside luxuries included leather upholstery, Tampico carpeting, deluxe floor mats, walnut wood appliques, dual power front reclining bucket seats with power lumbar support, a six-way power passenger seat, and front seatback pockets. American walnut wood found a place on the steering wheel, console, door trim and instrument panel. An optional touring suspension package (Goodyear Eagle GT high-performance P215/60R15 tires, rear stabilizer bar, stiffer front stabilizer bar and specially- tuned components) offered a firmer, better-controlled ride but included no special graphics or ornamentation.

I.D. DATA: All Cadillacs again had a 17-symbol Vehicle Identification Number (VIN), stamped on a metal tag attached to the upper left surface of the cowl, visible through the windshield. Coding was similar to 1985. Model year code changed to 'G' for 1986. Code '67' for convertible body was dropped. Engine coding was as follows: 'P' L4-121 TBI; 'W' V6-173 FI; '8' V8-249 DFI; 'Y' V8-307 4Bbl.

CIMARRON (FOUR/V-6)

Model Number	Body/Style Number	Body Type & Seating	Factory Price	Shipping Weight	Production Total
6J	G69	4-dr Sedan-5P	13128/13838	2514/2601	24,534

Price/Weight Note: Figure before the slash is for a Cimarron with four-cylinder engine, after slash for V-6.

SEVILLE (V-8)

6K	S69	4-dr Sedan-5P	26,756	3371	19,098

DEVILLE (FRONT-DRIVE)

6C	D47	2-dr Coupe-6P	19,669	3239	Note 1
6C	D69	4-dr Sedan-6P	19,990	3298	Note 2

FLEETWOOD (FRONT-DRIVE V-8)

6C	B47	2-dr Coupe-6P	23,443	N/A	Note 1
6C	B69	4-dr Sedan-6P	23,764	N/A	Note 2

Note 1: Total two-door DeVille/Fleetwood production, 36,350. Note 2: Total DeVille/Fleetwood four-door sedan production, 129,857.

FLEETWOOD SEVENTY-FIVE LIMOUSINE (V-8)

6C	H23	4-dr Limo-8P	33,895	3358	Note 3
6C	H33	4-dr Fml Limo-7P	35,895	3657	Note 3

Note 3: Total limousine production, 1,000.

FLEETWOOD BROUGHAM (REAR-DRIVE V-8)

6D	W69	4-dr Sedan-6P	21,265	3945	49,115

ELDORADO (V-8)

6E	L57	2-dr Coupe-5P	24,251	3291	21,342

ENGINES: BASE FOUR (Cimarron): Inline. OHV. Four-cylinder. Cast iron block and head. Displacement: 121 cu. in. (2.0 liters). Compression ratio: 9.3:1. Brake horsepower: 88 at 4800 R.P.M. Torque: 110 lbs.-ft. at 2400 R.P.M. Five main bearings. Hydraulic valve lifters. TBI. VIN Code: P. OPTIONAL V-6 (Cimarron): 60-degree, overhead-valve V-6. Cast iron block and head. Displacement: 173 cu. in. (2.8 liters). Bore & stroke: 3.50 x 2.99 in. Compression ratio: 8.5:1. Brake horsepower: 125 at 4800 R.P.M. Torque: 155 lbs.-ft. at 3600 R.P.M. Four main bearings. Hydraulic valve lifters. EFI. Chevrolet-built. VIN Code: W. BASE V-8 (Seville, DeVille, Fleetwood, Limo, Eldorado): 90-degree, overhead valve V-8. Cast iron block and head. Displacement: 249 cu. in. (4.1 liters). Bore & stroke: 3.47 x 3.31 in. Compression ratio: 8.5:1. Brake horsepower: 130 at 4200 R.P.M. Torque: 200 lbs.-ft. at 2200 R.P.M. Five main bearings. Hydraulic valve lifters. TBI. VIN Code: 8. BASE V-8 (Brougham): 90-degree, overhead valve V-8. Cast iron block and head. Displacement: 307 cu. in. (5.0 liters). Bore & stroke: 3.80 x 3.39 in. Compression ratio: 8.5:1. Brake horsepower: 140 at 3200 R.P.M. Torque: N/A. Five main bearings. Hydraulic valve lifters. Carburetor: 4Bbl. VIN Code: Y.

CHASSIS DATA: Wheelbase: (Cimarron) 101.2 in.; (Seville/Eldo) 108.0 in.; (DeV/Fleetwood) 110.8 in.; (Limo) 134.4 in.; (Brougham) 121.5 in. Overall length:- (Cimarron) 177.9 in.; (Seville/Eldo) 188.2 in.; (DeV/Fleetwood) 195.0 in.; (Limo) 218.6 in.; (Brghm) 221.0 in. Height:- (Cimarron) 52.0 in.; (Seville/Eldo) 53.7 in.; (DeV/F.W./Limo) 55.0 in.; (Brghm) 56.7 in. Width:- (Cimarron) 65.0 in.; (Seville) 70.9 in.; (DeV/F.W.) 71.7 in.; (Brghm) 75.3 in.; (Eldo) 71.3 in. Front Tread:- (Cimarron) 55.4 in.; (SeV/Eldo) 59.9 in.; (Limo) 60.3 in.; (Brghm) 61.7 in. Rear Tread:- (Cimarron) 55.2 in.; (SeV/Eldo) 59.9 in.; (Limo) 59.8 in.; (Brghm) 60.7 in. Standard Tires:- (Cimarron) P195/70R13; (SeV/Eldo) P205/70R14; (DeV/F.W.) P205/75R14.

TECHNICAL: Transmission: Five-speed, floor shift manual transmission standard on Cimarron four; four-speed manual on V-6. Cimarron optional three-speed Turbo Hydra-matic (THM125C) gear ratios: (1st) 2.84:1; (2nd) 1.60:1; (3rd) 1.00:1; (Rev) 2.07:1. Four-speed overdrive automatic (THM200-4R) standard on Brougham: (1st) 2.74:1; (2nd) 1.57:1; (3rd) 1.00:1; (4th) 0.67:1; (Rev) 2.07:1. Four-speed (THM440-T4) automatic on other models: (1st) 2.92:1; (2nd) 1.57:1; (3rd) 1.00:1; (4th) 0.70:1; (Rev) 2.38:1. Standard final drive ratio:- (Cimarron) N/A; (SeV/Eldo) 2.97:1; (DeV/F.W.) 2.97:1; (Brghm) 2.73:1. Steering:- power rack and pinion exc. Brougham, recirculating ball. Front suspension:- same as 1985 except (Eldo/SeV) MacPherson struts with dual path mounts, coil springs and stabilizer bar. Rear suspension:- same as 1985 except (Eldo/SeV) independent w/transverse leaf spring, struts, electronic level control. Brakes:- front disc, rear drum except Eldo/SeV, four-wheel disc. Fuel tank:- (Cimarron) 13.6 gal.; (Brghm) 20.7 gal.; (others) 18.0 gal.

DRIVETRAIN OPTIONS: 173 cu. in. (2.8-liter) EFI V 6 engine: Cimarron ($610). Four-speed manual transmission: Cimarron ($75 credit). Three- speed automatic trans.: Cimarron ($390). California emission equipment ($99). High-altitude emissions pkg.: Cimarron (NC). Engine block heater: Cimarron ($20); others ($45). Heavy-duty battery: Cimarron ($26); others ($40). Heavy-duty radiator: Cimarron ($45). Electronic level control: Brghm ($203). F72 heavy-duty ride suspension pkg. incl. electronic level control. FE2 touring suspension pkg.: DeVille ($695); w/Fleetwood pkg. ($375); Eldo ($200). FE2 touring suspension (15 in. alum. alloy wheels, P215/60R15 Goodyear Eagle GT hi-perf BSW tires, rear stabilizer bar, stiffer front stab. bar): Eldo/Seville ($155). Delco/Bilstein suspension system: Cimarron V-6 ($100).

OPTION PACKAGES: Cimarron D'Oro package ($975). Fleetwood package: cloth seats ($3150); leather ($3700). Fleetwood d'Elegance: cloth seating ($4445); leather ($4995). DeVille Touring Coupe or Touring Sedan package ($2880). Brougham d'Elegance pkg.: cloth seats ($1950); leather ($2500). Eldorado Biarritz: cloth ($3095); leather ($3495). Seville Elegante: cloth ($3595); leather ($3995). Black cambria cloth roof: DeV ($925). Formal cabriolet roof: DeV cpe ($698). Security option package: DeV/limo ($290); SeV/Eldo ($460); Brghm ($380).

DEVILLE/BROUGHAM/SEVENTY-FIVE/ELDORADO/SEVILLE CONVENIENCE/AP-PEARANCE OPTIONS: Astroroof ($1255); N/A on limo. Electronic cruise control: DeV/Brghm/limo ($195). Controlled-cycle wiper system: DeV/Brghm/limo ($60). Rear defogger w/heated outside mirrors ($170). Automatic door locks ($170) exc. limo. Remote fuel filler door release ($60). Garage door opener ($140-$165). Illuminated entry system ($80). Digital insrument cluster: DeV ($238). Cellular telephone: DeV ($2850); phone provision ($395). Six-way power passenger seat for dual comfort seats: DeV ($235). Two-position memory seat: DeV ($235); Brghm ($215). Six-way power passenger seat: Eldo/SeV/Brghm ($235). Power driver's seat recliner: DeV/Brghm ($95-$160). Power passenger seat recliner: DeV/Brghm ($95-$395). Power passenger seat recliner w/six-way power seat: Eldo/SeV ($330). Leather-trimmed steering wheel: DeV/Brghm/limo ($105). Tilt/telescope steering wheel: DeV/Brghm/limo ($195). Power trunk lid release: DeV/Brghm/limo ($195). Trunk release and pull-down ($80-$120). Theft deterrent system ($200). Twilight Sentinel: DeV/Brghm/limo ($85). Dimming Sentinel headlamp control ($130) exc.

Brougham. Guidematic headlamp control: Brghm ($95). Rear reading lights: Brghm ($33). Trumpet horn: DeV/Brghm/limo ($45). Electric remote-control outside mirrors: DeV/Brghm ($101). Twin lighted vanity mirrors ($140). Automatic day/night mirror ($80). Electronic- tuning AM/FM stereo radio w/cassette: Brghm ($299); w/cassette and CB ($577). ET AM/FM stereo radio w/cassette and graphic equalizer ($319) exc. Brougham. ET radio with cassette and Delco-GM/Bose music system ($895) exc. Brghm/limo. CB radio: DeV ($278). Power triband antenna: DeV/Brghm ($55). Firemist or Pearlmist paint ($240). Two-tone Seville paint ($600). Decklid/bodyside accent striping: DeV/Brghm ($55). Accent moldings: Eldo ($75). Color-keyed door edge guards ($19-$29). License frames, each ($15). Front license bracket: Eldo (NC). Dual comfort seats: DeV ($245). Leather seating area ($400-$550) exc. limo ($940). Carpeted floor mats: front ($45); rear ($25). Trunk mat ($25). Cloth trunk trim: Brghm ($860-$940). Aluminum alloy wheels: DeV ($115- $435); Seville Elegante (NC). Wire wheel covers: Eldo/SeV ($190); DeV/Brghm ($320-$400). Turbine vaned wheel covers: Brghm ($80). Puncture-sealing tires ($145-$190) exc. limo. P215/65R15 WSW tires: DeV ($66). P215/60R15 SBR BSW tires: Seville (NC). P215/60R15 SBR WSW: SeV/Eldo ($66).

CIMARRON CONVENIENCE/APPEARANCE OPTIONS: Vista Vent ($310). Garage door opener transmitter ($165); retainer ($25). Digital instrument cluster ($238). Twilight Sentinel ($85). Twin lighted visor vanity mirrors ($95). Electronic-tuning seek/scan AM/FM stereo radio w/cassette ($223); w/cassette and Delco-GM/Bose music system ($895). Delete radio ($151 credit). Lower bodyside accent moldings ($450). Door edge guards ($25). Rear license frame ($15). Decklid luggage rack ($130). Cloth seat trim ($100 credit). Carpeted rubber floor mats: front ($38); rear ($22). Trunk mat ($26). 14 in. aluminum alloy wheels ($40). P195/70R13 SBR WSW tires ($55). P205/60R14 SBR BSW tires ($94). P205/60R14 SBR RWL ($171); w/D'Oro ($77).

HISTORY: Introduced: September 26, 1985 except Eldorado/Seville, November 14, 1985; Fleetwood Brougham, February 13, 1986. Model year production: 281,296, including 3,628 with four- cylinder engine and 20,906 with V-6, for a 3.6 percent share of the industry total. Calendar year production: 319,031. Calendar year sales by U.S. dealers: 304,057. Model year sales by U.S. dealers: 300,053 for a 3.8 percent market share.

Historical Footnotes: Cadillac sales dropped a bit for the second year in a row, barely edging over 300,000, but that was enough to retain dominance among makers of luxury cars. E-body Eldorado production began at the new Hamtramck, Michigan plant in late 1985, but delays kept output below peak levels. As a result, Eldorado and Seville sales dropped by half. The rear-drive Fleetwood Brougham enjoyed a comeback of sorts, due to low gasoline prices and its upgraded V-8 engine. Front-drive DeVilles and Fleetwoods also gained in sales for the second year. Cimarron rose as well, but not by much. Cadillac clung to hopes that Cimarron would gain strength against new imports, such as Acura Legend, despite complaints that it was little more than a fancy Cavalier. At the upper end of the scale, the future held a new ultra- luxurious two-seater Allante, due out for 1987.

When Monte Carlo and the restyled Camaro appeared in 1970, few were surprised by their popularity. Similarly high expectations greeted the subcompact Vega when it emerged a year later, only to fizzle through half a dozen seasons, victim of unresolved technical difficulties (including its aluminum four-cylinder engine). Monza, an alternate subcompact, came to life for 1975. But Chevrolet's modest new Chevette for 1976 may have been most significant of all, heralding a trend toward small cars to rival the imports, which would eventually take over the industry. Based on GM's German-built Opel Kadett, Chevette even came in a two- passenger Scooter version, priced as low as $2899.

1980 Monte Carlo Landau Coupe (CP)

Full-size Chevrolets of 1976 were still mighty big, carrying V-8 engines up to 400 and 454 cu. in. displacement. Mid-sizes and Camaro, on the other hand, switched from a 350 to 305 cu. in. standard V-8. Nova compacts could have either a 305 or 350 V-8 instead of the basic inline six. Among the most noteworthy models was the Cosworth Vega with Twin Cam (16-valve) engine, in its final year. *Motor Trend* had named Monza Car of the Year for 1975. Monzas with the Spyder package draw the most interest today. So does the Nova Super Sport (SS) coupe and hatchback. Also of interest to enthusiasts: the last Chevelle Laguna S-3, sporting a "soft" aero front end and louvered coach windows. Camaro came in base or Luxury Touring (LT) trim, but the Z28 had faded away (temporarily).

1980 Citation X11 Club Coupe (CP)

In 1973, Chevrolet had turned away from the pillarless two-door hardtop, switching to the "Colonnade" design. This would be the final year for the true pillarless four-door hardtop in Impala/Caprice form. After a poor 1975, Chevrolet sales rose amply this year, but Oldsmobile's Cutlass was GM's best seller.

1981 Caprice Classic sedan (AA)

Full-size Chevrolets weren't quite full after their 1977 downsizing, as the 350 became Impala/Caprice's biggest V-8. Caprice earned the *Motor Trend* honors this year, as overall Chevrolet sales rose moderately — and full-size models considerably. A Borg-Warner four-speed gearbox went into some Camaros, which didn't change at first. Later in the year, though, the Z28 was back, carrying a four-barrel 350 V-8. Though not so potent as its forerunners, it attracted considerable attention. For its final season, Vega's Cosworth was gone, but twin GT packages were available. Chevette's Scooter added a back seat. Monza's Spyder came in two separate packages: one for appearance, another for performance.

1982 Camaro Z28 Sport Coupe (CH)

Downsizing hit the mid-size Malibu and Monte Carlo for 1978. Base engines were new too: a 200 cu. in. V-6 for Malibu, 231 V-6 (from Buick) for Monte. Chevrolet sales reached their third highest point ever for the model year, led by a whopping rise in Chevette interest. Monza continued in its previous form, and added the former Vega's hatchback and wagon. Both Spyder and GT packages were available, as was a new 196 cu. in. Buick-built V-6. Monza'a base four-cylinder engine came from Pontiac, but the 305 V-8 was Chevrolet's. Chevette supplemented the original two-door with a four-door hatchback, and lengthened its standard equipment list. Camaro's Z28 added slanted fender louvers, rear spoiler and hood air scoop.

Except for a new small-block 267 cu. in. V-8 available under Monte Carlo hoods, not much changed for 1979. A new Berlinetta replaced Camaro's Type LT, while Z28 featured new flared front wheel openings and air dam.

Full-size models switched from the old familiar inline six-cylinder engine to a new standard 229 cu. in. V-6 for 1980, and enjoyed an aero restyle. That news was minor, though, compared to the introduction of the Citation X-car. Widely praised at first, Chevrolet's first front-drive

model soon suffered a variety of recalls and charges of seriously flawed brakes—charges that were never fully resolved, even years later. For the moment, though, Citation found plenty of buyers, including nearly 25,000 for its sporty X-11 package. Monza Spyders were available again, but V-8 engines were not. Camaro's Z28 took on further bodily changes, this time rear fender flares and a rear-facing hood scoop. California Z28 fans couldn't have the 350 V-8. Both 267 and 305 V-8s were available in other Camaros, though, along with the new base V-6. Monte Carlos could now get Buick's turbocharged 231 cu. in. V-6, which delivered 55 more horsepower than the standard 229 cu. in. engine. Turbo-powered Chevrolets never quite took hold, as they did in other makes. Oldsmobile diesels were available in full-size wagons. Overall, Chevrolet sales declined by some 20 percent in this rough year for the industry.

Citation's X-11 package included a high-output V-6 engine for 1981, but the recalls were already having an impact on sales. Monte Carlo got a wedge-shape aero restyle, but little else was new. A diesel engine, supplied by Isuzu, became available in Chevettes, with five-speed gearbox. Sales slipped again—even worse for full-size models, which seemed in danger of extinction. Within the next couple of years, however, they would enjoy a rebirth of popularity.

1983 Cavalier Type 10 hatchback coupe (AA)

Front-wheel drive took on two additional forms for 1982: subcompact Cavalier and family-size Celebrity, both of which quickly became popular. A downsized Camaro looked even sleeker than its predecessor, if also a lot more expensive. It was named Car of the Year by *Motor Trend*. Powerplants ranged from the base Pontiac "Iron Duke" four (now fuel-injected), to 173 cu. in. V-6 and 305 V-8. More than 6,300 Indy 500 Commemorative Editions of the Z28 were built. Z28 Camaros could also get a Cross-Fire fuel-injected engine, churning out 165 horsepower.

Most noteworthy event of the 1983 model year was the arrival of a Cavalier convertible. A new high-output, 190-horsepower 305 V-8 became available under Camaro hoods. Monte Carlo added an SS model, which gained a strong following, also with a high-output 305 V-8. Only four-door full-size models were offered this year, but Caprice's coupe would return for '84. Five-speed gearboxes were available on Chevette, Cavalier and Camaro. Malibu, a long-standing nameplate, was in its final season. NHTSA's order to recall Citations for the alleged brake problems helped sales to plunge. Chevrolet sales went up somewhat, but largely as a result of increases in larger models.

A more powerful Monte Carlo SS lured youthful customers for 1984, with its wind-tunnel nose and lack of brightwork. Cross-Fire injection had lasted only two years as a Z28 option, but a four-barrel V-8 took its place. Camaro Berlinettas turned to a Corvette-inspired cockpit with digital instruments. A Eurosport option was added to Celebrity's possibilities; a Type 10 hatchback model to

1984 Celebrity Eurosport coupe (CP)

Cavalier's. So was a Celebrity station wagon. No more Chevette Scooters were built—hardly a major loss. Cavalier was America's best selling car, with Celebrity a strong second.

Excitement marked the 1985 model year, with the arrival of the IROC-Z Camaro. This Z28 option was styled like racing models, with foglamps, low air dam, and full-circle "ground effects" skirting. Three 305 cu. in. V-8s were available, including one with tuned-port fuel injection. A performance-oriented Z24 Cavalier was announced, but didn't arrive until later. Chevrolet's market share dropped by a percentage point, to 19 percent. Two new Chevrolet imports hit the market: the three-cylinder Sprint (from Suzuki) and four-cylinder Spectrum (from Isuzu). The new Astro van also appeared.

1985 Monte Carlo SS Sport Coupe (AA)

Citation finally bit the dust after 1985, but something quite different emerged: the joint-venture Nova, produced in partnership with Toyota. One more nameplate disappeared: Impala. Cavalier had its Z24, with port-injected 173 cu. in. V-6 engine; and an RS series replaced the former Type 10. Monte Carlo added an luxurious and stylish LS model. On the sales front, Celebrity took over Cavalier's spot as No. 1. Early in 1987, the Chevette dropped away. Even pioneers can't last forever, especially when front-drive had become the standard for small cars—and more than a few big ones.

As always, Chevrolet offered quite a selection of cars to tempt later collectors. All Camaros are pleasing, with Z28s the most desirable—even those that lacked the performance of earlier (and later) models. The recent IROC-Z has already attracted considerable attention. Monte Carlo SS coupes, especially the more stark looking, minimally-trimmed models, are likely to remain in demand. Rarest is Monte's SS Aerocoupe fastback, with only 200 built in 1986; but most enthusiasts have never even seen one. Surely a Cosworth Vega is worth hanging onto, while Monza Spyders may be too numerous to rise much in value. A V-8 Spyder may be more curiosity than collectible—an example of stuffing a full-size engine where it might not belong. In view of the imminent shrinking of engine sizes, one of the final 454 V-8s might be worth acquiring; too bad there weren't any '76 convertibles to put one in. A latter-day Cavalier ragtop might be nice to have a few years hence. Keep a Chevette in your garage? They played a powerful role in paving the way for small domestic cars, but it's hard to imagine one as truly collectible.

1976 CHEVROLET

Chevrolet's lineup was largely a carryover from 1975, with one big (actually small) exception: the new subcompact Chevette. Throughout the line, improved gas mileage was the year's primary theme. Chevrolet also reduced its total number of models. A new 305 cu. in. engine replaced the former 350 as base V-8 under Chevelle, Monte Carlo and Camaro hoods. Vega and Monza also got new engines this year. Most models could have optional low axle ratios. Rectangular headlamps, first offered on full-size 1975 models, were now stacked vertically on Malibu Classic and Monte Carlo. All Chevrolets had a new roll-over fuel spillage control system. Brake materials were improved. Monza offered a sporty new Spyder option package. Rust resistance got considerable attention this year. Chevettes were protected by 17 anti-corrosion methods including wax base spray; epoxy paint; front inner fender plastic liners; zinc coated cowl side panels, hood, roof side rails and rear quarter panels; zinc-rich primer; galvanized metal front side rails, front valance and rocker panels; and oil base coating on rear springs. Promoted for Vega was a zinc-rich pre-prime coating on door surfaces; Plastisol- sealed door edges; aluminum wax spray applied to inner door areas after painting; plus four-layer fender protection, zinc-coated steel for lower radiator support and front fenders, and galvanized steel rocker panels.

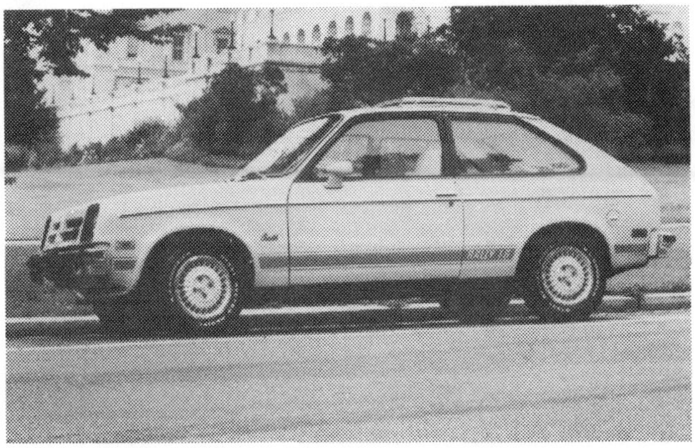

1976 Chevette Rally 1.6 hatchback coupe (CH)

CHEVETTE — SERIES 1T — FOUR — "A new kind of American car" was promised by Chevette's catalog, "international in design and heritage." Target market was buyers of Datsun B210, Toyota Corolla, and VW Rabbit. In addition to the basic four-passenger two-door hatchback, Chevrolet offered Sport, Woody and Rallye options, as well as a bare-bones two-passenger (no back seat) Scooter with a base price of just $2899. Chevette's design was based on GM's German-built Opel Kadett. Powered by a base 85 cu. in. (1.4-liter) four-cylinder overhead-cam engine, Chevette carried a fully synchronized four-speed manual transmission, rack-and-pinion steering, and front disc brakes. Chevrolet's new subcompact measured almost 17 inches shorter than Vega (formerly the smallest Chevrolet), and weighed over 600 pounds less (just under one ton). As for economy, EPA estimates with the base 1.4-liter engine and four-speed manual gearbox came to 28 MPG city and 40 MPG highway. And the optional 97.6 cu. in. (1.6-liter) OHC four was thriftier yet, reaching a 48 MPG highway estimate. Styling features included an aero-designed front spoiler and flush-type door handles. Chevette's simple grille consisted of four wide openings (two on each side) in an angled body-color panel. Front fenders held small marker lenses; rear quarters, similar red lenses. Round headlamps were recessed; park/signal lamps mounted below the bumper area. Front fenders held 'Chevette' script near rear edges. At the rear were "international" horizontal tri-color taillamps (red, amber and white). The full-width (48 in.) rear hatch had pneumatic supports. This was Chevrolet's first metric-measurement car, supplied with a simple self-servicing booklet. A built-in diagnostic connector (first one on a domestic car) helped do-it-yourselfers or mechanics analyze electrical system problems. The optional Four-Season air conditioner had its own diagnostic connector. Unibody construction plus a combined hood and grille gave easy underhood accessibility. Front fenders bolted on. High-strength bumpers were mounted on shock absorbers, which connected to solid underbody rails. The front suspension had a stabilizer bar, low-friction ball joints and high-caster geometry, mounted on a heavy-gauge crossmember. At the rear were variable-rate coil springs and torque tube axle. Chevette was the first Chevrolet to get a fingertip "Smart Switch" on the steering column to control headlamp dimmer, turn signals, lane-change and "flash-to-pass" signals, and wiper/washer. Up front were full-form, shell- type bucket seats; in back, a full-width seat with folding backrest. Body color choices were: antique white, silver, light or dark blue metallic, lime green, bright yellow, cream, burnt orange, medium orange, firethorn metallic, light red, black, buckskin, or dark green metallic. (Light blue metallic, lime green, burnt orange and light red were Chevette exclusives.) Soft vinyl upholstery came in black, dark blue, light buckskin or dark firethorn. Cloth-and-vinyl upholstery came in light buckskin or dark firethorn. The optional Custom interior was rattan-pattern vinyl in black, light buckskin, dark blue, dark firethorn or white; or Rutledge cloth-and- vinyl in the same colors (except white). Standard equipment included the 1.4-liter engine; four- speed manual gearbox with floor lever; blackwall tires on 13 x 5 in. disc wheels; heater/defroster; fuel gauge; courtesy light in windshield header; easy-access instrument panel; spare tire below cargo floor; mini do-it-yourself service manual; color-keyed wall-to-wall carpeting; fold-down rear seat; glove compartment with door latch; bright bumpers and trim moldings; and acoustical insulation. The Sport Coupe added bold sport stripes and black accents. The Rally Coupe package came with a 1.6-liter engine, special suspension with rear stabilizer bar, special instruments including tachometer and temperature gauge, sport shifter and steering wheel, passenger assist grip, Rally wheel covers, and black rocker panels. Woody Coupes had woodgrain vinyl body trim, custom interior with woodgrain vinyl accents on the instrument cluster, sport steering wheel, day/night mirror, bright window moldings, wheel trim rings, and deluxe grille with bright accents. The low-budget Scooter had only two bucket seats and less standard equipment, including an open glove compartment. It came only in light blue, antique white, cream, or light red. Chevette options included the larger 1.6-liter engine, AM/FM radio, twin sport mirrors, Four-Season air conditioning, sport steering wheel, deluxe bumpers with impact strips, bumper guards, rooftop luggage rack, rear defogger, custom exterior trim package, and swing-out rear quarter windows. Also optional: a sport shifter (with console), the $306 Woody package, and Rally equipment. Turbo Hydra-matic cost an extra $244.

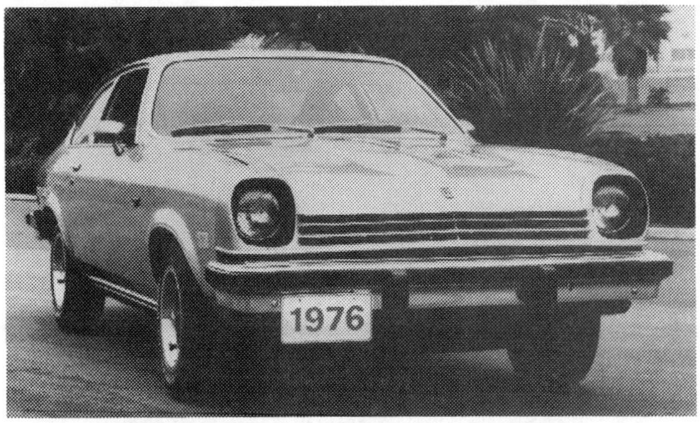

1976 Vega GT hatchback coupe (CH)

VEGA — SERIES 1H — FOUR — Chevrolet's first subcompact coupe, introduced in 1971, never quite managed to overcome its early so-so reputation. Vegas came in sport and hatchback coupe form, as well as a two-door station wagon and Estate wagon. The LX model was dropped this year. The base aluminum-block four added new hydraulic valve lifters, eliminating the need for tappet adjustment. Crankcase ventilation was improved to ease engine breathing. New valve stem seals improved overhead oil control. Instead of a catalytic converter, the base four used an air pump and manifold injection for emissions control. Torque arm rear suspension was new this year (introduced on the '75 Monza). Brakes used larger (91/2 x 2 in.) rear drums and new organo-metallic front disc pad material. Power brakes were optional. So was a new lightweight, aluminum-case four-speed manual gearbox, as well as a five-speed on the Cosworth twin-cam model (and others with the optional two- barrel engine). The four-speed came with a new 2.53:1 axle ratio, plus long 3.75:1 low-gear ratio. A new box-section design front cross-member added structural rigidity. Vega's new grille consisted of three wide louvered openings that reached almost to the recessed round headlamps, giving the car an ultra-wide appearance. Parking lamps sat behind the grille. At the back, new multi-color lights were divided into three top-to-bottom sections, with tiny square backup lenses in lower sections. (Wagons had narrower vertical taillamps.) Vega's unitized body had bolt-on front fenders. Body colors this year were antique white, silver, black, buckskin, cream, bright yellow, medium orange, and seven metallics: light or dark blue, firethorn, mahogany, lime green, medium saddle, and dark green. Both 140 cu. in. four-cylinder engines were called Dura- built: with one-barrel (70 horsepower) or two-barrel (84 horsepower) carburetion. Vegas rode 13 x 5 in. steel wheels, except 13 x 6 in. on the GT. Cosworths had 13 x 6 in. cast aluminum wheels. Standard equipment included the 140 cu. in. four with 1Bbl. carburetor, three-speed manual transmission (floor shift), electric fuel pump, heater/defroster, front bucket seats, and A78 x 13 blackwall tires. All models could have five-speed manual or Turbo Hydra-matic for the same $244 extra cost. All could get a new heavy-duty sealed Freedom battery. Vega's GT package included the two-barrel version of the 140 engine, F41 sport suspension, special instruments, woodgrain accents on instrument cluster, dual sport mirrors (left remote-controlled), black headlamp bezels, bright grille header moldings, 13 x 6 in. wheels with trim rings, and A70 x 13/B white-letter tires. Offered for both hatchback coupes and wagons, the GT package also included a sport steering wheel, belt and wheel opening moldings, adjustable driver's seatback, and black sill and lower bodyside moldings. Sport coupes could have a new Cabriolet appearance option. This would be the final season for the Cosworth Twin Cam Vega. Cosworths carried an aluminum 122 cu. in. engine developed by Chevrolet and Cosworth Engineering of England. It had twin overhead camshafts, 16 valves, electronic fuel injection and mechanical valve lifters, and developed 110 horsepower at 5600 R.P.M. Four-speed manual shift was standard. To boost performance, the axle ratio switched from the former 3.73:1 to a new 4.10:1. Cosworths came in nine colors with gold pinstriping. Included were special gold- color aluminum wheels; 'Cosworth Twin Cam' decals on rear and both sides; gold-colored wheel opening stripes; and end panel striping. Custom interiors came in black or white, with Cosworth insert in the sport steering wheel. Also standard: an 8000 R.P.M. tachometer and adjustable driver's seatback.

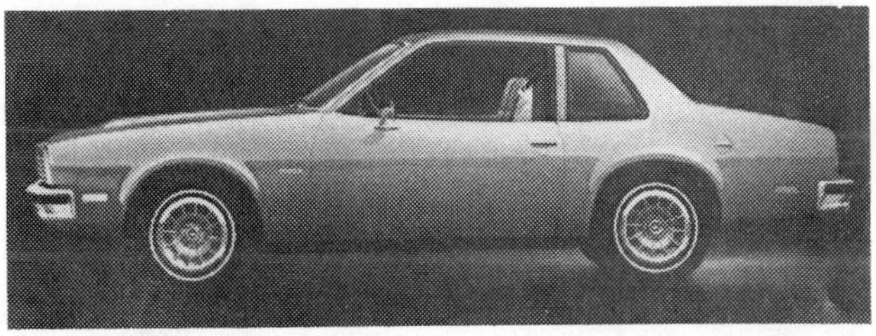

1976 Monza Town Coupe (CP)

MONZA — SERIES 1H — FOUR/V-8 — Monza's 2 + 2 hatchback had been named *Motor Trend* "Car of the Year" after introduction in 1975. Part way through that model year, the Town Coupe debuted, with much different notchback styling. Both returned for 1976, along with a formal Cabriolet version of the Town Coupe. The base Towne Coupe had large rear quarter windows, hard bumpers, plus a sound-deadening and acoustical package. The $256 Cabriolet option included opera-type rear quarter windows and a vinyl top that covered the rear half of the roof, plus bright moldings, sport equipment, and woodgrain steering wheel shroud. Hatchbacks had a low body-color grille: just two rows of four wide holes, with that pattern repeated below the bumper. On the solid panel above the grille was a round emblem, plus 'Chevrolet' lettering off toward the driver's side. Parking lamps with rounded outer lower edges sat below the bumper. An engine identification plaque was at the front of front fenders, above the marker lens; 'Monza 2+2' lettering farther back, at the cowl. Quad rectangular headlamps were inset into a soft, resilient urethane front- end skin. The hood sloped down between the headlamps, but contained a bulge farther back. The 2+2 had bright-trimmed wraparound taillamps that tapered to a point on the bodyside, with square backup lenses toward the center. Town Coupes had an entirely different front-end and side look, including bright chrome bumpers and single headlamp bezels. A classic grid grille (six holes wide) held hidden parking/signal lights. Rear bumper cover and rocker panels were body-colored. Monza body colors were cream, bright yellow, medium orange, black, buckskin, silver and antique white, plus metallic light or dark blue, firethorn, mahogany, lime green, saddle brown, and dark green. Refinements for the aluminum-block 140 cu. in. (2.3- liter) four included new hydraulic lifters for quieter running, new valve stem seals to improve oil control, and improved crankcase ventilation. That engine again had a 60,000-mile, five-year

1976 Monza 2+2 hatchback coupe (CP)

1976 Nova SS coupe (CP)

guarantee. Monza also offered options of a two-barrel version of the 140 four, a 262 cu. in. (4.3- liter) V-8, or even a 305 (5.0-liter) V-8. That big V-8 was smaller in size, yet considerably stronger in horsepower, than the 350 offered in 1975. No V-8s were available on the base Towne Coupe. The two-barrel four was included in Sport and Cabriolet packages. Transmission choices included a new four-speed manual gearbox with aluminum case for the four- cylinder engine, plus an economy five-speed that had been introduced during the 1975 model year. A new underbody lowered the floor hump between bucket seats by more than two inches. An all-new brake system included larger rear drums with increased torque capacity, a new vented front rotor, new front disc pad material, and front-to-rear proportioning. A muffler replaced the catalytic converter on the Town Coupe's base four. Models that retained converters lost their exhaust system resonators this year. All models had a new floor shift and parking brake console. The new lighter weight four-speed gearbox, used with four-cylinder engines, had a 3.75:1 low gear. Monza standard equipment included the 2.3-liter four with one-barrel carburetor, three-speed manual transmission, heater/defroster, bucket seats, cigarette lighter, front disc brakes, A78 x 13/B tires, and cut-pile carpeting. Hatchback 2+2 models included Euro-style finned wheel covers with GT center hub and bright nuts. Towne Coupes had bright metallic wheel covers. The 4.3-liter V-8 engine cost an extra $224. Four and five-speed manual gearboxes were optional, as was Turbo Hydra-matic. So were aluminum wheels, as well as a widened choice of entertainment options including AM/FM stereo radio and tape player. Inside, the 2+2 had a new deluxe "stitched" instrument panel pad, with woodgrain vinyl ornamentation color-keyed to the car interior. A two-spoke steering wheel had woodgrain vinyl insert. The 2+2 had knit cloth and vinyl upholstery in black, buckskin or firethorn; or all-vinyl in black, buckskin, firethorn or white. Town Coupes had sport cloth upholstery in black or buckskin. Cabriolet equipment for the Town Coupe included the padded vinyl roof in firethorn, mahogany, white, silver metallic, buckskin, or blue. Monza's Spyder package, available on the 2+2 or Town Coupe with sport equipment, had the two-barrel four; floor console; F41 suspension with large front and rear stabilizer bars and special shocks; wheel opening moldings; day/night mirror; sport steering wheel; distinctive Spyder identification; special instrumentation and stitched instrument panel pad with woodgrain vinyl accents; and BR70 or BR78 radial tires. Spyders required a five-speed manual gearbox or Turbo Hydra-matic. A total of 2,333 were produced. Town Coupes with Sport equipment had a black pillar applique with argent edges, ahead of large rear quarter windows. The package included body-colored finned wheel covers with argent painted edges; front stabilizer bar; plus body-contoured high-back front bucket seats. Knit cloth/vinyl upholstery came in black, buckskin or firethorn; all-vinyl in black, buckskin, firethorn or white.

pads and rear lining material, and larger-diameter rear cylinders. Air conditioners had a new seven-mode setting and maximum cooling position. Otherwise, changes were modest this year: altered fuel and exhaust system mountings, new interior colors and trim materials, and new instrument panel knobs. Nova's body colors were: medium orange, buckskin, cream, antique white, bright yellow, black and silver; plus metallic light or dark blue, firethorn, mahogany, lime green, saddle, and dark green. Regular Nova interiors came in three cloth and vinyl colors: black, buckskin or firethorn. All-vinyl colors were buckskin, blue or firethorn. Hatchbacks came only with all-vinyl interiors. Concours had three knit cloth and vinyl interiors: black, buckskin or firethorn. Or all-vinyl in buckskin or firethorn. White interiors were available in coupe and hatchback only. Optional: new high-pile deluxe carpeting. Standard equipment included the 250 cu. in. six-cylinder engine (one-barrel carb), three-speed manual shift, heater/defroster, front disc brakes, and cut-pile carpeting. Nova V-8s had power brakes. Four-speed wide-range manual shift cost $242, while a floor shift lever cost $29 extra. Both cabriolet and vinyl roofs were optional. So were heavy- duty and sport suspensions. The 350 cu. in. V-8 was available for $85 more than the standard 305 V-8. Nova Concours carried similar equipment but added bright moldings, front/rear bumper guards, full wheel covers, cigarette lighter, and FR78 x 14 steel-belted radial tires. Nova's Super Sport (SS) coupe and hatchback had a new black-finished diamond-mesh pattern grille with 'Nova SS' emblem, plus other black-accented trim. Styling features included black headlamp bezels, side window frame moldings; distinctive lower body side striping; Nova SS decals on fenders and rear end panel; dual black sport mirrors (left remote controlled); horizontal parking lamps with clear lenses; heavy-duty suspension; and four-spoke sport steering wheel. The $187 SS coupe package also included roof drip moldings, rally wheels with trim rings, and heavy-duty F40 front/rear suspension. All told, 7,416 SS Novas came off the line.

1976 Camaro Type LT coupe (CP)

CAMARO — SERIES 1F — SIX/V-8 — Chevrolet's sport coupe, in base or Type LT (Luxury Touring) form, looked similar to the 1975 version. The crosshatch grille was made up of thin bars peaked forward at the center, surrounded by a bright molding with rounded upper corners. Round, deeply recessed parking lamps sat between the grille and the recessed round headlamps. Front fenders held small side marker lenses. Taillamps with bright moldings wrapped around the side, tapering to a point. Small vertical backup lights were in the taillamp housings. Rectangular emblems sat on hood and deck. Type LT had a 'TYPE LT' nameplate on the right side of the bright rear end panel, but could also be spotted by its brushed aluminum applique across the full width of the rear end panel. LT seat trim now used vertical stitching for both cloth and vinyl upholstery (three knit cloth/vinyl choices or three all-vinyl). Standard sport coupes came with two cloth/vinyl interiors or four in all- vinyl. Styling features included a long hood and short deck, with swept-back roofline. Sport Coupes had new narrow bright rocker panel moldings, 14 x 6 in. wheels, contoured Strato- bucket front seats, cut-pile carpeting, padded vinyl-covered four-spoke steering wheel with crest, and a left outside mirror. Type LT added Hide-A-Way wipers and sport mirrors (left one remote-controlled), and 14 x 7 in. Rally wheels. Inside LT were a tachometer, clock, voltmeter and temp gauge, plus color-keyed steering wheel, glove compartment light, and simulated leather instrument panel trim. LT interiors also had special bucket seats with deep-contour backs and built-in padded armrests. A new small-block V-8 engine was available this year: a 305 cu. in. (5.0-liter) version that replaced the 350 as standard eight-cylinder engine. It came with either the standard or high-performance axle ratio. As before, the 250 cu. in. inline six was the base (Sport Coupe) powerplant, while a 350 (5.7-liter) V-8 with four-barrel carburetor was available for both models. Transmission choices were the same as in 1975, except that the four-speed manual gearbox came with a 2.85:1 low-gear ratio (formerly 2.54:1). Power brakes (front disc) were now standard with V-8s. Brake improvements included new front disc pad material and new rear linings, plus larger-diameter rear wheel cylinders. Base Sport Coupes had the standard inline six; LT the new 305 V-8. Standard equipment included a heater/defroster, variable-ratio power steering, finned rear brake drums, contoured Strato bucket seats, four-spoke steering wheel, and FR78 x 14 steel-belted radial tires. Three-speed manual transmission (floor shift) was standard. Turbo Hydra-matic was optional on all models, wide-range four-speed manual available for the optional 350 cu. in. engine (which cost $85 more than the 305). Both transmissions were priced at $260. Cruise-Master speed control was optional for the first time. Also available: Rally or styled wheels, sport suspension, power windows and door locks, Four-Season air conditioning, rear defogger, tinted glass, white-letter tires, front and rear spoilers, Positraction, two-position driver's seatback, and center console with storage area. This year's vinyl Sport Roof covered only the front, leaving a painted band exposed at the back. Of the 14 Camaro body colors this year, ten were new. Choices were: light or dark blue metallic, firethorn metallic, mahogany metallic, lime green or dark green metallic, buckskin, cream, bright yellow, medium orange or saddle metallic, black, silver, and antique white. Sport Coupes came with black or dark firethorn cloth/vinyl upholstery, or all-vinyl in black, white, dark firethorn or light buckskin. Type LT offered

1976 Nova Concours coupe (CH)

NOVA — SERIES 1X — SIX/V-8 — Nova Concours joined the lineup this year as top-of-the- line member of the compact family. Both 111 in. wheelbase models showed a new front-end look. Novas displayed a new six-row crosshatch grille (6 x 12 pattern) split in half by a heavier horizontal bar, with single round headlamps. Regular Novas had vertical amber parking lamp lenses at grille ends. Concours models added chrome trim around the headlamps and hood areas, as well as a special NC insignia and upright three-dimensional hood ornament. Concours' similar but bold grille had 24 square holes in two rows, each square containing 3 x 3 crosshatching, also with vertical parking lamps between grille and headlamps. Concours had a wide bright panel above the grille; regular Novas did not. Identifying features also included a fender nameplate, wheel cover insignia, and NC shield on the rear panel. Concours models also carried bumper guards and impact strips, bright moldings, plus dark-accented full-length bodyside louvers and rocker panel moldings. Inside, the Concours had rosewood-grain vinyl accents on the dash, steering wheel and upper door panels, along with identification on the right side of the instrument panel. A new 305 cu. in. engine became the basic V-8, replacing the former 262. Base engine continued to be the inline 250 cu. in. six. A four-barrel 350 V-8 was also optional again. Power brakes moved from the option list to standard equipment for V-8 Novas this year, and were available on six-cylinder models. Brake systems had new front disc

1976 Camaro Rally Sport coupe (CP)

three Dover knit cloth/vinyl choices (black, dark blue and dark firethorn) or all-vinyl in black, white or light buckskin. A Rally Sport package, available on both models, included low-gloss black finish on forward roof, hood, grille, header panel, headlamp bezels, upper fenders, rockers and rear panel, as well as Rally wheels. Tri-color striping separated the black-accented areas from the basic body color. The package also included bright headlamp trim, 'Rally Sport' decals on decklid and front fender, and argent paint. Rally Camaros came in white, silver, light blue metallic, firethorn metallic, or bright yellow body colors.

1976 Chevelle Malibu Classic Landau Coupe (CP)

CHEVELLE — SERIES 1A — SIX/V-8 — Two Chevelle series were offered for 1976, Malibu and Malibu Classic, plus (for the last time) the sportier Laguna S3. The Malibu Classic lineup included a Colonnade coupe and sedan, plus Landau coupe, two- and three-seat wagons, and two- or three-seat Estate wagons. Base Malibus came in coupe, sedan or wagon form (also two- or three-seat). Malibu Classic's restyled front end displayed new stacked rectangular headlamps, plus a lightweight diamond-pattern grille with script in lower corner, "classic" hood ornament, and new bumpers. Standard Malibus had a new horizontally-ribbed grille, but kept their single round headlamps with bright bezels. Both displayed a restyled rear end with tapered rear panel, and new horizontal rectangular taillamps and bumper in integrated design. Parking lamps were inset in the lower bumper. Landau coupes had new color-keyed paint stripes at front and rear, coach window styling, and distinctive vinyl roof. Malibu Classics had wide rocker panel moldings and window moldings, while base Malibus were plain. Biggest change in the powerplant parade was a new small-block 305 cu. in. (5.0-liter) standard V-8, which was supposed to emit fewer hydrocarbons as well as deliver better economy than the prior 350 V-8. Though the stroke of the 305 was the same as the 350, it was the only Chevrolet engine to have a 3.74 inch bore. Base engine was again the 250 cu. in. inline six, hooked to either three-speed manual or optional Turbo Hydra-matic. (V-8 Chevelles came only with automatic.) A 350 V-8 with two-barrel remained optional, as did a four-barrel 400 cu. in. V-8. Only in California was the four-barrel 350 offered. The big 454 was dropped as a Chevelle option this year. All Chevelles except the basic six-cylinder Malibu coupe and sedan now had standard power brakes. The brake system used new lining materials, plus larger rear drums in coupes and sedans. Standard equipment included the six-cylinder engine, three-speed manual (column) shift, front disc brakes, heater/defroster, cut-pile carpeting, lighter, hide-away wipers, and FR78 x 15/B steel-belted radial tires. Chevelle V-8s had a standard 305 engine and Turbo Hydra-matic, GR78 tires, as well as power brakes and steering. Wagons carried the 350 V-8. The Malibu Classic Landau added a vinyl roof, body-color sport mirrors (left remote-controlled), deluxe bumpers, dual horns, and full wheel covers. 70-series radial tires and sport suspension were available at extra cost. All models could have the 400 cu. in. V-8 powerplant for $148 or less. Of the 14 body colors this year, nine were new. Available were metallic light or dark blue, firethorn, mahogany, lime green, medium saddle, and dark green; plus cream, medium red, buckskin, cream gold, antique white, silver, and black. Interiors came in new knit vinyls as well as patterned cloths and expanded vinyls. Light buckskin, dark mahogany and lime white were new interior trim colors. Base Malibu interiors were sport cloth and vinyl, in black and buckskin. All-vinyl upholstery came in black, buckskin or blue, plus mahogany and white (with accents of black, lime or mahogany) for coupes only. Malibu Classic's interior was standard knit cloth and vinyl in black, blue or mahogany. (Coupes could have buckskin.) Or buyers could get all-vinyl in buckskin and blue, plus black, mahogany and white (with accents of black, blue, mahogany or lime) for coupe only. For its final season, the sporty Laguna S3 added the new Chevelle rear end but otherwise featured the same as in 1975. Laguna had an angled, aerodynamically styled "soft" urethane front end, louvered coach windows, sport mirrors (driver's side), rally wheels, color-keyed bumper impact strips, plus S3 identification on grille, front fenders and rear panel. Optional on Laguna: sport roof and sport striping. Inside was a round-dial instrument panel and woodgrain vinyl accents. The radial-tuned suspension had large-diameter stabilizer bars and revalved shock absorbers. Not available on Laguna bodies were light blue metallic, cream, medium saddle metallic, dark green metallic, medium red, buckskin, and cream gold. Laguna interiors were sport cloth and vinyl in black and buckskin; or all-vinyl in black, buckskin, blue and mahogany; plus white with accents of black, lime or mahogany.

MONTE CARLO — SERIES 1A — V-8 — Chevrolet's personal-luxury coupe, in the lineup since 1970, came in regular 'S' or Landau coupe form. New front-end styling focused on new vertically-stacked rectangular headlamps, plus an integrated-look bumper. This year's grille was made up of three wide segments, one above the other, each with internal crosshatching. Both parking and backup lamps were repositioned. Rounded horizontal parking lamps sat below the bumper. New tapered vertical taillamps had emblems in the center and small rectangular backup lenses below. A characteristic bodyside bulge tapered from front fenders into doors, continuing again on the rear quarters. Base engine was the 305 cu. in. (5.0-liter) V-8 with two-barrel carburetor; optional, either a 350 two-barrel or 400 four-barrel. Only in California was the 350 with four-barrel carb available. The 454 cu. in. V-8 available in 1975 was

1976 Monte Carlo Landau Coupe (CP)

dropped this year. Standard powertrain included Turbo Hydra-matic with a 2.73:1 axle ratio. Montes also had standard power steering and brakes, electric clock, hideaway wipers, cut-pile carpeting, full wheel covers, and 15x7 in. wheels with GR70 x 15/B steel-belted radial tires. The Landau model added a landau vinyl roof and body-color sport mirrors (left remote), visor vanity mirror, plus Turbine II wheels, pinstripe accents, dual horns, and landau body identification. The 350 cu. in. V-8 engines cost an extra $30 (two-barrel) or $85 (four-barrel); the 400 V-8, an extra $148. New to the option list: an electric rear window defogger. Of the 14 Monte body colors, nine were new. They included cream, buckskin, cream gold, medium red, white, black and silver; plus metallic mahogany, firethorn, medium saddle, lime green, light blue, dark blue, or dark green. Two-tones were available. Standard interiors had a full-foam bench seat; deep cut pile carpeting; color-keyed instrument panel and steering wheel; and tailored knit cloth or vinyl upholstery in choice of three shades. Optional swivel bucket seats could have rich velour fabric. Custom interiors came in velour, knit cloth or vinyl fabric; or three all-vinyl colors.

Impala S 4-Door Sedan.

1976 Impala S sedan (CP)

IMPALA/CAPRICE — SERIES 1B — V-8 — Full-size Chevrolets got new front styling and engine/brake refinements. For 1976 there were 13 models in two series (down from 17 in three series the year before). Bel Air sedans and wagons were dropped, as was the Caprice convertible. Impala's sport coupe was dropped; a new Impala sedan added. Impala's lineup now included a Custom coupe, Custom Landau coupe, sport sedan, four-door sedan, 'S' sedan, and station wagons (two or three seat). On the higher-priced Caprice Classic side, the choices were a coupe, sport sedan, four-door sedan, and Landau coupe; plus Caprice Estate station wagons (two or three seat). This would be the final year for the "true" pillarless four-door hardtop body. Impala refined its "swept back" front end look with round quad headlamps (as on the '75 Caprice). The grille had four full-width segments that appeared unconnected to each other. At the rear were triple-unit wraparound taillamps. The new Caprice front-end look featured new quad rectangular headlamps, plus a new grille with bold chrome horizontal and vertical bars and smaller inner bars. Both grilles repeated themselves in twin segments down in the front bumper. Both lines had hideaway windshield wipers. Caprice had wide bodyside moldings with color-keyed textured vinyl inserts (which could match the vinyl roof, if desired). Four V-8 choices were available: 350 cu. in. (5.7-liter) with two- or four-barrel carburetor; 400 V-8, (6.6-liter) 4Bbl.; and big 454 (7.4-liter) with 4Bbl. Three-speed Turbo Hydra-matic was standard with each engine. Wagons kept the 400 V-8 as standard powerplant. Like all Chevrolet engines, the 454 V-8 got revised ignition tuning and carburetor metering, plus refinements to improve economy and performance at low- and mid-range speeds. Some models with the 454 got different brake lining materials and heavier brake drums, plus a new brake pedal ratio. Standard Caprice equipment included the 350 V-8 with two-barrel, power steering and brakes, carpeting, heater/defroster, deluxe bumpers, and accent stripes.

1976 Caprice Classic Sport Sedan (CP)

Caprice also had rear fender skirts, a quiet sound group, electric clock, and GR78 x 15/B steel-belted radial tires. Wagons came with glide-away tailgate and LR78 x 15/C tires. Landau coupes added twin sport mirrors (left remote-controlled). The big 454 V-8 was optional on all models, priced from $223 to $375. Inside, Caprice Classic sported new bright steering wheel trim; plus new simulated rosewood accents on

instrument cluster, steering wheel, and above the glove compartment. Impala's standard equipment was similar to Caprice, but the low-budget 'S' version had bias-ply tires rather than radials, and less acoustical material. Impala 'S' also had no bodyside chrome strip or door window trim. Impala had a soft- rimmed steering wheel with cushioned center; but the same dash as Caprice, with simulated rosewood. Landau versions of both coupes had an elk-grain padded vinyl roof cover in choice of colors to complement the body. Also included: landau identification on quarter-window glass, body-colored wheel covers with landau markings, twin body- color sport mirrors, deluxe bumpers with impact strips, accent stripes and bright moldings. Sport sedans had a bright metal vinyl top molding. Of the 14 Caprice/Impala body colors, nine were new this year. The list included cream, antique white, silver, black, medium red, buckskin and cream gold; plus metallic light or dark blue, lime or dark green, medium saddle, firethorn, and mahogany. Impala upholstery was new standard knit cloth and vinyl in black, dark blue, or dark firethorn; or buckskin sport cloth. Caprice's knit cloth and vinyl came in black, dark blue, or dark mahogany. All-vinyl white trim was now available in the Caprice Classic coupe. Wagons added a cargo light as auxiliary lighting, while an illuminated visor vanity mirror was available on all models. Options included aluminum door edge guards.

I.D. DATA: Like other GM passenger cars, Chevrolets used a 13- symbol Vehicle Identification Number (VIN) displayed on the upper left surface of the instrument panel, visible through the windshield. The first digit ('1') indicates Chevrolet division. Next is a letter identifying the series (car line): 'B' Chevette; 'J' Chevette Scooter; 'V' Vega; 'M' Monza; 'R' Monza 2+2; 'X' Nova; 'Q' Camaro; 'S' Camaro Type LT; 'Y' Nova Concours; 'C' Chevelle Malibu; 'D' Malibu Classic; 'E' Laguna S3; 'H' Monte Carlo; 'L' Impala; 'N' Caprice Classic. Symbols 34 indicate body type: '08' Chevette 2-dr. hatchback coupe; '11' Vega 2-dr. notchback pillar coupe; '77' Vega 2-dr. hatchback coupe; '07' Monza hatchback pillar coupe; '17' Nova 2-dr. hatchback coupe; '27' 2-dr. notchback coupe; '87' Camaro 2-dr. hardtop sport coupe; '37' Chevelle 2-dr. notchback hardtop coupe; '47' Caprice/Impala 2-dr. notchback hardtop coupe; '57' Monte Carlo 2-dr. hardtop coupe; '69' 4-dr. (4-window) pillar sedan; '39' 4-dr. (4-window) hardtop sedan; '29' Chevelle 4-dr. sedan; '35' 4-dr. 2-seat station wagon; '45' 4-dr. 3-seat wagon; '15' Vega 2-dr. station wagon. Symbol five is the engine code: '1' L485 1Bbl.; 'E' L497.6 1Bbl.; 'O' L4122 EFI; 'A' L4140 1Bbl.; 'B' L4140 2Bbl.; 'D' L6250 1Bbl.; 'G' V8262 2Bbl.; 'Q' V8305 2Bbl.; 'L' V8350 2Bbl.; 'U' V8400 4Bbl.; 'S' V8454 4Bbl. Next is a code for model year ('6' 1976). Symbol seven denotes assembly plant: 'B' Baltimore, MD; 'C' South Gate, CA; 'D' Doraville, GA; 'J' Janesville, WI; 'K' Leeds, MO; 'U' Lordstown, OH; 'L' Van Nuys, CA; 'N' Norwood, OH; 'R' Arlington, TX; 'S' St. Louis, MO; 'T' Tarrytown, NY; 'W' Willow Run, MI; 'Y' Wilmington, DE; 'Z' Fremont, CA; '1' Oshawa, Ontario; '2' St. Therese, Quebec; '4' Scarborough, Canada. The last six digits are the sequential serial number. A Body Number Plate on the upper horizontal surface of the shroud (except X-bodies, on the vertical surface) identifies model year, car division, series, style, body assembly plant, body number, trim combination, modular seat code, paint code, and date build code. A three-symbol (sometimes two) code combined with a serial number identifies each engine. Inline sixes have that number on a pad at front right of block, at rear of distributor. On V-8s, it's on a pad at front right side of block. Chevette engine numbers are on a pad at right of block, below No. 1 spark plug. Vega numbers are on a pad at right side of block below No. 3 plug at head parting line.

CHEVETTE (FOUR)

Model Number	Body/Style Number	Body Type & Seating	Factory Price	Shipping Weight	Production Total
1T	B08	2-dr. Hatch-4P	3098	1924	178,007

CHEVETTE SCOOTER (FOUR)

1T	J08	2-dr. Hatch-4P	2899	1870	9,810

Chevette Production Note: 7,523 Chevettes were built for the Canadian market, called Acadians.

VEGA (FOUR)

1H	V11	2-dr. Spt Cpe-4P	2984	2443	27,619
1H	V77	2-dr. Hatch-4P	3099	2534	77,409
1H	V15	2-dr. Sta Wag-4P	3227	2578	46,114
1H	V15	2-dr. Est Wag-4P	3450	N/A	7,935

1976 Cosworth Vega hatchback coupe (CP)

COSWORTH VEGA (FOUR)

1H	V77	2-dr. Hatch-4P	6066	N/A	1,446

MONZA (FOUR/V-8)

1H	M27	2-dr. Twn Cpe-4P	3359	2625	46,735
1H	R07	2-dr. Hatch 2+2-4P	3727	2668	34,170

Monza Engine Note: Prices shown are for four-cylinder. Only 7,277 Towne Coupes and 10,085 hatchbacks had a V-8 engine, which cost an additional $224. Production totals include four-cylinder Monzas built in Canada.

NOVA (SIX/V-8)

1X	X27	2-dr. Cpe-6P	3248/3413	3188/3272	131,859
1X	X17	2-dr. Hatch-6P	3417/3579	3391/3475	18,719
1X	X69	4-dr. Sedan-6P	3283/3448	3221/3305	123,767

NOVA CONCOURS (SIX/V-8)

1X	Y27	2-dr. Cpe-6P	3795/3960	3324/3408	22,298
1X	Y17	2-dr. Hatch-6P	3972/4134	3401/3485	7,574
1X	Y69	4-dr. Sedan-6P	3830/3995	3367/3451	30,511

CAMARO (SIX/V-8)

1F	Q87	2-dr. Spt Cpe-4P	3762/3927	3421/3511	130,538
1F	S87	2-dr. LT Cpe-4P	-- /4320	-- /3576	52,421

CHEVELLE MALIBU (SIX/V-8)

1A	C37	2-dr. Col Cpe-6P	3636/4166	3650/3755	30,592
1A	C29	4-dr. Col Sed-6P	3671/4201	3729/3834	38,469
1A	C35	4-dr. Sta Wag-4P	-- /4543	-- /4238	13,581
1A	C35	4-dr. 3S Wag-9P	-- /4686	-- / N/A	2,984

CHEVELLE MALIBU CLASSIC (SIX/V-8)

1A	D37	2-dr. Col Cpe-6P	3926/4455	3688/3793	82,634
1A	D37	2-dr. Lan Cpe-6P	4124/4640	N/A	30,167
1A	D29	4-dr. Col Sed-6P	4196/4490	3827/3932	77,560
1A	D35	4-dr. Sta Wag-6P	-- /4776	-- /4300	24,635
1A	D35	4-dr. 3S Wag-9P	-- /4919	-- / N/A	11,617
1A	G35	4-dr. Est Wag-6P	-- /4971	-- /4326	5,518
1A	G35	4-dr. 3S Est Wag-6P	-- /5114	-- /N/A	6,386

Malibu Classic Engine Note: Only 672 Landau coupes, 5,791 regular coupes and 4,253 sedans had a six-cylinder engine.

LAGUNA S-3 (V-8)

1A	E37	2-dr. Col Cpe-5P	4622	3978	9,100

Laguna Production Note: Total includes 864 built in Canada.

MONTE CARLO (V-8)

1A	H57	2-dr. 'S' Cpe-6P	4673	3907	191,370
1A	H57	2-dr. Lan Cpe-6P	4966	N/A	161,902

FULL-SIZE CHEVROLETS IMPALA (V-8)

1B	L47	2-dr. Cust Cpe-6P	4763	4175	43,219
1B	L47	2-dr. Lan Cpe-6P	5058	N/A	10,841
1B	L69	4-dr. Sedan-6P	4706	4222	86,057
1B	L69	4-dr. 'S' Sed-6P	4507	N/A	18,265
1B	L39	4-dr. Spt Sed-6P	4798	4245	39,849
1B	L35	4-dr. Sta Wag-6P	5166	4912	19,657
1B	L45	4-dr. 3S Wag-9P	5283	4972	21,329

CAPRICE CLASSIC (V-8)

1B	N47	2-dr. Coupe-6P	5043	4244	28,161
1B	N47	2-dr. Lan Cpe-6P	5284	N/A	21,926
1B	N69	4-dr. Sedan-6P	5013	4285	47,411
1B	N39	4-dr. Spt Sed-6P	5078	4314	55,308
1B	N35	4-dr. Est Wag-6P	5429	4948	10,029
1B	N45	4-dr. 3S Est-6P	5546	5007	21,804

FACTORY PRICE AND WEIGHT NOTE: Where two prices and weights are shown, the figure to the left of the slash is for six-cylinder model, to right of slash for V-8 (except Monza, four-cylinder and V-8). **PRODUCTION NOTE:** Chevelle and full-size totals include models built in Canada.

ENGINE DATA: BASE FOUR (Chevette): Inline. Overhead cam. Four-cylinder. Cast iron block and head. Displacement: 85.0 cu. in. (1.4 liters). Bore & stroke: 3.23 x 2.61 in. Compression ratio: 8.5:1. Brake horsepower: 52 at 5200 R.P.M. Torque: 70 lbs.-ft. at 3600 R.P.M. Five main bearings. Hydraulic valve lifters. Carburetor: 1Bbl. Rochester 1ME. VIN Code: 1. **OPTIONAL FOUR** (Chevette): Inline. Overhead cam. Four-cylinder. Cast iron block and head. Displacement: 97.6 cu. in. (1.6 liters). Bore & stroke: 3.23 x 2.98 in. Compression ratio: 8.5:1. Brake horsepower: 60 at 4800 R.P.M. Torque: 82 lbs.-ft. at 3400 R.P.M. Five main bearings. Hydraulic valve lifters. Carburetor: 1Bbl. Roch. 1ME. VIN Code: E. **BASE FOUR** (Cosworth Vega): Inline vee-slanted. Dual overhead cam. Four-cylinder 16valve (four valves per cylinder). Cast aluminum alloy block and head. Displacement: 122 cu. in. (2.0 liters). Compression ratio: 8.0:1. Brake horsepower: 110 at 5600 R.P.M. Torque: 107 lbs.-ft. at 4800 R.P.M. Five main bearings. Solid valve lifters. Electronic fuel injection. VIN Code: O. **BASE FOUR** (Vega, Monza): Inline. Overhead cam. Four-cylinder. Aluminum block, cast iron head. Displacement: 140 cu. in. (2.3 liters). Bore & stroke: 3.50 x 3.63 in. Compression ratio: 8.0:1. Brake horsepower: 70 at 4400 R.P.M. Torque: 107 lbs.-ft. at 2400 R.P.M. Five main bearings. Hydraulic valve lifters. Carburetor: 1Bbl. Rochester 1MV. VIN Code: A. **OPTIONAL FOUR** (Vega, Monza): Same as 140 cu. in. four above, except Brake H.P.: 84 at 4400 R.P.M. Torque: 113 lbs.-ft. at 3200 R.P.M. Carb: 2Bbl. Holley 5210C. **BASE SIX** (Nova, Chevelle, Camaro): Inline. OHV. Six-cylinder. Cast iron block and head. Displacement: 250 cu. in. (4.1 liters). Bore & stroke: 3.88 x 3.53 in. Compression ratio: 8.5:1. Brake horsepower: 105 at 3800 R.P.M. Torque: 185 lbs.-ft. at 1200 R.P.M. Seven main bearings. Hydraulic valve lifters. Carburetor: 1Bbl. Roch. 1MV. VIN Code: D. **OPTIONAL V-8** (Monza): 90-degree, overhead valve V-8. Cast iron block and head. Displacement: 262 cu. in. (4.3 liters). Bore & stroke: 3.67 x 3.10 in. Compression ratio: 8.5:1. Brake horsepower: 110 at 3600 R.P.M. Torque: 195 lbs.-ft. at 2000 R.P.M. Five main bearings. Carburetor: 2Bbl. Roch. 2GC. VIN Code: G. **BASE V 8** (Monte Carlo); **OPTIONAL** (Monza, Nova, Camaro, Chevelle): 90-degree, overhead valve V-8. Cast iron block and head. Displacement: 305 cu. in. (5.0 liters). Bore & stroke: 3.74 x 3.48 in. Compression ratio: 8.5:1. Brake

horsepower: 140 at 3800 R.P.M. Torque: 245 lbs.-ft. at 2000 R.P.M. Five main bearings. Hydraulic valve lifters. Carburetor: 2Bbl. Roch. 2GC. VIN Code: Q. BASE V-8 (Chevelle wagon, Caprice, Impala); OPTIONAL (Chevelle, Monte Carlo): 90-degree, overhead valve V-8. Cast iron block and head. Displacement: 350 cu. in. (5.7 liters). Bore & stroke: 4.00 x 3.48 in. Compression ratio: 8.5:1. Brake horsepower: 145 at 3800 R.P.M. Torque: 250 lbs.-ft. at 2200 R.P.M. Five main bearings. Hydraulic valve lifters. Carburetor: 2Bbl. Roch. 2GC. VIN Code: V. OPTIONAL V-8 (Nova, Camaro, Chevelle, Monte Carlo, Caprice, Impala): Same as 350 cu. in. V-8 above, except four-barrel carburetor Brake H.P.: 165 at 3800 R.P.M. Torque: 260 lbs.-ft. at 2400 R.P.M. Carb: 4Bbl. Roch. M4MC. VIN Code: L. BASE V-8 (Caprice/Impala wagon); OPTIONAL (Chevelle, Monte Carlo, Caprice, Impala): 90-degree, overhead valve V-8. Cast iron block and head. Displacement: 400 cu. in. (6.6 liters). Bore & stroke: 4.13 x 3.75 in. Compression ratio: 8.5:1. Brake horsepower: 175 at 3600 R.P.M. Torque: 305 lbs.-ft. at 2000 R.P.M. Five main bearings. Hydraulic valve lifters. Carburetor: 4Bbl. Roch. M4MC. VIN Code: U. OPTIONAL V-8 (Caprice, Impala): 90-degree, overhead valve V-8. Cast iron block and head. Displacement: 454 cu. in. (7.4 liters). Bore & stroke: 4.25 x 4.00 in. Compression ratio: 8.25:1. Brake horsepower: 225 at 3800 R.P.M. Torque: 360 lbs.-ft. at 2400 R.P.M. Five main bearings. Hydraulic valve lifters. Carburetor: 4Bbl. Roch. M4ME. VIN Code: S.

CHASSIS DATA: Wheelbase: (Chevette) 94.3 in.; (Vega/Monza) 97.0 in.; (Camaro) 108.0 in.; (Nova) 111.0 in.; (Chevelle cpe) 112.0 in.; (Chevelle sed/wag, Monte Carlo) 116.0 in.; (Imp/Capr) 121.5 in.; (Imp/Capr wag) 125.0 in. Overall length: (Chvt) 158.7 in.; (Vega) 175.4 in.; (Monza twn cpe) 177.8 in.; (Monza hatch) 179.3 in.; (Camaro) 195.4 in.; (Nova) 196.7 in.; (Nova Concours) 197.7 in.; (Camaro) 195.4 in.; (Chevelle cpe) 205.3 in.; (Laguna) 207.3 in.; (Chevelle sed) 209.3 in.; (Chevelle wag) 215.2 in.; (Monte) 212.7 in.; (Imp/Capr) 222.9 in.; (Imp/Capr wag) 228.6 in. Height: (Chvt) 52.3 in.; (Vega spt cpe/wag) 51.8 in.; (Vega hatch) 50.0 in.; (Monza twn cpe) 49.8 in.; (Monza hatch) 50.2 in.; (Nova) 54.3 in.; (Camaro) 49.2 in.; (Chevelle/Laguna cpe) 53.1 in.; (Chevelle sed) 53.8 in.; (Chevelle wag) 55.7 in.; (Monte) 52.7 in.; (Imp/Capr cpe) 53.7 in.; (Imp/Capr sed) 54.4 in.; (Imp/Capr spt sed) 53.9 in.; (Imp/Capr 2S wag) 58.1 in.; (Imp/Capr 3S wag) 57.4 in. Width: (Chvt) 61.8 in.; (Vega/Monza) 65.4 in.; (Nova) 72.2 in.; (Camaro) 74.4 in.; (Chevelle) 76.6 in.; (Chevelle wag) 76.8 in.; (Monte) 77.6 in.; (Imp/Capr) 79.5 in. Front Tread: (Chvt) 51.2 in.; (Vega/Monza) 54.8 in.; (Nova/Camaro) 61.3 in.; (Camaro LT) 61.6 in.; (Chevelle) 61.5 in.; (Monte) 61.9 in.; (Imp/Capr) 64.1 in. Rear Tread: (Chvt) 51.2 in.; (Vega/Monza) 53.6 in.; (Nova) 59.0 in.; (Camaro) 60.0 in.; (Camaro LT) 60.3 in.; (Chevelle/Monte) 60.7 in.; (Imp/Capr) 64.0 in. Standard Tires: (Chvt) 155/8013B; (Vega/Monza) A78 x 13/B; (Nova) E78 x 14/B; (Nova Concours, Camaro) FR78 x 14/B; (Chevelle six) FR78 x 15/B; (Chevelle V-8) GR78 x 15/B; (Chevelle wag) HR78 x 15/B; (Monte) GR70 x 15/B; (Imp/Capr) G78 x 15/B; (Imp/Capr wag) LR78 x 15/C.

TECHNICAL: Transmission: Three-speed floor shift standard on Vega/Monza four and Camaro; column shift on Chevelle/Nova; floor shift available on Nova. Gear ratios: (1st) 3.11:1; (2nd) 1.84:1; (3rd) 1.00:1; (Rev) 3.22:1; except Nova V8350 (1st) 2.85:1; (2nd) 1.84:1; (3rd) 1.00:1; (Rev) 2.95:1. Four-speed floor shift standard on Chevette, optional on Vega/Monza four: (1st) 3.75:1; (2nd) 2.16:1; (3rd) 1.38:1; (4th) 1.00:1; (Rev) 3.82:1. Four-speed floor shift optional on Monza V-8, Cosworth: (1st) 3.11:1; (2nd) 2.20:1; (3rd) 1.47:1; (4th) 1.00:1; (Rev) 3.11:1. Four-speed floor shift optional on Nova/Camaro V8350: (1st) 2.85:1; (2nd) 2.02:1; (3rd) 1.35:1; (4th) 1.00:1; (Rev) 2.85:1. Five-speed floor shift on Vega/Monza: (1st) 3.10:1; (2nd) 1.89:1; (3rd) 1.27:1; (4th) 1.00:1; (5th) 0.80:1; (Rev) 3.06:1. Three-speed Turbo Hydra- matic standard on Chevelle V-8 and Monte/Caprice/Impala, optional on others. Gear ratios: (1st) 2.52:1; (2nd) 1.52:1; (3rd) 1.00:1; (Rev) 1.94:1 except Caprice/Impala w/V8454: (1st) 2.48:1; (2nd) 1.48:1; (3rd) 1.00:1; (Rev) 2.08:1. Chevette and Nova (exc. V8350) THM gear ratios: (1st) 2.74:1; (2nd) 1.57:1; (3rd) 1.00:1; (Rev) 2.07:1. Standard final drive ratio: (Chevette) 3.70:1 exc. 4.11:1 w/1.6 engine; (Vega) 2.92:1 exc. 2.53:1 w/4-spd, 2.93:1 w/5- spd, 2.92:1 or 3.42:1 w/auto.; (Cosworth Vega) 4.10:1; (Monza) 2.92:1 exc. 2.56:1 or 2.93:1 w/5-spd or auto., 3.42:1 w/2Bbl. four, 2.56:1 w/V-8; (Nova) 2.73:1 exc. 3.08:1 w/V8350, 2.73:1 or 3.08:1 w/auto.; (Camaro) 2.73:1 exc. 2.73:1 or 3.08:1 w/auto., 2.85:1 w/4-spd; (Chevelle) 2.73:1 exc. 2.73:1 or 3.08:1 w/auto.; (Monte) 2.73:1; (Caprice/Imp) 2.73:1 or 3.08:1. Steering: (Chevette) rack and pinion; (others) recirculating ball. Front Suspension: unequal length control arms, coil springs stabilizer bar. Rear Suspension: (Chevette) rigid axle, torque tube, longitudinal trailing radius arms, coil springs, transverse linkage bar; (Vega) rigid axle, lower trailing radius arms, upper oblique torque arms, coil springs, transverse linkage bar; (Monza) similar to Vega, with stabilizer bar; (Nova/Camaro) semi-elliptic leaf springs, stabilizer bar on Camaro; (others) rigid axle, lower trailing radius arms, upper oblique torque arms and coil springs, plus stabilizer bar on Laguna, Monte and Caprice Classic. Brakes: front disc, rear drum. Ignition: High energy electronic. Body construction: (Chvt/Vega/Monza) unitized; (Nova/Camaro) integral, with separate partial front box frame; (Chevelle/Monte/Impala/Caprice) perimeter box frame with cross-members. Fuel tank: (Chvt) 13 gal.; (Vega) 16 gal.; (Monza) 18.5 gal.; (Nova/Camaro) 21 gal.; (Chevelle/Monte) 22 gal.; (Imp/Capr) 26 gal.; (Imp/Capr wag) 22 gal.

DRIVETRAIN OPTIONS: Engines: 1.6-liter four: Chevette ($51). 140 cu. in., 2Bbl. four: Vega/Monza ($56). 262 cu. in., 2Bbl. V-8: Monza ($224). 350 cu. in., 2Bbl. V-8: Chevelle/Monte ($30). 350 cu. in., 4Bbl. V-8: Nova/Camaro/Chevelle/Monte ($85); Chevelle wag ($55); Imp/Caprice cpe/sed ($56). 400 cu. in., 4Bbl. V-8: Chevelle/Monte ($148); Chevelle wag ($118); Imp/Capr cpe/sed ($120). 454 cu. in., 4Bbl. V-8: Imp ($375); Caprice ($350); Imp/Capr wag ($223). Transmission/Differential: Four-speed manual shift: Vega/Monza ($60). Four-speed wide-range manual shift: Nova ($242); Camaro ($260). Five-speed manual shift: Vega/Monza ($244). Turbo Hydra-matic transmission: Chevette/Vega/Monza ($244); Nova/Camaro, Chevelle six ($260). Sport shifter w/console: Chevette ($40). Floor shift lever: Nova ($29). Positraction axle: Vega/Monza ($48); Nova/Camaro/Chevelle/Monte ($51); Imp/Capr ($55). High-altitude or highway axle ratio: Chvt/Vega/Monza ($12); Chevelle/Monte/Imp/Capr ($13). High- altitude axle ratio: Nova/Camaro ($13). Power Accessories: Power brakes: Chvt/Vega/Monza ($55); Nova/Camaro/Chevelle six ($58). Power steering (variable ratio): Vega/Monza ($120); Nova/Chevelle ($136). Suspension: F40 H.D. suspension: Nova ($6-$29); Chevelle/Monte/Imp/Capr ($18). F41 sport suspension: Vega ($141); Monza ($26); Nova/Camaro ($25-$32); Imp ($32); Caprice ($7). FE8 radial-tuned suspension: Chevelle ($27); Imp/Capr cpe/sed ($25). Superlift rear shock absorbers: Imp/Caprice ($44). Rear stabilizer bar: Chevette ($26). Other: Heavy-duty radiator ($25-$34). H.D. alternator (61amp): Chevelle/Monte/Imp/Capr ($27). H.D. battery ($15-$16). California emission certification ($50).

CHEVETTE/VEGA/MONZA CONVENIENCE/APPEARANCE OPTIONS: Option Packages: Woody package: Chevette ($306). Rally equipment: Chevette ($230-$251). GT pkg.: Vega hatch ($457); Vega wagon ($340-$429). Cabriolet equipment (vinyl roof, opera windows, bright moldings, woodgrain steering wheel shroud, sport equipment): Monza ($256). Sport equipment: Monza ($118). Spyder equipment: Monza Twn Cpe ($421-$430); Monza hatch ($333-$342). Quiet sound group: Chvt ($29- $39); Vega ($32-$43). Comfort/Convenience: Air conditioning ($424). Rear defogger ($66). Tinted glass ($44). Sport steering wheel ($15). Comfortilt steering wheel: Vega/Monza ($48). Special instrumentation: Chvt ($56); Vega ($72); Monza ($56-$72). Econominder gauge: Monza ($10-$26). Electric clock: Chvt/Monza ($16). Cigarette lighter: Chvt ($5). Glove compartment lock: Chvt ($3). Lighting and Mirrors: Aux. lighting: Vega ($15-$29); Monza ($15). Twin sport mirrors, left remote: Vega/Monza ($25). Driver's remote sport mirror: Chvt ($19). Twin remote sport mirrors: Chvt ($43). Day/night mirror ($7). Entertainment: Pushbutton AM radio ($70). Pushbutton AM/FM radio ($129). AM/FM stereo radio: Vega/Monza ($212). Stereo tape player w/AM radio: Monza ($196). Rear speaker ($20). Windshield antenna: Vega/Monza ($15); incl. w/radios. Exterior Trim: Vinyl roof: Chvt ($90). Swing-out windows: Chvt ($45); Vega cpe ($29-$35). Custom exterior: Chvt ($82); Vega ($59-$88). Decor group: Vega ($6-$34). Sport decor: Chvt ($77). Sport stripes: Vega ($76). Bodyside moldings ($36). Wheel opening moldings: Vega/Monza ($19). Side window reveal moldings: Chvt ($59). Door edge guards ($7). Roof carrier: Chvt/Vega ($53). Rear air deflector: Vega ($23). Deluxe bumpers, front/rear: Chvt ($27); Vega ($44). Deluxe bumpers w/guards: Monza ($60). Deluxe front bumper guards: Vega ($17). Deluxe bumper guards, front/rear: Chvt ($34-$61); Monza ($34). Interior Trim/Upholstery: Custom interior trim: Chevette ($152-$164). Console: Chvt ($16); Monza ($73). Bucket seats: Vega ($126-$158); Monza ($124-$140). Adjustable driver's seatback: Vega/Monza ($17). Load floor carpet: Chvt ($40). Color-keyed floor mats ($14). Front mats: Chvt ($8). Deluxe seatbelts ($15). Trunk mat: Monza ($10). Wheels and Tires: Aluminum wheels: Monza ($173-$204). Rally II wheels: Vega ($97). Wheel covers: Vega ($28). Sport wheel covers: Chvt ($36-$66). Wheel trim rings: Chvt ($30); Vega ($3-$30). 155/8013/B WSW: Chvt ($32). 155/8013/B SBR: Chvt ($99). 155/8013/B SBR WSW: Chvt ($131). 155/8013/B SBR WLT: Chvt ($145). A78 x 13/B WSW: Vega ($32); Monza ($26-$32). A78 x 13/B belted WSW: Vega ($53); Monza ($43-$53). BR78 x 13/B SBR: Vega ($34-$122); Monza ($98-$122). BR78 x 13/B SBR WSW: Vega ($66-$154); Monza ($123-$154). BR78 x 13/B SBR WLT: Vega ($80-$168); Monza ($135-$168). BR78 x 13/C SBR: Monza ($114- $146). BR78 x 13/C SBR WSW: Monza ($25-$178). BR78 x 13/C SBR WLT: Monza ($36-$192). BR70 x 13/B SBR WLT: Monza ($36-$46). Stowaway spare: Monza ($23).

NOVA/CAMARO/CHEVELLE/MONTE CARLO CONVENIENCE/APPEARANCE OPTIONS: Option Packages: SS equipment: Nova ($187). Rally Sport equipment: base Camaro ($260); Camaro LT ($173). Interior decor/quiet sound group: base Camaro ($53). Comfort/Convenience: Air conditioning ($452-$479). Rear defogger (forced-air): Nova/Camaro/Monte ($43); Chevelle ($43-$47). Rear defogger (electric): Monte ($77). Cruise- Master speed control: Nova/Chevelle/Monte ($73). Tinted glass: Nova/Camaro ($46); Chevelle ($49); Monte ($53). Sport steering wheel: base Nova, Chevelle ($16). Comfortilt steering wheel ($52). Six-way power seat: Chevelle/Monte ($124). Power windows ($99-$140). Power door locks: Nova/Chevelle ($62-$89); Camaro/Monte ($62). Power trunk release: Monte ($17). Power tailgate release: Chevelle 2S wag ($20). Electric clock: Nova/Camaro ($18); Chevelle ($19). Special instrumentation (incl. tach and console): Nova ($160); Concours ($89). Special instrumentation (incl. tach and dock): base Camaro ($92). Econominder gauge pkg.: Chevelle/Monte ($45). Econominder light: Nova ($16). Intermittent wipers: Nova/Monte ($28). Hide-a-way wipers: base Camaro ($22). Lighting, Horns and Mirrors: Aux. lighting ($21-$41). Dual horns: Nova/Camaro-/Chevelle ($6). Remote-control driver's mirror: Nova/Chevelle/Monte ($14). Twin sport mirrors, left remote ($27). Twin remote sport mirrors (body-color): Nova/Chevelle/Monte ($20-$46). Day/night mirror: Nova ($7). Visor vanity mirror: Chevelle/Monte ($4). Lighted visor mirror: Chevelle ($26); Monte ($23-$26). Entertainment: Pushbutton AM radio ($75). AM/FM radio: Nova/Camaro/Chevelle ($137); Monte ($146). AM/FM stereo radio ($226). Stereo 8track tape player w/AM radio: Nova/Camaro/Chevelle ($209); Monte ($225). Stereo tape player with AM/FM stereo radio ($324). Rear speaker ($21). Windshield antenna ($16); incl. w/radios. Exterior Trim: Electric sky roof: Monte ($370). Vinyl roof: Nova/Camaro ($96); Chevelle ($109); Monte ($129). Cabriolet roof: Nova ($150). Spoilers, front/rear: Camaro ($81). Exterior decor pkg.: Nova ($73); Chevelle ($19-$51). Custom appearance group: Nova Concours ($65-$75). Exterior style trim: Camaro ($58). Fashion-tone paint: Monte ($104-$233). Two-tone paint: Nova/Chevelle ($40). Swing-out rear side windows: Nova ($48). Bodyside moldings: Nova/Camaro-/Chevelle ($38); Nova Concours, Monte ($49). Door edge guards ($7-$11). Wheel opening moldings: Nova ($19). Roof drip moldings: base Nova, Camaro ($16). Bodyside pinstriping: Nova ($26). Sport stripes: Chevelle cpe/sed ($81). Rear window air deflector: Chevelle wag ($23). Roof carrier: Chevelle wag ($68). Deluxe bumpers: Chevelle/Monte ($29). Deluxe bumpers w/guards, front/rear: Nova ($63). Bumper guards, front/rear: Camaro/Chevelle/Monte ($36); Chevelle wag ($18). Interior Trim/Upholstery: Interior decor pkg.: base Nova ($25). Console: base Nova, Camaro/Chevelle/Monte ($71). Bench seat w/custom interior: base Nova ($180). Bucket seats: Nova ($255); Nova Concours ($204). Knit or sport cloth seats: Camaro, Chevelle wag ($20). Vinyl bucket seats: Chevelle ($20). Bucket seats w/knit cloth or vinyl: Chevelle ($102- $140); Monte ($140). Custom cloth bucket seats: Monte ($265). 50/50 reclining passenger seat: Monte ($273). Adj. driver's seatback: Camaro ($19). Litter container: Chevelle/Monte ($6). Deluxe carpet: Nova/Camaro ($32). Removable load-floor carpeting: Chevelle wag ($42). Color-keyed mats ($15). Deluxe seatbelts ($14-$20). Wheels and Tires: Custom styled wheels: Nova ($116); Nova Concours ($86); Camaro ($79-$116). Rally wheels: base Nova/Camaro ($60); Nova Concours ($38); Chevelle ($35-$60); Monte ($46). Wire wheel covers: Chevelle ($59-$89); Monte ($79); Monte Landau ($23 credit). Full wheel covers: base Nova, Camaro ($30). Deluxe wheel covers: Monte ($19). Wheel trim rings: base Nova ($33). E78 x 14/B BSW: Camaro ($84-$106 credit). E78 x 14/B WSW: base Nova ($26-$33); Camaro ($58-$73 redit). FR78 x 14/B SBR: base Nova ($84-$106). FR78 x 14/B SBR WSW: Nova ($112-$141); Nova Concours, Camaro ($28-$35); Chevelle six ($30-$37). FR78 x 14/B SBR WLT: Nova ($123- $155); Nova Concours, Camaro ($39-$49). GR78 x 15/B SBR WSW: Chevelle/Laguna V-8 ($30-$37). HR78 x 15/B SBR BSW: Chevelle/Laguna V-8 ($38). HR78 x 15/B SBR WSW: Chevelle/Laguna V-8 ($78); Chevelle wag ($40). GR70 x 15/B SBR BSW: Chevelle V-8 ($43-$54); Laguna ($14-$17). GR70 x 15/B SBR WSW: Chevelle V-8 ($73-$91); Laguna ($43-$54); Monte ($30-$37). GR70 x 15/B SBR WLT: Chevelle V-8 ($84-$105); Laguna ($55-$68). Stowaway spare: base Nova, Camaro ($15); Concours/Chevelle/Monte (NC). NOTE: Chevelle/Laguna GR70 tires included sport suspension.

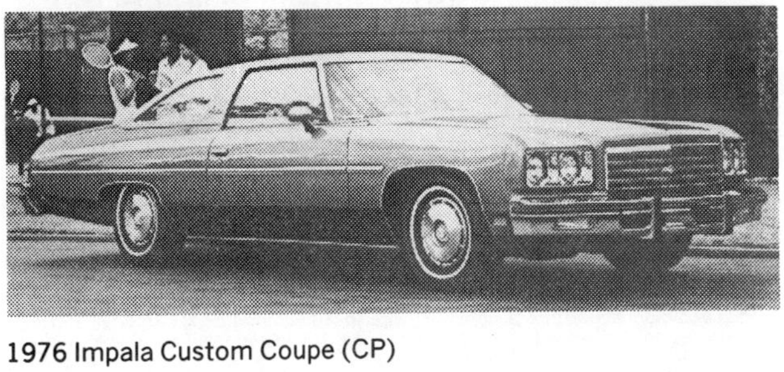

1976 Impala Custom Coupe (CP)

IMPALA/CAPRICE CONVENIENCE/APPEARANCE OPTIONS: Comfort/Convenience: Four season air cond. ($485). Comfortron auto-temp air cond. ($567). Rear defogger, forced-air ($44- $48). Cruise-Master speed control ($74). Tinted glass ($63). Comfortilt steering wheel ($53). Power door locks ($63-$90). Six-way power seat ($126). Power windows ($105-$159). Power trunk release ($17). Power tailgate: wag ($52). Electric clock: Imp ($19). Econominder gauge pkg. ($34). Intermittent wipers ($28). Quiet sound group ($33-$45). Lighting, Horns and Mirrors: Aux. lighting ($20-$37). Dome reading light ($14). Dual horns: Imp ($6). Driver's remote mirror ($14). Dual remote mirrors ($42). Dual remote body- color sport mirrors ($19-$47). Visor vanity mirror ($4). Lighted visor mirror ($26). Entertainment: Pushbutton AM radio ($76). AM/FM radio ($148). AM/FM stereo radio ($229). Stereo 8-track tape player w/AM radio ($228); with AM/FM stereo radio ($328). Rear speaker ($21). Windshield antenna ($16); incl. w/radios. Exterior Trim: Vinyl roof ($125-$150). Rear fender skirts ($33); std. on Caprice. Two-tone paint ($41) incl. bright outline moldings. Roof carrier: wag ($82). Bodyside moldings: wag ($39). Deluxe bodyside moldings: Imp ($25-$50). Door edge guards ($7-$11). Wheel opening moldings: Imp ($19); std. on cpe. Deluxe bumpers ($40). Bumper guards ($43). Interior Trim/Upholstery: 50/50 reclining passenger seat ($142). Deluxe load-floor carpet: wag ($61).

Removable load-floor carpet: wag ($43). Color-keyed mats ($15). Litter container ($6). Color-keyed deluxe seatbelts ($17-$20). Deluxe trunk trim ($35-$43). Wheels and Tires: Full wheel covers ($31). Wire wheel covers ($69-$100). G78 x 15/B WSW: cpe/sed ($37). HR78 x 15/B SBR BSW: Imp S ($132); others (NC). HR78 x 15/B SBR WSW: Imp S ($172); other cpe/sed ($41). LR78 x 15/C SBR BSW (NC); std. on wag. LR78 x 15/C SBR WSW ($47).

HISTORY: Introduced: Oct. 2, 1975. Model year production (U.S.): 1,920,200 (incl. Corvettes but not incl. 7,523 Acadians). Of total vehicles built for U.S. market, 411,883 were four-cylinder, 278,775 six, and 1,341,112 had a V-8. Calendar year production: 2,012,024 (incl. 47,425 Corvettes, 5,311 Acadians and 27,677 Sportvans). Calendar year sales by U.S. dealers: 2,104,142 for a 24.4 percent market share, down from almost 26 percent in 1975. (That total included 30,337 Sportvans and 41,673 Corvettes.) Model year sales by U.S. dealers: 2,077,119 (including 27,416 Sportvans and 41,027 Corvettes), up from 1,714,593 in 1975.

Historical Footnotes: Chevrolet hoped to sell 275,000 Chevettes in its initial season, taking 185,000 sales away from imports, to help the company into a strong year after poor sales in 1975. Only 1,686,062 Chevrolets had been built in calendar year 1975, the lowest total since 1970. Model year production was lower yet for 1975: just 1,614,491, far below the 2.4 million Chevrolets produced in model year 1973. As it turned out, neither Chevette nor Vega sold well in 1976. This year did indeed see a resurgence in sales, but GM's best seller was now the Olds Cutlass, not a Chevrolet. In fact, Chevrolet sales amounted to only 42.6 percent of the GM total—one of the lowest figures posted in recent years. Model year sales were up, however, by 21.1 percent over the 1975 total. Why? Because big cars continued to sell rather well. The new 305 cu. in. V-8 was particularly well received by the public. R.L. Lund was Chevrolet's General Manager. Appearing at the Detroit Auto Show was an experimental (but fully operational) Monza Super Spyder, crafted from a 1975 Monza 2 + 2. Powered by the Cosworth Twin Cam four and five-speed gearbox, it featured a hand-built fiberglass nose and tail panels, magnesium wheels, and fluorescent tube lighting up front. This was one more GM show car that never made it into production.

1977 CHEVROLET

Full-size Chevrolets were downsized for 1977, leading the first wave of shrinkage that would hit the entire domestic lineup in the next few years. The old reliable inline six and the 305 cu. in. V-8 each added five horsepower. At mid-year the renowned Camaro Z28 returned, adorned with graphics and carrying a four-barrel 350 V-8 under the hood. The one-barrel 140 cu. in. four and 262 V-8 were dropped. Intermittent wipers became optional on subcompact to compact models. A new "Pulse Air" system replaced air injection on Chevette, Vega and Monza fours.

1977 Chevette hatchback coupe (CH)

CHEVETTE — SERIES 1T — FOUR — As in its opening season, Chevette came in two models: standard four-passenger hatchback coupe, and Scooter. But this year, the Scooter added a standard back seat for the same four-passenger capacity (though the back seat could be deleted). The Woody option was dropped, but the Rally Sport was offered again. A new "Sandpiper" appearance package, available with white or yellow-gold body paint (a color not offered on other models) wasn't hard to spot with foot-long 'Sandpiper' decals on quarter panels. A custom interior included yellow-gold "Reef" vinyl seat trim with cloth insert, plus yellow-gold carpeting, instrument panel and door panels. Also in the package: a sport steering wheel, day/night mirror, and carpeted cargo area. Two engines were available again this year: the base 85 cu. in. (1.4-liter) four and bigger 97 cu. in. (1.6-liter). Both could have either standard four-speed manual gearbox or optional three-speed automatic. (In California and high-altitude regions, only the 1.6 was available.) The 1.4 gained five horsepower this year as a result of a larger carburetor flow capacity and revised hot air intake system. Positive carburetor outside air control also improved cold-weather driveability. The 1.4 had similar changes but a smaller power boost. New front disc brake pad and rear brake lining materials were meant to increase lining life. A smaller rear wheel cylinder was said to improve front-to-rear braking balance. Joining Chevette's option list: an intermittent "pulse" windshield wiper that operated either from the "smart switch" on the column or a separate dash control. Interiors had a new pattern of vinyl cloth, while custom interiors used perforated vinyl. Of the 14 Chevette body colors, nine were new: light lime, red, bright orange, light buckskin, and five metallics (silver, dark blue, brown, orange, and dark aqua). Carryover colors were white, black, firethorn metallic, light blue, and bright yellow.

VEGA — SERIES 1H — FOUR — For its seventh and final try at luring buyers, Vega again came in three body styles: notchback or hatchback coupe, plus station wagon and Estate wagon. The Cosworth Vega was gone. So were the GT Estate Wagon options and Cabriolet equipment package. This year's GT package came in two levels: one subtle, the other bold. The subtler one had a blacked-out trim theme with black paint around window openings, windshield and doors, plus black sport mirrors and wheels. For a more noticeable look, the alternate package featured bold horizontal stripes that broke along the bodyside to display huge 'Vega GT' lettering. It was hard to miss, since the lower-bodyside decal ran the full distance between wheel openings.

1977 Vega GT hatchback coupe (CP)

Standard engine was the 140 cu. in. (2.3-liter) Dura-Built four with two-barrel carburetor, plus four-speed manual gearbox. A five-speed manual and three-speed automatic transmission were available. The one-barrel carb engine and three-speed manual shift, formerly standard, were dropped this year. A new, simpler Pulse-Air manifold injection system was standard late in the base engine, replacing the Air Injection Reactor system. Vega was the only domestic production car with an all-aluminum engine block. Vega's standard interior added a color-keyed steering column, steering wheel, instrument cluster face, and parking brake cover. Of the 14 body colors this year, eight were new: dark blue, brown, orange, silver or dark aqua metallic; light buckskin; light lime; and bright orange. Carryover colors were white, black, firethorn metallic, light blue, red, and bright yellow. Vega's GT package included woodgrained dash accents, sport mirrors (left remote), black headlamp bezels, bright grille header molding, F41 sport suspension, Rally II wheels with trim rings and special center caps, black sill and lower bodyside moldings, gauge set (including tachometer and clock), and white-letter tires. The price was $401 for hatchbacks (including belt moldings) and $373 for wagons.

1977 Monza Sport Spyder hatchback coupe (CH)

MONZA — SERIES 1H — FOUR — Once again, Monza fielded a notchback Towne Coupe and a 2+2 hatchback, with no significant styling changes this year. Towne Coupes had a new rear look with functional tri-color taillamps. A Sport Front End Appearance option package, introduced late in the prior model year, gave Towne Coupes the same soft-fascia front end and rectangular headlamps as the 2+2, along with a rear bumper impact strip. Other carryover options: large rear quarter windows, or opera windows. The Cabriolet Equipment package was dropped, but a Cabriolet vinyl roof and opera windows remained available. Two intertwined all-new options were offered, however: the Monza Spyder appearance and performance packages. The appearance package included bold striping, front air dam and rear spoiler; plus satin black accents around window openings, headlamp openings and bezels, parking lamps, taillamps and grille louvers, as well as rocker panel, quarter, rear panel and fender areas. A large 'Spyder' script identification decal appeared on both doors. Dual side stripes came in black or gold, with Spyder lettering outlined in red, white or gold. The $199 package (for 2+2 only) also included black sport mirrors, black Rally II wheels and bright trim rings. Spyder's equipment package sold separately at $274. That one included an F41 suspension, console, sport steering wheel, sport mirrors, large Spyder emblem, hood header panel, modified front stabilizer and rear shocks, and BR70 x 13 radial tires. Other Monza options included aluminum wheels, Sport equipment and front-end appearance packages, front/rear spoilers, and an instrument set (including tachometer). Added to the option list: a digital clock over the glove box, angled toward the driver. Fourteen body colors were available, plus three new luxury cloth interior trims and four colors of vinyl trim. Both hatchback and Towne Coupe carried a standard 140 cu. in. (2.3-liter) Dura-Built four-cylinder engine, with four-speed manual transmission. A 305 cu. in. (5.0-liter) V-8 was also available, as were a five-speed manual gearbox and three-speed automatic. The 262 V-8 was gone. The standard 2+2 came with finned wheel covers.

1977 Nova Concours sedan (CH)

NOVA — SERIES 1X — SIX/V-8 — The basic Nova carried over its 1976 styling, offered again as a two-door coupe, two-door hatchback, or four-door sedan. Nova's grille had square holes in a 2 x 12 arrangement, with vertical parking lamps at outer ends. The upscale Concours had a new fine-mesh grille made up of many thin vertical bars, separated into four rows, intended to offer a massive look. Lower-profile parking lamps sat slightly inboard of grille ends. A new chromed center filler panel was meant to give an illusion of depth, in company with body molding, and bumper. Outer ends of the bumper filler panel were body-colored. Bright headlamp bezels were restyled, as were fender end caps. Concours also sported a stand-up hood ornament, new wide wheel opening moldings, and distinctive 'C' script insignias at front, side and rear, plus new triple rectangular taillamps. Inside, the Concours featured woodgrain appliques on door panels, instrument panel and steering wheel. Powerplant possibilities included 305 and 350 cu. in. V-8s as well as the standard inline six (250 cu. in.). Three- and four-speed manual gearboxes were available, along with three-speed automatic. Of the 14 Nova body colors, nine were new (all metallic): medium green, dark aqua, light blue, buckskin, light buckskin, orange, silver, brown, or dark blue. Antique white, black, red, bright yellow and firethorn metallic were repeated from 1976. A new Nova Rally option for coupe and hatchback was announced for mid-year availability, to replace the Super Sport. It consisted of a new chrome-plated, diamond-pattern grille with inset horizontal parking lamps and five-color 'Nova Rally' nameplate in the center. The name was repeated on fenders and decklid (above right taillamp). Rally models also had black headlamp bezels with bright edges plus white, black or gold tri-band striping along lower bodysides and rear end panel. Rally wheels were color-keyed to the stripes (but argent-finished when ordered with black striping).

1977 Camaro Type LT coupe (CH)

CAMARO — SERIES 1F — SIX/V-8 — Camaro changed little for 1977. The lineup included the standard Sport Coupe and luxury Type LT. A Rally Sport option came in three new contrasting accent colors for the satin black trim: medium gray, dark blue metallic, and buckskin metallic. Satin black treatment was found on Rally hood, front end, grille, headlamp bezels, forward roof section, rear end panel, and rocker panels. Otherwise, body color selection was the same as Nova: nine new colors and five carryovers. Inside was new cloth in the base interior. Type LT had new knit cloth and puffed-texture vinyl materials. The familiar inline 250 cu. in. (4.1-liter) six became the standard powerplant for Type LT this year. Optional were two V-8s: a 305 cu. in. (5.0-liter) and 350 (5.7-liter). Transmissions included the standard three-speed manual, four-speed manual, or three-speed automatic. Standard axle ratio for the V-8 with automatic changed from 2.73:1 to 2.56:1, to help boost gas mileage. The four-speed transmission shift pattern was revised this year. Reverse was now engaged by a rearward (toward the driver) lifting motion, rather than forward as before. A new refillable carbon-dioxide canister replaced the disposable froen-filled unit used to inflate the stowaway spare tire. Intermittent wipers joined the option list, and all Camaro wipers were hidden. Away from the lineup for two years, the high-performance Z28 returned as a 1977-1/2 model, debuting at the Chicago Auto Show. Special wide-profile radial tires were mounted on 15 x 7 in. mag-type wheels. Under the hood was a special 350 cu. in. V-8; atop it, an identifying decal. The chassis held front and rear stabilizer bars, special spring rates and quicker sterring. This new Z28 had body-color bumpers, spoilers, mirrors and wheels, plus a blackout grille, rear-end panel, rocker panels, moldings, headlamp bezels and taillamp bezels. Rounding out the Z28's appearance were rocker/wheelhouse stripes and emblems, and 'Z28' badge on the driver's side of the grille. Transmission was a Borg-Warner four-speed, and the "open" exhaust used dual resonators.

1977 Chevelle Malibu Classic Landau Coupe ((CH)

CHEVELLE MALIBU — SERIES 1A — SIX/V-8 — Chevelle dropped down to two series for 1977: Malibu and Malibu Classic. Two-door coupe, four-door sedan and station wagon bodies (two or three seat) were offered in both. The Laguna coupe and Malibu Classic Estate wagon were gone. Both series had new grilles and six-section taillamps this year. Malibu Classic's grille showed a vertical theme with many wide bars. Malibu's was a mesh pattern of many wide rectangles. As before, Classics had stacked rectangular headlamps, regular Malibu single round ones. Script was in the grille's lower corner (driver's side). Small horizontal rectangular parking lamps were again inset in the bumper. The Malibu coupe's rear side windows got "coach" style glass this year. Classic taillamps had fancier brightwork that reached down to the license plate, and rockers wore wide bright moldings. Station wagons had a standard 305 cu. in. (5.0-liter) V-8, and the Malibu Classic wagon held a 350 (5.7-liter) V-8, now

with four-barrel carb. The 400 V-8 was gone. Base engine for other bodies was the inline 250 six. Three-speed manual transmission was standard on six-cylinder models except the Malibu Classic sedan, which had Turbo Hydra-matic. Wagons also had automatic plus power brakes and steering. Also standard: heater/defroster, carpeting, lighter, and FR78 x 15/B fiberglass-belted radial tires (HR78 x 15/B steel-belted radials on wagons). The Classic Landau added a vinyl roof, deluxe front/rear bumpers, and full wheel covers. Coupes rode a 112-inch wheelbase, sedans and wagons 116- inch. Chevelle's design was all the way back to 1964. Of ten body colors, four were new this year. And of seven vinyl top colors, three were new. Six new trim colors were available for Malibu Classic, five for Malibu.

1977 Monte Carlo Landau Coupe (CH)

MONTE CARLO — SERIES 1A — V-8 — Personal-luxury Montes entered another year with a restyled, bold grille texture: still three separate rows, but eight holes across each one. Stacked rectangular headlamps continued, but horizontal rectangular parking lamps below the headlamps had a more square look. New wider taillamps had horizontal divider bars. End caps were also new. A new hood ornament on "flip-flop" pedestal carried the Monte Carlo crest surrounded by a bright ring. Fourteen body colors (nine new) were offered, plus seven interior trim fabrics (two new) and seven vinyl tops (two new). Monte's chassis had new front springs for a softer ride, plus improved corrosion protection. A radiator pressure relief cap improved cooling. Wheelbase was still 116 inches, length 212.7 inches. Again, the 305 cu. in. (5.0-liter) V-8 was the base engine. The 400 cu. in. V-8 was no longer available, but the 350 cu. in. (5.7-liter) V-8 with four- barrel was optional. Turbo Hydra-matic was standard with both engines. Standard equipment also included power steering and brakes, electric clock, hide-away wipers, deluxe wheel covers, heater/defroster, carpeting, lighter, inside hood release, wheel opening moldings, and GR70 x 15 steel-belted radial tires. The Landau coupe added a vinyl roof, dual body- color sport mirrors (left one remote-controlled), pinstriping, and Turbine II wheels.

1977 Impala Custom Coupe (CH)

IMPALA/CAPRICE CLASSIC — SERIES 1B — SIX/V-8 — Downsized full-size Chevrolet sedans were 5.5 inches shorter in wheelbase, 10.6 inches shorter overall and 4 inches narrowerbut 2.5 inches taller. Both Impala and Caprice kept their "big car" look and ample interior dimensions, but lost some 700 pounds. Impala's silhouette was more angular than before, with flatter side panels and a blunt front and rear look. Now they came with a base six- cylinder engine (the familiar inline 250 cu. in.) and smaller (305 cu. in.) base V-8 for better mileage. Wagons had the 305 as standard. All models could get a 350 cu. in. (5.7- liter) V-8 with four-barrel carburetor. A new diagnostic connector under the hood allowed up to 35 engine tests. Coupe/sedan fuel tanks shrunk from 26 to 21 gallons. The big 400 and 454 engines were gone, but full-size models could have an optional sport or heavy-duty suspension. Impala's 'S' model was dropped. So were sport sedans. All models now had pillars; the true hardtop had become a relic of the past. The rear-facing third seat for wagons was offered as a regular production option. The Landau coupe option emerged during the year. Of ten full-size body colors, four were new. Three new two-tone combinations were offered, along with seven vinyl top colors (three new). New interior trim came in six colors. Impalas had an 8 x 3 hole "eggcrate" grille pattern with center bowtie emblem, plus quad rectangular headlamps over quad park/signal lamps. Caprice's grille had a finer mesh pattern. Caprice also had wraparound marker lamps and small parking lamps inset down in the bumper. Back ends were similar, with taillamps in three side-by-side sections (outer one slightly angled). Caprice's version put backup lamps alongside the license plate. Caprice also displayed a stand- up hood ornament. Impala's new Custom coupe model had a distinctive back window treatment. Caprice wagons got a new two-way tailgate that opened either downward or to the side. Standard Impala/Caprice equipment included Turbo Hydra- matic transmission, power steering and brakes, heater/defroster, carpeting, cigarette lighter, windshield wipers, and FR78 x 15/B steel-belted radial tires. Wagons had HR78 x 15/B steel-belted tires and a power tailgate. Caprice Estate added an electric clock, dual horns, and quiet sound group.

I.D. DATA: Chevrolets again had a 13-symbol Vehicle Identification Number (VIN) on the upper left surface of the instrument panel, visible through the windshield. Coding

was similar to 1976. Body type codes '45' (three-seat station wagon) and '39' (full-size sport sedan) were dropped. Model year code changed to '7' for 1977. Engine codes 'N' (L4110), 'O' (L4122 EFI), 'G' (V8262), 'A' (L4140 1Bbl.) and 'S' (V8454) were dropped. The code for V8305 changed from 'Q' to 'U'.

CHEVETTE (FOUR)

Model Number	Body/Style Number	Body Type & Seating	Factory Price	Shipping Weight	Production Total
1T	B08	2-dr. Hatch-4P	3225	1958	120,278

CHEVETTE SCOOTER (FOUR)

1T	J08	2-dr. Hatch-4P	2999	1898	13,191

VEGA (FOUR)

1H	V11	2-dr. Coupe-4P	3249	2459	12,365
1H	V77	2-dr. Hatch-4P	3359	2522	37,395
1H	V15	2-dr. Sta Wag-4P	3522	2571	25,181
1H	V15	2-dr. Est Wag-4P	3745	N/A	3,461

MONZA (FOUR/V-8)

1H	M27	2-dr. Twn Cpe-4P	3560/3765	2580	34,133
1H	R07	2-dr. Hatch 2+2-4P	3840/4045	2671	39,215

NOVA (SIX/V-8)

1X	X27	2-dr. Cpe-6P	3482/3602	3139/3257	132,833
1X	X17	2-dr. Hatch-6P	3646/3766	3214/3335	18,048
1X	X69	4-dr. Sedan-6P	3532/3652	3174/3292	141,028

NOVA CONCOURS (SIX/V-8)

1X	Y27	2-dr. Cpe-6P	3991/4111	3285/3391	28,602
1X	Y17	2-dr. Hatch-6P	4154/4274	3378/3486	5,481
1X	Y69	4-dr. Sedan-6P	4066/4186	3329/3437	39,272

CAMARO (SIX/V-8)

1F	Q87	2-dr. Spt Cpe-4P	4113/4223	3369/3476	131,717
1F	S87	2-dr. LT Cpe-4P	4478/4598	3422/3529	72,787
1F	Q87	2-dr. Z28 Cpe-4P	-- /5170	-- / N/A	14,349

CHEVELLE MALIBU (SIX/V-8)

1A	C37	2-dr. Cpe-6P	3885/4005	3551/3650	28,793
1A	C29	4-dr. Sed-6P	3935/4055	3628/3727	39,064
1A	C35	4-dr. Sta Wag-6P	-- /4734	-- /4139	18,023
1A	C35	4-dr. 3S Wag-9P	-- /4877	-- / N/A	4,014

CHEVELLE MALIBU CLASSIC (SIX/V-8)

1A	D37	2-dr. Cpe-6P	4125/4245	3599/3698	73,739
1A	D37	2-dr. Lan Cpe-6P	4353/4473	N/A	37,215
1A	D29	4-dr. Sed-6P	4475/4595	3725/3824	76,776
1A	D35	4-dr. Sta Wag-6P	-- /5065	-- /4233	31,539
1A	D35	4-dr. 3S Wag-9P	-- /5208	-- / N/A	19,053

MONTE CARLO (V-8)

1A	H57	2-dr. 'S' Cpe-6P	4968	3852	224,327
1A	H57	2-dr. Lan Cpe-6P	5298	N/A	186,711

FULL-SIZE CHEVROLETS IMPALA (SIX/V-8)

1B	L47	2-dr. Cust Cpe-6P	4876/4996	3533/3628	55,347
1B	L47	2-dr. Lan Cpe-6P	N/A	N/A	2,745
1B	L69	4-dr. Sedan-6P	4901/5021	3564/3659	196,824
1B	L35	4-dr. Sta Wag-6P	-- /5289	-- /4042	37,108
1B	L35	4-dr. 3S Wag-9P	-- /5406	-- / N/A	28,255

CAPRICE CLASSIC (SIX/V-8)

1B	N47	2-dr. Coupe-6P	5187/5307	3571/3666	62,366
1B	N47	2-dr. Lan Cpe-6P	N/A	N/A	9,607
1B	N69	4-dr. Sedan-6P	5237/5357	3606/3701	212,840
1B	N35	4-dr. Est Wag-6P	-- /5617	-- /4088	22,930
1B	N35	4-dr. 3S Est-6P	-- /5734	-- / N/A	33,639

FACTORY PRICE AND WEIGHT NOTE: Where two prices and weights are shown, the figure to the left of the slash is for six-cylinder model, to right of slash for V-8 (except Monza, four-cylinder and V-8).

ENGINE DATA: BASE FOUR (Chevette): Inline. Overhead cam. Four-cylinder. Cast iron block and head. Displacement: 85.0 cu. in. (1.4 liters). Bore & stroke: 3.23 x 2.61 in. Compression ratio: 8.5:1. Brake horsepower: 57 at 5200 R.P.M. Torque: 71 lbs.-ft. at 3600 R.P.M. Five main bearings. Hydraulic valve lifters. Carburetor: 1Bbl. Rochester 1ME. VIN Code: 1. OPTIONAL FOUR (Chevette): Inline. Overhead cam. Four-cylinder. Cast iron block and head. Displacement: 97.6 cu. in. (1.6 liters). Bore & stroke: 3.23 x 2.98 in. Compression ratio: 8.5:1. Brake horsepower: 63 at 4800 R.P.M. Torque: 82 lbs.-ft. at 3200 R.P.M. Five main bearings. Hydraulic valve lifters. Carburetor: 1Bbl. Roch. 1ME. VIN Code: E. BASE FOUR (Vega, Monza): Inline. Overhead cam. Four-cylinder. Aluminum block and cast iron head. Displacement: 140 cu. in. (2.3 liters). Bore & stroke: 3.50 x 3.63 in. Compression ratio: 8.0:1. Brake horsepower: 84 at 4400 R.P.M. Torque: 117 lbs.-ft. at 2400 R.P.M. Five main bearings. Hydraulic valve lifters. Carburetor: 2Bbl. Holley 5210C. VIN Code: B. BASE SIX (Nova, Chevelle, Camaro, Impala, Caprice): Inline. OHV. Six-cylinder. Cast iron block and head. Displacement: 250 cu. in. (4.1 liters). Bore & stroke: 3.88 x 3.53 in. Compression ratio: 8.3:1. Brake horsepower: 110 at 3800 R.P.M. Torque: 195 lbs.-ft. at 1600 R.P.M. Seven main bearings. Hydraulic valve lifters. Carburetor: 1Bbl. Roch. 1ME. VIN Code: D. BASE V-8 (Monte Carlo, Malibu wagon, Impala/Caprice wagon); OPTIONAL (Monza, Nova, Chevelle, Camaro, Impala, Caprice): 90-degree, overhead valve V-8. Cast iron block and head. Displacement: 305 cu. in. (5.0 liters). Bore & stroke: 3.74 x 3.48 in. Compression ratio: 8.5:1. Brake horsepower: 145 at 3800 R.P.M. Torque: 245 lbs.-ft. at 2400 R.P.M. Five main bearings. Hydraulic valve lifters. Carburetor: 2Bbl. Roch. 2GC. VIN Code: U. BASE V-8 (Malibu Classic wagon); OPTIONAL (Nova, Camaro, Chevelle, Monte Carlo, Impala, Caprice): 90-degree, overhead valve V-8. Cast iron block and head. Displacement: 350 cu. in. (5.7 liters). Bore & stroke: 4.00 x 3.48 in. Compression ratio: 8.5:1. Brake horsepower: 170 at 3800 R.P.M. Torque: 270 lbs.-ft. at 2400 R.P.M. Five main bearings. Hydraulic valve lifters. Carburetor: 4Bbl. Roch. M4MC. VIN Code: L.

CHASSIS DATA: Wheelbase: (Chevette) 94.3 in.; (Vega/Monza) 97.0 in.; (Camaro) 108.0 in.; (Nova) 111.0 in.; (Chevelle cpe) 112.0 in.; (Chevelle sed/wag, Monte, Imp/Capr) 116.0 in. Overall length: (Chevette) 158.7 in.; (Vega) 175.4 in.; (Monza twn cpe) 177.8 in.; (Monza hatch) 179.3 in.; (Nova) 196.7 in.; (Nova Concours) 197.7 in.; (Camaro) 195.4 in.; (Chevelle cpe) 205.7 in.; (Chevelle sed) 209.7 in.; (Chevelle wag) 215.4 in.; (Monte) 213.3 in.; (Imp/Capr) 212.1 in.; (Imp/Capr wag) 214.7 in. Height: (Chevette) 52.3 in.; (Vega spt cpe/wag) 51.8 in.; (Vega hatch) 50.0 in.; (Monza twn cpe) 49.8 in.; (Monza hatch) 50.2 in.; (Nova) 53.6 in.; (Camaro) 49.2 in.; (Chevelle cpe) 53.4 in.; (Chevelle sed) 54.1 in.; (Chevelle wag) 55.8 in.; (Monte) 52.8 in.; (Imp/Capr cpe) 55.3 in.; (Imp/Capr sed) 56.0 in.; (Imp/Capr wag) 58.0 in. Width: (Chevette) 61.8 in.; (Vega/Monza) 65.4 in.; (Nova) 72.2 in.; (Camaro) 74.4 in.; (Chevelle) 76.9 in.; (Chevelle wag) 76.8 in.; (Monte) 77.6 in.; (Imp/Capr) 75.5 in.; (Imp/Capr wag) 79.1 in. Front Tread: (Chevette) 51.2 in.; (Vega/Monza) 54.8 in.; (Nova/Camaro) 61.3 in.; (Camaro LT) 61.6 in.; (Chevelle) 61.5 in.; (Monte) 61.9 in.; (Imp/Capr) 61.8 in.; (Imp/Capr wag) 62.2 in. Rear Tread: (Chevette) 51.2 in.; (Vega/Monza) 53.6 in.; (Nova) 59.0 in.; (Camaro) 60.0 in.; (Camaro LT) 60.3 in.; (Chevelle/Monte) 60.7 in.; (Imp/Capr) 60.8 in.; (Imp/Capr wag) 64.1 in. Standard Tires: (Chevette) 155/80 x 13/B; (Vega/Monza) A78 x 13/B; (Nova) E78 x 14/B; (Nova Concours, Camaro) FR78 x 14/B SBR; (Chevelle/Imp/Capr) FR78 x 15/B GBR; (Chevelle/ Imp/Capr wag) HR78 x 15/B SBR; (Monte) GR70 x 15.

TECHNICAL: Transmission: Three-speed manual transmission (column shift) standard on Chevelle; floor shift on Camaro. Gear ratios: (1st) 3.11:1; (2nd) 1.84:1; (3rd) 1.00:1; (Rev) 3.22:1. Four- speed floor shift standard on Chevette: (1st) 3.75:1; (2nd) 2.16:1; (3rd) 1.38:1; (4th) 1.00:1; (Rev) 3.82:1. Four-speed floor shift standard on Vega, Monza four: (1st) 3.11:1; (2nd) 2.20:1; (3rd) 1.47:1; (4th) 1.00:1; (Rev) 3.11:1. Four-speed floor shift standard on Monza V-8, optional on Nova/Camaro V8350: (1st) 2.85:1; (2nd) 2.02:1; (3rd) 1.35:1; (4th) 1.00:1; (Rev) 2.85:1. Five-speed floor shift available on Vega, Monza four: (1st) 3.40:1; (2nd) 2.08:1; (3rd) 1.39:1; (4th) 1.00:1; (5th) 0.80:1; (Rev) 3.36:1. Three-speed Turbo Hydra-matic standard on some Malibus, Monte Carlo and Caprice/Impala, optional on others. Automatic gear ratios: (1st) 2.52:1; (2nd) 1.52:1; (3rd) 1.00:1; (Rev) 1.94:1 except standard Caprice/Impala, Monza V-8, Chevette and Nova (V8305) ratios: (1st) 2.74:1; (2nd) 1.57:1; (3rd) 1.00:1; (Rev) 2.07:1. Standard final drive ratio: (Chevette) 3.70:1 exc. w/1.4- liter engine and automatic, 4.11:1; (Vega) 2.92:1; (Monza four) 3.42:1; (Monza V-8) 2.73:1; (Nova) 2.73:1; (Camaro) 2.73:1 exc. 2.56:1 w/V-8 and automatic; (Z28) 3.73:1; (Chevelle six) 2.73:1; (Chevelle V-8) 2.56:1; (Monte) 2.56:1; (Imp/Capr six) 2.73:1; (Imp/Capr V-8) 2.56:1. Steering: (Chevette) rack and pinion; (others) recirculating ball. Suspension/Body: same as 1976. Brakes: front disc, rear drum. Ignition: Electronic. Fuel tank: (Chevette) 13 gal.; (Vega) 16 gal.; (Monza) 18.5 gal.; (Nova/Camaro) 21 gal.; (Chevelle/Monte) 22 gal.; (Imp/Capr) 21 gal.; (Imp/Capr wag) 22 gal.

DRIVETRAIN OPTIONS: Engines: 1.6-liter four: Chevette ($55). 305 cu. in., 2Bbl. V-8: Monza ($205); Nova/Camaro, Chevelle/Imp/Caprice cpe/sed ($120). 350 cu. in., 4Bbl. V-8: Nova/Camaro/Chevelle ($210); Chevelle/Imp/Capr wag, Monte ($90); Imp/Capr cpe/sed ($210). Transmission/Differential: Four-speed manual shift: Nova/Camaro ($252). Five-speed manual shift: Vega/Monza ($248). Turbo Hydra-matic transmission: Chevette/Vega/Monza ($248); Nova/Camaro, Chevelle cpe/sed ($282). Sport shifter w/console: Chevette ($43). Floor shift lever: Nova ($31). Positraction axle: Vega/Monza ($50); Nova/Camaro/Chevelle/Monte ($54); Imp/Capr ($58). Highway axle ratio: Monza ($13). Performance axle ratio ($13-$14). Power Accessories: Power brakes: Chvt/Vega/Monza ($58); Nova, Camaro, Chevelle cpe/sed ($61). Power steering: Vega/Monza ($129); Nova, Chevelle cpe/sed ($146). Suspension: F40 H.D. suspension: Nova ($8-$31); Chevelle/Monte/Imp/Capr ($19). F41 sport susp.: Vega ($149); Monza ($28); Nova, Camaro, Chevelle/Imp/Capr cpe/sed ($36). Superlift rear shock absorbers: Imp/Capr ($47). Rear stabilizer bar: Chevette ($28). Other: Heavy-duty radiator ($27-$37). H.D. alternator (61- amp): Chevelle/Monte/Imp/Capr ($29). H.D. battery ($16- $17). California emission system ($70). High altitude emission system ($22).

CHEVETTE/VEGA/MONZA CONVENIENCE/APPEARANCE OPTIONS: Option Packages: Sandpiper pkg.: Chevette (N/A). Rally sport equipment: Chevette ($295-$321). GT pkg.: Vega hatch ($401); Vega wagon ($373). Sport equipment: Monza ($134). Sport front-end appearance pkg.: Monza ($118). Spyder equipment pkg.: Monza ($274). Spyder appearance pkg.: Monza ($199). Quiet sound group: Chvt ($31-$42); Vega ($34-$46). Comfort/Convenience: Air conditioning ($442). Rear defogger ($71). Tinted glass ($48). Sport steering wheel ($16). Comfortilt steering wheel: Vega/Monza ($50). Special instrumentation: Chvt ($60); Vega ($77); Monza ($60-$77). Econominder gauge: Monza ($28). Electric clock: Chvt/Monza ($17). Digital clock: Monza ($43). Cigarette lighter: Chvt ($5). Glove compartment lock: Chvt ($3). Intermittent wipers: Chvt/Vega ($28). Lighting, Horns and Mirrors: Aux. lighting: Chvt ($33- $38); Vega ($16-$31); Monza ($16-$20). Sport mirrors, left remote: Vega/Monza ($28). Twin remote sport mirrors: Chevette ($46). Driver's remote sport mirror: Chvt ($20). Day/night mirror ($8). Entertainment: AM radio ($67). AM/FM radio ($129). AM/FM stereo radio: Vega/Monza ($212). Stereo tape player w/AM radio: Vega/Monza ($196). Stereo tape player with AM/FM stereo radio: Vega/Monza ($304). Rear speaker ($22). Windshield antenna: Vega/Monza ($16); incl. w/radios. Exterior Trim: Sky roof: Vega/Monza ($210). Vinyl roof: Monza ($145) incl. opera windows. Spoilers, front/rear: Monza ($87). Swing-out windows: Chvt ($48); Vega cpe ($33-$39). Custom exterior: Chvt ($86); Vega ($62-$92). Decor group: Vega ($6-$36). Sport stripes: Vega ($80). Bodyside moldings ($38). Wheel opening moldings: Vega/Monza ($20). Side window reveal moldings: Chvt ($63). Door edge guards ($8). Roof carrier: Chvt/Vega ($56). Rear air deflector: Vega ($24). Deluxe bumpers, front/rear: Chvt ($29). Deluxe bumpers w/guards: Monza ($65). Deluxe front bumper guards: Vega ($18). Deluxe bumper guards, front/rear: Chvt ($36-$65); Monza ($36). Bumper rub strips, front/rear: Vega ($47). Interior Trim/Upholstery: Custom interior trim: Chevette ($151-$199); Vega ($139-$188). Console: Chvt ($17); Vega/Monza ($77). Bucket seats (plaid cloth): Chvt ($9-$18); Vega ($18). Knit cloth bucket seats: Monza ($18). Custom knit cloth bucket seats: Monza ($135-$151). Leather bucket seats: Monza ($213). Adjustable driver's seatback: Vega/Monza ($17). Folding rear

seat: Monza ($87). Rear seat delete: Chvt ($56 credit). Load floor carpet: Chvt ($43). Color-keyed floor mats ($15). Front mats: Chvt ($9). Deluxe seatbelts ($17). Wheels and Tires: Aluminum wheels: Monza ($186-$209). Rally II wheels: Vega ($74-$104). Wheel covers: Vega ($30). Deluxe wheel covers: Monza ($33). Sport wheel covers: Chevette ($71). Wheel trim rings: Chvt ($32); Vega ($2-$32). 155/8013/B WSW: Chvt ($38). 155/8013/B SBR: Chvt ($99). 155/8013/B SBR WSW: Chvt ($137). 155/8013/B SBR WLT: Chvt ($151). A78 x 13/B WSW: Vega ($38); Monza ($30-$38). BR78 x 13/B SBR: Vega ($35-$151); Monza ($94-$151). BR78 x 13/B SBR WSW: Vega ($73-$188); Monza ($124-$188). BR70 x 13/C SBR BSW: Monza (NC to $190). BR70 x 13/C SBR WSW: Monza ($30-$227). BR70 x 13/C SBR WLT: Vega ($126-$241); Monza ($42-$241). Conventional spare: Monza (NC).

NOVA/CAMARO/CHEVELLE/MONTE CARLO CONVENIENCE/APPEARANCE OPTIONS: Option Packages: Rally Sport equipment: base Camaro ($281); Camaro LT ($186). Estate equipment: Chevelle wag ($185). Interior decor/quiet sound group: base Camaro ($57). Comfort/Convenience: Air conditioning ($478-$507). Rear defogger, forced-air ($48). Rear defogger (electric): Monte ($82). Cruise-master speed control ($80). Tinted glass: Nova/Camaro ($50); Chevelle ($54); Monte ($58). Comfortilt steering wheel ($57). Six-way power seat: Chevelle/Monte ($137). Power windows ($108-$151). Power door locks: Nova/Chevelle ($68-$96); Camaro/Monte ($68). Power trunk release: Chevelle/Monte ($18). Power tailgate release: Chevelle 2S wag ($22). Electric clock: Nova, base Camaro ($19); Chevelle ($20). Special instrumentation (incl. tach and clock): Nova/Camaro ($99). Econominder gauge pkg.: Nova/Chevelle/Monte ($47). Intermittent wipers ($30). Lighting, Horns and Mirrors: Aux. lighting ($22-$44). Dual horns: Nova, base Camaro, Chevelle ($6). Remote-control driver's mirror: Nova/Chevelle/Monte ($15). Twin sport mirrors (left remote): Nova, base Camaro, Chevelle/Monte ($30). Twin remote sport mirrors: Chevelle/Monte ($21-$51). Day/night mirror: base Nova ($8). Visor vanity mirror: Chevelle/Monte ($4). Lighted visor mirror: Chevelle ($28); Monte ($24-$28). Entertainment: AM radio ($72). AM/FM radio: Nova/Camaro/Chevelle ($137); Monte ($146). AM/FM stereo radio ($226). Stereo tape player w/AM radio: Nova/Camaro/Chevelle ($209); Monte ($225). Stereo tape player with AM/FM stereo radio ($324). Rear speaker ($23). Windshield antenna ($17); incl. w/radios. Exterior Trim: Electric sky roof: Monte ($394). Vinyl roof: Nova/Camaro ($96); Chevelle ($111); Monte ($131). Cabriolet roof: Nova ($162). Spoilers, front/rear: Camaro ($87). Exterior decor pkg.: base Nova ($78); Chevelle ($20-$54). Custom appearance group: Nova Concours ($70-$81). Exterior style trim pkg.: Camaro ($61). Fashion-tone paint: Monte ($112). Two-tone paint: Nova, Chevelle cpe/sed ($43). Swing- out rear side windows: Nova ($52). Swing-out rear window: Chevelle 2S wag ($52). Bodyside moldings: Nova/Camaro/Chevelle ($40). Deluxe bodyside moldings: Nova Concours, Monte ($51). Door edge guards ($8-$12). Wheel opening moldings: base Nova ($20). Roof drip moldings: base Nova, Camaro ($17). Bodyside pinstriping: Nova ($28). Rear window air deflector: Chevelle wag ($26). Roof carrier: Chevelle wag ($71). Bumper rub strips: Chevelle/Monte ($32). Bumper rub strips and guards, front/rear: base Nova ($68). Bumper guards, front/rear: Camaro/Chevelle/Monte ($39); Chevelle wag ($20). Interior Trim/Upholstery: Interior decor pkg.: Nova ($27). Console: base Nova, Camaro/Chevelle/Monte ($75). Knit or plaid cloth bench seat: Nova ($20). Custom cloth interior: base Nova ($211). Custom vinyl interior: base Nova ($191). Vinyl bench seat: Monte ($20). Bench or notchback bench seat (sport cloth or vinyl): Chevelle ($20). Vinyl bucket seats: base Nova ($272); Chevelle ($109-$129); Monte ($169). Bucket seats (knit cloth): Nova Concours ($143-218). Sport cloth bucket seats: Camaro ($20). Monte custom 50/50 seating (reclining passenger): cloth ($293); vinyl ($313). Adj. driver's seatback: Camaro ($20). Litter container: Chevelle/Monte ($6). Load-floor carpeting: Chevelle wag ($45). Color-keyed mats ($16). Deluxe seatbelts ($16-$22). Deluxe trunk trim: Monte ($38). Wheels and Tires: Custom wheels: Camaro ($85-$125). Rally wheels: base Nova/Camaro ($65); Nova Concours ($42); Chevelle ($38-$65); Monte ($50). Wire wheel covers: base Nova ($108); Nova Concours ($75). Full wheel covers: base Nova, Camaro/Chevelle ($33). Deluxe wheel covers: Monte ($20). Sport wheel covers: Chevelle ($48-$81); Monte ($66). E78 x 14/B BSW: Camaro ($87-$107 credit). E78 x 14/B WSW: base Nova ($31-$39); Camaro ($56-$63 credit). FR78 x 14/B SBR: base Nova ($86-$107). FR78 x 14/B SBR WSW: base Nova ($119-$148); Nova Concours, Camaro ($33-$41). FR78 x 14/B SBR WLT: base Nova ($129-$161); Nova Concours, Camaro ($44-$55). FR78 x 15/B GBR WSW: Chevelle ($33-$41). FR78 x 15/B SBR BSW: Chevelle ($35-$45). FR78 x 15/B SBR WSW: Chevelle ($68-$86). GR78 x 15/B SBR BSW: Chevelle ($56-$71). GR78 x 15/B SBR WSW: Chevelle ($90-$114). HR78 x 15/B SBR BSW: Chevelle ($110). HR78 x 15/B SBR WSW: Chevelle ($157); Chevelle wag ($47). GR70 x 15/B SBR BSW: Chevelle ($74-$93). GR70 x 15/B SBR WSW: Chevelle ($108-$136); Monte ($34-$43). GR70 x 15/B SBR WLT: Chevelle ($119-$150). Stowaway spare: Nova w/o radials ($15); Camaro/Chevelle/Monte (NC).

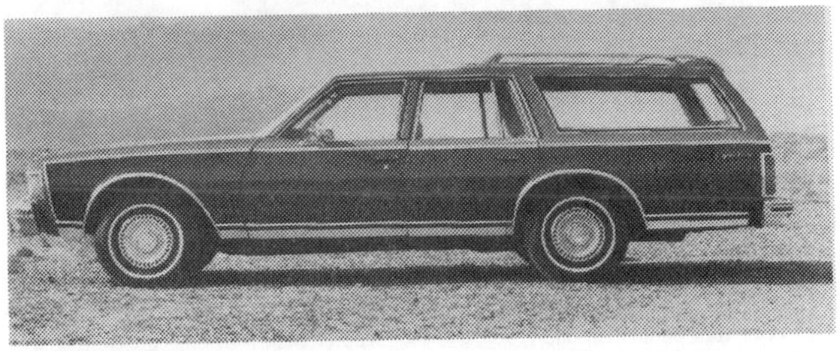

1977 Caprice Classic Estate Wagon (CH)

IMPALA/CAPRICE CONVENIENCE/APPEARANCE OPTIONS: Option Packages: Estate equipment: wag ($210). Value appearance group: bodyside and wheel opening moldings, full wheel covers ($69). Comfort/Convenience: Four season air cond. ($527). Comfortron auto-temp air cond. ($607). Rear defogger, forced-air: cpe/sed ($48). Rear defogger, electric ($83). Cruise-Master speed control ($84). Tinted glass ($69). Comfortilt steering wheel ($58). Power door locks ($70-$98). Six-way power driver's seat ($139). Power windows ($114-$171). Power trunk release ($18). Power tailgate lock: wag ($37). Electric clock: Imp ($20). Digital clock: Imp ($42); Caprice ($23). Econominder gauge pkg. ($47). Intermittent wipers ($30). Quiet sound group: Imp ($41). Lighting, Horns and Mirrors: Aux. lighting ($23-$38). Dome reading light ($15). Dual horns: Imp ($6). Driver's remote mirror ($15). Dual remote mirrors ($45). Dual sport mirrors, left remote ($30). Dual remote body-color sport mirrors ($51). Visor vanity mirror ($4). Lighted visor mirror ($28). Entertainment: AM radio ($73). AM/FM radio ($148). AM/FM stereo radio ($229). Stereo tape player w/AM radio ($228); with AM/FM stereo radio ($328). Rear speaker ($23). Power antenna ($57); w/radio ($40). Windshield antenna ($17); incl. w/radios. Exterior Trim: Vinyl roof ($135). Two-tone paint ($44). Custom two-tone ($99). Pinstriping ($31). Roof carrier: wag ($104). Bodyside moldings ($41). Door edge guards ($8-$12). Wheel opening moldings ($20). Roof drip moldings: Imp ($17). Bumper rub strips, front/rear ($66). Bumper guards ($46). Interior Trim/Upholstery: Vinyl bench seat: cpe/sed ($20). Knit or sport cloth bench seat: wag ($20). Knit cloth 50/50 seat: cpe/sed ($153). Knit or sport cloth 50/50 seat: wag ($173). Vinyl 50/50 seat ($153-$173). Special custom cloth 50/50 seat: cpe/sed ($285). Deluxe load-floor carpet: wag ($66). Deluxe cargo area carpet: wag ($95). Color-keyed mats ($16). Litter container ($6). Deluxe seatbelts ($19-$22). Deluxe trunk trim ($38). Wheel Covers: Full wheel covers ($34). Sport wheel covers: Imp ($82); Capr ($48). Coupe/Sedan Tires: FR78 x 15/B GBR WSW ($41). FR78 x 15/B SBR BSW ($45). FR78 x 15/B SBR WSW ($86). GR78 x 15/B SBR BSW ($71). GR78 x 15/B SBR WSW ($114). GR70 x 15/B SBR WSW ($136). Wagon Tires: HR78 x 15/B SBR WSW ($47).

HISTORY: Introduced: Sept. 30, 1976. Model year production (U.S.): 2,079,798 (incl. Corvettes but not incl. 3,299 Acadians). Of the total North American production for U.S. market, 263,829 had four-cylinder engines, 283,874 sixes, and 1,872,643 V-8s. Calendar year production: 2,135,942 (including 36,605 Sportvans, 46,345 Corvettes and 4,678 Acadians). Calendar year sales by U.S. dealers: 2,280,439 (incl. 36,609 Sportvans and 42,571 Corvettes) for a 25.1 percent market share. Full- size Chevrolets sold the best. Model year sales by U.S. dealers: 2,239,538 (incl. 39,640 Sportvans and 40,764 Corvettes).

Historical Footnotes: Caprice Classic, in its new downsized form, was voted *Motor Trend* "Car-of-the-Year" for 1977. That magazine considered Caprice "the most car you can get for your dollar" and applauded its "understated elegance." Model year sales rose by 8 percent over 1976, due largely to popular acceptance of the smaller full-sized models. Full-size sales rose by a healthy 38 percent, giving Chevrolet back the title of best selling passenger car in the industry (formerly held by Olds Cutlass). Calendar year production gained 4.5 percent. Only the discontinued Vega and soon-to-be-shrunk Malibu posted a loss for the calendar year. For the first time, Chevrolet began to supply other GM divisions with its 350 cu. in. V-8. Unfortunately, the installation of that V-8 in Oldsmobiles led eventually to class-action lawsuits and ultimate rebates to customers who felt they'd been cheated by not receiving a "real" Olds powerplant. In the four-cylinder engine marketplace, Pontiac's new cast iron "Iron Duke" powerplant was expected to tempt some customers away from Chevrolet with its all- aluminum 140 cu. in. four. But Chevrolet would soon obtain the Pontiac powerplant for its Monza. Chevette was the first serious attempt by a domestic automaker to compete against the smallest imports. That market began to fall, but Chevette remained a strong competitor. "It'll drive you happy" was Chevette's theme, and the rear-drive subcompact would hang around for another decade before being overrun by front-drive models. Monza's Spyder was thought by some observers to show revived Detroit interest in "muscle cars," though a Monza hardly seemed in the same league with some of the truly muscular beasts of the past.

1978 CHEVROLET

After downsizing of full-size models for 1977, the mid-size A body Malibu and Monte Carlo got the same treatment this year. Each was a foot shorter and 500-800 pounds lighter than equivalent 1977 models. Vega was dropped, but that line's hatchback and wagon continued under the Monza name. Chevrolet offered two new V-6 engines: a 200 cu. in. that was now standard on the downsized Malibu, and a 231 (supplied by Buick) for the Monte Carlo. Monza's new small V-8 (196 cu. in.) also originated at Buick. A new four, dubbed the "Iron Duke," came from Pontiac.

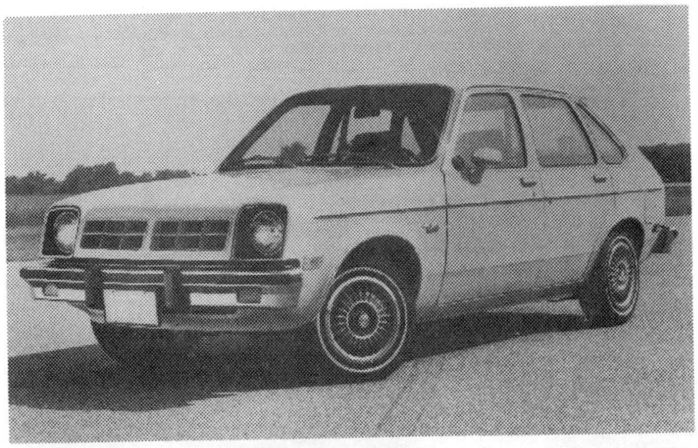

1978 Chevette hatchback sedan (CH)

CHEVETTE — SERIES 1T — FOUR — After two seasons as a two-door, Chevette added a six- window four-door hatchback sedan on a three-inch longer wheelbase. Rear legroom stretched five inches over the two- door's. Rear door glass in the sedan retracted only partly; side quarter glass was fixed. This year's grille used new molding treatments around each air inlet louver, plus single horizontal and double vertical bars through each opening. The result: a dozen large, boxy holes arranged in 3 x 2 pattern on each half of the angled panel. Grille moldings were argent on the Scooter coupe, bright chrome on other models. Small amber rectangular parking lamps were below the bumper rub strip; similar amber side marker lenses on front fenders. 'Chevette' script was on the front fender, just ahead of the door. Standard engine was now the 98 cu. in. (1.6-liter) overhead-cam four, rated 63 horsepower, replacing the smaller 1.4-liter of 1977. A high- output version (not available in California) had a bigger carburetor, revised manifolds, reduced exhaust back pressure, and higher-speed camshaft. Even though Chevette's price rose only modestly, 18 items that had been optional now became standard. Standard equipment (except on Scooter) now included a front spoiler, AM radio, center console with coin pocket, whitewall tires, wheel trim rings, bumper rub strips, bodyside and sill moldings, sport steering wheel, and cigarette lighter. The coupe had a swing-out rear window. Also standard: fully synchronized four-speed manual transmission, glove box lock, color-keyed dash, and carpeting. New options included tri-tone sport stripes (five color choices), and seven-position comfortilt steering wheel. Most automatic transmissions were produced at Strasbourg, identical to those used on European Chevettes. Body acoustics were revised for quieter road operation. Zincro-metal inner fender skirts and galvanized fender reinforcements joined the list of special corrosion-protection treatments. All-vinyl interiors came in black, blue, carmine, green or camel. Cloth/vinyl upholstery came in black, carmine or camel. Scooters were upholstered with all-vinyl or Sport cloth/vinyl, in black or camel. Optional Custom interiors were "Rattan" all-vinyl or "Darby" woven cloth/vinyl. Of the 14 body colors, ten were new this year.

MONZA — SERIES 1H — FOUR/V-6/V-8 — With the departure of Vega, the subcompact Monza line grew to seven two-door models in two groups. Monza took over two carryover Vega body styles: the hatchback and wagon. That gave the standard lineup an 'S' hatchback, 2+2 hatchback, coupe, and two station wagons. Monza's Sport series, repeating the soft fascia of 1977, came in two body types: sport coupe and 2+2 hatchback. Standard models had single round headlamps with restyled housings, black-accented bright grille and moldings with single crossbars and center bowtie emblem, new header panel, and bright steel bumpers. A new

1978 Monza S hatchback coupe (CH)

1978 Camaro Sport Coupe (CH)

body-colored filler strip at the rear closed the gap between bumper and body. Rear end of the wagon and hatchback coupe looked the same as their Vega predecessors, except for the steel bumper. Monza Sport displayed quad rectangular headlamps and the Euro-look soft fascia, restyled with new front cover and headlamp bezels. Bumper guards and strips (front and rear) switched to body color this year. Upper air intake slots were gone this year, replaced by a single wide opening over the bumper, with round emblem above. Separate 'Monza' block letters stood at the center of the thin, full-width grille opening. Engine choices were the new base 151 cu. in. (2.5-liter) four; new optional 196 cu. in. (3.2-liter) V-6; and optional 305 cu. in. (5.0-liter) V-8. All three had two-barrel carburetors. Both new engines came from other GM divisions. California Monzas carried a 231 cu. in. V-6 rather than the 196, and the four came only with automatic shift. Fours and the V6196 weren't available in high-altitude areas. The V-8 was available only in notchback or 2+2 models. The new base engine replaced the former aluminum 140 cu. in. four, which had its share of troubles. The 151 had a cast iron head, block and manifolds, with two-barrel two- stage carburetor. The new 196 V-6 also used cast iron construction. The California V-6 was similar but with larger bore. Transmissions were the standard four-speed manual or optional five-speed (available for four or V-6 engine). Turbo Hydra-matic was available for all engines. The acoustical package was upgraded this year, with full hood insulation. Front disc brakes had ventilated rotors. New GT coupe equipment packages featured 'GT' striping and BR70 x 13/C tires. Spyder performance equipment for the Sport 2+2 hatchback included special-handling suspension and BR70 x 13/C tires. V-8 versions had dual exhaust outlets. A 'Spyder' nameplate went on front fender; emblems on hood header and rear keylock cover. A companion Spyder appearance package could again be ordered separately. A new Estate package was offered for station wagons.

The forward roof section, hood surface and front header (to below the grille opening) were black metallic. Tri-color striping separated those black surfaces from the basic body color. 'Rally Sport' decals were on front fenders and decklid. Standard engine was the 250 cu. in. inline six, now rated 110 horsepower, with three-speed manual transmission. Optional: 305 and 350 V-8s, now with base four-speed manual gearbox. California Camaros only came with automatic, while high-altitude buyers could get only the 350 V-8 and automatic. The six had improved exhaust system isolation this year. An aluminum intake manifold helped cut the 305 V-8's weight by 35 pounds. Chassis had improved front frame reinforcements. And the brake-pressure differential switch was now made of nylon. All axle ratios were lowered in an attempt to boost gas mileage. Body colors this year were white, silver, black, light or bright blue, orange-yellow, bright yellow, dark blue- green, camel, dark camel, saffron, light red, and carmine. New Rally wheels came in all body colors. Camaros had new standard cloth seat trim, a new door trim design, and could have new optional aluminum wheels. Also joining the option list: a Tbar twin hatch roof with tinted glass lift-out roof panels, operated by a single latch on each panel. A total of 9,875 Troofs were installed this year. The high-performance Z28 added a new pointed hood panel air scoop with black throat, functional slanted front-fender air louvers, body-color rear spoiler, modified body striping, and the simulated string-wrapped steering wheel. Powerplant was the 350 (5.7-liter) V-8 with four-barrel and dual exhaust outlets, putting out 170 or 185 horsepower. Z28s had a 3.42:1 or 3.73:1 axle ratio, special handling suspension, and GR70 x 15/B white-letter tires. Suspension revisions this year increased front-end rigidity and limited transverse movement of the rear axle. A 'Z28' decal was below the air louvers.

1978 Nova Custom sedan (CH)

1978 Malibu Classic Landau Coupe (CH)

NOVA — SERIES 1X — SIX/V-8 — A new Nova Custom series combined the 1977 Concours body trim with the custom interior option. Otherwise, appearance was unchanged except for new colors, trims, emblems, and steering wheel. A two-door coupe and four-door sedan came in both levels, plus a two-door hatchback coupe in basic Nova dress only. The list of optional body moldings was expanded. A new front seatbelt retractor system provided greater rear seat comfort and more convenient operation. The "Nova Rally" coupe appearance option package for the Custom coupe was similar to the 1977 version, but the grille nameplate was deleted. Custom models were identified by a modified block-letter 'Nova Custom' emblem on front fender. Styling features included a massive-look grille made of thin vertical bars, inset low-profile vertical parking lamps, chromed headlamp bezels, bright wide hood edge moldings, and tri-section taillamps. The former Concours' stand-up hood ornament did not continue. Small horizontal side marker lenses were again near the front of front fenders. New colors this year were silver, light camel, bright blue metallic, camel or dark camel metallic, saffron metallic, and carmine metallic. Carried over: black, white, light blue or green metallic, dark blue-green metallic, bright yellow, and light red. Standard engine was the inline 250 cu. in. (4.1-liter) six with three-speed manual transmission. Optional: 305 cu. in. (5.0-liter) and 350 cu. in. (5.7-liter) V-8s. Four-speed manual transmission was required with the 305 V-8, while automatic was mandatory with the 350 V-8. California Novas came only with automatic. Novas could even be ordered with a police package, offering handling that some compared to a Camaro Z28. Nova's Rally Equipment package included striping at lower bodyside, rear end panel and over wheel openings; a chromed diamond-pattern grille; black headlamp bezels; Rally nameplates; and 14 x 6 in. (or 14 x 7 in.) Rally wheels.

CAMARO — SERIES 1F — SIX/V-8 — Though unchanged in basic design, Camaros managed a fresh look with a new body-colored soft nose section and rear bumper. The new design used the same cellular urethane as Corvette, to replace the former aluminum face bar and spring bumper system. Camaro's grille was similar to 1977, but with fewer horizontal bars and larger holes (ten rows across), and a deeper repeated lower section below the narrow bumper. At the rear were wedge-shaped wraparound taillamps with inboard amber directional signal lamps and clear backup lamps. Rally Sport became a model this year rather than an option, with new paint striping. Both standard and Type LT Rally Sport coupe models had a bold contrasting paint scheme.

MALIBU — SERIES 1A — V-6/V-8 — New-size Malibus rode a 108 inch wheelbase and averaged 193 inches overallthat was 12-1/2 to 22 inches shorter than 1977 equivalents. This year's editions were narrower, too, but as tall as before. Slimmer doors and reduced bodyside curvature helped keep interior space ample. Broad glass area improved visibility. Rear armrests in sedans and wagons were now recessed into back door trim panels, so door glass was fixed rather than movable. Somehow, the newly shrunken Malibus managed to offer more interior and luggage space. Shell-type seats helped add head/leg room. Coupes lost 550 pounds, wagons closer to half a ton. Models included a two-door coupe, four-door sedan, and four-door (two-seat) station wagon, in both Malibu and Malibu Classic series. A Malibu Classic Landau coupe was available. So was an Estate option for the Malibu Classic wagon. The old Chevelle name faded away this year. Both Malibus had a new wide, chrome-plated plastic grille in horizontally-oriented lattice style, with 'Chevrolet' block lettering in the upper molding. Vertical rectangular parking lamps sat between the grille and single chrome-bezel rectangular headlamps. Bright steel bumpers had horizontal sculpture lines. Tapered, angled amber side marker lamps stood at front fender tips. 'Malibu' or 'Malibu Classic' identification was at the rear of quarter panels. Both models had bright roof drip moldings and wheel covers. Six-window sedans had large pivoting quarter vent windows. At the rear were large tri-section taillamps, level with the license plate, with outboard lenses wrapping around to form side markers. (Wagon taillamps sat in the back bumper.) A 'Chevrolet' block-letter nameplate was on the lower right of the decklid. Malibu Classic added extra rear moldings and bright taillamp trim, plus wheel opening moldings (also on Malibu wagon). Standard powerplant was a new Chevrolet 200 cu. in. (3.3-liter) V-6, derived from the popular small-block V-8. The new engine had a cast iron block and cylinder heads, new "Dualjet" carburetor, and lightweight aluminum intake manifold. New dynamic balancing was supposed to ensure smooth running. California models, though, required a 231 V-6. Standard transmission was the three-speed manual, except in California where the otherwise optional Turbo Hydra-matic was mandatory. An optional 305 cu. in. (5.0-liter) V-8 could have either four-speed manual or automatic. Wagons in high- altitude areas had to have the four-barrel 350 cu. in. V-8. A new vertical-style instrument panel, mounted well forward, helped to enhance the spacious feeling. A separate module held radio/heater controls and instruments. Plug-in components and a swing-down glove compartment made behind- dash servicing easier. The dimmer switch moved to the turn- signal lever. A new ventilation system delivered outside air under all driving conditions, whether power assisted or ram vented. Sedans and wagons had standard swing-out rear vent windows. Drivers had a delta-spoke soft vinyl steering wheel. Wagons had a much wider cargo opening than before, plus a split tailgate instead of the previous swing-up version. As in full-size wagons, storage compartments were in the rear

quarter trim panels, just inside the tailgate. The new Malibus used a full perimeter frame to keep their "big car" ride. The chassis featured coil springs all around, a single-piece propeller shaft, lower rear axle ratios, relay-type steering, and front disc (rear drum) brakes. The new fuel tank held 17.5 gallons. Malibu rode radial-ply tires on 14 inch wheels. All had a modular mini-enersorber bumper system. A new temporary spare tire saved 15 pounds and allowed greater trunk space. Fourteen tuned rubber body mounts helped keep road noise down. In addition to 14 solid colors, five custom two-tone combinations were optional: dark blue and light blue metallic; gold and light camel; carmine and dark carmine metallic; green and light green metallic; and silver with medium gray accent. Standard equipment included heater/defroster, carpeting, bright windshield and back window reveal moldings, bright belt side moldings, front stabilizer bar, Freedom battery, and P185/75R14 fiberglass- belted radial tires (wagons had P195/75R14). Malibu Classic added dual horns. Malibu Classic Landau had a vinyl roof, bodyside striping, rally wheels, and sport wheel covers. Power brakes and steering, V-8 engines and Turbo Hydra-matic were optional.

1978 Monte Carlo Sport Coupe (CH)

MONTE CARLO — SERIES 1A — V-6/V-8 — The third-generation Monte, according to Chevrolet, was "reengineered to meet the need for modern levels of vehicle efficiency" to provide "a new dimension in affordable luxury." Weight was cut by over 800 pounds. Overall length shrunk by 12.9 inches, wheelbase by nearly 8 inches (down to 108.1), while height rose slightly. Even so, interior dimensions managed to grow instead of shrink. The downsized version displayed a more formal roofline with sweeping fender and body lines (but lacking the former body bulges), much larger quarter windows, and frameless door glass. Single bright-bezeled rectangular headlamps sat between large parking lamps (which wrapped around to amber marker lamps) and the bright, fine-mesh grid-pattern grille. At the rear were distinctive five-segment taillamps. Lower body contours retained the look of former Montes. Large, soft bumper impact areas held bright impact strips. Up front was a standup header emblem and 'Monte Carlo' script nameplate. Nameplates were also on front fenders; nameplate with bowtie emblem on decklid; Monte crest on the sail panel. Basic mechanical (and bodily) changes were similar to Malibu. The new standard 231 cu. in. (3.8-liter) V-6 engine with two-barrel carburetor was claimed to deliver 24 percent better gas mileage than the former base V-8. Sole V-8 option this year was the 305 cu. in. (5.0-liter). Base transmission was three-speed manual, with four-speed manual and automatic available. The V-8 came with automatic, but could have four-speed manual. Automatics were required in California. For improved handling, Monte got a special frame, front and rear stabilizer bars, and P205/70R14 steel-belted radial tires. The new body used aluminum inner and outer decklid panels to save weight. Rear brake drums were finned aluminum. Improved corrosion protection included zincro-metal, aluminum, galvanized metal, zinc priming, anti-corrosion dip, plus special sealers and coatings. Front and rear bumper reinforcement bars were aluminum. The new integrated-look outer covering was injection-molded and pliable, finished in body color. Monte's standard interior used a bench seat with split back, in vinyl or woven cloth. Optional: a 55/45 split bench seat (velour or vinyl), or vinyl buckets with individual adjustments. Standard equipment included the 231 V-6, three- speed manual transmission, manual front disc brakes, electric clock, day/night mirror, dual horns, bright wheel opening and roof drip moldings, bumper impact strips, front and rear stabilizer bars, heater/defroster, and carpeting. Body colors this year were white, silver, black, light blue, light camel, or nine metallics: light or dark blue, light or medium green, camel, dark camel, saffron, carmine, or dark carmine. A new Landau model had a vinyl half-roof with unique white-metalized rear quarter window treatment, sport mirrors, special wheel covers, wide sill moldings, lower body applique, upper body pinstriping, and 'Landau' nameplates with decorative crest. As before, Landaus came with standard automatic transmission, power brakes and steering. Added to the option list; a twin hatch sunroof with removable tinted glass panels. Still available was the power-operated steel sunroof.

1978 Impala Sport Coupe (CH)

IMPALA/CAPRICE CLASSIC — SERIES 1B — SIX/V-8 — Apart from revised front and rear styling treatments, the full-size Chevrolets were carryovers from their 1977 downsizing. Impalas carried a new horizontal-bar grille, with bowtie above rather than on the grille itself. Caprice's version had a lattice crosshatch pattern (with fewer divider bars than before). Taillamps and moldings were also restyled. Both Caprice and Impala were available in two-door coupe, four-door sedan and four-door station wagon (two- or three-seat) body styles. Powertrains were the same as 1977, except for reduced axle ratios to achieve greater economy. Standard engine was again the 250 cu. in. (4.1-liter) inline six, with both 305 and 350 V-8s available. The six now had an integral distributor cap and coil, while the 305 V-8 lost 35 pounds as a result of a new aluminum intake manifold. A larger power brake booster reduced pedal effort. Of the 14 standard body colors, ten were new this year. In addition to styling differences, Caprice added a few items of standard equipment absent on Impalas. They included a

1978 Caprice Classic sedan (CH)

dual-note horn, full wheel covers, wheel opening moldings, clock, interior lighting, and fold-down center armrest on sedans. The Caprice Classic Landau coupe, introduced during the 1977 model year, was continued this year. That appearance package included an elk-grain forward vinyl top with bright rear-edge molding, sport mirrors, wire wheel covers with Landau hub identification, accent striping, and belt moldings painted to match the vinyl top. Roof panels held a Landau nameplate. New options this year: new wheel trim covers for Impala, an electrically-powered sliding steel sunroof for coupes and sedans, and 40-channel CB built into AM/FM radio.

I.D. DATA: As before, Chevrolet used a 13-symbol Vehicle Identification Number (VIN) displayed on the upper left surface of the instrument panel, visible through the windshield. The first digit ('1') indicates Chevrolet division. Next is a letter identifying the series (car line): 'B' Chevette; 'J' Chevette Scooter; 'M' Monza; 'R' Monza Sport; 'X' Nova; 'Y' Nova Custom; 'Q' Camaro; 'S' Camaro Type LT; 'Y' Nova Concours; 'T' Malibu; 'W' Malibu Classic; 'Z' Monte Carlo; 'L' Impala; 'N' Caprice Classic. Symbols 34 indicate body type: '08' 2-dr. (4-pass.) hatchback coupe; '07' 2-dr. (2+2) hatchback coupe; '77' 2-dr. hatchback coupe; '17' Nova 2-dr. (6- pass.) hatchback coupe; '27' 2-dr. coupe or notchback coupe; '87' 2-dr. (4-pass.) sport coupe; '37' 2-dr. (6- pass.) sport coupe; '47' 2-dr. (6-pass.) coupe; '19' 4- dr. (6-pass.) sedan; '68' 4-dr. (4-pass.) hatchback sedan; '69' 4-dr. (6-pass.) sedan; '15' 2-dr. (4-pass.) station wagon; '35' 4-dr. station wagon. Symbol five is the engine code: 'E' L497.6 1Bbl.; 'J' L497.6 H.O.; 'V' L4151 2Bbl.; 'C' V6196 2Bbl.; 'M' V6200 2Bbl.; 'A' V6231 2Bbl.; 'D' L6250 1Bbl.; 'U' V8305 2Bbl.; 'L' V8350 4Bbl. Next is a code for model year ('8' 1978). Symbol seven denotes assembly plant: 'B' Baltimore, MD; 'C' South Gate, CA; 'D' Doraville, GA; 'J' Janesville, WI; 'K' Leeds, MO; 'U' Lordstown, OH; 'L' Van Nuys, CA; 'N' Norwood, OH; 'R' Arlington, TX; 'S' St. Louis, MO; 'T' Tarrytown, NY; 'W' Willow Run, MI; 'Y' Wilmington, DE; 'Z' Fremont, CA; '1' Oshawa, Ontario. The last six digits are the sequential serial number. A Body Number Plate on the upper horizontal surface of the shroud (except X-bodies, on the vertical surface) identifies model year, car division, series, style, body assembly plant, body number, trim combination, modular seat code, paint code, and date build code. A two- or three-symbol code (combined with a serial number) identifies each engine. Chevette engine numbers are on a pad at right of block, below No. 1 spark plug. Pontiac (151) fours have a number pad at the right side of the block, by distributor shaft hole. On sixes, the pad is at the right side of the block, to rear of distributor. On V-8s, that pad is just forward of the right cylinder head.

CHEVETTE (FOUR)

Model Number	Body/Style Number	Body Type & Seating	Factory Price	Shipping Weight	Production Total
1T	B08	2-dr. Hatch Cpe-4P	3354	1965	118,375
1T	B68	4-dr. Hatch Sed-4P	3764	2035	167,769

CHEVETTE SCOOTER (FOUR)

1T	J08	2-dr. Hatch Cpe-4P	2999	1932	12,829

Chevette Production Note: 11,316 Chevettes were built for sale in Canada as Acadians.

MONZA (FOUR/V-6/V-8)

1H	M07	2-dr. Hatch 2+2-4P	3609	2732	36,227
1H	M77	2-dr. 'S' Hatch-4P	3527	2643	2,326
1H	M27	2-dr. Cpe-4P	3462	2688	37,878
1H	M15	2-dr. Sta Wag-4P	3698	2723	24,255
1H	M15/YC6	2-dr. Est Wag-4P	3932	N/A	2,478

1978 Monza Sport Coupe (CH)

105

MONZA SPORT (FOUR/V-6/V-8)

1H	R27	2-dr. Spt Cpe-4P	3930	2730	6,823
1H	R07	2-dr. Hatch 2+2-4P	4077	2777	28,845

Monza Engine Note: Prices shown are for four-cylinder engine. The 196 cu. in. V-6 cost $130 extra; a 231 V-6, $170. Monza could also have a 305 V-8 for $320 over the four-cylinder price. A total of 41,995 Monzas had a V6196 installed, and 16,254 a 231 V-6. Only 9,478 had a V-8 engine.

NOVA (SIX/V-8)

1X	X27	2-dr. Cpe-6P	3702/3887	3132/3277	101,858
1X	X17	2-dr. Hatch-6P	3866/4051	3258/3403	12,665
1X	X69	4-dr. Sedan-6P	3777/3962	3173/3318	123,158

NOVA CUSTOM (SIX/V-8)

1X	Y27	2-dr. Cpe-6P	3960/4145	3261/3396	23,953
1X	Y69	4-dr. Sedan-6P	4035/4220	3298/3443	26,475

CAMARO (SIX/V-8)

1F	Q87	2-dr. Spt Cpe-4P	4414/4599	3300/3425	134,491
1F	Q87/Z85	2-dr. Rally Cpe-4P	4784/4969	N/A	11,902

CAMARO TYPE LT (SIX/V-8)

1F	S87	2-dr. Spt Cpe-4P	4814/4999	3352/3477	65,635
1F	S87/Z85	2-dr. Rally Cpe-4P	5065/5250	N/A	5,696

CAMARO Z28 (V-8)

1F	Q87	2-dr. Spt Cpe-4P	-- /5604	-- / N/A	54,907

MALIBU (V-6/V-8)

1A	T27	2-dr. Spt Cpe-6P	4204/4394	3001/3138	27,089
1A	T19	4-dr. Sed-6P	4279/4469	3006/3143	44,426
1A	T35	4-dr. Sta Wag-6P	4516/4706	3169/3350	30,850

MALIBU CLASSIC (V-6/V-8)

1A	W27	2-dr. Spt Cpe-6P	4461/4651	3031/3167	60,992
1A	W27/Z03	2-dr. Lan Cpe-6P	4684/4874	N/A	29,160
1A	W19	4-dr. Sed-6P	4561/4651	3039/3175	102,967
1A	W35	4-dr. Sta Wag-6P	4714/4904	3196/3377	63,152

Malibu Engine Note: Only 8,930 Malibus had the 231 V-6 engine, and only 802 had the 350 V-8 (code LM1).

MONTE CARLO (V-6/V-8)

1A	Z37	2-dr. Spt Cpe-6P	4785/4935	3040/3175	216,730
1A	Z37/Z03	2-dr. Lan Cpe-6P	5678/5838	N/A	141,461

IMPALA (SIX/V-8)

1B	L47	2-dr. Spt Cpe-6P	5208/5393	3511/3619	33,990
1B	L47/Z03	2-dr. Lan Cpe-6P	5598/5783	N/A	4,652
1B	L69	4-dr. Sedan-6P	5283/5468	3530/3638	183,161
1B	L35	4-dr. Sta Wag-6P	-- /5777	-- /4037	40,423
1B	L35/AQ4	4-dr. 3S Wag-8P	-- /5904	-- /4071	28,518

CAPRICE CLASSIC (SIX/V-8)

1B	N47	2-dr. Spt Cpe-6P	5526/5711	3548/3656	37,301
1B	N47/Z03	2-dr. Lan Cpe-6P	5830/6015	N/A	22,771
1B	N69	4-dr. Sedan-6P	5626/5811	3578/3680	203,837
1B	N35	4-dr. Sta Wag-6P	-- /6012	-- /4079	24,792
1B	N35/AQ4	4-dr. 3S Wag-8P	-- /6151	-- /4109	32,952

FACTORY PRICE AND WEIGHT NOTE: Where two prices and weights are shown, the figure to the left of the slash is for six-cylinder model, to right of slash for V-8. **BODY/STYLE NO. NOTE:** Some models are actually option packages. Figure after the slash (e.g., Z03) is the number of the option package that comes with the model listed.

ENGINE DATA: BASE FOUR (Chevette): Inline. Overhead cam. Four-cylinder. Cast iron block and head. Displacement: 97.6 cu. in. (1.6 liters). Compression ratio: 8.6:1. Brake horsepower: 63 at 4800 R.P.M. Torque: 82 lbs.-ft. at 3200 R.P.M. Five main bearings. Hydraulic valve lifters. Carburetor: 1Bbl. Rochester 1ME. VIN Code: E. OPTIONAL FOUR (Chevette): Same as above except Brake H.P.: 68 at 5000 R.P.M. Torque: 84 lbs.-ft. at 3200 R.P.M. VIN Code: J. BASE FOUR (Monza): Inline. Overhead valve. Four-cylinder. Cast iron block. Displacement: 151 cu. in. (2.5 liters). Bore & stroke: 4.00 x 3.00 in. Compression ratio: 8.3:1. Brake horsepower: 85 at 4400 R.P.M. Torque: 123 lbs.-ft. at 2800 R.P.M. Five main bearings. Hydraulic valve

lifters. Carburetor: 2Bbl. Holley 5210C. VIN Code: V. OPTIONAL V-6 (Monza): 90-degree, overhead-valve V-6. Cast iron block and head. Displacement: 196 cu. in. (3.2 liters). Bore & stroke: 3.50 x 3.40 in. Compression ratio: 8.0:1. Brake horsepower: 90 at 3600 R.P.M. Torque: 165 lbs.-ft. at 2000 R.P.M. Four main bearings. Hydraulic valve lifters. Carburetor: 2Bbl. Rochester 2GE. VIN Code: C. BASE V-6 (Malibu): 90-degree, overhead-valve V-6. Cast iron block and head. Displacement: 200 cu. in. (3.3 liters). Bore & stroke: 3.50 x 3.48 in. Compression ratio: 8.2:1. Brake horsepower: 95 at 3800 R.P.M. Torque: 160 lbs.-ft. at 2000 R.P.M. Four main bearings. Hydraulic valve lifters. Carburetor: 2Bbl. Rochester 2GC. VIN Code: M. BASE V-6 (Monte Carlo); OPTIONAL (Monza, Malibu): 90-degree, overhead-valve V-6. Cast iron block and head. Displacement: 231 cu. in. (3.8 liters). Bore & stroke: 3.80 x 3.40 in. Compression ratio: 8.0:1. Brake horsepower: 105 at 3400 R.P.M. Torque: 185 lbs.-ft. at 2000 R.P.M. Four main bearings. Hydraulic valve lifters. Carburetor: 2Bbl. Rochester 2GE. VIN Code: A. BASE SIX (Nova, Camaro, Impala, Caprice): Inline. Cast iron block and head. Displacement: 250 cu. in. (4.1 liters). Bore & stroke: 3.88 x 3.53 in. Compression ratio: 8.1:1. Brake horsepower: 110 at 3800 R.P.M. Torque: 190 lbs.-ft. at 1600 R.P.M. Seven main bearings. Hydraulic valve lifters. Carburetor: 1Bbl. Rochester 1ME. VIN Code: D. BASE V-8 (Impala/Caprice wagon); OPTIONAL (Monza, Nova, Camaro, Malibu, Monte Carlo, Impala, Caprice): 90-degree, overhead valve V-8. Cast iron block and head. Displacement: 305 cu. in. (5.0 liters). Bore & stroke: 3.74 x 3.48 in. Compression ratio: 8.4:1. Brake horsepower: 145 at 3800 R.P.M. Torque: 245 lbs.-ft. at 2400 R.P.M. Five main bearings. Hydraulic valve lifters. Carburetor: 2Bbl. Rochester 2GC. VIN Code: U. BASE V-8 (Camaro Z28); OPTIONAL (Nova, Camaro, Malibu wagon, Impala, Caprice): 90-degree, overhead valve V-8. Cast iron block and head. Displacement: 350 cu. in. (5.7 liters). Bore & stroke: 4.00 x 3.48 in. Compression ratio: 8.2:1. Brake horsepower: 170 at 3800 R.P.M. Torque: 270 lbs.-ft. at 2400 R.P.M. Five main bearings. Hydraulic valve lifters. Carburetor: 4Bbl. Rochester M4MC. VIN Code: L. OPTIONAL V-8 (Camaro Z28): Same as 350 V-8 above but Brake H.P.: 185 at 4000 R.P.M. Torque: 280 lbs.-ft. at 2400 R.P.M.

CHASSIS DATA: Wheelbase: (Chevette 2-dr.) 94.3 in.; (Chvt 4-dr.) 97.3 in.; (Monza) 97.0 in.; (Camaro) 108.0 in.; (Nova) 111.0 in.; (Malibu/Monte) 108.1 in.; (Caprice/Imp) 116.0 in. Overall length: (Chevette 2-dr.) 159.7 in.; (Chvt 4-dr.) 162.6 in.; (Monza) 178.0-179.3 in.; (Nova) 196.7 in.; (Camaro) 197.6 in.; (Malibu) 192.7 in.; (Monte) 200.4 in.; (Caprice/Imp) 212.1 in.; (Impala wag) 214.7 in. Height: (Chevette 2-dr.) 52.3 in.; (Chvt 4-dr.) 53.3 in.; (Monza cpe) 49.8 in.; (Monza hatch) 50.2 in.; (Monza wag) 51.8 in.; (Nova 2-dr.) 52.7 in.; (Nova 4dr.) 53.6 in.; (Camaro) 49.2 in.; (Malibu cpe) 53.3 in.; (Malibu sed) 54.2 in.; (Malibu wag) 54.5 in.; (Monte) 53.9 in.; (Capr/Imp cpe) 55.3 in.; (Capr/Imp sed) 56.0 in.; (Capr/Imp wag) 58.0 in. Width: (Chevette) 61.8 in.; (Monza) 65.4 in.; (Nova) 72.2 in.; (Camaro) 74.5 in.; (Malibu/Monte) 71.5 in.; (Malibu wag) 71.2 in.; (Capr/Imp) 76.0 in.; (Capr/Imp wag) 79.1 in. Front Tread: (Chevette) 51.2 in.; (Monza) 54.8 in.; (Nova/Camaro) 61.3 in.; (Camaro LT) 61.6 in.; (Malibu/Monte) 58.5 in.; (Capr/Imp) 61.8 in.; (Capr/Imp wag) 62.2 in. Rear Tread: (Chevette) 51.2 in.; (Monza) 53.6 in.; (Nova) 59.0 in.; (Camaro) 60.0 in.; (Camaro LT) 60.3 in.; (Malibu/Monte) 57.8 in.; (Capr/Imp) 60.8 in.; (Capr/Imp wag) 64.1 in. Standard Tires: (Chevette) P155/80 x 13; (Monza) A78 x 13; (Monza wag) B78 x 13; (Nova) E78 x 14; (Camaro) FR78 x 14/B SBR; (Malibu) P185/75R14 GBR; (Malibu wag) P195/75R14 GBR; (Imp/Capr) FR78 x 15 GBR; (Imp/Capr wag) HR78 x 15 SBR; (Monte) P205/70R14 SBR.

1978 Camaro Z28 Sport Coupe (CP)

TECHNICAL: Transmission: Three-speed manual transmission (floor shift) standard on Camaro, Nova and Monte Carlo six. Gear ratios: (1st) 3.50:1; (2nd) 1.81:1; (3rd) 1.00:1; (Rev) 3.62:1. Four-speed floor shift standard on Chevette: (1st) 3.75:1; (2nd) 2.16:1; (3rd) 1.38:1; (4th) 1.00:1; (Rev) 3.82:1. Four-speed floor shift optional on Monza four and Monte V-6: (1st) 3.50:1; (2nd) 2.48:1; (3rd) 1.66:1; (4th) 1.00:1; (Rev) 3.50:1. Four-speed floor shift standard on Nova (V8350) and Camaro V-8, optional on Chevette, Monza, Monte: (1st) 2.85:1; (2nd) 2.02:1; (3rd) 1.35:1; (4th) 1.00:1; (Rev) 2.85:1. Camaro Z28 four-speed floor shift: (1st) 2.64:1; (2nd) 1.75:1; (3rd) 1.34:1; (4th) 1.00:1; (Rev) 2.55:1. Five-speed floor shift available on Monza V-6: (1st) 3.40:1; (2nd) 2.08:1; (3rd) 1.39:1; (4th) 1.00:1; (5th) 0.80:1; (Rev) 3.36:1. Three-speed Turbo Hydra-matic standard on Caprice/Impala, optional on others. Gear ratios: (1st) 2.52:1; (2nd) 1.52:1; (3rd) 1.00:1; (Rev) 1.94:1 except standard Caprice/Impala V-8, Monza V-6, Malibu six and Monte (V8305) ratios: (1st) 2.74:1; (2nd) 1.57:1; (3rd) 1.00:1; (Rev) 2.07:1. Chevette/Monza four automatic trans.: (1st) 2.40:1; (2nd) 1.48:1; (3rd) 1.00:1; (Rev) 1.92:1. Standard final drive ratio: (Chevette) 3.70:1; (Monza four) 2.73:1 exc. 3.23:1 w/5spd; (Monza V-8) 2.73:1 w/5spd or auto.; (Monza V-6) 3.08:1 w/4spd, 2.29:1 w/auto.; (Nova) 2.73:1 exc. 3.08:1 w/V-8 and auto.; (Camaro six) 2.73:1; (Camaro V-8) 3.08:1; (Camaro Z28) 3.42:1 or 3.73:1; (Malibu) 2.73:1 exc. 2.29:1 w/V-8; (Malibu wag) 2.41:1; (Monte V-6) 2.93:1 w/3spd, 2.56:1 w/auto.; (Monte V-8) 2.73:1 w/4spd, 2.29:1 w/auto.; (Capr/Imp six) 2.73:1; (Capr/Imp V-8) 2.41:1; (Capr/Imp wag) 2.56:1. Steering/Suspension/Body: same as 1976-77. Brakes: front disc, rear drum. Fuel tank: (Chevette) 12.5 gal.; (Monza cpe) 18.5 gal.; (Monza hatch/wag) 15 gal.; (Nova/Camaro) 21 gal.; (Malibu/Monte) 17.5 gal.; (Malibu wag) 18 gal.; (Capr/Imp wag) 22 gal.

DRIVETRAIN OPTIONS: Engines: 1.6-liter H.O. four: Chevette ($55). 196 cu. in. V-6: Monza ($130). 231 cu. in. V-6: Monza ($170); Malibu ($40). 305 cu. in., 2Bbl. V-8: Monza ($320); Nova/Camaro ($185); Malibu ($190); Monte ($150); Imp/Caprice cpe/sed ($185). 350 cu. in., 4Bbl. V-8: Nova/Camaro ($300); Malibu wag ($305); Imp/Capr cpe/sed ($300); Imp/Capr wag ($115). Transmission/Differential: Four-speed manual shift: Nova/Camaro/Malibu/Monte ($125). Close-ratio four-speed manual shift: Camaro (NC). Five-speed manual shift: Monza ($175). Turbo Hydra-matic: Chevette/Monza ($270); Nova/Camaro/Malibu/Monte ($307); Camaro Z28 ($45). Sport shifter: Chvt ($28). Positraction axle: Monza ($59); Nova/Camaro ($60); Malibu/Monte ($60); Imp/Capr ($63). Performance axle ratio ($14-$17). Power Accessories: Power brakes: Chvt/Monza ($66); Nova/Camaro/Malibu cpe/sed ($69). Power steering: Monza ($134); Nova/Malibu/Monte ($152). Suspension: F40 H.D. suspension: Nova ($9-$33); Malibu cpe/sed, Monte/Imp/Capr cpe/sed ($20). F41 sport suspension: Monza ($30); Nova ($41); Camaro, Malibu/Imp/Capr cpe/sed ($38). Heavy duty shock absorbers: Malibu ($50). Rear stabilizer bar: Chvt ($30). Other: Heavy-duty radiator ($29-$31) exc. Imp/Capr ($40). H.D. alternator (61-amp): Malibu/Monte/Imp/Capr ($31). H.D. battery ($17-$18). California emission system ($75) exc. Monza four ($100). High altitude emission system ($33).

CHEVETTE/MONZA CONVENIENCE/APPEARANCE OPTIONS: Option Packages: Spyder equipment pkg.: Monza ($252). Spyder appearance pkg.: Monza ($216). Quiet sound group: Chvt ($33-$45); Monza ($24-$34). Comfort/Convenience: Air conditioning ($470). Rear defogger, electric ($79). Tinted glass ($54). Sport steering wheel: Monza ($17). Comfortilt steering wheel: Monza ($62). Special instrumentation: Chvt ($64); Monza ($64-$82). Electric clock ($18). Digital clock: Monza ($45). Cigarette lighter: Scooter ($5). Intermittent wipers ($30). Lighting, Horns and Mirrors: Aux. lighting: Chvt ($34-$35); Monza ($17-$33). Twin sport mirrors, left remote: Monza ($31). Driver's remote sport mirror: Chvt ($22). Twin remote sport mirrors: Chvt ($49). Day/night mirror ($9). Entertainment: AM radio ($71); std. on base Chevette. AM/FM radio: Chvt ($68); Scooter/Monza ($139). AM/FM stereo radio: Monza ($215). Stereo tape player w/AM radio: Monza ($216). Stereo tape player with AM/FM stereo radio: Monza ($308). Rear speaker ($23). Windshield antenna: Monza ($24); incl. w/radios. Exterior Trim: Sky roof ($215). Cabriolet vinyl roof: Monza ($153) incl. opera windows. Spoilers, front/rear: Monza ($93). Swing-out windows: Chvt ($51) but std. on base; Monza ($42). Custom exterior (wheel opening, side window and rocker panel moldings): Chvt ($99). Tri-tone sport stripes: Chvt ($67); w/o bodyside moldings ($27). Bodyside moldings ($40); std. on base Chevette. Wheel opening moldings: Monza ($21). Side window reveal moldings: Chvt ($67). Door edge guards ($11-$18). Roof carrier: Chvt ($60). Rear air deflector: Monza ($26). Deluxe bumpers, front/rear: Scooter ($33). Bumper guards, front/rear: Chvt ($38-$71); Monza ($38). Interior Trim/Upholstery: Console: Monza ($77). Bucket seats (sport cloth): Chvt ($10-$19); Monza ($19). Custom Chevette bucket seats: cloth ($170); vinyl ($151). Custom vinyl bucket seats: Monza (NC to $192). Custom sport cloth bucket seats: Monza ($19-$211). Adjustable driver's seatback: Monza ($19). Folding rear seat: Monza ($93) but std. on 2+2. Rear seat delete: Chvt ($56 credit). Load floor carpet: Chvt ($46). Color-keyed floor mats ($18). Deluxe seatbelts ($19). Wheels and Tires: Aluminum wheels: Monza ($178-$258). Rally II wheels: Monza ($43-$80). Styled gold wheels: Monza ($101- $181). Deluxe wheel covers: Monza ($37). Sport wheel covers: Chvt ($42). Wheel trim rings: Scooter ($34). 155/8013/B WSW: Scooter ($43). 155/8013/B SBR: Chvt ($62); Scooter ($105). 155/8013/B SBR WSW: Chvt ($105); Scooter ($148). 155/8013/B SBR WLT: Chvt ($120); Scooter ($163). B78 x 13 WSW: Monza (NC to $19). BR78 x 13 SBR BSW: Monza ($65-$117). BR78 x 13 SBR WSW: Monza ($125-$160). BR70 x 13 SBR BSW: Monza (NC to $157). BR70 x 13 SBR WSW: Monza ($132-$200). BR70 x 13 SBR WLT: Monza ($47-$215). Conventional spare: Monza (NC).

NOVA/CAMARO/MALIBU/MONTE CARLO CONVENIENCE/APPEARANCE OPTIONS: Option Packages: Rally equipment: Nova cpe ($199). Estate equipment: Malibu wag ($235). Interior decor/quiet sound group: Camaro ($61); std. on LT. Quiet sound group: Malibu ($46). Security pkg.: Malibu wag ($35). Comfort/Convenience: Air conditioning: Nova/Camaro ($508- $539); Malibu/Monte ($544). Rear defogger, forced-air ($51). Rear defogger (electric): Malibu/Monte ($92). Cruise-master speed control ($90). Tinted glass: Nova/Camaro ($56); Malibu/Monte ($62). Comfortilt steering wheel ($69). Six-way power seat: Malibu/Monte ($151). Power windows: Nova ($118- $164); Camaro/Monte ($124); Malibu ($124-$172). Power door locks: Nova/Malibu ($74-$112); Camaro/Monte ($80). Power trunk release: Malibu/Monte ($21). Electric clock: Nova, base Camaro ($20); Malibu ($21). Special instrumentation: Nova, base Camaro ($106); Malibu ($118); Monte ($97). Econominder gauge pkg.: Nova ($50). Gauge pkg.: Malibu ($53); Monte ($32). Intermittent wipers ($32). Lighting, Horns and Mirrors: Aux. lighting ($28-$52). Dome reading light: Malibu/Monte ($16). Dual horns: Nova, base Camaro, Z28, base Malibu ($7). Remote-control driver's mirror: Nova/Malibu/Monte ($16). Twin sport mirrors (left remote): Nova, base Camaro, Malibu/Monte ($33). Twin remote sport mirrors: Malibu/Monte ($57); Monte Lan ($24). Day/night mirror: Nova ($9). Visor vanity mirror: Malibu/Monte ($4). Lighted visor mirror: Malibu ($37); Monte ($33-$37). Entertainment: AM radio ($77-$79). AM/FM radio: Nova/Camaro/Malibu ($149); Monte ($154). AM/FM stereo radio ($229). Stereo tape player w/AM radio: Nova/Camaro ($229); Malibu/Monte ($233). Stereo tape player with AM/FM stereo radio ($328). Rear speaker ($24). Dual front speakers: Malibu/Monte ($20). Windshield antenna ($25); incl. w/radios. Power antenna: Malibu/Monte ($45). Exterior Trim: Removable glass roof panels: Camaro/Monte ($625). Power sky roof: Malibu cpe/sed, Monte ($499). Vinyl roof: Nova ($97); Camaro ($102); Malibu ($116); Monte ($131). Cabriolet roof: Nova ($179). Rear spoiler: Camaro/LT ($55). Style trim pkg.: Camaro ($70). Two-tone paint: Nova ($46); Malibu ($62-$110). Swing-out rear side windows: Nova ($56). Bodyside moldings: Nova/Camaro ($42). Deluxe bodyside moldings: Nova/Malibu/Monte ($53). Door edge guards ($11- $18). Bright rocker moldings and extensions: Nova ($37). Bright sill moldings: Monte ($44). Wheel opening moldings: Nova/Malibu ($21). Wide wheel opening moldings: Nova ($39). Side window sill moldings: Monte ($31). Side window reveal moldings: Nova/Malibu ($41). Roof drip moldings: Nova ($18); Camaro ($23). Bodyside pinstriping: Nova ($30); Malibu ($48); Monte ($33). Rear window air deflector: Malibu wag ($28). Roof carrier: Malibu wag ($85). Bumper rub strips: Malibu/Monte ($36). Bumper rub strips and guards, front/rear: Nova ($73). Bumper guards, front/rear: Malibu ($40). Interior Trim/Upholstery: Interior decor pkg.: base Nova ($29). Console ($80). Vinyl bench seat: Malibu cpe/sed, Monte ($24). Sport cloth bench seat: Nova ($21). Custom vinyl bench seat: Nova (NC). Custom vinyl bucket seats: Nova ($110). Vinyl bucket seats: Malibu cpe/sed, Monte ($110). Custom vinyl bucket seats: Camaro Z28 ($294). Sport cloth bucket seats: Camaro ($21). Custom cloth or sport cloth bucket seats: Camaro LT ($21); Z28 ($315). Knit cloth 50/50 seating: Malibu cpe/sed ($164). Vinyl 50/50 seating: Malibu cpe/sed ($188); Malibu wag ($164). Monte custom 55/45 seating: cloth ($340); vinyl ($364). Adj. driver's seatback: Camaro ($21). Litter container: Malibu/Monte ($6). Color-keyed mats ($20). Deluxe seatbelts ($19-$21). Deluxe trunk trim: Malibu/Monte ($41). Wheels and Tires: Aluminum wheels: Camaro ($180-$265). Custom styled wheels: Camaro ($91-$133). Rally wheels: Nova ($69); Camaro ($85) but std. on LT; Malibu ($41-$78); Malibu Lan (NC); Monte ($41). Color-keyed Rally wheels: Nova ($82). Full wheel covers: Nova, Camaro, Malibu cpe/sed ($37). Sport wheel covers (silver or gold): Malibu ($49-$86). Wire wheel covers: Nova ($120); Malibu ($60-$146); Monte ($109); Monte Landau ($60). E78 x 14/B BSW: Camaro ($90-$113 credit). E78 x 14/B WSW: Nova ($36-$44); Camaro ($55-$69 credit). FR78 x 14/B SBR: Nova ($91-$113). FR78 x 14/B SBR WSW: Nova ($128-$159); Camaro ($37-$46). FR78 x 14/B SBR WLT: Nova ($140-$174); Camaro ($49-$61). P185/75R14 GBR WSW: Malibu cpe/sed ($37). P195/75R14 SBR WSW: Malibu cpe/sed ($96); Malibu wag ($78). P205/75R14 SBR WSW: Malibu cpe/sed ($148). P195/75R14 GBR WSW: Malibu wag ($39). P205/75R14 SBR WLT: Malibu cpe/sed ($160). P205/70R14 SBR WSW: Monte ($42). Stowaway spare: Nova ($17); Camaro (NC).

IMPALA/CAPRICE CONVENIENCE/APPEARANCE OPTIONS: Option Packages: Estate equipment: wag ($235). Value appearance group: bodyside and wheel opening moldings, full wheel covers ($73). Comfort/Convenience: Four season air cond. ($569). Comfortron auto-temp air cond. ($655). Rear defogger, forced-air: wag ($51). Rear defogger, electric ($94). Cruise-Master speed control ($95). Tinted glass ($76). Comfortilt steering wheel ($70). Power door locks ($82-$114). Six-way power driver's seat ($151). Power windows ($130-$190). Power trunk release ($21). Power tailgate lock: wag ($40). Electric clock: Imp ($21). Digital clock: Imp ($49); Caprice ($28). Econominder gauge pkg. ($50). Intermittent wipers ($32). Quiet sound group: Imp ($51-$55). Lighting, Horns and Mirrors: Aux. lighting ($32-$46). Dual horns: Imp ($7). Driver's remote mirror ($16). Dual remote mirrors ($48). Dual sport mirrors, left remote ($33). Dual remote body-color sport mirrors ($57) exc. Lan ($24). Visor vanity mirror ($4). Lighted visor mirror ($37). Entertainment: AM radio ($80). AM/FM radio ($160). AM/FM stereo radio ($232). Stereo tape player with AM/FM radio ($250); with AM/FM stereo radio ($332). AM/FM/CB radio and power antenna ($498). Rear speakers ($24). Dual front speakers ($20). Power antenna ($45). Windshield antenna ($25); incl. w/radios. Exterior Trim: Power sky roof: cpe/sed ($595). Vinyl roof: cpe/sed ($142). Two-tone paint ($47). Custom two-tone ($115). Pinstriping ($33). Roof carrier ($110). Color-keyed bodyside moldings ($43). Door edge guards ($11-$18). Wheel opening moldings: Imp ($21). Bumper rub strips, front/rear ($50). Bumper guards ($46). Interior Trim/Upholstery: Vinyl bench seat: cpe/sed ($24). Knit cloth 50/50 seat: cpe/sed ($224). Sport cloth 50/50 seat: wag ($248). Vinyl 50/50 seat ($224-$248). Special custom cloth 50/50 seat: cpe/sed ($365). Deluxe load-floor carpet: wag ($71). Deluxe cargo area carpet: wag ($102). Color-keyed mats ($20). Litter container ($6). Color-keyed seatbelts ($21-$24). Deluxe trunk trim ($44). Wheel Covers: Full wheel covers ($38). Sport wheel covers: Imp ($88); Caprice ($50). Coupe/Sedan Tires: FR78 x 15/B GBR WSW ($46). FR78 x 15/B SBR BSW ($48). FR78 x 15/B SBR WSW ($94). GR78 x 15/B SBR WSW ($124). GR70 x 15/B SBR WSW ($147). Wagon Tires: HR78 x 15/B SBR WSW ($52).

HISTORY: Introduced: Oct. 6, 1977. Model year production (U.S.): 2,197,861 (incl. Corvettes but not incl. 11,316 Acadians). The North American total of 2,474,547 units for the U.S. market included 381,394 four-cylinder engines, 521,162 sixes and 1,571,991 V-8s. Chevrolet reported a total of 2,252,111 passenger cars shipped. Calendar year production: 2,347,327 (including 30,150 Sportvans, 48,522 Corvettes and 13,585 Acadians). Calendar year sales by U.S. dealers: 2,349,781 (incl. 43,582 Sportvans and 42,247 Corvettes) for a 25.3 percent market share. Model year sales by U.S. dealers: 2,342,035 (incl. 43,594 Sportvans and 43,106 Corvettes).

Historical Footnotes: Model year sales rose by 4.6 percent (from 2,239,538 to 2,342,035), making 1977 the third highest year in Chevrolet history. After two sluggish years, Chevette seemed to finally catch on, showing a whopping 71 percent sales gain. The freshly downsized Malibu and Monte Carlo took a while to get moving in sales. But the full-size (downsized in '77) Caprice and Impala continued to move well, taking 22.5 percent of the company's sales. In recent years, other GM divisions had been using more shared components and body style offerings. Chevrolet continued to retain more individuality, at least for the time eing. The new 200 cu. in. V-6 was built at Chevrolet's Tonawanda, New York plant. However, the 231 cu. in. V-6 came from Buick, as did the 196 V-8. And 151 cu. in. four-cylinder engines were supplied by Pontiac. Late in the model year, a handful of Chevettes came off the line with a passive restraint systemthe first examples on a domestic automobile.

1979 CHEVROLET

This was primarily a carryover year, with some engine changes, horsepower boosts (and losses) and appearance restyles, but nothing drastic. The 305 cu. in. V-8 managed to lose 15 horsepower, down to 130. Biggest news would actually be the mid-year introduction of the new Citation X- car as an early 1980 model—the first front-drive Chevrolet— which replaced the Nova.

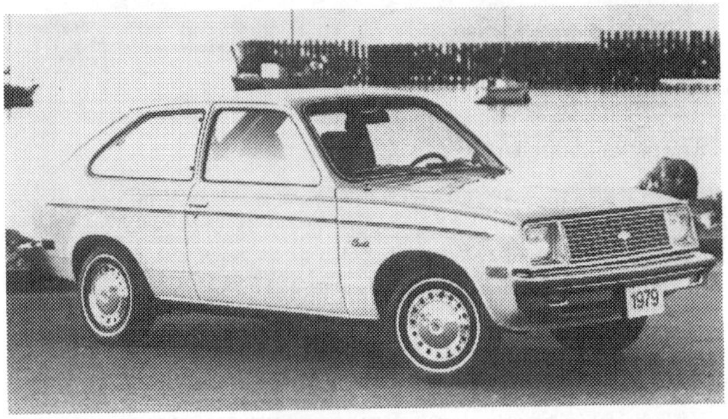

1979 Chevette hatchback coupe (CP)

CHEVETTE — SERIES 1T — FOUR — Chevrolet's subcompact got a new front-end look including a "real" separate brightwork crosshatch grille insert with bright/black bowtie emblem in the center, rather than the previous slots in a body-colored panel. Also new: a shorter hood and single recessed rectangular headlamps with bright bezels. Parking lamps remained down below the bumper rub strips. Bumpers, rub strips and valance panel were the same as in 1978. A driver's side lower duct increased air flow to the interior. The low-budget Scooter carried no bodyside trim. Standard tires were now glass-belted radials. A new two-stage carburetor, tuned intake manifold, valve port refinements, heavier pistons and improved EGR valve added to the driveability and gas mileage of the standard 7.6 cu. in. (1.6-liter) four. A trapped vacuum spark system gave it better cold-start qualities. Axle ratio was again 3.70:1 with either the standard or high-output engine, coupled to standard four-speed manual or optional three-speed automatic transmission. The formerly optional 4.11:1 ratio was dropped. A new F41 Sport Suspension option replaced the previous rear stabilizer bar option. It included a larger front stabilizer bar and bushings, plus a new and bigger eyeless- type rear stabilizer with new bushings and linkage. Steel- belted radial tires were required with the package. Other new options included an AM/FM stereo radio with three speakers, and a pair of sport mirrors (left one remote-controlled and the right one convex). The twin-remote sport mirror option was dropped. Chevettes kept their full coil suspension with torque tube drive. All Chevettes had a front stabilizer bar, Delco Freedom battery, heater/defroster, front bucket seats, and courtesy dome light. All but the Scooter also had an AM radio, fold-down back seat, color-keyed instrument panel, sport steering wheel, mini console, bumper impact strips, and cigarette lighter. Standard models had whitewall 155/80R13 glass-belted radial tires; Scooters wore blackwalls. Coupes (except Scooter) had swing-out rear windows.

MONZA — SERIES 1H — FOUR/V-6/V-8 — Though unchanged in appearance, Monza added a few horsepower to the base 151 cu. in. (2.5-liter) four-cylinder engine, supplied by Pontiac. That engine had a redesigned cross-flow cylinder head and new Varajet two-stage, two- barrel carburetor. That meant a triple-venturi first stage and air valve secondary for power-on-demand. A new aluminum intake manifold cut weight. The engine was now all-metric design, with a new replaceable-element air cleaner. Optional engines: a 196 cu. in. (3.2-liter) V-6 on all models, a 231 cu. in. (3.8-liter) V-6, plus a 305 cu. in. (5.0-liter) V-8 available on all except the 'S' hatchback coupe and wagon. Four-cylinder and V-6 models could have standard four- speed manual, optional five-speed manual, or automatic transmission. The V-8, which had a new Dualjet carburetor, came with four-speed manual or optional three-speed automatic. Monza interiors sported new front seats and a sport steering wheel. The Value Series got a new interior look with new seat design and upgraded vinyl and cloth fabrics. Corrosion protection was improved on rear compartment pan and door panels (inner/outer). Bodyside moldings were standard. New radio choices were available. As in 1978, the Sport 2+2's grille was just one wide, squat opening stretching to fender

1979 Monza coupe (CH)

tips, while the standard coupe carried a crossbar grille. All Monzas had energy-absorbing bumpers, standard A78 x 13 whitewall tires and full wheel covers, high-back bucket seats, heater/defroster, carpeting, AM radio, color-keyed instrument panel, tinted glass, center dome light, and cigarette lighter. All except the standard coupe held an interior console. Only 225 Monzas had a performance axle ratio installed this year, while 5,004 came with a five-speed transmission and 683 came with aluminum wheels. The Monza Spyder appearance package included front/rear spoilers; lower striping with Spyder name; black headlamp, parking light and belt moldings; black taillamp openings, sport mirrors and rear end panel; black lower body treatment from front to rear wheel openings; black windshield, back window, door and quarter-window moldings; and Rally II wheels. To add a bit of performance to looks, the separate Spyder equipment package included an F41 suspension, BR70 x 13/C radial tires and modified front stabilizer and rear shocks, as well as a day/night mirror. Spyder emblems went on the hood header panel and rear keylock cover. A total of 9,679 Spyder equipment packages were produced, and 8,670 appearance packages.

1979 Nova coupe (AA)

NOVA — SERIES 1X — SIX/V-8 — For its final year in the lineup, the compact Nova carried a new horizontally-ribbed grille, with single rectangular headlamps and inset clear vertical rectangular park/signal lamps with chrome bezels. The 'Chevrolet' insignia was on the heavy top bar of the grille. Separate 'Nova' letters stood on fender sides, somewhat forward of the door, in line with bodyside moldings. Two-door coupe and four-door bodies were again available in base or Custom series, along with the Nova hatchback coupe. Base engine continued to be the 250 cu. in. (4.1-liter) inline six, with optional 305 V-8. That V-8 actually lost 15 horsepower this year. Again, the three-speed manual transmission was standard with the six, four-speed with V-8 Novas. Turbo Hydra-matic was optional on both. Only in California or high altitude was the 350 four-barrel V-8 offered. A new steering column lock was supposed to thwart thieves. Rally wheels had a smaller center hub area with new Chevrolet bowtie emblem and chrome-accented vents. They were available separately, or as part of the Nova Rally option. A total of 2,299 Rally Novas were produced this year. Only 616 Novas came with a four-speed gearbox, 792 with the F41 sport suspension, and 303 with a performance axle ratio. Nova standard equipment included a built-in windshield radio antenna, heater/defroster, carpeting, locking glove compartment, manual steering and brakes, Freedom battery, and E78 x 14 blackwall tires. Nova Custom added a set of interior extras: cigarette lighter, glove box light, bright instrument cluster accents, bright front door courtesy light switch, and day/night mirror. Nova's Rally Sport Equipment package included lower bodyside and wheel opening stripes, a chrome diamond-pattern grille, black headlamp bezels, parking lamp accents, Rally wheels with trim rings and bright center hubs, and Rally nameplates.

1979 Camaro Rally Sport coupe (CP)

CAMARO — SERIES 1F — SIX/V-8 — A new Berlinetta version, promoted as the "new way to take your pulse," took the place of the former Type LT Camaro. Berlinettas had body pinstriping, a bright grille, and black rocker panels. Camaros got a new instrument panel and anti-theft steering column. The performance Z28 had new flared front wheel openings as well as a three-piece front air dam that wrapped around the sides, up into wheel openings. Z28 also had a blackout front end with center grille emblem. Its identifying decal moved from the front fender to the door. Both Z28 and Rally Camaros had a standard rear spoiler (but 81 examples were produced without one). The spoiler was a common option on other models. New radio options included a CB, cassette player or clock built into an AM/FM stereo. Both mast and windshield antennas were available. The base 250 cu. in. (4.1-liter) inline six had a lower axle ratio this year to raise gas mileage. Both 305 and 350 cu. in. V-8s were available. Only

1979 Camaro Berlinetta Sport Coupe (CH)

2,438 Camaros were produced with a performance axle ratio, while 33,584 had the optional removable glass roof panels. Camaro standard equipment included power steering, Delco Freedom battery, front stabilizer bar, concealed two-speed windshield wipers, carpeting, heater/defroster, front bucket seats, center dome light, four-spoke sport steering wheel, day/night mirror, and FR78 x 14 steel-belted radial tires. The Berlinetta added whitewall tires on color-keyed custom styled wheels, body-color sport mirrors (left one remote- controlled), dual pinstripes, chrome headlamp bezels, soft fascia bumper systems (front and rear), bright windshield and back window moldings, and argent rear-panel applique. Camaro Z28 came with a standard 350 cu. in. four-barrel V-8; four-speed close-ratio manual gearbox; simulated hood air scoop (bolt-on, with black throat); black windshield and back window moldings; plus two-tone striping on front fenders and flares, air dam, door panels and rear deck panel. Also on Z28: front fender air louvers; body-color spoilers (front and rear); black grille, headlamp/taillamp bezels, rear end panel, and license mount; body-color sport mirrors, door handle inserts and back bumper; and white-letter P225/70R15 steel-belted tires on body-color 7 in. wheels.

1979 Malibu Classic Landau Coupe (CP)

MALIBU — SERIES 1A — V-6/V-8 — Buyers may have been promised "a fresh new slice of apple pie," but mid-size Chevrolets didn't change much this year. Both Malibu and Malibu Classic had a new checkered-look horizontally-divided grille, along with new taillamps, for their second season in downsized form. The grille was actually in four horizontal sections, each one divided into two rows. Parking lamps and single rectangular headlamps were structured as in 1978. Base engine was again the 200 cu. in. (3.3-liter) V-6, with an optional 305 cu. in. (5.0-liter) V-8. But one other option was added: a small-block 267 cu. in. (4.4-liter) V-8. Like other Chevrolet engines, Malibu's gained improvements in the EGR system and cold-trapped spark control system. Malibu came in Landau and sport coupe form, as well as sedans, Classic and Estate wagons. There was also a Special Equipment Order police car this year, succeeding the popular Nova police vehicle that had come into existence during the 1973-74 energy crisis. A total of 849 Malibus were built with the optional power sky roof, while 8,300 had the F41 sport suspension and 1,903 carried the MM4 four-speed transmission. Standard equipment included the 200 cu. in. V-6, three-speed manual shift, High Energy ignition, front stabilizer bar, heater/defroster, concealed wipers, inside day/night mirror, inside hood release, and locking glove compartment. Malibu Classic and Landau added dual horns and a special acoustical package. Malibu Classic models now carried an identifying script on the dashboard. Malibu Landau had a vinyl roof and silver sport wheel covers. Wagons had power brakes, wheel opening moldings, and full wheel covers.

1979 Monte Carlo Sport Coupe (CH)

MONTE CARLO — SERIES 1A — V-6/V-8 — Monte had a new grille with tight crosshatch pattern this year. Restyled wraparound angular side marker lamps and park/signal lamps were housed in a single bright bezel with horizontal divider bars. Taillamps were divided into three sections by vertical bars, with backup lenses in the section nearest the center. Body changes also included wide, bright lower body molding extensions. Landau models showed a new canopy-type roof with bright moldings behind the rear quarter windows. Seats had new cloth and vinyl fabrics. Like Malibu, Monte added a new engine possibility: the small-block 267 cu. in. (4.4-liter) V-8. Base engine was still the 200 cu. in. (3.3-liter) V-6. Also optional: a 231 V-6 and 305 V-8. All Montes came with standard front/rear stabilizer bars, heater/defroster, concealed wipers, electric clock, day/night mirror, locking glove compartment, dual horns, and P205/70R14 steel-belted radial tires. The 200 cu. in. V-6 and three-speed manual shift were standard, with manual brakes and steering. Monte Landaus had an automatic transmission, power brakes and steering, vinyl canopy roof, bodyside and rear striping, bright body sill moldings, visor vanity mirror (right side), and twin sport mirrors (left remote- controlled). A total of 7,830 Montes came with the optional power sky roof; 10,764 with removable glass roof panels.

1979 Caprice Classic sedan (CH)

IMPALA/CAPRICE CLASSIC — SERIES 1B — SIX/V-8 — Full-size appearance changes for 1979 included front and rear refinements plus more subtle differences in side view. Impalas, as usual, had several styling differences to separate them from the costlier Caprice: a new "ladder" style grille with wide, squat holes; restyled park/signal lamps (inset in the bumper); narrow side marker lamps with horizontal dividers; and front fender end caps. Otherwise, the two full-size models remained similar, available in the same body styles: Sport coupe, Landau coupe, four-door sedan, and two- or three-seat wagon. Impala cost about $300 less than Caprice. Caprice's new grille, with wide-hole crosshatch pattern, was separated into ten side-by-side segments by dominant vertical bars. As before, the pattern repeated in slots below the bumper rub strip. Front fender extensions were reinforced fiberglass, molded continuously with the grille header for a full-width, flowing appearance. Front side marker lamps now had horizontal strip dividers. At the rear, Caprice had wider three-section taillamp clusters with a central Caprice crest. Backup lenses sat below each taillamp cluster. Both Impala and Caprice rear side marker lamps were restyled, with horizontal grid detailing. Both continued their quad rectangular headlamps. Base engine remained the 250 cu. in. (4.1-liter) inline six, which added five horsepower this year and ran a lower axle ratio than before. Wagons carried a standard 305 cu. in. (5.0-liter) V-8, which dropped from 145 to 130 horsepower. New, paler body colors were offered this year, including soft blues, greens and browns. Radios could have built-in tape players or CB transceivers. All full-size Chevrolets came with automatic transmission, power steering and brakes, Freedom battery, front stabilizer bar, heater/defroster, concealed two-speed wipers, carpeting, inside hood release, day/night mirror, locking glove compartment, and FR78 x 15 fiberglass-belted blackwall radial tires. Coupes had automatic front seatback locks. Caprice Classic added dual horns and wheel opening moldings. Caprice Classic Landau coupe added twin sport mirrors (left remote-controlled), a vinyl roof, and bodyside pinstriping. Impala's Landau coupe added a vinyl roof, wheel opening moldings, and bodyside pinstriping.

I.D. DATA: Chevrolet again used a 13-symbol Vehicle Identification Number (VIN), on a pad atop the dashboard, visible through the windshield. Coding was similar to 1978. Under Series, code 'S' now indicated Camaro Berlinetta rather than LT. Code '77' under body/style was dropped. Model year code changed to '9' for 1979. Engine codes were as follows: 'E' L4-97.6 2Bbl.; 'O' L4-97.6 H.O.; 'V' L4-151 2Bbl.; 'C' V6196 2Bbl.; 'A' V6200 2Bbl.; 'M' V6200 2Bbl.; 'A' V6231 2Bbl.; 'D' L6250 1Bbl.; 'J' V8267 2Bbl.; 'G' V8305 2Bbl.; 'H' V8305 4Bbl.; 'L' V8350 4Bbl. Under assembly plants, code '2' for St. Therese, Quebec was dropped; code 'A' for Lakewood, GA added.

CHEVETTE (FOUR)

Model Number	Body/Style Number	Body Type & Seating	Factory Price	Shipping Weight 1978	Production Total
1T	B08	2-dr. Hatch Cpe-4P	3794		136,145
1T	B68	4-dr. Hatch Sed-4P	3914	2057	208,865

CHEVETTE SCOOTER (FOUR)

1T	J08	2-dr. Hatch Cpe-4P	3299	1929	24,099

MONZA (FOUR/V-6/V-8)

1H	M07	2-dr. Hatch 2+2-4P	3844	2630	56,871
1H	M27	2-dr. Cpe-4P	3617	2577	61,110
1H	M15	2-dr. Sta Wag-4P	3974	2631	15,190

MONZA SPORT (FOUR/V-6/V-8)

1H	R07	2-dr. Hatch 2+2-4P	4291	2676	30,662

Monza Engine Note: Prices shown are for four-cylinder engine. The 196 cu. in. V-6 cost $160 extra; the 305 V-8 cost $395. Only 8,180 Monzas had a V-8 engine.

NOVA (SIX/V-8)

1X	X27	2-dr. Cpe-6P	3955/4190	3135/3265	36,800
1X	X17	2-dr. Hatch-6P	4118/4353	3264/3394	4,819
1X	X69	4-dr. Sedan-6P	4055/4290	3179/3309	40,883

NOVA CUSTOM (SIX/V-8)

1X	Y27	2-dr. Cpe-6P	4164/4399	3194/3324	7,529
1X	Y69	4-dr. Sedan-6P	4264/4499	3228/3358	7,690

CAMARO (SIX/V-8)

1F	Q87	2-dr. Spt Cpe-4P	4677/4912	3305/3435	111,357
1F	Q87/Z85	2-dr. Rally Cpe-4P	5073/5308	N/A	19,101

CAMARO BERLINETTA (SIX/V-8)

1F	S87	2-dr. Spt Cpe-4P	5396/5631	3358/3488	67,236

CAMARO Z28 (V-8)

1F	Q87/Z28	2-dr. Spt Cpe-4P	-- /6115	-- / N/A	84,877

MALIBU (V-6/V-8)

1A	T27	2-dr. Spt Cpe-6P	4398/4588	2983/3111	41,848
1A	T19	4-dr. Sed-6P	4498/4688	2988/3116	59,674
1A	T35	4-dr. Sta Wag-6P	4745/4935	3155/3297	50,344

MALIBU CLASSIC (V-6/V-8)

1A	W27	2-dr. Spt Cpe-6P	4676/4866	3017/3145	60,751
1A	W27/Z03	2-dr. Lan Cpe-6P	4915/5105	N/A	25,213
1A	W19	4-dr. Sed-6P	4801/4991	3024/3152	104,222
1A	W35	4-dr. Sta Wag-6P	4955/5145	3183/3325	70,095

MONTE CARLO (V-6/V-8)

1A	Z37	2-dr. Spt Cpe-6P	4995/5185	3039/3169	225,073
1A	Z37/Z03	2-dr. Lan Cpe-6P	5907/6097	N/A	91,850

Malibu/Monte Carlo Engine Note: V-8 prices are for the small-block 267; the 305 V-8 cost $105 more. Only 3,812 Malibus had the 350 V-8 (code LM1).

1979 Impala Sport Coupe (CP)

IMPALA (SIX/V-8)

1B	L47	2-dr. Spt Cpe-6P	5497/5732	3495/3606	26,589
1B	L47/Z03	2-dr. Lan Cpe-6P	5961/6196	N/A	3,247
1B	L69	4-dr. Sedan-6P	5597/5832	3513/3624	172,717
1B	L35	4-dr. Sta Wag-6P	-- /6109	-- /4013	39,644
1B	L35/AQ4	4-dr. 3S Wag-8P	-- /6239	-- /4045	28,710

CAPRICE CLASSIC (SIX/V-8)

1B	N47	2-dr. Spt Cpe-6P	5837/6072	3535/3649	36,629
1B	N47/Z03	2-dr. Lan Cpe-6P	6234/6469	N/A	21,824
1B	N69	4-dr. Sedan-6P	5962/6197	3564/3675	203,017
1B	N35	4-dr. Sta Wag-6P	-- /6389	-- /4056	23,568
1B	N35/AQ4	4-dr. 3S Wag-8P	-- /6544	-- /4088	32,693

FACTORY PRICE AND WEIGHT NOTE: Where two prices and weights are shown, the figure to the left of the slash is for six-cylinder model, to right of slash for V-8. Body/Style No. Note: Some models are actually option packages. Figure after the slash (e.g., Z03) is the number of the option package that comes with the model listed.

ENGINE DATA: BASE FOUR (Chevette): Inline. Overhead cam. Four-cylinder. Cast iron block and head. Displacement: 97.6 cu. in. (1.6 liters). Bore & stroke: 3.23 x 2.98 in. Compression ratio: 8.6:1. Brake horsepower: 70 at 5200 R.P.M. Torque: 82 lbs.-ft. at 2400 R.P.M. Five main bearings. Hydraulic valve lifters. Carburetor: 2Bbl. Holley 5210C. VIN Code: E. OPTIONAL HIGH-OUTPUT FOUR (Chevette): Same as above

except Brake H.P.: 74 at 5200 R.P.M. Torque: 88 lbs.-ft. at 2800 R.P.M. VIN Code: O. BASE FOUR (Monza): Inline. Overhead valve. Four-cylinder. Cast iron block. Displacement: 151 cu. in. (2.5 liters). Bore & stroke: 4.00 x 3.00 in. Compression ratio: 8.3:1. Brake horsepower: 90 at 4000 R.P.M. Torque: 128 lbs.-ft. at 2400 R.P.M. Five main bearings. Hydraulic valve lifters. Carburetor: 2Bbl. Rochester 2SE. VIN Code: V. OPTIONAL V-6 (Monza): 90-degree, overhead-valve V-6. Cast iron block and head. Displacement: 196 cu. in. (3.2 liters). Bore & stroke: 3.50 x 3.40 in. Compression ratio: 8.0:1. Brake horsepower: 105 at 4000 R.P.M. Torque: 160 lbs.-ft. at 2000 R.P.M. Four main bearings. Hydraulic valve lifters. Carburetor: 2Bbl. Rochester M2ME. VIN Code: C. BASE V-6 (Malibu, Monte Carlo): 90-degree, overhead-valve V-6. Cast iron block and head. Displacement: 200 cu. in. (3.3 liters). Bore & stroke: 3.50 x 3.48 in. Compression ratio: 8.2:1. Brake horsepower: 94 at 4000 R.P.M. Torque: 154 lbs.-ft. at 2000 R.P.M. Four main bearings. Hydraulic valve lifters. Carburetor: 2Bbl. Rochester M2ME. VIN Code: M. OPTIONAL V-6 (Monza, Malibu, Monte Carlo): 90-degree, overhead-valve V-6. Cast iron block and head. Displacement: 231 cu. in. (3.8 liters). Bore & stroke: 3.80 x 3.40 in. Compression ratio: 8.0:1. Brake horsepower: 115 at 3800 R.P.M. Torque: 190 lbs.-ft. at 2000 R.P.M. Four main bearings. Hydraulic valve lifters. Carburetor: 2Bbl. Rochester M2ME. VIN Code: A. BASE SIX (Nova, Camaro, Impala, Caprice): Inline. OHV. Six-cylinder. Cast iron block and head. Displacement: 250 cu. in. (4.1 liters). Bore & stroke: 3.88 x 3.53 in. Compression ratio: 8.0:1. Brake horsepower: 115 at 3800 R.P.M. Torque: 200 lbs.-ft. at 1600 R.P.M. Seven main earings. Hydraulic valve lifters. Carburetor: 1Bbl. Rochester 1ME. VIN Code: D. OPTIONAL V-8 (Malibu, Monte Carlo); 90-degree, overhead valve V-8. Cast iron block and head. Displacement: 267 cu. in. (4.4 liters). Bore & stroke: 3.50 x 3.48 in. Compression ratio: 8.2:1. Brake horsepower: 125 at 3800 R.P.M. Torque: 215 lbs.-ft. at 2400 R.P.M. Five main bearings. Hydraulic valve lifters. Carburetor: 2Bbl. Rochester M2MC. VIN Code: J. BASE V-8 (Impala/Caprice wagon); OPTIONAL (Monza, Nova, Camaro, Impala, Caprice): 90-degree, overhead valve V-8. Cast iron block and head. Displacement: 305 cu. in. (5.0 liters). Bore & stroke: 3.74 x 3.48 in. Compression ratio: 8.4:1. Brake horsepower: 130 at 3200 R.P.M. Torque: 245 lbs.-ft. at 2000 R.P.M. Five main bearings. Hydraulic valve lifters. Carburetor: 2Bbl. Rochester M2MC. VIN Code: G. OPTIONAL V-8 (Malibu, Monte Carlo): 90-degree, overhead valve V-8. Cast iron block and head. Displacement: 305 cu. in. (5.0 liters). Bore & stroke: 3.74 x 3.48 in. Compression ratio: 8.4:1. Brake horsepower: 160 at 4000 R.P.M. Torque: 235 lbs.-ft. at 2400 R.P.M. Five main bearings. Hydraulic valve lifters. Carburetor: 4Bbl. Rochester M4MC. VIN Code: H. OPTIONAL V-8 (Nova, Malibu wagon, Impala, Caprice): 90-degree, overhead valve V-8. Cast iron block and head. Displacement: 350 cu. in. (5.7 liters). Bore & stroke: 4.00 x 3.48 in. Compression ratio: 8.2:1. Brake horsepower: 165-170 at 3800 R.P.M. Torque: 260-270 lbs.-ft. at 2400 R.P.M. Five main bearings. Hydraulic valve lifters. Carburetor: 4Bbl. Rochester M4MC. VIN Code: L. BASE V-8 (Camaro Z28); OPTIONAL (Camaro): Same as 350 V-8 above but Brake H.P.: 175 at 4000 R.P.M. Torque: 270 lbs.-ft. at 2400 R.P.M.

CHASSIS DATA: Dimensions same as 1978, except Chevette Scooter overall length, 158.8 in. New Camaro Berlinetta had same dimensions as prior Type LT. Chevette tires were now 155/80R13 GBR.

TECHNICAL: Transmission: Three-speed manual transmission standard on Camaro, Nova, and Malibu/Monte six. Gear ratios: (1st) 3.50:1; (2nd) 1.89:1; (3rd) 1.00:1; (Rev) 3.62:1. Four-speed floor shift standard on Chevette: (1st) 3.75:1; (2nd) 2.16:1; (3rd) 1.38:1; (4th) 1.00:1; (Rev) 3.82:1. Four-speed floor shift standard on Monza four and V-6: (1st) 3.50:1; (2nd) 2.48:1; (3rd) 1.66:1; (4th) 1.00:1; (Rev) 3.50:1. Four-speed floor shift standard on Monza/Camaro/Nova (V8305) and Camaro 350, optional on Malibu/Monza/Monte: (1st) 2.85:1; (2nd) 2.02:1; (3rd) 1.35:1; (4th) 1.00:1; (Rev) 2.85:1. Four-speed on Malibu V8267: (1st) 3.11:1; (2nd) 2.20:1; (3rd) 1.47:1; (4th) 1.00:1; (Rev) 3.11:1. Camaro Z28 four-speed floor shift: (1st) 2.64:1; (2nd) 1.75:1; (3rd) 1.34:1; (4th) 1.00:1; (Rev) 2.55:1. Five-speed floor shift available on Monza: (1st) 3.40:1; (2nd) 2.08:1; (3rd) 1.39:1; (4th) 1.00:1; (5th) 0.80:1; (Rev) 3.36:1. Three-speed Turbo Hydra- matic standard on Monte Carlo Landau and Caprice/Impala, optional on others. Gear ratios: (1st) 2.52:1; (2nd) 1.52:1; (3rd) 1.00:1; (Rev) 1.93:1 except Caprice/Impala V8305, Monza four and some Malibu six ratios: (1st) 2.74:1; (2nd) 1.57:1; (3rd) 1.00:1; (Rev) 2.07:1. Chevette four automatic trans.: (1st) 2.40:1; (2nd) 1.48:1; (3rd) 1.00:1; (Rev) 1.92:1. Standard final drive ratio: (Chevette) 3.70:1; (Monza four) 2.73:1 or 2.93:1 w/4-spd, 3.08:1 w/5-spd, 2.73:1 w/auto.; (Monza V-6) 2.73:1 exc. 2.93:1 w/5-spd; (Monza V-8) 3.08:1 w/4-spd, 2.29:1 w/auto.; (Nova) 2.56:1 w/six, 3.08:1 w/V-8 and 4-spd, 2.41:1 w/V-8 and auto.; (Camaro six) 2.56:1; (Camaro V-8) 3.08:1 w/4spd, 2.41:1 or 3.08:1 w/auto.; (Z28) 3.73:1 w/4spd, 3.42:1 w/auto.; (Malibu six) 2.73:1; (Malibu V-8) 2.29:1 exc. 2.73:1 w/auto.; (Malibu V-8 wag) 2.56:1 or 2.41:1; (Monte V-6) 2.73:1 or 2.41:1; (Monte V-8) 2.29:1; (Capr/Imp six) 2.56:1; (Capr/Imp V-8) 2.41:1 exc. Steering: (Chevette) rack and pinion; (others) recirculating ball. Suspension/Body: same as 1976-78. Brakes: front disc, rear drum. Fuel tank: (Chevette) 12.5 gal.; (Monza) 18.5 gal.; (Monza wag) 15 gal.; (Nova/Camaro) 21 gal.; (Malibu/Monte) 18.1 gal.; (Caprice/Imp) 20.7 gal.; (Caprice/Imp wag) 22 gal.

DRIVETRAIN OPTIONS: Engines: 1.6-liter H.O. four: Chevette ($60). 196 cu. in., 2Bbl. V-6: Monza ($160). 231 cu. in., 2Bbl. V-6: Monza ($200); Malibu ($40); Monte ($30). 267 cu. in., 2Bbl. V-8: Malibu/Monte ($190). 305 cu. in., 2Bbl. V-8: Monza ($395); Nova/Camaro ($235); Imp/Caprice cpe/sed ($235). 305 cu. in., 4Bbl. V-8: Malibu/Monte ($295). 350 cu. in., 4Bbl. V-8: Nova/Camaro ($360); Malibu wag ($360); Imp/Capr cpe/sed ($360); Imp/Capr wag ($125). Transmission/Differential: Four-speed manual shift: Nova (NC); Camaro/Malibu ($135). Close-ratio four-speed manual: Camaro (NC). Five-speed manual shift: Monza ($175). Turbo Hydra-matic: Chvt/Monza ($295); Nova/Camaro/Malibu/Monte ($335); Camaro Z28 ($59). Sport shifter: Chvt ($30). Positraction axle: Monza ($60); Nova/Camaro ($64); Malibu/Monte ($65); Imp/Capr ($68). Performance axle ratio: Monza ($17); Nova/Camaro/Malibu/Monte ($18); Imp/Capr ($19). Power Accessories: Power brakes: Chvt/Monza ($71); Nova/Camaro/Monte, Malibu cpe/sed ($76). Power steering: Monza ($146); Nova/Malibu/Monte ($163). Suspension: F40 H.D. susp.: Nova ($11-$36); Malibu cpe/sed, Monte ($22); Imp/Capr ($23). F41 sport susp.: Chvt ($33); Monza ($31); Nova ($45); Camaro, Malibu cpe/sed ($41); Imp/Capr cpe/sed ($42). Superlift rear shock absorbers: Imp/Capr ($56). Front stabilizer bar: Monza ($27). Other: Heavy-duty radiator ($31-$33) exc. Imp/Capr ($42). H.D. alternator (63-amp): Malibu/Monte ($5-$33); Imp/Capr ($34). H.D. battery ($19-$21). California emission system ($83) exc. Monza four ($150). High altitude emission ($35).

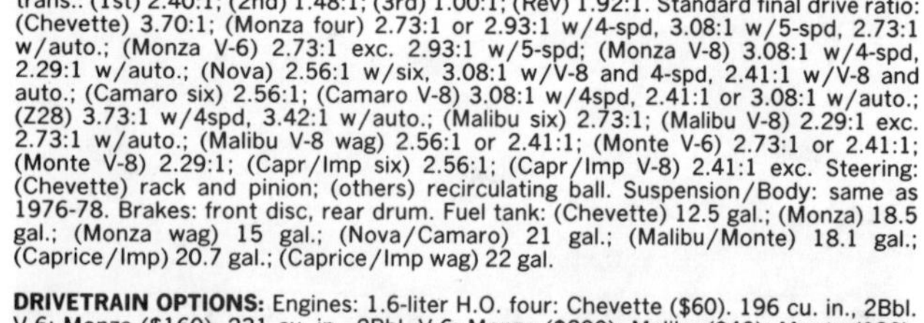

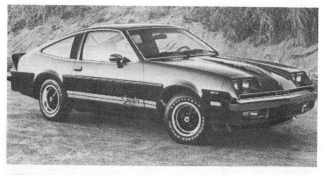

1979 Monza Sport Spyder 2+2 hatchback (CH)

CHEVETTE/MONZA CONVENIENCE/APPEARANCE OPTIONS: Option Packages: Spyder equipment pkg.: Monza ($164). Spyder appearance pkg.: Monza ($231). Quiet sound group: Chvt ($35-$47); Monza ($29-$39). Auto. shoulder belt convenience group: Chvt ($144-$166). Deluxe appointment group (quiet sound, aux. lighting, clock): Chvt ($94-$137). Comfort/Convenience: Air conditioning ($496). Rear defogger, electric ($87). Tinted glass: Chvt ($60). Comfortilt steering wheel ($68). Special instrumentation (incl. tach): Chvt ($67); Monza ($50-$88). Electric clock ($21). Digital clock: Monza ($49). Cigarette lighter: Scooter ($7). Intermittent wipers ($35). Lighting and Mirrors: Aux. lighting: Chvt ($37-$44); Monza ($20-$37). Driver's remote sport mirror: Chvt ($25). Twin sport mirrors, left remote ($40). Day/night mirror ($10). Entertainment: AM radio: Scooter ($74). AM/FM radio: Chvt/Monza ($74); Scooter ($148). AM/FM stereo radio ($148). AM/FM stereo radio w/digital clock: Monza ($299). Stereo tape player w/AM radio: Monza ($159). Cassette or 8track player with AM/FM stereo radio: Monza ($242). Rear speaker ($23). Exterior Trim: Removable sunroof: Monza ($180). Cabriolet vinyl roof: Monza ($156) incl. opera windows. Spoilers, front/rear: Monza ($97). Deluxe exterior (wheel opening, side window and rocker panel moldings): Chvt ($104). Tri-tone sport stripes: Chvt ($70). Sport striping: Monza wag ($84). Bodyside moldings: Scooter ($40). Wheel opening moldings: Monza ($21). Side window reveal moldings: Chvt ($67). Door edge guards ($12-$19). Roof carrier ($65). Rear air deflector: Monza ($28). Deluxe bumpers, front/rear: Scooter ($37). Bumper guards, front/rear: Chvt ($41-$78); Monza ($42); std. on wag. Interior Trim/Upholstery: Console: Monza cpe ($75). Bucket seats (sport cloth): Chvt ($11-$21). Knit cloth bucket seats: Monza ($21). Custom Chevette interior pkg. w/bucket seats: cloth ($181); vinyl ($160). Custom vinyl bucket seats: Monza ($159) exc. Sport (NC). Custom cloth bucket seats: Monza ($180) exc. Sport ($21). Folding rear seat: Monza ($97) but std. on 2+2. Rear seat delete: Chvt ($51 credit). Load floor carpet: Chvt ($21). Color-keyed floor mats ($21). Automatic shoulder belts: Chvt ($50). Deluxe seatbelts ($21). Wheels and Tires: Rally II wheels: Monza ($45-$88). Color- keyed deluxe wheel covers: Monza ($13-$43). Sport wheel covers: Chvt ($45). Wheel trim rings: Scooter ($37). 155/8013 GBR WSW: Scooter ($37). 155/8013 SBR BSW: Chvt ($11); Scooter ($42). 155/8013 SBR WSW: Chvt ($42); Scooter ($79). 155/8013 SBR WLT: Chvt ($55); Scooter ($92). B78 x 13 WSW: Monza ($19) exc. wag. (NC). BR70 x 13 SBR BSW: Monza ($137) exc. Spyder/wag (NC). BR70 x 13 SBR WSW: Monza ($138- $189). BR70 x 13 SBR WLT: Monza ($50-$205).

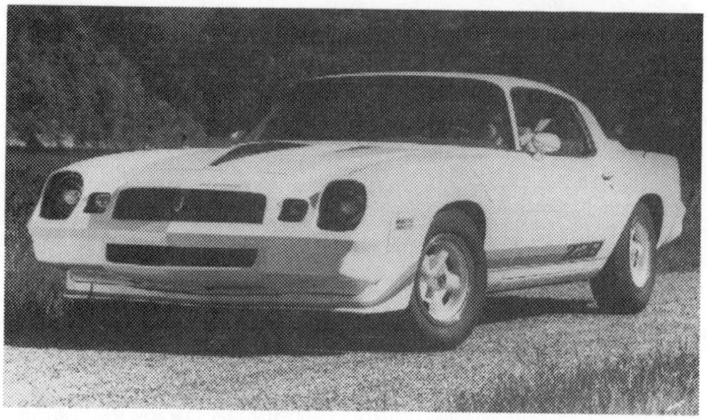

1979 Camaro Z28 Sport Coupe (CH)

NOVA/CAMARO/MALIBU/MONTE CARLO CONVENIENCE/APPEARANCE OPTIONS: Option Packages: Rally equipment: Nova ($211). Estate equipment: Malibu wag ($258). Interior decor/quiet sound group: Camaro ($64); std. on Berlinetta. Quiet sound group: Malibu ($51). Value appearance group (roof drip, side window and wheel opening moldings): Nova ($79). Security pkg.: Malibu wag ($37). Comfort/Convenience: Air conditioning: Nova/Camaro ($529- $562); Malibu/Monte ($562). Rear defogger (forced-air): Nova/Malibu ($55). Rear defogger (electric): Camaro/Malibu/Monte ($99). Cruise-master speed control ($103). Tinted glass: Camaro ($64); Malibu/Monte ($70). Comfortilt steering wheel ($75). Six-way power driver's seat: Malibu/Monte ($163). Power windows: Nova ($126-$178); Camaro/Monte ($132); Malibu ($132-$187). Power door locks: Nova/Malibu ($80-$120); Camaro/Monte ($86). Power trunk release: Malibu/Monte ($24). Power tailgate release: Malibu wag ($25). Electric clock: Nova, base Camaro ($23); Malibu ($23). Special instrumentation: Nova, base Camaro ($112); Malibu ($125); Monte ($102). Econominder gauge pkg.: Nova ($53). Gauge pkg.: Malibu ($57); Monte ($34). Intermittent wipers ($38). Lighting, Horns and Mirrors: Aux. lighting ($31-$56). Dome reading light: Malibu/Monte ($20). Dual horns: Nova/Camaro, base Malibu ($9). Remote-control driver's mirror: Nova/Malibu/Monte ($18). Twin sport mirrors (left remote): Nova, base Camaro, Malibu/Monte ($43). Twin remote sport mirrors: Malibu/Monte ($68); Monte Lan ($25). Day/night mirror: Nova ($11). Visor vanity mirror: Malibu/Monte ($5). Lighted visor mirror: Malibu ($40); Monte ($35-$40). Entertainment: AM radio ($82-$85). AM/FM radio ($158). AM/FM stereo radio ($232). AM/FM stereo radio w/digital clock: Nova/Malibu ($395); Camaro ($372-$395). Stereo tape player w/AM radio ($244-$248). Stereo 8track tape player with AM/FM stereo radio ($335). Cassette player with AM/FM stereo radio ($341). AM/FM/CB radio: Camaro/Malibu/Monte ($489). AM/FM stereo radio w/CB: Camaro/Malibu/Monte ($570). Rear speaker ($25). Dual front speakers: Malibu/Monte ($21). Windshield antenna ($27); incl. w/radios. Power antenna: Camaro/Malibu/Monte ($47). Exterior Trim: Removable glass roof panels: Camaro/Monte ($655). Power sky roof: Malibu cpe/sed, Monte ($529). Vinyl roof: Nova ($99); Camaro ($112); Malibu ($116); Monte ($131). Cabriolet roof: Nova ($190). Rear spoiler: Camaro Berlinetta ($58). Style trim pkg.: Camaro ($73). Two-tone paint: Nova ($55); Malibu ($67-$115); Monte ($120-$160). Swing-out rear side windows: Nova ($59). Bodyside moldings: Nova/Camaro ($43). Deluxe bodyside moldings: Nova/Malibu/Monte ($53). Door edge guards ($13-$21). Bright rocker moldings and extensions: Nova ($15-$37). Bright sill moldings: Monte ($44). Wheel opening moldings: Nova, Malibu cpe/sed ($23). Wide wheel opening moldings: Nova ($39). Side window sill moldings: Monte ($33). Side window reveal moldings: Nova/Malibu ($41). Roof drip moldings: Nova ($20); Camaro ($24). Bodyside pinstriping: Nova ($30); Malibu ($48); Monte ($40). Rear window air deflector: Malibu wag ($30). Roof carrier: Malibu wag ($90). Bumper rub strips: Malibu ($41). Bumper rub strips and guards, front/rear: Nova ($79). Bumper guards, front/rear: Malibu ($46). Interior Trim/Upholstery: Interior decor pkg.: base Nova ($31). Console ($80). Vinyl bench seat: Malibu cpe/sed, Monte ($26). Sport cloth bench seat: Nova ($23); Malibu (NC). Knit cloth bench seat: Malibu wag ($28). Custom vinyl bench seat: Nova (NC). Custom vinyl bucket seats: Nova ($85); Camaro ($307). Vinyl bucket seats: Malibu cpe/sed, Monte ($85). Cloth bucket seats: Monte ($85). Sport cloth bucket seats: Camaro ($23). Custom knit cloth bucket seats: Camaro Berlinetta ($23); base Camaro ($330). Knit cloth 50/50 seating: Malibu cpe/sed ($172); Malibu wag ($198). Vinyl 50/50 seating: Malibu cpe/sed ($198); Malibu wag ($172). Custom cloth 55/45 seating: Monte ($368). Adj. driver's seatback: Camaro ($23). Litter container: Malibu/Monte ($8). Color-keyed mats ($23). Deluxe load-floor carpet: Malibu ($70). Deluxe seatbelts ($21-$23). Deluxe trunk trim: Malibu/Monte ($43). Wheels and Tires: Aluminum wheels: Camaro ($172-$315). Custom styled wheels: Camaro ($100-$143). Rally wheels: Nova ($88); Camaro ($93) but std. on Rally; Malibu ($47-$90); Monte

($47). Wire wheel covers: Nova ($130); Malibu ($65-$160); Monte ($117); Monte Landau ($65). Full wheel covers: Nova/Camaro/Malibu ($43). Sport wheel covers (silver or gold): Malibu ($52-$95). E78 x 14 BSW: Camaro ($95-$119 credit). E78 x 14 WSW: Nova ($38-$47); Camaro ($58-$72 credit). FR78 x 14 SBR: Nova ($96-$119). FR78 x 14 SBR WSW: Nova ($135-$168); Camaro ($40-$49). FR78 x 14 SBR WLT: Nova ($148-$184); Camaro ($52-$65); Berlinetta ($13-$16). P185/75R14 GBR WSW: Malibu cpe/sed ($40). P195/75R14 GBR WSW: Malibu wag ($41). P195/75R14 SBR WSW: Malibu cpe/sed ($102). P205/70R14 SBR WSW: Monte ($44); Malibu cpe/sed ($149). Stowaway spare: Nova ($19); Camaro (NC).

IMPALA/CAPRICE CONVENIENCE/APPEARANCE OPTIONS: Option Packages: Estate equipment: wag ($262). Value appearance group: bodyside and wheel opening moldings, full wheel covers ($87). Comfort/Convenience: Four season air cond. ($605). Comfortron auto-temp air cond. ($688). Rear defogger, forced-air: cpe/sed ($57). Rear defogger, electric ($101). Cruise-Master speed control ($108). Tinted glass ($84). Comfortilt steering wheel ($77). Power door locks ($88-$122). Six-way power driver's seat ($166). Power windows ($122-$205). Power trunk release ($25). Power tailgate lock: wag ($40). Electric clock: Imp ($24). Digital clock: Imp ($55); Caprice ($31). Gauge pkg. ($54). Intermittent wipers ($39). Quiet sound group: Imp ($56). Lighting, Horns and Mirrors: Aux. lighting ($35-$50). Dual horns: Imp ($10). Driver's remote mirror ($19). Dual remote mirrors ($56). Dual sport mirrors, left remote ($44). Dual remote sport mirrors, body-color ($69) exc. Lan ($25). Visor vanity mirror ($6). Lighted visor mirror ($41). Entertainment: AM radio ($87). AM/FM radio ($161). AM/FM stereo radio ($236); w/digital clock, Imp ($401). Stereo tape player with AM radio ($265); with AM/FM stereo radio ($340). Cassette player with AM/FM stereo ($346). AM/FM/CB radio and power antenna ($503). AM/FM stereo with CB and power antenna ($578). Rear speaker ($26). Dual front speakers ($22). Power antenna ($48). Windshield antenna ($28); incl. w/radios. Exterior Trim: Power sky roof: cpe/sed ($625). Vinyl roof: cpe/sed ($145). Two-tone paint ($56). Custom two-tone ($87- $120). Pinstriping ($33). Color-keyed bodyside moldings ($44). Door edge guards ($14-$21). Wheel opening moldings ($23). Bumper rub strips ($56). Bumper guards ($52). Interior Trim/Upholstery: Vinyl bench seat: cpe/sed ($27). Sport or knit cloth bench seat: wag ($27). Vinyl 50/50 seat ($240-$267). Knit cloth 50/50 seat: cpe/sed ($240); wag ($267). Special custom cloth 50/50 seat: cpe/sed ($397). Deluxe load-floor carpet: wag ($75). Deluxe cargo area carpet: wag ($107). Color-keyed mats ($24). Litter container ($8). Color-keyed seatbelts ($24-$27). Deluxe trunk trim ($46). Wheel Covers: Full wheel covers ($44). Sport wheel covers: Imp ($98); Caprice ($54). Wire wheel covers ($120). Coupe/Sedan Tires: FR78 x 15 GBR WSW ($49). FR78 x 15 SBR BSW ($52). FR78 x 15 SBR WSW ($101). GR78 x 15 SBR WSW ($131). GR70 x 15 SBR WSW ($155). Wagon Tires: HR78 x 15 SBR WSW ($55).

HISTORY: Introduced: Sept. 28, 1978. Model year production (U.S.): 2,153,036 (incl. Corvettes but not incl. 44,927 Acadians and early 1980 Citations). Calendar year production: 2,238,226 (including 22,056 Sportvans, 48,568 Corvettes and 17,133 Acadians). Calendar year sales by U.S. dealers: 2,158,839 (incl. 30,630 Sportvans and 38,631 Corvettes) for a 25.9 percent market share. Model year sales by U.S. dealers: 2,257,751 (incl. 33,819 Sportvans and 39,816 Corvettes, plus 273,720 early 1980 Citations.)

Historical Footnotes: Chevrolet fared rather well this year, despite a general slowdown in the auto industry. Chevettes sold particularly well. Sales of small cars were mandatory if the division expected to reach the CAFE limit of 19 mile-per- gallon fuel economy. Chevrolet built a non-production version of a 1979 turbo injected Chevette, to study optimal performance, economy and driveability.

1980 CHEVROLET

Chevettes had a new rear-end look for 1980. An aero restyling cut the weight of full-size models. Otherwise, apart from the new front-wheel drive Citation, this was a carryover year, devoted more to technical improvements than appearance changes. The old reliable inline six-cylinder engine was gone, replaced by a V-6. Over the past few years, the entire Chevrolet line had been downsized, signaling the beginning of a new era of smaller, lighter, fuel-efficient automobiles. This year also marked the first appearance of a diesel V-8, produced by Oldsmobile and installed (for an extra $915) in full-size station wagons.

1980 Chevette hatchback coupe (AA)

CHEVETTE — SERIES 1T — FOUR — Chevette gained a new aero-styled rear end this year. Restyled rear quarters held four-lens wraparound taillamps with larger, square backup lenses. Instead of the straight angled hatch of prior years, this year's version bent several inches above the taillamps to create a more vertical rear-end look. A Chevrolet badge was on the hatch, just above the right taillamp. The grille had a new Chevrolet emblem and rectangular headlamps. Also new: a round fuel filler door, revised license plate light, improved pressure-proportioning brake system, and new passive restraint system (a two-piece lap/shoulder belt setup). Once again, Chevette came with either a standard or high-output 1.6-liter engine, both with four-speed fully-synchronized manual transmission (or optional automatic). The standard overhead-cam four had a staged two-barrel carburetor, "tuned" aluminum intake manifold, and special valve porting. The high-output version had a high-speed camshaft and dual-takedown exhaust manifold. Chevettes came in 13 body colors this

year: black, gray, red, red orange, white, bright yellow, and a selection of metallics: bright blue, dark blue, light blue, light camel, dark claret, dark green, or silver. Five two-tone combinations were available (except on the stripped-down Scooter). New to Chevette's option list: improved-wear steel- belted radial tires. Interiors held body-contoured, full foam front bucket seats that reclined (except Scooter's). Standard vinyl bucket seats came in black, camel, blue or carmine color (Scooter only in black or camel). Cloth bucket seats were available, as was a Custom interior in five two-tone combinations. All Chevettes had a built-in diagnostic connector, standard 155/80R13 glass-belted radial tires (whitewall except Scooter), "smart switch" on the steering column, Freedom battery, rack-and-pinion steering, and full coil suspension. Front disc brakes had audible wear sensors. Improved automatic-transmission driveshaft balancing this year was meant to reduce noise. Chevette's flow-through ventilation system was redesigned for increased defroster airflow. Ball joints had a visible wear indicator. Bolt-on front fenders had plastic inner shields. Standard equipment (except on Scooters) also included an AM radio, center console, wheel trim rings, bodyside and sill moldings, brushed aluminum instrument panel moldings, lighter, glove box lock, sport steering wheel, color-keyed seat/shoulder belts, and right door jamb dome light switch. All models had vinyl-coated headliner, courtesy dome light, day/night mirror, cut-pile carpeting, front stabilizer bar, bumper guards and rub strips, high-pressure compact spare tire, and removable load floor carpet.

1980 Monza Sport Spyder 2+2 hatchback coupe (CH)

MONZA — SERIES 1H — FOUR/V-6 — Apart from new black taillamp bezels and black grille center bars, Monza changed little this year. A restyled front air dam was integrated with wheel openings. Bumper guards were now standard. Emblems had a new finish. Bodyside moldings were sliced off at an angle to allow for new striping. The Spyder option included new hood decals and body stripes. Models included the 2+2 Sport hatchback, regular hatchback coupe, and notchback sedan. The station wagon was dropped, along with the V-8 option and green body color availability. Engine choices this year were the base 151 cu. in. (2.5-liter) four, or optional Buick 231 cu. in. (3.8- liter) V-6. Standard equipment included four-speed floor shift, manual front disc/rear drum brakes, A78 x 13 whitewall tires, front bucket seats, bumper guards (front/rear), vinyl bodyside moldings, AM radio, tinted glass, sport steering wheel, lighter, day/night mirror, carpeting, and Freedom battery. Monza's 2+2 hatchback added bumper rub strips, bright door frame and belt moldings, console, folding back seat, and bright/black rear quarter window moldings. The Monza Sport hatchback 2+2 with slope-back soft front end and bright-bezeled rectangular headlamps came with all the basic equipment, plus a black front air dam; bright/black windshield reveal molding; black wiper arms/blades; console; folding back seat; soft door trim panels with driver's side map pocket and armrest; bright door frame and belt moldings; body-color bumper rub strips and guards; bright/black rear quarter window and back window moldings; full wheel covers; bright-trimmed wraparound taillamps; and body-color rear end panel. This year's Spyder equipment package, priced at $521, included Rally II wheels, front/rear spoilers, stripes with Spyder inserts, F41 suspension, BR70 x 13/C blackwall tires, modified front stabilizer bar and rear shock absorbers, and a Spyder emblem on the hood header panel. Black accents went on headlamps, parking lamps and belt moldings; taillamp openings; lower rocker panel, quarter panel and front fenders; plus windshield, rear window, quarter window and door moldings. The package also included sport mirrors. A total of 7,589 Spyder packages were installed.

1980 Citation hatchback sedan (CP)

CITATION — SERIES 1X — FOUR/V-6 — Long before the model year began, in spring 1979, Chevrolet introduced the all-new front-drive Citation, described as "the most thoroughly tested new car in Chevy history." Chevrolet's General Manager Robert D. Lund called it "an affordable, functional family-type vehicle which is space efficient, economical to operate, comfortable and serviceable." Citation was claimed to offer "the exterior dimensions of a subcompact, the operating economy of a compact with a V-8, the interior room of a mid-size car and as much luggage capacity as many full-size sedans." Weighing about 2,500 pounds, it was 20 inches shorter and 800 pounds lighter than the compact Nova it replaced. Coupe, hatchback coupe and hatchback sedan models were offered, plus a sporty X11 option on both two-door models. Citation's front-drive chassis held a MacPherson strut front suspension with transverse-mounted engine and transmission, computer-selected coil springs, front

1980 Citation Club Coupe (CP)

and rear stabilizer bars, and rack-and-pinion steering. The variable-rate rear suspension used rubber jounce bumpers as load-carrying springs. Citation's mini-frame construction mounted the powertrain on a separate, bolt-on "cradle" that also served as a mount for the front suspension. In addition to producing a quieter ride, this design allowed easy servicing by replacing the entire engine/powertrain module. Standard engine was a cast iron 151 cu. in. (2.5-liter) four, rated 90 horsepower, supplied by Pontiac. Chevrolet produced the optional powerplant: the industry's first transverse-mounted V-6, a compact 60-degree 173 cu. in. (2.8-liter) design made of cast iron. That engine could fit into the same underhood area as a four. Both engines used two-stage Varajet carburetors that metered fuel into the combustion chambers according to driving needs, increasing flow when passing. Citation had single rectangular headlamps, wraparound amber marker lamps, and vertical parking lamps behind the honeycomb grille with center Chevrolet emblem. On two-tone models, bodyside moldings separated the upper and lower colors, with pinstriping on upper bodysides and fenders. A Citation nameplate was on the forward end of front fenders. Wide three-section taillamps included backup lamps in the center sections. Bodies came in 14 standard colors: beige, black, cinnabar, gray, red, silver, white, and yellow; plus six metallics (dark or light blue, light or medium camel, dark claret, or dark green). Thirteen two-tone combinations were also available. Six interior color trims were available in two trim levels. Standard vinyl bench seats came in black, camel, carmine or green. Custom vinyl and Sport and knit cloths were available, on bench or bucket seats. Citation was designed with easy servicing in mind. The cylinder head, oil pan, water pump, rear main bearing seal and engine front cover could all be removed without taking the engine out of the car. And even if it did have to come out, the mini-frame "cradle" made that job easier. Only eight bolts had to be removed, and suspension components loosened, to gain clearance for extracting the engine/transaxle unit. Both the engine and transaxle were removable separately too: the engine upward, transaxle downward. Since clutch repair on front-drives could be a problem, manual shift Citations had a constant-tension clutch cable to minimize the risk of early failure. Ball bearings at front and rear wheels were lifetime lubricated. Servicing of other components was also simplified, including the instrument panel cluster, taillamps, heater, and starter. Front fenders bolted onto the unitized body.

1980 Citation X11 hatchback coupe (CP)

Standard equipment included a four-speed manual transaxle with overdrive fourth gear, front disc/rear drum brakes (diagonal dual-braking), P185/80R13 glass-belted radial tires, front/rear stabilizer bars, compact spare tire, steel bumpers, concealed hatchback luggage compartment, dome light, and column-mounted turn signal/dimmer/wiper/washer control. Also standard: an inside hood release; locking glove box; inertia seatback latches; color-coded sliding door locks; and glass-belted radial tires. All except the base H11 coupe also had bright rocker panel, wheel opening and drip moldings; a cigarette lighter and ashtray; and pushbutton AM radio. Options included side window reveal moldings, tinted glass, remote swing-out side windows, bodyside pinstriping, full wheel covers, intermittent wipers, roof rack, tilt steering, electric rear defogger, reclining passenger seat, removable pop-up sunroof, plus bumper guards and rub strips. The X11 sport package for hatchback and club coupe included a black-accented grille; black accents on headlamp bezels, taillamps, rocker panels, door lock pillars and rear license plate pocket; decal stripes; rear spoiler; pinstriping; bright side window moldings; body-color sport mirrors; rally wheel trim; sport steering wheel; sport suspension; bumper rub strips; and white-letter P205/70R13 steel-belted radial tires. Large X11 identification was behind the door and on rear panel. X11 models could also have bucket seats, console, and special instrumentation (including tachometer, voltmeter, temp and oil pressure gauges). A total of 24,852 X11 equipment packages were installed this year.

1980 Camaro Z28 Sport Coupe (CP)

112

CAMARO — SERIES 1F — V-6/V-8 — Camaro entered 1980 wearing a new grille with tighter crosshatch pattern and offering a revised engine selection. A lighter, more economical 229 cu. in. (3.8-liter) V-6 rated 115 horsepower replaced the old familiar 250 cu. in. inline six as standard powerplant. (California Camaros carried a 231 V-6.) There was also a new 267 cu. in. (4.4-liter) optional V-8 rated 120 horsepower, plus a 305 V-8 and the Z28 350 V-8 (not available in California). Automatic transmissions had a new torque converter clutch to eliminate slippage. Rally Sport Camaros came with an all-black "thin-line" grille, while Berlinetta carried a bright grille in the same style. The standard Sport Coupe grille had an emblem in the upper corner; Berlinetta had one in the center. Berlinettas had new standard wire wheel covers. Z28 grilles had a pattern of horizontal bars, with large 'Z28' emblem in the upper corner. Z28, billed as "the maximum Camaro," also had a new (functional) hood air-intake scoop facing to the rear, with an electrically-activated flap that opened when stepping hard on the gas. A side fender port let out hot engine air, and boosted pickup at the same time. Also new to Z28: rear fender flares. Body colors this year were white, black, silver, gold, red, bright blue, dark blue, bright yellow, lime green, red orange, bronze, charcoal, dark brown, and dark claret. Standard Camaro equipment included the 229 cu. in. V-6 engine, three-speed manual transmission, P205/705R14 SBR tires, body-color front/rear bumper covers, bucket seats, console, day/night mirror, and cigarette lighter. The Berlinetta coupe had whitewall tires; bright headlamp bezels, upper/lower grille, windshield and window reveal moldings; black rocker panels; dual horns; electric clock; special instruments; quiet sound group; sport mirrors; and wire wheel covers. Z28 came with P225/70R15 white-letter tires on body-color 15 x 7 in. wheels; black headlamp bezels, upper/lower grille, and reveal moldings; sport mirrors; body-color front spoiler and front flares; a hood scoop decal; front fender louvers; rear spoiler; plus sport suspension, power brakes and four-speed manual shift. Camaro's Rally Sport package included a rear spoiler, sport suspension, black rocker panels, black grille, black headlamp bezels, bright reveal moldings, sport mirrors, plus color-keyed Rally wheels.

1980 Malibu Sport Coupe (AA)

MALIBU — SERIES 1A — V-6/V-8 — Though similar to the previous edition, Malibu sported a brighter, lightweight grille for 1980, made up of narrow vertical bars and divided by two subdued horizontal bars. Its nameplate was again in the lower corner (driver's side). Headlamps, parking lamps and side marker lamps all grew larger. At the rear were three-section wraparound taillamps with side marker lamps. New base engine was the 229 cu. in. (3.8-liter) V-6, with either a 267 (4.4-liter) or 305 (5.0-liter) V-8 optional. Wagons carried the 305 as standard; the big 350 was out of the lineup. Models included the two-door coupe, four-door sedan and four-door wagon; plus a Classic Landau. An Estate wagon package was optional. Malibu had a new, precisely controlled windshield washer (similar to Corvette's). Joining the option list: Rally wheels. The optional automatic transmission could now have a lock-up torque converter clutch. Only 202 Malibus came with a four-speed manual transmission. Malibu standard equipment included three-speed manual floor shift, front stabilizer bar, P185/75R14 tires, windshield and back window reveal moldings, roof drip moldings, day/night mirror, lighter, concealed wipers, and locking glove box. Wagons had P195/75R14 tires. Malibu Classic models added a standup hood ornament; wide wheel opening moldings; bright decklid and end cap moldings; dual horns; and full wheelcovers. The Landau coupe had sport wheel covers as well as bodyside and rear pinstriping.

1980 Monte Carlo Turbo T-top coupe (AA)

MONTE CARLO — SERIES 1A — V-6/V-8 — Monte wore a wider-spaced, heavier looking eggcrate grille this year, with 16 holes across in four rows. Also new were quad rectangular headlamps above wide rectangular parking lamps. Wraparound side marker lamps were replaced by separate horizontal lenses just ahead of the wheel, below 'Monte Carlo' script. New base engine was the Chevrolet-built 229 cu. in. (3.8-liter) V-6. But this year's option list included Buick's turbocharged 231 cu. in. V-6 that delivered 170 horsepower (compared to 115 from the base engine). Also available: 267 cu. in. (4.4-liter) and 305 (5.0-liter) V-8s, rated 120 and 155 horsepower respectively. Three-speed manual shift was dropped, so all Montes now carried three-speed Turbo Hydra-matic as well as power brakes and steering. Turbo models had a special hood with raised dome and identifying decal. A total of 13,839 turbo engines were installed for the model year. Standard Monte equipment included dual horns, day/night mirror, lighter, concealed wipers, front/rear stabilizer bars, and P205/70R14 steel-belted radial tires; plus moldings for window reveals, wheel openings, decklid, roof drip, and lower bodyside. New options: high-intensity halogen headlamps and a T-roof.

1980 Impala sedan (AA)

IMPALA/CAPRICE CLASSIC — SERIES 1B — V-6/V-8 — In an attempt to boost gas mileage, both full-size models got a lighter weight standard engine: a 229 cu. in. (3.8-liter) V-6 with Dualjet carburetor and aluminum manifold. That powerplant replaced the old inline six. Wagons came with a standard 267 cu. in. (4.4-liter) V-8, also with Dualjet carburetor, introduced a year earlier on mid-sizes. For the first time, wagons could get an optional 350 cu. in. (5.7-liter) Oldsmobile-built diesel V-8 (except in California). All models could also get a 305 cu. in. (5.0-liter) gas V-8 with four-barrel. Sleek new aerodynamic styling on full-size models showed a lower hood, higher rear deck and restyled sides, along with a 100-pound weight loss. Impala's restyled grille had vertical bars over smaller segments. Caprice gained a new eggcrate grille design and three-lens taillamp assembly (with working center light). The new taillamp rear-end panel was removable. Unlike prior versions, the grille pattern was not repeated down in the bumper area. Landau models gained new roof moldings. Also new were a one-piece door beam, aluminum components in radiators and wagon bumpers, high-pressure easy-rolling tires, side-lift frame jack, and a 25-gallon fuel tank (formerly 21) to boost cruising range. Automatic transmissions added a new lockup torque converter clutch. New options included self-sealing tires, plus cornering lamps that worked with turn signals when headlamps were lit. EPA ratings of 18 MPG city, 26 highway, were the highest ever for a full-size Chevrolet. Reaching a step further, in mid-year an economy Impala emerged: the first full-size gas- engine car to achieve a 20 MPG city estimate. A total of 1,612 cars carried the special economy equipment package, while 13,843 had a diesel engine under the hood. Full-size models came in 14 body colors: beige, black, cinnabar, gray, silver, white, and yellow; plus metallic dark or light blue, light or medium camel, dark claret, or dark green. Ten two-tone combinations were offered, along with seven vinyl top colors. Standard front bench seats had cloth upholstery, but vinyl was available. Caprice could get an optional 50/50 split front seat. Standard equipment included Turbo Hydra-matic, power front disc/rear drum brakes, power steering, easy-roll steel- belted radial tires, acoustical headlining, one-piece carpeting, front stabilizer bar, and new compact spare tire. Full-size models had a built-in engine diagnostics connector, foot parking brake, cigarette lighter, heater/defroster, luggage compartment light, Freedom battery, and column lever for turn signal and dimmer.

1980 Caprice Classic sedan (AA)

I.D. DATA: For the last time, Chevrolet used a 13-symbol Vehicle Identification Number (VIN), visible through the windshield on the driver's side. The first digit ('1') indicates Chevrolet division. Next is a letter identifying the series (car line): 'B' Chevette; 'J' Chevette Scooter; 'M' Monza; 'R' Monza Sport; 'H' Citation coupe; 'X' Citation; 'Q' Camaro; 'S' Camaro Berlinetta; 'T' Malibu; 'W' Malibu Classic; 'Z' Monte Carlo; 'L' Impala; 'N' Caprice Classic. Symbols 34 indicate body type: '08' 2-dr. hatchback coupe; '07' 2-dr. (2+2) hatchback coupe; '11' 2-dr. notchback; '27' 2-dr. coupe; '87' 2-dr. (4-pass.) sport coupe; '37' 2-dr. (6-pass.) sport coupe; '47' 2-dr. (6-pass.) coupe; '19' 4-dr. (6- window) notchback sedan; '68' 4-dr. (6-window) hatchback sedan; '69' 4-dr. (4-window) notchback sedan; '35' 4-dr. station wagon. Symbol five is the engine code: '9' L497.6 2Bbl.; 'O' L497.6 H.O.; 'V' L4151 2Bbl.; '5' L4151 2Bbl.; 'K' V6229 2Bbl.; 'A' V6231 2Bbl.; '3' Turbo V6231 4Bbl.; '7' V6173 2Bbl.; 'J' V8267 2Bbl.; 'H' V8305 4Bbl.; 'L' V8350 4Bbl; 'N' V8350 diesel. Next is a code for model year ('A' 1980). Symbol seven denotes assembly plant: 'A' Lakewood, GA; 'B' Baltimore, MD; 'C' South Gate, CA; 'D' Doraville, GA; 'J' Janesville, WI; 'K' Leeds, MO; 'U' Lordstown, OH; 'L' Van Nuys, CA; 'N' Norwood, OH; 'R' Arlington, TX; 'S' St. Louis, MO; 'T' Tarrytown, NY; 'W' Willow Run, MI; 'Y' Wilmington, DE; 'Z' Fremont, CA; '6' Oklahoma City, OK; '1' Oshawa, Ontario. The last six digits are the sequential serial number. A Body Number Plate on the upper horizontal surface of the shroud identifies model year, car division, series, style, body assembly plant, body number, trim combination, modular seat code, paint code, roof option, and build date code. Citations have a body style I.D. plate on the front tie bar, behind the right headlamp. A two- or three-symbol code (combined with a serial number) identifies each engine. Chevette engine numbers are on a pad at right of block, below No. 1 spark plug. Pontiac (151) fours have a number pad at the right side of the block, by distributor shaft hole. On sixes, the pad is at the right side of the block, to rear of distributor. On V-8s, that pad is just forward of the right cylinder head. Citation fours have an engine code on a pad at the left front of cylinder block, below the hood; and an engine unit/code number label on timing cover. Citation V-6s have an engine unit/code label at rear (or front) of right rocker cover.

CHEVETTE (FOUR)

Model Number	Body/Style Number	Body Type & Seating	Factory Price	Shipping Weight	Production Total
1T	B08	2-dr. Hatch Cpe-4P	4289	1989	146,686
1T	B68	4-dr. Hatch Sed-4P	4418	2048	261,477

CHEVETTE SCOOTER (FOUR)

1T	J08	2-dr. Hatch Cpe-4P	3782	1985	40,998

1980 Monza 2+2 hatchback coupe (CP)

MONZA (FOUR/V-6)

1H	M07	2-dr. Hatch 2+2-4P	4497/4722	2672	53,415
1H	M27	2-dr. Cpe-4P	4184/4409	2617	95,469

MONZA SPORT (FOUR/V-6)

1H	R07	2-dr. Hatch 2+2-4P	4921/5146	2729	20,534

Monza Production Note: Figures do not include units built in fall 1980 as part of extended model year.

CITATION (FOUR/V-6)

1X	H11	2-dr. Cpe-5P	4491/4716	2391/2428	42,909
1X	X11	2-dr. Club Cpe-5P	4905/5130	2397/2434	100,340
1X	X08	2-dr. Hatch Cpe-5P	5032/5257	2417/2454	210,258
1X	X68	4-dr. Hatch Sed-5P	5153/5378	2437/2474	458,033

Citation Production Note: Figures include 187,229 Citations produced during the 1979 model year as early '80s.

CAMARO (V-6/V-8)

1F	P87	2-dr. Spt Cpe-4P	5499/5679	3218/3346	68,174
1F	P87/Z85	2-dr. Rally Cpe-4P	5916/6096	N/A	12,015

1980 Camaro Berlinetta Sport Coupe (AA)

CAMARO BERLINETTA (V-6/V-8)

1F	S87	2-dr. Spt Cpe-4P	6262/6442	3253/3381	26,679

CAMARO Z28 (V-8)

1F	P87/Z28	2-dr. Spt Cpe-4P	--/7121	N/A	45,137

MALIBU (V-6/V-8)

1A	T27	2-dr. Spt Cpe-6P	5133/5313	2996/3117	28,425
1A	T19	4-dr. Sed-6P	5246/5426	3001/3122	67,696
1A	T35	4-dr. Sta Wag-6P	5402/5582	3141/3261	30,794

MALIBU CLASSIC (V-6/V-8)

1A	W27	2-dr. Spt Cpe-6P	5439/5619	3027/3148	28,425
1A	W27/Z03	2-dr. Lan Cpe-6P	5688/5868	N/A	9,342
1A	W19	4-dr. Sed-6P	5567/5747	3031/3152	77,938
1A	W35	4-dr. Sta Wag-6P	5654/5834	3167/3387	35,730

MONTE CARLO (V-6/V-8)

1A	Z37	2-dr. Spt Cpe-6P	6163/6343	3104/3219	116,580
1A	Z37/Z03	2-dr. Lan Cpe-6P	6411/6591	N/A	32,262

IMPALA (V-6/V-8)

1B	L47	2-dr. Spt Cpe-6P	6180/6360	3344/3452	10,756
1B	L69	4-dr. Sedan-6P	6289/6469	3360/3468	70,801
1B	L35	4-dr. Sta Wag-6P	-- /6780	-- /3892	11,203
1B	L35/AQ4	4-dr. 3S Wag-8P	-- /6925	-- /3924	6,767

CAPRICE CLASSIC (V-6/V-8)

1B	N47	2-dr. Spt Cpe-6P	6579/6759	3376/3484	13,919
1B	N47/Z03	2-dr. Lan Cpe-6P	7029/7209	N/A	8,857
1B	N69	4-dr. Sedan-6P	6710/6890	3410/3518	91,208
1B	N35	4-dr. Sta Wag-6P	-- /7099	-- /3930	9,873
1B	N35/AQ4	4-dr. 3S Wag-8P	-- /7266	-- /3962	13,431

FACTORY PRICE AND WEIGHT NOTE: Where two prices and weights are shown, the figure to the left of the slash is for six-cylinder model, to right of slash for the 267 cu. in. V-8 (305 V-8 cost $115 more). For Monza and Citation, prices and weights to left of slash are four-cylinder, to right for V-6 engine. All models had at least two price rises during the model year. The new Citation had an ample increase even before introduction. **BODY/STYLE NO. NOTE:** Some models are actually option packages. Figure after the slash (e.g., Z03) is the number of the option package that comes with the model listed.

ENGINE DATA: BASE FOUR (Chevette): Inline. Overhead cam. Four-cylinder. Cast iron block and head. Displacement: 97.6 cu. in. (1.6 liters). Bore & stroke: 3.23 x 2.98 in. Compression ratio: 8.6:1. Brake horsepower: 70 at 5200 R.P.M. Torque: 82 lbs.-ft. at 2400 R.P.M. Five main bearings. Hydraulic valve lifters. Carburetor: 2Bbl. Holley 5210C. VIN Code: 9. OPTIONAL HIGH-OUTPUT FOUR (Chevette): Same as above except Brake H.P.: 74 at 5200 R.P.M. Torque: 88 lbs.-ft. at 2800 R.P.M. VIN Code: O. BASE FOUR (Monza): Inline. Overhead valve. Four-cylinder. Cast iron block. Displacement: 151 cu. in. (2.5 liters). Bore & stroke: 4.00 x 3.00 in. Compression ratio: 8.2:1. Brake horsepower: 86 at 4000 R.P.M. Torque: 128 lbs.-ft. at 2400 R.P.M. Five main bearings. Hydraulic valve lifters. Carburetor: 2Bbl. Rochester 2SE. VIN Code: V. BASE FOUR (Citation): Same as 151 cu. in. four above except Brake H.P.: 90 at 4000 R.P.M. Torque: 134 lbs.-ft. at 2400 R.P.M. VIN Code: 5. OPTIONAL V-6 (Citation): 60-degree, overhead-valve V-6. Cast iron block and head. Displacement: 173 cu. in. (2.8 liters). Bore & stroke: 3.50 x 3.00 in. Compression ratio: 8.5:1. Brake horsepower: 115 at 4800 R.P.M. Torque: 145 lbs.-ft. at 2400 R.P.M. Four main bearings. Hydraulic valve lifters. Carburetor: 2Bbl. Rochester 2SE. VIN Code: 7. BASE V-6 (Camaro, Malibu, Monte Carlo, Impala, Caprice): 90-degree, overhead-valve V-6. Cast iron block and head. Displacement: 229 cu. in. (3.8 liters). Bore & stroke: 3.74 x 3.48 in. Compression ratio: 8.6:1. Brake horsepower: 115 at 4000 R.P.M. Torque: 175 lbs.-ft. at 2000 R.P.M. Four main bearings. Hydraulic valve lifters. Carburetor: 2Bbl. Rochester M2ME. VIN Code: K. OPTIONAL V-6 (Monza); alternate for models above: 90-degree, overhead-valve V-6. Cast iron block and head. Displacement: 231 cu. in. (3.8 liters). Bore & stroke: 3.80 x 3.40 in. Compression ratio: 8.0:1. Brake horsepower: 110 at 3800 R.P.M. Torque: 190 lbs.-ft. at 2000 R.P.M. Four main bearings. Hydraulic valve lifters. Carburetor: 2Bbl. Rochester M2ME. VIN Code: A. TURBOCHARGED V-6; OPTIONAL (Monte Carlo): Same as 231 cu. in. V-6 above, except 4Bbl. Rochester M4ME carburetor Brake H.P.: 170 at 4000 R.P.M. Torque: 265 lbs.- ft. at 2400 R.P.M. VIN Code: 3. OPTIONAL V-8 (Camaro, Malibu, Monte Carlo, Impala, Caprice): 90-degree, overhead valve V-8. Cast iron block and head. Displacement: 267 cu. in. (4.4 liters). Bore & stroke: 3.50 x 3.48 in. Compression ratio: 8.3:1. Brake horsepower: 120 at 3600 R.P.M. Torque: 215 lbs.-ft. at 2000 R.P.M. Five main bearings. Hydraulic valve lifters. Carburetor: 2Bbl. Rochester M2ME. VIN Code: J. OPTIONAL V-8 (Camaro, Malibu, Monte Carlo, Impala, Caprice): 90-degree, overhead valve V-8. Cast iron block and head. Displacement: 305 cu. in. (5.0 liters). Bore & stroke: 3.74 x 3.48 in. Compression ratio: 8.6:1. Brake horsepower: 155 at 4000 R.P.M. Torque: 240 lbs.-ft. at 1600 R.P.M. Five main bearings. Hydraulic valve lifters. Carburetor: 4Bbl. Rochester M4ME. VIN Code: H. BASE V-8 (Camaro Z28): 90-degree, overhead valve V-8. Cast iron block and head. Displacement: 350 cu. in. (5.7 liters). Bore & stroke: 4.00 x 3.48 in. Compression ratio: 8.2:1. Brake horsepower: 190 at 4200 R.P.M. Torque: 280 lbs.-ft. at 2400 R.P.M. Five main bearings. Hydraulic valve lifters. Carburetor: 4Bbl. Rochester M4ME. VIN Code: L. DIESEL V-8; OPTIONAL (Impala/Caprice wagon): 90-degree, overhead valve V-8. Cast iron block and head. Displacement: 350 cu. in. (5.7 liters). Bore & stroke: 4.06 x 3.39 in. Compression ratio: 22.5:1. Brake horsepower: 105 at 3200 R.P.M. Torque: 205 lbs.-ft. at 1600 R.P.M. Five main bearings. Hydraulic valve lifters. Fuel injection. VIN Code: N.

CHASSIS DATA: Vheelbase: (Chevette 2-dr.) 94.3 in.; (Chvt) 97.3 in.; (Monza) 97.0 in.; (Citation) 104.9 in.; (Camaro) 108.0 in.; (Malibu/Monte) 108.1 in.; (Capr/Imp) 116.0 in. Overall length: (Chvt 2-dr.) 161.9 in.; (Chvt 4-dr.) 164.9 in.; (Monza) 179.9 in.; (Cit) 176.7 in.; (Camaro) 197.6 in.; (Malibu) 192.7 in.; (Malibu wag) 193.4 in.; (Monte) 200.4 in.; (Capr/Imp) 212.1 in.; (Capr/Imp wag) 215.1 in. Height: (Chvt) 52.3 in.; (Monza cpe) 50.1 in.; (Monza hatch) 50.2 in.; (Cit) 53.1 in.; (Camaro) 49.2 in.; (Malibu cpe) 53.3 in.; (Malibu sed) 54.2 in.; (Malibu wag) 54.5 in.; (Monte) 53.9 in.; (Capr/Imp cpe) 55.3 in.; (Capr/Imp sed) 55.9 in.; (Capr/Imp wag) 57.7 in. Vidth: (Chvt) 61.8 in.; (Monza) 65.4 in.; (Cit) 68.3 in.; (Camaro) 74.5 in.; (Malibu/Monte) 71.5 in.; (Malibu wag) 71.2 in.; (Capr/Imp) 75.3 in.; (Capr/Imp wag) 79.3 in. Front Tread: (Chvt) 51.2 in.; (Monza) 54.8 in.; (Cit) 58.7 in.; (Camaro) 61.3 in.; (Berlinetta) 61.6 in.; (Malibu/Monte) 58.5 in.; (Capr/Imp) 61.8 in.; (Capr/Imp wag) 62.2 in. Rear Tread: (Chvt) 51.2 in.; (Monza) 53.6 in.; (Cit) 57.0 in.; (Camaro) 60.0 in.; (Berlinetta) 60.3 in.; (Malibu/Monte) 57.8 in.; (Capr/Imp) 60.8 in.; (Capr/Imp wag) 64.1 in. Standard Tires: (Chvt) P155/80R13 GBR; (Monza) A78 x 13; (Cit) P185/80R13 GBR; (Camaro) P205/75R14 SBR; (Malibu) P185/75R14/B GBR; (Malibu wag) P195/75R14/B GBR; (Imp/Caprice) P205/75R15/B SBR; (Imp/Capr wag) P225/75R15/B SBR; (Monte) P205/70R14/B SBR.

TECHNICAL: Transmission: Three-speed manual transmission standard on Camaro and Malibu V-6. Gear ratios: (1st) 3.50:1; (2nd) 1.89:1; (3rd) 1.00:1; (Rev) 3.62:1. Four-speed floor shift standard on Chevette: (1st) 3.75:1; (2nd) 2.16:1; (3rd) 1.38:1; (4th) 1.00:1; (Rev) 3.82:1. Four-speed floor shift standard on Monza: (1st) 3.50:1; (2nd) 2.48:1; (3rd) 1.66:1; (4th) 1.00:1; (Rev) 3.50:1. Citation four-speed floor shift: (1st) 3.53:1; (2nd) 1.96:1; (3rd) 1.24:1; (4th) 0.81:1; (Rev) 3.42:1. Four-speed floor shift optional on Camaro/Malibu V8305: (1st) 2.85:1; (2nd) 2.02:1; (3rd) 1.35:1; (4th) 1.00:1; (Rev) 2.85:1. Four-speed on Camaro V8350: (1st) 3.42:1; (2nd) 2.28:1; (3rd) 1.45:1; (4th) 1.00:1; (Rev) 3.51:1. Three-speed Turbo Hydra-matic standard on Monte Carlo and Caprice/Impala, optional on others. Automatic gear ratios: (1st) 2.52:1; (2nd) 1.52:1; (3rd) 1.00:1; (Rev) 1.93:1 except Caprice/Impala V6/V8267, Monza four, Malibu V-6 and Monte ratios: (1st) 2.74:1; (2nd) 1.57:1; (3rd) 1.00:1; (Rev) 2.07:1. Chevette automatic trans.: (1st) 2.40:1; (2nd) 1.48:1; (3rd) 1.00:1; (Rev) 1.92:1. Citation auto. trans.: (1st) 2.84:1; (2nd) 1.60:1; (3rd) 1.00:1; (Rev) 2.07:1. Standard final drive ratio: (Chevette) 3.70:1; (Monza four) 2.73:1; (Monza V-6) 2.93:1; (Citation) 3.34:1; (Camaro V-6) 2.73:1; (Camaro V-8) 2.56:1; (Malibu V-6) 2.73:1; (Malibu V8) 2.29:1; (Malibu V-8 wag) 2.41:1; (Monte V-6) 2.41:1; (Monte V-8) 2.29:1; (Caprice/Imp V-6) 2.73 :1; (Caprice/Imp V-8) 2.41:1; (Caprice/Imp wag) 2.56:1. Steering: (Chevette/Citation) rack and pinion; (others) recirculating ball. Front Suspension: (Citation) MacPherson struts and coil springs; (others) control arms, coil springs and stabilizer bar. Rear Suspension: (Corvette) rigid axle, torque tube, longitudinal trailing radius arms, transverse linkage bar, coil springs and stabilizer bar; (Citation) rigid axle, trailing arm, control arms and stabilizer arm; (Camaro) rigid axle, semi-elliptic leaf springs and stabilizer bar; (others) rigid axle, lower trailing radius arms, upper oblique torque arms and coil springs, plus stabilizer bar on Monte and full-size. Brakes: front disc, rear drum. Body construction: (Chevette/Citation) unibody; (Camaro) unibody with separate partial box frame; (others) separate body and perimeter box frame. Fuel tank: (Chvt) 12.5 gal.; (Monza) 18.5 gal.; (Citation) 14 gal.; (Camaro) 21 gal.; (Malibu/Monte) 18.1 gal.; (Malibu wag) 18.2 gal.; (Capr/Imp) 25 gal.; (Capr/Imp wag) 22 gal.

DRIVETRAIN OPTIONS: Engines: 1.6-liter H.O. four: Chevette ($60). 173 cu. in., 2Bbl. V-6: Citation ($225). 231 cu. in., 2Bbl. V-6: Monza ($225). Turbo 231 cu. in., 4Bbl. V-6: Monte ($500). 267 cu. in., 2Bbl. V-8: Camaro/Malibu/Monte/Imp/Caprice ($180). 305 cu. in., 4Bbl. V-8: Camaro/Malibu/Monte/Imp/Capr ($295); Imp/Capr wag ($115); Z28 ($50 credit). Diesel 350 cu. in. V-8: Imp/Capr wag ($915). Transmission/Differential: Four-speed manual shift: Camaro ($144); Malibu (N/A). Turbo Hydra-matic: Chvt/Monza ($320); Citation ($337); Camaro/Malibu ($358); Camaro Z28 ($63). Sport shifter: Chvt ($32). Limited-slip differential: Monza ($64); Camaro ($68); Malibu/Monte ($69); Imp/Capr ($73). Performance axle ratio: Monza ($18); Camaro/Malibu/Monte ($19); Imp/Capr ($20). Power Accessories: Power brakes: Chvt/Monza/Citation ($76); Camaro ($81). Power steering: Monza ($158); Citation/Malibu ($174). Suspension: F40 H.D. susp.: Citation ($21); Monte ($24). F40 H.D. shock absorbers: Imp/Capr ($25). F41 sport susp.: Chvt ($35); Monza ($33); Citation ($27); Camaro ($41); Imp/Capr cpe/sed ($45). Inflatable rear shock absorbers: Imp/Capr ($59). Front stabilizer bar: Monza ($29). Other: Heavy-duty radiator: Monza ($33). H.D. cooling: Chvt ($31-$58); Cit ($32-$59); Camaro/Malibu/Monte ($36-$63) Imp/Capr ($37-$64). Engine block heater: Imp/Capr wag ($16). H.D. alternator (63-amp): Malibu ($6-$35). H.D. alternator (70-amp): Cit ($11-$43); Monte ($32-$67); Imp/Capr ($33-$68). H.D. battery ($20-$22) exc. diesel ($44). California emission system ($250) exc. diesel ($83).

CHEVETTE/MONZA CONVENIENCE/APPEARANCE OPTIONS: Option Packages: Spyder equipment pkg.: Monza ($521). Quiet sound group: Chvt ($38-$50); Monza ($32-$42). Comfort/Convenience: Air conditioning ($531). Rear defogger, electric ($95). Tinted glass: Chvt ($64). Comfortilt steering wheel ($73). Tachometer: Chvt ($67). Gauge pkg. (incl. tach): Monza ($71-$94). Electric clock ($23). Cigarette lighter: Scooter ($8). Intermittent wipers ($37). Lighting and Mirrors: Aux. lighting: Chvt ($40-$41); Monza ($21-$27). Twin sport mirrors, left remote ($43). Driver's remote sport mirror: Chvt ($27). Entertainment: AM radio: Scooter ($79). AM/FM radio: Chvt/Monza ($64); Scooter ($143). AM/FM stereo radio ($101). AM/FM stereo radio w/digital clock: Monza ($252). Stereo 8track tape player w/AM radio: Monza ($154). 8track player with AM/FM: Monza ($176). Cassette player with AM/FM stereo radio: Monza ($188). Rear speaker ($18). Radio delete: Monza ($52 credit). Exterior Trim: Removable sunroof: Monza ($193). Cabriolet vinyl roof: Monza ($165) incl. opera windows. Spoilers, front/rear: Monza ($124). Deluxe exterior (wheel opening, side window and rocker panel moldings): Chvt ($112-$119). Exterior decor pkg. (wheel opening and side window moldings, wheel covers, luggage carrier): Monza ($139-$154). Two-tone paint: Chvt ($110). Sport stripes ($75). Bodyside moldings: Scooter ($43). Wheel opening moldings: Monza ($22). Side window reveal moldings: Chvt ($70-$77). Door edge guards ($13-$20). Roof carrier: Chvt ($70). Interior Trim/Upholstery: Console: Monza cpe ($80). Cloth bucket seats: Chvt ($12-$23); Monza ($23). Custom Chevette interior pkg. w/bucket seats: cloth ($183); vinyl ($160). Custom vinyl bucket seats: Monza ($170) exc. Sport (NC). Custom cloth bucket seats: Monza ($193) exc. Sport ($23). Folding rear seat: Monza ($104) but std. on 2+2. Rear seat delete: Chvt ($54 credit). Color-keyed floor mats ($22). Automatic seat/shoulder belts: Chvt ($65). Wheels and Tires: Rally II wheels: Monza ($48-$94). Color- keyed deluxe wheel covers: Monza ($14-$46). Sport wheel covers: Chvt ($48). Wheel trim rings: Scooter ($40). P155/8013/B GBR WSW: Scooter ($43). P175/7013/B SBR BSW: Chvt ($53); Scooter ($95). P175/7013/B SBR WSW: Chvt ($95); Scooter ($137). P175/7013/B SBR WLT: Chvt ($109); Scooter ($152). B78 x 13/B WSW: Monza ($18). BR70 x 13/C SBR BSW: Monza ($154) exc. Sport ($116). BR70 x 13/C SBR WSW: Monza ($158-$196). BR70 x 13/C SBR WLT: Monza ($57-$211).

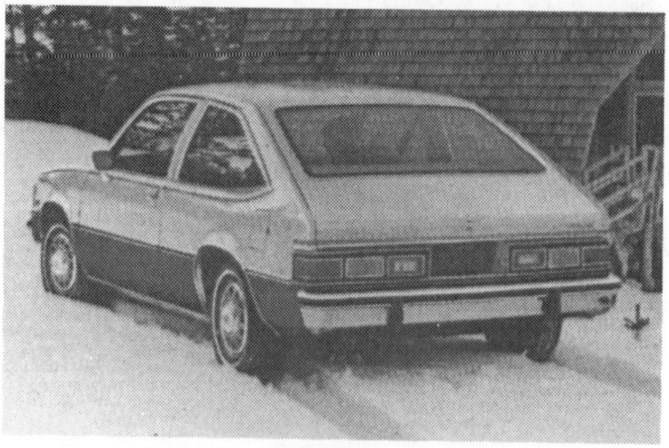

1980 Citation hatchback coupe (CP)

CITATION CONVENIENCE/APPEARANCE OPTIONS: Option Packages: X11 sport equipment pkg. ($501). Deluxe exterior pkg. ($102-$144). Quiet sound group ($52). Quiet sound/rear decor pkg. ($72). Comfort/Convenience: Air cond. ($564). Rear defogger, electric ($101). Cruise control ($105). Tinted glass ($70). Sport steering wheel (NC to $20). Comfortilt steering wheel ($75). Power windows ($133-$189). Power remote swing-out windows ($91). Power door locks ($87-$123). Gauge pkg. w/clock ($70). Special instruments incl. tachometer ($109). Electric clock ($25). Cigarette lighter: cpe ($8). Intermittent wipers ($39). Lighting, Horns and Mirrors: Aux.

lighting ($41). Right door light switch: cpe ($8). Dual horns ($9). Driver's remote mirror ($18). Dual sport mirrors, left remote ($43). Entertainment: AM radio: cpe ($79). AM/FM radio: cpe ($143); others ($64). AM/FM stereo radio: cpe ($180); others ($101). 8track player with AM/FM stereo: cpe ($255); others ($176). Cassette player with AM/FM stereo: cpe ($267); others ($188). CB with AM/FM stereo: cpe ($492); others ($413). Rear speaker ($18). Dual front/rear speakers ($40). Windshield antenna ($25); incl. w/radios. Radio delete ($52 credit). Exterior Trim: Removable sunroof ($240). Two-tone paint ($148) incl. pinstriping and bodyside moldings. Bodyside pinstriping ($32). Bodyside moldings ($43-$47). Bright rocker panel moldings: cpe ($20). Wheel opening moldings: cpe ($43). Door edge guards ($13-$20). Side window reveal moldings ($41-$65). Roof carrier ($86). Bumper guards ($45). Bumper rub strips ($40). Interior Trim/Upholstery: Console ($80). Reclining passenger seatback ($42-$70). Sport cloth bench seat ($23). Custom knit cloth bench seat ($189-$239). Custom vinyl bench seat ($166-$216). Custom bucket seats: knit cloth ($278-$328); vinyl ($255-$305). Locking glove compartment ($8). Color-keyed mats ($25). Wheels and Tires: Full wheel covers ($43). Wire wheel covers ($113-$156). Wheel trim rings ($35-$78). Rally wheel trim ($35-$78). P185/80R13/B GBR WSW ($45). P185/80R13/B SBR BSW ($49). P185/80R13/B SBR WSW ($93). P205/70R13/B SBR WSW ($182). P205/70R13/B SBR WLT ($196).

1980 Monte Carlo Sport Coupe (CP)

CAMARO/MALIBU/MONTE CARLO CONVENIENCE/APPEARANCE OPTIONS: Option Packages: Estate equipment: Malibu wag ($276). Interior decor/quiet sound group: Camaro ($68); std. on Berlinetta. Quiet sound group: Malibu ($55). Value appearance group: Malibu ($120-$129). Comfort/Convenience: Air cond.: Camaro ($566); Malibu/Monte ($601). Rear defogger (forced-air): Malibu cpe/sed ($59). Rear defogger, electric ($107). Cruise control ($112). Tinted glass: Camaro ($68); Malibu/Monte ($75). Comfortilt steering wheel ($81). Six-way power driver's seat: Malibu/Monte ($175). Power windows: Camaro/Monte ($143); Malibu ($143-$132). Power door locks: Malibu ($93-$132); Camaro/Monte ($93). Power trunk release: Monte ($26). Electric clock: base Camaro, Malibu ($25). Gauge pkg.: Monte ($41). Gauge pkg. w/tach: base Camaro ($120); Malibu ($134); Monte ($109). Gauge pkg. w/clock: Malibu ($66). Intermittent wipers ($41). Lighting, Horns and Mirrors: High-intensity high-beam headlamps: Monte ($26). Aux. lighting: Camaro ($33-$40); Malibu ($33-$60); Monte ($33). Dual horns: Camaro, base Malibu ($10). Remote-control driver's mirror: Malibu/Monte ($19). Twin sport mirrors (left remote): base Camaro, Malibu/Monte ($46). Twin remote sport mirrors: Malibu ($73); Monte ($48-$73). Visor vanity mirror: Monte ($6). Lighted visor mirror: Monte ($37-$43). Entertainment: AM radio ($97). AM/FM radio ($153). AM/FM stereo radio ($192). AM/FM stereo radio w/digital clock: Malibu ($353); Camaro ($328-$353). Stereo 8track tape player w/AM radio ($249). Stereo 8track tape player with AM/FM stereo radio ($272). Cassette player with AM/FM stereo radio ($285). AM/FM/CB radio ($473). AM/FM stereo radio w/CB ($525). Rear speaker ($20). Dual front speakers: Monte ($14). Dual front and rear speakers: Malibu/Monte ($43). Windshield antenna ($27); incl. w/radios. Power antenna ($51). Exterior Trim: Removable glass roof panels: Camaro/Monte ($695). Power sky roof: Monte ($561). Vinyl roof: Malibu ($124); Monte ($140). Rear spoiler: Camaro Berlinetta ($62). Style trim pkg.: Camaro ($78). Two-tone paint: Malibu ($72-$123); Monte ($148-$171). Bodyside moldings:

1980 Malibu Classic Landau Coupe (CP)

Camaro ($46). Deluxe bodyside moldings: Malibu/Monte ($57). Door edge guards ($14-$22). Bright sill moldings: Monte ($47). Wheel opening moldings: Malibu cpe/sed ($25). Side window sill moldings: Monte ($35). Side window reveal moldings: Malibu ($47). Roof drip moldings: Camaro ($26). Bodyside pinstriping: Malibu ($51); Monte ($42). Rear window air deflector: Malibu wag ($32). Roof carrier: Malibu wag ($96). Bumper rub strips: Malibu ($44). Bumper guards, front/rear: Malibu ($49). Interior Trim/Upholstery: Console: Malibu cpe/sed, Monte ($86). Cloth bench seat: Malibu cpe/sed, Monte ($28). Cloth bench seat: Malibu wag ($244). Custom vinyl bench seat: Malibu wag ($64). Cloth 50/50 seating: Malibu ($184-$244). Vinyl 50/50 seating: Malibu ($212-$244). Vinyl bucket seats: Camaro ($25). Cloth bucket seats: Camaro ($25); Malibu cpe/sed, Monte ($91). Custom vinyl bucket seats: base Camaro ($328). Custom cloth bucket seats: Berlinetta ($353); base Camaro ($353). Monte custom 55/45 seating: cloth ($366); vinyl ($394). Adj. driver's seatback: Camaro ($25). Litter container: Monte ($9). Color-keyed mats: Camaro/Malibu/Monte ($25). Deluxe load-floor carpet: Malibu wag ($75). Deluxe trunk trim: Monte ($46). Wheels and Tires: Aluminum wheels: Camaro ($184-$337). Custom styled wheels: Camaro ($107-$153). Rally wheels: Camaro ($100); Monte ($50-$96); Malibu ($50-$102). Wire wheel covers: Malibu cpe/sed ($118); Malibu wag ($96). P205/75R14 SBR WSW: Camaro ($51-$65); Malibu cpe/sed ($171). P205/70R14/B SBR WLT: Malibu cpe/sed ($185). Stowaway spare: Camaro (NC).

IMPALA/CAPRICE CONVENIENCE/APPEARANCE OPTIONS: Option Packages: Estate equipment: wag ($280). Value appearance group: Imp ($96). Comfort/Convenience: Four season air cond. ($647). Comfortron auto-temp air cond. ($738). Rear defogger, forced-air: cpe/sed ($61). Rear defogger, electric ($109). Cruise control ($118). Tinted glass ($90). Comfortilt steering wheel ($83). Power door locks ($95-$135). Six-way power driver's seat ($179). Power windows ($149-$221). Power trunk release ($27). Power tailgate lock: wag ($43). Electric clock: Imp ($26). Digital clock: Imp ($59). Caprice ($33). Gauge pkg.: Imp ($58). Intermittent wipers ($42). Quiet sound group: Imp ($29). Caprice ($33). Lighting, Horns and Mirrors: High-intensity high-beam headlamps ($27). Cornering lamps ($50). Aux. lighting ($37-$54). Dual horns: Imp ($11). Driver's remote mirror ($20). Dual remote mirrors ($60). Dual sport mirrors, left remote ($47). Dual remote body-color sport mirrors ($27-$74). Visor vanity mirror ($7). Lighted visor mirror ($44). Entertainment: AM radio ($99). AM/FM radio ($156). AM/FM stereo radio ($195); w/digital clock ($358-$384). Stereo 8track tape player with AM radio ($253); with AM/FM stereo radio ($276). Cassette player with AM/FM stereo ($289). AM/FM/CB radio and power antenna ($480). AM/FM stereo w/CB and power antenna ($533). Rear speaker ($21). Dual front/rear speakers ($44). Power antenna ($52). Windshield antenna; incl. w/radios. Exterior Trim: Power sky roof ($670). Vinyl roof: cpe/sed ($155). Roof carrier: wag ($123). Two-tone paint ($60). Custom two-tone ($128). Pinstriping ($35). Bodyside moldings ($48). Door edge guards ($15-$22). Wheel opening moldings ($15-$22). Bumper rub strips, front/rear ($60). Bumper guards ($56). Interior Trim/Upholstery: Vinyl bench seat: cpe/sed ($29). Cloth 50/50 seat ($229-$276). Vinyl 50/50 seat ($247-$276). Custom cloth 50/50 seat: cpe ($412); sed ($437). Deluxe load-floor carpet: wag ($80). Deluxe cargo area carpet: wag ($114). Color-keyed mats: front ($15); rear ($11). Litter container ($9). Deluxe trunk trim ($49). Wheel Covers: Full wheel covers ($47). Sport covers: Imp ($105); Caprice ($58). Custom covers: Imp ($125); Caprice ($78). Wire covers: Caprice ($128). Cloth ($114). Wire wheel covers: Caprice ($128). Tires: P205/75R15 SBR WSW ($51). P215/75R15 SBR WSW ($82). P225/70R15 SBR WSW ($124). Wagon Tires: P225/75R15/B SBR WSW ($55). Puncture-sealant tires ($85).

HISTORY: Introduced: Oct. 11, 1979 except Citation, April 19, 1979 and Corvette, Oct. 25, 1979. Model year production (U.S.): 2,017,054 (incl. Corvettes and early 1980 Citations, but not incl. 19,631 Acadians). Calendar year production: 1,737,336 (including 44,190 Corvettes and 18,958 Acadians). Calendar year sales by U.S. dealers: 1,747,534 for a 26.6 percent market share. Model year sales by U.S. dealers: 1,831,953 (incl. 37,471 Corvettes, but not incl. 273,720 early 1980 Citations).

Historical Footnotes: While auto sales fell overall this year, Chevrolet remained GM's top seller (hardly a surprise). Model year sales dropped 20 percent, however. Chevette sales went up a bit, but other models declined. Camaro fell by nearly 44 percent, while full-size models by about 40 percent. Full-size Chevrolet production fell by a whopping 66.3 percent. Only Chevette fared notably better than in 1979. The decline in full-size sales caused production to halt at South Gate, California and St. Louis plants. Only the Janesville, Wisconsin facility continued to build full-size models. South Gate would be the site for production of the 1982 J-cars. Monzas, which still sold fairly well, continued to roll out of the plant at Lordstown, Ohio. Although Citation would soon be plagued by complaints and recalls, it was popular from the start. Chevrolet hoped the new front-drive would appeal to "a whole new generation of car buyers with values and attitudes far different from their parents and even their older brothers and sisters," declared General Manager Robert Lund. Those "new values" buyers for whom a car was "a functional part of their lives" would soon "revolutionize the marketplace." Citation had first been conceived in 1974, when fuel economy was uppermost in engineers' minds. Instead of being evolutionary, as was nearly always the case in earlier periods, it was designed from the ground up. The Chevrolet 60-degree V-6 engine built for Citation at Tonawanda, New York was also distributed to the other GM division builders of X-bodied vehicles.

1981 CHEVROLET

Monza left the lineup this year, but the vacancy would soon be filled by the new (1982) front-drive Cavalier. Opening prices for 1981 were even higher compared to 1980 than 1980 was to '79—up by as much as $1500. Monte Carlo got an aerodynamic restyle, while other models changed their front-end look. For the first time, a four-speed overdrive automatic transmission was installed on full-size Chevrolets with the 5.0-liter V-8. All GM automatic transmissions now had the lockup torque converter that had been introduced on some 1980 models. It offered a direct flywheel-to-driveshaft connection in one or two gears. All gas-engine models had GM's new Computer Command Control that adjusted the air/fuel mixture and spark timing to compensate for driving conditions, altitude, temperature and barometric pressure. It also included self-diagnostic features.

1981 Chevette hatchback sedan (AA)

CHEVETTE — SERIES 1T — FOUR — Immodestly billed as "America's most popular subcompact," Chevette wore a new contemporary flush-mounted windshield with black outline molding. Also new: sporty argent-finish styled steel wheels and a bright-accented black grille. Standard powerplant was again the 98 cu. in. (1.6- liter) four, now with Computer Command Control to monitor the engine and reduce emissions. All models except the low-budget Scooter had a sport shifter in the floor console. Standard coupes had swing-out rear quarter windows, but Scooter's were fixed. A Rally trim option was available. For the first time, power steering was available

115

with automatic transmission and air conditioning a lot of work for that little 1.6 engine to perform. Halogen headlamps and a rear wiper/washer were new options. Body colors were beige, black, red, white, bright yellow, and nine metallics: medium or light brown, champagne, silver, light or dark blue, maroon, dark green, or burnt orange. The custom interior included high contoured bucket seats up front, upholstered in cloth or vinyl. Standard equipment included the 1.6-liter engine, four-speed manual transmission, maintenance-free battery, energy-absorbing bumpers, front stabilizer bar, diagnostic connector, two-speed wipers, bumper guards and rub strips, day/night mirror, mini-console, vinyl interior, dome light, and P155/8013 fiberglass-belted whitewall tires. Scooter had blackwall tires and lacked various pieces of equipment standard on other models: an AM radio, bodyside moldings, color-keyed seat/shoulder belts, color-keyed instrument panel, sport steering wheel, lighter, and reclining front bucket seats.

1981 Citation hatchback sedan (AA)

CITATION — SERIES 1X — FOUR/V-6 — Named *Motor Trend* "Car of the Year" for 1980, Citation was described (ironically, in view of imminent recalls and troubles) as the "most successful new car ever introduced." Following its huge introductory fanfare as an early 1980 model, Citation changed little for its second full year. The notchback coupe was dropped, so only hatchbacks remained: two-door or four-door. Citation had a 'Chevrolet' nameplate on the decklid, and 'Citation' nameplate at forward end of front fenders. Styling features included a body-color front valance panel, bright hood and windshield moldings, bright bumpers with body-color end caps, wide rocker panel moldings, and pinstriping on decklid and quarter panels. The new bright chrome grille was arranged in a looser 8 x 4 hole pattern, with bowtie emblem in the center. Below was a new slotted air dam. Body colors this year were beige, black, red, white, and bright yellow; plus metallic light or dark blue, light or medium brown, champagne, dark green, maroon, burnt orange, or silver. Cloth or vinyl interiors came in beige, black, dark blue, camel or maroon (vinyl also in champagne). Engine choices again were the base 151 cu. in. (2.5-liter) four or 60-degree 173 cu. in. (2.8-liter) V-6, both with new Computer Command Control. The V-6 also added Electric Early Fuel Evaporation to improve emissions, by supplying electric current to a heater grid in the carburetor bore for better cold starts and warmup. (1980 carburetor bases were heated by exhaust.) Engines also had a new Electronic Spark Timing system (ESC), plus a new Freedom II battery. Citation tires now took 30 psi air pressure. Engines offered improved service accessibility. A revised X11 package, which was mostly for looks in 1980, now included a high-output (135 horsepower) version of the V-6 engine. Chevrolet claimed that the X11 Citation package "gives you goose bumps." Carrying a Z09 RPO code and $1498 price tag, it included (for starters) a rear spoiler, body-color bumpers with black rub strips, tachometer, 'X11' decal on doors and rear spoiler, power brakes, and 'High Output 660' emblem on door. All Camaros got a space-saving P215/60R14 steel-belted radials on 14 x 6.5 inch aluminum alloy wheels. A special lightweight fiberglass-reinforced, sheet-molded compound hood had a molded-in air inlet and 'High Output 660' emblem to show that the performance V-6 was underneath. Aero drag rated only 0.4. The X11 package also included low-drag, semi-metallic brake linings; a dual-snorkel air cleaner; quick-ratio rack-and-pinion steering; sport steering wheel; special instruments; twin sport mirrors; and larger-diameter exhaust with dual tailpipes. The high-output V-6 had bigger valves, revised valve timing with higher lift and longer duration for better high-end volumetric efficiency, and an aluminum intake manifold. It produced 135 horsepower at 5400 R.P.M., and 145 lbs.-ft. of torque at 2400. The F41 sport suspension included larger-diameter stabilizer bars, higher-rate springs and firmer bushings, plus a numerically higher axle ratio. X11 also had black window moldings, headlamp bezels, and pillar louvers; black-accented grille and rocker panel moldings; and bucket seats. Also joining the option list were halogen headlamps and an automatic speed control with new "resume" feature, plus a reclining driver's seat backrest. Bucket seats could now be ordered with the standard interior. Citation's standard equipment included four-speed manual transmission, front stabilizer bar, P185/80R13 glass-belted radial tires on styled steel wheels, compact spare tire, two-speed wipers, bright roof drip moldings, pushbutton AM radio, day/night mirror, color-keyed steering wheel and seat/shoulder belts, and cut-pile carpeting.

1981 Camaro Berlinetta Sport Coupe (CP)

CAMARO — SERIES 1F — V-6/V-8 — Rally Sport left the Camaro lineup this year, leaving only the base Sport Coupe, Berlinetta, and performance Z28. Not much changed, beyond the new Computer Command Control on all engines. Power brakes, formerly standard only on the Z28, were now universal. All Camaros got a space-saving compact spare tire (formerly an option) and lighter weight Freedom II battery, plus new low-drag front disc brakes. Optional automatic transmissions added a lockup

torque converter clutch in third gear. The Z28's torque converter clutch was computer-controlled in both second and third gears. The basic Camaro coupe had an argent grille split (as before) into upper and lower sections, plus wraparound taillamps. Berlinetta's grille was bright-accented argent. Berlinetta came with a standard Quiet Sound Group including inner roof layer of sound-absorbing materials and inside roof covering of soft foam-backed headlining. Special paint and striping emphasized its "sculptured lines." Stripes came in silver, black, blue, beige, gold or red. Berlinetta identification was on the grille header panel, side pillars, and deck lid. Body sills were black (bright on the basic sport coupe). Base engine for both the standard sport coupe and posher Berlinetta remained the 229 cu. in. (3.8-liter) V-6 with three-speed manual transmission. Both 267 cu. in. (4.4-liter) and 305 cu. in. (5.0-liter) V-8s were optional, but required either four-speed or automatic. Z28 had a standard four-speed 305 V-8 engine, with new wide-ratio four-speed manual transmission (optional on others). That gearbox's 3.42:1 low-gear ratio delivered both economy and low-end performance, hooked to 3.42:1 axle ratio. Z28 Camaros could also get a 350 cu. in. (5.7-liter) V-8 at no charge, but with automatic only. Even California Camaro fans could now get the 5.7-liter V-8 in their Z28s again. Camaro Z28 included a front air dam, front fender flares and air louvers, hood scoop with decal, rear spoiler, P225/70R15 raised white-letter tires on body-color 15 x 7 in. sport wheels, and contour bucket seats. Z28's distinctive grille was body-colored with horizontal bars. There was 'Z28' identification on the driver's side of the grille, and a decal on doors. Other Z28 features included black headlamp/taillamp bezels, rear end panel, license plate opening, parking light bezels, sill moldings, window and windshield moldings; plus tri-tone striping on the rear spoiler and lower bodyside, as well as on front air dam and fender flares. Front and rear bumper covers were body-color urethane. Z28's solenoid-activated hood air intake actually drew in air. So did its fender air scoops. Seven Z28 striping colors were available: silver, charcoal, blue, dark gold, gold, red and orange. Base Camaro sport coupes had the 229 V-6, three-speed manual transmission, power steering and brakes, P205/75R14 steel-belted radial tires, front stabilizer bar, multi-leaf rear springs, concealed two-speed wipers, front bucket seats with console, dome light, four-spoke sport steering wheel, day/night mirror, and body-colored bumpers. Berlinetta added whitewall tires and wire wheel covers, a gauge package (including tachometer), dual horns, sport mirrors (left-hand remote), and electric clock; plus moldings for door pillar, upper fender, hood panel, belt and roof drip. Z28 also included heavy-duty cooling, clock, gauge package, and sport mirrors. Standard colors were black, red, white, and bright yellow; plus metallic bright blue, light or dark blue, dark brown, charcoal, gold, maroon, orange or silver. Cloth or vinyl interiors came in beige, black, dark blue, camel, red or silver. Halogen headlamps were a new option. Camaro's basic body dated back to 1970, but downsizing would come for 1982.

1981 Malibu Classic sedan (AA)

MALIBU — SERIES 1A — V-6/V-8 — Although the mid-size Malibu didn't change drastically this year, it got several appearance alterations. The four-door sedan (now marketed as a "sport sedan") got a dramatically restyled, squarish formal roofline and back window section. (The profile looked similar to that of the 1980 Buick Century.) The new grille with prominent horizontal bars had bright upper and lower moldings that extended the full width of the front end. Malibu also had new headlamp bezels, triple-unit taillights, and side marker lenses. Argent taillamp bezels had black accents. Full wheel covers were restyled, while the revised dash had a new glossy-black applique. Also new: high-pressure easy-roll tires, Delco maintenance-free Freedom II battery, and a jack that lifted the car from the side. Front ends held single rectangular headlamps. 'Chevrolet' nameplates were on the lower part of the grille (driver's side), as well as on the decklid (passenger side). 'Malibu' nameplates adorned the rear of quarter panels. Classic Landau coupes had a 'Landau' emblem on the 'B' pillar. Malibu had an ornament with Chevrolet crest. Malibu Classic had a stand-up hood ornament and front door pull straps. Body colors were beige, black, cream and white; plus metallic light or dark blue, light or medium brown, jade green, light jade green, maroon, light maroon, silver, or champagne. Cloth and vinyl interiors came in camel, champagne, dark blue, jade or maroon; custom interiors could also have beige. Power steering was now standard. As before, Malibu came in coupe, sedan or station wagon form, plus a Landau coupe. Halogen headlamps were now optional. Standard engine again was the 229 cu. in. (3.8-liter) V-6, with three-speed manual or optional automatic transmission. Both optional V-8s (267 and 305 cu. in.) came only with automatic. The bigger one was available only in wagons (and in California Malibus). Basic Malibu equipment included power brakes, compact spare tire, front stabilizer bar, concealed two-speed wipers, day/night mirror, and locking glove compartment. Malibu Classic models had dual horns and side window reveal moldings (except coupe). The Malibu Classic Landau coupe added a vinyl roof and body pinstriping, plus silver wheel covers. Wagons had wheel opening moldings. Cloth upholstery was standard except for wagons, which used vinyl.

1981 Monte Carlo Sport Coupe (CP)

MONTE CARLO — SERIES 1A — V-6/V-8 — Monte's A-Special body got a major aerodynamic restyle this year, including a lowered hood and slightly higher rear deck. The new "subtle wedge shape" was claimed to cut wind drag by 10 percent. High-pressure radial tires helped boost gas mileage. The standard automatic transmission had a torque converter clutch controlled by the CCC system, for lockup in third gear. High-pressure (35 psi) tires cut rolling resistance. Also new: Freedom II battery and side-lift frame jack. Coil springs were computer selected to match a specific car's weight and equipment (but softer to compensate for the higher-pressure tires). New cast aluminum wheels were available. Wide rectangular parking lamps moved to the outer ends of the bumper, well below the quad rectangular headlamps and in line with the license plate. Body-color front/rear bumpers blended into fender sides. Wide lower bodyside moldings ran the full car length. Side marker lamps were recessed into lower moldings (front and rear). Cornering lamps were optional this year. A 'Monte Carlo' nameplate was on the front of the front fender. The crosshatch grille with bright chrome bars was arranged in a 6 x 3 pattern of large holes. 'Monte Carlo' script was on the 'B' pillar (or 'Landau' nameplate and crest for Landau coupes). Monte colors were the same as Malibu. As before, base engine was the 229 cu. in. (3.8-liter) V-6, with optional turbocharged 231 cu. in. V-6 or a 267 cu. in. (4.4-liter) V-8. The 305 V-8 was now sold only in California. Standard equipment was similar to 1980, including automatic transmission, power steering and brakes, P195/75R14 steel-belted radial tires, compact spare tire, dual horns, concealed two-speed wipers, body-color bumpers, electric clock, locking glove compartment, body-color bumpers, and lighter. Also standard: wide lower bodyside, roof drip, rear quarter window and wheel opening moldings. Monte's Landau coupe added a vinyl roof, dual sport mirrors (driver's remote-controlled), a passenger visor mirror, side window sill moldings, 55/45 front seat, and body pinstriping.

1981 Impala Sport Coupe (CP)

IMPALA/CAPRICE CLASSIC — SERIES 1B — V-6/V-8 — Impala's three-section argent-finished grille this year had strong horizontal bars and recessed vertical divider bars, forming large holes in an 8 x 3 pattern, with bowtie emblem in the center. Parking/turn signal lights were in the bumper. At the rear were three-unit bright-accented taillamps on deck lid. An 'Impala' nameplate stood on the pillar behind the rear door. Caprice had a plain crosshatch grille this year, plus new side marker lamps, header moldings and headlamp bezels. Otherwise, the two looked much the same, though Caprice differed from Impala also in interior trim and option choices. Priced higher, however, Caprice (according to Chevrolet) "speaks of success. But not of excess." Both had tri-section taillamps, but Caprice's were bigger and added narrow vertical backup lamps alongside the license plate. Impala's small square backup lenses sat in each center taillamp section.

1981 Caprice Classic Landau Coupe (CP)

Fourteen solid body colors were offered: beige, black, cream and white, plus 10 metallics (light and dark blue, light and medium brown, champagne, light jade green, jade green, light maroon, maroon and silver). Nine two-tone combinations and seven vinyl top colors were available. Cloth interior colors were beige, dark blue, camel, champagne, jade and maroon. Vinyl came in all except beige. Caprice offered "richly elegant" velour upholstery. Full-size models with an optional 305 cu. in. (5.0- liter) V-8 got the new four-speed overdrive automatic transmission this year. The three-speed automatic continued with V-6 powerplants: standard 229 cu. in. (3.8-liter) in coupes and sedans. Wagons carried a standard 267 cu. in. (4.4-liter) V-8. Both transmissions had a computer-controlled torque converter clutch, which substituted a mechanical link for the customary fluid coupling in both third and fourth gears. A 350 cu. in. (5.7-liter) Oldsmobile diesel was offered again in wagons. Other changes included an easy-to-check plastic master cylinder reservoir, reduced-drag front disc brakes, Freedom II battery, new side-lift frame jack, and a "resume speed memory" for the optional cruise control. Corrosion protection at the underbody and fenders was improved, including durable Elpo dip plus frame assemblies immersed in hot-melt wax. A new compact spare was mounted on a 16 in. wheel. Easy-roll tires were standard, puncture-sealant tires available. Both Impala and Caprice had standard 229 V-6 engine (267 V-8 in wagons) and automatic transmission, plus power brakes and steering, concealed two-speed wipers, color-keyed steering wheel and carpeting, day/night mirror, and locking glove compartment. Impala lacked standard dual horns, an electric clock, electric clock, wheel opening moldings, stand-up hood ornament, and quiet sound group. The Caprice Classic Landau coupe had wire wheel covers, a vinyl roof, body pinstriping, and dual sport mirrors (driver's remote-controlled). Wagons had vinyl upholstery; sedans and coupes cloth.

I.D. DATA: Chevrolet, like all GM passenger cars, got a new 17- symbol Vehicle Identification Number (VIN) this year. As before, it was on the upper left surface of the instrument panel, visible through the windshield. The first symbol indicates country ('1' U.S.A.; '2' Canada). The second symbol denotes manufacturer ('G' General Motors). Symbol three indicates car make ('1' Chevrolet; '7' GM of Canada. Symbol four is restraint system ('A' non-passive; 'B' automatic belts; 'C' inflatable restraint). Symbol five is the car line/series: 'B' Chevette; 'J' Chevette Scooter; 'X' Citation; 'P' Camaro; 'S' Camaro Berlinetta; 'T' Malibu; 'W' Malibu Classic; 'Z' Monte Carlo; 'L' Impala; 'N' Caprice Classic. Symbols six and seven indicate body type: '08' 2-dr. hatchback coupe; '27' 2-dr. notchback coupe; '37' 2-dr. hardtop coupe; '47' 2-dr. hardtop coupe; '87' 2-dr. sport coupe; '68' 4-dr. hatchback sedan; '69' 4-dr. notchback sedan; '35' 4-dr. station wagon. Symbol eight is the engine code: '9' L4-98 2Bbl.; '5' L4-151 2Bbl.; 'X' V6173 2Bbl.; 'Z' V6173 H.O.; 'K' V6229 2Bbl.; 'A' V6231 2Bbl.; '3' Turbo V6231 4Bbl.; 'J' V8267 2Bbl.; 'H' V8305 4Bbl.; 'L' V8350 4Bbl.; 'N' Diesel V8350. Next comes a check digit. Symbol ten indicates model year ('B' 1981). Symbol eleven is assembly plant: 'A' Lakewood; 'B' Baltimore; 'D' Doraville, GA; 'J' Janesville, WI; 'K' Leeds, MO; 'L' Van Nuys, CA; 'N' Norwood, OH; 'R' Arlington, TX; 'S' St. Louis; 'T' Tarrytown, NY; 'W' Willow Run, MI; 'Y' Wilmington, DE; 'Z' Fremont, CA; '1' Oshawa, Ontario; '6' Oklahoma City. The final six digits make up the sequential serial number for output from each assembly plant. Body Number Plates and engine identification code locations were similar to 1980.

CHEVETTE (FOUR)

Model Number	Body/Style Number	Body Type & Seating	Factory Price	Shipping Weight	Production Total
1T	B08	2-dr. Hatch Cpe-4P	5255	2000	114,621
1T	B68	4-dr. Hatch Sed-4P	5394	2063	250,616

CHEVETTE SCOOTER (FOUR)

1T	J08	2-dr. Hatch Cpe-4P	4695	1945	55,211

CITATION (FOUR/V-6)

1X	X08	2-dr. Hatch Cpe-5P	6270/6395	2404/2459	113,983
1X	X68	4-dr. Hatch Sed-5P	6404/6529	2432/2487	299,396

CAMARO (V-6/V-8)

1F	P87	2-dr. Spt Cpe-4P	6780/6830	3222/3392	62,614

CAMARO BERLINETTA (V-6/V-8)

1F	S87	2-dr. Spt Cpe-4P	7576/7626	3275/3445	20,253

CAMARO Z28 (V-8)

1F	P87	2-dr. Spt Cpe-4P	-- /8263	N/A	43,272

MALIBU (V-6/V-8)

1A	T27	2-dr. Spt Cpe-6P	6498/6548	3037/3199	15,834
1A	T69	4-dr. Sed-6P	6614/6664	3028/3194	60,643
1A	T35	4-dr. Sta Wag-6P	6792/6842	3201/3369	29,387

MALIBU CLASSIC (V-6/V-8)

1A	W27	2-dr. Spt Cpe-6P	6828/6878	3065/3227	14,255
1A	W27/Z03	2-dr. Lan Cpe-6P	7092/7142	N/A	4,622
1A	W69	4-dr. Sed-6P	6961/7011	3059/3225	80,908
1A	W35	4-dr. Sta Wag-6P	7069/7119	3222/3390	36,798

MONTE CARLO (V-6/V-8)

1A	Z37	2-dr. Spt Cpe-6P	7299/7349	3102/3228	149,659
1A	Z37/Z03	2-dr. Lan Cpe-6P	8006/8056	N/A	38,191

IMPALA (V-6/V-8)

1B	L47	2-dr. Spt Cpe-6P	7129/7179	3326/3458	6,067
1B	L69	4-dr. Sedan-6P	7241/7291	3354/3486	60,090
1B	L35	4-dr. Sta Wag-6P	-- /7624	-- /3897	11,345
1B	L35/AQ4	4-dr. 3S Wag-8P	-- /7765	-- / N/A	8,462

CAPRICE CLASSIC (V-6/V-8)

1B	N47	2-dr. Spt Cpe-6P	7534/7584	3363/3495	9,741
1B	N47/Z03	2-dr. Lan Cpe-6P	7990/8040	N/A	6,615
1B	N69	4-dr. Sedan-6P	7667/7717	3400/3532	89,573
1B	N35	4-dr. Sta Wag-6P	-- /7948	-- /3940	11,184
1B	N35/AQ4	4-dr. 3S Wag-8P	-- /8112	-- / N/A	16,348

FACTORY PRICE AND WEIGHT NOTE: Where two prices and weights are shown, the figure to the left of the slash is for six-cylinder model, to right of slash for V-8 (267 and 305 V-8 were each $50 extra). For Citation, prices and weights to left of slash are four-cylinder, to right of slash for V-6 engine. All models had at least one price rise during the model year, except Chevette, which enjoyed a $100 price cut. **BODY/STYLE NO. NOTE:** Some models were actually option packages. Code after slash (e.g., Z03) is the number of the option package that comes with the model listed.

ENGINE DATA: BASE FOUR (Chevette): Inline. Overhead cam. Four-cylinder. Cast iron block and head. Displacement: 97.6 cu. in. (1.6 liters). Bore & stroke: 3.23 x 2.98 in. Compression ratio: 8.6:1. Brake horsepower: 70 at 5200 R.P.M. Torque: 82 lbs.-ft. at 2400 R.P.M. Five main bearings. Hydraulic valve lifters. Carburetor: 2Bbl. Holley 5210C. VIN Code: 9. BASE FOUR (Citation): Inline. Overhead valve. Four-cylinder. Cast iron block. Displacement: 151 cu. in. (2.5 liters). Bore & stroke: 4.00 x 3.00 in. Compression ratio: 8.2:1. Brake horsepower: 84 at 4000 R.P.M. Torque: 125 lbs.-ft. at 2400 R.P.M. Five main bearings. Hydraulic valve lifters. Carburetor: 2Bbl. Rochester 2SE. Pontiac-built. VIN Code: 5. OPTIONAL V-6 (Citation): 60-degree, overhead-valve V-6. Cast iron block and head. Displacement: 173 cu. in. (2.8 liters). Bore & stroke: 3.50 x 2.99 in. Compression ratio: 8.5:1. Brake horsepower: 110 at 4800 R.P.M. Torque: 145 lbs.-ft. at 2400 R.P.M. Four main bearings. Hydraulic valve lifters. Carburetor: 2Bbl. Rochester 2SE. VIN Code: X. HIGH-OUTPUT V-6 (Citation): Same as 173 cu. in. V-6 above except C.R.: 8.9:1. Brake H.P.: 135 at 5400 R.P.M. Torque: 145 lbs.-ft. at 2400 R.P.M. VIN Code: Z. BASE V-6 (Camaro, Malibu, Monte Carlo, Impala, Caprice): 90-degree, overhead-valve V-6. Cast iron block and head. Displacement: 229 cu. in. (3.8 liters). Bore & stroke: 3.74 x 3.48 in. Compression ratio: 8.6:1. Brake horsepower: 110 at 4200 R.P.M. Torque: 170 lbs.-ft. at 2000 R.P.M. Four main bearings. Hydraulic valve lifters. Carburetor: 2Bbl. Rochester 2ME. VIN Code: K. CALIFORNIA V-6 (for models above): 90-degree, overhead-valve V-6. Cast iron block and head. Displacement: 231 cu. in. (3.8 liters). Bore & stroke: 3.80 x 3.40 in. Compression ratio: 8.0:1. Brake horsepower: 110 at 3800 R.P.M. Torque: 190 lbs.-ft. at 1600 R.P.M. Four main bearings. Hydraulic valve lifters. Carburetor: 2Bbl. Rochester E2ME. Buick-built. VIN Code: A. TURBOCHARGED V-6; OPTIONAL (Monte Carlo): Same as 231 cu. in. V-6 above, except 4Bbl. Rochester E4ME carburetor Brake H.P.: 170 at 4000 R.P.M. Torque: 275 lbs.- ft. at 2400 R.P.M. VIN Code: 3. BASE V-8 (Caprice/Impala wagon); OPTIONAL (Camaro, Malibu, Monte Carlo, Impala, Caprice): 90-degree, overhead valve V-8. Cast iron block and head. Displacement: 267 cu. in. (4.4 liters). Bore & stroke: 3.50 x 3.48 in. Compression ratio: 8.3:1. Brake horsepower: 115 at 4000 R.P.M. Torque: 200 lbs.-ft. at 2400 R.P.M. Five main bearings. Hydraulic valve lifters. Carburetor: 2Bbl. Rochester 2ME. VIN Code: J. OPTIONAL V-8 (Camaro, Malibu, Monte Carlo, Impala, Caprice): 90-degree, overhead valve V-8. Cast iron block and head. Displacement: 305 cu. in. (5.0 liters). Bore & stroke: 3.74 x 3.48 in. Compression ratio: 8.6:1. Brake horsepower: 150 at 3800 R.P.M. Torque: 240 lbs.-ft. at 2400 R.P.M. Five main bearings. Hydraulic valve lifters. Carburetor: 4Bbl. Rochester 4ME. VIN Code: H. BASE V-8 (Camaro Z28): Same as 305 cu. in. V-8 above except Brake H.P.: 165 at 4000 R.P.M. Torque: 245 lbs.-ft. at 2400 R.P.M. M4ME carburetor. OPTIONAL V-8 (Camaro Z28): 90-degree, overhead valve V-8. Cast iron block and head. Displacement: 350 cu. in. (5.7 liters). Bore & stroke: 4.00 x 3.48 in. Compression ratio: 8.2:1. Brake horsepower: 175 at 4000 R.P.M. Torque: 275 lbs.-ft. at 2400 R.P.M. Five main bearings. Hydraulic valve lifters. Carburetor: 4Bbl. Rochester 4ME. VIN Code: L. DIESEL V-8; OPTIONAL (Impala/Caprice): 90-degree, overhead valve V-8. Cast iron block and head. Displacement: 350 cu. in. (5.7 liters). Bore & stroke: 4.057 x 3.385 in. Compression ratio: 22.5:1. Brake horsepower: 105 at 3200 R.P.M. Torque: 200 lbs.-ft. at 1600 R.P.M. Five main bearings. Hydraulic valve lifters. Fuel injection. Olds- built. VIN Code: N.

CHASSIS DATA: Vheelbase: (Chevette 2-dr.) 94.3 in.; (Chvt 4-dr.) 97.3 in.; (Citation) 104.9 in.; (Camaro) 108.0 in.; (Malibu/Monte Carlo) 108.1 in.; (Caprice/Imp) 116.0 in. Overall length: (Chvt 2-dr.) 161.9 in.; (Chvt 4-dr.) 164.9 in.; (Cit) 176.7 in.; (Camaro) 197.6 in.; (Malibu) 192.7 in.; (Malibu wag) 193.4 in.; (Monte) 200.4 in.; (Capr/Imp) 212.1 in.; (Capr/Imp wag) 215.1 in. Height: (Chvt) 52.9 in.; (Cit) 53.1 in.; (Camaro) 49.2 in.; (Malibu) 55.7 in.; (Malibu wag) 55.8 in.; (Monte) 53.9 in.; (Capr/Imp cpe) 54.6 in.; (Capr/Imp sed) 55.2 in.; (Capr/Imp wag) 57.1 in. Vidth: (Chvt) 61.8 in.; (Cit) 68.3 in.; (Camaro) 74.5 in.; (Malibu) 72.3 in.; (Malibu wag) 71.9 in.; (Monte) 71.8 in.; (Capr/Imp) 75.3 in.; (Capr/Imp wag) 79.3 in. Front Tread: (Chvt) 51.2 in.; (Cit) 58.7 in.; (Camaro) 61.3 in.; (Camaro Berlinetta) 61.6 in.; (Malibu/Monte) 58.5 in.; (Capr/Imp) 61.8 in.; (Capr/Imp wag) 62.2 in. Rear Tread: (Chvt) 51.2 in.; (Cit) 57.0 in.; (Camaro) 60.0 in.; (Camaro Berlinetta) 60.3 in.; (Malibu/Monte) 57.8 in.; (Capr/Imp) 60.8 in.; (Capr/Imp wag) 64.1 in. Standard Tires: (Chvt) P155/80R13 GBR; (Cit) P185/80R13 GBR; (Camaro) P205/75R14 SBR; (Camaro Z28) P225/70R15 WLT; (Malibu) P185/75R14 GBR; (Malibu wag) P195/75R14 GBR; (Monte) P195/75R14 SBR; (Imp/Capr) P205/75R15 SBR; (Imp/Capr wag) P225/75R15 SBR.

TECHNICAL: Transmission: Three-speed manual transmission standard on Camaro V-6. Gear ratios: (1st) 3.50:1; (2nd) 1.89:1; (3rd) 1.00:1; (Rev) 3.62:1. Four-speed floor shift standard on Chevette: (1st) 3.75:1; (2nd) 2.16:1; (3rd) 1.38:1; (4th) 1.00:1; (Rev) 3.82:1. Citation four-speed floor shift: (1st) 3.53:1; (2nd) 1.95:1; (3rd) 1.24:1; (4th) 0.81:1; (Rev) 3.42:1. Four-speed on Camaro V8305: (1st) 3.42:1; (2nd) 2.28:1; (3rd) 1.45:1; (4th) 1.00:1; (Rev) 3.51:1. Three-speed Turbo Hydra-matic standard on Monte Carlo and Caprice/Impala, optional on others. Gear ratios: (1st) 2.52:1; (2nd) 1.52:1; (3rd) 1.00:1; (Rev) 1.93:1 except Caprice/Impala V6231/V8305, Camaro V6229 and Monte V6231 ratios: (1st) 2.74:1; (2nd) 1.57:1; (3rd) 1.00:1; (Rev) 2.07:1. Base Chevette automatic trans.: (1st) 2.40:1; (2nd) 1.48:1; (3rd) 1.00:1; (Rev) 1.92:1. Citation auto. trans.: (1st) 2.84:1; (2nd) 1.60:1; (3rd) 1.00:1; (Rev) 2.07:1. Standard final drive ratio: (Chevette) 3.70:1; (Scooter) 3.36:1; (Citation) 3.32:1 w/manual, 2.84:1 w/auto.; (Camaro V-6) 2.73:1; (Camaro V-8) 2.56:1; (Camaro V8350) 3.08:1; (Z28) 3.42:1 w/4spd; (Malibu) 2.73:1 w/manual and V-6, 2.41:1 w/auto. and V-6, 2.29:1 w/V-8; (Monte V-6) 2.41:1; (Monte V8267) 2.73:1; (Monte V8305) 2.29:1; (Caprice/Imp V-6) 2.73:1; (Caprice/Imp V-8) 2.41:1. Steering: (Chevette/Citation) rack and pinion; (others) recirculating ball. Suspension/Body: same as 1980. Brakes: front disc, rear drum. Fuel tank: (Chvt) 12.5 gal.; (Cit) 14 gal.; (Camaro) 21 gal.; (Malibu) 18.1 gal.; (Monte) 18.1 gal.; (Capr/Imp) 25 gal.; (Capr/Imp wag) 22 gal.

DRIVETRAIN OPTIONS: Engines: 173 cu. in., 2Bbl. V-6: Citation ($125). Turbo 231 cu. in., 4Bbl. V-6: Monte ($750). 267 cu. in., 2Bbl. V-8: Camaro/Malibu/Monte/Imp/Caprice ($50). 305 cu. in., 4Bbl. V-8: Camaro/Malibu/Monte/Imp/Capr ($50); Imp/Capr wag (NC). 350 cu. in., 4Bbl. V-8: Z28 (NC). Diesel 350 cu. in. V-8: Imp/Capr wag ($695). Transmission/Differential: Four-speed manual shift: Camaro ($141). Three-speed automatic: Chevette ($335); Citation/Camaro/Malibu ($349); Camaro Z28 ($61). Four-speed overdrive automatic trans.: Imp/Capr ($162). Limited-slip differential: Camaro/Malibu/Monte ($67); Imp/Capr ($71). Performance axle ratio: Camaro/Malibu/Monte ($19). Power Accessories: Power brakes: Chvt/Cit ($79). Power steering: Chvt ($164); Cit ($168). Suspension: F40 H.D. susp.: Cit/Malibu/Monte/Imp/Capr ($23). F41 sport susp.: Chvt ($37); Cit ($39); Camaro ($33); Malibu/Monte/Imp/Capr cpe/sed ($43). Inflatable rear shock absorbers: Imp/Capr ($57). Other: H.D. cooling ($34-$61). Engine block heater: Imp/Capr wag ($16). H.D. alternator (63-amp): Malibu ($6-$34). H.D. alternator (70-amp): Cit ($11-$45); Monte/Imp/Capr ($32-$66). H.D. battery ($20) exc. diesel ($40). California emission system ($46).

CHEVETTE CONVENIENCE/APPEARANCE OPTIONS: Comfort/Convenience: Air conditioning ($531). Rear defogger, electric ($102). Tinted glass ($70). Comfortilt steering wheel ($78). Tachometer ($70). Electric clock ($23). Cigarette lighter: Scooter ($8). Intermittent wipers ($41). Rear wiper/washer ($100). Quiet sound group ($40-$52). Lighting and Mirrors: Halogen headlamps ($36). Aux. lighting: Chvt ($42-$43). Twin sport mirrors, left remote ($43). Driver's remote sport mirror ($29). Entertainment: AM radio: Scooter ($78). AM/FM radio ($64); Scooter ($142). AM/FM stereo radio ($100). Rear speaker ($19). Exterior Trim: Deluxe exterior: wheel opening, side window and rocker panel moldings ($118-$125). Two-tone paint ($116). Sport stripes ($78). Bodyside moldings: Scooter ($42). Side window reveal moldings ($69-$76). Door edge guards ($13-$21). Roof carrier ($74). Interior Trim/Upholstery: Cloth bucket seats ($16-$28). Custom bucket seats: cloth ($249); vinyl ($221). Rear seat delete ($50 credit). Color-keyed floor mats ($23). Vheels and Tires: Rally wheel trim ($52). P175/7013 SBR BSW: Chvt ($60); Scooter ($108). P175/7013 SBR WSW: Chvt ($108); Scooter ($155). P175/7013 SBR WLT: Chvt ($124); Scooter ($172).

CITATION CONVENIENCE/APPEARANCE OPTIONS: Option Packages: X11 sport equipment pkg. ($1498). Deluxe exterior pkg. ($117-$151). Quiet sound/rear decor pkg. ($75). Comfort/Convenience: Air cond. ($585). Rear defogger, electric ($107). Cruise control w/resume ($123). Tinted glass ($75). Sport steering wheel (NC to $21). Comfortilt steering wheel ($81). Power windows ($140-$195). Remote swing-out windows ($95). Power door locks ($93-$132). Gauge pkg. w/clock ($73). Special instruments incl. tachometer ($114). Electric clock ($23). Intermittent wipers ($41). Lighting, Horns and Mirrors: Halogen headlamps ($34). Aux. lighting ($43). Dual horns ($10). Driver's remote mirror ($19). Dual sport mirrors, left remote ($47). Entertainment: AM/FM radio ($64). AM/FM stereo radio ($100). Rear speaker ($19). Dual rear speakers ($28); incl. w/stereo radio. Windshield antenna ($10). Power antenna ($47). Radio delete ($51 credit). Exterior Trim: Removable sunroof ($246). Two-tone paint ($155) incl. pinstriping and bodyside moldings. Bodyside pinstriping ($34). Roof carrier ($90). Bodyside moldings ($44). Door edge guards ($13-$21). Side window reveal moldings ($41-$50). Bumper guards ($48). Bumper rub strips ($43). Interior Trim/Upholstery: Console ($86). Reclining driver or passenger seatback ($41-$69). Sport cloth bench seat ($28). Custom cloth or vinyl bench seat ($391). Vinyl bucket seats ($91-$116). Sport cloth bucket seats ($119-$144). Custom cloth or vinyl bucket seats ($482-$507). Color-keyed mats ($25). Vheels and Tires: Full wheel covers ($46). Wire wheel covers ($117-$163). Wheel trim rings ($50). Rally wheel trim ($36- $82). P185/80R13 GBR WSW ($51). P185/80R13 SBR BSW ($54). P185/80R13 SBR WSW ($105). P205/70R13 SBR WSW ($206). P205/70R13 SBR WLT ($222).

CAMARO/MALIBU/MONTE CARLO CONVENIENCE/APPEARANCE OPTIONS: Option Packages: Estate equipment: Malibu wag ($271). Interior decor/quiet sound group: Camaro ($67). Quiet sound group: Malibu ($54). Security pkg.: Malibu wag ($39). Comfort/Convenience: Air cond.: Camaro ($560); Malibu/Monte ($585). Rear defogger, electric ($107). Cruise control w/resume ($132). Tinted glass ($75). Comfortilt steering wheel ($81). Six-way power driver's seat: Malibu/Monte ($173). Power windows: Camaro/Monte ($140); Malibu ($140- $195). Power door locks: Malibu ($93-$132); Camaro/Monte ($93). Power trunk release: Monte ($27). Electric clock: base Camaro, Malibu ($23). Gauge pkg. w/tach: base Camaro ($118). Gauge pkg. w/clock and trip odometer: Malibu ($80). Gauge pkg. w/trip odometer: Monte ($55). Intermittent wipers ($41). Lighting, Horns and Mirrors: Halogen headlamps: Camaro/Malibu ($36). Halogen high-beams: Monte ($27). Cornering lamps: Monte ($48). Aux. lighting: Camaro ($33-$39); Malibu ($33- $59); Monte ($33). Dual horns: Camaro, base Malibu ($10). Remote-control driver's mirror: Malibu/Monte ($19). Twin sport mirrors (left remote): base Camaro, Malibu/Monte ($47). Twin remote sport mirrors: Malibu ($73); Monte ($26-$73). Visor vanity mirror: Monte ($6). Lighted visor mirror: Monte ($36-$42). Entertainment: AM radio ($90). AM/FM radio ($142). AM/FM stereo radio ($178). Stereo 8track tape player with AM/FM stereo radio ($252). Cassette player with AM/FM stereo radio ($264). AM/FM stereo radio w/CB ($487). Rear speaker ($19). Dual rear speakers: Malibu/Monte ($28). Windshield antenna ($25); incl. w/radios. Power antenna ($47). Exterior Trim: Removable glass roof panels: Camaro/Monte ($695). Power sky roof: Monte ($561). Vinyl roof: Malibu cpe ($115); Malibu sed ($124); Monte ($130). Cabriolet vinyl roof: Malibu ($171). Padded opera roof: Monte ($232). Rear spoiler: Camaro ($60). Style trim pkg.: Camaro ($76). Two- tone paint: Malibu ($71-$121); Monte ($134-$188). Bodyside moldings: Camaro ($44). Deluxe bodyside moldings: Malibu/Monte ($53). Door edge guards: Camaro/Malibu ($13- $21). Wheel opening moldings: Malibu cpe/sed ($25). Side window sill moldings: Monte ($34). Side window reveal moldings: Malibu ($44). Roof drip moldings: Camaro ($25). Bodyside pinstriping: Malibu ($50); Monte ($54). Rear window air deflector: Malibu wag ($32). Roof carrier: Malibu ($96). Bumper rub strips: Malibu ($43). Bumper guards, front/rear: Malibu ($48). Interior Trim/Upholstery: Custom interior (55/45 seating, center armrest, custom door panels and seats): Monte ($201- $387). Custom door/quarter trim panels: Monte ($27). Console: Malibu cpe/sed, Monte ($86). Vinyl bench seat: Malibu cpe/sed, Monte ($28). Cloth bench seat: Malibu wag ($28). Custom vinyl bench seat: Malibu wag ($63). Cloth 55/45 seating: Malibu ($181-$241); Monte ($208). Vinyl 55/45 seating: Malibu ($209-$241); Monte ($236); Monte Landau ($28). Vinyl bucket seats: Malibu cpe/sed ($91); Monte ($118). Cloth bucket seats: Camaro ($28); Malibu cpe/sed ($91); Monte ($118). Custom vinyl bucket seats: base Camaro ($322). Custom cloth bucket seats: Berlinetta ($28); base Camaro ($350). Adj. driver's seatback: Camaro ($23). Color- keyed mats ($25). Deluxe load-floor carpet: Malibu wag ($74). Deluxe trunk trim: Monte ($44). Vheels and Tires: Aluminum wheels: Camaro ($180-$331); Monte ($264-$319). Custom styled 14x7 wheels: Camaro ($151). Rally wheels: Camaro ($99); Malibu ($49-$95); Monte ($49); Malibu Classic Landau (NC). Full wheel covers: Camaro/Malibu ($46). Sport wheel covers (silver or gold): Malibu ($55- $101). Wire wheel covers: Malibu ($80-$181); Monte ($80- $135). Wheel cover locks: Berlinetta/Malibu/Monte ($34). P185/75R14 GBR WSW: Malibu cpe/sed ($48). P195/75R14 GBR WSW: Malibu wag ($51). P195/75R14 SBR WSW: Malibu cpe/sed ($125); Malibu wag ($102); Monte ($51). P205/75R14 SBR WSW: Camaro ($54). P205/75R14 SBR WLT: Camaro ($69); Berlinetta ($15). P205/70R14 SBR WSW: Monte ($107); Malibu cpe/sed ($183). P205/70R14 SBR WLT: Malibu cpe/sed ($198).

IMPALA/CAPRICE CONVENIENCE/APPEARANCE OPTIONS: Option Packages: Estate equipment: wag ($271). Value appearance group: bodyside and wheel opening moldings, full wheel covers ($93). Comfort/Convenience: Air cond. ($625). Comfortron auto-temp air cond. ($708). Rear defogger, blower: cpe/sed ($59). Rear defogger, electric ($107). Cruise control w/resume ($135). Tinted glass ($87). Comfortilt steering wheel ($81). Power door locks ($93-$132). Six-way power driver's seat ($173). Power windows ($143-$211). Power trunk release ($27). Power tailgate lock: wag ($43). Electric clock: Imp ($25). Digital clock: Imp ($59); Caprice ($36). Gauge pkg. w/trip odometer ($56). Intermittent wipers ($41). Quiet sound group: Imp ($58). Lighting, Horns and Mirrors: Halogen high-beam headlamps ($27). Cornering lamps ($48). Aux. lighting ($36-$57). Dual horns: Imp ($10). Driver's remote mirror ($19). Dual remote mirrors ($58). Dual sport mirrors, left remote ($47). Dual remote body-color sport mirrors ($26-$73). Visor vanity mirror ($6). Lighted visor mirror ($42). Entertainment: AM radio ($90). AM/FM radio ($142). AM/FM stereo radio ($178). Stereo 8track tape player with AM/FM stereo radio ($252). Cassette player with AM/FM stereo ($264). AM/FM stereo with CB and power antenna ($487). Rear speaker ($19). Dual rear speakers ($28). Power antenna ($47). Windshield antenna ($25); incl. w/radios. Exterior Trim: Power sky roof: cpe/sed ($650). Vinyl roof ($142). Roof carrier: wag ($119). Two-tone paint ($58). Custom two-tone ($124). Pinstriping ($34). Color-keyed bodyside moldings ($44). Door edge guards ($13-$21). Wheel opening moldings: Imp ($25). Bumper rub strips, front/rear ($58). Bumper guards ($54). Interior Trim/Upholstery: Vinyl bench seat: cpe/sed ($28). Cloth bench seat: wag ($28). Cloth 50/50 seat ($222-$268). Vinyl 50/50 seat ($240-$268). Custom cloth 50/50 seat: cpe ($400); sed ($424). Deluxe load-floor carpet: wag ($77). Deluxe cargo area carpet: wag ($114). Color-keyed mats: front ($15); rear ($10). Deluxe trunk trim ($55). Vheel Covers: Full wheel covers ($46). Sport wheel covers: Imp ($102); Caprice ($56). Custom wheel covers: Imp ($121); Capr ($75). Wire wheel covers: Capr ($135). Wire wheel cover locks ($34). Coupe/Sedan Tires: P205/75R15 SBR WSW ($54). P215/75R15 SBR WSW ($86). P225/70R15 SBR WSW ($132). Wagon Tires: P225/75R15 SBR WSW ($58). Puncture-sealant tires ($85-$105).

HISTORY: Introduced: Sept. 25, 1980. Model year production (U.S.): 1,582,575 (incl. Corvettes but not incl. 20,363 Acadians or early '82 Cavaliers). Of total production for U.S. market, 744,977 were four-cylinder, 590,984 sixes, and 392,632 V-8s. A total of 49,791 diesels and 3,027 turbos were installed. Calendar year production: 1,307,526 (including 27,990 Corvettes and 18,098 Acadians, but not incl. 139,837 early '82 Cavaliers). Calendar year sales by U.S. dealers: 1,442,281, for a 23.3 percent market share. Model year sales by U.S. dealers: 1,522,536 (incl. 33,414 Corvettes but not incl. 43,855 early 1982 Cavaliers).

Historical Footnotes: Sales had been expected to take an upturn for 1981, but fell far short of expectations, dropping by about 265,000 for the model year (even including early '82 Cavaliers). And 1980 had hardly been a big year either. Only Chevette sold better in 1981 than 1980 (but only slightly). Citation had been the company's best seller for 1980, setting a first-year sales record for General Motors. But second-year sales slipped along with the other models. Full-size Chevrolets sold so poorly that there was speculation they would soon be dropped. Even with sagging sales, prices were raised at mid-year. Incentives (including rebates and reduced finance rates) were announced, but failed to bring in enough customers.

1982 CHEVROLET

1982 Cavalier Cadet sedan (CH)

Two all-new models (subcompact Cavalier and compact Celebrity) and a major restyle highlighted 1982. Biggest news was the downsized Camaro, even racier than before, which debuted with the family-size Celebrity in January 1982. Some hefty price increases arrived this year too. Opening prices for the restyled Camaros were $976 to $1810 higher than 1981 equivalents. The remaining Malibu models rose by well over a thousand dollars. Unlike some years in this era, though, Chevrolets endured only a $15 price hike during the model year. On the mechanical front, Pontiac's four-cylinder engine (used in Citation, Camaro and Celebrity) added fuel injection. The fact that Malibu now wore a grille similar to full-size models helped fuel rumors that the big Chevrolets were doomed. But reports of their imminent demise proved premature.

1982 Chevette hatchback sedan (AA)

CHEVETTE — SERIES 1T — FOUR — Both gas and diesel engines were offered on the subcompact Chevette this year. The 1.8-liter four-cylinder diesel, coupled to a new five-speed manual transmission, rated 40 MPG city and 55 MPG highway in EPA estimates. It was offered under both coupe and sedan hoods (but not Scooter), priced as a separate model rather than an option. The overhead-cam, 51-horsepower diesel had actually became available late in the 1981 model year, in limited numbers. Built by Isuzu, it had a cross-flow cylinder head and lightweight Bosch distributor-type fuel pump/injection system. The low-budget Scooter came in four-door hatchback form this year, as well as the carryover two-door (priced just under $5000). The four-door cost $241 more. Standard gasoline engine was the 1.6-liter four, with four-speed manual transmission. A new five-speed gearbox was also available, as well as automatic. The five-speed had been added as a late '81 option. Compression ratio of the gas engine rose from 8.6:1 in 1981 to 9.2:1 this year, as a redesigned cylinder head forced the air/fuel mixture into the combustion chamber with a more efficient swirling motion. Standard equipment (except on Scooters) included an AM radio, color-keyed instrument panel, reclining front bucket seats, transmission floor control, and sport steering wheel. Chevettes did not change in appearance.

wheels, and flush-mount windshield; plus black grille, headlamp and parking lamp bezels. Body colors were white, black, light yellow, beige and red; plus metallic silver, light or dark blue, bright blue, light or dark jade, gold, maroon, or charcoal. After its first half-season, Cavalier got several powertrain changes (mainly in axle ratios and electronic control module) by the time the 1982 model year began. Carburetion and ignition calibration for models with air conditioning was revised to improve cold startups and low-speed response, using a new microchip. Models with air conditioning and automatic transmission got a 3.18:1 final drive ratio, while manual-shift Cavaliers switched from 2.96:1 to 3.32:1 after the start of the full model year. Automatic transmissions were modified too. As the model year began, Cavalier also got a full-width, three-passenger back seat (with optional split folding back), becoming a five-passenger vehicle rather than four. A bigger (2.0-liter), 90-horsepower four was announced, but arrived later. Cavalier's standard equipment included four-speed manual transaxle, P175/80R13 GBR tires on rally steel wheels, AM radio, electric side/rear window defoggers, lighter, digital clock, reclining front bucket seats, trip odometer, console, day/night mirror, color-keyed carpeting, locking glove compartment, front stabilizer bar, bodyside moldings, and bumper rub strips. Hatchbacks also had a gauge package and fold-down rear seat; wagons the fold-down seat and air deflector. Cavalier CL added power steering, AM/FM radio, whitewall tires, sport wheel covers, sport mirrors (left remote), tinted glass, rear stabilizer bar, gauges, intermittent wipers, leather-wrapped steering wheel, and halogen headlamps. CL hatchbacks had a tachometer and rear wiper/washer.

1982 Citation coupe (CH)

CITATION — SERIES 1X — FOUR/V-6 — Electronic fuel injection became standard this year on the base 151 cu. in. (2.5-liter) four, supplied by Pontiac. This produced an estimated 4 MPG mileage increase. Also new were high-pressure (35 psi) easy-roll tires, geometry-tuned suspension, and a relocated rack-and-pinion steering mount. Citation again came in two-door and four-door hatchback form, along with an H11 five-passenger coupe. The high-performance two-door X11 package was offered again, including the HO 600 engine (a 135-horsepower version of the 2.8-liter V-6) and modified suspension components. Citation had a new horizontal grille for 1982, shaped similar to the 1981 crosshatch version. Eight body colors were new. New vinyl upholstery went on standard seats. Interiors came in three new trim colors: charcoal, jadestone, and redwood. New options included automatic speed control for use with manual transmission. The automatic transmission got a lockup torque converter clutch for high gear. The X11 sport equipment package included the high-output V-6 engine, power brakes, sport mirrors, rear spoiler, bucket seats, P215/60R14 tires on aluminum wheels, special instruments, sport steering wheel, F41 sport suspension, and bumper rub strips.

1982 Cavalier hatchback coupe (CP)

CAVALIER — SERIES 1J — FOUR Introduced on May 21, 1981 as an early '82 model, the new front-drive four-passenger Chevrolet was described as subcompact on the outside, with compact roominess inside. It was also called a "high-content vehicle" with an ample load of standard equipment, including radio, power brakes, reclining bucket seats, stabilizer bar, and remote trunk/hatch/tailgate release. Four models were offered: two-door and four-door sedans, two-door hatchback, and four-door wagon. Cavaliers came in three series: low-budget Cadet, base, and CL. Sole engine at first was a transverse-mounted 112 cu. in. (1.8-liter) four, rated 88 horsepower, with four-speed (overdrive) manual transmission. EPA ratings reached 30 MPG (city). A 2.0-liter four was announced, but arrived later. Cavaliers had a low, horizontal-style grille with bowtie emblem in the solid panel above. Single recessed rectangular headlamps flanked vertical park/signal lamps. Taillamps were split into two sections by a horizontal divider. Base Cavaliers had integrated bright bumper systems with black/argent rub strips; PlastisolR lower body stone chip protection; black wipers; amber rear turn signal lamps; bright hood molding and grille bars; a styled black outside mirror; body-color wraparound bumper end caps; and bodyside moldings. Rally wheels held trim rings. 'Cavalier' nameplates were on front fenders. Hatchbacks came with a flush-mount back window, soft-fascia front-end panel, wide-base Rally

1982 Camaro Berlinetta Sport Coupe (CH)

119

CAMARO — SERIES 1F — FOUR/V-6/V-8 — An all-new Camaro arrived late in the model year, still rear-wheel drive but in a lighter-weight fastback form. In Chevrolet's words, the new version "captures the essence of the contemporary American performance expression." Offered again in three models, but with a contemporary aerodynamic shape and "aircraft-inspired interior," Camaro weighed some 470 pounds less than in 1981, though it was still no lightweight. The new body was nearly 10 inches shorter, riding a 101 inch wheelbase (down from 108). The fuel filler door was now on the quarter panel (driver's side), with a hatch release lock behind the license plate. Camaros had a new lift-up hatch back window. Standard Sport Coupe engine was now Pontiac's 151 cu. in. (2.5-liter), 90-horsepower "Iron Duke" four with electronic fuel injection. Options: a variant of Citation's 173 cu. in. (2.8-liter) V-6 rated 102 horsepower, or a four- barrel carbureted 305 cu. in. (5.0-liter) V-8 that produced 145 horsepower. The V-6 was standard in Berlinetta; V-8 standard in Z28. But the Z28 could also have an optional Cross-Fire fuel-injected 305 V-8, rated 165 horsepower, for an extra $450. That version was marked by a 'Cross Fire Injection' decal below the 'Z28' identifier (just behind the front wheel housing), plus operating air inlets. Camaro's optional three-speed automatic transmission had a torque converter lockup clutch. A four-speed manual gearbox was now standard on the base Camaro, so the old three-speed was gone for good. Four-wheel disc brakes were now available with V-8 engines. Inside, a new console held glove box, parking brake lever, and controls for heater, optional stereo radio and air conditioning. The instrument panel was black-finished to minimize reflections. Twin speedometer needles showed both MPH and kilometers per hour. Interior space was similar to before, even though outside dimensions had shrunk. The rear seat's backrest folded down, turning the rear section into a cargo area, accessible through the new hatch. For an extra $611, Z28s could have a new "Conteur" seat option from Lear- Siegler, with six adjustments (backrest bolster, thigh support, cushion bolster, lumbar and recliner). A six-way power seat was now optional on all models. Each model had its own styling features, including specific front air dam and rear fascia. All Camaros had deeply recessed quad rectangular headlamps and tri-color wraparound taillamps (not far removed from prior designs). Camaro's fastback profile included a compound Sshaped glass hatch. The flush-mounted windshield's 62-degree rake helped produce a 0.368 drag coefficientone of the lowest ever tested by GM. Z28's front end had no upper grille opening, while its "ground effects" air dams reached lower to the ground. Z28s also rode special five-spoke aluminum wheels. Body colors for 1982 were white, silver, black, red, maroon, charcoal, light or dark blue, light or dark jade, gold, or dark gold. The new Camaro's body was unitized construction, but with bolt-on front sheetmetal. Rear coils replaced the old leaf springs. The rear suspension now consisted of a longitudinal torque tube, short control arms ahead of the solid axle, and lateral track rod. Front suspension used modified MacPherson struts with coil springs and stabilizer bar. Z28s and the F41 sport suspension added a link-type rear stabilizer bar. Base Sport Coupe standard equipment included four-speed manual shift, power brakes and steering, front stabilizer bar, dual black sport mirrors, black windshield molding, concealed wipers, body-color wheels with hubcaps and P195/75R14 GBR tires, reclining front bucket seats, and a day/night mirror. Berlinetta added P205/70R14 SBR tires, body pinstriping, body-color sport mirrors, black-accented lower body (with stripe), gold-accented aluminum spoke wheels, and higher-level acoustic package. Camaro Z28 equipment included five-spoke aluminum wheels (gold or charcal accented) with P215/65R15 white-letter tires, a rear stabilizer bar, specially-tuned suspension, dual mufflers and tailpipes, body-color sport mirrors, front air dam, "ground effects" rocker molding area, and rear deck spoiler. Twin air scoops rode the special Z28 hood. A total of 6,360 Indy 500 Commemorative Editions of the Z28 were built this year, marking the use of a Camaro as Indy pace car. All the replicas had a silver/blue body, Indy 500 logos, red-accented silver aluminum wheels and Goodyear Eagle GT white-letter tires. Blue cloth/silver vinyl interiors held the Lear-Siegler Conteur driver's seat, along with special instruments, leather-wrapped steering wheel and AM/FM stereo radio. Chevrolet dealers were entitled to order one special edition apiece.

CELEBRITY — SERIES 1A — FOUR/V-6 — The new front-wheel drive family sedan was designed to combine small-car economy with "big-car ride, comfort and style." When buying a Celebrity, declared Chevrolet general manager Robert D. Lund, customers wouldn't find that "they sacrificed comfort, space and prestige" for the sake of economy. Though roughly the same size inside as the Malibu it soon would replace, Celebrity weighed some 500 pounds less and stood a foot shorter in overall length. Wheelbase was identical to Citation's, but Celebrity measured almost a foot longer (188.3 inches overall). Celebrity came in two- door and four-door sedan form, with three five-passenger interior trim levels (base, CS and CL). The wedge-shape design (low nose and high deck) resulted from extensive wind- tunnel testing. Celebrity's 0.38 aero drag coefficient was the lowest rating ever for a mass-produced GM sedan. Celebrity wasn't introduced until after the first of the year, on January 14, 1982. Standard powertrain was a fuel- injected 151 cu. in. (2.5-liter) four-cylinder engine with three-speed automatic transaxle, which produced EPA estimates of 25 MPG city and 40 highway. Both gas and diesel V-6 engines were announced: a 173 cu. in. (2.8-liter) gasoline model and 4.3-liter diesel. But the diesel's appearance was delayed for a year. Gasoline models had an on-board computer system that included self-diagnostics. Celebrity's front end was similar to Cavalier, with a solid panel above the low grille; but the 8x4 hole crosshatch grille held a bowtie emblem in its center. Celebrity also carried quad rectangular headlamps over horizontal park/signal lamps. Wide tri-section taillamps stretched from license plate opening to quarter panel, divided by a horizontal bar. Celebrity came in a dozen solid colors plus six two- tones. Solids were white, light and dark blue, light and dark metallic jadestone or sandstone, light and dark metallic redwood, slate gray, silver metallic, and charcoal metallic. Two-tones were slate gray/silver metallic; dark blue/light blue metallic; dark blue/pastel sandstone; light/dark jadestone metallic; pastel sandstone/light redwood metallic; or dark/light redwood metallic. Cloth or vinyl interior trim came in slate gray, dark blue, jadestone, sandstone, doeskin and redwood. Standard equipment included the four-cylinder engine, power brakes, power rack-and-pinion steering, pushbutton AM radio, maintenance-free battery, front stabilizer bar, chrome bumpers with black rub strips and body-color end caps, and P185/80R13 GBR tires with full wheel covers. Also standard: black side window frames, bright drip and bodyside moldings, front bench seat with fixed armrest, side window defoggers, day/night mirror, and locking glove compartment.

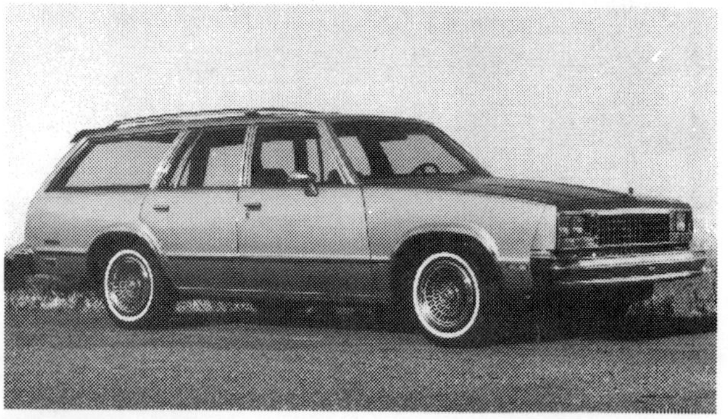

1982 Malibu Classic station wagon (CH)

MALIBU CLASSIC — SERIES 1A — V-6/V-8 — This year's Malibu had a distinctive crosshatch grille similar to Caprice, flanked by quad rectangular headlamps that stood over horizontal quad park/signal lamps. A dozen body colors were available, with either cloth or vinyl interiors. A four-door sport sedan and four-door wagon were the only models. Base engine was the 229 cu. in. (3.8-liter) V-6. But Malibus could also have either the 267 cu. in. (4.4- liter) or 305 cu. in. (5.0-liter) gas V-6, or a choice of diesels: 4.3-liter V-6 or the big 5.7-liter V-8 from Oldsmobile. The small diesel, which arrived later in the model year, was Chevrolet's first V-6 version (actually produced by Oldsmobile). It had roller hydraulic valve lifters, a serpentine belt system, venturi-shaped prechamber, and a torque-pulse compensator for smoother power flow. The diesel had aluminum cylinder heads, intake manifold, water outlet and oil pump body. Base Malibus were gone, leaving only the Classic, in only sedan and station wagon form. Standard equipment included automatic transmission, power brakes and steering, notchback front bench seats with folding armrests, dual horns, front stabilizer bar, full wheel covers, and stand-up hood ornament. Bodies displayed a bright wide upper grille molding, bright back window and windshield reveal moldings, bright sill and roof drip moldings, and wide wheel opening moldings. Circular instrumentation was similar to Monte Carlo's. Inside were a lighter, dome light and day/night mirror. Sedans had bright decklid and end cap moldings, plus black-accented bright taillamp trim.

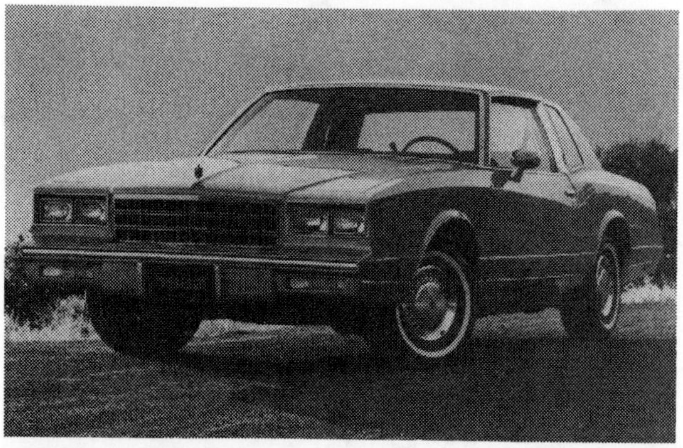

1982 Monte Carlo Sport Coupe (CH)

MONTE CARLO — SERIES 1A — V-6/V-8 — A finely-textured crosshatch grille set off Monte's front end this year, divided into three sections by two horizontal bars. Quad rectangular headlamps sat alongside the grille, but wide parking lamps were recessed low in the bumper. The body carried on Monte's "subtle wedge shape," now available in a dozen solid body colors and six two-tones. The Landau coupe was dropped, leaving only one coupe model. Interiors could have either cloth or vinyl trim. A passenger- side mirror was now standard, and a fixed-mast radio antenna replaced the former windshield antenna. Monte rode high- pressure (35 psi) tires and stopped with low-drag brakes. Standard engine remained the 229 cu. in. (3.8-liter) V-6. Two gasoline V-8s were also available: 267 and 305 cu. in. So were a pair of diesels: either the new V-6 or the big Oldsmobile V-8. The turbo V-6 was out. Montes had standard automatic transmission, power brakes and steering, plus P195/75R14 SBR tires on 6 in. wheels. Also standard: body- color bumpers, bright roof drip and windshield reveal moldings, twin bright outside mirrors, bright lower bodyside and quarter window reveal moldings, a stand-up hood ornament, full wheel covers, wheel opening moldings, bright decklid and end cap moldings, full-width front seat with folding armrest, dome light, day/night mirror, dual horns, lighter, and trunk mat.

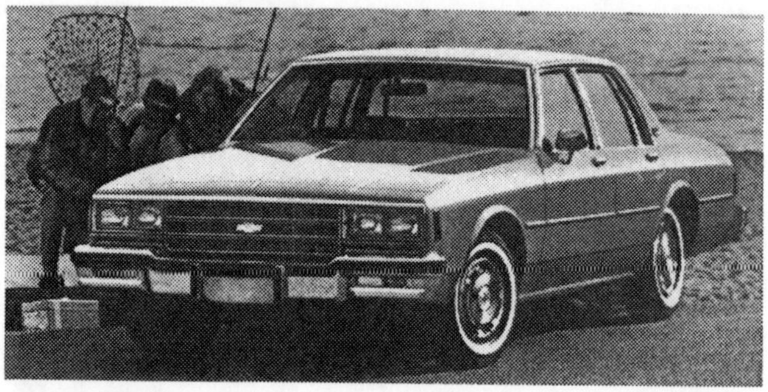

1982 Impala sedan (CP)

IMPALA/CAPRICE CLASSIC — SERIES 1B — V-6/V-8 — Full-size Chevrolets looked about the same for 1982, but came in fewer models. The Caprice Landau coupe and Impala sport coupe were dropped. Only the three-seat Caprice wagon was offered, along with the sport coupe and four-door sedan. Impala's lineup included the sedan and twin wagons. Oldsmobile's 350 cu. in. (5.7-liter) diesel V-8 was now available on all models, not just the station wagon. Standard engine was the 229 cu. in. (3.8-liter) V-6, with three-speed automatic. Wagons had the 267 cu. in. (4.4-liter) V-8, which cost $70 extra on other models. Optional four-speed overdrive automatic boosted gas mileage on the optional 267 cu. in. (4.4-liter) or 305 (5.0-liter) gas engines. Impala had an argent grille, Caprice a chrome-plated grille. Impala lacked a stand-up hood ornament and had thinner rocker moldings. Its front side marker lenses stood slightly back from fender tips, while Caprice's wrapped around. Standard equipment included three-speed automatic transmission, power brakes and steering, two-speed wipers, front stabilizer bar, bright windshield reveal and roof drip moldings, bright window reveal and frame moldings, day/night mirror, lighter, and one-piece carpeting. Caprice also included full wheel covers, wheel opening moldings, carpeted lower door panels, headlamp-on reminder, dual horns, and bright wide sill moldings. Wagons had a power tailgate window and locking side compartment.

I.D. DATA: Chevrolet's 17-symbol Vehicle Identification Number (VIN) was again on the upper left surface of the instrument panel, visible through the windshield. Coding is similar to 1981, but the following codes were added: Under car line/series (symbol five), code 'D' Cavalier; 'E' Cavalier hatch; 'W' both Celebrity and Malibu. Under body type (symbols six and seven), code '19' 4-dr. sedan; code '77' 2-dr. hatchback coupe. Symbol eight is the engine code: 'C' L4-98 2Bbl.; 'D' L4-111 diesel; 'R' or '2' L4-151

FI: 'X' or '1' V6173 2Bbl.; 'Z' V6173 H.O.; 'K' V6229 2Bbl.; 'V' Diesel V6262. 'J' V8267 2Bbl.; 'H' V8305 4Bbl.; '7' V8305 CFI; 'N' Diesel V8350. Model year (symbol ten) changed to 'C' for 1982. Codes combined with a serial number are also stamped on the engine. Chevette codes are on the right side of the block, below No. 1 plug. Cavalier's are on a pad on the right side of the block (facing the car), below the head. Pontiac 151 fours have coding on a pad at the left front of the block, below the head; or on a flange at left rear, above the starter. The V6173 is coded on the block at the front of the right head, or on the left rocker cover. Other V-6s and V-8s have coding stamped on the left side of the bell housing flange.

CHEVETTE (FOUR)

Model Number	Body/Style Number	Body Type & Seating	Factory Price	Shipping Weight	Production Total
1T	B08	2-dr. Hatch Cpe-4P	5513	2002	51,431
1T	B68	4-dr. Hatch Sed-4P	5660	2063	111,661

CHEVETTE SCOOTER (FOUR)

1T	J08	2-dr. Hatch Cpe-4P	4997	1957	31,281
1T	J68	4-dr. Hatch Sed-4P	5238	2004	21,742

CHEVETTE DIESEL (FOUR)

1T	B08/Z90	2-dr. Hatch Cpe-4P	6579	N/A	4,874
1T	B68/Z90	4-dr. Hatch Sed-4P	6727	N/A	11,819

Chevette Production Note: Totals do not include Chevette diesels (4,252 coupes and 8,900 sedans) produced during the 1981 model year.

1J	D27	2-dr. Coupe-5P	6966	2298	30,245
1J	E77	2-dr. Hatch Cpe-5P	7199	2364	22,114
1J	D69	4-dr. Sedan-5P	7137	2345	52,941
1J	D35	4-dr. Sta Wag-5P	7354	2405	30,853

1982 Cavalier station wagon (CP)

CAVALIER CADET (FOUR)

1J	D27/Z11	2-dr. Coupe-5P	6278	N/A	2,281
1J	D69/Z11	4-dr. Sedan-5P	6433	N/A	9,511
1J	D35/Z11	4-dr. Sta Wag-5P	6704	N/A	4,754

CAVALIER CL (FOUR)

1J	D27/Z12	2-dr. Coupe-5P	7944	2315	6,063
1J	E77/Z12	2-dr. Hatch Cpe-5P	8281	2381	12,792
1J	D69/Z12	4-dr. Sedan-5P	8137	2362	15,916
1J	D35/Z12	4-dr. Sta Wag-5P	8452	2422	7,587

CITATION (FOUR/V-6)

1X	H11	2-dr. Coupe-5P	6297/6515	2404/2468	9,102
1X	X08	2-dr. Hatch Cpe-5P	6754/6972	2413/2477	29,613
1X	X68	4-dr. Hatch Sed-5P	6899/7024	2447/2511	126,932

CAMARO (V-6/V-8)

1F	P87	2-dr. Spt Cpe-4P	7755/7925	2846/3025	78,761

CAMARO BERLINETTA (V-6/V-8)

1F	S87	2-dr. Spt Cpe-4P	9266/9436	2880/3094	39,744

CAMARO Z28 (V-8)

1F	P87	2-dr. Spt Cpe-4P	--/9700	--/3005	63,563

Camaro Engine Note: Prices and weights before slash are for V-6 engine, after slash for V-8. Base Camaro Sport Coupes were also available with a four-cylinder engine, priced at $7631 and weighing 2770 pounds. The Z28 could have an optional CFI V-8 for an additional $450. **Z28 Production Note:** A total of 6,360 Indy 500 Commemorative Editions were built, in addition to standard Z28s. Chevrolet figures also show over 1,300 Z28E hatchback models for export.

CELEBRITY (FOUR/V-6)

1A	W27	2-dr. Coupe-5P	8313/8438	2609/2669	19,629
1A	W19	4-dr. Sedan-5P	8463/8588	2651/2711	72,701

MALIBU CLASSIC (V-6/V-8)

1A	W69	4-dr. Spt Sed-6P	8137/8207	3097/3228	70,793
1A	W35	4-dr. Sta Wag-6P	8265/8335	3247/3387	45,332

MONTE CARLO (V-6/V-8)

1A	Z37	2-dr. Spt Cpe-6P	8177/8247	3116/3245	92,392

IMPALA (V-6/V-8)

1B	L69	4-dr. Sedan-6P	7918/7988	3368/3492	47,780
1B	L35	4-dr. Sta Wag-6P	--/8516	--/3938	10,654
1B	L35/AQ4	4-dr. 3S Wag-8P	--/8670	--/N/A	6,245

CAPRICE CLASSIC (V-6/V-8)

1B	N47	2-dr. Spt Cpe-6P	8221/8291	3380/3500	11,999
1B	N69	4-dr. Sedan-6P	8367/8437	3417/3541	86,126
1B	N35/AQ4	4-dr. 3S Wag-9P	--/9051	--/4019	25,385

FACTORY PRICE AND WEIGHT NOTE: For Citation and Celebrity, prices and weights to left of slash are for four-cylinder, to right for V-6 engine. For Camaro, Malibu, Monte Carlo and full-size models, figures to left of slash are for six-cylinder model, to right of slash for V-8 (267 and 305 V-8 were each $70 extra). Diesel engines cost considerably more (see option prices). **BODY/STYLE NO. NOTE:** Some models were actually option packages. Code after the slash (e.g., AQ4) is the number of the option package that comes with the model listed.

ENGINE DATA: BASE FOUR (Chevette): Inline. Overhead cam. Four-cylinder. Cast iron block and head. Displacement: 98 cu. in. (1.6 liters). Bore & stroke: 3.23 x 2.98 in. Compression ratio: 9.2:1. Brake horsepower: 65 at 5200 R.P.M. Torque: 80 lbs.-ft. at 3200 R.P.M. Five main bearings. Hydraulic valve lifters. Carburetor: 2Bbl. Holley 6510C. VIN Code: C. DIESEL FOUR (Chevette): Inline. Overhead cam. Four-cylinder. Cast iron block and head. Displacement: 111 cu. in. (1.8 liters). Bore & stroke: 3.31 x 3.23 in. Compression ratio: 22.0:1. Brake horsepower: 51 at 5200 R.P.M. Torque: 72 lbs.-ft. at 2000 R.P.M. Five main bearings. Solid valve lifters. Fuel injection. VIN Code: D. BASE FOUR (Cavalier): Inline. Overhead valve. Four-cylinder. Cast iron block and head. Displacement: 112 cu. in. (1.8 liters). Bore & stroke: 3.50 x 2.91 in. Compression ratio: 9.0:1. Brake horsepower: 88 at 5100 R.P.M. Torque: 100 lbs.-ft. at 2800 R.P.M. Five main bearings. Hydraulic valve lifters. Carburetor: 2Bbl. Rochester E2SE. VIN Code: G. BASE FOUR (Citation, Celebrity, Camaro): Inline. Overhead valve. Four-cylinder. Cast iron block and head. Displacement: 151 cu. in. (2.5 liters). Bore & stroke: 4.00 x 3.00 in. Compression ratio: 8.2:1. Brake horsepower: 90 at 4000 R.P.M. Torque: 132 lbs.-ft. at 2800 R.P.M. Five main bearings. Hydraulic valve lifters. Throttle-body fuel injection. Pontiac-built. VIN Code: R or 2. BASE V-6 (Camaro Berlinetta); OPTIONAL (Citation, Celebrity, Camaro): 60-degree, overhead-valve V-6. Cast iron block and head. Displacement: 173 cu. in. (2.8 liters). Bore & stroke: 3.50 x 2.99 in. Compression ratio: 8.5:1. Brake horsepower: 102-112 at 4800 R.P.M. (Camaro, 102). Torque: 142-145 lbs.-ft. at 2400 R.P.M. (Camaro, 142). Four main bearings. Hydraulic valve lifters. Carburetor: 2Bbl. Rochester E2SE. VIN Code: X or 1. HIGH-OUTPUT V-6 (Citation): Same as 173 cu. in. V-6 above except C.R.: 8.9:1. Brake H.P.: 135 at 5400 R.P.M. Torque: 145 lbs.- ft. at 2400 R.P.M. VIN Code: Z. BASE V-6 (Malibu, Monte Carlo, Impala, Caprice): 90-degree, overhead-valve V-6. Cast iron block and head. Displacement: 229 cu. in. (3.8 liters). Bore & stroke: 3.74 x 3.48 in. Compression ratio: 8.6:1. Brake horsepower: 110 at 4200 R.P.M. Torque: 170 lbs.-ft. at 2000 R.P.M. Four main bearings. Hydraulic valve lifters. Carburetor: 2Bbl. Rochester E2ME. VIN Code: K. DIESEL V-6 (Malibu, Monte Carlo): 90-degree, overhead-valve V-6. Cast iron block and aluminum head. Displacement: 262 cu. in. (4.3 liters). Bore & stroke: 4.057 x 3.385 in. Compression ratio: 22.5:1. Brake horsepower: 85 at 3600 R.P.M. Torque: 165 lbs.-ft. at 1600 R.P.M. Four main bearings. Hydraulic valve lifters. Fuel injection. VIN Code: V. BASE V-8 (Caprice/Impala wagon); OPTIONAL (Malibu, Monte Carlo, Impala, Caprice): 90-degree, overhead valve V-8. Cast iron block and head. Displacement: 267 cu. in. (4.4 liters). Bore & stroke: 3.50 x 3.48 in. Compression ratio: 8.3:1. Brake horsepower: 115 at 4000 R.P.M. Torque: 205 lbs.-ft. at 2400 R.P.M. Five main bearings. Hydraulic valve lifters. Carburetor: 2Bbl. Rochester E2ME. VIN Code: J. BASE V-8 (Camaro Z28): 90-degree, overhead valve V-8. Cast iron block and head. Displacement: 305 cu. in. (5.0 liters). Bore & stroke: 3.74 x 3.48 in. Compression ratio: 8.6:1. Brake horsepower: 145 at 4000 R.P.M. Torque: 240 lbs.-ft. at 2000 R.P.M. Five main bearings. Hydraulic valve lifters. Carburetor: 4Bbl. Rochester E4ME. VIN Code: H. OPTIONAL V-8 (Camaro Z28): Same as 305 cu. in. V-8 above with dual CFI Brake H.P.: 165 at 4200 R.P.M. Torque: 240 lbs.-ft. at 2400 R.P.M. VIN Code: 7. DIESEL V-8 (Impala, Caprice): OPTIONAL (Impala/Caprice): 90-degree, overhead valve V-8. Cast iron block and head. Displacement: 350 cu. in. (5.7 liters). Bore & stroke: 4.057 x 3.385 in. Compression ratio: 22.5:1. Brake horsepower: 105 at 3200 R.P.M. Torque: 200 lbs.-ft. at 1600 R.P.M. Five main bearings. Hydraulic valve lifters. Fuel injection. Olds- built. VIN Code: N.

CHASSIS DATA: Wheelbase: (Chevette 2-dr.) 94.3 in.; (Chvt 4-dr.) 97.3 in.; (Cavalier) 101.2 in.; (Citation/Celebrity) 104.9 in.; (Camaro) 101.0 in.; (Malibu/Monte Carlo) 108.1 in.; (Caprice/Imp) 116.0 in. Overall length: (Chvt 2-dr.) 161.9 in.; (Chvt 4-dr.) 164.9 in.; (Cav cpe) 170.4 in.; (Cav hatch) 173.5 in.; (Cav sed) 172.4 in.; (Cav wag) 173.0 in.; (Cit) 176.7 in.; (Camaro) 187.8 in.; (Celeb) 188.3 in.; (Malibu) 192.7 in.; (Malibu wag) 193.3 in.; (Monte) 200.4 in.; (Imp/Capr) 212.2 in.; (Imp/Capr wag) 215.1 in. Height: (Chvt) 52.9 in.; (Cav cpe) 52.0 in.; (Cav sed) 53.9 in.; (Cav wag) 54.4 in.; (Cit) 53.9 in.; (Camaro) 50.0 in.; (Celeb) 53.7 in.; (Malibu) 55.7 in.; (Malibu wag) 55.8 in.; (Monte) 54.3 in.; (Imp/Capr sed) 56.4 in.; (Imp/Capr wag) 58.1 in. Width: (Chvt) 61.8 in.; (Cav cpe) 66.0 in.; (Cav sed/wag) 66.3 in.; (Cit) 68.3 in.; (Camaro) 72.8 in.; (Celeb) 69.3 in.; (Celeb sed) 68.8 in.; (Malibu) 71.9 in.; (Malibu wag) 71.9 in.; (Monte) 71.8 in.; (Imp/Capr) 75.3 in.; (Imp/Capr wag) 79.3 in. Front Tread: (Chvt) 51.2 in.; (Cav) 55.4 in.; (Cit) 58.7 in.; (Camaro) 60.7 in.; (Celeb) 58.7 in.; (Malibu/Monte) 57.8 in.; (Imp/Capr) 61.8 in.; (Imp/Capr wag) 62.2 in. Rear Tread: (Chvt) 51.2 in.; (Cav) 55.2 in.; (Cit/Celeb) 57.0 in.; (Camaro) 61.6 in.; (Malibu/Monte) 57.8 in.; (Imp/Capr) 60.8 in.; (Imp/Capr wag) 64.1 in. Standard Tires: (Chvt) P155/80R13 GBR; (Cav) P175/80R13 GBR; (Cit/Celeb) P185/80R13 GBR; (Camaro) P195/75R14 GBR; (Camaro Berlinetta) P205/70R14 GBR; (Camaro Z28) P215/65R15 GBR; (Malibu) P185/75R14 GBR; (Malibu wag) P195/75R14 SBR; (Monte) P195/75R14 SBR; (Imp/Capr) P205/75R15 SBR; (Imp/Capr wag) P225/75R15 SBR. Wheel size: (Camaro) 14 x 6 in.; (Berlinetta) 14 x 7 in.; (Z28) 15 x 7 in.

TECHNICAL: Transmission: Four-speed floor shift standard on Chevette: Gear ratios (1st) 3.75:1; (2nd) 2.16:1; (3rd) 1.38:1; (4th) 1.00:1; (Rev) 3.82:1. Four-speed floor shift on four-cylinder Cavalier/Citation: (1st) 3.53:1; (2nd) 1.95:1; (3rd) 1.24:1; (4th) 0.81:1 or 0.73:1; (Rev) 3.42:1. Citation H.O. V-6 four- speed manual trans.: (1st) 3.31:1; (2nd) 1.95:1; (3rd) 1.24:1; (4th) 0.81:1; (Rev) 3.42:1. Camaro four/V-6 four-speed manual trans.: (1st) 3.50:1; (2nd) 2.48:1; (3rd) 1.66:1; (4th) 1.00:1; (Rev) 3.50:1. Four-speed on Camaro V8305: (1st) 3.42:1; (2nd) 2.28:1; (3rd) 1.45:1; (4th) 1.00:1; (Rev) 3.51:1. Camaro V8305 TBI four-speed manual trans.: (1st) 2.88:1; (2nd) 1.91:1: (3rd) 1.33:1; (4th) 1.00:1; (Rev) 2.78:1. Chevette five-speed manual shift: (1st) 3.76:1; (2nd) 2.18:1; (3rd) 1.36:1; (4th) 1.00:1; (5th) 0.86:1; (Rev) 3.76:1. Three-speed Turbo Hydra-matic standard on Monte Carlo and Caprice/Impala, optional on others. Automatic gear ratios: (1st) 2.52:1; (2nd) 1.52:1; (3rd) 1.00:1; (Rev) 1.93:1 except Caprice/Impala V6231/V8305, Camaro and Malibu/Monte diesel V-6: (1st) 2.74:1; (2nd) 1.57:1; (3rd) 1.00:1; (Rev) 2.07:1. Chevette automatic trans.: (1st) 2.40:1; (2nd) 1.48:1; (3rd) 1.00:1; (Rev) 1.92:1. Cav/Cit/Celebrity auto. trans.: (1st) 2.84:1; (2nd) 1.60:1; (3rd) 1.00:1; (Rev) 2.07:1. Four-speed overdrive automatic transmission on Caprice/Impala: (1st) 2.74:1; (2nd) 1.57:1; (3rd) 1.00:1; (4th) 0.67:1; (Rev) 2.07:1. Four-speed overdrive automatic on Capr/Imp w/V-6: (1st) 3.06:1; (2nd) 1.63:1; (3rd) 1.00:1; (4th) 0.70:1; (Rev) 2.29:1. Standard final drive ratio: (Chevette) 3.36:1; (Cavalier) 3.32:1 w/manual, 2.84:1 w/auto.; (Cav wag) 3.65:1; (Citation) 3.32:1 w/4-speed, 2.84:1 w/auto. exc. H.O. V-6, 3.65:1 w/4- spd, 3.33:1 w/auto.; (Camaro four) 3.42:1 w/4-spd, 3.08:1 w/auto.; (Camaro V-6) 3.23:1 w/4spd, 3.08:1 w/auto.; (Camaro V-8) 2.73:1; (Camaro "Cross-Fire" V-8) 3.23:1 w/4spd, 2.23:1 w/auto. exc. (Z28) 2.93:1. (Celebrity) 2.84:1; (Malibu V-6) 2.41:1; (Malibu V-8) 2.29:1; (Malibu wag) 2.73:1 w/V-6, 2.56:1 w/V8267, 2.41:1 or 2.73:1 w/V8305; (Monte V-6) 2.41:1; (Monte V-8) 2.29:1; (Capr/Imp V-6) 2.73:1; (Capr/Imp V-8) 2.41:1 or 2.73:1 exc. 3.08:1 w/4-spd and V8305. Steering: (Cavalier/Chevette/Citation/Celebrity) rack and pinion; (others) recirculating ball. Front suspension: (Chevette/Cavalier/Citation/Celeb) MacPherson struts, lower control arms, coil springs, stabilizer bar; (Camaro) modified MacPherson struts, control arms, coil springs, stabilizer bar; (Malibu/Monte/Capr/Imp) upper and lower control arms, coil springs, stabilizer bar. Rear suspension: (Chevette) rigid axle, coil springs, trailing links; (Cavalier) beam axle, trailing arms, variable-rate coil springs; (Citation) beam "twist" axle, trailing arms, control arms, stabilizer bar; (Celeb) beam "twist" axle, trailing arms, coil springs, Panhard rod, stabilizer bar; (Camaro) torque arm, solid axle, lower control arms, track bar and coil springs, plus link-type rear stabilizer bar for F41 sport suspension and Z28; (Malibu/Monte/Capr/Imp) coil springs, four-link live axle, lower trailing radius arms and upper oblique torque arms, plus stabilizer bar on some models. Brakes: front disc, rear drum. Four-wheel discs available with Camaro V-8. Body construction: (Chvt/Cav/Cit/Celeb) unit; (Camaro) unitized with partial front frame and bolt-on front sheetmetal; (Malibu/Monte/Capr/Imp) separate body and frame. Fuel tank: (Chvt) 12.5 gal.; (Cav) 14 gal.; (Cit) 15.9 gal.; (Camaro) 16 gal.; (Celeb) 15.7 gal.; (Celeb V-6) 16.4 gal.; (Malibu) 18.1 gal.; (Malibu wag) 18.2 gal.; (Monte) 18.1 gal.; (Capr/Imp) 25 gal.; (Capr/Imp wag) 22 gal.

DRIVETRAIN OPTIONS: Engines: 173 cu. in., 2Bbl. V-6: Citation, base Camaro, Celeb ($125). 267 cu. in., 2Bbl. V-8: Malibu/Monte/Imp/Caprice ($70). 305 cu. in., 4Bbl. V-8: Camaro ($295); Berlinetta ($170); Malibu wag, Monte/Imp/Capr ($70); Imp/Capr wag (NC). 305 cu. in., dual CFI V-8: Camaro ($450). Diesel 260 cu. in. V-6: Celeb ($775). Diesel 350 cu. in. V-8: Malibu/Monte/Imp/Capr ($825); Imp/Capr wag ($653). Transmission/Differential: Three-speed automatic trans.: Chevette ($380); Cavalier ($370); Citation/Camaro ($396); Camaro Z28 ($72). Four-speed overdrive automatic trans.: Imp/Capr ($172). Limited-slip differential: Camaro/Malibu/Monte ($76); Imp/Capr ($80). Special final drive ratio (2.84:1 or 3.18:1): Cavalier ($20). Performance axle ratio: Camaro, Malibu/Imp/Capr wag ($21). Power Accessories: Power brakes: Chvt/Cit ($93). Power four- wheel disc brakes: Camaro ($179). Power steering: Chvt ($190); Cav ($180); Cit ($195). Suspension: F40 H.D. suspension: Cit/Celeb/Monte/Imp/Capr ($26). F41 sport suspension: Cav ($10-$46); Cit/Celeb ($33); Camaro/Monte/Imp/Capr cpe/sed ($49). Rear stabilizer bar: Cavalier ($36). Inflatable rear shock absorbers: Imp/Capr wag ($64). Other: H.D. radiator: Cavalier ($37-$65). H.D. cooling: Chvt/Cit/Camaro/Celeb/Malibu/Monte/Imp/Capr ($40-$70). Cold climate pkg.: Malibu/Monte/Imp/Capr diesel ($99). Diesel engine and fuel line heater: Celeb ($49). H.D. battery: Cav ($22); others ($25) exc. diesel ($50). California emission system: Chvt/Cit/Malibu/Monte/Imp/Capr (N/A); Cav ($46); Camaro/Celeb($65); Celeb diesel ($205).

CHEVETTE CONVENIENCE/APPEARANCE OPTIONS: Comfort/Convenience: Air conditioning ($595). Rear defogger, electric ($120). Tinted glass ($82). Comfortilt steering wheel ($95). Quartz electric clock ($32). Cigarette lighter: Scooter ($10). Rear wiper/washer ($117). Quiet sound group ($48-$60). Lighting and Mirrors: Halogen headlamps ($10). Aux. lighting ($41-$42). Twin sport mirrors, left remote ($50). Driver's remote sport mirror ($33). Entertainment: AM radio: Scooter ($78). AM/FM radio ($75); Scooter ($153). AM/FM stereo radio ($106). Rear speaker ($20). Radio delete ($51 credit). Exterior Trim: Deluxe exterior ($131-$138). Two-tone paint ($133). Sport stripes ($89). Bodyside moldings: Scooter ($45). Door edge guards ($15-$25). Roof carrier ($87). Interior Trim/Upholstery: Cloth bucket seats ($16-$28). Custom cloth bucket seats ($160). Rear seat delete ($50 credit). Color-keyed floor mats ($25). Wheels and Tires: Rally wheel trim ($59). P155/80R13 SBR WSW ($51). P175/70R13 SBR WSW ($122) exc. Scooter ($173).

CAVALIER CONVENIENCE/APPEARANCE OPTIONS: Comfort/Convenience: Air cond. ($625). Cruise control w/resume ($145-$155). Tinted glass: base ($82). Six-way power driver's seat ($183). Comfortilt steering wheel ($88). Power windows ($152-$216). Power door locks ($99-$142). Remote swing-out side windows ($55). Gage pkg. ($46). Special instruments ($78-$124). Intermittent wipers ($44). Rear wiper/washer ($109). Lighting, Horns and Mirrors: Halogen headlamps: base ($38). Aux. lighting ($72-$81). Dual sport mirrors, left remote ($51). Dual electric remote sport mirrors ($79-$130). Right visor mirror ($7). Lighted visor mirror ($38-$45). Entertainment: AM/FM radio: base ($64). AM/FM stereo radio ($100) exc. CL ($36). AM/FM stereo radio w/8track player ($179) exc. CL ($115). AM/FM stereo radio w/cassette ($217) exc. CL ($153). Rear speaker ($20-$32); dual ($30-$42). Radio delete ($71-$138 credit). Exterior Trim: Removable sunroof ($261). Two-tone paint ($164). Pinstriping ($53). Sport striping ($95). Wheel opening moldings ($26). Door edge guards ($14-$22). Roof carrier ($98). Bumper guards ($51). Interior Trim/Upholstery: Cloth bucket seats ($28). Color- keyed mats: front ($15); rear ($10). Cargo area cover ($60). Vheels and Tires: Aluminum wheels ($272-$317). P175/80R13 GBR WSW ($55). P195/70R13 SBR BSW ($133) exc. CL ($78). P195/70R13 SBR WSW ($188) exc. CL ($133). P195/70R13 SBR WLT ($205) exc. CL ($150). Puncture-sealant tires ($94).

CITATION/CELEBRITY CONVENIENCE/APPEARANCE OPTIONS: Option Packages: X11 sport equipment pkg.: Citation ($1744). Deluxe exterior pkg.: Citation ($118-$169). Exterior molding pkg. (rocker panel and wheel opening moldings): Celeb ($53). Max. efficiency pkg. (rear spoiler and decals): Cit ($42). Quiet sound/rear decor pkg.: Cit ($87). Comfort/Convenience: Air cond. ($675). Rear defogger, electric ($125). Cruise control ($155-$165). Tinted glass ($88). Comfortilt steering wheel ($95). Six-way power driver's seat: Celeb ($197). Power windows ($165-$235). Remote swing-out side windows: Cit ($108). Power door locks ($106-$152). Gauge pkg. w/clock: Cit ($104). Gauge pkg. w/trip odometer: Celeb ($64). Electric clock: Cit ($32). Digital clock: Celeb ($60). Intermittent wipers ($47). Lighting, Horns and Mirrors: Halogen high-beam headlamps: Celeb ($10). Aux. lighting: Cit ($50). Dual horns: Cit ($12). Driver's remote mirror ($22). Dual sport mirrors, left remote ($55). Dual remote mirrors: Celeb ($86). Entertainment: AM/FM radio ($75-$82). AM/FM stereo radio ($106-$118). AM/FM stereo w/8track: Celeb ($282). AM/FM stereo w/cassette: Celeb ($277). Dual rear speakers ($30); incl. w/stereo radio. Windshield antenna: Cit ($12). Power antenna: Cit ($55). Radio delete ($56 credit). Exterior Trim: Removable sunroof: Cit ($275). Vinyl roof: Celeb ($140). Two-tone paint: Cit ($176) incl. pinstriping and bodyside moldings; Celeb ($148). Bodyside pinstriping: Cit ($39); Celeb ($57). Bodyside moldings: Cit ($47). Door edge guards ($15-$25). Bumper guards ($56-$60). Bumper rub strips: Cit ($50). Interior Trim/Upholstery: Console ($100). Reclining driver and passenger seatbacks ($96). Sport cloth bench seat: Cit ($28). Custom cloth or vinyl bench seat: Cit ($418). Sport cloth bucket seats: Citation ($131-$160) exc. w/X11 (NC). Custom cloth bucket seats: Cit ($397-$534). Vinyl bench seat: Celeb ($28). Celebrity custom bench seat: cloth ($109-$179); vinyl ($137-$207). Celebrity 45/45 seating: cloth ($133); vinyl ($161). Special custom cloth 45/45 seat: Celeb ($399- $459). Color-keyed mats: front ($16); rear ($11). Vheels and Tires: Full wheel covers: Cit ($52). Sport wheel covers: Celeb ($62). Wire wheel covers: Celeb ($153). Wheel cover locks: Celeb ($39). Rally wheels: Cit ($41-$93); Celeb ($153). P185/80R13 GBR WSW ($58). P185/80R13 SBR BSW ($64). P185/80R13 SBR WSW ($122). P205/70R13 SBR BSW: Celeb ($179). P205/70R13 SBR WSW: Celeb ($245). P205/70R13 SBR WLT: Cit ($267). P185/75R14 SBR WSW: Celeb ($157). P215/60R14 SBR WLT: Citation X11 ($92). Puncture-sealant tires ($106).

CAMARO/MALIBU/MONTE CARLO CONVENIENCE/APPEARANCE OPTIONS: Option Packages: Estate equipment: Malibu wag ($307). Quiet sound group: Camaro ($72-$82). Security pkg.: Malibu wag ($44). Comfort/Convenience: Air cond. ($675). Rear defogger, electric ($125). Cruise control ($155-$165). Tinted glass ($88). Comfortilt steering wheel ($95). Six-way power driver's seat: Camaro/Monte ($197). Power windows: Camaro/Monte ($165); Malibu ($235). Power door locks: Malibu ($152); Camaro/Monte ($106). Power trunk release: Monte ($32). Power hatch release: Camaro ($32). Power tailgate window release: Malibu wag ($33). Electric clock: base Camaro, Malibu/Monte ($32). Digital clock: Berlinetta/Z28 ($28). Gauge pkg. w/trip odometer: Malibu/Monte ($95). Special instruments: base Camaro ($149). Intermittent wipers ($47). Rear wiper/washer: Camaro ($117). Lighting, Horns and Mirrors: Halogen high-beam headlamps ($10). Cornering lamps: Monte ($55). Aux. lighting: Camaro ($52); Malibu/Monte ($38). Dual horns: Camaro ($12). Remote- control driver's mirror: Malibu ($22). Twin sport mirrors (left remote): base Camaro, Monte ($48); Malibu ($55). Twin remote sport mirrors: Monte ($79). Twin electric remote sport mirrors: Camaro ($89-$137). Lighted visor mirror: Monte ($48). Entertainment: AM radio: Camaro/Monte ($111). AM/FM radio: ($165-$172). AM/FM stereo radio: Camaro ($258-$282); Malibu/Monte ($196). Stereo 8track tape player with AM/FM stereo radio: Camaro ($390-$446); Malibu/Monte ($282). Cassette player with AM/FM stereo radio: Camaro ($385-$441); Malibu/Monte ($283). Dual rear speakers: Camaro ($30-$54); Malibu/Monte ($30). Fixed mast antenna ($41); incl. w/radios. Power antenna ($55). Exterior Trim: Removable glass roof panels: Camaro/Monte ($790). Landau vinyl roof: Monte ($232). Rear spoiler: Camaro ($69). Two-tone paint: Malibu ($138); Monte ($214). Bodyside moldings: Camaro ($47). Deluxe bodyside moldings: Malibu/Monte ($57). Door edge guards ($15-$25). Side window sill and rear hood moldings: Monte ($45). Roof drip moldings: Camaro ($29). Bodyside pinstriping: Malibu ($57); Monte ($61). Rear window air deflector: Malibu wag ($36). Roof carrier: Malibu wag ($115). Bumper rub strips: Malibu ($50). Bumper guards, front/rear: Malibu ($56). Interior Trim/Upholstery: Vinyl bench seat: Malibu cpe/sed, Monte ($28). Cloth bench seat: Malibu wag ($28). Custom cloth bench seat: Malibu sed, Monte ($358). Cloth or vinyl 55/45 seating: Malibu/Monte ($133-$161). Cloth bucket seats: Camaro ($28). Custom cloth or vinyl bucket seats: base Camaro/Z28 ($299). Cloth LS contour bucket seats: Camaro ($312). Custom cloth LS contour bucket seats: Camaro ($611). Color-keyed mats: Malibu/Monte ($27); Camaro front ($16); Camaro rear ($11). Deluxe load-floor carpet: Malibu wag ($84). Deluxe trunk trim: Camaro ($164); Monte ($47). Vheels and Tires: Aluminum wheels: Monte ($362). Rally wheels: Camaro ($112); Malibu/Monte ($56). Full wheel covers: Camaro ($52). Sport wheel covers (silver or gold): Malibu ($62). Wire wheel covers: Malibu/Monte ($153). Wheel cover locks: Malibu/Monte ($39). P185/75R14 GBR WSW: Malibu cpe/sed ($58). P195/75R14 GBR WSW: Camaro, Malibu wag ($62). P195/75R14 SBR BSW: Camaro ($65). P195/75R14 SBR WSW: Camaro ($127); Malibu cpe/sed ($151); Malibu wag ($123); Monte ($62). P205/70R14 SBR BSW: base Camaro ($123). P205/70R14 SBR WSW: Camaro ($189); Berlinetta ($66); Monte ($124). P205/70R14 SBR WLT: Camaro ($211). Puncture-sealant tires: Malibu/Monte ($105).

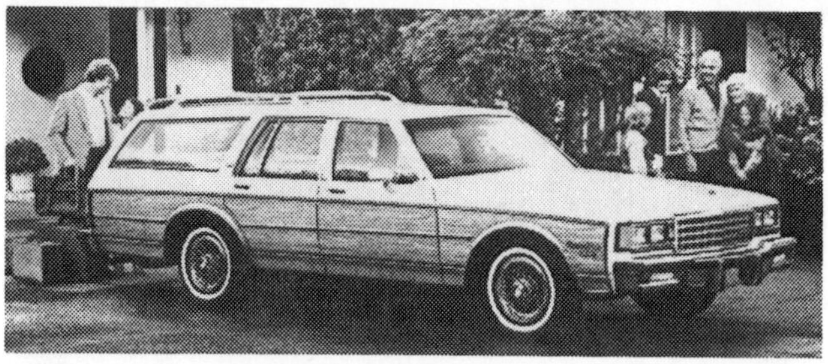

1982 Caprice Classic Estate Wagon (CP)

IMPALA/CAPRICE CONVENIENCE/APPEARANCE OPTIONS: Option Packages: Estate equipment: wag ($307). Value appearance group: bodyside and wheel opening moldings, full wheel covers ($113). Comfort/Convenience: Air cond. ($695). Rear defogger, electric ($125). Cruise control ($155). Tinted glass ($102). Comfortilt steering wheel ($95). Power door locks ($106- $152). Six-way power driver's seat ($197). Power windows ($165-$240). Power trunk release ($32). Power tailgate lock: wag ($49). Electric clock: Imp ($32). Digital clock: Imp ($66); Caprice ($34). Gauge pkg. w/trip odometer ($64). Intermittent wipers ($47). Quiet sound group: Imp ($66-$72). Lighting and Mirrors: Halogen high-beam headlamps ($10). Cornering lamps ($55). Aux. lighting ($42-$64). Driver's remote mirror ($22). Dual remote mirrors ($65). Dual sport mirrors, left remote ($55). Dual remote body-color sport mirrors ($86). Lighted visor mirror ($48). Entertainment: AM radio ($99). AM/FM radio ($153). AM/FM stereo radio ($184). Stereo 8track tape player with AM/FM stereo radio ($270). Cassette player with AM/FM stereo ($271). Dual rear speakers ($30). Power antenna ($55). Windshield antenna ($29); incl. w/radios. Exterior Trim: Vinyl roof: cpe/sed ($165). Roof carrier: wag ($140). Two-tone paint ($65). Custom two-tone ($141). Pinstriping ($39). Color-keyed bodyside moldings ($51). Door edge guards ($15-$25). Bumper rub strips, front/rear ($66). Bumper guards ($62). Interior Trim/Upholstery: Vinyl bench seat: cpe/sed ($28). Cloth bench seat: wag ($28). Cloth 50/50 seat ($238-$285). Custom cloth 50/50 seat: cpe ($428); sed ($452). Deluxe load- floor carpet: wag ($89). Deluxe cargo area carpet: wag ($129). Color-keyed mats: front ($16); rear ($11). Deluxe trunk trim ($59). Vheels and Tires: Full wheel covers ($52). Sport wheel covers: Imp ($115); Caprice ($63). Wire wheel covers ($153). Wire wheel cover locks ($39). P205/75R15 SBR WSW: cpe/sed ($66). P225/70R15 SBR WSW: cpe/sed ($159). P225/75R15 SBR WSW: wag ($71). Puncture-sealant tires ($106-$131).

HISTORY: General introduction was Sept. 24, 1981 but Cavalier debuted May 21, 1981; Chevette/Citation/Corvette on Dec. 12, 1981; and Camaro/Celebrity not until Jan. 14, 1982. Model year production (U.S.): 1,131,748 (incl. Corvettes and early '82 Cavaliers but not incl. 10,655 Acadians). Total production for the U.S. market was made up of 524,694 four-cylinder, 356,314 sixes, and 351,518 V-8s. A total of 48,654 diesels were installed. Calendar year production (U.S.): 1,004,244 (including 22,838 Corvettes plus Acadians, but not incl. 139,837 early '82 Cavaliers). Calendar year sales by U.S. dealers: 1,260,620, for a 21.8 percent market share. Model year sales by U.S. dealers: 1,234,988 (incl. 22,086 Corvettes but not incl. 43,855 early 1982 Cavaliers), for a 22.3 percent share.

Historical Footnotes: Cavalier debuted in a national media preview in Washington, DC, amid sales predictions of 345,000 for 1982. Production began slowly and sales proved disappointing, even after early delivery shortages were remedied. Additional assembly plants (at Leeds and Janesville) were prepared to begin Cavalier production in spring 1982. Chevrolet called 1982 the "year of the diesel." Diesel power was now available on Chevettes, Caprice/Impalas, Malibus and Monte Carlos, and soon would arrive on the new Celebrity. Of the 14 engine sizes available this year in cars and light trucks, five were diesels. General manager Robert D. Lund estimated that over 300,000 Chevrolet vehicles built in 1982 might have diesel engines. That prediction turned out to be overly optimistic. Within a couple of years the highly-touted diesel powerplant would begin to fade away, victim of driveability problems, stable gasoline prices, and general lack of customer interest. In one illuminating survey that held portents of the future, Chevrolet discovered that nearly 37 percent of Camaros purchased in 1980 were bought by women. That was higher than any other Chevrolet passenger car, and well above the industry average of 24.5 percent. Twin slogans for the restyled Camaro also suggested what was to come as the decade unrolled. "Excess is out. Efficiency is in" predicted the rising emphasis on fuel-efficiency and modest size. "Brute power is out. Precision is in" seemed to toll the death knell for the big V-8, but it would be around for some time yet.

1983 CHEVROLET

After the three major new product introductions for 1982, this year focused on powertrain refinements for performance and economy. Changes included new five-speed manual gearboxes available for Camaro, Chevette and Cavalier, plus a bigger Cavalier engine. All Citations could get the high-output (135 horsepower) V-6 this year. Mid-year arrivals included a Cavalier convertible, notchback Citation X11, and available four-speed manual transaxle in Celebrity. But the most notable news of all was probably the reworked 1984 Corvette, which debuted in spring and missed the '83 model year completely.

1983 Chevette S hatchback coupe (AA)

CHEVETTE — SERIES 1T — FOUR — Chevette enjoyed a rather dramatic restyling this year, gaining a deep front air dam that flowed into flared wheel housings, body-color bumpers (but black on Scooters), and a number of blackout body trim pieces. Even so, apart from a higher position of front side marker lamps and front fender script, basic appearance was quite similar to before. Scooters, priced as low as $4997, gained reclining front bucket seats as standard. Chevette's crosshatch grille sported a familiar bowtie emblem in its center. A new 'Chevette S' sport decor package included black and red accents, special wheel trim rings, black grille, black headlamp bezels, and black wheels. Red accents went on bodyside moldings and nameplates. The sport package came in five body colors, others in ten. Four interior colors were offered. Two four-cylinder engine choices were available (1.6-liter gas and 1.8-liter diesel), plus three transmissions: four- and five-speed manual, and three-speed automatic. Five-speed was standard with the diesel, and offered for the first time with the gas engine (though it had been announced earlier). Scooter equipment included a color-keyed front air dam, black steel bumpers with end caps and guards, black grille, dome lamp, day/night mirror, black moldings (windshield, hatch window reveal, roof drip), vinyl reclining front bucket seats, front stabilizer, and styled steel wheels. Standard models added color-keyed bumpers, lighter, mini console, locking glove box, black grille with argent accent, color-keyed dash, black bodyside and rocker moldings, and an AM radio. Diesel Chevettes had standard power brakes.

1983 Cavalier coupe (JG)

CAVALIER — SERIES 1J — FOUR — Appearance was similar to 1982, but a modified standard equipment list allowed significant price cuts to the subcompact Cavalier. The new base prices ($5888 to $6633) were $389 to $1868 lower than equivalent 1982 values. But quite a few items that had been standard now joined the option list. Seven models and three trim levels were available. Top-of-the-line was now the CS, while CL became an option package (priced at $577 to $696), containing many of the former CL series items. The budget-priced Cadet series was dropped, along with the base hatchback coupe. All Cavaliers had beige/charcoal instrument panels and consoles, replacing the former brushed aluminum/woodgrain. Two-door CS models got a new easy-entry passenger seat that slid forward automatically when folded down for access to the back. Standard equipment remaining in the list included radial tires, power brakes, front stabilizer bar, vinyl reclining front bucket seats, and side window defoggers. Cavaliers came in ten body colors and five interior colors. On the mechanical side, Cavalier became Chevrolet's first front-drive with a five-speed manual transaxle available. It offered two overdrive ratios (0.92:1 in fourth and 0.75:1 in fifth gear), plus a 3.91:1 first gear ratio. Four-speed overdrive manual remained standard, with three-speed automatic optional. Also new was a bigger (2.0-liter) fuel-injected engine with higher compression and torque. A "cyclonic" cylinder head gave faster fuel burning. New, "more aggressive" axle ratios boosted performance. A new convertible arrived later in the model year (January), built by American Sunroof in Lansing, Michigan. Produced in limited numbers, it was the first Chevrolet ragtop since 1975. Cavalier's new standard equipment list included bright bumpers with black/argent rub strips, black grille, black left-hand outside mirror, day/night inside mirror, console with rear ashtray and coin tray, four-spoke charcoal steering wheel, styled steel wheels with P175/80R13 GBR tires, compact spare tire, two-speed wiper/washers, and black moldings (glass and drip). CS models added a lighter, locking glove compartment, halogen headlamps, color-keyed dash, AM radio, three-spoke color-keyed steering wheel, black/argent bodyside moldings, and bright side window moldings. CS hatchbacks also had color-keyed bumpers, fold-down rear seat and special instruments; all but hatchbacks had a bright grille rather than the standard black. The new Cavalier convertible carried tinted glass, power steering, power windows, and twin sport mirrors (left remote). Added to the option list were an electric rear defogger, power hatch or trunk release, electronic-tuning radios, split folding rear seatback, and black/argent bodyside moldings.

1983 Citation hatchback coupe (JG)

CITATION — SERIES 1X — FOUR/V-6 — Little changed on Citation except for upgraded front seats and a restyled instrument panel. Interiors held new low-back front seats with adjustable headrests. Of the five interior colors, maroon and dark brown were new. Maroon was also a new addition to the body color selection. Base engine was still the fuel-injected 151 cu. in. (2.5-liter) four. The high-output V-6 was now optional on all models, not just as part of the X11 option package. Citation was still offered as a two-door hatchback, two-door notchback, or four-door hatchback. Joining the option list this year was a Sport Decor package that included exterior graphics, rear spoiler, rally wheels, color-keyed bumpers, and sport mirrors. The X11 package was again offered for the two-door hatchback, and later in the model year, for the notchback as well. It included special graphics, a bubble hood with nameplates, and high-output V-6 engine. Because of equipment changes, the package cost about $700 less than in 1982. The revised X11 also included bucket seats, sport mirrors, rear spoiler, P215/60R14 SBR tires on 14 in. aluminum alloy wheels, black grille, nameplates, sport steering wheel, power brakes, F41 sport suspension, modified exhaust, color-keyed bumpers with rub strips, sport decal, and black moldings (windshield, window and drip). Price tag was now $998, and 1,934 were installed.

1983 Camaro Z28 T-top Sport Coupe (JG)

CAMARO — SERIES 1F — V-6/V-8 — Camaro's looks changed little this year after the 1982 aero restyle, but more powertrain combinations were available. Engine choices were as before: base 151 cu. in. (2.5-liter) fuel-injected four on the Sport Coupe, Berlinetta's standard 173 cu. in. (2.8-liter) V-6, and two 305 cu. in. (5.0-liter) V-8s. Standard V-8 was carbureted, but Z28 could have the Cross-Fire fuel-injected version. Camaros with the CFI engine had functional dual air intake hood scoops. Five-speed overdrive manual was now optional on the base Sport Coupe, standard on others. New four-speed overdrive automatic (with lockup torque converter) was also available. A new high-output 305 V-8 engine with revised cam and four-barrel carburetor arrived late in the model year, developing 190 horsepower. A total of 3,223 H.O. V-8s were installed in Camaros this year. Optional "Contour" multi-adjustment driver's seats got matching passenger seats. Stereo radios offered electronic tuning. Z28 had new three-tone upholstery featuring multiple Camaro logos. Body colors this year were white, black and red, plus seven metallics: silver, light or dark blue, light or dark brown, charcoal, and dark gold. Maroon was dropped from the body color list, and brown replaced maroon as an interior choice; but colors otherwise remained the same as before. Camaros again had a rear glass hatch, reclining front bucket seats, and standard power steering. Joining the option list: a rear compartment cover to hide cargo. Optional mats were now carpeted instead of plain rubber.

1983 Celebrity CL sedan (AA)

CELEBRITY — SERIES 1A — FOUR/V-6 — Arriving late this year, the luxury aerodynamic five-passenger family car got the diesel V-6 option (announced earlier) for the first time. A new four-speed overdrive automatic transmission also joined the mid-year option list. Chevrolet's biggest front-drive kept its standard 151 cu. in. (2.5-liter) fuel-injected four, with optional 2.8-liter gas V-6 as well as the diesel. Standard equipment included automatic transmission, power brakes and steering. Interiors came in five colors and two CL trim levels, one with 45/45 seating. A center console was optional. Ten body colors were offered. All radio options now had electronic tuning and the eight-track tape players were dropped, but little else changed.

MALIBU — SERIES 1A — V-6/V-8 — This would be the final season for the rear-drive six-passenger Malibu, whose family-carrying duties were being taken over by the front-drive Celebrity. Base engine was the 229 cu. in. (3.8-liter) V-6, with V-6 and V-8 diesels available as well as the 305 gas V-8. Only two bodies were offered: four-door sedan and four-door wagon. The Malibu Classic nameplate was dropped (replaced by the luxury CL option), so only one series remained this year, stressing economy. Notchback bench or 55/45 split front seats with fold-down armrests came in cloth or vinyl. Several trim items were added to the option list, including rocker panel and wheel opening moldings. Malibu's standard equipment included power brakes and steering, automatic transmission, locking glove compartment, lighter, dome light, compact spare tire, front stabilizer bar, and two-speed wiper/washers. Bodies held bright sill, rear window and windshield reveal, roof drip and belt moldings.

1983 Monte Carlo CL Sport Coupe (AA)

MONTE CARLO — SERIES 1A — V-6/V-8 — Monte's front end gained a bolder, more aggressive look with its new large-segmented (bigger holes) crosshatch grille. Both gas and diesel V-6 and V-8 engines were available, but the small-block 267 cu. in. gas V-8 was dropped, replaced by the 305 cu. in. (5.0-liter) V-8. For the first time in three years, the 305 V-8 was available under both Malibu and Monte Carlo hoods. Standard engine was the 229 cu. in. (3.8-liter) V-6. Monte came in ten body colors and five interior colors, in two trim levels (including a luxury CL option). A revived interest in rear-drive mid-sizes kept Monte in the lineup, offering six-passenger coupe roominess. Standard equipment included power brakes and steering, full wheel covers, front stabilizer bar, body-color bumpers, bright windshield and quarter-window reveal moldings, twin bright mirrors, chromed headlamp bezels, bright lower bodyside moldings, wheel opening and roof drip moldings, dual horns, and a stand-up hood ornament. Montes rode P195/75R14 SBR tires and carried a compact spare. Inside was a full-width front seat with folding armrest, door pull straps, leather-like dash applique, day/night mirror, color-keyed steering wheel, locking glove compartment, lighter, and courtesy lights. In addition to the base model, a new Monte Carlo SS coupe joined the lineup late in the season, powered by a high-output version of the carbureted 305 cu. in. V-8.

1983 Caprice Classic sedan (JG)

IMPALA/CAPRICE CLASSIC — SERIES 1B — V-6/V-8 — Continuing demand kept the twin full-size Chevrolets around, but they lost a number of models this year. All that remained of the Impala name was a four-door sedan, while Caprice fielded a sedan and nine-passenger (three-seat) station wagon. No two-door models were left. Base sedan engine remained the 229 cu. in. (3.8-liter) V-6. The Caprice wagon continued with the 305 cu. in. (5.0-liter) V-8. Options included the 305 gas V-8, 350 diesel V-8, new four-speed overdrive automatic transmission with 0.79:1 top gear, and a higher-number (3.08:1) axle ratio. The 267 cu. in. V-8 was gone. Black was again offered as one of the ten possible body colors, after being unavailable in 1982. Interior trims came in five colors: dark blue, light green, silver, maroon, and dark brown. Caprice sedans cold have a CL luxury interior package. Impala standard equipment included three-speed automatic transmission, power brakes and steering, cloth bench seat, day/night mirror, two-speed wiper/washers, front stabilizer bar, trunk mat, lighter, and lights for dome, trunk and glove compartment. Impala also wore bright rood drip, windshield and back window reveal, window frame, door frame and lower bodyside moldings. Caprice added overdrive automatic transmission, a quartz electric clock, dual horns, full wheel covers, wheel opening moldings, bright wide lower bodyside moldings, dash and ashtray lights, and a headlamps-on warning buzzer. Wagons had a power tailgate window. Caprice sedans had cloth seats, wagons vinyl.

I.D. DATA: Chevrolets again had a 17-symbol Vehicle Identification Number (VIN) on the upper left surface of the instrument panel, visible through the windshield. Symbol one indicates country: '1' U.S.A.; '2' Canada. Next is a manufacturer code: 'G' General Motors. Symbol three is car make: '1' Chevrolet; '2' GM of Canada. Symbol four denotes restraint system: 'A' non-passive (standard); 'B' passive (automatic belts); 'C' passive (inflatable). Symbol five is car line/series: 'B' Chevette; 'J' Chevette Scooter; 'D' Cavalier; 'E' Cavalier hatchback; 'H' Citation coupe; 'X' Citation; 'P' Camaro; 'S' Camaro Berlinetta; 'W' Celebrity or Malibu; 'Z' Monte Carlo; 'L' Impala; 'N' Caprice. Symbols six-seven reveal body type: '08' 2-dr. hatch coupe; '11' 2-dr. notchback coupe; '27' 2-dr. notchback coupe (or convertible); '37' special 2-dr. notch coupe; '77' 2-dr. hatch coupe; '87' 2-dr. sport coupe; '19' 4-dr. 6-window notchback sedan; '68' 4-dr. hatch sedan; '69' 4-dr. 4-window notchback sedan; '35' 4-dr. station wagon. Next is the engine code: 'C' L498 2Bbl.; 'D' L4111 diesel; 'P' L4121 FI; 'R' or '2' L4151 FI; 'X' or '1' V6173 2Bbl.; 'Z' H.O. V6173; 'K' or '9' V6229 2Bbl.; 'T' or 'V' V6262 diesel; 'H' V8305 4Bbl.; 'S' V8305 FI; 'N' V8350 diesel. Next is a check digit, followed by 'D' for model year 1983. Symbol eleven indicates assembly plant: 'B' Baltimore; 'J' Janesville, WI; 'L' Van Nuys, CA; 'N' Norwood, OH; 'R' Arlington, TX; 'T' Tarrytown, NY; 'X' Fairfax, KS; 'Y' Wilmington, DE; '1' Oshawa, Ontario; '6' Oklahoma City, OK; '7' Lordstown, OH. The final six digits are the sequential serial number. Engine number coding is similar to 1982.

CHEVETTE (FOUR)

Model Number	Body/Style Number	Body Type & Seating	Factory Price	Shipping Weight	Production Total
1T	B08	2-dr. Hatch Cpe-4P	5469	2029	37,537
1T	B68	4-dr. Hatch Sed-4P	5616	2090	81,297

CHEVETTE SCOOTER (FOUR)

1T	J08	2-dr. Hatch Cpe-4P	4997	1971	33,488
1T	J68	4-dr. Hatch Sed-4P	5333	2040	15,303

CHEVETTE DIESEL (FOUR)

1T	B08/Z90	2-dr. Hatch Cpe-4P	6535	N/A	439
1T	B68/Z90	4-dr. Hatch Sed-4P	6683	N/A	1,501

CAVALIER (FOUR)

1J	C27	2-dr. Coupe-5P	5888	2315	23,028
1J	C69	4-dr. Sedan-5P	5999	2335	33,333
1J	C35	4-dr. Sta Wag-5P	6141	2395	27,922

CAVALIER CS (FOUR)

1J	D27	2-dr. Coupe-5P	6363	2305	22,172
1J	E77	2-dr. Hatch Cpe-5P	6549	2370	25,869
1J	D69	4-dr. Sedan-5P	6484	2357	52,802
1J	D35	4-dr. Sta Wag-5P	6633	2417	32,834
1J	D27/Z08	2-dr. Conv. Cpe-5P	10990	N/A	627

CITATION (FOUR/V-6)

1X	H11	2-dr. Coupe-5P	6333/6483	2394/2457	6,456
1X	X08	2-dr. Hatch Cpe-5P	6788/6938	2403/2466	14,323
1X	X68	4-dr. Hatch Sed-5P	6934/7084	2442/2505	71,405

CAMARO (V-6/V-8)

1F	P87	2-dr. Spt Cpe-4P	8186/8386	2878/3035	63,806

CAMARO BERLINETTA (V-6/V-8)

1F	S87	2-dr. Spt Cpe-4P	9881/10106	2864/3056	27,925

CAMARO Z28 (V-8)

1F	P87	2-dr. Spt Cpe-4P	--/10336	--/3061	62,100

Camaro Engine Note: Prices and weights before slash are for V-6 engine, after slash for V-8. Base Camaro Sport Coupes were also available with a four-cylinder engine, priced at $8036 and weighing 2803 pounds. The Z28 could have an optional CFI V-8 for an additional $450. **Z28 Production Note:** Chevrolet production figures also show 550 Z28E hatchback sport coupes built for export.

CELEBRITY (FOUR/V-6)

1A	W27	2-dr. Coupe-5P	8059/8209	2629/2689	19,221
1A	W19	4-dr. Sedan-5P	8209/8359	2649/2709	120,608

MALIBU CLASSIC (V-6/V-8)

1A	W69	4-dr. Spt Sed-6P	8084/8309	3106/3214	61,534
1A	W35	4-dr. Sta Wag-6P	8217/8442	3249/3376	55,892

MONTE CARLO (V-6/V-8)

1A	Z37	2-dr. Spt Cpe-6P	8552/8777	3128/3236	91,605

MONTE CARLO 'SS' (V-8)

1A	Z37/Z65	2-dr. Spt Cpe-6P	-- /10249	-- /3242	4,714

IMPALA (V-6/V-8)

1B	L69	4-dr. Sedan-6P	8331/8556	3356/3460	45,154

CAPRICE CLASSIC (V-6/V-8)

1B	N69	4-dr. Sedan-6P	8802/9027	3402/3506	122,613
1B	N35	4-dr. 3S Wag-9P	-- /9518	-- /3975	53,028

FACTORY PRICE AND WEIGHT NOTE: For Citation and Celebrity, prices and weights to left of slash are for four-cylinder, to right for V-6 engine. For Camaro, Malibu, Monte Carlo and full-size models, figures to left of slash are for six-cylinder model, to right of slash for 305 cu. in. V-8. Diesel V-6 and V-8 engines cost considerably more (see option prices). **BODY/STYLE NO. NOTE:** Some models were actually option packages. Code after the slash (e.g., Z65) is the number of the option package that comes with the model listed.

ENGINE DATA: BASE FOUR (Chevette): Inline. Overhead cam. Four-cylinder. Cast iron block and head. Displacement: 98 cu. in. (1.6 liters). Bore & stroke: 3.23 x 2.98 in. Compression ratio: 9.0:1. Brake horsepower: 65 at 5200 R.P.M. Torque: 80 lbs.-ft. at 3200 R.P.M. Five main bearings. Hydraulic valve lifters. Carburetor: 2Bbl. VIN Code: C. DIESEL FOUR (Chevette): Inline. Overhead cam. Four-cylinder. Cast iron block and head. Displacement: 111 cu. in. (1.8 liters). Bore & stroke: 3.31 x 3.23 in. Compression ratio: 22.0:1. Brake horsepower: 51 at 5200 R.P.M. Torque: 72 lbs.-ft. at 2000 R.P.M. Five main bearings. Solid valve lifters. Fuel injection. VIN Code: D. BASE FOUR (Cavalier): Inline. Overhead valve. Four-cylinder. Cast iron block and head. Displacement: 121 cu. in. (2.0 liters). Bore & stroke: 3.50 x 3.15 in. Compression ratio: 9.3:1. Brake horsepower: 88 at 4800 R.P.M. Torque: 110 lbs.-ft. at 2400 R.P.M. Five main bearings. Hydraulic valve lifters. Throttle-body fuel injection. VIN Code: P. BASE FOUR (Citation, Celebrity, Camaro): Inline. Overhead valve. Four-cylinder. Cast iron block and head. Displacement: 151 cu. in. (2.5 liters). Bore & stroke: 4.00 x 3.00 in. Compression ratio: 8.2:1. Brake horsepower: 92 at 4000 R.P.M. Torque: 134 lbs.-ft. at 2800 R.P.M. Five main bearings. Hydraulic valve lifters. Throttle-body fuel injection. Pontiac-built. VIN Code: R exc. (Camaro) 2. BASE V-6 (Camaro Berlinetta); OPTIONAL (Citation, Celebrity, Camaro): 60-degree, overhead-valve V-6. Cast iron block and head. Displacement: 173 cu. in. (2.8 liters). Bore & stroke: 3.50 x 2.99 in. Compression ratio: 8.5:1. Brake horsepower: 112 at 4800 R.P.M. (Camaro, 107 at 4800). Torque: 145 lbs.-ft. at 2100 R.P.M. Four main bearings. Hydraulic valve lifters. Carburetor: 2Bbl. Rochester E2SE. VIN Code: X exc. (Camaro) 1. HIGH-OUTPUT V-6 (Citation): Same as 173 cu. in. V-6 above except C.R.: 8.9:1. Brake H.P.: 135 at 5400 R.P.M. Torque: 145 lbs.- ft. at 2400 R.P.M. VIN Code: Z. BASE V-6 (Malibu, Monte Carlo, Impala, Caprice): 90-degree, overhead-valve V-6. Cast iron block and head. Displacement: 229 cu. in. (3.8 liters). Bore & stroke: 3.74 x 3.48 in. Compression ratio: 8.6:1. Brake horsepower: 110 at 4000 R.P.M. Torque: 190 lbs.-ft. at 1600 R.P.M. Four main bearings. Hydraulic valve lifters. Carburetor: 2Bbl. Rochester E2ME. VIN Code: K or 9. (NOTE: California models used a Buick 231 V-6.) DIESEL V-6 (Malibu, Celebrity, Monte Carlo): 90-degree, overhead-valve V-6. Cast iron block and head. Displacement: 262 cu. in. (4.3 liters). Bore & stroke: 4.057 x 3.385 in. Compression ratio: 22.8:1. Brake horsepower: 85 at 3600 R.P.M. Torque: 165 lbs.-ft. at 1600 R.P.M. Four main bearings. Hydraulic valve lifters. Fuel injection. VIN Code: T or V. BASE V-8 (Camaro Z28, Impala/Caprice wagon): OPTIONAL (Camaro, Malibu, Monte Carlo, Impala, Caprice): 90-degree, overhead valve V-8. Cast iron block and head. Displacement: 305 cu. in. (5.0 liters). Bore & stroke: 3.74 x 3.48 in. Compression ratio: 8.6:1. Brake horsepower: 150 at 4000 R.P.M. Torque: 240 lbs.-ft. at 2400 R.P.M. Five main bearings. Hydraulic valve lifters. Carburetor: 4Bbl. Rochester E4ME. VIN Code: H. HIGH-OUTPUT V-8 (Monte Carlo SS); OPTIONAL (Camaro): Same as 305 cu. in. V-8 above, except Brake H.P.: 175 at 4800 R.P.M. Torque: 235 lbs.-ft. at 3200 R.P.M. OPTIONAL FUEL-INJECTED V-8 (Camaro Z28): Same as 305 cu. in. V-8 above, with dual CFI Brake H.P.: 175 at 4200 R.P.M. Torque: 250 lbs.-ft. at 2800 R.P.M. VIN Code: S. DIESEL V-8; OPTIONAL (Malibu, Monte Carlo, Impala/Caprice): 90-degree, overhead valve V-8. Cast iron block and head. Displacment: 350 cu. in (5.7 liters). Bore & stroke: 4.057 x 3.385 in. Compression ratio: 22.5:1. Brake horsepower: 105 at 3200 R.P.M. Torque: 200 lbs.-ft. at 1600 R.P.M. Five main bearings. Hydraulic valve lifters. Fuel injection. Olds-built. VIN Code: N.

CHASSIS DATA: Dimensions and tires were virtually identical to 1982, except for slight growth in overall length of Cavalier coupe to 170.9 in.

TECHNICAL: Transmission: Four-speed floor shift standard on Chevette: Gear ratios (1st) 3.75:1; (2nd) 2.16:1; (3rd) 1.38:1; (4th) 1.00:1; (Rev) 3.82:1. Four-speed floor shift on Cavalier/Citation: (1st) 3.53:1; (2nd) 1.95:1; (3rd) 1.24:1; (4th) 0.81:1 or 0.73:1; (Rev) 3.42:1. Citation H.O. V-6 four- speed manual trans.: (1st) 3.31:1; (2nd) 1.95:1; (3rd) 1.24:1; (4th) 0.81:1; (Rev) 3.42:1. Camaro four/V-6 four- speed manual trans.: (1st) 3.50:1; (2nd) 2.48:1; (3rd) 1.66:1; (4th) 1.00:1; (Rev) 3.50:1. Cavalier five-speed manual: (1st) 3.91:1; (2nd) 2.04:1; (3rd) 1.33:1; (4th) 0.92:1; (5th) 0.75:1; (Rev) 3.50:1. Camaro four/V-6 five- speed manual: (1st) 3.50:1; (2nd) 2.14:1; (3rd) 1.36:1; (4th) 1.00:1; (5th) 0.78:1; (Rev) 3.39:1. Camaro V8305 five-speed manual: (1st) 2.95:1; (2nd) 1.94:1; (3rd) 1.34:1; (4th) 1.00:1; (5th) 0.73:1; (Rev) 2.76:1. Chevette five-speed manual shift: (1st) 3.76:1; (2nd) 2.18:1; (3rd) 1.36:1; (4th) 1.00:1; (5th) 0.86:1; (Rev) 3.76:1. Three-speed Turbo Hydra- matic standard on Celebrity, Malibu, Monte Carlo and Caprice/Impala. Malibu/Monte/Caprice/Imp gear ratios: (1st) 2.52:1; (2nd) 1.52:1; (3rd) 1.00:1; (Rev) 1.93:1. Camaro four/V-6 and Malibu/Monte diesel V-6: (1st) 2.74:1; (2nd) 1.57:1; (3rd) 1.00:1; (Rev) 2.07:1. Chevette automatic trans.: (1st) 2.40:1; (2nd) 1.48:1; (3rd) 1.00:1; (Rev) 1.92:1. Cavalier/Citation/Celebrity auto. trans.: (1st) 2.84:1; (2nd) 1.84:1; (3rd) 1.00:1; (Rev) 2.07:1. Four-speed overdrive automatic transmission on Caprice/Impala: (1st) 2.74:1; (2nd) 1.57:1; (3rd) 1.00:1; (4th) 0.67:1; (Rev) 2.07:1. Four-speed overdrive automatic on Camaro V8305, Caprice/Imp diesel: (1st) 3.06:1; (2nd) 1.63:1; (3rd) 1.00:1; (4th) 0.70:1; (Rev) 2.29:1. Standard final drive ratio: (Chevette) 3.36:1; (Cavalier) 3.32:1 exc. 2.83:1 w/5spd and 3.18:1 w/auto.; (Citation four) 2.42:1 or 2.39:1; (Cit V-6) 2.69:1 or 2.53:1; (Cit H.O. V-6) 2.96:1 or 3.06:1; (Camaro V-6) 3.42:1 w/5spd, 3.08:1 or 3.23:1 w/auto.; (Camaro V-8) 3.73:1 w/5spd, 3.08:1 or 2.93:1 w/auto.; (Z28) 3.23:1; (Celeb four) 2.39:1; (Celeb V-6) 2.84:1; (Malibu/Monte V-6) 2.41:1; (Malibu/Monte V-8) 2.29:1; (Caprice/Imp V-6) 2.56:1 or 2.73:1; (Caprice/Imp V-8) 2.41:1, 2.73:1 or 2.93:1. Steering: (Cavalier/Chevette/Citation/Celebrity) rack and pinion; (others) recirculating ball. Suspension/Brakes/Body: same as 1982. Fuel tank: (Chvt) 12.5 gal.; (Cav) 14 gal.; (Cit) 15.9 gal.; (Camaro) 16.2 gal. exc. 15.8 with four-cyl. or CFI V-8; (Celeb) 15.7 gal. approx.; (Malibu/Monte) 18.1 gal.; (Capr/Imp) 25 gal.; (Capr/Imp wag) 22 gal.

DRIVETRAIN OPTIONS: Engines: 173 cu. in., 2Bbl. V-6: Citation, base Camaro, Celeb ($150). H.O. 173 cu. in., 2Bbl. V-6: Citation ($300). 305 cu. in., 4Bbl. V-8: Camaro ($350); Berlinetta ($225); Malibu/Monte, Imp/Caprice sed ($225). H.O. 305 cu. in., 4Bbl. V-8: Camaro ($505). 305 cu. in. CFI V-8: Camaro Z28 ($450). Diesel 260 cu. in. V-6: Celeb/Monte, Malibu sed ($500). Diesel 350 cu. in. V-8: Malibu/Monte/Imp/Caprice ($700); Caprice wag ($525). Transmission/Differential: Three-speed automatic trans.: Chevette/Cavalier ($395); Chvt diesel ($380); Citation/Camaro ($425); Berlinetta ($195). Five-speed manual trans.: Chevette/Cavalier ($75); base Camaro ($125). Four- speed overdrive automatic trans.: base Camaro ($525); Berlinetta/Z28 ($295); Imp/Caprice ($175). Limited-slip differential: Camaro/Malibu/Monte/Imp/Capr ($95). Performance axle ratio Chvt/Cav/Camaro/Malibu/Monte, Imp/Capr wag ($21). Power Accessories: Power brakes: Chevette ($95); Citation ($100). Power four-wheel disc brakes: Camaro V-8 ($179). Power steering: Chvt/Cav ($199); Cit ($210). Suspension: F40 H.D. susp.: Cav/Cit/Celeb/Malibu/Monte/Imp/Capr ($26). F41 sport suspension: Cit/Celeb ($33); Cav/Camaro/Monte, Imp/Capr sed ($49). Rear stabilizer bar: Cavalier ($36). Inflatable rear shock absorbers: Caprice wag ($64). Other: H.D. cooling ($40-$70). Cold climate pkg.: Malibu/Monte/Imp/Capr diesel ($99). Diesel engine and fuel line heater: Celeb ($49). H.D. battery ($25) exc. diesel ($50). California emission system ($75) exc. diesel ($215).

CHEVETTE CONVENIENCE/APPEARANCE OPTIONS: Option Packages: Sport decor pkg.: black grille, headlamp bezels and wheels; bodyside moldings, trim rings and decals ($95). Deluxe exterior: side window reveal moldings, argent wheels and trim rings ($150-$165). Comfort/Convenience: Air conditioning ($625). Rear defogger, electric ($125). Tinted glass ($90). Comfortilt steering wheel ($99). Cigarette lighter: Scooter ($10). Rear wiper/washer ($117). Lighting and Mirrors: Aux. lighting ($41-$42). Twin sport mirrors, left remote ($51). Driver's remote sport mirror ($33). Entertainment: AM radio: Scooter ($83). AM/FM radio ($82); Scooter ($165). AM/FM stereo radio ($109). Radio delete ($51 credit). Exterior Trim: Two-tone paint ($133). Sport stripes ($89). Bodyside moldings: Scooter ($45). Door edge guards ($15-$25). Interior Trim/Upholstery: Cloth bucket seats ($28). Custom cloth bucket seats ($130). Color-keyed floor mats ($25). Wheels and Tires: Wheel trim rings ($52). P155/80R13 GBR WSW ($51). P175/70R13 SBR BSW ($119). P175/70R13 SBR WSW ($173).

CAVALIER CONVENIENCE/APPEARANCE OPTIONS: Option Packages: CL equipment pkg.: custom interior, quiet sound group, visor mirror, leather-wrapped steering wheel, sport mirrors and wheel covers, warning chimes ($577-$696). Comfort/Convenience: Air cond. ($625). Cruise control w/resume ($170). Rear defogger, electric ($125). Tinted glass ($90). Six-way power driver's seat ($210). Comfortilt steering wheel ($99). Power windows ($180-$255). Power door locks ($120-$170). Remote swing-out side windows ($55). Power hatch or trunk release ($40). Power liftgate release ($35). Gauge pkg. w/trip odometer ($69). Special instruments incl. tach ($70-$139). Lighter: base ($14). Intermittent wipers ($49). Rear wiper/washer ($117). Lighting, Horns and Mirrors: Halogen headlamps ($10). Aux. lighting ($72-$95). Dual sport mirrors, left remote ($51). Dual electric remote sport mirrors ($89-$137). Right visor mirror ($7). Entertainment: AM/FM radio: base ($112). AM/FM stereo radio ($171) exc. CS ($82). Electronic-tuning AM/FM stereo radio w/clock ($277) exc. CS ($177). Electronic-tuning AM/FM stereo radio w/cassette ($377) exc. CS ($277). Electronic-tuning AM/FM stereo seek/scan radio w/cassette and clock ($555) exc. CS ($455). Dual rear speakers ($30-$42); premium ($25). Fixed-mast antenna: base ($41) but incl. w/radios. Radio delete ($56 credit). Exterior Trim: Removable sunroof ($295). Two-tone paint ($176). Pinstriping ($53). Sport striping ($95). Bodyside moldings, black/argent ($45). Wheel opening moldings ($30). Door edge guards ($15-$25). Roof carrier ($98). Bumper guards ($56). Interior Trim/Upholstery: Cloth bucket seats ($28). Split-folding rear seatback ($50). Color-keyed mats: front ($15); rear ($10). Cargo area cover ($64). Wheels and Tires: Aluminum wheels ($272-$369). Wheel trim rings ($52). P175/80R13 GBR WSW ($54). P195/70R13 SBR BSW ($169). P195/70R13 SBR WSW ($231). P195/70R13 SBR WLT ($253).

CITATION/CELEBRITY CONVENIENCE/APPEARANCE OPTIONS: Option Packages: X11 sport equipment pkg.: Citation ($998). Sport decor pkg. (rear spoiler, rally wheels, sport mirrors, color-keyed bumpers w/rub strips, decal): Citation ($299). Deluxe exterior pkg.: Cit ($118-$218). Exterior molding pkg. (rocker panel and wheel opening moldings): Celeb ($53). Value appearance group: Cit ($55-$63). Quiet sound group: Cit cpe ($43). Quiet sound/rear decor pkg.: Cit ($92). Comfort/Convenience: Air conditioning ($725). Rear defogger, electric ($135). Cruise control w/resume ($170). Tinted glass ($105). Sport steering wheel: Cit ($22). Comfortilt steering wheel ($105). Six-way power driver's seat: Celeb ($210). Power windows ($180-$255). Remote swing-out side windows: Cit ($108). Power door locks ($120-$170). Gauge pkg. w/clock and trip odometer: Cit ($104). Gauge pkg. w/tachometer: Cit ($149). Gauge pkg. w/trip odometer: Celeb ($64). Electric clock: Cit ($35). Digital clock: Celeb ($39). Lighter: Cit cpe ($10). Intermittent wipers ($49). Lighting, Horns and Mirrors: Halogen high-beam headlamps: Celeb ($10). Aux. lighting ($50). Dual horns: Cit ($12). Driver's remote mirror ($22). Dual sport mirrors, left remote ($59). Dual remote mirrors: Celeb ($89). Entertainment: AM radio: Cit cpe ($83). AM/FM radio: Cit hatch, Celeb ($82); Cit cpe ($165). AM/FM stereo radio: Cit ($109) exc. cpe ($192). AM/FM stereo w/cassette: Cit ($209) exc. cpe ($292). Celebrity electronic-tuning AM/FM stereo radio w/clock ($177); w/cassette ($277); with seek/scan and cassette ($455). Dual rear speakers ($30); incl. w/stereo radio. Premium dual rear speakers: Celeb ($25) but incl. with seek/scan radio. Radio delete ($56 credit). Exterior Trim: Vinyl roof: Celeb ($155). Two-tone paint: Cit ($176-$184) incl. pinstriping and bodyside moldings; Celeb ($148). Bodyside pinstriping: Cit ($39-$47); Celeb ($57). Bodyside moldings: Cit ($55). Door edge guards ($15-$25). Bumper guards ($56). Bumper rub strips: Cit ($50). Interior Trim/Upholstery: Console ($100). Reclining driver and passenger seatbacks: Celeb ($90). Sport cloth bench seat: Cit ($28). Custom trim w/cloth bench seat: Cit ($467). Vinyl bench seat: Celeb ($28). Celebrity custom bench seat: cloth ($179-$250); vinyl ($109-$207). Celebrity 45/45 seating: cloth ($100); custom cloth ($250-$330). Sport cloth bucket seats: Cit ($221-$250). Custom trim w/cloth bucket seats: Cit ($467-$492). Color-keyed mats: front ($17); rear ($12). Deluxe seatbelts: Cit cpe ($26). Wheels and Tires: Full wheel covers: Cit ($52). Sport wheel covers: Celeb ($63). Wire wheel covers: Celeb ($153). Wheel cover locks: Celeb ($39). Rally wheels: Cit ($60-$112); Celeb ($56). P185/80R13 GBR WSW ($58). P185/80R13 SBR BSW ($65). P185/80R13 SBR WSW ($123). P195/74R14 GBR WSW: Celeb ($129). P195/75R14 SBR WSW: Celeb ($194). P205/70R13 SBR WSW: Celeb ($245). P205/70R13 SBR WLT: Cit ($267). P215/60R14 SBR WLT: Citation X11 ($92). Puncture-sealant tires: Celeb ($106).

CAMARO/MALIBU/MONTE CARLO CONVENIENCE/APPEARANCE OPTIONS: Option Packages: Estate equipment: Malibu wag ($307). Quiet sound group: Camaro ($72-$82); Malibu ($66). Security pkg.: Malibu wag ($44). Comfort/Convenience: Air cond. ($725). Rear defogger, electric ($135). Cruise control w/resume ($170). Tinted glass ($105). Comfortilt steering wheel ($105). Six-way power driver's seat:

1983 Monte Carlo SS Sport Coupe (JG)

Camaro/Monte ($210). Power windows: Camaro/Monte ($180); Malibu ($255). Power door locks: Malibu ($170); Camaro/Monte ($120). Power trunk opener: Monte ($40). Power hatch release: Camaro ($40). Power tailgate window release: Malibu wag ($40). Electric clock: base Camaro, Malibu/Monte ($35). Digital clock: base Camaro ($39). Gauge pkg. w/trip odometer: Malibu/Monte ($95). Special instruments incl. tach: base Camaro ($149). Intermittent wipers ($49). Rear wiper/washer: Camaro ($120). Lighting, Horns and Mirrors: Halogen high-beam headlamps ($10). Cornering lamps: Monte ($55). Aux. lighting: Camaro ($52); Malibu ($49-$56); Monte ($28). Dual horns: Camaro/Malibu ($12). Remote-control driver's mirror: Malibu ($22). Twin sport mirrors (left remote): base Camaro, Monte ($51); Malibu ($59). Twin remote sport mirrors: Monte ($81). Twin electric remote sport mirrors: Camaro ($89-$137). Entertainment: AM radio ($112). AM/FM radio ($171). AM/FM stereo radio ($198). Cassette player with AM/FM stereo radio: Malibu/Monte ($298). Camaro electronic-tuning AM/FM stereo radio w/clock ($267-$302); w/cassette and clock ($367-$402); w/cassette and seek/scan ($520-$555). Dual rear speakers ($30). Fixed mast antenna ($41); incl. w/radios. Power antenna: Camaro/Monte ($60). Exterior Trim: Removable glass roof panels: Camaro/Monte ($825). Landau vinyl roof: Monte ($240). Rear spoiler: Camaro ($69). Two-tone paint: Malibu ($138); Monte ($214). Bodyside moldings, black: Camaro ($55). Deluxe bodyside moldings: Malibu/Monte ($57). Rocker panel moldings: Malibu ($25). Wheel opening moldings: Malibu ($30). Side window reveal moldings: Malibu ($44). Door edge guards ($15-$25). Side window sill moldings: Monte ($45). Roof drip moldings: Camaro ($29). Bodyside pinstriping: Malibu ($57); Monte ($61). Rear window air deflector: Malibu wag ($36). Roof carrier: Malibu wag ($125). Bumper rub strips: Malibu ($50). Bumper guards: Malibu ($56). Interior Trim/Upholstery: Vinyl bench seat: Monte ($28). Cloth bench seat: Malibu ($28). Custom cloth bench seat: Malibu ($161); Monte ($358). Custom vinyl bench seat: Malibu ($133). Cloth or vinyl 55/45 seating: Malibu ($233-$261); Monte ($133-$161). Cloth bucket seats: Camaro ($28). Custom cloth or vinyl bucket seats: base Camaro ($299); Z28 ($227). Cloth LS conteur bucket seats: Camaro ($375). Custom cloth LS conteur bucket seats: Camaro ($650). Color-keyed mats: Malibu/Monte ($27); Camaro front ($20); Camaro rear ($15). Cargo area cover: Camaro ($64). Deluxe load-floor carpet: Malibu wag ($84). Deluxe trunk trim: Camaro ($164); Monte ($47). Wheels and Tires: Aluminum wheels: Monte ($362). Rally wheels: Camaro ($112); Malibu ($108); Monte ($56). Full wheel covers: Camaro/Malibu ($52). Sport wheel covers: Malibu ($115). Wire wheel covers: Malibu ($190); Monte ($153). Wheel cover locks: Monte ($39). P185/75R14 GBR WSW: Malibu sed ($58). P195/75R14 GBR WSW: Camaro, Malibu wag ($62). P195/75R14 SBR BSW: Camaro ($64). P195/75R14 SBR WSW: Camaro ($126); Malibu sed ($151); Malibu wag ($122); Monte ($62). P205/70R14 SBR BSW: base Camaro ($123). P205/70R14 SBR WSW: Camaro ($189); Berlinetta ($66); Monte ($124). P205/70R14 SBR WLT: Camaro ($211). P205/75R14 SBR BSW: Malibu ($95). P205/75R14 SBR WSW: Malibu ($151).

IMPALA/CAPRICE CONVENIENCE/APPEARANCE OPTIONS: Option Packages: Estate equipment: wag ($307). Value appearance group: bodyside and wheel opening moldings, full wheel covers ($118). Comfort/Convenience: Air cond. ($725). Rear defogger, electric ($135). Cruise control w/resume ($170). Tinted glass ($105). Comfortilt steering wheel ($105). Power door locks ($170). Six-way power driver's seat ($210). Power windows ($255). Power trunk opener ($40). Power tailgate lock: wag ($49). Electric clock: Imp ($35). Digital clock: Imp ($66); Caprice ($34). Gauge pkg. w/trip odometer ($64). Intermittent wipers ($49). Quiet sound group: Imp ($66). Lighting and Mirrors: Halogen high-beam headlamps ($10). Cornering lamps ($55). Aux. lighting ($32-$42). Driver's remote mirror ($22). Dual remote mirrors ($65). Dual sport mirrors, left remote ($59). Dual remote body-color sport mirrors ($89). Lighted visor mirror ($48). Entertainment: AM radio ($112). AM/FM radio ($171). AM/FM stereo radio ($198). Cassette player with AM/FM stereo ($298). Dual rear speakers ($30). Power antenna ($60). Windshield antenna ($29); incl. w/radios. Exterior Trim: Vinyl roof: sed ($180). Roof carrier: wag ($150). Custom two-tone paint ($141). Pinstriping ($39). Bodyside moldings ($55). Door edge guards ($25). Bumper rub strips ($66). Bumper guards ($62). Interior Trim/Upholstery: Vinyl bench seat: sed ($28). Cloth bench seat: wag ($28). Cloth 50/50 seat ($257-$285). Custom cloth 50/50 seat: sed ($452). Deluxe load-floor carpet: wag ($89). Deluxe cargo area carpet: wag ($129). Color-keyed mats: front ($17); rear ($12). Deluxe trunk trim ($59). Wheels and Tires: Full wheel covers ($52). Sport wheel covers: Imp ($115); Caprice ($63). Wire wheel covers ($153). Wire wheel cover locks ($39). P205/75R15 SBR WSW: sed ($66). P225/70R15 SBR WSW: sed ($159). P225/75R15 SBR WSW: wag ($71). Puncture-sealant tires ($106-$132).

HISTORY: Introduced: Sept. 23, 1982 exc. Camaro Nov. 8, 1982. Model year production (U.S.): 1,012,649 (incl. Corvettes but not incl. 11,640 Acadians). Total production for U.S. market was made up of 500,305 four-cylinder, 350,722 sixes and 374,668 V-8s. A total of 12,480 diesels were installed. Calendar year production (U.S.): 1,294,184 (including 28,174 Corvettes). Calendar year sales by U.S. dealers: 1,347,447 (incl. 28,144 Corvettes), for a 19.8 percent market share. Model year sales by U.S. dealers: 1,306,951 (incl. 25,891 Corvettes) for a 20.2 percent share.

Historical Footnotes: The nation's economic condition may have improved during 1983, but Chevrolet's status remained shaky. Model year sales rose by close to six percent, but domestic cars in general fared far betterup by nearly 17 percent. Both at Chevrolet and in the industry generally, most of that increase came from mid- and full-size models. Robert C. Stempel, Chevrolet's general manager, promoted a new "pricing strategy which finds more than half of Chevrolet's 1983 passenger car models carrying lower sticker prices than they did in '82." Some of the reduction, though, was due to elimination of formerly standard equipmenta practice that would become common in the years ahead. Citation sales fell sharply, down from a healthy 321,023 in 1981 and so-so 209,545 in 1982 to a piddling 116,460 this year. No doubt, the well-publicized recall of 1980 models contributed to much of the decline. NHTSA had ordered that recall for alleged brake problems as this model year began. That action would soon change popular opinion of the Xcar in general and Citation in particular. A week-long sales seminar at the Citation plant at Tarrytown, New York this year couldn't do much for sales if the buying public truly turned against the Xcar. The newer Cavalier and Celebrity performed better, showing ample sales gains, partly as a result of marketing Cavalier as a sporty economy car. Far fewer Chevette diesels were sold than in 1982: only 1,940 total. Camaro was named *Motor Trend* "Car of the Year" for 1982. In a GM reshuffling, Chevrolet became part of the new Chevrolet-Pontiac-GM of Canada Group, which was to emphasize small cars. That group was headed by Lloyd E. Reuss, formerly Buick's general manager. Robert C. Stempel of Chevrolet moved over to the new Buick-Oldsmobile-Cadillac group, which focused on large cars. Robert D. Burger then became Chevrolet's general manager.

126

1984 CHEVROLET

This year saw the arrival of only one new body style, the Celebrity station wagon, along with a "re-launching" of the troubled Xcar (as Citation II). Malibu was dropped, its role as a mid-size family car having been usurped by the front-drive Celebrity. Scooter was gone too, but Monte Carlo added a high-performance SS model to lure enthusiasts and Celebrity fielded a Eurosport option. Otherwise, 1984 was mainly a year for engineering changes.

1984 Chevette CS hatchback sedan (CP)

CHEVETTE — SERIES 1T — FOUR — Except for a new passenger door map pocket, the rear-drive subcompact showed virtually no change for 1984. Once again, Chevette came with either a 1.6-liter gasoline four or a 1.8-liter diesel, which could (according to Chevrolet) deliver fuel mileage in the 60 MPG neighborhood. Diesels added a fuel-line heater. Both two-door and four-door hatchbacks were again available, in two trim levels. Joining the option list: new chrome bumpers and sport wheel covers. The stripped-down Scooter was abandoned, but Chevettes still came in two series: base and CS. Base Chevettes came with black bumpers (with guards and end caps), vinyl reclining front bucket seats, fold-down rear seat, front stabilizer bar, four-speed manual transmission, two-speed wipers, styled steel wheels, and a passenger map pocket. Chevette CS added color-keyed bumpers, a cigarette lighter, mini-console, AM radio, and black bodyside moldings. Diesels included a five-speed transmission and power brakes. Chevette's CS Sport Decor package (price $95) included a black grille, black headlamps with red accents, bodyside moldings, black bumper with end caps, and black styled wheels with bright trim rings and decals. A Custom Exterior package included black window frames with narrow bright side window moldings, plus argent styled steel wheels with trim rings. CS displayed a 'Chevette' nameplate ahead of front doors; base models did not.

1984 Cavalier sedan (CP)

CAVALIER — SERIES 1J — FOUR — Cavalier's new wind-tunnel-tuned front end got a new grille, quad headlamps and bumper this year. The crosshatch-pattern grille, tapered inward at the base, had a Chevrolet bowtie in the center and occupied the entire opening, with no solid upper panel as before. Wide rectangular park/signal lamps moved down below the rub strips in the body-colored bumpers. Quad rectangular headlamps were recessed. Cavaliers now came in eight body colors and four interior colors. Sedans and wagons came in base or CS trim, but the base/CS two-door coupe and hatchback were dropped. The sporty Type 10, initially offered only in hatchback form, added the convertible and two-door notchback coupe to its body list. Type 10 models carried their special nameplates on bodysides, just ahead of the rear wheels. CS Cavaliers wore an identifier just ahead of the front door. More examples of the convertible, offered in limited number during 1983, were expected to find buyers this year. A total of 5,161 Cavaliers are reported to have come with an Olympic Special Appearance package. Cavalier's standard suspension got larger-diameter stabilizer bars and softer front bushings. The rear stabilizer bar on the optional F41 sport suspension was also larger in diameter. Standard equipment included power brakes, four-speed manual transaxle (with overdrive), argent grille, charcoal instrument panel, bright window moldings, color-keyed bumpers, vinyl front reclining bucket seats, front stabilizer bar, and four-spoke charcoal steering wheel. P175/80R13 GBR tires rode styled steel wheels. Type 10 added a black grille, color-keyed dash with black trim plate, cigarette lighter and ashtray light, AM radio,

1984 Cavalier CS station wagon (CP)

three-spoke color-keyed steering wheel, glove compartment lock, black window moldings, and bodyside moldings. Cavalier CS models had a bright grille. Convertible equipment was similar to Type 10 but with tinted glass, warning chimes, bright rocker panel moldings, power steering and windows, and dual black sport mirrors (left remote-controlled). An optional CL Custom Interior package included modified door and quarter trim, custom reclining seats with adjustable head restraints, and fender nameplates. On the Type 10 hatchback, it also included a leather steering wheel and split folding seat. This year's options added a leather-wrapped steering wheel and rear window louvers, plus a rear spoiler and sport wheel covers.

1984 Citation II X11 hatchback coupe (AA)

CITATION II — SERIES 1X — FOUR/V-6 — Chevrolet's X-car got a slightly different name this year, supposedly in response to the many improvements it had received during the preceding three years. But renamed or not, it was still essentially a carryover. All-season steel-belted radial tires were standard on all models. New body badges identified engines. Engine mounts were revised to reduce vibration at idle. The high-performance X11 equipment package, offered on both notchback and hatchback coupes, attempted to capitalize on a good record in SCCA showroom stock racing. Citation again came with a 151 cu. in. (2.5-liter) four-cylinder engine or optional V-6. Standard equipment included bright bumpers and grille, day/night mirror, four-speed manual transmission, styled steel wheels, two-speed wiper/washers, low-back vinyl bench front seat, locking glove box, and bright windshield and fender moldings. Hatchbacks also had a lighter, AM radio, black back window molding, rocker panel and wheel opening moldings. The X11 package included P215/60R14 SBR tires on cast aluminum wheels, hood scoop, sport suspension, color-keyed bumpers with black rub strips, power brakes, AM radio; and on hatchbacks, a cigarette lighter and removable cargo cover. Package price was $981 for an X11 hatchback, or $911 when installed on the coupe.

1984 Camaro Berlinetta Sport Coupe (CP)

CAMARO — SERIES 1F — V-6/V-8 — Berlinetta gained the most attention this year. That model's new "space-age instrumentation" included digital readouts, a pivoting pedestal-mounted radio, and dual adjustable fingertip control pods that could be moved close to the steering wheel. The Corvette-inspired cockpit also sported a roof console, plus adjustable low-back seats. A digital display ahead of the driver showed road speed (miles or kilometers per hour) plus odometer or engine speed. An adjoining vertical-bar tachometer flashed more urgently as engine speed increased, while a monitor farther to the right signaled low fluid levels or other trouble spots. At the left were conventional needle-type gauges. The twin pods contained switches for lights and instrument displays, plus wiper and climate control. Other pushbutton controls were in the floor console, while the overhead console contained a swivel map light and

1984 Camaro Z28 T-top Sport Coupe (CP)

small storage pouch. A remote-controlled, electronically-tuned AM/FM stereo radio with digital clock was standard; tape player and graphic equalizer optional. The radio could swivel for easy operation by either the driver or passenger. Buttons for optional cruise control were on Berlinetta's steering wheel, not the column. Berlinettas could be spotted by their gold-colored body trim. On the mechanical side, Cross-Fire Injection was dropped, but the Z28 could have an optional high-output 5.0-liter engine (RPO code L69) rated 190 horsepower, hooked to either five-speed manual or four-speed automatic transmission. That H.O. V-8 (introduced in spring 1983) was the most powerful carbureted engine offered in a Chevrolet. It had a higher-lift, longer-duration camshaft, retuned valve system, and 9.5:1 compression. The H.O. engine also had a specially-calibrated Rochester Quadrajet carb, dual-snorkel cold-air intake, large-diameter exhaust and tailpipes, and wide-mouth (Corvette-type) catalytic converter. Steel-belted radial tires were now made standard on the Sport Coupe with four-cylinder engine, thus standard on all Camaros. All except Z28 now carried fourth-generation All-Season tires. Once again, 173 cu. in. (2.8-liter) V-6 and 305 cu. in. (5.0-liter) V-8 engines were available. The three-speed automatic transmission was dropped, replaced by a four-speed overdrive unit. A hydraulic clutch was now used with all manual gearboxes. The base Camaro Sport Coupe still came with a choice of four, six or eight cylinder power. Camaro's basic "grille" hardly qualified for that name, consisting of no more than three side-by-side slots in the front panel flanked by rectangular headlamps. The Z28 didn't even have those slots in its upper panel, but displayed subtle '5.0-Liter H.O.' badges on its back bumper and rocker panels (and air cleaner), plus dual tailpipes at the back. Base Sport Coupe equipment was similar to 1983, now with SBR tires and color-keyed front/rear bumpers with black accents. Body colors were the same as 1983, but added Dark Gold. In addition to the electronic instrumentation and roof console, Berlinetta equipment included an AM/FM stereo electronic-tuning radio, digital clock, hood and sail panel decals, lockable fuel filler door, sport aluminum hood, dual horns, five-speed manual gearbox, smooth-ride suspension, intermittent wipers, and custom vinyl reclining front bucket seats with adjustable head restraints. Berlinettas carried color-keyed sport mirrors and lower accent body paint with striping. Their 14 x 7 in. wheels were gold/aluminum finned. Z28 equipment was similar to 1983. Other models could have Berlinetta's roof console for an extra $50, while a locking rear storage cover cost $80.

1984 Celebrity station wagon (AA)

CELEBRITY — SERIES 1A — FOUR/V-6 — Like Cavalier, the mid-size Celebrity boasted a new front-end design this year. The taller grille wore a center bowtie emblem and filled the entire space, lacking the solid upper panel of the prior version. Its top was roughly aligned with the top of the headlamps, and the crosshatch pattern was made up of thin vertical slots with two horizontal divider bars. New police and taxi packages were based on the standard four-door sedan platform. A new four-door station wagon came with either two seats or a rear-facing third seat, and a rear opening wider than the Malibu that it replaced. Eurosport versions of each body style included specially-tuned suspension, unique blackout trim, and special decals. The Eurosport name was on front doors, in block letters. A high-output 173 cu. in.

1984 Celebrity Eurosport sedan (AA)

127

(2.8-liter) V-6 engine, similar to Citation's but with slightly less horsepower, became optional on coupes and sedans. Only 2,945 of them were installed this year. A four-speed manual gearbox was offered for the first time, standard equipment with the base four (or V-6 diesel). Also new: four-speed overdrive automatic with V-6 engines. Celebrity's standard equipment included chrome bumpers with end caps and black rub strips (with white inserts), side window defoggers, black left mirror, AM radio, front and rear stabilizer bars, power steering, and full wheel covers. Also standard: two-passenger vinyl front bench seat with folding center armrest, black windshield/window moldings, bright headlamp bezels, wide bodyside moldings, and a concealed spare tire. Wagons had a three-passenger vinyl bench front seat, power brakes, tailgate-ajar light, and hidden floor stowage area. The Eurosport package included an F41 sport suspension, sport steering wheel, P195/7514 SBR tires on 6 in. rally wheels, red accent striping, blackout decor, black bodyside moldings, and red-finish nameplates. The price was $226 for coupe or sedan, $191 on wagons. A total of 26,844 Eurosport packages were installed for the year.

1984 Monte Carlo Sport Coupe (CP)

MONTE CARLO — SERIES 1G — V-6/V-8 — Two options returned to Monte Carlo's lineup this year: bucket seats and a console. Also joining the list was the four-speed overdrive automatic transmission. With the loss of Malibu, Monte remained the only rear-drive mid-size Chevrolet. The diesel V-6 engine was dropped, but the V-8 diesel remained available with a $700 price tag. The high-output 305 cu. in. (5.0-liter) V-8 in the high-performance Monte Carlo SS (added to the lineup in spring 1983) got a boost to 180 horsepower to become what Chevrolet called a "street version of current NASCAR point leader." The SS powertrain also consisted of a high-stall-speed automatic transmission, dual exhausts, 3.42:1 axle ratio, and low-profile Goodyear Eagle GT white-letter P215/65R15 tires on 7 in. rally wheels. Cleanly styled SS Montes carried no body brightwork and wore a wind-tunnel-tuned nose plus a rear spoiler, producing a drag coefficient of just .375. The simple, slightly-angled blackout grille was flanked by quad rectangular headlamps. Wide recessed parking/signal lamps sat below the bumper rub strips. Monte SS bodies were painted only in dark metalic blue or white. Large door decals identified the SS, which also displayed an easy-to-spot "ground effects" front panel. Base Monte standard equipment included power brakes and steering, three-speed automatic transmission, cloth-upholstered bench seats with folding armrest, P195/75R14 SBR tires, compact spare tire, full wheel covers, wheel opening and roof drip moldings, dual chrome mirrors, dual horns, two-speed wiper/washers, and courtesy lights. Monte Carlo SS eliminated the wheel opening moldings but added gauges, black roof drip moldings, a rear spoiler, tachometer, sport suspension, and sport mirrors (left remote). A total of 7,281 Montes had the optional removable glass roof panels.

1984 Impala Sport Coupe (CP)

IMPALA/CAPRICE CLASSIC — SERIES 1B — V-6/V-8 — After a year's absence, the Caprice Classic two-door coupe returned for 1984. The coupe and wagon came only in Caprice Classic trim, while sedans were sold under both Caprice and Impala names. Standard engine was again the 229 cu. in. (3.8-liter) V-6, with 305 cu. in. (5.0-liter) gas V-8 or 5.7-liter diesel optional. External appearance was unchanged. The wiper/washer controls moved from the dashboard to the turn signal lever. Optional cruise control gained incremental acceleration/deceleration, which allowed speed changes down to just 1 MPH at a time. Gas-engine wagons had standard heavy-duty suspension, while diesel wagons had standard four-speed overdrive automatic transmission. Impala's standard equipment included the V-6 engine, power brakes and steering, three-speed automatic transmission, front stabilizer bar, full wheel covers, cloth bench seat, padded door trim panels, trunk mat, day/night mirror, and bright moldings (windshield, door frame and roof drip). Also dome, trunk and glove box lights. Caprice equipment was similar, but added a folding center armrest, quartz clock, wheel opening moldings, color-keyed steering wheel with woodgrain insert, headlamps-on warning buzzer, and lower-carpeted door trim panels with pull straps. Caprice sport coupes and sedans had bumper rub strips. Wagons had vinyl bench seating plus the overdrive automatic transmission. A Landau equipment package with vinyl roof cost an extra $306.

I.D. DATA: Coding of the 17-symbol Vehicle Identification Number (VIN) was similar to 1983. Symbol five (car line/series) was now: 'J' base Chevette; 'B' Chevette CS; 'C' Cavalier; 'D' Cavalier CS; 'E' Cavalier Type 10; 'H' Citation coupe; 'X' Citation; 'P' Camaro; 'S' Camaro Berlinetta ; 'W' Celebrity ; 'G' Monte Carlo; 'L' Impala; 'N' Caprice. Body type (symbols six-seven) added code '47' for full-size 2-dr. sport coupe. Code 'S' for V8305 FI engine was dropped. Code 'G' for H.O. V8305 4Bbl. was added. The model year code changed to 'E' for 1984.

CHEVETTE (FOUR)

Model Number	Body/Style Number	Body Type & Seating	Factory Price	Shipping Weight	Production Total
1T	J08	2-dr. Hatch Cpe-4P	4997	1988	66,446
1T	J68	4-dr. Hatch Sed-4P	5333	2051	28,466

CHEVETTE CS (FOUR)

1T	B08	2-dr. Hatch Cpe-4P	5489	2032	47,032
1T	B68	4-dr. Hatch Sed-4P	5636	2091	94,897

CHEVETTE DIESEL (FOUR)

1T	J08/Z90	2-dr. Hatch Cpe-4P	5500	N/A	1,495
1T	J68/Z90	4-dr. Hatch Sed-4P	5851	N/A	1,180

CHEVETTE CS DIESEL (FOUR)

1T	B08/Z90	2-dr. Hatch Cpe-4P	5999	N/A	1,000
1T	B68/Z90	4-dr. Hatch Sed-4P	6161	N/A	3,384

CAVALIER (FOUR)

1J	C69	4-dr. Sedan-5P	6222	2320	90,023
1J	C35	4-dr. Sta Wag-5P	6375	2392	50,718

CAVALIER CS (FOUR)

1J	D69	4-dr. Sedan-5P	6666	2334	110,295
1J	D35	4-dr. Sta Wag-5P	6821	2405	58,739

1984 Cavalier Type 10 convertible (AA)

CAVALIER TYPE 10 (FOUR)

1J	E27	2-dr. Coupe-5P	6477	2300	103,204
1J	E77	2-dr. Hatch Cpe-5P	6654	2350	44,146
1J	E27/Z08	2-dr. Conv. Cpe-4P	11299	2515	5,486

CITATION II (FOUR/V-6)

1X	H11	2-dr. Coupe-5P	6445/6695	2382/2454	4,936
1X	X08	2-dr. Hatch Cpe-5P	6900/7150	2399/2471	8,783
1X	X68	4-dr. Hatch Sed-5P	7046/7296	2435/2507	83,486

1984 Camaro Z28 5.0L HO T-top Sport Coupe (CP)

CAMARO (V-6/V-8)

1F	P87	2-dr. Spt Cpe-4P	8245/8545	2907/3091	127,292

CAMARO BERLINETTA (V-6/V-8)

1F	S87	2-dr. Spt Cpe-4P	10895/11270	2919/3157	33,400

CAMARO Z28 (V-8)

1F	P87	2-dr. Spt Cpe-4P	-- /10620	-- /3107	100,416

Camaro Engine Note: Prices and weights before slash are for V-6 engine, after slash for V-8. Base Camaro Sport Coupes were also available with a four-cylinder engine, priced at $7995 and weighing 2813 pounds. The Z28 could have an optional high-output V-8 for an additional $530. **Z28 Production Note:** Chevrolet production figures also show 478 Z28E hatchback sport coupes.

CELEBRITY (FOUR/V-6)

1A	W27	2-dr. Coupe-5P	7711/7961	2587/2719	29,191
1A	W19	4-dr. Sedan-5P	7890/8140	2623/2755	200,259
1A	W35	4-dr. Sta Wag-5P	8214/8464	2771/2894	48,295
1A	W35/AQ4	4-dr. 3S Wag-8P	8429/8679	N/A	31,543

MONTE CARLO (V-6/V-8)

1G	Z37	2-dr. Spt Cpe-6P	8936/9311	3085/3200	112,730

MONTE CARLO 'SS' (V-8)

1G	Z37/Z65	2-dr. Spt Cpe-6P	-- /10700	-- /3336	24,050

IMPALA (V-6/V-8)

1B	L69	4-dr. Sedan-6P	8895/9270	3352/3450	55,296

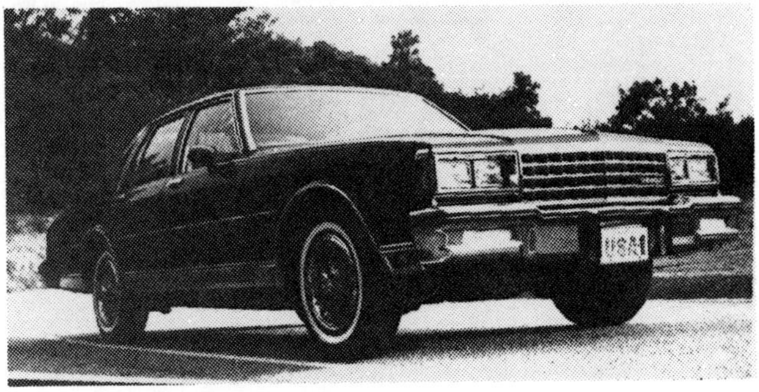

1984 Caprice Classic sedan (CP)

CAPRICE CLASSIC (V-6/V-8)

1B	N47	2-dr. Spt Cpe-6P	9253/9628	3363/3461	19,541
1B	N69	4-dr. Sedan-6P	9399/9774	3396/3494	135,970
1B	N35	4-dr. 3S Wag-8P	-- /10210	-- /3952	65,688

FACTORY PRICE AND WEIGHT NOTE: For Citation and Celebrity, prices and weights to left of slash are for four-cylinder, to right for V-6 engine. For Camaro, Monte Carlo and full-size models, figures to left of slash are for six-cylinder model, to right of slash for 305 cu. in. V-8. Celebrity diesel V-6 cost $250 more than gas V-6. Diesel V-8 was $325 more than gas V-8. **BODY/STYLE NO. NOTE:** Some models were actually option packages. Code after the slash (e.g., Z65) is the number of the option package that comes with the model listed.

ENGINE DATA: BASE FOUR (Chevette): Inline. Overhead cam. Four-cylinder. Cast iron block and head. Displacement: 98 cu. in. (1.6 liters). Bore & stroke: 3.23 x 2.98 in. Compression ratio: 9.0:1. Brake horsepower: 65 at 5200 R.P.M. Torque: 80 lbs.-ft. at 3200 R.P.M. Five main bearings. Hydraulic valve lifters. Carburetor: 2Bbl. VIN Code: C. DIESEL FOUR (Chevette): Inline. Overhead cam. Four-cylinder. Cast iron block and head. Displacement: 111 cu. in. (1.8 liters). Bore & stroke: 3.31 x 3.23 in. Compression ratio: 22.0:1. Brake horsepower: 51 at 5000 R.P.M. Torque: 72 lbs.-ft. at 2000 R.P.M. Five main bearings. Solid valve lifters. Fuel injection. VIN Code: D. BASE FOUR (Cavalier): Inline. Overhead valve. Four-cylinder. Cast iron block and head. Displacement: 121 cu. in. (2.0 liters). Bore & stroke: 3.50 x 3.15 in. Compression ratio: 9.3:1. Brake horsepower: 88 at 4800 R.P.M. Torque: 110 lbs.-ft. at 2400 R.P.M. Five main bearings. Hydraulic valve lifters. Throttle-body fuel injection. VIN Code: P. BASE FOUR (Citation, Celebrity, Camaro): Inline. Overhead valve. Four-cylinder. Cast iron block and head. Displacement: 151 cu. in. (2.5 liters). Bore & stroke: 4.00 x 3.00 in. Compression ratio: 9.0:1. Brake horsepower: 92 at 4000 R.P.M. Torque: 132 lbs.-ft. at 2800 R.P.M. Five main bearings. Hydraulic valve lifters. Throttle-body fuel injection. Pontiac-built. VIN Code: R exc. (Camaro) 2. BASE V-6 (Camaro Berlinetta); OPTIONAL (Citation, Celebrity, Camaro): 60-degree, overhead-valve V-6. Cast iron block and head. Displacement: 173 cu. in. (2.8 liters). Bore & stroke: 3.50 x 2.99 in. Compression ratio: 8.5:1. Brake horsepower: 112 at 4800 R.P.M. (Camaro, 107 at 4800). Torque: 145 lbs.-ft. at 2100 R.P.M. Four main bearings. Hydraulic valve lifters. Carburetor: 2Bbl. VIN Code: X exc. (Camaro) 1. HIGH-OUTPUT V-6; OPTIONAL (Citation, Celebrity): Same as 173 cu. in. V-6 above except C.R.: 8.9:1. Brake H.P.: 135 at 5400 R.P.M. (Celebrity, 130 H.P.). Torque: 145 lbs.-ft. at 2400 R.P.M. VIN Code: Z. BASE V-6 (Monte Carlo, Impala, Caprice): 90-degree, overhead-valve V-6. Cast iron block and head. Displacement: 229 cu. in. (3.8 liters). Bore & stroke: 3.74 x 3.48 in. Compression ratio: 8.6:1. Brake horsepower: 110 at 4000 R.P.M. Torque: 190 lbs.-ft. at 1600 R.P.M. Four main bearings. Hydraulic valve lifters. Carburetor: 2Bbl. VIN Code: 9. (NOTE: California models used a Buick 231 V-6.) DIESEL V-6 (Celebrity): 90-degree, overhead-valve V-6. Cast iron block and head. Displacement: 262 cu. in. (4.3 liters). Bore & stroke: 4.057 x 3.385 in Compression ratio: 22.8:1. Brake horsepower: 85 at 3600 R.P.M. Torque: 165 lbs.-ft. at 1600 R.P.M. Four main bearings. Hydraulic valve lifters. Fuel injection. VIN Code: T. BASE V-8 (Camaro Z28, Caprice wagon): OPTIONAL (Camaro, Monte Carlo, Impala, Caprice): 90-degree, overhead valve V-8. Cast iron block and head. Displacement: 305 cu. in. (5.0 liters). Bore & stroke: 3.74 x 3.48 in. Compression ratio: 8.6:1. Brake horsepower: 150 at 4000 R.P.M. Torque: 240 lbs.-ft. at 2400 R.P.M. Five main bearings. Hydraulic valve lifters. Carburetor: 4Bbl. VIN Code: H. HIGH-OUTPUT V-8 (Monte Carlo SS): Same as 305 cu. in. V-8 above, except Brake H.P.: 180 at 4800 R.P.M. Torque: 235 lbs.-ft. at 3200 R.P.M. VIN Code: G. HIGH-OUTPUT V-8; OPTIONAL (Camaro Z28): Same as 305 cu. in V-8 above, except C.R.: 9.5:1. Brake H.P.: 190 at 4800 R.P.M. Torque: 240 lbs.-ft. at 3200 R.P.M. VIN Code: G. DIESEL V-8; OPTIONAL (Monte Carlo, Impala/Caprice): 90-degree, overhead valve V-8. Cast iron block and head. Displacement: 350 cu. in (5.7 liters). Bore & stroke: 4.057 x 3.385 in. Compression ratio: 22.1:1. Brake horsepower: 105 at 3200 R.P.M. Torque: 200 lbs.-ft. at 1600 R.P.M. Five main bearings. Hydraulic valve lifters. Fuel injection. Olds-built. VIN Code: N.

CHASSIS DATA: Wheelbase: (Chevette 2-dr.) 94.3 in.; (Chvt 4-dr.) 97.3 in.; (Cavalier) 101.2 in.; (Citation/Celebrity) 104.9 in.; (Camaro) 101.0 in.; (Monte Carlo) 108.0 in.; (Imp/Caprice) 116.0 in. Overall length: (Chvt 2-dr.) 161.9 in.; (Chvt 4-dr.) 164.9 in.; (Cav cpe/conv) 172.4 in.; (Cav sed) 174.3 in.; (Cav wag) 174.5 in.; (Cit) 176.7 in.; (Camaro) 187.8 in.; (Celeb) 188.3 in.; (Celeb wag) 190.8 in.; (Monte) 200.4 in.; (Monte SS) 202.4 in.; (Impala) 212.2 in.; (Caprice sed) 212.8 in.; (Capr wag) 215.1 in. Height: (Chvt) 52.8 in.; (Cav cpe) 51.9 in.; (Cav hatch) 51.7 in.; (Cav conv) 52.7 in.; (Cav sed) 53.8 in.; (Cav wag) 54.3 in.; (Cit) 53.9 in.; (Camaro) 50.0 in.; (Camaro Z28) 50.3 in.; (Celeb) 53.9 in.; (Celeb wag) 54.3 in.; (Monte) 54.4 in.; (Monte SS) 55.0 in.; (Imp/Capr sed) 56.4 in.; (Capr wag) 58.1 in. Width: (Chvt) 61.8 in.; (Cav cpe/conv) 66.0 in.; (Cav sed/wag) 66.3 in.; (Cit) 68.3 in.; (Camaro) 72.8 in.; (Celeb) 69.3 in.; (Monte) 71.8 in.; (Imp/Capr) 75.4 in.; (Capr wag) 79.3 in. Front Tread: (Chvt) 51.2 in.; (Cav) 55.4 in.; (Cit/Celeb) 58.7 in.; (Camaro) 60.7 in.; (Monte) 58.5 in.; (Imp/Capr) 61.7 in.; (Caprice wag) 62.2 in. Rear Tread: (Chvt) 51.2 in.; (Cav) 55.2 in.; (Cit/Celeb) 57.0 in.; (Camaro) 61.6 in.; (Monte) 57.8 in.; (Imp/Capr) 60.7 in.; (Caprice wag) 64.1 in. Standard Tires: (Chvt) P155/80R13 GBR; (Cav) P175/80R13 GBR; (Cit/Celeb) P185/80R13 SBR; (Celeb wag) P185/75R14 SBR; (Camaro) P195/75R14 SBR; (Camaro Berlinetta) P205/70R14 SBR; (Camaro Z28) P215/65R15 WLT SBR; (Monte) P195/75R14 SBR; (Monte SS) P215/65R15; (Imp/Capr) P205/75R15 SBR; (Caprice wag) P225/75R15 SBR.

TECHNICAL: Transmission: Four-speed floor shift standard on Chevette. Gear ratios (1st) 3.75:1; (2nd) 2.16:1; (3rd) 1.38:1; (4th) 1.00:1; (Rev) 3.82:1. Four-speed floor shift on Cavalier/Citation/Celebrity: (1st) 3.53:1; (2nd) 1.95:1; (3rd) 1.24:1; (4th) 0.81:1 or 0.73:1; (Rev) 3.42:1. Citation H.O. V-6 four-speed manual trans.: (1st) 3.31:1; (2nd) 1.95:1; (3rd) 1.24:1; (4th) 0.81:1; (Rev) 3.42:1. Camaro four four-speed manual trans.: (1st) 3.50:1; (2nd) 2.48:1; (3rd) 1.66:1; (4th) 1.00:1; (Rev) 3.50:1. Cavalier five-speed manual: (1st) 3.91:1; (2nd) 2.15:1; (3rd) 1.33:1; (4th) 0.92:1; (5th) 0.74:1; (Rev) 3.50:1. Camaro four five-speed manual: (1st) 3.76:1; (2nd) 2.18:1; (3rd) 1.42:1; (4th) 1.00:1; (5th) 0.86:1; (Rev) 3.76:1. Camaro V-6 five-speed manual: (1st) 3.50:1; (2nd) 2.14:1; (3rd) 1.36:1; (4th) 1.00:1; (5th) 0.78:1; (Rev) 3.39:1. Camaro V8305 five-speed manual.: (1st) 2.95:1; (2nd) 1.94:1; (3rd) 1.34:1; (4th) 1.00:1; (5th) 0.73:1; (Rev) 2.76:1. Chevette five-speed manual shift: (1st) 3.76:1; (2nd) 2.18:1; (3rd) 1.36:1; (4th) 1.00:1; (5th) 0.86:1; (Rev) 3.76:1. Three-speed Turbo Hydra- matic standard on Monte Carlo and Imp/Caprice: (1st) 2.74:1; (2nd) 1.57:1; (3rd) 1.00:1; (Rev) 2.07:1. Monte/Imp/Caprice w/V6229: (1st) 2.52:1; (2nd) 1.52:1; (3rd) 1.00:1; (Rev) 1.93:1. Chevette auto. trans.: (1st) 2.40:1; (2nd) 1.48:1; (3rd) 1.00:1; (Rev) 1.92:1. Cav/Cit/Celeb auto. trans.: (1st) 2.84:1; (2nd) 1.60:1; (3rd) 1.00:1; (Rev) 2.07:1. Four-speed overdrive automatic on Imp/Caprice: (1st) 2.74:1; (2nd) 1.57:1; (3rd) 1.00:1; (4th) 0.67:1; (Rev) 2.07:1. Four-speed overdrive automatic on Celebrity: (1st) 2.92:1; (2nd) 1.57:1; (3rd) 1.00:1; (4th) 0.70:1; (Rev) 2.38:1. Four-speed overdrive automatic on Camaro: (1st) 3.06:1; (2nd) 1.63:1; (3rd) 1.00:1; (4th) 0.70:1; (Rev) 2.29:1. Standard final drive ratio: (Chevette) 3.36:1 or 3.62:1; (Cavalier) 3.32:1 or 4.10:1 w/4spd, 3.83:1 w/5spd or 3.73:1 w/auto.; (Citation four) 3.32:1 or 3.65:1 exc. 2.39:1 or 2.84:1 w/auto.; (Cit V-6) 3.32:1 exc. 2.53:1 w/auto.; (Cit H.O. V-6) 3.65:1 exc. 3.33:1 w/auto.; (Camaro four) 3.42:1 exc. 3.73:1 w/auto. or 5spd; (Camaro V-6) 3.42:1 w/5spd, 3.20:1 w/auto.; (Camaro V-8) 3.20:1 or 3.78:1 w/5spd, 3.08:1 or 3.73:1 w/auto.; (Z28) 3.20:1 w/auto.; (Celebrity four) 3.65:1 exc. 2.39:1 w/auto.; (Celeb V-6) 2.84:1 or 3.06:1; (Celeb H.O. V-6) 3.33:1; (Monte V-6) 2.41:1 or 2.73:1; (Monte V-8) 3.42:1 or 3.73:1; (Monte H.O. V-8) 3.42:1 or 3.73:1; (Monte SS) 3.42:1; (Imp/Caprice V-6) 2.73:1 or 3.23:1; (Imp/Capr V-8) 2.73:1 or 3.08:1. Steering, Suspension, Brakes and Body: same as 1982-83. Fuel tank: (Chvt) 12.2 gal.; (Cav) 13.6 gal.; (Cit four) 14.6 gal.; (Cit V-6) 15.1 gal.; (Camaro four) 15.5 gal.; (Camaro V-6) 16.2 gal.; (Celeb four) 15.7 gal.; (Celeb V-6) 16.4 gal.; (Monte) 18.1 gal.; (Imp/Capr) 25 gal.; (Caprice wag) 22 gal.

DRIVETRAIN OPTIONS: Engines: 173 cu. in., 2Bbl. V-6: Citation, base Camaro, Celeb ($250). H.O. 173 cu. in., 2Bbl. V-6: Citation ($400). 305 cu. in., 4Bbl. V-8: Camaro ($550); Berlinetta ($375); Monte, Imp/Caprice cpe/sed ($375). H.O. 305 cu. in., 4Bbl. V-8: Camaro Z28 ($530). Diesel 260 cu. in. V-6: Celeb ($500). Diesel 350 cu. in. V-8: Monte/Imp/Caprice ($700). Transmission/Differential: Five-speed manual trans.: Chevette/Cavalier ($75); base Camaro ($125). Three-speed automatic trans.: Chevette/Cavalier ($395); Chvt diesel ($380); Citation/Celeb ($425). Four-speed overdrive automatic trans.: base Camaro ($525); Berlinetta/Z28 ($295); Celeb (N/A); Monte, Imp/Capr cpe/sed ($175). Limited-slip differential: Camaro/Monte/Imp/Capr ($95). Performance axle ratio ($21). Power Accessories: Power brakes: Chevette ($95); Citation, Celeb cpe/sed ($100). Power four-wheel disc brakes: Camaro V-8 ($179). Power steering: Chvt/Cav ($204); Cit ($215). Suspension: F40 H.D. susp.: Cav/Cit/Celeb/Monte/Imp/Capr ($26). F41 sport suspension: Cit/Celeb ($33); Cav ($44-$49); Camaro/Monte, Imp/Capr cpe/sed ($49). Inflatable rear shock absorbers: Celeb/Caprice wag ($64). Other: H.D. cooling ($40-$70). Engine block heater ($20). Cold climate pkg.: Monte/Imp/Caprice diesel ($99). Diesel engine and fuel line heater: Celeb ($49). H.D. battery ($26) exc. diesel ($52). California emission system ($99).

CHEVETTE CONVENIENCE/APPEARANCE OPTIONS: Option Packages: Sport decor pkg.: black grille, headlamp bezels and wheels; bodyside moldings, trim rings and decals ($95). Deluxe exterior: side window reveal moldings, argent wheels and trim rings ($152-$167). Comfort/Convenience: Air conditioning ($630). Rear defogger, electric ($130). Tinted glass ($95). Comfortilt steering wheel ($104). Cigarette lighter: Scooter ($10). Lighting and Mirrors: Twin sport mirrors, left remote ($53). Driver's remote sport mirror ($34). Entertainment: AM radio: Scooter ($83). AM/FM radio ($82); Scooter ($165). AM/FM stereo radio ($109). Radio delete ($51 credit). Exterior Trim: Two-tone paint ($133). Rear spoiler ($69). Bodyside moldings: Scooter ($45). Door edge guards ($15-$25). Chrome bumpers ($25). Interior Trim/Upholstery: Cloth bucket seats ($28). Custom cloth bucket seats ($130). Color-keyed floor mats ($25). Wheels and Tires: Sport wheel covers ($97). Wheel trim rings ($52). P155/80R13 GBR WSW ($51). P175/70R13 SBR BSW ($119). P175/70R13 SBR WSW ($173).

CAVALIER CONVENIENCE/APPEARANCE OPTIONS: Option Packages: CL equipment pkg.: custom interior w/reclining seats, quiet sound group, three-spoke leather-wrapped steering wheel, custom door/quarter trim ($275-$375); incl. split folding rear seat on hatch/wagon. Comfort/Convenience: Air cond. ($630). Cruise control ($175). Rear defogger, electric ($130). Tinted glass ($95). Six-way power driver's seat ($215). Leather-wrapped steering wheel ($74-$95). Comfortilt steering wheel ($99). Power windows ($185-$260). Power door locks ($125-$175). Power hatch or trunk release ($40). Power liftgate release ($35). Gauge pkg. w/trip odometer ($69). Special instruments incl. tach ($139). Lighter: base ($14). Intermittent wipers ($50). Rear wiper/washer ($120). Lighting and Mirrors: Halogen headlamps ($10). Aux. lighting ($72-$95). Dual sport mirrors, left remote ($53). Right visor mirror ($7). Entertainment: AM radio: base ($112). AM/FM radio ($171) exc. CS/10 ($82). Electronic-tuning AM/FM stereo radio: CS/10 ($177). Elect.-tuning AM/FM stereo radio w/clock ($277) exc. CS/10 ($177). Elect.-tuning AM/FM stereo radio

w/cassette ($377) exc. CS/10 ($277). Elect.-tuning AM/FM stereo seek/scan radio w/cassette, equalizer and clock ($605) exc. CS/10 ($505). Dual rear speakers ($30-$42); premium ($25). Fixed-mast antenna: base ($41) but incl. w/radios. Radio delete ($56 credit). Exterior Trim: Removable sunroof ($300). Rear spoiler ($69). Rear window louvers ($199). Pinstriping ($53). Sport striping ($95). Bodyside moldings, black/argent ($45). Wheel opening moldings ($30). Wheel opening and rocker panel moldings ($55). Door edge guards ($15-$25). Roof carrier ($105). Bumper guards ($56). Interior Trim/Upholstery: Cloth or CS bucket seats ($28). Split-folding rear seatback ($50). Color-keyed mats: front ($15); rear ($10). Cargo area cover ($69). Wheels and Tires: Aluminum wheels ($369). Sport wheel covers w/black wheels ($97). Wheel trim rings ($52). P175/80R13 GBR WSW ($54). P195/70R13 SBR BSW ($169). P195/70R13 SBR WSW ($231). P195/70R13 SBR WLT ($253).

CITATION/CELEBRITY CONVENIENCE/APPEARANCE OPTIONS: Option Packages: X11 sport equipment pkg.: Citation ($919- $981). Eurosport pkg.: Celeb cpe/sed ($226); wag ($191). Sport decor pkg. (rear spoiler, rally wheels, sport mirrors, color-keyed bumpers w/rub strips, decal): Citation ($249). Deluxe exterior pkg.: Cit ($68-$168). Exterior molding pkg. (black rocker panel and wheel opening moldings): Celeb ($55). Value appearance group: Cit ($55-$63). Quiet sound group: Cit cpe ($43). Quiet sound/rear decor pkg.: Cit ($92). Security pkg.: Celeb wag ($44). Comfort/Convenience: Air cond. ($725-$730). Rear defogger, electric ($140). Cruise control ($175). Tinted glass ($110). Sport steering wheel: Cit ($22). Comfortilt steering wheel ($110). Six-way power driver's seat: Celeb ($215). Power windows ($185-$260). Remote swing-out side windows: Cit ($108). Power door locks ($125-$175). Citation gauge pkg. w/clock and trip odometer ($104); w/tachometer ($149). Gauge pkg. w/trip odometer: Celeb ($64). Electric clock: Cit ($35). Digital clock: Celeb ($39). Lighter: Cit cpe ($10). Intermittent wipers ($50). Rear wiper/washer: Celeb ($120). Lighting, Horns and Mirrors: Halogen high-beam headlamps: Celeb ($10). Aux. lighting: Cit ($50); Celeb ($43-$57). Dome reading lamp: Celeb ($24). Dual horns: Cit ($12). Driver's remote mirror ($23). Dual sport mirrors, left remote ($61). Dual remote mirrors: Celeb ($91). Entertainment: AM radio: Cit cpe ($83). AM/FM radio: Cit hatch, Celeb ($82); Cit cpe ($165). AM/FM stereo radio: Cit ($109) exc. cpe ($192). AM/FM stereo w/cassette: Cit ($209) exc. cpe ($292). Celebrity electronic-tuning AM/FM stereo radio w/clock ($177); w/cassette ($277); with seek/scan, equalizer and cassette ($505). Dual rear speakers ($30); incl. w/stereo radio. Premium dual rear speakers: Celeb ($25) but incl. with elect. tuning radio. Radio delete ($56 credit). Exterior Trim: Vinyl roof: Celeb ($160). Two-tone paint: Cit ($176-$184) incl. pinstriping and bodyside moldings; Celeb ($148). Bodyside pinstriping: Cit ($39-$47); Celeb ($57). Bodyside moldings: Cit ($55). Door edge guards ($15-$25). Rear window air deflector: Celeb wag ($40). Swing-out quarter vent windows: Celeb ($75). Swing-out tailgate: Celeb ($105). Roof carrier: Celeb wag ($105). Bumper guards ($56). Bumper rub strips: Cit ($50). Citation Interior Trim/Upholstery: Console ($105). Sport cloth bench seat ($28). Custom trim w/cloth bench seat ($195); w/custom cloth bucket seats ($367-$392). Sport cloth bucket seats ($221-$250). Color-keyed mats: front ($17); rear ($12). Deluxe seatbelts: cpe ($26). Celebrity Interior Trim/Upholstery: Console ($105). Reclining driver and passenger seatbacks ($90). Two-pass. vinyl front bench seat: cpe/sed ($28). Three-pass. vinyl front bench seat: sed ($78). Three-pass. cloth front bench seat ($28-$50). CL custom cloth 45/45 seat ($250-$330). CL three-pass. custom bench seating: vinyl ($229); cloth ($257). CL two- pass. custom cloth bench seating ($109-$179). 45/45 cloth seating ($100). Cloth bucket seats ($147). Color-keyed mats: front ($17); rear ($12). Deluxe luggage area trim: wag ($40). Citation Wheels/Tires: Rally wheels ($56). P185/80R13 SBR WSW ($58). P205/70R13 SBR WLT ($202). P215/60R14 SBR WLT: X11 ($92). Celebrity Wheels/Tires: Aluminum wheels ($306-$362). Sport wheel covers ($65). Wire wheel covers ($159). Wheel cover locks ($39). Rally wheels ($56). P185/80R13 SBR WSW ($58). P185/75R14 SBR BSW ($36). P185/75R14 SBR WSW ($58-$94). P195/70R14 SBR BSW ($28). P195/75R14 SBR BSW ($31-$67). P195/75R14 SBR WSW ($93-$129). P205/70R13 SBR WSW ($180).

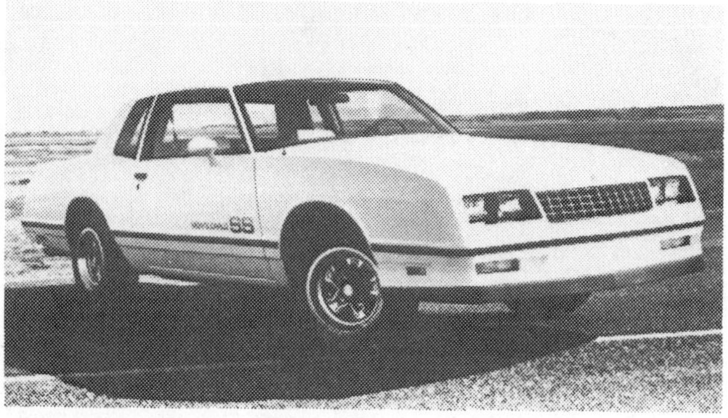

1984 Monte Carlo SS Sport Coupe (CP)

CAMARO/MONTE CARLO CONVENIENCE/APPEARANCE OPTIONS: Comfort/Convenience: Air conditioning ($730). Rear defogger, electric ($140). Cruise control ($175-$185). Tinted glass ($110). Comfortilt steering wheel ($110). Six-way power driver's seat ($215). Power windows ($185). Power door locks ($125). Power trunk opener: Monte ($40). Power hatch release: Camaro ($40). Electric clock ($35). Gauge pkg. w/trip odometer: Monte ($95). Gauge pkg. incl. tach: Camaro ($149). Intermittent wipers ($50). Rear wiper/washer: Camaro ($120). Quiet sound group: Camaro ($72-$82). Lighting, Horns and Mirrors: Halogen high-beam headlamps ($10). Cornering lamps: Monte ($55). Aux. lighting: Camaro ($37-$72); Monte ($28). Dual horns: Camaro ($12). Twin sport mirrors (left remote): base Camaro, Monte ($53). Twin remote sport mirrors: Monte ($83); SS ($30). Twin electric remote sport mirrors: Camaro ($91-$139). Entertainment: AM radio ($112). AM/FM radio ($171). AM/FM stereo radio: Monte ($198). Cassette player with AM/FM stereo radio: Monte ($298). Camaro electronic-tuning AM/FM stereo radio ($263); w/clock ($267-$302); w/cassette and clock ($367-$402); w/cassette, clock and seek/scan ($570-$605). Dual rear speakers ($30). Fixed mast antenna ($41); incl. w/radios. Power antenna ($60). Exterior Trim: Removable glass roof panels ($825). Landau vinyl roof: Monte ($245). Rear spoiler: Camaro ($69). Two- tone paint: Monte ($214). Bodyside moldings, black: Camaro ($55). Deluxe bodyside moldings: Monte ($57). Door edge guards ($15). Side window sill moldings: Monte ($45). Roof drip moldings: Camaro ($29). Bodyside pinstriping: Monte ($61). Interior Trim/Upholstery: Console: Camaro ($50); Monte ($105). Vinyl bench seat: base Monte ($28). Cloth 55/45 seating: base Monte ($133). Cloth bucket seats: Camaro ($28); Monte ($147). Custom cloth or vinyl bucket seats: base Camaro ($359); Z28 ($287). Custom cloth CL 55/45 seating: base Monte ($385). Cloth LS contour bucket seats: Camaro ($375). Custom cloth LS contour bucket seats: Camaro ($650). Mats w/carpeted inserts: Camaro front ($20); Camaro rear ($15). Color-keyed mats: Monte ($27). Cargo area cover: Camaro ($69). Deluxe trunk trim: Camaro ($164); Z28 ($84). Locking rear storage cover: Camaro ($80). Wheels and Tires: Aluminum wheels: Monte ($362). Rally wheels: Camaro ($112); Monte ($56). Full wheel covers: Camaro ($52). Wire wheel covers: Monte ($159). Wheel cover locks: Monte ($39). P195/75R14 GBR WSW: Camaro ($62). P195/75R14 SBR WSW: Monte ($62). P205/70R14 SBR BSW: base Camaro ($58). P205/70R14 SBR WSW: Camaro ($124); Berlinetta ($66); Monte ($124). P205/70R14 SBR WLT: Camaro ($146). P215/65R15 SBR BSW: Z28 ($92 credit).

IMPALA/CAPRICE CONVENIENCE/APPEARANCE OPTIONS: Option Packages: Estate equipment: wag ($307). Landau equipment pkg.: vinyl roof, sport mirrors and reveal moldings ($306). Comfort/Convenience: Air cond. ($730). Rear defogger, electric ($140). Cruise control ($175). Tinted glass ($110). Comfortilt steering wheel ($110). Power door locks ($125- $175). Six-way power driver's seat ($215). Power windows ($185-$260). Power trunk opener ($40). Power tailgate lock: wag ($50). Electric clock: Imp ($35). Digital clock: Imp ($66); Caprice ($34). Gauge pkg. w/trip odometer ($64). Intermittent wipers ($50). Quiet sound group: Imp ($66). Lighting and Mirrors: Halogen high-beam headlamps ($10). Cornering lamps ($55). Aux. lighting ($32-$42). Driver's remote mirror ($23). Dual remote mirrors ($67). Dual sport mirrors, left remote ($61). Dual remote body-color sport mirrors ($91) exc. Landau ($30). Lighted visor mirror ($48). Entertainment: Same as 1983. AM radio ($112). AM/FM radio ($171). AM/FM stereo radio ($198). Cassette player with AM/FM stereo ($298). Dual rear speakers ($30). Power antenna ($60). Windshield antenna ($29); incl. w/radios. Exterior Trim: Vinyl roof: sed ($185). Roof carrier: wag ($110). Custom two-tone paint ($141). Pinstriping ($39). Bodyside moldings ($55). Door edge guards ($15-$25). Rear window air deflector: wag ($40). Bumper rub strips ($66). Bumper guards ($62). Interior Trim/Upholstery: Reclining passenger seatback ($45). Vinyl bench seat: Imp sed ($28). Cloth bench seat: wag ($28). Cloth 50/50 seating: Caprice ($195-$225). Deluxe load-floor carpet: wag ($89). Deluxe cargo area carpet: wag ($129). Color-keyed mats: front ($17); rear ($12). Deluxe trunk trim ($59). Wheels and Tires: Sport wheel covers ($65). Wire wheel covers ($159). Wire wheel cover locks ($39). P205/75R15 SBR WSW: cpe/sed ($66). P225/70R15 SBR WSW: cpe/sed ($159). P225/75R15 SBR WSW: wag ($71). Puncture-sealant tires ($106-$132).

HISTORY: Introduced: Sept. 22, 1983. Model year production (U.S.): 1,658,868 (incl. Corvettes but not incl. 18,314 Acadians). Total production for the U.S. market included 871,578 four- cylinder, 466,797 sixes and 507,774 V-8s. A total of 11,452 diesels were installed. Calendar year production (U.S.): 1,471,462 (including 35,661 Corvettes). Calendar year sales by U.S. dealers: 1,565,143 (incl. 30,424 Corvettes) for a 19.7 percent market share. Model year sales by U.S. dealers: 1,585,902 (incl. 27,986 Corvettes) for a 20.1 percent share.

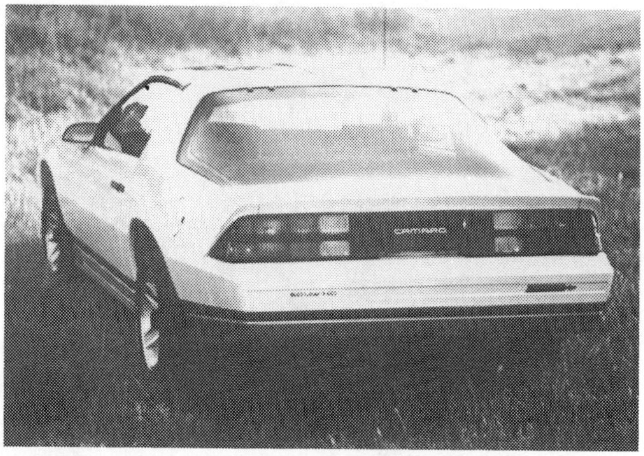

1984 Camaro Z28 5.0L HO T-top Sport Coupe (CP)

Historical Footnotes: Model year sales finished nearly 23 percent higher than the 1983 result, with all lines (except Citation) performing well. Sales of that forlorn Xcar fell by more than half. As demand for Citations slowed, production was halted at the Oklahoma plant and cut to one shift at Tarrytown, New York. Cavalier continued as America's best selling car, with Celebrity not far behind. Two new imports, Sprint (built by Suzuki) and Spectrum (by Isuzu) would soon give Chevrolet another toehold on the rising small-car market. Sprint went on sale late in the 1984 model year, Spectrum later, both as '85 models. To help plan for the enthusiast's market, surveys revealed that nearly two-thirds of Camaro buyers were under age 35. *Road & Track* magazine called the '84 Camaro one of the dozen top enthusiast cars, and it tied with Trans Am for best Sports GT in its price league. The International Race of Champions returned to the racing circuit during 1984, after a three-year absence. Co- sponsored by Chevrolet, Anheuser-Busch, Goodyear and True Value Hardware, the races would put a dozen of the world's top drivers behind the wheel of identically-prepared Camaro Z28s. That IROC racing series had begun in 1974 using Porsches, then switched to Camaros. With heavy TV coverage, this year's races would draw considerable attention to Camaro and perhaps help pave the way for the soon-to-come IROCZ production models. On another level, Chevrolet hosted a traveling Chevy Sports Hall of Fame show in urban shopping malls this year, as part of greatly increased advertising and promotional expenditures.

1985 CHEVROLET

Chevrolet claimed this year to offer "America's highest- mileage car, America's fastest car...America's most popular full-size car and America's most popular car, regardless of size." Still, 1985 was a year of refinement and evolution rather than revolution. But several intriguing models and engines were announced, including the new IROCZ Camaro, performance Z24 Cavalier, and 4.3-liter V-6 engine with fuel injection. That 130-horsepower powerplant was the standard eight in Caprice and Monte Carlo, intended to tempt V-8 fans who might appreciate a bit better gas mileage. Also new was a multi-port fuel-injected version of the 2.8-liter V-6, identified by 'MFI' logo when installed in a Cavalier, Celebrity, Citation II or Camaro. Unfortunately, the Z24 Cavalier didn't actually arrive until the 1986 model year, nearly a year later than scheduled. The old reliable 305 cu. in. (5.0-liter) V-8 got a boost in compression ratio and new Electronic Spark Control.

CHEVETTE — SERIES 1T — FOUR — In the face of a flurry of front-drive subcompacts, Chevette hung on with rear-wheel drive. Little changed this year, except that the base Chevette was dropped, leaving only the CS version, again in two- or four-door hatchback form. Base powertrain remained the 1.6-liter gas four with four-speed manual transmission. The diesel four was still available, but only a handful were sold. A five-speed manual gearbox was now available on all models (formerly only on two-doors without air conditioning). Diesels could no longer get automatic. Of the 10 body colors, eight were new this year. Also new: Custom two-tone combinations.

1985 Chevette CS hatchback sedan (CP)

Four-doors now had standard Custom Cloth front bucket seats. New bodyside moldings had argent inserts. Returning to the option list was a Z13 Sport Decor graphic package, including black grille, bumpers and wheels, plus black bodyside moldings with red inserts.

1985 Cavalier sedan (AA)

CAVALIER — SERIES 1J — FOUR/V-6 — Two-door Cavaliers got new taillamps, wheels and hubcaps, plus a new steering wheel. An upshift light was added to manual-gearbox models. Base models had upgraded seats. The lineup again included two-door notchbacks and hatchbacks, four-door sedans and wagons, plus the convertible. The convertible officially became a separate line this year, rather than an option package. Both Type 10 and convertible models got a "cockpit" styled instrument panel, with switches in control pods at the sides of the cluster. Cavaliers also got new interior trim colors and "Star Wars" instrumentation. Of the dozen body colors, ten were new this year. Cavaliers again had a crosshatch-pattern grille, angled inward at the base with bowtie emblem in the middle, and flanked by recessed quad rectangular headlamps. Parking lights were below the bumper rub strips. The base 121 cu. in. (2.0-liter) four, rated 85 horsepower, got refinements to improve durability and economy. But the biggest news for Cavalier was the availability of a 2.8-liter V-6 with multi-port fuel injection. Arriving later in the season, the V-6 was rated 125 horsepower, standard with the announced Z24 sports package but available in all models. That Z24 package, scheduled for spring 1985 arrival, was to include flared rocker panels, specific fascia, rally wheels, and digital instruments. But it didn't actually appear until the 1986 model year. Cavalier standard equipment included four-speed manual (overdrive) transmission, power brakes, front/rear ashtrays, color-keyed bumpers with black/argent rub strips, side window defogger, day/night mirror, front stabilizer bar, styled steel wheels, fixed quarter windows, black windshield and back window moldings, and vinyl reclining bucket seats. Type 10 Cavaliers included black/red bumper rub strips, lighter, black grille, AM radio, color-keyed sport steering wheel, black/red bodyside moldings, plus black window and belt moldings. CS equipment, though similar to Type 10, included black/argent bodyside moldings and a bright grille. Convertibles came with a power top, power windows (drop-down rear quarter), black/argent bumper rub strips, tinted glass, black sport mirrors, and bright rocker panel moldings. Convertible interiors held cloth or vinyl custom reclining bucket seats.

1985 Citation II X11 hatchback coupe (AA)

CITATION II — SERIES 1X — FOUR/V-6 — All the final Citations were hatchbacks, as the notchback coupe was dropped this year. Xcars had been plagued by problems, including court battles, largely for alleged brake flaws on the 1980 models. A new dashboard included a horizontal-style radio. Electronic-tuning models were now available, with or without a cassette tape player. A dozen body colors were offered (nine new this year). Citation's X11 package now included a 130-horsepower 173 cu. in. (2.8-liter) V-6 with multi-port fuel injection. That powerplant was also available separately, in all models. The base 151 cu. in. (2.5-liter) four added hydraulic roller valve lifters this year, while the carbureted 2.8 V-6 continued in its prior form. The X11 package also included power brakes, sport steering wheel, sport cloth bucket seats, domed hood with air inlet, body-color bumpers, X11 decals, rear deck spoiler, F41 sport suspension, and P215/60R14 SBR tires on newly-styled Rally wheels. Black headlamp bezels, grille, B-pillar/window frames and taillamp frames completed the package. Aluminum wheels were optional.

1985 Camaro IROC-Z T-top Sport Coupe (AA)

CAMARO — SERIES 1F — FOUR/V-6/V-8 — Most appealing to connoisseurs was the new IROCZ, styled along the lines of the racing models that performed in the International Race of Champions and with a nod to Corvette. IROCZ was packaged as a Z28 option. In appearance, it could be spotted by twin foglamps inset in the grille opening (alongside the license plate mount), a low front air dam, ornamental hood louvers, and striping at rocker panel level. IROCZ had a solid angled front panel between deeply recessed quad headlamps, with parking lamps just below the crease line. Deep body-color "ground effects" skirting encircled the entire car. Special 16 x 8 in. aluminum wheels held Corvette-inspired P245/50VR16 Goodyear Eagle GT unidirectional tires. Near the base of each door were large 'IROCZ' decals. The IROCZ chassis featured Delco/Bilstein rear shock absorbers, special struts and springs, special rear stabilizer, and reinforced front frame rails. The IROCZ could have any of three 305 cu. in. (5.0-liter) V-8s: standard four-barrel with five-speed manual gearbox (four-speed overdrive automatic available), a high-output L69 carbureted V-8 with five-speed, or the new LB9 tuned-port fuel injection (TPI) version. The TPI came only with four-speed automatic. Individually-tuned runners channeled incoming air to each cylinder in the TPI V-8, while computer-controlled port injectors delivered precisely-metered fuel. In limited-production IROCZ dress, the factory claimed a 060 MPH time in the seven-second area, and 15-second quarter-mile acceleration times. "Ordinary" Z28s could have only the standard or TPI versions, not the carbureted H.O. Z28s in general had a selection of changes in appearance details, including grille and parking lamps, deeper ground-effects rocker panels, hood louvers, deeper chin spoiler, three-element taillamps, larger rear bumper fascia, and new body nameplates. Inside were new speedometer graphics and tachometer. Berlinetta got a new standard 173 cu. in. (2.8-liter) V-6 with multi-port fuel injection and only one option: the carbureted 5.0-liter V-8. Also new were body graphics and subtly-patterned interior fabrics. The base Sport Coupe again came with either a four, V-6 or V-8 engine under the hood. Like the Z28, it had new body styling, a wider selection of optional sound systems with electronic-tuning radios, and revised optional instrument cluster graphics. All Camaros had new "wet arm" windshield wipers, with washer outlets mounted on the blades. The double-needle speedometer was abandoned. Split rear seatbacks were a new option, and cast aluminum wheels (standard on Z28) were available on the base Camaro. Body colors this year were white, silver, copper, red maroon, black, medium gray, dark or bright blue, yellow or light yellow, and light brown.

1985 Celebrity Eurosport sedan (AA)

CELEBRITY — SERIES 1F — FOUR/V-6 — Like other models, Celebrity got a new optional 173 cu. in. (2.8-liter) V-6 with multi-port fuel injection, available on all models. Also optional: a carbureted 2.8 and a 4.3-liter V-6 diesel, plus the standard 151 cu. in. (2.5-liter) four. All models now had 14 in. wheels and standard power brakes. Gas engines had new hydraulic mounts, plus the availability of four-speed overdrive automatic transmission. The Eurosport option package added gas-charged shock absorbers. Of the dozen body colors, nine were new this year. Station wagons could get a new woodgrain Estate Package. Coupes and sedans could be ordered with a new Celebrity Classic padded vinyl roof. Interior trim styles and colors were also new. The lineup continued as a two-door coupe, four-door sedan, and two- or three-seat wagons. The Eurosport package included black-finish body hardware with red accents, specific nameplates (inside and out), Rally wheels, red-accented bodyside molding rub strips, sport steering wheel, special F41 sport suspension, and gas-charged front struts and rear shocks. 'Eurosport' block lettering was at the forward edge of front doors; a '2.8FI' engine identifier on the decklid.

1985 Monte Carlo Sport Coupe (CP)

MONTE CARLO — SERIES 1G — V-6/V-8 — Under the hood of standard Montes was a new base 262 cu. in. (4.3-liter) V-6. Chevrolet claimed that the new 4.3 V-6 would be as economical as the prior carbureted 3.8, and nearly as "frisky" as a V-8. Standard Sport Coupes got new cloth interior trim and five new interior colors, plus new standard wheel covers. Still, the Monte Carlo SS, "cousin to the Grand National stock cars" on the NASCAR circuit, received the strongest promotion. Formerly offered only in white or blue body colors, this year's SS came in silver, maroon, white or black. Interiors could be gray or maroon, either bench or bucket style. This street version of the NASCAR racing car had special instruments, sport suspension, rear spoiler, sport mirrors and steering wheel, plus P215/65R15 white-letter radial tires on special rally wheels. Apart from 'Monte Carlo SS' lettering on the doors and decklid, the body was nearly devoid of ornamentation. The blackout grille was a simple crosshatch pattern, flanked by recessed quad rectangular headlamps with deeply inset park/signal lamps below the forward crease line. Taillamp lenses sat nearly flush with the decklid panel. Monte SS again carried a high-output (RPO code L69) version of the familiar 305 cu. in. (5.0-liter) V-8, now with four-speed overdrive automatic transmission. SS mufflers grew in capacity; axles got larger ring gears. Removable black roof panels were to become available on SS later in the model year.

1985 Caprice Classic Landau Sport Coupe (AA)

IMPALA/CAPRICE CLASSIC — SERIES 1B — V-6/V-8 — Full-size Chevrolets had some changes to produce a more controlled ride, plus an economical new 262 cu. in. (4.3-liter) V-6 engine rated 130 horsepower. That new base engine was described as "a standard V-6 that acts like a V-8." All full-size models now wore fourth-generation All-Season tires. Four-speed overdrive automatic was available across the board. For the last time, the 5.7-liter diesel V-8 was optional (except in California). The lineup again included Caprice Classic two-door, four-door and station wagon, plus the four-door Impala sedan. Interiors received their most extensive reworking since 1977, all presumably to give a more contemporary, less stodgy look and feel. Wagons again came with a standard 305 cu. in. (5.0-liter) V-8, which was optional in other models. This year, it got a boost in compression (and horsepower), plus a new exhaust system. Caprice added a bold crosshatch grille, parking lamps inset into the bumper, wraparound cornering lamps, and quad rectangular headlamps. A 'Caprice Classic' script was at the forward end of front fenders. Impalas had standard AM radio, folding front center armrest, power brakes and steering, three-speed automatic transmission, lighter, padded door panels, argent grille, day/night mirror, cloth bench seats, full wheel covers, two-speed wiper/washers, and bright moldings. Caprice added a quartz clock, dual horns, wheel opening and lower bodyside moldings, headlamps-on buzzer, and bumper rub strips (except wagons). Wagons included vinyl bench seating, a locking side compartment, heavy-duty front/rear suspension, power liftgate window, and overdrive automatic transmission, along with the V-8 engine.

I.D. DATA: Chevrolets again had a 17-symbol Vehicle Identification Number (VIN) on the upper left surface of the instrument panel, visible through the windshield. Symbol one indicates country: '1' U.S.A.; '2' Canada. Next is a manufacturer code: 'G' General Motors. Symbol three is car make: '1' Chevrolet; '7' GM of Canada. Symbol four denotes restraint system: 'A' non-passive (standard); 'B' passive (automatic belts); 'C' passive (inflatable). Symbol five is car line/series: 'B' Chevette; 'C' Cavalier; 'D' Cavalier CS; 'E' Cavalier Type 10; 'X' Citation; 'P' Camaro; 'S' Camaro Berlinetta; 'W' Celebrity; 'Z' Monte Carlo; 'L' Impala; 'N' Caprice. Symbols six-seven reveal body type: '08' 2-dr. hatch coupe; '27' 2-dr. notchback coupe (or convertible); '37' special 2-dr. notch coupe; '47' full-size 2-dr. sport coupe; '77' 2-dr. hatch coupe; '87' 2-dr. notchback coupe; '19' 4-dr. 6-window notchback sedan; '68' 4-dr. 6-window hatch sedan; '69' 4-dr. 4-window notchback sedan; '35' 4-dr. station wagon. Next is the engine code: 'C' L498 2Bbl.; 'D' L4111 diesel; 'P' L4121 FI; 'R' or 'Z' L4151 FI; 'X' V6173 2Bbl.; 'S' or 'W' V6173 MFI; 'Z' V6262 FI; 'T' V6262 diesel; 'H' V8305 4Bbl.; 'G' H.O. V8305 4Bbl.; 'F' V8305 TPI; 'N' V8350 diesel. Next is a check digit, followed by 'F' for model year 1985. Symbol eleven indicates assembly plant: 'B' Baltimore; 'J' Janesville, WI; 'L' Van Nuys, CA; 'N' Norwood, OH; 'R' Arlington, TX; 'T' Tarrytown, NY; 'X' Fairfax, KS; 'Y' Wilmington, DE; '1' Oshawa, Ontario; '6' Oklahoma City, OK; '7' Lordstown, OH. The final six digits are the sequential serial number. Engine number coding is similar to 1981-84.

CHEVETTE CS (FOUR)

Model Number	Body/Style Number	Body Type & Seating	Factory Price	Shipping Weight	Production Total
1T	B08	2-dr. Hatch Cpe-4P	5340	2032	57,706
1T	B68	4-dr. Hatch Sed-4P	5690	2091	65,128

CHEVETTE CS DIESEL (FOUR)

1T	B08/Z90	2-dr. Hatch Cpe-4P	5850	N/A	203
1T	B68/Z90	4-dr. Hatch Sed-4P	6215	N/A	462

CAVALIER (FOUR)

1J	C69	4-dr. Sedan-5P	6477	2320	86,597
1J	C35	4-dr. Sta Wag-5P	6633	2392	34,581

CAVALIER CS (FOUR)

1J	D69	4-dr. Sedan-5P	6900	2334	93,386
1J	D35	4-dr. Sta Wag-5P	7066	2405	33,551

CAVALIER TYPE 10 (FOUR)

1J	E27	2-dr. Coupe-5P	6737	2300	106,021
1J	E77	2-dr. Hatch Cpe-5P	6919	2350	25,508
1J	E27/Z08	2-dr. Conv. Cpe-4P	11693	2515	4,108

Cavalier Engine Note: A V-6 engine became available during the model year, priced at $560.

CITATION II (FOUR/V-6)

1X	X08	2-dr. Hatch Cpe-5P	6940/7200	2399/2471	7,443
1X	X68	4-dr. Hatch Sed-5P	7090/7350	2435/2507	55,279

CAMARO (V-6/V-8)

1F	P87	2-dr. Spt Cpe-4P	8698/8998	2907/3091	97,966

CAMARO BERLINETTA (V-6/V-8)

1F	S87	2-dr. Spt Cpe-4P	11060/11360	2919/3157	13,649

CAMARO Z28 (V-8)

1F	P87	2-dr. Spt Cpe-4P	--/11060	--/3107	68,199

Camaro Engine Note: Prices and weights before slash are for V-6 engine, after slash for V-8. Base Camaro Sport Coupes were also available with a four-cylinder engine, priced at $8363 and weighing 2813 pounds. The Z28 could have an optional fuel-injected or carbureted (IROCZ) high-output V-8 for an additional $695. **Z28 IROCZ Production Note:** A total of 21,177 Z28s had the IROCZ performance package (RPO Code B4Z). Chevrolet production figures also show 204 Z28E hatchback sport coupes.

CELEBRITY (FOUR/V-6)

1A	W27	2-dr. Coupe-5P	8102/8362	2587/2719	29,010
1A	W19	4-dr. Sedan-5P	8288/8548	2623/2755	239,763
1A	W35	4-dr. Sta Wag-5P	8479/8739	2771/2894	45,602
1A	W35/AQ4	4-dr. 3S Wag-8P	8699/8959	N/A	40,547

MONTE CARLO (V-6/V-8)

1G	Z37	2-dr. Spt Cpe-6P	9540/9780	3085/3093	83,573

MONTE CARLO 'SS' (V-8)

1G	Z37/Z65	2-dr. Spt Cpe-6P	--/11380	--/3336	35,484

IMPALA (V-6/V-8)

1B	L69	4-dr. Sedan-6P	9519/9759	3352/3366	53,438

CAPRICE CLASSIC (V-6/V-8)

1B	N47	2-dr. Spt Cpe-6P	9888/10128	3363/3377	16,229
1B	N69	4-dr. Sedan-6P	10038/10278	3396/3410	139,240
1B	N35	4-dr. 3S Wag-8P	--/10714	--/3952	55,886

FACTORY PRICE AND WEIGHT NOTE: For Citation and Celebrity, prices and weights to left of slash are for four-cylinder, to right for V-6 engine. For Camaro, Monte Carlo and full-size models, figures to left of slash are for six-cylinder model, to right of slash for 305 cu. in. V-8. Celebrity diesel V-6 cost the same as gas V-6. Diesel V-8 for Caprice/Impala was also priced the same as gas V-8. Optional engine prices rose during the model year. **BODY/STYLE NO. NOTE:** Some models were actually option packages. Code after the slash (e.g., Z65) is the number of the option package that comes with the model listed.

ENGINE DATA: BASE FOUR (Chevette): Inline. Overhead cam. Four-cylinder. Cast iron block and head. Displacement: 98 cu. in. (1.6 liters). Bore & stroke: 3.23 x 2.98 in. Compression ratio: 9.0:1. Brake horsepower: 65 at 5200 R.P.M. Torque: 80 lbs.-ft. at 3200 R.P.M. Five main bearings. Hydraulic valve lifters. Carburetor: 2Bbl. VIN Code: A. DIESEL FOUR (Chevette): Inline. Overhead cam. Four-cylinder. Cast iron block and head. Displacement: 111 cu. in. (1.8 liters). Bore & stroke: 3.31 x 3.23 in. Compression ratio: 22.0:1. Brake horsepower: 51 at 5000 R.P.M. Torque: 72 lbs.-ft. at 2000 R.P.M. Five main bearings. Fuel injection. VIN Code: B. BASE FOUR (Cavalier): Inline. Overhead valve. Four-cylinder. Cast iron block and head. Displacement: 121 cu. in. (2.0 liters). Bore & stroke: 3.50 x 3.15 in. Compression ratio: 9.0:1. Brake horsepower: 85 at 4800 R.P.M. Torque: 110 lbs.-ft. at 2400 R.P.M. Five main bearings. Hydraulic valve lifters. Throttle-body fuel injection. VIN Code: P. BASE FOUR (Citation, Celebrity, Camaro): Inline. Overhead valve. Four-cylinder. Cast iron block and head. Displacement: 151 cu. in. (2.5 liters). Bore & stroke: 4.00 x 3.00 in. Compression ratio: 9.0:1. Brake horsepower: 92 at 4400 R.P.M. (Camaro, 88 at 4400). Torque: 134 lbs.-ft. at 2800 R.P.M. (Camaro, 132 at 2800). Five main bearings. Hydraulic valve lifters. Throttle-body fuel injection. Pontiac-built. VIN Code: R exc. (Camaro) 2. OPTIONAL V-6 (Citation, Celebrity): 60-degree, overhead-valve V-6. Cast iron block and head. Displacement: 173 cu. in. (2.8 liters). Bore & stroke: 3.50 x 2.99 in. Compression ratio: 8.5:1. Brake horsepower: 112 at 4800 R.P.M. Torque: 145 lbs.-ft. at 2100 R.P.M. Four main bearings. Hydraulic valve lifters. Carburetor: 2Bbl. VIN Code: X. HIGH-OUTPUT V-6 (Camaro Berlinetta); OPTIONAL (Cavalier, Citation, Camaro, Celebrity): Same as 173 cu. in. V-6 above except with multi-port fuel injection C.R.: 8.9:1. Brake H.P.: 135 at 5100 R.P.M. (Cavalier, 125 at 4800; Citation/Celebrity, 130 at 4800). Torque: 165 lbs.-ft. at 3600 R.P.M. (Cavalier/Citation/Celeb, 155 at 3600). VIN Code: W exc. (Camaro) S. BASE V-6 (Monte Carlo, Impala, Caprice): 90-degree, overhead-valve V-6. Cast iron block and head. Displacement: 262 cu. in. (4.3 liters). Bore & stroke: 4.00 x 3.48 in. Compression ratio: 9.3:1. Brake horsepower: 130 at 3600 R.P.M. Torque: 210 lbs.-ft. at 2000 R.P.M. Four main bearings. Hydraulic valve lifters. Fuel injection. VIN Code: Z. DIESEL V-6 (Celebrity): 90-degree, overhead-valve V-6. Cast iron block and head. Displacement: 262 cu. in. (4.3 liters). Bore & stroke: 4.057 x 3.385 in. Compression ratio: 22.8:1. Brake horsepower: 85 at 3600 R.P.M. Torque: 165 lbs.-ft. at 1600 R.P.M. Four main bearings. Hydraulic valve lifters. Fuel injection. VIN Code: T. BASE V-8 (Camaro Z28, Caprice wagon): OPTIONAL (Camaro, Monte Carlo, Impala, Caprice): 90-degree, overhead valve V-8. Cast iron block and head. Displacement: 305 cu. in. (5.0 liters). Bore & stroke: 3.74 x 3.48 in. Compression ratio: 9.5:1. Brake horsepower: 155 at 4200 R.P.M. (Monte, 150 at 4000; Caprice/Imp, 165 at 4200). Torque: 245 lbs.-ft. at 2000 R.P.M. (Monte, 240 at 2000; Caprice/Imp, 245 at 2400). Five main bearings. Hydraulic valve lifters. Carburetor: 4Bbl. VIN Code: H. HIGH-OUTPUT V-8 (Monte Carlo SS): Same as 305 cu. in. V-8 above, except Brake H.P.: 180 at 4800 R.P.M. Torque: 235 lbs.-ft. at 3200 R.P.M. VIN Code: G. OPTIONAL HIGH-OUTPUT V-8 (Camaro Z28/IROC-Z): Same as 305 cu. in. V-8 above, except Brake H.P.: 190 at 4800 R.P.M. Torque: 240 lbs.-ft. at 3200 R.P.M. RPO Code: L69. VIN Code: G. OPTIONAL HIGH-OUTPUT V-8 (Camaro Z28/IROC-Z): Same as 305 cu. in. V-8 above, but with tuned port fuel injection Brake H.P.: 215 at 4400 R.P.M. Torque: 275 lbs.-ft. at 3200 R.P.M. RPO Code: LB9. VIN Code: F. DIESEL V-8; OPTIONAL (Impala/Caprice): 90-degree, overhead valve V-8. Cast iron block and head. Displacement: 350 cu. in. (5.7 liters). Bore & stroke: 4.057 x 3.385 in. Compression ratio: 22.1:1. Brake horsepower: 105 at 3200 R.P.M. Torque: 200 lbs.-ft. at 1600 R.P.M. Five main bearings. Hydraulic valve lifters. Fuel injection. Olds- built. VIN Code: N.

CHASSIS DATA: Wheelbase: (Chevette 2-dr.) 94.3 in.; (Chvt 4-dr.) 97.3 in.; (Cavalier) 101.2 in.; (Citation/Celeb) 104.9 in.; (Camaro) 101.0 in.; (Monte Carlo) 108.0 in.; (Imp/Caprice) 116.0 in. Overall length: (Chvt 2-dr.) 161.9 in.; (Chvt 4-dr.) 164.9 in.; (Cav cpe/conv) 172.4 in.; (Cav sed) 174.3 in.; (Cav wag) 174.5 in.; (Cit) 176.7 in.; (Camaro) 188.0 in.; (Camaro Z28) 192.0 in.; (Celeb) 188.3 in.; (Celeb wag) 190.8 in.; (Monte) 200.4 in.; (Monte SS) 202.4 in.; (Imp/Capr sed) 212.8 in.; (Caprice wag) 215.1 in. Height: (Chvt) 52.8 in.; (Cav cpe) 50.2 in.; (Cav conv) 52.7 in.; (Cav sed) 52.1 in.; (Cav wag) 52.8 in.; (Cit) 53.9 in.; (Camaro) 50.0 in.; (Camaro Z28) 50.3 in.; (Celeb) 54.1 in.; (Celeb wag) 54.3 in.; (Monte) 54.4 in.; (Monte SS) 54.9 in.; (Imp/Capr sed) 56.4 in.; (Caprice wag) 58.2 in. Width: (Chvt) 61.8 in.; (Cav cpe/conv) 66.0 in.; (Cav sed/wag) 66.3 in.; (Cit) 68.3 in.; (Camaro) 72.8 in.; (Celeb) 69.3 in.; (Monte) 71.8 in.; (Imp/Capr) 75.4 in.; (Caprice wag) 79.3 in. Front Tread: (Chvt) 51.2 in.; (Cav) 55.4 in.; (Cit/Celeb) 58.7 in.; (Camaro) 60.7 in.; (Camaro Berlinetta/Z28) 60.0 in.; (Monte) 58.5 in.; (Imp/Capr) 61.7 in.; (Caprice wag) 62.2 in. Rear Tread: (Chvt) 51.2 in.; (Cav) 55.2 in.; (Cit/Celeb) 57.0 in.; (Camaro) 61.6 in.; (Camaro Berlinetta/Z28): 60.9 in.; (Monte) 57.8 in.; (Imp/Capr) 60.7 in.; (Caprice wag) 64.1 in. Standard Tires: (Chvt) P155/80R13 GBR; (Cav) P175/80R13 GBR; (Cav Type 10) P215/60R14 SBR; (Cit) P185/80R13 SBR; (Celeb) P185/75R14 SBR; (Camaro) P195/75R14 SBR; (Camaro Berlinetta) P205/70R14 SBR; (Camaro Z28) P215/65R15 WLT SBR; (Monte) P195/75R14 SBR; (Monte SS) P215/65R15 SBR; (Imp/Capr) P205/75R15 SBR; (Caprice wag) P225/75R15 SBR.

TECHNICAL: Transmission: Four-speed floor shift standard on Chevette: Gear ratios (1st) 3.75:1; (2nd) 2.16:1; (3rd) 1.38:1; (4th) 1.00:1; (Rev) 3.82:1. Four-speed floor shift on Cavalier/Citation/Celebrity: (1st) 3.53:1; (2nd) 1.95:1; (3rd) 1.24:1; (4th) 0.81:1 or 0.73:1; (Rev) 3.42:1. Citation V-6 FI and Cavalier V-6 four-speed manual trans.: (1st) 3.31:1; (2nd) 1.95:1; (3rd) 1.24:1; (4th) 0.90:1; (Rev) 3.42:1. Camaro four four-speed manual trans.: (1st) 3.50:1; (2nd) 2.48:1; (3rd) 1.66:1; (4th) 1.00:1; (Rev) 3.50:1. Cavalier five-speed manual: (1st) 3.73:1; (2nd) 2.15:1; (3rd) 1.33:1; (4th) 0.92:1; (5th) 0.74:1; (Rev) 3.50:1. Camaro four five-speed manual: (1st) 3.76:1; (2nd) 2.18:1; (3rd) 1.42:1; (4th) 1.00:1; (5th) 0.86:1; (Rev) 3.76:1. Camaro V-6 five-speed manual: (1st) 3.50:1; (2nd) 2.14:1; (3rd) 1.36:1; (4th) 1.00:1; (5th) 0.78:1; (Rev) 3.39:1. Camaro V-8 five-speed manual.: (1st) 2.95:1; (2nd) 1.94:1; (3rd) 1.34:1; (4th) 1.00:1; (5th) 0.73:1; (Rev) 2.76:1. Chevette five-speed manual shift: (1st) 3.76:1; (2nd) 2.18:1; (3rd) 1.36:1; (4th) 1.00:1; (5th) 0.86:1; (Rev) 3.76:1. Three-speed Turbo Hydra- matic standard on Monte Carlo and Imp/Caprice: (1st) 2.74:1; (2nd) 1.57:1; (3rd) 1.00:1; (Rev) 2.07:1. Chevette automatic trans.: (1st) 2.40:1; (2nd) 1.48:1; (3rd) 1.00:1; (Rev) 1.92:1. Cavalier/Citation/Celebrity auto. trans.: (1st) 2.84:1; (2nd) 1.60:1; (3rd) 1.00:1; (Rev) 2.07:1. Four-speed overdrive automatic transmission on Monte Carlo: (1st) 2.74:1; (2nd) 1.57:1; (3rd) 1.00:1; (4th) 0.67:1; (Rev) 2.07:1. Four-speed overdrive automatic on Celebrity: (1st) 2.92:1; (2nd) 1.57:1; (3rd) 1.00:1; (4th) 0.70:1; (Rev) 2.38:1. Four-speed overdrive automatic on Camaro/Capr/Imp: (1st) 3.06:1; (2nd) 1.63:1; (3rd) 1.00:1; (4th) 0.70:1; (Rev) 2.29:1. Standard final drive ratio: (Chevette) 3.36:1 or 3.62:1; (Cavalier) 3.32:1 on notchback, 3.65:1 on others exc. 3.83:1 w/5-spd, 3.18:1 or 3.43:1 w/auto., 3.65:1 w/V-6 and 4-spd; (Citation) 3.32:1 w/4spd, 2.39:1 or 2.53:1 w/auto.; (Cit H.O. V-6) 3.65:1 w/4spd, 2.84:1 or 3.18:1 w/auto.; (Camaro four) 3.73:1; (Camaro V-6) 3.42:1; (Camaro V-8) 3.23:1 exc. 3.08:1 w/auto.; (Camaro TPI V-8) 3.23:1; (Camaro H.O. V-8) 3.73:1; (Celebrity four) 3.65:1 w/4spd, 2.39:1 w/auto.; (Celeb V-6) 2.84:1 or 3.06:1; (Monte) 2.29:1 or 2.41:1; (Monte H.O. V-8) 3.73:1; (Imp/Caprice V-6) 2.56:1 or 3.08:1; (Imp/Capr V-8) 2.73:1 or 3.08:1. Steering/Suspension/Brakes/Body: same as 1982-84. Fuel tank: (Chvt) 12.2 gal.; (Cav) 13.6 gal.; (Cit) 14.6 or 15.1 gal.; (Camaro) 15.5 or 16.2 gal.; (Celeb) 15.7 or 16.4 gal.; (Monte) 17.6 or 18.1 gal.; (Imp/Capr) 25 gal.; (Caprice wag) 22 gal.

DRIVETRAIN OPTIONS: (Note: Prices of many options rose soon after the model year began.) Engines: 173 cu. in., 2Bbl. V-6: Cavalier ($560); Citation ($260); base Camaro ($335) Celeb ($260). H.O. 173 cu. in., 2Bbl. V-6: Citation/Celeb ($435). 305 cu. in., 4Bbl. V-8: Camaro ($635); Berlinetta ($300); Monte, Imp/Caprice cpe/sed ($240). H.O. 305 cu. in., 4Bbl. V-8: Camaro IROCZ ($680). 350 cu. in., TPI V-8: Camaro Z28 ($680). Diesel 260 cu. in. V-6: Celeb ($260). Diesel 350 cu. in. V-8: Imp/Caprice ($240) exc. wag (NC). Transmission/Differential: Five-speed manual trans.: Chevette/Cavalier ($75); Camaro (NC). Three-speed automatic trans.: Chevette/Cavalier ($425); Citation/Celeb ($425). Four-speed overdrive automatic trans.: Camaro ($395); Celeb ($600); base Monte, Imp/Caprice cpe/sed ($175). Limited-slip differential: Camaro/Monte/Imp/Capr ($95). Performance axle ratio ($21). Power Accessories: Power brakes: Chevette ($100); Citation ($100). Power four-wheel disc brakes: Camaro V-8 ($179). Power steering: Chevette/Cavalier ($215); Citation ($215). Suspension: F40 H.D. susp.: Cav/Cit/Celeb/Imp/Capr ($26). F41 sport susp.: Cit ($33); Cav ($44-$49); Camaro/Monte, Imp/Capr cpe/sed ($49). Inflatable rear shock absorbers: Celeb/Caprice wag ($64). Other: H.D. cooling ($40-$70). Engine block heater ($20). Cold climate pkg.: Imp/Capr diesel ($99). Diesel engine and fuel line heater: Celeb ($49). H.D. battery ($26) exc. diesel ($52). California emission system ($99).

CHEVETTE CONVENIENCE/APPEARANCE OPTIONS: Option Packages: Sport decor pkg.: black grille, wheels, bodyside moldings, bumpers; black trim w/red accents ($95). Custom exterior: black window moldings, styled argent wheels and bright trim rings ($152-$167). Comfort/Convenience: Air conditioning ($645). Rear defogger, electric ($135). Tinted glass ($99). Comfortilt steering wheel ($115). Lighting and Mirrors: Twin sport mirrors, left remote ($53). Driver's remote sport mirror ($34). Entertainment: AM/FM radio ($82). AM/FM stereo radio ($109). Radio delete ($51 credit). Exterior Trim: Two-tone paint ($133). Rear spoiler (N/A). Door edge guards ($15-$25). Chrome bumpers ($25). Interior Trim/Upholstery: Cloth bucket seats: cpe ($28). Custom cloth bucket seats: cpe ($130). Color-keyed floor mats ($25). Wheels and Tires: Sport wheel covers ($45-$97). Wheel trim rings ($52). P155/80R13 GBR WSW ($51). P175/70R13 SBR BSW ($118). P175/70R13 SBR WSW ($172).

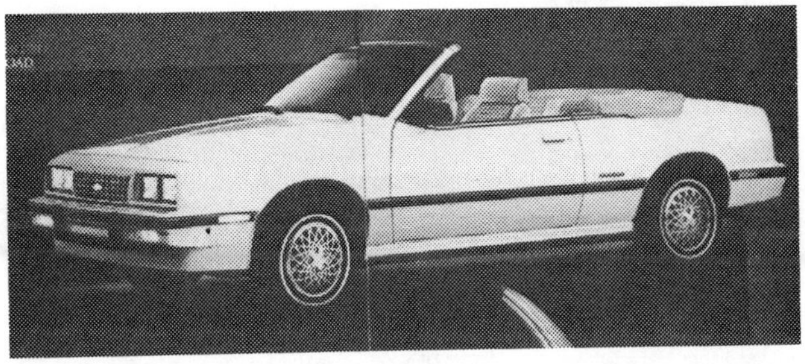

1985 Cavalier Type 10 convertible (CP)

CAVALIER CONVENIENCE/APPEARANCE OPTIONS: Option Packages: CL custom interior pkg.: reclining seats w/adj. head restraints, quiet sound group, sport steering wheel, console (for manual shift), custom door/quarter trim ($251-$325); incl. split folding rear seat on hatch/wagon. Comfort/Convenience: Air cond. ($645). Cruise control w/resume ($175). Rear defogger, electric ($135). Tinted glass ($99). Six-way power driver's seat ($225). Black sport steering wheel ($22-$40). Comfortilt steering wheel ($115). Power windows ($195-$270). Power door locks ($130-$180). Power hatch or trunk release ($40). Power liftgate release ($40). Electronic instrument cluster ($295). Gauge pkg. w/trip odometer ($69); incl. tach ($139). Digital clock: 10/conv. ($39). Lighter: base ($14). Intermittent wipers ($50). Rear wiper/washer ($125). Lighting and Mirrors: Halogen headlamps ($25). Aux. lighting ($43-$95). Dual black sport mirrors, left remote ($53). Right visor mirror ($7). Entertainment: AM radio: base ($112). AM/FM radio ($82) exc. base ($171). Electronic-tuning AM/FM stereo radio ($138) exc. base ($238); w/clock ($177) exc. base ($277); with seek/scan (N/A). Electronic-tuning AM/FM stereo seek/scan radio w/cassette ($319) exc. base ($419). Electronic-tuning AM stereo/FM seek/scan radio w/cassette, equalizer and clock ($494-$504) exc. base ($594). Dual rear speakers ($30-$42); premium ($25). Extended-range sound system: 10/Z24/conv. ($35). Fixed-mast antenna: base ($41) but incl. w/radios. Radio delete ($56 credit). Exterior Trim: Removable sunroof ($310). Rear spoiler: Type 10 ($69). Rear window louvers: Type 10 hatch ($199). Custom two-tone paint: CS ($176); Type 10 ($123). Pinstriping ($53). Bodyside moldings, black ($45). Wheel opening moldings: conv. ($30). Wheel opening and rocker panel moldings ($55). Door edge guards ($15-$25). Wagon roof carrier ($105). Bumper guards ($56). Interior Trim/Upholstery: Cloth or sport cloth reclining bucket seats ($28). Custom CL reclining bucket seats: CS/10/conv. (NC). Split-folding rear seatback: wag/hatch ($50). Color-keyed mats: front ($18); rear ($15). Cargo area cover: wag/hatch ($69). Wheels and Tires: Aluminum wheels, 13 x 5.5 in. ($285); 14 x 6 in. (N/A). Styled 14 in. wheels: 10/conv. ($52). Sport wheel covers ($97). Wheel trim rings ($52). P175/80R13 SBR WSW ($54). P195/70R13 SBR BSW ($104). P195/70R13 SBR WSW ($166). P195/70R13 SBR RWL ($188). P215/60R14 SBR BSW: 10/conv. ($246). P215/60R14 SBR RWL: 10/conv. ($338); Z24 ($92).

CITATION/CELEBRITY CONVENIENCE/APPEARANCE OPTIONS: Option Packages: X11 sport equipment pkg.: Citation ($941). Eurosport pkg.: Celeb ($199). Sport decor pkg. (rear spoiler, rally wheels, sport mirrors, color-keyed bumpers w/rub strips, black grille and moldings, black-accent trim, decal): Citation cpe ($249). Exterior molding pkg. (rocker panel and wheel opening moldings): Celeb ($55). CL custom interior (deluxe door trimw/cloth insert, custom cloth seats, rear ashtray, custom steering wheel): Citation cpe, reclining bucket seats ($392); Citation sed, bench seat ($195). Quiet sound/rear decor pkg.: Cit ($92). Security pkg.: Celeb wag ($44). Comfort/Convenience: Air conditioning ($730). Rear defogger, electric ($140). Cruise control ($175). Tinted glass ($110). Sport steering wheel: Cit ($22). Comfortilt steering wheel ($110). Six-way power driver's seat: Celeb ($215). Power windows ($185-$260). Power door locks ($125-$175). Power trunk or liftgate release: Celeb ($40). Gauge pkg. w/trip odometer: Cit ($69); Celeb ($64). Gauge pkg. w/tachometer: Cit ($149). Digital clock: Celeb ($39). Intermittent wipers ($50). Rear wiper/washer: Celeb ($120). Lighting, Horns and Mirrors: Halogen headlamps: Celeb ($22). Aux. lighting: Cit ($50); Celeb ($43-$57). Dome reading lamp: Celeb ($24). Dual horns ($12). Driver's remote mirror ($23). Dual sport mirrors, left remote ($61). Dual remote sport mirrors: Celeb ($91). Entertainment: AM/FM radio ($82). Electronic-tuning AM/FM stereo radio ($138); w/clock ($177); w/cassette, clock and seek/scan ($319). Electronic-tuning AM stereo/FM radio w/clock, seek/scan, equalizer and cassette: Celeb ($504). Dual rear speakers ($30). Extended-range rear speakers: Celeb ($35). Radio delete ($56 credit). Exterior Trim: Removable sunroof: Celeb ($300). Padded vinyl roof: Celeb ($270). Two-tone paint: Cit ($176) incl. pinstriping and bodyside moldings; Celeb ($148). Bodyside pinstriping: Cit ($39); Celeb ($57). Bodyside moldings, black: Cit ($55). Side window reveal moldings: Cit ($45-$55). Door edge guards ($15-$25). Rear window air deflector: Celeb wag ($40). Rear quarter vent windows: Celeb ($75). Swing-out tailgate: Celeb wag ($105). Decklid or roof (wagon) luggage carrier: Celeb ($100-$105). Bumper guards ($56). Bumper rub strips: Cit ($50). Interior Trim/Upholstery: Console ($105). Reclining driver and passenger seatbacks: Celeb ($90). Cloth bench seat: Cit ($28). Reclining cloth bucket seats: Cit ($243). Celebrity cpe/sed vinyl front bench seat: two-pass. ($28). Celebrity sed vinyl front bench seat: three-pass. ($78). Celebrity three-pass. cloth front bench seat ($28-$50). Celebrity CL three-pass. custom bench seating: vinyl ($229); cloth ($229- $257). Celebrity CL two-pass. custom cloth bench seating ($109-$179). Celebrity 45/45 cloth seating ($100). Celebrity CL custom cloth 45/45 seat ($250-$330). Cloth bucket seats: Celeb ($147). Color-keyed mats: front ($17); rear

($12). Deluxe trunk or wagon luggage area trim: Celeb ($40-$47). Wheels and Tires: Aluminum wheels: Cit ($306); Celeb ($306- $362). Sport wheel covers: Celeb ($65). Locking wire wheel covers: Celeb ($190). Rally wheels ($56). P185/80R13 SBR WSW: Cit ($58). P185/75R14 SBR WSW: Celeb ($58). P195/70R14 Eagle GT SBR BSW: Celeb ($60). P195/75R14 SBR BSW: Celeb ($30). P195/75R14 SBR WSW: Celeb ($92). P205/70R13 SBR WLT: Cit ($202). P215/60R14 SBR WLT: Cit ($92).

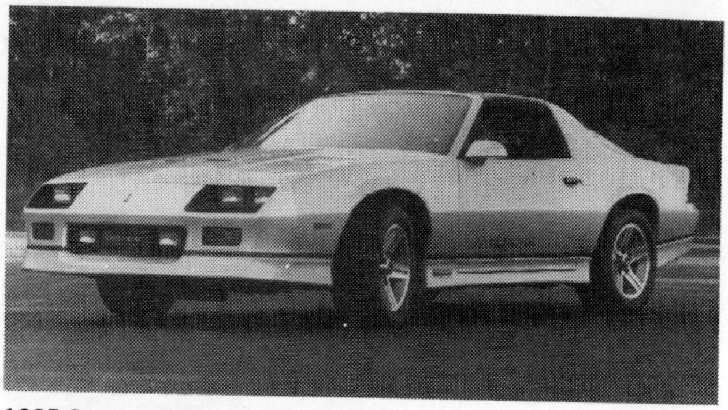

1985 Camaro Z28 Sport Coupe (CP)

CAMARO/MONTE CARLO CONVENIENCE/APPEARANCE OPTIONS: Option Packages: IROC-Z sport equipment pkg.: Camaro Z28 ($659). Comfort/Convenience: Air conditioning ($730). Rear defogger ($140). Cruise control w/resume ($175-$185). Tinted glass ($110). Comfortilt steering wheel ($110). Six-way power driver's seat ($215). Power windows ($185). Power door locks ($125). Power trunk opener: Monte ($40). Power hatch release: Camaro ($40). Electric clock ($35). Gauge pkg. w/trip odometer: Monte ($95). Gauge pkg. incl. tach: base Camaro ($149). Intermittent wipers ($50). Rear wiper/washer: Camaro ($120). Quiet sound group: Camaro ($72-$82). Lighting, Horns and Mirrors: Halogen headlamps ($22). Cornering lamps: Monte ($55). Aux. lighting: Camaro ($37- $72); Monte ($28). Dual horns: Camaro ($12). Twin sport mirrors (left remote): base Camaro, Monte ($53). Twin remote sport mirrors: Monte ($83); SS ($30). Twin electric remote sport mirrors: Camaro ($91-$139). Entertainment: AM/FM radio ($82). AM/FM stereo radio: Monte ($109). Cassette player with AM/FM stereo radio: Monte ($198). Electronic-tuning AM/FM stereo radio: base Camaro/Z28 ($173); w/clock ($177-$212); w/cassette, clock and seek/scan ($319-$354). Camaro seek/scan AM stereo/FM w/cassette, equalizer and clock ($469-$504). Seek/scan AM/FM stereo w/remote control: Berlinetta ($242). Dual rear speakers ($30). Power antenna ($60). Radio delete: Camaro ($56 credit); Berlinetta ($256 credit). Exterior Trim: Removable glass roof panels ($825). Landau vinyl roof: Monte ($245). Rear spoiler: Camaro ($69). Two- tone paint: Monte ($214). Bodyside moldings, black: Camaro ($55). Deluxe vinyl bodyside moldings: Monte ($57). Door edge guards ($15). Side window sill moldings: Monte ($45). Bodyside pinstriping: Monte ($61). Interior Trim/Upholstery: Console: Monte ($105). Roof console: Camaro/Z28 ($50). Vinyl bench seat: base Monte ($28). Cloth 55/45 seating: base Monte ($133). Cloth bucket seats: Camaro ($28); Monte ($147). Custom cloth bucket seats: base Camaro/Z28 ($359). Custom cloth CL 55/45 seating: base Monte ($385). Custom cloth LS conteur bucket seats: Camaro Z28 ($650). Split folding back seat: Camaro ($50). Mats w/carpeted inserts: Camaro front ($20); rear ($15). Color- keyed mats: Monte front ($17); rear ($12). Cargo area cover: Camaro ($69). Deluxe trunk trim: Camaro ($164); Z28 ($84). Locking rear storage cover: base Camaro ($80). Wheels and Tires: Aluminum wheels: Monte ($362); Camaro ($225); std. Z28. Rally wheels: base Camaro ($112); Monte ($56). Full wheel covers: base Camaro ($52). Locking wire wheel covers: Monte ($159). P195/75R14 SBR WSW: base Camaro ($62). P195/75R14 SBR WSW: Monte ($62). P205/70R14 SBR BSW: base Camaro ($58). P205/70R14 SBR WSW: Camaro ($124); Berlinetta ($66); Monte ($124). P205/70R14 SBR WLT: base Camaro ($146). P235/60VR15 SBR BSW: Z28 ($85).

IMPALA/CAPRICE CONVENIENCE/APPEARANCE OPTIONS: Option Packages: Estate equipment: wag ($307). Landau equipment pkg.: vinyl roof, sport mirrors and reveal moldings ($306). Comfort/Convenience: Air cond. ($730). Rear defogger, electric ($140). Cruise control ($175). Tinted glass ($110). Comfortilt steering wheel ($110). Power door locks ($125- $175). Six-way power driver's seat ($215). Power windows ($185-$260). Power trunk opener ($40). Power tailgate lock: wag ($50). Electric clock: Imp ($35). Gauge pkg. w/trip odometer ($64). Intermittent wipers ($50). Quiet sound group: Imp ($66). Lighting and Mirrors: Halogen headlamps ($22). Cornering lamps ($55). Aux. lighting ($32-$42). Driver's remote mirror ($23). Dual remote mirrors ($67). Dual sport mirrors, left remote ($61). Dual remote color-keyed sport mirrors ($91) exc. Landau ($30). Lighted right visor mirror ($48). Entertainment: AM/FM radio ($82). Electronic-tuning AM/FM stereo radio ($138); w/clock ($142-$177); w/cassette and seek/scan ($264-$319); w/cassette, seek/scan, equalizer and clock ($394-$464). Dual rear speakers ($30); extended-range ($35). Power antenna ($60). Radio delete ($56 credit). Exterior Trim: Vinyl roof: sed ($185). Roof carrier: wag ($110). Custom two-tone paint ($141). Pinstriping ($39). Bodyside moldings ($55). Wheel opening moldings: Imp ($30). Door edge guards ($15-$25). Rear window air deflector: wag ($40). Bumper rub strips ($66). Bumper guards ($62). Interior Trim/Upholstery: Reclining passenger seatback ($45). Vinyl bench seat: Imp sed ($28). Cloth bench seat: wag ($28). Cloth 50/50 seating: Caprice ($195-$225). Deluxe load-floor carpet: wag ($89). Deluxe cargo area carpet: wag ($129). Color-keyed mats: front ($17); rear ($12). Mats w/carpet insert: front ($25); rear ($20). Deluxe trunk trim ($59). Wheels and Tires: Sport wheel covers ($65). Wire wheel covers: Caprice ($159). Wire wheel cover locks ($39). P205/75R15 SBR WSW: cpe/sed ($66). P225/70R15 SBR WSW: cpe/sed ($157). P225/75R15 SBR WSW: wag ($71). Puncture- sealant tires ($105-$130).

HISTORY: General introduction was Oct. 2, 1984 but Camaro/Cavalier debuted on November 8 and Chevette on Nov. 21. The new imported subcompact Sprint was introduced on May 30, 1984 and the Sprint on November 15. Model year production (U.S.): 1,415,097 (incl. Corvettes but not incl. early '86 Novas and 8,992 Acadians). Of total production for sale in U.S., 695,893 were four-cylinder, 449,156 six, and 420,410 V-8. A total of 2,167 diesels were installed. Calendar year production (U.S.): 1,708,970 (including 46,304 Corvettes). Calendar year sales by U.S. dealers: 1,600,200 (incl. 37,956 Corvettes), for a 19.5 percent market share. Model year sales by U.S. dealers: 1,595,504 (incl. 37,878 Corvettes), for a 19.0 percent share.

Historical Footnotes: Model year sales rose only slightly over 1984, due mainly to the popularity of Cavalier and Celebrity, which ranked 1st and 3rd in the national ranking. Even so, Chevrolet's market share dropped a a full percentage point, down to 19 percent. Only 5,485 Cavalier convertibles had been built in the 1984 model year, but production was even lower in 1985. Prices rose a fairly modest 2.3 percent for 1985. (Chevette was cut in price, by $121 to $183.) Chevettes and Cavaliers arrived a bit late as the 1984 model year was extended to take advantage of their stronger CAFE fuel economy ratings. Chevrolet was the only GM division not receiving either a new C-body or N-body car this year. This year's ad theme was "Today's Chevrolet" and focused on the new IROC-Z and awaited Cavalier Z24, as well as the multi-port fuel-injection V-6 engine. The new subcompact Japanese imports, Spectrum and Sprint, arrived to give Chevrolet a stronger grasp on the small-car market. The three-cylinder Sprint (from Suzuki) debuted on the west coast in May 1984. Spectrum (built by Isuzu) arrived in November 1984, first sold only on the east coast. The new California-built Nova, a joint venture by Chevrolet and Toyota, would arrive as an early '86 model. Its initial sales looked good, requiring the addition of a second shift to the plant in Fremont, California by winter 1985. Also contributing to Chevrolet's versatility in the marketplace was the new Astro passenger van, intended to compete with the twin Chrysler mini-vans. A prototype "Customer Communications Systems" began test operation at selected Chevrolet dealerships. Prospects could view the benefits of Chevrolet ownership via touch-screen computer videodisc with bold graphics. A "Commitment to Excellence" program provided enhanced pre-delivery inspection of each new car sold by a dealer, an orientation drive by the saleperson, and customer benefit package mailed to the owner after purchase.

1986 CHEVROLET

Chevrolet's ill-fated Citation Xcar finally bit the dust, but its place in the lineup was taken up by the new subcompact Nova, produced in a joint venture between Chevrolet and Toyota. The rear-drive Chevette was still hanging on, but its days were numbered. Front-drive had become the rule for small carsand quite a few large ones as well. On the sporty front, Cavalier's Z24 package finally arrived, creating an obvious small-scale rival to the Camaro Z28. And for peak performance, the IROCZ package returned for the Z28. Monte Carlo added a new luxury model, but the Impala name dropped out of the Chevrolet list after nearly three decades of service. Diesel engines left the lineup, except for a handful installed in Chevettes.

CHEVETTE — SERIES 1T — FOUR — A new bowtie emblem went on Chevette's grille this year and one new body color (yellow beige) was offered. New Custom seat cloth became standard on the four-door, optional on the two-door. All-season P155/80R13 SBR blackwall tires were made standard. As before, the 1.6-liter four and four-speed manual gearbox were standard, with diesel four and three-speed automatic available. Diesels were no longer available in California. A $95 Sport Decor package included a black grille and bumpers, black bodyside moldings with red inserts, and black wheels; plus red 'Chevette S' and 'Chevrolet' decals on front fender and hatch. Though antiquated in mechanical design, the rear-drive Chevette was promoted not only as an entry-level car, but as a vehicle for fleets and light delivery.

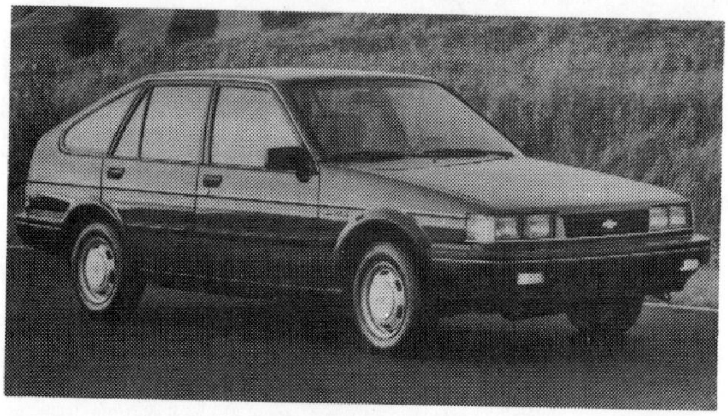

1986 Nova hatchback sedan (CH)

NOVA — SERIES 1S — FOUR — Produced in a joint venture between Chevrolet and Toyota, the five-passenger front-drive subcompact Nova went on sale in June 1985 in half the states. For the full 1986 model year, it was made available nationwide, and a four-door hatchback joined the original four-door notchback sedan. Riding a 95.7 inch wheelbase, Nova weighed about 200 pounds less than an equivalent Cavalier. Hatchbacks had split- folding rear seats, for carrying both passengers and cargo. Nova wore a black crosshatch grille with three horizontal divider bars and seven vertical divider bars, with center bowtie emblem. Wraparound cornering lamps flanked quad rectangular headlamps, with parking lamps inset low in the bumper. The original 97 cu. in. (1.6-liter) four-cylinder engine rated 70 horsepower, while the full-year version added four more. New engine mounts were meant to reduce idle shake, and the optional air conditioner got a larger compressor. A five-speed manual (overdrive) transaxle was standard, with three-speed automatic available. Standard equipment included power brakes, rack-and- pinion steering, AM radio, black bumpers with silver stripe, side window defoggers, cloth door panels with map pockets, full console, and a locking fuel filler door. Also standard: tinted glass, temperature gauge, locking glove box, day/night mirror, black left mirror (remote-controlled), temporary spare tire, trip odometer, cloth/vinyl low-back reclining front bucket seats, and an audible warning system. Argent styled wheels held P155/80R13 SBR blackwall tires. Wiper/washers had a mist cycle. Bodies carried narrow black bodyside, roof drip and windshield moldings. Hatchbacks had a black rear spoiler. Nova's option list was unusually small: just a series of packages rather than individual items. Step-up CL option packages each included a set of extras, in addition to the items indicated in the option lists. Those extra features included a custom cloth interior, wide bodyside moldings, bright belt and roof drip moldings, black door frames and rocker panels, console with storage box, trunk carpet and light, tilt steering column, remote trunk and fuel filler door openers, right visor vanity mirror, soft steering wheel, driver's seat with vertical adjustment and lumbar support, and passenger assist grips.

CAVALIER — SERIES 1J — FOUR/V-6 — After nearly a year's delay, Cavalier's new Z24 performance package (obviously inspired by Camaro's Z28) finally arrived to become a highlight of 1986. Offered in either two-door coupe or two-door hatchback form, it carried a 173 cu. in. (2.8-liter) V-6 with multi-port fuel injection, four-speed manual transaxle, 14 in. Eagle GT radial tires on Rally wheels, and sports package with all-around ground- effects skirting similar to Z28. A cockpit-style instrument panel displayed "Star Wars" electronic instrumentation. Control pods sat on each side of the steering wheel. The simple Z24 grille had four horizontal bars, with bowtie emblem at the center. Park/signal lamps sat at bumper level, below the quad rectangular headlamps. Also new this year was the sporty RS series (replacing the former Type 10). This one had standard F41 sport suspension, power steering, All-Season radial tires, and a distinctive exterior look. 'Cavalier RS' and engine identifier badges were red. Five different RS bodies were offered: four-door sedan and wagon, two-door coupe and hatchback, and the convertible. Base and CS Cavaliers came in four-door sedan or wagon form, as well as two-door bodies. A new Electronic Control Module reduced current drain when the car was idle, and included improved self-diagnostic features. New options this year were a decklid rack (for notchback coupes and sedans), plus new seat cloth and door panel trim for the CL custom interior. Base

1986 Cavalier Z24 coupe (CP)

Cavaliers had standard power brakes, color-keyed bumpers with rub strips, full console with storage, side window defoggers, an argent grille, black left-hand mirror, day/night mirror, compact spare tire, two-speed wiper/washer, and front stabilizer bar. Styled steel argent wheels held P175/80R13 SBR tires. Cavaliers had bright belt, drip, door and window moldings; plus black windshield and back window moldings. Cavalier CS added an AM radio and fixed-mast antenna, lighter, locking glove box, bright grille, and black bodyside moldings. RS models had black bumper rub strips with red accents, a cockpit-style console, power steering, black sport steering wheel, sport suspension, wheel trim rings, red-accented black bodyside moldings, and a set of black moldings (drip, rocker panel, belt, door, window). Convertibles lacked some of those moldings but included a boot cover, tinted glass, and front/rear courtesy lights. Z24 added an air dam, electronic instrument cluster, tachometer and trip odometer, dual black sport mirrors, and black bodyside and drip moldings.

1986 Camaro Sport Coupe (CP)

CAMARO — SERIES 1F — V-6/V-8 — Base Camaro Sport Coupes could take on the tone of the famed Z28 this year. When ordered with either optional engine (2.8-liter V-6 or 5.0-liter V-8), the base coupe also came equipped with a sport suspension, P215/65R15 blackwall tires on 15 x 7 in. styled steel wheels, and sport-tone exhaust. Even four-cylinder Camaros got the sport suspension and 14 in. styled wheels. With V-6 power, a five-speed manual gearbox was included (four-speed automatic optional). With a V-8 option, the four-speed automatic was installed. Appearance changes this year included black accents on headlamps and front fascia vents, lower body stripes (with black or charcoal finish below), black sport mirrors, and Rally wheels. Sport Coupe taillamps had a new black accent band. New 'Chevrolet' lettering replaced the Camaro name on rear fascia. New Sport Coupe standard equipment included styled wheels with trim rings, raised-letter SBR tires, retuned exhaust system with dual tailpipes, black sport mirrors, blackout rockers and fascia, and special stripes. An upshift indicator was added to manual-gearbox models. All Camaros got an air conditioning cutout switch, for use when full power was needed. The full-opening rear hatch had a new automatic closure. All Camaros had wet-arm windshield wipers. New standard items included an automatic rear hatch pulldown latch, plus softer-feel leather for steering wheel, shift lever and parking brake lever. Five engines were available: the "Iron Duke" four (from Pontiac), MFI 173 cu. in. (2.8-liter) V-6, standard 305 cu. in. (5.0-liter) V-8, high-output carbureted 5.0 V-8, and Tuned-port injection 5.0 V-8. Bodyside moldings now came in eight colors or black (black only on Sport Coupe).

1986 Camaro IROC-Z Sport Coupe (CH)

All 12 body colors (eight of them new) were applied using a new basecoat/clearcoat process. New to the option list were halogen foglamps (as on the IROCZ), available on all models; an automatic day/night mirror; color-keyed bodyside moldings; and an AM radio with digital clock. The top-performance IROC-Z, introduced a year earlier, was virtually unchanged except for new colors. Same with Z28 in general, except for new colors on lower panels and accent stripes. IROCZ had no grille opening at all in the front, but two foglamps alongside the license plate opening and parking lamps farther outboard. Quad rectangular headlamps were deeply recessed, flanking a solid angled body panel with tiny emblem in the center. Base Sport Coupe standard equipment included an AM radio, power steering and brakes, five-speed manual transmission, front/rear stabilizer bars, cockpit-style instrument panel, center console with stowage, side window defoggers, remote-controlled left mirror, day/night inside mirror, vinyl reclining front bucket seats, and tape stripes. P205/70R14 SBR all-season tires (P215/65R15 with V-6 or V-8) rode Rally steel wheels with trim rings.

Bodies had black lower body accent, plus black windshield and drip moldings and color-keyed bumpers. Berlinetta added an electronic-tuning AM/FM stereo radio with digital clock, dual horns, electronic instruments, locking rear storage cover, dome and map lights, color-keyed sport mirrors (left remote), intermittent wipers, roof console, full wheel covers, and a tachometer. Bodies showed color-keyed lower accent paint with striping; interiors held custom cloth reclining front bucket seats. Standard Berlinetta tires were P205/70R14 SBR. Berlinetta lacked rocker panel moldings and a rear stabilizer bar. Z28 added an air dam, gauge package, color-keyed sport mirrors, visor vanity mirror (passenger), AM radio with digital clock, rear spoiler, leather-wrapped steering wheel, tachometer, and P215/65R15 tires on color-keyed aluminum wheels. The IROCZ Sport Equipment package (RPO code B4Z, for Z28) included P245/50VR16 Goodyear Eagle GT tires on 16 in. aluminum wheels, halogen foglamps, and special suspension components: special front struts and springs, rear springs, larger-diameter stabilizer bar, and Delco/Bilstein gas-filled shock absorbers. IROCZ also had front frame reinforcement and specific steering gear valving. All that plus body-color lower ground-effect panels, door panel decals, and lower-body accent stripes.

1986 Celebrity sedan (CH)

CELEBRITY — SERIES 1A — FOUR/V-6 — Celebrity wore a new finely-louvered grille with center bowtie emblem for a new front-end lookthe most notable styling revision since the family mid-size was introduced in 1982. New wraparound side marker lamps flowed past the quad rectangular headlamps, with prominent bright bezels surrounding the entire assembly. New full wheel covers were standard. 'Celebrity' lettering was on the front door, engine identification at the forward end of front fenders, small parking lamps below the bumper rub strip. The new rear-end look consisted of three rectangular lamps, with side marker lamps included in the outboard unit. A new three-passenger front seat gave Celebrity six-passenger capacity rather than the previous five. At mid-year, a landau roof coupe option became available. Diesel engines were gone, and Celebrity's base prices were up by over $600. Standard engine was the 151 cu. in. (2.5-liter) four, with either carbureted or multi-port fuel injected 173 cu. in. (2.8-liter) V-6 optional. A new valve cover and gaskets improved oil sealing in all engines. Modified exhaust systems improved noise isolation. A fully galvanized floor pan was added at mid-year. A new variable-displacement air conditioning compressor for four-cylinder models was designed for quieter, more economical operation. New options included 55/45 front seating, a tachometer, AM radio with digital clock, and passenger visor mirror (standard or illuminated). Wagons could have an Estate package for $325. Both coupes and sedans could have a padded vinyl roof for $270. Celebrity Eurosports came in three new solid colors: silver metallic, light brown metallic, and black. Grilles, wheels and moldings matched the body color. The $225 Eurosport package included a sport suspension, sport steering wheel, P195/75R14 SBR tires on Rally wheels with trim rings, bodyside moldings with red accent stripes, color-accented bumper rub strips, and gas shock absorbers. Red 'Eurosport' nameplates on the doors made the model easy to identify.

1986 Monte Carlo SS Sport Coupe (CP)

MONTE CARLO — SERIES 1G — V-6/V-8 — Monte was moderately restyled for 1986, and a new luxury LS model joined the base and SS coupes after the start of the model year. Standard Montes kept their 1985-style grilles and quad rectangular headlamps, but the LS was different. An aerodynamic LS front end held wide flush-mount composite headlamps and a wide-look finely-crosshatched grille with 11 vertical dividers and distinctive center crest emblem. Parking lamps (also wide) sat below the bumper rub strips. Engine identification was on the forward end of the front fender. The LS had wide and bright bodyside moldings, semi-wraparound taillamps, and restyled standard wheels. All Montes got new aerodynamic sport mirrors (black on base model, body-color optional). Sport Coupe and LS Montes got new wheel covers. Retuned suspensions used harder bushings and stiffer shock valving. Inside was a new color-keyed two-spoke steering wheel. P205/70R14 tires with improved rolling resistance were optional on the Sport Coupe. Delco 2000 Series electronically-tuned radios were on the option list. Also optional: a tachometer and passenger visor vanity mirror (plain or illuminated). Monte Carlo had new aluminum wheels, plus gas-pressure shock absorbers (front and rear). Engine choices were the same as 1985: 262 cu. in. (4.3-liter) V-6 or 305 cu. in. (5.0-liter) V-8, with a high-output, 180-horsepower 305 under SS hoods. All Monte Carlos had standard power brakes and steering, three-speed overdrive automatic (four-speed on SS), AM radio with digital clock, cloth bench seats, dual black mirrors, dual-note horn, full wheel covers, color-keyed bumpers, and front stabilizer bar. Bodies held bright wheel opening, belt, window/windshield reveal, lower bodyside and roof drip moldings. Monte Carlo SS had a rear spoiler, black sport steering wheel, tachometer, black grille and moldings, sport mirrors (left remote-controlled), gauge package, and P215/65R15 white-letter tires. Rarest of the SS Montes is the striking Aerocoupe fastback. Only 200 were builta tiny fraction of Monte Carlo output.

1986 Caprice Classic sedan (CP)

CAPRICE CLASSIC — SERIES 1B — V-6/V-8 — With a history dating back to 1958, the Impala name departed this year, but a new Caprice Classic Brougham Sedan joined the full-size lineup (at the top). Three other Classic models were offered (two-door sport coupe, four-door sedan and four-door wagon), plus a basic lower-priced four-door Caprice sedan. All models had the same, somewhat rounded front-end look this year. That included a new grille and bumper filler panel, flush-mounted crest, and new bezels for headlamps and marker lamps. Coupes and sedans also had restyled tri-section taillamps in a full-width end panel, plus a new filler panel and bumper rub strip. Each taillamp section was split horizontally. Base prices were $700-$800 higher than in 1985. Four-speed overdrive automatic was now optional with the base 262 cu. in. (4.3-liter) V-6 engine. The diesel V-8 was dropped, but the 305 cu. in. (5.0-liter) gasoline V-8 remained optional (standard on wagons). Engines used a new polyV alternator drive belt. Power window and seat controls moved to the top of new front door armrest extensions. The new Brougham Sedan package included a full vinyl roof, cloth 55/45 pillow-style front seats with center armrest, front-door dome/map and warning lights, bright brushed metal center pillar applique, and 'Brougham' identification. Standard equipment on the basic Caprice sedan included an AM radio, power brakes and steering, three-speed automatic transmission, full wheel covers, folding front center armrest, cloth bench seats, day/night mirror, front stabilizer bar, two-speed wiper/washers, bright moldings (roof drip, windshield, belt and sill), and lower carpet door trim panels. Caprice Classic added a quartz clock, cloth- insert door trim panels, dual-note horn, wheel opening and bright wide lower bodyside moldings, and headlamps-on buzzer. Coupes and sedans had bumper rub strips. Wagons had a power tailgate window, heavy-duty suspension, and overdrive automatic transmission. Caprice and Pontiac's Parisienne were the last traditional rear-drive full-size family sedans left in the GM lineup, regularly threatened with extinction but continuing to find quite a few buyers.

I.D. DATA: Chevrolets again had a 17-symbol Vehicle Identification Number (VIN) on the upper left surface of the instrument panel, visible through the windshield. Symbol one indicates country: '1' U.S.A.; '2' Canada. Next is a manufacturer code: 'G' General Motors. Symbol three is car make: '1' Chevrolet; '7' GM of Canada. Symbol four denotes restraint system: 'A' non-passive (standard); 'B' passive (automatic belts); 'C' passive (inflatable). Symbol five is car line/series: 'B' Chevette; 'K' Nova; 'C' Cavalier; 'D' Cavalier CS; 'E' Cavalier RS; 'F' Cavalier Z24; 'P' Camaro; 'S' Camaro Berlinetta; 'W' Celebrity; 'Z' Monte Carlo; 'L' Impala; 'N' Caprice. Symbols six-seven reveal body type: '08' 2-dr. hatch coupe; '27' 2-dr. notchback coupe; '37' special 2-dr. notch coupe; '47' full-size 2-dr. sport coupe; '67' 2-dr. convertible coupe; '77' 2-dr. hatch coupe; '87' 2-dr. sport coupe; '19' 4- dr. 6-window notchback sedan; '68' 4-dr. 6-window hatch sedan; '69' 4-dr. 4-window notchback sedan; '35' 4-dr. station wagon. Next is the engine code: 'C' L498 2Bbl.; '4' L497 2Bbl.; 'D' L4111 diesel; 'P' L4121 FI; 'R' or '2' L4151 FI; 'X' V6173 2Bbl.; 'S' or 'W' V6173 MFI; 'Z' V6262 FI; 'H' or 'Y' V8305 4Bbl.; 'G' H.O. V8305 4Bbl.; 'F' V8305 TPI. Next is a check digit, followed by 'G' for model year 1986. Symbol eleven indicates assembly plant: 'B' Baltimore; 'J' Janesville, WI; 'L' Van Nuys, CA; 'N' Norwood, OH; 'R' Arlington, TX; 'T' Tarrytown, NY; 'X' Fairfax, KS; 'Y' Wilmington, DE; '1' Oshawa, Ontario; '6' Oklahoma City, OK; '7' Lordstown, OH. The final six digits are the sequential serial number. Engine number coding is similar to 1981-85.

CHEVETTE CS (FOUR)

Model Number	Body/Style Number	Body Type & Seating	Factory Price	Shipping Weight	Production Total
1T	B08	2-dr. Hatch Cpe-4P	5645	2022	48,756
1T	B68	4-dr. Hatch Sed-4P	5959	2083	54,164

CHEVETTE CS DIESEL (FOUR)

1T	B08/Z90	2-dr. Hatch Cpe-4P	6152	2194	124
1T	B68/Z90	4-dr. Hatch Sed-4P	6487	2255	200

NOVA (FOUR)

1S	K19	4-dr. Sedan-4P	7435	2016	124,961
1S	K68	4-dr. Hatch Sed-4P	7669	2057	42,788

Nova Production Note: An additional 27,943 Nova sedans were built late in the 1985 model year, placed on sale in June 1986.

CAVALIER (FOUR/V-6)

1J	C27	2-dr. Coupe-5P	6706/7316	2231/2351	57,370
1J	C69	4-dr. Sedan-5P	6888/7498	2274/2394	86,492
1J	C35	4-dr. Sta Wag-5P	7047/7657	2344/2464	30,490

CAVALIER CS (FOUR/V-6)

1J	D77	2-dr. Hatch Cpe-5P	7373/7983	2287/2407	8,046
1J	D69	4-dr. Sedan-5P	7350/7960	2306/2426	89,168
1J	D35	4-dr. Sta Wag-5P	7525/8135	2355/2475	23,101

CAVALIER RS (FOUR/V-6)

1J	E27	2-dr. Coupe-5P	7640/8250	2257/2377	53,941
1J	E77	2-dr. Hatch Cpe-5P	7830/8440	2319/2439	7,504
1J	E69	4-dr. Sedan-5P	7811/8451	2299/2419	17,361
1J	E35	4-dr. Sta Wag-5P	7979/8589	2371/2491	6,252
1J	E67	2-dr. Conv. Cpe-4P	12530/13140	-- /2376	5,785

CAVALIER Z24 (V-6)

1J	F27	2-dr. Spt Cpe-5P	-- /8878	-- /2451	36,365
1J	F77	2-dr. Hatch Cpe-5P	-- /9068	-- /2513	10,226

CAMARO (V-6/V-8)

1F	P87	2-dr. Spt Cpe-4P	9285/9685	2912/3071	99,517

CAMARO BERLINETTA (V-6/V-8)

1F	S87	2dr. Spt Cpe-4P	11902/12302	2983/3162	4,479

CAMARO Z28 (V-8)

1F	P87/Z28	2-dr. Spt Cpe-4P	-- /11902	-- /3121	38,547

CAMARO IROC-Z (V-8)

1F	P87/B4Z	2-dr. Spt Cpe-4P	-- /12561	N/A	49,585

Camaro Engine Note: Prices and weights before slash are for V-6 engine, after slash for V-8. Base Camaro Sport Coupes were also available with a four-cylinder engine, priced at $8935 and weighing 2781 pounds. **Z28 Production Note:** Chevrolet production figures also show 91 Z28E hatchback sport coupes built for export. IROC-Z was actually a $659 option package for the Z28, not a separate model.

CELEBRITY (FOUR/V-6)

1A	W27	2-dr. Coupe-6P	8735/9170	2609/2720	29,223
1A	W19	4-dr. Sedan-6P	8931/9366	2638/2749	291,760
1A	W35	4-dr. Sta Wag-6P	9081/9516	2790/2881	36,655
1A	W35/AQ4	4-dr. 3S Wag-8P	9313/9748	N/A	47,245

MONTE CARLO (V-6/V-8)

1G	Z37	2-dr. Spt Cpe-6P	10241/10631	3046/3120	50,418
1G	Z37/Z09	2-dr. LS Cpe-6P	10451/10841	3046/3170	27,428

MONTE CARLO 'SS' (V-8)

1G	Z37/Z65	2-dr. Spt Cpe-6P	— /12466	— /3293	41,164
1G	Z37/Z65	2-dr. Aerocpe-6P	— /14191	— /3440	200

CAPRICE (V-6/V-8)

1B	L69	4-dr. Sedan-6P	10243/10633	3399/3499	50,751

CAPRICE CLASSIC (V-6/V-8)

1B	N47	2-dr. Spt Cpe-6P	10635/11025	3411/3511	9,869
1B	N69	4-dr. Sedan-6P	10795/11185	3428/3528	67,772
1B	N69/B45	4-dr. Brghm-6P	11429/11819	N/A	69,320
1B	N69/B45	4-dr. LS Brghm-6P	N/A	N/A	2,117
1B	N35	4-dr. 3S Wag-8P	-- /11511	-- /3977	45,183

FACTORY PRICE AND WEIGHT NOTE: For Cavalier and Celebrity, prices and weights to left of slash are for four-cylinder, to right for V-6 engine. For Camaro, Monte Carlo and Caprice, figures to left of slash are for six-cylinder model, to right of slash for 305 cu. in. V-8. **BODY/STYLE NO. NOTE:** Some models were actually option packages. Code after the slash (e.g., B45) is the number of the option package that comes with the model listed.

ENGINE DATA: BASE FOUR (Chevette): Inline. Overhead cam. Four-cylinder. Cast iron block and head. Displacement: 98 cu. in. (1.6 liters). Bore & stroke: 3.23 x 2.98 in. Compression ratio: 9.0:1. Brake horsepower: 65 at 5200 R.P.M. Torque: 80 lbs.-ft. at 3200 R.P.M. Five main bearings. Hydraulic valve lifters. Carburetor: 2Bbl. VIN Code: C. **DIESEL FOUR** (Chevette): Inline. Overhead cam. Four-cylinder. Cast iron block and head. Displacement: 111 cu. in. (1.8 liters). Bore & stroke: 3.31 x 3.23 in. Compression ratio: 22.0:1. Brake horsepower: 51 at 5000 R.P.M. Torque: 72 lbs.-ft. at 2000 R.P.M. Five main bearings. Solid valve lifters. Fuel injection. VIN Code: D. **BASE FOUR** (Nova): Inline. Overhead cam. Four-cylinder. Cast iron block and head. Displacement: 97 cu. in. (1.6 liters). Bore & stroke: 3.19 x 3.03 in. Compression ratio: 9.0:1. Brake horsepower: 74 at 5200 R.P.M. Torque: 86 lbs.-ft. at 2800 R.P.M. Solid valve lifters. Carburetor: Aisan 2Bbl. VIN Code: 4. **BASE FOUR** (Cavalier): Inline. Overhead valve. Four-cylinder. Cast iron block and head. Displacement: 121 cu. in. (2.0 liters). Bore & stroke: 3.50 x 3.15 in. Compression ratio: 9.0:1. Brake horsepower: 85 at 4800 R.P.M. Torque: 110 lbs.-ft. at 2400 R.P.M. Five main bearings. Hydraulic valve lifters. Throttle-body fuel injection. VIN Code: P. **BASE FOUR** (Celebrity, Camaro): Inline. Overhead valve. Four-cylinder. Cast iron block and head.

136

Displacement: 151 cu. in. (2.5 liters). Bore & stroke: 4.00 x 3.00 in. Compression ratio: 9.0:1. Brake horsepower: 92 at 4400 R.P.M. (Camaro, 88 at 4400). Torque: 134 lbs.-ft. at 2800 R.P.M. (Camaro, 130 at 2800). Five main bearings. Hydraulic valve lifters. Throttle-body fuel injection. Pontiac-built. VIN Code: R or 2. OPTIONAL V-6 (Celebrity) 60-degree, overhead-valve V-6. Cast iron block and head. Displacement: 173 cu. in (2.8 liters). Bore & stroke: 3.50 x 2.99 in. Compression ratio: 8.0:1. Brake horsepower: 112 at 4800 R.P.M. Torque: 145 lbs.-ft. at 2100 R.P.M. Four main bearings. Hydraulic valve lifters. Carburetor: 2Bbl. VIN CODE: X. HIGH-OUTPUT V-6 (Camaro Berlinetta, Cavalier Z24): OPTIONAL (Cavalier, Camaro, Celebrity): Same as 173 cu. in. V-6 above except multi-port fuel injection C.R.: 8.5:1 (Camaro 8.9:1). Brake H.P.: 135 at 5100 R.P.M. (Cavalier, 120 at 4800; Celebrity, 125 at 4800). Torque: 160 lbs.-ft. at 3900 R.P.M. (Cavalier, 155 at 3600; Celeb. 160 at 3600). VIN Code: W or S. BASE V-6 (Monte Carlo, Caprice): 90-degree, overhead-valve V-6. Cast iron block and head. Displacement: 262 cu. in. (4.3 liters). Bore & stroke: 4.00 x 3.48 in. Compression ratio: 9.3:1. Brake horsepower: 140 at 4000 R.P.M. Torque: 225 lbs.-ft. at 2000 R.P.M. Four main bearings. Hydraulic valve lifters. Fuel injection. VIN CODE: Z. BASE V-8 (Camaro Z28. Caprice wagon): OPTIONAL (Camaro, Monte Carlo, Caprice): 90-degree, overhead valve V-8. Cast iron block and head. Displacement: 305 cu. in. (5.0 liters). Bore & stroke: 3.74 x 3.48 in. Compression ratio: 9.5:1. Brake horsepower: 155 at 4200 R.P.M. (Monte, 150 at 4000; Caprice, 165 at 4200, Z28, 165 at 4400). Torque: 245 lbs.-ft. at 2000 R.P.M. (Monte, 240 at 2000; Caprice, 245 at 2400; Z28, 250 at 2000). Five main bearings. Hydraulic valve lifters. Carburetor: 4Bbl. VIN Code: H exc. (Caprice) Y. HIGH-OUTPUT V-8 (Monte Carlo SS); Same as 305 cu. in. V-8 above, except Brake H.P.: 180 at 4800 R.P.M. Torque: 225 lbs.-ft. at 3200 R.P.M. VIN Code: G. OPTIONAL HIGH-OUTPUT V-8 (Camaro Z28/IROC-Z): Same as 305 cu. in V-8 above, except Brake H.P.: 190 at 4800 R.P.M. Torque: 240 lbs.-ft. at 3200 R.P.M. VIN Code: G. OPTIONAL HIGH-OUTPUT V-8 (Camaro Z28/IROC-Z): Same as 305 cu. in V-8 above, but with tuned port fuel injection Brake H.P.: 190 at 4000 R.P.M. Torque: 285 lbs.-ft. at 2800 R.P.M. VIN Code: F.

CHASSIS DATA: Wheelbase: (Chevette cpe) 94.3 in.; (Chvt sed) 97.3 in.; (Nova) 95.7 in.; (Cavalier) 101.2 in.; (Celebrity) 104.9 in.; (Camaro) 101.0 in.; (Monte Carlo) 108.0 in.; (Caprice) 116.0 in. Overall length: (Chvt cpe) 161.9 in.; (Chvt sed) 164.9 in.; (Nova) 166.3 in.; (Cav cpe/conv) 172.4 in.; (Cav sed) 174.3 in.; (Cav wag) 174.5 in.; (Camaro) 188.0 in.; (Camaro Z28) 192.0 in.; (Celeb) 188.3 in.; (Celeb wag) 190.8 in.; (Monte) 200.4 in.; (Monte SS) 202.4 in.; (Monte LS) 203.3 in.; (Caprice cpe) 212.8 in.; (Capr sed) 212.2 in.; (Capr wag) 215.1 in. Height: (Chvt) 52.8 in.; (Nova) 52.7 in.; (Cav cpe) 50.2 in.; (Cav conv) 52.7 in.; (Cav sed) 52.1 in.; (Cav wag) 52.8 in.; (Camaro) 50.0 in.; (Camaro Z28) 50.3 in.; (Celeb) 54.1 in.; (Celeb wag) 54.3 in.; (Monte) 54.4 in.; (Monte SS) 54.9 in.; (Caprice) 56.4 in.; (Caprice wag) 58.2 in. Width: (Chvt) 61.8 in.; (Nova) 64.4 in.; (Cav cpe/conv) 66.0 in.; (Cav sed/wag) 66.3 in.; (Camaro) 72.8 in.; (Celeb) 69.3 in.; (Monte) 71.8 in.; (Caprice) 75.4 in.; (Capr wag) 79.3 in. Front Tread: (Chvt) 51.2 in.; (Nova) 56.1 in.; (Cav) 55.4 in.; (Celeb) 58.7 in.; (Camaro) 60.7 in.; (Camaro Z28) 60.0 in.; (Monte) 58.5 in.; (Caprice) 61.7 in.; (Capr wag) 2.2 in. Rear Tread: (Chvt) 51.2 in.; (Nova) 55.3 in.; (Cav) 55.2 in.; (Celeb) 57.0 in.; (Camaro) 61.6 in.; (Camaro Z28): 60.9 in.; (Monte) 57.8 in.; (Caprice) 60.7 in.; (Capr wag) 64.1 in. Standard Tires: (Chvt/Nova) P155/80R13 SBR; (Cav) P175/80R13 SBR; (Cav RS) P195/70R13 SBR; (Cav Z24) P215/60R14 SBR; (Celeb) P185/75R14 SBR; (Celeb Eurosport) P195/75R14 SBR; (Camaro) P205/70R14 SBR; (Camaro Z28) P215/65R15 SBR; (Camaro IROCZ) P245/50VR16 SBR; (Monte) P195/75R14 SBR; (Monte SS) P215/65R15 SBR; (Caprice) P205/75R15 SBR; (Caprice wag) P225/75R15 SBR.

TECHNICAL: Transmission: Four-speed manual shift standard on Chevette and Celebrity. Four-speed overdrive manual shift standard on Cavalier. Five-speed manual shift standard on Chevette diesel, Nova, Camaro. Three-speed Turbo Hydra-matic standard on Monte Carlo and Caprice: (1st) 2.74:1; (2nd) 1.57:1; (3rd) 1.00:1; (Rev) 2.07:1. Chevette automatic trans.: (1st) 2.40:1; (2nd) 1.48:1; (3rd) 1.00:1; (Rev) 1.92:1. Nova auto. trans.: (1st) 2.30:1; (2nd) 1.55:1; (3rd) 1.00:1; (Rev) 2.81:1. Cavalier/Celebrity auto. trans.: (1st) 2.84:1; (2nd) 1.60:1; (3rd) 1.00:1; (Rev) 2.07:1. Four-speed overdrive automatic transmission on Monte Carlo: (1st) 2.74:1; (2nd) 1.57:1; (3rd) 1.00:1; (4th) 0.67:1; (Rev) 2.07:1. Four-speed overdrive automatic on Celebrity: (1st) 2.92:1; (2nd) 1.56:1; (3rd) 1.00:1; (4th) 0.70:1; (Rev) 2.38:1. Four-speed overdrive automatic on Camaro/Caprice: (1st) 3.06:1; (2nd) 1.63:1; (3rd) 1.00:1; (4th) 0.70:1; (Rev) 2.29:1. Standard final drive ratio: (Chevette) 3.36:1; (Nova) 3.72:1 w/5spd, 3.42:1 w/auto.; (Cavalier four) 3.32:1 w/4spd, 3.83:1 w/5spd, 3.18:1 w/auto.; (Cavalier V-6) 3.65:1 w/4spd, 3.18:1 w/auto.; (Camaro four) 3.73:1; (Camaro V-6) 3.42:1; (Camaro V-8) 2.73:1 or 3.23:1; (Celebrity four) 3.65:1 w/4spd, 2.39:1 w/auto.; (Celeb V-6) 2.84:1 or 3.06:1; (Celeb wag) 2.84:1; (Monte V-6) 2.29:1 or 2.41:1; (Monte V-8) 2.41:1 or 3.73:1; (Caprice V-6) 2.56:1; (Capr V-8) 2.73:1. Steering: (Cavalier/Chevette/Nova/Celebrity) rack and pinion; (others) recirculating ball. Front Suspension: (Chevette/Monte/Caprice) unequal-length control arms, coil springs, stabilizer bar; (Nova) MacPherson struts w/coil springs and lower control arms; (Cavalier/Camaro/Celeb) MacPherson struts with coil springs, lower control arms and stabilizer. Rear Suspension: (Chevette) rigid axle and torque tube w/four links and track bar, coil springs, stabilizer; (Nova) fully independent MacPherson struts, dual links, coil springs and stabilizer bar; (Cavalier) semi-independent with beam axle, trailing arms, coil springs, stabilizer available; (Camaro) rigid axle and torque tube with longitudinal control arms, Panhard rod, coil springs and stabilizer; (Celeb) beam twist axle with integral stabilizer, trailing arms, Panhard rod and coil springs; (Monte/Caprice) rigid axle with four links, control arms, coil springs, stabilizer available. Brakes: front disc, rear drum; four-wheel discs available on Camaro V-8. Body construction: unibody except (Camaro) unibody with partial frame; (Monte/Caprice) separate body and frame. Fuel tank: (Chvt) 13.2 gal.; (Cav) 13.6 gal.; (Camaro) 15.5 gal.; (Camaro V-8) 16.2 gal.; (Celeb) 15.7 or 16.4 gal.; (Monte) 17.6 or 18.1 gal.; (Capr) 24.5 gal.; (Capr wag) 22 gal.

DRIVETRAIN OPTIONS: Engines: 173 cu. in., 2Bbl. V-6: Cavalier ($670); base Camaro ($350); Celeb ($435). 173 cu. in., MFI V-6: Celeb ($560). 305 cu. in., 4Bbl. V-8: base Camaro ($750); Berlinetta ($400); base Monte, Caprice cpe/sed ($390). H.O. 305 cu. in., 4Bbl. V-8: Camaro Z28 ($695). 350 cu. in., TPI V-8: Camaro Z28 ($695). Transmission/Differential: Five-speed manual trans.: Chevette/Cavalier ($75). Three-speed automatic trans.: Chevette ($425); Cavalier ($465); Celeb ($490). Four-speed overdrive auto. trans.: Camaro ($465); Celeb ($665); base Monte, Caprice cpe/sed ($175). Limited-slip differential: Camaro/Monte/Caprice ($100). Performance axle ratio ($21). Power Accessories: Power brakes: Chevette ($100). Power four- wheel disc brakes: Camaro V-8 ($179). Power steering: Chvt/Cav ($215). Suspension: F40 H.D. susp.: Cav/Celeb/Caprice ($26). F41 sport susp.: Cav ($44-$49); Monte, Caprice cpe/sed ($49). Inflatable rear shock absorbers: Celeb/Caprice wag ($64). Other: H.D. cooling ($40-$70). Engine block heater ($20). H.D. battery ($26). California emission system ($99).

CHEVETTE CONVENIENCE/APPEARANCE OPTIONS: Option Packages: Sport Decor pkg.: black grille, headlamps bezels, bodyside moldings w/red accents; black bumpers; black wheels w/bright trim rings and red decals ($95). Custom exterior: black window moldings, styled argent wheels and bright trim rings ($152-$167). Comfort/Convenience: Air conditioning ($645). Rear defogger, electric ($135). Tinted glass ($99). Comfortilt steering wheel ($115). Lighting and Mirrors: Twin sport mirrors, left remote ($53). Driver's remote sport mirror ($34). Entertainment: AM/FM radio ($82). AM/FM stereo radio ($109). Radio delete ($51 credit). Exterior Trim: Two-tone paint ($133). Door edge guards ($15- $25). Chrome bumpers ($25). Interior Trim/Upholstery: Cloth bucket seats: cpe ($28). Custom cloth bucket seats: cpe ($130). Color-keyed floor mats ($25). Wheels and Tires: Sport wheel covers ($45-$97). Wheel trim rings ($52). P155/80R13 SBR WSW ($51).

NOVA CONVENIENCE/APPEARANCE OPTIONS: Nova had only one individual option: two-tone paint ($176). All other options came in packages, as follows. Pkg. 1: Five-speed trans., AM radio, P155/80R13 BSW tires (NC). Pkg. 2: Pkg. 1 plus power steering and automatic trans. ($610). Pkg. 3: Pkg. 1 plus air conditioning, electronic-tuning AM/FM stereo seek/scan radio w/digital clock, dual mirrors (left remote), power steering, electric rear defogger and halogen headlamps ($1180). Pkg. 4: Same as pkg. 3 plus automatic trans. ($1575). Pkg. 5: Automatic trans., P155/80R13 tires, AM/FM with clock, power steering and air cond. ($1525). CL Pkg. 1: Five-speed trans., air cond., P155/80R13 BSW tires, seek/scan AM/FM stereo radio with digital clock, dual mirrors (left remote), power steering, rear defogger, halogen headlamps and Custom CL features ($1730). CL Pkg. 2: Same as CL 1 plus automatic trans. ($2125). CL Pkg. 3: Same as CL 1 plus AM/FM stereo radio w/cassette player and clock, aluminum wheels, P175/70R13 SBR BSW tires, intermittent wipers, cruise control and (on hatchback) rear wiper/washer ($2515-$2640). CL Pkg. 4: Same as CL 3, but with automatic trans. and P155/80R13 tires, plus power door locks ($2620-$2745).

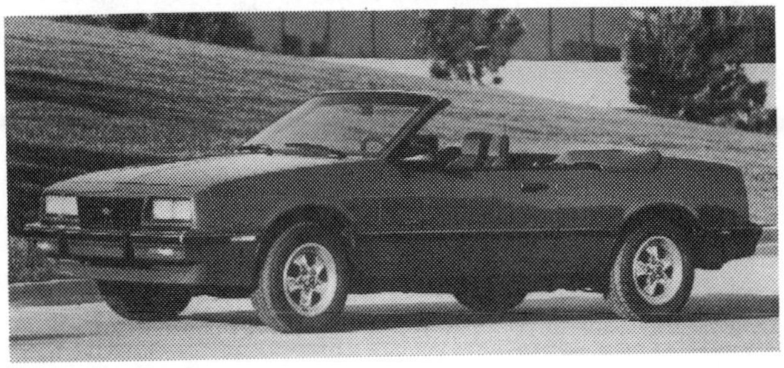

1986 Cavalier RS convertible (CH)

CAVALIER CONVENIENCE/APPEARANCE OPTIONS: Option Packages: CL custom interior pkg.: reclining bucket seats, quiet sound group, sport steering wheel, console, custom door/quarter trim w/carpet inserts, fender nameplates ($251-$325); incl. split folding rear seat on hatch/wagon. Comfort/Convenience: Air cond. ($645). Cruise control w/resume ($175). Rear defogger, electric ($135). Tinted glass ($99). Six-way power driver's seat ($225). Black sport steering wheel ($22-$40). Comfortilt steering wheel ($115). Power windows ($195-$270). Power door locks ($130-$180). Power hatch or trunk release ($40). Power liftgate release ($40). Electronic instrument cluster ($295). Gauge pkg. w/trip odometer ($69); incl. tach ($139). Digital clock: RS/Z24. ($39). Lighter: base ($14). Intermittent wipers ($50). Rear wiper/washer ($125). Lighting and Mirrors: Halogen headlamps ($25). Aux. lighting ($43-$95). Dual black sport mirrors, left remote ($53). Entertainment: AM radio: base ($112). Electronic-tuning seek/scan AM/FM stereo radio ($158) exc. base ($258); w/clock ($197) exc. base ($297); w/cassette ($319) exc. base ($419). Electronic-tuning AM stereo/FM seek/scan radio w/cassette, equalizer and clock ($494-$504) exc. base ($594). Premium dual rear speakers ($25). Extended-range sound system: RS/Z24/conv. ($35). Fixed-mast antenna: base ($41) but incl. w/radios. Radio delete ($56 credit). Exterior Trim: Removable sunroof ($310). Rear spoiler: RS/Z24 ($69). Rear window louvers ($199). Custom two-tone paint: CS ($176); RS ($123). Pinstriping ($53). Bodyside moldings, black: base ($45). Wheel opening moldings, black: conv. ($30). Wheel opening and rocker panel moldings ($55). Door edge guards ($15-$25). Wagon roof carrier ($105). Decklid luggage rack ($100). Bumper guards ($56). Interior Trim/Upholstery: Cloth reclining bucket seats: base/CS ($28). Sport cloth reclining bucket seats: Z24 (NC). Custom CL cloth bucket seats: CS/RS/Z24 (NC). Custom CL vinyl bucket seats: RS/Z24 (NC). Split-folding rear seatback: wag/hatch ($50). Color-keyed mats: front ($18); rear ($15). Cargo area cover: wag/hatch ($69). Deluxe seat/shoulder belts: base ($26). Wheels and Tires: Aluminum wheels, 13 in. ($233-$285); 14 in., Z24 ($173). Rally 14 in. wheels: conv. ($56). Sport wheel covers ($45-$97). Wheel trim rings: base/CS ($52). P175/80R13 SBR WSW: base/CS ($54). P195/70R13 SBR BSW: base/CS ($104). P195/70R13 SBR WSW: base/CS ($166). P195/70R13 SBR RWL: base/CS ($188); RS ($84). P215/60R14 SBR BSW: RS ($142). P215/60R14 SBR RWL: RS ($234); Z24 ($92).

CELEBRITY/CAPRICE CONVENIENCE/APPEARANCE OPTIONS: Option Packages: Eurosport pkg.: Celeb ($225). Estate equipment: Capr wag ($307). Landau equipment (vinyl roof, sport mirrors and reveal moldings): Capr ($306). Exterior molding pkg. (rocker panel and wheel opening moldings): Celeb ($55). Security pkg.: Celeb wag ($44). Quiet sound group: base Capr ($66). Comfort/Convenience: Air cond. ($750). Rear defogger, electric ($145-$150). Cruise control ($175). Tinted glass ($115). Comfortilt steering wheel ($115). Six-way power driver's seat ($215-$225). Power windows ($195-$270). Power door locks ($130-$180). Power trunk or liftgate release ($40). Power tailgate lock: Capr wag ($50). Gauge pkg. w/trip odometer ($64). Tachometer: Celeb ($90). Quartz clock: base Capr ($39). Intermittent wipers ($50). Rear wiper/washer: Celeb ($125). Lighting, Horns and Mirrors: Halogen headlamps ($25). Cornering lamps: Capr ($55). Aux. lighting: Celeb ($51-$67); Capr ($32-$42). Dome reading lamp: Celeb ($24). Dual horns: Celeb ($12). Driver's remote mirror ($23). Dual sport mirrors, left remote ($61). Dual remote sport mirrors ($91) exc. Capr Lan ($30). Right visor mirror: Celeb ($7). Lighted visor mirror ($50). Entertainment: AM radio w/digital clock: Celeb ($39). Electronic-tuning seek/scan AM/FM stereo radio ($158); w/clock ($162-$197); w/cassette, clock and seek/scan ($284- $319). Seek/scan AM/FM stereo radio w/casssette, equalizer and clock: Capr ($394-$464). Seek/scan AM stereo/FM radio w/clock, equalizer and cassette: Celeb ($504). Extended-range rear speakers ($35). Power antenna: Capr ($65). Radio delete ($56 credit). Exterior Trim: Removable sunroof: Celeb ($310). Padded vinyl roof: Celeb ($270). Vinyl roof: Capr sed ($185). Two-tone paint ($141-$148). Bodyside pinstriping ($39-$57). Bodyside moldings: Capr ($55). Wheel opening moldings: base Capr ($30). Door edge guards ($15-$25). Rear window air deflector: wag ($40). Rear quarter vent windows: Celeb ($75). Swing-out tailgate: Celeb wag ($105). Decklid luggage carrier: Celeb ($100). Roof carrier: wag ($105-$110). Bumper rub strips: Capr ($66). Bumper guards ($56-$62). Celebrity Interior: Console ($110). Reclining passenger seatback ($45); both ($90). Cloth bench seat: wag ($28). Vinyl bench seat: cpe/sed ($28). Cloth 55/45 seat ($133). CL custom cloth 45/45 seat ($200-$330). CL custom cloth 55/45 seating ($305-$435). Cloth reclining bucket seats ($147). Color-keyed rubber mats: front ($17); rear ($12). Carpeted mats: front ($25); rear ($20). Deluxe trunk or wagon luggage area trim ($40-$47). Caprice Interior: Reclining passenger seatback: Classic ($45). Vinyl bench seat: base sed ($28). Cloth bench seat: wag ($28). Cloth 50/50 seating: Classic ($195-$225). Vinyl 50/50 seating ($195). Deluxe load-floor carpet: wag ($89). Deluxe cargo area trim: wag ($129). Mats w/carpet insert: front ($25); rear ($20). Deluxe trunk trim ($59). Celebrity Wheels/Tires: Aluminum wheels ($306-$362). Sport wheel covers ($65). Locking wire wheel covers ($199). Rally wheels ($56). P185/75R14 SBR WSW ($58). P195/70R14 Eagle GT SBR BSW: Eurosport ($80). P195/75R14 SBR BSW ($30). P195/75R14 SBR WSW ($92). Caprice Wheels/Tires: Sport wheel covers ($65). Wire wheel covers w/locks ($199). P205/75R15 SBR WSW: cpe/sed ($66). P225/70R15 SBR WSW: cpe/sed ($157). P225/75R15 SBR WSW: wag ($71). Puncture-sealant tires ($115-$140).

CAMARO/MONTE CARLO CONVENIENCE/APPEARANCE OPTIONS: Option Packages: IROCZ sport equipment pkg.: Camaro Z28 ($659). Comfort/Convenience: Air cond. ($750). Rear defogger (electric) ($145). Cruise control w/resume ($175-$185). Tinted glass ($115). Comfortilt steering wheel ($115). Six- way power driver's seat ($225). Power windows ($195). Power door locks ($130). Power trunk opener: Monte ($40). Power hatch release: Camaro ($40). Tachometer: Monte ($90). Gauge pkg. w/trip odometer: Monte ($69). Gauge pkg. incl. tach: base Camaro ($149). Intermittent wipers ($50). Rear wiper/washer: Camaro ($125). Quiet sound group:

Camaro ($82). Lighting, Horns and Mirrors: Halogen headlamps ($25). Halogen foglamps: Camaro ($60). Aux. lighting: Camaro ($37-$72); Monte ($28). Dual horns: Camaro ($12). Twin sport mirrors (left remote): Monte ($53). Twin remote sport mirrors: Monte ($83); SS ($30). Twin electric remote sport mirrors: Camaro ($91). Automatic day/night mirror: Camaro ($80). Right visor mirror: Monte ($7); lighted ($50). Entertainment: AM radio w/digital clock: base ($39). Electronic-tuning seek/scan AM/FM stereo radio: base Camaro ($193); Electronic-tuning seek/scan AM/FM stereo radio w/clock: Camaro ($197-$232); w/cassette and clock ($319-$354); w/AM stereo and cassette ($469-$504). Seek/scan AM/FM stereo w/remote control and cassette: Berlinetta ($242) Monte seek/scan electronic-tuning AM/FM stereo radio ($158); w/clock ($197); w/cassette ($319); with AM stereo and cassette ($494). Premium rear speakers: Monte ($25). Power antenna: Camaro ($60). Radio delete ($56 credit). Exterior Trim: Removable glass roof panels: Camaro ($846); Monte ($875). Landau vinyl roof: Monte ($245). Rear spoiler: Camaro ($69). Rear window louvers: Camaro ($210). Two-tone paint: Monte ($214). Bodyside moldings, black: Camaro ($55). Deluxe vinyl bodyside moldings: Monte ($57). Door edge guards ($15). Side window sill moldings: Monte ($45). Bodyside pinstriping: Monte ($61). Interior Trim/Upholstery: Console: Monte ($110). Roof console: Camaro/Z28 ($50). Vinyl bench seat: Monte ($28). Cloth 55/45 seating: base Monte ($133). Cloth bucket seats: Camaro ($28); Monte ($147). Custom cloth bucket seats: base Camaro/Z28 ($359). Custom cloth CL 55/45 seating: base Monte ($385). Split folding back seat: Camaro ($50). Mats w/carpeted inserts: front ($20); rear ($15). Cargo area cover: Camaro ($69). Deluxe trunk trim: Camaro ($164); Z28 ($84). Locking rear storage cover: Z28 ($80). Wheels and Tires: Aluminum wheels: Monte ($362); Berlinetta ($225). Wheel locks: Berlinetta/Z28 ($16). Rally wheels: Monte ($56). Locking wire wheel covers: Monte ($199). P195/70R14 SBR BSW Eagle GT: Berlinetta ($80). P195/75R14 SBR WSW: Monte ($62). P205/70R14 SBR WSW: Berlinetta ($66); Monte ($124). P215/65R15 SBR BSW: Z28 ($92 credit). P215/65R15 SBR RWL: Camaro four ($92). P235/60VR15 SBR BSW: Z28 ($85).

HISTORY: Introduced: Oct. 3, 1985. Model year production (U.S.): 1,564,303 (incl. Corvettes but not incl. 21,643 Acadians). Total production for sale in U.S. consisted of 867,823 four- cylinder, 433,461 sixes, and 448,221 V-8s. Only 588 leftover diesels were installed. Calendar year production (U.S.): 1,518,794 (including 28,410 Corvettes). Calendar year sales by U.S. dealers: 1,558,476, for a 19.5 percent market share. Model year sales by U.S. dealers: 1,587,024 (incl. 35,969 Corvettes) for a 19.7 percent share.

Historical Footnotes: The new joint-venture Nova, produced by Chevrolet and Toyota, helped Chevrolet sales come close to the 1985 figure. Total sales still dropped a bit for the model year. Even so, Chevrolet's domestic market share managed to grow somewhat. A total of 170,661 Novas were sold during the full model year, but Cavalier and Celebrity were still the top sellers. Actually, Celebrity pulled ahead and made No. 1 this year. As Nova production increased, the outmoded rear-drive Chevette's days were numbered─especially when Chevrolet announced in late 1985 that the Lakewood, Georgia plant that assembled Chevettes would be converted to rear-drive production. Chevette sales shrunk to 75,761, prompting a price cut for 1987 and abandonment early in that model year. With the new Nova (based on Toyota's Corolla) and the twin Japanese imports sold under the Chevrolet banner (Spectrum and Sprint), Chevrolet offered a total of five small cars. Chevrolet's general manager Robert D. Burger predicted that subcompacts and smaller would "account for nearly 40 percent of total car sales in this country in 1986." The company was especially interested in attracting first-time, younger buyers, who might later want to move up to a "better" Chevrolet model. In addition to the small-car lineup, Chevrolet claimed to have America's fastest car (Corvette), most popular car (Cavalier), most popular mid- and full-size cars (Celebrity and Caprice), and favorite sporty 2+2 (Camaro). Low-interest loans (7.7 percent) were offered by GM late in the 1985 model year, and 8.8 percent rates arrived for 1986. One Illinois dealer opened experimental operations in a shopping mall, in an attempt to lure buyers who might otherwise be missed. A Women's Marketing Committee was formed to develop approaches to attract female buyers, whose role in auto purchasing was gaining steadily by the mid-1980s. Among other innovations was a pre-approved credit plan for women customers, through General Motors Acceptance Corporation. Dealers also held "Car Care Clinics" for women. Nova's manufacturing facility was called New United Motor Manufacturing, Inc. (NUMMI), located at Fremont, California.

By 1976, Corvette's shapely aerodynamic body was eight years old. Yet it would remain in this form for half a dozen more years, attracting performance-minded drivers even though the engine choices were far milder than they had been. After all, what else was there? As Chevrolet proclaimed, Corvette was "America's only true production sports car." Only the Stingray coupe body remained for 1976, as convertible Corvettes became extinct. Removable roof panels would be the closest one could come to open-topped motoring. Corvettes remained fiberglass-bodied, of course; but this year a partial steel underbody was added. Customers had a choice of wide- or close-ratio four-speed gearboxes, and the standard or special (L82) 350 cu. in. V-8 engine. The latter engine, installed in 5,720 cars, had finned aluminum rocker covers and special cylinder heads. Sales hit a record level.

1977 Corvette coupe (CH)

Next year, the Stingray name faded away, but not much else changed. Less than 16 percent of Corvettes came with either the close-ratio or wide-ratio four-speed transmission — a figure typical of this period. Most customers, it seemed, wanted Corvette's performance — but didn't wish to shift for themselves.

1978 Corvette Indy Pace Car (Tom and Cheryl Kell)

An aero restyling of the basic body arrived for Corvette's 25th anniversary year, adding a fastback roofline and large wraparound back window. The high-performance (L82) V-8 added horsepower with a new dual-snorkel air-intake system and lower-restriction exhaust components. Nearly one-third of this year's Corvettes sported optional Silver Anniversary two-tone silver paint. Even more striking were the Indy Pace Car

replicas, with black-over-silver paint and a host of extras. They sold for well above retail at the time, and remain among the more desirable Corvettes today.

1979 Turbo Corvette concept car (CP)

Some of those Pace Car features found their way onto standard models for 1979, including bolt-on spoilers and lightweight bucket seats. Both the base and special V-8s now had the dual-snorkel intake. Production slid upward for the model year, but sales slipped a bit. Another modest restyling came in 1980, lowering the hood profile and recessing the grille (and taking off some weight). Lift-off roof panels were made of microscopic glass beads. Front and rear spoilers were now molded into place. Corvette 350 cu. in. V-8s produced as much as 230 horsepower, but speedometers now peaked at 85 MPH.

In another weight-cutting move, a fiberglass-reinforced Monoleaf rear spring was installed on automatic-transmission models in 1981. A new-190 horsepower, 350 cu. in. (5.7-liter) engine had cast magnesium rocker covers and stainless steel exhaust manifolds. In an attempt to keep up with a rising problem, the theft alarm added a starter interrupt.

A new Corvette was in the works, but the 1982 version had some strong points of its own: essentially, a strong new drivetrain in the last of the old bodies. The "Cross Fire" fuel-injected V-8 used throttle-body injectors, but produced only 10 more horsepower (200) than the former version. For the first time since 1955, all Corvettes had automatic shift. A built-to-order Collector Edition featured silver-beige metallic paint and a frameless glass hatch. That was the first 'vette to carry a price tag above $20,000. Sales sagged dramatically, perhaps because customers were waiting for the next (sixth) generation.

1984 Corvette coupe (OCW)

No Corvettes at all were built for the 1983 model year, but the aerodynamic '84 edition (debuting in spring 1983) was worth the wait. The buff books fawned over it with superlatives. Technical changes included an aluminum driveshaft and fiberglass springs. A new transmission was offered—four-speed manual with automatic overdrive in top three gears—but only one in eight Corvettes carried it. The overdrive was locked out during hard acceleration. This year's dual-injector V-8 produced 205 horsepower. One other little change: Corvette's price tag soared past the $23,000 mark.

Horsepower jumped by 25 for 1985, with a new tuned-port fuel-injected 350 V-8. Next year, a convertible arrived— first open Corvette since 1975. Anti-lock braking also became standard, as did a new VATS anti-theft system. Four-speed overdrive automatic was standard, but a four-speed manual (overdrive in top three gears) cost no more. A switch to aluminum heads for the TPI engine produced a few problems, so early models kept the old cast iron heads. All convertibles (roadsters)

1986 Corvette Indy Pace Car convertible (CH)

were sold as Indy Pace Cars. It can easily be said that all Corvettes are collectible, yet some more so than others. The 1978 Pace Car Replica is one; the '82 Collector Edition another. Neither qualifies as rare, though, as quite a few were produced. No doubt, strong demand will keep the '86 convertible on the desirable list.

1976 CORVETTE

1976 Corvette coupe (CP)

STINGRAY — SERIES Y — V-8 — Unlike some advertisers, Chevrolet was correct in billing the fiberglass-bodied Corvette as "America's only true production sports car." The big-block V-8 had disappeared after 1974, leaving a 350 cu. in. (5.7-liter) small-block as the powerplant for all Corvettes in the next decade. Two V-8s were offered this year, both with four-barrel carburetor. The base L48 version now developed 180 horsepower (15 more than in 1975). An optional L82 V-8 produced 210. That one had special heads with larger valves, impact-extruded pistons, and finned aluminum rocker covers. The standard V-8 drove a new, slightly lighter weight automatic transmission: the Turbo Hydra-matic 350, which was supposed to improve shifting at wide-open throttle. Optional engines kept the prior Turbo Hydra-matic 400, but with a revised torque converter. A wide-range four-speed manual gearbox (with 2.64:1 first gear ratio) was standard; close-ratio version available at no extra cost. A new Carburetor Outside Air Induction system moved intake from the cowl to above the radiator. The convertible was dropped this year, so only the Stingray coupe remained, with twin removable roof panels. A partial steel underbody replaced the customary fiberglass, to add strength and improve shielding from exhaust system heat. A new one-piece bar Corvette nameplate was on the rear, between twin-unit taillamps (which were inset in the bumper cover). Of the ten body colors, eight were Corvette exclusives. This year's colors were red, silver, Classic white, bright yellow, bright blue, dark green, buckskin, dark brown, mahogany, and orange flame. Corvettes had side marker lights with reflectors, parking lamps that went on with headlamps, lane-change turn signals, and two-speed wiper/washers. Inside was a new, smaller-diameter four-spoke sports steering wheel with crossed-flags medallion, which came from Vega. Not everyone appreciated its lowly origin, so it lasted only this year. A grained vinyl trimmed instrument panel (with stitched seams) held a 160 MPH speedometer with trip odometer, and 7000 R.P.M. electronic tachometer. A key lock in left front fender set the anti-theft alarm. Corvettes had fully independent suspension and four-wheel disc brakes. Wide GR70 SBR tires rode 15 x 8 in. wheels. A total of 5,368 Corvettes had the FE7 Gymkhana suspension installed; 5,720 came with the L82 V-8; and 2,088 had the M21 four-speed close-ratio manual gearbox. Cast aluminum wheels were a new option, installed on 6,253 cars. Standard equipment included bumper guards, flush retracting headlamps, Soft-Ray tinted glass, Hide-A-Way wipers, wide-view day/night mirror, and center console with lighter and ashtray. Behind the seatbacks were three carpeted storage compartments. Bucket seats had textured-vinyl upholstery and deep-pleated saddle-stitched seat panels (black, dark firethorn, light buckskin or white). Interior leather trim was now available in seven colors. Like other GM vehicles, Corvette had a 13-symbol Vehicle Identification Number (VIN) atop the dashboard, visible through the windshield on the driver's side. The VIN appears in the form: 1Z37()6S4()()()(). The '1' indicates Chevrolet divisiion; 'Z' is Corvette series; '37' body type (2-dr. sport coupe). Fifth symbol is an engine code: 'L' base L48 V-8 and 'X' optional L82 V-8. Next is model year: '6' 1976. The letter 'S' indicates assembly plant (St. Louis). Finally comes a six-digit sequential serial number, starting with 400001. That sequential serial number is repeated on the engine block itself, stamped on a pad just ahead of the cylinder head on the right (passenger) side, combined with a three-letter identification suffix. Cast into the top rear (right side) of the block is a date built code. The first letter of that four-symbol code shows the month the block was cast. The next number (or numbers) reveals the day of the month, while the final digit indicates year.

CORVETTE

Model Number	Body/Style Number	Body Type & Seating	Factory Price	Shipping Weight	Production Total
1Y	Z37	2-dr. Cpe-2P	7605	3445	46,558

ENGINE DATA: BASE V-8: 90-degree, overhead valve V-8. Cast iron block and head. Displacement: 350 cu. in. (5.7 liters). Bore & stroke: 4.00 x 3.48 in. Compression ratio: 8.5:1. Brake horsepower: 180 at 4000 R.P.M. Torque: 270 lbs.-ft. at 2400 R.P.M. Five main bearings. Hydraulic valve lifters. Carburetor: 4Bbl. Rochester M4MC. RPO Code: L48. VIN Code: L. OPTIONAL V-8: Same as above, except Compression ratio: 9.0:1. Brake horsepower: 210 at 5200 R.P.M. Torque: 255 lbs.-ft. at 3600 R.P.M. RPO Code: L82. VIN Code: X.

CHASSIS DATA: Wheelbase: 98.0 in. Overall length: 185.2 in. Height: 48.0 in. Width: 69.0 in. Front Tread: 58.7 in. Rear Tread: 59.5 in. Wheel Size: 15 x 8 in. Standard Tires: GR70 x 15.

TECHNICAL: Transmission: Four-speed fully synchronized manual transmission (floor shift) standard. Gear ratios: (1st) 2.64:1; (2nd) 1.75:1; (3rd) 1.34:1; (4th) 1.00:1; (Rev) 2.55:1. Close-ratio four-speed fully synchronized manual trans. optional: (1st) 2.43:1; (2nd) 1.61:1; (3rd) 1.23:1; (4th) 1.00:1; (Rev) 2.35:1. Three-speed automatic optional: (1st) 2.52:1; (2nd) 1.52:1; (3rd) 1.00:1; (Rev) 1.94:1. Three-speed automatic ratios with L82 engine: (1st) 2.48:1; (2nd) 1.48:1; (3rd) 1.00:1; (Rev) 2.08:1. Standard

---

final drive ratio: 3.36:1 w/4spd, 3.08:1 w/auto. exc. with optional L82 engine 3.55:1 w/4spd, 3.55:1 or 3.70:1 with close-ratio four-speed, or 3.36:1 w/auto. Positraction standard. Steering: recirculating ball. Front Suspension: unequal-length control arms with ball joints, coil springs and stabilizer bar. Rear Suspension: independent with trailing-link, transverse semi-elliptic leaf spring. Brakes: Four-wheel disc (11.75 in. disc dia.). Ignition: HEI electronic. Body construction: Separate fiberglass body and box-type ladder frame with cross-members. Fuel tank: 18 gal.

CORVETTE OPTIONS: Special L82 350 cu. in., 4Bbl. V-8 engine ($481). Close-ratio four-speed manual transmission (NC). Turbo Hydra-matic (NC); but ($134) w/L82 V-8. High-altitude or highway axle ratio ($13). Gymkhana suspension ($35). Power brakes ($59). Power steering ($151). Heavy-duty battery ($16). California emissions system ($50). Four Season air cond. ($523). Rear defogger ($78). Tilt/telescopic steering wheel ($95). Power windows ($107). Map light ($10). Pushbutton AM/FM radio ($187). AM/FM stereo radio ($281). Vinyl interior (NC). Custom interior ($164). Aluminum wheels ($299). GR70 x 15/B SBR WSW tires ($37). GR70 x 15/B SBR WLT ($51).

HISTORY: Introduced: Oct. 2, 1975. Model year production: 46,558. Calendar year production: 47,425. Calendar year sales by U.S. dealers: 41,673. Model year sales by U.S. dealers: 41,027.

Historical Footnotes: Though largely a carryover from 1975, Corvette set a new sales record. Basic design dated back to 1968.

1977 CORVETTE

1977 Corvette coupe (OCW)

SERIES Y — V-8 — Since the Stingray front-fender nameplate departed this year, Chevrolet's sports car no longer had a secondary title. Changes were fairly modest this year, mainly hidden (such as steel hood reinforcement) or inside. New crossed-flags emblems stood between the headlamps, and on the fuel filler door. A thinner blacked-out pillar gave windshield and side glass a more integrated look. Corvette's console was restyled in an aircraft-type cluster design, with individual-look gauges. A voltmeter replaced the former ammeter. "Door ajar" and "headlamp up" warning lights were abandoned. New heater/air conditioning controls, ashtray and lighter were on the horizontal surface. A recessed pocket was now behind the shift lever. Power window switches moved to the new console. The manual shift lever was almost an inch higher, with shorter travel. Automatic transmission levers added a pointer, and both added a new black leather boot. A shorter steering column held a multi-function control lever. This year's steering wheel had a leather-wrapped rim. Of the ten body colors, seven were new and eight exclusive to Corvette. Colors were: Classic white, black, medium red and silver, plus Corvette dark or light blue, orange, dark red, tan or yellow. The Custom interior, formerly an extra-cost option, was now standard. "Dynasty" horizontal-ribbed cloth upholstery was framed with leather (the first cloth trim offered on Corvette), or buyers could have the customary all-leather seat panels. Leather came in ten colors, cloth in six. Two new trim colors were available: red and blue. Door panel inserts were satin finish black instead of the prior woodgrain. Both instrument panel and door trim lost their embossed stitch lines. New padded sunshades could swivel to side windows. Passenger-side roof pillars held a soft vinyl coat hook. Powertrains were the same as in 1976, but power brakes and steering were now standard. A total of 6,148 Chevrolets came with the special L82 V-8 engine under the hood, while 7,269 had optional Gymkhana suspension. Only 5,743 Corvettes had the M20 four-speed manual gearbox, and 2,060 the M26 close-ratio four-speed. And just 289 came with trailering equipment. New options included AM/FM stereo radio with tape player, cruise control (for automatic only), and a luggage carrier that could hold the roof panels. Glass roof panels were announced, but delayed for another year.

1977 Corvette coupe (CP)

141

CORVETTE

Model Number	Body/Style Number	Body Type & Seating	Factory Price	Shipping Weight	Production Total
1Y	Z37	2-dr. Cpe-2P	8648	3448	49,213

ENGINE DATA: BASE V-8: 90-degree, overhead valve V-8. Cast iron block and head. Displacement: 350 cu. in. (5.7 liters). Bore & stroke: 4.00 x 3.48 in. Compression ratio: 8.5:1. Brake horsepower: 180 at 4000 R.P.M. Torque: 270 lbs.-ft. at 2400 R.P.M. Five main bearings. Hydraulic valve lifters. Carburetor: 4Bbl. Rochester M4MC. RPO Code: L48. VIN Code: L. OPTIONAL V-8: Same as above, except C.R.: 9.0:1. B.H.P.: 210 at 5200 R.P.M. Torque: 255 lbs.-ft. at 3600 R.P.M. bearings. RPO Code: L82. VIN Code: X.

CHASSIS DATA: Wheelbase: 98.0 in. Overall length: 185.2 in. Height: 48.0 in. Width: 69.0 in. Front Tread: 58.7 in. Rear Tread: 59.5 in. Standard Tires: GR70x15.

TECHNICAL: Transmission: Four-speed manual transmission (floor shift) standard. Gear ratios: (1st) 2.64:1; (2nd) 1.75:1; (3rd) 1.34:1; (4th) 1.00:1; (Rev) 2.55:1. Close-ratio four-speed manual trans. optional: (1st) 2.43:1; (2nd) 1.61:1; (3rd) 1.23:1; (4th) 1.00:1; (Rev) 2.35:1. Three-speed automatic optional: (1st) 2.48:1; (2nd) 1.48:1; (3rd) 1.00:1; (Rev) 2.08:1. Standard final drive ratio: 3.36:1. Steering/Suspension-/Body: same as 1976. Brakes: Four-wheel disc. Ignition: Electronic. Fuel tank: 17 gal.

CORVETTE OPTIONS: L82 350 cu. in., 4Bbl. V 8 engine ($495). Close-ratio four- speed manual transmission (NC). Turbo Hydra-matic (NC); but ($146) w/L82 V-8. Highway axle ratio ($14). Gymkhana suspension ($38). Heavy-duty battery ($17). Trailer towing equipment ($83). California emissions system ($70). High- altitude emissions ($22). Air conditioning ($553). Rear defogger ($84). Cruise-master speed control ($88). Tilt/telescopic leather steering wheel ($165). Power windows ($116). Convenience group ($22). Sport mirrors, left remote ($36). AM/FM radio ($187). AM/FM stereo radio ($281); with stereo tape player ($414). Luggage carrier/roof panel ($73). Color-keyed floor mats ($22). Aluminum wheels ($321). GR70 x 15/B SBR WL tires ($57).

HISTORY: Introduced: Sept. 30, 1976. Model year production: 49,213 (Chevrolet inititially reported 49,034 units). Calendar year production: 46,345. Calendar year sales by U.S. dealers: 42,571. Model year sales by U.S. dealers: 40,764.

1978 CORVETTE

1978 Corvette Silver Anniversary coupe (CH)

SERIES Y — V-8 — To mark Corvette's 25th anniversary, the 1978 model got a major aerodynamic restyling with large wraparound back window and a fastback roofline. This was the first restyle since 1968. Two special editions were produced, one well known and the other little more than an optional paint job. New tinted glass lift-out roof panels were wired into the standard anti-theft system. A 24-gallon "fuel cell" replaced the former 17-gallon tank, filling space made available by a new temporary spare tire. Six of the ten body colors were new this year. Seven interiors were available (four new). Inside was a restyled, padded instrument panel with face-mounted round instruments and a new locking glove box (to replace the former map pocket). The restyled interior had more accessible rear storage area, with a roll shade to hide luggage. The wiper/washer control moved from the steering column back to the instrument panel, but turn signal and dimmer controls remained on the column. Door trim was now cut-and-sew design with soft expanded vinyl (or cloth). As in 1977, seats had leather side bolsters, with either leather or cloth seating area in a fine rib pattern. Corvette's optional L82 high-performance 350 V-8 reached 220 horsepower, as a result of a new dual-snorkel cold-air intake system, larger-diameter exhaust and tailpipes, and lower-restriction mufflers. The automatic transmission used with the option V-8 lost weight and had a low-inertia, high-stall torque converter. Base engines used a Muncie four-speed manual gearbox with higher first/second gear ratios than before; the performance V-8 used a close-ratio Borg-Warner. Axle ratios in California and at high altitude switched from 3.08:1 to 3.55:1. A total of 12,739 optional L82 engines were installed, while 3,385 Corvettes had the M21 four-speed close-ratio gearbox and 38,614 had automatic. Glass roof panels, promised earlier, actually became available this year. What Chevrolet described as "aggressive" 60-series white-letter tires joined the option list for the first time. An optional AM/FM/CB stereo radio used a tri- band power antenna on the rear deck. Each of this year's Corvettes could have Silver Anniversary emblems on the nose and rear deck. A total of 15,283 displayed the $399 special two-tone silver paint option: silver metallic on top, with charcoal silver on the lower body. Pinstripes accentuated fender upper profiles, wheel openings, front fender vents, hood, and rear license cavity. Interiors were also silver. Various other options were required, including aluminum

wheels. For a considerably higher price, buyers could have the Limited Edition replica of the Indy Pace Car with distinctive black-over-silver paint and red accent striping. Equipment in this "Indy Package" (RPO code Z78) included a special silver interior with new lightweight highback seats, special front/rear spoilers, P255/60R15 white-letter tires on alloy wheels, and lift-off glass canopy roof panels. It contained nearly all Corvette options, plus special decals (unless the customer specified that they be omitted). Upholstery was silver leather, or leather with smoke (gray) cloth inserts.

I.D. DATA: Corvette's 13-symbol Vehicle Identification Number (VIN), visible through the windshield, altered its coding a bit this year. The VIN appears in the form: 1Z87()8S()()()()(). The '1' indicates Chevrolet divisiion; 'Z' is Corvette series; '87' body type (2-dr. sport coupe). Fifth symbol is an engine code: 'L' base L48 V-8 and 'H' optional L82 V-8. Next is model year: '8' 1978. The letter 'S' indicates assembly plant (St. Louis). Finally comes a six-digit sequential serial number, starting with 400001 for standard model but 900001 for Pace Car replicas. This step was taken to make it more difficult to produce counterfeit pace cars. As before, the serial number is repeated on the engine block itself, stamped on a pad just ahead of the cylinder head on the right side. A date built code is also cast into the top rear (right side) of the block. The first letter of that four-symbol code shows the month the block was cast. The next number(s) reveal the day of the month, while the final digit indicates year.

1978 Corvette Limited Edition Indy Pace Car (IMSC)

CORVETTE

Model Number	Body/Style Number	Body Type & Seating	Factory Price	Shipping Weight	Production Total
1Y	Z87	2-dr. Cpe-2P	9446	3401	40,271

CORVETTE LIMITED EDITION (PACE CAR REPLICA)

1Y	Z87/Z78	2-dr. Cpe-2P	13653	N/A	6,501

ENGINE DATA: BASE V-8: 90-degree, overhead valve V-8. Cast iron block and head. Displacement: 350 cu. in. (5.7 liters). Bore & stroke: 4.00 x 3.48 in. Compression ratio: 8.2:1. Brake horsepower: 185 at 4000 R.P.M. Torque: 280 lbs.-ft. at 2400 R.P.M. Five main bearings. Hydraulic valve lifters. Carburetor: 4Bbl. RPO Code: L48. VIN Code: L. OPTIONAL V-8: Same as above, except C.R.: 8.9:1. B.H.P.: 220 at 5200 R.P.M. Torque: 260 lbs.-ft. at 3600 R.P.M. RPO Code: L82. VIN Code: H.

CHASSIS DATA: Wheelbase: 98.0 in. Overall length: 185.2 in. Height: 48.0 in. Width: 69.0 in. Front Tread: 58.7 in. Rear Tread: 59.5 in. Wheel size: 15 x 8 in. Standard Tires: P225/70R15 SBR. Optional Tires: P225/60R15.

TECHNICAL: Transmission: Four-speed manual transmission (floor shift) standard. Gear ratios: (1st) 2.85:1; (2nd) 2.02:1; (3rd) 1.35:1; (4th) 1.00:1; (Rev) 2.85:1. Close-ratio four-speed manual available at no extra charge: (1st) 2.43:1; (2nd) 1.61:1; (3rd) 1.23:1; (4th) 1.00:1; (Rev) 2.35:1. Three-speed automatic optional: (1st) 2.52:1; (2nd) 1.52:1; (3rd) 1.00:1; (Rev) 1.94:1. Standard final drive ratio: 3.36:1 w/4spd, 3.08:1 w/auto. exc. L82 V-8, 3.70:1 w/4spd and 3.55:1 w/auto. Steering/Suspension/Body: same as 1976-77. Brakes: Four-wheel disc (11.75 in. disc dia.). Ignition: Electronic. Fuel tank: 24 gal.

CORVETTE OPTIONS: L82 350 cu. in., 4Bbl. V-8 engine ($525). Close-ratio four- speed manual transmission (NC). Turbo Hydra-matic (NC). Highway axle ratio ($15). Gymkhana suspension ($41). Heavy- duty battery ($18). Trailer towing equipment inc. H.D. radiator and Gymkhana pkg. ($89). California emissions system ($75). High-altitude emissions ($33). Air conditioning ($605). Rear defogger, electric ($95). Cruise-master speed control ($99). Tilt/telescopic leather steering wheel ($175). Power windows ($130). Convenience group ($84). Sport mirrors, left remote ($40). AM/FM radio ($199). AM/FM stereo radio ($286); with stereo tape player ($419). AM/FM stereo radio w/CB and power antenna ($638). Power antenna ($49). 25th anniversary paint ($399). Aluminum wheels ($340). P225/70R15/B SBR WL tires ($51). P225/60R15/B SBR WL tires ($216).

HISTORY: Introduced: Oct. 6, 1977. Model year production: 46,772 (but some industry sources have reported a total of 47,667). Calendar year production: 48,522. Calendar year sales by U.S. dealers: 42,247. Model year sales by U.S. dealers: 43,106.

Historical Footnotes: The limited-edition Pace Car replica was created to commemorate the selection of Corvette as Pace Car for the 62nd Indy 500 race on May 28, 1978. A production run of 2,500 was planned. But so many potential buyers who saw it at the New York Auto Show in February wanted one that the goal quickly expanded to 6,500 roughly one for every Chevrolet dealer. Buyers also had to endure a selection of "Forced RPOs," meaning items installed at the factory whether wanted or not. Those mandatory extras included power windows, air conditioning, sport mirrors, tilt/telescope steering, rear defogger, AM/FM stereo with either an 8-track tape player or CB radio, plus power door locks and a heavy-duty battery. Before long, the original $13,653 list price meant little, as speculators eagerly paid double that amount and more. A year later, as is usually the case, the price retreated to around original list. Even though so many were built, it's still a desirable model. Dave McLellan was now head of engineering for Corvettes, working on the next generation.

1979 CORVETTE

1979 Corvette coupe (CH)

1979 Corvette coupe (CP)

SERIES Y — V-8 — "The Corvette evolution continues," declared this year's catalog. Not much of that evolution was visible, however, after the prior year's massive restyle. Under the hood, the base engine got the dual-snorkel air intake introduced in 1978 for the optional L82 V-8. That added 10 horsepower. The L82 V-8 had a higher-lift cam, special heads with larger valves and higher compression, impact-extruded pistons, forged steel crankshaft, and finned aluminum rocker covers. The "Y" pipe exhaust system had new open-flow mufflers, while the automatic transmission got a higher numerical (3.55:1) rear axle ratio. All Corvettes now had the highback bucket seats introduced on the 1978 limited-edition Indy Pace Car. A high pivot point let the seat backrest fold flat on the passenger side, level with the luggage area floor. An AM/FM radio was now standard. Of ten body colors, only one (dark green metallic) was new this year. The others were Classic white, black and silver, plus Corvette dark or light blue, yellow, light beige, red, and dark brown. Interiors came in black, red, light beige, dark blue, dark brown, oyster, or dark green. Corvettes had black roof panel and window moldings. Bolt-on front and rear spoilers (also from the Pace Car) ecame available. Buyers who didn't want the full Gymkhana suspension could now order heavy-duty shocks alone. Standard equipment included the L48 V-8 with four-barrel carb, either automatic transmission or four-speed manual gearbox (close-ratio version available), power four-wheel disc brakes, and limited-slip differential. Other standards: tinted glass; front stabilizer bar; concealed wipers/washers; day/night inside mirror; wide outside mirror; anti-theft alarm system; four-spoke sport steering wheel; electric clock; trip odometer; heater/defroster; bumper guards; and luggage security shade. Tires were P225/70R15 steel-belted radial blackwalls on 15 x 8 in. wheels. Corvettes had four-wheel independent suspension. Bucket seats came with cloth/leather or all-leather trim. The aircraft-type console held a 7000 R.P.M. tachometer, voltmeter, oil pressure, temp and fuel gauges. Seat inserts could have either leather or cloth trim.

I.D. DATA: Coding of the 13-symbol Vehicle Identification Number (VIN) was similar to 1978. Engine codes changed to '8' base L48 and '4' optional L82. Model year code changed to '9' for 1979. Serial numbers began with 400001.

1979 Corvette coupe (CP)

CORVETTE

Model Number	Body/Style Number	Body Type & Seating	Factory Price	Shipping Weight	Production Total
1Y	Z87	2-dr. Spt Cpe-2P	10220	3372	53,807

ENGINE DATA: BASE V-8: 90-degree, overhead valve V-8. Cast iron block and head. Displacement: 350 cu. in. (5.7 liters). Bore & stroke: 4.00 x 3.48 in. Compression ratio: 8.2:1. Brake horsepower: 195 at 4000 R.P.M. Torque: 285 lbs.-ft. at 3200 R.P.M. Five main bearings. Hydraulic valve lifters. Carburetor: 4Bbl. RPO Code: L48. VIN Code: 8. OPTIONAL V-8: Same as above, except C.R.: 8.9:1. B.H.P.: 225 at 5200 R.P.M. Torque: 270 lbs.-ft. at 3600 R.P.M. RPO Code: L82. VIN Code: 4.

CHASSIS DATA: Wheelbase: 98.0 in. Overall length: 185.2 in. Height: 48.0 in. Width: 69.0 in. Front Tread: 58.7 in. Rear Tread: 59.5 in. Wheel Size: 15 x 8 in. Standard Tires: P225/70R15 SBR. Optional Tires: P225/60R15.

TECHNICAL: Transmission: Four-speed manual transmission (floor shift) standard. Gear ratios: (1st) 2.85:1; (2nd) 2.02:1; (3rd) 1.35:1; (4th) 1.00:1; (Rev) 2.85:1. Close-ratio four-speed manual trans. optional: (1st) 2.43:1; (2nd) 1.61:1; (3rd) 1.23:1; (4th) 1.00:1; (Rev) 2.35:1. Three-speed automatic optional: (1st) 2.52:1; (2nd) 1.52:1; (3rd) 1.00:1; (Rev) 1.93:1. Standard final drive ratio: 3.36:1 w/4spd, 3.55:1 w/auto. Steering: Recirculating ball. Front Suspension: Control arms, coil springs and stabilizer bar. Rear Suspension: Independent with single transverse leaf spring and lateral struts. Brakes: Four-wheel disc (11.75 in. disc dia). Ignition: Electronic. Body construction: Fiberglass, on separate frame. Fuel tank: 24 gal.

CORVETTE OPTIONS: L82 350 cu. in., 4Bbl. V-8 engine ($565). Close-ratio four-speed manual transmission (NC). Turbo Hydra-matic (NC). Highway axle ratio ($19). Gymkhana suspension ($49). H.D. shock absorbers ($33). Heavy-duty battery ($21). Trailer towing equipment inc. H.D. radiator and Gymkhana suspension ($98). California emissions system (N/A). High-altitude emissions (N/A). Four season air cond. ($635). Rear defogger, electric ($102). Cruise-master speed control ($113). Tilt/telescopic leather-wrapped steering wheel ($190). Power windows ($141). Power windows and door locks ($272). Convenience group ($94). Sport mirrors, left remote ($45). AM/FM stereo radio ($90); with 8track or cassette player ($228-$234). AM/FM stereo radio w/CB and power antenna ($439). Dual rear speakers ($52). Power antenna ($52). Removable glass roof panels ($365). Aluminum wheels ($380). P225/70R15 SBR WL tires ($54). P225/60R15 Aramid-belted radial WL tires ($226).

HISTORY: Introduced: Sept. 25, 1978. Model year production: 53,807 (Chevrolet initially reported a total of 49,901 units.) Calendar year production: 48,568. Calendar year sales by U.S. dealers: 38,631. Model year sales by U.S. dealers: 39,816.

Historical Footnotes: For what it's worth, 7,949 Corvettes this year were painted in Classic White, while 6,960 carried silver paint. Only 4,385 Corvettes had the MM4 four-speed manual gearbox, while 4,062 ran with the close-ratio M21 version.

1980 CORVETTE

1980 Corvette coupe (CP)

SERIES Y — V-8 — Corvette lost close to 250 pounds in a more streamlined restyle. Hood and doors were lighter, glass thinner. Bodies held new fiberglass bumper structures. Lift-off roof panels were made of lightweight, low-density microscopic glass beads. Body panels were urethane-coated. Weight cuts also hit the powertrain. The differential housing and supports were made of aluminum. The 350 cu. in. (5.7-liter) V-8 had a new aluminum intake manifold, while California 305 (5.0- liter) V-8s had a stainless exhaust manifold. Hoods showed a new low profile. The front bumper had an integrated lower air dam, and the bumper cover now extended to wheel openings. Two-piece front cornering lamps worked whenever the lights were switched on. A deeply recessed split grille held integral parking lamps. Front fender air vents contained functional black louvers. New front/rear spoilers were molded in, integrated with bumper caps, no longer the bolt-on type. New emblems included an engine identifier for the optional L82 V-8. Turbo Hydra-matic transmissions added a lockup torque converter that engaged at about 30 MPH, while the four-speed manual got new gear ratios. California 'vettes could only have a 305 V-8 and automatic this year. The base V-8 lost five horsepower, while the optional version gained five. New standard equipment this year included the formerly optional power windows, tilt/telescopic steering wheel, and Four Season air conditioner. Rally wheels held P225/70R15/B blackwall SBR tires with trim rings and center caps. Body colors were: black, silver, red, yellow, white, dark green, dark blue, dark claret, dark brown, or frost beige. Interiors came in black, red, oyster, claret, dark blue, or doeskin. Dashes held a new 85 MPH speedometer. Only two storage bins stood behind the seat, where three used to be.

1980 Corvette coupe (CP)

I.D. DATA: Coding of the 13-symbol Vehicle Identification Number (VIN) was similar to 1978-79. Engine codes were '8' base L48 V-8, '6' optional L82 V-8, and 'H' California V-8. Model year code changed to 'A' for 1980. Serial numbers began with 400001.

CORVETTE

Model Number	Body/Style Number	Body Type & Seating	Factory Price	Shipping Weight	Production Total
1Y	Z87	2-dr. Cpe-2P	13140	3206	40,614

ENGINE DATA: BASE V-8: 90-degree, overhead valve V-8. Cast iron block and head. Displacement: 350 cu. in. (5.7 liters). Bore & stroke: 4.00 x 3.48 in. Compression ratio: 8.2:1. Brake horsepower: 190 at 4200 R.P.M. Torque: 280 lbs.-ft. at 2400 R.P.M. Five main bearings. Hydraulic valve lifters. Carburetor: 4Bbl. RPO Code: L48. VIN Code: 8. OPTIONAL V-8: Same as above, except C.R.: 9.0:1. B.H.P.: 230 at 5200 R.P.M. Torque: 275 lbs.-ft. at 3600 R.P.M. RPO Code: L82. VIN Code: 6. CALIFORNIA V-8: 90-degree, overhead valve V-8. Cast iron block and head. Displacement: 305 cu. in. (5.0 liters). Bore & stroke: 3.74 x 3.48 in. Compression ratio: 8.5:1. Brake horsepower: 180 at 4200 R.P.M. Torque: 255 lbs.-ft. at 2000 R.P.M. Five main bearings. Hydraulic valve lifters. Carburetor: 4Bbl. Roch. M4ME. RPO Code: LG4. VIN Code: H.

CHASSIS DATA: Wheelbase: 98.0 in. Overall length: 185.3 in. Height: 48.1 in. Width: 69.0 in. Front Tread: 58.7 in. Rear Tread: 59.5 in. Wheel size: 15 x 8 in. Standard Tires: P225/70R15/B SBR. Optional Tires: P255/60R15/B.

TECHNICAL: Transmission: Four-speed manual transmission (floor shift) standard. Gear ratios: (1st) 2.88:1; (2nd) 1.91:1; (3rd) 1.33:1; (4th) 1.00:1; (Rev) 2.78:1. Three-speed Turbo Hydra-matic optional: (1st) 2.52:1; (2nd) 1.52:1; (3rd) 1.00:1; (Rev) 1.93:1. Standard final drive ratio: 3.07:1 w/4spd, 3.55:1 w/auto.. Steering/Suspension/Body/Brakes: same as 1979. Fuel tank: 24 gal.

1980 Corvette coupe (CP)

CORVETTE OPTIONS: L82 350 cu. in., 4Bbl. V-8 engine ($595). 305 cu. in., 4Bbl. V-8 ($50 credit). Turbo Hydra-matic (NC). Gymkhana suspension ($55). H.D. shock absorbers ($35). Heavy-duty battery ($22). Trailer towing equipment incl. H.D. radiator and Gymkhana suspension ($105). California emissions system ($250). Rear defogger, electric ($109). Cruise-master speed control ($123). Power door locks ($140). AM/FM stereo radio ($46); with 8track ($155); w/cassette player ($168). AM/FM stereo radio w/CB and power antenna ($391). Dual rear speakers ($31). Power antenna ($56). Radio delete ($126 credit). Removable glass roof panels ($391). Roof panel carrier ($125). Aluminum wheels ($407). P225/70R15/B SBR WL tires ($62). P255/60R15/B SBR WL tires ($426).

HISTORY: Introduced: Oct. 25, 1979. Model year production: 40,614 (but Chevrolet reported a total of 40,564 units). Calendar year production: 44,190. Model year sales by U.S. dealers: 37,471.

Historical Footnotes: Production continued at the St. Louis plant, but a new GMAD operation at Bowling Green, Kentucky was planned to begin production of the next-generation Corvettes. Chevrolet engineers released a TurboVette that used a Garrette AiResearch turbocharger and fuel injection, but press people who drove it discovered performance more sluggish than a regular L82 V-8 could dish out. Only 5,726 Corvettes had the MM4 four-speed manual gearbox. And only 5,069 carried the special L82 engine. A total of 9,907 had the Gymkhana suspension.

144

1981 CORVETTE

Corvette Coupe

1981 Corvette coupe (JAG)

SERIES Y — V-8 — Probably the most significant change this year was hidden from view. Corvettes with Turbo Hydra-matic had a new fiberglass-reinforced Monoleaf rear spring that weighed just eight pounds (33 pounds less than the multi-leaf steel spring it replaced). Obviously, it also eliminated interleaf friction. Manual-shift models kept the old spring, as did those with optional Gymkhana suspension. Side glass was thinner, in a further attempt to cut weight. A new L81 version of the 350 cu. in. V-8 arrived this year, rated 190 horsepower, with lightweight magnesium rocker covers. New stainless steel free-flow exhaust manifolds weighed 14 pounds less than the previous cast iron. A new thermostatically-controlled auxiliary electric fan boosted cooling, and allowed use of a smaller main fan. Air cleaners had a new chromed cover. Computer Command Control controlled fuel metering as well as the torque converter lockup clutch, which operated in second and third gears. Manual transmission was available in all 50 states, the first time in several years that Californians could have a stick shift. A quartz crystal clock was now standard. Corvette's standard anti-theft alarm added a starter interrupt device. Joining the option list: a six-way power seat. Electronic- tuning radios could have built-in cassette or 8track tape players, or a CB transceiver. Body colors this year were black, white, red, yellow, beige, and five metallics: silver, dark or bright blue, maroon, or charcoal. Four two-tone combinations were available. Interiors came in black, red, silver, rust, camel or blue. Corvette's ample standard equipment list included either four-speed manual or automatic transmission (same price), four-wheel power disc brakes, limited-slip differential, power steering, tinted glass, twin remote-control sport mirrors, and concealed two-speed wipers. Also standard: halogen high-beam retractable headlamps, air conditioning, power windows, tilt/telescope leather-wrapped steering wheel, tachometer, AM/FM radio, trip odometer, courtesy lights, and a luggage compartment security shade. Buyers had a choice of cloth/vinyl or leather/vinyl upholstery. Corvettes rode P225/70R15 steel-belted radial blackwall tires on 15 x 8 in. wheels. The optional Gymkhana suspension (price $54) was also included with the trailer towing package.

1981 Corvette coupe (OCW)

I.D. DATA: Corvettes had a new 17-symbol Vehicle Identification Number (VIN), again visible through the windshield on the driver's side. The VIN took the form: 1G1AY8764B()()()()()(). The '1G1' portion indicates U.S.A., General Motors, Chevrolet Division, and non-passive restraint system. 'Y' denotes Corvette series. '87' indicates 2-door sport coupe body style. '6' is the engine code. '4' is a check digit. Model year 1981 is revealed by the 'B'. Next is a code for assembly plant: either 'S' for St. Louis or '5' for Bowling Green. The last six digits are the sequential serial number, starting with 400001 for St. Louis models and 100001 for Corvettes built at Bowling Green, Kentucky. As before, the serial number is repeated on the engine block, stamped on a pad just ahead of the cylinder head on the right side. A date built code is also cast into the top rear (right side) of the block. The first letter of that four-symbol code shows the month the block was cast. The next number(s) reveal the day of the month, while the final digit indicates year.

CORVETTE

Model Number	Body/Style Number	Body Type & Seating	Factory Price	Shipping Weight	Production Total
1Y	Y87	2-dr. Cpe-2P	15248	3179	40,606

ENGINE DATA: BASE V-8: 90-degree, overhead valve V-8. Cast iron block and head. Displacement: 350 cu. in. (5.7 liters). Bore & stroke: 4.00 x 3.48 in. Compression ratio: 8.2:1. Brake horsepower: 190 at 4200 R.P.M. Torque: 280 lbs.-ft. at 1600 R.P.M. Five main bearings. Hydraulic valve lifters. Carburetor: 4Bbl. RPO Code: L81. VIN Code: 6.

CHASSIS DATA: Wheelbase: 98.0 in. Overall length: 185.3 in. Height: 48.1 in. Width: 69.0 in. Front Tread: 58.7 in. Rear Tread: 59.5 in. Wheel Size: 15 x 8 in. Standard Tires: P225/70R15 SBR. Optional Tires: P225/60R15.

TECHNICAL: Transmission: Four-speed manual trans. (floor shift) standard. Gear ratios: (1st) 2.88:1; (2nd) 1.91:1; (3rd) 1.33:1; (4th) 1.00:1; (Rev) 2.78:1. Three-speed Turbo Hydra- matic optional: (1st) 2.52:1; (2nd) 1.52:1; (3rd) 1.00:1; (Rev) 1.93:1. Standard final drive ratio: 2.72:1 w/4spd, 2.87:1 w/auto. Steering/Suspension/Body/Brakes: same as 1979-80. Fuel tank: 24 gal.

CORVETTE OPTIONS: Turbo Hydra-matic (NC). Performance axle ratio ($19). Gymkhana suspension ($54). H.D. shock absorbers ($35). Trailer towing equipment incl. H.D. radiator and Gymkhana suspension ($104). California emissions system ($48). Rear defogger, electric ($109). Cruise-master speed control w/resume ($141). Six-way power driver's seat ($173). Power door locks ($135). AM/FM stereo radio ($95). Electronic- tuning AM/FM stereo radio with 8track ($385); w/cassette player ($423); w/8track and CB ($709); w/cassette and CB ($747). Power antenna ($52). Radio delete ($118 credit). Removable glass roof panels ($391). Roof panel carrier ($124). Aluminum wheels ($404). P225/70R15 SBR WL tires ($67). P255/60R15 SBR WL tires ($460).

HISTORY: Introduced: Sept. 25, 1980. Model year production: 40,606 (but Chevrolet first reported a total of 40,593 units). Calendar year production: 27,990. Model year sales by U.S. dealers: 33,414.

Historical Footnotes: Of the total output this model year, 8,995 Corvettes came out of the new plant at Bowling Green, Kentucky, which began production in June 1981. Despite some weak years in the industry, Corvette sales remained strong through this period.

1982 CORVETTE

1982 Corvette coupe (CH)

SERIES Y — V-8 — For the first time since 1955, no stick shift Corvettes were produced. Every one had four-speed automatic, now with lockup in every gear except first. Under the hood, though, was a new kind of 350 cu. in. V-8 with Cross-Fire fuel injection. Twin throttle-body injectors with computerized metering helped boosted horsepower to 200 (10 more than 1982), and cut emissions at the same time. This was the first fuel-injected Corvette in nearly two decades, and a much different breed now that mini-computerization had arrived. In the gas tank was a new electric fuel pump. Externally, this final verion of the big Corvettes changed little. But this year's Collector Edition displayed quite a few special features, highlighted by a frameless glass lift-up hatch instead of the customary fixed backlight. Unique silver-beige metallic paint was accented by pinstripes and fading shadow treatment on hood, fenders and doors, plus distinctive cloisonne emblems. Special finned wheels were similar to the cast aluminum wheels dating back to 1967 (finale for the last prior Corvette era). Removable glass roof panels had special bronze color and solar screening. Crossed-flags emblems read "Corvette Collector Edition" around the rim. Inside was a matching silver-beige metallic interior with multi-tone leather seats and door trim. Even the hand-sewn leather-wrapped steering wheel kept the theme color, and its leather-covered horn button had a cloisonne emblem. Tires were P255/60R15 Goodyear SBR WLT Eagle GT. Back to non-collector models, standard body colors were white, red and black, plus metallic charcoal, silver, silver blue, silver green, dark blue, bright blue, gold, or dark claret. Four two-tones were available. Interiors came in dark red, charcoal, dark blue, camel, silver grey, silver beige, or silver green. Standard equipment included power brakes and steering, P225/70R15/B SBR tires on steel wheels with center hub and trim rings, cornering lamps, front fender louvers, halogen high-beam retractable headlamps, dual remote sport mirrors, and tinted glass. The body-color front bumper had a built-in air dam. Also standard: luggage security shade, air conditioning, pushbutton AM/FM radio, concealed wipers, power windows, time-delay dome/courtesy lamps, headlamp-on reminder, lighted visor vanity mirror, tilt/telescoping leather-wrapped steering wheel, 7000 R.P.M. tachometer, analog clock with sweep second hand, day/night mirror, lighter, and trip odometer. Bucket seats could be all cloth or leather-trimmed.

I.D. DATA: Coding of the 17-symbol Vehicle Identification Number (VIN) was similar to 1981, but several of the codes changed. The VIN took the form: 1G1AY()()8()C51()()()()(). For symbols 67 (body type), '87' standard model and '07' Collector Edition. The next symbol ('8') is the engine code. Next is a check digit: '6' for standard model, '1' for Collector. Model year code 'C' 1982, and '5' indicates the new Bowling Green assembly plant. Six-digit sequential serial numbers began with 100001.

CORVETTE

Model Number	Body/Style Number	Body Type & Seating	Factory Price	Shipping Weight	Production Total
1Y	Y87	2-dr. Spt Cpe-2P	18290	3213	18,648

1982 Corvette Collector Edition coupe (JAG)

CORVETTE COLLECTOR EDITION

1Y	Y07	2-dr. Hatch Cpe-2P	22537	3222	6,759

ENGINE DATA: BASE V-8: 90-degree, overhead valve V-8. Cast iron block and head. Displacement: 350 cu. in. (5.7 liters). Bore & stroke: 4.00 x 3.48 in. Compression ratio: 9.0:1. Brake horsepower: 200 at 4200 R.P.M. Torque: 285 lbs.-ft. at 2800 R.P.M. Five main bearings. Hydraulic valve lifters. Cross-fire fuel injection (twin TBI). RPO Code: L83. VIN Code: 8.

CHASSIS DATA: Wheelbase: 98.0 in. Overall length: 185.3 in. Height: 48.4 in. Width: 69.0 in. Front Tread: 58.7 in. Rear Tread: 59.5 in. Wheel Size: 15 x 8 in. Standard Tires: P225/70R15 SBR (Collector Edition, P255/60R15).

TECHNICAL: Transmission: THM 700R4 four-speed overdrive automatic (floor shift). Gear ratios: (1st) 3.06:1; (2nd) 1.63:1; (3rd) 1.00:1; (4th) 0.70:1; (Rev) 2.29:1. Standard final drive ratio: 2.72:1 exc. 2.87:1 w/aluminum wheels. Steering: Recirculating ball (power assisted). Front Suspension: Upper/lower Aarms, coil springs, stabilizer bar. Rear Suspension: Fully independent with half-shafts, lateral struts, control arms, and transverse leaf spring. Brakes: Power four-wheel discs (11.75 in. dia.). Ignition: Electronic. Body construction: Separate fiberglass body and ladder-type steel frame. Fuel tank: 24 gal.

CORVETTE OPTIONS: Four-speed manual trans. (NC). Gymkhana suspension ($61). H.D. cooling ($57). California emissions system (N/A). Rear defogger, electric ($129). Cruise control w/resume ($165). Six-way power driver's seat ($197). Power door locks ($155). Twin electric remote-control sport mirrors ($125). AM/FM stereo radio ($101). Electronic-tuning AM/FM stereo radio with 8track ($386); w/cassette player ($423); w/cassette and CB ($755) exc. ($458) on Collector Edition. Power antenna ($60). Radio delete ($124 credit). Removable glass roof panels ($443). Roof panel carrier ($144). Custom two-tone paint ($428) w/lower body accents and multi-color striping. Aluminum wheels ($458). P225/70R15 SBR WL tires ($80).

HISTORY: Introduced: Dec. 12, 1981. Model year production: 25,407. Calendar year production: 22,838. Model year sales by U.S. dealers: 22,086.

Historical Footnotes: All Corvettes now came from the factory at Bowling Green, Kentucky. Production fell dramatically this year, reaching the lowest total since 1967. No doubt, some buyers preferred to wait for the next generation to arrive. Still, this was the end of the big 'vette era: "An enthusiast's kind of Corvette. A most civilized one," according to the factory catalog. Road & Track called it "truly the last of its series," thougn one with an all-new drivetrain. The Collector Edition earned the dubious distinction of being the first Corvette to cost more than $20,000. They were built to order, rather than according to a predetermined schedule. Special VIN plates were used, to prevent swindlers from turning an ordinary 'vette into a special edition (which had happened all too often with the Pace Car replicas of 1978).

1984 CORVETTE

1984 Corvette coupe (CP)

SERIES Y — V-8 — The eagerly-awaited sixth-generation Corvette for the eighties missed the 1983 model year completely, but arrived in spring 1983 in an all-new form. An aerodynamic exterior featuring an "acute" windshield rake (64 degrees) covered a series of engineering improvements. A one-piece, full width fiberglass roof (no T-bar) was removable; transparent acrylic lift-off panel with solar screen optional. At the rear was a frameless glass back window/hatch, above four round taillamps. Hidden headlamps were joined by clear, integrated halogen foglamps and front cornering lamps. Dual sport mirrors were electrically remote-controlled. The unit body (with partial front frame) used a front-hinged "clamshell" hood with integral twin-duct air intake. Sole engine was again the L83 350 cu. in. (5.7-liter) V-8 with Cross-Fire fuel injection. Stainless steel headers led into its exhaust system. Air cleaner and valve train had cast magnesium covers. After being unavailable in the 1982 model, a four-speed manual gearbox returned as the standard transmission (though not until January 1984). A four-plus- three speed automatic, with computer-activated overdrive in every gear except 1st, was offered at no extra cost. It used a hydraulic clutch. Overdrive was locked out during rigorous acceleration above specified speeds, and when a console switch was activated. Under the chassis were an aluminum driveshaft, forged aluminum suspension arms, and fiberglass transverse leaf springs. Power rack-and-pinion steering and power four-wheel disc brakes were standard. Optional Goodyear 50-series "uni-directional" tires were designed for mounting on a specific wheel. Inside, an electronic instrument panel featured both analog and digital LCD readouts, in either English or metric measure. A Driver Information System between speedometer and tach gave a selection of switch-chosen readings. At the driver's left was the parking brake. Body colors were red, black, white, and seven metallics: gold, light or medium blue, light bronze, dark bronze, silver or gray. Two-tone options were light/medium blue, silver/gray, and light/dark bronze. Standard interiors came in graphite, blue, bronze, saddle or gray cloth; optional leather in graphite, saddle, bronze, dark red or gray. Corvette's ample standard equipment list included an advanced (and very necessary) theft-prevention system with starter-interrupt. Other standard equipment: air conditioning, power windows, electronic-tuning seek/scan AM/FM stereo radio with digital clock, reclining bucket seats, leather-wrapped tilt/telescope steering wheel, luggage security shade, and side window defoggers.

1984 Corvette coupe (OCW)

I.D. DATA: Coding of the 17-symbol Vehicle Identification Number (VIN), visible through the windshield, was similar to prior models. The VIN took the form: 1G1AY078()E5100001. The '1G1A' portion indicates U.S.A., General Motors, Chevrolet Division, and non-passive restraint system (standard seatbelts). 'Y' denotes Corvette series. '07' indicates 2-door hatchback coupe body style. '8' is the engine code. Next is a check digit, followed by 'E' for the 1984 model year and '5' for the Bowling Green, KY assembly plant. Finally comes the six- digit sequential serial number, starting with 100001. Engine identification numbers again were stamped on a pad on the block, at the front of the right cylinder head. That number reveals assembly plant, date built, and a three- letter engine code.

CORVETTE

Model Number	Body/Style Number	Body Type & Seating	Factory Price	Shipping Weight	Production Total
1Y	Y07	2-dr. Hatch Cpe-2P	23360	3088	51,547

Note: Of the total production, 240 Corvettes were modified for use with leaded gasoline (for export).

ENGINE DATA: BASE V-8: 90-degree, overhead valve V-8. Cast iron block and head. Displacement: 350 cu. in. (5.7 liters). Bore & stroke: 4.00 x 3.48 in. Compression ratio: 9.0:1. Brake horsepower: 205 at 4200 R.P.M. Torque: 290 lbs.-ft. at 2800 R.P.M. Five main bearings. Hydraulic valve lifters. Dual TBI (CFI). RPO Code: L83. VIN Code: 8.

CHASSIS DATA: Wheelbase: 96.2 in. Overall length: 176.5 in. Height: 46.7 in. Width: 71.0 in. Front Tread: 59.6 in. Rear Tread: 60.4 in. Wheel Size: 15 x 7 in. Standard Tires: P215/65R15. Optional Tires: Eagle P255/50VR16 on 16 x 8 in. wheels.

TECHNICAL: Transmission: THM 700-R4 four-speed overdrive automatic (floor shift) standard. Gear ratios: (1st) 3.06:1, (2nd) 1.63:1, (3rd) 1.00:1, (4th) 0.70:1, (Rev) 2.29:1. Four-speed manual transmission optional: (1st) 2.88:1, (2nd) 1.91:1, (3rd) 1.33:1, (4th) 1.00:1, (overdrive) 0.67:1, (Rev) 2.78:1. Standard final drive ratio: 2.73:1 w/auto., 3.07:1 w/4spd (3.31:1 optional). Steering: Rack and pinion (power-assisted). Front Suspension: Single fiberglass composite monoleaf transverse spring with unequal-length aluminum control arms and stabilizer bar. Rear Suspension: Fully independent five-link system with transverse fiberglass single-leaf spring, aluminum upper/lower trailing links, and strut/tie rod assembly. Brakes: Four-wheel power disc. Body construction: Unibody with partial front frame. Fuel tank: 20 gal.

CORVETTE OPTIONS: Four-speed overdrive manual trans. (NC). California emission system ($75). Performance axle ratio ($22). Performance handling pkg.: H.D. springs/shocks, front/rear stabilizers, special bushings and P255/50VR16 tires on 16 x 91/2 in. wheels ($600). Delco/Bilstein shock absorbers ($189). Engine oil cooler ($158). H.D. cooling ($57). Rear defogger system incl. mirrors ($160). Electronic cruise control w/resume ($185). Six-way power driver's seat ($210). Power door locks ($165). Electronic-tuning AM/FM stereo radio with seek/scan, clock and cassette player ($153). DelcoGM/Bose music system: AM/FM seek/scan stereo radio w/clock, cassette and four speakers ($895). CB radio ($215). Radio delete ($276 credit). Lift-off transparent roof panels ($595). Custom two-tone paint ($428) w/lower body accents. Custom adj. sport cloth bucket seats ($625). Leather bucket seats ($400). P255/50VR16 SBR BSW tires on 16 in. aluminum wheels ($561).

HISTORY: Introduced: March 25, 1984. Model year production: 51,547 (in extended model year). Calendar year production: 35,661. Calendar year sales by U.S. dealers: 30,424. Model year sales by U.S. dealers: 53,877 (including 25,891 sold during the 1983 model year).

Historical Footnotes: Car and Driver called the new Corvette "the most advanced production car on the planet." Motor Trend described it as "the best-handling production car in the world, regardless of price." Heady praise indeed. During its year-and-a-half model run, orders poured in well ahead of schedule, even though the new edition cost over $5000 more than the 1982 version. The body offered the lowest drag coefficient of any Corvette: just 0.341. Testing at GM's Proving Grounds revealed 0.95G lateral acceleration—the highest ever for a production car. Only 6,443 Corvettes had a four-speed manual transmission, and only 410 came with a performance axle ratio, but 3,729 had Delco/Bilstein shocks installed.

1985 CORVETTE

1985 Corvette coupe (CP)

SERIES Y — V-8 — Two details marked the 1985 Corvette as different from its newly-restyled 1984 predecessor: a 'Tuned Port Injection' nameplate on fender molding, and straight tailpipes at the rear. That nameplate identified a new 350 cu. in. (5.7-liter) V-8 under the hood, with port fuel injection and a 230- horsepower rating. Peak torque reached 330 lbs.ft, compared to 290 from the prior Cross-Fire V-8. City fuel economy ratings went up too. Otherwise, the only evident change was a slight strengthening in the intensity of the red and silver body colors. Corvette's smoothly sloped nose, adorned by nothing other than the circular emblem, held retracting halogen headlamps. Wide parking/signal lamps nearly filled the space between license plate and outer edge. Wide horizontal side marker lenses were just ahead of the front wheels. The large air cleaner of '82 was replaced by an elongated plenum chamber with eight curved aluminum runners. Mounted ahead of the radiator, it ducted incoming air into the plenum through a Bosch hot-wire mass airflow sensor. Those tuned runners were meant to boost power at low to medium R.P.M., following a principle similar to that used for the tall intake stacks in racing engines. Electronic Spark Control sensed knocking and adjusted timing to fit fuel octane. Under the chassis, the '85 carried a reworked suspension (both standard and optional Z51) to soften the ride without losing control. The Z51 handling package now included 9.5-inch wheels all around, along with Delco-Bilstein gas-charged shock absorbers and heavy-duty cooling. Stabilizer bars on the Z51 were thicker. Spring rates on both suspensions were reduced. Cast aluminum wheels held P255/50VR16 Eagle GT tires. Master cylinders used a new large-capacity plastic booster. Manual gearboxes drove rear axles with 8.5-inch ring gears. Instrument cluster graphics had a bolder look. Roof panels added more solar screening. An optional leather- trimmed sport seat arrived at mid-year. Corvette standard equipment included an electronic information center, air conditioning, limited-slip differential, power four-wheel disc brakes, power steering, cornering lamps, and seek/scan AM/FM stereo radio with four speakers and automatic power antenna. Also standard: a lighter, digital clock, tachometer, intermittent wipers, halogen foglamps, and side window defoggers. Corvettes had contour high-back cloth bucket seats, power windows, a trip odometer, theft-deterrent system with starter interrupt, compact spare tire, dual electric remote-control sport mirrors, and tinted glass. Bodies held black belt, windshield and bodyside moldings, plus color-keyed rocker panel moldings. Four-speed overdrive automatic transmission was standard, with four-speed manual (overdrive in three gears) available at no extra cost.

1985 Corvette coupe (CP)

1985 Corvette coupe (CP)

I.D. DATA: Coding of the 17-symbol Vehicle Identification Number (VIN) was similar to 1984. Model year code changed to 'F' for 1985.

CORVETTE

Model Number	Body/Style Number	Body Type & Seating	Factory Price	Shipping Weight	Production Total
1Y	Y07	2-dr. Hatch Cpe-2P	24873	3088	39,729

ENGINE DATA: BASE V-8: 90-degree, overhead valve V-8. Cast iron block and head. Displacement: 350 cu. in. (5.7 liters). Bore & stroke: 4.00 x 3.48 in. Compression ratio: 9.0:1. Brake horsepower: 230 at 4000 R.P.M. Torque: 330 lbs.-ft. at 3200 R.P.M. Five main bearings. Hydraulic valve lifters. Tuned-port fuel injection. RPO Code: L98. VIN Code: 8.

CHASSIS DATA: Wheelbase: 96.2 in. Overall length: 176.5 in. Height: 46.4 in. Width: 71.0 in. Front Tread: 59.6 in. Rear Tread: 60.4 in. Wheel Size: 16 x 8.5 in. Standard Tires: P255/50VR16 SBR.

TECHNICAL: Transmission: THM 700R4 four-speed overdrive automatic standard. Gear ratios: (1st) 3.06:1; (2nd) 1.63:1; (3rd) 1.00:1; (4th) 0.70:1; (Rev) 2.29:1. Four-speed overdrive manual transmission available at no extra charge: (1st) 2.88:1; (2nd) 1.91:1; (3rd) 1.33:1; (4th) 1.00:1; (Rev) 2.78:1; planetary overdrive ratios: (2nd) 1.28:1; (3rd) 0.89:1; (4th) 0.67:1. Standard final drive ratio: 3.07:1 or 2.73:1. Steering/Suspension/BrakesBody: same as 1984. Fuel tank: 20.0 gal.

CORVETTE OPTIONS: Four-speed overdrive manual trans. (NC). California emission system ($99). Performance axle ratio ($22). Delco/Bilstein shock absorbers ($189). H.D. cooling ($225). Performance handling pkg. (Z51): H.D. springs and front/rear stabilizers, Delco/Bilstein shocks and H.D. cooling ($470). Rear defogger system incl. mirrors ($160). Electronic cruise control w/resume ($185). Six-way power driver's seat ($215). Power door locks ($170). Electronic-tuning AM/FM stereo radio with seek/scan, clock and cassette player ($122). DelcoGM/Bose music system: AM/FM seek/scan stereo radio w/clock, cassette and four speakers ($895). Radio delete ($256 credit). Lift-off transparent roof panels ($595). Custom two-tone paint ($428) w/lower body accents. Custom adj. sport cloth bucket seats ($625). Leather bucket seats ($400).

HISTORY: Introduced: October 2, 1984. Model year production: 39,729. Calendar year production: 46,304. Calendar year sales by U.S. dealers: 37,956. Model year sales by U.S. dealers: 37,878.

Historical Footnotes: Chevrolet claimed a 17 percent reduction in 0-60 MPH times with the TPI powerplant. To save weight, Corvettes used not only the fiberglass leaf springs front and rear, but over 400 pounds of aluminum parts (including steering/suspension components and frame members). A total of 14,802 Corvettes had the Z51 performance handling package installed, 9,333 had Delco/Bilstein shocks ordered separately, and only 9,576 had a four-speed manual transmission. Only 16 Corvettes are listed as having a CB radio, and only 82 with an economy rear axle ratio.

1986 CORVETTE

1986 Corvette Indy Pace Car convertible (CH)

SERIES Y — V-8 — One new body style and an engineering development were the highlights of 1986. Corvette added a convertible during the model year, the first since 1975. And computerized anti-lock braking system (ABS) was made standard. During hard braking, the system (based on a Bosch ABS II design) detected any wheel that was about to lock, then altered braking pressure in a pulsating action to prevent

lockup from happening. Drivers could feel the pulses in the pedal. This safety innovation helped the driver to maintain traction and keep the car under directional control, without skidding, even on slick and slippery surfaces. Corvette's engine was the same 350 cu. in. (5.7-liter) 230-horsepower, tuned-port fuel-injected V-8 as 1985, but with centrally-positioned copper-core spark plugs this year. New aluminum cylinder heads had sintered metal valve seats and increased intake port flow, plus higher (9.5:1) compression. The engine had an aluminum intake manifold with tuned runners, magnesium rocker covers, and outside-air induction system. Both four-plus-three manual and four-speed overdrive automatic transmissions were available, now with an upshift indicator light on the instrument cluster. Three monolith atalytic converters in a new dual exhaust system kept emissions down during warmup. Cast alloy wheels gained a new raised hub emblem and a brushed-aluminum look. The instrument cluster was tilted to cut glare. The sport seat from 1985 was made standard this year, with leather optional. Electronic air conditioning, announced earlier, arrived as a late option. Otherwise, standard equipment was similar to 1985. A new electronic Vehicle Anti-Theft System (VATS) was also made standard. A small electrically-coded pellet was embedded in the ignition key, while a decoder was hidden in the car. When the key was placed in the ignition, its resistance code was "read." Unless that code was compatible, the starter relay wouldn't close and the Electronic Control Module wouldn't activate the fuel injectors. Corvettes came in one new solid color this year (yellow), plus a white/silver metallic two-tone. Carryover body colors were white, black, bright red, silver metallic, medium gray metallic, and gold metallic. New this year were five metallics: medium blue, silver beige, copper, medium brown, and dark red. Corvette's back end held four round recessed lenses, with 'Corvette' block letters in the center. The license plate sat in a recessed housing. Cloth seats had lateral support and back-angle adjustments. Roadsters (convertibles) had a manual top with velour inner liner. The yellow console button that ordinarily controlled Corvette's hatch release opened a fiberglass panel ehind the seats to reveal the top storage area. Cast alloy 16 x 8-1/2 in. aluminum alloy wheels held unidirectional P255/50VR16 Goodyear Eagle GT SBR tires.

I.D. DATA: Coding of the 17-symbol Vehicle Identification Number (VIN) was similar to 1984-85, but body type codes were now either '07' for hatchback coupe or '67' for the new convertible. Model year code changed to 'G' for 1986.

1986 Corvette coupe (CMD)

CORVETTE

Model Number	Body/Style Number	Body Type & Seating	Factory Price	Shipping Weight	Production Total
1Y	Y07	2-dr. Hatch Cpe-2P	27027	3086	27,794
1Y	Y67	2-dr. Conv. Cpe-2P	32032	N/A	7,315

ENGINE DATA: BASE V-8: 90-degree, overhead valve V-8. Cast iron block and head. Displacement: 350 cu. in. (5.7 liters). Bore & stroke: 4.00 x 3.48 in. Compression ratio: 9.5:1. Brake horsepower: 230 at 4000 R.P.M. Torque: 330 lbs.-ft. at 3200 R.P.M. Five main bearings. Hydraulic valve lifters. Tuned-port fuel injection. RPO Code: L98. VIN Code: 8.

CHASSIS DATA: Wheelbase: 96.2 in. Overall length: 176.5 in. Height: 46.4 in. Width: 71.0 in. Front Tread: 59.6 in. Rear Tread: 60.4 in. Wheel Size: 16 x 8.5 in. (9.5 in. wide with optional Z51 suspension). Standard Tires: P245/50VR16 or P255/50VR16 SBR.

TECHNICAL: Transmission: THM 700R4 four-speed overdrive automatic transmission standard. Gear ratios: (1st) 3.06:1; (2nd) 1.63:1; (3rd) 1.00:1; (4th) 0.70:1; (Rev) 2.29:1. Four-speed manual overdrive transmission available at no extra charge. Standard final drive ratio: 3.07:1 w/manual, 2.59:1 or 3.07:1 w/auto. Steering/Suspension: same as 1984-85. Brakes: Anti-lock; power four-wheel disc. Ignition: Electronic. Body construction: Fiberglass; separate ladder frame with cross-members. Fuel tank: 20.0 gal.

CORVETTE OPTIONS: Four-speed overdrive manual trans. with upshift indicator (NC). California emission system ($99). Performance axle ratio ($22). Performance handling pkg. (Z51): H.D. springs and front/rear stabilizers, Delco/Bilstein shocks, H.D. radiator and boost fan, engine cooler and P255/50VR16 Eagle BSW tires ($470). Delco/Bilstein shock absorbers ($189). H.D. radiator ($40). Radiator boost cooling fan ($75). Engine oil cooler ($110). Custom feature pkg.: rear defogger, dual heated electric remote mirrors, map lights, console lighting ($195). Electronic air cond. ($150). Rear defogger system incl. mirrors ($165). Electronic cruise control w/resume ($185). Six-way power driver's seat ($225). Power door locks ($175). Electronic-tuning AM/FM stereo radio with seek/scan, clock and cassette player ($122). DelcoGM/Bose music system: AM/FM seek/scan stereo radio w/clock, cassette and four speakers ($895). Radio delete ($256 credit). Removable roof panel ($595); dual panels ($895) incl. blue or bronze transparent panel. Custom two-tone paint ($428) w/lower body accents. Leather bucket seats ($400). Leather adj. sport bucket seats ($1025).

HISTORY: Introduced: October 3, 1985. Model year production: 35,109. Calendar year production (U.S.): 28,410. Model year sales by U.S. dealers: 35,969.

Historical Footnotes: Styled like the Corvette roadster that would serve as '86 Indy Pace Car, the new convertible went on sale late in the model year. The actual pace car was bright yellow, differing from showroom models only in its special track lights. Chevrolet considered "pace car" to be synonymous with "open top," so all convertibles were considered pace car models. Special decals were packed in the car, but not mounted. Corvette's was the only street-legal vehicle to pace the Indy race since 1978 (also a Corvette). Instead of a conversion by an outside company, as had become the practice for most 1980s ragtops, Corvette's roadster was built by Chevrolet, right alongside the coupe. Problems with cracking of the new aluminum cylinder heads meant first '86 models had old cast iron heads. Those difficulties soon were remedied. As many potential buyers observed, the new anti-theft system would require half an hour's work to overcome, which would dissuade thieves who are typically in a hurry. A total of 6,242 Corvettes had removable roof panels installed, and 12,821 came with the Z51 performance handling package. Only 6,835 Corvettes carried the MM4 four-speed manual transmission.

While all American-built cars shrunk in size and power over the 1976-86 decade, none changed more than Chrysler. Riding a 124-inch wheelbase, on a platform introduced two years earlier, the '76 Chrysler Newport and New Yorker Brougham carried on the long tradition of luxury (and excess). Both continued the pillarless four-door hardtop a little longer, while Town & Country wagons displayed their own brand of deluxe styling. Imperial, the poshest of all, had been dropped after 1975; but New Yorker slipped neatly into its niche with an increase in luxury extras. New Yorker's engine was the huge 440 cu. in. V-8, producing 205 horsepower. Chryslers, then, were big and expensive. With one exception, that is: the Canadian-built Cordoba coupe, introduced in 1975. It cost as much as a Newport, but sat on a 115-inch wheelbase. Engine choices reached up to a high-performance 400 V-8, rated 240 horsepower, and Cordoba sold better than all other Chrysler put together. Strong promotion by actor Ricardo Montalban didn't hurt. Still, overall sales slipped downward, as they had in 1975.

The following year brought another surprise: the luxury mid-size LeBaron, smallest Chrysler ever, added as a 1977½ model. Designed as a rival to Cadillac's Seville and Lincoln's new Versailles (as well as Mercedes), LeBaron was actually a derivative of the Dodge Aspen/Plymouth Volare duo. No matter, though; Seville and Versailles had origins in "lesser" models too. LeBaron offered one unique mechanical change, turning the familiar Chrysler torsion bars from their customary position to transverse mounting. While Cordoba sales sagged a bit, both the new LeBaron and carryover full-size models performed well in the marketplace.

1978 LeBaron Medallion coupe (JG)

Full-size Chryslers kept their ample dimensions for 1978, even though GM models had been downsized a year earlier. The big Town & Country station wagon was dropped, but its name continued on a smaller LeBaron version. New Yorker Broughams could have a Salon decor package with silver paint and vinyl roof, while TorqueFlite transmissions added a lockup torque converter. Strong LeBaron sales couldn't keep the corporate total from slipping downward.

All-new Newport/New Yorker four-doors emerged for 1979, reduced to 118.5 inch wheelbase. Both the 400 and 440 cu. in. V-8s disappeared, leaving a 360 as the biggest engine. Newport actually came with a standard

Slant Six. Both models still managed to look big, even though they lost over 800 pounds. New Yorkers featured hidden headlamps, and could have a Fifth Avenue Edition option, highlighted by cream/beige body paint. Cordoba brought the '300' nameplate back to life temporarily on an option package with 195-horsepower engine, but it was a pale imitation of past 300 glories. While the smaller full-size models sold better than their predecessors, Cordoba slipped again.

A revised 1980 Cordoba dropped down to 112.7 inch wheelbase—same as LeBaron—and carried a standard six-cylinder engine. Most desirable example might be the Corinthian Edition, especially with a high-output V-8 under the hood. LeBaron adopted a luxurious Fifth Avenue package similar to New Yorker's, with formal roofline and carriage roof, but only 654 were installed. This was a tough year for the industry as a whole, but worse yet for Chrysler, whose financial troubles were beginning to get plenty of publicity. Sales fell by one-third. Among other troubles, Chrysler just wasn't responding to the public demand for greater fuel efficiency. . Lee Iacocca was now in charge, though. As just about everyone in the world became aware over the next few years, his adminstration managed to turn things around for Chrysler, with the help of government-guaranteed loans that were paid back in full much sooner than many had predicted.

Another Canadian-built model appeared the next year, reviving a familiar name. The ultra-luxurious "bustleback" Imperial carried a modest engine, though: a fuel-injected 318 V-8. In fact, that was now the biggest engine in the Chrysler lineup. In an attempt to attract a few younger customers, Cordoba turned to a more sporty 'LS' model with 300-style crossbar grille and "soft" front end. Most prospects seemed to resist the temptation. At the upper end of the scale was the latest Fifth Avenue version of the New Yorker, with just about every extra on its equipment list.

New Yorkers turned to a smaller platform for 1982 (LeBaron's old one, actually, as that model took a new form). The Newport name was gone. LeBaron was now front-wheel-drive, with a four-cylinder engine under the hood—a trend that would continue through the coming years. Most tempting was the new LeBaron convertible—first American to return to ragtop production after the demise of Cadillac's soft-top Eldorado in '76. A fair number of the posh Imperials had been sold in 1981, but the total slipped close to 2,300 this year. An 'FS' package (for Frank Sinatra) might make a rather rare collectible one day, but didn't do much for Imperial sales at the time.

Traditionalists might be forgiven for failing to recognize Chryslers as the 1980s continued. LeBaron got a standard five-speed gearbox for 1983—though its new Town & Country convertible brought back memories of T&C ragtops in the 1940s. In a shuffling of nameplates, the rear-drive model was now called New Yorker Fifth Avenue. How come? Because there was another New Yorker now: front-drive, along with a related E Class model. Attracting considerable publicity, not all of it favorable, was the new Voice Alert system—the car that talked. Some observers felt it talked too much, or about

the wrong things. Next year, it added a shutoff switch. Even the new Executive sedan and limousine turned to front-wheel drive and four-cylinder power, vastly removed from the last previous limos back in 1970.

Imperial did not return for 1984, but a sporty new Laser hatchback coupe appeared, near twin to Dodge's Daytona and a far cry from past Chryslers. Adding further surprise, a turbocharged four-cylinder engine became available, not only on Laser but under LeBaron, E Class and New Yorker hoods. Fifth Avenue was the last remaining rear-drive, with the old 318 cu. in. V-8 engine.

Yet another model joined up the next year: the LeBaron GTS performance-oriented sedan, also available with turbo power. Model year sales rose again, just as they had in '84. Both the new GTS and old rear-drive Fifth Avenue found surprising numbers of customers. That rear-drive had to pay a gas guzzler tax in 1986, but remained a strong contender for sales. Limousines had standard turbocharged four-cylinder engines—and what a shock that must have been to potential customers who'd not followed Chrysler's changes over the past few years.

Which Chryslers might collectors find worth a glance? Cordobas had their fans and foes when new, but the 1980 and later models, in particular, seem to look better all the time. Corinthian Editions and special roofs may be the best bets. Early LeBaron convertibles probably are worth hanging onto. The slow-selling 1981-83 Imperial didn't appeal to everyone's taste, but could easily become collectible. A "Sinatra" edition would be the rarest. Lasers? Maybe not yet, but a turbocharged XT wouldn't be the worst example to keep in a garage for a while. Then too, holding onto one of those final big guzzlers of 1976-78 might not be a bad idea.

1976 Chrysler

None of the Chrysler models displayed notable change in appearance for 1976. The luxury Imperial had been dropped at the end of the '75 model year; but New Yorker and, to a lesser extent, Newport were upgraded to take over its niche in the market. Both Newport and New Yorker still offered a real (pillarless) four-door hardtop, along with some big V-8 engines. Late in the 1976 model year, an Electronic Lean Burn System was introduced on all 400 and 440 cu. in. V-8s. A miniature computer absorbed data from sensors on throttle position, engine R.P.M., manifold vacuum and coolant temperature, then continually adjusted spark timing for the leanest (most economical) mixture. Lean Burn engines were available everywhere except California. An optional trailer towing package included large side mirrors.

1976 Cordoba two-door hardtop (CC)

CORDOBA — SERIES SS — V-8 — Chrysler's personal-luxury coupe, billed as "the small Chrysler," appeared for 1975. This year it gained a new fine-line vertical grille texture, along with new standard full-length bodyside and decklid tape stripes with filigree inserts. The grille was made up of thin vertical bars, with pattern continued in bumper slots below. Separate 'Chrysler' letters stood on its upper header molding, while front fenders held a 'Cordoba' nameplate and medallion. The stand-up hood ornament displayed a Cordoba crest. Round park/signal lamps were between the grille and headlamps. At the sides were small three-section front and rear side marker lenses. Vertical rectangular taillamps each were split by a vertical divider bar with emblem. Backup lamps were mounted in the back bumper. The rear license plate housing was recessed. Cordoba script was on the decklid; Cordoba medallions on wheel covers. Cordoba had standard opera windows and opera lamps, full wheel opening moldings, bright aluminum windshield moldings, bright roof drip and window moldings, bright belt and hood rear moldings, bright sill moldings, plus bumper guards and rub strips. Seven body colors were new: Saddle Tan, plus metallic Jamaican Blue, Jade Green, Caramel Tan, Light Chestnut, Vintage Red Sunfire, and Deep Sherwood Sunfire. Also available were (metallic) Silver Cloud, Platinum, Astral Blue, Starlight Blue, Bittersweet, Inca Gold, and Spanish Gold; plus Rallye Red, Yellow Blaze, Golden Fawn, Spinnaker White, and Formal Black. Interior colors were blue, red, green, black and gold, along with tan (new this year). Base engine was a 400 cu. in. V-8. Either a 360 or 318 V-8 was available at no extra cost. Standard equipment included power steering and brakes, three-speed TorqueFlite automatic, GR78 x 15 SBR WSW tires, digital clock, dual horns, and front/rear sway bars. New Brazilian Rosewood woodtone trim arrived on instrument panel and door panels. The dash held gauges for alternator, temperature, oil pressure and fuel, plus an LED low-fuel warning. Dials had new graphics, metric readings, and bright bezels. A new three-spoke deep-dish steering wheel held a Cordoba medallion and horn switches on spokes. Optional: a new two-spoke tilt wheel. A new optional 60/40 front seat had dual seatback recliners and folding center armrest. Other options included power front seats and door locks, electric decklid release, manual sunroof, automatic speed control, tachometer, and space-saving spare tire.

1976 Newport two-door hardtop (JG)

150

NEWPORT — SERIES CL/CM — V-8 — Three body styles were offered in the Newport line: hardtop coupe, hardtop sedan, and four-door sedan. Newport Custom had some distinctive styling features, extra equipment, and a price tag about $400 higher. All full-size models rode a 124 in. wheelbase. Newport had a chrome-plated grille with an undivided crosshatch pattern and a medallion on the driver's side. 'Chrysler' lettering was on its upper header molding. Side-by-side round quad headlamps sat in squarish bright housings. Fender tips held wraparound park/marker lenses, outboard of the headlamps. 'Chrysler' script was also on the decklid; Newport nameplates on front fenders. Recessed vertical taillamps were made up of two side-by-side segments that extended down into a notch in the bumper, with small backup lamps directly below (inset into bumper). Newport had bright headlamp bezels and hood rear-edge molding, bright windshield and back window moldings, bright roof drip rail and pillar moldings, plus bright wheel opening moldings with black paint-fill. Front bumper guards were standard (rear optional). Deluxe wheel covers highlighted standard HR78 x 15 SBR blackwall tires. Seats had a standard front folding center armrest. Base engine was a 400 cu. in. V-8 with 2Bbl. carburetor (4Bbl. in California). Both 360 and 440 cu. in. V-8s were available. Newport Custom's new grille had a fine crosshatch pattern divided by one vertical and two horizontal bars into six sections, with bright upper header containing 'CHRYSLER' letters. The bumper had two small slots, alongside a center license plate housing. A Griffin medallion was on the stand-up hood ornament and the fuel filler door. 'Newport Custom' nameplates were on front fenders. Bodysides displayed full-length dual paint stripes. New wide horizontal taillamps each were split by a horizontal divider bar. Standard Custom features included bright sill, decklid and quarter extension moldings; plus bright door upper frame moldings on the four-door sedan. Base Newports had wheel lip moldings only; Customs had both sill transition and wheel lip moldings. Standard Custom 50/50 split-bench front seats had front/rear folding center armrests. A three-spoke steering wheel was new this year. Among the optional items were rear wheel-opening skirts. Body colors were: Powder Blue, Sahara Beige, Saddle Tan, Golden Fawn, Spinnaker White, and Formal Black; plus metallic Silver Cloud, Platinum, Astral Blue, Starlight Blue, Vintage Red, Bittersweet, Jade Green, Tropic Green, Deep Sherwood, Moondust, Dark Chestnut, Inca Gold, and Spanish Gold.

1976 Town & Country station wagon (JG)

TOWN & COUNTRY WAGON — SERIES CP — V-8 — Front-end appearance of the full-size station wagon was the same as Newport Custom. The grille was divided into six rectangular sections by chrome moldings, with pattern continued in openings in the bumper. A new two-spoke steering wheel had woodtone accents. Molded fiberglass formed the headliner. Wiper-arm mounted windshield washer jets were standard. Options included a heated doorgate window defroster, lighted passenger vanity mirror, and an automatic height control system that adjusted rear shock absorbers using air pressure. Base engine was a 440 cu. in. V-8; optional, a 400 V-8. Standard tires were LR78 x 15 steel-belted radials.

1976 New Yorker Brougham four-door hardtop (CC)

NEW YORKER BROUGHAM — SERIES CS — V-8 — In taking over the role of the departed Imperial, the New Yorker Brougham got a luxury front end with concealed headlamps, plus unique rear end styling. The four-door sedan was dropped, but New Yorker came in two-door or four-door hardtop form. The Imperial-like "waterfall" grille had a pattern of thin vertical bars that wrapped over the top (and was repeated within twin bumper slots below), divided into two sections by a body-color vertical element. Clear park/signal lamps rode the fender tips. The front license plate was bumper-mounted, below the left headlamp cover. Large horizontal front side marker lenses sat low in fenders. On the hood was a stand-up medallion. Vertical taillamps extended down into bumper tips. 'Chrysler' lettering was on the driver's side headlamp cover; 'New Yorker' on front fenders; 'Chrysler New Yorker' on the decklid. Rear roof pillars displayed a 'Brougham' medallion. Broughams had rear wheel skirts with bright lower moldings, bright front wheel opening moldings, dual full-length bodyside accent stripes, and unique wheel covers. The driver's mirror was remote-controlled. Standard engine was a 4Bbl. 440 cu. in. V-8; standard tires JR78 x 15 steel-belted radial whitewalls. Wheelbase was the same as Newport's: 124 inches. Standard fittings included a digital clock, 65-amp alternator, color-keyed shag carpeting, rear reading lamps and lavalier straps. Cornering lamps were among the many options.

I.D. DATA: Chrysler's 13-symbol Vehicle Identification Number (VIN) was on the upper left corner of the instrument panel, between the wiper pivot and 'A' post, visible through the windshield. Symbol one indicates Car Line: 'S' Cordoba; 'C' other Chrysler. Symbol two is Price Class: 'S' Special; 'L' Low; 'M' Medium; 'P' Premium. The next two symbols denote body type: '22' 2dr. pillared hardtop coupe; '23' 2-dr. hardtop coupe; '41' 4-dr. sedan; '43' 4-dr. hardtop; '45' two-seat station wagon; '46' three-seat wagon. Symbol five is the engine code: 'G' V8318 2Bbl.; 'K' V8360 2Bbl.; 'M' V8400 2Bbl.; 'N' V8400 4Bbl.; 'P' Hi-perf. V8400 4Bbl.; 'T' V8440 4Bbl. Next is the model year code: '6' 1976. Symbol seven indicates assembly plant: 'A' Lynch Road (Detroit); 'D' Belvidere, Illinois; 'R' Windsor, Ontario. The last six digits make up the sequential serial number. An abbreviated version of the VIN is also stamped on the engine block (on a pad to rear of right engine mount) and on the transmission housing. Serial numbers for 318 and 360 cu. in. engines are coded as follows: first letter series (model year); second assembly plant; next three digits indicate displacement (cu. in.); next one or two letters denote model; next four digits show the build date; and final four digits are the engine sequence number. Coding of 400 and 440 cu. in. engines is: first letter series (model year); next three digits are displacement; next one or two letters indicate model; next four digits show the build date; and the final digit reveals the shift on which the engine was built. Information on over/undersized parts is stamped on 318/360 engines at the left front of the block, just below the head; on 400 V-8, just ahead of the No. 2 cylinder, next to the distributor; and on left bank pad of 440 V-8, adjacent to front tappet rail. A Vehicle Safety Certification Label that shows (among other data) the date of manufacture is attached to the rear facing of the driver's door.

CORDOBA (V-8)

Series Number	Body/Style Number	Body Type & Seating	Factory Price	Shipping Weight	Production Total
SS	22	2-dr. HT Cpe-6P	5392	3957	167,618

Production Note: All Cordobas were built in Canada.

NEWPORT (V-8)

CL	23	2-dr. HT Cpe-6P	5076	4431	2,916
CL	41	4-dr. Sed-6P	4993	4415	12,926
CL	43	4-dr. HT Sed-6P	5147	4500	3,448

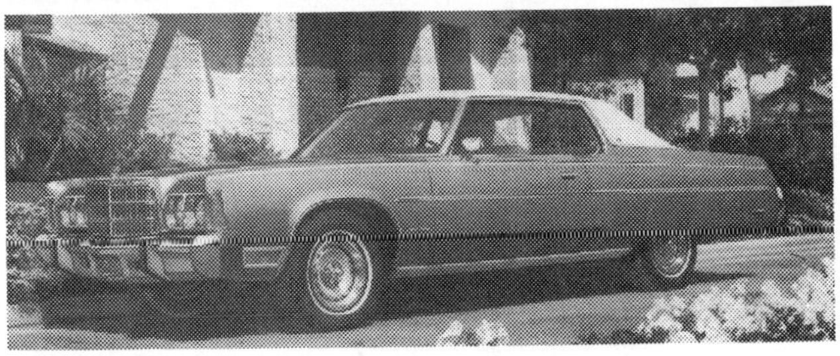

1976 Newport Custom two-door hardtop (CC)

NEWPORT CUSTOM (V-8)

CM	23	2-dr. HT Cpe-6P	5479	4483	3,855
CM	41	4-dr. Sed-6P	5407	4457	9,448
CM	43	4-dr. HT Sed-6P	5576	4547	6,497

TOWN & COUNTRY STATION WAGON (V-8)

CP	45	4-dr. 2S Wag-6P	6084	4982	1,271
CP	46	4-dr. 3S Wag-8P	6244	5002	3,227

NEW YORKER BROUGHAM (V-8)

CS	23	2-dr. HT Cpe-6P	6641	4752	9,748
CS	43	4-dr. HT Sed-6P	6737	4832	23,984

ENGINE DATA: OPTIONAL V-8 (Cordoba): 90-degree, overhead valve V-8. Cast iron block and head. Displacement: 318 cu. in. (5.2 liters). Bore & stroke: 3.91 x 3.31 in. Compression ratio: 8.5:1. Brake horsepower: 150 at 4000 R.P.M. Torque: 255 lbs.-ft. at 1600 R.P.M. Five main bearings. Hydraulic valve lifters. Carburetor: 2Bbl. Carter BBD8069S (or BBD8099S). VIN Code: G. OPTIONAL V-8 (Cordoba, Newport): 90-degree, overhead valve V-8. Cast iron block and head. Displacement: 360 cu. in. (5.9 liters). Bore & stroke: 4.00 x 3.58 in. Compression ratio: 8.4:1. Brake horsepower: 170 at 4000 R.P.M. Torque: 280 lbs.-ft. at 2400 R.P.M. Five main bearings. Hydraulic valve lifters. Carburetor: 2Bbl. Holley R7364A (Carter TQ9055S in Calif.). VIN Code: K. BASE V-8 (Cordoba, Newport); OPTIONAL (N.Y. Brougham): 90-degree, overhead valve V-8. Cast iron block and head. Displacement: 400 cu. in. (6.6 liters). Bore & stroke: 4.34 x 3.38 in. Compression ratio: 8.2:1. Brake horsepower: 175 at 4000 R.P.M. Torque: 300 lbs.-ft. at 2400 R.P.M. Five main bearings. Hydraulic valve lifters. Carburetor: 2Bbl. Holley R7366A. VIN Code: M. OPTIONAL HIGH-PERFORMANCE V-8 (Cordoba): Same as 400 cu. in. V-8 above, except with Carter TQ9054S 4Bbl. carburetor B.H.P.: 240 at 4400 R.P.M. Torque: 325 lbs.-ft. at 3200 R.P.M. VIN Code: P. OPTIONAL LEAN BURN V-8 (all models): Same as 400 cu. in. V-8 above, except with Electronic Lean Burn System and 4Bbl. Carter TQ9064S or TQ9097S carburetor B.H.P.: 210 at 4400 R.P.M. Torque: 305 lbs.-ft. at 3200 R.P.M. VIN Code: N. BASE V-8 (Town & Country, N.Y. Brougham); OPTIONAL (Newport): 90-degree, overhead valve V-8. Cast iron block and head. Displacement: 440 cu. in. (7.2 liters). Bore & stroke: 4.32 x 3.75 in. Compression ratio: 8.2:1. Brake horsepower: 205 at 3600 R.P.M. Torque: 320 lbs.-ft. at 2000 R.P.M. Five main bearings. Hydraulic valve lifters. Carburetor: 4Bbl. Carter TQ9058S (TQ9059S in Calif.). VIN Code: T.

CHASSIS DATA: Wheelbase: (Cordoba) 115.0 in.; (others) 124.0 in. Overall length: (Cordoba) 215.3 in.; (Newport) 227.1 in.; (Newport Cust) 226.6 in.; (T&C wag) 227.7 in.; (N.Y. Brghm) 232.7 in. Height: (Cord.) 52.6 in.; (Newpt HT cpe/sed) 54.4 in.; (Newpt sed) 55.2 in.; (T&C) 57.6 in.; (N.Y. Brghm) 54.5 in. Width: (Cord.) 77.1 in.; (Newpt cpe) 79.7 in.; (Newpt 4 dr.) 79.5 in.; (T&C) 79.4 in.; (N.Y. Brghm cpe) 79.7 in.; (N.Y. Brghm sed) 79.5 in. Front Tread: (Cord.) 61.9 in.; (others) 64.0 in. Rear Tread: (Cord.) 62.0 in.; (others) 63.4 in. Wheel size: 15 x 5.5 in. exc. (T&C, N.Y. Brghm) 15 x 6.5 in. Standard Tires: (Cord.) GR78 x 15 WSW; (Newpt) HR78 x 15; (T&C) LR78 x 15; (N.Y. Brghm) JR78 x 15.

TECHNICAL: Transmission: TorqueFlite three-speed automatic standard. Gear ratios: (1st) 2.45:1; (2nd) 1.45:1; (3rd) 1.00:1; (Rev) 2.22:1. Standard final drive ratio: 2.71:1. Steering: recirculating ball, power-assisted. Suspension: (Cordoba) front torsion bars, rear asymmetrical leaf springs and front/rear sway bars; (others) front torsion bars, sway bar and lower trailing links, and rear asymmetrical leaf springs. Brakes: Front disc, rear drum (power-assisted). Ignition: Electronic. Body construction: Unibody. Fuel tank: (Cordoba) 25.5 gal.; (Newpt/N.Y. sedan) 26.5 gal.; (T&C wag) 24.0 gal.

DRIVETRAIN OPTIONS: Engines: 400 cu. in., 4Bbl. V-8 w/single exhaust: Cordoba ($45); Newpt/Cust ($45); N.Y., T&C (NC). 400 cu. in., 4Bbl. V-8 w/dual exhaust: Cordoba ($96). 440 cu. in., 4Bbl. V-8: Newpt ($184). Transmission/Differential: Sure grip differential: Cordoba ($54); others ($58). Optional axle ratio ($15). Suspension: Heavy-duty susp. ($20-$27). H.D. shock absorbers ($7) exc. Cordoba. Automatic height control ($100) exc. Cordoba. Other: Light trailer towing pkg.: Cord. ($74); Heavy trailer towing pkg.: Cord. ($298).

CORDOBA CONVENIENCE/APPEARANCE OPTIONS: Option Packages: Easy-order pkg. ($856). Comfort/Convenience: Air conditioning ($490). Strato ventilation ($20). Rear defroster ($81). Automatic speed control ($77). Power bench seat ($130). Power driver's bucket or 60/40 seat ($130). Power windows ($104). Power door locks ($65). Power decklid release ($19). Tilt steering wheel ($59). Tinted glass ($52). Tinted windshield ($38). Tachometer ($62). Lighting and Mirrors: Remote-control left mirror ($15). Dual remote chrome mirrors ($29-$44). Dual sport remote mirrors: painted or chrome ($37-$52). Entertainment: AM radio ($79); w/8track stereo tape player ($119-$220). AM/FM radio ($71-$149). AM/FM stereo radio ($153-$254); w/8track stereo tape player ($256-$357). Search tune AM/FM stereo radio ($213-$314). Rear speaker ($22) w/radio. Exterior Trim: Sunroof, manual ($311). Full vinyl roof ($115) exc. ($15) w/easy-order pkg. Landau vinyl roof ($100). Vinyl side molding ($40). Door edge guards ($7). Undercoating ($30). Interior Trim/Upholstery: Console ($18). Castilian velour cloth/vinyl bench seat w/armrest ($18). Velour cloth/vinyl 60/40 split bench seat w/dual recliners ($124). Leather bucket seats ($196). Wheels and Tires: Wire wheel covers ($62). Styled wheels ($113). HR78 x 15 SBR WSW tires ($25). GR70 x 15 SBR RWL ($37). Space-saver spare (NC).

NEWPORT/NEW YORKER/T&C CONVENIENCE/APPEARANCE OPTIONS: Option Packages: St. Regis pkg. (padded canopy boar-grain vinyl roof w/formal opera windows): Newpt Cust, N.Y. ($455- $598). Light pkg.: Newpt ($75); T&C ($37). Basic group: Newpt ($894); T&C ($950); N.Y. ($698). Easy order pkg.: Newpt ($1245-$1268); T&C ($1370); N.Y. ($1327). Town & Country pkg.: T&C ($122). Deluxe sound insulation pkg. ($41). Comfort/Convenience: Air cond. ($533). Auto-temp air cond. ($618) exc. ($85) w/option pkg. Rear defroster ($82) exc. T&C. Auto. speed control ($83). Power six-way bench seat: Newpt ($132). Power six-way 50/50 driver's seat ($132) exc. base Newpt. Power six-way 50/50 driver/passenger seat ($132-$264) exc. Newpt. Power windows ($167). Power door locks ($66-$95). Luxury steering wheel ($17). Tilt/telescope steering wheel ($83-$100). Tinted glass ($66). Electric clock: Newpt ($21). Digital clock ($24-$45). Lighting and Mirrors: Cornering lamps ($43). Remote-control driver's mirror ($15). Remote passenger mirror: N.Y. ($30). Dual remote mirrors ($45) exc. N.Y. Lighted vanity mirror ($43). Entertainment: AM radio ($99). AM/FM radio ($62-$161). Search tune AM/FM stereo radio ($197-$318). AM/FM stereo w/8track tape player ($57-$375). Rear speaker ($22). Power antenna ($42) w/radio. Exterior Trim: Power sunroof ($754-$897). Vinyl roof ($143). Vinyl side molding ($47). Door edge protectors ($8-$13). Upper door frame moldings: Newpt sed ($29). Interior Trim/Upholstery. Vinyl bench seat trim: Newpt ($31). Castilian velour cloth/vinyl seat trim: Newpt ($84). Highlander cloth/vinyl 50/50 bench seat trim: Newpt Cust ($49). Leather 50/50 bench seat: N.Y. ($210). Wheels and Tires: Chrome styled wheels ($147); N/A T&C. Premier wheel covers ($45). HR78 x 15 WSW ($43). JR78 x 15 WSW ($31-$74). LR78 x 15 WSW ($36-$110).

HISTORY: Introduced: October 16, 1975. Model year production: Chrysler reported total shipments of 244,938 units (incl. Canadian- built Cordobas). Calendar year production: (U.S.) 127,466; (Canadian Cordoba) 200,986. Calendar year sales by U.S. dealers: 277,809 (incl. 175,456 Cordobas) for a 3.2 percent share of the market. Model year sales by U.S. dealers: 278,233 (incl. 180,938 Cordobas).

Historical Footnotes: Sales slipped this year, just as they had in 1975. Cordoba had sold well that year, however, and continued to find a lot of buyers in '76. In fact, more Cordobas were sold than all other Chryslers put together, and the personal- luxury coupe ranked second only to Chevrolet's Monte Carlo in that league. Movie stars pushing Chrysler products helped Cordoba at its debut and later. Also on the promotional scene, Chrysler produced a TV commercial with Jack Jones singing "What a beautiful New Yorker." That may have helped almost 40,000 Broughams find buyers for the 1976 model year, well above the 1975 total. In mid-year 1975, Chrysler-Plymouth Divison had added the imported Arrow, built by Mitsubishi in Japan.

1977 Chrysler

Most Chrysler V-8s now had a Lean Burn engine using computer-controlled electronic spark advancea forerunner of the fully computerized controls that soon would become standard in the industry. Introduced first on the 400 cu. in. V-8 during 1976, Lean Burn was offered this year on the 360, 400 and 440 V-8s; and later in the season, also the 318. For the first time, a Lean Burn (440 cu. in.) was announced for California Chryslers. One goal was to meet emissions standards without a catalytic converter. But because of stricter standards, Lean Burn engines had to add a catalytic converter anyway. Also new this year was a more powerful version of the reliable 225 slant six, dubbed the "Super Six."

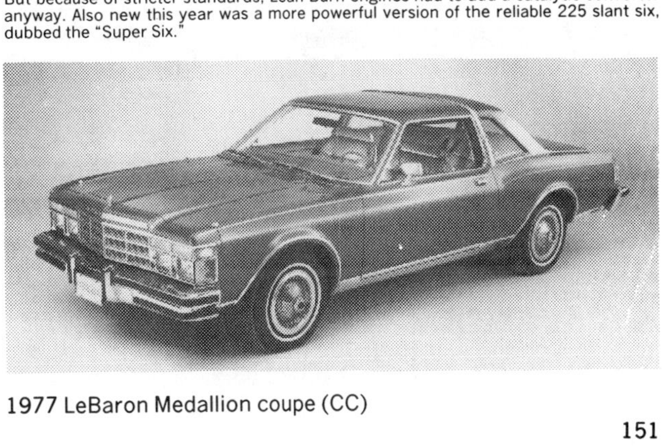

1977 LeBaron Medallion coupe (CC)

LEBARON — SERIES FH/FP — V-8 — As part of its attempt to recapture a greater share of the luxury market, Chrysler introduced the M-body LeBaron luxury mid-size as a 1977-1/2 model. The Medallion, in particular, emphasized luxury interior detailing. LeBaron was intended to rival Cadillac Seville, Lincoln Versailles, and Mercedes-Benz. Dodge Diplomat was its mate. Arriving at Chrysler-Plymouth dealers in May 1977, it was called a "new-size" Chrysler; a "leaner, lighter Chrysler" for the modern era; and "the beginning of a totally new class of automobiles." Wheelbase (112.7 in.) was identical to Plymouth Volare, and LeBaron even shared some Volare components. LeBaron, in fact, was the smallest (and lightest) Chrysler ever produced. The suspension used transverse torsion bars in front, with leaf-spring (live axle) rear. LeBaron's profile was highlighted by a long hood and sleek deck. Up front, its grille was made up of thin horizontal bars, split into an 8 x 4 pattern of wide rectangular holes by three vertical and two horizontal divider bars. Amber quad parking lamps stood directly above the quad rectangular headlamps, and both continued around the sides to meet two-section side marker lenses. The solid round stand-up hood ornament held a crest. Two-door (fixed-pillar) coupe and four-door sedan bodies were offered. LeBaron's coupe had longer door windows than Plymouth Volare, but smaller rear quarter windows. The back window showed a slight "vee" peak at center. Inside was a standard 60/40 split-bench front seat in choices of trim that ranged up to soft Corinthian leather. Medallion sedans had a padded vinyl roof, three overhead assist handles, rear vanity lamps with mirrors, and velour/vinyl or leather upholstery with fold-down center armrest. A curved left-hand dashboard section put radio and heat controls near the driver. Fuel, alternator and temperature gauges were included. Standard equipment included a 318 cu. in. V-8 with Electronic Lean Burn system, TorqueFlite automatic transmission, power brakes and steering, radial tires, and such extras as overhead reading lamps. Options included a Landau roof, 15 in. forged aluminum wheels, lighted vanity mirror, air conditioning, vinyl roof, cruise control, electric rear defroster, tilt steering, power seats, power windows, power door locks, and a sliding steel sunroof.

1977 Cordoba two-door hardtop (CC)

CORDOBA — SERIES S — V-8 — New front and rear styling arrived on Cordoba, which was called "the most successful car ever to carry the Chrysler nameplate." A new formal-look grille had a very fine crosshatch pattern dominated by vertical bars, with 'Chrysler' lettering in its header. As before, the pattern repeated in bumper slots. Otherwise, the front end (and overall) appearance didn't change drastically. Opera windows had a more rectangular shape. New taillamps were similar to 1976 but now recessed, with a different crest. Backup lamps again were inset in bumper slots, close to bumper guards. Interiors held five lights and standard plush Verdi velour cloth/vinyl split-bench seating with center armrest. Standard engine was the Lean Burn 400 cu. in. V-8 with 4Bbl. carburetor; optional, a 318 V-8. California and high-altitude Cordobas could have a 360 V-8. GR78 x 15 glass-belted radial blackwall tires rode 5.5 in. wheels. Cordoba colors were Claret Red, Golden Fawn, Jasmine Yellow and Spinnaker White; plus metallic Silver Cloud, Cadet Blue, Starlight Blue Sunfire, Vintage Red Sunfire, Jade Green, Forest Green Sunfire, Burnished Copper, Russet Sunfire, Caramel Tan, Light Chestnut, Coffee Sunfire, Inca Gold, Spanish Gold, or Formal Black Sunfire. Joining the option list were two new roof styles. The Crown landau roof in padded elk-grain vinyl had unique opera windows and back window, lighted by a slender band across the top. A new T-bar roof had lift-out tinted glass panels. Also available: a manual sunroof, plus Halo or Landau vinyl roof with opera windows and slim opera lamps. Interior options included an all-vinyl bench seat or Corinthian leather buckets, along with 60/40 reclining seats in Checkmate cloth or Verdi velour. New this year was a tilt steering wheel with hand-stitched Corinthian leather-covered rim.

1977 Newport four-door hardtop (CC)

NEWPORT — SERIES CL — V-8 — Moderate front and rear restyling hit Chrysler's lower-rung full-size, while its Custom model was discontinued. Upgrading of the base Newport put it closer to the Custom's trim level. Newport's new classic-style grille (borrowed from the former Custom) had wide, bright surround moldings. The new wide horizontal taillamps also came from Custom, and the hood ornament was new. Otherwise, appearance was largely unchanged. Newport's rear bumpers had rubber-covered steel corner guards. A four-door pillarless hardtop remained available. The two-door hardtop could have a St. Regis decor package with padded Seneca grain vinyl canopy roof (forward half), formal opera windows, and color-keyed moldings for roof and opera windows. Base engine was the 400 cu. in. Lean Burn V-8. Standard inside was a cloth/vinyl split-back bench seat with folding center armrest. An optional 50/50 Williamsburg cloth bench seat had vinyl accents. Full-size body colors were: Wedgewood Blue, Mojave Beige, Golden Fawn, Jasmine Yellow, and Spinnaker White; plus metallic Silver Cloud, Cadet Blue, Starlight Blue Sunfire, Vintage Red Sunfire, Jade Green, Forest Green Sunfire, Burnished Copper, Russet Sunfire, Coffee Sunfire, Moondust, Inca Gold, Spanish Gold, and Formal Black Sunfire.

TOWN & COUNTRY WAGON — SERIES CP — V-8 — Station wagons duplicated Newport's front-end styling and wraparound taillamps, but came with standard 440 cu. in. Lean Burn V-8. The three-way doorgate had a power window and automatic lock. A roof air deflector was standard. Inside was all-vinyl 50/50 bench seating. Wagons rode standard blackwall LR78 x 15 steel-belted radial tires, but weren't available in California or high-altitude areas. Options included wheelhouse opening skirts.

1977 New Yorker Brougham four-door hardtop (CC)

NEW YORKER BROUGHAM — SERIES CS — V-8 — The luxury Brougham continued its "classic" appearance and "Torsion-Quiet" ride with little change. Both two-door and four-hardtop styles were still available. 50/50 seating came in Cortez ribbed cord and crushed velour. Instrument panels displayed simulated rosewood accents, while interiors held front and rear armrests. Standard equipment included a digital clock, remote-control left mirror, reading lamps, built-in pillows on rear pillars, and lavaliere straps (on four-door). Options included a power sunroof, electric rear defroster, new vent windows (four-door), and lighted vanity mirror. The optional St. Regis group consisted of a formal Seneca grain padded vinyl canopy (forward-half) roof, opera windows, and color-keyed molding trim for roof and opera windows. Only the St. Regis could have Burnished Silver metallic paint.

I.D. DATA: Chrysler's 13-symbol Vehicle Identification Number (VIN) was on the upper left corner of the instrument panel, between the wiper pivot and 'A' post, visible through the windshield. Symbol one indicates Car Line: 'F' LeBaron; 'S' Cordoba; 'C' other Chrysler. Symbol two is Price Class: 'S' Special; 'L' Low; 'H' High; 'P' Premium. The next two symbols denote body type: '22' 2dr. pillared hardtop coupe; '23' 2-dr. hardtop coupe; '41' 4-dr. sedan; '43' 4-dr. hardtop; '45' two-seat station wagon; '46' three-seat wagon. Symbol five is the engine code: 'G' V8318 2Bbl.; 'K' V8360 2Bbl.; 'N' V8400 2Bbl.; 'T' V8440 4Bbl. Next is the model year code: '7' 1977. Symbol seven indicates assembly plant: 'D' Belvidere, Illinois; 'R' Windsor, Ontario. The last six digits make up the sequential serial number. Engine number coding and locations are the same as 1976.

LEBARON (V-8)

Series Number	Body/Style Number	Body Type & Seating	Factory Price	Shipping Weight	Production Total
FH	22	2-dr. Cpe-6P	5066	3510	7,280
FH	41	4-dr. Sed-6P	5224	3555	12,600

LEBARON MEDALLION (V-8)

FP	22	2-dr. Cpe-6P	5436	3591	14,444
FP	41	4-dr. Sed-6P	5594	3645	11,776

CORDOBA (V-8)

SP	22	2-dr. HT Cpe-6P	5368	N/A	Note 1
SS	22	2-dr. HT Cpe-6P	5418	4004	163,138

Note 1: Figure shown includes all Cordobas, which were built in Canada.

NEWPORT (V-8)

CL	23	2-dr. HT Cpe-6P	5374	4354	10,566
CL	41	4-dr. Sed-6P	5280	4372	32,506
CL	43	4-dr. HT Sed-6P	5433	4410	14,808

TOWN & COUNTRY STATION WAGON (V-8)

CP	45	4-dr. 2S Wag-6P	6461	4935	1,930
CP	46	4-dr. 3S Wag-8P	6647	4961	5,345

NEW YORKER BROUGHAM (V-8)

CS	23	2-dr. HT Cpe-6P	7090	4676	16,875
CS	43	4-dr. HT Sed-6P	7215	4739	45,252

ENGINE DATA: BASE V-8 (LeBaron); **OPTIONAL** (Cordoba): 90-degree, overhead valve V-8. Cast iron block and head. Displacement: 318 cu. in. (5.2 liters). Bore & stroke: 3.91 x 3.31 in. Compression ratio: 8.5:1. Brake horsepower: 145 at 4000 R.P.M. Torque: 245 lbs.-ft. at 1600 R.P.M. Five main bearings. Hydraulic valve lifters. Carburetor: 2Bbl. Carter BBD8133S (Cordoba); BBD8142S or R7990A (LeBaron). VIN Code: G. **OPTIONAL V-8** (Cordoba, Newport): 90-degree, overhead valve V-8. Cast iron block and head. Displacement: 360 cu. in. (5.9 liters). Bore & stroke: 4.00 x 3.58 in. Compression ratio: 8.4:1. Brake horsepower: 155 at 3600 R.P.M. Torque: 275 lbs.-ft. at 2000 R.P.M. Five main bearings. Hydraulic valve lifters. Carburetor: 2Bbl. Holley 2245. VIN Code: K.

Note: A 4Bbl. V8360 was available in California and high- altitude areas, rated 170 horsepower. BASE V-8 (Cordoba, Newport); OPTIONAL (N.Y. Brougham, T&C): 90-degree, overhead valve V-8. Cast iron block and head. Displacement: 400 cu. in. (6.6 liters). Bore & stroke: 4.34 x 3.38 in. Compression ratio: 8.2:1. Brake horsepower: 190 at 3600 R.P.M. Torque: 305 lbs.-ft. at 3200 R.P.M. Five main bearings. Hydraulic valve lifters. Carburetor: 4Bbl. Carter TQ9102S. Electronic Lean Burn System. VIN Code: N. BASE V-8 (Town & Country, N.Y. Brougham); OPTIONAL (Newport): 90-degree, overhead valve V-8. Cast iron block and head. Displacement: 440 cu. in. (7.2 liters). Bore & stroke: 4.32 x 3.75 in. Compression ratio: 8.2:1. Brake horsepower: 195 at 3600 R.P.M. Torque: 320 lbs.-ft. at 2000 R.P.M. Five main bearings. Hydraulic valve lifters. Carburetor: 4Bbl. Carter TQ9078S. Electronic Lean Burn System. VIN Code: T.

CHASSIS DATA: Wheelbase: (LeBaron) 112.7 in.; (Cordoba) 115.0 in.; (others) 124.0 in. Overall length: (LeB cpe) 204.1 in.; (LeB sed) 206.1 in.; (Cord.) 215.3 in.; (Newport) 226.6 in.; (T&C wag) 227.7 in.; (N.Y. Brghm) 231.0 in. Height: (LeB cpe) 53.3 in.; (LeB sed) 55.3 in.; (Cord.) 52.6 in.; (Newpt 2-dr. HT) 54.3 in.; (Newpt sed) 55.1 in.; (Newpt 4-dr. HT) 54.4 in.; (T&C) 57.0 in.; (N.Y. Brghm) 54.5 in. Width: (LeB cpe) 73.5 in.; (LeB sed) 72.8 in.; (Cord.) 77.1 in.; (Newpt/N.Y. cpe) 79.7 in.; (Newpt/N.Y. sed) 79.5 in.; (T&C) 79.4 in. Front Tread: (LeB) 60.0 in.; (Cord.) 61.9 in.; (others) 64.0 in. Rear Tread: (LeB) 58.5 in.; (Cord.) 62.0 in.; (others) 63.4 in. Wheel size: 15 x 5.5 in. exc. (N.Y. Brghm) 15 x 6.0 in.; (T&C) 15 x 6.5 in. Standard Tires: (LeB) FR78 x 15 polysteel; (Cord.) GR78 x 15 GBR BSW; (Newpt) HR78 x 15 SBR BSW; (T&C) LR78 x 15 SBR WSW; (N.Y. Brghm) JR78 x 15 SBR WSW.

TECHNICAL: Transmission: TorqueFlite three-speed automatic standard. Gear ratios: (1st) 2.45:1; (2nd) 1.45:1; (3rd) 1.00:1; (Rev) 2.22:1. Standard final drive ratio: 2.71:1 exc. (LeB) 2.76:1; (Cord. V8318) 2.45:1; (N.Y. Brghm) 3.2:1. Steering: recirculating ball, power-assisted. Suspension: (Cordoba) front torsion bars, rear asymmetrical leaf springs and front/rear sway bars; (others) front torsion bars and sway bar, rear asymmetrical leaf springs. Brakes: Front disc, rear drum (power-assisted). Ignition: Electronic. Body construction: Unibody. Fuel tank: (LeB) 19.5 gal.; (Cordoba) 25.5 gal.; (Newpt/N.Y. sedan) 26.5 gal.; (T&C wag) 24.0 gal.

DRIVETRAIN OPTIONS: Engines: 318 or 360 cu. in. V-8: Cordoba (NC). 360 or 400 cu. in. V-8: Newpt/N.Y. (NC). 440 cu. in., 4Bbl. V-8: Newpt ($196). Transmission/Differential: Sure grip differential: Cordoba ($57); others ($61). Optional axle ratio ($16). Suspension: Heavy-duty susp. ($20-$27). H.D. shock absorbers ($7) exc. T&C. Automatic height control ($109) exc. Cordoba. Other: Light trailer towing pkg.: Cord. ($79); Newpt, T&C ($80). Heavy trailer towing pkg.: Cord. ($316); Newpt/N.Y./T&C ($321). Fuel pacer system ($22). Long-life battery: Cord. ($31); N.Y., T&C ($32). Engine block heater ($18) exc. Cordoba. California emission system ($74-$95). High-altitude emission system ($23-$24).

CORDOBA CONVENIENCE/APPEARANCE OPTIONS: Option Packages: Easy-order pkg. ($1110). Light pkg. ($26). Comfort/Convenience: Air conditioning ($518). Rear defroster ($86). Automatic speed control ($84). Power bench seat ($143). Power driver's bucket or 60/40 seat ($143). Power windows ($113). Power door locks ($71). Power decklid release ($21). Leather steering wheel ($36). Tilt steering wheel ($59). Tinted glass ($57). Tinted windshield ($40). Tachometer ($66). Digital clock ($47). Locking gas cap ($7). Lighting and Mirrors: Remote-control left mirror ($16). Dual remote chrome mirrors ($31-$47). Dual sport remote mirrors: painted or chrome ($39-$55). Lighted vanity mirror ($45). Entertainment: AM radio ($76). AM/FM radio ($74-$149). AM/FM stereo radio ($134-$234); w/8track stereo tape player ($232-$332). Search tune AM/FM stereo radio ($214-$314). Rear speaker ($24). Exterior Trim: T-Bar roof w/lift-out panels ($605). Crown landau elk-grain vinyl roof w/over-the-top illuminated lamp band ($579-$733). Sunroof, manual ($330). Full vinyl roof ($116) exc. ($5) w/easy-order pkg. Landau vinyl roof ($112). Vinyl side molding ($42). Door edge guards ($8). Bumper rub strips ($32). Bodyside tape stripes ($42). Decklid tape stripe ($21). Undercoating ($32). Interior Trim/Upholstery: Console ($18). Vinyl bench seat ($29). Velour/vinyl 60/40 bench seat w/armrest and recliners ($132). Cloth/vinyl 60/40 bench seat w/Checkmate trim, armrest and recliners ($152). Leather bucket seats ($208). Color-keyed floor mats ($18). Pedal dress-up ($9). Trunk dress-up ($45). Wheels and Tires: Wire wheel covers ($73). Styled wheels ($120). GR78 x 15 GBR WSW (NC to $43). GR78 x 15 SBR WSW ($50-$93). HR78 x 15 SBR WSW tires ($77-$120). GR70 x 15 fiber-belt RWL ($40-$82). Conventional spare tire (NC).

NEWPORT/NEW YORKER/T&C CONVENIENCE/APPEARANCE OPTIONS: Option Packages: St. Regis pkg. (padded canopy seneca-grain vinyl roof w/formal opera windows): Newpt, N.Y. ($455-$600). Light pkg.: Newpt ($80); T&C ($39). Basic group: Newpt ($939); T&C ($999); N.Y. ($730). Easy order pkg.: Newpt ($1305); T&C ($1429); N.Y. ($1384). Town & Country pkg.: T&C ($128). Deluxe sound insulation pkg.: Newpt ($43). Comfort/Convenience: Air cond. ($560). Auto-temp air cond. ($645) exc. ($85) w/option pkg. Rear defroster ($87). Auto. speed control ($88). Power six-way bench seat: Newpt ($145). Power six-way 50/50 driver's seat ($146). Power six-way 50/50 driver/passenger seat ($145-$290). Power windows ($179) exc. N.Y. Power door locks ($72-$102). Power decklid release ($21). Luxury steering wheel ($18) exc. N.Y. Tilt/telescope steering wheel ($88-$106). Tinted glass ($72). Electric clock: Newpt ($22). Digital clock ($26-$48). Deluxe wiper/washer pkg.: Newpt ($17). Locking gas cap ($8). Lighting and Mirrors: Cornering lamps ($46). Remote-control driver's mirror ($16) exc. N.Y. Remote passenger mirror: N.Y. ($31). Dual remote mirrors ($32-$48) exc. N.Y. Lighted vanity mirror ($46). Entertainment: AM radio ($99). AM/FM radio ($62-$161). Search tune AM/FM stereo radio ($195-$318); std. on N.Y. AM/FM stereo w/8track tape player ($31-$349). Rear speaker ($25). Power antenna ($44). Exterior Trim: Power sunroof w/vinyl roof ($764-$908). Vinyl roof ($145). Manual vent windows: 4dr. ($43). Vinyl side moldings ($48). Wheelhouse opening skirts: Newpt ($46). Door edge protectors ($9-$14). Upper door frame moldings: Newpt 4dr. ($31). Rear bumper guards: T&C ($24). Undercoating ($37) exc. N.Y. Interior Trim/Upholstery: Vinyl bench seat trim: Newpt ($33). Cloth 50/50 bench seat: Newpt ($127). Vinyl 50/50 bench seat: Newpt ($141). Leather 50/50 bench seat: N.Y. ($223). Color- keyed floor mats ($20). Trunk dress-up ($24-$45). Wheels and Tires: Chrome styled wheels ($156); N/A T&C. Premier wheel covers ($48). HR78 x 15 WSW (NC to $48). JR78 x 15 WSW ($32-$80). LR78 x 15 WSW ($38-$118). Conventional spare tire (NC).

LEBARON OPTIONS LeBaron arrived late in the model year. Options were similar to those offered during the complete 1978 model year; see that listing below.

HISTORY: Introduced: October 1, 1976. Model year production: 336,520 (incl. Canadian-built Cordobas). Calendar year production (U.S.): 247,063. Calendar year sales by U.S. dealers: 317,012 for a 3.5 percent share of the market. Model year sales by U.S. dealers: 302,629 (incl. 147,814 Cordobas).

Historical Footnotes: Impressive model year sales were led by a strong start for the new LeBaron. Newport/New Yorker sales also rose, unlike those of the full-size Plymouth. Cordoba declined, however. Sales for the Chrysler-Plymouth Divison enjoyed only a slight increase, even though production jumped by some 22 percent. The LeBaron name had enjoyed a long, if sporadic history at Chrysler, stretching back to 1933 when the company took over the Briggs body company. But LeBaron-bodied Chryslers had been built even before that time.

1978 Chrysler

Major technical news for 1978 was the arrival of a new lockup torque converter for the TorqueFlite automatic transmission. Direct drive cut in at about 27-31 MPH. All V-8 engines now had Electronic Lean Burn, including the California four-barrel 318. The newest electronic sound system was an AM/FM stereo with foot-operated floor switch search-tune capability. Also new: a 40-channel CB transceiver built into AM or AM/FM stereo radios. Chrysler and Plymouth were trimmed in weight to boost fuel economy. Many parts were redesigned with aircraft-type lightening holes in steel panels. Models weighed an average 300 pounds less than their predecessors of 1977. Corrosion protection included the use of one-side galvanized sheet steel for front fenders and door outer panels of compacts and mid-sizes; also in door outer panels of standard-size cars. Big Chrysler wagons dropped out of the lineup, but LeBaron added a new wagon to carry on the Town & Country name.

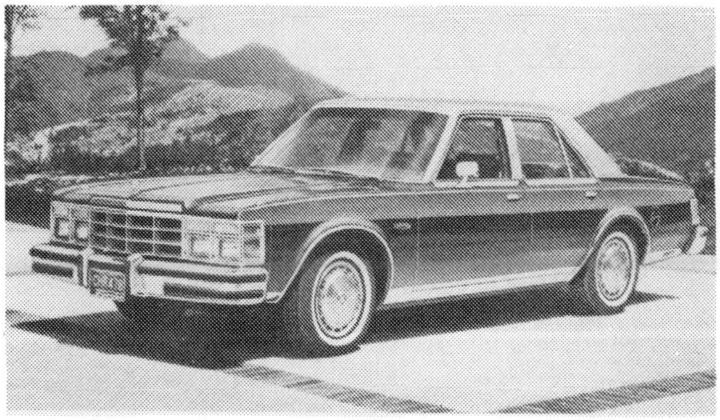

1978 LeBaron S four-door sedan (JG)

LEBARON — SERIES F — SIX/V-8 — A Town & Country station wagon joined the two-door coupe and four-door sedan that had been introduced in spring 1977, on the same 112.7 in. wheelbase. LeBaron had first appeared with a standard 318 cu. in. V-8; but for full year 1978 the 225 cu. in. Super Six became standard, with either a 318 or 360 V-8 optional. Overdrive-4 manual transmission was standard with both the six and 318 V-8. A new low-budget 'S' series was priced about $200 lower than base LeBarons. LeBaron's grille had bold rectangular openings framing fine horizontal chromed bars. 'Chrysler' lettering was on the bright upper grille molding. Quad side-by-side rectangular headlamps sat directly below rectangular parking lamps. Chromed headlamp/parking lamp framing wrapped around to car sides to frame amber marker lamps and cornering lamp lenses. On the hood was a stand-up eagle ornament. Opera lamps were standard on two-doors; padded full vinyl roof on four-doors. Wraparound taillamps held eagle medallions. Door pull straps were standard, as were power brakes and steering. The step-up Medallion added center-pillar assist handles (two-door),

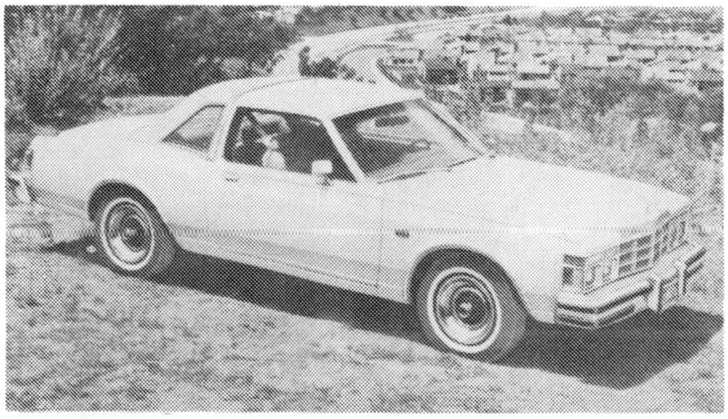

1978 LeBaron coupe (JG)

door courtesy lights, rear pillar vanity mirrors with lamps (four- door), and a map reading lamp. LeBaron tires were FR78 x 15 glass-belted radial blackwalls. Marine teakwood woodtone bodyside and liftgate trim on the new Town & Country wagon was framed with simulated white ash moldings. Authentic grain patterns and simulated finger- locking joints enhanced its effect. Wide sill moldings and wheel opening moldings were available if the "wood" exterior was deleted. The carpeted cargo compartment held stainless- steel skid strips. 'LeBaron' script was on front fenders and tailgate, 'Chrysler' block letters on the liftgate, a Chrysler eagle on cornering lamp lenses. A Town & Country nameplate stood on quarter panels, and a LeBaron medallion on 'C' pillars. Rear bumper guards held protective inserts. Bright moldings went on the windshield, quarter windows, liftgate window, roof drip rail, belt, and door upper frame. New 60/40 thin front seats with center armrests were standard on wagon and Medallion.

CORDOBA — SERIES SS — V-8 — The personal-luxury Cordoba coupe featured a new front end look, highlighted by vertically-stacked rectangular headlamps that replaced the former round units. The plainer square crosshatch pattern of the new finely-meshed, forward- jutting chrome grille continued in twin bumper slots below. 'Chrysler' lettering again appeared in the grille header. At the corners of front-fender end panels were combined park/signal/marker lamps (clear/amber/clear). 'Cordoba' script stood just ahead of the door, accompanied by a round emblem. The see-thru stand-up hood ornament consisted of a round insignia inside a five-sided frame. This year's decklid showed a sharper character line. Taillamps with round Cordoba crest were larger, and the back bumper was new. The license plate no longer extended down into the back bumper notch. Rear side marker lamps consisted of two side-by-side elements instead of one tri-section unit. Cordoba also had new wide

full-length sill moldings, plus front and rear bumper guards. Nine new colors were offered. The full list included: Dove Gray, Classic Cream, Spinnaker White and Formal Black; plus metallic Pewter Gray, Charcoal Gray Sunfire, Cadet Blue, Starlight Blue Sunfire, Tapestry Red Sunfire, Mint Green, Augusta Green Sunfire, Caramel Tan, and Sable Tan Sunfire. Inside was a new thin split-back bench seat with folding center armrest. Standard upholstery choices were Cortez ribbed cloth and Whittier cloth. Two new interior trim colors were offered: Dove Gray and Canyon Red. Instrument panel inserts were simulated Brazilian rosewood, with circular dials and miles/kilometers speedometer display. New to Cordoba was an optional 318 cu. in. V-8 with Lean Burn. Standard engine was the Lean Burn 360, with 360 also optional. A new 'S' model, priced $200 lower than the base Cordoba, amounted to 7.7 percent of total production. New options included cornering lamps and a factory-installed power sunroof. Also available: the Crown and T-bar roofs introduced in 1977, a cream-colored vinyl roof, three-spoke steering wheel with Corinthian leather-wrapped rim, forged aluminum wheels, and premium wheel covers with classic hex-nut hub and Cordoba crest. New optional low-back bucket seats came in Corinthian leather or Cortez cloth. An all-vinyl bench seat and cloth/vinyl 60/40 split-bench seats also were available.

1978 Newport coupe (CC)

NEWPORT — SERIES CL — V-8 — Both the Newport sedan and Town & Country wagon were dropped for 1978, but the T & C name emerged on the new LeBaron wagon. Newport's appearance changed little. The Lean Burn 400 cu. in. V-8 with four-barrel was now standard on both Newport and New Yorker Brougham. Newports could also have a 360 V-8. Both full-size Chryslers had six new body colors. The complete list included: Formal Black, Jasmine Yellow, Golden Fawn, Dove Gray, and Spinnaker White; plus metallic Starlight Blue Sunfire, Cadet Blue, Spanish Gold, Charcoal Gray Sunfire, Pewter Gray, Tapestry Red Sunfire, Mint Green, and Augusta Green Sunfire. The new lock-up torque converter in third gear was standard with 400 V-8s (and 360 in California), but not available with trailer-assist option, or for high altitudes. The standard Cambridge cloth/vinyl split-back bench seat had a fold-down center armrest; all-vinyl was available. New optional sill moldings enhanced the body lines. Also joining the option list was geometric-design Tuscany textured velour fabric with Newport's 50/50 optional front seat, premium wheel covers, a digital clock, and two new vinyl roof colors (red and silver). A St. Regis padded formal roof and trim was available for the Newport coupe.

1978 New Yorker Brougham four-door hardtop (CC)

NEW YORKER BROUGHAM — SERIES CS — V-8 — Luxury Broughams got a new segmented grille and modified bodyside styling, along with the six new body colors and two new optional vinyl roofs offered on both full-size models. Once again, the grille held concealed headlamps. The new divided grille, similar to the 1977 design, held a broadband top and wide center divider; but vertical bars on each side of the divider separated the tighter pattern into four sections. Along Brougham bodysides, new double tape stripes followed the lower body character lines; and at the rear, a dual tape stripe accented the decklid and matched the new side stripes. Bright vertical accent lines appeared on lens centers of the dual-element taillamps. Rearview mirrors and door handles had color-keyed accents, while the driver's mirror displayed Chrysler script. Intermittent wipers and a digital clock were now standard. Power windows continued as standard. Floating-pillow 50/50 seats were upholstered in Verdi crushed velour, with fold-down armrests. Four-doors had lavaliere straps in back and a reclining passenger seat. Rear pillars held integral pillows. The 400 cu. in. V-8 replaced the Brougham's previous 440, which was still an option this year. For $631, four-door Broughams could get an optional Salon decor package with special high-gloss silver crystal metallic paint, silver vinyl roof, formal back window, body and deck stripes, leather-covered steering wheel, and aluminum fascia road wheels. Nearly 6 percent of New Yorkers carried the Salon package. New optional wheel covers displayed brushed-finish centers and simulated hex nuts.

I.D. DATA: Chrysler's 13-symbol Vehicle Identification Number (VIN) again was on the upper left corner of the instrument panel, between the wiper pivot and 'A' post, visible through the windshield. Symbol one indicates Car Line: 'F' LeBaron; 'S' Cordoba; 'C' Newport/New Yorker. Symbol two is Price Class: 'S' Special; 'L' Low; 'M' Medium; 'H' High; 'P' Premium. The next two symbols denote body type: '22' 2-dr. pillared hardtop coupe; '23' 2-dr. hardtop coupe; '41' 4-dr. sedan; '43' 4-dr. hardtop; '45' two-seat station wagon. Symbol five is the engine code: 'D' L6225 2Bbl.; 'C' L6225 1Bbl. (Calif.); 'G' V8318 2Bbl.; 'K' V8360 2Bbl.; 'J' V8360 4Bbl. (Calif.); 'L' H.O. V8360 4Bbl.; 'N' V8400 4Bbl.; 'T' V8440 4Bbl. Next is the model year code: '8' 1978. Symbol seven indicates assembly plant: 'C' Jefferson; 'G' St. Louis; 'R' Windsor, Ontario. The last six digits make up the sequential serial number. Engine number coding is similar to 1976-77.

154

LEBARON (SIX/V-8)

Series Number	Body/Style Number	Body Type & Seating	Factory Price	Shipping Weight	Production Total
FH	22	2-dr. Cpe-6P	5114/5290	3420/3505	15,999
FH	41	4-dr. Sed-6P	5270/5446	3465/3550	22,215

LEBARON 'S' (SIX/V-8)

FM	22	2-dr. Cpe-6P	4894/5080	3335/3415	2,101
FM	41	4-dr. Sed-6P	5060/5246	3400/3485	2,101

LEBARON MEDALLION (SIX/V-8)

FP	22	2-dr. Cpe-6P	5484/5660	3495/3580	29,213
FP	41	4-dr. Sed-6P	5640/5816	3550/3635	35,259

1978 LeBaron Town & Country station wagon (JG)

LEBARON TOWN & COUNTRY (SIX/V-8)

FH	45	4-dr. Sta Wag-6P	5672/5848	3600/3685	21,504

LeBaron Price & Weight Note: Figures before the slash are for six-cylinder engine, after the slash for lowest-priced V-8 engine.

1978 Cordoba coupe (CC)

CORDOBA (V-8)

SS	22	2-dr. HT Cpe-6P	5750	4021	108,054

CORDOBA 'S' (V-8)

SS	22	2-dr. HT Cpe-6P	5550	N/A	Note 1

Note 1: Figure shown above includes both base and 'S' Cordobas, all of which were built in Canada.

NEWPORT (V-8)

CL	23	2-dr. HT Cpe-6P	5727	4394	5,987
CL	43	4-dr. HT Sed-6P	5802	4460	24,089

NEW YORKER BROUGHAM (V-8)

CS	23	2-dr. HT Cpe-6P	7591	4619	9,624
CS	43	4-dr. Pill. HT-6P	7715	4669	26,873

ENGINE DATA: BASE SIX (LeBaron): Inline, overhead valve six-cylinder. Cast iron block and head. Displacement: 225 cu. in. (3.7 liters). Bore & stroke: 3.40 x 4.12 in. Compression ratio: 8.4:1. Brake horsepower: 110 at 3600 R.P.M. Torque: 180 lbs.-ft. at 2000 R.P.M. Four main bearings. Solid valve lifters. Carburetor: 2Bbl. Carter BBD. VIN Code: D.

Note: California and high-altitude LeBarons had a 1Bbl. six- cylinder engine rated 90 horsepower. OPTIONAL V-8 (LeBaron, Cordoba): 90-degree, overhead valve V-8. Cast iron block and head. Displacement: 318 cu. in. (5.2 liters). Bore & stroke: 3.91 x 3.31 in. Compression ratio: 8.5:1. Brake horsepower: 140 at 4000 R.P.M. Torque: 245 lbs.-ft. at 1600 R.P.M. Five main bearings. Hydraulic valve lifters. Carburetor: 2Bbl. Carter BBD or Holley. Electronic Lean Burn. VIN Code: G. BASE V-8 (Cordoba 'S'); OPTIONAL (other models): 90-degree, overhead valve V-8. Cast iron block and head. Displacement: 360 cu. in. (5.9 liters). Bore & stroke: 4.00 x 3.58 in. Compression ratio: 8.4:1. Brake horsepower: 155 at 3600 R.P.M. Torque: 270 lbs.-ft. at 2400 R.P.M. Five main bearings. Hydraulic valve lifters. Carburetor: 2Bbl. Holley. Electronic Lean Burn. VIN Code: K.

Note: A 4Bbl. V8360 was available in California and high- altitude areas, rated 170 horsepower. A heavy-duty 4Bbl. was also available, without Lean Burn, rated 175 H.P. BASE V-8 (Cordoba, Newport, New Yorker); OPTIONAL (Cordoba 'S'): 90-degree, overhead valve V-8. Cast iron block and head. Displacement: 400 cu. in. (6.6 liters). Bore & stroke: 4.34 x 3.38 in. Compression ratio: 8.2:1. Brake horsepower: 190 at 3600 R.P.M. Torque: 305 lbs.-ft. at 3200 R.P.M. Five main bearings. Hydraulic valve lifters. Carburetor: 4Bbl. Carter TQ. Electronic Lean Burn System. VIN Code: N. OPTIONAL V-8 (Newport, New Yorker): 90-degree, overhead valve V-8. Cast iron block and head. Displacement: 440 cu. in. (7.2 liters). Bore & stroke: 4.32 x 3.75 in. Compression ratio: 8.2:1. Brake horsepower: 195 at 3600 R.P.M. Torque: 320 lbs.-ft. at 2000 R.P.M. Five main bearings. Hydraulic valve lifters. Carburetor: 4Bbl. Carter TQ. Electronic Lean Burn System. VIN Code: T.

CHASSIS DATA: Wheelbase: (LeBaron) 112.7 in.; (Cordoba) 114.9 in.; (others) 123.9 in. Overall length: (LeB cpe) 204.1 in.; (LeB sed) 206.1 in.; (LeB wag) 202.8 in.; (Cord.) 215.8 in.; (Newport) 227.1 in.; (N.Y.) 231.0 in. Height: (LeB cpe) 53.3 in.; (LeB sed) 55.3 in.; (LeB wag) 55.7 in.; (Cord.) 53.1 in.; (Newpt/N.Y.) 54.7 in. Width: (LeB cpe) 73.5 in.; (LeB sed/wag) 73.3 in.; (Cord.) 77.1 in.; (Newpt/N.Y. cpe) 79.7 in.; (Newpt/N.Y. sed) 79.5 in. Front Tread: (LeB) 60.0 in.; (Cord.) 61.9 in.; (others) 64.0 in. Rear Tread: (LeB) 58.5 in.; (Cord.) 62.0 in.; (others) 63.4 in. Wheel size: 15 x 5.5 in. Standard Tires: (LeB) FR78 x 15 GBR BSW; (Cord.) FR78 x 15 GBR BSW; (Newpt) GR78 x 15 BSW; (N.Y.) HR78 x 15 SBR WSW.

TECHNICAL: Transmission: Overdrive4 manual trans. standard on LeBaron cpe/sed. Gear ratios: (1st) 3.09:1; (2nd) 1.67:1; (3rd) 1.00:1; (4th) 0.71:1; (Rev) 3.00:1. TorqueFlite three-speed automatic standard (optional on LeBaron): (1st) 2.45:1; (2nd) 1.45:1; (3rd) 1.00:1; (Rev) 2.22:1. Standard final drive ratio: (LeB) 3.23:1, 2.94:1 or 2.45:1; (Cord.) 2.45:1; (Newpt/N.Y.) 2.71:1. Steering: recirculating ball, power-assisted. Suspension: (LeBaron) front transverse torsion bars with control arms and anti-sway bar, rigid rear axle with semi- elliptic leaf springs, (Cordoba) front torsion bars, rear asymmetrical leaf springs and front/rear sway bars; (Newport/N.Y.) front torsion bars and sway bar, rear asymmetrical leaf springs. Brakes: Front disc, rear drum (power-assisted). Ignition: Electronic. Body construction: Unibody. Fuel tank: (LeB) 19.5 gal.; (Cordoba) 25.5 gal.; (Newpt/N.Y. sedan) 26.5 gal.

DRIVETRAIN OPTIONS: Engines: 318 cu. in., 2Bbl. V-8: LeBaron ($176); Cordoba (NC). 318 cu. in., 4Bbl. V-8: LeB ($221). 360 cu. in., 2Bbl. V-8: LeB ($285). H.D. 360 cu. in., 2Bbl. V-8: LeB ($345). 360 cu. in., 4Bbl. V-8: LeB ($330); Cordoba (NC); Cordoba 'S' ($45); Newpt/N.Y. (NC). H.D. 360 cu. in., 4Bbl. V-8: LeB ($481); Cordoba ($102); Cordoba 'S' ($195). 400 cu. in. V-8: Cordoba 'S' ($94). H.D. 400 cu. in. V-8: Cordoba ($128); Cordoba 'S' ($222). 440 cu. in., 4Bbl. V-8: Newpt ($207). Transmission/Differential: Automatic trans.: LeB ($165). Sure grip differential: LeB/Cord. ($62); others ($68). Suspension: Heavy-duty susp. ($26-$28). H.D. shock absorbers ($7) exc. LeB. Automatic height control: Newpt/N.Y. ($122). Other: Heavy-duty trailer assist pkg.: LeB ($154); Cord. ($183); Newpt/N.Y. ($184). Long-life battery ($33-$34). Engine block heater: Newpt/N.Y. ($19). California emission system ($79-$80). High-altitude emission system ($34-$35).

LEBARON CONVENIENCE/APPEARANCE OPTIONS: Option Packages: Basic equipment pkg. ($1055-$1219). Light pkg. ($69-$80). Deluxe wiper/washer pkg. ($41). Deluxe insulation pkg. ($9-$80). Comfort/Convenience: Air conditioning ($563). Rear defroster $91). Automatic speed control ($94). Power seat ($155). Power windows ($129-$179). Power door locks ($83-$116). Power decklid or tailgate release ($22-$23). Luxury steering wheel ($19). Leather-wrapped steering wheel ($57). Tilt steering wheel ($71). Tinted glass ($65). Digital clock ($50). Locking gas cap ($7). Lighting and Mirrors: Cornering lamps ($48). Remote-control left mirror ($17); right ($33). Dual remote chrome mirrors ($33-$56). Lighted vanity mirror ($48). Entertainment: AM radio ($81). AM/CB radio ($333-$414). AM/FM radio ($81-$161). AM/FM stereo radio ($157-$237); w/CB ($490- $570). AM/FM stereo w/8track player ($256-$336). Search tune AM/FM stereo radio ($284-$365). Rear speaker ($25). Power antenna ($46). Exterior Trim: T-Bar roof w/lift-out panels ($643). Power sunroof: metal ($626); glass ($788). Landau vinyl roof ($137). Vinyl bodyside molding ($44). Front bumper guards ($21). Door edge guards ($11-$20). Decklid tape stripe ($23). Luggage rack: wag ($89). Air deflector: wag ($29). Undercoating ($24). Interior Trim/Upholstery: Vinyl bench seat ($48). Cloth 60/40 seat: wag ($140). Leather 60/40 seat ($270-$410). Color-keyed floor mats ($22). Color-keyed seatbelts ($16). Pedal dress-up ($10). Wheels and Tires: Wire wheel covers ($58-$99). Premier wheel covers ($41). Forged aluminum wheels ($208-$248). FR78 x 15 GBR WSW ($48). FR78 x 15 SBR WSW ($57-$106). Conventional spare tire (NC).

CORDOBA CONVENIENCE/APPEARANCE OPTIONS: Option Packages: Basic equipment pkg. ($1053). Light pkg. ($28). Comfort/Convenience: Air cond. ($563). Rear defroster ($91). Automatic speed control ($94). Power seat ($155). Power windows ($129). Power door locks ($83). Power decklid release ($24). Leather-wrapped steering wheel ($38). Tilt steering wheel ($71). Tinted glass ($65). Tinted windshield ($42). Tachometer ($70). Digital clock ($50). Deluxe wipers ($34). Locking gas cap ($7). Lighting and Mirrors: Cornering lamps ($48). Remote-control left mirror ($17). Dual remote chrome mirrors ($33-$50). Dual sport remote mirrors: painted or chrome ($41-$58). Lighted vanity mirror ($48). Entertainment: Same as LeBaron. Exterior Trim: T-Bar roof w/lift-out panels ($643). Crown landau elk-grain vinyl roof w/over-the-top illuminated lamp band ($668-$785). Power sunroof ($516). Full vinyl roof ($121) exc. ($5) w/easy-order pkg. Landau vinyl roof ($117). Vinyl bodyside molding ($44). Door edge guards ($11). Bumper rub strips ($35). Bodyside tape stripes ($45). Decklid tape stripe ($23). Undercoating ($34). Interior Trim/Upholstery: Console ($58). Vinyl bench seat ($31). Velour/vinyl 60/40 bench seat w/armrest and recliner ($140). Velour/vinyl bucket seats w/armrest and dual recliners ($70). Leather bucket seats ($270). Color-keyed floor mats ($22). Color-keyed seatbelts ($16). Pedal dress-up ($10). Trunk dress-up ($47). Wheels and Tires: Wire wheel covers ($99). Premium wheel covers ($41). Styled wheels ($248). GR78 x 15 GBR BSW ($21). GR78 x 15 GBR WSW (NC to $48). GR78 x 15 SBR WSW ($57-$106). HR78 x 15 SBR WSW tires ($83-$131). GR60 x 15 Aramid-belt RWL ($219-$267). Conventional spare tire (NC).

NEWPORT/NEW YORKER CONVENIENCE/APPEARANCE OPTIONS: Option Packages: New Yorker Salon pkg.: 4-dr. ($631). St. Regis pkg.: padded canopy seneca-grain vinyl roof w/formal opera windows and trim-off moldings ($493-$642). Light pkg.: Newpt ($85). Basic group: Newpt ($1222); N.Y. ($1084). Deluxe sound insulation pkg.: Newpt ($46). Comfort/Convenience: Air cond. ($602). Auto-temp air cond. ($693) exc. ($91) w/option pkg. Rear defroster ($98). Auto. speed control ($99). Power driver's seat ($157); both ($314). Power windows: Newpt ($198). Power door locks ($84-$118). Power decklid release ($24). Luxury steering wheel: Newpt $19). Tilt/telescope steering wheel ($100-$119). Tinted glass ($79). Electric clock: Newpt ($23). Digital clock: Newpt ($51). Deluxe wiper/washer pkg.: Newpt ($42). Locking gas cap ($9). Lighting and Mirrors: Cornering lamps ($49). Remote-control driver's mirror: Newpt ($17). Remote passenger mirror: N.Y. ($33). Dual remote mirrors: Newpt ($33-$51). Lighted vanity mirror ($49). Entertainment: AM radio ($103). AM/CB radio ($337-$440). AM/FM radio ($70-$173). AM/FM stereo radio w/CB ($484-$587). AM/FM stereo w/8track tape player ($197-$353). Search tune AM/FM stereo radio ($181-$369). Rear speaker ($26). Power antenna ($47). Exterior Trim: Power sunroof w/vinyl roof ($763-$912). Vinyl roof ($149). Manual vent windows: 4dr. ($46). Vinyl side moldings ($50). Sill moldings ($29). Wheelhouse opening skirts ($49). Door edge protectors ($12-$20). Bodyside tape stripe: Newpt ($46). Undercoating: Newpt ($40). Interior Trim/Upholstery: Vinyl bench seat trim: Newpt ($35). Cloth 50/50 bench seat: Newpt ($135). Vinyl 50/50 bench seat: Newpt ($150). Leather 50/50 bench seat: N.Y. ($274). Color- keyed floor mats ($24). Color-keyed seatbelts: Newpt ($17). Trunk dress-up ($27-$48). Wheels and Tires: Chrome styled wheels ($140). Premier wheel covers ($50). HR78 x 15 BSW ($25). HR78 x 15 WSW (NC to $51). JR78 x 15 WSW ($52-$103). Conventional spare tire (NC).

HISTORY: Introduced: October 7, 1977. Model year production: 303,019 (incl. Canadian-built Cordobas). Calendar year production (U.S.): 236,504. Calendar year sales by U.S. dealers: 298,892. Model year sales by U.S. dealers: 304,608 (incl. 112,560 Cordobas).

Historical Footnotes: Chrysler-Plymouth model year sales slumped by 10 percent for 1978. Sales of full-size Chryslers slipped by 35 percent. Only LeBaron made a good showing, with sales up handsomely: from just 41,536 in a short 1977 model year to 118,583 in full-year '78. This was the final year for big Chryslers, which would be replaced for 1979 by new R-body versions.

1979 Chrysler

Full-size Chryslers finally departed, their place taken over by the new R-body versions. These downsized Newport/New Yorker four-door pillared hardtops on 118.5 in. wheelbase still carried six passengers and were "engineered to provide big-car ride and handling while incorporating many new weight-saving materials for fuel efficiency." Efficiency, in fact, was this year's Chrysler/Plymouth byword. The 400 and 440 cu. in. V-8s were dropped, while the 318 and 360 were lightened. More models now came with slant six-cylinder engines (which had a new two-piece aluminum intake manifold). Newport/New Yorker were the first domestic Chrysler cars to use chrome-plated stamped aluminum bumpers, which saved 50-60 pounds. All models had aluminum and plastic master cylinders. Engines had lightweight radiators. All domestic Chrysler products had a diagnostic connector this year, on the left wheelhouse. That was to be used in conjunction with Chrysler's electronic engine performance analyzer. The 360 V-8 included a new 430-amp maintenance-free battery. Improved anti-corrosion protection including many more body panels of galvanized steel.

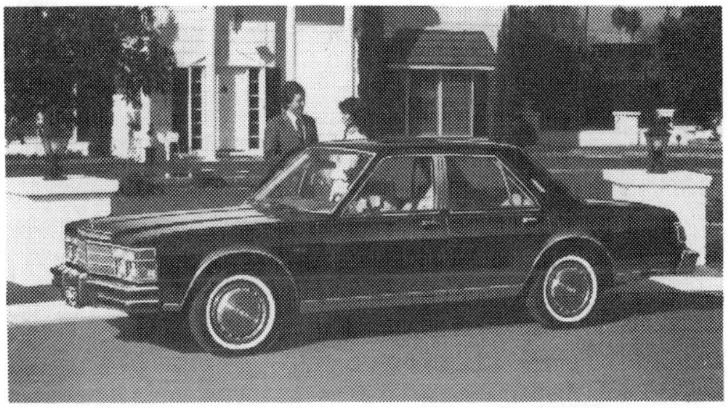

1979 LeBaron sedan (CC)

LEBARON — SERIES F — SIX/V-8 — LeBaron's lineup was revised to include base, high-line Salon, and premium Medallion models. A new chrome-plated grille had bold, rectangular openings formed by one vertical and two horizontal divider bars, enclosing a pattern of fine vertical chromed bars. Quad rectangular parking lamps again stood directly over quad rectangular headlamps. Framing for headlamps and parking lamps wrapped around fenders to contain the amber marker lamps and cornering lamp lenses. A distinctive round eagle ornament stood on the hood. Medallion 'C' pillars held a new opera lamp. New wide wraparound three- segment taillamps held bright eagle medallions in the center squares. Backup lamps were set into the bumper, while large 'Chrysler' block letters went on the panel between the taillamps. Sculptured-look quarter panels on two-doors curved downward just to the rear of the door. Rectangular opera windows with two-door vinyl roofs followed the body slope at their base. Salon models had new standard bodyside accent tape stripes. Medallions added deck lower panel accent striping. Salon/Medallion four-doors had a full padded vinyl roof with brushed stainless center pillar moldings. Town & Country wagons again had teakwood-grain woodtone appliques with simulated white ash moldings (woodtone could be deleted). Base engine was the one-barrel 225 cu. in. slant six; two-barrel Super Six optional (except in California). Both 318 and 360 cu. in. V-8s were available. Overdrive-4 manual transmission was standard with the one-barrel six. TorqueFlite with lock-up torque converter came with normal- duty V-8s (and 225 2Bbl. without air conditioning). Power brakes and steering were standard, as was a compact spare tire (except on wagons). All models had woodtone trim on instrument cluster and glovebox door. All but the base model had door-pull straps. Door courtesy lights were standard on Medallion; center-pillar assist handles on Medallion two-doors. Salon and Medallion two-doors had windshield header reading lamps; Medallion added map-reading lamps. Added to LeBaron's option list were halogen headlamps and new wire wheel covers. Two- and four-door Salons could have cloth/vinyl bucket seats with center cushion and folding center armrest. A new Landau vinyl roof with rectangular opera windows

was available on two-doors. A total of 1,936 LeBarons had the Sport appearance package installed. That package included a three-spoke steering wheel, color-keyed remote sport mirrors, and sport wheels. LeBaron body colors were: Dove Gray, Chianti Red, Spinnaker White, Formal Black and Light Cashmere; plus metallic Cadet Blue, Ensign Blue, Teal Frost, Regent Red Sunfire, Teal Green Sunfire, and Sable Tan Sunfire. Wagons could also get Medium Cashmere Metallic.

1979 Cordoba two-door hardtop (CC)

CORDOBA — SERIES SS — V-8 — A bold new vertically-textured grille, with thin vertical strips and heavy frame surround, repeated its pattern in twin bumper slots of Cordoba, billed as "the contemporary classic." Stacked quad rectangular headlamps appeared again, along with combined parking/turn signal/side marker lights mounted at corners of the front-end panel. 'Chrysler' letters were recessed into the grille header. Front fenders held Cordoba nameplates and medallions. On the hood was a stand-up ornament. Chrysler script and a Cordoba nameplate also went on the decklid. Large taillamps displayed a distinctive crest. In addition to opera windows and lamps, Cordobas held an ample array of brightwork, including full wheel opening moldings and wide lower sill moldings (plus fender and quarter extensions). Seven body colors were new. The list included: Dove Gray, Nightwatch Blue, Chianti Red, Light Cashmere, Spinnaker White and Formal Black; plus metallic Frost Blue, Teal Frost, Teal Green Sunfire, Regent Red Sunfire, and Sable Tan Sunfire. Three new trim colors were available: Midnight Blue, Teal Green, and Cashmere. The standard split-back bench seat had a folding center armrest. Woodtone trimmed the instrument panel, and there was a new standard High-Low heater/defroster. Joining the option list were semi-automatic temperature-control air conditioning, two new aluminum wheel styles, and a Roadability package. New two-tone paint treatments could be ordered with Crown and Landau vinyl roofs. Halogen headlamps and wire wheel covers also were available. A new $527 Special Appearance package included two-tone paint, accent stripes, square-cornered opera windows, black nerf stripes, dual remote sport mirrors (color-keyed to lower body), leather-wrapped three-spoke steering wheel, and Aramid-belted radial tires with gold/white sidewalls. (Sill molding extensions were deleted.) Only 693 Cordobas

1979 Cordoba 300 two-door hardtop (JG)

came with the Crown roof. One noteworthy late addition to the option list was a Cordoba "300" package (RPO Code A74) that included bucket seats, blacked-out crossbar grille with medallion, special trim, and the 195-horsepower 360 cu. in. V-8 engine. A total of 3,811 Cordobas had that package installed, for a price of $2040. This was the first use of the 300 nameplate since 1971, though the new version hardly rivalled the performance of its predecessors. Available only with Spinnaker white body paint, the package included red/white/blue bodyside and decklid striping, white sport remote mirrors, front fender louvers, '300' quarter-window decals with decorative bar below, and white bumper guards and rub strips. Inside were red leather bucket seats, an engine-turned dash applique, tachometer, and leather-wrapped steering wheel. The 300 had a special handling suspension, plus GR60 x 15 OWL Aramid-belted radial tires on aluminum wheels with a '300' medallion in each hub.

1979 Newport sedan (CC)

NEWPORT — SERIES TH — SIX/V-8 — Both Newport and the posher New Yorker shrunk considerably in size with their new R-bodies. Like the related Dodge St. Regis, they rode a 118.5 in. wheelbase and lost over 800 pounds, but both kept much of their "heavy" appearance. No two-door models remained in the new size. Newport's angled-back front end held a distinctive grille and exposed quad rectangular headlamps. The grille contained tight (3 x 3) crosshatching within larger crosshatch sections, in an overall 8 x 4 hole pattern. The grille molding was curved at the lower corners, but square at the top. Small amber side markers aligned with parking lamps, back just slightly on fenders; clear lenses were farther down, just ahead of each wheel. Wide wraparound taillamps were split by horizontal divider bars. Widely-spaced 'Chrysler' letters stood on the decklid. Newport had a chromed square stand-up hood ornament. Large "contemporary" windows held tinted glass. Interior trim came in three new colors (Midnight Blue, Teal Green and Cashmere) plus carryover Canyon Red and Dove Gray. Newport's split-back bench seat held Riviera cloth-and-vinyl trim and a folding center armrest. All-vinyl was available, as were 60/40 seats. A multi-function control lever on the steering column handled turn signals, dimmer, and wiper/washer. The two-spoke steering wheel had woodtone trim. There was a new high-low heater/defroster. In the trunk was a compact spare tire. Base engine (except in California) was the 225 cu. in. slant six, with optional 318 or 360 cu. in. V-8. An Open Road handling package was optional. Seven new body colors were offered: five metallics and two solids. Colors were: Dove Gray, Formal Black, Nightwatch Blue, Spinnaker White, Light Cashmere; plus metallic Teal Frost, Regent Red Sunfire, Sable Tan Sunfire, Medium Cashmere, Frost Blue, and Teal Green Sunfire.

1979 New Yorker sedan (CC)

NEW YORKER — SERIES TP — V-8 — Concealed headlamps were the most noticeable difference between the downsized New Yorker and its less expensive Newport mate. Though 9.5 inches shorter than before, New Yorker had a long, flat hood and distinctive grille with massive chrome header, plus a limousine-like rear area with fixed quarter windows. A Landau vinyl roof was standard (including rear-door opera windows and lamps). So were body-color door handle inserts, chromed aluminum bumper guards with protective pads, and a jeweled square hood ornament (Newport's was chrome). Headlamp bezels and front-fender end caps were made of soft urethane. Front fenders held louvers, just ahead of the door. The vertical-look grille used a pattern of many vertical bars that made up 16 sections across, with two subdued horizontal dividers. A heavy bright grille header wrapped over the top, reaching back to the hood opening. The new taillamp design reached all the way across the rear end in five sections, with 'New Yorker' block lettering in the center. Flag-type outside mirrors were standard. Colors were the same as Newport except for Light Cashmere. Inside was a standard 60/40 split bench seat with Richton cloth-and-vinyl trim and folding center armrest. Leather was available. Rear seats had a folding center armrest, plus assist straps and reading lamps. A digital clock was standard. So was a three-spoke luxury steering wheel with woodtone rim insert. A far cry from the old 440 cu. in. V-8 versions, the contemporary New Yorker had a

1979 New Yorker Fifth Avenue sedan (CC)

standard 360 (or optional 318). TorqueFlite was standard. A total of 16,113 New Yorkers came with the optional Fifth Avenue Edition package, with two-tone Designer's Cream-on-Beige paint treatment and medium beige accent stripes. Called "the most exclusive Chrysler you can own," Fifth Avenue displayed a unique pentastar hood ornament, wire wheel covers, whitewall radials with gold accent stripes, and color-keyed Laredo grain vinyl landau roof. Special edge-lighted quarter windows had 'Fifth Avenue' nomenclature instead of the standard New Yorker opera lamps. The color-coordinated theme extended to driftwood appliques on instrument and door trim panels. The leather-wrapped steering wheel had an inlaid pentastar emblem. Fifth Avenue's unique Champagne interior included garnish moldings, instrument panel, crash pad, package shelf, headlining, and 'C' pillar trim; plus light Champagne leather 60/40 split bench seat. All this added as much as $1500 to New Yorker's price tag.

I.D. DATA: Chrysler's 13-symbol Vehicle Identification Number (VIN) again was on the upper left corner of the instrument panel, between the wiper pivot and 'A' post, visible through the windshield. Symbol one indicates Car Line: 'F' LeBaron; 'S' Cordoba; 'T' Newport/New Yorker. Symbol two is Price Class: 'S' Special; 'L' Low; 'M' Medium; 'H' High; 'P' Premium. The next two symbols denote body type: '22' 2dr. pillared hardtop coupe; '41' 4-dr. sedan; '42' 4- dr. pillared hardtop; '45' two-seat station wagon. Symbol five is the engine code: 'C' L6225 1Bbl.; 'D' L6225 2Bbl.; 'G' V8318 2Bbl.; 'K' V8360 2Bbl.; 'L' V8360 4Bbl. Next is the model year code: '9' 1979. Symbol seven indicates assembly plant: 'A' Lynch Road; 'F' Newark; 'G' St. Louis; 'R' Windsor, Ontario. The last six digits make up the sequential serial number. An

abbreviated version of the VIN is also stamped on the engine block, on a pad below No. 6 spark plug (six-cylinder) or to rear of right engine mount (V-8). Six-cylinder engine numbers are at right front of block, below cylinder head; V-8, at left front of block below head. Six-cylinder coding is: first letter series; next three digits are displacment; next one or two letters indicate model; next four digits show the build date; and the final digit reveals the shift on which the engine was built. Serial numbers for V-8 engines are coded as follows: first letter series (model year); second assembly plant; next three digits indicate displacement (cu. in.); next one or two letters denote model; next four digits show the build date; and final four digits are the engine sequence number.

LEBARON (SIX/V-8)

Series Number	Body/Style Number	Body Type & Seating	Factory Price	Shipping Weight	Production Total
FM	22	2-dr. Cpe-6P	5024/5260	3270/3365	Note 1
FM	41	4-dr. Sed-6P	5122/5358	3330/3425	Note 1

Note 1: Total coupe/sedan production, 25,019.

LEBARON SALON (SIX/V-8)

FH	22	2-dr. Cpe-6P	5261/5497	3285/3385	Note 2
FH	41	4-dr. Sed-6P	5489/5725	3350/3450	Note 2

Note 2: Total coupe/sedan production, 35,906.

LEBARON MEDALLION (SIX/V-8)

FP	22	2-dr. Cpe-6P	5735/5971	3345/3440	Note 3
FP	41	4-dr. Sed-6P	5963/6199	3425/3520	Note 3

Note 3: Total coupe/sedan production, 35,475.

1979 LeBaron Town & Country station wagon (JG)

LEBARON TOWN & COUNTRY (SIX/V-8)

FH	45	4-dr. Sta Wag-6P	5955/6191	3585/3675	17,463

CORDOBA (V-8)

SS	22	2-dr. HT Cpe-6P	5995	3680	73,195

1979 Cordoba 300 two-door hardtop (JG)

CORDOBA 300 (V-8)

SP	22	2-dr. HT Cpe-6P	7666	N/A	Note 4

Note 4: Cordoba 300 was actually an option package, installed on 3,811 Cordobas. Figure shown above includes both standard and 300 Cordobas, all of which were built in Canada.

NEWPORT (SIX/V-8)

TH	42	4-dr. Pill. HT-6P	6089/6328	3484/3573	60,904

NEW YORKER (V-8)

TP	42	4-dr. Pill. HT-6P	8631	3727	43,636

FACTORY PRICE & WEIGHT NOTE: Figures to left of slash are for six- cylinder engine, to right of slash for the least expensive V-8.

ENGINE DATA: BASE SIX (LeBaron): Inline, overhead valve six-cylinder. Cast iron block and head. Displacement: 225 cu. in. (3.7 liters). Bore & stroke: 3.40 x 4.12 in. Compression ratio: 8.4:1. Brake horsepower: 100 at 3600 R.P.M. Torque: 165 lbs.-ft. at 1600 R.P.M. Four main bearings. Solid valve lifters. Carburetor: 1Bbl. Holley 1945 (R8917A). VIN Code: C. BASE SIX (Newport); OPTIONAL (LeBaron): Same as above, but with Carter BBD 2Bbl. carburetor Brake H.P.: 110 at 3600 R.P.M. Torque: 180 lbs.-ft. at 2000 R.P.M. VIN Code: D. OPTIONAL V-8 (all models): 90-degree, overhead valve V-8. Cast iron block and head. Displacement: 318 cu. in. (5.2 liters). Bore & stroke: 3.91 x 3.31 in. Compression ratio: 8.5:1. Brake horsepower: 135 at 4000 R.P.M. Torque: 250 lbs.-ft. at 1600 R.P.M. Five main bearings. Hydraulic valve lifters. Carburetor: 2Bbl. Holley 2280 (R8448A). VIN Code: G. BASE V-8 (New Yorker); OPTIONAL (other models): 90-degree, overhead valve V-8. Cast iron block and head. Displacement: 360 cu. in. (5.9 liters). Bore & stroke: 4.00 x 3.58 in. Compression ratio: 8.4:1. Brake horsepower: 150 at 3600 R.P.M. Torque: 265 lbs.-ft. at 2400 R.P.M. Five main bearings. Hydraulic valve lifters. Carburetor: 2Bbl. Holley 2245. VIN Code: K. HIGH-OUTPUT V-8; OPTIONAL (all models): Same as 360 cu. in. V-8 above, but with 4Bbl. Carter TQ carburetor Compression ratio: 8.0:1. Brake H.P.: 195 at 4000 R.P.M. Torque: 280 lbs.-ft. at 2400 R.P.M. VIN Code: L.

CHASSIS DATA: Wheelbase: (LeBaron) 112.7 in.; (Cordoba) 114.9 in.; (Newport/N.Y.) 118.5 in. Overall length: (LeB cpe) 204.1 in.; (LeB sed) 206.1 in.; (LeB wag) 202.8 in.; (Cord.) 215.8 in.; (Newport) 220.2 in.; (N.Y.) 221.5 in. Height: (LeB cpe) 53.0 in.; (LeB sed) 55.3 in.; (LeB wag) 55.7 in.; (Cord.) 52.1 in.; (Newpt/N.Y.) 54.5 in. Width: (LeB cpe) 73.5 in.; (LeB sed/wag) 72.8 in.; (Cord./Newpt/N.Y.) 77.1 in. Front Tread: (LeB) 60.0 in.; (others) 61.9 in. Rear Tread: (LeB) 58.5 in.; (others) 62.0 in. Standard Tires: (LeB) FR78 x 15; (Cord.) FR78 x 15 GBR BSW; (Newpt) P195/75R15 GBR BSW; (N.Y.) P205/75R15 GBR WSW.

TECHNICAL: Transmission: Overdrive4 manual trans. (floor shift) standard on LeBaron cpe/sed (exc. in Calif.). Gear ratios: (1st) 3.09:1; (2nd) 1.67:1; (3rd) 1.00:1; (4th) 0.71:1; (Rev) 3.00:1. TorqueFlite three-speed automatic standard (optional on LeBaron): (1st) 2.45:1; (2nd) 1.45:1; (3rd) 1.00:1; (Rev) 2.22:1. Standard final drive ratio: (LeB six) 3.23:1 or 2.94:1 exc. 2.76:1 or 2.71:1 w/auto.; (LeB V-8) 2.47:1, 2.45:1 or 3.21:1; (Cord. V8318) 2.71:1; (Cord. V8360) 2.45:1 or 3.21:1; (Newpt six) 2.94:1; (Newpt V-8) 2.45:1 or 3.21:1; (N.Y.) 2.45:1 exc. (H.D. V8360) 3.21:1. Steering: recirculating ball, power-assisted. Suspension: (LeBaron) front transverse torsion bars with control arms and anti-sway bar, rigid rear axle with semi- elliptic leaf springs; (others) longitudinal front torsion bars and anti-sway bar, rear asymmetrical leaf springs. Brakes: Front disc, rear drum (power-assisted). Ignition: Electronic. Body construction: Unibody. Fuel tank: (LeB) 19.5 gal.; (others) 21 gal.

DRIVETRAIN OPTIONS: Engines: 225 cu. in., 2Bbl. six: LeB (NC). 318 cu. in., 2Bbl. V-8: LeBaron ($236); Newpt ($239). 318 cu. in., 4Bbl. V-8: LeB ($296); Cord. ($61); Newpt ($300). 360 cu. in., 2Bbl. V-8: LeB ($426); Cord. ($191); Newpt ($432). 360 cu. in., 4Bbl. V-8: LeB ($487); Cord. ($251); Newpt ($493-$664); N.Y. ($61-232). H.D. 360 cu. in., 4Bbl. V-8: LeB ($655); Cordoba ($420); Newpt ($664); N.Y. ($232). Transmission/Differential: Automatic trans.: LeB ($193). Sure grip differential: LeB/Cord. ($67); others ($72). Optional axle ratio ($20). Suspension: Heavy-duty susp. ($28). H.D. shock absorbers ($8) exc. LeB. Other: Heavy-duty trailer assist pkg.: LeB ($170); Cord. ($150); Newpt/N.Y. ($152). Long-life battery ($35). California emission system ($87).

LEBARON CONVENIENCE/APPEARANCE OPTIONS: Option Packages: Basic group ($1130-$1385). Sport appearance pkg. ($110-$219). Spring sport special pkg. (landau roof, cloth/vinyl bucket seats, sport wheels/mirrors): Salon cpe ($261). Light pkg. ($72-$84). Deluxe wiper/washer pkg. ($47). Deluxe insulation pkg. ($10-$93). Comfort/Convenience: Air conditioning ($584). Rear defroster ($98). Automatic speed control ($107). Power seat ($167). Power windows ($137-$194). Power door locks ($89-$124). Power decklid or tailgate release ($25). Luxury steering wheel ($20). Leather-covered steering wheel ($40-$60). Tilt steering wheel ($58-$77). Tinted glass ($73). Digital clock ($56). Locking gas cap ($7). Lighting, Horns and Mirrors: Halogen headlamps ($26). Cornering lamps ($51). Dual horns ($9). Remote-control left mirror ($19). Remote right mirror: Medallion ($35). Dual remote chrome mirrors ($35-$54). Dual remote sport mirrors ($48-$67). Lighted vanity mirror ($50). Day/night mirror: base ($12). Entertainment: AM radio ($87). AM/CB radio ($287-$373). AM/FM radio ($80-$167). AM/FM stereo radio ($154-$240); w/CB ($440- $527). AM/FM stereo w/8track player ($256-$343). Search tune AM/FM stereo radio ($281-$368). Rear speaker ($26). Power antenna ($48). Exterior Trim: T-Bar roof: cpe ($675). Power glass sunroof ($827). Landau vinyl roof: cpe ($148). Full vinyl roof: base sed ($165). Vinyl bodyside molding ($45). Front bumper guards ($24). Bumper rub strips ($37). Door edge guards ($13-$22). Luggage rack: wag ($94). Air deflector: wag ($30). Undercoating ($25-$36). Interior Trim/Upholstery: Vinyl bench seat ($50-$67). Cloth 60/40 seat: wag ($175). Leather 60/40 seat ($283-$430). Cloth/vinyl bucket seats: Salon ($110). Color-keyed floor mats ($25). Color-keyed seatbelts ($20). Pedal dress-up ($10). Wheels and Tires: Wire wheel covers ($111-$300). Deluxe wheel covers: base ($45). Premium wheel covers ($45-$90). Forged aluminum wheels ($116-$305). FR78 x 15 WSW ($50-$110). Conventional spare tire (NC).

CORDOBA CONVENIENCE/APPEARANCE OPTIONS: Option Packages: '300' pkg. ($2040). Basic group ($1089- $1125). Crown roof two-tone paint pkg. ($777-$971). Special appearance pkg. ($527). Two-tone paint pkg. ($158). Roadability pkg. ($29). Light pkg. ($29). Comfort/Convenience: Air conditioning ($584). Auto-temp air cond. ($628) exc. w/option pkg. ($44). Rear defroster ($98). Automatic speed control ($107). Power seat ($167). Power windows ($137). Power door locks ($89). Power decklid release ($26). Leather-wrapped steering wheel: two-spoke ($77); three-spoke ($40). Tilt steering wheel ($77). Tinted glass ($73). Tinted windshield ($47). Tachometer ($73). Digital clock ($56). Deluxe wipers ($40). Locking gas cap ($7). Lighting and Mirrors: Halogen headlamps ($26). Cornering lamps ($51). Remote-control left mirror ($19). Dual remote chrome mirrors ($35-$54). Dual sport remote mirrors: painted or chrome ($48-$67). Lighted vanity mirror ($50). Entertainment: Same as LeBaron, plus: AM radio w/8track player ($166-$252). Exterior Trim: T-Bar roof w/lift-out panels ($675). Crown landau laredo grain vinyl roof w/illuminated lamp band and "frenched" antenna ($691-$823). Power sunroof ($546). Landau vinyl roof ($132). Vinyl bodyside molding ($45). Door edge guards ($13). Bumper rub strips ($37). Bodyside tape stripes ($29). Decklid tape stripe ($24). Undercoating ($36). Interior Trim/Upholstery: Console ($60). Vinyl bench seat ($32). Velour/vinyl 60/40 bench seat w/armrest and recliner ($147). Leather bucket seats ($283). Color-keyed floor mats ($25). Color-keyed seatbelts ($20). Pedal dress-up ($10). Trunk dress-up ($47). Wheels and Tires: Wire wheel covers ($211-$255). Premium wheel covers ($45). Aluminum wheels w/trim rings ($213). Forged aluminum wheels ($260). Aluminum fascia wheels ($164). FR78 x 15 WSW ($50). GR78 x 15 BSW ($22). GR78 x 15 WSW ($22- $72). HR78 x 15 WSW ($87-$160). GR60 x 15 RWL ($230-$302). Conventional spare tire (NC).

NEWPORT/NEW YORKER CONVENIENCE/APPEARANCE OPTIONS: Option Packages: Fifth Avenue Edition pkg.: N.Y. ($1307- $1500). Basic group: Newpt ($1176); N.Y. ($1098). Open road handling pkg. ($194-$216). Two-tone paint pkg. ($160). Light pkg. ($91-$96). Comfort/Convenience: Air cond. ($628). Automatic air cond. ($673) exc. ($45) w/option pkg. Rear defroster ($105). Auto. speed control ($112). Power seat ($170). Power windows ($212). Power door locks ($126). Power decklid release ($27-$35). Luxury steering wheel: Newpt ($20); N.Y. ($60). Leather-covered steering wheel ($41-$60). Digital clock: Newpt ($57). Locking gas cap ($9). Lighting and Mirrors: Halogen headlamps ($27). Cornering lamps ($51). Remote-control driver's mirror: Newpt ($20). Remote passenger mirror: N.Y. ($24). Dual remote mirrors: Newpt ($24-$44). Lighted vanity mirror ($50). Entertainment: AM radio ($106). AM/CB radio ($215-$396). AM/FM radio ($76-$182). AM/FM stereo radio ($71-$253); w/CB ($361-$543). AM/FM stereo w/8track tape player ($179-$360). Search tune AM/FM stereo radio ($191-$372). Rear speaker ($28). Power antenna ($50). Exterior Trim: Power glass sunroof ($993). Vinyl roof: Newpt ($152). Vinyl side moldings ($51). Bumper guards: Newpt ($60). Door edge protectors ($23). Bodyside/tailamp tape stripes: Newpt ($72). Undercoating ($30). Interior Trim/Upholstery: Vinyl split-back bench seat: Newpt ($33). Cloth 60/40 bench seat: Newpt ($149). Vinyl 60/40 bench seat: Newpt ($181). Leather 60/40 bench seat: N.Y. ($287). Color-keyed floor mats ($26). Color-keyed seatbelts: Newpt ($21). Pedal dress-up ($10). Trunk dress-up ($67). Litter container ($8). Wheels and Tires: Wire wheel covers ($259). Premier wheel covers ($54). Aluminum wheels ($175); w/trim rings ($216). P195/75R15 WSW ($51). P205/75R15 WSW ($23-$134). P225/70R15 WSW ($24-$75). Conventional spare tire (NC).

HISTORY: Introduced: Oct. 5, 1978. Model year production: 291,598 (incl. Canadian-built Cordobas). Calendar year production (U.S.): 181,427. Calendar year sales by U.S. dealers: 248,840. Model year sales by U.S. dealers: 277,749 (incl. 70,970 Cordobas).

Historical Footnotes: Division sales fell for the 1979 model year, by more than 8 percent (including the three Plymouth-badged imports). Cordoba sales slipped by 37 percent, but full-size Chryslers rose nearly 24 percent. Production for the model year dropped 12 percent. Weight-cutting had become a major theme. The heaviest Chrysler product weighed less than 3,900 pounds at the curb. As part of modernizing the old Lynch Road assembly plant, the use of lead solder was curtailed, thus eliminating the risk of lead poisoning. Synthetic solder was used instead. Many Chrysler, Dodge and Plymouth models had become quite alike in recent years, often differing from each other in little other than nameplate. Dodge's Magnum XE, for instance, was a near twin to Chrysler's Cordoba, but sold far fewer copies. Lee Iacocca was determined, as one of his many goals, to give Dodge Division back its separate identity, in an attempt to tweak sales of each brand.

1980 Chrysler

Cordoba got a fresh restyle this year and new model designations, while other models were largely carried over or given modest styling changes. LeBaron added a base station wagon and lower-priced Special sedan. New Yorker's Fifth Avenue edition was offered again this year, while Cordoba's 300 faded away after a short rebirth.

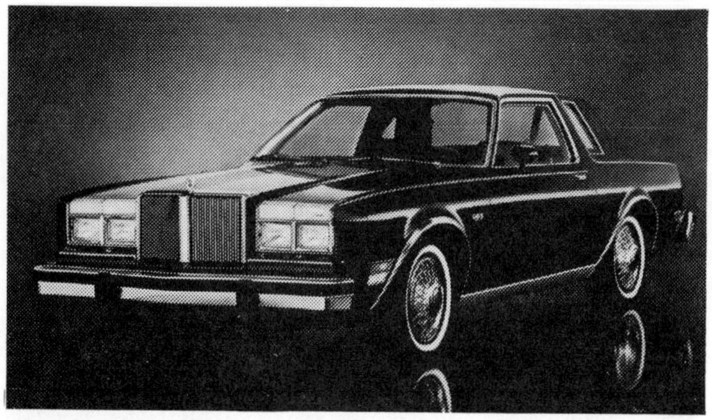

1980 LeBaron coupe (JG)

LEBARON — SERIES F — SIX/V-8 — A new grille made up of thin, close-together vertical strips was split in two by a wide vertical divider between the sections. Distinctive quad parking/signal lamps sat directly above quad rectangular headlamps and wrapped over fender tops. Above the grille was an eagle hood ornament. Amber-over-clear side marker lenses stood just ahead of each front wheel opening, angled to follow its shape. A 'LeBaron' nameplate was just ahead of the door. Narrow vertical red lenses sat above backup lamps at quarter panel tips, while wide taillamps with center emblems reached the license plate opening. LeBaron had sharper fenderline creases this year, as well as a revised, more squared-off roofline. Two-door models shrunk in length, now riding a 108.7 in. wheelbase rather than the 112.7 in. platform used by sedans and wagons. Base two-doors included bright windshield, back window, roof drip, belt, center pillar, quarter window, wheel opening, and wide sill moldings. Woodtoning adorned the instrument panel, two-spoke steering wheel, and door trim panels. Standard equipment included front bumper guards, hubcaps, TorqueFlite transmission, power steering and brakes, two-speed wipers, and trip odometer. Salon added a day/night mirror, dual horns, deluxe wheel covers, and bodyside accent stripes. The top-of-the-line Medallion added a landau or full padded vinyl roof with opera lamps, and sill molding extensions, plus warning chimes and left remote mirror. New to the option list was the illuminated entry system, with halo lamps around door locks. Auto-temp air conditioning also was available. Station wagons came with or without the simulated white ash moldings and teakwood applique. The new non-wood base wagon was available for a lower price. LeBaron colors were: Baron Red; Light Cashmere; Spinnaker White; Nightwatch Blue; Formal Black; Light Heather Gray; Natural Suede Tan; plus metallic Burnished Silver, Mocha Brown, Light Heather Gray, Frost Blue, Teal Frost, Teal Tropic Green, and Crimson Red. An LS Limited package was offered on the two-door coupe only, with unique classic diamond-mesh wire grille texture and integral eagle medallion in the upper center of the grille frame (protruding into each section). Quarter window glass showed LS ornamentation. Unique two-tone paint made hood, roof front and a narrow band surrounding front windows the same color as that on lower bodyside, while the rest of the car was a second color. Quarter and back window moldings were painted. Instead of a nameplate, a set of vertical (non- functional) fender louvers was mounted just ahead of the door. Inside were high-back cloth bucket seats. Wire wheel covers, dual remote mirrors, three-spoke steering wheel, P205/75R15 steel-belted radial whitewalls, and a brushed- finish instrument cluster bezel were among many LS Limited extras. An LS package was similar, but without the two-tone. A total of 948 LeBarons had the LS Coupe package, while 2,257 carried the LS Limited Coupe option. Chrysler also borrowed from New Yorker to produce a luxury Fifth Avenue package for LeBaron, which debuted at mid-year. A total of 654 were installed. Fifth Avenues had a different formal-look roofline with padded carriage roof and blanked rear quarter windows in the back doors, thin opera lamps in a wrapover roof band at the front of the vinyl portion, and a smaller "frenched" back window. The package also included wire wheel covers.

CORDOBA — SERIES S — SIX/V-8 — The restyled second-generation personal-luxury coupe actually became a close relative to LeBaron, riding the same 112.7 in. wheelbase. Though shaped similar to the prior version, the new Cordoba had a more formal appearance. It was also smaller6 in. shorter and over 4 in. narrower. For the first time, Cordoba came with a standard six-cylinder engine, with V-8 optional. Notable among the changes was a switch to single recessed rectangular headlamps. Cordoba's vertical-style grille had seven primary ribs, plus many vertical strips in between. 'Chrysler' block letters were inset in the grille header molding. Horizontally-ribbed clear parking lamps stood between grille and headlamps. The stand-up hood ornament held a Cordoba replica "coin" (Franklin Minted). Amber/clear side marker lenses sat low, just ahead of wheels. A grooved bodyside accent stretched from front to rear, up and over the wheel openings. A deeply sculptured lower accent line reached from front to rear bumper tips. 'Cordoba' script and minted medallion were on each front fender, ahead of the door. Full- length striping was higher up, above the door handle. Sill moldings were standard. Tri-lens taillamps consisted of three wide elements on each side, trimmed with a pair of horizontal strips. Backup lamps were alongside the license plate. 'Chrysler' block lettering was on decklid center; 'Cordoba' script on passenger side. Rear quarter extensions had a pointy (razor-edge) look. Slim opera lamps were angled to match the pillar angle. Standard equipment included TorqueFlite automatic, power brakes and steering, two-spoke steering wheel with woodtone insert, front/rear bumper guards and rub strips, coat hooks, tinted glass, bi-level heater/defroster, AM radio, dual horns, keyless door locking, and day/night mirror. Also standard: a chrome driver's outside mirror, opera windows, compact spare tire, two-speed wiper/washers, and deluxe wheel covers with P195/75R15 GBR WSW tires. Colors were White, Natural Suede Tan, Light Cashmere, Baron Red, Formal Black, Nightwatch Blue, and Light Heather Gray; plus metallic Light Heather Gray, Burnished Silver, Frost Blue, Crimson Red, and Mocha Brown. A Cabriolet roof option gave a convertible look, with fabric-like canvas that even covered the triangular quarter windows. New optional leather/vinyl bucket seats had a center cushion and folding center armrest. Cordoba Crown added a padded landau vinyl roof; brushed finish up-and-over roof molding; color-keyed vinyl roof termination and opera window moldings; opera lamps; "Frenched" back windows with no exposed moldings; wide sill moldings with rear extensions; and Premier wheel covers. The Crown Corinthian Edition had Black Walnut metallic or Designer's Cream-on-Beige paint treatment. The black version had gold accent stripes and black walnut reptile-grain padded landau vinyl roof. Cream/beige Corinthians showed medium beige accent stripes and light beige Laredo-grain padded landau vinyl roof. Inside was cashmere 60/40 leather/vinyl seating and a leather-wrapped tilt steering wheel. Also included: 'Corinthian Edition' identification; dual chrome remote mirrors; intermittent wipers; wire wheel covers and wide whitewall P205/75R15 Goodyear tires. A total of 305 Cordobas came with the Crown special edition package, while 2,069 were Corinthian Edition.

NEWPORT — SERIES TH — SIX/V-8 — Following its 1979 downsizing, Chrysler's "friend of the family" showed no significant change this year beyond a new pentastar stand-up hood ornament. Optional this year were an illuminated entry system and forged aluminum wheels. An Open Road Handling package included Firm-Feel suspension (heavy- duty sway bars front/rear, heavy-duty torsion bars and springs, H.D. shocks); special Firm-Feel power steering; and P225/70R15 wide whitewall SBR tires on wide rims. Solid colors for 1980 were: Light Heather Gray, Nightwatch Blue, Baron Red, Light Cashmere, Natural Suede Tan, Formal Black and Spinnaker White; plus metallic Light Heather Gray, Frost Blue, Teal Frost, Teal Tropic Green, Crimson Red, and Mocha Brown. Newport had five two-tones available.

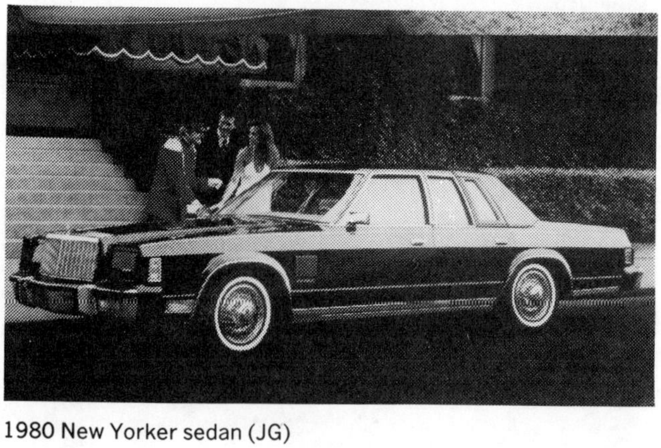

1980 New Yorker sedan (JG)

NEW YORKER — SERIES TP — V-8 — No major changes went on New Yorker in its year-old downsized form. 'Chrysler' block letters again were on the driver's side headlamp cover. Clear wide parking lamps were inset into the bumper. New Yorker had a pentastar hood ornament. Full-width taillamps had their outer segments recessed. Colors were the same as Newport, except for Light Cashmere. Six two-tones were offered. Fifth Avenue, promoted as "The One and Only," had new small tri-sectioned amber marker lenses near front fender tips, plus larger horizontal lenses farther down. The Fifth Avenue Edition package included Black Walnut metallic or Designer's Cream/Beige paint; leather-and-vinyl trimmed 60/40 split-back bench seat in Champagne color; beige/cashmere bodyside accent tape stripes (gold stripes with black walnut body); and padded landau beige Bancroft-grain vinyl roof (black walnut reptile-grain with black body). Edge-lighted quarter windows displayed 'Fifth Avenue' script. Also included: simulated front fender louvers; color-keyed bumper guards and protective strips; P205/75R15 SBR wide WSW tires; wire wheel covers; light package; tilt steering; intermittent wipers; leather-covered steering wheel; Driftwood appliques on instrument panel and trim; and Champagne interior trim. A total of 3,608 Fifth Avenue packages were installed, along with 386 Fifth Avenue Special Editions.

I.D. DATA: For the last time, Chrysler had a 13-symbol Vehicle Identification Number (VIN) on the upper left corner of the instrument panel, between the wiper pivot and 'A' post, visible through the windshield. Coding was similar to 1979. Engine code 'D' for 2Bbl. six was dropped. Model year code changed to 'A' for 1980. The Newark assembly plant (code F) switched to Aspen/Volare production. Engine number codes again were stamped on the block.

LEBARON (SIX/V-8)

Series Number	Body/Style Number	Body Type & Seating	Factory Price	Shipping Weight	Production Total
FM	22	2-dr. Cpe-6P	5948/6178	3220/3300	8,000
FM	41	4-dr. Sed-6P	6103/6333	3300/3385	8,391
FM	45	4-dr. Sta Wag-6P	6305/6535	3455/3535	1,865

LEBARON SPECIAL (SIX)

FL	41	4-dr. Sed-6P	5995/--	3260/--	3,139

1980 LeBaron Salon LS Limited coupe (CC)

LEBARON SALON (SIX/V-8)

FH	22	2-dr. Cpe-6P	6229/6459	3230/3310	10,575
FH	41	4-dr. Sed-6P	6348/6578	3325/3405	10,980

LEBARON MEDALLION (SIX/V-8)

FP	22	2-dr. Cpe-6P	6783/6888	3285/3360	5,955
FP	41	4-dr. Sed-6P	6888/7118	3400/3485	8,500

1980 LeBaron Town & Country wagon (JG)

LEBARON TOWN & COUNTRY (SIX/V-8)

FH	45	4-dr. Sta Wag-6P	6894/7124	3525/3610	6,074

CORDOBA (SIX/V-8)

SH	22	2-dr. HT Cpe-6P	6601/6831	3270/3355	26,333

CORDOBA 'LS' (SIX/V-8)

SS	22	2-dr. HT Cpe-6P	6745/6840	3270/3365	3,252

CORDOBA CROWN (SIX/V-8)

SP	22	2-dr. HT Cpe-6P	7051/7281	3320/3400	16,821

NEWPORT (SIX/V-8)

TH	42	4-dr. Pill. HT-6P	6849/7082	3545/3630	10,872

NEW YORKER (V-8)

TP	42	4-dr. Pill. HT-6P	10459	3810	10,166

FACTORY PRICE & WEIGHT NOTE: Figures to left of slash are for six- cylinder engine, to right of slash for the least expensive V-8. All models had a series of price rises during the model year.

ENGINE DATA: BASE SIX (LeBaron, Cordoba, Newport): Inline, overhead valve six-cylinder. Cast iron block and head. Displacement: 225 cu. in. (3.7 liters). Bore & stroke: 3.40 x 4.12 in. Compression ratio: 8.4:1. Brake horsepower: 90 at 3600 R.P.M. Torque: 160 lbs.-ft. at 1600 R.P.M. Four main bearings. Solid valve lifters. Carburetor: 1Bbl. Holley 1945 (R8831A). VIN Code: C. BASE V-8 (New Yorker): OPTIONAL (all models): 90-degree, overhead valve V-8. Cast iron block and head. Displacement: 318 cu. in. (5.2 liters). Bore & stroke: 3.91 x 3.31 in. Compression ratio: 8.5:1. Brake horsepower: 120 at 3600 R.P.M. Torque: 245 lbs.-ft. at 1600 R.P.M. Five main bearings. Hydraulic valve lifters. Carburetor: 2Bbl. Carter BBD. VIN Code: G. Note: A 4Bbl. 318 rated 155 H.P. was available in California. OPTIONAL V-8 (Newport, New Yorker): 90-degree, overhead valve V-8. Cast iron block and head. Displacement: 360 cu. in. (5.9 liters). Bore & stroke: 4.00 x 3.58 in. Compression ratio: 8.4:1. Brake horsepower: 130 at 3200 R.P.M. Torque: 255 lbs.-ft. at 2000 R.P.M. Five main bearings. Hydraulic valve lifters. Carburetor: 2Bbl. Carter BBD. VIN Code: K. HIGH-OUTPUT V-8 (Cordoba): Same as 360 cu. in. V-8 above, but with 4Bbl. Carter TQ9244S carburetor Compression ratio: 8.0:1. Brake H.P.: 185 at 4000 R.P.M. Torque: 275 lbs.-ft. at 2000 R.P.M. VIN Code: L.

CHASSIS DATA: Wheelbase: (LeBaron cpe) 108.7 in.; (LeB sed/wag) 112.7 in.; (Cordoba) 112.7 in.; (Newport/N.Y.) 118.5 in. Overall length: (LeB cpe) 201.2 in.; (LeB sed) 205.2 in.; (LeB wag) 205.5 in.; (Cord.) 209.8 in.; (Cord. LS) 209.5 in.; (Newport) 220.2 in.; (N.Y.) 221.5 in. Height: (LeB cpe) 53.4 in.; (LeB sed) 55.3 in.; (LeB wag) 55.5 in.; (Cord.) 53.3 in.; (Newpt/N.Y.) 54.5 in. Width: (LeB) 74.2 in.; (Cord.) 72.7 in.; (Newpt/N.Y.) 77.6 in. Front Tread: (LeB/Cord.) 60.0 in.; (Newpt/N.Y.) 61.9 in. Rear Tread: (LeB/Cord.) 59.5 in.; (Newpt/N.Y.) 62.0 in. Standard Tires: (LeB/Cord./Newpt) P195/75R15 GBR WSW; (N.Y.) P205/75R15 SBR WSW.

TECHNICAL: Transmission: TorqueFlite three-speed automatic standard. Six-cylinder gear ratios: (1st) 2.74:1; (2nd) 1.54:1; (3rd) 1.00:1; (Rev) 2.22:1. V-8 ratios: (1st) 2.45:1; (2nd) 1.45:1; (3rd) 1.00:1; (Rev) 2.22:1. Standard final drive ratio: (LeB/Cord. six) 2.76:1; (LeB/Cord. V-8) 2.47:1; (Newpt six) 2.94:1; (Newpt/N.Y. V-8) 2.45:1. Steering: recirculating ball, power-assisted. Suspension: (LeBaron/Cordoba) front transverse torsion bars with control arms and anti-sway bar, rigid rear axle with semi-elliptic leaf springs; (others) longitudinal front torsion bars and anti-sway bar, rear leaf springs. Brakes: Front disc, rear drum (power-assisted). Ignition: Electronic. Body construction: Unibody. Fuel tank: (LeB/Cord.) 18 gal.; (Newpt/N.Y.) 21 gal.

DRIVETRAIN OPTIONS: Engines: 318 cu. in., 2Bbl. V-8: LeBaron/Cord. ($230); Newpt ($233). 318 cu. in. 4Bbl. V-8: LeB/Cord. ($291); Newpt ($295); N.Y. (NC). 360 cu. in., 2Bbl. V-8: Newpt ($457); N.Y. (NC). Axle/Suspension: Sure grip differential ($71-$77). Heavy-duty susp. ($28-$30). H.D. shock absorbers ($8) exc. LeB. Other: Heavy-duty trailer assist pkg.: Newpt/N.Y. ($258). Max. cooling: LeB/Cord. ($37-$63); Newpt/N.Y. ($77-$104). Long-life battery ($36). California emission system ($254).

LEBARON CONVENIENCE/APPEARANCE OPTIONS: Option Packages: Fifth Avenue pkg. (N/A). LS Limited coupe pkg.: Salon ($353-$421). LS Limited coupe pkg.: Salon ($954-$974). Sport appearance pkg. ($166-$290). Two-tone paint pkg. ($162). Handling pkg. ($151). Protection group ($61-$70). Deluxe insulation pkg. ($10-$110). Comfort/Convenience: Air conditioning ($623). Auto-temp air cond. ($673) exc. w/option pkg. ($50). Rear defroster ($106). Automatic speed control ($116). Power seat ($179). Power windows ($148-$209). Power door locks ($96-$136). Power decklid or tailgate release ($27). Illuminated entry system ($58). Luxury steering wheel ($20). Leather-covered steering wheel ($41-$61). Tilt steering wheel ($63-$83). Tuff steering wheel ($36-$56). Tinted glass ($78). Liftgate wiper/washer: wag ($69). Digital clock ($60). Locking gas cap ($8). Lighting, Horns and Mirrors: Halogen headlamps ($41). Cornering lamps ($55). Dual horns ($10). Remote-control left mirror ($20). Remote right mirror: Medallion ($41). Dual remote chrome mirrors ($41-$61). Dual remote sport mirrors ($56-$76). Lighted vanity mirror ($51). Day/night mirror: base ($12). Entertainment: AM radio ($99). AM/FM radio ($63-$162). AM/FM stereo radio ($101-$200); w/CB ($383-$482). AM/FM stereo w/8track player ($181-$280); w/cassette ($240-$339). Search tune AM/FM stereo radio ($227-$326). Rear speaker ($21). Power antenna ($52). Exterior Trim: T-Bar roof: cpe ($715). Power glass sunroof ($871). Upper door frame moldings: base wag ($10). Rear bumper guards ($36). Door edge guards ($14-$23). Luggage rack: wag ($100). Air deflector: wag ($32). Undercoating ($25). Interior Trim/Upholstery: Console: Salon cpe ($109). Vinyl split-back bench seat ($51-$69). Vinyl 60/40 seating: Salon ($230). Vinyl 60/40 seat: Salon/wag ($212-$281). Cloth 60/40 seat: Salon/wag ($160-$281). Leather 60/40 seat ($371-$619). Cloth/vinyl bucket seats: Salon cpe ($103). Color- keyed floor mats: front ($26); rear ($21). Color-keyed seatbelts ($27). Pedal dress-up ($10). Trunk dress-up ($49). Cargo area carpet: base wag ($75); w/stowage bins ($101). Cargo security cover: wag ($61). Wheels and Tires: Wire wheel covers ($114-$308). Deluxe wheel covers: base ($48). Premium wheel covers ($45-$138). Premier wheel covers ($45-$93). Styled wheels ($101-$194). Forged aluminum wheels ($72-$380). P205/75R15 SBR WSW ($89). P205/75R15 Aramid-belted white/gold sidewall ($86-$135). Conventional spare tire ($27).

CORDOBA CONVENIENCE/APPEARANCE OPTIONS: Option Packages: Corinthian Edition: Crown ($1203-$1818). Basic group ($889-$1082). Cabriolet roof pkg. ($624-$950). Cabriolet roof two-tone pkg. ($745-$1071). Sport appearance pkg. ($171-$191). Two-tone paint pkg. ($73-$172). Sport handling pkg. ($192). Roadability pkg. ($29). Protection pkg. ($61). Light pkg. ($104). Comfort/Convenience: Air conditioning ($623). Auto-temp air cond. ($675) exc. w/option pkg. ($52). Rear defroster ($106). Automatic speed control ($116). Power seat ($179). Power windows ($148). Power door locks ($96). Power decklid release ($28-$44). Illuminated entry system ($58). Luxury steering wheel ($22). Leather-wrapped steering wheel ($39-$61). Tilt steering wheel ($61-$83). Tuff steering wheel ($34-$56). Digital clock ($60). Intermittent wipers ($43). Locking gas cap ($8). Lighting, Horns and Mirrors: Halogen headlamps ($41). Cornering lamps ($55). Reading lamp ($21). Triad horns ($22). Remote-control left mirror ($20). Dual remote mirrors ($57- $77). Lighted vanity mirror ($51). Entertainment: AM/FM radio ($63). AM radio w/8track ($156). AM/FM stereo ($101); w/CB ($383); w/8track ($181); w/cassette ($240). Search tune AM/FM stereo radio ($227). Rear speaker ($21). Power antenna ($52). Radio delete ($56 credit). Exterior Trim: T-Bar roof ($715). Power sunroof ($787). Landau vinyl roof ($141). Vinyl bodyside molding ($48). Door edge guards ($14). Bodyside/decklid tape stripes ($74). Hood tape stripe ($25). Undercoating ($25). Interior Trim/Upholstery: Console ($66). Vinyl bucket seats ($103). Leather bucket seats: Crown ($455). Color-keyed floor mats: front ($26); rear ($21). Color-keyed seatbelts ($27). Pedal dress-up ($10). Trunk dress-up ($49). Wheels and Tires: Wire wheel covers ($170-$262). Premium wheel covers ($216-$334). Forged aluminum wheels ($46-$92). P205/75R15 GBR WSW ($22). P205/75R15 SBR WSW ($89). P205/75R15 Aramid-belted gold-band WSW ($175). P215/70R15 RWL SBR ($114). Conventional spare tire ($27).

NEWPORT/NEW YORKER CONVENIENCE/APPEARANCE OPTIONS: Option Packages: Fifth Avenue Edition pkg.: N.Y. ($1120- $1300). Fifth Avenue Special Edition ($1881-$2092). Basic group: Newpt ($1203); N.Y. ($242). Open road handling pkg.: Newpt ($269); N.Y. ($177). Two-tone paint pkg. ($168). Light pkg. ($81-$87). Comfort/Convenience: Air cond. ($670). Auto-temp air cond.: Newpt ($720); N.Y. ($50). Rear defroster ($113). Auto. speed control ($122). Power seat ($183). Power windows: Newpt ($228). Power door locks ($139). Power decklid release ($30- $46). Illuminated entry system ($62). Luxury steering wheel: Newpt ($20). Leather-covered steering wheel: Newpt ($62); N.Y. ($42). Tilt steering: Newpt ($85); N.Y. ($65). Digital clock: Newpt ($61). Locking gas cap ($9). Lighting, Horns and Mirrors: Halogen headlamps ($42). Cornering lamps ($55). Triad horns ($22). Remote-control driver's mirror: Newpt ($21). Remote passenger mirror: N.Y. ($31). Dual remote mirrors: Newpt ($31-$52). Lighted vanity mirror ($53). AM radio: Newpt ($106). AM/FM radio: Newpt ($58-$164). AM/FM stereo radio: Newpt ($103-$209). AM/FM stereo w/8track tape player: Newpt ($181-$287); N.Y. ($78). AM/FM stereo

w/cassette: Newpt ($241-$347); N.Y. ($138). AM/FM stereo w/CB: Newpt ($389-$495); N.Y. ($286). Search tune AM/FM stereo radio: Newpt ($224-$330); N.Y. ($121). Rear speaker ($22). Power antenna ($54). Exterior Trim: Power glass sunroof ($1053). Full vinyl roof: Newpt ($162). Vinyl side moldings ($55). Bumper guards: Newpt ($62). Door edge protectors ($24). Bodyside/tailamp tape stripes: Newpt ($74). Undercoating ($31). Interior Trim/Upholstery: Vinyl split-back bench seat: Newpt ($34). Cloth/vinyl 60/40 bench seat: Newpt ($152). Vinyl 60/40 bench seat: Newpt ($186). Leather 60/40 bench seat: N.Y. ($432). Color-keyed floor mats: front ($26); rear ($21). Color-keyed seatbelts: Newpt ($27). Pedal dress-up ($10). Trunk dress-up: Newpt ($70). Litter container ($9). Wheels and Tires: Wire wheel covers ($266). Premier wheel covers: Newpt ($44). Premium wheel covers ($91). Forged aluminum wheels ($336). P205/75R15 SBR WSW ($92). P205/75R15 white/gold Aramid-belted ($87-$179). P225/70R15 SBR WSW ($93- $186). Conventional spare tire ($27).

HISTORY: Introduced: October 1, 1979. Model year production: 130,923 (incl. Canadian-built Cordobas). Calendar year production (U.S.): 82,463. Calendar year sales by U.S. dealers: 142,245. Model year sales by U.S. dealers: 151,752 (incl. 50,580 Cordobas).

Historical Footnotes: The newly restyled Cordoba lost some 350 pounds and over 2 inches of wheelbase, but wasn't exactly a hot seller in its modestly shrunken form. Even LeBaron, so popular at first and newly restyled, dropped by 43 percent in sales for the 1980 model year. Chrysler's financial troubles had become all too well known by the public, which doubtless had an impact on sales this yearespecially since some fresh models were expected for 1981. Apart from Omni and Horizon, and the captive imports, Chrysler Corporation wasn't capitalizing on the rising public clamor for fuel efficiency either. Thus, sales for model year 1980 dropped by one-third from the 1979 figure. Full-size Chryslers fared worse yet, slipping by some 61 percent. Production for the model year fell by 38 percent for the CP Division. Starting this year, the Plymouth Voyager passenger van was considered a truck for statistical purposes, thus affecting sales/production figures. Early in 1980, the Hamtramck (Michigan) assembly plant shut down.

1981 Chrysler

Changes were minimal for 1981, as Chrysler fans awaited the arrival of a front-drive model for '82. This year, the renowned Imperial name returned on a new bustleback luxury model, built in Windsor, Ontario. Under Chrysler hoods, the Slant Six engine added hydraulic valve lifters. Actually, the biggest change may have been the disappearance of the 360 cu. in. V-8, leaving the 318 as the largest powerplant offered by Chrysler. That one came in two- and four-barrel versions.

LEBARON — SERIES F — SIX/V-8 — Interior modifications and some new body colors were the extent of appearance change for LeBaron, which was promoted as a mid-size vehicle. A two-door coupe was added to the low- budget Special line. LeBaron also came in base, Salon, and Medallion trim, along with the fake wood Town & Country wagon. Thicker primer, more (one-side) galvanized and precoated steel increased corrosion resistance. Full and landau vinyl roof options were added. Standard equipment included TorqueFlite automatic transmission, power brakes and steering, P195/75R15 glass- belted radial whitewall tires, cigarette lighter, locking glove compartment, belt and drip rail moldings, wheel lip moldings, driver's side remote-control mirror, deluxe wheel covers, sill moldings, front bumper guards, and courtesy lamps. LeBaron Salon added dual horns, day/night inside mirror, and upper door frame moldings (four-doors). Medallion added premier wheel covers, a padded vinyl roof, luxury steering wheel, and trunk dress-up items.

1981 Cordoba LS coupe (CC)

CORDOBA — SERIES S — SIX/V-8 — After its 1980 restyle, Cordoba was carried over with little change. The shift pattern of the wide-ratio automatic transmission was modified for smoother acceleration in city driving. Cordobas had a transverse torsion bar front suspension (like LeBaron) and rear leaf springs. High-strength steel bumpers were new this year. Standard cloth/vinyl 60/40 seats had a folding center armrest. Leather/vinyl buckets were optional. Cordoba solid colors were: Light Heather Gray, Nightwatch Blue, Mahogany Starmist, Graphic Red, Spice Tan Starmist, Baron Red, Pearl White, Formal Black and Light Cashmere; plus metallic Daystar Blue or Burnished Silver. Three two-tones were offered. The Corinthian came in Mahogany Starmist or Formal Black, or three two-tones. A sporty new 'LS' model with "soft" front end was aimed at the youth market. It carried a crossbar blackout grille like that formerly used on the 300: just a body-colored horizontal/vertical crossbar with round 'LS' emblem in the center. Below the bumper rub strips were two thin slots. Unlike standard Cordobas, 'LS' had both headlamps and adjoining parking lamps set in a recessed housing. At the rear were body-colored taillamp bezels instead of the customary chrome. High-back vinyl bucket seats were standard, along with dual painted remote-control mirrors. Trim included thin red/white/blue bodyside and decklid accent stripes. In addition to a Special Edition padded vinyl landau roof, Cordoba's Corinthian Edition had a leather-wrapped rim two-spoke steering wheel with Cordoba "coin" insert. Also included: Corinthian Edition rear pillar identification; color-keyed bumper guards and rub strips; color-keyed door handle tape inserts; remote chrome mirrors; wire wheel covers; plus bodyside and decklid accent stripes. A total of 1,957 Cordobas had the Corinthian Edition package installed. A total of 998 had the simulated convertible top package, while 334 had that package with two-tone paint. A new vinyl roof featured covered-over opera windows and a small back window.

1981 Newport sedan (CC)

NEWPORT — SERIES TH — SIX/V-8 — Newport didn't look much different from 1980, but its grille now showed a simple tight crosshatch pattern with vertical elements dominant; no more pattern within a pattern. A 430-amp maintenance-free battery was now standard. Base engine remained the 225 cu. in. slant six, now with hydraulic lifters, with 318 cu. in. V-8 optional. This year's colors were Nightwatch Blue, Light Heather Gray, Pearl White, Baron Red, Light Cashmere, Formal Black; plus metallic Daystar Blue, Heather Mist, or Coffee Brown. Mahogany Starmist cost extra.

1981 New Yorker sedan (CC)

NEW YORKER — SERIES TP — V-8 — Like its less expensive full-size mate, New Yorker got a new grille; this one made up of all thin vertical bars of identical width. Otherwise, little was new or different. Base engine was the 318 cu. in. V-8. Options included Heavy-Duty and Open Road Handling packages. A total of 3,747 New Yorkers are reported to have had the Fifth Avenue package installed, while 347 are listed with an S/E version. Fifth Avenues included nearly all available optional equipment, and came in three two-tone combinations, as well as solid Nightwatch Blue. An optional Carriage Roof package included a sunroof, aluminum wheels, four-barrel 318 cu. in. V-8, and Sure-Grip axle. In fact, those were the only options available on the Fifth Avenue, either individually or in package form. Chrysler called it a "completely equipped luxury car."

1981 Imperial coupe (CC)

IMPERIAL — SERIES YS — V-8 — Striking in design and fully loaded with equipment, the new limited-production "bustleback" Imperial weighed nearly two tons, even though it was close to two feet shorter than the last previous (1975) Imperial. With no options available apart from a $1044 power moonroof, the two-door pillared hardtop coupe carried a price tag of $18,311. Buyers had several no-extra-cost choices, though: clearcoat paint; Mark Cross leather (or cloth) upholstery; digital electronic instruments; and a selection of AM/FM stereo systems. A "classic" vertical grille was accompanied by hidden headlamps. The bustle trunk, begging comparison with Cadillac's Seville, looked hugealmost like it was tacked on. Powerplant was a new fuel-injected 318 cu. in. V-8 with 8.5:1 compression, rated 140 horsepower at 4000 R.P.M. The suspension consisted of transverse torsion bars in front and leaf springs (live axle) in back. The basic platform was based on Cordoba's, but special chassis design and acoustics created what was described as "the quietest car in Chrysler history." Imperials wore the new Goodyear Arriva tires with low rolling resistance. The lengthy standard equipment list included TorqueFlite, semi-automatic air conditioning, automatic speed control, accent stripes, chimes, crystal hood ornament, digital clock (with date), electronic instrumentation, leather-wrapped steering wheel, tinted glass, tilt steering, and much more. A total of 148 Imperials came with a "Sinatra" package. Its availability wasn't surprising, since Frank Sinatra did a TV commercial for the car. Top-notch quality control was used in Imperial's assembly process, including a 5-1/2 mile road test.

I.D. DATA: Chrysler had a new 17-symbol Vehicle Identification Number (VIN) on the upper left corner of the instrument panel, again visible through the windshield. The first digit indicates Country: '1' U.S.A.; '2' Canada. The second symbol is Make: 'C' Chrysler; 'A' Imperial. Third is Vehicle Type: '3' passenger car; '7' truck. The next symbol ('B') indicates manual seatbelts. Symbol five is Car Line: 'M' LeBaron; 'J' Cordoba; 'R' Newport/New Yorker; 'Y' Imperial. Symbol six is Series: '2' Low; '3' Medium; '4' High'; '5' Premium; '6' Special. Symbol seven is Body Style: '2' 2-dr. coupe or HT coupe; '6' 4- dr. sedan; '7' 4-dr. pillared hardtop; '9' 4-dr. wagon. Eighth is the Engine Code: 'E' L6-225 1Bbl.; 'K' V8318 2Bbl.; 'M' V8318 4Bbl.; 'J' V8318 EFI. Next comes a check digit: 0 through 9 (or X). Symbol ten indicates Model Year: 'B' 1981. Symbol eleven is Assembly Plant: 'A' Lynch Road; 'G' St. Louis; 'R' Windsor, Ontario. The last six digits make up the sequential serial number, starting with 100001. An engine identification number is stamped on a pad at the right of the block on six-cylinder engines, below No. 6 spark plug. On V-8s, that pad is on the right of the block to the rear of the engine mount. An engine serial number is on the right of the block below No. 1 spark plug on six-cylinder engines, and on the left front corner of the block below the cylinder head on V-8s. A Body Code Plate is on the upper radiator support, left front fender shield, or wheelhousing.

LEBARON (SIX/V-8)

Series Number	Body/Style Number	Body Type & Seating	Factory Price	Shipping Weight	Production Total
FM	45	4-dr. Sta Wag-6P	7346/7408	3470/3590	2,136

LEBARON SPECIAL (SIX/V-8)

FL	22	2-dr. Cpe-6P	6672/6734	N/A	Note 1
FL	41	4-dr. Sed-6P	6495/6557	3275/ --	Note 1

Note 1: Total production, 11,890.

LEBARON SALON (SIX/V-8)

FH	22	2-dr. Cpe-6P	7263/7325	3200/3325	Note 2
FH	41	4-dr. Sed-6P	7413/7475	3305/3430	Note 2

Note 2: Total Salon production, 17,485.

LEBARON MEDALLION (SIX/V-8)

FP	22	2-dr. Cpe-6P	7768/7830	3255/3380	Note 3
FP	41	4-dr. Sed-6P	7917/7979	3355/3490	Note 3

Note 3: Total Medallion production, 7,635.

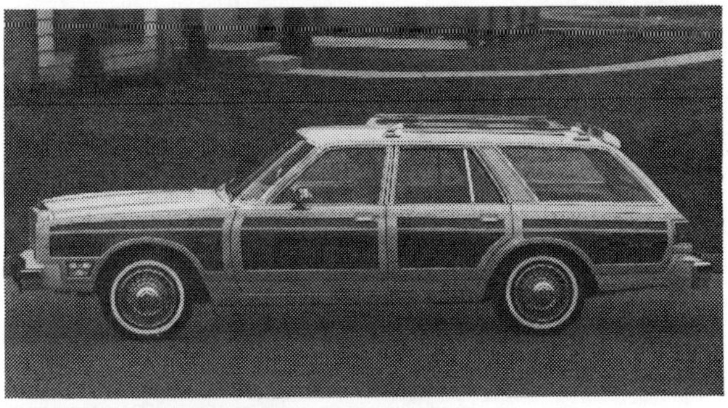

1981 LeBaron Town & Country wagon (CC)

LEBARON TOWN & COUNTRY (SIX/V-8)

FH	45	4-dr. Sta Wag-6P	8008/8070	3545/3665	3,987

CORDOBA (SIX/V-8)

SP	22	2-dr. HT Cpe-6P	7969/8033	3355/3495	12,978

CORDOBA 'LS' (SIX/V-8)

SS	22	2-dr. HT Cpe-6P	7199/7263	3300/3420	7,315

NEWPORT (SIX/V-8)

TH	42	4-dr. Pill. HT-6P	7805/7869	3515/3635	3,622

NEW YORKER (V-8)

TP	42	4-dr. Pill. HT-6P	10463	3805	6,548

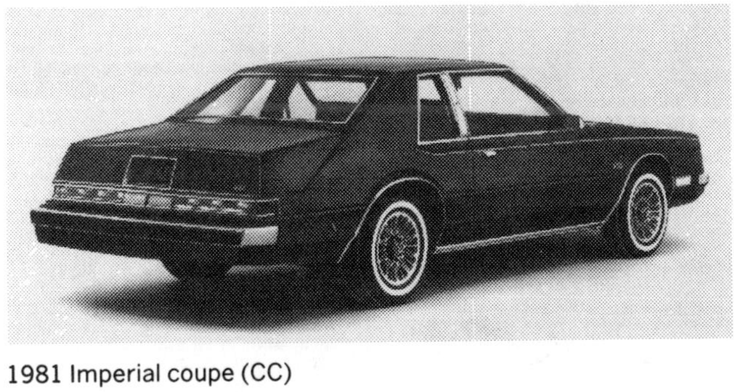

1981 Imperial coupe (CC)

IMPERIAL (V-8)

YS	22	2-dr. HT Cpe-6P	18311	3870	7,225

FACTORY PRICE & WEIGHT NOTE: Figures to left of slash are for six- cylinder engine, to right of slash for the least expensive V-8.

MODEL NUMBER NOTE: Some sources identify models using the new VIN data to indicate Car Line, Price Class and Body Style. Example: LeBaron station wagon (FM45) has the equivalent number CM39, which translates to LeBaron line, Medium price class, and station wagon body. See I.D. Data section for breakdown.

ENGINE DATA: BASE SIX (LeBaron, Cordoba, Newport): Inline, overhead valve six-cylinder. Cast iron block and head. Displacement: 225 cu. in. (3.7 liters). Bore & stroke: 3.40 x 4.12 in. Compression ratio: 8.4:1. Brake horsepower: 85 at 3600 R.P.M. Torque: 165 lbs.-ft. at 1600 R.P.M. Four main bearings. Hydraulic valve lifters. Carburetor: 1Bbl. Holley 1945 (R9253A). VIN Code: E. BASE V-8 (New Yorker); OPTIONAL (all models): 90-degree, overhead valve V-8. Cast iron block and head. Displacement: 318 cu. in. (5.2 liters). Bore & stroke: 3.91 x 3.31 in. Compression ratio: 8.5:1. Brake horsepower: 130 at 4000 R.P.M. Torque: 230 lbs.-ft. at 2000 R.P.M. Five main bearings. Hydraulic valve lifters. Carburetor: 2Bbl. Carter BBD 8291S. VIN Code: K. OPTIONAL V-8 (Newport, New Yorker, and California LeBaron/Cordoba): Same as 318 cu. in. V-8 above, but with Carter TQ9283S 4Bbl. carburetor B.H.P.: 165 at 4000 R.P.M. Torque: 240 lbs.-ft. at 2000 R.P.M. VIN Code: M. IMPERIAL V-8: Same as 318 cu. in. V-8 above, but with electronic fuel injection B.H.P.: 140 at 4000 R.P.M. Torque: 240 lbs.-ft. at 2000 R.P.M. VIN Code: J.

CHASSIS DATA: Wheelbase: (LeBaron cpe) 108.7 in.; (LeB sed/wag) 112.7 in.; (Cordoba/Imperial) 112.7 in.; (Newport/N.Y.) 118.5 in. Overall length: (LeB cpe) 201.7 in.; (LeB sed) 205.7 in.; (LeB wag) 206.0 in.; (Cord.) 210.1 in.; (Cord. LS) 209.5 in.; (Newport) 220.2 in.; (N.Y.) 221.5 in.; (Imperial) 213.3 in. Height: (LeB cpe) 53.3 in.; (LeB sed) 55.3 in.; (LeB wag) 55.5 in.; (Cord./Imp.) 53.2 in.; (Newpt/N.Y.) 54.5 in. Width: (LeB) 74.2 in.; (Cord./Imp.) 72.7 in.; (Newpt/N.Y.) 77.6 in. Front Tread: (LeB/Cord./Imp.) 60.0 in.; (Newpt/N.Y.) 61.9 in. Rear Tread: (LeB/Cord./Imp.) 59.5 in.; (Newpt/N.Y.) 62.0 in. Standard Tires: (LeB/Cord./Newpt) P195/75R15 GBR WSW; (N.Y./Imp.) P205/75R15 SBR WSW.

TECHNICAL: Transmission: TorqueFlite three-speed automatic standard. Gear ratios: (1st) 2.74:1; (2nd) 1.54:1 or 1.55:1; (3rd) 1.00:1; (Rev) 2.22:1. Standard final drive ratio: (LeB) 2.76:1, 2.26:1 or 2.45:1; (Cord.) 2.76:1; (Newpt six) 2.94:1; (Newpt/N.Y./Imp. V-8) 2.24:1; (Newpt/N.Y. V-8 4Bbl.) 2.45:1. Steering: recirculating ball, power-assisted. Suspension: (LeBaron/Cordoba/Imperial) front transverse torsion bars with control arms and anti-sway bar, rigid rear axle with semi-elliptic leaf springs; (Newport/New Yorker) longitudinal front torsion bars with lower trailing links and anti-sway bar, rear leaf springs. Brakes: Front disc, rear drum (power-assisted). Ignition: Electronic. Body construction: Unibody. Fuel tank: (LeB/Cord./Imp.) 18 gal.; (Newpt/N.Y.) 21 gal.

DRIVETRAIN OPTIONS: Engines: 318 cu. in., 2Bbl. V-8: LeBaron/Cord/Newpt ($62). 318 cu. in., 4Bbl. V-8: LeB/Cord./Newpt ($62), N.Y. (NC). Axle/Suspension: Sure grip differential ($75-$114) exc. LeB wag ($70). Heavy-duty susp. ($27-$29). H.D. shock absorbers ($8) exc. LeB. Other: Heavy-duty trailer assist pkg.: Newpt/N.Y. ($246). H.D. cooling: LeB/Cord./Newpt ($127). Long-life battery ($35- $39). California emission system ($46).

LEBARON CONVENIENCE/APPEARANCE OPTIONS: Option Packages: Basic group ($937-$1125). Sport appearance pkg. ($154-$258). Two-tone paint pkg. ($158). Handling pkg. ($163). Protection group ($58-$67). Light pkg. ($85-$99). Deluxe insulation pkg. ($10-$109). Comfort/Convenience: Air conditioning ($606). Auto-temp air cond. ($656) exc. w/option pkg. ($50). Rear defroster ($107). Automatic speed control ($136). Power seat ($177). Power windows ($145-$202). Power door locks ($96-$136). Power decklid or tailgate release ($29). Illuminated entry system ($57). Luxury steering wheel ($39). Leather-covered steering wheel ($21-$60). Tilt steering wheel ($83). Sport steering wheel ($16-$55). Tinted glass ($78). Deluxe wiper/washer ($51). Liftgate wiper/washer: wag ($82). Digital clock ($56). Locking gas cap ($8). Lighting, Horns and Mirrors: Halogen headlamps ($40). Cornering lamps ($54). Dual horns ($10). Remote-control left mirror ($20). Remote right mirror ($41). Dual remote chrome mirrors ($41-$61). Dual remote sport mirrors ($56-$76). Lighted vanity mirror ($50). Day/night mirror ($13). Entertainment: AM radio ($92). AM/FM radio ($59-$151). AM/FM stereo radio ($94-$186); w/CB ($355-$447). AM/FM stereo w/8track player ($169-$261); w/cassette ($223-$315). Search tune AM/FM stereo radio ($211-$303). Rear speaker ($21). Radio upgrade w/dual speakers ($26). Premium speaker pkg. ($93). Power antenna ($49). Exterior Trim: T-Bar roof: cpe ($695). Power glass sunroof ($865). Full vinyl roof: sed ($131). Padded landau vinyl roof: Salon cpe ($173). Starmist paint ($55). Vinyl bodyside moldings ($43). Upper door frame moldings ($38). Rear bumper guards ($25). Door edge guards ($13-$22). Bodyside tape stripe: base wag ($50). Hood tape stripe ($24). Luggage rack: wag ($98). Air deflector: wag ($31). Undercoating ($25). Interior Trim/Upholstery: Console: Salon cpe ($108). Center cushion: Salon cpe ($42). Vinyl split-back bench seat ($50- $68). Vinyl 60/40 split bench seat w/recliner ($208-$276). Cloth 60/40 seat: wag ($208-$276). Cloth/vinyl 60/40 seat: Salon ($226). Leather 60/40 seat ($364-$608). Cloth/vinyl bucket seats: Salon cpe ($101). Color-keyed floor mats: front ($25); rear ($20). Pedal dress-up ($10). Trunk dress-up ($47). Cargo area carpet: base wag ($74); w/stowage bins ($25-$99). Cargo security cover: wag ($60). Wheels and Tires: Wire wheel covers ($106-$249). Premium wheel covers: Medallion ($43-$88). Premier wheel covers ($45). Styled wheels ($98-$143). Forged aluminum wheels ($183-$326). P205/75R15 SBR WSW ($101). Conventional spare tire ($39).

CORDOBA CONVENIENCE/APPEARANCE OPTIONS: Option Packages: Corinthian Edition ($765-$888). Basic group ($791-$908). Cabriolet roof pkg. ($517-$634). Cabriolet roof two-tone pkg. ($615-$732). LS Decor pkg. ($450). Two-tone paint pkg. ($73-$170). Sport handling pkg. ($139-$240). Roadability pkg. ($31). Protection pkg. ($68). Light pkg. ($117). Comfort/Convenience: Air conditioning ($606). Auto-temp air cond. ($654) exc. w/option pkg. ($48). Rear defroster ($107). Automatic speed control ($136). Power seat ($177). Power windows ($145). Power door locks ($96). Power decklid release ($28-$43). Illuminated entry system ($57). Luxury steering wheel (NC). Leather-covered steering wheel ($39) exc. LS (NC). Tilt steering wheel ($83). Sport steering wheel ($34); std. on LS. Digital clock ($59). Intermittent wipers ($43). Locking gas cap ($8). Lighting, Horns and Mirrors: Halogen headlamps ($40). Cornering lamps ($54). Reading lamp ($20). Triad horns ($22). Remote-control left mirror ($20). Dual remote mirrors ($57- $77). Lighted vanity mirror ($50). Entertainment: AM/FM radio ($59). AM/FM stereo ($95); w/CB ($355); w/8track ($169); w/cassette ($223). Search tune AM/FM stereo radio ($211). Rear speaker ($20). Radio upgrade w/dual speakers ($26). Premium speaker pkg. ($93). Power antenna ($49). Radio delete ($85 credit). Exterior Trim: T-Bar roof ($695). Power sunroof ($758). Crown Special Edition landau vinyl roof ($268). Landau vinyl roof ($131). Premium paint ($68). Vinyl bodyside molding ($45). Sill moldings: LS ($30). Wheel lip moldings: LS ($26). Door edge guards ($13). Deluxe rear bumper guards: LS ($25). Bodyside/decklid tape stripes ($72). Hood tape stripe ($25). Undercoating ($25). Interior Trim/Upholstery: Console ($66-$108). Center cushion w/armrest ($42). Cloth/vinyl bucket seats: LS ($91). Leather bucket seats ($447-$540). Color-keyed floor mats: front ($25); rear ($20). Pedal dress-up ($11). Trunk dress-up ($47). Litter container ($10). Wheels and Tires: Wire wheel covers ($160-$206). Premium wheel covers ($46). Forged aluminum wheels ($237-$283). P205/75R15 GBR WSW ($27). P205/75R15 SBR WSW ($101). P215/70R15 SBR WSW ($60-$161). P215/70R15 RWL SBR: LS (NC to $157). Conventional spare tire ($39).

NEWPORT/NEW YORKER CONVENIENCE/APPEARANCE OPTIONS: Option Packages: Fifth Avenue Edition pkg.: N.Y. ($1822). Basic group: Newpt ($993); N.Y. ($156). Open road handling pkg.: Newpt ($281); N.Y. ($180). Carriage roof pkg.: N.Y. ($854). Light pkg.: Newpt ($103). Comfort/Convenience: Air cond.: Newpt ($646). Auto-temp air cond.: Newpt ($692) exc. w/option pkg. ($46). Rear defroster ($112). Auto. speed control ($139). Power seat ($179). Power windows: Newpt ($218). Power door locks ($138). Power decklid release ($30-$45). Illuminated entry system ($60). Luxury steering wheel ($39). Leather-covered steering wheel: Newpt ($60); N.Y. ($41). Tilt steering ($84). Digital clock: Newpt ($62). Intermittent wipers ($44). Locking gas cap ($9). Lighting, Horns and Mirrors: Halogen headlamps ($41). Cornering lamps ($54). Triad horns ($22). Remote-control driver's mirror: Newpt ($21). Remote passenger mirror: N.Y. ($30). Dual remote mirrors: Newpt ($30-$51). Lighted vanity mirror ($52). Entertainment: AM radio: Newpt ($97). AM/FM radio: Newpt ($54-$151). AM/FM stereo radio: Newpt ($95-$192). AM/FM stereo w/8track tape player: Newpt ($166-$263); N.Y. ($71); Fifth Ave. (NC). AM/FM stereo w/cassette: Newpt ($221-$318); N.Y. ($126); Fifth Ave. (NC). AM/FM stereo w/CB: Newpt ($356-$453); N.Y. ($261); Fifth Ave. (NC). Search tune AM/FM stereo radio: Newpt ($206-$303); N.Y. ($111); Fifth Ave. (NC). Rear speaker ($21). Radio upgrade w/dual speakers: Newpt ($26). Premium speaker pkg. ($95). Power antenna ($50). Exterior Trim: Power glass sunroof ($934). Special paint ($68). Vinyl side moldings ($54). Bumper guards: Newpt ($60). Door edge protectors ($23). Undercoating ($31). Interior Trim/Upholstery: Vinyl split-back bench seat: Newpt ($34). Cloth/vinyl 60/40 bench seat: Newpt ($148). Leather 60/40 bench seat: N.Y. ($376). Color-keyed floor mats: front ($25); rear ($20). Pedal dress-up ($11). Trunk dress-up: Newpt ($65). Litter container ($10). Wheels and Tires: Wire wheel covers ($251). Premium turbine wheel covers ($86). Forged aluminum wheels ($321) exc. Fifth Ave. ($70). P205/75R15 SBR WSW ($101). P225/70R15 SBR WSW ($91-$192). Conventional spare tire ($39).

IMPERIAL OPTIONS Imperial had only one extra-cost option, the Moonroof ($1044).

HISTORY: Introduced: October 13, 1980. Model year production: 80,821 (incl. Canadian-built Cordobas and Imperials). Calendar year production (U.S.): 57,315. Calendar year sales by U.S. dealers: 90,616. Model year sales by U.S. dealers: 105,584.

Historical Footnotes: Chrysler's model year sales shrunk considerably, though sales for the Chrysler-Plymouth Division rose 9 percent. But since 1980 was such a terrible year, even that rise wasn't so impressive. At the end of 1980, LeBaron production ceased as the Lynch Road plant in Detroit shut down. For 1982, the LeBaron name would return in front-drive form. Ads claimed that "It's Time for Imperial," yet only 6,368 of the new luxury coupes found buyers for the model year, which was more limited production than the "new Chrysler Corporation" had in mind.

1982 Chrysler

Newport left the lineup this year, while New Yorker went to a smaller platform. LeBaron emerged in an all-new form, with front-wheel drive. In addition to the coupe, sedan and Town & Country wagon, that series added a convertible—the first domestic-built ragtop since the '76 Cadillac Eldorado.

1982 LeBaron convertible (CC)

LEBARON — SERIES C — FOUR — Chrysler's first front-drives came in standard and Medallion trim, in two-door coupe or four-door sedan body styles. Though nearly two feet shorter and 800 pounds lighter, the new versions still carried six passengers, but managed up to 26 MPG city (40 highway) in EPA gas mileage ratings. Wheelbase was now 99.9 in. An overhead-cam 135 cu. in. (2.2-liter) Trans-4 engine was standard, with four-speed manual transaxle. The single powerplant option was a Mitsubishi-built Silent Shaft 156 cu. in. (2.6-liter) overhead-cam four. An automatic transaxle was also available. Front suspension used MacPherson Iso-Struts with linkless sway bar, while the rear held a flex arm beam axle with trailing links and coil springs. Power rack-and-pinion steering was standard. Related to the Dodge 400, the CV-bodied mid-size LeBaron was based on the recently-introduced K-car, but more posh. Dimensions, drivetrains and dash were the same as Dodge Aries/Plymouth Reliant. LeBaron's sharply-angled, formal-look grille (similar to Imperial's) consisted of thin vertical bars, with an upper header that wrapped over the top and held a pentastar hood ornament. The grille pattern continued in a wide slot below the bumper rub strip. Quad rectangular recessed headlamps were used. Small parking lamps sat down in the bumper. Amber and red side marker lenses were in the front and rear bumper strip extensions. Clear cornering lamps (optional) went below the amber lenses. Overall, LeBaron displayed a rather angular, upright profile devoid of curves, but sharply angled at the front fender tips and with protruding bumper. Wide taillamps reached from license plate opening to decklid edge, with bright molding and backup lamps above. The decklid a held pentastar emblem in its center, plus 'Chrysler' and 'LeBaron' lettering. Two-door coupes had opera windows, while back doors of four-door sedans had blanked (covered) windows at the rear. LeBaron standard equipment included power brakes and steering, four-speed manual transaxle, a padded vinyl roof, digital clock, bumper rub strips, lighter, chimes, electric cooling fan, pentastar hood ornament, dual horns, and day/night inside mirror. Also standard: dual chrome outside mirrors, AM radio, P185/70R14 SBR WSW tires, and deluxe wheel covers. Medallion added halogen headlamps, a light/gauge alert group, dual mirrors, bodyside stripes, premium color-keyed wheel covers, and trunk dress-up items. LeBaron colors were: Formal Black, Morocco Red, Light Blue Crystal, Sterling Silver Crystal, Nightwatch Blue, Goldenrod Tan Crystal, Manila Cream, Spice Tan

metallic, Pearl White, Charcoal Gray metallic, and Mahogany metallic; plus four two-tones. Two notable additions arrived at mid-year. LeBaron's Town & Country wagon had simulated wood (plastic) trim on bodysides and liftgate, similar to prior T&C wagons. Its standard engine was the 2.6-liter four with automatic transmission. Also standard: a crystal hood ornament, plus vinyl front bucket seats with folding center armrest. Also appearing was a LeBaron convertible. Both were converted from two-door coupe bodies by Cars & Concepts in Brighton, Michigan. Ragtops had a small back window and wide rear quarters. Equipment included vinyl bucket seats, standard automatic transaxle, center console, color-keyed remote-control mirrors, and power top with tailored boot. For extra dollars, buyers could have a Mark Cross convertible whose many standard features included the 2.6-liter engine, distinctive Mark Cross leather/vinyl bucket seats and rear bench seat, plus air conditioning, automatic transmission, power windows and door locks, and remote decklid release. Not every body color was available on convertibles or Town & Country wagons.

1982 Cordoba LS coupe (CC)

CORDOBA — SERIES S — SIX/V-8 — This year's Cordoba appeared much like the 1981 edition, but without 'Cordoba' script and medallion on front fenders. A new standard padded vinyl landau roof came in nine colors, highlighted by an up-and-over molding with brushed finish. Standard 60/40 seating had new cloth/vinyl trim, with folding center armrest and passenger seatback recliner. Optional: a seek/scan AM/FM stereo radio. Halogen headlamps and dual remote mirrors were now standard. Galvanized steel was used extensively for body panels. Base engine again was the 225 cu. in. slant six, with 318 V-8 optional. A wide-ratio automatic transmission with lockup torque converter was standard. The sporty LS, called the "very affordable" Cordoba, also looked much the same. Priced nearly $1000 lower, the LS was said to have "more youthful styling" rather than "upscale sophistication," with a "wickedly slanted grille." Inside were high-back vinyl bucket seats. Options included the convertible-like cabriolet roof, plus cloth/vinyl bucket seats with folding center armrest. Standard Cordoba colors were: Royal Red Crystal, Goldenrod Crystal, Light Auburn Crystal, Pearl White, Sterling Silver Crystal, Formal Black, Glacier Blue Crystal, Nightwatch Blue, and Manila Cream; plus metallic Charcoal Gray, Mahogany, or Spice Tan. Cordoba LS came in Morocco Red, Nightwatch Blue, Formal Black, Pearl White, or Burnished Silver metallic. A total of 1,612 Cordobas had the cabriolet roof.

1982 New Yorker Fith Avenue sedan (CC)

NEW YORKER — SERIES FS — SIX/V-8 — While retaining rear-wheel drive, a revised New Yorker four-door rode a new smaller platform with 112.7 in. wheelbase (8 inches shorter than before). It was actually LeBaron's old M-body, viewed as mid- rather than full-size. The former R-body versions (including Newport) had been dropped early in 1981. Plymouth's Gran Fury was a close relative. Base engine now was the 225 cu. in. (3.7-liter) slant six, with 318 V-8 optional. Standard equipment included semi-automatic air conditioning, bumper guards and rub strips, lighter, digital clock, automatic transmission, power brakes/steering, tinted glass, dual horns, halogen headlamps, AM radio, twin remote-control mirrors, decklid and bodyside striping, and a trip odometer. Wide parking lamps stood directly over quad rectangular headlamps. The upright rectangular grille was made up of thin vertical bars with a heavier center bar, plus two subdued horizontal dividers. The grille surrounding molding extended outward at the base, to fender tips. Above the grille and parking lamps was a heavy bright horizontal molding, just ahead of the hood (which held a Pentastar hood ornament). New Yorkers no longer had concealed headlamps. Vertical front fender louvers were just ahead of the door; small horizontal amber marker lenses just ahead of front wheels. At the rear were wide wraparound taillamps, while the padded vinyl landau roof held a small formal "frenched" back window. 'New Yorker' script appeared in the portion of the padded top that extended into the backs of the rear doors. Standard cloth/vinyl 60/40 individually adjustable seats had a folding center armrest and passenger seatback recliner. New Yorker's rather modest option list included an electronic-tuning AM/FM stereo radio, leather-covered steering wheel, and forged aluminum wheels. Body colors were: Goldenrod Crystal Coat, Nightwatch Blue, Charcoal Gray metallic, Formal Black, Morocco Red, Sterling Silver Crystal, Manogany metallic, and Pearl White. Nearly four-fifths of the New Yorkers shipped were Fifth Avenue Edition. That $1647 option package included loose-pillow 60/40 seats in Corinthian leather or velvet cloth, with folding center armrest and passenger seatback recliner; plus power seat, windows, door locks, and decklid release. The standard tilt steering column held a leather-wrapped wheel. Also standard: 'Fifth Avenue' identification on rear door plug, 318 V-8 engine, illuminated entry system, lighted vanity visor mirror, power antenna, AM/FM stereo radio, automatic speed control, hood stripe, and intermittent wipers.

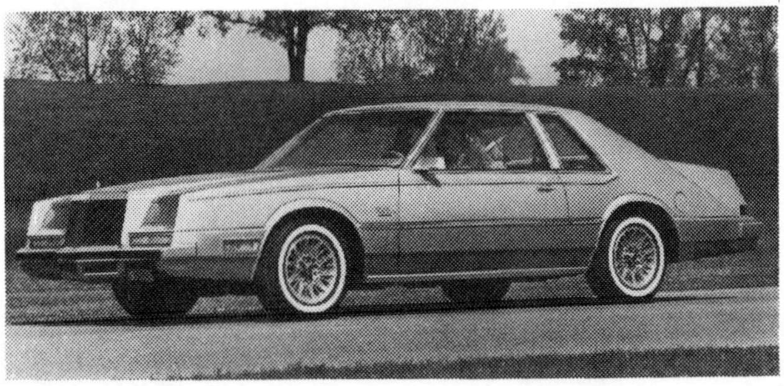

1982 Imperial coupe (CC)

IMPERIAL — SERIES YS — V-8 — Suffering a shortage of sales, the mid-size luxury Imperial coupe changed little for 1982. Now priced at $20,988, it had a vast list of standard equipment and virtually no options. Customers could select body color, seat covering, sound system, and wheel type. Standard engine again was the 318 cu. in. (5.2-liter) V-8 with electronic fuel injection. New interiors held Kimberley velvet cloth upholstery in choice of six colors. Crystal Coat paint came in three new colors: Sterling Silver, Golden Tan, and Light Blue. Only 2,329 Imperials were built in the model year, 279 of which had the "FS" Sinatra package. That one had special paint and emblemseven a set of 8-track tapes with Frank's top hits in a special console.

I.D. DATA: Chrysler again had a 17-symbol Vehicle Identification Number (VIN) on the upper left corner of the instrument panel, visible through the windshield. Coding changed somewhat with the revised model lineup. The first digit indicates Country: '1' U.S.A.; '2' Canada. The second symbol is Make: 'C' Chrysler; 'A' Imperial. Third is Vehicle Type: '3' passenger car; '7' truck. The next symbol ('B') indicates manual seatbelts. Symbol five is Car Line: 'C' LeBaron; 'S' Cordoba; 'F' New Yorker; 'Y' Imperial. Symbol six is Series: '4' High'; '5' Premium; '6' Special. Symbol seven is Body Style: '2' 2-dr. coupe or HT coupe; '5' 2-dr. convertible coupe; '6' 4-dr. sedan; '9' 4-dr. wagon. Eighth is the Engine Code: 'B' L4-135 2Bbl.; 'D' L4-156 2Bbl.; 'E' L6-225 1Bbl.; 'K' V8318 2Bbl.; 'M' V8318 4Bbl.; 'J' V8318 EFI. Next comes a check digit: 0 through 9 (or X). Symbol ten indicates Model Year: 'C' 1982. Symbol eleven is Assembly Plant: 'C' Detroit; 'G' St. Louis; 'F' Newark, DE; 'R' Windsor, Ontario. The last six digits make up the sequential serial number, starting with 100001. An engine identification number is stamped on the rear face of the block of the 2.2-liter four, directly beneath the cylinder head (left side of car). On the 2.6-liter four, that number is on the left side of the block, between the core plug and the rear face of the block (radiator side). Six- cylinder identification numbers, as before, are on the right of the block, below No. 6 spark plug; V-8s, on right of block to rear of engine mount. An engine serial number with parts replacement data is just below the identification number on the 2.2 engine; and on right front of the 2.6 block, adjacent to exhaust manifold stud. Serial numbers are on the right of the block below No. 1 spark plug on six-cylinder engines, and on the left front corner of the block below the cylinder head on V-8s. A Body Code Plate is on the upper radiator support, left front fender shield, or wheelhousing.

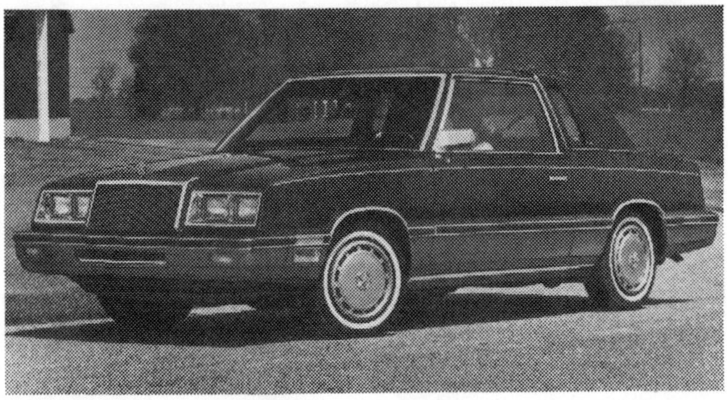

1982 LeBaron coupe (CC)

LEBARON (FOUR)

Series Number	Body/Style Number	Body Type & Seating	Factory Price	Shipping Weight	Production Total
CH	22	2-dr. Cpe-6P	8143	2470	14,295
CH	41	4-dr. Sed-6P	8237	2455	19,619
CH	27	2-dr. Conv.-4P	11698	2565	3,045
LEBARON MEDALLION (FOUR)					
CP	22	2-dr. Cpe-6P	8408	2475	12,856
CP	41	4-dr. Sed-6P	8502	2465	22,915
CP	27	2-dr. Conv.-4P	13998	2615	9,780
LEBARON TOWN & COUNTRY (FOUR)					
CP	45	4-dr. Sta Wag-5P	9425	2660	7,809
CORDOBA (SIX/V-8)					
SP	22	2-dr. HT Cpe-6P	9197/9267	3370/3520	11,762
CORDOBA 'LS' (SIX/V-8)					
SS	22	2-dr. HT Cpe-6P	8258/8328	3315/3465	3,136
NEW YORKER (SIX/V-8)					
FS	41	4-dr. Sed-6P	10781/10851	3510/3655	50,509
IMPERIAL (V-8)					
YS	22	2-dr. HT Cpe-6P	20988	3945	2,329

FACTORY PRICE & WEIGHT NOTE: Figures to left of slash are for six- cylinder engine, to right of slash for 318 V-8.

MODEL NUMBER NOTE: Some sources identify models using the new VIN data to indicate Car Line, Price Class and Body Style. Example: LeBaron coupe (CH22) has the equivalent number CC42, which translates to LeBaron line, High price class, and coupe body. See I.D. Data section for breakdown.

ENGINE DATA: BASE FOUR (LeBaron): Inline, overhead cam four-cylinder. Cast iron block; aluminum head. Displacement: 135 cu. in. (2.2 liters). Bore & stroke: 3.44 x 3.62 in. Compression ratio: 8.5:1. Brake horsepower: 84 at 4800 R.P.M. Torque: 111 lbs.-ft. at 2400 R.P.M. Five main bearings. Hydraulic valve lifters. Carburetor: 2Bbl. Holley 6520 or 5220. VIN Code: B. BASE FOUR (LeBaron Town & Country); OPTIONAL (other LeBarons): Inline, overhead cam four-cylinder. Cast iron block; aluminum head. Displacement: 156 cu. in. (2.6 liters). Bore & stroke: 3.59 x 3.86 in. Compression ratio: 8.2:1. Brake horsepower: 92 at 4500 R.P.M. Torque: 131 lbs.-ft. at 2500 R.P.M. Five main bearings. Solid valve lifters. Carburetor: 2Bbl. Mikuni. VIN Code: D. BASE SIX (Cordoba, New Yorker): Inline, overhead valve six-cylinder. Cast iron block and head. Displacement: 225 cu. in. (3.7 liters). Bore & stroke: 3.40 x 4.12 in. Compression ratio: 8.4:1. Brake horsepower: 90 at 3600 R.P.M. Torque: 160 lbs.-ft. at 1600 R.P.M. Four main bearings. Hydraulic valve lifters. Carburetor: 1Bbl. Holley 1945 or 6145. VIN Code: E. OPTIONAL V-8 (Cordoba, New Yorker): 90-degree, overhead valve V-8. Cast iron block and head. Displacement: 318 cu. in. (5.2 liters). Bore & stroke: 3.91 x 3.31 in. Compression ratio: 8.5:1. Brake horsepower: 130 at 4000 R.P.M. Torque: 230 lbs.-ft. at 2000 R.P.M. Five main bearings. Hydraulic valve lifters. Carburetor: 2Bbl. Carter BBD. VIN Code: K. CALIFORNIA V-8 (Cordoba, New Yorker): Same as 318 cu. in. V-8 above, but with Carter TQ 4Bbl. carburetor B.H.P.: 165 at 4000 R.P.M. Torque: 240 lbs.-ft. at 2000 R.P.M. VIN Code: M. IMPERIAL V-8: Same as 318 cu. in. V-8 above, but with electronic fuel injection B.H.P.: 140 at 4000 R.P.M. Torque: 245 lbs.-ft. at 2000 R.P.M. VIN Code: J.

CHASSIS DATA: Wheelbase: (LeBaron) 99.9 in.; (Cordoba/New Yorker/Imperial) 112.7 in. Overall length: (LeB) 179.7 in.; (LeB wag) 179.8 in.; (Cord.) 210.1 in.; (Cord. LS) 209.6 in.; (N.Y.) 206.7 in.; (Imperial) 213.4 in. Height: (LeB cpe) 52.6 in.; (LeB sed) 53.0 in.; (LeB wag) 52.7 in.; (LeB conv.) 54.1 in.; (Cord./Imp.) 53.2 in.; (N.Y.) 55.3 in. Width: (LeB) 68.5 in.; (Cord./Imp.) 72.7 in.; (N.Y.) 74.2 in. Front Tread: (LeB) 57.6 in.; (Cord./N.Y./Imp.) 60.0" in. Rear Tread: (LeB) 57.0 in.; (Cord./N.Y./Imp.) 59.5 in. Standard Tires: (LeB) P185/70R14 SBR WSW; (Cord.) P195/75R15 GBR WSW; (N.Y./Imp.) P205/75R15 SBR WSW.

TECHNICAL: Transmission: Four-speed manual trans. standard on LeBaron. Gear ratios: (1st) 3.29:1; (2nd) 1.89:1; (3rd) 1.21:1; (4th) 0.88:1; (Rev) 3.14:1. TorqueFlite three-speed automatic optional on LeBaron: (1st) 2.69:1; (2nd) 1.55:1; (3rd) 1.00:1; (Rev) 2.10:1. TorqueFlite standard on other models: (1st) 2.74:1; (2nd) 1.54:1 or 1.55:1; (3rd) 1.00:1; (Rev) 2.22:1. Standard final drive ratio: (LeB) 2.69:1 exc. 2.78:1 w/auto.; (Cord.) 2.94:1; (N.Y. six) 2.94:1; (N.Y. V-8) 2.2:1; (Imp.) 2.20:1. Steering: (LeBaron) rack and pinion; (others) recirculating ball, power-assisted. Suspension: (LeBaron) MacPherson Iso-Struts and linkless sway bar in front, flex arm beam axle with trailing links and coil springs at the rear, (others) front torsion bars and anti- sway bar, rear leaf springs; stabilizer bar on Imperial. Brakes: Front disc, rear drum (power-assisted). Ignition: Electronic. Body construction: Unibody. Fuel tank: (LeB) 13 gal.; (Cord./N.Y./Imp.) 18 gal.

DRIVETRAIN OPTIONS: Engines: 2.6-liter four: LeBaron ($171). 318 cu. in. V-8: Cord./N.Y. ($70). Transmission/Suspension: Auto. trans.: LeB ($396). Heavy-duty susp. ($26-$31). Rear sway bar: Cord. ($34). Other: H.D. cooling: LeB/Cord ($141). H.D. 500-amp battery ($43). California emission system ($65).

LEBARON CONVENIENCE/APPEARANCE OPTIONS: Option Packages: Easy-order packages (N/A). Mark Cross pkg. ($861). Two-tone paint ($170-$269). Light/gauge alert group ($79). Comfort/Convenience: Air conditioning ($676). Rear defroster ($125). Automatic speed control ($155). Power seat ($197). Power windows ($165-$235). Power door locks ($106-$152). Power decklid release ($32). Leather-wrapped or sport steering wheel ($50). Tilt steering wheel ($95). Tinted glass ($88). Deluxe wipers ($47). Lighting and Mirrors: Halogen headlamps ($15). Cornering lamps ($57). Reading lamp ($24). Dual remote mirrors: base ($55). Lighted vanity mirror ($50). Entertainment: AM/FM stereo radio ($106); w/CB ($364); w/8track player ($192). Electronic-tuning AM/FM stereo radio $250); w/cassette ($455). Radio upgrade w/dual speakers ($27). Premium speaker pkg. ($126). Radio delete ($56 credit). Exterior Trim: Glass sunroof ($275). Crystal coat paint ($99). Front or rear bumper guards ($23). Sill moldings ($23). Door edge guards ($15-$25). Bodyside tape stripe: base ($48). Undercoating ($39). Vinyl lower body protection ($39). Interior Trim/Upholstery: Console ($100). Center armrest ($59). Vinyl bucket seats: base ($92). Cloth/vinyl bucket seats: Medallion ($151). Leather bucket seats: Medallion ($414). Color-keyed floor mats: front ($25); rear ($20). Trunk dress-up ($51). Cargo area tonneau cover: wag ($64). Wheels and Tires: Wire wheel covers ($244-$257). Cast aluminum wheels ($344-$357). Conventional spare tire ($51).

CORDOBA CONVENIENCE/APPEARANCE OPTIONS: Option Packages: Basic group ($552-$1205). Cabriolet roof pkg. ($554). Protection pkg. ($107-$137). Light pkg. ($137-$159). Comfort/Convenience: Air conditioning ($731). Rear defroster ($125). Automatic speed control ($155). Power seat ($197). Power windows ($165). Power door locks ($106). Power decklid release ($32-$49). Illuminated entry system ($72). Leather- wrapped steering wheel ($50). Tilt steering wheel ($95). Sport steering wheel: LS ($50). Digital clock ($61). Intermittent wipers ($47). Lighting, Horns and Mirrors: Cornering lamps ($57). Triad horns ($25). Lighted vanity mirror ($58). Entertainment: AM/FM radio ($106). AM/FM stereo w/CB ($364); w/8track ($192). Electronic-tuning AM/FM stereo w/cassette ($455). Search-tune AM/FM stereo radio ($239). Radio upgrade w/dual speakers ($28). Premium speaker pkg. ($126). Power antenna ($55). Radio delete ($56 credit). Exterior Trim: T-Bar roof ($790). Landau vinyl roof: LS ($157). Crystal coat paint ($99). Sill moldings: LS ($34). Wheel lip moldings: LS ($30). Bodyside/decklid tape stripes: LS ($72). Bodyside/decklid/hood tape stripe ($96). Undercoating ($39). Interior Trim/Upholstery: Console ($75-$124). Center armrest ($49). Cloth/vinyl bucket seats: LS ($103). Leather bucket seats ($499). Trunk dress-up ($60). Wheels and Tires: Wire wheel covers ($216). Premium wheel covers ($53). Forged aluminum wheels ($323). P205/75R15 SBR WSW ($116). P215/70R15 SBR RWL ($182). Conventional spare tire ($51).

NEW YORKER CONVENIENCE/APPEARANCE OPTIONS: Option Packages: Fifth Avenue Edition ($1647). Protection group ($66). Comfort/Convenience: Auto. speed control ($155). Power seat ($197). Power door locks ($152). Power decklid release ($32). Illuminated entry system ($72). Leather-covered steering wheel ($50). Tilt steering ($95). Intermittent wipers ($47). Lighted vanity mirror ($58). Entertainment: AM/FM stereo radio ($106); w/CB ($258-$364); w/8track ($86-$192). Electronic-tuning AM/FM stereo w/cassette ($349-$455). Search-tune AM/FM stereo radio ($133- $239). Radio upgrade w/dual speakers ($28). Premium speaker pkg. ($126). Power antenna ($55). Exterior Trim: Power glass sunroof ($982). Crystal coat paint ($99). Hood tape stripe ($27). Undercoating ($39). Interior Trim/Upholstery: Cloth 60/40 bench seat (NC). Leather 60/40 bench seat ($306). Wheels and Tires: Wire wheel covers ($170). Forged aluminum wheels ($101-$271). Conventional spare tire ($51).

IMPERIAL OPTIONS: Imperial had only one extra-cost option, the Sinatra Edition ($1078). Customers could choose among several no-cost options: cloth/vinyl or leather split bench seat; AM/FM stereo w/CB, 8track or cassette; and wire wheel covers or cast aluminum wheels.

HISTORY: Introduced: October 14, 1981 except LeBaron, Oct. 29, 1981 and LeBaron convertible, April 1982. Model year production: 158,055 (incl. Canadian-built Cordobas, Imperials and New Yorkers). Calendar year production (U.S.): 114,443. Calendar year sales by U.S. dealers: 178,970. Model year sales by U.S. dealers: 152,436.

Historical Footnotes: Although the Chrysler-Plymouth Division gained in market share this year, model year sales declined. The new front- drive LeBaron sold considerably better than its rear-drive predecessor of 1981, partly as a result of interest in the new convertible. Cordoba sales fell by nearly half, but New Yorker made a strong showing in its shrunken form. At the modernized St. Louis assembly plant, selected LeBaron two-doors were subjected to a special Quality Assurance Program. One in three cars was given a three-mile road test, then underwent a thorough inspection.

1983 Chrysler

After a year in service, Chrysler's own Trans-4 2.2- liter four-cylinder engine added 10 horsepower by means of reworked manifolds and recalibrated fuel/spark control. Compression also got a boost, to 9.0:1. LeBaron got a new standard five-speed manual gearbox. In a slightly confusing shuffle of nameplates, the rear-drive M-body was called New Yorker Fifth Avenue this year, while the new E-body got the plain New Yorker (and E Class) badge. Electronic Voice Alert became optional on LeBaron and E Class/New Yorker. "Message Center" lights warned of such maladies as an open door or low fuel level, on a car diagram. The EVA system added audio warnings for the 11 monitored functions. Not everyone appreciated the intrusive voice, which would be modified for 1984. LeBaron added a Town & Country convertible with fake wood paneling like the T&C wagon, similar to the simulated wood convertibles of the same name three decades earlier. The wood-look ragtop, in fact, was advertised as "Re-introducing an American classic." An Executive sedan and limousine became available, stretched out from front-drive LeBaron coupes. The five-seat Executive sedan rode a 124.3 in. wheelbase. A seven-passenger Limousine with jump seats and electric division window had a 131.3 in. wheelbase. These were the first limos since the Imperials of 1970. Chrysler production totals show that only two LeBarons had the A89 limo package.

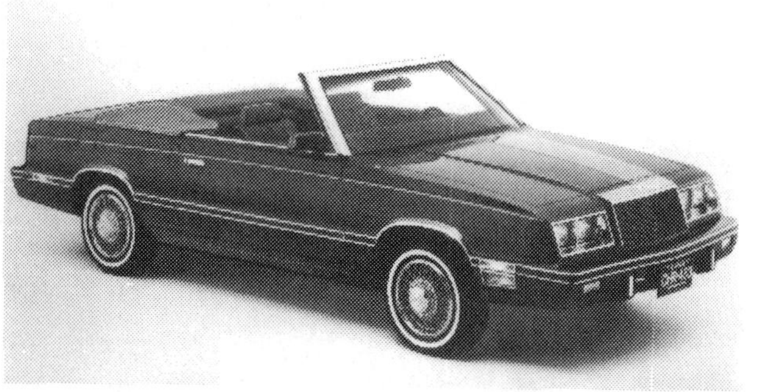

1983 LeBaron convertible (CP)

LEBARON — SERIES C — FOUR — Only one trim level was offered by the front-drive LeBaron in its second year, as the upper-level Medallion was dropped. LeBaron was essentially a posher version of the Kcar (Dodge Aries and Plymouth Reliant). New standard equipment included halogen headlamps, a tethered gas cap, and "ram air" heater/vent system with outlets on the dashboard. Brake rotors grew this year, and rear drum brakes became self-adjusting. The manual transaxle (standard only on coupes) gained a gear, offering five forward speeds instead of four. The convertible came in base, luxury Mark Cross, and (a little later) Town & Country form, with fake wood trim. Electronic Voice Alert was standard on the Mark Cross ragtop and T&C wagon. Door latches were made quieter, with sound- deadening materials. Appearance changed little for 1983. LeBaron had a formal- looking sloped grille with thin vertical bars and slightly wider center vertical bar, plus a pentastar hood ornament. Clear rectangular parking lights set into the bumper, where the grille pattern repeated in a grille-width center slot. Bright bodyside moldings with vinyl inserts extended into partial (upper half) wheel opening moldings. Low-back vinyl bucket seats with adjustable head restraints and dual recliners were standard in coupe and convertible. They came in silver, red, beige, brown or (convertible only) red/white. Standard in four-doors and Town & Country was a cloth bench seat with center armrests, in blue, silver, red, beige, or brown. Body colors were: Black, Crimson Red, Glacier Blue Crystal Coat, Silver Crystal Coat, Nightwatch Blue, Beige Crystal Coat, Pearl White, Charcoal Gray Metallic, and Sable Brown. Black and Crimson Red were not available with Mark Cross package on convertible; Glacier Blue, Silver, Nightwatch Blue and Charcoal Gray not available on any convertible. Glacier and Nightwatch Blue were unavailable on Town & Country. LeBaron's standard equipment also included an AM radio, digital clock, roll-resistant SBR whitewalls, luxury wheel covers, carpeted trunk floor, luxury two-spoke color-keyed steering wheel, power brakes, power rack-and-pinion steering, electronic digital clock, cloth-covered headliner, and inside hood release. Two-door coupes also had a padded vinyl landau roof. All models except the coupe had standard TorqueFlite automatic transmission. Convertibles had a center console, color-keyed dual remote mirrors, power top with zip-down window and weather-seal sides, plus tailored top boot. The standard 2.2-liter OHC four had chrome valve stems, alloy valve seats, and moly-faced compression rings. A new optional electronic travel computer displayed fuel used, trip mileage, average speed, and cruising range. The Mark Cross convertible added a host of extras: air conditioning, Mitsubishi-built Silent Shaft 2.6 OHC four, special low-back Corinthian leather bucket seats with console and freestanding center armrest, leather-wrapped steering wheel, vinyl door trim inserts and Mark Cross medallions, front/rear bumper guards, cornering lamps, upper body accent stripes, and wire wheel covers. Electronic Voice Alert, electronic-tuning AM/FM stereo radio, tilt steering column, power windows and door locks, power decklid release, automatic speed control, deluxe wipers, and Travel Computer also were Mark Cross standards. A Mark Cross package on other models included a 50/50 leather bench seat with dual armrests and recliners; vinyl door trim panels with leather inserts and medallions; leather-wrapped steering wheel; Electronic Voice Alert; and Travel Computer cluster.

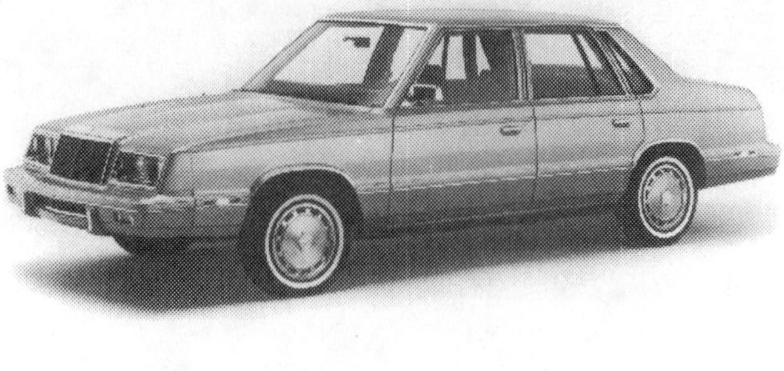

1983 E Class sedan (CC)

E CLASS/NEW YORKER — SERIES T — FOUR — Chrysler's new front-drive, mid-size E-body came with a new and an old name: E Class (first called Gran LeBaron) and, arriving a bit later, the upper-level New Yorker. A three- inch stretch of the K-car wheelbase provided the platform. To avoid confusion with the former rear-drive, that one was now called New Yorker Fifth Avenue. Both new models were six- window four-door sedans. New Yorker seated five; E Class, six. E Class featured a vertical-bar grille like that used on LeBaron and Imperial. New Yorkers carried a similar "waterfall" grille with larger header molding. New Yorker also had a formal, limousine-like roofline with wide rear quarters, heavily padded at the rear in landau style, covering the narrow windows. A brushed-finish wrapover roof band held opera lamps, while front fenders had small louvers and cornering lamps. Standard were bright moldings around sills, lower doors and wheel openings. Base engine on both models was the Trans-4 2.2-liter four. Three-speed TorqueFlite had wide-ratio gearing (high- ratio 1st and 2nd for improved pickup and economy). Optional was the Mitsubishi-built 2.6-liter four. Both had an Iso- Strut front suspension with integral linkless antisway bar, rubber-isolated from the body. At the rear was a beam axle with trailing arm, coil springs, track bar, and torsion-tube anti-roll control. Electronic Voice Alert was standard on both models; a Travel Computer on New Yorker. E Class standard equipment included: power brakes and steering, AM radio, dual horns, lighter, color-keyed wheel covers, halogen headlamps, power decklid release, digital lock, and dual chrome mirrors. Cloth bench seats had a center armrest and adjustable headrests. The fuel filler door opened from inside the car. In addition to a padded landau roof, New Yorker added tinted glass, cornering and opera lamps, remote-control mirrors, bright sill and quarter-window moldings, bodyside and deck tape stripes, intermittent wipers, and locking wire wheel covers. New Yorkers had cloth-upholstered 50/50 reclining bench seating with storage pockets in back and separate armrests. A crystalline pentastar hood ornament was standard. E Class rode P185/70R14 steel-belted radial whitewall tires, while New Yorker's were P185/75R14. New Yorker body colors were: Charcoal Metallic, Nightwatch Blue, Bright Silver Crystal Coat, Beige Crystal Coat, Glacier Blue Crystal Coat, Crimson Red, Sable Brown, Black, and Pearl White. A $696 Mark Cross package included plush leather-and- vinyl seats in four color choices, plus unique door trim panels with piped inserts; leather-wrapped luxury steering wheel; and special identification.

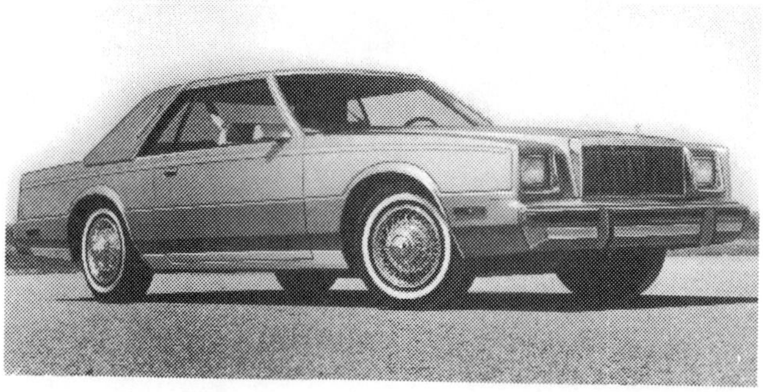

1983 Cordoba coupe (CC)

CORDOBA — SERIES S — SIX/V-8 — For its final year, Cordobe enjoyed little change beyond a switch from amber/clear to amber front side marker lenses and a new crystalline pentastar hood ornament. The low-budget LS model was dropped, leaving just one coupe choice. A new standard 60/40 split-bench seat had a passenger seatback recliner. Optional again was the Cabriolet simulated convertible roof, but only 899 Cordobas had one installed. Premium wheel covers were revised. Wide taillamps each were arranged in three rows, with vertical backup lamps between taillamps and license plate. Colors this year were: Nightwatch Blue, Glacier Blue Crystal Coat, Black, Silver or Beige Crystal Coat, Crimson Red, Sable Brown, Pearl White, and Charcoal Gray metallic. Cordoba's ample standard equipment list included the 225 cu. in. (3.7-liter) slant six engine, power brakes and steering, wide-ratio TorqueFlite automatic transmission, and Special Edition padded landau vinyl roof with brushed-finish roof band and opera lamps. Also standard: a cigarette lighter, digital clock, bumper guards and rub strips, tinted glass, dual horns, halogen headlamps, dual remote-control chrome mirrors, sill moldings with rear extensions, and sport wheel covers. The standard AM radio could be deleted. As before, the 318 cu. in. (5.2-liter) V-8 was optional.

NEW YORKER FIFTH AVENUE — SERIES FS — SIX/V-8 — What had for several years been a luxury option now became a full-fledged model, as the Fifth Avenue name was added to the rear-drive New Yorker. Chrysler described it as "a car with charisma" with an "aristocratic grille." Unchanged this year, that upright grille consisted of narrow vertical bars with somewhat thicker center bar, plus two horizontal divider bars. Simulated vertical front fender louvers appeared again. The formal padded vinyl landau roof had a unique backlight. 'Fifth Avenue Edition' script went on the rear-door portion of the padded vinyl top, just behind the bright brushed-finish wrapover roof molding. That molding held optional electroluminescent opera lamps. Up front was a new pentastar hood ornament. Inside, a two-spoke steering wheel. Premium wheel covers were standard; wire covers optional. Once again, a 225 cu. in. (3.7-liter) slant six was the base engine, with 318 V-8 the sole option. Standard equipment included three-speed automatic transmission, air conditioning, power windows, power steering/brakes, digital clock, dual remote mirrors, bodyside and decklid accent stripes, and tinted glass. Fifth Avenue colors were: Beige Crystal Coat, Nightwatch Blue, Charcoal Gray metallic, Formal Black, Crimson Red, Silver Crystal Coat, Sable Brown, and Pearl White. An $1870 Luxury Equipment package added a heavy-duty battery, V-8 engine, illuminated entry system, lighted right visor vanity mirror,

electroluminescent opera lamps, power door locks and decklid release, power driver's seat, AM/FM stereo radio, 60/40 leather seats, automatic speed control, intermittent wipers, and wire wheel covers.

1983 Imperial coupe (CC)

IMPERIAL — SERIES YS — V-8 — "A singular statement of car and driver." That's how the factory catalog described the luxury Imperial coupe, now in its third (and last) year. Changes were minimal to the sculptured-look bustleback body, apart from new colors. The Sinatra edition was abandoned. Price was cut by $2300, down to $18,688, and Imperials offered an extended warranty; yet only 1,427 were produced this year. Concealed headlamps stood above wide parking lamps in Imperial's angled front end. The forward-peaked grille had a bright upper header molding. Upholstery came in Mark Cross 60/40 Corinthian leather or Kimberley velvet. As before, the fuel-injected 318 cu. in. (5.2-liter) V-8 was standard.

I.D. DATA: Chrysler again had a 17-symbol Vehicle Identification Number (VIN) on the upper left corner of the instrument panel, visible through the windshield. Coding changed somewhat with the revised model lineup. The first digit indicates Country: '1' U.S.A.; '2' Canada. The second symbol is Make: 'C' Chrysler; 'A' Imperial. Third is Vehicle Type: '3' passenger car; '7' truck. The next symbol ('B') indicates manual seatbelts. Symbol five is Car Line: 'C' LeBaron; 'T' E Class and New Yorker (front-drive); 'S' Cordoba; 'F' New Yorker Fifth Avenue (rear- drive); 'Y' Imperial. Symbol six is Series: '4' High; '5' Premium; '6' Special. Symbol seven is Body Style: '1' 2-dr. sedan; '2' 2-dr. HT coupe; '5' 2-dr. convertible coupe; '6' 4-dr. sedan; '9' 4-dr. wagon. Eighth is the Engine Code: 'C' L4-135 2Bbl.; 'G' L4-156 2Bbl.; 'H' L6-225 1Bbl.; 'P' V8318 2Bbl.; 'N' V8318 EFI. Next comes a check digit. Symbol ten indicates Model Year: 'D' 1983. Symbol eleven is Assembly Plant: 'C' Detroit; 'F' Newark; 'G' St. Louis; 'R' Windsor, Ontario. The last six digits make up the sequential serial number, starting with 100001. Engine number coding is similar to 1982.

LEBARON (FOUR)

Series Number	Body/Style Number	Body Type & Seating	Factory Price	Shipping Weight	Production Total
CP	22	2-dr. Cpe-6P	8514	2430	18,331
CP	41	4-dr. Sed-6P	8790	2480	30,869
CP	27	2-dr. Conv.-4P	12800	2470	9,891

LEBARON TOWN & COUNTRY (FOUR)

CP	45	4-dr. Sta Wag-5P	9731	2600	10,994

1983 LeBaron Mark Cross Town & Country convertible (CC)

LEBARON MARK CROSS CONVERTIBLE (FOUR)

CP	27	2-dr. Conv.-4P	14595	N/A	Note 1
CP	27	2-dr. T&C Conv.-4P	15595	N/A	Note 1

Note 1: Mark Cross and Mark Cross Town & Country convertibles are included in base convertible total above. A total of 1,520 T&C convertible packages were installed, plus 5,441 Mark Cross convertible packages.

E CLASS (FOUR)

TH	41	4-dr. Sed-6P	9341	2525	39,258

1983 New Yorker (JG)

NEW YORKER (FOUR)

TP	41	4-dr. Sed-5P	10950	2580	33,832

CORDOBA (SIX/V-8)

SP	22	2-dr. HT Cpe-6P	9580/9805	3380/3515	13,471

1983 New Yorker Fifth Avenue sedan (CC)

NEW YORKER FIFTH AVENUE (SIX/V-8)

FS	41	4-dr. Sed-6P	12487/12712	3540/3690	83,501

IMPERIAL (V-8)

YS	22	2-dr. HT Cpe-6P	18688	3910	1,427

1983 Executive sedan (top); limousine (Bottom)

EXECUTIVE (FOUR)

CP	48	4-dr. Sed-5P	18900	N/A	N/A
CP	49	4-dr. Limo-7P	21900	N/A	N/A

FACTORY PRICE & WEIGHT NOTE: Figures to left of slash are for six- cylinder engine, to right of slash for 318 V-8.

MODEL NUMBER NOTE: Some sources identify models using the new VIN data to indicate Car Line, Price Class and Body Style. Example: LeBaron coupe (CP22) has the equivalent number CC51, which translates to LeBaron line, Premium price class, and two-door body. See I.D. Data section for breakdown.

ENGINE DATA: BASE FOUR (LeBaron, E Class, New Yorker): Inline, overhead cam four-cylinder. Cast iron block; aluminum head. Displacement: 135 cu. in. (2.2 liters). Bore & stroke: 3.44 x 3.62 in. Compression ratio: 9.0:1. Brake horsepower: 94 at 5200 R.P.M. Torque: 117 lbs.-ft. at 3200 R.P.M. Five main bearings. Hydraulic valve lifters. Carburetor: 2Bbl. Holley 6520. **OPTIONAL FOUR** (LeBaron, E Class, New Yorker).

Inline, overhead cam four-cyliner. Cast iron block; aluminum head. Displacement: 156 cu. in. (2.6 liters). Bore & stroke: 3.59 x 3.86 in. Compression ratio: 8.2:1. Brake horsepower: 93 at 4500 R.P.M. Torque: 132 lbs.-ft. at 2500 R.P.M. Five main bearings. Solid valve lifters. Carburetor: 2Bbl. Mikuni. BASE SIX (Cordoba, Fifth Ave.): Inline, overhead valve six-cylinder. Cast iron block and head. Displacement: 225 cu. in (3.7 liters). Bore & stroke: 3.40 x 4.12 in. Compression ratio: 8.4:1. Brake horsepower: 90 at 3600 R.P.M. Torque: 165 lbs.-ft. at 1600 R.P.M. Four main bearings. Hydraulic valve lifters. Carburetor: 1Bbl. Holley 1945. OPTIONAL V-8 (Cordoba, Fifth Ave.): 90-degree, overhead valve V-8. Cast iron block and head. Displacement: 318 cu. in. (5.2 liters). Bore & stroke: 3.91 x 3.31 in. Compression ratio: 8.5:1. Brake horsepower: 130 at 4000 R.P.M. Torque: 230 lbs.-ft. at 1600 R.P.M. Five main bearings. Hydraulic valve lifters. Carburetor: 2Bbl. Carter BBD. IMPERIAL V-8; Same as 318 cu. in V-8 above, but with electronic fuel injection B.H.P.: 140 at 4000 R.P.M. Torque: 245 lbs.-ft. at 2000 R.P.M.

CHASSIS DATA: Wheelbase: (LeBaron) 100.3 in.; (E Class/N.Y.) 103.3 in.; (Cordoba/Fifth Ave./Imperial) 112.7 in. Overall length: (LeB) 179.6 in.; (LeB wag) 179.8 in.; (E Class/N.Y.) 185.7 in.; (Cord.) 210.1 in.; (Fifth Ave.) 206.7 in.; (Imperial) 213.3 in. Height: (LeB cpe) 52.6 in.; (LeB sed) 53.0 in.; (LeB wag) 52.7 in.; (LeB conv.) 54.1 in.; (Cord./Imp.) 53.2 in.; (E Class/N.Y.) 53.9 in.; (Fifth Ave.) 55.3 in. Width: (LeB) 68.5 in.; (E Class/N.Y.) 68.0 in.; (Cord./Imp.) 72.7 in.; (Fifth Ave.) 74.2 in. Front Tread: (LeB/E Class/N.Y.) 57.6 in.; (Cord./Fifth Ave./Imp.) 60.0 in. Rear Tread: (LeB/E Class/N.Y.) 57.0 in.; (Cord./Fifth Ave./Imp.) 59.5 in. Standard Tires: (LeB/E Class) P185/70R14 SBR WSW; (New Yorker) P185/75R14 SBR WSW; (Cord.) P195/75R15 GBR WSW; (Fifth Ave./Imp.) P205/75R15 SBR WSW.

TECHNICAL: Transmission: Five-speed manual trans. standard on LeBaron. Gear ratios: (1st) 3.29:1; (2nd) 1.89:1; (3rd) 1.21:1; (4th) 0.88:1; (5th) 0.72:1; (Rev) 3.14:1. TorqueFlite three-speed automatic optional on LeBaron, standard on E Class and New Yorker: (1st) 2.69:1; (2nd) 1.55:1; (3rd) 1.00:1; (Rev) 2.10:1. TorqueFlite standard on other models: (1st) 2.74:1; (2nd) 1.54:1; (3rd) 1.00:1; (Rev) 2.22:1. Standard final drive ratio: (LeB) 2.57:1 exc. 2.78:1 w/auto.; (LeB conv.) 3.02:1; (E Class) 3.02:1; (New Yorker) 2.78:1 or 3.02:1; (Cord./Fifth Ave. six) 2.94:1; (Fifth Ave. V-8) 2.26:1; (Imp.) 2.24:1. Steering: (LeBaron/E Class/New Yorker) rack and pinion; (others) recirculating ball, power-assisted. Suspension: (LeBaron/E Class/New Yorker) MacPherson Iso- Struts and linkless sway bar in front, flex arm beam axle with trailing links and coil springs at the rear; (others) front torsion bars and anti-sway bar, rear leaf springs. Brakes: Front disc, rear drum (power-assisted). Ignition: Electronic. Body construction: Unibody. Fuel tank: (LeB/E Class/N.Y.) 13 gal.; (Cord./Fifth Ave./Imp.) 18 gal.

DRIVETRAIN OPTIONS: Engines: 2.6-liter four: LeBaron/E Class/New Yorker ($259). 318 cu. in. V-8: Cord./Fifth Ave. ($225). Transmission/Suspension: Auto. trans.: LeB ($439). Heavy-duty susp.: Cord. ($36); Fifth Ave. ($26). Sport suspension: LeB/E Class/N.Y. ($55). Rear sway bar: Cord. ($36). Other: H.D. cooling: LeB/E Class/N.Y. ($141). H.D. 500-amp battery ($43). California emission system ($75).

LEBARON CONVENIENCE/APPEARANCE OPTIONS: Option Packages: Mark Cross A61 pkg. ($963-$1232). Easy-order package A91 ($577-$645); A92 ($2022-$2147). Two-tone paint ($176). Comfort/Convenience: Air conditioning ($732). Rear defroster ($137). Automatic speed control ($174). Travel computer ($206). Audible message center ($63). Power seat ($210). Power windows ($180-$255). Power door locks ($120-$170). Power decklid or liftgate release ($40). Leather-wrapped or sport steering wheel ($50). Tilt steering wheel ($105). Tinted glass ($105). Intermittent wipers ($52). Lighting and Mirrors: Cornering lamps ($60). Reading lamp ($24). Dual remote mirrors ($57). Dual power remote mirrors ($47-$104). Lighted vanity mirror ($50). Entertainment: AM/FM stereo radio ($109). Electronic-tuning AM/FM stereo radio ($263); w/cassette ($402) exc. Mark Cross conv. (NC). Premium speaker pkg. ($126). Radio delete ($56 credit). Exterior Trim: Front or rear bumper guards ($23). Sill moldings (NC to $24). Door edge protectors ($15-$25). Luggage rack: wag ($106). Bodyside tape stripe ($42). Undercoating ($41). Vinyl lower body protection (NC to $39). Interior Trim/Upholstery: Console ($100). Center armrest ($59). Cloth/vinyl bucket seats: cpe/conv. ($160). Color- keyed floor mats: front ($25); rear ($20). Trunk dress-up ($51). Wheels and Tires: Wire wheel covers ($257). Cast aluminum wheels ($357) but (NC) w/Mark Cross conv.

E CLASS AND NEW YORKER CONVENIENCE/APPEARANCE OPTIONS: Option Packages: Protection group: E Class ($64-$120). Easy- order pkg.: E Class ($676 or $2196). Mark Cross pkg. ($696). California/Hawaii Advantage: E Class ($1409). Comfort/Convenience: Air cond. ($732). Rear defroster ($138). Auto. speed control ($174). Travel computer: E ($206). Power windows ($255). Power door locks ($170). Power seat ($210). Tinted glass: E ($104). Leather-wrapped steering wheel ($50). Tilt steering ($105). Intermittent wipers: E ($52). Lighting and Mirrors: Cornering lamps: E ($60). Dual remote mirrors: E ($57). Dual power remote mirrors: E ($107). Lighted vanity mirror ($58). Entertainment: Same as LeBaron. Exterior: Two-tone paint: E ($170). Bodyside and deck stripe: E ($63). Sill moldings: E ($23). Front or rear bumper guards ($28). Door edge protectors ($25). Vinyl lower body protection: E ($39). Undercoating ($41). Interior: Vinyl split bench seat: E (NC). Cloth 50/50 bench seat: E ($267). Color-keyed mats: front ($25); rear ($20). Trunk dress-up: E ($51). Wheels and Tires: Wire wheel covers: E ($244). Cast aluminum wheels: E ($363); N.Y. ($119). Conventional spare ($63).

CORDOBA CONVENIENCE/APPEARANCE OPTIONS: Option Packages: Basic group ($1121). Premium equipment ($2471). Cabriolet roof pkg. ($587). Protection group ($114). Light pkg. ($143). Comfort/Convenience: Air conditioning ($787). Rear defroster ($138). Automatic speed control ($174). Power seat ($199). Power windows ($180). Power door locks ($120). Power decklid release ($40). Illuminated entry system ($75). Leather- wrapped steering wheel ($53). Tilt steering wheel ($99). Intermittent wipers ($52). Lighting, Horns and Mirrors: Cornering lamps ($60). Triad horns ($27). Lighted vanity mirror ($61). Entertainment: AM/FM radio ($109). Electronic-tuning AM/FM stereo ($154-$263); w/cassette ($293-$402). Radio upgrade w/dual speakers ($28). Premium speaker pkg. ($126). Power antenna ($60). Radio delete ($56 credit). Exterior: Bodyside/decklid/hood tape stripe ($98). Undercoating ($41). Interior: Console ($75). Leather bucket seats ($529). Trunk dress-up ($48). Wheels and Tires: Wire wheel covers ($244). Premium wheel covers ($57). Forged aluminum wheels ($107). P205/75R15 SBR WSW ($116). P215/70R15 SBR RWL ($66-$182). Conventional spare tire ($63).

NEW YORKER FIFTH AVENUE CONVENIENCE/APPEARANCE OPTIONS: Option Packages: Luxury equipment ($1870). Protection group ($70). Comfort/Convenience: Auto. speed control ($170). Power seat ($199). Power door locks ($159). Power decklid release ($40). Illuminated entry system ($75). Leather-covered steering wheel ($53). Tilt steering ($99). Intermittent wipers ($49). Lighted vanity mirror ($61). Entertainment: Same as Cordoba. AM/FM stereo radio ($109). Electronic-tuning AM/FM stereo ($154-$263); w/cassette ($293- $402). Radio upgrade w/dual speakers ($28). Premium speaker pkg. ($126). Power antenna ($60). Exterior: Power glass sunroof ($1041). Hood tape stripe ($29). Undercoating ($41). Interior: Cloth 60/40 bench seat (NC). Leather 60/40 bench seat ($356). Wheels and Tires: Wire wheel covers ($170). Michelin WSW tires (NC). Conventional spare tire ($63).

IMPERIAL OPTIONS Apart from the California emission system ($75), Imperial had no extra-cost options. Customers could choose among several no-cost options: cloth/vinyl or leather 60/40 split bench seat; electronic-tuning AM/FM stereo w/cassette; and wire wheel covers or cast aluminum wheels.

HISTORY: Introduced: October 1, 1982. Model year production: 241,574 (incl. Canadian-built Cordobas, Fifth Avenues and Imperials). Calendar year production (U.S.): 234,203. Calendar year sales by U.S. dealers: 262,037. Model year sales by U.S. dealers: 243,664.

Historical Footnotes: Chrysler-Plymouth sales went up 20.2 percent for the 1983 model year, due largely to success of the new E-cars. Fifth Avenue (formerly New Yorker) sales jumped over 50 percent, to 77,700. Cordoba sales fell, prompting its dismissal from the line, despite a resurgence of interest in cars of that league. Imperial was dropped too, never having found enough buyers even for a limited-production model. Production of rear-drive intermediates (including Fifth Avenue) moved from Windsor, Ontario to St. Louis during 1983. LeBaron's base convertible price was cut in January, from $12,800 down to just $10,995. Late in 1982, Kenyon & Eckhardt Inc. was appointed the exclusive Chrysler-Plymouth ad agency. Vice-President of Marketing Joseph A. Campana wanted to promote an "image of engineered-in value," with Chryslers for "luxury and class," Plymouth for economy. Chrysler Corp. was in better financial shape, reaching a market share over 10 percent again for 1982, and paying back its highly-publicized loan. At year's end, NHTSA was investigating alleged carburetor defects on 1.8 million Chrysler Corp. vehicles with 1.7 and 2.2-liter engines. Up to this point, Chrysler had an impressively low record of mandated recalls.

1984 Chrysler

Both Cordoba and Imperial left the lineup this year, while a new Laser hatchback sport coupe was added. The 2.2- liter four-cylinder engine switched from carburetion to single-point, throttle-body electronic fuel injection, though early models still carried carburetors. All radios had electronic tuning. Laser XE offered Chrysler's LCD electronic dashboard. Electronic Voice Alert was improved, to make more useful audio comments—and added a shutoff switch in the glove compartment. In the performance department, a turbocharged version of the 2.2 engine, rated 140 horsepower, became available on Laser, LeBaron and E Class/New Yorker. Front-drive fuel tanks grew from 13 to 14 gallons.

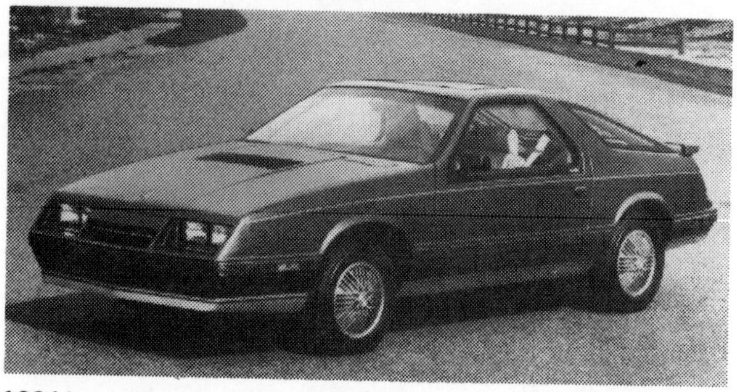

1984 Laser hatchback coupe (CC)

LASER — SERIES GC — FOUR — Chrysler described its new front-drive hatchback Laser coupe as "a definitive statement of motion technlogy." The all-new aerodynamic design featured a front air dam, plus flush windshield and glass for reduced drag. Dodge's Daytona was nearly identical. Four-passenger Laser bodies held recessed quad headlamps, with recessed parking lamps below the bumper rub strips. The minimalist grille consisted of one large slot that occupied half the angled upper panel, with two additional slots below (inboard of the parking lamps). Above was a laydown pentastar hood ornament. Louvers appeared atop the hood, on a modest bulge between its side creases. Small horizontal side marker lenses were just below the bodyside moldings. A 'Laser' decal went below the outside mirror, along the bodyside stripe. 'Turbo' identification (if applicable) was at base of window, just above the door handle. A 'Chrysler' nameplate was on the left side of the hatch; 'Laser' on the right side. A red Electronic Fuel Injection decal went on the door window frame. A new "dual path" upper Iso-Strut mount in the front suspension was designed to send shock absorber loads in one direction, spring loads in another. The rear suspension used gas-charged shock absorbers, plus a large-diameter tubular sway bar inside the rear axle. A track bar was mounted alongside. Power brakes and quick-ratio rack-and-pinion steering were standard. The five-speed close-ratio manual transaxle featured a reworked linkage. Laser equipment also included a console, digital clock built into AM radio, leather-wrapped steering wheel, lighter, side window demisters, halogen headlamps, optical horn (pass/flash), dual horns, dual mirrors (left remote), rear spoiler, intermittent wipers, and premium wheel covers. Low-back cloth bucket seats had dual recliners. Turbocharging of the 2.2-liter engine was available on both the base Laser and the performance Laser XE. Developed from a Garrett AiResearch unit, the turbocharger delivered 7.5 psi maximum boost. Multi-point fuel injection used Bosch injectors at each cylinder. Turbos had a water-cooled turbine end-shaft bearing, hotter cam, bigger oil pump, low- restriction exhaust, plus tighter piston rings and seals. Dished-top pistons cut compression down to 8.1:1. The turbo was rated 142 horsepower at 5600 R.P.M. A total of 32,538 Lasers had the AGT Turbo package. Laser XE also included a standard cloth/vinyl "enthusiast" driver's seat with air-filled bladders for adjustable (inflatable) thigh/lumbar support, plus tilt steering wheel. Other XE extras were an 11-function Electronic Navigator, illuminated entry system, electronic instrument cluster, dual electric remote mirrors, and AM/FM radio. Standard Laser tires were P185/70R14 blackwall steel- belted radials on 5.5 in. wheels. XE had the same size raised black-letter tires on cast aluminum wheels. A Special Handling Suspension available on XE included higher-rate springs and control arm rear bushings, gas-charged front shocks and Iso-Struts. Laser colors were: Beige Crystal Coat, Gunmetal Blue Pearl Coat, Black, and Radiant Silver Crystal Coat (plus Garnet Red or Mink Brown Pearl Coat at extra cost). XE came in black. Six two-tone combinations were offered.

LEBARON — SERIES KC — FOUR — Unchanged up front, LeBaron carried a revised rear end with wraparound taillamps that were taller than before, with horizontal trim strips. Vertical backup lamps were inboard, next to the license plate opening. Full wheel opening moldings and body sill moldings also were new this year. The full padded vinyl roof again extended into upper rear doors. T&C wagons had a new standard roof rack. Under the hood, the new turbocharged engine was available, while the base 2.2- liter version added fuel injection. Once again, the Mitsubishi-built 2.6-liter four was optional, making three choices in all. Inside was a new luxury two-spoke steering wheel and instrument cluster with dark butterfly walnut woodtone accents, plus a new padded top for the instrument panel. Digital clocks were built into all the new electronic-tuning radios, including the standard AM version (which could be deleted for credit). Wide-ratio TorqueFlite was the standard transmission. Coupes had cloth high-back bucket seats; four- doors and the T&C wagon, a cloth/vinyl front bench seat with folding center armrest. Body colors were: Crimson Red, Garnet Red Pearl, Mink Brown Pearl, Beige Crystal, Gunmetal Blue Pearl, Black, Charcoal Pearl,

Radiant Silver Crystal, and White. Two two-tone combinations were offered. Convertibles had larger (full-width) back seats, glass back windows (formerly plastic), power rear-quarter windows, and a new roof latch mechanism. The T&C version with fake wood trim was offered again, as was the Mark Cross Edition. The Mark Cross convertible added an electronic instrument cluster with electronic speedometer and odometer, analog fuel/voltage/oil/temp gauges, and graphic message center, along with low-back leather bucket seats, power driver's seat, and an illuminated entry system. A total of 5,401 non-convertible LeBarons carried a Mark Cross option package (code AFC). That one included included a leather/vinyl 50/50 front seat with dual armrests, center consolettes, and seatback recliners; plus door trim panels with leather-like inserts and Mark Cross medallions, and leather-wrapped steering wheel.

1984 E Class sedan (CC)

E CLASS/NEW YORKER — SERIES ET — FOUR — New Yorker's appearance was similar to 1983, but new wraparound taillamps had five thick, bright horizontal trim strips that stretched all the way from license plates around the quarter panel. The new "waterfall" grille also was similar to the 1983 version, but its bright surrounding molding now extended outward beneath the headlamps. Saddle-type belt moldings and full wheel opening moldings were new. New Yorker's padded vinyl landau roof held coach lamps and a bright roof band. Standard wire wheel covers had integral locks. Suspension improvements included recalibrated spring rates, redesigned spring seats, new jounce bumpers, and new dual path bushings; plus new standard all-weather P185/75R14 SBR tires with wide whitewalls. New pillow-style 50/50 front seats in luxury cloth featured driver/passenger recliners, dual armrests, storage consolettes, seatback and cushion pockets. Leather/vinyl seating was optional. New Yorkers had roof-mounted passenger assist handles and C-pillar courtesy/reading lamps. Power windows became standard this year. Door panels and dash had dark butterfly walnut woodtone accents and bright trim. A new electronic instrument cluster displayed oil pressure, voltage, fuel, and temperature, plus a digital speedometer. A Visual Message Center was standard on New Yorker, while a new optional Electronic Navigator showed MPG, driving range and such at the touch of a button. The standard electronic-tuning AM radio held a digital clock. Body colors were: Crimson Red, Garnet Red Pearl, Mink Brown Pearl, Beige Crystal, Nightwatch Blue, Gunmetal Blue Pearl, Black, Charcoal Metallic Pearl, Radiant Silver Crystal, and White. E Class was the stepdown version of the front-drive Ebody, priced $2600 lower and carrying less equipment (but an extra passenger). Its sharply-angled grille was made up of many evenly-spaced vertical bars, topped by a heavy bright header that wrapped over the top, toward the hood. The grille pattern continued in a wide slot below the bumper rub strip. E Class had a stand-up crystalline pentastar hood ornament, recessed quad rectangular headlamps, and small horizontal parking lamps set into the bumper (below the rub strip). Appearance was similar to New Yorker, but in six-window design rather than four. New Yorker-style full-width wraparound taillamps had thinner bright horizontal trim strips. Backup lamps were a continuation of the taillamps, alongside the license plate opening. Standard equipment included power brakes and steering, three-speed automatic transaxle, graphic message center, halogen headlamps, and concealed two-speed wipers. Also standard: door armrests, bumper rub strips, lighter, AM radio with digital clock, coat hooks, power fuel filler door release, dual horns, day/night mirror, dual mirrors (left remote), and premium wheel covers. E Class came in: Crimson Red, Garnet Red Pearl, Mink Brown Pearl, Beige Crystal, Nightwatch Blue, Black, Charcoal Gray Clear, Radiant Silver Crystal, White, and Gunmetal Blue Pearl. Two two-tones were available. Standard interior was a cloth bench seat with center armrest in blue, silver, red or beige. Base engine for both front-drive models remained the Trans-4 2.2-liter, now with fuel injection; but a turbocharged version also was offered. So was the Mitsubishi 2.6-liter four. Cast aluminum wheels were available on both, as was an illuminated entry system.

1984 Fifth Avenue sedan (CC)

FIFTH AVENUE — SERIES MFS — V-8 — The last rear-drive Chrysler dropped the New Yorker name completely this year. Appearance changes were modest. Its grille now consisted of vertical bars with no horizontal dividers. Full-width wraparound taillamps weren't as tall as New Yorker's, with subtle trim and small horizontal backup lenses. As in 1983, between the taillamps was a separate rectangular panel with 'Chrysler' block-letter nameplate. The license plate again was down in the back bumper. Fifth Avenue front fenders again displayed non-functional louvers. 'Chrysler' identification went on the driver's side mirror. The padded vinyl formal landau roof had its unique backlight and brushed-finish transverse roof molding. Sill moldings had front and rear extensions. Bodyside and decklid accent stripes were standard. After several years with six-cylinder power (which most buyers ignored), the 318 cu. in. V-8 became the sole engine. Chrysler touted Fifth Avenue as having "45 luxury features as standard equipment." The new standard AM radio had a digital readout and digital clock. Silver sputter chrome treatment went on instrument panel overlays. Cloth/vinyl 60/40 front seats with individual adjustments came in silver, dark blue, red or beige. Halogen headlamps came with time-delay switches. Trunk and

map/dome reading lamps were standard. Options included a power glass sunroof and new cast aluminum wheels. A Luxury Equipment Package included such extras as illuminated entry, automatic speed control, tilt steering, opera lamps, and power driver's seat. Fifth Avenue colors were: Radiant Silver Crystal Coat, Beige Crystal Coat, Crimson Red, Sable Brown, Charcoal Gray Pearl Coat, Nightwatch Blue, Black, or White.

1984 Executive limousine (CC)

EXECUTIVE — SERIES KCP — FOUR — An Executive sedan and limousine, announced earlier, were now official parts of the Chrysler lineup and listed in production totals. Conversions were done by ASC Corporation, near Chrysler's St. Louis assembly plant, adding 13 to 24 inches to a K-body platform. Roof, floorpan, sill and roof rail sections were added, along with a B-pillar. Sill areas were reinforced; front suspension strengthened; brakes enlarged. This produced what Chrysler called "traditional limousine characteristics in a modern, efficient size." Seven-passenger limos rose a 131 in. wheelbase and were 220.5 in. long (much smaller and lighter than a Cadillac). Wheelbase of the five-passenger Executive Sedan was 124 in. Both Executives carried the Mitsubishi-built 2.6-liter four and automatic transaxle.

I.D. DATA: Chrysler again had a 17-symbol Vehicle Identification Number (VIN) on the upper left corner of the instrument panel, visible through the windshield. Coding changed somewhat with the revised model lineup. The first digit indicates Country: '1' U.S.A.; '2' Canada. The second symbol is Make: 'C' Chrysler. Third is Vehicle Type: '3' passenger car. The next symbol ('B') indicates manual seatbelts. Symbol five is Car Line: 'A' Laser; 'C' LeBaron and New Yorker (front-drive); 'F' Fifth Avenue. Symbol six is Series: '4' High'; '5' Premium; '6' Special. Symbol seven is Body Style: '1' 2-dr. coupe; '3' 4-dr. sedan; '4' 2-dr. hatchback 22; '5' 2-dr. convertible coupe; '6' 4-dr. sedan; '7' 4-dr. limousine; '9' 4-dr. wagon. Eighth is the Engine Code: 'D' L4-135 EFI; 'E' Turbo L4135 EFI; 'G' L4-156 2Bbl.; 'P' V8318 2Bbl. Next comes a check digit. Symbol ten indicates Model Year. 'E' 1984. Symbol eleven is Assembly Plant. 'C' Detroit, 'F' Newark, 'G' or 'X' St. Louis. The last six digits make up the sequential serial number, starting with 100001. Engine number coding is similar to 1982-83.

LASER (FOUR)

Series Number	Body/Style Number	Body Type & Seating	Factory Price	Shipping Weight	Production Total
GCH	24	2-dr. Hatch-4P	8648	2525	33,976

LASER XE (FOUR)

GCP	24	2-dr. Hatch-4P	10546	2545	25,882

1984 LeBaron convertible (CC)

LEBARON (FOUR)

KCP	22	2-dr. Cpe-6P	8783	2445	24,963
KCP	41	4-dr. Sed-6P	9067	2495	47,664
KCP	27	2-dr. Conv.-4P	11595	2530	16,208

LEBARON TOWN & COUNTRY (FOUR)

KCP	45	4-dr. Sta Wag-5P	9856	2610	11,578

1984 LeBaron Mark Cross Town & Country convertible (JG)

LEBARON MARK CROSS CONVERTIBLE (FOUR)

KCP	27	2-dr. Conv.-4P	15495	N/A	Note 1
KCP	27	2-dr. T&C Conv.-4P	16495	N/A	Note 1

Note 1: Mark Cross and Mark Cross Town & Country convertibles are included in base convertible total above. A total of 1,105 T&C convertible packages (code AFG) were installed, plus 8,275 Mark Cross convertible packages (code AFD).

E CLASS (FOUR)

ETH	41	4-dr. Sed-6P	9565	2530	32,237

1984 New Yorker sedan (CC)

NEW YORKER (FOUR)

ETP	41	4-dr. Sed-5P	12179	2675	60,501

FIFTH AVENUE (V-8)

MFS	41	4-dr. Sed-6P	13990	3660	79,441

EXECUTIVE (FOUR)

KCP	48	4-dr. Sed-5P	18975	2945	196
KCP	49	4-dr. Limo-7P	21975	N/A	594

MODEL NUMBER NOTE: Some sources identify models using the new VIN data to indicate Car Line, Price Class and Body Style. Example: base Laser (GCH24) has the equivalent number CA44, which translates to Laser line, High price class, and hatchback body. See I.D. Data section for breakdown.

ENGINE DATA: BASE FOUR (Laser, LeBaron, E Class, New Yorker): Inline, overhead cam four-cylinder. Cast iron block; aluminum head. Displacement: 135 cu. in. (2.2 liters). Bore & stroke: 3.44 x 3.62 in. Compression ratio: 9.0:1. Brake horsepower: 99 at 5600 R.P.M. Torque: 121 lbs.-ft. at 3200 R.P.M. Five main bearings. Hydraulic valve lifters. Electronic fuel injection. TURBOCHARGED FOUR (Laser, LeBaron, E Class, New Yorker): Same as 135 cu. in. four above, but with turbocharger Compression ratio: 8.1:1. B.H.P.: 140 at 5200 R.P.M. (142 at 5600 w/manual shift). Torque: 160 lbs.-ft. at 3600 R.P.M. BASE FOUR (Executive); OPTIONAL (LeBaron, E Class, New Yorker): Inline, overhead cam four-cylinder. Cast iron block; aluminum head. Displacement: 156 cu. in. (2.6 liters). Bore & stroke: 3.59 x 3.86 in. Compression ratio: 8.7:1. Brake horsepower: 101 at 4800 R.P.M. Torque: 140 lbs.-ft. at 2800 R.P.M. Five main bearings. Solid valve lifters. Carburetor: 2Bbl. Mikuni. Built by Mitsubishi. BASE V-8 (Fifth Avenue): 90-degree, overhead valve V-8. Cast iron block and head. Displacement: 318 cu. in. (5.2 liters). Bore & stroke: 3.91 x 3.31 in. Compression ratio: 8.7:1. Brake horsepower: 130 at 4000 R.P.M. Torque: 235 lbs.-ft. at 1600 R.P.M. Five main bearings. Hydraulic valve lifters. Carburetor: 2Bbl. Carter BBD.

CHASSIS DATA: Wheelbase: (Laser) 97.0 in.; (LeBaron) 100.3 in.; (E Class/N.Y.) 103.3 in.; (Fifth Ave.) 112.7 in.; (Executive) 124.0 in.; (Limo) 131 in. Overall length: (Laser) 175.0 in.; (LeB) 179.8 in.; (LeB wag) 179.9 in.; (E Class) 187.2 in.; (N.Y.) 185.7 in.; (Fifth Ave.) 206.7 in.; (Exec.) 203.4 in.; (Limo) 220.5 in. Height: (Laser) 50.3 in.; (LeB cpe) 52.6 in.; (LeB sed) 53.0 in.; (LeB wag) 52.7 in.; (LeB conv.) 54.1 in.; (E Class/N.Y.) 52.9 in.; (Fifth Ave.) 55.3 in.; (Exec.) 55.0 in.; (Limo) 69.3 in.; (LeB/Exec.) 68.5 in.; (E Class/N.Y.) 68.3 in.; (Fifth Ave.) 74.2 in. Front Tread: (Laser/LeB/E Class/N.Y./Exec.) 57.6 in.; (Fifth Ave.) 60.0 in. Rear Tread: (Laser/Exec.) 57.2 in.; (LeB/E Class/N.Y.) 57.0 in.; (Fifth Ave.) 59.5 in. Standard Tires: (Laser/LeB/E Class) P185/70R14 SBR WSW; (Laser XE) P185/70R14 SBR RWL; (New Yorker/Exec.) P185/75R14 SBR WSW; (Fifth Ave.) P205/75R15 SBR WSW.

TECHNICAL: Transmission: Five-speed manual trans. standard on Laser/LeBaron. Gear ratios: (1st) 3.29:1; (2nd) 2.08:1; (3rd) 1.45:1; (4th) 1.04:1; (5th) 0.72:1; (Rev) 3.14:1. TorqueFlite three-speed automatic optional on Laser/LeBaron, standard on E Class and New Yorker: (1st) 2.69:1; (2nd) 1.55:1; (3rd) 1.00:1; (Rev) 2.10:1. TorqueFlite standard on Fifth Ave.: (1st) 2.74:1; (2nd) 1.54:1; (3rd) 1.00:1; (Rev) 2.22:1. Standard final drive ratio: (Laser) 2.57:1 exc. 3.22:1 or 3.02:1 w/auto.; (LeB) 2.57:1 exc. 3.02:1 w/auto.; (E Class/N.Y.) 3.02:1 exc. 2.94:1 (Exec.) 3.02:1. Steering: (Laser/LeBaron/E Class/New Yorker) rack and pinion; (others) recirculating ball, power-assisted. Suspension: (Laser) dual-path Iso-Strut front with anti-sway bar, trailing arm rear with tubular sway bar inside rear axle and track bar alongside, plus gas-charged shock absorbers; (LeBaron/E Class/New Yorker) MacPherson Iso-Struts and linkless sway bar in front, flex arm beam axle with trailing links and coil springs at the rear; (Fifth Ave.) front torsion bars and anti-sway bar, rear leaf springs. Brakes: Front disc, rear drum (power-assisted). Ignition: Electronic. Body construction: Unibody. Fuel tank: (Laser/LeB/E Class/N.Y.) 14 gal.; (Fifth Ave.) 18 gal.

DRIVETRAIN OPTIONS: Engines: 2.6-liter four: LeBaron/E Class/New Yorker ($271). Turbo 2.2-liter four: LeB/E Class/New Yorker ($610). Transmission/Suspension: Auto. trans.: Laser/LeB ($439). Heavy-duty susp.: Fifth Ave. ($27). Sport susp.: E Class/N.Y. ($57). Handling susp.: Laser XE ($102). European handling pkg.: LeB ($57). Other: H.D. cooling: LeB/E Class/N.Y. ($141). H.D. 500-amp battery ($44). California emission system ($99).

LASER CONVENIENCE/APPEARANCE OPTIONS: Option Packages: Turbo pkg.: base ($934); XE ($872). Basic group ($1194-$1319). Cargo trim/quiet sound: base ($154). Light group: base ($97). Comfort/Convenience: Air conditioning ($737). Rear defroster ($143-$168). Automatic speed control ($179). Electronic navigator: base ($272). Electronic voice alert: base ($66). Power seat ($215). Power windows ($185). Power door locks ($125). Tinted glass ($110). Illuminated entry system ($75). Tilt steering wheel ($110). Dual power remote mirrors: base ($48). Entertainment: AM/FM stereo radio: base ($125). Premium electronic-tuning seek/scan AM/FM stereo ($160-$285); w/cassette ($299-$424). Premium speaker pkg. ($126). Radio

delete ($56 credit). Exterior: Removable glass sunroof ($322). Pearl coat paint: base ($40). Interior: Low-back vinyl bucket seats: base (NC). Low-back cloth/vinyl bucket seats: base ($362). Low-back leather bucket seats: base ($929); XE ($567). Front/rear mats ($45). Wheels: 15 in. aluminum wheels: XE (NC). 14 in. aluminum wheels: base ($316).

LEBARON CONVENIENCE/APPEARANCE OPTIONS: Option Packages: Mark Cross A61 pkg. ($833-$1000). Easy-order package AAA ($476-$631); AAB ($1827-$1982). Two-tone paint ($232). Comfort/Convenience: Air conditioning ($737). Rear defroster ($143). Automatic speed control ($179). Electronic voice alert ($66). Power seat ($215). Power windows ($185-$260). Power door locks ($125-$175). Power decklid or liftgate release ($40). Illuminated entry ($75). Leather-wrapped steering wheel ($50). Tilt steering wheel ($110). Tinted glass ($110). Intermittent wipers ($53). Lighting and Mirrors: Cornering lamps ($60). Dual remote mirrors ($59). Dual power remote mirrors ($48-$107). Lighted vanity mirror ($58). Entertainment: Electronic-tuning AM/FM stereo radio ($125); w/cassette and seek/scan ($424) exc. Mark Cross conv. (NC). Premium seek/scan AM/FM stereo radio ($285). Premium speaker pkg. ($126). Radio delete ($56 credit). Exterior Trim: Front and rear bumper guards ($56). Pearl coat paint ($40). Vinyl bodyside moldings ($55). Bodyside tape stripe ($45). Undercoating ($43). Interior Trim/Upholstery: Console ($105). Center armrest ($61). Cloth/vinyl bench seat: cpe (NC). Vinyl bucket seats: wag (NC). Cloth/vinyl bucket seats: sed ($166). Color-keyed floor mats: cpe front ($25); both ($45). Trunk dress-up ($51). Wheels and Tires: Wire wheel covers ($215). Cast aluminum wheels ($322) but (NC) w/Mark Cross conv. Conventional spare ($83).

E CLASS AND NEW YORKER CONVENIENCE/APPEARANCE OPTIONS: Option Packages: Luxury equipment: N.Y. ($2622). Protection group: E Class ($81). Easy-order pkg.: E Class ($710 or $1965); N.Y. ($1143). Comfort/Convenience: Air cond. ($737). Rear defroster ($143). Auto. speed control ($179). Electronic navigator: N.Y. ($272). Electronic voice alert: E ($66). Power windows ($260). Power seat ($215). Tinted glass: E ($110). Illuminated entry ($75). Leather-wrapped steering wheel ($50). Tilt steering ($110). Intermittent wipers: E ($53). Lighting and Mirrors: Cornering lamps: E ($60). Dual power remote mirrors: E ($82). Lighted vanity mirror ($58). Entertainment: Same as LeBaron. Exterior: Two-tone paint: E ($232). Pearl coat paint ($40). Bodyside stripe: E ($45). Bodyside molding ($55). Front and rear bumper guards ($56). Door edge protectors ($25). Undercoating ($43). Interior: Vinyl bench seat: E (NC). Cloth 50/50 bench seat: E ($278). Leather 50/50 seats: N.Y. ($395). Color-keyed mats ($45). Trunk dress-up: E ($51). Wheels and Tires: Wire wheel covers: E ($215). Cast aluminum wheels: E ($322); N.Y. ($107). Conventional spare ($83).

FIFTH AVENUE CONVENIENCE/APPEARANCE OPTIONS: Option Packages: Luxury equipment ($1915). Protection group ($70). Comfort/Convenience: Auto. speed control ($179). Power seat ($175-$215); dual ($430). Power door locks ($175). Power decklid release ($40). Illuminated entry system ($75). Leather-wrapped steering wheel ($60). Tilt steering ($110). Intermittent wipers ($53). Lighted vanity mirror ($58). Entertainment: AM/FM stereo radio ($125). Premium seek/scan AM/FM stereo ($125-$250); w/cassette ($264-$389). Premium speaker pkg. ($126). Power antenna ($60). Exterior Trim: Power sunroof ($1041). Hood tape stripe ($29). Undercoating ($43). Interior Trim/Upholstery: Cloth 60/40 bench seat (NC). Leather 60/40 bench seat ($379). Wheels and Tires: Wire wheel covers ($197). Cast aluminum wheels ($47-$244). Conventional spare tire ($93).

EXECUTIVE SEDAN/LIMOUSINE OPTIONS: AM/FM stereo radio w/cassette: sed ($139). Leather bucket seats ($950-$1075). Wire wheel covers: sed ($263). Cast aluminum wheels: sed ($370).

HISTORY: Introduced: October 2, 1983. Model year production: 333,240. Calendar year production: 403,699. Calendar year sales by U.S. dealers: 328,499. Model year sales by U.S. dealers: 314,438 (incl. a few leftover Cordobas and Imperials).

Historical Footnotes: Lasers were built at St. Louis, on the same line as LeBaron and Reliant. Chrysler-Plymouth model year sales (including imports) rose 15 percent, due largely to initially strong Laser sales (52,073 for the model year). The front- drive New Yorker saw a sales rise of 67 percent; LeBaron a less dramatic 20 percent. Calendar year production for the Division rose by 38 percent over 1983, reaching 1,247,826. Workers put in considerable overtime to keep pace. Chrysler's sixth U.S. passenger car plant opened near year's end at Sterling Heights, Michigan, to produce the new LeBaron GTS and Dodge Lancer. The five-year, 50,000-mile warranty was extended late in the year to include light-duty trucks. Turbos were most in demand on Lasers (and Dodge Daytonas), making Chrysler No. 1 in turbo production. Chrysler claimed that Laser outperformed "the vast majority of sports cars sold in the U.S." The car was marketed against Firebird and Nissan 280ZX. This was Chrysler's 60th anniversary year.

1985 Chrysler

Chrysler's turbocharged 2.2-liter engine added an electronic wastegate control that varied maximum boost from 7.2 to 9.0 psi. More notable than that was the arrival of yet another new model: the LeBaron GTS four-door liftback performance sedan. Billed as "new midsize." GTS was intended to combine European look and feel with American-style roominess.

1985 Laser XE hatchback coupe (CC)

LASER — SERIES GC — FOUR—After reasonably good sales in its first year, Laser returned with only modest revisions. They included the improved turbo engine option (now rated 146 horsepower), new undercoating, and two new body colors. The close-ratio five- speed gearbox had a new "dual rail" shift linkage. Laser XE now had standard cast aluminum wheels with 205/60HR15 tires. Fuel and hatch door releases moved from the console glovebox to outside the driver's seat. Laser's suspension included nitrogen-charged rear shock absorbers. A European handling suspension (optional on XE) added front gas shocks. Standard engine was the 2.2-liter Trans-4 with EFI. Cloth/vinyl low-back bucket seats had dual recliners and inertia latches. All-vinyl upholstery was available on the base Laser; Mark Cross Corinthian leather optional on both base and XE. An "enthusiast" seat was optional (standard on XE). Base Lasers had a Rallye cluster of analog gauges, including tachometer, plus a Graphic Message Center. Non-turbo models included an upshift indicator light. XE again had an electronic cluster with quick-read digital speedometer, odometer, and

1985½ Laser XT hatchback coupe (CC)

trip odometer; plus an analog tachometer and gauge set. XE's standard Electronic Monitor displayed a two- line message on-screen, reporting on up to 21 functions and conditions, both visually and by "voice." Electronic Navigator was another XE standard. AM radio was standard on Laser; AM/FM stereo on XE. Turbo versions had functional hood louvers to release turbocharger heat, plus equal-length driveshafts to help reduce "torque steer." Both models had a functional front air dam and rear spoiler. Standard equipment also included a center console, driver's side footrest, digital clock, black remote-control mirrors, side window demisters, and inside hood release. Base Lasers came in six solid colors (Crystal or Pearl Coat); XE either in black or a choice of six two- tones. A total of 3,452 Lasers are reported to have added an XI performance package (code AGB), which wasn't available early in the year.

1985 LeBaron convertible (CC)

LEBARON — SERIES KC — FOUR — No more five-speed LeBarons could be ordered, as TorqueFlite automatic became the standard transmission. Appearance was similar to 1984, except for a new grille. It had the same overall shape but now was split into eight side- by-side sections (each made up of vertical strips), divided in half by a center bar. The grille pattern repeated in a wide slot below the bumper rub strip. As before, the full padded vinyl roof extended to the rear section of the back door on four-doors, which made for a narrow door window and private back seat area. Coupes, sedans and convertibles had new bodyside stripes. LeBaron's lineup was unchanged: four-door sedan, two- door coupe, convertible (standard or Town & Country), and T&C station wagon. Standard engine was the Trans-4 2.2-liter with fuel injection. Mitsubishi's MCA-JET Silent Shaft 2.6-liter four was standard on T&C, optional on others. Also optional on all body styles including (for the first time) the Town & Country wagon: the turbo 2.2, with new electronic wastegate control. Front suspension consisted of dual-path Iso-Struts and anti-sway bar. The rear beam axle used trailing arms and coil springs. Sport/handling suspension was recommended with the turbo four. Coupes had a new full-length console between the high- back cloth bucket seats, with storage for coins and cups (or tape cassettes). Sedans had a cloth bench seat. Convertibles had sporty low-back vinyl bucket seats with fixed center armrest/console. New heat (and air conditioning) controls allowed more precise settings. Intermittent wipers were now standard. Body colors were: Garnet Red, Mink Brown, Gold Dust, Cream, Gunmetal Blue, Ice Blue, Black, Radiant Silver, White, or Nightwatch Blue (all either Crystal or Pearl coat). Two two-tones were available. LeBaron's Mark Cross package added leather bucket seats and vinyl door trim panels with designer medallions, plus a leather-wrapped steering wheel, electronic instrument cluster, Ultimate Sound system radio, and locking wire wheel covers (or cast aluminum wheels). A total of 4,817 AFC Mark Cross packages were installed. Popular Equipment and Luxury Equipment Discount packages delivered a load of options without having to pay full price for each one.

LEBARON GTS — SERIES HC — FOUR — Chrysler's new H-bodied five-passenger hatchback sport sedan, with a drag coefficient of only 0.37, might be viewed almost as a four-door Laser. Dodge's Lancer was its near twin. The aero-styled six-window design featured a low- profile front end and 'delicately sloped' hood, aero-wrap flush-mounted windshield, and short deck. That hood, whose slope actually appeared somewhat sharp, led into a squat grille made up of evenly-spaced vertical bars, with center pentastar badge. Grille sides were slightly angled to match the housings for the quad rectangular headlamps. Wide parking lamps were inset into the bumper, below

1985 LeBaron GTS Sport Sedan (CC)

the rub strip. Full- width horizontally-ribbed wraparound taillamps had backup lamps at the inner ends, adjoining the license plate opening. On the decklid was 'Chrysler' and 'LeBaron GTS' lettering, plus a center pentastar emblem. Aircraft-style doors protruded slightly into the roof and held semi-flush side windows. GTS also had bright-edged black bodyside moldings and side striping. 'Turbo' lettering (if applicable) went on front fenders. Gas-charged dual path front Iso-Struts and rear shocks were part of the standard GTS road-touring suspension, which had large-diameter solid front and tubular rear anti-sway bars. Quick-ratio power steering and power brakes in a diagonally-split system were standard. Base engine was the 2.2-liter four with electronic fuel injection. The turbocharged 2.2 was optional. A close-ratio five-speed manual transaxle was standard, with upshift light on the non- turbo engine. High Line (base) models included a mechanical instrument cluster with analog gauges. Premium (LS) models featured an electronic cluster with digital speedometer/odometer and trip odometer, plus electronic analog display of engine speed, voltage, oil pressure, temperature and fuel level. Standard equipment on the base model included an AM/FM stereo electronic-tuning radio with digital clock, side window demisters, halogen headlamps, map pockets in front doors, remote-control driver's mirror, bodyside moldings, low-back cloth/vinyl bucket seats with recliners and one-piece rear folding seatback, P185/70R14 SBR tires, and two-speed wiper/washer. The Premium (LS) model added an intermittent wiper/washer, liftback and rear fascia striping, wheel opening and door frame surround striping, low-back cloth/vinyl front bucket seats with recliners and 60/40 split rear folding seatbacks, time-delay headlamp switch, driver's left footrest, and armrest console with storage bin and rear seat courtesy light. Low-back bucket seats had recliners and adjustable headrests. Both models had a fold-down rear seatback, but the LS version was split. Remote controls opened the liftback and fuel filler door. LeBaron GTS colors were: Black Crystal Coat, Gunmetal Blue Pearl Coat, Ice Blue Crystal Coat, Nightwatch Blue Crystal Coat, Desert Bronze Pearl Coat, Mink Brown Pearl Coat, Cream Crystal Coat, Gold Dust Crystal Coat, Garnet Red Pearl Coat, and Radiant Silver Crystal Coat. (Some colors cost extra.) Two special price packages were offered: Popular Equipment and Luxury Equipment. Also optional were two Sport Handling Suspension packages. The standard one, installed on 3,143 cars, included P195/70R14 RBL performance tires. Sport II package came with P205/60R14 RBL tires on cast aluminum 15 in. wheels. That one went on 12,436 GTS models. A total of 11,779 cars had the AGT Turbo Sport I package, which included the turbocharged engine and 14 in. aluminum wheels.

1985 New Yorker sedan (CC)

NEW YORKER — SERIES ET — FOUR — Only the New Yorker name remained on the front-drive Ebody, which changed little except for three new body colors. The E Class sedan of 1983-84 joined the Plymouth stable as a new Caravelle. Standard engine switched from the 2.2-liter Trans-4 to the MCA-Jet Silent Shaft 2.6-liter four with three-speed automatic. A turbocharged 2.2-liter was optional. Appearance was just about identical to 1984, but with three new body colors. A new cloth-covered overhead storage console held reading/courtesy lamps and two storage compartments. Rear seat headrests were new. So were cornering lamps, a 400-amp maintenance-free battery, and remote-control fuel filler door and decklid releases. Body colors were: Black, Ice Blue, Nightwatch Blue, Cream, Gold Dust, Radiant Silver or White Crystal Coat; and Gunmetal Blue, Mink Brown or Garnet Red Pearl Coat. New Yorker had an aerodynamically slanted hood, "classic" grille, quad halogen headlamps, decorative (non- functional) front fender louvers, and bodyside/decklid accent stripes. Locking wire wheel covers and steel-belted radial whitewalls were standard. New heater/air conditioner controls offered more choices for directing heated/cooled air. New Yorkers had a standard electronic instrument cluster and graphic message center, plus AM radio with digital clock. Power seats were now available for both passenger and driver. Other options: Electronic Navigator, and a new AM stereo/FM stereo Ultimate Sound radio with graphic equalizer. A Luxury Equipment Discount Package included such extras as the turbo engine, air conditioning, electric rear defroster, Electronic Navigator, and leather 50/50 power seats; plus a compass and outside-temperature digital readout for the overhead console.

FIFTH AVENUE — SERIES MFS — V-8 — Chrysler's last rear-drive model looked just about identical to the 1984 version, except that this year's rear- end trim panel between the taillamps appeared darker. Fifth Avenue's distinctive formal roofline continued with a revised landau padded vinyl roof that again extended into the rear of the back door, plus familiar up-and-over roof molding ahead of the vinyl. Inside were velvet cloth 60/40 pillow front seats, with leather/vinyl optional. Standard equipment

1985 Fifth Avenue sedan (CC)

included auto-temp control air conditioning, rear defroster, power windows, tinted glass, AM radio, and dual chrome remote mirrors. A Luxury Equipment Package included power door locks and decklid release, illuminated entry, AM/FM stereo radio with power antenna, intermittent wipers, and other extras. Colors this year were Crimson Red, Gold Dust, Nightwatch Blue, Radiant Silver, White or Black Crystal Coat; and Mink Brown or Gunmetal Blue Pearl Coat. Sole powertrain was the 318 cu. in. (5.2-liter) V-8 and TorqueFlite transmission. That engine now had roller tappets and higher compression (9.0:1) for a boost of 10 horsepower. Fifth Avenue's suspension consisted of transverse front torsion bars and anti-sway bar, plus rear leaf springs. New standard equipment included a 400-amp battery and tethered gas filler cap. Joining the option list: Ultimate Sound stereo and, later, a trim package with two-tone paint and vinyl roof.

EXECUTIVE — SERIES KCP — FOUR — Only the long-wheelbase (131 in.) front-drive limousine remained in the Executive series; the five-passenger sedan was dropped. This limo measured "only" 210.8 inches in length and carried a standard Mitsubishi-built MCA-Jet 2.6-liter engine and automatic transaxle. New this year: an Ultimate Sound AM stereo/FM stereo system with graphic equalizer and cassette player. Separate illuminated entry systems worked with front and rear compartments. Under the hood was a new 500-amp maintenance-free battery. Front seatbacks held new storage pockets. Limos had two rear-facing jump seats, plus a standard divider window with power-operated sliding glass. Two colors were new: Gunmetal Blue and Black Crystal Coat.

I.D. DATA: Chrysler again had a 17-symbol Vehicle Identification Number (VIN) on the upper left corner of the instrument panel, visible through the windshield. Coding changed somewhat with the revised model lineup. The first digit indicates Country: '1' U.S.A.; '2' Canada. The second symbol is Make: 'C' Chrysler. Third is Vehicle Type: '3' passenger car. The next symbol ('B') indicates manual seatbelts. Symbol five is Car Line: 'A' Laser; 'C' LeBaron (and Executive limo); 'H' LeBaron GTS; 'T' New Yorker; 'F' Fifth Avenue. Symbol six is Series: '4' High'; '5' Premium; '6' Special. Symbol seven is Body Style: '1' 2-dr. coupe; '2' 4-dr. limousine; '4' 2-dr. hatchback 22; '5' 2-dr. convertible coupe; '6' 4-dr. sedan; '8' 4-dr. hatchback; '9' 4-dr. wagon. Eighth is the Engine Code: 'D' L4-135 EFI; 'E' Turbo L4135 EFI; 'G' L4-156 2Bbl.; 'P' V8318 2Bbl. Next comes a check digit. Symbol ten indicates Model Year: 'F' 1985. Symbol eleven is Assembly Plant: 'C' Detroit; 'F' Newark, DE; 'G' or 'X' St. Louis; 'N' Sterling Hts. MI. The last six digits make up the sequential serial number, starting with 100001. Engine number coding is similar to 1982-84.

LASER (FOUR)

Series Number	Body/Style Number	Body Type & Seating	Factory Price	Shipping Weight	Production Total
GCH	24	2-dr. Hatch-4P	8854	2525	32,673

LASER XE (FOUR)

GCP	24	2-dr. Hatch-4P	10776	2545	18,193

LEBARON (FOUR)

KCP	22	2-dr. Cpe-5P	9460	2445	24,970
KCP	41	4-dr. Sed-6P	9309	2495	43,659
KCP	27	2-dr. Conv.-4P	11889	2530	16,475

1985 LeBaron Town & Country wagon (JG)

LEBARON TOWN & COUNTRY (FOUR)

KCP	45	4-dr. Sta Wag-5P	10363	2610	7,711

1985 LeBaron Mark Cross Town & Country convertible (JG)

LEBARON MARK CROSS CONVERTIBLE (FOUR)

KCP	27	2-dr. Conv.-4P	15994	N/A	Note 1
KCP	27	2-dr. T&C Conv.-4P	16994	N/A	Note 1

Note 1: Mark Cross and Mark Cross Town & Country convertibles are included in base convertible total above. A total of 595 T&C convertible packages (code AFG) were installed, plus 6,684 Mark Cross convertible packages (code AFD).

LEBARON GTS (FOUR)

HCH	44	4-dr. Spt Sed-5P	9024	N/A	33,176
HCP	44	4-dr. LS Sed-5P	9970	N/A	27,607

NEW YORKER (FOUR)

ETP	41	4-dr. Sed-5P	12865	N/A	60,700

FIFTH AVENUE (V-8)

MFS	41	4-dr. Sed-6P	13978	3660	109,971

1985 Executive limousine (CC)

EXECUTIVE (FOUR)

KCP	49	4-dr. Limo-7P	26318	N/A	759

MODEL NUMBER NOTE: Some sources identify models using the new VIN data to indicate Car Line, Price Class and Body Style. Example: base Laser (GCH24) has the equivalent number CA44, which translates to Laser line, High price class, and hatchback body. See I.D. Data section for breakdown.

ENGINE DATA: BASE FOUR (Laser, LeBaron, LeBaron GTS): Inline, overhead cam four-cylinder. Cast iron block; aluminum head. Displacement: 135 cu. in. (2.2 liters). Bore & stroke: 3.44 x 3.62 in. Compression ratio: 9.0:1. Brake horsepower: 99 at 5600 R.P.M. Torque: 121 lbs.-ft. at 3200 R.P.M. Five main bearings. Hydraulic valve lifters. Electronic fuel injection. TURBOCHARGED FOUR (Laser, LeBaron, LeBaron GTS, New Yorker): Same as 135 cu. in. four above, but with turbocharger Compression ratio: 8.1:1. B.H.P.: 146 at 5200 R.P.M. Torque: 168 lbs.-ft. at 3600 R.P.M. BASE FOUR (New Yorker, Executive Limousine); OPTIONAL (LeBaron): Inline, overhead cam four-cylinder. Cast iron block; aluminum head. Displacement: 156 cu. in. (2.6 liters). Bore & stroke: 3.59 x 3.86 in. Compression ratio: 8.7:1. Brake horsepower: 101 at 4800 R.P.M. Torque: 140 lbs.-ft. at 2800 R.P.M. Five main bearings. Solid valve lifters. Carburetor: 2Bbl. Mikuni. BASE V-8 (Fifth Avenue): 90-degree, overhead valve V-8. Cast iron block and head. Displacement: 318 cu. in. (5.2 liters). Bore & stroke: 3.91 x 3.31 in. Compression ratio: 9.0:1. Brake horsepower: 140 at 3600 R.P.M. Torque: 265 lbs.-ft. at 1600 R.P.M. Five main bearings. Hydraulic valve lifters. Carburetor: 2Bbl.

CHASSIS DATA: Wheelbase: (Laser) 97.0 in.; (LeBaron) 100.3 in.; (LeB T&C) 100.4 in.; (LeBaron GTS) 103.1 in.; (N.Y.) 103.3 in.; (Fifth Ave.) 112.7 in.; (Executive) 131.3 in. Overall length: (Laser) 175.0 in.; (LeB) 179.1 in.; (Exec.) 210.8 in.; (LeB conv.) 180.7 in.; (GTS) 180.4 in.; (N.Y.) 185.1 in.; (Fifth Ave.) 206.7 in.; (Exec.) 210.8 in. Height: (Laser) 50.3 in.; (LeB cpe) 52.7 in.; (LeB sed) 52.9 in.; (LeB wag) 53.2 in.; (LeB conv.) 53.7 in.; (GTS) 53.0 in.; (N.Y.) 53.1 in.; (Exec.) 55.3 in.; (Fifth Ave.) 55.3 in. Width: (Laser) 69.3 in.; (LeB/N.Y.) 68.0 in.; (GTS) 68.3 in.; (Fifth Ave.) 74.2 in.; (Exec.) 67.9 in. Front Tread: (Laser/LeB/GTS/N.Y./Exec.) 57.6 in.; (Fifth Ave.) 60.0 in. Rear Tread: (Laser/LeB/GTS/N.Y./Exec.) 57.2 in.; (Fifth Ave.) 59.5 in. Standard Tires: (Laser/LeB) P185/70R14 SBR WSW; (Laser XE) P205/60HR15 SBR RBL; (GTS) P185/70R14 SBR BSW; (New Yorker/Exec.) P185/75R14 SBR WSW; (Fifth Ave.) P205/75R15 SBR WSW.

TECHNICAL: Transmission: Five-speed manual trans. standard on Laser/GTS. Gear ratios: (1st) 3.29:1; (2nd) 2.08:1; (3rd) 1.45:1; (4th) 1.04:1; (5th) 0.72:1; (Rev) 3.14:1. TorqueFlite three-speed automatic optional on Laser/GTS, standard on LeBaron and New Yorker: (1st) 2.69:1; (2nd) 1.55:1; (3rd) 1.00:1; (Rev) 2.10:1. TorqueFlite standard on Fifth Ave.: (1st) 2.74:1; (2nd) 1.54:1; (3rd) 1.00:1; (Rev) 2.22:1. Standard final drive ratio: (Laser/GTS) 2.57:1 exc. 3.02:1 w/auto.; (LeB/N.Y./Exec.) 3.02:1; (Fifth Ave.) 2.26:1. Steering: (Laser/LeBaron/GTS/New Yorker) rack and pinion; (others) recirculating ball, power-assisted. Suspension: (Laser/GTS) Dual-path Iso-Strut front, trailing arm rear with front/rear sway bars and gas-charged rear shock absorbers; (LeBaron/New Yorker) Dual-path Iso-Struts and linkless sway bar in front, beam axle with trailing arms and coil springs at the rear; (Fifth Ave.) transverse front torsion bars and anti-sway bar, rear leaf springs. Brakes: Front disc, rear drum (power-assisted). Ignition: Electronic. Body construction: Unibody. Fuel tank: (Laser/LeB/GTS/N.Y.) 14 gal.; (Fifth Ave.) 18 gal.

DRIVETRAIN OPTIONS: Engines: 2.6-liter four: LeBaron/New Yorker ($282). Turbo 2.2- liter four: LeB/GTS/N.Y. ($634). Turbo pkg.: Laser ($1002); Laser XE ($907); GTS ($1141); GTS LS ($1091). Transmission/Suspension: Auto. trans.: Laser/GTS ($457). Heavy-duty susp.: Fifth Ave. ($27). Euro handling susp.: Laser XE ($106); LeB/N.Y. ($59). Sport handling pkg.: GTS ($122). Sport II handling pkg.: GTS ($644-$694) exc. ($187) w/turbo pkg. Other: H.D. cooling: Fifth Ave. ($156). H.D. 500-amp battery ($46). California emission system ($103).

LASER CONVENIENCE/APPEARANCE OPTIONS: Option Packages: Luxury equipment: base ($1186). Popular equipment: base ($793). Cargo trim/quiet sound: base ($72-$180). Light group: base ($138). Protection pkg. ($92). Comfort/Convenience: Air conditioning ($766). Rear defroster ($149-$175). Automatic speed control ($186). Electronic voice alert and navigator: base ($377). Power seat ($224). Power windows ($192). Power door locks ($130). Tinted glass ($114). Illuminated entry system ($78). Tilt steering wheel: base ($114). Liftgate wiper/washer ($125). Dual power remote mirrors: base ($50). Entertainment: AM/FM stereo radio: base ($166). AM/FM stereo w/cassette ($274-$440). Premium memory scan AM/FM stereo w/cassette ($465-$631). Radio delete ($56 credit). Exterior: Removable glass sunroof ($335). Pearl coat paint: base ($42). Interior: Low-back vinyl bucket seats: base ($25). Low-back cloth/vinyl bucket seats: base ($376). Low-back leather/vinyl bucket seats: base ($966); XE ($590). Wheels/Tires: 14 in. aluminum wheels: base ($335). P195/70R14 SBR RBL: base ($95). Conventional spare: base ($86-$97).

LEBARON CONVENIENCE/APPEARANCE OPTIONS: Option Packages: Mark Cross AFC pkg. ($866-$1040). Luxury pkg. ($1227-$1496). Popular equipment ($646-$1104). Comfort/Convenience: Air conditioning ($766). Rear defroster ($149). Automatic speed control ($186). Power seat ($224). Power windows ($192-$270). Power door locks ($130-$182). Power decklid or liftgate release ($42). Illuminated entry ($78). Leather-wrapped steering wheel ($52). Tilt steering wheel ($114). Tinted glass ($114). Lighting and Mirrors: Cornering lamps ($62). Dual remote mirrors ($59). Dual power remote mirrors ($85). Lighted vanity mirror ($60). Entertainment: Electronic-tuning AM/FM stereo radio ($130); w/cassette and seek/scan ($310-$440). Premium seek/scan AM/FM stereo radio ($501-$631). Radio delete ($56 credit). Exterior: Front/rear bumper guards ($58). Pearl coat paint ($42). Two-tone paint ($194). Bodyside moldings ($57). Undercoating ($45). Interior: Console ($145). Center armrest ($63). Cloth/vinyl bench seat: cpe (NC). Vinyl bucket seats: wag (NC). Cloth/vinyl bucket seats. sed ($173). Color-keyed floor mats: conv. front ($26); other front/rear ($47). Trunk dress-up ($53). Wheels and Tires: Wire wheel covers ($225). Cast aluminum wheels ($110-$335) but (NC) w/Mark Cross conv. Conventional spare ($86).

LEBARON GTS CONVENIENCE/APPEARANCE OPTIONS: Option Packages: Electronic feature pkg. (voice alert/navigator): LS ($398); w/illuminated entry ($536). Luxury equipment ($1101-$1314). Popular equipment ($480- $693). Light pkg. ($76). Comfort/Convenience: Air cond. ($766). Rear defroster ($149). Auto. speed control ($186). Power seat ($224). Power windows ($270). Power door locks ($182). Illuminated entry: LS ($78). Tinted glass ($114). Leather-wrapped steering wheel ($52- $95). Tilt steering ($114). Gauge set: LS (NC). Premium sound insulation: base ($45). Intermittent wipers: base ($55). Liftgate wiper/washer ($125). Lighting and Mirrors: Dual remote mirrors ($67). Dual power remote mirrors ($48-$115). Lighted visor vanity mirror ($60). Entertainment: Seek/scan AM/FM stereo w/cassette ($316). Memory scan AM/FM stereo w/cassette ($507). Radio delete: base ($152 credit). Exterior: Removable glass sunroof ($335). Pearl coat paint ($42). Undercoating ($45). Interior: Console: base ($82). Folding center armrest ($45). Leather/vinyl bucket seats: LS ($590). Color-keyed floor mats ($47). Wheels/Tires: Cast aluminum wheels, 14 or 15 in. ($335-$385). Styled steel wheels ($12-$62). P185/70R14 SBR WSW ($60). P195/70R14 SBR RBL ($95). P205/60HR15 SBR RBL ($187-$282).

NEW YORKER CONVENIENCE/APPEARANCE OPTIONS: Option Packages: Luxury equipment ($3220). Comfort/Convenience: Air cond. ($766). Rear defroster ($149). Auto. speed control ($186). Electronic navigator ($283). Power door locks ($182). Power seat ($224). Illuminated entry ($78). Leather-wrapped steering wheel ($52). Tilt steering ($114). Lighted vanity mirror ($60). Entertainment: Same as LeBaron, plus: Premium speakers ($131). Exterior: Pearl coat paint ($42). Bodyside molding ($57). Door edge protectors ($26). Undercoating ($45). Interior: Leather/vinyl 50/50 seats ($411). Color-keyed mats ($47). Wheels/Tires: Cast aluminum wheels ($110). Conventional spare ($86).

FIFTH AVENUE CONVENIENCE/APPEARANCE OPTIONS: Option Packages: Luxury equipment ($1782-$1915). Protection group ($132). Comfort/Convenience: Auto. speed control ($186). Power seat ($224). Power door locks ($182). Power decklid release ($42). Illuminated entry system ($78). Leather-wrapped steering wheel ($62). Tilt steering ($114). Intermittent wipers ($55). Underhood light ($16). Lighted vanity mirror ($60). Entertainment: AM/FM stereo radio ($130). AM/FM stereo w/cassette ($274-$404). Memory scan AM/FM stereo w/cassette ($465-$595). Power antenna ($62). Exterior: Power glass sunroof ($1083). Hood tape stripes ($30). Undercoating ($45). Interior: Cloth 60/40 bench seat (NC). Leather/vinyl 60/40 bench seat ($394). Wheels/Tires: Wire wheel covers ($205). Cast aluminum wheels ($49-$254). Conventional spare tire ($97).

EXECUTIVE LIMOUSINE OPTIONS Clearcoat paint ($42). Leather bucket seats ($1118).

HISTORY: Introduced: October 2, 1984 except LeBaron GTS, January 2, 1985. Model year production: Chrysler reported total factory shipments of 375,894 units. Calendar year production: 414,193. Calendar year sales by U.S. dealers: 375,880. Model year sales by U.S. dealers: 373,088.

Historical Footnotes: Strongest model year sales in eight years was good news for the Chrysler-Plymouth Division. The total came to 752,203, which was 18 percent over 1984 and not so far from the 828,315 cars sold in 1977. This was the third year in a row to produce a sales rise. The rear-drive Fifth Avenue sold nicely, at 112,137 units (up by 43 percent and well over corporate predictions). V-8 engines attracted quite a few buyers. LeBaron GTS also sold beyond expectations, finding 55,740 customers. GTS production began in late '84 at the new Sterling Heights, Michigan plant, which Chrysler had bought from Volkswagen. A Laser turbo turned in a 0-50 time of 5.8 seconds, as recorded by the U.S. Auto Club. That same organization claimed that LeBaron GTS surpassed BMW 528e and Mercedes 190E in their tests. Chrysler was an official sponsor of the U.S. Equestrian Team, which accounted for a focus on horses in the LeBaron catalog.

1986 Chrysler

A new 153 cu. in. (2.5-liter) Chrysler-built overhead- cam four-cylinder engine replaced the Mitsubishi 2.6 in most front-drive models. Rated 100 horsepower at 4800 R.P.M., the new four had fuel injection and a longer stroke than the 2.2. Twin nodular iron balance shafts counter-rotated at twice crankshaft speed. The 2.5 was standard on New Yorker, Laser XE, and T&C wagon; optional on Laser, LeBaron and GTS. New single-point fuel injection with a low-pressure (15 psi) fuel regulator arrived on all fours, with new speed compensating feature for smoother idling. Its Electronic Control Unit not only adjusted the air/fuel mixture and spark timing, but kept a record of engine operations to spot malfunctions. A new air cleaner housing on four-cylinder engines was easier to remove, while a labyrinth distributor was smaller in size with fewer parts. The "fast-burn" cylinder head on 2.2 and 2.5 fours was modified to speed combustion and improve idling. On-board diagnostics was part of all 2.2-liter engines. New Electronic Vehicle Height Control that adjusted the rear suspension to keep the car at proper height regardless of load was standard on LeBaron Town & Country, optional in New Yorker's Luxury Equipment package. New child safety rear door locks were standard on LeBaron GTS; intermittent rear wipers optional on Laser and LeBaron GTS. A microcomputer regulated incoming air temperature on New Yorker's optional Automatic Temperature Control. Four-way adjustable head restraints were available on New Yorker, Laser and GTS. All models had a new center high-mounted stop lamp, and all front-drives had "Precision- feel" power steering that was introduced in 1985.

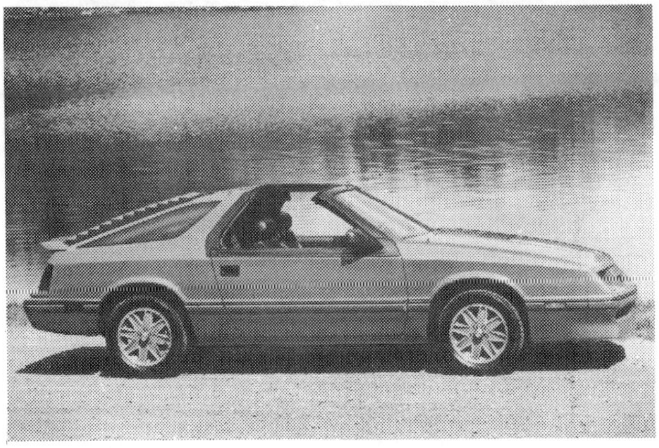

1986 Laser XT hatchback coupe (CC)

LASER — SERIES GC — FOUR — Three Laser price classes were offered this year: base, XE and a new XT. The base model had 14 in. all-season SBR tires and sport wheel covers; XE rode P205/60HR15 special- handling raised-black-letter tires on 15 in. cast aluminum wheels. Also on XE: an adjustable steering column, electronic instrumentation, 21-feature electronic monitor, Electronic Navigator, and "enthusiast" performance bucket seats with new four-way head restraints. XE's electronic instrumentation featured multicolor graphics including quick-read digital speedometer, odometer and trip odometer, plus analog tach and engine readouts. A five-speed manual transaxle was standard. The new 2.5-liter four was standard on XE, while base Lasers came with the 2.2 four. Laser XT, which was actually a performance option package, added aerodynamics components, new P225/50VR15 uni- directional tires, turbo engine and boost gauge, and performance suspension. Its dash displayed gauges and a graphic message center, but not the Navigator. The turbocharged four had multi-point fuel injection and produced 146 horsepower, with boost beginning at just 1200 R.P.M. XT's close-ratio five-speed transaxle with overdrive fifth gear had a higher-capacity clutch. A total of 6,989 Lasers had the XT package installed. Laser's grille was a simple 4 x 2 pattern of wide holes set in a slot at the lower portion of the grille panel, flanked by quad rectangular headlamps. Parking lamps were below, well outside the twin air slots. Except for bodyside moldings with inserts, rather than the ribbed look of 1985, this year's Laser didn't change too much in appearance. Lasers had a rear spoiler and full-wrap lower front fascia with low-profile air dam; XE added lower bodyside sill spoilers. Colors were: Garnet Red Pearl Coat, Golden Bronze Pearl Coat, Ice Blue, White, Black, Radiant Silver, Gold Dust, and Gunmetal Blue Pearl Coat. Laser XT also came in Flash Red. A total of 4,966 Lasers carried the new T-bar roof that included two removable tinted glass panels with keyed locks, offered in a package with power windows and larger aero-look power mirrors. A "Sun, Sound & Shade" package included sunroof, AM stereo/FM stereo radio with cassette, and black rear window louvers.

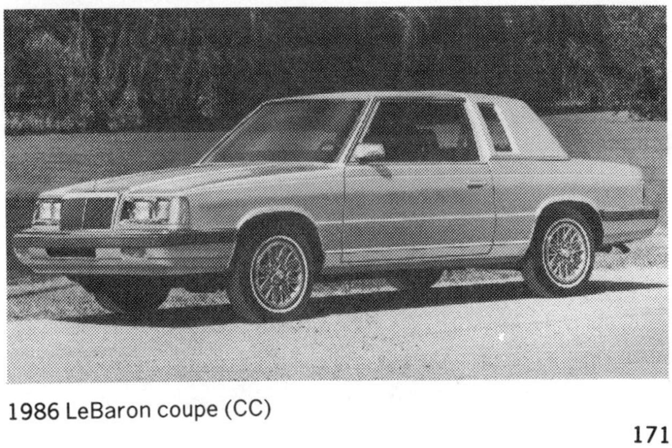

1986 LeBaron coupe (CC)

LEBARON — SERIES KC — FOUR — Changes focused on LeBaron's front end, which was moderately restyled with a new grille texture and header. The grille now consisted of thin vertical bars separated by a wider center bar. Large wraparound marker lamps now flanked the quad rectangular headlamps. Front bumper and soft fascia were new. So were the taillamps, rear end caps, and decklid. LeBarons had a new electro-mechanical instrument cluster and message center, plus a new AM stereo/FM stereo radio. Standard wheel covers were new. So were the padded landau roof on four-door sedans, as well as low-travel power window and door lock switches. Base engine remained the 2.2-liter four, with standard automatic transaxle. Optional: either the turbocharged 2.2 or new 2.5-liter four. Three convertibles were offered: base, Mark Cross Edition, and Town & Country (with decklid luggage rack). A total of 3,941 non-convertible LeBarons had the Mark Cross package. Standard equipment included a dual-note horn, locking glove box, power rack-and-pinion steering, two-spoke luxury steering wheel, upper bodyside accent stripes, P185/70R14 SBR whitewall tires, intermittent wipers, tinted glass, and day/night inside mirror. Town & Country wagons included automatic load leveling, roof luggage rack, front anti-sway bar, and simulated woodgrain bodyside paneling. Convertibles had dual remote-control mirrors.

1986 LeBaron GTS Sport Sedan (CC)

LEBARON GTS — SERIES HC — FOUR — Little change was evident on Chrysler's sport performance sedan in its second year. Air conditioning was now standard on the Premium (HCP44) model, while both had tinted glass. New this year were rear-door child safety locks, an electro-mechanical 125 MPH speedometer, and four-way adjustable front head restraints. Power door lock and window switches also were new. A modified "fast-burn" cylinder head went on the standard 2.2-liter four-cylinder engine. Both the turbo 2.2 and new 2.5-liter four were optional. Manual five-speed transaxle remained standard. GTS showed a steeply raked windshield (58 degrees), rounded contours, and high decklid. The six-window design had flush windshield and liftback glass and semi-flush side glass, plus snug-fit "aircraft" doors. Body colors were: Garnet Red, Dark Cordovan, Light Rosewood Mist, Golden Bronze or Gunmetal Blue Pearl Coat; Light Cream; Ice Blue; Black; Radiant Silver; or Gold Dust. Three two-tone options were offered on base models only. An electromechanical instrument cluster with analog gauges was standard on the High Line (base) model; full electronic cluster on Premium model, with digital speedometer/odometer and trip odometer readouts plus an analog tachometer and gauge set. Both had an incandescent message center that displayed a car outline with warning lights for such maladies as door/liftback ajar and low washer fluid. The standard AM stereo/FM stereo radio had a built-in digital clock and electronic tuning. Options included a 10-function Electronic Navigator and 10-function Electronic Voice Alert system. An optional center folding armrest and cushion package added space for a sixth passenger. Base models had low-back cloth/vinyl bucket seats; LS had upgraded cloth or optional leather. Standard suspension included dual-path upper Iso-Strut mounts, constant camber trailing arm-beam rear axle, large-diameter tubular rear sway bar, plus gas front struts and rear shocks. Two Sport Handling packages were available. Package I included Goodyear Eagle GT P195/70R14 blackwalls, higher-control struts/shocks, performance-tuned spring rates, and higher-capacity compact spare tire. Sport Handling Package II added P205/60R15 Eagle GT tires on 15 in. aluminum wheels.

1986 New Yorker sedan (CC)

NEW YORKER — SERIES ET — FOUR — Only a few changes were evident from the front of the front-drive New Yorker. Opera lamps moved from the vinyl roof to the up-and-over trim molding, while side marker lenses were absent from rear quarter panels. New rear styling included decklid panels, moldings, and full-width taillamps that combined side marker lamps and reflectors. Also new: a soft bumper fascia, bumper guards with license plate lamps, accent stripes, electro-luminescent opera lamps, and vinyl roof moldings. Narrower wraparound taillamps now had only two thin horizontal trim strips that stretched across the full width of the rear end, as there was no longer a recessed license plate housing between them. Front fenders still held louvers, and a pair of louver sets sat on the hood, at either side of the center crease. Colors were: Dark Cordovan, Light Rosewood Mist, Golden Bronze or Gunmetal Blue Pearl Coat; plus Light Cream, Ice Blue, Black, Radiant Silver, or White. New electronic instrumentation included a cluster containing a digital speedometer and odometer, vertical-bar gauges with red warning segments for oil/voltage/temp/fuel, warning lamps, and diagnostics. A trip computer revealed trip miles, trip fuel efficiency, instant fuel efficiency, distance to empty tank, and elapsed time. New plush velvet cloth 50/50 pillow front seats had dual armrests and recliners, plus four-way head restraints. The forward console was new. Electronic automatic temperature control was new, while electronic load leveling became optional. Standard engine was the new 2.5-liter four with balance shafts, while a turbocharged 2.2 was optional.

FIFTH AVENUE — SERIES MFS — V-8 — New body colors were offered on the rear-drive Fifth Avenue, including three two-tones. But that was about the extent of the changes for 1986. Standard equipment included the 318 cu. in. (5.2-liter) V-8 engine, TorqueFlite transmission, power brakes and steering, air conditioning, P205/75R15 steel-belted radial whitewalls, hood ornament, tinted glass, fender louvers, and AM radio with digital clock. Also standard: electric rear window defroster, tethered fuel filler cap, dual-note horn, courtesy lights, wheel opening and belt moldings, vinyl padded landau roof, bodyside/decklid tape stripes, and premium wheel covers. Colors were White, Radiant Silver, Crimson Red, Gold Dust, and Nightwatch Blue; plus Gunmetal Blue or Mink Brown Pearl Coat. Three two-tone combinations were available at extra cost. Standard 60/40 seats were velvet cloth; Corinthian leather with vinyl trim optional. A new Luxury Equipment Discount package included power 60/40 Corinthian leather seats, power door locks, power antenna, digital AM/FM stereo radio, power decklid release, illuminated entry, automatic speed control, and tilt steering column.

1986 Executive limousine (CC)

EXECUTIVE — SERIES KCP — FOUR — Chrysler's front-drive limousine, measuring under 211 inches overall, had a standard turbocharged 2.2-liter four-cylinder engine and the same front-end appearance as New Yorker. This year it got new decklid panels, rear bumper fascia, and end caps. The plush cloth interior had a pillowed back seat with center armrest (leather front seats optional). Air conditioning had five rear vents. Standard equipment included heavy-duty suspension, electro-luminescent opera lamps, rear compartment console, and glamour light module.

I.D. DATA: As before, Chrysler's 17-symbol Vehicle Identification Number (VIN) was on the upper left corner of the instrument panel, visible through the windshield. Coding was similar to 1985. Engine code 'G' was dropped; code 'K' (L4-153 FI) added. Model year code changed to 'G' for 1986. Engine number coding was similar to 1982-85.

LASER (FOUR)

Series Number	Body/Style Number	Body Type & Seating	Factory Price	Shipping Weight	Production Total
GCH	24	2-dr. Hatch-4P	9364	2560	21,123

LASER XE (FOUR)

GCP	24	2-dr. Hatch-4P	11501	2665	15,549

LASER XT (FOUR)

GCP	24/AGB	2-dr. Hatch-4P	11854	2695	Note 1

Note 1: A total of 6,989 Lasers had the XT package (RPO code AGB).

1986 LeBaron convertible (CC)

LEBARON (FOUR)

KCP	22	2-dr. Cpe-5P	9977	2475	24,761
KCP	41	4-dr. Sed-6P	10127	2500	40,116
KCP	27	2-dr. Conv.-4P	12695	2565	19,684

LEBARON TOWN & COUNTRY (FOUR)

KCP	45	4-dr. Sta Wag-5P	11370	2660	6,493

LEBARON MARK CROSS CONVERTIBLE (FOUR)

KCP	27	2-dr. Conv.-4P	16595	N/A	Note 1	
KCP	27	2-dr. T&C Conv.-4P	17595	N/A	Note 1	

Note 1: Mark Cross and Mark Cross Town & Country convertibles are included in base convertible total above. A total of 501 T&C convertible packages (RPO code AFG) were installed, plus 6,905 Mark Cross convertible packages (code AFD).

LEBARON GTS (FOUR)

HCH	44	4-dr. Spt Sed-5P	9754	2605	42,841

LEBARON GTS PREMIUM (FOUR)

HCP	44	4-dr. Spt Sed-5P	11437	2695	30,716

NEW YORKER (FOUR)

ETP	41	4-dr. Sed-5P	13409	2655	51,099

1986 Fifth Avenue sedan (CC)

FIFTH AVENUE (V-8)

MFS	41	4-dr. Sed-6P	14910	3655	104,744

EXECUTIVE (FOUR)

KCP	49	4-dr. Limo-7P	27495	3155	138

MODEL NUMBER NOTE: Some sources identify models using the new VIN data to indicate Car Line, Price Class and Body Style. Example: base Laser (GCH24) has the equivalent number CA44, which translates to Laser line, High price class, and hatchback body. See I.D. Data section for breakdown.

ENGINE DATA: BASE FOUR (Laser, LeBaron, LeBaron GTS): Inline, overhead cam four-cylinder. Cast iron block; aluminum head. Displacement: 135 cu. in. (2.2 liters). Bore & stroke: 3.44 x 3.62 in. Compression ratio: 9.5:1. Brake horsepower: 97 at 5200 R.P.M. Torque: 122 lbs.-ft. at 3200 R.P.M. Five main bearings. Hydraulic valve lifters. Electronic fuel injection. **TURBOCHARGED FOUR: BASE** (Laser, LeBaron, LeBaron GTS, New Yorker): Same as 135 cu. in. four above, but with turbocharger Compression ratio: 8.1:1. B.H.P.: 146 at 5200 R.P.M. Torque: 170 lbs.-ft. at 3600 R.P.M. **OPTIONAL** (Laser XE, LeBaron T&C wagon, New Yorker). **BASE FOUR** (Laser, LeBaron, LeBaron GTS): Inline, overhead cam four-cylinder. Cast iron block; aluminum head. Displacement: 153 cu. in. (2.5 liters). Bore & stroke: 3.44 x 4.09 in. Compression ratio: 9.0:1. Brake horsepower: 100 at 4800 R.P.M. Torque: 136 lbs.-ft. at 2800 R.P.M. Five main bearings. Hydraulic valve lifters. Electronic fuel injection. **BASE V-8** (Fifth Avenue): 90-degree, overhead valve V-8. Cast iron block and head. Displacement: 318 cu. in. (5.2 liters). Bore & stroke: 3.91 x 3.31 in. Compression ratio: 9.0:1. Brake horsepower: 140 at 3600 R.P.M. Torque: 265 lbs.-ft. at 1600 R.P.M. Five main bearings. Hydraulic valve lifters. Carburetor: 2Bbl.

CHASSIS DATA: Wheelbase: (Laser) 97.0 in.; (LeBaron) 100.3 in.; (LeB conv.) 100.4 in.; (LeBaron GTS) 103.1 in.; (N.Y.) 103.3 in.; (Fifth Ave.) 112.6 in.; (Limousine) 131.3 in. Overall length: (Laser) 175.0 in.; (LeB) 179.2 in.; (GTS) 180.4 in.; (N.Y.) 187.2 in.; (Fifth Ave.) 206.7 in.; (Limo) 210.7 in. Height: (Laser) 50.4 in.; (LeB cpe) 52.5 in.; (LeB sed/conv.) 52.9 in.; (LeB wag) 53.2 in.; (GTS) 53.0 in.; (N.Y.) 53.1 in.; (Fifth Ave.) 55.1 in.; (Limo) 53.6 in. Width: (Laser) 69.3 in.; (LeB/N.Y.) 68.0 in.; (GTS) 68.3 in.; (Fifth Ave.) 68.0 in. Front Tread: (Laser/LeB/GTS/N.Y./Limo) 57.6 in.; (Fifth Ave.) 60.5 in. Rear Tread: (Laser) 57.6 in.; (LeB/GTS/N.Y./Exec.) 57.2 in.; (Fifth Ave.) 60.0 in. Standard Tires: (Laser/LeB) P185/70R14 SBR WSW; (Laser XE) P205/60HR15 SBR RBL; (GTS) P185/70R14 SBW; (New Yorker/Exec.) P185/75R14 SBR WSW; (Fifth Ave.) P205/75R15 SBR WSW.

TECHNICAL: Specifications same as 1985.

DRIVETRAIN OPTIONS: Engines: 2.5-liter four: LeBaron/GTS ($279). Turbo 2.2-liter four: LeB/GTS/N.Y. ($628). Turbo pkg.: Laser ($993); Laser XE ($733). Transmission/Suspension: Auto. trans.: Laser/GTS ($478). Heavy-duty susp.: Fifth Ave. ($27). Euro handling susp.: LeB/N.Y. ($58). Sport Handling pkg.: GTS ($580-$642). Sport Handling pkg. II: GTS ($27-$688). Other: Maintenance-free 500-amp battery ($45). California emission system ($102).

LASER CONVENIENCE/APPEARANCE OPTIONS: Option Packages: Luxury equipment: XE ($1572-$1583). Popular equipment ($332-$436); w/air cond. ($937-$1066). Sun/sound/shade pkg. ($639). Protection pkg. ($90). Comfort/Convenience: Air conditioning ($780). Rear defroster ($152-$188). Automatic speed control ($184). Electronic navigator: base ($280). Power driver's seat ($232). Power windows ($201). Power door locks ($134). Tilt steering wheel ($118). Liftgate wiper/washer ($129). Dual power remote mirrors: base ($58). Entertainment: AM stereo/FM stereo w/cassette ($251). Ultimate sound radio w/cassette ($216-$467). Exterior: Removable glass sunroof ($342). Pearl coat paint: base ($41). Interior: Low-back cloth/vinyl bucket seats: base ($404). Low-back leather/vinyl bucket seats: base ($988); XE ($584). Wheels/Tires: 14 in. aluminum wheels: base ($332). P195/70R14 SBR RBL: base ($95). Conventional spare ($85).

LEBARON CONVENIENCE/APPEARANCE OPTIONS: Option Packages: Mark Cross AFC pkg. ($1040). Luxury equipment ($1087-$1278). Popular equipment ($1087). Deluxe convenience ($302). Power convenience ($335-$463). Center console pkg. ($206). Interior light pkg.: cpe/sed ($137). Protection pkg. ($115). Cold weather pkg.: cpe/sed ($197). Comfort/Convenience: Air conditioning ($780). Power seat ($232). Power decklid or liftgate release ($41). Illuminated entry ($77). Leather-wrapped steering wheel ($52). Dual power remote mirrors ($88). Lighted vanity mirror ($60). Entertainment: Seek/scan AM stereo/FM stereo radio w/cassette ($436). Ultimate sound AM stereo/FM stereo w/cassette ($652). Exterior: Front/rear bumper guards: wag ($58). Pearl coat paint ($41). Two-tone paint: cpe ($193). Undercoating ($44). Interior: Vinyl bucket seats: conv. (NC). Cloth/vinyl bucket seats: cpe/sed ($171). Color-keyed floor mats: conv. front ($26); other front/rear ($46). Trunk dress-up ($53). Wheels/Tires: Wire wheel covers ($180). Cast aluminum wheels ($101-$281) but (NC) w/Mark Cross conv. Conventional spare ($85).

LEBARON GTS CONVENIENCE/APPEARANCE OPTIONS: Option Packages: Electronic feature pkg. incl. voice alert/navigator ($348-$393). Luxury equipment ($688-$1078). Popular equipment ($667-$1503). Deluxe convenience ($118-$302). Power convenience ($463). Highline upgrade: base ($125). Protection pkg. ($90). Cold weather pkg. ($197). Comfort/Convenience: Air cond. ($780). Power driver's seat ($232). Leather-wrapped steering wheel ($52-$94). Liftgate wiper/washer ($129). Lighting and Mirrors: Dual remote mirrors ($66). Dual power remote mirrors ($115). Lighted visor vanity mirror ($60). Entertainment: Premium AM stereo/FM stereo w/cassette ($293). Ultimate sound AM stereo/FM stereo w/cassette ($509). Exterior: Removable glass sunroof ($342). Pearl coat paint ($41). Two-tone paint: base ($233). Interior: Console and armrest: base ($81). Folding center armrest ($44). Leather low-back bucket seats: premium ($583). Wheels/Tires: Cast aluminum wheels: 14 in. ($333-$381); 15 in. ($580-$642). Styled steel wheels ($14-$62). P185/70R14 SBR WSW ($60). P195/70R14 SBR RBL ($95). Conventional spare ($85).

NEW YORKER CONVENIENCE/APPEARANCE OPTIONS: Option Packages: Luxury equipment ($3413). Deluxe convenience pkg. ($302). Comfort/Convenience: Automatic air cond. ($927). Power door locks ($185). Power seat ($232). Illuminated entry ($77). Leather-wrapped steering wheel ($52). Twin lighted vanity mirrors ($120). Entertainment: AM stereo/FM stereo w/cassette ($287). Ultimate sound radio w/cassette ($503). Power antenna ($67). Exterior: Pearl coat paint ($41). Bodyside molding ($57). Undercoating ($44). Interior: Cloth 50/50 bench seat (NC). Leather 50/50 seats ($407). Color-keyed mats ($46). Wheels/Tires: Wire wheel covers ($181). Cast aluminum wheels ($110-$291). Conventional spare ($85).

FIFTH AVENUE CONVENIENCE/APPEARANCE OPTIONS: Option Packages: Luxury equipment ($1817-$1947). Two-tone paint pkg. ($153-$474). Protection group ($131). Comfort/Convenience: Auto. speed control ($184). Power seat ($232); dual ($232-$464). Power door locks ($185). Power decklid release ($41). Illuminated entry system ($77). Leather-wrapped steering wheel ($62). Tilt steering ($118). Intermittent wipers ($55). Lighted vanity mirror ($60). Entertainment: AM stereo/FM stereo radio ($149); w/seek scan and cassette ($251-$400). Ultimate sound AM stereo/FM stereo w/cassette ($497-$616). Power antenna ($67). Exterior: Power glass sunroof ($1108). Pearl coat paint ($41). Hood tape stripes ($30). Undercoating ($44). Interior: Cloth 60/40 bench seat (NC). Leather/vinyl 60/40 bench seat ($390). Wheels/Tires: Wire wheel covers (NC or $212). Cast aluminum wheels ($39-$251). Conventional spare tire ($96).

HISTORY: Introduced: October 1, 1985. Model year production: 357,264. Calendar year production: 368,638. Calendar year sales by U.S. dealers: 353,888. Model year sales by U.S. dealers: 370,544.

Historical Footnotes: Chrysler retained one note of notoriety, offering the only domestic cars that had to pay a gas guzzler penalty of $500 apiece. The V-8 Fifth Avenue couldn't manage the required 22.5 MPG minimum this year. This was especially ironic since Chrysler had been the only member of the Big Three to meet the original CAFE standards for 1986. Plymouth's Gran Fury also failed the test. Laser sales fell considerably for 1986 (down to 31,458 from a healthy 54,758 in model year 1985). Dodge's Daytona did better. LeBaron GTS, on the other hand, sold almost 16,000 more copies this model year than in its first season. Fifth Avenues sold rather well, even with their gas guzzler reputation (and penalty). Overall Chrysler-Plymouth sales rose 3 percent, to 775,025 units (including 69,402 imports). Incentives were big news this year. Chrysler and Plymouth would become separate divisions for the 1987 model year. A Maserati-built two-seat sport coupe was shown at auto shows during 1986, scheduled for 1987 release as a Chrysler product (but not actually available until 1988).

173

Recalls plagued Dodge's new Aspen, introduced for 1976 as compact replacement for the venerable Dart (which hung on one more year). Sales never took off like Dart's had, either. While performance wasn't forgotten in the Dodge camp, the high-potency Chargers and Challengers were mainly memories. Four hardtop coupe models (or option packages) carried on the Charger and Daytona nameplates, with a 240-horsepower, 400 cu. in. V-8 possible underhood; but such temptations wouldn't last much longer. Aspen's R/T package, on the other hand, could combine with a 360 V-8, on a lighter-weight coupe chassis. Dart's model selection reached out for fuel economy with a Dart Lite package, which sounded more like a new brand of beer. Pillarless hardtops were still available from Dodge, but top-line mid-sizes displayed opera windows. Full-size Monacos and Royal Monacos were the only models to offer the big 440 V-8. While model-year sales rose in '76, they hardly matched the record set three years earlier. Compacts were finding plenty of customers, but the bigger Dodges were losing appeal.

1978 Aspen R/T coupe (JG)

Monaco became the name for mid-sizes in 1977, as the well-known Coronet badge disappeared. Full-sizes kept the "Royal" prefix. Aspen coupes could have not only the former R/T package, but a Super R/T, as well as a T-Bar roof or sunroof. Those Aspens are most likely to appeal to collectors. So might the sporty Daytona package, which went on 5,225 Charger SE models. Dodge's new Diplomat, mid-size at the time, would still be around a decade later as the last remaining "big" rear-drive model.

1978 Diplomat wagon (JG)

174

Subcompacts, not full-size models, were the big news in 1978, though. As the biggest Dodges faded away, the L-body Omni (and near-twin Plymouth Horizon) arrived—first of the American-built front-drives. Few realized at the time that Omni signaled a major trend, paving the way for front-wheel drive to virtually take over the marketplace over the next decade. Sporty Aspens came in additional forms this time: R/T (again), R/T Sport Pak and Super Coupe, along with a Street Kit Car. Farther up the line, the Magnum XE, with its distinctive slat-style grille, took over from Daytona as the sporty mid-size. Magnum's GT package might be the one to look over now. Monaco had a couple of special packages, too—an 'SS' and Gran Coupe—but those hardly rivaled the appeal of a Magnum.

1980 Diplomat Sport Coupe (D)

Important as Omni was, it didn't help Dodge sales enough as the 1970s ended. Totals fell slightly in both 1978 and '79, then far lower for the '80 model year. Big Dodges were gone for 1979, replaced by a new and lighter St. Regis. A front-drive 024 coupe joined the original Omni sedan. Not many Aspens carried the R/T package this year, but quite a few were Sunrise Coupes. Among other moves, new Chrysler chairman Lee Iacocca tried to promote a wider gulf between Dodge and the Chrysler-Plymouth Division.

1981 Omni hatchback sedan (D)

Mirada, similar in appearance to the restyled Chrysler Cordoba but with slat grille, claimed the personal-luxury coupe niche from Magnum XE for 1980. Mirada's CMX package— especially one with high-output 360 cu. in. V-8

and dual exhausts — is the one to seek out today. Aspen R/T and new 024 DeTomaso options may not seem as attractive to latter-day enthusiasts, but are comparatively rare. Fewer are likely to grow excited by the sight of a Touring Edition St. Regis or a Diplomat 'S' coupe.

Excitement isn't the word that comes to mind for Aries, either, which entered the Dodge lineup for 1981, along with the related Plymouth Reliant. Yet this front-drive compact sedan worked wonders for Dodge sales and reputation. *Motor Trend* gave it Car of the Year honors. Omni added a stripped-down "Miser" and a step-up Euro-Sedan. More appealing nowadays, though, might be the subcompact coupe's option choices: the rather rare De Tomaso, and the new Charger 2.2 package, both with 2.2-liter engine. Aries' popularity helped Dodge sales rise by a healthy amount.

St. Regis didn't return for 1982, victim of sagged sales; and Diplomat came only in four-door sedan form. Charger was the name on the subcompact coupe's performance edition—hardly a rival to its predecessors with that badge, but appealing in its own way. Aries' chassis was stretched a bit to produce the new 400 series, which even included a convertible—something not seen in Dodge ranks since 1971.

Charger performance took a leap upward with the addition of a (Carroll) Shelby edition for 1983. A 107-horsepower four, after all, could propel a lightweight subcompact coupe quite nicely. Mirada was in its final year, but another numbered front-drive Dodge model arrived: the 600 sedan. "Talking dashboards" available on 400 and 600 were not universally loved. Sales looked good this year as Dodge's market share rose.

Next year, the 600 nameplate went on former 400 models and the 600 ES (Euro-Sport) came with gas-filled shocks. Dodge had a much different, smaller-scale offering for performance-minded prospects, though: the

1986 Daytona Turbo Z C/S hatchback coupe (D)

new Daytona, available with 142-horsepower turbocharged engine in regular or Turbo Z trim. Performance also came in tiny packages: not only the Shelby Charger, but a new Omni GLH option. With Mirada gone, Diplomat was the only rear-drive Dodge remaining, popular mainly with police agencies. After a long life, the old Slant Six engine was retired.

Just as Daytona had been near twin to Chrysler's Laser, the new Lancer for 1985 was closely related to LeBaron GTS. Turbo power was now standard on the Shelby Charger, and available under Omni GLH hoods as well as in larger models. Model-year sales hit their highest peak since 1978, and rose again for 1986 (but only with the help of captive import sales).

Performance fans tend to overlook Omni's GLH, described as "ferocious" and a "savage." Whether truly collectible or not, they serve as interesting examples of potent power in lightweight packages. Shelby Chargers are perhaps more likely to attract collector interest, if only for their name. Other recent possibilities that may hold future appeal: the 600 ES Turbo convertible, Daytona Turbo Z, and Mirada CMX.

1976 DODGE

Dodge's model lineup was similar to that offered in 1975, but this would be the final year for the venerable Dodge Dart. Its place would be taken up by the new Aspen compact, which debuted this year. Dodge covered much of the market with its model lineup, which included the mid-size Coronet, a selection of four Charger specialty coupes, and the full-size Monaco and Royal Monaco. Fuel mileage got a major push this year, with axle ratios geared in that direction. Chrysler's Electronic Lean Burn System went on all 400 and 440 cu. in. V-8s. Its miniature computer received data from sensors on throttle position, engine R.P.M., manifold vacuum, and coolant temperature; then adjusted spark timing to produce the leanest air/fuel mixture. Monaco was the only Dodge to have a 440 cu. in. V-8 option. Engines destined for California Dodges differed in horsepower and/or carburetor configuration from those offered in the other 49 states. Pillarless hardtops were still available, but top-line mid-sizes had opera windows.

1976 Dart sedan (D)

DART — SERIES L — SIX/V-8 — "The value car" came in four models for 1976, with no change in styling. Most of them could have either the base 225 cu. in. Slant Six, or a 318 or 360 cu. in. V-8 engine. Coupes rode a 108 in. wheelbase, while 111 in. was used for two-door hardtops and four-door sedans. Dart Sport was the cheapest; others were the Swinger, Swinger Special, and Dart Sedan. Several variants also were available. Single round headlamps set into the ends of Dart's full-width grille, made up of horizontal bars. Wide parking lamps were inset into the recessed portion of the grille on each side, just inboard of the headlamps. The full-width grille header (which surrounded the entire headlamp/grille unit) contained 'Dodge' block lettering. The grille's center came to a slight forward peak. At the rear were twin rectangular taillamps at each end of a full-width trim panel, wrapping slightly around the quarter panels. Dart Lite was the name for a Sport with fuel economy package, 150 pounds lighter than its mate. The economy Slant Six had an aluminum intake manifold and modified engine block. Aluminum was used for bumper reinforcements, as well as hood and decklid inner panels. An Overdrive4 transmission was used, with 2.94:1 axle ratio (2.76:1 with automatic). Lites also carried a shorter option list. Cloth/vinyl bench seats were standard on Swinger Special and Sport. A Decorator package containing low-back vinyl seats, Boca Raton cloth inserts, woodgrained dash and deluxe steering wheel was optional on Sport. A Custom package for the Dart sedan included deluxe cloth/vinyl seats, rear armrests, woodgrain dash, plus special moldings, nameplates and appliques. Dart Sport offered a Convertriple option: sunroof and fold-down rear seat (with security panel) that converted the rear seat and trunk into a carpeted cargo area. Also optional: the Overdrive4 transmission, manual sunroof, and Rallye wheels. A Special Edition package (RPO code A76) went on 7.3 percent of Darts.

1976 Aspen Special Edition coupe (D)

ASPEN — SERIES N — SIX/V-8 — Dart's new replacement was was dubbed "the family car of the future." Like the similar Fbodied Plymouth Volare, it arrived as a mid-year entry. Three bodies were offered: four-door sedan, semi-fastback coupe with large triangular quarter windows, and four-door wagon with one-piece liftgate. (That was the first compact wagon since 1966.) The two-door coupe rode a 108.5 in. wheelbase, while the four-door sedan and wagon measured 112.5 in. Three trim levels were offered: standard, Custom and SE. Coupes carried five passengers; others six.

Aspen used a new transverse (crosswise) torsion bar front suspension, rather than the conventional longitudinal torsion bars. Fully isolated from the body shell, it was supposed to give a "big car" ride. Leaf springs provided the rear suspension. Base engine was the 225 cu. in. Slant Six. Optional: 318 and 360 cu. in. V-8s. An Overdrive4 floor-shift transmission was available, to replace the standard three-speed. Four axle ratios were available, as was three-speed TorqueFlite automatic. Front disc brakes were power-assisted on wagons and V-8 models. Aspen's grille was made up of horizontal strips, with a wide center portion that protruded forward. A bright upper header molding held inset 'Dodge' block letters. Single round headlamps sat in square, bright housings. Parking lamps set into the bumper, below the headlamps, while the bumper center pushed forward to match the grille shape. Front fenders held 'Aspen' nameplates, ahead of the door. Small horizontal side marker lamps went on front fenders, roughly in line with wheel opening tops. The windshield had narrow roof pillars. Wide horizontal rectangular taillamps were directly above similarly-shaped but shorter backup lamps, in a single unit, set at ends of a wide trim panel with 'Dodge' lettering in the center. The license plate was mounted at the bumper. An 'Aspen' nameplate was on the decklid. Base Aspen coupes had low-back cloth-vinyl bench seats; the sedan and wagon used vinyl. Standard equipment included a heater/defroster, hubcaps, drip moldings, driver's mirror, armrests, two-speed wipers, three-spoke steering wheel, plus windshield and backlight moldings. Coupes and wagons had quarter-window moldings. Aspen's Custom coupe could have either standard Oxford vinyl bench seats or optional sporty buckets. Custom sedans had a standard cloth/vinyl bench seat or optional all-vinyl. Custom models also added rear armrests with ashtrays, a rear deck applique, wide bodyside moldings, belt moldings, cigarette lighter, and woodgrained dash. Special Edition models held a 60/40 split vinyl seat with dual recliners and center armrest. Coupes had special body striping and a formal landau vinyl roof with opera windows. Other coupes had much larger triangular rear windows. Special Edition wagons had lockable stowage compartments in side panels. SE models also included dual horns, a woodgrained glovebox door with lock, TorqueFlite transmission, color-keyed wide vinyl bodyside moldings, full wheel lip moldings, hood paint stripe, hood ornament and windsplit molding, day/night mirror, and electric clock. Sedans added a vinyl roof. Body colors were: Big Sky Blue, Spitfire Orange, Claret Red, Parchment, Saddle Tan, Harvest Gold, Eggshell White, and Black; plus metallic Silver Cloud, Jamaican Blue, Jade Green, Tropic Green, Deep Sherwood, Caramel Tan, Cinnamon, and Spanish Gold. Aspen's R/T coupe package had a blackout grille with bright moldings and 'R/T' medallion, special body and decklid striping, large 'R/T' decal just ahead of the rear wheel, and Rallye road wheels with wide E70 x 14 raised white-letter tires. The R/T rear end looked different, with much wider upper taillamps above the narrower backup lamps and no center trim panel. Twin wide stripes ran across the deck and through the full bodyside length. R/T Aspens came with either the 318 or 360 cu. in. V-8 engine. The R/T package was popular, installed on 79 percent of the 7,916 V-8 powered NL29 coupes.

1976 Coronet sedan (D)

CORONET — SERIES W — SIX/V-8 — Dodge's mid-size four-door, with 117.5 in. wheelbase, showed little body change for 1976. Coronet's split grille had a body-color center divider, like the base Charger coupe (below). Each side contained a crosshatch pattern dominated by three horizontal bars. Single round headlamps sat in square housings. Curved-side amber parking lamps were mounted in the bumper, below the headlamps. Wide horizontal taillamps were set into the back bumper, with backup lenses in the center of each unit and a recessed license plate housing in the middle. A 'Dodge' nameplate was on the decklid and grille; 'Coronet' script on front fenders. Decklids had a center crease. Coronets had a hood ornament in this, their final year. Only sedan and wagon bodies were offered. Wagons had a standard 360 cu. in. V-8, while the sedan was powered by a 225 cu. in. Slant Six or optional 318 V-8. The standard cloth/vinyl front bench seat came in five color choices. Brougham added a velour and vinyl front seat with center armrest and deluxe wheel covers, plus a distinctive hood ornament. Minor instrument changes included speedometer calibration in miles and kilometers. New to the option list: tilt steering. V-8s could have a no-cost optional 2.45:1 axle for extended cruising.

1976 Charger Special Edition coupe (D)

CHARGER — SERIES W — SIX/V-8 — Formerly part of the Coronet line, the Charger nameplate went on four separate hardtop coupe models or packages this year: base Charger and Charger Sport, plus the Charger Special Edition and Daytona (listed separately below). The basic Charger had a split blackout grille. Each side had a bright surrounding molding and three horizontal dividers over a subdued fine-mesh pattern. Between them was a body-color divider. A 'Dodge' nameplate sat on the driver's side of the grille. Single round headlamps rested in square housings. Horizontal amber parking lamps with curved edges were inset into the bumper. 'Charger' script on front fenders, just ahead of the door. Vertical taillamps sat at fender tips, each with a vertical divider. Standard Charger equipment included a heater/defroster, single

horn, day/night mirror, two-speed wipers, hubcaps, and woodgrain (simulated) dash trim; plus moldings for backlight, windshield, belt, hood rear edge, decklid, taillamp surround, drip, bodyside, and partial wheel lips. A low-back vinyl bench seat was standard, cloth/vinyl optional. Bucket seats were available in all-vinyl or cloth/vinyl. A canopy vinyl roof with louvered quartered windows was optional. Charger Sport had color-keyed vinyl insert bodyside moldings. Sport models also added dual horns and deluxe wheel covers, plus 'Sport' nameplates and medallions on rear roof pillars. Standard velour seats had a fold-down center armrest, but all-vinyl bucket seats were offered at no extra charge. In addition to the canopy vinyl roof with louvered windows, a halo vinyl roof that stood back from standard hardtop coupe windows was available. Charger/Sport body colors were: Powder Blue, Bright Red, Yellow Blaze, Golden Fawn, Black, or Eggshell White; plus metallic Silver Cloud, Jamaican Blue, Vintage Red, Bittersweet, Jade Green, Tropic Green, Deep Sherwood, Caramel Tan, Moondust, Cinnamon, Inca Gold, and Spanish Gold. New options included a 60/40 bench seat and tilt steering wheel.

1976 Charger Sport Coupe (D)

CHARGER SE — SERIES X — V-8 — Dodge's sporty SE, introduced in 1975, featured a Cordoba-like appearance, with round parking lamps between the grille and single round headlamps. Sheetmetal differed from the basic Charger. The SE grille consisted of just two horizontal and three vertical divider bars over a horizontal pattern. That pattern repeated in bumper slots below. Near front fender tips were small vertical side marker lenses, split into three sections. Louvers were optional for the narrow opera windows. The instrument panel had simulated rosewood trim. Standard bucket seats were upholstered in Oxford vinyl in black, blue, green, gold, red, tan or white. Base engine was the 318 cu. in. V-8. Charger SE was meant to rival Chevrolet's Monte Carlo and Ford's Elite. Daytona was actually an option package that was installed on 17.3 percent of SE models, featuring two-tone paint treatments with special body taping. Dual sport mirrors and bodyside moldings were color-keyed. Daytona decals stood on doors, fenders and decklid. The black-textured grille had bright accents in a 6 x 4 hole pattern, with horizontal bars dominant. A 'Dodge' nameplate was on the driver's side of the grille. Round parking lamps stood between the grille and single round headlamps, as on the SE, and the grille pattern was repeated in a wide bumper slot below. Underneath was a standard rear sway bar, plus whitewall steel-belted radials. Wraparound taillamps protruded along the quarter panel tips, but extended inward to the edge of the protruding decklid. Each taillamp held a horizontal divider strip. Backup lamps were inset into the bumper, roughly halfway in toward the center. Daytonas had plain, small opera windows. Distinctive two-tone paint treatments put the accent color on hood, deck and roof front, as well as the lower body. "Charger Daytona" lettering was low on the bodyside. Standard Daytona equipment included dual horns, power steering, TorqueFlite, hood ornament, and wheel lip moldings. Options included a 360 or 400 cu. in. V-8 and floor-shift TorqueFlite. A "Tuff" steering wheel was optional, along with urethane-styled road wheels. Standard interior was all-vinyl front bucket seats in red, black, blue and white. Daytona/SE colors were similar to base Chargers, but included Platinum metallic, Astral Blue metallic, Starlight Blue metallic, Saddle Tan, and Light Chestnut metallic. Powder Blue, Tropic Green, Moondust and Cinnamon were not available. The Daytona package cost only $345. A Brougham package that cost even less went on nearly 48 percent of Charger SE models.

1976 Royal Monaco Brougham formal hardtop (D)

MONACO — SERIES D — SIX/V-8 — Full-size Dodges split into several levels: basic Monaco, Royal Monaco, and Royal Monaco Brougham (introduced in 1975). Monaco came in four-door sedan or two-seat wagon form. The more costly Royal Monacos came with two-door hardtop and four-door sedan bodies, and either a two- or three-seat wagon. Wagons rode a 124 in. wheelbase; others 122 in. All could be spotted by their hidden headlamps. Royal Monaco's grille was a curious upright design in tight crosshatch pattern, with flat horizontal elements that contained columns of rounded vertical pieces. The bottom row extended outward on each side, below the concealed headlamp doors. The grille pattern repeated in bumper slots below. On the driver's side headlamp door was a 'Royal Monaco' script. At the fender tips were wraparound marker lenses. Royal Monaco taillamps were just above recessed openings in the bumper top. Each rectangular unit consisted of two tri-section red lenses on either side of a square center backup lamp. The license plate mounting was on the bumper, below a center hump. Between the taillamp was a trim panel with 'Royal Monaco' italic lettering. Standard equipment included TorqueFlite automatic transmission, power steering and brakes, and V-8 engine. Monaco had a standard 318 cu. in. V-8; Royal Monaco a 360 cu. in.; and Royal Monaco Brougham (and all wagons) the 400 cu. in. V-8. A 440 cu. in. V-8 was optional on all models. Monaco sedans had standard cloth/vinyl upholstery. Royal Monaco offered true hardtop styling with roll-down quarter windows. Other coupes had opera windows. Royal Monaco Brougham added opera windows, vinyl roof, and individually adjustable 50/50 front seats. A 'Diplomat' package for the Royal Monaco Brougham two-door hardtop included a landau vinyl roof, opera windows, and distinctive steel roof band.

I.D. DATA: Dodge's 13-symbol Vehicle Identification Number (VIN) was on the upper left corner of the instrument panel, visible through the windshield. Symbol one indicates car line: 'L' Dart; 'N' Aspen; 'W' Coronet; 'X' Charger SE; 'D' Monaco. Symbol two is series (price class): 'L' low; 'H' high; 'P' premium; 'M' medium; 'S' special. Symbols 3-4 show body type: '22' 2-dr. pillared hardtop; '23' 2-dr. hardtop; '29', 2-dr. special; '41' 4-dr. sedan; '45' two-seat station wagon; '46' three-seat wagon. Symbol five is the engine code: 'C' L6225; 'G' V8318 2Bbl.; 'J' V8360 4Bbl.; 'L' Hi-perf. V8360 4Bbl.; 'M' V8400 2Bbl.; 'N' V8400 4Bbl.; 'P' Hi-perf. V8400 4Bbl.; 'T' V8440 4Bbl. Symbol six is the model year code: '6' 1976. Symbol seven indicates assembly plant: 'A' Lynch Road; 'B' Hamtramck, MI; 'C' Jefferson; 'D' Belvidere, IL; 'F' Newark, DE; 'G' St. Louis; 'R' Windsor, Ontario. The final six digits make up the sequential serial number, starting with 100001. An abbreviated version of the VIN is also stamped on a pad on the engine block: below No. 6 spark plug on six-cylinder engines, and to rear of right engine mount on V-8s. Serial numbers for 318 and 360 cu. in. V-8s are coded as follows: first letter series (model year); second assembly plant; next three digits displacement (cu. in.); next one or two letters model; next four digits show build date; and final four digits are the engine sequence number. Coding of other engines is: first letter series (model year); next three digits displacement; next one or two letters model; next four digits build date; and the final digit reveals the shift on which the engine was built. Information on over/undersized parts is stamped on six-cylinder engines on the joint face at right corner, adjacent to No. 1 cylinder; on 318/360 V-8s, at left front of block just below the head; on 400 V-8, just ahead of No. 2 cylinder, next to distributor; and on 440 V-8, on left bank pad adjacent to front tappet rail. A Vehicle Safety Certification Label that displays (among other data) the date of manufacture is attached to the rear facing of the driver's door. A Body Code Plate is on the left front fender side shield, wheel housing, or left side of upper radiator support.

DART (SIX/V-8)

Model Number	Body/Style Number	Body Type & Seating	Factory Price	Shipping Weight	Production Total
LL	41	4-dr. Sedan-6P	3268/3405	3070/ --	27,849

DART SPORT FASTBACK (SIX/V-8)

LL	29	2-dr. Spt Cpe-6P	3233/3370	2990/ --	13,642

DART SWINGER (SIX/V-8)

LH	23	2-dr. HT Cpe-6P	3485/3622	3035/ --	8,937

DART SWINGER SPECIAL (SIX/V-8)

LL	23	2-dr. HT Cpe-6P	3312/3449	3050/ --	3,036

ASPEN (SIX/V-8)

NL	29	2-dr. Spt Cpe-5P	3336/3501	3160/3285	22,249
NL	41	4-dr. Sedan-6P	3371/3536	3190/3315	13,981
NL	45	4-dr. Sta Wag-6P	3658/3771	3560/3650	33,265

ASPEN CUSTOM (SIX/V-8)

NH	29	2-dr. Spt Cpe-5P	3518/3683	3170/3295	21,064
NH	41	4-dr. Sedan-6P	3553/3718	3200/3325	28,632

ASPEN SPECIAL EDITION (SIX/V-8)

NP	29	2-dr. Spt Cpe-5P	4413/4526	3375/3490	18,604
NP	41	4-dr. Sedan-6P	4400/4513	3410/3530	21,323
NH	45	4-dr. Sta Wag-6P	3988/4222	3565/3695	30,782

CORONET (SIX/V-8)

WL	41	4-dr. Sedan-6P	3700/3938	3625/3860	10,853
WL	45	4-dr. Sta Wag-6P	-- /4625	-- /4285	1,840
WL	46	4-dr. 3S Wag-9P	-- /4767	-- /4350	3,039

CORONET BROUGHAM (SIX/V-8)

WH	41	4-dr. Sedan-6P	3989/4227	3645/3875	12,831

CORONET CRESTWOOD STATION WAGON (V-8)

WH	45	4-dr. 2S Wag-6P	-- /5014	-- /4285	1,092
WH	46	4-dr. 3S Wag-9P	-- /5156	-- /4360	2,154

CHARGER (SIX/V-8)

WL	23	2-dr. HT Cpe-6P	3666/3904	3595/3830	6,613
WH	23	2-dr. Spt HT-6P	3955/4193	3600/3835	10,811

CHARGER SPECIAL EDITION (V-8)

XS	22	2-dr. HT Cpe-5P	4763	3945	35,337

MONACO (V-8)

DM	41	4-dr. Sedan-6P	4388	4160	3,686
DM	45	4-dr. Sta Wag-6P	4948	4910	597

ROYAL MONACO (V-8)

DH	23	2-dr. HT Cpe-6P	4778	4280	1,591
DH	41	4-dr. Sedan-6P	4763	4325	9,049
DH	45	4-dr. Sta Wag-6P	5241	4915	547
DH	46	4-dr. 3S Wag-9P	5364	4950	1,006

ROYAL MONACO BROUGHAM (V-8)

DP	29	2-dr. Formal HT-6P	5382	4430	2,742
DP	41	4-dr. Sedan-6P	5211	4520	3,890
DP	46	4-dr. 3S Wag-9P	5869	4995	1,873

FACTORY PRICE AND WEIGHT NOTE: Prices and weights to left of slash are for six-cylinder, to right for V-8 engine. **PRODUCTION NOTE:** In addition to the figures shown, a total of 3,852 Coronet and 2,426 Monaco police four-door sedans were shipped.

ENGINE DATA: BASE SIX (Dart, Aspen, Coronet, Charger): Inline, overhead-valve six. Cast iron block and head. Displacement: 225 cu. in. (3.7 liters). Bore & stroke: 3.40 x 4.12 in. Compression ratio: 8.4:1. Brake horsepower: 100 at 3600 R.P.M. Torque: 170 lbs.-ft. at 1600 R.P.M. Four main bearings. Solid valve lifters. Carburetor: 1Bbl. Holley 1945 (R7356A). VIN Code: C. BASE V-8 (Charger SE, Monaco); OPTIONAL (Dart, Aspen, Coronet, Charger): 90-degree, overhead valve V-8. Cast iron block and head. Displacement: 318 cu. in. (5.2 liters). Bore & stroke: 3.91 x 3.31 in. Compression ratio: 8.5:1. Brake horsepower: 150 at 4000 R.P.M. Torque: 255 lbs.-ft. at 1600 R.P.M. Five main bearings. Hydraulic valve lifters. Carburetor: 2Bbl. Carter BBD 8068S or 8069S. VIN Code: G. BASE V-8 (Coronet wagon, Royal Monaco); OPTIONAL V-8 (Aspen, Coronet, Charger/SE, Monaco): 90-degree, overhead valve V-8. Cast iron block and head. Displacement: 360 cu. in. (5.9 liters). Bore & stroke: 4.00 x 3.58 in. Compression ratio: 8.4:1. Brake horsepower: 170 at 4000 R.P.M. Torque: 280 lbs.-ft. at 2400 R.P.M. Five main bearings. Hydraulic valve lifters. Carburetor: 2Bbl. Holley 2245 (R7364A). VIN Code: K. CALIFORNIA V-8: Same as 360 cu. in. V-8 above, except with Carter TQ 4Bbl. carburetor Brake H.P.: 175 at 4000 R.P.M. Torque: 270 lbs.-ft. at 1600 R.P.M. VIN Code: J. OPTIONAL V-8 (Dart): Same as 360 V-8 above, with Carter TQ9002S 4Bbl. carburetor, except Brake H.P. 220 at 4400 R.P.M. Torque: 280 lbs.-ft. at 3200 R.P.M. VIN Code: L. BASE V-8 (Royal Monaco Brougham, Monaco/Royal Monaco wagon); OPTIONAL V-8 (Coronet, Charger, SE, Monaco, Royal Monaco): 90-degree, overhead valve V-8. Cast iron block and head. Displacement: 400 cu. in. (6.6 liters). Bore & stroke: 4.34 x 3.38 in. Compression ratio: 8.2:1. Brake horsepower: 175 at 4000 R.P.M. Torque: 300 lbs.-ft. at 2400 R.P.M. Five main bearings. Hydraulic valve lifters. Carburetor: 2Bbl. Holley 2245 (R7366A). VIN Code: M. CALIFORNIA V-8: Same as 400 cu. in. V-8 above, with Carter TQ9056S 4Bbl. carburetor Brake H.P.: 185 at 3600 R.P.M. Torque: 285 lbs.- ft. at 3200 R.P.M. VIN Code: N. OPTIONAL V-8 (Monaco, Royal Monaco): Same as 400 cu. in. 4Bbl. V-8 above, except Carter TQ9064S carburetor Brake H.P.: 210 at 4400 R.P.M. Torque: 305 lbs.-ft. at 3200 R.P.M. OPTIONAL V-8 (Coronet, Charger/SE, Royal Monaco Brougham): Same as 400 4Bbl. V-8 above, with Carter TQ9054S carburetor and dual exhausts Brake H.P.: 240 at 4400 R.P.M. Torque: 325 lbs.-ft. at 3200 R.P.M. VIN Code: P. OPTIONAL V-8 (Monaco, Royal Monaco): 90-degree, overhead valve V-8. Cast iron block and head. Displacement: 440 cu. in. (7.2 liters). Bore & stroke: 4.32 x 3.75 in. Compression ratio: 8.2:1. Brake horsepower: 205 at 3600 R.P.M. Torque: 320 lbs.-ft. at 2000 R.P.M. Five main bearings. Hydraulic valve lifters. Carburetor: 4Bbl. Carter TQ9058S. VIN Code: T.

CHASSIS DATA: Wheelbase: (Dart) 111.0 in.; (Dart Sport) 108.0 in.; (Aspen cpe) 108.5 in.; (Aspen sed/wag) 112.5 in.; (Coronet) 117.5 in.; (Coronet/Charger HT cpe) 115.0 in.; (Monaco) 121.5 in.; (Monaco wag) 124.0 in. Overall Length: (Dart) 203.4 in.; (Dart Sport) 200.9 in.; (Aspen cpe) 197.5 in.; (Aspen sed/wag) 201.5 in.; (Coronet sed) 218.4 in.; (Coronet wag) 225.6 in.; (Charger/Sport) 213.7 in.; (Charger SE) 215.3 in.; (Monaco) 225.7 in.; (Monaco wag) 229.5 in. Height: (Dart 2-dr.) 53.0 in.; (Dart 4-dr.) 54.0 in.; (Dart Sport) 53.4 in.; (Aspen cpe) 53.1 in.; (Aspen sed/wag) 54.8 in.; (Coronet sed) 54.0 in.; (Coronet wag) 55.8 in.; (Charger) 52.6 in.; (Monaco 2-dr.) 54.1 in.; (Monaco 4-dr.) 54.8 in.; (Monaco wag) 57.6 in. Width: (Dart) 69.8 in.; (Dart Sport) 71.7 in.; (Aspen) 72.8 in.; (Coronet sed) 77.7 in.; (Coronet wag) 78.8 in.; (Charger/Sport) 77.7 in.; (Charger SE) 77.1 in.; (Monaco) 79.8 in.; (Monaco wag) 79.4 in. Front Tread: (Dart) 59.2 in.; (Aspen) 60.0 in.; (Coronet/Charger) 61.9 in.; (Monaco) 64.0 in. Rear Tread: (Dart) 55.6 in.; (Aspen) 58.5 in.; (Coronet/Charger) 62.0 in.; (Coronet wag) 63.4 in.; (Monaco) 63.4 in. Wheel size: (Dart) 14 x 4.5 in.; (Aspen cpe/sed) 14 x 5.5 in.; (Charger) 14 x 5.0 in.; (Charger SE) 15 x 5.5 in.; (Coronet) 14 x 5.0 in. exc. wag, 6.0 in. (Monaco) 15 x 5.5 in. exc. wag, 6.5 in. Standard Tires: (Dart six) 6.95 x 14; (Dart V-8) D78x14; (Aspen) D78 x 14 BSW exc. wag, F78 x 14 glass-belted; (Coronet) F78 x 14 exc. wag, H78 x 14; (Charger) F78 x 14 BSW; (Charger SE) G78 x 15 BSW glass-belted exc. Daytona, GR78 x 15 WSW; (Monaco) GR78 x 15 exc. wag, LR78 x 15; (Royal Monaco) HR78 x 15 exc. wag, LR78 x 15.

TECHNICAL: Transmission: Three-speed manual transmission (column shift) standard on Dart, Aspen, Coronet and Charger. Gear ratios: (1st) 3.08:1; (2nd) 1.70:1; (3rd) 1.00:1; (Rev) 2.90:1 exc. six-cylinder Dart: (1st) 2.99:1; (2nd) 1.75:1; (3rd) 1.00:1; (Rev) 3.17:1. Column or floor lever on Dart/Aspen. Four-speed overdrive manual gearbox available on Dart/Aspen: (1st) 3.09:1; (2nd) 1.67:1; (3rd) 1.00:1; (4th) 0.73:1; (Rev) 3.00:1. Three-speed automatic standard on Charger SE and Monaco, optional on others. Gear ratios: (1st) 2.45:1; (2nd) 1.45:1; (3rd) 1.00:1; (Rev) 2.22:1. Floor lever available for all exc. Monaco. Standard final drive ratio: (Dart six) 3.23:1 exc. 3.21:1 w/overdrive, various ratios w/auto.; (Dart V8318) 2.45:1 exc. 2.94:1 or 3.21:1 w/overdrive, various ratios w/auto.; (Dart V8360) 2.94:1 w/auto.; (Aspen six) 3.23:1 exc. 2.76:1 w/auto., 2.94:1 in wag.; (Aspen V8318) 2.45:1 exc. 2.94:1 w/4spd; (Aspen V8360) 2.76:1 exc. 2.71:1 in wagon; (Coronet/Charger six) 3.21:1 w/3spd, 2.94:1 w/auto.; (Coronet/Charger V-8) 2.94:1 w/3spd, 2.71:1 or 3.21:1 w/auto; (Charger SE) 2.71:1; (Monaco) 2.71:1. Steering: Recirculating ball. Suspension: (Dart) longitudinal front torsion bars w/lower trailing links, semi-elliptic rear leaf springs w/rigid axle; (Aspen) transverse front torsion bars and anti-sway bar, asymmetrical semi-elliptic rear leaf springs; (others) longitudinal front torsion bars and anti-sway bar, semi- elliptic reaf leaf springs; rear anti-sway bar on Charger SE. Brakes: Front disc, rear drum exc. Dart six, front/rear drum. Ignition: Electronic. Body construction: (Dart) unibody; (Aspen/Monaco) unibody w/front auxiliary frame; (Coronet/Charger) unibody w/isolated front crossmembers. Fuel tank: (Dart) 16 gal.; (Aspen) 18 gal.; (Coronet) 25.5 gal. exc. wag, 20 gal.; (Charger six) 20.5 gal.; (Charger V-8) 25.5 gal.; (Monaco) 26.5 gal. exc. wag, 24 gal.

DRIVETRAIN OPTIONS: Engines: 360 cu. in., 2Bbl. V-8: Aspen ($50); Charger/SE, Coronet ($54); Monaco ($55). 360 cu. in., 4Bbl. V-8: Charger/SE, Coronet ($99) exc. wag ($45); Monaco ($100); Royal Monaco ($45). 360 cu. in., 4Bbl. V-8 w/dual exhaust: Dart Spt ($376). 400 cu. in., 2Bbl. V-8: Charger/SE, Coronet ($102) exc. wag ($48); Monaco ($104); Royal Monaco ($49). 400 cu. in., 4Bbl. V-8: Charger/SE, Coronet ($147) exc. wag ($93); Monaco ($149); Royal Monaco ($94); Monaco Brghm/wag ($45). 400 cu. in., 4Bbl. V-8 w/dual exhaust: Charger/SE, Coronet ($198) exc. wag ($144). 440 cu. in., 4Bbl. V-8: Monaco ($273); Royal Monaco ($218); Monaco Brghm/wag ($169). Transmission/Differential: Three-speed manual trans. w/floor shift: Dart/Aspen ($28). Four-speed overdrive manual trans. w/floor lever: Dart/Aspen ($127). TorqueFlite auto. trans.: Dart/Aspen ($250); Charger/Coronet ($273). Sure Grip differential: Dart/Aspen ($49); Charger/SE/Coronet ($54); Monaco ($58). Optional axle ratio: Aspen ($13); Charger/SE/Coronet/Monaco ($15). Brakes and Steering: Manual front disc brakes: Dart six ($25). Power front disc brakes ($56-$81) but std. w/Aspen V-8; Charger/Coronet ($61). Power steering: Dart/Aspen ($131); Charger/Coronet six ($143). Suspension: Automatic height control: Monaco ($100). Front sway bar: Dart ($14). H.D. susp.: Dart/Aspen ($9-$23); Charger/SE/Coronet ($25); Monaco ($18-$25). H.D. shock absorbers: Charger/-SE/Coronet/Monaco ($7). Other: Long-life battery: Monaco ($30). Engine temp and oil pressure gauge: Monaco ($20). Trailer towing pkg.: Dart/Aspen ($68). Light trailer towing pkg.: Charger/SE/Coronet ($298); Monaco ($75). Heavy trailer towing pkg.: Charger/SE/Coronet ($345); Monaco ($302).

DART/ASPEN CONVENIENCE/APPEARANCE OPTIONS: Option Packages: Dart decorator trim pkg. ($178). Dart Special Edition pkg. ($291-$438). Dart exterior decor pkg.: Spt ($84). Dart interior decor group: Spt ($92). Dart radial tire roadability pkg. ($17). Dart custom pkg.: base ($176- $218). Dart Lite pkg.: Spt ($68). Dart overdrive decor pjkg.: Spt ($19). Aspen R/T pkg.: base cpe ($196). Aspen R/T decor group: base cpe/sed ($95). Aspen two-tone paint pkg.: Cust cpe ($158). Light pkg. ($33). Deluxe insulation pkg. ($23- $51). Easy order pkg. ($604-$772) exc. Aspen SE ($221). Protection group ($18-$27). Comfort/Convenience: Air cond. ($431). Rear defogger, blower- type ($41). Rear defroster, electric ($74). Automatic speed control: Aspen ($70). Power seat: Aspen ($119). Power windows: Aspen ($95-$135). Power door locks: Aspen ($60-$86). Tinted windshield ($35); all windows ($44). Luxury steering wheel ($15-$26). Tilt steering wheel: Aspen ($54). Electric clock: Aspen ($18). Inside hood release ($11). Horns and Mirrors: Dual horns ($6). Remote left mirror ($14). Dual sport mirrors, left remote: Dart ($15-$29). Dual remote mirrors: Aspen ($27-$40). Dual remote sport mirrors: Aspen ($33-$47). Day/night mirror ($7). Entertainment: AM radio ($72). AM/FM radio ($65-$137). AM/FM stereo radio: Aspen ($160-$233). Rear speaker ($20). Exterior Trim: Manual sunroof: Dart Spt, Aspen cpe ($186). Full vinyl roof: Dart Spt, Aspen sed ($17-$92). Canopy vinyl roof: Dart Spt ($76). Halo vinyl roof: Aspen cpe ($92-$107). Landau vinyl roof: Aspen cpe ($45-$137). Vinyl bodyside moldings ($18-$37). Belt moldings: Aspen ($15). Door edge protectors ($7-$11). Upper door frame moldings: sed ($27). Wheel lip moldings ($18). Drip rail molding: Dart ($15). Sill moldings: Dart ($16). Tape stripe (up/over): Dart Spt ($44). Bumper guards ($35). Rear air deflectors: Aspen wag ($22). Luggage rack: Aspen wag ($65). Interior Trim/Upholstery: Console: Dart Spt, Aspen cpe ($68). Cloth/vinyl bench seat: Dart sed ($64). Vinyl bench seat: Dart cpe ($64); Aspen wag ($32). Split-back vinyl bench seat: Dart ($105). Cloth 60/40 split bench seat: Aspen SE ($51). Vinyl 60/40 split bench seat: Aspen SE wag ($114). Vinyl bucket seats: Dart Spt ($87-$150); Swinger ($128); Aspen ($87-$119). Carpets: Dart ($22). Cargo area carpets and bins: Aspen wag ($45). Wheels and Tires: Rallye wheels ($36-$66). Deluxe wheel covers ($29). Premier wheel covers: Aspen ($25-$54). Wire wheel covers: Aspen ($32-$86). 6.95 x 14 WSW: Dart (NC to $32). D78 x 14 BSW: Dart ($16). D78 x 14 WSW: Dart (NC to $75); Aspen (NC to $32). DR78 x 14 WSW: Dart ($85-$132). E78 x 14 BSW: Aspen ($16). E78 x 14 WSW: Dart ($16-$63); Aspen (NC to $75). E70 x 14 RWL: Dart ($61-$109); Aspen ($61-$93). ER78 x 14 WSW: Dart ($23-$148); Aspen ($85-$132). F78 x 14 BSW: Aspen ($44-$60). F78 x 14 WSW: Aspen (NC to $96). FR78 x 14 WSW: Aspen ($41-$153). GR78 x 14 WSW: Aspen ($75-$110).

CORONET/CHARGER/CHARGER SE CONVENIENCE/APPEARANCE OPTIONS: Option Packages: Charger SE Daytona pkg. ($345). Charger SE Brougham pkg. ($287-$303). Easy order pkg.: Charger SE ($1027); others ($347-$870). Luxury equipment pkg. ($1369- $1739) exc. SE. Exterior decor pkg. ($92-$175) exc. SE. Deluxe insulation pkg. ($55) exc. SE. Light pkg. ($24-$45). Comfort/Convenience: Air cond. ($490). Rear defroster, electric ($81). Automatic speed control ($77). Tinted windshield ($38); all windows ($52). Power seat ($130). Power windows ($104-$147). Power tailgate window: wag ($41). Power door locks ($65-$94). Power decklid release: SE ($19). Luxury steering wheel ($17). Tilt steering wheel ($59). Tachometer ($62). Electric clock ($20) exc. SE. Digital clock: SE ($45). Inside hood release ($12) exc. SE. Horns and Mirrors: Dual horns ($6) exc. SE. Left remote mirror ($15). Dual remote mirrors ($29-$44). Dual sport styled remote mirrors ($37-$52). Entertainment: AM radio ($79). AM/FM radio ($71-$149). AM radio w/8track tape player($48-$220). AM/FM stereo radio ($83-$254); w/8track ($186-$357). Search tune AM/FM stereo radio: Charger SE ($214-$314). Rear speaker ($22). Exterior Trim: Manual sunroof: cpe ($311). Full vinyl roof ($15-$115). Landau vinyl roof: Charger SE ($100). Canopy vinyl roof: HT cpe ($83). Canopy vinyl roof w/louvered quarter window: HT cpe ($32-$115). Vinyl bodyside moldings ($20-$40). Sill moldings: sed/wag ($25). Door edge protectors ($7-$13). Performance hood treatment: HT cpe ($28) exc. SE. Hood/deck stripes: Charger SE ($40). Hood stripe ($20). Bodyside stripes: HT cpe ($40). Side/deck rally stripe: HT cpe ($20). Air deflector: base wag ($24). Auto-lock tailgate: wag ($35). Luggage rack: wag ($71). Bumper guards ($38); front only, sed/wag ($19). Undercoating ($30). Interior Trim/Upholstery: Console: HT cpe ($18). 60/40 split bench seats: HT cpe cloth/vinyl, sedan velour/vinyl or wagon vinyl ($124). Vinyl bucket seats: base HT cpe ($206). Cloth/vinyl bucket seats w/sun gold trim: HT cpe ($31-$237). Cargo area carpet: base wag ($28). Charger SE Upholstery: Console ($90). Cloth/vinyl bench seat ($72). Velour/vinyl bench seat ($89). Velour/vinyl 60/40 bench seat w/recliners ($196). Wheels and Tires: Rallye wheels ($43-$75). Styled wheels ($113-$145). Deluxe wheel covers ($32) exc. SE. Wire wheel covers ($62-$94). F78 x 14 WSW (NC to $39). G78 x 14 BSW ($19). G78 x 14 WSW (NC to $58). H78 x 14 BSW ($32-$40). H78 x 14 WSW (NC to $83). G70 x 14 RWL ($53-$110). GR78 x 15 WSW ($111-$169). HR78 x 15 WSW ($111-$194). GR70 x 15 RWL ($164- $221). NOTE: optional tires do not apply to Charger SE.

MONACO CONVENIENCE/APPEARANCE OPTIONS: Option Packages: Luxury equipment pkg. ($1509-$1836). Wagon pkg. ($63). Deluxe sound insulation pkg. ($41). Comfort/Convenience: Air cond. ($504); auto-temp ($590) exc. ($85) w/luxury pkg. Rear defroster, electric ($82). Automatic speed control ($78). Power seat ($132). Power windows ($110- $167). Power door locks ($66-$95). Tinted glass ($66). Luxury steering wheel ($17). Tilt/telescope steering wheel ($83- $100). Electric clock ($20). Digital clock ($25-$45). Lighting, Horns and Mirrors: Cornering lights: Royal ($43). Dual horns ($6). Remote left mirror ($15). Dual remote mirrors ($30-$45). Day/night mirror ($8). Entertainment: AM radio ($80). AM/FM radio ($76-$155). AM radio w/8track tape player ($62-$239). AM/FM stereo radio ($80-$257); w/8track stereo tape ($184-$362). Rear speaker ($22). Exterior Trim: Sunroof w/vinyl roof ($627-$758). Door edge protectors ($8-$13). Upper door frame moldings: base ($29). Bumper guards ($45). Rear air deflector: base wag ($25). Auto-lock tailgate: wag ($35). Luggage rack: wag ($86). Wheels and Tires: Styled chrome wheels ($77-$147). Deluxe wheel covers ($32). Premium wheel covers ($38-$70). G78 x 15 WSW ($39). GR78 x 15 BSW ($99). GR78 x 15 WSW (NC to $158). HR78 x 15 BSW ($22 to $121). HR78 x 15 WSW (NC to $164). JR78 x 15 WSW ($31-$195). L78 x 15 WSW ($49). LR78 x 15 BSW ($99). LR78 x 15 WSW (NC to $148).

HISTORY: Introduced: October 16, 1975. Model year production: Chrysler reported a total of 359,163 passenger cars shipped. Total production for the U.S. market of 336,381 units included 163,307 six-cylinder and 173,074 V-8s. Calendar year production (U.S.): 547,916 (incl. 50,946 Sportsman vans). Calendar year sales by U.S. dealers: 478,960, for a 5.6 percent share of the market. Model year sales by U.S. dealers: 421,122 (not incl. 47,383 Colts and 42,303 Sportsman vans).

Historical Footnotes: The new Aspen, built at half of Chrysler's six U.S. final assembly plants, sold well. Over a third of Aspens sold were station wagons. The combination of Dart and Aspen amounted to some 54 percent of total sales, as mid-size and full-size models were losing ground. Sales for the model year were up 26.7 percent, but well under the 1973 record. (Figures include the imported Colt and Sportsman van). That Colt had a new 2.0-liter four, in addition to the standard 1.6-liter powerplant. Charger SE was made only at Windsor, Ontario. Before too long, both Aspen and its sister Plymouth Volare would be subjected to a succession of recalls, to achive one of the worst recall records of their era.

1977 DODGE

Several Dodge nameplates changed this year, but not much else. This would be the final year for the full-size Royal Monaco. The Coronet name was gone, as all mid-sizes were now called Monaco. Full-size Dodges now fell under the Royal Monaco banner. Charger SE had its own identity again, as the basic Charger name was dropped. Dart had disappeared during the 1976 model year. A new model joined the lineup at mid-year: the upper-level compact Diplomat, kin to Chrysler's new LeBaron. Electronic Lean Burn was now on the 360 cu. in. V-8 as well as bigger versions. The familiar Slant Six appeared in an additional form with two-barrel carburetor, called "Super Six." Aspen again offered an R/T package. Aspen coupes could have an optional T-Bar roof as well as a sunroof.

1977 Aspen R/T coupe (D)

ASPEN — SERIES N — SIX/V-8 — Introduced for the 1976 model year, the compact Aspen changed little in appearance this year. Again, it came in base, Custom, and Special Edition dress. Base engine was the 1Bbl. 225 cu. in. Slant Six, except for wagons which carried the new 2Bbl. Super Six. Optional were 318 and 360 cu. in. V-8s. Base coupes had cloth/vinyl bench seating; sedans and wagons had all vinyl. Custom coupes added all-vinyl seats, special bodyside moldings, woodgrained instrument panel, lighter, and rear armrests. Custom sedans had standard Revere cloth/vinyl bench seating in blue, green, red, parchment or tan. Special Edition Aspens carried 60/40 vinyl reclining seats with fold-down center armrest (same colors as Custom), door pull straps, glass-belted radial tires, power brakes and steering. Otherwise, standard equipment was similar to 1976. A T-Bar roof with removable panels was optional on all coupes. Aspen's R/T package was offered again, along with an R/T Super Pak. The basic package included a floor-shift three-speed manual transmission, E70 x 14 RWL tires on Rallye wheels, blackout grille, bold stripes, and 'R/T' decals between doors and rear wheel openings. Super Pak added front and rear spoilers, special tape stripes that included an 'R/T' insignia on the rear spoiler, wheel opening flares, and louvered rear quarter windows. Both could have a 360 2Bbl. or the 360 4Bbl. with Electronic Lean Burn. R/T was Dodge's only "performance" model. A total of 4,465 Aspen coupes had the R/T package, while 2,284 carried the Super R/T package.

1977 Diplomat coupe (D)

DIPLOMAT — SERIES G — V-8 — Classed as a "premium specialty intermediate," the new Diplomat arrived as a mid-year addition, offered in base and Medallion form. Riding a 112.7 in. wheelbase, the M-bodied Diplomat was closely related to the similarly new Chrysler LeBaron. Described in the catalog as "fiendishly seductive," Diplomat was also promoted for its "manageable new size," suggesting the start of the downsizing that was soon to arrive. Two bodies were offered: a fixed-pillar coupe and four-door sedan. Underneath the unibody design were transverse front torsion bars, plus a leaf-spring rear (live axle). Diplomat's upright grille showed a tight crosshatch pattern, divided into four side-by-side sections by three wider vertical strips. 'Dodge' block lettering highlighted the driver's side of the grille header. Side-by-side quad rectangular headlamps stood directly above quad rectangular park/signal lamps, which continued into twin-lensed (clear/amber) wraparound side marker lamps. (LeBaron's layout was just the opposite, with headlamps below.) 'Diplomat' lettering went on the front fender, ahead of the door. Wide wraparound taillamps were divided into three side-by-side sections, the outer one wrapping onto the quarter panel. Each taillamp unit also contained a bright horizontal divider bar, making six sections in all. Backup lamps were near the ends of the bumper, with license plate housing in the center. A 'Diplomat' nameplate sat on the right side of the decklid, just above the taillamp. 'Dodge' lettering stood below the decklid, on a center panel between the taillamps on base Diplomats; or above the lock on Medallion's center decklid extension. Rather large opera windows were four-sided, in a curious shape with sharp corners. Four-door sedans had standard fully padded vinyl roofs, available in seven colors. A landau roof was optional on two-doors. Back windows were slightly peaked at the center. Inside, the modular instrument panel had woodtone applique and

deeply-inset gauges. A curved left section of the dash put radio and heat controls near the driver. Fuel, alternator and temp gauges were displayed. Two-door models had reading lamps in the windshield header. Base Diplomats had cloth/vinyl bench seating. Medallion offered standard cloth/velour 60/40 seating, with leather/vinyl optional. Standard were door-pillar assist handles, plenty of courtesy lamps, and premium wheel covers. Base engine was the 318 cu. in. Lean Burn V-8 with TorqueFlite automatic transmission, power steering and brakes. Standard equipment also included FR78 x 15 GBR blackwall tires, space-saving spare tire, stand-up hood ornament, wide rocker moldings and extensions, and dual horns. Medallion added a remote-control driver's mirror and trunk dress-up package, wheel opening moldings, dual chrome quarter-window stripes (two-doors), bodyside tape accent stripes (two-doors), and lower deck accent stripes (four-door). Thirteen body colors were available: Dove Gray, Classic Cream, and Eggshell White; plus metallic Pewter Gray, Charcoal Gray Sunfire, Cadet Blue, Starlight Blue Sunfire, Tapestry Red Sunfire, Mint Green, Augusta Green Sunfire, Caramel Tan, Sable Tan Sunfire, and Black Sunfire. Vinyl roofs came in silver, blue, red, green, tan, white, or black. Options included air conditioning, vinyl roof, cruise control, electric rear defroster, tilt steering, power windows, power seats, power door locks, and sliding steel sunroof. The Slant Six engine could be ordered as a credit option.

1977 Monaco Brougham coupe (D)

MONACO — SERIES W — SIX/V-8 — After a long history at Dodge, the Coronet name disappeared, but its place in the mid-size lineup was taken over by Monaco. Wheelbase was the same as Coronet: 115 in. for two-doors, 117.5 for four-doors. Base and Brougham trim levels were offered, with two-door hardtop, four-door or Crestwood station wagon bodies. Most noticeable in appearance were the new vertically stacked quad headlamps, which replaced former round units. The split grille consisted of two side-by-side inserts, separated by a vertical divider. Each rectangular half was divided into a 3 x 2 pattern; and each of these sections showed an internal crosshatch pattern. Parking lights were in the bumper, below the headlamps. 'Monaco' script was on front fenders. Small side marker lenses at front and rear aligned with each wheel opening top (considerably higher than Royal Monaco). Each small wraparound taillamp was divided by two thin horizontal strips into three segments. The license plate was mounted in a recess that dipped down into the bumper and into a notch at the lower decklid. Backup lamps were in the bumper; their outer edges were angled. Coupes had opera windows and a wide rear roof pillar. Base engine was the new 2Bbl. Super Six. Optional: a 318 cu. in. V-8, or 360 or 400 V-8 with Lean Burn. Standard equipment included power brakes, and simulated woodgrain instrument panel accents.

1977 Charger SE Daytona coupe (D)

CHARGER SE — SERIES X — V-8 — With the abandonment of the Coronet name, Charger switched from a sub-model (as in 1975-76) to a separate model. Appearance was basically the same as 1976, but Charger's grille now showed a tight crosshatch pattern divided into three rows by two wide horizontal bars. As before, the pattern repeated in bumper slots. Charger still carried round parking lights and headlamps, revealing its relationship to Chrysler's Cordoba. Standard engine was the 318 cu. in. V-8, with TorqueFlite three-speed automatic. Both 360 and 400 cu. in. V-8s were optional. Charger had front torsion bars and rear leaf springs, with front and rear sway bars. Vinyl bucket seats were standard; corduroy/vinyl optional. Power brakes and steering also were standard. Charger SE wore GR78 x 15 glass-belted radial tires. Options included a T-Bar roof, with removable glass panel that could be stored in the trunk. A total of 2,937 Chargers had a Spring Special package (RPO code A58). More significant, 5,225 Charger SEs carried the sporty Daytona package. Daytona was basically similar to 1976, with 'Charger Daytona' decals on front fender and door. A new (and weird) "eye-catching" two-tone treatment put accent color at the front and rear of bodysides. That color extended into the door but left a center patch of basic color between, which also ran forward and back beneath the accented sections. Accent color was also on the forward roof. Four two-tone combinations were offered. Wraparound taillamps held two body-color horizontal divider strips. Daytona also had decklid, roof and cowl striping.

ROYAL MONACO — SERIES D — V-8 — Last of the traditional full-size Dodges, this year's Royal Monaco came in seven models: base and Brougham hardtop coupe, four-door sedan, or station wagon (two- or three- seat). Appearance was the same as 1976, except for new rear bumper corner guards (required by Federal standards). The two-door was one of the last remaining "true" (pillarless) hardtops. The lower portion of Royal Monaco's grille extended outward below the concealed headlamps. Low side marker lights stood just ahead of wheel openings. Wide taillamps were made up of

three squarish sections, with two vertical divider bars in each taillamp square and backup lenses in the center. Base engine was the 318 cu. in. V-8, but Broughams carried the 360 V-8 and wagons the 400. Optional: the big 440 cu. in. V-8. Standard equipment included TorqueFlite automatic transmission, power steering and brakes, and an inside hood release. Also standard: two front ashtrays, cigarette lighter, glovebox coin holder, wheel lip and door frame moldings, two-speed wipers, cloth/vinyl bench seats, fiberglass-belted radial tires, and hubcaps. Brougham added glovebox and instrument panel lighting, courtesy lights, a split-back vinyl front bench seat with center armrest, hood stripes, and body accent stripes. Brougham sedans had upper door frame moldings.

I.D. DATA: Dodge's 13-symbol Vehicle Identification Number (VIN) was on the upper left corner of the instrument panel, visible through the windshield. Symbol one indicates car line: 'N' Aspen; 'G' Diplomat; 'W' Monaco; 'X' Charger SE; 'D' Royal Monaco. Symbol two is series (price class): 'L' low; 'M' medium; 'H' high; 'P' premium; 'S' special. Symbols 3-4 show body type: '22' 2-dr. pillared hardtop; '23' 2-dr. hardtop; '29' 2-dr. coupe; '41' 4-dr. sedan; '45' two-seat station wagon; '46' three-seat wagon. Symbol five is the engine code: 'C' L6225 1Bbl.; 'D' L6225 2Bbl.; 'G' V8318; 'K' V8360 2Bbl.; 'L' Hi- perf. V8360 4Bbl.; 'N' V8400 4Bbl.; 'T' V8440 4Bbl. Symbol six is the model year code: '7' 1977. Symbol seven indicates assembly plant: 'A' Lynch Road; 'B' Hamtramck, MI; 'D' Belvidere, IL; 'F' Newark, DE; 'G' St. Louis; 'R' Windsor, Ontario. The final six digits make up the sequential serial number, starting with 100001. Engine number coding, Safety Certification Label and Body Code Plate are the same as 1976.

ASPEN (SIX/V-8)

Model Number	Body/Style Number	Body Type & Seating	Factory Price	Shipping Weight	Production Total
NL	29	2-dr. Spt Cpe-5P	3582/3752	3180/3290	24,378
NL	41	4-dr. Sedan-6P	3631/3801	3235/3345	25,838
NL	45	4-dr. Sta Wag-6P	3953/4037	3445/3540	59,458

ASPEN CUSTOM (SIX/V-8)

NH	29	2-dr. Spt Cpe-5P	3764/3934	3185/3295	26,389
NH	41	4-dr. Sedan-6P	3813/3983	3240/3350	40,455

ASPEN SPECIAL EDITION (SIX/V-8)

NP	29	2-dr. Spt Cpe-5P	4317/4430	3375/3480	15,908
NP	41	4-dr. Sedan-6P	4366/4479	3440/3545	21,522
NH	45	4-dr. Sta Wag-6P	4283/4488	3450/3585	52,064

DIPLOMAT (V-8)

GH	22	2-dr. Cpe-6P	4943	3510	12,335
GH	41	4-dr. Sedan-6P	5101	3560	8,092

DIPLOMAT MEDALLION (V-8)

GP	22	2-dr. Cpe-6P	5313	3615	9,155
GP	41	4-dr. Sedan-6P	5471	3675	4,631

MONACO (SIX/V-8)

WL	23	2-dr. HT Cpe-6P	3911/4172	3630/3860	10,368
WL	41	4-dr. Sedan-6P	3988/4249	3655/3890	15,433
WL	45	4-dr. Sta Wag-6P	-- /4724	-- /4335	3,037
WL	46	4-dr. 3S Wag-9P	-- /4867	-- /4395	4,297

MONACO BROUGHAM (SIX/V-8)

WH	23	2-dr. HT Cpe-6P	4146/4408	3635/3870	11,405
WH	41	4-dr. Sedan-6P	4217/4478	3665/3900	14,908

MONACO CRESTWOOD STATION WAGON (V-8)

WH	45	4-dr. 2S Wag-6P	-- /5224	-- /4330	1,341
WH	46	4-dr. 3S Wag-9P	-- /5367	-- /4405	2,895

MONACO SPECIAL (SIX/V-8)

WS	23	2-dr. HT Cpe-6P	3995/4256	N/A	N/A

CHARGER SPECIAL EDITION (V-8)

XS	22	2-dr. HT Cpe-5P	5098	3895	36,204

ROYAL MONACO (V-8)

DM	23	2-dr. HT Cpe-6P	4731	4050	1,901
DM	41	4-dr. Sedan-6P	4716	4125	9,491
DM	45	4-dr. Sta Wag-6P	5353	4905	1,333

ROYAL MONACO BROUGHAM (V-8)

DH	23	2-dr. Formal HT-6P	5011	4205	6,348
DH	41	4-dr. Sedan-6P	4996	4270	18,361
DH	45	4-dr. Sta Wag-6P	5607	4900	906
DH	46	4-dr. 3S Wag-9P	5730	4935	3,493

FACTORY PRICE AND WEIGHT NOTE: Prices and weights to left of slash are for six-cylinder, to right for V-8 engine. **PRODUCTION NOTE:** In addition to the figures shown, a total of 4,963 Monaco and 2,206 Royal Monaco police four-door sedans were shipped.

ENGINE DATA: BASE SIX (Aspen): Inline, overhead-valve six. Cast iron block and head. Displacement: 225 cu. in. (3.7 liters). Bore & stroke: 3.40 x 4.12 in. Compression ratio: 8.4:1. Brake horsepower: 100 at 3600 R.P.M. Torque: 170 lbs.-ft. at 1600 R.P.M. Four main bearings. Solid valve lifters. Carburetor: 1Bbl. Holley 1945 (R7764A). VIN Code: C. BASE SIX (Aspen wagon, Monaco); OPTIONAL (Aspen): Same as 225 cu. in. six above, but with 2Bbl. Carter BBD 8086S carburetor Horsepower: 110 at 3600 R.P.M. Torque: 180 lbs.-ft. at 2000 R.P.M. VIN Code: D. BASE V-8 (Diplomat, Charger SE, Royal Monaco); OPTIONAL (Aspen, Monaco): 90-degree, overhead valve V-8. Cast iron block and head. Displacement: 318 cu. in. (5.2 liters). Bore & stroke: 3.91 x 3.31 in. Compression ratio: 8.5:1. Brake horsepower: 145 at 4000 R.P.M. Torque: 245 lbs.-ft. at 1600 R.P.M. Five main bearings. Hydraulic valve lifters. Carburetor: 2Bbl. Carter BBD 8093S or 8094S. VIN Code: G. BASE V-8 (Monaco wagon, Royal Monaco Brougham); OPTIONAL V-8 (Aspen, Monaco, Charger SE, Royal Monaco): 90-degree, overhead valve V-8. Cast iron block and head. Displacement: 360 cu. in. (5.9 liters). Bore & stroke: 4.00 x 3.58 in. Compression ratio: 8.4:1. Brake horsepower: 155 at 3600 R.P.M. Torque: 275 lbs.-ft. at 2000 R.P.M. Five main bearings. Hydraulic valve lifters. Carburetor: 2Bbl. Holley 2245 (R7671A). VIN Code: K. OPTIONAL V-8 (Aspen): Same as 360 cu. in. V-8 above, but with Carter TQ 4Bbl. carburetor and Lean Burn system Compression: 8.0:1. Horsepower: 175 at 4000 R.P.M. Torque: 275 lbs.-ft. at 2000 R.P.M. VIN Code: L. BASE V-8 (Royal Monaco wagon); OPTIONAL (Charger SE, Monaco, Royal Monaco): 90-degree, overhead valve V-8. Cast iron block and head. Displacement: 400 cu. in. (6.6 liters). Bore & stroke: 4.34 x 3.38 in. Compression ratio: 8.2:1. Brake horsepower: 190 at 3600 R.P.M. Torque: 305 lbs.-ft. at 3200 R.P.M. Five main bearings. Hydraulic valve lifters. Carburetor: 4Bbl. Carter TQ9102S. VIN Code: N. OPTIONAL V-8 (Royal Monaco): 90-degree, overhead valve V-8. Cast iron block and head. Displacement: 440 cu. in. (7.2 liters). Bore & stroke: 4.32 x 3.75 in. Compression ratio: 8.2:1. Brake horsepower: 195 at 3600 R.P.M. Torque: 320 lbs.-ft. at 2000 R.P.M. Five main bearings. Hydraulic valve lifters. Carburetor: 4Bbl. Carter TQ9078S. VIN Code: T.

CHASSIS DATA: Wheelbase: (Aspen cpe) 108.7 in.; (Aspen sed/wag) 112.7 in.; (Diplomat) 112.7 in.; (Charger/Monaco cpe) 115.0 in.; (Monaco sed) 117.4 in.; (Monaco wag) 117.5 in.; (Royal Monaco) 121.4 in.; (Royal wag) 124.0 in. Overall length: (Aspen cpe) 197.5 in.; (Aspen sed/wag) 201.5 in.; (Diplo cpe) 204.1 in.; (Diplo sed) 206.1 in.; (Monaco cpe) 213.7 in.; (Monaco sed) 218.4 in.; (Monaco wag) 225.6 in.; (Charger SE) 215.3 in.; (Royal Monaco) 225.7 in.; (Royal wag) 229.5 in. Height: (Aspen cpe) 53.3 in.; (Aspen sed) 55.0 in.; (Aspen wag) 55.2 in.; (Diplo cpe) 53.3 in.; (Diplo sed) 55.3 in.; (Monaco sed) 54.0 in.; (Monaco wag) 55.8 in.; (Monaco/Charger SE cpe) 52.6 in.; (Royal Monaco 2-dr.) 54.1 in.; (Royal 4- dr.) 54.8 in.; (Royal wag) 56.9 in. Width: (Aspen) 72.8 in.; (Diplo cpe) 73.5 in.;. (Diplo sed) 72.8 in.; (Monaco) 77.7 in.; (Monaco wag) 78.8 in.; (Charger SE) 77.1 in.; (Royal Monaco) 79.8 in.; (Royal wag) 79.4 in. Front Tread: (Aspen/Diplo) 60.0 in.; (Monaco/Charger) 61.9 in.; (Royal Monaco) 64.0 in. Rear Tread: (Aspen/Diplo) 58.5 in.; (Monaco/Charger) 62.0 in.; (Monaco wag) 63.4 in.; (Royal Monaco) 63.4 in. Wheel size: (Aspen cpe/sed) 14 x 5.5 in.; (Diplo) 15 x 5.5 in.; (Charger SE) 15 x 5.5 in.; (Monaco/Royal) 15 x 5.5 in. exc. wag, 6.5 in. Standard Tires: (Aspen) D78 x 14 BSW exc. DR78 x 14 GBR BSW on SE cpe/sed, E78 x 14 or ER78 x 14 with V-8, and F78 x 14 on wagon; (Diplo) FR78 x 15 GBR; (Monaco) F78 x 15 exc. wag, H78 x 15; (Monaco V8400) G78 x 15 exc. wagon, H78 x 15; (Charger SE) GR78 x 15; (Royal Monaco) GR78 x 15 exc. wag, LR78 x 15.

TECHNICAL: Transmission: Three-speed manual transmission (column shift) standard on Aspen and Monaco. Gear ratios: (1st) 3.08:1; (2nd) 1.70:1; (3rd) 1.00:1; (Rev) 2.90:1. Column or floor lever on Aspen; column on Monaco. Four-speed overdrive manual gearbox available on Aspen: (1st) 3.09:1; (2nd) 1.67:1; (3rd) 1.00:1; (4th) 0.73:1; (Rev) 3.00:1. TorqueFlite three-speed automatic standard on other models, optional on all. Gear ratios: (1st) 2.45:1; (2nd) 1.45:1; (3rd) 1.00:1; (Rev) 2.22:1. Floor lever available for all exc. Royal Monaco. Standard final drive ratio: (Aspen six) 3.23:1 exc. 2.76:1 w/auto., 2.94:1 in wag.; (Aspen V8318) 2.94:1 exc. 2.71:1 w/auto.; (Aspen V8360) 2.45:1 exc. 2.71:1 in wagon, 3.23:1 w/Lean Burn 4Bbl.; (Diplomat) 2.7:1; (Monaco six) 3.21:1 w/3spd, 2.94:1 w/auto.; (Monaco V-8) 2.94:1 w/3spd but 2.71:1, 2.45:1 or 3.21:1 w/auto; (Charger SE) 2.71:1 except 2.45:1 w/V8360; (Royal Monaco) 2.71:1. Steering: Recirculating ball. Suspension: (Aspen/Diplomat) isolated transverse front torsion bars and anti-sway bar, semi-elliptic rear leaf springs; (others) longitudinal front torsion bars w/lower trailing links and anti-sway bar, semi-elliptic rear leaf springs; rear anti-sway bar on Charger SE. Brakes: Front disc, rear drum. Ignition: Electronic. Body construction: (Diplomat) unibody; (Aspen/Royal Monaco) unibody w/front auxiliary frame; (Monaco/Charger) unibody w/isolated front crossmembers. Fuel tank: (Aspen) 18 gal. exc. V-8 or wagon, 20 gal.; (Diplomat) 19.5 gal.; (Monaco) 25.5 gal. exc. wag, 20 gal.; (Charger SE) 25.5 gal.; (Royal Monaco) 26.5 gal. exc. wag, 24 gal. and V8318, 20.5 gal.

DRIVETRAIN OPTIONS: Engines: 225 cu. in., 2Bbl. six: Aspen ($38). 360 cu. in., 2Bbl. V-8: Aspen ($53); Charger SE, Monaco ($57); Royal ($58). 360 cu. in., 4Bbl. V-8: Aspen cpe ($219-$241); Charger SE, Monaco ($105) exc. wag ($47); Royal ($106); Royal Brghm ($48). 400 cu. in., 4Bbl. V-8: Charger SE, Monaco ($156) exc. wag ($98); Royal Monaco ($158); Royal Brghm ($99). 440 cu. in., 4Bbl. V-8: Royal Monaco ($289); Royal Brghm ($231); Royal wag ($132). Transmission/Differential: Three-speed manual trans. w/floor shift: Aspen ($30). Four-speed overdrive manual trans. w/floor lever: Aspen ($134). TorqueFlite auto. trans.: Aspen ($270); Monaco ($295). Sure Grip differential: Aspen ($52); Charger SE/Monaco ($57). Optional axle ratio: Aspen ($14); Charger SE/Monaco/Royal ($16). Brakes and Steering: Power front disc brakes: Aspen six ($59). Power steering: Aspen ($134); Monaco six ($153). Suspension: Automatic height control: Royal Monaco ($109). H.D. susp.: Aspen ($23); Charger SE ($25); Monaco, Royal ($18-$25). H.D. shock absorbers: Charger SE/Monaco/Royal ($7).

Other: Long-life battery ($29-$32). Fuel pacer system ($18- $36). Engine block heater: Royal ($18). Engine temp and oil pressure gauge: Royal Monaco ($21). Trailer towing pkg.: Aspen ($72). Light trailer towing pkg.: Charger SE/Monaco ($79); Royal ($80). Heavy trailer towing pkg.: Charger/Monaco ($316); Royal ($321). California emission system ($67-$75). High-altitude emission system ($21-$24).

ASPEN CONVENIENCE/APPEARANCE OPTIONS: Option Packages: R/T pkg.: base cpe ($184-$207). R/T decor group: base cpe ($82-$101). R/T "Super Pak": base cpe ($318). Two-tone paint pkg.: Cust/SE cpe ($120-$158). Light pkg. ($35). Deluxe insulation pkg. ($35-$65). Easy order pkg. ($594-$801). Fold-down rear seat pkg. ($110). Protection group ($19-$28). Comfort/Convenience: Air cond. ($454). Rear defogger, blower- type ($45); electric ($79). Automatic speed control ($77). Power seat ($131). Power windows ($104-$145). Power door locks ($65-$92). Tinted windshield ($37); all windows ($48). Luxury steering wheel ($28). Tuff steering wheel ($7-$35). Tilt steering wheel ($54). Electric clock ($19). Inside hood release ($11).

Deluxe wipers ($9). Lighter: base ($6). Locking gas cap ($6). Locking glovebox ($5). Horns and Mirrors: Dual horns ($6). Remote left mirror ($15). Dual remote mirrors ($28-$43). Dual remote sport mirrors ($35-$50). Day/night mirror ($8). Entertainment: AM radio ($69). AM/FM radio ($67-$137). AM/FM stereo radio ($145-$215); w/8track player ($235-$304). Exterior: T-Bar roof: cpe ($540-$554). Manual sunroof: cpe ($198). Full vinyl roof: sed ($92). Halo vinyl roof: cpe ($92-$107). Landau vinyl roof: cpe ($56-$148). Vinyl bodyside moldings ($19-$38). Belt moldings ($15). Door edge protectors ($8-$12). Upper door frame moldings: sed ($28). Wheel lip moldings ($19). Bumper guards ($37); rub strips ($30). Rear air deflector: wag ($25). Luggage rack: wag ($68). Undercoating ($30). Interior: Console: cpe ($72). Vinyl bench seat: base wag ($34). Cloth 60/40 split bench seat: SE ($54); SE wag ($198). Vinyl 60/40 split bench seat: wag ($121-$155). Vinyl bucket seats: cpe ($92-$126). Rear armrest w/ashtray: base ($11). Color-keyed mats ($16). Cargo area carpets: wag ($47). Wheels and Tires: Rallye wheels ($32-$68). Chrome wheels ($51-$119). Deluxe wheel covers ($32). Premium wheel covers ($25-$57). Wire wheel covers ($42-$99). Space-saving spare tire ($41).

DIPLOMAT CONVENIENCE/APPEARANCE OPTIONS: Option Packages: Easy-order pkg. Deluxe insulation pkg. Light pkg. Heavy-duty (trailering) pkg. Comfort/Convenience: Air conditioning. Rear defroster, electric. Automatic speed control. Power bench seat (base only). Power 60/40 split-bench seat, driver's side (Medallion). Power windows. Power door locks. Power decklid release. Tinted glass. Luxury three-spoke steering wheel. Tilt steering wheel. Digital clock. Deluxe wiper/washer. Locking gas cap. Lighting and Mirrors: Cornering lights. Remote driver's mirror (std. on Medallion). Remote passenger mirror (Medallion only). Dual remote-control mirrors (base only). Lighted vanity mirror. Entertainment: AM, AM/FM, and AM/FM stereo radios. AM/FM stereo with 8track tape player. Rear speaker. Exterior: Power sunroof (steel or glass). Front bumper guards. Door edge protectors. Undercoating. Interior: Color-keyed floor mats. Pedal dress-up (std. on Medallion). Wheels: Premium wheel covers (std. on Medallion). Wire wheel covers. Forged aluminum wheels.

CHARGER SE CONVENIENCE/APPEARANCE OPTIONS: Option Packages: Daytona pkg. ($166). Easy order pkg. ($987). Light pkg. ($26). Comfort/Convenience: Air cond. ($518). Rear defroster, electric ($86). Automatic speed control ($84). Tinted windshield ($40); all windows ($57). Power seat ($143). Power windows ($113). Power door locks ($71). Power decklid release ($21). Luxury steering wheel ($18). Padded leather steering wheel ($53). Tilt steering wheel ($59). Tachometer ($66). Digital clock ($47). Locking gas cap ($7). Deluxe wipers ($10). Mirrors: Left remote mirror ($16). Dual remote mirrors ($31- $47). Dual sport styled remote mirrors ($39-$55). Lighted vanity mirror ($45). Entertainment: AM radio ($76). AM/FM radio ($74-$149). AM/FM stereo radio ($134-$234); w/8track ($232-$332). Search tune AM/FM stereo radio ($214-$314). Rear speaker ($24). Exterior: T-Bar roof ($605). Manual sunroof ($330). Full vinyl roof ($5-$116). Landau vinyl roof ($112). Quarter window louvers (NC) w/vinyl roof. Vinyl bodyside moldings ($42). Door edge protectors ($9). Hood/deck stripes ($42). Bodyside stripes ($42). Undercoating ($32). pholstery: Console ($18-$94). Cloth/vinyl bench seat ($76). Velour/vinyl 60/40 bench seat ($208). Corduroy/vinyl bucket seats ($137). Center front cushion ($76). Color-keyed mats ($18). Trunk dress-up ($45). Wheels and Tires: Rallye wheels ($45). Styled wheels ($120). Wire wheel covers ($73). GR78 x 15 GBR WSW ($43). GR78 x 15 SBR WSW ($50-$93). HR78 x 15 SBR WSW ($77-$120). GR70 x 15 RWL ($40-$82). Conventional spare tire (NC).

MONACO CONVENIENCE/APPEARANCE OPTIONS: Option Packages: Luxury equipment pkg.: Brghm/Crestwood ($1461-$1792). Easy-order pkg. ($350-$872). Roadability pkg.: V-8 HT/sed ($33). Deluxe insulation pkg.: six-cyl. ($62). Light pkg. ($41-$48). Comfort/Convenience: Air cond. ($518). Rear defroster, electric ($86). Auto. speed control: V-8 ($84). Power windows ($113-$158). Power tailgate window: wag ($44). Power door locks ($71-$101). Power seat ($143). Auto-lock tailgate: wag ($37). Tinted glass ($57); windshield only ($40). Luxury steering wheel ($18). Tilt steering wheel ($59). Electric clock ($21). Deluxe wipers ($10). Inside hood release ($13). Locking gas cap ($7). Horns and Mirrors: Dual horns: base ($6). Remote driver's mirror ($16). Dual chrome remote mirrors ($31-$47). Dual sport remote mirrors, chrome or painted: HT ($39-$55). Entertainment: AM radio ($76). AM/FM radio ($74-$149). AM/FM stereo ($61-$234); w/8track tape player ($159-$332). Rear speaker ($24). Exterior: Manual sunroof: HT ($330). Full vinyl roof ($116) exc. Brghm HT ($22). Canopy vinyl roof: HT ($95). Canopy roof w/opera windows ($22-$116). Vinyl bodyside molding: base ($42). Belt moldings: base HT ($16). Door edge protectors ($8-$14). Sill moldings: sed, base wag ($27). Upper door frame moldings: base sed/wag ($31). Deck tape stripes: HT ($21). Bodyside tape stripes: HT ($42). Bumper rub strips: front ($16); front/rear, HT ($32). Luggage rack: wag ($75). Undercoating ($32). Interior: Console: Brghm HT ($18). Vinyl bench seat: base ($45). Cloth/vinyl 60/40 bench seat: HT/Crestwood ($132). Velour/vinyl 60/40 seat: Brghm sed ($132). Vinyl 60/40 seat: Crestwood, Brghm sed ($132). Cloth/vinyl bucket seats: Brghm HT ($32). Color-keyed mats ($18). Pedal dress-up ($9). Trunk dress-up: sed ($45). Wheels and Tires: Deluxe wheel covers ($35). Wire wheel covers ($73-$108). Rallye wheels ($45-$80). Styled wheels ($119-$154).

ROYAL MONACO CONVENIENCE/APPEARANCE OPTIONS: Option Packages: Diplomat pkg.: Brghm HT ($646-$834). Luxury equipment pkg. ($1876-$1969). Easy-order pkg. ($508-$581). Wagon pkg. ($67). Light pkg. ($69-$82). Deluxe sound insulation pkg. ($43). Comfort/Convenience: Air cond. ($546); auto-temp ($630) exc. ($83) w/luxury pkg. Rear defroster, electric ($87). Automatic speed control ($88). Power seat ($145). Power windows ($119- $179). Power door locks ($72-$102). Auto-lock tailgate: wag ($37). Decklid release ($21). Tinted glass ($72). Luxury steering wheel ($18). Tilt/telescope steering wheel ($88- $106). Electric clock ($21). Digital clock ($27-$48). Deluxe wiper/washer ($17). Locking gas cap ($8). Lighting, Horns and Mirrors: Cornering lights: Brghm ($46). Dual horns ($6). Remote left mirror ($16). Dual remote mirrors ($31-$48). Day/night mirror: base ($9). Entertainment: AM radio ($77). AM/FM radio ($79-$155). AM/FM stereo radio ($58-$237); w/8track stereo tape ($157-$337). Rear speaker ($25). Exterior: Power sunroof w/vinyl roof ($626-$768). Full vinyl roof ($60-$141). Canopy vinyl roof w/opera windows: HT ($141). Vinyl bodyside moldings ($22). Manual vent windows: sed ($43). Door edge protectors ($9-$14). Upper door frame moldings: base sed ($31). Rear air deflector: base wag ($28). Luggage rack: wag ($104). Assist handles: wag ($24). Rear bumper step pads: wag ($15). Undercoating ($33). Interior: Vinyl bench seat: base sed ($22). Cloth/vinyl bench seat: base wag ($59). Cloth/vinyl 50/50 bench seat: Brghm ($198). Vinyl 50/50 bench seat: Brghm wag ($198). Color-keyed mats ($18). Trunk dress-up ($45). Wheels and Tires: Chrome wheels ($81-$156). Deluxe wheel covers ($35). Premier wheel covers ($39-$74).

HISTORY: Introduced: October 1, 1976. Model year production: Chrysler reported a total of 449,559 passenger cars shipped. Total North American production for the U.S. market of 512,229 units (incl. 62,512 Sportsman vans) consisted of 181,083 six-cylinder and 331,146 V-8s. Calendar year production (U.S.): 450,871 (not incl. 46,362 Sportsman vans). Calendar year sales by U.S. dealers: 413,297 (plus 45,380 Sportsman vans). Model year sales by U.S. dealers: 418,644 (not incl. 69,963 Colts and 45,841 Sportsman vans).

Historical Footnotes: Dodge sales rose 5 percent for model year 1977, while production leaped 23 percent (though production fell for the calendar year). Aspen sales went up by 44 percent, reaching 254,532. Diplomat, introduced during the '77 model year, found 23,912 buyers even in the short period. The related Chrysler LeBaron also sold well from the start. Dodge's Mitsubishi-built Colt, imported from Japan, was selling well too, rising 47 percent for the model year after introduction of a smaller, cheaper version. An economy Colt version was added (slightly smaller).

1978 DODGE

Biggest news for 1978 was the January debut of the new front-drive subcompact Omni (and twin Plymouth Horizon). This was also the final year for big Dodges. Aspen, Diplomat and Monaco lost weight this year in their windshields, inner body panels, interior trim, and bumpers. Electronic Lean Burn was not only on many V-8s now, but even installed on the new subcompact Omni four. A new lock-up torque converter on many TorqueFlite transmissions engaged when shifted into third gear, and disengaged below about 30 MPH (or when the transmission downshifted). It was intended to minimize slippage. All Dodge models had unibody construction. Differences between California and 49-state engines peaked in the late 1970s. Variants such as a four-barrel carbureted version of the 318 cu. in. V-8 were offered strictly for California and/or high-altitude regions.

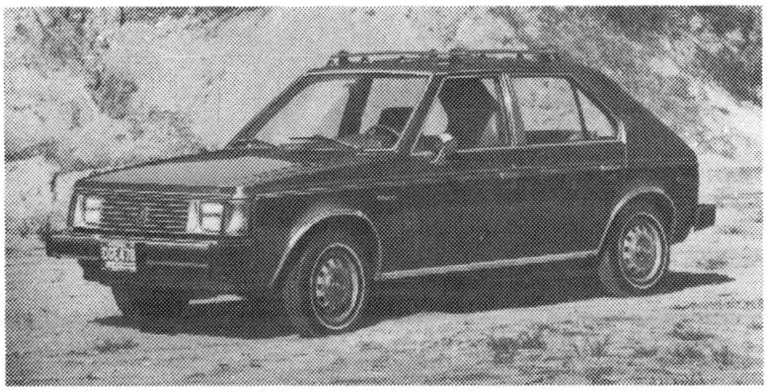

1978 Omni hatchback sedan (D)

OMNI — SERIES ZL — FOUR — Omni "does it all." That's what the factory sales catalog promised, at any rate, to prospective buyers of Dodge's new subcompact four-door hatchback. This was the first front-wheel drive subcompact manufactured in America. The 99 in. wheelbase, L-body design was shared by Plymouth's Horizon, which differed in little more than grille appearance. Omni's rectangular grille was made up of horizontal bars only, with a center medallion. Single rectangular headlamps were recessed, and flanked by amber wraparound park/signal lamps. Above the driver's side headlamp was 'Dodge' lettering. 'Omni' lettering went on the front fender, ahead of the door. At the rear, large rectangular three-row taillamps (upper rows red, bottom row amber on the outside with clear backup lens inside) wrapped around slightly onto the quarter panels. The license plate holder sat in the center of the back panel, below the lift-up hatch. Under the hood was a transverse-mounted overhead-cam four-cylinder engine with 104.7 cu. in. (1.7-liter) displacement. The engine actually came from Volkswagen, but was enlarged and modified to meet Chrysler's requirements. Both the cylinder head and intake manifold were aluminum. It drove a standard four-speed manual transaxle, but TorqueFlite automatic was available. Front suspension was an Iso-Strut design with coil springs and anti-sway bar. At the rear were trailing-arm independent coil springs with integral anti-sway provision. Rack-and-pinion steering was used. Tires were P155/80R13

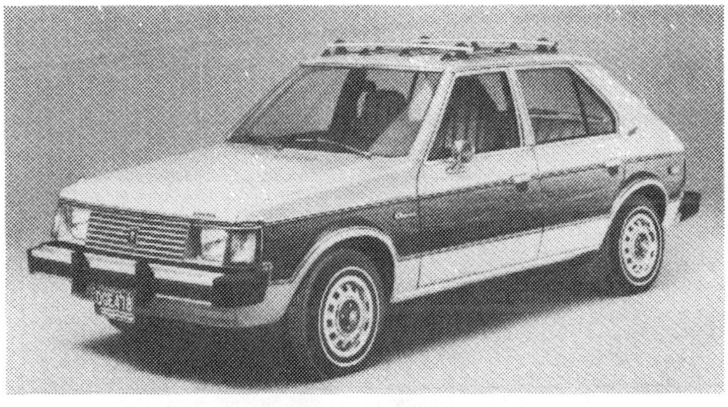

1978 Omni Premium hatchback sedan (JG)

glass-belted radial whitewalls. Standard equipment included bodyside moldings with black vinyl inserts, four-speed transmission, lighter, door armrests, color-keyed visors, two coat hooks, folding rear shelf security panel, built-in diagnostics connector, three-spoke steering wheel, manual disc/drum brakes, and cut-pile carpeting. Colors were: Spitfire Orange, Sunrise Orange, Light Mocha Tan, Yellow Blaze, Eggshell White, and Black; plus metallic Tapestry Red Sunfire, Caramel Tan, Citron, Augusta Green Sunfire, Regatta Blue, Starlight Blue Sunfire, and Pewter Gray. Five two-tone paint and tape options were available. Standard high-back vinyl bucket seats came in blue, tan, red or black. Optional cloth/vinyl upholstery was red or black. A Custom Interior Package could have all-vinyl high- back seats, either solid color or two-tone. A Premium Interior Package included dual reclining seatbacks, upholstered in embossed vinyl or suedelike cloth. On the dashboard was a mile/kilometer speedometer, ammeter, and temperature gauge. An AM radio and inside hood release were standard. A multi-function steering column lever controlled turn signals, dimmer, and wiper/washer with standard pulse- wipe. Options included a roof rack, AM/FM stereo radio, remote-control mirrors, air conditioning, rear defroster and wiper/washer, and power brakes. Basic Omnis had a bright grille, bright bumpers with rub strips, plus bright windshield and liftgate window moldings. A Custom Package added bright trim to hood, fender, wheel lip, door sill, and roof drip rail. The Premium Exterior Package added bright accents on door frames, belt, and center pillars; plus full-length bodyside and liftgate moldings, and Rallye wheel hubs with bright acorn nuts. Inside were a three-spoke simulated woodgrain steering wheel, visor vanity mirror (passenger), and premium door trim panels. One step further along was the Premium Wood-Grained Package, with simulated wood applique on bodysides and lower liftgate.

1978 Aspen sedan (JG)

ASPEN — SERIES N — SIX/V-8 — Similar in overall appearance to the 1977 version, this year's compact Aspen sported a revised front end. The new, narrower one-piece grille was made up of horizontal bars, but without the former recessed side portions. Instead, those twin areaa between grille and headlamps were occupied by square amber parking lamps, each with two horizontal trim strips. (Parking lamps had previously been in the bumper.) Round headlamps were again recessed in bright square housings. Rear appearance changed too, with revised taillamps. Each rectangular unit, about one-third the car width (with backup lamps toward the center of the car) was split by two horizontal trim strips that continued across the center trim panel. That panel displayed 'Dodge' block letters in the center row. As before, the standard model had no bodyside molding. This year's Aspen weighed less, as a result of changes in the windshield, inner body panels, headlining materials, and brakes. Ten new body colors were offered: Bright Canyon Red, Tapestry Red Sunfire metallic, Citron and Cadet Blue metallic, Caramel Tan and Mint Green metallic, Augusta Green Sunfire metallic, Classic Cream, Black, and Pewter Gray metallic. Eggshell White, Spitfire Orange, Starlight Blue Sunfire metallic and Light Mocha Tan were carried over. Only one trim level was offered, rather than the three choices of 1977. Instead, option packages allowed buyers to modify their Aspens. As before, two-door coupe, four-door sedan, and two-seat wagon bodies were available. Base engine was the one-barrel Slant Six, though wagons carried the two- barrel Super Six version. Three-speed

1978 Aspen station wagon (JG)

manual shift was standard; four-speed available. TorqueFlite automatic transmissions (optional) added a new lock-up torque converter. Aspen's sporty coupes were offered again, in three versions: Super Coupe, R/T, and R/T Sport Pak. The Super Coupe (arriving later in the season) included dark brown body paint with black-finish hood, front fender tops, headlamps, wiper arms, front/rear bumpers, and remote-control racing mirrors. Bodyside and roof tape striping was included, along with wheel flares, front/rear spoilers, quarter-window louvers, GR60 x 15 Aramid fiber-belted RWL radial tires on 8 in. GT wheels, heavy-duty suspension with rear anti-sway bar, and the 360 cu. in. four-barrel V-8. The basic R/T had FR78 x 14 GBR BSW tires on Rallye wheels; heavy-duty suspension; red grille treatment; multi-color bodyside, hood and rear tape stripes; R/T decals and grille medallion; rocker panel moldings with black paint below; and dual remote racing mirrors. The R/T Sport Pak added a front spoiler, wheel flares, quarter-window louvers, rear-deck spoiler, and full- length tricolor stripes on white or black body. The R/T package (RPO Code A57) went on 3.2 percent of Aspen coupes, while Super Coupes (code A67) amounted to 1.1 percent. R/T Sport Pak (code A66) was installed on 1.3 percent of Aspen coupes. A Sunrise package went on 7.5 percent, and rarest of the lot is the Street Kit Car, with an installation rate of only 0.3 percent.

1978 Diplomat Medallion coupe (JG)

DIPLOMAT — SERIES G — SIX/V-8 — Introduced during the 1977 model year, Diplomat added a four-door station wagon for its first full season. Offered only in base trim, the wagon had wraparound horizontally- divided taillamps, simulated teakwood-grain body panels, a shorter rear end, wide back pillars, and an all-vinyl split-

1978 Diplomat S sedan (JG)

back bench seat with fold-down center armrest. Appearance of the two-door coupe and four-door sedan did not change, but a low-priced 'S' series was added to the original base and Medallion selection. Diplomats had a large grille, quad rectangular headlamps, and wraparound taillamps, plus full wheelhouse plastic splash shields. TorqueFlite and a 318 V-8 had been standard in the first Diplomats, but this year's edition switched to the new 225 cu. in. two-barrel Super Six, coupled to four-speed manual overdrive gearbox. Automatic and V-8 power were now optional. A thin-back bench seat was standard. Options included a 40- channel CB transceiver/stereo radio, and a search-tune stereo radio.

1978 Charger SE coupe (JG)

CHARGER SE — SERIES XP — V-8 — Appearance of the Dodge's carryover coupe did not change for 1978. Charger's front end still revealed its Cordoba relationship. Standard engine was the 318 cu. in. 5.2-liter V-8 with Electronic Lean Burn, hooked to TorqueFlite three- speed automatic (now with a lock-up torque converter). Options reached all the way to the 400 cu. in. (6.6-liter) four-barrel V-8. Standard equipment included power steering, cloth bench seat, dual horns, and rear anti-sway bar. Door outer panels were one-sided galvanized metal. Joining the option list was a power sliding metal sunroof, as well as a T-Bar roof with removable tinted-glass panels. A new optional wiper gave intermittent operation. Thin-back bucket seats were also available. Other options: forged aluminum wheels and a three-spoke leather-wrapped steering wheel.

1978 Magnum XE coupe (JG)

MAGNUM XE — SERIES XS — V-8 — In another attempt to capture the performance-minded market, Dodge added a second sporty hardtop coupe to join Charger SE, replacing the abandoned Daytona. Ads called Magnum "the totally personal approach to driving excitement." Distinctive aero-inspired front-end styling featured quad rectangular headlamps behind horizontally-scored clear covers, which retracted when lights were switched on. The headlamp units extended outward to encompass wraparound parking/signal lenses. The grille merely consisted of four big, wide slots with thin bright trim on the body-colored horizontal divider bars. The thin outer grille molding extended outward on each side, a bit below the headlamps, to wrap around the fenders below the marker lenses. 'Magnum' block letters and a medallion stood on front fenders, ahead of the door. Narrow opera windows could be plain or display twin horizontal louvers (available at no charge with vinyl roof). Twin bulges in each door extended into front fenders and quarter panels. At the rear were wraparound taillamps with horizontal trim strips. Four roof styles were optional: full or landau vinyl, T-Bar, or a power-operated sunroof. Base engine was the Lean Burn 318 cu. in. V-8 with TorqueFlite three-speed automatic. Power steering and brakes were standard, as were thin-back low-profile vinyl bucket seats with adjustable head restraints. Cloth 60/40 seating and leather/vinyl buckets were available. Magnum's Gran Touring package, arriving later, included color-keyed polyurethane fender flares

that blended into the body, plus heavy-duty shock absorbers. GT Magnums rode GR60 x 15 Aramid fiber-belted radial tires with raised white letters on 7 in. wheels with functional trim rings, deep-dish trim rings, a bright centerpiece, and bright lug nuts. Inside, the Gran Touring had engine-turned instrument panel appliques, a two-spoke leather-wrapped steering wheel, and firm-feel power steering. GT colors were: Classic Cream, Eggshell White, Bright Canyon Red, Black, and metallic Pewter Gray, Starlight Blue Sunfire, or Tapestry Red Sunfire. Other Magnums could also have Charcoal Gray Sunfire metallic, Dove Gray, Cadet Blue or Mint Green metallic, Augusta Green or Sable Tan Sunfire metallic, or Caramel Tan metallic. GT packages (RPO Code A75) were installed in 1.8 percent of Magnums, and the model as a whole sold far better than Charger.

MONACO — SERIES W — SIX/V-8 —

When the traditional full-size Royal Monaco was dropped, Monaco became the biggest Dodge, even though the hardtop rode a mid-size 115 in. wheelbase and sedans/wagons measured just over 117 in. Monaco came in base or luxury Brougham trim, including two station wagon series (standard and Crestwood). An 'SS' package, installed on 20.5 percent of the base Monaco coupes, featured tri-color striping and vinyl bucket seats with center armrest. Base engine was the two-barrel Super Six with three-speed manual column shift. Power brakes were standard. Two- or three-seat wagons carried the 360 cu. in. V-8 with TorqueFlite, and added power steering. The automatic transmission now had a lock-up torque converter. Monacos had vertically stacked headlamps and a split horizontal-style grille, each section containing one dominant horizontal and two vertical bars. Hardtops had new wraparound taillamps. Regency cloth/vinyl bench seats were standard. Options included aluminum-fascia wheels, and AM or AM/FM stereo radios with built-in CB transceivers. Sedans could get a full vinyl roof; two-door hardtops a halo roof or canopy roof, the latter with or without opera windows. A Gran Coupe package was installed on 19.1 percent of the total production. Available only V-8 powered, it included a halo vinyl roof, bodyside accent stripes, cloth/vinyl bucket seats, luxury steering wheel, color-keyed seatbelts, hood ornament with windsplit molding, sill moldings, G78 x 15 whitewalls, and dual sport remote mirrors (chromed or painted).

I.D. DATA:

Dodge's 13-symbol Vehicle Identification Number (VIN) was on the upper left corner of the instrument panel, visible through the windshield. Symbol one indicates car line: 'Z' Omni; 'N' Aspen; 'G' Diplomat; 'W' Monaco; 'X' Charger SE or Magnum XE. Symbol two is series (price class): 'L' low; 'M' medium; 'H' high; 'P' premium; 'S' special. Symbols 3-4 show body type: '22' 2-dr. pillared hardtop; '23' 2-dr. hardtop; '29' 2-dr. coupe; '41' 4-dr. sedan; '44' 4-dr. hatchback; '45' two-seat station wagon; '46' three-seat wagon. Symbol five is the engine code: 'A' L4105; 'C' L6225 1Bbl.; 'D' L6225 2Bbl.; 'G' V8318; 'K' V8360 2Bbl.; 'J' V8360 4Bbl.; 'L' Hi-perf. V8360 4Bbl.; 'N' V8400 4Bbl.; 'P' Hi- perf. V8400 4Bbl. Symbol six is the model year code: '8' 1978. Symbol seven indicates assembly plant: 'A' Lynch Road; 'B' Hamtramck, MI; 'D' Belvidere, IL; 'F' Newark, DE; 'G' St. Louis; 'R' Windsor, Ontario. The final six digits make up the sequential serial number, starting with 100001. Six/V-8 engine number coding is similar to 1976-77. The engine number for the new Omni four-cylinder is located on a pad, just above the fuel pump. As before, a Vehicle Safety Certification Label that displays (among other data) the date of manufacture is attached to the rear facing of the driver's door. A Body Code Plate is on the left front fender side shield, wheel housing, or left side of upper radiator support.

OMNI (FOUR)

Model Number	Body/Style Number	Body Type & Seating	Factory Price	Shipping Weight	Production Total
ZL	44	4-dr. Hatch-4P	3976	2145	70,971

ASPEN (SIX/V-8)

NL	29	2-dr. Spt Cpe-5P	3747/3917	3135/3255	48,311
NL	41	4-dr. Sedan-6P	3865/4035	3175/3295	64,320
NL	45	4-dr. Sta Wag-6P	4207/4336	3405/3490	53,788

DIPLOMAT (SIX/V-8)

GH	22	2-dr. Cpe-6P	4991/5167	3420/3550	11,294
GH	41	4-dr. Sedan-6P	5147/5323	3465/3505	12,951
GH	45	4-dr. Sta Wag-6P	5486/5660	3555/3640	10,906

DIPLOMAT 'S' (SIX/V-8)

GM	22	2-dr. Cpe-6P	4771/4957	3315/3400	1,655
GM	41	4-dr. Sedan-6P	4937/5123	3395/3480	1,667

DIPLOMAT MEDALLION (SIX/V-8)

GP	22	2-dr. Cpe-6P	5361/5537	3495/3580	11,986
GP	41	4-dr. Sedan-6P	5517/5693	3550/3635	10,841

CHARGER SE (V-8)

XP	22	2-dr. HT Cpe-6P	5307	3895	2,735

MAGNUM XE (V-8)

XS	22	2-dr. HT Cpe-6P	5448	3895	47,827

MONACO (SIX/V-8)

WL	23	2-dr. HT Cpe-6P	4230/4406	3610/3865	7,509
WL	41	4-dr. Sedan-6P	4310/4385	3635/3885	16,333
WL	45	4-dr. Sta Wag-6P	--/5043	--/4310	1,665
WL	46	4-dr. 3S Wag-8P	--/5186	--/4375	2,544

MONACO 'SS' (SIX/V-8)

WL	23	2-dr. HT Cpe-6P	4322/4498	N/A	N/A

Note 1: Production included in base HT Coupe total above (approximately 1,540 'SS' packages were installed).

MONACO BROUGHAM (SIX/V-8)

WH	23	2-dr. HT Cpe-6P	4476/4652	3615/3870	4,727
WH	41	4-dr. Sedan-6P	4527/4703	3650/3900	6,937

MONACO CRESTWOOD STATION WAGON (V-8)

WH	45	4-dr. 2S Wag-6P	--/5486	--/4305	668
WH	46	4-dr. 3S Wag-8P	--/5629	--/4380	1,588

FACTORY PRICE AND WEIGHT NOTE: Prices and weights to left of slash are for six-cylinder, to right for V-8 engine.

ENGINE DATA: BASE FOUR (Omni): Inline, overhead-cam four-cylinder. Cast iron block; aluminum head. Displacement: 104.7 cu. in. (1.7 liters). Bore & stroke: 3.13 x 3.40 in. Compression ratio: 8.2:1. Brake horsepower: 75 at 5600 R.P.M. Torque: 90 lbs.-ft. at 3200 R.P.M. Five main bearings. Solid valve lifters. Carburetor: 2Bbl. Holley 5220. VIN Code: A. **BASE SIX (Aspen):** Inline, overhead-valve six. Cast iron block and head. Displacement: 225 cu. in. (3.7 liters). Bore & stroke: 3.40 x 4.12 in. Compression ratio: 8.4:1. Brake horsepower: 100 at 3600 R.P.M. Torque: 170 lbs.-ft. at 1600 R.P.M. Four main bearings. Solid valve lifters. Carburetor: 1Bbl. Holley 1945. VIN Code: C. **BASE SIX** (Aspen wagon, Diplomat, Monaco); **OPTIONAL** (Aspen): Same as 225 cu. in. six above, but with 2Bbl. Carter BBD carburetor. Horsepower: 110 at 3600 R.P.M. Torque: 180 lbs.- ft. at 2000 R.P.M. VIN Code: D. **BASE V-8** (Charger SE, Magnum XE); **OPTIONAL** (Aspen, Diplomat, Monaco): 90-degree, overhead valve V-8. Cast iron block and head. Displacement: 318 cu. in. (5.2 liters). Bore & stroke: 3.91 x 3.31 in. Compression ratio: 8.5:1. Brake horsepower: 140 at 4000 R.P.M. Torque: 245 lbs.-ft. at 1600 R.P.M. Five main bearings. Hydraulic valve lifters. Carburetor: 2Bbl. Carter BBD. VIN Code: G. **BASE V-8** (Monaco wagon); **OPTIONAL V-8** (Aspen, Diplomat, Charger SE, Magnum XE, Monaco): 90-degree, overhead valve V-8. Cast iron block and head. Displacement: 360 cu. in. (5.9 liters). Bore & stroke: 4.00 x 3.58 in. Compression ratio: 8.4:1. Brake horsepower: 155 at 3600 R.P.M. Torque: 270 lbs.-ft. at 2400 R.P.M. Five main bearings. Hydraulic valve lifters. Carburetor: 2Bbl. Holley 2245. VIN Code: K. **OPTIONAL V-8** (Aspen): Same as 360 cu. in. V-8 above, but with Carter TQ 4Bbl. carburetor C.R.: 8.0:1. Horsepower: 175 at 4000 R.P.M. Torque: 260 lbs.-ft. at 2400 R.P.M. VIN Code: J. **OPTIONAL V-8** (Charger SE, Magnum XE, Monaco): 90-degree, overhead valve V-8. Cast iron block and head. Displacement: 400 cu. in. (6.6 liters). Bore & stroke: 4.34 x 3.38 in. Compression ratio: 8.2:1. Brake horsepower: 190 at 3600 R.P.M. Torque: 305 lbs.-ft. at 3200 R.P.M. Five main bearings. Hydraulic valve lifters. Carburetor: 4Bbl. Carter TQ. VIN Code: N. **HIGH-OUTPUT V-8** (Charger SE, Magnum XE, Monaco): Heavy-duty version of 400 cu. in. V-8 above. Specs N/A. VIN Code: P.

CHASSIS DATA: Wheelbase: (Omni) 99.2 in.; (Aspen cpe) 108.7 in.; (Aspen sed/wag) 112.7 in.; (Diplomat) 112.7 in.; (Charger/Magnum/Monaco cpe) 114.9 in.; (Monaco sed) 117.4 in.; (Monaco wag) 117.5 in. Overall length: (Omni) 163.2 in.; (Aspen cpe) 197.2 in.; (Aspen sed/wag) 201.2 in.; (Diplo cpe) 204.1 in.; (Diplo sed) 206.1 in.; (Diplo wag) 202.8 in.; (Charger) 215.3 in.; (Magnum) 215.8 in.; (Monaco cpe) 213.2 in.; (Monaco sed) 218.0 in.; (Monaco wag) 225.1 in. Height: (Omni) 53.4 in.; (Aspen cpe) 53.3 in.; (Aspen sed) 55.3 in.; (Aspen wag) 55.7 in.; (Diplo cpe) 53.3 in.; (Diplo sed) 55.3 in.; (Diplo wag) 55.7 in.; (Charger/Magnum cpe) 52.9 in.; (Magnum) 53.1 in.; (Monaco sed) 54.3 in.; (Monaco wag) 56.9 in. Width: (Omni) 66.2 in.; (Aspen) 73.3 in.; (Diplo cpe) 73.5 in.;. (Charger/Magnum) 77.1 in.; (Monaco) 77.7 in.; (Monaco wag) 78.8 in. Front Tread: (Omni) 55.5 in.; (Aspen/Diplo) 60.0 in.; (Charger/Magnum/Monaco) 61.9 in. Rear Tread: (Omni) 55.1 in.; (Aspen/Diplo) 58.5 in.; (Charger/Mag/Monaco) 62.0 in.; (Monaco wag) 63.4 in. Wheel size: (Omni) 13 x 4.5 in.; (Aspen cpe/sed) 14 x 5.0 in. exc. wagon, 14 x 5.5 in.; (Diplo/Chgr/Magnum) 15 x 5.5 in.; (Monaco) 15 x 5.5 in. exc. wagon, 15 x 6.5 in. Standard Tires: (Omni) P155/80R13 GBR WSW; (Aspen) D78 x 14 BSW exc. wag, F78 x 14; (Diplo) FR78 x 15 GBR BSW; (Charger/Magnum) FR78 x 15 GBR BSW; (Monaco) F78 x 15 BSW exc. wag, H78 x 15.

TECHNICAL: Transmission: Three-speed manual transmission standard on Aspen, Monaco six. Gear ratios: (1st) 3.08:1; (2nd) 1.70:1; (3rd) 1.00:1; (Rev) 2.90:1. Floor lever on Aspen; column on Monaco. Four-speed manual (floor lever) standard on Omni: (1st) 3.45:1; (2nd) 1.94:1; (3rd) 1.29:1; (4th) 0.97:1; (Rev) 3.17:1. Four-speed overdrive manual gearbox available on Aspen, standard on Diplomat: (1st) 3.09:1; (2nd) 1.67:1; (3rd) 1.00:1; (4th) 0.73:1; (Rev) 3.00:1. TorqueFlite three- speed automatic standard on other models, optional on all. Gear ratios: (1st) 2.45:1; (2nd) 1.45:1; (3rd) 1.00:1; (Rev) 2.22:1. Floor lever available for all. Omni TorqueFlite gear ratios: (1st) 2.47:1; (2nd) 1.47:1; (3rd) 1.00:1; (Rev) 2.10:1. Standard final drive ratio: (Omni) 3.48:1; (Aspen six) 3.23:1; (Aspen V-8) 2.94:1; (Aspen 8360) 2.45:1 or 3.21:1; (Aspen wag) 3.21:1; (Diplomat six) 3.23:1; (Diplo V-8) 2.94:1 or 2.45:1; (Diplo V-8 wag) 2.71:1; (Charger/Magnum) 2.71:1 except 2.45:1 w/V8360/400, 3.21:1 w/hiperf. V8400; (Monaco six) 3.21:1; (Monaco V-8) 2.71:1; (Monaco V8360) 2.45:1 or 2.71:1. Steering: (Omni) rack and pinion; (others) recirculating ball.

Suspension: (Omni) Iso-Strut independent coil front w/anti- sway bar, trailing arm independent coil rear w/integral anti- sway; (Aspen/Diplomat) isolated transverse front torsion bars and anti-sway bar, semi-elliptic rear leaf springs; (others) longitudinal front torsion bars w/lower trailing links and anti-sway bar, semi-elliptic rear leaf springs; rear anti- sway bar on Charger SE/Magnum XE. Brakes: Front disc, rear drum. Ignition: Electronic. Body construction: (Omni) unibody; (Aspen/Diplomat) unibody w/front auxiliary frame; (Monaco/Charger/Magnum) unibody w/isolated front crossmembers. Fuel tank: (Omni) 13 gal.; (Aspen six) 18 gal.; (Aspen V-8/wag) 19.5 gal.; (Diplomat) 19.5 gal.; (Charger/Magnum) 25.5 gal.; (Monaco six) 20.5 gal.; (Monaco V-8) 25.5 gal. exc. wag, 20 gal.

DRIVETRAIN OPTIONS: Engines: 225 cu. in., 2Bbl. six: Aspen ($41). 318 cu. in., 2Bbl. V-8: Aspen ($170); Diplomat/Monaco ($176). 318 cu. in., 4Bbl. V-8 (Calif.): Aspen cpe/sed ($439-$463); Aspen wag ($399); Chgr/Mag ($45); Diplo/Monaco ($221). 360 cu. in., 2Bbl. V-8: Aspen cpe/sed ($275); Aspen wag ($234); Chgr/Mag ($109); Diplomat/Monaco ($285). H.D. 360 cu. in., 2Bbl. V-8: Aspen sed ($332); Aspen wag ($292); Diplo ($345). 360 cu. in., 4Bbl. V-8: Aspen cpe ($439-$463); Diplo ($330); Charger/Magnum ($154); Monaco ($330) exc. wag. H.D. 360 cu. in., 4Bbl. V-8: Charger/Magnum ($305); Diplo/Monaco ($481). 400 cu. in., 4Bbl. V-8: Chgr/Mag ($203); Monaco ($379) exc. wag ($94). H.D. 400 cu. in., 4Bbl. V-8: Chgr/Mag ($330); Monaco ($507) exc. wag ($222). Transmission-/Differential: Four-speed overdrive manual trans. w/floor lever: Aspen ($142). TorqueFlite auto. trans.: Omni ($303); Aspen ($293); Diplo ($165); Monaco ($320). Sure Grip differential: Aspen ($56); Diplo/Chgr/Mag/Monaco ($62). Optional axle ratio: Aspen ($15). Brakes and Steering: Power front disc brakes: Omni ($68); Aspen cpe/sed ($66). Power steering: Omni ($148); Aspen ($145); Monaco HT/sed ($159). Suspension: H.D. susp.: Aspen ($24); Diplo/Charger/Magnum ($26); Monaco ($19-$26). Sport susp.: Omni ($24). H.D. shock absorbers: Chgr/Mag/Monaco ($7). Other: Long-life battery ($30-$33). H.D. trailer towing pkg.: Aspen sed/wag ($150); Diplo ($154); Chgr/Mag ($183); Monaco ($157). California emission system ($72-$79). High-altitude emission system ($31-$34).

183

OMNI CONVENIENCE/APPEARANCE OPTIONS: Option Packages: Classic two-tone paint pkg. ($73-$107). Custom exterior pkg. ($71). Premium exterior pkg. ($167). Custom interior pkg. ($62-$82). Premium interior pkg. ($214- $242). Premium woodgrain pkg. ($312). Popular equipment group ($250). Light pkg. ($44). Comfort/Convenience: Air cond. ($493). Tinted glass ($56). Tinted windshield ($41). Luxury steering wheel ($15). Electric clock w/trip odometer ($26). Rear wiper/washer ($59). Locking gas cap ($7). Glovebox lock ($5). Horns and Mirrors: Dual horns ($7). Remote left mirror ($16). Dual remote mirrors ($30-$46). Day/night mirror ($9). Entertainment: AM/FM radio ($74). AM/FM stereo radio ($143). Exterior: Full vinyl roof ($93). Moldings: belt ($16); drip ($18); sill ($19); upper door frame ($30); wheel lip ($27). Door edge protectors ($20). Bumper guards ($41). Multi-color tape stripe ($78). Luggage rack ($81). Undercoating ($31). Interior: Console: storage ($21); shift lever ($30). Cloth/vinyl bucket seats ($21). Cargo area carpet ($43). Color-keyed floor mats ($26). Wheels and Tires: Wheel trim rings ($36). Rallye wheels ($36- $73). Bright rallye hubs ($37). 165/75 x 13 GBR WSW ($16). 165/75 x 13 SBR WSW ($48). Conventional spare tire ($12-$24).

ASPEN CONVENIENCE/APPEARANCE OPTIONS: Option Packages: Super Coupe pkg. ($1351-$1420). "Street Kit Car" pkg.: cpe ($1085). R/T pkg.: cpe ($289). R/T decor group: cpe ($51). R/T "Sport Pak": cpe ($340-$499). Special Edition wagon woodgrain group ($221). Special Edition interior pkg. ($180-$483). Special Edition exterior pkg. ($128-$157). Sunrise pkg.: cpe ($77). Sunrise decor pkg.: cpe ($170-$186). Custom exterior pkg. ($73-$86). Custom interior pkg. ($144-$224). Basic group ($653-$655). Value bonus pkg. A ($229); B ($656-$673). Two-tone paint pkg.: cpe ($188). Two- tone decor pkg. ($62). Light pkg. ($44). Deluxe insulation pkg. ($38-$47). Protection group ($28-$35). Comfort/Convenience: Air cond. ($484). Rear defogger, blower- type ($48); electric ($83). Automatic speed control ($86). Power seat ($142). Power windows ($113-$157). Power door locks ($71-$98). Power tailgate release: wag ($21). Tinted windshield ($39); all windows ($53). Luxury steering wheel ($29). Tuff steering wheel ($37). Tilt steering wheel ($65). Digital clock ($46). Inside hood release ($12). Intermitent wipers ($31). Lighter ($6). Locking gas cap ($7). Locking glovebox ($5). Horns and Mirrors: Dual horns ($6). Remote left mirror ($16). Dual remote mirrors ($30-$46). Dual remote sport mirrors ($38-$53). Day/night mirror ($9). Entertainment: AM radio ($74); w/8track player ($143-$217); w/CB ($305-$379). AM/FM radio ($74-$148). AM/FM stereo radio ($143-$217); w/8track player ($234-$308); w/CB ($448-$522). Rear speaker ($23). Exterior: T-Bar roof: cpe ($572). Full vinyl roof: sed ($93). Halo vinyl roof: cpe ($93-$109). Landau vinyl roof: cpe ($164). Vinyl bodyside moldings ($40). Belt moldings ($16). Door edge protectors ($10-$18). Upper door frame moldings: sed/wag ($30). Wheel lip moldings ($20). Bumper guards ($39); rub strips ($31). Rear air deflector: wag ($27). Luggage rack: wag ($81). Undercoating ($21-$31). Interior: Console: cpe ($55). Vinyl bucket seats ($102). Cloth/vinyl bucket seats ($160). Rear armrest ($11). Color- keyed mats ($20). Color-keyed seatbelts ($15). Cargo area carpets and stowage bin: wag ($50). Pedal dress-up ($9). Trunk dress-up ($43). Wheels and Tires: Rallye wheels ($33-$72). Styled wheels ($55-$127). Deluxe wheel covers ($36). Premium wheel covers ($36-$71). Wire wheel covers ($91-$127). D78 x 14 WSW. DR78 x 14 GBR BSW. DR78 x 14 GBR WSW. E78 x 14 GBR BSW. E78 x 14 GBR WSW. ER78 x 14 GBR BSW. ER78 x 14 GBR WSW. ER78 x 14 SBR WSW. FR70 x 14 RWL Aramid-belted. FR78 x 14 GBR BSW. FR78 x 14 GBR WSW. FR78 x 14 SBR WSW. GR78 x 14 SBR WSW. Space-saving spare tire: cpe/sed (NC). Conventional spare tire (NC).

DIPLOMAT CONVENIENCE/APPEARANCE OPTIONS: Option Packages: Basic group ($1055-$1219). Deluxe insulation pkg. ($9-$80). Light pkg. ($69-$80). Comfort/Convenience: Air cond. ($563). Rear defroster ($91). Auto. speed control ($94). Power seat ($155). Power windows ($129-$179). Power door locks ($83-$116). Power decklid/tailgate release ($22-$23). Tinted glass ($65). Luxury steering wheel ($19). Leather-covered steering wheel ($57). Tilt steering wheel ($71). Digital clock ($50). Deluxe wiper/washer ($41). Locking gas cap ($7). Lighting and Mirrors: Cornering lights ($48). Remote driver's mirror: base ($17). Remote passenger mirror: Medallion ($33). Dual remote-control mirrors: base ($33-$50). Lighted vanity mirror ($48). Entertainment: AM radio ($81); w/CB ($333-$414). AM/FM radio ($81-$161). AM/FM stereo ($157-$237); w/ 8track tape player ($256-$336); w/CB ($490-$570). Search-tune AM/FM stereo ($284-$365). Rear speaker ($25). Power antenna ($46). Exterior: T-Bar roof: cpe ($643). Power sunroof: metal ($626); glass ($788). Landau vinyl roof: cpe ($137). Vinyl bodyside moldings ($44). Front bumper guards ($21). Hood tape stripe: Medallion ($23). Door edge protectors ($11-$20). Air deflector: wag ($29). Luggage rack: wag ($89). Woodgrain: wag (NC). Undercoating ($24). Interior: Vinyl bench seat: base cpe/sed ($48). Cloth 60/40 seat: wag ($140). Leather 60/40 seat: wag ($410); Medallion ($270). Color-keyed floor mats ($22). Color-keyed seatbelts: base ($16). Pedal dress-up: base ($10). Wheels/Tires: Premium wheel covers: base ($41). Wire wheel covers ($58-$99). Forged aluminum wheels ($208-$248). FR78 x 15 GBR WSW ($48). FR78 x 15 SBR WSW ($57-$106). Conventional spare (NC).

CHARGER SE/MAGNUM XE CONVENIENCE/APPEARANCE OPTIONS: Option Packages: Gran Touring 'GT' pkg.: Magnum ($497). Basic group: Charger ($1030); Magnum ($988). Light pkg. ($28). Comfort/Convenience: Air cond. ($563). Rear defroster, electric ($91). Automatic speed control ($94). Tinted windshield ($42); all windows ($65). Power seat ($155). Power windows ($129). Power door locks ($83). Power decklid release ($23). Luxury steering wheel ($19). Leather steering wheel ($57). Tilt steering wheel ($71). Tachometer ($70). Digital clock ($50). Locking gas cap ($7). Deluxe wipers ($34). Mirrors: Left remote ($17). Dual remote ($33-$50). Dual sport remote ($41-$58). Lighted vanity ($48). Entertainment: AM radio ($81); w/8track player ($157-$237); w/CB ($333-$414). AM/FM radio ($81-$161). AM/FM stereo radio ($157-$237); w/8track ($256-$336); w/CB ($490-$570). Search- tune AM/FM stereo ($284-$365). Rear speaker ($25-$26). Power antenna ($46). Exterior: T-Bar roof ($643). Power sunroof ($516). Full vinyl roof ($5-$121). Landau vinyl roof ($117). Quarter window louvers: Magnum (NC) w/vinyl roof. Fender-mount turn signals: Mag ($15). Vinyl bodyside moldings ($44). Wheel lip moldings: Mag ($98). Door edge protectors ($11). Bumper rub strips: Mag ($35). Hood/deck or bodyside stripes: Mag ($45). Wheel lip tape stripes: Mag ($23). Undercoating ($34). Interior: Console ($58-$90). Velour/vinyl 60/40 bench seat: Mag ($216). Vinyl bucket seats: Chgr ($187). Velour/vinyl bucket seats: Mag ($146). Leather bucket seats: Mag ($346). Center front cushion: Mag ($41). Color-keyed mats ($22). Color-keyed seatbelts ($16). Trunk dress-up ($47). Pedal dress-up ($10). Wheels and Tires: Aluminum-fascia wheels: Magnum ($87). Styled wheels ($248). Wire wheel covers ($99). GR78 x 15 GBR BSW ($21). GR78 x 15 GBR WSW ($48). GR78 x 15 SBR WSW ($57- $106). HR78 x 15 SBR WSW ($83-$131). GR60 x 15 RWL Aramid- belted ($219-$267). Conventional spare tire (NC).

MONACO CONVENIENCE/APPEARANCE OPTIONS: Option Packages: Gran Coupe pkg. ($686). Basic group ($254- $739). Value pkg. ($168-$214). Roadability pkg.: V-8 HT/sed ($35). Deluxe insulation pkg.: six-cyl. ($32-$68). Light pkg. ($43-$51). Comfort/Convenience: Air cond. ($563). Rear defroster, electric ($91). Auto. speed control: V-8 ($94). Power windows ($129-$179). Power tailgate window: wag ($46). Power door locks ($83-$116). Power seat ($155). Auto-lock tailgate: wag ($38). Tinted glass ($65); windshield only ($42). Luxury steering wheel ($19). Tilt steering wheel ($71). Electric clock ($22). Deluxe wipers ($34). Inside hood release ($13). Locking gas cap ($7). Horns and Mirrors: Dual horns: base ($7). Remote driver's mirror ($17). Dual chrome remote mirrors ($33-$50). Dual sport remote mirrors, chrome or painted: HT ($41-$58). Entertainment: AM radio ($81); w/8track player ($157-$237); w/CB ($333-$414). AM/FM radio ($81-$161). AM/FM stereo ($157- $237); w/8track tape player ($256-$336); w/CB ($490-$570). Rear speaker ($25). Exterior: Full vinyl roof: sed ($121). Halo vinyl roof: HT ($121). Canopy vinyl roof: HT ($100). Canopy roof w/opera windows ($121). Vinyl bodyside molding: base ($22-$44). Wide bodyside molding: Crestwood (NC). Belt moldings: base HT ($17). Door edge protectors ($11-$20). Sill moldings: sed, base wag ($25). Upper door frame moldings: base sed/wag ($33). Wheel lip moldings: sed ($22). Deck stripes: HT ($23). Tri-color bodyside stripes: HT ($45). Bumper rub strips: front ($17); front/rear, HT ($35). Air deflector: wag ($29). Luggage rack: wag ($89). Undercoating ($34). Interior: Console: Brghm HT ($58). Vinyl bench seat: base ($48); Brghm sed ($31). Cloth/vinyl 60/40 bench seat: Brghm ($140). Vinyl 60/40 seat: Crestwood ($140). Color-keyed mats ($22). Color-keyed seatbelts ($16). Wheels and Tires: Deluxe wheel covers ($39). Wire wheel covers ($99-$138). Aluminum-fascia wheels ($87-$126). F78 x 15 WSW ($48). G78 x 15 BSW ($21). G78 x 15 WSW ($21-$69). H78 x 15 BSW ($45). H78 x 15 WSW ($47-$95). GR78 x 15 SBR WSW ($130-$178). GR60 x 15 RWL Aramid-belted ($327-$376). 215 x 15 SBR WSW ($109-$204). Space-saving spare tire (NC).

HISTORY: Introduced: October 7, 1977. Model year production: Chrysler reported a total of 391,223 passenger cars shipped. Total North American production for the U.S. market of 424,934 units (incl. 30,599 Sportsman vans) included 71,000 four- cylinder, 129,659 six-cylinder and 224,275 V-8s. Calendar year production (U.S.): 412,821 (not incl. 33,220 Sportsman vans). Calendar year sales by U.S. dealers: 398,219 (plus 44,376 Sportsman vans). Model year sales by U.S. dealers: 398,151 (not incl. 47,931 Colts, 14,196 Challengers and 46,292 Sportsman vans).

Historical Footnotes: This was not a great sales year for either Dodge or Plymouth. Dodge ranked No. 8, just behind Plymouth, with model year sales down 5 percent. Production fell even further, by 21 percent. A sporty new Challenger model, imported from Japan, was expected to help sales. Omni's engine block came from Volkswagenwerk AG in Germany, but was modified at Chrysler. That meant lengthening its stroke and adding a Lean Burn system. Manual gearboxes also came from Volkswagen, while automatics were Chrysler- made. Omni reached a composite (city/highway) EPA mileage figure of 30 MPG. Dodge ads in this era featured the Sherlock Holmes character.

1979 DODGE

Two nameplates left the lineup this year: Charger and Monaco. Magnum XE remained as Dodge's sporty performance coupe, while a new rear-drive St. Regis filled the big-car spot. That new R-bodied St. Regis, though, weighed some 700 pounds less than the full-size Dodges of a few years earlier. The average Dodge, in fact, weighed 160 pounds less this year, in an attempt to boost gas mileage. Omni added a new two-door 024 coupe to match the original four-door hatchback. Sixes and V-8s had aluminum intake manifolds. A new diagnostic connector on all models helped isolate electrical problems. A 430-amp maintenance-free battery was included with the 360 cu. in. V-8 on Aspen, Diplomat and St. Regis, and available on Omnis. A 500-amp battery was optional with all sixes and V-8s. Batteries had a new test indicator. Both Aspen and Diplomat continued to use the unique transverse torsion bar front suspension, while all rear-drives had multi-leaf rear springs. Omni and St. Regis had new sill- mounted jack pads for use with a scissors jack. A new compact spare tire arrived on Aspen, Diplomat and St. Regis coupes and sedans. TorqueFlite transmissions with all normal-duty V-8s (and some sixes) had the direct-drive lock-up torque converter clutch, introduced a year earlier.

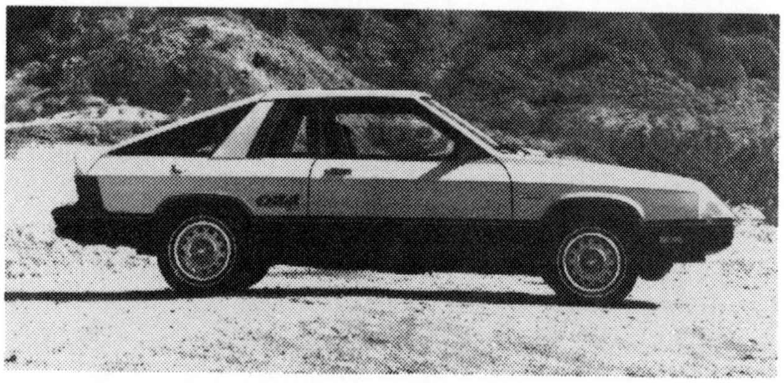

1979 Omni 024 hatchback coupe (D)

OMNI/024 — SERIES ZL — FOUR — Four-door Omnis looked the same as they had in their opening season of 1978. Body features included single rectangular headlamps, combined park/signal/marker lamps with bright accents in leading edges of front fenders, tri-color taillamp lenses with bright accents, and rear side marker lamps in quarter panels. Omnis had black vinyl bodyside moldings and bumper rub strips. Inside were standard high- back vinyl bucket front seats and a deep-dish three-spoke steering wheel, plus a rear bench seat with fold-down seatback. An electric rear defroster and AM radio were standard. So were the folding rear shelf security panel and a multi-function control lever on column. This year's solid colors were: Nightwatch Blue, Chianti Red, Flame Orange, Light Cashmere, Black, or Eggshell White; plus metallic Ensign Blue, Cadet Blue, Turquoise, Teal Green Sunfire, Teal Frost, Medium Cashmere, and Pewter Gray. Six two-tones also were offered. Standard engine was again the 1.7-liter four with four- speed transaxle. High-strength aluminum bumpers helped cut weight. Omni options included a custom equipment package, premium interior package (vinyl seats with head restraints and passenger seatback recliner), maintenance-free battery, sunroof, and locking glove box. In addition to the four-door econobox, however, Omni now offered a two-door hatchback 22 coupe, dubbed 024, on a wheelbase 2.5 inches shorter (96.7 in.) than the sedan. The six-window design included a narrow quarter window just to the rear of the door window, plus a sharply angled far-rear window that followed the line of the hatch. 024 had an aero- shaped, soft-feel molded urethane front end (including grille, bumper facing and fender caps) and a soft urethane rear bumper fascia, plus a sports suspension. Its grille was a simple set of wide horizontal slots, three on each side, in the sloping body-color panel, with 'Dodge' lettering above on the driver's side. Single rectangular headlamps were deeply recessed, with parking lamps recessed down below the bumper strip area. Large curved slots flanked the front license plate. An 'Omni 024' nameplate adorned front fenders, ahead of the door. Amber side marker lamps were on front fenders. Bodysides displayed dual pinstripes, plus a black aero driver's mirror. 024 also had belt, drip rail, sill and wheel lip moldings, along with black wiper arms and blades. Nearly full-width, bright-accented tri-color taillamps were red on the outside (wrapping onto quarter panels), then amber, with clear backup lenses toward the center. Each taillamp was divided by a pair of horizontal ribs. Solid body colors were the same as for the four-door Omni, along with Bright Yellow. Three two-tones were offered, plus three with the Sport package. Like the basic Omni, 024 had front-wheel drive and an Iso-Strut front suspension. A transverse-mounted four- cylinder engine and four-speed manual gearbox provided the power. Whitewall tires and wheel trim rings were standard; bumper rub strips optional. Inside were high-back all-vinyl bucket seats with integral head restraints, and a rear bench seat with fold-down seatback. Cloth/vinyl upholstery was optional. Standard equipment included an AM/FM radio, remote power liftgate release, electric rear defroster, glovebox lock, multi-function column

lever, deep-dish three-spoke steering wheel, and simulated woodgrain instrument panel. A Sport package included black accent striping with reflective red accents at the taillamp area, louvered quarter window applique, black bumper rub strips, black backlight and quarter window moldings, black belt moldings, and black windshield molding. Also included: dual black remote sport mirrors, four-spoke black sport steering wheel, Rallye instrument cluster (incl. tachometer), body-color wheels with bright trim rings, and large '024' decals on forward edges of quarter panels and rear spoiler. A total of 15,369 two-door Omnis had the Sport package, while 4,156 carried the Rallye package.

1979 Aspen "Sunrise" coupe (D)

ASPEN — SERIES NL — SIX/V-8 — As in 1978, Aspen came in only one trim level, but Custom and Special Edition packages were available. Coupe, sedan and station wagon bodies were offered, all looking about the same as the '78 versions. Aspen's grille had bright horizontal and vertical bars. Two-segment taillamps had red outboard lenses and clear (backup) lenses inboard. New body colors included: Teal Green Sunfire and Teal Frost metallic, Light Cashmere, Medium Cashmere metallic, Chianti Red, Regent Red Sunfire metallic, Ensign Blue metallic, and (coupe only) Light Yellow. On the dash was a new 85 MPH speedometer. Standard three-speed manual transmission was available only with a floor lever and one-barrel 225 cu. in. six. TorqueFlite had a lock-up torque converter clutch, except on wagons with the two-barrel six and some 360 cu. in. V-8s. Six-cylinder models used a new, quieter air conditioner compressor. A high-pressure compact spare tire became standard on coupe and sedan. Also new: an aluminum intake manifold, and aluminum/plastic master cylinder and ignition lock housing. A diagnostic connector allowed hookup to an electronic engine performance analyzer. New options included a Sunrise Coupe package with tape striping, R/T package, Sport Wagon package with flared wheel openings, bucket seats, and aluminum wheels. A total of 75 Aspens had the R/T package, while 8,159 had the Sunrise coupe package. A 40-channel CB was optional on all models, with AM or AM/FM stereo.

1979 Diplomat coupe (D)

DIPLOMAT — SERIES G — SIX/V-8 — Once again, seven Diplomat models were offered. They included a new medium-price base two- and four-door; high-line two- and four-door (now called Salon); premium models, again called Medallion; and Salon station wagon. Appearance was similar to before, but with modifications. Diplomat's new chromed grille had bold, rectangular openings framing fine vertical bars. It was divided into an 8 x 3 overall pattern, with crosshatching in each section and a heavy upper header. Quad rectangular parking lamps were mounted just above quad rectangular headlamps. Chromed framing for headlamps and parking lamps wrapped around bodysides, to frame the amber marker/cornering lenses with Diplomat crest. On the hood was a distinctive crest ornament. At the rear were restyled two-segment wraparound taillamps. Each consisted of four sections, arranged 2 x 2 and separated by a vertical trim bar. At closer glance, each of the four sections was split in two horizontally. Backup lamps again were mounted in the bumper. Salon two/four-doors had new bodyside accent tape stripes. Medallions had bodyside, decklid and deck lower panel accent stripes. A padded full vinyl roof was standard on Salon and Medallion four-doors. A restyled Landau vinyl roof with rectangular opera window was optional on two-doors. Medallions had a map/courtesy reading lamp, as well as rear-pillar vanity mirrors with lamps on the four-door. Wagons displayed teakwood-grain woodtone appliques with light woodtone stripes on bodysides and liftgate (which could be deleted). New cloth/vinyl bucket seats were optional on Salon. Other new options: halogen headlamps and wire wheel covers. Eleven body colors were available for coupes and sedans, seven for wagons. Choices were: Dove Gray, Chianti Red, Black, Light Cashmere, Eggshell White, and metallic Cadet Blue, Ensign Blue, Regent Red Sunfire, Sable Tan Sunfire, Teal Frost, Teal Green Sunfire, and Medium Cashmere (wagons only). Overdrive-4 manual transmission was standard with the 1Bbl. Slant Six. TorqueFlite had a lock-up clutch in all normal-duty V-8s and the two-barrel six (two-doors) without air conditioning. The electric choke heater was redesigned to improve cold-weather startup; the Slant Six carburetor revised; and the oil-change interval doubled. Power brakes and steering were standard on all Diplomats. A total of 594 Diplomats had the Sport Appearance package, while only 72 were reported to have the heavy-duty package.

1979 Magnum XE coupe (D)

MAGNUM XE — SERIES XS — V-8 — Modest appearance changes, notably new taillamps, hit the Magnum in its second year. With Charger out of the lineup, it remained the only Dodge performance coupe model. New wraparound two-segment taillamps had bright horizontal ribs to match the front styling. Magnum's sloping, aero-look front end featured a grille with widely-spaced horizontal bars and transparent, sealed (retractable) covers over quad headlamps. Parking/signal/marker lamps wrapped around the corners of front fender extensions behind a curved transparent cover. Horizontal ribs on that cover (and headlamp covers) blended with horizontal grille bars. Front fenders and decklid held bold 'Magnum' block letters. XE medallions went on front fenders and headlamp lenses. The 'Dodge' name was on the driver's side headlamp cover and decklid. Raised, sculptured sections on front fenders and rear quarter panels extended into doors. Wheel covers showed XE center medallions. New body colors included Nightwatch Blue, Teal Green, and Light Cashmere. Fourteen solid colors and four two-tones were available. Inside were low-back vinyl bucket seats, front/rear ashtrays, cigarette lighter, woodtone instrument panel trim, and two-spoke padded steering wheel. Standard TorqueFlite had a lock-up torque converter (except with heavy-duty 360 V-8 or 3.2:1 axle). Base engine was the 318 cu. in. V-8. New options included a unique two-tone paint package and Roadability package. Magnum was considered roughly equivalent to Chrysler's 300, but cost about the same as a base Cordoba. Magnum's Gran Touring (GT) package was offered again, with bold fender flares, GR60 x 15 Aramid-belted tires on raised white letters on 15 x 7 in. wheels, leather-wrapped three-spoke steering wheel, and engine-turned instrument panel applique to replace the standard woodtone. GT medallions highlighted front fenders. The package also included firm-feel suspension and power steering. A total of 1,670 Magnums had the GT package (RPO Code A75).

1979 St. Regis sedan (D)

ST. REGIS — SERIES EH — SIX/V-8 — Dodge's new "full size" four-door model would actually have been considered a mid-size a couple of years earlier. In fact, it was now called a "regular size" or family-size, with a design that had its roots in the departed Monaco. Though it offered a big-car look, St. Regis rode a 118.5 in. wheelbase and weighed 700 pounds less than prior full-size models. Chromed aluminum bumpers were one of many weight-cutting features. The R-body design, referred to as a "four-door pillared hardtop," was related to Chrysler's Newport and New Yorker. Basic grille shape was similar to Magnum's, but with a much different pattern of wide segments and a thick, bright header. The unusual pattern of the swing-away chrome grille was made up of separate small wide rectangles, arranged in six columns and seven rows. A pair of wider rectangular elements extended outward at the base, below the headlamps, to wrap around front fenders. Transparent headlamp doors with embossed horizontal ribs (similar to Magnum) swung down when lights were switched on. Wide parking lamps were inset in the bumper. Marker lenses mated with the headlamp covers. Separate cornering lamps (if ordered) were farther down on the fender, ahead of the wheel openings. Standard equipment included the two-barrel Slant Six engines, power steering and brakes, TorqueFlite three-speed automatic, tinted glass, a trip odometer, and aero flat-type mirrors. St. Regis colors were: Dove Gray, Frost Blue metallic, Nightwatch Blue, Teal Frost metallic, Teal Green or Regent Red Sunfire metallic, Light Cashmere, Medium Cashmere metallic, Sable Tan Sunfire metallic, Eggshell White, and Black; plus four two-tones. Three saxony interior trim colors were offered: Midnight Blue, Teal Green, and Cashmere; plus carryover Canyon Red and Dove Gray. A multi-switch lever on the steering column controlled turn signals, dimmer and wiper/washer. St. Regis had a two-spoke steering wheel with woodtone trim, new hi/lo heater/defroster, and compact spare tire. Bumper guards were optional. So was the 360 cu. in. V-8, which wouldn't be around too much longer. Other options included power windows and driver's seat, search-tune AM/FM stereo radio with digital display, 40-channel CB with AM or AM/FM stereo radio, intermittent wipers, cornering lamps, power glass sunroof, leather-wrapped or tilt steering wheel, trailer towing package, and wire wheel covers or aluminum wheels. An Open Road Handling Package had firm-feel suspension and power steering, like that on police cars. A total of 640 St. Regis models came with the handling package.

185

I.D. DATA: Dodge's 13-symbol Vehicle Identification Number (VIN) was on the upper left corner of the instrument panel, visible through the windshield. Symbol one indicates car line: 'Z' Omni/024; 'N' Aspen; 'G' Diplomat; 'X' Magnum XE; 'E' St. Regis. Symbol two is series (price class): 'L' low; 'M' medium; 'H' high; 'P' premium; 'S' special. Symbols 3-4 show body type: '22' 2-dr. pillared hardtop; '24' 2- dr. hatchback; '29' 2-dr. coupe; '41' 4-dr. sedan; '42' 4-dr. pillared hardtop; '44' 4-dr. hatchback; '45' two- seat station wagon. Symbol five is the engine code: 'A' L4105; 'C' L6225 1Bbl.; 'D' L6225 2Bbl.; 'G' V8318 2Bbl.; 'K' V8360 2Bbl.; 'L' V8360 4Bbl. Symbol six is the model year code: '9' 1979. Symbol seven indicates assembly plant: 'B' Hamtramck, MI; 'D' Belvidere, IL; 'F' Newark, DE; 'G' St. Louis; 'R' Windsor, Ontario. The final six digits make up the sequential serial number, starting with 100001. An abbreviated version of the VIN is also stamped on a pad on the engine block: below No. 6 spark plug on six- cylinder engines, and to rear of right engine mount on V-8s. Serial numbers for V-8s are coded as follows: first letter series (model year); second assembly plant; next three digits displacement (cu. in.); next one or two letters model; next four digits show build date; and final four digits are the engine sequence number. Omni's engine number is on a pad just above the fuel pump. Information on over/undersized parts is stamped on six-cylinder engines on the joint face at right corner, adjacent to No. 1 cylinder; on 318/360 V-8s, at left front of block just below the head. A Body Code Plate is on the left front fender side shield, wheel housing, or left side of upper radiator support.

OMNI (FOUR)

Model Number	Body/Style Number	Body Type & Seating	Factory Price	Shipping Weight	Production Total
ZL	44	4-dr. Hatch-4P	4122	2135	71,556

OMNI 024 (FOUR)

ZL	24	2-dr. Hatch 22-4P	4482	2195	46,781

ASPEN (SIX/V-8)

NL	29	2-dr. Cpe-5P	3968/4184	3050/3170	Note 1
NL	41	4-dr. Sedan-6P	4069/4285	3115/3235	Note 1
NL	45	4-dr. Sta Wag-6P	4445/4661	3325/3435	33,086

Note 1: Total Aspen coupe/sedan production, 88,268.

DIPLOMAT (SIX/V-8)

GM	22	2-dr. Cpe-6P	4901/5137	3270/3365	Note 2
GM	41	4-dr. Sedan-6P	4999/5235	3330/3425	Note 2

Note 2: Total production, 13,929.

DIPLOMAT SALON (SIX/V-8)

GH	22	2-dr. Cpe-6P	5138/5374	3285/3385	Note 3
GH	41	4-dr. Sedan-6P	5366/5602	3350/3450	Note 3
GH	45	4-dr. Sta Wag-6P	5769/6005	3545/3630	7,785

Note 3: Total coupe/sedan production, 17,577.

DIPLOMAT MEDALLION (SIX/V-8)

GP	22	2-dr. Cpe-6P	5612/5848	3345/3440	Note 4
GP	41	4-dr. Sedan-6P	5840/6076	3425/3520	Note 4

Note 4: Total Medallion production, 12,394.

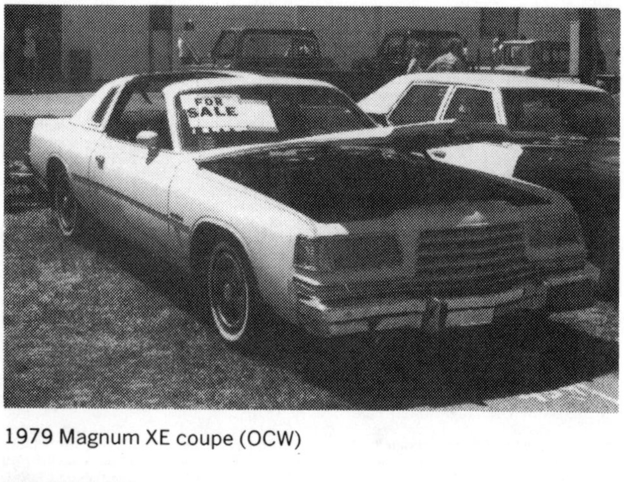

1979 Magnum XE coupe (OCW)

MAGNUM XE (V-8)

XS	22	2-dr. HT Cpe-6P	5709	3675	25,367

ST. REGIS (SIX/V-8)

EH	42	4-dr. Pill. HT-6P	6216/6455	3565/3640	34,434

FACTORY PRICE AND WEIGHT NOTE: Prices and weights to left of slash are for six-cylinder, to right for V-8 engine.

ENGINE DATA: BASE FOUR (Omni): Inline, overhead-cam four-cylinder. Cast iron block; aluminum head. Displacement: 104.7 cu. in. (1.7 liters). Bore & stroke: 3.13 x 3.40 in. Compression ratio: 8.2:1. Brake horsepower: 70 at 5200 R.P.M. Torque: 85 lbs.-ft. at 2800 R.P.M. Five main bearings. Solid valve lifters. Carburetor: 2Bbl. Holley 5220. VIN Code: A. BASE SIX (Aspen, Diplomat): Inline, overhead-valve six. Cast iron block and head. Displacement: 225 cu. in. (3.7 liters). Bore & stroke: 3.40 x 4.12 in. Compression ratio: 8.4:1. Brake horsepower: 100 at 3600 R.P.M. Torque: 165 lbs.-ft. at 1600 R.P.M. Four main bearings. Solid valve lifters. Carburetor: 1Bbl. Holley 1945. VIN Code: C. BASE SIX (St. Regis); OPTIONAL (Aspen, Diplomat): Same as 225 cu. in. six above, but with 2Bbl. Carter BBD carburetor Horsepower: 110 at 3600 R.P.M. Torque: 180 lbs.- ft. at 2000 R.P.M. VIN Code: D. BASE V-8 (Magnum XE); OPTIONAL (Aspen, Diplomat, St. Regis): 90-degree, overhead valve V-8. Cast iron block and head. Displacement: 318 cu. in. (5.2 liters). Bore & stroke: 3.91 x 3.31 in. Compression ratio: 8.5:1. Brake horsepower: 135 at 4000 R.P.M. Torque: 250 lbs.-ft. at 1600 R.P.M. Five main bearings. Hydraulic valve lifters. Carburetor: 2Bbl. Holley 2280 (R8448A). VIN Code: G. OPTIONAL V-8 (Diplomat, Magnum XE, St. Regis): 90-degree, overhead valve V-8. Cast iron block and head. Displacement: 360 cu. in. (5.9 liters). Bore & stroke: 4.00 x 3.58 in. Compression ratio: 8.4:1. Brake horsepower: 150 at 3600 R.P.M. Torque: 265 lbs.-ft. at 2400 R.P.M. Five main bearings. Hydraulic valve lifters. Carburetor: 2Bbl. Holley 2245. VIN Code: K. OPTIONAL V-8 (Aspen cpe, Diplomat, Magnum, St. Regis): Same as 360 cu. in. V-8 above, but with Carter TQ 4Bbl. carburetor C.R.: 8.0:1. Horsepower: 195 at 4000 R.P.M. Torque: 280 lbs.-ft. at 2400 R.P.M. VIN Code: L.

CHASSIS DATA: Wheelbase: (Omni) 99.2 in.; (024) 96.7 in.; (Aspen cpe) 108.7 in.; (Aspen sed/wag) 112.7 in.; (Diplomat) 112.7 in.; (Magnum) 114.9 in.; (St. Regis) 118.5 in. Overall length: (Omni) 164.8 in.; (024) 172.7 in.; (Aspen cpe) 197.2 in.; (Aspen sed/wag) 201.2 in.; (Diplo cpe) 204.1 in.; (Diplo sed) 206.1 in.; (Diplo wag) 202.8 in.; (Magnum) 215.8 in.; (St. R.) 220.2 in. Height: (Omni) 53.7 in.; (024) 51.4 in.; (Aspen cpe) 53.3 in.; (Aspen sed) 55.3 in.; (Aspen wag) 55.7 in.; (Diplo cpe) 53.0 in.; (Diplo sed) 55.3 in.; (Diplo wag) 55.7 in.; (Magnum) 53.1 in.; (St. R.) 54.5 in. Width: (Omni) 66.2 in.; (024) 66.0 in.; (Aspen) 72.8 in.; (Diplo cpe) 73.5 in.;. (Diplo sed/wag) 72.8 in.; (Magnum) 77.1 in.; (St. R.) 77.1 in. Front Tread: (Omni/024) 56.0 in.; (Aspen/Diplo) 60.0 in.; (Magnum/St. Regis) 61.9 in. Rear Tread: (Omni/024) 55.6 in.; (Aspen/Diplo) 58.5 in.; (Mag/St. R.) 62.0 in. Standard Tires: (Omni) P155/80R13 GBR WSW; (024) P165/75R13 GBR WSW; (Aspen) D78 x 14 exc. wag, ER78 x 14; (Diplo/Magnum) FR78 x 15 GBR BSW; (St. R.) P195/75R15 GBR BSW.

TECHNICAL: Transmission: Three-speed manual trans. (floor lever) standard on Aspen six. Gear ratios: (1st) 3.08:1; (2nd) 1.70:1; (3rd) 1.00:1; (Rev) 2.90:1. Four-speed manual (floor lever) standard on Omni: (1st) 3.45:1; (2nd) 1.94:1; (3rd) 1.29:1; (4th) 0.97:1; (Rev) 3.17:1. Overdrive4 manual gearbox standard on Diplomat, available on Aspen: (1st) 3.09:1; (2nd) 1.67:1; (3rd) 1.00:1; (4th) 0.71:1; (Rev) 3.00:1. TorqueFlite three-speed automatic standard on other models, optional on all. Gear ratios: (1st) 2.45:1; (2nd) 1.45:1; (3rd) 1.00:1; (Rev) 2.22:1. Floor lever available for all. Omni TorqueFlite gear ratios: (1st) 2.47:1; (2nd) 1.47:1; (3rd) 1.00:1; (Rev) 2.10:1. Standard final drive ratio: (Omni) 3.37:1 w/4spd, 3.48:1 w/auto.; (Aspen/Diplo six) 3.23:1; (Aspen V-8) 2.47:1 or 2.45:1; (Magnum) 2.71:1 except 2.45:1 w/V8360 or 3.21:1 w/4Bbl. V8360; (St. R. six) 2.94:1; (St. R. V-8) 2.45:1 exc. 3.2:1 w/4Bbl. V8360. Steering: (Omni) rack and pinion; (others) recirculating ball.

Suspension: (Omni) Iso-Strut independent coil front w/anti- sway bar, trailing arm independent coil rear w/integral anti- sway; (Aspen/Diplomat) isolated transverse front torsion bars and anti-sway bar, semi-elliptic rear leaf springs; (others) longitudinal front torsion bars w/anti-sway bar, semi- elliptic rear leaf springs. Brakes: Front-disc, rear drum. Ignition: Electronic. Body construction: Unibody. Fuel tank: (Omni) 13 gal.; (Aspen six) 18 gal.; (Aspen V-8/wag) 19.5 gal.; (Diplomat) 19.5 gal.; (Magnum/St. R.) 21 gal.

DRIVETRAIN OPTIONS: Engines: 225 cu. in., 2Bbl. six: Aspen ($43); Diplo (NC). 318 cu. in., 2Bbl. V-8: Aspen ($216); Diplomat ($236); St. Regis ($239). 318 cu. in., 4Bbl. V-8 (Calif.): Aspen ($271); Diplo ($296); Mag ($61); St. R. ($300). 360 cu. in., 2Bbl. V-8: Diplo ($426); Mag ($191); St. R. ($432). 360 cu. in., 4Bbl. V-8 (Calif.): Diplo ($487); Mag ($251); St. R. ($493). H.D. 360 cu. in., 4Bbl. V-8: Aspen ($575-$600); Diplo ($655); Magnum ($420); St. R. ($664). Transmission/Differential: Four-speed overdrive manual trans. w/floor lever: Aspen six ($149). TorqueFlite auto. trans.: Omni/Aspen ($319); Diplo ($193). Sure Grip differential: Aspen ($61); Diplo/Mag/St. R. ($67). Optional axle ratio: Omni/Aspen ($18); others ($20). Brakes and Steering: Power front disc brakes: Omni/Aspen ($72). Power steering: Omni/Aspen ($156). Suspension: H.D. susp.: Omni 4dr., Aspen ($25); Diplo/Mag/St. R. ($28). Sport susp.: 024 ($41). H.D. shock absorbers: Mag/St. R. ($8). Other: Long-life battery: Omni ($20); others ($32-$35). H.D. trailer assist pkg.: Aspen sed/wag ($157); Diplo ($170); Mag ($150); St. R. ($152). California emission system ($79-$88).

OMNI/024 CONVENIENCE/APPEARANCE OPTIONS: Option Packages: Sport pkg.: 024 ($278-$340). Rallye equipment pkg.: 024 ($177-$352). Sport/Classic two-tone paint pkg.: 4dr. ($114-$164). Custom exterior pkg.: 4dr. ($74). Premium exterior pkg. ($78-$199). Custom interior pkg.: 4dr. ($79-$101). Premium interior pkg. ($146-$270). Premium woodgrain pkg.: 4dr. ($290-$507). Popular equipment group ($267-$279). Light pkg. ($31-$46). Comfort/Convenience: Air cond. ($507). Tinted glass ($61). Tinted windshield ($43). Luxury steering wheel: 4dr. ($18). Rallye instrument cluster: 024 ($76). Electric clock w/trip odometer ($28). Rear wiper/washer: 4dr. ($62). Locking gas cap ($7). Locking glovebox ($5). Horns and Mirrors: Dual horns ($9). Remote left mirror: 024 ($17). Dual remote mirrors: 4dr. ($32-$49). Dual sport remote mirrors: 024 ($61). Day/night mirror ($11). Entertainment: AM/FM radio: 4dr. ($73). AM/FM stereo radio ($67-$141). Rear speaker: 024 ($24). Exterior Trim: Removable glass sunroof ($176). Rear spoiler: 024 ($53). Flip-out quarter windows: 024 ($54). Moldings, 4dr.: belt ($16); drip ($18); sill ($20); upper door frame ($31); wheel lip ($28). Black vinyl bodyside molding: 024 ($41). Door edge protectors ($12-$20). Bumper guards: 4dr. ($43). Bumper rub strips: 024 ($34). Multi-color tape stripe: 4dr. ($82). Luggage rack ($86). Undercoating ($33). Interior: Console: storage ($22); shift lever ($32). Cloth/vinyl bucket seats: 024 ($22-$52). Tonneau cover: 024 ($44). Cargo area dress-up ($43). Color-keyed floor mats ($27). Color-keyed seatbelts ($31). Wheels and Tires: Wheel trim rings: 4dr. ($41). Deluxe wheel covers (NC). Cast aluminum wheels ($165-$246). Rallye wheels ($39-$80). Bright rallye hubs ($39). 165/75R13 WSW ($17). 165/75R13 SBR WSW ($34-$51). 175/75R13 WSW ($51-$68). 185/70R13 OWL ($136). Conventional spare tire ($13-$25).

ASPEN CONVENIENCE/APPEARANCE OPTIONS: Option Packages: R/T pkg.: cpe ($651). Sport pkg.: cpe ($630). Handling/performance pkg.: cpe ($218). Special Edition wagon woodgrain group ($232). Special Edition interior pkg. ($275-$499). Special Edition exterior pkg. ($100-$165). Sunrise pkg.: cpe ($30-$60). Sunrise decor pkg.: cpe ($90). Custom exterior pkg. ($75-$89). Custom interior pkg. ($162-$196). Basic group ($626-$712). Two-tone paint pkg. ($142). Two-tone decor pkg. ($65-$96). Light pkg. ($46). Deluxe insulation pkg. ($39-$50). Protection group ($30-$38). Comfort/Convenience: Air cond. ($507). Rear defogger, blower- type ($52); electric ($90). Automatic speed control ($98). Power seat ($153). Power windows ($120-$169). Power door locks ($76-$106). Power liftgate release: wag ($23). Tinted windshield ($43); all windows ($61). Luxury steering wheel ($31). Tuff steering wheel ($8-$39). Tilt steering wheel ($32-$71). Digital clock ($51). Inside hood release ($13). Intermitent wipers ($36). Lighter ($7). Locking gas cap ($7). Locking glovebox ($5).

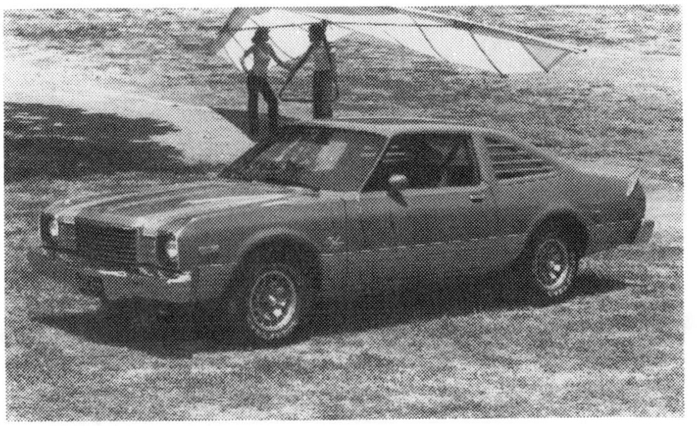

1979 Aspen R/T coupe (D)

Horns and Mirrors: Dual horns ($9). Remote left mirror ($17). Dual remote mirrors ($32-$49). Dual remote sport mirrors ($44-$61). Day/night mirror ($11). Entertainment: AM radio ($79); w/8track player ($152-$231); w/CB ($262-$342). AM/FM radio ($73-$153). AM/FM stereo radio ($141-$220); w/8track player ($235-$314); w/CB ($403-$482). Rear speaker ($24). Exterior: T-Bar roof: cpe ($600). Full vinyl roof: sed ($95). Halo vinyl roof: cpe ($95-$111). Landau vinyl roof: cpe ($174). Vinyl bodyside moldings ($41). Belt moldings ($16). Door edge protectors ($12-$20). Upper door frame moldings: sed/wag ($34). Wheel lip moldings ($22). Hood strobe stripe: cpe ($42). Bumper guards ($43); rub strips ($34). Rear air deflector: wag ($28). Luggage rack: wag ($86). Undercoating ($23-$33). Interior: Console: cpe/wag ($55-$95). Vinyl bench seat: sed ($30). Vinyl bucket seats ($107). Center cushion w/armrest: cpe ($39). Rear armrest ($12). Color-keyed mats ($23). Color- keyed seatbelts ($18). Cargo area carpets and stowage bin: wag ($53). Pedal dress-up ($9). Trunk dress-up ($43). Wheels and Tires: Cast aluminum wheels ($144-$280). Styled wheels ($94-$136). Deluxe wheel covers ($41). Premium wheel covers ($37-$79). Wire wheel covers ($94-$136). D78 x 14 WSW ($45). DR78 x 14 BSW ($56). DR78 x 14 WSW ($56-$101). ER78 x 14 BSW ($75). ER78 x 14 WSW ($45-$119). FR70 x 14 OWL ($129- $248). FR78 x 14 WSW ($72-$192). Conventional spare tire (NC).

DIPLOMAT CONVENIENCE/APPEARANCE OPTIONS: Option Packages: Sport appearance pkg. ($110-$219). Basic group ($1130-$1385). Deluxe insulation pkg. ($10-$93). Light pkg. ($72-$84). Comfort/Convenience: Air conditioning ($584). Rear defroster, electric ($98). Automatic speed control ($107). Power seat ($167). Power windows ($137-$194). Power door locks ($89- $124). Power decklid/tailgate release ($26). Tinted glass ($73). Luxury steering wheel ($20). Leather-covered steering wheel ($40-$60). Tilt steering wheel ($58-$77). Digital clock ($56). Deluxe wiper/washer ($47). Locking gas cap ($7). Lighting, Horns and Mirrors: Halogen headlamps ($26). Cornering lights ($51). Dual horns: base ($9). Remote driver's mirror: base/Salon ($19). Remote passenger mirror: Medallion ($35). Dual remote-control mirrors: base/Salon ($35-$54). Dual remote sport mirrors ($48-$67). Lighted vanity mirror ($50). Day/night mirror: base ($12). Entertainment: AM radio ($87); w/CB ($287-$373). AM/FM radio ($80-$167). AM/FM stereo ($154-$240); w/ 8track tape player ($256-$343); w/CB ($440-$527). Search-tune AM/FM stereo ($281-$368). Rear speaker ($26). Power antenna ($48). Exterior: T-Bar roof: cpe ($675). Power glass sunroof ($827). Full vinyl roof: base sed ($165). Landau vinyl roof: cpe ($148). Vinyl bodyside moldings ($45). Front bumper guards ($24). Bumper rub strips ($37). Hood tape stripe: Medallion ($24). Door edge protectors ($13-$22). Air deflector: wag ($30). Luggage rack: wag ($94). Undercoating ($25-$36). Interior: Vinyl bench seat: cpe/sed ($50-$67). Cloth 60/40 seat: wag ($175). Leather 60/40 seat: wag ($430); Medallion ($283). Cloth/vinyl bucket seats: Salon ($110). Color-keyed floor mats ($25). Color-keyed seatbelts ($20). Pedal dress-up ($10). Wheels/Tires: Deluxe wheel covers: base ($45). Premium wheel covers: base ($45-$90). Wire wheel covers ($111-$300). Forged aluminum wheels ($116-$305). FR78 x 15 GBR WSW ($50). FR78 x 15 SBR WSW ($60-$110). Conventional spare (NC).

MAGNUM XE CONVENIENCE/APPEARANCE OPTIONS: Option Packages: Gran Touring pkg. ($528-$601). Basic group ($1018-$1054). Two-tone paint pkg. ($203-$221). Roadability pkg. ($29). Light pkg. ($29). Comfort/Convenience: Air cond. ($584); auto-temp ($628) exc. ($44) w/option pkg. Rear defroster, electric ($98). Automatic speed control ($107). Tinted windshield ($47); all windows ($73). Power seat ($167). Power windows ($137). Power door locks ($89). Power decklid release ($26). Luxury steering wheel ($20). Leather-covered steering wheel ($60). Tilt steering wheel ($77). Tachometer ($73). Digital clock ($56). Locking gas cap ($7) Deluxe wipers ($40). Lighting and Mirrors: Halogen headlamps ($26). Left remote mirror ($19). Dual remote mirrors ($35-$54). Dual sport remote mirrors ($48-$67). Lighted vanity mirror ($50). Entertainment: AM radio ($87); w/8track player ($166-$252); w/CB ($287-$373). AM/FM radio ($80-$167). AM/FM stereo radio ($154-$240); w/8track ($256-$343); w/CB ($440-$527). Search- tune AM/FM stereo ($281-$368). Rear speaker ($26). Power antenna ($48). Exterior: T-Bar roof ($675). Power sunroof ($546). Landau vinyl roof ($132). Fender-mount turn signals ($16). Vinyl bodyside moldings ($45). Wheel lip flares ($102). Door edge protectors ($13). Bumper rub strips ($37). Hood/deck or bodyside stripes ($47). Wheel lip tape stripes ($24). Undercoating ($36). Interior: Console ($60-$103). Cloth/vinyl 60/40 bench seat ($226). Leather bucket seats ($363). Center front cushion ($43). Color-keyed mats ($25). Color-keyed seatbelts ($20). Trunk dress-up ($47). Pedal dress-up ($10). Wheels and Tires: Aluminum-fascia wheels ($93-$164). Aluminum wheels w/trim rings ($142-$213). Forged aluminum wheels ($189-$260). Premier wheel covers ($45). FR78 x 15 WSW ($50). GR78 x 15 BSW ($22). GR78 x 15 WSW ($22-$72). HR78 x 15 SBR WSW ($87-$160). GR60 x 15 RWL ($230-$302). Conventional spare tire (NC).

ST. REGIS CONVENIENCE/APPEARANCE OPTIONS: Option Packages: Basic group ($1176). Two-tone paint pkg. ($160). Open road handling pkg. ($216). Light pkg. ($96). Comfort/Convenience: Air cond. ($628); auto-temp ($673) exc. ($45) w/option pkg. Rear defroster, electric ($107). Auto. speed control ($112). Power windows ($212). Power door locks ($126). Power seat ($170). Power decklid release ($27-$35). Luxury steering wheel ($20). Leather-covered steering wheel ($60). Tilt steering wheel ($79). Digital clock ($57). Deluxe wipers ($41). Locking gas cap ($9). Lighting and Mirrors: Halogen headlamps ($27). Cornering lights ($51). Remote driver's mirror ($20). Dual chrome remote mirrors ($24-$44). Lighted vanity mirror ($50). Entertainment: AM radio ($106); w/CB ($290-$396). AM/FM radio ($76-$182). AM/FM stereo ($147-$253); w/8track tape player ($254-$360); w/CB ($437-$543). Search-tune AM/FM stereo ($266-$372). Rear speaker ($28). Power antenna ($50). Exterior: Power glass sunroof ($993). Full vinyl roof ($152). Vinyl bodyside molding ($51). Door edge protectors ($23). Bodyside/hood tape stripes ($72). Bumper guards ($60). Undercoating ($30). Interior: Vinyl 60/40 bench seat ($33). Color-keyed mats ($26). Color-keyed seatbelts ($21). Pedal dress-up ($10). Trunk dress-up ($67). Litter container ($8). Wheels and Tires: Premier wheel covers ($54). Wire wheel covers ($259). Aluminum wheels ($175). Aluminum wheels w/trim rings ($216). P195/75R15 WSW ($51). P205/75R15 BSW ($23). P205/75R15 WSW ($23-$134). P225/70R15 WSW ($24-$75). Conventional spare tire (NC).

HISTORY: Introduced: October 5, 1978. Model year production: Chrysler reported a total of 351,177 passenger cars shipped. Total North American production for the U.S. market of 336,979 units (not incl. 25,451 Sportsman vans) included 115,733 four-cylinder, 105,520 six-cylinder, and 115,726 V-8s. Calendar year production: 366,387 (not incl. 17,067 Sportsman vans). Calendar year sales by U.S. dealers: 342,925 (plus 24,917 Sportsman vans). Model year sales by U.S. dealers: 371,003 (not incl. 60,646 Colts, 16,920 Challengers and 32,070 Sportsman vans).

Historical Footnotes: Model year sales slipped by more than 5 percent for 1979, with big cars faring the worst. Sales of the new downsized St. Regis fell well below expectations. Omni, on the other hand, found quite a few buyers: 120,218 this year. But a shortage of engines kept Dodge from meeting the rising demand for small cars. Production for model year 1979 dropped even more. For the first time, though, Dodge outsold Plymouth for the model year (including imports). Many rebates were offered during this period (except on Omni/Horizon). On the import front, a new Colt two-door hatchback was added. Colt/Challenger sales amounted to an impressive 16 percent of Dodge's total. After this year, captive imports (Colt/Challenger) could no longer be counted in the figures to meet CAFE standards. Dodge Division, like the parent Chrysler Corporation, faced enormous financial problems that would eventually require federal loan guarantees. Lee Iacocca, the new corporate chairman, pushed for a sharper distinction between Dodge and the Chrysler-Plymouth Divison, as had been the case years before.

1980 DODGE

One new nameplate joined the lineup for 1980: the two- door Mirada, a replacement for the specialty Magnum XE. Otherwise, this was a year mainly of waiting for the new front-drive Aries, which would replace the rear-drive Aspen for 1981.

OMNI/024 — SERIES ZL — FOUR — Both the four-door hatchback sedan and two-door 024 coupe changed little in appearance this year. The sedan's grille consisted of six wide holes, each divided by another horizontal strip, making a 5 x 13 pattern of thin, wide holes. In the grille's center was a rectangular crest badge. Wraparound park/signal lamps had amber lenses. 'Dodge' letters stood above the left headlamp; 'Omni' lettering ahead of doors and on the hatch. Taillamps wrapped around slightly. Their tri-section design had two red segments, with the bottom split between clear and amber. Individually adjustable bucket seats were standard on the four-door, in cashmere or black. Powerplant was still the VW-built 1.6-liter four. Standard equipment included tinted glass, electric rear defroster, and trip odometer. New options: intermittent wipers and automatic speed control. Halogen headlamps also were available. Though they looked drastically different, the sport coupe was mechanically identical to the sedan. As before, the Omni sedan came in base form, or could be ordered with optional Custom or Premium interior and exterior packages, or a Premium Woodgrain Exterior package. 024 could have a Premium Exterior package with bright and black rub strips, bodyside and rear tape stripes, and whitewalls; or a Sport Appearance package with black molding accents and blackout lower body paint, '024' decals, black mirrors, rear spoiler, Rallye wheels and whitewalls. Body colors this year were: Graphic Blue, Baron Red, Natural Suede Tan, Light Cashmere, Nightwatch Blue, Formal Black, Bright Yellow, and Spinnaker White; plus metallic Mocha Brown, Frost Blue, Teal Tropic Green, Crimson Red, and Burnished Silver. Four two-tones were available on the sedan, three on the coupe, and four on the coupe with Sport package. A new De Tomaso sport coupe package came in graphic red or bright yellow body color with black accents, highlighted by a front air dam, wheel flares, vertically-louvered rear quarter windows, rear spoiler, cast aluminum wheels, and bright brushed transverse roof band. 'De Tomaso' badges were easy to spot on bodyside, spoiler, and windshield top. Inside De Tomaso were black bucket seats, a Rallye gauge cluster, leather-wrapped sport steering wheel and shift knob, plus 'De Tomaso' identificaton on front floor mats and a special dash plaque. Apart from a special sport suspension and wider (P185/70R13) Aramid-belted tires, though, De Tomaso's chassis was the same as the standard coupe. A total of 1,333 Omni coupes came with the De Tomaso package.

ASPEN — SERIES N — SIX/V-8 — This would be Aspen's final year, as a new front-drive Dodge compact was soon to arrive. Aspen's new full-width grille now had only three horizontal didider elements, which made it look like four separate sections (one above the other). Single rectangular headlamps were new. Basic lineup was the same as before: two-door coupe, four-door sedan, and four-door wagon. In addition, a new Special series (coupe and sedan only) was offered, sporting minimal chrome trim but with automatic transmission, power steering and wheel lip moldings. Otherwise, standard equipment was similar to 1979. Base engine was again the 225 cu. in. Slant Six, with 318 cu. in. V-8 optional. A Sport Wagon option package, introduced in 1979, included an air dam, wheel arch flares, bucket seats, tape stripes, and styled wheels. The R/T coupe package, installed on only 285 Aspens, had a blackout front end treatment, black drip moldings, new tape-stripe graphics, and painted wheels. Aspen's Sunrise package came with plaid bucket seats, deluxe wheel covers, and new body/decklid tape stripes. A total of 11,542 Aspens had the Premier package.

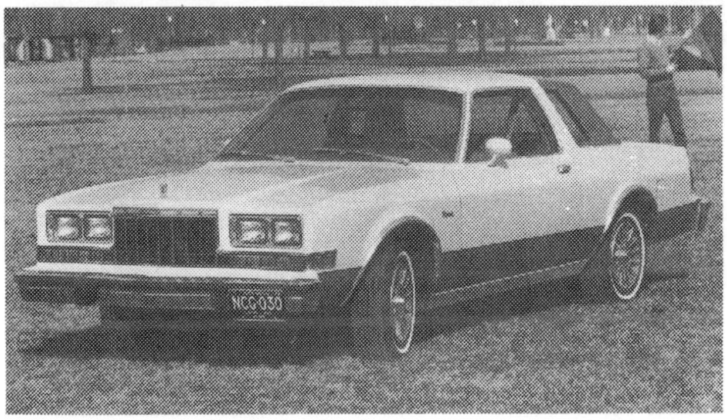

1980 Diplomat Sport Coupe (D)

DIPLOMAT — SERIES G — SIX/V-8 — Though similar in overall apperance to the 1979 version, Diplomat enjoyed a restyle this year, with squared-off fenders and a formal-look roofline. Models included a two- door coupe, four-door sedan and four-door wagon, in base and Salon dress. Coupes and sedans also came in top-line

Medallion form. Added a bit later was a new Special Sport Coupe. Available only with Slant Six engine, it had two-tone paint, wheel lip moldings, dual sport remote mirrors, belt moldings, luxury steering wheel, and deluxe wheel covers. The lowest-priced wagon lacked woodgrain side paneling. Two-door models now rode a shorter (108.7 in.) wheelbase; sedans and wagons measured 112.7 inches again. Wheelbases, in fact, were identical to Aspen's. Diplomat's new grille showed a fine-mesh pattern, separated into eight side-by-side vertical sections with bright framing around each one. Similarly-patterned, smaller sections extended outward below the quad rectangular headlamps, to wrap around the front fenders. Those smaller sections held segmented parking lamps at the front and sectioned marker lenses at the side. As before, the hood was creased on each side. Fenderline creases were sharper. 'Diplomat' lettering sat on front fenders, ahead of the door. Full-width taillamps wrapped around the quarter panels and held backup lenses toward the center of the car. The license plate mounted in a recessed housing between the taillamps. The revised roofline was most noticeable in the coupe body, which had a more horizontal look and narrow opera windows to the rear of fairly wide 'B' pillars. Standard equipment included cloth/vinyl bench seating, 225 cu. in. six-cylinder engine, power brakes and steering, TorqueFlite, multi-function steering column switch, trip odometer, temp/fuel/alternator gauges, inside hood release, whitewall radial tires, and protective bumper rub strips. Also standard: a bright hood ornament; bright windshield, back window, quarter window and roof drip moldings; tinted quarter-window (coupe) glass; bright driver's mirror; front bumper guards and hubcaps. Diplomat Salon added bright belt, sill, center pillar and wheel opening moldings, plus dual horns. Medallion came with bodyside and deck accent stripes, remote driver's mirror, and padded landau or full vinyl roof, plus crushed velour 60/40 seating. Body colors were: Baron Red, Light Cashmere, Eggshell White, Nightwatch Blue, Black, Light Heather Gray, and Natural Suede Tan; plus metallic Burnished Silver, Mocha Brown, Light Heather Gray, Frost Blue, Teal Frost, Teal Tropic Green and Crimson Red. New two-tone paint combinations were available. A new 'S' package for the Salon coupe cost $549 to $569. It included dual remote sport mirrors, bold body stripes, high-back cloth bucket seats, luxury steering wheel, and brushed-aluminum finish instrument cluster cover, door moldings and glovebox door insert. Also included: halogen headlamps and P205/75R15 steel-belted radial whitewall tires on color-keyed wheels. A total of 2,188 Diplomats had the S package. Salon coupes could also have a console for $109.

MIRADA — SERIES X — SIX/V-8 — New this year, Mirada served as replacement for the departed Magnum XE coupe. Its side view showed off what was described as a "striking roof motif" and aerodynamic profile (the latter a phrase that would soon come to describe just about any vehicle that wasn't squarely upright). Mirada was over 6 inches shorter than Magnum, and some 400 pounds lighter. And whereas Magnum had been V-8 powered, Mirada carried a base Slant Six; a 318 cu. in. V-8 was optional. As before, this was Dodge's version of the Chrysler Cordoba, which was also reworked this year. Mirada featured a soft front fascia with sloping, slat- style grille, single rectangular headlamps, and simulated front fender louvers. The grille consisted of four wide slots separated by five bright horizontal strips, each of which bent back at the ends to meet the angled front panel. A horizontal lip sat ahead of each headlamp's base. On front fenders were small horizontal side marker lenses, just ahead of the wheel opening and aligned with the bumper strip. A set of four angled louvers stood ahead of the door. 'Mirada' lettering was below the bodyside crease line. A 'CMX' nameplate (if applicable) sat below that lettering. Bodysides displayed sculptured-look creases near the top and bottom, as well as down the middle. Miradas had sharp-cornered opera windows at the far rear, plus a grooved bright band alongside the smaller forward quarter windows. Each rectangular taillamp had three horizontal trim strips, with backup lenses toward the center of the car. Though large, the taillamps didn't extend either to quarter panel tips or the license plate opening. The license plate housing was recessed, below the decklid (which held 'Mirada' lettering). Inside was a brushed-metal instrument panel that held a set of gauges. Standard equipment included the 225 cu. in. Slant Six, TorqueFlite, power steering and brakes, multi-function steering column lever, high-back vinyl bucket seats, AM radio, lighter, tinted glass, and dual horns. Also standard: chrome driver's side mirror, two-spoke padded steering wheel with brushed aluminum applique, compact spare tire, trip odometer, premier wheel covers, P195/75R15 GBR WSW tires, and two-speed wiper/washers. Body colors were: Light Heather Gray, Nightwatch Blue, Baron Red, Natural Suede Tan, Eggshell White, Black and Light Cashmere, plus metallic Light Heather Gray, Frost Blue, Crimson Red, Mocha Brown, and Burnished Silver. Two models were offered: standard and 'S' version, as well as a CMX package. A high-performance 360 cu. in. V-8 with dual exhausts was optional with that CMX package, which also included an up-and-over roof accent molding, color-keyed bumper strips with bright insert, front fender nameplates, dual remote mirrors, unique bodyside tape stripes, forged aluminum ten-spoke wheels, and larger (P205) whitewall tires. CMX came only in Baron Red, Nightwatch Blue, Frost Blue, or Burnished Silver. Options also included a cabriolet simulated-convertible roof, AM/FM stereo with cassette player, automatic speed control, intermittent wipers, illuminated entry system, forged aluminum wheels, and turbine wheel covers. A total of 5,384 Miradas had the CMX package, while 936 had the convertible-style roof (and only 7 of those were on the XS22 model).

1980 St. Regis sedan (D)

ST. REGIS — SERIES EH — SIX/V-8 — Little change was evident in Dodge's "regular size" four-door, except for side trim and striping. Full-width taillamps stretched from the license plate to wrap around quarter panels, each lens divided into a crosshatch pattern. Sculptured lines included notable twin bodyside creases that stretched full length. Again, St. Regis had transparent headlamp covers and a distinctive grille made up of small rectangles. Standard interior held a split-back bench seat with folding center armrest of Verdi II cloth/vinyl (or optional Oxford all-vinyl). 60/40 seating was also available. Standard equipment included the 225 cu. in. Slant Six, power brakes and steering, three-speed TorqueFlite, tinted glass, two-speed wiper/washers, two-spoke steering wheel with woodgrain trim, flag-type mirrors, dual horns, lighter, bumper rub strips, and temp/alternator/fuel gauges. Also available: both the 318 and 360 cu. in. V-8 engines, as well as an illuminated entry system. St. Regis had a new high- strength steel back bumper. A new Touring Edition was availble, priced at $1677 and up. The package included a padded full vinyl roof with special medallion inset into the rear post, a formal backlight, unique body pinstriping, cornering lamps, dual remote chrome mirrors, and bright rear sill extensions. Wide whitewall SBR tires rode

forged aluminum ten-spoke wheels, color-keyed in red or gold to match the interior. Inside was red or cashmere 60/40 leather seating, plus a leather-wrapped tilt steering wheel, power windows, and door courtesy lights. The instrument cluster cover held a Featherwood woodgrain- textured applique. A total of 438 St. Regis models had the Touring Edition package, while 222 had the aSpecial Promotional Package (RPO Code A84).

I.D. DATA: Dodge's 13-symbol Vehicle Identification Number (VIN) was on the upper left corner of the instrument panel, visible through the windshield. Symbol one indicates car line: 'Z' Omni/024; 'N' Aspen; 'G' Diplomat; 'X' Mirada; 'E' St. Regis. Symbol two is series (price class): 'E' economy; 'L' low; 'M' medium; 'H' high; 'P' premium; 'S' special. Symbols 3-4 show body type: '22' 2-dr. special coupe or 'B' pillared hardtop; '24' 2-dr. hatchback; '29' 2-dr. coupe; '41' 4-dr. sedan; '42' 4-dr. 'B' pillared hardtop; '44' 4-dr. hatchback; '45' two-seat station wagon. Symbol five is the engine code: 'A' L4105; 'C' L6225 1Bbl.; 'G' V8318 2Bbl.; 'K' V8360 2Bbl.; 'L' V8360 4Bbl. Symbol six is the model year code: 'A' 1980. Symbol seven indicates assembly plant: 'A' Lynch Road; 'B' Hamtramck, MI; 'D' Belvidere, IL; 'F' Newark, DE; 'G' St. Louis; 'R' Windsor, Ontario. The final six digits make up the sequential serial number, starting with 100001. Engine number coding and locations are similar to 1978-79.

OMNI (FOUR)

Model Number	Body/Style Number	Body Type & Seating	Factory Price	Shipping Weight	Production Total
ZL	44	4-dr. Hatch-4P	4925	2095	67,279

OMNI 024 (FOUR)

ZL	24	2-dr. Hatch 22-4P	5271	2135	51,731

ASPEN (SIX/V-8)

NL	29	2-dr. Cpe-5P	4742/4953	3110/3260	9,454
NL	41	4-dr. Sedan-6P	4859/5070	3165/3320	20,938
NL	45	4-dr. Sta Wag-6P	5101/5312	3340/3480	12,388

ASPEN SPECIAL (SIX)

NE	29	2-dr. Cpe-5P	4977	3155	9,684
NE	41	4-dr. Sedan-6P	4994	3210	14,854

DIPLOMAT (SIX/V-8)

GM	22	2-dr. Cpe-6P	5681/5911	3220/3300	4,213
GM	41	4-dr. Sedan-6P	5832/6062	3300/3385	5,671
GM	45	4-dr. Sta Wag-6P	5971/6201	3455/3535	1,569

DIPLOMAT SPECIAL SPORT (SIX)

GL	22	2-dr. Cpe-6P	5995	3130	2,597

DIPLOMAT SALON (SIX/V-8)

GH	22	2-dr. Cpe-6P	5997/6227	3230/3310	5,778
GH	41	4-dr. Sedan-6P	6119/6349	3325/3405	4,251
GH	45	4-dr. Sta Wag-6P	6661/6891	3485/3565	2,104

DIPLOMAT MEDALLION (SIX/V-8)

GP	22	2-dr. Cpe-6P	6551/6781	3285/3360	2,103
GP	41	4-dr. Sedan-6P	6698/6928	3400/3485	2,086

MIRADA (SIX/V-8)

XH	22	2-dr. HT Cpe-6P	6364/6594	3280/3360	27,165

MIRADA 'S' (SIX/V-8)

XS	22	2-dr. HT Cpe-6P	6645/6740	3280/3375	1,468

ST. REGIS (SIX/V-8)

EH	42	4-dr. Pill. HT-6P	6724/6957	3565/3650	14,010

FACTORY PRICE AND WEIGHT NOTE: Prices and weights to left of slash are for six-cylinder, to right for V-8 engine. Prices for 318 cu. in. V-8 engines dropped during the model year, to under $100.

ENGINE DATA: BASE FOUR (Omni): Inline, overhead-cam four-cylinder. Cast iron block; aluminum head. Displacement: 104.7 cu. in. (1.7 liters). Bore & stroke: 3.13 x 3.40 in. Compression ratio: 8.2:1. Brake horsepower: 65 at 5200 R.P.M. Torque: 85 lbs.-ft. at 2400 R.P.M. Five main bearings. Solid valve lifters. Carburetor: 2Bbl. Holley 5220. VIN Code: A. **BASE SIX** (Aspen, Diplomat, Mirada, St. Regis): Inline, overhead-valve six. Cast iron block and head. Displacement: 225 cu. in. (3.7 liters).

Bore & stroke: 3.40 x 4.12 in. Compression ratio: 8.4:1. Brake horsepower: 90 at 3600 R.P.M. Torque: 160 lbs.-ft. at 1600 R.P.M. Four main bearings. Solid valve lifters. Carburetor: 1Bbl. Holley 1945. VIN Code: C. OPTIONAL V-8 (Aspen, Diplomat, Mirada, St. Regis): 90-degree, overhead valve V-8. Cast iron block and head. Displacement: 318 cu. in. (5.2 liters). Bore & stroke: 3.91 x 3.31 in. Compression ratio: 8.5:1. Brake horsepower: 120 at 3600 R.P.M. Torque: 245 lbs.-ft. at 1600 R.P.M. Five main bearings. Hydraulic valve lifters. Carburetor: 2Bbl. Carter BBD. VIN Code: G. OPTIONAL V-8 (St. Regis): 90-degree, overhead valve V-8. Cast iron block and head. Displacement: 360 cu. in. (5.9 liters). Bore & stroke: 4.00 x 3.58 in. Compression ratio: 8.4:1. Brake horsepower: 150 at 3600 R.P.M. Torque: 265 lbs.-ft. at 2400 R.P.M. Five main bearings. Hydraulic valve lifters. Carburetor: 2Bbl. Carter BBD. VIN Code: K. OPTIONAL V-8 (Mirada): Same as 360 cu. in. V-8 above, but with Carter TQ 4Bbl. carburetor C.R.: 8.0:1. Horsepower: 185 at 4000 R.P.M. Torque: 275 lbs.-ft. at 2000 R.P.M. VIN Code: L.

CHASSIS DATA: Wheelbase: (Omni) 99.2 in.; (024) 96.7 in.; (Aspen/Diplomat cpe) 108.7 in.; (Aspen/Diplo sed/wag) 112.7 in.; (Mirada) 112.7 in.; (St. Regis) 118.5 in. Overall length: (Omni) 164.8 in.; (024) 173.3 in.; (Aspen cpe) 200.3 in.; (Aspen sed/wag) 204.3 in.; (Diplo cpe) 201.2 in.; (Diplo sed) 205.2 in.; (Diplo wag) 205.5 in.; (Mirada) 209.5 in.; (St. R.) 220.2 in. Height: (Omni) 53.5 in.; (024) 51.2 in.; (Aspen cpe) 53.6 in.; (Aspen sed) 55.3 in.; (Aspen wag) 55.5 in.; (Diplo cpe) 53.4 in.; (Diplo sed) 55.3 in.; (Diplo wag) 55.5 in.; (Mirada) 53.3 in.; (St. R.) 54.5 in. Width: (Omni) 65.8 in.; (024) 66.7 in.; (Aspen) 72.4 in.; (Diplo) 74.2 in.; (Mirada) 72.7 in.; (St. R.) 77.6 in. Front Tread: (Omni/024) 56.1 in.; (Aspen/Diplo/Mirada) 60.0 in.; (Magnum/St. Regis) 61.9 in. Rear Tread: (Omni/024) 55.6 in.; (Aspen/Diplo/Mirada) 59.5 in.; (St. R.) 62.0 in. Standard Tires: (Omni) P155/80R13 GBR WSW; (024) P175/75R13 GBR WSW; (Aspen) P195/75R14; (Diplo) P195/75R15 GBR BSW; (Mirada/St. R.) P195/75R15 GBR WSW.

TECHNICAL: Transmission: Three-speed manual trans. (floor lever) standard on Aspen six. Gear ratios: (1st) 3.08:1; (2nd) 1.70:1; (3rd) 1.00:1; (Rev) 2.90:1. Four-speed manual (floor lever) standard on Omni: (1st) 3.45:1; (2nd) 1.94:1; (3rd) 1.29:1; (4th) 0.97:1; (Rev) 3.17:1. Overdrive4 manual gearbox available on Aspen: (1st) 3.09:1; (2nd) 1.67:1; (3rd) 1.00:1; (4th) 0.71:1; (Rev) 3.00:1. TorqueFlite three-speed automatic standard on other models, optional on all. V-8 gear ratios: (1st) 2.45:1; (2nd) 1.45:1; (3rd) 1.00:1; (Rev) 2.22:1. Six-cylinder: (1st) 2.74:1; (2nd) 1.54:1; (3rd) 1.00:1; (Rev) 2.22:1. Omni TorqueFlite gear ratios: (1st) 2.47:1; (2nd) 1.47:1; (3rd) 1.00:1; (Rev) 2.10:1. Standard final drive ratio: (Omni) 3.37:1 w/4spd, 3.48:1 w/auto.; (Aspen six) 3.23:1 w/manual, 2.76:1 or 2.71:1 w/auto.; (Aspen Special) 2.76:1; (Aspen V-8) 2.47:1 exc. wag, 2.45:1; (Diplo six) 2.76:1; (Diplo wag) 2.94:1; (Diplo V-8) 2.47:1 exc. wag, 2.45:1; (Mirada six) 2.76:1; (Mirada V-8) 2.47:1; (Mirada V8360) 2.94:1; (St. R. six) 2.94:1; (St. R. V-8) 2.45:1. Steering: (Omni) rack and pinion; (others) recirculating ball. Susp.: (Omni) MacPherson strut w/anti-sway bar, trailing arm independent coil rear w/integral anti-sway; (Aspen/Diplomat/Mirada) transverse front torsion bars and anti-sway bar, semi-elliptic rear leaf springs; (St. Regis) longitudinal front torsion bars w/anti- sway bar, semi-elliptic rear leaf springs. Brakes: Front disc, rear drum. Ignition: Electronic. Body construction: Unibody. Fuel tank: (Omni) 13 gal.; (Aspen) 18 gal.; (Aspen wag) 19.5 gal.; (Diplomat/Mirada) 18 gal.; (St. Regis) 21 gal.

DRIVETRAIN OPTIONS: Engines: 318 cu. in., 2Bbl. V-8: Aspen ($211); Diplomat/Mirada ($230); St. Regis ($233). 318 cu. in., 4Bbl. V-8 (Calif.): Aspen ($266); Diplo/Mirada ($291); St. R. ($295). 360 cu. in., 2Bbl. V-8: St. R. ($457). 360 cu. in., 4Bbl. V-8: Mirada CMX ($545). Transmission/Differential: Four-speed overdrive manual trans. w/floor lever: Aspen six ($153). TorqueFlite auto. trans.: Omni/Aspen ($340). Sure Grip differential: Aspen ($63); Diplo ($71); Mirada ($72); St. R. ($77). Brakes and Steering: Power front disc brakes: Omni/Aspen ($77). Power steering: Omni ($161); Aspen ($166). Suspension: H.D. susp.: Omni 4dr., Aspen ($26); Diplo/Mirada ($28); St. R. ($30). Sport susp.: 024 ($43). H.D. shock absorbers: Mirada/St. R. ($8). Other: Long-life battery: Omni ($21); others ($33-$36). H.D. trailer assist pkg.: St. R. ($258). Max. cooling: Aspen ($34- $58); Diplo/Mirada ($37-$63); St. R. ($77-$104). California emission system ($254).

OMNI/024 CONVENIENCE/APPEARANCE OPTIONS: Option Packages: De Tomaso pkg.: 024 ($1484-$1575). Sport pkg.: 024 ($340-$431). Sport/Classic two-tone paint pkg. ($131-$137). Custom exterior pkg.: 4dr. ($101). Premium exterior pkg. ($126-$207). Custom interior pkg. ($89-$112). Premium interior pkg. ($239-$355). Premium woodgrain pkg.: 4dr. ($300-$344). Popular equipment group ($267-$273). Comfort/Convenience: Air cond. ($541). Automatic speed control ($101). Power liftgate release: 024 ($24). Luxury steering wheel: 4dr. ($18). Sport steering wheel ($18-$40). Rallye instrument cluster w/tachometer ($65). Intermittent wipers ($38). Rear wiper/washer: 4dr. ($63). Lighter ($8). Locking gas cap ($7). Locking glovebox: 4dr. ($5). Lighting, Horns and Mirrors: Halogen headlamps ($37). Dual horns ($9). Remote left mirror: 4dr. ($19). Dual remote mirrors: 4dr. ($38-$57). Dual sport remote mirrors: 024 ($69). Day/night mirror ($11). Entertainment: AM/FM radio: 4dr. ($58). AM/FM stereo radio ($35-$93). Rear speaker: 024 ($19). Exterior: Removable glass sunroof ($182). Rear spoiler: 024 ($55). Moldings, 4dr.: belt ($17); drip ($19); sill ($21); upper door frame ($32); wheel lip ($29). Vinyl bodyside molding: 024 ($44). Door edge protectors ($13-$21). Bumper guards: 4dr. ($45). Bumper rub strips: 024 ($35). Multi- color tape stripe: 4dr. ($72). Hood/bodyside/deck stripe: 4dr. ($45). Bodyside/deck stripe: 024 ($31). Luggage rack ($90). Undercoating ($34). Lower body protective coating ($31). Interior: Console: storage ($22); shift lever ($33). Cloth/vinyl bucket seats: 024 ($22). Vinyl bucket seats: 4dr. Vinyl bucket seats w/recliner: 024. Tonneau cover: 024 ($46). Cargo area carpet ($31). Cargo area dress-up ($45). Floor mats: front ($24); front/rear ($42). Color-keyed seatbelts ($23). Wheels and Tires: Wheel trim rings: 4dr. ($44). Deluxe wheel covers: 4dr. ($44); 024 (NC). Cast aluminum wheels ($171- $254). Rallye wheels ($39-$83). P165/75R13 WSW ($17). P175/75R13 WSW ($43). P175/75R13 SBR WSW ($78-$86). P185/70R13 Aramid-belted BSW ($45-$131). P185/70R13 Aramid- belted OWL ($106-$192). Conventional spare tire ($13-$26).

ASPEN CONVENIENCE/APPEARANCE OPTIONS: Option Packages: R/T pkg.: cpe ($586). Sport appearance pkg.: cpe ($192-$254). Handling/performance pkg.: base cpe/wag ($385). Wagon Sport pkg. ($721). Special Edition pkg. ($513- $814). Sunrise Coupe pkg. ($155). Custom pkg. ($258-$386). Basic group: base ($246-$403). Two-tone paint pkg.: base cpe/sed ($148). Light pkg. ($46). Deluxe insulation pkg. ($40-$51). Protection group ($56-$64). Comfort/Convenience: Air cond. ($543). Rear defogger, blower- type ($53); electric ($97). Automatic speed control ($106). Power seat ($163). Power windows ($130-$183). Power door locks ($83-$117). Power liftgate release: wag ($24). Tinted windshield ($44); all windows ($66). Luxury steering wheel ($32). Tuff steering wheel ($24-$56). Tilt steering wheel ($44-$76). Digital clock ($55). Inside hood release ($13). Intermitent wipers ($39). Tailgate wiper/washer: wag ($64). Lighter ($8). Locking gas cap ($7). Locking glovebox ($6). Lighting, Horns and Mirrors: Halogen headlamps ($37). Dual horns ($10). Remote left mirror ($18). Dual remote mirrors ($36-$54). Dual remote sport mirrors ($50-$68). Day/night mirror ($11). Entertainment: AM radio ($90); w/8track player ($143-$233). AM/FM radio ($58-$148). AM/FM stereo radio ($93-$183); w/8track player ($166-$256); w/cassette ($220-$310); w/CB ($351-$441). Rear speaker ($19). Delete AM radio ($51 credit). Exterior: T-Bar roof: cpe ($614). Full vinyl roof: sed ($97). Landau vinyl roof: cpe ($161-$178). Vinyl bodyside moldings ($44). Belt moldings ($17). Door edge protectors ($13-$21). Upper door frame moldings: sed/wag ($34). Wheel lip moldings: base ($24). Sill moldings: Special ($28). Bumper rub strips ($36). Rear air deflector: wag ($28). Luggage rack ($91). Undercoating ($23-$34). Interior: Console: cpe/wag ($34-$99). Vinyl bench seat: sed ($30). Vinyl bucket seats ($110). Cloth/vinyl bench seat. Cloth/vinyl bucket seats. Vinyl bucket seats w/cushion and center armrest. 60/40 seating (cloth or vinyl). Center cushion w/armrest: cpe/wag ($44). Rear armrest w/ashtray ($12). Color-keyed mats: front ($24); rear ($19). Color-keyed seatbelts ($23). Cargo area carpets: wag ($69); w/stowage bin ($93). Cargo security cover: wag ($46). Pedal dress-up ($9). Trunk dress-up ($45). Wheels and Tires: Cast aluminum wheels ($133-$287). Styled spoke wheels ($110-$154). Deluxe wheel covers ($44). Premium wheel covers ($37-$81). Wire wheel covers ($106-$150). P195/75R14 GBR WSW ($49). P205/75R14 SBR WSW ($84-$133). FR70 x 14 Aramid-belted OWL ($150-$199). Conventional spare tire ($25).

DIPLOMAT CONVENIENCE/APPEARANCE OPTIONS: Option Packages: 'S' pkg.: Salon cpe ($549-$569). Sport appearance pkg. ($166-$290). Basic group ($961-$1267). Two- tone paint pkg. ($162). Handling pkg. ($151). Deluxe insulation pkg. ($10-$110). Light pkg. ($85-$98). Protection group ($61-$70). Comfort/Convenience: Air conditioning ($623); auto-temp ($673) but ($50) w/option pkg. Rear defroster, electric ($106). Auto. speed control ($116). Power seat ($179). Power windows ($148-$209). Power door locks ($96-$136). Power decklid/tailgate release ($27). Illuminated entry system ($58). Tinted glass ($78). Luxury steering wheel ($20). Tuff steering wheel ($36-$56). Leather-covered steering wheel ($41-$61). Tilt steering wheel ($63-$83). Digital clock ($60). Deluxe wiper/washer ($51). Liftgate wiper/washer: wag ($69). Locking gas cap ($8). Lighting, Horns and Mirrors: Halogen headlamps ($41). Cornering lights ($55). Dual horns: base ($10). Remote driver's mirror: base/Salon ($20). Remote passenger mirror: Medallion ($41). Dual remote-control mirrors: base/Salon ($41-$61). Dual remote sport mirrors ($56-$76). Lighted vanity mirror ($51). Day/night mirror: base ($12). Entertainment: AM radio ($99). AM/FM radio ($63-$162). AM/FM stereo ($101-$200); w/ 8track tape player ($181-$280); w/cassette ($240-$339); w/CB ($383-$482). Search-tune AM/FM stereo ($227-$326). Rear speaker ($21). Power antenna ($52). Exterior: T-Bar roof: cpe ($715). Power glass sunroof ($871). Full vinyl roof: base/Salon sed ($129). Landau vinyl roof: base/Salon cpe ($176). Vinyl bodyside moldings ($46). Belt moldings: base ($21). Upper door frame moldings: base wag ($40). Wheel lip moldings: base ($26). Door edge protectors ($14-$23). Rear bumper guards ($25). Hood tape stripe ($24). Bodyside stripe ($50). Bodyside/decklid stripe: Salon ($73). Air deflector: wag ($32). Luggage rack: wag ($100). Undercoating ($25). Interior: Console: Salon cpe ($109). Vinyl bench seat: base/Salon ($51-$69). Cloth 60/40 seat: wag, Salon cpe ($160- $281). Vinyl 60/40 seat: base wag, Salon ($212-$281). Cloth/vinyl 60/40 seat: Salon sed ($230). Leather 60/40 seat ($371-$619). Cloth/vinyl bucket seats: Salon cpe ($103). Color-keyed floor mats: front ($26); rear ($21). Cargo area carpet: base wag ($75); w/stowage bins ($101). Cargo security cover: wag ($61). Color-keyed seatbelts ($27). Pedal dress-up ($10). Trunk dress-up ($49). Wheels and Tires: Deluxe wheel covers: base ($48). Premier wheel covers ($45-$93). Premium wheel covers ($45-$138). Wire wheel covers ($114-$308). Forged aluminum wheels ($118-$380). Styled wheels ($101-$194). P205/75R15 SBR WSW ($89). P205/75R15 Aramid-belted white/gold ($86-$175). Conventional spare ($27).

MIRADA CONVENIENCE/APPEARANCE OPTIONS: Option Packages: CMX pkg. ($614-$1426). Cabriolet roof pkg. ($738-$950). Basic group ($958-$1034). Sport handling pkg. ($192). Roadability pkg. ($29). Light pkg. ($104). Protection pkg. ($61). Comfort/Convenience: Air cond. ($623); auto-temp ($675) exc. ($52) w/option pkg. Rear defroster, electric ($106). Automatic speed control ($116). Power seat ($179). Power windows ($148). Power door locks ($96). Power decklid release ($28-$44). Illuminated entry system ($58). Luxury steering wheel ($22). Tuff steering wheel ($56). Leather-covered steering wheel ($61). Tilt steering wheel ($83). Digital clock ($60). Locking gas cap ($8). Intermittent wipers ($43). Lighting, Horns and Mirrors: Halogen headlamps ($41). Cornering lights ($55). Reading lamp ($21). Triad horns ($22). Left remote mirror ($20). Dual remote mirrors, chrome or painted ($57-$77). Lighted vanity mirror ($51). Entertainment: AM radio w/8track player ($156). AM/FM radio ($63). AM/FM stereo radio ($101); w/8track ($181); w/cassette ($240); w/CB ($383). Search-tune AM/FM stereo ($227). Rear speaker ($21). Power antenna ($52). Delete radio ($56 credit). Exterior: T-Bar roof ($715). Power sunroof ($787). Landau vinyl roof ($141). Vinyl bodyside moldings ($48). Wheel lip moldings ($26). Sill moldings ($30). Door edge protectors ($14). Bumper guards, rear ($25); rub strips ($20). Bodyside tape stripes ($51). Undercoating ($25). Interior: Console ($66-$109). Cloth/vinyl 60/40 bench seat ($232). Leather bucket seats ($550). Center front cushion ($43). Color-keyed mats: front ($26); rear ($21). Color-keyed seatbelts ($27). Trunk dress-up ($49). Pedal dress-up ($10). Wheels and Tires: Forged aluminum wheels ($334). Premium wheel covers ($92). P205/75R15 GBR WSW ($22). P205/75R15 SBR WSW ($89). P205/75R15 Aramid-belted white/gold ($86-$175). P215/70R15 SBR RWL ($25-$114). Conventional spare tire ($27).

ST. REGIS CONVENIENCE/APPEARANCE OPTIONS: Option Packages: Touring Edition pkg. ($1677-$1904). Two-tone paint pkg. ($168). Open Road handling pkg. ($269). Comfort/Convenience: Air cond. ($670); auto-temp ($720) exc. ($50) w/option pkg. Rear defroster, electric ($113). Auto. speed control ($122). Power windows ($228). Power door locks ($139). Power seat ($183). Power decklid release ($30-$46). Illuminated entry system ($62). Luxury steering wheel ($20). Leather-covered steering wheel ($62). Tilt steering wheel ($85). Digital clock ($61). Intermittent wipers ($44). Locking gas cap ($9). Lighting, Horns and Mirrors: Halogen headlamps ($42). Cornering lights ($55). Triad horns ($22). Remote driver's mirror ($21). Dual remote mirrors ($31-$52). Lighted vanity mirror ($53). Entertainment: AM radio ($106). AM/FM radio ($58-$164). AM/FM stereo ($103-$209); w/8track tape player ($181-$287); w/cassette ($241-$347); w/CB ($389-$495). Search-tune AM/FM stereo ($224-$330). Rear speaker ($22). Power antenna ($54). Exterior: Power glass sunroof ($1053). Full vinyl roof ($162). Vinyl bodyside molding ($55). Door edge protectors ($24). Bodyside tape stripes ($49). Bumper guards ($62). Undercoating ($31). Interior: Vinyl bench seat ($34). Vinyl 60/40 bench seat ($186). Cloth/vinyl 60/40 seat ($152). Leather 60/40 seat ($528). Color-keyed mats: front ($26); rear ($21). Color- keyed seatbelts ($27). Pedal dress-up ($10). Trunk dress-up ($70). Litter container ($9). Wheels and Tires: Premier wheel covers ($44). Premium wheel covers ($91). Wire wheel covers ($266). Forged aluminum wheels ($336). P205/75R15 SBR WSW ($92). P205/75R15 Aramid- belted white/gold ($179). P225/70R15 ($186). Conventional spare tire ($27).

HISTORY: Introduced: October 1, 1979. Model year production: Chrysler reported a total of 259,343 passenger cars shipped. Total North American production for the U.S. market of 258,792 units included 119,014 four-cylinder, 94,489 six-cylinder, and 45,289 V-8s. Calendar year production (U.S.): 269,446. Calendar year sales by U.S. dealers: 266,460. Model year sales by U.S. dealers: 325,036 (incl. 54,313 Colts and 13,059 Challengers). Note: Beginning this year, Sportsman vans were counted as trucks rather than passenger cars in production/sales figures.

Historical Footnotes: Dodge sales slipped drastically for the model year, down over 32 percent, though the Division at lest beat Plymouth again. Aspen and full-size models made the worst showing, but every model posted a decline. Rebates and incentive programs during the year didn't help enough. A weak national economy was hurting car sales nationwide. In fact, 1980 was considered the worst year ever for the domestic auto industry. Production also fell sharply, down from 418,215 in 1979 to just 286,703 this year. Dodge (and Chrysler as a whole) was pinning much of its hopes on the new-for-1981 Kcar. All through this dark period, Chrysler Corp. was instituting economy measures, including the purchase of more components from outside sources. Thus, Dodge workers endured not only layoffs but some plant closings.

1981 DODGE

At last, the long-awaited Chrysler front-drive compacts arrived, holding out a promise of improved sales. The company promoted fuel economy and six-passenger capacity for both Dodge Aries and its K-car twin, the Plymouth Reliant. The new 2.2-liter Trans-4 engine that powered Aries was the first Chrysler-built four-cylinder since the 1930s. Its overhead-cam design featured an aluminum head and cast iron block. The new four produced 84 horsepower at 4800 R.P.M., and 111 pound-feet of torque at 2800. It also became available as an Omni option. Also offered as an Aries option was a 2.6-liter four, built by Mitsubishi. On the subcompact level, Omni added a stripped "Miser" edition to both the two-door and four-door models. Also new: a Euro-Sedan package for the Omni sedan. Otherwise, the lineup remained much the same as in 1980. The old familiar Slant Six engine finally added hydraulic valve lifters. Omni managed to grow from its original four-passenger seating to a claimed five-passenger capacity, without gaining in size.

1981 Omni 024 hatchback coupe (D)

OMNI/024 — SERIES Z — FOUR — Although basic sedan appearance changed little, Omni's revised grille had only four bright horizontal divider bars (formerly five) over a fine-mesh pattern. A new vertical divider bar at the center replaced the former emblem. Tri-section wraparound taillamps were similar to 1978-80, with clear bottom sections. Some formerly standard equipment (such as tinted glass and a rear defroster) was now made optional. Two new variants of interest appeared: a Euro-Sedan and Miser, aimed at two different portions of the market. The Euro-Sedan package included blacked-out accent trim, P175/75R13 SBR tires on cast aluminum wheels, a Sport interior with corded-cloth front bucket seats, Rallye instrument cluster with tachometer and clock, four-spoke sport steering wheel, and carpeted cargo area. A total of 557 sedans had the Euro-Sedan package (RPO code A69). Miser managed a 28 MPG (43 highway) EPA estimate because of its lower weight, special engine calibrations, and 2.6:1 overall drive ratio. Misers also had a limited equipment list. Newly optional was the Chrysler-built 135 cu. in. (2.2-liter) Trans4 engine, made available during the model year instead of the standard 104.7 cu. in. (1.7-liter) four. Revised four-speed overdrive manual transaxle gearing came only with the larger engine; TorqueFlite automatic was available with both. Standard Omni interior had high-back vinyl bucket seats in blue, cashmere, red or black (Miser only cashmere and black). Body colors for 1980 were: Black, Sunlight Yellow, Graphic Yellow, Pearl White, Ginger, Baron Red, Graphic Red, Spice Tan Starmist, Nightwatch Blue, Vivid Blue Starmist, and metallic Burnished Silver, Daystar Blue, or Glencoe Green. Three two-tone combinations were offered. Options included a Tri-Lite sunroof, automatic speed control, intermittent wiper system, air conditioning, roof rack, and rear wiper/washer. AM/FM stereo radios were available with either 8-track or cassette, and Dolby noise reduction. Two-door 024 coupes were no longer listed in the same factory catalog as the Omni sedan, but remained part of the family. Coupe appearance changed little this year. 024's grille, consisting of three slots on each side of the sloping panel (each slot split by twin vertical dividers), looked a bit like a set of side-by-side stepladders. Turismo and De Tomaso packages were offered again, but revised a bit. The De Tomaso option, installed on 619 vehicles, included the new 2.2-liter engine and 14 in. wheels. A total of 7,306 coupes had a new Charger 2.2 package (RPO code A54), which cost $399 extra. That one included a hood scoop, quarter-window appliques, fender exhausters, 3.13:1 gearing with four-speed (2.71:1 w/automatic), rear spoiler, high-back bucket seats, P195/60R14 SBR RWL tires, and 'Charger 2.2' tape graphics. Basic 024 models could have either cast aluminum or Rallye 14 in. wheels as an option.

1981 Aries coupe (D)

ARIES — SERIES D — FOUR — The eagerly-awaited compact K-car came in two-door, four-door or station wagon form, in Custom and SE trim as well as the base model. Carrying six passengers on a front-wheel drive chassis, Aries was a near twin to Plymouth Reliant. The two looked very similar, but Plymouth used a more formal grille pattern. A simple slat-style grille (not unlike Mirada's) consisted of four wide, bright horizontal bars and a thin, subdued vertical divider set farther back. On the body-colored upper header panel was 'Dodge' block lettering. Vertical rectangular parking

lamps sat between the grille and single rectangular headlamps. A single frame on each side enclosed parking lamps, headlamps and large amber-lensed marker lamps at front fender tips. 'Aries' lettering sat just ahead of the door, and on the rear panel just above the right taillamp. The letter 'K' to identify the K-car stood alongside that lettering at the rear. On each side were tri-section taillamps consisting of two outer red lenses and an inner backup lens, adjoining the license plate mount. Bodyside moldings followed the same line from front to back, meeting the bumper rub strips. Aries' unibody design was much shorter and lighter than the Aspen it replaced, and its shape was more aerodynamic. At 99.6 inches, wheelbase was shorter than GM's new X-car, though overall size was similar. The suspension used Iso-Struts with coil springs at the front, and coil springs at the rear with a beam axle and trailing arms. Aries had front and rear anti-roll control, and rack-and-pinion steering. The K-car managed a 25 MPG EPA estimate (41 highway). Base engine was a transverse-mounted 135 cu. in. (2.2-liter) transverse-mounted overhead-cam four, called the Trans-4. Built by Chrysler, it had hydraulic valve lifters and an electronic feedback carburetor. The 2.2 came with standard four-speed overdrive manual transaxle, or optional TorqueFlite. For added performance, a Mitsubishi hemi Silent Shaft 156 cu. in. (2.6-liter) engine was available, with three-valve MCA-JET cylinder head. Also used in the imported Challenger coupe, that one came only with automatic. Standard equipment included an electric engine fan, fiberglass-belted radial tires, compact spare tire, bumper rub strips, wide bodyside moldings, drip rail moldings, cloth/vinyl bench seat, multi-function steering column lever, AM radio, lighter, day/night mirror, front/rear ashtrays, dome light, and carpeting. Four-doors and wagons had back door vent windows. Two-doors (sometimes referred to as coupes, but usually as sedans) had quarter-window louvers. Aries Special Edition (SE) had woodtone door panel and dash appliques plus dual horns, upper door frame moldings, remote-control driver's mirror, belt moldings, deluxe wheel covers, and cloth bench seat. Wagons in each series had power brakes. Body colors were: Nightwatch Blue, Baron Red, Graphic Red, Sunlight Yellow, Spice Tan Starmist, Pearl White, Formal Black and Natural Suede Tan; plus metallic Burnished Silver, Daystar Blue, Light Seaspray Green, or Glencoe Green. Designed with easy servicing in mind, K-cars had an ample option list. Extras included 14 in. tires and wheels, air conditioning, digital clock, automatic transmission, speed control, AM/FM stereo radio with cassette player and Dolby sound, remote-control right mirror, power steering, and six-way power seat. A total of 537 Aries sedans had the simulated convertible roof.

1981 Diplomat four-door sedan (D)

DIPLOMAT — SERIES G — SIX/V-8 — Following its 1980 restyle, Diplomat received no significant appearance change this year. Diplomat's model lineup was slightly revised, though, adding a new Sport Coupe to replace the former base two-door. No base sedan was announced at first. Both two- and four-door models came in mid-level Salon and upper-notch Medallion trim. Wagons came in the base or Salon level. The Sport Coupe included bright windshield, center pillar, rear quarter window, backlight and wheel opening moldings, as well as rocker panel moldings. It featured a two-tone paint treatment with landau effect (accent color on the lower body and rear roof). Sport Coupes also had bodyside and deck accent stripes, sport wheel covers, front bumper guards, front/rear bumper rub strips, and dual remote chrome sport mirrors. Diplomat's Salon included a remote driver's mirror and deluxe wheel covers, plus bright moldings for windshield, center pillar, back window, roof drip, quarter window, belt, sill and wheel openings. Medallions added a padded vinyl roof as well as bodyside and deck accent stripes. Salon and Medallion also had dual horns and a day/night inside mirror. Diplomat body colors were: Pearl White, Light Cashmere, Baron Red, Nightwatch Blue, Light Heather Gray, Black, Spice Tan Starmist, Mahogany Starmist, and Graphic Red; plus metallic Burnished Silver, Daystar Blue, Glencoe Green, or Light Seaspray Green. Four two-tone combinations were offered. New hydraulic valve lifters went on the standard Slant Six engine. Standard equipment included wide-ratio TorqueFlite three-speed automatic, along with power steering and brakes. Radio and tape player options were improved this year. Thicker primer coats and increased use of galvanized steel (and plastics) was intended to improve corrosion resistance, as well as cut weight. Like the related Chrysler LeBaron, Diplomat was now promoted as a mid-size.

1981 Mirada "Cabriolet" hardtop coupe (D)

MIRADA — SERIES X — SIX/V-8 — Dodge's distinctively-styled coupe appeared about the same this year, with its wide slat grille in an angled front end. As in 1980, large vertical rectangular parking lamps sat back from the grille in the same housing as the adjoining single rectangular headlamps. Non-functional angled fender louvers again were standard. For the first time, the base 225 cu. in. Slant Six had hydraulic valve lifters. Standard equipment included an AM radio, wide-ratio TorqueFlite three-speed automatic, trip odometer, brushed aluminum dash applique, gauges, cloth/vinyl

bucket seats, and locking glove box. Options included the 318 cu. in. V-8, Sport Handling or Roadability packages, leather-wrapped steering wheel, sunroof, wire wheel covers, and forged aluminum wheels. The 318 V-8 added a three-way catalyst emission control and electronic feedback carburetor this year, while Mirada's back bumper switched from aluminum to high-strength steel. Mirada's CMX package was offered again, including a simulated convertible top (tan, dark blue, dark red, black or white), P205/75R15 whitewall tires, black bumper rub strips with bright inserts, front fender CMX nameplates, and color- keyed rear bumper guards. CMX came in Baron Red, Nightwatch Blue, Pearl White, Graphic Red, Black, Light Cashmere, Silver, Spice Tan Starmist, or Daystar Blue metallic. Standard Miradas could also be painted Light Heather Gray or Mahogany Starmist. A total of 1,683 CMX packages were installed. The simulated convertible top was no longer offered separately.

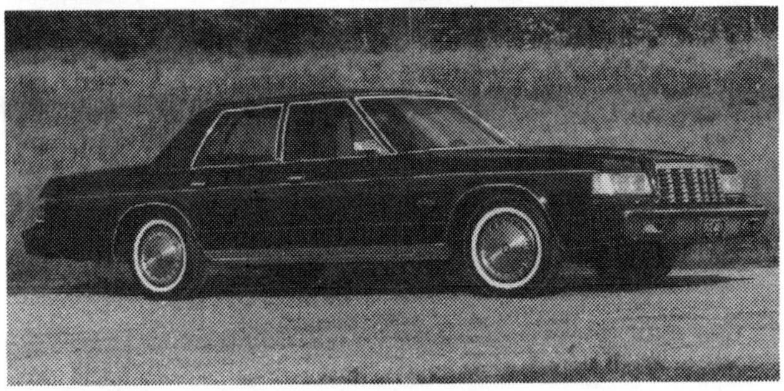

1981 St. Regis four-door pillared hardtop (D)

ST. REGIS — SERIES E — SIX/V-8 — Essentially unchanged in appearance, St. Regis was promoted as having more standard equipment this year, but the list revealed nothing startling. The current list included bumper rub strips, a two-spoke steering wheel, trip odometer, lane-change turn signals, and twin outside mirrors. St. Regis came with a full-length padded vinyl roof, bodyside accent stripes, cloth/vinyl seat trim with folding front center armrest, premier wheel covers and steel-belted whitewall tires, power brakes and steering, TorqueFlite automatic transmission, and tinted glass. This year's colors were: Pearl White, Mahogany Starmist, Light Cashmere, Black, Light Heather Gray, Nightwatch Blue, Baron Red, and metallic Heather Mist, Daystar Blue, or Coffee Brown. As before, only one model was offered: a formal-look four-door pillared hardtop sedan. Both the base Slant Six and optional 318 V-8 had improved catalytic emission control. Corrosion resistance was improved through use of a thicker primer coat and specially treated chrome. Like the related Plymouth Gran Fury, St. Regis remained popular with families, but its days were numbered anyway. The Touring Edition was dropped this year, so buyers had no option packages available other than a Basic Group priced at $1010.

I.D. DATA: Dodge had a new 17-symbol Vehicle Identification Number (VIN) on the upper left corner of the instrument panel, again visible through the windshield. The first digit indicates Country: '1' U.S.A.; '2' Canada. The second symbol is Make: 'B' Dodge. Third is Vehicle Type: '3' passenger car; '7' truck. The next symbol ('B') indicates manual seatbelts. Symbol five is Car Line: 'L' Omni; 'K' Aries; 'M' Diplomat; 'J' Mirada; 'R' St. Regis. Symbol six is Series (price class): '1' Economy; '2' Low; '3' Medium; '4' High'; '5' Premium; '6' Special. Symbol seven is Body Style: '1' 2-dr. sedan; '2' 2-dr. specialty hardtop; ''4' 2-dr. 22 hatchback; '6' 4-dr. sedan; '7' 4-dr. pillared hardtop; '8' 4-dr. hatchback; '9' 4-dr. wagon. Eighth is the Engine Code: 'A' L4105 2Bbl.; 'B' L4135 2Bbl.; 'D' L4156 2Bbl.; 'E' L6-225 1Bbl.; 'K' V8318 2Bbl.; 'M' V8318 4Bbl. Next comes a check digit: 0 through 9 (or X). Symbol ten indicates Model Year: 'B' 1981. Symbol eleven is Assembly Plant: 'A' Lynch Road; 'C' Jefferson; 'D' Belvidere, IL; 'F' Newark, DE; 'G' or 'X' St. Louis; 'R' Windsor, Ontario. The last six digits make up the sequential serial number, starting with 100001. Four-cylinder engine identification numbers are on the rear face of the block, directly under cylinder head (left side in vehicle) except for 2.6-liter, which is on left side of block between core plug and rear face of block (radiator side). Engine serial numbers (for parts replacement) are located on the block as follows: 1.7-liter, above fuel pump; 2.2-liter, on rear face just below head (below identification number); 2.6-liter, on right front of block adjacent to exhaust manifold stud. Six-cylinder engine identification numbers are stamped on a pad at the right of the block, below No. 6 spark plug. On V-8s, that pad is on the right of the block to the rear of the engine mount. An engine serial number is on the right of the block below No. 1 spark plug on six-cylinder engines, and on the left front corner of the block below the cylinder head on V-8s. A Body Code Plate is on the left upper radiator support, left front fender side shield, or wheelhousing.

OMNI (FOUR)

Model Number	Body/Style Number	Body Type & Seating	Factory Price	Shipping Weight	Production Total
ZL	24	2-dr. 024 Hatch-4P	6149	2205	35,983
ZL	44	4-dr. Hatch-5P	5690	2130	41,056

OMNI MISER (FOUR)

ZE	24	2-dr. Hatch 22-4P	5299	2137	Note 1
ZE	44	4-dr. Hatch-5P	5299	2060	Note 1

Note 1: Total Miser production, 37,819.

ARIES (FOUR)

DL	21	2-dr. Sedan-6P	5880	2305	Note 2
DL	41	4-dr. Sedan-6P	5980	2300	Note 2

Note 2: Total coupe/sedan production, 47,679.

ARIES CUSTOM (FOUR):

DH	21	2-dr. Sedan-6P	6315	2315	Note 3
DH	41	4-dr. Sedan-6P	6448	2310	Note 3
DH	45	4-dr. Sta Wag-6P	6721	2375	31,380

Note 3: Total Custom coupe/sedan production, 46,792.

ARIES SPECIAL EDITION (FOUR)

DP	21	2-dr. Sedan-6P	6789	2340	Note 4
DP	41	4-dr. Sedan-6P	6933	2340	Note 4
DP	45	4-dr. Sta Wag-6P	7254	2390	9,770

Note 4: Total Special Edition coupe/sedan production, 20,160.

DIPLOMAT (SIX/V-8)

GL	22	2-dr. Spt Cpe-6P	6495/6557	3210/3335	Note 5
GL	41	4-dr. Spt Sed-6P	6672/6734	3275/3400	Note 5
GM	45	4-dr. Sta Wag-6P	7089/7151	3470/3590	1,806

Note 5: Total Sport Coupe and sedan production, 4,608.

DIPLOMAT SALON (SIX/V-8)

GH	22	2-dr. Cpe-6P	7134/7196	3200/3325	Note 6
GH	41	4-dr. Sedan-6P	7268/7330	3305/3430	Note 6
GH	45	4-dr. Sta Wag-6P	7670/7732	3505/3625	1,206

Note 6: Total Salon coupe/sedan production, 15,023.

DIPLOMAT MEDALLION (SIX/V-8)

GP	22	2-dr. Cpe-6P	7645/7707	3255/3380	Note 7
GP	41	4-dr. Sedan-6P	7777/7839	3365/3490	Note 7

Note 7: Total Medallion coupe/sedan production, 1,527.

MIRADA (SIX/V-8)

XS	22	2-dr. HT Cpe-6P	7700/7764	3290/3410	11,899

ST. REGIS (SIX/V-8)

EH	42	4-dr. Pill. HT-6P	7674/7738	3535/3640	5,388

FACTORY PRICE AND WEIGHT NOTE: Prices and weights to left of slash are for six-cylinder, to right for V-8 engine. **MODEL NUMBER NOTE:** Some sources identify models using the new VIN data to indicate Car Line, Price Class and Body Style. Example: Aries four- door (DL41) has the equivalent number K26, which translates to Aries line, Low price class, and four-door sedan body. See I.D. Data section for breakdown.

ENGINE DATA: BASE FOUR (Omni): Inline, overhead-cam four-cylinder. Cast iron block; aluminum head. Displacement: 104.7 cu. in. (1.7 liters). Bore & stroke: 3.13 x 3.40 in. Compression ratio: 8.2:1. Brake horsepower: 63 at 5200 R.P.M. Torque: 83 lbs.-ft. at 2400 R.P.M. Five main bearings. Solid valve lifters. Carburetor: 2Bbl. Holley 6520 (R9052A). VIN Code: A. BASE FOUR (Aries); OPTIONAL (Omni): Inline, overhead-cam four-cylinder. Cast iron block; aluminum head. Displacement: 135 cu. in. (2.2 liters). Bore & stroke: 3.44 x 3.62 in. Compression ratio: 8.5:1. Brake horsepower: 84 at 4800 R.P.M. Torque: 111 lbs.-ft. at 2800 R.P.M. Five main bearings. Hydraulic valve lifters. Carburetor: 2Bbl. Holley 6520 (R9060A). VIN Code: B. OPTIONAL FOUR (Aries): Inline, overhead-cam four-cylinder. Cast iron block; aluminum head. Displacement: 156 cu. in. (2.6 liters). Bore & stroke: 3.59 x 3.86 in. Compression ratio: 8.2:1. Brake horsepower: 92 at 4500 R.P.M. Torque: 131 lbs.-ft. at 2500 R.P.M. Five main bearings. Solid valve lifters. Carburetor: 2Bbl. Mikuni. VIN Code: D. BASE SIX (Diplomat, Mirada, St. Regis): Inline, overhead-valve six. Cast iron block and head. Displacement: 225 cu. in. (3.7 liters). Bore & stroke: 3.40 x 4.12 in. Compression ratio: 8.4:1. Brake horsepower: 85 at 3600 R.P.M. Torque: 165 lbs.-ft. at 1600 R.P.M. Four main bearings. Hydraulic valve lifters. Carburetor: 1Bbl. Holley 1945 (R9253A). VIN Code: E. OPTIONAL V-8 (Diplomat, Mirada, St. Regis): 90-degree, overhead valve V-8. Cast iron block and head. Displacement: 318 cu. in. (5.2 liters). Bore & stroke: 3.91 x 3.31 in. Compression ratio: 8.5:1. Brake horsepower: 130 at 4000 R.P.M. Torque: 230 lbs.-ft. at 2000 R.P.M. Five main bearings. Hydraulic valve lifters. Carburetor: 2Bbl. Carter BBD 8291S. VIN Code: K. OPTIONAL V-8 (St. Regis): Same as 318 cu. in. V-8 above, but with 4Bbl. Carter TQ 9293S carburetor Horsepower: 165 at 4000 R.P.M. Torque: 240 lbs.- ft. at 2000 R.P.M. VIN Code: M.

CHASSIS DATA: Wheelbase: (Omni) 99.1 in.; (024) 96.6 in.; (Aries) 99.6 in.; (Diplomat cpe) 108.7 in.; (Diplo sed/wag) 112.7 in.; (Mirada) 112.7 in.; (St. Regis) 118.5 in. Overall Length: (Omni) 164.8 in.; (024) 174.0 in.; (Aries sed) 176.0 in.; (Aries wag) 176.2 in.; (Diplo cpe) 201.7 in.; (Diplo sed) 205.7 in.; (Diplo wag) 206.0 in.; (Mirada) 209.5 in.; (St. R.) 220.2 in. Height: (Omni) 53.1 in.; (024) 51.2 in.; (Aries 2dr.) 52.4 in.; (Aries 4dr.) 52.7 in.; (Aries wag) 52.8 in.; (Diplo cpe) 53.3 in.; (Diplo sed) 55.3 in.; (Diplo wag) 55.5 in.; (Mirada) 53.2 in.; (St. R.) 54.5 in. Width: (Omni) 65.8 in.; (024) 66.7 in.; (Aries) 68.6 in.; (Diplo) 74.2 in.; (Mirada) 72.7 in.; (St. R.) 77.6 in. Front Tread: (Omni/024) 56.1 in.; (Aries) 57.6 in.; (Diplo/Mirada) 60.0 in.; (St. Regis) 61.9 in. Rear Tread: (Omni/024) 55.6 in.; (Aries) 57.0 in.; (Diplo/Mirada) 59.5 in.; (St. R.) 62.0 in. Standard Tires: (Omni) P155/80R13 GBR WSW; (024) P175/75R13 GBR; (Aries) P175/75R13 GBR BSW; (Diplo/Mirada/St. R.) P195/75R15 GBR WSW.

TECHNICAL: Transmission: Four-speed manual (floor lever) standard on Omni. Gear ratios: (1st) 3.45:1; (2nd) 1.94:1; (3rd) 1.29:1; (4th) 0.97:1; (Rev) 3.17:1. Four-speed manual (floor lever) standard on Aries and Omni w/2.2-liter engine: (1st) 3.29:1; (2nd) 1.89:1; (3rd) 1.21:1; (4th) 0.88:1; (Rev) 3.14:1. TorqueFlite three-speed automatic standard on other models, optional on all. Omni 1.7-liter and Aries gear ratios: (1st) 2.69:1; (2nd) 1.55:1; (3rd) 1.00:1; (Rev) 2.10:1. Diplomat/Mirada/St. Regis: (1st) 2.74:1; (2nd) 1.54:1; (3rd) 1.00:1; (Rev) 2.22:1. Omni 2.2-liter: (1st) 2.47:1; (2nd) 1.47:1; (3rd) 1.00:1; (Rev) 2.10:1. Standard final drive ratio: (Omni) 3.37:1 w/4spd, 3.48:1 w/auto.; (Omni Miser) 2.6:1; (Omni w/2.2-liter four) 2.69:1 w/4spd, 2.78:1 w/auto.; (Aries) 2.69:1 w/4spd, 2.78:1 w/auto.; (Diplo six) 2.76:1; (Diplo wag) 2.94:1; (Diplo V-8) 2.26:1; (Diplo V-8 wag) 2.45:1; (Mirada six) 2.76:1; (Mirada V-8) 2.26:1; (St. R. six) 2.94:1; (St. R. V-8 2Bbl.) 2.24:1; (St. R. V-8 4Bbl.) 2.45:1. Steering: (Omni/Aries) rack and pinion; (others) recirculating ball. Suspension: (Omni) Iso-Strut independent coil front w/anti- sway bar, trailing arm semi-independent coil rear w/integral anti-sway; (Aries) Iso-Strut front w/coil springs, flex-arm beam rear axle w/trailing links and coil springs; (Diplomat/Mirada) transverse front torsion bars and anti-sway bar, semi-elliptic rear leaf springs; (St. Regis) longitudinal front torsion bars w/anti-sway bar, semi- elliptic rear leaf springs. Brakes: Front disc, rear drum. Ignition: Electronic. Body construction: Unibody. Fuel tank: (Omni/Aries) 13 gal.; (Diplomat/Mirada) 18 gal.; (St. Regis) 21 gal.

DRIVETRAIN OPTIONS: Engines: 2.2-liter four: Omni ($104). 2.6-liter four: Aries ($159). 318 cu. in. V-8: Diplomat/Mirada/St. Regis ($62). Transmission/Differential: TorqueFlite auto. trans.: Omni ($359); Aries ($360). Sure Grip differential: Diplo ($70-$109); Mirada ($110); St. R. ($114). Brakes and Steering: Power front disc brakes: Omni/Aries ($82). Power steering: Omni ($165); Aries ($174). Suspension: H.D. susp.: Omni 4dr. ($28); Aries ($23); Diplo/Mirada ($27); St. R. ($29). Sport susp.: 024 ($46). H.D. shock absorbers: Mirada/St. R. ($8). Other: Long-life battery: Omni ($23); others ($36-$38). H.D. trailer assist pkg.: St. R. ($253). Max. engine cooling ($127). California emission system ($46).

OMNI/024 CONVENIENCE/APPEARANCE OPTIONS: Option Packages: De Tomaso pkg.: 024 ($1511-$1866). Euro- Sedan pkg.: 4dr. ($613-$865). Charger 2.2 pkg.: 024 ($399). Charger 2.2 two-tone paint pkg. ($151). Sport appearance pkg.: 024 ($331-$435). Sport/Classic two-tone paint pkg. ($111-$164). Sport interior pkg. ($147-$200). Custom exterior pkg.: 4dr. ($188). Premium exterior pkg.: 024 ($92-$166); 4dr. ($250-$290). Premium interior pkg. ($212-$311). Popular equipment group ($423-$477). Light pkg. ($49). Comfort/Convenience: Air cond. ($554). Rear defroster, electric ($102). Automatic speed control ($136). Power liftgate release: 024 ($27). Tinted windshield: 4dr. ($45). Tinted glass ($71). Luxury steering wheel: 024 ($20). Sport steering wheel: 4dr. ($23-$43). Leather-wrapped steering wheel ($17-$60). Rallye instrument cluster w/tachometer ($70- $100). Electric clock w/trip odometer ($30). Intermittent wipers ($42). Rear wiper/washer: 4dr. ($83). Locking gas cap ($8). Light/Horn/Mirror: Halogen lamps($40). Two horns($10). Remote l. mirror: 4dr. ($20). Remote right mirror, black: 4dr. ($41). Dual remote chrome mirrors: 4dr. ($41-$60). Dual sport remote mirrors: 024 ($74). Entertainment: AM radio: Miser ($92). AM/FM radio ($59-$151). AM/FM stereo radio ($94-$186); w/8track player ($168-$260); w/cassette ($223-$315). Rear speaker: 024 ($20). Exterior: Removable glass sunroof ($213). Rear spoiler: 024 ($59). Starmist paint ($49). Moldings, 4dr.: belt ($19); drip ($21); upper door frame ($35); wheel lip ($32). Black vinyl bodyside molding ($46). Door edge protectors ($13-$23). Bumper guards: 4dr. ($48). Multi-color tape stripe: 4dr. ($99). Hood/bodyside/deck stripe: 4dr. ($48). Bodyside/deck stripe: 024 ($34). Luggage rack ($92). Undercoating ($37). Lower body protective coating ($34). Interior: Console: storage ($24); shift lever ($36). Cloth/vinyl bucket seats ($25). Tonneau cover: 024 ($49). Cargo area carpet ($34); w/sound insulation ($15-$49). Floor mats: front ($25); rear ($18). Color-keyed seatbelts ($25). Wheels and Tires: Wheel trim rings: 4dr. ($48). Deluxe wheel covers: 4dr. ($48). Cast aluminum 13 in. wheels: 4dr. ($215-$263). Cast aluminum 14 in. wheels: 024 ($175). 13 in. Rallye wheels: 4dr. ($40-$88). 14 in. Rallye wheels: 024 (NC). P155/80R13 WSW: 4dr. ($52). P165/75R13 WSW: 4dr. ($33-$85). P175/75R13 GBR WSW: 024 ($58). P175/75R13 SBR BSW: 4dr. ($17-$102). P175/75R13 SBR WSW: 4dr. ($89-$174). P185/70R13 SBR BSW: 024 ($116-$174). P195/60R14 SBR BSW: 024 ($79-$137). P195/60R14 SBR RWL: 024 ($39-$205). Conventional spare tire ($39).

ARIES CONVENIENCE/APPEARANCE OPTIONS: Option Packages: Basic group ($701-$784). Light pkg. ($75- $83). Protection group ($95-$103). Comfort/Convenience: Air cond. ($605). Rear defroster ($107). Auto. speed control ($132). Power seat ($173). Power door locks ($93-$132). Power decklid/liftgate release ($27). Tinted windshield ($48); all windows ($75). Luxury steering wheel ($46). Sport steering wheel ($7-$53). Tilt steering wheel ($81). Digital clock ($59). Intermitent wipers ($41). Tailgate wiper/washer: wag ($82). Locking gas cap ($7). Lighting, Horns and Mirrors: Halogen headlamps ($36). Dual horns ($10). Remote left mirror ($19). Remote right mirror: SE ($49). Dual remote mirrors ($49-$68). Vanity mirror ($5). Entertainment: AM radio: base ($90). AM/FM radio ($64-$150). AM/FM stereo radio ($100); w/8track player ($174); w/cassette ($224); w/CB ($361). Rear speaker ($19). Dual front speakers ($25) w/mono radio. Premium speakers ($92). Delete AM radio ($85 credit). Exterior: Glass sunroof ($246). Full vinyl roof: 4dr. ($131). Canopy vinyl roof: 2dr. ($131). Spice Tan Starmist paint ($55). Door edge protectors ($13-$20). Upper door frame moldings ($58-$67). Sill moldings ($20). Bumper guards, front or rear ($24). Luggage rack ($90). Special sound insulation ($75). Undercoating ($37). Vinyl lower body protection ($34). Interior: Vinyl bench seat ($27). Vinyl bucket seats ($51-$78) but (NC) on SE. Cloth bucket seats: SE ($91). Color- keyed mats: front ($25); rear ($19). Tonneau cover: wag ($50). Pedal dress-up ($9). Trunk dress-up ($45). Wheels and Tires: Styled wheels ($36-$82). Deluxe wheel covers ($46). Luxury wheel covers ($36-$82). P175/75R13 GBR wide WSW ($51). P185/70R13 SBR wide WSW ($124-$175). P185/65R14 GBR wide WSW ($82-$133). P185/65R14 SBR wide WSW ($136-$187). Conventional spare tire ($39).

DIPLOMAT CONVENIENCE/APPEARANCE OPTIONS: Option Packages: Sport appearance pkg. ($154-$238). Appearance pkg.: spt cpe (NC). Basic group ($937-$1147). Two- tone paint pkg. ($158). Handling pkg. ($163). Deluxe insulation pkg. ($10-$109). Light pkg. ($85-$99). Protection group ($58-$67). Comfort/Convenience: Air conditioning ($606); auto-temp ($656) but ($50) w/option pkg. Rear defroster, electric ($107). Auto. speed control ($136). Power seat ($177). Power windows ($145-$202). Power door locks ($96-$136). Power decklid/tailgate release ($29). Illuminated entry system ($57). Tinted glass ($78). Luxury steering wheel ($39). Sport steering wheel ($16-$55). Leather-covered steering wheel ($21-$60). Tilt steering wheel ($83). Digital clock ($56). Deluxe wiper/washer ($51). Liftgate wiper/washer: wag ($82). Locking gas cap ($8). Lighting, Horns and Mirrors: Halogen headlamps ($40). Cornering lights ($54). Dual horns: base ($10). Remote passenger mirror ($41). Dual remote sport mirrors ($56). Lighted vanity mirror ($50). Day/night mirror: base ($13). Entertainment: AM radio ($92). AM/FM radio ($59-$151). AM/FM stereo ($94-$186); w/ 8track tape player ($169-$261); w/cassette ($223-$315); w/CB ($355-$447). Search-tune AM/FM stereo ($211-$303). Rear speaker ($20). Dual front speakers ($26). Premium speakers ($93). Power antenna ($49). Exterior: T-Bar roof: cpe ($695). Power glass sunroof ($865). Full vinyl roof: Salon ($131). Landau padded vinyl roof: base/Salon cpe ($173). Starmist paint ($55). Vinyl bodyside moldings ($43). Belt moldings: base wag ($21). Upper door frame moldings: base wag ($38). Door edge protectors ($13- $22). Rear bumper guards ($25). Hood tape stripe ($24). Bodyside stripe ($50). Bodyside/decklid stripe: Salon ($72). Air deflector: wag ($31). Luggage rack: wag ($98). Undercoating ($25). Interior: Console: Salon ($108). Vinyl bench seat: spt cpe, base wag ($69); Salon ($50). Cloth 60/40 seat: wag ($208- $276). Vinyl 60/40 seat: base wag, Salon ($208-$276). Cloth/vinyl 60/40 seat: Salon ($226). Leather 60/40 seat: wag, Medallion ($364-$608). Cloth/vinyl bucket seats: Salon cpe ($101). Center armrest cushion: Salon ($42). Color-keyed floor mats: front ($25); rear ($20). Cargo area carpet: base wag ($74); w/stowage bins ($25-$99). Cargo security cover: wag ($60). Pedal dress-up ($10). Trunk dress-up ($47). Wheels and Tires: Premier wheel covers ($45). Premium wheel covers ($43-$88). Wire wheel covers ($106-$249). Forged aluminum wheels ($183-$326). Styled wheels ($98-$143). Conventional spare ($39).

MIRADA CONVENIENCE/APPEARANCE OPTIONS: Option Packages: CMX pkg. ($780). Basic group ($922). Sport handling pkg. ($139-$240). Roadability pkg. ($31). Light pkg. ($117). Protection pkg. ($68). Comfort/Convenience: Air cond. ($606); auto-temp ($654) exc. ($48) w/option pkg. Rear defroster, electric ($107). Auto. speed control ($136). Power seat ($177). Power windows ($145). Power door locks ($96). Power decklid release ($28-$43). Illuminated entry system ($57). Luxury steering wheel (NC). Leather-covered two-spoke steering wheel (NC). Tilt steering wheel ($83). Digital clock ($59). Locking gas cap ($8). Intermittent wipers ($43). Lighting, Horns and Mirrors: Halogen headlamps ($40). Cornering lights ($54). Reading lamp ($20). Triad horns ($22). Lighted vanity mirror ($50). Entertainment: AM/FM radio ($59). AM/FM stereo radio ($95); w/8track ($169); w/cassette ($211); w/CB ($355). Search-tune AM/FM stereo ($223). Rear speaker ($20). Dual front speakers ($26). Premium speakers ($93). Power antenna ($49). Delete radio ($85 credit). Exterior: T-Bar roof ($695). Power sunroof ($758). Landau vinyl roof ($131). Premium paint ($68). Vinyl bodyside moldings ($45). Wheel lip moldings ($26). Sill moldings ($30). Door edge protectors ($13). Bumper guards, rear ($25); rub strips ($20). Hood/deck tape stripes ($50). Undercoating ($25). Interior: Console ($66-$108). Vinyl bucket seats ($42). Leather bucket seats ($451-$493). Center cushion w/armrest ($42). Color-keyed mats: front ($25); rear ($20). Trunk dress-up ($47). Pedal dress-up ($11). Litter container ($10). Wheels and Tires: Forged aluminum wheels ($238-$329). Premium wheel covers ($91). Wire wheel covers ($161-$252). P205/75R15 GBR WSW ($27). P205/75R15 SBR WSW ($101). P215/70R15 SBR WSW ($56-$161). P215/70R15 SBR RWL ($60-$157). Conventional spare tire ($39).

ST. REGIS CONVENIENCE/APPEARANCE OPTIONS: Option Packages: Open Road handling pkg. ($281). Basic group ($993). Light pkg. ($103). Comfort/Convenience: Air cond. ($646); auto-temp ($692) exc. ($46) w/option pkg. Rear defroster, electric ($112). Auto. speed control ($139). Power windows ($218). Power door locks ($138). Power seat ($179). Power decklid release ($30-$45). Illuminated entry system ($60). Luxury steering wheel ($39). Leather-covered steering wheel ($60). Tilt steering wheel ($84). Digital clock ($62). Intermittent wipers ($44). Locking gas cap ($9). Lighting, Horns and Mirrors: Halogen headlamps ($41). Cornering lights ($54). Triad horns ($22). Remote driver's mirror ($21). Dual remote mirrors ($30-$51). Lighted vanity mirror ($51). Entertainment: AM radio ($97). AM/FM radio ($54-$151). AM/FM stereo ($95-$192); w/8track tape player ($166-$263); w/cassette ($221-$318); w/CB ($356-$453). Search-tune AM/FM stereo ($206-$303). Rear speaker ($21). Dual front speakers ($26). Premium speakers ($95). Power antenna ($50). Exterior: Power glass sunroof ($934). Special paint ($68). Vinyl bodyside molding ($51). Door edge protectors ($23). Bumper guards ($60). Undercoating ($31). Interior: Vinyl bench seat ($34). Cloth/vinyl 60/40 bench seat ($148). Color-keyed mats: front ($25); rear ($20). Pedal dress-up ($11). Trunk dress-up ($65). Litter container ($10). Wheels and Tires: Premium wheel covers ($86). Wire wheel covers ($251). Forged aluminum wheels ($321). P205/75R15 SBR WSW ($101). P225/70R15 SBR WSW ($192). Conventional spare tire ($39).

HISTORY: Introduced: October 13, 1980. Model year production: Chrysler reported a total of 312,096 passenger cars shipped. Total North American production for the U.S. market of 356,513 units included 255,120 four-cylinder, 79,314 six-cylinder and 22,079 V-8s. Calendar year production (U.S.): 328,631. Calendar year sales by U.S. dealers: 305,757. Model year sales by U.S. dealers: 371,528 (incl. 41,288 imported Colts and 12,371 Challengers).

Historical Footnotes: At introduction time, the new Aries was priced several hundred dollars lower than competitive X-cars from GM. After slow early sales and amid plenty of publicity, Aries soon began to sell strongly. Aries' catalog headline, "America's not going to be pushed around anymore!" made clear Chrysler's attitude toward the new K-car as an import fighter. Also promoted was the fact that Chrysler had begun front-wheel drive production (of the Omni) two or three years earlier than GM and Ford. The new Omni "Miser" was intended to rival Ford's new Escort/Lynx. To help sell Omnis and some other models, many dealers even offered a 30-Day/1000-Mile Money-Back Guarantee. Model year sales rose by over 14 percent, due mainly to success of front-drive Dodge models, led by Aries. Over 81 percent of Dodges sold had front-drive, and Aries accounted for over two-fifths of the total. Even so, the final figure stood well below the 1979 level. St. Regis faded away at the end of 1980, largely because of minimal sales (only 7,556 for the model year). Model year production rose by 26 percent, again led by Aries which amounted to half the total. Dodge's share of the industry production total for calendar year 1981 was 5.3 percent (up from 4.2 percent in 1980).

1982 DODGE

Several models came and went this year. Diplomat lost its coupe and station wagon body styles, leaving only a four- door sedan. The renowned Charger name went on a performance version of the Omni-based subcompact coupe. Dodge added one all-new model: the 400, which was a stretched version of the K-car (Aries) but more luxurious. And the full-size St. Regis was gone. Compacts were getting more standard equipment without equivalent price rises. Engineering changes were aimed at a better ride and gas mileage. Biggest engine was the two-barrel 318 cu. in. V-8 (four-barrel in California). At mid-year the new 400 series added a convertible, a mate to Chrysler's LeBaron.

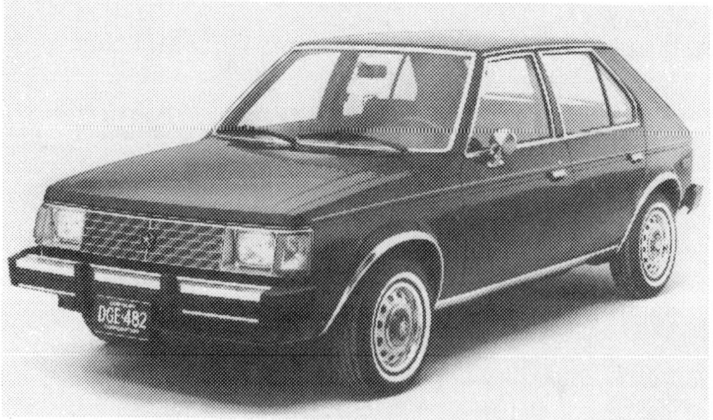

1982 Omni E Type hatchback sedan (D)

OMNI/024 — SERIES Z — FOUR — This year's Omni sedan looked similar to the 1981 version, but added a pentastar emblem atop the vertical divider of its horizontal-bar grille. 'Omni' lettering was no longer on the front fenders, though it remained on the hatch. A 'Dodge' nameplate was also on the hatch, as well as above the driver's side headlamp. The base Omni sedan was now called Custom. New standard equipment included a driver's remote outside mirror, dual horns, and bright wheel hub nuts. Euro-Sedan became a separate model, and the stripped-down Miser was offered again. Omni's chassis held a new linkless sway bar. At its rear were low-rate springs and retuned shocks, intended to give a softer ride and greater stability. A simplified catalytic converter was used; the dual-bed version dropped. The Custom held new standard cloth/vinyl Sport high-back bucket seats with integral headrests and dual recliners, plus a four-spoke color-keyed sport steering wheel and padded instrument panel with woodtone accents. Far fewer option packages were offered this year. New individual options included a lighted passenger vanity mirror and an engine block heater, as well as nerf strips. Reclining front seatbacks were

available. Standard engine was again the 1.7-liter OHC four, with 2.2 optional. Automatic TorqueFlite was available to replace the standard four-speed manual gearbox. Omni Miser returned with its specially calibrated 1.7-liter engine, four-speed manual transaxle, and 2.69:1 overall drive ratio. Miser's vinyl interior came in red, blue, cashmere or black. Standard fittings included a locking glove box, day/night mirror, remote driver's outside mirror, and inside hood release. Such extras as air conditioning and power steering weren't available on the Miser. Omni's sporty E-Type Euro-Sedan had blacked-out trim, dual black remote-control mirrors, bumper rub strips, special bodyside and mirror stripes, Rallye instrument cluster with tachometer and trip odometer, shift-lever console, and high-back cloth/vinyl bucket seats with recliners. This year's body colors were: Black, Pearl White, Graphic Yellow or Red, Morocco Red, and Manila Cream; plus metallic Charcoal Gray, Spice Tan, Medium Seaspray Green, Daystar Blue, Ensign Blue, Navy Blue, and Burnished Silver. Three two-tones were available. The 024 two-door hatchback coupe also came in Custom and Miser form again, marketed separately from the sedan. Custom coupes had thicker C-pillar appliques. New this year was a performance variant called Charger 2.2 (listed below).

1982 Omni Charger 2.2 hatchback coupe (D)

(OMNI) CHARGER 2.2 — SERIES Z — FOUR — Charger, a well-known name in Dodge performance-car history, returned to the Omni-based coupe with standard 135 cu. in. (2.2-liter) Trans4 engine. In addition to snappy performance, Charger offered an EPA mileage estimate of 26 MPG (41 highway). Appearance was similar to the basic 024, but more dramatic. Charger's grille consisted of six wide slots, three on each side, in a sharply-slanted front panel. Single rectangular headlamps were deeply recessed, with parking lamps below. At the front of the hood was a round laydown ornament with pentastar emblem. Bodies displayed easy-to-spot tape graphics, including large 'Charger 2.2' lettering as part of the bodyside and rear spoiler striping and a huge 'Charger 2.2' decal on the simulated hood scoop. Tape graphics came in several color combinations (red, black or gold), depending on the body color. A black lower body accent paint package was also available. On the fender just ahead of the door was a simulated front fender exhaust outlet. The sporty fastback roofline was similar to earlier 024s, except that the center side window did not come to a point at the rear. Two horizontal divider bars split each wide taillamp into three segments. Charger 2.2 standard equipment included manual front disc brakes, heater/defroster, AM radio, lighter, bumper rub strips, passenger and cargo area carpet, performance exhaust system, and tinted glass all around. Also standard: dual horns, padded instrument panel with woodtone applique, glovebox lock, power liftgate release, dual remote color-keyed mirrors, day/night inside mirror, black windshield and rear window moldings, black belt moldings, and a Sport suspension with rear anti-sway bar. Body colors were Black, Graphic Red, Pearl White, Burnished Silver metallic, and Ensign Blue metallic. Rallye steel wheels held P195/60R14 raised white-letter tires. Inside were Sport high-back reclining bucket seats upholstered in corded cloth/vinyl, plus a four-spoke steering wheel and Rallye instrument cluster (including tachometer, clock and trip odometer).

1982 Aries Special Edition coupe (D)

ARIES — SERIES D — FOUR — Except for a stand-up hood ornament and elimination of an 'Aries' nameplate from front fenders, the Dodge K-car didn't change much for its second season. Separate 'Dodge' letters stood above the slat-type grille. As before, vertical parking lamps were between the grille and single recessed headlamps, which connected with amber marker lenses. Lower bodyside moldings ran into the front and rear bumper strips for a unified look. Standard engine was again the 2.2-liter OHC Trans-4, with 2.6-liter Mitsubishi optional. The 2.2-liter four got a new cooling fan for improved fuel efficiency, plus a high-altitude compensator that adjusted spark advance electronically. Idle speed was modified, for smoother running. Silver/black was the underhood color scheme, and Aries had a new counterbalanced hood. Underneath was a new linkless front sway bar, with new geometry in the Iso-Strut suspension for better steering control on rough roads. As before, models included two-door and four-door sedans and a four-door wagon; in base, Custom and SE trim. Base Aries models had all-vinyl bench seats. Aries Custom had standard pleated cloth/vinyl bench seating in red, green, blue or cashmere. Custom also added door frame moldings, color-keyed quarter-window louvers, and bright taillamp accents. The Special Edition had cloth seats with a folding center armrest, plus power brakes and steering, a remote control driver's mirror, deluxe wheel covers, bright decklid molding, and Special Edition plaque on rear roof pillars. Aries colors for 1982 were: Black, Pearl White, Manila Cream, Nightwatch Blue, and Morocco Red; plus metallic Burnished Silver, Medium Seaspray Green, Spice Tan, Daystar Blue, Charcoal Gray,

Goldenrod Tan, and Light Seaspray Green. A new cabriolet roof package was offered for Custom and SE, but Chrysler reports that only 86 of the simulated convertible tops were installed. Also added to the option list: power front windows, center console (with manual shift), leather-covered steering wheel, Rallye wheels, and 14 in. cast aluminum wheels. Spring Special packages (RPO code A07) were installed on 2,082 Aries models.

1982 Dodge 400 convertible (D)

400 — SERIES V — FOUR — Riding a K-car chassis with 99.9 in. wheelbase, the sporty new mid-size front-drive "Super K" arrived first only in two-door form. Added at mid-year was a convertible model, similar to Chrysler's new LeBaron ragtop, converted from a coupe by Cars & Concepts in Brighton, Michigan. Dimensions, drivetrains, suspensions and dashboards were similar to Aries, but 400 had a body-color horizontal-bar grille like Mirada. Fenders held twin vertical louvers (simulated) at the cowl. The convertible had a small back window and wide rear quarters. The 135 cu. in. (2.2-liter) Trans4 served as base engine, with the Mitsubishi-built 156 cu. in. (2.6-liter) four optional (and standard on the convertible). Four-speed manual shift was standard, along with power brakes and rack-and-pinion steering. Three-speed TorqueFlite was optional. Tires were P185/70R14 steel-belted radials wide-whitewall tires. Better equipped than Aries, the 400 came with a standard AM radio, carpeting, door-ajar chimes, seatbelt and headlamps-on warnings, lighter, digital clock, dual horns, courtesy lights, locking glovebox, dual chrome mirrors, and day/night inside mirror. Moldings were provided for windshield, hood rear edge, lower deck, upper door frame, drip rail, partial wheel lip, and bodyside (color-keyed vinyl). Cloth/vinyl standard seats had a center armrest and door trim panels were carpeted. Also standard: a padded landau vinyl roof with color-keyed surround moldings and Frenched back window, luxury wheel covers, and luxury steering wheel. The instrument panel held a brushed-finish cluster with two-tone woodgrain treatment and padded top. LS added a velvet bench seat, halogen headlamps, light/gauge alert group, cornering lights, dual remote-controlled mirrors, and bodyside tape stripes.

1982 Diplomat Medallion sedan (D)

DIPLOMAT — SERIES G — SIX/V-8 — Only the four-door sedan remained in the Diplomat lineup, in Salon and Medallion trim. Both the coupe and station wagon were dropped. No base model was offered. Diplomat looked similar to the 1981 edition, with the same rectangular-element grille that extended outward at the base to enclose parking and marker lamps. With St. Regis gone, Diplomat was Dodge's biggest car and one of only two rear-drives. Salon had standard cushioned foam cloth/vinyl bench seats, while Medallion carried 60/40 seating. Both included folding center armrests. Standard equipment included the 225 cu. in. (3.7-liter) Slant Six engine, TorqueFlite three-speed automatic, power brakes and steering, glass-belted radial whitewalls, tinted glass, front bumper guards, bumper rub strips, and bright rear door glass division bar; plus moldings for windshield, belt, sill, wheel openings, and roof drip. Medallion added bright upper door frame moldings, a full vinyl roof with bright vinyl termination molding, map/dome reading light and headlamp switch with time delay, remote left mirror, and trunk dress-up equipment. This year's colors were: Black, Manila Cream, Morocco Red, Nightwatch Blue, and Pearl White; plus metallic Charcoal Gray, Spice Tan, Burnished Silver, and Daystar Blue. Automatic transmissions with the optional 318 cu. in. V-8 had a lock-up torque converter. A four-way power seat was available for the front passenger, as well as six-way for the driver. New to the option list: an electronic-tuning AM/FM stereo radio with cassette player. A total of 11,787 Police packages (RPO code A38) were installed on Diplomats. That was nearly half the total production.

MIRADA — SERIES X — SIX/V-8 — No significant appearance changes hit the Cordoba-related mid-size coupe, with its sleek profile and wide-slat grille. As before, rectangular parking lamps sat right next to the single rectangular headlamps in their set-back housings. Twin hood creases came forward to meet the grille sides. Mirada carried only modest bright ornamentation, but fenders again held angled simulated louvers above the 'Mirada' nameplates. Taillamps again held horizontal trim strips. The front end was made of flexible plastic. Body colors were: Morocco Red, Manila Cream, Nightwatch Blue, Black, and Pearl White; plus metallic Charcoal Gray, Mahogany, Daystar Blue, Burnished Silver, and Spice Tan. Standard Miradas had grooved-look moldings at the rear of the center side windows, which offered a simulated convertible top which offered a much different look. A T-Bar roof also was available. Base engine was again the 225 cu. in. Slant Six, with 318 V-8 optional.

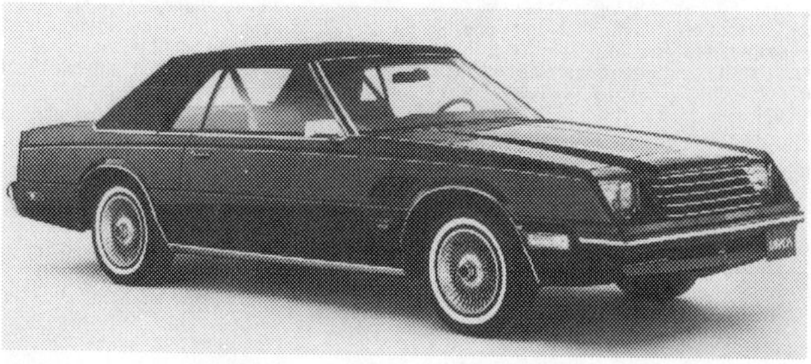

1982 Mirada "Cabriolet" hardtop coupe (D)

TorqueFlite three-speed automatic was standard. The instrument panel displayed round gauges. Standard high-back cloth Sport bucket seats could also have an optional center cushion and folding center armrest. Vinyl and leather/vinyl bucket seats were available, as was 60/40 seating. Also optional: a new electronic-tuning AM/FM stereo radio with cassette player, and a rear anti-sway bar. New standard equipment included halogen headlamps, rear bumper rub strips (formerly front only), and color-keyed two- spoke steering wheel. Mirada's CMX package included a sailcloth-textured simulated convertible vinyl top, bright touchdown moldings, front fender 'CMX' nameplates, color-keyed door handle inserts, premium wheel covers, and P205/75R15 SBR wide whitewall tires. A total of 1,474 CMX packages were installed.

I.D. DATA: Dodge's 17-symbol Vehicle Identification Number (VIN), as before, was on the upper left corner of the instrument panel, visible through the windshield. The first digit indicates Country: '1' U.S.A.; '2' Canada. The second symbol is Make: 'B' Dodge. Third is Vehicle Type: '3' passenger car; '7' truck. The next symbol ('B') indicates manual seatbelts. Symbol five is Car Line: 'Z' Omni; 'D' Aries; 'G' Diplomat; 'X' Mirada; 'V' 400. Symbol six is Series (price class): '1' Economy; '2' Low; '4' High'; '5' Premium; '6' Special. Symbol seven is Body Style: '1' 2-dr. sedan; '2' 2-dr. specialty hardtop; ''4' 2-dr. 22 hatchback; '5' 2-dr. convertible; '6' 4-dr. sedan; '8' 4-dr. hatchback; '9' 4-dr. wagon. Eighth is the Engine Code: 'A' L4105 2Bbl.; 'B' L4135 2Bbl.; 'D' L4156 2Bbl.; 'E' L6-225 1Bbl.; 'K' V8318 2Bbl. Next comes a check digit. Symbol ten indicates Model Year: 'C' 1982. Symbol eleven is Assembly Plant: 'C' Jefferson; 'D' Belvidere, IL; 'F' Newark, DE; 'G' or 'X' St. Louis; 'R' Windsor, Ontario. The last six digits make up the sequential serial number, starting with 100001. Engine number coding is the same as 1981.

OMNI CUSTOM (FOUR)

Model Number	Body/Style Number	Body Type & Seating	Factory Price	Shipping Weight	Production Total
ZH	24	2-dr. 024 Hatch-5P	6421	2205	11,287
ZH	44	4-dr. Hatch-5P	5927	2175	14,466

OMNI MISER (FOUR)

ZE	24	2-dr. 024 Hatch-5P	5799	2180	14,947
ZE	44	4-dr. Hatch-5P	5499	2110	16,105

OMNI EURO-SEDAN (FOUR)

ZP	44	4-dr. Hatch-5P	6636	2180	639

OMNI CHARGER 2.2 (FOUR)

ZP	24	2-dr. Hatch-5P	7115	2315	14,420

ARIES (FOUR)

DL	21	2-dr. Sedan-6P	5990	2315	10,286
DL	41	4-dr. Sedan-6P	6131	2310	28,561

ARIES CUSTOM (FOUR):

DH	21	2-dr. Sedan-6P	6998	2320	8,127
DH	41	4-dr. Sedan-6P	7053	2320	19,438
DH	45	4-dr. Sta Wag-6P	7334	2395	26,233

ARIES SPECIAL EDITION (FOUR)

DP	21	2-dr. Sedan-6P	7575	2365	1,374
DP	41	4-dr. Sedan-6P	7736	2385	4,269
DP	45	4-dr. Sta Wag-6P	8101	2470	6,375

400 (FOUR)

VH	22	2-dr. Cpe-6P	8043	2470	12,716
VH	41	4-dr. Sedan-6P	8137	N/A	3,595
VH	27	2-dr. Conv.-4P	12300	N/A	5,541

400 LS (FOUR)

VP	22	2-dr. Cpe-6P	8308	2475	6,727
VP	41	4-dr. Sedan-6P	8402	N/A	2,870

DIPLOMAT SALON (SIX/V-8)

GL	41	4-dr. Sedan-6P	7750/7820	3275/3415	19,773

DIPLOMAT MEDALLION (SIX/V-8)

GH	41	4-dr. Sedan-6P	8799/8869	3305/3445	3,373

MIRADA (SIX/V-8)

XS	22	2-dr. HT Cpe-5P	8619/8689	3305/3455	6,818

FACTORY PRICE AND WEIGHT NOTE: Prices and weights to left of slash are for six-cylinder, to right for V-8 engine. **MODEL NUMBER NOTE:** Some sources identify models using the new VIN data to indicate Car Line, Price Class and Body Style. Example: Aries four- door (DL41) has the equivalent number D26, which translates to Aries line, Low price class, and four-door sedan body. See I.D. Data section for breakdown.

ENGINE DATA: BASE FOUR (Omni): Inline, overhead-cam four-cylinder. Cast iron block; aluminum head. Displacement: 104.7 cu. in. (1.7 liters). Bore & stroke: 3.13 x 3.40 in. Compression ratio: 8.2:1. Brake horsepower: 63 at 4800 R.P.M. Torque: 83 lbs.-ft. at 2400 R.P.M. Five main bearings. Solid valve lifters. Carburetor: 2Bbl. Holley 6520. VIN Code: A. BASE FOUR (Aries, 400); OPTIONAL (Omni): Inline, overhead-cam four-cylinder. Cast iron block; aluminum head. Displacement: 135 cu. in. (2.2 liters). Bore & stroke: 3.44 x 3.62 in. Compression ratio: 8.5:1. Brake horsepower: 84 at 4800 R.P.M. Torque: 111 lbs.-ft. at 2400 R.P.M. Five main bearings. Hydraulic valve lifters. Carburetor: 2Bbl. Holley 6520 or 5220. VIN Code: B. OPTIONAL FOUR (Aries, 400): Inline, overhead-cam four-cylinder. Cast iron block; aluminum head. Displacement: 156 cu. in. (2.6 liters). Bore & stroke: 3.59 x 3.86 in. Compression ratio: 8.2:1. Brake horsepower: 92 at 4500 R.P.M. Torque: 131 lbs.-ft. at 2500 R.P.M. Five main bearings. Solid valve lifters. Carburetor: 2Bbl. Mikuni. VIN Code: D. BASE SIX (Diplomat, Mirada): Inline, overhead-valve six. Cast iron block and head. Displacement: 225 cu. in. (3.7 liters). Bore & stroke: 3.40 x 4.12 in. Compression ratio: 8.4:1. Brake horsepower: 90 at 3600 R.P.M. Torque: 160 lbs.-ft. at 1600 R.P.M. Four main bearings. Hydraulic valve lifters. Carburetor: 1Bbl. Holley 1945. VIN Code: E. OPTIONAL V-8 (Diplomat, Mirada): 90-degree, overhead valve V-8. Cast iron block and head. Displacement: 318 cu. in. (5.2 liters). Bore & stroke: 3.91 x 3.31 in. Compression ratio: 8.5:1. Brake horsepower: 130 at 4000 R.P.M. Torque: 230 lbs.-ft. at 2000 R.P.M. Five main bearings. Hydraulic valve lifters. Carburetor: 2Bbl. Carter BBD. VIN Code: K.

CHASSIS DATA: Wheelbase: (Omni) 99.1 in.; (024) 96.6 in.; (Aries/400) 99.9 in.; (Diplomat) 112.7 in.; (Mirada) 112.7 in. Overall Length: (Omni Miser) 162.6 in.; (Omni Cust) 164.8 in.; (Omni EType) 163.2 in.; (024) 174.0 in.; (Aries sed) 176.0 in.; (Aries wag) 176.2 in.; (400) 181.2 in.; (Diplomat) 205.7 in.; (Mirada) 209.6 in. Height: (Omni) 53.1 in.; (024) 50.8 in.; (Aries 2dr.) 52.3 in.; (Aries 4dr.) 52.7 in.; (Aries wag) 52.4 in.; (400 2dr.) 52.6 in.; (400 4dr.) 53.0 in.; (400 conv.) 54.1 in.; (Diplomat) 55.3 in.; (Mirada) 53.2 in. Width: (Omni) 65.8 in.; (024) 66.7 in.; (Aries) 68.6 in.; (400) 68.5 in.; (Diplo) 74.2 in.; (Mirada) 72.7 in. Front Tread: (Omni/024) 56.1 in.; (Aries/400) 57.6 in.; (Diplo/Mirada) 60.0 in. Rear Tread: (Omni/024) 55.6 in.; (Aries/400) 57.0 in.; (Diplo/Mirada) 59.5 in. Wheel size: (Omni/Aries) 13 x 5.5 in.; (024/400) 14 x 5.5 in.; (Diplo/Mirada) 15 x 5.5 in. Standard Tires: (Omni/Aries) P175/75R13 GBR BSW; (024) P195/60R14 SBR BSW; (400) P185/70R14 SBR; (Diplo/Mirada) P195/75R15 GBR WSW.

TECHNICAL: Transmission: Four-speed manual (floor lever) standard on Omni. Gear ratios: (1st) 3.45:1; (2nd) 1.94:1; (3rd) 1.29:1; (4th) 0.97:1; (Rev) 3.17:1. Four-speed manual (floor lever) standard on Aries, 400, Omni Miser, and Omni w/2.2-liter engine: (1st) 3.29:1; (2nd) 1.89:1; (3rd) 1.21:1; (4th) 0.88:1; (Rev) 3.14:1. TorqueFlite three-speed automatic standard on other models, optional on all. Omni, Aries and 400 gear ratios: (1st) 2.69:1; (2nd) 1.55:1; (3rd) 1.00:1; (Rev) 2.10:1. Diplomat/Mirada: (1st) 2.74:1; (2nd) 1.54:1; (3rd) 1.00:1; (Rev) 2.22:1. Standard final drive ratio: (Omni 4spd) 3.37:1; (Miser 4spd) 2.69:1; (Omni 2.2-liter 4spd) 3.13:1; (Omni auto.) 2.78:1; (Aries/400) 2.69:1 w/4spd, 2.78:1 w/auto.; (Diplo/Mirada six) 2.94:1; (Diplo/Mirada V-8) 2.20:1. Steering: (Omni/Aries/400) rack and pinion; (others) recirculating ball. Suspension: (Omni) Iso-Strut independent coil front w/anti- sway bar, trailing arm semi-independent coil rear w/integral anti-sway; (Aries/400) MacPherson strut front w/coil springs and anti-sway bar, flex-arm beam rear axle w/trailing arms, coil springs and anti-sway bar; (Diplomat/Mirada) transverse front torsion bars and anti-sway bar, semi-elliptic rear leaf springs. Brakes: Front disc, rear drum. Ignition: Electronic. Body construction: Unibody. Fuel tank: (Omni/Aries/400) 13 gal.; (Diplomat/Mirada) 18 gal.

DRIVETRAIN OPTIONS: Engines: 2.2-liter four: Omni ($112). 2.6-liter four: Aries/400 ($171). 318 cu. in., 2Bbl. V-8: Diplomat/Mirada ($70). Transmission: TorqueFlite auto. trans.: Omni/Aries/400 ($396). Brakes and Steering: Power front disc brakes: Omni/Aries ($93). Power steering: Omni ($190); Aries ($195). Suspension: H.D. susp.: Aries/Diplo ($26); 400 ($27); Mirada ($31). Sport susp.: 024 ($52). Rear sway bar: Mirada ($34). Other: Long-life battery: Omni ($26); others ($43). Engine block heater: Omni ($18). H.D. engine cooling ($141). California emission system ($65). High-altitude emission (NC).

OMNI/024 CONVENIENCE/APPEARANCE OPTIONS: Option Packages: Sport appearance pkg.: 024 ($138). Bright exterior accent group ($85-$121). Two-tone paint pkg. ($113- $186). Charger blackout graphics ($127). Light group ($74). Comfort/Convenience: Air cond. ($612). Rear defroster, electric ($120). Automatic speed control ($155). Tinted glass: 4dr. ($82). Rallye instrument cluster ($127). Electric clock w/trip odometer ($48). Intermittent wipers ($47). Rear wiper/washer: 4dr. ($117). Mirrors: Dual remote chrome: 4dr. ($47). Dual sport remote: 024 ($55). Lighted vanity ($50). Entertainment: AM radio: Miser ($78). AM/FM stereo radio ($106-$184); w/8track player ($192-$270); w/cassette ($242- $320). Exterior: Removable glass sunroof: 024 ($275). Rear spoiler: base 024 ($68). Black vinyl bodyside molding: 4dr. ($45). Bumper guards: 4dr. ($56). Front nerf strips: 4dr. ($25). Rear nerf strips ($25). Bodyside/deck stripe: 4dr. ($39). Luggage rack: 4dr. ($93). Undercoating ($39). Lower body protective coating ($39). Interior: Console, shift lever ($41). Cloth/vinyl bucket seats: Miser ($27). Vinyl bucket seats (NC) exc. Miser. Tonneau cover: 024 ($64). Cargo area carpet w/sound insulation ($56). Wheels and Tires: Deluxe wheel covers: 4dr. (NC). Luxury wheel covers (NC). Cast aluminum 14 in. wheels: 024 ($231). 13 in. Rallye wheels: Euro ($45). 14 in. Rallye wheels: 024 (NC). P175/75R13 WSW ($58). P175/75R13 SBR WSW ($134). P195/60R14 SBR BSW: 024 ($173). P195/60R14 SBR RWL: 024 ($257). Conventional spare tire ($51).

ARIES CONVENIENCE/APPEARANCE OPTIONS: Option Packages: Cabriolet roof pkg.: Cust/SE ($696). Light pkg. ($89-$98). Comfort/Convenience: Air cond. ($676). Rear defroster ($125). Automatic speed control ($155). Power seat ($197). Power front windows ($165). Power door locks ($106-$152). Power decklid/liftgate release ($32). Tinted glass ($88). Steering wheel: Luxury ($40); Sport ($50-$90); Leather-wrapped ($50- 90); Tilt ($95). Digital clock ($61). Intermitent wipers ($47). Liftgate wiper/washer: wag ($117). Lighting, Horns and Mirrors: Halogen headlamps ($41). Dual horns ($12). Remote left mirror ($22). Dual remote mirrors ($64-$86). Lighted vanity mirror, right ($50). Entertainment: AM radio: base ($78). AM/FM stereo radio ($106-$184); w/8track player ($192-$270); w/cassette ($242- $320); w/CB ($364-$442). Dual front speakers ($27). Premium speakers ($126). Delete AM radio ($56 credit). Exterior: Removable glass sunroof ($275). Full vinyl roof: 4dr. ($157). Padded landau roof: 2dr. ($157). Door edge protectors ($15-$25). Sill moldings ($23). Bumper guards, front or rear ($28). Bodyside tape stripe: 4dr. ($48). Luggage rack ($106). Special sound insulation ($87). Undercoating ($39). Vinyl lower body protection ($39). Interior: Console: Cust/SE ($100). Vinyl bench seat: Cust (NC). Cloth/vinyl bench seat: base ($31). Vinyl reclining bucket seats: Cust ($132-$151); SE

(NC). Cloth reclining bucket seats: Cust ($249-$270); SE ($98). Color-keyed mats: front ($25); rear ($20). Color-keyed seatbelts ($28). Tonneau cover: wag ($64). Trunk dress-up ($51). Wheels and Tires: Deluxe 13 in. wheel covers ($52). Luxury 14 in. wheel covers ($41-$93). 14 in. wire wheel covers ($257- $309). Rallye wheels, 13 or 14 in. ($41-$93). Cast aluminum 14 in. wheels ($357-$409). P175/75R13 GBR wide WSW ($58). P185/70R13 SBR wide WSW ($194). P185/70R14 GBR wide WSW ($207). Conventional spare tire ($51).

400 CONVENIENCE/APPEARANCE OPTIONS: Option Packages: Light/gauge alert group: base ($79). Sport appearance pkg. ($210-$309). Exterior appearance pkg. ($113- $212). Comfort/Convenience: Air cond. ($676). Rear defroster ($125). Auto. speed control ($155). Power windows ($165). Power door locks ($106). Power seat ($197). Power decklid release ($32). Tinted glass ($88). Sport steering wheel ($50). Leather- wrapped steering wheel ($51) but (NC) w/option pkg. Tilt steering wheel ($95). Deluxe wipers ($47). Lighting and Mirrors: Halogen headlamps: base ($15). Cornering lights: base ($57). Reading lamp: base ($24). Remote-control mirror: base ($55). Lighted vanity mirror ($50). Entertainment: AM/FM stereo ($106); w/8track tape player ($192); w/CB ($364). Electronic-tuning AM/FM stereo ($250); w/cassette ($455). Dual front speakers ($27). Premium speakers ($126). Radil delete ($56 credit). Exterior: Glass sunroof ($275). Crystal coat paint ($99). Two-tone paint: base ($113-$212). Sill moldings ($23). Door edge protectors ($15). Bodyside tape stripe ($48). Bumper guards, front or rear ($23). Undercoating ($39). Vinyl lower body protection ($39). Interior: Console ($100). Vinyl bucket seats w/dual recliners: base 2dr. ($92). Cloth/vinyl bucket seats: LS ($151). Leather bucket seats: LS ($263-$414). Center armrest ($59). Color-keyed mats: front ($25); rear ($20). Trunk dress-up: base ($51). Wheels/Tires: Wire wheel covers ($219). Cast aluminum wheels ($316). Conventional spare tire ($51).

DIPLOMAT CONVENIENCE/APPEARANCE OPTIONS: Option Packages: Basic group ($923-$1143). Light pkg. ($106- $139). Protection group ($119). Comfort/Convenience: Air cond. ($731). Rear defroster, electric ($125). Auto. speed control ($155). Power seat, each ($197). Power windows ($235). Power door locks ($152). Power decklid release ($32). Illuminated entry system ($72). Leather-wrapped steering wheel ($50). Tilt steering wheel ($95). Digital clock ($61). Intermittent wipers ($47). Mirrors: Remote driver's ($22). Dual remote chrome ($43-$65). Lighted vanity ($58). Entertainment: AM/FM stereo radio ($106); w/ 8track tape player ($192); w/CB ($364). Search-tune AM/FM stereo ($239). Electronic-tuning AM/FM stereo w/cassette ($455). Dual front speakers ($28). Premium speakers ($126). Power antenna ($55). Radio delete ($56 credit). Exterior: Power glass sunroof ($982). Full vinyl roof: Salon ($157). Vinyl bodyside moldings ($46). Upper door frame moldings: Salon ($41). Bodyside/deck/hood stripe ($109). Body sound insulation ($30). Undercoating ($39). Interior: Vinyl bench seat: Salon ($57). Leather 60/40 seat: Medallion ($416). Trunk dress-up ($50). Wheels and Tires: Premium wheel covers ($93). Wire wheel covers ($257). Forged aluminum wheels ($364). P205/75R15 SBR WSW ($116). Conventional spare ($51).

MIRADA CONVENIENCE/APPEARANCE OPTIONS: Option Packages: CMX pkg. ($935). Basic group ($1072-$1229). Light pkg. ($159). Protection pkg. ($137). Comfort/Convenience: Air cond. ($731). Rear defroster, electric ($125). Auto. speed control ($155). Power seat ($197); dual ($394). Power windows ($165). Power door locks ($106). Power decklid release ($32-$49). Illuminated entry system ($72). Sport steering wheel ($50). Leather-covered steering wheel ($50). Tilt steering wheel ($95). Digital clock ($61). Intermittent wipers ($47). Lighting, Horns and Mirrors: Cornering lights ($57). Triad horns ($25). Lighted vanity mirror ($58). Entertainment: AM/FM stereo radio ($106); w/8track ($192); w/CB ($364). Search-tune AM/FM stereo ($239). Electronic- tuning AM/FM stereo w/cassette ($455). Dual front speakers ($28). Premium speakers ($126). Power antenna ($55). Delete radio ($56 credit). Exterior: T-Bar roof ($790). Landau vinyl roof ($157). Wheel lip moldings ($30). Sill moldings ($34). Bodyside/hood/deck tape stripes ($96). Undercoating ($39). Interior: Console ($75-$124). Cloth/vinyl 60/40 seat ($202- $251). Vinyl bucket seats ($48). Leather bucket seats ($515- $564). Center armrest ($49). Trunk dress-up ($60). Wheels and Tires: Forged aluminum wheels ($270-$323). Premium wheel covers ($53). Wire wheel covers ($163-$216). P205/75R15 SBR WSW ($115). P215/70R15 SBR RWL ($66-$181). Conventional spare tire ($51).

HISTORY: Introduced: October 4, 1981 except 400, October 29; and 400 convertible, mid-April 1982. Model year production: Chrysler reported a total of 237,940 passenger cars shipped. Total North American production for the U.S. market of 272,407 units included 241,359 four-cylinder, 9,795 six-cylinder and 21,253 V-8s. Calendar year production (U.S.): 244,878. Calendar year sales by U.S. dealers: 261,105. Model year sales by U.S. dealers: 250,392 (not incl. 41,577 imported Colts and 14,340 Challengers).

Historical Footnotes: Model year sales slipped considerably, from 371,548 in 1981 (including captive imports) to just 306,309 in 1982. Nevertheless, Dodge's market share held almost steady at 4.0 percent. Figuring domestic models only, Dodge's share was 4.5 percent of the market (down from 4.8 percent). Only the imported Colt and Challenger showed a sales increase. Omni/024 sales dropped by 27 percent for the model year; rear-drive models by 44 percent. In fact, only 10 percent of Dodge sales were rear-drives (Mirada/Diplomat). Calendar year production fell by over 25 percent. *Motor Trend* had named Aries its 1981 Car of the Year. Aries was Dodge's top seller by far, but even its sales fell by 18 percent. The Charger 2.2 sales catalog directed customers to Direct Connection, Chrysler's Performance Parts Program, if they felt the need for additional dress-up items as well as mechanical components for off-road driving. In fall 1982, Batten, Barton, Durstine & Osborne Inc. was named Dodge's ad agency, taking over from Kenyon & Eckhardt Inc. (which had previously handled all Chrysler products). This was part of Chrysler vice-president of marketing Joseph A. Campana's strategy of giving Dodge Division a stronger independent identity. At mid-year a Rampage car/pickup debuted, based on the 024 design.

1983 DODGE

In the factory sales catalogs, Dodges were billed as "America's Driving Machines." All Omni-based coupes adopted the Charger nameplate this year, dropping the 024 designation. Dodge hoped to attract customers who might recognize the familiar name from the much larger performance- oriented models of the 1970s. A new high-performance Charger model, modified by Carroll Shelby, was aimed at younger buyers. This would be the final season for the rear-drive Mirada. One new model emerged late in 1982: a stretched version of the K-car, called 600. Chrysler's 2.2-liter Trans4 engine added 10 HP this year with a boost to 9.0:1 compression, reworked manifolds, and recalibrated fuel/spark control. Five-speed manual transmission was now standard on 400, optional on Omni/Charger/Aries. A "Message Center" displayed warning lights indicating door is open or fuel is low, on a car diagram. Electronic Voice Alert, optional on 400 and 600, added audio. The system monitored 11 functions. Galvanized sheet metal panels, pre-coated steel in critical areas, and a seven-step dip-and-spray process improved rust resistance.

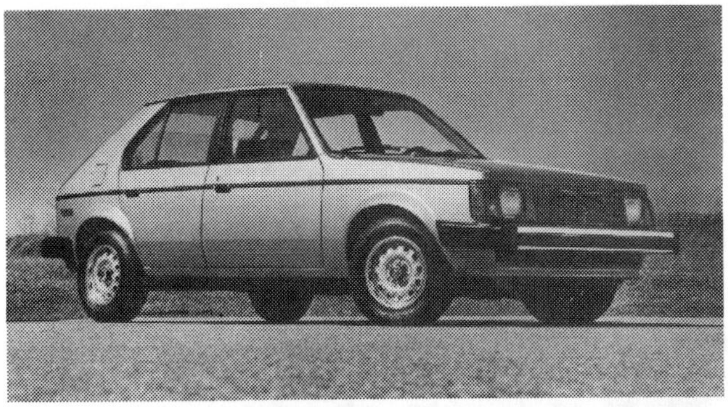

1983 Omni hatchback sedan (D)

OMNI — SERIES Z — FOUR — Appearance of Dodge's subcompact sedan was similar to 1982, but with red (upper) portions of taillamps split into separate side-by-side sections, rather than divided horizontally. Base Omnis were better equipped this year. New standard features included halogen headlamps, reclining bucket seats, a quartz clock, power brakes, and a trip odometer. Standard engine was again the 104.7 cu. in. (1.7- liter four) with four-speed manual transaxle. But a new 1.6- liter four (from Peugeot) took its place at mid-year. Omnis now had standard power front disc/self-adjusting rear drum brakes. Chrysler's pentastar sat in the center of the grille, which had one vertical bar and four horizontal bars forming 10 sections, plus subdued horizontal bars within each section. Amber parking/turn lamps wrapped around onto fenders. A 'Dodge' nameplate was on the left front lip of the hood. At the rear were small amber side reflectors. Omnis had full-length blackout bodyside moldings and new, longer bumper end caps. Interiors held standard reclining cloth-and-vinyl low- back premium bucket seats. All-vinyl buckets were available at no extra cost. Upholstery colors were: red, silver, dark blue/medium blue, or dark brown/beige. Standard equipment included wheel trim rings, a black outside mirror, vanity mirror, luggage compartment light, intermittent wipers, color-keyed four-spoke sport steering wheel, and P175/75R13 GBR tires. Base and Custom sedans were offered; the low- budget Miser was gone. So was the EType (Euro-Sedan). Omni Custom had dual reclining high-back sport bucket seats with integral headrests in cloth-and-vinyl (same colors as base model); woodgrain applique on instrument panel; wide whitewall GBR tires; deluxe wheel covers; cargo area carpeting and sound insulation; Body colors were: Silver Crystal Coat, Crimson Red, Charcoal Gray metallic, Black, Beige Crystal Coat, Glacier Blue Crystal Coat, Pearl White, and Graphic Red; Custom could also have Sable Brown or Nightwatch Blue. Two-tones (Custom only) were: Silver Crystal Coat/Charcoal Gray metallic; Glacier Blue Crystal Coat/Nightwatch Blue; Beige Crystal Coat/Sable Brown. Options included a new manual five-speed transaxle with 2.20:1 or 2.57:1 performance gear ratio. TorqueFlite automatic was available with the optional 2.2-liter engine. An optional Rallye cluster held a tachometer, trip odometer, quartz clock, alternator gauge, fuel gauge, temp and oil pressure lights, and brake system warning light. An electronic-tuning radio was now available, with or without a cassette player.

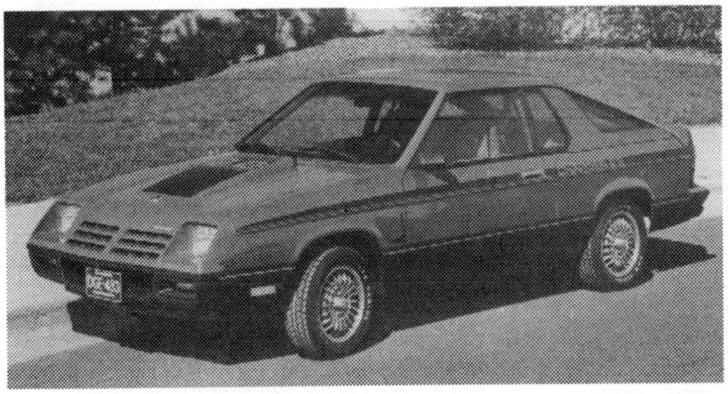

1983 Charger 2.2 hatchback coupe (D)

CHARGER/2.2 — SERIES Z — FOUR — A 'Charger' nameplate on wide pillars between the subcompact coupe's side windows demonstrated its name change this year. Coupes came in three levels: base model with standard 1.7-liter four and four-speed manual shift, Charger 2.2 with the Trans4 engine, and (as a mid-year addition) a new Shelby Charger performance model. The Miser edition was dropped. As with the Omni sedan, a 1.6-liter became the base engine at mid-year. Charger's front end featured a sharply sloped grille that was actually six simple horizontal slots, accompanied by tunneled halogen headlamps. Standard cloth- and-vinyl high-back bucket seats had integral headrests and reclining seatbacks. The back seat folded down. Upholstery colors were red, brown/beige, silver, black, and dark blue/medium blue. All-vinyl was available at no extra cost. A standard Rallye instrument cluster held an alternator gauge, temp/oil pressure warning light, fuel gauge, speedometer, tachometer, trip odometer, and quartz clock. Chargers had a color-keyed four-spoke sport steering wheel and P175/75R13 GBR tires. Body colors were: Glacier Blue Crystal Coat, Charcoal Gray Metallic, Crimson Red, Nightwatch Blue, Beige Crystal Coat, Pearl White, Black, Silver Crystal Coat, Sable Brown, or Graphic Red. Three two-tones were offered: Black/Burnished Silver metallic; Glacier Blue Crystal Coat/Nightwatch Blue; or Beige Crystal Coat/Sable Brown. Options includled the new five-speed manual transaxle, TorqueFlite automatic (which required the 2.2-liter engine), air conditioning (not with 1.6 engine), and a manual sun roof. Charger 2.2 was noticeable by its simulated hood scoop, topped by a large 'Charger 2.2' decal, and simulated front fender exhausters. Additional 'Charger 2.2' graphics in red, black or beige went on bodysides (to rear of door) and rear spoiler, along with black accent trim. Otherwise, appearance was similar to the base Charger, with a six-slot body grille (each slot containing twin vertical elements) topped by 'Dodge' nameplate and deep-set headlamps. Standard engine was the 135 cu. in. (2.2-liter) four with five-speed manual transaxle, with 10 more horsepower this year. Raised white letter low-profile P195/60R14 SBR tires rode 14 in. steel Rallye road wheels. Standard equipment included a performance exhaust (rather loud), firm-feel sport suspension, power brakes, cockpit-like interior with console, dual remote sport mirrors, front storage, and maintenance-free battery. Upholstery came in red, brown/beige, or black. High-back cloth-and-vinyl seats were like the base Charger; all-vinyl optional at no extra cost. Electronic-tuning radios, with or without cassette player, were newly optional. Charger 2.2 body colors were: Graphic Red, Pearl White, Black, Silver Crystal Coat, or Sable Brown. An optional Black graphics package consisted of flat black lower body paint, lower accent stripes on bodysides, and front/rear bumper rub

strips. It was available with silver, red or white body color. The heavily reworked Shelby Charger, developed at Santa Fe Springs, California, carried a high-performance 2.2-liter four rated 107 horsepower. Compression was boosted to 9.6:1, the camshaft revised, and exhaust restriction lessened. Shelby had a blue or silver body with contrasting stripes, a front air dam, rear roof appliques, rocker-panel (ground effects) extensions, rear lip spoiler, and special paint/tape treatment. Rather than the standard two-section quarter windows, Shelby had a one-piece design. Wide 15 in. aluminum wheels carried 50-series Eagle GT tires. Color-keyed bucket seats had a 'CS' logo. Gas/brake pedals were revised for heel/toe shifting. Five-speed manual shift was standard. So were heavy-duty shocks and higher-rate springs. All this effort paid off, as Shelby Chargers ran a claimed 0-60 time of 8.5 seconds.

1983 Aries Custom wagon (D)

ARIES — SERIES D — FOUR — Aries, according to the Dodge catalog, was "America's Family Driving Machine....The car that put America back on the road again." Appearance was just about the same as 1982, including the stand-up pentastar hood ornament, but with new bright metal accents. The grille consisted of five horizontal bars (including top and bottom bars) with 'Dodge' block letters on the body-color header above. Vertical rectangular clear parking lights sat between grille and headlamps, with amber cornering lamps on the outside. Integrated front and rear bumpers were intended to be part of its design, not 'hung' on as an afterthought. Only the wagon remained in the Custom series; sedans came in base or S.E. trim. Power brakes were now standard. So were brighter, longer-lasting halogen headlamps, as well as self-adjusting rear brakes, a tethered gas cap, and a maintenance-free battery. New optional air conditioning had bi-level cooling to eliminate "cold zones." Instrument panels had a new soft cover. A new flasher allowed signaling with headlamps when passing in daylight. Under the hood, the base 2.2-liter OHC engine got a horsepower boost from 84 to 94, to improve acceleration. That powerplant had chrome valve stems, cobalt alloy valve seats, moly-faced compression rings, and an electric thermo-controlled fan. Optional again was the 2.6-liter from Mitsubishi, on S.E. models as well as the Custom wagon. A new heater system improved air distribution, and there was a new maintenance-free battery. Four-speed manual transaxle was standard, five-speed overdrive optional. The five-speed used a cable shift linkage rather than the customary rod, which was supposed to shorten lever travel and improve its "feel." Three-speed TorqueFlite was standard with the 2.6-liter engine, optional with the 2.2-liter. Rack-and-pinion steering was power-assisted on the S.E. wagon. All-vinyl bench seats went in the standard interior, along with carpeted lower door trim panels. S.E. models had a plush new standard split-back all-cloth bench seat with fold- down center armrest, carpeted door trim panels with detailed woodtone inserts, and matching woodtone lower instrument panel trim. Two/four-door sedans had new rear quarter window louvers, bright decklid lower molding, and 'S.E.' pillar medallion. All S.E. models carried 10-ounce cut pile carpeting, a digital clock, dome light, cloth-covered headliner, day/night inside mirror, AM radio, and two-speed wiper/washers. S.E. wagons had woodgrain bodyside and liftgate appliques. Optional reclining cloth buckets and a center console with free-standing center armrest were available on the S.E. and Custom wagon. Standard upholstery colors were: brown/beige, dark/medium blue, or red. S.E. sedans could also have silver. Wagons could have the same colors in saddle vinyl. Upholstery options for base Aries were Kingsley cloth in brown/beige, Madison cloth in dark/medium blue, or red cloth-and-vinyl. Nine body colors were offered: Black, Nightwatch Blue, Charcoal Gray metallic, Pearl White, Silver Crystal Coat, Beige Crystal Coat, Crimson Red, Sable Brown, or Glacier Blue Crystal Coat. Also two-tone Charcoal Gray/Burnished Silver metallic. Three easy-order packages were available, along with a new electronic-tuning stereo radio option.

1983 Dodge 400 convertible (D)

400 — SERIES V — FOUR — Only one series was offered in the 400 line this year, as the original LS was dropped. A two-door coupe, four-door sedan and convertible were available again, the latter two having been added during the 1982 model year. A slat-style grille consisted of six wide, bright horizontal bars. Quad headlamps were mounted in separate, deeply recessed housings. Small parking lamps were below the bumper rub strip. Front fenders displayed twin vertical louvers. Bodyside moldings met with bumper strips at front and rear. Coupes had narrow opera windows, while the full vinyl roof on sedans extended to the rear portion of the back door, creating a narrow window shape. New standard equipment included a ram-air heat/vent system with an extra dash vent, tethered gas cap, wide rear bumper guards, self-adjusting rear brakes, and a maintenance- free battery. The ample list also included power

brakes and steering, bumper rub strips, digital clock, 2.2-liter Trans4 engine with electric fan, and halogen high/low beam headlamps. All models also had a pentastar hood ornament, dual horns, day/night mirror, dual outside chrome mirrors, color-keyed vinyl roof surround molding, AM radio, landau (coupe) or full (sedan) padded vinyl roof, and standard vinyl bucket seats with center armrest. Also standard: a two-spoke steering wheel, P185/70R14 SBR whitewall tires, two-speed wipers, deluxe wheel covers, and inside hood release. Bodies held bright moldings for belt, bodyside (with vinyl inserts), decklid, windshield, upper door frame, and drip rail. Convertibles included a console with center armrest, power top, visor vanity mirror, and dual color-keyed remote-control mirrors. The four-door and convertible had standard TorqueFlite transmission; two-doors came with a standard five-speed manual transaxle. The standard sedan interior held a Kimberley cloth bench seat with center armrest, while the coupe and convertible had low-back vinyl bucket seats with adjustable head restraints and seatback recliners. Body colors were: Black, Crimson Red, Nightwatch Blue, Sable Brown, and Pearl White; plus metallic Charcoal Gray, Beige Crystal Coat, Silver Crystal Coat, and Glacier Blue Crystal Coat. Two-door models could also have a choice of four two-tone paint packages; four-doors, three selections. New options included an Electronic Voice Alert System, to augment the standard message center. Also optional: an electronic travel computer cluster, tilt steering, power windows and door locks, air conditioning with new bi-level ventilation, automatic speed control, electronic-tuning AM/FM stereo radio with cassette player, and rear window defroster. Two easy-order packages were available, one for $640 and the other priced over $2100. A Roadability package included the Sport handling suspension (larger diameter sway bars, firm- feel power steering and special drive ratio) and P185/70R14 Goodyear Eagle GT SBR tires. Dodge's 400 was closely related to Chrysler LeBaron.

1983 Dodge 600 sedan (D)

600 — SERIES E — FOUR — Yet another front-drive joined the Dodge lineup this year (actually introduced late in 1982), the Ebodied 600 and more sporty 600 ES. According to Dodge, the 600 was a Euro- sport touring car that "begs to be driven." Wheelbase was 3 in. longer than the Kcar; 10 in. longer overall. The six- window, four-door sedan was a mate to Chrysler's E Class. A sculptured hood with pentastar stand-up hood ornament stood behind a grille with six bright horizontal bars, somewhat akin to Mirada and 400. Quad recessed rectangular halogen headlamps were used. Clear parking lights set into an integrated bumper. A wide slot in the front bumper was approximately grille width. Twin front fender louvers appeared just ahead of the front door. Unlike the Aries/400 back window, which was nearly vertical, the 600 version slanted somewhat. The rear end might remind some observers of Mercedes. Chassis and suspension were similar to Aries and 400: Iso-Strut front with linkless anti-sway bar and coil springs, and a flex-arm beam rear axle with trailing links and coil springs. Improved power brakes had bigger rotor and caliper assemblies; rear drums were now self-adjusting. An electronic feedback carburetor went on the standard 2.2-liter engine. Standard equipment included power brakes and steering, electric fuel filler door and decklid releases, dual bright mirrors, AM radio, and digital clock. The base 600 came with standard wide-ratio three-speed TorqueFlite; 600ES carried a standard manual five-speed transaxle. Mitsubishi's 2.6-liter four was optional. An "optical" horn let the driver blink lights when passing. Standard cloth-and- vinyl bench seats had a folding center armrest and adjustable head restraints. Interiors also held padded door trim panels with cloth and carpet inserts, woodtone bezels, full-length armrests, pull straps, and courtesy lamps. Interior colors were blue, silver, red, and beige. Silver, red or beige vinyl also was available. Also optional: cloth-and-vinyl 50/50 seating with dual armrests and recliners, center consolettes and seatback pockets in blue, silver, red, beige, or brown. Body colors were: Crimson Red, Glacier Blue Crystal Coat, Beige Crystal Coat, Charcoal metallic, and Bright Silver Crystal Coat. The base 600 could also get Pearl White, Sable Brown, Black, or Nightwatch Blue Crystal Coat. Two- tones included Sable Brown/Beige Crystal Coat, Nightwatch Blue/Glacier Blue Crystal Coat, and Black/Silver Crystal Coat. For a more dramatic look, the 600 ES displayed a blackout exterior including black moldings, outside mirrors, bodyside and decklid stripes, and outside door handle inserts. Inside were cloth-and-vinyl high-back bucket seats with integral head restraints and reclining backs, a center console with freestanding armrest (silver, red or beige), and sport steering wheel. Standard Electronic Voice Alert monitored 10 conditions: door ajar, brake on, low fuel, belts unbuckled, etc. A Sport Handling Suspension Package consisted of larger front/rear sway bars, higher-control shocks, firm-feel power steering with quicker ratio, and Goodyear SBR Eagle GT tires on aluminum wheels. Two easy-order packages were available, one for around $600 and the other over three times that figure.

1983 Diplomat Salon sedan (D)

DIPLOMAT — SERIES G — SIX/V-8 — Once again, Diplomat arrived only in four-door sedan form, in Salon and Medallion trim levels. Apart from four new body colors available, appearance was similar to 1982, including the same grille and stand-up pentastar hood ornament. The formal-style eight-section grille had cross- hatched segments within each vertical section. Six small squarish sections tapered outward toward the fender edge on each side, to join twin rectangular amber reflectors. 'Dodge' letters stood on the wide upper bar. Quad rectangular headlamps were used. 'Diplomat' insignias were on front fenders, ahead of the door. Standard engine was again the 225 cu. in. (3.7-liter) Slant Six, with 318 cu. in. V-8 optional. Diplomat's Salon included tinted glass, Sherwood woodtone trim on the instrument panel, cloth-and-vinyl bench seat with folding center armrest, power steering/brakes, and three-speed TorqueFlite. Upholstery colors were dark blue, red, beige, or silver. Optional: a beige vinyl bench seat. Medallion offered a more luxurious interior and formal roof styling. 60/40 cloth-and-vinyl seating had a folding center armrest and passenger recliner (dark blue, red, beige or silver), plus dress-up trunk. As for outside trim, Salon had bright windshield, roof drip, belt, sill and wheel opening moldings; bright rear door glass division bar; bumper protective rub strips; and front bumper guards. Medallion added bright upper door frame moldings, a full vinyl roof, and bright vinyl roof termination molding. Body colors were: Nightwatch Blue, Sable Brown, Crimson Red, Pearl White, Charcoal Gray metallic, Formal Black, Glacier Blue Crystal Coat, Beige Crystal Coat, and Silver Crystal Coat. Diplomat, it was said, was aimed at motorists who "couldn't afford to operate one of yesterday's behemoths." Most of its customers, though, were fleet buyers. A total of 13,106 Diplomats (over half the total production) had the Police package.

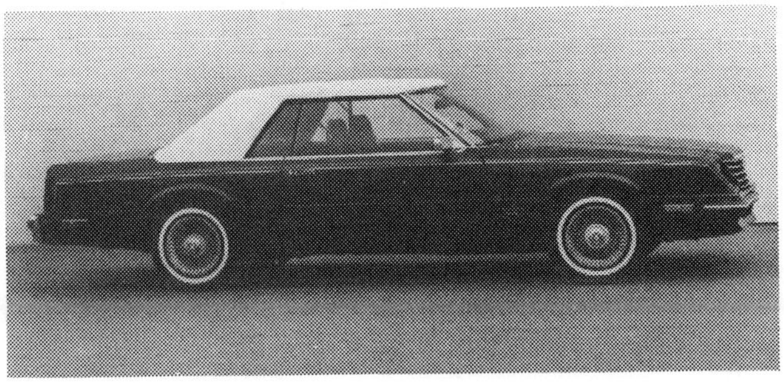

1983 Mirada "Cabriolet" hardtop coupe (D)

MIRADA — SERIES X — SIX/V-8 — For its final stab at attracting buyers, "America's sporty driving machine" kept the same eye-catching appearance as in 1982, but offered some new body colors. The factory catalog claimed that owning a rear-drive Mirada displayed "a clear statement of your personality." The familiar 225 cu. in. (3.7-liter) Slant Six was standard again, 318 cu. in. (5.2-liter) V-8 optional. All Miradas had three-speed TorqueFlite automatic and a "driver-oriented" dash filled with round gauges. Standard equipment included dual horns, inside hood release, color-keyed seat belts, power steering/brakes, and an AM radio. Mirada's chassis was the same as that used on the four- door Diplomat, but the resemblance stopped there. Mirada had a flexible plastic front end. A sculptured hood top merged into the sleek grille with five horizontal bars tipped by thin bright strips; half a dozen vertical bars sat well behind. Some observers compared Mirada's grille to that of the 1936-37 Cord. Vertical rectangular amber park/turn lights sat between headlamps and grille. An integrated front bumper held twin wide slots in its center. 'Mirada' block letters were evident at rear of front fenders; 'CMX' badge (if that package was included) immediately below. Both 'Dodge' and 'Mirada' letters could be seen on the decklid. Trim consisted of bright hood rear edge, fender edge, windshield, drip rail, belt, rear quarter side window, opera window, and rear window moldings; a bright/black wide- louvered up-and-over roof molding; and simulated (angled) front fender louvers. Also standard: bumper rub strips and tinted glass. Standard cloth-and-vinyl high-back bucket seats came in red, beige, dark blue, or silver. Optional cloth-and- vinyl 60/40 seats could be red, beige, dark blue or silver, with folding center armrest and passenger seat recliner. Also optional: leather-and-vinyl low-back bucket seats with center cushion and folding center armrest, in beige or silver. Body colors were: Glacier Blue Crystal Coat, Beige Crystal Coat, Silver Crystal Coat, Pearl White, Charcoal Gray metallic, Black, Nightwatch Blue, Sable Brown, or Crimson Red. The Optional CMX package included a sailcloth-textured vinyl simulated convertible roof; bright touchdown moldings; color-keyed door handle inserts; cloth-and-vinyl bucket seats with center armrest; premium wheel covers and P205/75R15 SBR WSW tires. A total of 1,841 Miradas had the CMX package, while 638 came with the Sport Equipment package (RPO code A76). Also optional: aluminum road wheels.

I.D. DATA: Dodge's 17-symbol Vehicle Identification Number (VIN), as before, was on the upper left corner of the instrument panel, visible through the windshield. The first digit indicates Country: '1' U.S.A.; '2' Canada. The second symbol is Make: 'B' Dodge. Third is Vehicle Type: '3' passenger car; '7' truck. The next symbol ('B') indicates manual seatbelts. Symbol five is Car Line: 'Z' Omni/Charger; 'D' Aries; 'E' 600; 'G' Diplomat; 'X' Mirada; 'V' 400. Symbol six is Series (price class): '1' Economy; '2' Low; '4' High'; '5' Premium; '6' Special. Symbol seven is Body Style: '1' 2-dr. sedan; '2' 2-dr. specialty hardtop; ''4' 2-dr. hatchback; '5' 2-dr. convertible; '6' 4-dr. sedan; '8' 4-dr. hatchback; '9' 4-dr. wagon. Eighth is the Engine Code: 'A' L498 2Bbl.; 'B' L4105 2Bbl.; 'C' L4135 2Bbl.; 'F' or '8' Shelby L4135 2Bbl.; 'G' L4156 2Bbl.; 'H' L6-225 1Bbl.; 'P' V8318 2Bbl. Next comes a check digit (0-9 or X). Symbol ten indicates Model Year: 'D' 1983. Symbol eleven is Assembly Plant: 'C' Jefferson (Detroit); 'D' Belvidere, IL; 'F' Newark, DE; 'G' or 'X' St. Louis; 'R' Windsor, Ontario. The last six digits make up the sequential serial number, starting with 100001. Engine numbers and Body Code Plates are in the same locations as 1981-82.

OMNI (FOUR)

Model Number	Body/Style Number	Body Type & Seating	Factory Price	Shipping Weight	Production Total
ZE	44	4-dr. Hatch-5P	5841	2165	33,264
ZE	44	4-dr. Hatch-5P	6071	2195	9,290

CHARGER (FOUR)

ZH	24	2-dr. Hatch-5P	6379	2210	22,535

CHARGER 2.2 (FOUR)

ZP	24	2-dr. Hatch-5P	7303	2330	10,448

SHELBY CHARGER (FOUR)

ZS	24	2-dr. Hatch-5P	8290	N/A	8,251

ARIES (FOUR)

DL	21	2-dr. Sedan-6P	6577	2300	14,218
DL	41	4-dr. Sedan-6P	6718	2300	51,783
DH	45	4-dr. Cust Wag-6P	7636	2410	29,228

ARIES SPECIAL EDITION (FOUR)

DH	21	2-dr. Sedan-6P	7260	2310	4,325
DH	41	4-dr. Sedan-6P	7417	2340	8,962
DP	45	4-dr. Sta Wag-6P	8186	2465	4,023

400 (FOUR)

VP	22	2-dr. Cpe-6P	8014	2430	11,504
VP	41	4-dr. Sedan-6P	8490	2480	9,560
VP	27	2-dr. Conv.-4P	12500	2475	4,888

400 Price Note: The convertible's price was cut sharply during the model year, down to $9995.

600 (FOUR)

EH	41	4-dr. Sedan—6P	8841	2525	21,065
EH	41	4-dr. ES sedan-6P	9372	2540	12,423

DIPLOMAT SALON (SIX/V-8)

GL	41	4-dr. Sedan-6P	8248/8473	3320/3455	21,368

DIPLOMAT MEDALLION (SIX/V-8)

GH	41	4-dr. Sedan-6P	9369/9594	3390/3525	3,076

MIRADA (SIX/V-8)

XS	22	2-dr. HT Cpe-5P	9011/9236	3310/3450	5,597

FACTORY PRICE AND WEIGHT NOTE: Prices and weights to left of slash are for six-cylinder, to right for V-8 engine. **MODEL NUMBER NOTE:** Some sources identify models using the new VIN data to indicate Car Line, Price Class and Body Style. Example: Aries four- door (DL41) has the equivalent number D26, which translates to Aries line, Low price class, and four-door sedan body. See I.D. Data section for breakdown.

ENGINE DATA: BASE FOUR (Omni, Charger): Inline, overhead-cam four-cylinder. Cast iron block; aluminum head. Displacement: 104.7 cu. in. (1.7 liters). Bore & stroke: 3.13 x 3.40 in. Compression ratio: 8.2:1. Brake horsepower: 63 at 4800 R.P.M. Torque: 83 lbs.-ft. at 2400 R.P.M. Five main bearings. Solid valve lifters. Carburetor: 2Bbl. Holley 6520. VIN Code: B. BASE FOUR (late Omni, Charger): Inline, overhead-cam four-cylinder. Cast iron block; aluminum head. Displacement: 97.3 cu. in. (1.6 liters). Bore & stroke: 3.17 x 3.07 in. Compression ratio: 8.8:1. Brake horsepower: 62 at 4800 R.P.M. Torque: 86 lbs.-ft. at 3200 R.P.M. Five main bearings. Solid valve lifters. Carburetor: 2Bbl. VIN Code: A. BASE FOUR (Charger 2.2, Aries, 400, 600); OPTIONAL (Omni, Charger): Inline, overhead-cam four-cylinder. Cast iron block; aluminum head. Displacement: 135 cu. in. (2.2 liters). Bore & stroke: 3.44 x 3.62 in. Compression ratio: 9.0:1. Brake horsepower: 94 at 5200 R.P.M. (Charger 2.2, 100 at 5200 R.P.M.). Torque: 111 lbs.-ft. at 2400 R.P.M. (Charger 2.2, 122 lbs.-ft. at 3200 R.P.M.). Five main bearings. Hydraulic valve lifters. Carburetor: 2Bbl. Holley 6520. VIN Code: C. BASE FOUR (Shelby Charger): Same as 135 cu. in. four above, except Compression ratio: 9.6:1. Horsepower: 107 at 5600 R.P.M. Torque: 127 lbs.-ft. at 3200 R.P.M. VIN Code: F. OPTIONAL FOUR (Aries, 400, 600): Inline, overhead-cam four-cylinder. Cast iron block; aluminum head. Displacement: 156 cu. in. (2.6 liters). Bore & stroke: 3.59 x 3.86 in. Compression ratio: 8.2:1. Brake horsepower: 93 at 4500 R.P.M. Torque: 132 lbs.-ft. at 2500 R.P.M. Five main bearings. Solid valve lifters. Carburetor: 2Bbl. Mikuni. Mitsubishi-built. VIN Code: G. BASE SIX (Diplomat, Mirada): Inline, overhead-valve six. Cast iron block and head. Displacement: 225 cu. in. (3.7 liters). Bore & stroke: 3.40 x 4.12 in. Compression ratio: 8.4:1. Brake horsepower: 90 at 3600 R.P.M. Torque: 165 lbs.-ft. at 1600 R.P.M. Four main bearings. Hydraulic valve lifters. Carburetor: 1Bbl. Holley 6145. VIN Code: H. OPTIONAL V-8 (Diplomat, Mirada): 90-degree, overhead valve V-8. Cast iron block and head. Displacement: 318 cu. in. (5.2 liters). Bore & stroke: 3.91 x 3.31 in. Compression ratio: 8.5:1. Brake horsepower: 130 at 4000 R.P.M. Torque: 230 lbs.-ft. at 1600 R.P.M. Five main bearings. Hydraulic valve lifters. Carburetor: 2Bbl. Carter BBD. VIN Code: P.

CHASSIS DATA: Wheelbase: (Omni) 99.1 in.; (Charger) 96.6 in.; (Aries) 100.1 in.; (400) 100.3 in.; (600) 102.9 in.; (Diplomat/Mirada) 112.7 in. Overall length: (Omni) 164.8 in.; (Chgr) 173.7 in.; (Aries sed) 176.0 in.; (Aries wag) 176.2 in.; (400) 181.2 in.; (600) 187.2 in.; (Diplomat) 205.7 in.; (Mirada) 209.5 in. Height: (Omni) 53.1 in.; (Chgr) 50.8 in.; (Aries 2dr.) 52.3 in.; (Aries 4dr.) 52.7 in.; (Aries wag) 52.4 in.; (400 2dr.) 52.5 in.; (400 4dr.) 52.9 in.; (400 conv.) 54.1 in.; (600) 53.9 in.; (Diplomat) 55.3 in.; (Mirada) 53.2 in. Width: (Omni) 65.8 in.; (Chgr) 66.7 in.; (Aries) 68.6 in.; (400) 68.5 in.; (600) 68.0 in.; (Diplo) 74.2 in.; (Mirada) 72.7 in. Front Tread: (Omni/Chgr) 56.1 in.; (Aries/400/600) 57.6 in.; (Diplo/Mirada) 60.0 in. Rear Tread: (Omni/Chgr) 55.6 in.; (Aries/400/600) 57.0 in.; (Diplo/Mirada) 59.5 in. Standard Tires: (Omni/Charger/Aries) P175/75R13 GBR; (Charger 2.2) P195/60R14 SBR RWL; (400) P185/70R14; (600) P185/70R14 SBR WSW; (600ES) P185/70R14 SBR RBL; (Diplo/Mirada) P195/75R15 GBR WSW.

TECHNICAL: Transmission: Four-speed manual (floor lever) standard on Omni/Charger w/1.7liter four. Gear ratios: (1st) 3.45:1; (2nd) 1.94:1; (3rd) 1.29:1; (4th) 0.97:1; (Rev) 3.17:1. Four- speed manual (floor lever) standard on other Omni/Charger and Aries: (1st) 3.29:1; (2nd) 1.89:1; (3rd) 1.21:1; (4th) 0.88:1; (Rev) 3.14:1. Five-speed manual standard on 400 and 600ES, optional on Omni/Charger/Aries: (1st) 3.29:1; (2nd) 1.89:1; (3rd) 1.21:1; (4th) 0.88:1; (5th) 0.72:1; (Rev) 3.14:1. TorqueFlite three-speed automatic standard on other models, optional on all. Front-wheel drive gear ratios: (1st) 2.69:1; (2nd) 1.55:1; (3rd) 1.00:1; (Rev) 2.10:1.

Diplomat/Mirada: (1st) 2.74:1; (2nd) 1.54:1; (3rd) 1.00:1; (Rev) 2.22:1. Standard final drive ratio: (Omni/Charger) 2.69:1 w/4spd, 2.59:1 or 2.20:1 w/5spd, 2.78:1 w/auto.; (Aries) 2.69:1 w/4spd, 2.20:1 w/5spd, 2.78:1 w/auto.; (400) 2.57:1 w/manual, 2.78:1 w/auto.; (400 w/2.6-liter) 2.78:1 or 3.02:1 w/auto.; (600) 2.57:1 w/5 spd, 2.78:1 w/auto., 3.02:1 w/2.6liter and auto.; (Diplo) 2.94:1; (Mirada six) 2.94:1; (Mirada V-8) 2.26:1. Steering: (Omni/Charger/Aries/400/600) rack and pinion; (others) recirculating ball. Suspension: (Omni/Charger) MacPherson Iso-Strut independent coil front w/anti-sway bar, trailing arm semi-independent coil rear w/beam axle and integral anti-sway; (Aries/400/600) Iso-Strut front w/coil springs and linkless anti-sway bar, and flex-arm beam rear axle w/trailing links, coil springs and anti-sway bar; (Diplomat/Mirada) transverse front torsion bars and anti-sway bar, semi-elliptic rear leaf springs. Brakes: Front disc, rear drum. Ignition: Electronic. Body construction: Unibody. Fuel tank: (Omni/Chgr/Aries/400/600) 13 gal.; (Diplomat/Mirada) 18 gal.

DRIVETRAIN OPTIONS: Engines: 2.2-liter four: Omni ($134). 2.6-liter four: Aries/400/600 ($259). 318 cu. in., 2Bbl. V-8: Diplomat/Mirada ($225). Transmission and Axle: Five-speed manual trans.: Omni/Chgr, Aries Cust/SE ($75). TorqueFlite auto. trans.: Omni/Aries/400/600 ($439). Performance axle: Omni/Chgr, Aries Cust/SE ($22). Steering and Suspension: Power steering: Omni/Aries ($214). H.D. susp.: Omni 4dr. ($34); Aries/Diplo ($26); Mirada ($36). Sport susp.: 400 2dr., 600 ($55). Rear sway bar: Mirada ($36). Other: H.D. battery ($43) exc. Omni/Chgr. H.D. engine cooling ($141). California emission system ($75). High-altitude emission (NC).

OMNI/CHARGER CONVENIENCE/APPEARANCE OPTIONS: Option Packages: Bright exterior accent group: Chgr ($64). Two-tone paint ($134-$155). Light group ($44-$62). Protection group ($125-$181). Cold weather group ($174). Comfort/Convenience: Air cond. ($632). Rear defroster, electric ($127). Automatic speed control ($174). Tinted glass: 4dr. ($90). Rallye instrument cluster: 4dr. ($79). Rear wiper/washer: 4dr. ($117). Mirrors: Dual remote: 4dr. ($48). Dual sport remote: Chgr ($56). Entertainment: AM radio ($83). AM/FM stereo radio ($109- $192). Electronic-tuning AM/FM stereo ($263-$346); w/cassette ($402-$485). Exterior: Removable glass sunroof: Chgr ($310). Rear spoiler: Chgr ($72). Black vinyl bodyside molding: 4dr. ($45). Luggage rack: 4dr. ($93). Interior: Console ($76-$84). Vinyl bucket seats (NC). Center armrest ($46). Tonneau cover: Chgr ($68). Cargo area carpet: Chgr ($41); w/sound insulation, base 4dr. ($59). Wheels and Tires: Deluxe wheel covers: Chgr (NC). Cast aluminum 14 in. wheels: Chgr ($250-$298). 13 in. Rallye wheels: 4dr. ($48). 14 in. Rallye wheels: Chgr ($48). P175/75R13 wide WSW: base ($59). P175/75R13 SBR BSW ($54). P175/75R13 SBR wide WSW ($81-$135). P195/60R14 SBR BSW: Chgr ($225). P195/60R14 SBR RWL: Chgr ($310); 2.2 ($85). Conventional spare tire ($63).

ARIES CONVENIENCE/APPEARANCE OPTIONS: Option Packages: Easy-order pkg. A91 ($132-$238); A92 ($761- $1203); A93 ($1607-$1943). Light pkg. ($93-$103). Security pkg. ($687-$810). Comfort/Convenience: Air cond. ($732). Rear defroster ($137). Auto. speed control ($174). Power driver's bucket seat ($210). Power windows ($180-$255). Power door locks ($120- $170). Power decklid/liftgate release ($40). Tinted glass ($105). Luxury steering wheel: base ($40). Tilt steering wheel ($105). Intermitent wipers ($52). Liftgate wiper/washer: wag ($117). Mirrors: Remote left ($22). Dual remote ($66-$88). Lighted vanity, right: Cust/SE ($50). Entertainment: AM radio: base ($78). AM/FM stereo radio ($109-$187). Electronic-tuning AM/FM stereo ($263-$341); w/cassette ($402-$480). Delete AM radio ($56 credit). Exterior: Full vinyl roof: 4dr. ($172). Padded landau roof: 2dr. ($177). Two-tone paint: 2dr. ($176). Door edge protectors ($15-$25). Sill moldings ($23). Bumper guards, front or rear ($28). Bodyside tape stripe ($48). Luggage rack: wag ($106). Special sound insulation ($43). Undercoating ($41). Vinyl lower body protection ($39). Interior: Vinyl bench seat: Cust/SE (NC). Cloth/vinyl bench seat: base ($31). Cloth bucket seats: Cust/SE ($156). Center armrest: Cust/SE ($63). Color-keyed mats: front ($25); rear ($20). Color-keyed seatbelts ($28). Tonneau cover: wag ($68). Trunk dress-up: base ($51). Wheels and Tires: Deluxe 13 in. wheel covers ($52). Luxury 13 in. wheel covers ($47-$99). P175/75R13 GBR wide WSW ($58). P185/70R13 SBR wide WSW ($194). P185/70R14 SBR wide WSW ($207). Conventional spare tire ($63).

400/600 CONVENIENCE/APPEARANCE OPTIONS: Option Packages: Sport appearance pkg.: 400 ($176-$218). Easy-order pkg. A ($556-$676); B ($1832-$2288). Roadability pkg.: 400 ($123). Protection pkg.: 600 ($64-$120). Comfort/Convenience: Air cond. ($732). Rear defroster ($137- $138). Auto. speed control ($174). Power windows ($180-$255). Power door locks ($120-$170). Power seat ($210). Power decklid release: 400 ($40). Tinted glass ($105). Audible message center ($63). Travel Computer cluster ($206). Sport steering wheel: 400 ($50). Leather-wrapped steering wheel ($50). Tilt steering wheel ($105). Intermittent wipers ($52). Lighting and Mirrors: Cornering lights ($60). Reading lamp: 400 ($24). Dual remote-control mirrors ($57); power ($104- $107). Lighted vanity mirror ($50-$58). Entertainment: AM/FM stereo radio ($109). Electronic-tuning AM/FM stereo ($263); w/cassette ($402). Premium speakers ($126). Radio delete ($56 credit). Exterior: Two-tone paint ($170-$176). Sill moldings ($23). Door edge protectors ($15-$25). Bodyside tape stripe: 400 ($42). Bodyside/deck stripes: 600 ($63). Bumper guards, front or rear ($23-$28). Undercoating ($41). Vinyl lower body protection ($39). Interior: Console: 400 sed ($100). Cloth/vinyl bench seat: 400 cpe (NC). Vinyl bench seat: 600 (NC). Cloth 50/50 bench seat: 600 ($267). Vinyl bucket seats w/dual recliners: 400 sed (NC). Cloth/vinyl bucket seats: 400 cpe/sed ($160). Center armrest: 400 ($59). Color-keyed mats: front ($25); rear ($20). Trunk dress-up ($51). Wheels/Tires: Wire wheel covers ($219). Cast aluminum wheels ($316-$336). Conventional spare tire ($63).

DIPLOMAT CONVENIENCE/APPEARANCE OPTIONS: Option Packages: Basic group ($1101-$1308). Light pkg. ($112- $147). Protection group ($132). Comfort/Convenience: Air conditioning, semi-auto ($787). Rear defroster, electric ($138). Auto. speed control ($174). Power seat, left: Salon ($199). Power windows ($255). Power door locks ($159). Power decklid release ($40). Illuminated entry system ($75). Leather-wrapped steering wheel ($53). Tilt steering wheel ($99). Digital clock ($64). Intermittent wipers ($52). Mirrors: Remote driver's: Salon ($23). Dual remote, chrome ($44-$67). Lighted vanity, right ($61). Entertainment: AM/FM stereo radio ($109). Electronic-tuning AM/FM stereo ($154-$263); w/cassette ($293-$402). Dual front speakers ($28). Premium speakers ($126). Power antenna ($60). Radio delete ($56 credit). Exterior: Power glass sunroof ($1041). Full vinyl roof: Salon ($172). Vinyl bodyside moldings ($57). Upper door frame moldings: Salon ($44). Bodyside/deck/hood stripe ($109). Body sound insulation: Salon ($43). Undercoating ($41). Interior: Vinyl bench seat: Salon ($60). Trunk dress-up: Salon ($54). Wheels/Tires: Premium wheel covers ($94). Wire wheel covers ($257). P205/75R15 SBR WSW ($123). Conventional spare ($63).

MIRADA CONVENIENCE/APPEARANCE OPTIONS: Option Packages: CMX pkg. ($982). Basic group ($1048-$1146). Light pkg. ($168). Protection pkg. ($146). Comfort/Convenience: Air cond., semi-auto ($787). Rear defroster, electric ($138). Auto. speed control ($174). Power seat ($199). Power windows ($180). Power door locks ($120). Power decklid release ($40-$58). Illuminated entry system ($75). Leather-wrapped steering wheel ($53). Tilt steering wheel ($99). Digital clock ($64). Intermittent wipers ($52). Lighting, Horns and Mirrors: Cornering lights ($60). Triad horns ($27). Lighted vanity mirror ($61). Entertainment: Same as Diplomat. Exterior: Wheel lip moldings ($30). Sill moldings ($34). Bodyside/hood/deck tape stripes ($98). Undercoating ($41). Interior: Console ($75-$124). Cloth/vinyl 60/40 seat ($217- $266). Leather bucket seats ($549-$598). Center armrest ($49). Trunk dress-up ($48). Wheels and Tires: Forged aluminum wheels ($270-$327). Premium wheel covers ($56). Wire wheel covers ($187-$244). P205/75R15 SBR WSW ($116); Michelins available. P215/70R15 SBR RWL ($66- $193). Conventional spare tire ($63).

HISTORY: Introduced: October 1, 1982. Model year production: Chrysler reported a total of 285,808 passenger cars shipped. Total North American production for the U.S. market of 334,505 units included 304,464 four-cylinder, 9,443 six-cylinder, and 20,598 V-8s. Calendar year production (U.S.): 358,602. Calendar year sales by U.S. dealers: 313,977. Model year sales by U.S. dealers: 309,056 (not incl. 34,701 Colts, 14,735 Challengers and 71 other imports).

Historical Footnotes: Like Chrysler Corp. as a whole, Dodge enjoyed an ample sales rise for model year 1983, gaining 17 percent. Dodge's newest model, the front-drive 400, showed the greatest gain, up one-third over the 1982 figure. Only the rear-drive Mirada slipped, and it dropped out of the lineup before the '84 model year. Dodge's market share rose to 4.8 percent, which gave it an eighth place ranking. A new assembly plant at Sterling Heights was purchased from Volkswagen of America this year, and readied for production of an anticipated Hbody compact. Dodges came with a 5-year/50,000-mile powertrain limited warranty (plus outer panel rust-through protection), applicable after the regular 12/12,000 warranty expired. It had a deductible, though. New Computer-Assisted Design and Manufacturing techniques were being used.

1984 DODGE

Two-door 400 Dodges were renamed 600 this year, joining the four-door of that name (or number). The 400 designation was abandoned. Daytona was the all-new model this year, aimed at the youth market. A 142-horsepower turbocharged engine was a major attraction. The new turbo was also available in the 600 series. Electronic Voice Alert was improved, to deliver more significant comments. Better yet, a shutoff switch in the glovebox allowed drivers who found the comments irritating to eliminate them completely. Later in the year, a fuel-injected 2.2-liter four, standard in the new Daytona, replaced the carbureted version. Mirada was dropped, making Diplomat the only rear-drive Dodge left, now available only with the 318 cu. in. V-8 engine. Radios now incorporated electronic tuning.

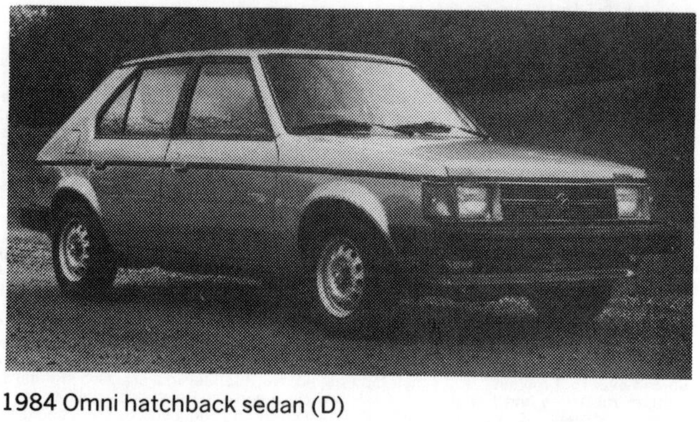

1984 Omni hatchback sedan (D)

OMNI — SERIES Z — FOUR — Touted as "the car that started the Dodge revolution," the Omni sedan came in base and step-up SE trim for 1984. Also available was a new GLH package, said to denote an Omni that "goes like h—-," carrying a hefty $1528 price tag. The base model's grille was similar in shape to 1983, but with more and thinner horizontal bars (all black except the two center ones). A pentastar emblem again went in its center. Omni displayed "Euro-type" blacked-out trim. Inside was a four-spoke sport steering wheel, plus a revised dashboard with gauges that looked easier to read. Unlike the base model, Omni SE had distinct bright door frame, belt, sill and liftgate window moldings, plus bodyside and liftgate moldings, deluxe wheel covers, and a body-color center pillar. SE was described as looking "American" because of its bright moldings and whitewall tires. Body colors were: Black, White, Graphic Red, Nightwatch Blue, Spice metallic, Charcoal metallic, Garnet Red pearl coat, and three crystal coats: Radiant Silver, Beige, or Glacier Blue. Three two- tones were available. Standard interiors had cloth/vinyl low- back bucket seats with dual recliners and adjustable headrests, and a fold-down back seat. SE held cloth/vinyl high-back bucket seats with dual recliners and integral headrests. The base 1.6-liter four-cylinder engine was offered only with four-speed manual shift. The optional 2.2-liter came with five-speed or automatic. Standard equipment included power brakes, halogen headlamps, intermittent wipers, and a tethered fuel cap. Omni SE had an electronic-tuning AM radio with digital clock. The 110-horsepower high-performance engine, formerly offered only on the Shelby Charger, was now available on all models for $256 extra. A total of 3,285 GLH performance packages (RPO code AGB) were installed on Omnis.

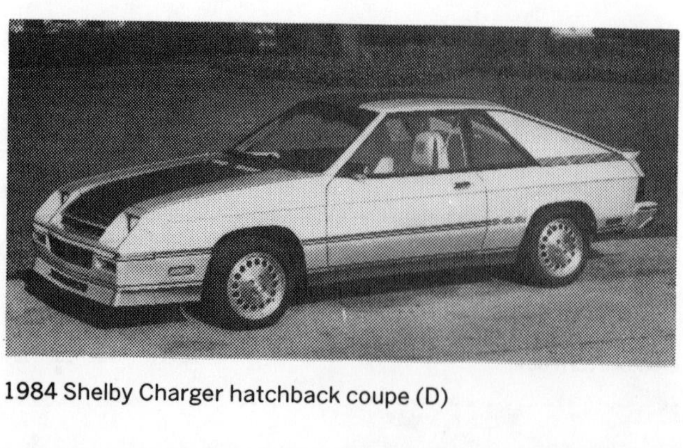

1984 Shelby Charger hatchback coupe (D)

CHARGER/2.2 — SERIES Z — FOUR — A restyled nose and simpler grille helped give Charger a different look this year. The sharply angled side window at the far rear was gone, leaving "only" two windows on each side for a more conventional appearance. A totally different grille consisted of just two wide slots between new quad rectangular halogen headlamps (formerly dual). Twin side-by- side slots were also evident below the bumper strip, along with parking lamps. A shallow depression in the hood held a laydown pentastar ornament. Grillework patterning to the rear of quarter windows ran back to the hatch, in line with window bases. Wraparound, horizontally-ribbed taillamp lenses held square backup lamps toward the license plate housing at the center. Taillamps also displayed black graphics. 'Dodge' and 'Charger' block lettering, plus a center pentastar, were on the rear panel. Charger 2.2. lost its simulated hood scoop. A 'Charger 2.2' decal (if applicable) was now on the upper quarter panel, where the rearward window used to be. Charger 2.2's quarter panels now looked similar to Shelby's. A new liftgate spoiler was standard on Charger 2.2, optional on the base coupe. Base engine remained the Peugeot 1.6-liter four, with four-speed manual transaxle. Options included the regular 2.2-liter four, as well as the high-performance edition (priced at $256). Power brakes and hatch release were standard, along with a color-keyed four-spoke sport steering wheel. Contoured cloth/vinyl low-back bucket seats had individually adjustable front seatback recliners. A redesigned, full-gauge Rallye instrument cluster included a tachometer and trip odometer. Body colors were: Black, White, Nightwatch Blue, Graphic Red, Charcoal or Spice metallic, Glacier Blue or Beige crystal coat, Radiant Silver crystal coat, or Garnet Red pearl coat. Four two-tones were offered. Shelby Charger's 2.2-liter engine gained a rephased camshaft and a compression boost to 9.6:1, as well as recalibrated electronics. It produced 110 horsepower at 5600 R.P.M. Overall top gear ratio switched from 2.57:1 to 2.78:1. Shelby added an aerodynamic front air dam, bodyside ground- effect spoilers, and unique "Porsche-like" rear spoiler, which helped produce a drag coefficient of only 0.37. Shelby also had a "free-breathing" exhaust, chrome valve cover, stiffer shocks/springs, 14:1 fast-ratio power steering, and low-profile 50-series Eagle GT speed-rated radial tires on 15 in. cast aluminum wheels. The gas pedal was redesigned for heel-and-toe shifting. Shelby had its own look with single headlamps and a grille made up of two wide slots: one above the bumper rub strip, the other below. The hood sloped downward onto the panel between the headlamps, with pentastar at the center. A 'Shelby' decal went on the bodyside, between door and rear wheel opening. As before, Shelby came only in Radiant Silver with Santa Fe Blue trim (or the reverse combination). High-back bucket seats with dual recliners and integral headrests were upholstered in blue and silver cloth with Shelby logo. This performance edition was named after Carroll Shelby, the famed racing car designer and driver. It cost about $2000 more than a base Charger. As for performance, Shelby was claimed to go 0-50 in 5.5 seconds and do the quarter-mile in under 16 seconds (based on National Hot Road Association testing of an '83 model).

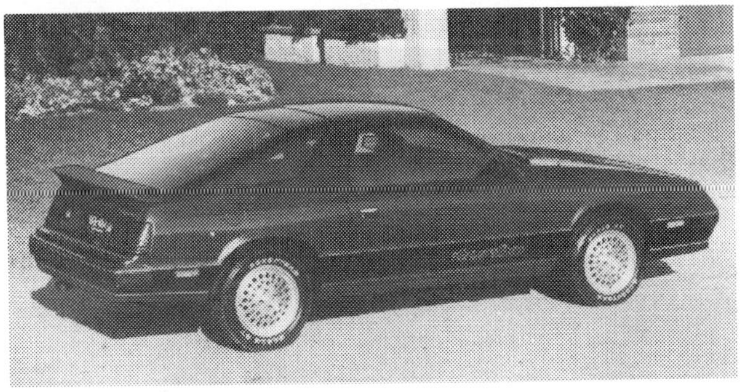

1984 Daytona Turbo hatchback coupe (D)

DAYTONA — SERIES GV — FOUR — Close kin to Chrysler's new Laser, the sporty new Daytona four-passenger coupe was created to draw youthful, performance-minded buyers. Essentially a variant of the Kcar, on a shorter wheelbase and developed as a G24 coupe, Daytona came with either a standard 2.2-liter four-cylinder engine (now fuel injected) or a new turbocharged edition. That was the first front-drive turbo. Rated 142 horsepower with multi-point fuel injection, the Daytona Turbo still managed an EPA mileage estimate of 22 MPG (35 highway). The base four produced 99 horsepower, with throttle-body fuel injection. Daytona Turbo had a close-ratio five-speed manual transaxle, performance seats, performance handling package, Goodyear Eagle GT tires, and aluminum wheels. It cost nearly $2000 more than a base Daytona. Stepping up further yet, buyers could choose a Turbo Z. A total of 9,422 of those packages (RPO code AGS) were installed, versus 4,194 for the "plain" Turbo package (code AGT). Turbo Z had two-tone paint and a deep air dam, ground-effects rocker extensions, tape stripes, bodyside moldings, and unique rear spoiler. Chrysler's Laser differed little, but Laser offered no Turbo Z equivalent. Developed by Garrett AIResearch, the turbocharger unit delivered 7.5 psi maximum boost and had a water-cooled turbine end-shaft bearing. Multi-point fuel injection used Bosch injectors at each cylinder. Dished-top pistons cut compression down to 8.0:1. Turbo engines had a detonation sensor and could use no-lead regular gasoline (though premium was recommended). They also had a racier camshaft, bigger oil pump, 2.5 in. low-restriction exhaust, and tighter internal sealing. Equal-length half-shafts helped reduce torque-steer during acceleration, to improve handling. Turbo dashes held analog gauges. Suspensions used gas-filled shocks, as well as higher spring rates than the Aries line. Turbos included a Performance Handling Package with firmer spring/shock rates, larger stabilizer bars, and 60-series 15 in. tires. Turbo seats also had inflatable lumbar/thigh support bolsters. All Daytonas had a center console, plus bucket seats in front and rear (really tight in the back). Chrysler claimed a 0-60 MPH acceleration time of 8.5 seconds or less with turbo and manual shift. Non-turbo Daytonas managed to hit 60 in about 10 seconds. Daytona's rivals included Porsche, Camaro/Firebird, and Datsun/Nissan 280ZX.

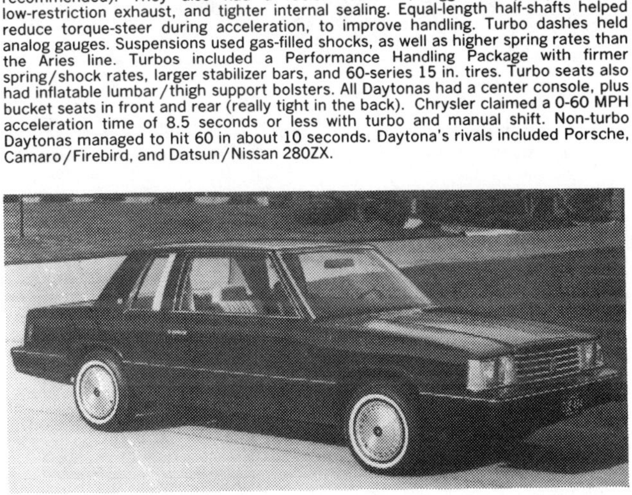

1984 Aries Special Edition coupe (D)

ARIES — SERIES D — FOUR — Revisions were modest on Dodge's front-drive compact Kcar sedans and wagons, offered in base and SE form (along with a Custom wagon). The new black-accented grille showed a similar pattern of bright horizontal bars, but added a large pentastar in the center instead of the former pentastar stand-up hood ornament. 'Dodge' block letters no longer stood above the grille. Taillamps kept their full-width design with three square sections on each side of the license plate housing, but now had horizontal ribbing (two horizontal strips across each section). Also, backup lenses (alongside the license plate) were larger than before. 'Dodge' and 'Aries' lettering was on the decklid, along with a center pentastar. Wagon taillamps were tri-section vertical wraparound style, with a small backup lens in the bottom section. Standard deluxe wheel covers were new. So was the instrument panel with a full set of gauges, including fuel/temp/voltage indicators and trip odometer. The gas tank grew from 13 to 14 gallons. New standard tires were P175/80R13 all-season steel-belted radial blackwalls. A multi-function control was on the steering column. Body colors this year were: Crimson Red, Pearl White, Nightwatch Blue, and Black; plus Beige, Glacier Blue, Charcoal or Radiant Silver crystal coat; or Garnet Red or Mink Brown pearl coat. Also a pair of two-tones. An all-vinyl bench seat went in the base interior. Aries SE sported an all-cloth split-back front bench seat with fold-down center armrests and adjustable head restraints. Base engine again was the 2.2-liter Trans4 with two- barrel carburetor. That engine had chrome valve stems, cobalt alloy valve seats, and moly-faced compression rings. A fuel- injected version was anticipated for later in the model year, but failed to materialize. Optional once more was the Mitsubishi-built 2.6-liter four, which gained 8 horsepower as a result of carburetor and ignition recalibration. A four- speed manual transaxle was standard again, with five-speed and TorqueFlite optional. New options included Rallye 13 in. and cast aluminum 14 in. wheels. Low-back cloth bucket seats were available. All radios had electronic-tuning and a built- in digital clock.

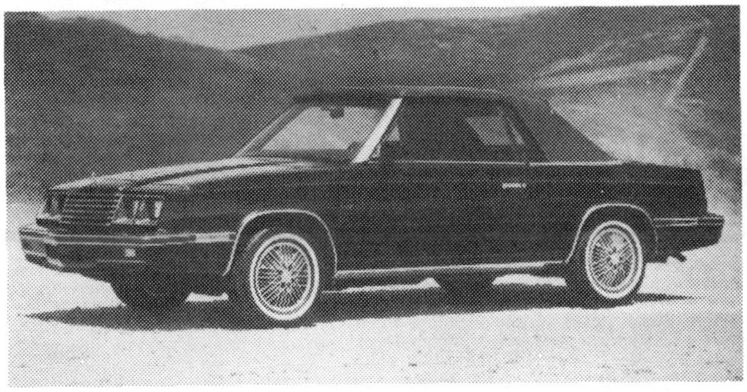

1984 Dodge 600 convertible (D)

600 COUPE/CONVERTIBLE — SERIES KV — FOUR —— Both the club coupe and convertible in this year's 600 series were actually the 400 models from 1983. Only the four- door sedan (listed below) carried over with the same designation as before. The coupe was promoted for its "classic elegance;" the convertible for "classic styling." The two-door front end looked the same as 1983, with a grille made up of horizontal strips and a wide empty slot below the bumper rub strip. Quad rectangular headlamps were recessed. Parking lamps stood below the bumper strip. Twin vertical fender louvers were standard again. New wide wraparound taillamps each were divided into six side-by-side sections, with backup lenses at the inner ends, next to the license plate housing. Each was also split horizontally by a divider bar that went all the way across the full width. On the decklid was 'Dodge' and '600' lettering and a center pentastar. The club coupe had a padded formal landau roof and narrow opera windows. Inside were high-back cloth/vinyl bucket seats (same as the 600 ES sedan but without a standard console). Base club coupe and convertible engine was the carbureted 2.2-liter four, but this year a turbocharged version was available, as well as the Mitsubishi-built 2.6- liter four. The 2.6 was offered only with automatic transmission. A five-speed manual transaxle was standard with 2.2-liter coupe engines, but convertibles came only with TorqueFlite. All models had an electronic-tuning AM radio with digital clock, but that unit could be deleted. Halogen headlamps were standard; cornering lamps optional. Inside was a new standard luxury steering wheel; underneath, a larger 14-gallon gas tank. Added to the option list: an illuminated entry system. Body colors were: Black, Crimson Red, Nightwatch Blue, and Pearl White; Garnet Red, Mink Brown or Gunmetal Blue pearl coat; Radiant Silver, Beige or Charcoal crystal coat. Two two-tones were offered. Not all colors were available on every model. Dodge claimed to have "brought back the American convertible to the American road," offering the lowest-priced ragtop on the domestic market. Convertibles had a wider back seat and tinted glass back window this year, along with new power side (quarter) windows. The soft top had narrower quarters, too. Vinyl low-back bucket seats had dual recliners and console. A visual message center on the dash was standard, as were dual remote color-keyed mirrors. A total of 1,786 ES Turbo convertibles (RPO code AGT) were produced in the 600 series. Not a bad figure, considering that the package cost a whopping $3378.

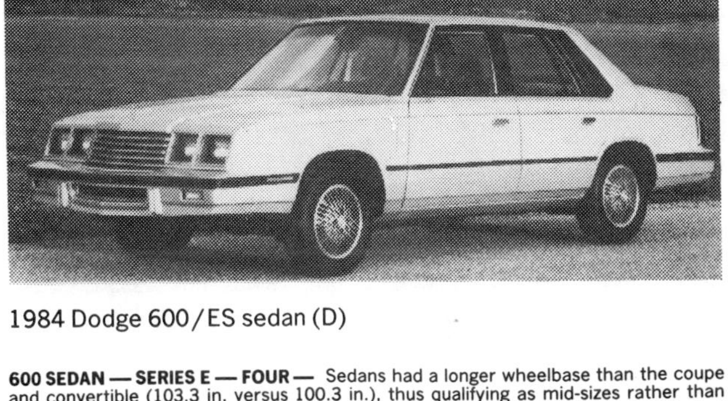

1984 Dodge 600/ES sedan (D)

600 SEDAN — SERIES E — FOUR — Sedans had a longer wheelbase than the coupe and convertible (103.3 in. versus 100.3 in.), thus qualifying as mid-sizes rather than compacts. Styling was similar, with the same slatted grille. On the decklid was 'Dodge' and '600' (or '600 ES') lettering, along with the center pentastar. The base sedan was promoted for its "sophistication," the 600ES for performance. Both models had a standard fuel-injected version of the 2.2-liter Trans4 engine, with both the 2.6- liter and turbo 2.2 optional. The base sedan came with TorqueFlite, whereas the 600ES could have either a five- speed manual or automatic gearbox. Kimberley cloth/vinyl bench seating was standard on the base sedan, with fold-down center armrest and adjustable head restraints. Billed as a "Euro-Sport" touring model, the 600ES came

with a standard Sport Handling Suspension Package that included gas-filled shocks and quicker power steering. A standard electronic instrument cluster included self-diagnostics and a distinctive digital tachometer. Blackout styling consisted of black moldings, black dual power remote- control mirrors, and black bodyside stripes. P185/70R14 SBR Goodyear Eagle GT tires with raised black letters rode cast aluminum wheels. Cloth/vinyl high-back bucket seats had integral head restraints and reclining seatbacks. The standard center console included a freestanding center armrest. Dark woodtone accented the instrument panel. Taillamps displayed two horizontal divider bars rather than one. Both 600 sedans had a power decklid release.

1984 Diplomat Salon sedan (D)

DIPLOMAT — SERIES G — V-8 — Once again, Diplomat proved most popular for fleet applications, since 10,330 Police packages were installed. This year, the familiar Slant Six finally disappeared. Only the 318 cu. in. V-8 was offered, with TorqueFlite three-speed automatic. Two models were available: basic Salon and, added later, a new SE (to replace the former Medallion). Salon appearance was similar to 1983. The grille again consisted of seven vertical bars and a heavy upper header, with a pattern of squares extending outward below the quad rectangular headlamps. Those squares held parking/signal lamps and wrapped around the fenders. A markedly different front end look for the new SE was highlighted by quad park/signal lamps *over* the quad rectangular headlamps, and a simple bright crossbar grille fronting a black pattern. Each of Diplomat's wide wraparound taillamps was subtly divided into four side-by-side sections, with backup lenses in inner sections alongside the license plate housing. Diplomat featured "classic" squared-off fenders and a formal-look roofline. All-season P205/75R15 wide-whitewall steel-belted radial tires were standard. Body colors were: Crimson Red, Formal Black, Sable Brown, White, and Nightwatch Blue; plus Charcoal Gray, Glacier Blue, Radiant Silver or Beige crystal coat. Salon's interior contained a cloth/vinyl bench seat with folding center armrest. SE turned to a cloth/vinyl 60/40 individually-adjustable seat with folding center armrest and passenger recliner. Also inside was a new luxury steering wheel, along with new black velvet-finish instrument panel bezels. An electronic-tuning AM radio with digital clock was now standard. SE Diplomats could have cast aluminum wheels.

I.D. DATA: Dodge's 17-symbol Vehicle Identification Number (VIN), as before, was on the upper left corner of the instrument panel, visible through the windshield. The first digit indicates Country: '1' U.S.A. The second symbol is Make: 'B' Dodge. Third is Vehicle Type: '3' passenger car; '7' truck. The next symbol ('B') indicates manual seatbelts. Symbol five is Car Line: 'Z' Omni/Charger; 'A' Daytona; 'D' Aries; 'E' 600 sedan; 'V' 600 coupe/convertible; 'G' Diplomat. Symbol six is Series (price class): '1' Economy; '2' Low; '4' High; '5' Premium; '6' Special. Symbol seven is Body Style: '1' 2-dr. sedan; '4' 2-dr. hatchback; '5' 2-dr. convertible; '6' 4-dr. sedan; '8' 4-dr. hatchback; '9' 4-dr. wagon. Eighth is the Engine Code: 'A' L498 2Bbl.; 'C' L4135 2Bbl.; 'D' L4135 FI; 'E' Turbo L4135 FI; 'F' or '8' Hi-perf. (Shelby) L4135 2Bbl.; 'G' L4156 2Bbl.; 'P' V8318 2Bbl. Next comes a check digit (0-9 or X). Symbol ten indicates Model Year: 'E' 1984. Symbol eleven is Assembly Plant: 'C' Jefferson (Detroit); 'D' Belvidere, IL; 'F' Newark, DE; 'G' or 'X' St. Louis. The last six digits make up the sequential serial number, starting with 100001. Engine numbers and Body Code Plates are in the same locations as 1981-83.

OMNI (FOUR)

Model Number	Body/Style Number	Body Type & Seating	Factory Price	Shipping Weight	Production Total
ZE	44	4-dr. Hatch-5P	5830	2095	54,584
ZH	44	4-dr. SE Hatch-5P	6148	2120	13,486

CHARGER (FOUR)

ZH	24	2-dr. Hatch-5P	6494	2160	34,763

CHARGER 2.2 (FOUR)

ZP	24	2-dr. Hatch-5P	7288	2305	11,949

SHELBY CHARGER (FOUR)

ZS	24	2-dr. Hatch-5P	8541	2350	7,552

DAYTONA (FOUR)

GVH	24	2-dr. Hatch-4P	8308	2520	21,916

DAYTONA TURBO (FOUR)

GVS	24	2-dr. Hatch-4P	10227	2630	27,431

ARIES (FOUR)

DL	21	2-dr. Sedan-6P	6837	2335	11,921
DL	41	4-dr. Sedan-6P	6949	2340	55,331
DH	45	4-dr. Cust Wag-6P	7736	2430	31,421

ARIES SPECIAL EDITION (FOUR)

DH	21	2-dr. Sedan-6P	7463	2345	4,231
DH	41	4-dr. Sedan-6P	7589	2375	12,314
DP	45	4-dr. Sta Wag-6P	8195	2480	4,814

600 COUPE/CONVERTIBLE (FOUR)

VP	22	2-dr. Cpe-5P	8376	2445	13,296
VP	27	2-dr. Conv.-4P	10595	2530	10,960

600 ES SEDAN (FOUR)

EH	41	4-dr. Sedan-6P	8903	2530	28,646
ES	41	4-dr. ES Sed-5P	9525	2530	8,735

DIPLOMAT SALON (V-8)

GL	41	4-dr. Sedan-6P	9180	3465	16,261

DIPLOMAT SE (V-8)

GP	41	4-dr. Sedan-6P	N/A	N/A	5,902

MODEL NUMBER NOTE: Some sources identify models using the VIN data to indicate Car Line, Price Class and Body Style. Example: Aries four-door (DL41) has the equivalent number D26, which translates to Aries line, Low price class, and four-door sedan body. See I.D. Data section for breakdown.

ENGINE DATA: BASE FOUR (Omni, Charger): Inline, overhead-cam four-cylinder. Cast iron block; aluminum head. Displacement: 97.3 cu. in. (1.6 liters). Bore & stroke: 3.17 x 3.07 in. Compression ratio: 8.8:1. Brake horsepower: 64 at 4800 R.P.M. Torque: 87 lbs.-ft. at 2800 R.P.M. Five main bearings. Solid valve lifters. Carburetor: 2Bbl. Holley 6520. VIN Code: A. BASE FOUR (Charger 2.2, Aries, 600); OPTIONAL (Omni, Charger): Inline, overhead-cam four-cylinder. Cast iron block; aluminum head. Displacement: 135 cu. in. (2.2 liters). Bore & stroke: 3.44 x 3.62 in. Compression ratio: 9.0:1. Brake horsepower: 96 at 5200 R.P.M. (Charger 2.2, 101 at 5200 R.P.M.). Torque: 119 lbs.-ft. at 3200 R.P.M. (Charger 2.2, 124 lbs.-ft. at 3200 R.P.M.). Five main bearings. Hydraulic valve lifters. Carburetor: 2Bbl. Holley 6520. VIN Code: C. BASE FOUR (Shelby Charger); OPTIONAL (Omni, Charger): Same as 135 cu. in. four above, except Compression ratio: 9.6:1. Horsepower: 110 at 5600 R.P.M. Torque: 129 lbs.-ft. at 3600 R.P.M. VIN Code: F. BASE FOUR (Daytona, 600 sedan): Same as 135 cu. in. fours above, but with electronic fuel injection Horsepower: 99 at 5600 R.P.M. Torque: 121 lbs.- ft. at 3200 R.P.M. VIN Code: D. TURBOCHARGED FOUR; BASE (Daytona Turbo); OPTIONAL (Daytona, 600): Same as 135 cu. in. four above, with EFI and turbocharger Compression: 8.0:1. Horsepower: 142 at 5600 R.P.M. Torque: 160 lbs.-ft. at 3200 R.P.M. VIN Code: E. OPTIONAL FOUR (Aries, 600): Inline, overhead-cam four-cylinder. Cast iron block; aluminum head. Displacement: 156 cu. in. (2.6 liters). Bore & stroke: 3.59 x 3.86 in. Compression ratio: 8.7:1. Brake horsepower: 101 at 4800 R.P.M. Torque: 140 lbs.-ft. at 2800 R.P.M. Five main bearings. Solid valve lifters. Carburetor: 2Bbl. Mikuni. Mitsubishi-built. VIN Code: G. BASE V-8 (Diplomat): 90-degree, overhead valve V-8. Cast iron block and head. Displacement: 318 cu. in. (5.2 liters). Bore & stroke: 3.91 x 3.31 in. Compression ratio: 8.5:1. Brake horsepower: 130 at 4000 R.P.M. Torque: 235 lbs.-ft. at 1600 R.P.M. Five main bearings. Hydraulic valve lifters. Carburetor: 2Bbl. Carter BBD. VIN Code: P. POLICE V-8 (Diplomat): Same as 318 cu. in. V-8 above, with 4Bbl. Carter TQ 9295 carburetor Horsepower: 165 at 4000 R.P.M. Torque: 240 lbs.- ft. at 2000 R.P.M.

CHASSIS DATA: Wheelbase: (Omni) 99.1 in.; (Charger) 96.6 in.; (Daytona) 97.0 in.; (Aries/600) 100.3 in.; (600 sedan) 103.3 in.; (Diplomat) 112.7 in. Overall Length: (Omni) 164.8 in.; (Chgr) 174.8 in.; (Daytona) 175.0 in.; (Aries) 176.0 in.; (600) 179.5 in.; (600 sedan) 187.4 in.; (Diplomat) 205.7 in. Height: (Omni) 53.0 in.; (Chgr) 50.8 in.; (Shelby) 50.2 in.; (Daytona) 50.3 in.; (Aries 2dr.) 52.3 in.; (Aries 4dr.) 52.7 in.; (Aries wag) 52.4 in.; (600 cpe) 52.6 in.; (600 conv.) 54.1 in.; (600 sedan) 52.9 in.; (Diplomat) 55.3 in. Width: (Omni) 66.2 in.; (Chgr) 66.7 in.; (Aries) 68.6 in.; (Daytona) 69.3 in.; (600) 68.5 in.; (600 sed) 68.3 in.; (Diplomat) 74.2 in. Front Tread: (Omni/Chgr) 56.1 in.; (Aries/Daytona/600) 57.6 in.; (Diplo) 60.0 in. Rear Tread: (Omni) 55.6 in.; (Chgr) 55.9 in.; (Aries/600) 57.0 in.; (Daytona) 57.2 in.; (Diplo) 59.5 in. Standard Tires: (Omni/Charger) P165/80R13 SBR; (Charger 2.2) P195/60R14 SBR RBL; (Shelby) P195/50R15 SBR RBL; (Daytona) P185/70R14; (Aries) P175/80R13 SBR; (600) P185/70R14 SBR; (600ES) P185/70R14 SBR RBL; (Diplomat) P205/75R15 SBR WSW.

TECHNICAL: Transmission: Four-speed manual (floor lever) standard on Omni/Charger and Aries: (1st) 3.29:1; (2nd) 1.89:1; (3rd) 1.21:1; (4th) 0.88:1; (Rev) 3.14:1. Five-speed manual standard on 600 two-door and Daytona, optional on Omni/Charger/Aries: (1st) 3.29:1; (2nd) 2.08:1; (3rd) 1.45:1; (4th) 1.04:1; (5th) 0.72:1; (Rev) 3.14:1. TorqueFlite three-speed automatic standard on Diplomat, optional on all other models. Diplomat gear ratios: (1st) 2.74:1; (2nd) 1.54:1; (3rd) 1.00:1; (Rev) 2.22:1. Other models: (1st) 2.69:1; (2nd) 1.55:1; (3rd) 1.00:1; (Rev) 2.10:1. Standard final drive ratio: (Omni/Charger) 2.69:1 w/4spd, 2.20:1 w/5spd, 3.02:1 w/auto.; (Omni/Chgr w/H.O. 2.2-liter) 2.78:1 w/5spd; (Daytona) 2.57:1 w/5spd, 3.22:1 or 3.02:1 w/auto.; (Aries) 2.69:1 w/4spd, 2.20:1 w/5spd, 2.78:1 or 3.02:1 w/auto.; (600) 2.57:1 w/5-spd, 3.02:1 w/auto.; (Diplo) 2.26:1. Steering: (Diplomat) recirculating ball; (others) rack and pinion. Suspension: (Omni/Chgr) MacPherson Iso-Strut independent coil front w/anti-sway bar, trailing arm semi-independent coil rear w/beam axle and integral anti-sway; (Daytona) Iso-Strut front w/anti-sway bar, rigid rear axle w/radius arms and track bar; (Aries/600) MacPherson Iso-Strut front w/coil springs and linkless anti-sway bar, flex-arm beam rear axle w/trailing links and transverse track bar; (Diplomat) transverse front torsion bars and anti-sway bar, semi- elliptic rear leaf springs. Brakes: Front disc, rear drum. Ignition: Electronic. Body construction: Unibody. Fuel tank: (Omni/Chgr) 13 gal.; (Daytona/Aries/600) 14 gal.; (Diplomat) 18 gal.

DRIVETRAIN OPTIONS: Engines: 2.2-liter four: Omni/Chgr ($134). Hi-perf. 2.2-liter four: Omni/Chgr ($256); Chgr 2.2 ($122). Turbocharged 2.2- liter four: base Daytona ($934); 600 ($610). 2.6-liter four: Aries/600 ($271). Transmission and Axle: Five-speed manual trans.: Omni/Chgr, Aries Cust/SE ($75). TorqueFlite auto. trans.: Omni/Chgr/Daytona/Aries, 600 cpe/ES ($439). High-altitude axle: Omni/Chgr/Aries ($22). Steering and Suspension: Power steering: Omni/Chgr/Aries, 600 conv. ($219). H.D. susp.: Omni 4dr. ($36); Aries wag, Diplo ($26). Sport handling susp.: 600 ($57) exc. conv. ($276). Other: H.D. battery: Aries/600/Diplo ($44). H.D. engine cooling: Omni/Chgr/Aries/600 ($141). California emission system ($99).

OMNI/CHARGER CONVENIENCE/APPEARANCE OPTIONS: Option Packages: GLH pkg.: base Omni ($1528). Light group ($38-$57). Protection group ($88-$144). Cold weather group ($180). Comfort/Convenience: Air cond. ($643). Rear defroster, electric ($132). Automatic speed control ($179). Tinted glass: Omni ($95). Rallye instrument cluster: Omni ($121). Rear wiper/washer: Omni ($120). Mirrors: Dual remote: Omni ($49). Dual black remote: Chgr ($57). Electronic-tuning Radios: AM: base ($113). AM/FM stereo ($125-$238). Seek/scan AM/FM stereo w/cassette ($264-$502). Exterior: Removable glass sunroof: Chgr ($315). Rear spoiler: base Chgr ($72). Pearl coat paint ($40). Two-tone paint ($151) exc. base Omni. Black vinyl bodyside molding: Omni ($45). Luggage rack: Omni ($100). Interior: Console ($79-$88). Low-back vinyl bucket seats: SE/Chgr (NC). High-back vinyl bucket seats: base Omni (NC). High-back cloth bucket seats: Chgr ($65). Center armrest ($48). Tonneau cover: Chgr ($69). Cargo area carpet ($43- $62).

Wheels and Tires: Cast aluminum 14 in. wheels: Chgr ($305); 2.2 ($255). 13 in. Rallye wheels ($50) exc. 2.2/Shelby. P165/80R13 SBR WSW: base ($59). P195/60R14 SBR RWL: base Chgr ($286); 2.2 ($22). P195/60R14 SBR RWL w/sport susp.: base Chgr ($308). Conventional spare tire ($63-$93).

DAYTONA CONVENIENCE/APPEARANCE OPTIONS: Option Packages: Turbo pkg.: base ($934). Turbo Z pkg.: Turbo model ($1277). Basic group ($1294-$1319). Cargo trim/quiet sound group: base ($154). Light group: base ($97). Comfort/Convenience: Air cond. ($737). Rear defroster ($143- $168). Auto. speed control ($179). Electronic navigator ($272). Electronic voice alert ($66). Power driver's seat ($215). Power windows ($185). Power door locks ($125). Illuminated entry system ($75). Tinted glass ($110). Tilt steering wheel ($110). Liftgate wiper/washer ($120). Dual power remote mirrors: base ($48). Electronic-tuning Radios: AM/FM stereo: base ($125) Seek/scan AM/FM stereo ($160-$285); w/cassette ($299-$424). Premium speakers ($126). Delete radio ($56 credit). Exterior: Removable glass sunroof ($322). Thin black bodyside molding: base ($55). Interior: Low-back vinyl bucket seats: base (NC). Low-back cloth/vinyl bucket seats w/adj. driver's lumbar/thigh support: base ($362). Low-back leather bucket seats w/adj. driver's lumbar/thigh support: base ($929); Turbo ($567). Front/rear mats ($45). Wheels/Tires: Aluminum wheels: base ($316). P185/70R14 RBL: base ($62); Turbo (NC). P185/70R14 RWL: base ($22-$84).

ARIES CONVENIENCE/APPEARANCE OPTIONS: Option Packages: Easy-order pkg. AAA ($130-$243); AAB ($795- $1235); AAC ($1594-$1947). Light pkg. ($70-$108). Comfort/Convenience: Air cond. ($737). Rear defroster ($143). Auto. speed control ($179). Power driver's bucket seat: Cust/SE ($215). Power windows ($185-$260). Power door locks ($125-$175). Power decklid/liftgate release ($40). Tinted glass ($110). Tilt steering wheel ($110). Intermittent wipers ($53). Liftgate wiper/washer: wag ($120). Mirrors: Remote left ($24). Dual remote ($88). Electronic-tuning Radios: AM: base ($113). AM/FM stereo ($125-$238). Seek/scan AM/FM stereo: Cust/SE ($250); w/cassette ($389). Delete AM radio ($56 credit). Exterior: Full vinyl roof: SE 4dr. ($179). Padded landau roof: 2dr. ($184). Two-tone paint ($184). Pearl coat paint ($40). Sill moldings ($26). Bumper guards, front/rear ($56). Bodyside tape stripe ($48). Luggage rack: wag ($106). Special sound insulation ($43). Undercoating ($43). Interior: Vinyl bench seat (NC). Cloth/vinyl bench seat: base ($31). Cloth bucket seats: Cust/SE ($161). Color-keyed mats ($45). Trunk dress-up: SE ($51). Wheels and Tires: Wire wheel covers, 14 in.: Cust/SE ($263). Luxury wheel covers, 13 in. ($48). Rallye wheels, 13 in. ($60). Cast aluminum wheels, 14 in.: Cust/SE ($370). P175/80R13 WSW ($58). P185/70R14 SBR wide WSW ($143). Conventional spare tire ($73-$83).

600 CONVENIENCE/APPEARANCE OPTIONS: Extra-cost option packages: 600 ES Turbo convertible ($3378). Easy- order pkg. A ($530-$710); B ($1570-$2013). Comfort/Convenience: Air cond. ($737). Rear defroster ($143). Auto. speed control ($179). Power windows ($185-$260). Power door locks ($125-$175). Power seat ($215). Power decklid release: 2dr. ($40). Illuminated entry system ($75). Tinted glass ($110). Electronic voice alert ($66). Leather-wrapped steering wheel ($50). Tilt steering wheel ($110). Intermittent wipers ($53). Lighting and Mirrors: Cornering lamps ($60). Dual remote- control mirrors ($59); power ($82-$107). Lighted vanity mirror ($58). Electronic-tuning Radios: AM/FM stereo ($125). Seek/scan AM/FM stereo ($285); w/cassette ($139-$424). Premium speakers ($126). Radio delete ($56 credit). Exterior: Two-tone paint ($232). Pearl coat paint ($40). Vinyl bodyside moldings ($55). Door edge protectors: sed ($25). Bodyside tape stripe ($45). Bumper guards ($56). Undercoating ($43). Interior: Cloth/vinyl bench seat: cpe (NC). Vinyl bench seat: sed (NC). Cloth 50/50 bench seat: sed ($278). Center armrest: cpe ($61). Color-keyed mats: front, conv. ($25); front/rear, others ($45). Trunk dress-up ($51). Wheels/Tires: Wire wheel covers, locking ($266). Cast aluminum wheels ($370). P185/70R14 SBR WSW: conv. ($58). Conventional spare tire ($83).

DIPLOMAT CONVENIENCE/APPEARANCE OPTIONS: Option Packages: Basic group ($1129-$1351). Light pkg. ($118- $153). Protection group ($133). Comfort/Convenience: Air conditioning, semi-auto ($792). Rear defroster, electric ($143). Auto. speed control ($179). Power seat, left: SE ($215). Power windows ($260). Power door locks ($175). Power decklid release ($40). Illuminated entry system ($75). Leather-wrapped steering wheel ($60). Tilt steering wheel ($110). Intermittent wipers ($53). Mirrors: Remote driver's: Salon ($24). Dual remote, chrome ($67). Lighted vanity, right ($58). Electronic-Tuning Radios: AM/FM stereo ($125). Seek/scan AM/FM stereo ($125-$250); w/cassette ($264-$389). Premium speakers ($126). Power antenna ($60). Radio delete ($39 credit). Exterior: Power glass sunroof ($1041). Full vinyl roof: Salon ($185). Vinyl bodyside moldings ($57). Upper door frame moldings: Salon ($46). Bodyside/deck/hood stripe: Salon ($109). Body sound insulation: Salon ($66). Undercoating ($43). Interior: Vinyl split-back bench seat: Salon ($60). Trunk dress-up ($57). Wheels/Tires: Premium wheel covers ($96). Wire wheel covers ($215-$263). Cast aluminum wheels: SE ($262). Conventional spare ($93).

HISTORY: Introduced: October 2, 1983. Model year production: Chrysler reported a total of 375,513 passenger cars shipped. Calendar year production: 465,885. Calendar year sales by U.S. dealers: 369,255. Model year sales by U.S. dealers: 353,954 (not incl. 35,113 Colts, 1,424 Challengers, 3,341 Conquests and 7,672 Colt Vistas).

Historical Footnotes: Prices rose less than 2 percent (average) as the 1984 model year began, though Aries jumped by 10 percent. On the other hand, the 600 convertible enjoyed a 12 percent price cut. Though full-size models were gaining renewed popularity, Dodge no longer had any such models to compete with. Diplomat, Dodge's largest model, sold mainly to police and taxi fleets. Model year sales edged over 400,000 this time, marking a 12 percent gain over 1983 (including import sales of four Mitsubishi models, which fell slightly). The new Daytona was a strong seller, arriving as an early 1984 model and finding over 42,000 buyers. Aries sales dropped 12 percent, though. On the import scene, a new Conquest replaced the Challenger, and there was a new Colt Vista wagon. Also new this year was the Caravan mini-van (described in the *Standard Catalog of American Trucks*). Nearly 70 percent of '84 Daytonas carried one of the turbo packages, helping to make Chrysler the leader in turbo sales among domestic producers. The 600 convertible sold fairly well too, though not as strongly as Chrysler's LeBaron version (or Ford's Mustang ragtop). Dodge/Chrysler's CAFE rating was right in line with government standards. The financial picture looked good too, with impressive earnings to offset those huge losses of a few years earlier. In October 1984, NHTSA launched an investigation into alleged stalling problems with various engines used in the Omni, Aries and 400: a total of 2.7 million Chrysler-built cars built between 1978 and 1984. Up to that point, Chrysler's recall record had been better than either GM or Ford.

1985 DODGE

"The revolution continues." So proclaimed Dodge's sales catalog, at any rate, as an all-new Hbodied Lancer joined the lineup. Similar to Chrysler's new LeBaron GTS, Lancer was built at the Sterling Heights, Michigan plant. The turbocharged four-cylinder engine, with 4 more horsepower than before, was now standard on Shelby Charger and optional on several models. A new electronic wastegate control varied maximum turbo boost from 7.2 to 9.0 psi. The close-ratio five-speed manual gearbox got a revised dual-rail selector mechanism. Omni/Charger, Aries, and 600 all had dual-path Iso-Strut front suspensions with a linkless anti-sway bar. Daytona also had the dual-path Iso-Struts, while the new Lancer used gas-charged struts and shocks. A number of items left the option lists, either becoming standard or dropping out completely. Ultimate Sound stereo systems with cassette player became optional, with provision for AM stereo as well as FM stereo reception. Model numbering now included a prefix letter to indicate body type.

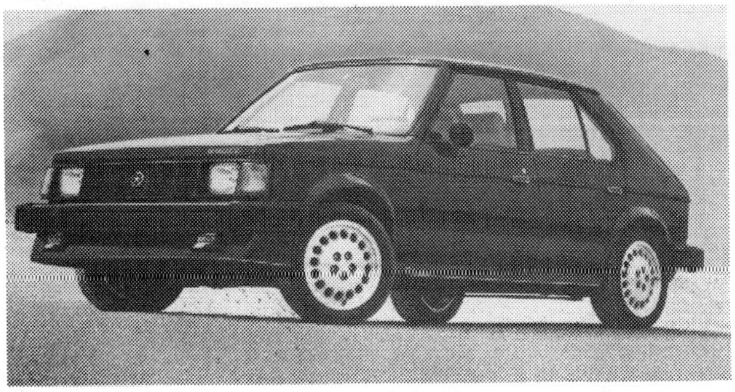

1985 Omni GLH hatchback sedan (D)

OMNI — SERIES LZ — FOUR — Not much changed on the Omni four-door hatchback. As before, base Omnis featured Euro-inspired blackout trim, while the SE sported bright metal trim. Standard engine was again the Peugeot-built 1.6 four with four-speed manual transaxle. "No more Mr. nice guy" was how Dodge described the performance-oriented Omni GLH. "This ferocious contender," it was said, "qualifies as one of the fastest production cars in America." Rather than being priced as an option, as in 1984, Omni GLH was given an actual list price of $7620 (over $1600 higher than base Omni). A total of 6,513 Omnis had the GLH package (RPO code AGB). Equipped somewhat like the Shelby Charger, GLH came with a high-output 110-horsepower 2.2-liter engine and five-speed manual gearbox, black grille and trim, air dam, sill spoilers, foglamps, and aluminum wheels. GLH could also have the turbocharged 2.2 engine.

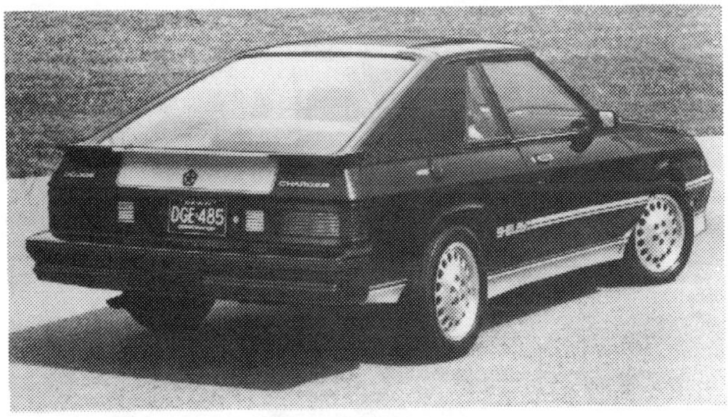

1985 Shelby Charger hatchback coupe (D)

CHARGER/2.2 — SERIES LZ — FOUR — Three versions made up the Charger series again: base Charger with standard 1.6-liter four, Charger 2.2 with the high-performance 2.2-liter engine (formerly in Shelby), and Shelby Charger, now carrying the turbocharged 2.2-liter. Styling of the standard Charger was the same as in 1984. Three body colors were new, as was one interior trim color. A four-speed transaxle remained standard in the base model. Low-back Embassy cloth bucket seats had individually adjustable front seatback recliners. Charger had a four-spoke sport steering wheel and Rallye full-gauge instrument cluster. Deluxe 13 in. wheel covers were new. So was a shift indicator on manual-gearbox models (except with turbo engine). In addition to the 110-horsepower engine and standard five-speed transmission, Charger 2.2 revealed a bold new look with fresh graphics. Charger 2.2 lost its wide bodyside moldings, but now had a performance-look air dam and fender extensions, plus side sill ground-effect spoilers. Rallye wheels were standard, with cast aluminum 14 in. wheels a new option. 'Charger 2.2' lettering no longer appeared to the rear of the quarter window, but as a portion of bodyside striping, just to rear of the door. A 'Charger 2.2' decal was also on the hatch, as part of its striping. Otherwise, appearance was similar to 1984. A Sun-Sound-Shade discount package included a

removable sunroof with vinyl storage bag, black rear window louvers, and electronic-tuning AM/FM stereo radio with digital clock. "Awe-inspiring" was Dodge's description of the Shelby Charger, now powered by a 2.2-liter four with Garrett AiResearch T3 turbocharger that delivered boost up to 8.0 psi. Appearance was about the same as 1984, but with 'Turbo' lettering on the side of the hood's bulge as well as hood louvers. The 146-horsepower engine had Chrysler/Bosch multi- point fuel injection. Shelby had a performance-geared close- ratio five-speed (overdrive) transaxle, 2.57:1 overall top gear ratio, gas-charged front struts and rear shocks, bigger rear drum brakes, and new standard P205/50VR15 speed-rated steel-belted radial tires. Premium high-back bucket seats displayed an embroidered Shelby logo. A Rallye instrument cluster held a 7000 R.P.M. tachometer and trip odometer. Shelby's wider gas pedal was positioned for heel/toe shifting. Shelby now carried a standard AM/FM stereo radio (formerly AM). Body colors this year were: Black, Ice Blue, Cream, Gold Dust, Graphic Red, Radiant Silver, Spice or White crystal coat; Charcoal or Garnet Red pearl coat. Three two-tones were available. Shelby Charger expanded to four two-tone combinations: Santa Fe Blue and Radiant Silver crystal coat (or vice versa), Black and Radiant Silver crystal coat, or Garnet Red pearl and Radiant Silver crystal coat. Charger's interior contained cloth/vinyl low-back bucket seats with reclining seatbacks, in charcoal/silver, blue, red or tan. Shelby had high-back full-contour premium bucket seats with integral head restraints, reclining seatbacks, and increased lateral support. Shelby upholstery came in blue/silver or charcoal/silver.

1985 Daytona hatchback coupe (D)

DAYTONA — SERIES GV — FOUR — Dodge's sporty hatchback coupe, with a distinctive wraparound rear spoiler, bodyside rocker panel extensions, molded front air dam and aircraft-style doors, was touted as "the ultimate moving experience." As in 1984, Daytona came in three versions: base, Turbo, and Turbo Z. Rather than being priced merely as an option package, Turbo Z was given its own list price this year, over $1300 higher than the standard Daytona Turbo. Changes this year included a switch to wider (P205/60HR15) raised-black-letter tires for the Turbo, a slightly more powerful turbo 2.2-liter engine, modified dual- rail shift linkage, and two new body colors. A new body-color three-piece wraparound rear spoiler, similar to that used on the '84 Turbo Z, now appeared on all Daytonas. Fuel filler door and hatch releases moved from the console glovebox to the sill alongside the driver's seat. Newly optional: an Ultimate Sound stereo system with graphic equalizer. As for performance, a Turbo four could match many six and V-8 coupes. A standard Graphic Message Center showed an incandescent display. Base Daytonas carried an AM radio; Turbos an AM/FM stereo and leather-wrapped steering wheel. Turbos also had black hood louvers and a handling suspension, plus cast aluminum 15 in. wheels, while base Daytonas rode P185/70R14 tires on 14 in. wheels. Turbo Z added a distinctive wraparound rear spoiler, lower body ground effects, and specially-molded front air dam. The Turbo Z package featured a unique front fascia and rear fascia that wrapped to wheel openings; integrated wide black bodyside moldings; black headlamp surround moldings; black bumper rub strips; front fascia extension; subtle accent tape striping; Turbo Z decal; dual electric aero-style remote mirrors; and rear sunvisors. Daytonas came in Black Crystal Coat or a choice of 10 pearl coat and crystal coat two-tone combinations. Turbo Z came only in Black or two two-tone possibilities. Standard Daytona interior had cloth low-back bucket seats with reclining seatbacks and adjustable head restraints in black, red, silver/charcoal, or light/medium tan. Turbo model Enthusiast driver's seats, with adjustable (pneumatic) lumbar and thigh support, were available in Corinthian leather as well as cloth. Turbos got much of the attention, but the base Daytona came with a standard fuel-injected 2.2-liter four. A new system retarded spark knock in one or more cylinders, instead of all four at once. A total of 8,023 Daytonas were reported to have the Turbo Z package (code AGS), while 3,539 had the Electronic Features Package I (code ADM) and 391 had the T- Bar roof package.

1985 Aries LE coupe (JG)

ARIES — SERIES KD — FOUR — A wider grille, tapered inward at its base, helped give Aries a much different front-end look in its first major facelift. Simple bright crossbars covered a subdued black pattern, with center pentastar emblem. Billed as having new "sweeping curves and softened lines," Aries' basic shape remained close to 1984, though truly more rounded with a slightly longer nose and higher deck. Plastic halogen headlamps had integral turn signals. Wraparound amber lenses served as

parking lamps, without the separate park lamps next to the grille as in 1984. Prior tri-section full-width taillamps changed to five sections this year, with backup lenses at the inner ends and new wraparound sections at the outside. As before, though, two horizontal ribs ran across each lens panel. Rear side marker lenses were now part of the bodyside molding, no longer separate as in 1984. New black bodyside moldings were integrated (continuous) with bumper rub strips. Bright moldings now surrounded the entire side- window segment, while each window held new black moldings. Also new were soft bumper coverings, black headlamp bezels, hood and decklid. Inside, a new soft padded cover topped the instrument panel. A new flat-face climate control panel eliminated protruding buttons, and door panels held new map pockets. The Custom wagon was dropped, but a whole new top-rung LE (Luxury Edition) series was added: sedans and the wagon. Aries gained standard equipment and more black trim this year. SE added an AM radio and intermittent wipers. LE added black sill moldings, wide black bodyside moldings with argent edge, and a trunk light. Wire wheel covers left the option list, as did vinyl roofs. Added to that list were electronic- tuning radios with AM stereo, reclining bucket seats with full-length console, and a heavy-duty suspension with gas- filled shocks. Base engine was the 2.2-liter four, with 2.6-liter optional. An electronic feedback carburetor was used. A four- speed manual transaxle was standard; five-speed and TorqueFlite available. Manual-shift models had a new upshift indicator light. Aries colors were: Black, Ice Blue, Nightwatch Blue, Cream, Gold Dust, Crimson Red, Radiant Silver, or White crystal coat; Gunmetal Blue, Mink Brown, or Garnet Red pearl coat. Base interiors held an all-vinyl bench seat with adjustable head restraints (split-back on two-door sedan). Aries LE and SE had cloth split-back bench seating with folding center armrest.

1985 Lancer ES hatchback sedan (D)

LANCER — SERIES HD — FOUR — Dodge's new hatchback six-window, four-door aero-styled touring sedan rode a 103.1 in. wheelbase, just a trifle shorter than the 600 sedan. Described as a "world-class automotive achievement," Lancer featured a front air dam, flush windshield and liftback glass, sloping hood with available (functional) turbo louvers, plus black bumper strips and bodyside moldings. Doors were aircraft-style (extending slightly into the roof), and the aerowrap windshield displayed a sharp 58-degree slant. Lancer had a black crossbar grille, as opposed to the bright vertical-bar grille used on the similar H-bodied Chrysler LeBaron GTS. Two trim levels were offered: base and ES. Standard engine was the fuel-injected 2.2-liter four, with turbocharged edition optional. With that option came a 'Turbo' nameplate on front fenders. A close-ratio five-speed gearbox was standard. TorqueFlite three-speed automatic was available with either engine. Remote cable releases operated the liftback and fuel door. Base Lancer dashboards held a Graphic Message Center and mechanical (analog) instrument cluster. La Corde II cloth upholstered, contoured low-back bucket seats had back wings and reclining seatbacks. Standard equipment also included power brakes, soft-fascia bumpers, warning chimes, side window demisters, tethered gas cap, halogen quad headlamps, bi-level Ram Air heater, front-door map pockets, driver's remote aero-style mirror, and a day/night inside mirror. Lancer had bright-edge belt moldings, narrow black bodyside moldings with bright edge, black windshield molding, multi- function steering column lever, AM/FM stereo radio with digital clock, power rack-and-pinion steering, and two-speed wipers. The padded instrument panel had an integral console. A heel-and-toe gas pedal went into manual-shift models. The road touring suspension used nitrogen-charged front dual-path Iso-Struts and rear shocks, with front/rear anti-sway bars and rear track support bar. P185/70R14 steel-belted radial tires were standard. Lancer's sportier ES added a black front air dam with black trim and bodyside moldings, along with both bodyside and liftback accent stripes. Sport bucket seats had reclining seatbacks; standard cloth, or available Corinthian leather. Seats offered adjustable lumbar and thigh support. A 60/40 split-back rear seat contained integral headrests. An electronic instrument cluster included fluorescent displays for digital speedometer/odometer/trip odometer, plus graphic flashing tachometer and graphic gauges. ES also had a Euro- sport steering wheel, P195/70R14 raised-black-letter tires on styled steel wheels, sport handling suspension, black upper door frame and pillar applique tape, black sill moldings, time-delay headlamp switch, and courtesy lights. All paints were crystal coat or pearl coat. Lancer colors were: Black, Ice Blue, Nightwatch Blue, Cream, Gold Dust and Radiant Silver crystal coat; Gunmetal Blue, Desert Bronze, Mink Brown and Garnet Red pearl coat. Three two-tone combinations were offered. Two "Sport Handling" suspension packages were available. The standard one, installed on 992 cars, included P185/70R14 all-season Goodyear Vector or Michelin XA4 tires. A Premium version added full electronic instrument cluster, rear headrests, and 60/40 fold-down rear seatback. That one is reported to have gone on 4,639 Lancers. A total of 4,581 Lancers carried the Turbo Sport I package (code AGT).

1985 Dodge 600/ES convertible (D)

600 SEDAN — SERIES EE — FOUR — Moving to the longer-wheelbase sedan, which measured the same as Chrysler's New Yorker, changes also were minimal. The 600ES Euro-style sedan was dropped, partly because of the new Lancer. But a 600SE edition replaced it, offering more luxury touches. Standard equipment was similar to the 600 coupe, but with front center armrest, assist handles, power decklid release, remote fuel filler door release, cloth/vinyl split-back bench seats, and bright/black rear quarter window moldings. No vinyl roof was included.

600 COUPE/CONVERTIBLE — SERIES KV — FOUR — Little change was evident in either the shorter- wheelbase two-door 600 or the longer sedan. New this year were upper bodyside accent stripes, improved seatbelt retractors, and a maintenance-free 400-amp battery. Both the carbureted 2.2-liter engine and five-speed transaxle were dropped. The club coupe had a formal roofline and Laredo- grain landau roof with opera windows. A total of 5,621 ES Turbo convertible packages (code AGT) were installed. The ES convertible carried P195/60VR15 SBR Eagle GT RBL tires, while other 600s had P185/70R14. Base engine was the fuel-injected 2.2-liter four with automatic transaxle. Mitsubishi's MCA-Jet 2.6-liter was optional again, along with a turbo 2.2. In addition to the turbocharged engine, the 600 ES Turbe featured leather upholstery.

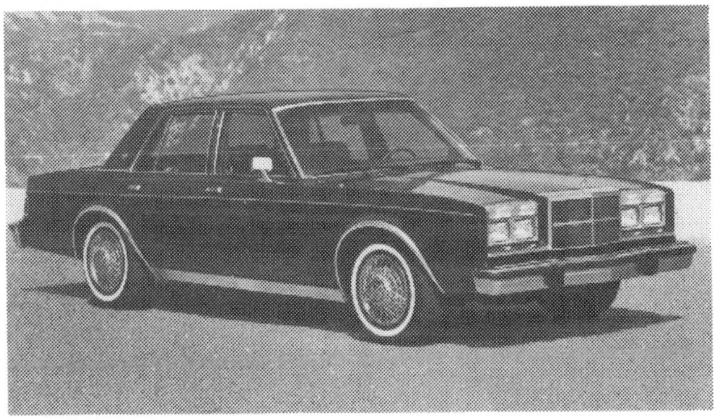

1985 Diplomat SE sedan (D)

DIPLOMAT — SERIES MG — V-8 — Changes to the biggest Dodge focused mainly on the standard 318 cu. in. (5.2-liter) V-8 engine. Compression jumped from 8.4:1 to 9.0:1, roller cam followers were installed, and horsepower rose by 10 (to 140). Two trim levels were offered: Salon and luxury SE (the latter added late in the 1984 model year), both four-door sedans only. SE had a distinctive quad crossbar grille, Laredo grain full vinyl roof, Gibson velour upholstery, door courtesy lights, dual remote-control mirrors, and improved sound insulation. Vinyl bodyside moldings were new this year. So was a new standard 400-amp maintenance-free battery. Lower bodyside panels were treated with a urethane protective coating to resist chips/corrosion. An electronic-tuning stereo radio with cassette player was a new option. Diplomat, a near twin to Plymouth's Gran Fury, continued to sell mainly to fleet operators (and large families). A total of 14,834 Diplomats had the Police package (code AHB).

I.D. DATA: Coding of Dodge's 17-symbol Vehicle Identification Number (VIN), on the upper left corner of the instrument panel visible through the windshield, is similar to 1984. Under Car Line, code 'X' (Lancer) was added. Model Year code changed to 'F' 1985. Code 'N' was added for the new assembly plant at Sterling Heights, MI. Engine numbers and Body Code Plates are in the same locations as 1981-84.

OMNI (FOUR)

Model Number	Body/Style Number	Body Type & Seating	Factory Price	Shipping Weight	Production Total
LZE	44	4-dr. Hatch-5P	5977	2095	54,229
LZH	44	4-dr. SE Hatch-5P	6298	2120	13,385

OMNI GLH (FOUR)

LZE	44/AGB	4-dr. Hatch-5P	7620	2320	6,513

CHARGER (FOUR)

LZH	24	2-dr. Hatch-5P	6584	2160	38,203

CHARGER 2.2 (FOUR)

LZP	24	2-dr. Hatch-5P	7515	2305	10,645

SHELBY CHARGER (FOUR)

LZS	24	2-dr. Hatch-5P	9553	2350	7,709

DAYTONA (FOUR)

GVH	24	2-dr. Hatch-4P	8505	2520	29,987

DAYTONA TURBO (FOUR)

GVS	24	2-dr. Hatch-4P	10286	2630	9,509

DAYTONA TURBO Z (FOUR)

GVS	24/AGS	2-dr. Hatch-4P	11620	N/A	8,023

ARIES (FOUR)

KDL	21	2-dr. Sedan-6P	6924	2335	9,428
KDL	41	4-dr. Sedan-6P	7039	2340	39,580

ARIES SE (FOUR)

KDM	21	2-dr. Sedan-6P	7321	2345	7,937
KDM	41	4-dr. Sedan-6P	7439	2375	23,920
KDH	45	4-dr. Sta Wag-6P	7909	2480	22,953

ARIES LE (FOUR)

KDH	21	2-dr. Sedan-6P	7659	2345	3,706
KDH	41	4-dr. Sedan-6P	7792	2375	5,932
KDP	45	4-dr. Sta Wag-6P	8348	2480	4,519

LANCER (FOUR)

HDH	44	4-Dr. Spt Hatch-5P	8713	N/A	30,567
HDS	44	4-dr. ES Hatch-5P	9690	N/A	15,286

600 COUPE/CONVERTIBLE (FOUR)

KVP	22	2-dr. Cpe-5P	9060	2445	12,670
KVP	27	2-dr. Conv.-4P	10889	2530	8,188
KVP	27/AGT	2-dr. ES Conv.-4P	13995	2530	5,621

600 SE SEDAN (FOUR)

EEH	41	4-dr. Sedan-6P	8953	2530	32,368

DIPLOMAT SALON (V-8)

MGL	41	4-dr. Sedan-6P	9399	3465	25,398

DIPLOMAT SE (V-8)

MGP	41	4-dr. Sedan-6P	10418	N/A	13,767

MODEL NUMBER NOTE: Some sources identify models using the VIN data to indicate Car Line, Price Class and Body Style. Example: Aries four-door (KDL41) has the equivalent number D26, which translates to Aries line, Low price class, and four-door sedan body. See I.D. Data section for breakdown.

ENGINE DATA: BASE FOUR (Omni, Charger): Inline, overhead-cam four-cylinder. Cast iron block; aluminum head. Displacement: 97.3 cu. in. (1.6 liters). Bore & stroke: 3.17 x 3.07 in. Compression ratio: 8.8:1. Brake horsepower: 64 at 4800 R.P.M. Torque: 87 lbs.-ft. at 2800 R.P.M. Five main bearings. Solid valve lifters. Carburetor: 2Bbl. Holley 6520. Peugeot-built. VIN Code: A. BASE FOUR (Aries); OPTIONAL (Omni, Charger): Inline, overhead-cam four-cylinder. Cast iron block; aluminum head. Displacement: 135 cu. in. (2.2 liters). Bore & stroke: 3.44 x 3.62 in. Compression ratio: 9.0:1. Brake horsepower: 96 at 5200 R.P.M. Torque: 119 lbs.-ft. at 3200 R.P.M. Five main bearings. Hydraulic valve lifters. Carburetor: 2Bbl. Holley 6520. VIN Code: C. BASE FOUR (Daytona, Lancer, 600); OPTIONAL (Aries): Same as 135 cu. in. four above, but with electronic fuel injection Horsepower: 99 at 5600 R.P.M. Torque: 121 lbs.- ft. at 3200 R.P.M. VIN Code: D. BASE FOUR (Omni GLH, Charger 2.2): High-performance carbureted version of 135 cu. in. four above Compression ratio: 9.6:1. Horsepower: 110 at 5600 R.P.M. Torque: 129 lbs.-ft. at 3600 R.P.M. VIN Code: F. TURBOCHARGED FOUR, BASE (Shelby Charger); OPTIONAL (Omni GLH, Daytona, Lancer, 600): Same as 135 cu. in. four above, with EFI and turbocharger Compression ratio: 8.1:1. Horsepower: 146 at 5200 R.P.M. Torque: 168 lbs.-ft. at 3600 R.P.M. VIN Code: E. OPTIONAL FOUR (Aries, 600): Inline, overhead-cam four-cylinder. Cast iron block; aluminum head. Displacement: 156 cu. in. (2.6 liters). Bore & stroke: 3.59 x 3.86 in. Compression ratio: 8.7:1. Brake horsepower: 101 at 4800 R.P.M. Torque: 140 lbs.-ft. at 2800 R.P.M. Five main bearings. Solid valve lifters. Carburetor: 2Bbl. Mikuni. Mitsubishi-built. VIN Code: G. BASE V-8 (Diplomat): 90-degree, overhead valve V-8. Cast iron block and head. Displacement: 318 cu. in. (5.2 liters). Bore & stroke: 3.91 x 3.31 in. Compression ratio: 8.7:1. Brake horsepower: 140 at 3600 R.P.M. Torque: 265 lbs.-ft. at 1600 R.P.M. Five main bearings. Hydraulic valve lifters. Carburetor: 2Bbl. Holley 6280. VIN Code: P.

NOTE: Dodge's police V-8 was the same as the above 318 cu. in. engine, except: Compression ratio: 8.0:1. Horsepower: 175 at 4000 R.P.M. Torque: 250 lbs.-ft. at 3200 R.P.M.

CHASSIS DATA: Wheelbase: (Omni) 99.1 inches.; (Charger) 96.5 inches; (Daytona) 97.0 inches; (Aries/600 coupe) 100.3 inches; (600 Sedan) 103.3 inches; (Lancer) 103.1 inches.; (Diplomat) 112.7 inches. Overall length: (Omni) 164.8 inches.; (Charger) 174.8 inches.; (Daytona) 175.0 inches; (Aeries) 178.6 inches; (Aeries wagon) 179.0 inches; (Lancer) 180.4 inches; (600 coupe) 180.7 inches; (600 sedan) 186.6 inches; (Diplomat) 205.7 inches. Height: (Omni) 53.0 inches; (Charger) 50.7 inches. (Shelby) 50.2 in.; (Daytona) 50.3 in.; (Aries 2dr.) 52.7 in.; (Aries 4dr.) 52.9 in.; (Aries wag) 53.2 in.; (Lancer) 53.0 in.; (600 cpe) 52.7 in.; (600 conv.) 53.7 in.; (600 sedan) 53.1 in.; (Diplomat) 55.3 in. Width: (Omni) 66.8 in.; (Chgr) 66.7 in.; (Aries/600) 68.0 in.; (Daytona) 69.3 in.; (Lancer) 68.3 in.; (Diplo) 74.2 in. Front Tread: (Omni/Chgr) 56.1 in.; (Aries/Daytona/Lancer/600) 57.6 in.; (Diplo) 60.0 in. Rear Tread: (Omni/Chgr) 55.7 in.; (Aries/Daytona/Lancer/600) 7.2 in.; (Diplo) 59.5 in. Standard Tires: (Omni/Charger) P165/80R13 SBR; (Charger 2.2) P195/60R14 SBR RBL; (Shelby) P205/50VR15 SBR RBL unidirectional; (Daytona) P185/70R14 SBR BSW; (Daytona Turbo) P205/60HR15 SBR RBL; (Aries) P175/80R13 SBR BSW; (Lancer) P185/70R14 SBR BSW; (Lancer ES) P195/70R14 SBR RBL; (600) P185/70R14 SBR; (600 ES conv.) P195/60VR15 SBR Eagle GT RBL; (Diplomat) P205/75R15 SBR WSW.

TECHNICAL: Transmission: Four-speed manual (floor lever) standard on Omni/Charger and Aries 2.2-liter: (1st) 3.29:1; (2nd) 1.89:1; (3rd) 1.21:1; (4th) 0.88:1; (Rev) 3.14:1. Five-speed manual standard on Omni/Charger 2.2-liter, Lancer and Daytona; optional on Aries: (1st) 3.29:1; (2nd) 2.08:1; (3rd) 1.45:1; (4th) 1.04:1; (5th) 0.72:1; (Rev) 3.14:1. TorqueFlite three- speed automatic standard on Diplomat, Aries 2.6-liter and 600; optional on all other models. Diplomat gear ratios: (1st) 2.74:1; (2nd) 1.54:1; (3rd) 1.00:1; (Rev) 2.22:1. Other models: (1st) 2.69:1; (2nd) 1.55:1; (3rd) 1.00:1; (Rev) 2.10:1. Standard final drive ratio: (Omni/Charger) 2.69:1 w/4spd, 2.20:1 or 2.78:1 w/5spd, 3.02:1 w/auto.; (Shelby) 2.57:1; (Daytona/Lancer) 2.57:1 w/5spd, 3.02:1 w/auto.; (Aries) 2.69:1 w/4spd, 2.20:1 w/5spd, 3.02:1 w/auto.; (600) 3.02:1; (Diplo) 2.26:1. Steering: (Diplomat) recirculating ball; (others) rack and pinion. Suspension: (Omni/Chgr) Dual path Iso-Strut independent coil front w/anti-sway bar, trailing arm semi-independent coil rear w/anti-sway bar on Charger 2.2 and Shelby; (Daytona) Dual path Iso-Strut front, trailing arm rear w/gas-charged shock absorbers, front/rear anti-sway bars; (Lancer) Dual path gas-charged front Iso-Struts, gas-charged rear shocks, front/rear anti-sway bars and rear track support bars; (Aries/600) Dual path Iso-Strut front w/coil springs and linkless anti-sway bar, beam rear axle w/trailing arms and coil springs; (Diplomat) transverse front torsion bars and anti-sway bar, semi-elliptic rear leaf springs. Brakes: Front disc, rear drum. Ignition: Electronic. Body construction: Unibody. Fuel tank: (Omni/Chgr) 13 gal.; (Daytona/Aries/Lancer/600) 14 gal.; (Diplomat) 18 gal.

DRIVETRAIN OPTIONS: Engines: 2.2-liter four: Omni/Chgr ($134). Turbocharged 2.2-liter four: Omni GLH ($872); base Daytona ($964); Lancer/600 ($610). 2.6-liter four: Aries/600 ($271). Transmission/Axle: Five-speed manual trans.: Omni/Chgr, Aries Cust/SE ($75). TorqueFlite auto. trans.: Omni/Chgr/Daytona/Aries ($439); Lancer ($464). High-altitude axle: Omni/Chgr/Aries ($22). Steering/Suspension: Power steering: Omni/Chgr/Aries, base 600 conv. ($219). H.D. susp.: Aries ($58); Diplo ($26). Sport handling susp.: 600 ($57) exc. base conv. ($276). Other: H.D. battery: Aries/600/Lancer/Diplo ($44). H.D. engine cooling: Omni/Chgr/Aries ($141). California emission system ($99).

OMNI/CHARGER CONVENIENCE/APPEARANCE OPTIONS: Option Packages: Sun/Sound/Shade pkg.: Shelby/2.2 ($512- $623). Auto. trans. discount pkg. ($765-$886). 2.2-liter engine and five-speed discount pkg. ($295-$408). Light group ($55-$88). Protection group ($88-$189). Comfort/Convenience: Air cond. ($643). Rear defroster ($132). Automatic speed control ($179). Rear wiper/washer: Omni ($120). Dual remote mirrors: Omni/SE ($49); Chgr ($57). Electronic-tuning Radios: AM: base ($113). AM/FM stereo ($125-$238). Seek/scan AM/FM stereo w/cassette ($264-$502). Ultimate sound stereo w/cassette: Chgr ($210-$712). Exterior: Removable glass sunroof: Chgr ($315). Rear spoiler: base Chgr ($72). Pearl coat paint ($40). Two-tone paint: SE/Chgr ($150). Interior: Low-back vinyl bucket seats ($31) exc. SE (NC). High-back cloth bucket seats ($107). Center armrest ($48). Tonneau cover: Chgr ($69). Cargo area carpet ($43-$62). Wheels and Tires: Cast aluminum 14 in. wheels: Chgr ($255- $305). P165/80R13 SBR WSW: base ($59). P195/60R14 SBR RWL: Chgr 2.2 ($22). P195/60R14 SBR RWL w/sport susp.: base Chgr ($350). Conventional spare tire ($63-$187).

DAYTONA CONVENIENCE/APPEARANCE OPTIONS: Option Packages: Equipment discount pkg.: Popular ($417-$763); Luxury ($1156-$1269). Electronic features pkg.: voice alert and navigator ($338-$362). Cargo trim/quiet sound group: base ($154-$173). Light group ($138). Protection pkg. ($88-$142). Comfort/Convenience: Air cond. ($737). Rear defroster ($143- $168). Auto. speed control ($179). Power driver's seat ($215). Power windows ($185). Power door locks ($125). Illuminated entry system ($75). Tinted glass ($110). Tilt steering wheel ($110). Liftgate wiper/washer ($120). Dual power remote mirrors ($48). Electronic-tuning Radios w/digital clock: AM/FM stereo: base ($160). Premium AM/FM stereo w/cassette ($264-$424). Ultimate sound seek/scan AM/FM stereo w/cassette ($474-$634). Delete radio ($56 credit). Exterior: Removable glass sunroof ($322). Interior: Low-back vinyl bucket seats: base ($31). Low-back cloth/vinyl bucket seats w/adj. driver's lumbar/thigh support: base ($362). Low-back leather bucket seats w/adj. driver's lumbar/thigh support: base ($929); Turbo ($567). Wheels/Tires: Aluminum wheels: base ($322). P195/70R14 RBL: base ($92). Conventional spare tire ($83-$93).

ARIES CONVENIENCE/APPEARANCE OPTIONS: Option Packages: Equipment pkg.: Basic, base ($247); Popular, LE/SE ($516-$603); Premium, LE ($742-$887). Light pkg. ($56- $119). Comfort/Convenience: Air cond. ($737). Rear defroster ($143). Auto. speed control ($179). Power windows ($185-$260). Power door locks ($125-$175). Tinted glass ($110). Tilt steering wheel ($110). Intermitent wipers ($53). Liftgate wiper/washer: wag ($120). Mirrors: Remote left ($24). Dual black remote ($64-$88). Electronic-tuning Radios: AM: base ($113). AM/FM stereo ($125-$238). Seek/scan AM/FM stereo w/cassette ($264-$389). Exterior: Pearl coat paint ($40). Sill moldings, black ($26). Bumper guards, front/rear ($56). Bodyside tape stripe ($48). Luggage rack: wag ($116). Special sound insulation: base ($43). Undercoating ($43). Interior: Vinyl bench seat: SE, wag ($31). Cloth/vinyl bench seat: base ($31). Cloth/vinyl bucket seats: SE ($284); LE, wag ($210). Color-keyed mats ($45). Trunk dress-up: SE ($51). Wheels/Tires: Deluxe wheel covers: base ($52). Luxury wheel covers: base ($48-$100). Styled 13 in. wheels ($12-$112). Cast aluminum wheels, 14 in.: SE/LE ($322-$370). P175/80R13 WSW ($58). P185/70R14 SBR BSW ($36-$94). P185/70R14 SBR WSW ($94-$152). Conventional spare tire ($73-$83).

LANCER CONVENIENCE/APPEARANCE OPTIONS: Option Packages: Turbo sport pkg. ($1098-$1397). Equipment discount pkg.: Popular ($509-$664); Luxury ($1102-$1257). Electronic features pkg. I: ES ($515); II ($382). Sport handling pkg.: base ($118). Sport handling pkg. II ($180- $668). Light pkg.: base ($76). Comfort/Convenience: Air cond. ($757). Rear defroster ($148). Auto. speed control ($179). Power windows ($270). Power door locks ($180). Power seat ($225). Illuminated entry system ($75). Tinted glass ($115). Mechanical instrument cluster: ES (NC). Tilt steering wheel ($110). Intermittent wipers ($53). Liftgate wiper/washer ($125). Mirrors: Dual black remote-control ($64); power ($48-$112). Lighted vanity, right ($58). Electronic-tuning Radios w/digital clock: Seek/scan AM stereo/FM stereo w/cassette ($305). Ultimate sound AM stereo/FM stereo w/cassette ($515). Radio delete ($152 credit). Exterior: Removable glass sunroof ($332). Two-tone paint ($210). Pearl coat paint ($40). Premium sound insulation: base ($43). Undercoating ($43). Interior: Leather bucket seats: ES ($566). Folding armrest: base ($43). Vinyl console/armrest: base ($79). Color-keyed mats ($45). Wheels and Tires: Styled 14 in. wheels: base ($60). Cast aluminum wheels, 14 in. or 15 in. ($310-$370) but (NC) w/base Turbo sport pkg. P185/70R14 SBR WSW ($58). P195/70R14 SBR RBL: base ($92). P205/60R15 SBR RBL ($180-$272). Conventional spare tire: base ($83).

600 CONVENIENCE/APPEARANCE OPTIONS: Option Packages: Equipment discount pkg.: Popular ($593- $1055); Luxury, cpe/sed ($1272-$1397). Protection pkg.: sed ($81). Comfort/Convenience: Air cond. ($757). Rear defroster ($143). Auto. speed control ($179). Power windows ($195-$270). Power door locks ($130-$180). Power seat ($225). Power decklid release: 2dr. ($40). Illuminated entry system ($75). Tinted glass ($115). Electronic voice alert: sed ($66). Euro/sport three-spoke steering wheel: cpe/conv. ($10). Leather-wrapped steering wheel ($50). Tilt steering wheel ($110). Lighting/Mirrors: Cornering lamps ($60). Dual power remote- control mirrors ($86). Lighted vanity mirror ($58). Electronic-tuning Radios w/digital clock: AM/FM stereo ($125). Seek/scan AM/FM stereo w/cassette ($299-$424). Ultimate sound stereo w/cassette ($210-$634). Premium speakers ($126). Radio delete ($56 credit). Exterior: Two-tone paint: cpe/sed ($187). Pearl coat paint ($40). Vinyl bodyside moldings ($55). Door edge protectors: sed ($25). Bumper guards ($56). Undercoating ($43). Interior: Cloth/vinyl bench seat: cpe (NC). Vinyl bench seat: sed ($31). Cloth 50/50 bench seat: sed ($287). Center armrest: cpe ($61). Color-keyed mats: front, conv. ($25); front/rear, others ($45). Trunk dress-up ($51). Wheels/Tires: Wire wheel covers, locking ($224). Cast aluminum wheels ($107-$322). P185/70R14 SBR WSW: conv. ($58). Conventional spare tire ($83).

DIPLOMAT CONVENIENCE/APPEARANCE OPTIONS: Option Packages: Equipment pkg.: Popular ($414-$537); Luxury, SE ($1868). Light pkg. ($120-$158). Comfort/Convenience: Air conditioning, semi-auto ($812). Rear defroster ($148). Auto. speed control ($179). Power seat, left: SE ($225). Power windows ($270). Power door locks ($180). Power decklid release ($40). Illuminated entry system ($75). Leather-wrapped steering wheel: SE ($60). Tilt steering wheel ($115). Intermittent wipers ($53). Mirrors: Remote driver's: Salon ($24). Dual remote, chrome ($67). Lighted vanity, right ($58). Electronic-Tuning Radios w/digital clock: AM/FM stereo ($125). Seek/scan AM/FM stereo w/cassette ($264-$389). Ultimate sound AM stereo/FM stereo w/cassette ($474-$599). Power antenna: SE ($65). Radio delete ($56 credit). Exterior: Power glass sunroof ($1076). Full vinyl roof: Salon ($185). Pearl coat paint ($40). Vinyl bodyside moldings ($57). Upper door frame moldings: Salon ($46). Body sound insulation: Salon ($66). Undercoating ($43). Interior: Vinyl split-back bench seat: Salon ($60). Trunk dress-up ($56). Wheels/Tires: Premium wheel covers: Salon ($96). Wire wheel covers: SE ($224). Cast aluminum wheels: SE ($262). Conventional spare ($93).

HISTORY: Introduced: October 2, 1984 except Lancer, January 2, 1985. Model year production: Chrysler reported a total of 440,043 passenger cars shipped. Of the 400,878 four-cylinder engines, 65,854 were turbos. Calendar year production: 482,388. Calendar year sales by U.S. dealers: 434,325. Model year sales by U.S. dealers: 438,494.

Historical Footnotes: Chrysler Corp. prices rose only an average 1.2 percent ($125) for 1985; half that amount on smaller Dodge models. The previous year's increases had been modest, too; far different from the hefty jumps of a few years earlier. Model year sales (including Japanese imports) reached the highest total since 1978, and 21 percent over the 1984 figure. Every domestic model except the 600 showed a sales rise for the model year, including Diplomat, which jumped from 21,932 in 1984 to 37,350 for a 70 percent increase. Plenty of buyers, it appeared, still craved a V-8 engine. The P-body Dodge Shadow (and Plymouth Sundance), scheduled for arrival in mid-1986, were originally intended to become the Omni/Horizon replacement. But renewed vigor in sales of those old L-bodies caused Chrysler Corp. to retarget the upcoming models into a higher price level of the market, between Omni and Aries.

1986 DODGE

No new models were introduced for 1986, but Dodge added a new engine to replace the Mitsubishi 2.6-liter four. Optional in Aries, Daytona, Lancer and 600, the 153 cu. in. (2.5-liter) fuel-injected four used two counter-rotating balance shafts to counteract the vibrations ordinarily inherent in four-cylinder powerplants. They were mounted in a cast aluminum housing beneath the crankshaft, in the oil pan. The engine produced 100 horsepower at 4800 R.P.M. An electronic control unit monitored engine operation and adjusted fuel/air mixture, timing, and emission control components. It even maintained a "diary" of operations that assisted in diagnosis if a fault were detected. The new engine was essentially a stroked variant of the 2.2-liter. The cylinder head of the 2.2-liter four was modified to hasten burning of the air/fuel mixture by creating turbulence, allowing gases to ignite closer to TDC. This allowed a compression jump to 9.5:1, without the need for higher-octane fuel. The same "fast-burn" head was used on the new 2.5-liter. New Chrysler/Bosch low-pressure single-point fuel injection operated at 14.7 psi (less than half the previous pressure); it was used in all Chrysler fours. All fours also had a new labyrinth distributor with fewer parts. Fuel-injected engines, and the carbureted 2.2, had on- board diagnostics that monitored 23 functions. All Dodges had the required center high-mounted stop lamp, either mounted inside the car and sealed against the backlight, built into a rear spoiler or, on convertibles, mounted in a separate pod attached to the decklid. On the less dramatic side, all Dodges except Omni/Charger got a new ignition key design. Intermittent rear window wipers became optional on Daytona and Lancer. All domestic front-drives now had the "precision- feel" power steering introduced in 1985.

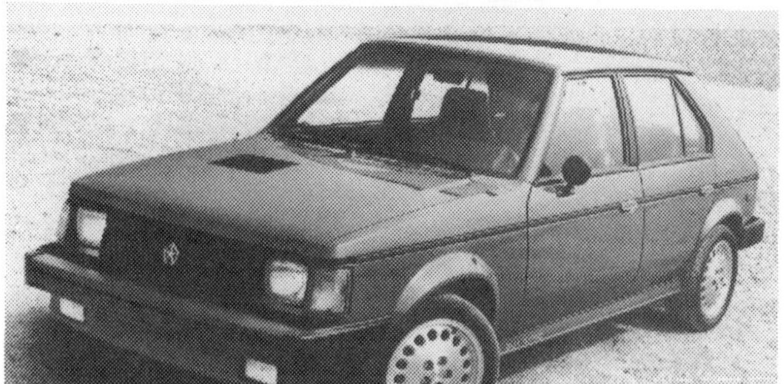

1986 Omni GLH Turbo hatchback sedan (D)

OMNI — SERIES LZ — FOUR — Buyers could choose either a "lean or mean" Omni. Even though the base Omni hatchback and step-up SE were sensible small cars, Omni GLH was described as "a well-behaved savage." Appearance of each model changed little this year, except for the newly-required center stop lamp, which was attached to the lower hatchback lip. As before, base Omni's Euro-styling included black grille, headlamp bezels and trim, while SE turned to bright body trim. Base engine was again the 1.6-liter Peugeot four, with four-speed manual transaxle; optional, the 2.2-liter with close-ratio five-speed manual or three-speed TorqueFlite. Manual transaxles included a shift indicator light. A Rallye instrument cluster held large analog gauges. This year's body colors were: Black, Ice Blue, Cream, Charcoal pearl coat, Gold Dust, Garnet Red pearl coat, Graphic Red, Radiant Silver, Spice, White, and Santa Fe Blue. Three two-tones were available only on Omni SE. Both models had standard cloth/vinyl low-back bucket seats, while SE's were the high-back design. SE also had standard P165/80R13 whitewall tires. National Hot Rod Association tests in 1984 had demonstrated that Omni GLH could hit 50 MPH in 5.75 seconds, and this year's version was expected to beat that figure. GLH came with the 110-horsepower, high-output 2.2-liter four, which had a chrome valve cover and performance exhaust; or optional 146-horsepower turbo edition. Close-ratio five- speed was standard, along with a higher final drive ratio. The GLH package included black bumpers, dual black remote mirrors, black front air dam with side extensions, black grille and headlamp

bezels, a black painted panel between taillamps, black side sill spoilers, dual Bosch foglamps integrated into front air dam, and GLH identification. Red striping went on the air dam and sill spoilers. Inside was an AM stereo/FM stereo radio with digital clock, and a heel-and- toe gas pedal. Speed-rated Eagle GT P195/50HR15 SBR tires rode 15 in. cast aluminum wheels. Trenton cloth high-back sport bucket seats were standard, and the special sport suspension used gas-charged front struts and rear shocks. Turbo GLH models also had a functional louvered hood and stainless steel exhaust, as well as a GLH Turbo decal on each sill spoiler and on passenger side of hatch. A total of 3,629 Omnis had the GLH performance package.

1986 Shelby Charger hatchback (D)

CHARGER/2.2 — SERIES LZ — FOUR — Like the closely-related Omni sedan, the shorter- wheelbase Charger showed no significant change for 1986 beyond the new center stop lamp. Once again, a base model, Charger 2.2 and Shelby Charger were offered. Base engine was the 1.6-liter with four-speed, while Charger 2.2 had a five-speed with its high-output (110 horsepower) 2.2-liter four, and Shelby carried a 146-horsepower turbo. A 2.2-liter engine rated 96 horsepower was also available for the base model. A shift indicator light, called Fuel Pacer, went on manual- transaxle models. Cloth/vinyl low-back bucket seats with recliners and adjustable head restraints made up the standard interior. Charger colors were: Black, Ice Blue, Charcoal pearl coat, Cream, Gold Dust, Garnet Red pearl coat, Graphic Red, Radiant Silver, Spice and White. Shelby came only in one of four two-tone combinations (silver/blue, blue/silver, silver/red, or silver/black); base Chargers had two two-tone options. In addition to turbo power, Shelby had gas-charged front Iso-struts and rear shocks, quick 14:1 steering, ventilated front disc brakes, large anti-sway bars, and 15 in. cast aluminum Shelby wheels holding P205/50VR15 blackwall Eagle GT SBR tires with unidirectional tread. Body features included a "turbo bulge" hood with louvers and special badges, aero front air dam, side sill spoilers, and functional rear spoiler. Cloth/vinyl high-back bucket seats were embroidered with the Carroll Shelby logo. A 1985 Shelby had managed 0-50 MPH in 5.34 seconds, in NHRA testing.

1986 Daytona Turbo Z hatchback coupe (D)

DAYTONA — SERIES GV — FOUR — For its third season, Daytona changed only modestly in appearance. This year's lineup consisted of a base model and the Turbo Z. The former "ordinary" Turbo model was dropped. Front and rear fascias were modified. New nerf extensions and integrated bodyside moldings now offered full 360-degree protection. Tinted glass became standard, as did new 14 in. cast aluminum wheels. Both models had a standard AM stereo/FM stereo radio with six speakers. New low-travel switches controlled optional power door locks, windows, rear defogger, and a new intermittent rear wiper/washer. There was also a new four-way adjustable head restraint. Base Daytonas had 14 in. cast aluminum wheels, a standard 2.2-liter four with fuel injection, and five-speed manual transaxle. The new 2.5-liter four with balancing shafts was optional, as was three-speed TorqueFlite. Daytona colors were: Black, Ice Blue, Radiant Silver, Golden Bronze or Garnet Red pearl coat, and White. Turbo Z came in Black, Flash Red, Radiant Silver, White, or Gunmetal Blue pearl coat. Daytona's Turbo Z showed a specially molded single-piece front air dam and functional three-piece rear spoiler. P205/60HR15 raised-black-letter Eagle GT tires rode distinctive 6 x 15 in. Shelby cast aluminum wheels. Turbo Z had standard wraparound front and rear fascias that extended to wheel openings; integrated wide bodyside moldings; accent tape striping; and 'Turbo Z' lettering below taillamp lenses. An Enthusiast driver's seat offered orthopedic support, especially in lumbar/thigh areas, using pneumatic adjustment. Turbo Z also added black functional hood louvers, a leather- wrapped Euro-sport steering wheel, lower bodyside sill spoilers, and a handling suspension with gas-charged struts and shocks. New this year was an optional C/S Handling Package (named for Carroll Shelby) for the Turbo Z. Priced at $189, it included solid 32 mm front and 28 mm rear anti-sway bars (standard bars were tubular), performance-tuned struts/shocks, and P225/50VR15 unidirectional speed-rated tires on unique C/S 6.5 x 15 in. cast aluminum wheels. A new optional T-Bar roof package had twin removable tinted glass panels and anti-theft locks. That package also included power windows and larger aero-look power mirrors. A total of 7,704 Daytonas had the C/S Handling Package, while 5,984 had the T- Bar roof package. The turbocharged engine was also optional on the base model. While the closely-related Chrysler Laser promoted luxury, Dodge focused more on performance with its Daytona.

ARIES K — SERIES KD — FOUR — A square 'K' emblem joined the 'Aries' lettering on the decklid, emphasizing the basic body type. Otherwise, Aries looked the same as in 1985. Base, SE and LE versions were offered. Base engine was the 2.2-liter four, now fuel- injected, with fully synchronized five-speed close-ratio transaxle. Optional: the new 2.5-liter, and TorqueFlite three-speed automatic. The four-speed gearbox was

1986 Aries K LE station wagon (D)

abandoned. Bodies included the two- and four-door sedan, and four-door station wagon. Base models had a standard all-vinyl bench seat (split- back on two-door sedan). LE had Kincaid and Classic cloth/vinyl split-back seating with folding center armrest and adjustable head restraints, and cloth door trim panels. SE also used cloth/vinyl, but with vinyl door trim panels. Bucket seats were available in SE/LE. An AM radio with digital clock and a remote driver's mirror were standard in SE, while Aries LE carried a standard AM stereo/FM stereo sound system. Base models had two-speed wipers and black narrow bodyside moldings. Both SE and LE switched to intermittent wipers and wide black bodyside moldings with argent stripe. Standard tires were P175/80R13 steel-belted radial blackwalls except LE, which carried P185/70R14. Aries K colors were: Black, Ice Blue, Gunmetal Blue pearl coat, Golden Bronze pearl coat, Dark Cordovan pearl coat, Light Cream, Gold Dust, Garnet Red pearl coat, Radiant Silver, and White. Revised discount option packages were available for SE/LE.

1986 Lancer ES hatchback sedan (D)

LANCER — SERIES HD — FOUR — Not much change was evident in the four-door hatchback Lancer, but its option list lost quite a few items. As in its opening season, base and ES versions were available. New this year were a refined electro-mechanical instrument cluster (including 125 MPH speedometer); tinted glass; passenger- assist straps; and child-proof safety rear door locks. Base Lancers had reclining low-back bucket seats in cloth/vinyl, with two-way headrest. ES carried new standard cloth/vinyl low-back reclining performance bucket seats with four-way adjustable head restraints and increased lateral support, plus intermittent wipers and new 14 in. styled road wheels. Standard 60/40 split-back rear seatbacks folded down. Engine choices included the base fuel-injected 2.2-liter four, new optional 2.5-liter, or turbocharged 2.2 rated 146 horsepower. Five-speed manual shift was standard; TorqueFlite optional (required with the 2.5-liter engine). Lancer body colors were: Garnet Red, Dark Cordovan, Light Rosewood Mist, Golden Bronze or Gunmetal Blue pearl coat; Gold Dust; Light Cream; Ice Blue; Black; and Radiant Silver. Three two-tone combinations were offered. An electronic instrument cluster with fluorescent displays was available only on ES. Base Lancers showed electro-mechanical analog gauges. An Electronic Navigator was optional only on ES. A road touring suspension was standard, but buyers had two step-up alternatives. Sport Handling Pkg. I included P195/70R14 SBR RBL tires and sport handling suspension. Package II added P205/60HR15 SBR RBL tires on cast aluminum wheels. A total of 2,508 ES Lancers had the Turbo Sport package (code AGT) installed. That one included black belt, door window frame, and quarter window moldings; P205/60HR15 SBR RBL tires on cast aluminum wheels; dual remote mirrors; lower bodyside and door window frame surround tape stripes; two-tone paint; and the turbo engine.

600 COUPE/CONVERTIBLE — SERIES KV — FOUR — Shaped similar to the prior version, 600 nevertheless had a significantly altered appearance with completely different grille and restyled back end. Front fender louvers were gone. The new crossbar grille contained a pentastar emblem attached to wide vertical and horizontal bars, over a black crosshatch pattern. The grille had a thick, bright upper header molding, with sides slightly tapered inward at the base. This year's front-end treatment used quad rectangular headlamps with side marker lamps and reflectors integral to the bezel. Amber park/signal lamps went into the front bumper, which was modified to hold air intake slots. A new soft bumper fascia had integral nerf rub strips with bright insert. A new square gas filler door replaced the former round one. Taillamps looked similar to 1985, but more tapered in their wraparound portion, with integral side markers and turn signals shining through new lenses. Also new: bright trunk lid and rear quarter extension moldings and bodyside accent stripes. A 'Turbo' badge (if applicable) went on front fenders, just below the bodyside molding line. On the dash, a new convenience light bar indicated door ajar, low fuel, low washer fluid, and trunk lid ajar. As before, the Club Coupe and convertible rode a shorter wheelbase than the 600 ES sedan (listed below). Also available was a 600 ES Turbo convertible. The option list lost a number of individual items, but added some new accessory packages. Base engine was the 2.2-liter four (fuel injected), with new 2.5-liter four or 2.2-liter turbo optional. The Club Coupe had a classic formal landau roof and opera windows, plus standard cloth front bench seat with folding center armrest. Convertibles carried Saddle Grain vinyl low-back reclining bucket seats. 600 body colors were: Garnet Red or Gunmetal Blue pearl coat, Radiant Silver, Black, Ice Blue, White, Nightwatch Blue, Dark Cordovan or Light Rosewood Mist pearl coat, Light Cream, or Golden Bronze pearl coat. One two-tone was offered on all models, another on Club Coupe only. Besides the turbocharged Trans4 2.2-liter engine, the 600 ES Turbo Convertible added a special sports/handling suspension. The package also included Corinthian leather/vinyl low-back bucket seats, aero dual remote mirrors, Euro/sport leather-wrapped steering wheel, electronic instrument cluster with tachometer, AM stereo/FM stereo radio with cassette player, accent tape striping, color-keyed protective rub strips, and black door handles. P195/60R15 Goodyear

Eagle GT SBR RBL tires went on Shelby cast aluminum wheels. Bodies displayed blackout exterior trim, plus a '600 ES' insignia on the decklid. A total of 4,759 ES Turbo convertibles were produced. Options this year included a padded vinyl landau roof with opera windows (coupe); narrow bodyside moldings color-keyed to bumper nerfs; and color-coordinated front/rear bumper guards. Several new discount packages were offered, including interior lighting, cold-weather protection, and power conveniences.

600 SEDAN — SERIES EE — FOUR — As before, the 600 sedan, though similar in appearance to coupe and convertible, qualified as a mid-size rather than compact by virtue of its longer wheelbase. Chassis was the same as Chrysler's New Yorker and Plymouth Caravelle. A base model was added to the former SE. New standard equipment on four-doors included an easier-to-read instrument cluster, plus 50/50 front seats (on SE only).

1986 Diplomat SE sedan (D)

DIPLOMAT — SERIES MG — V-8 — Offered again in Salon and SE dress, Diplomat carried on with minimal change apart from the newly required center stop lamp. Diplomat's interior used Sherwood woodtone trim and a padded instrument panel. Standard equipment included tinted glass and dual remote mirrors. Salons had a cloth/vinyl split-back front bench seat with folding center armrest. SE had all-cloth velour 60/40 front seating with folding center armrest and passenger recliner, plus a full vinyl roof and door courtesy lights. Colors this year were: Crimson Red, Ice Blue, Gold Dust, Nightwatch Blue, White, Radiant Silver, Black, and Mink Brown or Gunmetal Blue pearl coat. Sole engine remained the 318 cu. in. (5.2-liter) V-8 with two-barrel carburetor, but a four-barrel version was installed in Police Diplomats. A total of 10,372 Diplomats had the Police package. Three-speed TorqueFlite was standard. A standard lower body protective coating included stone-resistant urethane primer. Joining the option list was an AM stereo/FM stereo radio. A Luxury Equipment discount package for the SE cost $2010 extra. Virtually identical to Plymouth's Gran Fury, Diplomat was offered only as a four-door sedan.

I.D. DATA: Dodge's 17-symbol Vehicle Identification Number (VIN), as before, was on the upper left corner of the instrument panel, visible through the windshield. The first digit indicates Country: '1' U.S.A. The second symbol is Make: 'B' Dodge. Third is Vehicle Type: '3' passenger car; '7' truck. The next symbol ('B') indicates manual seatbelts. Symbol five is Car Line: 'Z' Omni/Charger; 'A' Daytona; 'D' Aries; 'E' 600 sedan; 'V' 600 coupe/convertible; 'X' Lancer; 'G' Diplomat. Symbol six is Series (price class): '1' Economy; '2' Low; '3' Medium; '4' High'; '5' Premium; '6' Special. Symbol seven is Body Style: '1' 2-dr. sedan; '4' 2-dr. hatchback; '5' 2-dr. convertible; '6' 4-dr. sedan; '8' 4-dr. hatchback; '9' 4-dr. wagon. Eighth is the Engine Code: 'A' L498 2Bbl.; 'C' L4135 2Bbl.; 'D' L4135 FI; 'E' Turbo L4135 FI; '8' Hi-perf. L4135 2Bbl.; 'K' L4153 FI; 'P' V8318 2Bbl. Next comes a check digit. Symbol ten indicates Model Year: 'G' 1986. Symbol eleven is Assembly Plant: 'C' Jefferson (Detroit); 'D' Belvidere, IL; 'F' Newark, DE; 'N' Sterling Heights, MI; 'G' or 'X' St. Louis. The last six digits make up the sequential serial number, starting with 100001. Engine numbers and Body Code Plates are in the same locations as 1981-85.

OMNI (FOUR)

Model Number	Body/Style Number	Body Type & Seating	Factory Price	Shipping Weight	Production Total
LZE	44	4-dr. Hatch-5P	6209	2100	61,812
LZH	44	4-dr. SE Hatch-5P	6558	2120	8,139

OMNI GLH (FOUR)

LZE	44/AGB	4-dr. Hatch-5P	7918	2295	3,629

CHARGER (FOUR)

LZH	24	2-dr. Hatch-5P	6787	2170	38,172

CHARGER 2.2 (FOUR)

LZP	24	2-dr. Hatch-5P	7732	2325	4,814

SHELBY CHARGER (FOUR)

LZS	24	2-dr. Hatch-5P	9361	2390	7,669

DAYTONA (FOUR)

GVH	24	2-dr. Hatch-4P	9013	N/A	26,771

DAYTONA TURBO (FOUR)

GVS	24	2-dr. Hatch-4P	11301	N/A	17,595

ARIES (FOUR)

KDL	21	2-dr. Sedan-6P	7184	2380	2,437
KDL	41	4-dr. Sedan-6P	7301	2390	14,445

ARIES SE (FOUR)

KDM	21	2-dr. Sedan-6P	7639	2400	9,084
KDM	41	4-dr. Sedan-6P	7759	2415	40,254
KDM	45	4-dr. Sta Wag-6P	8186	2470	17,757

ARIES LE (FOUR)

KDH	21	2-dr. Sedan-6P	8087	2440	2,475
KDH	41	4-dr. Sedan-6P	8207	2455	5,638
KDH	45	4-dr. Sta Wag-6P	8936	2560	5,278

LANCER (FOUR)

HDH	44	4-Dr. Spt Hatch-5P	9426	2610	34,009
HDS	44	4-dr. ES Hatch-5P	10332	2665	17,888

600 COUPE/CONVERTIBLE (FOUR)

KVP	22	2-dr. Club Cpe-6P	9577	2470	11,714
KVP	27	2-dr. Conv.-4P	11695	2535	11,678
KVP	27/AGT	2-dr. ES Conv.-4P	14856	2580	4,759

600/SE SEDAN (FOUR)

EEM	41	4-dr. Sedan-6P	9370	2535	16,235
EEH	41	4-dr. SE Sed-6P	10028	2545	15,291

DIPLOMAT SALON (V-8)

MGL	41	4-dr. Sedan-6P	10086	3475	15,469

DIPLOMAT SE (V-8)

MGP	41	4-dr. Sedan-6P	11166	3530	11,484

MODEL NUMBER NOTE: Some sources identify models using the VIN data to indicate Car Line, Price Class and Body Style. Example: Aries four-door (KDL41) has the equivalent number D26, which translates to Aries line, Low price class, and four-door sedan body. See I.D. Data section for breakdown.

ENGINE DATA: BASE FOUR (Omni, Charger): Inline, overhead-cam four-cylinder. Cast iron block; aluminum head. Displacement: 97.3 cu. in. (1.6 liters). Bore & stroke: 3.17 x 3.07 in. Compression ratio: 8.8:1. Brake horsepower: 64 at 4800 R.P.M. Torque: 87 lbs.-ft. at 2800 R.P.M. Five main bearings. Solid valve lifters. Carburetor: 2Bbl. Holley 6520. Peugeot-built. VIN Code: A. **OPTIONAL FOUR** (Omni, Charger): Inline, overhead-cam four-cylinder. Cast iron block; aluminum head. Displacement: 135 cu. in. (2.2 liters). Bore & stroke: 3.44 x 3.62 in. Compression ratio: 9.0:1. Brake horsepower: 96 at 5200 R.P.M. Torque: 119 lbs.-ft. at 3200 R.P.M. Five main bearings. Hydraulic valve lifters. Carburetor: 2Bbl. Holley 6520. VIN Code: C. **BASE FOUR** (Aries, Daytona, Lancer, 600): Same as 135 cu. in. four above, but with electronic fuel injection Compression ratio: 9.5:1. Horsepower: 97 at 5200 R.P.M. Torque: 122 lbs.-ft. at 3200 R.P.M. VIN Code: D. **BASE FOUR** (Omni GLH, Charger 2.2): High-performance carbureted version of 135 cu. in. four above Compression ratio: 9.6:1. Horsepower: 110 at 5600 R.P.M. Torque: 129 lbs.-ft. at 3600 R.P.M. VIN Code: 8. **TURBOCHARGED FOUR, BASE** (Shelby Charger, Daytona Turbo); **OPTIONAL** (Omni GLH, Daytona, Lancer, 600): Same as 135 cu. in. four above, with EFI and turbocharger Compression ratio: 8.1:1. Horsepower: 146 at 5200 R.P.M. Torque: 170 lbs.-ft. at 3600 R.P.M. VIN Code: E. **OPTIONAL FOUR** (Aries, Daytona, Lancer, 600): Inline, overhead-cam four-cylinder. Cast iron block; aluminum head. Displacement: 153 cu. in. (2.5 liters). Bore & stroke: 3.44 x 4.09 in. Compression ratio: 9.0:1. Brake horsepower: 100 at 4800 R.P.M. Torque: 136 lbs.-ft. at 2800 R.P.M. Five main bearings. Hydraulic valve lifters. Electronic fuel injection. VIN Code: K. **BASE V-8** (Diplomat): 90-degree, overhead valve V-8. Cast iron block and head. Displacement: 318 cu. in. (5.2 liters). Bore & stroke: 3.91 x 3.31 in. Compression ratio: 9.0:1. Brake horsepower: 140 at 3600 R.P.M. Torque: 265 lbs.-ft. at 1600 R.P.M. Five main bearings. Hydraulic valve lifters. Carburetor: 2Bbl. Holley 6280. VIN Code: P.

Note: Police V-8 was same as 318 cu. in. V-8 above, but with 4Bbl. Rochester carburetor Compression ratio: 8.0:1. Horsepower: 175 at 4000 R.P.M. Torque: 250 lbs.-ft. at 3200 R.P.M.

CHASSIS DATA: Wheelbase: (Omni) 99.1 in.; (Charger) 96.5 in.; (Daytona) 97.0 in.; (Aries/600) 100.3 in.; (Aries wag, 600 conv.) 100.4 in.; (600 sedan) 103.3 in.; (Lancer) 103.1 in.; (Diplomat) 112.6 in. Overall Length: (Omni) 163.2 in.; (Chgr) 174.8 in.; (Shelby) 174.7 in.; (Daytona) 175.0 in.; (Daytona Turbo Z) 176.9 in.; (Aries) 178.6 in.; (Aries wag) 179.0 in.; (Lancer) 180.4 in.; (600) 179.2 in.; (600 sedan) 185.2 in.; (Diplomat) 204.6 in. Height: (Omni) 53.0 in.; (Chgr) 50.7 in.; (Shelby) 50.2 in.; (Daytona) 50.4 in.; (Aries 2dr.) 52.5 in.; (Aries 4dr.) 52.9 in.; (Aries wag) 53.2 in.; (Lancer) 53.0 in.; (600 cpe) 52.5 in.; (600 conv.) 52.9 in.; (600 sedan) 53.1 in.; (Diplomat) 55.1 in. Width: (Omni) 66.8 in.; (Chgr) 66.6 in.; (Aries/600) 68.0 in.; (Daytona) 69.3 in.; (Lancer) 68.3 in.; (Diplo) 72.4 in. Front Tread: (Omni/Chgr) 56.1 in.; (Aries/Daytona/Lancer/600) 57.6 in.; (Diplo) 60.0 in. Rear Tread: (Omni/Chgr) 55.7 in.; (Aries/Daytona/Lancer/600) 57.2 in.; (Diplo) 59.5 in. Standard Tires: (Omni/Charger) P165/80R13 SBR BSW; (Charger 2.2) P195/60R15 SBR RBL; (Shelby) P205/50VR15 SBR RBL unidirectional; (Daytona) P185/70R14 SBR BSW; (Daytona Turbo) P205/60HR15 SBR RBL; (Aries) P175/80R13 SBR BSW; (Aries LE, Lancer) P185/70R14 SBR BSW; (Lancer ES) P195/70R14 SBR RBL; (600) P185/70R14 SBR; (Diplomat) P205/75R15 SBR WSW.

206

TECHNICAL: Transmission: Four-speed manual (floor lever) standard on Omni/Charger. Five-speed manual standard on Omni/Charger 2.2-liter, Aries, Lancer and Daytona. TorqueFlite three-speed automatic standard on Diplomat, Aries 2.5-liter and 600; optional on all other models. Diplomat gear ratios: (1st) 2.74:1; (2nd) 1.54:1; (3rd) 1.00:1; (Rev) 2.22:1. Other models: (1st) 2.69:1; (2nd) 1.55:1; (3rd) 1.00:1; (Rev) 2.10:1. Standard final drive ratio: (Omni/Charger) 2.69:1 w/4spd, 2.20:1 or 2.78:1 w/5spd, 2.78:1 or 3.02:1 w/auto.; (Omni GLH/Shelby turbo) 2.57:1; (Daytona/Lancer) 2.57:1 w/5spd, 3.02:1 w/auto. exc. (Daytona 2.5-liter) 3.02:1 w/5spd; (Aries) 2.20:1 w/5spd, 2.78:1 or 3.02:1 w/auto.; (600) 3.02:1; (Diplo) 2.26:1. Steering: (Diplomat) recirculating ball; (others) rack and pinion. Suspension: (Omni/Chgr) Dual path Iso-Strut independent coil front w/anti-sway bar, trailing arm semi-independent coil rear w/anti-sway bar on Charger 2.2; (Shelby) same as Omni/Chgr but gas-charged rear shocks and front/rear anti- sway bars; (Daytona) Dual path Iso-Strut front, trailing arm rear w/gas-charged shock absorbers, front/rear anti-sway bars; (Daytona Turbo) same as Daytona but gas-charged front Iso-Struts; (Lancer) Dual path gas-charged front Iso-Struts, gas-charged rear shocks, front/rear anti-sway bars; (Aries/600) Dual path Iso-Strut front w/coil springs and linkless anti-sway bar, beam rear axle w/trailing arms and coil springs; (Diplomat) transverse front torsion bars and anti-sway bar, semi-elliptic rear leaf springs. Brakes: Front disc, rear drum. Ignition: Electronic. Body construction: Unibody. Fuel tank: (Omni/Chgr) 13 gal.; (Daytona/Aries/Lancer/600) 14 gal.; (Diplomat) 18 gal.

DRIVETRAIN OPTIONS: Engines: 2.2-liter four: Omni/Chgr ($138). Turbocharged 2.2-liter four: Omni GLH ($898); base Daytona ($993); Lancer/600 ($628). 2.5-liter four: Aries/Lancer/600, base Daytona ($279). Transmission/Axle: Five-speed manual trans.: Omni/Chgr ($77). TorqueFlite auto. trans.: Omni/Chgr/Daytona-/Aries/Lancer ($478). High-altitude axle: Omni/Chgr/Aries ($23). Steering/Suspension: Power steering: Omni/Chgr/Aries, base 600 conv. ($226). H.D. susp.: Aries ($60); Diplo ($27). Sport handling susp.: 600 ($58) exc. base conv. ($284). Sport handling susp. w/14 in. tires: base Lancer ($122). Other: H.D. battery: Aries/600/Diplo ($45). H.D. engine cooling: Omni/Chgr ($145). California emission system ($102).

OMNI/CHARGER CONVENIENCE/APPEARANCE OPTIONS: Option Packages: Sun/Sound/Shade pkg.: Shelby/2.2 ($562- $634). Auto. trans. discount pkg. ($808-$933). 2.2-liter engine and five-speed discount pkg. ($304-$420). Light group ($52-$86). Protection group ($90-$194). Comfort/Convenience: Air cond. ($683). Rear defroster ($141). Automatic speed control ($184). Rear wiper/washer: Omni ($129). Dual remote mirrors: Omni/SE ($50); Chgr ($59). Electronic-tuning Radios: AM: base ($116). AM/FM stereo ($149-$265). Seek/scan AM/FM stereo w/cassette ($251-$516). Ultimate sound stereo w/cassette: Chgr ($216-$732). Exterior: Removable glass sunroof: Chgr ($335). Pearl coat paint ($41). Two-tone paint: SE/Chgr ($155). Interior: Low-back vinyl bucket seats ($32). High-back cloth bucket seats ($110). Center armrest ($49). Tonneau cover: Chgr ($71). Cargo area carpet ($44-$64). Wheels/Tires: Cast aluminum 14 in. wheels: Chgr ($263-$314). P165/80R13 SBR WSW: base ($61). P195/60R14 SBR RWL: base Chgr ($358); Chgr 2.2 ($23). Conventional spare tire ($65-$193).

DAYTONA CONVENIENCE/APPEARANCE OPTIONS: Option Packages: Sun/Sound/Shade discount pkg. ($639). Popular equipment discount pkg. ($260-$354); w/air ($840-$934). Electronic features pkg. w/navigator: base ($280); w/navigator and electronic instruments: Turbo ($600). Cargo trim/quiet sound group: Turbo ($239-$258). C/S handling pkg.: Turbo ($189). Protection pkg. ($90). Comfort/Convenience: Air cond. ($780). Rear defroster ($152- $188). Auto. speed control ($184). Power driver's seat ($232). Power windows ($201). Power door locks ($134). Tilt steering wheel ($118). Liftgate wiper/washer ($129). Dual power remote mirrors ($58). Electronic-tuning Radios w/digital clock: Premium AM/FM stereo w/cassette ($251). Ultimate sound AM/FM stereo w/cassette ($216-$467). Exterior: Removable glass sunroof ($342). Pearl coat paint ($41). Interior: Low-back cloth/vinyl bucket seats w/adj. driver's lumbar/thigh support: base ($404). Low-back leather bucket seats w/adj. driver's lumbar/thigh support: base ($988); Turbo ($584). Tires: P195/70R14 RBL: base ($95). Conventional spare ($85).

ARIES CONVENIENCE/APPEARANCE OPTIONS: Option Packages: Equipment pkg.: Basic, base ($256); Popular, LE/SE ($219-$702); Premium, LE ($758-$1076). Protection pkg. ($148). Comfort/Convenience: Air cond. ($780). Rear defroster ($152). Auto. speed control ($184). Power door locks ($134-$185). Tinted glass ($118). Tilt steering wheel ($118). Liftgate wiper/washer: wag ($129). Electronic-tuning Radios: AM stereo/FM stereo: base ($149- $265). AM stereo/FM stereo w/cassette: SE/LE ($251-$400). Exterior: Pearl coat paint ($41). Luggage rack: wag ($119). Interior: Vinyl bench seat: SE ($32); LE (NC). Cloth/vinyl bench seat: base ($32). Cloth/vinyl bucket seats: SE ($275); LE ($216). Wheels and Tires: Deluxe wheel covers: SE ($49). Cast aluminum wheels, 14 in.: LE ($332-$381). P175/80R13 WSW: base/SE ($60). P185/70R14 BSW: SE ($97). P185/70R14 WSW: SE ($157); LE ($60). Conventional spare tire ($75-$85).

LANCER CONVENIENCE/APPEARANCE OPTIONS: Option Packages: Turbo sport pkg.: ES ($413-$1415). Equipment discount pkg.: Popular ($667-$1839); Luxury ($688-$1078). Electronic features pkg.: ES ($637-$681). Deluxe convenience pkg. ($118-$302). Power convenience pkg. ($463). Highline upgrade pkg.: base ($125). Sport handling pkg. I with P195/70R14 tires ($118). Sport handling pkg. II with P205/60HR15 SBR RBL tires on 15 in. cast aluminum wheels ($180-$668). Cold weather pkg. ($197). Protection pkg. ($90). Comfort/Convenience: Air cond. ($760). Power seat ($232). Liftgate wiper/washer ($129). Electronic-tuning Radios w/digital clock: Premium AM stereo/FM stereo w/cassette ($293). Ultimate sound AM stereo/FM stereo w/cassette ($509). Exterior: Removable glass sunroof ($342). Two-tone paint ($216). Pearl coat paint ($41). Interior: Leather bucket seats: ES ($583). Folding cloth armrest: base ($44). Console/armrest: base ($81). Wheels and Tires: Styled 14 in. wheels: base ($62). Cast aluminum wheels, 14 in. or 15 in. ($319-$381). P195/70R14 SBR WSW ($60). P195/70R14 SBR: base ($95). Conventional spare tire: base ($85).

600 CONVENIENCE/APPEARANCE OPTIONS: Option Packages: Equipment discount pkg.: Popular ($382-$531); Luxury ($915-$1238). Deluxe convenience pkg. ($302). Power convenience pkg. ($335-$463). Interior illumination pkg.: cpe ($137). Center console pkg.: cpe ($208). Cold weather pkg.: cpe ($197). Protection pkg.: 2-dr. ($115). Light pkg.: base sed ($139). Comfort/Convenience: Air cond. ($780). Rear defroster ($152). Power seat ($232). Power decklid release: 2-dr. ($41). Illuminated entry system: conv. ($77). Leather-wrapped steering wheel ($52). Intermittent wipers ($55). Mirrors: Left remote: base sed ($25). Dual power remote- control: cpe ($88); sed ($88-$113). Lighted vanity, pair: sed ($120). Electronic-tuning Radios w/digital clock: AM stereo/FM stereo: base sed ($149). Seek/scan AM stereo/FM stereo w/cassette ($287-$436). Ultimate sound stereo w/cassette ($216-$652). Exterior: Two-tone paint: cpe ($193). Pearl coat paint ($41). Vinyl bodyside moldings: sed ($57). Bumper guards: sed ($58). Undercoating ($44). Interior: Cloth bucket seats: cpe ($171). Color-keyed mats: front, conv. ($26); front/rear, others ($46). Trunk dress-up ($53). Wheels and Tires: Wire wheel covers, locking: 2-dr. ($280). Cast aluminum wheels: 2-dr. ($381). P185/70R14 SBR WSW: conv. ($60). Conventional spare tire ($85).

DIPLOMAT CONVENIENCE/APPEARANCE OPTIONS: Option Packages: Equipment pkg.: Popular ($461-$588); Luxury, SE ($2010). Light pkg. ($93-$132). Protection group ($137). Comfort/Convenience: Air conditioning, semi-auto ($836). Rear defroster ($152). Auto. speed control ($184). Power seat, left: SE ($232). Power windows ($278). Power door locks ($185). Power decklid release ($41). Illuminated entry system: SE ($77). Leather-wrapped steering wheel: SE ($62). Tilt steering wheel ($118). Intermittent wipers ($55). Mirrors: Remote driver's: Salon ($25). Dual remote, chrome: Salon ($69). Lighted vanity, right: SE ($60). Electronic-Tuning Radios w/digital clock: AM stereo/FM stereo ($149). Seek/scan AM/FM stereo w/cassette ($467-$616). Ultimate sound AM stereo/FM stereo w/cassette ($467-$616). Power antenna: Salon ($67). Radio delete ($56 credit). Exterior: Power glass sunroof: Salon ($1108). Full vinyl roof: Salon ($191). Pearl coat paint ($41). Vinyl bodyside moldings: Salon ($59). Upper door frame moldings: Salon ($47). Body sound insulation: Salon ($68). Undercoating ($44). Interior: Vinyl split-back bench seat: Salon ($62). Trunk dress-up: Salon ($58). Wheels/Tires: Premium wheel covers: Salon ($231). Cast aluminum wheels: SE ($39-$270). Conventional spare ($96).

HISTORY: Introduced: October 1, 1985. Model year production: Chrysler reported a total of 404,496 passenger cars shipped. Of the four-cylinder engines, 66,272 were turbos. Calendar year production: 506,404. Calendar year sales by U.S. dealers: 456,777. Model year sales by U.S. dealers: 432,205 (not incl. imports or early '87 Dodge Shadows).

Historical Footnotes: Chrysler Corp. predicted a decline in domestic car sales for the model year. Yet Dodge Division beat the 1985 figure, posting the highest total since 1978. That rise was due largely to the three Mitsubishi-built imports, however (Colt, Colt Vista, and Conquest). Domestic sales declined a bit (down about 6,300) for the model year. Daytona expected to remain for 1987, even though sales were down, whereas Chrysler's Laser was to be dropped. Omni/Charger sales had been rather good during 1985 as a result of option discount packages and low-rate financing. Omni sales improved after the new "America" campaign, which included price cuts. Aries declined somewhat in model year sales, while Lancer rose by 20 percent. Diplomats were hit with a gas guzzler tax, yet sold fairly well, down only moderately for the model year. Dodge's market share for 1986 was 5.3 percent (not including the imports). High-performance versions of GLH, Charger and Daytona were tested on a track of the Chrysler Shelby Performance Center at Santa Fe Springs, California. Dodge, according to General Marketing Manager John Damoose, served as "the performance division of the Corporation."

No make offered a more complete line than Ford in 1976, from subcompact Pinto through full-size LTD and Thunderbird. Engines reached all the way up to a 460 cu. in. V-8, which would remain available through 1978. After

1976 Granada Sports Coupe (F)

five years in the lineup, Pinto was about to get some trouble in the form of serious accusations about fire hazards. Some hideous blazes had resulted from rear-end collisions. Less-vulnerable gas tanks were installed in Pintos built after 1976, but the adverse publicity hurt sales in subsequent years as well.

1977 Pinto three-door Runabout (F)

Maverick was in its next-to-last season, dangling a Stallion package in an attempt to lure youthful drivers. Pinto had one too, but both were for looks rather than action. Ford had high hopes for Granada, introduced in

1977 Granada Ghia coupe (F)

208

1975 with Mercedes-like styling and a four-wheel disc brake option. Torino and Elite made up the mid-size lineup. Thunderbird not only carried a 202-horsepower engine, but came in a selection of luxury paint options to dress up its huge body. Ford sales had shrunk in 1975, but rebounded somewhat this year, partly as a result of the new "California strategy" that delivered special option packages only to West Coast customers.

1978 Fairmont sedan (F)

The big T-Bird didn't last much longer, replaced for 1977 by a downsized edition that was actually a modification of the new LTD II. T-Bird cost far less in this form—but also carried less standard equipment and a modest 302 cu. in. V-8. Production soared far above the level of the last big 'bird. Torino and Elite both faded away, and Maverick was about to do so. Granada became the first American car to offer a standard four-speed (overdrive) gearbox. GM had downsized its full-size models, but LTD kept its immense dimensions until 1979.

1980 LTD Crown Victoria Country Squire station wagon (JG)

Few realized it at the time, but the basic structure of the new Fairmont for 1978 soon would serve as the basis for a whole line of FoMoCo rear-drive models. MacPherson struts held up Fairmont's front end—a suspension style that would grow more common as front-wheel drives arrived. Fairmont powerplants ran the gamut: four, six, or V-8. A Euro-styled ES edition became available, but most of the attention went to the Futura Sport Coupe, marked by wide B-pillars in a wraparound roofline reminiscent of Thunderbird's. Granada tried the Euro route too, with a blackout-trimmed ESS variant. Pinto's Cruising Wagon and Sports Rallye packages seemed less memorable, if practical. Thunderbird added a Town Landau model, but collectors are more likely to turn to the Diamond Jubilee Edition, offered this year only.

Two years after GM's downsizing of Caprice/Impala, Ford finally shrunk its LTD. Engines shrunk too, with a

302 V-8 standard and 351 the biggest. A luxurious Heritage model took the place of the single-year Diamond Jubilee T-Bird. Pinto added equipment and an ESS package and found more customers, while the smaller LTD had trouble in the sales department. LTD II never had caught on, and dropped away after '79. It was Thunderbird's turn for downsizing in 1980, as a modest 255 cu. in. standard V-8 went under the hood. Best bet for collectors: the Silver Anniversary T-Bird. The "Crown Victoria" name reappeared in the LTD roster this year, bringing back memories of the sharpest mid-1950s Ford. LTDs also had a new automatic overdrive transmission. Every Ford model endured a loss of sales, but so did most other domestic makes.

1981 Fairmont Futura sedan (JG)

Heralding a new Ford era, the front-wheel-drive Escort arrived for 1981, carrying a CHV (hemi) engine. Escort became Ford's best seller and, a year later, best-selling domestic model. Granada slimmed down to Fairmont size, with Fairmont's base four-cylinder engine. After two years powered by a 302 cu. in. V-8, LTD dropped to a 255. That wasn't the most startling engine change, however: Thunderbird now carried a standard six-cylinder powerplant.

1981 LTD coupe (JG)

Sporty performance seemed paramount for the 1982 model year, with the arrival not only of a Mustang GT but a two-seater EXP, based on the Escort platform. Ford now offered its own V-6 engine, while LTDs could get a 351 V-8 only if destined for police hands. T-Bird not only continued the base inline six, but made a 255 V-8 the biggest possibility. A 20 percent sales decline didn't harm Ford's market share, since other makes weren't finding too many customers either.

The massive Thunderbirds of the 1970s seemed fully forgotten as the tenth generation arrived for 1983. This one was loaded with curves—and before long, a possible turbocharged, fuel-injected four-cylinder engine. With close-ratio five-speed and "quadra-shock" rear suspension. T-Bird's Turbo Coupe became quite an attraction, helping sales to more than double. A little

1986 Tarus GL wagon (JG)

shuffling of names produced a "new" LTD (closely tied to the dropped Granada), while the big rear- drives became "LTD Crown Victoria."

Turbocharging even hit EXP and Escort GT for 1984. EXP altered its form, adding the "bubbleback" liftgate from the faded Mercury LN7. Another front-drive model joined up: the compact Tempo with High Swirl Combustion engine, a replacement for Fairmont. Both Tempo and Escort could be ordered with a Mazda-built diesel—a curious decision since diesels were on their way out in other makes. Led by Thunderbird, sales hit their highest point since 1979, but Escort lost the best-seller label to Chevrolet's Cavalier.

LTD continued its high-performance, V-8 engine LX touring sedan into 1985, which was generally a carryover year. Tempos now came with standard five-speed gearboxes. Incentive programs helped sales (and Ford's market share) to rise noticeably. A revised Escort emerged before the 1986 model year, including an attractive GT model with high-output engine.

Not many new models received as much publicity as the front-drive Taurus, leader of the 1986 pack. And few cars looked as different from the model they replaced than Taurus versus LTD. Plenty of customers liked Taurus's grille-free aero look, as did *Motor Trend* with its Car of the Year award. Overall sales fell, however, after three years of increases, leaving Ford with less than 12 percent of the total market (imports included).

1986 Escort LX sedan (JG)

Potentially collectible Fords include a number of the upper-level and special-edition Thunderbirds: Diamond Jubilee, Turbo Coupe, perhaps a recent Fila. Fans of little Fords may like the 1985-86 Escort GT, though plenty of them seem to be around. EXP never really caught the fancy of two- seater customers, and enthusiasts don't seem overly excited either. Fairmont and Granada had their strong points as new (and used) cars, but whether an ES blackout option or Futura roofline makes them desirable later on is another matter. Unfortunately, only Mustang offered a convertible during the 1976-86 period.

1976 FORD

1976 Maverick "Luxury Decor" sedan (F)

Not much was dramatically different at Ford for 1976, after some significant changes a year earlier. Full-size models had been restyled in 1975, gaining a Mercedes-like grille. The Granada mid-size was new that year, with obvious Mercedes styling touches, while the Elite name went on the former Gran Torino. Pillarless two-door hardtop models had faded away by 1975, replaced by a new six-window coupe style with fixed quarter windows and large opera windows. Installation of catalytic converters expanded for 1976, accompanied by ample gas mileage boosts. Fuel economy improvements this year resulted from revised carburetor calibrations and lower rear axle ratios. All models used no-lead gas. The model lineup was the same as 1975, except that Custom 500 (equivalent to LTD) was now available only to fleet buyers. Special Pinto (and Mustang) models were produced for West Coast consumption. Corporate body colors for 1976 were: Black, Silver metallic, Medium Slate Blue metallic, Candyapple Red, Dark Red, Bright Red, Medium Blue metallic, Bright Blue metallic, Bright Dark Blue metallic, Light Blue, Bright Medium Blue, Dark Yellow Green metallic, Dark Jade metallic, Light or Dark Green, Copper metallic, Medium Chestnut metallic, Dark Brown metallic, Saddle Bronze metallic, Tan, Yellow Orange, Bright ellow, Cream, Dark Yellow, Chrome Yellow, Light Gold, Light Jade, Medium Green Gold, Medium Ginger metallic, Dark Brown, Medium Orange metallic, Tangerine, and White. Additional colors were available on certain models, including Diamond Bright and Diamond Flare finishes, as well as three Crystal metallic colors.

1976 Pinto Stallion hatchback coupe (F)

PINTO — FOUR/V-6 — Ford's subcompact, introduced in 1971, had a new front-end look this year. Appearance changes included a new argent-painted eggcrate grille of one-piece corrosion-resistant plastic, bright bezels for the single round headlamps, bright front lip hood molding, and 'Ford' block letters centered above the grille. That new grille was peaked and angled forward slightly, with a tighter crosshatch pattern than before, and held square inset parking lamps. Backup lights were integral with the horizontal taillamps. Bodies held front and rear side marker lights. For the first time, standard interiors had a choice of all vinyl or sporty cloth-and-vinyl. Four new interior trim fabrics were offered, along with a new bright red interior color. Three four-passenger bodies were offered: two-door sedan, "three-door" Runabout hatchback, and two-door wagon. Wagons had flipper rear compartment windows and a liftgate-open warning light, as well as tinted glass. Major fuel economy improvements resulted from catalysts, new carburetor calibrations, and a lower (3.18:1) rear axle ratio with the standard 140 cu. in. (2.3-liter) OHC four and fully synchronized four-speed manual gearbox with floor shift lever. Optional was a 170.8 cu. in. (2.8-liter) two-barrel V-6, which came only with Cruise-O-Matic transmission. Pinto's front suspension used independent short/long arms with ball joints. At the rear were longitudinal semi-elliptic leaf springs with rubber Iso-clamps at the axle. Rear springs had four leaves except wagons, five leaves. Pinto had front disc/rear drum brakes, rack-and-pinion steering, and unibody construction. New this year was a low-budget Pony MPG two-door, wearing minimal chrome trim and plain hubcaps. The fuel economy leader Pinto, dubbed an "import fighter," had 3.00:1 axle ratio, a slip-clutch cooling fan, and new calibrations for the 2.3-liter engine. Pinto standard equipment included a heater/defroster with DirectAire ventilation, bucket seats, mini-console, inside hood release, dome light, glovebox, dual padded sunvisors, and B78x13 tires. Runabouts and wagons had a fold-down back seat and deluxe seatbelts. Six-cylinder models required automatic transmission. Runabouts had a carpeted load area. A new Squire option for Runabouts added simulated woodgrain vinyl paneling on bodyside and lower back panel, similar to the Squire wagon option. Squire also displayed bright surround and Bpillar moldings as well as belt, drip and window frame moldings. Targeting younger drivers was a sporty new Stallion option featuring special silver body paint and taping, black window and door moldings, and blacked-out wiper arms, hood, grille and lower back panel. Black tape treatment went on rocker panel and wheel lip areas; Stallion (horse) decals on front fenders. Stallion also included dual racing mirrors, styled steel wheels with trim rings, A70 x 13 tires with raised white letters, and a "competition" handling suspension. A Luxury Decor Group included woodtone instrument panel applique, custom steering wheel, passenger door courtesy light switch, and rear seat ashtray. Joining the individual option list this year were an AM radio with tape player, the half-vinyl roof, rocker panel moldings, and leather-wrapped steering wheel.

MAVERICK — SIX/V-8 — Initially scheduled for disappearance when the new Granada arrived in 1975, Maverick hung on a while longer as concern about the fuel crisis continued. This year's grille was a forward-slanting horizontal-bar design, split into two sections by a center vertical divider bar. Rectangular park/signal lamps were mounted in the bright argent front grille; backup lights integral with the taillamps. Single round headlamps continued. The front bumper held twin slots, and the hood showed a sculptured bulge. Inside was a new foot-operated parking brake. Front disc brakes were now standard. Base engine was the 200 cu. in. (3.3-liter) inline six with one-barrel carburetor. Options: 250 cu. in. six with one-barrel, or the 302 V-8 with two-barrel. All three came with either three-speed manual or automatic transmission. Maverick's fuel tank had grown from 16 to 19.2 gallons during the 1975 model year. Gas mileage was improved by lowering rear axle ratio to 2.79:1, recalibrating engines, and adding back-pressure modulation of the EGR system. The compact, unibodied Maverick used a ball-joint front suspension with short and long arms. Hotchkiss rear suspensions had longitudinal semi-elliptic (three-leaf) springs. Standard equipment included fully-synchronized three-speed column shift, C78 x 14 bias-ply tires, hubcaps, ventless windows with curved glass, front/rear side marker lights, European-type armrest with door pull assist handle, and lockable glovebox. A padded instrument

1976 Maverick Stallion coupe (F)

panel held two round cluster pods for gauges. Standard bench seats were trimmed in Random stripe cloth and vinyl. Two-doors had a flipper rear quarter window. A Stallion dress-up package, similar to Pinto's, included black grille and moldings; unique paint/tape treatment on hood, grille, decklid, lower body, and lower back panel; plus large Stallion decal on front quarter panel. The package also included dual outside mirrors, raised white-letter steel-belted radials on styled steel wheels, and "competition" suspension. Two-doors had a new optional three-quarter vinyl roof; four-doors, a "halo" vinyl roof. Other options included individually reclining bucket seats; paint stripes that extended along bodyside and over the roof (on vinyl-topped two-doors); and AM and AM/FM radios with stereo tape players.

1976 Granada Ghia sedan (F)

GRANADA — SIX/V-8 — Ford called Granada "the most successful new-car nameplate in the industry in 1975," after its debut. For 1976, fuel economy improved and the "precision-size" compact held a new standard vinyl bench seat and door trim, but not much changed otherwise. Granada's chromed grille showed a 6x5 pattern of wide holes, with a 2 x 2 pattern within each hole. On each side of the single round headlamps were small, bright vertical sections patterned like the grille. Wide-spaced 'Ford' letters stood above the grille. On the fender extensions were wraparound front parking lights and signal/marker lenses. Hoods held a stand-up ornament. Each wraparound tri-color horizontal-style taillamp was divided into an upper and lower section, with integral side marker lights. Backup lamps sat inboard of the taillamps. Sporting a tall, squared-off roofline and European-influenced design, the five-passenger Granada strongly resembed a Mercedes up front. Ford hardly hit that fact, bragging that "Its looks and lines remind you of the Mercedes 280 and the Cadillac Seville." Bodies featured bright wraparound bumpers, plus bright moldings on windshield, backlight, drip rail, door belt, door frame, and wheel lip. Two-door Granadas had distinctive opera windows. Four-doors had a bright center pillar molding with color-keyed insert. Two- and four-door sedans were offered, in base or Ghia trim. Standard equipment included a three-speed manual transmission, front disc/rear drum brakes, heater/defroster, inside hood release, burled walnut woodtone instrument panel appliques, anti-theft decklid lock, DR78 x 14 blackwall steel-belted radials, locking glovebox, two rear seat ashtrays, lighter, and full wheel covers. Base engine was the 200 cu. in. (3.3-liter) inline six with one-barrel carb. Optional: a 250 cu. in. six, 302 cu. in. V-8, and 351 cu. in. V-8. Granada Ghia added a Ghia ornament on the opera window glass; color-keyed bodyside molding with integral wheel lip molding; left-hand remote-control mirror; dual accent paint stripes on bodyside, hood and decklid; trunk carpeting; and lower back panel applique color-keyed to the vinyl roof. Inside Ghia was a "floating pillow" sew design on independent reclining or flight bench

seats, map pockets and assist handle on back of front seats, day/night mirror, and luxury steering wheel with woodtone applique on the rim. Under Ghia's hood was the larger 250 cu. in. six-cylinder engine. For economy, axle ratios were reduced to 2.75:1 and 2.79:1. Granada's front suspension used short/long control arms with ball joints and coil springs. At the rear were semi-elliptic four-leaf springs. Steering was the recirculating ball type. Four-wheel power disc brakes had become optional during the 1975 model year, along with Sure-Trak anti-skid brakes, power seats, Traction-Lok axle, power moonroof, and space- saver spare tire. Those continued for 1976. New options this year included speed control, tilt steering wheel, AM radio with stereo tape player, power door locks, and heavy-duty suspension. A Luxury Decor option (for four-door Ghia only) included black/tan two-tone paint, four-wheel disc brakes, lacy-spoke cast aluminum wheels, large Ghia badge on C-pillar, and front/rear bumper rub strips. Inside, that option had velour cloth and super-soft vinyl upholstery with larger door armrest, soft glovebox and ashtray doors, rear center armrest, console with warning lights, leather-wrapped steering wheel, and lighted visor vanity mirror. A Sports Sedan package for two-doors included a floor shift lever, special paint, color-keyed wheels, pinstripes, and leather- wrapped steering wheel. Mercury's Monarch was Granada's corporate twin, differing only in grille/taillamp design and trim details. Both evolved from the Maverick platform.

1976 Gran Torino two-door hardtop (F)

TORINO — V-8 — Nine models made up the mid-size Torino lineup this year: base, Gran Torino and Brougham two- and four-doors, and a trio of wagons. Gran Torino Sport was dropped. Two-doors rode a 114 in. wheelbase; four-doors measured 118 in. between hubs. The similar-size Elite was a separate model (below). Fuel economy was improved by recalibrating engine spark and back-pressure EGR, and lowering the rear axle ratio to 2.75:1. Five body colors were new. Torino and Gran Torino got a new saddle interior. Appearance was similar to 1975. Side-by-side quad round headlamps flanked a one-piece plastic grille with tiny crosshatch pattern, divided into six sections by vertical bars. Clear vertical parking lamps hid behind twin matching outer sections, making eight in all. 'Ford' block letters stood above the grille. Two-door Torinos retained the conventional pillarless design, while four-doors were referred to as "pillared hardtops." Bodies held frameless, ventless curved side glass. Standard engine was the 351 cu. in. (5.8-liter) V-8 with two-barrel carburetor and solid-state ignition. SelectShift Cruise-O-Matic, power front disc/rear drum brakes, power steering, and HR78 x 14 steel-belted radial tires were standard. Two V-8s were optional: a 400 cu. in. two-barrel and the big 460 four-barrel. Torino's front suspension used single lower control arms, strut bar and ball joints. Coil springs brought up the rear. Bodies sat on a separate torque box perimeter-type frame. Standard equipment included a cloth/vinyl front bench seat with adjustable head restraints, vinyl door trim panels, recessed door handles, day/night mirror, heater/defroster, and inside hood release. Broughams had a split bench seat. Torino and Gran Torino wore hubcaps; Broughams added wheel covers, as well as opera windows and a vinyl roof. Wagons had a three-way tailgate and locking storage compartment. Squire wagons added a power tailgate window, full wheel covers, and woodgrain paneling with side rails. New options included a bucket seat console (on Gran Torino two-door); opera windows for the base Torino two-door (as well as other models); and engine immersion heater. Also optional: an automatic parking brake release and electric decklid release.

1976 Elite two-door hardtop (F)

ELITE — V-8 — Although the Elite nameplate arrived just a year earlier, its body had been around a while longer, then called Gran Torino. Appearance changes were slight this year on the pillarless two-door Elite body, which rode a 114 in. wheelbase. Elite sported a "luxury" sectioned grille with vertical bars and horizontal center bar. Its floating eggcrate design formed a two-row, eight-column arrangement. Each of the 16 "holes" held a crosshatch pattern. The grille protruded forward in segments, and the bumper extended forward at its center and ends. A stand-up hood ornament held the Elite crest. Single round headlamps in square housings had bright bezels, while vertical parking/signal lamps sat in front fendertip extensions. Wide vinyl-insert bodyside moldings were color-keyed to the vinyl roof. Large wraparound taillamps had bright bezels and integral side marker lights (with red reflector on lower back panel applique). On the rear roof pillar were two tiny side-by-side opera windows, to the rear of regular quarter windows. Bodies also displayed bright tapered wide wheel lip moldings. Six body colors were new, while a stand-alone gold vinyl roof replaced the former brown. Either a full vinyl roof or a new half-vinyl version was available, at no extra charge. To boost gas milealge, the standard axle changed from 3.00:1 to 2.75:1. Standard equipment included the 351 cu. in. (5.8- liter) two-barrel V-8 with SelectShift Cruise-O-Matic, power steering and brakes, four-wheel coil springs, and HR78 x 15 SBR tires. The standard bench seat had Westminster pleated knit cloth and vinyl trim. Woodtone accented the instrument cluster/panel, steering wheel and door panels.

Also standard: front bumper guards, heater/defroster, DirectAire ventilation, clock, full wheel covers, and bright window moldings. An Interior Decor group included individually adjustable split bench seats with choice of cashmere-like cloth or all- vinyl trim, shag carpeting, visor vanity mirror, dual-note horn, and eight-pod instrument panel with tachometer. Bucket seats with console and floor shift became optional this year. Other new options: space-saver spare tire, turbine-spoke cast aluminum wheels, AM/FM stereo search radio, electric decklid release, automatic parking brake release, and engine immersion heater.

1976 LTD Landau four-door pillared hardtop (F)

FULL-SIZE LTD/CUSTOM 500 — V-8 — LTD was the only full-size Ford available to private buyers this year, as the Custom 500 badge went on fleet models only. The ten-model lineup included two- and four-door base, Brougham and Landau LTD models; Custom 500 four-door and wagon; and base and Country Squire LTD wagons. Four-doors were called "pillared hardtops." Landau and Country Squire models had hidden headlamps. Brougham and Landau two-doors carried half-vinyl roofs; four-doors got a "halo" vinyl roof. Front-end appearance changed slightly with a switch to dark argent paint on the secondary surface of the chromed grille. Otherwise, little change was evident other than a new wheel cover design. LTD's crosshatch grille peaked slightly forward. Headlamp doors held a horizontal emblem. Tri-section wraparound front parking/signal lenses stood at fender tips. On the hood was a stand-up ornament. Two-doors had a six-window design, with narrow vertical windows between the front and rear side windows. Vinyl-insert bodyside moldings were standard. All models had a reflective rear applique. Six body colors were new. At mid-year, Country Squire lost the long horizontal chrome strip along its woodgrain bodyside panel. Base engine was the two-barrel 351 cu. in. (5.8-liter) V-8, but wagons carried the 400 cu. in. engine. A 460 V-8 with dual exhausts was optional on all models. Standard equipment included power steering and brakes, SelectShift Cruise-O-Matic, steel-belted radials, power ventilation system, and front bumper guards. Brougham, Landau and wagon also had rear guards. Police models with the 460 V-8 and three-speed automatic had first-gear lockout. Front suspensions used single lower arms with strut bar and ball joints. At the rear were coil springs with three-link rubber cushion and track bar. Rear axle ratios changed to 2.75:1 and engines were recalibrated, in an attempt to boost gas mileage. Wagons had a fuel tank of only 21 gallons, versus 24.3 gallons on hardtops. An 8-gallon auxiliary tank was available. Wagons now had standard hydro-boost rear brakes. A parking brake warning light became standard on all models. Decklid and ignition switch locks offered improved anti-theft protection. Other new options: four-wheel power disc brakes, adjustable-level air shocks, dual-tone paint treatment (Brougham and Landau) in four combinations, and AM/FM search radio. Inside were standard full-width bench seats with cloth/vinyl trim; cut-pile carpeting; full-length padded armrests; and woodtone instrument panel and door appliques. LTD bodies held bright belt, drip and wheel lip moldings. Landau bodies held concealed headlamps, a convenience group, half vinyl roof (on two-door), front cornering lamps, wide color- keyed bodyside moldings, and unique narrow center pillar windows. Also on Landaus: padded door panels with woodtone accents, fold-down center armrests, and a digital clock.

1976 Thunderbird two-door hardtop (F)

THUNDERBIRD — V-8 — Apart from a trio of trim/paint Luxury Group packages, not much was new on the personal-luxury Thunderbird for 1976. T-Bird's bulged-out grille consisted of rectangular holes in a crosshatch pattern, with 'Thunderbird' block letters above. Quad round headlamps in squarish housings didn't fit snugly together but were mounted separately, with a little body- colored space between each pair. Large sectioned wraparound parking and cornering lamps stood at fender tips. T-Bird's opera windows were less tall than most, and narrow roll-down rear windows also were installed. Full-width segmented-design taillamps had four bulbs in each pod. Standard equipment included the big 460 cu. in. (7.5- liter) V-8 with four-barrel carburetor, SelectShift Cruise-O- Matic, 2.75:1 rear axle, SelectAire conditioner, vinyl roof, vinyl-insert bodyside moldings, JR78 x 15 steel-belted radials, power steering and brakes, power windows, and cornering lamps. Rear suspension, as before, was the "stabul" four-link system. Inside was a baby burled walnut woodtone instrument panel applique and new AM radio. Also standard: automatic parking brake release, and front and rear bumper guards with white insert rub strips, split bench seats with fold- down armrests, remote-control left mirror, full wheel covers, twin padded pull-down armrests, lined luggage area, and courtesy lights. New options included a power lumbar seat, AM/FM search radio, AM/FM quadrasonic 8track tape player, engine block heater, and Kasman cloth interior trim. An automatic headlamp dimmer was added to the Light Group. Also available: a power- operated moonroof made with one-way glass. The new Creme/Gold Luxury Group featured two-tone paint (gold

glamour paint on bodyside and creme accent on hood, deck, greenhouse and bodyside molding). Also included was a gold padded half-vinyl roof, deep-dish aluminum wheels, and gold Thunderbird emblem in opera window. Inside was a choice of two-tone Creme/Gold leather or gold media velour seating surface. The right-hand instrument panel was finished with gold applique. A Bordeaux Luxury Group included Bordeaux glamour paint, fully padded half-vinyl roof in silver or dark red, wide bodyside moldings to match the vinyl roof, dual hood and bodyside paint stripes, and simulated wire wheel covers. Inside was a choice of red leather or red media velour. There was also a Lipstick (red) package with white striping. Thunderbirds came in 21 colors, including the Luxury Group choices.

I.D. DATA: Ford's 11-symbol Vehicle Identification Number (VIN) is stamped on a metal tab fastened to the instrument panel, visible through the windshield. The first digit is a model year code ('6' 1976). The second letter indicates assembly plant: 'A' Atlanta, GA; 'B' Oakville, Ontario (Canada); 'E' Mahwah, NJ; 'G' Chicago; 'H' Lorain, Ohio; 'J' Los Angeles; 'K' Kansas City, MO; 'P' Twin Cities, Minn.; 'R' San Jose, CA; 'T' Metuchen, NJ; 'U' Louisville, KY; 'W' Wayne, MI; 'Y' Wixom, MI. Digits three and four are the body serial code, which corresponds to the Model Numbers shown in the tables below (e.g., '10' Pinto 2-dr. sedan). The fifth symbol is an engine code: 'Y' L4-140 2Bbl.; 'Z' V6170 2Bbl.; 'T' L6200 1Bbl.; 'L' L6250 1Bbl.; 'F' V8302 2Bbl.; 'H' V8351 2Bbl.; 'S' V8400 2Bbl.; 'A' V8460 4Bbl.; 'C' Police V8460 4Bbl. Finally, digits 6-11 make up the consecutive unit number of cars built at each assembly plant. The number begins with 100,001. A Vehicle Certification Label on the left front door lock face panel or door pillar shows the manufacturer, month and year of manufacture, GVW, GAWR, certification statement, VIN, body code, color code, trim code, axle code, transmission code, and domestic (or foreign) special order code.

PINTO (FOUR/V-6)

Model Number	Body/Style Number	Body Type & Seating	Factory Price	Shipping Weight	Production Total
10	62B	2-dr. Sedan-4P	3025/3472	2452/2590	92,264
10	62B	2-dr. Pony Sed-4P	2895/--	2450/--	Note 1
11	64B	2-dr. Hatch-4P	3200/3647	2482/2620	92,540
11	64B	2-dr. Sqr Hatch-4P	3505/3952	2518/2656	Note 2
12	73B	2-dr. Sta Wag-4P	3365/3865	2635/2773	105,328
12	73B	2-dr. Sqr Wag-4P	3671/4171	2672/2810	Note 2

Note 1: Pony production included in base sedan figure. **Note 2:** Squire Runabout hatchback and Squire Wagon production are included in standard Runabout and station wagon totals.

MAVERICK (SIX/V-8)

91	62A	2-dr. Sedan-4P	3117/3265	2763/2930	60,611
92	54A	4-dr. Sedan-5P	3189/3337	2873/3040	79,076

GRANADA (SIX/V-8)

82	66H	2-dr. Sedan-5P	3707/3861	3119/3226	161,618
81	54H	4-dr. Sedan-5P	3798/3952	3168/3275	187,923

GRANADA GHIA (SIX/V-8)

84	66K	2-dr. Sedan-5P	4265/4353	3280/3387	46,786
83	54K	4-dr. Sedan-5P	4355/4443	3339/3446	52,457

TORINO (V-8)

25	65B	2-dr. HT Cpe-6P	4172	3976	34,518
27	53B	4-dr. HT Sed-6P	4206	4061	17,394
40	71B	4-dr. Sta Wag-6P	4521	4409	17,281

1976 Gran Torino Brougham four-door pillared hardtop (F)

GRAN TORINO (V-8)

30	65D	2-dr. HT Cpe-6P	4461	3999	23,939
31	53D	4-dr. HT Sed-6P	4495	4081	40,568
42	71D	4-dr. Sta Wag-6P	4769	4428	30,596
43	71K	4-dr. Sqr Wag-6P	5083	4454	21,144

GRAN TORINO BROUGHAM (V-8)

32	65K	2-dr. HT Cpe-6P	4883	4063	3,183
33	53K	4-dr. HT Sed-6P	4915	4144	4,473

ELITE (V-8)

21	65H	2-dr. HT Cpe-6P	4879	4169	146,475

CUSTOM 500 (V-8)

52	60D	2-dr. Pill. HT-6P	N/A	N/A	7,037
53	53D	4-dr. Pill. HT-6P	4493	4298	23,447
72	71D	4-dr. Ranch Wag-6P	4918	4737	4,633

LTD (V-8)

62	60H	2-dr. Pill. HT-6P	4780	4257	62,844
63	53H	4-dr. Pill. HT-6P	4752	4303	108,168
74	71H	4-dr. Sta Wag-6P	5207	4752	30,237
74	71H	4-dr. DFRS Wag-10P	5333	4780	Note 3
76	71K	4-dr. Ctry Sqr-6P	5523	4809	47,379
76	71K	4-dr. DFRS Sqr-10P	5649	4837	Note 3

Note 3: Wagons with dual-facing rear seats (a $126 option) are included in standard station wagon and Country Squire wagon totals.

LTD BROUGHAM (V-8)

68	60K	2-dr. Pill. HT-6P	5299	4299	20,863
66	53K	4-dr. Pill. HT-6P	5245	4332	32,917

LTD LANDAU (V-8)

65	60L	2-dr. Pill. HT-6P	5613	4346	29,673
64	53L	4-dr. Pill. HT-6P	5560	4394	35,663

THUNDERBIRD (V-8)

87	65K	2-dr. HT Cpe-6P	7790	4808	52,935

FACTORY PRICE AND WEIGHT NOTE: For Maverick and Granada, prices and weights to left of slash are for six-cylinder, to right for V-8 engine. For Pinto, prices and weights to left of slash are for four-cylinder, to right for V-6 engine.

ENGINE DATA: BASE FOUR (Pinto): Inline. Overhead cam. Four-cylinder. Cast iron block and head. Displacement: 140 cu. in. (2.3 liters). Bore & stroke: 3.78 x 3.13 in. Compression ratio: 9.0:1. Brake horsepower: 92 at 5000 R.P.M. Torque: 121 lbs.-ft. at 3000 R.P.M. Five.00 main bearings. Hydraulic valve lifters. Carburetor: 2Bbl. Holley-Weber 9510. VIN Code: Y. OPTIONAL V-6 (Pinto): 60-degree, overhead-valve V-6. Cast iron block and head. Displacement: 170.8 cu. in. (2.8 liters). Bore & stroke: 3.66 x 2.70 in. Compression ratio: 8.7:1. Brake horsepower: 103 at 4400 R.P.M. Torque: 149 lbs.-ft. at 2800 R.P.M. Four main bearings. Solid valve lifters. Carburetor: 2Bbl. Motorcraft 9510 (D6ZE-BA). VIN Code: Z. BASE SIX (Maverick, Granada): Inline. Overhead valve. Six-cylinder. Cast iron block and head. Displacement: 200 cu. in. (3.3 liters). Bore & stroke: 3.68 x 3.13 in. Compression ratio: 8.3:1. Brake horsepower: 81 at 3400 R.P.M. Torque: 151 lbs.-ft. at 1700 R.P.M. Seven main bearings. Hydraulic valve lifters. Carburetor: 1Bbl. Carter YFA 9510. VIN Code: T. BASE SIX (Granada Ghia); OPTIONAL (Maverick, Granada): Inline. Overhead valve. Six-cylinder. Cast iron block and head. Displacement: 250 cu. in. (4.1 liters). Bore & stroke: 3.68 x 3.91 in. Compression ratio: 8.0:1. Brake horsepower: 87 at 3600 R.P.M. (Maverick/Ghia, 90 at 3000). Torque: 190 lbs.-ft. at 2000 R.P.M. (Ghia, 187 at 1900). Seven bearings. Hydraulic valve lifters. Carburetor: 1Bbl. Carter YFA 9510. VIN Code: L. OPTIONAL V-8 (Maverick, Granada): 90-degree, overhead valve V-8. Cast iron block and head. Displacement: 302 cu. in. (5.0 liters). Bore & stroke: 4.00 x 3.00 in. Compression ratio: 8.0:1. Brake horsepower: 138 at 3600 R.P.M. (Granada, 134 at 3600). Torque: 245 lbs.-ft. at 2000 R.P.M. (Granada, 242 at 2000). Five main bearings. Hydraulic valve lifters. Carburetor: 2Bbl. Ford 2150A 9510. VIN Code: F. BASE V-8 (Torino, Elite, LTD); OPTIONAL (Granada): 90-degree, overhead valve V-8. Cast iron block and head. Displacement: 351 cu. in. (5.8 liters). Bore & stroke: 4.00 x 3.50 in. Compression ratio: 8.0:1 (Torino, 8.1:1). Brake horsepower: 152 at 3800 R.P.M. (Torino, 154 at 3400). Torque: 274 lbs.-ft. at 1600 R.P.M. (Torino, 286 at 1800). Five main bearings. Hydraulic valve lifters. Carburetor: 2Bbl. Ford 2150A. VIN Code: H. BASE V-8 (500/LTD wagon); OPTIONAL (Torino, Elite, LTD): 90-degree, overhead valve V-8. Cast iron block and head. Displacement: 400 cu. in. (6.6 liters). Bore & stroke: 4.00 x 4.00 in. Compression ratio: 8.0:1. Brake horsepower: 180 at 3800 R.P.M. Torque: 336 lbs.-ft. at 1800 R.P.M. Five main bearings. Hydraulic valve lifters. Carburetor: 2Bbl. Ford 2150A. VIN Code: S. BASE V-8 (Thunderbird); OPTIONAL (Torino, Elite, LTD): 90-degree, overhead valve V-8. Cast iron block and head. Displacement: 460 cu. in. (7.5 liters). Bore & stroke: 4.36 x 3.85 in. Compression ratio: 8.0:1. Brake horsepower: 202 at 3800 R.P.M. Torque: 352 lbs.-ft. at 1600 R.P.M. Five main bearings. Hydraulic valve lifters. Carburetor: 4Bbl. Motorcraft 9510 or Ford 4350A 9510. VIN Code: A.

Note: A Police 460 cu. in. V-8 ws also available for LTD.

CHASSIS DATA: Wheelbase: (Pinto) 94.5 in.; (Pinto wag.) 94.8 in.; (Maverick 2dr.) 103.0 in.; (Maverick 4dr.) 109.9 in.; (Granada) 109.9 in.; (Torino) 114.0 in.; (Torino 4dr./wag.) 118.0 in.; (Elite) 114.0 in.; (Custom 500/LTD) 121.0 in.; (TBird) 120.4 in. Overall length: (Pinto) 169.0 in.; (Pinto wag) 178.8 in.; (Maverick 2dr.) 193.9 in.; (Granada) 197.7 in.; (Torino 2dr.) 213.6 in.; (Torino 4dr.) 217.6 in.; (Torino wag) 222.6 in.; (Elite) 216.1 in.; (LTD 2dr.) 223.9 in.; (LTD wag) 225.6 in.; (TBird) 225.7 in. Height: (Pinto) 50.6 in.; (Pinto wag) 52.0 in.; (Maverick) 52.9 in.; (Granada) 53.3-53.4 in.; (Torino 2dr.) 52.6 in.; (Torino 4dr.) 53.3 in.; (Torino wag) 54.9 in.; (Elite) 53.1 in.; (LTD 2dr.) 53.7 in.; (LTD 4dr.) 54.8 in.; (LTD wag) 56.7 in.; (TBird) 52.8 in. Width: (Pinto) 69.4 in.; (Pinto wag) 69.7 in.; (Maverick) 70.5 in.; (Granada) 74.0 in.; (Granada Ghia) 74.5 in.; (Torino) 78.5 in.; (Torino wag) 79.9 in.; (Elite) 78.5 in.; (LTD) 79.5 in.; (LTD wag) 79.9 in.; (TBird) 79.7 in. Front Tread: (Pinto) 55.0 in.; (Maverick) 56.5 in.; (Granada) 58.5 in.; (Torino) 63.4 in.; (LTD) 64.1 in.; (TBird) 62.9 in. Rear Tread: (Pinto) 55.8 in.; (Maverick) 56.5 in.; (Granada) 57.7 in.; (Torino wag) 64.3 in.; (Torino) 63.1 in.; (LTD) 64.3 in.; (TBird) 62.8 in. Standard Tires: (Pinto) A78 x 13 or B78 x 13; (Maverick) C78 x 14, except DR78 x 14 w/V-8 engine; (Granada) DR78 x 14; (Torino) HR78 x 14; (Elite) HR78 x 15; (LTD) HR78 x 15 exc. wagon, JR78 x 15; (TBird) JR78 x 15.

TECHNICAL: Transmission: Three-speed manual transmission (column shift) standard on Maverick/Granada. Gear ratios: (1st) 2.99:1; (2nd) 1.75:1; (3rd) 1.00:1; (Rev) 3.17:1. Four-speed floor shift standard on Pinto: (1st) 3.65:1; (2nd) 1.97:1; (3rd) 1.37:1; (4th) 1.00:1; (Rev) 3.66:1 or 3.95:1. Pinto station wagon: (1st) 4.07:1; (2nd) 2.57:1; (3rd) 1.66:1; (4th) 1.00:1; (Rev) 3.95:1. Select-Shift three-speed automatic standard on other models, optional on all; column lever but floor shift optional on Maverick, Granada, Torino and Elite (standard on Pinto). Pinto (L4140) automatic gear ratios: (1st) 2.47:1; (2nd) 1.47:1; (3rd) 1.00:1; (Rev) 2.11:1. Pinto (V-6)/Maverick/Granada/Torino (V8351)/Elite (V8351) auto. gear ratios: (1st) 2.46:1; (2nd) 1.46:1; (3rd) 1.00:1; (Rev) 2.20:1. Torino/Elite/LTD/TBird (V8400/460): ratios: (1st) 2.46:1; (2nd) 1.46:1; (3rd) 1.00:1; (Rev) 2.18:1. LTD (V8351): (1st) 2.40:1; (2nd) 1.47:1; (3rd) 1.00:1; (Rev) 2.00:1. Standard final drive ratio: (Pinto four) 3.18:1 w/4spd, 3.18:1 or 3.40:1 w/auto.; (Pinto Pony) 3.00:1; (Pinto V-6) 3.40:1; (Maverick) 2.79:1; (Granada) 2.79:1 or 2.75:1 w/3spd and 2.75:1, 3.00:1 or 3.07:1 w/auto.; (Torino/Elite) 2.75:1; (LTD/T-Bird) 2.75:1 exc. Police 460 V-8, 3.00:1. Steering: (Pinto) rack and pinion; (others) recirculating ball. Front Suspension: (Pinto) coil springs with short/long control arms, lower leading arms, and anti-sway bar on wagon; (Maverick/Granada) coil springs with short/long arms, lower trailing links and anti-sway bar; (Torino/Elite/LTD/Thunderbird) coil springs with single lower control arm, lower trailing links, strut bar and anti-sway bar. Rear Suspension: (Pinto/Maverick/Granada) rigid axle w/semi- elliptic leaf springs; (Torino/Elite) rigid axle w/lower trailing arms, upper oblique torque arms and coil springs; (LTD) rigid axle w/lower trailing radius arms, upper torque arms and coil springs, three-link w/track bar; (Thunderbird) "stabul" four-link system with coil springs and anti-sway bar. Brakes: Front disc, rear drum; four-wheel discs available on Granada, LTD and Thunderbird. Ignition: Electronic. Body construction: (Pinto/Maverick/Granada) unibody; (Torino/Elite/LTD) separate body and perimeter box frame; (Thunderbird) separate body and perimeter frame with torque box. Fuel tank: (Pinto) 13 gal.; (Pinto wag) 14 gal.; (Maverick/Granada) 19.2 gal.; (Torino/Elite) 26.5 gal.; (Torino wag) 21.3 gal.; (LTD) 24.3 gal. exc. wagon, 21 gal.; (TBird) 26.5 gal.

DRIVETRAIN OPTIONS: Engines: 250 cu. in., 1Bbl. six: Maverick/Granada ($96). 302 cu. in., 2Bbl. V-8: Granada ($154); Granada Ghia ($88). 351 cu. in., 2Bbl. V-8: Granada ($200); Granada Ghia ($134). 400 cu. in., 2Bbl. V-8: Torino/Elite/LTD ($100). 460 cu. in., 4Bbl. V-8: Torino/Elite ($292); LTD ($353); LTD wagon ($251). Dual exhaust: TBird ($72). Transmission/Differential: SelectShift Cruise-O-Matic: Pinto ($186); Maverick/Granada ($245). Floor shift lever: Maverick/Granada ($27). Traction-Lok differential: Granada ($48); Torino/Elite ($53); LTD ($54); TBird ($55). Optional axle ratio: Pinto/Maverick/Granada ($13); Torino/Elite/LTD/TBird ($14). Power Accessories: Power brakes: Pinto ($54); Maverick ($53); Granada ($57). Four-wheel power disc brakes: Granada ($210); LTD ($170); TBird ($184). Sure-Track brakes: Granada ($227); TBird ($378). Power steering: Pinto ($117); Maverick/Granada ($124). Suspension: H.D. susp.: Maverick ($16); Granada ($29); LTD ($18); TBird ($29). H.D. handling susp.: Torino ($18-$32); Elite ($92). Adjustable air shock absorbers: LTD ($43). Other: Engine block heater: Pinto/Maverick/Granada ($17); Torino/Elite/LTD/TBird ($18). H.D. battery: Maverick/Granada ($14); LTD ($17). H.D. electrical system: Torino ($29); Elite ($80). Extended-range fuel tank: LTD ($99). Trailer towing pkg. (light duty): Granada ($42); LTD ($53). Trailer towing pkg. (medium duty): Torino/Elite ($59); LTD ($46-$145). Trailer towing pkg. (heavy duty): Torino ($87-$121); Elite ($121); LTD ($132-$230); TBird ($92). California emission system: Maverick/Granada ($46); Torino/Elite/LTD/TBird ($50). High-altitude option: Torino/Elite/LTD/TBird ($13).

PINTO CONVENIENCE/APPEARANCE OPTIONS: Option Packages: Stallion option ($283). Luxury decor group ($241). Convenience light group ($70-$102). Protection group ($73-$134). Comfort/Convenience: Air conditioner ($420). Rear defroster, electric ($70). Tinted glass ($46). Leather-wrapped steering wheel ($33). Dual color-keyed mirrors ($42). Entertainment: AM radio ($71); w/stereo tape player ($192). AM/FM radio ($129). AM/FM stereo radio ($173). Exterior: Sunroof, manual ($230). Half vinyl roof ($125). Metallic glow paint ($54). Roof luggage rack ($52-$75). Rocker panel moldings ($19). Wheels: Forged aluminum wheels ($82-$172). Styled steel wheels ($92-$119). Wheel covers ($28). Trim rings ($29). Tires: A78 x 13 WSW. A70 x 13 RWL. B78 x 13 BSW/WSW. BR78 x 13 SBR BSW/WSW. BR70 x 13 RWL.

MAVERICK CONVENIENCE/APPEARANCE OPTIONS: Option Packages: Stallion option ($329). Exterior decor group ($99). Interior decor group ($106). Luxury decor group ($508). Luxury interior decor ($217). Deluxe bumper group ($28-$61). Convenience group ($34-$64). Protection group ($24-$39). Light group ($22-$34). Security lock group ($16). Comfort/Convenience: Air cond. ($420). Rear defogger ($40). Tinted glass ($45-$59). Fuel monitor warning light ($18). Dual color-keyed mirrors ($13-$25). Entertainment: AM radio ($71); w/tape player ($192). AM/FM radio ($128). AM/FM stereo radio ($210); w/tape player ($299). Exterior: Vinyl roof ($94). Metallic glow paint ($54). Lower bodyside paint ($55). Bodyside or bodyside-roof accent paint stripe ($27). Decklid luggage rack ($51). Rocker panel moldings ($19). Bumper guards, front or rear ($17). Interior: Reclining bucket seats ($147). Cloth bucket seat trim ($24). Vinyl seat trim ($25). Color-keyed deluxe seatbelts ($17). Wheels: Forged aluminum wheels ($98-$187). Styled steel wheels ($59-$89). Hubcap trim rings ($35) except (NC) with decor group. Tires: C78 x 14 WSW. BR78 x 14 BSW. CR78 x 14 BSW/WSW. DR78 x 14 BSW/WSW. DR70 x 14 RWL. Space-saver spare ($13) except (NC) with radial tires.

GRANADA CONVENIENCE/APPEARANCE OPTIONS: Option Packages: Sports sedan option ($482). Exterior decor group ($128). Interior decor group ($181). Luxury decor group ($642). Convenience group ($31-$75). Deluxe bumper group ($61). Light group ($25-$37). Protection group ($24-$39). Visibility group ($30-$47). Security lock group ($17). Comfort/Convenience: Air cond. ($437). Rear defogger ($43). Rear defroster, electric ($76). Fingertip speed control ($96). Power windows ($95-$133). Power door locks ($63-$88). Power four-way seat ($119). Tinted glass ($47). Leather- wrapped steering wheel ($14-$33). Luxury steering wheel ($18). Tilt steering wheel ($54). Fuel monitor warning light ($18). Digital clock ($40). Horns and Mirrors: Dual-note horn ($6). Color-keyed outside mirrors ($29-$42). Lighted visor vanity mirror ($40). Entertainment: AM radio ($71); w/tape player ($192). AM/FM radio ($142). AM/FM stereo radio ($210); w/tape player ($299). Exterior: Power moonroof ($786). Power sunroof ($517). Vinyl or half vinyl roof ($102). Metallic glow paint ($54). Bodyside/decklid paint stripes ($27). Bodyside/decklid accent moldings ($28). Black vinyl insert bodyside moldings ($35). Rocker panel moldings ($19). Decklid luggage rack ($33). Interior: Console ($65). Reclining seats ($60). Leather seat trim ($181). Deluxe cloth seat trim ($88). Trunk carpeting ($20). Trunk dress-up ($33). Color-keyed seatbelts ($17). Wheels: Styled steel wheels ($41-$60); w/trim rings ($76- $95). Lacy spoke aluminum wheels ($112-$207). Tires: E78 x 14 BSW/WSW. DR78 x 14 WSW. ER78 x 14 BSW/WSW. FR78 x 14 BSW/WSW. Space-saver spare (NC).

TORINO/ELITE CONVENIENCE/APPEARANCE OPTIONS: Option Packages: Squire Brougham option: Torino ($184). Interior decor group: Elite ($384). Accent group: Torino ($45). Deluxe bumper group ($50-$67). Light group ($41-$43). Convenience group: Tornio ($33-$84); Elite ($49). Protection group ($26-$42). Security lock group ($18). Comfort/Convenience: Air cond. ($420); w/auto-temp control ($520). Defroster, electric ($83). Fingertip speed control ($105). Tinted glass ($51-$55). Power windows ($104-$145). Power tailgate window: Torino wag ($43). Power door locks ($68-$109). Electric decklid release ($17). Six-way power seat ($130). Automatic seatback release ($30). Reclining passenger seat ($70). Leather-wrapped steering wheel ($36). Luxury steering wheel ($20). Tilt steering wheel ($59). Fuel sentry vacuum gauge ($13-$32). Fuel monitor warning light ($20). Electric clock: Torino ($18). Horns and Mirrors: Dual-note horn ($7). Remote driver's mirror, chrome ($14). Remote-control color-keyed mirrors ($32-$46). Lighted visor vanity mirror ($43). Entertainment: AM radio ($78). AM/FM stereo radio ($229); w/tape player ($326). AM/FM stereo search radio: Elite ($386). Dual rear speakers ($39). Exterior: Power moonroof: Elite ($859). Power sunroof ($545). Vinyl roof: Torino ($112); Elite (NC). Opera windows: Torino ($50). Fender skirts: Torino ($41). Rocker panel moldings ($26). Vinyl-insert bodyside moldings: Torino ($38). Metallic glow paint ($59). Dual accent paint stripes ($29). Bumper guards, front or rear: Torino ($18). Luggage rack: Torino ($82-$91). Interior: Bucket seats ($146) exc. Elite w/decor group (NC). Rear-facing third seat: Torino wag ($104). Vinyl bench seat trim: Torino ($22). Pleated vinyl bench seat trim ($22-$28). Duraweave vinyl seat trim: Torino ($55). Vinyl split bench seat: Torino (NC). Color-keyed seatbelts ($18). Trunk trim ($36). Wheels: Deluxe wheel covers: Torino ($37). Luxury wheel covers ($58-$95). Wire wheel covers: Elite ($99). Magnum 500 wheels w/trim rings: Torino ($141-$178). Turbine spoke cast aluminum wheels: Elite ($226). Torino Tires: H78 x 14 BSW/WSW. HR78 x 14 WSW. HR78 x 14 six- ply BSW/WSW. JR78 x 14 WSW. HR78 x 15 BSW/WSW. Space-saver spare (NC). Elite Tires: HR78 x 15 SBR WSW ($39). HR70 x 15 SBR WSW ($59). Space-saver spare (NC).

LTD CONVENIENCE/APPEARANCE OPTIONS: Option Packages: Landau luxury group ($472-$708). Brougham option: wagon ($396); Squire ($266). Harmony color group ($99). Convenience group ($97-$104). Light group ($76-$79). Deluxe bumper group ($41-$59). Protection group ($47-$78). Security lock group ($18). Comfort/Convenience: Air cond. ($353); w/auto-temp control ($486). Anti-theft alarm system ($566). Rear defogger ($43). Rear defroster, electric ($83). Fingertip speed control ($87-$107). Power windows ($108-$161). Power mini-vent and side windows ($232). Power door locks ($68-$109). Six-way power driver's seat ($132); driver and passenger ($259). Automatic seatback release ($30). Tinted glass ($64). Luxury steering wheel ($20). Tilt steering wheel ($59). Fuel monitor warning light ($20). Electric clock ($18). Digital clock ($25-$43). Lighting, Horns and Mirrors: Cornering lamps ($43). Dual-note horn ($6). Driver's remote mirror ($14). Entertainment: AM radio ($78). AM/FM stereo radio ($229); w/tape player ($326). AM/FM stereo search radio ($386). Dual rear speakers ($39). Exterior: Sunroof, manual ($632). Full vinyl roof ($126) exc. wagon ($151) and Brougham/Landau two-door (NC). Half vinyl roof ($126). Fender skirts ($42). Metallic glow paint ($59). Dual accent paint stripes ($29). Rocker panel moldings ($26). Vinyl-insert bodyside moldings ($41). Rear bumper guards ($18). Luggage rack ($82-$96). Interior: Dual-facing rear seats: wagon ($126). Split bench seat w/passenger recliner ($141). Leather interior trim ($222). All-vinyl seat ($22). Duraweave vinyl trim ($55). Recreation table ($58). Color-keyed seatbelts ($18). Deluxe cargo area ($83-$126). Lockable side stowage compartment ($43). Luggage area trim ($36). Wheels: Full wheel covers ($30). Deluxe wheel covers ($63- $93). Tires: H78 x 15 BSW/WSW. J78 x 15 BSW/WSW. HR78 x 15 WSW. JR78 x 15 BSW/WSW. LR78 x 15 BSW/WSW.

THUNDERBIRD CONVENIENCE/APPEARANCE OPTIONS: Option Packages: Bordeaux luxury group ($624-$700). Creme/gold luxury group ($717-$793). Lipstick luxury group ($337-$546). Turnpike group ($180). Convenience group ($84). Protection group ($79-$87). Light group ($164). Power lock group ($86). Security lock group ($18). Comfort/Convenience: Auto-temp control air cond. ($88). Anti- theft alarm system ($84). Rear defroster, electric ($99). Windshield/rear window defroster, electric ($355). Fingertip speed control ($120). Tinted glass ($29-$66). Power mini-vent windows ($79). Six-way power driver's seat ($132); driver and passenger ($250). Power lumbar support seats ($86). Reclining passenger seat ($70). Automatic seatback release ($30). Tilt steering wheel ($68). Fuel monitor warning light ($20). Lighting and Mirrors: Cornering lamps ($43). Lighted driver's visor vanity mirror ($43). Entertainment: AM/FM stereo radio ($145); w/tape player ($249). AM/FM stereo search radio ($298). AM/FM quadrasonic radio w/tape player ($382). Power antenna ($39). Exterior: Power moonroof ($879); sunroof ($716). Starfire paint ($204). Wide color-keyed vinyl-insert bodyside molding ($121). Dual bodyside/hood paint stripes ($33). Interior: Leather trim ($239). Kasman cloth trim ($96). Super-soft vinyl seat trim ($55). Trunk dress-up ($59). Wheels: Deluxe wheel covers ($67). Simulated wire wheel covers ($88) exc. with creme/gold group ($163 credit). Deep- dish aluminum wheels ($251) exc. with Bordeaux/lipstick luxury group ($163). Tires: JR78 x 15 SBR WSW ($41). LR78 x 15 SBR wide WSW ($59). Space-saver spare ($86).

HISTORY: Introduced: October 3, 1975. Model year production: 1,861,537 (incl. Mustangs). Total production for the U.S. market of 1,714,258 units (incl. Mustangs) consisted of 342,434 four- cylinder, 390,750 sixes and 981,074 V-8s. Calendar year production (U.S.): 1,459,109 (incl. Mustangs). Calendar year sales by U.S. dealers: 1,682,583 (incl. Mustangs); total sales gave Ford a 19.9 percent share of the market. Model year sales by U.S. dealers: N/A. NOTE: Totals do not include Club Wagons.

Historical Footnotes: Ford sales had declined sharply in the 1975 model year, down over 21 percent. That left Ford with only a 22 percent market share. Full-size models had sold best. Even the success of the Granada (new for 1975) hadn't been as great as anticipated. Continuing their interest in small, economical cars, Ford had introduced Pinto Pony and Mustang II MPG models late in the 1975 model year. Sales swung upward again for the 1976 model year, even though few major changes were evident in the lineup. Part of the reason was Ford's new "California strategy," which offered special option packages for West Coast buyers only, in an attempt to take sales away from the imports. It proved quite successful this year. Prices took a sizable jump as the model year began, then were cut back in January. Production fell for Pinto, Mustang II and Maverick in the 1976 model year, but overall production zoomed up almost 19 percent—especially due to Granada demand. Model year sales followed a similar pattern, up 18.5 percent for the year. Major changes in Ford personnel had taken place late in the 1975 model year. Henry Ford II, Lee Iacocca and B.E. Bidwell were the top Ford executives. Pinto was once described as "a car nobody loved, but everybody bought." This was the last year of the allegedly unsafe Pinto gas tank and filler neck, which had resulted in a number of highly publicized and grotesque accident-caused fires that led to massive product-liability lawsuits. The new Maverick Stallion was meant to look like a '60s muscle car, but offered no more performance than other Mavericks. Granada, on the other hand, had proven to be one of the fastest Fords, at least with a "Windsor" 351 cu. in. V-8 under its hood.

1977 FORD

Biggest news for 1977 was the downsizing of Thunderbird (which had actually grown a bit in the past few years). Torino and Elite were dropped, and Pinto restyled with a sportier look. Maverick hung on for one more season without change, and nothing dramatic happened to Granada or LTD. Later in the model year, though, a new Abodied LTD II replaced the abandoned Torino. On the mechanical side, Dura- Spark ignition was supposed to help meet the more stringent emissions standards.

PINTO — FOUR/V-6 — Revised front and rear styling hit Ford's subcompact, offered again in two-door sedan, "three-door" Runabout and station wagon form. Up front was a new "soft" nose with sloping hood and flexible fender extension and stone deflector assembly. The new horizontal-bar crosshatch grille, made of rigid plastic, tilted backward. Twin vertical rectangular park/signal lamps stood on each side of the bright grille, with recessed round headlamps at the outside. Soft urethane headlamp housings were taller than before, but the grille itself was narrower. As in the previous design, 'Ford' letters stood above the grille. At the rear of the two-door sedan and three-door Runabout were new, larger horizontal dual-lens taillamps. New extruded anodized aluminum bumpers went on the front and rear. New body colors were added, and a new vinyl roof grain was available. Runabouts had a new optional all-glass third

1977 Pinto three-door Runabout (F)

door. Inside was new cloth trim, optional on the base high-back bucket seats. A new lower (2.73:1) rear axle ratio went with the standard OHC 140 cu. in. (2.3-liter) four-cylinder engine, which hooked up to a wide-ratio four-speed manual gearbox. The low-budget Pony came with rack-and-pinion steering, front disc brakes, all-vinyl or cloth/vinyl high-back front bucket seats, mini-console, color-keyed carpeting, and argent hubcaps. The base two-door sedan included a color-keyed instrument panel and steering wheel, bright backlight trim, plus bright drip and belt moldings. Runabouts had a fold-down rear seat, rear liftgate, and rubber mat on the load floor. All models except the Pony could have a 170.8 cu. in. (2.8- liter) V-6 instead of the four. Pinto got a shorter manual-transmission shift lever to speed up gear-changes. A new Sports option included a tachometer, ammeter and temperature gauge, new soft-rim sports steering wheel, front stabilizer bar, higher-rate springs, and higher axle ratio. A new Cruising Wagon, styled along the lines of the Econoline Cruising Van, aimed at youthful buyers. It included a front spoiler, blanked rear quarters with glass portholes, styled wheels, Sports Rallye equipment, and carpeted rear section. Other major new options included a flip-up removable sunroof, manual four-way bucket seat, Runabout cargo area cover, two-tone paint, simulated wire wheel covers, and high-altitude option. An Interior Decor Group included Alpine cloth plaid trim on low-back bucket seats.

1977 Maverick coupe (F)

MAVERICK — SIX/V-8 — For its final season, Maverick changed little except for some new body and interior colors, two new vinyl roof colors, and a new vinyl-insert bodyside molding. New options included wire wheel covers, four-way manual bucket seats, and high- altitude option. The optional 302 V-8 got a new variable- venturi carburetor. All engines gained Dura-Spark ignition. There was also a new wide-ratio three-speed manual shift. Revised speedometers showed miles and kilometers. The Decor Group added a halo vinyl roof. Standard powerplant was the 200 cu. in. (3.3-liter) six; optional, either a 250 cu. in. six or 302 cu. in. V-8. Standard equipment included front disc brakes (manual), three-speed column-shift manual transmission, foot parking brake with warning light, and 19.2-gallon gas tank. The full- width bench seat had Random stripe cloth and vinyl trim. Also standard: color-keyed carpeting; armrests with door pull assist handle; flip-open rear quarter windows; and bright drip rail and wheel lip moldings.

1977 Granada sedan (JG)

GRANADA — SIX/V-8 — Styling of the Mercedes-emulating Granada remained similar to 1976, with nine new body colors available. According to Ford's catalog, that carryover design "Looks like cars costing three times as much." A new fully-synchronized four-speed manual transmission with overdrive fourth gear became standard, replacing the former three- speed. That made Granada the first domestic model to offer an overdrive four-speed as standard equipment (except in California,

1977 Granada Sports Coupe (F)

where it was unavailable). Actually, it was the old three-speed gearbox with an extra gear hooked on. Base engine was the 200 cu. in. (3.3-liter) inline six with Dura-Spark ignition. Also standard were front disc brakes, inside hood release, wiper/washer control on the turn signal lever, DR78 x 14 steel-belted radial tires, hood ornament, vinyl-trim bench seats, cigar lighter, and full wheel covers. The body sported window, drip, belt and wheel lip moldings. Two-doors displayed opera lamps. Granada Ghia added a left-hand remote-control mirror, wide color-keyed vinyl-insert bodyside moldings (integral with wheel lip moldings), flight bench seats, and unique wire-style wheel covers. Alternate engine choices were the 250 cu. in. inline six, 302 and 351 V-8. A new variable-venturi carburetor for the 302 V-8 was used only in California. Four basic models were offered: Granada and Ghia two- and four-door sedans. A Sport Coupe package with odense- grain half-vinyl roof became available later. It included white-painted styled steel wheels with bright trim rings, louvered opera window applique, color-keyed lower back panel applique, and rubber bumper guards (front/rear) with wide rub strips. Sport Coupes also had new taillamp lenses with black surround moldings; black wiper arms and window moldings; color-keyed sport mirrors; leather-wrapped sports steering wheel; and reclining bucket seats in simulated perforated vinyl. New Granada options included four-way manual bucket seats, automatic-temperature-control air conditioning, illuminated entry, front cornering lamps, simulated wire wheel covers, white lacy-spoke cast aluminum wheels, wide-band whitewall radials, electric trunk lid release, and high- altitude option.

1977 LTD II hardtop coupe (F)

LTD II — V-8 — Serving as a replacement for the abandoned Torino, the new A-bodied LTD II had similar dimensions, and long-hood styling that wasn't radically different. Wheelbase was 114 inches for the two-door, 118 inches for four-door models. Overall length ranged from 215.5 to 223.1 inches. The goal, according to Ford, was to combine "LTD's traditional high level of workmanship with Mustang's sporty spirit." A wide choice of models was offered: 'S', base and Brougham in two- door hardtop, four-door pillared hardtop or four-door wagon body styles (same selection as Torino). Wagons were offered only this year, and LTD II would last only into the 1979 model year. Among the more noticeable styling features were vertically-stacked quad rectangular headlamps, and doors with a straight beltline. Sharply-tapered opera windows on wide roof pillars stood to the rear of (and higher than) the regular quarter windows of two-doors (except for the 'S' model). Four-doors were also a six-window design. Wraparound parking/signal lamps were fendertip-mounted, and the hood ornament was new. The chrome-plated grille had a crosshatch pattern similar to the full-size LTD, but with a sharper peak. Angled, sharp-edged wraparound vertical taillamps stood at rear quarter panel tips. Inside, LTD II had new seat trim and sew styles, plus new-look door trim and instrument cluster. Standard engine dropped from the 351 of the last Torino to a 302 V-8, now with Dura-Spark ignition and a lower axle ratio. Standard equipment on the budget-priced 'S' included SelectShift automatic transmission; power steering and brakes; coolant recovery system; and Kirsten cloth/vinyl bench seat. The basic LTD II had Ardmore cloth/vinyl flight bench seat, deluxe door trim, rear panel applique, hood ornament, and rocker panel and wheel lip moldings. The top-line Brougham added Doral cloth/vinyl split bench seats, dual horns, electric clock, dual accent paint stripes, and wide color- keyed vinyl-insert bodyside moldings. Standard engine was the 302 cu. in. V-8 with two-barrel carb (351 in California) hooked to SelectShift Cruise-O- Matic. Important new options included the opera windows, illuminated entry, day/date quartz clock, sports steering wheel, cornering lamps, monaural AM/FM radio, stereo radio with quadrasonic tape player, wide whitewall radials, wire wheel covers, and (for two-doors) a half-vinyl roof. Announced for mid-year introduction was a Brougham Creme/Blue package, offered in Creme or dark blue metallic body color with creme or blue vinyl roof. Creme vinyl split-bench seats had blue accent straps and welts.

LTD/CUSTOM 500 — V-8 — Rivals may have shrunk their big cars, but Ford's remained fully full-size once again. According to the factory, that gave LTD a "wider stance, and more road-hugging weight." New colors and fabrics entered LTD interiors this year, but not much else was different. Powertrain changes included improved 351 and 400 cu. in. V-8s with new Dura- Spark ignition, as well as lower rear axle ratios and standard coolant recovery system. New options included illuminated entry, quadrasonic tape player, simulated wire wheel covers, forged aluminum wheels, and wide whitewall radial tires. LTD Brougham was dropped, but the top-rung Landau model took over its position in the pricing lineup. Six basic models were available: LTD and Landau two- and four-door, LTD wagon, and Country Squire wagon. As in 1976, the Custom 500 was for fleet buyers only. LTD's front end looked similar to 1976. A

1977 LTD Landau four-door pillared hardtop (F)

crosshatch grille had four horizontal divider bars and 15 vertical bars, with 'Ford' block letters across the upper header. Three-section wraparound parking/signal lamps stood at fender tips. Standard LTD equipment included a 351 cu. in. (5.8- liter) V-8 with Dura-Spark ignition, SelectShift automatic transmission, power brakes and steering, front bumper guards, Redondo cloth/vinyl bench seat, glovebox and ashtray lamps, hood ornament, and bright hubcaps. Vinyl-insert moldings highlighted door belt, drip, hood, rear, rocker panels, and wheel lips. Landau models added concealed headlamps, as well as an Ardmore cloth/vinyl flight bench seat, electric clock, half or full vinyl roof, rear bumper guards, full wheel covers, wide color-keyed bodyside moldings, and dual-note horn. A Landau Creme and Blue package was announced for mid- year, with choice of color combinations. Creme body color came with a creme or blue vinyl roof; dark blue body with creme or blue vinyl roof. Inside was a creme super-soft vinyl luxury group, and split bench seats with blue welts.

1977 Thunderbird Town Landau hardtop coupe (F)

THUNDERBIRD — V-8 — All-new sheetmetal and sharp downsizing to a 114 inch wheelbase helped concealed the fact that the shrunken Thunderbird was essentially an adaptation of the newly- introduced LTD II. Even if buyers noticed, they might not have cared, since T-Bird's price was also sharply cut by about $2700 from its 1976 level. However, this Thunderbird had less standard equipment and more options than before. Overall length was cut by 10 inches in this new "contemporary" package, ranking as mid- rather than full- size, but with the same six-passenger capacity. This year's side view was much different. A chrome wrapover roof molding with little beveled-glass opera windows stood on the wide, solid B-pillars between the door window and large far-rear coach window, with thin C-pillar. Both of those rear side windows sat higher than the door window. Distinctive features also included concealed headlamps behind large flip-up doors, and functional fender louvers. The chrome-plated crosshatch grille with bright surround molding was similar to the prior design, but with dominant horizontal bars. Park/signal lenses stood at front fender tips. At the rear were new tall, full-width taillamps and a sculptured decklid. A 'Thunderbird' nameplate stood on the deck section that extended down between the taillamps. The hinged grille's lower edge was designed to swing rearward under impact, to avoid damage from slow-speed collision. A smaller engine was installed this year: the 302 cu. in. (5.0-liter) V-8 with new Dura-Spark ignition; but California buyers got a 351 V-8. Both the 351 and 400 cu. in. V-8s were optional. To improve handling, Thunderbird had higher-rate rear springs, larger front stabilizer bar, and standard rear stabilizer bar. Standard fittings included HR78x15 steel-belted radial tires, SelectShift automatic transmission, power steering and brakes, coolant recovery system, Wilshire cloth/vinyl bench seats, AM radio, electric clock, wheel covers, and hood ornament. Moldings for roof wrapover, wheel lips, rocker panels, hood rear, and belt also were standard. Inside was a new five-pod instrument cluster with European-type graphics and simulated burled woodgrain. Sew style of the standard bench seat was new, with optional split-bench and bucket seats. Town Landau added an aluminum roof wrapover applique; unique stripes on upper bodysides, hood/grille opening panel, headlamp doors and decklid; accent paint on wheels and fender louvers; die-cast hood ornament with color-coordinated acrylic insert; and 'Town Landau' script silk-screened on opera windows. Also included: turbine-spoke cast aluminum wheels, dual sport mirrors, cornering lamps, Town Landau plaque at the right of the instrument panel, and an owner's nameplate in 22K gold finish. Major new options included an illuminated entry system, day/date quartz clock, leather-wrapped sports steering wheel, console, turbine-style cast aluminum wheels, automatic- temperature air conditioning, and front and rear vinyl roof. An optional Exterior Decor Group could accent T-Bird's wrapover roof treatment. An Interior Decor Group contained Ardmore and Kasman Knit cloth upholstery, fold-down center armrests, reclining passenger seat, passenger visor vanity mirror, and color-keyed seatbelts. A Silver/Lipstick feature package, announced for mid- year, featured Silver metallic or Lipstick Red body color with Silver or Lipstick Red vinyl roof. Inside was a Dove Grey all-vinyl decor group with either split-bench or bucket seats, with Lipstick Red accent straps and welts, Dove Grey door and quarter trim, and Lipstick carpet molding.

I.D. DATA: As before, Ford's 11-symbol Vehicle Identification Number (VIN) is stamped on a metal tab fastened to the instrument panel, visible through the windshield. Coding is similar to 1976. Model year code changed to '7' for 1977. Code 'Y' for Wixom assembly plant was dropped. One engine code was added: 'Q' modified V8351 2Bbl.

PINTO (FOUR/V-6)

Model Number	Body/Style Number	Body Type & Seating	Factory Price	Shipping Weight	Production Total
10	62B	2-dr. Sedan-4P	3237/3519	2315/2438	48,863
10	62B	2-dr. Pony Sed-4P	3099/--	2313/--	Note 1
11	64B	2-dr. Hatch-4P	3353/3635	2351/2474	74,237
12	73B	2-dr. Sta Wag-4P	3548/3830	2515/2638	79,449
12	73B	2-dr. Sqr Wag-4P	3891/4172	2552/2675	Note 2

Note 1: Pony production included in base sedan figure. **Note 2:** Squire Wagon production is included in standard station wagon total. **Pinto Production Note:** Totals include 22,548 Pintos produced as 1978 models but sold as 1977 models (6,599 two-door sedans, 8,271 hatchback Runabouts, and 7,678 station wagons).

MAVERICK (SIX/V-8)

91	62A	2-dr. Sedan-4P	3322/3483	2782/2947	40,086
92	54A	4-dr. Sedan-5P	3395/3556	2887/3052	58,420

GRANADA (SIX/V-8)

82	66H	2-dr. Sedan-5P	4022/4209	3124/3219	157,612
81	54H	4-dr. Sedan-5P	4118/4305	3174/3269	163,071

GRANADA GHIA (SIX/V-8)

84	66K	2-dr. Sedan-5P	4452/4639	3175/3270	34,166
83	54K	4-dr. Sedan-5P	4548/4735	3229/3324	35,730

LTD II (V-8)

30	65D	2-dr. HT Cpe-6P	4785	3789	57,449
31	53D	4-dr. Pill. HT-6P	4870	3904	56,704
42	71D	4-dr. Sta Wag-6P	5064	4404	23,237
43	71K	4-dr. Squire Wag-6P	5335	4430	17,162

LTD II 'S' (V-8)

25	65B	2-dr. HT Cpe-6P	4528	3789	9,531
27	53B	4-dr. Pill. HT-6P	4579	3894	18,775
40	71B	4-dr. Sta Wag-6P	4806	4393	9,636

LTD II BROUGHAM (V-8)

32	65K	2-dr. HT Cpe-6P	5121	3898	20,979
33	53K	4-dr. Pill. HT-6P	5206	3930	18,851

CUSTOM 500 (V-8)

52	60D	2-dr. Pill. HT-6P	N/A	N/A	4,139
53	53D	4-dr. Pill. HT-6P	N/A	N/A	5,582
72	71D	4-dr. Ranch Wag-6P	N/A	N/A	1,406

LTD (V-8)

62	60H	2-dr. Pill. HT-6P	5128	4190	73,637
63	53H	4-dr. Pill. HT-6P	5152	4240	160,255
74	71H	4-dr. Sta Wag-6P	5415	4635	90,711
76	71K	4-dr. Ctry Sqr-6P	5866	4674	Note 3

Note 3: Country Squire production, and that of wagons with dual-facing rear seats (a $134 option for both standard and Country Squire wagon), is included in basic wagon totals.

LTD LANDAU (V-8)

65	60L	2-dr. Pill. HT-6P	5717	4270	44,396
64	53L	4-dr. Pill. HT-6P	5742	4319	65,030

THUNDERBIRD (V-8)

87	60H	2-dr. HT Cpe-6P	5063	3907	318,140

THUNDERBIRD TOWN LANDAU (V-8)

87	60H	2-dr. HT Cpe-6P	7990	4104	Note 4

Note 4: Town Landau production is included in basic Thunderbird total.

FACTORY PRICE AND WEIGHT NOTE: For Maverick and Granada, prices and weights to left of slash are for six-cylinder, to right for V-8 engine. For Pinto, prices and weights to left of slash are for four-cylinder, to right for V-6 engine.

ENGINE DATA: BASE FOUR (Pinto): Inline. Overhead cam. Four-cylinder. Cast iron block and head. Displacement: 140 cu. in. (2.3 liters). Bore & stroke: 3.78 x 3.13 in. Compression ratio: 9.0:1. Brake horsepower: 89 at 4800 R.P.M. Torque: 120 lbs.-ft. at 3000 R.P.M. Five main bearings. Hydraulic valve lifters. Carburetor: 2Bbl. Motorcraft 5200. VIN Code: Y. OPTIONAL V-6 (Pinto): 60-degree, overhead-valve V-6. Cast iron block and head. Displacement: 170.8 cu. in. (2.8 liters). Bore & stroke: 3.66 x 2.70 in. Compression ratio: 8.7:1. Brake horsepower: 93 at 4200 R.P.M. Torque: 140 lbs.-ft. at 2600 R.P.M. Four main bearings. Solid valve lifters. Carburetor: 2Bbl. Motorcraft 2150. VIN Code: Z. BASE SIX (Maverick, Granada): Inline. Overhead valve. Six-cylinder. Cast iron block and head. Displacement: 200 cu. in. (3.3 liters). Bore & stroke: 3.68 x 3.13 in. Compression ratio: 8.5:1. Brake horsepower: 96 at 4400 R.P.M. Torque: 151 lbs.-ft. at 2000 R.P.M. Seven main bearings. Hydraulic valve lifters. Carburetor: 1Bbl. Carter YFA. VIN Code: T. BASE SIX (Granada Ghia); OPTIONAL (Maverick, Granada): Inline. Overhead valve. Six-cylinder. Cast iron block and head. Displacement: 250 cu. in. (4.1 liters). Bore & stroke: 3.68 x 3.91 in. Compression ratio: 8.1:1. Brake horsepower: 98 at 3400 R.P.M. Torque: 182 lbs.-ft. at 1800 R.P.M. Seven main bearings. Hydraulic valve lifters. Carburetor: 1Bbl. Carter YFA. VIN Code: L. BASE V-8 (LTD II, Thunderbird); OPTIONAL (Maverick, Granada): 90-degree, overhead valve V-8. Cast iron block and head. Displacement: 302 cu. in. (5.0 liters). Bore & stroke: 4.00 x 3.00 in. Compression ratio: 8.4:1. Brake horsepower: 130-137 at 3400-3600 R.P.M. (some Granadas, 122 at 3200). Torque: 243-245 lbs.-ft. at 1600-1800 R.P.M. (some Granadas, 237 at 1600). Five main bearings. Hydraulic valve lifters. Carburetor: 2Bbl. Motorcraft 2150. VIN Code: F. NOTE: Horsepower and torque ratings of the 302 V 8 varied slightly, according to model. OPTIONAL V-8 (LTD II, Thunderbird): 90-degree, overhead valve V-8. Cast iron block and head. Displacement: 351 cu. in. (5.8 liters). Bore & stroke: 4.00 x 3.50 in. Compression ratio: 8.3:1. Brake horsepower: 149 at 3200 R.P.M. Torque: 291 lbs.-ft. at 1600 R.P.M. Five main bearings. Hydraulic valve lifters. Carburetor: 2Bbl. Motorcraft 2150. Windsor engine. VIN Code: H. OPTIONAL V-8 (Granada): Same as 351 cu. in. V-8 above, but Brake H.P.: 135 at 3200 R.P.M. Torque: 275 lbs.-ft. at 1600 R.P.M. BASE V-8 (LTD II wagon, LTD); OPTIONAL (Granada Ghia, LTD II, Thunderbird): Same as 351 cu. in. V-8 above, but Compression: 8.0:1. Brake H.P.: 161 at 3600 R.P.M. Torque: 285 lbs.-ft. at 1800 R.P.M. VIN Code: Q. BASE V-8 (LTD wagon); OPTIONAL (LTD II, Thunderbird, LTD): 90-degree, overhead valve V-8. Cast iron block and head. Displacement: 400 cu. in. (6.6 liters). Bore & stroke: 4.00 x 4.00 in. Compression ratio: 8.0:1. Brake horsepower: 173 at 3800 R.P.M. Torque: 326 lbs.-ft. at 1600 R.P.M. Five main bearings. Hydraulic valve lifters. Carburetor: 2Bbl. Motorcraft 2150. VIN Code: S. OPTIONAL V-8 (LTD): 90-degree, overhead valve V-8. Cast iron block and head. Displacement: 460 cu. in. (7.5 liters). Bore & stroke: 4.36 x 3.85 in. Compression ratio: 8.0:1. Brake horsepower: 197 at 4000 R.P.M. Torque: 353 lbs.-ft. at 2000 R.P.M. Five main bearings. Hydraulic valve lifters. Carburetor: 4Bbl. Motorcraft 4350. VIN Code: A.

Note: A Police 460 cu. in. V-8 was also available for LTD.

CHASSIS DATA: Wheelbase: (Pinto) 94.5 in.; (Pinto wag) 94.8 in.; (Maverick 2dr.) 103.0 in.; (Maverick 4dr.) 109.9 in.; (Granada) 109.9 in.; (LTD II 2dr.) 114.0 in.; (LTD II 4dr./wag) 118.0 in.; (Custom 500/LTD) 121.0 in.; (TBird) 114.0 in. Overall Length: (Pinto) 169.0 in.; (Pinto wag) 178.8 in.; (Maverick 2dr.) 187.0 in.; (Maverick 4dr.) 193.9 in.; (Granada) 197.7 in.; (LTD II 2dr.) 215.5 in.; (LTD II 4dr.) 219.5 in.; (LTD II wag) 223.1 in.; (LTD) 224.1 in.; (LTD wag) 225.6 in.; (TBird) 215.5 in. Height: (Pinto) 50.6 in.; (Pinto wag) 52.0 in.; (Maverick) 53.4-53.5 in.; (Granada) 53.2-53.5 in.; (LTD II 2dr.) 52.6 in.; (LTD II 4dr.) 53.3 in.; (LTD II wag) 54.9 in.; (LTD 2dr.) 53.8 in.; (LTD 4dr.) 54.8 in.; (LTD wag) 56.7 in.; (TBird) 53.0 in. Width: (Pinto) 69.4 in.; (Pinto wag) 69.7 in.; (Maverick) 70.5 in.; (Granada) 74.0 in.; (Granada 4dr.) 74.5 in.; (LTD II) 78.0 in.; (LTD II wag) 79.6 in.; (LTD) 79.5 in.; (LTD wag) 79.9 in.; (TBird) 78.5 in. Front Tread: (Pinto) 55.0 in.; (Maverick) 56.5 in.; (Granada) 59.0 in.; (LTD II) 63.6 in. (LTD) 64.1 in. (TBird) 63.2 in. Rear Tread: (Pinto) 55.8 in.; (Maverick) 56.5 in.; (Granada) 57.7 in.; (LTD II) 63.5 in.; (LTD) 64.3 in. (TBird) 63.1 in. Standard Tires: (Pinto) A78 x 13; (Maverick) C78 x 14, except DR78 x 14 w/V-8 engine; (Granada) DR78 x 14 SBR BSW; (LTD II) HR78 x 14 SBR; (LTD) HR78 x 15 exc. wagon, JR78 x 15; (TBird) HR78 x 15 SBR BSW.

TECHNICAL: Transmission: Three-speed manual transmission (column shift) standard on Maverick. Gear ratios: (1st) 3.56:1; (2nd) 1.90:1; (3rd) 1.00:1; (Rev) 3.78:1. Four-speed overdrive manual standard on Granada: (1st) 3.29:1; (2nd) 1.84:1; (3rd) 1.00:1; (4th) 0.81:1; (Rev) 3.29:1. Four-speed floor shift standard on Pinto: (1st) 3.98:1; (2nd) 2.14:1; (3rd) 1.42:1; (4th) 1.00:1; (Rev) 3.99:1. Pinto station wagon: (1st) 3.65:1; (2nd) 1.97:1; (3rd) 1.37:1; (4th) 1.00:1; (Rev) 3.66:1. Select-Shift three-speed automatic standard on other models, optional on all. Pinto automatic gear ratios: (1st) 2.46-2.47:1; (2nd) 1.46-1.47:1; (3rd) 1.00:1; (Rev) 2.11:1 or 2.19:1. Maverick/Granada/LTD II/LTD/TBird gear ratios: (1st) 2.46:1; (2nd) 1.46:1; (3rd) 1.00:1; (Rev) 2.14:1 to 2.19:1. LTD II/LTD/TBird w/V8351 or V8400: (1st) 2.40:1; (2nd) 1.47:1; (3rd) 1.00:1; (Rev) 2.00:1. Standard final drive ratio: (Pinto four) 2.73:1 w/4spd, 3.18:1 w/auto.; (Pinto V-6) 3.00:1; (Maverick) 2.79:1 or 3.00:1; (Granada) 3.00:1 or 3.4:1; (LTD II) 2.50:1; (LTD) 2.47:1; (TBird) 2.50:1 exc. w/V8400, 3.00:1. Steering: (Pinto) rack and pinion; (others) recirculating ball. Front Suspension: (Pinto) coil springs with short/long control arms, lower leading arms, and anti-sway bar on wagon; (others) coil springs with control arms, lower trailing links and anti-sway bar. Rear Suspension: (Pinto/Maverick/Granada) rigid axle w/semi- elliptic leaf springs; (LTD II/Thunderbird) rigid axle w/lower trailing radius arms, upper oblique torque arms, coil springs and anti-sway bar; (LTD) rigid axle w/lower trailing radius arms, upper torque arms and coil springs, three-link w/track bar. Brakes: Front disc, rear drum; four-wheel discs available on Granada and LTD. Ignition: Electronic. Body construction: (Pinto/Maverick/Granada) unibody; (LTD II/LTD/TBird) separate body and perimeter box frame. Fuel tank: (Pinto) 13 gal.; (Pinto wag) 14 gal.; (Maverick/Granada) 19.2 gal.; (LTD II) 26 gal. exc. wag, 21.3 gal.; (LTD) 24.2 gal. exc. wagon, 21 gal.; (TBird) 26.5 gal.

DRIVETRAIN OPTIONS: Engines: 170 cu. in. V-6: Pinto ($289). 250 cu. in., 1Bbl. six: Maverick/Granada ($102). 302 cu. in., 2Bbl. V-8: Maverick ($161); Granada ($164). 351 cu. in., 2Bbl. V-8: Granada ($212); LTD II/TBird ($66). 400 cu. in., 2Bbl. V-8: LTD II/TBird ($155); LTD II wagon ($100); LTD ($107). 460 cu. in., 4Bbl. V-8: LTD ($297); LTD wagon ($189). Transmission/Differential: SelectShift Cruise-O-Matic: Pinto ($196); Maverick/Granada ($259). Floor shift lever: Granada ($28). Traction-Lok differential: LTD ($57); TBird ($54). Optional axle ratio: Pinto ($14); TBird ($14); LTD ($16). Power Accessories: Power brakes: Pinto ($58); Maverick ($57); Granada ($60). Four-wheel power disc brakes: Granada ($222); LTD ($180). Power steering: Pinto ($124); Maverick/Granada ($131). Suspension: H.D. susp.: Maverick ($17); Granada ($38); LTD ($20). Handling susp.: TBird ($79). H.D. handling susp.: LTD II ($9-$33). Adjustable air shock absorbers: LTD ($46). Other: H.D. battery: Pinto/Maverick ($16); LTD II/TBird ($17); LTD ($18). H.D. alternator: LTD II/TBird ($45). Trailer towing pkg. (heavy duty): LTD II ($93-$151); LTD ($125); TBird ($138). California emission system: Maverick/Granada ($48); LTD ($53); TBird ($70). High- altitude option: Pinto/Maverick/Granada ($39); LTD ($42); TBird ($22).

PINTO CONVENIENCE/APPEARANCE OPTIONS: Option Packages: Cruising wagon option, incl. bodyside tape stripe ($416). Sports rallye pkg. ($89). Exterior decor group ($122-$128). Interior decor group ($160). Convenience light group ($73-$108). Deluxe bumper group ($65). Protection group ($122-$142). Comfort/Convenience: Air conditioner ($446). Rear defroster, electric ($73). Tinted glass ($48). Dual sport mirrors ($45). Entertainment: AM radio ($76); w/stereo tape player ($204). AM/FM radio ($135). AM/FM stereo radio ($184). Exterior: Sunroof, manual ($243). Flip-up open air roof ($147). Half vinyl roof ($133). Glass third door ($13). Metallic glow paint ($58). Two-tone paint/tape treatment ($5- $51). Special paint/tape w/luggage rack: cruising wag ($58). Black narrow vinyl-insert bodyside moldings ($37). Roof luggage rack ($80). Rocker panel moldings ($20). Interior: Four-way driver's seat ($33). Load floor carpet ($23). Cargo area cover ($30). Wheels: Wire wheel covers ($79-$119). Forged aluminum wheels ($57-$183). Styled steel wheels ($98-$127). Wheel covers ($29). Tires: A78 x 13 WSW. A70 x 13 RWL. B78 x 13 BSW/WSW. BR78 x 13 BSW/WSW. BR70 x 13 RWL.

MAVERICK CONVENIENCE/APPEARANCE OPTIONS: Option Packages: Exterior decor group ($105). Interior decor group ($112). Deluxe bumper group ($65). Convenience group ($49-$67). Protection group ($34-$41). Light group ($36). Comfort/Convenience: Air cond. ($446). Rear defogger ($42). Tinted glass ($47-$63). Dual sport mirrors ($14-$27). Entertainment: AM radio ($76); w/tape player ($204). AM/FM radio ($135). AM/FM stereo radio ($222); w/tape player ($317). Exterior: Vinyl roof ($100). Metallic glow paint ($58). Wide vinyl-insert bodyside moldings ($64). Bumper guards, front and rear ($36). Interior: Four-way reclining driver's bucket seat ($33). Reclining vinyl bucket seats ($129). Cloth reclining bucket seats ($25). Vinyl seat trim ($27). Wheels: Wire wheel covers ($86-$119). Lacy spoke aluminum wheels ($218-$251). Styled steel wheels ($100-$131). Tires: C78 x 14 WSW ($33). CR78 x 14 SBR BSW ($89). CR78 x 14 SBR WSW ($121). DR78 x 14 SBR BSW ($89-$112). DR78 x 14 SBR WSW ($121-$144). Space-saver spare ($14) except (NC) with radial tires.

GRANADA CONVENIENCE/APPEARANCE OPTIONS: Option Packages: Sports coupe option ($483-$511). Interior decor group ($192). Luxury decor group ($618). Convenience group ($34-$80). Deluxe bumper group ($65). Light group ($27- $40). Cold weather group ($18-$64). Heavy-duty group ($16- $48). Protection group ($25-$41). Visibility group ($33-$49). Comfort/Convenience: Air cond. ($464); auto-temp ($505). Rear defogger ($46). Rear defroster, electric ($81). Fingertip speed control ($102). Illuminated entry system ($49). Power windows ($101-$141). Power door locks ($66-$93). Power decklid release ($17). Power four-way seat ($127). Tinted glass ($49). Tilt steering wheel ($58). Digital clock ($42). Lighting and Mirrors: Cornering lamps ($42). Dual sport mirrors ($30-$45). Lighted right visor vanity mirror ($42). Entertainment: AM radio ($76); w/tape player ($204). AM/FM radio ($151). AM/FM stereo radio ($222); w/tape player ($317). Exterior: Power moonroof ($833). Full or half vinyl roof ($108). Metallic glow paint ($58). Bodyside/decklid paint stripes ($28). Bodyside/decklid accent moldings ($29). Black vinyl insert bodyside moldings ($37). Rocker panel moldings ($20). Decklid luggage rack ($54). Interior: Console ($69). Four-way driver's seat ($33). Reclining seats ($64). Leather seat trim ($192). Cloth bench seat ($12). Cloth flight bench seat ($19). Deluxe cloth seat/door trim ($93). Color-keyed seatbelts ($18). Wheels: Deluxe wheel covers ($20) exc. Ghia (NC). Wire wheel covers ($65-$86). Styled steel wheels w/trim rings ($81- $101). Lacy spoke cast aluminum wheels ($119-$219). Tires: DR78 x 14 SBR WSW. ER78 x 14 SBR BSW/WSW. FR78 x 14 SBR BSW/WSW/wide WSW. Space-saver spare (NC).

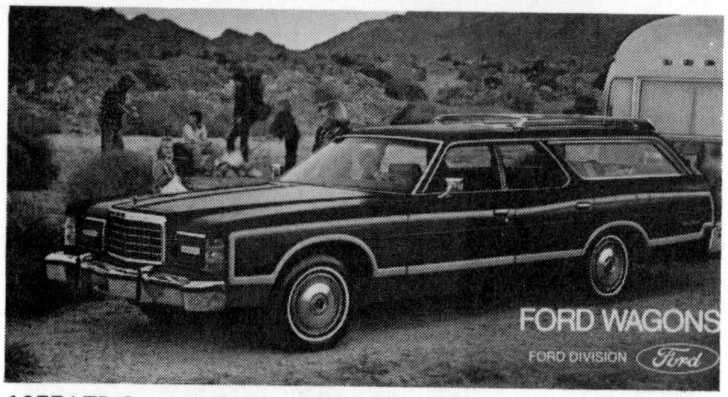

1977 LTD Country Squire wagon (JG)

LTD II CONVENIENCE/APPEARANCE OPTIONS: Option Packages: Squire Brougham option ($203). Sports instrumentation group ($103-$130). Exterior decor group ($225-$276). Accent group ($58). Deluxe bumper group ($72). Light group ($46-$49). Convenience group ($101-$132). Power lock group ($92-$125). Comfort/Convenience: Air cond. ($505); w/auto-temp control ($546). Rear defroster, electric ($87). Fingertip speed control ($93-$114). Illuminated entry system ($51). Tinted glass ($57). Power windows ($114-$158). Power tailgate window: wag ($43). Six-way power seat ($143). Leather-wrapped steering wheel ($39-$61). Tilt steering wheel ($63). Day/date clock ($20-$39). Lighting and Mirrors: Cornering lamps ($43). Remote driver's mirror, chrome ($14). Dual sport mirrors ($51). Entertainment: AM radio ($72). AM/FM radio ($132). AM/FM stereo radio ($192); w/tape player ($266); w/quadrasonic tape player ($399). AM/FM stereo search radio ($349). Dual rear speakers ($43). Exterior: Full vinyl roof ($111-$162). Half vinyl roof ($111). Opera windows ($51). Vinyl-insert bodyside moldings ($39). Metallic glow paint ($62). Two-tone paint ($49-$88). Dual accent paint stripes ($30). Luggage rack ($100). Interior: Bucket seats w/console ($158) exc. Brougham (NC). Rear-facing third seat: wag ($100). Vinyl seat trim ($22). Color-keyed seatbelts ($18). Wheels: Deluxe wheel covers ($36). Luxury wheel covers ($59- $95). Wire wheel covers ($99). Turbine spoke cast aluminum wheels ($234-$270). Tires: H78 x 14 SBR WSW ($45). HR78 x 14 wide-band WSW ($16- $61). JR78 x 14 SBR WSW ($26-$71). HR78 x 15 SBR WSW ($45).

LTD CONVENIENCE/APPEARANCE OPTIONS: Option Packages: Landau luxury group ($403-$563). Convenience group ($88-$136). Light group ($36-$38). Deluxe bumper group ($43-$63). Protection group ($50-$59). Comfort/Convenience: Air cond. ($514); w/auto-temp control ($600). Rear defogger ($46). Rear defroster, electric ($88). Fingertip speed control ($92-$113). Illuminated entry system ($54). Power windows ($114-$170). Power mini-vent and side windows ($246). Power door locks ($72-$116). Six-way power driver's seat ($139); driver and passenger ($275). Tinted glass ($68). Tilt steering wheel ($63). Electric clock ($20). Digital clock ($26-$46). Lighting and Mirrors: Cornering lamps ($46). Driver's remote mirror ($16). Lighted visor vanity mirror ($42-$46). Entertainment: AM radio ($83). AM/FM radio ($147). AM/FM stereo radio ($242); w/tape player ($346); w/quadrasonic tape player ($450). AM/FM stereo search radio ($409). Dual rear speakers ($42). Exterior: Full vinyl roof ($134) exc. Landau two-door (NC). Half vinyl roof ($134). Fender skirts ($45). Metallic glow paint ($63). Dual accent paint stripes ($30). Rocker panel moldings ($28). Vinyl-insert bodyside moldings ($43). Rear bumper guards ($20). Luggage rack ($101). Interior: Dual-facing rear seats: wagon ($134). Split bench seat w/passenger recliner ($149). Leather seat trim ($236). All-vinyl seat trim ($24). Duraweave vinyl trim ($59). Color- keyed seatbelts ($20). Lockable side stowage compartment ($46). Wheels: Full wheel covers ($32). Deluxe wheel covers ($67- $99). Wire wheel covers ($105-$137). Deep-dish aluminum wheels ($251-$283). Tires: HR78 x 15 SBR WSW. JR78 x 15 SBR BSW/WSW/wide WSW. LR78 x 15 SBR WSW.

THUNDERBIRD CONVENIENCE/APPEARANCE OPTIONS: Option Packages: Interior luxury group ($724). Exterior decor group ($317-$368). Interior decor group ($299). Deluxe bumper group ($72). Instrumentation group ($103-$111). Convenience group ($88-$96). Protection group ($43-$47). Light group ($46). Power lock group ($92). Comfort/Convenience: Air cond. ($505); auto-temp ($546). Rear defroster, electric ($87). Fingertip speed control ($93- $114). Illuminated entry system ($51). Tinted glass ($61). Power windows ($114). Six-way power seat ($143). Automatic seatback release ($32). Leather-wrapped steering wheel ($39- $61). Tilt steering wheel ($63). Day/date clock ($20). Lighting and Mirrors: Cornering lamps ($43). Driver's remote mirror, chrome ($14). Dual sport mirrors ($51). Lighted passenger visor vanity mirror ($42-$46). Entertainment: AM/FM radio ($59). AM/FM stereo radio ($120); w/tape player ($193); w/quadrasonic tape player ($326). AM/FM stereo search radio ($276). AM radio delete ($72 credit). Dual rear speakers ($43). Exterior: Power moonroof ($888). Vinyl roof, two-piece ($132). Metallic glow paint ($62). Two-tone paint ($49). Bright wide bodyside moldings ($39). Black vinyl-insert bodyside moldings ($39). Wide color-keyed vinyl-insert bodyside moldings ($51). Dual accent paint stripes ($39).

Interior: Bucket seats w/console ($158) exc. (NC) w/decor group. Leather seat trim ($241). Vinyl seat trim ($22). Color-keyed seatbelts ($18). Wheels: Wire wheel covers ($99) exc. w/decor group ($47 credit). Turbine spoke aluminum wheels ($88-$234). Tires: HR78 x 15 SBR WSW ($45). HR78 x 15 SBR wide WSW ($61). HR70 x 15 SBR WSW ($67). Space-saver spare (NC).

HISTORY: Introduced: October 1, 1976. Model year production: 1,840,427 (incl. Mustangs). Total passenger-car production for the U.S. market of 1,703,945 units (incl. Mustangs) included 236,880 four-cylinder, 262,840 sixes and 1,184,225 V-8s. Calendar year production (U.S.): 1,714,783 (incl. Mustangs). Calendar year sales by U.S. dealers: 1,824,035 (incl. Mustangs). Model year sales by U.S. dealers: 1,749,529 (incl. Mustangs).

NOTE: Totals above do not include Club Wagons, of which 32,657 were sold in the model year.

Historical Footnotes: Both the new LTD II and the shrunken Thunderbird were meant to rival Chevrolet's Monte Carlo and Pontiac Grand Prix. Far more T-Birds came off the line for 1977 than had their predecessors the year before: 301,787 of the new downsized versions versus just 48,196 of the '76 biggies. While Thunderbird's price was cut dramatically this year, LTD cost nearly 7 percent more than in 1976. Since gasoline prices weren't rising, Ford's lineup of relatively small cars wasn't doing as well as hoped. Slight price cuts of smaller models, after their 1977 introduction, didn't help. As a result, plants producing smaller Fords shut down nearly two months earlier for the '78 changeover than did those turning out full-size models. During the model year, Maverick production halted, to be replaced by the new Fairmont compact. A UAW strike against Ford during the model year didn't affect production much, as it was nearly identical to 1976 output. Since the California strategy of special models available on the West coast had been successful the year before, Ford continued that approach.

1978 FORD

Ford's diamond jubilee (75th anniversary) was celebrated for an entire year, topped off by the Diamond Jubilee Edition Thunderbird. New this year was the compact Fairmont, replacing the Maverick which had not been selling well. Granada gained a restyle since its first year since its 1975 debut. Thunderbird now offered a sports decor package. A Pulse Air or Thermactor II emissions control device replaced the complicated standard Thermactor air pump system.

1978 Pinto three-door hatchback (F)

PINTO — FOUR/V-6 — New body and interior colors made up most of the changes in Ford's rear-drive subcompact model. Pintos now carried split-cushion "bucket" style rear seats. New options included white-painted forged aluminum wheels and an accent stripe treatment in four color combinations. New interior colors were jade, tangerine and blue. Seven body colors were available, as well as vinyl roofs in jade or chamois. Pinto's model lineup was the same as before: two-door sedan, three-door hatchback Runabout, and station wagon. Base engine remained the 140 cu. in. (2.3-liter) overhead-cam four, with four-speed manual gearbox. The optional 2.8-liter V-6 engine got a new lightweight plastic fan. Optional power rack-and-pinion steering added a new variable-ratio system similar to that used on Fairmont/Zephyr. A Sports Rallye Package included a tachometer, sport steering wheel, front stabilizer bar, heavy-duty suspension, and 3.18:1 axle. The Rallye Apperaance package contained dual racing mirrors, black front spoiler, gold accent stripes, and blacked-out exterior moldings. The Cruising Wagon option returned, with front spoiler, graphic multi-colored paint striping, cargo area carpeting, styled steel wheels, dual sport mirrors, and steel side panels with round tinted porthole windows near the rear. At mid-year a panel delivery Pinto was added, with full-length flat cargo floor and metal side panels. Most regular production options were available on the panel Pinto (plus a rear-window security screen).

1978 Fairmont sedan (JG)

FAIRMONT — FOUR/SIX/V-8 — With the demise of Maverick came a new, more modern compact model. Fairmont and Zephyr (its corporate twin from Mercury) shared the new unitized "Fox" body/chassis platorm, which began development in the early 1970s and would later carry a number of other FoMoCo models. Fairmont was designed with an emphasis on efficiency and fuel economy, achieved by means of reduced weight and improved aerodynamics. At the same time, Ford wanted to make the best use of interior space, combining the economy of a compact with the spaciousness of a mid-size. Fairmont also offered easy serviceability and maintenance, with a roomy engine compartment and good accessibility. Styling was influenced by Ford's Ghia design studios in Turin, Italy, with clean, straightforward lines. Zephyr differed only in grille design and trim details. The standard Fairmont grille had two horizontal bars and one vertical divider over a subdued crosshatch pattern. Single rectangular headlamps flanked vertical rectangular signal lamps. A single bright molding surrounded the headlamps, park/signal lamps, and grille. Taillamps contained integral backup lamps. Doors and front seatbacks were thinner than Maverick's.

1978 Fairmont Futura Sport Coupe (F)

Fairmont also had a higher roofline and lower beltline. Under the chassis was a new suspension system using MacPherson struts and coil springs up front, and four-link coil spring design at the rear. Front coil springs were mounted on lower control arms instead of around the struts, as in other applications. Rack-and-pinion steering could have unique variable-ratio power assist at extra cost. Base engine was the 140 cu. in. (2.3-liter) "Lima" four, as used in Pintos and Mustangsthe first four-cylinder powerplant in a domestic Ford compact. Options included a 250 cu. in. (3.3-liter) inline six and 302 cu. in. (5.0-liter) V-8. A four-speed manual gearbox was standard, but V-8 models required automatic. Four-cylinder models had standard low- back bucket seats, while sixes and eights held a bench seat. Bodies sported bright grille, headlamp and parking lamp bezels; plus bright windshield, backlight and drip moldings. Standard equipment included B78 x 14 blackwall tires, hubcaps, and bright left-hand mirror. Wagons had CR78 x 14 tires. Wheelbase was 105.5 inches. The opening model lineup included two- and four-door sedans and a station wagon. An ES option (Euro styled), added later, displayed a blacked-out grille and cowl grille, rear quarter window louvers, black window frames and lower back panel, and turbine-spoked wheel covers. Also included: a sports steering wheel, color-keyed interior trim, and unique black instrument panel with gray engine turnings. Its specially-tuned suspension included a rear stabilizer bar. Vent louvers were also available as an individual option. A different looking Futura Sport Coupe, with roofline reminiscent of Thunderbird, joined the original sedans and wagon in December, touted as a sporty luxury model. Futura's unique styling features included quad rectangular headlamps above rectangular parking lamps, a large-pattern crosshatch grille, hood ornament, bright window frames, slanted rear end with wraparound taillamps, wide wrapover roof design, and horizontal louvers in center roof pillars. The coupe, which borrowed a subtitle formerly used on the 1960s Falcon, also added accent paint striping, black luggage area, full-length vinyl bodyside moldings with bright inserts, bright belt moldings, wheel lip moldings, and deluxe wheel covers. Inside, the five-passenger Futura had pleated vinyl bucket seats, woodtone appliques on the dash, and color-keyed seatbelts. William P. Benton, Ford's vice-president (and Ford Division General Manager) said Fairmont Futura "has the best fuel economy in its class, leg, shoulder and hip room of a mid-size car, and responsive handling, plus a rich new look and an array of luxury touches." Four-cylinder powered, with four-speed manual shift, it could deliver 26 MPG on the EPA scale. Options included a divided vinyl roof and seven two- tone combinations, plus color-keyed turbine wheel covers.

GRANADA — SIX/V-8 — Granada and its twin, the Mercury Monarch, took on a fresh look this year with new bright grilles, rectangular headlamps, parking lamps, front bumper air spoiler, wide rub strip moldings, new wraparound taillamps, and lower back panel appliques. Also new on two-doors were "twindow" opera windows split by a bright center bar. This was the first major restyle since the pair's 1974 debut, and the first quad rectangular headlamps in the Ford camp. The spoiler and hood-to-grille-opening panel seal, and revised decklid surface, helped reduce aerodynamic drag. The new crosshatch grille showed a tight pattern, split into sections by two horizontal dividers. A 'Ford' badge went on the lower driver's side of the grille. Rectangular headlamps stood above nearly-as-large rectangular parking lamps, both in a recessed housing. Two-door and four-door sedans were offered again, in base or Ghia trim. Granada Ghia had wide bodyside moldings. A new ESS (European Sports Sedan) option package included a blackout vertical grille texture as well as black rocker panels, door frames and bodyside moldings; black bumper guards and wide rub strips; and a unique interior. ESS had color-keyed wheel covers, a heavy-duty suspension, dual sport mirrors, decklid and hood pinstriping, leather-wrapped steering wheel, FR78 x 14 SBR tires, and individual reclining bucket seats. ESS also had unique half- covered, louvered quarter windows. Low on the cowl was an 'ESS' badge, above 'Granada' script. Other options included an AM/FM stereo with cassette tape player, and a 40-channel CB transceiver. Five new Granada colors were offered this year, and a valino vinyl roof came in three new color choices. The base 200 cu. in. six from 1977 was replaced by a 250 cu. in. (4.1-liter) version, with 302 cu. in. (5.0-liter) V-8 optional. The V-8 could now have a variable-venturi carburetor. The bigger 351 cu. in. V-8 was abandoned.

1978 LTDII Brougham hardtop coupe (F)

LTD II — V-8 — Station wagons left the LTD II lineup this year, since the new Fairmont line included a wagon. Otherwise, models continued as before in 'S', base and Brougham series. Broughams had a full-length bodyside trim strip. Standard engine was again the 302 cu. in. (5.0-liter) V-8 with Cruise- O-Matic transmission, power front disc brakes, and power steering. Options included the 351 and 400 cu. in. V-8 engines, a heavy-duty trailer towing package (for the 400 V-8), and a Sports Appearance package. Two-doors could either have a solid panel at the rear, or the extra (higher) far rear coach-style window. A new bumper front spoiler, hood-to-grille-opening panel seal, revised decklid surface, and new fuel tank air deflector were supposed to cut aerodynamic drag and boost economy. Bumper-to-fender shields were new, too. A revised low-restriction fresh-air intake went on V-8 engines. A new mechanical spark control system was limited to the 351M and 400 cu. in. V-8s. Newly optional this year: a 40-channel CB radio. Mercury Cougar was corporate twin to the LTD II.

1978 LTD Landau pillared sedan (F)

LTD/CUSTOM 500 — V-8 — Full-size Fords were carried over for 1978, with new body colors available but little change beyond a new front bumper spoiler, rear floorpan air deflector, and other aerodynamic additions. The decklid also was new. As before, LTD came in two-door or four-door pillared hardop form, as well as plain-bodyside and Country Squire (simulated wood paneled) station wagons. Custom 500 was the fleet model, sold in Canada. Station wagons could now have optional removable auxiliary cushions for the dual facing rear seats. Among the more than 70 options were new two-tone body colors for the LTD Landau. Air conditioners now allowed the driver to control heating and cooling. A downsized LTD would arrive for 1979, so this was a waiting season.

1978 Thunderbird Town Landau hardtop coupe (JG)

THUNDERBIRD — V-8 — Styling of Ford's personal luxury coupe was similar to that of the downsized 1977 model. Six new body colors, four vinyl roof colors, bold striped cloth bucket seat trim, and new russet interior trim were offered. But the biggest news was the limited-production Diamond Jubilee Edition, commemorating Ford's 75th anniversary. Billed as "the most exclusive Thunderbird you can buy," it included several items never before offered on a TBird. Diamond Jubilee had a unique monochromatic exterior in Diamond Blue metallic or Ember metallic; distinctive matching thickly-padded vinyl roof and color-keyed grille texture; unique quarter-window treatment; accent striping; jewel-like hood ornament; cast aluminum wheels; and bodyside moldings. 'Diamond Jubilee Edition' script went in the opera windows, a hand-painted 'D.J.' monogram on the door (with owner's initials). Also included were color-keyed bumper guard/rub strips and turbine aluminum wheels. Inside was unique "biscuit" style cloth split bench seat trim, leather-covered steering wheel, twin illuminated visor vanity mirrors, seatbelt warning chimes, "super sound" package, and other luxury options. Even the keys were special. Diamond Blue models had a blue luxury cloth interior; Ember bodies, a chamois-color interior. Standard features also included whitewall tires, AM/FM stereo search radio with power antenna, dual sport mirrors, manual passenger recliner, and a hand-stitched leather-covered instrument panel pad above the tachometer and gauge set. Finishing off the interior were ebony woodtone appliques, and 22K gold-finish owner's nameplate. Thunderbird's Town Landau, introduced as a mid-year 1977 model, continued in 1978. Its roofline displayed a brushed aluminum wrapover applique. Also included were pinstriping, script on the opera windows, a color-coordinated jewel-like hood ornament, cast aluminum wheels with accent paint, wide vinyl-insert bodyside moldings, six-way power driver's seat, power windows and door locks, cornering lamps, and interior luxury group. Town Landau came in 14 body colors. Standard fittings also included whitewall tires, accent stripes, lighted visor vanity mirror, and dual sport mirrors. Inside were crushed velour split bench seats with fold-down center armrests. Six velour trim colors were available, along with optional leather seating surfaces. Dashes held burled walnut woodtone appliques. Also on Town Landau: SelectAire conditioner, AM/FM stereo search radio, day/date clock, and trip odometer. Thunderbird's Sports Decor Group included a bold blackout grille, unique imitation decklid straps, paint stripes, twin remote mirrors, spoke-style wheels, and tan vinyl roof with color-keyed rear window moldings. New options included a power radio antenna and 40-channel CB. Standard engine remained the 302 cu. in. (5.0-liter) V-8 with SelectShift automatic, power steering and brakes. Both 351 and 400 cu. in. V-8s were optional. Cougar XR7 was Thunderbird's Mercury counterpart.

I.D. DATA: As before, Ford's 11-symbol Vehicle Identification Number (VIN) is stamped on a metal tab fastened to the instrument panel, visible through the windshield. Coding is similar to 1976-77. Model year code changed to '8' for 1978.

218

PINTO (FOUR/V-6)

Model Number	Body/Style Number	Body Type & Seating	Factory Price	Shipping Weight	Production Total
10	62B	2-dr. Sedan-4P	3336/3609	2337/2463	62,317
10	62B	2-dr. Pony Sed-4P	2995/--	2321/--	Note 1
11	64B	3-dr. Hatch-4P	3451/3724	2381/2507	74,313
12	73B	2-dr. Sta Wag-4P	3794/4067	2521/2637	52,269
12	73B	2-dr. Sqr Wag-4P	4109/4382	2555/2672	Note 2

Note 1: Pony production included in base sedan figure. **Note 2:** Squire Wagon production is included in standard station wagon total.

Pinto Production Note: Totals do not include 22,548 Pintos produced as 1978 models but sold as 1977s (see note following 1977 listing).

1978 Fairmont station wagon (JG)

FAIRMONT (FOUR/SIX)

93	36R	2-dr. Spt Cpe-5P	4044/4164	2605/2648	116,966
91	66B	2-dr. Sedan-5P	3589/3709	2568/2611	78,776
92	54B	4-dr. Sedan-5P	3663/3783	2610/2653	136,849
94	74B	4-dr. Sta Wag-5P	4031/4151	2718/2770	128,390

Fairmont Engine Note: Prices shown are for four-cylinder and six- cylinder engines. A V-8 cost $199 more than the six.

GRANADA (SIX/V-8)

81	66H	2-dr. Sedan-5P	4264/4445	3087/3177	110,481
82	54H	4-dr. Sedan-5P	4342/4523	3122/3212	139,305

GRANADA GHIA (SIX/V-8)

81	66K	2-dr. Sedan-5P	4649/4830	3147/3237	Note 3
82	54K	4-dr. Sedan-5P	4728/4909	3230/3320	Note 3

GRANADA ESS (SIX/V-8)

81	N/A	2-dr. Sedan-5P	4836/5017	3145/3235	Note 3
82	N/A	4-dr. Sedan-5P	4914/5095	3180/3270	Note 3

Note 3: Granada Ghia and ESS production is included in base Granada totals above.

LTD II (V-8)

30	65D	2-dr. HT Cpe-6P	5069	3773	76,285
31	53D	4-dr. Pill. HT-6P	5169	3872	64,133

LTD II 'S' (V-8)

25	65B	2-dr. HT Cpe-6P	4814	3746	9,004
27	53B	4-dr. Pill. HT-6P	4889	3836	21,122

LTD II BROUGHAM (V-8)

30	65K	2-dr. HT Cpe-6P	5405	3791	Note 4
31	53K	4-dr. Pill. HT-6P	5505	3901	Note 4

Note 4: Brougham production is included in LTD II totals above.

LTD LANDAU (V-8)

64	60L	2-dr. Pill. HT-6P	5898	4029	27,305
65	53L	4-dr. Pill. HT-6P	5973	4081	39,836

CUSTOM 500 (V-8)

52	60D	2-dr. Pill. HT-6P	N/A	N/A	1,359
53	53D	4-dr. Pill. HT-6P	N/A	N/A	3,044
72	71D	4-dr. Ranch Wag-6P	N/A	N/A	1,196

Production Note: Custom 500 was produced for sale in Canada. Totals include an LTD 'S' two-door and Ranch wagon for sale in U.S.

LTD (V-8)

62	60H	2-dr. Pill. HT-6P	5335	3972	57,466
63	53H	4-dr. Pill. HT-6P	5410	4032	112,392
74	71H	4-dr. Sta Wag-6P	5797	4532	71,285
74	71K	4-dr. Ctry Sqr-6P	6207	4576	Note 5

Note 5: Country Squire production, and that of wagons with dual-facing rear seats (a $143 option for both standard and Country Squire wagon), is included in basic wagon totals.

THUNDERBIRD (V-8)

87	60H	2-dr. HT Cpe-6P	5411	3907	333,757

THUNDERBIRD TOWN LANDAU (V-8)

87/607	60H	2-dr. HT Cpe-6P	8420	4104	Note 6

Note 6: Town Landau production is included in basic Thunderbird total.

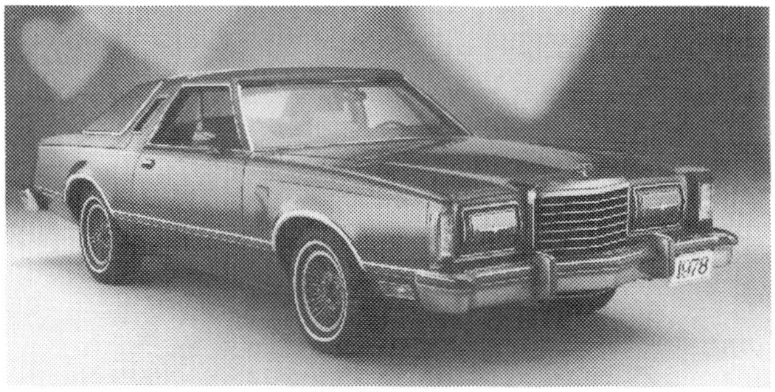

1978½ Thunderbird Diamond Jubilee hardtop coupe (F)

THUNDERBIRD DIAMOND JUBILEE EDITION (V-8)

87/603	60H	2-dr. HT Cpe-6P	10106	4200	18,994

FACTORY PRICE AND WEIGHT NOTE: Pinto/Fairmont prices and weights to left of slash are for four-cylinder, to right for six-cylinder engine. For Granada, prices and weights to left of slash are for six-cylinder, to right for V-8 engine.

ENGINE DATA: BASE FOUR (Pinto, Fairmont): Inline. Overhead cam. Four-cylinder. Cast iron block and head. Displacement: 140 cu. in. (2.3 liters). Bore & stroke: 3.78 x 3.13 in. Compression ratio: 9.0:1. Brake horsepower: 88 at 4800 R.P.M. Torque: 118 lbs.-ft. at 2800 R.P.M. Five main bearings. Hydraulic valve lifters. Carburetor: 2Bbl. Motorcraft 5200. VIN Code: Y. OPTIONAL V-6 (Pinto): 60-degree, overhead-valve V-6. Cast iron block and head. Displacement: 170.8 cu. in. (2.8 liters). Bore & stroke: 3.66 x 2.70 in. Compression ratio: 8.7:1. Brake horsepower: 90 at 4200 R.P.M. Torque: 143 lbs.-ft. at 2200 R.P.M. Four main bearings. Solid valve lifters. Carburetor: 2Bbl. Motorcraft 2150. VIN Code: Z. OPTIONAL SIX (Fairmont): Inline. Overhead valve. Six-cylinder. Cast iron block and head. Displacement: 200 cu. in. (3.3 liters). Bore & stroke: 3.68 x 3.13 in. Compression ratio: 8.5:1. Brake horsepower: 85 at 3600 R.P.M. Torque: 154 lbs.-ft. at 1600 R.P.M. Seven main bearings. Hydraulic valve lifters. Carburetor: 1Bbl. Carter YFA. VIN Code: T. BASE SIX (Granada): Inline. Overhead valve. Six-cylinder. Cast iron block and head. Displacement: 250 cu. in. (4.1 liters). Bore & stroke: 3.68 x 3.91 in. Compression ratio: 8.5:1. Brake horsepower: 97 at 3200 R.P.M. Torque: 210 lbs.-ft. at 1400 R.P.M. Seven main bearings. Hydraulic valve lifters. Carburetor: 1Bbl. Carter YFA. VIN Code: L. BASE V-8 (LTD II, Thunderbird, LTD); OPTIONAL (Fairmont, Granada): 90-degree, overhead valve V-8. Cast iron block and head. Displacement: 302 cu. in. (5.0 liters). Bore & stroke: 4.00 x 3.00 in. Compression ratio: 8.4:1. Brake horsepower: 134 at 3400 R.P.M. (Fairmont, 139 at 3600). Torque: 248 lbs.-ft. at 1600 R.P.M. (Fairmont, 250 at 1600). Five main bearings. Hydraulic valve lifters. Carburetor: 2Bbl. Motorcraft 2150. VIN Code: F. BASE V-8 (LTD wagon); OPTIONAL (LTD II, LTD): 90-degree, overhead valve V-8. Cast iron block and head. Displacement: 351 cu. in. (5.8 liters). Bore & stroke: 4.00 x 3.50 in. Compression ratio: 8.3:1. (LTD, 8.0:1). Brake horsepower: 144 at 3200 R.P.M. (LTD, 145 at 3400). Torque: 277 lbs.-ft. at 1600 R.P.M. (LTD, 273 at 1800). Five main bearings. Hydraulic valve lifters. Carburetor: 2Bbl. Motorcraft 2150. Windsor engine. VIN Code: H. OPTIONAL V-8 (LTD II, Thunderbird): Modified version of 351 cu. in. V-8 above Compression: 8.0:1. Brake H.P.: 152 at 3600 R.P.M. Torque: 278 lbs.-ft. at 1800 R.P.M. VIN Code: Q. OPTIONAL V-8 (LTD II, Thunderbird, LTD): 90-degree, overhead valve V-8. Cast iron block and head. Displacement: 400 cu. in. (6.6 liters). Bore & stroke: 4.00 x 4.00 in. Compression ratio: 8.0:1. Brake horsepower: 166 at 3800 R.P.M. (LTD, 160 at 3800). Torque: 319 lbs.-ft. at 1800 R.P.M. (LTD, 314 at 1800). Five main bearings. Hydraulic valve lifters. Carburetor: 2Bbl. Motorcraft 2150. VIN Code: S. OPTIONAL V-8 (LTD): 90-degree, overhead valve V-8. Cast iron block and head. Displacement: 460 cu. in. (7.5 liters). Bore & stroke: 4.36 x 3.85 in. Compression ratio: 8.0:1. Brake horsepower: 202 at 4000 R.P.M. Torque: 348 lbs.-ft. at 2000 R.P.M. Five main bearings. Hydraulic valve lifters. Carburetor: 4Bbl. Motorcraft 4350. VIN Code: A.

Note: A Police 460 cu. in. V-8 was also available for LTD.

CHASSIS DATA: Wheelbase: (Pinto) 94.5 in.; (Pinto wag) 94.8 in.; (Fairmont) 105.5 in.; (Granada) 109.9 in.; (LTD II 2dr.) 114.0 in.; (LTD II 4dr.) 118.0 in.; (Custom 500/LTD) 121.0 in.; (TBird) 114.0 in. Overall Length: (Pinto) 169.3 in.; (Pinto wag) 179.1 in.; (Fairmont) 193.8 in. exc. Futura coupe, 195.8 in.; (Granada) 197.7 in.; (LTD II 2dr.) 215.5 in.; (LTD II 4dr.) 219.5 in.; (LTD) 224.1 in.; (LTD wag) 225.7 in.; (LTD Landau) 226.8 in.; (TBird) 215.5 in. Height: (Pinto) 50.6 in.; (Pinto wag) 52.1 in.; (Fairmont) 53.5 in.; (Fairmont Futura cpe) 52.2 in.; (Fairmont wag) 54.7 in.; (Granada) 53.2-53.3 in.; (LTD II 2dr.) 52.6 in.; (LTD II 4dr.) 53.3 in.; (LTD 2dr.) 53.8 in.; (LTD 4dr.) 54.8 in.; (LTD wag) 56.7 in.; (TBird) 53.0 in. Width: (Pinto) 69.4 in.; (Pinto wag) 69.7 in.; (Fairmont) 71.0 in.; (Granada) 74.0 in.; (LTD II) 78.6 in.; (LTD) 79.5 in.; (LTD wag) 79.7 in.; (TBird) 78.5 in. Front Tread: (Pinto) 55.0 in.; (Fairmont) 56.6 in.; (Granada) 59.0 in.; (LTD II) 63.6 in. (LTD) 64.1 in. (TBird) 63.2 in. Rear Tread: (Pinto) 55.8 in.; (Fairmont) 57.0 in.; (Granada) 57.7 in.; (LTD II) 63.5 in.; (LTD) 64.3 in. (TBird) 63.1 in. Standard Tires: (Pinto) A78 x 13; (Fairmont) B78 x 14, except CR78 x 14 on wagon; (Granada) DR78 x 14 SBR BSW; (Granada Ghia) ER78 x 14; (LTD II) HR78 x 14 SBR BSW; (LTD) HR78 x 15 exc. wagon, JR78 x 15 and 2dr. w/V8302 engine, GR78 x 15; (TBird) HR78 x 15 SBR BSW.

TECHNICAL: Transmission: Three-speed manual transmission standard on Fairmont six. Gear ratios: (1st) 3.56:1; (2nd) 1.90:1; (3rd) 1.00:1; (Rev) 3.78:1. Four-speed overdrive manual standard on Granada: (1st) 3.29:1; (2nd) 1.84:1; (3rd) 1.00:1; (4th) 0.81:1; (Rev) 3.29:1. Four-speed floor shift standard on Pinto/Fairmont four: (1st) 3.98:1; (2nd) 2.14:1; (3rd) 1.42:1; (4th) 1.00:1; (Rev) 3.99:1. SelectShift three-speed automatic standard on other models, optional on all. Pinto/Fairmont four-cylinder automatic gear ratios: (1st) 2.47:1; (2nd) 1.47:1; (3rd) 1.00:1; (Rev) 2.11:1. LTD II/TBird w/V8351 or V8400: (1st) 2.40:1; (2nd) 1.47:1; (3rd) 1.00:1; (Rev) 2.00:1. Other models: (1st) 2.46:1; (2nd) 1.46:1; (3rd) 1.00:1; (Rev) 2.18:1 to 2.20:1. Standard final drive ratio: (Pinto) 2.73:1 w/4spd; (Fairmont) 3.08:1 or 2.73:1 w/manual, 2.47:1 w/auto.; (Granada) 3.00:1 w/4spd, 2.47:1 w/auto.; (LTD II) 2.75:1 or 2.50:1; (LTD) 2.75:1 or 2.47:1; (TBird) 2.75:1 w/V8302, 2.50:1 w/other V-8 engines. Steering: (Pinto/Fairmont) rack and pinion; (others) recirculating ball. Front Suspension: (Pinto) coil springs with short/long control arms, lower leading arms, and anti-sway bar on wagon; (Fairmont) MacPherson struts with coil springs mounted on lower control arms; (others) coil springs w/lower trailing links and anti-sway bar. Rear Suspension: (Pinto/Granada) rigid axle w/semi-elliptic leaf springs; (Fairmont) four-link coil springs; (LTD II/TBird) rigid axle w/lower trailing radius arms, upper oblique torque arms, coil springs and anti-sway bar; (LTD) rigid axle w/lower trailing radius arms, upper torque arms and coil springs, three-link w/track bar. Brakes: Front disc, rear drum; four-wheel discs available on Granada and LTD. Ignition: Electronic. Body construction: (Pinto/Fairmont/Granada) unibody; (LTD II/LTD/TBird) separate body and perimeter box frame. Fuel tank: (Pinto) 13 gal.; (Pinto wag) 14 gal.; (Fairmont) 16 gal.; (Granada) 18 gal.; (LTD II) 21 gal.; (LTD) 24.2 gal. exc. wagon, 21 gal.; (TBird) 21 gal.

DRIVETRAIN OPTIONS: Engines: 170 cu. in. V-6: Pinto ($273). 200 cu. in., 1Bbl. six: Fairmont ($120). 302 cu. in., 2Bbl. V-8: Fairmont ($319); Granada ($181). 351 cu. in., 2Bbl. V-8: LTD II/LTD/TBird ($157). 400 cu. in., 2Bbl. V-8: LTD II/LTD/TBird ($283); LTD wagon ($126). 460 cu. in., 4Bbl. V-8: LTD ($428); LTD wagon ($271). Transmission/Differential: SelectShift Cruise-O-Matic: Pinto ($281); Fairmont ($368); Fairmont wagon ($281); Granada ($193). Floor shift lever: Fairmont/Granada ($30). First-gear lockout delete: LTD/LTD II ($7). Traction-Lok differential: LTD II/TBird ($59); LTD ($62). Optional axle ratio: Pinto ($13); LTD ($14). Brakes & Steering: Power brakes: Pinto ($64); Fairmont/Granada ($63). Four-wheel power disc brakes: Granada ($300); LTD ($187-$197). Power steering: Pinto ($131); Fairmont ($140); Granada ($148). Semi-metallic front disc pads: LTD/LTD II ($8). Suspension: H.D. susp.: Granada ($27); LTD ($65); TBird ($20). Handling susp.: Fairmont ($30). H.D. handling susp.: LTD II ($36). Adjustable air shock absorbers: LTD ($50). Other: H.D. battery: Fairmont ($17); LTD II/LTD/TBird ($18). H.D. alternator: LTD II/LTD/TBird ($50). Trailer towing pkg. (heavy duty): LTD II/TBird ($184); LTD ($139). California emission system: Pinto/Fairmont/Granada ($69); LTD II/TBird ($75); LTD ($138-$295). High-altitude option (NC).

PINTO CONVENIENCE/APPEARANCE OPTIONS: Option Packages: Cruising wagon option ($365-$401). Cruising wagon paint/tape treatment ($59). Sports rallye pkg. ($76- $96). Rallye appearance pkg. ($176-$201). Exterior decor group ($30-$40). Interior decor group ($149-$181). Interior accent group ($28-$40). Convenience/light group ($81-$143). Deluxe bumper group ($70). Protection group ($83-$135). Comfort/Convenience: Air conditioner ($459). Rear defroster, electric ($77). Tinted glass ($53); windshield only ($25). Cigar lighter ($5). Trunk light ($5). Driver's sport mirror ($16). Dual sport mirrors ($49). Day/night mirror ($7). Entertainment: AM radio ($65); w/digital clock ($47-$119); w/stereo tape player ($119-$192). AM/FM radio ($48-$120). AM/FM stereo radio ($89-$161). Exterior: Flip-up open air roof ($167). Half vinyl roof ($125). Glass third door ($25). Metallic glow paint ($40). Two-tone paint/tape treatment ($40-$49). Accent tape stripe ($49-$59). Black narrow vinyl-insert bodyside moldings ($39). Bumper guards ($37). Roof luggage rack ($59). Rocker panel moldings ($22). Lower bodyside protection ($30). Interior: Four-way driver's seat ($33). Load floor carpet ($23). Cargo area cover ($25). Wheels: Wire wheel covers ($90). Forged aluminum wheels ($173-$252); white ($187-$265). Styled steel wheels ($78). Tires: A78 x 13 WSW. A70 x 13 RWL. B78 x 13 BSW/WSW. BR78 x 13 BSW/WSW. BR70 x 13 RWL.

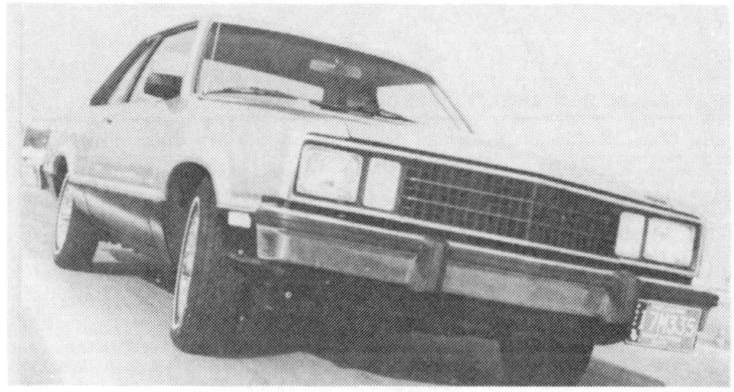

1978 Fairmont ES Sport Coupe (JG)

FAIRMONT CONVENIENCE/APPEARANCE OPTIONS: Option Packages: ES option: sedan ($300). Squire option ($365). Exterior decor group ($214). Exterior accent group ($96). Interior decor group ($176-$301). Interior accent group ($89-$94). Deluxe bumper group ($70). Convenience group ($29-$60). Appearance protection group ($36-$47). Light group ($35-$40). Comfort/Convenience: Air cond. ($465). Rear defogger ($47). Rear defroster, electric ($84). Tinted glass ($52); windshield only ($25). Sport steering wheel ($36). Electric clock ($18). Cigar lighter ($6). Interval wipers ($29). Liftgate wiper/washer: wag ($78). Trunk light ($4). Left remote mirror ($19). Dual bright mirrors ($13-$36). Day/night mirror ($8). Entertainment: AM radio ($72); w/8track tape player ($192). AM/FM radio ($120). AM/FM stereo radio ($176); w/8track or cassette player ($243). Exterior: Vinyl roof ($89-$124). Metallic

glow paint ($46). Two-tone paint ($42). Accent paint stripe ($30) exc. Futura (NC). Pivoting front vent windows ($37-$60). Rear quarter vent louvers ($33). Bodyside moldings ($39). Rocker panel moldings ($22). Bumper guards, front and rear ($37). Luggage rack ($72). Lower bodyside protection ($30-$42). Interior: Bucket seat, non-reclining ($72). Bench seat ($72 credit). Cloth seat trim ($19-$37). Vinyl seat trim ($22). Lockable side storage box ($19). Wheels: Hubcaps w/trim rings ($34) exc. Futura (NC). Deluxe wheel covers ($33). Turbine wheel covers ($33-$66). Wire wheel covers ($48-$114). Cast aluminum wheels ($210-$276). Tires: B78 x 14 WSW. BR78 x 14 BSW/WSW. C78 x 14 BSW/WSW. CR78 x 14 BSW/WSW. DR78 x 14 SBR BSW/WSW/RWL.

GRANADA CONVENIENCE/APPEARANCE OPTIONS: Option Packages: Luxury interior group ($476). Interior decor group ($211). Convenience group ($30-$89). Deluxe bumper group ($70). Light group ($30-$43). Cold weather group ($37- $54). Heavy-duty group ($37-$54). Protection group ($25-$43). Visibility group ($4-$58). Comfort/Convenience: Air cond. ($494); auto-temp ($535). Rear defogger ($47). Rear defroster, electric ($84). Fingertip speed control ($55-$102). Illuminated entry system ($49). Power windows ($116-$160). Power door locks ($76-$104). Power decklid release ($19). Auto. parking brake release ($8). Power four-way seat ($90). Tinted glass ($54); windshield only ($25). Tilt steering wheel ($58). Digital clock ($42). Lighting and Mirrors: Cornering lamps ($42). Trunk light ($4). Left remote mirror ($14). Dual remote mirrors ($31- $46). Dual sport mirrors ($42-$53). Day/night mirror ($8). Lighted right visor vanity mirror ($34). Entertainment: AM radio ($72); w/tape player ($192). AM/FM radio ($135). AM/FM stereo radio ($176); w/8track or cassette player ($243); w/quadrasonic tape ($365). AM/FM stereo search radio ($319). CB radio ($270). Exterior: Power moonroof ($820). Full or half vinyl roof ($102). Metallic glow paint ($46). Bodyside/decklid paint stripes ($29). Bodyside accent moldings ($33). Vinyl insert bodyside moldings ($39). Rocker panel moldings ($23). Interior: Console ($75). Four-way driver's seat ($33). Reclining seats (NC). Leather seat trim ($271). Flight bench seat (NC). Cloth flight bench seat ($54). Deluxe cloth seat/door trim: Ghia/ESS ($99). Color-keyed seatbelts ($19). Wheels: Deluxe wheel covers ($37) exc. Ghia/ESS (NC). Wire wheel covers ($59-$96). Styled steel wheels w/trim rings ($59-$96). Lacy spoke aluminum wheels ($205-$242); white ($218-$255). Tires: DR78 x 14 SBR WSW. ER78 x 14 SBR BSW/WSW. FR78 x 14 SBR BSW/WSW/wide WSW. Inflatable spare (NC).

LTD II CONVENIENCE/APPEARANCE OPTIONS: Option Packages: Sports appearance pkg. ($216-$363). Sports instrumentation group ($111-$138). Sports touring pkg. ($287- $434). Deluxe bumper group ($76). Light group ($49-$54). Convenience group ($107-$139). Power lock group ($100-$132). Front protection group ($46-$58). Comfort/Convenience: Air cond. ($543); w/auto-temp control ($588). Rear defroster, electric ($93). Fingertip speed control ($104-$117). Illuminated entry system ($54). Tinted glass ($62); windshield only ($28). Power windows ($126- $175). Power door locks ($71-$101). Six-way power seat ($149). Auto. parking brake release ($9). Leather-wrapped steering wheel ($51-$64). Tilt steering wheel ($70). Electric clock ($20). Day/date clock ($22-$42). Lighting, Horns and Mirrors: Cornering lamps ($46). Trunk light ($4). Dual-note horn ($7). Remote driver's mirror ($16). Dual chrome mirrors ($7). Dual sport mirrors ($29- $58). Lighted visor vanity mirror ($33-$37). Entertainment: AM radio ($79). AM/FM radio ($132). AM/FM stereo radio ($192); w/tape player ($266); w/quadrasonic tape player ($399). AM/FM stereo search radio ($349). CB radio ($295). Dual rear speakers ($46). Exterior: Full or half vinyl roof ($112). Opera windows ($51). Vinyl-insert bodyside moldings ($42). Wide bright bodyside moldings ($42). Rocker panel moldings ($29). Metallic glow paint ($62) exc. (NC) w/sports pkg. Two-tone paint ($53). Dual accent paint stripes ($33). Lower bodyside protection ($33). Interior: Bucket seats w/console ($211) exc. Brougham ($37). Vinyl seat trim ($24). Cloth/vinyl seat trim ($24). Front floor mats ($20). H.D. floor mats ($9). Color-keyed seatbelts ($21). Wheels: Deluxe wheel covers ($38). Luxury wheel covers ($62- $100). Wire wheel covers ($105-$143) exc. (NC) w/sports pkg. Cast aluminum wheels ($196-$301). Tires: HR78 x 14 SBR WSW ($46). HR78 x 14 wide-band WSW ($66). HR78 x 14 SBR RWL ($62). HR78 x 15 SBR WSW ($68). Inflatable spare (NC).

LTD CONVENIENCE/APPEARANCE OPTIONS: Option Packages: Landau luxury group ($457-$580). Convenience group ($96-$146). Light group ($26-$38). Deluxe bumper group ($50-$72). Protection group ($45-$53). Comfort/Convenience: Air cond. ($562); w/auto-temp control ($607). Rear defogger ($50). Rear defroster, electric ($93). Fingertip speed control ($104-$117). Illuminated entry system ($54). Power windows ($129-$188). Power door locks ($82- $153). Six-way power driver's seat ($149); driver and passenger ($297). Tinted glass ($75); windshield only ($28). Tilt steering wheel ($70). Auto. parking brake release ($8). Electric clock ($21). Digital clock ($28-$49). Lighting, Horns and Mirrors: Cornering lamps ($46). Trunk light ($4). Dual-note horn ($7). Driver's remote mirror ($16). Dual remote mirrors ($32-$47). Lighted visor vanity mirror ($33-$37). Entertainment: AM radio ($79). AM/FM radio ($132). AM/FM stereo radio ($192); w/tape player ($266); w/quadrasonic tape player ($399). AM/FM stereo search radio ($349). Dual rear speakers ($46). Exterior: Power moonroof ($896). Full vinyl roof ($141) exc. Landau two-door (NC). Half vinyl roof ($141). Metallic glow paint ($62). Dual accent paint stripes ($33). Rocker panel moldings ($29). Vinyl-insert bodyside moldings ($42). Rear bumper guards ($22). Luggage rack ($80). Interior: Dual-facing rear seats: wagon ($143). Split bench seat w/passenger recliner ($141-$233). Leather seat trim ($296). All-vinyl seat trim ($24). Duraweave vinyl trim ($50). H.D. floor mats ($9). Color-keyed seatbelts ($21). Lockable side stowage compartment ($33). Wheels: Full wheel covers ($38). Deluxe or color-keyed wheel covers ($61-$99). Wire wheel covers ($99-$137). Deep-dish aluminum wheels ($263-$301). Tires: GR78 x 15 SBR WSW. HR78 x 15 SBR BSW/WSW. JR78 x 15 SBR BSW/WSW/wide WSW. LR78 x 15 SBR WSW.

THUNDERBIRD CONVENIENCE/APPEARANCE OPTIONS: Option Packages: Sports decor group ($396-$446). Interior luxury group ($783). Exterior decor group ($332-$382). Interior decor group ($316). Deluxe bumper group ($76). Sports instrumentation group ($111-$118). Convenience group ($93-$103). Protection group ($46-$50). Light group ($49). Power lock group ($100). Sound insulation pkg. ($29). Comfort/Convenience: Air cond. ($543); auto-temp ($588) exc. special editions ($45). Rear defroster, electric ($93). Fingertip speed control ($104-$117). Illuminated entry system ($54). Tinted glass ($66); windshield only ($28). Power windows ($126). Six-way power seat ($149). Automatic seatback release ($33). Auto. parking brake release ($9). Leather- wrapped steering wheel ($51-$64). Tilt steering wheel ($70). Day/date clock ($22). Lighting and Mirrors: Cornering lamps ($46). Trunk light ($4). Driver's remote mirror, chrome ($16). Dual sport mirrors ($8-$58). Lighted visor vanity mirror ($33-$37). Entertainment: AM/FM radio ($53). AM/FM stereo radio ($113); w/tape player ($187); w/quadrasonic tape player ($320) exc. special editions ($50). AM/FM stereo search radio ($270). CB radio ($295). AM radio delete ($79 credit). Power antenna ($45). Dual rear speakers ($46). Exterior: Power moonroof ($691). Vinyl roof, two-piece ($138). Metallic glow paint ($62). Two-tone paint ($53). Dual accent paint stripes ($46). Bright wide bodyside moldings ($42). Vinyl bodyside moldings ($42). Wide color-keyed bodyside moldings ($54). Rocker panel moldings ($29). Bumper guards ($42). Interior: Bucket seats w/console ($211) exc. ($37) w/decor group. Leather/vinyl seat trim ($296). Vinyl seat trim ($24). Front floor mats ($20). Trunk trim ($39). Color-keyed seatbelts ($21). Wheels: Wire wheel covers ($105). Styled wheels ($146). Tires: GR78 x 15 WSW ($46). HR78 x 15 BSW ($22). HR78 x 15 SBR WSW ($20-$68). HR78 x 15 SBR wide WSW ($88). HR70 x 15 SBR WSW ($22-$90). Inflatable spare (NC).

HISTORY: Introduced: October 7, 1977 except Fairmont Futura Coupe, December 2, 1977. Model year production: 1,929,254 (incl. Mustangs). Total passenger-car production for the U.S. market of 1,777,291 units (incl. Mustangs) included 285,878 four- cylinder, 511,500 sixes and 979,913 V-8s. Calendar year production (U.S.): 1,698,136 (incl. Mustangs). Calendar year sales by U.S. dealers: 1,768,753 (incl. Mustangs). Model year sales by U.S. dealers: 1,830,417 (incl. Mustangs).

NOTE: Totals above do not include Club Wagons, of which 43,917 were sold in the model year; or imported Fiestas, which recorded sales of 81,273).

Historical Footnotes: Model year sales increased modestly for 1978, though production slipped a bit. Major recalls of more than 4 million vehicles, however (and investigations of many more), did Ford's reputation no good. Most serious were the Pintos recalled for gas tanks that might burst into flame, followed by automatic transmissions that were alleged to jerk suddenly from "park" to "reverse" (a situation that never was fully resolved). At this time, too, Ford president Lee Iacocca was replaced by Philip Caldwell; and Iacocca reemerged within a few months as the new head of Chrysler. The new compact Fairmont sold far better than its predecessor Maverick: 417,932 Fairmonts versus just 105,156 Mavericks sold in 1977. Fairmont sold even better as a first- year car than had Mustang when it was introduced. 1977 had been Thunderbird's best sales year, and it sold well in 1978 too. Granada and LTD II sales plummeted for the model year. Fairmont was "the most successful new-car nameplate ever introduced by a domestic manufacturer and Ford's top selling car line in 1978," said Walter S. Walla, Ford Division General Manager. It was also highly rated by the auto magazines. Readers of *Car and Driver* called it "most significant new American car for 1978." Computer-assisted design techniques had been used to develop the Fairmont/Zephyr duo, along with over 320 hours of wind-tunnel testing. Corporate Average Fuel Economy (CAFE) standards began this year. Automakers' fleets would be required to meet a specified average miles-per-gallon rating each year for the next decade, with 27.5 MPG the ultimate goal. Fairmont, in fact, was designed with the CAFE ratings in mind, which required that Fords average 18 MPG. This year's model introduction meetings had been held in the Detroit and Dearborn area for the first time since 1959. More than 15,000 dealers, general managers and spouses attended. The international emphasis was highlighted by a "flags of the world of Ford" display at the world headquarters, in a special ceremony. On the import front, Ford began to import the tiny front-wheel drive Fiesta from its German plant.

1979 FORD

Full-size Fords finally received their expected downsizing, two years later than equivalent General Motors models. Mustang (listed separately) also offered some big news for 1979 with a total restyle. Pinto got a more modest alteration, while Thunderbird switched grilles. CAFE standards rose from 18 to 19 MPG this year, prompting powertrain refinements. The 2.3-liter four on Pinto/Fairmont got an aluminum or plastic fan, oil filler cap and rear cover plate. The 2.8-liter V-6 got a new camshaft design. An aluminum intake manifold went on the 302 cu. in. V-8 in LTD and some Granadas. The 351 cu. in. V-8 ('W' version), optional in LTD, LTD II and Thunderbird, lost up to 40 pounds by switching to an aluminum intake manifold, water pump and rear cover.

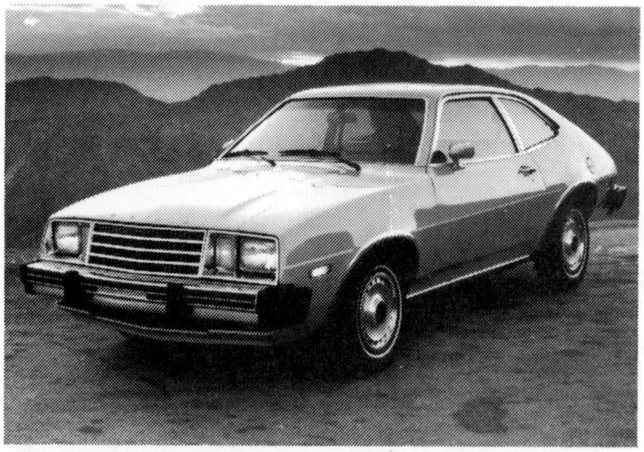

1979 Pinto three-door Runabout (F)

PINTO — FOUR/V-6 — Restyling brought the subcompact Pinto a new front-end look with single rectangular headlamps in bright housings, as well as a new sloping hood and fenders, and horizontal-style argent grille. Single vertical parking lamps stood inboard of the headlamps, which were recessed farther back than the parking lamps. The slat-style grille contained three horizontal divider bars. 'Ford' block letters stood at the hood front. New sculptured-look front/rear aluminum bumpers had black rub strips and end sections. Small backup lenses were at inner ends of the new sedan/Runabout horizontal-design taillamps, extending through the upper, center and lower sections. Full wheel covers took on a new design. Inside, a new instrument panel and pad held rectangular instrument pods. The redesigned cluster now included a speedometer graduated in miles and kilometers, fuel gauge, and warning lights with symbols. New body and interior colors were available. As before, two-door sedan, "three-door" hatchback Runabout and station wagon models were offered. A Cruising Package became optional on both Runabouts and wagons, featuring multi-color bodyside paint/tape treatment and black louvers on the wagon's liftgate window. There was also a new ESS option for sedans and Runabouts, with black grille and exterior accents, black-hinged glass third door, wide black bodyside moldings, and sports-type equipment. Other new options included lacy-spoke cast aluminum wheels, AM/FM stereo radio with cassette, separate light and convenience groups (formerly combined), heavy-duty battery, and a revised Exterior Decor group. Pinto's standard equipment list grew longer this year, adding an AM radio, power brakes, electric rear defroster, and tinted glass. The low-budget Pony lacked some of these extras. Standard engine remained the 140 cu. in. (2.3-liter) overhead-cam four, with four-speed gearbox; automatic and V-6 optional. Oil-change intervals were raised to 30,000 miles. The V-6 added a higher-performance camshaft, while V-6 automatic transmissions were meant to offer higher R.P.M. shift points to improve acceleration.

FAIRMONT — FOUR/SIX/V-8 — Appearance of the year-old compact didn't change this year. Model lineup included two-door and four-door sedans, a station wagon, and the uniquely-styled Futura coupe. Seven new body colors and four new vinyl roof colors were available. Availability of the distinctive tu-tone paint treatment was expanded to sedans, as well as the Futura. A four-speed overdrive manual

1979 Fairmont Squire wagon (F)

transmission with new single-rail shifter design replaced the former three-speed, with either the 200 cu. in. (3.3-liter) inline six or 302 cu. in. (5.0- liter) V-8. (V-8s formerly came only with automatic.) Base engine remained the 140 cu. in. (2.3-liter) four, with non- overdrive four-speed manual gearbox. The six was now offered on California wagons. Ignition and door locks were modified to improve theft- resistance. A lower axle ratio (2.26:1) came with the V-8 and automatic. Inside was a new dark walnut woodtone instrument cluster applique. New options included tilt steering, new- design speed control, performance instruments (including tachometer and trip odometer), ultra-fidelity premium sound system, remote decklid release, styled steel wheels with trim rings, and flip-up open-air roof. Wide vinyl-insert bodyside moldings were available on Futura. The Futura Sports Group included unique tape striping, charcoal argent grille and color-keyed turbine wheel covers, but dispensed with the usual hood ornament. Futura again sported a unique front end with quad rectangular headlamps, wrapover roof pillar, wide tapered Bpillars, and wraparound taillamps. Fairmont's ES package was offered again. It included a blackout grille, black cowl grille, bright belt moldings, black window frames and quarter window vent louvers, black/bright bodyside moldings, dual black sail-mount sport mirrors (left remote), turbine wheel covers, handling suspension with rear stabilizer bar, and 5.5 inch wheels.

1979 Granada Ghia coupe (F)

GRANADA — SIX/V-8 — Billed as "An American Classic" (playing on its Mercedes lookalike origins), Granada changed little for 1979. Few customers had chosen four-wheel disc brakes, so that option was dropped. Both the standard 250 cu. in. (3.3-liter) inline six and 302 cu. in. (5.0-liter) V-8 came with a four-speed overdrive manual gearbox that used a new enclosed single-rail shift mechanism. As before, two- and four-door sedans were produced, in base, Ghia or ESS trim. Four new body colors and two new vinyl roof colors were offered, along with a paint and tape treatment option. Base models got all-bright versions of the '78 Ghia wheel cover. A thin, contemporary wheel lip molding replaced Ghia's former wider moldings. Ghia seats had a new sew style, as well as all-vinyl door trim with carpeted lower panels. Leather/vinyl trim was now available with bucket seats in the Interior Decor group. New soft Rossano cloth became optional on the base flight bench seat. New Willshire cloth luxury trim was available. Bright moldings replaced the color-keyed moldings on the vinyl roof. A new lightweight aluminum intake manifold went on V-8s in four-doors. Electronic voltage regulators were new. Ignition locks offered improved theft-resistance. New options included tone-on-tone paint in five color combinations. Dropped were white lacy-spoke aluminum wheels, Traction-Lok axle, and the Luxury Interior Group. This year's ESS option was identified by 'Granada' script above the 'ESS' badge, rather than below, on the lower cowl. Granada ESS had blacked-out grille and exterior trim, color-keyed wheel covers and dual mirrors, decklid and hood pinstriping, individually reclining bucket seats with Euro headrests, and leather-wrapped steering wheel. Optional speed control for the ESS included a black leather-wrapped steering wheel.

1979 LTD II hardtop coupe (F)

LTD II — V-8 — Not enough buyers had found LTD II appealing, so this would be its third and final season. Not much was new this year, except for a redesigned front bumper spoiler, corrosion-resistant plastic battery tray, and electronic voltage regulator. Seven body colors were new, as were front and full vinyl roofs. Broughams had new interior fabric selections. All models had standard flight bench seating with fold-down center armrest. The 400 cu. in. V-8 option was abandoned. Base engine remained the 302 cu. in. (5.0-liter) V-8, with 351 V-8 optional. Automatic transmission was standard. A newly optional 27.5 gallon gas tank suggested that LTD II's economy problems hadn't quite been corrected by the use of a lighter weight front bumper this year, or by carburetor refinements. Rear bumper guards became standard, and the ignition lock was modified. The Sports Touring Package included two- tone paint with tape breaks on the bodyside/hood/lower back panel, as well as a grille badge and Magnum 500 wheels with HR78 x 14 RWL tires. A Sports Appearance Group for two-doors added the bold tri-color tape stripes. As before, two-door hardtop and four-door pillared hardtop bodies were offered, in base, Brougham or 'S' trim. The low-cost 'S' model had an upgraded bench seat and woodtone instrument panel applique this year.

1979 LTD Country Squire station wagon (F)

LTD — V-8 — Substantial downsizing made this year's LTD the ninth all-new full-size model in the company's history. Still built with body-on-frame construction, it was intended to be space- efficient as well as fuel-efficient, a result of over 270 hours of wind-tunnel testing. Riding a 114.4 inch wheelbase (7 inches shorter than before), the reduced LTD managed to increase its former interior space while shrinking on the outside. A conventionaL sedan design replaced the former pillared hardtop style. Door openings grew larger, and doors thinner. Both the cowl and hood were lower. So was the car's beltline. Glass area expanded. Overall, the new design was slightly taller and more boxy. Inside, LTD's seating position was higher. LTD's tighter crosshatch grille was split into two side- by-side sections by a narrow vertical divider, and topped by a wide upper bar. The grille looked flatter than before. 'Ford' letters went on the driver's side of the upper grille header. Base models displayed single rectangular headlamps with outboard fendertip signal lamps, while quad rectangular headlamps above rectangular park/signal lamps went on Landau and Squire models. Front marker lenses wrapped around fender sides, matching the headlamps and parking lamps. A tall, narrow ornament adorned the hood. Two-doors were four-window design with a slim coach-style quarter window. Landaus had new rear-pillar coach lamps. Country Squire wagons showed a new woodtone applique treatment. Large vertical rectangular taillamps were rather wide, each with a small backup lens below. The recessed license plate housing was in the decklid's center, with 'Ford' letters on left of decklid. Inside were thin-back seats with foam padding over flex-o-lator cushion support, and a four- spoke soft-rim steering wheel. A steering-column stalk held the dimmer, horn and wiper/washer controls. Door-lock plungers moved to the armrests to improve theft-resistance. Lockable side stowage compartments were standard on wagons. Base engine, except on wagons with California emissions, was the 302 cu. in. (5.0-liter) V-8. That engine had a new single accessory-drive belt operating the fan/water pump, alternator, and power steering pump. A variable-venturi carburetor became standard on both the 302 and the optional 351 V-8 engines. Up front was a new short/long Aarm coil spring front suspension with link-type stabilizer bar; at the rear, a new four-bar link coil spring setup. Front disc brakes used a new pin-slider design. LTD's option list still included speed control, tilt steering, automatic-temperature-control air conditioning, heavy-duty trailer towing package, and the 351 V-8, along with other popular extras. New options this year were: special handling suspension system, premium stereo sound, digital clock with time/date/elapsed time, flight bench seating with dual reclining seatbacks, power antenna, and 40-channel CB radio. Also available: window-frame-mounted mirrors, bumper rub strips, electronic AM/FM stereo search radio with Quadrasonic8 tape player, AM/FM stereo radio with cassette, tu-tone paint/tape treatment, and Exterior Accent Group. The Convenience Group added a trip odometer and low fuel/low washer fluid warning lights. A "resume" feature was added to the fingertip speed control; a left-hand recliner added to split bench seats. Options dropped included the 400 and 460 V-8 engines, Traction-Lok, four-wheel disc brakes, leather seat trim, color-keyed wheel covers, deep-dish aluminum wheels, and fender skirts.

1979 Thunderbird Heritage Edition hardtop coupe (F)

THUNDERBIRD — V-8 — A much bolder, heavier-looking box-texture grille greeted TBird customers this year. A large 4x4 grid pattern (just three horizontal and three vertical bars) stood in front of thin vertical bars. A new spoiler went below the front bumper. Clear fendertip parking lamps with adjoining amber marker lenses each held three horizontal divider strips. Separate large rectangular taillamps, replacing the

former full-width units, were essentially a rectangle within a rectangle, with TBird emblem in the center. A single backup lamp stood between them, centered over new standard rear bumper guards. Thunderbird also had a new electronic voltage regulator, and carburetor refinements on the standard 302 cu. in. (5.0-liter) V-8. Door and ignition locks were modified for theft protection. Eight body colors, five vinyl roof colors, and four interior trim colors were new. Standard seating was now the flight bench design with Rossano cloth seating surfaces and large fold-down front armrest. Front fenders held a vertical set of "louvers." Bodysides showed narrow opera windows, with large rear swept-back side windows. Headlamp covers held a wide insignia, plus 'Thunderbird' script on the left one. A posh new Heritage model replaced the Diamond Jubilee edition. 'Heritage' script went on the huge blank Cpillar, as that model had no large rear side window. Heritage had two monochromatic body color themes in maroon or light medium blue, with formal padded vinyl roof. Equipment included 36- ounce cut-pile carpeting, split bench seats in soft velour cloth (or optional leather seating surfaces), leather- wrapped steering wheel, sports instrument panel with tachometer and gauges, driver's lighted visor vanity mirror, and AM/FM stereo radio. Town Landau had a brushed aluminum wrapover applique, color-keyed hood ornament, cast aluminum wheels with accent paint, and wide vinyl-insert bodyside moldings. New options included an extended-range 27.5-gallon gas tank (standard on Town Landau and Heritage), AM/FM stereo radio with cassette, mud/stone deflectors, and ultra-soft leather/vinyl upholstery (for Heritage). Bucket seats and a console could be ordered separately, or as a no-cost extra with the Interior Decor Group.

I.D. DATA: Ford's 11-symbol Vehicle Identification Number (VIN) is stamped on a metal tab fastened to the instrument panel, visible through the windshield. The first digit is a model year code ('9' 1979). The second letter indicates assembly plant: 'A' Atlanta, GA; 'B' Oakville, Ontario (Canada); 'E' Mahwah, NJ; 'G' Chicago; 'H' Lorain, Ohio; 'J' Los Angeles; 'K' Kansas City, MO; 'S' St. Thomas, Ontario; 'T' Metuchen, NJ; 'U' Louisville, KY; 'W' Wayne, MI. Digits three and four are the body serial code, which corresponds to the Model Numbers shown in the tables below (e.g., '10' Pinto 2-dr. sedan). The fifth symbol is an engine code: 'Y' L4-140 2Bbl.; 'Z' V6170 2Bbl.; 'T' L6200 1Bbl.; 'L' L6250 1Bbl.; 'F' V8302 2Bbl.; 'H' V8351 2Bbl. Finally, digits 6-11 make up the consecutive unit number of cars built at each assembly plant. The number begins with 100,001. A Vehicle Certification Label on the left front door lock face panel or door pillar shows the manufacturer, month and year of manufacture, GVW, GAWR, certification statement, VIN, body code, color code, trim code, axle code, transmission code, and special order code.

PINTO (FOUR/V-6)

Model Number	Body/Style Number	Body Type & Seating	Factory Price	Shipping Weight	Production Total
10	62B	2-dr. Sedan-4P	3629/3902	2346/2446	75,789
10	41E	2-dr. Pony Sed-4P	3199/--	2329/--	Note 1
11	64B	3-dr. Hatch-4P	3744/4017	2392/2492	69,383
12	73B	2-dr. Sta Wag-4P	4028/4301	2532/2610	53,846
12	41E	2-dr. Pony Wag-4P	3633/--	N/A	Note 1
12	73B	2-dr. Sqr Wag-4P	4343/4616	2568/2646	Note 2

Note 1: Pony production included in base sedan and wagon figures. **Note 2:** Squire Wagon production is included in standard station wagon total.

1979 Fairmont Futura sedan (F)

FAIRMONT (FOUR/SIX)

93	36R	2-dr. Spt Cpe-5P	4071/4312	2546/2613	106,065
91	66B	2-dr. Sedan-5P	3710/3951	2491/2558	54,798
92	54B	4-dr. Sedan-5P	3810/4051	2544/2611	133,813
94	74B	4-dr. Sta Wag-5P	4157/4398	2674/2741	100,691

Fairmont Engine Note: Prices shown are for four-cylinder and six- cylinder engines. A V-8 cost $283 more than the six.

GRANADA (SIX/V-8)

81	66H	2-dr. Sedan-5P	4342/4625	3051/3124	76,850
82	54H	4-dr. Sedan-5P	4445/4728	3098/3169	105,526

GRANADA GHIA (SIX/V-8)

81/602	66K	2-dr. Sedan-5P	4728/5011	3089/3160	Note 3
82/602	54K	4-dr. Sedan-5P	4830/5113	3132/3203	Note 3

GRANADA ESS (SIX/V-8)

81/433	N/A	2-dr. Sedan-5P	4888/5161	3105/3176	Note 3
82/433	N/A	4-dr. Sedan-5P	4990/5273	3155/3226	Note 3

Note 3: Granada Ghia and ESS production is included in base Granada totals above.

1979 LTD Landau sedan (F)

LTD II (V-8)

30	65D	2-dr. HT Cpe-6P	5445	3797	18,300
31	53D	4-dr. Pill. HT-6P	5569	3860	19,781

LTD II 'S' (V-8)

25	65B	2-dr. HT Cpe-6P	5198	3781	834
27	53B	4-dr. Pill. HT-6P	5298	3844	9,649

Production Note: LTD 'S' was for fleet sale only.

LTD II BROUGHAM (V-8)

30	65K	2-dr. HT Cpe-6P	5780	3815	Note 4
31	53K	4-dr. Pill. HT-6P	5905	3889	Note 4

Note 4: Brougham production is included in LTD II totals above.

LTD (V-8)

62	66H	2-dr. Sedan-6P	5813	3421	54,005
63	54H	4-dr. Sedan-6P	5913	3463	117,730
74	74H	4-dr. Sta Wag-6P	6122	3678	37,955
74	74K	4-dr. Ctry Sqr-6P	6615	3719	29,932

LTD Production Notes: Production of wagons with dual-facing rear seats (a $145-$149 option for both standard and Country Squire wagon) is included in basic wagon totals. Totals also include production of Custom 500 models for Canadian market (2,036 two-doors, 4,567 four-doors and 1,568 wagons).

LTD LANDAU (V-8)

64	66K	2-dr. Sedan-6P	6349	3472	42,314
65	54K	4-dr. Sedan-6P	6474	3527	74,599

THUNDERBIRD (V-8)

87	60H	2-dr. HT Cpe-6P	5877	3893	284,141

THUNDERBIRD TOWN LANDAU (V-8)

87/607	60H	2-dr. HT Cpe-6P	8866	4284	Note 5

THUNDERBIRD HERITAGE EDITION (V-8)

87/603	60H	2-dr. HT Cpe-6P	10687	4178	Note 5

Note 5: Town Landau and Heritage production is included in basic Thunderbird total.

FACTORY PRICE AND WEIGHT NOTE: Pinto/Fairmont prices and weights to left of slash are for four-cylinder, to right for six-cylinder engine. For Granada, prices and weights to left of slash are for six-cylinder, to right for V-8 engine.

ENGINE DATA: BASE FOUR (Pinto, Fairmont): Inline. Overhead cam. Four-cylinder. Cast iron block and head. Displacement: 140 cu. in. (2.3 liters). Bore & stroke: 3.78 x 3.13 in. Compression ratio: 9.0:1. Brake horsepower: 88 at 4800 R.P.M. Torque: 118 lbs.-ft. at 2800 R.P.M. Five main bearings. Hydraulic valve lifters. Carburetor: 2Bbl. Motorcraft 5200. VIN Code: Y. OPTIONAL V-6 (Pinto): 60-degree, overhead-valve V-6. Cast iron block and head. Displacement: 170.8 cu. in. (2.8 liters). Bore & stroke: 3.66 x 2.70 in. Compression ratio: 8.7:1. Brake horsepower: 102 at 4400 R.P.M. Torque: 138 lbs.-ft. at 3200 R.P.M. Four main bearings. Solid valve lifters. Carburetor: 2Bbl. Motorcraft 2150 or 2700VV. VIN Code: Z. OPTIONAL SIX (Fairmont): Inline. Overhead valve. Six-cylinder. Cast iron block and head. Displacement: 200 cu. in. (3.3 liters). Bore & stroke: 3.68 x 3.13 in. Compression ratio: 8.5:1. Brake horsepower: 85 at 3600 R.P.M. Torque: 154 lbs.-ft. at 1600 R.P.M. Seven main bearings. Hydraulic valve lifters. Carburetor: 1Bbl. Carter YFA or Holley 1946. VIN Code: T. BASE SIX (Granada): Inline. Overhead valve. Six-cylinder. Cast iron block and head. Displacement: 250 cu. in. (4.1 liters). Bore & stroke: 3.68 x 3.91 in. Compression ratio: 8.6:1. Brake horsepower: 97 at 3200 R.P.M. Torque: 210 lbs.-ft. at 1400 R.P.M. Seven main bearings. Hydraulic valve lifters. Carburetor: 1Bbl. Carter YFA. VIN Code: L. BASE V-8 (LTD II, Thunderbird,

LTD); OPTIONAL (Fairmont, Granada): 90-degree, overhead valve V-8. Cast iron block and head. Displacement: 302 cu. in. (5.0 liters). Bore & stroke: 4.00 x 3.00 in. Compression ratio: 8.4:1. Brake horsepower: (LTD) 129 at 3600 R.P.M.; (LTD II/TBird) 133 at 3400; (Fairmont) 140 at 3600; (Granada) 137 at 3600. Torque: (LTD) 223 lbs.- ft. at 2600 R.P.M.; (LTD II/TBird) 245 at 1600; (Fairmont) 250 at 1800; (Granada) 243 at 2000. Five main bearings. Hydraulic valve lifters. Carburetor: 2Bbl. Motorcraft 2150 or 2700VV. VIN Code: F. OPTIONAL V-8 (LTD, Thunderbird): 90-degree, overhead valve V-8. Cast iron block and head. Displacement: 351 cu. in. (5.8 liters). Bore & stroke: 4.00 x 3.50 in. Compression ratio: 8.3:1. Brake horsepower: 135 or 142 at 3200 R.P.M. Torque: 286 lbs.-ft. at 1400 R.P.M. Five main bearings. Hydraulic valve lifters. Carburetor: 2Bbl. Motorcraft 7200VV. Windsor engine. VIN Code: H. OPTIONAL V-8 (LTD II, LTD, Thunderbird): Modified version of 351 cu. in. V-8 above Compression: 8.0:1. Brake H.P.: 151 at 3600 R.P.M. Torque: 270 lbs.-ft. at 2200 R.P.M. Carb: Motorcraft 2150.

CHASSIS DATA: Wheelbase: (Pinto) 94.5 in.; (Pinto wag) 94.8 in.; (Fairmont) 105.5 in.; (Granada) 109.9 in.; (LTD II 2dr.) 114.0 in.; (LTD II 4dr.) 118.0 in.; (LTD) 114.4 in.; (TBird) 114.0 in. Overall Length: (Pinto) 168.8 in.; (Pinto wag) 178.6 in.; (Fairmont) 193.8 in. exc. Futura coupe, 195.8 in.; (Granada) 197.8 in.; (LTD II 2dr.) 217.2 in.; (LTD II 4dr.) 221.2 in.; (LTD) 209.0 in.; (LTD wag) 212.9 in.; (TBird) 217.2 in. Height: (Pinto) 50.6 in.; (Pinto wag) 52.1 in.; (Fairmont) 53.5 in.; (Fairmont Futura cpe) 52.3 in.; (Fairmont wag) 54.4 in.; (Granada) 53.2 in.; (LTD II 2dr.) 52.6 in.; (LTD II 4dr.) 53.3 in.; (LTD) 54.5 in.; (LTD wag) 56.7 in.; (TBird) 52.8 in. Width: (Pinto) 69.4 in.; (Pinto wag) 69.7 in.; (Fairmont) 71.0 in.; (Granada) 74.0 in.; (LTD II) 78.6 in.; (LTD) 77.5 in.; (LTD wag) 79.3 in.; (TBird) 78.5 in. Front Tread: (Pinto) 55.0 in.; (Fairmont) 56.6 in.; (Granada) 59.0 in.; (LTD II) 63.6 in. (LTD) 62.2 in. (TBird) 63.2 in. Rear Tread: (Pinto) 55.8 in.; (Fairmont) 57.0 in.; (Granada) 57.7 in.; (LTD II) 63.5 in.; (LTD) 62.0 in. (TBird) 63.1 in. Standard Tires: (Pinto) A78 x 13; (Fairmont) B78 x 14, except CR78 x 14 on wagon; (Granada) DR78 x 14 SBR BSW; (Granada Ghia) ER78 x 14; (LTD II) HR78 x 14 SBR BSW; (LTD) FR78 x 14 SBR BSW exc. wagon, GR78 x 14; (TBird) GR78 x 15 SBR BSW.

TECHNICAL: Transmission: Four-speed manual standard on Pinto/Fairmont four: (1st) 3.98:1; (2nd) 2.14:1; (3rd) 1.42:1; (4th) 1.00:1; (Rev) 3.99:1. Four-speed overdrive manual standard on Fairmont/Granada six/V-8. Six-cylinder: (1st) 3.29:1; (2nd) 1.84:1; (3rd) 1.00:1; (4th) 0.81:1; (Rev) 3.29:1. V-8 ratios: (1st) 3.07:1; (2nd) 1.72:1; (3rd) 1.00:1; (4th) 0.70:1; (Rev) 3.07:1. Three-speed automatic standard on other models, optional on all. Pinto/Fairmont four-cylinder (and Fairmont six) gear ratios: (1st) 2.47:1; (2nd) 1.47:1; (3rd) 1.00:1; (Rev) 2.11:1. LTD II/TBird w/V8351: (1st) 2.40:1; (2nd) 1.47:1; (3rd) 1.00:1; (Rev) 2.00:1. Other models: (1st) 2.46:1; (2nd) 1.46:1; (3rd) 1.00:1; (Rev) 2.18:1 to 2.20:1. Standard final drive ratio: (Pinto) 2.73:1 or 3.08:1; (Fairmont) 3.08:1 exc. 2.73:1 w/six and auto., 2.26:1 w/V-8 and auto.; (Granada) 3.00:1 w/4spd; (LTD II) 2.75:1 or 2.47:1; (LTD) 2.26:1 exc. wag, 2.73:1 or 2.26:1; (TBird) 2.75:1 exc. w/V8351, 2.47:1. Steering: (Pinto/Fairmont) rack and pinion; (others) recirculating ball. Front Suspension: (Pinto) coil springs with short/long control arms, and anti-sway bar with V-6; (Fairmont) MacPherson struts with coil springs on lower control arms and link-type anti-sway bar; (Granada/LTD II/TBird) coil springs with short/long control arms and anti-sway bar; (LTD) long/short control arms w/coil springs and link-type stabilizer. Rear Suspension: (Pinto/Granada) rigid axle w/semi-elliptic leaf springs; (Fairmont) four-bar link coil springs; (LTD II/TBird) rigid axle w/lower trailing radius arms, upper oblique torque arms, coil springs and anti-sway bar; (LTD) rigid axle w/four-bar link and helical coil springs. Brakes: Front disc, rear drum. Ignition: Electronic. Body construction: (Pinto/Fairmont/Granada) unibody; (LTD II/LTD/TBird) separate body and perimeter box frame. Fuel tank: (Pinto) 11.7 gal.; (Pinto wag) 14 gal.; (Fairmont) 16 gal.; (Granada) 18 gal.; (LTD II) 21 gal.; (LTD) 19 gal. exc. wagon, 20 gal.; (TBird) 21 gal. exc. 27.5 gal. on Town Landau and Heritage.

DRIVETRAIN OPTIONS: Engines: 170 cu. in. V-6: Pinto ($273). 200 cu. in., 1Bbl. six: Fairmont ($241). 302 cu. in., 2Bbl. V-8: Fairmont ($524); Granada ($283). 351 cu. in., 2Bbl. V-8: LTD II/LTD/TBird ($263). Transmission/Differential: Cruise-O-matic trans.: Pinto ($307); Fairmont ($401); Fairmont wagon ($307); Granada ($307). Floor shift lever: Fairmont/Granada ($31). Traction- Lok differential: LTD II/TBird ($64). Optional axle ratio: Pinto ($13); LTD ($18). Brakes & Steering: Power brakes: Pinto/Fairmont/Granada ($70). Power steering: Pinto ($141); Fairmont ($149); Granada ($155). Suspension: H.D. susp.: Fairmont ($19-$25); Granada ($20); LTD II ($41); LTD/TBird ($22). Handling susp.: Fairmont ($41); LTD ($42). Adjustable air shock absorbers: LTD ($54). Other: H.D. battery ($18-$21). H.D. alternator: LTD II/LTD ($50). Engine block heater ($13-$14). Trailer towing pkg. (heavy duty): LTD ($161-$192). California emission system: Pinto ($69); Fairmont/Granada ($76); others ($83). High- altitude option ($33-$36).

PINTO CONVENIENCE/APPEARANCE OPTIONS: Option Packages: ESS pkg. ($236-$261). Cruising pkg. ($330- $566); tape delete ($55 credit). Sport pkg. ($96-$110). Exterior decor group ($20-$40). Interior decor group ($137- $207). Interior accent group ($5-$40). Convenience group ($24-$61). Deluxe bumper group ($52). Protection group ($33- $36). Light group ($25-$37). Comfort/Convenience: Air conditioner ($484). Rear defroster ($84). Tinted glass ($59). Cigar lighter ($5). Trunk light ($5). Driver's sport mirror ($18). Dual sport mirrors ($52). Day/night mirror ($10). Entertainment: AM radio: Pony ($65). AM radio w/digital clock ($47-$119); w/stereo tape player ($119-$192). AM/FM radio ($48-$120). AM/FM stereo radio ($89-$161); w/cassette player ($157-$222). Radio flexibility option ($90). Exterior: Flip-up open air roof ($199). Glass third door ($25). Metallic glow paint ($41). Two-tone paint/tape treatment ($76). Accent tape stripe ($76). Black narrow vinyl-insert bodyside moldings ($39). Premium bodyside moldings ($10-$48). Rear bumper guards ($19). Roof luggage rack ($63). Mud/stone deflectors ($23). Lower bodyside protection ($30). Interior: Four-way driver's seat ($35). Load floor carpet ($24). Cargo area cover ($28). Front floor mats ($18). Wheels: Wire wheel covers ($99). Forged aluminum wheels ($217-$289); white ($235-$307). Lacy spoke alum. wheels ($217-$289). Styled steel wheels ($54). Tires: A78 x 13 WSW ($43). BR78 x 13 BSW ($148); WSW ($191). BR70 x 13 RWL ($228).

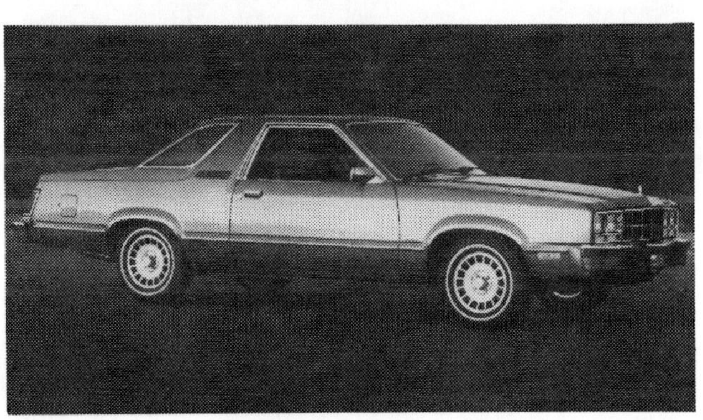

1979 Fairmont Futura Sport Coupe (F)

FAIRMONT CONVENIENCE/APPEARANCE OPTIONS: Option Packages: ES option ($329). Futura sports group ($102). Ghia pkg. ($207-$498). Squire option ($399). Exterior decor group ($223). Exterior accent group ($82). Interior decor group ($170-$311). Interior accent group ($80-$84). Instrumentation group ($77). Deluxe bumper group ($57). Convenience group ($33-$65). Appearance protection group ($36-$47). Light group ($27-$43). Comfort/Convenience: Air cond. ($484). Rear defogger ($51). Rear defroster, electric ($90). Fingertip speed control ($104-$116). Power windows ($116-$163). Power door locks ($73-$101). Power decklid release ($22). Power seat ($94). Tinted glass ($59); windshield only ($25). Sport steering wheel ($39). Tilt steering ($69-$81). Electric clock ($20). Cigar lighter ($7). Interval wipers ($35). Rear wiper/washer ($63). Map light ($7). Trunk light ($7). Left remote mirror ($17). Dual bright mirrors ($37-$43). Day/night mirror ($10). Entertainment: AM radio ($72); w/8track tape player ($192). AM/FM radio ($120). AM/FM stereo radio ($176); w/8track or cassette player ($243). Premium sound system ($67). Radio flexibility ($93). Exterior: Flip-up open air roof ($199). Full vinyl roof ($90). Metallic glow paint ($48). Two-tone paint ($51); special ($51-$207). Accent stripe ($28). Pivoting front vent windows ($48). Rear quarter vent louvers ($35). Vinyl bodyside moldings ($39); wide black vinyl ($41). Rocker panel moldings ($25). Bright window frames ($18). Bumper guards, rear ($20). Luggage rack ($76). Lower bodyside protection ($30-$42). Interior: Vinyl bucket seats, non-reclining ($72). Bench seat ($72 credit). Cloth/vinyl seat trim ($20-$42). Vinyl seat trim ($24). Front floor mats ($18). Lockable side storage box ($20). Wheels: Hubcaps w/trim rings ($37). Deluxe wheel covers ($37). Turbine wheel covers ($39-$76). Wire wheel covers ($50-$127). Styled steel wheels ($40-$116). Cast aluminum wheels ($251-$327). Tires: B78 x 14 WSW. BR78 x 14 BSW/WSW. C78 x 14 BSW/WSW. CR78 x 14 BSW/WSW. DR78 x 14 SBR BSW/WSW/RWL.

GRANADA CONVENIENCE/APPEARANCE OPTIONS: Option Packages: Interior decor group ($211). Convenience group ($35-$94). Deluxe bumper group ($78). Light group ($41- $46). Cold weather group ($30-$60). Heavy-duty group ($18- $60). Protection group ($24-$47). Visibility group ($5-$70). Comfort/Convenience: Air cond. ($514); auto-temp ($555). Rear defogger ($51). Rear defroster, electric ($90). Fingertip speed control ($104-$116). Illuminated entry system ($52). Power windows ($120-$171). Power door locks ($78-$110). Power decklid release ($22). Auto. parking brake release ($8). Power four-way seat ($94). Tinted glass ($64); windshield only ($25). Tilt steering wheel ($69). Digital clock ($47). Lighting and Mirrors: Cornering lamps ($43). Trunk light ($5). Left remote mirror ($17). Dual remote mirrors ($37- $54). Dual sport mirrors ($46-$63). Day/night mirror ($11). Lighted right visor vanity mirror ($36). Entertainment: AM radio ($72); w/tape player ($192). AM/FM radio ($135). AM/FM stereo radio ($176); w/8track or cassette player ($243); w/quadrasonic tape ($365). AM/FM stereo search radio ($319). CB radio ($270). Radio flexibility ($93). Exterior: Power moonroof ($899). Full or half vinyl roof ($106). Metallic glow paint ($48). Bodyside/decklid paint stripes ($36). Two-tone paint/tape ($163). Bodyside accent moldings ($43). Black vinyl insert bodyside moldings ($39). Rocker panel moldings ($25). Lower bodyside protection ($31). Interior: Console ($99). Four-way driver's seat ($34). Reclining seats (NC). Leather seat trim ($271). Flight bench seat (NC). Cloth/vinyl flight bench seat ($54). Deluxe cloth/vinyl trim (NC). Front floor mats ($18). Color-keyed seatbelts ($19). Wheels: Deluxe wheel covers ($41) exc. Ghia/ESS (NC). Wire wheel covers ($108) exc. Ghia/ESS ($67). Styled steel wheels w/trim rings ($83-$124). Cast aluminum wheels ($248-$289). Tires: DR78 x 14 SBR WSW. ER78 x 14 SBR BSW/WSW. FR78 x 14 SBR BSW/WSW/wide WSW. Inflatable spare (NC).

LTD II CONVENIENCE/APPEARANCE OPTIONS: Option Packages: Sports appearance pkg.: 2dr. ($301-$449). Sports instrumentation group ($121-$151). Sports touring pkg.: 2dr. ($379-$526). Deluxe bumper group ($63). Light group ($51-$57). Convenience group ($120-$155). Power lock group ($111-$143). Protection group ($49-$61). Comfort/Convenience: Air cond. ($562); w/auto-temp control ($607). Rear defroster, electric ($99). Fingertip speed control ($113-$126). Illuminated entry system ($57). Tinted glass ($70); windshield only ($28). Power windows ($132- $187). Six-way power seat ($163). Tilt steering wheel ($75). Electric clock ($22). Day/date clock ($22-$45). Lighting, Horns and Mirrors: Cornering lamps ($49). Dual-note horn ($9). Remote driver's mirror ($18). Dual sport mirrors ($9-$68). Lighted visor vanity mirror ($34-$39). Entertainment: AM radio ($79). AM/FM radio ($132). AM/FM stereo radio ($192); w/tape player ($266); w/quadrasonic tape player ($399). AM/FM stereo search radio ($349). CB radio ($295). Dual rear speakers ($46). Radio flexibility ($105). Exterior: Full or half vinyl roof ($116). Opera windows ($54). Vinyl-insert bodyside moldings ($42). Wide bright bodyside moldings ($42-$71). Rocker panel moldings ($29). Metallic glow paint ($64) exc. (NC) w/sports pkg. Two-tone paint ($82). Dual accent paint stripes ($33). Front bumper guards ($26). Mud/stone deflectors ($25). Lower bodyside protection ($33-$46). Interior: Bucket seats w/console ($211) exc. Brougham ($37). Vinyl seat trim ($26). Cloth/vinyl seat trim ($26). Front floor mats ($20). H.D. floor mats ($9). Color-keyed seatbelts ($22). Wheels/Tires: Deluxe wheel covers ($45). Luxury wheel covers ($66-$111). Wire wheel covers ($116-$161) exc. (NC) w/sports pkg. Cast aluminum wheels ($200-$361). HR78 x 14 SBR WSW ($47). GR78 x 15 SBR WSW ($48).

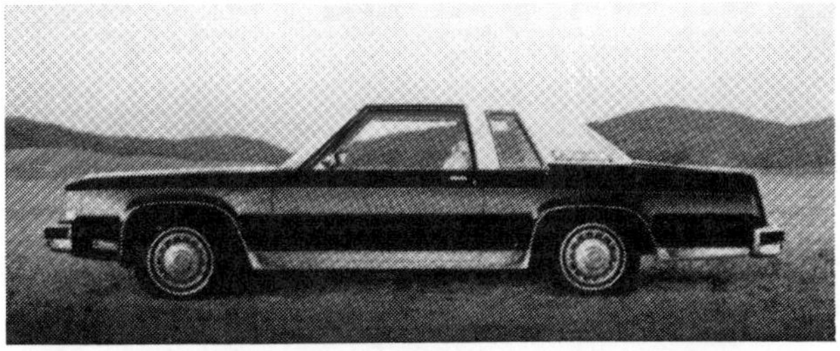

1979 LTD Landau sedan (JG)

LTD CONVENIENCE/APPEARANCE OPTIONS: Option Packages: Interior luxury group: Landau ($705); Country Squire ($758). Exterior accent group ($29-$66). Convenience group ($68-$99). Light group ($32-$41). Protection group ($46-$55). Comfort/Convenience: Air cond. ($597); w/auto-temp control ($642). Rear defogger ($57). Rear defroster, electric ($100). Fingertip speed control ($113-$126). Illuminated entry system ($57). Power windows ($137-$203). Power door locks ($87- $161). Power driver's seat ($164); driver and passenger ($329). Tinted glass ($83); windshield only ($28). Tilt steering wheel ($76). Auto. parking brake release ($8). Electric clock ($24). Digital clock ($32-$55). Lighting, Horns and Mirrors: Cornering lamps ($49). Trunk light ($4). Dual-note horn ($9). Driver's remote mirror, door or sail mount ($18). Dual remote mirrors ($37-$55). Lighted visor vanity mirror ($36-$41). Entertainment: AM radio ($79). AM/FM radio ($132). AM/FM stereo radio ($192); w/tape player ($266). AM/FM stereo search radio w/quadrasonic tape player ($432). CB radio ($295). Power antenna ($47). Dual rear speakers ($46). Deluxe sound pkg. ($55); luxury pkg. ($42). Premium sound system ($74-$158). Radio flexibility ($105). Exterior: Full or half vinyl roof ($143). Metallic glow paint ($64). Two-tone paint/tape ($86-$118). Hood striping ($14). Rocker panel moldings ($29). Vinyl-insert bodyside moldings ($43). Bumper guards, front or rear ($26). Bumper rub strips ($54). Luggage rack ($113). Lower bodyside protection ($33- $46).

Interior: Dual-facing rear seats: wagon ($145-$149). Flight bench seat ($99). Dual flight bench seat recliner ($58). Split bench seat w/passenger recliner ($187-$233). All-vinyl seat trim ($26). Duraweave vinyl trim ($52). Front floor mats ($20). H.D. floor mats ($9). Trunk trim ($41-$46). Color-keyed seatbelts ($24). Wheels: Full wheel covers ($52). Wire wheel covers ($64). Tires: FR78 x 14 WSW ($47). GR78 x 14 BSW ($30). GR78 x 14 WSW ($47-$77). HR78 x 14 (wagon): BSW ($30); WSW ($77). Conventional spare ($13).

THUNDERBIRD CONVENIENCE/APPEARANCE OPTIONS: Option Packages: Sports decor group ($459-$518). Interior luxury group ($816). Exterior decor group ($346-$405). Interior decor group ($322). Sports instrumentation group ($87-$129). Convenience group ($108-$117). Protection group ($49-$53). Light group ($51). Power lock group ($111). Luxury sound insulation ($30). Comfort/Convenience: Air cond. ($562); auto-temp ($607) exc. Twn Lan/Heritage ($607). Rear defroster ($99). Fingertip speed control ($113-$126). Illuminated entry system ($57). Tinted glass ($70); windshield only ($28). Power windows ($132). Six-way power seat ($163). Automatic seatback release ($36). Seatbelt warning chime ($22). Tilt steering wheel ($75). Day/date clock ($24). Lighting and Mirrors: Cornering lamps ($49). Driver's remote mirror, chrome ($18). Dual sport mirrors ($9-$68). Lighted visor vanity mirror ($34-$39). Entertainment: AM/FM radio ($53). AM/FM stereo radio ($113); w/tape player ($187); w/quadrasonic tape player ($320) exc. Twn Lan/Heritage ($50). AM/FM stereo search radio ($270). CB radio ($295). AM radio delete ($79 credit). Power antenna ($47). Dual rear speakers ($46). Radio flexibility ($105). Exterior: TRoof ($747). Power moonroof ($691). Vinyl roof, two-piece ($132). Metallic glow paint ($64). Two-tone paint ($82). Dual accent paint stripes ($46). Bright wide bodyside moldings ($42). Vinyl bodyside moldings ($42). Wide color-keyed vinyl bodyside moldings ($53). Rocker panel moldings ($29). Bumper rub strips ($37). Mud/stone deflectors ($25). Lower bodyside protection ($33-$46). Interior: Bucket seats w/console ($211) exc. ($37) w/decor group. Leather seat trim ($243-$309). Vinyl seat trim ($26). Front floor mats ($20). Trunk trim ($43). Color-keyed seatbelts ($22). Wheels/Tires: Wire wheel covers ($118). Styled wheels ($166). Cast aluminum wheels ($150-$316). GR78 x 15 WSW ($47). HR78 x 15 BSW ($25). HR78 x 15 WSW ($72). HR70 x 15 WSW ($29-$100). Inflatable spare (NC).

HISTORY: Introduced: October 6, 1978. Model year production: 1,835,937 (incl. Mustangs). Total passenger-car production for the U.S. market of 1,670,106 units (incl. Mustangs) included 448,627 four-cylinder, 485,842 sixes and 735,637 V-8s. Calendar year production (U.S.): 1,345,427 (incl. Mustangs). Calendar year sales by U.S. dealers: 1,499,098 (incl. Mustangs). Model year sales by U.S. dealers: 1,541,600 (incl. Mustangs).

NOTE: Totals above do not include Club Wagons, of which 42,449 were sold in the model year; or imported Fiestas, which recorded sales of 77,733.

Historical Footnotes: To attempt to meet the CAFE requirement of 19 MPG gas mileage this year, Ford pushed sales of the new downsized LTD. Buyers seemed to want the big V-8 rather than economical fours and sixes, prompting Ford to increase the price of the V-8 model. LTD sales fell rather sharply, putting the reduced-size model far behind Caprice/Impala. LTD II production ceased in January 1979, amid flagging sales. Sales declined considerably for model year 1979, down 15 percent. A gasoline crisis in mid-year didn't help; but mainly, Ford had lagged behind other companies in downsizing its big-car lineup. Pinto sales were good, even though the outmoded design couldn't truly rival the new subcompacts. And sales of the new Mustang were most impressive—nearly 70 percent above the final figure for its second-generation predecessor. A replacement for the Pinto was scheduled for 1981, dubbed "Erika." That would, of course, be changed to Escort by the time the new front-drive subcompact was introduced. Not until then would Ford have a true rival to Chevrolet's Chevette. Lee Iacocca had been fired by Henry Ford II soon after the model year began. Philip Caldwell then became president.

1980 FORD

Ford's emphasis this year lay in economy, highlighted by its new lockup overdrive automatic transmission. The 1980 CAFE goal for automakers' fleets was 20 MPG (up from 19 MPG in 1979). Thunderbird was the star of the lineup in its new downsized form. LTD II was gone, and Pinto was in its final season. On the powerplant front, a turbocharged four was announced as a Fairmont option, but didn't quite materialize, presumably due to mechanical difficulties. A smaller (255 cu. in.) V-8 replaced the former 302 as a Fairmont option, and became standard on the new mid-size TBird. LTD's new automatic overdrive transmission boasted an economy improvement of 19 percent over a comparable 1979 model.

1980 Pinto three-door hatchback (JG)

PINTO — FOUR — All Pintos had four-cylinder engines for 1980, as the optional V-6 disappeared. The standard 140 cu. in. (2.3-liter) four received improvements to boost its highway gas mileage. Styling was virtually identical to 1979, with seven new body colors and three new interior trim colors available. The low-budget Pony now wore steel-belted radial tires. Batteries were maintenance-free, and cars carried a restyled scissors jack. Radios played a Travelers' Advisory band, and the station wagon's Cruising Package option was revised. This was Pinto's final season, as the new front-drive Escort was ready for production. The Rallye Pack option, introduced late in 1979 on hatchback and wagon, was expanded this year. Model lineup contined as before: two-door sedan, "three-door" hatchback Runabout, two-door station wagon, and Pony sedan or wagon. Pony lacked the base model's tinted glass, rear defroster,

AM radio, bumper rub strips, and vinyl-insert bodyside moldings, as well as bright window frame, belt and 'B' pillar moldings. Pinto's ESS package included a charcoal grille and headlamp doors, black windshield and backlight moldings, dual black racing mirrors, glass third door with black hinges, blackout paint treatment, black wheel lip moldings, 'ESS' fender insignia, and black window frames. The price was $281 to $313.

1980 Fairmont sedan (JG)

FAIRMONT — FOUR/SIX/V-8 — Powerplants were the major news in the Fairmont arena this year. Most notable was the announcement of a turbocharged four, but evidently that one never quite made production. A new 255 cu. in. (4.2-liter) V-8 did, though, replacing the former 302 option. It was available only with automatic. Both the 255 and the 200 cu. in. (3.3-liter) inline six had a new lightweight starter. Base engine remained the 140 cu. in. (2.3-liter) four, with four-speed manual gearbox. Manual-shift transmissions had a new self-adjusting clutch. New high-pressure P-metric steel-belted radial tires became standard on all models. Maintenance-free battery were standard, while all radios added a Travelers' Advisory band. Fairmont came in nine new body colors and two new two-tone color schemes (with accent color in the bodyside center). A four-door sedan joined the Futura coupe at mid-year, wearing the unique Futura crosshatch grille. Futuras had standard halogen headlamps (except where prohibited by state laws). Otherwise, styling was similar to 1978-79. The Futura coupe had a woodgrain dash applique, quad halogen headlamps, trunk light, bright window frame moldings, vinyl bodyside moldings, and wheel lip and door belt moldings. The Futura sports group, priced at $114, included color-keyed turbine wheel covers, charcoal/argent grille, and youth-oriented tape stripes; the customary hood ornament, louvers and accent stripe were deleted. The optional sport steering wheel switched from brushed aluminum to black finish. Fairmont's $378 ES sedan option package included a blackout grille, front/rear rub strips, black cowl grille, black window frames and quarter window vent louvers, and vinyl-insert bodyside moldings. Also included: dual black remote sport mirrors, turbine wheel covers, black sport steering wheel, rear bumper guards, handling suspension, and black lower back panel.

1980 Granada Ghia sedan (F)

GRANADA — SIX/V-8 — Apart from seven new body colors and three new vinyl roof colors, little changed on the compact Granada sedans. A new lightweight starter went under the hood, a better scissors jack in the trunk, and Ardmore cloth upholstery on the seats. Maintenance-free batteries were standard. Joining the option list were a heavy-duty 54-amp battery, mud/stone guards, and revised electronic search stereo radios and tape players. "Tu-tone" paint cost $180. Standard engine was the 250 cu. in. (4.1-liter) inline six, with 302 cu. in. (5.0-liter) V-8 optional. California Granadas required the new 255 cu. in. V-8. Granada came in two- or four-door sedan form again: base, Ghia or ESS trim. Granada Ghia carried dual body/hood/decklid accent stripes, black/argent lower back panel applique, left remote mirror, wide vinyl-insert bodyside moldings, and burled walnut woodtone door trim. The sporty Granada ESS held a blacked-out grille. dual remote mirrors, black bodyside moldings with bright inserts, black rocker panel paint, hood/decklid paint stripes, bucket seats with chainmail vinyl inserts, leather-wrapped steering wheel, louvered opera window applique, and wide wheel lip moldings.

1980 LTD Crown Victoria sedan (F)

1980 LTD Crown Victoria Country Squire station wagon (JG)

LTD — V-8 — Reshuffling of the model lineup hit the full-size line for 1980. This year's selection included budget-priced LTD 'S', base LTD, and LTD Crown Victoria sedans. An 'S' edition also joined the LTD (plain-body) and Country Squire (woodgrain) station wagon choices. Crown Victoria (same name as the mid-1950s high-line Ford) replaced the former Landau as top-of-the-line sedan. A new four-speed automatic transmission with overdrive top gear became optional on all models with the 351 cu. in. (5.8-liter) V-8, and carried the same stroke as the base 302 (5.0-liter) V-8. Also new this year: standard P-metric radial tires with higher pressure, standard maintenance-free battery, and halogen headlamps (except LTD 'S'). Crown Victoria and Country Squire carried a new wide hood ornament design, while standard LTDs had no ornament at all. Country Squire wagons had simulated woodgrain panels with planking lines. New black rocker panel moldings and lower bright moldings with rear extensions went on the Crown Victoria. So did a new rear half-vinyl roof with "frenched" seams and brushed aluminum roof wrapover moldings. Both LTD and Crown Vic sedans displayed new decklid tape stripes. Front bumper guards were standard. New options included the Traction-Lok axle; cast aluminum wheels; auto-headlamp on/off/delay system; leather-wrapped luxury steering wheel; and electronic stereo search radio with cassette player and Dolby sound. Appearance was similar to 1979. Each checkerboard grille section had a 15 x 7 hole pattern (30 across), topped by a heavy upper header bar. 'S' had a different front end and grille, with round headlamps and parking lamps inset into the grille. Other models showed quad headlamps. Bodyside beltline striping was higher this year. Two-door opera windows had a more vertical look. LTD had three police packages available: 302 cu. in. V-8, regular 351 V-8, and high-output 351 (with dual exhausts and modified camshaft). Police packages included heavy-duty alternators, a 2.26:1 axle for the 5.0 liter (3.08:1 for the 5.8 liter), 71 ampere-hour battery, heavy-duty power brakes, 140 MPH speedometer, heavy-duty suspension, GR70 x 15 blackwall police radials, and conventional spare tire. Police automatic transmissions had a first-gear lockout and oil cooler.

1980 Thunderbird Silver Anniversary hardtop coupe (F)

THUNDERBIRD — V-8 — For its 25th year in the lineup, Thunderbird got a new size and a new standard engine. This year's version rode a 108.4 inch wheelbase (formerly 114) and carried a standard 255 cu. in. (4.2-liter) V-8. That engine had the same stroke as the 302 V-8 (now optional), but a smaller bore. For the first time in a decade and a half, this TBird also wore a unitized body, essentially a stretch of the Fairmont platform. Instead of the former six-passenger capacity, the ninth-generation edition was intended for just four. It weighed over 700 pounds less than before. Modified MacPherson struts made up the front suspension, with four-bar-link coil springs at the rear. Thunderbird had power-assisted, variable-ratio rack-and-pinion steering. Axle ratios were lowered, to boost mileage. A new four-speed overdrive automatic transmission was optional with the 302 V-8. Styling features included traditional concealed headlamps, full-width wraparound taillamps, a lower beltline, unique (but traditional) wraparound parking lamps, and a strong mid-bodyside sculpture theme. Single opera windows to the rear of a wrapover roof band on the solid wide C pillars held a Thunderbird emblem. At front and rear were soft color-keyed urethane bumper systems. The eggcrate grille showed an 8 x 6 "hole" pattern, with the pattern repeated in a bumper slot below. Trim panels on the headlamp covers extended outward and around the fender sides to contain side marker lenses. Taillamp panels had a notch at the center, and wide Thunderbird emblem on each lens. Base and Town Landau models were offered at first. Town Landau added air conditioning, autolamp delay system, tinted glass, jewel-like hood ornament, electronic instrument cluster, cornering lamps, dual remote mirrors, and owner's nameplate with 22K gold finish. Also included: upper bodyside/hood/grille paint/tape striping, AM/FM stereo search radio, padded half-vinyl roof with wrapover band and coach lamps, power driver's seat, power windows, and turbine-spoke cast aluminum wheels. A Silver Anniversary model, added at mid-year, came in a selection of color combinations: Silver Anniversary Glow (with black wrapover band and silver vinyl roof, or silver band and black roof); Black (silver wrapover band and black vinyl roof, or black wrapover and silver roof); Light Grey (silver wrapover band and black vinyl roof); Red Glow (silver wrapover and red vinyl roof); Midnight Blue metallic (silver wrapover band and midnight blue vinyl roof); or Black Silver Glow two-tone (silver wrapover and black vinyl roof). All Silver Anniversary models had Dove Grey interiors, plus standard automatic overdrive transmission. Three distinct roof treatments were available: base, Exterior Luxury Group (on Town Landau), and Silver Anniversary. TBirds also had new high-pressure P-metric radial tires, maintenance-free battery, new spare tire, new wheels and covers, new two-tier instrument panel, and a four-spoke soft-rim steering wheel. Dual seatback recliners went on all split bench seats. Sculptured window-frame-mounted mirrors were optional. Other new options were: electronic instrument cluster including digital speedometer; TR type low-profile wide aspect ratio tires on cast aluminum wheels with special suspension tuning; keyless entry system; electronic garage door opener; diagnostic warning light system; six-speaker premium sound system; and flip-up removable moon roof. Many of these extras were standard on Town Landau and/or Silver Anniversary. Thunderbird's mate over at Mercury was the Cougar XR7.

I.D. DATA: As before, Ford's 11-symbol Vehicle Identification Number (VIN) is stamped on a metal tab fastened to the instrument panel, visible through the windshield. Coding is the same as 1979, except engine codes (symbol five) changed as follows: 'A' L4-140 2Bbl.; 'A' turbo L4140 2Bbl.; 'B' L6200 1Bbl.; 'C' L6250 1Bbl.; 'D' V8255 2Bbl.; 'F' V8302 2Bbl.; 'G' V8351 2Bbl. Model year code changed to '0' for 1980.

PINTO (FOUR)

Model Number	Body/Style Number	Body Type & Seating	Factory Price	Shipping Weight	Production Total
10	62B	2-dr. Sedan-4P	4223	2385	84,053
10	41E	2-dr. Pony Sed-4P	3781	2377	Note 1
11	64B	3-dr. Hatch-4P	4335	2426	61,842
12	73B	2-dr. Sta Wag-4P	4622	2553	39,159
12	41E	2-dr. Pony Wag-4P	4284	2545	Note 1
12/604	73B	2-dr. Sqr Wag-4P	4937	2590	Note 2

Note 1: Pony production included in base sedan and wagon figures. Panel deliver Pintos also were produced. **Note 2:** Squire Wagon production is included in standard station wagon total.

1980 Fairmont Squire wagon (F)

FAIRMONT (FOUR/SIX)

91	66B	2-dr. Sedan-5P	4435/4604	2571/--	45,074
92	54B	4-dr. Sedan-5P	4552/4721	2599/--	143,118
94	74B	4-dr. Sta Wag-5P	4721/4890	2722/--	77,035

FAIRMONT FUTURA (FOUR/SIX)

93	36R	2-dr. Spt Cpe-5P	4837/5006	2612/--	51,878
92	N/A	4-dr. Sedan-5P	5070/5239	N/A	5,306

Fairmont Engine Note: Prices shown are for four-cylinder and six-cylinder engines. A 255 cu. in. V-8 cost $119 more than the six.

1980 Granada sedan (JG)

GRANADA (SIX/V-8)

81	66H	2-dr. Sedan-5P	4987/5025	3063/3187	60,872
82	54H	4-dr. Sedan-5P	5108/5146	3106/3230	29,557

GRANADA GHIA (SIX/V-8)

81/602	66K	2-dr. Sedan-5P	5388/5426	3106/3230	Note 3
82/602	54K	4-dr. Sedan-5P	5509/5547	3147/3271	Note 3

GRANADA ESS (SIX/V-8)

81/933	N/A	2-dr. Sedan-5P	5477/5515	3137/3261	Note 3
82/933	N/A	4-dr. Sedan-5P	5598/5636	3178/3302	Note 3

Note 3: Granada Ghia and ESS production is included in base Granada totals above. Granada Engine Note: Prices shown are for six-cylinder and V8255 engines. A 302 cu. in. V-8 cost $150 more than the 255 V-8.

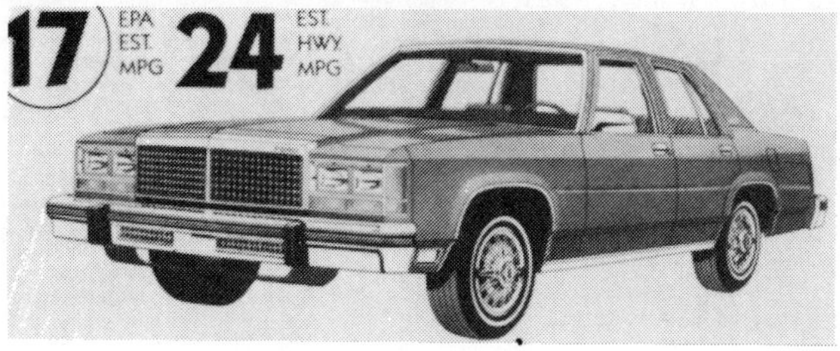
17
EPA
EST
MPG
24
EST
HWY
MPG

1980 LTD sedan (JG)

LTD (V-8)

62	66H	2-dr. Sedan-6P	6549	3447	15,333
63	54H	4-dr. Sedan-6P	6658	3475	51,630
74	74H	4-dr. Sta Wag-6P	7007	3717	11,718

LTD 'S' (V-8)

N/A	66D	2-dr. Sedan-6P	N/A	N/A	553
61	54D	4-dr. Sedan-6P	6320	2464	19,283
72	74D	4-dr. Sta Wag-6P	6741	3707	3,490

LTD CROWN VICTORIA (V-8)

64	66K	2-dr. Sedan-6P	7070	3482	7,725
65	54K	4-dr. Sedan-6P	7201	3524	21,962
76	74K	4-dr. Ctry Sqr-6P	7426	3743	9,868

LTD Production Note: Production of wagons with dual-facing rear seats (a $146-$151 option for both standard and Country Squire wagon) is included in basic wagon totals.

THUNDERBIRD (V-8)

87	66D	2-dr. HT Cpe-4P	6432	3118	156,803

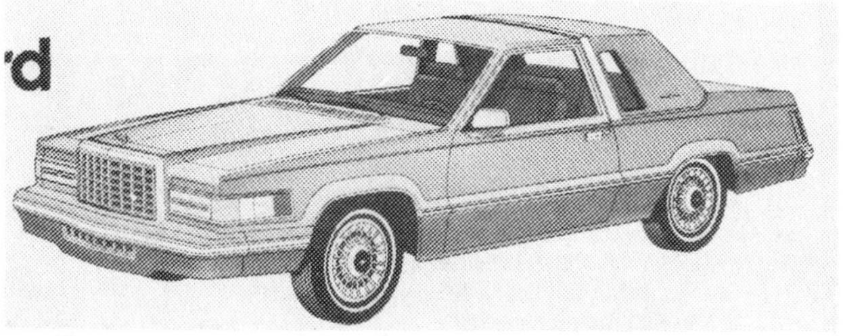
'd

1980 Thunderbird Town Landau hardtop coupe (JG)

THUNDERBIRD TOWN LANDAU (V-8)

87/607	66D	2-dr. HT Cpe-4P	10036	3357	Note 4

THUNDERBIRD SILVER ANNIVERSARY (V-8)

87/603	66D	2-dr. HT Cpe-4P	11679	3225	Note 4

Note 4: Town Landau and Silver Anniversary production is included in basic Thunderbird total.

FACTORY PRICE AND WEIGHT NOTE: Fairmont prices and weights to left of slash are for four-cylinder, to right for six-cylinder engine. Granada prices and weights to left of slash are for six-cylinder, to right for 255 cu. in. V-8 engine.

ENGINE DATA: BASE FOUR (Pinto, Fairmont): Inline. Overhead cam. Four-cylinder. Cast iron block and head. Displacement: 140 cu. in. (2.3 liters). Bore & stroke: 3.78 x 3.13 in. Compression ratio: 9.0:1. Brake horsepower: 88 at 4600 R.P.M. Torque: 119 lbs.-ft. at 2600 R.P.M. Five main bearings. Hydraulic valve lifters. Carburetor: 2Bbl. Motorcraft 5200. VIN Code: A. OPTIONAL SIX (Fairmont): Inline. Overhead valve. Six-cylinder. Cast iron block and head. Displacement: 200 cu. in. (3.3 liters). Bore & stroke: 3.68 x 3.13 in. Compression ratio: 8.6:1. Brake horsepower: 91 at 3800 R.P.M. Torque: 160 lbs.-ft. at 1600 R.P.M. Seven main bearings. Hydraulic valve lifters. Carburetor: 1Bbl. Holley 1946. VIN Code: B. BASE SIX (Granada): Inline. Overhead valve. Six-cylinder. Cast iron block and head. Displacement: 250 cu. in. (4.1 liters). Bore & stroke: 3.68 x 3.91 in. Compression ratio: 8.6:1. Brake horsepower: 90 at 3200 R.P.M. Torque: 194 lbs.-ft. at 1660 R.P.M. Seven main bearings. Hydraulic valve lifters. Carburetor: 1Bbl. Carter YFA. VIN Code: C. BASE V-8 (Thunderbird); OPTIONAL (Fairmont, Granada): 90-degree, overhead valve V-8. Cast iron block and head. Displacement: 255 cu. in. (4.2 liters). Bore & stroke: 3.68 x 3.00 in. Compression ratio: 8.8:1. Brake horsepower: (Fairmont) 119 at 3800 R.P.M.; (TBird) 115 at 3800. Torque: (Fairmont) 194 lbs.-ft. at 2200 R.P.M.; (TBird) 194 at 2200. Five main bearings. Hydraulic valve lifters. Carburetor: 2Bbl. Motorcraft 2150. VIN Code: D. BASE V-8 (LTD, Thunderbird Silver Anniversary); OPTIONAL (Granada, Thunderbird): 90-degree, overhead valve V-8. Cast iron block and head. Displacement: 302 cu. in. (5.0 liters). Bore & stroke: 4.00 x 3.00 in. Compression ratio: 8.4:1. Brake horsepower: (LTD) 130 at 3600 R.P.M.; (TBird) 131 at 3600; (Granada) 134 at 3600. Torque: (LTD) 230 lbs.-ft. at 1600 R.P.M.; (TBird) 231 at 1600; (Granada) 232 at 1600. Five main bearings. Hydraulic valve lifters. Carburetor: 2Bbl. Motorcraft 2150 or 2700VV. VIN Code: F. OPTIONAL V-8 (LTD): 90-degree, overhead valve V-8. Cast iron block and head. Displacement: 351 cu. in. (5.8 liters). Bore & stroke: 4.00 x 3.50 in. Compression ratio: 8.3:1. Brake horsepower: 140 at 3400 R.P.M. Torque: 265 lbs.-ft. at 2000 R.P.M. Five main bearings. Hydraulic valve lifters. Carburetor: 2Bbl. Motorcraft 7200VV. Windsor engine. VIN Code: G.

NOTE: A high-output version of the 351 cu. in. V-8 was available for police use.

CHASSIS DATA: Wheelbase: (Pinto) 94.5 in.; (Pinto wag) 94.8 in.; (Fairmont) 105.5 in.; (Granada) 109.9 in.; (LTD) 114.3 in.; (TBird) 108.4 in. Overall Length: (Pinto) 170.8 in.; (Pinto wag) 180.6 in.; (Fairmont) 195.5 in. exc. Futura coupe, 197.4 in.; (Granada) 199.7 in.; (LTD) 209.3 in.; (LTD wag) 215.0 in.; (TBird) 200.4 in. Height: (Pinto) 50.5 in.; (Pinto wag) 52.0 in.; (Fairmont) 52.9 in.; (Fairmont Futura cpe) 51.7 in.; (Fairmont wag) 54.2 in.; (Granada) 53.2-53.3 in.; (LTD) 54.7 in.; (LTD wag) 57.4 in.; (TBird) 53.0 in. Width: (Pinto) 69.4 in.; (Pinto wag) 69.7 in.; (Fairmont) 71.0 in.; (Granada) 74.5 in.; (LTD) 77.5 in.; (LTD wag) 79.3 in.; (TBird) 74.1 in. Front Tread: (Pinto) 55.0 in.; (Fairmont) 56.6 in.; (Granada) 59.0 in.; (LTD) 62.2 in. (TBird) 58.1 in. Rear Tread: (Pinto) 55.8 in.; (Fairmont) 57.0 in.; (Granada) 57.7 in.; (LTD) 62.0 in. (TBird) 57.0 in. Standard Tires: (Pinto) BR78 x 13 SBR exc. Pony, A78 x 13; (Fairmont) P175/75R14; (Granada) DR78 x 14 SBR BSW exc. Ghia, ER78 x 14 and ESS, FR78 x 14; (LTD) P205/75R14 BSW exc. wagon, P215/75R14; (TBird) P185/75R14 SBR BSW.

TECHNICAL: Transmission: Four-speed manual standard on Pinto/Fairmont four: (1st) 3.98:1; (2nd) 2.14:1; (3rd) 1.42:1; (4th) 1.00:1; (Rev) 3.99:1. Four-speed overdrive manual standard on Fairmont/Granada six: (1st) 3.29:1; (2nd) 1.84:1; (3rd) 1.00:1; (4th) 0.81:1; (Rev) 3.29:1. Three-speed automatic standard on other models, optional on all. Pinto/Fairmont four-cylinder gear ratios: (1st) 2.47:1; (2nd) 1.47:1; (3rd) 1.00:1; (Rev) 2.11:1. Other models: (1st) 2.46:1; (2nd) 1.46:1; (3rd) 1.00:1; (Rev) 2.18:1 to 2.20:1. Four-speed overdrive automatic available on Thunderbird w/V8302 and LTD: (1st) 2.47:1; (2nd) 1.47:1; (3rd) 1.00:1; (4th) 0.67:1; (Rev) 2.00:1. Standard final drive ratio: (Pinto) 3.08:1 w/4spd; (Fairmont) 3.08:1 exc. 2.73:1 w/six and auto., 2.26:1 w/V-8 and auto.; (Granada) 3.00:1 w/4spd, 2.79:1 w/V-8 and auto.; (LTD) 2.26:1 exc. wag 2.73:1, and 3.08:1 w/4spd overdrive auto.; (TBird) 2.26:1 exc. w/4spd auto., 3.08:1. Steering: (Pinto/Fairmont/TBird) rack and pinion; (others) recirculating ball. Front Suspension: (Pinto) coil springs with short/long control arms, and anti-sway bar with V-6; (Fairmont) MacPherson struts with coil springs on lower control arms and link-type anti-sway bar; (Granada) coil springs with short/long control arms and anti-sway bar; (LTD) long/short control arms w/coil springs and link-type stabilizer; (Thunderbird) modified MacPherson struts. Rear Suspension: (Pinto/Granada) rigid axle w/semi-elliptic leaf springs; (Fairmont/TBird) four-bar link coil springs; (LTD) rigid axle w/four-bar link and helical coil springs. Brakes: Front disc, rear drum. Ignition: Electronic. Body construction: (Pinto/Fairmont/Granada/TBird) unibody; (LTD) separate body and perimeter box frame. Fuel tank: (Pinto) 13 gal. exc. wag, 14; (Fairmont) 16 gal.; (Granada) 18 gal.; (LTD) 19 gal.; (TBird) 17.5 gal.

DRIVETRAIN OPTIONS: Engines: Turbo 140 cu. in. four: Fairmont ($481). 200 cu. in. six: Fairmont ($169). 255 cu. in. V-8: Fairmont ($288); Granada ($38). 302 cu. in. V-8: Granada ($188); TBird ($150). 351 cu. in. V-8: LTD ($150). Transmission/Differential: Select-shift auto. trans.: Pinto/Fairmont/Granada ($340). Four-speed overdrive automatic trans.: LTD/TBird ($138). Floor shift lever: Fairmont/Granada ($38). Traction-Lok differential: LTD ($69). Optional axle ratio: Pinto/Fairmont ($15); LTD ($19). Brakes/Steering/Suspension: Power brakes: Pinto/Fairmont/Granada ($78). Power steering: Pinto ($160); Fairmont/Granada ($165). H.D. susp.: Granada/LTD/TBird ($23). Handling susp.: Fairmont ($44); LTD ($43). Adjustable air shock absorbers: LTD ($55). Other: H.D. battery ($20-$21). Engine block heater ($15). Trailer towing pkg., heavy duty: LTD ($164-$169). California emission system: Pinto/Fairmont ($253); Granada ($275); LTD ($235); TBird ($238). High-altitude option ($36).

PINTO CONVENIENCE/APPEARANCE OPTIONS: Option Packages: ESS pkg. ($281-$313). Cruising pkg. ($355- $606); tape delete ($70 credit). Rally pack: hatch ($369); wagon ($625). Sport pkg. ($103-$118). Exterior decor group ($24-$44). Interior decor group ($165-$238). Interior accent group ($5-$50). Convenience group ($26-$118). Protection group ($36-$40). Light group ($41). Comfort/Convenience: Air conditioner ($538). Rear defroster, electric ($96). Tinted glass ($65). Cigar lighter ($8). Trunk light ($5). Driver's remote mirror ($18). Dual sport mirrors ($58). Day/night mirror ($11). Entertainment: AM radio: Pony ($80). AM/FM radio ($65-$145). AM/FM stereo radio ($103-$183); w/cassette player ($191- $271). Radio flexibility option ($60). Exterior: Flip-up open air roof ($206-$219). Glass third door ($31). Metallic glow paint ($45). Two-tone paint/tape ($80). Accent tape stripe ($80). Black narrow vinyl-insert bodyside moldings ($43). Premium bodyside moldings ($11-$54). Bumper rub strips ($34). Roof luggage rack ($71). Mud/stone deflectors ($25). Lower bodyside protection ($34). Interior: Four-way driver's seat ($38). Load floor carpet ($28). Cargo area cover ($30). Front floor mats ($19). Wheels/Tires: Wire wheel covers ($104). Forged aluminum wheels ($225-$300); white ($256-$331). Lacy spoke alum. wheels ($225-$300). Styled steel wheels ($56). BR78 x 13 WSW ($50). BR70 x 13 RWL ($87).

FAIRMONT CONVENIENCE/APPEARANCE OPTIONS: Option Packages: ES option ($378). Futura sports group ($114). Ghia pkg.: Futura cpe ($193); std. sedan ($566). Squire option ($458). Exterior decor group ($260). Exterior accent group ($95). Interior decor group ($184-$346). Interior accent group ($110-$115). Instrument cluster ($85). Convenience group ($29-$51). Appearance protection group ($46-$53). Light group ($30-$48). Comfort/Convenience: Air cond. ($571). Rear defroster, electric ($101). Fingertip speed control ($116-$129). Power windows ($135-$191). Power door locks ($88-$125). Power decklid release ($25). Power seat ($111). Tinted glass ($71). Sport steering wheel ($43). Leather-wrapped steering wheel ($44). Tilt steering ($78-$90). Electric clock ($25). Cigar lighter ($8). Interval wipers ($39). Rear wiper/washer ($79). Left remote mirror ($19). Dual bright remote mirrors ($54-$60). Entertainment: AM radio ($93). AM/FM radio ($145). AM/FM stereo radio ($183). w/8track player ($259); w/cassette player ($271). Premium sound system ($94). Radio flexibility ($63). Exterior: Flip-up open air roof ($219). Full or half vinyl roof ($118). Metallic glow paint ($54). Two-tone paint ($56); metallic ($154-$169). Accent stripe ($33). Pivoting front vent windows ($50). Rear quarter vent louvers ($41). Vinyl-insert bodyside moldings ($44); wide black vinyl ($45). Rocker panel moldings ($30). Bright window frames ($24). Bumper guards, rear ($23). Bumper rub strips ($40). Luggage rack ($88). Mud/stone deflectors ($25). Lower bodyside protection ($34-$48). Interior: Non-reclining bucket seats ($31-$50). Bench seat ($50 credit). Cloth/vinyl seat trim ($28-$44). Vinyl seat trim ($25). Front floor mats ($19). Lockable side storage box ($23). Wheels/Tires: Hubcaps w/trim rings ($41). Deluxe wheel covers ($41). Turbine wheel covers ($43); argent ($43-$84). Wire wheel covers ($74-$158). Styled steel wheels ($49-$133). Cast aluminum wheels ($268-$351). P175/75R14 WSW ($50). P185/75R14 BSW ($31); WSW ($81); RWL ($96). Conventional spare ($37).

GRANADA CONVENIENCE/APPEARANCE OPTIONS: Option Packages: Interior decor group ($243). Convenience group ($39-$108). Light group ($46-$51). Cold weather group ($31-$65). Heavy-duty group ($20-$65). Protection group ($29- $53). Visibility group ($6-$66). Comfort/Convenience: Air cond. ($571); auto-temp ($634). Rear defroster, electric ($101). Fingertip speed control ($116- $129). Illuminated entry system ($58). Power windows ($136- $193). Power door locks ($89-$125). Power decklid release ($25). Power four-way seat ($111). Tinted glass ($71). Tilt steering wheel ($78). Digital clock ($54). Lighting and Mirrors: Cornering lamps ($50). Dual remote mirrors ($41-$60). Dual sport mirrors ($50-$69). Lighted right visor vanity mirror ($41). Entertainment: AM radio ($93). AM/FM radio ($145). AM/FM stereo radio ($183); w/8track player ($259); w/cassette ($271). AM/FM stereo search

radio ($333); w/8track ($409); w/cassette and Dolby ($421). Radio flexibility ($63). Exterior: Power moonroof ($998). Full or half vinyl roof ($118). Metallic glow paint ($54). Bodyside/decklid paint stripes ($49). Two-tone paint/tape ($180). Bodyside accent moldings ($50). Black vinyl insert bodyside moldings ($44). Rocker panel moldings ($30). Bumper rub strips ($41). Mud/stone deflectors ($25). Lower bodyside protection ($34). Interior: Console ($110). Four-way driver's seat ($38). Reclining bucket seats (NC). Deluxe cloth/vinyl seat (NC). Flight bench seat (NC). Cloth/vinyl flight bench seat ($60). Leather seat trim ($277). Front floor mats ($19). Color-keyed seatbelts ($23). Wheels: Luxury wheel covers ($46) exc. Ghia (NC). Wire wheel covers ($119) exc. Ghia/ESS ($73). Styled steel wheels w/trim rings ($91-$138). Cast aluminum wheels ($275-$321). Tires: DR78 x 14 SBR WSW. ER78 x 14 SBR BSW/WSW. FR78 x 14 SBR BSW/WSW/wide WSW. Inflatable spare ($37).

LTD CONVENIENCE/APPEARANCE OPTIONS: Option Packages: Interior luxury group ($693-$741). Convenience group ($68-$98). Power lock group ($114-$166). Light group ($33-$43). Protection group ($48-$58). Comfort/Convenience: Air cond. ($606); w/auto-temp control ($669). Rear defroster, electric ($103). Fingertip speed control ($116). Illuminated entry system ($58). Power windows ($140-$208). Power door locks ($89-$120). Power driver's seat ($168); driver and passenger ($335). Tinted glass ($85). Autolamp on/off delay ($63). Leather-wrapped steering wheel ($44). Tilt steering wheel ($78). Auto. parking brake release ($10). Electric clock ($24). Digital clock ($38-$61). Seatbelt chime ($23). Interval wipers ($40). Lighting, Horns and Mirrors: Cornering lamps ($48). Trunk light ($5). Dual-note horn ($10). Driver's remote mirror ($19). Dual remote mirrors ($38-$56). Lighted right visor vanity mirror ($35-$41); pair ($42-$83). Entertainment: AM radio ($93). AM/FM radio ($145). AM/FM stereo radio ($183); w/8track tape player ($259); w/cassette ($271). AM/FM stereo search radio ($333); w/8track ($409); w/cassette ($421). CB radio ($316). Power antenna ($49). Dual rear speakers ($40). Premium sound system ($94). Radio flexibility ($66). Exterior: Full or half vinyl roof ($145). Metallic glow paint ($65). Two-tone paint/tape ($75). Dual accent paint stripes ($33). Hood striping ($14). Pivoting front vent windows ($50). Rocker panel moldings ($29). Vinyl-insert bodyside moldings ($45). Bumper guards, rear ($26). Bumper rub strips ($56). Luggage rack ($115). Lower bodyside protection ($34- $46). Interior: Dual-facing rear seats: wagon ($146-$151). Flight bench seat ($56). Leather split bench seat ($349). Dual flight bench seat recliners ($55). Split bench seat w/ recliners ($173-$229). All-vinyl seat trim ($28). Duraweave vinyl trim ($50). Front floor mats ($19); front/rear ($30). Trunk trim ($46-$51). Trunk mat ($14). Color-keyed seatbelts ($24). Wheels/Tires: Luxury wheel covers ($70). Wire wheel covers ($138). Cast aluminum wheels ($310). P205/75R14 WSW ($50). P215/75R14 BSW ($29); WSW ($50-$79). P225/75R14 WSW ($79- $107). P205/75R15 WSW ($55-$87). Conventional spare ($37).

THUNDERBIRD CONVENIENCE/APPEARANCE OPTIONS: Option Packages: Exterior luxury group ($489). Interior luxury group ($975). Exterior decor group ($359). Interior decor group ($348). Protection group ($39-$43). Light group ($35). Power lock group ($113). Comfort/Convenience: Air cond. ($571); auto-temp ($634) exc. Twn Lan/Anniv. ($63). Rear defroster ($101). Fingertip speed ontrol ($116-$129). Illuminated entry system ($58). Keyless entry ($106-$119). Garage door opener w/lighted vanity mirrors ($130-$171). Autolamp on/off delay ($63). Tinted glass ($71); windshield only ($29). Power windows ($136). Four-way power seat ($111). Six-way power driver's seat ($166). Auto. parking brake release ($10). Leather-wrapped steering wheel ($44). Tilt steering wheel ($78). Electronic instrument cluster ($275-$313). Diagnostic warning lights ($50). Digital clock ($38). Interval wipers ($39). Lighting, Horns and Mirrors: Cornering lamps ($50). Trunk light ($5). Dual-note horn ($9). Driver's remote mirror, chrome ($18). Dual remote mirrors ($69). Lighted right visor vanity mirror ($35-$41). Entertainment: AM/FM radio ($53). AM/FM stereo radio ($90); w/8track player ($166); w/cassette ($179). AM/FM stereo search radio ($240); w/8track ($316) exc. Twn Lan/Anniv. ($76); w/cassette ($329) exc. Twn Lan/Anniv. ($89). CB radio ($316). AM radio delete ($81 credit). Power antenna ($49). Dual rear speakers ($38). Premium sound system ($119-$150). Radio flexibility ($66). Exterior: Flip-up open-air roof ($219). Vinyl half roof ($133). Metallic glow paint ($60). Two-tone paint/tape ($106- $163). Dual accent bodyside paint stripes ($40). Hood/bodyside paint stripes ($16-$56). Wide vinyl bodyside moldings ($54). Wide door belt moldings ($31-$44). Rocker panel moldings ($30). Mud/stone deflectors ($25). Lower odyside protection ($34-$46). Interior: Bucket seats w/console ($176) exc. (NC) w/decor group. Recaro buckets w/console ($166-$254) exc. Twn Lan (NC). Leather seat trim ($318-$349). Vinyl seat trim ($26). Front floor mats ($19). Trunk trim ($44). Color-keyed seatbelts ($23). Wheels/Tires: Wire wheel covers ($50-$138). Luxury wheel covers ($88). P195/75R14 BSW ($26); WSW ($50). TR WSW tires on alum. wheels: base ($441-$528). Conventional spare ($37).

HISTORY: Introduced: October 12, 1979. Model year production: 1,167,581 (incl. Mustangs). Total passenger-car production for the U.S. market of 1,048,044 units (incl. Mustangs) included 426,107 four-cylinder, 334,298 sixes and 287,639 V-8s. Of the fours, 1,158 were Fairmont turbos (and 12,052 Mustang turbos). Calendar year production (U.S.): 929,639 (incl. Mustangs). Calendar year sales by U.S. dealers: 1,074,675 (incl. Mustangs). Model year sales by U.S. dealers: 1,124,192 (incl. Mustangs, but not incl. 68,841 imported Fiestas).

NOTE: Starting this year, Club Wagons (vans) were no longer classed as passenger cars.

Historical Footnotes: Early in 1980, the "Erika" subcompact to come for 1981 was renamed Escort (and Mercury Lynx). Sales for the model year fell over 28 percent, touching every car in the lineup but headed by LTD's 43 percent drop. LTD was advertised during this period as rivaling Rolls-Royce for smooth, quiet ride qualities. The restyled and downsized Thunderbird didn't find many buyers either. Two assembly plants closed during 1980, at Mahwah, New Jersey and Los Angeles. Still, Ford expected to spend $2 billion for expansion and retooling at other domestic acilities. Foremost hope for the future was the new Escort being readied for 1981 introduction. Philip E. Benton became head of the Ford Division, following the retirement of Walter S. Walla.

1981 FORD

The new front-wheel drive Escort "world car" arrived for 1981, to assist Ford in reaching a healthy share of subcompact buyers. Granada had all-new sheetmetal with shorter wheelbase and length, but claimed six-passenger capacity. Fairmont Futura added a wagon, while there was a new top-of-the-line Thunderbird. Several Ford models could be ordered with either a four, six or eight-cylinder engine. New base powertrain for the full-size LTD was the small (255 cu. in.) V-8. Corporate body colors for 1981 were: Black, Bright Bittersweet, Candyapple Red, Medium or Bright Red, Light Medium Blue, Medium Dark Brown, Bright Yellow, Cream, Chrome Yellow, Tan, Antique Cream, Pastel Chamois, Fawn, and White. Also available was a selection of metallics including: Silver, Medium Grey, Light Pewter, Medium Pewter, Maroon, Dark Blue, Bright Blue, Medium Dark Spruce, Dark Brown, Dark Pine, and Dark Cordovan. Some Ford products also could choose from up to nine "Glamour" colors and 16 clearcoat polish paint selections.

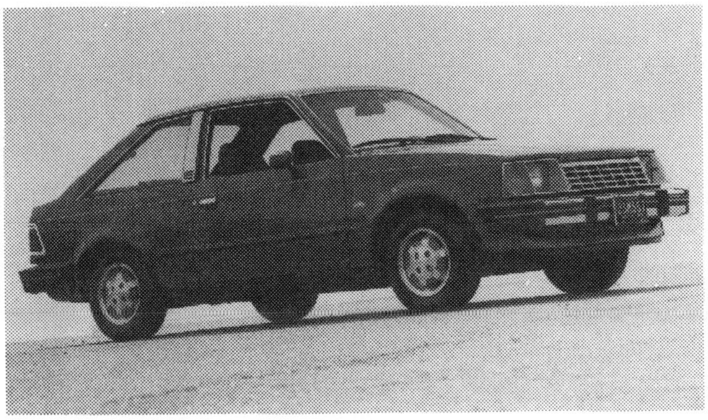

1981 Escort GLX three-door hatchback (F)

ESCORT — FOUR — Because it evolved from Ford's international experience, the new front-wheel-drive Escort was called a "world car." It was also dubbed "international" size, as Ford's attempt to rival the imports. A $3 billion development program had been initiated in the early 1970s to produce Escorts for sale both in the U.S. and Europe. The engine alone cost $1 billion to develop. The U.S. version of the all-new overhead-cam, Compound Valve Hemispherical (CVH) engine had to meet federal emissions standards, too. The transverse-mounted engine was called hemi-head because of its hemispherical-shaped combustion chambers, calling to mind some far more muscular hemis of past decades. Displacing just 97.6 cu. in., it was the smallest engine in American Ford history. Cylinder head and intake manifold were aluminum. The CVH design put the spark plug close to the center of the combustion chamber. Escort had many maintenance-free features, including self-adjusting brakes, lubed-for-life wheel bearings and front suspension, preset carb mixtures, hydraulic valve lifters, fixed caster and camber settings at the front end, and self-adjusting clutches. Ford General Manager Phillip E. Benton Jr. said "all of the Escort's major components and systems such as the engine, transaxle...suspension and body were especially designed for the car, with no carryover parts or components." "Three-door" hatchback and four-door liftgate bodies were offered. Both were 65.9 inches wide, on a 94.2 inch wheelbase. Five trim levels included base, L, GL, GLX, and sporty SS. Escort's four-speed manual transaxle was fully synchronized. with wide-ratio gearing. Optional three-speed automatic used a new split-torque design in intermediate and high, which divided torque between the converter and a direct mechanical hookup to the dual driveshafts. Escort had four- wheel independent suspension, rack-and-pinion steering, standard halogen headlamps, maintenance-free battery, fluidic windshield washer, and inertia seatback release. Front suspension used MacPherson struts with strut-mounted coil springs and a stabilizer bar. At the rear were independent trailing arms with modified MacPherson struts and coil springs, mounted on stamped lower control arms. P-metric (P155/80R) radial tires rode 13 in. steel wheels, with cast aluminum wheels optional. The hatchback Escort was 7 inches shorter than the old Pinto Runabout, while the wagon was 15 inches shorter than the Pinto version. Seats were higher than Pinto's, and glass area greatly enlarged. Escort's eggcrate grille had a 7 x 4 hole pattern. Recessed single rectangular headlamps sat in bright housings. Outboard were wraparound park/signal lamps. Wraparound taillamps were angled at the front edge. Backup lamps stood inboard, toward the license plate housing. 'Ford' and 'Escort' lettering went on the hatch lid, below large sloping, curved

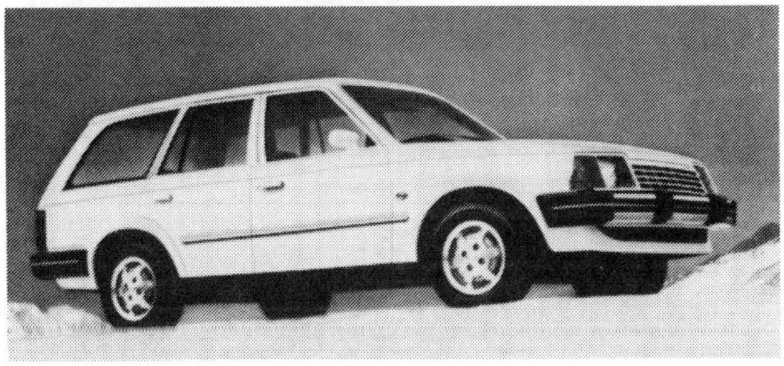

1981 Escort GLX four-door Liftgate (JG)

hatch glass. Wagons had vertical wraparound taillamps and a less-sloped rear window. Standard equipment for the base Escort included an AM radio, two-speed wipers, lighter, three-speed heater/defroster, inside hood release, high-back vinyl front bucket seats, bench-type folding rear seat, argent grille, bright bumpers, door-mounted driver's mirror, day/night mirror, courtesy lights, and semi-styled steel wheels with black hub covers and lug covers. Bright moldings went on the windshield surround, drip rail, and rear window surround. Escort L added bright headlamp housings, a bright grille, bright driver's mirror, matte black rocker panel paint, bodyside paint stripe, and bright belt molding. Escort GL included deluxe bumper rub strips and end caps, bright window frame moldings, vinyl-insert bodyside moldings with argent stripe, bright wheel hub covers and trim rings, bright lower back surround molding, high-back reclining bucket seats, four-spoke "soft feel" steering wheel, consolette, visor vanity mirror, and rear ashtrays. Escort GLX added dual color-keyed remote-control sport mirrors, bumper guards, low-back reclining bucket seats, woodtone instrument cluster applique, console with graphic warning display, digital clock, roof grab handles, locking glovebox, styled steel wheels with bright trim rings, interval wipers, and P165/80R13 blackwall SBR tires. Escort SS included black bumpers, argent stripe bumper end caps, black grille and headlamp housings, blackout moldings and rocker panel paint, dual black remote sport mirrors, bodyside/rear tape striping with decal, styled steel wheels with bright trim rings and argent hub covers, high-back reclining vinuyl bucket seats, handling suspension, and instrumentation group. Options included a console with graphic display module, intermittent wipers, and pivoting front vent windows. Gas mileage estimates reached 30 MPG city and 44 MPG highway. Early criticisms from the press and elsewhere prompted Ford to deliver a number of running changes right from the start, in an attempt to increase the car's refinement. First-year versions suffered several recalls. Mercury Lynx was Escort's corporate twin.

FAIRMONT — FOUR/SIX/V-8 — In addition to the usual sedans and Futura coupe, Fairmont delivered a station wagon this year under the Futura badge. The four-door, steel-sided wagon had Futura's quad rectangular headlamps and distinctive grille, as well as body brightwork and an upgraded interior. Squire (woodgrain) trim was available at extra cost. Fairmonts also added new standard equipment, including

1981 Fairmont sedan (F)

power front disc brakes, bucket seats, deluxe sound package to reduce road noise, dual-note horn, bright window frames, visor vanity mirror, glovebox lock, and rear seat ashtray. The option list expanded to include a console with diagnostic warning lights and digital clock (as on Mustang), illuminated entry system, Traction-Lok rear axle (V-8 only), lighted visor vanity mirror, and Michelin TR type tires. Both the 200 cu. in. (3.3-liter) six and 255 cu. in. (4.2-liter) V-8 now had a viscous-clutch fan drive. Base engine remained the 140 cu. in. (2.3-liter) four, with four-speed manual gearbox. The elusive turbo four was no longer listed as a possibility. Neither was the six with four-speed manual gearbox. That four-speed now had a self-adjusting clutch. Fairmont's base four-cylinder produced EPA estimates of 34 MPG highway and 23 MPG city. Fairmont's new grille had a tight crosshatch pattern, with two horizontal dividers to split it into three rows, each two "holes" high. As before, large vertical parking lamps stood inboard of the rectangular headlamps. Wide (non-wraparound) taillamps had vertical ribbing, with backup lenses at inner ends. Four-doors had a six-window design with narrow quarter windows that tapered to a point at the top. Wagons carried vertical wraparound taillamps, with backup lenses alongside the license plate.

1981 Granada GLX sedan (F)

GRANADA — FOUR/SIX/V-8 — For its final two years in the lineup, Granada received an aerodynamic restyle that was supposed to deliver a 21 percent improvement in fuel economy. Ford called it "the industry's most changed American-built sedan for 1981." This Granada was 3 inches shorter than its predecessor, but with more leg, hip and shoulder room inside, and more luggage space. Wheelbase was Fairmont-sized. In fact, Granada's chassis was based on the familiar "Fox" platform, with coil springs all around. The fully unitized body weighed 400 pounds less than the 1980 version. Drag coefficient rated a low 0.44. Under this year's hood was a standard 140 cu. in. (2.3-liter) OHC four, as in Fairmont and Mustang, with four-speed manual shift. Also available: the 200 cu. in. (3.3-liter) inline six and 255 cu. in. (4.2-liter) V-8. Automatic

1981 Granada GL coupe (JG)

was standard with the bigger engines. New for 1981 was a MacPherson strut front suspension, a pin-slider front disc brake system, front bucket seats on all models, revised instrument panel with two-pod instrument cluster, and stalk-mounted controls for turn signals, horn, dimmer, and wiper. P-metric steel-belted radial tires rode 14 in. stamped steel wheels. Granada also sported halogen headlamps. Three Granada series were offered: L, GL, and GLX (replacing base, Ghia and ESS). As before, body styles included only the two- and four-door sedans. The new upright bright grille had a tight crosshatch pattern with wide slots in 10 x 10 hole arrangement, with 'Ford' lettering on the upper header bar (driver's side). Quad rectangular headlamps were

used, with wraparound marker lenses and small horizontal amber parking lamps set in the front bumper. Wide taillamps (full-width except for the recessed license plate area) had backup lamps halfway toward the center. Each taillamp was divided into an upper and lower segment. Pinstripes flowed along the hood creases, and there was a stand-up see-through hood ornament. A small square badge was mounted ahead of the front door. Mercury Cougar was Granada's corporate companion.

1981 LTD coupe (JG)

LTD — V-8 — Full-size Fords no longer carried a standard full-size engine. LTD's new standard powertrain consisted of the 255 cu. in. (4.2-liter) V-8 and automatic overdrive transmission, which had been introduced in 1980 as an option on LTD and Thunderbird. That transmission also featured a lockup clutch torque converter. Three-speed automatic was abandoned. Two other V-8s were optional: 302 cu. in. (5.0-liter) or 351 cu. in. (5.8-liter), both with two-barrel carburetors. The latter produced 145 horsepower. A high-output 351 delivering 20 more horsepower was available only for police cars. LTD's lineup included four-door sedans in base, 'S' and Crown Victoria trim; two-door sedans in base and Crown Vic; and four-door wagons in all three series. Switching to a smaller base powerplant didn't seem to help mileage enormously, as the EPA estimate was a modest 16 MPG. New standard equipment included halogen headlamps on 'S' models, and separate ignition and door keys. Remote mirrors were now door-mounted rather than sail-mounted. Joining the option list were puncture-resistant tires and a convex remote-control passenger mirror. Country Squire switched from a seatbelt buzzer to chime. Appearance was the same as 1980. Taillamps had vertical ribbing, with small backup lenses below. The license plate was recessed in the decklid. Rear marker lenses followed the angle of quarter panel tips.

1981 Thunderbird Heritage hardtop coupe (F)

THUNDERBIRD — V-8 — Some TBird enthusiasts were doubtless shocked by the news: this year's edition carried a standard six-cylinder engine. The old familiar inline six at that, displacing just 200 cu. in. (3.3-liter). It came with standard SelectShift automatic. (Actually, the inline six had become a credit option during the 1980 model year.) The formerly standard 255 cu. in. (4.2-liter) V-8 became optional, as was a 302 cu. in. (5.0-liter) engine and automatic overdrive transmission for either V-8. Base models were better trimmed this year. In fact, all models offered items that had formerly been part of the Exterior Luxury Group. New standard equipment included halogen headlamps, viscous fan clutch, vinyl-insert bodyside moldings, wide door belt moldings, remote control left mirror, and deluxe color-keyed seatbelts. Automatic-temperature-control air conditioners added a defog mode. Three Thunderbird series were offered: base, Town Landau, and Heritage (replacing the former Silver Anniversary model). Town Landau also added equipment, including luxury wheel covers and a color-keyed wrapover band with small opera windows for the rear half-vinyl roof (similar to the treatment used on the 1980 Silver Anniversary TBird). Heritage carried a standard 255 cu. in. V-8. Appearance was similar to 1980, except that the front bumper no longer held a lower grille pattern. Huge full-width taillamps held Thunderbird emblems on each side. The decklid protruded halfway between each taillamp half. The license plate sat in a recessed opening low on the bumper. With wrapover roof band, opera windows were tiny. New options included a convertible-like Carriage Roof, Traction-Lok axle, pivoting front vent windows, convex remote mirror (passenger side), and self-sealing puncture-resistant tires.

I.D. DATA: Ford had a new 17-symbol Vehicle Identification Number (VIN), again stamped on a metal tab fastened to the instrument panel, visible through the windshield. Symbols one to three indicates manufacturer, make and vehicle type: '1FA' Ford passenger car. The fourth symbol ('B') denotes restraint system. Next comes a letter 'P', followed by two digits that indicate body type: Model Number, as shown in left column of tables below. (Example: '91' Fairmont two-door sedan.) Symbol eight indicates engine type: '2' L498 2Bbl.; 'A' L4-140 2Bbl.; 'B' L6200 1Bbl.; 'D' V8255 2Bbl.; 'F' V8302 2Bbl.; 'G' V8351 2Bbl. Next is a check digit. Symbol ten indicates model year ('B' 1981). Symbol eleven is assembly plant: 'A' Atlanta, GA; 'B' Oakville, Ontario (Canada); 'G' Chicago; 'H' Lorain, Ohio; 'K' Kansas City, MO; 'X' St. Thomas, Ontario; 'T' Metuchen, NJ; 'U' Louisville, KY; 'W' Wayne, MI. The final six digits make up the sequence number, starting with 100001. A Vehicle Certification Label on the left front door lock face panel or door pillar shows the manufacturer, month and year of manufacture, GVW, GAWR, certification statement, VIN, and codes for such items as body type, color, trim, axle, transmission, and special order information.

1981 Escort three-door hatchback (JG)

ESCORT (FOUR)

Model Number	Body/Style Number	Body Type & Seating	Factory Price	Shipping Weight	Production Total
05	61D	3-dr. Hatch Sed-4P	5158	1962	Note 1
08	74D	4-dr. Liftgate-4P	5731	2074	Note 1
05/60Q	61D	3-dr. L Hatch-4P	5494	1964	Note 1
08/60Q	74D	4-dr. L Liftgate-4P	5814	2075	Note 1
05/60Z	61D	3-dr. GL Hatch-4P	5838	1987	Note 1
08/60Z	74D	4-dr. GL Lift-4P	6178	2094	Note 1
05/602	61D	3-dr. GLX Hatch-4P	6476	2029	Note 1
08/602	74D	4-dr. GLX Lift-4P	6799	2137	Note 1
05/936	61D	3-dr. SS Hatch-4P	6139	2004	Note 1
08/936	74D	4-dr. SS Lift-4P	6464	2114	Note 1

Note 1: Total Escort production came to 192,554 three-door hatchbacks and 128,173 four-door liftbacks. Breakdown by trim level not available.

Escort Body Type Note: Hatchback Escorts are variously described as two- or three-door; Liftgate models are sometimes referred to as station wagons.

FAIRMONT (FOUR/SIX)

20	66	2-dr. 'S' Sed-5P	5701/5914	N/A	N/A
20	66B	2-dr. Sedan-5P	6032/6245	2564/2617	23,066
21	54B	4-dr. Sedan-5P	6151/6364	2614/2667	104,883
23	74B	4-dr. Sta Wag-5P	6384/6597	2721/2788	59,154

1981 Fairmont Futura Squire station wagon (JG)

FAIRMONT FUTURA (FOUR/SIX)

22	36R	2-dr. Coupe-5P	6347/6560	2619/2672	24,197
21/605	54B	4-dr. Sedan-5P	6361/6574	2648/2701	Note 2
23/605	74B	4-dr. Sta Wag-5P	6616/6829	2755/2822	Note 2

Note 2: Production totals listed under base Fairmont sedan and wagon also include Futura models.

GRANADA (FOUR/SIX)

26	66D	2-dr. L Sedan-5P	6474/6687	2707/2797	35,057
27	54D	4-dr. L Sedan-5P	6633/6848	2750/2840	86,284
26/602	66D	2-dr. GL Sed-5P	6875/7088	2728/2818	Note 3
27/602	54D	4-dr. GL Sed-5P	7035/7248	2777/2867	Note 3
26/933	66D	2-dr. GLX Sed-5P	6988/7201	2732/2822	Note 3
27/933	54D	4-dr. GLX Sed-5P	7148/7361	2784/2874	Note 3

Note 3: Granada GL and GLX production is included in base Granada totals above.

Fairmont/Granada Engine Note: Prices shown are for four- and six-cylinder engines. A 255 cu. in. V-8 cost $50 more than the six.

1981 LTD Country Squire station wagon (JG)

LTD (V-8)

32	66H	2-dr. Sedan-6P	7607	3496	6,279
33	54H	4-dr. Sedan-6P	7718	3538	35,932
38	74H	4-dr. Sta Wag-6P	8180	3719	10,554
39	74K	4-dr. Ctry Sqr-6P	8640	3737	9,443

LTD 'S' (V-8)

31	54D	4-dr. Sedan-6P	7522	3490	17,490
37	74D	4-dr. Sta Wag-6P	7942	3717	2,465

LTD CROWN VICTORIA (V-8)

34	66K	2-dr. Sedan-6P	8251	3496	11,061
35	54K	4-dr. Sedan-6P	8384	3538	39,139

LTD Production Note: Production of wagons with dual-facing rear seats (a $143 option) is included in basic wagon totals.

THUNDERBIRD (SIX/V-8)

42	66D	2-dr. HT Cpe-4P	7551/7601	3004/3124	86,693

1981 Thunderbird Town Landau hardtop coupe (JG)

THUNDERBIRD TOWN LANDAU (SIX/V-8)

42/60T	66D	2-dr. HT Cpe-4P	8689/8739	3067/3187	Note 4

THUNDERBIRD HERITAGE (V-8)

42/607	66D	2-dr. HT Cpe-4P	11355	3303	Note 4

Note 4: Town Landau and Heritage production is included in basic Thunderbird total.

MODEL NUMBER NOTE: Some sources include a prefix 'P' ahead of the two-digit model number. **FACTORY PRICE AND WEIGHT NOTE:** Fairmont/Granada prices and weights to left of slash are for four-cylinder, to right for six-cylinder engine. Thunderbird prices and weights to left of slash are for six-cylinder, to right for V-8 engine.

ENGINE DATA: BASE FOUR (Escort): Inline. Overhead cam. Four-cylinder. Cast iron block; aluminum head. Displacement: 97.6 cu. in. (1.6 liters). Bore & stroke: 3.15 x 3.13 in. Compression ratio: 8.8:1. Brake horsepower: 65 at 5200 R.P.M. Torque: 85 lbs.-ft. at 3000 R.P.M. Five main bearings. Hydraulic valve lifters. Carburetor: 2Bbl. Holley-Weber 5740. VIN Code: 2. BASE FOUR (Fairmont, Granada): Inline. Overhead cam. Four-cylinder. Cast iron block and head. Displacement: 140 cu. in. (2.3 liters). Bore & stroke: 3.78 x 3.13 in. Compression ratio: 9.0:1. Brake horsepower: 88 at 4600 R.P.M. Torque: 118 lbs.-ft. at 2600 R.P.M. Five main bearings. Hydraulic valve lifters. Carburetor: 2Bbl. Holley 6500. VIN Code: A. BASE SIX (Thunderbird); OPTIONAL (Fairmont, Granada): Inline. Overhead valve. Six-cylinder. Cast iron block and head. Displacement: 200 cu. in. (3.3 liters). Bore & stroke: 3.68 x 3.13 in. Compression ratio: 8.6:1. Brake horsepower: 88 at 3800 R.P.M. Torque: 154 lbs.-ft. at 1400 R.P.M. Seven main bearings. Hydraulic valve lifters. Carburetor: 1Bbl. Holley 1946. VIN Code: B. BASE V-8 (LTD); OPTIONAL (Fairmont, Granada, Thunderbird): 90-degree, overhead valve V-8. Cast iron block and head. Displacement: 255 cu. in. (4.2 liters). Bore & stroke: 3.68 x 3.00 in. Compression ratio: 8.2:1. Brake horsepower: 115 at 3400 R.P.M.; (LTD, 120 at 3400). Torque: 195 lbs.-ft. at 2200 R.P.M.; (LTD, 205 at 2600). Five main bearings. Hydraulic valve lifters. Carburetor: 2Bbl. Motorcraft 2150 or 7200VV. VIN Code: D. OPTIONAL V-8 (LTD, Thunderbird): 90-degree, overhead valve V-8. Cast iron block and head. Displacement: 302 cu. in. (5.0 liters). Bore & stroke: 4.00 x 3.00 in. Compression ratio: 8.4:1. Brake horsepower: 130 at 3400 R.P.M. Torque: 235 lbs.-ft. at 1600 R.P.M.; (LTD, 235 at 1800). Five main bearings. Hydraulic valve lifters. Carburetor: 2Bbl. Motorcraft 2150 or 7200VV. VIN Code: F. OPTIONAL V-8 (LTD): 90-degree, overhead valve V-8. Cast iron block and head. Displacement: 351 cu. in. (5.8 liters). Bore & stroke: 4.00 x 3.50 in. Compression ratio: 8.3:1. Brake horsepower: 145 at 3200 R.P.M. Torque: 270 lbs.-ft. at 1800 R.P.M. Five main bearings. Hydraulic valve lifters. Carburetor: 2Bbl. Motorcraft 7200VV. Windsor engine. VIN Code: G.

NOTE: A high-output version of the 351 cu. in. V-8 was available. Brake H.P.: 165 at 3600 R.P.M. Torque: 285 lbs.-ft. at 2200 R.P.M.

CHASSIS DATA: Wheelbase: (Escort) 94.2 in.; (Fairmont/Granada) 105.5 in.; (LTD) 114.3 in.; (TBird) 108.4 in. Overall Length: (Escort hatch) 163.9 in.; (Escort Lift) 165.0 in.; (Fairmont) 195.5 in. exc. Futura coupe, 197.4 in.; (Granada) 196.5 in.; (LTD) 209.3 in.; (LTD wag) 215.0 in.; (TBird) 200.4 in. Height: (Escort) 53.3 in.; (Fairmont) 52.9 in.; (Fairmont Futura 2dr.) 51.7 in.; (Fairmont wag) 54.2 in.; (Granada) 53.0 in.; (LTD) 54.7 in.; (LTD wag) 57.4 in.; (TBird) 53.0 in. Width: (Escort) 65.9 in.; (Fairmont/Granada) 71.0 in.; (LTD) 77.5 in.; (LTD wag) 79.3 in.; (TBird) 74.1 in. Front Tread: (Escort) 54.7 in.; (Fairmont/Granada) 56.6 in.; (LTD) 62.2 in.; (TBird) 58.1 in. Rear Tread: (Escort)

56.0 in.; (Fairmont/Granada) 57.0 in.; (LTD) 62.0 in. (TBird) 57.0 in. Standard Tires: (Escort) P155/80R13 SBR BSW; (Fairmont/Granada) P175/75R14 SBR BSW; (LTD) P205/75R14 SBR WSW exc. wagon, P215/75R14; (TBird) P195/75R14 SBR WSW.

TECHNICAL: Transmission: Four-speed manual standard on Fairmont/Granada four: (1st) 3.98:1; (2nd) 2.14:1; (3rd) 1.42:1; (4th) 1.00:1; (Rev) 3.99:1. Four-speed manual transaxle standard on Escort: (1st) 3.58:1; (2nd) 2.05:1; (3rd) 1.21:1; (4th) 0.81:1; (Rev) 3.46:1. Three-speed automatic standard on other models, optional on all. Gear ratios on Fairmont/Granada four, Fairmont six and some TBirds: (1st) 2.47:1; (2nd) 1.47:1; (3rd) 1.00:1; (Rev) 2.11:1. Other models: (1st) 2.46:1; (2nd) 1.46:1; (3rd) 1.00:1; (Rev) 2.19:1. Four-speed overdrive automatic standard on LTD, available on Thunderbird V-8: (1st) 2.40:1; (2nd) 1.47:1; (3rd) 1.00:1; (4th) 0.67:1; (Rev) 2.00:1. Standard final drive ratio: (Escort) 3.59:1 w/4spd, 3.31:1 w/auto.; (Fairmont/Granada) 3.08:1 exc. 2.73:1 w/six, 2.26:1 w/V-8; (LTD) 3.08:1. (TBird) 2.73:1 w/six and auto., 2.26:1 w/255 V-8 and 3spd auto., 3.08:1 w/4-spd automatic. Drive Axle: (Escort) front; (others) rear. Steering: (LTD) recirculating ball; others (rack and pinion). Front Suspension: (Escort/Granada) MacPherson strut-mounted coil springs with lower control arms and stabilizer bar; (Fairmont/Thunderbird) modified MacPherson struts with lower control arms, coil springs and link-type anti-sway bar; (LTD) long/short control arms w/coil springs and link-type stabilizer bar. Rear Suspension: (Escort) independent trailing arms w/modified MacPherson struts and coil springs on lower control arms; (Fairmont/Granada/LTD) four-link live axle with coil springs; (Thunderbird) four-link live axle system with coil springs and anti-sway bar. Brakes: Front disc, rear drum. Ignition: Electronic. Body construction: (LTD) separate body and frame; (others) unibody. Fuel tank: (Escort) 10 gal.; (Fairmont/Granada) 14 or 16 gal.; (LTD) 20 gal.; (TBird) 18 gal.

DRIVETRAIN OPTIONS: Engines: 200 cu. in. six: Fairmont/Granada ($213). 255 cu. in. V-8: Fairmont/Granada ($263); TBird ($50). 302 cu. in. V-8: TBird ($91) exc. Heritage ($41); LTD sedan ($41). 351 cu. in. V-8: LTD sedan ($83); LTD wagon ($41). H.O. 351 cu. in. V-8: LTD ($139-$180). Transmission/Differential: Automatic transaxle: Escort ($344). Select-shift auto. trans.: Fairmont/Granada ($349). Four-speed overdrive automatic trans.: TBird ($162). Floor shift lever: Fairmont/Granada ($43). Traction-Lok differential: Fairmont/Granada/TBird ($67); LTD ($71). Optional axle ratio: Escort ($15); Granada ($16). Brakes/Steering/Suspension: Power brakes: Escort ($79). Power steering: Escort ($163); Fairmont/Granada ($168). H.D. susp.: Fairmont/Granada ($22); LTD/TBird ($23). Handling susp.: Escort ($37); Fairmont/LTD ($45). Adjustable air shock absorbers: LTD ($57). Other: H.D. battery ($20). H.D. alternator: LTD ($46). Extended-range gas tank: Escort ($32). Engine block heater ($16). Trailer towing pkg., heavy duty: LTD ($176). California emission system ($46). High-altitude option ($38).

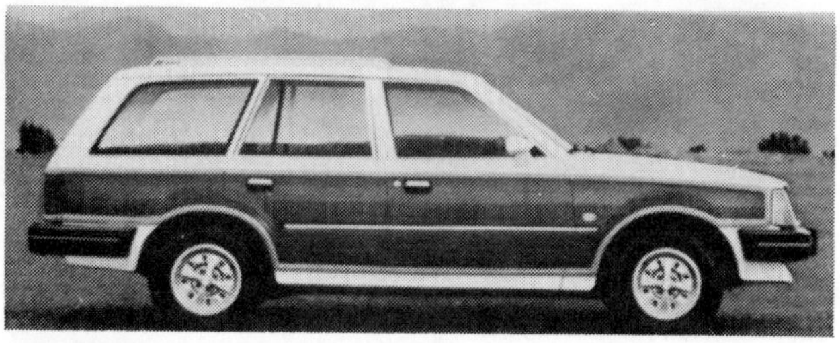

1981 Escort GLX Squire wagon (JG)

ESCORT CONVENIENCE/APPEARANCE OPTIONS: Option Packages: Squire wagon pkg. ($256). Instrument group ($77). Protection group ($49). Light group ($39). Comfort/Convenience: Air conditioner ($530). Rear defroster, electric ($102). Fingertip speed control ($132). Tinted glass ($70); windshield only ($28). Digital clock ($52). Intermittent wipers ($41). Rear wiper/washer ($100). Dual remote sport mirrors ($56). Entertainment: AM/FM radio ($63). AM/FM stereo radio ($100); w/cassette player ($187). Dual rear speakers ($37). Premium sound ($91). AM radio delete ($61 credit). Exterior: Flip-up open air roof ($154-$228). Metallic glow paint ($45). Two-tone paint/tape ($104). Front vent windows, pivoting ($55). Remote quarter windows ($95). Vinyl-insert bodyside moldings ($41). Bumper guards, front or rear ($23). Bumper rub strips ($34). Roof luggage rack ($74). Roof air deflector ($26). Lower bodyside protection ($60). Interior: Console ($98). Low-back reclining bucket seats ($30). Reclining front seatbacks ($55). Cloth/vinyl seat trim ($28); vinyl (NC). Deluxe seatbelts ($23). Wheels/Tires: Wheel trim rings ($44). Aluminum wheels ($193- $330). P155/80R13 WSW ($55). P165/80R13 BSW ($19); WSW ($55- $74).

FAIRMONT CONVENIENCE/APPEARANCE OPTIONS: Option Packages: Squire option ($200). Interior luxury group ($232-$256). Instrument cluster ($88). Appearance protection group ($50). Light group ($43). Comfort/Convenience: Air cond. ($585). Rear defroster, electric ($107). Fingertip speed control ($132). Illuminated entry ($60). Power windows ($140-$195). Power door locks ($93-$132). Remote decklid release ($27). Power seat ($122). Tinted glass ($76); windshield only ($29). Leather-wrapped steering wheel ($49). Tilt steering ($80-$93). Electric clock ($23). Interval wipers ($41). Rear wiper/washer ($85). Lighting and Mirrors: Map light ($9); dual-beam ($13). Trunk light ($6). Left remote mirror ($15). Dual bright remote mirrors ($55). Lighted visor vanity mirror ($43). Entertainment: AM/FM radio ($51). AM/FM stereo radio ($88); w/8track player ($162); w/cassette player ($174). Twin rear speakers ($37). Premium sound system ($91). Radio flexibility ($61). AM radio delete ($61 credit). Exterior: Flip-up open air roof ($228). Full or half vinyl roof ($115). Metallic glow paint ($55). Two-tone paint ($128- $162). Accent paint stripe ($34). Pivoting front vent windows ($55). Liftgate assist handle: wag ($16). Rocker panel moldings ($30). Bumper guards, rear ($23). Bumper rub strips ($43). Luggage rack: wagon ($90). Lower bodyside protection ($37-$49). Interior: Console ($168). Bench seat ($24 credit). Cloth seat trim ($28-$54). Flight bench seat (NC); w/vinyl trim ($26). Front floor mats ($18-$20). Locking storage box ($24). Deluxe seatbelts ($23). Wheels/Tires: Wire wheel covers ($76-$117). Styled steel wheels ($52-$94). P175/75R14 WSW ($55). P185/75R14 WSW ($86). P190/65R390 BSW on TRX alum. wheels ($470-$512). Conventional spare ($39).

GRANADA CONVENIENCE/APPEARANCE OPTIONS: Option Packages: Interior sport group ($282-$295). Light group ($45). Cold weather group ($67). Protection group ($51). Comfort/Convenience: Air cond. ($585). Rear defroster ($107). Fingertip speed control ($89-$132). Illuminated entry system ($60). Power windows ($140-$195). Power door locks ($93- $132). Power decklid release ($27). Power flight bench seat ($122); split bench ($173). Tinted glass ($76); windshield only ($29). Steering wheel: sport ($26-$39); leather-wrapped ($49); tilt ($80-$94). Electric clock ($23). Interval wipers ($41). Lighting and Mirrors: Cornering lamps ($51). Map light ($13). Trunk light ($6). Remote right mirror ($52). Lighted right visor vanity mirror ($43). Entertainment: AM/FM radio ($51). AM/FM stereo radio ($88); w/8track player ($162); w/cassette ($174). Premium sound ($91). Radio flexibility ($61). AM radio delete ($61 credit). Exterior: Flip-up open-air roof ($228). Full or half vinyl roof ($115). Metallic glow paint ($55). Bodyside/decklid paint stripes ($50). Two-tone paint ($146-$162). Pivoting front vent windows ($55). Vinyl insert bodyside moldings ($45). Bumper guards, rear ($23). Bumper rub strips ($43). Mud/stone deflectors ($26). Lower bodyside protection ($37). Interior: Console ($168). Split bench seat: GL/GLX ($178). Cloth seat trim ($45-$62). Flight bench seat (NC). Front floor mats ($18-$20). Color-keyed seatbelts ($23). Wheels/Tires: Luxury wheel covers: L ($43); GL/GLX (NC). Wire wheel covers ($124); GL/GLX ($80). Cast aluminum wheels ($308-$350). P175/75R14 WSW ($55). P185/75R14 BSW ($32); WSW ($86); RWL ($102). 190/65R390 BSW on TRX aluminum wheels ($468-$512). Conventional spare ($39).

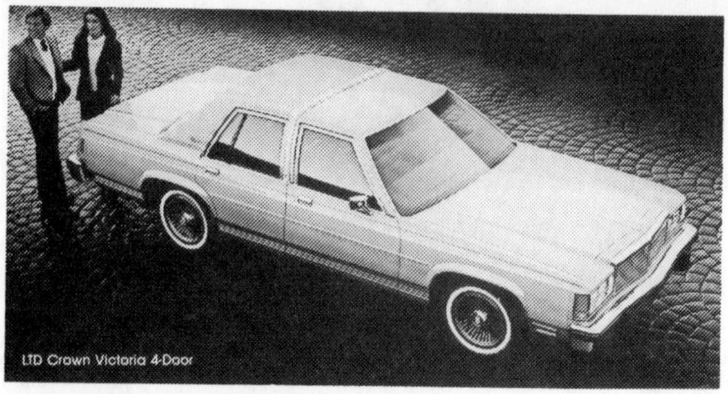

1981 LTD Crown Victoria sedan (JG)

LTD CONVENIENCE/APPEARANCE OPTIONS: Option Packages: Interior luxury group ($693-$765). Convenience group ($70-$101). Power lock group ($93-$176). Light group ($37). Protection group ($57). Comfort/Convenience: Air cond. ($624); w/auto-temp control ($687). Rear defroster, electric ($107). Fingertip speed control ($135). Illuminated entry system ($59). Power windows ($143-$211). Power driver's seat ($173); driver and passenger ($346). Tinted glass ($87); windshield only ($29). Autolamp on/off delay ($65). Leather-wrapped steering wheel ($45). Tilt steering wheel ($80). Auto. parking brake release ($10). Electric clock ($23). Digital clock ($40-$63). Seatbelt chime ($23). Interval wipers: fleet only ($41). Lighting and Mirrors: Cornering lamps ($48). Remote right mirror ($39). Lighted right visor vanity mirror ($38); pair ($43-$80). Entertainment: AM/FM radio ($51). AM/FM stereo radio ($88); w/8track tape player ($162) exc. Crown Vic ($74); w/cassette ($174) exc. Crown Vic ($87). AM/FM stereo search radio ($234) exc. Crown Vic ($146); w/8track ($221-$309); w/cassette ($233-$321). Power antenna ($48). Dual rear speakers ($39). Premium sound system ($116-$146). Radio flexibility ($65). AM radio delete ($61 credit). Exterior: Full or half vinyl roof ($141). Metallic glow paint ($67). Two-tone paint/tape ($44-$78). Dual accent paint stripes ($34). Hood striping ($15). Pivoting front vent windows ($55). Rocker panel moldings: Ctry Squire ($29). Vinyl-insert bodyside moldings ($44). Bumper guards, rear ($27). Bumper rub strips ($46). Luggage rack ($84). Lower bodyside protection ($34-$46). Interior: Dual-facing rear seats: wagon ($146). Cloth/vinyl flight bench seat ($59). Leather seating ($361). Dual flight bench seat recliners ($56). Cloth/vinyl split bench seating ($178-$237). All-vinyl seat trim: Crown Vic/Ctry Squire ($28); Duraweave vinyl ($54). Front floor mats ($20). Trunk trim ($45). Wheels/Tires: Luxury wheel covers ($72). Wire wheel covers ($135). Cast aluminum wheels ($338). P215/75R14 WSW ($30). P225/75R14 WSW ($30-$61). P205/75R15 WSW ($10-$40); puncture- resistant ($95-$125). Conventional spare ($39).

THUNDERBIRD CONVENIENCE/APPEARANCE OPTIONS: Option Packages: Interior luxury group ($1039) exc. Town Landau ($584). Exterior decor group ($341). Interior decor group ($349). Protection group ($45). Light group ($30). Power lock group ($120). Comfort/Convenience: Air cond. ($585); auto-temp ($652) exc. Twn Lan/Heritage ($67). Rear defroster ($107). Fingertip speed control ($132). Illuminated entry system ($60). Keyless entry ($122). Garage door opener w/lighted vanity mirrors ($134-$177). Autolamp on/off delay ($65). Tinted glass ($76); windshield only ($29). Power windows ($140). Four-way power seat ($122). Six-way power driver's seat ($173). Auto. parking brake release ($10). Leather-wrapped steering wheel ($45). Tilt steering wheel ($80). Electronic instrument cluster ($282-$322). Diagnostic warning lights: base ($51). Digital clock ($40). Interval wipers ($41). Lighting and Mirrors: Cornering lamps ($51). Remote right mirror ($52). Lighted right visor vanity mirror ($41). Entertainment: AM/FM radio ($51). AM/FM stereo radio ($88); w/8track player ($74-$162); w/cassette ($87-$174). AM/FM stereo search radio ($146-$234); w/8track ($221-$309) exc. Heritage ($74); w/cassette ($233-$321) exc. Heritage ($87). Power antenna ($48). Dual rear speakers ($37). Premium sound system ($116-$146). Radio flexibility ($65). AM radio delete ($61 credit). Exterior: Carriage roof ($902). Flip-up open-air roof ($228). Vinyl half roof ($130). Metallic glow paint ($70). Two-tone paint ($111-$180). Dual accent bodyside paint stripes: base ($41). Hood/bodyside paint stripes ($16-$57). Pivoting front vent windows ($55). Wide door belt moldings ($45). Rocker panel moldings ($30). Mud/stone deflectors ($26). Lower bodyside protection ($34-$48). Interior: Bucket seats w/console ($182) exc. (NC) w/decor group. Recaro bucket seats w/console ($376-$461) exc. Heritage ($213). Leather seat trim ($359). Vinyl seat trim ($28-$29). Front floor mats ($13); carpeted ($20). Trunk trim ($44). Wheels/Tires: Wire wheel covers ($38-$135). Luxury wheel covers ($98). Self-sealing tires ($85). TR WSW tires on alum. wheels ($428-$563). Conventional spare ($39).

HISTORY: Introduced: October 3, 1980. Model year production: 1,054,976 (incl. Mustangs). Total passenger-car production for the U.S. market of 1,030,915 units (incl. Mustangs) included 531,507 four-cylinder, 287,673 sixes and 211,735 V-8s. (Total includes 71,644 early '82 EXPs, all four-cylinder.) Calendar year production (U.S.): 892,043 (incl. Mustangs). Calendar year sales by U.S. dealers: 977,220 (incl. Mustangs). Model year sales by U.S. dealers: 1,058,044 (incl. Mustangs, 27,795 leftover Pintos and 41,601 early '82 EXPs, but not incl. 47,707 imported Fiestas).

Historical Footnotes: Escort quickly managed to become the best-selling Ford model, selling 284,633 examples. Obviously, Escort was primed to compete with Chevrolet's five-year-old Chevette. Otherwise, sales slumped somewhat. The restyled and downsized Granada sold better than in 1980, however, finding 105,743 buyers. Total model year sales were down over 7 percent, but that wasn't so bad considering the 28 percent decline from 1979 to 1980 (which also saw Ford/Lincoln/Mercury's market share shrink to a record low 16.5 percent). Mustang didn't sell nearly as well as hoped, even with a series of rebates offered during the year, dropping 29.5 percent for the model year. Model year production was closer to the 1980 figure, down just over 3 percent as opposed to a whopping 39 percent decline in the previous season. Calendar year production and sales both fell too, but not to a shocking level. This was a bad year all around for the industry. Car prices and interest rates had been rising steadily during this inflationary period, while the country also remained in a recession economy. Escort evolved from the "Erika" project, which first began in 1972. The goal: to produce a car that could be revised to suit both European and American tastes, using parts that could either be provided locally or imported. Both a 1.3-liter and 1.6-liter engine were planned, but only the bigger one found its way under domestic Escort hoods. Ford spent some $640 million to renovate its Dearborn, Michigan plant to manufacture Escort's 1.6-liter CVH engine. The engines were also built at a Ford facility in Wales. Additional future production was planned for Lima, Ohio, and for a new plant to be built in Mexico. The 1981 CAFE goal was 22 MPG.

1982 FORD

In addition to the new high-performance Mustang GT, 1982 brought a new two-seater EXP to the Ford fold, the first two-passenger model since the '55 Thunderbird. Escort added a four-door hatchback sedan, while Granada added a station wagon. Otherwise, 1982 was largely a carryover year. Ford's first domestic V-6 engine became available this year in Granada and Thunderbird. Weighing only a few pounds more than a four, it had an aluminum head, intake manifold and front cover. Ford's famous script returned this year after a long absence, in the form of a blue oval emblem at the front and rear of each model. Fairmont/Granada/Thunderbird sixes now had lockup torque converters in their SelectShift automatics, which worked in all three forward speeds. The government's fuel economy (CAFE) standard this year was 24 MPG.

1982 Escort GLX five-door hatchback (JG)

ESCORT — FOUR — A new four-door hatchback sedan joined Escort's initial "three-door" (actually two-door) hatchback and four-door liftback wagon. Base and SS wagons were dropped. L, GL and GLX Escorts now had bright headlamp housings. Power front disc brakes had become standard on wagons late in the 1981 model year, and continued this year. New stainless steel wheel trim rings (formerly stamped aluminum) arrived on GL, GLX and GT models. Escort had a new low-restriction exhaust and larger (P165/80R13) tires in all series. Ford's oval script emblem replaced 'Ford' block letters on the liftgate, which also held 'Escort' lettering. An electric hatch release was now standard on GLX hatchbacks (optional elsewhere). There was a running change in the four-speed manual transaxle, with different third and fourth gear ratios. Third gear changed from 1.23:1 to 1.36:1, and fourth from 0.81:1 to 0.95:1. Air-conditioned models included a switch that disconnected the unit for an instant when the gas pedal was floored. Like other Ford models, this year's Escort also displayed the blue script oval up front. Otherwise, appearance was similar to 1981. Base Escorts had an argent painted grille, wraparound amber parking lamps, single rectangular halogen headlamps, short black bumper end caps, semi-styled steel wheels with black and argent hub covers, and black wheel nut covers. Sedans had wraparound tri-color taillamps; red taillamps went on wagons. Inside were vinyl high-back front bucket seats, a black two-spoke steering wheel, black instrument panel with ashtray, bronzetone cluster, and color-keyed soft-feel pad. Escort L added bright headlamp doors, bright grille with integral Ford oval, brushed center-pillar applique, matte black rocker panels, bodyside paint stripes, black taillamp extensions, an 'L' badge on the liftgate, and blackout front end. Escort GL added deluxe bumper end caps and rub strips, 'GL' badge in back, front air dam, vinyl-insert bodyside moldings with argent insert, and bright window frame and lower back surround moldings. Inside, the GL had high-back reclining bucket seats and a four-spoke soft-feel color-keyed steering wheel. GLX stepped upward with interval wipers, dual color-keyed remote sport mirrors, 'GLX' badge, front and rear bumper guards, low-back reclining bucket seats in GLX vinyl or cloth/vinyl, woodtone instrument cluster applique, P165/80R13 tires, and console with graphic warning display. Escort GT (formerly SS) added a handling suspension, black bumpers with deluxe rub strips and deluxe end caps, front air dam, roof grab handles, black grille and headlamp doors, and Ford oval on the black grille's header bar. Blackout treatment went on windshield molding, drip moldings, quarter window and door frames, quarter window moldings, dual remote sport mirrors, door handles and lock covers, center pillar applique, rocker panels, belt and back window moldings, lower back surround molding, and taillamp extensions. Bodyside and rear end tape stripes showed an identifying decal. New options included shearling and leather (or leather alone) seat inserts, and an AM/FM stereo with 8-track player. The optional Squire exterior now had lighter-color walnut woodtone trim. Escorts had a larger (11.3 gallon) gas tank this year. EPA ratings reached 31 MPG city (47 MPG highway) on the base Escort with four-speed.

1982 EXP three-door hatchback (F)

EXP — FOUR — First shown at the Chicago Auto Show, then introduced in April as an early '82 model, EXP was the first two-seater Ford offered in 25 years. Comparing EXP to the original Thunderbird, Ford Division General Manager Louis E. Lataif said: "We're introducing another two-seater with the same flair, but the EXP will be a very affordable, very fuel efficient car matched to the lifestyles of the eighties." For comparison, the sporty new coupe weighed a thousand pounds less than the original Thunderbird. EXP was also 2 inches lower and 5 inches shorter. EXP's rakish non-boxy body rode an Escort/Lynx 94.2 inch wheelbase, with that car's front-drive running gear, four-wheel independent suspension, and dashboard. EXP was longer, lower and narrower than Escort. Performance wasn't (yet) its strong suit, however, since EXP weighed about 200 pounds more than Escort but carried the same small engine. Standard features included steel-belted radial tires, power front disc/rear drum brakes, halogen headlamps, rack-and-pinion steering, reclining high-back bucket seats, four-spoke sport steering wheel, and easy-to-read instrument panel and console with full instrumentation. Underhood was the 97.6 cu. in. (1.6-liter) CVH

engine with standard four-speed overdrive manual transaxle. Several standard equipment additions were incorporated as a running change. They included tinted glass, an electronic day/date digital clock, power liftgate release, maintenance-free 48 ampere-hour battery, engine compartment light, ashtray light, and headlamps-on warning buzzer. Both EXP and Mercury's LN7, its corporate cousin, had a sharply-sloped windshield, wheel arches with prominent lips, and wide bodyside moldings not far below the top of the wheel opening line. Biggest difference was in the back end. Ford's coupe was a notchback with lift-up hatch, while Mercury's LN7 fielded a big "bubbleback" back window. EXP's minimalist grille consisted merely of twin side-by-side slots in the sloped front panel (LN7 had ten). Single quad hedlamps sat in "eyebrow" housings. Large wraparound taillamps came to a point on the quarter panel. Parking lamps stood in the bumper, well below the headlamps. Priced considerably higher than Escort, EXP carried an ample list of standard equipment. It included power brakes, tachometer, engine gauges, full carpeting, electric back-window defroster, power hatchback release, digital clock, and cargo area security shade. Manual-transaxle models had a sport-tuned exhaust. Automatic models had a wide-open-throttle cutout switch for the optional air conditioning compressor clutch. A rather modest option list included a flip-up open-air roof, premium stereo system, and leather (or shearling and leather) seating surfaces. An optional TR handling package included special wheels and Michelin TRX tires in P165/70R365 size, and a larger-diameter front stabilizer bar. Shock valving, spring rates and caster/camber settings were modified for firmer ride and tighter handling. As the full model year began, Ford offered an optional (no-extra-cost) 4.05:1 final drive ratio for better performance. Later came a close-ratio gearbox with 3.59:1 final drive ratio, intended for the same purpose. Finally, in March 1982, an 80-horsepower edition of the CVH four became available. It had higher (9.0:1) compression, a bigger air cleaner intake, lower-restriction exhaust and dual-outlet exhaust manifold, larger carburetor venturis, and higher-lift camshaft.

1982 Fairmont Futura sedan (JG)

FAIRMONT FUTURA — FOUR/SIX — All Fairmont models acquired the Futura name this year as the lineup shrunk to a single series: just a two- and four-door sedan, and sport coupe. The station wagon was dropped, and the 255 cu. in. (4.2-liter) V-8 was available only in police and taxi packages. Base engine was the 140 cu. in. (2.3-liter) four, with 3.3-liter inline six optional. Optional SelectShift automatic with the six included a new lockup torque converter. Fairmont's new front end look featured a bold grille with strong divider forming a 6x2 grid, with each "hole" containing a tight internal crosshatch pattern. Quad rectangular headlamps now stood above quad park/signal lamps, like LTD but without its wraparound side marker lenses. Instead, Fairmont had small marker lenses set low on front fenders. The rear held the same vertically-ribbed taillamps as before. Front fenders held a Futura badge. Deluxe wide lower bodyside moldings met partial wheel lip moldings. Interiors held new high-gloss woodtone door trim and instrument panel appliques (formerly walnut). In back was a new deep-well trunk. AM radios added dual front speakers, and a new flash-to-pass feature was added to the headlamp lever. There was also a new gas cap tether. The former optional sweep-hand electric clock switched to quartz-type, and the available extended-range fuel tank held 20 gallons (formerly 16). Discontinued options were the leather-wrapped steering wheel, vinyl front floor mats, and right lighted visor vanity mirror.

1982 Granada GL Squire station wagon (JG)

GRANADA — FOUR/SIX/V-6 — Following its major restyle and downsizing for 1981, Granada looked the same this year but added a pair of station wagons (L and GL series). New station wagon options included a luggage rack, two-way liftgate (with flip-up window), rear wiper/washer, and Squire package. Fuel filler caps were now tethered. Flash-to-pass control on the steering column was new this year. Sedans could get an optional extended-range fuel tank. No more V-8s went under Granada hoods. A new optional "Essex" 232 cu. in. (3.8-liter) V-6 producing 112 horsepower was said to offer V-8 power; and it weighed just 4 pounds more than the base 140 cu. in. (2.3-liter) four. An inline six also remained available (standard on wagons). The V-6 got an EPA rating of 19 MPG city and 26 MPG highway. A new torque converter clutch providing a direct connection became standard on SelectShift automatic for the six and V-6 engines. This would be Granada's final season, but its basic design carried on in the form of a restyled LTD.

LTD — V-8 — After a long history, the 351 cu. in. (5.8-liter) V-8 no longer was available for private full-size Fords, but continued as an option for police models. Little changed to this year's LTD lineup, apart from seven new body colors. Ford ovals were added to front grilles and rear decklids (or tailgates). All monaural radios had dual

1982 LTD Crown Victoria sedan (JG)

front speakers and wiring for rear speakers. The sweep-hand clock added quartz operation. A new medium-duty trailer towing option replaced the former heavy-duty one. New optional wire wheel covers incorporated a locking feature. Base engine was a 255 cu. in. (4.2-liter) V-8; optional, the 302 cu. in. (5.0-liter) V-8. Also optional for 1982 was a Tripminder computer that combined a trip odometer with quartz clock to show vehicle speed, real or elapsed time, and fuel flow. Touching buttons could display instant or average MPG, amount of fuel used, trip mileage, average trip speed, and total trip time. Thunderbird could also get one. With 114.3 inch wheelbase, LTD was the biggest Ford. Wide amber parking lamps stood below quad headlamps. Amber marker lenses had a large section above a smaller one, to follow the line of the headlamp/parking lamp. The fine checkerboard grille pattern was divided by a vertical center bar, with Ford oval at driver's side. An 'Automatic Overdrive' badge went ahead of the door. Vertically ribbed taillamps held 'LTD' lettering, with small backup lamps below the taillamps. 'LTD' letters also decorated the 'C' pillar.

1982 Thunderbird Heritage hardtop coupe (JG)

THUNDERBIRD — SIX/V-6/V-8 — Engine choices grew smaller yet on the '82 Thunderbird, as the familiar 302 cu. in. (5.0-liter) V-8 was abandoned. The 200 cu. in. (3.3-liter) inline six became standard on base 'birds, new 232 cu. in. (3.8-liter) V-6 optional, with 255 cu. in. (4.2-liter) V-8 the biggest that could be bought. SelectShift transmission with the inline six had a new lockup torque converter. Three models were offered again: base, Town Landau, and Heritage. TBird's gas tank grew from 18 to 21 gallons. Exterior trim had more black-accented areas. A new optional Tripminder computer not only showed time and speed, but figured and displayed elapsed time, distance traveled, average or present MPG, fuel used, and average speed. There was a new wire wheel cover option with locking feature, and a new luxury vinyl roof option (standard on Town Landau). Appearance was similar to 1981, with the same huge taillamps. Concealed headlamps again had a clear lens-like trim panel on each cover, which extended outward far around the fender to form large wraparound signal/marker lenses. Those lenses were all clear except for an amber section toward the wheel. The crosshatch grille had an 8 x 6 pattern of wide holes. 'Thunderbird' lettering was set in the grille header. A wide see-through hood ornament held a Thunderbird insignia. That emblem also highlighted lenses and back pillars.

I.D. DATA: Ford's 17-symbol Vehicle Identification Number (VIN) again was stamped on a metal tab fastened to the instrument panel, visible through the windshield. The first three symbols ('1FA') indicate manufacturer, make and vehicle type. The fourth symbol ('B') denotes restraint system. Next comes a letter 'P', followed by two digits that indicate body type: Model Number, as shown in left column of tables below. (Example: '05' Escort two-door hatchback.) Symbol eight indicates engine type: '2' L498 2Bbl.; 'A' L4-140 2Bbl.; 'B' or 'T' L6200 1Bbl.; '3' V6232 2Bbl.; 'D' V8255 2Bbl.; 'F' V8302 2Bbl.; 'G' V8351 2Bbl. Next is a check digit. Symbol ten indicates model year ('C' 1982). Symbol eleven is assembly plant: 'A' Atlanta, GA; 'B' Oakville, Ontario (Canada); 'G' Chicago; 'H' Lorain, Ohio; 'K' Kansas City, MO; 'X' St. Thomas, Ontario; 'Z' St. Louis, MO; 'R' San Jose, CA; 'T' Edison, NJ; 'W' Wayne, MI. The final six digits make up the sequence number, starting with 100001. A Vehicle Certification Label on the left front door lock face panel or door pillar shows the manufacturer, month and year of manufacture, GVW, GAWR, certification statement, VIN, and codes for such items as body type, color, trim, axle, transmission, and special order information.

ESCORT (FOUR)

Model Number	Body/Style Number	Body Type & Seating	Factory Price	Shipping Weight	Production Total
05	61D	2-dr. Hatch-4P	5462	1920	Note 1
06	58D	4-dr. Hatch-4P	5668	N/A	Note 1
05	61D	2-dr. L Hatch-4P	6046	1926	Note 1
06	58D	4-dr. L Hatch-4P	6263	2003	Note 1
08	74D	4-dr. L Sta Wag-4P	6461	2023	Note 1
05	61D	2-dr. GL Hatch-4P	6406	1948	Note 1
06	58D	4-dr. GL Hatch-4P	6622	2025	Note 1
08	74D	4-dr. GL Sta Wag-4P	6841	2043	Note 1
05	61D	2-dr. GLX Hatch-4P	7086	1978	Note 1
06	58D	4-dr. GLX Hatch-4P	7302	2064	Note 1
08	74D	4-dr. GLX Sta Wag-4P	7475	2079	Note 1
05	61D	2-dr. GT Hatch-4P	6706	1963	Note 1

Note 1: Total Escort production came to 165,660 two-door hatchbacks, 130,473 four-door hatchbacks, and 88,999 station wagons. Breakdown by trim level not available. Bodies are sometimes referred to as three-door and five-door.

EXP (FOUR)

01	67D	3-dr. Hatch Cpe-2P	7387	2047	98,256

FAIRMONT FUTURA (FOUR/SIX)

22	36R	2-dr. Spt Cpe-5P	6517/7141	2597/2682	17,851
20	66B	2-dr. Sedan-5P	5985/6619	2574/2659	8,222
21	54B	4-dr. Sedan-5P	6419/7043	2622/2707	101,666

GRANADA (FOUR/SIX/V-6)

26	66D	2-dr. L Sedan-5P	7126/7750	2673/2791	12,802
27	54D	4-dr. L Sedan-5P	7301/7925	2705/2823	62,339
28	74D	4-dr. L Sta Wag-5P	--/7983	--/2965	45,182
26	66D	2-dr. GL Sed-5P	7543/8167	2699/2817	Note 2
27	54D	4-dr. GL Sed-5P	7718/8342	2735/2853	Note 2
28	74D	4-dr. GL Wag-5P	--/8399	--/2995	Note 2
26	66D	2-dr. GLX Sed-5P	7666/8290	2717/2835	Note 2
27	54D	4-dr. GLX Sed-5P	7840/8464	2753/2871	Note 2

Note 2: Granada GL and GLX production is included in basic Granada L totals above.

Fairmont/Granada Engine Note: Prices shown are for four- and six- cylinder engines. Six-cylinder price includes $411 for the required automatic transmission. A 232 cu. in. V-6 cost $70 more than the inline six in a Granada.

LTD (V-8)

32	66H	2-dr. Sedan-6P	8455	3496	3,510
33	54H	4-dr. Sedan-6P	8574	3526	29,776
38	74H	4-dr. Sta Wag-6P	9073	3741	9,294

LTD 'S' (V-8)

31	54D	4-dr. Sedan-6P	8312	3522	22,182
37	74D	4-dr. Sta Wag-6P	8783	3725	2,973

LTD CROWN VICTORIA (V-8)

34	66K	2-dr. Sedan-6P	9149	3523	9,287
35	54K	4-dr. Sedan-6P	9294	3567	41,405
39	74K	4-dr. Ctry Sqr-6P	9580	3741	9,626

THUNDERBIRD (SIX/V-8)

42	66D	2-dr. HT Cpe-4P	8492/8733	3000/3137	45,142

THUNDERBIRD TOWN LANDAU (SIX/V-8)

42/60T	66D	2-dr. HT Cpe-4P	9703/9944	3063/3200	Note 3

THUNDERBIRD HERITAGE (V-6/V-8)

42/607	66D	2-dr. HT Cpe-4P	12742/12742	3235/3361	Note 3

Note 3: Town Landau and Heritage production is included in basic Thunderbird total.

MODEL NUMBER NOTE: Some sources include a prefix 'P' ahead of the two- digit model number. **FACTORY PRICE AND WEIGHT NOTE:** Fairmont/Granada prices and weights to left of slash are for four-cylinder, to right for six-cylinder engine. Thunderbird prices and weights to left of slash are for inline six- cylinder, to right for V-8 engine. Thunderbird could also have a V-6 engine (standard on the Heritage) for the same price as the V-8.

ENGINE DATA: BASE FOUR (Escort, EXP): Inline. Overhead cam. Four-cylinder. Cast iron block and aluminum head. Displacement: 97.6 cu. in. (1.6 liters). Bore & stroke: 3.15 x 3.13 in. Compression ratio: 8.8:1. Brake horsepower: 70 at 4600 R.P.M. Torque: 89 lbs.-ft. at 3000 R.P.M. Five main bearings. Hydraulic valve lifters. Carburetor: 2Bbl. Motorcraft 740. VIN Code: 2. NOTE: An 80-horsepower high-output version of the 1.6-liter four arrived later in the model year. BASE FOUR (Fairmont, Granada): Inline. Overhead cam. Four-cylinder. Cast iron block and head. Displacement: 140 cu. in. (2.3 liters). Bore & stroke: 3.78 x 3.13 in. Compression ratio: 9.0:1. Brake horsepower: 86 at 4600 R.P.M. Torque: 117 lbs.-ft. at 2600 R.P.M. Five main bearings. Hydraulic valve lifters. Carburetor: 2Bbl. Holley 6500 or Motorcraft 5200. VIN Code: A. BASE SIX (Granada wagon, Thunderbird); OPTIONAL (Fairmont, Granada): Inline. Overhead valve. Six-cylinder. Cast iron block and head. Displacement: 200 cu. in. (3.3 liters). Bore & stroke: 3.68 x 3.13 in. Compression ratio: 8.6:1. Brake horsepower: 87 at 3800 R.P.M. Torque: 151-154 lbs.-ft. at 1400 R.P.M. Seven main bearings. Hydraulic valve lifters. Carburetor: 1Bbl. VIN Code: B or T. OPTIONAL V-6 (Granada, Thunderbird): 90-degree, overhead valve V-6. Cast iron block and aluminum head. Displacement: 232 cu. in. (3.8 liters). Bore & stroke: 3.80 x 3.40 in. Compression ratio: 8.65:1. Brake horsepower: 112 at 4000 R.P.M. Torque: 175 lbs.-ft. at 2000 R.P.M. Four main bearings. Hydraulic valve lifters. Carburetor: 2Bbl. Motorcraft 2150. VIN Code: 3. BASE V-8 (LTD); OPTIONAL (Thunderbird): 90-degree, overhead valve V-8. Cast iron block and head. Displacement: 255 cu. in. (4.2 liters). Bore & stroke: 3.68 x 3.00 in. Compression ratio: 8.2:1. Brake horsepower: 122 at 3400 R.P.M.; (TBird, 120 at 3400). Torque: 209 lbs.-ft. at 2400 R.P.M.; (TBird, 205 at 1600). Five main bearings. Hydraulic valve lifters. Carburetor: 2Bbl. Motorcraft 2150 or 7200VV. VIN Code: D. Note: The 255 cu. in. V-8 was also offered in Fairmont police cars. BASE V-8 (LTD wagon); OPTIONAL (LTD sedan): 90-degree, overhead valve V-8. Cast iron block and head. Displacement: 302 cu. in. (5.0 liters). Bore & stroke: 4.00 x 3.00 in. Compression ratio: 8.4:1. Brake

horsepower: 132 at 3400 R.P.M. Torque: 236 lbs.-ft. at 1800 R.P.M. Five main bearings. Hydraulic valve lifters. Carburetor: 2Bbl. Motorcraft 2150A or 7200VV. VIN Code: F. HIGH-OUTPUT POLICE V-8 (LTD): 90-degree, overhead valve V-8. Cast iron block and head. Displacement: 351 cu. in. (5.8 liters). Bore & stroke: 4.00 x 3.50 in. Compression ratio: 8.3:1. Brake horsepower: 165 at 3600 R.P.M. Torque: 285 lbs.-ft. at 2200 R.P.M. Five main bearings. Hydraulic valve lifters. Carburetor: 2Bbl. VV. VIN Code: G.

CHASSIS DATA: Wheelbase: (Escort/EXP) 94.2 in.; (Fairmont/Granada) 105.5 in.; (LTD) 114.3 in.; (TBird) 108.4 in. Overall Length: (Escort hatch) 163.9 in.; (Escort wagon) 165.0 in.; (EXP) 170.3 in.; (Fairmont) 195.5 in. exc. Futura oupe, 197.4 in.; (Granada) 196.5 in.; (LTD) 209.3 in.; (LTD wag) 215.0 in.; (LTD Crown Vic) 211.0 in.; (TBird) 200.4 in. Height: (Escort hatch) 53.1 in.; (Escort wag) 53.3 in.; (EXP) 50.5 in.; (Fairmont) 52.9 in.; (Futura cpe) 51.7 in.; (Granada) 53.0 in.; (Granada wag) 54.2 in.; (LTD) 54.7 in.; (LTD wag) 57.4 in.; (TBird) 53.3 in. Width: (Escort) 65.9 in.; (EXP) 63.0 in.; (Fairmont/Granada) 71.0 in.; (LTD) 77.5 in.; (LTD wag) 79.3 in.; (TBird) 74.1 in. Front Tread: (Escort/EXP) 54.7 in.; (Fairmont/Granada) 56.6 in.; (LTD) 62.2 in. (TBird) 58.1 in. Rear Tread: (Escort/EXP) 56.0 in.; (Fairmont/Granada) 57.0 in.; (LTD) 62.0 in. (TBird) 57.0 in. Standard Tires: (Escort/EXP) P165/80R13 SBR BSW; (Fairmont/Granada) P175/75R14 SBR BSW; (LTD) P205/75R14 SBR WSW exc. wagon, P215/75R14; (TBird) P195/75R14 SBR WSW.

TECHNICAL: Transmission: Four-speed manual standard on Fairmont/Granada four: (1st) 3.98:1; (2nd) 2.14:1; (3rd) 1.42:1; (4th) 1.00:1; (Rev) 3.99:1. Four-speed manual transaxle standard on Escort/EXP: (1st) 3.58:1; (2nd) 2.05:1; (3rd) 1.21:1 or 1.36:1; (4th) 0.81:1 or 0.95:1; (Rev) 3.46:1. Three-speed automatic standard on Fairmont/Granada and TBird six: (1st) 2.46:1 or 2.47:1; (2nd) 1.46:1 or 1.47:1; (3rd) 1.00:1; (Rev) 2.11:1 or 2.19:1. Escort/EXP three-speed automatic: (1st) 2.79:1; (2nd) 1.61:1; (3rd) 1.00:1; (Rev) 1.97:1. Four-speed overdrive automatic standard on LTD and Thunderbird V-6/V-8: (1st) 2.40:1; (2nd) 1.47:1; (3rd) 1.00:1; (4th) 0.67:1; (Rev) 2.00:1. Standard final drive ratio: (Escort/EXP) 3.59:1 w/4spd, 3.31:1 w/auto.; (Fairmont/Granada four) 3.08:1; (Fairmont/Granada six) 2.73:1; (Granada V-6) 2.47:1; (LTD) 3.08:1 exc. w/V8351, 2.73:1; (TBird six) 2.73:1; (TBird V-6/V-8) 3.08:1. Drive Axle: (Escort/EXP) front; (others) rear. Steering: (LTD) recirculating ball; (others) rack and pinion. Front Suspension: (Escort/EXP) MacPherson strut-mounted coil springs and stabilizer bar; (Fairmont/Granada/TBird) modified MacPherson struts with lower control arms, coil springs and anti-sway bar; (LTD) long/short control arms w/coil springs and stabilizer bar. Rear Suspension: (Escort/EXP) independent trailing arms w/modified MacPherson struts and coil springs on lower control arms; (others) four-link rigid axle with coil springs. Brakes: Front disc, rear drum; power assisted (except Escort). Ignition: Electronic. Body construction: (Escort/EXP/Fairmont/Granada/TBird) unibody; (LTD) separate body and frame. Fuel tank: (Escort/EXP) 11.3 gal.; (Fairmont/Granada) 16 gal.; (LTD) 20 gal.; (TBird) 21 gal.

DRIVETRAIN OPTIONS: Engines: H.O. 1.6-liter four: Escort ($57). Fuel-saver 1.6- liter four: Escort (NC). Fuel-saver 140 cu. in. four: Fairmont (NC). 200 cu. in. six: Fairmont/Granada ($213). 232 cu. in. V-6: Granada ($283) exc. wagon ($70); Thunderbird ($241). 255 cu. in. V-8: TBird ($241) exc. Heritage (NC). 302 cu. in. V-8: LTD sedan ($59). Transmission/Differential: Automatic transaxle: Escort/EXP ($411). Auto. transmission.: Fairmont/Granada ($411). Floor shift lever: Fairmont/Granada ($49). Traction-Lok differential: Fairmont/Granada/TBird ($76); LTD ($80). Optional axle ratio: Escort/EXP/Fairmont/Granada (NC). Brakes & Steering: Power brakes: Escort ($93). Power steering: Escort/EXP ($190); Fairmont/Granada ($195). Suspension: H.D. susp.: Granada ($24); LTD/TBird ($26). Handling susp.: Escort ($139-$187) exc. GLX ($41); Fairmont ($52); LTD ($49). TR performance susp. pkg.: EXP ($405) w/TR sport aluminum wheels; ($204) w/steel wheels. Other: H.D. battery ($22-$26). H.D. alternator: EXP ($27); LTD ($52). Extended-range gas tank: Fairmont/Granada ($46). Engine block heater ($17-$18). Trailer towing pkg., medium duty: LTD ($200-$251). California emission system ($64-$65). High-altitude emissions (NC).

ESCORT CONVENIENCE/APPEARANCE OPTIONS: Option Packages: Squire wagon pkg. ($293). Instrument group ($87). Appearance protection group ($55). Light group ($30). Comfort/Convenience: Air conditioner ($611). Rear defroster, electric ($120). Remote liftgate release ($30). Tinted glass ($82); windshield only ($32). Digital clock ($57). Interval wipers ($48). Rear wiper/washer ($117). Dual remote sport mirrors ($66). Entertainment: AM radio ($61). AM/FM radio ($76) exc. base ($137). AM/FM stereo radio ($106) exc. base ($167); w/cassette or 8track player ($184) exc. base ($245). Dual rear speakers ($39). Exterior: Metallic glow paint ($61). Two-tone paint/tape ($122-$161). Front vent windows, pivoting ($60). Remote quarter windows ($109). Vinyl-insert bodyside moldings ($45). Bumper guards, front or rear ($26). Bumper rub strips ($41). Luggage rack ($93). Roof air deflector ($29). Lower bodyside protection ($68). Interior: Console ($111). Low-back reclining bucket seats ($33-$98). High-back reclining bucket seats ($65). Cloth/vinyl seat trim ($29); vinyl (NC). Shearling/leather seat trim ($109-$138). Deluxe seatbelts ($24). Wheels/Tires: Wheel trim rings ($48). Aluminum wheels ($232- $377). P165/80R13 WSW ($58).

EXP CONVENIENCE/APPEARANCE OPTIONS: Comfort/Convenience: Appearance protection group ($48). Air conditioner ($611). Fingertip speed control ($151). Tinted glass ($82). Right remote mirror ($41). Entertainment: AM/FM radio ($76). AM/FM stereo radio ($106); w/cassette or 8track player ($184). Premium sound ($105). AM radio delete ($37 credit). Exterior: Flip-up open air roof ($276). Metallic glow paint ($51). Two-tone paint/tape ($122). Luggage rack ($93). Lower bodyside protection ($68). Interior: Low-back bucket seats ($33). Cloth/vinyl seat trim ($29); vinyl (NC). Leather seat trim ($138). Shearling/leather seat trim ($138). Wheels/Tires: Cast aluminum wheels ($232). P165/80R13 RWL ($72).

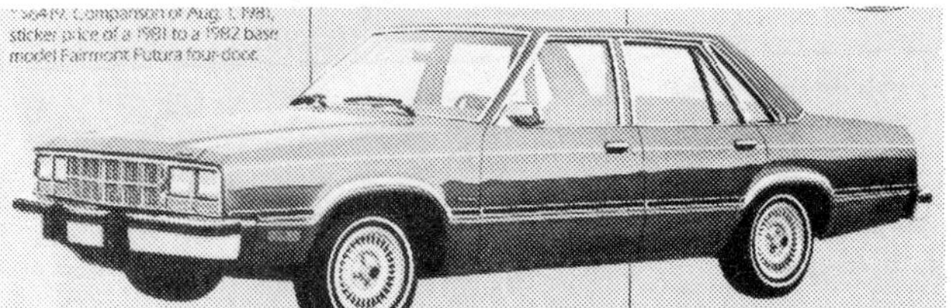

1982 Fairmont Futura sedan (JG)

FAIRMONT/GRANADA CONVENIENCE/APPEARANCE OPTIONS: Option Packages: Granada Squire option ($282). Interior luxury group: Fairmont ($282). Instrument cluster: Fairmont ($100). Cold weather group: Granada ($77). Appearance protection group ($57-$59). Light group ($49-$51). Comfort/Convenience: Air cond. ($676). Rear defroster, electric ($124). Fingertip speed control ($155). Illuminated entry ($68). Power windows ($165-$235). Power door locks ($106-$184). Remote decklid release: Fairmont ($32). Power seat: Fairmont ($139). Power split bench seat: Granada ($196). Tinted glass: Granada ($88). Tinted windshield ($32). Leather-wrapped steering wheel: Granada ($55). Tilt steering ($95). Quartz clock ($32). Interval wipers ($48). Liftgate wiper/washer: wagon ($99). Lighting and Mirrors: Cornering lamps: Granada ($59). Map light: Fairmont ($10); Granada dual-beam ($15). Trunk light ($7). Left remote mirror: Fairmont ($22). Dual bright remote mirrors: Fairmont ($65); right only, Granada ($60). Lighted right visor vanity mirror ($46); pair ($91). Entertainment: AM/FM radio ($39-$54). AM/FM stereo radio ($85); w/8track or cassette player ($172). Twin rear speakers: Fairmont ($39). Premium sound system ($105). AM radio delete ($61 credit). Exterior: Flip-up open air roof ($276). Full or half vinyl roof ($137-$140). Metallic glow paint ($63). Two-tone paint ($105-$144). Accent paint stripes ($39-$57). Pivoting front vent windows ($63). Two-way liftgate: wag ($105). Rocker panel moldings: Fairmont ($33). Protective bodyside moldings: Granada ($49). Bumper guards, rear ($28). Bumper rub strips ($50). Luggage rack: Granada ($115). Lower bodyside protection ($41). Interior: Console ($191). Vinyl flight bench seat: Fairmont ($29) w/interior luxury. Cloth/vinyl seat trim: Fairmont ($29). Vinyl seat trim: Granada ($29). Flight bench seat (NC). Split bench seat: Granada ($230). Front floor mats ($13-$22). Wheels/Tires: Luxury wheel covers: Granada ($49) exc. GL/GLX (NC). Wire wheel covers ($80-$152). Turbine wheel covers: Fairmont ($54). Styled steel wheels: Fairmont ($54-$107). Cast aluminum wheels: Granada ($348-$396). P175/75R14 WSW ($66). P185/75R14 BSW: Granada ($38). P185/75R14 WSW ($104) exc. wagon ($66). P185/75R14 RWL: Granada ($121) exc. wagon ($83). P190/65R390 BSW on TRX alum. wheels ($529-$583). Conventional spare ($51).

LTD CONVENIENCE/APPEARANCE OPTIONS: Option Packages: Interior luxury group ($727-$807). Convenience group ($90-$116). Power lock group ($106-$201). Light group ($43). Protection group ($67). Comfort/Convenience: Air cond. ($695); w/auto-temp control ($761). Rear defroster, electric ($124). Fingertip speed control ($155). Illuminated entry system ($68). Power windows ($165-$240). Power driver's seat ($198); driver and passenger ($395). Tinted glass ($102); windshield only ($32). Autolamp on/off delay ($73). Leather-wrapped steering wheel ($51). Tilt steering wheel ($95). Auto. parking brake release ($12). Tripminder computer ($215-$293). Quartz clock ($32). Digital clock ($46-$78). Seatbelt chime ($27). Interval wipers ($48). Lighting and Mirrors: Cornering lamps ($55). Remote right mirror ($43). Lighted right visor vanity mirrors ($46-$91). Entertainment: AM/FM radio ($41-$54). AM/FM stereo radio ($85); w/8track or cassette tape player ($172) exc. Crown Vic ($87). AM/FM stereo search radio ($232) exc. Crown Vic ($146); w/8track or cassette ($233-$318). Power antenna ($55). Dual rear speakers ($41). Premium sound system ($133- $167). AM radio delete ($61 credit). AM/FM delete: Crown Vic ($152 credit). Exterior: Full or half vinyl roof ($165). Metallic glow paint ($66). Two-tone paint/tape ($66-$105). Dual accent bodyside paint stripes ($39). Hood striping ($17). Pivoting front vent windows ($63). Rocker panel moldings ($32). Vinyl-insert bodyside moldings ($51). Bumper guards, rear ($30). Bumper rub strips ($52). Luggage rack ($104). Lower bodyside protection ($39-$52). Interior: Dual-facing rear seats: wagon ($167). Leather seating ($412). Dual flight bench seat recliners ($65). Split bench seating ($139-$204). All-vinyl seat trim ($28); Duraweave vinyl ($62). Front floor mats ($15-$21). Trunk trim ($49). Wheels/Tires: Luxury wheel covers ($82). 15 in. wheel covers ($49). Wire wheel covers ($152). Cast aluminum wheels ($384). P215/75R14 WSW ($36). P225/75R14 WSW ($36-$73). P205/75R15 WSW ($11-$47); puncture-resistant ($112-$148). Conventional spare ($51).

THUNDERBIRD CONVENIENCE/APPEARANCE OPTIONS: Option Packages: Interior luxury group ($1204) exc. Town Landau ($683). Exterior decor group ($385). Interior decor group ($372). Protection group ($51). Light group ($35). Power lock group ($138). Comfort/Convenience: Air cond. ($676); auto-temp ($754) exc. Heritage ($78). Rear defroster ($126). Fingertip speed control ($155). Illuminated entry system ($68). Keyless entry ($139). Tripminder computer ($215-$261). Autolamp on/off delay ($73). Tinted glass ($88); windshield only ($32). Power windows ($165). Six-way power driver's seat ($198). Auto. parking brake release ($12). Leather-wrapped steering wheel ($51). Tilt steering wheel ($95). Electronic instrument cluster ($321-$367). Diagnostic warning lights ($59). Digital clock ($46). Interval wipers ($48). Lighting and Mirrors: Cornering lamps ($59). Remote right mirror ($60). Lighted right visor vanity mirrors ($46-$91). Entertainment: AM/FM radio ($39-$54). AM/FM stereo radio ($85); w/8track or cassette player ($87-$172). AM/FM stereo search radio ($146-$232); w/8track or cassette ($318) exc. Twn Lan ($233) and Heritage ($87). Power antenna ($55). Dual rear speakers ($39). Premium sound system ($133-$167). AM radio delete ($61 credit). Exterior: Carriage roof ($766-$973). Flip-up open-air roof ($276). Vinyl rear half roof ($156-$320). Metallic glow paint ($80). Two-tone paint ($128-$206). Dual accent bodyside paint stripes ($49). Hood/bodyside paint stripes ($16-$65). Pivoting front vent windows ($63). Wide door belt moldings ($51). Rocker panel moldings ($33). Lower bodyside protection ($39-$54). Interior: Bucket seats w/console ($211) exc. (NC) w/decor group. Split bench seat ($208). Luxury split bench ($124). Recaro bucket seats w/console ($405-$523) exc. Heritage ($222). Leather seat trim ($409). Vinyl seat trim ($28-$30). Front floor mats, carpeted ($22). Trunk trim ($48). Wheels/Tires: Wire wheel covers ($45-$152). Luxury wheel covers ($107). Self-sealing tires ($106). TR WSW tires on alum. wheels ($490-$643). Conventional spare ($51).

HISTORY: Introduced: September 24, 1981 except EXP, April 9, 1981. Model year production: 1,035,063 (incl. Mustangs). Total production for the U.S. market of 888,669 units (incl. Mustangs) included 461,524 four-cylinder, 251,145 sixes and 176,000 V-8s. Calendar year production (U.S.): 690,655 (incl. Mustangs). Calendar year sales by U.S. dealers: 925,490 (incl. Mustangs). Model year sales by U.S. dealers: 888,633 (incl. Mustangs).

Historical Footnotes: Escort became the best selling domestic car this model year, finding 321,952 buyers (up over 13 percent from 1981). Still, total Ford Division sales for the model year declined by close to 20 percent: only 888,633 versus 1,105,751 in 1981. And 1981 had posted a loss as well. FoMoCo's market share held at the depressing 16.5 percent level of the prior year. *Car and Driver* readers had voted Escort "Most Significant New Domestic Car" for 1981, and it beat Chevrolet's Chevette this year. Granada gained sales in its recently downsized form, but other models did not. Mustang dropped by almost one-third, Fairmont and Thunderbird by more than 40 percent. EXP did not sell as well as hoped for after its spring 1981 debut, so within a couple of months incentives were being offered. Sales rose a bit later, partly due to a more peppy high- output EXP 1.6-liter engine that debuted in mid-year. Two new plants (San Jose, California and St. Thomas, Ontario) were assigned to assemble the Escort/EXP subcompacts. Escort was also assembled at Wayne, Michigan and Edison, New Jersey. Production of Thunderbird for the model year fell dramatically, by more than half. As the 1983 model year began, Ford offered what was then low-interest financing (10.75 percent rate) to customers who would buy one of the leftover '82 models. In January 1982, the UAW agreed to an alternating-shift arrangement at certain plants. Workers would work 10 days, then take 10 days off. That way, a skilled work force remained available for the day when increased production again became necessary. Ford's advertising theme at this time was: "Have you driven a Ford lately?"

1983 FORD

A dramatically modern 10th-generation Thunderbird showed the aero styling that was becoming the standard for sporty— and even luxury—models. Escort added a revised GT model, based on the European XR3. The high-output 1.6-liter four, added at mid-year 1982, could power both Escort and EXP. The new short-wheelbase LTD sedan was basically a rebodied Granada. The LTD nameplate also continued on the bigger LTD Crown Victoria.

1983 Escort GT three-door hatchback (F)

ESCORT — FOUR — America's best selling car in 1982 lost its base model this year, dropping to four series. That made Escort L the new base model, with stepups to GL, GLX, and a sporty GT. The new GT was said to be more akin to the high-performance XR3, which had been the image car of the European Escort line. Its 1.6-liter four had multi-port fuel injection. GT also carried five-speed manual shift with 3.73:1 final drive, a TR performance suspension with Michelin TRX tires, functional front and rear spoilers, molded wheel lip extensions (flares), and flared tailpipe extension. GT standards also included foglamps (below the bumper), flat black exterior trim, unique taillamp treatment, a new reclining sport seat, specially-tuned exhaust, special steering wheel, and console and full instrumentation featuring arc yellow graphics. GT was claimed to run 0-60 MPH in about 11 seconds. The high-output carbureted 97.6 cu. in. (1.6-liter) four, introduced as a 1982.5 option, continued available on any Escort except the GT. The base 1.6-liter had new fast-burn technology to improve fuel economy. Escort might have any of three suspension levels: base, handling, and TRX performance. All manual-shift models had a standard upshift indicator that showed when to shift into the next higher gear for best mileage. All Escorts now had all-season SBR tires and a larger (13-gallon) gas tank. Five-speed was available with either the high-output or EFI engine. Escort's Fuel-Saver package came with economy 3.04:1 final drive and wide- ratio four-speed gearbox. Apart from minor changes, appearance was the same as 1982. GL and GLX had a new wide bodyside molding with argent stripe (introduced at mid-year 1982). GLX no longer had front and rear bumper guards. GL now had standard low-back reclining bucket seats. All except L had a new locking gas filler door with inside release. Optional knit vinyl seat trim replaced regular vinyl on GL and GLX. New Escort options were: remote-controlled convex right-hand mirror, remote- release fuel filler door (standard on upper Escorts), and P175/80R13 tires. Other options included a luggage rack for hatchbacks, roof air deflector, shearling and leather seat trim, and dual rear speakers.

1983 EXP HO Sport Coupe (JG)

EXP — FOUR — This year's EXP looked the same, but had a wider choice of engines and transaxles. Standard powertrain was a refined 97.6 cu. in. (1.6-liter) four with two-barrel carburetor and fast-burn technology, hooked to four-speed manual transaxle with overdrive fourth gear. The high-output 1.6-liter introduced as a 1982.5 option was available with either automatic or a new five-speed gearbox. That engine produced 80 horsepower, versus 70 for the base four. Newly optional this year was a multi-port fuel-injected version of the four. Acceleration to 60 MPH was supposed to be cut by 3 seconds with the new powertrain. Five-speed gearboxes had a 100-amp alternator. Shift control for the optional automatic transaxle was revised to a straight-line pattern. EXP had a larger (13- gallon) gas tank. Interiors were more color-keyed this year, including the console and instrument panel (which had arc yellow gauge graphics); the former panel was black. Seats had a new sew style and more porous knit vinyl that would be cooler in summer. A remote-control locking fuel filler door was now standard. New options included a right-hand remote- control convex mirror, remote fuel door release, sport performance bucket seats, and P175/80R13 tires. Michelin TRX tires and TR wheels were now available with base suspension. The luggage rack, 4.05:1 drive ratio and conventional remote right mirror were deleted from the option list. As before, a Ford script oval stood above the twin grille slots. 'EXP' letters and Ford decorated the decklid. Small backup lenses were near inner ends of full- width wraparound taillamps.

FAIRMONT FUTURA — FOUR/SIX — For its final season, Fairmont continued with little change. The lineup had been simplified into a single series for the 1982 model year. This time, the 4.2-liter V-8 was dropped, leaving only a base four and optional inline six. The 140 cu. (2.3-liter) switched from 1Bbl. to 2Bbl. carburetion and added fast-burn technology and longer- reach spark plugs, plus a redesigned exhaust manifold. Two- and four-door sedans were offered again, along with a two-door coupe. A low-budget 'S' series also was introduced. The Traction-Lok axle was now available with TR- type tires. New options included a 100-amp alternator (LPO option). Flight bench seating and a headlamp-on warning buzzer were added to the interior luxury group. Dual rear speakers were discontinued as an option. Radios got a new look and graphics. In short, not much change. For 1984, the rear-drive Fairmont, which had sold quite well during its six-year life and remained popular with fleet and taxi buyers, would be replaced by the new front-drive Tempo.

LTD — FOUR/SIX/V-6 — The familiar LTD nameplate took on two forms for 1983: a new, smaller five-passenger model, and the old (larger) LTD Crown Victoria (listed below). This new LTD was built on the 'L' body shell. Among its features were gas-pressurized shocks and struts, as introduced in 1982 on the new Continental. LTD came in a single well-equipped series: just a four-door sedan and wagon. Sedans carried the 140 cu. in. (2.3-liter) four with four-speed as base powertrain; wagons, the 250 cu. in. (3.3-liter) inline six with three-speed automatic. A 3.8-liter "Essex" V-6 became optional, with four-speed overdrive automatic. So was a propane-powered four, intended to attract fleet buyers. The base 2.3-liter engine had a new single-barrel

1983 LTD four-door sedan (JG)

carburetor and fast-burn technology. LTD had flash-to-pass on the headlamp lever, as well as rack-and-pinion steering. Wheelbase was 105.5 inches, just like the Granada it replaced. In fact this was the familiar Fairmont platform, in yet another variant. Aerodynamic design features included a 60-degree rear-window angle, addition of a front valance and spoiler, and aero-styled decklid. Drag coefficient was claimed to be 0.38 (low for a sedan). LTD's sloping front end displayed a slanted grille that consisted of thin vertical strips dominated by three heavier horizontal divider bars. A Ford oval adorned the center of the heavy upper header bar. Quad rectangular headlamps were deeply recessed. Park lamps sat below the bumper strip; wraparound side markers at front fender tips. The sloping rear end held horizontal tri-color wraparound taillamps with upper and lower segments, and backup lenses halfway toward the center (similar to 1982 Granada). Standard wide vinyl-insert bodyside moldings met with bright partial wheel lip moldings. The instrument panel stemmed from the 1982 Thunderbird. Tire tread design was the wraparound European style, with all-season capability. Mercury Marquis was LTD's corporate twin. Both measured somewhere between compact and mid-size.

1983 LTD Country Squire station wagon (JG)

LTD CROWN VICTORIA — V-8 — Full-size Fords carried on with little change and a longer name. The model lineup first consisted of two- and four-door sedans and Country Squire (woodgrain) station wagon, in just one luxury level. Later came a low-budget 'S' pair of sedans and plain-bodied wagon. Base engine was the fuel-injected 302 cu. in. (5.0-liter) V-8 with four-speed overdrive automatic. Base tires grew one size, to P215/75R14. Country Squire now had a standard AM/FM radio. All models had a new fuel cap tether. The right-hand remote mirror option was now a convex type. A new, bolder double-crosshatch design grille had a 12x4 hole pattern with internal crosshatching in each hole, and a heavy upper header. The Ford script oval sat at the left portion of the grille. Quad rectangular headlamps stood above rectangular parking lamps, and the assembly continued around the fender tips to enclose signal/marker lenses. Sedans also had a new taillamp design. Country Squire had revised woodtone appearance without the former planking lines. New options included a remote-control locking fuel door, locking wire wheel covers, and new-generation electronic radios. Two trailer-towing packages were offered. Options deleted were dual rear speakers, monaural AM/FM radio, full and half vinyl roofs, seatbelt reminder chime, rear bumper guards, and dual flight bench recliner seats.

1983 Thunderbird hardtop coupe (F)

THUNDERBIRD — V-6/V-8 — In its tenth and smaller form, Thunderbird took on a striking aero look. "Conceived for today with an eye on tomorrow" was the way the factory catalog described it. The new version was built on the 'S' shell, with 104 inch wheelbase (down from 108). Extensive aerodynamic testing resulted in an air drag coefficient of 0.35 (lower than any tested domestic competitor in its class). Aero design features included concealed drip moldings, a sloping hood, tapered fenders and quarter panels, sharply raked windshield and backlight, contoured parking lamps, and integrated decklid spoiler. Inside, Thunderbird had a standard deep-well luggage

1983 Thunderbird Turbo coupe (JG)

compartment, assist straps, storage bins integral with door trim panels, and a console with padded armrest/lid. Engineering features of the new design included gas-pressurized, modified MacPherson struts at the front suspension and gas shocks at the four-bar-link rear. Base engine was the 232 cu. in. (3.8-liter) V-6 with SelectShift three-speed automatic and locking torque converter. Optional: a fuel-injected 302 cu. in. (5.0-liter) V-8 with four-speed overdrive automatic. The Town Landau series was deleted. So was the 4.2-liter V-8 and the inline six. Flash-to-pass became standard. So was variable-ratio, power rack-and-pinion steering. Much more curvaceous and smooth than former 'Birds, the new one had exposed quad rectangular halogen headlamps in deeply recessed housings, with cornering/marker lenses at the edge of each headlamp housing. Parking lamps were well below the front bumper strip. The sloping grille showed an eggcrate (8x6) pattern and heavy upper header. Full-width wraparound taillamps met the recessed license plate housing in a sloping back panel. Backup lenses stood near the center of each taillamp. Trim was minimal, with little of the former TBird's sculptured look. Wide bodyside moldings continued all around the car to meet the bumper rub strips. Options included electric remote outside mirrors, an automatic-dimming rear-view mirror, pivoting front vent windows, keyless entry, clearcoat metallic paint, remote locking fuel door, voice alert, and a canvas-wrapped emergency kit containing tools and first aid items (which stored in a quarter-panel well). Mercury Cougar was similar in design, but with a different side-window look. The new Thunderbird was expected to appeal to younger buyers than previous editions. All the more so a little later when the Turbo Coupe appeared. Louis E. Lataif spoke for Ford in calling it "the ultimate road machine—a complete high- performance package." The turbocharged 2.3-liter four was Ford's first use of a "blow-through" design. That put the turbocharger *ahead* of the throttle, giving faster response by maintaining slight pressure in the intake system. This helped overcome the low-speed lag of conventional turbos. The engine also had Bosch multi-port fuel injection, forged-aluminum pistons, an oil cooler, aluminum rocker covers, and the fourth generation (EECIV) of electronic engine control systems. Compression was cut to 8.0:1 from the usual 9.5:1. Standard was a five-speed manual transmission with performance-type close-ratio gearing. Fifth gear was a 0.86:1 overdrive. The shift linkage had a short throw between gears. Turbos had a 3.45:1 final drive ratio. A new Ford rear suspension called "quadra-shock" was offered for the first time on the Turbo Coupe. It was a special four-link coil spring system with two hydraulic axle dampers mounted horizontally toward the rear, between brackets on axle and body rail. Like other models, Turbo Coupe had gas-pressurized struts and shocks. The unique front fascia included two recessed Marchal foglamps. A wide charcoal-color bodyside molding and bumper rub strip system encircled the whole car. Headlamp housings were black. There was also a special fluted B pillar molding, and other charcoal or black accents. Goodyear Eagle P205/70HR14 blackwall performance tires rode unique aluminum wheels. Turbo Coupe's instrument panel was special black and brushed finish, including a tachometer with boost and overboost lights; plus a row of diagnostic warning lights and a digital clock. Controls for the dual electric mirrors were on the console. Standard fittings included a leather-wrapped steering wheel and shift knob, Traction-Lok axle, bodyside and decklid paint stripes, black door handles and lock bezels, and charcoal headlamp doors. Lear-Siegler articulated bucket seats had inflatable lumbar support along with open- mesh head restraints. Turbo Coupe's special handling suspension with performance tires was available on other models. Illuminated entry was now standard on the Heritage model, as were dual bright electric remote-control mirrors, electronic instruments, tinted glass, lighted vanity mirrors, and a premium sound system. Also included: tilt steering, digital clock, power locks, autolamp on/off/delay system, bodyside moldings, bumper rub strip extensions, wire wheel covers, a special grille ornament, and striping on hood, bodyside and decklid. Heritage seats wore velour cloth trim and a Thunderbird seatback emblem. Front seats held a Velcro- closed driver's map pocket. The instrument panel displayed Prima Vera woodtone appliques. Heritage had unique quarter windows and electro-luminescent coach lamps, Customers later received an anodized aluminum plaque with their signature.

I.D. DATA: Ford's 17-symbol Vehicle Identification Number (VIN) again was stamped on a metal tab fastened to the instrument panel, visible through the windshield. The first three symbols ('1FA') indicate manufacturer, make and vehicle type. The fourth symbol ('B') denotes restraint system. Next comes a letter 'P', followed by two digits that indicate body type: Model Number, as shown in left column of tables below. (Example: '04' Escort L two-door hatchback; the numbering system changed this year.) Symbol eight indicates engine type: '2' L498 2Bbl.; '4' H.O. L498 2Bbl.; '5' L498 EFI; 'A' L4-140 1Bbl.; 'D' Turbo L4140 EFI; 'X' L6200 1Bbl.; '3' V6232 2Bbl.; 'F' V8302 2Bbl.; 'G' V8351 2Bbl. Next is a check digit. Symbol ten indicates model year ('D' 1983). Symbol eleven is assembly plant: 'A' Atlanta, GA; 'B' Oakville, Ontario (Canada); 'G' Chicago; 'H' Lorain, Ohio; 'K' Kansas City, MO; 'X' St. Thomas, Ontario; 'Z' St. Louis, MO; 'R' San Jose, CA; 'T' Edison, NJ; 'W' Wayne, MI. The final six digits make up the sequence number, starting with 100001. A Vehicle Certification Label on the left front door lock face panel or door pillar shows the manufacturer, month and year of manufacture, GVW, GAWR, certification statement, VIN, and codes for such items as body type, color, trim, axle, transmission, and special order information.

ESCORT (FOUR)

Model Number	Body/Style Number	Body Type & Seating	Factory Price	Shipping Weight	Production Total
04	61D	2-dr. L Hatch-4P	5639	1932	Note 1
13	58D	4-dr. L Hatch-4P	5846	1998	Note 1
09	74D	4-dr. L Sta Wag-4P	6052	2026	Note 1
05	61D	2-dr. GL Hatch-4P	6384	1959	Note 1
14	58D	4-dr. GL Hatch-4P	6601	2025	Note 1
10	74D	4-dr. GL Sta Wag-4P	6779	2052	Note 1
06	61D	2-dr. GLX Hatch-4P	6771	1993	Note 1
15	58D	4-dr. GLX Hatch-4P	6988	2059	Note 1
11	74D	4-dr. GLX Sta Wag-4P	7150	2083	Note 1
07	61D	2-dr. GT Hatch-4P	7339	2020	Note 1

Note 1: Total Escort production came to 151,386 two-door hatchbacks, 84,649 four-door hatchback sedans, and 79,335 station wagons. Breakdown by trim level not available. Bodies are sometimes referred to as three- door and five-door.

EXP (FOUR)

01	67D	3-dr. Hatch Cpe-2P	6426	2068	19,697
01/301B	67D	3-dr. HO Cpe-2P	7004	N/A	Note 2
01/302B	67D	3-dr. HO Spt Cpe-2P	7794	N/A	Note 2
01/303B	67D	3-dr. Luxury Cpe-2P	8225	N/A	Note 2
01/304B	67D	3-dr. GT Cpe-2P	8739	N/A	Note 2

Note 2: Production of step-up models is included in basic EXP total above.

FAIRMONT FUTURA (FOUR/SIX)

37	36R	2-dr. Coupe-4P	6666/7344	2601/2720	7,882
35	66B	2-dr. Sedan-5P	6444/7122	2582/2701	3,664
36	54B	4-dr. Sedan-5P	6590/7268	2626/2745	69,287

FAIRMONT 'S' (FOUR)

35/41K	66B	2-dr. Sedan-5P	5985/6663	2569/2688	Note 3
36/41K	54B	4-dr. Sedan-5P	6125/6803	2613/2732	Note 3

Note 3: Fairmont 'S' production is included in Futura sedan totals above.

1983 LTD Brougham sedan (JG)

LTD (FOUR/SIX)

39	54D	4-dr. Sedan-5P	7777/8455	2788/2874	111,813
39/60H	54D	4-dr. Brghm-5P	8165/8843	2802/2888	Note 4
40	74D	4-dr. Sta Wag-5P	--/8577	--/2975	43,945

Note 4: Brougham production is included in basic sedan total.

Fairmont/LTD Engine Note: Prices shown are for four- and six-cylinder engines. Six-cylinder price includes $439 for the required automatic transmission. A 232 cu. in. V-6 cost $70 more than the inline six in an LTD.

LTD CROWN VICTORIA (V-8)

42	66K	2-dr. Sedan-6P	10094	3590	11,414
43	54K	4-dr. Sedan-6P	10094	3620	81,859
44	74K	4-dr. Ctry Sqr-6P	10253	3773	20,343
43/41K	54K	4-dr. 'S' Sed-6P	9130	N/A	Note 5
44/41K	74K	4-dr. 'S' Wag-6P	9444	N/A	Note 5
44/41E	74K	4-dr. Sta Wag-6P	10003	N/A	Note 5

Note 5: Production of 'S' models and basic station wagon is included in basic sedan and Country Squire totals above.

THUNDERBIRD (V-6/V-8)

46	66D	2-dr. HT Cpe-4P	9197/9485	2905/2936	121,999

THUNDERBIRD HERITAGE (V-6/V-8)

46/607	66D	2-dr. HT Cpe-4P	12228/12516	3027/ --	Note 6

THUNDERBIRD TURBO COUPE (FOUR)

46/934	66D	2-dr. HT Cpe-4P	11790	N/A	Note 6

Note 6: Turbo Coupe and Heritage production is included in basic Thunderbird total.

MODEL NUMBER NOTE: Some sources include a prefix 'P' ahead of the two- digit model number. **FACTORY PRICE AND WEIGHT NOTE:** Fairmont/LTD prices and weights to left of slash are for four-cylinder engine, to right for six-cylinder engine. Thunderbird prices and weights to left of slash are for V-6, to right for V-8 engine.

ENGINE DATA: BASE FOUR (Escort, EXP): Inline. Overhead cam. Four-cylinder. Cast iron block and aluminum head. Displacement: 98 cu. in. (1.6 liters). Bore & stroke: 3.15 x 3.13 in. Compression ratio: 8.8:1. Brake horsepower: 70 at 4600 R.P.M. Torque: 88 lbs.-ft. at 2600 R.P.M. Five main bearings. Hydraulic valve lifters. Carburetor: 2Bbl. Motorcraft 740. VIN Code: A. OPTIONAL FOUR (Escort, EXP): High-output version of 1.6-liter four above Horsepower: 80 at 5400 R.P.M. Torque: 88 lbs.-ft. at 3000 R.P.M. VIN Code: 4. BASE FOUR (Escort GT); OPTIONAL (Escort, EXP): Fuel-injected version of 1.6-liter four above Compression ratio: 9.5:1. Horsepower: 88 at 5400 R.P.M. Torque: 94 lbs.- ft. at 4200 R.P.M. VIN Code: 5. BASE FOUR (Fairmont, LTD): Inline. Overhead cam. Four-cylinder. Cast iron block and aluminum head. Displacement: 140 cu. in. (2.3 liters). Bore & stroke: 3.78 x 3.13 in. Compression ratio: 9.0:1. Brake horsepower: 90 at 4600 R.P.M. Torque: 122 lbs.-ft. at 2600 R.P.M. Five main bearings. Hydraulic valve lifters. Carburetor: 1Bbl. Carter YFA. VIN Code: A. NOTE: A 140 cu. in.

(2.3-liter) propane four was also available for LTD. TURBOCHARGED FOUR (Thunderbird Turbo Coupe): Same as 140 cu. in. four above, with fuel injection and turbocharger Compression ratio: 8.0:1. Horsepower: 142 at 5000 R.P.M. Torque: 172 lbs.-ft. at 3800 R.P.M. VIN Code: D. OPTIONAL SIX (Fairmont, LTD): Inline. Overhead valve. Six-cylinder. Cast iron block and head. Displacement: 200 cu. in. (3.3 liters). Bore & stroke: 3.68 x 3.13 in. Compression ratio: 8.6:1. Brake horsepower: 92 at 3800 R.P.M. Torque: 156 lbs.-ft. at 1400 R.P.M. Seven main bearings. Hydraulic valve lifters. Carburetor: 1Bbl. Holley 1946. VIN Code: X. BASE V-6 (Thunderbird); OPTIONAL (LTD): 90-degree, overhead valve V-6. Cast iron block and aluminum head. Displacement: 232 cu. in. (3.8 liters). Bore & stroke: 3.80 x 3.40 in. Compression ratio: 8.65:1. Brake horsepower: 110 at 3800 R.P.M. Torque: 175 lbs.-ft. at 2200 R.P.M. Four main bearings. Hydraulic valve lifters. Carburetor: 2Bbl. Motorcraft 2150 or 7200VV. VIN Code: 3. BASE V-8 (Crown Victoria); OPTIONAL (LTD, Thunderbird): 90-degree, overhead valve V-8. Cast iron block and head. Displacement: 302 cu. in. (5.0 liters). Bore & stroke: 4.00 x 3.00 in. Compression ratio: 8.4:1. Brake horsepower: 130 at 3200 R.P.M. Torque: 240 lbs.-ft. at 2000 R.P.M. Five main bearings. Hydraulic valve lifters. Electronic fuel injection. VIN Code: F. NOTE: Crown Victoria also announced a high-output version rated 145 horsepower at 3600 R.P.M., 245 lbs.-ft. at 2200 R.P.M. HIGH-OUTPUT POLICE V-8 (Crown Victoria): 90-degree, overhead valve V-8. Cast iron block and head. Displacement: 351 cu. in. (5.8 liters). Bore & stroke: 4.00 x 3.50 in. Compression ratio: 8.3:1. Brake horsepower: 165 at 3600 R.P.M. Torque: 290 lbs.-ft. at 2200 R.P.M. Five main bearings. Hydraulic valve lifters. Carburetor: 2Bbl. VV. VIN Code: G.

CHASSIS DATA: Wheelbase: (Escort/EXP) 94.2 in.; (Fairmont/LTD) 105.5 in.; (Crown Vic) 114.3 in.; (TBird) 104.0 in. Overall Length: (Escort) 163.9 in.; (Escort wagon) 165.0 in.; (EXP) 170.3 in.; (Fairmont) 195.5 in. exc. Futura coupe, 197.4 in.; (LTD) 196.5 in.; (Crown Vic) 211.1 in.; (Crown Vic wag) 215.0 in.; (TBird) 197.6 in. Height: (Escort) 53.3 in.; (EXP) 50.5 in.; (Fairmont) 52.9 in.; (Futura cpe) 51.7 in.; (LTD) 53.6 in.; (LTD wag) 54.3 in.; (Crown Vic) 55.3 in.; (Crown Vic wag) 56.8 in.; (TBird) 53.2 in. Width: (Escort/EXP) 65.9 in.; (Fairmont/LTD) 71.0 in.; (Crown Vic) 77.5 in.; (Crown Vic wag) 79.3 in.; (TBird) 71.1 in. Front Tread: (Escort/EXP) 54.7 in.; (Fairmont/LTD) 56.6 in.; (Crown Vic) 62.2 in. (TBird) 58.1 in. Rear Tread: (Escort/EXP) 56.0 in.; (Fairmont/LTD) 57.0 in.; (Crown Vic) 62.0 in. (TBird) 58.5 in. Standard Tires: (Escort/EXP) P165/80R13 SBR BSW; (Escort GT/EXP luxury cpe) P165/70R365 Michelin TRX; (Fairmont) P175/75R14 SBR BSW; (LTD) P185/75R14 SBR BSW; (Crown Vic) P215/75R14 SBR WSW; (TBird) P195/75R14 SBR WSW; (TBird Turbo Cpe) P205/70HR14. Tranmission: Four-speed manual standard on LTD: (1st) 3.98:1; (2nd) 2.14: 1; (3rd) 1.49:1; (4th) 1.00:1; (Rev) 3.99:1. Escort four-speed manual transaxle (1st) 3.23:1; (2nd) 1.90:1; (3rd) 1.23:1; (4th) 0.81:1; (Rev) 3.46:1. Four- speed manual on Escort/EXP: (1st) 3.58:1; (2nd) 2.05:1; (3rd) 1.23:1 or 1.36:1; (4th) 0.81:1 or 0.95:1; (Rev) 3.46:1. Five- speed manual on Escort/EXP: (1st) 3.60:1; (2nd) 2.12:1; (3rd) 1.39:1; (4th) 1.02:1; (5th) 1.02:1; (Rev) 3.62:1. (Note: separate final drive for 5th gear.) TBird Turbo Coupe five- speed: (1st) 4.03:1; (2nd) 2.37:1; (3rd) 1.50:1; (4th) 1.00:1; (5th) 0.86:1; (Rev) 3.76:1. TBird Turbo Coupe five- speed with 3.73:1 axle ratio: (1st) 3.76:1; (2nd) 2.18:1; (3rd) 1.36:1; (4th) 1.00:1; (5th) 0.86:1; (Rev) 3.76:1. Three-speed automatic standard on LTD and TBird six: (1st) 2.46:1 or 2.47:1; (2nd) 1.46:1 or 1.47:1; (3rd) 1.00:1; (Rev) 2.11:1 or 2.19:1. Escort/EXP three-speed automatic: (1st) 2.79:1; (2nd) 1.61:1; (3rd) 1.00:1; (Rev) 1.97:1. Four-speed overdrive automatic standard on LTD V-6, Crown Victoria and Thunderbird V-8: (1st) 2.40:1; (2nd) 1.47:1; (3rd) 1.00:1; (4th) 0.67:1; (Rev) 2.00:1. Standard final drive ratio: (Escort/EXP) 3.59:1 w/4spd, 3.04:1 w/fuel saver, 3.73:1 w/5spd, 3.31:1 w/auto.; (Fairmont) 3.08:1 exc. w/six, 2.73:1; (LTD four) 3.45:1; (LTD six) 2.73:1; (LTD V-6) 3.08:1; (Crown Vic) 3.08:1; (TBird) 3.45:1 w/5spd, 2.47:1 w/3spd automatic, 3.08:1 w/4spd auto. Drive Axle: (Escort/EXP) front; (others) rear. Steering: (Crown Vic) recirculating ball; (others) rack and pinion. Front Suspension: (Escort/EXP) MacPherson struts with lower control arms, coil springs and stabilizer bar; (Fairmont/LTD/TBird) modified MacPherson struts with lower control arms, coil springs and anti-sway bar; (Crown Vic) long/short control arms w/coil springs and stabilizer bar. LTD and TBird had gas-filled shock absorbers. Rear Suspension: (Escort/EXP) independent trailing arms w/modified MacPherson struts and coil springs on lower control arms; (Fairmont/LTD/Crown Vic) rigid axle w/four-link coil springs; (Thunderbird) four-link rigid axle with coil springs and electronic level control; (TBird Turbo Coupe) "quadra-shock" four-bar-link assembly with two hydraulic, horizontal axle dampers. Gas-filled shocks on LTD and TBird. Brakes: Front disc, rear drum; power assisted (except Escort). Ignition: Electronic. Body construction: (Crown Vic) separate body and frame; (others) unibody. Fuel tank: (Escort/EXP) 13.0 gal.; (Fairmont/LTD) 16.0 gal.; (Crown Vic) 18.0 gal.; (Crown Vic wagon) 18.5 gal.; (TBird) 21 gal.

DRIVETRAIN OPTIONS: Engines: H.O. 1.6-liter four: Escort ($70-$73); EXP GT ($70). Fuel-saver 1.6-liter four: Escort (NC). Turbo 140 cu. in. four: LTD ($896). 200 cu. in. six: Fairmont/LTD ($239). 232 cu. in. V-6: LTD ($309) exc. wagon ($70). 302 cu. in. V-8: Thunderbird ($288). Transmission/Differential: Close-ratio four-speed trans.: Escort (NC). Five-speed manual trans.: Escort ($76). Automatic transaxle: Escort/base EXP ($439) exc. GT and other EXP ($363). Select-shift auto. transmission.: Fairmont/LTD ($439). Overdrive auto. trans.: LTD ($615) exc. wagon ($176); Thunderbird ($176). Floor shift lever: Fairmont/LTD ($49). Traction-Lok differential: Fairmont/LTD/Crown Vic/TBird ($95). Optional axle ratio: Fairmont (NC). Brakes & Steering: Power brakes: Escort ($95). Power steering: Escort/EXP ($210); Fairmont/LTD ($218). Suspension: H.D. susp.: Fairmont ($24); Crown Vic/TBird ($26). Handling susp.: Escort ($199) exc. GLX ($41); Fairmont ($52); Crown Vic ($49). TR performance susp. pkg.: Escort ($41) w/Michelin TRX tires; EXP luxury or GT ($41). Other: H.D. battery ($26). H.D. alternator: EXP ($27). Extended-range gas tank: Fairmont/LTD ($46). Engine block heater ($17-$18). Trailer towing pkg., medium duty: Crown Vic ($200-$251); heavy duty ($251-$302). Trailer towing pkg.: TBird ($251). California emission system ($46-$76). High- altitude emissions (NC).

ESCORT CONVENIENCE/APPEARANCE OPTIONS: Option Packages: Squire wagon pkg. ($350). Instrument group ($87). Appearance protection group ($39). Light group ($43). Comfort/Convenience: Air conditioner ($624). Rear defroster, electric ($124). Fingertip speed control ($170). Tinted glass ($90); windshield only, LPO ($38). Digital clock ($57). Interval wipers ($49). Rear wiper/washer ($117). Dual remote sport mirrors ($67). Entertainment: AM radio: L ($61). AM/FM radio ($82) exc. L ($143). AM/FM stereo radio ($109) exc. base ($170); w/cassette or 8track player ($199) exc. L ($260). Premium sound ($117). Exterior: Flip-up open-air roof ($217-$310). Clearcoat metallic paint ($305). Metallic glow paint ($51). Two-tone paint/tape ($134-$173). Dual bodyside paint stripes ($39). Front vent windows, pivoting ($60). Remote quarter windows ($109). Vinyl-insert bodyside moldings ($45). Bumper guards, front or rear ($28). Bumper rub strips ($41). Luggage rack ($93). Lower bodyside protection ($68). Interior: Console ($111). Fold-down center armrest ($55). Low-back reclining bucket seats: L ($98). High-back reclining bucket seats: L ($65). Vinyl low-back reclining bucket seats: GL/GLX ($24). Vinyl high-back bucket seats: L ($24). Color- keyed front mats ($22). Wheels/Tires: Wheel trim rings ($54). Cast aluminum wheels ($226-$383). TR sport aluminum wheels ($568) exc. GLX ($411) and GT ($201). TR styled steel wheels ($210-$367). P165/80R13 SBR WSW ($59). P175/80R13 SBR BSW ($20); WSW ($78).

EXP CONVENIENCE/APPEARANCE OPTIONS: Comfort/Convenience: Air conditioner ($624). Rear defroster: base ($124). Tinted glass: HO ($90). Entertainment: AM/FM radio ($82). AM/FM stereo radio ($109); w/cassette or 8track player ($199) exc. luxury cpe ($90). Premium sound ($117). AM radio delete ($37 credit). AM/FM stereo delete: luxury cpe ($145 credit). AM/FM stereo/cassette delete: GT ($235 credit). Exterior: Flip-up open air roof ($310). Metallic glow paint ($51). Two-tone paint/tape ($146). Sport tape stripe ($41). Lower bodyside protection ($68). Interior: Low-back sport cloth or knit vinyl bucket seats (NC). Low-back sport performance seats ($173). Leather/vinyl seat trim ($144). Shearling low-back bucket seats ($227). Wheels: TR sport aluminum wheels: GT (NC).

FAIRMONT CONVENIENCE/APPEARANCE OPTIONS: Option Packages: Interior luxury group ($294). Instrument cluster ($100). Appearance protection group ($32-$60). Light group ($55). Comfort/Convenience: Air cond. ($724). Rear defroster, electric ($135). Fingertip speed control ($170). Illuminated entry ($82). Power windows ($180-$255). Power door locks ($120-$170). Remote decklid release ($40). Four-way power seat ($139). Tinted glass ($105). Tinted windshield ($38). Tilt steering ($105). Quartz clock ($35). Interval wipers ($49). Lighting and Mirrors: Trunk light ($7). Left remote mirror: S ($22). Dual bright remote mirrors: S ($68). Lighted visor vanity mirrors, pair ($100). Entertainment: AM radio: S ($61). AM/FM radio ($59-$120). AM/FM stereo radio ($109-$170); w/8track or cassette player ($199-$260). Premium sound system ($117). AM radio delete ($61 credit). Exterior: Flip-up open air roof ($310). Full or half vinyl roof ($152). Metallic glow paint ($63). Two-tone paint ($117- $156). Accent paint stripes: S ($39). Pivoting front vent windows ($63). Rocker panel moldings ($33). Bumper guards, rear ($28). Bumper rub strips ($50). Lower bodyside protection ($41). Interior: Console ($191). Cloth/vinyl seat trim ($35). Bench seat (NC). Front floor mats ($15-$24). Wheels/Tires: Wire wheel covers ($87-$152). Turbine wheel covers: S ($66). Styled steel wheels ($60-$126). Steel wheels, 5.5 in.: fleet LPO ($18-$74). P175/75R14 SBR WSW ($72). P185/75R14 BSW: fleet ($44). P185/75R14 WSW ($116). P190/65R390 Michelin BSW TRX ($535-$601).

LTD CONVENIENCE/APPEARANCE OPTIONS: Option Packages: Squire option ($282). Brougham decor option: wagon ($363). Power lock group ($170-$210). Cold weather group ($77). Appearance protection group ($60). Light group ($38). Comfort/Convenience: Air cond. ($724); auto-temp ($802). Rear defroster, electric ($135). Fingertip speed control ($170). Illuminated entry ($76). Autolamp on-off delay ($73). Power windows ($255). Six-way power driver's seat ($207); dual ($415). Tinted glass ($105). Tinted windshield: fleet ($38). Leather-wrapped steering wheel ($59). Tilt steering ($105). Electronic instrument cluster ($289-$367). Tripminder computer ($215-$293). Digital clock ($78). Diagnostic warning lights ($59). Auto. parking brake release ($12). Interval wipers ($49). Liftgate wiper/washer: wagon ($99). Lighting and Mirrors: Cornering lamps ($60). Map light: fleet ($15). Right remote convex mirror ($60). Lighted visor vanity mirrors ($51-$100). Entertainment: AM/FM radio ($59). AM/FM stereo radio ($109); w/8track or cassette player ($199). Electronic-tuning AM/FM stereo radio ($252); w/cassette ($396). Premium sound system ($117-$151). AM radio delete ($61 credit). Exterior: Flip-up open air roof ($310). Full vinyl roof ($152). Metallic glow paint ($63). Two-tone paint ($117). Pivoting front vent windows ($63). Two-way liftgate: wag ($105). Protective bodyside moldings, LPO ($49). Bumper guards, rear ($28). Bumper rub strips ($56). Luggage rack: wagon ($126). License frames ($9). Lower bodyside protection ($41). Interior: Console ($100). Vinyl seat trim ($35). Split bench seat (NC). Individual seats w/console ($61). Leather seat trim ($415). Front floor mats ($23). Wheels/Tires: Luxury wheel covers ($55). Wire wheel covers ($159-$198). Styled wheels ($178). Cast aluminum wheels ($402). P185/75R14 BSW ($38); WSW ($72). P195/75R14 WSW ($72- $116). Puncture-sealant P195/75R14 WSW ($228). Conventional spare ($63).

CROWN VICTORIA CONVENIENCE/APPEARANCE OPTIONS: Option Packages: Interior luxury group ($830-$911). Convenience group ($95-$116). Power lock group ($123-$220). Light group ($48). Protection group ($68). Comfort/Convenience: Air cond. ($724); w/auto-temp control ($802). Rear defroster, electric ($135). Fingertip speed control ($170). Illuminated entry system ($76). Power windows ($180-$255). Power driver's seat ($210); driver and passenger ($420). Remote fuel door lock ($24). Tinted glass ($105); windshield only, fleet ($38). Autolamp on/off delay ($73). Leather-wrapped steering wheel ($59). Tilt steering wheel ($105). Auto. parking brake release ($12). Tripminder computer ($215-$261). Quartz clock: S ($35). Digital clock ($61-$96). Interval wipers ($49). Lighting and Mirrors: Cornering lamps ($60). Remote right mirror ($43). Lighted visor vanity mirrors ($100). Entertainment: AM/FM stereo radio: S ($106); w/8track or cassette tape player ($112-$218). AM/FM stereo search radio ($166-$272); w/8track or cassette ($310-$416). Power antenna ($60). Premium sound system ($145-$179). AM radio delete: S ($61 credit). AM/FM delete ($152 credit). Exterior: Metallic glow paint ($77). Two-tone paint/tape ($78). Dual accent bodyside paint stripes: S ($39). Pivoting front vent windows ($63). Rocker panel moldings: Ctry Squire ($32). Vinyl-insert bodyside moldings ($55). Bumper rub strips ($52). Luggage rack: Ctry Sq ($110). License frames ($9). Lower bodyside protection ($39-$52). Interior: Dual-facing rear seats: Ctry Sq ($167). Leather seat trim ($418). Split bench seating ($139). All-vinyl seat trim ($34); Duraweave vinyl, wagon ($96). Carpeted floor mats ($33). Trunk trim ($49). Wheels/Tires: Luxury wheel covers ($88). 15 in. wheel covers: S ($49). Wire wheel covers ($159-$198). Cast aluminum wheels ($390). P225/75R14 WSW ($42-$43). P205/75R15 WSW ($17); puncture-resistant ($130). Conventional spare ($63).

THUNDERBIRD CONVENIENCE/APPEARANCE OPTIONS: Option Packages: Interior luxury group: base ($1170). Exterior accent group ($343). Luxury carpet group ($48-$72). Traveler's assistance kit ($65). Light group ($35). Power lock group ($172). Comfort/Convenience: Air cond. ($732); auto-temp ($802). Rear defroster ($135). Fingertip speed control ($170). Illuminated entry system ($82). Keyless entry ($163) exc. Heritage ($88). Anti-theft system ($159). Remote fuel door lock ($26). Tripminder computer ($215-$276). Autolamp on/off delay ($73). Tinted glass ($105); windshield only, LPO ($38). Power windows ($193). Six-way power driver's seat ($222); dual ($444). Auto. parking brake release ($12). Leather-wrapped steering wheel ($59). Tilt steering wheel ($105). Electronic instrument cluster ($321-$382). Electronic voice alert ($67). Diagnostic warning lights ($59). Digital clock ($61). Interval wipers ($49). Lighting and Mirrors: Cornering lamps ($68). Dual electric remote mirrors ($94). Electronic-dimming day/night mirror ($77). Lighted visor vanity mirrors, pair ($106). Entertainment: AM/FM stereo radio: base ($109); w/8track or cassette player ($199) exc. Turbo Cpe ($90). Electronic- tuning AM/FM stereo search radio ($144-$252); w/cassette ($396) exc. Turbo Cpe ($288) and Heritage ($144). Power antenna ($66). Premium sound system ($179). AM radio delete ($61 credit). Exterior: Flip-up open-air roof ($310). Clearcoat paint ($152). Two-tone paint/tape ($148-$218). Charcoal lower accent treatment: Turbo Cpe ($78). Hood paint stripe ($16). Dual accent bodyside/decklid paint stripes ($55). Hood/decklid/bodyside paint stripes ($71). Pivoting front vent windows ($76). Wide bodyside moldings: base ($57). Bright rocker panel moldings ($39). Bumper rub strip extensions ($52). License frames ($9). Lower bodyside protection ($39-$54). Interior: Articulated seats ($183-$427). Leather seat trim ($415-$659). Vinyl seat trim ($37). Front floor mats, carpeted ($22). Wheels/Tires: Wire wheel covers ($45-$159); locking ($84-$198) exc. Heritage ($20). Luxury wheel covers ($113). Styled wheels ($65-$178). Puncture-sealing tires ($124). P205/70R14 performance WSW ($62). P205/70HR14 performance BSW ($152). TRX performance BSW ($471-$649) exc. Turbo Cpe ($154). Conventional spare ($63).

HISTORY: Introduced: October 14, 1982 except Thunderbird, February 17, 1983 and Thunderbird Turbo Coupe, April 1, 1983. Model year production: 928,146 (incl. Mustangs). Total production for the U.S. market of 914,666 units (incl. Mustangs and 55,314 early '84 Tempos) included 423,532 four-cylinder, 313,353 sixes and 177,781 V-8s. That total included 12,276 turbo fours. Calendar year production (U.S.): 1,008,799 (incl. Mustangs). Calendar year sales by U.S. dealers: 1,060,314 (incl. Mustangs). Model year sales by U.S. dealers: 996,694 (incl. Mustangs and 70,986 early '84 Tempos).

Historical Footnotes: Once again, Escort was the best-selling car in the country. That helped Ford's model year sales to rise 12 percent over 1982, but the total stood well below the 1981 total of 1.1 million. Next in line for sales honors were the new smaller LTD and full-size LTD Crown Victoria. The new aero-styled T-Bird sold far more copies than its predecessor- -more than twice the 1982 total. Ford still ranked No. 2 in the domestic auto industry, but Oldsmobile had become a potent contender for that spot. Ford was judged second in the industry in quality, behind the Lincoln-Mercury division but ahead of rival GM and Chrysler. Low-rate (10.75 percent) financing was extended in December 1982 to include '83 models as well as the leftover 1982s. Continuing demand kept the big rear-drive Ford alive, as did improved fuel supplies. The new Tempo was introduced in May 1983, but as an early '84 model.

1984 FORD

Ford was trying hard to conquer the youth market— especially the affluent young motorist—with offerings like the SVO Mustang, Thunderbird Turbo Coupe, and new turbo EXP. Fairmont was gone after a six-year run, but the brand-new Tempo took its place in the compact market. Horn buttons returned to the steering wheel hub once again on most models. The inline six finally disappeared. The turbocharged 1.6-liter four, available for Escort and EXP, featured a high-lift camshaft and EEC-IV electronic controls. It delivered boost up to 8 PSI, raising horsepower by some 35 percent.

1984 Escort GL five-door hatchback (JG)

ESCORT — FOUR — Diesel power was the first big news under Ford subcompact hoods, as the company's first passenger-car diesel engine became available on both Escort and Tempo. Produced by Mazda, the 2.0-liter diesel four came with five-speed manual (overdrive) transaxle. A little later came a different kind of four: a turbocharged, fuel-injected version of Escort's 97.6 cu. in. (1.6-liter) engine, ready for the GT model. Turbos hooked up to a five-speed manual gearbox, in a package that included firmer suspension and special wheels/tires. Three other 1.6-liter engines were available: base carbureted, high-output, and fuel-injected. Model availability was revised. In addition to the carryover L and GL, and the sporty GT, there was a new LX (replacing GLX). LX had the fuel-injected four, TR suspension, blackout body trim, overhead console with digital clock, full instruments (including tach), and five-speed transaxle. Appearance changes were limited to details. Escort GT now sported black polycarbonate bumpers. Inside was a new soft-feel instrument panel with integral side-window demisters, and new steering wheel. Escort's horn button moved to the center of the steering wheel. A new-design rear seat, standard on GL, GT and LX, folded down to form a flatter load floor. Each side could fold independently. LX bodies showed dark moldings with "discreet" bright accents. Power ventilation replaced the "ram air" system. New Escort options were: overhead console with digital clock; floor console with graphic warning display module and covered storage area; new electronic radios; graphic equalizer; tilt steering; and power door locks. A lighted visor vanity mirror was added to the light group.

1984 EXP Turbo coupe (JG)

EXP — FOUR — Turbocharged power brought EXP a strong performance boost this year. The new turbo model had a unique front air dam and rear decklid spoiler, with easy-to-spot taped 'Turbo' nomenclature on doors and rear bumper. It also had two-tone paint with black lower section, unique Cpillar applique, black wheel flares, and black rocker panel moldings. The turbo package also included a tighter suspension with Koni shock absorbers, Michelin P185/65R365 TRX tires on new cast aluminum wheels, and five-speed manual transaxle. Base powertrain was upgraded to the high-output 1.6-liter engine, also mated to five-speed manual. EXP had a completely revised exterior. The silhouette was altered dramatically by adding a "bubbleback" liftgate. EXP also had new blackout taillamps, color-keyed bumper rub strips and mirrors, and a revised front air dam. Both the liftgate and taillamps came from Mercury's LN7, companion to EXP that was discontinued this year. Inside was a standard overhead console with digital clock, new instrument panel with performance cluster and tachometer, and new steering wheel with center horn control. Cloth low-back bucket seats became standard. Styled steel wheels were a new design. New options included a tilt steering wheel, electronic radios with graphic equalizer, clearcoat paint, and illuminated visor vanity mirror. Options deleted were: shearling and leather seat trims, AM/FM stereo with 8track, and AM/FM monaural radio. Both EXP and Escort had a new clutch/starter interlock system. New competitors for EXP included Honda's CRX and Pontiac Fiero.

1984 Tempo GLX coupe (JG)

TEMPO — FOUR — Ford's second front-drive model, replacement for the departed rear-drive Fairmont, arrived as an early '84 model, wearing what Ford called "rakish contemporary styling." General Manager Louis E. Lataif said "it continues the modern aerodynamic design theme established with the '83 Thunderbird, but with its own particular flair." Less enthusiastic observers sometimes referred to Tempo's aero shape as a "jellybean" design. Aircraft-type door configurations were indeed shared with the '83 Thunderbird. Door tops extended up into the roof to create a wraparound effect. That also eliminated the need for an exterior drip molding, and allowed easier entry/exit. Tempo's body-color plastic grille consisted of three horizontal slots, one above the other, with a Ford oval at the center of the middle one. Alongside the grille were single quad recessed nalogen headlamps. Tapered amber wraparound signal/marker lenses started at the outer end of each headlamp housing. Horizontal taillamps at ends of rear panels tapered down in a curve on the quarter panels. A bodyside "character line" ran just below the beltline, sweeping upward a bit at the back. The nose was sloped; the rear end stubby. Two- and four-door sedans were offered, on a 99.9 inch wheelbase, the latter with six-window design and rounded window corners. Tempo came in L, GL, and GLX trim. This was essentially a stretched version of Escort's chassis, but with a different suspension. A new 140 cu. in. (2.3-liter) HSC (high swirl combustion) four-cylinder engine was developed specially for Tempo. Displacement was identical to the familiar 2.3-liter four used in Fairmont/LTD, but bore/stroke dimensions differed in this OHV design, which actually evolved from the old inline six. This was the first production fast-burn engine, controlled by an EEC-IV onboard computer as used in the Thunderbird Turbo Coupe. The engine had 9.0:1 compression and was announced as producing 90 horsepower (though later sources give a lower rating). For this year only, a carburetor was used. Tempo could have either a close-ratio five-speed manual or automatic transaxle, or a Fuel Saver four-speed (which was standard). In addition to rack-and-pinion steering, Tempo had fully independent quadra-link rear suspension using MacPherson struts; also a MacPherson strut front suspension and stabilizer bar. Power front disc brakes were standard. Inside, Tempo had low-back bucket seats with cloth trim; color-keyed molded door trim panels with integral storage bins; a storage bin above the radio (on the instrument panel); color-keyed vinyl sunvisors with elastic band on driver's side; a carpeted package tray; and a consolette. An optional TR handling package included Michelin P185/65R365 TRX tires on new-design cast aluminum wheels, and a special handling suspension. Other notable options included a factory-installed anti-theft system, remote-release fuel filler door, illuminated entry, light-duty trailer towing package, and electronic AM/FM stereo search sound systems. Several changes were made for the full 1984 model year. Most noteworthy new 1984 feature was the addition of a 2.0-liter diesel option with five-speed manual overdrive. The horn button was relocated to the steering wheel; fuel tank enlarged; and two options were added (tachometer and sport performance seat). Mercury's Topaz was nearly identical except for trim and the list of options available.

1984 LTD/LX four-door sedan (JG)

LTD — FOUR/V-6 — Though basically unchanged after its 1983 debut, LTD received a few fresh touches that included argent accents on bodyside moldings and (optional) bumper rub strips, and a revised instrument panel woodtone applique. A new Aframe steering wheel with center horn button replaced the former four-spoke design. Headlamp doors now had dark argent paint, instead of light argent. Parking and turn lamp lenses switched from clear white to amber, and bulbs from amber to clear. Most noteworthy new body feature was the unique formal roof treatment added to the Brougham four-door sedan. It had a distinctive solid rear pillar and "frenched" back window treatment, and included a full Cambria cloth roof. The inline six-cylinder engine finally disappeared. Manual transmission with the base 140 cu. in. (2.3-liter) four was dropped. A 302 cu. in. (5.0-liter) EFI high-output V-8 was available only on police sedans. That made a 232 cu. in. (3.8-liter) V-6, now fuel-injected, the only regular option (standard on wagons). All engines added EECIV controls. Propane power was available again, but found few takers. Base and Brougham sedans were offered again, along with a station wagon. Base models could get some of Brougham's expanded standard trim as part of the Interior Luxury Group. Power steering and three-speed automatic were made standard, with four-speed automatic available in V-6 models. New LTD options included a flight bench seat (said to be the single most requested feature).

1984 LTD Crown Victoria sedan (JG)

237

1984 LTD Country Squire station wagon (JG)

LTD CROWN VICTORIA — V-8 — Crown Vic's new grille featured a light argent second surface, and a new optional Brougham roof for the four-door had a formal look. It included a padded full vinyl top, a more upright rear window with "frenched" treatment, and electro-luminiscent coach lamps on the center pillar. Interiors had a new vinyl pattern. Otherwise, the full- size Ford was a carryover, available again as a two- or four- door sedan, and pair of wagons. The Crown Victoria station wagon was just a Country Squire without simulated wood trim. The wide grille had a 12 x 4 hole crosshatch pattern (plus a 2 x 2 pattern within each segment). Wide amber parking lamps went below the quad headlamps. Amber signal/marker lenses consisted of a large lens above a small one. 'LTD Crown Victoria' lettering went ahead of the front door, just above the crease line. Sole standard engine was the 302 cu. in. (5.0-liter) fuel-injected V-8. The high- performance 351 cu. in. (5.8-liter) V-8 with variable-venturi carburetor was available only with police package.

1984 Thunderbird Elan hardtop coupe (JG)

THUNDERBIRD — FOUR/V-6/V-8 — Visible changes were few on Ford's personal luxury coupe, but the model lineup was revised. The Heritage series was renamed elan (Ford didn't capitalize the name). And a new Fila model was developed in conjunction with Fila Sports, Inc., an Italian manufacturer of apparel for active leisure sports (mainly tennis and skiing). Fila had exclusive light oxford gray over charcoal paint, with unique red and blue tape stripes emulating the graphics of the company's logo. Bright trim was minimal, with body-color grille and wheels, and charcoal windshield and backlight moldings. Inside, Fila had charcoal components. Articulated seats were trimmed in oxford white leather, with perforated leather inserts; or oxford gray luxury cloth with perforated cloth inserts. Turbo Coupe added charcoal greenhouse moldings and a new viscous clutch fan, as well as a starter/clutch interlock system

1984 Thunderbird Turbo coupe (JG)

and oil-temperature warning switch. All TBirds now had standard bumper rub strip extensions, and a modified appearance of the birds on taillamps. Electronic fuel injection went on the base 232 cu. in. (3.8-liter) V-6. Counterbalanced springs replaced the hood's prior prop rod. Steering wheels (except Turbo Coupe's) were now A frame design, with horn button in the center. Sole engine option was the 302 cu. in. (5.0-liter) fuel-injected V-8. Turbo Coupe retained the 140 cu. in. (2.3-liter) turbocharged four, but now came with automatic transmission as well as the five-speed manual gearbox. Each model had a slightly curved 8 x 6 hole crosshatch grille pattern with wide Thunderbird insignia in the tall header bar. Staggered, recessed quad headlamps flanked the grille. Amber (formerly clear) parking lamps were set into the bumper. Small amber wraparound marker lenses were used. 'Thunderbird' insignias went on back pillars. Mercury Cougar was mechanically identical, but a bit different in styling.

I.D. DATA: Ford's 17-symbol Vehicle Identification Number (VIN) again was stamped on a metal tab fastened to the instrument panel, visible through the windshield. The first three symbols ('1FA') indicate manufacturer, make and vehicle type. The fourth symbol ('B') denotes restraint system. Next comes a letter 'P', followed by two digits that indicate body type: Model Number, as shown in left column of tables below. (Example: '04' Escort L two-door hatchback). Symbol eight indicates engine type: '2' L498 2Bbl.; '4' H.O. L498 2Bbl.; '5' L498 EFI; '8' Turbo L498 FI; 'H' Diesel L4121; 'A' L4-140 1Bbl.; 'R' or 'J' HSC L4140 1Bbl.; '6' Propane L4140; 'W' Turbo L4140 EFI; '3' V6232 2Bbl.; 'F' V8302 2Bbl.; 'G' V8351 2Bbl. Next is a check digit. Symbol ten indicates model year ('E' 1984). Symbol eleven is assembly plant: 'A' Atlanta, GA; 'B' Oakville, Ontario (Canada); 'G' Chicago; 'H' Lorain, Ohio; 'K' Kansas City, MO; 'X' St. Thomas, Ontario; 'Z' St. Louis, MO; 'T' Edison, NJ; 'W' Wayne, MI. The final six digits make up the sequence number, starting with 100001. A Vehicle Certification Label on the left front door lock face panel or door pillar shows the manufacturer, month and year of manufacture, GVW, GAWR, certification statement, VIN, and code for such items as body type and color, trim, axle ratio, transmission, and special order data.

ESCORT (FOUR)

Model Number	Body/Style Number	Body Type & Seating	Factory Price	Shipping Weight	Production Total
04	61D	2-dr. Hatch-4P	5629	1981	Note 1
13	58D	4-dr. Hatch-4P	5835	2024	Note 1
04	61D	2-dr. L Hatch-4P	5885	1981	Note 1
13	58D	4-dr. L Hatch-4P	6099	2034	Note 1
09	74D	4-dr. L Sta Wag-4P	6313	2066	Note 1
05	61D	2-dr. GL Hatch-4P	6382	2033	Note 1
14	58D	4-dr. GL Hatch-4P	6596	2086	Note 1
10	74D	4-dr. GL Sta Wag-4P	6773	2115	Note 1
15	58D	4-dr. LX Hatch-4P	7848	2137	Note 1
11	74D	4-dr. LX Sta Wag-4P	7939	2073	Note 1

ESCORT GT (FOUR)

07	61D	2-dr. Hatch-4P	7593	2103	Note 1
07	61D	2-dr. Turbo Hatch-4P	N/A	2239	Note 1

Note 1: Total Escort production came to 184,323 two-door hatchbacks, 99,444 four-door hatchback sedans, and 88,756 station wagons. Breakdown by trim level not available. Bodies are sometimes referred to as three- door and five-door.

Diesel Engine Note: Diesel-powered Escorts came in L and GL trim, priced $558 higher than equivalent gasoline models.

EXP (FOUR)

01/A80	67D	3-dr. Hatch Cpe-2P	6653	2117	23,016
01/A81	67D	3-dr. Luxury Cpe-2P	7539	2117	Note 2
01/A82	67D	3-dr. Turbo Cpe-2P	9942	2158	Note 2

Note 2: Production of luxury and turbo coupe models is included in basic EXP total above.

1984 Tempo GLX sedan (JG)

TEMPO (FOUR)

18	66D	2-dr. L Sedan-5P	6936	2249	Note 3
21	54D	4-dr. L Sedan-5P	6936	2308	Note 3
19	66D	2-dr. GL Sed-5P	7159	2276	Note 3
22	54D	4-dr. GL Sed-5P	7159	2339	Note 3
20	66D	2-dr. GLX Sed-5P	7621	2302	Note 3
23	54D	4-dr. GLX Sed-5P	7621	2362	Note 3

Note 3: Total Tempo production came to 107,065 two-doors and 295,149 four-doors.

Diesel Engine Note: Diesel-powered Tempos cost $558 more than equivalent gasoline models.

LTD (FOUR/V-6)

39	54D	4-dr. Sedan-5P	8605/9014	2804/2881	154,173
39/60H	54D	4-dr. Brghm-5P	9980/10389	2812/2889	Note 4
40	74D	4-dr. Sta Wag-5P	--/9102	--/2990	59,569

Note 4: Brougham production is included in basic sedan total.

LTD CROWN VICTORIA (V-8)

42	66K	2-dr. Sedan-6P	10954	3546	12,522
43	54D	4-dr. Sedan-6P	10954	3587	130,164
44	74K	4-dr. Ctry Sqr-6P	11111	3793	30,803
43/41K	54K	4-dr. 'S' Sed-6P	9826	N/A	Note 5
44/41K	74K	4-dr. 'S' Wag-6P	10136	N/A	Note 5
44/41E	74K	4-dr. Sta Wag-6P	10861	N/A	Note 5

Note 5: Production of 'S' models and basic station wagon is included in basic sedan and Country Squire totals above.

THUNDERBIRD (V-6/V-8)

46	66D	2-dr. HT Cpe-4P	9633/10253	2890/3097	170,533
46/607	66D	2-dr. Elan Cpe-4P	12661/13281	2956/3163	Note 6
46/606	66D	2-dr. Fila Cpe-4P	14471/14854	3061/3268	Note 6

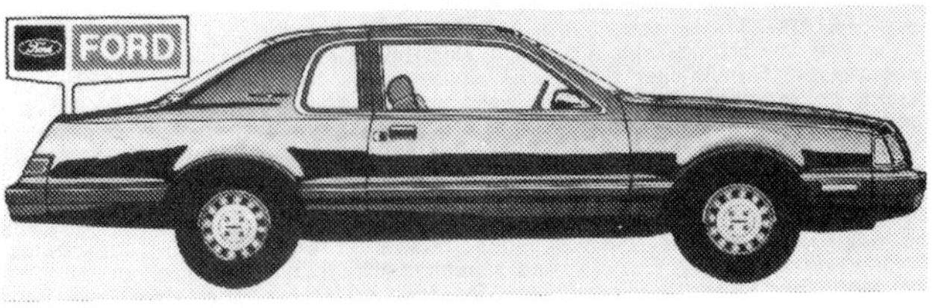

1984 Thunderbird hardtop coupe (JG)

THUNDERBIRD TURBO COUPE (FOUR)

46/934	66D	2-dr. HT Cpe-4P	12330	2938	Note 6

Note 6: Turbo Coupe and Elan/Fila production is included in basic Thunderbird total.

MODEL NUMBER NOTE: Some sources include a prefix 'P' ahead of the two- digit model number**FACTORY PRICE AND WEIGHT NOTE:** LTD prices and weights to left of slash are for four-cylinder, to right for V-6 engine. Thunderbird prices and weights to left of slash are for V-6, to right for V-8 engine.

ENGINE DATA: BASE FOUR (Escort): Inline. Overhead cam. Four-cylinder. Cast iron block and aluminum head. Displacement: 97.6 cu. in. (1.6 liters). Bore & stroke: 3.15 x 3.13 in. Compression ratio: 9.0:1. Brake horsepower: 70 at 4600 R.P.M. Torque: 88 lbs.-ft. at 2600 R.P.M. Five main bearings. Hydraulic valve lifters. Carburetor: 2Bbl. Motorcraft 740. VIN Code: 2. BASE FOUR (EXP); OPTIONAL (Escort): High-output version of 1.6-liter four above Horsepower: 80 at 5400 R.P.M. Torque: 88 lbs.-ft. at 3000 R.P.M. VIN Code: 4. BASE FOUR (Escort LX, GT); OPTIONAL (Escort, EXP): Fuel-injected version of 1.6-liter four above Horsepower: 84 at 5200 R.P.M. Torque: 90 lbs.-ft. at 2800 R.P.M. VIN Code: 5. TURBO FOUR (Escort, EXP): Same as 1.6-liter four above, with fuel injection and turbocharger Compression ratio: 8.0:1. Horsepower: 120 at 200 R.P.M. Torque: 120 lbs.-ft. at 3400 R.P.M. VIN Code: 8. DIESEL FOUR (Escort, Tempo): Inline. Overhead cam. Four-cylinder. Cast iron block and aluminum head. Displacement: 121 cu. in. (2.0 liters). Bore & stroke: 3.39 x 3.39 in. Compression ratio: 22.5:1. Brake horsepower: 52 at 4000 R.P.M. Torque: 82 lbs.-ft. at 2400 R.P.M. Five main bearings. Solid valve lifters. Fuel injection. VIN Code: H. BASE FOUR (Tempo): Inline. Overhead valve. Four-cylinder. Cast iron block and head. Displacement: 140 cu. in. (2.3 liters). Bore & stroke: 3.70 x 3.30 in. Compression ratio: 9.0:1. Brake horsepower: 84 at 4400 R.P.M. Torque: 118 lbs.-ft. at 2600 R.P.M. Five main bearings. Hydraulic valve lifters. Carburetor: 1Bbl. Holley 6149. High Swirl Combustion (HSC) design. VIN Code: R (U.S.) or J (Mexico). BASE FOUR (LTD): Inline. Overhead cam. Four-cylinder. Cast iron block and head. Displacement: 140 cu. in. (2.3 liters). Bore & stroke: 3.78 x 3.13 in. Compression ratio: 9.0:1. Brake horsepower: 88 at 4000 R.P.M. Torque: 122 lbs.-ft. at 2400 R.P.M. Five main bearings. Hydraulic valve lifters. Carburetor: 1Bbl. Carter YFA. VIN Code: A. PROPANE FOUR (LTD): Same as 140 cu. in. four above, but for propane fuel Compression ratio: 10.0:1. Brake horsepower: 88 at 4000 R.P.M. Torque: 122 lbs.-ft. at 2400 R.P.M. VIN Code: 6. TURBOCHARGED FOUR (Thunderbird Turbo Coupe): Same as 140 cu. in. four above, with fuel injection and turbocharger Compression ratio: 8.0:1. Horsepower: 145 at 4600 R.P.M. Torque: 180 lbs.-ft. at 3600 R.P.M. VIN Code: W. BASE V-6 (Thunderbird); OPTIONAL (LTD): 90-degree, overhead valve V-6. Cast iron block and aluminum head. Displacement: 232 cu. in. (3.8 liters). Bore & stroke: 3.80 x 3.40 in. Compression ratio: 8.7:1. Brake horsepower: 120 at 3600 R.P.M. Torque: 205 lbs.-ft. at 1600 R.P.M. Four main bearings. Hydraulic valve lifters. Throttle-body fuel injection. VIN Code: 3. BASE V-8 (Crown Victoria); OPTIONAL (Thunderbird): 90-degree, overhead valve V-8. Cast iron block and head. Displacement: 302 cu. in. (5.0 liters). Bore & stroke: 4.00 x 3.00 in. Compression ratio: 8.4:1. Brake horsepower: 140 at 3200 R.P.M. Torque: 250 lbs.-ft. at 1600 R.P.M. Five main earings. Hydraulic valve lifters. Electronic fuel injection (TBI). VIN Code: F. NOTE: Crown Victoria wagons had a high-output 302 cu. in. V-8 rated 155 horsepower at 3600 R.P.M., 265 lbs.-ft. at 2000 R.P.M. HIGH-OUTPUT POLICE V-8 (Crown Victoria): 90-degree, overhead valve V-8. Cast iron block and head. Displacement: 351 cu. in. (5.8 liters). Bore & stroke: 4.00 x 3.50 in. Compression ratio: 8.3:1. Brake horsepower: 180 at 3600 R.P.M. Torque: 285 lbs.-ft. at 2400 R.P.M. Five main bearings. Hydraulic valve lifters. Carburetor: 2Bbl. VV. VIN Code: G.

CHASSIS DATA: Wheelbase: (Escort/EXP) 94.2 in.; (Tempo) 99.9 in.; (LTD) 105.6 in.; (Crown Vic) 114.3 in.; (TBird) 104.0 in. Overall Length: (Escort) 163.9 in.; (Escort wagon) 165.0 in.; (EXP) 170.3 in.; (Tempo) 176.2 in.; (LTD) 196.5 in.; (Crown Vic) 211.1 in.; (Crown Vic wag) 215.0 in.; (TBird) 197.6 in. Height: (Escort) 53.3-53.4 in.; (EXP) 50.5 in.; (Tempo 2dr.) 2.5 in.; (Tempo 4dr.) 52.7 in.; (LTD) 53.6 in.; (LTD wag) 54.3 in.; (Crown Vic) 55.3 in.; (Crown Vic wag) 56.8 in.; (TBird) 53.2 in. Width: (Escort/EXP) 65.9 in.; (Tempo) 66.2 in.; (LTD) 71.0 in.; (Crown Vic) 77.5 in.; (Crown Vic wag) 79.3 in.; (TBird) 71.1 in. Front Tread: (Escort/EXP) 54.7 in.; (Tempo) 54.7 in.; (LTD) 56.6 in.; (Crown Vic) 62.2 in. (TBird) 58.1 in. Rear Tread: (Escort/EXP) 56.0 in.; (Tempo) 57.6 in.; (LTD) 57.0 in.; (Crown Vic) 62.0 in. (TBird) 58.5 in. Standard Tires: (Escort/EXP) P165/80R13 SBR BSW; (Escort GT) P165/70R365 Michelin TRX; (Escort Turbo GT) P185/65R365 Michelin TRX; (Tempo) P175/80R13 SBR BSW; (LTD) P185/75R14; (Crown Vic) P215/75R14 SBR WSW; (TBird) P195/75R14 SBR WSW; (TBird Turbo Cpe) P205/70HR14 BSW.

TECHNICAL: Transmission: Four-speed manual standard on Tempo: (1st) 3.23:1; (2nd) 1.92:1; (3rd) 1.23:1; (4th) 0.81:1; (Rev) 3.46:1. Escort four-speed manual transaxle: (1st) 3.23:1; (2nd) 1.90:1; (3rd) 1.23:1; (4th) 0.81:1; (Rev) 3.46:1. Alternate Escort four-speed manual: (1st) 3.58:1; (2nd) 2.05:1; (3rd) 1.23:1 or 1.36:1; (4th) 0.81:1 or 0.95:1; (Rev) 3.46:1. Five-speed manual on Escort/EXP/Tempo: (1st) 3.60:1; (2nd) 2.12:1; (3rd) 1.39:1; (4th) 1.02:1; (5th) 1.02:1; (Rev) 3.62:1. (Note: separate final drive for 5th gear.) Tempo diesel five-speed manual: (1st) 3.93:1; (2nd) 2.12:1; (3rd) 1.39:1; (4th) 1.02:1; (5th) 0.98:1; (Rev) 3.62:1. TBird Turbo Coupe five-speed: (1st) 4.03:1; (2nd) 2.37:1; (3rd) 1.50:1; (4th) 1.00:1; (5th) 0.86:1; (Rev) 3.76:1. Three-speed automatic standard on LTD: (1st) 2.46:1 or 2.47:1; (2nd) 1.46:1 or 1.47:1; (3rd) 1.00:1; (Rev) 2.11:1 or 2.19:1. Escort/EXP/Tempo three-speed automatic: (1st) 2.79:1; (2nd) 1.61:1; (3rd) 1.00:1; (Rev) 1.97:1. Four-speed overdrive automatic standard on LTD propane four, Crown Victoria and Thunderbird: (1st) 2.40:1; (2nd) 1.47:1; (3rd) 1.00:1; (4th) 0.67:1; (Rev) 2.00:1. Standard final drive ratio: (Escort/EXP) 3.59:1 w/4spd, 3.73:1 w/5spd, 3.31:1 w/auto., 3.52:1 w/diesel; (Tempo) 3.04:1 w/4spd, 3.33:1 w/5spd, 3.23:1 w/auto., 3.73:1 w/diesel; (LTD four) 3.27:1; (LTD V-6) 2.73:1 or 3.27:1; (LTD propane four) 3.08:1; (Crown Vic) 3.08:1; (TBird) 3.45:1 w/5spd, 2.73:1 w/3spd automatic and V-6, 3.27:1 w/4spd auto. and V-6, 3.08:1 w/4spd auto. and V-8, 3.73:1 w/turbo and auto. Drive Axle: (Escort/EXP/Tempo) front; (others) rear. Steering: (Crown Vic) recirculating ball; (others) rack and pinion. Front Suspension: (Escort/EXP) MacPherson struts with lower control arms, coil springs and stabilizer bar; (Tempo) MacPherson struts with stabilizer bar; (LTD/TBird) modified MacPherson struts with lower control arms, coil springs and anti-sway bar; (Crown Vic) long/short control arms w/coil springs and stabilizer bar. LTD and TBird had gas-filled struts. Rear Suspension: (Escort/EXP) independent trailing arms w/modified MacPherson struts and coil springs on lower control arms; (Tempo) fully independent quadra-link with MacPherson struts; (LTD/Crown Vic) rigid axle w/four-link coil springs; (Thunderbird) four-link rigid axle with coil springs and electronic level control; (TBird Turbo Coupe) "quadra-shock" four-bar-link assembly with two hydraulic, horizontal axle dampers. Gas-filled shocks on LTD and TBird. Brakes: Front disc, rear drum; power assisted (except Escort). Ignition: Electronic. Body construction: (Crown Vic) separate body and frame; (others) unibody. Fuel tank: (Escort/EXP) 13.0 gal.; (Tempo) 14.0 gal.; (LTD) 16.0 gal.; (Crown Vic) 20.0 gal.; (TBird) 21 gal.

DRIVETRAIN OPTIONS: Engines: Fuel-saver 1.6-liter four: Escort (NC). Propane 140 cu. in. four: LTD ($896). 232 cu. in. V-6: LTD ($409). 302 cu. in. V-8: Thunderbird ($383). Transmission/Differential: Five-speed manual trans.: Escort/Tempo ($76). Automatic transaxle: Escort ($439) exc. LX/GT and EXP ($363); Tempo ($439). Auto. transmission.: TBird Turbo Cpe ($315). Overdrive auto. trans.: LTD/TBird ($237). Traction-Lok differential: LTD/Crown Vic/TBird ($95). Brakes & Steering: Power brakes: Escort ($95). Power steering: Escort/EXP ($215); Tempo ($223). Suspension: H.D. susp.: Tempo (NC); Crown Vic/TBird ($26). Handling susp.: Escort L ($199); Escort GL ($95). Soft ride susp. pkg.: Tempo (NC). Other: H.D. battery ($27). H.D. alternator: EXP ($27); LTD ($52). Extended-range gas tank: LTD ($46). Engine block heater ($18). Trailer towing pkg.: LTD ($398); Crown Vic ($200-$251); TBird ($251). California emission system: Escort/EXP ($46); others ($99). High-altitude emissions (NC).

ESCORT CONVENIENCE/APPEARANCE OPTIONS: Option Packages: Squire wagon pkg. ($373). Instrument group ($87). Power door lock group ($124-$176). Light group ($67). Comfort/Convenience: Air conditioner ($643). Rear defroster, electric ($130). Fingertip speed control ($176). Tinted glass ($95); windshield only ($48). Tilt steering ($104). Overhead console w/digital clock ($82). Interval wipers ($50). Rear wiper/washer ($120) exc. LX ($46). Dual remote sport mirrors ($68). Entertainment: AM radio: L ($39). AM/FM radio ($82) exc. L ($121). AM/FM stereo radio ($109) exc. L ($148); w/cassette player ($204) exc. L ($243). Electronic-tuning AM/FM stereo ($252-$291); w/cassette ($396-$435). Graphic equalizer ($176). Premium sound ($117). Exterior: Flip-up open-air roof ($315). Clearcoat metallic paint (NC). Glamour paint ($51). Two-tone paint/tape ($134- $173). Dual bodyside paint stripes ($39). Front vent windows, pivoting ($63). Vinyl-insert bodyside moldings ($45). Bumper guards, front or rear ($28). Bumper rub strips ($48). Luggage rack ($100). Lower bodyside protection ($68). Interior: Console ($111). Vinyl seat trim ($24). Color-keyed front mats ($22). Wheels/Tires: Wheel trim rings ($54). Cast aluminum wheels ($279). TR aluminum wheels ($201). Styled steel wheels ($104 credit). P165/80R13 SBR WSW ($59). P175/80R13 SBR BSW (NC).

EXP CONVENIENCE/APPEARANCE OPTIONS: Comfort/Convenience: Air conditioner ($643). Fingertip speed control ($176). Tinted glass ($95). Tilt steering ($104). Lighted visor vanity mirror ($50). Entertainment: AM/FM stereo radio ($109); w/cassette player ($204) exc. luxury cpe ($95). Electronic-tuning AM/FM stereo ($252) exc. luxury cpe ($144) and Turbo ($49); w/cassette ($396) exc. luxury ($288) and Turbo ($193). Graphic equalizer ($176). Premium sound ($117). AM radio delete ($39 credit). AM/FM stereo delete: luxury cpe ($148 credit). AM/FM stereo/cassette delete: Turbo ($243 credit). Exterior: Flip-up open air roof ($315). Clearcoat paint ($161). Lower two-tone paint/tape ($146). Sport tape stripe ($41). Stripe delete (NC). Medium bodyside moldings ($45). Lower bodyside protection ($68). Interior: Low-back knit vinyl bucket seats (NC). Sport performance seats ($173). Front floor mats ($22). Wheels: TR aluminum wheels ($369). TR styled steel wheels ($168). Cast aluminum wheels ($238). P165/80R13 RWL ($90). P165/70R365 TRX (NC).

TEMPO CONVENIENCE/APPEARANCE OPTIONS: Option Packages: TR performance pkg. w/aluminum wheels ($366- $424). Sport appearance group: GL 2dr. ($299). Power lock group ($202-$254). Appearance protection group ($71). Light/convenience group ($50-$85). Comfort/Convenience: Air cond. ($743). Rear defroster, electric ($140). Fingertip speed control ($176). Illuminated entry ($82). Anti-theft system ($159). Power windows ($272). Power decklid release ($41). Six-way power seat ($224). Tinted glass ($110); windshield ($48). Tilt steering ($110). Sport instrument cluster ($71-$87). Digital clock ($61). Interval wipers ($50). Lighting and Mirrors: Left remote mirror ($23); right ($70). Dual sport remote mirrors ($93). Lighted visor vanity mirrors, pair ($100-$112). Entertainment: AM/FM radio ($59). AM/FM stereo radio ($109); w/cassette player ($204). Electronic-tuning AM/FM stereo ($252); w/cassette ($396). Premium sound system ($117). AM radio delete ($39 credit). Exterior: Flip-up open air roof ($315). Metallic glamour glow paint ($63). Black lower body accent paint ($78-$194). Narrow bodyside moldings ($61). Bumper guards, front/rear ($56). Bumper rub strips ($56). Interior: Console ($111). Fold-down front armrest ($55). Vinyl seat trim ($35). Carpeted front floor mats ($13). Trunk trim ($30). Wheels/Tires: Luxury wheel covers ($59). Styled steel wheels ($59) exc. GL/GLX (NC). P175/80R13 WSW ($72).

LTD CONVENIENCE/APPEARANCE OPTIONS: Option Packages: Squire option ($282). Brougham decor option: wagon ($363). Interior luxury group ($388). Power lock group ($213-$254). Cold weather group ($77). Light group ($38). Police pkg. ($859-$1387). Taxi pkg. ($860). H.D. fleet pkg. ($210). Comfort/Convenience: Air cond. ($743); auto-temp ($809). Rear defroster, electric ($140). Fingertip speed control ($176). Illuminated entry ($82). Autolamp on-off delay ($73). Power windows ($272). Six-way power driver's seat ($224); dual ($449). Tinted glass ($110). Tinted windshield ($48). Leather-wrapped steering wheel ($59). Tilt steering ($110). Electronic instrument cluster ($289-$367). Tripminder computer ($215-$293). Digital clock ($78). Diagnostic warning lights ($83). Interval wipers ($50). Liftgate wiper/washer: wagon ($99). Lighting and Mirrors: Cornering lamps ($68). Right remote convex mirror ($61). Lighted visor vanity mirrors ($57-$106). Entertainment: AM/FM stereo radio ($109); w/cassette player ($204). Electronic-tuning AM/FM stereo radio w/cassette ($396). Premium sound system ($151). AM radio delete ($39 credit). Exterior: Full vinyl roof ($152). Metallic glow paint ($63). Two-tone paint ($117). Pivoting front vent windows ($79). Two-way liftgate: wag ($105). Protective bodyside moldings ($55). Bumper guards, rear ($28). Bumper rub strips ($56). Luggage rack: wagon ($126). Lower bodyside protection ($41). Interior: Vinyl seat trim ($35). Split or flight bench seat (NC). Individual seats w/console ($61). Leather seat trim ($415). Front floor mats, carpeted ($23). Wheels/Tires: Luxury wheel covers ($55). Wire wheel covers ($165); locking ($204). Styled wheels ($178). Styled steel wheels w/trim rings ($54). P185/75R14 WSW ($72). P195/75R14 BSW ($38); WSW ($116). Puncture-sealant P195/75R14 WSW ($240). Conventional spare ($63).

LTD CROWN VICTORIA CONVENIENCE/APPEARANCE OPTIONS: Option Packages: Interior luxury group ($954-$1034). Convenience group ($109-$134). Power lock group ($140-$238). Light group ($48). Protection group ($68). Police pkg. ($279-$398). Comfort/Convenience: Air cond. ($743); w/auto-temp control ($809). Rear defroster, electric ($140). Fingertip speed control ($176). Illuminated entry system ($82). Power windows ($198-$272). Power driver's seat ($227); driver and passenger ($454). Remote fuel door lock ($35). Tinted glass ($110); windshield only ($48). Autolamp on/off delay ($73). Leather- wrapped steering wheel ($59). Tilt steering wheel ($110). Auto. parking brake release ($12). Tripminder computer ($215- $261). Digital clock ($61). Interval wipers ($50). Lighting and Mirrors: Cornering lamps ($68). Remote right mirror ($46). Lighted visor vanity mirrors ($106). Entertainment: AM/FM stereo radio: S ($106); w/cassette tape player ($112-$204). Electronic-tuning AM/FM stereo radio w/cassette ($166) exc. S ($416). Power antenna ($66). Premium sound system ($151-$179). Radio delete ($148 credit). Exterior: Metallic glow paint ($77). Two-tone paint ($117). Dual accent bodyside paint stripes ($39). Pivoting front vent windows ($79). Rocker panel moldings ($18-$38). Vinyl-insert bodyside moldings ($61). Bumper rub strips ($59). Luggage rack ($110). Lower bodyside protection ($39-$52). Interior: Dual-facing rear seats: Ctry Sq ($167). Leather seat trim ($418). Split bench seating ($139). All-vinyl seat trim ($34); Duraweave vinyl ($96). Carpeted front floor mats ($21). Trunk trim ($49). Wheels/Tires: Wire wheel covers ($165); locking ($204). Cast aluminum wheels ($390). P225/75R14 WSW ($42-$43). P205/75R15 WSW ($17); puncture-sealant ($178). P215/75R14 BSW ($66 credit). Conventional spare ($63).

1984 Thunderbird FILA hardtop coupe (JG)

THUNDERBIRD CONVENIENCE/APPEARANCE OPTIONS: Option Packages: Interior luxury group ($1223). Exterior accent group ($299). Luxury carpet group ($72). Traveler's assistance kit ($65). Light group ($35). Power lock group ($177). Comfort/Convenience: Air cond. ($743); auto-temp ($809). Rear defroster ($140). Fingertip speed control ($176). Illuminated entry system ($82). Keyless entry ($116-$198). Anti-theft system ($159). Remote fuel door lock ($37). Tripminder computer ($215-$276). Autolamp on/off delay ($73). Tinted glass ($110); windshield only ($48). Power windows ($198). Six-way power driver's seat ($227); dual ($454) exc. Fila ($227). Auto. parking brake release ($12). Leather-wrapped steering wheel ($59). Tilt steering wheel ($110). Electronic instrument cluster ($321-$382). Electronic voice alert ($67). Diagnostic warning lights ($89). Low oil warning light ($24). Digital clock: base ($61). Interval wipers ($50). Lighting and Mirrors: Cornering lamps ($68). Electro- luminescent coach lamps ($84). Dual electric remote mirrors ($86). Electronic-dimming day/night mirror ($77). Lighted visor vanity mirrors, pair ($106). Entertainment: AM/FM stereo radio: base ($109); w/cassette player ($204) exc. Turbo Cpe ($95). Electronic-tuning AM/FM stereo search radio ($144-$252); w/cassette ($396) exc. Turbo Cpe ($288) and Elan ($144). Power antenna ($66). Premium sound system ($179). AM radio delete ($39 credit). Exterior: Flip-up open-air roof ($315). Metallic clearcoat paint ($183). Two-tone paint/tape ($148-$218). Charcoal lower accent treatment ($78). Hood paint stripe ($16). Dual accent bodyside/decklid paint stripes ($55). Hood/decklid/bodyside paint stripes ($71). Pivoting front vent windows ($79). Wide bodyside moldings ($57). Rocker panel moldings ($39). License frames ($9). Lower bodyside protection ($39-$54). Interior: Articulated seats ($183-$427). Leather seat trim ($415). Vinyl seat trim ($37). Front floor mats, carpeted ($22). Wheels/Tires: Wire wheel covers, locking ($26-$204). Luxury wheel covers ($113). Styled wheels ($65-$178). Puncture- sealing tires ($124). P205/70R14 BSW (NC). P205/70R14 WSW ($62). P205/70HR14 performance BSW ($152). Cast aluminum TRX wheels w/BSW performance tires ($471-$649) exc. Turbo Cpe ($154). Conventional spare ($63).

HISTORY: Introduced: September 22, 1983 except Tempo, May 1983. Model year production: 1,496,997 (incl. Mustangs). Total production for the U.S. market of 1,294,491 units (incl. Mustangs) included 711,698 four-cylinder, 323,985 sixes and 258,808 V-8s. That total included 25,581 turbo fours and 24,879 diesel engines. Calendar year production (U.S.): 1,145,028 (incl. Mustangs). Calendar year sales by U.S. dealers: 1,300,644 (incl. Mustangs). Model year sales by U.S. dealers: 1,262,498 (incl. Mustangs).

Historical Footnotes: Sales hit their highest mark since 1979 for the model year. That was a 27 percent jump over 1983. Thunderbird showed the strongest rise. Escort lost its title as top- selling car in the nation to Chevrolet's Cavalier. EXP sales had never been promising, and declined again this year, even after the turbo edition had been offered. Escort/Tempo's 2.0- liter diesel, from Mazda Motor Corp., showed sluggish sales as well. As an indication of the importance placed upon advertising to the youth market, Edsel B. Ford II was named advertising manager in late 1983. Tempo design had begun in 1979 under a "Topaz" project (the name ultimately given to the Mercury version).

1985 FORD

Thunderbird enjoyed a modest restyle, but nothing too dramatic occurred for the 1985 model year. LTD had added a high-performance, V-8 powered LX touring sedan late in the '84 season, which continued this year. Base models were upgraded, now including as standard various popular items that were formerly optional. Such simplification of the model lineup cut production costs and (presumably) made selection easier for buyers. Manual gearboxes for Escort and Thunderbird were improved. Tempo now had a standard fuel- injected 2.3-liter four and five-speed transaxle, as well as a high-performance engine option.

1985 Escort GL five-door hatchback (JG)

ESCORT — FOUR — Reverse gear on both the four- and five-speed manual transaxle moved to a new position this year, intended to make shifting easier. On five-speeds, it moved from the upper left to the lower right. (The change began on Thunderbird Turbo Coupe and Mustang SVO for '84.) Mechanical radios had a new flat-face design. Starting in mid-year 1984, clearcoat paints were made available on the Escort L and GL. Otherwise, little was new on Ford's subcompact two- and four-door hatchbacks as the model year began. Later on, though, a restyled 1985.5 Escort appeared, powered by a new 1.9-liter four-cylinder engine. Standard engine for the first series was again

the CVH 97.6 cu. in. (1.6-liter) carbureted four, with four-speed gearbox. A high-output version was available, as well as one with electronic fuel injection and another with a turbocharger. The 2.0-liter diesel was offered again, too. Five-speed manual and three-speed automatic transmissions were available. Escort's three-row grille design had thin vertical bars across each row to form a crosshatch pattern, with Ford oval in the center. Base and L Escorts had a bright grille and blackout front-end treatment, halogen headlamps, heater/defroster, four-speed gearbox, rack-and-pinion steering, short black bumper end caps, bright bumpers, side window demisters, day/night mirror, and cloth/vinyl high-back reclining front bucket seats. Bright moldings went on the windshield surround, backlight, belt, headlamps and drip rail; color- keyed moldings on the A pillar. Escort L had a brushed aluminum B pillar applique. Wagons and diesels had standard power brakes. Escort GL added a front air dam, long black bumper end caps with argent stripe, remote locking fuel door, dual bodyside paint stripes, AM radio, low-back seats, and additional bright moldings. Escort LX included front/rear bumper guards, power brakes, blackout body treatment, digital clock, foglamps, locking glovebox, TR performance suspension and styled steel wheels, black tri-oval steering wheel, and five-speed manual tranxale. GT models carried wide black bodyside moldings with argent striping, dual black remote racing mirrors, power brakes, TR performance suspension, tape stripes and decals, five-speed transaxle, black wheel spats, remote liftgate release, foglamps, and sport-tuned exhaust. Turbo GT had aluminum TR wheels; non-turbos, steel wheels with bright trim rings. Turbos also had standard power steering.

EXP — FOUR — Like the Escort sedans, the two-seater EXP got a revised location for reverse gear (below 5th gear). Radios and cassette players showed a new flat-face design. Base engine was the fuel-injected 97.6 cu. in. (1.6-liter) four. The Turbo Coupe was available again, wearing aluminum wheels with low-profile performance tires and Koni shock absorbers. This was EXP's final season in its original form. Standard equipment included an AM rdio, tinted rear- window glass, halogen headlamps, digital clock, power brakes, tachometer, handling suspension, remote locking fuel door, black bumper rub strips, black left-hand remote sport mirror, and black moldings. Inside were low-back cloth/vinyl reclining bucket seats. EXP's Luxury Coupe added an AM/FM stereo radio, interval wipers, luxury cloth seats with four- way (manual) driver's side adjuster, remote liftgate release, dual remote mirrors, rear defroster, and tinted glass. Turbo Coupe included a front air dam, black rocker panel moldings, AM/FM stereo with cassette, lower tu-tone paint/tape treatment, power steering, TR suspension and aluminum wheels, wheel spats, and rear spoiler.

1985 Tempo Sport GL coupe (JG)

TEMPO — FOUR — Throttle-body fuel injection was added to Tempo's 2300 HSC (High Swirl Combustion) engine after a year of carburetion. A new high-output version had a new cylinder head and intake manifold, and drove a special 3.73:1 final drive ratio. Five-speed manual overdrive transaxles were now standard in all Tempo series, with revised reverse gear position (now below 5th gear). GL Tempos now had a sport instrument cluster, front center armrest, power lock group, illuminated entry, light convenience group, tinted glass, AM/FM stereo radio, power steering, and tilt steering wheel. Just before the '85 model year, the fuel tank grew from 14 to 15.2 gallons. There were new see-through reservoirs for brake, power steering and washer fluid levels. This year's instrument panel included side window demisters, plus contemporary flat-face radio design and a storage shelf. New options included graphic equalizer, clearcoat metallic paints, and styled road wheels (standard on GL and GLX).

1985 Tempo GLX sedan (JG)

Tempo again came in three series: L, GL and GLX. Base Tempos came with AM radio, cloth/vinyl reclining low-back bucket seats, bodyside accent stripes, dual decklid stripes (two-doors), power brakes, bright bumpers with black end caps, and black left-hand mirror. GL added a blackout back panel treatment, bumper end cap extensions, bumper rub strips, digital clock, map pocket, black bodyside moldings, styled wheels, interval wipers, and dual striping on four- door decklids. A high-performance Sport GL performance option included the high-output (HSO) engine, seven-spoke aluminum wheels with locking lug nuts, P185/70R14 blackwall tires, improved suspension components, dual remote mirrors, sport performance cloth seats, and grey bumpers with blue inserts.

LTD — FOUR/V-6 — Restyling gave LTD a new horizontal grille for its third season, plus new sedan taillamps. Otherwise, only minor trim changes were evident. The new grille had three horizontal bars, with the Ford script oval incorporated into the body. As before, the whole front end was angled, and displayed a large upper grille header bar. The new taillamps had a larger lighted area. LTD also had new black vinyl-clad bodyside moldings with argent accent stripe, and a new, smoother-looking brushed stainless B-pillar molding. Base models wore new deluxe wheel covers. The base 140 cu. in. (2.3-liter) engine added low-friction piston rings, with a boost in compression. Wagons had a standard 232 cu. in. (3.8-liter) V-6. Standard tires grew one size, to 195/75R14 all-season tread. New options included dual electric remote mirrors and black vinyl rocker panel moldings. Optional styled road wheels changed

color to light argent. Joining the base and Brougham sedan and LTD wagon later in the model year was a new high-performance LX touring sedan. It carried a high-output version of the fuel-injected 302 cu. in. (5.0-liter) V-8, coupled to four-speed overdrive automatic transmission and a 3.27:1 Traction-Lok rear axle. The performance sedan also had a special handling suspension with rear stabilzer bar, fast 15:1 steering gear, and Goodyear Eagle GT performance tires. LX had its own distinctive look, highlighted by body-color grille, charcoal and red-orange accents, twin chromed exhaust extensions, and styled road wheels. Inside LX was a center console with floor shifter, tachometer, and unique front bucket seats with inflatable lumbar support. Both base and Brougham sedans had an AM radio, SelectShift automatic transmission, locking glovebox, power brakes and steering, reclining split-bench seating with cloth upholstery, left-hand remote mirror, dual bodyside and hood accent stripes, and bright moldings. Brougham added a digital clock, light group, seatback map pockets, lighted visor vanity mirror (passenger), luxury cloth upholstery, automatic parking brake release, and luxury door trim panels with cloth inserts.

LTD CROWN VICTORIA — V-8 — Except for an aluminum front bumper on station wagons and some new body and vinyl roof colors, full-size Fords showed no significant body change. To improve the ride, Crown Vic got new gas-filled shock absorbers, pressurized with nitrogen. An ignition diagnostics monitor was added to the EEC-IV electronic engine controls. The horn control moved from the stalk to the center of the steering wheel. Flash-to-pass feature was added this year. A single key was now used for door and ignition locks. Lower bodyside panels now had urethane coating for extra corrosion protection. Model lineup for the biggest rear-drives remained the same: two- and four-door sedan (standard or 'S'), along with plain-bodied and Country Squire (woodgrain) wagons. The sole 302 cu. in. (5.0-liter) V-8 came, with fuel injection, came with four-speed automatic overdrive transmission. A new optional automatic load leveling suspension (available later in the model year) used an electronic sensor and air- adjustable rear shocks. With a heavy-duty trailer towing package, Crown Vic and Country Squire could again tow trailers up to 5,000 pounds. Standard equipment included chrome bumpers with guards, left-hand remote-control mirror, dual-note horn, cloth/vinyl reclining flight bench seating, power steering and brakes, and deluxe wheel covers. The budget-priced 'S' models lacked such items as the padded half (rear) vinyl roof, dual accent tape striping, quartz clock, brushed lower decklid applique, and various moldings. 'S' models had an AM radio; others an AM/FM stereo.

1985 Thunderbird Elan hardtop coupe (JG)

THUNDERBIRD — FOUR/V-6/V-8 — A new color-keyed grille and full-width wraparound taillamps with inboard backup lamps made up the evident changes on Ford's personal luxury coupe. There was also a new Thunderbird emblem, which appeared on taillamp lenses, C pillars and upper grille header. Inside was a new instru- instrument panel with digital speedometer and anolog gauges, door trim panels, and a third rear seatbelt. Standard interiors had a shorter center console, so three people could sit in back. Turbo Coupe's 140 cu. in. (2.3-liter) four- cylinder engine got electronic boost control and higher flow- rate fuel injectors for more power, water-cooled bearings, and a new five-speed gearbox with revised gear ratios. Standard tire size was now 205/70R14 except for Turbo Coupe, which wore performance 225/60VR15 tires on 7 inch wheels. Joining the option list were power front seat recliners for comfort and a graphic equalizer to improve audio entertainment. Fully electronic instruments were optional on all TBirds except the Turbo Coupe. Base 'birds had the standard 232 cu. in. (3.8-liter) V-6 with three-speed automatic transmission, power steering and brakes, mini spare tire, knit cloth 60/40 split bench reclining seats, AM/FM stereo radio, quartz clock, and bumper rub strips. Bright moldings went on the drip rail, windshield surround, backlight, and windows. Charcoal bodyside moldings had vinyl inserts. Thunderbird Elan added wide bodyside moldings, power windows, interval wipers, dual electric remote mirrors, diagnostic warning lights, digital clock, tinted glass, AM/FM stereo with cassette, decklid and bodyside accent stripes, and a light group. Fila included the autolamp delay system, speed control, leather-wrapped tilt steering wheel, four-speed overdrive automatic transmission, cast aluminum wheels, electronic-tuning radio with cassette, cornering lamps, power locks, illuminated entry, and articulated sport seats. The driver's seat had six-way power adjustment and power lumbar support. Fila also had a color- keyed grille instead of the usual brightwork, as well as charcoal paint with dark charcoal lower accents and charcoal windshield/backlight moldings.

I.D. DATA: Ford's 17-symbol Vehicle Identification Number (VIN) again was stamped on a metal tab fastened to the instrument panel, visible through the windshield. Coding was similar to 1984. Model year code changed to 'F' for 1985. Engine code 'W' for HSC L4140 FI was added; code '6' for propane fuel dropped. A Vehicle Certification Label on the left front door lock face panel or door pillar shows the manufacturer, month and year of manufacture, GVW, GAWR, certification statement, VIN, and codes for such items as body type, color, trim, axle, transmission, and special order information.

ESCORT (FOUR)

Model Number	Body/Style Number	Body Type & Seating	Factory Price	Shipping Weight	Production Total
04/41P	61D	2-dr. Hatch-4P	5620	1981	Note 1
13/41P	58D	4-dr. Hatch-4P	5827	2034	Note 1
04	61D	2-dr. L Hatch-4P	5876	1981	Note 1
13	58D	4-dr. L Hatch-4P	6091	2034	Note 1
09	74D	4-dr. L Sta Wag-4P	6305	2066	Note 1
05	61D	2-dr. GL Hatch-4P	6374	2033	Note 1
14	58D	4-dr. GL Hatch-4P	6588	2086	Note 1
10	74D	4-dr. GL Sta Wag-4P	6765	2115	Note 1
15	58D	4-dr. LX Hatch-4P	7840	2137	Note 1
11	74D	4-dr. LX Sta Wag-4P	7931	2073	Note 1

ESCORT GT (FOUR)

07	61D	2-dr. Hatch-4P	7585	2103	Note 1
07/935	61D	2-dr. Turbo Hatch-4P	8680	2239	Note 1

1985.5 ESCORT — Second Series (FOUR)

31	N/A	2-dr. Hatch-4P	5856	2089	Note 1
31	N/A	2-dr. L Hatch-4P	6127	2096	Note 1
36	N/A	4-dr. !. Hatch-4P	6341	2154	Note 1
34	N/A	4-dr. L Sta Wag-4P	6622	2173	Note 1
32	N/A	2-dr. GL Hatch-4P	6642	2160	Note 1
37	N/A	4-dr. GL Hatch-4P	6855	2214	Note 1
35	N/A	4-dr. GL Sta Wag-4P	7137	2228	Note 1

Note 1: Ford reported production of the second (1985.5) Escort series at 100,554 two-door hatchbacks, 48,676 four-door hatchback sedans, and 36,998 station wagons, but did not include the initial series. Other sources give total Escort production for the model year of 212,960 two- doors, 111,385 four-doors, and 82,738 wagons. Breakdown by trim level not available. Bodies are sometimes referred to as three-door and five- door.

Diesel Engine Note: Diesel-powered Escorts came in L and GL trim, priced $558 higher than equivalent gasoline models.

EXP (FOUR)

01/A80	67D	3-dr. Hatch Cpe-2P	6697	2117	26,462
01/A81	67D	3-dr. Luxury Cpe-2P	7585	2117	Note 2
01/A82	67D	3-dr. Turbo Cpe-2P	9997	N/A	Note 2

Note 2: Production of luxury and turbo coupe models is included in basic EXP total above.

TEMPO (FOUR)

18	66D	2-dr. L Sedan-5P	7052	2249	Note 3
21	54D	4-dr. L Sedan-5P	7052	2308	Note 3
19	66D	2-dr. GL Sed-5P	7160	2276	Note 3
22	54D	4-dr. GL Sed-5P	7160	2339	Note 3
20	66D	2-dr. GLX Sed-5P	8253	2302	Note 3
23	54D	4-dr. GLX Sed-5P	8302	2362	Note 3

Note 3: Total Tempo production came to 72,311 two-doors and 266,776 four-doors. A turbocharged Tempo GTX, priced at $9870, was announced but apparently not produced.

Diesel Engine Note: Diesel-powered Tempos cost $479 more than equivalent gasoline models.

LTD (FOUR/V-6)

39	54D	4-dr. Sedan-5P	8874/9292	2804/2881	162,884
39/60H	54D	4-dr. Brghm-5P	9262/9680	2812/2889	Note 4
40	74D	4-dr. Sta Wag-5P	--/9384	--/2990	42,642

LTD LX BROUGHAM (V-8)

39/938	54D	4-dr. Sedan-5P	11421	N/A	Note 4

Note 4: Brougham production is included in basic sedan total.

LTD CROWN VICTORIA (V-8)

42	66K	2-dr. Sedan-6P	11627	3546	13,673
43	54K	4-dr. Sedan-6P	11627	3587	154,612
44	74K	4-dr. Ctry Sqr-6P	11809	3793	30,825
43/41K	54K	4-dr. 'S' Sed-6P	10609	N/A	Note 5
44/41K	74K	4-dr. 'S' Wag-6P	10956	N/A	Note 5
44/41E	74K	4-dr. Sta Wag-6P	11559	N/A	Note 5

Note 5: Production of 'S' models and basic station wagon is included in basic sedan and Country Squire totals above.

Police Model Note: Crown Victoria 'S' police models sold for $10,929 with the 302 cu. in. V-8 and $11,049 with 351 cu. in. V-8. engine.

1985 Thunderbird Turbo coupe (JG)

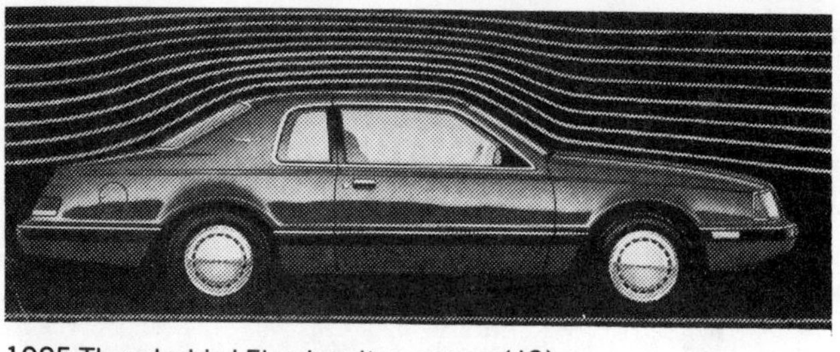

1985 Thunderbird Elan hardtop coupe (JG)

THUNDERBIRD (V-6/V-8)

46	66D	2-dr. HT Cpe-5P	10249/10884	2890/3097	151,851
46/607	66D	2-dr. Elan Cpe-5P	11916/12551	2956/3163	Note 6
46/606	66D	2-dr. Fila Cpe-5P	14974/15609	3061/3268	Note 6

THUNDERBIRD TURBO COUPE (FOUR)

46/934	66D	2-dr. HT Cpe-5P	13365	2938	Note 6

Note 6: Turbo Coupe and Elan/Fila production is included in basic Thunderbird total.

MODEL NUMBER NOTE: Some sources include a prefix 'P' ahead of the two- digit model number. **FACTORY PRICE AND WEIGHT NOTE:** LTD prices and weights to left of slash are for four-cylinder, to right for V-6 engine. Thunderbird prices and weights to left of slash are for V-6, to right for V-8 engine.

ENGINE DATA: BASE FOUR (Escort): Inline. Overhead cam. Four-cylinder. Cast iron block and aluminum head. Displacement: 97.6 cu. in. (1.6 liters). Bore & stroke: 3.15 x 3.13 in. Compression ratio: 9.0:1. Brake horsepower: 70 at 4600 R.P.M. Torque: 88 lbs.-ft. at 2600 R.P.M. Five main bearings. Hydraulic valve lifters. Carburetor: 2Bbl. Holley 740. VIN Code: 2. Note: Second Series Escorts, introduced at mid-year, carried a new 1.9-liter engine; see 1986 listing for specifications. BASE FOUR (EXP); OPTIONAL (Escort): High-output version of 1.6-liter four above Horsepower: 80 at 5400 R.P.M. Torque: 88 lbs.-ft. at 3000 R.P.M. VIN Code: 4. BASE FOUR (Escort LX/GT); OPTIONAL (Escort): Fuel-injected version of 1.6-liter four above Horsepower: 84 at 5200 R.P.M. Torque: 90 lbs.-ft. at 2800 R.P.M. VIN Code: 5. TURBO FOUR (Escort, EXP): Same as 1.6-liter four above, with fuel injection and turbocharger Compression ratio: 8.0:1. Horsepower: 120 at 5200 R.P.M. Torque: 120 lbs.-ft. at 3400 R.P.M. VIN Code: 8. DIESEL FOUR (Escort, Tempo): Inline. Overhead cam. Four-cylinder. Cast iron block and aluminum head. Displacement: 121 cu. in. (2.0 liters). Bore & stroke: 3.39 x 3.39 in. Compression ratio: 22.5:1. Brake horsepower: 52 at 4000 R.P.M. Torque: 82 lbs.-ft. at 2400 R.P.M. Five main bearings. Solid valve lifters. Fuel injection. VIN Code: H. BASE FOUR (Tempo): Inline. Overhead valve. Four-cylinder. Cast iron block and head. Displacement: 140 cu. in. (2.3 liters). Bore & stroke: 3.70 x 3.30 in. Compression ratio: 9.0:1. Brake horsepower: 86 at 4000 R.P.M. Torque: 124 lbs.-ft. at 2800 R.P.M. Five main bearings. Hydraulic valve lifters. Throttle-body fuel injection. High Swirl Combustion (HSC) design. VIN Code: X. OPTIONAL FOUR (Tempo): High-output version of HSC four above Horsepower: 100 at 4600 R.P.M. Torque: 125 lbs.-ft. at 3200 R.P.M. VIN Code: S. BASE FOUR (LTD): Inline. Overhead cam. Four-cylinder. Cast iron block and head. Displacement: 140 cu. in. (2.3 liters). Bore & stroke: 3.78 x 3.13 in. Compression ratio: 9.5:1. Brake horsepower: 88 at 4000 R.P.M. Torque: 122 lbs.-ft. at 2400 R.P.M. Five main bearings. Hydraulic valve lifters. Carburetor: 1Bbl. Carter YFA. VIN Code: A. PROPANE FOUR (LTD): Same as 140 cu. in. four above, but for propane fuel Compression ratio: 10.0:1. Brake horsepower: 88 at 4000 R.P.M. Torque: 122 lbs.-ft. at 2400 R.P.M. VIN Code: 6. TURBOCHARGED FOUR (Thunderbird Turbo Coupe): Same as 140 cu. in. four above, with fuel injection and turbocharger Compression ratio: 8.0:1. Horsepower: 155 at 4600 R.P.M. Torque: 190 lbs.-ft. at 2800 R.P.M. VIN Code: W. BASE V-6 (LTD wagon, Thunderbird); OPTIONAL (LTD): 90-degree, overhead valve V-6. Cast iron block and aluminum head. Displacement: 232 cu. in. (3.8 liters). Bore & stroke: 3.80 x 3.40 in. Compression ratio: 8.7:1. Brake horsepower: 120 at 3600 R.P.M. Torque: 205 lbs.-ft. at 1600 R.P.M. Four main bearings. Hydraulic valve lifters. Throttle-body fuel injection. VIN Code: 3. BASE V-8 (Crown Victoria); OPTIONAL (Thunderbird): 90-degree, overhead valve V-8. Cast iron block and head. Displacement: 302 cu. in. (5.0 liters). Bore & stroke: 4.00 x 3.00 in. Compression ratio: 8.4:1. Brake horsepower: 140 at 3200 R.P.M. Torque: 250 lbs.-ft. at 1600 R.P.M. Five main bearings. Hydraulic valve lifters. Electronic fuel injection (TBI). VIN Code: F. OPTIONAL HIGH-OUTPUT V-8 (Crown Victoria): Same as 302 cu. in. V-8 above, except Horsepower: 155 at 3600 R.P.M. Torque: 265 lbs.-ft. at 2000 R.P.M. BASE V-8 (LTD LX): Same as 302 cu. in. V-8, above, except Compression ratio: 8.3:1. Horsepower: 165 at 3800 R.P.M. Torque: 245 lbs.-ft. at 2000 R.P.M. HIGH-OUTPUT POLICE V-8 (Crown Victoria): 90-degree, overhead valve V-8. Cast iron block and head. Displacement: 351 cu. in. (5.8 liters). Bore & stroke: 4.00 x 3.50 in. Compression ratio: 8.3:1. Brake horsepower: 180 at 3600 R.P.M. Torque: 285 lbs.-ft. at 2400 R.P.M. Five main bearings. Hydraulic valve lifters. Carburetor: 2Bbl. 7200VV. VIN Code: G.

CHASSIS DATA: Wheelbase: (Escort/EXP) 94.2 in.; (Tempo) 99.9 in.; (LTD) 105.6 in.; (Crown Vic) 114.3 in.; (TBird) 104.0 in. Overall Length: (Escort) 163.9 in.; (Escort wagon) 165.0 in.; (EXP) 170.3 in.; (Tempo) 176.2 in.; (LTD) 196.5 in.; (Crown Vic) 211.0 in.; (Crown Vic wag) 215.0 in.; (TBird) 197.6 in. Height: (Escort) 53.3-53.4 in.; (EXP) 50.5 in.; (Tempo) 52.7 in.; (LTD) 53.8 in.; (LTD wag) 54.4 in.; (Crown Vic) 55.3 in.; (Crown Vic wag) 56.8 in.; (TBird) 53.2 in. Width: (Escort/EXP) 65.9 in.; (Tempo) 68.3 in.; (LTD) 71.0 in.; (Crown Vic) 77.5 in.; (Crown Vic wag) 79.3 in.; (TBird) 71.1 in. Front Tread: (Escort/EXP/Tempo) 54.7 in.; (LTD) 56.6 in.; (Crown Vic) 62.2 in. (TBird) 58.1 in. Rear Tread: (Escort/EXP) 56.0 in.; (Tempo) 57.6 in.; (LTD) 57.0 in.; (Crown Vic) 62.0 in. (TBird) 58.5 in. Standard Tires: (Escort/EXP) P165/80R13 SBR BSW; (Escort L) P175/80R13; (Escort LX/GT) P165/70R365 Michelin TRX; (Escort/EXP Turbo) P185/65R365 Michelin TRX; (Tempo) P175/80R13 SBR BSW; (LTD) P195/75R14 SBR BSW exc. LX and police, P205/70HR14 Goodyear Eagle BSW; (Crown Vic) P215/75R14 SBR WSW; (TBird) P205/70R14 SBR BSW; (TBird Turbo Cpe) P225/60VR15 performance BSW.

TECHNICAL: Transmission: Escort four-speed manual transaxle: (1st) 3.23:1; (2nd) 1.92:1; (3rd) 1.23:1; (4th) 0.81:1; (Rev) 3.46:1. Alternate Escort four-speed manual: (1st) 3.58:1; (2nd) 2.05:1; (3rd) 1.23:1; (4th) 0.81:1; (Rev) 3.46:1. Five- speed manual on Escort/EXP/Tempo: (1st) 3.60:1; (2nd) 2.12:1; (3rd) 1.39:1; (4th) 1.02:1; (5th) 1.02:1; (Rev) 3.62:1. (Note: separate final drive for 5th gear.) Escort/Tempo diesel five-speed manual: (1st) 3.93:1; (2nd) 2.12:1; (3rd) 1.39:1; (4th) 0.98:1; (5th) 0.98:1; (Rev) 3.62:1. TBird Turbo Coupe five-speed: (1st) 4.03:1; (2nd) 2.37:1; (3rd) 1.49:1; (4th) 1.00:1; (5th) 0.81:1; (Rev) 3.76:1. Three-speed automatic standard on LTD, Thunderbird turbo/V-6: (1st) 2.46:1 or 2.47:1; (2nd) 1.46:1 or 1.47:1; (3rd) 1.00:1; (Rev) 2.11:1 or 2.19:1. Escort/EXP/Tempo three-speed automatic: (1st) 2.79:1; (2nd) 1.61:1; (3rd) 1.00:1; (Rev) 1.97:1. Four- speed overdrive automatic standard on LTD V-6, Crown Victoria and Thunderbird: (1st) 2.40:1; (2nd) 1.47:1; (3rd) 1.00:1; (4th) 0.67:1; (Rev) 2.00:1. Standard final drive ratio: (Escort/EXP) 3.59:1 w/4spd, 3.73:1 w/5spd, 3.31:1 w/auto., 3.52:1 w/diesel; (Tempo) 3.33:1 w/5spd, 3.23:1 w/auto., 3.73:1 w/diesel or H.O. engine; (LTD four) 3.27:1; (LTD V-6) 2.73:1 w/3spd auto.; (Crown Vic) 3.08:1; (TBird) 3.45:1 w/turbo, 2.73:1 w/3spd automatic and V-6, 3.27:1 w/4spd auto. and V-6, 3.08:1 w/V-8. Drive Axle: (Escort/EXP/Tempo) front; (others) rear. Steering: (Crown Vic) recirculating ball; (others) rack and pinion. Front Suspension: (Escort/EXP/Tempo) MacPherson struts with lower control arms, coil springs and stabilizer bar; (LTD/TBird) modified MacPherson struts with lower control arms, coil springs and anti-sway bar; (Crown Vic) long/short control arms w/coil springs and stabilizer bar. LTD, Crown Vic and TBird had gas-filled struts/shocks. Rear Suspension: (Escort/EXP) independent trailing arms w/modified MacPherson struts and coil springs on lower control arms; (Tempo) fully independent quadra-link with MacPherson struts; (LTD/Crown Vic/TBird) rigid axle w/four- link coil springs; (TBird Turbo Coupe) "quadra-shock" four- bar-link assembly with two hydraulic, horizontal axle dampers. Gas-filled shocks on LTD, Crown Vic and TBird. Brakes: Front disc, rear drum; power assisted (except Escort). Ignition: Electronic. Body construction: (Crown Vic) separate body and frame; (others) unibody. Fuel tank: (Escort/EXP) 13.0 gal.; (Tempo) 15.2 gal.; (LTD) 16.0 gal.; (Crown Vic) 18.0 gal.; (Crown Vic wag) 18.5 gal.; (TBird) 20.6 gal.

DRIVETRAIN OPTIONS: Engines: H.O. 1.6-liter four: Escort ($73). 232 cu. in. V-6: LTD ($418). 302 cu. in. V-8: Thunderbird ($398). Transmission/Differential: Five-speed manual trans.: Escort ($76). Automatic transaxle: Escort ($439) exc. LX/GT and EXP ($363); Tempo ($266-$363). Auto. transmission.: TBird Turbo Cpe ($315). First gear lockout delete: LTD, Crown Vic 'S' ($7). Overdrive auto. trans.: TBird ($237). Traction-Lok differential: LTD/Crown Vic/TBird ($95). Brakes/Steering/Suspension: Power brakes: Escort ($95). Power steering: Escort/EXP ($215); Tempo ($223). H.D. susp.: Crown Vic/TBird ($26); LTD LPO ($43). Handling susp.: Escort L ($199); Escort GL ($95); Crown Vic ($49). Auto. load leveling: Crown Vic ($200). Other: H.D. battery ($27). H.D. alternator: Escort/EXP ($27). Extended-range gas tank: LTD ($46). Engine block heater ($18). Trailer towing pkg.: Crown Vic ($251-$302); TBird ($251). California emission system: Escort/EXP ($46); others ($99). High-altitude emissions (NC).

ESCORT CONVENIENCE/APPEARANCE OPTIONS: Option Packages: Squire wagon pkg. ($373). Instrument group ($87). Convenience group ($206-$341). Light group ($67). Comfort/Convenience: Air conditioner ($643). Rear defroster, electric ($139). High-capacity heater ($76). Fingertip speed control ($176). Power door locks ($124-$176). Tinted glass ($95); windshield only LPO ($48). Tilt steering ($104). Overhead console w/digital clock ($82). Interval wipers ($50). Rear wiper/washer ($120) exc. LX ($46). Dual remote sport mirrors ($68). Entertainment: AM radio: base/L ($39). AM/FM radio ($82) exc. base/L ($121). AM/FM stereo radio ($109) exc. base/L ($148); w/cassette player ($148) exc. base/L ($295). Electronic- tuning AM/FM stereo w/cassette ($409-$448). Premium sound ($138). Exterior: Flip-up open-air roof ($315). Clearcoat metallic paint ($91) exc. LX/GT (NC). Two-tone paint/tape ($134-$173). Dual bodyside paint stripes ($39). Front vent windows, pivoting ($63). Vinyl-insert bodyside moldings ($45). Bumper guards, front or rear ($28). Bumper rub strips ($48). Luggage rack: wag ($100). Interior: Console ($111). Vinyl seat trim ($24). Cloth/vinyl low-back bucket seats: L ($33). Color-keyed front mats ($22). Wheels/Tires: Wheel trim rings ($54). Cast aluminum wheels ($279). TR aluminum wheels: LX/GT ($201). Styled steel wheels fleet only ($104 credit). P165/80R13 SBR WSW ($59).

EXP CONVENIENCE/APPEARANCE OPTIONS: Comfort/Convenience: Air conditioner ($643). Fingertip speed control ($176). Tinted glass ($95). Tilt steering ($104). Lighted visor vanity mirror ($50). Entertainment: AM/FM stereo radio: base ($109); w/cassette player ($256) exc. luxury cpe ($148). Electronic-tuning AM/FM stereo w/cassette ($409) exc. luxury cpe ($300) and Turbo ($152). Premium sound ($138). AM radio delete ($39 credit). AM/FM stereo delete: luxury cpe ($148 credit). AM/FM stereo/cassette delete: Turbo ($295 credit). Exterior: Flip-up open air roof ($315). Clearcoat paint ($91). Lower two-tone paint/tape ($146). Paint/tape delete LPO (NC). Medium bodyside moldings: Turbo ($45). Lower bodyside protection ($68). Interior: Four-way driver's seat: base ($55). Low-back vinyl bucket seats: base (NC). Cloth sport performance seats: luxury cpe ($173). Front floor mats ($22). Wheels/Tires: TR aluminum wheels: luxury cpe ($370). TR styled steel wheels: luxury cpe ($168). Cast aluminum wheels: luxury cpe ($238). P165/80R13 RWL ($90). P165/70R365 Michelin TRX (NC).

TEMPO CONVENIENCE/APPEARANCE OPTIONS: Option Packages: Sport performance pkg.: GL ($900-$911). Power lock group ($202-$254). Luxury option group: GL/LX ($755-$855). Select option group: GL ($401). Comfort/Convenience: Air bag, driver's side: GL 4dr. fleet only ($815). Air cond. ($743). Rear defroster, electric ($140). Fingertip speed control: GL/GLX ($176). Power windows ($272). Power decklid release ($40). Remote fuel door release LPO ($26). Six-way power driver's seat ($224). Tinted glass ($110); windshield fleet ($48). Tilt steering: GL ($110). Sport instrument cluster ($87). Dual sport remote mirrors ($93). Entertainment: AM/FM stereo radio: L/GL ($109); w/cassette player ($148-$256). Electronic-tuning AM/FM stereo w/cassette ($152-$409). Graphic equalizer ($107-$218). AM radio delete ($39 credit). Exterior: Clearcoat paint ($91). Lower body accent paint ($78-$118). Interior: Vinyl seat trim LPO ($35). Leather seat trim: GLX ($300). Carpeted front floor mats fleet ($13). Wheels/Tires: Styled wheels: L ($73). P175/80R13 WSW ($72).

LTD CONVENIENCE/APPEARANCE OPTIONS: Option Packages: Squire option ($282). Interior luxury group: wagon ($388). Power lock group ($213-$254). Light group ($38). Police pkg. ($901-$1429). Taxi pkg. ($860). Comfort/Convenience: Air cond. ($743); auto-temp ($809). Fingertip speed control ($176). Illuminated entry ($82). Autolamp on-off delay ($73). Power windows ($272). Six-way power driver's seat ($224); dual ($449). Tinted glass ($110). Tinted windshield fleet ($48). Leather-wrapped steering wheel ($59). Tilt steering ($110). Tripminder computer ($215- $293). Digital clock ($78). Diagnostic warning lights ($89). Auto. parking brake release LPO ($12). Interval wipers ($50). Liftgate wiper/washer: wagon ($99). Lighting and Mirrors: Cornering lamps ($68). Right remote convex mirror ($61). Dual electric remote mirrors ($96). Lighted visor vanity mirrors ($57-$106). Entertainment: AM/FM stereo radio ($109); w/cassette player ($256). Electronic-tuning AM/FM stereo radio w/cassette ($409). Premium sound system ($138). AM radio delete ($39 credit). Exterior: Formal roof, cloth or vinyl ($848). Full vinyl roof ($152). Two-tone paint ($117). Pivoting front vent windows ($79). Two-way liftgate: wag ($105). Bright protective bodyside moldings w/vinyl insert ($55). Rocker panel moldings ($40). Bumper guards, rear ($28). Bumper rub strips ($56). Luggage rack: wagon ($126). Lower bodyside protection ($41). Interior: Vinyl seat trim ($35). Flight bench seat (NC). Front floor mats, carpeted ($23). Wheels/Tires: Luxury wheel covers ($55). Wire wheel covers, locking ($204). Cast aluminum wheels: LX ($224). Styled wheels ($178). Styled steel wheels w/trim rings fleet ($54). P195/75R14 WSW ($72). P205/70R14 WSW ($134). Puncture- sealant P195/75R14 WSW ($202). Conventional spare LPO ($63).

NOTE: Many LTD options listed above were not available for the LX Brougham.

LTD CROWN VICTORIA CONVENIENCE/APPEARANCE OPTIONS: Option Packages: Interior luxury group ($949-$1022). Convenience group ($109-$134). Power lock group ($140-$238). Light group ($48). Comfort/Convenience: Air cond. ($743); w/auto-temp control ($809). Rear defroster, electric ($140). Fingertip speed control ($176). Illuminated entry system ($82). Power windows ($198-$272). Power driver's seat ($227); driver and passenger ($454). Remote fuel door lock ($35). Tinted glass ($110); windshield only LPO ($48). Autolamp on/off delay ($73). Leather-wrapped steering wheel ($59). Tilt steering wheel ($110). Auto. parking brake release ($12). Tripminder computer ($215-$261). Quartz clock: S ($35). Digital clock ($61-$96). Interval wipers ($50). Lighting and Mirrors: Cornering lamps ($68). Remote right mirror ($46). Lighted visor vanity mirrors ($106). Entertainment: AM/FM stereo radio: S ($109); w/cassette tape player ($148-$256). Electronic-tuning AM/FM stereo radio

w/cassette ($300) exc. S LPO ($409). Power antenna ($66). Premium sound system ($168). Radio delete: AM ($39 credit); AM/FM ($148 credit). Exterior: Fully padded Brougham vinyl roof ($793). Two-tone paint/tape ($117). Dual accent bodyside paint stripes: S LPO ($39). Pivoting front vent windows ($79). Rocker panel moldings ($18-$38). Vinyl-insert bodyside moldings ($61). Bumper rub strips ($59). Luggage rack: wagon ($110). License frames ($9). Interior: Dual-facing rear seats: wagon ($167). Leather split bench seat ($418). Cloth/vinyl split bench seating ($139). All-vinyl seat trim ($34); Duraweave vinyl, wagon ($96). Carpeted front/rear floor mats ($33). Trunk trim ($37). Wheels/Tires: Wire wheel covers, locking ($204). Cast aluminum wheels ($390). P205/75R15 WSW ($17); puncture-sealant ($178). P215/70R15 WSW ($79). Conventional spare ($63).

THUNDERBIRD CONVENIENCE/APPEARANCE OPTIONS: Option Packages: Light group ($35). Power lock group ($213). Comfort/Convenience: Air cond. ($743); auto-temp ($905). Rear defroster ($140). Fingertip speed control ($176). Illuminated entry system ($82). Keyless entry ($116-$198). Anti-theft system ($159). Tripminder computer ($215-$276). Autolamp on/off delay ($73). Tinted glass ($110); windshield only LPO ($48). Power windows ($198). Six-way power driver's seat ($227); dual ($454) exc. Fila ($227). Dual power seat recliners ($189). Auto. parking brake release: base ($12). Leather-wrapped steering wheel ($59). Tilt steering wheel ($110). Electronic instrument cluster ($270-$330). Diagnostic warning lights ($89). Low oil warning light: base ($24). Digital clock: base ($61). Interval wipers ($50). Lighting and Mirrors: Cornering lamps ($68). Dual electric remote mirrors ($96). Electronic-dimming day/night mirror ($77). Lighted visor vanity mirrors, pair ($106). Entertainment: AM/FM stereo radio w/cassette player ($148). Electronic-tuning AM/FM stereo search radio w/cassette ($300) exc. Elan ($152). Power antenna ($66). Graphic equalizer ($252). Premium sound system ($168). AM/FM radio delete ($148 credit). Exterior: Flip-up open-air roof ($315). Metallic clearcoat paint ($183). Two-tone paint/tape ($163-$218). Hood paint stripe ($16). Dual accent bodyside/decklid paint stripes: base ($55). Hood/decklid/bodyside paint stripes: base ($71). Pivoting front vent windows ($79). Wide bodyside moldings: base ($57). Bright rocker panel moldings ($39). License frames ($9). Interior: Articulated sport seats ($183-$427). Heated seats ($157). Leather seat trim ($415). Vinyl seat trim: base ($37). Front floor mats, carpeted ($22). Wheels/Tires: Wire wheel covers, locking ($204). Cast aluminum wheels ($343). Styled wheels ($178). P205/70R14 WSW ($62). P215/70R14 WSW ($99). P215/70HR14 performance BSW ($215). Conventional spare ($63).

HISTORY: Introduced: October 4, 1984. Model year production: 1,265,221 (incl. Mustangs, but with incomplete Escort total from Ford). Total production for the U.S. market of 1,389,103 units (incl. Mustangs) included 828,320 four-cylinder, 270,461 sixes and 290,322 V-8s. That total included 24,708 turbo fours and 10,246 diesel engines. Calendar year production (U.S.): 1,098,532 (incl. Mustangs). Calendar year sales by U.S. dealers: 1,386,195 (incl. Mustangs). Model year sales by U.S. dealers: 1,443,993 (incl. Mustangs).

Historical Footnotes: Sales rose 14 percent for the 1985 model year, partly as a result of incentive programs late in the season. Ford's market share rose to a healthy 17.2 percent, up from 16 percent the year before. All seven series showed an increase, led by Escort which revealed a 21 percent rise. Tempo did well, too. Ford raised prices only 1.3 percent (average) this year, though Crown Victoria went up over 6 percent and Mustangs were actually cheaper.

1986 FORD

The new front-drive, mid-size Taurus was the big news for 1986. Its aerodynamic styling went considerably beyond the Tempo design, taking its cue from European Fords. Taurus hardly resembled the rear-drive LTD that it was meant to replace. Mercury's Sable was similar, but with its own set of body panels and features. A reworked Escort had appeared as a mid-year 1985 model, but the restyled EXP two-seater wouldn't arrive until later in this model year.

1986 Escort LX wagon (JG)

ESCORT — FOUR — This year's Escort actually arrived as a 1985.5 model, carrying a bigger (1.9-liter) four-cylinder engine under its hood. The model lineup was revised. An LX series replaced the former GL, and the temporarily-abandoned GT was reintroduced. Pony was the name for the base hatchback (same name as the low-budget Pinto of the late 1970s). "Official" diesel models were dropped, but the 2.0-liter diesel engine remained available as an option. A new two-slot body-color grille held the Ford script oval in the center of the single horizontal bar. Aero-style headlamps met the amber wraparound parking lenses. Wraparound taillamps had two horizontal ribs. Inside was a new black four-spoke steering wheel. Options included tilt steering, speed control, and an instrumentation group. Escort's base engine was carbureted, hooked to a four-speed manual transaxle. Automatic shift was optional. As before, Escort had four-wheel independent suspension. Pony had standard power brakes, day/night mirror, dome light, cloth/vinyl low-back reclining bucket seats, and P175/80R13 tires. Escort L added an AM radio and load floor carpet. LX included remote fuel door lock, remote liftgate release, wide vinyl bodyside moldings, bumper rub strips, and styled steel wheels. In addition to a high-output 1.9 liter engine with port fuel injection and five-speed manual transaxle, Escort GT had a performance suspension with new front and rear stabilizer bars, as well as P195/60HR15 tires on eight-spoke aluminum wheels. Also included: front and rear body-color partial fascias; foglamps; console with graphic display; leather-wrapped steering wheel; body-color wheel spats with integral rocker panel moldings; rear spoiler; and body-color narrow bodyside moldings. One easy-to-spot styling feature was GT's offset grille, with slots occuping just two-thirds of the panel instead of full-width. A 'GT' decal sat on the solid passenger side of the "grille" panel.

1986 Escort EXP Sport Coupe (F)

EXP — FOUR — After a brief absence from the lineup, the two-seater EXP returned in restyled form with a sleek new front-end design, including air dam and aero headlamps. Also new was a bubble-back styled rear hatch with integral spoiler. Otherwise, the new four-window coupe design looked similar to 1985 at the rear, but markedly different up front. Ford's blue script oval stood above a single-slot grille. Aero headlamps met wraparound marker lenses. Parking lamps were mounted below, in the bumper region, alongside a wide center slot. Large 'EXP' recessed lettering was easy to spot on the wide C pillar. Wraparound full-width taillamps (split by the license plate's recessed housing) were divided into upper/lower segments, and tapered downward to a point on each quarter panel. Luxury Coupe and Sport Coupe versions were offered, with 1.9-liter fast-burn four, five-speed manual transaxle, and four-wheel independent suspension. Luxury Coupe had the carbureted engine, along with a tachometer and trip odometer, reclining low-back bucket seats in cloth/vinyl (or all vinyl), AM/FM stereo radio, overhead console, and left remote mirror. A fuel-injected high-output version of the four went into the Sport Coupe, which also had special handling components, performance bucket seats, center console with graphic systems monitor, foglamps, dual electric mirrors, and low-profile 15 in. handling tires on cast aluminum wheels. Special Option Groups contained such items as speed control, flip-up open air•roof, and premium sound system.

1986 Tempo LX coupe (JG)

TEMPO — FOUR — After only two seasons in the lineup, Tempo got new front and rear styling. The new grille consisted simply of twin wide slots below a blue Ford oval in the sloping, body-colored center panel. Aerodynamic halogen headlamps continued outward to meet clear parking lamps, wrapping around to amber side marker lenses that tapered downward to a rounded "point." (The former Tempo had conventional recessed headlamps.) Tempo also had a color-keyed lower front valence panel. Wide, dark gray bodyside moldings held bright inserts. This year's taillamps were wraparound full-width style. Dark gray partial front and rear bumper covers had side extensions with bright insert. Completing the look were aero-style mirrors. Inside was a new-design four-spoke deep-dish steering wheel. A push-pull headlamp switch replaced the toggle unit. New door sill scuff plates were added. A new LX series replaced the GLX. Both GL and LX tires were upgraded to 14 inch size. Sport GL went to 15 inches, and had red interior accent colors to replace the former blue. New options included P185/70R14 whitewalls, decklid luggage rack, 2.0-liter diesel (except in California), and premium sound system. Diesel power was an option rather than a distinct model. Also available: a supplemental air bag restraint system, sport instrument cluster, and lower accent paint treatment. In addition to the basic GL and LX models, Select GL and Sport GL packages were offered. GL included full cloth reclining front bucket seats, power front disc/rear drum brakes, and such conveniences as interval wipers and a digital clock. Tempo LX included styled wheels, tilt steering, power door locks, a full array of courtesy lights, bright argent lower back panel applique, and AM/FM stereo radio (which could be deleted). A Select GL package added power steering, tinted glass, dual sail-mounted remote electric mirrors, and AM/FM stereo radio (also open to deletion for credit). Sport GL had a special handling suspension, as well as a high specific output (HSO) version of the standard 2300 HSC (high swirl combustion) four. All had a standard five-speed manual transaxle. Automatic was optional on GL and Select GL, as was the 2.0-liter diesel four with five-speed.

1986 Taurus LX sedan (JG)

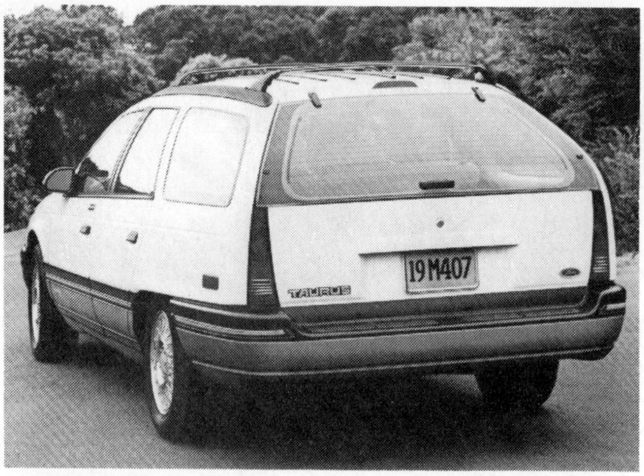

1986 Taurus GL wagon (JG)

TAURUS — FOUR/V-6 — Most striking of the aerodynamic new mid-size, front- drive Taurus's styling features was the lack of a grille. The solid body-colored panel between aero halogen headlamps held nothing other than a Ford oval, set in a larger oval opening. The only other opening up front was a wide center air-intake slot, far down between horizontally-ribbed bumper segments. Those wide single-section headlamps (with integrated turn signal lamps) continued around the fender side to meet small amber lenses. Clear side marker lenses were farther down, below the bodyside/bumper molding. The 'Taurus' nameplate (and model identification) went low on the door, in or just below the bodyside molding. At the rear were wraparound taillamps. Taurus wagons had narrow vertical taillamps, and center high-mount stoplamp above the liftgate. That distinctive liftgate design had a back window that tapered inward at the top. Taurus had flush- mounted glass all around, and shingled one-piece doors. Aero styling gave an impressive drag coefficient: as low as 0.33 for the sedan. Four series were offered: L, GL, LX, and (later) a sporty MT5, in six-window sedan or wagon form. Base engine was a new 153 cu. in. (2.5-liter) fuel-injected HSC four, though early models came only with the 183 cu. in. (3.0- liter) V-6. Later optional (standard on GL/LX and wagons), that V-6 had multi-port fuel injection. The 2.5-liter four could have a three-speed automatic transaxle with centrifugally locking clutch; the V-6 turned to a four-speed overdrive automatic transaxle. A five-speed manual transaxle was available only with the four. The four-cylinder engine was derived from Tempo's High Swirl Combustion design. Sedans had fully independent MacPherson strut suspension, front and rear. Wagons had independent short and long arm type rear suspension, which was more compact to add cargo space. Polycarbonate bumpers were corrosion-proof and resilient. The driver-oriented instrument panel featured a swept-away design with three analog backlit instrument clusters. An electronic cluster was optional. Tactile-type switches had raised or depressed sections so drivers could determine the function by touch. Windshield wipers had 20 in. blades and an articulated driver's side arm for a full wipe all the way to the pillar. Standard equipment included power brakes and steeering, gas-filled shocks and struts, all-season steel-belted radials, driver's side footrest, locking glovebox, dual-note horn, black left-hand remote mirror, AM radio, and reclining cloth flight bench seats. Wagons had a 60/40 split fold-down rear seat, cargo tie-downs, rear bumper step pad, and dual cargo area lights. MT5 came with five-speed manual transaxle and floor shift lever, and included interval wipers, electronic-tuning AM/FM stereo with digital clock, tinted glass, tachometer, dual electric remote mirrors, color-keyed rocker panel moldings, and bucket seats. MT5 sedans had blackout treatment on 'B' and 'C' pillars. Taurus GL was similar to MT5 but with four-speed automatic and without a tachometer. The top-ranked LX had air conditioning, remote fuel door release, cornering lamps, power locks, black/bright bodyside moldings, power cloth split bench seats with adjustable front lumbar support, tilt steering, power windows, and lighted visor vanity mirrors. Options included an Insta-Clear heated windshield, power moonroof, keyless entry, and electronic climate control. Wagons could get a rear-facing third seat, liftgate wiper/washer, and folding load floor extension that could also serve as a picnic table. Preferred Equipment Packages included such options as speed control, rear window defroster, air conditioning, and electronic entertainment systems. At first glance, Taurus looked very much like the related Mercury Sable, developed under the same program; but the sedans shared no sheetmetal at all. Wagons differed up front, but were the same from the windshield on back. The pair did share drivetrains and running gear, plus most equipment.

LTD — FOUR/V-6 — Ford's rear-drive mid-size was scheduled for abandonment at mid-year, now that the front-drive Taurus had arrived. For its final partial season, the 232 cu. in. (3.8-liter) V-6 became standard (though the four was listed as a credit option). The high-performance LX sedan didn't make the lineup this year, and not much was new apart from the newly required center high-mount stop lamp. Quite a few low-rate options were dropped, and the four-speed automatic overdrive transmission became optional. LTD was virtually identical to Mercury Marquis, both riding the old Granada platform. Models included base and Brougham sedans, and the base wagon.

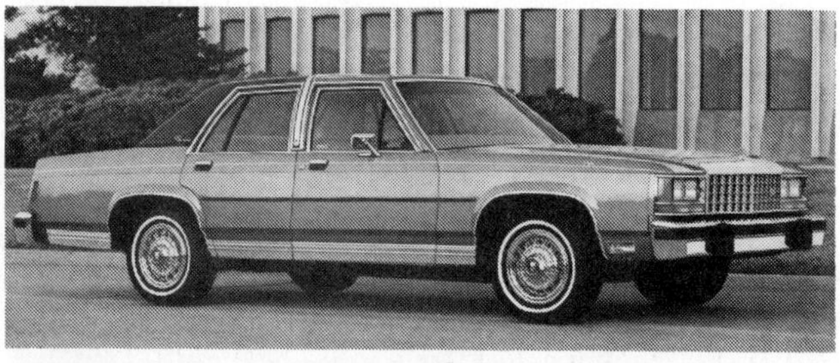

1986 LTD Crown Victoria sedan (JG)

LTD CROWN VICTORIA — V-8 — Big rear-drives had more than a spark of life remaining in Ford's plans. Crown Victoria added a new sedan and wagon series this year: the top-level LX and Country Squire LX. Each model incorporated a standard (previously optional) interior luxury group. LX had reclining split bench seats upholstered in velour cloth or vinyl (leather seating surfaces optional). Equipment included power windows and a digital clock, as well as a variety of luxury trim extras. Sequential multi-port fuel injection replaced the former central injection on the standard 302 cu. in. (5.0-liter) V-8 engine, which came with four-speed overdrive automatic. No options were available, except the 351 cu. in. V-8 for police models. The 302 got a number of internal changes, including fast-burning combustion chambers, higher compression, roller tappets, low-tension piston rings, and viscous clutch cooling fan. Wagons now had a mini spare tire rather than the conventional one. All series had automatic parking brake release, a tethered gas cap, and right-hand visor mirror. A rear bumper step pad became standard on wagons. The new high- mount brake lamp was mounted on the package tray on sedans, on tailgate of wagons. Standard equipment included an AM/FM stereo radio with four speakers, quartz clock, front/rear courtesy lights, cloth flight bench seat with dual recliners, and remote driver's mirror. Split bench seats were optional. P205/75R15 tires became standard this year. Seven exterior colors were new, along with five vinyl roof colors. Country Squire's simulated woodgrain panels switched from cherry to dark cherry. Optional this year were dual electric remote mirrors for LX and a conventional spare tire for wagons. Traction-Lok axle was now included with the heavy-duty trailer towing packages. Preferred Equipment Packages grouped such options as six-way power driver's seat, power lock group, and speed control. Styling was similar to 1985. Full-size Fords had an upright crosshatch grille with relatively large holes in a 12x4 pattern. Quad rectangular headlamps stood above amber park/signal lenses, and the whole assembly continued outward to meet twin amber lenses around the fender tips. The entire front end showed a straight-up, symmetrical design. Small marker lenses sat quite low on the front fenders, just ahead of wheel openings. Red rear side marker lenses were vertical, near quarter panel tips. In back, each squarish vertical taillamp consisted of four raised segments.

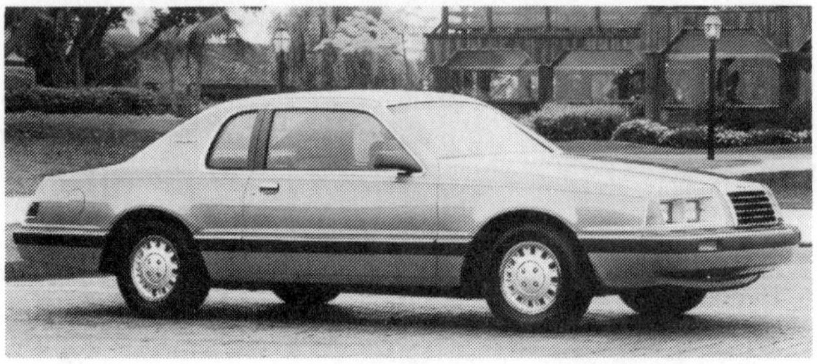

1986 Thunderbird hardtop coupe (JG)

THUNDERBIRD — FOUR/V-6/V-8 — Thunderbird dropped down to three models this year as the Fila series left the lineup. Both the base 232 cu. in. (3.8-liter) V-6 and optional 302 cu. in. (5.0-liter) V-8 engines now had viscous engine mounts (which had been standard on the 2.3-liter turbo in 1985). The V-8 switched to multi-port fuel injection and added roller tappets, low- tension piston rings, and fast-burn combustion chambers. P215/70R14 blackwalls were now standard (except on Turbo Coupe). V-6 models came with three-speed SelectShift automatic; V-8s with four-speed overdrive automatic. All models now had an electronic-tuning AM/FM stereo radio. Six body colors and three interior trim colors were new. Elan's interior cloth trim was revised for a plusher appearance. A woodtone instrument panel applique was added. Standard equipment included variable-ratio power rack- and-pinion steering, power front disc/rear drum brakes, and gas-pressurized shocks and struts. Inside were reclining cloth split bench seats. Thunderbird elan (accent over the e) had upgraded trim and such conveniences as power windows, dual electric remote mirrors, interval wipers, system sentry, a digital clock, and lighted visor mirrors. Turbo Coupe again carried the 2.3-liter turbocharged four, with five-speed close-ratio manual shift and special Goodyear performance tires. Articulated front sport seats adjusted several ways. New options were: power moonroof (delayed availability) and a collapsible spare tire (including a 12-volt air compressor that plugged into the lighter). Preferred Equipment Packages included such extras as illuminated entry, electronic instrument cluster, and a power lock group. Styling was similar to 1985. Recessed, staggered quad rectangular headlamps were flanked by amber wraparound signal/marker lenses at matching height. TBird's grille had four thin, bright horizontal bars over a blackout pattern. Small amber parking lamps were down in the bumper rub strip. Wraparound taillamps again held a Thunderbird emblem in each lens. Emblems also went on the Cpillar and grille header. Thunderbird was similar to Mercury's Cougar.

I.D. DATA: Ford's 17-symbol Vehicle Identification Number (VIN) again was stamped on a metal tab fastened to the instrument panel, visible through the windshield. The first three symbols ('1FA') indicate manufacturer, make and vehicle type. The fourth symbol ('B') denotes restraint system. Next comes a letter 'P', followed by two digits that indicate body type: Model Number, as shown in left column of tables below. (Example: '31' Escort L two-door hatchback). Symbol eight indicates engine type: '9' L4113 2Bbl.; 'J' H.O. L4113 FI; 'H' Diesel L4121; 'X' HSC L4140 FI; 'S' H.O. HSC L4140 FI; 'W' Turbo L4140 EFI; 'D' L4153 FI; 'U' V6183 FI; '3' V6232 2Bbl.; 'F' V8302 2Bbl.; 'G' V8351 2Bbl. Next is a check digit. Symbol ten indicates model year ('G' 1986). Symbol eleven is assembly plant: 'A' Atlanta, GA; 'B' Oakville, Ontario (Canada); 'G' Chicago; 'H' Lorain, Ohio; 'K' Kansas City, MO; 'X' St. Thomas, Ontario; 'T' Edison, NJ; 'W' Wayne, MI. The final six digits make up the sequence number, starting with 100001. A Vehicle Certification Label on the left front door lock face panel or door pillar shows the manufacturer, month and year of manufacture, GVW, GAWR, certification statement, VIN, and codes for such items as body type, color, trim, axle, transmission, and special order information.

ESCORT (FOUR)

Model Number	Body/Style Number	Body Type & Seating	Factory Price	Shipping Weight	Production Total
31/41P	N/A	2-dr. Pony Hatch-4P	6052	2089	Note 1
31	N/A	2-dr. L Hatch-4P	6327	2096	Note 1
36	N/A	4-dr. L Hatch-4P	6541	2154	Note 1
34	N/A	4-dr. L Sta Wag-4P	6822	2173	Note 1
32	N/A	2-dr. LX Hatch-4P	7284	2160	Note 1
37	N/A	4-dr. LX Hatch-4P	7448	2214	Note 1
35	N/A	4-dr. LX Sta Wag-4P	7729	2228	Note 1
33	N/A	2-dr. GT Hatch-4P	8112	2282	Note 1

Note 1: For the model year, a total of 228,013 two-door hatchbacks, 117,300 four-door hatchback sedans, and 84,740 station wagons were produced. Breakdown by trim level not available. Bodies are sometimes referred to as three-door and five-door.

EXP (FOUR)

01	N/A	2-dr. Spt Cpe-2P	7186	N/A	Note 2
01/931	N/A	2-dr. Luxury Cpe-2F	8235	N/A	Note 2

Note 2: Total EXP production was 30,978.

TEMPO (FOUR)

19	66D	2-dr. GL Sed-5P	7358	2363	Note 3
22	54D	4-dr. GL Sed-5P	7508	2422	Note 3
20	66D	2-dr. GLX Sed-5P	8578	2465	Note 3
23	54D	4-dr. GLX Sed-5P	8777	2526	Note 3

Note 3: Total Tempo production came to 69,101 two-doors and 208,570 four-doors.

TAURUS (FOUR/V-6)

29	54D	4-dr. L Sedan-6P	9645/10256	2749/2749	Note 4
30	74D	4-dr. L Sta Wag-6P	-- /10763	-- /3067	Note 4
29/934	54D	4-dr. MT5 Sed-6P	10276/ --	2759/ --	Note 4
30/934	74D	4-dr. MT5 Wag-6P	10741/ --	2957/ --	Note 4
29/60D	54D	4-dr. GL Sedan-6P	-- /11322	-- /2909	Note 4
30/60D	74D	4-dr. GL Wag-6P	-- /11790	-- /3108	Note 4
29/60H	54D	4-dr. LX Sedan-6P	-- /13351	-- /3001	Note 4
30/60H	74D	4-dr. LX Wag-6P	-- /13860	-- /3198	Note 4

Note 4: Total Taurus production came to 178,737 sedans and 57,625 station wagons.

LTD (FOUR/V-6)

39	54D	4-dr. Sedan-5P	9538/10032	2801/2878	58,270
39	54D	4-dr. Brghm-5P	9926/10420	2806/2883	Note 5
40	74D	4-dr. Sta Wag-5P	-- /10132	-- /2977	14,213

Note 5: Brougham production is included in basic sedan total.

LTD CROWN VICTORIA (V-8)

42	66K	2-dr. Sedan-6P	13022	3571	6,559
43	54K	4-dr. Sedan-6P	12562	3611	97,314
44	74K	4-dr. Ctry Sqr-6P	12655	3834	20,164
44/41E	74K	4-dr. Sta Wag-6P	12405	3795	Note 6
43/41K	54K	4-dr. 'S' Sed-6P	12188	3591	Note 6
44/41K	74K	4-dr. 'S' Wag-6P	12468	3769	Note 6

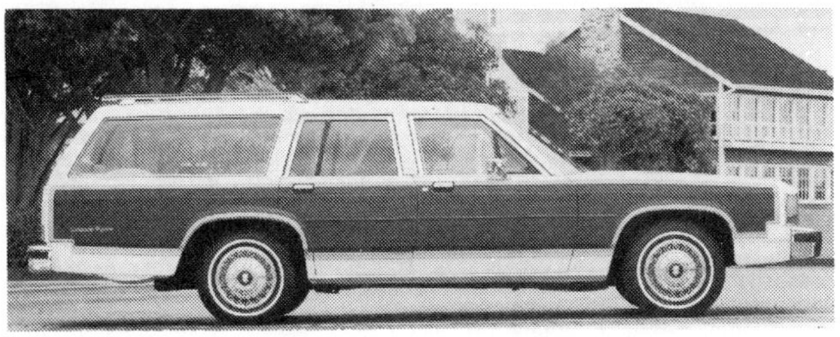

1986 LTD Crown Victoria Country Squire station wagon (JG)

LTD CROWN VICTORIA LX (V-8)

42/60H	66K	2-dr. Sedan-6P	13752	3608	Note 6
43/60H	54K	4-dr. Sedan-6P	13784	3660	Note 6
44/41E/ 60H	74K	4-dr. Sta Wag-6P	13567	3834	Note 6
44/60H	74K	4-dr. Ctry Sqr-6P	13817	3873	Note 6

Note 6: Production of 'S' and LX models and basic station wagon is included in basic sedan and Country Squire totals above.

Police Crown Victoria Note: A Police model (P43/41K/55A) 'S' sedan cost $11,813 with 302 cu. in. V-8, or $11,933 with 351 cu. in. V-8 engine.

THUNDERBIRD (V-6/V-8)

46	66D	2-dr. HT Cpe-5P	11020/11805	2923/3101	163,965
46	66D	2-dr. Elan Cpe-5P	12554/13339	2977/3155	Note 7

THUNDERBIRD TURBO COUPE (FOUR)

46	66D	2-dr. HT Cpe-5P	14143	3016	Note 7

Note 7: Turbo Coupe and Elan production is included in basic Thunderbird total.

MODEL NUMBER NOTE: Some sources include a prefix 'P' ahead of the two- digit model number. **FACTORY PRICE AND WEIGHT NOTE:** LTD and Taurus prices and weights to left of slash are for four-cylinder, to right for V-6 engine. Thunderbird prices and weights to left of slash are for V-6, to right for V-8 engine.

ENGINE DATA: BASE FOUR (Escort): Inline. Overhead cam. Four-cylinder. Cast iron block and aluminum head. Displacement: 113 cu. in. (1.9 liters). Bore & stroke: 3.23 x 3.46 in. Compression ratio: 9.0:1. Brake horsepower: 86 at 4800 R.P.M. Torque: 100 lbs.-ft. at 3000 R.P.M. Five main bearings. Hydraulic valve lifters. Carburetor: 2Bbl. Holley 740. VIN Code: 9. BASE FOUR (Escort GT); OPTIONAL (Escort): High-output, multi-port fuel-injected version of 1.9-liter four above Horsepower: 108 at 5200 R.P.M. Torque: 114 lbs.- ft. at 4000 R.P.M. VIN Code: J. DIESEL FOUR (Escort, Tempo): Inline. Overhead cam. Four-cylinder. Cast iron block and aluminum head. Displacement: 121 cu. in. (2.0 liters). Bore & stroke: 3.39 x 3.39 in. Compression ratio: 22.7:1. Brake horsepower: 52 at 4000 R.P.M. Torque: 82 lbs.-ft. at 2400 R.P.M. Five main bearings. Solid valve lifters. Fuel injection. VIN Code: H. BASE FOUR (Tempo): Inline. Overhead valve. Four-cylinder. Cast iron block and head. Displacement: 140 cu. in. (2.3 liters). Bore & stroke: 3.70 x 3.30 in. Compression ratio: 9.0:1. Brake horsepower: 86 at 4000 R.P.M. Torque: 124 lbs.-ft. at 2800 R.P.M. Five main bearings. Hydraulic valve lifters. Throttle-body fuel injection. High Swirl Combustion (HSC) design. VIN Code: X. OPTIONAL FOUR (Tempo): High-output version of HSC four above Horsepower: 100 at 4600 R.P.M. Torque: 125 lbs.-ft. at 3200 R.P.M. VIN Code: S. BASE FOUR (Thunderbird Turbo Coupe): Inline. Overhead cam. Four-cylinder. Cast iron block and head. Displacement: 140 cu. in. (2.3 liters). Bore & stroke: 3.78 x 3.13 in. Compression ratio: 8.0:1. Brake horsepower: 155 at 4600 R.P.M. (145 at 4400 with automatic). Torque: 190 lbs.-ft. at 2800 R.P.M. (180 at 3000 with automatic). Five main bearings. Hydraulic valve lifters. Port fuel injection. VIN Code: W. BASE FOUR (late Taurus): Inline. Overhead valve. Four-cylinder. Cast iron block and head. Displacement: 153 cu. in. (2.5 liters). Bore & stroke: 3.70 x 3.60 in. Compression ratio: 9.0:1. Brake horsepower: 88 at 4600 R.P.M. Torque: 130 lbs.-ft. at 2800 R.P.M. Five main bearings. Hydraulic valve lifters. Electronic fuel injection. VIN Code: D. BASE V-6 (Taurus LX/wagon); OPTIONAL (Taurus): 60-degree, overhead valve V-6. Cast iron block and head. Displacement: 183 cu. in. (3.0 liters). Bore & stroke: 3.50 x 3.10 in. Compression ratio: 9.25:1. Brake horsepower: 140 at 4800 R.P.M. Torque: 160 lbs.-ft. at 3000 R.P.M. Four main bearings. Hydraulic valve lifters. Multi-port fuel injection. VIN Code: U. BASE V-6 (LTD, Thunderbird): 90-degree, overhead valve V-6. Cast iron block and aluminum head. Displacement: 232 cu. in. (3.8 liters). Bore & stroke: 3.80 x 3.40 in. Compression ratio: 8.7:1. Brake horsepower: 120 at 3600 R.P.M. Torque: 205 lbs.-ft. at 1600 R.P.M. Four main bearings. Hydraulic valve lifters. Throttle-body fuel injection. VIN Code: 3. BASE V-8 (Crown Victoria); OPTIONAL (Thunderbird): 90-degree, overhead valve V-8. Cast iron block and head. Displacement: 302 cu. in. (5.0 liters). Bore & stroke: 4.00 x 3.00 in. Compression ratio: 8.9:1. Brake horsepower: 150 at 3200 R.P.M. Torque: 270 lbs.-ft. at 2000 R.P.M. Five main bearings. Hydraulic valve lifters. Sequential (port) fuel injection. VIN Code: F. HIGH-OUTPUT POLICE V-8 (Crown Victoria): 90-degree, overhead valve V-8. Cast iron block and head. Displacement: 351 cu. in. (5.8 liters). Bore & stroke: 4.00 x 3.50 in. Compression ratio: 8.3:1. Brake horsepower: 180 at 3600 R.P.M. Torque: 285 lbs.-ft. at 2400 R.P.M. Five main bearings. Hydraulic valve lifters. Carburetor: 2Bbl. VIN Code: G.

CHASSIS DATA: Wheelbase: (Escort/EXP) 94.2 in.; (Tempo) 99.9 in.; (Taurus) 106.0 in.; (LTD) 105.6 in.; (Crown Vic) 114.3 in.; (TBird) 104.0 in. Overall Length: (Escort) 166.9 in.; (Escort wagon) 168.0 in.; (EXP) 168.4 in.; (Tempo) 176.2 in.; (Taurus) 188.4 in.; (Taurus wag) 191.9 in.; (LTD) 196.5 in.; (Crown Vic) 211.0 in.; (Crown Vic wag) 215.0 in.; (TBird) 197.6 in. Height: (Escort) 53.3-53.5 in.; (EXP) 50.9 in.; (Tempo) 52.7 in.; (Taurus) 54.4 in.; (Taurus wag) 55.2 in.; (LTD) 53.8 in.; (LTD wag) 54.4 in.; (Crown Vic) 55.3 in.; (Crown Vic wag) 56.8 in.; (TBird) 53.2 in. Width: (Escort/EXP) 65.9 in.; (Tempo) 68.3 in.; (Taurus) 70.7 in.; (LTD) 71.0 in.; (Crown Vic) 77.5 in.; (Crown Vic wag) 79.3 in.; (TBird) 71.1 in. Front Tread: (Escort/EXP/Tempo) 54.7 in.; (Taurus) 61.5 in.; (LTD) 56.6 in.; (Crown Vic) 62.2 in. (TBird) 58.1 in. Rear Tread: (Escort/EXP) 56.0 in.; (Tempo) 57.6 in.; (Taurus) 60.5 in.; (Taurus wag) 59.9 in.; (LTD) 57.0 in.; (Crown Vic) 62.0 in. (TBird) 58.5 in. Standard Tires: (Escort Pony/L) P165/80R13 SBR BSW; (Escort L wag/LX) P175/80R13; (Escort GT) P195/60HR15 BSW; (EXP) P185/70R14 SBR; (Tempo) P185/80R14 SBR BSW; (Taurus) P195/70R14 BSW; (Taurus GL/LX) P205/70R14; (LTD) P195/75R14 BSW; (Crown Vic) P205/75R15 SBR WSW; (TBird) P215/70R14 SBR BSW; (TBird Turbo Cpe) P225/60VR15 Goodyear unidirectional "Gatorback" BSW.

TECHNICAL: Transmission: Four-speed manual transaxle standard on Escort Pony/L; five-speed standard on Escort LX/GT, EXP, Tempo, and Thunderbird Turbo Coupe. Gear ratios N/A. Three-speed automatic standard on LTD, Thunderbird turbo/V-6: (1st) 2.46:1 or 2.47:1; (2nd) 1.46:1 or 1.47:1; (3rd) 1.00:1; (Rev) 2.11:1 or 2.19:1. Taurus four/Escort/Tempo three-speed automatic: (1st) 2.79:1; (2nd) 1.61:1-1.62:1; (3rd) 1.00:1; (Rev) 1.97:1. Four-speed overdrive automatic standard on LTD V-6, Crown Victoria and Thunderbird: (1st) 2.40:1; (2nd) 1.47:1; (3rd) 1.00:1; (4th) 0.67:1; (Rev) 2.00:1. Taurus V-6 four-speed overdrive automatic: (1st) 2.77:1; (2nd) 1.54:1; (3rd) 1.00:1; (4th) 0.69:1; (Rev) 2.26:1. Standard final drive ratio: (Escort) 3.52:1 w/4spd, 2.85:1 w/fuel saver, 3.73:1 w/5spd, 3.23:1 w/auto., 3.52:1 w/diesel; (EXP) N/A; (Tempo) 3.23:1 exc. 3.73:1 w/diesel or H.O. engine; (Taurus four) 3.23:1; (Taurus V-6) 3.37:1; (LTD) 2.73:1 w/3spd auto., 3.27:1 w/4-spd auto.; (Crown Vic) 2.73:1; (TBird) 3.45:1 w/turbo, 2.73:1 w/3spd automatic and V-6, 3.27:1 w/4spd auto. and V-6, 3.08:1 w/V-8. Drive Axle: (Escort/EXP/Tempo/Taurus) front; (others) rear. Steering: (Crown Vic) recirculating ball; (others) rack and pinion. Front Suspension: (Escort/EXP/Tempo) MacPherson struts with lower control arms, coil springs and stabilizer bar; (EXP) N/A; (Taurus) MacPherson struts with control arms, coil springs and stabilizer bar; (LTD/TBird) modified MacPherson struts with lower control arms, coil springs and anti-sway bar; (Crown Vic) long/short control arms w/coil springs and stabilizer bar. LTD, Crown Vic and TBird had gas-filled struts/shocks. Rear Suspension: (Escort/EXP) independent trailing arms w/modified MacPherson struts and coil springs on lower control arms; (EXP) N/A; (Tempo) fully independent trailing quadra-link with MacPherson struts; (Taurus) MacPherson struts w/parallel suspension arms and coil springs; (Taurus wag) upper/lower control arms, coil springs and stabilizer bar; (LTD/Crown Vic/TBird) rigid axle w/four links and coil springs; (TBird Turbo Coupe) "quadra-shock" four-bar-link assembly with two hydraulic, horizontal axle dampers. Gas- filled shocks on LTD, Crown Vic and TBird. Brakes: Front disc, rear drum (power assisted). Ignition: Electronic. Body construction: (Crown Vic) separate body and frame; (others) unibody. Fuel tank: (Escort) 10.0 gal.; (Escort wag) 13.0 gal.; (EXP) N/A; (Tempo) 15.2 gal.; (Taurus/LTD) 16.0 gal.; (Crown Vic) 18.0 gal.; (Crown Vic wag) 18.5 gal.; (TBird) 20.6 gal.

DRIVETRAIN OPTIONS: Engines: Diesel 2.0-liter four: Escort ($591); Tempo ($509). 140 cu. in. four: LTD ($494 credit). 182 cu. in. V-6: Taurus L sed ($611). 302 cu. in. V-8: Thunderbird ($548). Transmission/Differential: Five-speed manual trans.: Escort ($76). Automatic transaxle: Escort ($466) exc. LX/GT and EXP ($390); Tempo ($448). Auto. transmission.: TBird Turbo Cpe ($315). Floor shift lever: Taurus GL/LX (NC). First gear lockout delete: Crown Vic ($7). Overdrive auto. trans.: TBird ($237); LTD ($245). Traction-Lok differential: LTD/Crown Vic/TBird ($100). Steering/Suspension: Power steering: Escort/EXP ($226); Tempo ($223). H.D. susp.: Escort/Taurus/-Crown Vic ($26); LTD ($43). Handling susp.: Crown Vic ($49). Auto. load leveling: Crown Vic ($200). Other: H.D. battery ($27). H.D. alternator: Escort/EXP ($27); Crown Vic ($54). Extended-range gas tank: Taurus/LTD ($46). Engine block heater ($18). Trailer towing pkg.: Crown Vic ($377-$389). California emission system: Escort/EXP ($46); others ($99). High-altitude emissions (NC).

ESCORT CONVENIENCE/APPEARANCE OPTIONS: Option Packages: Instrument group ($87). Climate control/convenience group ($742-$868). Premium convenience group ($306-$390). Protection convenience group ($131-$467). Select L pkg. ($397). Light group ($67). Comfort/Convenience: Air conditioner ($657). Rear defroster, electric ($135). Fingertip speed control ($176). Tinted glass ($99). Tilt steering ($115). Overhead console w/digital clock ($82). Interval wipers ($50). Rear wiper/washer ($126). Dual remote sport mirrors ($68). Entertainment: AM radio ($39). AM/FM stereo radio ($109) exc. base ($148); w/cassette player ($256) exc. base/L ($295) and GT ($148). Radio delete: L/LX ($39 credit); GT ($148 credit). Premium sound ($138). Exterior: Clearcoat paint ($91). Two-tone paint ($61-$156). Front vent windows, pivoting ($63). Wide vinyl bodyside moldings ($45). Bumper guards, front/rear ($56). Bumper rub strips ($48). Luggage rack: wag ($100). Interior: Console ($111). Vinyl seat trim ($24). Wheels/Tires: Bright wheel trim rings ($54). Styled wheels ($128-$195). P165/80R13 SBR WSW ($59). Full-size spare ($63).

EXP CONVENIENCE/APPEARANCE OPTIONS: Option Packages: Climate control/convenience group ($841- $868). Sun/Sound group ($612). Convenience group ($300-$455). Comfort/Convenience: Air conditioner ($657). Rear defroster ($135). Fingertip speed control ($176). Console w/graphic systems monitor ($111). Tinted glass ($99). Tilt steering ($115). Interval wipers ($50). Dual electric remote mirrors ($88). Lighted visor vanity mirror ($50). Entertainment: AM/FM stereo radio w/cassette player ($148). Premium sound ($138). Radio delete ($148 credit). Exterior: Flip-up open air roof ($315). Clearcoat paint ($91). Interior: Cargo area cover ($59). Vinyl seat trim ($24).

TEMPO CONVENIENCE/APPEARANCE OPTIONS: Option Packages: Sport GL pkg. ($934). Select GL pkg. ($340- $423). Power lock group ($207-$259). Power equipment group ($291-$575). Convenience group ($224-$640). Comfort/Convenience: Air bag restraint system ($815). Air cond. ($743). Rear defroster, electric ($145). Fingertip speed control ($176). Power windows ($207-$282). Six-way power driver's seat ($234). Tinted glass ($113); windshield ($48). Tilt steering ($115). Sport instrument cluster ($87). Dual electric remote mirrors ($111). Entertainment: AM/FM

stereo radio ($109); w/cassette player ($148-$256). Electronic-tuning AM/FM stereo w/cassette ($171-$279) exc. w/Sport GL pkg. ($23). Premium sound ($138). Radio delete ($39-$295 credit). Exterior: Clearcoat metallic paint ($91). Lower body accent paint ($78). Decklid luggage rack ($100). Interior: Console ($116). Front center armrest ($55). Leather seat trim ($300). Wheels/Tires: Styled wheels ($178). P185/70R14 WSW ($72).

TAURUS CONVENIENCE/APPEARANCE OPTIONS: Option Packages: Exterior accent group ($49-$99). Power lock group ($180-$221). Light group ($48-$51). Comfort/Convenience: Air cond. ($762). Electronic climate control air cond.: GL ($945); LX ($183). Rear defroster ($145). Insta-clear windshield ($250); N/A on MT5. Fingertip speed control ($176). Illuminated entry ($82). Keyless entry ($202). Power windows ($282). Six-way power driver's seat ($237); dual ($473). Remote fuel door release: MT5/GL ($37). Tinted glass: L ($115); windshield only LPO ($48). Leather-wrapped steering wheel ($59). Tilt steering ($115). Electronic instrument cluster ($305); N/A on MT5. Autolamp on/off delay ($73). Diagnostic warning lights ($89). Auto. parking brake release: L/GL ($12). Digital clock: L ($78). Interval wipers: L ($50). Rear wiper/washer: wag ($124). Lighting and Mirrors: Cornering lamps ($68). Dual electric remote mirrors: L ($59-$96). Dual lighted visor vanity mirrors ($104-$116). Entertainment: Electronic-tuning AM/FM stereo radio: L/MT5 ($157). Electronic-tuning AM/FM stereo w/cassette/Dolby ($127-$284). Power antenna ($71). Premium sound system ($168). Radio delete: L ($39 credit); others ($196 credit). Exterior: Power moonroof ($701). Clearcoat paint ($183). Bodyside/decklid paint stripe ($57). Rocker panel moldings: L ($55). Luggage rack delete: L wag LPO ($105 credit). Interior: Bucket seats (NC). Split bench seating: L ($276). Vinyl seat trim ($39). Leather seat trim: LX sed ($415). Rear-facing third seat: wag ($155). Reclining passenger seat ($45). Load floor extension: wag ($66). Cargo area cover: wag ($66). Carpeted floor mats ($43). Wheels/Tires: Luxury wheel covers ($65). Styled wheels, 14 in. ($113-$178). Cast aluminum wheels, 15 in. ($326-$390). P195/70R14 WSW ($72). P205/70R14 BSW ($38); WSW ($72-$110). P205/65R15 BSW ($46-$84); WSW ($124-$162). Conventional spare ($63).

LTD CONVENIENCE/APPEARANCE OPTIONS: Option Packages: Squire option ($282). Interior luxury group ($388). Power lock group ($218-$259). Light group ($38). Comfort/Convenience: Air cond. ($762). Rear defroster ($145). Fingertip speed control ($176). Autolamp on-off delay ($73). Power windows ($282). Six-way power driver's seat ($234). Tinted glass ($115). Tinted windshield ($48). Leather-wrapped steering wheel ($59). Tilt steering ($115). Digital clock ($78). Auto. parking brake release ($12). Interval wipers ($50). Lighting and Mirrors: Cornering lamps ($68). Right remote convex mirror ($61). Dual electric remote mirrors ($96). Lighted visor vanity mirrors ($57-$106). Entertainment: AM/FM stereo radio ($109); w/cassette player ($256). Premium sound system ($138). AM radio delete ($39 credit). Exterior: Full vinyl roof ($152). Clearcoat metallic paint ($183). Two-tone paint w/tape stripe ($117). Pivoting front vent windows ($79). Two-way liftgate: wag ($105). Rocker panel moldings ($40). Bumper guards, rear ($28). Bumper rub strips ($56). Luggage rack: wagon ($126). Lower bodyside protection ($41). Interior: Vinyl seat trim ($35). Flight or split bench seat (NC). Front floor mats, carpeted ($23). Wheels/Tires: Luxury wheel covers ($55). Wire wheel covers, locking ($212). Styled wheels ($178). Styled steel wheels w/trim rings ($54). P195/75R14 WSW ($72). P205/70R14 WSW ($134). Conventional spare ($63).

LTD CROWN VICTORIA CONVENIENCE/APPEARANCE OPTIONS: Option Packages: Convenience group ($109-$134). Power lock group ($143-$243). Light group ($48). Police pkg. ($291-$411). Comfort/Convenience: Air cond. ($762); w/auto-temp control ($828). Rear defroster, electric ($145). Fingertip speed control ($176). Illuminated entry system ($82). Power windows ($282). Power six-way driver's seat ($237); driver and passenger ($473). Tinted glass ($115); windshield only ($48). Autolamp on/off delay ($73). Leather-wrapped steering wheel ($59). Tilt steering wheel ($115). Tripminder computer ($215-$261). Quartz clock: S ($35). Digital clock ($61-$96). Interval wipers ($50). Lighting and Mirrors: Cornering lamps ($68). Remote

right convex mirror ($46). Dual electric remote mirrors ($100). Entertainment: AM/FM stereo radio: S ($109); w/cassette tape player ($148-$256). Electronic-tuning AM/FM stereo radio w/cassette ($300) exc. S ($409). Power antenna ($73). Premium sound system ($168). Radio delete: AM ($39 credit); AM/FM ($148 credit). Exterior: Brougham vinyl roof ($793). Two-tone paint/tape ($117). Dual accent bodyside stripes ($39). Pivoting front vent windows ($79). Rocker panel moldings ($18-$38). Vinyl- insert bodyside moldings ($61). Bumper rub strips ($59). Luggage rack: wagon ($110). Interior: Dual-facing rear seats: wagon ($167). Leather seat trim ($433). Reclining split bench seats ($144). All-vinyl seat trim ($35); Duraweave vinyl ($100). Carpeted front floor mats ($21); front/rear ($33). H.D. floor covering ($27). Wheels/Tires: Wire wheel covers, locking ($205). Cast aluminum wheels ($390). P205/75R15 puncture-sealant ($161). P215/70R15 WSW ($62). Conventional spare ($63).

THUNDERBIRD CONVENIENCE/APPEARANCE OPTIONS: Option Packages: Light group ($35). Power lock group ($220). Comfort/Convenience: Air cond. ($762); auto-temp ($924). Rear defroster ($145). Fingertip speed control ($176). Illuminated entry system ($82). Keyless entry ($198). Anti-theft system ($159). Tripminder computer ($215-$276). Autolamp on/off delay ($73). Tinted glass ($115); windshield only ($49). Power windows ($207). Six-way power driver's seat ($238); dual ($476). Dual power seat recliners ($189). Leather-wrapped steering wheel ($59). Tilt steering wheel ($115). Electronic instrument cluster ($270-$330). Diagnostic warning lights ($89). Digital clock ($61). Interval wipers ($50). Lighting and Mirrors: Cornering lamps ($68). Dual electric remote mirrors ($96). Lighted visor vanity mirrors, pair ($106). Entertainment: Power antenna ($71). Graphic equalizer ($218). Premium sound system ($168). AM/FM radio delete ($196 credit). Exterior: Power moonroof ($701). Metallic clearcoat paint ($183). Two-tone paint/tape ($163-$218). Dual accent paint stripes ($55). Pivoting front vent windows ($79). Wide bodyside moldings ($57). Interior: Articulated sport seats ($183). Leather seat trim ($415). Soft vinyl seat trim ($37). Front floor mats, carpeted ($22). Wheels/Tires: Wire wheel covers, locking ($212). Cast aluminum wheels ($343). Styled wheels ($178). P215/70R14 WSW ($62). Conventional spare ($63). Inflatable spare ($122).

HISTORY: Introduced: October 3, 1985 except Taurus, December 26, 1985 and EXP, mid-year. Model year production: 1,559,959 (incl. Mustangs). Total production for the U.S. market of 1,424,374 units (incl. Mustangs) included 845,607 four-cylinder, 380,402 sixes and 198,365 V-8s. That total included 23,658 turbo fours and 7,144 diesel engines. Calendar year production (U.S.): 1,221,956 (incl. Mustangs). Calendar year sales by U.S. dealers: 1,397,141 (incl. Mustangs). Model year sales by U.S. dealers: 1,332,097 (incl. Mustangs).

Historical Footnotes: Sales fell this model year, after three straight years of rises. Moreover, Ford's market share shrunk markedly (from 13.1 percent overall in 1985 to just 11.9 percent in '86). Ford's share when considering only domestic-built autos declined less sharply, from 17.2 percent down to 16.5 percent. Only Mustang showed a sales increase. Escort continued as America's best seller. The Escort/EXP duo found 416,147 buyers this year. Tempo was the second best-selling Ford, for the third year in a row. Crown Vic hung on because of continuing popularity of full-size rear-drives, partly due to moderated gas prices. Throughout the year, low-interest financing was offered, at record-breaking rates. Ford offered a new three-year unlimited mileage powertrain warranty (with deductibles). Because of production delays, the new Taurus (and related Mercury Sable) weren't introduced until December 1985. The new aero mid-size sold well, however. V-6 engines for Taurus were in short supply, keeping production from reaching an even higher level. Taurus was the result of a $3 billion development program, and was named *Motor Trend* Car of the Year. Even before production, it got a lot of publicity. Auto show attendees were even asked their opinions on whether Taurus should or should not have a conventional grille. (Those who preferred a solid panel eventually "won.") Ford claimed that a 1985 owner survey showed that "Ford makes the best-built American cars," based on reports of problems people had with 198184 models. Ford's main slogan at this time: "Quality is Job 1."

Disappointment was doubtless a common reaction among ponycar fans, when Mustang II replaced the former edition for 1974. Ford's claim that it was the "right car at the right time" may well have been accurate, especially in view of the gas crisis. Yet it was far removed from the original concept of a decade past—and farther yet from the scorching performance versions that greeted the early 1970s. Still, the new and smaller Mustang sold a lot better than its ample predecessor. Sales fell after the opening year, but remained well above the level of 1971-73.

1976 Mustang Cobra II 2+2 coupe (F)

As 1976 rolled around, Mustang came with a four, German-made V-6, or small-block (302 cu. in.) V-8 engine. The two-door hardtop had a restrained look, while the 2--2 hatchback showed more sporty lines. Ghia was the luxury edition, while Mach 1 sounded a lot more exciting than reality dictated. A silver Stallion appearance group added few thrills, and even the new blackout-trimmed Cobra II package was stronger on bold looks than performance.

Cobra II became more colorful by 1977, and a T-Roof became available, but not much changed otherwise. For its next (and final) season, Mustang II added a V-8 powered King Cobra selection with giant snake on the hood. Though ranking with collectible Mustangs, the King added little to Mustang's performance capability.

1980 Mustang "Carriage Roof" coupe (F)

Customers eagerly awaited the next Mustang, which took on a far different form—a design that was destined for long life. Notchback (two-door) and hatchback (three-door) bodies were offered again, but the new aero wedge shape could hardly be compared with Mustang II.

By year's end, five different engines had been installed under Mustang hoods: base four, carryover V-6, replacement inline six, 302 V-8, and a new turbocharged four. Both the turbo and V-8 produced 140 horsepower. The Cobra option package could have either engine. Sport and TRX packages helped Mustang's handling. To tempt contemporary customers and later collectors, about 6,000 Indy Pace Car replicas were produced. Sales zoomed upward for the model year, but slipped back close to pre-1979 levels later.

1982 Mustang 5.0L SVO coupe (F)

Cobra for 1980 adopted some styling touches from the Pace Car, including a slat-style grille, foglamps and hood scoop. While turbo power went up, the 302 cu. in. V-8 disappeared temporarily, replaced by a 255. A new carriage roof was designed to resemble a convertible, but the real thing would arrive a couple of years later. Not much changed for 1981, except for the availability of a new five-speed gearbox. But a year later the "Boss" 302 V-8 was back, stronger than before (while the turbo took a breather for one season). Mustang's revised model lineup now included a GT instead of the old Cobra option, yet sales declined for the third year in a row.

1984 Mustang SVO coupe (F)

The awaited convertible Mustang arrived for 1983, along with a restyled front and rear end. Replacing the V-8's carburetor with a four-barrel boosted horsepower up to 175. At the other end, the base four's carb switched

from two barrels to one. When the turbo emerged again, it had new multi-port fuel injection. Borg-Warner's close-ratio five-speed could help GT Mustangs hit 60 MPH in the seven-second neighborhood.

1984½ Mustang GT-350 20th Anniversary convertible (JG)

Several years earlier, Ford had formed a Special Vehicle Operations Department to oversee racing and limited-edition production. The first regular-production fruit of their labor appeared for 1984: the Mustang SVO, with an air-to-air intercooler on its turbocharged four-cylinder engine. SVO's five-speed had a Hurst linkage, wheels held big 16-inch tires, and it stopped with discs on all wheels. A non-intercooled turbo went into GT models. Sales edged upward again in 1984, and further yet in the next two years.

All Mustangs for 1985 sported a single-slot grille similar to SVO's. Roller tappets and a performance camshaft gave GT's carbureted 302 V-8 a 210-horsepower rating, 30 more than the fuel-injected V-8. Sequential fuel injection went into V-8s for 1986, adding 20 horsepower; but the four-barrel version faded away. SVO turbos now managed to produce 200 horsepower, ready for the Hurst-shifted five-speed.

Expensive when new, SVO is surely one of the Mustangs worth hanging onto. Far more exotic would be the McLaren Mustang, but only 250 were produced in 1981. A mid-1980s GT wouldn't be a bad choice either, with so many more available. Quite a few of the '79 Pace Car replicas went on sale, too, and might be worth a look. King Cobras of 1978 have attracted some interest, as have some of the "ordinary" Cobra versions. Of course, some people consider just about every Mustang to be worth owning, if not exactly collectible.

1976 MUSTANG

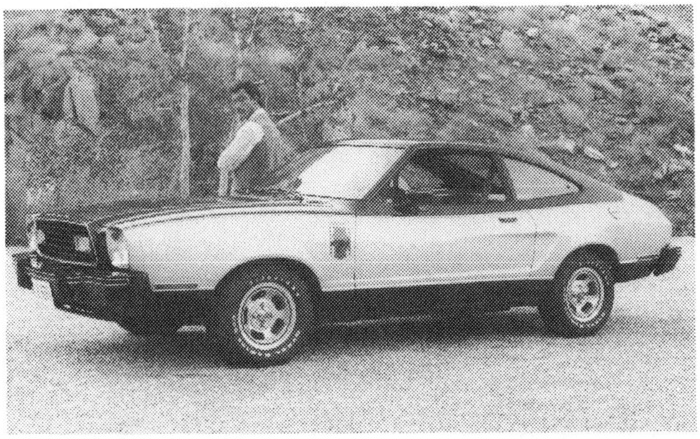

1976 Mustang II Stallion 2+2 coupe (F)

MUSTANG II — FOUR/V-6/V-8 — Restyled in a new smaller size in 1974, Mustang came in two basic body styles: a two-door hardtop and three-door 2+2 hatchback. The two-door was commonly referred to by Ford as a sedan rather than a coupe, which distinguished it from the old (larger) coupe design. The "three-door" model had only two doors for people, and was designated either a hatchback or fastback, both terms accurately describing the sloping lift-up rear design. Two-doors came in base or Ghia trim; fastbacks in base or Mach 1 form. Fastbacks had fold- down rear seats, while the hardtops displayed a formal-look roofline. An MPG series, carrying fewer standard items and a smaller price tag, had joined the Mustang lineup in mid-year 1975 and continued in 1976. This year's highlights included significant fuel economy gains, some new options, and a new sport exterior dress-up package for the 2+2 and Mach 1. The former horizontal stainless steel bumper inserts were replaced by black bumper rub strips with white stripes. The wiper/washer control had moved to the turn signal lever in mid-year 1975, and continued there this year. To improve economy, Mustang II got a lower optional 2.79:1 axle ratio. An optional wide-ratio transmission was available with that rear-end ratio. New options included sporty plaid trim on seating surfaces; expanded availability of Ghia luxury coupe colors; whitewall tires; and an AM radio with stereo tape player. Styling was similar to 1975, except for a new air scoop below the front bumper. Rectangular parking/signal lamps were inset right into the forward-slanting grille, which had a 14 x 6 hole crosshatch pattern. The grille was narrower at the top than at the base, with a traditional Mustang (horse) emblem in its center. Separate 'Ford' block letters stood above the grille, facing upward. Single round headlamps were recessed into squarish housings. The front bumper protruded forward in the center, matching the width of the grille. Rub strips wrapped only slightly onto the bumper sides. Door sheetmetal had a sculptured, depressed area that began near the back and extended for a short distance on the quarter panel, following the contour of the wheel opening. The curvaceous bodyside crease ran below the door handle. Two-doors had a 'B' pillar and conventional quarter window. Fastbacks had sharply tapered quarter windows that came to a point at the rear. Each European-style taillamp consisted of three side-by-side sections, with a small backup lens at the bottom of each center section and large amber turn signal lenses. Large 'Ford' block letters stood on the panel between the taillamps, above the license plate housing. Bodies had a a one-piece fiberglass-reinforced front end nd color-keyed urethane-coated bumpers. Standard features included wheel lip moldings, side marker lights with die-cast bezels, recessed door handles, and slim high-lustre exterior trim moldings. Inside were low-back all-vinyl front bucket seats with full-width head restraints, tachometer, speedometer, ammeter, fuel and temperature gauges, European- type armrests with integral pull handles, a two-spoke steering wheel, and lockable glovebox. Simulated burled walnut woodtone accents went on the instrument panel and shift knob. Mustang had a unitized body and chassis with front isolated mini-frame, Hotchkiss-type rear suspension, and rack-and-pinion steering. The rear suspension consisted of longitudinal semi-elliptic leaf springs (four leaves), while the independent front suspension used ball joints, a stabilizer bar, and compression-type struts. Standard engine was a 140 cu. in. (2.3-liter) four with four-speed floor shift. Optional: a 302 cu. in. (5.0-liter) V-8 with Cruise-O- Matic, or 171 cu. in. (2.8-liter) V-6 with four-speed manual. Mach 1 had the V-6 as standard. A four-speed manual gearbox became available with the V-8 later in the season. Front disc brakes were standard; power brakes (and steering) optional. Ghias included a quartz digital clock, bodyside molding, BR78 x 13 steel-belted radial whitewalls, padded half or full vinyl roof, hood ornament, dual remote mirrors, crushed velour seat surfaces, full console, and bodyside paint stripes. Mach 1 added the 2.8-liter V-6, dual remote racing mirrors, BR70 x 13 raised-white-letter tires on styled steel wheels, and rear tape and fender decals. Black paint went on lower bumpers, lower bodyside, and between rear taillamps. Ghias had wire-type wheel covers; Mach 1 included wheel trim rings. Three Luxury Groups were available: Silver, Tan Glow, and Silver Blue Glow (the latter two colors new this year). Two special option packages were offered: a new Stallion group intended to appeal to youthful buyers, and the more notorious Cobra II. The sporty silver Stallion package featured a two-tone paint and tape treatment (on fastback models); a large Stallion decal on front fenders (at the cowl); dual racing mirrors; styled steel wheels with raised- white-letter tires; and a competition suspension. Black paint highlighted the greenhouse, lower body, hood, grille, decklid, and lower back panel. On the ultimate option, large 'Cobra II' decal lettering at the door bottoms was easy to spot from a distance. Cobra II sported a black grille with cobra emblem, front air dam, simulated hood scoop, rear spoiler, and rocker-panel racing stripes. Dual wide stripes ran from the grille, over the hood and roof, onto the deck area. Front fenders displayed large cobra (snake) decals. Louvers covered the triangular flip-out quarter windows. Inside was a sport steering wheel and brushed-aluminum trim on dash and door panels, plus dual remote-control mirrors. Cobra II carried a standard V-6 ngine and four-speed, with raised-white-letter tires on styled steel wheels. Only one body color scheme was offered at first: white with blue striping.

I.D. DATA: Mustang's 11-symbol Vehicle Identification Number (VIN) is stamped on a metal tab fastened to the instrument panel, visible through the windshield. The first digit is a model year code ('6' 1976). The second letter indicates assembly plant: 'F' Dearborn, MI; 'R' San Jose, CA. Digits three and four are the body serial code, which corresponds to the Model Numbers shown in the tables below: '02' 2-dr. HT; '03' 3-dr. 22 hatchback; '04' Ghia 2-dr. HT; '05' Mach 1 3-dr. 22 hatchback. The fifth digit is an engine code: 'Y' L4-140 2Bbl.; 'Z' V6170 2Bbl.; 'F' V8302 2Bbl. Finally, digits 6-11 make up the consecutive unit number, starting with 100,001. A Vehicle Certification Label on the left front door lock face panel or door pillar shows the manufacturer, month and year of manufacture, GVW, GAWR, certification statement, VIN, body code, color code, trim code, axle code, transmission code, and domestic (or foreign) special order code.

MUSTANG II (FOUR/V-6)

Model Number	Body/Style Number	Body Type & Seating	Factory Price	Shipping Weight	Production Total
02	60F	2-dr. Notch Cpe-4P	3525/3791	2678/2756	78,508
03	69F	3-dr. 2+2 hatch-4P	3781/4047	2706/2784	62,312

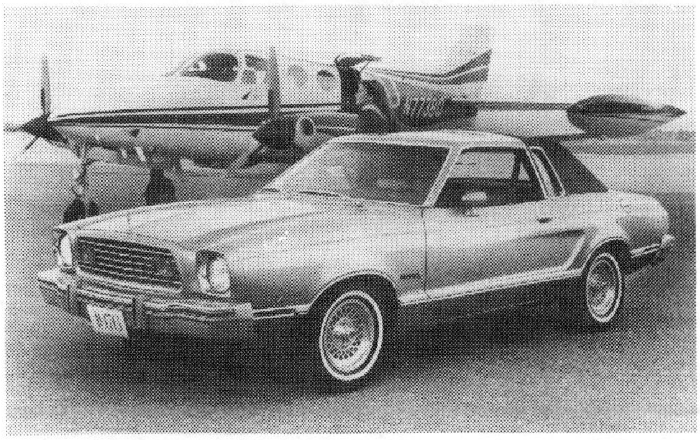

1976 Mustang II Ghia coupe (F)

MUSTANG GHIA (FOUR/V-6)

04	60H	2-dr. Notch Cpe-4P	3859/4125	2729/2807	37,515

MUSTANG MACH 1 (V-6/V-8)

05	69R	3-dr. 22 Hatch-4P	4209/4154	2822/ --	9,232

FACTORY PRICE/WEIGHT NOTE: Figures to left of slash are for four- cylinder engine, to right of slash for V-6 engine (Mach 1, V-6 and V-8). A V-8 engine on base or Ghia initially was priced $212 higher than the V-6, but later cost $54 less than a V-6.

ENGINE DATA: BASE FOUR: Inline, overhead cam, four-cylinder. Cast iron block and head. Displacement: 140 cu. in. (2.3 liters). Bore & stroke: 3.78 x 3.13 in. Compression ratio: 9.0:1. Brake horsepower: 92 at 5000 R.P.M. Torque: 121 lbs.-ft. at 3000 R.P.M. Five main bearings. Hydraulic valve lifters. Carburetor: 2Bbl. Holley-Weber 9510. VIN Code: Y. OPTIONAL V-6: 60-degree, overhead valve V-6. Cast iron block and head. Displacement: 170.8 cu. in. (2.8 liters). Bore & stroke: 3.66 x 2.70 in. Compression ratio: 8.7:1. Brake horsepower: 103 at 4400 R.P.M. Torque: 149 lbs.-ft. at 2800 R.P.M. Four main bearings. Solid valve lifters. Carburetor: 2Bbl. Holley-Weber 9510. German-built. VIN Code: Z. OPTIONAL V-8: 90-degree, overhead valve V-8. Cast iron block and head. Displacement: 302 cu. in. (5.0 liters). Bore & stroke: 4.00 x 3.00 in. Compression ratio: 8.0:1. Brake horsepower: 134 at 3600 R.P.M. Torque: 247 lbs.-ft. at 1800 R.P.M. Five main bearings. Hydraulic valve lifters. Carburetor: 2Bbl. Motorcraft 9510. VIN Code: F.

CHASSIS DATA: Wheelbase: 96.2 in. Overall length: 175.0 in. Height: (Notch cpe) 50.0 in.; (Hatch) 49.7 in. Width: 70.2 in. Front Tread: 55.6 in. Rear Tread: 55.8 in. Wheel Size: 13 x 5 in. Standard Tires: B78 x 13 exc. (Ghia) BR78 x 13; (Mach 1) BR70 x 13 RWL SBR. Sizes CR70 x 13 and 195/70R13 were available.

TECHNICAL: Transmission: Four-speed manual transmission (floor shift) standard. Gear ratios: (1st) 4.07:1; (2nd) 2.57:1; (3rd) 1.66:1; (4th) 1.00:1; (Rev) 3.95:1. Four-cylinder four-speed: (1st) 3.50:1; (2nd) 2.21:1; (3rd) 1.43:1; (4th) 1.00:1; (Rev) 3.38:1. Select-Shift three-speed automatic optional (initially standard on V-8). Four-cylinder: (1st) 2.47:1; (2nd) 1.47:1; (3rd) 1.00:1; (Rev) 2.11:1. V-6/V-8 automatic: (1st) 2.46:1; (2nd) 1.46:1; (3rd) 1.00:1; (Rev) 2.20:1. Standard final drive ratio: 2.79:1 w/4spd, 3.18:1 w/auto.; (V-6) 3.00:1; (V-8) 2.79:1. Steering: Rack and pinion. Front Suspension: Compression strut with lower trailing links, stabilizer bar and coil springs. Rear Suspension: Hotchkiss rigid axle w/semi-elliptic leaf springs (four leaves) and anti-sway bar. Brakes: Front disc, rear drum. Disc dia.: 9.3 in. outer, 6.2 in. inner. Drum dia.: 9.0 in. Ignition: Electronic. Body construction: Unibody w/front isolated mini-frame. Fuel tank: 13 gal.

DRIVETRAIN OPTIONS: Engines: 140 cu. in. four ($272 credit from base V-6 price). Transmission/Differential: Cruise-O-Matic trans. ($239). Optional axle ratio ($13). Traction-Lok differential ($48). Brakes/Steering/Suspension: Power brakes ($54). Power steering ($117). Competition suspension ($29-$191). Other: H.D. 53-amp battery ($14). Extended-range fuel tank ($24). Engine block heater ($17). California emission system ($49).

CONVENIENCE/APPEARANCE OPTIONS: Option Packages: Cobra II pkg. ($325). Cobra II modification pkg. ($287). Rallye package: Mach 1 ($163); 22/hardtop ($267-$399). Ghia luxury group ($177). Stallion option ($72). Exterior accent group ($169). Luxury interior group ($117). Convenience group ($35). Light group ($28-$41). Protection group ($36-$43). Comfort/Convenience: Air cond. ($420). Rear defroster, electric ($70). Tinted glass ($46). Leather-wrapped steering wheel ($33). Electric clock ($17). Digital clock ($40). Fuel monitor warning light ($18). Anti-theft alarm ($83). Security lock group ($16). Horns and Mirrors: Dual-note horn ($6). Color-keyed mirrors ($42). Entertainment: AM radio ($71); w/tape player ($192). AM/FM radio ($128). AM/FM stereo radio ($173); w/tape player ($299). Exterior: Glass moonroof ($470). Manual sunroof ($230). Vinyl roof ($86). Half-vinyl roof: Ghia (NC). Glamour paint ($54). Two-tone paint/tape ($84). Pinstriping ($27). Bumper guards, front/rear ($34). Color-keyed vinyl-insert bodyside molding ($60). Rocker panel moldings ($19). Pivoting rear quarter windows ($33). Decklid luggage rack ($51). Interior: Console ($71). Fold-down rear seat ($72). Velour cloth trim ($99). Color-keyed deluxe seatbelts ($17). Wheels and Tires: Cast aluminum spoke wheels ($96-$182). Forged aluminum wheels ($96-$182). Styled steel wheels: 22/HT ($51); Ghia (NC). Trim rings ($35). B78 x 13 BSW ($84). B78 x 13 WSW ($33-$52). BR78 x 13 BSW ($97). BR78 x 13 WSW ($33-$130 BR70 x 13 RWL ($30-$160). CR70 x 13 WSW ($10- $169). 195/70R13 WSW ($22-$191). 195/70R13 RWL ($12-$203). 195/70R13 wide WSW ($5-$208).

Introduced: October 3, 1975. Model year production (U.S.): 187,567. Total production for the U.S. market of 172,365 included 91,880 four-cylinder, 50,124 V-6, and 30,361 V-8 Mustangs. Calendar year production (U.S.): 183,369. Calendar year sales: 167,201. Model year sales by U.S. dealers: N/A.

Historical Footnotes: Mustang, America's best selling small specialty car, had been outselling Monza, Starfire and Skyhawk combined. The optional V-6, also used on the imported Mercury Capri, was made in Germany. A V-8 powered Cobra II could do 0-60 MPH in around 9 seconds.

1977 MUSTANG

1977 Mustang II Ghia coupe (F)

MUSTANG II — FOUR/V-6/V-8 — No significant styling changes were evident on Mustang for 1977, though new colors were offered and both four and V-6 engines lost power. As before, hardtop (notchback) and three- door fastback models were available. Simulated pecan replaced the burled walnut woodgrain interior appliques. California models used a variable-venturi carburetor. Joining the option list were simulated wire wheel covers, painted cast aluminum spoke wheels, a flip-up removable sunroof, four-way manual bucket seats, and high-altitude option. The bronze-tinted glass sunroof panels could either be propped partly open, or remove completely for storage in the trunk. That TBar roof package included a wide black band across the top (except with the Cobra II). Mustang's engine/transmission selection continued as before. Neither a V-6, nor a V-8 with four-speed manual gearbox, was offered in California. The basic two-door hardtop carried a standard 140 cu. in. (2.3-liter) four-cylinder engine with Dura-Spark ignition, four-speed manual gearbox, front disc brakes, color-keyed urethane bumpers, low-back bucket seats with vinyl trim, B78 x 13 tires, and full wheel covers. Mustang 2+2 hatchbacks included a front spoiler at no extra cost (which could be deleted), along with a sport steering wheel, styled steel wheels, B78 x 13 bias-belted raised-white-letter or 195R/70 whitewall tires, blackout grille, and brushed aluminum instrument panel appliques. Ghia added a half-vinyl roof, pinstripes, unique wheel covers, and bodyside moldings with color-keyed vinyl inserts. Ghia interiors could have Media Velour cloth with large armrests. Stepping up another notch, Mach 1 carried a standard 2.8-liter V-6 and sported a black paint treatment on lower bodyside and back panel. Also included: dual sport mirrors, Mach 1 emblem, and raised-white-letter BR70 x 13 (or 195R/70) steel-belted radial tires on styled steel wheels with trim rings. Cobra II changed its look after the model year began. Big new tri-color tape stripes went on the full bodyside and front spoiler, front bumper, hood, hood scoop, roof, decklid and rear

1977 Mustang Cobra II 2+2 coupe (F)

spoiler. 'Cobra II' block lettering was low on the doors at first, later halfway up as part of the huge center bodyside tape stripe. The decklid spoiler displayed a Cobra snake decal, and another snake highlighted the black grille. Early Cobras also had snake cowl decals. Flat black greenhouse moldings, vertical-style quarter-window louvers (without the snake) and rear-window louvers also became standard. So was a narrow band of flat black along the upper doors. Cobra II equipment also included dual black sport mirrors, rear-opening hood scoop, BR70 or 195/R70 x 13 RWL tires, and brushed

aluminum door trim inserts. The required power brakes cost extra. Cobra II was now offered in four color choices, not just the original white with blue striping. Selections were white body with red, blue or green stripes; or black with gold stripes. A new Rallye package included dual racing mirrors, heavy-duty springs and cooling, adjustable shocks, and rear stabilizer bar. Mustang's Sports Performance package included a 302 cu. in. V-8 with two-barrel carb, heavy-duty four-speed manual gearbox, power steering and brakes, and P195R/70 radial tires. Ghia's Sports Group was available with black or tan body, including a vinyl roof and many color-coordinated components in black or chamois color. Also included was a three-spoke sports steering wheel, cast aluminum wheels with chamois-color spokes, and trunk luggage rack with straps and buckles. The later-arriving 2+2 Rallye Appearance Package replaced the Stallion option. It included dual gold accent stripes on hood and bodysides; flat black wiper arms, door handles, lock cylinders, and antenna; dual black sport mirrors; and argent styled steel wheels with trim rings. A gold-color surround molding highlighted the black grille (which lost its horse emblem). Also included: gold taillamp accent moldings and dual gold accent stripes in bumper rub strips. A black front spoiler was a no-cost option. Black and Polar White body colors were offered with the package. Inside were black or white vinyl seats with gold ribbed velour Touraine cloth inserts and gold welting, and gold accent moldings on door panels.

I.D. DATA: As before, Mustang's 11-symbol Vehicle Identification Number (VIN) is stamped on a metal tab fastened to the instrument panel, visible through the windshield. Coding is similar to 1976. Model year code changed to '7' for 1977.

MUSTANG II (FOUR/V-6)

Model Number	Body/Style Number	Body Type & Seating	Factory Price	Shipping Weight	Production Total
02	60F	2-dr. Notch Cpe-4P	3702/3984	2627/2750	67,783
03	69F	3-dr. 2+2 Hatch-4P	3901/4183	2672/2795	49,161

MUSTANG GHIA (FOUR/V-6)

04	60H	2-dr. Notch Cpe-4P	4119/4401	2667/2790	29,510

MUSTANG MACH 1 (V-6/V-8)

05	69R	3-dr. 2+2 Hatch 4P	4332/4284	2785/ --	6,719

FACTORY PRICE/WEIGHT NOTE: Figures to left of slash are for four- cylinder engine, to right of slash are for V-6 engine (Mach 1, V-6 and V-8). A V-8 engine on base or Ghia initially was priced $234 higher than the V-6.

PRODUCTION NOTE: Totals shown include 20,937 Mustangs produced as 1978 models, but sold as 1977 models (9,826 model 02, 7,019 model 03, 3,209 Ghia, and 883 Mach 1).

ENGINE DATA: BASE FOUR: Inline, overhead cam, four-cylinder. Cast iron block and head. Displacement: 140 cu. in. (2.3 liters). Bore & stroke: 3.78 x 3.13 in. Compression ratio: 9.0:1. Brake horsepower: 89 at 4800 R.P.M. Torque: 120 lbs.-ft. at 3000 R.P.M. Five main bearings. Hydraulic valve lifters. Carburetor: 2Bbl. Motorcraft 5200. VIN Code: Y. OPTIONAL V-6: 60-degree, overhead valve V-6. Cast iron block and head. Displacement: 170.8 cu. in. (2.8 liters). Bore & stroke: 3.66 x 2.70 in. Compression ratio: 8.7:1. Brake horsepower: 93 at 4200 R.P.M. Torque: 140 lbs.-ft. at 2600 R.P.M. Four main bearings. Solid valve lifters. Carburetor: 2Bbl. Motorcraft 2150. German-built. VIN Code: Z. OPTIONAL V-8: 90-degree, overhead valve V-8. Cast iron block and head. Displacement: 302 cu. in. (5.0 liters). Bore & stroke: 4.00 x 3.00 in. Compression ratio: 8.4:1. Brake horsepower: 139 at 3600 R.P.M. Torque: 247 lbs.-ft. at 1800 R.P.M. Five main bearings. Hydraulic valve lifters. Carburetor: 2Bbl. Motorcraft 2150. VIN Code: F.

CHASSIS DATA: Wheelbase: 96.2 in. Overall length: 175.0 in. Height: (Notch cpe) 50.3 in.; (Hatch) 50.0 in. Width: 70.2 in. Front Tread: 55.6 in. Rear Tread: 55.8 in. Standard Tires: B78 x 13 exc. (Ghia) BR78 x 13; (Mach 1) BR70 x 13.

TECHNICAL: Transmission: Four-speed manual transmission (floor shift) standard. V-8 gear ratios: (1st) 2.64:1; (2nd) 1.89:1; (3rd) 1.34:1; (4th) 1.00:1; (Rev) 2.56:1. Four/V-6 four-speed: (1st) 3.50:1; (2nd) 2.21:1; (3rd) 1.43:1; (4th) 1.00:1; (Rev) 3.38:1. Select-Shift three-speed automatic optional. Four- cylinder: (1st) 2.47:1; (2nd) 1.47:1; (3rd) 1.00:1; (Rev) 2.11:1. V-8 automatic: (1st) 2.46:1; (2nd) 1.46:1; (3rd) 1.00:1; (Rev) 2.19:1. Standard final drive ratio: (four) 3.18:1; (V-6/V-8) 3.00:1. Steering/suspension/brakes/body: same as 1976. Fuel tank: 13 gal. exc. w/V-8, 16.5 gal.

DRIVETRAIN OPTIONS: Engines: 140 cu. in. four ($289 credit from base V-6 price). 170 cu. in. V-6 ($289). 302 cu. in. V-8 ($230). Other: Cruise-O-Matic trans. ($253). Power brakes ($58). Power steering ($124). H.D. battery ($16). California emission system ($52). High-altitude emissions ($39).

CONVENIENCE/APPEARANCE OPTIONS: Option Packages: Cobra II pkg. ($535). Sports performance pkg. ($451-$607) exc. Mach 1 ($163). Rallye package ($43- $88). Ghia sports group ($422). Exterior accent group ($216). Appearance decor group ($96-$152). Luxury interior group ($124). Convenience group ($37-$71). Light group ($29-$43). Protection group ($39-$46). Comfort/Convenience: Air cond. ($446). Rear defroster, electric ($73). Tinted glass ($48). Leather-wrapped steering wheel ($35-$49). Digital clock ($42). Dual sport mirrors ($45). Entertainment: AM radio ($76); w/tape player ($204). AM/FM radio ($135). AM/FM stereo radio ($184); w/tape player ($317). Exterior: Flip-up open air roof ($147). Manual sunroof ($243). Full vinyl roof ($90). Front spoiler (NC). Metallic glow paint ($58). Pinstriping ($28). Color-keyed vinyl-insert bodyside moldings ($64). Rocker panel moldings ($20). Decklid luggage rack ($54). Interior: Console ($76). Four-way driver's seat ($33). Fold-down rear seat ($77). Media velour cloth trim ($105). Color- keyed deluxe seatbelts ($18). Wheels and Tires: Wire wheel covers ($33-$86). Forged aluminum wheels ($102-$193). Lacy spoke aluminum wheels ($102-$193); white ($153-$243). Styled steel wheels ($37- $90). Trim rings ($37). B78 x 13 BSW/WSW. BR78 x 13 BSW/WSW. BR70 x 13 RWL. 195/70R13 WSW/white WSW/RWL.

HISTORY: Introduced: October 1, 1976. Model year production (U.S.): 153,173. Total production for the U.S. market of 141,212 included 71,736 four-cylinder, 33,326 V-6, and 36,150 V-8 Mustangs. Calendar year production (U.S.): 170,315. Calendar year sales: 170,659. Model year sales by U.S. dealers: 161,513.

Historical Footnotes: After a very strong showing following the 1974 restyle, Mustang sales had begun to sag somewhat in 1975 and '76. The Cobra packages looked dramatic, and performed well enough with a V-8, but Mustang couldn't find enough customers in this form. Production declined significantly this year. A four-cylinder Mustang with manual four-speed managed a 26 MPG city/highway rating in EPA estimates.

1978 MUSTANG

1978 Mustang coupe (JG)

MUSTANG II — FOUR/V-6/V-8 — New colors and interior trims made up most of the changes for 1978. The 2.8-liter V-6 got a plastic cooling fan. A new electronic voltage regulator gave longer-life reliability than the old electro-mechanical version. New this year was optional variable-ratio power steering, first introduced on the Fairmont. New inside touches included separate back-seat cushions, revised door and seat trim, new carpeting, and new tangerine color. Six new body colors added late in the 1977 model year were carried over this time. As before, clear rectangular horizontal parking lamps set into the crosshatch black grille. Angled outward at its base, that grille had a 14 x 6 hole pattern, with Mustang (horse) badge in the center. Separate 'Ford' letters stood above the grille. Single round headlamps continued this year. Engine choices were the same as in 1977. So were the two body styles: two-door hardtop (notchback) or "three-door" 22 fastback (hatchback). Base and Ghia notchback models were offered; base and Mach 1 hatchbacks. Standard equipment included the 140 cu. in. (2.3-liter) four-cylinder engine with electronic ignition, four-speed transmission, front disc brakes, rack-and-pinion steering, tachometer, and ammeter. Mustang's Cobra II package (for hatchback only) ontinued in the form introduced at mid-year in 1977. Tri-color tape stripes decorated bodysides and front spoiler, front bumper, hood, hood scoop, roof, decklid and rear spoiler. Huge 'Cobra' block letters went on the center bodyside tape stripe and decklid spoiler; a Cobra decal on the back spoiler; and Cobra II snake emblem on the black grille. The package also included flat black greenhouse moldings, black quarter-window and backlight louvers, black rocker panels and dual racing mirrors, a narrow black band along upper doors, rear-opening hood scoop, Rallye package, and flipper quarter windows (except with T-Roof option). Styled steel wheels with trim rings held BR70 RWL tires (195/70R with V-8, or with V-6 engine and air conditioner). King Cobra, new this year, might be viewed as a regular Cobra and more of the same, with plenty of striping and lettering. The King did without the customary bodyside striping, but sported a unique tape treatment including a giant snake decal on the hood and pinstriping on the greenhouse, decklid, wheel lips, rocker panels, belt, over-the-roof area, and around the side windows. Up front was a tough-looking spoiler. The 302 cu. in. (5.0-liter) V-8 was standard on the King, with four-speed transmission and power brakes/steering. A 'King Cobra' nameplate went on each door and the back spoiler; '5.0L' badge on the front hood scoop. King Cobra also had rear quarter flares, a black grille and moldings, and color-keyed dual sport mirrors. Raised-white-letter tires rode lacy spoke aluminum wheels with twin rings and Cobra symbol on the hubs. A Fashion Accessory Group, aimed at women, consisted of a four-way adjustable driver's seat, striped cloth seat inserts, illuminated entry, lighted driver's vanity visor mirror, coin tray, and door pockets. It came in nine body colors. The simulated convertible T-Roof, with dual removable tinted glass panels, was now entering its first full model year as an option on the 22 and Mach 1 hatchbacks. Mustang's Ghia sports group came with black, blue or chamois body paint and a chamois or black vinyl half-roof, along with vinyl-insert bodyside moldings and pinstripes. Aluminum wheels had chamois-color lacy spokes. Inside was all-vinyl chamois or black seat trim, black "engine-turned" dash appliques, and a leather-wrapped steering wheel.

I.D. DATA: As before, Mustang's 11-symbol Vehicle Identification Number (VIN) is stamped on a metal tab fastened to the instrument panel, visible through the windshield. Coding is similar to 1976-77. Model year code changed to '8' for 1978.

MUSTANG II (FOUR/V-6)

Model Number	Body/Style Number	Body Type & Seating	Factory Price	Shipping Weight	Production Total
02	60F	2-dr. Notch Cpe-4P	3555/3768	2608/2705	81,304
03	69F	3-dr. 22 Hatch-4P	3798/4011	2654/2751	68,408

MUSTANG GHIA (FOUR/V-6)

04	60H	2-dr. Notch Cpe-4P	3972/4185	2646/2743	34,730

MUSTANG MACH 1 (V-6/V-8)

05	69R	3-dr. 22 Hatch-4P	4253/4401	2733/--	7,968

FACTORY PRICE/WEIGHT NOTE: Figures to left of slash are for four-cylinder engine, to right of slash for V-6 engine (Mach 1, V-6 and V-8). A V-8 engine on base or Ghia initially was priced $148 higher than the V-6.

PRODUCTION NOTE: Totals shown do not include 20,937 Mustangs produced as 1978 models, but sold as 1977 models (see note with 1977 listing).

ENGINE DATA: BASE FOUR: Inline, overhead cam, four-cylinder. Cast iron block and head. Displacement: 140 cu. in. (2.3 liters). Bore & stroke: 3.78 x 3.13 in. Compression ratio: 9.0:1. Brake horsepower: 88 at 4800 R.P.M. Torque: 118 lbs.-ft. at 2800 R.P.M. Five main bearings. Hydraulic valve lifters. Carburetor: 2Bbl. Motorcraft 5200. VIN Code: Y. OPTIONAL V-6: 60-degree, overhead valve V-6. Cast iron block and head. Displacement: 170.8 cu. in. (2.8 liters). Bore & stroke: 3.66 x 2.70 in. Compression ratio: 8.7:1. Brake horsepower: 90 at 4200 R.P.M. Torque: 143 lbs.-ft. at 2200 R.P.M. Four main bearings. Solid valve lifters. Carburetor: 2Bbl. Motorcraft 2150. German-built. VIN Code: Z. OPTIONAL V-8: 90-degree, overhead valve V-8. Cast iron block and head. Displacement: 302 cu. in. (5.0 liters). Bore & stroke: 4.00 x 3.00 in. Compression ratio: 8.4:1. Brake horsepower: 139 at 3600 R.P.M. Torque: 250 lbs.-ft. at 1600 R.P.M. Five main bearings. Hydraulic valve lifters. Carburetor: 2Bbl. Motorcraft 2150. VIN Code: F.

CHASSIS DATA: Wheelbase: 96.2 in. Overall length: 175.0 in. Height: (Notch cpe) 50.3 in.; (Hatch) 50.0 in. Width: 70.2 in. Front Tread: 55.6 in. Rear Tread: 55.8 in. Standard Tires: B78 x 13 exc. (Ghia) BR78 x 13 SBR; (Mach 1) BR70 x 13 SBR RWL.

TECHNICAL: Transmission: Four-speed manual transmission (floor shift) standard. V-8 gear ratios: (1st) 2.64:1, (2nd) 1.89:1, (3rd) 1.34:1, (4th) 1.00:1, (Rev) 2.56:1. Four-cylinder four-speed: (1st) 3.50:1, (2nd) 2.21:1, (3rd) 1.43:1, (4th) 1.00:1, (Rev) 3.38:1. V-6 four-speed: (1st) 4.07:1, (2nd) 2.57:1, (3rd) 1.66:1, (4th) 1.00:1, (Rev) 3.95:1. Select-Shift three-speed automatic optional. Four-cylinder: (1st) 2.47:1, (2nd) 1.47:1, (3rd) 1.00:1, (Rev) 2.11:1. V-6/V-8 automatic: (1st) 2.46:1, (2nd) 1.46:1, (3rd) 1.00:1, (Rev) 2.19:1. Standard final drive ratio: (four) 3.18:1, (V-6) 3.00:1 w/4spd, 3.40:1 w/auto.; (V-8) 2.79:1. Steering/suspension/brakes/body: same as 1976-77. Fuel tank: 13 gal. exc. w/V-8 engine, 16.5 gal.

DRIVETRAIN OPTIONS: Engine/Transmission: 140 cu. in. four ($213 credit from base V-6 price). 170 cu. in. V-6 ($213). 302 cu. in. V-8 ($361) exc. Mach 1 ($148). Cruise-O-Matic trans. ($281). Brakes/Steering: Power brakes ($64). Power steering ($131). Other: Engine block heater ($12). California emission system ($69). High-altitude emissions (NC).

CONVENIENCE/APPEARANCE OPTIONS: Option Packages: Cobra II pkg.: hatch ($677-$700). King Cobra pkg.: hatch ($1253). Fashion accessory pkg.: 2dr. ($207). Rally package ($43-$93). Rally appearance pkg. ($163). Ghia sports group ($361). Exterior accent group: pinstripes, wide bodyside moldings, dual remote sport mirrors, and whitewalls on styled wheels ($163-$245). Appearance decor group: lower body two-tone, pinstripes, styled wheels, brushed aluminum dash applique ($128-$167). Luxury interior group ($149-$155). Convenience group: interval wipers, vanity and day/night mirrors, and pivoting rear quarter windows on hatchback ($34- $81). Light group ($40-$52). Appearance protection group ($24-$36). Comfort/Convenience: Air cond. ($459). Rear defroster, electric ($77). Tinted glass ($53). Leather-wrapped steering wheel ($34-$49). Digital clock ($43). Lighting and Mirrors: Trunk light ($4). Color-keyed driver's sport mirror ($16). Dual sport mirrors ($49). Day/night mirror ($7). Entertainment: AM radio ($72); w/tape player ($192). AM/FM radio ($120). AM/FM stereo radio ($161); w/8track or cassette tape player ($229). Exterior: TRoof "convertible" option ($587-$629). Full vinyl top open air roof ($167). Full vinyl roof ($99). Front spoiler ($8). Metallic glow paint ($40). Pinstriping ($30). Color-keyed bodyside moldings ($66). Rocker panel moldings ($22). Bumper guards, front and rear ($37). Lower bodyside protection ($30). Interior: Console ($75). Four-way driver's seat ($33). Fold-down rear seat ($90). Willshire cloth trim ($100). Ashton cloth/vinyl trim ($12). Color-keyed deluxe seatbelts ($18). Wheels and Tires: Wire wheel covers ($12-$90). Forged aluminum wheels ($173-$252); white ($187-$265). Lacy spoke aluminum wheels ($173-$252); white ($187-$265). Styled steel wheels ($59-$78). Trim rings ($39). B78 x 13 WSW. BR78 x 13 BSW/WSW. BR70 x 13 RWL. 195/70R13 WSW/wide WSW/RWL.

HISTORY: Introduced: October 7, 1977. Model year production: 192,410. Total production for the U.S. market of 173,423 units included 85,312 four-cylinder, 57,060 V-6, and 31,051 V-8 Mustangs. Calendar year production: 240,162. Calendar year sales by U.S. dealers: 199,760. Model year sales by U.S. dealers: 179,039.

Historical Footnotes: This would be the final year for Mustang II, as an all-new Mustang was planned for 1979. Although plenty of Mustangs were built during the 1974-78 period, Cobra II production was modest. King Cobra, offered only for 1978, is the rarest of the lot.

1979 MUSTANG

1979 Mustang Sport Option coupe (JG)

MUSTANG — FOUR/V-6/SIX/V-8 — All-new sheetmetal created what appeared to be an all-new Mustang for 1979. Its chassis came from Fairmont, though, shortened and modified to hold the new body metal. The familiar curved crease in the bodyside was gone. At a time when most cars were shrinking, the new Mustang managed to gain 4 inches in length—and 20 percent more passenger space. Soft urethane bumpers added to the illusion of length. Weight was down by some 200 pounds, however. The aerodynamic wedge design featured a sloping front and hood, and sculptured roofline. A lowered window line gave Mustang large glass area for improved visibility. As in the prior version, two-door notchback and three-door hatchback bodies were offered, in base and Ghia levels. There was also a Sport package, and a high-performance TRX package. As before, Ford generally referred to the two-door as a sedan, while the third door of the "three-door" was a hatch rather than an entry for people. The new hatchback did not have the sharply-angled fastback shape of the former Mustang. The notchback two-door did look more like a sedan than its predecessor, though enthusiasts still tend to view it as a coupe (especially since a convertible would appear on that body a few years later). Mercury Capri was similar, but offered only in hatchback form. Both bodies had sail-shaped quarter windows that were wider at the base, but the hatchback's were much narrower at the top, almost triangle-shaped.

251

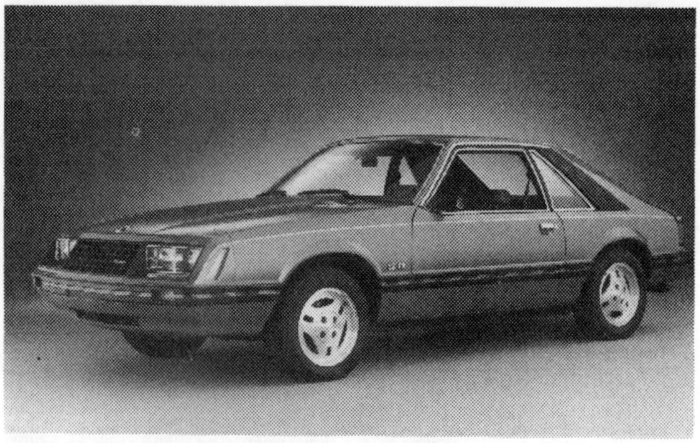

1979 Mustang 5.0L Sport Option coupe (F)

Both models had a set of tall louver-like ribs formed in a tapered panel on the 'C' pillar, angled to match the quarter window's rear edge, but the hatchback had one more of them. Staggered, recessed quad rectangular headlamps replaced the former single round units. The outer units sat a little farther back than the inner pair. The new black crosshatch grille (with 10 x 5 hole pattern) angled forward at the base and no longer held a Mustang badge. It did have 'Ford' lettering at the driver's side. Rectangular amber parking/signal lamps were mounted in the bumper, just below the outboard headlamps. Narrow amber front side marker lenses followed the angle of front fender tips. Well below the front bumper was an air scoop with five holes. On the hood, above the grille, was a round tri-color Mustang emblem. A '2.8' or '5.0' badge on front fenders, at the cowl ahead of the door, denoted a V-6 or V-8 engine under the hood. Taillamps were wider than before, now wrapping around each quarter panel. In addition to the German-built 170 cu. in. (2.8-liter) V-6 and 302 cu. in. (5.0-liter) V-8, both carried over from 1978, there was a new engine option: a turbocharged 140 cu. in. (2.3-liter) four. Base engine remained a non-turbo four. Later in the year, Ford's inline six replaced the V-6 as irst option above the base model. The turbo was also optional in other Mustangs. A V-8 model could have a new four-speed manual overdrive transmission, with "peppy" 3.07:1 first gear and 0.70:1 overdrive. A single (serpentine) belt now drove engine accessories. Mustang's new front suspension used a hydraulic shock strut to replace the conventional upper arm. Rear suspension was a new four-bar link-and-coil system, replacing the old leaf-spring Hotchkiss design. Two handling/suspension options were offered. The basic handling suspension with 14-inch radial tires included different spring rates and shock valving, stiffer bushings in front suspension and upper arm in the rear, and a special rear stabilizer bar. The second level package came with a Michelin TRX tire option, an ultra-low aspect ratio tire (390 MM) introduced on the European Granada. Its 15.35 inch size demanded special metric wheels. That package also included unique shock valving, increased spring rates, and wider front/rear stabilizer bars. All Mustangs had full instruments including tachometer, trip odometer, and gauges for fuel, oil pressure, alternator and temperature. Mustangs also had bucket seats, simulated woodgrain instrument panel applique, and stalk-mounted controls for horn, headlamp dimmer, and wiper/washer. At the chassis, standard equipment included rack-and-pinion steering, manual front disc brakes, and a front stabilizer ar. Also standard: vinyl door trim with carpeted lower panel, squeeze-open lockable glovebox, day/night mirror, lighter, black remote driver's mirror, and full wheel covers. Fastbacks had black rocker panel moldings, full wraparound bodyside moldings with dual accent stripe insert, and semi- styled wheels with black sport hub covers and trim rings. Quite a few options joined the list, including a sport-tuned exhaust, cruise control, tilt steering, leather seat trim, and interval windshield wipers. Ghia Mustangs used many color-keyed components including dual remote-control mirrors, quarter louvers, and bodyside molding inserts. Ghia also had turbine-style wheel covers, BR78 x 14 radial tires, pinstripes, body-color window frames, a 'Ghia' badge on decklid or hatch, low-back bucket seats with European-type headrests, and convenience pockets in color-keyed door panels. Interiors came in six leather colors and five of soft cloth. The costly ($1173) Cobra package included a 2.3-liter turbocharged four, turbo hood scoop with 'Turbo' nameplate, 190/65R x 390 TRX tires on metric forged aluminum wheels, and special suspension. A 302 cu. in. V-8 was available instead of the turbo. Cobras had blacked-out greenhouse trim, black lower bodyside tape treatment, and wraparound bodyside moldings with dual color-keyed inserts. Also included: color- keyed grille and quarter louvers, dual sport mirrors, black bumper rub strips with dual color-keyed inserts, an 8000 R.P.M. tachometer, engine-turned instrument cluster panel, sport-tuned exhaust, and bright tailpipe extension. Rocker panel moldings were deleted. Optional hood graphics cost $78 extra.

I.D. DATA: Mustang's 11-symbol Vehicle Identification Number (VIN) is stamped on a metal tab fastened to the instrument panel, visible through the windshield. The first digit is a model year code ('9' 1979). The second letter indicates assembly plant: 'F' Dearborn, MI; 'R' San Jose, CA. Digits three and four are the body serial code, which corresponds to the Model Numbers shown in the tables below: '02' 2-dr. notchback; '03' 3-dr. hatchback; '04' Ghia 2-dr. notchback; '05' Ghia 3-dr. hatchback. The fifth digit is an engine code: 'Y' L4-140 2Bbl.; 'W' turbo L4140 2Bbl.; 'Z' V6170 2Bbl.; 'T' L6200 (late); 'F' V8302 2Bbl. Finally, digits 6-11 make up the consecutive unit number, starting with 100,001. A Vehicle Certification Label on the left front door lock face panel or door pillar shows the manufacturer, month and year of manufacture, GVW, GAWR, certification statement, VIN, and codes for body type, color, trim, axle, transmission, and special order data.

MUSTANG (FOUR/V-6)

Model Number	Body/Style Number	Body Type & Seating	Factory Price	Shipping Weight	Production Total
02	66B	2-dr. Notch-4P	4071/4344	2431/2511	156,666
03	61R	3-dr. Hatch-4P	4436/4709	2451/2531	120,535

MUSTANG GHIA (FOUR/V-6)

04	66H	2-dr. Notch-4P	4642/4915	2539/2619	56,351
05	61H	3-dr. Hatch-4P	4824/5097	2548/2628	36,384

PRODUCTION NOTE: Approximately 6,000 Indy Pace Car Replicas were built, offered for sale at mid-year.

FACTORY PRICE/WEIGHT NOTE: Figures to left of slash are for four- cylinder engine, to right of slash for V-6 engine. A V-8 engine was priced $241 higher than the V-6.

ENGINE DATA: BASE FOUR: Inline, overhead cam, four-cylinder. Cast iron block and head. Displacement: 140 cu. in. (2.3 liters). Bore & stroke: 3.78 x 3.13 in. Compression ratio: 9.0:1. Brake horsepower: 88 at 4800 R.P.M. Torque: 118 lbs.-ft. at 2800 R.P.M. Five main bearings. Hydraulic valve lifters. Carburetor: 2Bbl. Motorcraft 5200. VIN Code: Y. TURBO FOUR: Same as 140 cu. in. four above, but with turbocharger Brake H.P.: 140 at 4800 R.P.M. Torque: N/A. Carburetor: 2Bbl. Holley 6500. VIN Code: W. OPTIONAL V-6: 60-degree, overhead valve V-6. Cast iron block and head. Displacement: 170.8 cu. in. (2.8 liters). Bore & stroke: 3.66 x 2.70 in. Compression ratio: 8.7:1. Brake horsepower: 109 at 4800 R.P.M. Torque: 142 lbs.-ft. at 2800 R.P.M. Four main bearings. Solid valve lifters. Carburetor: 2Bbl. Ford 2150 or Motorcraft 2700VV. German-built. VIN Code: Z. NOTE: A 200 cu. in. inline six became optional late in the model year; see 1980 listing for specifications. OPTIONAL V 8: 90-degree, overhead valve V-8. Cast iron block and head. Displacement: 302 cu. in. (5.0 liters). Bore & stroke: 4.00 x 3.00 in. Compression ratio: 8.4:1. Brake horsepower: 140 at 3600 R.P.M. Torque: 250 lbs.-ft. at 1800 R.P.M. Five main bearings. Hydraulic valve lifters. Carburetor: 2Bbl. Motorcraft 2150. VIN Code: F.

CHASSIS DATA: Wheelbase: 100.4 in. Overall length: 179.1 in. Height: 51.8 in. Width: 69.1 in. Front Tread: 56.6 in. Rear Tread: 57.0 in. Standard Tires: B78 x 13 BSW exc. (Ghia) BR78 x 14 SBR BSW.

TECHNICAL: Transmission: Four-speed manual (floor shift) standard on four-cylinder. Gear ratios: (1st) 3.98:1; (2nd) 2.14:1; (3rd) 1.42:1; (4th) 1.00:1; (Rev) 3.99:1. Turbo four-speed: (1st) 4.07:1; (2nd) 2.57:1; (3rd) 1.66:1; (4th) 1.00:1; (Rev) 3.95:1. Four-speed overdrive manual transmission standard on V-8. Gear ratios: (1st) 3.07:1; (2nd) 1.72:1; (3rd) 1.00:1; (4th) 0.70:1; (Rev) 3.07:1. Select-Shift three-speed automatic optional. Four-cylinder: (1st) 2.47:1; (2nd) 1.47:1; (3rd) 1.00:1; (Rev) 2.11:1. V-6/V-8 automatic: (1st) 2.46:1; (2nd) 1.46:1; (3rd) 1.00:1; (Rev) 2.18:1 or 2.19:1. Standard final drive ratio: 3.08:1 except 3.45:1 w/turbo, 2.47:1 w/V-8 and auto. (early models differed). Steering: Rack and pinion. Front Suspension: Modified MacPherson hydraulic shock struts with coil springs and stabilizer bar. Rear Suspension: Four-bar link and coil spring system; anti- sway bar with V-8. Brakes: Front disc, rear drum. Disc dia.: 9.3 in. (10.4 in. w/V-8). Rear drum dia.: 9 in. Ignition: Electronic. Body construction: unibody w/front isolated mini-frame. Fuel tank: 11.5 gal. exc. with V-6/V-8 engine, 12.5 gal.

DRIVETRAIN OPTIONS: Engine/Transmission: Turbo 140 cu. in. four ($542). 170 cu. in. V-6 ($273). 302 cu. in. V-8 ($514). Sport-tuned exhaust ($34). Automatic trans. ($307). Brakes & Steering: Power brakes ($70). Variable-ratio power steering ($141). Other: Handling suspension ($33). Engine block heater ($13). H.D. battery ($18). California emission system ($76). High- altitude emissions ($33).

CONVENIENCE/APPEARANCE OPTIONS: Option Packages: Cobra pkg. ($1173). Cobra hood graphics ($78). Sport option ($175). Exterior accent group ($72). Interior accent group ($108-$120). Light group ($25-$37). Protection group ($33-$36). Power lock group ($99). Comfort/Convenience: Air cond. ($484). Rear defroster, electric ($84). Fingertip speed control ($104-$116). Tinted glass ($59); windshield only ($25). Leather-wrapped steering wheel ($41-$53). Tilt steering wheel ($69-$81). Interval wipers ($35). Rear wiper/washer ($63). Lighting and Mirrors: Trunk light ($5). Driver's remote mirror ($18). Dual remote mirrors ($52). Entertainment: AM radio ($72); w/digital clock ($119); w/tape player ($192). AM/FM radio ($120). AM/FM stereo radio ($176); w/8track or cassette tape player ($243). Premium sound system ($67). Dual rear speakers ($42). Radio flexibility option ($90). Exterior: Flip-up open air roof ($199). Full vinyl roof ($102). Metallic glow paint ($41). Lower two-tone paint ($78). Bodyside/decklid pinstripes ($30). Wide bodyside moldings ($66). Narrow vinyl-insert bodyside moldings ($39). Rocker panel moldings ($24). Mud/stone deflectors ($23). Lower bodyside protection ($30). Interior: Console ($140). Four-way driver's seat ($35). Cloth seat trim ($20). Ghia cloth seat trim ($42). Accent cloth seat trim ($29). Leather seat trim ($282). Front floor mats ($18). Color-keyed deluxe seatbelts ($20). Wheels and Tires: Wire wheel covers ($60-$99). Turbine wheel covers ($10-$39). Forged metric aluminum wheels ($259-$298). Cast aluminum wheels ($251-$289). Styled steel wheels w/trim rings ($55-$94). B78 x 13 WSW ($43). C78 x 13 BSW ($25); WSW ($69). B78 x 14 WSW ($66). C78 x 14 BSW ($48). BR78 x 14 BSW ($124); WSW ($43-$167). CR78 x 14 WSW ($69-$192); RWL ($86- $209). TRX 190/65R 390 Michelin BSW ($117-$241). Tire Note: Lower prices are for Mustang Ghia.

HISTORY: Introduced: October 6, 1978. Model year production: 369,936. Total production for the U.S. market of 332,024 units included 181,066 four-cylinder (29,242 with turbocharger), 103,390 sixes, and 47,568 V-8 Mustangs. Calendar year production: 365,357. Calendar year sales by U.S. dealers: 304,053. Model year sales by U.S. dealers: 302,309.

Historical Footnotes: If the second-generation Mustang had lacked some of the pizazz of the original pony car, the "new breed" third- generation edition offered a chance to boost the car's image. The optional turbocharged 2.3-liter four was said to offer "V-8 performance without sacrificing fuel economy." In Ford tests, the Mustang turbo went 0-55 MPH in just over 8 seconds (a little quicker than a V-8). Gas mileage reached well into the 20s. A V-8 version was named pace car for the Indy 500, prompting the production of a Pace Car Replica later in the year. Ready for the 1980s, Mustang now offered a pleasing blend of American and European design. Of many styling proposals, the final one came from a team led by Jack Telnack of the Light Truck and Car Design Group. Plastic and aluminum components helped cut down the car's weight, and it was considerably roomier inside than the former Mustang II. Drag oefficient of 0.44 (for the fastback) was the best Ford had ever achieved. Customers must have liked the new version, as Mustang leaped from No. 22 to No. 7 in the sales race.

1980 MUSTANG

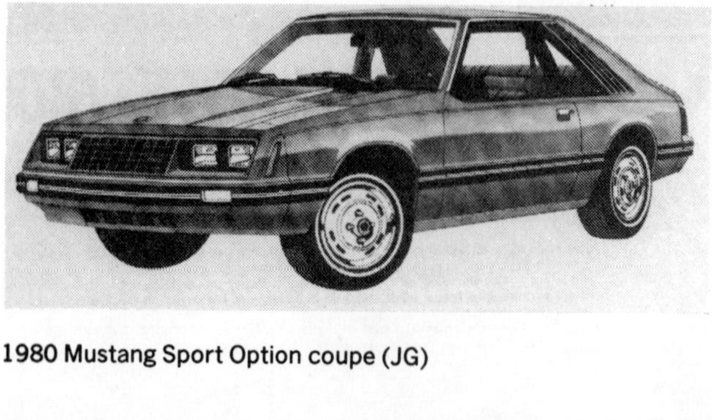

1980 Mustang Sport Option coupe (JG)

MUSTANG — FOUR/SIX/V-8 — Appearance of the modern, resized Mustang changed little in its second season, except for a new front/rear look on the sporty Cobra model. Two-door notchbacks also had an aerodynamic revision to their decklids. Mustang's taillamps consisted of five sections on each side, plus a backup lens section inboard (toward the license plate). A larger section at the outside wrapped around onto each quarter panel. Decklids held 'Ford' and 'Mustang' lettering. Bodyside moldings stretched all the way around the car, meeting bumper strips. Body striping came down ahead of the front marker lenses. Four-cylinder models had no fender identifier; others were marked with a liter figure. Base and Ghia models were offered again, in notchback or hatchback form. Base notchbacks had black bumper rub strips; hatchback bumpers had dual argent stripe inserts. Hatchbacks also had full wraparound, wide black bodyside moldings with dual argent inserts. Both models carried high-back vinyl bucket seats. Notchback rear pillar louvers were color-keyed, while the hatchback's were black. Ghia added low-back bucket seats with Euro-style headrests, a roof assist handle, color- keyed window frames, dual remote mirrors, pinstriping, 14 inch tires, turbine wheel covers, and Ghia insignia on decklid or hatch. Available again was the Cobra option, raised in price to $1482. Cobra's slat-style three-hole grille, hood scoop (with simulated rear opening), front air dam (with built-in foglamps) and rear spoiler were restyled with the '79 Indy Pace Car replica in mind. Cobra's tape treatment was also revised, and it carried the TRX suspension. Features included black lower Tu-Tone treatment, special bodyside and quarter window taping, dual black sport mirrors, sport-tuned exhaust with bright tailpipe extension, black bumper rub strips, 190/65R x 390 TRX tires on forged metric aluminum wheels, engine-turned instrument cluster panel with Cobra medallion, bodyside molding with dual color-keyed accent stripes, 8000 R.P.M. tach. and the turbo engine. 'Cobra' lettering went on quarter windows. A 255 cu. in. (4.-liter) V-8 replaced the former 302, but engines were otherwise the same as before. The 200 cu. in. (3.3-liter) inline six had replaced the former V-6 as a powerplant option during 1979. Both the non-turbocharged 2.3-liter four and inline six could have a four-speed manual gearbox (overdrive fourth with the six), while all engines could have automatic. All models now had high-pressure Pmetric radial tires and halogen headlamps. Maintenance-free batteries were standard, and radios added a Travelers' Advisory Band. Semi-metallic front disc brake pads were included with optional engines. Two suspension options were available: The standard package and a modified "Special Suspension System" that included Michelin TRX tires on special forged aluminum wheels. A new Carriage Roof option for the notchback model was supposed to resemble a convertible, even though the car had a solid 'B' pillar. It used diamond-grain vinyl. Other new options included a root luggage rack, cargo area cover (hatchback), liftback window louvers, and Recaro adjustable seatback bucket seats with improved thigh support. Inside door handles were relocated to the upper door.

I.D. DATA: As before, Mustang's 11-symbol Vehicle Identification Number (VIN) is stamped on a metal tab fastened to the instrument panel, visible through the windshield. Engine codes changed this year. The first digit is a model year code ('0' 1980). The second letter indicates assembly plant: 'F' Dearborn, MI; 'R' San Jose, CA. Digits three and four are the body serial code, which corresponds to the Model Numbers shown in the tables below: '02' 2-dr. notchback; '03' 3- dr. hatchback; '04' Ghia 2-dr. notchback; '05' Ghia 3-dr. hatchback. The fifth digit is an engine code: 'A' L4-140 2Bbl.; 'A' turbo L4140 2Bbl.; 'T' L6200 1Bbl.; 'D' V8255 2Bbl. Finally, digits 6-11 make up the consecutive unit number, starting with 100,001. A Vehicle Certification Label on the left front door lock face panel or door pillar shows the manufacturer, month and year of manufacture, GVW, GAWR, certification statement, VIN, and codes for body type and color, trim, axle, transmission, and special order information.

MUSTANG (FOUR/SIX)

Model Number	Body/Style Number	Body Type & Seating	Factory Price	Shipping Weight	Production Total
02	66B	2-dr. Notch-4P	4884/5103	2497/2532	128,893
03	61R	3-dr. Spt Hatch-4P	5194/5413	2531/2566	98,497

MUSTANG GHIA (FOUR/SIX)

04	66H	2-dr. Notch-4P	5369/5588	2565/2600	23,647
05	61H	3-dr. Hatch-4P	5512/5731	2588/2623	20,285

FACTORY PRICE/WEIGHT NOTE: Figures to left of slash are for four- cylinder engine, to right of slash for six-cylinder. A V-8 engine cost $119 more than the six.

ENGINE DATA: BASE FOUR: Inline, overhead cam, four-cylinder. Cast iron block and head. Displacement: 140 cu. in. (2.3 liters). Bore & stroke: 3.78 x 3.13 in. Compression ratio: 9.0:1. Brake horsepower: 88 at 4600 R.P.M. Torque: 119 lbs.-ft. at 2600 R.P.M. Five main bearings. Hydraulic valve lifters. Carburetor: 2Bbl. Motorcraft 5200. VIN Code: A. TURBO FOUR: Same as 140 cu. in. four above, but with turbocharger Brake H.P.: 150 at 4800 R.P.M. Torque: N/A. Carburetor: 2Bbl. Holley 6500. OPTIONAL SIX: Inline, overhead valve six-cylinder. Cast iron block and head. Displacement: 200 cu. in. (3.3 liters). Bore & stroke: 3.68 x 3.13 in. Compression ratio: 8.6:1. Brake horsepower: N/A. Torque: N/A. Seven main bearings. Hydraulic valve lifters. Carburetor: 2Bbl. Holley 1946. VIN Code: T. OPTIONAL V-8: 90-degree, overhead valve V-8. Cast iron block and head. Displacement: 255 cu. in. (4.2 liters). Bore & stroke: 3.68 x 3.00 in. Compression ratio: 8.8:1. Brake horsepower: 119 at 3800 R.P.M. Torque: 194 lbs.-ft. at 2200 R.P.M. Five main bearings. Hydraulic valve lifters. Carburetor: 2Bbl. Motorcraft 2150. VIN Code: D.

CHASSIS DATA: Wheelbase: 100.4 in. Overall length: 179.1 in. Height: 51.4 in. Width: 69.1 in. Front Tread: 56.6 in. Rear Tread: 57.0 in. Standard Tires: P185/80R13 BSW exc. (Ghia) P175/75R14.

TECHNICAL: Transmission: Four-speed manual (floor shift) standard on four-cylinder. Gear ratios: (1st) 3.98:1; (2nd) 2.14:1; (3rd) 1.42:1; (4th) 1.00:1; (Rev) 3.99:1. Turbo four-speed: (1st) 4.07:1; (2nd) 2.57:1; (3rd) 1.66:1; (4th) 1.00:1; (Rev) 3.95:1. Four-speed overdrive manual transmission standard on six. Gear ratios: (1st) 3.29:1; (2nd) 1.84:1; (3rd) 1.00:1; (4th) 0.81:1; (Rev) 3.29:1. Select-Shift three-speed automatic optional. Four-cylinder: (1st) 2.47:1; (2nd) 1.47:1; (3rd) 1.00:1; (Rev) 2.11:1. Turbo/six/V-8 automatic: (1st) 2.46:1; (2nd) 1.46:1; (3rd) 1.00:1; (Rev) 2.19:1. Standard final drive ratio: 3.08:1 w/four, 2.26:1 w/V-8 and auto., 3.45:1 w/turbo. Steering: Rack and pinion. Front Suspension: Modified MacPherson hydraulic shock struts with coil springs and stabilizer bar. Rear Suspension: Four-bar link and coil spring system. Brakes: Front disc, rear drum. Ignition: Electronic. Body construction: Unibody w/front isolated mini-frame. Fuel tank: 11.5 gal. exc. w/V-8 engine, 12.5 gal.

DRIVETRAIN OPTIONS: Engine/Transmission: Turbo 140 cu. in. four ($481). 200 cu. in. six ($219). 255 cu. in. V-8 ($338) exc. w/Cobra pkg. ($144 credit). Sport-tuned exhaust: V-8 ($38). Select-shift automatic trans. ($340). Optional axle ratio ($18). Brakes & Steering: Power brakes ($78). Power steering ($160). Other: Handling suspension ($35). Engine block heater ($15). H.D. battery ($20). California emission system ($253). High- altitude emissions ($36).

CONVENIENCE/APPEARANCE OPTIONS: Option Packages: Cobra pkg. ($1482). Cobra hood graphics ($88). Sport option: black rocker/belt moldings and door/window frames, full wraparound bodyside molding with dual argent stripe insert, sport wheel trim rings and steering wheel ($168-$186). Exterior accent group ($63). Interior accent group ($120-$134). Light group ($41). Appearance protection group ($38-$41). Power lock group ($113). Comfort/Convenience: Air cond. ($583). Rear defroster, electric ($96). Fingertip speed control ($116-$129). Tinted glass ($65); windshield only ($29). Leather-wrapped steering wheel ($44-$56). Tilt steering wheel ($78-$90). Interval wipers ($39). Rear wiper/washer ($79). Lighting and Mirrors: Trunk light ($5). Driver's remote mirror ($19). Dual remote mirrors ($58). Entertainment: AM radio ($93). AM/FM radio ($145). AM/FM stereo radio ($183); w/8track tape player ($259); w/cassette player ($271). Premium sound system ($94). Dual rear speakers ($38). Radio flexibility option ($63). Exterior: Flip-up open air roof ($204-$219). Carriage roof ($625). Full vinyl roof ($118). Metallic glow paint ($46). Lower two-tone paint ($88). Bodyside/decklid pinstripes ($34). Accent tape stripes ($19-$53). Hood scoop ($31). Liftgate louvers ($141). Narrow vinyl-insert bodyside moldings ($43); wide ($74). Rocker panel moldings ($30). Roof luggage rack ($86). Mud/stone deflectors ($25). Lower bodyside protection ($34). Interior: Console ($166). Four-way driver's seat ($38). Recaro high-back bucket seats ($531). Cloth/vinyl bucket seats ($21-$46). Vinyl low-back bucket seats (NC). Accent cloth/vinyl seat trim ($30). Leather low-back bucket seats ($345). Cargo area cover ($44). Front floor mats ($19). Color-keyed seatbelts ($23). Wheels and Tires: Wire wheel covers ($79-$121). Turbine wheel covers ($10-$43). Forged metric aluminum wheels ($313-$355). Cast aluminum wheels ($279-$321). Styled steel wheels w/trim rings ($61-$104). P185/80R13 WSW ($50). P175/75R14 BSW ($25); WSW ($50-$75). P185/75R14 BSW ($25-$49); WSW ($75-$100); RWL ($92-$117). TRX 190/65 x 390 BSW ($125-$250).

HISTORY: Introduced: October 12, 1979. Model year production: 271,322. Total production for the U.S. market of 241,064 units included 162,959 four-cylinder (12,052 with turbocharger), 71,597 sixes, and 6,508 V-8 Mustangs. Calendar year production: 232,517. Calendar year sales by U.S. dealers: 225,290. Model year sales by U.S. dealers: 246,008.

Historical Footnotes: Mustang's base 2.3-liter four-cylinder engine was said to deliver an ample boost in gas mileage this year. Short supplies of the German-made V-6 had prompted Ford to switch to the familiar inline six during the 1979 model year. After a whopping sales increase for 1979, Mustang slackened this year. Still, most observers felt the new model showed a vast improvement over the Mustang II and would give Ford another strong hold on the ponycar market.

1981 MUSTANG

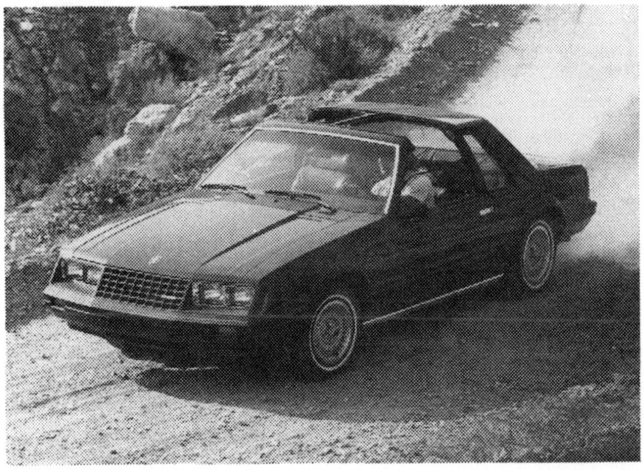

1981 Mustang T-top coupe (F)

MUSTANG — FOUR/SIX/V-8 — For Mustang's third season in this form, little change was evident. A variety of manual transmission ratios was offered, both four-speed and new five-speed. First offered only on four-cylinder models (standard or turbocharged), the five-speed cost an extra $152. Its fifth gear was an overdrive ratio, but the lower four did not offer close-ratio gearing. Some critics found fault with the five-speed's shift pattern, which put fifth gear right next to fourth. The standard 140 cu. in. (2.3-liter) four-cylinder overhead-camshaft engine was rated at 23 MPG city (34 highway) with four-speed manual gearbox. Two other engines (inline six and 255 cu. in. V-8) were optional, along with a total of seven transmissions. Turbocharged models no longer came with automatic shift. For identification, both 'Ford' and 'Mustang' block lettering stood on the hatch or decklid. As usual, Ford tended to describe the notchback two-door model as a "sedan," though most observers call it a coupe. Joining the option list was a TRoof with twin removable tinted glass panels, offered on either the two-door notchback or three-door hatchback. Other new options included reclining bucket seats (either high- or low-back), power windows, and remote right convex mirror. An optional console included a graphic display module that contained a digital clock with elapsed time, and warned of low fuel or washer level as well as inoperative lights. Mustangs could also get a Traction-Lok rear axle. Ghia was a separate model again, while Cobra was a $1588 option package. Cobra equipment was similar to 1979-80, including 190/65R x 390 TRX tires on forged metric aluminum wheel, an 8000 R.P.M. tachometer, lower two-tone paint, 'Cobra' tape treatment, hood scoop, sport-tuned exhaust, dual black sport mirrors, black bumper rub strips, bodyside moldings with dual accent stripes, and black greenhouse moldings. Cobra had a built-in front spoiler, black quarter- window louvers, Cobra medallion on dash and door trim, and a handling suspension. A V-8 engine could replace the standard turbo four, for a $346 credit. Taping could be deleted from the Cobra package, if desired, knocking $65 off the price; but the bold hood decal cost $85 extra. Offered

late in 1980 was the limited-production, much- modified McLaren Mustang, similar in appearance to the IMSA show car. McLaren had no grille, a low (and large) front spoiler, working hood scoops, prominent fender flares, and Firestone HPR radial tires on BBS alloy wheels. The variable- boost turbo engine produced 175 horsepower. A total of 250 McLarens were built, priced at $25,000.

I.D. DATA: Like other Ford products, Mustang had a new 17-symbol Vehicle Identification Number (VIN), again stamped on a metal tab fastened to the instrument panel, visible through the windshield. The first three symbols specify manufacturer, make and vehicle type: '1FA' Ford passenger car. Symbol four ('B') denotes restraint system. Next comes a letter 'P', followed by two digits that indicate body type: '10' 2-dr. notchback; '15' 3-dr. hatchback; '12' Ghia 2-dr. notchback; '13' Ghia 3-dr. hatchback. Symbol eight indicates engine type: 'A' L4-140 2Bbl.; 'A' turbo L4140 2Bbl.; 'T' L6200 1Bbl.; 'D' V8255 2Bbl. Next is a check digit. Symbol ten indicates model year ('B' 1981). Symbol eleven is assembly plant: 'F' Dearborn, MI; 'R' San Jose, CA. The final six digits make up the sequence number, starting with 100001. A Vehicle Certification Label on the left front door lock face panel or door pillar shows the month and year of manufacture, GVW, GAWR, VIN, and codes for body type and color, trim, axle, transmission, accessories, and special order information.

MUSTANG (FOUR/SIX)

Model Number	Body/Style Number	Body Type & Seating	Factory Price	Shipping Weight	Production Total
10	66B	2-dr. Notch-4P	6171/6384	2524/2551	77,458
15	61R	3-dr. Spt Hatch-4P	6408/6621	2544/2571	77,399

MUSTANG GHIA (FOUR/SIX)

12	66H	2-dr. Notch-4P	6645/6858	2558/2585	13,422
13	61H	3-dr. Hatch-4P	6729/6942	2593/2620	14,273

FACTORY PRICE/WEIGHT NOTE: Figures to left of slash are for four- cylinder engine, to right of slash for six-cylinder engine. A V-8 engine was priced $50 higher than the six.

ENGINE DATA: BASE FOUR: Inline, overhead cam, four-cylinder. Cast iron block and head. Displacement: 140 cu. in. (2.3 liters). Bore & stroke: 3.78 x 3.13 in. Compression ratio: 9.0:1. Brake horsepower: 88 at 4600 R.P.M. Torque: 118 lbs.-ft. at 2600 R.P.M. Five main bearings. Hydraulic valve lifters. Carburetor: 2Bbl. Motorcraft 5200 or Holley 6500. VIN Code: A. TURBO FOUR: Same as 140 cu. in. four above, but with turbocharger Brake H.P.: N/A. Torque: N/A. OPTIONAL SIX: Inline, overhead valve six-cylinder. Cast iron block and head. Displacement: 200 cu. in. (3.3 liters). Bore & stroke: 3.68 x 3.13 in. Compression ratio: 8.6:1. Brake horsepower: 94 at 4000 R.P.M. Torque: 158 lbs.-ft. at 1400 R.P.M. Seven main bearings. Hydraulic valve lifters. Carburetor: 2Bbl. Holley 1946. VIN Code: T. OPTIONAL V-8: 90-degree, overhead valve V-8. Cast iron block and head. Displacement: 255 cu. in. (4.2 liters). Bore & stroke: 3.68 x 3.00 in. Compression ratio: 8.2:1. Brake horsepower: 115 at 3400 R.P.M. Torque: 195 lbs.-ft. at 2200 R.P.M. Five main bearings. Hydraulic valve lifters. Carburetor: 2Bbl. Motorcraft 7200VV or 2150. VIN Code: D.

CHASSIS DATA: same as 1980.

TECHNICAL: Transmission: Four-speed manual (floor shift) standard on four-cylinder. Gear ratios: (1st) 3.98:1; (2nd) 2.14:1; (3rd) 1.42:1; (4th) 1.00:1; (Rev) 3.99:1. Turbo four-speed: (1st) 4.07:1; (2nd) 2.57:1; (3rd) 1.66:1; (4th) 1.00:1; (Rev) 3.95:1. Four-speed overdrive manual transmission standard on six. Gear ratios: (1st) 3.29:1; (2nd) 1.84:1; (3rd) 1.00:1; (4th) 0.81:1; (Rev) 3.29:1. Other models: (1st) 3.98:1; (2nd) 2.14:1; (3rd) 1.42:1; (4th) 1.00:1; (Rev) 3.99:1. Five-speed manual overdrive optional: (1st) 4.05:1; (2nd) 2.43:1; (3rd) 1.48:1; (4th) 1.00:1; (5th) 0.82:1; (Rev) 3.90:1. Turbo five- speed: (1st) 3.72:1; (2nd) 2.23:1; (3rd) 1.48:1; (4th) 1.00:1; (5th) 0.76:1; (Rev) 3.59:1. Select-Shift three-speed automatic optional: (1st) 2.46:1 or 2.47:1; (2nd) 1.46:1 or 1.47:1; (3rd) 1.00:1; (Rev) 2.11:1 or 2.19:1. Standard final drive ratio: (four) 3.08:1 exc. 3.45:1 w/5spd; (six) 3.45:1 w/4spd, 2.73:1 w/auto.; (V-8) 2.26:1. Steering: Rack and pinion. Front Suspension: Modified MacPherson struts with lower control arms, coil springs and stabilizer bar. Rear Suspension: Four-bar link and coil spring system with lower trailing arms and transverse linkage bar. Brakes: Front disc, rear drum. Ignition: Electronic. Body construction: Unibody. Fuel tank: 12.5 gal.

DRIVETRAIN OPTIONS: Engine/Transmission: Turbo 140 cu. in. four ($610). 200 cu. in. six ($213). 255 cu. in. V-8 ($263) exc. w/Cobra pkg. ($346 credit). Sport-tuned exhaust: V-8 ($39); w/turbo and auto. (NC). Five-speed manual trans. ($152). Select-shift automatic trans. ($349). Traction-Lok differential ($63). Optional axle ratio ($20). Brakes & Steering: Power brakes ($76). Power steering ($163). Other: Handling suspension ($43). Engine block heater ($16). H.D. battery ($20). California emission system ($46). High- altitude emissions ($38).

CONVENIENCE/APPEARANCE OPTIONS: Option Packages: Cobra pkg. ($1588); tape delete ($65 credit). Cobra hood graphics ($90). Sport option ($52-$72). Interior accent group ($126-$139). Light group ($43). Appearance protection group ($41). Power lock group ($93- $120). Comfort/Convenience: Air cond. ($560). Rear defroster, electric ($107). Fingertip speed control ($132). Power windows ($140). Tinted glass ($76); windshield only ($29). Leather-wrapped steering wheel ($49-$61). Tilt steering wheel ($80-$93). Interval wipers ($41). Rear wiper/washer ($85). Lighting and Mirrors: Trunk light ($6). Driver's remote mirror ($20). Dual remote mirrors ($56). Entertainment: AM/FM radio ($51). AM/FM stereo radio ($88); w/8track tape player ($162); w/cassette player ($174). Premium sound system ($91). Dual rear speakers ($37). Radio flexibility option ($61). AM radio delete ($61 credit). Exterior: TRoof ($874). Flip-up open air roof ($213-$228). Carriage roof ($644). Full vinyl roof ($115). Metallic glow paint ($48). Two-tone paint ($121-$155). Lower two-tone paint ($90). Pinstriping ($34). Accent tape stripes ($54). Hood scoop ($32). Liftgate louvers ($145). Rocker panel moldings ($30). Roof luggage rack ($90). Mud/stone deflectors ($26). Lower bodyside protection ($37). Interior: Console ($168). Recaro high-back bucket seats ($732). Cloth/vinyl bucket seats ($22-$48). Accent cloth/vinyl seat trim ($30). Leather low-back bucket seats ($359). Cargo area cover: hatch ($45). Front floor mats ($18- $20). Color-keyed seatbelts ($23). Wheels and Tires: Wire wheel covers ($77-$118). Turbine wheel covers ($10-$41). Forged metric aluminum wheels ($340). Cast aluminum wheels ($305). Styled steel wheels w/trim rings ($60-$101). P185/80R13 WSW ($49). P175/75R14 BSW ($24); WSW ($49-$73). P185/75R14 BSW ($24-$49); WSW ($73-$97); RWL ($90- $114). TRX 190/65R x 390 BSW ($122-$146).

HISTORY: Introduced: October 3, 1980. Model year production: 182,552. Total production for the U.S. market of 162,593 Mustangs included 101,860 four-cylinder, 55,406 sixes, and only 5,327 V-8 engines. Calendar year production: 153,719. Calendar year sales by U.S. dealers: 154,985. Model year sales by U.S. dealers: 173,329.

Historical Footnotes: Mustang prices rose sharply this year, as did those of other Ford products. The new TRoof met all federal body structure regulations, as a result of body modifications that included the use of H-shaped reinforcements. Both production and sales slipped considerably, but this was a weak period for the industry as a whole. Ford's Special Vehicle Operations department started up in September 1980, headed by Michael Kranefuss. Its goal: limited production performance cars and motorsport activities. Several racing Mustangs got factory assistance, including a turbo model driven in IMSA GT events and a TransAm model. A turbo-powered IMSA "concept car" with big Pirelli tires and huge fender flares toured the auto show circuit.

1982 MUSTANG

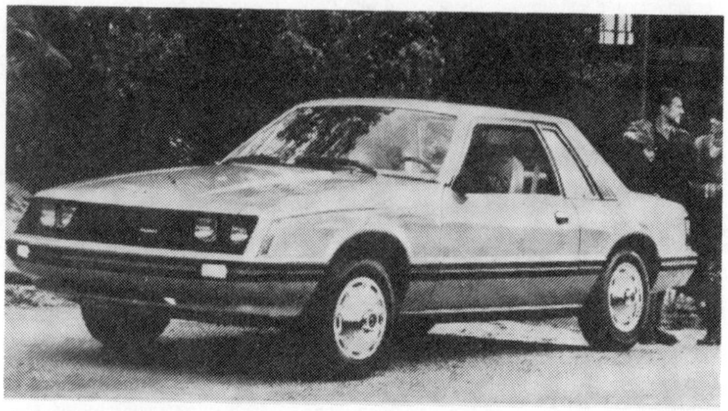

1982 Mustang 5.0L Sport Option coupe (JG)

MUSTANG — FOUR/SIX/V-8 — "The Boss is Back!" declared Ford ads. Biggest news of the year was indeed the return of the 302 cu. in. (5.0-liter) V-8, coupled with the temporary disappearance of the turbo four. Performance-oriented Mustangs could have a high-output 302 with four-speed manual overdrive transmission, a combination that had last been offered in 1979. This year's 302 V-8 had a bigger (356 CFM) two-barrel carburetor, larger- diameter (freer-flowing) exhaust system, and low-restriction air cleaner with dual inlets. That setup delivered considerably faster acceleration than the '79 version, able to hit 60 MPH in less than 8 seconds. Base engine was the 140 cu. in. (2.3-liter) four; also optional, a 255 cu. in. (4.2- liter) V-8, and 200 cu. in. inline six. A lockup torque converter (all three gears) was included on automatics with the inline six or small V-8 engine. A high-altitude emissions system was available with all engines. Appearance changed little for 1981, but model designations were revised. The new lineup included an L, GL, and GLX, as well as a GT that replaced the former Cobra option. Mustang L was the new base model, with full wheel covers, full wraparound bodyside moldings, and an AM radio. New standard equipment included seatbelts with tension relievers, a remote-control left-hand mirror, new flash-to- pass headlamp feature, and new screw-on gas cap tethered to the filler neck. There was also a switch to 14inch wheels with Pmetric (P175/75R14) steel-belted radial tires. Four- cylinder Mustangs with air conditioning had an electro-drive cooling fan. Radios had dual front speakers plus wiring for two more. Mustang's GT (first designated an SS) added P185/75R14 blackwall steel-belted radials on cast aluminum wheels, a handling suspension, dual black remote mirrors, and built-in foglamps. Styling features included body-colored front fascia with integral spoiler and air dam, three-slot grille, color- keyed rear spoiler, and body-color cowl grille. 'GT' identification went on the liftgate. Body-color headlamp frames replaced the black doors on other models. Black bodyside moldings had a black plastic insert and aluminum end caps. Equipment included a Traction-Lok differential, power brakes and steering, and a console with digital clock and diagnostic warning module. Blackout treatment continued on interior components. An optional TR performance package could enhance the handling qualities of all Mustang models. It included Michelin TRX tires on forged metric aluminum wheels, and a handling suspension with rear stabilizer bar.

I.D. DATA: Mustang's 17-symbol Vehicle Identification Number (VIN), stamped on a metal tab fastened to the instrument panel, is visible through the windshield. The first three symbols specify manufacturer, make and vehicle type: '1FA' Ford passenger car. Symbol four ('B') denotes restraint system. Next comes a letter 'P', followed by two digits that indicate body type: '10' 2-dr. notchback sedan; '16' 3-dr. hatchback; '12' GLX 2-dr. notchback; '13' GLX 3-dr. hatchback. Symbol eight indicates engine type: 'A' L4-140 2Bbl.; 'B' L6200 1Bbl.; 'D' V8255 2Bbl.; 'F' V8302 2Bbl. Next is a check digit. Symbol ten indicates model year ('C' 1982). Symbol eleven is assembly plant: 'F' Dearborn, MI. The final six digits make up the sequence number, starting with 100001. A Vehicle Certification Label on the left front door lock face panel or door pillar shows the month and year of manufacture, VIN, and codes for body type and color, trim, axle ratio, transmission, and special order information.

MUSTANG (FOUR/SIX)

Model Number	Body/Style Number	Body Type & Seating	Factory Price	Shipping Weight	Production Total
10	N/A	2-dr. L Notch-4P	6345/7062	2511/2635	Note 1
10	66B	2-dr. GL Notch-4P	6844/7468	2528/2652	45,316
16	61B	3-dr. GL Hatch-4P	6979/7390	2565/2689	69,348
12	66H	2-dr. GLX Notch-4P	6980/7604	2543/2667	5,828
13	61H	3-dr. GLX Hatch-4P	7101/7725	2579/2703	9,926

MUSTANG GT (V-8)

16	N/A	3-dr. Hatch-4P	-- /8308	-- /2629	Note 2

Note 1: Production of L model is included in GL total. Note 2: Ford figures include GT production in GL hatchback total above. Other industry sources report a total of 23,447 GT models produced.

FACTORY PRICE/WEIGHT NOTE: Figures to left of slash are for four- cylinder engine, to right of slash for six-cylinder. (The higher amount includes the cost of an automatic transmission.) A 255 cu. in. V-8 engine was priced $70 higher than the six; a 302 V-8 was $189 higher.

ENGINE DATA: BASE FOUR: Inline, overhead cam, four-cylinder. Cast iron block and head. Displacement: 140 cu. in. (2.3 liters). Bore & stroke: 3.78 x 3.13 in. Compression ratio: 9.0:1. Brake horsepower: 86 at 4600 R.P.M. Torque: 117 lbs.-ft. at 2600 R.P.M. Five main bearings. Hydraulic valve lifters. Carburetor: 2Bbl. Motorcraft 5200 or Holley 6500. VIN Code: A. OPTIONAL SIX: Inline, overhead valve six-cylinder. Cast iron block and head. Displacement: 200 cu. in. (3.3 liters). Bore & stroke: 3.68 x 3.13 in. Compression ratio: 8.6:1. Brake horsepower: 87 at 3800 R.P.M. Torque: 154 lbs.-ft. at 1400 R.P.M. Seven main bearings. Hydraulic valve lifters. Carburetor: 2Bbl. Holley 1946. VIN Code: B. OPTIONAL V-8: 90-degree, overhead valve V-8. Cast iron block and head. Displacement: 255 cu. in. (4.2 liters). Bore & stroke: 3.68 x 3.00 in. Compression ratio: 8.2:1. Brake horsepower: 120 at 3400 R.P.M. Torque: 205 lbs.-ft. at 1600 R.P.M. Five main bearings. Hydraulic valve lifters. Carburetor: 2Bbl. Motorcraft 2150 or 7200VV. VIN Code: D. OPTIONAL HIGH-OUTPUT V-8: 90-degree, overhead valve V-8. Cast iron block and head. Displacement: 302 cu. in. (5.0 liters). Bore & stroke: 4.00 x 3.00 in. Compression ratio: 8.3:1. Brake horsepower: 157 at 4200 R.P.M. Torque: 240 lbs.-ft. at 2400 R.P.M. Five main bearings. Hydraulic valve lifters. Carburetor: 2Bbl. Motorcraft 2150A. VIN Code: F.

CHASSIS DATA: Wheelbase: 100.4 in. Overall length: 179.1 in. Height: 51.4 in. Width: 69.1 in. Front Tread: 56.6 in. Rear Tread: 57.0 in. Standard Tires: P175/75R14 BSW exc. GT, P185/75R14.

TECHNICAL: Transmission: Four-speed manual (floor shift) standard on four-cylinder. Gear ratios: (1st) 3.98:1; (2nd) 2.14:1; (3rd) 1.49:1; (4th) 1.00:1; (Rev) 3.99:1. Four-speed overdrive manual transmission standard on V-8. Gear ratios: (1st) 3.07:1; (2nd) 1.72:1; (3rd) 1.00:1; (4th) 0.70:1; (Rev) 3.07:1. Five-speed manual overdrive optional: (1st) 3.72:1; (2nd) 2.23:1; (3rd) 1.48:1; (4th) 1.00:1; (5th) 0.76:1; (Rev) 3.59:1. Select-Shift three-speed automatic optional on four- cylinder, standard on six: (1st) 2.47:1; (2nd) 1.47:1; (3rd) 1.00:1; (Rev) 2.11:1. Converter clutch automatic available with six/V-8: (1st) 2.46:1; (2nd) 1.46:1; (3rd) 1.00:1; (Rev) 2.19:1. Standard final drive ratio: 2.73:1 except four w/5spd, 3.45:1; four w/auto. or 302 V-8 w/4spd, 3.08:1. Steering/Suspension/Brakes: same as 1981. Body construction: unibody. Fuel tank: 15.4 gal.

DRIVETRAIN OPTIONS: Engine/Transmission: 200 cu. in. six ($213). 255 cu. in. V-8 ($263) exc. w/GT ($57 credit). 302 cu. in. V-8 ($452) exc. w/TR performance pkg. ($402). Five-speed manual trans. ($196). Select-shift automatic trans. ($411). Traction-Lok differential ($76). Optional axle ratio (NC). Brakes/Steering/Suspension: Power brakes ($93). Power steering ($190). TR performance suspension pkg. ($533-$583) exc. GT ($105). Handling suspension ($50). Other: Engine block heater ($17). H.D. battery ($24). California emission system ($46). High-altitude emissions (NC).

CONVENIENCE/APPEARANCE OPTIONS: Option Packages: Light group ($49). Appearance protection group ($48). Power lock group ($139). Comfort/Convenience: Air cond. ($676). Rear defroster, electric ($124). Fingertip speed control ($155). Power windows ($165). Tinted glass ($88); windshield only ($32). Leather-wrapped steering wheel ($55). Tilt steering wheel ($95). Interval wipers ($48). Rear wiper/washer ($101). Lighting and Mirrors: Trunk light ($7). Remote right mirror ($41). Entertainment: AM/FM radio ($76). AM/FM stereo radio ($106); w/8track or cassette player ($184). Premium sound system ($105). Dual rear speakers ($39). AM radio delete ($61 credit). Exterior: TRoof ($1021). Flip-up open air roof ($276). Carriage roof ($734). Full vinyl roof ($137). Metallic glow paint ($54). Two-tone paint ($138-$177). Lower two-tone paint ($104). Accent tape stripes ($62). Hood scoop ($38). Liftgate louvers ($165). Black rocker panel moldings ($33). Lower bodyside protection ($41). Interior: Console ($191). Recaro high-back bucket seats ($834). Cloth/vinyl seats ($23-$51). Leather low-back bucket seats ($409). Cargo area cover ($51). Front floor mats, carpeted ($22). Wheels and Tires: Wire wheel covers ($91-$141). Cast aluminum wheels ($348-$398). Styled steel wheels w/trim rings ($72- $122). P175/75R14 WSW ($66). P185/75R14 BSW ($30); WSW ($66- $96); RWL ($85-$116).

HISTORY: Introduced: September 24, 1981. Model year production: 130,418. Total production for the U.S. market of 119,314 Mustangs included 54,444 four-cylinder, 37,734 sixes, and 27,136 V-8 engines. Calendar year production: 127,370. Calendar year sales by U.S. dealers: 119,526. Model year sales by U.S. dealers: 116,804.

Historical Footnotes: Option prices rose sharply this year, by around 20 percent on the average. Production of V-8 engines also rose sharply, with five times as many coming off the line as in 1981. Mustang sales declined by almost one-third this year. A convertible model was announced, but didn't appear until the 1983 model year.

1983 MUSTANG

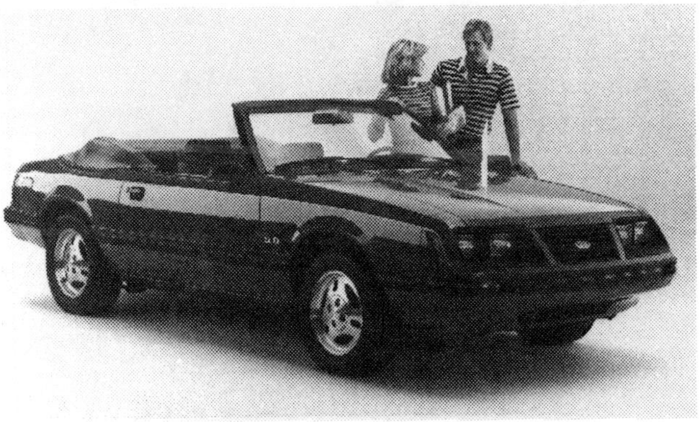

1983 Mustang GT 5.0L convertible (F)

MUSTANG — FOUR/V-6/V-8 — A restyled nose and rear end improved Mustang's aerodynamics, but the model was otherwise essentially a carryover for 1983. All Mustangs had a new angled-forward front end and new front fascia, with deeply recessed headlamp housings. A narrower grille design tapered inward slightly at the base, with a Ford oval in its center. Rectangular parking lamps stood at bumper level, as before, below the outboard headlamps. Taillamps continued the wraparound design, but in restyled form. The use of galvanized and zincrometal coatings was expanded. The high-output 302 cu. in. V-8 edition displayed a new hood scoop design. Most noteworthy, though, was the return of the ragtop. A new convertible (part of the GLX series) came with any powertrain except the 2.3-liter four with automatic. Unlike the Chrysler LeBaron, Mustang convertibles had a glass backlight and roll-down quarter windows, along with a power top. Engine choices changed considerably for (and during) 1983. A 232 cu. in. (3.8-liter) "Essex" V-6, offered in Mustang for the first time, delivered a 2-second improvement in 0-60 time over the previous 3.3-liter inline six. The high-output 302 cu. in. (5.0-liter) V-8 with four-speed manual continued this year, but a four-barrel carburetor replaced the former two-barrel. Horsepower jumped to 175 (formerly 157). The V-8 also got an aluminum intake manifold and freer exhaust flow. It was standard on the GT. The base 140 cu. in. (2.3-liter) four switched from two-barrel to single-barrel carburetion. Later in the season, a new 140 cu. in. OHC turbo arrived, with multi-port fuel injection. The last previous turbo four, in 1981, had been carbureted. Turbo models could not have air conditioning. Both the inline six and 255 cu. in. (4.2-liter) V-8 were dropped. A new manual five-speed gearbox, optional with the four, had Ford's U-shaped shift motion between fourth and fifth gear. A Borg-Warner T5 close-ratio five-speed arrived later for the GT's high-output 5.0-liter V-8, hooked to a 3.27:1 final drive. An upshift indicator light option (with manual transmission) was available, to show the most fuel-efficient shift points. All Mustang tires increased by at least one size, while the optional handling suspension got tougher anti-sway bars and retuned springs/shocks. It was now available without the formerly-required Michelin TRX tires. Joining the option list were: cloth sport performance low-back bucket seats; turbine wheel covers; restyled wire wheel covers; convex right-hand mirror; new special two-tone paint and tape treatment; and TRX tires and wheels without the TR performance suspension. Several options were deleted, including the rear wiper/washer, dual rear speakers, carriage roof, liftgate louvers, accent tape stripe, and Recaro seats. Standard equipment on the L (base) Mustang included black bumper rub strips, halogen headlamps, three-speed heater/defroster, woodtone instrument panel aplique, quarter- window louvers, black remote left mirror, AM radio, and four- spoke steering wheel with woodgrain insert. Also standard: four-speed manual gearbox, full wheel covers, argent accent striping, cigarette lighter, and high-back reclining bucket seats with vinyl upholstery. Mustang GL added black rocker panel, door and window frame moldings; dual accent bodyside pinstripes; a black sport steering wheel; lower-carpeted door trim panels; right visor vanity mirror; and low-back bucket seats. Mustang GLX came with dual bright remote-control mirrors, woodgrain-insert four-spoke steering wheel, bright rocker panel moldings, map pockets in the driver's door trim panel, and a light group. The GLX convertible included power brakes, tinted glass, dual black remote-control mirrors, black rocker moldings, and automatic transmission. Mustang GT carried a standard Traction-Lok rear axle, power brakes and steering, black grille, rear spoiler, black hood scoop, handling suspension, and five-speed manual gearbox. GT models could have Michelin TRX tires on cast aluminum wheels and a console with digital clock and diagnostic module, but no dual accent bodyside pinstriping. Black windshield, window and door frames completed the GT's appearance.

I.D. DATA: As before, Mustang's 17-symbol Vehicle Identification Number (VIN) was stamped on a metal tab fastened to the instrument panel, visible through the windshield. Symbols one to three specify manufacturer, make and vehicle type: '1FA' Ford passenger car. Symbol four ('B') denotes restraint system. Next comes a letter 'P', followed by two digits that indicate body type: '26' 2-dr. notchback sedan; '28' 3-dr. hatchback; '27' 2-dr. convertible. Symbol eight indicates engine type: 'A' L4-140 1Bbl.; 'D' turbo L4140 FI; '3' V6232 2Bbl.; 'F' V8302 4Bbl. Next is a check digit. Symbol ten indicates model year ('D' 1983). Symbol eleven is assembly plant: 'F' Dearborn, MI. The final six digits make up the sequence number, starting with 100001. A Vehicle Certification Label on the left front door lock face panel or door pillar shows the manufacturer, month and year of manufacture, GVW, GAWR, certification statement, VIN, and codes for body type, color, trim, axle, transmission, and special order information.

MUSTANG (FOUR/V-6)

Model Number	Body/Style Number	Body Type & Seating	Factory Price	Shipping Weight	Production Total
26	66B	2-dr. L Notch-4P	6727/7036	2532/2621	Note 1
26/60C	66B	2-dr. GL Notch-4P	7264/7573	2549/2638	Note 1
28/60C	61B	3-dr. GL Hatch-4P	7439/7748	2584/2673	Note 1
26/602	66B	2-dr. GLX Notch-4P	7398/7707	2552/2641	Note 1
28/602	61B	3-dr. GLX Hatch-4P	7557/7866	2587/2676	Note 1
27/602	N/A	2-dr. GLX Conv.-4P	-- /9449	-- /2759	Note 1

MUSTANG GT (V-8)

28/932	61B	3-dr. Hatch-4P	-- /9328	-- /2891	Note 1
27/932	N/A	2-dr. Conv.-4P	-- /13479	N/A	Note 1

MUSTANG TURBO GT (FOUR)

28/932	61B	3-dr. Hatch-4P	9714/ --	N/A	Note 1

Note 1: Ford reports total production of 33,201 two-doors, 64,234 hatchbacks, and 23,438 convertibles.

FACTORY PRICE/WEIGHT NOTE: Figures to left of slash are for four- cylinder engine, to right of slash for V-6. A 4Bbl. 302 cu. in. V-8 engine cost $1044 more than the V-6 ($595 more on the GLX convertible). The price of the GLX convertible jumped sharply after the model year began, to $12,467.

ENGINE DATA: BASE FOUR: Inline, overhead cam, four-cylinder. Cast iron block and head. Displacement: 140 cu. in. (2.3 liters). Bore & stroke: 3.78 x 3.13 in. Compression ratio: 9.0:1. Brake horsepower: 90 at 4600 R.P.M. Torque: 122 lbs.-ft. at 2600 R.P.M. Five main bearings. Hydraulic valve lifters. Carburetor: 1Bbl. Carter YFA. VIN Code: A. OPTIONAL TURBO FOUR: Same as 140 cu. in. four above, but with turbocharger and electronic fuel injection Compression ratio: 8.0:1. Brake H.P.: 142 at 5000 R.P.M. Torque: 172 lbs.-ft. at 3800 R.P.M. VIN Code: D. OPTIONAL V-6: 90-degree, overhead valve V-6. Cast iron block and aluminum head. Displacement: 232 cu. in. (3.8 liters). Bore & stroke: 3.80 x 3.40 in. Compression ratio: 8.7:1. Brake horsepower: 112 at 4000 R.P.M. Torque: 175 lbs.-ft. at 2600 R.P.M. Four main bearings. Hydraulic valve lifters. Carburetor: 2Bbl. Motorcraft 2150. VIN Code: 3. OPTIONAL V-8: 90-degree, overhead valve V-8. Cast iron block and head. Displacement: 302 cu. in. (5.0 liters). Bore & stroke: 4.00 x 3.00 in. Compression ratio: 8.3:1. Brake horsepower: 175 at 4000 R.P.M. Torque: 245 lbs.-ft. at 2400 R.P.M. Five main bearings. Hydraulic valve lifters. Carburetor: 4Bbl. Holley 4180. VIN Code: F.

CHASSIS DATA: Wheelbase: 100.4 in. Overall length: 179.1 in. Height: 51.9 in. Width: 69.1 in. Front Tread: 56.6 in. Rear Tread: 57.0 in. Standard Tires: P185/75R14 SBR BSW exc. GT, P205/70HR14 or Michelin P220/55R390 TRX.

TECHNICAL: Transmission: Four-speed manual (floor shift) standard on four-cylinder. Gear ratios: (1st) 3.98:1; (2nd) 2.14:1; (3rd) 1.49:1; (4th) 1.00:1; (Rev) 3.99:1. Four-speed overdrive manual transmission standard on V-8. Gear ratios: (1st) 3.07:1; (2nd) 1.72:1; (3rd) 1.00:1; (4th) 0.70:1; (Rev) 3.07:1. Five-speed manual overdrive optional: (1st) 3.72:1; (2nd) 2.23:1; (3rd) 1.48:1; (4th) 1.00:1; (5th) 0.76:1; (Rev) 3.59:1. Turbo five-speed: (1st) 4.03:1; (2nd) 2.37:1; (3rd) 1.50:1; (4th) 1.00:1; (5th) 0.86:1; (Rev) 3.76:1. Alternate turbo five-speed: (1st) 3.76:1; (2nd) 2.18:1; (3rd) 1.36:1; (4th) 1.00:1; (5th) 0.86:1; (Rev) 3.76:1. V-8 five-speed: (1st) 2.95:1; (2nd) 1.94:1; (3rd) 1.34:1; (4th) 1.00:1; (5th) 0.73:1; (Rev) 2.76:1. Select-Shift three-speed automatic optional on four-cylinder, standard on six: (1st) 2.47:1; (2nd) 1.47:1; (3rd) 1.00:1; (Rev) 2.11:1. V-6 ratios: (1st) 2.46:1; (2nd) 1.46:1; (3rd) 1.00:1; (Rev) 2.19:1. Standard final drive ratio: 3.08:1 w/4spd, 3.45:1 w/5spd, 3.08:1 or 2.73:1 w/auto. Steering: Rack and pinion. Front Suspension: Modified MacPherson struts with lower control arms and stabilizer bar. Rear Suspension: Rigid axle w/four-bar link and coil springs. Brakes: Front disc, rear drum. Ignition: Electronic. Body construction: Unibody. Fuel tank: 15.4 gal.

DRIVETRAIN OPTIONS: Engine/Transmission: 232 cu. in. V-6 ($309). 302 cu. in. V-8 ($1343) exc. conv. ($595). Five-speed manual trans. ($124). Select-shift automatic trans. ($439). Traction-Lok differential ($95). Optional axle ratio (NC). Brakes/Steering/Suspension: Power brakes ($93). Power steering ($202). Handling suspension ($252). Other: Engine block heater ($17). H.D. battery ($26). California emission system ($76). High-altitude emissions (NC).

CONVENIENCE/APPEARANCE OPTIONS: Option Packages: Sport performance pkg. ($196). Light group ($55). Appearance protection group ($60). Power lock group ($160). Comfort/Convenience: Air cond. ($724). Rear defroster, electric ($135). Fingertip speed control ($170). Power windows ($180). Tinted glass ($105); windshield only ($38). Leather-wrapped steering wheel ($59). Tilt steering wheel ($105). Interval wipers ($49). Remote right mirror ($44). Entertainment: AM/FM radio ($82). AM/FM stereo radio ($109); w/8track or cassette player ($199). Premium sound system ($117). AM radio delete ($61 credit). Exterior: TRoof ($1055). Flip-up open· air roof ($310). Metallic glow paint ($54). Two-tone paint ($150-$189). Liftgate louvers: hatch ($171). Rocker panel moldings ($33). Lower bodyside protection ($41). Interior: Console ($191). Cloth/vinyl seats ($29-$57). Leather low-back bucket seats ($415). Front floor mats, carpeted ($22). Wheels and Tires: Wire wheel covers ($98-$148). Turbine wheel covers (NC). Cast aluminum wheels ($354-$404). Styled steel wheels w/trim rings ($78-$128). P185/75R14 WSW ($72). P195/75R14 WSW ($108). P205/75R14 BSW ($224). TRX P220/55R390 BSW ($327-$551).

HISTORY: Introduced: October 14, 1982 except convertible, November 5, 1982. Model year production: 108,438. Total production for the U.S. market of 108,438 Mustangs included 27,825 four- cylinder, 47,766 sixes, and 32,847 V-8 engines. Calendar year production: 124,225. Calendar year sales by U.S. dealers: 116,976. Model year sales by U.S. dealers: 116,120.

Historical Footnotes: Mustang's convertible actually began life as a steel- topped notchback, modified by an outside contractor. The car itself was assembled at Dearborn, then sent to Cars & Concepts in Brighton, Michigan for installation of the top and interior trim. Mustang GT was said to deliver a seven-second 0-60 time (quickest of any standard domestic model), as well as cornering that matched exotic cars. All that plus fuel economy in the mid-20s.

1984 MUSTANG

1984 Mustang GT 5.0L HO Sport Coupe (JG)

MUSTANG — FOUR/V-6/V-8 — Performance-minded Mustangers enjoyed fresh temptation this year in the new SVO. Developed by Ford's Special Vehicle Operations department, SVO carried an air-to-air intercooler on its 140 cu. in. (2.3-liter) turbocharged, fuel-injected four-cylinder engine. That helped boost horsepower up to 175, and improve low-end performance. The SVO package included a Borg-Warner T5 five-speed manual gearbox with Hurst linkage, four-wheel disc brakes, performance suspension with adjustable Koni gas-filled shocks, P225/50VR16 Goodyear NCT tires on cast aluminum 16 x 7 in. wheels, and functional hood scoop. SVO could, according to Ford, hit 134 MPH and get to 60 MPH in just 7.5 seconds. Inside were multi-adjustable articulated leather bucket seats. SVO's shock absorbers and struts had three settings: cross-country (for front and rear), GT (front only), and competition

1984 Mustang 3.8L convertible (JG)

(front and rear). Four-wheel disc brakes were standard. SVO had a much different front-end look than the standard Mustang, with a "grille-less" front fascia and integrated foglamps. Just a single slot stood below the hood panel, which contained a Ford oval. Large single rectangular headlamps were deeply recessed, flanked by large wraparound lenses. A polycarbonate dual-wing rear spoiler was meant to increase rear-wheel traction, while rear-wheel "spats" directed airflow around the wheel wells. SVO's price tag was more than double that of a base Mustang. Offered in "three-door" hatchback form, SVO came only in black, silver metallic, dark charcoal metallic, or red metallic. Interiors were all charcoal. Only six major options were available for SVO, because it had so much standard equipment. Those were: air conditioning, power windows, power door locks, cassette player, flip-up sunroof, and leather seat trim.

1984 Mustang SVO coupe (JG)

Standard SVO equipment included an 8000 R.P.M. tachometer; quick-ratio power steering; Traction-Lok rear axle; leather-wrapped steering wheel, shift knob and brake handle; unique instrument panel appliques; narrow bodyside moldings; and unique C-pillar and taillamp treatments. A premium/regular fuel switch recalibrated the ignition instantly. Revised pedal positioning allowed "heel and toe" downshifting, and had a footrest for the left foot during hard cornering. Standard models looked the same as in 1983. Throughout the line were new steering wheels with center horn, new instrument panel appliques, and split folding rear seats. All manual transmissions now had a clutch/starter interlock, so the engine couldn't start unless the clutch was depressed. Mustang instrument panels had red lighting this year. Buyers could also select a more modest turbo model, without the intercooler. Mustang's GT Turbo had been introduced in spring 1983, and continued for '84. GT customers also had a choice of V-8 engines, and an available overdrive automatic transmission. The series lineup was simplified this year. The L series, previously two-door notchback only, was now also available in "three-door" hatchback form. GL and GLX models of 1983 were

gone, replaced by a single LX series. A convertible was offered again this year, in both LX and GT form. The GT series displayed a new front air dam, with road lamps available. GT also added gas-filled shock absorbers and a handling suspension. Elsewhere on the powerplant front, the optional 232 cu. in. (3.8-liter) V-6 switched to throttle-body fuel injection and gained more horsepower. A fuel-injected high-output 5.0-liter V-8 came with automatic overdrive transmission. A higher-output version of the four-barrel V-8, producing 205 horsepower, was announced for December arrival but delayed.

I.D. DATA: Mustang's 17-symbol Vehicle Identification Number (VIN) again was stamped on a metal tab fastened to the instrument panel, visible through the windshield. The first three symbols specify manufacturer, make and vehicle type: '1FA' Ford passenger car. Symbol four ('B') denotes restraint system. Next comes a letter 'P', followed by two digits that indicate body type: '26' 2-dr. notchback sedan; '28' 3-dr. hatchback; '27' 2-dr. convertible. Symbol eight indicates engine type: 'A' L4-140 1Bbl.; 'W' turbo L4140 FI; '3' V6232 FI; 'F' V8302 FI; 'M' V8302 4Bbl. Next is a check digit. Symbol ten indicates model year ('E' 1984). Symbol eleven is assembly plant: 'F' Dearborn, MI. The final six digits make up the sequence number, starting with 100001. A Vehicle Certification Label on the left front door lock face panel or door pillar shows the manufacturer, month and year of manufacture, GVW, GAWR, certification statement, VIN, and codes for body type and color, trim, axle, transmission, and special order information.

MUSTANG (FOUR/V-6)

Model Number	Body/Style Number	Body Type & Seating	Factory Price	Shipping Weight	Production Total
26	66B	2-dr. L Notch-4P	7098/7507	2538/2646	Note 1
28	61B	3-dr. L Hatch-4P	7269/7678	2584/2692	Note 1
26/602	66B	2-dr. LX Notch-4P	7290/7699	2559/2667	Note 1
28/602	61B	3-dr. LX Hatch-4P	7496/7905	2605/2713	Note 1
27/602	66B	2-dr. LX Conv.-4P	--/11849	--/2873	Note 1

L/LX Price/Weight Note: Figures to left of slash are for four-cylinder engine, to right of slash for V-6. A 4Bbl. 302 cu. in. V-8 engine cost $1165 more than the V-6 ($318 more on the LX convertible).

1984½ Mustang GT-350 20th Anniversary convertible (F)

MUSTANG GT (TURBO FOUR/V-8)

28/932	61B	3-dr. Hatch-4P	9762/9578	2753/2899	Note 1
27/932	66B	2-dr. Conv.-4P	13245/13051	2921/3043	Note 1

GT Price and Weight Note: Figures to left of slash are for turbo four, to right for V-8.

1984 Mustang SVO coupe (JG)

MUSTANG SVO (TURBO FOUR)

28/939	61B	3-dr. Hatch-4P	15596	2881	Note 1

Note 1: Ford reports total production of 37,680 two-doors, 86,200 hatchbacks and 17,600 convertibles.

ENGINE DATA: BASE FOUR: Inline, overhead cam, four-cylinder. Cast iron block and head. Displacement: 140 cu. in. (2.3 liters). Bore & stroke: 3.78 x 3.13 in. Compression ratio: 9.0:1. Brake horsepower: 88 at 4000 R.P.M. Torque: 122 lbs.-ft. at 2400 R.P.M. Five main bearings. Hydraulic valve lifters. Carburetor: 1Bbl. Carter YFA. VIN Code: A. OPTIONAL TURBO FOUR: Same as 140 cu. in. four above, but with turbocharger and electronic fuel injection Compression ratio: 8.0:1. Brake H.P.: 145 at 4600 R.P.M. Torque: 180 lbs.-ft. at 3600 R.P.M. VIN Code: W. SVO TURBO FOUR: Same as standard turbo four above, but Brake H.P.: 175 at 4400 R.P.M. Torque: 210 lbs.-ft. at 3000 R.P.M. OPTIONAL V-6: 90-degree, overhead valve V-6. Cast iron block and aluminum head. Displacement: 232 cu. in. (3.8 liters). Bore & stroke: 3.80 x 3.40 in. Compression ratio: 8.7:1. Brake horsepower: 120 at 3600 R.P.M. Torque: 205 lbs.-ft. at 1600 R.P.M. Four main bearings. Hydraulic valve lifters. Electronic fuel injection (TBI). VIN Code: 3. OPTIONAL V-8: 90-degree, overhead valve V-8. Cast iron block and head. Displacement: 302 cu. in. (5.0 liters). Bore & stroke: 4.00 x 3.00 in. Compression ratio: 8.3:1. Brake horsepower: 175 at 4000 R.P.M. Torque: 245 lbs.-ft. at 2200 R.P.M. Five main bearings. Hydraulic valve lifters. Carburetor: 4Bbl. Holley 4180C. VIN Code: M. OPTIONAL V-8: Fuel injected version of 302 cu. in. V-8 above. Brake H.P.: 165 at 3800 R.P.M. Torque: 245 lbs.-ft. at 2000 R.P.M. VIN Code: F.

NOTE: A high-output version of the carbureted V-8, rated 205 horsepower at 4400 R.P.M., was announced but delayed.

CHASSIS DATA: Wheelbase: 100.5 in. Overall length: 179.1 in. except SVO, 181.0 in. Height: 51.9 in. Width: 69.1 in. Front Tread: 56.6 in. except SVO, 57.8 in. Rear Tread: 57.0 in. except SVO, 58.3 in. Standard Tires: P185/75R14 SBR BSW exc. GT, P205/70HR14.

TECHNICAL: Transmission: Four-speed manual (floor shift) standard on four-cylinder. Gear ratios: (1st) 3.98:1; (2nd) 2.14:1; (3rd) 1.49:1; (4th) 1.00:1; (Rev) 3.99:1. Standard turbo five-speed: (1st) 4.03:1; (2nd) 2.37:1; (3rd) 1.50:1; (4th) 1.00:1; (5th) 0.86:1; (Rev) 3.76:1. Standard V-8 five-speed: (1st) 2.95:1; (2nd) 1.94:1; (3rd) 1.34:1; (4th) 1.00:1; (5th) 0.63:1; (Rev) 2.76:1. Select-Shift three-speed automatic optional on four-cylinder: (1st) 2.47:1; (2nd) 1.47:1; (3rd) 1.00:1; (Rev) 2.11:1. Four-speed overdrive automatic standard on V-6: (1st) 2.40:1; (2nd) 1.47:1; (3rd) 1.00:1; (4th) 0.67:1; (Rev) 2.00:1. Standard final drive ratio: (four) 3.08:1 w/4spd, 3.27:1 w/auto.; (V-6) 3.08:1; (V-8) 3.08:1 w/5spd, 2.73:1 w/3spd auto., 3.27:1 w/4spd auto.; (turbo) 3.45:1. Steering: Rack and pinion. Front Suspension: Modified MacPherson struts with lower control arms and stabilizer bar; SVO added adjustable gas-pressurized shocks. Rear Suspension: Rigid axle w/four-bar link and coil springs; SVO and GT Turbo added an anti-sway bar. Brakes: Front disc, rear drum except SVO, four-wheel disc brakes. Ignition: Electronic. Body construction: Unibody. Fuel tank: 15.4 gal.

DRIVETRAIN OPTIONS: Engine/Transmission: 232 cu. in. V-6 ($409). 302 cu. in. V-8 pkg. ($1574) exc. LX conv. ($727). Five-speed manual trans. (NC). Three-speed automatic trans. ($439). Four-speed overdrive auto. trans. ($551). Traction-Lok differential ($95). Optional axle ratio (NC). Brakes/Steering/Suspension: Power brakes ($93). Power steering ($202). Handling suspension ($252) exc. w/VIP pkg. ($50). Other: Engine block heater ($18). H.D. battery ($27). California emission system ($99). High-altitude option (NC).

CONVENIENCE/APPEARANCE OPTIONS: Option Packages: SVO competition preparation pkg.: delete air cond., power locks, AM/FM/cassette and power windows ($1253 credit). VIP pkg. for L/LX with AM/FM stereo or tilt wheel ($93); both ($196). VIP pkg. for GT ($110). 20th anniversary VIP pkg.: GT ($25-$144). Light/convenience group ($55-$88). Power lock group ($176). Comfort/Convenience: Air cond. ($743). Rear defroster, electric ($140). Fingertip speed control ($176). Power windows ($198). Tinted glass ($110). Tilt steering wheel ($110). Interval wipers ($50). Remote right mirror ($46). Entertainment: AM/FM stereo radio ($109); w/cassette player ($222) exc. SVO or w/VIP pkg. ($113). Premium sound system ($151). AM radio delete ($39 credit). Exterior: TRoof ($1074) exc. w/VIP pkg. ($760). Flip-up open air roof ($315). Metallic glow paint ($54). Two-tone paint: L/LX ($150-$189). Lower two-tone paint ($116). Liftgate louvers: hatch ($171). Rocker panel moldings ($39). Lower bodyside protection ($41). Interior: Console ($191). Articulated sport seats ($196). High-back vinyl bucket seats: L ($29); low-back, LX/GT ($29). Leather bucket seats ($189). Front floor mats, carpeted ($22). Wheels and Tires: Wire wheel covers ($98). Cast aluminum wheels ($354). Styled steel wheels w/trim rings ($78). P185/75R14 WSW ($72). P195/75R14 WSW ($108). P205/75R14 BSW ($224). TRX P220/55R390 BSW ($327-$551) exc. GT ($27 credit).

HISTORY: Introduced: September 22, 1983. Model year production: 141,480. Total production for the U.S. market of 129,621 Mustangs included 46,414 four-cylinder, 47,169 sixes, and 36,038 V-8 engines. Calendar year production: 140,338. Calendar year sales by U.S. dealers: 138,296. Model year sales by U.S. dealers: 131,762.

Historical Footnotes: Ford's Special Vehicle Operations Department had been formed in 1981 to supervise the company's renewed involvement in motorsports (among other duties), and to develop special limited-edition high-performance vehicles. SVO was the first of those offered as a production model. Motor Trend called SVO "the best driving street Mustang the factory has ever produced." Road & Track claimed that SVO "outruns the Datsun 280ZX, outhandles the Ferrari 308 and Porsche 944...and it's affordable." Its hefty price tag meant SVO was targeted toward more affluent, car-conscious consumers.

1985 MUSTANG

MUSTANG — FOUR/V-6/V-8 — Changes for 1985 focused mainly on Mustang's front end and mechanical matters. All models wore a new front-end look with a four-hole integral air dam below the bumper, flanked by low rectangular parking lamps. GT also had integral foglamps. A "grille" similar to SVO—essentially one wide slot with angled sides in a sloping front panel—appeared on all Mustangs. That panel displayed a Ford oval. Taillamps were full-width (except for the license plate opening), with backup lenses at the upper portion of each inner section. A Ford script oval stood above the right taillamp. Most Mustang exterior trim and accents switched from black to a softer charcoal shade. All models had new charcoal front and rear bumper rub strips and bodyside moldings. Also new: charcoal hood paint/tape treatment, a revised decklid decal, and GT nomenclature (where applicable) molded into the bodyside molding. The base L series was dropped, making LX the bottom-level Mustang. Standard LX equipment now included power brakes and steering, remote-control right-side mirror, dual-note horn, interval windshield wipers, and an AM/FM stereo radio. Also available were the GT and SVO, as well as LX and GT convertibles. As before, both notchback and hatchback odies were offered. New standard interior features included a console, low-back bucket seats, articulated sport seats (on GT), luxury door trim panels, and covered visor mirrors. The convertible's quarter trim panels were revised to accommodate a refined seatbelt system. Mechanical radio faces switched to a contemporary flat design. All Mustangs had larger tires this year, and added urethane lower bodyside protection. New GT tires were P225/60VR15 Goodyear Eagle

1985 Mustang Special Pursuit 5.0L coupe (JG)

unidirectional "Gatorbacks" on 15 x 7 in. cast aluminum wheels. Added to the option list: a new electronic AM/FM stereo radio with cassette player. The 140 cu. in. (2.3-liter) four remained standard, but buyers had quite a choice of other powerplants, as usual. Mustang GT's high-output carbureted 302 cu. in. (5.0-liter) V-8 gained a high-performance camshaft, plus roller tappets and a two-speed accessory drive system. That engine now produced 210 horsepower, while its mating five-speed manual gearbox had a tighter shift pattern and new gear ratios. The high-output, fuel-injected V-8 also gained strength, reaching 180 horsepower. The turbocharged SVO returned a little late, now wearing Eagle 50-series tires on 16-inch wheels. Both the 3.8-liter V-6 and 5.0-liter V-8 had a new oil warning light.

I.D. DATA: Mustang's 17-symbol Vehicle Identification Number (VIN) again was stamped on a metal tab fastened to the instrument panel, visible through the windshield. Coding was similar to 1984. Model year code changed to 'F' for 1985. Coding for the SVO turbocharged four changed to 'T'.

MUSTANG LX (FOUR/V-6)

Model Number	Body/Style Number	Body Type & Seating	Factory Price	Shipping Weight	Production Total
26/602	66B	2-dr. Notch-4P	6885/8017	2559/2667	Note 1
28/602	61B	3-dr. Hatch-4P	7345/8477	2605/2713	Note 1
27/602	66B	2-dr. Conv.-4P	--/11985	--/2873	Note 1

LX Price/Weight Note: Figures to left of slash are for four-cylinder engine, to right of slash for V-6 (including the price of the required automatic transmission). A 4Bbl. 302 cu. in. V-8 engine cost $561 more than the V-6 ($152 more on the LX convertible).

MUSTANG GT (V-8)

28/932	61B	3-dr. Hatch-4P	9885	2899	Note 1
27/932	66B	2-dr. Conv.-4P	13585	3043	Note 1

1985 Mustang SVO Turbo coupe (JG)

MUSTANG SVO (TURBO FOUR)

28/939	61B	3-dr. Hatch-4P	14521	2881	Note 1

Note 1: Ford reports total production of 56,781 two-doors, 84,623 hatchbacks and 15,110 convertibles.

ENGINE DATA: BASE FOUR: Inline, overhead cam, four-cylinder. Cast iron block and head. Displacement: 140 cu. in. (2.3 liters). Bore & stroke: 3.78 x 3.13 in. Compression ratio: 9.0:1. Brake horsepower: 88 at 4000 R.P.M. Torque: 122 lbs.-ft. at 2600 R.P.M. Five main bearings. Hydraulic valve lifters. Carburetor: 1Bbl. Carter YFA. VIN Code: A. SVO TURBO FOUR: Same as 140 cu. in. four above, but with turbocharger and electronic fuel injection Compression ratio: 8.0:1. Brake H.P.: 175 at 4400 R.P.M. Torque: 210 lbs.-ft. at 3000 R.P.M. VIN Code: T. OPTIONAL V-6: 90-degree, overhead valve V-6. Cast iron block and aluminum head. Displacement: 232 cu. in. (3.8 liters). Bore & stroke: 3.80 x 3.40 in. Compression ratio: 8.7:1. Brake

horsepower: 120 at 3600 R.P.M. Torque: 205 lbs.-ft. at 1600 R.P.M. Four main bearings. Hydraulic valve lifters. Electronic fuel injection (TBI). VIN Code: 3. OPTIONAL V-8: 0-degree, overhead valve V-8. Cast iron block and head. Displacement: 302 cu. in. (5.0 liters). Bore & stroke: 4.00 x 3.00 in. Compression ratio: 8.3:1. Brake horsepower: 180 at 4200 R.P.M. Torque: 260 lbs.-ft. at 2600 R.P.M. Five main bearings. Hydraulic valve lifters. Electronic fuel injection. VIN Code: F. OPTIONAL HIGH-OUTPUT V-8: Same as 302 cu. in. V-8 above, but with Holley 4Bbl. carburetor Brake H.P.: 210 at 4400 R.P.M. Torque: 270 lbs.- ft. at 3200 R.P.M. VIN Code: M.

CHASSIS DATA: Wheelbase: 100.5 in. Overall length: 179.3 in. except SVO, 180.8 in. Height: 52.1 in. Width: 69.1 in. Front Tread: 56.6 in. except SVO, 57.8 in. Rear Tread: 57.0 in. except SVO, 58.3 in. Standard Tires: P195/75R14 SBR WSW exc. GT, P225/60VR15 SBR BSW; and SVO, P225/50VR16 Eagle BSW.

TECHNICAL: Transmission: Four-speed manual (floor shift) standard on four-cylinder. Gear ratios: (1st) 3.98:1; (2nd) 2.14:1; (3rd) 1.42:1; (4th) 1.00:1; (Rev) 3.99:1. SVO turbo five-speed: (1st) 3.50:1; (2nd) 2.14:1; (3rd) 1.36:1; (4th) 1.00:1; (5th) 0.78:1; (Rev) 3.39:1. Standard V-8 five-speed: (1st) 3.35:1; (2nd) 1.93:1; (3rd) 1.29:1; (4th) 1.00:1; (5th) 0.68:1; (Rev) 3.15:1. Select-Shift three-speed automatic optional on four- cylinder: (1st) 2.47:1; (2nd) 1.47:1; (3rd) 1.00:1; (Rev) 2.11:1. V-6 three speed automatic: (1st) 2.46:1; (2nd) 1.46:1; (3rd) 1.00:1; (Rev) 2.19:1. Four-speed overdrive automatic standard on V-8: (1st) 2.40:1; (2nd) 1.47:1; (3rd) 1.00:1; (4th) 0.67:1; (Rev) 2.00:1. Standard final drive ratio: (four) 3.08:1 w/4spd, 3.27:1 w/auto.; (V-6) 2.73:1; (V-8) 3.08:1 w/5spd, 3.27:1 w/4spd auto.; (turbo) 3.45:1. Steering: Rack and pinion, power-assisted. Front Suspension: Modified MacPherson struts with lower control arms and stabilizer bar; SVO added adjustable gas- pressurized shocks. Rear Suspension: Rigid axle w/four-bar link and coil springs; GT/SVO added an anti-sway bar. Brakes: Front disc, rear drum (power-assisted) except SVO, four-wheel discs. Ignition: Electronic. Body construction: Unibody. Fuel tank: 15.4 gal.

DRIVETRAIN OPTIONS: Engine/Transmission/Suspension: 232 cu. in. V-6: LX ($439). 302 cu. in. V-8 engine: LX ($1000) exc. LX conv. ($152). Five-speed manual trans.: LX ($124). Three-speed automatic trans.: LX ($439). Four-speed overdrive auto. trans.: LX ($676); GT ($551). Traction-Lok differential ($95). Optional axle ratio (NC). Handling suspension: LX ($258). Other: Engine block heater ($18). H.D. battery ($27). California emission system ($99). High-altitude option (NC).

CONVENIENCE/APPEARANCE OPTIONS: Option Packages: SVO competition preparation pkg.: delete air cond., power locks, AM/FM stereo/cassette and power windows ($1417 credit). Light/convenience group ($55). Power lock group ($177-$210). Comfort/Convenience: Air cond. ($743). Rear defroster, electric ($140). Fingertip speed control ($176). Power windows ($198) exc. conv. ($272). Tinted glass ($110). Tilt steering wheel: LX ($110). Entertainment: AM/FM stereo radio w/cassette player: LX/GT ($148). Electronic AM/FM stereo w/cassette: LX/GT ($300). Premium sound system: LX/GT ($138). Radio delete ($148 credit). Exterior: TRoof: hatch ($1074). Flip-up open air roof: hatch ($315). Lower two-tone paint ($116). Single wing spoiler: SVO (NC). Interior: Console ($191). Low-back vinyl bucket seats: LX ($29). Leather sport performance bucket seats: LX conv. ($780); GT conv. ($415); SVO ($189). LX Wheels and Tires: Wire wheel covers ($98). Styled steel wheels ($178). P205/75R14 WSW ($109). P205/70VR14 BSW ($238). P225/60VR15 SBR BSW ($665).

HISTORY: Introduced: October 4, 1984. Model year production: 156,514. Total production for the U.S. market of 143,682 Mustangs included 79,885 four-cylinder, 18,334 sixes, and 45,463 V-8 engines. Calendar year production: 187,773. Calendar year sales by U.S. dealers: 157,821. Model year sales by U.S. dealers: 159,741.

Historical Footnotes: This year's GT proved that the V-8 had a future under Mustang hoods, even with the turbocharged SVO available. For one thing, the GT was a lot cheaper. It also performed more sedately than a turbo under ordinary conditions, yet was able to deliver impressive performance whenever needed. *Motor Trend* applauded the arrival of the potent 210-horsepower V-8 for delivering "lovely axle-creaking torque reminiscent of another time."

1986 MUSTANG

1986 Mustang GT convertible (JG)

MUSTANG — FOUR/V-6/V-8 — Model lineup was the same as in 1985: LX two-door sedan or hatchback (and convertible), GT hatchback and convertible, and SVO. LX had full bodyside striping, power brakes and steering, and such extras as interval wipers, luxury sound package, and an AM/FM stereo radio (which could be deleted for credit). Base engine remained the 140 cu. in. (2.3-liter) OHC four, with four-speed manual gearbox. V-8 engines now had sequential port fuel injection. The 232 cu. in. (3.8-liter) V-6 with throttle-body injection also was optional again, and standard on the LX convertible. Appearance was essentially the same as in 1985. The sloping center front-end panel held a Ford oval at the top, and a single wide opening below. Quad rectangular headlamps were deeply recessed. Parking lamps stood far down on the front end. Side marker lenses were angled to match the front fender tips. Taillamps were distinctly divided into upper and lower sections by a full-width divider bar. 'Mustang' lettering stood above the left taillamp, a Ford oval above the right. Three new body colors were offered. Turbine wheel covers switched from bright/argent to bright/black. Mustang's rear axle was upgraded to 8.7 inches with the standard 2.73:1 axle ratio (8.8 inch with others), for use with the 5.0-liter V-8. Viscous engine mounts were added on the 3.8-liter V-6 and the V-8, as used on the turbo four starting in mid-year 1985. One key now operated door locks and ignition.   The two-door LX notchback had its high-mount brake lamp added to the package tray; GT and SVO were modified to take it on the spoilers. Hatchback LX models added a spoiler to house that brake lamp, while LX and GT convertibles installed a luggage rack with integrated brake lamp. Preferred Equipment Packages included such items as air conditioning, styled wheels, and Premium Sound System. Mustang GT carried a new high-output 302 cu. in. (5.0- liter) V-8 with multi-port fuel injection. Rated 200 horsepower, with EECIV electronic engine controls, it was hooked to a five-speed manual (overdrive) transmission, or automatic overdrive. GT included a special suspension, Goodyear Eagle VR performance tires, quick-ratio power steering, and articulated front sport seats. The four-barrel V-8 was abandoned. All Mustang V-8s with five-speed manual also added an upshift indicator light. SVO, the "ultimate Mustang," carried a computer- controlled 200-horsepower 2.3-liter four with intercooled turbocharger and multi-port fuel injection. A five-speed transmission, with Hurst shifter that offered short, quick throws, was standard. So were disc brakes all around.

I.D. DATA: Mustang's 17-symbol Vehicle Identification Number (VIN) again was stamped on a metal tab fastened to the instrument panel, visible through the windshield. Coding was similar to 198485. Model year code changed to 'G' for 1986.

MUSTANG LX (FOUR/V-6)

Model Number	Body/Style Number	Body Type & Seating	Factory Price	Shipping Weight	Production Total
26	66B	2-dr. Notch-4P	7189/8153	2601/2722	Note 1
28	61B	3-dr. Hatch-4P	7744/8708	2661/2782	Note 1
27	66B	2-dr. Conv.-4P	--/12821	--/2908	Note 1

LX Price/Weight Note: Figures to left of slash are for four-cylinder engine, to right of slash (including the price of the required automatic transmission). A 302 cu. in. V-8 engine cost $1120 more than the four ($106 more on the LX convertible).

MUSTANG GT (V-8)

28	61B	3-dr. Hatch-4P	10691	2976	Note 1
27	66B	2-dr. Conv.-4P	14523	3103	Note 1

MUSTANG SVO (TURBO FOUR)

28/937	61B	3-dr. Hatch-4P	15272	3028	Note 1

Note 1: Ford reports total production of 106,720 two-doors (including convertibles) and 117,690 hatchbacks.

ENGINE DATA: BASE FOUR: Inline, overhead cam, four-cylinder. Cast iron block and head. Displacement: 140 cu. in. (2.3 liters). Bore & stroke: 3.78 x 3.13 in. Compression ratio: 9.5:1. Brake horsepower: 88 at 4200 R.P.M. Torque: 122 lbs.-ft. at 2600 R.P.M. Five main bearings. Hydraulic valve lifters. Carburetor: 1Bbl. Carter YFA. VIN Code: A. **SVO TURBO FOUR:** Same as 140 cu. in. four above, but with turbocharger and electronic fuel injection Compression ratio: 8.0:1. Brake H.P. at 5000 R.P.M. Torque: 240 lbs.-ft. at 3200 R.P.M. VIN Code: T. **OPTIONAL V-6:** 90-degree, overhead valve V-6. Cast iron block and aluminum head. Displacement: 232 cu. in. (3.8 liters). Bore & stroke: 3.80 x 3.40 in. Compression ratio: 8.7:1. Brake horsepower: 120 at 3600 R.P.M. Torque: 205 lbs.-ft. at 1600 R.P.M. Four main bearings. Hydraulic valve lifters. Electronic fuel injection (TBI). VIN Code: 3. **OPTIONAL V-8:** 90-degree, overhead valve V-8. Cast iron block and head. Displacement: 302 cu. in. (5.0 liters). Bore & stroke: 4.00 x 3.00 in. Compression ratio: 9.2:1. Brake horsepower: 200 at 4000 R.P.M. Torque: 285 lbs.-ft. at 3000 R.P.M. Five main bearings. Hydraulic valve lifters. Sequential fuel injection. VIN Code: M.

CHASSIS DATA: Wheelbase: 100.5 in. Overall length: 179.3 in. Height: 52.1 in. except SVO, 180.8 in. Height: 52.1 in. exc. conv., 51.9 in. Width: 69.1 in. Front Tread: 56.6 in. except SVO, 57.8 in. Rear Tread: 57.0 in. except SVO, 58.3 in. Standard Tires: P195/75R14 SBR WSW exc. GT, P225/60R15 SBR BSW; and SVO, P225/50VR16 "Gatorback" BSW.

TECHNICAL: Transmission: Four-speed manual (floor shift) standard on four-cylinder. Five-speed manual standard on turbo and V-8. Gear ratios N/A. Select-Shift three-speed automatic optional on four-cylinder, standard on V-6. Gear ratios: (1st) 2.47:1; (2nd) 1.47:1; (3rd) 1.00:1; (Rev) 2.11:1. V-6 three-speed automatic: (1st) 2.46:1; (2nd) 1.46:1; (3rd) 1.00:1; (Rev) 2.19:1. Four-speed overdrive automatic available with V-8: (1st) 2.40:1; (2nd) 1.47:1; (3rd) 1.00:1; (4th) 0.67:1; (Rev) 2.00:1. Standard final drive ratio: (four) 3.08:1 w/4spd, 3.27:1 w/auto.; (V-6) 2.73:1 w/auto, (V-8) 2.73:1 w/5spd, 3.27:1 w/4spd auto.; (turbo) 3.73:1. Steering: Rack and pinion, power-assisted. Front Suspension: Modified MacPherson struts with lower control arms and stabilizer bar; SVO added adjustable gas- pressurized shocks. Rear Suspension: Rigid axle w/four-bar link and coil springs; GT/SVO added an anti-sway bar and dual shocks on each side. Brakes: Front disc, rear drum (power-assisted) except SVO, four-wheel disc brakes. Ignition: Electronic. Body construction: Unibody. Fuel tank: 15.4 gal.

DRIVETRAIN OPTIONS: Engine/Transmission/Suspension: 232 cu. in. V-6: LX ($454). 302 cu. in. V-8 pkg. ($1120) exc. LX conv. ($106). Five-speed manual trans.: LX ($124). Three-speed automatic trans.: LX ($510); std. on conv. Four-speed overdrive auto. trans.: LX ($746); GT ($622). Other: Engine block heater ($18). H.D. battery ($27). California emission system ($102). High-altitude option (NC).

CONVENIENCE/APPEARANCE OPTIONS: Option Packages: SVO competition preparation pkg.: equipment deleted ($1451 credit). Light/convenience group ($55). Power lock group ($182-$215). Comfort/Convenience: Air cond. ($762). Rear defroster, electric ($145). Fingertip speed control ($176). Power windows ($207) exc. conv. ($282). Tinted glass ($115). Tilt steering wheel: LX ($115). Entertainment: AM/FM stereo radio w/cassette player: LX/GT ($148). Electronic seek/scan AM/FM stereo w/cassette: LX/GT ($300). Premium sound system ($138). Radio delete ($148 credit). Exterior: TRoof: hatch ($1100). Flip-up open air roof: hatch ($315). Lower charcoal accent paint ($116). Single wing spoiler: SVO (NC). Interior: Console w/clock and systems monitor ($191). Vinyl bucket seats: LX ($29). Articulated leather sport bucket seats: LX conv. ($807); GT conv. ($429). Leather seat upholstery: SVO ($189). LX Wheels and Tires: Wire wheel covers ($98). Styled steel wheels ($178). P205/75R14 WSW ($109). P225/60VR15 on cast aluminum wheels ($665).

HISTORY: Introduced: October 3, 1985. Model year production: 224,410. Total production for the U.S. market of 198,358 Mustangs included 107,340 four-cylinder, 38,422 sixes, and 52,596 V-8 engines. Calendar year production: 177,737. Calendar year sales by U.S. dealers: 167,699. Model year sales by U.S. dealers: 175,598.

Historical Footnotes: Mustang was the only Ford model to show a sales increase for 1986. Mercury's similar Capri would not return for another year, but Mustang was prepared to carry on in ordinary and high-performance trim. Turbocharging forced a hefty amount of horsepower out of SVO's small four-cylinder engine, delivering acceleration that rivaled big old V-8s.

Descriptions of Lincoln in 1976 and beyond sound more like they belong in a fashion magazine than an automobile catalog. Bill Blass? Givenchy? Pucci and Cartier? Each of those internationally known apparel designers put his name and ideas on a Designer Series "Mark" Lincoln. Each displayed the designer's signature on opera windows, as well as a golden plate on the dash. Affluent customers must have liked the idea, just as ordinary folks wore jeans with designer names on the back pocket. Lincoln sales leaped upward this year.

1976 Continental sedan (L)

As the era began, just two basic models made up the Lincoln lineup: Continental and Mark IV, both powered by FoMoCo's 460 cu. in. V-8. Mark was known not only for fashionable signatures, but for its Rolls-Royce style vertical-bar grille. Town Car and Town Coupe options added even greater luxury to Continentals.

1978 Versailles sedan (L)

Downsizing hit bodies and engines alike in 1977 as the 400 V-8 became standard, its big brother an option. Styling carried on traditional Lincoln cues, including hidden headlamps and simulated spare tire hump on the reduced Mark V coupe. Continentals adopted the Town Car name and added a Williamsburg special edition. Another breed of Lincoln arrived later in the year: the compact Versailles, ready to battle Cadillac's Seville on a Granada-size platform. Early Versailles models carried a standard 351 cu. in. V-8, but dropped to a 302 for 1978. In honor of Ford's 75th anniversary, Mark V put out a Diamond Jubilee Edition.

Collector's Series versions of both Continental and Mark-V joined up for 1979, as Versailles got a bit of restyling. The 400 cu. in. V-8 was now the largest Lincoln powerplant, as the big 460 cu. in disappeared. Further downsizing came in 1980, as Continental and the new Mark VI managed to look more alike than before. Mark's headlamps remained hidden, while Continental's were now exposed. Base engine for both was now the 302 V-8, with 351 an option—and even that choice would be gone

a year later. Marks came in both the customary Designer Series and a similarly luxurious Signature Series. Versailles, never able to attract enough buyers (perhaps because of its modest origins and high price), dropped out of the lineup after 1980.

1979 Collectors Series sedan / Continental Mark V coupe (JG)

An all-new Continental for 1982 weighed less than the old Versailles, and could even have a V-6 engine instead of the traditional Lincoln V-8. The former Continental design continued under the Town Car badge, as a four-door only. Mark-VI still offered three Designer models and a Signature Series. Continental added a pair of Designer models of its own for 1983 and dropped that V-6 engine choice. Lincoln sales climbed appreciably for the model year.

Mark VII took a dramatically different form for 1984: an aero-styled wedge shape, far removed from its Mark forerunners. It was also shorter. A Mark VII LSC model added capable handling to traditional Lincoln luxuries. Both Continental and Mark could get a turbodiesel engine—though not too many customers seemed to want one, and it didn't last long.

A performance Lincoln? That was the Mark VII LSC, adding more such extras for 1985, including big Eagle GT blackwall tires. Anti-lock braking became optional on both Mark and Continental, and standard the next year. All three models offered Designer and Signature Series. Town Car continued as the "big" conventional Lincoln, reaching record sales levels in 1985 and again in '86. Plenty of Lincoln buyers, it seemed, preferred the old familiar comforts.

Collectors have a huge selection of Designer Lincolns and other special editions to choose from—several for each model year. Mark coupes tend to attract more attention than the stodgier Continental/Town Car. Among recent models, the Mark VII LSC may not look like a Lincoln (or perform like one), but could be a good bet for the future. Versailles? An interesting idea that never caught on, which could become collectible on that basis alone. Like other Lincolns, it holds a lot of luxury and was especially well constructed.

1976 LINCOLN

Lincoln entered the mid-1970s with a pair of big luxury cars. Continental had received a significant facelift for 1975 and continued in that form this year. Mark IV also showed little change for 1976, but added a set of Designer models, signed by well-known names in the fashion world, to lure affluent buyers. Quite a few previously standard items were made optional for 1976, to keep base prices down.

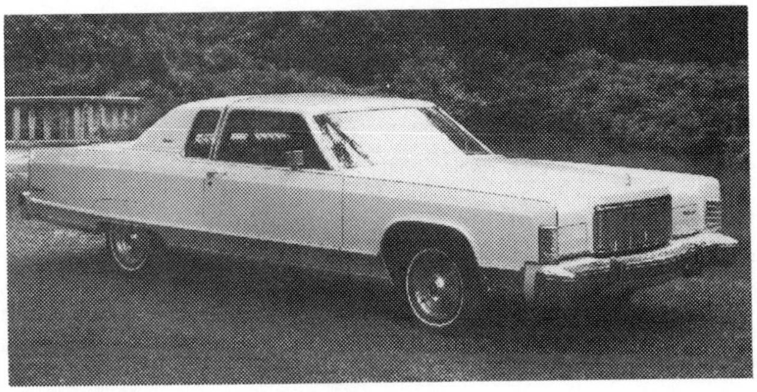

1976 Continental Town Coupe (L)

CONTINENTAL — V-8 — Not much changed in the Continental luxury lineup, which had been substantially redesigned a year earlier, except for several new options and some revisions in standard equipment. A number of former standard items became optional. As before, two body styles were produced: a traditional four-door sedan and distinctive coupe. Posher Town Car and Town Coupe packages also were offered. Wheelbase was 127.2 inches. Continental had a wide six-section vertical-bar grille, with pattern repeated in twin side-by-side bumper slots below. A nameplate decorated the door of the left concealed headlamp. Horizontally-ribbed wraparound park/signal lights stood at fender tips, with separate cornering lamps. The bright Continental star stand-up hood ornament had a fold- down feature. A gold Continental star was laminated into the glass of the two-door's large fixed quarter windows. Front doors held a plaque for owner's initials. Rear fender skirts had bright moldings. The vertical two-pod taillamp assembly had a bright frame and integral side marker light and reflector, with full-width red lower back panel applique. Continental also had bright 'Lincoln Continental' script and 'Lincoln' block letters. Four body colors were added, and the distinctive Jade Green interior was now available in all models. Inside was a standard Cartier-signed digital clock, and the instrument panel had a simulated burled walnut applique. Town Car had special identification on the front fender; Town Coupe, on rear pillar. Both had a vinyl roof and coach lamps on the center pillar, with a new roof band. Interiors had leather seating surfaces and vinyl upholstery. Above the glovebox door was a gold-color Lincoln Town Coupe or Town Car nameplate. For 1976, both Town Coupe and Town Car could be ordered with a coach roof in 14 color choices. It was a thickly-padded vinyl half-roof, rolled and tucked at the rear and quarter windows. A wide molding extended over the roof at the center pillar. Town Car and Town Coupe interiors had loose-pillow seating. Leather and vinyl bench seats were standard in both, with Twin Comfort Lounge seats optional in velour or leather and vinyl. Continental had a separate body on perimeter frame and helical coil spring rear suspension with three-link, rubber- insulated cushioned pivots. Sole engine was the big 460 cu. in. (7.5-liter) V-8. New options included two radio packages: AM/FM stereo search, and the same thing with quadrasonic tape player (an industry first). Forged aluminum wheels were also optional. So was a four-note horn. Four-doors had a new optional opera window set.

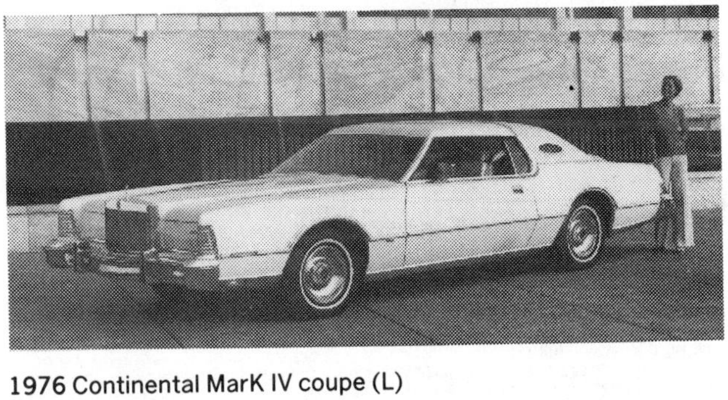

1976 Continental MarK IV coupe (L)

MARK IV — V-8 — Lincoln's personal luxury coupe rode a 120.4 inch wheelbase and its "classic" styling changed little this year. New trims and options were available, and the standard equipment list was altered. Most noteworthy, though, was the addition of four Designer Series models, each named for a famous fashion designer: Bill Blass, Cartier, Hubert de Givenchy, and Emilio Pucci. Appearance was similar to 1975, including the expected concealed headlamps. Mark's traditional radiator-style, classic-look grille was rather narrow, made up of thin vertical bars, with a heavy upper header bar that extended down along the grille sides. Its resemblance to Rolls-Royce was no accident. Above the grille was a bright Continental star stand-up hood ornament. Combination wraparound parking and turn signal lamps were inset in leading edges of front fenders. The padded halo vinyl roof had color-keyed surround moldings, with vinyl-clad color-keyed rear window molding. Tiny oval opera windows to the rear of the quarter windows, in the wide rear pillar, held Continental star ornaments. Identification consisted of 'Continental' block letters and script, as well as 'Mark IV' block letters and plaque. Doors displayed the buyer's initials. Bright rocker panel moldings and extensions were included. The simulated spare tire had 'Continental' lettering around the upper perimeter. Horizontal wraparound taillamps stood just above the bumper. Inside were standard Twin Comfort Lounge seats in cloth and vinyl. Mark had the same 460 cu. in. (7.5-liter) V-8 as Continental, with standard 2.75:1 rear axle ratio. A Traction-Lok differential was available, as was a new engine block heater. A number of formerly standard items were made optional, including an AM/FM stereo radio, power door locks, power decklid release, tilt steering column, speed control, paint stripes, and appearance protection group. There were four new optional luxury group interiors: gold/cream, red/rose, light jade/dark jade, and jade/white. Other new colors included dark jade (with a Versailles option), gold, and dove grey. Standard body colors were: black, dove grey, dark red, dark blue metallic, light blue, dark jade metallic, dark brown metallic, cream, tan, and white. Thirteen additional colors were optional. Turning to the Designer Series, the Cartier had dove grey body paint and a Valino grain landau vinyl roof; red and white paint/tape stripes; dove grey bodyside molding; and Twin Comfort Lounge seats in either dove grey Versailles cloth or grey leather seating surfaces. Opera windows carried the golden Cartier signature. Bill Blass had a blue metallic body, cream Normande grain landau vinyl roof, cream and gold paint/tape stripes, and either cream or dark blue bodyside moldings. Twin Comfort seats were either blue majestic cloth or blue leather, with cream accent straps and buttons. The Givenchy Mark displayed aqua blue (turquoise) Diamond Fire body paint, with white Normande grain landau vinyl roof, black and white paint/tape stripes, and white or aqua blue bodyside moldings. Twin Comfort seats wore aqua blue velour cloth or aqua blue leather. Dark red Moondust (burgundy) body paint went on the Pucci, which also had a silver Normande grain landau vinyl roof, silver and lipstick red custom paint/tape stripes, and red or silver bodyside moldings. Twin Comfort seats carried dark red majestic cloth. All four Designer editions had forged aluminum wheels. All had the designer's signature on the opera window, and on a 22K gold plate on the instrument panel (which also carried the owner's name).

I.D. DATA: Lincoln's 11-symbol Vehicle Identification Number (VIN) is stamped on a metal tab fastened to the instrument panel, visible through the windshield. The first digit is a model year code ('6' 1976). The second letter indicates assembly plant: 'Y' Wixom, MI. Digits three and four are the body serial code, which corresponds to the Model Numbers shown in the tables below: '81' Continental 2-dr. HT coupe; '82' Continental 4-dr. HT sedan; '89' Mark IV 2-dr. HT coupe. The fifth symbol is an engine code: 'A' V8460 4Bbl. Finally, digits 6-11 make up the consecutive unit number, starting with 800,001. A Vehicle Certification Label on the left front door lock face panel or door pillar shows the manufacturer, month and year of manufacture, GVW, GAWR, certification statement, VIN, body code, color code, trim code, axle code, transmission code, and domestic (or foreign) special order code.

CONTINENTAL (V-8)

Model Number	Body/Style Number	Body Type & Seating	Factory Price	Shipping Weight	Production Total
81	60B	2-dr. HT Cpe-6P	9142	5035	24,663
82	53B	4-dr. Sedan-6P	9293	5083	43,983

MARK IV (V-8)

89	65D	2-dr. HT Cpe-6P	11060	5051	56,110

ENGINE DATA: BASE V-8: 90-degree, overhead valve V-8. Cast iron block and head. Displacement: 460 cu. in. (7.5 liters). Bore & stroke: 4.36 x 3.85 in. Compression ratio: 8.0:1. Brake horsepower: 202 at 3800 R.P.M. Torque: 352 lbs.-ft. at 1600 R.P.M. Five main bearings. Hydraulic valve lifters. Carburetor: 4Bbl. Motorcraft 4350 (9510).

CHASSIS DATA: Wheelbase: (Continental) 127.2 in.; (Mark IV) 120.4 in. Overall Length: (Cont.) 232.9 in.; (Mark IV) 228.1 in. Height: (Cont. 2-dr.) 55.3 in.; (Cont. 4-dr.) 55.5 in.; (Mark IV) 53.5 in. Width: (Cont.) 80.3 in.; (Mark IV) 79.8 in. Front Tread: (Cont.) 64.3 in.; (Mark IV) 63.1 in. Rear Tread: (Cont.) 64.3 in.; (Mark IV) 62.6 in. Standard Tires: KR78 x 15 SBR WSW.

TECHNICAL: Transmission: Select-Shift three-speed manual transmission (column shift) standard. Gear ratios: (1st) 2.46:1; (2nd) 1.46:1; (3rd) 1.00:1; (Rev) 2.18:1. Standard final drive ratio: 2.75:1. Steering: Recirculating ball, power-assisted. Suspension: Independent front coil springs w/lower trailing links and anti-sway bar; rigid rear axle w/lower trailing radius arms, upper oblique torque arms, coil springs, and transverse linkage (anti-sway) bar. Brakes: Front disc, rear drum. Ignition: Electronic. Body construction: Separate body on perimeter-type (ladder) frame. Fuel tank: (Continental) 24.2 gal.; (Mark IV) 26.5 gal.

DRIVETRAIN OPTIONS: Differential: Higher axle ratio: Cont. ($33). Higher axle ratio w/dual exhausts: Mark ($87). Traction-Lok differential ($61). Brakes & Steering: Sure track brakes ($263). Four-wheel disc brakes: Cont. ($172). Other: Engine block heater ($19). Extended-range fuel tank: Cont. ($100). Trailer towing pkg. III: Mark ($127).

CONVENIENCE/APPEARANCE OPTIONS: Option Packages: Town Car option: Cont. ($731). Town Coupe option: Cont. ($731). Versailles option: Mark ($1033). Mark IV Designer series (Cartier, Blass or Pucci): leather ($1500); Versailles cloth ($2000). Mark IV Givenchy Designer series: leather or velour ($1500). Mark IV luxury group: gold-cream, red rose, dark/light jade, jade-white, saddle- white, lipstick-white, or blue diamond paint ($477-$552). Power lock convenience group ($87-$113). Appearance protection group ($53-$61). Headlamp convenience group ($101). Comfort/Convenience: Rear defroster, electric ($81). Quick- defroster: Mark ($360). Speed control ($117). Power vent windows ($80). Tilt steering wheel ($69). Fuel economy light ($27). Intermittent wipers ($28). Anti-theft alarm ($115). Security lock group ($11-$17). Lighting, Horn and Mirrors: Coach lamps: Cont. ($60). Four- note horn ($17). Right remote mirror ($31). Lighted visor vanity mirrors ($100). Entertainment: AM/FM stereo radio ($148); w/quadrasonic 8- track tape player ($387). AM/FM stereo radio w/tape player: Cont. ($288). Search-tune AM/FM stereo radio ($300). Exterior: Sunroof ($701). Moonroof ($885). Vinyl roof: Cont. ($168). Landau vinyl roof ($113-$512). Coach vinyl roof: Cont. Twn Car/Cpe ($333). Opera windows: Cont. ($84). Moondust paint ($147). Diamond fire paint ($193). Custom paint stripes ($29). Narrow vinyl-insert moldings ($41). Premium bodyside moldings ($113-$143). Interior: Leather interior: Cont. ($220); Mark ($235 credit). Velour seats: Cont. Twn Car/Cpe ($187 credit). Bench seat w/passenger recliner: Cont. ($76). Twin comfort seats: Cont. ($259); w/passenger recliner ($335). Power lumbar seat: Mark ($93). Passenger recliner seat: Mark ($76). Trunk trim option: Cont. ($61). Wheels and Tires: Luxury wheel covers: Cont. ($83). Forged aluminum wheels ($300). LR78 x 15 SBR WSW ($44). Space saver spare: Mark ($96).

HISTORY: Introduced: October 3, 1975. Model year production: 124,756. Calendar year production: 124,880. Calendar year sales by U.S. dealers: 122,003. Model year sales by U.S. dealers: 122,317.

Historical Footnotes: Sales rose by 43 percent for both Lincoln models in the 1976 model year. That made Continental the industry's most successful car (according to Lincoln-Mercury). Production of the new Versailles was scheduled to begin in April 1977, targeted to compete with Cadillac's Seville.

1977 LINCOLN

In the first wave of powerplant downsizing, the restyled Mark lost its big 460 cu. in. standard V-8 and switched to a modest 400 cu. in. version. Continental soon did likewise, keeping the big V-8 was an option. A whole new model arrived later in the season: the Versailles, based on the Ford Granada/Mercury Monarch platform but far most costly, ready to compete with Cadillac's Seville. Standard Continental/Mark colors were: black, dove grey, midnight blue, dark jade metallic, cream, cordovan metallic, light cordovan, and white. Optional: dark red, ice blue, ember, or cinnamon gold Moondust; and silver, black, yellow gold, light jade, or (Mark V only) rose Diamond Fire. Versailles introduced clearcoat paint to domestic cars.

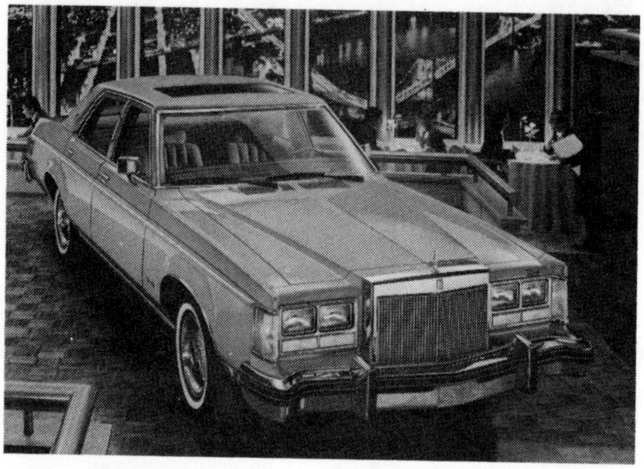

1977 Versailles sedan (JG)

VERSAILLES — V-8 — Lincoln hardly wanted to be left behind when Cadillac's new Seville was attracting plenty of customers. Versailles was its response, introduced very late in the model year (not until spring) as a 1977.5 model. The idea was to combine traditional Lincoln styling with a smaller, more efficient chassis. That was accomplished by turning to the compact Granada/Monarch platform, adding a number of luxury Lincoln touches and vastly improved quality control. Versailles had a radiator-style vertical-bar grille not unlike Continental's (with small emblem in the center of the upper header bar); quad rectangular (exposed) headlamps above clear quad parking/signal lamps; a decklid lid similar in shape to Mark V (with simulated spare tire bulge); and fully padded vinyl roof with "frenched" rear window. Clear wraparound and amber side marker lenses on front fenders matched the height of the headlamp/parking lamp housing and were enclosed by the same bright molding. A stand-up hood ornament featured the Continental star. Full-length high- lustre bodyside moldings had color-keyed vinyl inserts. On the center pillars were Continental-style coach lamps; up top, a padded vinyl roof with Valino pattern (six color choices). At the rear were simple wraparound horizontal taillamps. Forged aluminum wheels were uniquely styled. Versailles came in three metallic colors (cordovan, cinnamon gold and light silver), plus five non-metallic (white, midnight blue, wedgewood blue, light chamois, and midnight cordovan). A lower body two-tone option came in four colors: medium silver metallic, midnight blue, midnight cordovan, or cinnamon gold. Inside were standard flight bench seats, leather-covered armrests, a hand-wrapped leather instrument panel crash pad, and woodgrain cluster and trim panel appliques. Standard equipment included a collapsible spare tire, dual lighted vanity mirrors, digital clock from Cartier, AM/FM stereo search radio, and four-way power seat. A relatively small option list included an illuminated outside thermometer, tilt steering wheel, power decklid release, remote right-hand mirror, whitewalls, power door locks, speed control, forged aluminum wheels, leather/vinyl trim, visor-mounted garage door opener, glass moonroof, CB radio, and illuminated entry. Under the hood (at first) was a 351 cu. in. (5.8-liter) two-barrel V-8 with DuraSpark ignition and SelectShift automatic, hooked to standard 2.50:1 rear axle ratio. California versions carried a 302 cu. in. V-8, which would soon become standard everywhere. Versailles featured unibody construction and a lightweight aluminum hood. Front suspension consisted of helical coil springs (spring over upper arm) with ball joints and drag strut. The Hotchkiss rear had semi-elliptic leaf springs. Four-wheel power disc brakes were standard. Engineering features aimed at refinement and smooth, quiet ride. They included matched, balanced driveline parts, low-friction lower ball joints, double-isolated shocks, reinforced chassis areas, and plenty of insulation. Balanced forged aluminum wheels wore Michelin-X radials. Quality control at the plant was strengthened to the point of dynamometer testing of the engine/transmission, a rigorous water spray test to pinpoint body leaks, and a simulated road test. Bodies received the first clearcoat paint on a regular production car.

CONTINENTAL — V-8 — Model lineup of the big Continental was the same as 1976, including the posh Town Coupe and Town Car options. The restyled front end retained the "classic" vertical chrome- plated grille, but in a narrower form similar to Mark V, along with concealed headlamps and integral parking/turn signal lamps in front fender extensions. Otherwise, appearance was similar to 1976. The strong vertical theme was enhanced by crisp lines of the hood, front fenders, and parking lamps. Continentals had black bumper guard pads and rub strips, a bright stand-up hood ornament, cornering lamps, bright rocker moldings with rear quarter extension, bright full-length fender peak moldings, and rear fender skirts. Premium bodyside moldings had a new vinyl insert grain. Rear quarter windows on two-doors had a Continental star laminated into the glass. Rear ends displayed a full-width red reflective lower back panel applique, vertical two-pod taillamp assembly, and hinged Continental star on the decklid. Five body colors were new. Inside were new head restraints and two new interior colors, as well as a new high-gloss simulated walnut grain on instrument panel, steering wheel, and other components. New options included illuminated entry, fixed-glass moon roof, and CB radio. Base engine announced at first was the big old 460 cu. in. (7.5-liter) V-8, but a 400 cu. in. (6.6-liter) two-barrel V-8 engine with SelectShift automatic later became standard, the 460 four-barrel optional. New DuraSpark ignition gave higher spark plug voltage at startup and low idle speeds, which allowed the wider spark gap needed for burning modern (lean) mixtures. Town Car and Town Coupe added a new Valino grain full vinyl roof and center pillar; coach lamps; and 'Town Coupe' script on rear pillar (or 'Town Car' on front fender). Both had

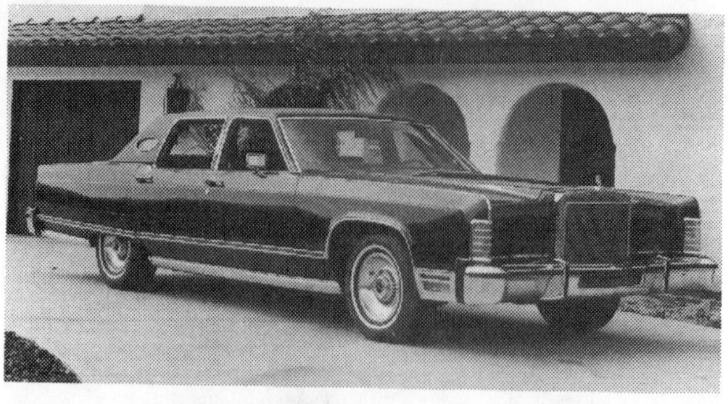

1977 Continental Town Car (L)

leather seating surfaces, with "loose pillow" design. They also had power vent windows and a six-way power seat. A new special edition also was announced: the Town Car Williamsburg series, in silver or cordovan. It combined two different shades of the same color to give a longer and lower appearance. The silver model had new medium grey metallic paint on bodysides, combined with silver diamond fire on hood, roof and rear deck. The cordovan model had new midnight cordovan bodyside paint, with cordovan metallic hood, roof and rear deck. The silver Williamsburg model also had a silver Valino grain full vinyl roof, dual silver paint stripes, and dove gray natural-grain leather-and-vinyl or media velour upholstery. Cordovan versions carried a cordovan Valino grain vinyl roof, cordovan paint stripes, and cordovan leather-and-vinyl or media velour upholstery. Both Williamsburgs had six-way power Twin Comfort Lounge seats, reclining passenger seat, power vent windows, personalized instrument panel nameplate, lighted visor vanity mirror, carpeted luggage compartment, and dual-beam dome/map lamp.

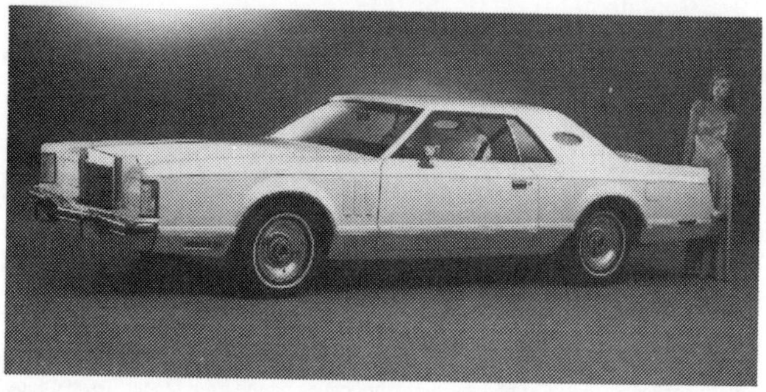

1977 Continental Mark V coupe (L)

MARK V — V-8 — A new Mark version arrived for 1977, similar to its predecessor but weighing more than 300 pounds less. Downsized, that is, but hardly drastically. Styling was described as "evolutionary," carrying on such familiar details as concealed headlamps, simulated-tire decklid hump, and little horizontal oval porthole windows on the sail panels (with Continental star laminated in the glass). But this version had all-new sheetmetal, grille, bumpers, functional triple fender louvers at the cowl, and vertical taillamps. The overall look was more angular than before, described as "sculptured styling." As before, Mark V had a "classic" (radiator-style) chrome-plated vertical-bar grille, with heavier upper header bar. Front bumper guards were farther apart. Vertical taillamps had thin horizontal trim strips. Mark also had a bright star stand-up hood ornament, blade-like vertical parking lamps, black bumper guard pads and rub strips, premium bodyside moldings with Corinthian grain vinyl insert (choice of color), cornering lamps, bright wheel lip moldings, and personalized owner's initials. The standard roof was painted metal. Interiors held Twin Comfort Lounge seats in pleated design with soft ultravelour fabric. The new instrument panel had a high-gloss walnut woodgrain applique, new lenses with cut crystal appearance, jewelry-like instrument faces, and new Cartier day/date clock. Other standard features included an AM/FM monaural radio with four speakers, power antenna, two- spoke steering wheel, automatic-temperature- control air conditioning, power windows and six-way driver's seat, tinted glass, and four lighted ashtrays with lighters. Standard Mark V colors were black, white, dove grey, midnight blue, dark jade metallic, cream, cordovan metallic, and light cordovan. Optional Moondust colors were dark red, ice blue, cinnamon gold, or ember. Optional Diamond Fire colors: black, rose, silver, light jade, or yellow gold. Base powerplant was reduced to a 400 cu. in. (6.6- liter) two-barrel V-8 with Dura-Spark ignition. Standard equipment included SelectShift three-speed automatic, four- wheel power disc brakes, Michelin steel-belted radial whitewalls, space-saver spare tire, and power steeering. The big 460 V-8 remained available as an option. Other new options included illuminated entry, heated left-hand remote mirror (packaged with electric rear defroster), turbine-style cast aluminum wheels, CB radio, and high-altitude option. Like its predecessor, Mark V was available in Designer models. Bill Blass had midnight blue paint; chamois-color landau vinyl roof with pigskin grain (full vinyl roof optional); pigskin-grain leather-and-vinyl interior in new chamois color; chamois or midnight blue bodyside molding; dual chamois paint stripes on bodyside and decklid, with Bill Blass insignia on front fender; Bill Blass name in opera window; and optional (no extra charge) 22K gold finished instrument panel nameplate with customer's name engraved. Turbine style cast aluminum wheels and six-way power passenger's seat also were included. Cartier's version was similar but with dove grey paint and landau vinyl roof, and dove grey leather-and-vinyl (or majestic velour) interior. Also dove grey bodyside moldings, and a single thin dark red bodyside paint stripe. Decklids held a Cartier interlockingC logo; opera windows, a Cartier signature. The Emilio Pucci model came in black Diamond Fire paint with white landau roof in Cayman grain patent-leather look. A white leather and vinyl interior had black components. Pucci also had black bodyside moldings, a three-quarter length bodyside tape stripe, and Pucci signature in the opera window. Mark's Givenchy edition was painted dark jade metallic, with a unique forward half-vinyl roof in chamois-color pigskin. Interiors were dark jade majestic cloth or leather and vinyl. Chamois-color bodyside moldings and dual paint stripes went on bodyside, hood and decklid. Hood and decklid stripes terminated in a double-G Givenchy insignia. There was also a series of luxury groups: cordovan, midnight blue/cream, gold/cream, light jade/dark jade, red/rose, and majestic velour.

I.D. DATA: Lincoln's 11-symbol Vehicle Identification Number (VIN) is stamped on a metal tab fastened to the instrument panel, visible through the windshield. The first digit is a model year code ('7' 1977). The second letter indicates assembly plant: 'Y' Wixom, MI; 'W' Wayne, MI. Digits three and four are the body serial code, which

corresponds to the Model Numbers shown in the tables below: '81' Continental 2-dr. HT coupe; '82' Continental 4-dr. sedan; '84' Versailles 4dr. sedan; '89' Mark V 2-dr. HT coupe. The fifth symbol is an engine code: 'H' V8351 2Bbl.; 'S' V8400 2Bbl.; 'A' V8460 4Bbl. Finally, digits 6-11 make up the consecutive unit number, starting with 800,001. A Vehicle Certification Label on the left front door lock face panel or door pillar shows the manufacturer, month and year built, GVW, GAWR, VIN, body code, color code, trim code, axle code, transmission code, and special order coding.

VERSAILLES (V-8)

Model Number	Body/Style Number	Body Type & Seating	Factory Price	Shipping Weight	Production Total
84	54M	4-dr. Sedan-5P	11500	3800	15,434

CONTINENTAL (V-8)

81	60B	2-dr. HT Cpe-6P	9474	4836	27,440
82	53B	4-dr. Sedan-6P	9636	4880	68,160

MARK V (V-8)

89	65D	2-dr. HT Cpe-6P	11396	4652	80,321

ENGINE DATA: BASE V-8 (Versailles): 90-degree, overhead valve V-8. Cast iron block and head. Displacement: 351 cu. in. (5.8 liters). Bore & stroke: 4.00 x 3.50 in. Compression ratio: 8.1:1. Brake horsepower: 135 at 3200 R.P.M. Torque: 275 lbs.-ft. at 1600 R.P.M. Five main bearings. Hydraulic valve lifters. Carburetor: 2Bbl. Motorcraft 2150. VIN Code: H. BASE V-8 (Mark V, later Continental): 90-degree, overhead valve V-8. Cast iron block and head. Displacement: 400 cu. in. (6.6 liters). Bore & stroke: 4.00 x 4.00 in. Compression ratio: 8.0:1. Brake horsepower: 179 at 4000 R.P.M. Torque: 329 lbs.-ft. at 1600 R.P.M. Five main bearings. Hydraulic valve lifters. Carburetor: 2Bbl. Motorcraft 2150. VIN Code: S. BASE V-8 (early Continental); OPTIONAL (Mark V): 90-degree, overhead valve V-8. Cast iron block and head. Displacement: 460 cu. in. (7.5 liters). Bore & stroke: 4.36 x 3.85 in. Compression ratio: 8.0:1. Brake horsepower: 208 at 4000 R.P.M. Torque: 356 lbs.-ft. at 2000 R.P.M. Five main bearings. Hydraulic valve lifters. Carburetor: 4Bbl. Motorcraft 4350. VIN Code: A.

CHASSIS DATA: Wheelbase: (Versailles) 109.9 in.; (Continental) 127.2 in.; (Mark V) 120.4 in. Overall Length: (Versailles) 200.9 in. (Cont.) 233.0 in. (Mark V) 230.3 in. Height: (Versailles) 54.1 in.; (Cont. 2-dr.) 55.0 in.; (Cont. 4-dr.) 55.2 in.; (Mark V) 53.0 in. Width: (Versailles) 74.5 in.; (Cont. 2-dr.) 79.7 in.; (Cont. 4-dr.) 80.0 in.; (Mark V) 79.7 in. Front Tread: (Versailles) 59.0 in.; (Cont.) 64.3 in.; (Mark V) 63.1 in. Rear Tread: (Versailles) 57.7 in.; (Cont.) 64.3 in.; (Mark V) 62.6 in. Standard Tires: (Versailles) N/A; (Continental) KR78 x 15 SBR WSW; (Mark V) JR78 x 15 SBR WSW.

TECHNICAL: Transmission: SelectShift three-speed manual transmission (column shift) standard. Gear ratios: (1st) 2.46:1; (2nd) 1.46:1; (3rd) 1.00:1; (Rev) 2.18:1. Standard final drive ratio: (Versailles) 2.50:1; (Continental) 2.75:1 except with V8460, 2.50:1; (Mark V) 3.00:1. Steering: Recirculating ball, power-assisted. Suspension: (Versailles) front spring over upper arm w/ball joints and drag struts and coil springs, Hotchkiss rear w/semi-elliptic leaf springs; (others) independent front coil springs w/lower trailing links and anti-sway bar; rigid rear axle w/lower trailing radius arms, upper oblique torque arms, coil springs, and transverse linkage (anti-sway) bar. Brakes: Four-wheel disc except Continental, front disc and rear drum. Ignition: Electronic. Body construction: (Versailles) unibody; (others) separate body on perimeter-type ladder frame. Fuel Tank: (Versailles) N/A; (Continental) 24.2 gal.; (Mark V) 26 gal.

DRIVETRAIN OPTIONS: 460 cu. in. V-8 engine: Mark ($133). Dual exhausts: Mark ($71). Higher axle ratio: Mark ($21). Traction-Lok differential ($65). Four-wheel disc (Sure Track) brakes: Cont. ($461). Sure Track brakes: Mark ($280). Engine block heater ($20). Trailer towing pkg.: Mark ($68-$89). California emission system ($54).

CONTINENTAL/MARK V CONVENIENCE/APPEARANCE OPTIONS: Option Packages: Town Car option: Cont. ($913). Town Coupe option: Cont. ($913). Williamsburg Limited Edition: Cont. (N/A). Mark Cartier Designer series: leather ($1600); cloth ($2100). Mark V Bill Blass or Emilio Pucci Designer series ($1600). Mark V Givenchy Designer series: leather vinyl ($1600); velour ($2100). Power lock convenience group ($92- $120). Appearance protection group ($57-$65). Headlamp convenience group ($107). Defroster group ($107). Interior light group ($106-$120). Comfort/Convenience: Rear defroster: Cont. ($86). Speed control ($124). Illuminated entry system ($55). Six-way power seat: Cont. ($139); w/recliner ($219) exc. ($81) with Town Car/Cpe. Reclining passenger seat: Mark ($139). Six-way power passenger seat: Mark ($143). Power lumbar seat: Mark ($187). Twin comfort power seats: Cont. ($354-$493). Power vent windows ($85). Tilt steering wheel ($73). Intermittent wipers: Cont. ($30). Lighting and Mirrors: Coach lamps: Cont. ($64). Right remote mirror ($33). Entertainment: AM/FM stereo radio ($143); w/quadrasonic 8- track tape player ($396). AM/FM stereo search radio ($304). CB radio ($285). Exterior: Fixed-glass moonroof: Cont. ($954). Power glass moonroof ($938). Steel roof: Mark ($271 credit). Coach roof: Cont. ($522) exc. ($285) with Town Car/Cpe. Full vinyl roof: Cont. ($178); Mark ($187) exc. ($271 credit) w/Designer series. Opera windows: Cont. ($89). Moondust paint ($155). Diamond fire paint ($205). Custom paint stripes ($31). Rocker panel moldings: Mark ($28). Narrow vinyl-insert moldings: Cont. ($44). Premium bodyside moldings: Cont. ($88). Interior: Leather interior trim: Mark ($252). Velour seats: Cont. Twn Car/Cpe ($198 credit). Wheels: Luxury wheel covers: Cont. ($88). Forged aluminum wheels: Cont. ($230-$318). Turbine spoke wheels: Cont. ($237- $325).

NOTE: Versailles option list not available; similar to 1978.

HISTORY: Introduced: October 1, 1976 except Versailles, March 28, 1977. Model year production: 191,355. Calendar year production: 211,439. Calendar year sales by U.S. dealers: 181,282. Model year sales by U.S. dealers: 164,208.

Historical Footnotes: Continental was the biggest car on the domestic market, as well as the worst guzzler. It weighed a whopping 5,000 pounds at the curb. The restyled Mark V sold strongly, up by one-third over the score of the last Mark IV. Versailles cost nearly three times as much as the related Mercury Monarch, and not everyone agreed that it was worth the extra price, even with the luxury features and tight construction. The new compact was 32 inches shorter and half a ton lighter than a Continental sedan but cost nearly $2000 more. Only 8,169 Versailles found buyers in its short opening season. Stretch limousines were offered by various manufacturers, including AHA Manufacturing Company in Mississauga, Ontario. That firm did a 12-inch stretch to 139 inch wheelbase, an 18-inch stretch to 145 inches, and even a massive 157 inch version.

Versailles turned to a smaller V-8 engine in its first complete season, while both Continental and Mark carried on with 400 and 460 cu. in. V-8s. Mark V offered a new Diamond Jubilee Edition to help commemorate FoMoCo's 75th anniversary.

1978 Versailles sedan (L)

VERSAILLES — V-8 — After beginning life in spring 1977 with a 351 cu. in. V-8, Versailles switched to a 302 cu. in. (5.0-liter) V-8 with variable-venturi carburetor for the 1978 model year. That engine had been formerly been installed in California Versailles. Appearance of the four-door sedan was nearly identical this year, and mechanical changes modest: just an improved power steering pump and new electronic engine control system. Versailles had a Continental-style grille, horizontal parking lamps, sculptured aluminum hood with bright Continental star ornament, center-pillar coach lamps, special forged aluminum wheels, and simulated spare tire on the decklid. The fully padded vinyl roof had a "frenched" rear window. Bumper guards had vertical rub strips and a wide horizontal rub strip. Bodies featured a clearcoat paint finish, as well as high-lustre wide upper bodyside moldings with vinyl insert. At the rear were horizontal wraparound taillamps and low-profile bumper guards. Inside touches included leather covering on the instrument panel, steering wheel and armrests. This year's colors were white, midnight blue, wedgewood blue, light chamois, cordovan metallic, light silver metallic, cinnamon gold metallic, dark red metallic, or medium silver metallic in two-tones only. There was a new wire wheel cover option, as well as a remote-mount 40-channel CB radio and lighted outside thermometer. SelectShift automatic transmission was standard, with a 2.50:1 axle ratio.

1978 Continental Town Car (L)

CONTINENTAL — V-8 — Not too much was new on the big Continental, except for different wheel covers. The sculptured bodyside got a new, more contemporary rear fender skirt and wheel lip molding (to match the rocker molding). Interiors had a new wide center folding armrest and revised door armrests. The instrument panel had a new high-gloss woodtone applique, as well as restyled knobs and controls and a padded glovebox door. The "classic" vertical-bar grille and concealed headlamps continued, as did the Town Coupe and Town Car option packages. This year's body colors were: black, white, midnight blue, wedgewood blue, midnight jade, cream, cordovan metallic, dark champagne, midnight cordovan, and dove grey. Optional glamour metallic colors were: dark red, silver, ice blue, light jade, light gold, crystal apricot, champagne, and cinnamon gold. The 400 cu. in. (6.6-liter) V-8 offered improved fuel economy with a low-restriction fresh-air intake, and a new mechanical spark control system. The 460 cu. in. (7.5-liter) V-8 was optional again, except in California. Under the hood was a new electronic voltage regulator and maintenance-free battery; on the dash, a low windshield washer fluid warning light. New options included an integral garage door opener, lighted outside thermometer, and wire wheel covers. The optional CB radio introduced in 1977 now had 40 channels.

263

1978 Continental Mark V coupe (L)

1978 Continental sedan (L)

MARK V — V-8 — Lincoln's personal luxury coupe was limited mainly to mechanical refinements and new standard wheel covers this year, but a special version was offered: the Diamond Jubilee Edition, to commemorate Ford's 75th anniversary. That one came in a choice of special Diamond Blue or Jubilee Gold clearcoat metallic paint. It had a Valino grain landau vinyl roof with matching Valino grain accent molding. Vertical grille bars were color-keyed to the body color, as was the unique hood ornament. There was also a special paint stripe on the hood. Front and rear bumper guard pads had horizontal rub strips color-keyed to the body color. Bright-edged fender louvers and coach lamps were included, and the special opera windows (very small oval, as usual) had 'Diamond Jubilee Edition' script and a simulated diamond chip laminated in the beveled glass. Turbine style cast aluminum wheels were color-keyed to the body. Unique bodyside paint striping was interrupted on the door by personalized customer's initials. On the decklid contour was distinctive Valino grain padded vinyl, with 'Continental' letters spelled out on the simulated spare tire cover. A Valino grain vinyl insert also went in the trunk lock cover. Inside were Diamond Jubilee leather/cloth bucket seats in unique sew style with power lumbar support, along with real and simulated ebony woodgrain inserts. Extras even went so far as unique keys with woodtone applique insert, plus a leather-bound owner's manual and a leather-bound tool kit. A leather-covered console held an umbrella. Diamond Jubilee had dual wide-band whitewall steel-belted radials, illuminated entry, interval wipers, tilt steering, and other extras. Two engines were offered again on Mark V: the 400 cu. in. (6.6-liter) V-8 with SelectShift and 2.75:1 rear axle, or the 460 V-8 with 2.50:1 rear axle. Body colors were: black, white, midnight blue, wedgewood blue, midnight jade, cream, cordovan metallic, dark champagne, light champagne, midnight cordovan, and dove grey. Moondust metallic colors were optional: dark red, light silver, ice blue, light jade, light gold, crystal apricot, and cinnamon gold. Joining the option list were a digital miles-to-empty indicator, integral garage door opener, lighted outside thermometer, wire wheel covers, and power retractable CB antenna. The four Designer Series were available again. Bill Blass sported midnight cordovan body color with light champagne landau vinyl roof in Valino grain. The Cartier edition came in light champagne body color with light champagne landau vinyl roof. (A standard metal-finished roof was offered at no extra cost; full vinyl roof at extra cost.) Both had light champagne bodyside moldings. Mark's Pucci edition came in light silver metallic body color, with black landau vinyl roof in Cayman grain for a patent-leather look. It had black bodyside moldings and unique paint/tri-tone tape stripes, plus Pucci logo. Givenchy came in midnight jade body color, with unique forward half- vinyl roof in light chamois color pigskin. Jade leather and vinyl interior trim had a unique broad lace insert in the seatback, embroidered in the double-G Givenchy logo. Bodyside moldings and dual paint stripes were chamois-colored on the Givenchy.

I.D. DATA: As before, Lincoln's 11-symbol Vehicle Identification Number (VIN) is stamped on a metal tab fastened to the instrument panel, visible through the windshield. Coding is similar to 1977. Model year code changed to '8' for 1978. Engine code 'H' (V8351) was replaced by 'F' (V8302 2Bbl.).

VERSAILLES (V-8)

Model Number	Body/Style Number	Body Type & Seating	Factory Price	Shipping Weight	Production Total
84	54M	4-dr. Sedan-5P	12529	3759	8,931

CONTINENTAL (V-8)

Model Number	Body/Style Number	Body Type & Seating	Factory Price	Shipping Weight	Production Total
81	60B	2-dr. HT Cpe-6P	9974	4659	20,977
82	53B	4-dr. Sedan-6P	10166	4660	67,110

MARK V (V-8)

Model Number	Body/Style Number	Body Type & Seating	Factory Price	Shipping Weight	Production Total
89	65D	2-dr. HT Cpe-6P	12099	4567	72,602

Mark V Production Note: Of the total shown, 5,159 were the Diamond Jubilee edition. A total of 16,537 Marks had one of the four Designer packages (8,520 Cartier, 3,125 Pucci, 917 Givenchy, and 3,975 Bill Blass).

ENGINE DATA: BASE V-8 (Versailles): 90-degree, overhead valve V-8. Cast iron block and head. Displacement: 302 cu. in. (5.2 liters). Bore & stroke: 4.00 x 3.00 in. Compression ratio: 8.4:1. Brake horsepower: 133 at 3600 R.P.M. Torque: 243 lbs.-ft. at 1600 R.P.M. Five main bearings. Hydraulic valve lifters. Carburetor: 2Bbl. variable-venturi Motorcraft 2150. VIN Code: F. **BASE V-8 (Continental, Mark V):** 90-degree, overhead valve V-8. Cast iron block and head. Displacement: 400 cu. in. (6.6 liters). Bore & stroke: 4.00 x 4.00 in. Compression ratio: 8.0:1. Brake horsepower: 166 at 3800 R.P.M. Torque: 319 lbs.-ft. at 1800 R.P.M. Five main bearings. Hydraulic valve lifters. Carburetor: 2Bbl. Motorcraft 2150. VIN Code: S. **OPTIONAL V-8 (Continental, Mark V):** 90-degree, overhead valve V-8. Cast iron block and head. Displacement: 460 cu. in. (7.5 liters). Bore & stroke: 4.36 x 3.85 in. Compression ratio: 8.0:1. Brake horsepower: 210 at 4200 R.P.M. Torque: 357 lbs.-ft. at 2200 R.P.M. Five main bearings. Hydraulic valve lifters. Carburetor: 4Bbl. Motorcraft 4350. VIN Code: A.

CHASSIS DATA: Wheelbase: (Versailles) 109.9 in.; (Continental) 127.2 in.; (Mark V) 120.4 in. Overall Length: (Versailles) 200.9 in.; (Cont.) 233.0 in.; (Mark V) 230.3 in. Height: (Versailles) 54.1 in.; (Cont. 2-dr.) 55.0 in.; (Cont. 4-dr.) 55.2 in.; (Mark V) 52.9 in. Width: (Versailles) 74.5 in.; (Cont. 2-dr.) 79.7 in.; (Cont. 4-dr.) 80.0 in.; (Mark V) 79.7 in. Front Tread: (Versailles) 59.0 in.; (Cont.) 64.3 in.; (Mark V) 63.2 in. Rear Tread: (Versailles) 57.7 in.; (Cont.) 64.3 in.; (Mark V) 62.6 in. Standard Tires: (Versailles) FR78 x 14 SBR WSW; (Continental) 225 x 15 SBR WSW; (Mark V) Michelin 225/230 x 15 SBR WSW.

TECHNICAL: Transmission: SelectShift three-speed manual transmission (column shift) standard. Gear ratios: (1st) 2.46:1 (2nd) 1.46:1; (3rd) 1.00:1; (Rev) 2.18:1. Standard final drive ratio: (Versailles) 2.50:1; (Continental/Mark V) 2.75:1 except with V8460, 2.50:1. Steering: Recirculating ball, power-assisted. Suspension/Brakes/Body: same as 1977. Fuel Tank: (Versailles) 19.2 gal.; (Continental) 24.2 gal.; (Mark V) 25 gal.

DRIVETRAIN OPTIONS: 460 cu. in. V-8 engine: Cont./Mark ($187). Dual exhausts: Cont./Mark ($75). Floor shift selector: Versailles ($33). Higher axle ratio: Cont. ($21). Traction-Lok differential: Cont./Mark ($67). Four-wheel disc (Sure Track) brakes: Cont. ($496). Sure Track brakes: Mark ($296). Engine block heater ($20). Trailer towing pkg.: Cont. ($33-$67). Class III trailer towing pkg.: Mark ($72-95). California emission system ($76). High-altitude option (NC).

VERSAILLES CONVENIENCE/APPEARANCE OPTIONS: Appearance protection group ($76). Reclining bucket seat group ($467). Power lock group ($147). Defroster group ($115). Rear defroster, electric ($88). Garage door opener ($87). Illuminated outside thermometer ($27). Tilt steering wheel ($77). AM/FM stereo radio w/8track tape player ($84 credit); w/quadrasonic 8track ($87). 40channel CB radio ($321). Power glass panel moonroof ($1027). Dual-shade paint ($59). Protective bodyside moldings ($48). Lower bodyside protection ($33). Leather interior trim ($295). Wire wheel covers (NC).

1978 Continental Mark V Diamond Jubilee coupe (L)

CONTINENTAL/MARK V CONVENIENCE/APPEARANCE OPTIONS: Option Packages: Mark V Diamond Jubille edition ($8000). Williamsburg Limited Edition: Cont. ($1525-$1725). Town Car option: Cont. ($1440). Town Coupe option: Cont. ($1440). Mark V Cartier Designer series: leather/vinyl or velour cloth ($1800). Mark V Emilio Pucci or Givenchy Designer series: leather/vinyl ($1800). Mark V Bill Blass Designer series: leather/vinyl ($1800); ultra-velour cloth ($1533). Mark V luxury groups ($680), but ($775) w/moondust paint. Power lock convenience group ($115-$147). Appearance protection group ($69-$76). Headlamp convenience group ($133). Defroster group ($115). Interior light group ($108-$127). Comfort/Convenience: Speed control ($127). Illuminated entry system ($63). Six-way power seat: Cont. ($151); w/recliner ($236). Reclining passenger seat: Mark ($85). Six-way power passenger seat: Mark ($151). Power lumbar seat: Mark ($107). Twin comfort power seats: Cont. ($547). Power vent windows ($89). Illuminated outside thermometer ($27). Miles-to-empty fuel indicator ($125). Garage door opener ($87). Tilt steering wheel ($77). Intermittent wipers ($35). Lighting and Mirrors: Coach lamps: Cont. ($63). Map/dome light ($19). Right remote mirror ($37). Entertainment: AM/FM stereo radio ($144); w/8track tape player ($203); w/quadrasonic 8-track player ($373). AM/FM stereo search radio ($287). 40channel CB radio ($321). Exterior: Fixed-glass moonroof: Cont. ($1027). Power glass panel moonroof ($1027). Landau vinyl roof: Mark ($484). Steel roof: Mark V Cartier ($261 credit). Coach roof: Cont. ($547) exc. ($269) with Town Car/Cpe or ($332) w/Williamsburg. Full vinyl roof: Cont. ($215); Mark ($223) exc. ($261 credit) w/Designer series. Opera windows: Cont. ($93). Moondust paint ($189). Custom paint stripes ($53). Rocker panel moldings: Mark ($29). Narrow vinyl-insert moldings: Cont. ($48). Premium bodyside moldings: Cont. ($128). Lower bodyside protection ($33). Interior: Leather interior trim ($267-$295). Velour seats (leather delete): Cont. Twn Car/Cpe ($200 credit). Wheels and Tires: Wire wheel covers ($233). Forged aluminum wheels ($333) exc. (NC) w/Designer Mark. Turbine spoke wheels ($333). Dual wide-band whitewall tires ($52).

HISTORY: Introduced: October 7, 1977. Model year production: 169,620. Calendar year production: 189,523. Calendar year sales by U.S. dealers: 188,487. Model year sales by U.S. dealers: 184,299.

Historical Footnotes: Although Versailles production for the model year dropped sharply, sales this year weren't too far short of twice the total in its first (brief) season: 15,061 versus 8,169. Continental sales rose somewhat for the model year (94,242 versus 83,125), while Mark V gained only modestly. To meet Lincoln-Mercury sales-weighted CAFE requirements, sales of the full-size models had to be held in check, but the company counted on Versailles in its second year.

1979 LINCOLN

Both Continental and Mark V added a new Collector's Series, but otherwise changed little for 1979. Versailles enjoyed a modest, though much-needed restyle, and was the first domestic model to get halogen headlamps. The big 460 cu. in. V-8 disappeared, making a 400 V-8 the biggest Lincoln powerplant.

1979 Versailles "Moon Roof" option sedan (JG)

1979 Versailles "Convertible" option sedan (JG)

VERSAILLES — V-8 — Subtle restyling added 8 inches to the Versailles roofline, giving it a more square, formal "town car" look. Topped with Valino grain vinyl, the roof was fully padded, with a "frenched" back window. Cavalry twill vinyl also was available, with convertible-style back window. New roof accents included a brushed stainless steel wrapover molding, and matching brushed-finish center-pillar appliques with restyled integral coach lamps. Quarter windows were enlarged and door frames revised, allowing wider back doors to open farther. Versailles also added padded vinyl over the simulated spare tire shape on the decklid contour, which carried 'Lincoln' block letters. Wide wraparound taillamps met that "spare." Versailles was the first domestic car with standard halogen headlamps, which cast a "whiter" light. The standard 302 cu. in. (5.0-liter) V-8 had been the first engine to be equipped with electronic engine control (EECI) and variable-venturi carburetor, and continued in that form. Standard equipment included such tempting touches as air conditioning, power windows, four-wheel disc brakes, and speed control. A new electronic AM/FM stereo radio had seek/scan and a Quadrasonic8 tape player. Wire wheel covers were a no-cost option, with aluminum wheels standard.

1979 Continental "Collectors Series" sedan (L)

CONTINENTAL — V-8 — Lincoln's big rear-drive was largely a carryover for 1979, though a Collector's Series was added. Lincoln-Mercury called it the "pinnacle of Lincoln Continental prestige." Some styling features came from the 1978 Mark V Diamond Jubilee Edition, including special paint and a gold-colored grille. Both Town Car and Town Coupe option packages were still available. Wheelbase contined at the lengthy 127 inches. Collector's Series Continentals offered a choice of white or midnight blue clearcoat metallic body paint, with coach roof color-keyed to the body (replacing the full vinyl roof that would otherwise be standard). Up front were gold-painted vertical grille bars. Turbine-style cast aluminum wheels were painted midnight blue between the spokes and the bodyside held unique paint stripes, along with premium lower bodyside moldings keyed to the body color. (Bodyside moldings on other Continentals had a Corinthian grain vinyl insert in customer's choice of color.) 'Collector's Series' script went on the lower corner of the rear pillar of that model. The customary 'Town Car' script on front fender was deleted, and the Collector's Series did not include opera windows. Collector's interior choices were luxury cloth or leather-and-vinyl seat trim in midnight blue. There was a woodtone applique insert in

the steering wheel rim and hub, and a unique hub ornament. Also included: plush midnight blue Tiffany cut-pile carpeting; leather-bound tool kit (containing tools); leather-bound owner's manual; umbrella; power mini-vent windows; illuminated entry; speed control; 63 ampere-hour maintenance-free battery; interval windshield wipers; and a remote-control garage door opener. A Williamsburg option for the Town Car was offered again, in a choice of seven dual-shade color combinations. Williamsburgs included a full vinyl roof, either leather-and-vinyl or velour interior, Twin Comfort Lounge seats, power vent windows, premium bodyside moldings, and so forth. Continental came with the 400 cu. in. (6.6-liter) two-barrel V-8, SelectShift automatic, and 2.47:1 rear axle. Interiors showed expanded use of woodtone appliques on the instrument panel, which added a fuel warning light to replace the former washer fluid light. A new electronic AM/FM stereo radio had digital frequency display.

1979 Continental Mark V "Bill Blass" coupe (L)

MARK V — V-8 — Like Continental, Mark V added a Collector's Series with golden grille this year, to replace the previous Diamond Jubilee Edition. It came with a choice of white or midnight blue clearcoat metallic paint. Standard Collector's equipment included a landau vinyl roof with matching accent moldings, gold-painted vertical grille bars, unique hood ornament and paint stripe, color-keyed front/rear bumper guard pads and horizontal rub strips, bright-edged fender louvers, and coach lamps. 'Collector's Series' script decorated the rear pillar. Turbine aluminum wheels were painted midnight blue between the spokes. A unique bodyside paint stripe was interrupted by the owner's initials on the door. Opera windows were deleted on the Collector's Series, but the decklid lock cover had a vinyl insert. Inside, Mark Collector's had midnight blue power bucket seats in unique sew style (or optional Twin Comfort Lounge seats in white or dark blue leather-and-vinyl). It also had a leather-covered instrument panel, ebony woodtone applique insert in steering wheel rim and hub, blue plush carpeting, leather-covered padded console, leather-bound tool kit and owner's manual, unique keys with woodtone applique insert, power vent windows, illuminated entry, interval wipers, and a number of other luxury touches.

1979 Continental Mark V "Luxury Group" coupe (L)

Otherwise, Mark V appearance chaned little. Padded vinyl now decorated the simulated spare tire on the decklid, which had 'Continental' lettering spaced around its rim. Mark V had only the 400 cu. in. (6.6-liter) two-barrel V-8, with 2.47:1 rear axle ratio. Not much else was different beyond new door/ignition locks and an improved heater. Four Designer Series were offered again, with modest revisions. Bill Blass had a distinctive two-tone paint treatment with hood, decklid and upper bodysides in white; lower bodysides and decklid contour in midnight blue metallic. A white carriage roof had a bright die-cast rear pillar ornament. (If ordered with optional full vinyl roof, the Bill Blass name was in the opera windows.) Blass also had dark blue bodyside moldings and dual gold paint stripes on bodysides and decklid, along with color-keyed turbine-style cast aluminum wheels. Cartier again came in the popular light champagne paint with matching landau vinyl roof, though a standard metal-finished roof was available at no extra cost. It had light champagne bodyside moldings, and a single thin, dark red paint stripe on bodysides. A Cartier interlocking-C logo went on the decklid, and Cartier signature in opera windows. Emilio Pucci's edition had turquoise metallic body paint, a full vinyl roof in midnight blue, white leather-and-vinyl interior trim with midnight blue accents, midnight blue bodyside moldings, Pucci signature in opera windows, and Pucci logo as part of the tri-tone tape stripes. Pucci also had wire wheel covers, whereas the other three had turbine-style cast aluminum wheels. The Givenchy model came in a new crystal blue metallic body paint with crystal blue front half-vinyl roof. Also included: dark crystal blue bodyside moldings and dual tape stripes on bodysides, hood and decklid. Those hood and decklid stripes terminated in a double-G logo. There was also the signature in opera windows. Designer models also had a new electronic-search AM/FM stereo radio with Quadrasonic8 tape player. Mark's Luxury Group series expanded to nine colors this year, up from seven in 1978. One of the new ones was white leather-and-vinyl seats with color-keyed components.

I.D. DATA: As before, Lincoln's 11-symbol Vehicle Identification Number (VIN) is stamped on a metal tab fastened to the instrument panel, visible through the windshield. Coding is similar to 1977-78. Model year code changed to '9' for 1979. Engine code 'A' (V8460) was dropped. Consecutive unit (sequence) numbers began with 600,001.

1979 Versailles "Valino Brougham" option sedan (JG)

VERSAILLES (V-8)

Model Number	Body/Style Number	Body Type & Seating	Factory Price	Shipping Weight	Production Total
84	54M	4-dr. Sedan-5P	12939	3684	21,007

CONTINENTAL (V-8)

81	60B	2-dr. HT Cpe-6P	10985	4639	16,142
82	53B	4-dr. Sedan-6P	11200	4649	76,458

MARK V (V-8)

89	65D	2-dr. HT Cpe-6P	13067	4589	75,939

PRICE NOTE: Collector's Series Continental and Mark V were listed as option packages, but also given initial prices as separate models: Continental $16,148 with leather interior, $15,936 with cloth; Mark V $21,326 with bucket seats, $20,926 with Twin Comfort seats.

ENGINE DATA: BASE V-8 (Versailles): 90-degree, overhead valve V-8. Cast iron block and head. Displacement: 302 cu. in. (5.2 liters). Bore & stroke: 4.00 x 3.00 in. Compression ratio: 8.4:1. Brake horsepower: 130 at 3600 R.P.M. Torque: 237 lbs.-ft. at 1600 R.P.M. Five main bearings. Hydraulic valve lifters. Carburetor: 2Bbl. variable-venturi Motorcraft 2150. VIN Code: F. BASE V-8 (Continental, Mark V): 90-degree, overhead valve V-8. Cast iron block and head. Displacement: 400 cu. in. (6.6 liters). Bore & stroke: 4.00 x 4.00 in. Compression ratio: 8.0:1. Brake horsepower: 159 at 3400 R.P.M. Torque: 315 lbs.-ft. at 1800 R.P.M. Five main bearings. Hydraulic valve lifters. Carburetor: 2Bbl. Motorcraft 2150. VIN Code: S.

CHASSIS DATA: Wheelbase: (Versailles) 109.9 in.; (Continental) 127.2 in.; (Mark V) 120.3 in. Overall Length: (Versailles) 201.0 in.; (Cont.) 233.0 in.; (Mark V) 230.3 in. Height: (Versailles) 54.1 in.; (Cont. 2-dr.) 55.2 in.; (Cont. 4-dr.) 55.4 in.; (Mark V) 53.1 in. Width: (Versailles) 74.5 in.; (Cont. 2-dr.) 79.6 in.; (Cont. 4-dr.) 79.9 in.; (Mark V) 79.7 in. Front Tread: (Versailles) 59.0 in.; (Cont.) 64.3 in.; (Mark V) 63.2 in. Rear Tread: (Versailles) 57.7 in.; (Cont.) 64.3 in.; (Mark V) 62.6 in. Standard Tires: (Versailles) FR78 x 14 SBR WSW; (Continental, Mark V) 225 x 15 SBR WSW.

TECHNICAL: Transmission: Select-Shift three-speed manual transmission (column shift) standard. Gear ratios: (1st) 2.46:1; (2nd) 1.46:1; (3rd) 1.00:1; (Rev) 2.18:1. Standard final drive ratio: 2.47:1. Steering/Suspension/Brakes/Body: same as 1977-78. Fuel Tank: (Versailles) 19.2 gal.; (Continental) 24.2 gal.; (Mark V) 25 gal.

DRIVETRAIN OPTIONS: Floor shift selector: Versailles ($36). Higher axle ratio: Cont./Mark ($23). Traction-Lok differential: Cont./Mark ($71). Sure Track disc brakes: Cont. ($525). Sure Track brakes: Mark ($313). H.D. battery: Cont. ($21). Engine block heater ($21). Trailer towing pkg.: Cont. ($71). Class III trailer towing pkg.: Mark ($84-$107). California emission system ($84). High-altitude option: Cont./Mark (NC).

1979 Versailles "French Window" option sedan (L)

VERSAILLES CONVENIENCE/APPEARANCE OPTIONS: Appearance protection group ($87). Reclining bucket seat group ($491). Power lock group ($155). Defroster group ($121). Rear defroster, electric ($101). Garage door opener ($92). Illuminated outside thermometer ($28). Tilt steering wheel ($81). AM/FM stereo radio w/standard 8track or cassette tape player ($168 credit). 40channel CB radio ($321). Power glass panel moonroof ($1088). Full vinyl or coach roof: Valino grain or Cavalry twill (NC). Dual-shade paint ($63). Protective bodyside moldings ($51). Premium bodyside moldings ($77). Lower bodyside protection ($35). Leather/vinyl interior trim ($312). Wire wheel covers (NC).

266

CONTINENTAL/MARK V CONVENIENCE/APPEARANCE OPTIONS: Option Packages: Collector's Series: Continental ($4736- $5163); Mark ($7859-$8259). Williamsburg Limited Edition: Cont. ($1617-$1829). Town Car option: Cont. ($1527). Town Coupe option: Cont. ($1527). Mark V Cartier Designer series: leather/vinyl or velour cloth ($1945). Mark V Emilio Pucci Designer series: leather/vinyl interior ($1525). Mark V Bill Blass Designer series: leather/vinyl interior w/carriage roof ($2775); w/full vinyl roof ($1809). Mark V Givenchy Designer series w/broadlace interior ($2145). Mark V luxury groups ($743), but w/moondust paint ($843). Power lock convenience group ($121-$156). Appearance protection group ($80-$91). Headlamp convenience group ($140). Defroster group ($121). Interior light group ($115-$135). Comfort/Convenience: Rear defroster ($101). Speed control ($140). Illuminated entry system ($65). Six-way power seat: Cont. ($160); w/recliner ($251). Reclining passenger seat: Mark ($91). Six-way power passenger seat: Mark ($159). Power lumbar seat: Mark ($113). Twin comfort power seats: Cont. ($580). Power vent windows ($95). Illuminated outside thermometer ($28). Miles-to-empty fuel indicator: Mark ($133). Garage door opener ($92). Tilt steering wheel ($81). Intermittent wipers ($40). Lighting and Mirrors: Coach lamps: Cont. ($67). Map/dome light ($20). Right remote mirror ($39). Entertainment: AM/FM stereo radio ($144); w/8track tape player ($203); w/cassette player ($203) exc. ($204 credit) w/Collector's. AM/FM stereo search radio w/quadrasonic 8track player ($407). 40channel CB radio ($321). Exterior: Fixed-glass moonroof: Cont. ($1088). Power glass panel moonroof ($1088) exc. ($555) w/Cont. Collector's. Carriage roof: Mark ($1201). Landau vinyl roof: Mark ($513). Coach roof: Cont. ($580) exc. ($285) with Town Car/Cpe or ($352) w/Williamsburg. Full vinyl roof: Cont. ($228); Mark ($236). Opera windows: Cont. ($99). Moondust paint ($201). Custom paint stripes ($56). Rocker panel moldings: Mark ($31). Narrow vinyl-insert moldings: Cont. ($136). Lower bodyside protection ($35). Interior: Leather interior trim ($312-$333): Cont. Twn Car/Cpe ($212 credit). Velour seats (leather delete): Cont. Twn Car/Cpe ($212 credit). Wheels and Tires: Wire wheel covers ($247). Forged aluminum wheels ($373). Turbine spoke wheels ($373). Dual wide-band whitewall tires ($54). Inflatable spare tire (NC).

HISTORY: Introduced: October 6, 1978. Model year production: 189,546. Calendar year production: 151,960. Calendar year sales by U.S. dealers: 131,271. Model year sales by U.S. dealers: 149,717.

Historical Footnotes: The big Continental was about to be replaced by a new smaller, lighter version. Sales fell for the model year, quite sharply for the two big Lincolns. Mark V sales had been more than double Cadillac Eldorado's, but the freshly-downsized Eldo threatened Lincoln's supremacy in that league.

1980 LINCOLN

Weights of both big Lincolns dropped considerably as Continental took on an all-new form and Mark VI was similarly redesigned. Each was nearly 800 pounds lighter than its predecessor. New suspensions kept the luxury ride, and both got a new deep-well trunk. Electronic engine control systems were standard on all Lincolns. So was a new four-speed automatic overdrive transmission, which had a mechanical lockup in (overdrive) fourth gear. Continental and Mark were more similar than before, essentially two versions of one modernized traditional design, with Mark the upscale edition. Both rode a "Panther" platform based on the 1979 LTD/Marquis. Base engines also shrunk, down to 302 cu. in. (5.0- liter) V-8, with 351 cu. in. (5.8-liter) V-8 optional. Other new technical features on both models included halogen headlamps, P-metric radial tires, and a fluidic windshield washer system. A new electronic instrument panel with message center was standard on Mark VI, optional on Continental. It included a digital speedometer, graphic fuel gauge, vehicle warning system and trip computer. Optional on both was keyless entry, operated by a panel of calculator-type pushbuttons in a preprogrammed sequence. All these changes applied to the upper Lincolns, as the smaller Versailles was in its final season.

1980 Versailles "French Window" sedan (JG)

1980 Versailles "Convertible" option sedan (L)

VERSAILLES — V-8 — Only a handful of changes hit the compact Lincoln sedan in its final year. Under the hood was a new starter; in the trunk, an improved jack. Five body colors were new, as well as three vinyl roof colors. So were standard Twin Comfort Lounge seats with recliners. Two Versailles options were dropped: the floor-mounted shift lever and the full vinyl roof. Standard engine was again the 302 cu. in. (5.0-liter V-8) with variable-venturi carburetor. The enlarged and ample standard equipment list included halogen headlamps, leather-wrapped steering wheel, six-way power driver's seat, auto-temp air conditioning, tinted glass, four-wheel disc brakes, new electronic AM/FM stereo search radio and day/date/elapsed time digital clock, and Michelin tires. Appearance was the same as 1979.

1980 Continental "Collectors Series" sedan (L)

CONTINENTAL — V-8 — For the first time in a decade, an all-new Lincoln arrived, featuring a formal roofline, wider swing-away grille, and full-width taillamps. Again built with separate body and frame construction, Continental lost close to 800 pounds. The aero-styled body was more than a foot shorter, now riding a 117.4 inch wheelbase. A traditional Lincoln "classic" chrome-plated grille was now flanked by exposed quad rectangular halogen headlamps, rather than the former concealed lights. The grille was wider than the former version, though not as tall. As before, its pattern repeated in a single bumper slot. Integral parking/turn signal lamps were in front fender extensions, with cornering lamps standard. Bright bumper guards had black pads, and black bumper rub strips held white accent stripes. On the hood was a bright Continental star ornament, bright rear edge molding, and paint stripes. At the rear was a full-width red reflective lower back panel applique (with bright surround molding), vertical taillamps with bright surround moldings, and bumper-mounted backup lamps. Power vent windows and a full vinyl roof with padded rear roof pillar were standard. Inside was a restyled three-pod instrument cluster with new engine temperature gauge. As before, two- and four-door models were offered. Town Car and Town Coupe had their script in the rear quarter window. Both had coach lamps, seatback robe cords, and map pockets. The Williamsburg Town Car series was replaced by individual dual-shade paint options. New dual-shade paint treatments came in five combinations: black with light pewter metallic, maroon with silver metallic, dark cordovan metallic with bittersweet metallic, dark blue metallic with light pewter metallic, or dark champagne metallic with medium fawn metallic. That dual-finish treatment included upper body paint stripes and premium bodyside moldings. The new standard 302 cu. in. (5.0-liter) V-8 had electronic fuel injection and third-generation electronic engine controls (EECIII). Standard four-speed automatic transmission (basically a three-speed with 0.67:1 overdrive gear tacked on) would slip into overdrive at about 35 MPH. A single poly "V" belt on the optional 351 cu. in. (5.8-liter) V-8 drove the water pump, fan, alternator, and power steering pump. Axle ratio was 3.08:1 with the 302 engine, 2.73:1 with the 351 (same as Mark VI). The big 400 cu. in. V-8 was gone. The new coil-spring front suspension used long and short arms, with a stabilizer bar. At the rear was a new four-link coil spring suspension. Michelin Pmetric steel-belted radials were standard. Gas cylinders eased opening of both hood and decklid. An electronic AM/FM stereo search radio was standard. New options included an electronic instrument cluster (with "message center" and 11-function monitor), keyless entry (with five door-mounted pushbuttons), Premium Sound System, and lacy-spoke aluminum wheels. Optional speed control added a "resume" feature.

MARK VI — V-8 — This year, a four-door sedan joined the customary Mark luxury coupe in its freshly downsized form. While the shrunken Mark rode a 114.4 inch wheelbase, though, the sedan's was 3 inches longer (same as Continental). The coupe lost 6 inches of wheelbase and 14 inches in overall length, as well as close to 700 pounds. Styling was undeniably Lincoln, evolved from Mark V, including Rolls-Royce style grille, oval opera windows on wide Cpillars (with Continental star), and easy-to-spot decklid bulge. While the similarly downsized Continental switched to exposed quad headlamps, Mark kept its hidden headlamps hidden behind closed (larger) doors. Body features included a fully padded vinyl roof with "frenched" rear window, wide bright stainless steel/aluminum rocker panel moldings, and standard power vent windows. Four-doors had center-pillar coach lamps. Front fender louvers had bright edges and a simulated adjuster. Premium bodyside moldings came with vinyl insert in choice of colors. Mark also had bright bumper guards with black pads, black bumper rub strips with white accent stripe, bright Continental star hood ornament, and a bright hood rear-edge molding. This year's taller vertical wraparound parking/signal lights stood again at fender tips. This year's vertical-bar grille pattern was repeated in a wide bumper slot below. Inside was a four-spoke color-keyed steering wheel. Base engine was now the 302 cu. in. (5.0-liter) V-8, with 351 cu. in. variable-venturi V-8 optional. Four-speed overdrive automatic was standard. Unequal-length A-arms replaced the former single arm with drag strut at the front suspension. The four-link rear suspension had shocks angled ahead of the axle. Standard electronic instruments could be deleted. In the trunk was a new mini spare tire. Once again, Mark VI two-doors came in four Designer Series. Bill Blass, painted dark blue metallic on the lower areas, with white upper accents, had a white carriage roof. Leather seating surfaces were midnight blue with white accents (or vice versa). Blass also had dark blue bodyside moldings, dual gold paint stripes on bodyside and decklid contour. Blass logo on rear roof pillar and decklid contour, and color-keyed lacy-spoke cast aluminum wheels. The light/medium pewter metallic Cartier, with medium pewter landau roof, had light pewter bodyside moldings and a single thin, dark red paint stripe on bodyside and decklid. A Cartier logo went on the decklid above the Mark VI script, and Cartier signature in the opera windows. Leather or luxury cloth seating came in light and medium pewter colors. Mark's light/medium fawn metallic Pucci had medium fawn bodyside moldings, tri-band bodyside and decklid contour tape stripes, Pucci signature in opera window, and Pucci logo on rearward fender louver. Givenchy offered bittersweet bodyside moldings, dual bittersweet hood tape stripes, and light fawn bodyside and decklid paint stripes with integral hood/decklid Givenchy logo. Givenchy lettering decorated the opera windows. Body paint was two-tone light fawn and bittersweet metallic, with full vinyl roof in light fawn. Twin Comfort Lounge seats with leather seating surfaces were bittersweet color, accented with Givenchy buttons on seatbacks. Givenchy had wire wheel covers. A new top-of-the-line Signature Series Mark VI (replacing the Collector's Edition) came in dark red or silver metallic paint on both two- and four-door bodies. It had a color-keyed Cavalry twill landau vinyl roof, color-keyed bumper rub strips, body-color accent on parking lamp lenses, vinyl roof wrapover molding with bright accents and

coach lamps, and two-tone bodyside and hood accent stripes. 'Signature Series' script went on the rear roof pillar, an owner's monogram on front door. The decklid contour had a padded vinyl treatment. Inside, Signature had dark red leather or cloth seating surfaces, an owner's Signature nameplate on the dash, and plush Allure carpeting on the floor, cowl side, lower doors, center pillar, and in the trunk. Many Mark VI options were standard on the Signature Series, including speed control, six-way power seats, driver and passenger recliners, keyless entry, and Premium Sound System.

I.D. DATA: Lincoln's 11-symbol Vehicle Identification Number (VIN) is stamped on a metal tab fastened to the instrument panel, visible through the windshield. The first digit is a model year code ('0' 1980). The second letter indicates assembly plant: 'Y' Wixom, MI; 'W' Wayne, MI. Digits three and four are the body serial code, which corresponds to the Model Numbers shown in the tables below: '81' Continental 2-dr. coupe; '82' Continental 4-dr. sedan; '84' Versailles 4dr. sedan; '89' Mark VI 2-dr. coupe; '90' Mark VI 4dr. sedan; '96' Mark VI Signature Series. The fifth symbol is an engine code: 'F' V8302 2Bbl. or EFI; 'G' V8351 2Bbl. Finally, digits 6-11 make up the consecutive unit number, starting with 600,001. A Vehicle Certification Label on the left front door lock face panel or door pillar shows the manufacturer, month and year built, GVW, GAWR, VIN, body code, color code, trim code, axle code, transmission code, and special order coding.

VERSAILLES (V-8)

Model Number	Body/Style Number	Body Type & Seating	Factory Price	Shipping Weight	Production Total
84	54M	4-dr. Sedan-6P	14674	3661	4,784

CONTINENTAL (V-8)

81	66D	2-dr. Coupe-6P	12555	3843	7,177
82	54D	4-dr. Sedan-6P	12884	3919	24,056

MARK VI (V-8)

89	66D	2-dr. Coupe-6P	15424	3892	20,647
90	54D	4-dr. Sedan-6P	15824	3988	18,244

MARK VI SIGNATURE SERIES (V-8)

96	66D	2-dr. Coupe-6P	20940	3896	N/A
96	54D	4-dr. Sedan-6P	21309	3993	N/A

ENGINE DATA: BASE V-8 (Versailles): 90-degree, overhead valve V-8. Cast iron block and head. Displacement: 302 cu. in. (5.2 liters). Bore & stroke: 4.00 x 3.00 in. Compression ratio: 8.4:1. Brake horsepower: 132 at 3600 R.P.M. Torque: 232 lbs.-ft. at 1400 R.P.M. Five main bearings. Hydraulic valve lifters. Carburetor: 2Bbl. Motorcraft 2150. VIN Code: F. **BASE V-8 (Continental, Mark VI):** Same as 302 cu. in. V-8 above, but with electronic fuel injection Brake H.P.: 129 at 3600 R.P.M. Torque: 231 lbs.-ft. at 2000 R.P.M. **OPTIONAL V-8 (Continental, Mark VI):** 90-degree, overhead valve V-8. Cast iron block and head. Displacement: 351 cu. in. (5.8 liters). Bore & stroke: 4.00 x 3.50 in. Compression ratio: 8.3:1. Brake horsepower: 140 at 3400 R.P.M. Torque: 265 lbs.-ft. at 2000 R.P.M. Five main bearings. Hydraulic valve lifters. Carburetor: 2Bbl. Motorcraft 7200VV. VIN Code: G.

CHASSIS DATA: Wheelbase: (Versailles) 109.9 in.; (Continental) 117.4 in.; (Mark VI 2dr.) 114.4 in.; (Mark VI 4dr.) 117.4 in. Overall length: (Versailles) 200.7 in.; (Cont.) 219.2 in.; (Mark 2dr.) 216.0 in.; (Mark 4dr.) 219.2 in. Height: (Versailles) 54.1 in.; (Cont./Mark 2dr.) 55.1 in.; (Cont./Mark 4dr.) 55.8 in. Width: (Versailles) 74.5 in.; (Cont./Mark) 78.1 in. Front Tread: (Versailles) 59.0 in.; (Cont./Mark) 62.2 in. Rear Tread: (Versailles) 57.7 in.; (Cont./Mark) 62.0 in. Standard Tires: (Versailles) FR78 x 14 SBR WSW; (Continental, Mark) Michelin P205/75R15 SBR WSW.

TECHNICAL: Transmission: SelectShift three-speed manual transmission (column shift) standard on Versailles. Gear ratios: (1st) 2.46:1; (2nd) 1.46:1; (3rd) 1.00:1; (Rev) 2.19;1. Four-speed automatic overdrive standard on Continental and Mark VI: (1st) 2.40:1; (2nd) 1.47:1; (3rd) 1.00:1; (4th) 0.67:1; (Rev) 2.00:1. Standard final drive ratio: (Versailles) 2.47:1; (Cont./Mark) 3.08:1 except 2.73:1 w/V8351. Steering: Recirculating ball, power-assisted. Suspension: (Versailles) front spring over upper arm w/ball joints and drag struts and coil springs, Hotchkiss rear w/semi-elliptic leaf springs; (Continental/Mark VI) long/short Aarm front w/coil springs and anti-sway bar, four-link coil spring rear. Brakes: (Versailles) four-wheel disc; (others) front disc and rear drum; all power-assisted. Ignition: Electronic. Body construction: (Versailles) unibody; (others) separate body and frame. Fuel Tank: (Versailles) 19.2 gal.; (others) 20.0 gal.

DRIVETRAIN OPTIONS: 351 cu. in. V-8 engine: Cont./Mark ($160). Optional axle ratio ($24). Traction-Lok differential: Cont./Mark ($110). H.D. battery: Cont./Mark ($23). Engine block heater ($23). Trailer towing pkg.: Cont. ($97-$137); Mark ($140-$180). California emission system ($253). High-altitude option: Versailles (NC).

VERSAILLES CONVENIENCE/APPEARANCE OPTIONS: Appearance protection group ($84-$88). Reclining bucket seat group ($416). Power lock group ($169). Defroster group ($132). Rear defroster, electric ($109). Garage door opener ($99). Illuminated outside thermometer ($31). Tilt steering wheel ($81). AM/FM stereo search radio w/8track tape player ($81); w/cassette player ($95). 40channel CB radio ($356). Power glass panel moonroof ($1128). Coach roof, Valino grain (NC). Dual-shade paint ($80). Protective bodyside moldings ($53). Premium bodyside moldings ($83). Lower bodyside protection ($35). Padded decklid applique delete (NC). Leather/vinyl interior trim ($416). Wire wheel covers (NC).

CONTINENTAL/MARK VI CONVENIENCE/APPEARANCE OPTIONS: Option Packages: Mark VI Signature Series ($5485-$5516). Fashion Accent series: Cont. ($600). Town Car option: Cont. ($1089). Town Coupe option: Cont. ($1089). Mark VI Cartier Designer series: leather/vinyl or luxury cloth interior ($2191). Mark VI Emilio Pucci Designer series ($2191). Mark VI Bill Blass Designer series w/carriage roof ($2809). Mark VI Givenchy Designer series ($1739). Mark VI luxury groups ($1044). Headlamp convenience group ($141). Defroster group ($132). Comfort/Convenience: Rear defroster ($109). Speed control ($149). Illuminated entry system ($67). Keyless entry ($253-$293). Power door locks ($103-$143). Remote decklid release ($27). Six-way power flight bench seat: Cont. ($171); w/recliners ($312). Reclining passenger seat: Mark ($91); both ($139). Twin comfort six-way power seats: Mark ($171). Twin comfort lounge power seats: Cont. ($1044-$1089) exc. ($45) with Town Car/Cpe. Electronic instrument panel: Cont. ($707); Mark ($707 credit). Garage door opener ($99). Leather-wrapped steering wheel ($47). Tilt steering wheel ($83). Intermittent wipers ($43). Lighting and Mirrors: Coach lamps: Cont. ($71). Touring lamps: Mark ($67). Right remote mirror ($44).

267

Lighted visor vanity mirror ($123). Entertainment: AM/FM stereo search radio w/cassette ($95) or 8track player ($81). 40channel CB radio ($356). Premium sound system ($160). Exterior: Power glass panel moonroof ($1128) exc. ($817-$888) w/Mark Signature. Carriage roof: Mark ($984). Landau vinyl roof: Mark ($240-$311). Coach vinyl roof: Cont. ($367) exc. ($296) with Town Car/Cpe. Moondust paint ($232). Dual-shade paint: Cont. ($360). Custom paint stripes: Mark ($53). Door edge guards ($16-$24). Premium bodyside moldings: Cont. ($144). Rocker panel molding delete: Mark ($76 credit). Padded decklid applique delete: Mark Signature (NC). License plate frames: rear ($8); front/rear ($16). Lower bodyside protection ($35). Interior: Leather interior trim: Cont. ($368-$435). Floor mats: front ($35); rear ($19). Trunk mat ($15). Wheels and Tires: Wire wheel covers ($255). Lacy spoke or turbine spoke aluminum wheels ($396) exc. Givenchy ($141). Wide-band whitewall tires ($36). Conventional spare tire ($40).

NOTE: Mark VI Signature Series was listed first as an option package (with prices shown above), then as a separate model.

HISTORY: Introduced: October 12, 1979. Model year production: 74,908. Calendar year production: 52,793. Calendar year sales by U.S. dealers: 69,704. Model year sales by U.S. dealers: 87,468.

Historical Footnotes: This was the final year for Versailles, which was expensive and guzzled. Its price rose once again, and sales fell to a mere 4,784 for the year. In fact, sales of all three models fell sharply. The total for Lincoln dropped 42 percent. Evidently, downsizing of the "big" Lincolns wasn't enough to attract customers in this difficult period for the industry.

1981 LINCOLN

Without changing appreciably in appearance, the Continental of 1980 became this year's "Town Car," adding more power/comfort choices. A new top-rung Signature Series was added. New options included wire-spoke aluminum wheels and self-sealing tires. Versailles was dropped after 1980 due to shrunken sales. So was the 351 cu. in. V-8, leaving only the fuel-injected 302 powerplant.

1981 Continental Town Car (L)

TOWN CAR — V-8 — Now called the Lincoln Town Car, the former Continental (downsized for 1980) aimed harder at connoisseurs of luxury motoring. Town Car had new standard Twin Comfort Lounge seats with six-way power driver's seat. Coach lamps and premium bodyside moldings were added as standard. Town Car came in 18 body colors: 11 standard, seven optional. Standard auto-temp air conditioning added a "mix" mode, while the optional electronic instrument panel included a message center with fuel economy data. New options were: self-sealing whitewalls; dual-shade paint colors with vinyl roof matching the upper bodyside; Class II trailer towing package; dual power remote mirrors; and wire-spoke aluminum wheels. Coach and carriage roofs were available. Base (indeed only) engine was the fuel- injected 302 cu. in. (5.0-liter) V-8, with four-speed automatic overdrive transmission and 3.08:1 rear axle. The 351 cu. in. V-8 disappeared. Appearance was similar to 1980, except that the grille pattern no longer repeated in a bumper slot. Both the two-door and four-door rode a 117.3 inch wheelbase. The new top-level Signature Series was posher yet. It included a coach roof, 'Signature Series' script on rear roof pillar (and instrument panel), six-way power Twin Comfort Lounge front seats in special "pillowed" sew style, seatback robe cords and map pockets, and padded center-pillar upper trim panel with lower carpeting.

1981 Continental Mark VI sedan (L)

268

MARK VI — V-8 — Six important options became standard this year: power door locks, power decklid release, intermittent wipers, tilt steering wheel, speed control, and right remote-control mirror. Mark's electronic instrument panel with message center had a new instantaneous fuel economy function. A mix mode was added to the standard automatic-temperature-control air conditioning. Four-doors had new dual-shade paint options. New options this year were: puncture-resistant self- sealing wide whitewalls; power remote mirrors; Class II trailer towing package; and wire-spoke aluminum wheels. The wire wheels and power mirrors became standard on Signature Series, which was otherwise a carryover. Two-doors could have a carriage roof in diamond-grain or Cambria fabric. Of the 21 body colors offered on Mark VI, seven were new: five new standard colors and two optional Moondust colors. Eleven colors in all were standard, eight optional (moondust), and two offered only on the Signature Series. New interior colors were: nutmeg, light fawn, medium fawn, and gold. Powertrain was the same as Town Car's: 302 cu. in. (5.0- liter) fuel-injected V-8 with four-speed overdrive automatic and 3.08:1 axle ratio. No other choices were available. Appearance was unchanged following the 1980 restyle. The Designer Series quartet was revised this year. Cartier came in medium pewter metallic body color. Its interior was luxury group sew style in choice of leather with vinyl or luxury cloth, pewter colored with Cartier logo buttons. The landau vinyl roof was medium pewter. Cartier had dark red accent stripes on bodyside and decklid, and medium pewter bodyside moldings. Standard wheels were color-keyed lacy-spoke aluminum. Mark's Givenchy model had its upper bodyside in black, lower bodyside in dark pewter. Leather with vinyl or luxury cloth interior was pewter colored, with Givenchy logo buttons. Also included: a black landau vinyl roof; red and gold dual accent stripes on hood, bodyside and decklid; black bodyside moldings; and new wire-spoke aluminum wheels. Pucci's edition came in medium fawn metallic, with light fawn interior and Pucci buttons on the seatbacks. It had a fawn full vinyl roof, tri-tone accent stripes on bodyside and decklid, light fawn bodyside moldings, and wire-spoke aluminum wheels. Finally, Bill Blass had its upper bodyside in dark blue metallic, lower bodyside in light fawn metallic. Interior was dark blue with light fawn bolsters and Blass seat buttons; carriage vinyl roof in midnight blue cloth. The Bill Blass had dual dark blue accent stripes on the bodyside, light fawn accent stripes on decklid contour, and light fawn bodyside moldings; plus color-keyed lacy-spoke aluminum wheels.

I.D. DATA: Lincoln had a new 17-symbol Vehicle Identification Number (VIN) this year, again fastened to the instrument panel, visible through the windshield. The first three symbols indicate manufacturer, make and vehicle type: '1LN' Lincoln; '1MR' Continental (Mark). The fourth symbol ('B') denotes restraint system. Next comes a letter 'P', followed by two digits that indicate body type: '93' 2dr. Town Car; '94' 4dr. Town Car; '95' 2dr. Mark VI; '96' 4dr. Mark VI. Symbol eight indicates engine type ('F' V8302). Next is a check digit. Symbol ten indicates model year ('B' 1981). Symbol eleven is assembly plant ('Y' Wixom, MI). The final six digits make up the sequence number, starting with 600001. A Vehicle Certification Label on the left front door lock face panel or door pillar shows the manufacturer, month and year built, GVW, GAWR, VIN, and codes for body type, color, trim, axle, transmission, and special order information.

1981 Continental Town Car (JG)

TOWN CAR (V-8)

Model Number	Body/Style Number	Body Type & Seating	Factory Price	Shipping Weight	Production Total
93	66D	2-dr. Coupe-5P	13707	3884	4,935
94	54D	4-dr. Sedan-6P	14068	3958	27,904

MARK VI (V-8)

95	66D	2-dr. Coupe-5P	16858	3899	18,740
96	54D	4-dr. Sedan-6P	17303	3944	17,958

MARK VI SIGNATURE SERIES (V-8)

95	66D	2-dr. Coupe-5P	22463	3990	N/A
96	54D	4-dr. Sedan-6P	22838	4035	N/A

ENGINE DATA: BASE V-8 (Town Car, Mark VI): 90-degree, overhead valve V-8. Cast iron block and head. Displacement: 302 cu. in. (5.2 liters). Bore & stroke: 4.00 x 3.00 in. Compression ratio: 8.4:1. Brake horsepower: 130 at 3400 R.P.M. Torque: 230 lbs.-ft. at 2200 R.P.M. Five main bearings. Hydraulic valve lifters. Electronic fuel injection. VIN Code: F.

CHASSIS DATA: Wheelbase: (2dr.) 114.3 in.; (4dr.) 117.3 in. Overall Length: (Town Car) 219.0 in.; (Mark 2dr.) 216.0 in.; (Mark 4dr.) 219.1 in. Height: (2dr.) 55.4 in.; (4dr.) 56.1 in. Width: 78.1 in. Front Tread: 62.2 in. Rear Tread: 62.0 in. Standard Tires: Michelin P205/75R15 SBR WSW.

TECHNICAL: Transmission: Four-speed automatic overdrive standard. Gear ratios: (1st) 2.40:1; (2nd) 1.47:1; (3rd) 1.00:1; (4th) 0.67:1; (Rev) 2.00:1. Standard final drive ratio: 3.08:1. Steering: Recirculating ball, power-assisted. Suspension: Upper/lower front control arms w/coil springs and anti-sway bar, four-link coil spring rear. Brakes: Front disc and rear drum, power-assisted. Ignition: Electronic. Body construction: Separate body and frame. Fuel Tank: 18 gal.

DRIVETRAIN OPTIONS: Traction-Lok differential ($108). H.D. battery ($22). Engine block heater ($22). Trailer towing pkg. ($141-$180). California emission system ($47).

CONVENIENCE/APPEARANCE OPTIONS: Option Packages: Town Car Signature Series ($1144). Mark VI Designer series: Cartier ($2031); Emilio Pucci ($2160); Bill Blass ($3015); Givenchy ($2372). Mark VI luxury groups ($1044). Headlamp convenience group ($149). Defroster group ($135). Comfort/Convenience: Speed control w/resume: Town Car ($153). Illuminated entry system ($67). Keyless entry: Town Car ($257-$294); Mark ($123). Power door locks: Town ($106-$143). Remote decklid release: Town Car ($27). Driver/passenger recliners: Mark ($138); passenger only ($90). Twin comfort six-way power seats: Mark ($170). Twin comfort lounge power seats: Town Car ($260). Twin comfort lounge power seats w/dual recliners: Town ($309) exc. ($48) w/Signature Series. Electronic instrument panel: Town ($706); Mark, delete ($706 credit). Garage door opener ($99). Leather-wrapped steering wheel ($47). Tilt steering wheel: Town ($83). Intermittent wipers: Town ($44). Lighting and Mirrors: Touring lamps: Mark ($67). Right remote mirror: Town ($46). Dual power remote mirrors: Town ($148); Mark ($99). Lighted visor vanity mirrors, pair ($126). Entertainment: AM/FM stereo search radio w/8track player ($81); w/cassette and Dolby ($95). 40channel CB radio ($356). Premium sound system ($160). Exterior: Power glass panel moonroof ($1122). Carriage roof, diamond-grain or cambria fabric: 2dr. ($984). Vinyl coach roof ($240-$315). Moondust paint ($236). Dual-shade paint: Town Car or Mark 4dr. ($246). Custom paint stripes: Mark ($53). Door edge guards ($16-$23). Rocker panel molding delete: Mark ($141 credit). License plate frames: rear ($9); front/rear ($16). Lower bodyside protection ($35). Interior: Leather interior trim: Town ($378-$440); Mark ($470). Floor mats: front ($35); rear ($20). Trunk mat ($16). Wheels and Tires: Wire spoke aluminum wheels ($756) exc. Blass/Cartier ($342). Lacy spoke aluminum wheels ($414) exc. Givenchy/Pucci ($342 credit). Turbine spoke aluminum wheels ($414) exc. Givenchy/Pucci ($342 credit) and Blass/Cartier (NC). Self-sealing whitewall tires ($105). Conventional spare tire ($39).

HISTORY: Introduced: October 3, 1980. Model year production: 69,537. Calendar year production: 64,185. Calendar year sales by U.S. dealers: 63,830. Model year sales by U.S. dealers: 65,248 (plus 334 leftover Versailles models).

Historical Footnotes: Sales were disappointing for the 1981 model year, down by some 25 percent. The Town Car at least came fairly close to its 1980 sales total, but Mark VI found more than 10,000 fewer buyers (down to 34,210).

1982 LINCOLN

A new, smaller Continental debuted this year, weighing less than the old Versailles. Three models now made up the Lincoln lineup: four-door Continental, four-door (Lincoln) Town Car, and Mark VI coupe.

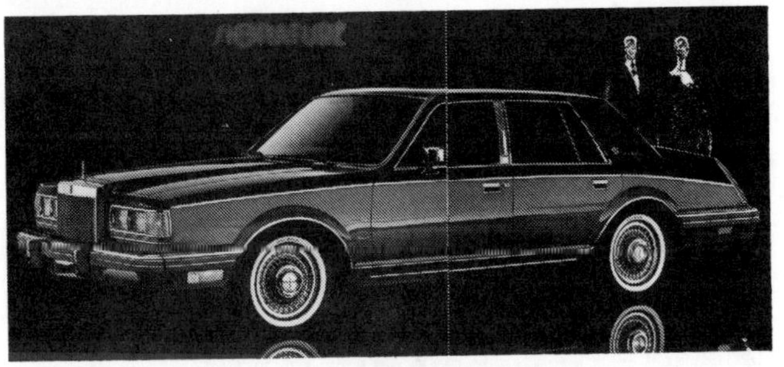

1982 Continental Signature Series sedan (JG)

CONTINENTAL — V-6/V-8 — An all-new "contemporary size" Continental took on the name used by Lincoln for four decades. This modern version rode a 108.7 inch wheelbase and weighed less than 3,600 pounds at the curb. It was 18 inches shorter and 500 pounds lighter than the former version. Base price of $21,302 was considerably higher than either the Town Car or Mark. Four-doored bodied only, Continental came in base model, Signature Series, and Givenchy Designer Series. Under the hood, the 302 cu. in. (5.0-liter) V-8 was standard, but a 232 cu. in. (3.8-liter) V-6 was now available as a no-cost option. Four-speed overdrive automatic was the standard transmission. Continental had variable-ratio power rack-and-pinion steering, four-wheel disc brakes, and a modified MacPherson strut front suspension with stabilizer bar. Nitrogen-pressurized shock absorbers went at all four corners (first time on a domestic car). Standard features included an electronic instrument panel with message center, all-electronic AM/FM stereo search radio, self-sealing steel- belted radials, speed control, illuminated entry, tilt steering, rear defroster, power door locks, power windows, power antenna, interval wipers, and dual power heated outside mirrors (with thermometer in the left one). Six-way power Twin Comfort Lounge front seats had manual recliners. The modest option list included keyless entry and a power glass moonroof. Styling was unmistakably Lincoln, starting with the traditional "classic" vertical-style grille and 'Continental' decklid treatment. Continental had front bumper guards, front and rear bumper rub strips with accent stripe, a Lincoln star hood ornament, and flush-mounted bright windshield molding. Each pair of exposed quad rectangular headlamps met wraparound signal lenses at the fender tips, with cornering and side marker lamps in a single housing. Bumper-mounted backup lamps stood on each side of the license plate bracket. 'Lincoln' script went on the decklid, 'Continental' script on front fenders. There was also a Lincoln Continental rear roof pillar ornament and rear side marker lamps. Front cornering and side marker lamps fit in a single housing. Forged aluminum wheels were standard. Continental's Signature Series had 'Signature Series' script on rear roof pillar, coach lamps in center roof pillar, and wire-spoke aluminum wheels. A bright/brushed full-length narrow upper bodyside molding replaced the standard accent stripe. The owner's identification kit included a signature plate for the instrument panel, and two sets of initials for the outside of front doors. Those items were sent directly to the buyer. The dual-shade

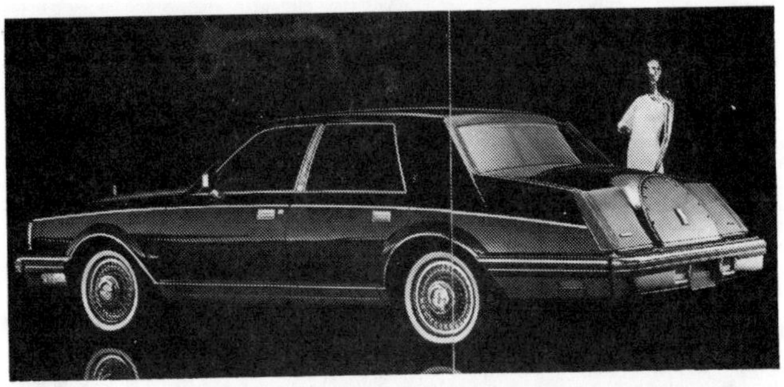

1982 Continental Givenchy Designer Series sedan (JG)

paint treatment on Signature Series came in three special color combinations. A Givenchy Designer Series had dual-shade paint in unique black/medium dark mulberry metallic. Givenchy's rear roof pillar ornament replaced the usual Lincoln Continental ornament and Signature Series script. There was also 'Givenchy' script in the rear quarter window glass. Interior was mulberry cloth luxury cloth or leather. Signature and Designer Series had a new trouble light mounted in the trunk.

MARK VI — V-8 — Appearance of Lincoln's personal luxury coupe and sedan was similar to 1981, with the exception of two new optional specialty roofs: a coach roof (rear half) for two-doors, and a full roof for four-doors. Specialty roofs included a large Cpillar, accented by small vertical quarter windows and slim coach lamps. Roof rear half and moldings could be covered in either Bayville grain vinyl, diamond grain vinyl, Valino vinyl, or Cambria cloth. As before, Mark had concealed headlamps, a simulated spare tire bulge on the decklid, and (on two-doors) tiny horizontal oval opera windows. Standard equipment was similar to 1981, including air conditioning, four-speed overdrive automatic, power brakes and steering, and the fuel-injected 302 cu. in. (5.0-liter) V-8. Eleven paint colors were added, along with three new dual-shade combinations. Both the Givenchy and Cartier Designer Series were scheduled to disappear, but Givenchy reappeared a bit later. The optional leather-wrapped steering wheel was no longer available. A dual exhaust system had become optional in late 1981 and continued this year. Mark's Signature Series came in 13 monotone paint colors, with color-keyed Valino grain coach roof. It also had color-keyed bumper rub strips with white accent stripes. Body-color accents went on parking lamp lenses, and 'Signature Series' script on the Cpillar. This year's Designer Series consisted only of a Bill Blass two-door and Pucci four-door (and later, a Givenchy two-door). The Bill Blass had a choice of three paint and roof treatments: two-tone white with red bodyside accent color, and white diamond-grain vinyl carriage roof; all-white paint with white diamond-grain vinyl carriage roof; or all- black with black Cambria cloth carriage roof. Blass also had black bodyside moldings and dual accent stripes, and double red accent stripes on the decklid contour. The Bill Blass logo went on C pillar and decklid. Mark VI Puccis came in two-tone pastel French vanilla on the top, pastel vanilla metallic on the bottom. The Bayville textured vinyl specialty full roof was pastel French vanilla colored. Bodyside accent stripes were dark brown with gold; decklid pinstripes dark brown with the Pucci logo. That Pucci logo in dark brown was also on the front fender, and on the instrument panel. The Givenchy Designer Series had a dual- shade paint treatment with black upper and medium dark pewter metallic lower, black Valino grain coach roof, and choice of pewter cloth or leather seat trim with Givenchy seat buttons. Givenchy also had black bodyside moldings; red and gold dual accent stripes on hood, bodyside and decklid; Givenchy logo on hood and decklid; 'Givenchy' lettering in opera window; an identification plaque on instrument panel; and wire-spoke aluminum wheels.

(LINCOLN) TOWN CAR — V-8 — Only a four-door Town Car was offered for 1982 (sometimes referred to as, simply, "Lincoln"). The two-door model was dropped. New this year was a Cartier Designer Series, joining the former Signature Series. Appearance was the same as 1981. Sole engine was the fuel-injected 302 cu. in. (5.0-liter) V-8, with electronic controls and four-speed overdrive automatic transmission. Town Car had a 3.08:1 rear axle ratio and an 18-gallon fuel tank. Power door locks were now standard, as was a remote- control decklid release (both formerly optional). Thirteen new paint colors were available. A dual exhaust system had joined the option list in mid-year 1981. The Signature Series added a coach roof, and 'Signature Series' script on the rear roof pillar. The new Cartier model featured two-tone paint: light pewter on top and opal on the bottom. It had a light pewter full vinyl roof in Bayville textured vinyl; opal bodyside moldings; opal and pewter in single red bodyside paint stripe; single red decklid paint stripe with Cartier logo in red tape; Cartier Designer logo in rear quarter windows; and turbine-spoke aluminum wheels. The instrument panel also carried the Cartier logo and identification. Cartier's interior was opal leather with light pewter luxury cloth (or leather in the insert area).

I.D. DATA: Lincoln again had a 17-symbol Vehicle Identification Number (VIN), fastened to the instrument panel, visible through the windshield. The first digit three symbols indicate manufacturer, make and vehicle type: '1LN' Lincoln; '1MR' Continental. The fourth symbol ('B') denotes restraint system. Next comes a letter 'P', followed by two digits that indicate body type: '94' 4dr. Town Car; '95' 2dr. Mark VI; '96' 4dr. Mark VI; '98' 4dr. Continental. Symbol eight indicates engine type: 'F' V8302; '3' V6232 2Bbl. Next is a check digit. Symbol ten indicates model year ('C' 1982). Symbol eleven is assembly plant ('Y' Wixom, MI). The final six digits make up the sequence number, starting with 600001. A Vehicle Certification Label on the left front door lock face panel or door pillar shows the manufacturer, month and year built, GVW, GAWR, VIN, and codes for body type, color, trim, axle, transmission, and special order information.

CONTINENTAL (V-6/V-8)

Model Number	Body/Style Number	Body Type & Seating	Factory Price	Shipping Weight	Production Total
98	54D	4-dr. Sedan-5P	21302	3512	23,908

CONTINENTAL SIGNATURE SERIES (V-6/V-8)

98/603	54D	4-dr. Sedan-5P	24456	3610	Note 1

CONTINENTAL GIVENCHY DESIGNER SERIES (V-6/V-8)

98/60M	54D	4-dr. Sedan-5P	24803	3610	Note 1

TOWN CAR (V-8)

94	54D	4-dr. Sedan-6P	16100	3936	35,069

1982 Continental sedan (JG)

TOWN CAR SIGNATURE SERIES (V-8)

94/60U	54D	4-dr. Sedan-6P	17394	3952	Note 1

TOWN CAR CARTIER DESIGNER SERIES (V-8)

94/605	54D	4-dr. Sedan-6P	18415	3944	Note 1

MARK VI (V-8)

95	66D	2-dr. Coupe-6P	19452	3879	11,532
96	54D	4-dr. Sedan-6P	19924	3976	14,804

MARK VI SIGNATURE SERIES (V-8)

95/603	66D	2-dr. Coupe-6P	22252	3888	Note 1
96/603	54D	4-dr. Sedan-6P	22720	3985	Note 1

MARK VI DESIGNER SERIES (V-8)

95/60M	66D	2-dr. Givenchy-6P	22722	3910	Note 1
95/60N	66D	2-dr. Blass-6P	23594	3910	Note 1
96/60P	54D	4-dr. Pucci-6P	23465	3970	Note 1

Note 1: Production of Signature and Designer Series is included in basic model totals.

Model Number Note: Some sources include a prefix 'P' ahead of the two- digit number; e.g., 'P98' for Continental.

ENGINE DATA: BASE V-8 (Mark VI, Town Car): 90-degree, overhead valve V-8. Cast iron block and head. Displacement: 302 cu. in. (5.2 liters). Bore & stroke: 4.00 x 3.00 in. Compression ratio: 8.4:1. Brake horsepower: 134 at 3400 R.P.M. Torque: 232 lbs.-ft. at 2200 R.P.M. Five main bearings. Hydraulic valve lifters. Electronic fuel injection. VIN Code: F. BASE V-8 (Continental): Same as 302 cu. in. V-8 above, but with 2Bbl. variable- venturi carburetor Brake H.P.: 131 at 3400 R.P.M. Torque: 229 lbs.-ft. at 1200 R.P.M. OPTIONAL V-6 (Continental): 90-degree, overhead valve V-6. Cast iron block and head. Displacement: 232 cu. in. (3.8 liters). Bore & stroke: 3.80 x 3.40 in. Compression ratio: 8.7:1. Brake horsepower: 112 at 4000 R.P.M. Torque: 175 lbs.-ft. at 2600 R.P.M. Four main bearings. Hydraulic valve lifters. Carburetor: 2Bbl. Motorcraft 2150. VIN Code: 3.

NOTE: Some sources list the V-6 as standard Continental engine, with the V-8 a no-cost option.

CHASSIS DATA: Wheelbase: (Continental) 108.7 in.; (Mark 2dr.) 114.3 in.; (Mark/Town 4dr.) 117.3 in. Overall Length: (Cont.) 201.2 in.; (Mark 2dr.) 216.0 in.; (Mark/Town 4dr.) 219.0 in. Height: (Cont.) 55.0 in.; (Mark 2dr.) 55.1 in.; (Mark 4dr.) 56.0 in.; (Town Car) 55.8 in. Width: (Cont.) 73.6 in.; (Mark/Town) 78.1 in. Front Tread: (Cont.) 58.4 in.; (Mark/Town) 62.2 in. Rear Tread: (Cont.) 59.0 in.; (Mark/Town) 62.0 in. Standard Tires: P205/75R15 SBR WSW.

TECHNICAL: Transmission: Four-speed automatic overdrive standard. Gear ratios: (1st) 2.40:1; (2nd) 1.47:1; (3rd) 1.00:1; (4th) 0.67:1; (Rev) 2.00:1. Standard final drive ratio: 3.08:1. Steering: (Continental) rack and pinion; (Mark/Town) recirculating ball; all power-assisted. Suspension: (Continental) modified MacPherson front struts with anti-sway bar, rigid rear axle with upper/lower trailing arms, and gas-pressurized shocks; (others) front control arms w/anti-sway bar, rigid four-link rear axle with lower trailing radius arms and oblique torque arms. Brakes: Front disc and rear drum, power-assisted; except Continental, four-wheel disc brakes. Ignition: Electronic. Body construction: (Continental) unibody; (others) separate body and box-type ladder frame. Fuel Tank: 18 gal. exc. Continental, 22.6 gal.

DRIVETRAIN OPTIONS: Dual exhaust system: Mark/Town ($83) but (NC) w/high-altitude emissions. Traction-Lok differential: Mark/Town ($128). H.D. battery ($28). Engine block heater ($26). Trailer towing pkg. ($223-$306). California emission system ($47). High-altitude emissions (NC).

CONTINENTAL CONVENIENCE/APPEARANCE OPTIONS: Appearance protection group ($47). Keyless entry ($141). Leather-wrapped steering wheel ($59). Dual lighted visor vanity mirrors ($146). Electronic AM/FM radio w/cassette or 8track ($107). Power glass moonroof ($1259). Color-keyed vinyl bodyside molding ($64). Two-tone paint ($298). Moondust paint ($257). Monotone paint: Signature ($298 credit). Leather interior trim ($535). Wire spoke aluminum wheels ($395).

MARK VI/TOWN CAR CONVENIENCE/APPEARANCE OPTIONS: Option Packages: Headlamp convenience group ($175). Defroster group ($151). Comfort/Convenience: Fingertip speed control: Town ($178). Illuminated entry system ($77). Keyless entry ($141). Twin comfort six-way power seats w/recliners: Mark ($354); w/passenger recliner only ($302). Twin comfort power seats w/passenger recliner: Town Car ($288); dual recliners ($340) exc. ($52) w/Signature Series. Electronic instrument panel: Town ($804); Mark, delete ($804 credit). Garage door opener ($110). Tilt steering wheel: Town ($96). Intermittent wipers: Town ($53). Lighting and Mirrors: Touring lamps: Mark ($78). Right remote mirror: Town ($59). Dual remote mirrors w/lighted left thermometer: Town ($173); Mark ($114). Lighted visor vanity mirrors, pair ($146). Entertainment: Electronic AM/FM stereo radio w/8track player ($107); w/cassette and Dolby ($107). 40channel CB radio ($356). Premium sound system ($181). Exterior: Power glass panel moonroof ($1259). Carriage roof: Mark 2dr. ($1057). Full specialty roof: Mark 4dr. ($640) exc. Signature ($368). Specialty coach roof: Mark 2dr. ($1028) exc. Signature ($757). Vinyl coach roof ($272-$357). Moondust paint ($257). Dual-shade paint ($298). Custom accent stripes ($62). Door edge guards ($19-$27). Rocker panel molding delete: Mark ($149 credit). License plate frames: rear ($11); front/rear ($20). Lower bodyside protection ($40). Interior: Leather interior trim: Town ($436-$498); Mark ($535). Floor mats w/carpet inserts: front ($41); rear ($23). Wheels and Tires: Wire wheel covers ($274) exc. Mark Pucci or Town Cartier ($191 credit), or Mark Blass/Givenchy ($586 credit). Wire spoke aluminum wheels ($860) exc. Mark Signature or Town Cartier ($395), or Mark Pucci ($465). Lacy spoke aluminum wheels ($465) exc. Mark Signature ($191), Town Cartier (NC), or Mark Givenchy/Blass ($465 credit). Turbine spoke aluminum wheels ($465) exc. Mark Signature ($191) and Mark Givenchy/Pucci ($395 credit). Self-sealing whitewall tires ($129). Conventional spare tire ($52).

HISTORY: Introduced: September 24, 1981 except Continental, Oct. 1, 1981. Model year production: 85,313. Calendar year production: 97,622. Calendar year sales by U.S. dealers: 93,068. Model year sales by U.S. dealers: 81,653.

Historical Footnotes: Lincoln sales climbed more than 25 percent for 1982— just about the same percentage that they'd declined in the previous model year. Of course, there were three models this year, as opposed to only two in 1981. Obviously, some buyers who might otherwise have chosen another model turned to the new Continental instead. In fact, Mark VI sales dropped considerably, from 34,210 to just 25,386. All Lincolns were built at Wixom, Michigan, a factory that put in considerable overtime to keep up with production. That production total rose sharply in 1982, up to 47,611 from just 26,651 for the prior calendar year. Lincolns had a 36-month, 36,000-mile warranty.

1983 LINCOLN

All three Lincoln models were mainly carryovers this year. Each came in a choice of Designer or Signature Series, as well as base models. Continental losts its short-lived V-6 option, but offered a long list of standard equipment.

1983 Continental sedan (OCW)

CONTINENTAL — V-8 — Bodies of Lincoln's mid-size "bustleback" four-door sedan showed virtually no change this year, except for an 'Electronic Fuel Injection' plaque on the front fender. That space previously held 'Continental' script. Continental now got the fuel-injected (TBI) version of the familiar 302 cu. in. (5.0-liter) V-8, formerly installed only in the big Lincolns. The 3.8-liter V-6 was discontinued. Four-speed automatic overdrive was again the standard transmission, with a lockup torque converter. A heavy-duty 68 ampere-hour battery was now standard. So was a locking fuel filler door with remote release. Digital electronic instruments were standard. Continental's chassis was actually the old rear- drive "Fox" platform, which originated with Fairmont/Zephyr and also appeared (with shorter wheelbase) in this year's new LTD and Marquis. Standard equipment included four-wheel power disc brakes, self-sealing P205/75R15 whitewall tires, tilt steering, power windows and door locks, speed control, tinted glass, intermittent wipers, cornering lamps, dual power heated mirrors (thermometer on driver's side), stereo search radio, and illuminated entry. Six-way power Twin Comfort Lounge seats were upholstered in Radcliffe cloth. An owner's identification kit included two plaques with owner's initials on front doors, and one for his or her signature on the dash. This year's base model was actually a revision of the Signature Series of 1982, leaving no Signature in the lineup. The Givenchy Designer Series returned again in revised form, joined by an all-new Valentino Designer model. Givenchy was painted Midnight Black and Platinum Mist, with tri-color (grey-blue, magenta, and charcoal) accent striping and unique wraparound roof. Twin Comfort Lounge seats had charcoal Radcliffe cloth or leather seating surfaces. Givenchy identification went on the rear pillar, dash, and quarter windows. Valentino came in a dual-shade combination of its own: Walnut Moondust over Golden Mist, with black and gold accent striping and Valentino logo on the bodyside. Gold decklid accent striping included the Valentino logo. Comfort Lounge seats had Desert Tan Radcliffe cloth or leather seating surfaces, both trimmed with walnut straps and buttons. Valentino also had a leather-wrapped steering wheel. Both Designer Series included coach lamps and cast aluminum wire wheels. A dozen new paint colors were offered this year on "ordinary" Continentals, and seven new dual-shade combinations. Standard colors were: Midnight Black, Cameo White, Platinum Mist, Scarlet Red, Aegean Green Mist, Pastel French Vanilla, Desert Tan, Light Desert Tan, Midnight Blue Mist, and Scarlet Mist. Five moondust colors were optional. Front and rear floor mats were now standard. New options included a three-channel garage door opener, coach lamps, automatic-dimming day/night mirror, and anti- theft alarm system. A bright brushed-aluminum upper bodyside molding option had been added in mid-year 1982.

MARK VI — V-8 — Some shuffling of the Designer Series occurred this year, but otherwise Mark was essentially a carryover with minimal change. Mark had a standard full vinyl roof with opera windows and limousine-style back window, front fender louvers (at the cowl), concealed halogen headlamps, and power vent windows. Standard engine was again the fuel-injected 302 cu. in. (5.0-liter) V-8, with four-speed overdrive automatic. A new all-electronic stereo search radio became standard, while a larger (71 ampere-hour) battery had been standard since mid-year 1982. The Givenchy Designer Series was dropped, as was the four-door specialty roof. But a four-door carriage roof was a new option. Other new options included an automatic dimming day/night mirror, anti-theft alarm, three- channel garage door opener, and locking wire wheel covers. Pucci's Designer Series was now available on both two- and four-door Marks. Body paint was Blue Flannel Mist, with carriage roof in dark blue Cambria cloth. Opera windows were deleted. Inside was a choice of Academy Blue cloth or leather seat trim. Pucci had a wide bright bodyside molding with Midnight Blue vinyl insert, silver sparkle bodyside accent stripes, silver sparkle decklid pinstripe and Pucci logo. 'Emilio Pucci' script went in the rear door quarter window. Pucci's logo also appeared in tape on fender and decklid. Also included: a Mark "star" on rear roof pillar, leather- wrapped steering wheel, and turbine-spoke aluminum wheels. The Bill Blass Designer Series came in two dual-shade combinations: Midnight Black upper and lower, and Light French Vanilla middle, with black Cambria cloth carriage roof; or Light French Vanilla upper/lower and Midnight Black in the middle, with Light French Vanilla Bayville textured vinyl carriage roof. Inside was a choice of French Vanilla cloth or leather seat inserts, with French Vanilla leather bolsters in Signature Series sew style. Midnight Black bodyside moldings, vanilla and black bodyside accent stripes, and vanilla or black decklid accent stripe with the Bill Blass logo were included. (That logo also was on the rear roof pillar and instrument panel.) Bill Blass also had a leather-wrapped steering wheel and wire-spoke aluminum wheels. Rocker panel moldings were deleted. Eleven new paint colors were available on base Marks, and seven new dual-shade combinations. Standard colors were the same as Continental's, except Antique Mahogany Mist replaced Scarlet.

LINCOLN (TOWN CAR) — V-8 — While many sources continued to refer to the traditional big Lincoln sedan as a Town Car, the factory catalog listed it as, simply, "Lincoln." Not much was new, apart from an all-electronic stereo search radio and heavy-duty battery. Eleven new body colors and seven dual-shade combinations were added, along with eight vinyl roof colors. Sole powertrain was again the fuel-injected 302 cu. in. (5.0-liter) V-8 with four-speed overdrive automatic, the same as Mark VI. Standard equipment included auto-temp air conditioning, power antenna, coach and cornering lamps, power side/vent windows, analog clock, remote decklid release, tinted glass, left remote mirror, and full vinyl roof. The Cartier Designer Series had a new Medium Charcoal Moondust over Platinum Mist dual-shade paint treatment. Up top was a Medium Charcoal Moondust padded full vinyl roof in Valino grain. Also included: silver metallic bodyside moldings, a single red bodyside accent stripe, single red decklid accent stripe with Cartier logo in red tape, Cartier designer logo in rear quarter windows, and turbine-spoke aluminum wheels. Cartier's interior was charcoal luxury cloth or leather. Cartier also had a fingertip speed control, and leather-wrapped steering wheel. 'Signature Series' script on the rear quarter pillar and instrument panel identified that model. Twin Comfort Lounge seats came in distinctively sewn Shubert cloth. The coach roof had a "frenched" backlight. Padded center pillars had lower carpeting.

I.D. DATA: Lincoln again had a 17-symbol Vehicle Identification Number (VIN), fastened to the instrument panel, visible through the windshield. The first three symbols indicate manufacturer, make and vehicle type: '1LN' Lincoln; '1MR' Continental. Symbol four ('B') denotes restraint system. Next comes a letter 'P', followed by two digits that indicate body type: '96' 4dr. Town Car; '97' 4dr. Continental; '98' 2dr. Mark VI; '99' 4dr. Mark VI. Symbol eight indicates engine type: 'F' V8302 EFI. Next is a check digit. Symbol ten indicates model year ('D' 1983). Symbol eleven is assembly plant ('Y' Wixom, MI). The final six digits make up the sequence number, starting with 600001. A Vehicle Certification Label on the left front door lock face panel or door pillar shows the manufacturer, month and year built, GVW, GAWR, VIN, and codes for body type, color, trim, axle, transmission, and special order data.

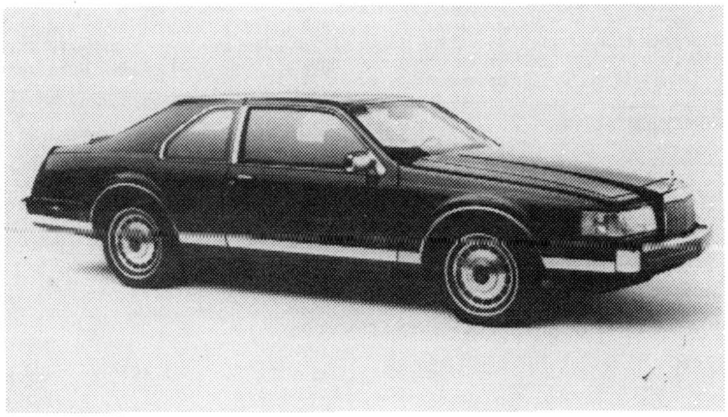

1983 Continental coupe (OCW)

CONTINENTAL (V-8)

Model Number	Body/Style Number	Body Type & Seating	Factory Price	Shipping Weight	Production Total
97	54D	4-dr. Sedan-5P	21201	3719	16,831

CONTINENTAL VALENTINO DESIGNER SERIES (V-8)

97/60R	54D	4-dr. Sedan-5P	22792	3757	Note 1

CONTINENTAL GIVENCHY DESIGNER SERIES (V-8)

97/60M	54D	4-dr. Sedan-5P	22792	3757	Note 1

TOWN CAR (V-8)

96	54D	4-dr. Sedan-6P	17139	4062	53,381

TOWN CAR SIGNATURE SERIES (V-8)

96/60U	54D	4-dr. Sedan-6P	18481	4078	Note 1

TOWN CAR CARTIER DESIGNER SERIES (V-8)

96/605	54D	4-dr. Sedan-6P	19817	4070	Note 1

MARK VI (V-8)

98	66D	2-dr. Coupe-6P	20445	4004	12,743
99	54D	4-dr. Sedan-6P	20933	4105	18,113

MARK VI SIGNATURE SERIES (V-8)

98/603	66D	2-dr. Coupe-6P	23340	4013	Note 1
99/603	54D	4-dr. Sedan-6P	23828	4114	Note 1

MARK VI DESIGNER SERIES (V-8)

98/60N	66D	2-dr. Blass-6P	24749	4035	Note 1
98/60P	66D	2-dr. Pucci-6P	24345	N/A	Note 1
99/60P	54D	4-dr. Pucci-6P	24623	4099	Note 1

Note 1: Production of Signature and Designer Series is included in basic model totals.

Model Number Note: Model numbers changed slightly this year. Some sources include a prefix 'P' ahead of the two-digit number; e.g., 'P97' for Continental.

ENGINE DATA: BASE V-8 (all models): 90-degree, overhead valve V-8. Cast iron block and head. Displacement: 302 cu. in. (5.2 liters). Bore & stroke: 4.00 x 3.00 in. Compression ratio: 8.4:1. Brake horsepower: 130 at 3200 R.P.M. Torque: 240 lbs.-ft. at 2000 R.P.M. Five main bearings. Hydraulic valve lifters. Throttle-body (electronic) fuel injection. VIN Code: F. OPTIONAL V-8 (Mark VI): Same as 302 cu. in. V-8 above, but Brake H.P.: 145 at 3600 R.P.M. Torque: 245 lbs.-ft. at 2200 R.P.M.

CHASSIS DATA: Wheelbase: (Continental) 108.6 in.; (Mark 2dr.) 114.3 in.; (Mark/Town 4dr.) 117.3 in. Overall Length: (Cont.) 201.2 in.; (Mark 2dr.) 216.0 in.; (Mark/Town 4dr.) 219.0 in. Height: (Cont.) 54.8 in.; (Mark 2dr.) 55.2 in.; (Mark 4dr.) 56.1 in.; (Town Car) 55.9 in. Width: (Cont.) 73.6 in.; (Mark/Town) 78.1 in. Front Tread: (Cont.) 58.4 in.; (Mark/Town) 62.2 in. Rear Tread: (Cont.) 59.0 in.; (Mark/Town) 62.0 in. Standard Tires: P205/75R15 SBR WSW (self-sealing on Continental).

TECHNICAL: Transmission: Four-speed automatic overdrive standard. Gear ratios: (1st) 2.40:1; (2nd) 1.47:1; (3rd) 1.00:1; (4th) 0.67:1; (Rev) 2.00:1. Standard final drive ratio: 3.08:1. Steering: (Continental) rack and pinion; (Mark/Town) recirculating ball; all power-assisted. Suspension: (Continental) modified MacPherson strut front with anti-sway bar and gas-pressurized shocks, rigid rear axle w/four links, coil springs and gas-pressurized shocks; (Mark/Town Car) short/long front control arms w/coil springs and anti-sway bar, rigid rear axle with four links and coil springs. Brakes: Front disc and rear drum, power-assisted; except Continental, four-wheel disc brakes. Ignition: Electronic. Body construction: (Continental) unibody; (Mark/Town) separate body and frame. Fuel Tank: 18 gal. exc. Continental, 22.3 gal.

DRIVETRAIN OPTIONS: Dual exhaust system ($83) but (NC) w/high-altitude emissions. Traction-Lok differential ($96-$160). Engine block heater ($26). Trailer towing pkg.: Mark/Town ($210-$306). California emission system ($75). High-altitude emissions (NC).

CONTINENTAL CONVENIENCE/APPEARANCE OPTIONS: Platinum luxury group: scarlet red interior, coach lamps, wire spoke aluminum wheels, brushed-aluminum bodyside moldings and leather-wrapped steering wheel ($656). Keyless entry ($89). Garage door opener ($140). Anti-theft alarm ($185). Leather-wrapped steering wheel ($99). Coach lamps ($88). Dual lighted visor vanity mirrors ($149). Automatic-dimming day/night mirror ($89). Electronic AM/FM radio w/cassette or 8track ($170). Power glass moonroof ($1289). Vinyl-insert bodyside molding ($64). Brushed-aluminum upper bodyside molding ($74). Two-tone paint ($320). Moondust paint ($263). License plate frames: rear ($11); front/rear ($20). Leather interior trim ($551). Wire spoke aluminum wheels ($395). Conventional spare tire ($97)

MARK VI/TOWN CAR CONVENIENCE/APPEARANCE OPTIONS: Option Packages: Appearance protection group ($30-$48). Headlamp convenience group ($178). Defroster group ($160). Comfort/Convenience: Fingertip speed control: Town ($188). Illuminated entry system ($77). Keyless entry ($165). Anti- theft alarm ($185). Twin comfort six-way power seats w/recliners: Mark ($357); w/passenger recliner only ($302). Twin comfort power seats w/passenger recliner: Town Car ($302); dual recliners ($357) exc. ($54) with Signature/Cartier. Electronic instrument panel: Town ($804); Mark, delete ($804 credit). Garage door opener ($140). Leather-wrapped steering wheel ($99). Tilt steering wheel: Town ($96). Interval wipers: Town ($60). Lighting and Mirrors: Touring lamps: Mark ($78). Right remote mirror: Town ($59). Dual power remote mirrors w/lighted left thermometer: Town ($174); Mark ($115). Lighted visor vanity mirrors, pair ($149). Automatic-dimming day/night mirror ($89). Entertainment: Electronic AM/FM stereo radio w/8track or cassette player ($170). 40channel CB radio ($356). Premium sound system ($194). Exterior: Power glass panel moonroof ($1289). Carriage roof ($1069-$1102) exc. Signature ($721-$726). Specialty coach roof: Mark 2dr. ($1073) exc. Signature ($779). Vinyl coach roof: Town ($343). Luxury Valino vinyl coach roof: Mark ($294-$381). Moondust paint ($263). Dual-shade paint ($320). Custom accent stripes: Mark ($62). Rocker panel molding delete: Mark ($149 credit). License plate frames: rear ($11); front/rear ($20). Lower bodyside protection ($40). Interior: Leather interior trim ($459-$551) exc. Town Cartier (NC). Floor mats w/carpet inserts: front ($41); rear ($25). Wheels and Tires: Wire wheel covers: Town ($293) exc. Cartier ($145 credit). Locking wire wheel covers ($330) exc. Mark Pucci or Town Cartier ($142 credit), or Mark Blass ($537 credit). Wire spoke aluminum wheels ($867) exc. Mark Pucci or Town Cartier ($395), or Mark Signature ($593). Lacy spoke aluminum wheels ($472) exc. Mark Signature ($191), Town Cartier or Mark Pucci (NC), or Mark Blass ($395 credit). Turbine spoke aluminum wheels ($472) exc. Mark Signature ($191) and Mark Blass ($395 credit). Self-sealing whitewall tires ($139). Conventional spare tire ($64).

HISTORY: Introduced: October 14, 1982. Model year production: 101,068. Calendar year production: 106,528. Calendar year sales by U.S. dealers: 101,574. Model year sales by U.S. dealers: 105,326.

Historical Footnotes: Sales rose sharply for the 1983 model year, reaching a total of 105,326 for the luxury trio (versus 81,653 the year before). Calendar year sales of the bigger Lincolns jumped even more, causing a second shift to be added at the Wixom, Michigan assembly plant. Continental now offered a 36/36,000 warranty on maintenance (free for the first year, with $50 deductible later). The full-line factory catalog referred to independent coachbuilders offering special limousine conversions.

1984 LINCOLN

The aero-styled Mark VII was all new for 1984, almost 6 inches shorter in wheelbase and nearly 400 pounds lighter than before. Aerodynamic features of the Mark VII included a sharply-raked windshield and hidden wipers. Continental alterations were far more modest, focused mainly on the front end. Lincoln added a turbocharged diesel option to both Mark VII and Continental this year, with the engine obtained from BMW. Mark also added an LSC model that combined improved handling with Lincoln's traditional luxury and riding qualities.

CONTINENTAL — SIX/V-8 — A new "aerodynamic" front end gave Continental a more modern look, though not radically different from the 198283 version. Rectangular quad headlamps again flanked a grille made up of thin vertical bars. But the front end had a slightly more sloped appearance, and the grille bars were separated into side-by-side sections. Rectangular parking/signal lamps stood immediately below the headlamps, and the wraparound marker lenses (now split into sections) extended farther back on the fender with an angled rear edge. Separate marker lenses below bumper level were no longer used. Two engine choices were offered this year: the standard gas 302 cu. in. (5.0-liter) V-8 with fuel injection, or the new 2.4-liter turbodiesel. The V-8 had a 3.08:1 axle ratio; the diesel a 3.73:1. Both were coupled to four-speed overdrive automatic transmissions. Electronic air suspension offered automatic level control. The fully electronic automatic-climate-control system featured a digital display, while the dash held an electronic odometer and digital fuel gauge with multi-color graphics. There was also a low oil level warning light and an overhead console, as well as new sew styles for the cloth and leather seat trim. Cast aluminum wheels were new. Revised instrument and door trim panels had real wood veneer appliques. Fold-away outside mirrors were used. Continental's Givenchy Designer Series had light blue and Midnight Blue glamour clearcoat metallic paint, with tri-color bodyside accent stripe applied at the break line between the two colors. There was a two-color decklid accent stripe with doubleG logo at the center. A rear roof pillar ornament was included. 'Givenchy' script went in the rear quarter window. Twin Comfort Lounge seats came in Admiral Blue luxury cloth (or optional leather at no extra cost). This year's Valentino Designer Series turned to Cabernet wine/medium charcoal glamour clearcoat metallic paint. It had a unique bodyside accent stripe and two-color decklid accent stripe, plus Valentino 'V' logo on the decklid. 'Valentino' script adorned the rear quarter window, and the rear roof pillar held a Valentino ornament. Twin Comfort Lounge seats were charcoal leather and mini-pleated cloth.

The 1984 Continental

1984 Continental Mark VII coupe (JG)

MARK VII — SIX/V-8 — Styling on the all-new "contemporary size premium" Lincoln retained traditional Mark cues, but on a dramatically different form. Aerodynamic appearance included aero headlamps, a wedge profile, and sloping back window. Lincoln described the new Mark as "the most airflow-efficient luxury car built in America, with a drag coefficient of 0.38." This edition was over a foot shorter than the Mark VI, mounted on the same chassis as the Continental sedan (downsized two years earlier). Some observers compared Mark VII's new design to Ford Thunderbird (logically enough) and even to Mercedes 380SEC. Mark had electronic air suspension with automatic three-way level control, nitra-cushion gas-pressurized front struts and rear shocks, and four-wheel power disc brakes. An all-new cockpit-style instrument panel had full electronics. The full-length floor console with gearshift lever included a lockable stowage bin in the armrest, while an overhead console held warning lights and dual-intensity courtesy/reading lamps. Base engine was the 302 cu. in. (5.0-liter) V-8 with EFI and EECIV, hooked to four-speed automatic overdrive transmission. Mark VII could also be ordered with a new inline turbodiesel with dual exhausts, suplied by BMW-Steyr. Power rack-and-pinion steering replaced the old recirculating-ball system. The modern Mark had integrated, flush-mounted aero headlamps that extended well back onto fenders to form marker lenses; a sharply-sloped windshield; wide color-keyed lower bodyside moldings; bright wheel lip and belt moldings; and large nearly-triangular quarter windows. Full-length upper bodyside dual-shade paint stripes were standard. The traditional decklid bulge, shaped as a simulated spare tire housing, was back again. So was an upright grille made up of thin vertical bars. Diesel models had a 'Turbo Diesel' badge on the decklid. Eleven new paint colors and six new interior trim colors were available. Standard equipment included front and rear stabilizer bars, tilt steering, speed control, power windows and door locks, locking gas door with remote release, electric rear defroster, and dual remote-control mirrors. Also standard: tinted glass, auto-temp air conditioning, six-way power driver's seat,

1984 Continental Mark VII coupe (JG)

272

electronic AM/FM stereo search radio, and P215/70R15 whitewall tires on cast aluminum wheels with center hub ornament. New options included heated driver and passenger seats, a compass/thermometer group for the header, handling package, and portable CB radio. Aimed at the European luxury coupe market, the new LSC Series had a standard handling package and 3.27:1 axle ratio. LSC had quicker-ratio power steering, high-performance P215/65R15 tires on 6 inch aluminum wheels, dark charcoal lower bodyside paint, foglamps, and leather upholstery. There was also a new Versace Designer Series, as well as the popular Bill Blass Designer Series. This year's Blass came in dual-shade clearcoat metallic paint: Goldenrod Glamour with Harvest Wheat. Exterior trim included two-tone cream/dark green bodyside and decklid accent stripes, along with the designer's signature in the quarter window and Bill Blass logo on the decklid. Upholstery was standard two-tone flax and gold ultra-soft leather (or cloth trim at no extra charge). The dash held a Bill Blass logo. Emanating from Gianni Versace of Milan, Italy (a designer of avant-garde clothing), the Mark Versace had a walnut glamour clearcoat metallic body with two-tone tan/bright blue accent stripes on bodyside and decklid, and tan stripes on the hood. Also included: a signature in the quarter window, and Versace logo on the instrument panel. Desert Tan ultra-soft leather went inside, in designer's sew style. Cloth inserts with leather bolster seat trim were available at no extra cost.

1984 Continental Town Car (JG)

TOWN CAR — V-8 — The traditional long-wheelbase Lincoln sedan kept its same form this year, with little change beyond new nitra- cushion gas-pressurized shocks. Tire size rose a notch, to P215/70R15. The dash held a low oil level warning light and revised electronic radio graphics. Full wheel covers were new. Twelve new paint colors and six new dual-shade combinations were offered. A 100-amp alternator had become optional in mid-year 1983. New this year: an optional power decklid pull-down. The optional power six-way driver's seat had a two-position programmable memory. Town Car came only with the 302 cu. in. (5.0-liter) fuel-injected V-8, four- speed overdrive automatic, and 3.08:1 axle. There was a Town Car Signature Series, and a Cartier Designer Series. The Cartier came in a new dual-shade paint treatment: Arctic White with platinum clearcoat metallic, with a new standard Arctic White coach Valino roof that included a "frenched" backlight. Cartier had premium bodyside moldings with platinum vinyl inserts, platinum and red bodyside tape striping, and a single red paint stripe on the decklid with Cartier logo in red tape. The Cartier logo was also laminated in the rear quarter window. Interiors had a choice of Dove Grey luxury cloth or leather upholstery. Town Car Signature had a coach roof, pleat-pillow upholstery, seatback straps and map pockets, and woodtone accents on doors and quarter trim panels.

I.D. DATA: Lincoln again had a 17-symbol Vehicle Identification Number (VIN), fastened to the instrument panel, visible through the windshield. The first three symbols indicate the manufacturer, make and vehicle type: '1LN' Lincoln; '1MR' Continental. Symbol four ('B') denotes restraint system. Next comes a letter 'P', followed by two digits that indicate body type: '96' 4dr. Town Car; '97' 4dr. Continental; '98' 2dr. Mark VII. Symbol eight indicates engine type: 'F' V8302 EFI; 'L' turbodiesel L6146. Next is a check digit. Symbol ten indicates model year ('E' 1984). Symbol eleven is assembly plant ('Y' Wixom, MI). The final six digits make up the sequence number, starting with 600001. A Vehicle Certification Label on the left front door lock face panel or door pillar shows the manufacturer, month and year built, GVW, GAWR, VIN, and codes for such items as body type, color, trim, axle, transmission, and special order data.

CONTINENTAL (V-8)

Model Number	Body/Style Number	Body Type & Seating	Factory Price	Shipping Weight	Production Total
97	54D	4-dr. Sedan-5P	21769	3719	30,468

CONTINENTAL VALENTINO DESIGNER SERIES (V-8)

97/60R	54D	4-dr. Sedan-5P	24217	3757	Note 1

CONTINENTAL GIVENCHY DESIGNER SERIES (V-8)

97/60M	54D	4-dr. Sedan-5P	24242	3757	Note 1

TOWN CAR (V-8)

96	54D	4-dr. Sedan-6P	18071	4062	93,622

TOWN CAR SIGNATURE SERIES (V-8)

96/60U	54D	4-dr. Sedan-6P	20040	4078	Note 1

TOWN CAR CARTIER DESIGNER SERIES (V-8)

96/605	54D	4-dr. Sedan-6P	21706	4070	Note 1

MARK VII (V-8)

98	63D	2-dr. Coupe-5P	21707	N/A	33,344

MARK VII LSC (V-8)

98/938	63D	2-dr. Coupe-5P	23706	N/A	Note 1

MARK VII VERSACE DESIGNER SERIES (V-8)

98/60P	63D	2-dr. Coupe-5P	24406	N/A	Note 1

MARK VII BILL BLASS DESIGNER SERIES (V-8)

98/60N	63D	2-dr. Coupe-5P	24807	N/A	Note 1

Note 1: Production of Signature and Designer Series is included in basic model totals.

Diesel Engine Note: A turbodiesel engine (RPO Code 99L) for Continental or Mark VII cost $1235 extra.

Model Number Note: Some sources include a prefix 'P' ahead of the two- digit number; e.g., 'P97' for Continental.

ENGINE DATA: BASE V-8 (all models): 90-degree, overhead valve V-8. Cast iron block and head. Displacement: 302 cu. in. (5.2 liters). Bore & stroke: 4.00 x 3.00 in. Compression ratio: 8.4:1. Brake horsepower: 140 at 3200 R.P.M. Torque: 250 lbs.-ft. at 1600 R.P.M. Five main bearings. Hydraulic valve lifters. Throttle-body (electronic) fuel injection. VIN Code: F. OPTIONAL V-8 (Town Car): Same as 302 cu. in. V-8 above, with dual exhausts Brake H.P.: 155 at 3600 R.P.M. Torque: 265 lbs.-ft. at 2000 R.P.M. OPTIONAL TURBODIESEL SIX (Continental, Mark VI): Inline, overhead-cam six-cylinder. Cast iron block and aluminum head. Displacement: 149 cu. in. (2.4 liters). Bore & stroke: 3.15 x 3.19 in. Compression ratio: 23.0:1. Brake horsepower: 115 at 4800 R.P.M. Torque: 155 lbs.-ft. at 2400 R.P.M. Four main bearings. Hydraulic valve lifters. Fuel injection. VIN Code: L.

CHASSIS DATA: Wheelbase: (Continental/Mark) 108.5 in.; (Town Car) 117.3 in. Overall Length: (Cont.) 200.7 in.; (Mark) 202.8 in.; (Town) 219.0 in. Height: (Cont.) 55.5 in.; (Mark) 54.0 in.; (Town) 55.9 in. Width: (Cont.) 73.6 in.; (Mark) 70.9 in.; (Town) 78.1 in. Front Tread: (Cont./Mark) 58.4 in.; (Town) 62.2 in. Rear Tread: (Cont./Mark) 59.0 in.; (Town) 62.0 in. Standard Tires: P215/70R15 SBR WSW exc. Mark LSC, P215/65R15 BSW.

TECHNICAL: Transmission: Four-speed automatic overdrive standard. Gear ratios: (1st) 2.40:1; (2nd) 1.47:1; (3rd) 1.00:1; (4th) 0.67:1; (Rev) 2.00:1. Turbodiesel ratios: (1st) 2.73:1; (2nd) 1.56:1; (3rd) 1.00:1; (4th) 0.73:1; (Rev) 2.09:1. Standard final drive ratio: 3.08:1 exc. turbodiesel, 3.73:1 and Mark VII LSC, 3.27:1. Steering: (Continental/Mark) rack and pinion; (Town Car) recirculating ball; all power-assisted. Suspension: (Continental/Mark) modified MacPherson strut front with anti-sway bar, rigid rear axle w/four links and anti-sway bar, electronically-controlled auto-leveling air springs and gas-pressurized shocks at front and rear; (Town Car) short/long front control arms w/coil springs and anti- sway bar, rigid rear axle with four links and coil springs, gas-pressurized front/rear shocks. Brakes: Four-wheel disc except (Town Car) front disc and rear drum; all power-assisted. Ignition: Electronic. Body construction: Unibody except (Town Car) separate body and frame. Fuel Tank: 22.3 gal. exc. Town Car, 18 gal.

DRIVETRAIN OPTIONS: Dual exhaust system: Town Car LPO ($82) but standard w/high-altitude emissions. Handling pkg.: Mark VII ($243). Traction-Lok differential ($96-$160). 100-amp alternator: Town ($62). Engine block heater ($26). Trailer towing pkg. ($209-$306). California emission system ($99). High-altitude emissions (NC).

CONTINENTAL CONVENIENCE/APPEARANCE OPTIONS: Compass/thermometer group ($191). Keyless entry ($122). Garage door opener ($140). Anti-theft alarm ($190). Power decklid pulldown ($79). Dual heated seats ($159). Dual power recliners ($191). Leather-wrapped steering wheel ($99). Coach lamps ($88). Foglamps ($158). Dual lighted visor vanity mirrors ($156). Automatic-dimming day/night mirror ($89). Electronic AM/FM radio w/cassette or 8track ($170). Premium sound system ($206). Portable CB radio ($154). Power glass moonroof ($1289). Vinyl-insert bodyside molding ($70). Brushed-aluminum upper bodyside molding ($74). Dual-shade paint ($320). Moondust paint ($263). License plate frames: rear ($11); front/rear ($22). Leather interior trim: Signature ($551); Givenchy (NC). Wire spoke aluminum wheels: Signature ($686). Forged aluminum wheels ($291) exc. Designer ($395 credit). Puncture-sealant tires ($180). Conventional spare tire ($121).

MARK VII/TOWN CAR CONVENIENCE/APPEARANCE OPTIONS: Option Packages: Headlamp/convenience group ($190). Compass/thermometer group: Mark ($191). Defroster group: Town ($165). Comfort/Convenience: Fingertip speed control: Town ($188). Illuminated entry system ($83). Keyless entry ($205). Anti- theft alarm ($190). Power decklid pulldown ($79). Six-way power seats w/dual recliners: Mark ($225); w/power recliners ($416) exc. Designer ($191). Twin comfort power seats w/passenger recliner: Town Car ($320); dual recliners ($374) exc. ($54) with Signature/Cartier. Dual heated seats: Mark ($159). Electronic instrument panel: Town ($804). Garage door opener ($140). Leather-wrapped steering wheel ($99). Tilt steering wheel: Town ($101). Vent windows: Mark ($73). Interval wipers: Town ($60). Lighting and Mirrors: Foglamps: Mark ($158). Right remote mirror: Town ($59). Dual power remote mirrors: Town ($177). Dual heated outside mirrors: Mark ($49). Lighted visor vanity mirrors, pair ($156). Automatic-dimming day/night mirror ($89). Entertainment: Electronic AM/FM stereo radio w/8track or cassette player ($170). CB radio: Town ($356). Portable CB: Mark ($154). Premium sound system ($206). Exterior: Power glass moonroof ($1289). Carriage roof: Town ($1069) exc. Town Signature ($726). Luxury Valino vinyl coach roof: Town ($343). Moondust paint ($263). Dual-shade paint: Town ($320). License plate frames: rear ($11); front/rear ($22). Interior: Leather interior trim ($459-$551) exc. Town Cartier (NC). Floor mats w/carpet inserts: front ($41); rear ($25). Wheels and Tires: Wire wheel covers: Town ($335) exc. Cartier ($137 credit). Wire spoke aluminum wheels: Town ($867) exc. Cartier ($395), or Signature ($532); Mark ($607-$686). Lacy spoke or turbine spoke aluminum wheels: Town ($472) exc. Signature ($137) or Cartier (NC). Forged aluminum wheels: Mark ($291) exc. Designer ($395 credit). Puncture-sealant whitewall tires ($180). Conventional spare tire: Town ($64); Mark ($121).

HISTORY: Introduced: November 10, 1983 except Town Car, Sept. 22, 1983. Model year production: 157,434. Calendar year production: 168,704. Calendar year sales by U.S. dealers: 151,475. Model year sales by U.S. dealers: 136,753.

Historical Footnotes: Lincoln sales rose 31 percent for the 1984 model year, while the all-new aero Mark VII gained a more modest number of customers. Continental, on the other hand, showed a whopping 71 percent sales gain. The new Mark VII design got extensive wind-tunnel testing at the Lockheed facility in Marietta, Georgia. Results were transmitted instantly to Ford engineers at Dearborn, who could then deduce the likely effect of modifications before the next trial. Mark VII's 0.38 drag coefficient was some 25 percent better than its predecessor, suggesting considerable gain in highway fuel economy. The federal government had first opposed the adoption of European-style aero headlamps, but Ford pressed the issue for two years (later joined by Chrysler) until permission was granted. That change in itself accounted for a 5 percent improvement in aero efficiency, as well as imparting a smooth look to the car's front end. *Ward's Yearbook* described the restyled Mark as "an aerodynamic showpiece."

1985 LINCOLN

Anti-lock brakes arrived as an option on Continental and Mark VII. The ABS system, supplied by the Teves company of Germany, was the first of its kind to be offered on a domestic auto. Electronic suspension became available on the Lincoln Town Car, which got a modest facelift. A mobile telephone became optional, anticipating the craze for cellular car phones that would soon arrive.

CONTINENTAL — SIX/V-8 — Biggest news for the four-door Continental was four-wheel anti-lock braking, standard on the two Designer Series with 5.0-liter V-8, and on all West Coast V-8 models. The system used a mini-computer to monitor all four wheels, and control braking pressure to prevent lockup during a hard stop. Otherwise, apart from a new hood ornament, no change was evident. Continental still had quad rectangular headlamps above rectangular parking lights, leading to sectioned wraparound lenses. Vertical taillamps and the familiar decklid bulge, with 'Continental' lettering around its perimeter and a center emblem, continued as before. Standard engine was the fuel-injected 302 cu. in. (5.0- liter) V-8, with BMW 2.4-liter turbo diesel optional once more (for the last time). A single serpentine accessory drive belt was added to the V-8. Four-speed overdrive automatic was the standard transmission. Standard equipment included auto- temp air conditioning, power four-wheel disc brakes and rack- and-pinion steering, power windows and door locks, electronic AM/FM stereo radio, cast aluminum wheels, overhead console, illuminated entry, tinted glass, and automatic level control. The electronic instrument panel had a message center and systems monitor. Givenchy and Valentino Designer Series were offered again, carrying the same new comfort/convenience package as Mark VII, with seven popular options. Givenchy came in dark rosewood clearcoat metallic paint with special bodyside accent stripe. It had exclusive decklid accent striping with a doubleG logo at the center, a rear roof pillar ornament, and 'Givenchy' script in the rear quarter window. Twin Comfort Lounge seats were upholstered in Mulberry Brown leather (or no-cost optional luxury cloth). Valentino was Midnight Black and Burnished Pewter clearcoat metallic. The unique bodyside and decklid accent stripe included a Valentino 'V' logo on the decklid. The designer's badge went on the rear pillar. Valentino's interior held Sand Beige leather and "vee" cloth seat trim.

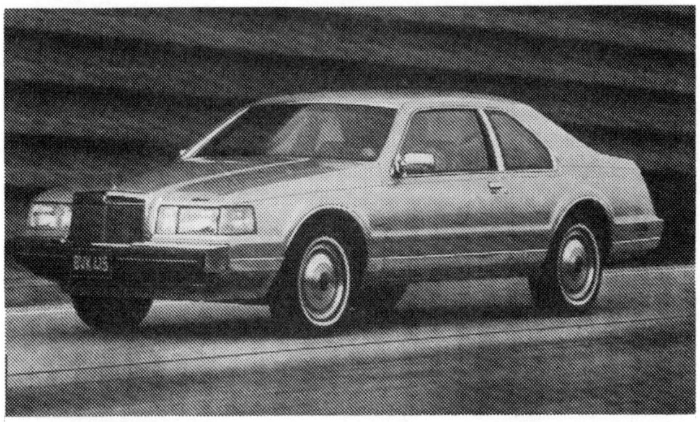

1985 Continental Mark VII coupe (JG)

MARK VII — SIX/V-8 — Like Continental, the Mark VII offered anti-lock braking this year. ABS was standard on the LSC, Bill Blass and Versace Series with 302 cu. in. (5.0-liter) V-8, as well as all V-8s in the five Pacific states. In fact, the two models had become quite similar after Mark's downsizing in 1984 to the Continental-size wheelbase. Mark added a new hood ornament, but not much else in appearance changes. Three engines were offered for Mark VII: the regular fuel-injected 5.0-liter V-8 with 2.73:1 axle; a high- performance V-8 (on LSC only) with 3.27:1 rear axle; and the 2.4-liter turbo diesel with 3.73:1 axle. All engines were coupled to four-speed overdrive automatic. V-8s had the new single serpentine accessory drive belt. The high-performance V-8 had a performance camshaft, tubular exhaust manifolds with dual exhausts, aluminum intake manifold, higher-flow- rate throttle body, and low-restriction air cleanerall giving significant acceleration improvement. LSC also had electronic air suspension with special handling components, including stiffer front and rear stabilizer bars, special struts and shocks, and special air springs. New multi-adjustment, articulated sport seats for passenger and driver, with six-way power adjustments, helped to enhance LSC's driver-oriented image. Leather was used extensively inside. LSC's tires were Goodyear Eagle GT P215/65R15 blackwalls with an "aggressive" tread pattern. Much of the regular Mark VII's brightwork was replaced with black or dark charcoal accents for the LSC. A "fluted" dark charcoal full-length lower bodyside molding, with the bodyside painted dark charcoal below the molding, was a distinguishing feature. Also unique to LSC: foglamps and special cast aluminum wheels with exposed lug nuts. Mark's Bill Blass edition came in Silver Sand clearcoat metallic with Burnished Pewter below the lower bodyside moldings. It had two-tone bodyside and decklid accent stripes, designer's name in quarter window, Bill Blass logo on the decklid, and standard Carob Brown leather trim upholstery (or UltraSuede fabric seating surfaces). Either one could have leather designer seat straps to no extra cost. Navy clearcoat metallic was now the color of the Versace Designer Series, with two-tone accent stripes on bodyside and decklid, designer's name in the quarter window, and Admiral Blue ultra-soft leather seats (or at no extra cost, cloth inserts with leather bolster seat trim). A Versace logo went on the dash and floor mats. Standard equipment on the base Mark included power four- wheel disc brakes, power rack-and-pinion steering, front and rear stabilizer bars, tinted glass, digital clock, automatic level control, power windows, cast aluminum wheels, speed control, and electronic AM/FM stereo radio. A new optional comfort/convenience package included eight popular options: power decklid pull-down, keyless entry, illuminated entry, illuminated visor vanity mirrors, six-way power seats (standard on LSC), stereo search radio with cassette, heated remote mirrors, and headlamp convenience system. That package was standard on the Bill Blass and Versace Designer Series.

TOWN CAR — V-8 — "Senior" Lincolns got a facelift for 1985, keeping the same basic (long wheelbase) body and separate chassis. Restyled wraparound parking/signal lamps were still in the front fender tips, outboard of (and separated from) quad rectangular headlamps. But the new grille texture had a tight crosshatch pattern, dominated by vertical bars. Taillamps were now angled slightly, each one divided into two side-by- side sections. Flush bumpers also added a more modern look. Body corners were more rounded, at front and rear. Base engine remained the 302 cu. in. (5.0-liter) EFI V-8 with four-speed automatic overdrive transmission. A higher-output

version of the V-8 also was announced. Standard equipment now included speed control, tilt steering, manual reclining seats, right remote-control mirror, and intermittent wipers. A single key now operated door locks and ignition. Seat upholstery fabrics and styles were new this year. The horn button returned to the steering wheel from its former turn-signal stalk location. Signature Series and Cartier Designer Series now had standard keyless entry with illuminated entry, stereo search radio with cassette, and Premium Sound System. The Cartier edition was now painted in Arctic White/Platinum clearcoat metallic, with Arctic White coach Valino vinyl roof and "frenched" backlight. Premium bodyside moldings had light charcoal vinyl inserts. Also included: platinum and red bodyside tape striping, and Cartier logo in red tape on the decklid. Cartier's logo also was laminated in the rear quarter window. Inside was a choice of gray luxury cloth or leather inserts with Oxford White leather bolsters. New options included an automatic-leveling rear suspension (with electronic sensors and air-adjustable shocks), and hands-free mobile phone. Town Car also offered the comfort/convenience package available on Mark VII, with seven popular options.

I.D. DATA: Lincoln again had a 17-symbol Vehicle Identification Number (VIN) fastened to the instrument panel, visible through the windshield. Coding is similar to 1984. Model year code changed to 'F' for 1985. One engine code was added: 'M' H.O. V8302 EFI.

CONTINENTAL (V-8)

Model Number	Body/Style Number	Body Type & Seating	Factory Price	Shipping Weight	Production Total
97/850A	54D	4-dr. Sedan-5P	22573	3719	28,253

CONTINENTAL VALENTINO DESIGNER SERIES (V-8)

97/865A	54D	4-dr. Sedan-5P	26078	3757	Note 1

CONTINENTAL GIVENCHY DESIGNER SERIES (V-8)

97/860A	54D	4-dr. Sedan-5P	25783	3757	Note 1

TOWN CAR (V-8)

96/700A	54D	4-dr. Sedan-6P	19047	4062	119,878

TOWN CAR SIGNATURE SERIES (V-8)

96/705A	54D	4-dr. Sedan-6P	22130	4078	Note 1

TOWN CAR CARTIER DESIGNER SERIES (V-8)

96/710A	54D	4-dr. Sedan-6P	23637	4070	Note 1

MARK VII (V-8)

98/800A	63D	2-dr. Coupe-5P	22399	N/A	18,355

MARK VII LSC (V-8)

98/805A	63D	2-dr. Coupe-5P	24332	N/A	Note 1

MARK VII VERSACE DESIGNER SERIES (V-8)

98/815A	63D	2-dr. Coupe-5P	26578	N/A	Note 1

MARK VII BILL BLASS DESIGNER SERIES (V-8)

98/810A	63D	2-dr. Coupe-5P	26659	N/A	Note 1

Note 1: Production of LSC, Signature and Designer Series is included in basic model totals.

Diesel Engine Note: A turbodiesel engine (RPO Code 99L) for Continental or Mark VII cost $1234 extra on base models, $772 extra for Designer Series or Mark VII LSC.

Model Number Note: Suffixes changed this year. Some sources include a prefix 'P' ahead of the basic two-digit number; e.g., 'P97' for Continental.

ENGINE DATA: BASE V-8 (all models): 90-degree, overhead valve V-8. Cast iron block and head. Displacement: 302 cu. in. (5.2 liters). Bore & stroke: 4.00 x 3.00 in. Compression ratio: 8.4:1. Brake horsepower: 140 at 3200 R.P.M. Torque: 250 lbs.-ft. at 1600 R.P.M. Five main bearings. Hydraulic valve lifters. Throttle-body (electronic) fuel injection. VIN Code: F. **OPTIONAL V-8** (Town Car): Same as 302 cu. in. V-8 above, with dual exhausts Brake H.P.: 155 at 3600 R.P.M. Torque: 265 lbs.-ft. at 2000 R.P.M. **BASE V-8** (Mark VII LSC): High-output version of 302 cu. in. V-8 above Compression ratio: 8.3:1. Brake H.P.: 180 at 4200 R.P.M. Torque: 260 lbs.-ft. at 2600 R.P.M. VIN Code: M. **OPTIONAL TURBODIESEL SIX** (Continental, Mark VI): Inline, overhead-cam six-cylinder. Cast iron block and aluminum head. Displacement: 149 cu. in. (2.4 liters). Bore & stroke: 3.15 x 3.19 in. Compression ratio: 23.0:1. Brake horsepower: 115 at 4800 R.P.M. Torque: 155 lbs.-ft. at 2400 R.P.M. Four main bearings. Hydraulic valve lifters. Fuel injection. VIN Code: L.

CHASSIS DATA: Wheelbase: (Continental/Mark) 108.5 in.; (Town Car) 117.3 in. Overall Length: (Cont.) 200.7 in.; (Mark) 202.8 in.; (Town) 219.0 in. Height: (Cont.) 55.6 in.; (Mark) 54.2 in.; (Town) 55.9 in. Width: (Cont.) 73.6 in.; (Mark) 70.9 in.; (Town) 78.1 in. Front Tread: (Cont./Mark) 58.4 in.; (Town) 62.2 in. Rear Tread: (Cont./Mark) 59.0 in.; (Town) 62.0 in. Standard Tires: P215/70R15 SBR WSW exc. Mark VII LSC, P215/65R15 BSW.

TECHNICAL: Transmission: Four-speed automatic overdrive standard. Gear ratios: (1st) 2.40:1; (2nd) 1.47:1; (3rd) 1.00:1; (4th) 0.67:1; (Rev) 2.00:1. Turbodiesel ratios: (1st) 2.73:1; (2nd) 1.56:1; (3rd) 1.00:1; (4th) 0.73:1; (Rev) 2.09:1. Standard final drive ratio: 3.08:1 exc. Mark VII, 2.73:1; Mark VII LSC, 3.27:1; and turbodiesel, 3.73:1. Steering/Suspension/Brakes/Body: same as 1984. Fuel Tank: 22.3 gal. exc. Town Car, 18 gal.

DRIVETRAIN OPTIONS: Dual exhaust system: Town Car ($83) but (NC) w/high-altitude emissions. Traction-Lok differential ($96-$160). 100-amp alternator: Town ($62). Engine block heater ($26). Trailer towing pkg.: Town ($223-$306). California emission system ($99). High-altitude emissions (NC).

CONTINENTAL/MARK VII CONVENIENCE/APPEARANCE OPTIONS: Comfort/convenience pkg.: Cont. ($932); Mark ($1293); Mark LSC ($1068). Compass/thermometer group ($191). Anti-theft alarm ($190). Mobile telephone ($2995-$3135). Dual power recliners ($191). Leather-wrapped steering wheel: Mark ($99). Automatic-dimming day/night mirror ($89). Electronic AM/FM radio w/cassette player and premium sound ($389). Power glass moonroof ($1289). Manual vent windows: Mark ($73). Vinyl-insert bodyside molding: Cont. ($70). Brushed-aluminum upper bodyside molding: Cont. ($74). Dual-shade paint: Cont. ($320). Glamour paint ($263). Leather interior trim ($551) exc. Cont. Givenchy (NC). Wire spoke aluminum wheels ($686). Forged or cast aluminum wheels ($291) exc. Designer ($395 credit). Puncture-sealant tires ($180).

TOWN CAR CONVENIENCE/APPEARANCE OPTIONS: Option Packages:Comfort/convenience pkg. ($607-$821). Headlamp convenience group ($190). Defroster group ($165). Comfort/Convenience: Keyless entry ($205). Anti-theft alarm ($190). Mobile telephone ($2995-$3135). Power decklid pulldown ($79). Twin comfort power seats ($225). Electronic instrument panel ($822). Leather-wrapped steering wheel ($99). Lighting and Mirrors: Dual power remote mirrors ($177). Lighted visor vanity mirrors, pair ($156). Automatic-dimming day/night mirror ($89). Entertainment: Electronic AM/FM stereo radio w/cassette player and premium sound ($389). Exterior: Power glass moonroof ($1289). Carriage roof ($1069) exc. Signature ($726). Luxury Valino vinyl coach roof ($343). Glamour paint ($268). Dual-shade paint ($320). Protective bodyside molding ($70). Interior: Leather interior trim ($459-$521) exc. Cartier (NC). Floor mats w/carpet inserts: front ($41); rear ($25). Wheels and Tires: Wire wheel covers ($335) exc. Cartier ($137 credit). Wire spoke aluminum wheels ($867) exc. Cartier ($395) or Signature ($532). Lacy spoke or turbine spoke aluminum wheels ($472) exc. Signature ($137) or Cartier (NC). Puncture-sealant whitewall tires ($180). Conventional spare tire ($64).

HISTORY: Introduced: October 4, 1984. Model year production: 166,486. Calendar year production: 163,077. Calendar year sales by U.S. dealers: 165,138. Model year sales by U.S. dealers: 165,012.

Historical Footnotes: Customers obviously had a craving for luxury motoring in the traditional style, as sales of Lincoln's Town Car reached a record level. A total of 116,015 found buyers, up a whopping 50 percent from the 1984 figure. The previous record of 94,242 had been set way back in 1978. Continental sales rose only slightly, while the Mark dropped sharply (down to just 20,198, versus 31,502 in the previous model year). The BMW-built turbodiesel found so few buyers that it was discontinued after 1985.

1986 LINCOLN

While option prices remained similar to their 1985 levels, the lists (especially for Continental and Mark VII) shrunk considerably. Both models had ample lists of standard equipment. Among other deletions, the slow-selling turbodiesel engine was dropped. Anti-lock braking became standard on all Continentals and Marks. The V-8 engine added sequential fuel injection, fast-burn combustion chambers, low-tension piston rings, and roller tappets, which delivered a boost in compression and horsepower.

1986 Continental sedan (JG)

CONTINENTAL — V-8 — Lincoln's short-wheelbase, five-passenger luxury four-door sedan showed no appearance change this year. Continental's grille was similar to Mark VII, made up of thin vertical bars with a slightly heavier center bar, and a wide upper header with inset center emblem. Recessed quad rectangular headlamps stood directly above amber-lensed park/signal lamps. The headlamp/park lamp moldings continued around fender tips to surround the large clear/amber marker and cornering lenses, with a molding that angled at the rear. After a couple of years of being branded, simply, "Continental," the mid-size sedan reverted to a "Lincoln" badge. The standard 302 cu. in. V-8 switched from throttle-body to sequential (multi-port) fuel injection, again hooked to four-speed overdrive automatic. The anti-lock, four-wheel disc braking system introduced in 1985 continued this year as standard. Electronic air suspension with level control was also standard. The turbodiesel option was abandoned during the '85 model year. Dropped for 1986 were the mobile phone

option and Valentino edition. This year's lineup consisted only of the base Continental and Givenchy Designer Series. Standard equipment included keyless entry (and illuminated entry), power decklid pull-down (and remote release), compass/thermometer group, power remote heated mirrors, rear defroster, tinted glass, power windows and door locks, speed control, gas-pressurized shock absorbers, front and rear stabilizer bars, power steering, and P215/70R15 WSW tires on cast aluminum wheels. Also standard: power mini-vent windows, interval wipers, coach lamps, bumper rub strips with argent stripes, dual bodyside and decklid stripes, and electronic instrument panel.

1986 Continental Mark VII coupe (JG)

MARK VII — V-8 — "The car you never expected from Lincoln." That's how the full-line catalog described Mark VII, now entering its third year in aero-styled shape. No significant changes were evident, other than the required high-mount center stop lamp. Mark's grille consisted of many thin vertical bars, dominated by seven slightly heavier vertical bars, with a heavy bright upper header and side surround molding. Inset into the center of the header was a tiny square emblem. Stretched from the grille edge to fender tips were large aero headlamps with integral parking/signal lamps, which met wraparound marker/cornering lenses. Above the left headlamp was 'Lincoln' lettering. Far below the bumper rub strips were LSC's standard foglamps. Three Marks were offered: base, Bill Blass Designer Series, and handling/performance LSC. The latter was powered by an improved high-output 302 cu. in. (5.0-liter) V-8 with sequential (multi-port) fuel injection, tubular exhaust headers and tuned intake manifold, now delivering 200 horsepower. Other models had a more modest 5.0-liter V-8, also driving a four-speed (overdrive) automatic transmission. All Mark VII models now had a standard anti-lock brake system (ABS), introduced on LSC a year earlier. Electronic air suspension with level control continued as standard. The Versace Designer Series was dropped. Formerly optional equipment that became standard this year included keyless entry, power decklid pull-down, Premium Sound System, and power front seat recliners. LSC added a new analog instrument cluster to replace the former electronic display. Standard equipment on base Marks included auto-temp air conditioning, power steering, tilt wheel, P215/70R15 WSW tires on cast aluminum wheels, compass/thermometer, rear defroster, side window defoggers, power windows and door locks, speed control, tinted glass, interval wipers, and AM/FM stereo with cassette player. LSC added dual exhausts with its high-output engine, a handling suspension, P215/65R15 blackwalls, wide bodyside moldings, lower bodyside accent paint, tachometer, and leather seat trim with perforated leather or cloth inserts. Bill Blass had unique lower bodyside clearcoat paint, two-color bodyside/decklid paint stripes, wire-spoke aluminum wheels, and leather or Ultra Suede seat trim.

1986 "Signature Series" Town Car (JG)

TOWN CAR — V-8 — Like its mates, the big four-door Lincoln added sequential fuel injection to its 302 cu. in. (5.0-liter) V-8. That engine also got higher compression, roller tappets, new piston rings, and revised combustion chambers. Town Car's standard equipment list grew, now including the formerly optional dual power remote mirrors, and a defroster group. Three models were fielded again: base Town Car, Signature Series, and Cartier Designer Series. Appearance was the same as 1985. Town Car's classic-look upright grille had a subdued crosshatch pattern dominated by seven vertical bright divider bars, with a bold and bright upper header bar that continued down the sides. The grille stood forward from the headlamp panel, with the space filled in by its wide, bright surrounding side moldings. Each pair of rectangular headlamps was surrounded by a strong, bright molding. Wraparound amber signal lenses were mounted in the fender extensions, with side marker lenses down below the bodyside moldings. Small 'Lincoln' block letters stood above the left headlamp; tiny 'Town Car' script at the cowl, just ahead of the front door. At the rear were vertical taillamps, with a horizontal rectangular backup lamp at the center. Standard equipment included power brakes and steering, rear defroster, auto-temp air conditioning, power windows and door locks, power vent windows, tinted glass, gas-pressurized shocks, speed control, tilt steering, P215/70R15 WSW tires, mini spare tire, full vinyl roof, heated power remote mirrors, and a four-speaker AM/FM stereo radio. Town Car Signature and Cartier both added keyless illuminated entry, a conventional spare tire, wide bright lower bodyside moldings, and six-speaker radio with cassette player and premium sound. Signature had two-color hood/bodyside accent paint stripes and wire wheel covers. Cartier featured dual red hood and single red bodyside/decklid paint stripes, and turbine-spoke aluminum wheels. Both had a half coach roof with wrapover molding and "frenched" back window.

I.D. DATA: Lincoln again had a 17-symbol Vehicle Identification Number (VIN), fastened to the instrument panel, visible through the windshield. The first three symbols indicate manufacturer, make and vehicle type: '1LN' Lincoln. Symbol four denotes restraint system. Next comes a letter 'P', followed by two digits that indicate body type: '96' 4dr. Town Car; '97' 4dr. Continental; '98' 2dr. Mark VII. Symbol eight indicates engine type: 'F' V8302 EFI; 'M' H.O. V8302 EFI. Next is a check digit. Symbol ten indicates model year ('G' 1986). Symbol eleven is assembly plant ('Y' Wixom, MI). The final six digits make up the sequence number, starting with 600001. A Vehicle Certification Label on the left front door lock face panel or door pillar shows the manufacturer, month and year built, GVW, GAWR, VIN, and codes for body, color, trim, axle, transmission, and special order data.

1986 Continental sedan (JG)

CONTINENTAL (V-8)

Model Number	Body/Style Number	Body Type & Seating	Factory Price	Shipping Weight	Production Total
97/850A	54D	4-dr. Sedan-5P	24556	3778	19,012

CONTINENTAL GIVENCHY DESIGNER SERIES (V-8)

97/860A	54D	4-dr. Sedan-5P	26837	3808	Note 1

TOWN CAR (V-8)

96/700B	54D	4-dr. Sedan-6P	20764	4038	117,771

TOWN CAR SIGNATURE SERIES (V-8)

96/705B	54D	4-dr. Sedan-6P	23972	4121	Note 1

TOWN CAR CARTIER DESIGNER SERIES (V-8)

96/710B	54D	4-dr. Sedan-6P	25235	4093	Note 1

MARK VII (V-8)

98/800A	63D	2-dr. Coupe-5P	22399	3667	20,056

MARK VII LSC (V-8)

98/805B	63D	2-dr. Coupe-5P	23857	3718	Note 1

MARK VII BILL BLASS DESIGNER SERIES (V-8)

98/810B	63D	2-dr. Coupe-5P	23857	3732	Note 1

Note 1: Production of LSC, Signature and Designer Series is included in basic model totals.

Model Number Note: Some sources include a prefix 'P' ahead of the basic two-digit number; e.g., 'P97' for Continental. Not all sources include the suffix after the slash.

ENGINE DATA: BASE V-8 (all models): 90-degree, overhead valve V-8. Cast iron block and head. Displacement: 302 cu. in. (5.2 liters). Bore & stroke: 4.00 x 3.00 in. Compression ratio: 8.9:1. Brake horsepower: 150 at 3200 R.P.M. Torque: 270 lbs.-ft. at 2000 R.P.M. Five main bearings. Hydraulic valve lifters. Sequential port (electronic) fuel injection. VIN Code: F. **OPTIONAL V-8 (Town Car):** Same as 302 cu. in. V-8 above, with dual exhausts Brake H.P.: 160 at 3400 R.P.M. Torque: 280 lbs.-ft. at 2200 R.P.M. **BASE V-8 (Mark VII LSC):** High-output version of 302 cu. in. V-8 above Compression ratio: 9.2:1. Brake H.P.: 200 at 4000 R.P.M. Torque: 285 lbs.-ft. at 3000 R.P.M. VIN Code: M.

275

1986 Continental Mark VII LSC coupe (JG)

CHASSIS DATA: Wheelbase: (Continental/Mark) 108.5 in.; (Town Car) 117.3 in. Overall Length: (Cont.) 200.7 in.; (Mark) 202.8 in.; (Town) 219.0 in. Height: (Cont.) 55.6 in.; (Mark) 54.2 in.; (Town) 55.9 in. Width: (Cont.) 73.6 in.; (Mark) 70.9 in.; (Town) 78.1 in. Front Tread: (Cont./Mark) 58.4 in.; (Town) 62.2 in. Rear Tread: (Cont./Mark) 59.0 in.; (Town) 62.0 in. Standard Tires: P215/70R15 SBR WSW exc. Mark LSC, P215/65R15 BSW.

TECHNICAL: Transmission: Four-speed automatic overdrive standard. Gear ratios: (1st) 2.40:1; (2nd) 1.47:1; (3rd) 1.00:1; (4th) 0.67:1; (Rev) 2.00:1. Standard final drive ratio: 2.73:1 exc. Mark VII LSC, 3.27:1; Town Car Signature/Cartier, 3.08:1. Steering/Suspension/Body: same as 1984-85. Brakes: Four-wheel disc except (Town Car) front disc and rear drum; all power-assisted; ABS (anti-lock) standard on Continental/Mark. Fuel Tank: 22.1 gal. exc. Town Car, 18 gal.

DRIVETRAIN OPTIONS: Dual exhaust system: Town Car LPO ($83) but standard w/high-altitude emissions. Traction-Lok differential ($101- $165). 100-amp alternator: Town ($67). Engine block heater ($26). Automatic load leveling: Town ($202). Trailer towing pkg.: Town ($159-$306). California emission system ($99).

CONTINENTAL/MARK VII CONVENIENCE/APPEARANCE OPTIONS: Anti-theft alarm ($200). Automatic-dimming day/night mirror ($89). Power glass moonroof ($1319). Vinyl-insert bodyside molding: Cont. ($70). Brushed-aluminum upper bodyside molding: Cont. ($74). Dual-shade paint: Cont. ($320). Glamour paint ($268). Leather interior trim ($551) exc. Cont. Givenchy (NC). Wire spoke aluminum wheels ($693) exc. Designer (NC). Geometric cast aluminum wheels ($298) exc. Designer ($395 credit). Puncture-sealant tires ($190).

TOWN CAR CONVENIENCE/APPEARANCE OPTIONS: Option Packages: Comfort/convenience pkg. ($698). Headlamp convenience group ($198). Comfort/Convenience: Keyless illuminated entry ($209). Anti-theft alarm ($200). Power decklid pulldown ($79). Six-way power passenger seat ($235). Electronic instrument panel ($822). Leather-wrapped steering wheel ($105). Lighting/Mirrors: Lighted visor vanity mirrors, pair ($156). Automatic-dimming day/night mirror ($89). Entertainment: Electronic AM/FM stereo radio w/cassette player and premium sound ($389). Exterior: Power glass moonroof ($1319). Carriage roof ($1069) exc. Signature ($726). Luxury Valino vinyl coach roof ($343). Glamour paint ($268). Dual-shade paint ($320). Protective bodyside molding ($70). Interior: Leather interior trim ($459-$521) exc. Cartier (NC). Floor mats w/carpet inserts: front ($43); rear ($25). Wheels and Tires: Wire wheel covers ($341) exc. Cartier ($137 credit) and Signature (NC). Wire spoke aluminum wheels ($873) exc. Cartier ($395) or Signature ($532). Lacy spoke or turbine spoke aluminum wheels ($478) exc. Signature ($137) or Cartier (NC). Puncture-sealant whitewall tires ($190). Conventional spare tire ($64).

HISTORY: Introduced: October 3, 1985. Model year production: 156,839. Calendar year production: 183,035. Calendar year sales by U.S. dealers: 177,584. Model year sales by U.S. dealers: 159,320.

Historical Footnotes: Town Car broke its model year sales record for the second year in a row, while Continental sales fell 31 percent. Mark VII sold just a trifle better than in 1985. The main reason for buying a Town Car, according to Lincoln, was "the aura of success it reflects upon its owners." Lincoln called Town Car "the roomiest passenger car in America" (not including wagons and vans), and touted its "regal bearing and formal elegance."

From the beginning, Mercury suffered an identity problem. Back in 1949, Mercury and Ford were two quite different automobiles. That difference faded somewhat later in the 1950s, but a revival began in the next decade. High- powered Cougars of the late '60s, in particular, renewed Merc's reputation for performance; and, to a lesser extent, for styling that expressed a separate identity.

1976 Comet "Custom Option" sedan (AA)

That difference didn't last. Through most of the 1976-86 period, Mercury was just, to put it bluntly, a plusher and pricier Ford. Sure, their grilles weren't identical, and trim details (even some overall lengths) varied. But down at chassis or engine level, and in the basic body structure, Mercury seemed to offer little that was new or original. What didn't come from Ford--notably styling in the bigger models--came from Lincoln. Style-wise, in fact, Mercury often looked more like a lesser Lincoln than an upscale Ford.

1978 Zephyr Z-7 coupe (M)

Much of the change was solidified earlier in the 1970s when Cougar switched from its role as a slightly bigger Mustang, and became a mid-size instead, closer to Thunderbird. By 1977, the XR-7 badge lost much of its significance. Rather than a singular sporty offering, that model became little more than just another coupe out of a baroquely-trimmed lot, styled after Lincoln Continental's Mark series. By 1980, Cougar grew even closer to T-Bird, hardly more than a clone, just as every other Mercury model had its Ford mate. Bobcat was basically a restyled Pinto, Monarch a fancier Granada, Zephyr nearly identical to Ford's Fairmont. And at the top of the size heap, Marquis and LTD had far more in common than

1979 Grand Marquis sedan (JG)

they had differences. This twin- model concept was known as "badge engineering," and Mercury was one of its most adept practitioners.

Actually, the biggest difference between the two makes may have occurred from 1975-78, when Mercury fielded a German-built Capri rather than turn to a variant of the reduced-size (domestically-built) Mustang II. Even when Mercury finally introduced its version of the all-new Mustang for 1979, it never quite captured the attention of enthusiasts in the same way as Ford's version. That was true even though the chassis was the same, engines the same, just about everything of consequence similar, if not precisely identical. When Ford V-8s were downsized from 302 to 255 cubic inches, so were Mercury's. Ford models add four-speed overdrive automatic, or switch from eight- to six-cylinder power? So do their Mercury counterparts, nearly always at the very same time. When LTD was sharply downsized in 1979, there was Mercury with a similarly shrunken Marquis.

1983½ Topaz CS sedan (JG)

Still, Mercury managed to survive these years and continues strong today. How did that happen? Well, Mercury was best at turning out mid-size and full-size models which, if not exactly thrilling, at least attracted a regular crop of traditional-minded buyers. Smaller Mercury models never seemed to catch on as well as

1986 Lynx GS wagon (JG)

1986 Grand Marquis Colony Park wagon (JG)

Ford's, but the biggies (and near-biggies) didn't fare badly. Perhaps the best example was the two-seater LN7, introduced in 1982. Ford's EXP, its corporate twin, didn't exactly set the marketplace ablaze; but Mercury's sales record was a disaster.

New-car buyers may have been willing to pay a few hundred dollars extra for a Mercury badge rather than a Ford name on their coupes or sedans, but collectors and enthusiasts might be more reluctant. When you're faced with a basically dull and repetitive lot, how can you select one worthy of hanging onto? Even the models that differed from Ford (or Lincoln) equivalents in some notable way, such as the bubble-back Capri introduced for 1983, aren't likely to send shivers down many people's spines. If you like a particular Mercury design better than its Ford mate, fine. Buy it, or keep it, or admire it. Otherwise, unless the Merc carries a markedly smaller price tag, there are few compelling reasons to pick it over a comparable Ford. Maybe it's silly, in view of their similarities, but Mustang and T-Bird are likely to draw more admiring glances than Capris and Cougars in like condition. Even an Escort GT seems to have a trifle more panache than Mercury's XR3, though if you squint your eyes you can hardly tell them apart.

1976 MERCURY

While the previous model year had brought the longest list of running changes in Lincoln-Mercury history, 1975 was largely a carryover year. The subcompact Bobcat and luxurious Grand Monarch Ghia had been introduced in mid-1975, along with the revised (imported) Capri II. Mercury would not offer a domestic-built cousin to Ford's Mustang until 1979. Otherwise, Mercury offered a model equivalent to each Ford product, typically differing more in body details than basic structure. A number of previously standard items were made optional for 1976 on full-size and luxury models, to keep base prices down. As in the industry generally, fuel economy was a major factor in planning the 1976 lineup. Mercury still offered some "real" pillarless two-door hardtops, but not for long.

1976 Bobcat MPG Runabout (AA)

BOBCAT (MPG) — FOUR/V-6 — Bobcat carried on in its first full season with two body styles: the "three-door" (actually two-door with hatch) Runabout, and a Villager station wagon. Bobcat rode a 94.5 inch wheelbase and had a base 140 cu. in. (2.3-liter) four- cylinder engine with four-speed manual gearbox. A 2.8-liter V-6 was optional. As with most Mercury models, Bobcat was essentially a Ford Pinto with a different hood and grille, and a fancier interior. Bobcat's distinctive grille, made up of thin vertical bars (slightly wider center bar) with bright surround molding, along with a domed hood, identified it as a member of the Lincoln-Mercury family. Large 'Mercury' block letters stood above the grille. Small square running/park/signal lamps with crossbar-patterned bright overlay sat between the single round headlamps and the grille, rather low, just above the bumper. Bodies held front and rear side marker lights, ventless door windows, and fixed quarter windows. Wide, bright wheel lip moldings and bright rocker panel moldings were standard. Also standard: bright windshield, drip rail, side window frame, lower back panel surround, door belt and rear window moldings. At the rear, each wide horizontal three-pod taillamp assembly held a red run/brake/signal light, white backup light and red reflector lens, with bright surround

1976 Bobcat Villager wagon (AA)

molding. Bright wheel covers were standard (styled steel wheels in California). Inside were all-vinyl high-back front bucket seats with integral head restraints. Villager had simulated rosewood-grain appliques with bright surround molding on bodyside and liftgate, a front- hinged center side window, and vertical taillamp assembly with integral backup lights and bright surround molding. The full-upswinging liftgate held fixed glass. New standard equipment included high-back bucket seats, revised door trim panels, and regular seatbelts. Deluxe low- back bucket seats became optional. Runabouts had a new optional simulated woodgrain applique for side and lower back panels. Woodgrain side panels were standard on the Villager wagon. Alpine plaid cloth interior trim in four colors replaced polyknit cloth as an interior option. Other new options included an AM radio with stereo tape player, interval-select wipers, sports vinyl roof with optional sports tape stripes, and engine block heater. Bobcat had rack-and-pinion steering, solid-state ignition, electro-coat primer, and unitized body construction. V-6 models came with power brakes.

COMET — SIX/V-8 — Introduced in 1971, the compact Comet had only minor changes at the front end and grille this year. New blackout paint went on the grille's vertical bars, and around headlamp doors and parking lamps. The wide protruding horizontal-rib center grille was accompanied by bright framed argent side grille panels with integral run/park/signal lamps. Exposed single headlamps now showed blackout housings. Two-doors had front-hinged rear quarter windows; four-doors, roll-down back windows. Both had ventless door windows, bright rocker panels and upper bodyside molding, and a bright gas cap with L-M crest and 'Comet' block letters. Identification was also provided by bright 'Comet' and 'Mercury' script. Two-pod color-keyed taillamp assemblies held integral backup lights. Inside was a two-pod instrument cluster with recessed instruments and a standard front bench seat. Comet's former GT edition was replaced by a Sports Accent Group that included

1976 Comet "Sports Accent" coupe (M)

wide lower bodyside moldings, lower body two-tone paint, dual racing mirrors, belt moldings, styled steel wheels with trim rings, and whitewalls. Two-doors could have an optional half-vinyl roof. A Custom option included new bucket seats, door trim and tinted glass. Five new body colors were offered, as well as a revised Custom interior. Alpine plaid was a new cloth seat trim. There was a new double-action foot-operated parking brake, and a new standard two-spoke steering wheel. Base engine was a 200 cu. in. inline six with one-barrel carb (250 cu. in. in California), with three-speed manual shift. A 302 cu. in. V-8 was optional. Comets had unitized body construction and standard bias-ply blackwall tires. Two- doors rode a 103 inch wheelbase; four-doors, 109.9 inches. Comet was a variant of Ford's Maverick.

1976 Monarch Ghia coupe (M)

MONARCH — SIX/V-8 — Close kin to Ford's Granada, Monarch was described as "precision-size," with 109.9 inch wheelbase. Three models were offered: base, Ghia, and top-rung Grand Monarch Ghia. Little changed this year, except for some engineering improvements that were supposed to improve ride and quiet sound levels inside. Monarch's bright upright grille was made up of thin vertical bars, with a slightly wider center divider bar. Above the grille were 'Mercury' block letters, and a stand-up hood ornament with Monarch 'M' crest and fold-down feature. Single round headlamps sat in color-keyed square frames. Large wraparound park/signal lamps with horizontal ribs were mounted in front fender tips. Bright full-length upper bodyside and decklid moldings were standard. Bright moldings also went on the windshield, full wheel lip, roof drip, and door frame. Full wheel covers displayed a center ornament, composed of three concentric circles on a circular field of red. Two-doors had opera windows. Four-doors included a bright center pillar molding. Three-pod taillamp assemblies included a tri-color lens with white backup lights, and amber-overlayed red brake and turn signal light. The textured back panel applique with bright 'Monarch' block lettering had an integral fuel filler door and hidden gas cap, color coordinated with body paint or vinyl roof. 'Mercury' script stood on the decklid. All-vinyl upholstery was standard. Flight bench seats were now standard in Monarch Ghia. Monarch had a standard 200 cu. in. one-barrel six with three-speed manual (fully synchronized) column shift. A 250 cu. in. inline six was optional, along with 302 and 351 cu. in. V-8s. Monarch used unibody construction. Four-leaf semi- elliptic rear springs were nearly 5 feet long and had stagger-mounted shock absorbers. A new base model had revised standard equipment, including a bench seat, different steering wheel, and revised door trim. Monarch Ghia added a bright driver's side remote mirror, wide odense grain bodyside molding and partial wheel lip molding, and distinctive Ghia wheel covers with simulated spoke motif and round red center ornament, highlighted by three bright concentric circles. A Ghia ornament adorned the opera window of two-doors, or rear pillar of four-doors. Also on Ghia: hood and decklid contour paint stripes, and a full- length upper bodyside paint stripe. A four-door luxury version (Grand Monarch Ghia) joined the lineup in late spring. That one added power windows, power steering, four-wheel power disc brakes, unique seat and door trim, and a fully padded Normande grain vinyl roof with frenched backlight. Bright 'Grand Monarch' script went on the lower fender. Also included on Grand Monarch: cast aluminum spoked wheels, a Normande grain vinyl center pillar pad, Ghia emblem on rear pillar, digital clock, whitewall tires, and unique taillamps. The 250 cu. in. six was standard. Buyers had a choice of saddle and white two-tone leather seating, dark red monotone leather, or dark red monotone cloth. (Leather seating was vinyl door trim.) New options were: console with warning lights (standard on Grand Monarch Ghia), power door locks, speed control, tilt steering, and automatic seatback release as part of the convenience group. Monarch's windshield wiper/washer control had moved to the steering column in mid-1975. Other mid-1975 changes included optional Sure-Track brakes, four-wheel disc brakes, and power seats.

1976 Montego MX Brougham sedan (AA)

1976 Montego MX coupe (AA)

1976 Grand Marquis Ghia sedan (AA)

MONTEGO — V-8 — This would be the final outing for Mercury's mid-size, offered in three series: Montego, Montego MX, and Montego MX Brougham. In addition to hardtop coupe and sedan models, two station wagons were available, including the simulated woodgrain-sided MX Villager. Five new body colors raised the total to 16. A landau vinyl roof option was available in six colors for two-doors. Another new option: Twin Comfort Lounge seats (with or without reclining feature) available on MX Brougham and Villager. A 351 cu. in. V-8 engine with SelectShift automatic transmission was standard on all Montegos; 400 and 460 cu. in. V-8 available. Quad round headlamps in bright rectangular frames were flanked by large combination run/park/turn signal lamps that followed the inner surface of the fendertip extensions. A rather narrow, forward-protruding grille carried both horizontal and vertical bars, with horizontal theme dominant. A bright 'Mercury' script went on the upper grille panel and decklid; L-M crest on grille panel and fuel filler door; bright 'Montego' script on lower front fender; and 'Montego' block letters on fuel door. Three-pod taillamp assemblies were used. Bright hubcaps were standard. Inside was a standard low-back front bench seat with adjustable head restraint, upholstered in cloth and vinyl. Standard equipment included power steering and brakes. Front bumper guards held rub strips. Montego MX added bright rocker panel moldings, dual upper body paint stripes, 'Montego MX' script on lower front fender, a lower back panel center surround molding, and bright/black 'Montego MX' name on instrument panel. MX Brougham had deluxe wheel covers with L-M crest in the center, over a brushed metal background with simulated spokes on outer circumference. Also on Broughams: bright upper body peak molding, bright plaque with 'Brougham' script on rear pillar, bright lower rear fender molding, and lower back panel box-textured applique with blackout paint and bright surround molding. Montego MX station wagons came with bright 'Montego' script and 'Mercury' block letters on the three-way tailgate, a vertical two-pod taillamp assembly, bright roof rear and quarter-window moldings, and bright tailgate belt molding. The top-line Villager wagon added full-length simulated woodgrain bodyside and tailgate paneling, surrounded by bright molding (partially black paint-filled). Also on Villager: bright front and rear partial wheel lip moldings, 'Montego MX' script on lower front fender, and Villager plaque. A power tailgate window was included. Montego also had a police package with choice of V-8 engines: 351 cu. in., 400 2Bbl., 460 cu. in. 4Bbl., or Police Interceptor 460 4Bbl. V-8 (with mechanical fuel pump, low-restriction air cleaner and exhaust, and engine oil cooler). Montego's front suspension used single lower arm drag struts and a link-type stabilizer bar. At the rear were helical coil springs in a four-link rubber-cushioned system.

MARQUIS — V-8 — Eight models in three series made up the full-size line: Marquis, Marquis Brougham, and Grand Marquis. Two wagons were offered, including a simulated woodgrain-sided Colony Park. A 400 cu. in. two-barrel V-8 with three-speed SelectShift was standard on all models. Power front disc/rear drum brakes and power steering were standard. Eight new body colors were added. Otherwise, this was basically a carryover year. Half a dozen separate side-by-side "boxes" made up the Marquis grille, each one holding a set of vertical ribs. Fender tips held large wraparound parking/turn signal/side marker lamps with horizontal lens ribbing. Quad headlamps were hidden behind doors with center emblems. The bright wreath stand-up hood ornament had a fold-down feature. 'Mercury' script stood on the upper grille panel; 'Marquis' script on front fender; a Marquis plaque on rear pillar; and 'Mercury' block letters on rear back panel. Two-doors had fixed quarter windows. Bright rocker panel and lower front/rear fender moldings were standard, along with bright wheel lip moldings. Deluxe wheel covers showed the L-M crest. Wraparound taillamps had horizontal ribs. A textured applique between taillamp assemblies was color-keyed to either the optional vinyl roof or the body color. Inside were low-back front bench seats, rear bench seats trimmed in new cloth and vinyl, and a two-spoke color-keyed steering wheel. Four-doors had a fold-down front seat center armrest (dual on two-doors). Simulated baby burl woodgrain adorned the instrument cluster, with a color-keyed applique over the glovebox door. Front bumper guards had black vertical protection strips. Marquis Brougham added such extras as a vinyl roof, rear fender skirts with bright hip moldings, electric clock, power windows, bright full-length fender peak molding, Brougham plaque on lower front fender, and remote-control driver's mirror. Distinctive Brougham wheel covers had a partially paint-filled Marquis plaque and slots in the outer circumference. The hinged decklid cover showed an L-M crest. Flight bench seats had adjustable low-profile head restraints and a single center folding armrest. Four-doors had rear door courtesy light switches, and a cigar lighter in the back-door armrest ashtrays. Grand Marquis included tinted glass, dual hood

1976 Cougar XR-7 Sports Coupe (M)

COUGAR XR-7 — V-8 — By the mid-1970s, Mercury's Cougar was a far different animal than the version that first appeared in 1967. Mid-size in dimensions, it had a big-car look and styling that emulated the Lincoln Continental Mark IV. Angled horizontal opera windows had been added for 1974, joining the vestigial small quarter windows. The two-door hardtop personal-luxury coupe came with plenty of standard equipment, including a landau vinyl roof and full instrumentation (including tachometer, clock, trip odometer, fuel gauge, ammeter, oil and temp gauges). Standard powerteam was a 351 cu. in. two-barrel V-8 with SelectShift Cruise-O-Matic. 400 cu. in. and 460 four-barrel V-8s were optional. Previously standard features, such as a luxury steering wheel, tinted glass, styled steel wheels with trim rings, and bucket seats with console, were made optional this year. New interior options included reclining Twin Comfort Lounge seats, with or without optional velour cloth trim; as well as a cream and gold two-tone interior for the Twin Comfort seats. Other new options: cast aluminum wheels, rocker panel moldings, engine block heater, and AM/FM stereo radio with search feature. A power-operated moon roof had been introduced as an option for 1975, with a sliding panel of tinted one-way glass that could be covered manually by an opaque shade that matched the headliner color and material. Cougar's narrow grille consisted of very thin vertical ribs with a dominant surround molding. Twin side-by-side slots were in the bumper, just below the grille, between the bumper guards. Matching side grilles held quad round headlamps, with parking/turn signal lamps in the front fender extensions. The bright Cougar stand-up hood ornament had a fold-down feature. 'Mercury' script went on both hood and deck. Side marker lights and reflectors were on the front fenders. Horizontal taillamps had integral backup lights, with bright vertical bars, bright partially black paint-filled surround molding, and red reflex rear fender applique. Rear side marker lights and reflectors were integral with taillamps. Lower bodyside moldings held color-keyed vinyl inserts. Side windows were ventless and frameless; quarter windows fixed. Bright Cougar ornaments were embedded in the opera window glass. Luxury wheel covers had an L-M crest and Cougar XR-7 ornament on the center hub.

1976 Marquis Brougham hardtop coupe (M)

and decklid paint stripes, full-length bodyside moldings with wide color-keyed vinyl insert, and gold Marquis crest on rear pillar and headlamp covers. Lower front fenders held 'Grand Marquis' script. Interiors held Twin Comfort lounge seats with dual center armrests and leather (or leather and velour) seating surfaces. A digital clock and dome lamp with dual-beam map lights were standard. Marquis station wagons had three-pod vertical taillamps, a bright tailgate belt molding, 'Mercury' block letters across the three-way tailgate, bright L-M crest on the tailgate, and a power back window. Seat upholstery was all vinyl. Rear bumper guards had black vertical rub strips. Colony Park wagons added simulated rosewood-grain paneling on bodyside and tailgate. They were also identified by 'Colony Park' script on lower rear fender, bright full-length fender peak moldings, and Brougham-style wheel covers. Flight bench seats had adjustable low-profile head restraints. New Marquis options included an AM/FM stereo search radio, landau vinyl roof, rocker panel moldings, engine block heater, and forged aluminum wheels. Base Marquis two-doors could get an automatic seatback release. A Tu-Tone group was available on Marquis Brougham and Grand Marquis two-doors. It gave a choice of two distinctive color combinations: tan and dark brown, or cream and gold. Two-tone interior trims in those packages also were available, with colors compatible to the body. The new optional vinyl half-roof for the two-door was offered in a wide range of colors, including two new ones: gold and medium red. There was a full-size Mercury police package, with 460 cu. in. four-barrel V-8 and dual exhausts, automatic transmission with auxiliary oil cooler, 3.00:1 axle ratio, four-wheel power disc brakes, and a list of heavy-duty equipment. It also included a 140 MPH speedometer. Low-gear lockout for the automatic was a limited-produciton option on the police packages. The packages also were available with other V-8s: 400 2Bbl. (single exhaust) and 460 4Bbl. PI with mechanical fuel pump and dual exhausts.

I.D. DATA: The 11-symbol Vehicle Identification Number (VIN) is stamped on a metal tab fastened to the instrument panel, visible through the windshield. The first digit is a model year code ('6' 1976). The second letter indicates assembly plant: 'A' Atlanta, GA; 'B' Oakville (Canada); 'E' Mahwah, NJ; 'H' Lorain, Ohio; 'K' Kansas City, MO; 'R' San Jose, CA; 'T' Metuchen, NJ; 'W' Wayne, MI; 'Z' St. Louis. Digits three and four are the body serial code, which corresponds to the Model Numbers shown in the tables below (e.g., '20' Bobcat 3-dr. Runabout). The fifth digit is an engine code: 'Y' L4-140 2Bbl.; 'Z' V6170 2Bbl.; 'T' L6200 1Bbl.; 'L' L6250 1Bbl.; 'F' V8302 2Bbl.; 'H' or 'Q' V8351 2Bbl.; 'S' V8400 2Bbl.; 'A' V8460 4Bbl. Finally, digits 6-11 make up the consecutive unit number of cars built at each assembly plant. The number begins with 500,001. A Vehicle Certification Label on the left front door lock face panel or door pillar shows the manufacturer, month and year of manufacture, GVW, GAWR, certification statement, VIN, body code, color code, trim code, axle code, transmission code, and domestic (or foreign) special order code.

1976 Bobcat MPG hatchback coupe (M)

BOBCAT MPG RUNABOUT (FOUR/V-6)

Model Number	Body/Style Number	Body Type & Seating	Factory Price	Shipping Weight	Production Total
20	64H	3-dr. Hatch-4P	3338/3838	2535/ --	28,905

BOBCAT MPG VILLAGER (FOUR/V-6)

22	73H	2-dr. Sta Wag-4P	3643/4143	2668/ --	18,731

COMET (SIX/V-8)

31	62B	2-dr. Fast Sed-4P	3250/3398	-- /2952	15,068
30	54B	4-dr. Sed-5P	3317/3465	-- /3058	21,006

MONARCH (SIX/V-8)

35	66H	2-dr. Sedan-4P	3773/3927	3111/3294	47,466
34	54H	4-dr. Sedan-5P	3864/4018	3164/3347	56,351

MONARCH GHIA (SIX/V-8)

38	66K	2-dr. Sedan-4P	4331/4419	3200/3383	14,950
37	54K	4-dr. Sedan-5P	4422/4510	3250/3433	27,056

MONARCH GRAND GHIA (SIX/V-8)

37	N/A	4-dr. Sedan-5P	5740/5828	3401/3584	Note 1

Note 1: Production included in basic Monarch Ghia total above.

MONTEGO (V-8)

03	65B	2-dr. HT-6P	4299	4057	2,287
02	53D	4-dr. HT Sed-6P	4343	4133	3,103

MONTEGO MX (V-8)

07	65D	2-dr. HT-6P	4465	4085	12,367
04	53D	4-dr. HT Sed-6P	4498	4133	12,666
08	71D	4-dr. Sta Wag-6P	4778	4451	5,012

MONTEGO MX BROUGHAM (V-8)

11	65K	2-dr. HT-6P	4621	4097	3,905
10	53K	4-dr. HT Sed-6P	4670	4150	5,043

MONTEGO MX VILLAGER (V-8)

18	71K	4-dr. Sta Wag-6P	5065	4478	6,412

COUGAR XR-7 (V-8)

93	65F	2-dr. HT Cpe-5P	5125	4168	83,765

MARQUIS (V-8)

66	65H	2-dr. HT-6P	5063	4436	10,450
63	53H	4-dr. Pill. HT-6P	5063	4460	28,212
74	71H	4-dr. 2S Sta Wag-6P	5275	4796	2,493
74	71H	4-dr. 3S Sta Wag-8P	5401	4824	Note 2

1976 Marquis Brougham Pillared Hardtop (AA)

MARQUIS BROUGHAM (V-8)

64	65K	2-dr. HT-6P	5955	4652	10,431
62	53K	4-dr. Pill. HT-6P	6035	4693	22,411

GRAND MARQUIS (V-8)

61	65L	2-dr. HT-6P	6439	4679	9,207
60	53L	4-dr. Pill. HT-6P	6528	4723	17,650

MARQUIS COLONY PARK (V-8)

76	71K	4-dr. 2S Sta Wag-6P	5590	4878	15,114
76	71K	4-dr. 3S Sta Wag-8P	5716	4906	Note 2

Note 2: Production totals for three-seat station wagons are included in two-seat figures.

FACTORY PRICE AND WEIGHT NOTE: For Comet and Monarch, prices and weights to left of slash are for six-cylinder, to right for V-8 engine. For Bobcat, prices/weights to left of slash are for four-cylinder, to right for V-6.

ENGINE DATA: BASE FOUR (Bobcat): Inline. Overhead cam. Four-cylinder. Cast iron block and head. Displacement: 140 cu. in. (2.3 liters). Bore & stroke: 3.78 x 3.13 in. Compression ratio: 9.0:1. Brake horsepower: 92 at 5000 R.P.M. Torque: 121 lbs.-ft. at 3000 R.P.M. Five main bearings. Hydraulic valve lifters. Carburetor: 2Bbl. Holley-Weber 9510 (D6EE-AA). VIN Code: Y. OPTIONAL V-6 (Bobcat): 60-degree, overhead-valve V-6. Cast iron block and head. Displacement: 170.8 cu. in. (2.8 liters). Bore & stroke: 3.66 x 2.70 in. Compression ratio: 8.7:1. Brake horsepower: 100 at 4600 R.P.M. Torque: 143 lbs.-ft. at 2600 R.P.M. Four main bearings. Hydraulic valve lifters. Carburetor: 2Bbl. Motorcraft 9510 (D6ZE-BA). VIN Code: Z. BASE SIX (Comet, Monarch): Inline. OHV. Six-cylinder. Cast iron block and head. Displacement: 200 cu. in. (3.3 liters). Bore & stroke: 3.68 x 3.13 in. Compression ratio: 8.3:1. Brake horsepower: 81 at 3400 R.P.M. Torque: 151 lbs.-ft. at 1700 R.P.M. Seven main bearings. Hydraulic valve lifters. Carburetor: 1Bbl. Carter YFA 9510 (D6BE-AA). VIN Code: T. BASE SIX (Monarch Ghia); OPTIONAL (Comet, Monarch): Inline. OHV. Six-cylinder. Cast iron block and head. Displacement: 250 cu. in. (4.1 liters). Bore & stroke: 3.68 x 3.91 in. Compression ratio: 8.0:1. Brake horsepower: 90 at 3000 R.P.M. (Monarch, 87 at 3000). Torque: 190 lbs.-ft. at 2000 R.P.M. (Monarch, 187 at 1900). Seven main bearings. Hydraulic valve lifters. Carburetor: 1Bbl. Carter YFA 9510. VIN Code: L. OPTIONAL V-8 (Comet, Monarch): 90-degree, overhead valve V-8. Cast iron block and head. Displacement: 302 cu. in. (5.0 liters). Bore & stroke: 4.00 x 3.00 in. Compression ratio: 8.0:1. Brake horsepower: 138 at 3600 R.P.M. (Monarch, 134 at 3600). Torque: 245 lbs.-ft. at 2000 R.P.M. (Monarch, 242 at 2000). Five main bearings. Hydraulic valve lifters. Carburetor: 2Bbl. Ford 2150A 9510 (D5DE-AFA). VIN Code: F. BASE V-8 (Montego, Cougar); OPTIONAL (Monarch): 90-degree, overhead valve V-8. Cast iron block and head. Displacement: 351 cu. in. (5.8 liters). Bore & stroke: 4.00 x 3.50 in. Compression ratio: 8.0:1. (Montego, 8.1:1). Brake horsepower: 152 at 3800 R.P.M. (or 154 at 3400). Torque: 274 lbs.-ft. at 1600 R.P.M. (or 286 at 1800). Five main bearings. Hydraulic valve lifters. Carburetor: 2Bbl. Ford 2150A 9510. VIN Code: H. BASE V-8 (Marquis); OPTIONAL (Cougar, Montego): 90-degree, overhead valve V-8. Cast iron block and head. Displacement: 400 cu. in. (6.6 liters). Bore & stroke: 4.00 x 4.00 in. Compression ratio: 8.0:1. Brake horsepower: 180 at 3800 R.P.M. Torque: 336 lbs.-ft. at 1800 R.P.M. Five main bearings. Hydraulic valve lifters. Carburetor: 2Bbl. Ford 2150A 9510. VIN Code: S. OPTIONAL V-8 (Cougar, Montego, Marquis): 90-degree, overhead valve V-8. Cast iron block and head. Displacement: 460 cu. in. (7.5 liters). Bore & stroke: 4.36 x 3.85 in. Compression ratio: 8.0:1. Brake horsepower: 202 at 3800 R.P.M. Torque: 352 lbs.-ft. at 1600 R.P.M. Five main bearings. Hydraulic valve lifters. Carburetor: 4Bbl. Motorcraft 9510 or Ford 4350A 9510. VIN Code: A.

CHASSIS DATA: Wheelbase: (Bobcat sed) 94.5 in.; (Bobcat wag) 94.8 in.; (Comet 2-dr.) 103.0 in.; (Comet 4-dr.) 109.9 in.; (Monarch) 109.9 in.; (Cougar) 114.0 in.; (Montego) 114.0 in.; (Montego wag) 118.0 in.; (Marquis) 124.0 in.; (Marquis wag) 121.0 in. Overall Length: (Bobcat sed) 169.0 in.; (Bobcat wag) 178.8 in.; (Comet 2-dr.) 189.5 in.; (Comet 4-dr.) 196.4 in.; (Monarch) 197.7 in.; (Cougar) 215.7 in.; (Montego 2-dr.) 215.7 in.; (Montego 4-dr.) 219.7 in.; (Montego wag) 224.4 in.; (Marquis) 229.0 in.; (Marquis wag) 228.3 in. Height: (Bobcat sed) 50.6 in.; (Bobcat wag) 52.0 in.; (Comet) 52.9 in.; (Monarch) 53.2-53.4 in.; (Cougar) 52.6 in.; (Montego 2.00dr.) 52.6 in.; (Montego 4dr.) 53.3 in.; (Montego wag) 54.9 in.; (Marquis 2-dr.) 53.7 in.; (Marquis 4-dr.) 54.7 in.; (Marquis wag) 56.9 in. Width: (Bobcat sed) 69.4 in.; (Bobcat wag) 69.7 in.; (Comet) 70.5 in.; (Monarch 2-dr.) 74.0 in. exc. Ghia, 74.5 in.; (Monarch 4-dr.) 74.1 in. exc. Ghia, 75.5 in.; (Cougar) 78.5 in.; (Montego) 78.6 in.; (Montego 4-dr./wag) 79.6 in.; (Marquis) 79.6 in.; (Marquis wag) 79.8 in. Front Tread: (Bobcat) 55.0 in.; (Comet) 56.5 in.; (Monarch) 58.5 in.; (Cougar) 63.4 in.; (Montego) 63.4 in.; (Marquis) 64.1 in. Rear Tread: (Bobcat) 55.8 in.; (Comet) 56.5 in.; (Monarch) 57.7 in.; (Cougar) 63.5 in.; (Montego) 63.5 in.; (Marquis) 64.3 in. Standard Tires: (Bobcat) A78 x 13 exc. V-6/wagon, B78 x 13; (Comet) C78 x 14 exc. V-8, CR78 x 14 or DR78 x 14; (Monarch) DR78 x 14 exc. V8351, ER78 x 14; (Cougar) HR78 x 14; (Montego) HR78 x 14; (Marquis) HR78 x 15 exc. wagon, JR78 x 15; (Colony Park) LR78 x 15.

TECHNICAL: Transmission: Three-speed manual transmission (column shift) standard on Comet/Monarch six and V8302. Gear ratios: (1st) 2.99:1; (2nd) 1.75:1; (3rd) 1.00:1; (Rev) 3.17:1. Four-speed floor shift standard on Bobcat. Gear ratios: (1st) 3.65:1; (2nd) 1.97:1; (3rd) 1.37:1; (4th) 1.00:1; (Rev) 3.66:1. Bobcat wagon: (1st) 4.07:1; (2nd) 2.57:1; (3rd) 1.66:1; (4th) 1.00:1; (Rev) 3.95:1. Select-Shift three-speed automatic (column lever) standard on Monarch V-8, Cougar, Montego and Marquis; optional on others. Floor lever optional on all except full-size. Bobcat L4140 automatic gear ratios: (1st) 2.47:1; (2nd) 1.47:1; (3rd) 1.00:1; (Rev) 2.11:1. Bobcat V-6/Comet/Monarch/Cougar V8351: (1st) 2.46:1; (2nd) 1.46:1; (3rd) 1.00:1;

2.20:1. Cougar V8400/460, Montego, full- size: (1st) 2.46:1; (2nd) 1.46:1; (3rd) 1.00:1; (Rev) 2.18:1. Standard final drive ratio: (Bobcat) 3.18:1 w/four, 3.00:1 w/V-6; (Comet) 2.79:1 w/3spd, 2.79:1 or 3.00:1 w/auto.; (Monarch) 2.79:1 w/3spd and 2.75:1, 3.00:1 or 3.07:1 w/auto.; (Cougar) 2.75:1; (Montego) 2.75:1; (Marquis) 2.75:1. Steering: (Bobcat) rack and pinion; (others) recirculating ball. Front Suspension: (Bobcat) coil springs with lower trailing arms, and anti-sway bar on wagon; (Montego) single lower arm drag strut w/coil springs and link-type anti-sway bar; (others) coil springs with short/long arms, lower trailing links and anti-sway bar. Rear Suspension: (Bobcat/Comet/Monarch) rigid axle w/semi- elliptic leaf springs; (Cougar) rigid axle w/lower trailing radius arms, upper oblique torque arms and coil springs; (Montego) four-link rubber-cushioned system w/coil springs; (Marquis) rigid axle w/lower trailing radius arms, upper torque arms and coil springs. Brakes: Front disc, rear drum. Ignition: Electronic. Body construction: (Bobcat/Comet/Monarch) unibody; (others) separate body on perimeter frame; Fuel tank: (Bobcat) 13 gal. exc. wagon, 14 gal.; (Comet) 19.2 gal.; (Monarch) 19.2 gal.; (Cougar) 26.5 gal.; (Montego) 21.3 gal.; (Marquis) 21 gal.

DRIVETRAIN OPTIONS: Engines: 250 cu. in., 1Bbl. six: Comet/Monarch ($96). 302 cu. in., 2Bbl. V-8: Monarch ($154); Monarch Ghia ($88). 351 cu. in., 2Bbl. V-8: Monarch ($200); Monarch Ghia ($134). 400 cu. in., 2Bbl. V-8: Montego/Cougar ($93). 460 cu. in., 4Bbl. V-8: Montego/Cougar ($292); Marquis ($212). Transmission/Differential: SelectShift Cruise-O-Matic: Bobcat ($186); Comet/Monarch ($245). Floor shift lever: Comet/Monarch ($27). Traction-Lok differential: Monarch ($48); Montego/Cougar ($53); Marquis ($54). Optional axle ratio: Bobcat/Comet/Monarch ($13); Montego/Cougar/Marquis ($14). Brakes/Steering: Power brakes: Bobcat ($54); Comet ($53); Monarch ($57). Four-wheel power disc brakes: Monarch ($210); Marquis ($170). Sure-Track brakes: Marquis ($217). Power steering: Bobcat ($117); Comet/Monarch ($124). Suspension: H.D. susp.: Comet ($17); Monarch ($29). Cross-country susp.: Montego/Cougar ($26). Adjustable air shock absorbers: Marquis ($46). Other: Engine block heater: Bobcat/Comet/Monarch ($17); Montego/Marquis/Cougar ($18). H.D. battery: Comet/Monarch ($14-$16); Marquis ($20). H.D. electrical system: Montego/Cougar ($37). Extended-range fuel tank: Marquis ($99). Trailer towing pkg. (light duty): Monarch ($42); Marquis ($53). Trailer towing pkg. (medium duty): Montego/Cougar ($59); Marquis ($46). Trailer towing pkg. (heavy duty): Montego ($82-$121); Cougar/Marquis ($132). Equalizer hitch: Marquis ($99). High-altitude option: Cougar ($13).

BOBCAT CONVENIENCE/APPEARANCE OPTIONS: Option Packages: Sports accent group ($116-$269). Convenience light group ($92). Appearance protection group ($35). Bumper protection ($64). Comfort/Convenience: Air conditioner ($420). Rear defroster, electric ($67). Tinted glass ($46). Interval wipers ($25). Entertainment: AM radio ($71); w/stereo tape player ($192). AM/FM radio ($128). AM/FM stereo radio ($173). Exterior: Sunroof, manual ($230). Sports vinyl roof ($86). Glamour paint ($54). Sports tape striping ($40). Hinged quarter windows ($34). Wide bodyside moldings ($60); narrow ($35). Rocker panel moldings ($19). Runabout woodgrain ($214). Roof luggage rack ($52-$75). Bumper guards ($34). Interior: Deluxe interior ($139). Alpine plaid seat trim ($30). Deluxe seatbelts ($17). Wheels and Tires: Forged aluminum wheels ($53-$136). Styled steel wheels ($48-$83). A78 x 13 WSW. A70 x 13 RWL. B78 x 13 BSW/WSW. BR78 x 13 SBR BSW/WSW. BR70 x 13 RWL.

COMET CONVENIENCE/APPEARANCE OPTIONS: Option Packages: Sports accent group ($235). Custom decor group ($496). Custom interior decor ($222). Bumper group ($30-$64). Convenience/visibility group ($43-$51). Appearance protection group ($8-$39). Security lock group ($16). Comfort/Convenience: Air cond. ($420). Rear defogger ($43). Tinted glass ($42). Fuel monitor warning light ($18). Interval wipers ($25). Entertainment: AM radio ($71); w/tape player ($192). AM/FM radio ($128). AM/FM stereo radio ($216); w/tape player ($299). Exterior: Vinyl roof ($89). Glamour paint ($54). Lower bodyside paint ($55). Tu-tone paint ($33). Bodyside molding ($35). Rocker panel moldings ($19). Decklid luggage rack ($51). Bumper guards, front ($17). Interior: Reclining bucket seats ($119). Alpine plaid seat trim ($30). Vinyl seat trim ($25). Color-keyed deluxe seatbelts ($17). Wheels and Tires: Forged aluminum wheels ($67-$192). Styled steel wheels ($60-$89). Deluxe wheel covers ($29). C78 x 14 WSW. BR78 x 14 BSW. CR78 x 14 BSW/WSW. DR78 x 14 BSW/WSW. DR70 x 14 RWL. Space-saver spare ($13) except (NC) with radial tires.

MONARCH CONVENIENCE/APPEARANCE OPTIONS: Option Packages: 'S' group ($482). Decor group ($181). Convenience group ($31-$75). Bumper group ($64). Light group ($25-$37). Protection group ($24-$39). Visibility group ($34- $47). Security lock group ($17). Comfort/Convenience: Air cond. ($437). Rear defogger ($43). Rear defroster, electric ($73). Fingertip speed control ($96). Power windows ($95-$133). Power door locks ($63-$88). Power four-way seat ($119). Tinted glass ($47). Leather- wrapped steering wheel ($14-$33). Luxury steering wheel ($18). Tilt steering wheel ($54). Fuel monitor warning light ($18). Digital clock ($40). Interval wipers ($25). Horns and Mirrors: Dual-note horn ($6). Dual racing mirrors ($29-$42). Lighted visor vanity mirror ($40). Entertainment: AM radio ($71); w/tape player ($192). AM/FM radio ($142). AM/FM stereo radio ($210); w/tape player ($299). Exterior: Power moonroof ($786). Power sunroof ($517). Full or landau vinyl roof ($102). Glamour paint ($54). Bodyside moldings ($35). Rocker panel moldings ($19). Decklid luggage rack ($51). Interior: Console ($65). Reclining bucket seats ($60). Leather seat trim ($181). Luxury cloth seat trim ($88) exc. (NC) w/Grand Ghia. Trunk carpeting ($20). Trunk dress-up ($33). Color-keyed seatbelts ($17). Wheels/Tires: Styled steel wheels ($35-$54); w/trim rings ($70-$89). Spoke aluminum wheels ($112-$201). E78 x 14 BSW/WSW. DR78 x 14 WSW. ER78 x 14 BSW/WSW. FR78 x 14 BSW/WSW. Space-saver spare (NC).

MONTEGO CONVENIENCE/APPEARANCE OPTIONS: Option Packages: Bumper group ($33-$53). Visibility light group ($82). Convenience group ($20-$66). Protection group ($18-$42). Security lock group ($18). Comfort/Convenience: Air cond. ($483); w/auto-temp control ($520). Defroster, electric ($80). Fingertip speed control ($101). Tinted glass ($53). Power windows ($104-$145). Power tailgate window: wag ($43). Power door locks ($68-$109). Electric decklid release ($17). Six-way power seat ($130). Leather-wrapped steering wheel ($36). Luxury steering wheel ($20). Tilt steering wheel ($59). Fuel sentry vacuum gauge ($34). Fuel monitor warning light ($20). Electric clock ($20). Interval wipers ($28). Horns and Mirrors: Dual-note horn ($7). Remote driver's mirror ($14). Dual racing mirrors ($36-$50). Entertainment: AM radio ($78). AM/FM stereo radio ($236); w/tape player ($339). Dual rear speakers ($39). Exterior: Full or landau vinyl roof ($112). Opera windows ($50). Rocker panel moldings ($26). Bodyside moldings ($38). Glamour paint ($59). Luggage rack ($82-$97). Interior: Twin comfort lounge seats ($164-$234). Polyknit trim ($50). Vinyl trim ($28). Rear-facing third seat: wag ($108). Trunk trim ($36). Wheels/Tires: Deluxe wheel covers ($32). Luxury wheel covers ($37-$68). Styled wheel ($66-$97). H78 x 14 BSW/WSW. HR78 x 14 BSW/WSW. HR78 x 14C BSW/WSW. JR78 x 14 WSW. Space-saver spare (NC).

COUGAR CONVENIENCE/APPEARANCE OPTIONS: Option Packages: Convenience group ($49-$57). Protection group ($34). Light group ($82). Bumper group ($53). Security lock group ($18). Comfort/Convenience: Air cond. ($483); auto-temp ($520). Rear defroster, electric ($80). Fingertip speed control ($101). Tinted glass ($53). Power seat ($130). Power windows ($104). Power door locks ($68). Electric trunk release ($17). Reclining passenger seat ($70). Leather-wrapped steering wheel ($36). Tilt steering wheel ($59). Fuel monitor warning light ($20). Interval wipers ($28). Driver's remote mirror ($14). Dual racing mirrors ($36-$50). Entertainment: AM radio ($78). AM/FM stereo radio ($236); w/tape player ($339). AM/FM stereo search radio ($386). Dual rear speakers ($39). Exterior: Power moonroof ($859); sunroof ($545). Full vinyl roof ($41). Glamour paint ($59). Bodyside molding ($38). Rocker panel moldikngs ($26). Interior: Twin comfort lounge seats ($86). Bucket seats w/console ($143). Leather trim ($222). Velour trim ($96). Trunk dress-up ($36). Wheels/Tires: Styled steel wheels ($93). Cast aluminum wheels ($199). HR78 x 14 SBR WSW ($39). HR78 x 15 SBR WSW ($62). HR70 x 15 WSW ($82). Space-saver spare (NC).

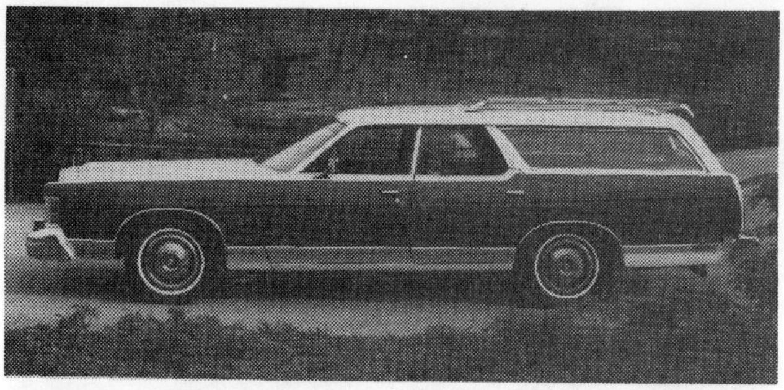

1976 Colony Park station wagon (AA)

MARQUIS CONVENIENCE/APPEARANCE OPTIONS: Option Packages: Grand Marquis option: Colony Park ($305). Tu-tone group ($59-$145). Lock convenience group ($86-$112). Light group ($83-$118). Bumper group ($33-$53). Protection group ($47-$55). Security lock group ($8-$18). Comfort/Convenience: Air cond. ($512); w/auto-temp control ($549). Anti-theft alarm system ($100-$105). Rear defroster, electric ($80). Fingertip speed control ($101). Power windows ($109-$162). Power vent windows ($79). Six-way power driver's seat ($132); driver and passenger ($257). Automatic seatback release ($30). Tinted glass ($66). Deluxe steering wheel ($20). Tilt steering wheel ($59). Fuel monitor warning light ($20). Electric clock ($20). Digital clock ($29-$49). Interval wipers ($28). Lighting and Mirrors: Cornering lamps ($41). Driver's remote mirror ($14). Entertainment: AM radio ($78). AM/FM stereo radio ($236); w/tape player ($339). AM/FM stereo search radio ($386). Dual rear speakers ($39). Power antenna ($39). Exterior: Power sunroof ($632). Full vinyl roof ($126) exc. wagon ($151). Landau vinyl roof ($126). Fender skirts ($41). Glamour metallic paint ($59). Paint stripes ($29). Rocker panel moldings ($26). Vinyl-insert bodyside moldings ($41). Luggage rack: wag ($82-$100). Interior: Twin comfort lounge seats ($86). Reclining passenger seat ($58). Dual-facing rear seats: wagon ($126). Vinyl bench seat ($26). Recreation table: wag ($58). Color- keyed seatbelts ($18). Front/rear mats ($33). Deluxe cargo area ($83-$126). Lockable side stowage compartment: wag ($43). Luggage area trim ($46). Wheels: Brougham wheel covers ($26). Luxury wheel covers ($50-$76). Forged aluminum wheels ($211-$237). Tires: HR78 x 15 WSW. JR78 x 15 BSW/WSW. LR78 x 15B BSW/WSW. LR78 x 15C WSW.

HISTORY: Introduced: October 3, 1975. Model year production: 482,714. Calendar year production (U.S.): 434,877. Calendar year sales by U.S. dealers: 418,749. Model year sales by U.S. dealers: 428,023.

Historical Footnotes: Lincoln-Mercury sales rose almost 24 percent for the 1976 model year, a far better showing than in 1975, which had posted a significant decline. Showing the strongest increase were Monarch and Marquis, rising by some 60 percent. At the smaller end of the Mercury spectrum, Comet fell by nearly 37 percent, while Montego (in its final season) showed a more moderate deline. Led by Monarch, model year production showed a gain of nearly 17 percent. Although General Motors was ready to downsize its full-size models, Ford/Mercury planned to keep its biggies for two more years, including the massive 400 and 460 cu. in. V-8s.

1977 MERCURY

Although the mid-size Montego disappeared, a broad new line of Cougars joined the XR-7. While XR7 competed with Grand Prix, Monte Carlo and Cordoba, the new standard Cougars became rivals to Olds Cutlass and Supreme, Pontiac LeMans, and Buick Century, retaining some of the distinctive sculptured XR7 styling. Engines had "second generation" DuraSpark electronic ignition that produced higher spark-plug voltage. Monarch added a four-speed gearbox (overdrive fourth gear) as standard equipment. Marquis carried on in full-size form, unlike the downsized GM big cars.

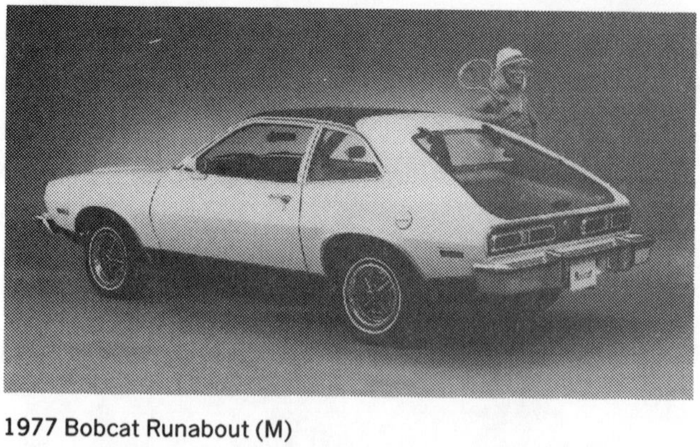

1977 Bobcat Runabout (M)

BOBCAT — FOUR/V-6 — Appearance and equipment of Mercury's subcompact changed little this year, except for new colors and trims. Runabouts could have a new optional all-glass third door (hatch). Bumpers were now bright-surfaced, extruded anodized aluminum, which helped cut weight by over 100 pounds. To improve ride/handling, shock absorbers were revalved, and rear-spring front eye bushings stiffened. New DuraSpark ignition offered higher voltage. Inside, the manual gearshift lever was shortened, while a new wide-ratio four-speed was offered. Rear axle ratios were lowered (numerically) too, to help gas mileage. Joining the option list were: a flip-up removable sunroof, manual four-way bucket seats, Sports Group (handling and instrumentation package), simulated wire wheel covers, and high-altitude option. That Sports Group included a tachometer, ammeter and temperature gauges, new soft-rim sports steering wheel, front stabilizer bar, and higher-rate springs. Bobcats had a domed hood, bright metal vertical-textured grille with surround molding, and clear

square park/signal lamps with crosshair bars, positioned between the grille and single round headlamps. Wide-spaced 'Bobcat' block letters stood above the grille. California versions had styled steel wheels, while 49-staters carried deluxe wheel covers. Standard equipment included a lighter, front/rear ashtrays, woodgrain instrument panel applique, wide wheel lip and rocker panel moldings, and manual front disc brakes. Bodies also carried bright side window frame and door belt moldings, and center pillar moldings. At the rear were horizontal tri- pod taillamps with a small backup light in the center of each unit. 'Bobcat' script went in the lower corner of the glass third door. Base engine again was the 140 cu. in. (2.3-liter) four with four-speed floor shift, with 2.8-liter V-6 available. Bias-ply A78 x 13 blackwalls were standard, except in California which required steel-belted radials. Contoured high-back bucket seats came in all-vinyl or Kirsten cloth and vinyl. An 'S' option group included gold-stripe treatment from hood to back panel, blackout trim, styled steel wheels with gold accents, dual racing mirrors, sports suspension with stabilizer bar, and the new glass third door. A Sports Accent Group included styled steel wheels with trim rings, special paint/tape, leather-wrapped steering wheel, deluxe bucket seats, and sound package.

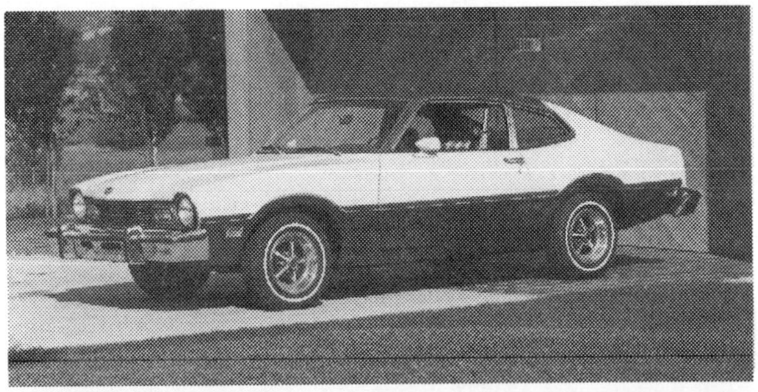

1977 Comet coupe (M)

COMET — SIX/V-8 — Not much changed in the compact Comet, which would not return for 1978. New body and interior colors were offered, along with two new vinyl roof colors. New options included simulated wire wheel covers, two-tone paint, four-way manual bucket seats, high-altitude emissions, and new Decor Groups. The new optional driver's bucket seat adjusted (manually) up and down as well as forward and back. All three engines were modified, including a new variable-venturi carburetor for the California 302 cu. in. V-8. All had improved-response throttle linkage and new DuraSpark ignition. Drivetrains held a new wide-ratio three-speed manual shift, while the 302 V-8 models had a more efficient torque converter. Comet's grille was peaked forward slightly, made up of thin horizontal bars with a dominant horizontal bar in the center and full-width lower grille molding. Aligned with the grille were surround moldings for the clear rectangular park/signal lenses, framed in argent side panels. Those moldings followed the curve of the single round headlamps at their outer edges. Blackout headlamp frames had argent beads. The entire front end had a full-width look. Amber side marker lenses were just ahead of the front wheels, below the bodyside molding. Front bumpers contained two side-by-side slots in the center. Each taillamp consisted of two separate pods. Two-doors had front-hinged rear quarter windows; four- doors, roll-down back door windows. Bright front/rear wheel lip moldings and rocker panel moldings were used, as well as bright upper bodyside and drip rail moldings. Hubcaps were standard, with C78 x 14 blackwall tires. Bright window frames and belt moldings became part of the optional exterior decor group. Several items, including lighter and rear ashtray, were put into a new interior decor group, which also included a deluxe steering wheel, cloth/vinyl or all-vinyl seat trim, and upgraded sound package. Five colors of vinyl were available in the standard interior. Standard equipment included the 200 cu. in. six, three-speed manual shift (but 250 six with automatic in California), lighted front ashtray, European-type armrests and door handles, glovebox, and dome light. The Custom option included a vinyl roof, whitewalls, bodyside paint stripes, full-length molding with color-keyed vinyl inserts, reclining front bucket seats, tinted glass, and leather-wrapped sports steering wheel. That option was billed as having "a little Cougar in it."

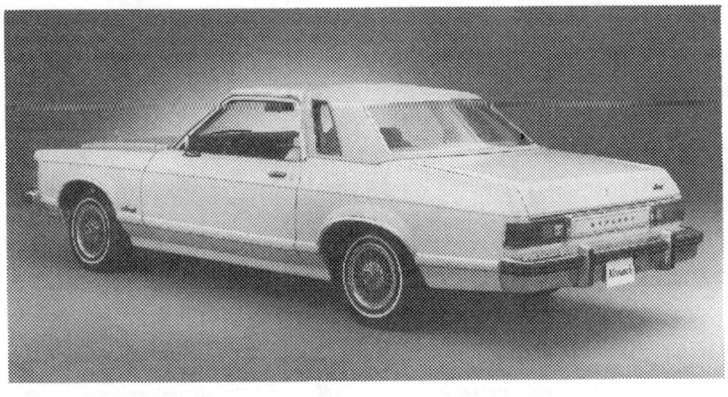

1977 Monarch Ghia coupe (M)

MONARCH — SIX/V-8 — "The precision size car with a touch of class." That's how Lincoln-Mercury described Monarch this year. Like other models, it carried a plaque on the dash proclaiming that it was "Ride-Engineered by Lincoln-Mercury." Appearance changed little, however, apart from some new body colors and option choices. New options included four-way manual bucket seats, automatic-temperature-control air conditioning, illuminated entry, front cornering lamps, simulated wire wheel covers, white lacy-spoke cast aluminum wheels, wide-band whitewall radial tires, high-altitude emissions, and electric trunk lid release. Several appearance options had debuted in mid-year 1976 and continued this year, including a landau half-vinyl roof, dual racing mirrors, and styled steel wheels. A new standard four-speed manual floor shift had fourth- gear overdrive. California 302 cu. in. V-8s had a new variable-venturi carburetor. Other mechanical changes included an improved-response throttle linkage; new Dura- Spark ignition; lower rear axle ratios; and new standard coolant recovery system. Monarch's grille was made up of thin vertical bars with bright surround molding and 'Mercury' block lettering above. Horizontally-ribbed park/signal lamps in front fender extensions turned into amber side marker lenses after wrapping around the fender. Twin side-by-side slots were in the front bumper's center. Single round headlamps were recessed in square bright housings. The unique stand-up hood ornament had seven tiny "knobs" atop a pillar within a circle. 'Monarch' script was on the lower cowl, just above the lower bodyside molding. Backup lenses stood at the inner ends of each square-styled tri-pod wraparound taillamp, with tri-color lenses. Two-doors had opera windows; four-doors, rear quarter windows. The textured back panel applique was color-keyed to either the body or vinyl roof. Front and rear full wheel lip moldings, full-length upper bodyside moldings, and bright window frame moldings were standard. Dashboards displayed a simulated burled walnut woodgrain applique. Base engine was again the 200 cu. in. inline six. Standard equipment also included front disc brakes, foot parking brake, blackwall SBR tires, full wheel covers, locking glovebox, and lighter. Monarch Ghia moved up to the 250 cu. in. six and added paint striping on hood contours and decklid, a tapered bodyside paint stripe (replacing the usual darts), and Ghia ornament on opera window of two-doors (rear pillar of four- doors). Full-length lower bodyside moldings had wide color- keyed vinyl inserts. Front and rear partial wheel lip moldings replaced the base Monarch's full wheel lip moldings. Ghia also included map pockets, color-keyed wheel covers (or wire wheel covers), carpeted trunk, day/night mirror, remote driver's mirror, inside hood release, and Flight Bench seat. An 'S' option group included a landau vinyl roof (two-door); goldtone paint/tape stripes on bodysides, hood and decklid; rocker panel moldings; dual remote racing mirrors; styled steel wheels with gold-color accents and trim rings; bucket seats; leather-wrapped steering wheel; heavy-duty suspension; and floor lever with optional automatic. Both models could have the optional 302 cu. in. V-8.

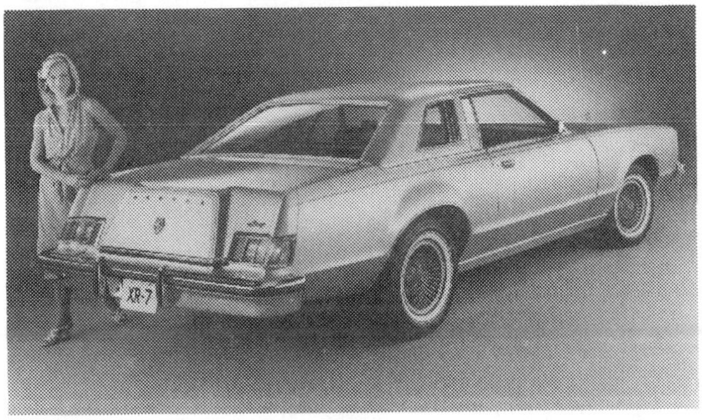

1977 Cougar XR-7 Sports Coupe (M)

COUGAR/XR-7 — V-8 — All-new styling hit Cougar's A-body shell for 1976, as the nameplate expanded to included a set of sedans and wagons as well as the usual XR7 hardtop coupe. Grille, grille opening panel, quad rectangular headlamps, and combination parking/turn signal lamps were all new. Cougar's rear end had new vertical taillamps, backup lights, decklid, quarter panel, and deck opening lower panel. Larger side glass and backlight improved visibility. XR-7 had distinctive new wraparound taillamps, plus a new decklid similar to the Mark V Lincoln. Viewed from the side, the two- and four-door models showed new doors and a straight beltline, as well as a new rear roof (plus optional opera windows). XR-7's profile showed a distinctive large opera window with louvers and a padded landau roof. Base and Villager wagons were offered. Base engine size was reduced from 351 to 302 cu. in., with new Dura-Spark ignition and lower rear axle ratio. Instrument clusters were revised on both Cougars. Air conditioner performance improved with a 40 percent airflow increase. XR7 had a larger-diameter front stabilizer bar, and an added rear stabilizer bar to improve handling. Appearance of the new models was similar to XR-7, but without the louvered opera windows. Taillamps were different, though: two-section vertical units at quarter panel tips, with small backup lenses at outer ends of a wide red center panel below the decklid. Cougar had a distinctive Continental-type swing-away grille made up of vertical bars, divided into two side-by- side sections (each containing three sections). A heavy surround molding positioned the grille well forward of the headlamps, and it extended slightly below the bumper. No bumper slots were used. Moldings above and below the quad rectangular headlamps continued outward to enclose the large fender-tip wraparound park/signal/marker lenses (which were amber at the rear). Above was a bright new stand-up Cougar hood ornament. The red reflective rear center applique in the lower back panel had a bright surround molding. Bright rocker panel moldings, full wheel lip moldings, roof drip rail and window frame moldings, and door belt moldings all were standard. Two-doors had rear quarter window moldings. Inside was a standard cloth and vinyl bench seat. Cougar Brougham added a full vinyl roof (on four-door), upper bodyside paint stripe, bright wide door belt molding, deluxe wheel covers, and Flight bench seat with folding armrest (cloth and vinyl or all vinyl). Opera windows had 'Brougham' script embedded in the glass. Full-length bright bodyside moldings with integral wheel lip moldings replaced the usual full wheel lip and rocker panel moldings. Mercury promoted the XR7 for its sweeping profile, accentuated by its sculptured rear decklid and accent stripes, calling it "bold" and "aggressive." Cougar XR-7 features included the sport-style roofline, fully padded landau vinyl roof. grille extension below the bumper, hood rear edge molding, full wheel lip and rocker panel moldings, and full wheel covers with unique Cougar center insert. Wide opera windows had a trio of vertical louvers at the forward end. Those were accompanied by a small frameless window just to the rear of the door window, in hardtop style. A Cougar ornament adorned the center pillar, while the rear end held a sculptured simulated-spare-tire decklid with lower molding and paint stripe, and 'Cougar' block lettering. Horizontal wraparound taillamps were divided into six sections by vertical strips, wrapping around quarter panel tips, with backup lenses in the second section from the inside. 'Mercury' script went just above the right taillamp. Flight Bench seating with decorative accent stripes came in Ashton cloth or Mateao vinyl. Cougar standard equipment included the 302 V-8 and SelectShift, power brakes and steering, HR78 x 14 tires, two- spoke color-keyed steering wheel, day/night mirror, and inside hood release. XR-7 equipment included HR78 x 15 SBR tires, landau vinyl roof, clock, walnut instrument panel appliques, day/night mirror, dual-note horn, and locking glovebox. Four new XR7 colors were available. Station wagons had a 351 cu. in. V-8, optional on other models. A 400 cu. in. V-8 also was available. Major new options included opera windows, illuminated entry, day/date clock, sports steering wheel, cornering lamps, monaural AM/FM radio, AM/FM stereo search radio, radio with quadrasonic tape player, wide whitewall radials, wire wheel covers, and (two-doors only) front and rear half-vinyl roof.

MARQUIS — V-8 — New body colors and interior fabrics accounted for most of the changes in Mercury's full-size line. Bright vinyl roof surround moldings replaced color-keyed vinyl moldings on Brougham and Grand Marquis. Grand Marquis had newly styled Twin Comfort lounge seats. New options included a power moonroof, illuminated entry, AM/FM stereo radio with quadrasonic8 tape player, simulated wire wheel covers, high- altitude emissions, and wide whitewall radials. The improved standard 400 cu. in. V-8 engine had Dura-Spark ignition and a new standard coolant recovery system, while the rear axle ratio was lowered (numerically). The Colony Park wagon was now a Brougham-level option package. As before, the upright grille consisted of six side-by- side sections, each with five vertical bars, surrounded by a bright molding. Concealed headlamps stood behind rectangular doors with rectangular trim molding and center crest emblem. 'Mercury' script went above the left headlamp. Horizontally- ribbed park/signal lamps stood at fender tips, wrapping around to amber side marker lenses. Front vertical bumper guards had black inserts. Bright rocker panel moldings included front extensions. Inside was a new "Ride-Engineered by Lincoln-Mercury" dash plaque. Front bench seats came in

Ardmore cloth and vinyl, with fold-down center armrest. Standard equipment included three-speed SelectShift, power steering and brakes, and HR78 x 15 blackwall steel-belted radials. Marquis Brougham added a full vinyl roof (on four-doors) or landau vinyl roof (two-doors) with bright surround moldings, fender skirts with bright molding, power windows, clock, and full-length upper body peak molding. Decklid lock covers showed the L-M crest. Flight bench seats came in Willshire cloth and vinyl with folding center armrest. Two- doors had automatic seatback release. Grand Marquis included the 460 4Bbl. V-8, SelectShift, power windows, tinted glass, vinyl roof, digital clock, automatic parking brake release, fender skirts, Twin Comfort Lounge seats, and hood/decklid paint stripes. The big 460 V-8 was not available in California.

I.D. DATA: As before, Mercury's 11-symbol Vehicle Identification Number (VIN) is stamped on a metal tab fastened to the instrument panel, visible through the windshield. Coding is similar to 1976. Model year code changed to '7' for 1977.

BOBCAT RUNABOUT/WAGON (FOUR/V-6)

Model Number	Body/Style Number	Body Type & Seating	Factory Price	Shipping Weight	Production Total
20	64H	3-dr. Hatch-4P	3438/3739	2369/ --	18,405
22	73H	2-dr. Sta Wag-4P	3629/3930	2505/ --	Note 1

BOBCAT VILLAGER (FOUR/V-6)

22	73H	2-dr. Sta Wag-4P	3771/4072	N/A	Note 1

Note 1: Total station wagon production was 13,047 units. Bobcat Runabout and wagon totals include 3,616 vehicles produced in 1978 but sold as 1977 models.

COMET (SIX/V-8)

31	62B	2-dr. Fast Sed-4P	3392/3544	-- /2960	9,109
30	54B	4-dr. Sed-5P	3465/3617	-- /3065	12,436

MONARCH (SIX/V-8)

35	66H	2-dr. Sedan-4P	4092/4279	3123/3277	44,509
34	54H	4-dr. Sedan-5P	4188/4375	3173/3327	55,592

MONARCH GHIA (SIX/V-8)

38	66K	2-dr. Sedan-4P	4659/4749	3244/3398	11,051
37	54K	4-dr. Sedan-5P	4755/4850	3305/3459	16,545

COUGAR (V-8)

91	65D	2-dr. HT Cpe-6P	4700	3811	15,910
90	53D	4-dr. Pill. HT-6P	4832	3893	15,256
92	71D	4-dr. Sta Wag-6P	5104	4434	4,951

1977 Cougar Brougham sedan (M)

COUGAR BROUGHAM (V-8)

95	65K	2-dr. HT Cpe-6P	4990	3852	8,392
94	53K	4-dr. Pill. HT-6P	5230	3946	16,946

COUGAR VILLAGER (V-8)

96	71K	4-dr. Sta Wag-6P	5363	4482	8,569

COUGAR XR-7 (V-8)

93	65L	2-dr. HT Cpe-6P	5274	3909	124,799

MARQUIS (V-8)

66	65H	2-dr. HT-6P	5496	4293	13,242
63	53H	4-dr. Pill. HT-6P	5496	4326	36,103
74	71H	4-dr. 2S Sta Wag-6P	5631	4628	20,363
74	71H	4-dr. 3S Sta Wag-8P	5794	N/A	Note 2

Note 2: Production total for three-seat station wagon is included in two-seat figure.

MARQUIS BROUGHAM (V-8)

64	65K	2-dr. HT-6P	6229	4350	12,237
62	53K	4-dr. Pill. HT-6P	6324	4408	29,411

GRAND MARQUIS (V-8)

61	65L	2-dr. HT-6P	6880	4516	13,445
60	53L	4-dr. Pill. HT-6P	6975	4572	31,231

FACTORY PRICE AND WEIGHT NOTE: For Comet and Monarch, prices and weights to left of slash are for six-cylinder, to right for V-8 engine. For Bobcat, prices/weights to left of slash are for four-cylinder, to right for V-6.

ENGINE DATA: BASE FOUR (Bobcat): Inline. Overhead cam. Four-cylinder. Cast iron block and head. Displacement: 140 cu. in. (2.3 liters). Bore & stroke: 3.78 x 3.13 in. Compression ratio: 9.0:1. Brake horsepower: 89 at 4800 R.P.M. Torque: 120 lbs.-ft. at 3000 R.P.M. Five main bearings. Hydraulic valve lifters. Carburetor: 2Bbl. Motorcraft 5200. VIN Code: Y. OPTIONAL V-6 (Bobcat): 60-degree, overhead-valve V-6. Cast iron block and head. Displacement: 170.8 cu. in. (2.8 liters). Bore & stroke: 3.66 x 2.70 in. Compression ratio: 8.7:1. Brake horsepower: 90-93 at 4200 R.P.M. Torque: 139-140 lbs.-ft. at 2600 R.P.M. Four main bearings. Hydraulic valve lifters. Carburetor: 2Bbl. Motorcraft 2150. VIN Code: Z. BASE SIX (Comet, Monarch): Inline. OHV. Six-cylinder. Cast iron block and head. Displacement: 200 cu. in. (3.3 liters). Bore & stroke: 3.68 x 3.13 in. Compression ratio: 8.5:1. Brake horsepower: 96 at 4400 R.P.M. Torque: 151 lbs.-ft. at 2000 R.P.M. Seven main bearings. Hydraulic valve lifters. Carburetor: 1Bbl. Carter YFA. VIN Code: T. BASE SIX (Monarch Ghia); OPTIONAL (Comet, Monarch): Inline. OHV. Six-cylinder. Cast iron block and head. Displacement: 250 cu. in. (4.1 liters). Bore & stroke: 3.68 x 3.91 in. Compression ratio: 8.0:1. Brake horsepower: 98 at 3400 R.P.M. Torque: 182 lbs.-ft. at 1800 R.P.M. Seven main bearings. Hydraulic valve lifters. Carburetor: 1Bbl. Carter YFA. VIN Code: L. BASE V-8 (Cougar); OPTIONAL (Comet, Monarch): 90-degree, overhead valve V-8. Cast iron block and head. Displacement: 302 cu. in. (5.0 liters). Bore & stroke: 4.00 x 3.00 in. Compression ratio: 8.4:1. Brake horsepower: 130-137 at 3400-3600 R.P.M. (some Monarchs, 122 at 3200). Torque: 242-245 lbs.-ft. at 1600-1800 R.P.M. (some Monarchs, 237 at 1600). Five main bearings. Hydraulic valve lifters. Carburetor: 2Bbl. Motorcraft 2150. VIN Code: F. OPTIONAL V-8 (Cougar, Monarch): 90-degree, overhead valve V-8. Cast iron block and head. Displacement: 351 cu. in. (5.8 liters). Bore & stroke: 4.00 x 3.50 in. Compression ratio: 8.3:1. Brake horsepower: 149 at 3200 R.P.M. Torque: 291 lbs.-ft. at 1600 R.P.M. Five main bearings. Hydraulic valve lifters. Carburetor: 2Bbl. Motorcraft 2150. Windsor engine. VIN Code: H. OPTIONAL V-8 (Monarch Ghia): Same as 351 cu. in. V-8 above, but Horsepower: 135 at 3200 R.P.M. Torque: 275 lbs.-ft. at 1600 R.P.M. BASE V-8 (Cougar wagon); OPTIONAL (Cougar): Same as 351 cu. in. V-8 above, but— Compression ratio: 8.0:1. Horsepower: 161 at 3600 R.P.M. Torque: 285 lbs.-ft. at 1800 R.P.M. VIN Code: Q. BASE V-8 (Marquis); OPTIONAL (Cougar): 90-degree, overhead valve V-8. Cast iron block and head. Displacement: 400 cu. in. (6.6 liters). Bore & stroke: 4.00 x 4.00 in. Compression ratio: 8.0:1. Brake horsepower: 173 at 3800 R.P.M. Torque: 328 lbs.-ft. at 1600 R.P.M. Five main bearings. Hydraulic valve lifters. Carburetor: 2Bbl. Motorcraft 2150. VIN Code: S. BASE V-8 (Grand Marquis); OPTIONAL (Marquis): 90-degree, overhead valve V-8. Cast iron block and head. Displacement: 460 cu. in. (7.5 liters). Bore & stroke: 4.36 x 3.85 in. Compression ratio: 8.0:1. Brake horsepower: 197 at 000 R.P.M. Torque: 353 lbs.-ft. at 2000 R.P.M. Five main bearings. Hydraulic valve lifters. Carburetor: 4Bbl. Motorcraft 4350. VIN Code: A.

CHASSIS DATA: Wheelbase: (Bobcat sed) 94.5 in.; (Bobcat wag) 94.8 in.; (Comet 2-dr.) 103.0 in.; (Comet 4-dr.) 109.9 in.; (Monarch) 109.9 in.; (Cougar 2dr.) 114.0 in.; (Cougar 4dr.) 118.0 in.; (Marquis) 124.0 in.; (Marquis wag) 121.0 in. Overall Length: (Bobcat sed) 169.0 in.; (Bobcat wag) 179.1 in.; (Comet 2-dr.) 189.4 in.; (Comet 4-dr.) 196.3 in.; (Monarch) 197.7 in.; (Cougar 2dr.) 215.5 in.; (Cougar 4dr.) 219.5 in.; (Cougar wag) 223.1 in.; (Marquis) 229.0 in.; (Marquis wag) 228.3 in. Height: (Bobcat sed) 50.6 in.; (Bobcat wag) 52.1 in.; (Comet) 52.9 in.; (Monarch) 53.2-53.3 in.; (Cougar) 52.6 in.; (Cougar 4dr.) 53.3 in.; (XR7) 53.0 in.; (Marquis 2-dr.) 53.7-53.8 in.; (Marquis 4-dr.) 54.7-54.8 in.; (Marquis wag) 56.9 in. Width: (Bobcat sed) 69.4 in.; (Bobcat wag) 69.5 in.; (Monarch 2-dr.) 74.0 in. exc. Ghia, 74.5 in.; (Monarch 4-dr.) 74.1 in.; (Cougar) 78.0 in.; (Marquis) 79.6 in.; (Marquis wag) 79.8 in. Front Tread: (Bobcat) 55.0 in.; (Comet) 56.5 in.; (Monarch) 59.0 in.; (Cougar) 63.6 in.; (Marquis) 64.1 in. Rear Tread: (Bobcat) 55.8 in.; (Comet) 56.5 in.; (Monarch) 57.7 in.; (Cougar) 63.5 in.; (Marquis) 64.3 in. Standard Tires: (Bobcat) A78 x 13 BSW exc. B78 x 13 w/V-6; (Comet) C78 x 14 BSW; (Monarch) DR78 x 14 BSW; (Cougar) HR78 x 14 BSW; (XR7) HR78 x 15 BSW; (Marquis) HR78 x 15; (Marquis wag) JR78 x 15.

TECHNICAL: Transmission: Three-speed manual transmission (column shift) standard on Comet six. Gear ratios: (1st) 3.56:1; (2nd) 1.90:1; (3rd) 1.00:1; (Rev) 3.78:1. Four-speed overdrive floor shift standard on Monarch: (1st) 3.29:1; (2nd) 1.84:1; (3rd) 1.00:1; (4th) 0.81:1; (Rev) 3.29:1. Four-speed floor shift standard on Bobcat sedan: (1st) 3.98:1; (2nd) 2.14:1; (3rd) 1.42:1; (4th) 1.00:1; (Rev) 3.99:1. Bobcat wagon: (1st) 3.65:1; (2nd) 1.97:1; (3rd) 1.37:1; (4th) 1.00:1; (Rev) 3.66:1. Select-Shift three-speed automatic (column lever) standard on Cougar and Marquis, optional on others. Bobcat L4140 automatic gear ratios: (1st) 2.47:1; (2nd) 1.47:1; (3rd) 1.00:1; (Rev) 2.11:1. Bobcat V-6/Comet/Monarch/Cougar/Marquis: (1st) 2.46:1; (2nd) 1.46:1; (3rd) 1.00:1; (Rev) 2.14:1 to 2.19:1. Some Cougar/Marquis: (1st) 2.40:1; (2nd) 1.47:1; (3rd) 1.00:1; (Rev) 2.00:1. Standard final drive ratio: (Bobcat) 2.73:1 w/4spd, 3.18:1 w/auto.; (Bobcat V-6) 3.00:1; (Comet) 3.00:1 w/3spd, 2.79:1 w/250 six and 3spd or any auto.; (Monarch) 3.40:1 w/200 six, 3.00:1 w/250 six or V-8, 2.47:1 w/auto.; (Cougar) 2.50:1 or 2.75:1; (Marquis) 2.47:1 w/V8400, 2.50:1 w/V8460. Steering: (Bobcat) rack and pinion; (others) recirculating ball. Front Suspension: (Bobcat) coil springs with short/long control arms, lower leading arms, and anti-sway bar on wagon; (Comet/Monarch/Cougar) coil springs with short/long arms, lower trailing links, strut bar and anti-sway bar; (XR7/Marquis) coil springs w/single lower control arms, lower trailing links, strut bar and anti-sway bar. Rear Suspension: (Bobcat/Comet/Monarch) rigid axle w/semi- elliptic leaf springs; (Cougar) rigid axle w/lower trailing radius arms, upper oblique torque arms and coil springs; (Marquis) rigid axle with upper/lower control arms and coil springs. Brakes: Front disc, rear drum. Ignition: Electronic. Body construction: (Bobcat/Comet/Monarch) unibody; (others) separate body on perimeter frame; Fuel tank: (Bobcat) 13 gal. exc. wagon, 14 gal.; (Comet) 19.2 gal.; (Monarch) 19.2 gal.; (Cougar) 26.0 gal.; (Marquis) 24.2 gal.

DRIVETRAIN OPTIONS: Engines: 170 cu. in. V-6: Bobcat ($301). 250 cu. in., 1Bbl. six: Comet/Monarch ($102). 302 cu. in., 2Bbl. V-8: Comet (N/A); Monarch ($93-$163). 351 cu. in., 2Bbl. V-8: Monarch ($142); Cougar ($66); Marquis (NC). 400 cu. in., 2Bbl. V-8: Cougar ($132); Cougar wag ($66); Marquis (NC). 460 cu. in., 4Bbl. V-8: Marquis ($225). Transmission/Differential: SelectShift Cruise-O-Matic: Bobcat ($197); Comet/Monarch ($259). Floor shift lever: Monarch ($28). Traction-Lok differential: Marquis ($57); Cougar ($54). Optional axle ratio: Cougar ($16); Marquis ($15). Brakes/Steering: Power brakes: Bobcat ($57); Comet ($56); Monarch ($60). Four-wheel power disc brakes: Monarch ($273); Marquis ($180). Power steering: Bobcat ($124); Comet/Monarch ($132). Suspension: H.D. susp.: Monarch ($31). Cross country pkg.: Cougar XR7/wag, Marquis ($27). Other: H.D. battery: Bobcat ($15); Comet ($17); Cougar ($18); Marquis ($21). H.D. alternator: Cougar/Marquis ($45). Engine block heater: Bobcat/Monarch ($18); Marquis ($18). Trailer towing pkg. (heavy duty): Cougar ($117-$157); Marquis ($188). California emission system: Bobcat ($52); Comet/Monarch ($49); Marquis ($53). High-altitude option: Bobcat/Monarch ($38); Marquis ($42).

BOBCAT CONVENIENCE/APPEARANCE OPTIONS: Option Packages: 'S' group ($115). Sports accent group ($285- $308). Sports instrument/handling group ($77-$89). Convenience light group ($68-$125). Bumper group ($68). Protection group ($37). Comfort/Convenience: Air conditioner ($446). Rear defroster, electric ($72). Tinted glass ($49). Driver's remote mirror ($14). Entertainment: AM radio ($75); w/stereo tape player ($203). AM/FM radio ($135). AM/FM stereo radio ($184). Exterior: Sunroof, manual ($244). Flip-up/removable moonroof ($147). Sports vinyl roof ($133). Glass third door ($13). Hinged quarter windows ($36). Glamour paint ($57). Narrow bodyside moldings ($37). Wide color-keyed bodyside moldings ($64). Roof luggage rack ($79). Rocker panel moldings ($20). Interior: Four-way bucket seat ($32). Plaid seat trim ($32). Deluxe interior trim ($147). Load floor carpet ($23). Cargo area cover ($34). Deluxe seatbelts ($18). Wheels/Tires: Wire wheel covers ($86). Forged aluminum wheels ($56-$144). Styled steel wheels ($88). Trim rings ($32). A78 x 13 WSW. B78 x 13 BSW/WSW. BR78 x 13 BSW/WSW. BR70 x 13 RWL.

COMET CONVENIENCE/APPEARANCE OPTIONS: Option Packages: Custom group ($609). Sports accent group ($249). Exterior decor group ($64). Interior decor group ($112). Custom interior ($296). Bumper group ($32-$68). Convenience/visibility group ($65-$80). Protection group ($9-$41). Comfort/Convenience: Air cond. ($46). Electric rear defogger ($46). Tinted window glass ($47). Dual racing mirrors ($14-$28). Entertainment: AM radio ($75); w/tape player ($203). AM/FM radio ($135). AM/FM stereo radio ($229); w/tape player ($317). Exterior: Vinyl roof ($95). Glamour paint ($57). Tu-tone paint ($59). Bodyside moldings ($37). Rocker panel moldings ($20). Interior: Four-way seat ($32). Reclining vinyl bucket seats ($156). Vinyl seat trim ($27). Plaid seat trim ($32). Deluxe seatbelts ($18). Wheels/Tires: Deluxe wheel covers ($31). Wire wheel covers ($22-$116). Cast aluminum wheels ($138-$233). Styled steel wheels ($64-$95). C78 x 14 WSW ($32). CR78 x 14 SBR BSW ($57- $89). CR78 x 14 SBR WSW ($89-$121). DR78 x 14 SBR BSW ($57- $112). DR78 x 14 SBR WSW ($89-$144). Space-saver spare ($14) except (NC) with radial tires.

MONARCH CONVENIENCE/APPEARANCE OPTIONS: Option Packages: 'S' group ($483-$511). Interior decor group ($192). Convenience group ($27-$79). Bumper group ($68). Light group ($40). Cold weather group ($18-$51). Heavy-duty group ($26-$51). Protection group ($26-$41). Visibility group ($4-$50). Comfort/Convenience: Air cond. ($464); auto-temp ($499). Rear defogger ($46). Rear defroster, electric ($78). Fingertip speed control ($98). Illuminated entry system ($50). Power windows ($101-$140). Power door locks ($66-$93). Power decklid release ($17). Power four-way seat ($126). Tinted glass ($50). Tilt steering wheel ($57). Digital clock ($42). Lighting and Mirrors: Cornering lamps ($40). Dual racing mirrors ($31-$45). Lighted right visor vanity mirror ($42). Entertainment: AM radio ($75); w/tape player ($203). AM/FM radio ($151). AM/FM stereo radio ($222); w/tape player ($317). Exterior: Power moonroof ($833). Full or landau vinyl roof ($109). Glamour paint ($57). Bodyside moldings ($37). Rocker panel moldings ($20). Decklid luggage rack ($54). Interior: Console ($69). Four-way seat ($32). Reclining bucket seats ($64). Leather seat trim ($192). Barletta cloth seat ($12). Luxury cloth trim ($93). Color-keyed seatbelts ($18). Wheels/Tires: Deluxe wheel covers ($31) exc. Ghia (NC). Wire wheel covers ($77-$86). Styled steel wheels w/trim rings ($74-$95). Cast aluminum wheels ($118-$213). White aluminum wheels ($138-$232). DR78 x 14 SBR WSW. ER78 x 14 SBR BSW/WSW. FR78 x 14 SBR BSW/WSW/wide WSW.

COUGAR CONVENIENCE/APPEARANCE OPTIONS: Option Packages: Sports instrumentation group ($130-$151). Appearance protection group ($42-$50). Bumper group ($68). Convenience group ($53-$130). Power lock group ($92-$121). Comfort/Convenience: Air cond. ($505); w/auto-temp control ($551). Rear defroster, electric ($82). Fingertip speed control ($78-$97). Illuminated entry system ($51). Tinted glass ($57). Power windows ($114-$158). Power tailgate window: wag ($47). Six-way power seat ($143). Leather-wrapped steering wheel ($61). Tilt steering wheel ($63). Day/date clock ($21-$42). Lighting and Mirrors: Cornering lamps ($50). Remote driver's mirror ($14). Dual racing mirrors ($51). Lighted visor vanity mirror ($42). Entertainment: AM radio ($79). AM/FM radio ($132). AM/FM stereo radio ($192); w/tape player ($266); w/quadrasonic tape player ($399). AM/FM stereo search radio ($349). Dual rear speakers ($42). Exterior: Power moonroof: XR7 ($934). Full vinyl roof ($111- $161). Landau vinyl roof ($111). Opera windows ($50). Bodyside moldings ($42). Rocker panel moldings ($26). Glamour paint ($63). Two-tone paint ($45-$66). Paint stripes ($33). Luggage rack: wag ($100). Interior: Twin comfort seats: XR7 ($141). Flight bench seat: wag ($66). Leather seat trim: XR7 ($241). Bucket seats w/console ($141-$207). Rear-facing third seat: wag ($113). Vinyl seat trim ($28). Color-keyed seatbelts ($18). Wheels/Tires: Deluxe wheel covers ($29). Luxury wheel covers ($32-$61). Wire wheel covers ($100-$129). Cast aluminum wheels ($211-$239). Styled wheels: XR7 ($146). Styled wheels w/trim rings ($72-$101). HR78 x 14 SBR WSW ($41-$68). HR78 x 14 wide-band WSW ($55). JR78 x 14 SBR WSW ($68). R7 Tires: HR78 x 15 WSW ($46-$61). HR70 x 15 WSW ($67).

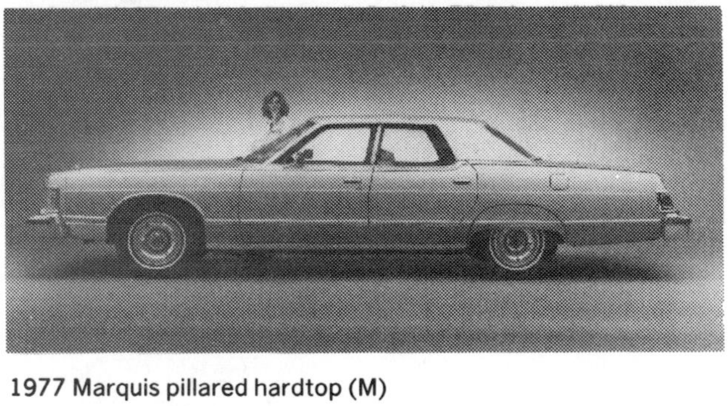

1977 Marquis pillared hardtop (M)

MARQUIS CONVENIENCE/APPEARANCE OPTIONS: Option Packages: Grand Marquis decor ($543). Colony Park option ($315). Tu-tone group ($63-$215). Lock/convenience group ($91-$134). Visibility light group ($46-$86). Protection group ($56). Comfort/Convenience: Air cond. ($543); w/auto-temp control ($582). Rear defroster, electric ($85). Fingertip speed control ($86-$107). Illuminated entry system ($54). Power windows ($116-$172). Power vent windows ($84). Six-way power driver's seat ($139); driver and passenger ($272). Tinted glass ($70). Tilt steering wheel ($63). Digital clock ($31- $52). Interval wipers ($29). Lighting and Mirrors: Cornering lamps ($43). Driver's remote mirror ($15). Lighted visor vanity mirror ($46). Entertainment: AM radio ($82). AM/FM radio (N/A). AM/FM stereo radio ($250); w/tape player ($360); w/quadrasonic tape player ($499). AM/FM stereo search radio ($409). Dual rear speakers ($42). Power antenna ($42). Exterior: Power moonroof ($926). Full vinyl roof ($134). Landau vinyl roof ($134). Fender skirts ($43). Glamour paint ($63). Paint stripes ($31). Rocker panel moldings ($28). Bodyside moldings ($40). Door edge guards ($8-$17). Rear bumper guards ($20). Luggage rack ($106). Interior: Dual-facing rear seats: wagon ($134). Twin comfort seats ($152). Vinyl seat trim ($28). Floor mats ($10). Deluxe seatbelts ($20). Lockable side stowage compartment ($46). Wheels/Tires: Luxury wheel covers ($81). Wire wheel covers ($105). Forged aluminum wheels ($251). HR78 x 15 SBR WSW. JR78 x 15 SBR BSW/WSW/wide WSW. LR78 x 15 SBR WSW.

HISTORY: Introduced: October 1, 1976. Model year production: 531,549 (including 3,616 Bobcats produced as 1978 models but sold as 1977s, but not incl. Canadian Bobcats). Calendar year production (U.S.): 583,055. Calendar year sales by U.S. dealers: 508,132. Model year sales by U.S. dealers: 475,211.

Historical Footnotes: Full-size and luxury models demonstrated a strong sales rise for the 1977 model year, while subcompacts (Bobcat and the imported Capri) declined by nearly 15 percent. That's how it was throughout the industry, though, as customers still craved big cars. The compact Comet and Monarch both declined substantially, while the full-size Marquis found 21 percent more buyers this year, leading the Lincoln-Mercury division in sales. Sales of the specialty Cougar XR7 jumped by 53 percent, from 78,497 in 1976 to an impressive 120,044 this season. The new Cougar models did better than the Montegos they replaced, showing an 18 percent sales rise. Fleet sales were becoming more significant for the Lincoln-Mercury division in the mid-1970s, as dealers pushed harder in their leasing/rental departments.

1978 MERCURY

Comet was gone, replaced by the new Zephyr—close relative of Ford's Fairmont. Based on the "Fox" platform, its chassis would serve as the basis for a variety of FoMoCo products in the coming years. Among its mechanical features were MacPherson struts in the front suspension. Mercury's German-import Capri was in its final season, soon to be replaced by a domestic version based on Mustang. Monarch enjoyed a modest restyle, while the big Marquis continued in its large-scale form for one more year.

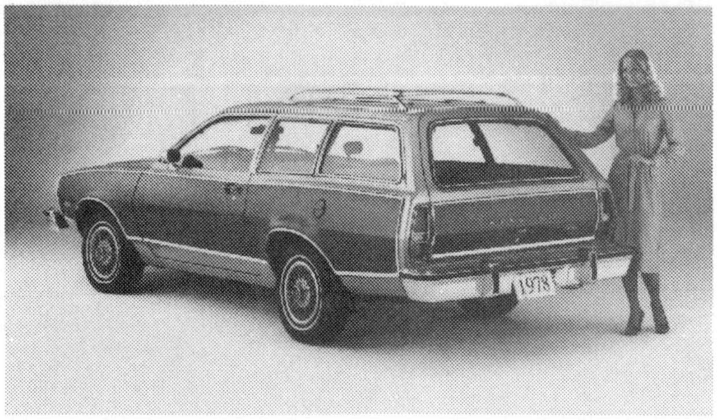

1978 Bobcat Villager station wagon (M)

BOBCAT — FOUR/V-6 — Subcompact appearance and equipment changed little this year, except for new body and interior colors. New options included white-painted aluminum wheels and a stripe treatment in four color combinations. The optional 2.8-liter V-6 had a new lightweight plastic fan. Optional power rack-and-pinion steering had a new variable-ratio system similar to Fairmont/Zephyr. Bobcat again had a domed hood, vertical-textured grille with surround moldings, bright-framed round headlamps, and aluminum bumpers. Combination park/signal lamps sat between the grille and headlamps. High-back front bucket seats came in all-vinyl or cloth and vinyl. The rear bench seat had new split bucket-style cushions. Runabout, station wagon and Villager models were offered. Standard equipment included the 140 cu. in. (2.3-liter) OHC four, four-speed manual gearbox, A78 x 13 BSW tires, full fender splash shields, front bucket seats, lighter, front/rear ashtrays, wide wheel lip and rocker panel moldings, wheel covers, and simulated woodgrain instrument panel applique. Power brakes and tinted glass became standard later. Wagons had a liftgate-open warning, high-back bucket seats, three-pod vertical taillamps, hinged rear-quarter windows, cargo area light, wheel lip and rocker panel moldings, and door-operated courtesy lights. Villager wagons added simulated rosewood appliques on bodyside and liftgate, and load floor carpeting.

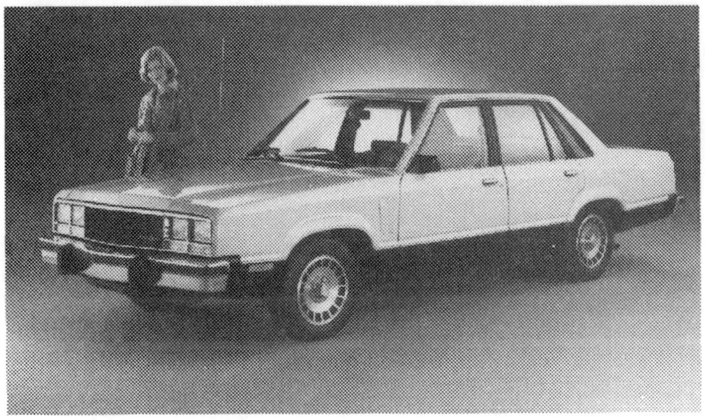

1978 Zephyr sedan (M)

ZEPHYR — FOUR/SIX/V-8 — Weighing some 300 pounds less than the Comet it replaced, the new Zephyr (and similar Ford Fairmont) came in two-door and four-door sedan form, along with a station wagon. Base engine was a 140 cu. in. (2.3-liter) four with four-speed manual gearbox. Options included both an inline six and small-block V-8. Sixes had three-speed shift. Zephyr had MacPherson strut front suspension with lower control arms, and four-link rear suspension with coil springs. Rack- and-pinion steering was used, and the body was unitized. A total of 13 body colors were available, as well as European- style trim. Quad rectangular headlamps stood directly above

quad clear-lensed park/signal lamps, in a clean front-end style that would become typical. Bright frames surrounded the headlamps and parking lamps. Zephyr's vertical-theme grille consisted of many very thin vertical bars, with 'Mercury' lettering on the driver's side. Bumpers were bright anodized aluminum. Body features also included a bright windshield molding, stand-up hood ornament, and upper bodyside dual accent paint stripes. Twin vertical front fender louvers decorated the cowl. Bright wheel lip, rocker panel, door belt and roof drip moldings were used. Wide horizontally-ribbed taillamps (five ribbed segments) had vertical backup lenses inside, adjoining the license plate recess. Two- and four- door sedans had a wide louver-like design at the rear of the quarter windows or rear door. Doors displayed a thin-line appearance. Low-back bucket seats were upholstered in Colton all-vinyl trim. Steering-column mounted controls operated the wiper/washer, horn, signals and dimmer. Standard equipment included the 2.3-liter OHC four, four-speed manual transmission, high/low ram air ventilation, front disc brakes, foot parking brake, low-back bucket seats (with four-cylinder), bench seats (other engines), woodtone cluster appliques, header-mounted dome lamp, and deluxe wheel covers. Four-doors and wagons had movable quarter windows. B78 x 14 blackwalls were standard except with V-8 engine, which required CR78 x 14. Zephyr's ES option displayed a different front-end look with blackout grille, black rear hood grille, and no hood ornament. ES also had black window frames and rear window ventilation louver, bright full-length lower bodyside moldings, black lower back panel, and styled wheel covers. Inside was a black three-spoke sports steering wheel, black instrument panel and pad, and full-width gunmetal gray instrument panel applique. Dual black outside mirrors were standard. The ES handling suspension included a rear stabilizer bar as well as modified spring rates and shock valving. Rocker panel moldings and upper bodyside paint stripes were deleted. Yet another form was evident on the Zephyr Z-7 sport coupe (kin to Fairmont's Futura Coupe). Most notable was the contemporary wrapover roof design, with very wide B-pillar that held a Z-7 ornament. Z7 also included hood tape stripes, upper bodyside tape stripes, full-length lower bodyside molding, bright window frames, and wraparound taillamps. Rocker panel moldings were deleted. Interiors contained pleated Corinthian vinyl seat trim and a woodtone dash applique. The Villager wagon had woodtone bodyside/tailgate appliques in medium cherry, with bright surround moldings and woodtone inserts. A Luxury Exterior Decor Group included dual accent hood paint stripes, deluxe bodyside protective molding, bright door frame and quarter window moldings, and dual mirrors (driver's remote).

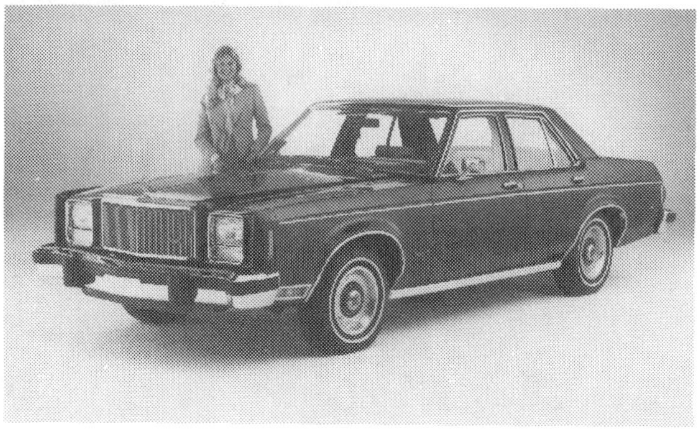

1978 Monarch pillared hardtop (M)

MONARCH — SIX/V-8 — Both Monarch and the closely related Ford Granada entered 1978 with a new look, including new grille, rectangular headlamps, parking lamps, front bumper air spoiler, wide wheel lip moldings, and lower back panel appliques. Two-doors also sported new "twindow" opera windows (two narrow side-by-side windows in the space one would ordinarily occupy). A new ESS option included black vertical grille texture, rocker panels, door frames and bodyside molding; black rubber bumper guards and wide rub strips; and a unique interior. Also optional: AM/FM stereo with cassette tape player and 40-channel CB. Monarch's spoiler and hood-to- grille-opening panel seal, and revised decklid surface, helped reduce aerodynamic drag. The 302 cu. in. V-8 with variable-venturi carburetor was now available. Single rectangular headlamps stood directly above large clear rectangular park/signal lamps, surrounded by a single bright molding. The vertical-bar grille was similar to 1977, but with a heavier upper header bar that reached to the hood top, with no block lettering above. 'Mercury' script went on the side of the grille, with 'Monarch' script again at the cowl area of front fenders. Narrow amber reflector lenses were set back from the front fender tips. Monarch's hood ornament consisted of a castle-like shape within a circle, with seven tiny "knobs" atop the inner segment. Bright front/rear full wheel lip moldings were used, along with a full-length upper bodyside molding. New full- width wraparound taillamps were three-pod design. The red reflective back panel applique held 'Monarch' lettering. Inside was an all-vinyl Flight bench seat. Under the hood, a standard 250 cu. in. (4.1-liter) inline six and four-speed manual overdrive gearbox with floor shift lever. Full wheel covers were standard, along with SBR blackwall tires, an inflatable spare tire, foot parking brake, column-mounted wiper/washer control, and burled woodtone instrument cluster. Monarch Ghia added wire wheel covers, paint stripes on hood and decklid contours, tapered bodyside paint stripes, remote-control driver's mirror, and Ghia ornament on two- door's front quarter panel (or four-door's rear pillar). Ghia's full-length lower bodyside molding had a wide odense grain color-keyed vinyl insert. Burled walnut woodtone accents went on the deluxe steering wheel and door trim panel. Extra conveniences included seatback map pockets, and rear door courtesy lamp switches on the four-door. Ghia also included a dual-note horn, padded door trim with lower carpeting, and driver's remote mirror. The new ESS (Euro-style) option package included a blackout grille; black wipers, black hood paint stripes, and front/rear bumper guards with horizontal rub strip. Also on ESS: bright wide wheel lip moldings, dual racing mirrors, color-keyed wheel covers, black/argent lower back appliques, black bodyside molding with bright mylar insert, black rocker panel paint treatment, and black side window surround moldings. Two-doors had a louvered opera window applique. ESS equipment included a leather-wrapped three-spoke sport steering wheel, day/night mirror, dual-note horn, Flight bench seat, FR78 x 14 BSW tires, and heavy-duty suspension.

COUGAR/XR-7 — V-8 — After just one year of availability, station wagons left the Cougar lineup, since the new Zephyr came in wagon form. Little appearance change was evident either on the basic or XR7 models. Brougham became an option package this year. A 40-channel CB transceiver became optional. A new front bumper air spoiler, hood-to-grille-opening panel seal and other alterations were supposed to reduce XR7 aerodynamic drag, thus improve gas mileage. A revised low-restriction fresh-air intake went on the 302 and larger V-8s. A new mechanical spark control system hit the 351 and 400 cu. in. V-8 engines. Basic Cougars were related to Ford's LTD II, while Cougar shared structural details with Thunderbird. As in 1977, Cougar's Continental-style grille extended slightly below the front bumper. Atop the hood was a bright new stand-up Cougar-head ornament. Signal/marker lamps in front fender extensions were said to "emphasize the wide stance and clean look." The twin-pod vertical taillamp assembly held integral side marker lights. A bright molding surrounded the red reflective rear center applique in the lower back panel. Standard

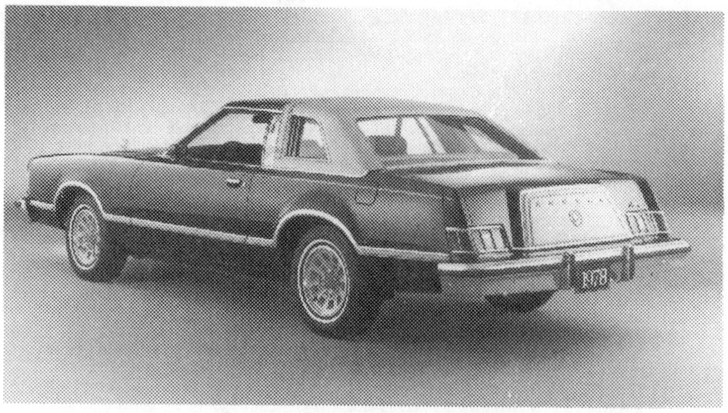

1978 Cougar XR-7 "Midnight/Chamois Decor" coupe (AA)

Cougar equipment included the 302 cu. in. V-8 and SelectShift three-speed automatic transmission, blackwall SBR tires, power brakes/steering, two-speed wipers, cloth/vinyl bench seat, simulated rosewood dash applique, full wheel lip moldings, bright backlight and windshield moldings, bright taillamp bezels with ornament, and 'Cougar' decklid script. Cougar Brougham added a full vinyl roof (on four-doors), full-length bright bodyside molding with integral wheel lip moldings, and opera windows with 'Brougham' script embedded in the glass. Also on Brougham: upper bodyside paint stripes, bright wide door belt moldings, electric clock, deluxe wheel covers, and Flight bench seat with folding center armrest. Cougar XR7 had a grille extension below the bumper, a hood rear edge molding, sport-style roofline with opera window and louvers, and fully padded landau vinyl roof. Its Flight bench seat came in a new sew style, with accent stripes in Rossano cloth or Mateao vinyl. XR7 had a rear stabilizer bar and 15 in. wheels. 'Cougar' block lettering went on the "sculptured" simulated-spare portion of the decklid. Horizontal wraparound taillamps were divided into five segments, three of them on the back panel with an integral backup lamp in one. Standard XR-7 equipment included the 302 cu. in. V-8, SelectShift, power brakes/steering, baby burl walnut woodtone instrument panel appliques, and day/night mirror. An XR-7 Decor Option included styled wheels, full-length bodyside molding with color-keyed vinyl inserts, color-keyed remote mirrors, Twin Comfort Lounge seats with recliner (or bucket seats with console), and hood stripes. A Midnight/Chamois Decor Option (available later) for XR-7 offered a half vinyl roof with vinyl crossover strap, padded 'Continental' type rear deck, and straight-through paint stripes; plus Midnight Blue and Chamois interior, with Tiffany carpeting.

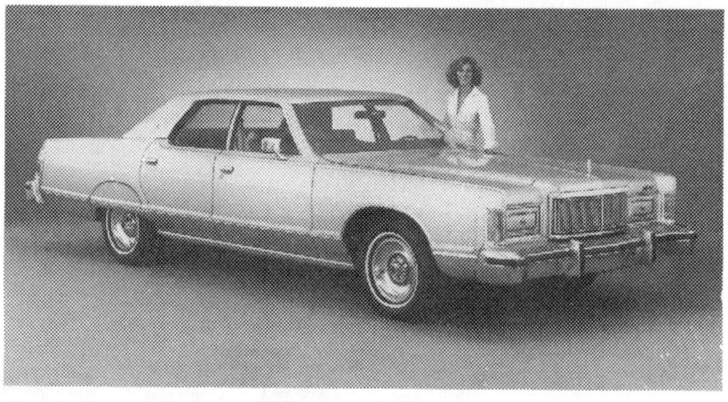

1978 Marquis pillared hardtop (M)

MARQUIS — V-8 — Full-size models were carryovers, with new body colors but little other change. Station wagons could now have optional removable auxiliary dual seat cushions. As before, they came in pillarless-look two-door hardtop style, and a narrow-pillar four-door. Standard equipment included the 351 cu. in. (5.8-liter) 2Bbl. V-8 (400 cu. in. engine in California and high-altitude areas), SelectShift three-speed automatic, power brakes/steering, HR78 x 15 SBR tires, bench seat in Althea cloth/vinyl, and fold-down center armrest. Marquis again featured a bright vertical box-textured grille, flanked by concealed headlamps with body-color textured pad and Marquis crest. The front end also displayed integral parking/signal/side marker lights, concealed wipers, and a bright stand-up hood ornament. Vertical front bumper guards had black inserts. Rear pillars held a Marquis plaque. Full wheel lip moldings and bright rocker panel moldings with front extensions were standard. Wraparound horizontal-ribbed taillamps had integral rear side marker lights, while the textured color-keyed rear center applique below the decklid had 'Mercury' block letters and little backup lamps at its ends. Marquis Brougham added a landau vinyl roof (two-door) or full vinyl roof (four-door), both with bright surround molding. The full vinyl roof was also available as a no-cost option on two-doors. Brougham also had power windows, fender skirts with bright molding, full-length upper body peak molding, and a decklid lock cover with L-M crest. Brougham wheel covers displayed slots around the circumference and a center crest emblem. Flight bench seats had a folding center armrest and automatic seatback release (on two-door). Moving all the way up, Grand Marquis had a vinyl roof, fender skirts, hood and decklid paint stripes, and a gold Marquis crest on the headlamp cover and the rear pillar. Full-length wide bodyside moldings had color-keyed vinyl inserts; rocker panel extensions and wheel lip moldings were deleted. 'Grand Marquis' script highlighted the decklid. Standard features included tinted glass, a digital clock, dual-beam dome/map light, and Twin Comfort lounge seats in Media velour with dual center folding armrests and headrests with vinyl welts.

I.D. DATA: As before, Mercury's 11-symbol Vehicle Identification Number (VIN) is stamped on a metal tab fastened to the instrument panel, visible through the windshield. Coding is similar to 1976-77. Model year code changed to '8' for 1978. One Canadian assembly plant was added: 'X' St. Thomas, Ontario.

BOBCAT RUNABOUT/WAGON (FOUR/V-6)

Model Number	Body/Style Number	Body Type & Seating	Factory Price	Shipping Weight	Production Total
20	64H	3-dr. Hatch-4P	3537/3810	2389/--	23,428
22	73H	2-dr. Sta Wag-4P	3878/4151	2532/--	Note 1

BOBCAT VILLAGER (FOUR/V-6)

22	73H	2-dr. Sta Wag-4P	4010/4283	N/A	Note 1

Note 1: Total station wagon production was 8,840 units.

ZEPHYR (FOUR/SIX)

31	66D	2-dr. Sed-5P	3742/3862	2572/2615	27,673
32	54D	4-dr. Sed-5P	3816/3936	2614/2657	47,334
36	74D	4-dr. Sta Wag-5P	4184/4304	2722/2765	32,596

ZEPHYR Z-7 (FOUR/SIX)

35	36R	2-dr. Spt Cpe-5P	4095/4215	2609/2652	44,569

Zephyr Engine Note: A V-8 engine cost $199 more than the six.

MONARCH (SIX/V-8)

35	66H	2-dr. Sedan-5P	4330/4511	3058/3130	38,939
34	54H	4-dr. Sedan-5P	4409/4590	3102/3174	52,775

COUGAR (V-8)

91	65D	2-dr. HT Cpe-6P	5009	3761	21,398
92	53D	4-dr. Pill. HT-6P	5126	3848	25,364

COUGAR XR-7 (V-8)

93	65L	2-dr. HT Cpe-6P	5603	3865	166,508

MARQUIS (V-8)

61	65H	2-dr. HT-6P	5764	4296	11,176
62	53H	4-dr. Pill. HT-6P	5806	4328	27,793
74	71K	4-dr. 2S Sta Wag-6P	5958	4578	16,883
74	71K	4-dr. 3S Sta Wag-8P	N/A	4606	Note 2

Note 2: Production total for three-seat station wagon is included in two-seat figure.

MARQUIS BROUGHAM (V-8)

63	65K	2-dr. HT-6P	6380	4317	10,368
64	53K	4-dr. Pill. HT-6P	6480	4346	26,030

GRAND MARQUIS (V-8)

65	65L	2-dr. HT-6P	7132	4342	15,624
66	53L	4-dr. Pill. HT-6P	7232	4414	37,753

FACTORY PRICE AND WEIGHT NOTE: Monarch prices and weights to left of slash are for six-cylinder, to right for V-8 engine. For Bobcat and Zephyr, prices/weights to left of slash are for four-cylinder, to right for V-6.

ENGINE DATA: BASE FOUR (Bobcat, Zephyr): Inline. Overhead cam. Four-cylinder. Cast iron block and head. Displacement: 140 cu. in. (2.3 liters). Bore & stroke: 3.78 x 3.13 in. Compression ratio: 9.0:1. Brake horsepower: 88 at 4800 R.P.M. Torque: 118 lbs.-ft. at 2800 R.P.M. Five main bearings. Hydraulic valve lifters. Carburetor: 2Bbl. Motorcraft 5200. VIN Code: Y. OPTIONAL V-6 (Bobcat): 60-degree, overhead-valve V-6. Cast iron block and head. Displacement: 170.8 cu. in. (2.8 liters). Bore & stroke: 3.66 x 2.70 in. Compression ratio: 8.7:1. Brake horsepower: 90 at 4200 R.P.M. Torque: 143 lbs.-ft. at 2200 R.P.M. Four main bearings. Hydraulic valve lifters. Carburetor: 2Bbl. Motorcraft 2150. VIN Code: Z. OPTIONAL SIX (Zephyr): Inline. OHV. Six-cylinder. Cast iron block and head. Displacement: 200 cu. in. (3.3 liters). Bore & stroke: 3.68 x 3.13 in. Compression ratio: 8.5:1. Brake horsepower: 85 at 3600 R.P.M. Torque: 154 lbs.-ft. at 1600 R.P.M. Seven main bearings. Hydraulic valve lifters. Carburetor: 1Bbl. Carter YFA. VIN Code: T. BASE SIX (Monarch): Inline. OHV. Six-cylinder. Cast iron block and head. Displacement: 250 cu. in. (4.1 liters). Bore & stroke: 3.68 x 3.91 in. Compression ratio: 8.5:1. Brake horsepower: 97 at 3200 R.P.M. Torque: 210 lbs.-ft. at 1400 R.P.M. Seven main bearings. Hydraulic valve lifters. Carburetor: 1Bbl. Carter YFA or Holley 1946. VIN Code: L. BASE V-8 (Cougar); OPTIONAL (Zephyr, Monarch): 90-degree, overhead valve V-8. Cast iron block and head. Displacement: 302 cu. in. (5.0 liters). Bore & stroke: 4.00 x 3.00 in. Compression ratio: 8.4:1. Brake horsepower: 134-139 at 3400-3600 R.P.M. Torque: 248-250 lbs.-ft. at 1600 R.P.M. Five main bearings. Hydraulic valve lifters. Carburetor: 2Bbl. Motorcraft 2150. VIN Code: F. BASE V-8 (Marquis); OPTIONAL (Cougar): 90-degree, overhead valve V-8. Cast iron block and head. Displacement: 351 cu. in. (5.8 liters). Bore & stroke: 4.00 x 3.50 in. Compression ratio: 8.3:1. Brake horsepower: 145-152 at 3400-3600 R.P.M. Torque: 273-278 lbs.-ft. at 1800 R.P.M. Five main bearings. Hydraulic valve lifters. Carburetor: 2Bbl. Motorcraft 2150. Windsor engine. VIN Code: H. OPTIONAL V-8 (Cougar, Marquis): 90-degree, overhead valve V-8. Cast iron block and head. Displacement: 400 cu. in. (6.6 liters). Bore & stroke: 4.00 x 4.00 in. Compression ratio: 8.0:1. Brake horsepower: 160-166 at 3800 R.P.M. Torque: 314-319 lbs.-ft. at 1800 R.P.M. Five main bearings. Hydraulic valve lifters. Carburetor: 2Bbl. Motorcraft 2150. VIN Code: S. BASE V-8 (Grand Marquis); OPTIONAL (Marquis): 90-degree, overhead valve V-8. Cast iron block and head. Displacement: 460 cu. in. (7.5 liters). Bore & stroke: 4.36 x 3.85 in. Compression ratio: 8.0:1. Brake horsepower: 202 at 4000 R.P.M. Torque: 348 lbs.-ft. at 2000 R.P.M. Five main bearings. Hydraulic valve lifters. Carburetor: 4Bbl. Motorcraft 4350. VIN Code: A.

CHASSIS DATA: Wheelbase: (Bobcat sed) 94.5 in.; (Bobcat wag) 94.8 in.; (Zephyr) 105.5 in.; (Monarch) 109.9 in.; (Cougar 2dr.) 114.0 in.; (Cougar 4dr.) 118.0 in.; (Marquis) 124.0 in.; (Marquis wag) 121.0 in. Overall Length: (Bobcat sed) 169.3 in.; (Bobcat wag) 179.8 in.; (Zephyr) 193.8 in.; (Z7) 195.8 in.; (Monarch) 197.7 in.; (Cougar 2dr.) 215.5 in.; (Cougar 4dr.) 219.5 in.; (Marquis) 229.0 in.; (Marquis wag) 227.1 in. Height: (Bobcat sed) 50.6 in.; (Bobcat wag) 52.1 in.; (Zephyr) 53.5 in.; (Zephyr wag) 54.7 in.; (Z7) 52.2 in.; (Monarch) 53.2-53.3 in.; (Cougar 2dr.) 52.6 in.; (Cougar 4dr.) 53.3 in.; (XR7) 52.9 in.; (Marquis 2-dr.) 53.7-53.8 in.; (Marquis 4-dr.) 54.7-54.8 in.; (Marquis wag) 56.9 in. Width: (Bobcat sed) 69.4 in.; (Bobcat wag) 69.7 in.; (Zephyr) 70.2 in.; (Monarch) 74.0 in.; (Cougar) 78.6 in.; (Marquis) 79.6-79.7 in. Front Tread: (Bobcat) 55.0 in.; (Zephyr) 56.6 in.; (Monarch) 59.0 in.; (Cougar) 63.6 in.; (XR7) 63.2 in.; (Marquis) 64.1 in. Rear Tread: (Bobcat) 55.8 in.; (Zephyr) 57.0 in.; (Monarch) 57.7 in.; (Cougar) 63.5 in.; (XR7) 63.1 in.; (Marquis) 64.3 in. Standard Tires: (Bobcat) A78 x 13 BSW; (Zephyr) B78 x 14 BSW; (Zephyr V-8) CR78 x 14; (Monarch) DR78 x 14 BSW; (Cougar) HR78 x 14 BSW; (XR7) HR78 x 15 BSW; (Marquis) HR78 x 15; (Marquis wag) JR78 x 15.

TECHNICAL: Transmission: Three-speed manual transmission (column shift) standard on Zephyr six. Gear ratios: (1st) 3.56:1; (2nd) 1.90:1; (3rd) 1.00:1; (Rev) 3.78:1. Four-speed overdrive floor shift standard on Monarch: (1st) 3.29:1; (2nd) 1.84:1; (3rd) 1.00:1; (4th) 0.81:1; (Rev) 3.29:1. Four-speed floor shift standard on Bobcat/Zephyr four: (1st) 3.98:1; (2nd) 2.14:1; (3rd) 1.42:1; (4th) 1.00:1; (Rev) 3.99:1. Select- Shift three-speed automatic (column lever) standard on Cougar and Marquis, optional on others. Bobcat L4140 automatic gear ratios: (1st) 2.47:1; (2nd) 1.47:1; (3rd) 1.00:1; (Rev) 2.11:1. Cougar/Marquis with V8351: (1st) 2.40:1; (2nd) 1.47:1; (3rd) 1.00:1; (Rev) 2.00:1. Other automatics: (1st) 2.46:1; (2nd) 1.46:1; (3rd) 1.00:1; (Rev) 2.18:1 to 2.20:1. Standard final drive ratio: (Bobcat) 2.73:1 w/four, 3.40:1 w/V-6; (Zephyr) 3.08:1 w/four, 2.73:1 w/six and 2.47:1 w/V-8; (Monarch) 3.00:1 w/six and 4spd, 2.47:1 w/auto.; (Cougar) 2.75:1 w/V8302, 2.50:1 w/V8351/400. (Marquis) 2.47:1 w/V8400, 2.50:1 w/V8460. Steering: (Bobcat/Zephyr) rack and pinion; (others) recirculating ball. Front Suspension: (Bobcat) coil springs with short/long control arms, lower leading arms, and anti-sway bar on wagon; (Zephyr) MacPherson struts w/coil springs mounted on lower control arm; (others) coil springs w/lower trailing links and anti-sway bar. Rear Suspension: (Bobcat/Monarch) rigid axle w/semi-elliptic leaf springs; (Zephyr) four-link w/coil springs; (Cougar/Marquis) rigid axle with upper/lower control arms and coil springs. Brakes: Front disc, rear drum. Ignition: Electronic. Body construction: (Bobcat/Zephyr/Monarch) unibody; (others) separate body on perimeter frame; Fuel tank: (Bobcat) 11.7 or 13 gal. exc. wagon, 14 gal.; (Zephyr) 16.0 gal.; (Monarch) 18.0 gal.; (Cougar) 21.0 gal.; (Marquis) 24.2 gal. exc. wagon, 21 gal.

DRIVETRAIN OPTIONS: Engines: 170 cu. in. V-6: Bobcat ($273). 200 cu. in., 1Bbl. six: Zephyr ($120). 302 cu. in., 2Bbl. V-8: Zephyr ($319); Monarch ($181). 351 cu. in., 2Bbl. V-8: Cougar ($157). 400 cu. in., 2Bbl. V-8: Cougar ($283); Marquis ($126). 460 cu. in., 4Bbl. V-8: Marquis ($271). Transmission/Differential: SelectShift Cruise-O-Matic: Bobcat/Zephyr ($281); Monarch ($193). Floor shift lever: Zephyr/Monarch ($30). First-gear lockout: Zephyr (NC). Traction-Lok differential: Cougar ($59); Marquis ($63). Optional axle ratio: Bobcat ($13); Marquis ($14). Brakes & Steering: Power brakes: Bobcat (N/A); Zephyr/Monarch ($63). Four-wheel power disc brakes: Monarch ($300); Marquis ($197). Power steering: Bobcat ($131); Zephyr ($140); Monarch ($148). Suspension: H.D. susp.: Monarch ($27). Handling susp.: Zephyr ($30). Cross-country susp.: Cougar ($20); Marquis ($26). Other: H.D. battery: Zephyr ($18); Cougar/Marquis ($20). H.D. alternator: Cougar/Marquis ($49). Engine block heater: Bobcat/Zephyr/Monarch ($12); Cougar ($13); Marquis ($21). Trailer towing pkg. (heavy duty): Cougar ($184); Marquis ($138). California emission system: Bobcat/Zephyr/Monarch ($69); Cougar/Marquis ($75). High-altitude option (NC).

BOBCAT CONVENIENCE/APPEARANCE OPTIONS: Option Packages: Sports accent group ($212-$235). Sports instrument/handling group ($90). Sports pkg. ($108). Convenience/light group ($72-$137). Bumper group ($70). Protection group ($40). Comfort/Convenience: Air conditioner ($459). Rear defroster, electric ($77). Tinted glass (NC). Driver's remote mirror ($14). Day/night mirror ($7). Entertainment: AM radio ($72); w/digital clock ($119); w/stereo tape player ($192). AM/FM radio ($120). AM/FM stereo radio ($161). Exterior: Flip-up/removable moonroof ($167). Sunroof ($259). Sports vinyl roof ($145). Glass third door ($25). Hinged quarter windows ($41). Glamour paint ($40). Narrow bodyside moldings ($39); wide ($67). Roof luggage rack ($59). Rocker panel moldings ($22). Lower bodyside protection ($30). Interior: Four-way bucket seat ($33). Load floor carpet ($23). Cargo area cover ($25). Deluxe interior ($158-$181). Deluxe seatbelts ($18). Wheels/Tires: Wire wheel covers ($20). Forged aluminum wheels ($128); white ($141). Styled steel wheels (NC). Trim rings ($34). BR78 x 13 WSW ($42). BR70 x 13 RWL ($77).

ZEPHYR CONVENIENCE/APPEARANCE OPTIONS: Option Packages: ES option ($180). Villager option ($169). Exterior decor group ($96). Interior decor group ($72). Luxury interior ($199-$289). Bumper protection group ($70). Convenience group ($36). Appearance protection group ($36- $43). Light group ($36-$40). Comfort/Convenience: Air cond. ($465). Rear defogger ($47). Rear defroster, electric ($84). Tinted glass ($52). Sport steering wheel ($36). Electric clock ($20). Cigar lighter ($6). Interval wipers ($29). Liftgate wiper/washer: wag ($78). Map light ($16). Trunk light ($6). Left remote mirror ($14). Dual mirrors ($14-$30). Day/night mirror ($7). Entertainment: AM radio ($72); w/8track tape player ($192). AM/FM radio ($120). AM/FM stereo radio ($176); w/8track or cassette player ($243). Exterior: Vinyl roof ($89). Glamour paint ($46). Two-tone paint ($42). Pivoting front vent windows ($54). Rear vent louvers ($33). Bodyside moldings ($39). Rocker panel moldings ($22). Bright window frames ($24-$29). Bumper guards, front and rear ($37). Luggage rack ($72). Lower bodyside protection ($30-$42). Interior: Bucket seats ($72). Cloth seat trim ($19-$37). Lockable side storage box ($19). H.D. mats ($8). Wheels/Tires: Styled wheel covers ($33). Wire wheel covers ($81). Aluminum wheels ($242). B78 x 14 WSW. BR78 x 14 BSW/WSW. C78 x 14 BSW/WSW. CR78 x 14 BSW/WSW. DR78 x 14 SBR BSW/WSW/RWL.

MONARCH CONVENIENCE/APPEARANCE OPTIONS: Option Packages: ESS option ($524). Ghia option ($426). Interior decor group ($211). Convenience group ($33-$89). Bumper protection group ($70). Light group ($43). Cold weather group ($36-$54). Heavy-duty group ($36-$54). Protection group ($29-$43). Visibility group ($7-$58). Comfort/Convenience: Air cond. ($494); auto-temp ($535). Rear defogger ($47). Rear defroster, electric ($84). Fingertip speed control ($102). Illuminated entry system ($49). Power windows ($116-$160). Power door locks ($76-$104). Power decklid release ($19). Auto. parking brake release ($8). Power four-way seat ($90). Tinted glass ($54). Tilt steering wheel ($58). Digital clock ($42). Lighting and Mirrors: Cornering lamps ($42). Trunk light ($6). Left remote mirror ($14). Right remote mirror ($31). Dual racing mirrors ($39-$53). Day/night mirror ($7). Lighted right visor vanity mirror ($34). Entertainment: AM radio ($72); w/tape player ($192). AM/FM radio ($135). AM/FM stereo radio ($176); w/8track or cassette player ($243); w/quadrasonic tape ($365). AM/FM stereo search radio ($319). CB radio ($270). Exterior: Power moonroof ($820). Full or landau vinyl roof ($102). Glamour paint ($46). Bodyside moldings ($39). Rocker panel moldings ($23). Lower bodyside protection ($30). Interior: Console ($75). Four-way seat ($33). Reclining bucket seats ($84). Leather seat trim ($271). Barletta cloth seat ($54). Luxury cloth seat/door trim ($99). Deluxe seatbelts ($19). Wheels: Deluxe wheel covers ($37) exc. Ghia/ESS (NC). Wire wheel covers ($59-$96). Styled steel wheels w/trim rings ($59-$96). Cast aluminum wheels ($146-$242); white ($159- $255). Tires: DR78 x 14 SBR WSW. ER78 x 14 SBR BSW/WSW. FR78 x 14 SBR BSW/WSW/wide WSW.

COUGAR CONVENIENCE/APPEARANCE OPTIONS: Option Packages: Brougham option ($271-$383). Midnight/chamois decor group: XR7 ($592). Sports instrumentation group ($100-$138). Decor group ($211-$461). Bumper protection group ($76). Light group ($51). Convenience group ($58-$139). Power lock group ($100-$132). Appearance protection group ($45-$53). Comfort/Convenience: Air cond. ($543); w/auto-temp control ($588). Rear defroster, electric ($93). Fingertip speed control ($99-$117). Illuminated entry system ($54). Tinted glass ($66). Power windows ($126-$175). Power seat ($149). Auto. parking brake release ($9). Leather-wrapped steering wheel ($64). Tilt steering wheel ($70). Day/date clock ($22- $42). Lighting, Horns and Mirrors: Cornering lamps ($46). Trunk light ($7). Dual-note horn ($7). Remote driver's mirror ($16). Dual racing mirrors ($58). Lighted visor vanity mirror ($37). Entertainment: AM radio ($79). AM/FM radio ($132). AM/FM stereo radio ($192); w/tape player ($266); w/quadrasonic tape player ($399). AM/FM stereo search radio ($349). CB radio ($295). Upgraded sound ($29). Dual rear speakers ($46). Power antenna ($42). Exterior: Power moonroof ($789). Front/landau vinyl roof ($112). Full vinyl roof ($112-$163). Opera windows ($51). Bodyside moldings ($42). Wide bodyside moldings: XR7 ($55). Rocker panel moldings: Brghm ($29). Glamour paint ($62). Two- tone paint ($41-$95). Paint striping ($33). Bumper guards ($42). Lower bodyside protection ($33). Interior: Twin comfort seats w/passenger recliner: XR7 ($175). Bucket seats w/console ($175-$247). Vinyl bench seat ($28). Leather seat: XR7 ($296). Trunk trim ($39). Color- keyed seatbelts ($21). Wheels/Tires: Deluxe wheel covers ($38). Luxury wheel covers ($30-$68). 15 in. wheel covers ($38). Wire wheel covers ($105-$143). Cast aluminum wheels ($118-$303). Styled wheels ($146). Styled wheels w/trim rings ($105-$143) exc. XR7. HR78 x 14 SBR WSW ($46). HR78 x 14 wide-band WSW ($66). HR78 x 15 SBR WSW ($68).

MARQUIS CONVENIENCE/APPEARANCE OPTIONS: Option Packages: Colony Park option ($547). Grand Marquis decor: wag ($559). Tu-tone group ($72-$151). Lock convenience group ($108-$161). Bumper protection group ($59). Appearance protection group ($50-$58). Visibility light group ($47-$96). Comfort/Convenience: Air cond. ($583); w/auto-temp control ($628). Rear defroster, electric ($93). Fingertip speed control ($101-$120). Illuminated entry system ($54). Power windows ($129-$188). Six-way power driver's seat ($149); driver and passenger ($297). Tinted glass ($75); windshield only ($36). Tilt steering wheel ($72). Digital clock ($26-$49). Interval wipers ($32). Lighting and Mirrors: Cornering lamps ($46). Driver's remote mirror ($16). Lighted visor vanity mirror ($33-$37). Entertainment: AM radio ($79). AM/FM stereo radio ($192); w/tape player ($266); w/quadrasonic tape player ($399). AM/FM stereo search radio ($349). Dual rear speakers ($46). Power antenna ($42). Exterior: Power moonroof ($896). Full or landau vinyl roof ($141). Fender skirts ($50). Glamour metallic paint ($62). Rocker panel moldings ($23). Narrow bodyside moldings ($42). Rear bumper guards: wag ($22). Luggage rack: wag ($80). Lower bodyside protection ($33). Interior: Dual-facing rear seats: wagon ($186). Twin comfort seats ($97); w/passenger recliner ($149). Reclining passenger seat ($63). Vinyl bench seat trim ($29). Deluxe floor mats ($36). Deluxe seatbelts ($21). Lockable side stowage compartment: wag ($49). Wheels/Tires: Luxury wheel covers ($55-$84). Wire wheel covers ($30-$109). Forged aluminum wheels ($236-$264). HR78 x 15 SBR WSW. JR78 x 15 SBR BSW/WSW/wide WSW. LR78 x 15 SBR WSW.

HISTORY: Introduced: October 7, 1977. Model year production: 635,051. Calendar year production (U.S.): 624,229. Calendar year sales by U.S. dealers: 579,498 (incl. 18,035 Capris). Model year sales by U.S. dealers: 571,118.

Historical Footnotes: Model year sales for Lincoln-Mercury division climbed 15 percent, led by Cougar's XR7, setting a new record for the second year in a row. This put LM surprisingly close to Buick in the sales race. A total of 152,591 Cougar XR7 models found buyers. Second best seller was the full-size Marquis, again demonstrating the continued appeal of big cars. Some of the sales, though, may well have been due to the fact that downsizing was expected for 1979, so this would be the last chance for big-car fans. The new compact Zephyr sold far better than had Comet in its final (1977) year. This was the final year for the imported Capri, as a domestic Mercury of that name (closely related to the Ford Mustang) was being readied for the '79 model year.

1979 MERCURY

Two all-new vehicles entered the Mercury stable for 1979: Capri and Marquis. The Capri nameplate moved from a German-made model to a clone of Ford's Mustang. The full-size Marquis was sharply downsized, losing some 800 pounds and 17 inches of overall length. A second generation of electronic controls (EEC-II) was now standard on Marquis with the optional 351W V-8. Bobcat got a significant styling change, with new front/rear appearance. Option availability expanded considerably, especially in Capri and Zephyr, which offered many more options than their predecessors, including speed control (available for first time with manual shift) and tilt steering. AM/FM stereo radios with cassette tape players, formerly offered only on Zephyr and Monarch, were now available in all models. Various engines had a new electronic voltage regulator.

1979 Bobcat "Sports Option" hatchback coupe (M)

288

BOBCAT — FOUR/V-6 — Rectangular headlamps and a new rakishly sloped, fine-patterned grille dominated by vertical bars gave Mercury's subcompact a fresh front-end look. The hood and front fenders also sloped more than before. Vertical-styled park/signal lamps were inboard of the single headlamps, in the same recessed housings. New front side marker lamps had no surround moldings. A new rear-end appearance on the Runabout included unique horizontal taillamps and exposed black third-door hinges; but the wagon retained its three-pod vertical configuration with integrated backup lights. Bright extruded aluminum bumpers had black rubber end caps. Villager wagons added new rosewood-grain bodyside appliques with simulated wood surround moldings. Inside was a new rectangular instrument cluster, with miles/kilometer speedometer. This was the first Bobcat restyle since its 1975 debut. Five new paint colors were offered. The optional V-6 had a higher-performance camshaft this year, and engines had a new electronic voltage regulator. Standard tires grew to BR78 x 13 steel-belted radials.

1979 Capri RS hatchback coupe (M)

CAPRI — FOUR/V-6/V-8 — No longer did Mercury have to do without a domestically-built equivalent to Ford's Mustang. Capri differed mainly in grille pattern and body details from the Ford ponycar. Unlike Mustang, though, the Mercury version came only in three-door hatchback body style. The company described the shape as a "linear, flowing look highlighted by a sloping roof, soft front and rear bumper coverings, and standard wide bodyside moldings... to create a wraparound effect." Two models were offered: base and Ghia, plus an R/S and Turbo R/S option. The latter included a turbocharged turbo four and TRX tires and suspension. TRX was one of three specially-tuned variants of the Zephyr-type suspension system. It came with new low-profile wide-aspect Michelin 190/65R390 TRX tires. Base engine was a 140 cu. in. (2.3-liter) four. Capri could also have a 2.8-liter V-6 or 302 cu. in. (5.0-liter) V-8. Only on Capri did the optional V-8 have a single belt accessory drive system. That engine also hooked to a four-speed manual overdrive transmission with new single-rail shift design, standard on all Capris. Capri featured a horizontal-bar black and bright grille, flanked by quad rectangular headlamps in bright frames. A sloping hood held color-keyed simulated (non-working) louvers. Wide black bodyside moldings with dual color-keyed center stripe accompanied partial wheel lip moldings. Body trim included upper bodyside paint stripes; black window frame moldings with black frames; black belt and cowl moldings; bright windshield, rear window and drip moldings; black wiper arms; and a black window-frame-mounted remote-control driver's mirror. Soft bumpers were color-keyed. Steel wheels came with hub covers and lug nuts. Large horizontal wraparound taillamps carried integral backup lights. On the mechanical front, Capri had a strut-type coil- spring front suspension with stabilizer, four-bar link coil- spring rear suspension, unitized body, and rack-and-pinion steering. Front high-back bucket seats carried pleated trim. Dashboards held a tachometer and gauges in woodtone cluster applique, with European ISO style identificaton symbols on controls. A three-spoke sport steering wheel was standard. Capri rode a 100.4 inch wheelbase and measured 179.1 inches in length. Standard tires were B78 x 13. Among Capri's new options were tilt steering and speed control (offered for the first time on a FoMoCo car with floor-shift automatic or manual). Capri Ghia came with BR78 x 14 radial tires, dual black remote-control outside mirrors, argent sport wheel covers, a light group, soft-rim sport steering wheel, low-back bucket seats with European headrests, door map pockets, and passenger assist handle on roof rail. Capri R/S option equipment included BR78 x 14 RWL tires and handling suspension; black grille, headlamp housings and quarter louvers; argent sport wheel covers; black greenhouse moldings; hood scoop; dual black window-frame-mounted remote mirrors; and bright tailpipe extension. Tape treatment on bodysides (over the wheels) substituted for the usual pinstripes. Inside were engine-turned instrument panel appliques and Ghia soft door trim panels. In addition to the turbocharged engine and TRX suspension, the Turbo R/S option included a sport-tuned exhaust and tailpipe extension, three- spoke TRX aluminum wheels, and low-back bucket seats with European headrests. Turbo models came only with four-speed manual.

1979 Zephyr sedan (M)

ZEPHYR — FOUR/SIX/V-8 — For its second year in Mercury's lineup, Zephyr looked the same but enjoyed a few mechanical improvements and extra options. Four-speed overdrive manual shift became standard this year for both the 200 cu. in. (3.3-liter) V-6 and 302 cu. in. (5.0-liter) V-8 engines. A new single-rail shift mechanism with enclosed linkage was supposed to eliminate the need for adjustments. California staton wagons could now get the 3.3-liter six. The 302 V-8 with SelectShift had reduced rear axle ratio, now 2.26:1. Options added to Zephyr during the 1978 model

year included power, seats, windows and door locks; plus a flip-up removable moonroof. New options this year included speed control, tilt steering, performance instruments, and electric trunk lid release. Eight body colors were new. A revised tone-on-tone paint treatment was available on sedans, and on Z-7 (except ES type, which had its own unique paint treatment). Zephyr police and taxi packages had been introduced during the 1978 model year. Zephyr had a vertical-design grille, quad rectangular headlamps in bright frames, bright rocker panel and wheel lip moldings, deluxe wheel covers, and upper bodyside dual paint stripes. Front bucket seats came with four-cylinder models, but bench seating with six/V-8. In addition to its unique wrapover roof design with wide center pillar, the Z-7 sport coupe added tinted rear window glass, large wraparound taillamps, special hood and bodyside tape stripes, full-length vinyl-insert bodyside molding, bright window frames, and pleated vinyl seat trim. Z-7 deleted the base model's rocker panel moldings. Zephyr wagons had tinted liftgate glass and a cargo area light. Villager wagons added woodtone bodyside and tailgate appliques in medium cherry color, with woodtone-insert bright surround moldings. On the option list, Zephyr ES added a handling suspension and bumper protection group; blackout grille treatment; dual black mirrors (driver's remote); and black cowl grille that was almost full hood width. ES also sported black window frames and rear window ventilation louvers, full-length bright lower bodyside molding, black lower back panel, styled wheel covers with unique all-bright treatment, and gray engine-turned instrument panel and cluster appliques. ES deleted the usual hood ornament, paint stripes, rocker panel and wheel lip moldings.

1979 Monarch Ghia sedan (M)

MONARCH — SIX/V-8 — Blackout paint treatment on the vertical-theme grille was Monarch's major body change this year. Bright vinyl roof moldings replaced the former color-keyed moldings. Engines had new electronic voltage regulators. A new single-rail shift four-speed manual overdrive transmission came in an aluminum case, and a new lightweight aluminum intake manifold went on the 302 cu. in. V-8 (installed in four-doors). Options dropped included four-wheel disc brakes, and Traction-Lok. Monarchs had single rectangular headlamps, a stand-up hood ornament, bright upper bodyside and wheel lip moldings, full wheel covers, and red reflectorized back panel applique with integral fuel filler door. Base engine was the 250 cu. in. inline six; standard tires, DR78 x 14 blackwall steel-belted radials. All-vinyl Flight Bench seating was standard, as was a burled woodtone instrument cluster. In addition to the base model, Ghia and ES option groups were available. The Ghia option group included a dual-note horn; day/night mirror; paint stripes on hood, upper bodyside and decklid; wire wheel covers; and wide odense grain vinyl bodyside moldings and partial wheel lip moldings. Lettering on the cowl read 'ESS Monarch' (formerly 'Monarch ESS') when that package was installed. The ESS group included FR78 x 14 blackwalls; black wipers and rocker panel treatment; black bodyside moldings with bright inserts; black window frames and center roof pillar; black hood and decklid paint stripes; and louvered opera window appliques (on two-door). Wide wheel lip moldings and color-keyed wheel covers also were included. Four-doors had a black division bar on the back door window. ESS did not have the standard upper bodyside moldings, and offered a choice of all-vinyl Flight bench seat or carryover bucket seats. A leather-wrapped sport steering wheel was standard.

1979 Cougar XR-7 Sports Coupe (M)

COUGAR/XR7 — V-8 — As before, two types of Cougars were available: basic two- and four-door pillared-hardtop models (in base or Brougham trim), and the personal-luxury XR7. Under Cougar's hood was a new electronic voltage regulator, plastic battery tray, and modified carburetor. Base engine was the 302 cu. in. (5.0-liter) V-8. Aerodynamic improvements including a modified under-the-front-bumper spoiler. XR7 had a new black/bright accented grille with body-color tape stripes and new horizontal-style wraparound taillamps (each with two horizontal chrome trim strips). Once again, the XR-7 grille included a lower extension below the front bumper. New color fabric was available for the XR7 Chamois Decor Group. Other models kept their 1978 styling. An extended-range fuel tank became optional. Standard Cougars had a vertical swing-grille, quad rectangular headlamps, wraparound amber parking lamps with integral side markers, stand-up hood ornament, full wheel lip moldings, and rocker panel moldings. Vertical taillamps had bright bezels and integral side markers. Equipment included SelectShift three-speed automatic, HR78 x 14 tires, power steering and brakes, and rear bumper guards. Cougar Brougham added opera windows; a full vinyl roof (on four-door); upper

bodyside paint stripes; deluxe wheel covers; full-length bright bodyside molding with integral wheel lip moldings; wide bright door belt moldings; and Flight bench seat with folding center armrest. Cougar XR-7 rode 15 in. wheels with GR78 x 15 BSW tires and carried a rear stabilizer bar. Also included; a dual-note horn; special wheel covers with Cougar insert; hood rear edge molding; unique C-pillar treatment and ornament; padded landau vinyl roof with louvered opera window; and the typical sculptured spare-tire decklid design with lower molding. Full wheel lip and rocker panel moldings replaced the usual full-length bright bodyside molding. Dashboards held a simulated walnut instrument cluster faceplate.

1979 Grand Marquis coupe (M)

MARQUIS — V-8 — Two years later than equivalent GM models, the full-size Mercury got its awaited downsizing, losing some 17 inches and over 800 pounds. The new aerodynamically-influenced body came in two- and four-door sedan form, along with station wagons. Underneath was a new long/short A-arm coil-spring front suspension and four-link coil-spring rear suspension. Standard powerplant was now a 302 cu. in. V-8 with variable-venturi carburetor (except wagons with California emissions, a 351 V-8). The big 400 and 460 V-8 engines were gone. Four-wheel disc brakes and Traction-Lok axle also left the option list, along with the power moonroof. Newly optional was an electronic AM/FM stereo search radio with quadrasonic8 tape player and premium sound system. Also joining the option list: an analog clock, digital clock with day/date and elapsed time, AM/FM stereo with cassette, 40-channel CB, and Grand Marquis package. Speed control option included a 'resume' feature. This smaller Marquis had a lower hood, cowl and beltline. The new vertical-theme grille consisted of six separate side-by-side box sections. Concealed headlamps were replaced by exposed quad rectangular headlamps, which led into wraparound park/signal/marker lenses. A new chrome trim strip appeared along the mid-bodyside. So did front fender louvers. At the rear were large horizontal wraparound taillamps with integral rear side marker lights. Vertical backup lamps were adjacent to the recessed rear license plate bracket. Four-doors had a bright rear door window divider bar. Bright rocker panel, belt, wheel lip, roof drip, windshield, rear window and hood rear edge moldings were standard. Doors were thinner and armrests smaller, adding interior space. A mini spare tire was now used. Under the hood, a new EECII electronic engine control system monitored six functions. Inside was a new four-spoke steering wheel. Flight bench seats were trimmed in Fontaine cloth or optional Ruffino vinyl. Standard equipment included three-speed automatic transmission, power steering and brakes, dual-note horn, bright full wheel covers, stand-up hood ornament, rear roof pillar louvers, and FR78 x 14 SBR blackwall tires. Marquis Brougham added power windows; a full vinyl roof (on four-door) or landau vinyl roof (two-door), bright door frames, hood and decklid paint stripes, deluxe wheel covers, analog clock, and remote driver's mirror. Wide bright lower bodyside moldings included the quarter panels. Two-door Broughams could have the full vinyl roof at no extra cost. The Grand Marquis option added tinted glass, coach lamps, bodyside paint stripes, and wide bright/black lower bodyside moldings. Twin Comfort lounge seats had dual center armrests and reclining passenger seat, upholstered in Kinvara cloth or optional leather and vinyl. Also included: a right visor vanity mirror, dome/dual-beam map light, and pull straps. Marquis wagons had a three-way tailgate and power tailgate window. The Colony Park wagon added full-length bodyside and tailgate rosewood woodtone appliques with bright and woodtone rails, remote driver's mirror, coach lamps, bright door frames, and deluxe wheel covers. Rocker panel and wheel lip moldings were deleted.

I.D. DATA: Mercury's 11-symbol Vehicle Identification Number (VIN) is stamped on a metal tab fastened to the instrument panel, visible through the windshield. The first digit is a model year code ('9' 1979). The second letter indicates assembly plant: 'E' Mahwah, NJ; 'F' Dearborn, MI; 'H' Lorain, Ohio; 'R' San Jose, CA; 'K' Kansas City, MO; 'S' St. Thomas, Ontario; 'T' Metuchen, NJ; 'Z' St. Louis, MO; 'W' Wayne, MI. Digits three and four are the body serial code, which corresponds to the Model Numbers shown in the tables below (e.g., '20' Bobcat hatchback Runabout). The fifth symbol is an engine code: 'Y' L4-140 2Bbl.; 'W' Turbo L4140 2Bbl.; 'Z' V6170 2Bbl.; 'T' L6200 1Bbl.; 'L' L6250 1Bbl.; 'F' V8302 2Bbl.; 'H' V8351 2Bbl. Finally, digits 6-11 make up the consecutive unit number of cars built at each assembly plant. The number begins with 600,001. A Vehicle Certification Label on the left front door lock face panel or door pillar shows the manufacturer, month and year of manufacture, GVW, GAWR, certification statement, VIN, body code, color code, trim code, axle code, transmission code, and special order code.

BOBCAT RUNABOUT/WAGON (FOUR/V-6)

Model Number	Body/Style Number	Body Type & Seating	Factory Price	Shipping Weight	Production Total
20	64H	3-dr. Hatch-4P	3797/4070	2474/--	35,667
22	73H	2-dr. Sta Wag-4P	4099/4372	2565/--	Note 1

BOBCAT VILLAGER (FOUR/V-6)

| 22 | 73H | 2-dr. Sta Wag-4P | 4212/4485 | N/A | Note 1 |

Note 1: Total station wagon production was 9,119 units. Engine Note: An automatic transmission was required with Bobcat V-6 engine, at a cost of $307 more.

CAPRI (FOUR/V-6)

| 14 | 61D | 3-dr. Fastbk-4P | 4481/4754 | 2548/-- | 92,432 |

CAPRI GHIA (FOUR/V-6)

16	61H	3-dr. Fastbk-4P	4845/5118	2645/ --	17,712

Capri Engine Note: A V-8 engine cost $241 more than the V-6.

ZEPHYR (FOUR/SIX)

31	66H	2-dr. Sed-5P	3870/4111	2516/2519	15,920
32	54D	4-dr. Sed-5P	3970/4211	2580/2583	41,316
36	74D	4-dr. Sta Wag-5P	4317/4558	2681/2684	25,218

ZEPHYR Z-7 (FOUR/SIX)

35	36R	2-dr. Spt Cpe-5P	4122/4363	2551/2554	42,923

Zephyr Engine Note: A V-8 engine cost $283 more than the six.

MONARCH (SIX/V-8)

33	66H	2-dr. Sedan-5P	4412/4695	3070/3150	28,285
34	54H	4-dr. Sedan-5P	4515/4798	3111/3191	47,594

COUGAR (V-8)

91	65D	2-dr. HT Cpe-6P	5379	3792	2,831
92	53D	4-dr. Pill. HT-6P	5524	3843	5,605

COUGAR XR-7 (V-8)

93	65L	2-dr. HT Cpe-6P	5994	3883	163,716

MARQUIS (V-8)

61	66H	2-dr. Sedan-6P	5984	3507	10,035
62	54H	4-dr. Sedan-6P	6079	3557	32,289
74	74H	4-dr. 2S Sta Wag-6P	6315	3775	5,994

MARQUIS COLONY PARK (V-8)

74	74H	4-dr. 2S Sta Wag-6P	7100	3800	13,758

Wagon Note: Dual facing rear seats for the base Marquis or Colony Park wagon were available for $193.

MARQUIS BROUGHAM (V-8)

63	66K	2-dr. Sedan-6P	6643	3540	10,627
64	54K	4-dr. Sedan-6P	6831	3605	24,682

GRAND MARQUIS (V-8)

65	66L	2-dr. Sedan-6P	7321	3592	11,066
66	54L	4-dr. Sedan-6P	7510	3659	32,349

FACTORY PRICE AND WEIGHT NOTE: Monarch prices and weights to left of slash are for six-cylinder, to right for V-8 engine. For Bobcat and Zephyr, prices/weights to left of slash are for four-cylinder, to right for V-6.

ENGINE DATA: BASE FOUR (Bobcat, Capri, Zephyr): Inline. Overhead cam. Four-cylinder. Cast iron block and head. Displacement: 140 cu. in. (2.3 liters). Bore & stroke: 3.78 x 3.13 in. Compression ratio: 9.0:1. Brake horsepower: 88 at 4800 R.P.M. Torque: 118 lbs.-ft. at 2800 R.P.M. Five main bearings. Hydraulic valve lifters. Carburetor: 2Bbl. Motorcraft 5200. VIN Code: Y. OPTIONAL TURBOCHARGED FOUR (Capri): Same as 140 cu. in. four above, but with turbocharger Horsepower: 140 at 4800 R.P.M. Torque: N/A. Carburetor: 2Bbl. Holley 6500. VIN Code: W. OPTIONAL V-6 (Bobcat, Capri): 60-degree, overhead-valve V-6. Cast iron block and head. Displacement: 170.8 cu. in. (2.8 liters). Bore & stroke: 3.66 x 2.70 in. Compression ratio: 8.7:1. Brake horsepower: 102 at 4400 R.P.M. (Capri, 109 at 4800). Torque: 138 lbs.-ft. at 3200 R.P.M. (Capri, 142 at 2800). Four main bearings. Hydraulic valve lifters. Carburetor: 2Bbl. Motorcraft 2150 or 2700VV. VIN Code: Z. OPTIONAL SIX (Zephyr): Inline. OHV. Six-cylinder. Cast iron block and head. Displacement: 200 cu. in. (3.3 liters). Bore & stroke: 3.68 x 3.13 in. Compression ratio: 8.5:1. Brake horsepower: 85 at 3600 R.P.M. Torque: 154 lbs.-ft. at 1600 R.P.M. Seven main bearings. Hydraulic valve lifters. Carburetor: 1Bbl. Carter YFA or Holley 1946. VIN Code: T. BASE SIX (Monarch): Inline. OHV. Six-cylinder. Cast iron block and head. Displacement: 250 cu. in. (4.1 liters). Bore & stroke: 3.68 x 3.91 in. Compression ratio: 8.6:1. Brake horsepower: 97 at 3200 R.P.M. Torque: 210 lbs.-ft. at 1400 R.P.M. Seven main bearings. Hydraulic valve lifters. Carburetor: 1Bbl. Carter YFA. VIN Code: L. BASE V-8 (Cougar, Marquis); OPTIONAL (Capri, Zephyr, Monarch): 90-degree, overhead valve V-8. Cast iron block and head. Displacement: 302 cu. in. (5.0 liters). Bore & stroke: 4.00 x 3.00 in. Compression ratio: 8.4:1. Brake horsepower: 129-140 at 3400-3600 R.P.M. Torque: 223-250 lbs.-ft. at 1600-2600 R.P.M. Five main bearings. Hydraulic valve lifters. Carburetor: 2Bbl. Motorcraft 2150 or 2700VV. VIN Code: F. OPTIONAL V-8 (Cougar, Marquis): 90-degree, overhead valve V-8. Cast iron block and head. Displacement: 351 cu. in. (5.8 liters). Bore & stroke: 4.00 x 3.50 in. Compression ratio: 8.3:1. Brake horsepower: 135-138 at 3200 R.P.M. Torque: 260-288 lbs.-ft. at 1400-2200 R.P.M. Five main bearings. Hydraulic valve lifters. Carburetor: 2Bbl. Motorcraft 7200VV. Windsor engine. VIN Code: H. OPTIONAL V-8 (Cougar): Modified version of 351 cu. in. V-8 above Compression ratio: 8.0:1. Horsepower: 151 at 3600 R.P.M. Torque: 270 lbs.-ft. at 2200 R.P.M. Carburetor: 2Bbl. Motorcraft 2150.

CHASSIS DATA: Wheelbase: (Bobcat) 94.5 in.; (Bobcat wag) 94.8 in.; (Capri) 100.4 in.; (Zephyr) 105.5 in.; (Monarch) 109.9 in.; (Cougar 2dr.) 114.0 in.; (Cougar 4dr.) 118.0 in.; (Marquis) 114.4 in. Overall Length: (Bobcat) 169.3 in.; (Bobcat wag) 179.8 in.; (Capri) 179.1 in.; (Zephyr) 193.8 in.; (Z7) 195.8 in.; (Monarch) 197.7 in.; (Cougar 2dr.) 215.5 in.; (Cougar 4dr.) 219.5 in. (Marquis) 212.0 in.; (Marquis wag) 217.7 in. Height: (Bobcat) 50.6 in.; (Bobcat wag) 52.1 in.; (Capri) 51.5 in.; (Zephyr) 53.5 in.; (Zephyr wag) 54.7 in.; (Z7) 52.2 in.; (Monarch) 53.2-53.3 in.; (Cougar 2dr.) 52.6 in.; (Cougar 4dr.) 53.3 in.; (XR7) 53.0 in.; (Marquis) 54.5 in.; (Marquis wag) 56.8 in. Width: (Bobcat) 69.4 in.; (Bobcat wag) 69.7 in.; (Capri) 69.1 in.; (Zephyr) 71.0 in.; (Monarch) 74.5 in.; (Cougar) 78.6 in.; (Marquis) 77.5 in.; (Marquis wag) 79.3 in. Front Tread: (Bobcat) 55.0 in.; (Capri) 56.6 in.; (Zephyr) 56.6 in.; (Monarch) 59.0 in.; (Cougar) 63.6 in.; (XR7) 63.2 in.; (Marquis) 62.2 in. Rear Tread: (Bobcat) 55.8 in.; (Capri) 57.0 in.; (Zephyr) 57.0 in.; (Monarch) 57.7 in.; (Cougar) 63.5 in.; (XR7) 63.1 in.; (Marquis) 62.0 in. Standard Tires: (Bobcat) BR78 x 13 SBR; (Capri) B78 x 13; (Capri Ghia) BR78 x 14; (Zephyr) B78 x 14 BSW; (Monarch) DR78 x 14; (Cougar) HR78 x 14; (XR7) GR78 x 15; (Marquis) FR78 x 14; (Marquis wag) GR78 x 14.

TECHNICAL: Transmission: Four-speed manual transmission standard on Capri; automatic optional (gear ratios N/A). Four-speed overdrive floor shift standard on Zephyr/Monarch six: (1st) 3.29:1; (2nd) 1.84:1; (3rd) 1.00:1; (4th) 0.81:1; (Rev) 3.29:1. Zephyr/Monarch V-8: (1st) 3.07:1; (2nd) 1.72:1; (3rd) 1.00:1; (4th) 0.70:1; (Rev) 3.07:1. Four-speed floor shift standard on Bobcat/Zephyr four: (1st) 3.98:1; (2nd) 2.14:1; (3rd) 1.42:1; (4th) 1.00:1; (Rev) 3.99:1. SelectShift three- speed automatic (column lever) standard on Cougar and Marquis, optional on others. Bobcat/Zephyr automatic gear ratios: (1st) 2.47:1; (2nd) 1.47:1; (3rd) 1.00:1; (Rev) 2.11:1. Other automatics: (1st) 2.46:1; (2nd) 1.46:1; (3rd) 1.00:1; (Rev) 2.18:1 to 2.20:1. Standard final drive ratio: (Bobcat) 2.73:1 w/4spd, 3.40:1 w/others; (Capri) 3.08:1 w/four or V-6, 3.45:1 w/turbo, 2.47:1 w/V-8 and auto.; (Zephyr) 3.08:1 exc. 2.73:1 w/six and auto., 2.26:1 w/V-8 and auto.; (Monarch) 3.00:1 w/4spd, 2.79:1 w/auto.; (Cougar) 2.75:1 w/V8302, 2.47:1 w/V8351. (Marquis) 2.26:1 exc. wagon, 2.73:1. Steering: (Bobcat/Capri/Zephyr) rack and pinion; (others) recirculating ball. Front Suspension: (Bobcat) coil springs with short/long control arms, lower leading arms, and anti-sway bar w/V-6; (Capri) modified MacPherson struts w/coil springs and anti- sway bar; (Zephyr) MacPherson struts w/coil springs mounted on lower control arm; (others) coil springs with long/short Aarms and anti-sway bar. Rear Suspension: (Bobcat/Monarch) rigid axle w/semi-elliptic leaf springs; (Capri/Zephy-r/Cougar) four-link w/coil springs; (Marquis) rigid axle with upper/lower control arms and coil springs. Brakes: Front disc, rear drum. Ignition: Electronic. Body construction: (Bobcat/Capri/Zephyr/Monarch) unibody; (others) separate body on perimeter frame; Fuel tank: (Bobcat) 11.7 gal. exc. 13 gal. w/V-6 and wagon 14 gal.; (Capri) 11.5 gal. w/four, others 12.5 gal.; (Zephyr) 16.0 gal.; (Monarch) 18.0 gal.; (Cougar) 21.0 gal.; (Marquis) 19 gal. exc. wagon, 20 gal.

DRIVETRAIN OPTIONS: Engines: Turbo 140 cu. in. four: Capri ($542). 170 cu. in. V-6: Bobcat/Capri ($273). 200 cu. in., 1Bbl. six: Zephyr ($241). 302 cu. in., 2Bbl. V-8: Capri ($514); Zephyr ($524); Monarch ($283). 351 cu. in., 2Bbl. V-8: Cougar/Marquis ($263). Sport-tuned exhaust: Capri ($34). Transmission/Differential: SelectShift Cruise-O-Matic: Bobcat/Capri/Monarch ($307); Zephyr ($307-$398). Floor shift lever: Zephyr/Monarch ($31). Traction-Lok differential: Cougar ($64). Optional axle ratio: Bobcat/Capri ($13); Marquis ($16). Brakes & Steering: Power brakes: Bobcat/Capri/Zephyr/Monarch ($70). Power steering: Bobcat/Capri ($141); Zephyr/Monarch ($149). Suspension: H.D. susp.: Monarch ($27); Marquis ($22). Sport handling susp.: Zephyr ($34). Handling pkg.: Marquis ($51). Cross-country susp.: Cougar ($22-$36). Radial sport susp.: Capri ($33). Load levelers: Marquis ($53-$67). Other: H.D. battery ($18-$21). Engine block heater ($13-$14) exc. Marquis ($21). Extended-range fuel tank: Cougar ($33). Trailer towing pkg. (heavy duty): Marquis ($146). California emission system ($76-$83). High-altitude option ($31-$36).

BOBCAT CONVENIENCE/APPEARANCE OPTIONS: Option Packages: Sports accent group ($223-$247). Sports instrument group ($94). Sport pkg. ($72). Deluxe interior ($158-$182). Interior accent group ($42). Convenience group ($55-$96). Appearance protection group ($41-$49). Light group ($33). Comfort/Convenience: Air conditioner ($484). Dual racing mirrors ($36-$52). Day/night mirror ($8. Entertainment: AM radio w/digital clock ($47). AM/FM radio ($48). AM/FM stereo radio ($89); w/tape player ($119); w/cassette player ($157). Radio flexibility option ($90). AM radio delete ($72 credit). Exterior: Flip-up/removable moonroof ($199). Glass third door ($25). Glamour paint ($41). Narrow bodyside moldings ($41). Deluxe bodyside moldings ($51). Rocker panel moldings ($24). Roof luggage rack: wag ($63). Mud/stone deflectors ($22). Lower bodyside protection ($30). Interior: Four-way bucket seat ($35). Load floor carpet ($24). Cargo area cover ($28). Wheels/Tires: Wire wheel covers ($33). Forged or cast aluminum wheels ($164); white forged ($177). BR78 x 13 ($43). BR70 x 13 RWL ($79).

CAPRI CONVENIENCE/APPEARANCE OPTIONS: Option Packages: RS option ($249). Turbo RS option ($1186). Interior accent group ($42-$108). Light group ($16-$28). Appearance protection group ($41-$45). Power lock group ($99). Comfort/Convenience: Air cond. ($484). Rear defroster, electric ($84). Fingertip speed control ($104). Tinted glass ($59); windshield only ($27). Leather-wrapped steering wheel ($36). Tilt steering wheel ($69). Interval wipers ($35). Rear wiper/washer ($63). Right remote mirror ($30). Entertainment: AM radio ($72); w/digital clock ($119). AM/FM radio ($120). AM/FM stereo radio ($176); w/8track or cassette tape player ($243). Premium sound system ($67). Dual rear speakers ($43). Radio flexibility option ($93). Exterior: Flip-up/removable moonroof ($199). Glamour paint ($41). Two-tone paint, black ($48). Rocker panel moldings ($24). Mud/stone deflectors ($22). Lower bodyside protection ($30). Interior: Console ($127). Four-way driver's seat ($35). Danbury or Bradford cloth w/vinyl seat trim ($20). Leather seat trim ($283). Color-keyed deluxe seatbelts ($20). Wheels and Tires: Wire wheel covers ($64). TRX or cast aluminum wheels ($240). Styled steel wheels w/trim rings ($65). B78 x 13 WSW ($43). C78 x 13 BSW ($22); WSW ($65). B78 x 14 WSW ($65). BR78 x 14 BSW ($125); WSW ($43-$168). CR78 x 14 WSW ($65-$190); RWL ($14-$204). TRX 190/65Rx390 Michelin BSW ($51-$241).

ZEPHYR CONVENIENCE/APPEARANCE OPTIONS: Option Packages: ES option ($237). Ghia option ($211-$428). Villager option ($195). Sports instrument group ($78). Exterior decor group ($102). Interior decor group ($72-$108). Luxury interior ($208-$323). Bumper protection group ($58). Convenience group ($31-$51). Appearance protection group ($48-$54). Light group ($35-$41). Comfort/Convenience: Air cond. ($484). Rear defogger ($51). Rear defroster, electric ($90). Speed control ($83-$104). Tinted glass ($59). Power windows ($116-$163). Power door locks ($78-$107). Power seat, four-way ($94). Electric trunk release ($22). Sport steering wheel ($39). Tilt steering ($48-$69). Electric clock ($20). Cigar lighter ($6). Interval wipers ($35). Liftgate wiper/washer: wag ($80). Lighting and Mirrors: Trunk light ($7). Left remote mirror ($17). Dual mirrors ($35). Day/night mirror ($8). Entertainment: AM radio ($72); w/8track tape player ($192). AM/FM radio ($120). AM/FM stereo radio ($176); w/8track or cassette player ($243). Premium sound ($67). Radio flexibility ($93). Exterior: Flip-up/removable moonroof ($199). Vinyl roof ($90). Glamour paint ($48). Two-tone paint ($81-$96). Pivoting front vent windows ($41). Rear vent louvers ($35). Bodyside moldings ($41). Deluxe wide bodyside moldings ($53). Rocker panel moldings ($24). Bright window frames ($25-$30). Bumper guards, rear ($20). Mud/stone deflectors ($22). Roof luggage rack ($76). Lower bodyside protection ($30-$42). Interior: Bucket seats ($72). Ardmore or Brodie cloth seat trim ($39). Kirsten cloth trim ($20). Lockable side storage box ($20). Wheels/Tires: Styled wheel covers ($41). Wire wheel covers ($52-$93). Aluminum wheels ($237-$278). Styled wheels ($54- $95). B78 x 14 WSW. BR78 x 14 BSW/WSW. C78 x 14 BSW/WSW. CR78 x 14 BSW/WSW. DR78 x 14 SBR BSW/WSW/RWL.

MONARCH CONVENIENCE/APPEARANCE OPTIONS: Option Packages: ESS option ($524). Ghia option ($425). Interior decor group ($211). Convenience group ($36-$94). Bumper protection group ($78). Light group ($46). Cold weather group ($57). Heavy-duty group ($57). Appearance protection group ($33-$51). Visibility group ($8-$64). Comfort/Convenience: Air cond. ($514); w/auto-temp ($555). Rear defogger ($51). Rear defroster, electric ($90). Fingertip speed control ($104). Illuminated entry system ($52). Power windows ($116-$163). Power door locks ($78-$107). Power decklid release ($22). Auto. parking brake release ($8). Power four-way seat ($94). Tinted glass ($64). Tilt steering wheel ($69). Digital clock ($45). Lighting and Mirrors: Cornering lamps ($45). Trunk light ($7). Dual racing mirrors ($42-$59). Lighted right visor vanity mirror ($37). Entertainment: AM radio ($72); w/tape player ($192). AM/FM radio ($135). AM/FM stereo radio ($176); w/8track or cassette player ($243); w/quadrasonic tape ($365). AM/FM stereo search radio ($319). CB radio ($270). Radio flexibility ($93). Exterior: Power moonroof ($849). Full or landau vinyl roof ($106). Glamour paint ($48). Tone-on-tone ($123). Bodyside moldings ($41). Rocker panel moldings ($24). Mud/stone deflectors ($22). Lower bodyside protection ($30). Interior: Console ($84). Four-way seat ($34). Leather seat trim ($283). Rossano cloth seat ($54). Willshire cloth trim ($104). Deluxe seatbelts ($20). Wheels/Tires: Deluxe wheel covers ($40) exc. Ghia/ESS (NC). Wire wheel covers ($69-$108). Styled steel wheels w/trim rings ($75-$114). Cast aluminum wheels ($170-$278). DR78 x 14 SBR WSW. ER78 x 14 SBR BSW/WSW. FR78 x 14 SBR BSW/WSW/wide WSW.

COUGAR CONVENIENCE/APPEARANCE OPTIONS: Option Packages: Brougham option ($266-$382). Brougham decor ($221). Chamois decor group: XR7 ($625). XR7 decor ($487). Sports instrumentation group ($105-$149). Bumper protection group ($63). Light group ($54). Convenience group ($62-$147). Power lock group ($111-$143). Appearance protection group ($66-$76). Comfort/Convenience: Air cond. ($562); w/auto-temp control ($607). Rear defroster, electric ($99). Fingertip speed control ($105-$125). Illuminated entry system ($57). Tinted glass ($70). Tilt steering wheel ($75). Day/date clock ($22-$46). Seatbelt chime: XR7 ($22). Lighting and Mirrors: Cornering lamps ($49). Remote driver's mirror ($18). Dual racing mirrors ($64). Lighted visor vanity mirror ($39). Entertainment: AM radio ($79). AM/FM radio ($132). AM/FM stereo radio ($192); w/tape or cassetteplayer ($266); w/quadrasonic tape player ($399). AM/FM stereo search radio ($349). CB radio ($295). Upgraded sound: XR7 ($30). Dual rear speakers ($47). Power antenna: XR7 ($47). Radio flexibility ($105). Exterior: Power moonroof ($789). Landau vinyl roof ($116). Full vinyl roof ($170). Opera windows: base ($54). Glamour paint ($64). Two-tone paint ($74-$128). Paint striping ($36). Narrow bodyside moldings ($45). Wide bodyside moldings ($58). Rocker panel moldings: Brghm ($29). Mud/stone deflectors ($24). Lower bodyside protection ($33). Interior: Twin comfort seats w/passenger recliner: XR7/Brghm ($184). Bucket seats w/console ($184-$259). Vinyl bench seat ($30). Flight bench seat ($75). Velour trim: XR7 ($208). Leather seat: XR7 ($309). Trunk trim ($42). Color-keyed seatbelts ($22). Wheels/Tires: Deluxe wheel covers ($43). Luxury wheel covers ($34-$78). Wire wheel covers ($118-$162). Cast aluminum wheels ($136-$345). Styled wheels: XR7 ($166). Styled wheels w/trim rings ($120-$163) exc. XR7. HR78 x 14 SBR WSW ($47). GR78 x 15 WSW ($47). HR78 x 15 SBR WSW ($71).

MARQUIS CONVENIENCE/APPEARANCE OPTIONS: Option Packages: Grand Marquis decor: Colony Park ($586). Convenience group ($78-$93). Lock convenience group ($91-$154). Visibility light group ($18-$47). Appearance protection group ($61-$71). Comfort/Convenience: Air cond. ($597); w/auto-temp control ($642). Rear defroster, electric ($100). Fingertip speed control ($111-$130). Illuminated entry system ($57). Power windows ($137-$203). Six-way power seat ($164); driver and passenger ($329). Tinted glass ($83). Tilt steering wheel ($76). Electric clock ($24). Digital clock ($36-$59). Seatbelt chimes ($22). Lighting and Mirrors: Cornering lamps ($49). Driver's remote mirror ($18). Right remote mirror ($38). Lighted visor vanity mirror ($41). Entertainment: AM radio ($79). AM/FM radio ($132). AM/FM stereo radio ($192); w/tape or cassette player ($266). CB radio ($295). Power antenna ($45). Dual rear speakers ($47). Premium sound system ($74-$158). Radio flexibility ($105). Exterior: Full or landau vinyl roof ($143). Glamous metallic paint ($64). Two-tone paint ($99-$129). Paint striping ($36). Hood striping: Colony Park ($20). Rocker panel moldings: Colony Park ($29). Narrow bodyside moldings ($45). Window frame moldings ($34-$39). Bumper guards, front or rear ($22). Bumper rub strips ($41). Luggage rack: wag ($86). Lower bodyside protection ($33). Interior: Dual-facing rear seats: wagon ($193). Twin comfort seats: Brghm/Colony ($101). Dual seat recliners ($44). Cloth seat trim: Colony ($42). Vinyl seat trim ($34). Polyknit flight bench seat trim: wag ($53). Leather twin comfort seat trim: Grand Marquis/Colony ($261). Trunk trim ($45). Spare tire cover ($13). Deluxe seatbelts ($24). Wheels/Tires: Luxury wheel covers ($64-$93). Wire wheel covers ($89-$118). FR78 x 14 WSW ($47). GR78 x 14 BSW ($23). GR78 x 14 WSW ($47-$71). HR78 x 14 (wagon): BSW ($23); WSW ($71). Conventional spare ($13).

HISTORY: Introduced: October 6, 1978. Model year production: 669,138. Calendar year production (U.S.): 509,450. Calendar year sales by U.S. dealers: 509,999. Model year sales by U.S. dealers: 540,526.

Historical Footnotes: Sales for the '79 model year fell by close to 10 percent for the Lincoln-Mercury division, as motorists worried more about gas mileage. The shrunken Marquis sold far fewer copies than its full-size predecessor of 1978. Model year production rose, however, partly as a result of the new domestically- built Capri; but calendar year production was down considerably. The turbocharger option in the new Capri was supposed to give Mercury a "sporty" image to add to its luxury role.

1980 MERCURY

A new four-speed overdrive automatic transmission, and some weight reductions in the engines, helped give Lincoln- Mercury models considerably better gas mileage. A turbo option was announced for Zephyr as a mid-year addition, but failed to materialize. Capri got a new five-speed gearbox option. Also arriving this year was a new (smaller) Cougar XR7 model. A new powerplant appeared: the 255 cu. in. V-8, replacing the 302 in some models.

BOBCAT — FOUR — Since the front-drive subcompact Lynx would appear for 1981, this would be Bobcat's final year. Little changed in appearance or equipment, apart from a new optional two-tone paint treatment and new sport option. Standard front/rear bumper guards moved inward by 4 inches. Five new paint colors were available. Bobcat again displayed a rakishly-angled, vertical- textured grille with single rectangular headlamps and vertical park/signal lamps in the same recessed housings. Styled steel wheels came with trim rings. Bodies held bright wide wheel lip moldings; bright rocker panel, side window frame and door belt moldings; and ventless front side windows. Horizontal taillamps had integral backup lights. Aluminum bumpers had black rubber end caps. High-back front bucket seats were standard. Equipment also included the 140 cu. in. (2.3-liter) four with four-speed manual shift; BR78 x 13 BSW tires; an AM radio (which could be deleted); tinted glass; rear window defroster; front and rear bumper guards with rub strips; and choice of all-vinyl or cloth and vinyl interior. Manual-shift models had a woodgrain shift knob. Two wagons were available

1980 Bobcat "Sport Option" hatchback coupe (M)

again: base and Villager (with full-length rosewood woodtone bodyside applique). New options included mud/stone deflectors, rear spoiler, and special paint/tape treatment. The new Sport option included a front air dam, rear spoiler, and special paint/tape treatment. It included large Bobcat decal lettering on the door as part of the wide stripe treatment. No V-6 engine was offered in this final season.

1980 Capri hatchback coupe (M)

CAPRI — FOUR/SIX/V-8 — Introduced for 1979, Mercury's equivalent to the Ford Mustang looked the same this year, but enjoyed a few mechanical changes. After the new model year began, the turbo engine was to be available with optional automatic as well as the standard four-speed manual shift. A new 255 cu. in. (4.2-liter) V-8 replaced the optional 302. An inline 200 cu. in. six became available late in the model year, replacing the former V-6 as first choice above the base 140 cu. in. (2.3- liter) four. Five-speed shifting became optional with the four at mid-year. New standard equipment included halogen headlamps and metric-size (P185/80R13) steel-belted radials. An AM radio was also made standard later. Wide-aspect, low- profile Michelin TRX tires were again optional. New options included a roof luggage carrier, concealed cargo compartment cover, tri-tone accent tape stripe, and Recaro bucket seats. Capris carried a black/bright horizontal-bar grille and quad rectangular headlamps in bright frames. Color-keyed louvers decorated the hood; black louvers went on the cowl. Semi-styled 13 in. steel wheels had trim rings. Extra-wide wraparound black bodyside moldings held dual color-keyed center stripes. The swing-up hatch had a bright window molding. High back bucket seats were pleated all-vinyl trim. Standard equipment included the 2.3-liter four with four-speed manual, inside hood release, front stabilizer bar, color-keyed bumpers, full fender splash shields, woodgrain instrument panel applique, full instrumentation (including tachometer), lighter, trip odometer, sport steering wheel, locking glovebox, day/night mirror, and a remote driver's mirror. Ghia added P175/75R14 SBR tires on 14 in. wheels, sport wheel covers, dual black remote mirrors, a Ghia badge, low- back bucket seats with European-style headrests, four-spoke steering wheel with woodtone insert, and a light group. Capri RS included a rear spoiler; non-functional hood scoop; black grille; black right-hand remote mirror; sport wheel covers; and upper bodyside dual accent paint striping. 'RS' tape identification went on the front fender, at the cowl. Blackout headlamp frames, windshield molding, window frame moldings, and third door window molding were RS standards. So was a simulated engine-turned instrument panel. P175/75R14 tires rode 14 in. wheels, with a radial sport suspension. Topping the line, the Turbo RS model had 'Turbo RS' tape identification on the front fender (at cowl); a bright 'Turbo' plaque on the hood scoop; sport-tuned exhaust; three- spoke 15.3 inch forged aluminum wheels; Michelin TRX 190/65R390 low-profile tires; 8000 R.P.M. tachometer; turbo function indicator lights on dash; and rally suspension. Low- back bucket seats had European-style headrests. Turbo engines had a dual bright tailpipe extension (optional with V-8).

1980 Zephyr Z-7 Sports Coupe (AA)

ZEPHYR — FOUR/SIX/V-8 — Biggest news for Zephyr was to be the availability of a turbocharged four-cylinder engine, but that prospect faded away. However, a new 255 cu. in. (4.2-liter) V-8 replaced the former 302. Zephyrs now had high-pressure P-metric SBR tires (P175/75R14) and new quad rectangular halogen headlamps. Manual-shift models had a new self-adjusting clutch. Standard front bumper guards were moved inward a little over 3 inches, but Zephyr was otherwise little changed. Styling features included bright frames around quad headlamp and quad park/signal lamps; a thin-vertical-bar grille; aluminum bumper (with front guards); upper bodyside dual accent stripes; dual front fender louvers; and deluxe wheel covers. Horizontal taillamps had integral backup lenses and bright bezels. Zephyrs had bright wheel lip and rocker panel moldings, bright door belt and roof drip moldings, and all-vinyl low-back bucket seats. Standard equipment included the 140 cu. in. (2.3-liter) four with four-speed manual shift, inside hood release, front stabilizer bar, woodgrain instrument cluster applique, Euro-style front door armrest, and a stand-up hood ornament. Zephyr's Z-7 sport coupe was noted for its contemporary wraparound roof design with upper bodyside accent stripe treatment that continued over the roof. Also standard on Z7: lower bodyside molding with black vinyl insert; bright wheel lip moldings and window frames; Z-7 ornament on wide center pillar; wraparound taillamps; pleated vinyl seat trim; and tinted rear window glass. The Villager wagon had woodtone bodyside paneling appliques. There was also a standard wagon. Ghia packages were available on all models, but the ES option was abandoned.

1980 Monarch Ghia sedan (AA)

MONARCH — SIX/V-8 — Styling remained the same as 1979, but eight new paint colors and three new tone-on-tone combinations were offered. New electronic chimes replaced the buzzer warning system. A new full-width aluminum lower back panel applique with black center replaced the former red reflective applique. Three new vinyl roof colors were available. Again, there was a base model, Ghia option group, and sporty ESS option group. Standard Monarchs had Flight bench seating with fold-down center armrest. Ghia and ESS had a choice of special sculptured Flight bench or bucket seats. Standard equipment included a 250 cu. in. (4.1-liter) inline six with four-speed manual overdrive and floor lever (automatics had column shift), DR78 x 14 BSW SBR tires, inside hood release, vinyl seat trim, lighter, burled woodgrain instrument cluster, locking glovebox, stand-up hood ornament, and full wheel covers. Moldings were included for windshield, wheel lip, backlight, drip, belt, door frame and decklid. Two-doors had opera windows. The optional 302 cu. in. (5.0-liter) V-8 was required in California. Monarch's Ghia option group included accent stripes on hood contours, tapered bodyside accent stripes, wire wheel covers, full-length lower bodyside molding with wide color-keyed vinyl insert, bright driver's remote mirror, accent stripes on decklid and decklid contours, and Ghia decklid ornament. Ghias rode ER78 x 14 tires and carried a dual-note horn, rear door courtesy light switches, vinyl seats, seatback map pockets, and day/night mirror. The ESS option group had black wipers, black hood accent stripes, front/rear bumper guards and horizontal rub strip, bright wide wheel lip moldings, dual racing mirrors, and color-keyed wheel covers. Also on ESS: black bodyside molding with bright mylar insert; black rocker panel paint; black side window surround moldings; louvered opera window applique (two-doors); black rear window division bar (four-doors); black decklid accent stripes; and FR78 x 14 tires. 'ESS' block lettering on front fenders (at cowl) replaced the former 'ESS Monarch' label.

1980 Cougar XR-7 Sports Coupe (AA)

COUGAR XR-7 — V-8 — Aerodynamic styling on an all-new and smaller unitized body changed Cougar substantially. So did a new standard 255 cu. in. (4.1-liter) V-8 instead of the former 302 (which was now optional). Also optional this year was new four-speed automatic overdrive transmission. The new Cougar weighed 700 pounds less than the old, and rode a shorter 108.4 inch wheelbase. More important, the base models were dropped, leaving only the XR7. Cougar now had a strut-type front suspension, four-bar link coil-spring rear suspension, standard variable-ratio power rack-and-pinion steering, sealed-beam halogen headlights, and P-metric SBR tires (P185/75R14 BSW). Keyless entry was a new option, using door-mounted pushbuttons to activate the door locks and trunk lid. Bodies featured distinctive deep bodyside sculpturing, color-keyed soft front/rear bumper coverings, new vertical-theme taillamps, a padded half-vinyl roof, quarter window louvers, all-new wheels and wheel covers. Passenger capacity dropped to four. Standard equipment included three-speed automatic transmission, power steering and brakes, dual-note horn, front and rear stabilizer bars, brake failure warning light, Flight bench seat, woodgrain instrument panel applique, trip odometer, front/rear center seat dividers, ashtray and glovebox lights, four-spoke steering wheel, analog clock, soft color-keyed bumpers, and quarter-window louvers. Cougar's upright vertical-bar grille with bright surround molding had its pattern repeated in a lower bumper grille opening. Quad rectangular halogen headlamps in bright housings led into wraparound marker lenses. Turn signals were bumper-mounted. Styling touches included a stand-up hood ornament, wide rocker moldings, wheel lip moldings, "frenched" rear window, and dual bodyside

accent stripes. Black door and quarter window frames had bright moldings. An optional Decor Group included such items as full-length wide bodyside moldings (with vinyl inserts to match the roof), hood and decklid accent stripes, bright sail-mount dual remote mirrors, and Twin Comfort lounge seats. A Sports Group (available later) had a striking two-tone treatment and low-profile TR type tires on cast aluminum wheels, with special suspension tuning. The Sports model also had Recaro bucket seats with cloth trim and lumbar/depth/shoulder support adjustment, and power windows. The Luxury Group added such extras as Michelin TRX whitewall tires on cast aluminum wheels, a 5.0-liter V-8, luxury half-vinyl roof, automatic overdrive transmission, split bench seat, electronic instruments, diagnostic warning light module, power windows, lighted visor mirror, quarter courtesy lamp, and hood/decklid paint stripes.

1980 Grand Marquis "Coach Roof" sedan (AA)

MARQUIS — V-8 — Downsized in 1979 to almost full-size, Marquis changed only slightly in appearance this year with new taillamp and lower back panel moldings. New paint combinations put the darker color on top. Halogen headlamps and P-metric (P205/75R14) radial tires were new. So were front bumper guards. Both the base 302 cu. in. (5.0-liter) V-8 and optional 351 cu. in. (5.8-liter) could have four-speed automatic overdrive transmission instead of the standard three-speed automatic. An improved EEC-III system was standard on 351 V-8s and California 302s. The Traction-Lok option reappeared. Two new versions of the electronic AM/FM stereo search radio, introduced on the '79 Marquis, were offered: plain or with cassette and Dolby. A mid-year 1979 option had been pivoting front vent windows. Joining the option list: turbine-spoke cast aluminum wheels. Again, two and four-door sedans in base, Brougham and Grand Marquis trim were offered, along with base and Colony Park wagons. A bright Marquis crest or 'Grand Marquis' script replaced the former louvers on rear roof pillar. Accent stripes were added to the fender louvers on Grand Marquis. Bodies had bright decklid edge and taillamp surround moldings, bright window frame and lower quarter extension moldings, and Wraparound parking lamps with integral side marker lights. Fender louvers and a wide center pillar were standard. Four-doors had a rear door window divider bar; two-doors, a fixed quarter window. At the back was a black lower back panel, bright rear window molding, horizontal wraparound taillamps with integral side marker lights, and bright decklid lower edge and taillamp surround molding. Flight bench seats had a fold-down center armrest and cloth and vinyl upholstery. Electronic chimes replaced the buzzer as seatbelt warning on Brougham, Grand Marquis and Colony Park. All steering wheels had a woodgrain insert. Two new luxury half-vinyl roofs were available: the standard coach roof on all Grand Marquis models (optional on Brougham); and a formal coach roof optional only on four-door Grand Marquis. Vinyl roofs later switched to smooth french seams and color-keyed back window moldings. Base Marquis standard equipment included power brakes and steering, dual-note horn, four-spoke steering wheel, woodgrain instrument panel applique, day/night mirror, front bumper guards and rub strips, and hood ornament. Brougham added hood accent stripes; full vinyl roof (four-door) or landau vinyl roof (two-door); driver's remote mirror; deluxe wheel covers; wide bright lower bodyside molding with quarter panel extensions; decklid accent stripes; power windows; dash and trunk courtesy lights; and 'Brougham' nameplate on decklid. Grand Marquis included coach lamps, wide bright/black lower bodyside moldings, upper bodyside accent stripes, black painted rocker panel flange, 'Grand Marquis' script on rear roof pillar, and 'Grand Marquis' decklid nameplate. Grand Marquis had standard tinted glass and Twin Comfort lounge seats with dual center folding armrests. Colony Park wagons had full-length bodyside rosewood woodtone appliques, with bright and woodtone rails; plus 'Colony Park' script on quarter panel. Both wagons carried P215/75R14 tires.

I.D. DATA: Mercury's 11-symbol Vehicle Identification Number (VIN) is stamped on a metal tab fastened to the instrument panel, visible through the windshield. Coding is the same as 1979, except engine codes (symbol five) changed as follows: 'A' L4-140 2Bbl.; 'A' Turbo L4140 2Bbl.; 'B' or 'T' L6200 1Bbl.; 'C' L6250 1Bbl.; 'D' V8255 2Bbl.; 'F' V8302 2Bbl.; 'G' V8351 2Bbl. Model year code changed to '0' for 1980.

BOBCAT RUNABOUT/WAGON (FOUR)

Model Number	Body/Style Number	Body Type & Seating	Factory Price	Shipping Weight	Production Total
20	64H	3-dr. Hatch-4P	4384	2445	28,103
22	73H	2-dr. Sta Wag-4P	4690	2573	Note 1

BOBCAT VILLAGER (FOUR)

22	73H	2-dr. Sta Wag-4P	4803	N/A	Note 1

Note 1: Total station wagon production was 5,547 units.

CAPRI (FOUR/SIX)

14	61D	3-dr. Fastbk-4P	5250/5469	2547/2585	72,009

CAPRI GHIA (FOUR/SIX)

16	61H	3-dr. Fastbk-4P	5545/5764	2632/2670	7,975

Capri Engine Note: A V-8 engine cost $119 more than the six.

292

ZEPHYR (FOUR/SIX)

31	66D	2-dr. Sed-5P	4582/4751	2605/2608	10,977
32	54D	4-dr. Sed-5P	4700/4869	2647/2650	40,399
36	74D	4-dr. Sta Wag-5P	4870/5039	2769/2772	20,341

ZEPHYR Z-7 (FOUR/SIX)

35	36R	2-dr. Spt Cpe-5P	4876/5045	2644/2647	19,486

Zephyr Engine Note: A V-8 engine cost $119 more than the six.

MONARCH (SIX/V-8)

33	66H	2-dr. Sedan-5P	5074/5262	3093/3160	8,772
34	54H	4-dr. Sedan-5P	5194/5382	3134/3227	21,746

Monarch Engine Note: Prices are for 302 cu. in. V-8; a 255 V-8 cost only $38 more than the six.

COUGAR XR-7 (V-8)

93	66D	2-dr. HT Cpe-4P	6569	3191	58,028

Cougar Engine Note: Price shown is for 255 cu. in. V-8; a 302 V-8 cost $150 more.

MARQUIS (V-8)

61	66H	2-dr. Sedan-6P	6134	3450	2,521
62	54H	4-dr. Sedan-6P	6722	3488	13,018
74	74H	4-dr. 2S Sta Wag-6P	7071	3697	2,407

MARQUIS BROUGHAM (V-8)

63	66K	2-dr. Sedan-6P	7298	3476	2,353
64	54K	4-dr. Sedan-6P	7490	3528	8,819

MARQUIS COLONY PARK (V-8)

76	74K	4-dr. 2S Sta Wag-6P	7858	3743	5,781

GRAND MARQUIS (V-8)

65	66L	2-dr. Sedan-6P	8075	3504	3,434
66	54L	4-dr. Sedan-6P	8265	3519	15,995

FACTORY PRICE AND WEIGHT NOTE: Monarch prices and weights to left of slash are for six-cylinder, to right for V-8 engine. For Capri and Zephyr, prices/weights to left of slash are for four-cylinder, to right for V-6.

ENGINE DATA: BASE FOUR (Bobcat, Capri, Zephyr): Inline. Overhead cam. Four-cylinder. Cast iron block and head. Displacement: 140 cu. in. (2.3 liters). Bore & stroke: 3.78 x 3.13 in. Compression ratio: 9.0:1. Brake horsepower: 88 at 4600 R.P.M. Torque: 119 lbs.-ft. at 2600 R.P.M. Five main bearings. Hydraulic valve lifters. Carburetor: 2Bbl. Motorcraft 5200. VIN Code: A. OPTIONAL TURBOCHARGED FOUR (Capri): Same as 140 cu. in. four above, but with turbocharger Horsepower: 150 at 4800 R.P.M. Torque: N/A. Carburetor: 2Bbl. Holley 6500. VIN Code: A. OPTIONAL SIX (Capri, Zephyr): Inline. OHV. Six-cylinder. Cast iron block and head. Displacement: 200 cu. in. (3.3 liters). Bore & stroke: 3.68 x 3.13 in. Compression ratio: 8.6:1. Brake horsepower: 91 at 3800 R.P.M. Torque: 160 lbs.-ft. at 1600 R.P.M. Seven main bearings. Hydraulic valve lifters. Carburetor: 1Bbl. Holley 1946. VIN Code: B. BASE SIX (Monarch): Inline. OHV. Six-cylinder. Cast iron block and head. Displacement: 250 cu. in. (4.1 liters). Bore & stroke: 3.68 x 3.91 in. Compression ratio: 8.6:1. Brake horsepower: 90 at 3200 R.P.M. Torque: 194 lbs.-ft. at 1660 R.P.M. Seven main bearings. Hydraulic valve lifters. Carburetor: 1Bbl. Carter YFA. VIN Code: C. BASE V-8 (Cougar); OPTIONAL (Capri, Zephyr): 90-degree, overhead valve V-8. Cast iron block and head. Displacement: 255 cu. in. (4.2 liters). Bore & stroke: 3.68 x 3.00 in. Compression ratio: 8.8:1. Brake horsepower: 115-119 at 3800 R.P.M. Torque: 191-194 lbs.-ft. at 2200 R.P.M. Five main bearings. Hydraulic valve lifters. Carburetor: 2Bbl. Motorcraft 2150. VIN Code: D. BASE V-8 (Marquis); OPTIONAL (Cougar, Monarch): 90-degree, overhead valve V-8. Cast iron block and head. Displacement: 302 cu. in. (5.0 liters). Bore & stroke: 4.00 x 3.00 in. Compression ratio: 8.4:1. Brake horsepower: 130-134 at 3600 R.P.M. Torque: 230-232 lbs.-ft. at 1600 R.P.M. Five main bearings. Hydraulic valve lifters. Carburetor: 2Bbl. Motorcraft 2150 or 2700VV. VIN Code: F. OPTIONAL V-8 (Marquis): 90-degree, overhead valve V-8. Cast iron block and head. Displacement: 351 cu. in. (5.8 liters). Bore & stroke: 4.00 x 3.50 in. Compression ratio: 8.3:1. Brake horsepower: 140 at 3400 R.P.M. Torque: 265 lbs.-ft. at 2000 R.P.M. Five main bearings. Hydraulic valve lifters. Carburetor: 2Bbl. Motorcraft 7200VV. VIN Code: G.

CHASSIS DATA: Wheelbase: (Bobcat) 94.5 in.; (Bobcat wag) 94.8 in.; (Capri) 100.4 in.; (Zephyr) 105.5 in.; (Monarch) 109.9 in.; (Cougar) 108.4 in.; (Marquis) 114.3 in. Overall Length: (Bobcat) 170.8 in.; (Bobcat wag) 180.6 in.; (Capri) 179.1 in.; (Zephyr) 195.5 in.; (Z7) 197.4 in.; (Monarch) 199.7 in.; (Cougar) 200.4 in.; (Marquis) 212.3 in.; (Marquis wag) 218.0 in. Height: (Bobcat) 50.5 in.; (Bobcat wag) 52.0 in.; (Capri) 51.4 in.; (Zephyr) 52.9 in.; (Zephyr wag) 54.2 in.; (Z7) 51.7 in.; (Monarch) 53.2-53.3 in.; (Cougar) 53.0 in.; (Marquis) 54.7 in.; (Marquis wag) 57.4 in. Width: (Bobcat) 69.4 in.; (Bobcat wag) 69.7 in.; (Capri) 69.1 in.; (Zephyr) 71.0 in.; (Monarch) 74.5 in.; (Cougar) 74.1 in.; (Marquis) 77.5 in.; (Marquis wag) 79.3 in. Front Tread: (Bobcat) 55.0 in.; (Capri) 56.6 in.; (Zephyr) 56.6 in.; (Monarch) 59.0 in.; (Cougar) 58.1 in.; (Marquis) 62.2 in. Rear Tread: (Bobcat) 55.8 in.; (Capri) 57.0 in.; (Zephyr) 57.0 in.; (Monarch) 57.7 in.; (Cougar) 57.0 in.; (Marquis) 62.0 in. Standard Tires: (Bobcat) BR78 x 13 SBR BSW; (Capri) P185/80R13 SBR; (Capri Ghia) P175/75R14; (Capri turbo) TRX 190/65R390. (Zephyr) P175/75R14 SBR; (Monarch) DR78 x 14 exc. Ghia, ER78 x 14; (Cougar) P184/75R14 SBR BSW; (Marquis) P205/75R14 SBR; (Marquis wag) P215/75R14.

TECHNICAL: Transmission: Four-speed overdrive floor shift standard on Capri/Zephyr/Monarch six: (1st) 3.29:1; (2nd) 1.84:1; (3rd) 1.00:1; (4th) 0.81:1; (Rev) 3.29:1. Four-speed floor shift standard on Bobcat/Capri/Zephyr four: (1st) 3.98:1; (2nd) 2.14:1; (3rd) 1.42:1; (4th) 1.00:1; (Rev) 3.99:1. Capri turbo: (1st) 4.07:1; (2nd) 2.57:1; (3rd) 1.66:1; (4th) 1.00:1; (Rev) 3.95:1. Select-Shift three-speed automatic standard on Cougar and Marquis, optional on others. Bobcat/Capri/Zephyr automatic gear ratios: (1st) 2.47:1; (2nd) 1.47:1; (3rd) 1.00:1; (Rev) 2.11:1. Other automatics: (1st) 2.46:1; (2nd) 1.46:1; (3rd) 1.00:1; (Rev) 2.18:1 to 2.20:1. Four-speed overdrive automatic standard on Cougar w/V8302: (1st) 2.47:1; (2nd) 1.47:1; (3rd) 1.00:1; (4th) 0.67:1; (Rev) 2.00:1. Standard final drive ratio: (Bobcat) 2.73:1 or 2.79:1 w/4spd, exc. 3.08:1 or 3.00:1 for wagon or either model with auto.; (Capri) 2.73:1 w/four and 4spd, 3.08:1 w/four and auto., 3.08:1 w/six and 4spd, 2.73:1 w/six and auto., 2.26:1 w/V-8 and auto., 3.45:1 w/turbo; (Zephyr) 3.08:1 exc. 2.73:1 w/six and auto., 2.26:1 w/V-8 and auto.; (Monarch) 3.00:1 w/4spd, 2.79:1 w/auto.; (Cougar) 2.26:1 exc. 3.08:1 w/V8302 and overdrive auto.; (Marquis) 2.26:1 exc. 3.08:1 w/V8302 and overdrive auto., 2.73:1 w/V8351; (Marquis wagon) 2.73:1 w/V8302. Steering: (Marquis) recirculating ball; (others) rack and pinion. Front Suspension: (Bobcat) coil springs with short/long control arms and lower leading arms; (Capri) modified MacPherson struts w/coil springs and anti-sway bar; (Zephyr) MacPherson struts w/coil springs mounted on lower control arm; (Cougar) MacPherson struts with anti-sway bar; (Marquis) coil springs with long/short Aarms and anti-sway bar. Rear Suspension: (Bobcat/Monarch) rigid axle w/semi-elliptic leaf springs; (Capri/Zephyr/Marquis) four-link w/coil springs; (Cougar) four-link with coil springs and anti-sway bar. Brakes: Front disc, rear drum. Ignition: Electronic. Body construction: (Marquis) separate body and frame; (others) unibody. Fuel tank: (Bobcat) 13 gal. exc. wagon, 14 gal.; (Capri) 11.5 gal. w/four, 11.9 w/turbo, others 12.5 gal.; (Zephyr) 14 or 16 gal.; (Monarch) 18.0 gal.; (Cougar) 17.5 gal.; (Marquis) 19 gal. exc. wagon, 20 gal.

DRIVETRAIN OPTIONS: Engines: Turbo 140 cu. in. four: Capri ($481). 200 cu. in. six: Capri ($219); Zephyr ($169). 255 cu. in. V-8: Capri ($338); Zephyr ($288); Monarch ($38). 302 cu. in. V-8: Monarch ($188); Cougar ($150). 351 cu. in. V-8: Marquis ($150). Sport-tuned exhaust: Capri ($38). Transmission/Differential: Five-speed manual trans.: Capri ($156). Select-shift auto. trans.: Bobcat/Capri/Zephyr/Monarch ($340). Four-speed overdrive automatic trans.: Marquis/Cougar ($138). Floor shift lever: Zephyr/Monarch ($38). Traction-Lok differential: Marquis ($106). Optional axle ratio: Bobcat/Capri/Zephyr/Marquis ($15). Brakes & Steering: Power brakes: Bobcat/Capri/Zephyr/Monarch ($78). Power steering: Bobcat/Capri ($160); Zephyr/Monarch ($165). Suspension: H.D. susp.: Monarch ($29); Cougar/Marquis ($23). Handling susp.: Capri/Zephyr ($35); Marquis ($51). Adjustable air shock absorbers: Marquis ($55). Other: H.D. battery ($19-$21). Engine block heater ($15). Trailer towing pkg., heavy duty: Marquis ($131-$168). California emission system ($238). High-altitude option ($36).

BOBCAT CONVENIENCE/APPEARANCE OPTIONS: Option Packages: Sport pkg. ($206). Sports accent group ($235-$263). Sports instrument group ($80-$111). Deluxe interior ($173-$200). Interior decor group ($50). Convenience group ($69-$111). Appearance protection group ($38-$41). Light group ($24-$36). Comfort/Convenience: Air conditioner ($538). Dual racing mirrors ($43-$60). Day/night mirror ($10). Entertainment: AM/FM radio ($65). AM/FM stereo radio ($103); w/cassette player ($191). AM radio delete ($76 credit). Exterior: Flip-up/removable moon roof ($219). Glass third door ($31). Glamour paint ($45). Tu-tone paint ($113). Narrow vinyl-insert bodyside moldings ($44). Wide black bodyside moldings ($54). Rocker panel moldings ($28). Roof luggage rack: wag ($71). Mud/stone deflectors ($25). Lower bodyside protection ($31). Interior: Four-way driver's seat ($38). Load floor carpet ($28). Cargo area cover ($30). Front floor mats ($19). Wheels/Tires: Wire wheel covers ($40). Forged or cast aluminum wheels ($185); white forged ($200). BR78 x 13 WSW ($50). BR70 x 13 RWL ($89).

CAPRI CONVENIENCE/APPEARANCE OPTIONS: Option Packages: RS option ($204). Turbo RS option ($1185). Interior accent group ($50-$120). Light group ($20-$33). Appearance protection group ($38-$41). Comfort/Convenience: Air cond. ($538). Rear defroster, electric ($96). Fingertip speed control ($129). Tinted glass ($65). Power door locks ($113). Leather-wrapped steering wheel ($44). Tilt steering wheel ($78). Interval wipers ($39). Rear wiper/washer ($76). Right remote mirror ($36). Entertainment: AM radio ($93). AM/FM radio ($145). AM/FM stereo radio ($183); w/8track tape player ($259); w/cassette player ($271). Premium sound system ($94). Dual rear speakers ($38). Exterior: Flip-up/removable moonroof ($219). Glamour glow paint ($46). Black lower Tu-tone paint ($56). Accent tape stripes: base ($53). Backlight louvers ($141). Rocker panel moldings ($28). Roof luggage rack ($86). Mud/stone deflectors ($25). Lower bodyside protection ($31). Interior: Console ($156). Four-way driver's seat ($38). Recaro bucket seats ($531). Cloth/vinyl bucket seats ($21). Accent cloth/vinyl seat trim ($21). Leather/vinyl bucket seats ($313). Cargo area cover ($34). Color-keyed seatbelts ($24). Wheels and Tires: Wire wheel covers ($89). Forged aluminum wheels ($279). Cast aluminum wheels ($279). Styled steel wheels w/trim rings ($68). P185/80R13 WSW ($50). P175/75R14 BSW (NC); WSW ($50). P185/75R14 BSW ($24); WSW ($74); RWL ($89). TRX 190/65 x 390 BSW ($150).

ZEPHYR CONVENIENCE/APPEARANCE OPTIONS: Option Packages: Ghia pkg.: Z7 ($254); sedan ($499); Villager ($373). Villager option ($226). Luxury exterior decor group ($126). Luxury interior group ($370). Interior accent group ($100). Sports instrument group ($85). Convenience group ($31-$55). Appearance protection group ($43-$53). Light group ($40-$48). Comfort/Convenience: Air cond. ($571). Rear defroster, electric ($101). Fingertip speed control ($108-$129). Power windows ($135-$191). Power door locks ($88-$125). Power decklid release ($25). Power seat ($111). Tinted glass ($71). Sport steering wheel ($43). Leather-wrapped steering wheel ($44). Tilt steering ($78-$99). Electric clock ($24). Cigar lighter ($6). Interval wipers ($39). Rear wiper/washer: wag ($91). Trunk light ($8). Dual bright sculptured remote mirrors ($60). Entertainment: AM radio ($93). AM/FM radio ($145). AM/FM stereo radio ($183); w/8track player ($259); w/cassette player ($271). Premium sound system ($94). Exterior: Flip-up/removable moonroof ($219). Vinyl roof ($118). Glamour paint ($54). Tu-tone paint ($88-$106). Pivoting front vent windows ($50). Rear window vent louvers ($41). Narrow vinyl-insert bodyside moldings ($44); wide black vinyl ($56). Rocker panel moldings ($28). Bright window frames ($24). Bumper guards, rear ($24). Bumper rub strips ($41). Luggage rack: wag ($86). Liftgate assist handle: wag ($13). Mud/stone deflectors ($25). Lower bodyside protection ($31-$44). Interior: Non-reclining bucket seats ($31-$50). Bench seat ($50 credit). Accent cloth seat trim ($40). Base cloth seat trim ($28). Lockable side storage box ($23). Wheels/Tires: Deluxe wheel covers ($41). Styled wheel covers ($46). Wire wheel covers ($120). Styled steel wheels ($99). Cast aluminum wheels ($310). P175/75R14 WSW ($50). P185/75R14 BSW ($24); WSW ($50-$74); RWL ($65-$89). Conventional spare ($37).

MONARCH CONVENIENCE/APPEARANCE OPTIONS: Option Packages: ESS group ($516). Ghia group ($476). Interior decor group ($234). Convenience group ($40). Light group ($51). Cold weather group ($65). Heavy-duty group ($65). Appearance protection group ($30-$53). Visibility group ($71). Comfort/Convenience: Air cond. ($571); auto-temp ($634). Rear defroster, electric ($101). Fingertip speed control ($129). Illuminated entry system ($58). Power windows ($136-$193). Power door locks ($89-$125). Power decklid release ($25). Power four-way seat ($111). Tinted glass ($71). Tilt steering wheel ($78). Auto. parking brake release ($10). Digital clock ($51). Lighting and Mirrors: Cornering lamps ($50). Dual racing mirrors ($49-$68). Lighted right visor vanity mirror ($41). Entertainment: AM radio ($93). AM/FM radio ($145). AM/FM stereo radio ($183); w/8track player ($259); w/cassette ($271). AM/FM stereo search radio ($333); w/8track ($409); w/cassette and Dolby ($421). CB radio ($313). Exterior: Power moonroof ($923). Full or landau vinyl roof ($118). Glamour paint ($54). Tone-on-tone paint ($138). Bodyside moldings ($44). Rocker panel moldings ($28). Bumper rub strips ($41). Mud/stone deflectors ($25). Lower bodyside protection ($31). Interior: Console ($93). Four-way driver's seat ($38).

Reclining bucket seats (NC). Luxury cloth seat ($108). Base cloth flight bench seat trim ($60). Leather seat trim ($313). Color-keyed seatbelts ($24). Wheels/Tires: Luxury wheel covers ($46) exc. Ghia/ESS (NC). Wire wheel covers ($74-$120). Styled steel wheels w/trim rings ($79-$125). Cast aluminum wheels ($190-$310). DR78 x 14 SBR WSW. ER78 x 14 SBR BSW/WSW. FR78 x 14 SBR BSW/WSW/wide WSW.

COUGAR XR-7 CONVENIENCE/APPEARANCE OPTIONS: Option Packages: Luxury group ($1987). Sports group ($1687). Decor group ($516). Appearance protection group ($43-$46). Light group ($35). Power lock group ($113). Comfort/Convenience: Air cond. ($571); auto-temp ($634). Rear defroster ($101). Fingertip speed control ($108-$129). Illuminated entry system ($58). Keyless entry ($231). Garage door opener w/lighted vanity mirrors ($171). Autolamp on/off delay ($63). Tinted glass ($71). Power windows ($136). Four- way power seat ($111). Six-way power driver's seat ($166). Auto. parking brake release ($10). Leather-wrapped steering wheel ($44). Tilt steering wheel ($78). Electronic instrument cluster ($313). Diagnostic warning lights ($50). Digital clock ($38). Seatbelt chimes ($23). Interval wipers ($39). Lighting and Mirrors: Cornering lamps ($50). Driver's remote mirror ($19). Dual remote mirrors ($60). Lighted right visor vanity mirror ($41). Entertainment: AM radio ($93). AM/FM radio ($145). AM/FM stereo radio ($183); w/8track player ($259); w/cassette ($271). AM/FM stereo search radio ($333); w/8track ($409); w/cassette ($421). CB radio ($313). Power antenna ($49). Dual rear speakers ($38). Premium sound system ($119-$150). Exterior: Flip-up/removable moonroof ($219). Luxury half vinyl roof ($125). Vinyl roof delete ($156 credit). Glamour paint ($65). Tu-tone paint ($96-$119). Hood/decklid stripes ($24). Manual vent windows ($50). Wide vinyl-insert bodyside moldings ($56). Rocker panel moldings ($28). Mud/stone deflectors ($25). Lower bodyside protection ($31-$44). Interior: Twin comfort lounge seats ($209). Bucket seats w/console ($176) exc. (NC) w/decor group. Leather seat trim ($303). Trunk trim ($43). Color-keyed seatbelts ($24). Wheels/Tires: Wire wheel covers ($50-$138). Luxury wheel covers ($88). P195/75R14 BSW ($24); WSW ($50). TR 220/55Rx390 WSW tires on alum. wheels: base ($442-$530). Conventional spare ($37).

MARQUIS CONVENIENCE/APPEARANCE OPTIONS: Option Packages: Grand Marquis decor: Colony Park ($581). Convenience group ($80-$98). Power lock group ($90-$164). Visibility light group ($19-$48). Appearance protection group ($51-$61). Comfort/Convenience: Air cond. ($606); w/auto-temp control ($669). Rear defroster, electric ($103). Fingertip speed control ($111-$133). Illuminated entry system ($58). Power windows ($140-$208). Six-way power driver's or bench seat ($168); driver and passenger ($335). Tinted glass ($85). Autolamp on/off delay ($63). Leather-wrapped steering wheel ($44). Tilt steering wheel ($78). Auto. parking brake release ($10). Electric clock ($25). Digital clock ($38-$63). Seatbelt chime ($23). Lighting and Mirrors: Cornering lamps ($50). Driver's remote mirror ($19); passenger's ($41). Lighted right visor vanity mirror ($35-$43). Entertainment: AM radio ($93). AM/FM stereo radio ($183); w/8track tape player ($259); w/cassette ($271). AM/FM stereo search radio ($333); w/8track ($409); w/cassette ($421). CB radio ($313). Power antenna ($49). Dual rear speakers ($38). Premium sound system ($94). Exterior: Full or landau vinyl roof ($145). Coach vinyl roof ($130). Glamour paint ($65). Tu-tone paint ($103-$131). Upper bodyside paint stripes ($36). Hood striping ($14). Hood/decklid paint stripes: base ($23). Pivoting front vent windows ($50). Rocker panel moldings: Colony Park ($29). Narrow bodyside moldings ($44). Bumper guards, rear ($24). Bumper rub strips ($41). Luggage rack: wag ($86-$118). Lower bodyside protection ($31-$44). Interior: Dual-facing rear seats: wagon ($199). Twin comfort seats ($104-$130). Leather seating ($303). Dual seat recliners ($56). All-vinyl seat trim ($34). Cloth trim: wag ($40). Duraweave vinyl trim: wag ($50). Trunk trim ($46). Trunk mat ($14). Color-keyed seatbelts ($25). Wheels/Tires: Luxury wheel covers ($66-$94). Wire wheel covers ($110-$138). Turbine-spoke cast aluminum wheels ($283- $310). P205/75R14 WSW. P215/75R14 BSW/WSW. P225/75R14 WSW. P205/75R15 WSW.

HISTORY: Introduced: October 12, 1979. Model year production: 347,711. Calendar year production (U.S.): 324,518. Calendar year sales by U.S. dealers: 330,852. Model year sales by U.S. dealers: 345,111.

Historical Footnotes: Lincoln-Mercury sales plunged 37 percent for the 1980 model year, drastically below predictions. This would be the final season for Bobcat and Monarch, which would be replaced by the new Lynx and revised Cougar. Bobcat was the slowest- selling Mercury model this year, with Monarch a close second. Sales of both dropped substantially. Plenty of leftover Monarchs remained when the new model year began. Best seller this year was the Zephyr, which found 85,946 buyers. Both sales and production fell sharply for the calendar year, down around 40 percent. Only four Mercury models were expected to reach or exceed the EPA's gas mileage standard, now 20 MPG. Mercury was still perceived as a big, heavy car, at a time when small, lightweight cars were taking over the market.

1981 MERCURY

The new Lynx and Cougar replaced Bobcat and Monarch, both of which had been selling poorly. Like Ford's Escort, Lynx was billed as a "world car." Two models got smaller base engines this year. Cougar XR7 dropped from the 255 cu. in. (4.2-liter) V-8 to a 200 cu. in. (3.3-liter) inline six, while Marquis went from a 5.0-liter V-8 down to 4.2 liters.

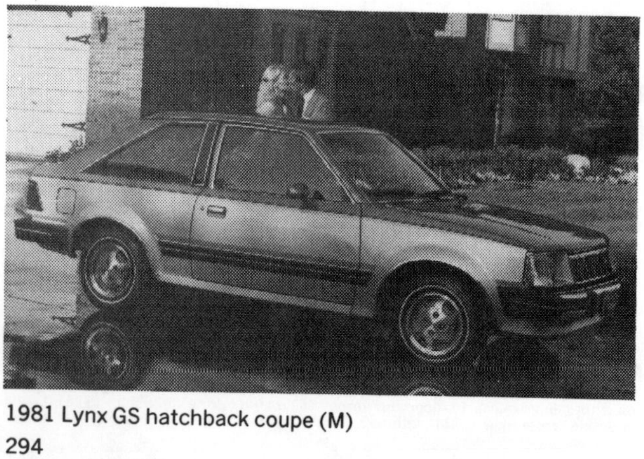

1981 Lynx GS hatchback coupe (M)

LYNX — FOUR — Heralding the coming trend toward front-wheel-drive was Mercury's new subcompact "world car," a close twin to Ford Escort. Lynx came in two models and five series: three-door hatchback and four-door liftgate wagon in standard, GL, GS or sporty RS; and with the Villager woodgrain option. The hatchback also came in a fifth, top-of-the-line LS series (a Lincoln-Mercury exclusive). Lynx had four-wheel fully independent suspension, a 97.6 cu. in. (1.6-liter) CVH (Compound Valve Hemispherical) engine, fully synchronized four-speed manual transaxle, and rack-and-pinion steering. Optional: a split-torque three- speed automatic transaxle. A smaller 1.3-liter engine was planned but abandoned. Front suspension consisted of MacPherson struts with strut-mounted coil springs, forged lower control arms, cast steering knuckle, and stabilizer bar. At the rear was an independent trailing-arm suspension with modified MacPherson struts and coil springs on stamped lower control arms. Both Escort and Lynx were designed for easy (and minimal) servicing. Many parts were secured with simple fasteners, including the radiator, fan shroud, oil pan, front fenders, bumpers, grilles, and doors. It was supposed to be easy to replace the battery, headlamps, and exhaust system. Fuses and most bulbs could be replaced without tools. The tight crosshatch-patterned grille was divided into six side-by-side sections by bright vertical bars. Clear wraparound park/signal lamps were outboard of the single rectangular halogen headlamps, which sat within argent housings. Styling included long black front/rear bumper end caps, standard semi-styled steel wheels with white trim rings, bodyside accent striping, and matte black rocker panel paint. Three-doors had high-gloss black center roof pillar appliques and wraparound horizontal taillamps. Four-doors had brushed aluminum center roof pillar appliques. Standard Lynx models had bright wheel lip, window frame, beltline and drip moldings; forward-folding rear bench seat; lighter; day/night mirror; AM radio; and P155/80R13 SBR blackwall tires with European-type wraparound tread patterns. Standard high-back front bucket seats had vinyl upholstery. Options included reclining high- or low-back bucket seats, console with graphic warning display, speed control, premium sound, digital clock, manual pivoting front vent windows, rear wiper/washer, and cast aluminum spoked wheels. Lynx GL added a black air dam, black bumper rub strips with argent accent stripe (front and rear), wide bodyside molding with argent accent stripe, GL badge on hatch or liftgate, and reclining high-back front bucket seats. GL three-door hatchbacks had a black lower back panel surround molding, and both models deleted the matte black rocker panel paint. Lynx GS had front and rear black rubber bumper guards and rub strips, reclining low-back bucket seats, cloth/vinyl seat trim, console with graphic warning display, full instrumentation, GS badge on hatch or liftgate, P165/80R13 SBR BSW tires, intermittent wipers, headlamps-on warning buzzer, and glovebox lock. Two-color upper bodyside accent striping replaced the standard single color. GS also had fully styled steel wheels with bright trim rings, argent hub covers and bright wheel nuts, and dual color-keyed remote mirrors. Lynx RS had a blackout grille with bright 'Mercury' plaque, black bumpers with black rub strip and argent accent stripe, black headlamp housings and windshield molding, and black air dam. Special RS accent stripe/decal treatment replaced the standard upper bodyside accent stripe. RS also had black dual remote mirrors, and blackout treatment on the 'B' pillar applique, 'C' pillar applique, drip and belt moldings, wheel lip moldings, door window frame and quarter window moldings. An RS badge went on the hatch or liftgate. RS also included a handling suspension with larger front stabilizer bar, heavy-duty shocks and stiffer springs, plus P165/80R13 blackwalls. Inside were high-back reclining front bucket seats and a console with graphic warning display. Top-line LS hatchbacks offered all the GS features, plus two-tone paint (four combinations available), hatch accent stripe, pleated velour seat trim, electric rear defroster, AM/FM stereo radio, and burled walnut woodtone appliques on the dash, radio panel and console.

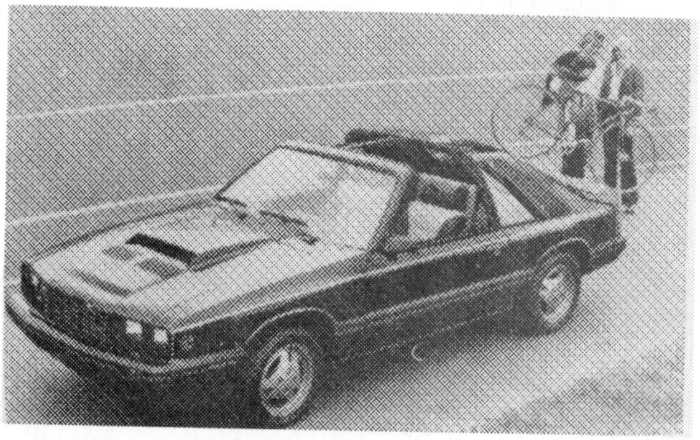

1981 Capri TRX T-Top coupe (JG)

CAPRI — FOUR/SIX/V-8 — Five possibilities greeted Capri customers this year: the base or GS model, RS option, Turbo RS, and Black Magic option. GS replaced the former Ghia. Five-speed manual overdrive became available with either the standard or turbo four-cylinder engine. For 1981, the 200 cu. in. inline six was available with standard four-speed manual overdrive transmission, as well as the optional automatic. Power brakes were now standard, along with 14 in. tires and wheels, and turbine wheel covers. Sport wheel covers were a no-cost option. An AM radio also was standard. New options included a Traction-Lok rear axle and power windows. An optional TRoof came with two removable tinted glass panels. Capri again displayed a black and bright horizontal grille theme with bright headlamp frames, color-keyed hood louvers, black cowl louvers, and black wiper arms. Standard equipment included the 140 cu. in. (2.3-liter) four and four- speed manual shift, and P175/75R14 SBR BSW tires. Powertrain choices included an inline 200 cu. in. (3.3-liter) six, and 255 cu. in. (4.2-liter) V-8, along with the turbo four. Turbos came only with manual shift, V-8s only with automatic. Both the V-8 and turbo had a dual bright tailpipe extension. Capri GS added black dual remote control mirrors, a light group, door map pocket, and four-spoke steering wheel with woodtone insert and GS badge. RS had a large (non-functional) hood scoop; black grille; black headlamp frames and windshield molding; dual black remote mirrors; upper bodyside dual accent stripe (which meant deleting the customary pinstripes); black window frame moldings; and black rear spoiler. RS also included a handling suspension, leather-wrapped steering wheel, and simulated engine-turned instrument panel. Turbo RS models were identified by 'Turbo RS' tape on the front fender, and a bright Turbo plaque on the hood scoop. They also featured a sport-tuned exhaust, three-spoke 15.3 inch forged aluminum wheels, 8000 R.P.M. tachometer, and Rally suspension. Black Magic sported black or white paint with gold accents. The option package included a smallish body-color hood scoop, gold paint on the grille's leading edge, body- color rear spoiler, and Rally suspension. Gold bodyside accent stripes replaced the standard upper bodyside pinstripes. Also included: black bodyside moldings with gold accent stripes; blackout window frame moldings; spoiler; and gold license plate frames. White cars with this option had white taillamp accents and quarter louvers. Black Magic also had Michelin TRX low-profile tires and three-spoke 15.3 inch forged metric aluminum wheels with gold-color finish. Inside were black engine-turned cluster, radio and right-hand appliques. Black vinyl seat trim had gold-color cloth inserts. Black Magic and Turbo models carried TRX 190/65R390 tires.

1981 Zephyr Z-7 Sports Coupe (M)

ZEPHYR — FOUR/SIX/V-8 — Not much changed in Zephyr's appearance, but new standard equipment included power (front disc/rear drum) brakes, narrow protective bodyside moldings, and deluxe sound insulation. A new GS option replaced the former Ghia, available on all except the base wagon. Traction-Lok was now available with the V-8. Inline sixes now required automatic. Also made standard: a glovebox lock and dual-note horn. Zephyr's gas tank grew to 16 gallons except for the four- cylinder, which stayed at 14. Low-back front bucket seats with pleated vinyl trim were standard on all models. Also standard: AM radio, day/night inside mirror, cigar lighter, rear ashtray, and right-hand visor vanity mirror. New options included a console, illuminated entry, and Michelin TRX tires on forged aluminum wheels. Base Zephyr sedans had dual front fender louvers, bright lower bodyside moldings with black vinyl insert, upper bodyside dual accent stripes, and front bumper guards. The vertical-theme grille was made up of thin vertical bars in a uniform pattern (no wider divider bar at any point). Quad rectangular headlamps stood over amber quad rectangular parking lamps. Low-back bucket seats had pleated vinyl trim. Zephyr's Z7 Sport Coupe retained its contemporary wrapover roof design, wraparound taillamps, and upper bodyside accent striping that continued over the roof. A Z-7 ornament was on the center pillar. It had no rocker panel moldings. Standard equipment included tinted rear window glass. Zephyr's GS option added dual accent stripes on the hood, rear quarter window moldings, protective bodyside moldings with integral partial wheel lip moldings, dual bright remote mirrors, and GS decklid badge. Both police and taxi packages were available.

1981 Cougar GS sedan (M)

COUGAR — FOUR/SIX/V-8 — Whereas the 1980 lineup had included only a Cougar XR7, basic Cougars returned this year in the form of a new mid-size five-passenger model, to replace the former Monarch. Two- and four-door sedans were offered, over 3.5 inches narrower than Monarch, but with more hip room in front and rear. Three trim levels were available: base, GS and LS (the latter actually option packages, not separate models). Base engine was now a 140 cu. in. (2.3-liter) four with four-speed manual gearbox. Standard tires: P175/75R14 SBR. The hybrid MacPherson strut front suspension placed the coil spring on the lower arm. At the rear: a four-bar link coil spring system. Rack-and-pinion steering with variable-ratio power assist was standard. Manual gearboxes had a self-adjusting clutch. Four-cylinder powered, the new Cougar managed an EPA estimate of 23 MPG (city), as opposed to just 19 for the six-cylinder Monarch it replaced. It also displayed a bit more aerodynamic styling. Cougar sedans had a bright grille with surround molding, made up of very thin vertical bars and a wider center bar, plus three subdued horizontal strips. Quad rectangular halogen headlamps stood in bright housings. Park/turn signal lamps were bumper-mounted. Body features included a Cougar hood ornament, bright bumper with flexible black end caps (front guards standard), bright windshield molding, wide lower bodyside molding with black tape insert and integral partial wheel lip moldings, and full-width wraparound taillamps with integral backups. A Cougar medallion went on the roof pillar, and there was a brushed center pillar applique as well as a color-keyed rear pillar louver applique. Low-back bucket seats were all-vinyl upholstery. A four-spoke color-keyed steering wheel and AM radio were standard. Basic equipment also included interval wipers, power brakes, dual-note horn, locking glovebox, visor vanity mirror, lighter, trunk mat, hood ornament, full wheel covers, and driver's remote mirror. A 200 cu. in. (3.3-liter) inline six and 255 cu. in. (4.2-liter) V-8 were optional, as was automatic transmission. Cougar GS added such items as hood/bodyside accent stripes, bumper rub strips with white accent stripes, lower bodyside molding with color-keyed vinyl insert, GS badge on front fender, rear bumper guards, upgraded vinyl bucket seat trim, and four-spoke steering wheel with woodtone insert. Cougar LS was available only as a four-door, including ribbed vinyl-insert color-keyed bodyside moldings, a rear half-vinyl roof with color-keyed back window molding, and special bright wheel lip moldings. Also on LS: special bodyside accent stripe, luxury wheel covers, bright passenger remote mirror, LS fender badge, Twin Comfort lounge front seats, cornering lamps, and a light group.

COUGAR XR-7 — SIX/V-8 — After years of V-8 power, XR7 dropped down to an inline six as standard engine. Both 255 cu. in. and 302 cu. in. V-8s were optional, however. Automatic overdrive transmission (introduced in 1980) was now available with both V-8s. The gas tank grew to 18 gallons. New options included puncture-resistant self-sealing tires, Traction-Lok, and pivoting vent windows. Options also

1981 Cougar XR-7 Sports Coupe (M)

included a flip-up removable glass moonroof and keyless entry. Appearance changes included a standard wide bodyside molding with color-keyed vinyl insert, and a wide bright/black belt molding that framed the lower edge of the door and quarter glass. The accent stripe was raised to belt level. Quarter window louvers were removed. The grille and bumper were revised, but still a vertical-bar grille style with bright surround molding. The color-keyed soft bumper covering had a bright insert. Bright rear moldings replaced the "frenched" window design. At the rear was a new standard decklid stripe, plus revised large vertical-theme taillamps (with integral backup lenses) and ornamentation. Later in the season, the vinyl roof wrapover molding was moved forward. New standard equipment included power brakes and variable-ratio power steering. Also standard: the 200 cu. in. (3.3-liter) inline six with automatic transmission, P195/75R14 SBR BSW tires, AM radio, dual-note horn, mini spare tire, halogen headlamps, stand-up hood ornament, upper bodyside paint stripe, analog clock, and half-vinyl roof with black belt molding. XR-7's GS option included hood accent stripes, bright right-hand remote mirror, Twin Comfort lounge seats, woodgrain steering wheel, and luxury wheel covers. LS added power windows and luxury interior trim, as well as door pull straps and electronic seatbelt warning chimes.

1981 Grand Marquis sedan (AA)

MARQUIS — V-8 — A new 255 cu. in. (4.2-liter) V-8, derived from the 302, was standard on base and Brougham Marquis this year. The 302 remained standard on Grand Marquis and on both wagons. The 255 came with automatic overdrive transmission, introduced for 1980 and made standard on all Marquis models for '81. Nine new paint colors were offered, with five new two-tones and three new vinyl roof colors. Among the new options were puncture-resistant self-sealing tires. The optional premium sound system added two more door-mount speakers, making six in all. A high-output 351 cu. in. (5.8-liter) V-8 was available with optional trailer towing or police packages. Tinted glass had become standard on the wagon's tailgate window in mid-year 1980. So had an AM radio on the base sedan and wagon; AM/FM on Brougham, Grand Marquis and Colony Park. For 1981, P205/75R14 SBR whitewalls were standard on all Marquis, and a coach roof on Brougham and Grand Marquis. Rear bumper guards were now standard on Grand Marquis. Appearance was similar to 1980, with a bright vertical- bar grille and quad rectangular halogen headlamps within bright headlamp/parking lamp surround moldings. Front bumper guards and a stand-up hood ornament were standard. Wraparound parking lamps had integral side markers, as did the horizontal wraparound taillamps. Twin fender louvers decorated each side of the car. Marquis Brougham added hood accent stripes, a coach vinyl roof, coach lamps, Brougham decklid nameplate, wide bright lower bodyside molding with quarter panel extensions, deluxe wheel covers, and power windows. The AM/FM stereo had two rear speakers. Twin Comfort lounge seats came in Brougham cloth and vinyl trim. Grand Marquis included tinted glass, wide bright/black lower bodyside molding, upper bodyside accent stripes, black rocker panel flanges, accent stripes on fender louvers, and rear bumper guards. Twin Comfort lounge seats were luxury cloth with dual center folding armrests. The Grand Marquis nameplate went on the rear roof pillar and decklid.

I.D. DATA: Mercury had a new 17-symbol Vehicle Identification Number (VIN), again stamped on a metal tab fastened to the instrument panel, visible through the windshield. Symbols one to three indicate manufacturer, make and vehicle type: '1ME' Mercury passenger car. The fourth symbol ('B') denotes restraint system. Next comes a letter 'P', followed by two digits that indicate body type: Model Number, as shown in left column of tables below. (Example: '31' Zephyr two-door sedan.) Symbol eight indicates engine type: '2' L498 2Bbl.; 'A' L4-140 2Bbl.; 'A' Turbo L4140 2Bbl.; 'B' or 'T' L6200 1Bbl.; 'D' V8255 2Bbl.; 'F' V8302 2Bbl.; 'G' V8351 2Bbl. Next is a check digit. Symbol ten indicates model year ('B' 1981). Symbol eleven is assembly plant: 'A' Atlanta, GA; 'F' Dearborn, MI; 'R' San Jose, CA; 'G' Chicago; 'H' Lorain, Ohio; 'K' Kansas City, MO; 'X' St. Thomas, Ontario; 'T' Metuchen, NJ; 'Z' St. Louis, MO; 'W' Wayne, MI. The final six digits make up the sequence number, starting with 600,001. A Vehicle Certification Label on the left front door lock face panel or door pillar shows the manufacturer, month and year of manufacture, GVW, GAWR, certification statement, VIN, and codes for such items as body type, color, trim, axle, transmission, and special order information.

295

LYNX (FOUR)

Model Number	Body/Style Number	Body Type & Seating	Factory Price	Shipping Weight	Production Total
63	61D	3-dr. Hatch-4P	5603	N/A	Note 1
65	74D	4-dr. Lift-4P	5931	N/A	Note 1
63	61D	3-dr. L Hatch-4P	5665	1935	Note 1
65	74D	4-dr. L Lift-4P	6070	2059	Note 1
63/60Z	61D	3-dr. GL Hatch-4P	5903	1957	Note 1
65/60Z	74D	4-dr. GL Lift-4P	6235	2074	Note 1
63/602	61D	3-dr. GS Hatch-4P	6642	1996	Note 1
65/602	74D	4-dr. GS Lift-4P	6914	2114	Note 1
63/603	61D	3-dr. LS Hatch-4P	7127	2004	Note 1
63/936	61D	3-dr. RS Hatch-4P	6223	1980	Note 1
65/936	74D	4-dr. RS Lift-4P	6563	2098	Note 1

Note 1: Total Lynx production, 72,786 three-door hatchbacks and 39,192 four-door liftgate models.

CAPRI (FOUR/SIX)

67	61D	3-dr. Fastbk-4P	6685/6898	2576/2603	51,786

CAPRI GS (FOUR/SIX)

68	61H	3-dr. Fastbk-4P	6867/7080	2623/2650	7,160

Capri Engine Note: A V-8 engine cost $50 more than the six.

1981 Zephyr Villager station wagon (JG)

ZEPHYR (FOUR/SIX)

70	66D	2-dr. Sed-5P	6103/6316	2532/2585	5,814
N/A	66D	2-dr. S Sed-5P	5769/5982	N/A	N/A
71	54D	4-dr. Sed-5P	6222/6435	2597/2650	34,334
73	74D	4-dr. Sta Wag-5P	6458/6671	2672/2725	16,283

ZEPHYR Z-7 (FOUR/SIX)

72	36R	2-dr. Spt Cpe-5P	6252/6465	2584/2637	10,078

COUGAR (FOUR/SIX)

76	66D	2-dr. Sedan-5P	6535/6748	2682/2772	10,793
77	54D	4-dr. Sedan-5P	6694/6907	2726/2816	42,860

Zephyr/Cougar Engine Note: A 255 cu. in. V-8 engine cost $50 more than the six.

COUGAR XR-7 (SIX/V-8)

90	66D	2-dr. HT Cpe-4P	7799/7849	3000/3137	37,275

R-7 Engine Note: Price shown is for 255 cu. in. V-8; a 302 V-8 cost $41 more.

MARQUIS (V-8)

81	54H	4-dr. Sedan-6P	7811	3493	10,392
87	74H	4-dr. 2S Sta Wag-6P	8309	3745	2,219

MARQUIS BROUGHAM (V-8)

82	66K	2-dr. Sedan-6P	8601	3513	2,942
83	54K	4-dr. Sedan-6P	8800	3564	11,744

MARQUIS COLONY PARK (V-8)

88	74K	4-dr. 2S Sta Wag-6P	9304	3800	6,293

GRAND MARQUIS (V-8)

84	66L	2-dr. Sedan-6P	9228	3533	4,268
85	54L	4-dr. Sedan-6P	9459	3564	23,780

FACTORY PRICE AND WEIGHT NOTE: Cougar XR7 prices and weights to left of slash are for six-cylinder, to right for V-8 engine. For Capri, Zephyr and Cougar, prices/weights to left of slash are for four-cylinder, to right for V-6.

ENGINE DATA: BASE FOUR (Lynx): Inline. Overhead cam. Four-cylinder. Cast iron block and aluminum head. Displacement: 97.6 cu. in. (1.6 liters). Bore & stroke: 3.15 x 3.13 in. Compression ratio: 8.8:1. Brake horsepower: 65 at 5200 R.P.M. Torque: 85 lbs.-ft. at 3000 R.P.M. Five main bearings. Hydraulic valve lifters. Carburetor: 2Bbl. Holley-Weber 5740. VIN Code: 2. **BASE FOUR (Capri, Zephyr, Cougar):** Inline. Overhead cam. Four-cylinder. Cast iron block and head. Displacement: 140 cu. in. (2.3 liters). Bore & stroke: 3.78 x 3.13 in. Compression ratio: 9.0:1. Brake horsepower: 88 at 4600 R.P.M. Torque: 118 lbs.-ft. at 2600 R.P.M. Five main bearings. Hydraulic valve lifters. Carburetor: 2Bbl. Holley 6500. VIN Code: A. **OPTIONAL TURBOCHARGED FOUR (Capri):** Same as 140 cu. in. four above, but with turbocharger Horsepower: N/A. Torque: N/A. Carburetor: 2Bbl. VIN Code: A. **BASE SIX (XR7); OPTIONAL (Capri, Zephyr, Cougar):** Inline. OHV. Six-cylinder. Cast iron block and head. Displacement: 200 cu. in. (3.3 liters). Bore & stroke: 3.68 x 3.13 in. Compression ratio: 8.6:1. Brake horsepower: 88-94 at 3800-4000 R.P.M. Torque: 154-158 lbs.-ft. at 1400 R.P.M. Seven main bearings. Hydraulic valve lifters. Carburetor: 1Bbl. Holley 1946. VIN Code: B or T. **BASE V-8 (Marquis); OPTIONAL (Capri, Zephyr, Cougar):** 90-degree, overhead valve V-8. Cast iron block and head. Displacement: 255 cu. in. (4.2 liters). Bore & stroke: 3.68 x 3.00 in. Compression ratio: 8.8:1. Brake horsepower: 115-120 at 3100-3400 R.P.M. Torque: 195-205 lbs.-ft. at 2000-2600 R.P.M. Five main bearings. Hydraulic valve lifters. Carburetor: 2Bbl. Motorcraft 2150 or 7200VV. VIN Code: D. **OPTIONAL V-8 (XR7, Marquis):** 90-degree, overhead valve V-8. Cast iron block and head. Displacement: 302 cu. in. (5.0 liters). Bore & stroke: 4.00 x 3.00 in. Compression ratio: 8.4:1. Brake horsepower: 130 at 3400 R.P.M. Torque: 235 lbs.-ft. at 1600 R.P.M. Five main bearings. Hydraulic valve lifters. Carburetor: 2Bbl. Motorcraft 2150 or 2700VV. VIN Code: F. **OPTIONAL V-8 (Marquis):** 90-degree, overhead valve V-8. Cast iron block and head. Displacement: 351 cu. in. (5.8 liters). Bore & stroke: 4.00 x 3.50 in. Compression ratio: 8.3:1. Brake horsepower: 145 at 3200 R.P.M. Torque: 270 lbs.-ft. at 1800 R.P.M. Five main bearings. Hydraulic valve lifters. Carburetor: 2Bbl. Motorcraft 7200VV. VIN Code: G.

NOTE: A police version of the 351 V-8 was available, rated 165 horsepower at 3600 R.P.M. and 285 lbs.-ft. at 2200 R.P.M.

CHASSIS DATA: Wheelbase: (Lynx) 94.2 in.; (Capri) 100.4 in.; (Zephyr) 105.5 in.; (Cougar) 105.5 in.; (XR7) 108.4 in.; (Marquis) 114.3 in. Overall Length: (Lynx) 163.9 in.; (Lynx lift) 165.0 in.; (Capri) 179.1 in.; (Zephyr) 195.5 in.; (Z7) 197.4 in.; (Cougar) 196.5 in.; (XR7) 200.4 in.; (Marquis) 212.3 in.; (Marquis wag) 218.0 in. Height: (Lynx) 53.3 in.; (Capri) 51.4 in.; (Zephyr) 52.9 in.; (Zephyr wag) 54.2 in.; (Z7) 51.7 in.; (Cougar) 53.0 in.; (XR7) 53.2 in.; (Marquis) 54.7 in.; (Marquis wag) 57.4 in. Width: (Lynx) 65.9 in.; (Capri) 69.1 in.; (Zephyr) 71.0 in.; (Cougar) 68.7 in.; (XR7) 74.1 in.; (Marquis) 77.5 in.; (Marquis wag) 79.3 in. Front Tread: (Lynx) 54.7 in.; (Capri) 56.6 in.; (Zephyr/Cougar) 56.6 in.; (XR7) 58.1 in.; (Marquis) 62.2 in. Rear Tread: (Lynx) 56.0 in.; (Capri) 57.0 in.; (Zephyr/Cougar) 57.0 in.; (XR7) 57.0 in.; (Marquis) 62.0 in. Standard Tires: (Lynx) P155/80R13; (Capri) P175/75R14; (Capri turbo) TRX 190/65R390. (Zephyr/Cougar) P175/75R14 SBR; (XR7) P195/75R14 SBR BSW; (Marquis) P205/75R14 SBR; (Marquis wag) P215/75R14.

TECHNICAL: Transmission: Four-speed manual standard on Lynx. Gear ratios: (1st) 3.58:1; (2nd) 2.05:1; (3rd) 1.21:1; (4th) 0.81:1; (Rev) 3.46:1. Four-speed floor shift standard on Capri/Zephyr/Cougar four: (1st) 3.98:1; (2nd) 2.14:1; (3rd) 1.42:1; (4th) 1.00:1; (Rev) 3.99:1. Four-speed overdrive floor shift standard on Capri six: (1st) 3.29:1; (2nd) 1.84:1; (3rd) 1.00:1; (4th) 0.81:1; (Rev) 3.29:1. Capri turbo four-speed: (1st) 4.07:1; (2nd) 2.57:1; (3rd) 1.66:1; (4th) 1.00:1; (Rev) 3.95:1. Capri five-speed: (1st) 4.05:1; (2nd) 2.43:1; (3rd) 1.48:1; (4th) 1.00:1; (5th) 0.82:1; (Rev) 3.90:1. Capri turbo five-speed: (1st) 3.72:1; (2nd) 2.23:1; (3rd) 1.48:1; (4th) 1.00:1; (5th) 0.76:1; (Rev) 3.59:1. Select-Shift three-speed automatic standard on XR7, optional on others. Gear ratios: (1st) 2.46:1 or 2.47:1; (2nd) 1.46:1 or 1.47:1; (3rd) 1.00:1; (Rev) 2.11:1 to 2.19:1. Lynx three-speed automatic: (1st) 2.80:1; (2nd) 1.60:1; (3rd) 1.00:1; (Rev) 1.97:1. Four-speed overdrive automatic on XR7/Marquis: (1st) 2.40:1; (2nd) 1.47:1; (3rd) 1.00:1; (4th) 0.67:1; (Rev) 2.00:1. Standard final drive ratio: (Lynx) 3.59:1 w/4spd, 3.31:1 w/auto.; (Capri four/turbo) 3.08:1 w/4spd, 3.45:1 w/5spd; (Capri six) 3.08:1 w/4spd, 2.73:1 w/5spd; (Capri V-8) 2.26:1; (Zephyr) 3.08:1 exc. 2.73:1 w/six, 2.26:1 w/V-8; (Cougar) 2.73:1 w/six, 2.26:1 w/V8255 and auto., 3.08:1 w/V-8 and 4-spd auto.; (Marquis) 3.08:1 exc. 2.73:1 w/high-output 351 V-8 and 4spd auto. Steering: (Marquis) recirculating ball; (others) rack and pinion. Front Suspension: (Lynx) MacPherson strut-mounted coil springs w/lower control arms and stabilizer bar; (Capri) modified MacPherson struts w/coil springs and anti-sway bar; (Zephyr/Cougar) MacPherson struts w/coil springs mounted on lower control arm and anti-sway bar; (Marquis) coil springs with long/short Aarms and stabilizer bar. Rear Suspension: (Lynx) independent trailing arms w/modified MacPherson struts and coil springs on lower control arms; (Capri/Zephyr/Cougar/Marquis) four-link w/coil springs; (XR7) four-link with coil springs and anti-sway bar. Brakes: Front disc, rear drum. Ignition: Electronic. Body construction: (Marquis) separate body and frame; (others) unibody. Fuel tank: (Lynx) 10 gal.; (Capri) 12.5 gal.; (Zephyr) 16 gal. exc. 14 gal. w/four; (Cougar) 16 gal.; (XR7) 18 gal.; (Marquis) 19 gal. exc. wagon, 20 gal.

DRIVETRAIN OPTIONS: Engines: Turbo 140 cu. in. four: Capri ($610). 200 cu. in. six: Capri/Zephyr/Cougar ($213). 255 cu. in. V-8: Capri/Zephyr/Cougar ($263); XR7 ($50). 302 cu. in. V-8: Cougar XR7 ($91); Marquis ($41). 351 cu. in. V-8: Marquis ($83); Grand Marquis 4dr., wagon ($41). H.O. 351 cu. in. V-8: Marquis ($139-$180). Sport-tuned exhaust: Capri ($39). Transmission/Differential: Five-speed manual trans.: Capri ($152). Automatic transaxle: Lynx ($344). Select-shift auto. trans.: Capri/Zephyr/Cougar ($349). Four-speed overdrive automatic trans.: Cougar XR7 ($162). Floor shift lever: Zephyr/Cougar ($43). Traction-Lok differential: Capri/Zephyr/Cougar/XR7 ($67); Marquis ($71). Brakes & Steering: Power brakes: Lynx ($79). Power steering: Capri ($163); Zephyr ($168); Cougar ($161). Suspension: H.D. susp.: Marquis ($22); Cougar XR7 ($23). Handling susp.: Lynx ($37); Zephyr ($45); Capri/Marquis ($43). Load levelers: Marquis ($57). Other: H.D. battery ($20). Extended-range gas tank: Lynx ($32). Engine block heater ($16). Trailer towing pkg., heavy duty: Marquis ($176-$206). California emission system ($46). High-altitude option ($35-$36).

LYNX CONVENIENCE/APPEARANCE OPTIONS: Option Packages: Villager woodtone option: GL/GS ($224). Appearance protection group ($49). Light group ($39). Comfort/Convenience: Air conditioner ($530). Rear defroster, electric ($102). Fingertip speed control ($132); windshield only ($28). Tinted glass ($70); windshield only ($28). Intermittent wipers ($41). Rear wiper/washer ($100). Dual remote sport mirrors ($56). Entertainment: AM/FM radio ($63). AM/FM stereo radio ($100); w/cassette player ($87-$187). Dual rear speakers ($37). Premium sound ($91). AM radio delete ($61 credit). Exterior: Flip-up/open air roof ($154-$228). Glamour paint ($45). Tu-tone paint ($91). Front vent windows, pivoting ($55). Vinyl-insert bodyside

moldings ($41). Bumper guards, front or rear ($23). Bumper rub strips ($34). Roof luggage rack ($74). Roof air deflector ($26). Lower bodyside protection ($60). Interior: Console ($98). Low-back reclining bucket seats ($30). Reclining front seatbacks ($55). Cloth/vinyl seat trim ($28); vinyl (NC). Deluxe seatbelts ($23). Wheels/Tires: Cast aluminum spoke wheels ($193-$279). P155/80R13 WSW ($55). P165/80R13 BSW ($19); WSW ($55-$74).

CAPRI CONVENIENCE/APPEARANCE OPTIONS: Option Packages: Black magic option ($644). RS option ($234). Turbo RS option ($1191). Light group ($43). Appearance protection group ($41). Comfort/Convenience: Air cond. ($560). Rear defroster, electric ($107). Fingertip speed control ($132). Power windows ($140). Power door locks ($93). Tinted glass ($76). Leather-wrapped steering wheel ($49). Tilt steering wheel ($80-$93). Interval wipers ($41). Rear wiper/washer ($85). Right remote mirror ($37). Entertainment: AM/FM radio ($51). AM/FM stereo radio ($88); w/8track tape player ($162); w/cassette player ($174). Premium sound system ($91). Dual rear speakers ($37). Radio flexibility option ($61). AM radio delete ($61 credit). Exterior: TRoof ($874). Flip-up/open air roof ($213-$228). Glamour paint ($48). Tu-tone paint ($57-$110). Gold accent stripes ($54). Liftgate louvers ($145). Rocker panel moldings ($30). Roof luggage rack ($90). Mud/stone deflectors ($26). Lower bodyside protection ($37). Interior: Console ($168). Recaro bucket seats ($610). Accent cloth/vinyl seat trim ($22). Leather/vinyl seat trim ($359). Front floor mats ($18). Wheels and Tires: Wire wheel covers ($80). Sport wheel covers (NC). Forged metric aluminum wheels ($340). Cast aluminum wheels ($305). Styled steel wheels w/trim rings ($63). P175/75R14 WSW ($55). P185/75R14 BSW (N/A); WSW ($82); RWL ($102). TR 190/65Rx390 BSW ($128).

ZEPHYR CONVENIENCE/APPEARANCE OPTIONS: Option Packages: Villager option ($229). GS option ($327- $383). Instrument cluster ($88). Appearance protection group ($50). Light group ($43). Comfort/Convenience: Air cond. ($585). Rear defroster, electric ($107). Fingertip speed control (N/A). Illuminated entry ($60). Power windows ($140-$195). Power door locks ($93-$132). Remote decklid release ($27). Power seat ($122). Tinted glass ($76). Leather-wrapped steering wheel ($49). Tilt steering ($80-$93). Electric clock ($23). Interval wipers ($41). Rear wiper/washer: wag ($110). Lighting and Mirrors: Dual-beam map light ($13). Trunk light ($6). Left remote mirror ($15). Dual remote mirrors ($55). Lighted visor vanity mirror ($43). Entertainment: AM/FM radio ($51). AM/FM stereo radio ($88); w/8track player ($162); w/cassette player ($174). Twin rear speakers ($37). Premium sound system ($91). Radio flexibility ($61). AM radio delete ($61 credit). Exterior: Flip-up/open air roof (N/A). Full vinyl roof ($115). Glamour paint ($55). Tu-tone paint ($90-$110). Pivoting front vent windows ($55). Tailgate assist handle: wag ($16). Wide vinyl bodyside moldings: Z7 ($55). Rocker panel moldings ($30). Bumper guards, rear ($23). Bumper rub strips ($43). Luggage rack: wagon ($90). Lower bodyside protection ($37-$49). Interior: Console ($168). Bench seat ($24 credit). Cloth/vinyl seat trim ($28). Vinyl trim: Z7 ($26). Front floor mats ($18). Locking storage box ($24). Deluxe seatbelts ($23). Wheels/Tires: Wire wheel covers ($117). Styled steel wheels ($48); w/trim rings ($94). P175/75R14 WSW ($55). P185/75R14 WSW ($86). TR 190/65R390 BSW on TRX alum. wheels ($512). Conventional spare ($39).

COUGAR CONVENIENCE/APPEARANCE OPTIONS: Option Packages: GS option ($371). LS option ($972). Light group ($45). Cold weather group ($67). Appearance protection group ($45). Comfort/Convenience: Air cond. ($585). Rear defroster ($107). Fingertip speed control ($126). Illuminated entry system ($60). Six-way power twin comfort seats ($162). Four-way power flight bench seat ($122). Power windows ($140-$195). Power door locks ($93-$132). Remote decklid release ($27). Tinted glass ($76). Tilt steering wheel ($96). Electric clock ($23). Interval wipers ($41). Lighting and Mirrors: Cornering lamps ($51). Lighted right visor vanity mirror ($43). Entertainment: AM/FM radio ($51). AM/FM stereo radio ($88); w/8track player ($162); w/cassette ($174). Premium sound ($91). Dual rear speakers ($37). Radio flexibility ($61). AM radio delete ($61 credit). Exterior: Flip-up open-air roof ($228). Full or landau vinyl roof ($115). Glamour paint ($55). Tu-tone paint ($66-$162). Bodyside moldings ($45). Bumper rub strips ($41). Mud/stone deflectors ($26). Lower bodyside protection ($37). Interior: Console ($168). Twin comfort seats ($168). Cloth seat trim ($45-$62). Leather seat trim ($340). Deluxe seatbelts ($24). Wheels/Tires: Luxury wheel covers: base ($43). Wire wheel covers ($80-$124). Aluminum wheels ($306-$350). P175/75R14 WSW. P185/75R14 BSW/WSW/RWL. TR on aluminum wheels. Conventional spare.

COUGAR XR7 CONVENIENCE/APPEARANCE OPTIONS: Option Packages: LS option ($715). GS option ($320) exc. ($96) w/LS option. Appearance protection group ($45). Light group ($30). Power lock group ($120). Comfort/Convenience: Air cond. ($585); auto-temp ($652). Rear defroster ($107). Fingertip speed control ($105-$132). Illuminated entry system ($60). Keyless entry ($227). Garage door opener w/lighted vanity mirrors ($177). Autolamp on/off delay ($65). Tinted glass ($76). Power windows ($140). Four- way power seat ($122). Six-way power driver's seat ($173). Auto. parking brake release ($10). Leather-wrapped steering wheel ($45). Tilt steering wheel ($80). Electronic instrument cluster ($322). Diagnostic warning lights ($51). Seatbelt chimes ($23). Digital clock ($40). Interval wipers ($41). Lighting and Mirrors: Cornering lamps ($51). Remote right mirror ($52). Lighted right visor vanity mirror ($41). Entertainment: AM/FM radio ($51). AM/FM stereo radio ($88); w/8track player ($162); w/cassette ($174). AM/FM stereo search radio ($224); w/8track ($309); w/cassette ($321). Power antenna ($48). Dual rear speakers ($37). Premium sound system ($116-$146). Radio flexibility ($65). AM radio delete ($61 credit). Exterior: Carriage roof ($772). Flip-up/open-air roof ($228). Luxury rear vinyl half roof ($165). Vinyl roof delete ($130 credit). Glamour paint ($70). Tu-tone paint ($99). Hood paint stripes ($16). Pivoting front vent windows ($55). Rocker panel moldings ($30). Mud/stone deflectors ($26). Lower bodyside protection ($48). Interior: Bucket seats w/console ($182) exc. (NC) with GS/LS. Recaro bucket seats ($528). Twin comfort lounge seats w/recliners ($215). Leather seat trim ($359). Vinyl seat trim ($28). Front floor mats ($13). Trunk trim ($44). Wheels: Wire wheel covers ($93). Luxury wheel covers ($43).

MARQUIS CONVENIENCE/APPEARANCE OPTIONS: Option Packages: Grand Marquis decor: Colony Park ($491). Convenience group ($70-$101). Power lock group ($93-$176). Light group ($22-$37). Appearance protection group ($57). Comfort/Convenience: Air cond. ($624); w/auto-temp control ($687). Rear defroster, electric ($107). Fingertip speed control ($135). Illuminated entry system ($59). Power windows: base 4dr. ($211). Power seat ($173). Six-way power seats w/recliners ($229). Power twin comfort seats: base ($402). Tinted glass ($87). Autolamp on/off delay ($65). Leather-wrapped steering wheel ($45). Tilt steering wheel ($80). Electric clock ($23). Digital clock ($40-$63). Seatbelt chime ($23). Lighting and Mirrors: Cornering lamps ($49). Remote right mirror ($39). Lighted right visor vanity mirror ($38). Entertainment: AM/FM stereo radio ($88); w/8track tape player ($74) exc. base ($162); w/cassette ($87) exc. base ($174). AM/FM stereo search radio ($146) exc. base ($234); w/tape player ($233-$321). CB radio ($305). Power antenna ($48). Dual rear speakers ($37). Premium sound system ($116). Radio flexibility ($65). AM radio delete ($61 credit). Exterior: Coach vinyl roof: Brghm ($567). Full vinyl roof: base sed ($141). Glamour paint ($67). Tu-tone paint ($100-$134). Paint stripes ($34). Hood striping ($15). Pivoting front vent windows ($55). Rocker panel moldings: Colony Park ($27). Bodyside moldings ($44). Bumper rub strips ($46). Luggage rack: wag ($84). Lower bodyside protection ($46). Interior: Dual-facing rear seats: wagon ($146). Cloth twin comfort seats: wag ($39). Leather twin comfort seating ($361). Duraweave flight bench seats: wag ($54). Vinyl seat trim ($28). Deluxe seatbelts ($24). Trunk trim ($45). Wheels/Tires: Luxury wheel covers ($45-$72). Wire wheel covers ($112-$139). P215/75R14 WSW. P225/75R14 WSW. P205/75R15 WSW/puncture-resistant. Conventional spare.

HISTORY: Introduced: October 3, 1980. Model year production: 389,999. Calendar year production (U.S.): 363,970. Calendar year sales by U.S. dealers: 339,550. Model year sales by U.S. dealers: 354,335 (including 5,730 leftover Bobcats and 13,954 early '82 LN7 models).

Historical Footnotes: After a terrible 1980, the Lynx arrived to give Mercury new hope. First-year sales were heartening, totaling the highest figure since the Comet appeared back in 1960. Model year sales fell only slightly, as a result of the Lynx success. Calendar year sales and production both rose, as did model year production. Cougar XR7 scored far weaker and well below expectations, but the new smaller standard Cougar did better, finding many more buyers than it had a year earlier wearing a Monarch badge. Sales of the full-size Marquis fell, but not drastically. The new LN7, kin to Ford's EXP, debuted in April 1981 but as an early '82 model.

1982 MERCURY

A new four-door Lynx was introduced this year. So was a close-ratio manual transaxle option for both Lynx and the new LN7 two-seater, which arrived in April 1981. Cougar added a station wagon model, and an optional lightweight 232 cu. in. (3.8-liter) V-6 with aluminum heads and plastic rocker arms. Several models had a new lockup torque converter in the SelectShift automatic transmission. A high-output 302 cu. in. (5.0-liter) V-8 became standard on the Capri RS, optional on other Capris.

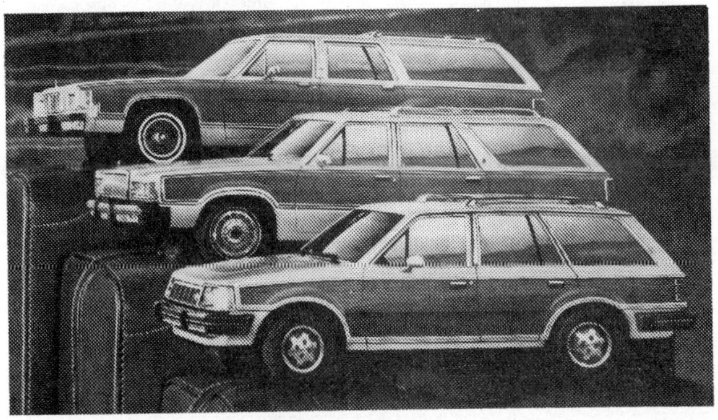

1982 Lynx GL Villager station wagon (JG)

LYNX — FOUR — A new five-door (actually four "people" doors) hatchback model joined the original two-door hatchback and four-door wagon, but appearance was the same as the original 1981 version. Lynx had quickly become Mercury's best seller. As for mileage, the EPA rating with the base 97.6 cu. in. (1.6- liter) four was 31 city and 47 highway. That CVH engine got a new reduced-restriction exhaust system. The gas tank grew to 11.3 gallons this year, and P165/80R13 tires replaced the former P155 size, but not much else changed. Not until mid- year, at any rate, when a number of mechanical improvements were announced. A high-output 1.6-liter engine was added to the option list in mid-year. So was a new sport close-ratio manual transaxle with higher numerical gear ratios in third and fourth gear, and smaller steps between second and third, and third and fourth. The H.O. powerplant had a higher-lift cam, less-restrictive muffler, stainless steel tubular exhaust header, less-restrictive air intake system, and larger carburetor venturi. Both engines came with a 3.59:1 drive axle ratio (3.31:1 with three-speed automatic).

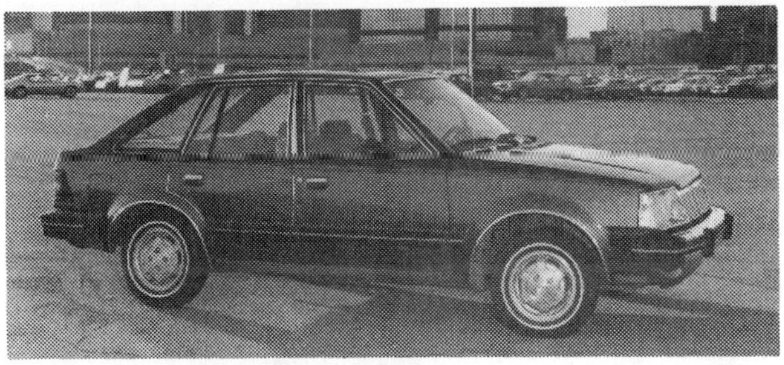

1982 Lynx LS hatchback sedan (M)

LN7 — FOUR — Even though Lynx was essentially a carryover this year, the two-seater derived from its basic chassis was brand new. Wearing a "bubbleback" third-door treatment, the LN7 coupe displayed an aerodynamic design with 0.34 drag coefficient. The front-wheel drive chassis had four-wheel, fully independent suspension. Powertrain was the same as Lynx: 1.6- liter Compound Valve Hemispherical (CVH) OHC engine with four-speed manual transaxle (overdrive fourth). Mechanically, LN7 was identical to Ford's new EXP. Mercury's version was considered the more radical of the pair, though, as a result of its large wraparound "bubbleback" back window. Both EXP and LN7 had sizable wheel lips, wide bodyside moldings, and steep windshield angle. Large sloped taillamps wrapped around to a point on each quarter panel. Single rectangular halogen headlamps sat in black "eyebrow" housings. Park/signal lamps were mounted below the bumper strip. The LN7 grille consisted of 10 small slots (in two rows) in a sloping body-color panel, versus just two on EXP. Wide black bodyside moldings had argent accent striping. So did the soft black front and rear bumpers. LN7 had dual black door-mounted remote sport mirrors, and a single-color dual bodyside paint stripe. The slotted front fascia held a cat-head ornament, while rear pillars were vertically-louvered. Black paint treatment went on the front pillar, quarter window frame, door frame, and rocker panels. An ample standard equipment list included power brakes, electric rear defroster, AM radio, full performance instrumentation, power liftgate release, self-adjusting clutch linkage, throaty tuned exhaust (with manual shift), interval wipers, and full tinted glass. LN7 also had bright exposed dual exhausts, reclining low-back bucket seats with vinyl trim, tachometer, trip odometer, and temperature gauge. A console held the ammeter, oil pressure gauge and other indicators. Tires were P165/80R13 blackwall steel-belted radials with European-type wraparound tread pattern, on styled steel wheels with trim rings.

1982 Capri L hatchback coupe (CP)

CAPRI — FOUR/SIX/V-8 — Changes in Mercury's variant of Mustang were mainly mechanical this year. Both the optional 200 cu. in. (3.3-liter) inline six with SelectShift automatic, and 255 cu. in. (4.2-liter) V-8, had a new lockup torque converter for the automatic transmission. A new powerteam also was available: the 302 cu. in. (5.0-liter) V-8 with four-speed manual overdrive. That high-output 5.0-liter V-8 had new camshaft timing, low-restriction air cleaner with dual air inlets, large-venturi carburetor, and low-restriction sporty-tuned exhaust. Five-speed manual overdrive with the base 140 cu. in. (2.3-liter) four-cylinder engine later became optional in 45 states. A new base series was added, so the prior base model with console was now Capri L. Selection consisted of base, L, GS, RS, and Black Magic models. This year's gas tank held 15.4 gallons. Flash-to-pass was added to the stalk, and the new screw-on gas cap had a tether. Rear pillar louvers were now body-colored, except for the RS, which had black ones. A console with graphic warning display was now standard on all except the base model. Base Capris had a black and bright horizontal-style grille, front and rear bumpers with color-keyed soft urethane cover, extra-wide wraparound black bodyside molding with dual color-keyed center stripes, turbine wheel covers, upper bodyside pinstripes, black driver's side remote mirror, black and bright window frames, black cowl louver, and color-keyed hood louvers. High-back bucket seats had reclining seatbacks and pleated vinyl trim. Tires were P175/75R14 SBR blackwalls. Capri L had low-back bucket seats, a passenger-side visor vanity mirror, upgraded door trim, console with graphic warning display, and 'L' badge. GS included dual black remote mirrors, 'GS' badge, light group, four-spoke steering wheel with woodtone insert, and driver's door map pocket. Capri RS had a large non-functional hood scoop, black grille, black headlamp frames and windshield molding, dual black remote mirrors, upper bodyside dual accent tape striping, 'RS' tape identification on front fender, black window frame moldings, rear spoiler, and black "third door" window molding. Several revisions hit the RS later on, including a '5.0' badge on the side, dual bright tailpipe outlets, and Rallye suspension with TR performance package replacing the original handling suspension. It also came with Traction-Lok axle, P185/75R14 blackwalls, and power steering. Capri's Black Magic was offered again, with either black or white body color and gold accents. It had a small body-color hood scoop, gold paint on leading edge of grille, and other gold and black trim. Black Magic included a gold cat's head on the fender, and gold license plate frame at the back. Also included: a body-color rear spoiler, Michelin TRX tires on forged metric aluminum wheels with gold-color finish, and rallye suspension. A fuel economy calibration option (with four-cylinder) was added, to attract the economy-minded buyer. It had a feedback fuel system, four-speed manual shift, and 2.73:1 axle (to replace the standard 3.08:1).

1982 Zephyr sedan (CP)

ZEPHYR — FOUR/SIX/V-8 — Not much was new on the Zephyr compact, but the two-door sedan and station wagon were dropped. That left only a two-door (Z7) sport coupe and four-door sedan. Both came in base or GS trim. A new locking torque converter was added to the automatic transmission with optional inline six and 255 cu. in. (4.2-liter) V-8. That V-8 was available only with police and taxi packages. There was a new tethered gas cap and new deep-well trunk design. Tires were P175/75R14 blackwalls. Sedan interiors were upgraded to Z7 level by adding luxury door trim panels, high-gloss woodtone instrument panel appliques, and color-keyed seatbelts. A fuel economy calibration version of the base 140 cu. in. (2.3-liter) four replaced the standard 3.08:1 axle with a 2.73:1, as a no-extra-cost option with restricted options list. It was supposed to deliver 40 MPG on the highway, 25 overall in EPA estimates. Z7 again had the wrapover roof design with broad center pillar and thin rear pillar, no rocker panel moldings, Z7 ornament on the center pillar, and wraparound taillamps. Also standard: tinted rear window glass. GS models had dual accent stripes on the hood, protective bodyside moldings with integral partial wheel lip moldings, a 'GS' badge on the decklid, and dual bright remote mirrors. Rocker panel moldings were deleted from the four-door sedan with GS option.

1982 Cougar LS sedan (CP)

COUGAR — SIX/V-6 — For its second season in this Monarch-based body style, Cougar added a new station wagon model and lost the prospect of V-8 power. Wagons came in either GS or Villager form; sedans were either GS or LS. GS was now the basic level. Passenger capacity increased from five to six, because of the new standard Flight bench seat. Base engine was now the 200 cu. in. (3.3-liter) inline six. SelectShift automatic with locking torque converter was now standard. Manual shift was dropped. An AM radio with dual speakers was now standard. A tether was added to the gas cap, and the tank grew to 16 gallons. Flash-to-pass was added later to the steering column stalk control, while 'GS' badges went on fenders. A rear bumper sight shield was added. Hood and bodyside accent stripes were now standard, along with color-keyed vinyl-insert bodyside moldings. Cougar had a unitized body, strut-type front suspension with spring on lower arm, variable-ratio power-assist rack-and-pinion steering, and four-bar link rear suspension. Cougar LS added unique hood accent stripes that extended across the grille opening panel; bumper rub strips with white accent stripes; ribbed vinyl color-keyed bodyside molding; special bright wheel lip moldings; rear bumper guards; and luxury wheel covers with cat's head center insert. 'LS' badges went on front fenders. LS also added Twin Comfort lounge seats, whereas the GS had a Flight bench seat. The GS station wagon had a bodyside paint stripe in a straight-through design with no kickup, which did not extend onto the liftgate. The Villager wagon deleted the hood accent stripes and had medium rosewood woodtone bodyside paneling appliques. 'Villager' script went on the liftgate and the 'GS' badge was deleted from front fenders. Options included an all-new 232 cu. in. (3.8-liter) V-6, power lock group, and extended-range fuel tank. Options dropped: the floor shifter, console, mud/stone deflectors, and radio flexibility.

1982 Cougar XR-7 Sports Coupe (CP)

COUGAR XR-7 — SIX/V-6/V-8 — No longer available on this year's personal-luxury XR7 was the 302 cu. in. V-8 engine. Three choices were offered, though: base 200 cu. in. (3.3-liter) inline six, new optional aluminum-head 232 cu. in. (3.8-liter) V-6, and 255 cu. in. (4.2-liter) V-8. The two-door hardtop body came in GS and upscale LS form, as the former base model dropped out. Gas tanks grew from 18 to 21 gallons. Four-speed automatic overdrive transmission was standard with the V-6 or V-8, while the base inline six had SelectShift three-speed automatic with a lockup torque converter clutch. Looking at appearance changes, black vinyl-insert bodyside moldings replaced the former color-keyed moldings. Black bumper stripes with white accent stripes replaced bright rub strips. A new half-vinyl roof design with wide black accent and wrapover molding arrived this year. That molding blended into the door belt moldings to give a unified look. The analog clock was now quartz-type. New options included a Tripminder computer. XR7 GS had a vertical-bar grille with bright surround molding, color-keyed soft bumper covering with black rub strips (including white accent stripes), quad rectangular halogen headlamps, amber wraparound park/signal lamps, hood/decklid accent stripes, and upper bodyside paint stripe. Large vertical-theme taillamps had integral backup lenses. Twin Comfort lounge seats had fold-down center armrests and dual recliners. Power brakes and variable-ratio rack-and-pinion steering were standard. Also standard: AM radio, halogen headlamps, and P195/75R14 SBR whitewalls. LS added dual bright remote window-frame-mounted mirrors and luxury wheel covers, plus power windows and tinted glass.

1982 Marquis Brougham sedan (CP)

MARQUIS — V-8 — Full-size Mercury models didn't look much different, but dropped their fender louvers. The former bumper-slot grille extensions were deleted too, replaced by slotless bumpers. Decklid lock covers were replaced with a bezel and ornament. A 302 cu. in. (5.0-liter) V-8 became standard on the Brougham and Grand Marquis four-door this year. Base engine on other models was the 255 cu. in. (4.2-liter) V-8. The 351 cu. in. high-output V-8 was now available only with the police package. All models had four-speed automatic overdrive transmission. AM radios now included two instrument-panel speakers. Electric clocks became quartz. The CB radio option was deleted, as were the radio flexibility option and manual load levelers. One noteworthy new option was a Tripminder computer, which had a multi-function digital clock. It could also compute and display such trip-related information as distance traveled, average speed, instantaneous and trip-average fuel economy, and gallons of fuel consumed. Also joining the option list: a Class II Trailer Towing package, rated up to 3,500 pounds. As before, Marquis had a bright vertical-bar theme grille, front bumper guards, quad rectangular halogen headlamps with bright headlamp/parking lamp surround moldings, and stand-up hood ornament. Wraparound front parking lamps had integral side markers. Bodies also showed a wide center pillar, rear door window divider bar, black lower back panel with vertical backup lamps adjacent to the recessed license plate bracket, and horizontal wraparound taillamps with integral side marker lights. Marquis rode P205/75R14 steel-belted radial whitewalls and carried a mini spare tire. Marquis Brougham added a rear half vinyl roof, coach lamps, hood accent stripes, 'Brougham' decklid nameplate, deluxe wheel covers, and wide bright lower bodyside molding with quarter-panel extensions. Inside were Twin Comfort lounge seats in cloth/vinyl. Four-door Broughams had a standard 302 V-8 with variable venturi carburetor. Also standard: an AM/FM stereo radio and power windows. Grand Marquis had upper bodyside accent stripes, wide bright/black lower

bodyside molding, black painted rocker panel flange, nameplate on rear roof pillar and decklid, rear bumper guards, tinted glass, dual-beam dome light, and Twin Comfort seats in luxury cloth. Grand Marquis four-doors carried the 302 V-8. There was still a base Marquis station wagon, and a Colony Park wagon with full-length bodyside rosewood woodtone applique. Wagons had the 302 V-8 and P215/75R14 SBR whitewalls.

I.D. DATA: Mercury's 17-symbol Vehicle Identification Number (VIN) was stamped on a metal tab fastened to the instrument panel, visible through the windshield. Symbols one to three indicates manufacturer, make and vehicle type: '1ME' Mercury passenger car. The fourth symbol ('B') denotes restraint system. Next comes a letter 'P', followed by two digits that indicate body type: Model Number, as shown in left column of tables below. (Example: '71' Zephyr four- door sedan.) Symbol eight indicates engine type: '2' L498 2Bbl.; 'A' L4-140 2Bbl.; 'B' or 'T' L6200 1Bbl.; '3' V6232 2Bbl.; 'D' V8255 2Bbl.; 'F' V8302 2Bbl.; 'G' V8351 2Bbl. Next is a check digit. Symbol ten indicates model year ('C' 1982). Symbol eleven is assembly plant: 'A' Atlanta, GA; 'F' Dearborn, MI; 'R' San Jose, CA; 'G' Chicago; 'H' Lorain, Ohio; 'K' Kansas City, MO; 'X' St. Thomas, Ontario; 'Z' St. Louis, MO; 'W' Wayne, MI; or Edison, NJ. The final six digits make up the sequence number, starting with 600001. A Vehicle Certification Label on the left front door lock face panel or door pillar shows the manufacturer, month and year of manufacture, GVW, GAWR, certification statement, VIN, and codes for such items as body type, color, trim, axle, transmission, and special order information.

LYNX (FOUR)

Model Number	Body/Style Number	Body Type & Seating	Factory Price	Shipping Weight	Production Total
63	61D	3-dr. Hatch-4P	5502	1924	Note 1
64	58D	5-dr. Hatch-4P	5709	1986	Note 1
63	61D	3-dr. L Hatch-4P	6159	1932	Note 1
64	58D	5-dr. L Hatch-4P	6376	1994	Note 1
65	74D	4-dr. L Sta Wag-4P	6581	2040	Note 1
63/60Z	61D	3-dr. GL Hatch-4P	6471	1927	Note 1
64/60Z	58D	5-dr. GL Hatch-4P	6688	1989	Note 1
65/60Z	74D	4-dr. GL Sta Wag-4P	6899	2040	Note 1
63/602	61D	3-dr. GS Hatch-4P	7257	1963	Note 1
64/602	58D	5-dr. GS Hatch-4P	7474	2025	Note 1
65/602	74D	4-dr. GS Sta Wag-4P	7594	2062	Note 1
63/603	61D	3-dr. LS Hatch-4P	7762	1952	Note 1
64/603	58D	5-dr. LS Hatch-4P	7978	2014	Note 1
65/603	74D	4-dr. LS Sta Wag-4P	8099	2052	Note 1
63/936	61D	3-dr. RS Hatch-4P	6790	1961	Note 1

Note 1: Total Lynx production, 54,611 three-door hatchbacks, 40,713 five-door hatchbacks, and 23,835 four-door liftgate station wagons.

LN7 (FOUR)

61	67D	3-dr. Hatch Cpe-2P	7787	2059	35,147

CAPRI (FOUR/SIX)

67	61D	3-dr. Fastbk-4P	6711/7245	N/A	Note 2
67	61D	3-dr. L Fastbk-4P	7245/7869	2591/ --	Note 2

CAPRI BLACK MAGIC (FOUR/SIX)

67	61D	3-dr. Fastbk-4P	7946/8570	2562/2676	Note 2

CAPRI RS (V-8)

67	61D	3-dr. Fastbk-4P	8107	2830	Note 2

CAPRI GS (FOUR/SIX)

68	61H	3-dr. Fastbk-4P	7432/8056	2590/2704	Note 2

Note 2: Total Capri production was 31,525, plus 4,609 GS-level models.

Capri Engine Note: Six-cylinder prices include cost of the required automatic transmission. A 255 cu. in. V-8 engine cost $70 more than the six; a 302 V-8, $189-$239 more.

ZEPHYR (FOUR/SIX)

71	54D	4-dr. Sed-5P	6411/7035	2630/2750	31,698
71/602	54D	4-dr. GS Sed-5P	6734/7358	2643/2763	Note 3

ZEPHYR Z-7 (FOUR/SIX)

72	36R	2-dr. Spt Cpe-5P	6319/6943	2627/2747	7,394
72/602	36R	2-dr. GS Cpe-5P	6670/7294	2637/2757	Note 3

Note 3: Production of GS models is included in basic totals.

Zephyr Engine Note: Six-cylinder prices include cost of the required automatic transmission. A V-8 cost $70 more than the six.

COUGAR (SIX/V-6)

76	66D	2-dr. GS Sed-6P	7983/8053	2937/2941	6,984
77	54D	4-dr. GS Sed-6P	8158/8228	2980/2983	30,672
78	74D	4-dr. GS Wag-6P	8216/8286	3113/3116	19,294
76	66D	2-dr. LS Sed-6P	8415/8485	2973/2976	Note 4
77	54D	4-dr. LS Sed-6P	8587/8657	3022/3025	Note 4

Cougar Engine Note: V-6 engine required power steering (not incl. in above prices).

COUGAR XR-7 (SIX/V-8)

90	66D	2-dr. GS Cpe-4P	9094/9235	3152/3289	16,867
90/60H	66D	2-dr. LS Cpe-4P	9606/9847	3161/3298	Note 4

Note 4: Production of LS models is included in GS totals.

Engine Note: A V-6 cost the same as a V-8 under XR7 hoods.

MARQUIS (V-8)

81	54H	4-dr. Sedan-6P	8674	3734	9,454
87	74H	4-dr. 2S Sta Wag-6P	9198	3880	2,487

MARQUIS BROUGHAM (V-8)

82	66K	2-dr. Sedan-6P	9490	3693	2,833
83	54K	4-dr. Sedan-6P	9767	3776	15,312

MARQUIS COLONY PARK (V-8)

88	74K	4-dr. 2S Sta Wag-6P	10252	3890	8,004

GRAND MARQUIS (V-8)

84	66L	2-dr. Sedan-6P	10188	3724	6,149
85	54L	4-dr. Sedan-6P	10456	3809	32,918

FACTORY PRICE AND WEIGHT NOTE: Cougar prices and weights to left of slash are for inline six-cylinder, to right for V-6 engine. For Capri/Zephyr, prices/weights to left of slash are for four-cylinder, to right for V-6.

ENGINE DATA: BASE FOUR (Lynx, LN7): Inline. Overhead cam. Four-cylinder. Cast iron block and aluminum head. Displacement: 97.6 cu. in. (1.6 liters). Bore & stroke: 3.15 x 3.13 in. Compression ratio: 8.8:1. Brake horsepower: 70 at 4600 R.P.M. Torque: 89 lbs.-ft. at 3000 R.P.M. Five main bearings. Hydraulic valve lifters. Carburetor: 2Bbl. Motorcraft 740. VIN Code: 2. BASE FOUR (Capri, Zephyr): Inline. Overhead cam. Four-cylinder. Cast iron block and head. Displacement: 140 cu. in. (2.3 liters). Bore & stroke: 3.78 x 3.13 in. Compression ratio: 9.0:1. Brake horsepower: 86 at 4600 R.P.M. Torque: 117 lbs.-ft. at 2600 R.P.M. Five main bearings. Hydraulic valve lifters. Carburetor: 2Bbl. Holley 6500 or Motorcraft 5200. VIN Code: A. BASE SIX (Cougar, XR7); OPTIONAL (Capri, Zephyr): Inline. OHV. Six-cylinder. Cast iron block and head. Displacement: 200 cu. in. (3.3 liters). Bore & stroke: 3.68 x 3.13 in. Compression ratio: 8.6:1. Brake horsepower: 87 at 3800 R.P.M. Torque: 151-154 lbs.-ft. at 1400 R.P.M. Seven main bearings. Hydraulic valve lifters. Carburetor: 1Bbl. Holley 1946. VIN Code: B or T. OPTIONAL V-6 (Cougar, XR7): 90-degree, overhead valve V-6. Cast iron block and aluminum head. Displacement: 232 cu. in. (3.8 liters). Bore & stroke: 3.80 x 3.40 in. Compression ratio: 8.65:1. Brake horsepower: 112 at 4000 R.P.M. Torque: 175 lbs.-ft. at 2000 R.P.M. Four main bearings. Hydraulic valve lifters. Carburetor: 2Bbl. Motorcraft 2150. VIN Code: 3. BASE V-8 (Marquis); OPTIONAL (Capri, Zephyr, XR7): 90-degree, overhead valve V-8. Cast iron block and head. Displacement: 255 cu. in. (4.2 liters). Bore & stroke: 3.68 x 3.00 in. Compression ratio: 8.2:1. Brake horsepower: 120-122 at 3400 R.P.M. Torque: 205-209 lbs.-ft. at 1600-2400 R.P.M. Five main bearings. Hydraulic valve lifters. Carburetor: 2Bbl. Motorcraft 2150 or 7200VV. VIN Code: D. BASE V-8 (Marquis Brougham, Grand Marquis 4dr.); OPTIONAL (Marquis): 90-degree, overhead valve V-8. Cast iron block and head. Displacement: 302 cu. in. (5.0 liters). Bore & stroke: 4.00 x 3.00 in. Compression ratio: 8.4:1. Brake horsepower: 132 at 3400 R.P.M. Torque: 236 lbs.-ft. at 1800 R.P.M. Five main bearings. Hydraulic valve lifters. Carburetor: 2Bbl. Motorcraft 2150A or 7200VV. VIN Code: F. OPTIONAL V-8 (Capri): High-output version of 302 cu. in. V-8 above Compression ratio: 8.3:1. Horsepower: 157 at 4200 R.P.M. Torque: 240 lbs.-ft. at 2400 R.P.M. POLICE V-8 (Marquis): 90-degree, overhead valve V-8. Cast iron block and head. Displacement: 351 cu. in. (5.8 liters). Bore & stroke: 4.00 x 3.50 in. Compression ratio: 8.3:1. Brake horsepower: 165 at 3600 R.P.M. Torque: 285 lbs.-ft. at 2200 R.P.M. Five main bearings. Hydraulic valve lifters. Carburetor: VV. VIN Code: G.

CHASSIS DATA: Wheelbase: (Lynx/LN7) 94.2 in.; (Capri) 100.4 in.; (Zephyr) 105.5 in.; (Cougar) 105.5 in.; (XR7) 108.4 in.; (Marquis) 114.3 in. Overall Length: (Lynx) 163.9 in.; (Lynx lift) 165.0 in.; (LN7) 170.3 in.; (Capri) 179.1 in.; (Zephyr) 195.5 in.; (Z7) 197.4 in.; (Cougar) 196.5 in.; (XR7) 200.4 in.; (Marquis) 212.3 in.; (Marquis wag) 218.0 in. Height: (Lynx) 53.3 in.; (LN7) 50.5 in.; (Capri) 51.4 in.; (Zephyr) 52.9 in.; (Z7) 51.7 in.; (Cougar) 53.0 in.; (Cougar wag) 54.3 in.; (XR7) 53.2 in.; (Marquis) 55.1 in.; (Marquis wag) 57.2 in. Width: (Lynx/LN7) 65.9 in.; (Capri) 69.1 in.; (Zephyr) 71.0 in.; (Cougar) 71.0 in.; (XR7) 74.1 in.; (Marquis) 77.5 in.; (Marquis wag) 79.3 in. Front Tread: (Lynx/LN7) 54.7 in.; (Capri) 56.6 in.; (Zephyr/Cougar) 56.6 in.; (XR7) 58.1 in.; (Marquis) 62.2 in. Rear Tread: (Lynx/LN7) 56.0 in.; (Capri) 57.0 in.; (Zephyr/Cougar) 57.0 in.; (XR7) 57.0 in.; (Marquis) 62.0 in. Standard Tires: (Lynx/LN7) P165/80R13; (Capri) P175/75R14; (Zephyr/Cougar) P175/75R14 SBR; (XR7) P195/75R14 SBR WSW; (Marquis) P205/75R14 SBR; (Marquis wag) P215/75R14.

TECHNICAL: Transmission: Four-speed manual standard on Lynx. Gear ratios: (1st) 3.58:1; (2nd) 2.05:1; (3rd) 1.21:1 or 1.36:1; (4th) 0.81:1 or 0.95:1; (Rev) 3.46:1. Four-speed floor shift standard on Capri/Zephyr four: (1st) 3.98:1; (2nd) 2.14:1; (3rd) 1.42:1; (4th) 1.00:1; (Rev) 3.99:1. Four-speed overdrive floor shift standard on Capri V-8: (1st) 3.07:1; (2nd) 1.72:1; (3rd) 1.00:1; (4th) 0.70:1; (Rev) 3.07:1. Capri four-cylinder five-speed: (1st) 3.72:1; (2nd) 2.23:1; (3rd) 1.48:1; (4th) 1.00:1; (5th) 0.76:1; (Rev) 3.59:1. SelectShift three-speed automatic standard on Cougar and XR7 six, optional on others. Gear ratios: (1st) 2.46:1 or 2.47:1; (2nd) 1.46:1 or 1.47:1; (3rd) 1.00:1; (Rev) 2.11:1 to 2.19:1. Lynx three-speed automatic: (1st) 2.79:1; (2nd) 1.61:1; (3rd) 1.00:1; (Rev) 1.97:1. Four-speed overdrive automatic on XR7/Marquis: (1st) 2.40:1; (2nd) 1.47:1; (3rd) 1.00:1; (4th) 0.67:1; (Rev) 2.00:1. Standard final drive ratio: (Lynx/LN7) 3.59:1 w/4spd, 3.31:1 w/auto.; (Capri four) 3.08:1 w/4spd or auto., 3.45:1 w/5spd; (Capri six/V-8) 2.73:1; (Capri V-8 w/4spd auto.) 3.08:1; (Zephyr) 3.08:1 exc. 2.73:1 w/six or V-8; (Cougar) 2.73:1 w/six, 2.47:1 with V-6; (XR7) 2.73:1 w/six, 3.08:1 with V-6/V-8. (Marquis) 3.08:1 exc. 2.73:1 w/police 351 V-8. Steering: (Marquis) recirculating ball; (others) rack and pinion. Front Suspension: (Lynx/LN7) MacPherson strut-mounted coil springs w/lower control arms and stabilizer bar; (Capri) modified MacPherson struts w/coil springs and anti-sway bar; (Zephyr/Cougar) MacPherson struts w/coil springs mounted on lower control arm and anti-sway bar; (Marquis) coil springs with long/short Aarms and anti-sway bar. Rear Suspension: (Lynx/LN7) independent trailing arms w/modified MacPherson struts and coil springs on lower control arms; (Capri/Zephyr/Cougar/Marquis) four-link w/coil springs; (XR7) four-link with coil springs and anti-sway bar. Brakes: Front disc, rear drum. Ignition: Electronic. Body construction: (Marquis) separate body and frame; (others) unibody. Fuel tank: (Lynx/LN7) 11.3 gal.; (Capri) 15.4 gal.; (Zephyr) 16 gal.; (Cougar) 16 gal.; (XR7) 21 gal.; (Marquis) 20 gal.

DRIVETRAIN OPTIONS: Engines: 200 cu. in. six: Capri/Zephyr ($213). 232 cu. in. V-6: Cougar ($70); Cougar XR7 ($241). 255 cu. in. V-8: Capri/Zephyr ($283); Capri RS ($57 credit); Cougar XR7 ($241). 302 cu. in. V-8: Capri ($402-$452); Marquis sedan ($59). Transmission/Differential: Five-speed manual trans.: Capri ($196). Automatic transaxle: Lynx/LN7 ($411). Auto. transmission.: Capri/Zephyr ($411). Floor shift lever: Zephyr ($49). Traction-Lok differential: Capri/Zephyr/Cougar/XR7 ($76); Marquis ($80). Optional axle ratio: Lynx/LN7/Capri/Zephyr (NC). Brakes & Steering: Power brakes: Lynx ($93). Power steering: Lynx/LN7/Capri ($190); Zephyr/Cougar ($195). Suspension: H.D. susp.: Zephyr/Cougar ($24); Marquis/Cougar XR7 ($26). Handling susp.: Lynx ($41); Capri ($50); Zephyr ($52); Marquis ($49). Other: H.D. battery ($24-$26). H.D. alternator: LN7 ($27). Extended-range gas tank: Zephyr/Cougar ($46). Engine block heater ($17-$18). Trailer towing pkg., medium duty: Marquis ($200-$251). California emission system ($46-$65). High- altitude emissions (NC).

LYNX CONVENIENCE/APPEARANCE OPTIONS: Option Packages: Villager woodtone pkg.: GL/GS/RS wag ($259). Instrument group ($87). Appearance protection group ($55). Light group ($43). Comfort/Convenience: Air conditioner ($611). Speed control ($151). Remote liftgate release ($30). Tinted glass ($82); windshield only ($32). Digital clock ($57). Interval wipers ($48). Rear wiper/washer ($117). Dual remote sport mirrors ($66). Entertainment: AM radio delete ($61 credit). AM/FM radio ($76). AM/FM stereo radio ($106); w/cassette or 8track player ($184) exc. LS ($78). Premium sound ($105). Dual rear speakers ($39). Exterior: Flip-up open air roof ($183-$276). Glamour paint ($61) exc. RS. Tu-tone paint ($122) exc. RS. Front vent windows ($60). Narrow bodyside moldings ($45). Bumper guards, front or rear ($26). Bumper rub strips: base/L ($41). Luggage rack ($93). Roof air deflector ($29). Lower bodyside protection ($68). Interior: Console ($111). Low-back reclining bucket seats ($33-$98). High-back reclining bucket seats ($65). Cloth/vinyl seat trim ($29). Vinyl trim: GS (NC). Shearling/leather seat trim ($59-$138). Deluxe seatbelts ($24). Wheels/Tires: Aluminum wheels ($232-$329). P165/80R13 WSW ($58).

LN7 CONVENIENCE/APPEARANCE OPTIONS: Comfort/Convenience: Appearance protection group ($48). Air conditioner ($611). Fingertip speed control ($151). Entertainment: AM/FM radio ($76). AM/FM stereo radio ($106); w/cassette or 8track player ($184). Premium sound ($105). AM radio delete ($37 credit). Exterior: Flip-up open air roof ($276). Glamour paint ($51). Tu-tone paint ($122). Luggage rack ($93). Lower bodyside protection ($68). Interior: Vinyl high-back reclining seats (NC). Cloth/vinyl seat trim ($29). Leather seat trim ($138). Shearling/leather seat trim ($138). Wheels/Tires: Cast aluminum spoke wheels ($232). P165/80R13 RWL ($72).

CAPRI CONVENIENCE/APPEARANCE OPTIONS: Option Packages: TR performance pkg. ($483-$533). Light group ($49). Appearance protection group ($48). Power lock group ($139). Comfort/Convenience: Air cond. ($676). Rear defroster, electric ($124). Fingertip speed control ($155). Power windows ($165). Tinted glass ($88). Leather-wrapped steering wheel ($55). Tilt steering wheel ($95). Interval wipers ($48). Rear wiper/washer ($101). Remote right mirror ($41). Entertainment: AM/FM radio ($76). AM/FM stereo radio ($106); w/8track or cassette player ($184). Premium sound system ($105). Dual rear speakers ($39). AM radio delete ($61 credit). Exterior: TRoof ($1021). Flip-up/open air roof ($276). Carriage roof ($734). Full vinyl roof ($137). Glamour paint ($54). Tu-tone paint ($66-$124). Gold accent stripes ($62). Hood scoop ($72). Liftgate louvers ($165). Rocker panel moldings ($33). Lower bodyside protection ($41). Interior: Recaro bucket seats ($834). Cloth/vinyl seats: base ($23). Cloth/vinyl accent trim: L/RS ($34). Leather/vinyl seats ($409). Wheels and Tires: Wire wheel covers ($91). Cast aluminum wheels ($348). Styled steel wheels w/trim rings ($72). P175/75R14 WSW ($66). P185/75R14 BSW ($30); WSW ($66-$96); RWL ($85-$116).

ZEPHYR/COUGAR CONVENIENCE/APPEARANCE OPTIONS: Option Packages: Cougar Villager option: wag ($282). Power lock group: Cougar ($138-$184). Instrument cluster: Zephyr ($100). Cold weather group: Cougar ($77). Appearance protection group ($57-$59). Light group ($49-$51). Comfort/Convenience: Air cond. ($676). Rear defroster, electric ($124). Fingertip speed control ($155). Illuminated ntry ($68). Power windows ($165-$235). Power door locks: Zephyr ($106-$152). Four-way power seat ($139). Six-way power seats: Cougar ($196). Remote decklid release: Zephyr ($32). Tinted glass ($88). Leather-wrapped steering wheel: Cougar ($55). Tilt steering ($95). Quartz clock ($32). Interval wipers ($48). Liftgate wiper/washer: wagon ($99). Lighting and Mirrors: Cornering lamps: Cougar ($59). Map light: Cougar ($15). Trunk light: Zephyr ($7). Left remote mirror: Zephyr ($22). Dual bright remote mirrors: Zephyr ($65). Right remote mirror: Cougar ($60). Lighted right visor vanity mirror ($46); pair ($91). Entertainment: AM/FM radio ($54). AM/FM stereo radio ($85); w/8track or cassette player ($172). Twin rear speakers: Zephyr ($39). Premium sound system ($105). AM radio delete ($61 credit). Exterior: Flip-up open air roof ($276). Full or half vinyl roof ($137-$140). Glamour paint ($63). Tu-tone paint ($82- $105). Pivoting front vent windows ($63). Two-way liftgate: wag ($105). Rocker panel moldings: Zephyr Z7/GS ($33). Protective bodyside moldings: Cougar ($49). Wide bodyside moldings: Zephyr Z7 ($59). Bumper guards, rear ($28). Bumper rub strips ($50). Luggage rack: wagon ($115). Lower bodyside protection ($41). Interior: Console: Zephyr ($191). Twin comfort seats: Cougar ($204). Cloth/vinyl seat trim: Zephyr ($29). Vinyl seat trim ($29). Leather trim: Cougar LS ($409). Flight bench seat: Zephyr (NC). Floor mats: Zephyr ($13). Wheels/Tires: Luxury wheel covers: Cougar ($49). Wire wheel covers ($104-$152). Styled steel wheels: Zephyr ($54); w/trim rings ($107). Cast aluminum wheels: Cougar ($348-$396). P175/75R14 WSW ($66). P185/75R14 BSW: Cougar ($38). P185/75R14 WSW ($104) exc. wagon ($66). P185/75R14 RWL: Cougar ($121) exc. wagon ($83). TR BSW on alum. wheels ($534-$583). Conventional spare ($51).

COUGAR XR7 CONVENIENCE/APPEARANCE OPTIONS: Option Packages: Appearance protection group ($51). Light group ($35). Power lock group ($138). Comfort/Convenience: Air cond. ($676); auto-temp ($754). Rear defroster ($126). Fingertip speed control ($155). Illuminated entry system ($68). Keyless entry ($277). Tripminder computer ($215-$261). Autolamp on/off delay ($73). Tinted glass ($88). Power windows ($165). Six-way power driver's seat ($198). Auto. parking brake release ($12). Leather-wrapped steering wheel ($51). Tilt steering wheel ($95). Electronic instrument cluster ($367). Diagnostic warning lights ($59). Seatbelt chimes ($27). Digital clock ($46). Interval wipers ($48). Lighting and Mirrors: Cornering lamps ($59). Remote right mirror ($60). Lighted right visor vanity mirrors ($91). Entertainment: AM/FM radio ($54). AM/FM stereo radio ($85); w/8track or cassette player ($172). AM/FM stereo search radio ($232); w/8track or cassette ($318). Power antenna ($55). Dual rear speakers ($39). Premium sound system ($133- $167). AM radio delete ($61 credit). Exterior: Carriage roof ($885). Flip-up open-air roof ($276). Vinyl rear half roof ($187). Vinyl roof delete ($156 credit). Glamour paint ($80). Tu-tone paint ($112). Pivoting front vent windows ($63). Rocker panel moldings ($33). Lower bodyside protection ($54). Interior: Bucket seats w/console (NC). Recaro bucket seats w/console ($523). Leather seat trim ($409). Vinyl seat trim ($28). Trunk trim ($48). Wheels/Tires: Wire wheel covers ($99-$152). Luxury wheel covers: GS ($54). Self-sealing tires ($106). TR tires on alum. wheels ($589-$643). Conventional spare ($51).

MARQUIS CONVENIENCE/APPEARANCE OPTIONS: Option Packages: Grand Marquis decor: Colony Park ($555). Convenience group ($90-$116). Power lock group ($106-$201). Light group ($27-$43). Appearance protection group ($67). Comfort/Convenience: Air cond. ($695); w/auto-temp control ($761). Rear defroster, electric ($124). Fingertip speed control ($155). Illuminated entry system ($68). Power windows ($240). Six-way power flight bench seat: base ($198); reclining ($262). Six-way power twin comfort driver's seat w/recliners ($262); driver and passenger ($460). Tinted glass ($102). Autolamp on/off delay ($73). Leather-wrapped steering wheel ($51). Tilt steering wheel ($95). Tripminder computer ($215-$293). Quartz clock ($32). Digital clock ($46-$78). Seatbelt chime ($27). Lighting and Mirrors: Cornering lamps ($55). Remote right mirror ($43). Lighted right visor vanity mirrors ($91). Entertainment: AM/FM stereo radio ($85-$172); w/8track or cassette tape player ($87-$172). AM/FM stereo search radio ($146-$232); w/8track or cassette ($233-$318). Power antenna ($55). Dual rear speakers ($41). Premium sound system ($133- $167). AM radio delete ($61 credit). AM/FM delete ($152 credit). Exterior: Formal vinyl coach roof: Brghm/Grand 4dr. ($638). Full vinyl roof: base sed ($165). Vinyl roof delete ($71 credit). Glamour paint ($77). Tu-tone paint ($117-$156). Dual accent bodyside stripes ($39). Hood striping ($17). Pivoting front vent windows ($63). Rocker panel moldings ($32). Vinyl- insert bodyside moldings ($51). Bumper guards, rear ($30). Bumper rub strips ($52). Luggage rack ($104). Lower bodyside protection ($39-$52). Interior: Dual-facing rear seats: wagon ($167). Twin comfort lounge seats: base ($139). All-vinyl seat trim: base ($28). Cloth seat trim: wag ($41). Duraweave trim: wag ($62). Leather seating: Grand Marquis ($412). Dual seatback recliners ($65). Trunk trim ($49). Wheels/Tires: Luxury wheel covers ($52-$82). Wire wheel overs ($123-$152). Cast aluminum wheels ($355-$384). P215/75R14 WSW ($36). P225/75R14 WSW ($36-$73). P205/75R15 WSW ($11-$47); puncture-resistant ($112-$148). Conventional spare ($51).

HISTORY: Intro: September 24, 1981 except LN7, April 9, 1981. Production: 380,506. Calendar year production (U.S.): 315,798. Calendar year sales by U.S. dealers: 327,140. Model year sales by U.S. dealers: 319,697 (not including 13,954 early '82 LN7 models sold during 1981 model year).

Historical Footnotes: Sales slumped again this model year, but not so dramatically as in 1981. Mercury's 6.6 percent decline was well under the 16 percent plunge experienced by the domestic auto industry as a whole. The full-size Marquis found more buyers this year, up by almost one-third. Lynx sales proved disappointing, falling well behind the slow-moving EXP, even when the new high-output engine became available. Some observers felt the two-seater's performance didn't match its sporty looks, accounting for lack of buyer interest. In a *Road & Track* test, LN7 took 15 seconds to hit 60 MPH, which wasn't quite sparkling performance for a sporty lightweight. Zephyr and XR-7 sales fell sharply, while the standard Cougar gained a little. Lynx production dropped quite a bit, causing Ford to plan a shutdown of its San Jose, California plant in 1983.

1983 MERCURY

A total restyle hit XR-7, which changed its name to, simply, Cougar. Its aerodynamic design managed a 0.40 drag coefficient. A bubble-back hatchback was added to Capri, along with more engine choices. Two vehicles now carried the Marquis badge: a derivation of the former four-door Cougar on 105.5 inch wheelbase, and Grand Marquis with a 114.3 in. wheelbase. The smaller one had nitrogen-pressurized gas shocks and new sheetmetal. The new front-drive Topaz, replacing the Zephyr, arrived in spring 1983 as an early '84 model.

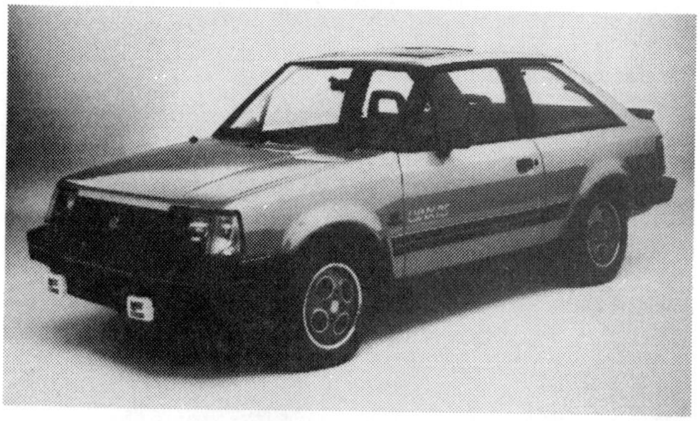

1983 Lynx R8 hatchback coupe (OCW)

LYNX — FOUR — Mercury's best seller took on a new grille and striping this year, offering a broader selection of engines. The powertrain list included the base 1.6-liter carbureted four with four-speed manual or three-speed automatic; a fuel- injected 1.6; or high-output 1.6. A simplified model lineup included L, GS and LS. Base models and GL were dropped. The new grille had thin vertical bars, as before, but only two wider vertical divider bars (formerly five). The grille emblem moved from the side to the center. Otherwise, appearance was similar to 1982. Interiors were revised, with standard full-width cloth seat trim. Hatchbacks had a removable rear package shelf. Manual-shift models added an upshift indicator light. A high-mileage model (with economy gearing) was available everywhere except California. All except L now had a standard remote-locking fuel filler door. The fuel tank grew to 13 gallons. Standard equipment on Lynx L included four-speed manual shift, P165/80R13 SBR BSW tires on semi-styled steel wheels, four-spoke color-keyed steering wheel, compact spare tire, cloth/vinyl high-back bucket front seats (folding rear bench seat), four-speed heater/defroster, consolette, cargo area cover, and dome lamp. Bright bumpers showed black end caps. Wagons had power brakes. Lynx GS added a black front air dam, AM radio, passenger assist handles, carpeted lower door trim panels, locking gas filler door, power hatch release, dual visor vanity mirrors, two-color upper bodyside accent paint stripes, reclining cloth/vinyl low-back bucket seats with head restraints, and wide bodyside moldings with argent accent stripe. Rocker panel moldings were deleted. Black bumper end caps and rub strips had argent accent stripes. Lynx LS included styled steel wheels, an AM/FM stereo radio, dual remote sport mirrors, velour cloth low-back bucket seats, burled walnut appliques, digital clock, console with graphic warning display, electric back window defroster, and instrument group. The three-door RS now carried a fuel- injected four and five-speed gearbox, plus TR sport suspension and wheels, and Michelin P165/70R365 blackwall TRX tires. Also included with RS: an AM radio, black wheel spats, tape decals, front/rear spoilers, dual black remote sport mirrors, cloth reclining sport bucket seats, black bumper guards and end caps, black console, foglamps, locking fuel filler door, instrument group, and black steering wheel. Wide black bodyside moldings had argent accent stripes. Black moldings were used on the rocker panels, drip, belt, wheel lip, windshield, windows, and lower back panel surround. Blackout treatment extended to the grille, louvered center pillar applique, front roof pillar, wheel housings, dash and license plate area.

LN7 — FOUR — In an attempt to defeat claims of substandard performance, the two-passenger LN7 could now have a high- output version of the CVH 1.6-liter four, hooked to a five- speed manual gearbox. A multi-port fuel-injected four also was available, to improve idling and low-end torque. New options included a four-way adjustable driver's seat and shift indicator light. The gas tank was now 13-gallon. Standard LN7 equipment included the basic 98 cu. in. four with five-speed manual shift, P165/80R13 SBR BSW tires, power brakes, AM radio, C-pillar louvers, black sport steering wheel, interval wipers, digital clock, and electric rear defroster. Also standard: a console, cargo area cover, remote-lock fuel filler door, tachometer, tinted glass, power liftgate release, dual remote black mirrors, and color-keyed scuff plates. Black windshield surround, backlight and wide bodyside moldings were used. Black bumpers had argent stripe and soft fascia. Black paint treatment was evident on the A-pillar, quarter windows, door frames, rocker panels, and back license plate area. Sport models had an AM/FM stereo radio; Grand Sport and RS, an AM/FM stereo with cassette player. Models with the TR package had P165/70Rx365 Michelin BSW tires.

CAPRI — FOUR/V-6/V-8 — Mercury's version of the ponycar distanced itself from Mustang with a new "bubbleback" hatchback design. This year's grille used only one bright horizontal divider bar to separate the pattern into an upper and lower section, unlike the previous multi-bar form. Wraparound taillamps now reached the license plate recess. New standard equipment included a cargo cover. Instruments got more legible graphics. Under Capri hoods, the high-output 302 cu. in. (5.0- liter) V-8 switched from a two- to a four-barrel carburetor and added horsepower. A Borg-Warner five-speed was to be offered with the H.O. engine later in the model year. First step-up engine above the base 140 cu. in. (2.3-liter) four was now the "Essex" 232 cu. in. (3.8-liter) V-6. The base engine changed from a two-barrel to one-barrel carb. A turbo four was announced for spring 1983 arrival (similar to the turbo offered in 1979-81, but fuel-injected). Manual-shift models now had an upshift indicator light. Standard tires grew one size and took on all-season tread. RS tires grew two sizes. Standard Capri equipment included the 140 cu. in. (2.3- liter) four with four-speed manual shift, P185/75R14 SBR BSW tires, power brakes, AM radio, tachometer, trip odometer, aero wheel covers, black bumper rub strips, cargo area cover, black remote driver's mirror, day/night mirror, and halogen headlamps. Extra-wide wraparound black bodyside moldings had dual color-keyed stripes. Bright moldings went on the windshield and roof drip; black molding on the back window; black/bright on window frames. Interiors held high-back vinyl bucket seats with reclining seatbacks (fold-down rear seat), black sport steering wheel, and woodtone dash applique. Capri L added a digital clock, console with graphic warning display, center armrest, low-back bucket seats, and right visor vanity mirror. GS included a woodtone-insert four- spoke steering wheel, black right-hand remote mirror, luxury cloth seats, map pocket, and light group. Capri RS added a Traction-Lok axle, P205/70R14 SBR BSW tires, power steering, leather-wrapped steering wheel, handling suspension, upper bodyside dual accent stripes, tape striping, black windshield and window frame moldings, black right-hand remote mirror, non-working hood scoop, black grille, and black brushed instrument panel. Black Magic came with P220/55R390 Michelin TRX tires on gold 15.3 inch forged metric aluminum wheels, a handling suspension, black leather-wrapped steering wheel, power steering, black hood scoop, black bodyside and window frame moldings, and black right-hand remote mirror. Reclining black vinyl low-back bucket seats had gold cloth inserts. Styling features included gold-accent bodyside taping, and gold accents on fender, grille edge, hood and license frames. Crimson Cat added TR cast aluminum wheels, 'Crimson Cat' tape treatment, sport steering wheel, and dual remote mirrors.

ZEPHYR — FOUR/SIX — Facing its last year in the lineup, Zephyr changed little. The base 140 cu. in (2.3-liter) four now had a one- barrel carburetor instead of two barrels. Manual-shift models had an optional upshift indicator light. The 4.2-liter V-8 was dropped, but Zephyrs could still have a 200 cu. in. (3.3- liter) inline six with locking torque converter in the automatic transmission. The optional Traction-Lok differential could now be ordered with TR-type tires. As in 1982, two trim levels were offered: base and GS, in four-door sedan or sporty coupe form. The Fairmont/Zephyr chassis/body design would continue as the downsized Ford LTD/Mercury Marquis (introduced this year). Zephyr standard equipment included the 2.3-liter four with four-speed manual gearbox, power brakes, deluxe wheel covers, P175/75R14 SBR BSW tires, AM radio, day/night mirror, vinyl low-back bucket seats, two-spoke color-keyed steering wheel, dual upper bodyside accent stripes, front bumper guards, dome lamp, and trunk mat. Bright moldings went on the windshield, back window, roof drip, wheel lip, door belt, rocker panels, and side window frames. Narrow lower bodyside moldings had black inserts. Zephyr's Z7 Sport Coupe added tinted rear window glass, and deleted rocker panel moldings. GS models (Z-7 or sedan) included dual hood accent stripes, four-spoke steering wheel, luxury cloth Flight bench seating, dual bright remote mirrors, and protective bodyside and integral partial wheel lip moldings (no rocker panel moldings).

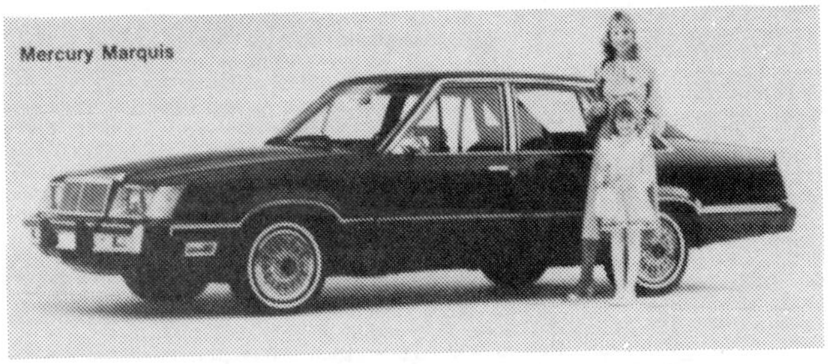

1983 Marquis Brougham sedan (JG)

MARQUIS — FOUR/SIX/V-6 — Mercury borrowed the rear-drive "Fox" platform to create a new mid-size model bearing the Marquis badge. To avoid confusion, the big one was now called Grand Marquis. This smaller Marquis was basically the former Cougar sedan (and wagon), but with new sheetmetal and redone interior, and a more aero look. It was a six-window design, offered in Two trim levels: base and Brougham. Marquis was closely related to Ford's new LTD, but with a different grille and taillamps. The sloped grille was made up of thin vertical bars with a wider center bar, heavy bright surround molding, and nameplate on the lower driver's side. Quad rectangular headlamps were used, with park/signal lamps mounted in the bumper. Wide taillamps had horizontal ribbing, and the profile showed a 60-degree backlight angle. Marquis used the same drivetrains as LTD, including an optional propane four. Nitrogen gas-pressurized front struts and rear shocks were used. Front suspension had modified MacPherson struts; rear, a four-bar link arrangement. Standard tires were one size bigger than the '82 Cougar. A tethered gas cap was new. A contoured split-front bench seat with individual recliners was standard on automatic-tranmission models. New options included an electronic instrument cluster, six-way power seats, and locking wire wheel covers. A sunroof and extended- range gas tank also were offered. Standard Marquis equipment included a 140 cu. in. (2.3- liter) four with four-speed manual gearbox, AM radio, power brakes, deluxe full wheel covers, P185/75R14 BSW tires, black front bumper guards, lighter, locking glovebox, three-speed heater/defroster, dual-note horn, and trunk mat. A bright remote driver's mirror, day/night mirror, and right visor vanity mirror were standard. Cloth-upholstered Twin Comfort Lounge seats came with seatback recliners. Also included: a mini spare tire and luxury steering wheel with woodtone insert. Dual accent stripes went on hood and upper bodysides. Moldings appeared on window frames, wheel lip, belt, back window, license plate bracket, roof drip and windshield. Bodyside moldings were color-keyed vinyl. Wagons came with the inline 200 cu. in. (3.3-liter) six and automatic shift, tinted liftgate glass, cargo area light, and fold-down rear seat. Marquis Brougham added an illuminated passenger visor vanity mirror, digital clock, electronic warning chimes, full-length armrest, trunk carpeting, and extra interior lights.

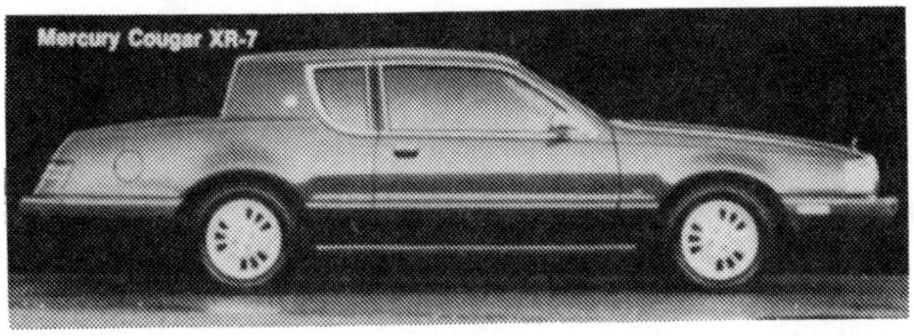

1983 Cougar XR-7 Sports Coupe (JG)

COUGAR — V-6/V-8 — Like the closely related Thunderbird, Cougar enjoyed a major restyle. Foremost difference between the two was Cougar's notchback formal appearance with upright backlight and upswept quarter-window shape. TBird had a rounded backlight. Cougar also had a different grille design made up of thin vertical bars. Otherwise, Cougar (no longer called XR-7) looked much like its mate, with rounded contours, sloping front end and raked windshield, and an aero drag coefficient not too much worse than Thunderbird's. Extended- height doors curved inward at the top. Wipers and drip moldings were concealed. Body dimensions dropped a bit, as did Cougar's weight. Cougar's rear-drive "Fox" chassis had coil springs all around. New this year were gas-pressurized shock absorbers. Only two engine choices were offered: base 232 cu. in. (3.8- liter) V-6 or (later) the 302 cu. in. V-8 with throttle-body fuel injection. Four-speed overdrive automatic transmission was optional. Standard Cougar equipment included three-speed automatic transmission, power brakes and steering, AM radio, bumper rub strips, center pillar applique, console with storage bin, analog clock, locking glovebox, hood ornament, brushed instrument panel, and driver's remote mirror. Sport cloth bucket seats included reclining seatbacks. Also standard: a mini spare tire, decklid and bodyside accent stripes, deluxe wheel covers, and P195/75R14 WSW SBR tires. Bright moldings went on the grille surround, concealed drip, door frames, windshield, backlight, and belt. Charcoal lower bodyside moldings had bright accents. Cougar LS added a woodtone instrument panel applique, 'LS' fender badge, tinted glass, coach lamps, dual power remote mirrors, bright rocker panel moldings, luxury cloth seat trim, power windows, luxury wheel covers, hood accent stripes, steering wheel with woodtone insert, and luxury door trim. New options included an anti-theft alarm, emergency kit, and locking fuel filler door. Articulated sport seats and a voice-alert system also joined the option selection.

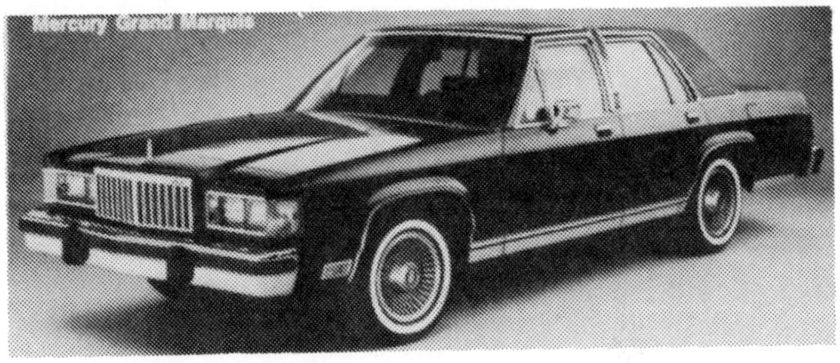

1983 Grand Marquis LS sedan (JG)

GRAND MARQUIS — V-8 — Still selling well, the biggest Mercury carried on with a revised nameplate and modified grille style. This version, shaped similar to its predecessor, consisted of rather heavy bright vertical bars and a wider center bar, with bright surround molding. Sedans also carried new full-width wraparound taillamps with horizontal ribbing. Backup lenses adjoined the license plate opening, at the inner ends of each taillamp. Grand Marquis came in base and LS trim, in the same three bodies as before: two- and four-door sedan, and four- door Colony Park wagon. Sole engine was the 302 cu. in. (5.0- liter) V-8, now with throttle-body fuel injection. Four-speed overdrive automatic transmission was standard. Sedan tires grew one size. New options included a remote locking fuel filler door and locking wire wheel covers. Marquis was similar to Ford's similarly renamed LTD Crown Victoria, sharing drivetrains and suspension. Standard Grand Marquis equipment included a coach vinyl roof, coach lamps, power windows, power brakes and steering, AM/FM stereo radio, cloth/vinyl Twin Comfort lounge seats, mini spare tire with cover, color-keyed steering wheel, bright wheel covers, bumper guards, analog clock, and dual- note horn. The instrument panel was argent with woodtone applique. Bright moldings went on rocker panels, belt, window frames, wheel lips, taillamps, hood rear edge, windshield, roof drip, grille and parking lamp surround. Wide lower bodyside moldings were used, with color-keyed quarter and rear window moldings. Accent stripes went on the hood and upper bodyside. Grand Marquis LS added tinted glass, luxury cloth Twin Comfort seats, full-length armrests, door pull straps, woodtone applique on door trim panels, front seatback map pocket, dual-beam dome lamp, and a right visor vanity mirror. Colony Park wagons had a three-way tailgate with power tinted window, vinyl-trimmed Twin Comfort seats, conventional spare tire, lockable stowage compartment, woodtone aplique on bodyside and tailgate, bumper step pad, bright/black tailgate window moldings, and bright/woodtone bodyside applique surround moldings. Wagons had no rocker panel, lower bodyside or wheel lip moldings.

I.D. DATA: Mercury's 17-symbol Vehicle Identification Number (VIN) was stamped on a metal tab fastened to the instrument panel, visible through the windshield. Symbols one to three indicates manufacturer, make and vehicle type: '1ME' Mercury passenger car. The fourth symbol ('B') denotes restraint system. Next comes a letter 'P', followed by two digits that indicate body type: Model Number, as shown in left column of tables below. (Example: '86' Zephyr four- door sedan.) Symbol eight indicates engine type: '2' L498 2Bbl.; '4' H.O. L498 2Bbl.; '5' L498 FI; 'A' L4-140 2Bbl.; 'D' Turbo L4140 2Bbl.; 'X' L6200 1Bbl.; '3' V6232 2Bbl.; 'F' V8302 2Bbl.; 'G' V8351 2Bbl. Next is a check digit. Symbol ten indicates model year ('D' 1983). Symbol eleven is assembly plant: 'A' Atlanta, GA; 'F' Dearborn, MI; 'G' Chicago; 'H' Lorain, Ohio; 'K' Kansas City, MO; 'R' San Jose, CA; 'W' Wayne, MI; 'X' St. Thomas, Ontario; 'Z' St. Louis, MO; and Edison, NJ. The final six digits make up the sequence number, starting with 600001. A Vehicle Certification Label on the left front door lock face panel or door pillar shows the manufacturer, month and year of manufacture, GVW, GAWR, certification statement, VIN, and codes for such items as body type, color, trim, axle, transmission, and special order information.

LYNX (FOUR)

Model Number	Body/Style Number	Body Type & Seating	Factory Price	Shipping Weight	Production Total
54	61D	3-dr. L Hatch-4P	5751	1922	Note 1
55	58D	5-dr. L Hatch-4P	5958	1984	Note 1
60	74D	4-dr. L Sta Wag-4P	6166	2026	Note 1
55	61D	3-dr. GS Hatch-4P	6476	1948	Note 1
66	58D	5-dr. GS Hatch-4P	6693	2010	Note 1
61	74D	4-dr. GS Sta Wag-4P	6872	2050	Note 1
58	61D	3-dr. LS Hatch-4P	7529	1950	Note 1
68	58D	5-dr. LS Hatch-4P	7746	2012	Note 1
63	74D	4-dr. LS Sta Wag-4P	7909	2050	Note 1
57	61D	3-dr. RS Hatch-4P	7370	1997	Note 1
65/934	58D	5-dr. LTS Hatch-4P	7334	1920	Note 1

Note 1: Total Lynx production, 40,142 three-door hatchbacks, 28,461 five-door hatchbacks, and 19,192 four-door liftgate station wagons.

LN7 (FOUR)

51/A80	67D	3-dr. Hatch Cpe-2P	7398	2076	4,528
51/A8C	67D	3-dr. RS Hatch-2P	8765	N/A	Note 2

LN7 SPORT (FOUR)

51/A8A	67D	3-dr. Hatch Cpe-2P	8084	N/A	Note 2

LN7 GRAND SPORT (FOUR)

51/A8B	67D	3-dr. Hatch Cpe-2P	8465	N/A	Note 2

Note 2: Total LN7 production is included in figure above.

CAPRI (FOUR/V-6)

79/41P	61D	3-dr. Fastbk-4P	7156/7465	2589/2697	Note 3
79	61D	3-dr. L Fastbk-4P	7711/8020	2615/2723	Note 3

CAPRI CRIMSON CAT (FOUR/V-6)

79	61D	3-dr. Fastbk-4P	8525/8834	N/A	Note 3

CAPRI BLACK MAGIC (FOUR/SIX)

79/932	61D	3-dr. Fastbk-4P	8629/8938	2597/2705	Note 3

CAPRI GS (FOUR/SIX)

79/602	61H	3-dr. Fastbk-4P	7914/8223	N/A	Note 3

CAPRI RS (V-8)

79	61D	3-dr. Fastbk-4P	9241	2894	Note 3

Note 3: Total Capri production was 25,376.

Capri Engine Note: Six-cylinder prices do not include cost of the required automatic transmission ($439). A high-output 302 cu. in. V-8 engine cost $1034 more than the V-6 on L or GS; $866 more on Black Magic.

ZEPHYR (FOUR/SIX)

86	54D	4-dr. Sed-5P	6545/6774	2630/2750	21,732
86/602	54D	4-dr. GS Sed-5P	7311/7550	2696/2881	Note 4

ZEPHYR Z-7 (FOUR/SIX)

87	36R	2-dr. Spt Cpe-5P	6442/6681	2627/2747	3,471
87/602	36R	2-dr. GS Cpe-5P	7247/7486	2690/2810	Note 4

Zephyr Price Note: Six-cylinder prices do not include cost of the required automatic transmission ($439).

MARQUIS (FOUR/SIX)

89	54D	4-dr. Sedan-5P	7893/8132	N/A	50,169
90	74D	4-dr. Sta Wag-5P	--/8693	N/A	17,189

MARQUIS BROUGHAM (FOUR/SIX)

89	54D	4-dr. Sedan-5P	8202/8441	N/A	Note 4
90	74D	4-dr. Sta Wag-5P	--/8974	N/A	Note 4

Note 4: Brougham production is included in basic totals above.

Marquis Engine Note: A V-6 engine cost $70 more than the inline six on sedan.

302

1983 Cougar XR-7 Sports Coupe (OCW)

COUGAR (V-6/V-8)

92	66D	2-dr. Cpe-4P	9521/9809	2911/--	75,743
92/603	66D	2-dr. LS Cpe-4P	10850/11138	2911/--	Note 5

Note 5: Production of LS models is included in base or GS totals.

GRAND MARQUIS (V-8)

93	66K	2-dr. Sedan-6P	10654	3607	11,117
95	54K	4-dr. Sedan-6P	10718	3761	72,207
93/60H	66K	2-dr. LS Sed-6P	11209	3607	Note 6
95/60H	54K	4-dr. LS Sed-6P	11273	3761	Note 6

GRAND MARQUIS COLONY PARK (V-8)

94	74K	4-dr. 2S Sta Wag-6P	10896	3788	12,394

Note 6: LS production is included in basic Grand Marquis totals.

FACTORY PRICE AND WEIGHT NOTE: Cougar prices and weights to left of slash are for V-6, to right for V-8 engine. For Capri/Zephyr/Marquis, prices/weights to left of slash are for four-cylinder, to right for inline six (or V-6).

ENGINE DATA: BASE FOUR (Lynx, LN7): Inline. Overhead cam. Four-cylinder. Cast iron block and aluminum head. Displacement: 97.6 cu. in. (1.6 liters). Bore & stroke: 3.15 x 3.13 in. Compression ratio: 8.8:1. Brake horsepower: 70 at 4600 R.P.M. Torque: 88 lbs.-ft. at 2600 R.P.M. Five main bearings. Hydraulic valve lifters. Carburetor: 2Bbl. Motorcraft 740. VIN Code: 2. OPTIONAL FOUR (Lynx, LN7): High-output version of 1.6-liter engine above Horsepower: 80 at 5400 R.P.M. Torque: 88 lbs.-ft. at 3000 R.P.M. VIN Code: 4. OPTIONAL FOUR (Lynx, LN7): Fuel-injected version of 1.6-liter engine above Compression ratio: 9.5:1. Horsepower: 88 at 5400 R.P.M. Torque: 94 lbs. - ft. at 4200 R.P.M. VIN Code: 5. BASE FOUR (Capri, Zephyr, Marquis): Inline. Overhead cam. Four-cylinder. Cast iron block and head. Displacement: 140 cu. in. (2.3 liters). Bore & stroke: 3.78 x 3.13 in. Compression ratio: 9.0:1. Brake horsepower: 90 at 4600 R.P.M. Torque: 122 lbs.-ft. at 2600 R.P.M. Five main bearings. Hydraulic valve lifters. Carburetor: 1Bbl. Carter YFA. VIN Code: A. OPTIONAL TURBOCHARGED FOUR (Capri): Same as 140 cu. in. four above, but with turbocharger Compression ratio: 8.0:1. Horsepower: 142 at 5000 R.P.M. Torque: 172 lbs.-ft. at 3800 R.P.M. VIN Code: D. NOTE: Propane four was available for Marquis. OPTIONAL SIX (Zephyr, Marquis): Inline. OHV. Six-cylinder. Displacement: 200 cu. in. (3.3 liters). Bore & stroke: 3.68 x 3.13 in. Compression ratio: 8.6:1. Brake horsepower: 92 at 3800 R.P.M. Torque: 156 lbs.-ft. at 1400 R.P.M. Seven main bearings. Hydraulic valve lifters. Carburetor: 1Bbl. Holley 1946. VIN Code: X. BASE V-6 (Cougar); OPTIONAL (Marquis): 90-degree, overhead valve V-6. Cast iron block and aluminum head. Displacement: 232 cu. in. (3.8 liters). Bore & stroke: 3.80 x 3.40 in. Compression ratio: 8.65:1. Brake horsepower: 110-112 at 3800-4000 R.P.M. Torque: 175 lbs.-ft. at 2200-2600 R.P.M. Four main bearings. Hydraulic valve lifters. Carburetor: 2Bbl. Motorcraft 2150 or 7200VV. VIN Code: 3. BASE V-8 (Grand Marquis); OPTIONAL (Cougar): 90-degree, overhead valve V-8. Cast iron block and head. Displacement: 302 cu. in. (5.0 liters). Bore & stroke: 4.00 x 3.00 in. Compression ratio: 8.4:1. Brake horsepower: 130 at 3200 R.P.M. Torque: 240 lbs.-ft. at 2000 R.P.M. Five main bearings. Hydraulic valve lifters. Fuel injection. VIN Code: F. OPTIONAL V-8 (Grand Marquis): Carbureted version of 302 cu. in. V-8 above Compression ratio: 8.4:1. Horsepower: 145 at 3800 R.P.M. Torque: 245 lbs.-ft. at 2200 R.P.M. OPTIONAL V-8 (Capri): High-output version of 302 cu. in. V-8 above Compression ratio: 8.3:1. Horsepower: 175 at 4000 R.P.M. Torque: 245 lbs.-ft. at 2400 R.P.M. Carburetor: 4Bbl. Holley 4180. POLICE V-8 (Grand Marquis): 90-degree, overhead valve V-8. Cast iron block and head. Displacement: 351 cu. in. (5.8 liters). Bore & stroke: 4.00 x 3.50 in. Compression ratio: 8.3:1. Brake horsepower: 165 at 3600 R.P.M. Torque: 290 lbs.-ft. at 2200 R.P.M. Five main bearings. Hydraulic valve lifters. Carburetor: 2Bbl. VV. VIN Code: G.

CHASSIS DATA: Wheelbase: (Lynx/LN7) 94.2 in.; (Capri) 100.4 in.; (Zephyr/Marquis) 105.5 in.; (Cougar) 104.0 in.; (Grand Marquis) 114.3 in. Overall Length: (Lynx) 163.9 in.; (Lynx lift) 165.0 in.; (LN7) 170.3 in.; (Capri) 179.1 in.; (Zephyr) 195.5 in.; (Z7) 197.4 in.; (Marquis) 196.5 in.; (Cougar) 197.6 in.; (Grand Marquis) 214.0 in.; (Grand Marquis wag) 218.0 in. Height: (Lynx) 53.3 in.; (LN7) 50.5 in.; (Capri) 51.9 in.; (Zephyr) 52.9 in.; (Z7) 51.7 in.; (Marquis) 53.6 in.; (Marquis wag) 54.3 in.; (Grand Marquis) 55.2 in.; (Grand Marquis wag) 56.8 in. Width: (Lynx/LN7) 65.9 in.; (Capri) 69.1 in.; (Zephyr/Marquis) 71.0 in.; (Cougar) 71.1 in.; (Grand Marquis wag) 79.3 in. Front Tread: (Lynx/LN7) 54.7 in.; (Capri) 56.6 in.; (Zephyr/Marquis) 56.6 in.; (Cougar) 58.1 in.; (Grand Marquis) 62.0 in. Rear Tread: (Lynx/LN7) 56.0 in.; (Capri) 57.0 in.; (Zephyr/Marquis) 57.0 in.; (Cougar) 58.5 in.; (Grand Marquis) 62.0 in. Standard Tires: (Lynx/LN7) P165/80R13; (Capri) P185/75R14; (Capri RS) P205/70R14; (Zephyr) P175/75R14; (Marquis) P185/75R14; (Cougar) N/A; (Grand Marquis) P215/75R14 SBR.

TECHNICAL: Transmission: Four-speed manual standard on Lynx. Gear ratios: (1st) 3.58:1; (2nd) 2.05:1; (3rd) 1.23:1; (4th) 0.81:1 or 0.95:1; (Rev) 3.46:1. Alternate Lynx four- speed: (1st) 3.23:1; (2nd) 1.90:1; (3rd) 1.23:1; (4th) 0.81:1; (Rev) 3.46:1. Four-speed floor shift standard on Capri/Marquis four: (1st) 3.98:1; (2nd) 2.14:1; (3rd) 1.42:1 or 1.49:1; (4th) 1.00:1; (Rev) 3.99:1. Four-speed standard on Capri V-8: (1st) 3.07:1; (2nd) 1.72:1; (3rd) 1.00:1; (4th) 0.70:1; (Rev) 3.07:1. Lynx/LN7 five-speed manual: (1st) 3.60:1; (2nd) 2.12:1; (3rd) 1.39:1; (4th) 1.02:1; (5th) 1.02:1; (Rev) 3.62:1. Capri four-cylinder five-speed: (1st) 3.72:1; (2nd) 2.23:1; (3rd) 1.48:1; (4th) 1.00:1; (5th) 0.76:1; (Rev) 3.59:1. Capri V-8 five-speed manual:

(1st) 2.95:1; (2nd) 1.94:1; (3rd) 1.34:1; (4th) 1.00:1; (5th) 0.73:1; (Rev) 2.76:1. Capri turbo five-speed manual: (1st) 4.03:1; (2nd) 2.37:1; (3rd) 1.50:1; (4th) 1.00:1; (5th) 0.86:1; (Rev) 3.76:1. Alternate Capri turbo five-speed manual: (1st) 3.76:1; (2nd) 2.18:1; (3rd) 1.36:1; (4th) 1.00:1; (5th) 0.86:1; (Rev) 3.76:1. SelectShift three-speed automatic standard on Capri/Cougar/Marquis six, optional on others. Gear ratios: (1st) 2.46:1 or 2.47:1; (2nd) 1.46:1 or 1.47:1; (3rd) 1.00:1; (Rev) 2.11:1 to 2.19:1. Lynx three- speed automatic: (1st) 2.79:1; (2nd) 1.61:1; (3rd) 1.00:1; (Rev) 1.97:1. Four-speed overdrive automatic on Cougar/Marquis/Grand Marquis: (1st) 2.40:1; (2nd) 1.47:1; (3rd) 1.00:1; (4th) 0.67:1; (Rev) 2.00:1. Standard final drive ratio: (Lynx/LN7) 3.59:1 w/4spd, 3.73:1 w/5spd, 3.31:1 w/auto.; (Capri four) 3.08:1 w/4spd or auto., 3.45:1 w/5spd; (Capri V-6) 2.73:1; (Capri V-8) 3.08:1 w/4spd; (Capri turbo) 3.45:1; (Zephyr four) 3.08:1; (Zephyr six) 2.73:1; (Marquis) 3.45:1 w/four, 2.73:1 w/six, 3.08:1 w/V-8; (Cougar) 2.47:1 w/3spd auto., 3.08:1 with 4spd auto.; (Grand Marquis) 3.08:1. Steering: (Grand Marquis) recirculating ball; (others) rack and pinion. Front Suspension: (Lynx/LN7) MacPherson strut-mounted coil springs w/lower control arms and stabilizer bar; (Capri/Zephyr/Cougar/Marquis) modified MacPherson struts w/coil springs and anti-sway bar; (Grand Marquis) coil springs with long/short Aarms and anti-sway bar. Rear Suspension: (Lynx/LN7) independent trailing arms w/modified MacPherson struts and coil springs on lower control arms; (Capri/Zephyr/Cougar/Marquis/Grand Marquis) four-link w/coil springs. Brakes: Front disc, rear drum. Ignition: Electronic. Body construction: (Grand Marquis) separate body and frame; (others) unibody. Fuel tank: (Lynx/LN7) 13 gal.; (Capri) 15.4 gal.; (Zephyr) 16 gal.; (Marquis) 16 gal.; (Cougar) 21 gal.; (Grand Marquis) 18 gal.; (Grand Marquis wag) 18.5 gal.

DRIVETRAIN OPTIONS: Engines: H.O. 1.6-liter four: Lynx ($70-$73); LN7 RS ($70). Fuel-injected 1.6-liter four: Lynx LS ($367); Lynx LTS ($294). Propane 140 cu. in. four: Marquis ($896). 200 cu. in. six: Zephyr/Marquis ($239). 232 cu. in. V-6: Capri/Marquis ($309) exc. wagon ($70). 302 cu. in. V-8: Capri L/GS ($1343); Capri Black Magic ($866); Capri Redline ($1118); Cougar ($288). Transmission/Differential: Close-ratio four-speed trans.: Lynx (NC). Five-speed manual trans.: Lynx ($76). Automatic transaxle: Lynx ($439) exc. LTS/RS ($363); LN7 ($363). Select-shift auto. transmission.: Capri/Zephyr/Marquis ($439). Overdrive auto. trans.: Marquis ($615) exc. wagon ($176); Cougar ($176). Floor shift lever: Zephyr/Marquis ($49). First-gear lockout delete: Zephyr ($9). Traction-Lok differential: Capri/Zephyr/Marquis/Grand Marquis/Cougar ($95). Optional axle ratio: Capri/Zephyr (NC). Brakes & Steering: Power brakes: Lynx ($95). Power steering: Lynx/LN7 ($210); Capri ($202); Zephyr/Marquis ($218). Suspension: H.D. susp.: Zephyr/Marquis ($24); Grand Marquis/Cougar ($26). Handling susp.: Lynx L/GS ($145); Lynx LS ($41); Zephyr ($52); Grand Marquis ($49). Handling susp. pkg.: Capri ($252). TR performance susp.: Lynx ($41). TR sport susp.: LN7 ($41). Other: H.D. battery ($26). H.D. alternator: LN7 ($27). Extended-range gas tank: Zephyr/Marquis ($46). Engine block heater ($17-$18). Trailer towing pkg., medium duty: Grand Marquis ($200-$251); heavy duty ($251-$302). Trailer towing pkg.: Cougar ($251). California emission system ($46-$76). High-altitude emissions (NC).

LYNX CONVENIENCE/APPEARANCE OPTIONS: Option Packages: TR performance pkg. ($185-$515). Villager woodtone pkg. ($316). Instrument group ($87). Light group ($43). Comfort/Convenience: Air conditioner ($624). Rear defroster, electric ($124). Fingertip speed control ($170). Tinted glass ($90); windshield only ($38). Digital clock ($57). Interval wipers ($49). Rear wiper/washer ($117). Dual remote sport mirrors ($67). Entertainment: AM radio ($61). AM/FM radio ($82) exc. L ($143). AM/FM stereo radio ($109) exc. L ($170); w/cassette or 8track player ($199) exc. L ($260), LS ($90). Premium sound ($117). Exterior: Flip-up open-air roof ($217-$310). Clearcoat metallic paint: RS ($305). Glamour paint ($51). Tu-tone paint ($134-$173). Dual bodyside paint stripes ($39). Front vent windows, pivoting ($60). Remote quarter windows ($109). Vinyl-insert bodyside moldings ($45). Bumper guards, front or rear ($28). Bumper rub strips ($48). Luggage rack ($93). Lower bodyside protection ($68). Interior: Console ($111). Fold-down center armrest ($55). Low-back reclining bucket seats ($98). High-back reclining bucket seats ($65). Vinyl seats ($24). Wheels/Tires: Cast aluminum wheels ($226-$329). P165/80R13 SBR WSW ($59).

LN7 CONVENIENCE/APPEARANCE OPTIONS: Comfort/Convenience: Air conditioner ($624). Entertainment: AM/FM radio ($82). AM/FM stereo radio ($109); w/cassette or 8track player ($199) exc. Sport ($90). Premium sound ($117). AM radio delete ($37 credit). AM/FM stereo delete ($145 credit). AM/FM stereo/cassette delete ($352 credit). Exterior: Flip-up open air roof ($310). Glamour paint ($51). Two-tone paint/tape ($146). Sport tape stripe ($41). Lower bodyside protection ($68). Interior: Cloth, sport cloth or knit vinyl bucket seats (NC). Sport seats ($173). Leather low-back seat trim ($144). Shearling low-back bucket seats ($227).

CAPRI CONVENIENCE/APPEARANCE OPTIONS: Option Packages: Light group ($55). Appearance protection group ($60). Power lock group ($160). Comfort/Convenience: Air cond. ($724). Rear defroster, electric ($135). Fingertip speed control ($170). Power windows ($180). Tinted glass ($105); windshield only ($38). Leather-wrapped steering wheel ($59). Tilt steering wheel ($105). Interval wipers ($49). Remote right mirror ($44). Entertainment: AM/FM radio ($82). AM/FM stereo radio ($109); w/8track or cassette player ($199). Premium sound system ($117). AM radio delete ($61 credit). Exterior: TRoof ($1055). Flip-up open air roof ($310). Glamour paint ($54). Two-tone paint ($78-$137). Rocker panel moldings ($33). Lower bodyside protection ($41). Interior: Console ($191). Cloth/vinyl seats ($29-$40). Leather/vinyl seats ($415). Sport seats ($196). Front floor mats, carpeted ($22). Wheels and Tires: Wire wheel covers ($98). Turbine wheel covers (NC). Cast aluminum wheels ($345). Styled steel wheels w/trim rings ($78). P185/75R14 WSW ($72). P195/75R14 WSW ($108). P205/75R14 BSW ($224). TRX P220/55R390 BSW ($327- $551).

ZEPHYR CONVENIENCE/APPEARANCE OPTIONS: Option Packages: Instrument cluster ($100). Appearance protection group ($32-$60). Light group ($55). Comfort/Convenience: Air cond. ($724). Rear defroster, electric ($135). Fingertip speed control ($170). Illuminated entry ($82). Power windows ($180-$255). Power door locks ($120-$170). Remote decklid release ($40). Four-way power seat ($139). Tinted glass ($105). Tinted windshield ($38). Tilt steering ($105). Quartz clock ($35). Interval wipers ($49). Lighting and Mirrors: Map light ($10). Trunk light ($7). Left remote mirror ($22). Dual bright remote mirrors ($68). Lighted visor vanity mirrors, pair ($106). Entertainment: AM/FM radio ($59). AM/FM stereo radio ($109); w/8track or cassette player ($199). Premium sound system ($117). AM radio delete ($61 credit). Exterior: Flip-up open air roof ($310). Full or half vinyl roof ($152). Glamour paint ($63). Two-tone paint ($117). Pivoting front vent windows ($63). Wide bodyside moldings ($59). Rocker panel moldings ($39). Bumper guards, rear ($28). Bumper rub strips ($50). Lower bodyside protection ($41). Interior: Console ($191). Bucket seats ($21). Cloth/vinyl seat trim ($35). Bench seat (NC). Front floor mats, carpeted ($24). Front/rear rubber mats ($15). Wheels/Tires: Wire wheel covers ($152). Styled steel wheels ($66). Styled steel wheels w/trim rings ($126). Steel wheels, 5.5 in. ($18); H.D. ($74). P175/75R14 SBR WSW ($72). P185/75R14 WSW ($116). TR BSW on aluminum wheels ($601). Conventional spare ($63).

MARQUIS CONVENIENCE/APPEARANCE OPTIONS: Option Packages: Woodtone option ($282). Heavy-duty pkg. ($210). Power lock group ($170-$210). Cold weather group ($77). Appearance protection group ($60). Light group ($38). Comfort/Convenience: Air cond. ($724); auto-temp ($802). Rear defroster, electric ($135). Fingertip speed control ($170). Illuminated entry ($76). Autolamp on-off delay ($73). Power windows ($255). Six-way power driver's seat ($207); dual ($415). Tinted glass ($105). Tinted windshield ($38). Leather-wrapped steering wheel ($59). Tilt steering ($105). Electronic instrument cluster ($289-$367). Tripminder computer ($215-$293). Digital clock ($78). Diagnostic warning lights ($59). Auto. parking brake release ($12). Interval wipers ($49). Liftgate wiper/washer: wagon ($99). Lighting and Mirrors: Cornering lamps ($60). Map light ($15). Right remote convex mirror ($60). Lighted visor vanity mirrors ($51-$100). Entertainment: AM/FM radio ($59). AM/FM stereo radio ($109); w/8track or cassette player ($199). Electronic-tuning AM/FM stereo radio ($252); w/cassette ($396). Premium sound system ($117-$151). AM radio delete ($61 credit). Exterior: Flip-up open air roof ($310). Full vinyl roof ($152). Glamour paint ($63). Two-tone paint ($117). Pivoting front vent windows (N/A). Two-way liftgate: wag ($105). Protective bodyside moldings (N/A). Bumper guards, rear ($28). Bumper rub strips ($56). Luggage rack: wagon ($126). Lower bodyside protection ($41). Interior: Console ($100). Vinyl seat trim ($35). Individual seats w/console ($61). Leather seat trim ($415). Front floor mats ($23). Wheels/Tires: Luxury wheel covers ($55). Wire wheel covers ($159); locking ($198). Styled wheels w/trim rings ($54). Cast aluminum wheels ($402). P185/75R14 BSW ($38); WSW ($72). P195/75R14 WSW ($72-$116). Puncture-sealant P195/75R14 WSW ($240). Conventional spare ($63).

COUGAR CONVENIENCE/APPEARANCE OPTIONS: Option Packages: Luxury carpet group ($72). Traveler's assistance kit ($65). Light group ($35). Power lock group ($172). Comfort/Convenience: Air cond. ($737); auto-temp ($802). Rear defroster ($135). Fingertip speed control ($170). Illuminated entry system ($82). Keyless entry ($163). Anti-theft system ($159). Remote fuel door lock ($26). Tripminder computer ($215-$276). Autolamp on/off delay ($73). Tinted glass ($105); windshield only ($38). Power windows ($193). Six-way power driver's seat ($222); dual ($444). Auto. parking brake release ($12). Leather-wrapped steering wheel ($59). Tilt steering wheel ($105). Electronic instrument cluster ($382). Electronic voice alert ($67). Diagnostic warning lights ($59). Digital clock ($61). Interval wipers ($49). Lighting and Mirrors: Cornering lamps ($68). Electro- luminescent coach lamps ($84). Dual electric remote mirrors ($94). Electronic-dimming day/night mirror ($77). Lighted visor vanity mirrors, pair ($106). Entertainment: AM/FM stereo radio ($109); w/8track or cassette player ($199). Electronic-tuning AM/FM stereo search radio ($252); w/cassette ($396). Power antenna ($66). Premium sound system ($179). AM radio delete ($61 credit). Exterior: Flip-up open-air roof ($310). Luxury vinyl rear half roof ($240). Clearcoat metallic paint ($152). Two-tone paint: LS ($148-$163). Hood striping ($16). Pivoting front vent windows ($76). Rocker panel moldings ($39). License frames ($9). Lower bodyside protection ($39-$54). Interior: Articulated sport seats ($427) exc. LS ($183). Leather seat trim ($415-$659). Vinyl seat trim ($34). Front floor mats, carpeted ($22). Wheels/Tires: Wire wheel covers, locking ($84-$198). Luxury wheel covers ($113). Puncture-sealing tires ($124). P205/70R14 WSW ($62). P205/70HR14 performance BSW ($152). 220/55R390 TRX performance tires on aluminum wheels ($499- $649). Conventional spare ($63).

GRAND MARQUIS CONVENIENCE/APPEARANCE OPTIONS: Option Packages: Grand Marquis LS decor ($616). Convenience group ($95-$116). Power lock group ($123-$220). Light group ($30-$48). Comfort/Convenience: Air cond. ($724); w/auto-temp control ($802). Rear defroster, electric ($135). Fingertip speed control ($170). Illuminated entry system ($76). Power driver's seat ($210); driver and passenger ($420). Remote fuel door lock ($24). Tinted glass ($105); windshield only ($38). Autolamp on/off delay ($73). Leather-wrapped steering wheel ($59). Tilt steering wheel ($105). Tripminder computer ($261). Digital clock ($61). Lighting and Mirrors: Cornering lamps ($60). Remote right mirror ($43). Lighted visor vanity mirrors ($100). Entertainment: AM/FM stereo radio w/8track or cassette tape player ($112). AM/FM stereo search radio ($166); w/8track or cassette ($310). Power antenna ($60). Premium sound system ($145-$179). AM/FM delete ($152 credit). Exterior: Formal coach vinyl roof ($650). Glamour paint ($77). Two-tone paint ($129). Pivoting front vent windows (N/A). Rocker panel moldings ($32). Vinyl-insert bodyside moldings ($55). Bumper rub strips ($52). Luggage rack ($110). Lower bodyside protection ($39-$52). Interior: Dual-facing rear seats: wag ($167). Cloth trim ($48). Leather seat trim ($418). Duraweave vinyl seat trim ($96). Carpeted front floor mats ($21). Wheels/Tires: Luxury wheel covers ($59). Wire wheel covers ($129); locking ($168). Cast aluminum wheels ($361). P225/75R14 WSW ($42-$43). P205/75R15 WSW ($17); puncture- resistant ($130). Conventional spare ($63).

HISTORY: Introduced: September 23, 1982 or October 14, 1982 except Cougar, February 17, 1983. Model year production: 381,721. Calendar year production (U.S.): 432,353. Calendar year sales by U.S. dealers: 409,433. Model year sales by U.S. dealers: 357,617 (not incl. 21,745 early '84 Topaz models).

Historical Footnotes: Grand Marquis was Mercury's best seller for the '83 model year, taking over that spot from the subcompact Lynx. Model year sales jumped nearly 40 percent for the big full- size model. The two-seater LN7 never had found an adequate number of customers, and dropped out after 1983. Ford's similar EXP hung on longer. Capri sales declined a bit, but remained strong enough to carry on. Only about 30 percent of Capris had V-8 power. Topaz, introduced spring as an early '84, found 21,745 buyers in just the few months before the full model year began. Sales were helped by Hertz, which bought 15,200 Tempo/Topaz models for its rental fleet. Cougar sold quite well with its new "reverse-curve" back window styling, though analysts thought the design inferior to Thunderbird's aero- look. Mercury discovered that 40 percent of them were bought by women. Production of Marquis and Grand Marquis rose sharply, adding jobs at the Chicago and St. Louis plants. For the first time, both large and small cars (front-drive Escort/Lynx and rear-drive Grand Marquis) were produced on the same assembly (at St. Thomas, Ontario). Mercury's market share rose from 5.5 percent to 6.1 percent in two years, with credit taken by Lincoln-Mercury General Manager Gordon B. MacKenzie, who took over in 1981. However, MacKenzie soon left Mercury to return to his former spot at Ford of Europe. The new General Manager was Robert L. Rewey Jr.

1984 MERCURY

Mercury's factory sales catalog promised "a new direction in automotive technology." That meant cars that were exciting to drive, pleasing to the eye, "combining innovative design, aerodynamic styling and meticulous engineering." Highlight of the year was the arrival of the front-wheel-drive Tempo compact, which actually emerged as an early '84 model. A diesel four-cylinder engine was available on Lynx and Topaz. Turbos were optional on Lynx and Capri, and standard on the revived Cougar XR-7. Due to sluggish sales, the two-seater LN7 was abandoned.

LYNX — FOUR — "The quality-built small car." So went Mercury's claim for the subcompact Lynx, now in its fourth season. Three- door, five-door and wagon bodies were offered again, with little appearance change. Wraparound taillamps with two horizontal ribs came to a point at their forward limit on the rear quarter panel. Trim levels ran from base and L to GS, sporty RS, RS Turbo, and top-rung LTS (five-door only). Base engine remained the 1.6-liter CVH four, with four-speed manual transaxle. New this year: an optional 2.0-liter diesel engine with five-speed transaxle. Lynx had a "lubed-for-life" chassis, self-adjusting brakes and clutch, rack-and-pinion steering, fully independent suspension, and maintenance-free battery. A new full-width flat-folding rear seat went into L models; new split-folding rear seat on others. Instrument panels and interiors were revised, including new side-window defoggers. The RS Turbo had a fuel-injected turbocharged engine, five-speed manual overdrive transaxle, special suspension with Koni shocks and TR sport cast aluminum wheels with Michelin 185/60R365 TRX traction compound tires, plus power steering and brakes. New options included a tilt steering wheel, power door locks, overhead console with digital clock and map lights, electronic stereo search radio, and graphic equalizer. Also available: air conditioning, electric rear window defroster, flip-up/open-air roof, tinted glass, and Premium Sound System.

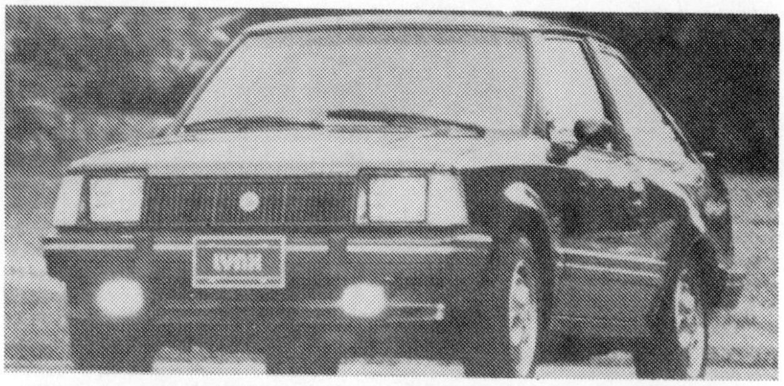

1984 Lynx GS hatchback coupe (JG)

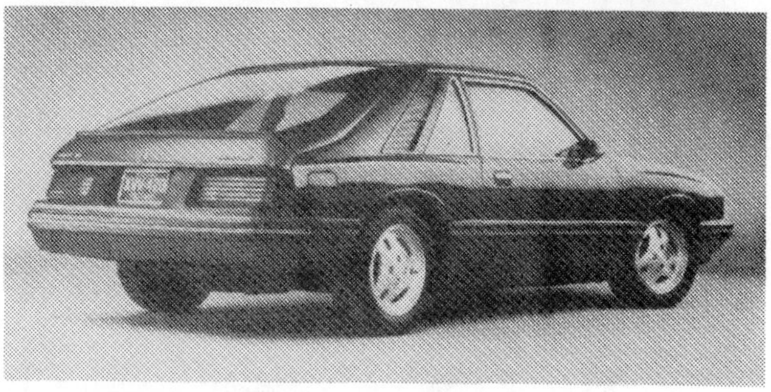

1984 Capri GS hatchback coupe (JG)

CAPRI — FOUR/V-6/V-8 — A simplified Capri model lineup included the base GS, high-performance RS, and RS Turbo. Base, L, Black Magic, and Crimson Cat models were dropped. Promoting the Capri turbo, Mercury's factory catalog insisted that "automotive technology didn't became less exhilirating with the passing of the old muscle cars—it merely became more intelligent." The turbocharged four, introduced in 1983 on Mustang GT and TBird Turbo Coupe, produced 145 horsepower at 4600 R.P.M. (60 percent more than standard four). It was hooked to a five-speed manual overdrive transmission and Traction-Lok axle. Capri RS or GS could have a High Output 302 cu. in. (5.0-liter) V-8 with either fuel injection or four-barrel. The four-barrel version (on RS) had a 2.5 inch diameter exhaust and dual outlets, cast aluminum rocker arm covers, and high-lift camshaft. The fuel-injected V-8 now came with automatic overdrive transmission. Fuel injection was added to the 232 cu. in. (3.8-liter) V-6, optional on GS. All Capris had a split rear searback, with each side folding separately. Instrument panels were revised, now with red backlighting. New steering wheels put the horn button on the hub rather than the column stalk. Gas-pressurized shocks were used at front and rear. Bodies had extra-wide wraparound black bodyside moldings with dual color-keyed stripes, bright roof drip and windshield moldings, black rear window molding, and black/bright window frame moldings. Wraparound horizontally- ribbed taillamps were used, and the rear license plate fit in a recessed opening. Standard front seats were cloth/vinyl reclining low-back buckets. Capri had color-keyed hood and rear pillar louvers, and black cowl louvers. The instrument panel was grey suede painted, with applique. Bumpers had integral black rub strips. GS standard equipment included four-speed manual shift, power brakes, turbine wheel covers, trip odometer, tachometer, three-oval black sport steering wheel, integral rear spoiler, AM radio, black left remote mirror, day/night mirror, and dual visor vanity mirrors. Also standard: a dual-note horn, halogen headlamps, locking glovebox, temp/amp/oil gauges, lighter, digital clock, cargo area cover, and console with graphic warning display and stowage bin. Capri RS added a front air dam, power steering, wrapped steering wheel, five-speed manual gearbox, handling suspension, Traction-Lok axle, foglamps, and locking fuel filler door. Styling features included a black right remote mirror, black grille, black rear pillar louver, and tu-tone black/grey instrument panel. RS had black windshield, roof rip and window frame moldings. Turbo RS added identifying decals on fenders and decklid, sport-tuned exhaust with bright tailpipe extension, a hood scoop, cast aluminum valve covers, and heavy-duty battery.

TOPAZ — FOUR — Taking up the rising tide toward front-wheel-drive, Mercury introduced its second model, the compact Topaz, closely tied to Ford's Tempo. Two- and four-door sedans, replacements for the departed Zephyr, carried five passengers. Riding a wheelbase under 100 inches (actually a stretched Lynx platform), Topaz tipped the scales at about 2,200 lbs. The aerodynamically-styled body had a horizontal- bar grille with center emblem. Single rectangular headlamps met amber wraparound front side marker lenses. Euro-style wraparound taillamps tapered downward on each quarter panel. Two-doors had decklid stripes and dual bodyside accent stripes, and a black B pillar molding. Both bodies had a lower back panel applique with argent accents. Two trim levels were offered: GS and LS. Both had standard lower bodyside protection. Color-keyed bodyside moldings were wide in Pacific states, narrow elsewhere. Standard GS features included bright upper/lower grille bars, and window frame, belt, rear window surround and windshield moldings. Bumpers had color-keyed end caps and rub strips. Base engine was a 140 cu. in. (2.3-liter) 2300 HSC (High Swirl Combustion) four with EEC-IV. Displacement was the same as the four that had been around for some years, but bore and stroke were not. This was a different design, derived from the inline six. The standard four-speed manual overdrive transaxle (five-speee in Pacific states) had a self-adjusting clutch. A 2.0-liter diesel also was offered, with five-speed transaxle. Topaz had rack-and-pinion steering and a parallel four-bar-link independent rear suspension. A firm-handling suspension was standard. Interiors held contoured front seats, a locking glovebox, and a color-keyed consolette. Door trim panels were carpeted on the lower section, with built-in storage bins. Cloth/vinyl low-back reclining bucket seats were standard. Standard GS equipment included polycast wheels, two- speed wiper/washer, AM radio (AM/FM in Pacific states), power brakes, lighter, temp gauge, ammeter, locking glovebox, dual- note horn, four-speed heater/defroster, halogen headlamps, color-keyed instrument panel applique, dual color-keyed rmeote mirrors, day/night mirror, and dual visor vanity mirrors. The radio could be deleted for credit. Topaz LS added passenger assist handles, a swivel map light, interval wipers, dual color bodyside accent stripes, color-keyed wide bodyside moldings, decklid moldings (four-door), comfort/convenience group, digital clock, and color-keyed umper end cap extensions. Pacific-state models also had power steering, power door locks, power windows, dual lighted visor vanity mirrors, console with graphic warning display, and illuminated entry. The special Western State Package, adding standard equipment, was offered only in California, Oregon, Washington, Alaska and Hawaii.

MARQUIS — FOUR/V-6 — Descended from the old Cougar, the rear-drive Marquis changed little for its second season. Three-speed SelectShift automatic was now the standard transmission, and the inline six option was dropped. A fuel-injected 232 cu. in. (3.8- liter) V-6 was standard in wagons, optional in sedans. Power steering became standard, and the horn button returned to the center hub of the steering wheel. Gas-pressurized shocks were standard. Thin vertical bars made up the Marquis grille. Angled clear/amber side marker lenses continued back from the housing that contained the quad rectangular headlamps. Amber parking lamps were built into the bumper. Separate clear horizontal rectangular marker lenses were below the bodyside molding, just ahead of the front wheel. At the rear were wraparound taillamps. Front seatbacks had individual recliners. An extra-cost front bench seat expanded capacity to six passengers. Marquis Brougham had Twin Comfort lounge seats with dual recliners and individual fold-down center armrests. Cloth upholstery was standard; vinyl or leather seating surfaces optional. Options included an Electronic Instrument Cluster with Tripminder computer, auto-temp air conditioner, power lock group, and Premium Sound System. Marquis wagons had a standard liftgate-open warning light and cargo area lamp.

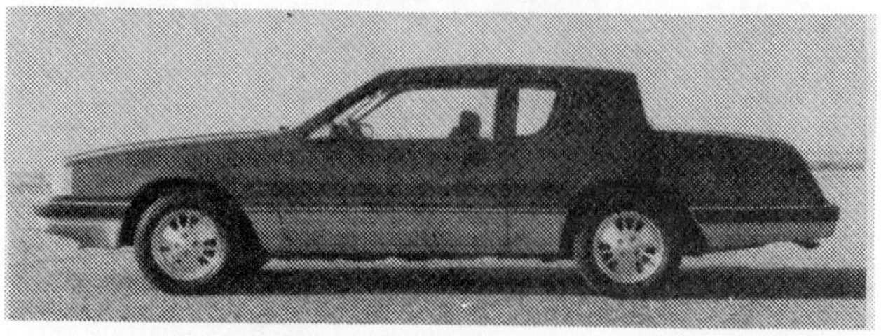

1984 Cougar XR-7 Sports Coupe (JG)

COUGAR/XR-7 — FOUR/V-6/V-8 — Following a year out of the lineup, the XR7 name returned this year on a turbocharged Cougar—Mercury's version of the Thunderbird Turbo Coupe. XR7 had a standard five-speed manual or optional (extra cost) three-speed automatic transmissin, along with a handling suspension, high-performance tires, and a tachometer. Turbo models featured Quadra-Shock rear suspension, with two horizontal dampers. Fuel injection went on the basic Cougar's 232 cu. in. (3.8-liter) base V-6 engine. Standard automatic transmissions had a lock-up torque converter. The 302 cu. in. (5.0-liter) V-8 was optional. All engines now had EEC-IV electronic controls. The horn button moved to the center hub of the new steering wheel. Nitrogen gas-pressurized front struts and rear shocks were standard. So was variable-ratio power rack- and-pinion steering. Appearance was similar to 1983, with upswept quarter- window design and wide rear pillars with round emblem. Cougars had deeply recessed quad rectangular headlamps. Wraparound amber side marker lenses extended from the same housing. An optional Electronic Instrument Cluster contained a digital speedometer, graphic fuel gauge, and digital clock. Base Cougars came with automatic transmission, AM radio, bright wheel covers, power brakes and steering, driver's remote mirror, reminder chimes, analog clock, lighter, full console with padded lid, and mini spare tire. Bright moldings went on the grille surround, belt, concealed drip, quarter and back windows, door frames, windshield, and bodyside (with charcoal vinyl insert). Bodies displayed a center pillar applique, charcoal bumper rub strips with extensions, and decklid and upper bodyside accent stripes. Cougar LS added a woodtone applique instrument panel, tinted glass, coach lamps, dual black power remote mirrors, bright rocker panel moldings, power windows, and hood accent stripes. LS also had standard luxury cloth 40/40 seats and a passenger visor vanity mirror. In addition to the turbo engine, Cougar XR-7 had a Traction-Lok axle, tachometer, heavy-duty (54-amp) battery, charcoal floor console with Oxford Grey armrest pad, Oxford Grey headliner, charcoal instrument panel, power windows, and silver metallic polycast wheels. Also on XR7: Oxford Grey tri-band lower tape striping, black leather-wrapped four- spoke steering wheel, clearcoat metallic paint with lower accent, and color-keyed rear window moldings. Seats were Oxford Grey cloth sport buckets.

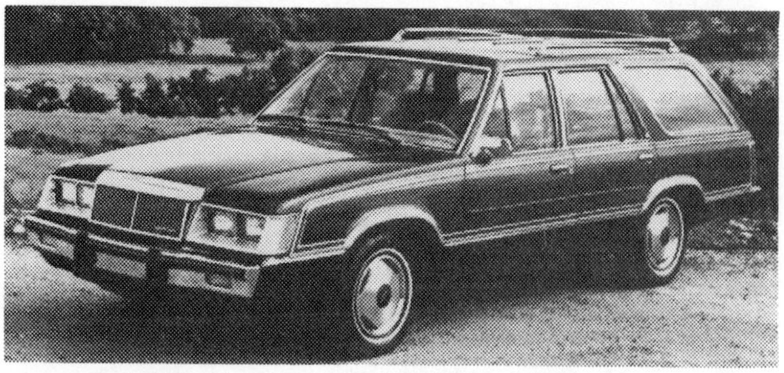

1984 Marquis Colony Park station wagon (OCW)

GRAND MARQUIS — V-8 — Immodestly described as an "American classic," the full-size (by modern standards, at any rate) Grand Marquis continued with little change, carrying six passengers. Sole engine was the 302 cu. in. (5.0-liter) V-8 with EFI and EEC- IV, coupled to four-speed automatic overdrive. Base and LS trim levels were availble in the two- and four-door sedans. LS had Twin Comfort lounge seats in luxury cloth or optional leather. As before, the upright grille was made up of six vertical bars on each side of a slightly wider center divider bar. Surround moldings of the recessed quad headlamps continued to meet clear park/signal lights at the fender tips, which wrapped around the fenders to a narrow amber lens at the rear. Wraparound horizontally-ribbed taillamps were used. Colony Park and Colony Park LS wagons both had a three- way tailgate with power window, locking stowage compartment, and load floor carpeting. Twin Comfort lounge seats had standard vinyl upholstery, with cloth and knitted vinyl optional; cloth standard on Colony Park LS. Dual-facing optional rear seats held two passengers (for a total of eight). A heavy-duty suspension package included bigger front stabilizer bar, heavy-duty springs and revalved shocks. The heavy-duty (Class III) Trailer Towing Package that could haul 5,000 pounds included a heavy-duty radiator, auxiliary power steering and transmission oil coolers.

I.D. DATA: Mercury's 17-symbol Vehicle Identification Number (VIN) was stamped on a metal tab fastened to the instrument panel, visible through the windshield. Symbols one to three indicates manufacturer, make and vehicle type: '1ME' Mercury passenger car. The fourth symbol ('B') denotes restraint system. Next comes a letter 'P', followed by two digits that indicate body type: Model Number, as shown in left column of tables below. (Example: '54' base Lynx three-door hatchback.) Symbol eight indicates engine type: '2' L498 2Bbl.; '4' H.O. L498 2Bbl.; '5' L498 EFI; '8' Turbo L498 FI; 'H' Diesel L4121; 'A' L4-140 1Bbl.; 'R' or 'J' HSC L4140 1Bbl.; '6' Propane L4140; 'W' Turbo L4140 EFI; '3' V6232 2Bbl. or FI; 'F' V8302 2Bbl. or FI; 'M' V8302 4Bbl.; 'G' V8351 2Bbl. Next is a check digit. Symbol ten indicates model year ('E' 1984). Symbol eleven is assembly plant: 'A' Atlanta, GA; 'B' Oakville, Ontario

(Canada); 'F' Dearborn, MI; 'G' Chicago; 'H' Lorain, Ohio; 'K' Kansas City, MO; 'W' Wayne, MI; 'X' St. Thomas, Ontario; 'Z' St. Louis, MO; and Edison, NJ. The final six digits make up the sequence number, starting with 600001. A Vehicle Certification Label on the left front door lock face panel or door pillar shows the month and year of manufacture, GVW, GAWR, VIN, and codes for such items as body type, color, trim, axle, transmission, and special order information.

LYNX (FOUR)

Model Number	Body/Style Number	Body Type & Seating	Factory Price	Shipping Weight	Production Total
54	61D	3-dr. Hatch-4P	5758	1928	Note 1
65	58D	5-dr. Hatch-4P	5965	1984	Note 1
54	61D	3-dr. L Hatch-4P	6019	1922	Note 1
65	58D	5-dr. L Hatch-4P	6233	N/A	Note 1
60	74D	4-dr. L Sta Wag-4P	6448	N/A	Note 1
55	61D	3-dr. GS Hatch-4P	6495	1948	Note 1
66	58D	5-dr. GS Hatch-4P	6709	N/A	Note 1
61	74D	4-dr. GS Sta Wag-4P	6887	N/A	Note 1
57	61D	3-dr. RS Hatch-4P	7641	N/A	Note 1
68/934	58D	5-dr. LTS Hatch-4P	7879	1920	Note 1

LYNX TURBO (FOUR)

57	61D	3-dr. RS Hatch-4P	8728	1997	Note 1

Note 1: Total Lynx production, 38,208 three-door hatchbacks, 21,090 five-door hatchbacks, and 16,142 four-door liftgate station wagons.

CAPRI GS (FOUR/V-6)

79	61D	3-dr. Fastbk-4P	7758/8167	2615/2723	Note 2

Capri Engine Note: Six-cylinder price does not include cost of the required automatic transmission ($439). The high-output 302 cu. in. V-8 engine cost $1165 more than the V-6.

CAPRI RS TURBO (FOUR)

79	61D	3-dr. Fastbk-4P	9822	2894	Note 2

CAPRI RS (V-8)

79	61D	3-dr. Fastbk-4P	9638	2894	Note 2

Note 2: Total Capri production was 20,642.

TOPAZ (FOUR)

72	66D	2-dr. GS Sedan-5P	7469	2329	32,749
75	54D	4-dr. GS Sedan-5P	7469	2413	96,505
73	66D	2-dr. LS Sedan-5P	7872	2353	Note 3
76	54D	4-dr. LS Sedan-5P	7872	2434	Note 3

Note 3: Production of LS models is included in GS totals.

Diesel Engine Note: A diesel model Topaz cost $8027 (GS) or $8429 (LS).

MARQUIS (FOUR/V-6)

89	54D	4-dr. Sedan-5P	8727/9136	2796/--	91,808
90	74D	4-dr. Sta Wag-5P	--/9224	--/2996	16,004

1984 Marquis Brougham sedan (JG)

MARQUIS BROUGHAM (FOUR/V-6)

89	54D	4-dr. Sedan-5P	9030/9439	2796/--	Note 4
90	74D	4-dr. Sta Wag-5P	--/9498	N/A	Note 4

Note 4: Brougham production is included in basic totals above.

COUGAR (V-6/V-8)

92	66D	2-dr. Cpe-4P	9978/10361	2912/--	131,190
92/603	66D	2-dr. LS Cpe-4P	11265/11648	2941/--	Note 5

Cougar Engine Note: The V-8 engine required a four-speed automatic transmission at $237 extra.

COUGAR XR-7 (TURBO FOUR)

92/934	66D	2-dr. Cpe-4P	13065	2900	Note 5

Note 5: Production of LS and XR-7 is included in basic total above.

1984 Grand Marquis LS sedan (JG)

GRAND MARQUIS (V-8)

93	66K	2-dr. Sedan-6P	11576	3607	13,657
95	66K	4-dr. Sedan-6P	11640	3761	117,739
93/60H	66K	2-dr. LS Sed-6P	12131	3607	Note 6
95/60H	54K	4-dr. LS Sed-6P	12195	3761	Note 6

GRAND MARQUIS COLONY PARK (V-8)

94	74K	4-dr. Sta Wag-6P	11816	3788	17,421

Note 6: LS production is included in basic Grand Marquis totals.

FACTORY PRICE AND WEIGHT NOTE: Cougar prices and weights to left of slash are for V-6, to right for V-8 engine. For Capri/Marquis, prices/weights to left of slash are for four-cylinder, to right for V-6.

ENGINE DATA: BASE FOUR (Lynx): Inline. Overhead cam. Four-cylinder. Cast iron block and aluminum head. Displacement: 97.6 cu. in. (1.6 liters). Bore & stroke: 3.15 x 3.13 in. Compression ratio: 9.0:1. Brake horsepower: 70 at 4600 R.P.M. Torque: 88 lbs.-ft. at 2600 R.P.M. Five main bearings. Hydraulic valve lifters. Carburetor: 2Bbl. Motorcraft 740. VIN Code: 2. OPTIONAL FOUR (Lynx): High-output version of 1.6-liter engine above Horsepower: 80 at 5400 R.P.M. Torque: 88 lbs.-ft. at 3000 R.P.M. VIN Code: 4. OPTIONAL FOUR (Lynx): Fuel-injected version of 1.6-liter engine above Compression ratio: 9.5:1. Horsepower: 84 at 5200 R.P.M. Torque: 90 lbs.-ft. at 2800 R.P.M. VIN Code: 5. TURBO FOUR (Lynx): Same as 1.6-liter four above, with fuel injection and turbocharger Compression ratio: 8.0:1. Horsepower: 120 at 5200 R.P.M. Torque: 120 lbs.-ft. at 3400 R.P.M. VIN Code: 8. DIESEL FOUR (Lynx, Topaz): Inline. Overhead cam. Four cylinder. Cast iron block and aluminum head. Displacement: 121 cu. in. (2.0 liters). Bore & stroke: 3.39 x 3.39 in. Compression ratio: 22.5:1. Brake horsepower: 52 at 4000 R.P.M. Torque: 82 lbs.-ft. at 2400 R.P.M. Solid valve lifters. Fuel injection. VIN Code: H. BASE FOUR (Topaz): Inline. Overhead valve. Four-cylinder. Cast iron block and head. Displacement: 140 cu. in. (2.3 liters). Bore & stroke: 3.70 x 3.30 in. Compression ratio: 9.0:1. Brake horsepower: 84 at 4400 R.P.M. Torque: 118 lbs.-ft. at 2600 R.P.M. Five main bearings. Hydraulic valve lifters. Carburetor: 1Bbl. Holley 6149. High Swirl Combustion (HSC) design. VIN Code: R (U.S.) or J (Mexico). BASE FOUR (Capri, Marquis): Inline. Overhead cam. Four-cylinder. Cast iron block and head. Displacement: 140 cu. in. (2.3 liters). Bore & stroke: 3.78 x 3.13 in. Compression ratio: 9.0:1. Brake horsepower: 88 at 4000 R.P.M. Torque: 122 lbs.-ft. at 2400 R.P.M. Five main bearings. Hydraulic valve lifters. Carburetor: 1Bbl. Carter YFA. VIN Code: A. BASE TURBO FOUR (Cougar XR-7); OPTIONAL (Capri): Same as 140 cu. in. four above, but with turbocharger Compression ratio: 8.0:1. Horsepower: 145 at 4600 R.P.M. (Capri, 175 at 4400 R.P.M.). Torque: 180 lbs.-ft. at 3800 R.P.M. (Capri, N/A). VIN Code: W. NOTE: Propane four was available for Marquis. BASE V-6 (Cougar); OPTIONAL (Capri, Marquis): 90-degree, overhead valve V-6. Cast iron block and aluminum head. Displacement: 232 cu. in. (3.8 liters). Bore & stroke: 3.80 x 3.40 in. Compression ratio: 8.65:1. Brake horsepower: 120 at 3600 R.P.M. Torque: 205 lbs.-ft. at 1600 R.P.M. Four main bearings. Hydraulic valve lifters. Carburetor: 2Bbl. (or fuel-injected). VIN Code: 3. BASE V-8 (Grand Marquis); OPTIONAL (Cougar): 90-degree, overhead valve V-8. Cast iron block and head. Displacement: 302 cu. in. (5.0 liters). Bore & stroke: 4.00 x 3.00 in. Compression ratio: 8.4:1. Brake horsepower: 140 at 3200 R.P.M. Torque: 250 lbs.-ft. at 1600 R.P.M. Five main bearings. Hydraulic valve lifters. Fuel injection. VIN Code: F. OPTIONAL V 8 (Grand Marquis): Carbureted version of 302 cu. in. V-8 above Compression ratio: 8.4:1. Horsepower: 155 at 3600 R.P.M. Torque: 265 lbs.-ft. at 2000 R.P.M. OPTIONAL V-8 (Capri): Fuel-injected version of 302 cu. in. V-8 above Compression ratio: 8.3:1. Horsepower: 165 at 4000 R.P.M. Torque: 245 lbs.-ft. at 2200 R.P.M. OPTIONAL V-8 (Capri): High-output version of 302 cu. in. V-8 above Compression ratio: 8.3:1. Horsepower: 175 at 4000 R.P.M. Torque: 245 lbs.-ft. at 2200 R.P.M. Carburetor: 4Bbl. Holley 4180C. VIN Code: M. NOTE: High-output version rated 205 H.P. was announced but delayed. POLICE V-8 (Grand Marquis): 90-degree, overhead valve V-8. Cast iron block and head. Displacement: 351 cu. in. (5.8 liters). Bore & stroke: 4.00 x 3.50 in. Compression ratio: 8.3:1. Brake horsepower: 180 at 3600 R.P.M. Torque: 285 lbs.-ft. at 2400 R.P.M. Five main bearings. Hydraulic valve lifters. Carburetor: 2Bbl. VV. VIN Code: G.

CHASSIS DATA: Wheelbase: (Lynx) 94.2 in.; (Capri) 100.5 in.; (Topaz) 99.9 in.; (Marquis) 105.6 in.; (Cougar) 104.0 in.; (Grand Marquis) 114.3 in. Overall Length: (Lynx) 163.9 in.; (Capri) 179.1 in.; (Topaz) 176.5 in.; (Marquis) 196.5 in.; (Cougar) 197.6 in.; (Grand Marquis) 214.0 in.; (Grand Marquis wag) 218.0 in. Height: (Lynx)

53.3 in.; (Capri) 51.9 in.; (Topaz 2dr.) 52.5 in.; (Topaz 4dr.) 52.7 in.; (Marquis) 53.6 in.; (Marquis wag) 54.3 in.; (Cougar) 53.4 in.; (Grand Marquis) 55.2 in.; (Grand Marquis wag) 56.8 in. Width: (Lynx) 65.9 in.; (Capri) 69.1 in.; (Topaz) 66.2 in.; (Marquis) 71.0 in.; (Cougar) 71.1 in.; (Grand Marquis) 77.5 in.; (Grand Marquis wag) 79.3 in. Front Tread: (Lynx) 54.7 in.; (Capri) 56.6 in.; (Topaz) 54.7 in.; (Marquis) 56.6 in.; (Cougar) 58.1 in.; (Grand Marquis) 62.2 in. Rear Tread: (Lynx) 56.0 in.; (Capri/Marquis) 57.0 in.; (Topaz) 57.6 in.; (Cougar) 58.5 in.; (Grand Marquis) 62.0 in. Standard Tires: (Lynx) P165/80R13; (Lynx RS/LTS) 165/70R365 Michelin TRX; (Capri) P185/75R14; (Capri RS) P205/70R14; (Topaz) P175/80R13; (Marquis) P185/75R14; (Cougar) P185/75R14; (XR7) P205/70HR14; (Grand Marquis) P215/75R14 SBR WSW.

TECHNICAL: Transmission: Four-speed manual standard on Lynx/Topaz; five- speed manual or three-speed automatic optional. Four-speed manual standard on Capri; five-speed manual, three-speed or four-speed automatic optional. SelectShift three-speed automatic standard on Cougar/Marquis; four-speed overdrive optional. Five-speed manual standard on Cougar XR7. Four- speed overdrive automatic standard on Grand Marquis. Gear ratios same as equivalent Ford models; see Ford/Mustang listings. Standard final drive ratio: (Lynx) 3.59:1 w/4spd, 3.73:1 w/5spd, 3.31:1 w/auto., 3.52:1 w/diesel; (Capri four) 3.08:1 w/4spd, 3.27:1 w/auto.; (Capri V-6) 3.08:1; (Capri V-8) 3.08:1 w/5spd, 2.73:1 w/auto., 3.27:1 w/4spd auto.; (Capri turbo) 3.45:1; (Topaz) 3.04:1 w/4spd, 3.23:1 w/5spd or auto., 3.73:1 w/diesel; (Marquis) 3.08:1, 3.27:1 or 2.73:1; (Cougar V-6) 2.73:1 w/3spd auto., 3.27:1 with 4spd auto.; (Cougar V-8) 3.08:1; (Cougar XR7 turbo) 3.45:1 w/5spd, 3.73:1 w/auto.; (Grand Marquis) 3.08:1. Steering: (Grand Marquis) recirculating ball; (others) rack and pinion. Front Suspension: (Lynx) MacPherson strut-mounted coil springs w/lower control arms and stabilizer bar; (Topaz) MacPherson struts w/stabilizer bar; (Capri/Cougar/Marquis) modified MacPherson struts w/coil springs and anti-sway bar; (Grand Marquis) coil springs with long/short Aarms and anti- sway bar. Rear Suspension: (Lynx) independent trailing arms w/modified MacPherson struts and coil springs on lower control arms; (Topaz) fully independent quadra-link w/MacPherson struts; (Capri/Cougar/Marquis/Grand Marquis) four-link w/coil springs. Brakes: Front disc, rear drum. Ignition: Electronic. Body construction: (Grand Marquis) separate body and frame; (others) unibody. Fuel tank: (Lynx) 13 gal.; (Capri) 15.4 gal.; (Topaz) 15.2 gal.; (Marquis) 16 gal.; (Cougar) 20.6 gal.; (Grand Marquis) 18 gal.; (Grand Marquis wag) 18.5 gal.

DRIVETRAIN OPTIONS: Engines: Fuel-saver 1.6-liter four: Lynx (NC). H.O. 1.6-liter four: Lynx ($73). Propane 140 cu. in. four: Marquis ($896). 232 cu. in. V-6: Capri/Marquis ($409). 302 cu. in. V-8: Capri ($1372-$1574); Cougar ($383). Transmission/Differential: Five-speed manual trans.: Lynx/Topaz ($76). Automatic transaxle: Lynx ($439) exc. LTS/RS ($363); Topaz ($439). Auto. transmission.: Capri ($439). Overdrive auto. trans.: Capri ($551); Marquis/Cougar ($237). Traction-Lok differential: Capri/Marquis/Grand Marquis/Cougar ($95). Brakes & Steering: Power brakes: Lynx ($95). Power steering: Lynx ($215); Capri ($202); Topaz ($223). Suspension: H.D. susp.: Topaz (NC); Marquis ($43); Grand Marquis/Cougar ($26). Handling susp.: Lynx L ($145); Lynx GS ($41); Grand Marquis ($49). Handling susp. pkg.: Capri ($252) exc. w/VIP pkg. ($50). Soft ride susp. pkg.: Topaz (NC). Other: H.D. battery ($27). Engine block heater ($18). Trailer towing pkg.: Grand Marquis ($200-$302); Cougar ($251). California emission system: Lynx ($46); others ($99). High- altitude emissions (NC).

LYNX CONVENIENCE/APPEARANCE OPTIONS: Option Packages: Villager woodtone pkg. ($339). Instrument group ($87). Power door lock group ($124-$176). Light group ($67). Comfort/Convenience: Air conditioner ($643). Rear defroster, electric ($130). Fingertip speed control ($176). Tinted glass ($95); windshield only ($48). Tilt steering ($104). Overhead console w/digital clock ($82). Interval wipers ($50). Rear wiper/washer ($120). Dual remote sport mirrors ($68). Entertainment: AM radio ($39). AM/FM stereo radio ($109) exc. L ($148); w/cassette player ($204) exc. L ($243). Electronic- tuning AM/FM stereo w/cassette ($396-$435). Premium sound ($117). Radio delete ($39 credit). Exterior: Flip-up open-air roof ($315) exc. Villager ($215). Clearcoat metallic paint (NC). Glamour paint ($51). Dual bodyside paint stripes ($39). Front vent windows, pivoting ($63). Vinyl-insert bodyside moldings ($45). Bumper guards, front or rear ($28). Bumper rub strips ($48). Luggage rack ($100). Lower bodyside protection ($68). Interior: Console ($111). Vinyl seat trim ($24). Wheels/Tires: Wheel trim rings ($54). TR aluminum wheels: LTS/RS ($201). Styled steel wheels ($104 credit). P165/80R13 SBR WSW ($59). P175/80R13 SBR BSW (NC).

CAPRI CONVENIENCE/APPEARANCE OPTIONS: Option Packages: Light group ($55-$88). Power lock group ($177). Comfort/Convenience: Air cond. ($743). Rear defroster, electric ($140). Fingertip speed control ($176). Power windows ($198). Tinted glass ($110). Tilt steering wheel ($110). Interval wipers ($50). Remote right mirror ($46). Entertainment: AM/FM stereo radio ($109); w/cassette player ($222) exc. w/VIP pkg. ($113). Premium sound system ($151). AM radio delete ($39 credit); AM/FM ($148 credit). Exterior: TRoof ($874-$1074). Flip-up open air roof ($315). Glamour paint ($54). Lower bodyside protection ($41). Interior: Sport seats ($196). Vinyl low-back seats ($29). Wheels and Tires: Wire wheel covers ($98). P195/75R14 WSW ($108). P205/70HR14 BSW ($224). TRX 220/55R390 BSW in performance pkg. ($327-$551).

TOPAZ CONVENIENCE/APPEARANCE OPTIONS: Option Packages: TR performance pkg. w/aluminum wheels ($293). Power lock group ($202-$254). Appearance protection group ($71). Light/convenience group ($50-$70). Comfort/Convenience: Air cond. ($743). Rear defroster, electric ($140). Fingertip speed control ($176). Illuminated entry ($82). Anti-theft system ($159). Power windows ($272). Power decklid release ($40). Six-way power seat ($224). Tinted glass ($110); windshield ($48). Tilt steering ($110). Digital clock ($61). Interval wipers ($50). Lighted visor vanity mirrors, pair ($100). Entertainment: AM/FM stereo radio ($109); w/cassette player ($204). Electronic-tuning AM/FM stereo ($252); w/cassette ($396). Premium sound system ($117). AM radio delete ($39 credit). Exterior: Flip-up open air roof ($315). Metallic glamour glow paint ($63). Black lower body accent paint ($78-$133). Bumper guards, front/rear ($56). Interior: Console ($111). Fold-down front armrest ($55). Vinyl seat trim ($35). Carpeted front floor mats ($13). Trunk trim ($30). Tires: P175/80R13 WSW ($72).

MARQUIS CONVENIENCE/APPEARANCE OPTIONS: Option Packages: Woodtone option ($282). Power lock group ($213-$254). Cold weather group ($77). Light group ($38). Police pkg. ($859-$1387). H.D. pkg. ($210). Comfort/Convenience: Air cond. ($743); auto-temp ($809). Rear defroster, electric ($140). Fingertip speed control ($176). Illuminated entry ($82). Autolamp on-off delay ($73). Power windows ($272). Six-way power driver's seat ($224); dual ($449). Tinted glass ($110). Tinted windshield ($48). Leather-wrapped steering wheel ($59). Tilt steering ($110). Electronic instrument cluster ($289-$367). Tripminder computer ($215-$293). Digital clock ($78). Diagnostic warning lights ($89). Auto. parking brake release ($12). Interval wipers ($50). Liftgate wiper/washer: wagon ($99). Lighting and Mirrors: Cornering lamps ($68). Right remote convex mirror ($61). Lighted visor vanity mirrors ($57-$106). Entertainment: AM/FM stereo radio ($109); w/cassette player ($204). Electronic-tuning AM/FM stereo radio w/cassette ($396). Premium sound system ($117-$151). AM radio delete ($39 credit). Exterior: Carriage roof ($848). Full vinyl roof ($152). Glamour paint ($63). Two-tone paint ($117). Pivoting front vent windows ($79). Two-way liftgate: wag ($105). Protective bodyside moldings ($55). Bumper guards, rear ($28). Bumper rub strips ($56). Luggage rack: wagon ($126). Lower bodyside protection ($41). Interior: Vinyl seat trim ($35). Individual seats w/console ($61). Leather seat trim ($415). Front floor mats, carpeted ($23). Wheels/Tires: Luxury wheel covers ($55). Wire wheel covers, locking ($204). Polycast wheels ($178). Styled steel wheels w/trim rings ($54). P185/75R14 WSW ($72). P195/75R14 BSW ($38); WSW ($116). Puncture-sealant P195/75R14 WSW ($240). Conventional spare ($63).

COUGAR CONVENIENCE/APPEARANCE OPTIONS: Option Packages: Luxury carpet group ($72). Traveler's assistance kit ($65). Light group ($35). Power lock group ($177). Comfort/Convenience: Air cond. ($743); auto-temp ($809). Rear defroster ($140). Fingertip speed control ($176). Illuminated entry system ($82). Keyless entry ($198). Anti-theft system ($159). Remote fuel door lock ($37). Tripminder computer ($215-$276). Autolamp on/off delay ($73). Tinted glass ($110); windshield only ($48). Power windows ($198). Six-way power driver's seat ($227); dual ($454). Auto. parking brake release ($12). Leather-wrapped steering wheel ($59). Tilt steering wheel ($110). Electronic instrument cluster ($382). Diagnostic warning lights ($89). Digital clock ($61). Interval wipers ($49). Lighting and Mirrors: Cornering lamps ($68). Electro-luminiscent coach lamps ($84). Dual electric remote mirrors ($96). Electronic-dimming day/night mirror ($77). Lighted visor vanity mirrors, pair ($106). Entertainment: AM/FM stereo radio ($109); w/cassette player ($204). Electronic-tuning AM/FM stereo search radio ($252); w/cassette ($396). Power antenna ($66). Premium sound system ($179). AM radio delete ($39 credit). Exterior: Luxury vinyl half rear roof ($245). Flip-up open-air roof ($315). Metallic clearcoat paint ($183). Hood accent striping ($16). Pivoting front vent windows ($79). Rocker panel moldings ($39). License frames ($9). Lower bodyside protection ($39-$54). Interior: Articulated seats ($183-$427). Leather seat trim ($415). Vinyl seat trim ($37). Front floor mats, carpeted ($22). Wheels/Tires: Wire wheel covers, locking ($90-$204). Luxury wheel covers ($113). Polycast wheels ($65-$178). P195/75R14 puncture-sealing tires ($124). P205/70R14 BSW (NC). P205/70R14 WSW ($62). P205/70HR14 performance BSW ($152). Cast aluminum TRX wheels w/BSW performance tires ($535-$649) exc. XR7 ($318).

GRAND MARQUIS CONVENIENCE/APPEARANCE OPTIONS: Option Packages: LS decor: Colony Park ($621). Convenience group ($109-$134). Power lock group ($140-$238). Light group ($30-$48). Comfort/Convenience: Air cond. ($743); w/auto-temp control ($809). Rear defroster, electric ($140). Fingertip speed control ($176). Illuminated entry system ($82). Power driver's seat ($227); driver and passenger ($454). Remote fuel door lock ($35). Tinted glass ($110); windshield only ($48). Autolamp on/off delay ($73). Leather-wrapped steering wheel ($59). Tilt steering wheel ($110). Tripminder computer ($261). Digital clock ($61). Interval wipers ($50). Lighting and Mirrors: Cornering lamps ($68). Remote right mirror ($44). Lighted visor vanity mirrors ($106). Entertainment: Electronic-tuning AM/FM stereo radio w/cassette ($166). Power antenna ($66). Premium sound system ($151- $179). Radio delete ($148 credit). Exterior: Formal vinyl coach roof: 4dr. ($650). Glamour paint ($77). Two-tone paint ($129). Pivoting front vent windows ($79). Rocker panel moldings ($18-$38). Vinyl-insert bodyside moldings ($61). Bumper rub strips ($59). Luggage rack ($104). Lower bodyside protection ($39-$52). Interior: Dual-facing rear seats: wagon ($167). Cloth twin comfort seats ($48). Leather seat trim ($418). All-vinyl seat trim ($34); Duraweave vinyl ($96). Carpeted front floor mats ($21). Wheels/Tires: Wire wheel covers, locking ($174). Cast aluminum wheels ($361). P225/75R14 WSW ($42-$43). P205/75R15 WSW ($17); puncture-sealant ($178). P215/75R14 BSW ($66 credit). Conventional spare ($63).

NOTE: Many value option packages were offered for each Mercury model.

HISTORY: Introduced: September 22, 1983 except Topaz, April 1983. Model year production: 613,155. Calendar year production (U.S.): 461,504. Calendar year sales by U.S. dealers: 527,198. Model year sales by U.S. dealers: 529,300 (including early '84 Topaz models).

Historical Footnotes: A giant sales leap highlighted the 1984 model year, up about one-third from 484,688 (including 21,745 early Topaz models) to 644,308. Marquis sales rose dramatically, and Cougar wasn't so far from doubling (up 82 percent). Big and luxury models seemed to be doing well, as was the case in the industry as a whole. Lynx and Capri sales slipped notably, though not drastically. LN7 was dropped in 1984, as it had never found a significant number of buyers. Only a few leftovers were sold during the 1984 model year. Lincoln-Mercury now had its own import: the sporty Merkur XR4Ti, from Ford Werke AG in West Germany, rivaling BMW, Audi and Volvo. It was actually sold under a separate franchise.

1985 MERCURY

Cougar got a modest facelift this year, including grille, taillamps and dash. Grand Marquis offered an electronic suspension system. A fuel-injected four-cylinder engine and five-speed manual transaxle were made standard on Topaz. Lynx was a carryover at introduction time, but a Second Series arrived at mid-year, with a larger (1.9-liter) engine under the hood.

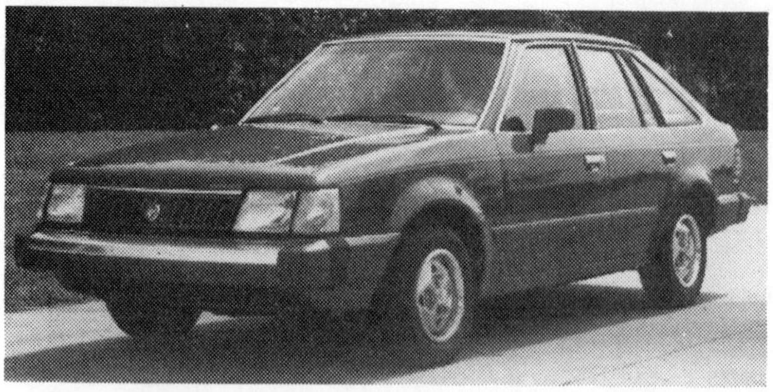

1985 Lynx hatchback sedan (CP)

LYNX — FOUR — Since a Second Series Lynx with larger (1.9-liter) CVH four-cylinder engine would arrive as a 1985.5 model, the early carryover version continued with fewer models and engine possibilities. Only the three-door base model survived, along with GS and LS editions. The RS (three-door) and LTS (five-door) were dropped. Also dropped was the port fuel-injected 1.6 engine, leaving only the carbureted version. A new shift pattern for the five-speed transaxle put reverse below fifth gear, instead of by itself at the upper left. All except the base three-door now had power brakes. An AM/FM stereo radio was now standard on GS. The 2.0-liter diesel engine was available again, but turbos faded away. Base Lynx standard equipment included the two-barrel four-cylinder engine, four-speed manual transaxle, P165/80R13 SBR BSW tires on semi-styled steel wheels with bright trim rings, color-keyed door scuff plates, compact spare tire, cargo area cover, consolette, side window demisters, dome light, and day/night mirror. Bright bumpers had black end caps. Cloth reclining high-back

bucket seats were standard. So was a 10-gallon fuel tank. Lynx L added power brakes, an AM radio, black carpeting, 13-gallon fuel tank, black rocker panel paint, and cloth reclining low-back bucket seats. Pacific state models had a five-speed manual transaxle, AM/FM stereo and an instrument group. GS models included a black front air dam, AM/FM stereo radio, styled steel wheels, high-output engine, five-speed transaxle, dual-color upper bodyside accent paint stripes, and color-keyed lower back panel carpeting. Also on GS: a locking glovebox, remote fuel filler door lock/release, and power hatch release. Wide bodyside moldings had argent accent striping, and rocker panels had no black paint. See 1986 listing for description of the Second Series Lynx.

1985 Capri GS hatchback coupe (CP)

CAPRI — FOUR/V-6/V-8 — Appearance of Mercury's Mustang clone was similar to 1984. As usual, Capri had a different grille than Mustang, and horizontal louvers at the rear of the quarter window rather than vertical. Biggest styling difference, though, was the "bubbleback" glass hatch. Roller tappets were added to the 302 cu. in. (5.0-liter) V-8, standard in the RS (later changed to 5.0L name), along with a higher-performance camshaft and two-speed accessory drive. The five-speed manual gearbox got tighter gear ratios and shorter lever travel. Capri GS continued with a standard 140 cu. in. (2.3-liter) four. Other choices included the 232 cu. in. (3.8-liter) V-6, and fuel-injected or four-barrel V-8. The turbo four was scheduled to reappear, but didn't make it. Both the V-6 and V-8 had a low oil level warning light. Bodies now had charcoal highlights. Standard equipment was added, including an electric rear-window defroster, tinted glass, power steering, interval wipers, and tilt steering. Capri GS standard equipment included the 140 cu. in. four with four-speed manual gearbox, P195/75R14 SBR BSW tires, turbine wheel covers, power windows, tachometer, integral rear spoiler, power brakes, charcoal bumper rub strips, digital clock, console with graphic warning display, and charcoal dual remote mirrors. Capri's charcoal grille had bright edges. Extra-wide wraparound charcoal bodyside moldings were used. Bodies also had dual fender and quarter panel pinstripes, lower bodyside protection, and color-keyed bumpers. Color-keyed louvers went on the hood, rear pillar and quarter panel; charcoal louvers on the cowl. Capri 5.0L included the V-8 engine, P205/70R14 tires, five-speed gearbox, cast aluminum wheels, handling suspension, three-oval black sport steering wheel, foglamps, locking remote gas filler door, front air dam, Traction-Lok, and dual exhausts. Bodies featured a charcoal lower bodyside paint treatment, charcoal moldings and grille, and charcoal rear pillar and quarter panel louvers. Tu-tone articulated sport seats offered adjustable thigh support.

1985 Topaz LS sedan (CP)

TOPAZ — FOUR — Changes to the front-drive compact in its second year were mainly mechanical. Throttle-body fuel injection was added to the standard 140 cu. in. (2.3-liter) four. A new expanded option, the GS Sports Group, included a high-output four with new cylinder head and intake manifold, offered only with manual shift. All manual transaxles were now five-speed, with a new shift pattern (reverse moved from upper left to lower right position). Standard equipment now included power steering, tinted glass, and AM/FM stereo, leaving fewer items on the option list. A restyled instrument panel included a package tray and side window defoggers. Child-proof rear door locks were new. Joining the option list: leather seat trim, and a graphic equalizer for audio fans. Topaz had more standard equipment than Tempo—and more yet in Western states. Another difference between the two was Topaz's vertical-style wraparound taillamps, which connected with a full-width ribbed horizontal bar. Topaz GS standard equipment included the five-speed manual transaxle, P175/80R13 SBR BSW tires on polycast aluminum wheels, handling suspension, and tachometer. Styling features included dual bodyside accent stripes, decklid stripes (two-door), dual sport remote mirrors, color-keyed bumper end caps and rub strips, and a black grille. Wide bodyside moldings were color-keyed. Cloth/vinyl low-back reclining bucket seats were standard, along with vinyl lower bodyside protection, consolette, side window demisters, and power brakes. Topaz LS equipment included AM/FM stereo with cassette player, power windows, interval wipers, dual lighted visor vanity mirrors, and tilt steering. LS also had three assist handles, a digital clock, console, remote decklid release, electric rear window defroster, power door locks, illuminated entry, and remote gas filler door lock/release. New optional leather seat trim came only in charcoal.

MARQUIS — FOUR/V-6 — Apart from a revised grille, little change was evident on Mercury's rear-drive mid-size (nearly identical to Ford LTD), redesigned in 1983 on the former Cougar platform. This year's grille had fewer (and wider) vertical bars, and a center bar that was wider yet. New wide wraparound taillamps had horizontal ribbing in a two-tiered, all-red design. The base 140 cu. in. (2.3-liter) four added low-friction rings and gained compression. Standard tires increased to P195/75R14 size, with P205/70R14 newly optional. A high-output V-8 package also was announced, equivalent to LTD's LX model, but failed to appear. A four-door sedan and wagon came in base or Brougham trim. Wagons had a standard 232 cu. in. (3.8-liter) V-6. Standard Marquis equipment included automatic transmission, AM radio, cloth reclining Twin Comfort lounge seats, black front bumper guards, remote driver's mirror, power brakes and steering, and a mini spare tire. Dual hood and upper bodyside accent stripes were used. Wide color-keyed vinyl bodyside moldings had argent striping. Marquis Brougham added a digital clock, lighted passenger visor vanity mirror, luxury cloth reclining Twin Comfort seats, light group, and luxury interior touches. New options included rocker panel moldings, dual power remote mirrors, and Brougham Flight bench seating.

1985 Marquis sedan (CP)

1985 Cougar XR-7 coupe (CP)

COUGAR — FOUR/V-6/V-8 — Two years after its massive restyling, Cougar got a modest facelift. The new grille, styled à la Mercedes, had two horizontal bars and one vertical bar. Its basic shape, though, wasn't much different than before. Taillamps also were revised. A restyled instrument cluster contained a digital speedometer, plus analog fuel and temperature gauges. A full electronic display was optional. XR7 carried an all-analog cluster, and switched to 15 inch wheels. The 60/40 split bench front seat came with a consolette (not full console). Flatter back seat cushions now held three people. A soft-feel dashboard held side-window defoggers. The turbocharged four-cylinder engine in XR7 was modified for smoother, quiet running, and added horsepower. Five-speed gearboxes got a tighter shift pattern. New standard tires were P205/70R14 on basic models, P225/60VR15 for the XR7. Base models had a standard 232 cu. in. (3.8-liter) V-6 with SelectShift three-speed automatic (four-speed available); or optional 302 V-8 with four-speed overdrive automatic. Standard equipment also included power brakes and steering, four-speaker AM/FM stereo radio, cloth/vinyl reclining Twin Comfort lounge seats, bumper rub strips with extensions, analog clock, side defoggers, and dual-note horn. Upper bodyside accent stripes were standard. Bright moldings went on belt, drip, door frame, quarter and back windows, and windshield. Lower bodyside moldings had charcoal vinyl inserts. Cougar LS added power windows, hood accent stripes, cloth seat trim, bright rocker panel moldings, dual power remote mirrors, tinted glass, coach lamps, and trunk carpeting. XR7 included the turbocharged four with five-speed gearbox, P225/60VR15 performance Goodyear Gatorback BSW tires on cast aluminum wheels, handling suspension, Traction-Lok axle, front air dam, foglamps, and color-keyed dual power remote mirrors. Inside were Oxford Grey cloth sport bucket seats, a black sport steering wheel, digital clock, and charcoal console. Oxford Grey tri-band lower tape stripes, tinted glass, and charcoal moldings were standard on XR7.

1985 Grand Marquis sedan (CP)

GRAND MARQUIS — V-8 — Full-size rear-drives didn't have to change much each year to attract buyers. This year was no exception. Gas-pressurized front struts and rear shocks became standard. The horn button moved from the steering-column stalk to the hub, and a flash-to-pass feature was added. One key now worked both ignition and door locks. An ignition diagnostic monitor was added to EEC-IV engine control. Lower bodysides added chip-resistant urethane coating. Late in the model year, electronic rear leveling was to be made optional. As before, the full-size selection included a two- and four-door sedan, and four-door wagon. Standard equipment included the 302 cu. in. (5.0-liter) V-8 with automatic overdrive transmission, P215/75R14 SBR WSW tires, power brakes/steering, power windows, analog quartz clock, driver's remote mirror, and AM/FM stereo radio. Body features included upper bodyside accent stripes, a coach vinyl roof, bumper guards, and coach lamps. Color-keyed moldings went on quarter windows and roof wraparound of two-doors, and on the rear window; other moldings were bright, including wide lower bodyside moldings. Cloth reclining Twin Comfort lounge seats were standard. Grand Marquis LS added luxury cloth Twin Comfort seats, tinted glass, a folding center rear armrest, dual-beam dome light, and woodtone-applique door trim panels. Colony Park wagons had P215/75R14 WSW tires, conventional spare tire, three-way tailgate with power window, full-length bodyside/rail/tailgate woodtone applique, and vinyl Twin Comfort seats. Mercury's 17-symbol Vehicle Identification Number (VIN) was stamped on a metal tab fastened to the instrument panel, visible through the windshield. Symbols one to three indicates manufacturer, make and vehicle type: '1ME' Mercury passenger car. The fourth symbol ('B') denotes restraint system. Next comes a letter 'P', followed by two digits that indicate body type: Model Number, as shown in left column of tables below. (Example: '72' Topaz GS two-door sedan). Symbol eight indicates engine type: '2' L498 2Bbl.; '4' H.O. L498 2Bbl.; 'H' Diesel L4121; 'A' L4-140 1Bbl.; 'X' HSC L4140 1Bbl.; 'S' H.O. L4140 FI; 'W' Turbo L4140 EFI; '3' V6232

DRIVETRAIN OPTIONS: Engines: H.O. 1.6-liter four: Lynx ($73). 232 cu. in. V-6: Capri ($439); Marquis sedan ($418). 302 cu. in. V-8: Capri ($1238); Cougar ($398). Transmission/Differential: Five-speed manual trans.: Lynx L ($76); Capri GS w/V-8 (NC). Automatic transaxle: Lynx L ($439); Lynx GS ($363); Topaz ($363). SelectShift auto. trans.: Capri ($439); Cougar XR7 ($315). Overdrive auto. trans.: Capri ($551-$676); Cougar ($237). Traction-Lok differential: Marquis/Grand Marquis/Cougar ($95). Brakes & Steering: Power brakes: Lynx ($95). Power steering: Lynx ($215). Suspension: H.D. susp.: Cougar base/LS, Grand Marquis ($26); Marquis LPO ($43). Auto. load leveling: Grand Marquis ($200). Other: H.D. battery ($27). Extended-range gas tank: Marquis sedan ($46). Engine block heater ($18). Trailer towing pkg.: Grand Marquis ($251-$302); Cougar ($251) exc. XR7. California emission system: Lynx ($46); others ($99). High- altitude emissions (NC).

LYNX CONVENIENCE/APPEARANCE OPTIONS: Option Packages: Comfort/convenience group ($259-$384). Comfort/Convenience: Air conditioner ($643). Rear defroster, electric ($130). Fingertip speed control ($176). Power door locks ($124-$176). Tinted glass ($95). Tilt steering ($104). Console w/graphic warning display ($111). Rear wiper/washer ($120). Entertainment: AM/FM stereo radio ($109) exc. base ($148); w/cassette player ($148-$295). Graphic equalizer ($218). Exterior: Clearcoat metallic paint ($91). Two-tone paint ($134-$173). Dual bodyside stripes: L ($39). Black vinyl- insert bodyside moldings ($45). Bumper guards, front or rear ($28). Bumper rub strips ($48) exc. base. Luggage rack: wag ($100). Interior: Vinyl seat trim ($24). Tires: P165/80R13 SBR WSW ($59).

NOTE: Many options were not available on base Lynx.

CAPRI CONVENIENCE/APPEARANCE OPTIONS: Option Packages: TR performance pkg. P220/55VR390 TRX tires on aluminum wheels w/handling suspension: GS ($565) exc. w/V-8 ($377). Power lock group ($177). Comfort/Convenience: Air cond. ($743). Fingertip speed control ($176). Entertainment: Electronic AM/FM stereo w/cassette ($300). Premium sound system ($138). Radio delete ($148 credit). Exterior: TRoof ($1074). Flip-up open air roof ($315). Interior: Low-back vinyl bucket seats: GS ($29). GS Wheels and Tires: Wire wheel covers ($98). Polycast steel wheels ($178). P205/75R14 WSW ($109).

TOPAZ CONVENIENCE/APPEARANCE OPTIONS: Option Packages: Sports group: GS ($439). Comfort/convenience pkg.: GS ($320-$706). TR performance pkg.: P185/65R365 Michelin TRX tires on cast aluminum wheels w/handling suspension ($293). Power lock group ($188-$254). Comfort/Convenience: Air cond. ($743). Rear defroster, electric ($140). Fingertip speed control ($176). Power windows: GS LPO ($272). Six-way power driver's seat LPO ($224). Tilt steering: GS ($110). Entertainment: AM/FM stereo radio w/cassette player: GS ($148). Electronic-tuning AM/FM stereo w/cassette ($78-$300). Graphic equalizer ($218). Exterior: Clearcoat paint ($91). Lower body accent paint ($78). Interior: Vinyl reclining bucket seat trim LPO ($35). Leather seat trim ($300). Wheels/Tires: Styled wheels: GS LPO ($59). P175/80R13 WSW ($72). Conventional spare ($63).

MARQUIS CONVENIENCE/APPEARANCE OPTIONS: Option Packages: Woodtone option: wagon ($282). Power lock group ($213-$254). Light group: base ($38). Comfort/Convenience: Air cond. ($743). Rear defroster ($140). Fingertip speed control ($176). Illuminated entry ($82). Autolamp on-off delay ($73). Power windows ($272). Six-way power driver's seat ($224). Tinted glass ($110). Leather- wrapped steering wheel ($59). Tilt steering ($110). Digital clock: base ($78). Auto. parking brake release LPO ($12). Interval wipers ($50). Lighting and Mirrors: Cornering lamps ($68). Right remote convex mirror ($61). Dual electric remote mirrors ($96). Lighted visor vanity mirrors ($57-$106). Entertainment: AM/FM stereo radio ($109); w/cassette player ($256). Electronic-tuning AM/FM stereo radio w/cassette ($409). AM radio delete ($39 credit). Exterior: Full vinyl roof ($152). Two-tone paint ($117). Pivoting front vent windows ($79). Two-way liftgate: wag ($105). Rocker panel moldings ($40). Bumper guards, rear ($28). Black bumper rub strips w/argent stripe ($56). Luggage rack: wagon ($126). Interior: Vinyl seat trim ($35). Flight bench seat: base (NC). Front floor mats, carpeted ($23). Wheels/Tires: Luxury wheel covers ($55). Wire wheel covers, locking ($204). Polycast wheels ($178). Styled steel wheels w/trim rings fleet ($54). P195/75R14 WSW ($72). P205/70R14 WSW ($134). Conventional spare LPO fleet ($63).

COUGAR CONVENIENCE/APPEARANCE OPTIONS: Option Packages: Headlamp convenience group ($176). Light group ($35). Power lock group ($213). Comfort/Convenience: Air cond. ($743); auto-temp ($905). Rear defroster ($140). Fingertip speed control ($176). Illuminated entry system ($82). Keyless entry ($198). Tinted glass: base ($110). Power windows: base ($198). Six-way power driver's seat ($227); dual ($454). Dual power seat recliners: base/LS ($189). Auto. parking brake release: base/LS ($12). Leather- wrapped steering wheel ($59). Tilt steering wheel ($110). Electronic instrument cluster ($330); N/A XR7. Diagnostic warning lights ($89). Low oil warning light LPO ($24). Digital clock ($61). Interval wipers ($50). Lighting and Mirrors: Cornering lamps ($68). Dual electric remote mirrors: base ($96). Lighted visor vanity mirrors, pair ($106). Entertainment: AM/FM stereo radio w/cassette player ($148). Electronic-tuning AM/FM stereo search radio w/cassette ($300). Power antenna ($66). Graphic equalizer ($252). Premium sound system ($168). AM/FM radio delete ($148 credit). Exterior: Padded half vinyl roof: base/LS ($245). Metallic clearcoat paint ($183). Two-tone paint/tape: base ($163). Hood accent stripe: base ($16). Pivoting front vent windows ($79). Interior: Heated seats ($157). Leather/vinyl seat trim ($415). Vinyl seat trim: base ($37). Front floor mats, carpeted ($22). Wheels/Tires (except XR7): Wire wheel covers, locking ($204). Polycast wheels ($178). P205/70R14 BSW ($62 credit). P215/70R14 WSW ($37). P215/70HR14 performance BSW ($152). Conventional spare ($63).

GRAND MARQUIS CONVENIENCE/APPEARANCE OPTIONS: Option Packages: LS decor: Colony Park ($621). Convenience group ($109-$134). Power lock group ($176-$273). Light group ($30-$48). Comfort/Convenience: Air cond. ($743); w/auto-temp control ($809). Rear defroster, electric ($140). Fingertip speed control ($176). Illuminated entry system ($82). Power driver's seat ($227); driver and passenger ($454). Tinted glass ($110). Autolamp on/off delay ($73). Leather-wrapped steering wheel ($59). Tilt steering wheel ($110). Tripminder computer ($261). Digital clock ($61). Lighting and Mirrors: Cornering lamps ($68). Remote right convex mirror ($46). Lighted visor vanity mirrors ($106). Entertainment: AM/FM stereo radio w/cassette tape player ($148). Electronic-tuning AM/FM stereo radio w/cassette ($300). Power antenna ($66). Premium sound system ($168). AM/FM radio delete ($148 credit). Exterior: Formal coach vinyl roof ($650). Two-tone paint/tape ($129). Hood accent stripes ($18). Pivoting front vent windows ($79). Rocker panel moldings ($18-$38). Narrow vinyl- insert bodyside moldings ($61). Bumper rub strips ($59). Luggage rack: wagon ($110). License frames ($9). Interior: Dual-facing rear seats: wagon ($167). Leather seat trim: LS ($418). All-vinyl seat trim ($34). Cloth trim: wagon ($48). Carpeted front/rear floor mats LPO fleet ($33). Wheels/Tires: Wire wheel covers, locking ($174). Turbine spoke cast aluminum wheels ($361). P205/75R15 WSW ($17); puncture-sealant ($178). P215/70R15 WSW ($79). Conventional spare ($63).

HISTORY: Introduced: October 4, 1984. Model year production: 541,276 (including only mid-year Lynx models). Calendar year production (U.S.): 374,535. Calendar year sales by U.S. dealers: 519,059. Model year sales by U.S. dealers: 555,021.

Historical Footnotes: Grand Marquis sold the best since record-setting 1978, reaching 145,242 buyers (up from 131,515 in 1984). Cougar sales rose about 13 percent; Topaz a bit; Marquis down just a hair. Capri was not doing at all well, finding only 16,829 customers. The imported Merkur wasn't strong either, in its first (short) season. Front-drive may have been the wave of the future by the mid-1980s, but Lincoln-Mercury's rear- drives were doing quite well, not yet ready for retirement.

1986 MERCURY

A new aero-styled Sable, close kin to Ford Taurus, suffered a delayed introduction but replaced the old Marquis (which hung on for this model year). Lynx added a sporty equivalent to Escort's GT. All Lynx models now carried the 1.9-liter engine.

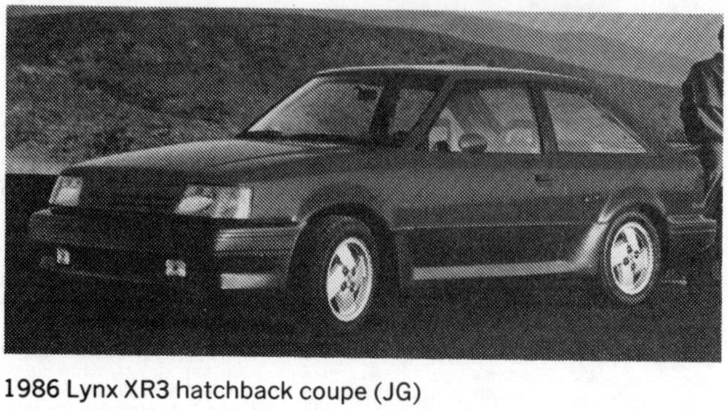

1986 Lynx XR3 hatchback coupe (JG)

LYNX — FOUR — A sporty new XR3 hatchback, similar to Ford's Escort GT, joined the Lynx line, which had arrived in revised form at mid-year 1985. The former 1.6-liter CVH engine had been reworked to reach 1.9-liter displacement. XR3 carried a standard high-output version with multi-port fuel injection, plus 15 inch performance radial tires on aluminum wheels, an asymmetrical grille (again like Escort), foglamps, wheel spats, rocker panel moldings, rear spoiler, and front air dam. Standard five-speed manual or optional three-speed automatic were the two transmission choices. Base, L and GS models were offered, in three- or five-door (actually two and four) hatchback or wagon body styles. The diesel engine option returned (with five-speed gearbox). Lynx carried a new four-spoke steering wheel and new wraparound bumper end treatment, as well as a larger-diameter front stabilizer bar. The 1985.5 Lynx restyle had incorporated new front-end styling and headlamps, along with a revised rear end. Aero headlamps extended outward from the squat angled grille, made up of thin vertical bars with a round center emblem. Above the grille on the driver's side was 'Mercury' block lettering. The headlamps met wraparound park/signal/marker lenses that were amber colored. Horizontally-ribbed, wraparound full-width taillamps extended outward from the recessed rear license plate opening. Small integral, squarish backup lenses were part of each assembly. 'Lynx' lettering (and model identification) went above the left taillamps; 'Mercury' lettering above the right one. Standard Lynx equipment included the 1.9-liter OHC four- cylinder engine, four-speed manual transaxle, power brakes, P175/80R13 BSW SBR tires, semi-styled steel wheels with bright trim rings and argent hub covers with black lug nuts, high-mount rear stoplamp, and black driver's mirror. Bumper end caps extended to wheel openings. Interiors contained low- back reclining front seats with cloth upholstery, a flat- folding rear seat, soft-feel instrument panel, and grained- finish glovebox with coin slots. Lynx L added an AM radio (which could be deleted for credit), bright hood molding, bright hub covers and lug nuts, matte black rocker panel paint, and dual bodyside paint stripes. GS added a five-speed manual transaxle, AM/FM stereo radio, locking fuel filler door with remote release, body- color rocker panels, styled steel wheels, bumper rub strips, wide bodyside molding, roof grab handles, dual visor vanity mirrors, and fold-down front center armrest. XR3's minimalist grille consisted of two slots, one above the other, occuping just two-thirds of the body-color front panel, with 'XR3' identification on the other side. XR3 also had an aerodynamic front air dam with built-in foglamps. Equipment included the high-output engine, P195/60HR15 BSW SBR Goodyear Eagle unidirectional tires on cast aluminum wheels, power steering, overhead console with digital clock, foglamps, full console with graphic warning display, and an instrument group (including tachometer). Also part of XR3: a leather-wrapped steering wheel, cloth sport seats, dual remote mirrors, blackout greenhouse treatment, Midnight Smoke lower bodyside treatment, body-color spoiler, and narrow bodyside moldings.

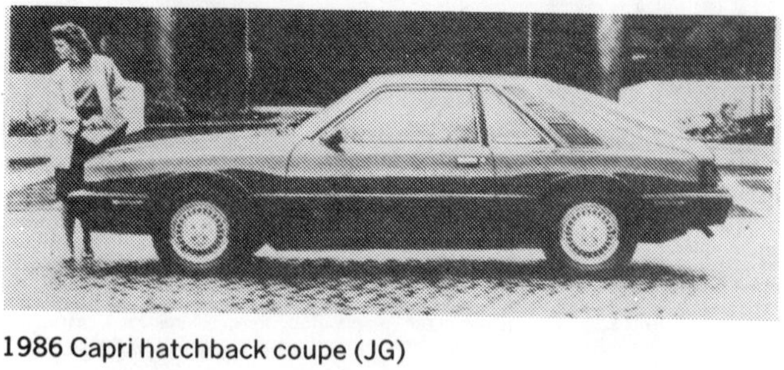

1986 Capri hatchback coupe (JG)

CAPRI — FOUR/V-6/V-8 — Changes to Mercury's ponycar went mostly under the hood for 1986. The 302 cu. in. (5.0-liter) V-8 added sequential fuel injection, along with roller tappets, new rings, a knock sensor, and tuned intake/exhaust manifolds. Carbureted V-8s were gone. So was the turbo four, which hadn't even arrived for 1985, though it had been announced. Capri's simple model lineup was the same this year: just GS and 5.0L, the latter signifying V-8 power. Capri's ample standard equipment list meant few options were available. Standard equipment included the 140 cu. in. (2.3-liter) four with four-speed manual gearbox, power brakes/steering, tinted glass, interval wipers, electric back window defroster, AM/FM stereo radio, tilt steering, and power windows. GS also had aero wheel covers, upper bodyside paint stripes, a black remote driver's mirror, tachometer and trip odometer, console with graphic warning display, digital clock, and passenger visor vanity mirror. Low-back front bucket seats had cloth upholstery. Options included the 232 cu. in. (3.8-liter) V-6 and three-speed automatic. Capri 5.0 added the 302 cu. in. V-8 and five-speed overdrive manual gearbox, P225/60VR15 tires, hood scoop (non-working), Traction-Lok differential, handling suspension, black brushed-finish dash applique, black remote passenger mirror, upper bodyside dual accent tape stripes, blackout body tgrim, and twin bright tailpipe outlets.

FI; 'F' V8302 2Bbl. or FI; 'M' V8302 4Bbl.; 'G' V8351 2Bbl. Next is a check digit. Symbol ten indicates model year ('F' 1985). Symbol eleven is assembly plant: 'A' Atlanta, GA; 'B' Oakville, Ontario (Canada); 'F' Dearborn, MI; 'G' Chicago; 'H' Lorain, Ohio; 'K' Kansas City, MO; 'W' Wayne, MI; 'X' St. Thomas, Ontario; 'Z' St. Louis, MO; and Edison, NJ. The final six digits make up the sequence number, starting with 600001. A Vehicle Certification Label on the left front door lock face panel or door pillar shows the manufacturer, month and year of manufacture, GVW, GAWR, certification statement, VIN, and codes for such items as body type, color, trim, axle, transmission, and special order information.

LYNX (FOUR)

Model Number	Body/Style Number	Body Type & Seating	Factory Price	Shipping Weight	Production Total
54/41P	61D	3-dr. Hatch-4P	5750	1922	Note 1
54	61D	3-dr. L Hatch-4P	6170	1985	Note 1
65	58D	5-dr. L Hatch-4P	6384	2050	Note 1
60	74D	4-dr. L Sta Wag-4P	6508	2076	Note 1
55	61D	3-dr. GS Hatch-4P	6707	2054	Note 1
66	58D	5-dr. GS Hatch-4P	6921	2121	Note 1
61	74D	4-dr. GS Sta Wag-4P	6973	2137	Note 1

Diesel Engine Note: Lynx diesel models cost $558 more (L) or $415 more (GS).

1985.5 LYNX (FOUR)

51	61D	3-dr. Hatch-4P	5986	2060	Note 1
51	61D	3-dr. L Hatch-4P	6272	2060	Note 1
63	58D	5-dr. L Hatch-4P	6486	2106	Note 1
58	74D	4-dr. L Sta Wag-4P	6767	2141	Note 1
52	61D	3-dr. GS Hatch-4P	6902	2149	Note 1
64	58D	5-dr. GS Hatch-4P	7176	2192	Note 1
59	74D	4-dr. GS Sta Wag-4P	7457	2215	Note 1

Note 1: Total Lynx production for the 1985.5 model year, 20,515 three- door hatchbacks, 11,297 five-door hatchbacks, and 6,721 four-door liftgate station wagons. Further information not available.

CAPRI GS (FOUR/V-6)

79	61D	3-dr. Fastbk-4P	7944/8383	2615/2723	Note 2

Capri Engine Note: Six-cylinder price does not include cost of the required automatic transmission ($439). The high-output 302 cu. in. V-8 engine cost $799 more than the V-6.

CAPRI RS/5.0L (V-8)

79	61D	3-dr. Fastbk-4P	10223	N/A	Note 2

Note 2: Total Capri production was 18,657.

TOPAZ (FOUR)

72	66D	2-dr. GS Sedan-5P	7767	2313	18,990
75	54D	4-dr. GS Sedan-5P	7767	2368	82,366
73	66D	2-dr. LS Sedan-5P	8931	2335	Note 3
76	54D	4-dr. LS Sedan-5P	8980	2390	Note 3

Note 3: Production of LS models is included in GS totals.

Diesel Engine Note: A diesel model Topaz cost $8246 (GS) or $9410- $9459 (LS).

MARQUIS (FOUR/V-6)

89	54D	4-dr. Sedan-5P	8996/9414	2755/ --	91,465
90	74D	4-dr. Sta Wag-5P	-- /9506	-- /2978	12,733

MARQUIS BROUGHAM (FOUR/V-6)

89/60H	54D	4-dr. Sedan-5P	9323/9741	2849/ --	Note 4
90/60H	74D	4-dr. Sta Wag-5P	-- /9805	N/A	Note 4

Note 4: Brougham production is included in basic totals above.

COUGAR (V-6/V-8)

92	66D	2-dr. Cpe-5P	10650/11048	2931/ --	117,274
92/603	66D	2-dr. LS Cpe-5P	11850/12248	2961/ --	Note 5

Cougar Engine Note: The V-8 engine required a four-speed automatic transmission at $237 extra.

COUGAR XR-7 (TURBO FOUR)

92/934	66D	2-dr. Cpe-5P	13599	2947	Note 5

Note 5: Production of LS and XR-7 is included in basic total above.

GRAND MARQUIS (V-8)

93	66K	2-dr. Sedan-6P	12240	3607	10,900
95	54K	4-dr. Sedan-6P	12305	3761	136,239
93/60H	66K	2-dr. LS Sed-6P	12789	3607	Note 6
95/60H	54K	4-dr. LS Sed-6P	12854	3761	Note 6

GRAND MARQUIS COLONY PARK (V-8)

94	74K	4-dr. Sta Wag-6P	12511	3788	14,119

Note 6: LS production is included in basic Grand Marquis totals.

FACTORY PRICE AND WEIGHT NOTE: Cougar prices and weights to left of slash are for V-6, to right for V-8 engine. For Capri/Marquis, prices/weights to left of slash are for four-cylinder, to right for V-6.

ENGINE DATA: BASE FOUR (Lynx): Inline. Overhead cam. Four-cylinder. Cast iron block and aluminum head. Displacement: 97.6 cu. in. (1.6 liters). Bore & stroke: 3.15 x 3.13 in. Compression ratio: 9.0:1. Brake horsepower: 70 at 4600 R.P.M. Torque: 88 lbs.-ft. at 2600 R.P.M. Five main bearings. Hydraulic valve lifters. Carburetor: 2Bbl. Holley 740. VIN Code: 2. NOTE: Second Series Lynx, introduced at mid-year, used a new 1.9-liter four; see 1986 listing for specifications. OPTIONAL FOUR (Lynx): High-output version of 1.6 liter engine above Horsepower: 80 at 5400 R.P.M. Torque: 88 lbs.-ft. at 2600 R.P.M. VIN Code: 4. DIESEL FOUR (Lynx, Topaz): Inline. Overhead cam. Four-cylinder. Cast iron block and aluminum head. Displacement: 121 cu. in. (2.0 liters). Bore & stroke: 3.39 x 3.39 in. Compression ratio: 22.5:1. Brake horsepower: 52 at 4000 R.P.M. Torque: 82 lbs.-ft. at 2400 R.P.M. Five main bearings. Solid valve lifters. Fuel injection. VIN Code: H. BASE FOUR (Topaz): Inline. Overhead valve. Four-cylinder. Cast iron block and head. Displacement: 140 cu. in. (2.3 liters). Bore & stroke: 3.70 x 3.30 in. Compression ratio: 9.0:1. Brake horsepower: 86 at 4000 R.P.M. Torque: 122 lbs.-ft. at 2800 R.P.M. Five main bearings. Hydraulic valve lifters. Fuel injection (TBI). High Swirl Combustion (HSC) design. VIN Code: X. OPTIONAL FOUR (Topaz): High-output version of 140 cu. in. HSC four above Horsepower: 100 at 4600 R.P.M. Torque: 125 lbs.-ft. at 3200 R.P.M. VIN Code: S. BASE FOUR (Capri, Marquis): Inline. Overhead cam. Four-cylinder. Cast iron block and head. Displacement: 140 cu. in. (2.3 liters). Bore & stroke: 3.78 x 3.13 in. Compression ratio: 9.0:1. Brake horsepower: 88 at 4200 R.P.M. Torque: 122 lbs.-ft. at 2600 R.P.M. Five main bearings. Hydraulic valve lifters. Carburetor: 1Bbl. Carter YFA. VIN Code: A. BASE TURBO FOUR (Cougar XR7): Same as 140 cu. in. four above, but with turbocharger Compression ratio: 8.0:1. Horsepower: 155 at 4600 R.P.M. Torque: 190 lbs.-ft. at 2800 R.P.M. VIN Code: W. BASE V-6 (Cougar); OPTIONAL (Capri, Marquis): 90-degree, overhead valve V-6. Cast iron block and aluminum head. Displacement: 232 cu. in. (3.8 liters). Bore & stroke: 3.80 x 3.40 in. Compression ratio: 8.65:1. Brake horsepower: 120 at 3600 R.P.M. Torque: 205 lbs.-ft. at 1600 R.P.M. Four main bearings. Hydraulic valve lifters. Fuel-injected. VIN Code: 3. BASE V-8 (Grand Marquis); OPTIONAL (Cougar): 90-degree, overhead valve V-8. Cast iron block and head. Displacement: 302 cu. in. (5.0 liters). Bore & stroke: 4.00 x 3.00 in. Compression ratio: 8.4:1. Brake horsepower: 140 at 3200 R.P.M. Torque: 250 lbs.-ft. at 2000 R.P.M. Five main bearings. Hydraulic valve lifters. Fuel injection. VIN Code: F. OPTIONAL V-8 (Grand Marquis): High-output version of 302 cu. in. V-8 above Compression ratio: 8.4:1. Horsepower: 180 at 3600 R.P.M. Torque: 265 lbs.-ft. at 2000 R.P.M. OPTIONAL V-8 (Capri): High-output version of 302 cu. in. V-8 above Compression ratio: 8.3:1. Horsepower: 180 at 4200 R.P.M. Torque: 260 lbs.-ft. at 2600 R.P.M. OPTIONAL V-8 (Capri): High-output version of 302 cu. in. V-8 above Compression ratio: 8.3:1. Horsepower: 210 at 4400 R.P.M. Torque: 270 lbs.-ft. at 3200 R.P.M. Carburetor: 4Bbl. Holley. VIN Code: M.

NOTE: Police 351 cu. in. V-8 remained available for Grand Marquis.

CHASSIS DATA: Wheelbase: (Lynx) 94.2 in.; (Capri) 100.5 in.; (Topaz) 99.9 in.; (Marquis) 105.6 in.; (Cougar) 104.0 in.; (Grand Marquis) 114.3 in. Overall Length: (Lynx) 163.9 in.; (Lynx wag) 165.0 in.; (Capri) 179.3 in.; (Topaz) 176.5 in.; (Marquis) 196.5 in.; (Cougar) 197.6 in.; (Grand Marquis) 211.0 in.; (Grand Marquis wag) 215.0 in. Height: (Lynx) 53.3-53.4 in.; (Capri) 52.1 in.; (Topaz) 52.7 in.; (Marquis) 53.8 in.; (Marquis wag) 54.4 in.; (Cougar) 53.4 in.; (Grand Marquis) 55.2 in.; (Grand Marquis wag) 56.8 in. Width: (Lynx) 65.9 in.; (Capri) 69.1 in.; (Topaz) 68.3 in.; (Marquis) 71.0 in.; (Cougar) 71.1 in.; (Grand Marquis) 77.5 in.; (Grand Marquis wag) 79.3 in. Front Tread: (Lynx) 54.7 in.; (Capri) 56.6 in.; (Topaz) 54.7 in.; (Marquis) 56.6 in.; (Cougar) 58.1 in.; (Grand Marquis) 62.2 in. Rear Tread: (Lynx) 56.0 in.; (Capri/Marquis) 57.0 in.; (Topaz) 57.6 in.; (Cougar) 58.5 in.; (Grand Marquis) 62.0 in. Standard Tires: (Lynx) P165/80R13; (Capri) P195/75R14; (Capri 5.0L) P225/60VR15; (Topaz) P175/80R13; (Marquis) P195/75R14; (Cougar) P205/75R14; (XR7) P225/60VR15; (Grand Marquis) P215/75R14 SBR WSW.

TECHNICAL: Transmission: Four-speed manual standard on Lynx; five- speed manual or three-speed automatic optional. Four-speed manual standard on Capri; five-speed manual standard on Capri 5.0L; three-speed or four-speed automatic optional. Five-speed manual standard on Topaz; three-speed automatic optional. SelectShift three-speed automatic standard on Cougar/Marquis; four-speed overdrive optional. Five-speed manual standard on Cougar XR7. Four-speed overdrive automatic standard on Grand Marquis. Gear ratios same as equivalent Ford models; see Ford/Mustang listings. Standard final drive ratio: (Lynx) 3.59:1 w/4spd, 3.73:1 w/5spd, 3.31:1 w/auto., 3.52:1 w/diesel; (Capri four) 3.08:1 w/4spd, 3.27:1 w/auto.; (Capri V-6) 2.73:1 w/5spd or auto., 3.27:1 w/4spd.; (Capri four/V-8) 3.45:1; (Topaz) 3.33:1 w/5spd, 3.23:1 w/auto., 3.73:1 w/diesel or FI four; (Marquis) 3.27:1 or 2.73:1; (Cougar V-6) 2.73:1 w/3spd auto., 3.27:1 with w/auto.; (Cougar V-8) 3.08:1; (Cougar XR7 turbo) 3.45:1; (Grand Marquis) 3.08:1. Steering: (Grand Marquis) recirculating ball; (others) rack and pinion. Front Suspension: (Lynx/Topaz) MacPherson strut-mounted coil springs w/lower control arms and stabilizer bar; (Capri/Cougar/Marquis) modified MacPherson struts w/lower control arms, coil springs and anti-sway bar; (Grand Marquis) coil springs with long/short Aarms and anti-sway bar. Rear Suspension: (Lynx) independent trailing arms w/modified MacPherson struts and coil springs on lower control arms; (Topaz) fully independent quadra-link w/MacPherson struts; (Capri/Cougar/Marquis/Grand Marquis) four-link w/coil springs. Brakes: Front disc, rear drum. Ignition: Electronic. Body construction: (Grand Marquis) separate body and frame; (others) unibody. Fuel tank: (Lynx) 10 gal. exc. wag. 13 gal.; (Capri) 15.4 gal.; (Topaz) 15.2 gal.; (Marquis) 16 gal.; (Cougar) 20.6 gal.; (Grand Marquis) 18 gal.; (Grand Marquis wag) 18.5 gal.

1986 Topaz sedan (JG)

TOPAZ — FOUR — Two years after its debut, the front-drive Topaz deserved a change or two. They came in the form of revised front-end styling with aero headlamps, a new grille, and body-color bumpers. Standard tires grew to P185/70R14 size with all-season tread, on 14 inch wheels. Four-way adjustable head restraints were new. The base GS model also got a new standard touring suspension with gas-filled struts. A push/pull headlamp switch replaced the rocker switch, and the wiper/washer control moved from the stalk to the instrument panel. The Sport Group option included new 6 in. aluminum wheels with 15 inch tires, and its high-output engine came only with five-speed manual. Diesel power remained available. The new aerodynamic body featured softly rounded edges and aircraft-inspired doors, with windshield and back window slanted nearly 60 degrees. The sloping front panel contained a single air intake slot, below a bright, horizontally-ribbed upper panel with center round emblem and 'Mercury' lettering on the driver's side. A series of six air intake slots went below the bumper strip. Aero headlamps extended outward to meet wraparound park/signal lenses and amber side markers. At the rear were tall wraparound taillamps. A drag coefficient of 0.36 was recorded for the four-door. Inside was a new four-spoke steering wheel; outside, sail-mounted dual power remote mirrors. Front suspension again used MacPherson struts, with a parallel four-bar arrangement at the back. Standard GS equipment included the HSC 2.3-liter four, five-speed manual transaxle, power brakes and steering, full wheel covers, low-back cloth reclining front seats, tachometer, AM/FM stereo radio (which could be deleted), side-window demisters, and color-keyed consolette. Dark Smoke bumper rub strips had bright inserts. Other body features: an acrylic grille applique with bright/argent accents, Dark Smoke cowl grille, bright windshield moldings, and black leather arms. The optional GS Sport Group added Michelin TRX BSW tires on TR cast aluminum wheels with locking lug nuts, and special handling components, along with a high specific output (HSO) version of the 2.3-liter four. A revised intake manifold, higher-lift camshaft, larger cylinder head and other modifications boosted horsepower by 16 percent over the standard engine. It also got a new cast aluminum rocker cover. GS Sport Group also included a graphic display alert module, red inserts in bodyside moldings and bumper rub strips, Dark Smoke greenhouse moldings, and black leather- wrapped steering wheel. Topaz LS included a Touring suspension with gas-filled struts, full console, power windows and door locks, dual lighted visor vanity mirrors, dual-color accent stripes, argent lower taillamp molding, woodgrain instrument cluster accents, and illuminated entry.

1986 Sable LS sedan (JG)

SABLE — FOUR/V-6 — Like Ford's new mid-size Taurus, the closely-related Sable lacked a conventional grille. Unlike Taurus with its mostly solid "grille" panel, Sable sported an illuminated plastic light bar between flush headlamps. Those headlamps extended outward to meet park/signal lamps, and wrap around the fenders into side marker lenses. Below the front bumper rub strip was a set of many vertical slots, arranged in four sections. Bodyside moldings followed a straight line from front to back, above horizontal ribbing in the center segment. At the rear were wide wraparound taillamps (wider than Taurus). Surprisingly, sedans shared no sheetmetal at all. Wagons shared body parts only to the rear of the windshield. The first Sables came only with 181 cu. in. (3.0- liter) fuel-injected V-6 and four-speed overdrive automatic, but a 151 cu. in. (2.5-liter) four and new three-speed automatic would become standard later. Sable's standard cluster included a tachometer and temp gauge. Gas shock absorbers were used in the fully independent suspension. Sable offered seating for six. Two trim levels were offered, GS and LS, in four-door sedan and station wagon form. Standard GS equipment included the 2.5-liter four and three-speed automatic, power brakes/steering, cornering lamps, bumper rub strips, driver's remote mirror, side-window defoggers, passenger assist handles, tachometer, trip odometer, P205/70R14 tires, and a day/night mirror. Wagons used the 3.0-liter V-6 engine and four-speed automatic. Interiors contained a cloth Flight bench seat with driver's side recliner, and fold-down center front armrest. Sable LS added the V-6 engine and four-speed automatic, power windows, remote decklid release, remote gas door release, digital clock, intermittent wipers, dual power remote mirrors, diagnostic

1986 Sable LS wagon (JG)

310

warning lights, and AM/FM stereo radio. Twin Comfort lounge seats had dual recliners and power lumbar support adjusters. Urethane lower door and rocker panel coating was included. Taurus/Sable came from a $3 billion development program that began in 1980. In early tests, Sable demonstrated an even lower coefficient of drag than Taurus: 0.29 versus 0.32, partly because Sable had two inches more rear overhang.

1986 Marquis sedan (JG)

MARQUIS — FOUR/V-6 — With the new Sable getting all the attention, the car it replaced was almost overlooked. In fact, quite a few examples were sold in this, its final season. The holdover rear-drive mid-size came with a base 140 cu. in. (2.3-liter) four or optional 232 cu. in. (3.8-liter) V-6. Appearance was the same as 1985.

1986 Cougar XR-7 coupe (JG)

COUGAR — FOUR/V-6/V-8 — Mercury's two-door personal-luxury coupe again came in three levels: GS, LS, and the turbocharged XR7. Appearance was similar to 1985. Cougar still displayed an upswept quarter-window design, which was its most notable difference from the closely-related Thunderbird. Base powerplant was the 232 cu. in. (3.8-liter) V-6, with three-speed automatic. The optional 302 cu. in. (5.0-liter) V-8 had new sequential (multi-point) fuel injection and other improvements. Standard tires grew wider, to P215/70R14 size. For the third year in a row, counterbalanced hood springs were promised to replace the prop rod. A standard electronic-tuning stereo radio replaced the manual-tuning version. New options included a power moonroof (arriving later), seven-band graphic equalizer, and inflatable spare tire (complete with air compressor). Standard equipment included power steering/brakes, halogen heeadlamps, AM/FM stereo, driver's remote mirror, bodyside/decklid accent stripes, vinyl-insert bodyside moldings, analog quartz clock, console, four-spoke steering wheel, and brushed instrument panel applique. Individual cloth/vinyl front seats came with recliners. Cougar LS added tinted glass, power windows, remote passenger mirror, rocker panel moldings, hood accent striping, digital clock, velour upholstery, lighted right visor vanity mirror, and woodtone dash applique. Cougar XR7 included the turbo four with five- speed manual, handling suspension, P205/70HR14 BSW tires on polycast wheels, leather-wrapped steering wheel, tinted glass, and Traction-Lok differential.

1986 Grand Marquis LS sedan (JG)

GRAND MARQUIS — V-8 — Mercury's most popular model, the big rear-drive sedan (and wagon) enjoyed mostly mechanical changes for 1986. The standard 302 cu. in. (5.0-liter) V-8 gained sequential port fuel injection and other internal changes, including roller lifters and tuned intake manifold, with low-tension rings and higher compression ratio. Standard tires grew from 14 to 15 inch diameter. Wagons now had a compact spare tire (conventional option). Gas caps were tethered. Standard equipment included four-speed overdrive automatic, P215/75R15 whitewalls, AM/FM stereo, wide lower bodyside moldings, power windows, vinyl roof, power brakes/steering, rocker panel and wheel lip moldings, Flight bench seat, gas-filled shocks, hood/decklid paint stripes, and an analog clock. Grand Marquis LS added a visor vanity mirror and luxury interior touches. Colony Park wagons had the woodgrain bodyside and tailgate applique, three-way tailgate with power window, fold-down rear seat, and conventional spare tire. Mercury's 17-symbol Vehicle Identification Number (VIN) was stamped on a metal tab fastened to the instrument panel, visible through the windshield. Symbols one to three indicate manufacturer, make and vehicle type: '1ME' Mercury passenger car. The fourth symbol ('B') denotes restraint system. Next comes a letter 'P', followed by two digits that indicate body type: Model Number, as shown in left column of tables below. (Example: '72' Topaz GS two- door sedan.) Symbol eight indicates engine type: '9' L4113 2Bbl.; 'J' H.O. L4113 MFI; 'H' Diesel L4121; 'A' L4- 140 1Bbl.; 'X' HSC L4140 Fl; 'S' H.O. L4140 Fl; 'W' Turbo L4140 EFI; 'D' L4153 Fl; '3' V6232 Fl; 'U' V6183 Fl; 'F' V8302 Fl; 'M' H.O. V8302 Fl; 'G' Police V8351 2Bbl. Next is a check digit. Symbol ten indicates model year ('G' 1986).

Symbol eleven is assembly plant: 'A' Atlanta, GA; 'B' Oakville, Ontario (Canada); 'F' Dearborn, MI; 'G' Chicago; 'H' Lorain, Ohio; 'K' Kansas City, MO; 'W' Wayne, MI; 'X' St. Thomas, Ontario; and Edison, NJ. The final six digits make up the sequence number, starting with 600001. A Vehicle Certification Label on the left front door lock face panel or door pillar shows the manufacturer, month and year of manufacture, GVW, GAWR, certification statement, VIN, and codes for such items as body type, color, trim, axle, transmission, and special order information.

LYNX (FOUR)

Model Number	Body/Style Number	Body Type & Seating	Factory Price	Shipping Weight	Production Total
51	61D	3-dr. Hatch-4P	6182	2060	Note 1
51	61D	3-dr. L Hatch-4P	6472	2060	Note 1
63	58D	5-dr. L Hatch-4P	6886	2106	Note 1
58	74D	4-dr. L Sta Wag-4P	6987	2141	Note 1
52	61D	3-dr. GS Hatch-4P	7162	2149	Note 1
64	58D	5-dr. GS Hatch-4P	7376	2192	Note 1
59	74D	4-dr. GS Sta Wag-4P	7657	2215	Note 1
53	61D	3-dr. XR3 Hatch-4P	8193	2277	Note 1

Note 1: Total Lynx production, 45,880 three-door hatchbacks, 26,512 five-door hatchbacks, and 13,580 four-door liftgate station wagons.

Diesel Engine Note: Lynx diesel models cost $591-$667 more than a gas engine.

CAPRI GS (FOUR/V-6)

79	61D	3-dr. Fastbk-4P	8331/8785	2692/2808	Note 2

Capri Engine Note: Six-cylinder price does not include cost of the required automatic transmission ($510). The high-output 302 cu. in. V-8 engine cost $1330 more than the V-6.

CAPRI 5.0L (V-8)

79	61D	3-dr. Fastbk-4P	10950	3055	Note 2

Note 2: Total Capri production was 20,869.

1986 Topaz coupe (JG)

TOPAZ (FOUR)

72	66D	2-dr. GS Sedan-5P	8085	2313	15,757
75	54D	4-dr. GS Sedan-5P	8235	2368	62,640
73	66D	2-dr. LS Sedan-5P	9224	2335	Note 3
76	54D	4-dr. LS Sedan-5P	9494	2390	Note 3

Diesel Engine Note: A diesel engine cost $509 more than the gasoline- powered Topaz.

SABLE GS (FOUR/V-6)

87	54D	4-dr. Sedan-6P	10700/11311	2812/2812	71.707
88	74D	4-dr. Sta Wag-6P	-- /12574	3092	23,931

SABLE LS (V-6)

87	54D	4-dr. Sedan-6P	11776	2812	Note 3
88	74D	4-dr. Sta Wag-6P	13068	3092	Note 3

Note 3: Production of Topaz and Sable LS models is included in GS totals.

MARQUIS (FOUR/V-6)

89	54D	4-dr. Sedan-6P	9660/10154	2883/2935	24,121
90	74D	4-dr. Sta Wag-6P	-- /10254	-- /2987	4,461

MARQUIS BROUGHAM (FOUR/V-6)

89/60H	54D	4-dr. Sedan-6P	10048/10542	2895/2947	Note 4
90/60H	74D	4-dr. Sta Wag-6P	-- /10613	-- /2999	Note 4

Note 4: Brougham production is included in basic totals above.

1986 Cougar LS coupe (JG)

COUGAR (V-6/V-8)

92	66D	2-dr. Cpe-4P	11421/11969	2918/3096	135,909
92	66D	2-dr. LS Cpe-4P	12757/13305	2918/3096	Note 5

Cougar Engine Note: The V-8 engine required a four-speed automatic transmission at $237 extra.

COUGAR XR-7 (TURBO FOUR)

92	66D	2-dr. Cpe-4P	14377	3015	Note 5

Note 5: Production of LS and XR-7 is included in basic total above.

GRAND MARQUIS (V-8)

93	66K	2-dr. Sedan-6P	13480	3730	5,610
95	54K	4-dr. Sedan-6P	13504	3672	93,919
93/60H	66K	2-dr. LS Sed-6P	13929	3730	Note 6
95/60H	54K	4-dr. LS Sed-6P	13952	3672	Note 6

GRAND MARQUIS COLONY PARK (V-8)

94	74K	4-dr. Sta Wag-6P	13724	3851	9,891

Note 6: LS production is included in basic Grand Marquis totals.

FACTORY PRICE AND WEIGHT NOTE: Cougar prices and weights to left of slash are for V-6, to right for V-8 engine. For Capri/Marquis/Sable, prices/weights to left of slash are for four-cylinder, to right for V-6.

ENGINE DATA: BASE FOUR (Lynx): Inline. Overhead cam. Four-cylinder. Cast iron block and aluminum head. Displacement: 113 cu. in. (1.9 liters). Bore & stroke: 3.23 x 3.46 in. Compression ratio: 9.0:1. Brake horsepower: 86 at 4800 R.P.M. Torque: 100 lbs.-ft. at 3000 R.P.M. Five main bearings. Hydraulic valve lifters. Carburetor: 2Bbl. Holley 740. VIN Code: 9. OPTIONAL FOUR (Lynx): High-output, multi-port fuel injected version of 1.9-liter engine above Horsepower: 108 at 5200 R.P.M. Torque: 114 lbs.-ft. at 4000 R.P.M. VIN Code: J. DIESEL FOUR (Lynx, Topaz): Inline. Overhead cam. Four-cylinder. Cast iron block and aluminum head. Displacement: 121 cu. in. (2.0 liters). Bore & stroke: 3.39 x 3.39 in. Compression ratio: 22.7:1. Brake horsepower: 52 at 4000 R.P.M. Torque: 82 lbs.-ft. at 2400 R.P.M. Five main bearings. Solid valve lifters. Fuel injection. VIN Code: H. BASE FOUR (Topaz): Inline. Overhead valve. Four-cylinder. Cast iron block and head. Displacement: 140 cu. in. (2.3 liters). Bore & stroke: 3.70 x 3.30 in. Compression ratio: 9.0:1. Brake horsepower: 86 at 4600 R.P.M. Torque: 124 lbs.-ft. at 2800 R.P.M. Five main bearings. Hydraulic valve lifters. Fuel injection (TBI). High Swirl Combustion (HSC) design. VIN Code: X. OPTIONAL FOUR (Topaz): High-output version of 140 cu. in. HSC four above Horsepower: 100 at 4600 R.P.M. Torque: 125 lbs.-ft. at 3200 R.P.M. VIN Code: S. BASE FOUR (Capri, Marquis): Inline. Overhead cam. Four-cylinder. Cast iron block and head. Displacement: 140 cu. in. (2.3 liters). Bore & stroke: 3.78 x 3.13 in. Compression ratio: 9.5:1. Brake horsepower: 88 at 4200 R.P.M. Torque: 122 lbs.-ft. at 2600 R.P.M. Five main bearings. Hydraulic valve lifters. Carburetor: 1Bbl. Carter YFA. VIN Code: A. BASE TURBO FOUR (Cougar XR-7): Same as 140 cu. in. four above, but with turbocharger Compression ratio: 8.0:1. Horsepower: 155 at 4600 R.P.M. (145 at 4400 with automatic). Torque: 190 lbs.-ft. at 2800 R.P.M. (180 at 3000 w/automatic). VIN Code: W. BASE FOUR (Sable): Inline. Overhead valve. Four-cylinder. Cast iron block and head. Displacement: 153 cu. in. (2.5 liters). Bore & stroke: 3.70 x 3.60 in. Compression ratio: 9.0:1. Brake horsepower: 88 at 4600 R.P.M. Torque: 130 lbs.-ft. at 2800 R.P.M. Five main bearings. Hydraulic valve lifters. Fuel injection (TBI). VIN Code: D. BASE V-6 (Sable LS, wagon); OPTIONAL (Sable): 60-degree, overhead valve V-6. Cast iron block and head. Displacement: 183 cu. in. (3.0 liters). Bore & stroke: 3.50 x 3.10 in. Compression ratio: 9.25:1. Brake horsepower: 140 at 4800 R.P.M. Torque: 160 lbs.-ft. at 3000 R.P.M. Four main bearings. Hydraulic valve lifters. Multi-port fuel injection. VIN Code: U. BASE V-6 (Cougar); OPTIONAL (Capri, Marquis): 90-degree, overhead valve V-6. Cast iron block and aluminum head. Displacement: 232 cu. in. (3.8 liters). Bore & stroke: 3.80 x 3.40 in. Compression ratio: 8.7:1. Brake horsepower: 120 at 3600 R.P.M. Torque: 205 lbs.-ft. at 1600 R.P.M. Four main bearings. Hydraulic valve lifters. Fuel-injected. VIN Code: 3. BASE V-8 (Grand Marquis); OPTIONAL (Cougar): 90-degree, overhead valve V-8. Cast iron block and head. Displacement: 302 cu. in. (5.0 liters). Bore & stroke: 4.00 x 3.00 in. Compression ratio: 8.9:1. Brake horsepower: 150 at 3200 R.P.M. Torque: 270 lbs.-ft. at 2000 R.P.M. Five main bearings. Hydraulic valve lifters. Sequential fuel injection. VIN Code: F. OPTIONAL V-8 (Capri): High-output version of 302 cu. in. V-8 above Compression ratio: 9.2:1. Horsepower: 200 at 4000 R.P.M. Torque: 285 lbs.-ft. at 3000 R.P.M. VIN Code: M.

NOTE: Police 351 cu. in. V-8 remained available for Grand Marquis, rated 180 horsepower at 3600 R.P.M., 285 lbs.-ft. at 2400 R.P.M.

CHASSIS DATA: Wheelbase: (Lynx) 94.2 in.; (Capri) 100.5 in.; (Topaz) 99.9 in.; (Sable) 106.0 in.; (Marquis) 105.6 in.; (Cougar) 104.0 in.; (Grand Marquis) 114.3 in. Overall Length: (Lynx) 166.9 in.; (Capri) 168.0 in.; (Topaz) 179.3 in.; (Sable) 190.9 in.; (Sable wag) 191.9 in.; (Marquis) 196.5 in.; (Cougar) 197.6 in.; (Grand Marquis) 214.0 in.; (Grand Marquis wag) 218.0 in. Height: (Lynx) 53.3-53.5 in.; (Capri) 52.1 in.; (Topaz) 52.7 in.; (Sable) 54.2 in.; (Sable wag) 55.1 in.; (Marquis) 53.8 in.; (Marquis wag) 54.4 in.; (Cougar) 53.4 in.; (Grand Marquis) 55.2 in.; (Grand Marquis wag) 56.8 in. Width: (Lynx) 65.9 in.; (Capri) 69.1 in.; (Topaz) 68.3 in.; (Sable) 70.7 in.; (Marquis) 71.0 in.; (Cougar) 71.1 in.; (Grand Marquis) 77.5 in.; (Grand Marquis wag)

79.3 in. Front Tread: (Lynx) 54.7 in.; (Capri) 56.6 in.; (Topaz) 54.7 in.; (Sable) 61.6 in.; (Marquis) 56.6 in.; (Cougar) 58.1 in.; (Grand Marquis) 62.2 in. Rear Tread: (Lynx) 56.0 in.; (Capri/Marquis) 57.0 in.; (Topaz) 57.6 in.; (Sable) 60.5 in.; (Sable wag) 59.9 in.; (Cougar) 58.5 in.; (Grand Marquis) 62.0 in. Standard Tires: (Lynx) P165/80R13; (XR3) P195/60HR15; (Capri) P195/75R14; (Capri 5.0L) P225/60VR15; (Topaz) P185/70R14; (Sable) P205/70R14; (Marquis) P195/75R14; (Cougar) P215/70R14; (XR7) P225/60VR15 Goodyear "Gatorback;" (Grand Marquis) P205/75R15 SBR WSW.

TECHNICAL: Transmission: Four-speed manual standard on Lynx; five-speed manual or three-speed automatic optional. Four-speed manual standard on Capri; five-speed manual standard on Capri 5.0L; three-speed or four-speed automatic optional. Five-speed manual standard on Topaz; three-speed automatic optional. SelectShift three-speed automatic standard on Cougar/Marquis; four-speed overdrive optional (standard on Cougar V-8). Three-speed automatic standard on Sable four; four-speed on Sable V-6. Five-speed manual standard on Cougar XR7. Four- speed overdrive automatic standard on Grand Marquis. Gear ratios same as equivalent Ford models; see Ford/Mustang listings. Standard final drive ratio: (Lynx) 3.52:1 w/4spd, 3.73:1 w/5spd, 3.23:1 w/auto., 3.52:1 w/diesel; (Capri four) 3.08:1 w/4spd, 3.27:1 w/auto.; (Capri V-6) 2.73:1; (Capri V-8) 2.73:1 w/5spd or auto., 3.27:1 w/4spd auto.; (Topaz) 3.33:1 w/5spd, 3.23:1 w/auto., 3.73:1 w/diesel or FI four; (Sable) 3.23:1 w/four, 3.37:1 w/V-6; (Marquis) 3.27:1 or 2.73:1; (Cougar V-6) 2.73:1 w/3spd auto., 3.27:1 with 4spd auto.; (Cougar V-8) 3.08:1; (Cougar XR7 turbo) 3.45:1; (Grand Marquis) 2.73:1. Steering: (Grand Marquis) recirculating ball; (others) rack and pinion. Front Suspension: (Lynx/Topaz) MacPherson strut-mounted coil springs w/lower control arms and stabilizer bar; (Capri/Cougar/Marquis) modified MacPherson struts w/lower control arms, coil springs and anti-sway bar; (Sable) MacPherson struts w/control arm, coil springs and anti-sway bar; (Grand Marquis) coil springs with long/short Aarms and anti-sway bar. Rear Suspension: (Lynx) independent trailing arms w/modified MacPherson struts and coil springs on lower control arms; (Topaz) fully independent quadra-link w/MacPherson struts; (Sable) MacPherson struts w/coil springs, parallel suspension arms and anti-sway bar; (Capri/Cougar/Marquis/Grand Marquis) four-link w/coil springs. Brakes: Front disc, rear drum. Ignition: Electronic. Body construction: (Grand Marquis) separate body and frame; (others) unibody. Fuel tank: (Lynx) 10 gal. exc. wag, 13 gal.; (Capri) 15.4 gal.; (Topaz) 15.2 gal.; (Sable) 16 gal.; (Marquis) 16 gal.; (Cougar) 20.6 gal.; (Grand Marquis) 18 gal.; (Grand Marquis wag) 18.5 gal.

DRIVETRAIN OPTIONS: Engines: Diesel 2.0-liter four: Lynx ($591); Topaz ($509). 182 cu. in. V-6: Sable (N/A). 232 cu. in. V-6: Capri ($454); Marquis ($494). 302 cu. in. V-8: Capri ($1784); Cougar ($548). Transmission/Differential: Five-speed manual trans.: Lynx ($76). Automatic transaxle: Lynx L ($466); Lynx GS ($390); Topaz ($448) exc. w/GS sport group ($350). Three-speed auto. transmission.: Capri ($510); Cougar XR7 ($315). Floor shift lever: Sable sedan (NC). Overdrive auto. trans.: Capri GS ($746); Capri 5.0L ($622); Sable GS ($611); Cougar/Marquis ($237). Traction-Lok differential: Marquis/Grand Marquis/Cougar ($100). Steering/Suspension: Power steering: Lynx ($226). H.D. susp.: Lynx/Sable/Grand Marquis ($26); Sable LPO ($26); Marquis ($43). Auto. load leveling: Grand Marquis ($200). Other: H.D. battery ($27). H.D. alternator: Lynx ($27). Extended-range gas tank: Sable/Marquis ($46). Engine block heater ($18). Trailer towing pkg.: Grand Marquis ($377-$389). California emission system: Lynx/EXP ($46); others ($99). High-altitude emissions (NC).

LYNX CONVENIENCE/APPEARANCE OPTIONS: Option Packages: Comfort/convenience pkg. ($298) exc. XR3 ($117) and diesel ($211). Climate control group ($791-$818). Comfort/Convenience: Air conditioner ($657). Rear defroster, electric ($135). Fingertip speed control ($176). Tinted glass ($99). Tilt steering ($115). Console w/graphic systems monitor ($111). Rear wiper/washer ($126). Dual remote mirrors ($68). Entertainment: AM/FM stereo radio: L ($109); base ($148). AM/FM stereo w/cassette player: L ($256); base ($295); GS/XR3 ($148). Radio delete: AM ($39 credit); AM/FM ($148 credit). Premium sound ($138). Exterior: Clearcoat paint ($91). Two-tone paint ($156). Wide vinyl bodyside moldings ($45). Bumper guards, front/rear ($56). Bumper rub strips ($48). Luggage rack: wag ($100). Interior: Vinyl seat trim ($24). Wheels/Tires: Styled wheels ($128). P165/80R13 SBR WSW ($59). Full-size spare ($63).

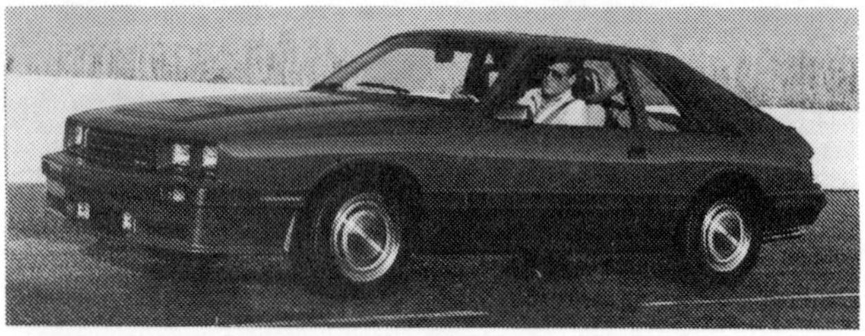

1986 Capri 5.0L hatchback coupe (JG)

CAPRI CONVENIENCE/APPEARANCE OPTIONS: Option Packages: Power lock group ($182). Comfort/Convenience: Air cond. ($762). Fingertip speed control ($176). Entertainment: Electronic seek/scan AM/FM stereo w/cassette ($300). Premium sound system ($138). Radio delete ($148 credit). Exterior: TRoof ($1100). Flip-up open air roof ($315). Interior: Vinyl bucket seats ($29). Wheels and Tires: Wire wheel covers ($98). Polycast wheels ($178). P205/70R14 WSW ($112).

TOPAZ CONVENIENCE/APPEARANCE OPTIONS: Option Packages: GS sport group ($610). Comfort/convenience pkg. ($330). Convenience group ($246). Power lock group ($141-$259). Comfort/Convenience: Air bag restraint system ($815). Air cond. ($743). Rear defroster, electric ($145). Fingertip speed control ($176). Power windows ($207-$282). Six-way power driver's seat ($234). Tilt steering ($115). Entertainment: AM/FM stereo radio w/cassette player ($148). Electronic-tuning AM/FM stereo w/cassette ($161-$309). Premium sound ($138). Radio delete ($148-$295 credit). Exterior: Clearcoat metallic paint ($91). Lower body accent paint ($78-$118). Interior: Vinyl seat trim ($35). Leather seat trim ($300). Wheels/Tires: Polycast wheels ($178). P185/70R14 WSW ($72).

SABLE CONVENIENCE/APPEARANCE OPTIONS: Option Packages: Power lock group ($186-$257). Light group ($48-$51). Comfort/Convenience: Air cond. ($762). Electronic climate control air cond. ($945). Rear defroster ($145). Heated windshield ($250). Fingertip speed control ($176). Keyless entry ($202). Power windows ($282). Six-way power driver's seat ($237); dual ($473). Tinted glass ($115); windshield only LPO ($48). Leather-wrapped steering wheel ($59). Tilt steering ($115). Electronic instrument cluster ($305). Autolamp on/off delay ($73). Auto. parking brake release: GS ($12). Digital clock: GS ($78). Interval wipers: GS ($50). Rear wiper/washer: wag ($124). Dual lighted visor vanity mirrors: GS ($99). Entertainment: AM/FM stereo w/cassette ($127). Power antenna ($71). Premium sound system ($168). Radio delete LPO ($196 credit). Exterior: Power moonroof ($701). Vent windows ($79). Clearcoat paint ($183). Bodyside accent paint ($57). Luggage rack delete: wag LPO ($105 credit). Interior: Cloth twin comfort reclining seats: GS ($195). Vinyl seat trim: GS ($39). Leather seat trim: LS ($415). Rear- facing third seat: wag ($155). Reclining passenger seat: GS ($45). Picnic tray: wagon ($66). Carpeted floor mats ($43). Wheels/Tires: Polycast wheels ($66). Aluminum wheels ($335). P205/70R14 WSW ($72). P205/65R15 BSW ($46); WSW ($124). Conventional spare ($63).

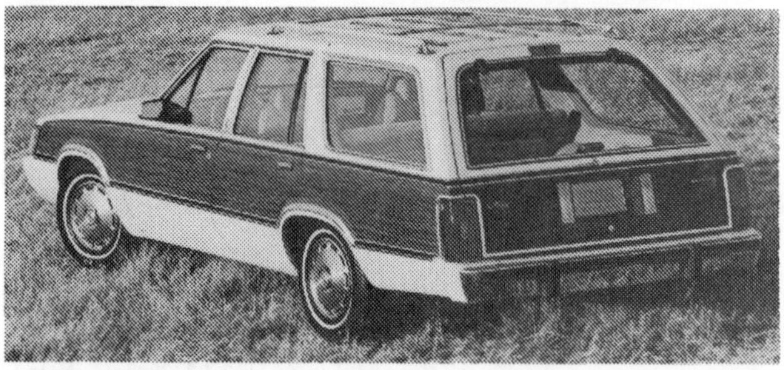

1986 Marquis Brougham Villager wagon (JG)

MARQUIS CONVENIENCE/APPEARANCE OPTIONS: Option Packages: Woodtone option ($282). Interior luxury group ($388). Power lock group ($218-$259). Light group ($38). Comfort/Convenience: Air cond. ($762). Rear defroster ($145). Fingertip speed control ($176). Autolamp on-off delay ($73). Power windows ($282). Six-way power driver's seat ($234). Tinted glass ($115). Leather-wrapped steering wheel ($59). Tilt steering ($115). Digital clock ($78). Auto. parking brake release ($12). Lighting and Mirrors: Cornering lamps ($68). Right remote convex mirror ($61). Dual electric remote mirrors ($96). Lighted visor vanity mirrors ($57-$106). Entertainment: AM/FM stereo radio ($109); w/cassette player ($256). AM radio delete ($39 credit). Exterior: Full vinyl roof ($152). Clearcoat metallic paint ($183). Two-tone paint w/tape stripe ($117). Pivoting front vent windows ($79). Two-way liftgate: wag ($105). Rocker panel moldings ($40). Bumper guards, rear ($28). Bumper rub strips ($56). Luggage rack: wagon ($126). Interior: Vinyl seat trim ($35). Flight bench seat (NC). Front floor mats, carpeted ($23). Wheels/Tires: Luxury wheel covers ($55). Wire wheel covers, locking ($212). Polycast wheels ($178). Styled steel wheels w/trim rings ($54). P195/75R14 WSW ($72). P205/70R14 WSW ($134). Conventional spare ($63).

COUGAR CONVENIENCE/APPEARANCE OPTIONS: Option Packages: Headlamp convenience group ($176). Light group ($35). Power lock group ($220). Comfort/Convenience: Air cond. ($762); auto-temp ($924). Rear defroster ($145). Fingertip speed control ($176). Illuminated entry system ($82). Keyless entry ($198). Tinted glass ($115). Power windows ($207). Six-way power driver's seat ($238); dual ($476). Dual power seat recliners ($189). Leather-wrapped steering wheel ($59). Tilt steering wheel ($115). Electronic instrument cluster ($330). Diagnostic warning lights ($89). Low-oil alert ($24). Digital clock ($61). Auto. parking brake release ($12). Interval wipers ($50). Lighting and Mirrors: Cornering lamps ($68). Dual electric remote mirrors ($96). Lighted visor vanity mirrors, pair ($106). Entertainment: Electronic-tuning AM/FM stereo w/cassette ($127). Power antenna ($71). Graphic equalizer ($218). Premium sound system ($168). AM/FM radio delete ($196 credit). Exterior: Power moonroof ($701). Luxury vinyl rear half roof ($245). Metallic clearcoat paint ($183). Two-tone paint ($163). Hood accent stripes ($16). Pivoting front vent windows ($79). Interior: Leather seat trim ($415). Vinyl seat trim ($37). Front floor mats, carpeted ($22). Wheels/Tires: Wire wheel covers, locking: base ($212); LS ($90). TRX cast aluminum wheels: base ($612); LS ($490). Polycast wheels: base ($178); LS ($56). P215/70R14 BSW ($62 credit). P215/70HR14 performance BSW ($116). Conventional spare ($63). Inflatable spare ($122).

GRAND MARQUIS CONVENIENCE/APPEARANCE OPTIONS: Option Packages: LS decor ($521). Convenience group ($109- $134). Power lock group ($178-$278). Light group ($30-$48). Comfort/Convenience: Air cond. ($762); w/auto-temp control ($828). Rear defroster, electric ($145). Fingertip speed control ($176). Illuminated entry system ($82). Power six-way driver's seat ($237); driver and passenger ($473). Tinted glass ($118). Autolamp on/off delay ($73). Leather-wrapped steering wheel ($59). Tilt steering wheel ($115). Tripminder computer ($261). Digital clock ($61). Lighting and Mirrors: Cornering lamps ($68). Dual electric remote mirrors ($100). Lighted visor vanity mirrors ($109). Entertainment: AM/FM stereo radio w/cassette tape player ($148). Electronic-tuning AM/FM stereo radio w/cassette ($300). Power antenna ($71). Premium sound system ($168). AM/FM radio delete ($148 credit). Exterior: Formal coach vinyl roof ($650). Two-tone paint/tape ($129). Hood accent stripes ($18). Pivoting front vent windows ($79). Rocker panel moldings ($18-$38). Narrow vinyl- insert bodyside moldings ($61). Bumper rub strips ($59). License frames ($9). Luggage rack: wagon ($110). Interior: Dual-facing rear seats: wagon ($167). Cloth seat trim ($54). All-vinyl seat trim ($34). Leather seat trim ($418). Carpeted front floor mats ($21); front/rear ($33). Wheels/Tires: Wire wheel covers, locking ($176). Turbine spoke cast aluminum wheels ($361). P205/75R15 puncture- sealant ($161). P215/70R15 WSW ($62). Conventional spare ($63).

HISTORY: Introduced: October 3, 1985. Model year production: 791,149. Calendar year production (U.S.): 359,002. Calendar year sales by U.S. dealers: 491,782. Model year sales by U.S. dealers: 474,612.

Historical Footnotes: Every model in the Mercury lineup slipped in the sales race this year. Availability of the new Sable was limited at first, and production flaws (later recalls) were a problem. Rear-drive luxury was still promoted, despite the new front-drive models. Cougar was Lincoln-Mercury's Number One seller, and Capri finally dropped out.

Even more than its General Motors mates, Oldsmobile presented a curious mixture of family-car comforts and performance-model possibilities. Ranking third in the sales race through the late 1970s, no one could deny Oldsmobile's popularity in the marketplace — especially when the mid-size Cutlass edged out Chevrolet to become America's best seller. Nearly half a million people purchased a Cutlass in 1976. Not as widely known or thought about was the Olds relation to the NASCAR circuit and its penchant for producing some uniquely memorable (and collectible) models.

1978 Ninety-Eight Regency sedan (O)

Heralding a trend toward smaller scale and efficiency that would become universal, Olds introduced a small-block 260 cu. in. V-8 in 1975 for the compact Omega. Still, the luxury Ninety-Eight and front-drive Toronado carried a standard 455 cu. in. V-8 in 1976. That one wouldn't last another year, but the 403 V-8 hung on through 1979. Inline sixes disappeared after 1976, replaced by V-6s. Full-size Delta 88 and Ninety-Eight models were cut down to "family size" in 1977 and the mid-size Cutlass line endured similar shrinkage the next year.

1977 Cutlass 442 colonnade coupe (O)

Cutlass offered a rather bewildering model lineup of Supremes, Broughams, Salons and Calais coupes through these years. Fuel-efficiency improvements included the use of a four-cylinder engine in the subcompact Starfire and a V-6 in Omega, Cutlass and Delta 88. Only Toronado carried the biggest (403) V-8, as standard equipment, in both its Brougham and upscale XS/XSR edition.

With the arrival of its 350 cu. in. diesel V-8 in 1978 (a little later than expected), Oldsmobile soon became king of diesel power in America. The gasoline crisis of 1973-74

1982 Cutlass Ciera coupe (JG)

still smoldered in motorists' minds and diesel fuel seemed a likely candidate to help ease future shortages. Unfortunately, the diesel was not an original creation, but derived from a conventional gasoline-powered V-8. While its internal components and seals were beefed up, it seemed that not quite enough "beef" was used.

Diesels sold well in their early years and were adopted by all other GM makes before long. V-6 versions also were placed on the market. Eventually, though, customers complained about mechanical problems, which led to legal actions and horrid publicity. Diesels hung on until 1985, but sales diminished steadily. If new-car buyers at the time were advised to steer clear of diesels (once their flaws had been noted), the same advice generally holds for collectors today. Diesels have long been listed at sharply reduced prices in the used-car price guides for good reason. On the other hand, accepting a diesel under the hood could be one way to obtain an attractive model that would otherwise be well out of pocketbook reach.

1983 Ninety-Eight Regency Brougham sedan (AA)

On the gas-engine front, Olds, like other GM divisions, came with a number of non-Olds engines in the late 1970s. Later, this would lead to lawsuits from customers who felt cheated by a Chevrolet-powered Olds.

Toronado had hung on in full-size form through 1977-78, but couldn't avoid a downsized body transplant. Though smaller on the outside, the resized Toro still offered plenty of room inside. Over a million Oldsmobiles were sold in the 1979 model year, which was the second best total ever. Cutlass again ranked as America's best seller, but the fastback Cutlass models never achieved the popularity of the conventional notchback design.

Omega turned to front-wheel drive for 1980 as the Olds version of Chevrolet's Citation X-car. Engine shrinkage continued with a 307 cu. in. V-8 now standard in Ninety-Eight and Toronado, instead of the former 350. Tighter emissions standards were becoming a problem for the diesel, especially in California.

1984 Custom Cruiser station wagon (AA)

1986 Calais sedan (AA)

Hefty price rises in the early 1980s came despite the fact that sales had slumped badly. Inflationary pressures, it seemed, took precedence over the previous year's sales total at Oldsmobile and elsewhere. Gas mileage concerns remained prominent in 1981, which brought a new four-speed (overdrive fourth) automatic transmission, as well as more use of lock-up torque converter clutches that minimized slippage. Full-size models had a more aerodynamic look. Ninety-Eight and Toronado no longer carried a standard V-8, but switched to a base V-6. Nearly one in five Oldsmobiles was diesel-powered.

1984 Hurst/Olds coupe (AA)

Going along with the rising popularity of front-wheel drive, Oldsmobile introduced a much different Cutlass for 1982: the Ciera. Rear-drive Cutlasses remained in the lineup, however. A subcompact front-drive Firenza also appeared. Of greatest interest to enthusiasts, then and now, is the Hurst/Olds variant of the rear-drive Cutlass coupe, offered in 1983-84. Its appearance marked the 15th anniversary of the first Hurst/Olds in 1968. Not everyone had kind words to say about the car's "Lightning Rod" shifter for the automatic transmission, which some considered gimmicky. Even so, a Hurst/Olds is one model worth seeking out. Far more available than a Hurst/Olds, if less dramatic, is one of the 4-4-2 option packages offered on Cutlass coupes in the late 1970s.

For 1984, fans who wanted extra handling qualities as well as styling had a selection of ES models to choose from. Toronado offered a Caliente option; Cutlass Ciera, a Holiday coupe. In its efforts to attract younger (presumably the most desirable) customers, Olds turned to a front-drive Calais for 1985. Luxury-minded buyers had a far different and contemporary Ninety-Eight available. A year later, both Toronado and Delta 88 switched to front-drive. Despite a few weak years earlier in the decade, Olds generally kept a strong hold on the number three spot in sales, which topped a million in each year from 1984 to '86.

At first glance, apart from the relatively rare Hurst/Olds and more familiar 4-4-2, Oldsmobile doesn't seem to offer a wide variety to collectors. A closer look at the option packages reveals a slightly different story, highlighted by the Toronado XS options at the upper end, Starfire GT and Firenza packages at the small end and Delta 88 Holiday Coupes in the middle. Then too, there's the Indy Pace Car edition of Delta 88, of which 2,401 were built in 1977.

1976 OLDSMOBILE

Six car lines made up the 1976 Oldsmobile lineup: 34 models in all. This year brought a new Omega Brougham and Cutlass Supreme Brougham series. The Omega Salon, base Cutlass and Delta 88 Royale convertible were dropped. To boost economy, powerplants included an improved 260 cu. in. V-8 and a recalibrated Toronado engine. A lighter weight (7.5 inch) axle became standard on Omega, and a five-speed overdrive gearbox optional on some models. Body colors for 1976 Oldsmobile included: silver, light or dark blue, lime, red, mahogany, saddle, or dark green metallic; white; buckskin; cream; and black. All models except Starfire and Omega could have yellow or red. Starfire and Omega could have bright yellow or red-orange.

1976 Starfire GT hatchback coupe (O)

STARFIRE — SERIES 3H — V-6 — Riding a 97 inch wheelbase and measuring 179.3 inches in length, the subcompact four-passenger Starfire came in base and SX sport coupe form. As in 1975, quad rectangular headlamps stood in a soft plastic front-end panel that flexed with the energy-absorbing front bumper, returning to original shape after minor impact. Starfire's grille was made up of two narrow slots, side-by-side, with 'Oldsmobile' script on the driver's side (just above the grille opening). An Oldsmobile insignia adorned the center of the sloping front panel. Another (larger) grille slot was visible below the bumper rub strip. Park/signal lights were below the bumper, alongside the bumper slot. Omega's rear hatchback door opened to a carpeted load floor, which could be extended by folding the back seat forward. Inside were standard high-back front bucket seats with vinyl trim and a new instrument panel. Standard again was the 231 cu. in. (3.8-liter) V-6, with floor-shift four-speed manual gearbox. Optional: Turbo Hydra-matic and new manual five-speed (overdrive). Starfire tires were B78 x 13 blackwalls. SX offered a higher trim level, with cloth or vinyl upholstery, along with BR78 x 13 steel-belted radial tires, wheel opening moldings, and custom sport steering wheel. The Starfire GT option (introduced in mid-1975) included special hood and side stripes to complement the body color, Starfire Rallye wheels, raised-white-letter tires, tachometer, clock and gauges. Doors held a very large 'Starfire GT' decal, as part of the striping that extended from the very front to the very rear of the car.

1976 Omega Brougham coupe (O)

OMEGA/F85 — SERIES 3X — SIX/V-8 — Joining the low-budget F85 and base compact Omega this year was a new Brougham (replacing the former Salon). Vertical rectangular parking lamps were now mounted in outboard ends of a new full-width, chrome-plated grille. That grille was made up of many narrow vertical bars, split into four side-by-side sections. A wider bright vertical bar in the center held an Oldsmobile emblem, and script went on lower driver's side of the grille. Single round headlamps were mounted in square housings. A bumper slot was visible between the front guards. On the cowl was good-size 'Omega' script. Omega SX had an 'SX' decal on the lower cowl. The rear-end panel between the taillamps was restyled to give a full-width look (except F85). Omegas carried six passengers. Brougham had new interior fabrics and trim, with choice of standard bench seat or optional front buckets, in cloth or vinyl upholstery, along with a special stand-up hood emblem. The sporty SX option (on standard coupe or hatchback) included special wheel discs and bodyside decals, rocker panel and wheel opening moldings, sports-styled mirrors, Rallye suspension, and custom sport steering wheel. Base engine was a 250 cu. in. inline six; optional, a 260 two-barrel V-8 and a 350 V-8 with either two- or four- barrel carburetion. Three-speed manual shift was standard. A new five-speed overdrive floor-shift manual gearbox was available in all Omegas with the 260 V-8. Its higher (numerical) first gear ratio and overdrive fifth gear helped mileage.

CUTLASS S/SUPREME — SERIES 3A — SIX/V-8 — The Cutlass name encompassed quite a few mid-size Oldsmobile models, with varying appearance and characteristics. The list included Cutlass S, Cutlass Supreme, Cutlass Salon, and new Cutlass Supreme Brougham. The base model of 1975 was dropped, making S the base level. Two distinct coupe styles were available: sporty fastback Cutlass S, with new sloping front end; and formal-look Cutlass Supreme, Supreme Brougham, and Salon. New front ends featured wide horizontal parking/signal lamps below the quad rectangular headlamps. Hoods and front fenders also were new. Bodies were referred to as

1976 Cutlass Supreme colonnade coupe (O)

"Colonnade" hardtops. Cutlass S had a bold, vertical-bar twin-section grille design in the sloping front-end panel. The grille had a vertical appearance at the base, sweeping back at roughly a 45-degree angle, following the slope of the front-end panel, with fewer segments than the other Cutlass grilles. On the panel between the grille sections was an emblem. Quad headlamps were recessed. A wide slot in the front bumper was roughly grille-width. Coupes had large triangular quarter windows. Cutlass S again offered the 442 appearance/handling option, with distinctive new stripes and decals, large '442' decals at the forward portion of lower doors, and FE2 rally suspension. Salon/Supreme/Brougham used a wrapover twin grille with narrow vertical bars to give a more formal appearance. The grille pattern continued up over the top, back toward the hood). Following the usual Olds custom, the grille was split into two sections with a body-color vertical divider between them. Each section was also divided into two segments. 'Oldsmobile' script went on the driver's side of the grille. Quad rectangular headlamps stood over wide, clear parking lamps. In the bumper was a wide, grille-width slot. 'Cutlass Supreme Brougham' script decorated the lower cowl. Standard Cutlass engine included a 250 cu. in. (3.3- liter) inline six-cylinder engine, three-speed column-shift manual transmission, front disc/rear drum brakes power steering, woodgrain vinyl instrument panel trim, and FR78 x 15 blackwall steel-belted radial tires. Salon had a 260 cu. in. V-8 and Turbo Hydra-matic, and GR78 x 15 whitewalls. All models except S coupe/sedan and Supreme coupe had power brakes. Supreme Broughams had 60/40 divided front bench seats, with the loose-pillow look introduced on the 98 Regency. A new five-speed overdrive floor-shift manual gearbox became avilable on S, Supreme, Salon and Brougham models with the small-block (260) V-8. The V-8 was recalibrated to boost mileage, including a new spark switching valve to better match spark advance characteristics to engine speed and load. A new removable hatch roof option was offered on Supreme, Salon and Brougham coupes. Twin tinted glass roof panels could be removed and stored in the trunk.

CUTLASS SUPREME AND VISTA CRUISER — SERIES 3A — V-8 — Styled along the same lines as Cutlass coupes and sedans, the Supreme Cruiser and Vista Cruiser had a standard 350 cu. in. (5.7-liter) four-barrel V-8 and Turbo Hydra- matic. Options reached all the way to the 455 cu. in. four- barrel V-8. Two seats were standard, with a third seat available. Wagon tires were HR78 x 15 blackwalls.

1976 Delta 88 Royale Crown landau coupe (O)

DELTA 88 — SERIES 3B — V-8 — Like other full-size models, Delta 88 rode a 124 inch wheelbase. Two models were offered: base and Royale, both in two- or four-door hardtop body styles (a style that soon would disappear). Design was similar to 1975, with a few refinements, led by new quad rectangular headlamps. A four- opening aluminum grille consisted of two sections on each side of a wide body-color divider, which held a rectangular emblem. Each section contained vertical bars. 'Oldsmobile' script went on the driver's side of the grille. Wide rectangular park/signal lamps were below the headlamps, which continued into amber side marker lenses. Parking lamps wrapped around the front fenders. The front bumper held two slots. 'Delta 88' script was on the cowl. Wraparound taillamps were squarish in shape, with a bright square trim element and emblem in each lens center. Across the panel below the decklid were 'Oldsmobile' block letters. Base Delta 88 engine was the 350 cu. in. (5.7-liter) four-barrel V-8, with Turbo Hydra-matic. Optional: a 455 cu. in. V-8. Standard equipment also included vari-ratio power steering, power brakes, electronic message center, chrome wheel covers, inside hood release, plush-pile carpeting, ashtray and overhead courtesy lamps, HR78 x 15 BSW SBR tires, and automatic front-door courtesy switches. Bright metal moldings were used for rocker panels, drip rails and wheel openings. Royale added velour interior, color-coordinated protective bodyside moldings, courtesy and glovebox lights, and bright metal brake and gas pedal accents. A new Crown Landau option for the Delta Royale coupe included a padded landau vinyl roof with 6inch wide stainless steel band across the top. Crown Landau also had color-keyed wheel covers, a stand-up hood ornament, and Royale emblem on the rear-quarter inner panel.

CUSTOM CRUISER — SERIES 3B — V-8 — Full-size wagons looked like Ninety-Eights up front, with a two-section upright grille. Each section contained a checkered pattern, separated by the typical body-color panel with emblem. 'Oldsmobile' script stood at the lower driver's side of the grille. Quad rectangular headlamps went above wide rectangular park/signal lamps. Twin bumper slots were visible alongside the license plate. 'Custom Cruiser' script decorated the cowl. Backup lenses were separate, mounted inboard of the upright taillamps. Two-seat wagons held six passengers, but a third seat brought capacity up to nine. Custom Cruiser carried standard a 455 cu. in. V-8 with Turbo Hydra-matic, new semi-automatic load leveling, and LR78 x 15 BSW SBR tires. Wheelbase was 127 inches.

1976 Ninety-Eight Regency sedan (O)

NINETY-EIGHT — SERIES 3C — V-8 — Luxury and Regency editions of the full-size Ninety- Eight were offered, in two-door hardtop coupe or four-door hardtop sedan form. Four-doors had an extra window (like an opera window) behind the back door window. A landau roof option for the coupe gave it a huge-looking opera window. Like the Custom Cruiser, Ninety-Eights had a dual-section eggcrate-design grille, with new front-end panel, front bumper and wraparound horizontal parking lamps. Amber marker lenses aligned with the headlamps wrapped around the fender sides. Separate clear cornering lamps had horizontal ribs. Vertical taillamps were decorated with a small emblem in each lens. Tiny backup lamps stood alongside the license plate, on a panel that also contained small red lenses next to the taillamps. Standard Ninety-Eight equipment included a 455 cu. in. Rocket V-8 engine with four-barrel carb, Turbo Hydra-matic, vari-ratio power steering, power brakes, power driver's seat, driver's door armrest control console, electronic message center, electric clock, fold-down center armrests, front ashtray, and JR78 x 15 blackwall steel-belted radials. Rear fender skirts and bumper impact strips also were standard. A new 2.41:1 axle ratio became available, to boost highway gas mileage.

1976 Toronado coupe (O)

TORONADO — SERIES 3E — V-8 — The front-wheel-drive Toronado's revised look included grille bars with a wide chrome face, new gold/black stand-up hood ornament, and bodyside moldings to complement the body color. Toro's carburetion, ignition and EGR systems were calibrated to improve economy and driveability. New this year: a semi-automatic leveling system. The grille consisted of just two horizontal bars, low on the front end, below a deep hood front panel with 'Toronado' block lettering. Vertical park/signal lamps stood at fender tips, separate from the quad rectangular headlamps. Twin bumper slots went below the headlamps, outboard of the guards. At the rear tips of quarter panels, where taillamp lenses seemed appropriate, were body-color segments and an ornamental emblem. Instead, the taillamps were horizontal, one set of lenses along a trim strip at the decklid's lower edge (three lenses on each side), with small backup lenses on the same strip next to the license plate mounting. Two additional wide red lenses were positioned forward of the decklid, next to the back window. Standard engine was the four-barrel 455 cu. in. Rocket V-8, with Turbo Hydra-matic. Equipment included JR78 x 15 steel-belted radials, vari-ratio power steering, power front disc/rear drum brakes with new semi-metallic pads and linings, power windows, message center, driver's door onsole, digital clock, front ashtray, and glovebox lights, and inside hood release. Brougham or Custom interiors were available.

I.D. DATA: The 13-symbol Vehicle Identification Number (VIN) was located on the upper left surface of the instrument panel, visible through the windshield. The first digit is '3', indicating Oldsmobile division. Next is a letter indicating series: 'T' Starfire; 'D' Starfire SX; 'S' Omega F85; 'B' Omega; 'E' Omega Brougham; 'G' Cutlass S; 'J' Cutlass Supreme or Vista Cruiser; 'M' Cutlass Supreme Brougham ; 'K' Cutlass Salon; 'H' Cutlass Supreme Cruiser; 'L' Delta 88; 'N' Delta 88 Royale; 'Q' Custom Cruiser; 'R' Custom Cruiser (woodgrain trim); 'V' Ninety- Eight Luxury; 'X' Ninety-Eight Regency; 'Y' Toronado Custom; 'Z' Toronado Brougham. Next come two digits that denote body type: '07' Starfire coupe; '17' Omega 2-dr. hatchback coupe; '27' Omega 2-dr. pillar coupe; '37' 2- dr. Colonnade or HT coupe; '57' 2-dr. Colonnade coupe or HT coupe; '29' 4-dr. Colonnade HT sedan; '39' 4-dr. HT (4- window) sedan; '69' 4-dr. thin-pillar (4-window) sedan; '35' 4-dr. 2-seat wagon; '45' 4-dr. 3-seat wagon. The fifth symbol is a letter indicating engine code: 'C' V6-231 2Bbl.; 'D' L6-250 1Bbl.; 'F' V8-260 2Bbl.; 'H', 'J' or 'R' V8-350 4Bbl.; 'S' V8-455 4Bbl.; 'T' V8-455 4Bbl. The sixth symbol denotes model year ('6' 1976). Next is a plant code: '2' Ste. Therese, Quebec (Canada); 'L' Van Nuys, Calif.; 'G' Framingham, Mass.; 'D' Doraville, Georgia; 'M' Lansing, Mich.; 'W' Willow Run, Mich.; 'R' Arlington, Texas; 'C' Southgate, Calif.; 'X' Fairfax, Kansas; 'E' Linden, New Jersey. The final six digits are the sequential serial number, which began with 100001. Engine numbers were stamped on the right front of the block (Buick-built V8350), on the block next to the distributor (Chevrolet inline six), or on the oil filler tube (Oldsmobile engines). A body number plate on the shroud identified model year, car division, series, style, body assembly plant, body number, trim combination, modular seat code, paint code, and date built code.

STARFIRE SPORT (V-6)

Model Number	Body/Style Number	Body Type & Seating	Factory Price	Shipping Weight	Production Total
3H	T07	2-dr. Spt Cpe-4P	3882	2888	8,305

STARFIRE SX (V-6)

3H	D07	2-dr. Spt Cpe-4P	4062	2919	20,854

OMEGA F-85 (SIX/V-8)

3X	S27	2-dr. Cpe-6P	3390/3480	3171/3320	3,918

OMEGA (SIX/V-8)

3X	B27	2-dr. Cpe-6P	3485/3575	3174/3323	15,347
3X	B17	2-dr. Hatch Cpe-6P	3627/3717	3248/3397	4,497
3X	B69	4-dr. Sed-6P	3514/3604	3196/3345	20,221

OMEGA BROUGHAM (SIX/V-8)

3X	E27	2-dr. Cpe-6P	3675/3765	3178/3327	5,363
3X	E17	2-dr. Hatch Cpe-6P	3817/3907	3258/3407	1,235
3X	E69	4-dr. Sed-6P	3704/3794	3212/3361	7,587

CUTLASS 'S' (SIX/V-8)

3A	G37	2-dr. Col HT Cpe-6P	3999/4194	3608/3771	59,179
3A	G29	4-dr. Col HT Sed-6P	4033/4228	3690/3853	34,994

Production Note: A total of 964 'S' coupes had the 260 cu. in. V-8 and five-speed manual transmission.

CUTLASS SUPREME (SIX/V-8)

3A	J57	2-dr. Col HT Cpe- 6	4291/4486	3637/3800	186,647
3A	J29	4-dr. Col HT Sed-6	4415/4610	3730/3893	37,112

Production Note: A total of 862 Supreme coupes had the 260 cu. in. V-8 and five-speed manual transmission.

CUTLASS SUPREME CRUISER (V-8)

3A	H35	4-dr. 2S Sta Wag-6P	4923	4333	13,964
3A	H35	4-dr. 3S Sta Wag-8P	5056	4370	Note 1

CUTLASS VISTA CRUISER (V-8)

3A	J35	4-dr. 2S Sta Wag-6P	5041	4333	20,560
3A	J35	4-dr. 3S Sta Wag-8P	5174	4370	Note 1

Note 1: Three-seat wagon production is included in two-seat totals.

CUTLASS SUPREME BROUGHAM (SIX/V-8)

3A	M57	2-dr. Col HT Cpe- 5	4580/4775	3668/3831	91,312

CUTLASS SALON (V-8)

3A	K57	2-dr. Col HT Cpe-5P	4890	3829	48,440
3A	K29	4-dr. Col HT Sed-5P	4965	3949	7,921

DELTA 88 (V-8)

3B	L57	2-dr. HT Cpe-6P	4975	4243	7,204
3B	L39	4-dr. HT Sed-6P	5038	4336	9,759
3B	L69	4-dr. Town Sed-6P	4918	4279	17,115

DELTA 88 ROYALE (V-8)

3B	N57	2-dr. HT Cpe-6P	5146	4263	33,364
3B	N39	4-dr. HT Sed-6P	5217	4368	52,103
3B	N69	4-dr. Town Sed-6P	5078	4294	33,268

Production Note: A total of 4,360 Royales had the Crown Landau option (code Y61).

CUSTOM CRUISER (V-8)

3B	Q35	4-dr. 2S Sta Wag-6P	5563	5002	2,572
3B	Q45	4-dr. 3S Sta Wag-9P	5705	5062	3,626

CUSTOM CRUISER — Woodgrain Trim (V-8)

3B	R35	4-dr. 2S Sta Wag-6P	5719	5009	3,849
3B	R45	4-dr. 3S Sta Wag-9P	5861	5071	12,269

NINETY-EIGHT LUXURY (V-8)

3C	V37	2-dr. HT Cpe-6P	6271	4501	6,056
3C	V39	4-dr. HT Sedan-6P	6419	4633	16,802

NINETY-EIGHT REGENCY (V-8)

3C	X37	2-dr. HT Cpe-6P	6544	4535	26,282
3C	X39	4-dr. HT Sedan-6P	6691	4673	55,339

TORONADO CUSTOM (V-8)

3E	Y57	2-dr. HT Cpe-6P	6891	4620	2,555

TORONADO BROUGHAM (V-8)

3E	Z57	2-dr. HT Cpe-6P	7137	4729	21,749

Production Note: 140 Toronado motor home chassis also were produced.

FACTORY PRICE AND WEIGHT NOTE: For Omega and Cutlass, prices and weights to left of slash are for six-cylinder, to right for V-8 engine.

ENGINE DATA: BASE V-6 (Starfire): 90-degree, overhead-valve V-6. Cast iron block and head. Displacement: 231 cu. in. (3.8 liters). Bore & stroke: 3.80 x 3.40 in. Compression ratio: 8.0:1. Brake horsepower: 105 at 3400 R.P.M. Torque: 185 lbs.ft. at 2000 R.P.M. Four main bearings. Hydraulic valve lifters. Carburetor: 2Bbl. Rochester 2GC. VIN Code: C. BASE SIX (Omega, Cutlass): Inline. OHV. Six-cylinder. Cast iron block and head. Displacement: 250 cu. in. (4.1 liters). Bore & stroke: 3.88 x 3.53 in. Compression ratio: 8.25:1. Brake horsepower: 105 at 3800 R.P.M. Torque: 185 lbs.ft. at 1200 R.P.M. Seven main bearings. Hydraulic valve lifters. Carburetor: 1Bbl. Rochester. VIN Code: D. BASE V-8 (Cutlass Salon); OPTIONAL (Omega, Cutlass): 90-degree, overhead valve V-8. Cast iron block and head. Displacement: 260 cu. in. (4.3 liters). Bore & stroke: 3.50 x 3.39 in. Compression ratio: 8.0:1. Brake horsepower: 110 at 3400 R.P.M. Torque: 205 lbs.ft. at 1600 R.P.M. Five main bearings. Hydraulic valve lifters. Carburetor: 2Bbl. Rochester. VIN Code: F. OPTIONAL V-8 (Omega): 90-degree, overhead valve V-8. Cast iron block and head. Displacement: 350 cu. in. (5.7 liters). Bore & stroke: 3.80 x 3.85 in. Compression ratio: 8.0:1. Brake horsepower: 140 at 3200 R.P.M. Torque: 280 lbs.ft. at 1800 R.P.M. Five main bearings. Hydraulic valve lifters. Carburetor: 2Bbl. Rochester 2GC. OPTIONAL V-8 (Omega): Same as 350 cu. in. V-8 above, with 4Bbl. Rochester 4MV carburetor Horsepower: 155 at 3400 R.P.M. BASE V-8 (Delta 88, Cutlass Supreme/Vista Cruiser wagon); OPTIONAL (Cutlass): 90-degree, overhead valve V-8. Cast iron block and head. Displacement: 350 cu. in. (5.7 liters). Bore & stroke: 4.06 x 3.39 in. Compression ratio: 8.5:1. Brake horsepower: 170 at 3800 R.P.M. Torque: 275 lbs.ft. at 2400 R.P.M. Five main bearings. Hydraulic valve lifters. Carburetor: 4Bbl. Rochester. VIN Code: R. BASE V-8 (Ninety-Eight, Custom Cruiser); OPTIONAL (Cutlass, Delta 88): 90-degree, overhead valve V-8. Cast iron block and head. Displacement: 455 cu. in. (7.5 liters). Bore & stroke: 4.13 x 4.25 in. Compression ratio: 8.5:1. Brake horsepower: 190 at 3400 R.P.M. Torque: 350 lbs.ft. at 2000 R.P.M. Five main bearings. Hydraulic valve lifters. Carburetor: 4Bbl. Rochester. VIN Code: S. BASE V-8 (Toronado): Same as 455 cu. in. V-8 above, except B.H.P.: 215 at 3600 R.P.M. Torque: 370 lbs.ft. at 2400 R.P.M. Carburetor: 4Bbl. Rochester. VIN Code: T.

CHASSIS DATA: Wheelbase: (Starfire) 97.0 in.; (Omega) 111.0 in.; (Cutlass 2dr.) 112.0 in.; (Cutlass 4dr.) 116.0 in.; (Cutlass Supreme wag) 116.0 in.; (Delta 88) 124.0 in.; (NinetyEight) 127.0 in.; (Custom Crsr) 127.0 in.; (Toronado) 122.0 in. Overall Length: (Starfire) 179.3 in.; (Omega) 199.6 in.; (Cutlass 2dr.) 211.7 in.; (Cutlass 4dr.) 215.7 in.; (Cutlass Supreme wag) 219.9 in.; (Delta 88) 226.7 in.; (Ninety-Eight) 232.2 in.; (Custom Crsr) 231.0 in.; (Toro) 227.6 in. Height: (Starfire) 50.2 in.; (Omega 2dr.) 53.4 in.; (Omega 4dr.) 54.3 in.; (Cutlass 2dr.) 53.4 in.; (Cutlass 4dr.) 54.1 in.; (Cutlass Supreme wag) 55.5 in.; (Delta 88 2dr.) 3.4 in.; (Delta 88 4dr.) 54.5 in.; (Ninety-Eight 2dr.) 54.2 in.; (Ninety-Eight 4dr.) 54.7 in.; (Custom Crsr) 57.1 in.; (Toro) 53.2 in. Width: (Starfire) 65.4 in.; (Omega) 72.9 in.; (Cutlass 2dr.) 76.2 in.; (Cutlass 4dr.) 76.7 in.; (Cutlass Supreme wag) 77.7 in.; (Delta 88) 80.0 in.; (Ninety-Eight) 80.0 in.; (Custom Crsr) 80.0 in.; (Toro) 79.7 in. Front Tread: (Starfire) 54.7 in.; (Omega) 61.3 in.; (Cutlass) 61.1 in.; (Delta 88/Ninety-Eight) 63.7 in.; (Custom Crsr) 63.3 in.; (Toro) 63.6 in. Rear Tread: (Starfire) 53.6 in.; (Omega) 59.0 in.; (Cutlass) 60.7 in.; (Delta 88/Ninety-Eight) 64.0 in.; (Custom Crsr) 63.7 in.; (Toro) 63.5 in. Standard Tires: (Starfire) B78 x 13; (Starfire SX) BR78 x 13; (Omega) E78 x 14; (Cutlass) FR78 x 15; (Cutlass Supreme wag) HR78 x 15; (Cutlass Salon) GR78 x 15; (Delta 88) HR78 x 15; (Ninety-Eight) JR78 x 15; (Custom Crsr) LR78 x 15; (Toronado) JR78 x 15.

TECHNICAL: Transmission: Three-speed manual transmission (column shift) standard on Omega/Cutlass six or V8260. Gear ratios: (1st) 3.11:1; (2nd) 1.84:1; (3rd) 1.00:1; (Rev) 3.22:1. Four-speed floor shift standard on Starfire: (1st) 3.11:1; (2nd) 2.20:1; (3rd) 1.47:1; (4th) 1.00:1; (Rev) 3.11:1. Five-speed manual optional on Starfire, and on Omega/Cutlass coupe with V8260. Three-speed Turbo Hydra-matic standard on other models, optional on all. Floor selector lever available on Omega/Cutlass. Starfire, Omega/Cutlass six or V8260/350 THM gear ratios: (1st) 2.52:1; (2nd) 1.52:1; (3rd) 1.00:1; (Rev) 1.93:1. Cutlass (V8455)/Delta 88/Ninety-Eight/Toro THM: (1st) 2.48:1; (2nd) 1.48:1; (3rd) 1.00:1; (Rev) 2.08:1. Standard final drive ratio: (Starfire) 2.56:1; (Omega) 2.73:1 exc. 2.56:1 w/V8350; (Cutlass) 2.73:1 w/six, 3.08:1 w/V8260, 2.56:1 w/V8350 or V8455; (Cutlass Crsr) 2.73:1 w/V8350, 2.56:1 w/V8455; (Delta 88) 2.73:1 exc. 2.56:1 w/V8455; (Custom Crsr) 2.73:1; (Ninety-Eight) 2.56:1; (Toronado) 2.73:1. Steering: Recirculating ball. Front Suspension: (Starfire) coil springs w/lower trailing links and anti-sway bar; (Toronado); longitudinal torsion bars w/anti-sway bar; (others) coil springs w/control arms and anti-sway bar. Rear Suspension: (Starfire) rigid axle w/coil springs, lower trailing radius arms, upper torque arms, transverse linkage bar and anti-sway bar; (Omega) rigid axle w/semi-elliptic leaf springs; (others) rigid axle w/coil springs, lower trailing radius arms and upper torque arms. Semi-automatic leveling on Toronado. Brakes: Front disc, rear drum. Ignition: Electronic. Body construction: (Starfire) unibody; (Omega) unibody w/separate front partial frame; (others) separate body on perimeter frame. Fuel tank: (Starfire) 18.5 gal.; (Omega) 21 gal.; (Cutlass) 22 gal.; (Cutlass Supreme wag) 22 gal.; (Delta 88) 26 gal.; (Ninety-Eight) 26 gal.; (Custom Crsr wag) 22 gal.; (Toronado) 26 gal.

DRIVETRAIN OPTIONS: Engines: 260 cu. in. V-8: Omega/Cutlass ($90). 350 cu. in. 2Bbl. V-8: Omega ($140). 350 cu. in. 4Bbl. V-8: Omega ($195); Cutlass ($195) exc. Salon ($112). 455 cu. in. V-8: Cutlass ($321) exc. Salon ($238); Cutlass wag ($126); Delta 88 ($147). Transmission/Differential: Five-speed manual floor shift: Starfire ($244); Omega ($262). Turbo Hydra-matic: Starfire ($244); Omega ($262); Cutlass ($262-$286) exc. Salon/wag ($24). Floor shift lever, three-speed manual: Omega ($28). Anti-spin axle: Starfire/Omega/Cutlass ($51); full-size ($54). Brakes/Steering: Power disc brakes: Starfire ($55); Omega, Cutlass S ($58); Power steering: Starfire ($120); Omega ($136). Suspension: Driver-controlled leveling system: Cutlass ($85); full-size ($86). Rallye susp. pkg.: Omega ($15-$20). H.D. susp.: Cutlass ($23); full-size ($23). Firm ride shock absorbers: Cutlass/88/98 ($6). Superlift rear shocks: Cutlass ($45); full-size ($46). Rear stabilizer bar: Starfire ($16). Other: High-capacity cooling: Cutlass ($18). High-capacity radiator: Starfire/Omega ($18). H.D. battery: Starfire ($15). Maintenance-free battery: full-size ($28). High-capacity alternator: full-size ($43). Engine block heater ($12) exc. Starfire. California emissions equipment: Starfire/Omega/Cutlass ($50).

STARFIRE CONVENIENCE/APPEARANCE OPTIONS: Option Packages: GT pkg. ($290-$391). Aux. lighting group ($12). Comfort/Convenience: Four season air cond. ($452). Rear defogger ($66). Soft ray tinted glass ($44). Tilt steering ($48). Fuel economy meter ($25). Electric clock ($16). Sport mirrors ($27). Entertainment: AM radio ($71). AM radio w/stereo tape player ($197). AM/FM radio ($134). AM/FM stereo radio ($219). Rear speakers ($20). Exterior: Accent stripe ($24). Protective bodyside moldings ($39). Bright door edge moldings ($8). Bright wheel opening moldings: base ($18). Roof luggage rack ($54). Interior: Sports console ($73). Driver's seatback adjuster ($17). Front/rear floor mats ($14). Deluxe seatbelts ($15). Wheels and Tires: Super stock III wheels ($74-$84). Deluxe wheel covers ($39). Wheel trim rings ($33). B78 x 13 WSW. BR78 x 13 BSW/WSW/RWL.

OMEGA CONVENIENCE/APPEARANCE OPTIONS: Option Packages: SX pkg.: base hatch/cpe ($171). Convenience group ($26-$28). Comfort/Convenience: Four season air cond. ($452). Forced-air defogger ($43). Cruise control ($73). Soft ray tinted glass ($46). Power windows ($99-$140). Power door locks ($62-$89). Custom sport steering wheel ($34). Tilt steering ($52). Tachometer/voltage/temp gauges ($6). Fuel economy meter ($25). Electric clock ($18). Lighter: F85 ($5). Locking gas cap ($7). Horns and Mirrors: Dual horns ($6). Remote driver's mirror ($14). Sport mirrors ($26). Entertainment: AM radio ($75). AM radio w/stereo tape player ($209). AM/FM radio ($137). AM/FM stereo radio ($233); w/tape player ($337). Rear speakers ($20). Exterior: Vinyl roof ($91). Landau vinyl roof ($150). Two- tone paint ($35). Accent stripe ($23). Swing-out rear quarter vent windows ($48). Bright roof drip moldings ($16). Rocker panel moldings ($15). Protective bodyside moldings ($37). Bright wheel opening moldings ($17). Bright door edge moldings ($8-$12). Bright window frame moldings: F85 ($20). Bumper guards ($63). Bumper rub strips ($29). Roof luggage rack: wag ($71). Interior: Sports console ($71). Bucket seats ($79). Aux. front or rear floor mats ($7). Deluxe seatbelts ($15). Wheels and Tires: Super stock III wheels ($78-$89). Deluxe wheel covers ($32). Wire wheel covers ($111). E78 x 14 WSW. ER78 x 14 BSW/WSW. FR78 x 14 RWL SBR.

CUTLASS CONVENIENCE/APPEARANCE OPTIONS: Option Packages: 442 appearance/handling package: S cpe ($134). Special option pkg.: S cpe ($239-$250). Convenience group ($25-$31). Comfort/Convenience: Four season air cond. ($476); tempmatic ($513). Rear defogger ($77). Cruise control ($73). Twilight sentinel ($45). Soft ray tinted glass ($50). Six-way power seat ($124). Power windows ($99-$140). Power door locks ($62- $89). Power trunk release ($17). Custom sport steering wheel ($34). Tilt steering ($52). Instrument panel cluster ($35). Pulse wipers ($28). Fuel economy meter ($25). Electric clock ($20). Locking gas cap ($7). Lighting, Horns and Mirrors: Dome reading lamps ($15). Sport mirrors ($26). Remote driver's mirror ($14). Remote passenger mirror ($28). Lighted visor vanity mirror ($39). Entertainment: AM radio ($79). AM radio w/stereo tape player ($213). AM/FM radio ($142). AM/FM stereo radio ($233); w/tape player ($337). Rear speakers ($20). Exterior: Hatch roof ($550). Vinyl roof ($109). Landau vinyl roof: cpe ($109). Special solid-color paint ($125-$171). Two- tone paint ($31-$40); special ($154-$208); Firemist ($216). Accent stripe ($23). Swing-out rear quarter vent windows: wag ($48). Protective bodyside moldings ($44). Bright rocker panel and wheel opening moldings: S ($34). Bright door edge moldings ($8-$12). Special front bumper ($18). Special rear bumper: wag ($18). Bumper guards ($36); front only ($18). Rear air deflector: wag ($24). Rear storage lock/trim: wag ($14). Interior: Sports console ($71). Divided front seat: Supreme, Vista ($86). Swivel bucket seat: S cpe ($79). Aux. front or rear floor mats ($8). Trunk mat ($10). Cargo floor carpeting: Crsr ($22). Deluxe seatbelts ($15-$18). Wheels and Tires: Super stock II or III wheels ($64-$89). H.D. wheels ($10-$12). Deluxe wheel covers ($32). Wire wheel covers ($103-$120). FR78 x 15 WSW. GR78 x 15 BSW/WSW. HR78 x 15 WSW (wagon).

FULL SIZE (DELTA 88/NINETY-EIGHT/CUSTOM CRUISER/TORONADO) CONVENIENCE/APPEARANCE OPTIONS: Option Packages: Crown Landau pkg.: 88 Royale cpe ($598). Appearance option: Toro ($281). Illumination pkg. ($49). Comfort/Convenience: Air cushion restraint system (N/A). Four season air cond. ($512); tempmatic ($549). Rear defogger, electric ($78). Cruise control ($79). Theft-deterrent system ($115). Soft ray tinted glass ($64). Six-way power seat ($126) exc. 98 bench or driver's seat ($98). Power door locks ($63-$90). Power windows: 88/wag ($159). Power glide-away tailgate: wag ($52). Power trunk lid release ($17). Tilt steering ($53). Tilt/telescope steering wheel: 98/Toro ($95). Trip odometer/safety sentinel ($19). Electric clock ($20) exc. 98/Toro. Digital clock ($22-$43). Pulse wiper ($28). Locking gas cap ($7). Lighting, Horns and Mirrors: Cornering lamps ($41). Twilight sentinel ($41-$46). Electric monitoring lamp ($43). Courtesy/warning front-door lamps: 88 Royale ($25). Dome/reading lamps ($15). Sports mirrors: 88/wag ($26). Remote driver's mirror: 88/wag ($14). Remote passenger mirror ($28). Lighted visor vanity mirror ($40). Entertainment: AM radio ($92). AM radio w/stereo tape player ($228). AM/FM radio ($153). AM/FM stereo radio ($236); w/tape player ($341). Exterior: Vinyl roof ($136-$150). Landau vinyl roof: 98 cpe ($150). Halo vinyl roof: 98 cpe ($162). Special paint ($128- $173). Two-tone paint: 88/wag ($35-$48); special ($203-$216). Shadow-tone paint: Toro ($239). Protective bodyside moldings ($29-$45). Bright window frame moldings: 88 twn sed ($26). Bright door edge moldings ($8-$12). Bumper guards: 88/98 ($36). Front bumper guards: wag ($18). Roof luggage carrier: wag ($94). Rear storage area lock: wag ($14). Interior: Divided front seat w/twin controls: Royale/Luxury cpe/sed ($87); Royale twn sed/Cust Crsr ($126). Aux. floor mats, front or rear ($8-$11). Aux. front/mats w/carpet inserts ($36-$43). Nylon carpeting ($61). Litter container ($6). Trunk mat ($10). Deluxe seatbelts: wag ($15-$18). Wheels and Tires: Wire wheel covers: 88 ($69-$104). H.D. wheels: 88 ($12). HR78 x 15 WSW: 88 ($41). JR78 x 15 WSW: 98/Toro ($38-$44). JR78 x 15 wide WSW: 98/Toro ($48-$60). LR78 x 15 WSW: wag ($47).

HISTORY: Introduced: September 25, 1975. Model year production: 874,618. Calendar year production: 964,425. Calendar year sales by U.S. dealers: 900,611. Model year sales by U.S. dealers: 851,433.

Historical Footnotes: Cutlass managed to become the best-selling American automobile in 1976, pulling ahead of Chevrolet. Close to half a million customers chose a Cutlass (486,845 to be precise). Total Oldsmobile sales rose dramatically, markedly exceeding the company's early prediction, with each model posting an increase (though Starfire and Toronado rose only slightly). Overall, Oldsmobile ranked No. 3 in sales.

1977 OLDSMOBILE

Although the same six models appeared in Oldsmobile's lineup for 1977, the total number of models declined by six. A V-6 engine replaced the familiar inline six. As in much of the industry, fuel-efficiency got considerable attention this year, along with engineering improvements. Most notable, though, was the first wave of downsizing: this time of full- size models, reduced to "family size." A hardtop sedan was added to the Cutlass Supreme Brougham line, but taken away from Cutlass Salon. The basic Cutlass Supreme Cruiser faded away, leaving only one model. Toronado announced an XSR model, which changed its name to XS as production began. A number of smaller, more fuel-efficient engines went into use: a 140 cu. in. four in Starfire; 231 cu. in. V-6 in Omega/Cutlass/Delta; 260 cu. in. V-8 in Cutlass Salon; 350 V-8 in wagons and 98;

and a 403 in Toro. The big 455 cu. in. V-8 was abandoned. Lighter weight blocks and heads were used, too, along with lighter Turbo Hydra-matic 200 transmissions on some Starfires, Omegas and Delta 88s. Delta 88/98 models had new diagnostics for electrical-system analysis. Full-size model instruments could be removed from the passenger side by taking off a trim cover. Oldsmobile bodies carried more wax coating, zinc plating, zinc-rich primers, zincrometal and improved paints for better corrosion resistance.

1977 Starfire 8X hatchback coupe (O)

STARFIRE — SERIES 3H — FOUR/V-6 — A new grille with vertical ports went into Starfire's restyled front end, along with a larger emblem between the grille sections. Vertical slots made up the grille pattern in the sloping body-color front panel, which was upright at the front. Block lettering replaced the former Oldsmobile script. Deeply recessed, quad rectangular headlamps again were mounted in a soft plastic front-end panel, which flexed with the energy-absorbing front bumper. Amber park/signal lamps were mounted below the bumper. Wide wraparound taillamps came to a sharp point on quarter panels, with small backup lenses at inner ends of each taillamp. The rear hatchback lifted to reveal a carpeted load floor. A space-saver spare tire (with inflator bottle) fit in the right rear quarter well, concealed by a soft trim tire cover. Base engine was now the 140 cu. in. (2.3-liter) four; optional, the 231 cu. in. (3.8-liter) V-6. Four-speed manual gearbox with floor lever was standard. Only one body style was offered: a four-passenger sport coupe with high-back front bucket seats. Base Starfires had vinyl trim and a new interior door design. Carpeting and woodgrain moldings replaced the former map pockets. SX had upgraded trim in cloth or vinyl, with SBR tires, wheel opening moldings, and custom sport steering wheel. Bias-belted tires remained standard on the base model. Starfire's GT option was available again, including the V-6 engine, Rallye wheels, raised-white-letter tires, and tachometer, clock and gauges on the dash. Special hood and bodyside stripes (black, white or gold) complemented the body color.

1977 Omega coupe (O)

OMEGA/F85 — SERIES 3X — V-6/V-8 — Shaping of Omega's front end was similar to 1976, but the grille now displayed an eggcrate (crosshatch) pattern instead of the former vertical bars. Single headlamps appeared again, with parking lamps mounted in the grille's outboard ends. A body-color bumper center filler was used. Model lineup was the same: F85, standard Omega, and Brougham. New taillamps had a flush, full-width appearance. They stretched from the recessed license plate to the outside and wrapped around onto the quarter panel. Square backup lenses were at the center of each lens set. Inside was a new instrument panel and steering wheel. Standard engine was the 231 cu. in. (3.8-liter) V-6, with 260 cu. in. (4.3-liter) V-8 optional. In California and high-altitude areas, the option was a 350 cu. in. V-8 instead. As before, the sporty SX option was available on coupe and hatchback coupe, including special bodyside and wheel opening decals, rocker panel and wheel opening moldings, sports styled mirrors, Rallye suspension, and padded-rim custom sport steering wheel.

1977 Cutlass Supreme colonnade coupe (O)

CUTLASS S/SUPREME/SALON — SERIES 3A — V-6/V-8 — As in 1976, quad rectangular headlamps on the Cutlass mid-sizes stood above horizontal parking lamps with bright bezel. Once again, different grilles were used on S and Supreme/Salon models, accenting the sportiness of Cutlass S and the more formal image of Supreme and Salon. Cutlass S had a front end with vertical-bar twin-section wrapover grille style similar in concept to the 1976 version, with bold, bright dividers forming eight wide "holes" on each side. But the front vertical segment was taller, wrapping back nearly horizontally along the top. The former version followed an angled front panel. At the rear again were dual stacked taillamps. Once again, Cutlass S could have the 442 appearance/handling option, with special striping, specific front-end panel, and dual grilles with a series of narrow horizontal bars that carried upward and rearward into the front-end panel. Cutlass Supreme/Brougham/Salon (and Vista Cruiser) had a new grille with vertical bars similar to 1976, but accented with four heavier divider bars on each side. Coupes added a bright molding to the lower part of the rear-end panel. Coupe/sedan taillamps had new vertical lenses and bezels. All Cutlasses had a restyled instrument panel. The clock moved to the right side and a rectangular air outlet replaced the former round units on the passenger side. Base engine was the 231 cu. in. (3.8-liter) V-6, but the Salon (except in California and high-altitude) had the 260 cu. in. (4.3-liter) V-8 instead. That one was optional on other models. The removable hatch roof was optional again on coupes, redesigned with improved latching. Two tinted glass roof panels could be stored in the trunk.

CUTLASS VISTA CRUISER — SERIES 3A — V-8 — Vista Cruisers had the 350 cu. in. (5.7-liter) V-8, optional on other Cutlass models, as standard equipment. Like the others, it could get the 403 cu. in. (6.6-liter) V-8 as an option. Front-end styling was the same as Supreme.

1977 Delta 88 Royale pillared coupe (O)

DELTA 88 — SERIES 3B — V-6/V-8 — A total redesign hit the Delta 88, which now qualified as "family-size" (whatever that might mean). The new version made more efficient use of interior space. Redesigned front/rear seats actually helped back-seat knee and leg room to increase, even though the car grew smaller on the outside. Models included the base Delta 88 and Royale, in two-door pillar coupe and four-door town sedan body styles. Front-end design was similar to the former full-size appearance, with twin-segment grille. But each of the four grille sections now contained thin horizontal strips. An Olds emblem decorated the center divider panel. Quad rectangular headlamps stood above matching clear quad horizontal park/turn lamps. Headlamps didn't quite reach the fender tips, and no wraparound markers were used in the new design. A separate small amber lens (and clear cornering lens) went ahead of the front wheel: amber above the molding, clear below. Royale kept its standard colored bodyside molding, with extended rocker molding on the rear quarter; but the sail panel emblem was new this year. Royales also had a stand-up Rocket emblem. Both models had wide horizontal taillamps that extended to the license plate opening, with backup and side marker lamps forming an integral, brightly-framed unit at the outer ends (backups at quarter-panel tips). New Oldsmobile block lettering went on the deck lid. Royale models had a swing lock cover. Inside was a new instrument panel, seats, steering wheels, and door trim panels. Standard engine was the 231 cu. in. (3.8-liter) V-6 with Turbo Hydra-matic. Three V-8s were optional: 260 cu. in. (4.3-liter), 350 cu. in. (5.7-liter), and 403 cu. in. (6.6- liter). The small-block V-8 was not available in California or high-altitude regions. Standard equipment included power front disc/rear drum brakes, power steering, FR78 x 15 fiberglass-belted radial tires, ashtray and overhead courtesy lamps, electronic message center, carpeted lower doors, and chrome wheel covers. Royale added a custom sport bench front seat with fold-down center armrest, velour upholstery, glovebox lamp, bright metal pedal accents, stand-up hood ornament, protective bodyside moldiings, and bumper impact strips.

CUSTOM CRUISER — SERIES 3B — V-8 — Cruiser wagons had the same front end and wheelbase as Delta 88 Royale (11 inches shorter in wheelbase than 1976). Carpeting went on the floor and lower sidewalls in the cargo area. A new tailgate could be opened like a regular door, with the glass either up or down; or hinged down after the glass was lowered, to produce a flat area for easier loading. An electric tailgate window was standard. Engines were the same as Ninety-Eight. Custom Cruiser wagons came with two seats, or with optional rear-facing third seat. Either one could have optional bodyside moldings, or deluxe woodgrain treatment.

1977 Ninety-Eight Regency landau coupe (O)

NINETY-EIGHT — SERIES 3C — V-8 — Like the Delta 88, the posher Ninety-Eight was sharply downsized, but to a 119 inch wheelbase (3 inches longer than 88). Four models were offered again: two-door coupe and four- door sedan, in Luxury and Regency series. This year's grille had a very bright, chrome-plated look with broad framework and bright center divider with recessed Ninety-Eight emblem. Each of the two sections contained a tight eggcrate (crosshatch) pattern. As before, quad rectangular headlamps stood above quad park/turn lamps. Separate marker lenses were used. Both models had specific sail panel identification. Regency sedans included an exterior sail panel light. Vertical taillamps in rear-quarter end caps included a Rocket emblem in each lens, and vertical divider. Long horizontal backup lights with

rear reflex, at the decklid's lower edge, extended to the license plate opening on each side. Decklids held new Oldsmobile block lettering. An all-new instrument panel held relocated controls and gauges. New 55/45 divided front seating with dual controls was standard on Regency, available on Luxury models. Standard engine was the 350 cu. in. (5.7-liter) four-barrel V-8 with Turbo Hydra-matic; optional, the 403 cu. in. (6.6-liter) V-8. Standard equipment included power brakes, steering and windows, two-way power seat, GR78 x 15 blackwall steel-belted radial tires, driver's door armrest control console, electronic message centers, electric clock, fold-down center armrests, and bumper impact strips. Regency added velour upholstery, a divided front seat with dual controls, digital clock, and front seatback pouches.

1977 Toronado XSR coupe (O)

TORONADO — SERIES 3E — V-8 — Appearance of the front-drive Oldsmobile was basically similar to 1976, but the grille had a different look. Still squat, it was nonetheless taller than before, now displaying a wide-hole rectangular eggcrate pattern (10 x 4 hole) instead of the former horizontal strips. Quad headlamps now stood above quad park/signal lamps, and identifying lamps instead of parking lights went into each front fender tip. Inboard of bumper guards were small slots. A small 'Oldsmobile' nameplate went above the grille on the driver's side, replacing the former full-width lettering. Horizontal amber/clear marker/cornering lenses were mounted ahead of the front wheel panel. In addition to the basic Brougham, Toro offered a new XSR (changed to XS) model that had a restyled roof section with panoramic wraparound back window. Twin electrically- operated glass panels were above the driver and passenger seats, which slid inboard and could be stowed (one above the other) in the center roof section. XS/XSR had special identification and wheel covers. Standard this year was a 403 cu. in. (6.6-liter) V-8 with Turbo Hydra-matic. All Toros had electronic spark timing (EST) with an on-board microprocessor that continuously adjusted ignition timing, and monitored engine vacuum, coolant temperature and engine speed. Standard equipment included power front disc/rear drum brakes, power steering, electric windows, air conditioning, maintenance-free battery, velour upholstery, digital clock, Four Season air conditioning, cornering lamps, inside day/night mirror, lower front bumper guards, and bumper impact strips. Bright metal moldings decorated the roof, window sill, rocker panel and wheel openings. Bodies held color-coordinated protective moldings. Tires were JR78 x 15 blackwall steel-belted radials.

I.D. DATA: The 13-symbol Vehicle Identification Number (VIN) was located on the upper left surface of the instrument panel, visible through the windshield. The first digit is '3', indicating Oldsmobile division. Next is a letter indicating series: 'T' Starfire; 'D' Starfire SX; 'S' Omega F85; 'B' Omega; 'E' Omega Brougham; 'G' Cutlass S; 'J' Cutlass Supreme or Vista Cruiser; 'M' Cutlass Supreme Brougham; 'K' Cutlass Salon; 'H' Cutlass Supreme Cruiser; 'L' Delta 88; 'N' Delta 88 Royale; 'Q' Custom Cruiser; 'V' Ninety-Eight Luxury; 'X' Ninety-Eight Regency; 'Z' Toronado Brougham; 'W' Toronado XS/XSR. Next come two digits that denote body type: '07' Starfire coupe; '17' Omega 2-dr. hatchback coupe; '27' Omega 2-dr. pillar coupe; '37' 2-dr. Colonnade or HT coupe; '57' 2-dr. Colonnade coupe or HT coupe; '29' 4-dr. HT sedan; '39' 4- dr. HT (4-window) sedan; '69' 4-dr. thin-pillar (4-window) sedan; '35' 4-dr. 2-seat wagon; '45' 4-dr. 3-seat wagon. The fifth symbol is a letter indicating engine code: 'B' L4140 2Bbl.; 'A' or 'C' V6-231 2Bbl.; 'F' V8-260 2Bbl.; 'U' V8-305 2Bbl.; 'R' V8-350 4Bbl.; 'L' Omega V8-350 4Bbl.; 'K' V8-403 4Bbl. The sixth symbol denotes model year ('7' 1977). Next is a plant code: '2' Ste. Therese, Quebec (Canada); 'L' Van Nuys, Calif.; 'G' Framingham, Mass.; 'D' Doraville, Georgia; 'M' Lansing, Mich.; 'W' Willow Run, Mich.; 'R' Arlington, Texas; 'C' Southgate, Calif.; 'X' Fairfax, Kansas; 'E' Linden, New Jersey. The final six digits are the sequential serial number, which began with 100001. Engine numbers were stamped on the right front of the block (Buick-built engines), on the right side (Chevrolet- built V-8), or on the oil filler tube (Oldsmobile engines). Four-cylinder engine numbers were on a pad at right of block, above the starter. A body number plate on the shroud identified model year, car division, series, style, body assembly plant, body number, trim combination, modular seat code, paint code, and date built code.

STARFIRE (FOUR/V-6)

Model Number	Body/Style Number	Body Type & Seating	Factory Price	Shipping Weight	Production Total
3H	T07	2-dr. Spt Cpe-4P	3802/3942	--/2808	4,910

STARFIRE SX (FOUR/V-6)

3H	D07	2-dr. Spt Cpe-4P	3999/4139	--/2836	14,181

OMEGA F-85 (V-6/V-8)

3X	S27	2-dr. Cpe-6P	3653/3998	3109/3258	2,241

OMEGA (V-6/V-8)

3X	B27	2-dr. Cpe-6P	3740/3785	3127/3276	18,611
3X	B17	2-dr. Hatch Cpe-6P	3904/3949	3196/3345	4,739
3X	B69	4-dr. Sed-6P	3797/3842	3162/3311	21,723

OMEGA BROUGHAM (V-6V-8)

3X	E27	2-dr. Cpe-6P	3934/3979	3151/3300	6,478
3X	E17	2-dr. Hatch Cpe-6P	4104/4149	3228/3377	1,189
3X	E69	4-dr. Sed-6P	3994/4039	3188/3337	9,003

CUTLASS 'S' (V-6/V-8)

3A	G37	2-dr. Col HT Cpe-6	4350/4395	3535/3680	70,155
3A	G29	4-dr. Col HT Sed-6	4386/4431	3618/3763	42,923

CUTLASS SUPREME (V-6/V-8)

3A	J57	2-dr. Col HT Cpe-6	4609/4714	3565/3710	242,874
3A	J29	4-dr. Col HT Sed-6	4733/4778	3666/3811	37,929

CUTLASS SUPREME CRUISER (V-8)

3A	H35	4-dr. 2S Sta Wag-6P	N/A	4218	14,838

CUTLASS VISTA CRUISER (V-8)

3A	J35	4-dr. 2S Sta Wag-6P	5242	4273	25,816

CUTLASS SUPREME BROUGHAM (V-6/V-8)

3A	M57	2-dr. HT Cpe-5P	4968/5013	3584/3729	124,712
3A	M29	4-dr. HT Sed-6P	5032/5077	3692/3837	16,738

CUTLASS SALON (V-8)

3A	K57	2-dr. Col HT Cpe-5P	5268	3787	56,757

DELTA 88 (V-6/V-8)

3B	L37	2-dr. Cpe-6P	5144/5189	3431/3561	8,788
3B	L69	4-dr. Town Sed-6P	5204/5249	3472/3602	26,084

DELTA 88 ROYALE (V-6/V-8)

3B	N37	2-dr. Cpe-6P	5362/5407	3440/3570	61,138
3B	N69	4-dr. Town Sed-6P	5432/5477	3496/3626	117,571

Production Note: A total of 2,401 Indy Pace Car replicas (W44) were built, which cost $914 more than the base model.

CUSTOM CRUISER (V-8)

3B	Q35	4-dr. 2S Sta Wag-6P	5922	4064	32,827
3B	N/A	4-dr. 3S Sta Wag-8P	N/A	4095	Note 1

Note 1: Three-seat production is included in two-seat total.

NINETY-EIGHT LUXURY (V-8)

3C	V37	2-dr. Cpe-6P	6808	3753	5,058
3C	V69	4-dr. Town Sedan-6P	6785	3807	14,323

NINETY-EIGHT REGENCY (V-8)

3C	X37	2-dr. Cpe-6P	6948	3767	32,072
3C	X69	4-dr. Town Sedan-6P	7132	3840	87,970

TORONADO BROUGHAM (V-8)

3E	Z57	2-dr. Cpe-6P	8133	4634	31,371

TORONADO XS/XSR (V-8)

3E	W57	2-dr. Cpe-6P	11132	4688	2,713

Production Note: 176 Toronado chassis also were produced. Oldsmobile production totals listed separately one XSR coupe (W57).

FACTORY PRICE AND WEIGHT NOTE: For Omega, Cutlass and Delta 88, prices and weights to left of slash are for six-cylinder, to right for V-8 engine. For Starfire, prices/weights to left are for four-cylinder, to right for V-6.

ENGINE DATA: BASE FOUR (Starfire): Inline, overhead-cam four-cylinder. Aluminum block. Displacement: 140 cu. in. (2.3 liters). Bore & stroke: 3.50 x 3.63 in. Compression ratio: 8.0:1. Brake horsepower: 84 at 4400 R.P.M. Torque: 117 lbs.ft. at 2400 R.P.M. Five main bearings. Hydraulic valve lifters. Carburetor: 2Bbl. Holley 5210C. VIN Code: B. **BASE V-6** (Omega, Cutlass, Delta 88); OPTIONAL (Starfire): 90-degree, overhead-valve V-6. Cast iron block and head. Displacement: 231 cu. in. (3.8 liters). Bore & stroke: 3.80 x 3.40 in. Compression ratio: 8.0:1. Brake horsepower: 105 at 3400 R.P.M. Torque: 185 lbs.ft. at 2000 R.P.M. Four main bearings. Hydraulic

valve lifters. Carburetor: 2Bbl. Rochester 2GC. VIN Code: A or C. BASE V-8 (Cutlass Salon); OPTIONAL (Omega, Cutlass, Delta 88): 90-degree, overhead valve V-8. Cast iron block and head. Displacement: 260 cu. in. (4.3 liters). Bore & stroke: 3.50 x 3.39 in. Compression ratio: 7.5:1. Brake horsepower: 110 at 3400 R.P.M. Torque: 205 lbs.ft. at 1800 R.P.M. Five main bearings. Hydraulic valve lifters. Carburetor: 2Bbl. Rochester. VIN Code: F. OPTIONAL V-8 (Omega): 90-degree, overhead valve V-8. Cast iron block and head. Displacement: 305 cu. in. (5.0 liters). Bore & stroke: 3.74 x 3.48 in. Compression ratio: 8.5:1. Brake horsepower: 145 at 3800 R.P.M. Torque: 245 lbs.ft. at 2400 R.P.M. Five main bearings. Hydraulic valve lifters. Carburetor: 2Bbl. VIN Code: U. OPTIONAL V-8 (Omega): 90-degree, overhead valve V-8. Cast iron block and head. Displacement: 350 cu. in. (5.7 liters). Bore & stroke: 4.00 x 3.48 in. Compression ratio: 8.5:1. Brake horsepower: 170 at 3800 R.P.M. Torque: 270 lbs.ft. at 2400 R.P.M. Five main bearings. Hydraulic valve lifters. Carburetor: 4Bbl. Rochester M4MC. VIN Code: L. BASE V-8 (98, Vista/Custom Cruiser wagon); OPTIONAL (Cutlass, Delta 88): 90-degree, overhead valve V-8. Cast iron block and head. Displacement: 350 cu. in. (5.7 liters). Bore & stroke: 4.06 x 3.39 in. Compression ratio: 8.0:1. Brake horsepower: 170 at 3800 R.P.M. Torque: 275 lbs.ft. at 2000 R.P.M. Five main bearings. Hydraulic valve lifters. Carburetor: 4Bbl. Rochester. VIN Code: R. BASE V-8 (Toronado); OPTIONAL (Cutlass, Delta 88, 98): 90-degree, overhead valve V-8. Cast iron block and head. Displacement: 403 cu. in. (6.6 liters). Bore & stroke: 4.35 x 3.39 in. Compression ratio: 8.0:1. Brake horsepower: 185 at 3600 R.P.M. (Toro, 200 at 3600). Torque: 320 lbs.ft. at 2200 R.P.M. (Toro, 330 at 2400). Five main bearings. Hydraulic valve lifters. Carburetor: 4Bbl. Rochester. VIN Code: K.

CHASSIS DATA: Wheelbase: (Starfire) 97.0 in.; (Omega) 111.0 in.; (Cutlass cpe) 112.0 in.; (Cutlass sed) 116.0 in.; (Cutlass wag) 116.0 in.; (Delta 88) 116.0 in.; (NinetyEight) 119.0 in.; (Custom Crsr) 116.0 in.; (Toronado) 122.0 in. Overall Length: (Starfire) 179.3 in.; (Omega) 199.6 in.; (Cutlass cpe) 209.6 in.; (Cutlass sed) 215.2 in.; (Cutlass wag) 219.9 in.; (Delta 88) 217.5 in.; (Ninety-Eight) 220.4 in.; (Custom Crsr) 217.1 in.; (Toro) 227.5 in. Height: (Starfire) 50.2 in.; (Omega cpe) 53.8 in.; (Omega sed) 54.7 in.; (Cutlass cpe) 53.4 in.; (Cutlass sed) 54.1 in.; (Cutlass wag) 55.5 in.; (Delta 88 cpe) 54.5 in.; (Delta 88 sed) 55.7 in.; (Ninety-Eight cpe) 55.5 in.; (Ninety-Eight sed) 56.6 in.; (Custom Crsr) 58.0 in.; (Toro) 3.2 in. Width: (Starfire) 65.4 in.; (Omega) 72.9 in.; (Cutlass cpe) 76.2 in.; (Cutlass sed) 76.7 in.; (Cutlass wag) 77.7 in.; (Delta 88) 76.8 in.; (Ninety-Eight) 76.8 in.; (Custom Crsr) 79.8 in.; (Toro) 80.0 in. Front Tread: (Starfire) 54.7 in.; (Omega) 61.3 in.; (Cutlass) 61.0-61.1 in.; (Delta 88/Ninety-Eight) 61.7 in.; (Custom Crsr) 62.1 in.; (Toro) 63.6 in. Rear Tread: (Starfire) 53.6 in.; (Omega) 59.0 in.; (Cutlass) 60.7 in.; (Delta 88/Ninety-Eight) 60.7 in.; (Custom Crsr) 64.1 in.; (Toro) 63.5 in. Standard Tires: (Starfire) A78 x 13; (Starfire SX) BR78 x 13; (Omega) E78 x 14; (Cutlass) FR78 x 15; (Cutlass wag) HR78 x 15; (Cutlass Salon) GR78 x 15; (Delta 88) FR78 x 15; (Ninety- Eight) GR78 x 15; (Custom Crsr) HR78 x 15; (Toronado) JR78 x 15.

TECHNICAL: Transmission: Three-speed manual transmission (column shift) standard on Omega/Cutlass V-6. Gear ratios: (1st) 3.11:1; (2nd) 1.84:1; (3rd) 1.00:1; (Rev) 3.22:1. Four-speed floor shift standard on Starfire, and on Cutlass V-6 or V8260: (1st) 3.11:1; (2nd) 2.20:1; (3rd) 1.47:1; (4th) 1.00:1; (Rev) 3.11:1. Five-speed manual optional on Starfire: (1st) 3.40:1; (2nd) 2.08:1; (3rd) 1.39:1; (4th) 1.00:1; (5th) 0.80:1; (Rev) 3.36:1. Five-speed manual on Omega with V8260 and Cutlass coupe with V-6: (1st) 3.10:1; (2nd) 1.89:1; (3rd) 1.27:1; (4th) 1.00:1; (5th) 0.84:1; (Rev) 3.06:1. Three-speed Turbo Hydra-matic standard on other models, optional on all. Standard final drive ratio: (Starfire) 3.42:1; (Omega) 3.08:1; (Cutlass S/Supreme) 3.08:1; (Cutlass Salon/Brghm) 2.73:1; (Cutlass Cruiser) 2.73:1; (Delta 88) 2.73:1; (Custom Crsr) 2.73:1; (Ninety-Eight) 2.41:1; (Toronado) 2.73:1. Steering: Recirculating ball. Front Suspension: (Starfire) coil springs w/lower trailing links and anti-sway bar; (Toronado); longitudinal torsion bars w/anti-sway bar; (others) coil springs w/control arms and anti-sway bar. Rear Suspension: (Starfire) rigid axle w/coil springs, lower trailing radius arms, upper torque arms, transverse linkage bar and anti-sway bar; (Omega) rigid axle w/semi-elliptic leaf springs; (others) rigid axle w/coil springs, lower trailing radius arms and upper torque arms. Brakes: Front disc, rear drum. Ignition: Electronic. Body construction: (Starfire) unibody; (Omega) unibody w/separate front partial frame; (others) separate body on perimeter frame. Fuel Tank: (Starfire) 18.5 gal.; (Omega) 21 gal.; (Cutlass) 22 gal.; (Cutlass wag) 22 gal.; (Delta 88) 21 gal.; (Ninety- Eight) 24.5 gal.; (Custom Crsr wag) 22 gal.; (Toronado) 26 gal.

DRIVETRAIN OPTIONS: Engines: 231 cu. in. V-6: Starfire ($140). 260 cu. in. V-8: Omega/Cutlass/88 ($45). 305 cu. in. 2Bbl. V-8: Omega ($65). 350 cu. in. 4Bbl. V-8: Omega/Cutlass/88 ($155) exc. Vista ($110). 403 cu. in. V-8: Cutlass ($220) exc. Salon ($175); Cutlass Vista wag ($65); Delta 88 ($220); 98/Custom Crsr ($65). Transmission/Differential: Five-speed manual floor shift: Starfire ($248); Cutlass ($282). Turbo Hydra-matic: Starfire ($248); Omega/Cutlass ($282). Anti-spin axle: Starfire ($51); Omega/Cutlass ($54); full-size ($57). Brakes/Steering: Power brakes: Starfire ($58); Omega ($61). Power steering: Starfire ($127); Omega ($144). Suspension: Driver-controlled leveling system: Cutlass/Vista ($90); full-size ($91). Rallye susp. pkg.: Omega/Cutlass ($27). H.D. susp.: Cutlass ($24); 88/98 ($24); Vista/Toro ($18). Firm ride shock absorbers: Cutlass/88/98 ($7). Superlift rear shocks: Cutlass/Vista ($48); full-size ($49). Rear stabilizer bar: Starfire ($17). Other: High-capacity cooling: Omega ($19-$54); Cutlass ($19- 66); full-size ($6-$24). High-capacity radiator: Starfire ($18). H.D. battery: Starfire ($16); full-size ($18). High- capacity alternator: Cutlass/Vista/full-size ($46). Trailer wiring: Cutlass/full-size ($20-$32). Engine block heater ($13) exc. Starfire. California emissions equipment ($70). High-altitude emissions ($22).

STARFIRE CONVENIENCE/APPEARANCE OPTIONS: Option Packages: GT pkg. ($451-$567). Aux. lighting group ($13). Comfort/Convenience: Air cond. ($442). Rear defogger, electric ($71). Tinted glass ($48). Tilt steering ($50). Tach/volt/temp gauges ($56). Electric clock ($18). Sport mirrors ($29). Tilt inside mirror ($8). Entertainment: AM radio ($71). AM/FM radio ($134). AM/FM stereo radio ($219); w/tape player ($316). Rear speakers ($20). Windshield antenna ($23). Exterior: Accent stripe ($25). Protective bodyside moldings ($40). Door edge moldings ($9). Wheel opening moldings: base ($19). Interior: Sports console ($77). Driver's seatback adjuster ($18). Front/rear floor mats ($15). Deluxe seatbelts ($15). Wheels and Tires: Super stock III wheels ($74-$84). Deluxe wheel covers ($41). A78 x 13 WSW. B78 x 13 WSW. BR78 x 13 BSW/WSW/RWL. Conventional spare (NC).

OMEGA CONVENIENCE/APPEARANCE OPTIONS: Option Packages: SX pkg.: base hatch/cpe ($187). Convenience group ($28-$29). Comfort/Convenience: Air cond. ($478). Forced-air rear defogger ($48). Cruise control ($80). Tinted glass ($50). Power windows ($108-$151). Power door locks ($68-$96). Custom sport steering wheel ($36). Tilt steering ($57). Tachometer/voltage/temp gauges ($98). Electric clock ($21). Lighter: F85 ($6). Pulse wipers ($30). Horns and Mirrors: Dual horns ($7). Remote driver's mirror ($15). Sport mirrors ($28). Tilt inside mirror: F85 ($8). Entertainment: AM radio ($75). AM/FM radio ($137). AM/FM stereo radio ($233); w/tape player ($337). Rear speakers ($20). Windshield antenna ($23). Exterior: Full vinyl roof ($93). Landau vinyl roof: cpe ($162). Two-tone paint ($42). Accent stripe ($24). Swing-out rear quarter vent windows ($51). Roof drip moldings ($17). Rocker panel moldings ($16). Protective bodyside moldings ($38). Wheel opening moldings ($18). Door edge moldings ($9- $13). Window frame moldings: F85 ($21). Bumper guards ($67). Bumper rub strips ($29). Interior: Sports console ($75). Bucket seats ($84). Aux. front or rear floor mats ($8). Deluxe seatbelts ($15). Wheels and Tires: Custom sport wheels ($78-$89). E78 x 14 WSW. ER78 x 14 BSW/WSW. FR78 x 14 RWL SBR. Stowaway spare ($17).

CUTLASS CONVENIENCE/APPEARANCE OPTIONS: Option Packages: 442 appearance/handling package: S cpe ($169). Convenience group ($24-$34). Comfort/Convenience: Four season air cond. ($499); tempmatic ($538). Rear defogger, electric ($82). Cruise control ($80). Tinted glass ($54). Six-way power driver's or bench seat ($137). Power windows ($108-$151). Power door locks ($68- $96). Power trunk release ($18). Tilt steering ($57). Instrument panel cluster ($37). Fuel economy meter ($27). Trip odometer ($11). Electric clock ($21). Digital clock ($46). Pulse wipers ($30). Lighting and Mirrors: Dome reading lamps ($16). Sport mirrors ($28). Remote driver's mirror ($15). Remote passenger mirror ($30). Lighted visor vanity mirror ($41). Entertainment: AM radio ($79). AM/FM radio ($142). AM/FM stereo radio ($233); w/tape player ($337); w/CB radio ($453). CB radio ($195). Rear speakers ($21). Windshield antenna ($23). Power antenna ($42). Exterior: Hatch roof w/removable glass panels ($587). Full vinyl roof ($111). Landau vinyl roof: cpe ($111). Special solid-color paint ($133-$182). Two-tone paint ($42); special ($175-$219); Firemist ($229). Woodgrain paneling: Vista ($134). Accent stripe ($24). Swing-out rear quarter vent windows: wag ($51). Protective bodyside moldings ($45). Rocker panel and wheel opening moldings: S ($36). Door edge moldings ($9-$13). Special front or rear bumper ($19). Bumper guards ($38); front only ($19). Rear air deflector: wag ($25). Rear storage lock/trim: wag ($15). Roof luggage rack: wag ($75). Interior: Sports console ($75). Rear-facing third seat: wagon ($152). Divided front seat: Supreme, Vista ($91). Bucket seats: S cpe ($84). Aux. front or rear floor mats ($9). Carpeted front mats ($21); rear (17). Litter container ($7). Trunk mat ($11). Cargo floor carpeting: Vista ($23). Deluxe seatbelts ($15-$19). Wheels and Tires: Super stock II or III wheels ($64-$89). H.D. wheels ($10-$13). Deluxe wheel covers ($34). Wire wheel covers ($103-$120). FR78 x 15 BSW/WSW SBR. FR78 x 15 WSW GBR. GR78 x 15 BSW/WSW SBR. GR70 x 15 RWL SBR. Stowaway spare ($17).

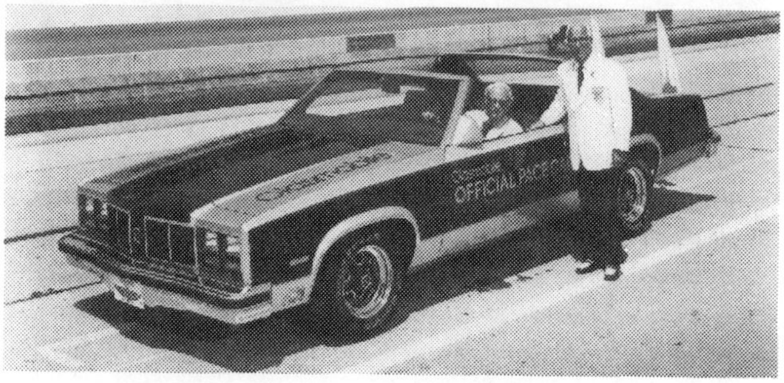

1977 Delta 88 T-top coupe Indy Pace Car (IMSC)

FULL SIZE (DELTA 88/NINETY-EIGHT/CUSTOM CRUISER/TORONADO) CONVENIENCE/APPEARANCE OPTIONS: Option Packages: Appearance option: Toro ($300). Illumination pkg. ($52) exc. Toro. Convenience group ($10-$35). Reminder pkg. ($44). Comfort/Convenience: Four season air cond. ($539); tempmatic ($578) exc. Toro ($39). Rear defogger, electric ($83). Cruise control ($84). Tinted glass ($69). Six-way power bench or driver's seat: 88/wag ($139); 98 ($109). Six-way power passenger seat ($139) except 88. Power door locks ($70-$98) exc. wag ($131). Power door locks w/seatback release: Toro ($96). Power windows: 88/wag ($114-$171). Power trunk lid release ($18). Tilt steering ($58). Tilt/telescope steering wheel: 98/Toro ($101). Special instrument cluster: Toro ($37). Trip odometer ($11) exc. Toro. Fuel economy meter ($27) exc. Toro. Electric clock: 88/wag ($21). Digital clock: 88/wag ($46); 98 ($23). Pulse wiper ($30). Lighting and Mirrors: Cornering lamps ($44) exc. Toro. Twilight sentinel ($42). Electric monitoring lamp: 98/Toro ($46). Courtesy/warning lamps: 88 Royale ($27). Dome/reading lamps ($16). Sport mirrors: 88/wag ($23-$28). Remote driver's mirror: 88/wag ($15). remote driver's mirror w/thermometer ($25-$39). Remote passenger mirror ($25-$30). Lighted visor vanity mirror ($42) exc. Toro. Entertainment: AM radio ($92) ex. Toro. AM/FM radio ($153). AM/FM stereo radio ($236); w/tape player ($341). AM/FM stereo radio w/digital clock: 98/Toro ($341-$364). AM/FM stereo w/CB ($459); N/A on wagon. CB radio ($197); N/A on wagon. Windshield antenna ($23). Power antenna ($42). Rear speaker ($21). Exterior: Electric astroroof ($898). Electric sunroof ($734). Full vinyl roof ($138-$179). Landau vinyl roof: 88/98 cpe ($166-$179); Toro XSR ($258). Special paint ($135-$184). Two-tone magic mirror paint: 88 cpe ($51). Firemist paint ($232). Lower bodyside paint: 88 ($100). Accent striping: 88/98 ($24). Woodgrain paneling: wag ($172). Protective bodyside moldings ($40-$46). Door edge moldings ($9-$13). Bumper guards: 88/98/wag ($38). Special rear bumper: Toro ($13). Rear bumper step: wag ($15). Roof luggage carrier: wag ($125). Tailgate lock release: wag ($30). Interior: Divided front seat w/twin controls: Royale/Luxury ($92); wag ($134). Third seat: wagon ($175). Reclining passenger seat ($55-$79) exc. Toro. Custom leather trim: 98 Regency ($204). Aux. floor mats, front or rear ($9-$12). Aux. mats w/carpet inserts: front ($21); rear ($17). Aux. floor mats w/carpet inserts: Toro ($46). Litter container ($7). Trunk mat ($11). Deluxe seatbelts: 88/wag ($16-$19). Wheels and Tires: Deluxe wheel covers ($39) exc. Toro. Wire wheel covers ($104) exc. Toro. Custom chrome wheels: 88/98 ($100-$117). Custom sport chrome wheels: 88 ($100-$117). H.D. wheels: 88/98 ($10-$13). FR78 x 15 BSW: 88 ($36-$45); WSW ($69-$86). FR78 x 15 WSW GBR: 88 ($33-$41). GR78 x 15 WSW: 98 ($34-$43); wide WSW ($48-$60). HR78 x 15 WSW: wag ($47). JR78 x 15 WSW: Toro ($40-$50). JR78 x 15 wide WSW: Toro ($54-$67). Stowaway spare (NC) exc. Toro.

HISTORY: Introduced: September 30, 1976. Model year production: 1,135,909. Calendar year production: 1,079,836. Calendar year sales by U.S. dealers: 977,046. Model year sales by U.S. dealers: 1,135,909.

Historical Footnotes: Once again, Oldsmobile hit the No. 3 position in sales, exceeding one million for the first time. Cutlass again led the pack, and also played a role in NASCAR racing. Like other GM divisions, Oldsmobile promoted its freshly downsized big cars for their space- and fuel-efficiency. Diesel power was expected to become available in mid-year, but delayed until model year 1978 so the current state of emissions standards could be evaluated. Abandonment of the 455 cu. in. V-8 would be just the beginning of a continual reduction of engine displacement in the years ahead.

1978 OLDSMOBILE

Following the full-size downsizing of 1977, the mid-size Cutlass line got similar treatment, shrinking to 108.1 inch wheelbase. Cutlass coupes and sedans lost an average of 657 pounds, (60 of them saved by a new frame design). Certain 260 cu. in. V-8s lost 38 pounds by switching to an aluminum intake manifold and lighter-weight exhaust manifolds. Many Cutlass and 88 hoods had aluminum panels. Some Cutlass models used aluminum brake drums. Cutlass also had new plug-in instrument panel components. In other major news, a diesel engine of 350 cu. in. (5.7-liter) displacement became available as an option on Delta 88, Ninety-Eight and Custom Cruiser models. Derived from the gas 350, many components were strengthened to handle the higher diesel compression—but not strengthened enough, in view of problems that developed with GM diesels. Tests revealed a fuel mileage gain of up to 25 percent with the diesel over comparable gas engines. That was no small matter at a time when memories of the gas crisis were still quite fresh, and further crises seemed imminent.

1978 Starfire GT hatchback coupe (O)

STARFIRE — SERIES 3H — FOUR/V-6/V-8 — Appearance of Oldsmobile's subcompact was similar to 1977. The grille was made up of vertical bars, with soft front end and quad rectangular headlamps. At the rear: a lift-up hatchback, opening to a carpeted load floor. Base engine this year was Pontiac's "Iron Duke" 151 cu. in. (2.5-liter) four; optional, either a 231 cu. in. (3.8-liter) V-6 or 305 cu. in. (5.0-liter) V-8. Both base and SX models could have the GT option (RPO code Y74). It came with V-6 engine, GT stripe (black, white or metallic gold) to complement the body color, Rallye wheels, raised-white-letter tires, and a tachometer. A total of 905 GT option were installed on base Starfires, 2,299 on SX. New this year was a Firenza package (RPO code Y65), 2,523 of which were installed on Starfire SX models. Intended to deliver a "sports car" look, this package included a special front air dam, rear spoiler, front/rear wheel opening flares, sport mirrors, wide-oval tires on star spoke wheels, rally suspension, and large 'Firenza' decal lettering on the door. Special paint treatment consisted of black lower bodysides with red accent striping that continued into the front and rear bumper. Firenze came in white, black, silver or bright red body colors.

1978 Omega coupe (O)

OMEGA — SERIES 3X — V-6/V-8 — Five models remained in the compact Omega lineup, as both the low-budget F85 and Brougham hatchback dropped out. Omega's front end displayed a new single-unit, six-section horizontal-bar (three sections on each side) grille with large surround moldings. Each section contained thin horizontal strips. Parking lamps again were mounted in outboard ends of the grille, within the same framework. Single headlamps appeared again, as did the flush taillamps that showed a full-length look. Bumper rub strips were optional. Base engine was the 231 cu. in. V-6 with three-speed column shift. Optional: the 305 cu. in. V-8 (in California and high-altitude, the 350 V-8). Both the standard and hatchback coupe again could have the SX sporty option, with special bodyside decals, rocker panel and wheel opening moldings, sports mirrors, Rallye suspension, and custom sport steering wheel. Topping the line this season was the LS option, billed as "Oldsmobile's small luxury limousine." It was a Brougham sedan option, including the V-6 engine, automatic transmission, air conditioning, AM/FM stereo, painted wheel covers, special lower bodyside accent paint, 'LS' sail panel emblems, and so forth. A total of 1,198 LS packages (RPO code Y61) went into four-door Broughams.

1978 Cutlass Supreme Brougham coupe (O)

CUTLASS — SERIES 3A — V-6/V-8 — Eight models made up the resized Cutlass mid-size series: coupe and sedan in fastback Salon and Salon Brougham form; Supreme, Calais and Supreme Brougham coupe; and two-seat Cruiser wagon. Styling differed among the models, especially in the grille pattern and shape. Cutlass models used an independent front suspension with wishbone-type upper and lower control arms, coil springs and link-type stabilizer. At the rear was a conventional four-link design with coil springs mounted atop the axle tube, and shock absorbers behind the axle. All Cutlass models carried a standard 231 cu. in. (3.8-liter) V-6 with two-barrel

carb. Three-speed manual shift was standard. Options included 260 and 305 cu. in. V-8s. Wagons had standard automatic transmission, and high-altitude versions could get a 350 cu. in. V-8. Gas tanks shrunk to 17.5 gallons (18.2 on wagons) and trunks held a new compact spare tire. Restyled instrument panels put the speedometer, gauges and other items in a pod directly in a driver's side pod. The headlamp dimmer was now part of the turn signal lever. All had single rectangular headlamps alongside clear vertical park/turn lamps (in the same housing). Cutlass Salon used a four-section eggcrate (crosshatch-pattern) upright grille surrounded by bright moldings. Coupes had frameless door glass; sedans had door frames with bright window frame scalp moldings. Across the bottom of the decklid was a full-length lower molding. Salon Brougham's grille was an eight-section upright vertical eggcrate (four sections on each side). A stand-up Olds emblem went on the front end panel. Hoods had a center molding. Wide lower moldings were used on front fenders, doors, quarter panels, and behind the rear quarters. Sedan window frames were black. Brougham looked the same as Salon at the rear, except for a wide lower decklid molding with horizontal simulated reflex band. As before, the sporty 442 appearance/handling option on Salon and Salon Brougham coupes was availbale. It had a blacked-out grille and wide '442' stripe along the lower sides and decklid bottom. Supreme had a traditional Olds dual vertical six-element grille that wrapped over the front-end panel. Thin vertical bars were split into three sections on each side of the body-colored center divider. A molding extended below the headlamp housing, across the bottom of the front-end panel, to give a full-width look. Standard features included a stand-up Olds emblem and hood center molding. No bumper slots were used. At Supreme's rear, single-unit vertical taillamps at protruding quarter-panel tips were surrounded by bright moldings, with a lighted center Oldsmobile emblem and backup lights at each side of the license plate opening. The decklid held a narrow full-width lower molding. Supreme Brougham had the regular Supreme front end, but with a Brougham name on brushed chrome background of the front-end panel. Broughams had wide belt moldings, bright drip moldings, wheel opening and rocker panel moldings, and wide lower moldings on front fenders, doors, quarters, and rear of rear quarters. Cutlass Calais was built on a Supreme body, but with its own wrapover vertical eggcrate-style grille and stand-up Olds emblem. Vertical bars appeared dominant in the crosshatch grille pattern. Calais features included wide belt moldings and wide lower moldings on front fenders, doors, quarters and rear of rear quarters, plus a body lock pillar applique. Cutlass Cruiser had the same front-end look as Salon Brougham, with standard wheel opening, rocker panel, drip and window moldings. Optional woodgrained vinyl had bright surrounding moldings as well as wide lower moldings on front fenders, doors and quarter panels. Cutlass standard equipment included a heater/defroster, lighter, day/night mirror, and rocker panel and wheel opening moldings (except base Salon). Cutlass Cruiser had power brakes and automatic transmission. Salon models had chrome wheels and P185/75R14 glass-belted radial tires; Salon Brougham, P195/75R14. Supreme and Calais wore P195/75R14 steel-belted radials.

1978 Delta 88 landau coupe (O)

DELTA 88 — SERIES 3B — V-6/V-8 — A new 88 dual three-segment eggcrate grille used two horizontal divider bars in each section to form three rows, all over a crosshatch pattern. A stand-up front-end emblem was standard. Royale included a hood center molding. The new front-end panel included amber wraparound front side markers, in the same frame as the quad headlamps and quad park/signal lamps. Two-pillar coupe and four-door town sedan bodies were offered, in base and Royale trim. Restyled wide wraparound taillamps put tiny narrow backup lights at the center of each lamp section, rather than at the outboard end. Each taillamp unit continued around and onto the quarter panel side. The small lenses at quarter-panel tips contained tiny emblems. Royale had standard front/rear bumper rub strips with white stripes. Base engine was the 231 cu. in. V-6 with automatic transmission. Optional: a 260 cu. in. or 350 cu. in. V-8, 350 cu. in. diesel V-8, and 403 gas V-8. Standard equipment included chrome wheel covers, power steering and brakes, front/rear ashtrays, lighter, day/night mirror, and moldings for rocker panels, wheel openings and roof drip. Royale also had protective bodyside moldings, sport front seat with center armrest, and front/rear bumper rub strips with white stripes.

1978 Delta 88 Custom Cruiser (O)

CUSTOM CRUISER — SERIES 3B — V-8 — The full-size Cruiser wagon had the Delta 88 grille and wheelbase, but its own front-end panel. The 350 V-8 was standard; diesel or 403 V-8 optional. Equipment included automatic transmission, power tailgate window, power brakes and steering, lighter, spare tire extractor, bumper impact strips, bench front seat with center armrest, and cargo area carpeting.

1978 Ninety-Eight Regency Diesel sedan (O)

NINETY-EIGHT — SERIES 3C — V-8 — Appearance of the Ninety-Eight was similar to 1977, but the grille had a looser crosshatch pattern (wider-spaced bars forming larger holes). New amber wraparound side marker lenses went into leading edges of front fenders, in the same frame as quad headlamps and parking/signal lamps. Regency had a new stand-up front-end emblem. A hood center molding was standard. New dual paint striping including a full-length upper and lower stripe was available. Redesigned taillamps eliminated the former red reflex from around the backup lights, and had no vertical divider. On the Regency, bright lower moldings now ran from the license plate opening to the taillamp bezels. Four models were offered again: coupe and sedan in Luxury or Regency trim. Regency had two leather and vinyl interiors available. Base engine was the 350 cu. in. (5.7- liter) V-8 with automatic; optional, either a 350 diesel or 403 gas V-8. Standard equipment also included power steering and brakes, GR78 x 15 blackwall steel-belted radial tires, bumper impact strips, bench seats with center armrest, power windows, lighter, electric clock, and two-way power driver's seat. Regency included a digital clock and 55/45 front bench seat with dual controls.

1978 Toronado Brougham coupe (O)

TORONADO — SERIES 3E — V-8 — Front-end appearance of the front-drive Olds was similar to 1977, but the grille now contained a vertical-bar design instead of an eggcrate pattern, with a bright bead around each grille opening. Gray bumper rub strips with twin white stripes were standard. Rear quarter side markers were part of the standard color-coordinated bodyside moldings. Rear bumper vertical pads had a simulated reflex with Olds emblems. Toronado's XS model was actually an option package this year. A standard microprocessor sensing and automatic regulation (MISAR) system monitored and adjusted ignition timing in response to engine vaccum and speed, and coolant temperature. Standard engine was the 403 cu. in. four-barrel V-8. Also standard: Turbo Hydra-matic, power brakes/steering, power windows, velour upholstery, digital clock, Four Season air conditioning, and cornering lamps.

I.D. DATA: Oldsmobile's 13-symbol Vehicle Identification Number (VIN) was located on the upper left surface of the instrument panel, visible through the windshield. The first digit is '3', indicating Oldsmobile division. Next is a letter indicating series: 'T' Starfire; 'D' Starfire SX; 'B' Omega; 'E' Omega Brougham; 'G' Cutlass Salon; 'J' Cutlass Salon Brougham; 'R' Cutlass Supreme; 'M' Cutlass Supreme Brougham ; 'K' Cutlass Calais; 'H' Cutlass Cruiser; 'L' Delta 88; 'N' Delta 88 Royale; 'Q' Custom Cruiser; 'V' Ninety-Eight Luxury; 'X' Ninety-Eight Regency; 'Z' Toronado Brougham; 'W' Toronado XS. Next come two digits that denote body type: '07' Starfire coupe; '17' Omega 2dr. hatchback coupe; '27' Omega 2dr. pillar coupe; '37' 2dr. coupe; '47' 2dr. coupe; '57' 2dr. coupe; '87' 2dr. coupe; '09' 4dr. sedan; '69' 4dr. sedan; '35' 4dr. 2seat wagon. The fifth symbol is a letter indicating engine code: 'V' L4151 2Bbl.; 'A' V6231 2Bbl.; 'F' V8260 2Bbl.; 'U' V8305 2Bbl.; 'H' V8305 4Bbl.; 'R' V8350 4Bbl.; 'L' Omega V8350 4Bbl.; 'N' diesel V8350; 'K' V8403 4Bbl. The sixth symbol denotes model year ('8' 1978). Next is a plant code: '2' Ste. Therese, Quebec (Canada); 'G' Framingham, Mass.; 'D' Doraville, Georgia; 'M' Lansing, Mich.; 'W' Willow Run, Mich.; 'R' Arlington, Texas; 'C' Southgate, Calif.; 'X' Fairfax, Kansas; 'E' Linden, New Jersey; '7' Lordstown, Ohio. The final six digits are the sequential serial number, which began with 100,001. Engine numbers were stamped on the right front of the block (Buick-built engines), on the right side (Chevrolet- built V-8), or on the oil filler tube or left valve cover (Oldsmobile engines). Four-cylinder engine numbers were on a pad at right front, near the distributor shaft. A body number plate on the shroud identified model year, car division, series, style, body assembly plant, body number, trim combination, modular seat code, paint code, and date built code.

STARFIRE (FOUR/V-6)

Model Number	Body/Style Number	Body Type & Seating	Factory Price	Shipping Weight	Production Total
3H	T07	2-dr. Spt Cpe-4P	3925/4095	--/2786	9,265

STARFIRE SX (FOUR/V-6)

3H	D07	2-dr. Spt Cpe-4P	4131/4301	--/2790	8,056

OMEGA (V-6/V-8)

3X	B27	2-dr. Cpe-6P	3973/4123	3105/3262	15,632
3X	B17	2-dr. Hatch Cpe-6P	4138/4288	3171/3328	4,084
3X	B69	4-dr. Sed-6P	4048/4198	3143/3300	19,478

OMEGA BROUGHAM (V-6/V-8)

3X	E27	2-dr. Cpe-6P	4179/4329	3126/3283	3,798
3X	E69	4-dr. Sed-6P	4254/4404	3167/3324	7,125

CUTLASS SALON (V-6/V-8)

3A	G87	2-dr. Cpe-6P	4408/4508	3056/3187	21,198
3A	G09	4-dr. Sed-6P	4508/4608	3070/3201	29,509

CUTLASS SALON BROUGHAM (V-6/V-8)

3A	J87	2-dr. Cpe-6P	4696/4796	3017/3148	10,741
3A	J09	4-dr. Sed-6P	4796/4896	3121/3252	21,902

CUTLASS SUPREME (V-6/V-8)

3A	R47	2-dr. Cpe-6P	4842/4942	3161/3295	240,917

CUTLASS CRUISER (V-6/V-8)

3A	H35	4-dr. 2S Sta Wag-6	5242/5342	3213/3402	44,617

CUTLASS SUPREME BROUGHAM (V-6/V-8)

3A	M47	2-dr. Cpe-6P	5247/5347	3138/3269	117,880

CUTLASS (SUPREME) CALAIS (V-6/V-8)

3A	K47	2-dr. Cpe-5P	5195/5295	3146/3277	40,842

DELTA 88 (V-6/V-8)

3B	L37	2-dr. Cpe-6P	5483/5583	3404/3588	17,469
3B	L69	4-dr. Town Sed-6P	5559/5659	3449/3633	25,322

DELTA 88 ROYALE (V-6/V-8)

3B	N37	2-dr. Cpe-6P	5707/5807	3415/3599	68,469
3B	N69	4-dr. Town Sed-6P	5807/5907	3477/3661	131,430

CUSTOM CRUISER (V-8)

3B	Q35	4-dr. 2S Sta Wag-6P	6324	4045	34,491
3B	Q35	4-dr. 3S Sta Wag-8P	N/A	4095	Note 1

Note 1: Three-seat production is included in two-seat total.

NINETY-EIGHT LUXURY (V-8)

3C	V37	2-dr. Cpe-6P	7064	3753	2,956
3C	V69	4-dr. Sedan-6P	7241	3805	9,136

NINETY-EIGHT REGENCY (V-8)

3C	X37	2-dr. Cpe-6P	7427	3767	28,573
3C	X69	4-dr. Sedan-6P	7611	3836	78,100

TORONADO BROUGHAM (V-8)

3E	Z57	2-dr. HT Cpe-6P	8889	4624	22,362

TORONADO XS (V-8)

3E	W57	2-dr. Cpe-6P	N/A	N/A	2,453

Production Note: Toronado XS was actually an option package. 545 Toronado chassis also were produced.

FACTORY PRICE AND WEIGHT NOTE: For Omega, Cutlass and Delta 88, prices and weights to left of slash are for six-cylinder, to right for V-8 engine. For Starfire, prices/weights to left are for four-cylinder, to right for V-6.

ENGINE DATA: BASE FOUR (Starfire): Inline, overhead-valve four-cylinder. Cast iron block and head. Displacement: 151 cu. in. (2.5 liters). Bore & stroke: 4.00 x 3.00 in. Compression ratio: 8.3:1. Brake horsepower: 85 at 4400 R.P.M. Torque: 123 lbs.ft. at 2800 R.P.M. Five main bearings. Hydraulic valve lifters. Carburetor: 2Bbl. Holley 5210C. Pontiac-built. VIN Code: V. BASE V-6 (Omega, Cutlass, Cutlass wagon, Delta 88); OPTIONAL (Starfire): 90-degree, overhead-valve V-6. Cast iron block and head. Displacement: 231 cu. in. (3.8 liters). Bore & stroke: 3.80 x 3.40 in. Compression ratio: 8.0:1. Brake horsepower: 105 at 3400 R.P.M. Torque: 185 lbs.ft. at 2000 R.P.M. Four main bearings. Hydraulic valve lifters. Carburetor: 2Bbl. Rochester 2GE. Buick-built. VIN Code: A. OPTIONAL V-8 (Cutlass, Cutlass wagon, Delta 88): 90-degree, overhead valve V-8. Cast iron block and head. Displacement: 260 cu. in. (4.3 liters). Bore & stroke: 3.50 x 3.39 in. Compression ratio: 7.5:1. Brake horsepower: 110 at 3400 R.P.M. Torque: 205 lbs.ft. at 1800 R.P.M. Five main bearings. Hydraulic valve lifters. Carburetor: 2Bbl. Rochester 2GC. VIN Code: F. OPTIONAL V-8 (Starfire, Omega,Cutlass): 90-degree, overhead valve V-8. Cast iron block and head. Displacement: 305 cu. in. (5.0 liters). Bore & stroke: 3.74 x 3.48 in. Compression ratio: 8.4:1. Brake horsepower: 145 at 3800 R.P.M. Torque: 245 lbs.ft. at 2400 R.P.M. Five main bearings. Hydraulic valve lifters. Carburetor: 2Bbl Rochester 2GC. Chevrolet-built. VIN Code: U. OPTIONAL V-8 (Cutlass): Same as 305 cu. in. V-8 above, with four-barrel carburetor. Horsepower: 160 at 4000 R.P.M. Torque: 235 lbs.-ft. at 2400 R.P.M. VIN Code: H. OPTIONAL V-8 (California/high-altitude Omega, Cutlass Cruiser): 90-degree, overhead valve V-8. Cast iron block and head. Displacement: 350 cu. in. (5.7 liters). Bore & stroke: 4.00 x 3.48 in. Compression ratio: 8.2:1. Brake horsepower: 160 at 3800 R.P.M. Torque: 260 lbs.ft. at 2400 R.P.M. Five main bearings. Hydraulic valve lifters. Carburetor: 4Bbl. Rochester M4MC. Chevrolet-built. VIN Code: L. BASE V-8 (98, Custom Cruiser wagon); OPTIONAL (Delta 88): 0-degree, overhead valve V-8. Cast iron block and head. Displacement: 350 cu. in. (5.7 liters). Bore & stroke: 4.06 x 3.39 in. Compression ratio: 7.9:1. Brake horsepower: 170 at 3800 R.P.M. Torque: 275 lbs.ft. at 2000 R.P.M. Five main bearings. Hydraulic valve lifters. Carburetor: 4Bbl. Rochester M4MC. VIN Code: R. BASE V-8 (Toronado); OPTIONAL (Delta 88, 98, Custom Cruiser): 90-degree, overhead valve V-8. Cast iron block and head. Displacement: 403 cu. in. (6.6 liters). Bore & stroke: 4.35 x 3.39 in. Compression ratio: 7.9:1. Brake horsepower: 185 at 3600 R.P.M. (Toro, 190 at 3600). Torque: 320 lbs.ft. at 2000 R.P.M. (Toro, 325 at 2000). Five main bearings. Hydraulic valve lifters. Carburetor: 4Bbl. Rochester M4MC. VIN Code: K. DIESEL V-8 (Delta 88, 98, Custom Cruiser): 90-degree, overhead valve V-8. Cast iron block and head. Displacement: 350 cu. in. (5.7 liters). Bore & stroke: 4.06 x 3.39 in. Compression ratio: 22.5:1. Brake horsepower: 120 at 3600 R.P.M. Torque: 220 lbs.ft. at 1600 R.P.M. Five main bearings. Hydraulic valve lifters. Fuel injection. VIN Code: N.

1978 Delta 88 Royale sedan (O)

CHASSIS DATA: Wheelbase: (Starfire) 97.0 in.; (Omega) 111.0 in.; (Cutlass) 108.1 in.; (Delta 88) 116.0 in.; (98) 119.0 in.; (Custom Crsr) 116.0 in.; (Toronado) 122.0 in. Overall Length: (Starfire) 179.3 in.; (Omega) 199.6 in.; (Cutlass Supreme cpe) 200.1 in.; (Cutlass Salon) 197.7 in.; (Cutlass wag) 197.6 in.; (Delta 88) 217.5 in.; (98) 220.4 in.; (Custom Crsr) 217.1 in.; (Toro) 227.5 in. Height: (Starfire) 50.2 in.; (Omega cpe) 53.8 in.; (Omega sed) 54.7 in.; (Cutlass cpe) 53.4 in.; (Cutlass sed) 54.2 in.; (Cutlass wag) 54.5 in.; (Delta 88 cpe) 54.5 in.; (Delta 88 4dr.) 55.2 in.; (98) 55.5 in.; (Custom Crsr) 57.2 in.; (Toro) 53.2 in. Width: (Starfire) 65.4 in.; (Omega) 72.9 in.; (Cutlass cpe) 71.3 in.; (Cutlass sed) 71.9 in.; (Cutlass wag) 71.7 in.; (Delta 88) 76.8 in.; (98) 76.8 in.; (Custom Crsr) 79.8 in.; (Toro) 80.0 in. Front Tread: (Starfire) 54.7 in.; (Omega) 61.9 in.; (Cutlass) 58.5 in.; (Delta 88/98) 61.7 in.; (Custom Crsr) 62.1 in.; (Toro) 63.7 in. Rear Tread: (Starfire) 53.6 in.; (Omega) 59.6 in.; (Cutlass) 57.7 in.; (Delta 88/98) 60.7 in.; (Custom Crsr) 64.1 in.; (Toro) 63.6 in. Standard Tires: (Starfire) A78 x 13; (Starfire SX) BR78 x 13; (Omega) E78 x 14; (Cutlass Supreme/Calais) P195/75R14; (Cutlass Salon) P185/75R14; (Cutlass wag) P195/75R14; (Delta 88) FR78 x 15; (98) GR78 x 15; (Custom Crsr) HR78 x 15; (Toronado) JR78 x 15.

TECHNICAL: Transmission: Three-speed manual transmission standard on Omega and Cutlass V-6. Four-speed floor shift standard on Starfire V-6 and Omega/Cutlass V8305. Five-speed manual optional on Starfire, and Omega/Cutlass V8260. Three-speed Turbo Hydra-matic standard on other models, optional on all. Standard final drive ratio: (Starfire) 2.73:1; (Omega) 3.08:1; (Cutlass) 2.93:1; (Cutlass Cruiser) 2.73:1; (Delta 88) 2.73:1; (Custom Crsr) 2.73:1; (98) 2.41:1; (Toronado) 2.73:1. Steering: Recirculating ball. Front Suspension: (Starfire) coil springs w/lower trailing links and anti-sway bar; (Toronado) longitudinal torsion bars w/anti-sway bar; (others) coil springs w/control arms and anti-sway bar. Rear Suspension: (Starfire) rigid axle w/coil springs, lower trailing radius arms, upper torque arms, transverse linkage bar and anti-sway bar; (Omega) rigid axle w/semi-elliptic leaf springs; (others) rigid axle w/coil springs, lower trailing radius arms and upper torque arms. Semi-automatic leveling on Toronado. Brakes: Front disc, rear drum. Ignition: Electronic. Body construction: (Starfire) unibody; (Omega) unibody w/separate front partial frame; (others) separate body on perimeter frame. Fuel Tank: (Starfire) 18.5 gal.; (Omega) 21 gal.; (Cutlass) 17.5 gal.; (Cutlass wag) 18.2 gal.; (Delta 88) 21 or 25.3 gal.; (98) 25.3 gal.; (Custom Crsr wag) 22 gal.; (Toronado) 26 gal.

DRIVETRAIN OPTIONS: Engines: 231 cu. in. V-6: Starfire ($170). 260 cu. in. V-8: Cutlass/88($100). 305 cu. in. 2Bbl. V-8: Starfire ($320); Starfire w/GT pkg. ($150); Omega/Cutlass ($150). 305 cu. in. 4Bbl. V-8: Omega/Cutlass ($200). 350 cu. in. 4Bbl. V-8: Omega ($265); Cutlass Crsr ($265). 403 cu. in. V-8: Delta 88 ($330); 98/Custom Crsr ($65). Diesel 350 cu. in. V-8: 88 ($850); 98/Custom Crsr ($740). Transmission/Differential: Four-speed floor shift: Omega/Cutlass ($125). Five-speed manual floor shift: Starfire ($175). Turbo Hydra-matic: Starfire (N/A); Omega/Cutlass ($307). Limited-slip differential: Starfire ($56); Omega/Cutlass ($60); 88 ($64). Power steering: Starfire (N/A); Omega/Cutlass ($152). Brakes/Steering: Power brakes: Omega/Cutlass ($66); Omega ($69). Power disc brakes: Omega/Cutlass ($69-$300). Suspension: Rallye susp. pkg.: Omega/Cutlass ($29). H.D. susp.: full-size ($19-$25). Firm ride shock absorbers: Cutlass/88/98 ($7). Superlift rear shocks: Cutlass/88/98 ($52). Rear stabilizer bar: Starfire ($18). Automatic load leveling: Cutlass/88/98 ($116). Load leveling: Toro ($96). Other: High-capacity cooling ($20-72). High-capacity radiator: Starfire ($19). H.D. battery ($17-$20). High-capacity alternator: Cutlass/full-size ($49). Trailer wiring: Cutlass/full-size ($21-$34). Engine block heater ($14) exc. Starfire. California emissions equipment ($75-$100). High- altitude emissions ($33).

1978 Cutlass Cruiser station wagon (O)

OPTION PACKAGES: Starfire GT pkg. ($504-$627). Omega LS pkg.: Brougham sedan ($1943). Omega SX pkg.: base hatch/cpe ($201). Cutlass 442 appearance/handling pkg.: Salon cpe ($260); Salon Brghm ($111). Toronado XS pkg. ($2700).

MAJOR CONVENIENCE/APPEARANCE OPTIONS: Four Season air conditioner ($470-$581). Tempmatic air conditioning: Cutlass/88/98 ($584-$626); Toro ($45). Power seat ($120-$151); N/A Starfire. Power windows ($118-$190); N/A Starfire. Cornering lamps: Cutlass/88/98 ($45). Twilight sentinel: 88/98/Toro ($45). Power astroroof: Cutlass/88/98/Toro ($699-$978). Power sliding metal sunroof: Cutlass/88/98/Toro ($499-$778). Removable glass panel roof: Cutlass ($625). Sliding glass panel roof: Starfire ($215). Landau vinyl roof ($168-$268); N/A Starfire. Full vinyl roof ($79-$187); N/A Starfire. Firemist paint: Cutlass/88/98/Toro ($165). Rear-facing third seat: Custom Cruiser ($186).

HISTORY: Introduced: October 6, 1977. Model year production: 1,015,805. Calendar year production (U.S.): 910,254. Calendar year sales by U.S. dealers: 1,006,344. Model year sales by U.S. dealers: 952,151. A total of 33,841 diesel-powered Oldsmobiles were produced in the model year.

Historical Footnotes: As usual, Olds occupied the No. 3 spot in sales. Oldsmobiles came with quite a variety of engines at this time, from Buick, Chevrolet and Pontiac as well as its own plants. This phenomenon, which pervaded the GM camp, eventually led to some consumer dissatisfaction and even lawsuits from those who felt cheated. The new diesel V-8 engine proved quite popular, and would soon find its way under hoods of other GM vehicles, making Olds a leader in diesel power. In a continuing attempt to improve rust resistance, one-side electro-galvanized steel was used on Oldsmobile door outer panels and outer quarter panels.

1979 OLDSMOBILE

A redesigned front-drive Toronado was the year's major news, smaller but with more head/leg room. A new 260 cu. in. (4.3-liter) diesel V-8 joined the original 350 diesel, making diesel power available on 19 of Oldsmobile's 26 models. It was available with either automatic transmission or five-speed manual. Both diesel V-8 engines adopted a fast-start system that "nearly eliminates the need to wait while the glow plugs warm the air in the pre-chamber." The car was supposed to start at zero degrees in about six seconds, whereas the 1978 diesel took a full minute.

1979 Starfire hatchback coupe (O)

STARFIRE — SERIES 3H — FOUR/V-6 — Not only did the Olds subcompact look a little different this year, it felt somewhat different. Up front was a new four-element vertical-bar grille in body color, in a new hard fiberglass-reinforced sloping front-end panel. And a hard rear end replaced the soft one of 1978. The new grille contained four sections of thin vertical bars. Park/signal lamps were now behind the outer grille segments. Single quad recessed headlamps provided the illumination on this year's model, and small horizontal amber marker lenses went ahead of each front wheel. Base and SX two-door sport coupes had a hatchback rear and fold-down back seat. Standard engine was the 151 cu. in. (2.5-liter) four. The GT package was optional again, with bodyside and hood paint stripes (black, white or metallic gold) and 'GT' lettering. That package included a 231 cu. in. (3.8-liter) V-6 engine, Rallye wheels, raised-white-letter tires, tachometer, clock and temperature gauge. The Firenza option, introduced late in the 1978 model year, also reappeared, installed on 3,873 Starfire SX models. It included a special front air dam, rear spoiler, flared front/rear wheel openings, sport mirrors, wide oval tires on sport wheels, and Rallye suspension. Firenzas had special paint, with Firenza identification on the lower paint stripe.

1979 Omega Brougham coupe (O)

OMEGA — SERIES 3X — V-6/V-8 — Not many Oldsmobiles entered a new year without at least a revised grille, and Omega was no exception. This one had four sections on each side, each contained a set of thin vertical bars. Amber vertical park/signal lamps stood at the outboard ends of the grille (in the same framework). Single round headlamps were used again. Base Omegas came in pillar (notchback) coupe, hatchback coupe, and four-door sedan form; Brougham as a pillar coupe and sedan. Standard engine was a 231 cu. in. (3.8-liter) V-6. The SX option on base Omega coupe and hatchback included rocker panel and wheel opening moldings, special wheel opening and bodyside decals, sport styled wheels, Rallye suspension, and custom sport steering wheel. An LS option package for Brougham sedans included automatic transmission, Four Season air conditioner, 'LS' sail-panel emblem, painted wheel covers, and special paint scheme with accent stripes.

1979 Cutlass Calais landau coupe (AA)

CUTLASS — SERIES 3A — V-6/V-8 — As usual, Cutlass models could be differentiated mainly by their grille appearance. Nine models this year included a Salon and Salon Brougham coupe and sedan; Supreme, Calais and Supreme Brougham coupe; Cutlass Cruiser wagon; and new Cruiser Brougham. Base Cutlass engine was the 231 cu. in. (3.8-liter) V-6. Coupes and sedans could have a 260 cu. in. (4.3-liter) diesel V-8. Cutlass Cruisers could get the larger 350 diesel V-8. Cutlass Salon had a six-segment grille; Salon Brougham a twelve-segment. Both back ends had dual vertical taillamps. The Salon grille had three sections on each side, and amber vertical (formerly clear) park/signal lamps in the same frame as single rectangular headlamps. Salon Brougham's grille had six side-by-side sections on each side of the body-color divider, instead of four as in 1978. Supreme and Supreme Brougham had a four-element vertical-bar type grille that wrapped over the front-end panel. Calais now sported an upright twin rectangular-bar type grille with eggcrate pattern, replacing the former wrapover design. All three formal coupes had the same back end with vertical taillamps divided by a bright center. Cutlass Cruiser had the same front end as Cutlass Salon, while Cruiser Brougham shared grilles with the Salon Brougham. Salon and Salon Brougham coupes could again have the 442 appearance/handling package, which included '442' paint striping and lettering on lower bodyside and decklid, bucket seats, sports console, Rallye suspension, and blacked- out grille. 409 Supremes had a five-speed gearbox and the LV8 engine; 267 had the five-speed and LF7 engine. A total of 38,672 Cutlass diesels were produced. Cutlass Calais announced a Hurst/Olds option (RPO code W30). It would include a 350 cu. in. (5.7-liter) four-barrel V-8 and automatic transmission. The car body had special black and gold (or white and gold) paint, gold aluminum sport wheels, and gold sport mirrors. Also included: raised-white-letter tires, sport console with Hurst shifter, power steering and brakes, digital clock, ride/handling package, sport steering wheel, full instrumentation, and contour reclining front bucket seats. A total of 2,499 were built.

1979 Delta 88 coupe (AA)

DELTA 88 — SERIES 3B — V-6/V-8 — Overall Delta 88 appearance was similar to 1978, and the front end had the same basic design. But this year's grille contained thin horizontal strips along with three vertical divider bars on each side, to form four sections. Wraparound side markers carried a new design. Base and Royale models were offered again, in two-door hardtop coupe and four-door town sedan. Base engine was a 231 cu. in. (3.8-liter) V-6 with automatic; optional, the 350 cu. in. diesel V-8. A total of 48,879 diesels were produced. Reviving an old name, a sporty Holiday 88 coupe was offered this year on the base model. It included a T-handle floor shifter, Rallye suspension, sports console, sport steering wheel, front bucket seats, dual sport mirrors, custom wheel covers, and special Holiday 88 emblem on the sail panel.

CUSTOM CRUISER — SERIES 3B — V-8 — The full-size wagon was available plain, or with a deluxe option that included woodgrain treatment. Two seats were standard, with rear-racing third seat optional. Standard engine was the 350 cu. in. (5.7-liter) gas V-8; optional, the 350 diesel.

1979 Ninety-Eight Regency sedan (O)

NINETY-EIGHT — SERIES 3C — V-8 — Even though the Ninety-Eight front end looked basically the same as before, each grille side now contained a solid crosshatch pattern (with no dividers). The back end was similar too, but backup lenses were much smaller, now mounted alongside the license plate at inner ends of a decorative panel. A two-door hardtop coupe and four-door sedan came in Luxury and Regency series. Standard engine was a 350 cu. in. (5.7-liter) V-8; optional, the 350 diesel, of which 21,231 were produced. A total of 1,999 models came with an LS package (RPO code Y68). Standard Ninety-Eight equipment included power brakes/steering, power windows, two-way power driver's seat, clock, fold-down center armrests, and courtesy lamps. Regency included a loose-cushion-look interior with velour upholstery, divided front seat with dual controls, digital clock, and front seatback pouches.

1979 Toronado Diesel coupe (O)

TORONADO — SERIES 3E — V-8 — Toronado got a substantial downsizing this year along with an ample price hike. Wheelbase dropped to 114 inches, length to 205.6 (down from 122 and 227.5 in 1978). Even the car's width was reduced by close to 9 inches. Still front-drive, Toro had a new steering linkage and power steering gear to improve tight maneuvering. Turning diameter was cut by over 3 feet. The shrunken model weighed over 900 pounds less than its predecessor, and carried four passengers. Standard engine was a 350 cu. in. (5.7-liter) V-8; optional, the 350 diesel. A total of 8,040 diesel Toronados were produced. Gas mileage was estimated to be about 3 MPG better than before (city). The rectangular shape of grille openings was repeated in the quad headlamps, and balanced by long horizontal park and turn signal lamps. 'Toronado' lettering extended across the front-end panel, above the grille. Toronado displayed a formal roofline. Small, fixed rear quarter windows were covered when the landau or full vinyl roof was ordered. A Toronado emblem went on the sail panel (except when replaced by optional opera lamps). Long horizontal taillamps and backup lamps extended from the decklid's edge to the license plate opening. 'Toronado' lettering stretched across the decklid. A flush-mounted windshield was meant to produce smooth airflow. The back window was flush-fitted, installed from inside the car, allowing smaller reveal moldings. A fiber optic system lit the center Toronado nameplate, ashtray and lighter, cruise control, rear defogger and light switches. The steering column held a combination dimmer/signal control. The new instrument panel had a vinyl pad that offered what was described as the look and feel of leather. Standard automatic leveling adjusted car height by electric compression, with an electronic height sensor controlling air pressure in the rear shock absorbers. A rear stabilizer bar was standard. Other standard Toronado equipment included air conditioning, automatic transmission, six-way power driver's seat, divided front seat, side window defoggers, power windows, remote driver's mirror, automatic level control, AM/FM stereo radio, digital clock, stowaway spare tire, power antenna, SBR whitewall tires, cornering lamps, power brakes/steering, door courtesy/warning lights, and a temperature gauge. New options included reclining front seats, opera lamps, illuminated door locks and interior, Rallye suspension, and fiber-optic lamp monitors.

I.D. DATA: Oldsmobile's 13-symbol Vehicle Identification Number (VIN) was located on the upper left surface of the instrument panel, visible through the windshield. The first digit is '3', indicating Oldsmobile division. Next is a letter indicating series: 'T' Starfire; 'D' Starfire SX; 'B' Omega; 'E' Omega Brougham; 'G' Cutlass Salon; 'J' Cutlass Salon Brougham; 'R' Cutlass Supreme; 'M' Cutlass Supreme Brougham ; 'K' Cutlass Calais; 'G' Cutlass Cruiser; 'H' Cutlass Cruiser Brougham; 'L' Delta 88; 'N' Delta 88 Royale; 'Q' Custom Cruiser; 'V' Ninety-Eight Luxury; 'X' Ninety-Eight Regency; 'Z' Toronado Brougham. Next come two digits that denote body type: '07' Starfire hatch coupe; '17' Omega 2dr. hatchback coupe; '27' Omega 2dr. notch coupe; '37' 2dr. coupe; '47' 2dr. coupe; '57' 2dr. coupe; '87' 2dr. plain-back coupe; '09' 4dr. 6window sedan; '69' 4dr. 4window notch sedan; '35' 4dr. 2seat wagon. The fifth symbol is a letter indicating engine code: 'V' L4151 2Bbl.; 'A' V6231 2Bbl.; 'F' V8260 2Bbl.; 'P' diesel V8260; 'Y' V8301 2Bbl.; 'G' V8305 2Bbl.; 'R' V8305 4Bbl.; 'L' Omega V8350 4Bbl.; 'N' diesel V8350; 'K' V8403 4Bbl. The sixth symbol denotes model year ('9' 1979). Next is a plant code: '2' Ste. Therese, Quebec (Canada); 'G' Framingham, Mass.; 'D' Doraville, Georgia; 'M' Lansing, Mich.; 'W' Willow Run, Mich.; 'R' Arlington, Texas; 'X' Fairfax, Kansas; 'E' Linden, New Jersey; '7' Lordstown, Ohio. The final six digits are the sequential serial number, which began with 100,001. Engine numbers were stamped on the front of the right rocker cover, or top of left cover (Buick-built engines), on the front of the right cover (Chevrolet-built

V-8), at the front of either rocker cover (Pontiac V-8), or on the left rocker cover (Oldsmobile engines). Four-cylinder engine numbers were on a pad at right front, near the distributor shaft. A body number plate on the shroud identified model year, car division, series, style, body assembly plant, body number, trim combination, modular seat code, paint code, and date built code.

STARFIRE (FOUR/V-6)

Model Number	Body/Style Number	Body Type & Seating	Factory Price	Shipping Weight	Production Total
3H	T07	2-dr. Spt Cpe-4P	4095/4295	2690/ --	-13,144

STARFIRE SX (FOUR/V-6)

3H	D07	2-dr. Spt Cpe-4P	4295/4495	2703/ --	7,155

Starfire Engine Note: A V-8 engine cost $195 more than the V-6.

OMEGA (V-6/V-8)

3X	B27	2-dr. Cpe-6P	4181/4376	3080/3210	4,806
3X	B17	2-dr. Hatch Cpe-6P	4345/4540	3157/3287	956
3X	B69	4-dr. Sed-6P	4281/4476	3118/3248	5,826

OMEGA BROUGHAM (V-6/V-8)

3X	E27	2-dr. Cpe-6P	4387/4582	3091/3221	1,078
3X	E69	4-dr. Sed-6P	4487/4682	3149/3279	2,145

CUTLASS SALON (V-6/V-8)

3A	G87	2-dr. Cpe-6P	4623/4763	3060/3175	8,399
3A	G09	4-dr. Sed-6P	4723/4863	3080/3195	20,266

CUTLASS SALON BROUGHAM (V-6/V-8)

3A	J87	2-dr. Cpe-6P	4907/5047	3100/3215	3,617
3A	J09	4-dr. Sed-6P	5032/5172	3127/3242	18,714

1979 Hurst/Olds coupe (O)

CUTLASS SUPREME (V-6/V-8)

3A	R47	2-dr. Cpe-6P	5063/5203	3091/3206	277,944

CUTLASS SUPREME BROUGHAM (V-6/V-8)

3A	M47	2-dr. Cpe-6P	5492/5632	3116/3231	137,323

CUTLASS CALAIS (V-6/V-8)

3A	K47	2-dr. Cpe-5P	5491/5631	3122/3237	43,780

CUTLASS CRUISER (V-6/V-8)

3A	G35	4-dr. 2S Sta Wag-6P	4980/5120	3201/3361	10,755
3A	H35	4-dr. Brghm Wag-6P	5517/5657	3245/3405	42,953

DELTA 88 (V-6/V-8)

3B	L37	2-dr. Cpe-6P	5782/5922	3462/3639	16,202
3B	L69	4-dr. Sed-6P	5882/6022	3488/3665	25,424

1979 Delta 88 Royale sedan (O)

DELTA 88 ROYALE (V-6/V-8)

3B	N37	2-dr. Cpe-6P	6029/6169	3471/3648	60,687
3B	N69	4-dr. Sed-6P	6154/6294	3513/3690	152,626

CUSTOM CRUISER (V-8)

3B	Q35	4-dr. 2S Sta Wag-6P	6742	4042	36,648
3B	Q35	4-dr. 3S Sta Wag-8P	6935	N/A	Note 1

Note 1: Three-seat production is included in two-seat total.

NINETY-EIGHT LUXURY (V-8)

3C	V37	2-dr. Cpe-6P	7492	3806	2,104
3C	V69	4-dr. Sedan-6P	7673	3850	6,720

NINETY-EIGHT REGENCY (V-8)

3C	X37	2-dr. Cpe-6P	7875	3810	29,965
3C	X69	4-dr. Sedan-6P	8063	3885	91,862

TORONADO BROUGHAM (V-8)

3E	Z57	2-dr. HT Cpe-4P	10112	3731	50,056

FACTORY PRICE AND WEIGHT NOTE: For Omega, Cutlass and Delta 88, prices and weights to left of slash are for six-cylinder, to right for V-8 engine. For Starfire, prices/weights to left are for four-cylinder, to right for V-6.

1979 Cutlass 442 coupe (O)

ENGINE DATA: BASE FOUR (Starfire): Inline, overhead-valve four-cylinder. Cast iron block and head. Displacement: 151 cu. in. (2.5 liters). Bore & stroke: 4.00 x 3.00 in. Compression ratio: 8.3:1. Brake horsepower: 85 at 4400 R.P.M. Torque: 123 lbs.ft. at 2800 R.P.M. Five main bearings. Hydraulic valve lifters. Carburetor: 2Bbl. Rochester 2SE. Pontiac-built. VIN Code: V. BASE V-6 (Omega, Cutlass, Cutlass wagon, Delta 88); OPTIONAL (Starfire): 90-degree, overhead-valve V-6. Cast iron block and head. Displacement: 231 cu. in. (3.8 liters). Bore & stroke: 3.80 x 3.40 in. Compression ratio: 8.0:1. Brake horsepower: 115 at 3800 R.P.M. Torque: 190 lbs.ft. at 2000 R.P.M. Four main bearings. Hydraulic valve lifters. Carburetor: 2Bbl. Rochester M2ME. Buick-built. VIN Code: A. OPTIONAL V-8 (Cutlass, Cutlass wagon, Delta 88): 90-degree, overhead valve V-8. Cast iron block and head. Displacement: 260 cu. in. (4.3 liters). Bore & stroke: 3.50 x 3.39 in. Compression ratio: 7.5:1. Brake horsepower: 105 at 3600 R.P.M. Torque: 205 lbs.ft. at 1800 R.P.M. Five main bearings. Hydraulic valve lifters. Carburetor: 2Bbl. Rochester M2MC. VIN Code: F. DIESEL V-8 (Cutlass): 90-degree, overhead valve V-8. Cast iron block and head. Displacement: 260 cu. in. (4.3 liters). Bore & stroke: 3.50 x 3.39 in. Compression ratio: 22.5:1. Brake horsepower: 90 at 3600 R.P.M. Torque: 160 lbs.ft. at 1600 R.P.M. Five main bearings. Hydraulic valve lifters. Fuel injection. VIN Code: P. OPTIONAL V-8 (Delta 88): 90-degree, overhead valve V-8. Cast iron block and head. Displacement: 301 cu. in. (4.9 liters). Bore & stroke: 4.00 x 3.00 in. Compression ratio: 8.2:1. Brake horsepower: 135 at 3800 R.P.M. Torque: 240 lbs.ft. at 1600 R.P.M. Hydraulic valve lifters. Carburetor: 2Bbl. Rochester M2MC. Pontiac-built. VIN Code: Y. OPTIONAL V-8

(Starfire, Omega): 90-degree, overhead valve V-8. Cast iron block and head. Displacement: 305 cu. in. (5.0 liters). Bore & stroke: 3.74 x 3.48 in. Compression ratio: 8.4:1. Brake horsepower: 130 at 3200 R.P.M. Torque: 245 lbs.ft. at 2000 R.P.M. Five main bearings. Hydraulic valve lifters. Carburetor: 2bbl. Rochester M2MC. Chevrolet-built. VIN Code: G. OPTIONAL V-8 (Cutlass): Same as 305 cu. in. V-8 above, with four-barrel Rochester M4MC carburetor Horsepower: 160 at 4000 R.P.M. Torque: 235 lbs.-ft. at 2400 R.P.M. VIN Code: H. OPTIONAL V-8 (California/high-altitude Omega, Cutlass Cruiser): 90-degree, overhead valve V-8. Cast iron block and head. Displacement: 350 cu. in. (5.7 liters). Bore & stroke: 4.00 x 3.48 in. Compression ratio: 8.5:1. Brake horsepower: 160 at 3800 R.P.M. Torque: 260 lbs.ft. at 2400 R.P.M. Five main bearings. Hydraulic valve lifters. Carburetor: 4Bbl. Rochester M4MC. Chevrolet-built. VIN Code: L. BASE V-8 (98, Custom Cruiser wagon, Toronado); OPTIONAL (Delta 88): 90-degree, overhead valve V-8. Cast iron block and head. Displacement: 350 cu. in. (5.7 liters). Bore & stroke: 4.06 x 3.39 in. Compression ratio: 8.0:1. Brake horsepower: 160-165 at 3800 R.P.M. Torque: 270-275 lbs.ft. at 2000 R.P.M. Five main bearings. Hydraulic valve lifters. Carburetor: 4Bbl. VIN Code: R. OPTIONAL V-8 (98, Custom Cruiser): 90-degree, overhead valve V-8. Cast iron block and head. Displacement: 403 cu. in. (6.6 liters). Bore & stroke: 4.35 x 3.39. in. Compression ratio: 7.8:1. Brake horsepower: 175 at 3600 R.P.M. Torque: 310 lbs.ft. at 2000 R.P.M. Five main bearings. Hydraulic valve lifters. Carburetor: 4Bbl. Rochester M4MC. VIN Code: K. DIESEL V-8 (Cutlass Cruiser, Delta 88, 98, Custom Cruiser, Toronado): 90-degree, overhead valve V-8. Cast iron block and head. Displacement: 350 cu. in. (5.7 liters). Bore & stroke: 4.06 x 3.39 in. Compression ratio: 22.5:1. Brake horsepower: 125 at 3600 R.P.M. Torque: 225 lbs.ft. at 1600 R.P.M. Five main bearings. Hydraulic valve lifters. Fuel injection. VIN Code: N.

CHASSIS DATA: Wheelbase: (Starfire) 97.0 in.; (Omega) 111.0 in.; (Cutlass) 108.1 in.; (Delta 88) 116.0 in.; (98) 119.0 in.; (Custom Crsr) 116.0 in.; (Toronado) 114.0 in. Overall Length: (Starfire) 179.6 in.; (Omega) 199.6 in.; (Cutlass Supreme/Calais cpe) 200.1 in.; (Cutlass Salon) 197.7 in.; (Cutlass wag) 197.6 in.; (Delta 88) 217.5 in.; (98) 220.4 in.; (Custom Crsr) 217.1 in.; (Toro) 205.6 in. Height: (Starfire) 50.2 in.; (Omega cpe) 53.8 in.; (Omega sed) 54.7 in.; (Cutlass) 53.4-54.2 in.; (Cutlass wag) 54.5 in.; (Delta 88 cpe) 54.5 in.; (Delta 88 4dr.) 55.2 in.; (98 cpe) 55.5 in.; (98 sed) 55.5 in.; (Custom Crsr) 57.2 in.; (Toro) 54.2 in. Width: (Starfire) 65.4 in.; (Omega) 72.9 in.; (Cutlass) 71.3- 71.9 in.; (Cutlass wag) 71.7 in.; (Delta 88) 76.8 in.; (98) 76.8 in.; (Custom Crsr) 79.8 in.; (Toro) 71.4 in. Front Tread: (Starfire) 54.7 in.; (Omega) 61.9 in.; (Cutlass) 58.5 in.; (Delta 88/98) 61.7 in.; (Custom Crsr) 62.1 in.; (Toro) 59.3 in. Rear Tread: (Starfire) 53.6 in.; (Omega) 59.6 in.; (Cutlass) 57.7 in.; (Delta 88/98) 60.7 in.; (Custom Crsr) 64.1 in.; (Toro) 60.0 in. Standard Tires: (Starfire) A78 x 13; (Starfire SX) BR78 x 13; (Omega) E78 x 14; (Cutlass Supreme/Calais) P195/75R14; (Cutlass Salon) P185/75R14; (Cutlass wag) P195/75R14; (Delta 88) FR78 x 15; (98) GR78 x 15; (Custom Crsr) HR78 x 15; (Toronado) P205/75R15.

TECHNICAL: Transmission: Three-speed manual transmission standard on Omega and Cutlass. Four-speed floor shift standard on Starfire, Omega V8305 and Cutlass. Five-speed manual optional on Starfire/Cutlass. Three-speed Turbo Hydra-matic standard on other models, optional on all. Standard final drive ratio: (Starfire) 2.73:1; (Omega) 3.08:1; (Cutlass) 2.93:1; (Cutlass Cruiser) 2.73:1; (Delta 88) 2.73:1; (Custom Crsr) 2.41:1; (98) 2.41:1; (Toronado) 2.41:1. Steering: Recirculating ball. Front Suspension: (Starfire) coil springs w/lower trailing links and anti-sway bar; (Toronado) longitudinal torsion bars w/anti-sway bar; (others) coil springs w/control arms and anti-sway bar. Rear Suspension: (Starfire) rigid axle w/coil springs, lower trailing radius arms, upper torque arms, transverse linkage bar and anti-sway bar; (Omega) rigid axle w/semi-elliptic leaf springs; (Toronado) independent w/coil springs, longitudinal trailing arms and automatic leveling; (others) rigid axle w/coil springs, lower trailing radius arms and upper torque arms. Brakes: Front disc, rear drum. Ignition: Electronic. Body construction: (Starfire) unibody; (Omega) unibody w/separate front partial frame; (others) separate body on perimeter frame. Fuel Tank: (Starfire) 18.5 gal.; (Omega) 20.3 gal.; (Cutlass) 18.1 gal.; (Cutlass wag) 18.2 gal.; (Delta 88) 20.7 or 25 gal.; (98) 25.0 gal.; (Custom Crsr wag) 22 gal.; (Toronado) 20 gal.

1979 Starfire Firenza hatchback coupe (O)

DRIVETRAIN OPTIONS: Engines: 231 cu. in. V-6: Starfire ($200). 260 cu. in. V-8: Cutlass/88 ($140). Diesel 260 cu. in. V-8: Cutlass ($735). 301 cu. in. 2Bbl. V-8: Delta 88 ($195). 305 cu. in. 2Bbl. V-8: Starfire ($395). Starfire w/GT pkg. ($195): Omega ($195). 305 cu. in. 4Bbl. V-8: Cutlass ($255). 350 cu. in. 4Bbl. V-8: Omega/Cutlass Crsr/88 ($320). 403 cu. in. V-8: 98/Custom Crsr ($70). Diesel 350 cu. in. V-8: Cutlass Crsr/88 ($895); 98/Custom Crsr ($785); Toronado ($395). Engine oil cooler: Cutlass ($40). Transmission/Differential: Four-speed floor shift: Omega/Cutlass ($135). Five-speed manual floor shift: Starfire ($175); Cutlass ($310). Turbo Hydra-matic: Starfire ($295); Omega/Cutlass ($335). Limited-slip differential: Starfire ($60); Omega/Cutlass ($64); 88/98 ($68). Brakes/Steering: Power brakes: Starfire ($71); Omega/Cutlass ($76). Power four-wheel disc brakes: Toro ($205). Power steering: Starfire/Omega/Cutlass ($163). Suspension: Rallye susp. pkg.: Omega ($43); Cutlass ($37); Toro ($28). H.D. susp.: Cutlass/88/98 ($25); Custom Crsr ($10). Firm ride shock absorbers: Cutlass/88/98 ($7). Superlift rear shocks: Cutlass/88/98 ($54-$55). Automatic load leveling: Cutlass/88/98 ($120). Other: High-capacity cooling ($21-$92). High-capacity radiator: Starfire ($20); Omega ($21). H.D. battery ($18- $21). High-capacity alternator: Cutlass/full-size ($49). Trailer wiring: Cutlass/full-size ($22-$35). Engine block heater ($15). California emissions equipment ($83). High- altitude emissions ($35).

OPTION PACKAGES: Starfire GT pkg. ($447-$577). Firenza sport pkg.: Starfire ($375). Omega LS pkg.: Brougham sedan ($2078). Omega SX pkg.: base hatch/cpe ($231). Cutlass 442 appearance/handling pkg.: Salon cpe ($276); Salon Brghm ($122). Delta 88 Holiday coupe pkg.: base ($288). Sport paint pkg.: Cutlass Supreme/Calais cpe ($181).

MAJOR CONVENIENCE/APPEARANCE OPTIONS: Four Season air conditioner ($496-$605). Tempmatic air conditioning: Cutlass/88/98 ($602-$650); Toro ($45). Power seat ($135-$166); N/A Starfire. Power windows ($126-$205); N/A Starfire. Twilight sentinel: Cutlass/88/98/Toro ($47). Cornering lamps: Cutlass/88/98 ($49). Power astroroof: Cutlass/88/98/Toro ($729-$998). Power sliding metal sunroof: Cutlass/88/98/Toro ($529-$798). Removable glass panel roof: Cutlass ($655). Removable glass panel sunroof: Starfire ($180). Landau vinyl roof ($178-$200); N/A Starfire. Full vinyl roof ($79-$145); N/A Starfire. Woodgrain vinyl bodyside/tailgate paneling: Cutlass/Custom Cruiser wagon ($243-$261). Rear-facing third seat: Custom Cruiser ($193).

HISTORY: Introduced: September 28, 1978. Model year production: 1,068,155. Calendar year production (U.S.): 1,007,996. Calendar year sales by U.S. dealers: 949,488. Model year sales by U.S. dealers: 1,000,673.

Historical Footnotes: Sales topped the million mark, making 1979 the second biggest model year ever for Oldsmobile. Cutlass accounted for well over half the total, reaching over 536,000 customers. Once again, Cutlass was America's best seller, with Supreme alone taking over four-fifths of the sales. The fastback Cutlass models did not fare nearly as well. Full-size sales dropped, but not nearly as much as some other makes. Part of the reason was the availability of the diesel engine, which was gaining quite a few fans.

1980 OLDSMOBILE

Eye-popping price rises and a new front-wheel-drive Omega highlighted the 1980 model year. A new 5.0-liter gas V-8 was to be the base engine in Ninety-Eight and Toronado, and optional in Eighty-Eight. It was derived from the 350 cu. in. (5.7-liter) engine, with a smaller bore. The 403 cu. in. (6.6-liter V-8) was dropped this year. New poppet-type injector nozzles on diesels were smaller and did not require fuel return lines, and delivered a finer spray.

1980 Starfire Firenza hatchback coupe (AA)

STARFIRE — SERIES 3H — FOUR/V-6 — Oldsmobiles' subcompact barely qualified for inclusion in this year's lineup, as it was dropped in December 1979. For its brief final season, little change was evident, and no V-8 engine was available.

1980 Omega Brougham coupe (AA)

OMEGA — SERIES 3X — FOUR/V-6 — A far different X-bodied Omega, much lighter (and more expensive), joined the Olds lineup this year. This one was front-wheel-drive, with a transverse-mounted 151 cu. in. (2.5-liter) four-cylinder engine. Wheelbase was 6 inches shorter than the former Omega, 18.5 inches shorter overall. Omega carried five passengers. Weighing some 750 pounds less than prior Omegas, it was a clone of the Chevrolet Citation, thus closely related to Buick and Pontiac models as well. Four models were offered: coupe and sedan, in base or Brougham trim. Unlike other GM makes, Oldsmobile did not offer a hatchback coupe. A sporty SX option was available. A dual vertical-bar grille extended above and below the headlamps, wrapping up into the front-end panel. Vertical park/turn signal lamps stood between the single rectangular headlamps and the grille. Centered on the front-end panel was a red Oldsmobile emblem. 'Oldsmobile' block letters went on the left grille section. Anodized aluminum bumpers could have optional bumper guards and rub strips. 'Omega' block letters were on the sail panel of all models, while Broughams added a sail panel emblem. Omega Brougham had a stand-up hood ornament and hood center molding, as well as rocker panel and wheel opening moldings. Hood, rocker, wheel and front-end panel moldings were optional on base Omegas. Wide lower rocker panel moldings were optional on both. Large chrome- bordered vertical wrap-over taillamps had a center Oldsmobile emblem. Backup lamps were at the bottom of taillamps. 'Oldsmobile' block letters went on the lower right corner of the rear-end panel. Broughams had a bright lower rear-end panel molding and license plate opening molding, and a decklid lock ornament. Four-door Broughams had a bright brushed

center pillar applique, which was optional on base models. All Omegas had bright side window frame moldings. Base Omegas had a narrow bead belt molding, while Broughams had a wide belt molding. Sedan rear-quarter windows rolled down; coupes had fixed rear quarter windows. Base models had hubcaps; Broughams had wheel covers. Fourteen body colors were offered. Speedometer, clock and light switch were plug-in type for easier servicing. The glovebox top snapped out to service the right side of the instrument panel. Doors locked via a sliding lever below the door handle, to improve theft- resistance. Standard equipment included four-speed manual floor shift, rack-and-pinion steering, low-drag front disc brakes, maintenance-free wheel bearings, P185/80R13 glass- belted radial tires, self-adjusting clutch, Freedom battery, AM radio, inside hood release, day/night mirror, and bench seats. Brougham added a custom bench seat with fold- down center armrest. Options included a 2.8-liter V-6, six-way seat adjusters (for either bucket or bench seats), reclining front seatbacks, removable glass sunroof, electric rear window defogger, combination dome and dual-lens reading lamp, digital clock, pushbutton AM/FM stereo with cassette player (or with 40channnel CB transceiver). Coupes could have an optional landau top with covered back window, and all could get a full vinyl roof with bright back window reveal moldings. Omega's SX option came in 10 colors on the base coupe and sedan. The package included black grille bars; black lower body color; blacked-out window frames, headlamp doors, taillamp bezels and side markers; and black bumpers and fillers. Also included: a one-piece body-color decklid spoiler, sport mirrors, special wheel trim, and decal stripes.

1980 Cutlass Supreme landau coupe (AA)

CUTLASS — SERIES 3A — V-6/V-8 — Ten Cutlass models were available this year, including three new notchback sedans. They replaced the Cutlass Salon and Salon Brougham four-doors. The lineup included Cutlass Salon and Salon Brougham coupe, Cutlass sedan, Cutlass LS sedan, Cutlass Supreme and Supreme Brougham coupe, Cutlass Brougham sedan, Cutlass Calais coupe, Cutlass Cruiser, and Cruiser Brougham wagon. For the first time, opera lamps were optional, on LS and Brougham sedans. Each side of Salon's grille contained three vertical bars over a series of horizontal bars. Single headlamps were outboard of park/signal lamps. Salon continued the fastback styling. The Calais grille was an eggcrate design (5 x 4 hole pattern on each side) similar to 1979, but with a narrower center divider segment. This year's version also featured quad rectangular headlamps, along with wide park/signal lamps mounted in the bumper. Cutlass Brougham and LS carried a grille similar to Calais, but with single headlamps. Cutlass Calais could get the 442 (W30) option with either black or white body paint, W30 and 442 identification, gold accent stripes, and gold-painted grille, pillar, hood and top. The package also included sport aluminum wheels with raised-white-letter tires, sport mirrors, and the 350 cu. in. (5.7-liter) four-barrel V-8 with automatic transmission. The 350 V-8 was not available in any other Cutlass. A total of 886 442 packages installed. A total of 6,000 custom appearance packages (RPO code Y68) from American Sunroof installed on Supremes. Oldsmobile has also estimated that 3-8 simulated convertible tops (code W44) were installed. This year, 46,990 Cutlass diesels were produced.

1980 Delta 88 Royale coupe (AA)

DELTA 88 — SERIES 3B — V-6/V-8 — Substantial restyling targeted Delta 88 for 1980, including softer side feature lines, a longer front end, and shorter back end. Park/turn signal lamps went into the bumper, allowing a lower front end (and reduced aero drag). Other aerodynamic improvements included flatter wheel covers, rounded front corners, and a small spoiler added to the decklid. A straighter backlight angle helped to produce a more formal appearance. This year's grille had four sections on each side, with three vertical dividers over a pattern of narrow vertical bars. Quad headlamps and wraparound front side marker lenses were used. At the rear were large wraparound taillamps with emblems in their lenses. Base, Royale, and Royale Brougham models were offered in two body styles: two-door coupe or four-door sedan. A Holiday 88 coupe option (RPO code Y78) was installed in 3,547 vehicles. It included contour bucket front seats, a sports console with shifter, sport mirrors, custom sport steering wheel, special emblems, and special color-keyed wheel covers. A total of 49,087 diesel 88s were built this year. Standard equipment included a 231 cu. in. (3.8-liter) V-6 with automatic transmission, P205/75R15 steel-belted radial tires, bumper guards and impact strips, wheel covers and wheel opening moldings, lighter, day/night mirror, and power brakes/steering.

CUSTOM CRUISER — SERIES 3B — V-8 — This year's full-size wagon adopted the Delta 88's grille and front-end look. Standard engine was a 307 cu. in. (5.0-liter) four-barrel V-8 with automatic transmission.

1980 Ninety-Eight Regency sedan (AA)

NINETY-EIGHT — SERIES 3C — V-8 — Restyling of the Ninety-Eight was similar to that performed for Delta 88, with softened side feature lines and aerodynamic improvements. Each side of the split eggcrate grille contained a 5 x 4 pattern. Quad headlamps extended outward into wraparound marker lenses. Wide park/signal lamps were bumper-mounted. Cornering lamps were mounted low on the front fenders. 'Ninety Eight' script went on the cowl, just below the bodyside molding. Vertical taillamps sat at quarter-panel tips. Three models were offered: Luxury sedan, and Regency coupe and sedan. Standard equipment included fender skirts, a 307 cu. in. (5.0-liter) V-8 engine with four-barrel carb, automatic transmission, P215/75R15 steel-belted radial tires, bumper guards and impact strips, dual remote-control mirrors, power windows and driver's seat, rocker panel and wheel opening moldings, and electric clock. Regency included an AM/FM stereo radio and digital clock. A total of 18,446 diesel models were produced.

TORONADO — SERIES 3E — V-8 — A new grille gave Toro a slightly different appearance for its second season in downsized form. The basic front end was similar to 1979, but the grille consisted only of horizontal bars (no vertical dividers). Moreover, those bars extended outward to the fender tips and contained the parking/signal lamps. Quad rectangular headlamps were used. 'Toronado' block letters reached across the upper grille panel and the decklid. Horizontal taillamps had small backup lenses next to the rear license plate. Standard equipment included a 307 cu. in. (5.0-liter) V-8 with automatic transmission, AM/FM stereo radio, power antenna, rocker panel and wheel opening moldings, level control, power six-way driver's seat, and power windows. Tires were P205/75R15 steel-belted radial whitewalls. Also standard: power door locks, air conditioning, digital clock, and side window defrosters. Toro's weight was cut by over 100 pounds through the use of many lighter weight components, including the alternator, an aluminum intake manifold, compact spare tire, and aluminum bumper reinforcements. A new sport coupe option, Toronado XSC, included a special ride/handling package, bucket seats with console, leather-wrapped steering wheel, voltmeter and oil pressure gauge. A total of 12,362 diesel models were built.

I.D. DATA: Oldsmobile's 13-symbol Vehicle Identification Number (VIN) was located on the upper left surface of the instrument panel, visible through the windshield. The first digit is '3', indicating Oldsmobile division. Next is a letter indicating series: 'T' Starfire; 'D' Starfire SX; 'B' Omega; 'E' Omega Brougham; 'G' Cutlass/Salon; 'J' Cutlass Salon Brougham; 'R' Cutlass Supreme; 'M' Cutlass Supreme Brougham; 'K' Cutlass Calais; 'G' Cutlass Cruiser; 'H' Cutlass Cruiser Brougham; 'L' Delta 88; 'N' Delta 88 Royale; 'Y' Delta 88 Royale Brougham; 'P' Custom Cruiser; 'V' Ninety-Eight Luxury; 'X' Ninety- Eight Regency; 'Z' Toronado Brougham. Next come two digits that denote body type: '07' Starfire hatch coupe; '37' 2dr. coupe; '47' 2dr. coupe; '57' 2dr. coupe; '87' 2dr. plain-back coupe; '69' 4dr. 4window notch sedan; '35' 4dr. 2seat wagon. The fifth symbol is a letter indicating engine code: '5' L4151 2Bbl.; '7' V6173 2Bbl.; 'A' V6231 2Bbl.; 'F' V8260 2Bbl.; 'S' V8265 2Bbl.; 'H' V8305 4Bbl.; 'Y' V8307 4Bbl.; 'R' V8350 4Bbl.; 'N' diesel V8350. The sixth symbol denotes model year ('A' 1980). Next is a plant code: '2' Ste. Therese, Quebec (Canada); 'G' Framingham, Mass.; 'D' Doraville, Georgia; 'M' Lansing, Mich.; 'W' Willow Run, Mich.; 'R' Arlington, Texas; 'X' Fairfax, Kansas; 'E' Linden, New Jersey; '7' Lordstown, Ohio. The final six digits were the sequential serial number, which began with 100,001. Engine numbers were stamped on the front of the right rocker cover, or top of left cover (Buick-built engines), on the front of the right cover (Chevrolet-built V-8), on label at front or rear of right rocker cover (Chevrolet V-6), or on the left rocker cover (Oldsmobile engines). Four-cylinder engine numbers were on a pad at right front of block, near the distributor shaft; or left front, below cylinder head. A body number plate on the shroud identified model year, car division, series, style, body assembly plant, body number, trim combination, modular seat code, paint code, and date built code.

STARFIRE (FOUR/V-6)

Model Number	Body/Style Number	Body Type & Seating	Factory Price	Shipping Weight	Production Total
3H	T07	2-dr. Spt Cpe-4P	4750/4975	2656/ --	-Note 1

STARFIRE SX (FOUR/V-6)

3H	D07	2-dr. Spt Cpe-4P	4950/5175	2668/ --	8,237

Note 1: Production included in SX total.

OMEGA (FOUR/V-6)

3X	B37	2-dr. Cpe-5P	5100/5325	2400/2439	28,267
3X	B69	4-dr. Sed-5P	5266/5491	2427/2466	42,172

OMEGA BROUGHAM (FOUR/V-6)

3X	E37	2-dr. Cpe-5P	5380/5605	2432/2471	21,595
3X	E69	4-dr. Sed-5P	5530/5755	2459/2498	42,289

CUTLASS/SALON (V-6/V-8)

3A	G87	2-dr. Salon Cpe-6P	5372/5552	3065/3214	3,429
3A	G69	4-dr. Sed-6P	5532/5712	3069/3218	36,923

CUTLASS SALON BROUGHAM (V-6/V-8)

3A	J87	2-dr. Cpe-6P	5662/5842	3065/3214	965

CUTLASS SUPREME (V-6/V-8)

3A	R47	2-dr. Cpe-6P	6252/6432	3190/3339	169,597
3A	R69	4-dr. LS Sed-6P	6353/6533	3179/3328	86,868

CUTLASS SUPREME BROUGHAM (V-6/V-8)

3A	M47	2-dr. Cpe-6P	6691/6871	3201/3350	77,875
3A	M69	4-dr. Sed-6P	6776/6956	3206/3355	52,462

CUTLASS CALAIS (V-6/V-8)

3A	K47	2-dr. Cpe-5P	6716/6896	3201/3350	26,269

CUTLASS CRUISER (V-6/V-8)

3A	G35	4-dr. 2S Sta Wag-6	5978/6158	3263/3423	7,815
3A	H35	4-dr. Brghm Wag-6	6377/6557	3300/3460	22,791

DELTA 88 (V-6/V-8)

3B	L37	2-dr. Cpe-6P	6457/6637	3325/3465	6,845
3B	L69	4-dr. Sed-6P	6552/6732	3358/3498	15,285

DELTA 88 ROYALE (V-6/V-8)

3B	N37	2-dr. Cpe-6P	6716/6896	3333/3473	39,303
3B	N69	4-dr. Sed-6P	6864/7044	3336/3476	87,178

DELTA 88 ROYALE BROUGHAM (V-6/V-8)

3B	Y37	2-dr. Cpe-6P	7079/7259	3333/3473	Note 2
3B	Y69	4-dr. Sed-6P	7160/7340	3336/3476	Note 2

Note 2: Production included in 88 Royale totals above.

CUSTOM CRUISER (V-8)

3B	P35	4-dr. 2S Sta Wag-6P	7443	3910	17,067
3B	P35	4-dr. 3S Sta Wag-8P	7651	3940	Note 3

Note 3: Three-seat production is included in two-seat total.

NINETY-EIGHT LUXURY (V-8)

3C	V69	4-dr. Sedan-6P	9113	3789	2,640

NINETY-EIGHT REGENCY (V-8)

3C	X37	2-dr. Cpe-6P	9620	3811	12,391
3C	X69	4-dr. Sedan-6P	9742	3832	58,603

TORONADO BROUGHAM (V-8)

3E	Z57	2-dr. Cpe-4P	11361	3627	43,440

FACTORY PRICE AND WEIGHT NOTE: For Cutlass and Delta 88, prices and weights to left of slash are for six-cylinder, to right for V-8 engine. For Starfire/Omega, prices/weights to left are for four-cylinder, to right for V-6.

ENGINE DATA: BASE FOUR (Starfire, Omega): Inline, overhead-valve four-cylinder. Cast iron block and head. Displacement: 151 cu. in. (2.5 liters). Bore & stroke: 4.00 x 3.00 in. Compression ratio: 8.2:1. Brake horsepower: 85 at 4400 R.P.M. (Omega, 90 at 4000). Torque: 128 lbs.ft. at 2400 R.P.M. (Omega, 134 at 2400). Five main bearings. Hydraulic valve lifters. Carburetor: 2Bbl. Rochester 2SE. Pontiac-built. VIN

Code: 5. OPTIONAL V-6 (Omega): 60-degree, overhead-valve V-6. Cast iron block and aluminum head. Displacement: 173 cu. in. (2.8 liters). Bore & stroke: 3.50 x 3.00 in. Compression ratio: 8.5:1. Brake horsepower: 115 at 4800 R.P.M. Torque: 145 lbs.ft. at 2400 R.P.M. Four main bearings. Hydraulic valve lifters. Carburetor: 2Bbl. Rochester 2SE. Chevrolet-built. VIN Code: 7. BASE V-6 (Cutlass, Delta 88); OPTIONAL (Starfire): 90-degree, overhead-valve V-6. Cast iron block and head. Displacement: 231 cu. in. (3.8 liters). Bore & stroke: 3.80 x 3.40 in. Compression ratio: 8.0:1. Brake horsepower: 110 at 3800 R.P.M. Torque: 190 lbs.ft. at 1600 R.P.M. Four main earings. Hydraulic valve lifters. Carburetor: 2Bbl. Rochester M2ME. Buick-built. VIN Code: A. OPTIONAL V-8 (Cutlass): 90-degree, overhead valve V-8. Cast iron block and head. Displacement: 260 cu. in. (4.3 liters). Bore & stroke: 3.50 x 3.39 in. Compression ratio: 7.5:1. Brake horsepower: 105 at 3400 R.P.M. Torque: 195 lbs.ft. at 1600 R.P.M. Five main bearings. Hydraulic valve lifters. Carburetor: 2Bbl. Rochester M2MC. VIN Code: F. OPTIONAL V-8 (Delta 88): 90-degree, overhead valve V-8. Cast iron block and head. Displacement: 265 cu. in. (4.3 liters). Bore & stroke: 3.75 x 3.00 in. Compression ratio: 8.3:1. Brake horsepower: 120 at 3600 R.P.M. Torque: 210 lbs.ft. at 1800 R.P.M. Five main bearings. Hydraulic valve lifters. Carburetor: 2Bbl. Rochester 2SE. VIN Code: S. BASE V-8 (98, Toronado); OPTIONAL (Delta 88): 90-degree, overhead valve V-8. Cast iron block and head. Displacement: 307 cu. in. (5.0 liters). Bore & stroke: 3.80 x 3.39 in. Compression ratio: 8.0:1. Brake horsepower: 150 at 3600 R.P.M. Torque: 245 lbs.ft. at 1600 R.P.M. Five main bearings. Hydraulic valve lifters. Carburetor: 4Bbl. Rochester M4MC. VIN Code: Y. OPTIONAL V-8 (Cutlass): 90-degree, overhead valve V-8. Cast iron block and head. Displacement: 305 cu. in. (5.0 liters). Bore & stroke: 3.74 x 3.48 in. Compression ratio: 8.6:1. Brake horsepower: 155 at 4000 R.P.M. Torque: 240 lbs.ft. at 1600 R.P.M. Five main bearings. Hydraulic valve lifters. Carburetor: 4Bbl. Rochester M4MC. Chevrolet-built. VIN Code: H. OPTIONAL V-8 (Delta 88, 98, Toronado): 90-degree, overhead valve V-8. Cast iron block and head. Displacement: 350 cu. in. (5.7 liters). Bore & stroke: 4.06 x 3.39 in. Compression ratio: 8.0:1. Brake horsepower: 160 at 3600 R.P.M. Torque: 270 lbs.ft. at 1600 R.P.M. Five main bearings. Hydraulic valve lifters. Carburetor: 4Bbl. Rochester E4MC. VIN Code: R. DIESEL V-8 (Cutlass, Delta 88, 98, Custom Cruiser): 90-degree, overhead valve V-8. Cast iron block and head. Displacement: 350 cu. in. (5.7 liters). Bore & stroke: 4.06 x 3.39 in. Compression ratio: 22.5:1. Brake horsepower: 105 at 3200 R.P.M. Torque: 205 lbs.ft. at 1600 R.P.M. Five main bearings. Hydraulic valve lifters. Fuel injection. VIN Code: N.

CHASSIS DATA: Wheelbase: (Starfire) 97.0 in.; (Omega) 104.9 in.; (Cutlass) 108.1 in.; (Delta 88) 116.0 in.; (98) 119.0 in.; (Custom Crsr) 116.0 in.; (Toronado) 114.0 in. Overall Length: (Starfire) 179.6 in.; (Omega) 181.8 in.; (Cutlass) 199.1 in.; (Cutlass Supreme) 200.9 in.; (Cutlass wag) 198.4 in.; (Delta 88) 218.4 in.; (98) 221.4 in.; (Custom Crsr) 219.4 in.; (Toro) 206.0 in. Height: (Starfire) 50.2 in.; (Omega) 51.9 in.; (Cutlass) 53.0-54.1 in.; (Cutlass wag) 54.3 in.; (Delta 88 cpe) 54.1 in.; (Delta 88 sed) 54.7 in.; (98) 55.3 in.; (Custom Crsr) 56.6 in.; (Toro) 52.5 in. Width: (Starfire) 65.4 in.; (Omega) 69.8 in.; (Cutlass) 71.3- 71.9 in.; (Cutlass wag) 71.8 in.; (Delta 88) 76.3 in.; (98) 76.3 in.; (Custom Crsr) 79.8 in.; (Toro) 71.4 in. Front Tread: (Starfire) 54.7 in.; (Omega) 58.7 in.; (Cutlass) 58.5 in.; (Delta 88/98) 61.7 in.; (Custom Crsr) 62.1 in.; (Toro) 59.3 in. Rear Tread: (Starfire) 53.6 in.; (Omega) 57.0 in.; (Cutlass) 57.7 in.; (Delta 88/98) 60.7 in.; (Custom Crsr) 64.1 in.; (Toro) 60.0 in. Standard Tires: (Starfire) A78 x 13; (Starfire SX) BR78 x 13; (Omega) P185/80R13; (Cutlass) P185/75R14; (Cutlass Supreme/Brghm/Calais) P195/75R14; (Cutlass wag) P195/75R14; (Delta 88) P205/75R15; (98) P215/75R15; (Custom Crsr) P225/75R15; (Toronado) P205/75R15.

TECHNICAL: Transmission: Three-speed manual transmission standard on Cutlass (except LS/Brougham/Calais, automatic standard). Four-speed floor shift standard on Starfire/Omega. Three- speed Turbo Hydra-matic standard on other models, optional on all. Standard final drive ratio: Axle ratios not available. Steering: (Omega) rack and pinion; (others) recirculating ball. Front Suspension: (Starfire) coil springs w/lower trailing links and anti-sway bar; (Omega) MacPherson struts w/lower controls arms and coil springs; (Toronado) longitudinal torsion bars w/anti-sway bar; (others) coil springs w/control arms and anti-sway bar. Rear Suspension: (Starfire) rigid axle w/coil springs, lower trailing radius arms, upper torque arms, transverse linkage bar and anti-sway bar; (Omega) coil springs and lower control arms; (Toronado) independent with coil springs, longitudinal trailing arms and automatic leveling; (others) rigid axle w/coil springs, lower trailing radius arms and upper torque arms. Brakes: Front disc, rear drum. Ignition: Electronic. Body construction: (Starfire/Omega) unibody; (others) separate body on perimeter frame. Fuel Tank: (Starfire) 18.5 gal.; (Omega) 14 gal.; (Cutlass) 18.0 gal.; (Cutlass wag) 18.2 gal.; (Delta 88) 25 gal.; (98) 25 gal.; (Custom Crsr wag) 22 gal.; (Toronado) 21 gal.

DRIVETRAIN OPTIONS: Engines: 173 cu. in. V-6: Omega ($225). 231 cu. in. V-6: Starfire ($225). 260 cu. in. V-8: Cutlass ($180). 265 cu. in. V-8: Cutlass ($180). 307 cu. in. V-8: Cutlass ($295). 305 cu. in. V-8: Cutlass ($295). 305 cu. in. 4Bbl. V-8: 88 ($425). Custom Crsr/98/Toro ($130). Diesel 350 cu. in. V-8: Cutlass/88 ($960); 98/Custom Crsr ($860); Toronado ($860). Transmission/Differential: Turbo Hydra-matic: Starfire ($320); Omega ($337); Cutlass ($358). Limited-slip differential: Starfire ($65); Cutlass ($70); 88/98 ($74). Brakes/Steering: Power brakes: Starfire/Omega ($76). Power four-wheel disc brakes: Toro ($232). Power steering: Starfire ($158); Omega ($164); Cutlass ($174). Suspension: Rallye susp. pkg.: Cutlass/88 ($40). Omega ($20). Performance H.D. susp.: Omega/Cutlass/88/98 ($27). Custom Crsr ($12). Superlift rear shocks: Omega ($55). Automatic load leveling: Cutlass/88/98 ($145). Other: High-capacity cooling ($22-$75). High-capacity radiator ($15-$52). H.D. battery ($20-$21) exc. diesel ($42). Engine block heater ($16).

OPTION PACKAGES: Starfire GT pkg. ($496-$644). Firenza sport pkg.: Starfire ($427). Omega SX pkg.: base ($262-$303). Cutlass 442 appearance/handling pkg.: Calais ($1425). Delta 88 Holiday coupe pkg.: base ($295). Toronado XSC sport pkg. ($331). Designer interior pkg.: Cutlass Supreme/Brghm ($181).

MAJOR CONVENIENCE/APPEARANCE OPTIONS: Four Season air conditioner ($531-$647). Tempmatic air conditioning: Cutlass/88/98 ($651-$697); Toro ($50). Power seat ($148-$179). Power windows ($133-$221); N/A Starfire. Twilight sentinel: Cutlass/88/98/Toro ($50). Cornering lamps: Cutlass/88/98 ($53). Power astroroof w/sliding glass panel: Cutlass/88/98/Toro ($773-$1058). Power sliding metal sunroof: Cutlass/88/98/Toro ($561-$848). Removable glass roof panels: Cutlass ($695). Removable glass panel sunroof: Starfire/Omega ($193-$240). Landau vinyl roof ($175-$213); N/A Starfire. Full vinyl roof: Omega/Cutlass/88/98 ($116-$174). Rear-facing third seat: Custom Cruiser ($208).

HISTORY: Introduced: October 11, 1979 except Omega, April 19, 1979. Model year production: 910,306. Calendar year production (U.S.): 783,230. Calendar year sales by U.S. dealers: 820,681. Model year sales by U.S. dealers: 825,526.

Historical Footnotes: Oldsmobile's fleet fuel economy average was 21.1 MPG (35 percent better than the 15.6 MPG in 1975). Hopes for the diesel engine were stymied somewhat by shifting emissions regulations. Federal standards were relaxed a bit as the model year began, but California presented more of a problem. The smaller (4.2-liter) diesel was abandoned after a brief life in some 1979 models. Still, diesel V-8 production rose sharply this year, up some 73 percent over the 1979 level. Production of the gasoline 350 V-8, on the other hand, declined badly and it would not last long in the powerplant lineup. Following a marvelous 1979 model year in the sales race, Oldsmobile slipped considerably for 1980. But then, so did most other makes. Cutlass remained America's popularity champ.

1981 OLDSMOBILE

Substantial price rises greeted Oldsmobile buyers once again. With the demise of Sunbird early in the 1980 model year, only five lines were offered this time. Cutlass Salon and Salon Brougham coupes were dropped. Cutlass Supreme was restyled to cut aero drag by 15 percent. Fuel mileage gains came from a new four-speed automatic transmission, expanded use of lock-up torque converter clutches, low-drag brakes, higher-pressure tires, better aerodynamics (especially full-size), more on-board computers, and engine downsizing. Lock-up torque converter clutches were standard on all Olds models with automatic except Omega and Toronado. Four-speed automatic was standard on Ninety-Eight and Custom Cruiser, and Delta 88 with 5.0-liter V-8; optional on 88s with 4.3-liter engine. It had 0.67:1 overdrive fourth gear. All gas engines now had computer command control, with an electronic carburetor control to maintain constant air/fuel ratio. Only seven engines were available this year, versus ten in 1980 (and quite a few more in prior years, when a proliferation of 49-state, California and high-altitude powerplants had been the rule). Only 88/98, Toro and Custom Cruiser had the 5.0-liter V-8. A 4.1-liter V-6 was now standard in Ninety-Eight and Toro—the first V-6 in either of those models. This year, 19 of the 23 Olds models could have 5.7-liter diesel (but 5.0-liter was the biggest gas engine). Diesels added roller valve lifters, among other internal changes. An electronic control module (ECM), a little black box in the passenger compartment, controlled the engine of all gas models. It monitored coolant temperature, manifold pressure, transmission gear, R.P.M., idle speed, oxygen in exhaust, and other functions. A diagnostic system and "Check Engine" warning light were part of the computerized system. The Sport Omega was the first use of flex injected-molded fenders in an Oldsmobile. That model also used a soft front and rear fascia, as did the newly restyled Cutlass Supreme coupe bumpers.

1981 Omega sedan (AA)

OMEGA — SERIES 3X — FOUR/V-6 — Added options were the biggest news for the front-drive Omega in its second year. Four special styling options were announced: SX, Sport Omega, ES2500, and ES2800. A total 696 sport packages (RPO code Y78) were installed. As before, a coupe and sedan came in base or Brougham trim. This year's grille was a curious wrapover design. Not only did the pattern wrap slightly over onto the hood area, but the wrapover portion extended outward, above the single headlamps. The basic style was similar to before, but with a pattern of thin vertical bars accented by three horizontal dividers instead of vertical elements alone. Park/signal lamps were bumper-mounted. The sporty ES version a carried a non-wrapover blacked-out grille.

1981 Cutlass Calais T-top coupe (AA)

CUTLASS — SERIES 3A — V-6/V-8 — Eight models this year included Cutlass and Cutlass LS sedan, Cutlass Supreme and Supreme Brougham coupe, Brougham sedan, Calais, Cruiser, and Cruiser Brougham. Cutlass Supreme had all-new styling and improved aerodynamics. A soft-fascia front end extended to the bumper rub strip. The new swing-away grille displayed an eggcrate pattern on each side (4 x 6 hole arrangement). But the bottom two rows of the grille angled forward at the base, toward the bumper. Quad headlamps were used. Park and turn signal lamps were in the lower bumper, which also held twin slots. Supreme's side view showed a tapered look, with lowered front end and slightly higher decklid. The side feature line was softened and covered the body's length, with a flush-mounted quarter window. Wheel opening moldings were standard. Supreme's rear-end panel wrapped down to provide a soft covering for the upper bumper, with a chrome lower bar. Narrow two-section vertical taillamps wrapped up and over in typical Oldsmobile style. The base Cutlass sedan and Cutlass Cruiser had the same new grille. Cutlass LS, Brougham and Cruiser Brougham had their own grille and new quad headlamps with park/signal lamps in the bumper. This upright grille had five vertical bars on each side of a wide, bright center divider. Headlamp framing extended to wraparound side marker lights. Identifying script went on the cowl. Taillamps were wider than Supreme's and didn't reach the top of the quarter panel. Standard equipment included a 231 cu. in. (3.8-liter) V-6, column-shift automatic transmission, power brakes, and stand-up hood ornament. Calais had specially painted wheel covers and front/rear stabilizer bars. Supreme coupes included rocker panel moldings. Tires were P195/75R14 steel-belted blackwalls. A total of 15,000 appearance packages (RPO code Y68) were installed.

1981 Delta Royale Brougham coupe (AA)

DELTA 88 — SERIES 3B — V-6/V-8 — Each side of 88's new rectangular segmented grille contained an 8 x 2 pattern of bold holes. Quad rectangular headlamps led into side marker lenses. Park/signal lamps were set into the bumper. Rear ends had a small decklid spoiler, as on all full-size Olds models. Large angular wraparound taillamps displayed two horizontal trim strips. Six models were offered: coupe or sedan in base, Royale or Royale Brougham trim. Standard Delta 88 equipment included a 231 cu. in. (3.8-liter) V-6 with automatic transmission, power brakes and steering, front/rear armrests, bumper guards, stand-up hood ornament, bumper impact strips, rocker panel and wheel opening moldings, lighter, walnut-grained instrument panel, dome lamp, wheel covers, and P205/75R15 steel-belted radial blackwalls. Royale added bodyside moldings and a custom sport bench seat with center armrest. Brougham coupes had opera lamps; both Broughams had belt reveal moldings. A total 1,637 Holiday coupe packages (RPO code Y78) were installed on base 88 models.

CUSTOM CRUISER — SERIES 3B — V-8 — The full-size wagon had the same grille design as Delta 88, but came with V-8 power only. Standard engine was the 5.0-liter V-8, with four-speed overdrive automatic transmission.

1981 Ninety-Eight Regency Brougham sedan (AA)

NINETY-EIGHT — SERIES 3C — V-6/V-8 — Front-end appearance of this year's Ninety-Eight was similar to Delta 88, but the grille had two vertical and one horizontal bars on each side, over a tight crosshatch pattern. That gave each side six major sections, with a recessed eggcrate design. The rear end carried a small decklid spoiler. Taillamps were much narrower than 88's. Three models were available: Luxury sedan, and Regency coupe or sedan. Standard Ninety-Eight equipment included a 252 cu. in. (4.1-liter) V-8 and four-speed overdrive automatic transmission, power brakes and steering, power windows, bumper guards and impact strips, electric clock, fender skirts, dome reading lamp, and remote-control outside mirrors. Also standard: rocker panel and wheel opening moldings, belt reveal and roof drip moldings, two-way power seat, and P215/75R15 steel-belted radial whitewalls. Regency added an AM/FM stereo radio, digital clock, opera lamps, and divided front seat with twin controls.

1981 Toronado coupe (AA)

TORONADO — SERIES 3E — V-6/V-8 — Little changed in the front-drive Toronado. A Brougham coupe was the standard model, with sporty XSC package available. As before, the streamlined grille extended across the entire width of the car. Park and turn lamps were hidden behind the grille, below the quad rectangular headlamps. Long horizontal taillamps and backup lamps extended from the decklid's edge to the license plate opening. A total of 3,959 XSC packages (RPO code Y78) were installed. Toronado's standard equipment included a 252 cu. in. (4.1 liter) V-6 and automatic transmission, automatic level control, power brakes and steering, air conditioning, bumper guards and impact strips, digital clock, side window defogger, power windows and door locks, and halogen headlamps. Also included: cornering lamps, rocker panel and wheel opening moldings, AM/FM stereo radio, power antenna, six-way power driver's seat, remote-control mirrors, tinted glass, and P205/75R15 steel-belted whitewalls.

329

I.D. DATA: A new 17-symbol Vehicle Identification Number (VIN) was located on the upper left surface of the instrument panel, visible through the windshield. The first three symbols ('1G3') indicate Oldsmobile division. Symbol four denotes restraint type: 'A' manual (active) belts. Symbol five is car line/series: 'B' Omega; 'E' Omega Brougham; 'G' Cutlass Salon; 'J' Cutlass Salon Brougham; 'R' Cutlass Supreme; 'M' Cutlass Supreme Brougham ; 'K' Cutlass Calais; 'G' Cutlass Cruiser; 'H' Cutlass Cruiser Brougham; 'L' Delta 88; 'N' Delta 88 Royale; 'Y' Delta 88 Royale Brougham; 'P' Custom Cruiser; 'V' Ninety-Eight Luxury; 'X' Ninety-Eight Regency; 'Z' Toronado Brougham. Next come two digits that denote body type: '37' 2-dr. coupe; '47' 2dr. coupe; '57' 2-dr. coupe; '69' 4-dr. 4window notch sedan; '35' 4dr. 2seat wagon. Symbol eight is a letter for engine code: '5' L4151 2Bbl.; 'X' V6173 2Bbl.; 'A' V6231 2Bbl.; '4' V6252 4Bbl.; 'F' V8260 2Bbl.; 'Y' V8307 4Bbl.; 'N' diesel V8350. Next comes a check digit, followed by a code for model year: ('B' 1981). Symbol eleven is the assembly plant code: '2' Ste. Therese, Quebec (Canada); 'G' Framingham, Mass.; 'D' Doraville, Georgia; 'M' Lansing, Mich.; 'W' Willow Run, Mich.; 'R' Arlington, Texas; 'X' Fairfax, Kansas; 'E' Linden, New Jersey. The final six digits are the sequential serial number, starting with 100,001. Engine numbers were stamped on the front of the right rocker cover, or top of left cover (Buick-built engines), on label at front or rear of right rocker cover (Chevrolet-built engines), or on the left rocker cover (Oldsmobile engines). Four- cylinder engine numbers were on a pad at left or right front of block. A body number plate on the upper right cowl identified model year, series, style, body assembly plant, body number, trim combination, modular seat code, paint code, date built code, and option codes.

OMEGA (FOUR/V-6)

Model Number	Body/Style Number	Body Type & Seating	Factory Price	Shipping Weight	Production Total
3X	B37	2-dr. Cpe-5P	6343/6468	2414/2464	27,323
3X	B69	4-dr. Sed-5P	6514/6639	2444/2494	51,715

OMEGA BROUGHAM (FOUR/V-6)

3X	E37	2-dr. Cpe-5P	6700/6825	2437/2487	19,260
3X	E69	4-dr. Sed-5P	6855/6980	2474/2524	49,620

CUTLASS (V-6/V-8)

3A	G69	4-dr. Sed-6P	6955/7005	3127/3283	25,580

CUTLASS SUPREME (V-6/V-8)

3A	R47	2-dr. Cpe-6P	7484/7534	3137/3290	187,875

CUTLASS LS (V-6/V-8)

3A	R69	4-dr. Sed-6P	7652/7702	3160/3313	84,272

CUTLASS SUPREME/BROUGHAM (V-6/V-8)

3A	M47	2-dr. Supr Cpe-6P	7969/8019	3162/3315	93,855
3A	M69	4-dr. Sed-6P	8100/8150	3166/3319	53,952

CUTLASS CALAIS (V-6/V-8)

3A	K47	2-dr. Cpe-5P	8004/8054	3151/3304	4,105

CUTLASS CRUISER (V-6/V-8)

3A	G35	4-dr. 2S Sta Wag-6	7418/7468	3293/3445	31,926
3A	H35	4-dr. Brghm Wag-6	7725/7775	3286/3448	Note 1

Note 1: Brougham production included in basic total.

DELTA 88 (V-6/V-8)

3B	L37	2-dr. Cpe-6P	7429/7479	3401/3570	3,330
3B	L69	4-dr. Sed-6P	7524/7574	3427/3596	10,806

DELTA 88 ROYALE (V-6/V-8)

3B	N37	2-dr. Cpe-6P	7693/7743	3405/3574	41,682
3B	N69	4-dr. Sed-6P	7842/7892	3446/3615	104,124

DELTA 88 ROYALE BROUGHAM (V-6/V-8)

3B	Y37	2-dr. Cpe-6P	8058/8108	3435/3604	Note 2
3B	Y69	4-dr. Sed-6P	8141/8191	3480/3649	Note 2

Note 2: Production included in 88 Royale totals above.

CUSTOM CRUISER (V-8)

3B	P35	4-dr. 2S Sta Wag-6P	8452	3950	18,956

NINETY-EIGHT LUXURY (V-6/V-8)

3C	V69	4-dr. Sedan-6P	9951/9951	3661/3822	1,957

NINETY-EIGHT REGENCY (V-6/V-8)

3C	X37	2-dr. Cpe-6P	10440/10440	3655/3816	13,696
3C	X69	4-dr. Sedan-6P	10558/10558	3714/3875	74,017

TORONADO BROUGHAM (V-6/V-8)

3E	Z57	2-dr. Cpe-5P	12148/12148	3567/3696	42,604

FACTORY PRICE AND WEIGHT NOTE: Prices and weights to left of slash are for six-cylinder, to right for V-8 engine except Omega, to left for four-cylinder and to right for V-6.

ENGINE DATA: BASE FOUR (Omega): Inline, overhead-valve four-cylinder. Cast iron block and head. Displacement: 151 cu. in. (2.5 liters). Bore & stroke: 4.00 x 3.00 in. Compression ratio: 8.2:1. Brake horsepower: 90 at 4000 R.P.M. Torque: 125 lbs.ft. at 2400 R.P.M. Five main bearings. Hydraulic valve lifters. Carburetor: 2Bbl. Rochester. Pontiac-built. VIN Code: 5. OPTIONAL V-6 (Omega): 60-degree, overhead-valve V-6. Cast iron block and aluminum head. Displacement: 173 cu. in. (2.8 liters). Bore & stroke: 3.50 x 3.00 in. Compression ratio: 8.5:1. Brake horsepower: 110 at 4800 R.P.M. Torque: 145 lbs.ft. at 2400 R.P.M. Four main bearings. Hydraulic valve lifters. Carburetor: 2Bbl. Rochester. Chevrolet-built. VIN Code: X. BASE V-6 (Cutlass, Delta 88): 90-degree, overhead-valve V-6. Cast iron block and head. Displacement: 231 cu. in. (3.8 liters). Bore & stroke: 3.80 x 3.40 in. Compression ratio: 8.0:1. Brake horsepower: 110 at 3800 R.P.M. Torque: 190 lbs.ft. at 1600 R.P.M. Four main bearings. Hydraulic valve lifters. Carburetor: 2Bbl. Rochester 2ME. Buick-built. VIN Code: A. BASE V-6 (98, Toronado): 90-degree, overhead-valve V-6. Cast iron block and head. Displacement: 252 cu. in. (4.1 liters). Bore & stroke: 3.96 x 3.40 in. Compression ratio: 8.0:1. Brake horsepower: 125 at 4000 R.P.M. Torque: 205 lbs.ft. at 2000 R.P.M. Four main bearings. Hydraulic valve lifters. Carburetor: 4Bbl. Rochester M4MC. Buick-built. VIN Code: 4. OPTIONAL V-8 (Cutlass, Delta 88): 90-degree, overhead valve V-8. Cast iron block and head. Displacement: 260 cu. in. (4.3 liters). Bore & stroke: 3.50 x 3.39 in. Compression ratio: 7.5:1. Brake horsepower: 105 at 3600 R.P.M. Torque: 190 lbs.ft. at 1600 R.P.M. Five main bearings. Hydraulic valve lifters. Carburetor: 2Bbl. Rochester 2MC. VIN Code: F. OPTIONAL V-8 (Delta 88, 98, Toronado): 90-degree, overhead valve V-8. Cast iron block and head. Displacement: 307 cu. in. (5.0 liters). Bore & stroke: 3.80 x 3.38 in. Compression ratio: 8.0:1. Brake horsepower: 140 at 3800 R.P.M. Torque: 240 lbs.ft. at 1600 R.P.M. Five main bearings. Hydraulic valve lifters. Carburetor: 4Bbl. Rochester M4ME. VIN Code: Y. DIESEL V-8 (Cutlass, Delta 88, 98, Custom Cruiser, Toronado): 90-degree, overhead valve V 8. Cast iron block and head. Displacement: 350 cu. in. (5.7 liters). Bore & stroke: 4.06 x 3.39 in. Compression ratio: 22.5:1. Brake horsepower: 105 at 3200 R.P.M. Torque: 200 lbs.ft. at 1600 R.P.M. Five main bearings. Hydraulic valve lifters. Fuel injection. VIN Code: N.

CHASSIS DATA: Wheelbase: (Omega) 104.9 in.; (Cutlass) 108.1 in.; (Delta 88) 116.0 in.; (98) 119.0 in.; (Custom Crsr) 116.0 in.; (Toronado) 114.0 in. Overall Length: (Omega) 181.8 in.; (Cutlass sed) 199.1 in.; (Cutlass Calais/Supreme) 200.0 in.; (Cutlass wag) 198.2 in.; (Delta 88) 218.1 in.; (98) 221.1 in.; (Custom Crsr) 220.3 in.; (Toro) 206.0 in. Height: (Omega) 53.7 in.; (Cutlass) 54.9-55.9 in.; (Cutlass wag) 56.2 in.; (Delta 88 cpe) 56.0 in.; (Delta 88 sed) 56.7 in.; (98) 57.2 in.; (Custom Crsr) 58.5 in.; (Toro) 54.6 in. Width: (Omega) 69.8 in.; (Cutlass) 71.9 in.; (Cutlass wag) 71.9 in.; (Delta 88) 76.3 in.; (98) 76.3 in.; (Custom Crsr) 79.8 in.; (Toro) 71.4 in. Front Tread: (Omega) 58.7 in.; (Cutlass) 58.5 in.; (Delta 88/98) 61.7 in.; (Custom Crsr) 62.1 in.; (Toro) 59.3 in. Rear Tread: (Omega) 57.0 in.; (Cutlass) 57.7 in.; (Delta 88/98) 60.7 in.; (Custom Crsr) 64.1 in.; (Toro) 60.0 in. Standard Tires: (Omega) P185/80R13; (Cutlass) P185/75R14; (Cutlass Supreme/Brghm/Calais) P195/75R14; (Cutlass wag) P195/75R14; (Delta 88) P205/75R15; (98) P215/75R15; (Custom Crsr) N/A; (Toronado) P205/75R15.

TECHNICAL: Transmission: Three-speed manual transmission standard on Cutlass sedan (except LS/Brougham/, automatic standard). Four-speed floor shift standard on Omega. Three-speed Turbo Hydra-matic standard on other models, optional on all. Four- speed automatic overdrive standard on 98, optional on 88. Standard final drive ratio: (Omega) 3.32:1 w/4spd, 2.53:1 w/auto.; (Cutlass V-6) 3.08:1 w/3spd, 2.41:1 w/auto.; (Cutlass V-8) 2.29:1; (Cutlass Cruiser) 2.73:1 w/V-6, 2.41:1 w/V8260, 2.29:1 w/V8307 or diesel; (Delta 88) 2.73:1 w/V-6, 2.56:1 w/V8260, 2.41:1 w/V8307 or diesel; (Custom Crsr) 2.73:1; (98) 3.23:1 w/V-6, 2.73:1 w/V8307, 2.41:1 w/diesel; (Toronado) 2.93:1 w/V-6, 2.41:1 w/V8307. Steering: (Omega) rack and pinion; (others) recirculating ball. Front Suspension: (Omega) MacPherson struts w/coil springs and lower control arms; (Toronado) longitudinal torsion bars w/anti-sway bar; (others) coil springs w/control arms and anti-sway bar. Rear Suspension: (Omega) rigid axle w/lower control arms, trailing arm and coil springs; (Toronado) independent with coil springs, longitudinal swinging trailing arms and automatic leveling; (others) rigid axle w/coil springs, lower trailing radius arms and upper torque arms. Brakes: Front disc, rear drum. Ignition: Electronic. Body construction: (Omega) unibody; (others) separate body on perimeter frame. Fuel Tank: (Omega) 14 gal.; (Cutlass) 18.1 gal.; (Cutlass wag) 18.1 gal.; (Delta 88) 25 gal.; (98) 25 gal.; (Custom Crsr wag) 22 gal.; (Toronado) 21 gal.

DRIVETRAIN OPTIONS: Engines: 173 cu. in. V-6: Omega ($125). 260 cu. in. V-8: Cutlass/88 ($50). 307 cu. in. 4Bbl. V-8: Cutlass wag ($50); 88 ($203); 98/Toro (NC). Diesel 350 cu. in. V-8: Cutlass/88 ($695); 98/Custom Crsr ($542); Toronado ($695). Transmission/Differential: Turbo Hydra-matic: Omega/Cutlass ($349). Overdrive automatic: 88 (NC). Limited-slip differential: Cutlass/88/98 ($69). Brakes/Steering: Power brakes: Omega ($69). Power four-wheel disc brakes: Toro ($215). Power steering: Omega ($168). Suspension: Firm ride/handling pkg.: Omega ($32); Cutlass/88/98 ($24-$39); 98 ($24). Superlift rear shocks: Omega ($54). Automatic load leveling: 88/98 ($142). Other: High-capacity cooling ($24-$74). High-capacity radiator: Cutlass/88 ($21); 98/Toro ($21-$32). High-capacity alternator: Omega ($49); Cutlass/88 ($27-$75); 98/Toro ($27). H.D. battery ($20) exc. diesel ($40). Engine block heater ($16). Trailer wiring harness ($23-$24). California emissions ($46) exc. diesel ($182).

OPTION PACKAGES: Omega ES pkg.: Brghm sedan ($895-$1020). Omega sport pkg.: base cpe ($669). Omega SX pkg.: base cpe ($358). Delta 88 Holiday coupe pkg.: base ($271). Toronado XSC sport pkg. ($310).

MAJOR CONVENIENCE/APPEARANCE OPTIONS: Four Season air conditioner ($585-$625). Tempmatic air conditioning: Cutlass/88 ($635-$675); 98/Toro ($50). Cruise control ($132-$135). Power seat ($146-$173). Power windows ($140-$221). Cornering lamps: 88/98 ($51). Twilight sentinel: 98/Toro ($49). Power astroroof w/sliding glass panel: Cutlass/88/98/Toro ($773-$995). Power sliding metal sunroof: Cutlass ($561-$848). Removable glass roof panels: Cutlass ($695). Glass panel sunroof: Omega ($246). Landau vinyl roof ($173-$195). Full vinyl roof: Omega/88/98 ($115-$159). Rear- facing third seat: Custom Cruiser ($190).

HISTORY: Introduced: September 25, 1980. Model year production: 940,655. Calendar year production (U.S.): 838,333. Calendar year sales by U.S. dealers: 848,739. Model year sales by U.S. dealers: 882,505.

Historical Footnotes: Sales began to rise again this year, but still fell far short of the million level achieved two years earlier. Cutlass, however, continued as the most popular car in the country. Diesel engine production rose dramatically, but not all of them went under Oldsmobile hoods. Still, over 18 percent of Oldsmobiles sold were now diesel-powered. A steady decline in engine sizes meant the gas V-6 was now dominant over the V-8 at the production level. Over half of the engines built in 1980 had been gas V-8s, but less than one-third this year. Fleet fuel economy was estimated at 22.5 MPG (1.2 higher than 1980).

1982 OLDSMOBILE

In addition to five returning models, a new front-drive Cutlass Ciera joined the Olds lineup in late fall, displaying a contemporary aero appearance. Fleet fuel economy estimate was 25.3 MPG (up nearly 3 MPG from 1981). To boost mileage further, Oldsmobile took several steps, starting with more use of torque converter lock-up clutches (on all V-6 engines, and on all fours by mid-year). Throttle-body fuel injection became standard on the 151 cu. in. (2.5-liter) four. Automatic overdrive transmissions were standard on 98 and Toronado, and 88 with V-8 power. Optional in Cutlass Ciera was a new 181 cu. in. (3.0-liter) V-6 engine. A new V-6 diesel weighed over 150 pounds less than the V-8 diesel, and was supposed to give Cutlass Supreme fuel mileage of 36 MPG on the highway. All models except the compact Omega could have diesel power.

1982 Firenza hatchback coupe (AA)

FIRENZA — SERIES 3J — FOUR — Riding a 101.2 inch wheelbase, the subcompact front-drive, five-passenger Firenza hatchback carried a transverse-mounted 112 cu. in. (1.8-liter) four-cylinder engine and four-speed manual transaxle. It was introduced in March 1982, to replace the abandoned Starfire as Oldsmobile's subcompact offering. Coupe and sedan bodies were offered, in base or SX/LX trim. Coupes had swing-out rear quarter windows. Optional powerplant was a 121 cu. in. (2.0-liter) four. Firenza had no conventional grille above the bumper, but only a sloping solid center panel between deeply recessed quad headlamps. Parking/signal lamps were positioned between each headlamp pair. Below the bumper were sets of vertical ribbed slots on both sides. A 'Firenza' nameplate stood high on the cowl. Large taillamps with Olds emblems wrapped just slightly onto quarter panels. Hatchbacks had a small decklid spoiler. Standard Firenza equipment included an AM radio, side window defogger, sport console, passenger assist grips, power brakes, day/night mirror, reclining cloth/vinyl front bucket seats, and compact spare tire. Coupes had a folding back seat and Rallye wheels with stainless steel trim rings. Sedans included deluxe wheel covers. The SX coupe added a Rallye instrument cluster. Both LX and SX included bodyside moldings, velour bucket seats, power steering, and color-keyed outside mirrors (driver's remote-controlled).

OMEGA — SERIES 3X — FOUR/V-6 — Four compact Omega models were offered: base and Brougham coupe and sedan, along with ES2500 and ES2800 options. Styling changes included a new, slightly sloping front end with a grille containing 5 x 4 eggcrate-patterned segments on each side of the divider. Park and turn signal lamps were recessed behind the grille, with single headlamps at the outboard sides. Dual-lens taillamps contained integral vertical backup lights with Olds emblem. Taillamps gave a lower appearance, not reaching the decklid top. A new ESC option on Brougham coupe featured "continental" styling and lightweight flex fenders. Omega had new fluidic windshield wipers, a larger gas tank, and match-mounted tires with pressure increased to 35 PSI. A new high-output 2.8-liter V-6 became optional in Omega ES, with free-flow exhaust, improved cylinder head port design, and high-output camshaft. The base 151 cu. in. (2.5-liter) four switched to throttle-body fuel injection. A standard 173 cu. in. (2.8-liter) V-6 was optional. Four-speed manual or automatic transmissions were available with each engine.

1982 Cutlass Ciera sedan (JG)

CUTLASS CIERA — SERIES 3A — FOUR/V-6 — As advertised, this aerodynamically-styled A-body compact was the first Cutlass model with front-wheel drive. Ciera's twin-section grille had an eggcrate pattern (5 x 6 hole arrangement) similar to Omega's on each side of the wide center divider panel, which held an Oldsmobile emblem. Framework around the recessed quad rectangular headlamps continued around the front fender sides to enclose clear/amber marker lenses. Thin horizontal park/signal lamps were mounted right along the bumper rub strip. At the rear were large wraparound taillamps. Ciera came in base, Brougham and LS trim. Brougham coupes and sedans had a divided front seat with loose-pillow look. At the cowl was a small multi-color international-style nameplate, below a 'Cutlass Ciera' nameplate. Standard engine was a 151 cu. in. (2.5-liter) four, with optional 181 cu. in. (3.0-liter) V-6. Also optional: a 4.3-liter diesel. Ciera standard equipment included an AM radio, four-speed manual transaxle, P185/80R13 blackwall glass-belted radial tires, deluxe wheel covers, power steering, and bench seat. Brougham added lower bodyside moldings, pillar applique moldings (on sedan), and sport bench seat with fold-down armrest. Base models had rocker panel moldings. All except the base coupe had wheel opening moldings and rocker panel moldings.

CUTLASS SUPREME — SERIES 3G — V-6/V-8 — The mid-size lineup included Cutlass Supreme coupe and sedan, Supreme Brougham coupe and sedan, Calais coupe, and Cruiser wagon. As usual, Cutlass grilles varied depending on the model. Sedans and wagons had a new square eggcrate grille. Cutlass Supreme coupes displayed a specific vertical grille with body-colored dividers. Supreme Brougham and Calais had an eggcrate grille with two vertical body-colored bars in each side. Coupes had a sloping front end with soft fascia front panel that extended to the rub strip. Their rear end panel wrapped down to provide a soft covering for the upper bumper. Sedans had a different rear-end look, including three-segment taillamps at outboard sides of the back panel. Each model had quad headlamps, and park/turn signal lamps were mounted in the lower bumper. Base engine was the 231 cu. in. (3.8-liter) V-6; optional, the 260 cu. in. (4.3-liter) V-8 or 5.7-liter diesel. Coupes and sedans could get the new 4.3-liter diesel V-6, while wagons came with an optional 5.0-liter V-8 engine.

DELTA 88 — SERIES 3B — V-6/V-8 — A new grille made up of thin horizontal bars was the major change on 88. Framework around the quad rectangular headlamps extended into wraparound side markers. Large wraparound taillamps had single lenses divided into three segments, with horizontal ribbing. Backup lenses stood alongside the license plate mounting. Five models were offered: Delta 88 sedan, Royale coupe and sedan, and Royale Brougham coupe and sedan. A multi-function lever controlled the turn signal, wiper, dimmer and optional cruise control (with resume). Base engine was the 231 cu. in. (3.8-liter) V-6; optional, a 260 cu. in. (4.3-liter) V-8, 5.0-liter V-8, and 5.7-liter diesel.

CUSTOM CRUISER — SERIES 3B — V-8 — Full-size wagons had a standard 307 cu. in. (5.0-liter) V-8 with four-barrel carburetor, and optional big diesel V-8. Little changed this year.

1982 Ninety-Eight Regency Brougham sedan (JG)

NINETY-EIGHT REGENCY — SERIES 3C — V-6/V-8 — Not much changed in Ninety-Eight appearance, apart from a new checkered lattice-design grille, divided as usual into two separate sections. Three models were available: Regency coupe and sedan, and new Regency Brougham sedan. Regency Brougham had lower body and bodyside moldings, sail panel emblem, a vinyl padded roof, locking wire wheel covers, convenience group, halogen headlamps, cornering lamps, and deluxe interior components. A multi-function lever controlled the turn signal, wiper, dimmer, and optional cruise control (with resume). A 252 cu. in. (4.1-liter) V-6 was standard, with 307 cu. in. (5.0-liter) gas V-8 and 5.7-liter diesel optional.

1982 Toronado coupe (JG)

TORONADO — SERIES 3E — V-6/V-8 — Toro's new chrome/argent grille was similar to the previous design, stretching to the fender tips, but had extra horizontal bars this year. A single-piece nameplate emblem replaced the former individual letters. Only one model was offered: the Brougham coupe, with standard 252 cu. in. (4.1-liter) V-6. Optional: either a 307 cu. in. (5.0-liter) V-8 or 350 diesel. A new memory seat option (on no other model) gave two memory positions on the six-way power seat. Pushing a button moved the seat to one of its pre-set locations. The new optional 2000 series radio had separate bass and treble controls, balance and fader controls, automatic loudness, and increased power output.

I.D. DATA: Oldsmobile's 17-symbol Vehicle Identification Number (VIN) again was located on the upper left surface of the instrument panel, visible through the windshield. The first three symbols ('1G3') indicate Oldsmobile division. Symbol four denotes restraint type: 'A' manual (active) belts. Symbol five is car line/series: 'C' Firenza; 'D' Firenza SX/LX; 'B' Omega; 'E' Omega Brougham; 'G' Cutlass Ciera; 'J' Cutlass Ciera LS; ''M' Cutlass Ciera Brougham; 'R' Cutlass Supreme; 'M' Cutlass Supreme Brougham; 'K' Cutlass Calais; 'H' Cutlass Cruiser; 'L' Delta 88; 'N' Delta 88 Royale; 'Y' Delta 88 Royale Brougham; 'P' Custom Cruiser; 'X' Ninety-Eight Regency;

'W' Ninety-Eight Regency Brougham; 'Z' Toronado Brougham. Next come two digits that denote body type: '27' 2dr. coupe; '37' 2dr. coupe; '47' 2dr. coupe; '57' 2dr. coupe; '77' 2dr. coupe; '19' 4dr. sedan; '69' 4dr. 4window notch sedan; '35' 4dr. 2seat wagon. Symbol eight is a letter for engine code: 'G' L4112 2Bbl.; 'B' L4122 2Bbl.; 'R' L4151 FI; 'X' V6173 2Bbl.; 'E' V6181 2Bbl.; 'A' V6231 2Bbl.; '4' V6252 4Bbl.; '8' V8260 2Bbl.; 'T' or 'V' diesel 6262; 'Y' V8307 4Bbl.; 'N' diesel V8350. Next comes a check digit, followed by a code for model year: ('C' 1982). Symbol eleven is the assembly plant code: '2' Ste. Therese, Quebec (Canada); 'D' Doraville, Georgia; 'M' Lansing, Mich.; 'W' Willow Run, Mich.; 'X' Fairfax, Kansas; 'E' Linden, New Jersey; 'Z' Fremont. The final six digits are the sequential serial number, starting with 100,001. Engine numbers were stamped on the front of the right rocker cover, or top of left cover (Buick-built engines), on label at front or rear of right rocker cover (Chevrolet V-6), or on the left rocker cover (Oldsmobile engines). Four- cylinder engine numbers were on a pad at left or right front of block. A body number plate on the upper right cowl identified model year, series, style, body assembly plant, body number, trim combination, modular seat code, paint code, date built code, and option codes.

FIRENZA (FOUR)

Model Number	Body/Style Number	Body Type & Seating	Factory Price	Shipping Weight	Production Total
3J	C77	2-dr. S cpe-5P	7413	N/A	8,894
3J	C69	4-dr. Sedan-5P	7448	N/A	9,256
3J	D77	2-dr. SX cpe-5P	8159	N/A	6,017
3J	D69	4-dr. LX sed-5P	8080	N/A	5,941

OMEGA (FOUR/V-6)

3X	B37	2-dr. Cpe-5P	7388/7513	2437/2489	12,140
3X	B69	4-dr. Sed-5P	7574/7699	2470/2522	29,548

OMEGA BROUGHAM (FOUR/V-6)

3X	E37	2-dr. Cpe-5P	7722/7847	2461/2513	9,430
3X	E69	4-dr. Sed-5P	7891/8016	2501/2553	26,351

CUTLASS CIERA (FOUR/V-6)

3A	G27	2-dr. Cpe-5P	8847/8972	2577/2660	5,185
3A	G19	4-dr. Sed-5P	8997/9122	2596/2679	9,717
3A	J27	2-dr. LS Cpe-5P	8968/9093	2583/2666	10,702
3A	J19	4-dr. LS Sed-5P	9157/9282	2587/2652	29,322

CUTLASS CIERA BROUGHAM (FOUR/V-6)

3A	M27	2-dr. Cpe-5P	9397/9522	2585/2668	12,518
3A	M19	4-dr. Sed-5P	9599/9724	2588/2653	33,876

CUTLASS SUPREME (V-6/V-8)

3G	R47	2-dr. Cpe-6P	8588/8658	3136/3232	89,617
3G	R69	4-dr. Sed-6P	8712/8782	3197/3252	60,053

CUTLASS SUPREME BROUGHAM (V-6/V-8)

3G	M47	2-dr. Cpe-6P	9160/9230	3163/3259	59,592
3G	M69	4-dr. Sed-6P	9255/9325	3222/3277	34,717

CUTLASS CALAIS (V-6/V-8)

3G	K47	2-dr. Cpe-5P	9379/9449	3198/3273	17,109

CUTLASS CRUISER (V-6/V-8)

3G	H35	4-dr. Sta Wag-6P	8905/8975	3338/3479	20,363

DELTA 88 (V-6/V-8)

3B	L69	4-dr. Sed-6P	8603/8673	3425/3556	8,278

DELTA 88 ROYALE (V-6/V-8)

3B	N37	2-dr. Cpe-6P	8733/8803	3402/3533	41,382
3B	N69	4-dr. Sed-6P	8894/8964	3440/3571	105,184

DELTA 88 ROYALE BROUGHAM (V-6/V-8)

3B	Y37	2-dr. Cpe-6P	9202/9272	3437/3568	Note 1
3B	Y69	4-dr. Sed-6P	9293/9363	3473/3604	Note 1

Note 1: Production included in 88 Royale totals above.

CUSTOM CRUISER (V-8)

3B	P35	4-dr. Sta Wag-6P	9614	3909	19,367

NINETY-EIGHT REGENCY (V-6/V-8)

3C	X37	2-dr. Cpe-6P	12117/12117	3648/3817	11,832
3C	X69	4-dr. Sedan-6P	12294/12294	3705/3821	79,135
3C	W69	4-dr. Brghm-6P	13344/13344	3751/3867	Note 2

Note 2: Production included in basic sedan total.

TORONADO BROUGHAM (V-6/V-8)

3E	Z57	2-dr. Cpe-5P	14462/14462	3584/3705	33,928

FACTORY PRICE AND WEIGHT NOTE: Prices and weights to left of slash are for six-cylinder, to right for V-8 engine except Omega/Ciera, to left for four-cylinder and to right for V-6.

ENGINE DATA: BASE FOUR (Firenza): Inline, overhead-valve four-cylinder. Cast iron block and head. Displacement: 112 cu. in. (1.8 liters). Bore & stroke: 3.50 x 2.91 in. Compression ratio: 9.0:1. Brake horsepower: 88 at 5100 R.P.M. Five main bearings. Hydraulic valve lifters. Carburetor: 2Bbl. Rochester E2SE. VIN Code: G. **OPTIONAL (Firenza):** Inline, overhead-valve four-cylinder. Cast iron block and head. Displacement: 122 cu. in. (2.0 liters). Bore & stroke: 3.50 x 3.14 in. Compression ratio: 9.0:1. Brake horsepower: 90 at 5100 R.P.M. Torque: 111 lbs.ft. at 2700 R.P.M. Five main bearings. Hydraulic valve lifters. Carburetor: 2Bbl. Rochester E2SE. VIN Code: B. **BASE FOUR (Omega, Cutlass Ciera):** Inline, overhead-valve four-cylinder. Cast iron block and head. Displacement: 151 cu. in. (2.5 liters). Bore & stroke: 4.00 x 3.00 in. Compression ratio: 8.2:1. Brake horsepower: 90 at 4000 R.P.M. Torque: 134 lbs.ft. at 2400 R.P.M. Five main bearings. Hydraulic valve lifters. Fuel injection (TBI). Pontiac-built. VIN Code: R. **OPTIONAL V-6 (Omega):** 60-degree, overhead-valve V-6. Cast iron block and aluminum head. Displacement: 173 cu. in. (2.8 liters). Bore & stroke: 3.50 x 3.00 in. Compression ratio: 8.5:1. Brake horsepower: 112 at 5100 R.P.M. Torque: 148 lbs.ft. at 2400 R.P.M. Four main bearings. Hydraulic valve lifters. Carburetor: 2Bbl. Rochester E2SE. Chevrolet-built. VIN Code: X. NOTE: A high-output 173 cu. in. V-6 was available Compression ratio: 8.9:1. Horsepower: 130 at 5400 R.P.M. Torque: 145 lbs.ft. at 2400 R.P.M. **OPTIONAL V-6 (Cutlass Ciera):** 90-degree, overhead-valve V-6. Cast iron block and head. Displacement: 181 cu. in. (3.0 liters). Bore & stroke: 3.80 x 2.66 in. Compression ratio: 8.45:1. Brake horsepower: 110 at 4800 R.P.M. Torque: 145 lbs.ft. at 2000 R.P.M. Four main bearings. Hydraulic valve lifters. Carburetor: 2Bbl. Rochester E2ME. VIN Code: E. **BASE V-6 (Cutlass Supreme, Delta 88):** 90-degree, overhead-valve V-6. Cast iron block and head. Displacement: 231 cu. in. (3.8 liters). Bore & stroke: 3.80 x 3.40 in. Compression ratio: 8.0:1. Brake horsepower: 110 at 3800 R.P.M. Torque: 190 lbs.ft. at 1600 R.P.M. Four main earings. Hydraulic valve lifters. Carburetor: 2Bbl. Rochester E2ME. Buick-built. VIN Code: A. **BASE V-6 (98, Toronado):** 90-degree, overhead-valve V-6. Cast iron block and head. Displacement: 252 cu. in. (4.1 liters). Bore & stroke: 3.96 x 3.40 in. Compression ratio: 8.0:1. Brake horsepower: 125 at 4000 R.P.M. Torque: 205 lbs.ft. at 2000 R.P.M. Four main bearings. Hydraulic valve lifters. Carburetor: 4Bbl. Rochester E4ME. Buick-built. VIN Code: 4. **OPTIONAL V-8 (Cutlass, Delta 88):** 90-degree, overhead valve V-8. Cast iron block and head. Displacement: 260 cu. in. (4.3 liters). Bore & stroke: 3.50 x 3.38 in. Compression ratio: 7.5:1. Brake horsepower: 100 at 3600 R.P.M. Torque: 190 lbs.ft. at 1600 R.P.M. Five main bearings. Hydraulic valve lifters. Carburetor: 2Bbl. Rochester E2ME. VIN Code: 8. **DIESEL V-6 (Cutlass Ciera, Cutlass Supreme):** 90-degree, overhead-valve V-6. Cast iron block and head. Displacement: 262 cu. in. (4.3 liters). Bore & stroke: 4.06 x 3.38 in. Compression ratio: 21.6:1. Brake horsepower: 85 at 3600 R.P.M. Torque: 165 lbs.ft. at 1600 R.P.M. Five main bearings. Hydraulic valve lifters. Fuel injection. VIN Code: T or V. **BASE V-8 (Custom Cruiser); OPTIONAL (Cutlass Supreme, Delta 88, 98, Toronado):** 90-degree, overhead valve V-8. Cast iron block and head. Displacement: 307 cu. in. (5.0 liters). Bore & stroke: 3.80 x 3.38 in. Compression ratio: 8.0:1. Brake horsepower: 140 at 3600 R.P.M. Torque: 240 lbs.ft. at 1600 R.P.M. Five main bearings. Hydraulic valve lifters. Carburetor: 4Bbl. Rochester M4MC. VIN Code: Y. **DIESEL V-8 (Cutlass Supreme, Delta 88, 98, Custom Cruiser, Toronado):** 90-degree, overhead valve V-8. Cast iron block and head. Displacement: 350 cu. in. (5.7 liters). Bore & stroke: 4.06 x 3.39 in. Compression ratio: 21.6:1. Brake horsepower: 105 at 3200 R.P.M. Torque: 200 lbs.ft. at 1600 R.P.M. Five main bearings. Hydraulic valve lifters. Fuel injection. VIN Code: N.

CHASSIS DATA: Wheelbase: (Firenza) 101.2 in.; (Omega/Ciera) 104.9 in.; (Cutlass) 108.1 in.; (Delta 88) 116.0 in.; (98) 119.0 in.; (Custom Crsr) 116.0 in.; (Toronado) 114.0 in. Overall Length: (Firenza cpe) 174.3 in.; (Firenza sed) 176.2 in.; (Omega) 182.8 in.; (Ciera) 188.4 in.; (Cutlass sed) 199.1 in.; (Cutlass Supreme cpe) 200.0 in.; (Cutlass wag) 200.4 in.; (Delta 88) 218.1 in.; (98) 221.1 in.; (Custom Crsr) 220.3 in.; (Toro) 206.0 in. Height: (Firenza cpe) 51.7 in.; (Firenza sed) 53.7 in.; (Omega) 53.7 in.; (Ciera) 54.1 in.; (Cutlass Supreme) 54.9- 55.9 in.; (Delta 88 cpe) 56.0 in.; (Delta 88 sed) 56.7 in.; (98) 57.2 in.; (Custom Crsr) 58.5 in.; (Toro) 54.6 in. Width: (Firenza) 65.0 in.; (Omega) 69.8 in.; (Ciera) 69.5 in.; (Cutlass) 71.6-71.9 in.; (Cutlass wag) 71.8 in.; (Delta 88) 76.3 in.; (98) 76.3 in.; (Custom Crsr) 79.8 in.; (Toro) 71.4 in. Front Tread: (Firenza) 55.4 in.; (Omega/Ciera) 58.7 in.; (Cutlass) 58.5 in.; (Delta 88/98) 61.7 in.; (Custom Crsr) 62.1 in.; (Toro) 59.3 in. Rear Tread: (Firenza) 55.2 in.; (Omega/Ciera) 57.0 in.; (Cutlass) 57.7 in.; (Delta 88/98) 60.7 in.; (Custom Crsr) 64.1 in.; (Toro) 60.0 in. Standard Tires: (Firenza) P175/80R13; (Omega/Ciera) P185/80R13; (Cutlass) P185/75R14; (Cutlass Supreme) P195/75R14; (Delta 88) P205/75R15; (98) P215/75R15; (Custom Crsr) P225/75R15; (Toronado) P205/75R15.

TECHNICAL: Transmission: Four-speed floor shift standard on Firenza/Omega. Gear ratios: (1st) 3.53:1; (2nd) 1.95:1; (3rd) 1.24:1; (4th) 0.73:1 or 0.81:1; (Rev) 3.42:1. Three-speed Turbo Hydra-matic standard on Cutlass/88. Four-speed automatic overdrive standard on Custom Cruiser/98/Toronado. Standard final drive ratio: (Firenza) 3.65:1; (Omega) 3.32:1 w/4spd, 2.39:1 w/auto.; (Omega V-6) 3.32:1 w/4spd, 2.53:1 w/auto.; (Ciera) 2.39:1 or 2.53:1; (Cutlass) 2.41:1 w/V-6, 2.29:1 w/V-8, 2.41:1 w/V-6 diesel; (Cutlass Cruiser) 2.73:1 w/V-6, 2.41:1 w/V8260, 2.29:1 w/V8307 or diesel; (Delta 88) 2.73:1 w/V-6, 2.56:1 w/V8260, 2.93:1 w/diesel; (Custom Crsr) 2.73:1 exc. 2.93:1 w/diesel; (98) 3.23:1 w/V-6, 2.73:1 w/V8307, 2.93:1 w/diesel; (Toronado) 3.15:1 w/V-6, 2.73:1 w/V-8, 2.93:1 w/diesel. Steering: (Firenza/Omega/Ciera) rack and pinion; (others) recirculating ball. Front Suspension: (Firenza) MacPherson struts w/coil springs and anti-sway bar; (Omega/Ciera) MacPherson struts w/coil springs; (Toronado) longitudinal torsion bars w/anti- sway bar; (others) coil springs w/control arms and anti-sway bar. Rear Suspension: (Firenza) coil springs w/trailing crank arms; (Omega/Ciera) coil springs w/trailing arms; (Toronado) independent with coil springs, longitudinal trailing arms and automatic leveling; (others) rigid axle w/coil springs, lower trailing radius arms and upper torque arms. Brakes: Front disc, rear drum. Ignition: Electronic. Body construction: (Firenza/Omega/Ciera) unibody; (others) separate body and frame. Fuel tank: (Firenza) 14 gal.; (Omega) 14.2 gal.; (Ciera) 14.5 or 15.7 gal.; (Cutlass) 18.1 gal.; (Cutlass wag) 18.2 gal.; (Delta 88) 25 gal.; (98) 25 gal.; (Custom Crsr wag) 22 gal.; (Toronado) 21.1 gal.

DRIVETRAIN OPTIONS: Engines: 121 cu. in. four: Firenza ($50). 173 cu. in. V-6: Omega ($125). 181 cu. in. V-6: Ciera ($125). 260 cu. in. V-8: Cutlass/88 ($70). Diesel 262 cu. in. V-6: Cutlass/Ciera ($775). 307 cu. in. 4Bbl. V-8: Cutlass wag ($70); 88 ($70); 98/Toro (NC). Diesel 350 cu. in. V-8: Cutlass/88/98/Custom Crsr/Toronado ($825). Transmission/Differential: Turbo Hydra-matic: Firenza ($370); Omega ($396). Limited-slip differential: Cutlass/88/98 ($80). Brakes/Steering: Power steering: Firenza ($180). Suspension: Firm ride/handling pkg. ($28-$46). Automatic load leveling: Ciera/88/98 ($165). Other: High-capacity cooling ($30-$83). High-capacity radiator ($24) exc. Firenza/Omega. High-capacity alternator ($35-$85) exc. Firenza. H.D. battery ($22-$25) exc. diesel ($50). Engine block heater ($19). Block/fuel line heater ($49). Trailer wiring ($28) exc. Firenza/Omega. California emissions ($46) exc. diesel ($205).

OPTION PACKAGES: Omega ES pkg.: Brghm sedan ($896-$1146).

MAJOR CONVENIENCE/APPEARANCE OPTIONS: Four Season air conditioner ($675-$695). Tempmatic air conditioning: Cutlass/88 ($730-$750); 98/Toro ($50). Cruise control ($155-$165). Power seat ($178-$197). Power windows ($165-$240). Twilight sentinel: 98/Toro ($57). Cornering lamps: 88/98 ($57). Power astroroof w/sliding glass panel: Cutlass/88/98/Toro ($875-$1125). Removable glass roof panels: Cutlass ($790). Glass panel sunroof: Omega/Ciera ($275). Landau vinyl roof ($195-$225). Full vinyl roof: Omega/Ciera/88/98 ($140-$180). Rear-facing third seat: Custom Cruiser ($215).

HISTORY: Introduced: September 24, 1981 except Omega, December 12, 1981; Cutlass Ciera, January 14, 1982; and Firenza, March 4, 1982. Model year production: 789,454. Calendar year production (U.S.): 759,637. Calendar year sales by U.S. dealers: 799,585. Model year sales by U.S. dealers: 759,000.

Historical Footnotes: The year began with more price leaps. Sales slipped for the 1982 model year, even below the depressed 1980 level. Only 88 and 98 sold better than in 1981, and not by much.

1983 OLDSMOBILE

For later enthusiasts, if not for the ordinary buyer at the time, the biggest Oldsmobile news of 1983 had to be the reappearance of a Hurst/Olds option on a Cutlass coupe. All told, the lineup consisted of 30 models, including two new Firenza wagons. Four special appearance options also were available. A new 1.8-liter OHC four (with new five-speed manual shift) became available for Firenza, which otherwise had a standard 2.0-liter with four-speed manual. Both could have automatic. The 260 cu. in. (4.3-liter) gas V-8 offered in 1982 on Cutlass Supreme and 88 was dropped. Four-speed automatic transmissions expanded in usage, becoming available on Cutlass Ciera with a 3.0-liter V-6 or 4.3 diesel V-6 after mid-year. Three-speed automatic with diesel engine was dropped for Custom Cruiser and 98, making four-speed automatic standard in all full-size wagons and the 98. Mechanical changes to cut weight included a smaller alternator with plastic fan on diesels and the 5.0-liter gas V-8, and a stainless steel exhaust manifold and aluminum water pump on the transverse-mounted V-6 diesel.

1983 Firenza hatchback coupe (O)

FIRENZA — SERIES 3J — FOUR — Appearance changed little in Firenza's second season. The five-passenger, front-wheel drive Jbody subcompact came in six models, including two new wagons: Cruiser and LX Cruiser. Standard wagon equipment included a tailgate-ajar warning lamp. Wagon options included rear wiper/washer, two-tone paint, simulated woodgrain, and accent stripe. All Firenzas had a standard floor console and reclining front bucket seats, as well as a fold-down rear seat. Split-folding rear seats were available in coupe or wagon. Standard seat trim was vinyl or cloth, with deluxe trim available in velour. New base engine was a 122 cu. in. (2.0-liter) four with TBI, with four-speed manual transmission. It was actually the original 1.8-liter powerplant from Chevrolet, but stroked a bit to reach the larger displacement. Five-speed manual and three-speed automatic were available. Optional engine: the new 1.8-liter OHC four with fuel injection, from GM of Brazil, with either automatic or five-speed. Firenza equipment included four-speed manual transaxle, power brakes, bumper moldings, sport console, side window defogger, wheel opening and belt reveal moldings, AM radio, and P175/80R13 glass-belted blackwalls. SX added a Rallye instrument cluster and Rallye trim wheels. SX and LS (and Cruiser Brougham) included power steering, velour reclining front bucket seats, rocker panel moldings, and color-keyed mirrors (driver's remote).

OMEGA — SERIES 3X — FOUR/V-6 — A tighter crosshatch pattern (6 x 12 hole arrangement) replaced the former looser design on Omega's eggcrate grille, but otherwise appearance was similar to 1982. Aerodynamic patch mirrors, with housings faired into the door window surrounds, replaced the usual chrome mirrors. The standard driver's mirror was black; optional dual mirrors were body-color. Rear-end appearance was the same as 1982. Four models were offered: coupe and sedan, in base or Brougham trim. Inside was a new two-tone instrument panel. Brushed pewter or brushed bronze complemented the interior color. New side-window defoggers went in the radio speaker grilles and front defroster grilles. A locker headlamp control replaced the former push-pull switch, and a headlamp-on warning was standard. Standard bench seats now had low backs and separate headrests, and a fold-down armrest. Base engine was the 151 cu. in. (2.5-liter) four with standard four-speed manual or optional automatic. Optional: a 173 cu. in. (2.8-liter) V-6, manual or automatic shift. A high-output 2.8 V-6 was available with the ES option, expected to hit 60 in about 11 seconds. The high-output engine could have a four-speed manual

1983 Omega coupe (AA)

transmission, for a little extra swiftness. An ES or ESC (European Sport Coupe) appearance package added a "continental" look with blacked-out grille; wraparound bumpers with integral scoop; and black headlamp bezels, taillamp bezels, door frames, quarter window and rocker panel moldings. The package also included a firm ride/handling package, custom sport steering wheel, styled polycast wheels with trim rings, and blackwall tires.

1983 Cutlass Ciera sedan (AA)

CUTLASS CIERA — SERIES 3A — FOUR/V-6 — Appearance of the front-drive mid-size, introduced in early 1982, was similar this year except for a revised rear-end panel molding and taillamp treatment. Coupe and sedan bodies were offered, in LS and Brougham series. The former base models were dropped. New optional electro-luminescent opera lamps were available on either coupe or sedan. An optional console now included a coin holder and T-shifter lever. An electronic instrument cluster was available (Oldsmobile's first). It included a digital speedometer, bar-graph fuel and temperature gauges, low fuel indicator, trip odometer, and English/metric switch. Base engine was the 151 cu. in. (2.5-liter) four with automatic. Optional: a 181 cu. in. (3.0-liter) V-6 or 4.3-liter diesel V-6. Optional engines came with three- or four-speed automatic (the latter available later in the model year). Cutlass Ciera offered an ES package, similar to Omega's, on any model. It included blacked-out grille bars, headlamp housings and rear-end treatment, as well as black bumper rub strips and bodyside moldings. Oversize SBR blackwall tires were used, with specially-designed wheel covers. Reclining bucket seats, console with floor shifter, sport steering and gauge package with tachometer were standard. So was an F41 firm ride/handling suspension package. The ES package came in five body colors.

1983 Cutlass Supreme coupe (O)

CUTLASS SUPREME — SERIES 3G — V-6/V-8 — Changes on the mid-size rear-drive Cutlass focused on the grille, which, as usual, differed from model to model. Coupes had new sloping-forward rectangular-patterned grilles with bright vertical bars and recessed horizontal bars. The grille followed the sharply-split angle of the front panel, which contained an identification nameplate below the left headlamp. Sedans and wagons had a new upright square-pattern grille, and their rectangular headlamp framing extended outward to meet wraparound marker lenses. Coupes had no such side markers. Six models were offered: Supreme and Supreme Brougham coupe and sedan, Calais coupe, and Cutlass Cruiser wagon. Calais had a unique look with black headlamp doors, amber parking lamp lenses, and standard paint striping. Optional Calais bodyside moldings were black. Base engine on Supreme and Cruiser was the 231 cu. in. (3.8-liter) V-6, with either a 307 cu. in. (5.0-liter) gas V-8 optional. Supreme coupes and sedans could also get the 4.3-liter diesel V-6. All models had a three-speed automatic transmission. The 260 cu. in. gas V-8 was dropped. Cutlass Supreme standard equipment included automatic transmission, power brakes and steering, bright wheel covers, P195/75R14 blackwall SBR tires, bumper rub strips with integral guards, and cloth or vinyl custom sport bench seat with fold-down center armrest. Moldings went at wheel openings, rocker panels, roof drip and hood center. Supreme Brougham added a convenience group, velour divided front seat, wide door/fender moldings, and woodgrain dash. Calais came with front

1983 Hurst/Olds 15th Anniversary coupe (O)

and rear stabilizer bars, bodyside accent stripes, color-keyed Super Stock wheels, sport mirrors (left remote), halogen headlamps, sport console with floor shift lever, and contour reclining front bucket seats. Saving the best for last, about 2,500 Hurst/Olds options were produced on Cutlass Calais coupe bodies, painted black/silver. Red and silver stripes went on upper bodysides and the front-end panel. A specially-tuned 307 cu. in. (5.0-liter-V-8) was rated at 180 horsepower, producing 245 lbs.-ft. of torque. It had a dual-snorkel air cleaner with chrome cover, special 70-degree secondary air valve travel, and dual exhausts. Four-speed automatic with special shift calibration and torque converter ratio, plus a Hurst "Lightning Rod" shifter, fed a 3.73:1 rear axle. The grille was black/argent. Shadow-lettered Hurst/Olds decals decorated doors and decklid. Sail panels and dash carried a 15th anniversary Hurst/Olds medallion. 15 in. chrome/argent wheels held Goodyear Eagle GT tires. Inside extras included reclining bucket seats, quartz clock, tachometer. Also on Hurst/Olds: air conditioning with wide-open-throttle lockout, front lower air dam, decklid spoiler, and hood scoop. Hurst/Olds, according to the factory, could manage 0-60 MPH in 8.5 seconds.

DELTA 88 — SERIES 3B — V-6/V-8 — Hardly a year went by without a grille change on most Oldsmobile models, and that was the extent of the change for 88. The new one consisted of horizontal bars divided into three sections on each side of the traditional wide divider. Six models were offered: base sedan, Royale coupe and sedan, and Royale Brougham coupe and sedan. Base engine was the 231 cu. in. (3.8-liter) V-6, with optional 307 cu. in. (5.0- liter) gas V-8 or 5.7 diesel. Both gas and diesel V-8s could have either three- or four-speed automatic. Base 88 standard equipment included power steering and brakes, driver's remote mirror, bumper guards and rub strips, lighter, P205/75R15 blackwall SBR tires, and compact spare tire. Bodies held bright rocker panel, wheel opening and roof drip moldings. Royale added a velour custom sport bench seat with center armrest and color-keyed bodyside moldings. Brougham included a divided velour bench seat, belt reveal molding, convenience group, and opera lamps (on coupe).

CUSTOM CRUISER — SERIES 3B — V-8 — The full-size wagon was similar to Ninety-Eight, but wore its own grille with 3 x 3 arrangement of segments on each side, and horizontal strips within each segment. Custom Cruiser had a standard 307 cu. in. (5.0-liter) V-8 with four- speed automatic.

1983 Ninety-Eight Regency Brougham coupe (AA)

NINETY-EIGHT REGENCY — SERIES 3C — V-6/V-8 — This year's Ninety-Eight grille had a tighter crosshatch pattern but the traditional Olds look, not terribly different from 1982. The nameplate was now on the left (driver's) side of the grille, not above it. Three models were offered: Regency coupe and sedan, and Regency Brougham sedan. Base engine was the 252 cu. in. (4.1-liter) V-6 with four-speed overdrive automatic. Optional: a 307 cu. in. (5.0-liter) gas V-8 or 5.7-liter diesel V-8. Four-speed automatic was standard with both V-8s. Standard Ninety-Eight equipment included power brakes and steering, tinted glass, Four Season air conditioner, bumper guards and impact strips, digital clock, power windows and door locks, rear fender skirt, dual remote-control mirrors, P215/75R15 whitewalls, and compact spare tire. A divided front seat had dual controls, velour upholstery and two-way power driver's side. Regency Brougham added a fully padded vinyl roof, tilt steering, locking wire wheel covers, lower bodyside moldings, and halogen high-beam headlamps, and cornering lamps.

TORONADO — SERIES 3E — V-6/V-8 — Engine selection on the personal-luxury front-drive coupe was the same as Ninety-Eight. Essentially a carryover, Toro changed a bit at the grille. The panel above the full- width grille added a center emblem and lost its nameplate (which moved onto the grille itself). a new optional sound system from Delco/Bose, rated 100 watts, included an electronic-tuning radio/cassette player with Dolby noise reduction, dynamic noise reduction, and custom-equalized sound. Toronado standard equipment included the 252 cu. in. (4.1-liter) V-6 with four-speed

1983 Toronado Brougham coupe (AA)

overdrive automatic, power steering and brakes, AM/FM electronic-tuning stereo radio, speed control (with resume feature), tilt steering wheel, power windows, Four Season air conditioning, power antenna (in front fender), and digital clock. Also standard: power door locks, side window defoggers, automatic leveling, dual remote-control mirrors, and P205/75R15 steel-belted radial whitewalls.

I.D. DATA: Oldsmobile's 17-symbol Vehicle Identification Number (VIN) again was located on the upper left surface of the instrument panel, visible through the windshield. The first three symbols ('1G3') indicate Oldsmobile division. Symbol four denotes restraint type: 'A' manual (active) belts. Symbol five is car line/series: 'C' Firenza; 'D' Firenza SX/LX; 'B' Omega; 'E' Omega Brougham; 'J' Cutlass Ciera LS; ''M' Cutlass Ciera Brougham; 'R' Cutlass Supreme; 'M' Cutlass Supreme Brougham; 'K' Cutlass Calais; 'H' Cutlass Cruiser; 'L' Delta 88; 'N' Delta 88 Royale; 'Y' Delta 88 Royale Brougham; 'P' Custom Cruiser; 'X' Ninety-Eight Regency; 'W' Ninety-Eight Regency Brougham; 'Z' Toronado Brougham. Next come two digits that denote body type: '27' 2dr. coupe; '37' 2dr. coupe; '47' 2dr. coupe; '57' 2dr. coupe; '77' 2dr. coupe; '19' 4dr. sedan; '69' 4dr. 4window notch sedan; '35' 4dr. 2seat wagon. Symbol eight is a letter for engine code: '0' L4112 Fl; 'P' L4121 Fl; 'R' L4151 Fl; 'X' V6173 2Bbl.; 'Z' H.O. V6173 2Bbl.; 'E' V6181 2Bbl.; 'A' V6231 2Bbl.; '4' V6252 4Bbl.; 'T' or 'V' diesel V6262; 'Y' V8307 4Bbl.; '9' Hurst/Olds V8307 4Bbl.; 'N' diesel V8350. Next comes a check digit, followed by a code for model year: ('D' 1983). Symbol eleven is the assembly plant code: '2' Ste. Therese, Quebec (Canada); 'D' Doraville, Georgia; 'M' Lansing, Mich.; 'W' Willow Run, Mich.; 'X' Fairfax, Kansas; 'E' Linden, New Jersey; 'K' Leeds, Missouri. The final six digits are the sequential serial number, starting with 300,001 (except 88/98 built at Lansing, 700,001). Engine numbers were stamped on the front of the right rocker cover, or top of left cover (Buick-built engines), on label at front or rear of right rocker cover (Chevrolet V-6), or on the left rocker cover (Oldsmobile engines). Four- cylinder engine numbers were on a pad at left or right front of block. A body number plate on the upper right cowl identified model year, series, style, body assembly plant, body number, trim combination, modular seat code, paint code, date built code, and option codes.

FIRENZA (FOUR)

Model Number	Body/Style Number	Body Type & Seating	Factory Price	Shipping Weight	Production Total
3J	C77	2-dr. S cpe-5P	7007	2374	8,208
3J	C69	4-dr. S sed-5P	7094	2353	11,278
3J	D77	2-dr. SX cpe-5P	7750	2410	3,767
3J	D69	4-dr. LX sed-5P	7646	2372	5,067

FIRENZA CRUISER (FOUR)

3J	C35	4-dr. Sta Wag-5P	7314	2429	7,460
3J	D35	4-dr. LX Wag-5P	7866	2453	4,972

OMEGA (FOUR/V-6)

3X	B37	2-dr. Cpe-5P	7478/7628	2423/2487	6,448
3X	B69	4-dr. Sed-5P	7676/7826	2461/2533	24,287

OMEGA BROUGHAM (FOUR/V-6)

3X	E37	2-dr. Cpe-5P	7767/7917	2454/2518	5,177
3X	E69	4-dr. Sed-5P	7948/8098	2486/2558	18,014

CUTLASS CIERA LS (FOUR/V-6)

3A	J27	2-dr. Cpe-5P	8703/8853	2596/2698	12,612
3A	J19	4-dr. Sed-5P	8892/9042	2630/2733	66,731

CUTLASS CIERA BROUGHAM (FOUR/V-6)

3A	M27	2-dr. Cpe-5P	9183/9333	2621/2723	17,088
3A	M19	4-dr. Sed-5P	9385/9535	2655/2758	73,219

CUTLASS SUPREME (V-6/V-8)

3G	R47	2-dr. Cpe-6P	8950/9175	3155/3339	107,946
3G	R69	4-dr. Sed-6P	9103/9328	3196/3380	56,347

CUTLASS SUPREME BROUGHAM (V-6/V-8)

3G	M47	2-dr. Cpe-6P	9589/9814	3192/3376	60,025
3G	M69	4-dr. Sed-6P	9719/9944	3230/3414	28,451

CUTLASS CALAIS (V-6/V-8)

3G	K47	2-dr. Cpe-5P	9848/10073	3237/3421	19,660

CUTLASS CRUISER (V-6/V-8)

3G	H35	4-dr. Sta Wag-6P	9381/9606	3342/3537	22,037

DELTA 88 (V-6/V-8)

3B	L69	4-dr. Sed-6P	9084/9309	3426/3537	8,297

DELTA 88 ROYALE (V-6/V-8)

3B	N37	2-dr. Cpe-6P	9202/9427	3403/3511	54,771
3B	N69	4-dr. Sed-6P	9363/9588	3466/3623	132,683

DELTA 88 ROYALE BROUGHAM (V-6/V-8)

3B	Y37	2-dr. Cpe-6P	9671/9896	3428/3539	Note 1
3B	Y69	4-dr. Sed-6P	9762/9987	3466/3648	Note 1

Note 1: Production included in 88 Royale totals above.

CUSTOM CRUISER (V-8)

3B	P35	4-dr. Sta Wag-6P	10083	3932	25,243

NINETY-EIGHT REGENCY (V-6/V-8)

3C	X37	2-dr. Cpe-6P	12943/13018	3655/3814	13,816
3C	X69	4-dr. Sedan-6P	13120/13195	3708/3867	105,948
3C	W69	4-dr. Brghm-6P	14170/14245	3748/3907	Note 2

Note 2: Production included in basic sedan total.

TORONADO BROUGHAM (V-6/V-8)

3E	Z57	2-dr. Cpe-5P	15252/15327	3593/3758	39,605

FACTORY PRICE AND WEIGHT NOTE: Prices and weights to left of slash are for six-cylinder, to right for V-8 engine except Omega/Ciera, to left for four-cylinder and to right for V-6.

ENGINE DATA: BASE FOUR (Firenza): Inline, overhead-valve four-cylinder. Cast iron block and head. Displacement: 121 cu. in. (2.0 liters). Bore & stroke: 3.50 x 3.14 in. Compression ratio: 9.3:1. Brake horsepower: 86 at 4900 R.P.M. Torque: 110 lbs.ft. at 3000 R.P.M. Five main bearings. Hydraulic valve lifters. Electronic fuel injection. VIN Code: P. **OPTIONAL FOUR (Firenza):** Inline, overhead-cam four-cylinder. Cast iron block and head. Displacement: 112 cu. in. (1.8 liters). Bore & stroke: 3.34 x 3.11 in. Compression ratio: 9.0:1. Brake horsepower: 84 at 5200 R.P.M. Torque: 102 lbs.ft. at 2800 R.P.M. Five main bearings. Hydraulic valve lifters. Electronic fuel injection. VIN Code: O. **BASE FOUR (Omega, Cutlass Ciera):** Inline, overhead-valve four-cylinder. Cast iron block and head. Displacement: 151 cu. in. (2.5 liters). Bore & stroke: 4.00 x 3.00 in. Compression ratio: 8.2:1. Brake horsepower: 90 at 4000 R.P.M. Torque: 134 lbs.ft. at 2400 R.P.M. Five main bearings. Hydraulic valve lifters. Fuel injection (TBI). Pontiac-built. VIN Code: R. **OPTIONAL V-6 (Omega):** 60-degree, overhead-valve V-6. Cast iron block and aluminum head. Displacement: 173 cu. in. (2.8 liters). Bore & stroke: 3.50 x 3.00 in. Compression ratio: 8.5:1. Brake horsepower: 112 at 4800 R.P.M. Torque: 145 lbs.ft. at 2100 R.P.M. Four main bearings. Hydraulic valve lifters. Carburetor: 2Bbl. Rochester E2SE. Chevrolet-built. VIN Code: X. **OPTIONAL V-6 (Omega):** High-output version of 173 cu. in. V-6. Horsepower: 130 at 5400 R.P.M. Torque: 145 lbs.ft. at 2400 R.P.M. VIN Code: Z. **OPTIONAL V-6 (Cutlass Ciera):** 90-degree, overhead-valve V-6. Cast iron block and head. Displacement: 181 cu. in. (3.0 liters). Bore & stroke: 3.80 x 2.66 in. Compression ratio: 8.45:1. Brake horsepower: 110 at 4800 R.P.M. Torque: 145 lbs.ft. at 2000 R.P.M. Four main bearings. Hydraulic valve lifters. Carburetor: 2Bbl. Rochester E2ME. VIN Code: E. **BASE V-6 (Cutlass Supreme, Delta 88):** 90-degree, overhead-valve V-6. Cast iron block and head. Displacement: 231 cu. in. (3.8 liters). Bore & stroke: 3.80 x 3.40 in. Compression ratio: 8.0:1. Brake horsepower: 110 at 3800 R.P.M. Torque: 190 lbs.ft. at 1600 R.P.M. Four main bearings. Carburetor: 2Bbl. Rochester. Buick-built. VIN Code: A. **BASE V-6 (98, Toronado):** 90-degree, overhead-valve V-6. Cast iron block and head. Displacement: 252 cu. in. (4.1 liters). Bore & stroke: 3.96 x 3.40 in. Compression ratio: 8.0:1. Brake horsepower: 125 at 4000 R.P.M. Torque: 205 lbs.ft. at 2000 R.P.M. Four main bearings. Hydraulic valve lifters. Carburetor: 4Bbl. Rochester. Buick-built. VIN Code: 4. **DIESEL V-6 (Cutlass Ciera, Cutlass Supreme):** 90-degree, overhead valve V-8. Cast iron block and head. Displacement: 262 cu. in. (4.3 liters). Bore & stroke: 4.06 x 3.38 in. Compression ratio: 22.5:1. Brake horsepower: 85 at 3600 R.P.M. Torque: 165 lbs.ft. at 1600 R.P.M. Five main bearings. Hydraulic valve lifters. Fuel injection. VIN Code: T or V. **BASE V-8 (Custom Cruiser); OPTIONAL (Cutlass Supreme, Delta 88, 98, Toronado):** 90-degree, overhead valve V-8. Cast iron block and head. Displacement: 307 cu. in. (5.0 liters). Bore & stroke: 3.80 x 3.38 in. Compression ratio: 8.0:1. Brake horsepower: 140 at 3600 R.P.M. Torque: 240 lbs.ft. at 1600 R.P.M. Five main bearings. Hydraulic valve lifters. Carburetor: 4Bbl. VIN Code: Y. **OPTIONAL HURST/OLDS V-8 (Cutlass Calais):** Same as 307 cu. in. V-8 above, but Compression ratio: 8.0:1. Horsepower: 180 at 4000 R.P.M. Torque: 245 lbs.ft. at 3200 R.P.M. VIN Code: 9. **DIESEL V-8 (Cutlass Supreme, Delta 88, 98, Custom Cruiser, Toronado):** 90-degree, overhead valve V-8. Cast iron block and head. Displacement: 350 cu. in. (5.7 liters). Bore & stroke: 4.06 x 3.39 in. Compression ratio: 22.5:1. Brake horsepower: 105 at 3200 R.P.M. Torque: 200 lbs.ft. at 1600 R.P.M. Five main bearings. Hydraulic valve lifters. Fuel injection. VIN Code: N.

CHASSIS DATA: Wheelbase: (Firenza) 101.2 in.; (Omega/Ciera) 104.9 in.; (Cutlass) 108.1 in.; (Delta 88) 116.0 in.; (98) 119.0 in.; (Custom Crsr) 116.0 in.; (Toronado) 114.0 in. Overall Length: (Firenza cpe) 174.3 in.; (Firenza sed) 176.2 in.; (Firenza wag) 175.7 in.; (Omega) 182.8 in.; (Ciera) 188.4 in.; (Cutlass Supreme) 200.0-200.4 in.; (Cutlass wag) 200.4 in.; (Delta 88) 218.1 in.; (98) 221.1 in.; (Custom Crsr) 220.3 in.; (Toro) 206.0 in. Height: (Firenza cpe) 50.8 in.; (Firenza sed) 52.8 in.; (Firenza wag) 53.9 in.; (Omega) 54.8 in.; (Ciera) 55.1 in.; (Cutlass Supreme cpe) 55.6 in.; (Cutlass Supreme sed) 56.6 in.; (Cutlass wag) 56.9 in.; (Delta 88 cpe) 56.8 in.; (Delta 88 sed) 57.5 in.; (98) 58.0 in.; (Custom Crsr) 59.1 in.; (Toro) 55.9 in. Width: (Firenza) 65.0 in.; (Omega) 69.8 in.; (Ciera) 69.5 in.; (Cutlass cpe) 71.6 in.; (Cutlass sed) 71.9 in.; (Cutlass wag) 71.8 in.; (Delta 88) 76.3 in.; (98) 76.3 in.; (Custom Crsr) 79.8 in.; (Toro) 71.4 in. Front Tread: (Firenza) 55.4 in.; (Omega/Ciera) 58.7 in.; (Cutlass) 58.5 in.; (Delta 88/98) 61.7 in.; (Custom Crsr) 62.1 in.; (Toro) 59.3 in. Rear Tread: (Firenza) 55.2 in.; (Omega/Ciera) 57.0 in.; (Cutlass) 57.7 in.; (Delta 88/98) 60.7 in.; (Custom Crsr) 64.1 in.; (Toro) 60.0 in. Standard Tires: (Firenza) P175/80R13; (Omega/Ciera) P185/80R13; (Cutlass Supreme) P195/75R14; (Delta 88) P205/75R15; (98) P215/75R15; (Custom Crsr) P225/75R15; (Toronado) P205/75R15.

TECHNICAL: Transmission: Four-speed floor shift standard on Firenza/Omega. Gear ratios: (1st) 3.53:1; (2nd) 1.95:1; (3rd) 1.24:1; (4th) 0.73:1 or 0.81:1; (Rev) 3.42:1 or 3.50:1. Five- speed manual trans. optional on Firenza: (1st) 3.91 in.; (2nd) 2.15:1; (3rd) 1.45:1; (4th) 1.03:1; (5th) 0.74:1; (Rev) 3.50:1. Three-speed Turbo Hydra-matic standard on Cutlass/Ciera/88. Four-speed automatic overdrive standard on Custom Cruiser/98/Toronado. Standard final drive ratio: (Firenza) 4.10:1 w/4spd, 3.83:1 w/5spd, 3.18:1 w/auto.; (Omega) 3.32:1 w/4spd, 2.39:1 w/auto.; (Omega V-6) 3.32:1 w/4spd, 2.53:1 w/auto.; (Omega H.O. V-6) 3.65:1 w/4spd, 3.06:1 w/auto.; (Ciera) 2.39:1 w/four, 2.53:1 w/V-6; (Cutlass) 2.41:1 except 2.29:1 w/diesel V-8, 3.73:1 with Hurst/Olds option; (Cutlass Cruiser) 2.73:1 w/V-6, 2.29:1 w/V8307 or diesel; (Delta 88) 2.73:1 w/V-6, 2.41:1 w/V-8; (98) 3.23:1 w/V-6, 2.73:1 w/V8307, 2.93:1 w/diesel; (Toronado) 3.00:1 w/V-6, 2.73:1 w/V-8, 2.93:1 w/diesel. Steering: (Firenza/Omega/Ciera) rack and pinion; (others) recirculating ball. Front Suspension: (Firenza/Omega/Ciera) MacPherson struts w/coil springs, lower control arms and anti-sway bar; (Toronado) torsion bars w/anti-sway bar; (others) coil springs with upper/lower control arms and anti-sway bar. Rear Suspension: (Firenza) beam axle w/coil springs, trailing arms and anti-sway bar; (Omega/Ciera) beam axle with integral anti-sway, coil springs and Panhard rod; (Toronado) independent with coil springs, semi-trailing arms, anti-sway bar and automatic leveling; (others) rigid axle w/coil springs, lower trailing radius arms and upper torque arms (four-link). Brakes: Front disc, rear drum. Ignition: Electronic. Body construction: (Firenza/Omega/Ciera) unibody; (others) separate body and frame. Fuel tank: (Firenza) 14 gal.; (Omega) 14.6 gal.; (Ciera) 15.7 gal.; (Cutlass) 18.1 gal.; (Delta 88) 25 gal.; (98) 25 gal.; (Custom Crsr wag) 22 gal.; (Toronado) 21.1 gal.

DRIVETRAIN OPTIONS: Engines: 112 cu. in. four: Firenza ($50). 173 cu. in. V-6: Omega ($150). 181 cu. in. V-6: Ciera ($150). Diesel 262 cu. in. V-6: Cutlass/Ciera ($500). 307 cu. in. 4Bbl. V-8: Cutlass/88 ($75); 98/Toro ($75). Diesel 350 cu. in. V-8: Cutlass/88/98/Custom Crsr/Toronado ($700). Transmission/Differential: Five-speed manual trans.: Firenza ($395). Turbo Hydra-matic: Firenza ($395); Omega ($425). Four- speed overdrive auto.: 88 ($175). Limited-slip differential: Cutlass/88/98 ($95). Limited-slip differential w/air shocks: Hurst/Olds Calais ($159). Steering/Suspension: Power steering: base Firenza ($199). Firm ride/handling pkg. ($30-$49). Automatic load leveling: Ciera/88/98 ($165). Other: High-capacity cooling ($40-$70). High-capacity radiator ($30) exc. Firenza/Omega. H.D. battery ($25) exc. diesel ($50). Engine block heater ($19). Block/fuel line heater ($49) exc. Firenza/Omega. Trailer wiring ($30) exc. Firenza/Omega. California emissions ($75) exc. diesel ($215).

OPTION PACKAGES: Omega ESC pkg.: Brghm coupe ($851-$1151). Omega ES pkg.: Brghm coupe ($896-$1196). Ciera ES pkg. ($752-$897). Hurst/Olds pkg.: Calais coupe ($1997).

MAJOR CONVENIENCE/APPEARANCE OPTIONS: Four Season air conditioner ($625-$725). Tempmatic air conditioning: 88 ($780); 98/Toro ($55). Cruise control ($170). Power seat ($185-$210). Power windows ($180-$255). Twilight sentinel: 98/Toro ($60). Cornering lamps: 88/98 ($60). Power astroroof w/sliding glass panel: Cutlass/88/98/Toro ($895- $1195). Removable glass roof panels: Cutlass ($825). Glass panel sunroof: Firenza/Omega/Ciera ($295). Landau vinyl roof ($215-$240). Full vinyl roof: Omega/Ciera/Cutlass/88 ($155- $180). Rear-facing third seat: Custom Cruiser ($220).

HISTORY: Introduced: September 23, 1982. Model year production: 939,157. Calendar year production (U.S.): 1,050,846. Calendar year sales by U.S. dealers: 1,007,559. Model year sales by U.S. dealers: 955,243.

Historical Footnotes: The first Hurst/Olds model had appeared 15 years earlier, in 1968. This version would return for 1984.

1984 OLDSMOBILE

ES models were promoted this year for their styling and handling. One more ES option was offered this year: on Firenza sedan. Toronado had a new Caliente option, and Cutlass Ciera had a Holiday coupe. A new barometric sensor in the 5.0-liter V-8 altered spark advance, air/fuel ratio and EGR calibration. A similar sensor in diesels adjusted injection timing and EGR calibration. Other improvements also were made to diesels, but that seemed a losing battle as their popularity had dwindled. Oldsmobile still pushed the the 4.3- liter diesel, though, for its allegedly quiet running and economy. Diesel V-8s were no longer available in California, but the V-6 was.

1984 Firenza GT hatchback coupe (AA)

335

FIRENZA — SERIES 3J — FOUR — A new front-end look, intended to add more Olds "character," made air intake strips below the bumper full-width, stretching all the way across. A new color-matched grille, urethane-molded, could deform in a minor impact, yet return to original shape. Wraparound side marker lenses now connected to the headlamp frames. Firenza was promoted toward younger customers for its sporty, fun-to-drive qualities. Manual-shift models included an upshift indicator light, to help drivers attain maximum gas mileage. Wagons added an optional cargo area cover that could store behind the back seat. Six models were offered: S hatchback coupe, base four-door sedan, SX hatchback coupe, LX four-door sedan, Cruiser wagon, and LX Cruiser wagon. SX and LX could be identified by their wide bumper fascia molding. The S hatchback coupe could get a GT package (RPO code WJ4), of which 2,312 were produced. A total of 1,125 ES packages (code W47) were installed on base sedans, 1,008 on LX sedans. Base engine was Chevrolet's 2.0-liter four; optional, a 1.8-liter OHC four from GM of Brazil. Firenza ES offered "international" styling with blacked-out moldings and minimal brightwork. Black appliques went on the sail panel, with black sport mirrors. Wide black bumper fascia moldings (front/rear) and black rocker panel moldings were used. Polycast wheels were offered. Three ES body colors were offered: silver, light royal blue, or light maple metallic. GT showed the same updated front end as other Firenzas. This year, GT included not only the spectra red and silver paint scheme offered in 1983, but also a white and silver version. Polycast sport wheels and black accents were included. Inside, GT's instrument panel was highlighted by red beading, which also accented the subtle checkered gray fabric seat inserts.

1984 Omega ES sedan (AA)

OMEGA — SERIES 3X — FOUR/V-6 — Changes were modest for the compact front-drive. A new flush-look bumper treatment this year was possible through use of thermoplastic olifin bumper end caps. Omega's new grille consisted of horizontal strips. Park/signal lamps were now vertical, mounted between the grille and headlamps. Manual-shift models included an upshift indicator light. New tread design on standard SBR all-season tires improved snow/wet traction, but kept noise down. Four models were available: base and Brougham, coupe and sedan. Engines were the same as 1983: base 151 cu. in. (2.5-liter) four; optional 2.8 V-6 (standard or high-output). Brougham sedans could have an ES package (RPO code W48), featuring an "international" theme similar to Firenza's. The revised grille had a blacked-out treatment. Three colors were available: silver, light royal blue, and light maple metallic. Only 224 of the ES packages were installed.

1984 Cutlass Ciera coupe (AA)

CUTLASS CIERA — SERIES 3A — FOUR/V-6 — Ciera gained a bit of an appearance update front and rear. This year's grille was similar to before, but the twin sections now consisted of thin vertical bars. Each model now had six-passenger capacity, with divided bench and custom bench seats. New 14 inch wheels had bigger standard tires. Coupes had a wide center pillar. Inside, a new center console contained a storage area under the armrest. An optional auto calculator could be installed in the console. Four-speed automatic was to become standard with the 231 cu. in. (3.8-liter) V-6 and optional with the V-6 diesel after start of production. This transmission was designed for transverse-mounted front-drives. It had an integral four- speed design, using two planetary gear sets instead of the usual three in rear-drives. Five models were offered: LS coupe and four-door sedan, Brougham coupe and sedan, and new Cruiser two-seat wagon. The new wagon actually had more cargo capacity than rear-drive Cutlass wagons, and could hold a 4 x 8 foot plywood sheet. The wide tailgate opened upward with one motion, and the back window was separately hinged. Wagon options included accent striping or two-tone paint, sunroof, simulated woodgrain trim, and roof rack. An optional rear-facing third seat gave eight-passenger capacity, including a rear-pillar assist handle. Wagons had working rear vent windows and a rear step pad. Coupes and sedans could have an ES package (RPO code W48) with larger 14 inch SBR BSW tires and a decklid luggage rack. ES also had black belt reveal and drip moldings, and black door handle accents. Brougham coupes could have a Holiday coupe package, which offered a unique profile with padded vinyl landau top and opera windows. The option was identified by special script and emblem on the sail panel. Opera lamps were available. Base engine was the 151 cu. in. (2.5-liter) four with automatic; optional, a 3.0-liter gas V-6 or 4.3-liter V-6. Four-speed automatic was available with either V-6. Newly optional this year: Buick's 3.8-liter V-6 with multi-port fuel injection.

CUTLASS SUPREME — SERIES 3G — V-6/V-8 — New grilles and revised taillamps were the most noticeable changes on rear-drive mid-size models. This year's coupe grille had a sweep-forward design similar to before, but with seven sections of vertical bars on each side of the divider. Sedan grilles had large holes in a 4 x 3 pattern, with the same headlamp design as 1983: quad headlamps meeting wraparound side marker lenses. All-season SBR tires had a new tread design. Joining the option list: chrome sport wheels. Five models were offered: Supreme and Brougham coupe and

1984 Cutlass Supreme coupe (AA)

four-door sedan, and Calais coupe (which could get the Hurst/Olds package). The Cutlass Cruiser wagon was dropped, since Cutlass Ciera now had a wagon. Four-speed overdrive automatic was available with all engines except the base 231 cu. in. (3.8-liter) V-6. A total of 3,500 Hurst/Olds limited-edition options (RPO code W40) were installed on Calais. Bodies were silver with black lower body paint, with red and black accent stripes on upper bodysides and the front-end panel. Silver, red and black accent stripes separated the two-tone paint, and also appeared on bumper rub strips. Hurst/Olds included a black front lower air dam, a hood scoop, and a silver decklid spoiler. The modified 5.0-liter V-8 had specific carburetion, a dual-snorkel, chrome-covered air cleaner, and low-restriction dual-outlet mufflers. The engine produced 180 horsepower at 4000 R.P.M., along with 245 lbs.-ft. of torque at 3200 R.P.M. Four-speed overdrive automatic was used, hooked to the Hurst Lightning Rod shifter, which allowed control of upshifts and downshifts. Hurst/Olds' firm ride/handling package included unequal-length front control arms with 1.25 inch diameter anti-sway bar. At the rear was a rigid axle with trailing links and 7/8 inch anti-sway bar. Superlift air shocks were used. Tires were 15 inch Goodyear Eagle GT, on chrome/argent wheels with red accent stripes.

1984 Eighty-Eight landau coupe (AA)

DELTA 88 — SERIES 3B — V-6/V-8 — Promoted as the best selling full-size domestic, and as a family car, Delta 88 sported a new grille (as usual) and restyled taillamps, but was otherwise little changed. Five models made the lineup: Royale and Royale Brougham coupe and sedan, plus the Custom Cruiser wagon (two-seat or optional rear-facing third seat). Base engine was the 231 cu. in. (3.8-liter) V-6. This year's grille sections contained short horizontal strips to form eight segments on each side. As before, the quad rectangular headlamps extended to meet wraparound side marker lenses, with park/signal lamps down in the bumper. Wraparound taillamps had vertical ribbings, divided into upper and lower segments.

1984 Ninety-Eight Regency Brougham sedan (AA)

NINETY-EIGHT REGENCY — SERIES 3C — V-8 — A tightly-patterned crosshatch grille was the major change for Ninety-Eight, along with new wire wheel cover designs and new bodyside moldings. Vertical taillamps held emblems on their lenses. Wide twin-section backup lamps were used. Models included the Regency coupe and sedan, and Regency Brougham sedan. The 4.1-liter V-6 was dropped, making the 307 cu. in. (5.0-liter) V-8 standard. No diesel V-8 was available in California.

TORONADO — SERIES 3E — V-6/V-8 — A new Caliente package was available for Toro customers who craved something different. Caliente had a padded landau roof and stainless steel crown molding, accented with Toronado emblem. Full-length, bright bodyside molding highlighted the car's feature line. Bodysides also held a wide, ridged lower molding. Standard equipment included dual electric remote mirrors, locking wire wheel covers, leather-wrapped sport steering wheel, and electronic instrument panel cluster. Leather seat trim was standard, sheepskin inserts optional. A total of 5,007 Caliente (RPO code WJ8) packages were installed. Toros in general had a revised front end. The new grille contained bright horizontal bars, with a color-coordinated band running the full width of the front end. Unlike former versions, park and turn signal lamps were exposed this year. Optional electronic instruments had blue fluorescent digital speed displays, plus bar graphs for fuel level and temperature. An Optional voice system warned of problems in overheating, low oil pressure and charging failures, and gave advice. Base engine was the 252 cu. in. (4.1-liter) V-6; optional, either a 307 cu. in. (5.0-liter) gas V-8 or 350 diesel V-8.

I.D. DATA: Oldsmobile's 17-symbol Vehicle Identification Number (VIN) again was located on the upper left surface of the instrument panel, visible through the windshield. The first three symbols ('1G3') indicate Oldsmobile division. Symbol four denotes restraint type: 'A' manual (active) belts. Symbol five is car line/series: 'C' Firenza; 'D' Firenza SX/LX; 'B' Omega; 'E' Omega Brougham; 'J' Cutlass Ciera LS; "M' Cutlass Ciera Brougham; 'J' Cutlass Ciera LS Cruiser; R' Cutlass Supreme; 'M' Cutlass Supreme Brougham ; 'K' Cutlass Calais; 'L' Delta 88; 'N' Delta 88 Royale; 'Y' Delta 88 Royale Brougham; 'V' Delta 88 Royale Brougham LS; 'P' Custom Cruiser; 'G' Ninety-Eight Regency; 'H' Ninety-Eight Regency Brougham; 'Z' Toronado Brougham. Next come two digits that denote body type: '27' 2dr. coupe; '37' 2dr. coupe; '47' 2dr. coupe; '57' 2dr. coupe; '77' 2dr. coupe; '19' 4dr. sedan; '69' 4dr. 4window notch sedan; '35' 4dr. 2seat wagon. Symbol eight is a letter for engine code: '0' L4112 FI; 'P' L4121 FI; 'R' L4151 FI; 'X' V6173 2Bbl.; 'Z' H.O. V6173 2Bbl.; 'E' V6181 2Bbl.; 'A' V6231 2Bbl.; '4' V6252 4Bbl.; 'T' or 'V' diesel V6262; 'Y' V8307 4Bbl.; '9' Hurst/Olds V8307 4Bbl.; 'N' diesel V8350. Next comes a check digit, followed by a code for model year: ('E' 1984). Symbol eleven is the assembly plant code: '2' Ste. Therese, Quebec (Canada); 'D' Doraville, Georgia; 'G' Framingham, Mass.; 'M' Lansing, Mich.; 'W' Willow Run, Mich.; 'X' Fairfax, Kansas; 'E' Linden, New Jersey; 'R' Arlington, Texas; 'K' Leeds, Missouri; and Detroit. The final six digits are the sequential serial number, starting with 300,001 (except 88/98 built at Lansing, 700,001). Engine numbers were stamped on the front of the right rocker cover, or top of left cover (Buick-built engines), on label at front or rear of right rocker cover (Chevrolet V-6), or on the left rocker cover (Oldsmobile engines). Four- cylinder engine numbers were on a pad at left or right front of block. A body number plate on the upper right cowl identified model year, series, style, body assembly plant, body number, trim combination, modular seat code, paint code, date built code, and option codes.

FIRENZA (FOUR)

Model Number	Body/Style Number	Body Type & Seating	Factory Price	Shipping Weight	Production Total
3J	C77	2-dr. S cpe-5P	7214	2390	13,811
3J	C69	4-dr. Sedan-5P	7301	2393	34,564
3J	D77	2-dr. SX cpe-5P	7957	2437	4,179
3J	D69	4-dr. LX sed-5P	7853	2438	11,761

FIRENZA CRUISER (FOUR)

3J	C35	4-dr. Sta Wag-5P	7521	2439	12,389
3J	D35	4-dr. LX Wag-5P	8073	2457	5,771

OMEGA (FOUR/V-6)

3X	B37	2-dr. Cpe-5P	7634/7884	2431/2503	5,242
3X	B69	4-dr. Sed-5P	7832/8082	2461/2540	21,571

OMEGA BROUGHAM (FOUR/V-6)

3X	E37	2-dr. Cpe-5P	7923/8173	2448/2520	5,870
3X	E69	4-dr. Sed-5P	8104/8354	2482/2561	20,303

CUTLASS CIERA LS (FOUR/V-6)

3A	J27	2-dr. Cpe-5P	9014/9264	2611/2714	14,887
3A	J19	4-dr. Sed-5P	9203/9453	2650/2753	99,182

CUTLASS CIERA BROUGHAM (FOUR/V-6)

3A	M27	2-dr. Cpe-5P	9519/9769	2637/2740	22,687
3A	M19	4-dr. Sed-5P	9721/9971	2676/2779	102,667

CUTLASS SUPREME (V-6/V-8)

3G	R47	2-dr. Cpe-6P	9376/9751	3133/3328	132,913
3G	R69	4-dr. Sed-6P	9529/9904	3184/3361	62,136

CUTLASS SUPREME BROUGHAM (V-6/V-8)

3G	M47	2-dr. Cpe-6P	10015/10390	3171/3366	87,207
3G	M69	4-dr. Sed-6P	10145/10520	3214/3391	37,406

CUTLASS CALAIS (V-6/V-8)

3G	K47	2-dr. Cpe-5P	10274/10649	3209/3404	24,893

Production Note: Cutlass Supreme and Calais totals include Canadian production for U.S. market.

CUTLASS CIERA LS CRUISER (FOUR/V-6)

3G	J35	4-dr. Sta Wag-5P	9551/9801	2824/2927	41,816

DELTA 88 ROYALE (V-6/V-8)

3B	N37	2-dr. Cpe-6P	9939/10314	3380/3566	23,387
3B	N69	4-dr. Sed-6P	10051/10426	3419/3605	87,993

DELTA 88 ROYALE BROUGHAM (V-6/V-8)

3B	Y37	2-dr. Cpe-6P	10408/10783	3413/3599	41,913
3B	Y69	4-dr. Sed-6P	10499/10874	3449/3635	89,450
3B	V69	4-dr. LS Sed-6P	13854/14229	N/A	17,064

CUSTOM CRUISER (V-8)

3B	P35	4-dr. Sta Wag-6P	10839	4033	34,061

NINETY-EIGHT REGENCY (V-8)

3C	G37	2-dr. Cpe-6P	13974	3829	7,855
3C	G69	4-dr. Sedan-6P	14151	3886	26,919
3C	H69	4-dr. Brghm-6P	15201	3937	42,059

TORONADO BROUGHAM (V-6/V-8)

3E	Z57	2-dr. Cpe-6P	16107/16332	3612/3795	48,100

FACTORY PRICE AND WEIGHT NOTE: Prices and weights to left of slash are for six-cylinder, to right for V-8 engine except Omega/Ciera, to left for four-cylinder and to right for V-6.

ENGINE DATA: BASE FOUR (Firenza): Inline, overhead-valve four-cylinder. Cast iron block and head. Displacement: 121 cu. in. (2.0 liters). Bore & stroke: 3.50 x 3.14 in. Compression ratio: 9.3:1. Brake horsepower: 88 at 4800 R.P.M. Torque: 110 lbs.ft. at 2400 R.P.M. Five main bearings. Hydraulic valve lifters. Electronic fuel injection. VIN Code: P. OPTIONAL FOUR (Firenza): Inline, overhead-cam four-cylinder. Cast iron block and head. Displacement: 112 cu. in. (1.8 liters). Bore & stroke: 3.34 x 3.11 in. Compression ratio: 9.0:1. Brake horsepower: 82 at 5200 R.P.M. Torque: 102 lbs.ft. at 2800 R.P.M. Five main bearings. Hydraulic valve lifters. Electronic fuel injection. VIN Code: O. BASE FOUR (Omega, Cutlass Ciera): Inline, overhead-valve four-cylinder. Cast iron block and head. Displacement: 151 cu. in. (2.5 liters). Bore & stroke: 4.00 x 3.00 in. Compression ratio: 8.2:1. Brake horsepower: 92 at 4000 R.P.M. Torque: 134 lbs.ft. at 2800 R.P.M. Five main bearings. Hydraulic valve lifters. Fuel injection (TBI). Pontiac-built. VIN Code: R. OPTIONAL V-6 (Omega): 60-degree, overhead-valve V-6. Cast iron block and aluminum head. Displacement: 173 cu. in. (2.8 liters). Bore & stroke: 3.50 x 3.00 in. Compression ratio: 8.5:1. Brake horsepower: 112 at 4800 R.P.M. Torque: 145 lbs.ft. at 2100 R.P.M. Four main bearings. Hydraulic valve lifters. Carburetor: 2Bbl. Chevrolet-built. VIN Code: X. OPTIONAL V-6 (Omega): High-output version of 173 cu. in. V-6 above Compression ratio: 8.9:1. Horsepower: 130 at 5400 R.P.M. Torque: 145 lbs.-ft. at 2400 R.P.M. VIN Code: Z. OPTIONAL V-6 (Cutlass Ciera): 90-degree, overhead-valve V-6. Cast iron block and head. Displacement: 181 cu. in. (3.0 liters). Bore & stroke: 3.80 x 2.66 in. Compression ratio: 8.4:1. Brake horsepower: 110 at 4800 R.P.M. Torque: 145 lbs.ft. at 2600 R.P.M. Four main bearings. Hydraulic valve lifters. Carburetor: 2Bbl. VIN Code: E. BASE V-6 (Cutlass Supreme, Delta 88): 90-degree, overhead-valve V-6. Cast iron block and head. Displacement: 231 cu. in. (3.8 liters). Bore & stroke: 3.80 x 3.40 in. Compression ratio: 8.0:1. Brake horsepower: 110 at 3800 R.P.M. Torque: 190 lbs.ft. at 1600 R.P.M. Four main bearings. Hydraulic valve lifters. Carburetor: 2Bbl. Buick- built. VIN Code: A. BASE V-6 (Toronado): 90-degree, overhead-valve V-6. Cast iron block and head. Displacement: 252 cu. in. (4.1 liters). Bore & stroke: 3.96 x 3.40 in. Compression ratio: 8.0:1. Brake horsepower: 125 at 4000 R.P.M. Torque: 205 lbs.ft. at 2000 R.P.M. Four main bearings. Hydraulic valve lifters. Carburetor: 4Bbl. Buick- built. VIN Code: 4. DIESEL V-6 (Cutlass Ciera, Cutlass Supreme): 90-degree, overhead valve V-8. Cast iron block and head. Displacement: 262 cu. in. (4.3 liters). Bore & stroke: 4.06 x 3.38 in. Compression ratio: 22.8:1. Brake horsepower: 85 at 3600 R.P.M. Torque: 165 lbs.ft. at 1600 R.P.M. Five main bearings. Hydraulic valve lifters. Fuel injection. VIN Code: T or V. BASE V-8 (Custom Cruiser); OPTIONAL (Cutlass Supreme, Delta 88, Toronado): 90-degree, overhead valve V-8. Cast iron block and head. Displacement: 307 cu. in. (5.0 liters). Bore & stroke: 3.80 x 3.38 in. Compression ratio: 8.0:1. Brake horsepower: 140 at 3600 R.P.M. Torque: 240 lbs.ft. at 1600 R.P.M. Five main earings. Hydraulic valve lifters. Carburetor: 4Bbl. Rochester. VIN Code: Y. OPTIONAL HURST/OLDS V-8 (Cutlass Calais): Same as 307 cu. in. V-8 above, but Compression ratio: 8.0:1. Horsepower: 180 at 4000 R.P.M. Torque: 245 lbs.-ft. at 3200 R.P.M. VIN Code: 9. DIESEL V-8 (Cutlass Supreme, Delta 88, 98, Custom Cruiser, Toronado): 90-degree, overhead valve V-8. Cast iron block and head. Displacement: 350 cu. in. (5.7 liters). Bore & stroke: 4.06 x 3.39 in. Compression ratio: 22.7:1. Brake horsepower: 105 at 3200 R.P.M. Torque: 200 lbs.ft. at 1600 R.P.M. Five main bearings. Hydraulic valve lifters. Fuel injection. VIN Code: N.

CHASSIS DATA: Wheelbase: (Firenza) 101.2 in.; (Omega/Ciera) 104.9 in.; (Cutlass) 108.1 in.; (Delta 88) 115.9 in.; (98) 119.0 in.; (Custom Crsr) 115.9 in.; (Toronado) 114.0 in. Overall Length: (Firenza cpe) 173.3 in.; (Firenza sed) 176.1 in.; (Firenza wag) N/A; (Omega) 182.8 in.; (Ciera) 188.4 in.; (Ciera wag) 191.0 in.; (Cutlass Supreme) 200.0-200.4 in.; (Delta 88) 218.1 in.; (98) 221.1 in.; (Custom Crsr) 220.3 in.; (Toro) 206.0 in. Height: (Firenza cpe) 51.1 in.; (Firenza sed) 53.7 in.; (Firenza wag) 55.2 in.; (Omega) 53.7 in.; (Ciera) 54.1 in.; (Cutlass Supreme cpe) 54.9 in.; (Cutlass Supreme sed) 55.9 in.; (Delta 88 cpe) 56.0 in.; (Delta 88 sed) 56.7 in.; (98) 57.2 in.; (Custom Crsr) 58.5 in.; (Toro) 54.6 in. Width: (Firenza) 65.0 in.; (Omega) 69.8 in.; (Ciera) 69.5 in.; (Cutlass cpe) 71.6; (Cutlass sed) 71.9 in.; (Delta 88) 76.3 in.; (98) 76.3 in.; (Custom Crsr) 79.8 in.; (Toro) 71.4 in. Front Tread: (Firenza) 55.3 in.; (Omega/Ciera) 58.7 in.; (Cutlass) 58.5 in.; (Delta 88/98) 61.7 in.; (Custom Crsr) 62.1 in.; (Toro) 59.3 in. Rear Tread: (Firenza) 55.1 in.; (Omega/Ciera) 57.0 in.; (Cutlass) 57.7 in.; (Delta 88/98) 60.7 in.; (Custom Crsr) 64.1 in.; (Toro) 60.0 in. Standard Tires: (Firenza) P175/80R13; (Omega) P185/80R13; (Ciera) P185/75R14; (Cutlass Supreme) P195/75R14; (Delta 88) P205/75R15; (98) P215/75R15; (Custom Crsr) P225/75R15; (Toronado) P205/75R15.

TECHNICAL: Transmission: Four-speed floor shift standard on Firenza/Omega. Gear ratios: (1st) 3.53:1; (2nd) 1.95:1; (3rd) 1.24:1; (4th) 0.73:1 or 0.81:1; (Rev) 3.42:1 or 3.50:1. Five- speed manual trans. optional on Firenza: (1st) 3.91 in.; (2nd) 2.15:1; (3rd) 1.45:1; (4th) 1.03:1; (5th) 0.74:1; (Rev) 3.50:1. Three-speed Turbo Hydra-matic standard on Cutlass/Ciera/88. Four-speed automatic overdrive standard on Custom Cruiser/98/Toronado. Standard final drive ratio: (Firenza) 4.10:1 w/4spd, 3.45:1 w/5spd, 3.18:1 w/auto.; (Omega) 3.32:1 w/4spd, 2.39:1 w/auto.; (Omega V-6) 3.32:1 w/4spd, 2.53:1 w/auto.; (Omega H.O. V-6) 3.65:1 w/4spd, 3.33:1 w/auto.; (Ciera) 2.84:1 w/four, 2.53:1 w/V-6, 3.06:1 or 2.84:1 w/V-6 and 4spd auto.; (Cutlass) 2.41:1 except 2.56:1 w/V-8 and 4spd auto., 3.73:1 with Hurst/Olds option; (Delta 88) 2.73:1 w/V-6, 2.41:1 w/V-8; (98) 2.73:1 exc. 2.93:1 w/diesel; (Toronado) 3.15:1 w/V-6, 2.73:1 w/V-8, 2.93:1 w/diesel. Steering: (Firenza/Omega/Ciera) rack and pinion; (others) recirculating ball. Front Suspension: (Firenza/Omega/Ciera) MacPherson struts w/coil springs, lower control arms and anti-sway bar; (Toronado); torsion bars w/anti-sway bar; (others) coil springs with upper/lower control arms and anti-sway bar. Rear Suspension: (Firenza) beam axle w/coil springs, trailing arms and anti-sway bar; (Omega/Ciera) beam axle with integral anti-sway, coil springs and Panhard rod; (Toronado) independent with coil springs, semi-trailing arms, anti-sway

bar and automatic leveling; (others) rigid axle w/coil springs, lower trailing radius arms and upper torque arms (four-link). Brakes: Front disc, rear drum. Ignition: Electronic. Body construction: (Firenza/Omega/Ciera) unibody; (others) separate body and frame. Fuel tank: (Firenza) 14 gal.; (Omega) 14.6 or 15.1 gal.; (Ciera) 15.7 gal.; (Cutlass) 18.2 or 19.8 gal.; (Delta 88) 25 gal.; (98) 25 gal.; (Custom Crsr wag) 22 gal.; (Toronado) 21 gal.

1984 Toronado Caliente coupe (AA)

DRIVETRAIN OPTIONS: Engines: 112 cu. in. four: Firenza ($50). 173 cu. in. V-6: Omega ($250). H.O. 173 cu. in. V-6: Omega Brghm sed ($400). 181 cu. in. V-6: Ciera ($250). Diesel 262 cu. in. V-6: Cutlass/Ciera ($500). 307 cu. in. 4Bbl. V-8: Cutlass/88 ($375); Toro ($225). Diesel 350 cu. in. V-8: Cutlass/88/98/Toronado ($700). Transmission/Differential: Five-speed manual trans.: Firenza ($75). Turbo Hydra-matic: Firenza ($395); Omega ($425). Four-speed overdrive auto.: Cutlass/88 ($175). Limited-slip differential: Cutlass/88/98 ($95). Steering/Suspension: Power steering: base Firenza ($204). Firm ride/handling pkg. ($30-$49). Automatic load leveling: Ciera/88/98 ($175). Other: High-capacity cooling ($40-$70) except Firenza. High-capacity radiator: Cutlass/88/98/Toro ($30). H.D. battery ($26) exc. diesel ($52). Engine block heater ($18). Block/fuel line heater ($49). Trailer wiring: 88/98/Toro ($30). California emissions ($99).

OPTION PACKAGES: Firenza GT pkg.: S cpe ($695). Firenza ES pkg.: base sedan ($450); LX sedan ($375). Omega ES pkg.: Brghm sedan ($675). Ciera Holiday coupe pkg.: Brghm ($565). Ciera ES pkg. ($696-$851). Hurst/Olds pkg.: Calais coupe ($1997). Toronado Caliente pkg. ($2195).

MAJOR CONVENIENCE/APPEARANCE OPTIONS: Four Season air conditioner ($630-$730). Tempmatic air conditioning: 88 ($785); 98/Toro ($55). Cruise control ($175). Power seat ($178-$215). Power windows ($185-$260). Twilight sentinel: Toro ($60). Cornering lamps: 88/98 ($60). Power astroroof w/sliding glass panel: Cutlass ($895); 88/98/Toro ($1195). Removable glass roof panels: Cutlass ($825). Glass panel sunroof: Firenza/Omega/Ciera ($215-$245). Full vinyl roof: Omega/Ciera/Cutlass/88 ($160-$185). Full padded vinyl roof: Cutlass ($245). Rear-facing third seat: Cutlass/Custom Cruiser ($215-$220).

HISTORY: Introduced: September 22, 1983. Model year production: 1,179,656. Calendar year production (U.S.): 1,065,528. Calendar year sales by U.S. dealers: 1,056,053. Model year sales by U.S. dealers: 1,098,685.

Historical Footnotes: A "special feel in an Oldsmobile" was a promotional theme this year, suggesting quality, value, prestige, pride of ownership, and confidence in the name. Also emphasized was the "Oldsmobile difference." Oldsmobile was still trying to reach second place in sales.

1985 OLDSMOBILE

One new model joined up this year: the Calais, measuring between subcompact (Firenza) and Cutlass Ciera dimensions, intended to attract younger drivers. Omega dropped out, victim of the series of Xcar recalls and problems. Anticipating the federal standard of 1986, an optional high-mount stoplight went on Cutlass Ciera, Calais and Ninety-Eight Regency.

FIRENZA — SERIES 3J — FOUR/V-6 — Firenza looked the same up front, but gained a revised look at the rear-end this year. It also gained the possibility of V-6 power. A multi-port fuel-injected 173 cu. in. (2.8-liter) V-6 from Chevrolet became optional instead of the base 2.0-liter four (also Chevrolet's). The 130-horsepower V-6 was standard on GT. GT was claimed to deliver a 0-60 MPH time of 9 seconds with four-speed manual, 9.5 with automatic. To get the V-6 into a Firenza compartment, a serpentine belt system was used, along with a bubble hood. The grille area expanded too, to deliver added cooling. Also optional was a 1.8-liter four from GM of Brazil. Coupe, sedan and wagon bodies were available, along with sporty GT and sophisticated ES options. A total of 498 GT packages (RPO code W54) were installed, and 863 ES packages. ES had blacked-out body moldings and polycast wheels.

1985 Calais Indy Pace Car convertible (AA)

338

CALAIS — SERIES 3N — FOUR/V-6 — Though retaining traditional Olds styling cues, the new Nbody Calais coupe featured a sporty, contemporary design with formal roofline. Front-wheel drive was used, and the car held five passengers. Calais was similar to the new Buick Somerset Regal and Pontiac Grand Am. Two trim levels were offered, intended to appeal to the "style-conscious, quality-oriented, younger car buyer." Calais displayed a wedge shape with soft rounded lines. The hood extended all the way to the windshield, eliminating the cowl panel. The grille consisted of thin vertical bars with a smaller-than-usual center divider that contained no emblem. Rectangular headlamps were used, with park/signal lamps set into the front bumper. 'Calais' script went on the leading edges of doors, just above the bodyside molding. No "tulip" rear-end panel was used between the rear window and decklid. Door hinges were bolted on rather than welded. A zincrometal decklid outer panel was used, with a galvanized steel inner panel. Base coat/clear coat paint gave a high-gloss finish. Interiors held standard front bucket seats and console. Light and wiper switches went on pods at steering wheel sides. Optional analog gauges and electronic instruments were available. Base engine was the 151 cu. in. (2.5-liter) four with TBI and roller lifters, with five-speed manual or three-speed automatic. Optional: a 3.0-liter V-6 with multi-port fuel injection, only with automatic. Optional were wire wheels or all-new aluminum wheels (a Calais exclusive). A total of 2,998 "500" packages were installed on the base coupe, and 6,763 Special Edition models (code WK5) were produced.

1985 Cutlass Ciera Holiday coupe (AA)

CUTLASS CIERA — SERIES 3A — FOUR/V-6 — A more aerodynamic front end was evident on this year's Ciera. The small-crosshatch eggcrate grille sections had more of a slope, and wraparound side marker lenses a more rounded shape. As before, wide park/signal lights were in the bumper strip. Wraparound taillamps had rounded tops. Very wide backup lights were mounted in a panel with center 'Oldsmobile' nameplate. An energy-absorbing back bumper used a polyethylene honeycomb with roll-form beam. The rear license was bumper-mounted. Optional: a high-mount stoplight. Models included an LS and Brougham coupe and sedan, and Cruiser wagon. The base 151 cu. in. (2.5-liter) four added roller lifters. Options included a 3.0-liter V-6, new 3.8-liter PFI V-6, and diesel V-6 (with new aluminum head). Three specialty options were offered: GT, ES, and Holiday Coupe. A total of 1,084 GT packages (RPO code W45), 3,101 ES packages (code W48) and 9,836 Holiday coupe packages were installed. GT models had the 3.8-liter V-6 as well as special trim and suspension. Ciera standard equipment included a 151 cu. in. (2.5-liter) fuel-injected four, power rack-and-pinion steering, power brakes, AM radio, velour custom bench seat, automatic transmission, and P185/75R14 SBR all-season blackwalls. Bodies held bright belt beveal and roof drip moldings, and black window frame moldings. Cruiser had wheel opening and rocker panel moldings. Ciera Brougham added a convenience group, bright rocker panel and wheel opening moldings, and 55/45 divided bench seat.

1985 Cutlass Ciera sedan (JG)

CUTLASS SUPREME — SERIES 3G — V-6/V-8 — Replacing the Hurst/Olds option after two years in the lineup was a 442 package, with high-output V-8, and special paint and suspension. The 442 name had been retired for a while. A total of 3,000 442 packages (RPO code W42) were produced. Features include a '442' door decal, 3.73:1 rear axle, super stock wheels and Eagle GT tires. Otherwise, the Cutlass line displayed a revised front-end treatment. Coupe grilles continued the sloping forward shape, with crosshatch patterns on each side but split into three side-by-side segments. Sedan grilles were upright again, made up of thin horizontal strips divided into four side-by-side sections. As before, sedans had wraparound side marker lenses and park/signal lights down in the bumper. Standard Supreme equipment included a 231 cu. in. (3.8-liter) V-6, three-speed automatic transmission, power brakes and steering, cloth/vinyl custom bench seat, AM radio, P195/75R14 blackwall SBR tires, bumper guards and rub strips, and bright wheel covers. Bright moldings went on rocker panels, wheel openings, windshield, hood center, and roof drip area. Brougham added 55/45 divided frontseat, wide bodyside moldings, belt reveal moldings, convenience group, and reading lamp; rocker panel moldings were deleted from the Brougham coupe. The sporty Salon included front and rear stabilizer bars, color-keyed Super Stock wheels, specific bodyside accent paint stripes, leather-wrapped steering wheel, contour reclining front bucket seats, sport console (with floor shift), Rallye instruments, and color-keyed sport mirrors. Salon also had wheel opening and wide bodyside moldings. Optional engine were the diesel V-6 or V-8, and 307 cu. in. (5.0-liter) gas V-8, which added roller lifters this year along with other internal modifications.

DELTA 88 — SERIES 3B — V-6/V-8 — As usual, Delta 88 sported a new grille: this one with four rows on each side. And this year's back end displayed elongated backup lamps between the taillamps and license plate. Brougham and Brougham LS models were offered, the latter with a 4 x 5 "hole" eggcrate pattern grille. Base engine remained the Buick-built 231 cu. in. (3.8-liter) V-6. Optional: a 307 cu. in. (5.0-liter) gas V-8, now with roller lifters; and 5.7-liter diesel. Added standard equipment included an AM/FM stereo radio and all-season SBR tires. The Custom Cruiser wagon was

1985 Delta 88 Brougham coupe (JG)

available again (V-8 powered). Standard 88 equipment included three-speed automatic, power brakes/steering, custom cloth bench seat, AM/FM stereo radio, bumper guards and rub strips, left remote mirror, and woodgrain dash. Bright moldings were used for rocker panels, wheel openings, bodyside, windshield, and roof drip rail. Royale Brougham added a 55/45 divided seat, belt reveal moldings, convenience group, and opera lamps (on coupe). Delta 88 LS included a four-speed overdrive automatic transmission, power windows, wire wheel covers (with locks), tilt steering, lower bodyside moldings, six-way power driver's seat, air conditioning, digital clock, tinted glass, opera lamps, dual color-keyed remote mirrors, and power door locks. Tires were P205/75R15 blackwall SBR except LS, P215/75R15 whitewalls. Standard Cruiser equipment included a 307 cu. in. (5.0- liter) V-8, four-speed automatic, AM/FM stereo, power brakes/steering, 55/45 divided bench seat (vinyl or velour), power tailgate window, driver's remote mirror, and P225/75R15 blackwall SBR tires. An all-new Delta 88 was expected for 1986.

1985 Ninety-Eight landau coupe (AA)

NINETY-EIGHT REGENCY — SERIES 3C — V-6 — After a long history as a big rear-drive luxury model, Ninety-Eight now switched to front-drive, though still able to carry six passengers. Introduced as an early 1985, the far different Ninety-Eight came in coupe and sedan form, base and Regency trim. Aero styling highlights included a sloping hood and curved decklid, rounded edges, bumpers flush to bodyside, and flush-mounted windshield and backlight. The windshield flowed into flush side door glass, with only a narrow black molding visible at the windshield (the pillar was under the glass). This version was 15 inches shorter than its predecessor, weighing 570 to 635 pounds less. But inside dimensions were nearly identical to the 1984 rear-drive. Dual grilles were separated by a chrome center post with "rocket" emblem. Quad rectangular headlamps and the grille were surrounded by bright housings. Amber side marker lenses were integral with the headlamp housings. A soft fascia covered the upper portion of the bright bumpers. Crystal- lensed parking lamps were horizontally-mounted in the front bumper. Both bumpers had a black rub strip with white stripe. Ninety-Eight's traditional formal roofline continued, with small sail panel area. Opera lamps were standard. Coupes had a landau vinyl roof; sedans, a full vinyl roof. Sedans also had a pillar applique. Narrow vertical taillamps held rocket emblem accents. Wide horizontal backup lamps extended from the taillamps to the license plate opening. Regency models had polished stainless steel wheel covers. Regency Brougham carried aero-profile simulated wire wheel covers. Inside, a split-bench seat had lumbar, lateral back and cushion support, with six-way power driver's seat. Two-position memory was optional, as was six-way power for the passenger seat and manual recliner. Power windows were standard. An optional auto calculator (available with the optional electronic instrument cluster) showed 12 functions including time, date, trip distance, elapsed time, estimated distance and time of arrival, distance since fill-up, and average fuel economy. A voice synthesis system alert also was included. Options included an automatic day/night mirror and power remote mirrors. The standard carbureted 181 cu. in. (3.0-liter) V-6 was transverse-mounted, with four-speed overdrive automatic transmission. Broughams had a standard 3.8-liter V-6 with multi-port fuel injection. A 4.3-liter diesel V-6 also was available. Ninety-Eight's chassis featured fully independent suspension. For corrosion protection, the floor pan was galvanized, and all body panels except the roof had either galvanized zinc or special pre-coatings on inside surfaces.

1985 Toronado Caliente coupe (AA)

TORONADO — SERIES 3E — V-8 — Only a V-8 engine powered Toronados this year, as the former V-6 hadn't found enough buyers. Appearance changed little. Toro's grille was similar to before, a full-width dual-segment design with park/signal lamps at the outside; but tiny crosshatch patterning was visible through each center portion. The standard 307 cu. in. (5.0-liter) V-8 had new roller lifters, new exhaust manifold, and other internal changes. Standard equipment included four-speed overdrive automatic, power brakes/steering, Four Season air conditioner, power windows, digital clock, tinted glass, automatic leveling, AM/FM stereo radio with electronic tuning, six-way power driver's seat, and P205/75R15 whitewalls. Also standard: cornering lamps, dual remote mirrors, speed control, and bright body moldings. A 350 cu. in. diesel V-8 was available for the last time. A total of 7,342 Caliente packages (RPO code WJ8) were produced this year. Each one had a padded landau vinyl roof, stainless steel crown, bright bodyside and lower bodyside moldings, special front-end panel emblem, dual power mirrors, tempmatic air conditioning, leather-wrapped steering wheel, wire wheel covers, and electronic instrument panel.

I.D. DATA: Oldsmobile's 17-symbol Vehicle Identification Number (VIN) again was located on the upper left surface of the instrument panel, visible through the windshield. The first three symbols ('1G3') indicate Oldsmobile division. Symbol four denotes restraint type: 'A' manual (active) belts. Symbol five is car line/series: 'C' Firenza; 'D' Firenza SX/LX; 'F' Calais; 'T' Calais Supreme; 'J' Cutlass Ciera LS; ''M' Cutlass Ciera Brougham; 'J' Cutlass Ciera LS Cruiser; 'R' Cutlass Supreme; 'M' Cutlass Supreme Brougham ; 'K' Cutlass Salon; 'L' Delta 88; 'N' Delta 88 Royale; 'Y' Delta 88 Royale Brougham; 'V' Delta 88 Royale Brougham LS; 'P' Custom Cruiser; 'X' Ninety-Eight Regency; 'W' Ninety-Eight Regency Brougham; 'Z' Toronado Brougham. Next come two digits that denote body type: '11' 2dr. notchback sedan; '27' 2dr. coupe; '37' 2dr. coupe; '47' 2dr. coupe; '57' 2dr. coupe; '77' 2dr. coupe; '19' 4dr. sedan; '69' 4dr. 4window notch sedan; '35' 4dr. 2seat wagon. Symbol eight is a letter for engine code: '0' L4112 FI; 'P' L4121 FI; 'R' L4151 FI; 'W' V6173 FI; 'E' V6181 2Bbl.; 'L' V6181 FI; 'A' V6231 2Bbl.; '3' V6231 FI; 'T' diesel V6262; 'Y' V8307 4Bbl.; '9' Hurst/Olds V8307 4Bbl.; 'N' diesel V8350. Next comes a check digit, followed by a code for model year: ('F' 1985). Symbol eleven is the assembly plant code: '2' Ste. Therese, Quebec (Canada); 'D' Doraville, Georgia; 'G' Framingham, Mass.; 'M' Lansing, Mich.; 'P' Pontiac, Mich.; 'E' Linden, New Jersey; 'R' Arlington, Texas; and 'K' Leeds, Missouri. (Oldsmobiles were also built in Detroit; Orion, Michigan; Wilmington, Delaware; and Wentzville, Missouri.) The final six digits are the sequential serial number. Engine numbers were stamped on the front of the right rocker cover, or top of left cover (Buick-built engines), on label at front or rear of right rocker cover (Chevrolet V-6), or on the left rocker cover (Oldsmobile engines). Four- cylinder engine numbers were on a pad at left or right front of block. A body number plate on the upper right cowl identified model year, series, style, body assembly plant, body number, trim combination, modular seat code, paint code, date built code, and option codes.

FIRENZA (FOUR/V-6)

Model Number	Body/Style Number	Body Type & Seating	Factory Price	Shipping Weight	Production Total
3J	C77	2-dr. S cpe-5P	7588/8148	2390/ --	5,842
3J	C69	4-dr. Sedan-5P	7679/8239	2393/ --	25,066
3J	D77	2-dr. SX cpe-5P	8395/8955	2437/ --	1,842
3J	D69	4-dr. LX sed-5P	8255/8815	2438/ --	7,563

FIRENZA CRUISER (FOUR/V-6)

3J	C35	4-dr. Sta Wag-5P	7898/8458	2439/ --	6,291
3J	D35	4-dr. LX Wag-5P	8492/9052	2457/ --	2,436

CALAIS (FOUR/V-6)

3N	F27	2-dr. Cpe-5P	8499/9059	2431/2503	49,545

CALAIS SUPREME (FOUR/V-6)

3N	T27	2-dr. Cpe-5P	8844/9404	2448/2520	56,695

CUTLASS CIERA LS (FOUR/V-6)

3A	J27	2-dr. Cpe-6P	9307/9567	2611/2714	13,396
3A	J19	4-dr. Sed-6P	9497/9757	2650/2753	118,575

CUTLASS CIERA BROUGHAM (FOUR/V-6)

3A	M27	2-dr. Cpe-6P	9787/10047	2637/2740	20,476
3A	M19	4-dr. Sed-6P	9998/10258	2676/2779	112,441

CUTLASS CIERA CRUISER (FOUR/V-6)

3G	J35	4-dr. Sta Wag-6P	9858/10118	2824/2927	38,225

CUTLASS SUPREME (V-6/V-8)

3G	R47	2-dr. Cpe-6P	9797/10087	3133/3328	75,045
3G	R69	4-dr. Sed-6P	9961/10251	3184/3361	43,085

CUTLASS SUPREME BROUGHAM (V-6/V-8)

3G	M47	2-dr. Cpe-6P	10468/10758	3171/3366	58,869
3G	M69	4-dr. Sed-6P	10602/10892	3214/3391	28,741

CUTLASS SALON (V-6/V-8)

3G	K47	2-dr. Cpe-6P	10770/11060	3209/3404	17,512

DELTA 88 ROYALE (V-6/V-8)

3B	N37	2-dr. Cpe-6P	10488/11053	3380/3566	15,002
3B	N69	4-dr. Sed-6P	10596/11161	3419/3605	69,641

DELTA 88 ROYALE BROUGHAM (V-6/V-8)

3B	Y37	2-dr. Cpe-6P	10968/11533	3413/3599	31,891
3B	Y69	4-dr. Sed-6P	11062/11627	3449/3635	72,103
3B	V69	4-dr. LS Sed-6P	-- /14331	N/A	30,239

CUSTOM CRUISER (V-8)

3B	P35	4-dr. Sta Wag-6P	11627	4033	22,889

NINETY-EIGHT REGENCY (V-6)

3C	X11	2-dr. Sedan-6P	14725	3684	4,734
3C	X69	4-dr. Sedan-6P	14665	3733	43,697

NINETY-EIGHT REGENCY BROUGHAM (V-6)

3C	W11	2-dr. Sedan-6P	15932	3784	9,704
3C	W69	4-dr. Sedan-6P	15864	4059	111,297

TORONADO BROUGHAM (V-8)

3E	Z57	2-dr. Cpe-5P	16798	3612	42,185

FACTORY PRICE AND WEIGHT NOTE: Prices and weights to left of slash are for six-cylinder, to right for V-8 engine except Firenza/Calais/Ciera, to left for four-cylinder and to right for V-6.

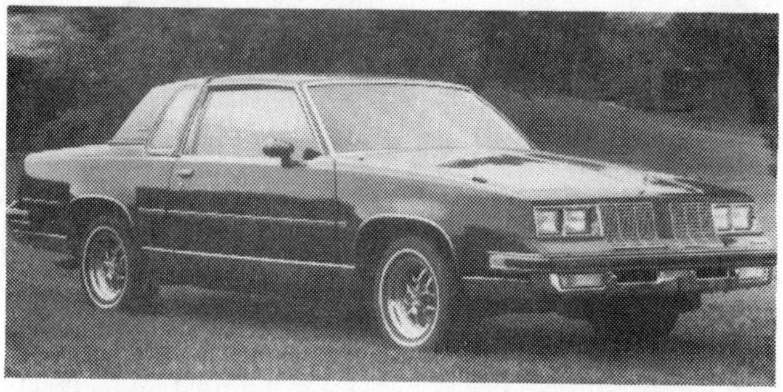

1985 Cutlass Supreme coupe (JG)

ENGINE DATA: BASE FOUR (Firenza): Inline, overhead-valve four-cylinder. Cast iron block and head. Displacement: 121 cu. in. (2.0 liters). Bore & stroke: 3.50 x 3.14 in. Compression ratio: 9.3:1. Brake horsepower: 88 at 4800 R.P.M. Torque: 110 lbs.ft. at 2400 R.P.M. Five main bearings. Hydraulic valve lifters. Electronic fuel injection. VIN Code: P. OPTIONAL FOUR (Firenza): Inline, overhead-cam four-cylinder. Cast iron block and aluminum head. Displacement: 112 cu. in. (1.8 liters). Bore & stroke: 3.34 x 3.11 in. Compression ratio: 9.0:1. Brake horsepower: 82 at 5200 R.P.M. Torque: 102 lbs.ft. at 2800 R.P.M. Five main bearings. Hydraulic valve lifters. Electronic fuel injection. VIN Code: O. BASE FOUR (Calais, Cutlass Ciera): Inline, overhead-valve four-cylinder. Cast iron block and head. Displacement: 151 cu. in. (2.5 liters). Bore & stroke: 4.00 x 3.00 in. Compression ratio: 8.2:1. Brake horsepower: 92 at 4400 R.P.M. Torque: 134 lbs.ft. at 2800 R.P.M. Five main bearings. Hydraulic valve lifters. Fuel injection (TBI). Pontiac-built. VIN Code: R. OPTIONAL V-6 (Firenza): 60-degree, overhead-valve V-6. Cast iron block and aluminum head. Displacement: 173 cu. in. (2.8 liters). Bore & stroke: 3.50 x 3.00 in. Compression ratio: 8.9:1. Brake horsepower: 130 at 4800 R.P.M. Torque: 150 lbs.ft. at 2400 R.P.M. Four main bearings. Hydraulic valve lifters. Electronic fuel injection. Chevrolet-built. VIN Code: W. BASE V-6 (98); OPTIONAL V-6 (Cutlass Ciera): 90-degree, overhead-valve V-6. Cast iron block and head. Displacement: 181 cu. in. (3.0 liters). Bore & stroke: 3.80 x 2.66 in. Compression ratio: 8.4:1. Brake horsepower: 110 at 4800 R.P.M. Torque: 145 lbs.ft. at 2600 R.P.M. Four main bearings. Hydraulic valve lifters. Carburetor: 2Bbl. Rochester E2SE. VIN Code: E. OPTIONAL V-6 (Calais): Same as 181 cu. in. V-6 above, with fuel injection Compression ratio: 9.0:1. Horsepower: 125 at 4900 R.P.M. Torque: 150 lbs.-ft. at 2400 R.P.M. VIN Code: L. BASE V-6 (Calais, Delta 88): 90-degree, overhead-valve V-6. Cast iron block and head. Displacement: 231 cu. in. (3.8 liters). Bore & stroke: 3.80 x 3.40 in. Compression ratio: 8.0:1. Brake horsepower: 110 at 3800 R.P.M. Torque: 190 lbs.ft. at 1600 R.P.M. Four main bearings. Hydraulic valve lifters. Carburetor: 2Bbl. Rochester E2ME. Buick-built. VIN Code: A. BASE V-6 (Cutlass Supreme, Delta 88, 98 Brougham); OPTIONAL (Ciera LS/Brougham, 98): Same as 231 cu. in. V-6 above, but with fuel injection Horsepower: 125 at 4400 R.P.M. Torque: 195 lbs.-ft. at 2000 R.P.M. VIN Code: 3. DIESEL V-6 (Cutlass Ciera, Cutlass Supreme, 98): 90-degree, overhead valve V-8. Cast iron block and head. Displacement: 262 cu. in. (4.3 liters). Bore & stroke: 4.06 x 3.38 in. Compression ratio: 22.8:1. Brake horsepower: 85 at 3600 R.P.M. Torque: 165 lbs.ft. at 1600 R.P.M. Five main bearings. Hydraulic valve lifters. Fuel injection. VIN Code: T. BASE V-8 (Delta 88 LS, Custom Cruiser, Toronado); OPTIONAL (Cutlass Supreme, Delta 88): 90-degree, overhead valve V-8. Cast iron block and head. Displacement: 307 cu. in. (5.0 liters). Bore & stroke: 3.80 x 3.38 in. Compression ratio: 8.0:1. Brake horsepower: 140 at 3600 R.P.M. (Cutlass, 140 at 3200). Torque: 240 lbs.ft. at 1600 R.P.M. (Cutlass, 255 at 2000). Five main bearings. Hydraulic valve lifters. Carburetor: 4Bbl. Rochester 4MC. VIN Code: Y. OPTIONAL HURST/OLDS V-8 (Cutlass Calais): Same as 307 cu. in. V-8 above, but Compression ratio: 9.0:1. Horsepower: 180 at 4000 R.P.M. Torque: 245 lbs.-ft. at 3200 R.P.M. VIN Code: 9. DIESEL V 8 (Cutlass Supreme, Delta 88, Custom Cruiser, Toronado): 90-degree, overhead valve V-8. Cast iron block and head. Displacement: 350 cu. in. (5.7 liters). Bore & stroke: 4.06 x 3.39 in. Compression ratio: 22.7:1. Brake horsepower: 105 at 3200 R.P.M. Torque: 200 lbs.ft. at 1600 R.P.M. Five main bearings. Hydraulic valve lifters. Fuel injection. VIN Code: N.

CHASSIS DATA: Wheelbase: (Firenza) 101.2 in.; (Calais) 103.4 in.; (Ciera) 104.9 in.; (Cutlass) 108.1 in.; (Delta 88) 115.9 in.; (98) 110.8 in.; (Custom Crsr) 115.9 in.; (Toronado) 114.0 in. Overall Length: (Firenza cpe) 174.3 in.; (Firenza sed) 176.2 in.; (Firenza wag) 176.2 in.; (Calais) 177.5 in.; (Ciera) 190.0-190.3 in.; (Ciera wag) 194.4 in.; (Cutlass Supreme) 200.0-200.4 in.; (Delta 88) 218.1 in.; (98) 196.1 in.; (Custom Crsr) 220.3 in.; (Toro) 206.0 in. Height: (Firenza cpe) 51.7 in.; (Firenza sed) 53.7 in.; (Firenza wag) 55.2 in.; (Calais) 52.5 in.; (Ciera) 54.1 in.; (Ciera wag) 54.5 in.; (Cutlass Supreme cpe) 54.9 in.; (Cutlass Supreme sed) 55.9 in.; (Delta 88 cpe) 56.0 in.; (Delta 88 sed) 56.7 in.; (98) 55.0 in.; (Custom Crsr) 58.5 in.; (Toro) 54.6 in. Width: (Firenza) 65.0 in.; (Calais) 66.9 in.; (Ciera) 69.5 in.; (Cutlass cpe) 71.6; (Cutlass sed) 71.9 in.; (Delta 88) 76.3 in.; (98) 71.4 in.; (Custom Crsr) 79.8 in.; (Toro) 71.4 in. Front Tread: (Firenza) 55.4 in.; (Calais) 55.5 in.; (Ciera) 58.7 in.; (Cutlass) 58.5 in.; (Delta 88) 61.7 in.; (98) 60.3 in.; (Custom Crsr) 62.1 in.; (Toro) 59.3 in. Rear Tread: (Firenza) 55.2 in.; (Calais) 55.2 in.; (Ciera) 57.0 in.; (Cutlass) 57.7 in.; (Delta 88) 60.7 in.; (98) 59.8 in.; (Custom Crsr) 64.1 in.; (Toro) 60.0 in. Standard Tires: (Firenza) P175/80R13; (Calais) P185/80R13; (Ciera) P185/75R14; (Cutlass Supreme) P195/75R14; (Delta 88) P205/75R15; (98) P205/75R14; (Custom Crsr) P225/75R15; (Toronado) P205/75R15.

TECHNICAL: Transmission: Four-speed floor shift standard on Firenza four. Gear ratios: (1st) 3.53:1; (2nd) 1.95:1; (3rd) 1.24:1; (4th) 0.81:1; (Rev) 3.42:1. Four-speed on Firenza V-6: (1st) 3.31:1; (2nd) 1.95:1; (3rd) 1.24:1; (4th) 0.90:1; (Rev) 3.42:1. Five-speed manual trans. standard on Calais: (1st) 3.73:1; (2nd) 2.04:1; (3rd) 1.45:1; (4th) 1.03:1; (5th) 0.74:1; (Rev) 3.50:1. Five-speed manual trans. optional on Firenza: (1st) 3.91 in.; (2nd) 2.15:1; (3rd) 1.45:1; (4th) 1.03:1; (5th) 0.74:1; (Rev) 3.50:1. Three-speed Turbo Hydra- matic standard on Cutlass/Ciera/88. Four-speed automatic overdrive standard on Custom Cruiser/98/Toronado. Standard final drive ratio: (Firenza) 3.65:1 w/4spd, 3.45:1 w/5spd, 3.18:1 w/auto.; (Calais) 3.35:1 w/5spd, 2.84:1 w/auto.; (Ciera) 2.84:1 w/four, 2.53:1 w/V6181, 2.84:1 w/V6231; (Cutlass) 2.41:1 w/V-6, 2.14:1 w/V-8; (Delta 88) 2.73:1; (98) 3.06:1 w/V6181, 2.84:1 w/V6231, 3.06:1 w/diesel; (Toronado) 2.73:1 except 2.93:1 w/diesel. Steering: (Firenza/Calais/Ciera/98) rack and pinion; (others) recirculating ball. Front Suspension: (Firenza/Calais/Ciera/98) MacPherson struts w/coil springs, lower control arms and anti-sway bar; (Toronado); torsion bars w/anti-sway bar; (others) coil springs with upper/lower control arms and anti-sway bar. Rear Suspension: (Firenza) beam axle w/coil springs, trailing arms and anti-sway bar; (Calais) semi-independent w/coil springs and trailing arms; (Ciera) beam axle with integral anti-sway, coil springs and Panhard rod; (98) independent w/struts, coil springs, lower control arms, anti-sway bar and automatic level control; (Toronado) independent with coil springs, semi-trailing arms, anti-sway bar and automatic leveling; (others) rigid axle w/coil springs, lower trailing radius arms and upper torque arms (four-link). Brakes: Front disc, rear drum. Ignition: Electronic. Body construction: (Firenza/Calais/Ciera/98) unibody; (others) separate body and frame. Fuel tank: (Firenza) 14 gal.; (Calais) 13.6 gal.; (Ciera) 16.6 gal.; (Cutlass) 18.1 gal.; (Delta 88) 27 gal.; (98) 18 gal.; (Custom Crsr wag) 22 gal.; (Toronado) 21.1 gal.

DRIVETRAIN OPTIONS: Engines: 112 cu. in. four: Firenza ($50). 173 cu. in. V-6: Firenza ($560). 181 cu. in. V-6: Calais ($560); Ciera ($260). 231 cu. in. V-6: Ciera ($520); 98 ($260). Diesel 262 cu. in. V-6: Cutlass/Ciera/98 ($260); 98 Brghm (NC). 307 cu. in. 4Bbl. V-8: Cutlass/88 ($390). Diesel 350 cu. in. V-8: Cutlass/88/ ($390); Custom Crsr/Delta LS/Toro (NC). Transmission/Differential: Five-speed manual trans.: Firenza ($75). Turbo Hydra-matic: Firenza ($425). Four-speed overdrive auto.: Ciera/88 ($175). Limited-slip differential: Cutlass/88 ($100). Steering/Suspension: Power steering: base Firenza ($215). Firm ride/handling pkg. ($30-$49). Automatic load leveling: Ciera/88 ($180). Other: High-capacity cooling ($40-$70). High-capacity radiator: Ciera/Cutlass/88/98/Toro ($30). H.D. battery ($26) exc. diesel ($52); N/A on Calais. Engine block heater ($18). Block/fuel line heater ($49). California emissions ($99).

OPTION PACKAGES: Firenza GT pkg.: S cpe (N/A). Firenza ES pkg. ($595-$1555). Calais 500 pkg.: base ($1595). Ciera ES pkg.: LS sedan ($895). Ciera Holiday coupe pkg.: Brghm ($565). Ciera GT pkg.: LS cpe ($3295). Cutlass Salon 442 pkg. ($1175). Toronado Caliente pkg. ($1970).

MAJOR CONVENIENCE/APPEARANCE OPTIONS: Four Season air conditioner ($645-$750). Tempmatic air conditioning: 88 ($805); 98 ($125); Toro ($55). Cruise control ($175). Power seat ($178-$225). Power windows ($195-$270). Twilight sentinel: 98/Toro ($60). Cornering lamps: 88/98 ($60). Power astroroof w/sliding glass panel: Cutlass ($925); 88/98/Toro ($1230). Removable glass roof panels: Cutlass ($850). Glass panel sunroof: Firenza/Calais/Ciera ($310). Landau vinyl roof: Ciera/Cutlass/88/98/Toro ($215-$245). Full vinyl roof: Ciera/Cutlass/88 ($160-$185). Full padded vinyl roof: Cutlass/98 ($245). Rear-facing third seat: Cutlass/Custom Cruiser ($215-$220).

HISTORY: Introduced: October 2, 1984 except Firenza, November 8, 1984 and Ninety-Eight, April 5, 1984. Model year production: 1,192,549. Calendar year production (U.S.): 1,168,982. Calendar year sales by U.S. dealers: 1,066,122. Model year sales by U.S. dealers: 1,087,675.

Historical Footnotes: The new Ninety-Eight was called "the most thoroughly tested vehicle ever introduced by the division." A thousand of the first production models were driven by engineers to study possible problems. Assembly included such "tricks" as video- camera and gamma ray inspection of sheetmetal parts. Front and rear outer panels were formed in the same draw die, so beltlines and feature lines would match precisely. A red Firenza concept car with metallic silver lower rocker panels was shown to the auto press, with chassis modification based on SCCA off-road production class rally racing. It had a more rakish Cpillar angle than normal and an integral rear spoiler.

1986 OLDSMOBILE

All-new front-drive Delta 88 and Toronado models highlighted the year for Oldsmobile. There were also new body styles for Firenza (notchback coupe) and Calais (sedan). Special features available included anti-lock braking (ABS) and an FE3 suspension.

FIRENZA — SERIES 3J — FOUR/V-6 — Front appearance of the Olds subcompact was similar to 1985, with a revised full-width lower grille made up of horizontal bars. At the rear was a new body-color panel. The SX hatchback was dropped, but a new notchack coupe added. This year's lineup included a base coupe and sedan; S hatchback coupe; LC coupe; GT hatchback coupe; LX sedan; and Cruiser two-seat wagon. Firenza was promoted as an affordable entry-level car, with coupes targeted at young drivers and women. A Firenza GT replaced the upscale hatchback. GT had a 173 cu. in. (2.8-liter) V-6 with manual shift, 14 inch low- profile Eagle GT tires, and a handling package. Oldsmobile claimed a 0-60 MPH time of 10 seconds. Base engine was the 122 cu. in. (2.0-liter) four. Options: 112 cu. in. (1.8- liter) four and 173 cu. in. (2.8-liter) V-6. Standard Firenza equipment included the 2.0-liter four with four-speed manual transaxle, bright wheel opening moldings, swing-out rear quarter windows, full-length console, AM radio, contoured reclining front bucket seats, LX/LC added a decklid lock, bright rocker panel moldings, dual mirrors (driver's remote), and power

1986 Firenza GT hatchback coupe (AA)

steering. LC included leather-wrapped steering wheel and full instruments. GT hatchback added P205/60R14 Eagle GT tires on aluminum wheels, a 2.8-liter V-6 with multipoint fuel injection, two- tone paint, instrument cluster with tachometer, leather-wrapped steering wheel, FE3 handling suspension, and velour interior.

CALAIS — SERIES 3N — FOUR/V-6 — Introduced as a coupe in 1985, Calais now added a four- door sedan. Four models were offered: base and Supreme trim level, in coupe and sedan bodies. Two new specialty models arrived: a sophisticated ES sports sedan, and sporty GT coupe. The ES sedan had aero composite headlamps as well as blacked-out rocker panels, bumpers, moldings and mirrors. Equipment included the FE3 firm ride /handling suspension, 14 in. styled aluminum wheels and Eagle GT tires. Also rallye instrument cluster. GT featured composite headlamps, aero rocker panels, specific front and rear fascias, two-tone paint, FE3 suspension, 14 in. styled aluminum wheels, and Eagle GT tires. A 3.0-liter V-6 was optional. Both ES and GT included front bucket seats, integral rear headrests, and rallye gauge cluster. This year's Calais grille had vertical bars and an Olds rocket emblem. Specialty models showed a completely different front-end look with their aero headlamps, and full-width horizontal strips that extended outward below the headlamps and through the lower portion of the grille panel. (The upper center panel was solid, but GT had a center emblem.) Optional this year: column shift for the extra-cost automatic (not available on other N-cars). Base engine was a fuel-injected 151 cu. in. (2.5-liter four). Optional: 181 cu. in. (3.0-liter) V-6 with PFI (automatic required). Calais standard equipment included power brakes and steering, P185/80R13 SBR blackwall tires, stand-up hood ornament, wheel opening and rocker panel moldings, tinted glass, full-length console, electronic-tuning AM/FM stereo radio with seek/scan and digital clock, and reclining front bucket seats. Supreme added deluxe bodyside moldings and body-color mirrors (driver's remote), as well as a lamp/convenience group and roof rail courtesy lamp.

1986 Cutlass Ciera GT coupe (AA)

CUTLASS CIERA — SERIES 3A — FOUR/V-6 — Five models made up this year's Ciera selection: S coupe, base sedan, SL coupe, Brougham sedan, and Cruiser two-seat wagon (available with rear-facing third seat). The GT package was available for S coupe and base sedan. GT and ES models had a new standard 231 cu. in. (3.8-liter) V-6 with sequential fuel injection, three-coil ignition and roller valve lifters. Also included: a new FE3 handling performance package. GT equipment package was offered for Ciera S and on Ciera four-door sedan, including halogen headlamps, integral front air dam with foglamps, and aero fascia and rocker panel treatments, as well as specially-styled leather bucket seats, leather-wrapped steering wheel, and rallye gauges. GT models had a 3.8-liter V-6 with dual-outlet exhaust and console- mounted four-speed overdrive automatic transmission. Also included: the FE3 handling package with styled aluminum wheels and Eagle GT tires. Ciera's grille now showed a 7 x 3 pattern of wide holes, but in a shape similar to before. Base engine once again was Pontiac's "Iron Duke" 151 cu. in. (2.5-liter) four. Newly optional: Chevrolet's 2.8-liter V-6 with MFI (replacing the former carbureted 3.0-liter V-6). The diesel 4.3-liter V-6 had been dropped in spring 1985. In March 1986, a 1986.5 Cutlass Ciera coupe became available, along with four new mid-year "specialty" models. They had an all-new roofline with sloping back window and revised Cpillar design, for a European profile. No other GM division offered this styling. Two trim levels were offered: S and SL.

1986 Cutlass Supreme sedan (AA)

CUTLASS SUPREME — SERIES 3G — V-6/V-8 — Rear-drive mid-size appearance was similar to 1985, except for a 5 x 5 hole pattern in the sedan's upright eggcrate grille. Sporty Salon and 442 models had a contemporary front-end look with aero composite headlamps. Five models were offered: Supreme coupe and sedan, Supreme Brougham coupe and sedan, and Salon coupe (with 442 package available). Base engine was Buick's 231 cu. in. (3.8-liter) V-6, now with sequential fuel injection. Optional: the 307 cu. in. (5.0-liter) four-barrel V-8.

1986 Delta 88 coupe (AA)

DELTA 88 — SERIES 3H — V-6 — Ninety-Eight had switched to contemporary front-drive for 1985. Now it was 88's turn. The all-new coupe and sedan bodies featured soft lines and rounded edges, but traditional Olds semi-notchback roofline and split grille. Coupes had a rounded backlight and sloping roofline, aimed at younger buyers who wanted roominess as well as style. Four models were offered: Royale coupe and sedan, and Royale Brougham coupe and sedan. Twin narrow grilles in a sloping panel stood alongside a wide center body-color divider with emblem. A nameplate went on the left grille section. Wide park/signal lamps were below the bumper strips. Also below the bumper was a single air intake slot. Recessed headlamps met shapely wraparound side marker lenses. Taillamps were flush-mounted to follow the back panels and wrapped around the quarter panel slightly, with upper and lower lens sections. Small backup lenses stood below the rear bumper strip. Standard engine was a 181 cu. in. (3.0-liter) V-6; optional, a 231 cu. in. (3.8-liter) V-6.

CUSTOM CRUISER — SERIES 3B — V-8 — Now that Delta 88 and Ninety-Eight were front-drive, the old rear-drive wagon became a model on its own. Two-seat wagons with six-passenger capacity were standard, with a rear-facing third seat available to add space for two more. Wagons came only with four-barrel 307 cu. in. (5.0-liter) V-8 and four-speed overdrive automatic. No more diesel engines were available. Custom Cruiser was similar to Buick Estate, Chevrolet Caprice Classic and Pontiac Parisienne wagons.

NINETY-EIGHT REGENCY — SERIES 3C — V-6 — Not too much changed for the front-drive Ninety-Eight in its second season. The most notable addition was on the option list: anti-lock braking, the first such offering on an Oldsmobile. Sensors at each wheel detected wheel speed changes. Then, a computer altered the pressure applied at each wheel to prevent lockup and potential skids. Ninety-Eight had recessed quad headlamps and wraparound side marker lenses, with wide park/signal lamps down below the bumper strip. Twin intake slots were in the bumper. The sloping grille consisted of very tight crosshatch sections. Cornering lamps stood very low on the front fenders. Vertical taillamps with emblems wrapped slightly around onto each quarter panel. Four models were offered: Regency and Regency Brougham coupe and sedan. Sole engine was the 231 cu. in. (3.8-liter) V-6, now with sequential fuel injection. Options included an FE3 handling package. A new luxury Grande option package for Broughams included aero composite headlamps, classic eggcrate grille, leather interior and leather-wrapped steering wheel. Optional on Grande: sueded pigskin interior with suede sport steering wheel and a storage console. About 3,000 Grandes were expected to be produced, all at Orion, Michigan.

1986 Toronado coupe (JG)

TORONADO — SERIES 3E — V-6 — Since this was Toro's 20th anniversary, an all-new design arrived. The sleek new front end had concealed headlamps integral with the grille design for an aerodynamic look. Headlamp doors moved below the lamps when they were switched on. Drag coefficient of 0.36 was 35 percent better than the 1985 model. This version was 18 inches shorter and 550 pounds lighter than its predecessor, but carried six passengers. Toro's wedge silhouette featured a low sloping hood, upwardly curving rear fascia, and high rear deck. The lower roof sloped gently into a slightly rounded backlight. Taillamps consisted of a full-width horizontal bar. Front sheetmetal panels were rounded, and all glass was flush- mounted. With headlamps closed, the front end showed full- width horizontal strips on each side of the center divider (which contained an emblem). A four-section air intake was in the bumper area, with park/signal lamps in the bumper strip. Internal seals replaced drip moldings. Wheel covers were flatter and more flush. For corrosion protection, all inner and outer body panels were now two-sided galvanized steel. A new stainless steel exhaust system was used, with modular welded construction instead of clamps. In the engine compartment, all wires were covered (and protected) by rigid plastic channels. Toronado had rackandpinion steering, and four-wheel low- drag disc brakes. Front suspension was MacPherson struts with single lower control arm and microcellular urethane jounce bumpers. Standard (and only) engine was a 231 cu. in. (3.8- liter) V-6 with four-speed overdrive automatic. No engine options were available, but the V-6 actually delivered more horsepower than the former V-8. A power driver's seat was standard. Ample electronics were used in Toronado, to provide convenience, information, safety and servicing ease. It offered the first "body computer" in an Olds, receiving information from sensors throughout the car to control instruments, message center and optional voice control system, as well as engine functions. A message center alerted the driver to problems, with 26 diagnostic and 11 trip monitor messages. A system monitor let the driver check if the car was in proper running condition. Toro's heat/vent/air conditioning system could be fully automatic or manually controlled. A special 20th anniversary Toronado was offered at mid- year. It came in a choice of two paint schemes, with specific striping, leather-wrapped steering wheel, leather seats with pigskin inserts, and P215/60R15 tires on special 15 x 6 inch aluminum wheels. Multi-colored 20th anniversary emblems went on the hood and sail panels. The model also included a personalized registration plaque.

I.D. DATA: Oldsmobile's 17-symbol Vehicle Identification Number (VIN) again was located on the upper left surface of the instrument panel, visible through the windshield. The first three symbols ('1G3') indicate Oldsmobile division. Symbol four denotes restraint type: 'A' manual (active) belts. Symbol five is car line/series: 'C' Firenza; 'D' Firenza LC/LX; 'F' Calais; 'T' Calais Supreme; 'J' Cutlass Ciera LS; 'M' Cutlass Ciera Brougham; 'R' Cutlass Supreme; 'M' Cutlass Supreme Brougham ; 'K' Cutlass Salon; 'L' Delta 88; 'N' Delta 88 Royale; 'Y' Delta 88 Royale Brougham; 'P' Custom Cruiser; 'X' Ninety-Eight Regency; 'W' Ninety-Eight Regency Brougham; 'Z' Toronado Brougham. Next come two digits that denote body type: '11' 2dr. notchback sedan; '27' 2dr. coupe; '37' 2dr. coupe; '47' 2dr. coupe; '57' 2dr. coupe; '77' 2dr. hatch coupe; '19' 4dr. sedan; '69' 4dr. 4window notch sedan; '35' 4dr. 2seat wagon. Symbol eight is a letter for engine code: '0' L4112 FI; 'P' L4121 FI; 'R' L4151 FI; 'X' V6173 2Bbl; 'W' V6173 FI; 'L' V6181 FI; 'A' V6231; 'Y' V8307 4Bbl. Next comes a check digit, followed by a code for model year: ('G' 1986). Symbol eleven is the assembly plant code: 'D' Doraville, Georgia; 'G' Framingham, Mass.; 'M' Lansing, Mich.; 'P' Pontiac, Mich.; 'W' Willow Run, Mich.; 'E' Linden, New Jersey; 'R' Arlington, Texas; 'K' Leeds, Missouri; '1' Oshawa, Ontario; '2' Ste. Therese, Quebec. (Oldsmobiles were also built in Hamtramck, Detroit and Orion, Mich.; and at Wentzville, Missouri.) The final six digits are the sequential serial number. Engine numbers were stamped on the front of the right rocker cover, or top of left cover (Buick-built engines), on label at front or rear of right rocker cover (Chevrolet V-6), or on the left rocker cover (Oldsmobile engines). Four- cylinder engine numbers were on a pad at left front of block, below cylinder head. A body number plate on the upper right cowl identified model year, series, style, body assembly plant, body number, trim combination, modular seat code, paint code, date built code, and option codes.

FIRENZA (FOUR)

Model Number	Body/Style Number	Body Type & Seating	Factory Price	Shipping Weight	Production Total
3J	C27	2-dr. Cpe-5P	7782	2276	12,003
3J	C77	2-dr. S Hatch-5P	7941	2329	2,531
3J	D27	2-dr. LC Cpe-5P	8611	2328	2,867
3J	C69	4-dr. Sedan-5P	8035	2330	18,437
3J	D69	4-dr. LX sed-5P	8626	2361	4,415

FIRENZA CRUISER (FOUR)

3J	C35	4-dr. Sta Wag-5P	8259	2387	5,416

FIRENZA GT (V-6)

3J	D77	2-dr. Hatch Cpe-5P	9774	2509	1,032

CALAIS (FOUR/V-6)

3N	F27	2-dr. Cpe-5P	9283/10358	2415/2527	52,726
3N	F69	4-dr. Sed-5P	9478/10553	2481/2593	40,393

CALAIS SUPREME (FOUR/V-6)

3N	T27	2-dr. Cpe-5P	9668/10743	2426/2538	33,060
3N	T69	4-dr. Sed-5P	9863/10938	2484/2596	25,128

CUTLASS CIERA LS (FOUR/V-6)

3A	J27	2-dr. Cpe-6P	10153/10588	2651/2708	9,233
3A	J37	2-dr. S Cpe-6P	10619/11054	N/A	16,281
3A	J19	4-dr. Sed-6P	10354/10789	2694/2751	144,466
3G	J35	4-dr. Sta Wag-6P	10734/11169	2853/2912	35,890

CUTLASS CIERA BROUGHAM (FOUR/V-6)

3A	M27	2-dr. Cpe-6P	10645/11080	2667/2724	11,534
3A	M37	2-dr. SL Cpe-6P	10868/11303	2667/2724	12,525
3A	M19	4-dr. Sed-6P	10868/11303	2724/2781	123,027

CUTLASS SUPREME (V-6/V-8)

3G	R47	2-dr. Cpe-6P	10698/11238	3123/3283	79,654
3G	R69	4-dr. Sed-6P	10872/11412	3173/3321	41,973

CUTLASS SUPREME BROUGHAM (V-6/V-8)

3G	M47	2-dr. Cpe-6P	11408/11948	3153/3313	55,275
3G	M69	4-dr. Sed-6P	11551/12091	3201/3349	24,646

CUTLASS SALON (V-6/V-8)

3G	K47	2-dr. Cpe-6P	11728/12268	3175/3335	9,608

DELTA 88 ROYALE (V-6)

3H	N37	2-dr. Cpe-6P	12760	3046	13,696
3H	N69	4-dr. Sed-6P	12760	3091	88,564

DELTA 88 ROYALE BROUGHAM (V-6)

3H	Y37	2-dr. Cpe-6P	13461	3075	23,697
3H	Y69	4-dr. Sed-6P	13461	3116	108,344

CUSTOM CRUISER (V-8)

3B	P35	4-dr. Sta Wag-6P	13416	4004	21,073

NINETY-EIGHT REGENCY (V-6)

3C	X11	2-dr. Sedan-6P	16062	3179	803
3C	X69	4-dr. Sedan-6P	15989	3215	23,717

NINETY-EIGHT REGENCY BROUGHAM (V-6)

3C	W11	2-dr. Sedan-6P	17052	3196	5,007
3C	W69	4-dr. Sedan-6P	16979	3232	95,045

TORONADO BROUGHAM (V-6)

3E	Z57	2-dr. Cpe-5P	19418	3216	15,924

FACTORY PRICE AND WEIGHT NOTE: Cutlass Supreme prices and weights to left of slash are for six-cylinder, to right for V-8 engine; others, to left for four-cylinder and to right for V-6.

ENGINE DATA: BASE FOUR (Firenza): Inline, overhead-valve four-cylinder. Cast iron block and head. Displacement: 121 cu. in. (2.0 liters). Bore & stroke: 3.50 x 3.14 in. Compression ratio: 9.3:1. Brake horsepower: 88 at 4800 R.P.M. Torque: 110 lbs.ft. at 2400 R.P.M. Five main bearings. Hydraulic valve lifters. Electronic fuel injection. VIN Code: P. **OPTIONAL FOUR (Firenza):** Inline, overhead-cam four-cylinder. Cast iron block and aluminum head. Displacement: 112 cu. in. (1.8 liters). Bore & stroke: 3.34 x 3.11 in. Compression ratio: 9.0:1. Brake horsepower: 84 at 5200 R.P.M. Torque: 98 lbs.ft. at 2800 R.P.M. Five main bearings. Hydraulic valve lifters. Electronic fuel injection. VIN Code: O. **BASE FOUR (Calais, Cutlass Ciera):** Inline, overhead-valve four-cylinder. Cast iron block and head. Displacement: 151 cu. in. (2.5 liters). Bore & stroke: 4.00 x 3.00 in. Compression ratio: 8.2:1. Brake horsepower: 92 at 4400 R.P.M. Torque: 132-134 lbs.ft. at 2800 R.P.M. Five main bearings. Hydraulic valve lifters. Fuel injection (TBI). Pontiac-built. VIN Code: R. **OPTIONAL V-6 (Firenza):** 60-degree, overhead-valve V-6. Cast iron block and aluminum head. Displacement: 173 cu. in. (2.8 liters). Bore & stroke: 3.50 x 3.00 in. Compression ratio: 8.9:1. Brake horsepower: 130 at 4800 R.P.M. Torque: 160 lbs.ft. at 3600 R.P.M. Four main bearings. Hydraulic valve lifters. Electronic fuel injection. Chevrolet-built. VIN Code: W. **OPTIONAL V-6 (Cutlass Ciera):** Carbureted version of 173 cu. in. V-6 above Compression ratio: 8.5:1. Horsepower: 112 at 4800 R.P.M. Torque: 145 lbs.-ft. at 2100 R.P.M. Carburetor: 2Bbl. VIN Code: X. **BASE V-6 (Delta 88):** 90-degree, overhead-valve V-6. Cast iron block and head. Displacement: 181 cu. in. (3.0 liters). Bore & stroke: 3.80 x 2.66 in. Compression ratio: 9.0:1. Brake horsepower: 125 at 4900 R.P.M. Torque: 150 lbs.ft. at 2400 R.P.M. Four main bearings. Hydraulic valve lifters. Electronic fuel injection. VIN Code: L. **BASE V-6 (Cutlass Supreme):** 90-degree, overhead-valve V-6. Cast iron block and head. Displacement: 231 cu. in. (3.8 liters). Bore & stroke: 3.80 x 3.40 in. Compression ratio: 8.0:1. Brake horsepower: 110 at 3800 R.P.M. Torque: 190 lbs.ft. at 1600 R.P.M. Four main bearings. Hydraulic valve lifters. Carburetor: 2Bbl. Rochester E2ME. Buick-built. VIN Code: A. **BASE V-6 (Ninety-Eight, Toronado); OPTIONAL (Cutlass Ciera, Delta 88):** Same as 231 cu. in. V-6 above, but with sequential fuel injection Horsepower: 140 at 4400 R.P.M. (Ciera/Delta 88, 150 at 4400). Torque: 200 lbs.-ft. at 2000 R.P.M. **BASE V-8 (Custom Cruiser); OPTIONAL (Cutlass Supreme):** 90-degree, overhead valve V-8. Cast iron block and head. Displacement: 307 cu. in. (5.0 liters). Bore & stroke: 3.80 x 3.38 in. Compression ratio: 8.0:1. Brake horsepower: 140 at 3200 R.P.M. Torque: 255 lbs.ft. at 2000 R.P.M. Five main bearings. Hydraulic valve lifters. Carburetor: 4Bbl. Rochester E4MC. VIN Code: Y.

CHASSIS DATA: Wheelbase: (Firenza) 101.2 in.; (Calais) 103.4 in.; (Ciera) 104.9 in.; (Cutlass) 108.1 in.; (Delta 88) 110.8 in.; (98) 110.8 in.; (Custom Cruiser) 115.9 in.; (Toronado) 108.0 in. Overall Length: (Firenza cpe) 174.3 in.; (Firenza sed) 176.2 in.; (Firenza wag) 176.2 in.; (Calais) 178.8 in.; (Ciera) 190.3 in.; (Ciera wag) 194.4 in.; (Cutlass Supreme) 200.0- 200.4 in.; (Delta 88) 196.0 in.; (98) 196.4 in.; (Custom Crsr) 220.3 in.; (Toro) 187.9 in. Height: (Firenza cpe) 51.7 in.; (Firenza sed) 53.7 in.; (Firenza wag) 55.2 in.; (Calais) 53.3 in.; (Ciera) 54.1 in.; (Ciera wag) 54.5 in.; (Cutlass Supreme cpe) 54.9 in.; (Cutlass Supreme sed) 55.9 in.; (Delta 88 cpe) 54.5-54.6 in.; (98) 55.1 in.; (Custom Crsr) 58.5 in.; (Toro) 52.9 in. Width: (Firenza) 65.0 in.; (Calais) 66.9 in.; (Ciera) 69.5 in.; (Cutlass cpe) 71.6; (Cutlass sed) 71.9 in.; (Delta 88) 72.1 in.; (98) 71.4 in.; (Custom Crsr) 79.8 in.; (Toro) 70.7 in. Front Tread: (Firenza) 55.4 in.; (Calais) 55.5 in.; (Ciera) 58.7 in.; (Cutlass) 58.5 in.; (Delta 88) 60.3 in.; (98) 60.3 in.; (Custom Crsr) 62.1 in.; (Toro) 59.9 in. Rear Tread: (Firenza) 55.2 in.; (Calais) 55.2 in.; (Ciera) 57.0 in.; (Cutlass) 59.8 in.; (Delta 88) 60.7 in.; (98) 59.8 in.; (Custom Crsr) 64.1 in.; (Toro) 59.9 in. Standard Tires: (Firenza) P175/80R13; (Calais) P185/80R13; (Ciera) P185/75R14; (Cutlass Supreme) P195/75R14; (Delta 88) P205/75R14; (98) P205/75R14; (Custom Crsr) P225/75R15; (Toronado) P205/70R14.

TECHNICAL: Transmission: Four-speed floor shift standard on Firenza. Five-speed manual trans. standard on Calais, optional on Firenza: Three-speed Turbo Hydra-matic standard on Cutlass/Ciera. Four-speed automatic overdrive standard on Delta 88/Custom Cruiser/98/Toronado. Standard final drive ratio: (Firenza) 3.65:1 w/4spd w/5spd, 3.18:1 w/auto.; (Calais) 3.35:1 w/5spd, 2.84:1 w/auto.; (Ciera) 2.84:1 except 3.06:1 w/V6173 and 4spd auto.; (Cutlass) 2.41:1 w/V-6, 2.14:1 w/V-8, 3.73:1 w/V-8 and 4spd auto.; (Delta 88) 3.06:1 w/V6181, 2.73:1 w/V6231; (98) 2.84:1; (Toronado) 2.84:1. Steering: (Cutlass/Custom Cruiser) recirculating ball; (others) rack and pinion. Front Suspension: (Firenza/Calais/Ciera/88/98) MacPherson struts w/coil springs, lower control arms and anti-sway bar; (Toronado) MacPherson struts w/link control arm and anti- sway bar; (Cutlass/Custom Crsr) coil springs with upper/lower control arms. Rear Suspension: (Firenza) beam axle w/coil springs, trailing arms and anti-sway bar; (Calais) semi-independent w/coil springs and trailing arms; (Ciera) beam axle with integral anti-sway, coil springs and Panhard rod; (88) independent w/struts, coil springs and anti-sway bar; (98) independent w/struts, coil springs, lower control arms, anti-sway bar and automatic level control; (Toronado) independent with transverse leaf spring, control arms and automatic leveling; (Cutlass/Custom Crsr) rigid axle w/coil springs, lower trailing radius arms and upper torque arms (four-link). Brakes: Front disc, rear drum except Toronado, four-wheel disc. Ignition: Electronic. Body construction: (Cutlass/Custom Cruiser) separate body and frame; (others) unibody. Fuel tank: (Firenza/Calais) 13.6 gal.; (Ciera) 16.6 gal.; (Cutlass) 18.1 gal.; (Delta 88) 18 gal.; (98) 18 gal.; (Custom Crsr wag) 22 gal.; (Toronado) 18 gal.

DRIVETRAIN OPTIONS: Engines: 112 cu. in. four: Firenza ($50). 173 cu. in. 2Bbl. V-6: Ciera ($435). 173 cu. in. FI V-6: Ciera ($560). 181 cu. in. V-6: Calais ($610). 307 cu. in. 4Bbl. V-8: Cutlass ($540). Transmission/Differential: Five-speed manual trans.: Firenza ($75). Turbo Hydra-matic: Firenza/Calais ($465). Four-speed overdrive auto.: Ciera/Cutlass ($175). Column shift: Calais ($110 credit). Limited-slip differential: Cutlass/Custom Cruiser ($100). Steering/Suspension: Power steering: base Firenza ($215). Firm ride/handling pkg. ($30-$49). Automatic load leveling: Ciera/88/Custom Crsr ($180). Other: High-capacity cooling ($40-$70). High-capacity radiator: Cutlass/Custom Crsr/88/98/Toro ($30). Wiring harness: Custom Crsr/98 ($30). Engine block heater ($18). California emissions ($99).

OPTION PACKAGES: Calais GT pkg.: base cpe ($1350). Calais ES pkg.: base sed ($995). Calais sport appearance pkg. ($150-$195). Ciera ES pkg.: base sedan ($1992). Ciera Holiday coupe pkg.: Brghm ($680). Ciera GT pkg.: base cpe ($3330). Cutlass Salon 442 pkg. ($2075). 98 premium interior: Brghm ($975).

MAJOR CONVENIENCE/APPEARANCE OPTIONS: Four Season air conditioner ($645-$750). Tempmatic air conditioning: 88 ($805); 98 ($125); Custom Crsr ($55). Cruise control ($175). Power seat ($178-$225). Power windows ($195-$270). Electronic instrument panel: Ciera/Calais/98 ($83-$299). Twilight sentinel: 98 ($60). Cornering lamps: 98 ($60). Power astroroof w/sliding glass panel: Cutlass ($925); 98 ($1230). Removable glass roof panels: Cutlass ($850). Glass panel sunroof: Firenza/Calais/Ciera ($310). Landau vinyl roof: Ciera/Cutlass ($245). Full vinyl roof: Ciera/Cutlass ($160). Full padded vinyl roof: Cutlass/98 ($245). Rear-facing third seat: Cutlass/Custom Cruiser ($215-$220).

HISTORY: Introduced: October 3, 1985 except 88 and Toronado, November 14, 1985 and Calais, August 28, 1985. Model year production: 1,157,990. Calendar year production (U.S.): 927,173. Calendar year sales by U.S. dealers: 1,059,390. Model year sales by U.S. dealers: 1,067,819.

Historical Footnotes: Olds had ranked No. 3 in sales through the past decade. Now, for the third year in a row, sales hit the million mark. Ciera was the best selling Oldsmobile by a comfortable margin over the new front-drive Delta 88. Sales of the reworked Toronado, however, reached only half their 1985 level. The two Cutlass lines amounted to nearly half of Olds sales.

Through most of its early life, Plymouth was thought of as a kind of kid brother to Dodge: same shape, same engines, similar models appealing to ordinary families. Starting with the Fifties Fury, however, Plymouth also turned to performance, eventually turning out such eye-openers as the 1970 Superbird with six-barrel carburetion, and a selection of potent Barracudas. Those were gone by 1976, and Plymouth seemed (with one or two exceptions) to have reverted to its family motorcar origins—and would soon lose most of its familiar names.

1976 Feather Duster two-door hardtop (CM)

The selection of Valiant and Duster models was still around, but scheduled for replacement by the new Volare (twin to Dodge's Aspen). Volare's Road Runner coupe package came with a 318 cu. in. V-8, floor shift and heavy-duty suspension, but hardly rivaled earlier models with that name. Basically, it was one more family car. So was the mid-size Fury, restyled a year before, which offered one of the last pillarless two-door hardtop designs. Fury could have a 240- horsepower, 400 cu. in. V-8, while the full-size Gran Fury's optional 440 rated just 205 horsepower.

1976 Volare Custom coupe (JG)

Fury got another restyle for 1977, while the biggest Plymouths carried on for just one more year. Volare was the big seller in Plymouth's lineup. A selection of option packages helped, including the Road Runner and Sun Runner, plus a Super Pak with spoilers and louvered quarter windows. Super Coupe and a Street Kit Car were

1978 Horizon four-door hatchback (CM)

added to the Volare list for 1978, and a Gran Coupe to Fury's options. But the biggest event was the introduction of the subcompact Horizon. Like Dodge's nearly-identical Omni, Horizon had front-wheel drive and a transverse-mounted four-cylinder engine. The 440 V-8 was dropped as a Fury selection, and the name itself faded away before the 1979 model year. In fact, only two Plymouths were left by then: Horizon and Volare. A new TC3 hatchback coupe joined the Horizon sedan, though, with Sport and Rallye packages available. Volare coupes could still get a four-barrel 360 cu. in. V-8, and the Road Runner extras.

Gran Fury returned for 1980, but in a new and shorter form. Volares weren't selling well, and this would be their final try. A Turismo package was now available for the Horizon TC3 coupe, including blackout moldings and a rear spoiler. Plymouth sales were augmented by three captive imports: Arrow, Champ and Sapporo.

1979 Duster SE coupe (OCW)

Reliant was Plymouth's version of the new front-drive K-car, introduced for 1981. Economy-minded Miser models were added to the Horizon and TC3·list. TC3 had its Turismo option again, and Horizon a Euro-Sedan package. Gran Fury dropped down to a single model, and was downsized to a 112.7 inch wheelbase for 1982. That

version would remain in the lineup through the 1980s, appealing mainly to fleets and larger families. Gran Fury sedans sold to police departments carried a four-barrel high-performance version of the V-8 engine. The Turismo 2.2 variant of TC3 came with a 2.2- liter engine. Model year sales slumped considerably—but they had risen substantially the year before, so all was just about even. Not until 1985 would a notable increase occur.

1979 Duster SE coupe (OCW)

Horizon and Turismo engines for 1983 were smaller than before: 97 cu. in. (1.6-liter) Peugeot-built versions, as opposed to the former 105 fours. Their optional powerplant was the 2.2-liter Trans-4, which began life as Reliant's base selection. The TC3 nameplate was dropped, as were the Miser and Euro-Sedan variants of the Plymouth subcompacts. Reliants could now have a five-speed manual transaxle.

It was almost like losing an old friend when the Slant Six engine dropped out, before the 1984 model year. But it

1986 Gran Fury four-door sedan (CM)

just didn't fit in with the trend toward front-drive. Gran Fury carried on with only the 318 cu. in. V-8, adding roller lifters in 1985. Horizon showed the strongest sales rise for '84, but Gran Fury took the honors the next year. Also in 1985 came a new Plymouth: the front-drive Caravelle (which was actually a Chrysler E Class). The Turismo 2.2 got some performance-oriented styling features. In 1986, a brand new fuel-injected 2.5 liter engine replaced the Mitsubishi-built four as an option for Reliant and Caravelle.

This wasn't the greatest period for collectible Plymouths. Road Runner Volares? Passable, but not the most thrilling choice. Other Volare variants? Worth a look, but probably not worth traveling cross-country to find one. Even the moderately performance-oriented Turismo subcompact coupes were just adaptations of the Dodge design, not unique to Plymouth. No, Plymouth fanciers might do best to look to an earlier era—or switch to Dodge, which had a few more models of interest to choose from.

1976 PLYMOUTH

Plymouth's lineup for 1976 included compact Valiants and Volares, the mid-size Fury, and full-size Gran Fury. This would be the final year for the Valiant group (which included Duster and Scamp), as the new Volare prepared to take over their spot. The familiar 225 cu. in. Slant Six engine was standard on all except Gran Fury, with a selection of optional V-8s available. The big 400 and 440 cu. in. V-8s had Chrysler's Electronic Lean Burn System. Its mini-computer gathered data from sensors on throttle position, engine R.P.M., manifold vacuum and coolant temperature, and adjusted ignition timing for the leanest (most economical) air/fuel mixture.

1976 Volare "Road Runner" coupe (OCW)

1976 Silver Duster two-door hardtop (JG)

VALIANT/DUSTER/SCAMP — SERIES V — SIX/V-8 — Like the closely related Dodge Dart series, Valiant reached back to 1960 origin. For its final year, Plymouth's compact lineup included the Duster hardtop (semi-fastback) coupe on a 108 in. wheelbase, plus a Scamp hardtop and Valiant sedan on 111 in. wheelbases. The wide-look front end had a grille made up of many wide crosshatch elements, which stretched the full width between single round headlamps in squarish housings. Slightly rounded rectangular park/signal lamps sat in the grille insert. The center portion of that grille insert protruded forward slightly, and had a vertical rectangular emblem in the middle. On the thicker center portion of the upper header bar was 'Plymouth' block lettering. Duster's clean-look rear end held horizontal rectangular taillamps that reached to the quarter panel tips, surrounded by bright moldings and with a thin horizontal divider across each housing. Backup lenses were at the inner ends of each taillamp housing. Duster's bodyside sloped upward to the rear of the door, giving the

VOLARE — SERIES H — SIX/V-8 — Introduced this year as a replacement for the doomed Valiant, Volare was billed as "the new small car with the accent on comfort." Like the similar F-bodied Dodge Aspen, it debuted at mid-year. Base, Custom and top-rung Premier models were offered. Two-door coupes rode a 108.5 in. wheelbase, while four-door sedans and four-door station wagons measured 112.5 in. Volare had a new Isolated Transverse Suspension System, with transverse-mounted front torsion bars and anti- sway bar, separated from the chassis by two sets of rubber mounts. This system of crosswise torsion bars (rather than the usual longitudinal mounting) was claimed to give a "big- car ride." Base engine was the 225 cu. in. Slant Six; 318 or 360 cu. in. V-8 optional, with TorqueFlite transmission. Overdrive four-speed manual shift also was available, instead of the standard three-speed. All Volares had standard front disc brakes; wagons and V-8s had power brakes. Volare's grille consisted of tiny squares arranged in three rows, divided by a vertical center bar. Single round headlamps sat in recessed square housings. Unusually large, clear park/signal lamps were recessed between the grille and headlamps. Volare's hood was higher in the center to match the grille width, sloping downward at the sides to meet the signal lamps. 'Volare' script was on front fenders, ahead of the door. Small horizontal amber side marker lenses stood on front fenders, near the headlamps. A horizontal strip divided each rectangular taillamp into upper and lower segments. A trim panel of the same height as the taillamps stretched between them. Backup lenses were at the inner end of each taillamp housing. Standard two- door Volares had large triangular quarter windows. A Landau vinyl roof, standard on Volare Premier, included square-look opera windows. Wagons had a large one-piece liftgate. Standard equipment included drip moldings, quarter- window reveal moldings, heater/defroster, and dome light. Volare Custom added a cigarette lighter, woodgrain instrument cluster trim, pleated vinyl or cloth/vinyl bench seats, rear deck lower applique, belt molding, B-pillar molding (on coupes), bodyside and partial wheel lip moldings, and

1976 Valiant Scamp two-door hardtop (JG)

quarter windows a tapered look. Scamp had a different back end appearance, with horizontal taillamps that wrapped slightly around the quarter panels and contained a horizontal divider bar. A sizable bright trim strip containing 'Plymouth' block letters on a darker panel ran between the taillamps. Scamp's side view was also different, with triangular, older-style quarter windows. The Valiant series offered torsion-bar front suspension, electric choke assist, hubcaps, fuel and temperature gauges, an ammeter, dome lamp switch, amd unibody construction. V-8 models had front disc brakes; sixes kept drum brakes all around. V-8s also had front bumper guards. Duster had swing- out rear quarter windows; Scamp's were the roll-down type. Valiant sedans included vent windows. Duster held five passengers on standard cloth/vinyl bench seats. Valiant's base model could add a Custom or Brougham trim package. Brougham added such touches as simulated woodgrain inserts on the instrument panel, day/night mirror, and velour upholstery. Brougham packages were installed on 5.8 percent of hardtop and sedan models. Base engine was the old familiar 225 cu. in. Slant Six. A 318 cu. in. V-8 was optional. So was a 360 cu. in. V-8 (except in California), available only with TorqueFlite automatic transmission. Plymouth engines now had electronic ignition. Three-speed manual shift was standard, with four- speed overdrive optional. Body colors were: Powder Blue, Rallye Red, Sahara Beige, Yellow Blaze, Golden Fawn, Spinnaker White, and Formal Black; plus metallic Silver Cloud, Jamaican Blue, Vintage Red, Jade Green, Deep Sherwood, Caramel Tan, Cinnamon, Inca Gold, or Spanish Gold. A SpaceMaker option allowed the rear seat to fold down. Also among the options was a Fuel Pacer System, designed to conserve fuel. An optional Silver Duster decor package included unique bodyside stripes that twisted upward at the rear to meet the taillamps, and another stripe between the taillamp housings. It also included wheel moldings and a red interior. The Feather Duster fuel economy package turned to lightweight aluminum components, including the intake manifold, hood and deck inner panels, as well as economy (long) axle ratios. The overdrive manual gearbox was mounted in an aluminum case. More than 22 percent of Duster coupes had the Feather Duster package, which had a limited option list. Scamp's Special was also aimed at economy buyers. Base Scamps had all-vinyl bench seating. Scamp Brougham went the other direction with velour cloth/vinyl upholstery, woodgrain instrument panel inserts, a hood ornament, wide sill moldings, and hood/deck accent stripes.

1976 Volare "Road Runner" coupe (JG)

rear armrests. Volare Premier added TorqueFlite, power steering, day/night mirror, electric clock, dual horns, locking glovebox, color-keyed vinyl insert bodyside moldings, bodyside accent tape stripes, hood ornament and accent stripe, premium wheel covers, and a carpeted trunk. Inside was a 60/40 split bench seat with dual reclining seatbacks, carpeted lower door panels, door pull-handles, and luxury three-spoke steering wheel. Premier coupes had a landau vinyl roof; sedans a full vinyl roof. Premier wagons had standard woodgrain bodyside appliques. Body colors for Volare were: Big Sky Blue, Spitfire Orange, Claret Red, Sahara Beige, Saddle Tan, Harvest Gold, Spinnaker White, and Formal Black. Metallic colors were: Silver Cloud, Jamaican Blue, Jade or Tropic Green, Deep Sherwood, Caramel Tan, Cinnamon, and Spanish Gold. Two-tone combinations arranged the colors in a way that looked almost like a three-tone. Performance-minded buyers could select a Volare Road Runner coupe package (like Dodge's Aspen R/T), which included a 318 cu. in. V-8, heavy-duty suspension, three-speed floor shift, and sporty interior trim. A hefty 83.8 percent of the 8,769 HL29 Volares with V-8 engine had the Road Runner package (code A57), while 21.7 percent carried the A66 Super Pak.

FURY — SERIES R — SIX/V-8 — Restyled for 1975, Plymouth's mid-size (descended from the old Satellite) entered this year with little change. The model lineup included a base two-door hardtop (true pillarless design) and four-door sedan; Salon four-door; Sport two-door hardtop; plus Suburban and Sport Suburban station wagons. Fury was closely related to Dodge's Coronet and Charger. The Road Runner performance package was announced again as a Fury option, but that name went on a Volare variant instead. Fury coupes rode a 115 in. wheelbase, while sedans and wagons measured 117.5 in. between hubs. Fury's grille consisted of many thin vertical bars, separated into a dozen sections by 11 dominant vertical dividers. Outer sections actually contained the parking lamps. Single round headlamps in squarish housings sat farther back than the grille. 'Plymouth' lettering was above the grille on the driver's side. Front fenders held 'Fury' script, just ahead of the door. Just inside the quarter panel tips of base and Sport Fury two-door models were vertical taillamps, surrounded by bright moldings, angled slightly inward. The triple-crease decklid had a sculptured look and 'Plymouth' block lettering. A recessed license plate housing extended into the

1976 Fury four-door sedan (JG)

bumper and lower decklid. Fury sedans had a different rear end, with large tri- section horizontal taillamps inset into the bumper. The license plate was deeply recessed in a housing built entirely into the bumper. Salon's decklid also had only a single crease running down its center, plus 'Plymouth' block lettering. On the decklid's side was a small 'Salon' script. A velour/vinyl seat with folding center armrest was standard on Salon, as was a hood ornament. The Fury Sport two-door hardtop was not a "true" hardtop, but displayed opera windows. It had standard tape stripes and styled wheels, plus a standard 318 cu. in. V-8 engine. All-vinyl bucket seats with folding center armrest were a no-cost option to replace the standard velour split- back seating. The

1976 Fury Sport Coupe (CM)

soft-touch steering wheel was new this year. Fury Sport could have optional louvered quarter windows with a canopy vinyl roof. Actually, that simply meant it had two skinny side-by-side opera window openings instead of one, in a design obviously meant for appearance rather than visibility. Base engine was the 225 cu. in. Slant Six. Optional: 318, 360 and 400 cu. in. V-8s. Wagons came with a standard 360 V-8 and automatic transmission, plus power steering and brakes. Standard equipment on the base Fury included hubcaps, F78 x 14 blackwall tires (H78 x 14 on wagons), front and rear armrests, sill moldings, decklid lower molding, dome light, lighter, heater/defroster, Torsion-Bar suspension with anti- sway bar, three-speed fully synchronized transmission (column shift), tuned exhaust system, and locking glovebox. Sedans and wagons had rear bumper guards. Fury Sport added deluxe wheel covers, dual horns, bodyside stripes, a bench seat with center armrest, premium door trim panels with pull handles, hood rear edge molding, hood ornament, and 'Sport' name on the C-pillar. Fury Salon added the hood ornament, Salon nameplate and crest, deluxe wheel covers, velour split-seat with center armrest, dual horns, and luxury door trim panels with pull handles. Newly optional this year was 60/40 split-bench seating with dual reclining seatbacks.

1976 Gran Fury Custom four-door sedan (JG)

GRAN FURY — SERIES P — V-8 — Full-size Plymouths changed little this year, except for a revised grille and parking lamp treatment. Dodge's Monaco was its near twin. The grille insert's crosshatch pattern was divided into four rows by three dominant horizontal dividers, each with 14 "holes" across and peaked forward at the center. Separate, large 'Plymouth' block letters stood above the grille, on the panel ahead of the hood. Vertical rectangular parking/signal lamps were between the grille and single round headlamps, mounted in square housings. A single bright molding surrounded both headlamps and parking lamps. Twin slots were in the front bumper, outboard of the bumper guards. Gran Fury came in base, Custom, or Brougham trim. Suburban wagons rode a 124 in. wheelbase, while the coupe and sedan measured 121.5 in. A 318 cu. in. V-8 was standard on the base sedan (available at no cost on others); Customs had a 360 cu. in. V-8; and Broughams a 400 V-8. Both 400 and 440 cu. in. V-8 engines were offered as options. Standard equipment also included TorqueFlite automatic transmission, power brakes and steering, and heater/defroster. Broughams and Sport Suburbans had an electric clock and deluxe wheel covers. Wagons had a two-way tailgate and (optional) rear- facing third seat. Standard tires were G78 x 15 blackwalls; GR78 x 15 steel-belted radials on Brougham; LR78 x 15 steel- belted radials on Sport Suburban. The unibodied Gran Fury was lighter in weight than full-size Fords and Chevrolets, both of which used separate body/frame construction.

I.D. DATA: Plymouth's 13-symbol Vehicle Identification Number (VIN) was on the upper left corner of the instrument panel, visible through the windshield. Symbol one indicates car line: 'V' Valiant; 'H' Volare; 'R' Fury; 'P' Gran Fury. Symbol two is series (price class): 'L' low; 'M' medium; 'H' high; 'P' premium. Symbols 3-4 show body type: '23' 2-dr. hardtop coupe; '29' 2-dr. special coupe; '41' 4-dr. sedan; '45' two-seat station wagon; '46' three-seat wagon. Symbol five is the engine code: 'C' L6225; 'G' V8318; 'K' V8360 2Bbl.; 'J' V8360 4Bbl.; 'L' Hi- perf. V8360 4Bbl.; 'M' V8400 2Bbl.; 'N' V8400 4Bbl.; 'P' Hi-perf. V8400 4Bbl.; 'T' V8440 4Bbl. Symbol six is the model year code: '6' 1976. Symbol seven indicates assembly plant: 'A' Lynch Road; 'B' Hamtramck, MI; 'C' Jefferson; 'D' Belvidere, IL; 'F' Newark, DE; 'G' St. Louis. The final six digits make up the sequential serial number, starting with 100001. An abbreviated version of the VIN is also stamped on a pad on the engine block: below No. 6 spark plug on six- cylinder engines, and to rear of right engine mount on V-8s. Serial numbers for 318 and 360 cu. in. V-8s are coded as follows: first letter series (model year); second assembly plant; next three digits displacement (cu. in.); next one or two letters model; next four digits show build date; and final four digits are the engine sequence number. Coding of other engines is: first letter (model year); next three digits displacment; next one or two letters model; next four digits build date; and the final digit reveals the shift on which the engine was built. Information on over/undersized parts is stamped on six- cylinder engines on the joint face at right corner, adjacent to No. 1 cylinder; on 318/360 V-8s, at left front of block just below the head; on 400 V-8, just ahead of No. 2 cylinder, next to distributor; and on 440 V-8, on left bank pad adjacent to front tappet rail. A Vehicle Safety Certification Label that displays (among other data) the date of manufacture is attached to the rear facing of the driver's door. A Body Code Plate is on the left front fender side shield, wheel housing, or left side of upper radiator support.

1976 Valiant Brougham four-door sedan (JG)

VALIANT (SIX/V-8)

Model Number	Body/Style Number	Body Type & Seating	Factory Price	Shipping Weight	Production Total
VL	41	4-dr. Sedan-6P	3251/3388	3050/ --	32,901

(VALIANT) SCAMP (SIX/V-8)

Model Number	Body/Style Number	Body Type & Seating	Factory Price	Shipping Weight	Production Total
VH	23	2-dr. HT Cpe-6P	3485/3622	3020/ --	5,147
VL	23	2-dr. Spec HT-6P	3312/3449	3020/ --	3,308

(VALIANT) DUSTER (SIX/V-8)

Model Number	Body/Style Number	Body Type & Seating	Factory Price	Shipping Weight	Production Total
VL	29	2-dr. Spt Cpe-5P	3216/3353	2975/ --	26,688

VOLARE (SIX/V-8)

Model Number	Body/Style Number	Body Type & Seating	Factory Price	Shipping Weight	Production Total
HL	29	2-dr. Spt Cpe-5P	3324/3489	3160/3285	30,191
HL	41	4-dr. Sedan-6P	3359/3524	3190/3315	19,186
HL	45	4-dr. Sta Wag-6P	3646/3759	3560/3650	40,497

VOLARE CUSTOM (SIX/V-8)

Model Number	Body/Style Number	Body Type & Seating	Factory Price	Shipping Weight	Production Total
HH	29	2-dr. Spt Cpe-5P	3506/3671	3170/3295	27,656
HH	41	4-dr. Sedan-6P	3541/3706	3200/3325	32,765

1976 Volare Premier coupe (CM)

VOLARE PREMIER (SIX/V-8)

HP	29	2-dr. Spt Cpe-5P	4402/4515	3375/3490	27,442
HP	41	4-dr. Sedan-6P	4389/4502	3410/3530	33,080
HH	45	4-dr. Sta Wag-6P	3976/4210	3565/3695	44,191

FURY (SIX/V-8)

RL	23	2-dr. HT Cpe-6P	3629/3867	3590/3830	11,341
RL	41	4-dr. Sedan-6P	3663/3901	3625/3860	18,006
RL	45	4-dr. 2S Wag-6P	--/4588	--/4285	3,765
RL	46	4-dr. 3S Wag-9P	--/4730	--/4350	3,810

1976 Fury Salon four-door sedan (JG)

FURY SPORT/SUBURBAN (SIX/V-8)

RH	23	2-dr. HT Cpe-6P	3918/4156	3595/3835	23,312
RH	41	4-dr. Salon Sed-6P	3952/4109	3645/3875	16,768
RH	45	4-dr. 2S Wag-6P	--/4977	--/4285	1,567
RH	46	4-dr. 3S Wag-9P	--/5119	--/4360	3,143

GRAN FURY (V-8)

PM	41	4-dr. Sedan-6P	4349	4140	5,560
PM	45	4-dr. 2S Wag-6P	4909	4880	1,046

GRAN FURY CUSTOM/SUBURBAN (V-8)

PH	23	2-dr. HT Cpe-6P	4730	4265	1,513
PH	41	4-dr. Sedan-6P	4715	4305	12,088
PH	45	4-dr. 2S Wag-6P	5193	4895	1,018
PH	46	4-dr. 3S Wag-9P	5316	4940	1,700

1976 Gran Fury Brougham coupe (JG)

GRAN FURY BROUGHAM (V-8)

PP	29	2-dr. HT Cpe-6P	5334	4400	1,823
PP	41	4-dr. Sedan-6P	5162	4435	1,869

GRAN FURY SPORT SUBURBAN (V-8)

PP	46	4-dr. 3S Wag-9P	5761	4975	1,794

FACTORY PRICE AND WEIGHT NOTE: Prices and weights to left of slash are for six-cylinder, to right for V-8. **PRODUCTION NOTE:** In addition to totals shown, 4,427 Fury and 7,953 Gran Fury police four-door sedans were shipped this year.

ENGINE DATA: BASE SIX (Valiant/Scamp/Duster, Volare, Fury): Inline, overhead-valve six-cylinder. Cast iron block and head. Displacement: 225 cu. in. (3.7 liters). Bore & stroke: 3.40 x 4.12 in. Compression ratio: 8.4:1. Brake horsepower: 100 at 3600 R.P.M. Torque: 170 lbs.-ft. at 1600 R.P.M. Four main bearings. Solid valve lifters. Carburetor: 1Bbl. Holley 1945 (R7356A). VIN Code: C. BASE V-8 (Gran Fury); OPTIONAL (all others): 90-degree, overhead valve V-8. Cast iron block and head.

Displacement: 318 cu. in. (5.2 liters). Bore & stroke: 3.91 x 3.31 in. Compression ratio: 8.5:1. Brake horsepower: 150 at 4000 R.P.M. Torque: 255 lbs.-ft. at 1600 R.P.M. Five main bearings. Hydraulic valve lifters. Carburetor: 2Bbl. Carter BBD 8068S or 8069S. VIN Code: G. BASE V-8 (Fury wagon, Gran Fury Custom); OPTIONAL (Volare, Fury, base Gran Fury): 90-degree, overhead valve V-8. Cast iron block and head. Displacement: 360 cu. in. (5.9 liters). Bore & stroke: 4.00 x 3.58 in. Compression ratio: 8.4:1. Brake horsepower: 170 at 4000 R.P.M. Torque: 280 lbs.-ft. at 2400 R.P.M. Five main bearings. Hydraulic valve lifters. Carburetor: 2Bbl. Holley 2245 (R7364A). VIN Code: K. OPTIONAL V-8 (Valiant/Duster/Scamp): Same as 360 cu. in. V-8 above, but with Carter TQ9002S 4Bbl. carburetor Horsepower: 220 at 4400 R.P.M. Torque: 280 lbs.- ft. at 3200 R.P.M. VIN Code: L. BASE V-8 (Fury/Gran Fury wagon, Gran Fury Brougham); OPTIONAL (Fury, Gran Fury): 90-degree, overhead valve V-8. Cast iron block and head. Displacement: 400 cu. in. (6.6 liters). Bore & stroke: 4.34 x 3.38 in. Compression ratio: 8.2:1. Brake horsepower: 175 at 4000 R.P.M. Torque: 300 lbs.-ft. at 2400 R.P.M. Five main bearings. Hydraulic valve lifters. Carburetor: 2Bbl. Holley 2245 (R7366A). VIN Code: M. OPTIONAL V-8 (Gran Fury): Same as 400 cu. in. V-8 above, but with Carter TQ9064S 4Bbl. carburetor Horsepower: 210 at 4400 R.P.M. Torque: 305 lbs.- ft. at 3200 R.P.M. VIN Code: N. OPTIONAL V-8 (Fury): Same as 400 cu. in. V-8 above, but with Carter TQ9054S 4Bbl. carburetor Horsepower: 240 at 4400 R.P.M. Torque: 325 lbs.- ft. at 3200 R.P.M. VIN Code: P. OPTIONAL V-8 (Gran Fury): 90-degree, overhead valve V-8. Cast iron block and head. Displacement: 440 cu. in. (7.2 liters). Bore & stroke: 4.32 x 3.75 in. Compression ratio: 8.2:1. Brake horsepower: 205 at 3600 R.P.M. Torque: 320 lbs.-ft. at 2000 R.P.M. Five main bearings. Hydraulic valve lifters. Carburetor: 4Bbl. Carter TQ9058S. VIN Code: T.

CHASSIS DATA: Wheelbase: (Duster) 108.0 in.; (Volare cpe) 108.5 in.; (Valiant/Scamp) 111.0 in.; (Volare sed/wag) 112.5 in.; (Fury cpe) 115.0 in.; (Fury sed/wag) 117.5 in.; (Gran Fury) 121.5 in.; (Gran Fury wag) 124.0 in. Overall length: (Duster) 197.0 in.; (Volare cpe) 197.5 in.; (Valiant/Scamp) 199.6 in.; (Volare sed/wag) 201.5 in.; (Fury cpe) 213.7 in.; (Fury sed) 218.4 in.; (Fury wag) 224.2 in.; (Gran Fury) 222.4 in.; (Gran Fury wag) 226.4 in. Height: (Duster) 53.4 in.; (Valiant) 54.0 in.; (Scamp) 53.0 in.; (Volare cpe) 53.1 in.; (Volare sed/wag) 54.8 in.; (Fury cpe) 52.6 in.; (Fury sed) 53.9 in.; (Gran Fury cpe) 54.1 in.; (Gran Fury sed) 54.8 in.; (Gran Fury wag) 57.6 in. Width: (Duster) 71.7 in.; (Valiant/Scamp) 71.0 in.; (Volare) 72.8 in.; (Fury) 77.7 in.; (Fury wag) 78.8 in.; (Gran Fury) 79.8 in.; (Gran Fury wag) 79.4 in. Front Tread: (Valiant) 59.2 in.; (Volare) 60.0 in.; (Fury) 61.9 in.; (Gran Fury) 64.0 in. Rear Tread: (Valiant) 55.6 in.; (Volare) 58.5 in.; (Fury) 62.0 in. exc. wag, 63.4 in.; (Gran Fury) 63.4 in. Standard Tires: (Valiant six) 6.95 x 14 BSW; (Valiant V8318) D78 x 14 BSW; (Valiant V8360) E70 x 14 BSW; (Volare) D78 x 14, E78 x 14 or F78 x 14 BSW; (Fury) F78 x 14 or G78 x 14 BSW; (Fury wag) H78 x 14 BSW; (Gran Fury) GR78 x 15 exc. Brghm, HR78 x 15 and wagon, LR78 x 15.

TECHNICAL: Transmission: Three-speed manual transmission (column or floor shift) standard on all except Gran Fury. Gear ratios: (1st) 3.08:1; (2nd) 1.70:1; (3rd) 1.00:1; (Rev) 2.90:1, except Valiant six: (1st) 2.99:1; (2nd) 1.75:1; (3rd) 1.00:1; (Rev) 3.17:1. Four-speed overdrive available on Valiant/Volare: (1st) 3.09:1; (2nd) 1.67:1; (3rd) 1.00:1; (4th) 0.73:1; (Rev) 3.00:1. Three-speed automatic standard on Gran Fury (column shift) optional on others (column or floor lever). Gear ratios: (1st) 2.45:1; (2nd) 1.45:1; (3rd) 1.00:1; (Rev) 2.22:1. Standard final drive ratio: (Valiant/Duster six) 3.21:1 exc. 2.76:1 w/auto.; (Valiant/Duster V-8) 2.45:1 w/3spd, 2.94:1 w/4spd, 2.45:1 or 2.76:1 w/auto., 2.94:1 w/V8360; (Volare six) 3.23:1 w/3spd, 3.21:1 w/4spd, 2.71:1 w/auto.; (Volare V-8) 2.45:1 w/3spd, 2.94:1 w/4spd, 2.45:1 w/auto.; (Volare V8360) 2.76:1 w/4spd; (Fury) 2.94:1 exc. 3.21:1 w/six and 3spd, 2.71:1 w/V-8 and auto.; (Gran Fury) 2.71:1. Steering: Recirculating ball. Suspension: (Volare) isolated transverse front torsion bars, semi-elliptic rear leaf springs; (others) longitudinal front torsion bars, semi-elliptic rear leaf springs; front anti- sway bar on all except Valiant. Brakes: Front disc, rear drum except Valiant six, front/rear drum. Ignition: Electronic. Body construction: (Valiant/Duster/Volare/Fury) unibody; (Gran Fury) unibody w/auxiliary front frame. Fuel tank: (Valiant) 16 gal.; (Volare) 18 gal.; (Fury) 25.5 gal. exc. 20.5 gal. on wagons and six-cyl. models; (Gran Fury) 26.5 gal. exc. wagon, 24 gal.

DRIVETRAIN OPTIONS: Engines: 318 cu. in. 2Bbl. V-8: Gran Fury (NC). 360 cu. in., 2Bbl. V-8: Volare ($50); Fury ($54); base Gran Fury sedan ($55). 360 cu. in., 4Bbl. V-8: Fury ($99); Fury wag ($45); base Gran Fury ($100); Gran Fury Cust ($45). 360 cu. in., 4Bbl. V-8 w/dual exhaust: Duster ($392). 400 cu. in. 2Bbl. V-8: Fury ($102); Fury wag ($48); base Gran Fury ($104); Gran Fury Cust ($49). 400 cu. in. 4Bbl. V-8: Fury ($147); Fury wag ($93); base Gran Fury ($149); Gran Fury Cust ($94); Gran Fury Brghm, wag ($45). 400 cu. in. 4Bbl. V-8 w/dual exhaust: Fury ($198); Fury wag ($144). 440 cu. in., 4Bbl. V-8: base Gran Fury ($273); Gran Fury Cust ($218); Gran Fury Brghm, wag ($169). Transmission/Differential: TorqueFlite: Valiant/Scamp/Duster/Volare ($250); Fury ($273). Four-speed manual trans. w/floor lever: Valiant/Scamp/Duster/Volare ($127). Three-speed floor shifter: Valiant/Scamp/Duster/Volare ($28). Sure grip differential: Valiant/Scamp/Duster/Volare ($13); Fury ($54); Gran Fury ($58). Optional axle ratio: Valiant/Scamp/Duster/Volare ($13); Fury ($15). Gran Fury 3.21 axle ratio ($15); 2.45:1 ratio (NC). Power Accessories: Power steering: Valiant/Scamp/Duster/Volare ($131); Fury ($143). Power brakes: Valiant/Scamp/Duster/Volare ($56-$81). Front disc brakes (manual): Valiant/Scamp/Duster six ($25). Suspension: H.D. susp.: Valiant/Scamp/Duster-/Volare ($9-$23); Fury ($25); Gran Fury ($18-$25). Automatic height control: Gran Fury ($100). H.D. shock absorbers: Fury/Gran Fury ($7). Front sway bar: Valiant/Scamp/Duster ($14). Other: Trailer towing pkg.: Valiant/Scamp/Duster-/Volare ($68); Fury: light ($74); heavy ($298). Gran Fury trailer towing pkg.: light ($75); heavy ($302). Fuel pacer system: Valiant/Scamp/Duster-/Volare ($19-$34). Long-life battery: Valiant/Scamp/Duster/Volare ($27); Fury ($29); Gran Fury ($30). California emission system: Valiant/Scamp/Duster/Volare ($53); Fury ($58).

VALIANT/SCAMP/DUSTER CONVENIENCE/APPEARANCE OPTIONS: Option Packages: Silver Duster trim pkg.: Duster ($178). Feather Duster pkg.: Duster ($51). Brougham pkg.: Scamp ($291). Easy-order pkg. ($698-$772). Space maker pak: Duster ($104). Custom pkg.: Valiant ($176-$218). Radial tire roadability pkg. ($17). Exterior decor group: Duster ($84). Interior decor group: Duster ($92). Light pkg. ($33). Deluxe insulation pkg. ($23-$51). Protection group: Valiant ($22-$27). Comfort/Convenience: Air cond. ($431). Rear defogger, blower- type ($41); electric ($74). Tinted glass ($44). Tinted windshield ($35). Luxury steering wheel ($15-$26). Tuff steering wheel ($7-$33). Inside hood release ($11). Three-speed wipers ($8). Lighter ($6). Glovebox lock ($4). Locking gas cap ($6). Horns and Mirrors: Dual horns ($6). Remote driver's mirror ($14). Dual chrome sport mirrors, left remote: Duster ($15- $29). Day/night mirror ($7). Entertainment: AM radio ($72). AM/FM radio ($65-$137). Rear speaker ($20). Exterior Trim: Manual sunroof: Duster ($186). Full vinyl roof ($17-$92). Canopy vinyl roof: Duster ($76). Vinyl bodyside molding ($18-$37). Bodyside tape stripe: Duster ($32). Bumper guards, front/rear: six-cyl. ($35). Bumper guards, rear: V-8 ($17). Door edge protectors ($7-$11). Drip rail moldings ($16). Sill moldings ($16). Upper door frame moldings: Valiant ($17). Wheel lip moldings ($18). Undercoating ($28). Interior Trim/Upholstery: Console: Duster ($68). Vinyl split- back bucket seat: Valiant ($105). Cloth/vinyl bench seat: Valiant ($64). Vinyl bench seat: Duster ($64). Vinyl bucket seats: Duster ($87-$150); Scamp ($125). Carpeting ($25). Color-keyed mats ($15). Wheels and Tires: Deluxe wheel covers ($29). Rallye wheels ($36-$66). 6.95 x 14 WSW ($32). D78 x 14 BSW ($16). D78 x 14 WSW ($16-$75). DR78 x 14 WSW ($85-$132). E78 x 14 WSW ($16-$63). E70 x 14 RWL ($61-$109). ER78 x 14 WSW ($23-$148).

VOLARE CONVENIENCE/APPEARANCE OPTIONS: Option Packages: Road Runner pkg.: base cpe ($205). Road Runner decor group: base cpe ($95). Two-tone paint pkg.: base cpe ($205). Easy-order pkg. ($221-$757). Space maker pak: cpe ($104). Light pkg. ($33). Protection group ($18-$27). Deluxe insulation pkg. ($23-$51). Comfort/Convenience: Air cond. ($431). Rear defogger, blower- type ($41); electric ($74). Automatic speed control ($70). Power seat ($119). Power windows ($95-$135) exc. wag. Power door locks ($60-$86) exc. wag. Tinted glass ($44). Tinted windshield ($35). Luxury steering wheel ($26). Tuff steering wheel ($54). Tilt steering wheel ($54). Three-speed wipers ($8). Electric clock ($18). Inside hood release ($11). Glovebox lock ($4). Lighter: base ($6). Locking gas cap ($6). Horns and Mirrors: Dual horns ($6). Remote left-hand mirror ($14). Dual remote mirrors ($27-$40). Dual remote sport mirrors ($33-$47). Day/night mirror ($7). Entertainment: AM radio ($72). AM/FM radio ($65-$137). AM/FM stereo radio ($160-$233). Rear speaker ($54). Exterior Trim: Manual sunroof: cpe ($186). Full vinyl roof: sed ($92). Canopy vinyl roof: cpe ($76-$90). Landau vinyl roof: cpe ($62-$137). Vinyl bodyside moldings ($18-$37). Belt moldings: base ($15). Door edge protectors ($7-$11). Upper door frame moldings: base sed- ($27). Wheel lip moldings: base ($18). Bumper guards, front/rear ($35). Protective bumper rub strips ($28). Air deflector: wag ($22). Luggage rack: wag ($65). Undercoating ($28). Interior Trim/Upholstery: Console ($68). Rear armrest w/ashtray: base ($10). Vinyl bench seat: base wag ($32). Cloth 60/40 seat: Premier ($51). Vinyl 60/40 seat w/recliners: Premier wag ($114). Vinyl bucket seats: cpe ($87-$119). Cargo area carpets/stowage bin: base wag ($45). Wheels and Tires: Deluxe wheel covers ($29). Premium wheel covers ($25-$54). Wire wheel covers ($32-$86). Rallye wheels ($36-$66). Styled wheels ($47-$113). D78 x 14 WSW ($32). E78 x 14 BSW ($16). E78 x 14 WSW ($16-$75). ER78 x 14 WSW ($85-$132). E70 x 14 RWL ($61-$93). F78 x 14 BSW ($44-$60). F78 x 14 WSW ($36-$96). FR78 x 14 WSW ($41-$153). GR78 x 14 WSW ($75-$110).

FURY CONVENIENCE/APPEARANCE OPTIONS: Option Packages: Easy order pkg. ($347-$870). Luxury equipment pkg.: Sport/Salon ($1393-$1779). Exterior decor pkg.: HT ($72-$155). Light pkg. ($38-$45). Deluxe insulation pkg.: six-cyl. ($55). Comfort/Convenience: Air cond. ($490). Rear defroster, electric ($81). Automatic speed control ($77). Power seat ($130). Power windows ($147). Power tailgate window: wag ($41). Auto-lock tailgate: wag ($83). Power door locks ($65- $94). Tinted glass ($52). Tinted windshield ($38). Strato ventilation ($20). Three-speed wipers ($9). Luxury steering wheel ($17). Tuff steering wheel ($54). Tilt steering wheel ($59). Inside hood release ($12). Tachometer ($42-$62). Electric clock ($20). Locking gas cap ($6). Horns and Mirrors: Dual horns ($8). Remote left mirror ($15). Dual chrome remote mirrors ($29-$44). Dual sport remote mirrors, painted or chrome ($37-$52). Entertainment: AM radio ($79); w/8track stereo tape player ($48-$220). AM/FM radio ($71-$149). AM/FM stereo radio ($83- $254); w/8track ($186-$357). Rear speaker ($22). Exterior Trim: Manual sunroof: HT ($311). Full vinyl roof ($115); w/easy-order ($32). Canopy vinyl roof: HT ($83). Canopy vinyl roof w/louvered quarter windows: HT ($115); w/easy-order ($32). Vinyl bodyside moldings ($40). Hood/deck tape stripes: HT ($40). Door edge protectors ($7-$13). Bumper guards, front: sed/wag ($19). Bumper guards, front/rear: HT ($38). Bumper strips, front: sed/wag ($15). Bumper strips, front/rear: HT ($31). Air deflector: wag ($24). Luggage rack: wag ($71). Undercoating ($30). Interior Trim/Upholstery: Console: Sport HT ($18). Vinyl bench seat: base ($42). Cloth/vinyl bucket seats: Sport HT ($31). Cloth/vinyl 60/40 bench seat: Sport HT ($124). Velour/vinyl 60/40 bench seat: Salon sed ($124). Vinyl 60/40 bench seat: Salon sed, Sport wag ($124). Pedal dress-up ($8). Trunk dress-up ($8). Color-keyed mats ($43). Cargo area carpet: wag ($28). Wheels and Tires: Deluxe wheel covers ($32). Wire wheel covers ($62-$94). Rallye wheels ($43-$75). Styled wheels ($113-$145). F78 x 14 WSW ($39). G78 x 14 BSW ($19). G78 x 14 WSW ($39-$58). H78 x 14 BSW ($22-$40). H78 x 14 WSW ($25-$83). G70 x 14 RWL ($53-$110). GR78 x 15 WSW ($130-$169). HR78 x 15 WSW ($111-$181). GR70 x 15 RWL ($164-$203).

GRAN FURY CONVENIENCE/APPEARANCE OPTIONS: Option Packages: Easy order pkg. ($347-$522). Luxury equipment pkg. ($1488-$1811); N/A base. Light pkg. ($55-$74). Wagon pkg.: Sub ($63). Deluxe sound insulation pkg.: base/Cust HT/sed ($41). Comfort/Convenience: Air cond. ($504). Auto-temp air cond. ($15-$85). Rear defroster, electric ($82). Automatic speed control ($78). Power seat ($132). Power windows ($110-$167). Auto-lock tailgate: wag ($35). Power door locks ($66-$95). Tinted glass ($66). Deluxe wiper/washer pkg. ($16). Luxury steering wheel ($17). Tilt/telescope steering wheel ($83- $100). Gauges, temp & oil pressure ($23). Electric clock ($20). Digital clock ($25-$45). Horns and Mirrors: Remote left mirror ($15). Dual remote mirrors ($30-$45). Day/night mirror ($8). Entertainment: AM radio ($80); w/8track stereo tape player ($62-$239). AM/FM radio ($76-$155). AM/FM stereo radio ($80- $257); w/8track ($184-$362). Rear speaker ($22). Exterior Trim: Sunroof w/vinyl roof ($627-$758). Vinyl roof ($131). Vinyl bodyside moldings ($22-$31). Door edge protectors ($8-$13). Upper door frame moldings: 4dr. ($29). Bumper guards, rear ($23). Air deflector: base wag ($25). Assist handles: wag ($23). Luggage rack: wag ($86). Rear bumper step pads: wag ($14). Interior Trim/Upholstery: Vinyl bench seat: HT/sed ($28) exc. Brghm. Vinyl bench seat w/center armrest: Cust ($43). Wheels and Tires: Deluxe wheel covers ($32). Premier wheel covers ($38-$70). G78 x 15 WSW ($39). GR78 x 15 BSW ($99). GR78 x 15 WSW ($39-$138). HR78 x 15 BSW ($22-$121). HR78 x 15 WSW ($25-$164). JR78 x 15 WSW ($56-$195). L78 x 15 ($49). LR78 x 15 BSW ($99). LR78 x 15 WSW ($148).

HISTORY: Introduced: October 16, 1975. Model year production: Chrysler reported a total of 445,555 passenger cars shipped. Total North American passenger-car production for the U.S. market of 459,512 units included 221,765 six-cylinder and 237,747 V-8s. Calendar year production (U.S.): 658,019. Calendar year sales by U.S. dealers: 532,197 (not incl. 12,974 Voyagers). Model year sales by U.S. dealers: 515,347 (not incl. 20,769 imported Arrows and 13,009 Voyager vans).

Historical Footnotes: The new Volares (and Dodge Aspens) turned out to be the most recalled models of their day. Among other failings, their unibodies were notably prone to rusting. The Aspen/Volare duo was meant to rival Ford's Granada and Mercury Monarch. In mid-year 1975 a new Arrow subcompact, manufactured by Mitsubishi in Japan, had been added to the Plymouth line.

1977 PLYMOUTH

The Valiant bunch left the lineup this year, leaving the year-old Volare as Plymouth's compact offering. A two-barrel version of the Slant Six engine, dubbed Super Six, was now available. It was standard on Volare wagons and Fury, optional on other Volares. The big 440 cu. in. V-8 engine was back once more as a Gran Fury option, and Electronic Lean Burn went on the 360 V-8 as well as the bigger ones. Volare again offered a Road Runner option package, though its performance hardly ranked with earlier versions of that name. Volare's coupe could have an optional T-Bar roof as well as a sunroof.

VOLARE — SERIES H — SIX/V-8 — For its second year in the Plymouth lineup, Volare looked identical to the 1976 version, again with large, clear-lensed parking/signal lamps between the single headlamps and grille. Eight new body colors were offered. The list included: French Racing Blue, Spitfire Orange, Spinnaker White, Yellow Blaze, Light Mocha Tan, and Mojave Beige; plus metallic Silver Cloud, Regatta

1977 Volare station wagon (CM)

Blue, Starlight Blue Sunfire, Vintage Red Sunfire, Jade Green, Forest Green Sunfire, Formal Black Sunfire, Spanish Gold, Caramel Tan, or Russet Sunfire. Nine two-tone combinations also were available (formerly just three). Standard equipment included a heater/defroster, drip moldings, bright grille surround moldings, dome light, and quarter-window reveal moldings. Base Volares had low-back cloth/vinyl bench seating; Customs used pleated all-vinyl (or cloth/vinyl) with rear armrests and woodgrain instrument cluster inserts. Customs also added a rear deck lower applique, belt moldings, B-pillar molding (coupe) and cigarette lighter, as well as partial wheel lip moldings. Premiers had power brakes and steering, day/night mirror, clock, dual horns, bodyside and hood accent tape stripes, premium wheel covers, vinyl 60/40 split-bench seats, a chrome grille insert, hood medallion, and color-keyed vinyl bodyside moldings. The optional canopy vinyl roof had up-and-over stripes. Base engine was the 1Bbl. 225 cu. in. Slant Six, with three-speed manual shift. Options included a 2Bbl. Super Six (for $38 extra), rated 10 horsepower higher; a 318 cu. in. V-8; Overdrive-4 manual transmission; or a 2Bbl. 360 cu. in. V-8 with automatic. Wagons came with either the Super Six, 318 cu. in. V-8, or 360 V-8. Volare coupes could get a 4Bbl. 360 V-8, rated 175 horsepower. Power brakes were standard with V-8 models. Volare's Road Runner featured an identifying decal on doors, along the lower bodyside stripe, plus E70 x 14 raised- letter tires, heavy-duty suspension, Rallye wheels, blackout grille, and special "Beep-Beep" horn. A total of 4,585 Volares had the

1977 Volare Road Runner coupe (CM)

Road Runner package, while 2,390 were Super Road Runners. New Fun Runner option packages were offered for the coupe, including a "Sun Runner" and a "Front Runner" Super Pak that came with front and rear spoilers, louvered quarter windows, and flared wheel openings. The Front Runner came only in Spitfire Orange, with orange/yellow/black tape stripe. "Super Pak" cost $318 on the base coupe. A Space Maker Pak allowed the rear seat to fold down. There was also a new T-Bar roof option with removable glass panels.

1977 Fury Salon sedan (CM)

FURY — SERIES R — SIX/V-8 — A major restyle hit Plymouth's mid-size, along with cousin Dodge Monaco. Fury's revised front-end look was highlighted by new vertically-stacked quad rectangular headlamps that replaced the former single round units. The overall grille shape was similar to 1976, but had a heavier bright surrounding molding with 'Plymouth' block letters inset in the upper header. The grille pattern was altered too, now consisting of two rows of small vertical-style segments. Park/signal lamps were built into the bright front bumper, in half-curved openings below the headlamps. Small side marker lenses sat roughly midway between wheel openings and front fender tips. 'Fury' fender script was just ahead of the door. The Fury Sport two-door rode a 115 in. wheelbase; Salon sedan was 117.4 in. As in 1976, Fury Sport (and the base two- door) had a different rear-end appearance than sedans, with

vertical taillamps at quarter panel tips and a recessed license plate opening that extended down into the bumper, plus sculptured-look decklid with 'Plymouth' block lettering. 'Sport' script stood on the wide C-pillar, behind the swooping molding that accompanied the canopy roof's opera windows. Those optional opera windows were now single units instead of the extremely narrow side-by-side versions offered for 1976. Fury sedan's back end looked similar to 1976, with tri-section taillamps set into large rear bumper slots; but each tri-color (red/clear/amber) unit had a larger center backup lens, no longer inset into a red panel. The base Fury came in two-door hardtop or four-door (thin-pillar) sedan form, with standard Regency cloth/vinyl bench seat. Fury Sport's standard interior had crushed velour and vinyl split-back bench seats with folding center armrest. Engine choices included the new standard Super Six (2Bbl.), 318 cu. in. V-8, 360 V-8, or Electronic Lean Burn 400 V-8 rated 190 horsepower. All models had power brakes. Three-speed manual shift was standard on the base Fury with 318 cu. in. V-8; TorqueFlite on the six-cylinder model (except in California and at high altitudes). Standard equipment included bumper guards, hubcaps, F78 x 15 blackwall tires, wheel opening moldings, lighter, dome light, lockable glovebox, and heater/defroster. Sedans had front and rear armrests; hardtops a decklid lower molding. Fury Sport added dual horns, hood rear edge and belt moldings, sill moldings, and hood ornament. Fury Salon included a hood ornament, Salon nameplate and crest, plush velour split-back bench seat, upper door frame moldings, deck molding, and dual horns. Fury colors were: Wedgewood Blue, Rallye Red, Spinnaker White, Golden Fawn, and Jasmine Yellow; plus metallic Silver Cloud, Cadet Blue, Stalight Blue Sunfire, Vintage Red Sunfire, Jade Green, Forest Green Sunfire, Formal Black Sunfire, Spanish or Inca Gold, Moondust, Coffee Sunfire, Russet Sunrire, or Burnished Copper. A total of 2,079 Fury models had the Police package, while 1,150 had a Taxi package.

1977 Gran Fury Brougham coupe (CM)

GRAN FURY — SERIES P — V-8 — Gran Fury dropped the Custom line, but added a base two-door hardtop. This would be the last year for the long (121.5 and 124 in.) wheelbase models. Base engine was the 318 cu. in. V-8, but Broughams had the 360 cu. 2Bbl. in. V-8, and wagons carried a 400 cu. in. 4Bbl. V-8. Also optional was a 440 V-8 rated 195 horsepower. Gran Fury could have a full vinyl roof, or a canopy vinyl roof with opera windows, for the same price. A sunroof was available again. Also on the option list were manual vent windows and chrome wheels. Appearance was virtually identical to 1976. Standard equipment included TorqueFlite automatic transmission, power brakes and steering, heater/defroster, carpeting, and electronic ignition. Base hardtops and sedans had G78 x 15 glass-belted radial tires; Broughams wore HR78 x 15; Suburban wagons had L78 x 15; and top-line Sport Suburban wagons carried LR78 x 15 tires. Steel-belted radials were optional. Sport Suburban wagons had either two or three seats; base Suburban, just two. Gran Fury now weighed some 450 pounds more than a freshly downsized Chevrolet Caprice. Nothing startling was new this year: just a lighter (yet heftier) battery; improved ignition switch and wiring harness; and new TorqueFlite torque converter.

I.D. DATA: Plymouth's 13-symbol Vehicle Identification Number (VIN) was on the upper left corner of the instrument panel, visible through the windshield. Symbol one indicates car line: 'H' Volare; 'R' Fury; 'P' Gran Fury. Symbol two is series (price class): 'L' low; 'M' medium; 'H' high; 'P' premium. Symbols 3-4 show body type: '23' 2-dr. hardtop coupe; '29' 2-dr. special coupe; '41' 4-dr. sedan; '45' two-seat station wagon; '46' three-seat wagon. Symbol five is the engine code: 'C' L6225 1Bbl.; 'D' L6225 2Bbl.; 'G' V8318 2Bbl.; 'K' V8360 2Bbl.; 'L' V8360 4Bbl.; 'N' V8400 4Bbl.; 'T' V8440 4Bbl. Symbol six is the model year code: '7' 1977. Symbol seven indicates assembly plant: 'A' Lynch Road; 'B' Hamtramck, MI; 'D' Belvidere, IL; 'F' Newark, DE; 'G' St. Louis. The final six digits make up the sequential serial number, starting with 100001. Engine number coding and Body Code Plate locations are the same as 1976. As before, a Vehicle Safety Certification Label that displays (among other data) the date of manufacture is attached to the rear facing of the driver's door.

VOLARE (SIX/V-8)

Model Number	Body/Style Number	Body Type & Seating	Factory Price	Shipping Weight	Production Total
HL	29	2-dr. Spt Cpe-5P	3570/3740	3180/3480	32,264
HL	41	4-dr. Sedan-6P	3619/3789	3235/3545	36,688
HL	45	4-dr. Sta Wag-6P	3941/4025	3445/3585	70,913

1977 Volare Custom coupe (CM)

1977 Volare Premier sedan (CM)

VOLARE CUSTOM (SIX/V-8)

HH	29	2-dr. Spt Cpe-5P	3752/3922	3185/3295	30,230
HH	41	4-dr. Sedan-6P	3801/3971	3240/3350	45,130

VOLARE PREMIER (SIX/V-8)

HP	29	2-dr. Spt Cpe-5P	4305/4418	3375/3480	17,852
HP	41	4-dr. Sedan-6P	4354/4467	3440/3545	26,050
HH	45	4-dr. Sta Wag-6P	4271/4476	3450/3585	68,612

FURY/SUBURBAN (SIX/V-8)

RL	23	2-dr. HT Cpe-6P	3893/4154	3625/3855	11,909
RL	41	4-dr. Sedan-6P	3944/4205	3655/3890	20,103
RL	45	4-dr. 2S Wag-6P	--/4687	--/4335	5,626
RL	46	4-dr. 3S Wag-9P	--/4830	--/4390	5,141

1977 Fury Sport Coupe (CM)

FURY SPORT/SALON (SIX/V-8)

RH	23	2-dr. Sport HT-6P	4132/4394	3630/3865	24,385
RH	41	4-dr. Salon Sed-6P	4185/4446	3665/3900	22,188
RH	45	4-dr. 2S Wag-6P	--/5192	--/4330	1,827
RH	46	4-dr. 3S Wag-9P	--/5335	--/4400	3,634

GRAN FURY (V-8)

PM	23	2-dr. HT Cpe-6P	4692	4070	1,504
PM	41	4-dr. Sedan-6P	4697	4145	10,162
PM	45	4-dr. 2S Wag-6P	5315	4885	1,442

GRAN FURY BROUGHAM (V-8)

PH	23	2-dr. HT Cpe-6P	4963	4190	3,242
PH	41	4-dr. Sedan-6P	4948	4250	15,021

GRAN FURY SPORT SUBURBAN (V-8)

PH	45	4-dr. 2S Wag-6P	5558	4880	1,194
PH	46	4-dr. 3S Wag-9P	5681	4925	3,600

FACTORY PRICE AND WEIGHT NOTE: Prices and weights to left of slash are for six-cylinder, to right for V-8 engines. **PRODUCTION NOTE:** In addition to totals shown, 793 Volare (Model HK41), 7,204 Fury and 6,236 Gran Fury (Model PK41) police four-door sedans were shipped this year.

ENGINE DATA: BASE SIX (Volare): Inline, overhead-valve six-cylinder. Cast iron block and head. Displacement: 225 cu. in. (3.7 liters). Bore & stroke: 3.40 x 4.12 in. Compression ratio: 8.4:1. Brake horsepower: 100 at 3600 R.P.M. Torque: 170 lbs.-ft. at 1600 R.P.M. Four main bearings. Solid valve lifters. Carburetor: 1Bbl. Holley 1945 (R7764A). VIN Code: C. BASE SIX (Volare wagon, Fury); OPTIONAL (Volare): Same as 225 cu. in. six above, but with 2Bbl. Carter BBD 8086S carburetor Horsepower: 110 at 3600 R.P.M. Torque: 180 lbs.-ft. at 2000 R.P.M. VIN Code: D. BASE V-8 (Gran Fury); OPTIONAL (Volare, Fury): 90-degree, overhead valve V-8. Cast iron block and head. Displacement: 318 cu. in. (5.2 liters). Bore & stroke: 3.91 x 3.31 in. Compression ratio: 8.5:1. Brake horsepower: 145 at 4000 R.P.M. Torque: 245 lbs.-ft. at 1600 R.P.M. Five main bearings. Hydraulic valve lifters. Carburetor: 2Bbl. Carter BBD 8093S or 8094S.

VIN Code: G. BASE V-8 (Fury wagon, Gran Fury Brougham); OPTIONAL (Volare, Fury, Gran Fury): 90-degree, overhead valve V-8. Cast iron block and head. Displacement: 360 cu. in. (5.9 liters). Bore & stroke: 4.00 x 3.58 in. Compression ratio: 8.4:1. Brake horsepower: 155 at 3600 R.P.M. Torque: 275 lbs.-ft. at 2000 R.P.M. Five main bearings. Hydraulic valve lifters. Carburetor: 2Bbl. Holley 2245 (R7671A). VIN Code: K. OPTIONAL V-8 (Volare): Same as 360 cu. in. V-8 above, but with Carter TQ 4Bbl. carburetor Horsepower: 175 at 4000 R.P.M. Torque: 275 lbs.- ft. at 2000 R.P.M. VIN Code: L. BASE V-8 (Gran Fury wagon); OPTIONAL (Fury, Gran Fury/Brougham): 90-degree, overhead valve V-8. Cast iron block and head. Displacement: 400 cu. in. (6.6 liters). Bore & stroke: 4.34 x 3.38 in. Compression ratio: 8.2:1. Brake horsepower: 190 at 3600 R.P.M. Torque: 305 lbs.-ft. at 3200 R.P.M. Five main bearings. Hydraulic valve lifters. Carburetor: 4Bbl. Carter TQ 9102S. VIN Code: N. OPTIONAL V-8 (Gran Fury): 90-degree, overhead valve V-8. Cast iron block and head. Displacement: 440 cu. in. (7.2 liters). Bore & stroke: 4.32 x 3.75 in. Compression ratio: 8.2:1. Brake horsepower: 195 at 3600 R.P.M. Torque: 320 lbs.-ft. at 2000 R.P.M. Five main bearings. Hydraulic valve lifters. Carburetor: 4Bbl. Carter TQ 9101S. VIN Code: T.

CHASSIS DATA: Wheelbase: (Volare cpe) 108.7 in.; (Volare sed/wag) 112.7 in.; (Fury cpe) 115.0 in.; (Fury sed/wag) 117.4 in.; (Gran Fury) 121.4 in.; (Gran Fury wag) 124.0 in. Overall length: (Volare cpe) 197.5 in.; (Volare sed/wag) 201.5 in.; (Fury cpe) 213.7 in.; (Fury sed) 218.4 in.; (Fury wag) 225.6 in.; (Gran Fury) 222.4 in.; (Gran Fury wag) 226.4 in. Height: (Volare cpe) 53.3 in.; (Volare sed) 55.0 in.; (Volare wag) 55.2 in.; (Fury cpe) 52.6 in.; (Fury sed) 54.0 in.; (Fury wag) 55.8 in.; (Gran Fury cpe) 54.1 in.; (Gran Fury sed) 54.8 in.; (Gran Fury wag) 56.9 in. Width: (Volare) 72.8 in.; (Fury) 77.7 in.; (Fury wag) 78.8 in.; (Gran Fury) 79.8 in.; (Gran Fury wag) 79.4 in. Front Tread: (Volare) 60.0 in.; (Fury) 61.9 in.; (Gran Fury) 64.0 in. Rear Tread: (Volare) 58.5 in.; (Fury) 62.0 in. exc. wag, 63.4 in.; (Gran Fury) 63.4 in. Standard Tires: (Volare six/V8318) D78 x 14; (Volare V8360) E78 x 14; (Volare Premier six) DR78 x 14 GBR BSW; (Volare Premier V-8) ER78 x 14 GBR BSW; (Volare wag) F78 x 14 BSW; (Fury) F78 x 15; (Fury V8440) G78 x 15; (Fury wag) H78 x 15; (Gran Fury) GR78 x 15 exc. (V8440) HR78 x 15 and wagon, LR78 x 15.

TECHNICAL: Transmission: Three-speed manual transmission standard on all Volare and Fury V-8 (column shift on Fury, column or floor on Volare). Gear ratios: (1st) 3.08:1; (2nd) 1.70:1; (3rd) 1.00:1; (Rev) 2.90:1. Four-speed overdrive available on Volare: (1st) 3.09:1; (2nd) 1.67:1; (3rd) 1.00:1; (4th) 0.73:1; (Rev) 3.00:1. Three-speed automatic standard on Fury six and Gran Fury (column shift), optional on others (column or floor lever). Gear ratios: (1st) 2.45:1; (2nd) 1.45:1; (3rd) 1.00:1; (Rev) 2.22:1. Standard final drive ratio: (Volare six) 3.23:1 w/3spd, 3.2:1 w/4spd, 2.7:1 w/auto.; (Volare V8318) 2.94:1 w/manual, 2.7:1 w/auto.; (Volare V8360) 2.45:1; (Volare wag) 3.21:1, 2.94:1 or 2.71:1; (Fury six) 2.94:1; (Fury V8318) 2.94:1 w/3spd, 2.71:1 w/auto.; (Fury V8360/400) 2.45:1; (Gran Fury) 2.71:1. Steering: Recirculating ball. Suspension: (Volare) isolated transverse front torsion bars, semi-elliptic rear leaf springs; (others) longitudinal front torsion bars, semi-elliptic rear leaf springs; front anti- sway bar on all. Brakes: Front disc, rear drum. Ignition: Electronic. Body construction: (Volare/Fury) unibody; (Gran Fury) unibody w/auxiliary front frame. Fuel tank: (Volare) 18 gal. exc. V-8/wagon, 20 gal.; (Fury) 25.5 gal. exc. 20 gal. on wagons; (Gran Fury) 26.5 gal. exc. wagon, 24 gal. and V8318, 20.5 gal.

DRIVETRAIN OPTIONS: Engines: 225 cu. in., 2Bbl. six: Volare cpe/sed ($38). 360 cu. in., 2Bbl. V-8: Volare ($53); Fury ($57); base Gran Fury HT/sed ($58). 360 cu. in., 4Bbl. V-8: Volare cpe ($219-$241); Fury ($105); Fury wag ($47); base Gran Fury ($106); Gran Fury Brghm ($48). 400 cu. in., 4Bbl. V-8: Fury wag ($98); base Gran Fury ($158); Gran Fury Brghm ($99). 440 cu. in., 4Bbl. V-8: base Gran Fury ($289); Gran Fury Brghm ($231); Gran Fury wag ($132). Transmission/Differential: TorqueFlite: Volare ($270); Fury ($295). Four-speed manual trans. w/floor lever: Volare ($134). Three-speed floor shifter: Volare ($30). Sure grip differential: Volare ($52); Fury ($57); Gran Fury ($61). Optional axle ratio: Volare ($14); Fury/Gran Fury ($16). Power Accessories: Power steering: Volare ($140); Fury six ($153). Power brakes: base Volare cpe/sed ($59). Suspension: H.D. susp.: Volare ($23); Fury/Gran Fury ($18-$25). Automatic height control: Gran Fury ($109). H.D. shock absorbers: Fury/Gran Fury ($7). Other: Trailer towing pkg.: Volare ($72). Fury trailer towing pkg.: light ($79); heavy ($316). Gran Fury trailer towing pkg.: light ($80); heavy ($321). Fuel pacer system: Volare ($20-$33); Fury ($22-$36); Gran ($22). Engine block heater: Gran Fury ($18). Long-life battery: Volare ($29); Fury ($31); Gran ($32). California emission system ($67-$75). High- altitude emission system ($21-$24).

VOLARE CONVENIENCE/APPEARANCE OPTIONS: Option Packages: Road Runner pkg.: base cpe ($193-$216). Road Runner decor group: base cpe ($82-$101). Road Runner "Super Pak": base cpe ($318). Two-tone paint pkg.: cpe ($120-$177). Easy-order pkg. ($594-$801). Space maker pak: cpe ($110). Light pkg. ($35). Protection group ($19-$28). Deluxe insulation pkg. ($35-$65). Comfort/Convenience: Air cond. ($454). Rear defogger, blower- type ($45); electric ($79). Automatic speed control ($77). Power seat ($131). Power windows ($104-$145). Power door locks ($65-$92). Tinted glass ($48). Tinted windshield ($37). Luxury steering wheel ($28). Tuff steering wheel ($7-$35). Tilt steering wheel ($54). Deluxe wipers ($9). Electric clock ($19). Inside hood release ($11). Glovebox lock ($5). Lighter: base ($6). Locking gas cap ($6). Horns and Mirrors: Dual horns ($6). Remote left-hand mirror ($15). Dual remote mirrors ($28-$43). Dual remote sport mirrors ($35-$50). Day/night mirror ($8). Entertainment: AM radio ($69). AM/FM radio ($67-$137). AM/FM stereo radio ($145-$215); w/8track tape player ($235-$304). Rear speaker ($22). Exterior: T-Bar roof ($540-$554). Manual sunroof: cpe ($198). Full vinyl roof: sed ($92). Canopy vinyl roof: cpe ($87-$101). Landau vinyl roof: cpe ($62-$148). Vinyl bodyside moldings ($19-$38). Belt moldings: base ($15). Door edge protectors ($8-$12). Upper door frame moldings: sed ($28). Wheel lip moldings: base ($19). Bumper guards, front/rear ($37). Protective bumper rub strips ($30). Air deflector: wag ($25). Luggage rack: wag ($68). Undercoating ($30). Interior: Console ($72). Rear armrest w/ashtray: base ($11). Vinyl bench seat: base wag ($34). Cloth 60/40 seat: Premier ($54); Cust wag ($198). Vinyl 60/40 seat w/recliners: wag ($121-$155). Vinyl bucket seats: cpe ($92-$126). Color-keyed mats ($16). Cargo area carpets/stowage bin: base wag ($47). Wheels and Tires: Deluxe wheel covers ($32). Premium wheel covers ($25-$57). Wire wheel covers ($42-$99). Rallye wheels ($32-$68). Chrome wheels ($51-$119). D78 x 14 WSW ($37). DR78 x 14 BSW ($51-$88). E78 x 14 BSW ($17). E78 x 14 WSW ($17- $54). ER78 x 14 BSW ($67). ER78 x 14 WSW ($67-$135). E70 x 14 RWL ($63-$101). FR78 x 14 BSW ($85). FR78 x 14 WSW ($87- $155). Space-saving spare tire ($41).

FURY CONVENIENCE/APPEARANCE OPTIONS: Option Packages: Easy order pkg. ($350-$872). Luxury equipment pkg.: Sport/Salon ($1461-$1837). Roadability pkg.: V-8 ($33). Light pkg. ($41-$48). Deluxe insulation pkg.: six- cyl. ($62). Comfort/Convenience: Air cond. ($518). Rear defroster, electric ($86). Automatic speed control ($84). Power seat ($143). Power windows ($113-$158). Power tailgate window: wag ($44). Auto-lock tailgate: wag ($37). Power door locks ($71- $101). Tinted glass ($57). Tinted windshield ($40). Deluxe wipers ($10). Luxury steering wheel ($18). Tilt steering wheel ($59). Inside hood release ($13). Electric clock ($21). Locking gas cap ($7). Horns and Mirrors: Dual horns ($6). Remote left mirror ($16). Dual chrome remote mirrors ($31-$47). Dual sport remote mirrors, painted or chrome ($39-$55). Entertainment: AM radio ($76). AM/FM radio ($74-$149). AM/FM stereo radio ($61-$234); w/8track ($159-$332). Rear speaker ($24). Exterior: Manual sunroof: HT ($330). Full vinyl roof ($116) exc. Sport w/option pkg. ($22). Canopy vinyl roof: HT ($95). Canopy vinyl roof w/louvered quarter windows: HT ($116) exc. w/option pkg. ($22). Narrow bodyside moldings: base ($42). Wide bodyside moldings: Spt/Salon ($45). Hood tape stripe: sed ($21). Hood/deck tape stripes: HT ($42). Bodyside tape stripes: Spt ($42). Belt molding: base HT ($16). Sill moldings: base ($27). Upper door frame moldings: base sed/wag ($31). Door edge protectors ($8-$14). Bumper strips, front: sed/wag ($16). Bumper strips, front/rear: HT ($32). Air deflector: wag ($27). Luggage rack: wag ($75). Undercoating ($32). Interior: Console: Sport HT ($18). Vinyl bench seat: base ($45). Cloth/vinyl bucket seats: Sport ($32). 60/40 seat ($132). Pedal dress-up ($9). Trunk dress-up: sed ($45). Color-keyed mats ($18). Wheels and Tires: Deluxe wheel covers ($35). Wire wheel covers ($73-$108). Rallye wheels ($45-$80). Styled wheels ($119-$154). F78 x 15 WSW ($43). G78 x 15 BSW ($20). G78 x 15 WSW ($20-$63). H78 x 15 BSW ($43-$70). H78 x 15 WSW ($27- $90). G70 x 15 RWL ($56-$119). GR78 x 15 WSW ($103-$165). GR70 x 15 RWL ($159-$222). 215 x 15 WSW ($103-$192).

GRAN FURY CONVENIENCE/APPEARANCE OPTIONS: Option Packages: Easy order pkg. ($457-$530). Luxury equipment pkg.: Brghm ($1826-$1922). Light pkg. ($66-$79). Wagon pkg. ($67). Deluxe sound insulation pkg.: HT/sed ($43). Comfort/Convenience: Air cond. ($546). Auto-temp air cond. ($630) exc. w/option pkg. on Brhgm ($83). Rear defroster, electric ($87). Automatic speed control ($88). Power seat ($145). Power windows ($119-$179). Auto-lock tailgate: wag ($37). Power decklid release ($21). Tinted glass ($72). Deluxe wiper/washer pkg. ($17). Luxury steering wheel ($18). Tilt/telescope steering wheel ($88-$106). Gauges, temp & oil pressure ($21). Electric clock ($21). Digital clock ($27- $48). Locking gas cap: cpe/sed ($8). Horns and Mirrors: Dual horns ($6). Remote left mirror ($16). Dual remote mirrors ($31-$48). Day/night mirror ($9). Entertainment: AM radio ($77). AM/FM radio ($79-$155). AM/FM stereo radio ($58-$237); w/8track ($157-$337). Rear speaker ($25). Exterior: Sunroof w/vinyl top ($627-$768). Full vinyl roof ($141). Canopy vinyl roof w/opera windows ($141). Manual vent windows ($43). Vinyl bodyside moldings ($23). Door edge protectors ($9-$14). Upper door frame moldings: sed/wag ($31). Bumper guards, rear: wag ($24). Air deflector: base wag ($28). Assist handles: wag ($24). Luggage rack: wag ($104). Rear bumper step pads: wag ($15). Undercoating ($33). Interior: Cloth/vinyl bench seat: Spt wag ($59). Vinyl bench seat: sed ($29). Vinyl bench seat w/center armrest: Brghm ($45). Cloth/vinyl 50/50 seat: Brghm ($198). Vinyl 50/50 seat: Spt wag ($198). Carpeting: wag ($26). Color-keyed mats ($18). Trunk dress-up ($45). Wheels and Tires: Deluxe wheel covers ($35). Premier wheel covers ($39-$74). Chrome wheels ($81-$156).

HISTORY: Introduced: October 1, 1976. Model year production: Chrysler reported a total of 472,910 passenger cars shipped. Total North American passenger-car production for the U.S. market of 473,748 units included 219,335 six-cylinder and 254,413 V-8s. Calendar year production (U.S.): 492,063. Calendar year sales by U.S. dealers: 444,063 (not incl. 13,767 Voyagers). Model year sales by U.S. dealers: 459,995 (not incl. 51,849 imported Arrows and 13,842 Voyager vans).

Historical Footnotes: This was the final year for the full-size Gran Fury, which slipped considerably in sales after once ranking No. 1 in the Plymouth lineup. Dodge/Plymouth mid-sizes not only looked alike at this time; they were assembled together. Volare sold strongly in 1977, reaching a total of 318,555 versus 239,528 in its opening year.

1978 PLYMOUTH

Biggest news this year was the new Plymouth Horizon, a twin to Dodge Omni, the first front-drive subcompacts built in America. No less significant was the abandonment of the Gran Fury badge, though it would return later in another (smaller) form. A rather long list of 318, 360 and 400 cu. in. V-8s was optional, standard and heavy-duty, some available only in California and/or high-altitude regions. The big 440 V-8 was gone. Automatic transmissions added a lockup torque converter that cut in at about 2731 MPH.

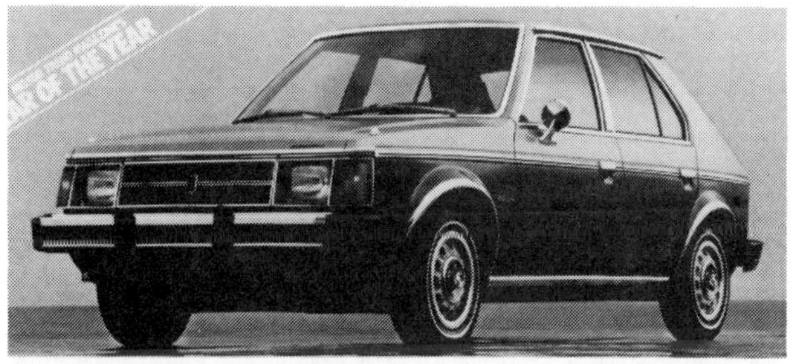

1978 Horizon four-door hatchback (JG)

HORIZON — SERIES M — FOUR— Plymouth's new L body front-wheel drive subcompact, near twin to the Dodge Omni, had four doors and carried four passengers, with a liftgate (hatch) at the back. The two models differed mainly in grille appearance. Horizon's grille showed a tight crosshatch pattern with horizontal divider bar and center shield-style emblem. Framing for the single rectangular headlamps, slightly recessed, extended outward to encircle wraparound amber park/signal lamps. Small 'Plymouth' block letters sat above the left headlamp. 'Horizon' script was on front fenders, and on passenger side of the liftgate. Taillamps consisted of fairly large wraparound red units at the outside, with smaller amber lens inside, above the matching clear backup lens. Small horizontal marker reflectors went on quarter panels, just ahead of the taillamps. Bodyside moldings continued around the back of the car. Sole engine was a transverse-mounted Lean Burn 104.7 cu. in. (1.7-liter) overhead-cam four, with standard four-speed manual shift. Engines came from Volkswagen, enlarged to the 1.7-liter displacement. In fact, the car itself had a VW Rabbit-like appearance. Horizon had rack-and-pinion steering, an Iso-Strut front suspension with anti-sway bar, plus "anti- sway characteristics" built into the trailing-arm, coil- spring beam axle rear suspension. Standard equipment included black vinyl bodyside moldings, bucket seats, AM radio, lighter, door dome light switch, folding rear shelf panel, fold-down rear seat, ammeter, temperature gauge, bin-type glovebox, heater/defroster, three-spoke steering wheel, roll-down rear- door windows, multi-function steering column lever, and two- speed wiper/washers. Also standard: argent styled sport wheels with P155/80R13 glass-belted radial whitewall tires, anodized aluminum bumpers with protective strips, and stainless steel exhaust pipe. Options included a stereo radio, power steering, Torqueflite transmission, roof rack, remote-control mirrors, air conditioning, and tinted glass. A selection of exterior and interior packages also was offered, essentially groupings of conventional add-ons. Body colors were: Sunrise Orange, Spitfire Orange, Formal Black, Spinnaker White, Yellow Blaze, and Light Mocha Tan; plus metallic Pewter Gray, Regatta Blue, Starlight Blue Sunfire, Tapestry Red Sunfire, Caramel Tan, Augusta Green Sunfire, and Mint Green. Five "classic" two-tone combinations were available.

1978 Volare four-door sedan (CM)

VOLARE — SERIES H — SIX/V-8 — While Volare dropped down to a single series, an ample selection of option packages allowed buyers to vary their Volares considerably. They included Super Coupe and Street Kit Car packages that added over $1000 to the coupe price, plus the cheaper Road Runner and Fun Runner. A two-door coupe, four-door sedan and two-seat station wagon made up the selection. Volare had a new "waffle-look" grille pattern, along with revised taillamps and trim. Otherwise, little change was evident. Bumpers were now built of high-strength steel to cut weight. Other weight reductions occurred in tires, glass and brakes, as well as the engine and air conditioner. "Super Pak" coupes added such extras as spoilers and wheel arch flares, along with black paint, special striping, heavy-duty suspension, and the 360 cu. in. 4Bbl. V-8. Standard engine was again the 225 cu. in. Slant Six, with 318 or 360 V-8 optional. Wagons had the two-barrel Super Six, as well as power brakes. Three-speed manual shift was standard; four-speed and TorqueFlite (with new lockup clutch) optional. Coupes and sedans had D78 x 14 blackwall tires; wagons, F78 x 14 glass-belted tires. New optional thin-back front bucket seats had headrests and a center armrest. Also joining the option list: AM and AM/FM stereo radios with built-in CB transceivers. Galvanized metal and plastic front splash shields were now used to try and cut rusting.

1978 Fury Sport Coupe (CM)

FURY — SERIES R — SIX/V-8 — Plymouth's full-size Gran Fury disappeared, but the mid-size lineup amounted to eight models: base two-door hardtop and sedan, Sport hardtop, Salon sedan, plus Suburban and Sport Suburban wagons with either two or three seats. Styling was the same as 1977, though new thin-back front seats offered more knee room in back. Base engine was the 225 cu. in., 2Bbl. Super Six; optional, a 318 cu. in. (5.2-liter) Lean Burn V-8. Wagons had a standard 360 cu. in. (5.9-liter) Lean Burn or optional 400 Lean Burn V-8, also available on other models. Three-speed manual transmission was standard on six-cylinder models, but V-8s had TorqueFlite. Automatic transmissions added a lock-up torque converter. Standard equipment also included power brakes, power steering (on V-8 models), front/rear bumper guards, day/night mirror, locking glovebox, and F78 x 15 blackwall tires. Wagons had H78 x 15 tires. The Salon four-door added shag carpet, door trim panels, and a hood ornament with center molding. On the option list, a Fury Gran Coupe package was available for $686. So was a halo vinyl roof, as well as the canopy and full vinyl tops. Both AM and AM/FM stereo radios could have a built-in CB transceiver or tape player. Aluminum-fascia wheels and wire wheel covers were offered as options.

I.D. DATA: Plymouth's 13-symbol Vehicle Identification Number (VIN) again was on the upper left corner of the instrument panel, visible through the windshield. Symbol one indicates car line: 'M' Horizon; 'H' Volare; 'R' Fury. Symbol two is series (price class): 'L' low; 'H' high. Symbols 3-4 show body type: '23' 2-dr. hardtop coupe; '29' 2-dr. special coupe; '41' 4-dr. sedan; '44' 4-dr. hatchback; '45' two-seat station wagon; '46' three-seat wagon. Symbol five is the engine code: 'A' L4105 2Bbl.; 'C' L6225 1Bbl.; 'D' L6225 2Bbl.; 'G' V8318 2Bbl.; 'K' V8360 2Bbl.; 'J' V8360 4Bbl.; 'N' V8400 4Bbl. Symbol six is the model year code: '8' 1978. Symbol seven indicates assembly plant: 'A' Lynch Road; 'B' Hamtramck, MI; 'D' Belvidere, IL; 'F' Newark, DE. The final six digits make up the sequential serial number, starting with 100001. Six-cylinder/V-8 engine number coding is similar to 1976-77. Engine numbers for the new Horizon four-cylinder are on a pad just above the fuel pump. As before, a Vehicle Safety Certification Label that displays (among other data) the date of manufacture is attached to the rear facing of the driver's door. A Body Code Plate is on the left front fender side shield, wheel housing, or left side of upper radiator support.

HORIZON (FOUR)

Model Number	Body/Style Number	Body Type & Seating	Factory Price	Shipping Weight	Production Total
ML	44	4-dr. Hatch-4P	3976	2145	95,817

VOLARE (SIX/V-8)

HL	29	2-dr. Spt Cpe-5P	3735/3905	3140/3255	61,702
HL	41	4-dr. Sedan-6P	3853/4020	3175/3295	85,365
HL	45	4-dr. Sta Wag-6P	4195/4324	3405/3490	70,728

FURY/SUBURBAN (SIX/V-8)

RL	23	2-dr. HT Cpe-6P	4212/4388	3600/3855	9,473
RL	41	4-dr. Sedan-6P	4292/4468	3635/3885	28,245
RL	45	4-dr. 2S Wag-6P	--/5024	--/4310	3,328
RL	46	4-dr. 3S Wag-9P	--/5167	--/4370	3,342

1978 Fury Salon sedan (CM)

FURY SPORT/SALON (SIX/V-8)

RH	23	2-dr. Sport HT-6P	4452/4628	3610/3860	9,736
RH	41	4-dr. Salon Sed-6P	4527/4703	3645/3900	12,976

FURY SPORT SUBURBAN (V-8)

RH	45	4-dr. 2S Wag-6P	--/5482	--/4300	1,106
RH	46	4-dr. 3S Wag-9P	--/5625	--/4375	2,117

FACTORY PRICE AND WEIGHT NOTE: Prices and weights to left of slash are for six-cylinder, to right for V-8 engine.

ENGINE DATA: BASE FOUR (Horizon): Inline, overhead-cam four-cylinder. Cast iron block; aluminum head. Displacement: 104.7 cu. in. (1.7 liters). Bore & stroke: 3.13 x 3.40 in. Compression ratio: 8.2:1. Brake horsepower: 75 at 5600 R.P.M. Torque: 90 lbs.-ft. at 3200 R.P.M. Solid valve lifters. Five main bearings. Carburetor: 2Bbl. Holley 5220. VIN Code: A. BASE SIX (Volare): Inline, overhead-valve six-cylinder. Cast iron block and head. Displacement: 225 cu. in. (3.7 liters). Bore & stroke: 3.40 x 4.12 in. Compression ratio: 8.4:1. Brake horsepower: 100 at 3600 R.P.M. Torque: 170 lbs.-ft. at 1600 R.P.M. Solid valve lifters. Four main bearings. Carburetor: 1Bbl. Holley 1945. VIN Code: C. BASE SIX (Volare wagon, Fury); OPTIONAL (Volare): Same as 225 cu. in. six above, but with 2Bbl. Carter BBD 8086S carburetor Horsepower: 110 at 3600 R.P.M. Torque: 180 lbs.-ft. at 2000 R.P.M. VIN Code: D. OPTIONAL V-8 (Volare, Fury): 90-degree, overhead valve V-8. Cast iron block and head. Displacement: 318 cu. in. (5.2 liters). Bore & stroke: 3.91 x 3.31 in. Compression ratio: 8.5:1. Brake horsepower: 140 at 4000 R.P.M. Torque: 245 lbs.-ft. at 1600 R.P.M. Five main bearings. Hydraulic valve lifters. Carburetor: 2Bbl. Carter BBD. VIN Code: G. BASE V-8 (Volare wagon); OPTIONAL (Volare, Fury): 90-degree, overhead valve V-8. Cast iron block and head. Displacement: 360 cu. in. (5.9 liters). Bore & stroke: 4.00 x 3.58 in. Compression ratio: 8.4:1. Brake horsepower: 155 at 3600 R.P.M. Torque: 270 lbs.-ft. at 2400 R.P.M. Five main bearings. Hydraulic valve lifters. Carburetor: 2Bbl. Holley 2245. VIN Code: K. OPTIONAL V-8 (Volare): Same as 360 cu. in. V-8 above, but with Carter TQ 4Bbl. Carburetor Horsepower: 175 at 4000 R.P.M. Torque: 260 lbs.-ft. at 2400 R.P.M. VIN Code: J. OPTIONAL V-8 (Fury): 90-degree, overhead valve V-8. Cast iron block and head. Displacement: 400 cu. in. (6.6 liters). Bore & stroke: 4.34 x 3.38 in. Compression ratio: 8.2:1. Brake horsepower: 190 at 3600 R.P.M. Torque: 305 lbs.-ft. at 3200 R.P.M. Five main bearings. Hydraulic valve lifters. Carburetor: 4Bbl. Carter TQ. VIN Code: N.

CHASSIS DATA: Wheelbase: (Horizon) 99.2 in.; (Volare cpe) 108.7 in.; (Volare sed/wag) 112.7 in.; (Fury cpe) 114.9 in.; (Fury sed) 117.4 in.; (Fury wag) 117.5 in. Overall Length: (Horizon) 163.2 in.; (Volare cpe) 197.2 in.; (Volare sed/wag) 201.2 in.; (Fury cpe) 213.2 in.; (Fury sed) 218.0 in.; (Fury wag) 225.1 in. Height: (Horizon) 53.4 in.; (Volare cpe) 53.3 in.; (Volare sed) 55.3 in.; (Volare wag) 55.7 in.; (Fury cpe) 52.9 in. (Fury sed) 54.3 in.; (Fury wag) 56.4 in. Width: (Horizon) 66.2 in.; (Volare) 73.3 in.; (Fury) 77.7 in.; (Fury wag) 78.8 in. Front Tread: (Horizon) 55.5 in.; (Volare) 60.0 in.; (Fury) 61.9 in. Rear Tread: (Horizon) 55.1 in.; (Volare) 58.5 in.; (Fury) 62.0 in. exc. wag, 63.4 in. Standard Tires: (Horizon) P155/80R13 GBR WSW; (Volare) D78 x 14 BSW; (Volare wag) F78 x 14 BSW; (Fury) F78 x 15; (Fury wag) H78 x 15.

TECHNICAL: Transmission: Three-speed manual transmission standard on Volare and Fury six (column shift on Fury, floor on Volare). Gear ratios: (1st) 3.08:1; (2nd) 1.70:1; (3rd) 1.00:1; (Rev) 2.90:1. Four-speed overdrive available on Volare: (1st) 3.09:1; (2nd) 1.67:1; (3rd) 1.00:1; (4th) 0.71:1; (Rev) 3.00:1. Four-speed manual (floor shift) standard on Horizon: (1st) 3.45:1; (2nd) 1.94:1; (3rd) 1.29:1; (4th) 0.97:1; (Rev) 3.17:1. TorqueFlite three-speed automatic standard on Fury V-8, optional on others. Volare/Fury gear ratios: (1st) 2.45:1; (2nd) 1.45:1; (3rd) 1.00:1; (Rev) 2.22:1. Horizon gear ratios: (1st) 2.47:1; (2nd) 1.47:1; (3rd) 1.00:1; (Rev) 2.10:1. Standard final drive ratio: (Horizon) 3.48:1; (Volare six) 3.23:1 w/3spd, 2.76:1, 2.71:1 or 2.94:1 w/auto.; (Volare V8318) 2.94:1 w/manual, 2.47:1 or 2.45:1 w/auto.; (Volare V8360) 2.45:1 or 3.21:1 w/manual, 2.71:1 w/auto.; (Fury six) 3.21:1 w/manual, 2.71:1 w/auto.; (Fury V-8) 2.71:1 w/auto.; (Fury V8360) 2.45:1 w/auto.; (Fury V8360 wag) 2.71:1. Steering: (Horizon) rack and pinion; (others) recirculating ball. Suspension: (Horizon) Iso-Strut independent coil front w/anti-sway bar, independent trailing arm coil rear w/integral anti-sway; (Volare) isolated transverse front torsion bars w/anti-sway bar, semi-elliptic rear leaf springs; (Fury) longitudinal front torsion bars w/anti-sway bar, semi-elliptic rear leaf springs. Brakes: Front disc, rear drum. Ignition: Electronic. Body construction: Unibody. Fuel tank: (Horizon) 13 gal.; (Volare) 18 gal. exc. V-8/wagon, 19.5 gal.; (Fury) 25.5 gal. exc. wagon, 20 gal.

DRIVETRAIN OPTIONS: Engines: 225 cu. in., 2Bbl. six: Volare cpe/sed ($41). 318 cu. in., 2Bbl. V-8: Volare cpe/sed ($170); Volare wag ($129); Fury ($176). 318 cu. in., 4Bbl. V-8: Calif. Volare ($172-213); Calif. Fury ($221). 360 cu. in., 2Bbl. V-8: Volare cpe/sed ($275); Volare wag ($234); Fury ($285). H.D. 360 cu. in., 2Bbl. V-8: Volare sed ($332); Volare wag ($292). 360 cu. in., 4Bbl. V-8: Volare cpe ($439-463); high-altitude/Calif. Fury ($330-481); high-alt./Calif. Fury wag ($45). 400 cu. in., 4Bbl. V-8: Fury HT/sed ($379); Fury wag ($94). H.D. 400 cu. in., 4Bbl. V-8: Fury HT/sed ($507); Fury wag ($222). Transmission/Differential: TorqueFlite: Horizon ($303); Volare ($293); Fury ($320). Four-speed manual trans. w/floor lever: Volare ($142). Sure grip differential: Volare ($56); Fury ($62). Optional axle ratio: Volare ($15). Power Accessories: Power steering: Horizon ($148); Volare ($145); Fury ($159). Power brakes: Horizon ($68); Volare ($66). Suspension: H.D. susp.: Volare ($24); Fury ($24). Sport susp.: Volare ($24). H.D. shock absorbers: Fury ($7). Other: Trailer towing pkg.: Volare ($150); Fury ($157). Long- life battery: Volare ($30); Fury ($33). California emission system ($72-79). High-altitude emission system ($31-$34).

HORIZON CONVENIENCE/APPEARANCE OPTIONS: Option Packages: Classic two-tone paint pkg. ($73-$107). Custom exterior pkg. ($71). Premium exterior pkg. ($167). Custom interior pkg. ($62-$82). Premium interior pkg. ($214-$242). Premium woodgrain pkg. ($312). Popular equipment group ($250). Light pkg. ($44). Comfort/Convenience: Air cond. ($493). Rear defroster ($80). Tinted glass ($56). Tinted windshield ($41). Luxury steering wheel ($15). Electric clock w/trip odometer ($26). Rear wiper/washer ($59). Locking gas cap ($7). Glovebox lock ($5). Horns and Mirrors: Dual horns ($7). Remote left mirror ($16). Dual remote mirrors ($30-$46). Day/night mirror ($9). Entertainment: AM/FM radio ($74). AM/FM stereo radio ($143). Exterior: Full vinyl roof ($93). Moldings: belt ($16); drip ($18); sill ($19); upper door frame ($30); wheel lip ($27). Door edge protectors ($20). Bumper guards ($41). Multi-color tape stripe ($66). Luggage rack ($81). Undercoating ($31). Interior: Console: storage ($21); shift lever ($30). Cloth/vinyl bucket seats ($21). Cargo area carpet ($43). Color-keyed floor mats ($26). Wheels and Tires: Wheel trim rings ($36). Rallye wheels ($36- $73). Bright rallye hubs ($37). 165/75 x 13 GBR WSW ($16). 165/75 x 13 SBR WSW ($48). Conventional spare tire ($12-$24).

VOLARE CONVENIENCE/APPEARANCE OPTIONS: Option Packages: Super Coupe pkg. ($1348-$1417). Street Kit Car pkg. ($1085). Road Runner pkg. ($289). Road Runner decor group: cpe ($51). Road Runner Sport Pak: cpe ($411-$499). Fun Runner Coupe pkg. ($77). Fun Runner decor pkg. ($180). Custom exterior pkg. ($73-$86). Custom interior pkg. ($144-$224). Premium exterior pkg. ($108-$138). Premium interior pkg. ($180-$483). Premier wagon woodgrain group ($221). Two-tone paint pkg.: cpe ($188). Two-tone decor pkg.: cpe ($62). Basic group ($653-$655). Light pkg. ($44). Protection group ($28-$35). Deluxe insulation pkg. ($35-$38). Comfort/Convenience: Air cond. ($484). Rear defogger, blower- type ($48); electric ($83). Automatic speed control ($86). Power seat ($142). Power windows ($113-$157). Power door locks ($71-$98). Tinted glass ($65). Tinted windshield ($39). Tilt steering wheel ($65). Intermittent wipers ($31). Digital clock ($46). Inside hood release ($12). Locking glovebox ($5). Lighter ($6). Locking gas cap ($7). Horns and Mirrors: Dual horns ($7). Remote left-hand mirror ($16). Dual remote mirrors ($30-$46). Dual remote sport mirrors: cpe ($37-$53). Day/night mirror ($9). Entertainment: AM radio ($74); w/8track player ($143-$217); w/CB ($305-$379). AM/FM radio ($74-$148). AM/FM stereo radio ($143-$217); w/8track tape player ($234-$308); w/CB ($448- $522). Rear speaker ($23). Exterior: T-Bar roof: cpe ($572). Full vinyl roof: sed ($93). Halo vinyl roof: cpe ($93-$109). Landau vinyl roof: cpe ($164). Vinyl bodyside moldings ($40). Belt moldings ($16). Door edge protectors ($10-$18). Upper door frame moldings: sed/wag ($30). Wheel lip moldings ($20). Bumper guards, front/rear ($39). Protective bumper rub strips ($32). Undercoating ($21-$31). Interior: Console: cpe ($55). Cloth/vinyl bucket seats: cpe ($160). Vinyl bucket seats: cpe ($102). Rear armrest ($11). Color-keyed mats ($20). Pedal dress-up ($9). Trunk dress-up ($43). Color-keyed seatbelts ($15). Wheels and Tires: Deluxe wheel covers ($36). Premium wheel covers ($36-$71). Wire wheel covers ($91-$127). Rallye wheels ($33-$72). Styled wheels ($55-127). D78 x 14 WSW ($42). DR78 x 14 BSW ($54-$88). DR78 x 14 WSW ($42-$96). E78 x 14 BSW ($18). E78 x 14 WSW ($18-$60). ER78 x 14 GBR BSW ($18-$71). ER78 x 14 GBR WSW ($18-$113). F78 x 14 BSW ($86-$145). F78 x 14 WSW ($44). FR78 x 14 GBR BSW ($25-$73). FR78 x 14 GBR WSW ($25-$117). FR78 x 14 SBR WSW ($57-$149). FR70 x 14 Aramid-belt RWL ($127-$237). GR78 x 14 SBR WSW ($76-$120). Space-saving or conventional spare tire (NC).

FURY CONVENIENCE/APPEARANCE OPTIONS: Option Packages: Gran Coupe pkg.: HT ($686). Basic group ($254-$739). Light pkg. ($42-$51). Deluxe insulation pkg.: six-cyl. ($66). Roadability pkg. ($35). Comfort/Convenience: Air cond. ($563). Rear defroster, electric ($91). Automatic speed control ($94). Power seat ($155). Power windows ($129-$179). Power tailgate window: wag ($46). Auto-lock tailgate: wag ($38). Power door locks ($83- $116). Tinted glass ($83). Tinted windshield ($42). Deluxe wipers ($34). Luxury steering wheel ($19). Tilt steering wheel ($71). Inside hood release ($13). Electric clock ($22). Locking gas cap ($7). Horns and Mirrors: Dual horns ($7). Remote left mirror ($17). Dual chrome remote mirrors ($33-$450. Dual sport remote mirrors, painted or chrome ($41-$58). Entertainment: AM radio ($81); w/8track player ($157-$237); w/CB ($333-$414). AM/FM radio ($81-$161). AM/FM stereo radio ($157-$237); w/8track ($256-$336); w/CB ($490-$570). Rear speaker ($25). Exterior Trim: Halo vinyl roof: HT ($121). Full vinyl roof ($121). Canopy vinyl roof: HT ($100). Canopy vinyl roof w/louvered quarter windows: HT ($121). Narrow bodyside moldings ($44). Wide bodyside moldings ($48). Hood tape stripe: sed ($23). Hood/deck tape stripes: HT ($45). Belt molding: base HT ($17). Sill moldings: base sed/wag ($28). Wheel lip moldings: base sed ($22). Upper door frame moldings: base sed/wag ($33). Door edge protectors ($11-$20). Bumper strips, front: sed/wag ($17). Bumper strips, front/rear: HT ($35). Air deflector: wag ($29). Luggage rack: wag ($89). Undercoating ($34). Interior: Console: Sport HT ($58). Vinyl bench seat: base ($48); Salon ($31). Vinyl bucket seats: Sport HT (NC). Cloth/vinyl 60/40 seat: Spt/Salon ($140). Vinyl 60/40 seat: Spt wag ($140). Color-keyed mats ($22). Color-keyed seatbelts ($16). Wheels and Tires: Deluxe wheel covers ($39). Wire wheel covers ($99-$138). Aluminum-fascia wheels ($87-$126). F78 x 15 WSW ($48). G78 x 15 BSW ($21). G78 x 15 WSW ($21-$69). H78 x 15 BSW ($45). H78 x 15 WSW ($47-$95). GR78 x 15 SBR WSW ($130-$178). GR60 x 15 Aramid-belted RWL ($327-$376). 215 x 15 SBR WSW ($109-$204).

HISTORY: Introduced: October 7, 1977. Model year production: Chrysler reported a total of 383,935 passenger cars shipped. Total North American passenger-car production for the U.S. market of 385,068 units included 95,854 four-cylinder, 170,105 six- cylinder, and 119,109 V-8s. Calendar year production (U.S.): 443,619. Calendar year sales by U.S. dealers: 404,371 (not incl. 13,895 Voyagers). Model year sales by U.S. dealers: 393,368 (not incl. 36,693 imports and 14,138 Voyager vans).

Historical Footnotes: A poor year for sales, 1978 was also the final year for big cars from Chrysler Corp. Plymouth ranked No. 7 in production, just ahead of Dodge. Production of the new Horizon at the Belvidere, Illinois plant began in November 1977. Chrysler thus became the first domestic automaker to build a front-drive subcompact. Volare sales dropped by 29 percent for the model year, due partly to success of the new Chrysler LeBaron. Fury faded away during the '78 model year, as had the Gran Fury before it. A new sporty Plymouth Sapporo to match the Dodge Challenger was now being imported from Mitsubishi in Japan.

1979 PLYMOUTH

After more than two decades in the lineup, the Fury name faded away, shrinking the Plymouth selection to just two models and a single (low) price class. A new Horizon-based hatchback coupe, on a shorter wheelbase but 8 in. longer overall, was called Horizon TC3. Volare added a sports equipment package, but not much else.

1979 Horizon four-door hatchback (CM)

HORIZON/TC3 — SERIES M — FOUR— "Horizons Unlimited," promised the 1979 factory sales catalog. Not quite, but Plymouth's front-drive subcompact now came in two forms: four-door hatchback and new two-door TC3 coupe. They were equivalent to Dodge's Omni and 024, respectively. Similar in design and basic equipment, the coupe and sedan differed significantly in appearance and size. TC3 rode a shorter wheelbase (96.7 in. versus 99.2 in. for the four-door), but the same basic chassis structure. Both models had Iso-Strut front suspension and rack-and- pinion steering. TC3 was promoted as "sporty," making use of a term that would, a few years later, become trendy throughout the industry. Four-door appearance was unchanged. TC3 had a grille consisting of five wide horizontal slots in a sloped body-color panel that extended forward from the hood. Above the grille on the driver's side was 'Plymouth' block lettering, just like the four-door. Single rectangular headlamps sat in recessed, trim-free housings. The inner fender lines extended back from the inner edge of the headlamp housings, so the hood was a bit lower than the fenders. Partly-curved parking/signal lamps were recess- mounted in the bumper area. Front side marker lenses were just ahead of the front wheels. 'Horizon' script sat on front fenders. TC3 had a six-window design, with a conventional quarter window just to the rear of the door, plus a triangular window at the very back that followed the sharp slope of the

1979 Horizon TC3 two-door hatchback (CM)

liftgate. Standard TC3 equipment included dual bodyside pinstripes, bright moldings, wheel trim rings, AM/FM radio, electric rear window defroster, woodgrain instrument panel applique, luxury steering wheel, electric remote hatchback release, vinyl bucket front seats, and fold-down rear seat. Tires were P165/75R13 glass-belted radial whitewalls. Larger steel-belted radials were available, as were Aramid-belted tires with outline white letters. Sport and Rallye TC3 packages were available, along with a "woody" look option for the four-door. The TC3 Sport Appearance package included a rear spoiler, blackout exterior treatment, 'TC3' decals, louvered quarter window appliques, painted Rallye wheels, and four-spoke steering wheel. A Rallye instrument cluster contained a tachometer and trip odometer. A total of 14,709 coupes had the Sport package, while 4,154 carried the Rallye package. Cast aluminum wheels also were available. So were flip-out quarter windows. Four-door standard equipment included an AM radio, electric rear-window defroster, lighter, whitewalls, and vinyl bodyside moldings. Both models carried the 104.7 cu. in. (1.7-liter) four with standard four-speed manual shift. Power steering, power brakes and TorqueFlite automatic were optional. Body colors this year were: Formal Black, Nightwatch Blue, Flame Orange, Light Cashmere, Chianti Red, and Spinnaker White; plus metallic Pewter Gray, Cadet Blue, Ensign Blue, Teal Frost, Teal Green Sunfire, Turquoise, or Medium Cashmere. TC3 could also have Bright Yellow, and both models had a choice of two-tones.

1979 Duster coupe (CM)

VOLARE — SERIES H — SIX/V-8 — Not much changed in Plymouth's compact, offered again with a base 225 cu. in. Slant Six engine and single-barrel carburetor. Volare's coupe could have a four-barrel 360 cu. in. V-8, rated 195 horsepower, for a price of $575 to $600. Otherwise, the standard engine upgrades for Volare were the two-barrel Slant Six ($41) and two-barrel 318 V-8 ($216). Volare six had a standard three-speed manual transmission with floor lever, with option of the four-speed overdrive unit ($149 extra). Volare V-8 came with TorqueFlite, and could get an optional maintenance-free battery. Only one trim level was offered, with sport coupe, four-door sedan or four- door station wagon body style. An electric choke heater was supposed to improve cold-weather startup. Galvanized metal body panels were installed to help protect against rust. The Duster name returned on a coupe package that cost only $30 (or $60 with quarter-window louvers). The Duster package included five-spoke painted wheels, two-tone paint, accent tape, performance options, louvered quarter windows, headlamp doors, and a rear deck spoiler. A Duster decor package added another $90. The wagon Sport package, priced considerably higher ($630), included a front air dam, tape stripes, blacked-out grille, and bucket seats. A total of 1,122 Volares had the Road Runner package (RPO code A57), which was also more costly. Cast aluminum wheels were optional this year.

I.D. DATA: Plymouth's 13-symbol Vehicle Identification Number (VIN) again was on the upper left corner of the instrument panel, visible through the windshield. Symbol one indicates car line: 'M' Horizon; 'H' Volare. Symbol two is series (price class): 'L' low. Symbols 3-4 show body type: '29' 2-dr. sport coupe; '41' 4-dr. sedan; '44' 4-dr. hatchback; '45' two-seat station wagon. Symbol five is the engine code: 'A' L4105 2Bbl.; 'C' L6225 1Bbl.; 'D' L6225 2Bbl.; 'G' V8318 2Bbl.; 'J' V8360 4Bbl. Symbol six is the model year code: '9' 1979. Symbol seven indicates assembly plant: 'B' Hamtramck, MI; 'D' Belvidere, IL; 'F' Newark, DE. The final six digits make up the sequential serial number, starting with 100001. Engine number coding is similar to 1976-78. As before, a Vehicle Safety Certification Label that displays (among other data) the date of manufacture is attached to the rear facing of the driver's door. A Body Code Plate is on the left front fender side shield, wheel housing, or left side of upper radiator support.

HORIZON (FOUR)

Model Number	Body/Style Number	Body Type & Seating	Factory Price	Shipping Weight	Production Total
ML	44	4-dr. Hatch-4P	4122	2135	86,214

HORIZON TC3 (FOUR)

ML	24	2-dr. Hatch 22-4P	4482	2195	54,249

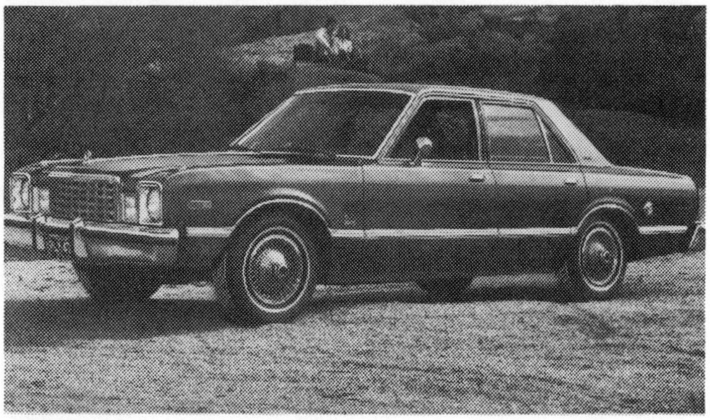

1979 Volare Premier sedan (CM)

VOLARE (SIX/V-8)

HL	29	2-dr. Spt Cpe-5P	3956/4172	3050/3170	Note 1
HL	41	4-dr. Sedan-6P	4057/4273	3115/3235	Note 1
HL	45	4-dr. Sta Wag-6P	4433/4649	3325/3435	44,085

Note 1: Total coupe/sedan production, 134,734.

FACTORY PRICE AND WEIGHT NOTE: Prices and weights to left of slash are for six-cylinder, to right for V-8 engine.

ENGINE DATA: BASE FOUR (Horizon): Inline, overhead-cam four-cylinder. Cast iron block; aluminum head. Displacement: 104.7 cu. in. (1.7 liters). Bore & stroke: 3.13 x 3.40 in. Compression ratio: 8.2:1. Brake horsepower: 70 at 5200 R.P.M. Torque: 85 lbs.-ft. at 2800 R.P.M. Five main bearings. Solid valve lifters. Carburetor: 2Bbl. Holley 5220. VIN Code: A. BASE SIX (Volare): Inline, overhead-valve six-cylinder. Cast iron block and head. Displacement: 225 cu. in. (3.7 liters). Bore & stroke: 3.40 x 4.12 in. Compression ratio: 8.4:1. Brake horsepower: 100 at 3600 R.P.M. Torque: 165 lbs.-ft. at 1600 R.P.M. Four main bearings. Solid valve lifters. Carburetor: 1Bbl. Holley 1945. VIN Code: C. OPTIONAL SIX (Volare): Same as 225 cu. in. six above, but with 2Bbl. Carter BBD carburetor Horsepower: 110 at 3600 R.P.M. Torque: 180 lbs.- ft. at 2000 R.P.M. VIN Code: D. OPTIONAL V-8 (Volare): 90-degree, overhead valve V-8. Cast iron block and head. Displacement: 318 cu. in. (5.2 liters). Bore & stroke: 3.91 x 3.31 in. Compression ratio: 8.5:1. Brake horsepower: 135 at 4000 R.P.M. Torque: 250 lbs.-ft. at 1600 R.P.M. Five main bearings. Hydraulic valve lifters. Carburetor: 2Bbl. Holley 2280. VIN Code: G. OPTIONAL V-8 (Volare): 90-degree, overhead valve V-8. Cast iron block and head. Displacement: 360 cu. in. (5.9 liters). Bore & stroke: 4.00 x 3.58 in. Compression ratio: 8.0:1. Brake horsepower: 195 at 4000 R.P.M. Torque: 280 lbs.-ft. at 2400 R.P.M. Five main bearings. Hydraulic valve lifters. Carburetor: 4Bbl. Carter TQ. VIN Code: J.

CHASSIS DATA: Wheelbase: (Horizon) 99.2 in.; (TC3) 96.7 in.; (Volare cpe) 108.7 in.; (Volare sed/wag) 112.7 in. Overall Length: (Horizon) 164.8 in. incl. optional bumper guards; (TC3) 172.7 in.; (Volare cpe) 197.2 in.; (Volare sed/wag) 201.2 in. Height: (Horizon) 53.7 in.; (TC3) 51.4 in.; (Volare cpe) 53.3 in.; (Volare sed) 55.3 in.; (Volare wag) 55.7 in. Width: (Horizon) 66.2 in.; (TC3) 66.0 in.; (Volare) 72.8 in. Front Tread: (Horizon/TC3) 56.0 in.; (Volare) 60.0 in. Rear Tread: (Horizon/TC3) 55.6 in.; (Volare) 58.5 in. Standard Tires: (Horizon) P155/80R13 GBR WSW; (TC3) P165/75R13 GBR WSW; (Volare) D78 x 14; (Volare wag) F78 x 14.

TECHNICAL: Transmission: Three-speed manual trans. (floor lever) standard on Volare six. Gear ratios: (1st) 3.08:1; (2nd) 1.70:1; (3rd) 1.00:1; (Rev) 2.90:1. Four-speed overdrive available on Volare six: (1st) 3.09:1; (2nd) 1.67:1; (3rd) 1.00:1; (4th) 0.71:1; (Rev) 3.00:1. Four-speed manual (floor shift) standard on Horizon: (1st) 3.45:1; (2nd) 1.94:1; (3rd) 1.29:1; (4th) 0.97:1; (Rev) 3.17:1. TorqueFlite three-speed automatic standard on Volare V-8, optional on others. Volare gear ratios: (1st) 2.45:1; (2nd) 1.45:1; (3rd) 1.00:1; (Rev) 2.22:1. Horizon gear ratios: (1st) 2.47:1; (2nd) 1.47:1; (3rd) 1.00:1; (Rev) 2.10:1. Standard final drive ratio: (Horizon/TC3) 3.37:1 w/4 spd, 3.46:1 w/auto.; (Volare six) 3.23:1 w/3spd, 3.23:1 or 3.21:1 w/4spd, 2.71:1 or 2.76:1 w/auto.; (Volare V8318) 2.47:1 or 2.45:1; (Volare V8360) 2.71:1; (Volare wag) 2.94:1, 3.21:1 or 2.45:1. Steering: (Horizon) rack and pinion; (others) recirculating ball. Suspension: (Horizon/TC3) Iso-Strut independent coil front w/anti-sway bar, independent trailing arm coil rear w/integral anti-sway; (Volare) isolated transverse front torsion bars w/anti-sway bar, semi-elliptic rear leaf springs. Brakes: Front disc, rear drum. Ignition: Electronic. Body construction: Unibody. Fuel tank: (Horizon/TC3) 13 gal.; (Volare) 18 gal. exc. V-8/wagon, 19.5 gal.

DRIVETRAIN OPTIONS: Engines: 225 cu. in., 2Bbl. six: Volare ($43). 318 cu. in., 2Bbl. V-8: Volare ($216). 318 cu. in., 4Bbl. V-8: Calif. Volare ($271). 360 cu. in., 4Bbl. V-8: Volare ($575-$600). Transmission/Differential: TorqueFlite: Horizon/Volare ($319); Four-speed manual trans. w/floor lever: Volare ($149). Sure grip differential: Volare ($61). Optional axle ratio ($18). Power Accessories: Power steering ($155-$156). Power brakes ($72). Suspension: H.D. susp.: Horizon 4dr. ($25); Volare ($25). Sport susp.: TC3 ($41). Other: Trailer assist pkg.: Volare ($157). Maintenance-free battery: Horizon ($20). Long-life battery: Volare ($32). California emission system ($79).

HORIZON/TC3 CONVENIENCE/APPEARANCE OPTIONS: Option Packages: Rallye equipment pkg.: TC3 ($177-$352). Sport pkg.: TC3 ($278-$340). Sport/Classic two-tone paint pkg. ($114-$164). Custom exterior pkg.: 4dr. ($74). Premium exterior pkg.: TC3 ($78); 4dr. ($122-$199). Custom interior pkg.: 4dr. ($79-$101). Premium interior pkg. ($146-$270). Premium woodgrain pkg.: 4dr. ($290-$331). Popular equipment group ($267-$279). Light pkg. ($31-$46). Comfort/Convenience: Air cond. ($507). Tinted glass ($61). Tinted windshield ($43). Luxury steering wheel: 4dr. ($18). Rallye instrument cluster: TC3 ($76). Electric clock w/trip odometer ($28). Rear wiper/washer ($62). Locking gas cap ($7). Locking glovebox: 4dr. ($5). Horns and Mirrors: Dual horns ($9). Remote left mirror: 4dr. ($17). Dual remote mirrors: 4dr. ($32-$49). Dual remote sport mirrors: TC3 ($61). Day/night mirror ($11). Entertainment: AM/FM radio: 4dr. ($73). AM/FM stereo radio: 4dr. ($141); TC3 ($67). Rear speaker: TC3 ($24). Exterior: Removable glass sunroof ($176). Rear spoiler: TC3 ($53). Flip-out quarter windows: TC3 ($54). Black vinyl bodyside moldings: TC3 ($41). Moldings (4dr.): belt ($16); drip rail ($18); upper door frame ($31); wheel lip ($28); sill ($20). Door edge protectors ($12-$20). Bumper guards: 4dr. ($43). Bumper rub strips: TC3 ($34). Multi-color tape stripe: 4dr. ($70). Luggage rack ($86). Undercoating ($33). Interior: Console: storage ($22); shift lever ($32). Cloth/vinyl bucket seats: TC3 ($22-$52). Vinyl or cloth/vinyl bucket seats: 4dr. (N/A). Tonneau cover: TC3 ($44). Cargo area dress-up ($43). Color-keyed floor mats ($27). Color- keyed seatbelts ($31). Wheels and Tires: Wheel trim rings: 4dr. ($41). Deluxe wheel covers: 4dr. ($41). Cast aluminum wheels ($165-$246). Rallye wheels ($39-$80). Bright rallye hubs ($39). 165/75R13 GBR WSW ($17). 165/75R13 SBR WSW ($34-$51). 175/75R13 WSW ($51-$68). 185/70R13 OWL: TC3 ($136). Conventional spare tire ($13-$25).

VOLARE CONVENIENCE/APPEARANCE OPTIONS: Option Packages: Road Runner pkg.: cpe ($651). Sport pkg.: wag ($630). Handling/performance pkg.: cpe ($218). Duster Coupe pkg. ($30); w/quarter window louvers ($60). Duster decor pkg.: cpe ($90). Custom exterior pkg. ($75-$89). Custom interior pkg. ($151-$196). Premium exterior pkg. ($79-$144). Premium interior pkg. ($275-$499). Premier wagon woodgrain group ($232). Two-tone paint pkg. ($142). Two-tone decor pkg. ($78-$96). Basic group ($626-$712). Light pkg. ($46). Protection group ($30-$38). Deluxe insulation pkg. ($39-$50). Comfort/Convenience: Air cond. ($507). Rear defogger, blower- type ($52); electric ($90). Automatic speed control ($98). Power seat ($153). Power windows ($120-$169). Power door locks ($79-$106). Power liftgate release: wag ($23). Tinted glass ($61). Tinted windshield ($43). Luxury steering wheel ($31). Tuff steering wheel ($8-$39). Tilt steering wheel ($32-$71). Intermittent wipers ($36). Digital clock ($51). Inside hood release ($13). Locking glovebox ($5). Lighter ($7). Horns and Mirrors: Dual horns ($9). Remote left-hand mirror ($17). Dual remote mirrors ($32-$49). Dual remote sport mirrors: cpe ($44-$61). Day/night mirror ($11). Entertainment: AM radio ($79); w/8track player ($152-$231); w/CB ($262-$342). AM/FM radio ($73-$153). AM/FM stereo radio ($141-$220); w/8track tape player ($235-$314); w/CB ($403- $482). Rear speaker ($24). Exterior: T-Bar roof: cpe ($600). Full vinyl roof: sed ($95). Halo vinyl roof: cpe ($95-$111). Black vinyl bodyside moldings ($41). Belt moldings ($18). Door edge protectors ($12-$20). Upper door frame moldings: sed/wag ($31). Wheel lip moldings ($22). Hood strobe stripe: cpe ($42). Air deflector: wag ($28). Luggage rack: wag ($86). Bumper guards, front/rear ($43). Protective bumper rub strips ($34). Undercoating ($23-$33). Interior: Console: cpe/wag ($55-$95). Vinyl bench seat: sed ($30). Vinyl bucket seats: cpe/wag ($107). Center cushion w/armrest: cpe ($39). Rear armrest ($12). Cargo area carpet w/stowage bins: wag ($53). Color-keyed mats ($23). Pedal dress-up ($9). Trunk dress-up ($43). Color-keyed seatbelts ($18). Wheels and Tires: Deluxe wheel covers ($41). Premium wheel covers ($37-$79). Wire wheel covers ($94-$136). Cast aluminum wheels ($144-$280). Styled wheels ($94-$136). D78 x 14 WSW ($45). DR78 x 14 BSW ($56). DR78 x 14 WSW ($56-$101). ER78 x 14 BSW ($75). ER78 x 14 WSW ($45-$119). FR78 x 14 wide WSW ($72-$192). FR70 x 14 OWL ($129-$248). Conventional spare tire (NC).

HISTORY: Introduced: October 5, 1978. Model year production: Chrysler reported a total of 319,282 passenger cars shipped. Total North American passenger-car production for the U.S. market of 311,008 units included 137,635 four-cylinder, 139,797 six- cylinder, and 33,576 V-8s. Calendar year production (U.S.): 358,863 (not incl. 4,874 Voyagers). Calendar year sales by U.S. dealers: 317,258 (not incl. 8,265 Voyagers). Model year sales by U.S. dealers: 337,895 (not incl. 59,576 imports and 10,653 Voyagers).

Historical Footnotes: Weight-cutting had become a major theme. The heaviest Chrysler product weighed less than 3,900 pounds at the curb. All models had aluminum and plastic master cylinders. All sixes and V-8s had lightweight radiators. To boost gas mileage, the big 400 and 440 cu. in. V-8s were abandoned. Plymouth added another import: the Champ hatchback coupe. The subcompact imports (Arrow/Sapporo/Champ) helped Chrysler meet this year's CAFE standards, but couldn't be counted for 1980 requirements. Horizon sales rose by almost 58 percent for the 1979 model year, but total volume was the lowest ever.

1980 PLYMOUTH

Two years after leaving the lineup, the Gran Fury nameplate returned, but on a shorter wheelbase than before. This would be Volare's final year, as the new K-car was being readied for 1981 introduction.

1980 Volare station wagon (CM)

1980 Horizon four-door hatchback (CM)

HORIZON/TC3 — SERIES M — FOUR— Neither the subcompact four-door hatchback sedan nor TC3 two-door sport coupe changed in appearance. New options included automatic speed control, halogen headlamps, and intermittent windshield wipers. Also available: a Tri-Lite sunroof with flip-up or removable glass panel. Both four-passenger models again had the standard 104.7 cu. in. (1.7-liter) four-cylinder engine and four-speed manual transaxle. Four-doors had a standard AM radio, tinted glass, three-spoke steering wheel, rear defroster, electric clock, and trip odometer. They could also have a selection of Premium and Custom exterior and interior packages to dress up the basic design. Standard vinyl bucket seats came in cashmere or black. The option list included a Premium Woodgrain package that added woodgrain appliques along bodysides and the lower liftgate panel. A total of 1,701 Horizon coupes had a new Turismo package that cost around $1200. That package included cast aluminum wheels, rear spoiler, blackout moldings, low-back vinyl premium bucket

1980 TC3 Horizon two-door hatchback (CM)

seats, and bright solid-color paint. A TC3 Sport Appearance Package included a 'TC3' decal between door and rear wheel opening. Coupe options also included quick-ratio power steering, power brakes, rear spoiler, and premium interior. Body colors were: Graphic Blue, Graphic Red, Baron Red, Natural Suede Tan, Light Cashmere, Nightwatch Blue, Formal Black, Bright Yellow, Spinnaker White, and a selection of metallics: Mocha Brown, Burnished Silver, Crimson Red, Teal Tropic Green, or Frost Blue. Four-doors could also have four two-tone combinations; TC3 had three; the TC3 Sport Package, four two-tones.

VOLARE — SERIES H — SIX/V-8— For its final year in the Dodge lineup, Volare sported a new symmetrical crosshatch grille in five-row pattern, with large 'Plymouth' block letters inset into the upper header bar. Parking lamps again stood between grille and headlamps, but were narrower than earlier versions. Front side marker lenses were now vertical, at corner of fender, aligned with new single rectangular headlamps (formerly horizontal and set farther back). Halogen headlamps became optional. Two-doors had triangular sail-shaped quarter windows. Horizontal-style taillamps each were split into four sections: two narrow vertical lenses flanking wider red and white recessed lenses. Between the taillamps was a panel containing 'Plymouth' block lettering. 'Volare' script was on the decklid as well as front fenders. Volare ornamentation was new, and a landau vinyl top joined the option list. Base engine was again the 225 cu. in. Slant Six, with 318 cu. in. (5.2-liter) V-8 optional. Three-speed manual transmission was standard, as were cloth/vinyl bench seats. Volare body colors were: Natural Suede Tan, Baron Red, Graphic Red (coupe only), Nightwatch Blue, Light Cashmere, Formal Black, and Spinnaker White; plus metallic Burnished Silver, Crimson Red, Teal Tropic Green, Frost Blue, Teal Frost, and Mocha Brown. Three two-tones were offered. A new optional AM/FM stereo came with a cassette player and Dolby noise reduction. Quite a selection of option packages was available. The modestly-priced Duster Coupe package included colorful new bodyside and decklid tape stripes, 'Plymouth' front fender nameplates, and plaid cloth/vinyl high-back bucket seats. The Premier package's vinyl top covered up the standard triangular windows, showing wide, squarish opera-type windows instead. Premier coupes and sedans also had wheel opening and sill moldings, hood accent stripes, bodyside stripes, a stand-up hood medallion, rear lower deck applique, driver's remote mirror, day/night mirror, dual horns, and woodtone instrument panel. Wagons with a Premier package had woodtone trim on bodysides and tailgate, along with woodtone instrument panel cluster and glovebox door. A new Custom package included (among other extras) dual horns, an inside hood release, wheel lip and sill moldings, and belt

moldings. Volare's Road Runner package included a black grille, headlamp doors and parking lamp surround; black anodized moldings; dual remote sport mirrors; bright sill moldings with black surround; body accent stripes; rear spoiler; and unique gas cap. 'Road Runner' decals went on front fenders and spoiler; 'Plymouth' on the spoiler. Eight-spoke wheels with stainless steel ornamentation held P195/75R14 blackwall tires. Underneath was a heavy-duty suspension; inside, vinyl bucket seats and a "Tuff" steering wheel. The Sport Wagon package included wheel-opening flares, front air dam, tape stripe, and black-highlight grille; plus dual body-colored sport mirrors, "Tuff" three-spoke steering wheel, and eight-spoke road wheels. A total of 5,586 Duster coupe packages (RPO code A42) were installed, while 496 Volares had the Road Runner package and 12,644 the Premier package. In addition to the base two- and four-door models, and a station wagon, Volare offered a new Special series. For a slightly higher price, the buyer got an automatic transmission, power steering, cloth/vinyl bench seat, whitewalls, deluxe wheel covers, bodyside tape stripes, and wheel opening moldings. Specials came only with the Slant Six engine.

1980 Gran Fury four-door sedan (CM)

GRAN FURY — SERIES J — SIX/V-8— Out of the lineup for two years, Gran Fury was back again in downsized form, fully restyled on a 118.5 in. wheelbase. The four-door pillared hardtop had a long hood and a bold, blacked-out grille in 8 x 4 checkerboard pattern with chrome header. Recessed, side-by-side quad rectangular headlamps stood over wide parking lamps. Wide horizontal taillamps wrapped around the quarter panels. Unlike the old Gran Fury, this R bodied version carried a base Slant Six engine with TorqueFlite automatic transmission. The 318 cu. in. two-barrel V-8 was optional. So was a 360 cu. in. V-8, required with the heavy-duty package. California models had a four-barrel 318 V-8. Turn signals and other controls went on the steering column. The suspension used front torsion bars with an anti-sway bar. Gran Fury was similar to Chrysler's Newport and Dodge St. Regis, and sold mainly to fleet buyers. Base and Salon versions were offered. Among the options was a heavy-duty trailer towing assist package. Only 31 Gran Fury models are reported to have had the optional handling package. Standard equipment included power steering and brakes, P195/75R15 glass-belted radial whitewall tires, tinted glass, dual flag mirrors, dual horns, cigarette lighter, day/night inside mirror, and inside hood release. Belt, drip and wheel opening moldings were included. Gran Fury Salon added protective bumper rub strips, sill moldings, and deluxe wheel covers.

I.D. DATA: Plymouth's 13-symbol Vehicle Identification Number (VIN) again was on the upper left corner of the instrument panel, visible through the windshield. Symbol one indicates car line: 'M' Horizon; 'H' Volare; 'J' Gran Fury. Symbol two is series (price class): 'E' economy; 'L' low; 'H' high. Symbols 3-4 show body type: '29' 2-dr. sport coupe; '41' 4-dr. sedan; '42' 4-dr. pillared hardtop; '44' 4-dr. hatchback; '45' two-seat station wagon. Symbol five is the engine code: 'A' L4105 2Bbl.; 'C' L6225 1Bbl.; 'G' V8318 2Bbl.; 'K' V8360 2Bbl. Symbol six is the model year code: 'A' 1980. Symbol seven indicates assembly plant: 'A' Lynch Road; 'B' Hamtramck, MI; 'D' Belvidere, IL; 'F' Newark, DE. The final six digits make up the sequential serial number, starting with 100001. Engine number coding is similar to 1976-79. As before, a Vehicle Safety Certification Label that displays (among other data) the date of manufacture is attached to the rear facing of the driver's door. A Body Code Plate is on the left front fender side shield, wheel housing, or left side of upper radiator support.

HORIZON (FOUR)

Model Number	Body/Style Number	Body Type & Seating	Factory Price	Shipping Weight	Production Total
ML	44	4-dr. Hatch-4P	4925	2135	85,751

HORIZON TC3 (FOUR)

Model Number	Body/Style Number	Body Type & Seating	Factory Price	Shipping Weight	Production Total
ML	24	2-dr. Hatch 22-4P	5271	2095	59,527

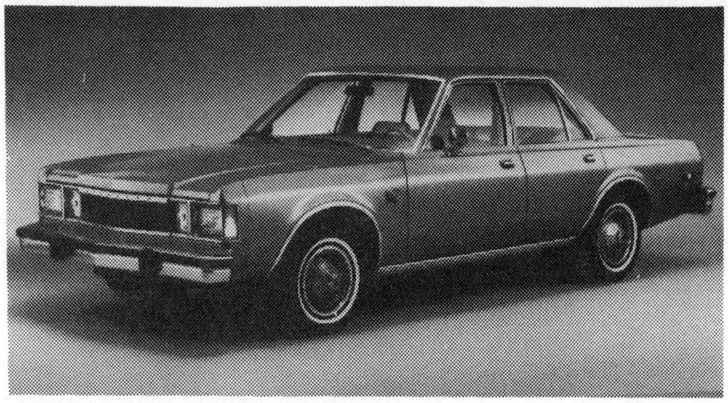

1980 Volare four-door sedan (CM)

VOLARE (SIX/V-8)

HL	29	2-dr. Spt Cpe-5P	4730/4941	3110/3260	14,453
HL	41	4-dr. Sedan-6P	4847/5058	3165/3320	25,768
HL	45	4-dr. Sta Wag-6P	5089/5300	3340/3480	16,895

VOLARE SPECIAL (SIX)

HE	29	2-dr. Cpe-5P	4977/ --	3155/ --	12,334
HE	41	4-dr. Sedan-6P	4994/ --	3210/ --	20,613

GRAN FURY (SIX/V-8)

JL	42	4-dr. Pill. HT-6P	6280/6513	3520/3605	12,576

GRAN FURY SALON (SIX/V-8)

JH	42	4-dr. Pill. HT-6P	6711/6944	3545/3630	2,024

FACTORY PRICE AND WEIGHT NOTE: Prices and weights to left of slash are for six-cylinder, to right for V-8 engine.

ENGINE DATA: BASE FOUR (Horizon/TC3): Inline, overhead-cam four-cylinder. Cast iron block; aluminum head. Displacement: 104.7 cu. in. (1.7 liters). Bore & stroke: 3.13 x 3.40 in. Compression ratio: 8.2:1. Brake horsepower: 65 at 5200 R.P.M. Torque: 85 lbs.-ft. at 2400 R.P.M. Five main bearings. Solid valve lifters. Carburetor: 2Bbl. Holley 5220. VIN Code: A. BASE SIX (Volare, Gran Fury): Inline, overhead-valve six-cylinder. Cast iron block and head. Displacement: 225 cu. in. (3.7 liters). Bore & stroke: 3.40 x 4.12 in. Compression ratio: 8.4:1. Brake horsepower: 90 at 3600 R.P.M. Torque: 160 lbs.-ft. at 1600 R.P.M. Four main bearings. Solid valve lifters. Carburetor: 1Bbl. Holley 1945. VIN Code: C. OPTIONAL V-8 (Volare, Gran Fury): 90-degree, overhead valve V-8. Cast iron block and head. Displacement: 318 cu. in. (5.2 liters). Bore & stroke: 3.91 x 3.31 in. Compression ratio: 8.5:1. Brake horsepower: 120 at 3600 R.P.M. Torque: 245 lbs.-ft. at 1600 R.P.M. Five main bearings. Hydraulic valve lifters. Carburetor: 2Bbl. Carter BBD. VIN Code: G. Note: High-altitude models could have a 4Bbl. V8 318 rated 155 H.P. at 4000 R.P.M. OPTIONAL V-8 (Gran Fury): 90-degree, overhead valve V-8. Cast iron block and head. Displacement: 360 cu. in. (5.9 liters). Bore & stroke: 4.00 x 3.58 in. Compression ratio: 8.4:1. Brake horsepower: 130 at 3200 R.P.M. Torque: 255 lbs.-ft. at 2000 R.P.M. Five main bearings. Hydraulic valve lifters. Carburetor: 2Bbl. Carter BBD. VIN Code: K.

CHASSIS DATA: Wheelbase: (Horizon) 99.2 in.; (TC3) 96.7 in.; (Volare cpe) 108.7 in.; (Volare sed/wag) 112.7 in.; (Gran Fury) 118.5 in. Overall Length: (Horizon) 164.8 in. incl. optional bumper guards; (TC3) 172.8 in.; (Volare cpe) 200.3 in.; (Volare sed/wag) 204.3 in.; (Gran Fury) 220.2 in. Height: (Horizon) 53.4 in.; (TC3) 51.1 in.; (Volare cpe) 53.6 in.; (Volare sed) 55.3 in.; (Volare wag) 55.5 in.; (Gran Fury) 54.5 in. Width: (Horizon) 65.8 in.; (TC3) 66.7 in.; (Volare) 72.4 in.; (Gran Fury) 77.6 in. Front Tread: (Horizon/TC3) 56.1 in.; (Volare) 60.0 in.; (Gran Fury) 61.9 in. Rear Tread: (Horizon/TC3) 55.6 in.; (Volare) 59.5 in.; (Gran Fury) 62.0 in. Standard Tires: (Horizon) P155/80R13 GBR WSW; (TC3) P175/75R13 GBR BSW; (Volare) P195/75R14 GBR BSW; (Gran Fury) P195/75R15 GBR WSW.

TECHNICAL: Transmission: Three-speed manual trans. (floor lever) standard on Volare six. Gear ratios: (1st) 3.08:1; (2nd) 1.70:1; (3rd) 1.00:1; (Rev) 2.90:1. Four-speed overdrive available on Volare six: (1st) 3.09:1; (2nd) 1.67:1; (3rd) 1.00:1; (4th) 0.71:1; (Rev) 3.00:1. Four-speed manual (floor shift) standard on Horizon/TC3: (1st) 3.45:1; (2nd) 1.94:1; (3rd) 1.29:1; (4th) 0.97:1; (Rev) 3.17:1. TorqueFlite three- speed automatic standard on Gran Fury, optional on others. Six-cylinder gear ratios: (1st) 2.74:1; (2nd) 1.54:1; (3rd) 1.00:1; (Rev) 2.22:1. V-8 ratios: (1st) 2.45:1; (2nd) 1.45:1; (3rd) 1.00:1; (Rev) 2.22:1. Horizon ratios: (1st) 2.47:1; (2nd) 1.47:1; (3rd) 1.00:1; (Rev) 2.10:1. Standard final drive ratio: (Horizon/TC3) 3.37:1 w/4spd, 3.48:1 w/auto.; (Volare six) 3.23:1 w/3spd, 3.23:1 or 3.21:1 w/4spd, 2.76:1 or 2.71:1 w/auto.; (Volare Special) 2.76:1; (Volare V-8) 2.47:1 or 2.24:1 w/auto.; (Volare wag) 3.21:1 or 2.45:1; (Gran Fury six) 2.94:1; (G. Fury V-8) 2.45:1. Steering: (Horizon) rack and pinion; (others) recirculating ball. Suspension: (Horizon/TC3) Iso-Strut independent coil front w/anti-sway bar, independent trailing arm coil rear w/integral anti-sway; (Volare) isolated transverse front torsion bars w/anti-sway bar, semi-elliptic rear leaf springs; (Gran Fury) longitudinal front torsion bars, semi- elliptic rear leaf springs. Brakes: Front disc, rear drum. Ignition: Electronic. Body construction: Unibody. Fuel tank: (Horizon/TC3) 13 gal.; (Volare) 18 gal.; (Gran Fury) 21 gal.

DRIVETRAIN OPTIONS: Engines: 318 cu. in., 2Bbl. V-8: Volare ($211); Gran Fury ($233). 318 cu. in., 4Bbl. V-8: Calif. Volare ($266); G. Fury ($295). 360 cu. in., 2Bbl. V-8: G. Fury ($457). Transmission/Differential: TorqueFlite: Horizon ($322-$340); Volare ($340). Four-speed manual trans. w/floor lever: Volare ($153). Sure grip differential: Volare ($63); G. Fury ($77). Power Accessories: Power steering: Horizon ($161); Volare ($166). Power brakes: Horizon/Volare ($77). Suspension: H.D. susp.: Horizon 4dr., Volare ($26); G. Fury ($30). Sport susp.: TC3 ($43). H.D. shock absorbers: G. Fury ($8). Other: Trailer assist pkg.: G. Fury ($258). Maintenance-free battery: Horizon ($21). Long-life battery: Volare ($33); G. Fury ($36). Max. cooling: Volare ($34-$58); G. Fury ($77- $104). California emission system ($254).

HORIZON/TC3 CONVENIENCE/APPEARANCE OPTIONS: Option Packages: Turismo pkg.: TC3 ($1199-$1227). Sport pkg.: TC3 ($340-$431). Sport/Classic two-tone paint pkg. ($131- $137). Custom exterior pkg.: 4dr. ($101). Premium exterior pkg. ($126-$207). Custom interior pkg.: 4dr. ($89-$112). Premium interior pkg. ($239-$355). Premium woodgrain pkg.: 4dr. ($300-$344). Popular equipment group ($267-$273). Comfort/Convenience: Air cond. ($541). Auto. speed control ($101). Luxury steering wheel: 4dr. ($18). Sport steering wheel ($18-$40). Rallye instrument cluster w/tach: TC3 ($65). Intermittent wiper ($38). Rear wiper/washer: 4dr. ($63). Lighter ($8). Locking gas cap ($7). Locking glovebox: 4dr. ($5). Lighting, Horns and Mirrors: Halogen headlamps ($37). Dual horns ($9). Remote left mirror: 4dr. ($19). Dual remote mirrors: 4dr. ($38-$57). Dual remote sport mirrors: TC3 ($69). Day/night mirror ($11). Entertainment: AM/FM radio: 4dr. ($58). AM/FM stereo radio: 4dr. ($93); TC3 ($35). Rear speaker: TC3 ($19). Exterior: Removable glass sunroof ($182). Rear spoiler: TC3 ($55). Black vinyl bodyside moldings: TC3 ($44). Moldings (4dr.): belt ($17); drip rail ($19); sill ($21); upper door frame ($32); wheel lip ($29). Door edge protectors ($13-$21). Bumper guards: 4dr. ($45). Bumper rub strips: TC3 ($35). Hood/bodyside/deck tape stripe: 4dr. ($45). Bodyside/deck stripe: TC3 ($31). Luggage rack ($90). Undercoating ($34). Lower body coating ($31). Interior: Console: storage ($22); shift lever ($33). Cloth/vinyl bucket seats: TC3 ($22-$53). Vinyl or cloth/vinyl bucket seats: 4dr. (NC). Bucket seats w/passenger recliner: TC3 (NC). Tonneau cover: TC3 ($46). Cargo area carpet; ($31); dress-up ($45). Color-keyed floor mats: front ($24); front/rear ($42). Color-keyed seatbelts ($23). Wheels and Tires: Wheel trim rings: 4dr. ($44). Deluxe wheel covers: 4dr. ($44). Cast aluminum wheels ($171-$254). Rallye wheels ($39-$83). P165/75R13 WSW: 4dr. ($17). P165/75R13 WSW: TC3 ($43). P175/75R13 SBR WSW ($78-$86). P185/70R13 Aramid BSW: TC3 ($45-$131). P185/70R13 Aramid OWL: TC3 ($106-$192). Conventional spare tire ($13-$26).

VOLARE CONVENIENCE/APPEARANCE OPTIONS: Option Packages: Road Runner pkg.: cpe ($586). Wagon Sport pkg. ($721). Sport appearance pkg. ($192-$254). Handling/performance pkg.: cpe/wag ($385). Duster Coupe pkg. ($155). Custom pkg. ($258-$386). Premier pkg. ($513-$814). Two-tone paint pkg. ($148). Basic group ($246-$403). Light pkg. ($46). Protection group ($56-$64). Deluxe insulation pkg. ($40-$51). Comfort/Convenience: Air cond. ($543). Rear defogger, blower- type ($53); electric ($97). Automatic speed control ($106). Power seat ($163). Power windows ($130-$183). Power door locks ($83-$117). Power liftgate release: wag ($24). Tinted glass ($66). Tinted windshield ($44). Luxury steering wheel: wag ($32). Tuff steering wheel ($24-$56). Tilt steering wheel ($20-$76). Intermittent wipers ($39). Tailgate wiper/washer: wag ($64). Digital clock ($55). Inside hood release ($10). Locking glovebox ($6). Lighter ($8). Locking gas cap ($7). Lighting, Horns and Mirrors: Halogen headlamps ($37). Dual horns ($10). Remote left-hand mirror ($18). Dual remote mirrors ($36-$54). Dual remote sport mirrors ($50-$68). Day/night mirror ($11). Entertainment: AM radio ($90); w/8track player ($143-$233). AM/FM radio ($58-$148). AM/FM stereo radio ($93-$183); w/8track tape player ($166-$256); w/cassette ($220-$310); w/CB ($351-$441). Rear speaker ($19). Radio delete ($51 credit). Exterior: T-Bar roof: cpe ($614). Full vinyl roof: sed ($97). Landau vinyl roof: cpe ($161-$178). Black vinyl bodyside moldings ($44). Belt moldings ($17). Door edge protectors ($13-$21). Upper door frame moldings: sed/wag ($34). Wheel lip moldings ($24). Air deflector: wag ($28). Luggage rack: wag ($91). Protective bumper rub strips ($36). Undercoating ($23-$34). Interior: Console: cpe/wag ($34-$99). Vinyl bench seat: sed ($30). Vinyl bucket seats: cpe/wag ($110). Center cushion w/armrest: cpe/wag ($44). Rear armrest ($12). Cargo area carpet: wag ($69); w/stowage bins ($93). Cargo security cover: wag ($46). Color-keyed mats: front ($24); rear ($19). Pedal dress-up ($9). Trunk dress-up ($45). Color-keyed seatbelts ($23). Wheels and Tires: Deluxe wheel covers ($44). Premium wheel covers ($37-$81). Wire wheel covers ($106- $150). Cast aluminum wheels ($133-$287). Styled spoke wheels ($110-$154). P195/75R14 GBR WSW ($49). P205/75R14 SBR WSW ($84-$133). FR70 x 14 Aramid OWL ($150-$199). Conventional spare tire ($25).

GRAN FURY CONVENIENCE/APPEARANCE OPTIONS: Option Packages: Basic group ($1203). Two-tone paint pkg. ($168). Open Road handling pkg. ($269). Light pkg. ($87). Comfort/Convenience: Air conditioning ($670); auto-temp ($720) but ($50) w/option pkg. Rear defroster, electric ($113). Auto. speed control ($122). Power seat ($183). Power windows ($228). Power door locks ($139). Power decklid release ($30-$46). Illuminated entry system ($62). Luxury steering wheel ($20). Leather-covered steering wheel ($62). Tilt steering wheel ($85). Digital clock ($61). Intermittent wipers ($44). Locking gas cap ($9). Lighting, Horns and Mirrors: Halogen headlamps ($42). Cornering lights ($55). Triad horns ($22). Remote driver's mirror ($21). Dual remote-control mirrors ($31-$52). Lighted vanity mirror ($53). Entertainment: AM radio ($106). AM/FM radio ($58-$164). AM/FM stereo ($103-$209); w/ 8track tape player ($181-$287); w/cassette ($241-$347); w/CB ($389-$495). Search-tune AM/FM stereo ($224-$330). Rear speaker ($22). Power antenna ($54). Exterior: Power glass sunroof ($1053). Full vinyl roof ($162). Vinyl bodyside moldings ($55). Sill moldings: base ($31). Bumper guards ($62). Bumper rub strips: base ($41). Bodyside tape stripe ($49). Undercoating ($31). Interior: Vinyl bench seat ($34). Color-keyed floor mats: front ($26); rear ($21). Color-keyed seatbelts ($27). Pedal dress-up ($10). Trunk dress-up ($70). Litter container ($9). Wheels and Tires: Deluxe wheel covers: base ($49). Premier wheel covers ($44-$93). Premium wheel covers ($91-$140). Wire wheel covers ($266-$315). Forged aluminum wheels ($336-$385). P205/75R15 SBR WSW ($92). P205/75R15 Aramid-belted white/gold ($179). P225/70R15 SBR WSW ($186). Conventional spare ($27).

HISTORY: Introduced: October 1, 1979. Model year production: Chrysler reported a total of 249,941 passenger cars shipped. Total North American production for the U.S. market of 249,629 units included 145,284 four-cylinder, 82,165 six-cylinder, and 22,180 V-8s. Calendar year production: 287,065. Calendar year sales by U.S. dealers: 251,312. Model year sales by U.S. dealers: 239,627 (not incl. 57,598 imported Arrow/Champs and 10,311 Sapporos).

Historical Footnotes: Horizon TC3 was the only Chrysler-Plymouth domestic model to register a sales gain for the 1980 model year. Volare, which had sold well when introduced a few years earlier, slipped considerably (down over 50 percent this year). That loss resulted from its unimpressive fuel mileage, the popularity of GM's new X-cars, and the expectation of a "better" front-drive Dodge/Plymouth model for 1981. Even an aggressive advertising campaign and offers of rebates didn't help Volare much.

1981 PLYMOUTH

Both Plymouth and Dodge gained a new front-drive compact: the Reliant (and Aries) Kcar, powered by a base 2.2-liter Trans4 engine. That aluminum-head, overhead-cam engine was the first four produced by Chrysler since the 1930s. It produced 84 horsepower and had 8.5:1 compression. Optional on Reliant was a 2.6-liter four, built by Mitsubishi in Japan. Elsewhere in the lineup, the subcompact coupe was now called just TC3, rather than Horizon TC3. Both the Horizon sedan and TC3 coupe added Miser models. All Plymouths had thick primer, precoated steel and plastic to improve corrosion resistance. A new 17-symbol Vehicle Identification Number was initiated this year. The electronic feedback carburetor, used in California models for 1980, was now in all fours and V-8s.

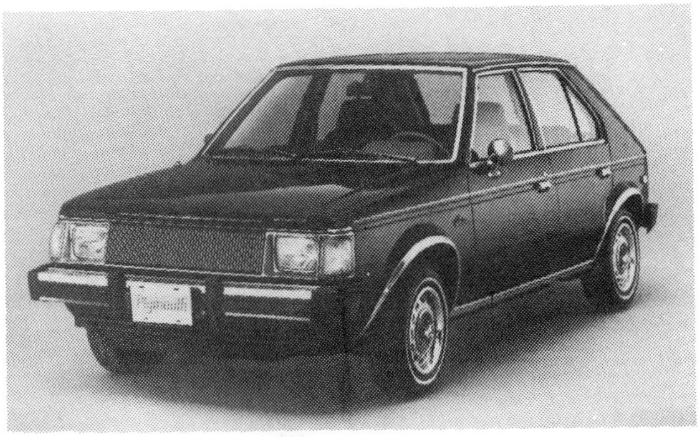

1981 Horizon four-door hatchback (CM)

HORIZON — SERIES M — FOUR — The subcompact four-door's previous crosshatch-pattern grille was replaced by a simple pattern of thin vertical bars, running full width between the headlamps, unadorned by any emblem. As before, small 'Plymouth' block lettering was above the left headlamp. Single headlamps and wraparound parking/marker lamps were similar to 1980, though Plymouth promoted the parking lamps as new this year. As before, front fenders held 'Horizon' script. New two-color taillamps (red/clear) put turn signal, stop and taillamp functions in a single bulb. New interiors came in saddle grain vinyl, plus optional LaCorde and Monteverdi II cloth. Seven body colors were new. Tinted glass and a rear-window defroster, formerly standard, now became optional. Also added to the option list: a leather-wrapped steering wheel, and AM/FM stereo with cassette or 8track player. Various option packages were available too. Horizon wasn't any bigger than before, but passenger capacity as noted in the factory catalog grew from four to five. This year marked the first appearance of Miser, lighter in weight, with a specially calibrated 104.7 cu. in. (1.7- liter) engine and 2.6:1 overall top gear ratio. Reliant's new 135 cu. in. (2.2-liter) Trans4 engine became optional on Horizon, but the 1.7 was standard. Body colors were: Ginger, Nightwatch Blue, Sunlight White, Graphic Yellow, Pearl White, Graphic Red, Formal Black, and Baron Red; plus metallic Glencoe Green, Daystar Blue, and Burnished Silver. Vivid Blue Starmist and Spice Tan Starmist were offered at extra cost. Three two-tones were available (except on Miser). With a price tag of $591 to $839, Horizon's Euro-Sedan package included blackout trim, moldings and bumpers; P175/75R13 SBR blackwall tires on cast aluminum wheels; and new bodyside stripes. Inside was a Rallye instrument cluster with tachometer, clock and trip odometer; four-spoke sport steering wheel; and LaCorde cloth/vinyl bucket seats. Mechanically, however, the Euro-Sedan offered nothing special beyond a stiffer suspension. A total of 2,483 cars had either the Euro or Turismo (coupe) package, which carried RPO code A69.

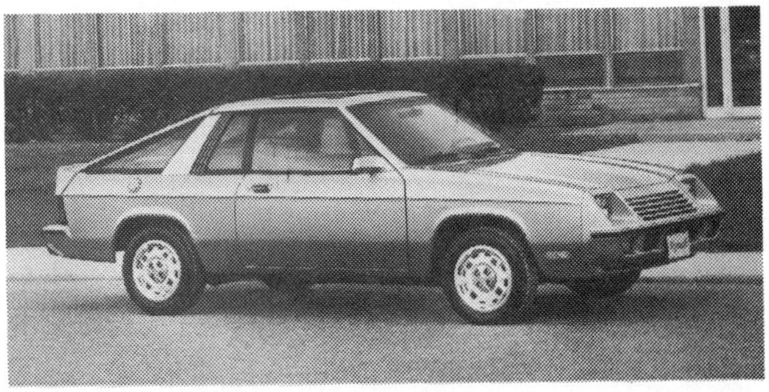

1981 Horizon TC3 two-door coupe (CM)

TC3 — SERIES M — FOUR — For the first time, the subcompact two-door coupe veered away from its Horizon connection, billed simply as 'TC3.' Appearance was virtually unchanged from 1980, though official passenger capacity was enlarged to five (while size remained the same). TC3's grille again consisted of five wide slots in a sloped body-color panel, each row divided into six wide "holes." 'Plymouth' block lettering was on front fenders, just above the crease line. New TC3 Misers had the small 1.7-liter four under the hood, but standard models switched to the new Trans-4 2.2- liter. Misers had standard vinyl high-back front bucket seats and tinted glass all around. Standard tires were P175/75R13 glass-belted radials, but TC3 could have optional P195/60R14 steel-belted tires, either blackwall or with raised white letters. Priced at $135 to $518, the Turismo package came with P195/60R14 SBR tires on steel Rallye wheels, Sport bucket front seats, Rallye instruments (tachometer, trip odometer and clock), and a four-spoke steering wheel. Also included: bodyside and rear spoiler identification, front fascia and wheel opening stripes, black moldings and bumper strips, and dual remote sport mirrors. Turismo had no 'TC3' nameplates, sill moldings, or wheel opening moldings. Solid TC3 body colors were the same as Horizon. Four two-tones were available, plus four with the Sport Appearance package. That option also included black moldings, a rear spoiler, P195/60R14 tires on Rallye wheels, 'TC3' quarter panel and spoiler identification, and Rallye instruments among its list of extras.

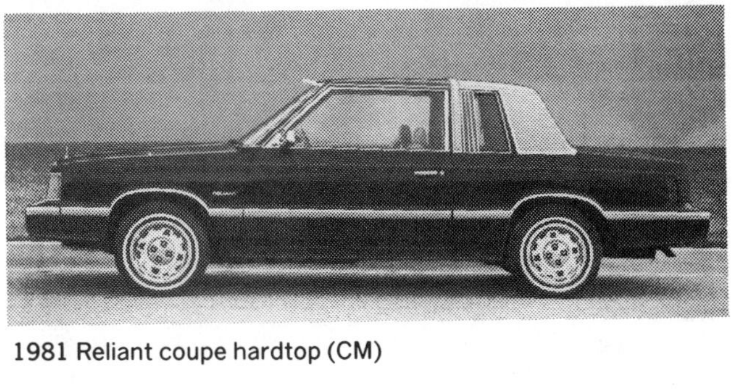

1981 Reliant coupe hardtop (CM)

RELIANT K — SERIES P — FOUR — Plymouth's new K-body front-drive six-passenger compact, referred to as the Kcar, was a near twin to the new Dodge Aries. Promoting fuel economy, Plymouth described Reliant as "The American way to beat the pump." The EPA gave Reliant a city rating of 25 MPG with manual shift. Mounted on a 99.6 in. wheelbase, Reliant was almost half a ton lighter and two feet shorter than Volare, with a squarish basic shape. Reliant's bright grille displayed a tiny crosshatch pattern, divided into eight larger sections by three horizontal bars and one vertical bar. A thin upper header molding had 'Plymouth' lettering on the driver's side. Clear vertical parking lamp lenses stood between bright-bezeled, single recessed rectangular headlamps and the grille. Amber side marker lenses extended rearward from the edge of the headlamp housings. 'Reliant' nameplates went on front fenders. Thin vertical marker lenses were at the rear edges of quarter panels. Reliant's soft color-keyed bumper wasn't a separate unit, but blended into the bodyside, with moldings that reached all around the car and served as protective bumper strips. Reliant's new Trans-4 135 cu. in. (2.2-liter) engine weighed 298 pounds. It had same-side intake/exhaust valve porting and self-adjusting hydraulic lifters. An Electronic Fuel Control System used seven sensors and a tiny computer to adjust spark timing and air/fuel mixture. Optional was a Silent Shaft 156 cu. in. (2.6-liter) engine from Mitsubishi, which had a three-valve MCA-JET cylinder head with hemispherical combustion chambers. That engine was used in the imported Sapporo coupe. Both engines had five main bearings and an aluminum head, plus two-barrel carburetor and single overhead camshaft. The 2.2-liter rated 84 horsepower; the 2.6 produced 92. Both were transverse mounted. The fully synchronized manual gearbox included an overdrive fourth gear; three-speed TorqueFlite was available (standard with the 2.6-liter engine). An open back end in the four-speed's one-piece die-cast aluminum case would allow easy conversion to five-speed gearing in the future. Chrysler had designed Reliant's Iso-Strut front suspension, with 1 in. diameter front anti-sway bar. A three-point system of trailing links positioned the flex-arm beam rear suspension, which included a transverse track bar. Rack-and-pinion steering was used. A steering column-mounted lever held controls for turn signals, dimmer, wiper/washer (and optional speed control). Two-door and four-door sedan and four-door station wagon bodies were offered; in base, Custom or Special Edition trim. There was no base wagon. Inside the base two-door was a cloth/vinyl split-back bench seat in cashmere color only. Reliant Custom had a standard cloth/vinyl bench seat in light blue, light green, red or cashmere; Custom wagons had an all- vinyl bench seat. SE held cloth bench seating in the same colors. Options included contoured vinyl bucket seats. Standard Custom equipment included blackwall fiberglass- belted radial tires, color-keyed protective bumper rub strips and wide vinyl bodyside moldings, AM radio, lighter, glovebox lock, deluxe steering wheel, and day/night mirror. Also standard: an electric engine cooling fan, front disc brakes, high-pressure compact spare tire, woodtone instrument panel accents, dome light, rear door vent windows, and trunk mat. Wagons had power brakes. The base two-door had bright windshield moldings, bright headlamp bezels and grille surround, and came only in tan, white or black. It lacked the otherwise standard AM radio and other extras. Reliant Custom two-doors added quarter-window louvers. SE added bright decklid and window moldings, deluxe wheel covers, a Special Edition plaque on roof pillars, and body accent stripes. SE models also included dual horns, upper door frame moldings, belt moldings, and remote-control driver's mirror. SE wagons had woodtone bodyside and liftgate appliques, while SE sedans displayed bodyside accent stripes. Reliant body colors were: Nightwatch Blue, Sunlight Yellow, Baron Red, Graphic Red, Natural Suede Tan, Formal Black, and Pearl White; plus metallic Burnished Silver, Daystar Blue, Light Seaspray Green, and Glencoe Green. Spice Tan Starmist cost extra. Vinyl roofs came in seven colors. Reliants were built for easy servicing, with such features as self-adjusting clutch linkage and cables, self- adjusting hydraulic tappets (2.2-liter), and easy-access drive belts and instrument panel. In addition to TorqueFlite, options included power brakes and steering, power decklid release, power seats, power door locks, tilt steering, automatic speed control, air conditioning, and color-keyed bodyside moldings. Also available: halogen headlamps, roof rack, flip-up sunroof, cargo tonneau cover, digital clock, bucket seats, and electric rear defroster. A total of 15,803 Reliants (9,097 sedans and 6,706 wagons) had a Spring Prom package installed.

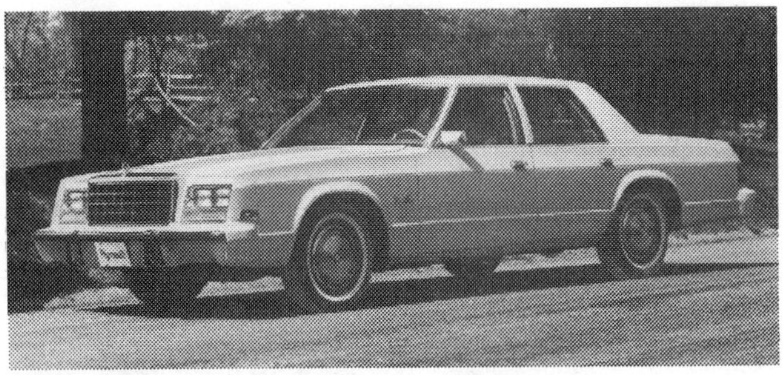

1981 Gran Fury sedan

GRAN FURY — SERIES J — SIX/V-8— Only one Gran Fury model remained this year, as the Salon disappeared. Since fleet buyers continued to buy, the last remaining rear-drive Plymouth hung on longer. Not much changed in the four-door pillared hardtop body, apart from improved corrosion protection and a better optional (rear) radio speaker. Gran Fury's blacked-out grille consisted of rectangles within rectangles, with a huge chrome upper header. Horizontal taillamps wrapped around the rear quarter panels to serve also as side markers. Base engine once again was the 225 cu. in. Slant Six, with 318 cu. in. V-8 optional. Only 468 Gran Fury models had a six-cylinder engine installed.

I.D. DATA: Like other domestic makes, Plymouth had a new 17-symbol Vehicle Identification Number (VIN) on the upper left corner of the instrument panel, again visible through the windshield. The first digit indicates Country: '1' U.S.A. The second symbol is Make: 'P' Plymouth. Third is Vehicle Type: '3' passenger car. The next symbol ('B') indicates manual seatbelts. Symbol five is Car Line: 'L' Horizon; 'K' Reliant; 'R' Gran Fury. Symbol six is Series (price class): '1' Economy; '2' Low; '4' High'; '5' Premium. Symbol seven is Body Style: '1' 2-dr. sedan; '4' 2-dr. 22 hatchback; '6' 4-dr. sedan; '7' 4-dr. pillared hardtop; '8' 4-dr. hatchback; '9' 4-dr. wagon. Eighth is the Engine Code: 'A' L4105 2Bbl.; 'B' L4135 2Bbl.; 'D' L4156 2Bbl.; 'E' L6-225 1Bbl.; 'K' V8318 2Bbl.; 'M' V8318 4Bbl. Next comes a check digit: 0 through 9 (or X). Symbol ten indicates Model Year: 'B' 1981. Symbol eleven is Assembly Plant: 'A' Lynch Road; 'C' Jefferson; 'D' Belvidere, IL; 'F' Newark, DE. The last six digits make up the sequential serial number, starting with 100001. Four-cylinder engine identification numbers are on the rear face of the block, directly under cylinder head (left side in vehicle) except for 2.6-liter, which is on left side of block between core plug and rear face of block (radiator side). Engine serial numbers (for parts replacement) are located on the block as follows: 1.7-liter, above fuel pump; 2.2-liter, on rear face just below head (below identification number); 2.6-liter, on right front of block adjacent to exhaust manifold stud. Six-cylinder engine identification numbers are stamped on a pad at the right of the block, below No. 6 spark plug. On V-8s, that pad is on the right of the block to the rear of the engine mount. An engine serial number is on the right of the block below No. 1 spark plug on six-cylinder engines, and on the left front corner of the block below the cylinder head on V-8s. A Body Code Plate is on the left upper radiator support, left front fender side shield, or wheelhousing.

HORIZON (FOUR)

Model Number	Body/Style Number	Body Type & Seating	Factory Price	Shipping Weight	Production Total
ML	44	4-dr. Hatch-5P	5690	2130	58,547

HORIZON MISER (FOUR)

ME	44	4-dr. Hatch-5P	5299	2060	Note 1

TC3 (FOUR)

ML	24	2-dr. Hatch-5P	6149	2205	36,312

TC3 MISER (FOUR)

ME	24	2-dr. Hatch-5P	5299	2137	Note 1

Note 1: Total Miser production, 44,922.

RELIANT (FOUR)

PL	21	2-dr. Sedan-6P	5880	2305	Note 2
PL	41	4-dr. Sedan-6P	5980	2300	Note 2

Note 2: Total base Reliant production, 58,093.

RELIANT CUSTOM (FOUR)

PH	21	2-dr. Sedan-6P	6315	2315	Note 3
PH	41	4-dr. Sedan-6P	6448	2310	Note 3
PH	45	4-dr. Sta Wag-6P	6721	2375	40,830

Note 3: Total Custom production, 13,587 coupes/sedans.

RELIANT SPECIAL EDITION (FOUR)

PP	21	2-dr. Sedan-6P	6789	2340	Note 4
PP	41	4-dr. Sedan-6P	6933	2340	Note 4
PP	45	4-dr. Sta Wag-6P	7254	2390	10,670

Note 4: Total Reliant SE production, 28,457 coupes/sedans.

GRAN FURY (SIX/V-8)

JL	42	4-dr. Pill. HT-6P	7387/7451	3485/3610	7,719

FACTORY PRICE AND WEIGHT NOTE: Gran Fury price and weight to left of slash is for six-cylinder, to right for V-8 engine. **MODEL NUMBER NOTE:** Some sources identify models using the new VIN data to indicate Car Line, Price Class and Body Style. Example: base Reliant four-door (PL41) has the equivalent number K26, which translates to Reliant line, Low price class, and four-door sedan body. See I.D. Data section for breakdown.

ENGINE DATA: BASE FOUR (Horizon, TC3): Inline, overhead-cam four-cylinder. Cast iron block; aluminum head. Displacement: 104.7 cu. in. (1.7 liters). Bore & stroke: 3.13 x 3.40 in. Compression ratio: 8.2:1. Brake horsepower: 63 at 5200 R.P.M. Torque: 83 lbs.-ft. at 2400 R.P.M. Five main bearings. Solid valve lifters. Carburetor: 2Bbl. Holley 6520. VIN Code: A. BASE FOUR (Reliant, late TC3); OPTIONAL (Horizon, TC3 Miser): Inline, overhead-cam four-cylinder. Cast iron block; aluminum head. Displacement: 135 cu. in. (2.2 liters). Bore & stroke: 3.44 x 3.62 in. Compression ratio: 8.5:1. Brake horsepower: 84 at 4800 R.P.M. Torque: 111 lbs.-ft. at 2800 R.P.M. Five main bearings. Hydraulic valve lifters. Carburetor: 2Bbl. Holley 6520. VIN Code: B. OPTIONAL FOUR (Reliant): Inline, overhead-cam four-cylinder. Cast iron block; aluminum head. Displacement: 156 cu. in. (2.6 liters). Bore & stroke: 3.59 x 3.86 in. Compression ratio: 8.2:1. Brake horsepower: 92 at 4500 R.P.M. Torque: 131 lbs.-ft. at 2500 R.P.M. Five main bearings. Solid valve lifters. Carburetor: 2Bbl. Mikuni. VIN Code: D. BASE SIX (Gran Fury): Inline, overhead-valve six. Cast iron block and head. Displacement: 225 cu. in. (3.7 liters). Bore & stroke: 3.40 x 4.12 in. Compression ratio: 8.4:1. Brake horsepower: 85 at 3600 R.P.M. Torque: 165 lbs.-ft. at 1600 R.P.M. Four main bearings. Hydraulic valve lifters. Carburetor: 1Bbl. Holley 1945. VIN Code: E. OPTIONAL V-8 (Gran Fury): 90-degree, overhead valve V-8. Cast iron block and head. Displacement: 318 cu. in. (5.2 liters). Bore & stroke: 3.91 x 3.31 in. Compression ratio: 8.5:1. Brake horsepower: 130 at 4000 R.P.M. Torque: 230 lbs.-ft. at 2000 R.P.M. Five main bearings. Hydraulic valve lifters. Carburetor: 2Bbl. Carter BBD 8291S. VIN Code: K. OPTIONAL V-8 (Gran Fury): Same as 318 cu. in. V-8 above, but with Carter TQ 9283S 4Bbl. carburetor Horsepower: 165 at 4000 R.P.M. Torque: 240 lbs.- ft. at 2000 R.P.M. VIN Code: M.

CHASSIS DATA: Wheelbase: (Horizon) 99.1 in.; (TC3) 96.6 in.; (Reliant) 99.6 in.; (Gran Fury) 118.5 in. Overall Length: (Horizon) 164.8 in. incl. optional bumper guards; (TC3) 173.5 in.; (Reliant) 176.0 in.; (Reliant wag) 176.2 in.; (Gran Fury) 220.2 in. Height: (Horizon) 53.1 in.; (TC3) 50.8 in.; (Reliant 2dr.) 52.4 in.; (Reliant 4-dr.) 52.7 in.; (Reliant wag) 52.8 in.; (Gran Fury) 54.5 in. Width: (Horizon) 65.8 in.; (TC3) 66.7 in.; (Reliant) 68.6 in.; (Gran Fury) 77.6 in. Front Tread: (Horizon/TC3) 56.1 in.; (Reliant) 57.6 in.; (Gran Fury) 61.9 in. Rear Tread: (Horizon/TC3) 55.6 in.; (Reliant) 57.0 in.; (Gran Fury) 62.0 in. Standard Tires: (Horizon) P155/80R13 GBR BSW; (TC3/Reliant) P175/75R13 GBR BSW; (Gran Fury) P195/75R15 GBR WSW.

TECHNICAL: Transmission: Four-speed manual (floor shift) standard on Horizon/TC3: (1st) 3.45:1; (2nd) 1.94:1; (3rd) 1.29:1; (4th) 0.97:1; (Rev) 3.17:1. Four-speed manual (floor shift) standard on Reliant and Horizon/TC3 w/2.2-liter engine: (1st) 3.29:1; (2nd) 1.89:1; (3rd) 1.21:1; (4th) 0.88:1; (Rev) 3.14:1. TorqueFlite three-speed automatic standard on Gran Fury, optional on others. Gran Fury gear ratios: (1st) 2.74:1; (2nd) 1.54:1; (3rd) 1.00:1; (Rev) 2.22:1. Horizon/TC3/Reliant ratios: (1st) 2.69:1; (2nd) 1.55:1; (3rd) 1.00:1; (Rev) 2.10:1. Horizon/TC3 w/2.2-liter engine: (1st) 2.47:1; (2nd) 1.47:1; (3rd) 1.00:1; (Rev) 2.10:1. Standard final drive ratio: (Horizon/TC3) 3.37:1 w/4spd, 3.48:1 w/auto.; (Horizon/TC3 Miser) 2.6:1 w/4spd; (Horizon/TC3 w/2.2-liter four) 2.69:1 w/4spd, 2.7:1 w/auto.; (Reliant) 2.69:1 w/4spd, 2.78:1 w/auto.; (Gran Fury six) 2.94:1; (G. Fury V-8 2Bbl.) 2.24:1; (G. Fury V-8 4Bbl.) 2.45:1. Steering: (Horizon/TC3/Reliant) rack and pinion; (Gran Fury) recirculating ball. Suspension: (Horizon/TC3) Iso-Strut independent coil front w/anti-sway bar, independent trailing arm coil rear w/integral anti-sway; (Reliant) Iso-Strut front, flex-beam rear axle w/trailing links and coil springs; (Gran Fury) front torsion bars, rear leaf springs. Brakes: Front disc, rear drum. Ignition: Electronic. Body construction: Unibody. Fuel Tank: 13 gal. exc. (Gran Fury) 21 gal.

DRIVETRAIN OPTIONS: Engines: 2.2-liter four: Horizon/TC3 ($104) exc. in California (NC). 2.6-liter four: Reliant ($159). 318 cu. in. V-8, 2Bbl. or 4Bbl.: Gran Fury ($64). Transmission/Differential: TorqueFlite: Horizon/TC3 ($359); Reliant ($360). Sure grip differential: G. Fury ($114). Power Accessories: Power steering: Horizon/TC3 ($165); Reliant ($174). Power brakes: Horizon/TC3/Reliant ($82). Suspension: H.D. susp.: Horizon 4dr. ($28); Reliant ($23); G. Fury ($29). Sport susp.: TC3 ($46). H.D. shock absorbers: G. Fury ($8). Other: Trailer assist pkg.: G. Fury ($246). 430-amp battery: Horizon/TC3 ($23). 500-amp battery: Reliant/G. Fury ($38). Max. cooling ($127). California emission system ($46).

HORIZON/TC3 CONVENIENCE/APPEARANCE OPTIONS: Option Packages: Euro-Sedan pkg.: 4-dr. ($613-$865). Turismo pkg.: TC3 ($275-$655). Sport appearance pkg.: TC3 ($331- $435). Sport/Classic two-tone paint pkg. ($111-$164). Custom exterior pkg.: 4dr. ($188). Premium exterior pkg.: 4dr. ($250-$290); TC3 ($92-$166). Premium interior pkg. ($212- $311). Sport interior pkg. ($146-$196). Popular equipment group ($423-$477). Light pkg. ($49). Comfort/Convenience: Air cond. ($554). Rear defroster, electric ($102). Auto. speed control ($136). Tinted glass: 4dr. ($71). Tinted windshield: 4dr. ($45). Power liftgate release: TC3 ($27). Luxury steering wheel: 4dr. ($20). Sport steering wheel ($23-$43). Leather-wrapped steering wheel ($17-$60). Rallye instrument cluster w/tach ($70-$100). Electric clock w/trip odometer ($30). Intermittent wiper ($42). Rear wiper/washer: 4dr. ($83). Locking gas cap ($8). Lighting, Horns and Mirrors: Halogen headlamps ($40). Dual horns ($10). Remote left mirror, chrome: 4dr. ($20). Remote right mirror, black: 4dr. ($41). Dual remote mirrors, chrome: 4dr. ($41-$60). Dual remote sport mirrors: TC3 ($74). Day/night mirror: Miser ($13). Entertainment: AM radio: Miser ($92). AM/FM radio ($59-$151). AM/FM stereo radio ($94-$186); w/8track player ($168-$260); w/cassette ($223-$315). Radio upgrade ($14-$25). Rear speaker: TC3 ($20). Exterior: Glass sunroof ($213). Rear spoiler: TC3 ($59). Starmist paint ($49). Black vinyl bodyside moldings ($46). Moldings (4dr.): belt ($19); drip rail ($21); upper door frame ($35); wheel lip ($32). Door edge protectors ($13-$23). Bumper guards: 4dr. ($48). Hood/bodyside/deck tape stripe: 4dr. ($48). Bodyside/deck stripe: TC3 ($34). Multi-color bodyside stripe: 4dr. ($99). Luggage rack ($92). Undercoating ($37). Lower body coating ($34). Interior: Console: storage ($24); shift lever ($36). Cloth/vinyl bucket seats ($25). Tonneau cover: TC3 ($49). Cargo area carpet; ($34); w/sound insulation ($15-$49). Color-keyed floor mats: front ($25); rear ($18). Color-keyed seatbelts ($25). Wheels and Tires: Wheel trim rings: 4dr. ($48). Deluxe wheel covers: 4dr. ($48); TC3 (NC). Cast aluminum wheels, 13 in.: 4dr. ($215-$263); 14 in., TC3 ($175). Rally wheels, 13 in.: 4dr. ($40-$88); 14 in., TC3 (NC). P155/80R13 WSW: 4dr. ($52). P165/75R13 WSW: 4dr. ($33-$85). P175/75R13 SBR BSW: 4dr. ($17-$102). P175/75R13 SBR WSW: 4dr. ($89-$174). P175/75R13 GBR WSW: TC3 ($58). P185/70R13 SBR WSW: TC3 ($116- $174). P195/60R14 SBR BSW: TC3 ($79-$137). P195/60R14 SBR RWL: TC3 ($68-$205). Conventional spare tire ($39).

RELIANT CONVENIENCE/APPEARANCE OPTIONS: Option Packages: Basic group ($709-$784). Light pkg. ($75- $83). Protection group ($95-$103). Comfort/Convenience: Air cond. ($605). Rear defroster ($107). Automatic speed control ($132). Power seat ($173). Power door locks ($93-$132). Power decklid/liftgate release ($27). Tinted windshield ($48); all windows ($75). Luxury steering wheel: Cust ($46). Sport steering wheel: Cust ($53); SE ($7). Tilt steering wheel ($81). Digital clock ($59). Intermitent wipers ($41). Tailgate wiper/washer: wag ($82). Locking gas cap ($7). Lighting, Horns and Mirrors: Halogen headlamps ($36). Dual horns ($10). Remote left mirror ($19). Remote right mirror: SE ($49). Dual remote mirrors ($49-$68). Vanity mirror ($5). Entertainment: AM radio: base ($90); AM/FM radio ($64-$154). AM/FM stereo radio ($100); w/8track player ($174); w/cassette ($224); w/CB ($361). Rear speaker ($19). Dual front speakers ($25) w/mono radio. Premium speakers ($92). Delete AM radio ($85 credit). Exterior: Glass sunroof ($246). Full vinyl roof: 4dr. ($131). Landau vinyl roof: 2dr. ($131). Spice Tan Starmist paint ($55). Door edge protectors ($13-$21). Upper door frame moldings ($58-$67). Sill moldings ($20). Bumper guards, front or rear ($24). Luggage rack ($90). Special sound insulation ($75). Undercoating ($37). Vinyl lower body protection ($34). Interior: Console ($86). Vinyl bench seat: Cust ($27). Vinyl bucket seats ($51-$78) but (NC) on SE. Cloth bucket seats: SE ($91). Color-keyed mats: front ($25); rear ($19). Tonneau cover: wag ($50). Pedal dress-up ($9). Trunk dress-up ($45). Wheels and Tires: Rallye wheels ($36-$82). Deluxe wheel covers ($46). Luxury wheel covers ($36-$82). P175/75R13 GBR wide WSW ($51). P185/70R13 SBR wide WSW ($124-$175). P185/65R14 GBR wide WSW ($82-$133). P185/65R14 SBR wide WSW ($136-$187). Conventional spare tire: wag ($39).

GRAN FURY CONVENIENCE/APPEARANCE OPTIONS: Option Packages: Basic group ($993). Open Road handling pkg. ($281). Light pkg. ($103). Comfort/Convenience: Air conditioning ($646); auto-temp ($692) but ($46) w/option pkg. Rear defroster, electric ($112). Auto. speed control ($139). Power seat ($179). Power windows ($218). Power door locks ($138). Power decklid release ($30-$45). Illuminated entry system ($60). Luxury steering wheel ($39). Leather-covered steering wheel ($60). Tilt steering wheel ($84). Digital clock ($62). Intermittent wipers ($44). Locking gas cap ($9). Lighting, Horns and Mirrors: Halogen headlamps ($41). Cornering lights ($54). Triad horns ($22). Remote driver's mirror ($21). Dual remote-control mirrors ($30-$51). Lighted vanity mirror ($51). Entertainment: AM radio ($97). AM/FM radio ($54-$151). AM/FM stereo ($95-$192); w/ 8track tape player ($166-$263); w/cassette ($221-$318); w/CB ($356-$453). Search-tune AM/FM stereo ($206-$303). Dual front speakers ($26). Rear speaker ($21). Premium speakers ($95). Power antenna ($50). Exterior: Power glass sunroof ($934). Vinyl bodyside moldings ($51). Sill moldings ($31). Door edge protectors ($23). Bumper guards ($60). Bumper rub strips ($41). Bodyside tape stripe ($47). Undercoating ($31). Interior: Vinyl split-back bench seat ($69). Cloth/vinyl 60/40 bench seat ($182). Color-keyed floor mats: front ($25); rear ($20). Pedal dress-up ($11). Trunk dress-up ($65). Litter container ($10). Wheels and Tires: Deluxe wheel covers ($48). Premier wheel covers ($90). Premium wheel covers ($134). Wire wheel covers ($299). Forged aluminum wheels ($369). P205/75R15 SBR WSW ($101). P225/70R15 SBR WSW ($192). Conventional spare ($39).

HISTORY: Introduced: October 2, 1980 except Horizon/Gran Fury, October 16. Model year production: Chrysler reported a total of 348,985 passenger cars shipped. Total North American production for the U.S. market of 389,306 units included 310,101 four-cylinder, 71,209 six-cylinder, and 7,996 V-8s. Calendar year production: 363,702. Model year sales by U.S. dealers: 341,082 (not incl. 41,300 imported Champ/Arrows and 12,709 Sapporos).

Historical Footnotes: Reliants were produced in Detroit (at the Jefferson Ave. plant) and at Newark, Delaware. Not surprisingly, Reliant was the top seller for the model year, amounting to nearly two- fifths of total Chrysler-Plymouth Division sales. Almost three-fourths of the cars sold by CP were front-wheel drive (including the Japanese imports). The revived Gran Fury (and similar Rbodied Chrysler Newport) left the lineup soon after the model year began, only to return for 1982 with a totally different body on a shorter wheelbase.

1982 PLYMOUTH

Gran Fury took on a whole new, downsized form this year, but the rest of the Plymouth lineup enjoyed only engine/chassis refinements. Engine fans offered greater energy-efficiency, and a linkless sway bar was added to front-drive suspensions. Counterbalanced hoods replaced the old prop rods. New electronic-tuning radios had seek/scan, and new seat fabrics appeared. New roll-down back window mechanisms were offered, along with new inertia-recliner bucket seats. Compacts added more standard equipment, without corresponding price rises.

1982 Horizon four-door hatchback (CM)

HORIZON — SERIES M — FOUR — Except for modest revisions, Horizon appearance was the same as 1981. The grille had the same pattern of thin vertical bars, but added the Chrysler pentastar in the center. 'Horizon' script no longer appeared on front fenders, but remained on the hatch. Underneath was a new linkless front anti-sway bar. As usual, Horizon was nearly identical to Dodge's Omni, right down to the option list. Both were rated for five-passenger seating, but in a tight squeeze. Both served as Chrysler's "import fighters." Base, Custom, and E-Type Horizons were available this year. Horizon's EPA highway rating gained 2 MPG, as a result of changes in the catalytic converter and emissions control system. A base Miser reached an estimated 35 MPG city and 52 highway, with base 1.7-liter engine and four-speed manual. Customs had new corded cloth/vinyl Sport high-back bucket seats with dual recliners. Standard equipment included a color-keyed four-spoke sport steering wheel, deluxe wheel covers, bright body moldings, and woodgrain-trim instrument panel. Horizon Miser, offered again this year, carried a specially calibrated 1.7-liter four with four-speed manual transaxle and 2.69:1 overall top gear ratio. Miser had simpler trim and a smaller option selection. New vinyl high-back bucket seats and color-keyed seatbelts came in four colors. New standard Miser equipment also included a glovebox lock, day/night mirror, bright wheel hubs/nuts, and remote-control driver's mirror. Dual horns were standard. An optional light group included halogen headlamps, map/courtesy light, ignition switch light with time-delay, plus glovebox, ashtray and cargo area lights. A new blackout-trimmed E-Type (Euro-style) Horizon included Rallye instrumentation with tachometer, trip odometer, quartz clock, gauges, and a brake warning light. Standard high-back Sport bucket seats in corded cloth/vinyl had dual seatback recliners; optional, all-vinyl low-back buckets. A shift-lever console was included. Black moldings went on EType's windshield, liftgate window, drip rail and belt. Also standard: black upper door frames and center pillars; dual black remote-control mirrors with tape stripes; black door-handle inserts; and black bumpers with protective rub strips. Tape stripes ran from front to rear wheel openings. A four-speed manual transaxle with special 3.13:1 performance overall top gear ratio hooked up to either the standard 1.7-liter or optional 2.2-liter Trans-4 engine (2.2 standard in California). ETypes were supposed to lure younger drivers. Thirteen body colors were available. They included: Formal Black, Graphic Red, Morocco Red, Pearl White, Manila Cream, and Graphic Yellow (except E-Type); plus metallic Daystar Blue, Ensign Blue, Burnished Silver, Navy Blue, Spice Tan, Charcoal Gray, and Medium Seaspray Green. Three two-tones were offered on Custom only.

1982 Horizon TC3 coupe (CM)

TC3 — SERIES M — FOUR — Side appearance of the subcompact two-door coupe was similar to 1981, except that 'Plymouth' block lettering on front fenders was dropped. Also, the center side window was made smaller, now triangular-shaped rather than squarish as before. The 'C' pillar also grew wider, giving a wider appearance this year. Up front was a new front-end design with soft-fascia nose. TC3's body-color grille now consisted of 16 large square holes in the sloped panel, arranged in two rows of eight each. Below the bumper rub strip were three large slots. As before, 'Plymouth' block lettering stood above the driver's side of the grille, but a new round emblem also appeared at the hood front. Like Horizon, the TC3 carried a new linkless anti-sway bar and new single catalytic converter. Black wiper arms were installed, and a variety of items that had been optional became standard. They included a power hatchback release, deluxe sound insulation, and tape stripes. Three price levels were offered: Miser, Custom and Turismo. Rated optimistically at five-passenger capacity, TC3 had a rear seat that folded down to create nearly 34

cubic feet of cargo space. The Custom model had a new quarter-window applique and standard Rallye road wheels, plus standard cloth/vinyl high-back Sport bucket seats with integral headrests and dual seatback recliners. TC3 Miser's design, though similar to the Custom, had much narrower C-pillars, allowing for a wider quarter window. Misers carried standard vinyl high-back bucket seats and a specially calibrated 1.7-liter four to deliver up to 51 MPG on the highway in EPA estimates. TC3 solid colors were the same as Horizon's. Four two-tones were offered on TC3 Custom; three more with the Sport Appearance package. A TC3 Turismo was offered this year, with equipment similar to the Horizon E-Type. Turismo had a claimed 0-50 time of 7 seconds with standard 2.2-liter engine and 3.13:1 overall top gear ratio. A performance exhaust system was optional. Many black accents highlighted Turismo's apperance, along with a rear spoiler, special tape striping and graphics, and low-profile blackwall steel-belted radial tires on 14 in. steel Rallye wheels (with bright hubs and trim rings). Inside was a Rallye instrument cluster and cloth/vinyl Sport bucket seats, or optional low-back Premium bucket seats. Buyers were also directed to Direct Connection, Chrysler's Performance Parts Program, as a source for such extras as air dams, wheels and engine chrome, along with off-road camshafts and pistons and an off-road suspension kit. Graphic Yellow body color wasn't available on Turismo. A separate factory sales catalog was distributed later for the Turismo 2.2. Though similar in appearance to the standard Turismo, the ultimate coupe showed special graphics including a 'Turismo' decal between door and rear wheel opening, large '2.2' decal on the 'C' pillar, and two-color bodyside striping. Turismo 2.2 also added a simulated hood scoop and rear spoiler, dual remote-control sport mirrors, and P195/60R14 SBR blackwall tires on 14 in. Rallye wheels. A special sport suspension included heavy-duty shock absorbers and rear anti-sway bar. Naturally, the 2.2-liter engine was standard, with a "throaty" performance exhaust system. Turismo 2.2 came in five body colors: Morocco Red, Charcoal Gray metallic, Burnished Silver metallic, Black, or Pearl White. All graphics matched the narrow upper body stripe colors. A total of 3,208 cars had the Turismo 2.2 package.

1982 Reliant coupe (CM)

RELIANT — SERIES P — FOUR — Changes in Plymouth's front-drive compact focused on engineering refinements rather than style for its second year in the lineup. Four-doors had new roll-down rear windows. Like other front-drives, Reliant added a linkless anti-sway bar in the front suspension. A counterbalanced hood replaced the former prop style. The 2.2-liter engine got new silver/black paint on the outside, a reworked intake manifold and repositioned camshaft on the inside. The engine fan was quieter, and the fuel-control computer was reworked to modify idle speed. Disc brake rotors were new. Base engine again was the 135 cu. in. (2.2-liter) four; optional, the Mitsubishi 156 cu. in. (2.6-liter), available only with automatic transmission. New options included power front windows, a Euro-style center console (with manual shift), lighted vanity mirror, bodyside tape stripes, wire wheel covers, and 14 in. cast aluminum wheels. Seven models included a base four-door sedan; Custom and SE two-and four-door sedans; and four-door (two-seat) wagon. Recliner bucket seats were optional in Custom and SE models. SE had new cloth/vinyl bench seating with center armrest; rosewood instrument panel and door trim appliques; and power brakes/steering.

1982 Gran Fury sedan (CM)

GRAN FURY — SERIES B — SIX/V-8— Once again, the Gran Fury name went on a smaller model. This Mbodied four-door sedan, riding a 112.7 in. wheelbase, stood 14.5 in. shorter than its predecessor and some 230 pounds lighter. Actually, it was the '81 rear-drive LeBaron, which had been replaced by a new front-drive version. Gran Fury's grille lacked the usual eggcrate look. Instead, it showed what was described as "bold vertical lines (full depth) ...against a silvered background" to give a massive look. The standard seat, with center armrest, was upholstered in Madison cloth. Vinyl was available too. Upholstery colors were silver, blue, red, and cashmere. Body colors included Spice Tan, Daystar Blue, Nightwatch Blue, Manila Cream, Charcoal Gray, Morocco Red, Silver, White, and Black. Options included two new electronic-tuning AM/FM stereo radios made by Chrysler, with seek/scan to replace the prior search provision. One included a stereo cassette player with Dolby noise reduction. Engines were the same as before: either a 225 cu. in. Slant Six or 318 cu. in. V-8, both with TorqueFlite three-speed automatic transmission.

I.D. DATA: Plymouth again had a 17-symbol Vehicle Identification Number (VIN) on the upper left corner of the instrument panel, visible through the windshield. The first digit indicates Country: '1' U.S.A. The second symbol is Make: 'P' Plymouth. Third is Vehicle Type: '3' passenger car. The next symbol ('B') indicates manual seatbelts. Symbol five is Car Line: 'M' Horizon; 'P' Reliant; 'B' Gran Fury. Symbol six is Series (price class): '1' Economy; '2' Low; '4' High'; '5' Premium. Symbol seven is Body Style: '1' 2-dr. sedan; '4' 2-dr. 22 hatchback; '6' 4-dr. sedan; '8' 4-dr. hatchback; '9' 4-dr. wagon. Eighth is the Engine Code: 'A' L4105 2Bbl.; 'B' L4135 2Bbl.; 'D' L4156

2Bbl.; 'E' L6-225 1Bbl.; 'K' V8318 2Bbl.; 'M' V8318 4Bbl. Next comes a check digit: 0 through 9 (or X). Symbol ten indicates Model Year: 'C' 1982. Symbol eleven is Assembly Plant: 'C' Jefferson; 'D' Belvidere, IL; 'F' Newark, DE; 'R' Windsor, Ontario. The last six digits make up the sequential serial number, starting with 100001. Engine number and Body Code Plate locations are the same as 1981.

Model Number	Body/Style Number	Body Type & Seating	Factory Price	Shipping Weight	Production Total
HORIZON CUSTOM (FOUR)					
MH	44	4-dr. Hatch-5P	5927	2175	17,315
HORIZON MISER (FOUR)					
ME	44	4-dr. Hatch-5P	5499	2110	19,102
HORIZON EURO-SEDAN (FOUR)					
MP	44	4-dr. Hatch-5P	6636	2180	779
TC3 CUSTOM (FOUR)					
MH	24	2-dr. Hatch-5P	6421	2205	12,889
TC3 MISER (FOUR)					
ME	24	2-dr. Hatch-5P	5799	2180	18,359
TC3 TURISMO (FOUR)					
MP	24	2-dr. Hatch-5P	7115	2315	6,608
RELIANT (FOUR)					
PL	21	2-dr. Sedan-6P	5990	2315	12,026
PL	41	4-dr. Sedan-6P	6131	2310	37,488
RELIANT CUSTOM (FOUR)					
PH	21	2-dr. Sedan-6P	6898	2320	12,403
PH	41	4-dr. Sedan-6P	7053	2320	29,980
PH	45	4-dr. Sta Wag-6P	7334	2395	32,501
RELIANT SPECIAL EDITION (FOUR)					
PP	21	2-dr. Sedan-6P	7575	2365	2,536
PP	41	4-dr. Sedan-6P	7736	2385	4,578
PP	45	4-dr. Sta Wag-6P	8101	2470	7,711
GRAN FURY SALON (SIX/V-8)					
BL	41	4-dr. Sedan-6P	7750/7820	3275/ --	18,111

FACTORY PRICE AND WEIGHT NOTE: Gran Fury price and weight to left of slash is for six-cylinder, to right for V-8. **MODEL NUMBER NOTE:** Some sources identify models using the new VIN data to indicate Car Line, Price Clas and Body Style. Example: base Reliant four-door (PL41) has the equivalent number P26, which translates to Reliant line, Low price class, and four-door sedan body. See I.D. Data section for breakdown.

ENGINE DATA: BASE FOUR (Horizon, TC3): Inline, overhead-cam four-cylinder. Cast iron block; aluminum head. Displacement: 104.7 cu. in. (1.7 liters). Bore & stroke: 3.13 x 3.40 in. Compression ratio: 8.2:1. Brake horsepower: 63 at 5200 R.P.M. Torque: 83 lbs.-ft. at 2400 R.P.M. Five main bearings. Solid valve lifters. Carburetor: 2Bbl. Holley 6520. VIN Code: A. BASE FOUR (Reliant, TC3 Turismo); OPTIONAL (Horizon, TC3): Inline, overhead-cam four-cylinder. Cast iron block; aluminum head. Displacement: 135 cu. in. (2.2 liters). Bore & stroke: 3.44 x 3.62 in. Compression ratio: 8.5:1. Brake horsepower: 84 at 4800 R.P.M. Torque: 111 lbs.-ft. at 2400 R.P.M. Five main bearings. Hydraulic valve lifters. Carburetor: 2Bbl. Holley 6520 or 5220. VIN Code: B. OPTIONAL FOUR (Reliant): Inline, overhead-cam four-cylinder. Cast iron block; aluminum head. Displacement: 156 cu. in. (2.6 liters). Bore & stroke: 3.59 x 3.86 in. Compression ratio: 8.2:1. Brake horsepower: 92 at 4500 R.P.M. Torque: 131 lbs.-ft. at 2500 R.P.M. Five main bearings. Solid valve lifters. Carburetor: 2Bbl. Mikuni. VIN Code: D. BASE SIX (Gran Fury): Inline, overhead-valve six. Cast iron block and head. Displacement: 225 cu. in. (3.7 liters). Bore & stroke: 3.40 x 4.12 in. Compression ratio: 8.4:1. Brake horsepower: 90 at 3600 R.P.M. Torque: 160 lbs.-ft. at 1600 R.P.M. Four main bearings. Hydraulic valve lifters. Carburetor: 1Bbl. Holley 1945. VIN Code: E. OPTIONAL V-8 (Gran Fury): 90-degree, overhead valve V-8. Cast iron block and head. Displacement: 318 cu. in. (5.2 liters). Bore & stroke: 3.91 x 3.31 in. Compression ratio: 8.5:1. Brake horsepower: 130 at 4000 R.P.M. Torque: 230 lbs.-ft. at 2000 R.P.M. Five main bearings. Hydraulic valve lifters. Carburetor: 2Bbl. Carter BBD. VIN Code: K. CALIFORNIA V-8 (Gran Fury): Same as 318 cu. in. V-8 above, but with Carter TQ 4Bbl. carburetor Horsepower: 165 at 4000 R.P.M. Torque: 240 lbs.-ft. at 2000 R.P.M. VIN Code: M.

CHASSIS DATA: Wheelbase: (Horizon) 99.1 in.; (TC3) 96.6 in.; (Reliant) 99.9 in.; (Gran Fury) 112.7 in. Overall Length: (Horizon) 162.6 in.; (Horizon E-Type) 163.2 in.; (TC3) 173.7 in.; (TC3 Turismo) 174.1 in.; (Turismo 2.2) 174.2 in.; (Reliant) 176.0 in.; (Reliant wag) 176.2 in.; (Gran Fury) 205.7 in. Height: (Horizon) 53.1 in.; (TC3) 50.8 in.; (Reliant 2dr.) 52.3 in.; (Reliant 4-dr.) 52.7 in.; (Reliant wag) 52.4 in.; (Gran Fury) 55.3 in. Width: (Horizon) 65.8 in.; (TC3) 66.7 in.; (Reliant) 68.6 in.; (Gran Fury) 74.2 in. Front Tread: (Horizon/TC3) 56.1 in.; (Reliant) 57.6 in.; (Gran Fury) 60.0 in. Rear Tread: (Horizon/TC3) 55.6 in.; (Reliant) 57.0 in.; (Gran Fury) 59.5 in. Standard Tires: (Horizon/TC3) P175/75R13 GBR BSW; (Turismo) P195/60R14 SBR RBL; (Reliant) P175/75R13 GBR; (Gran Fury) P195/75R15 GBR.

TECHNICAL: Transmission: Four-speed manual (floor shift) standard on Horizon/TC3: (1st) 3.45:1; (2nd) 1.94:1; (3rd) 1.29:1; (4th) 0.97:1; (Rev) 3.17:1. Four-speed manual (floor shift) standard on Reliant, Horizon/TC3 Miser, and Horizon/TC3 w/2.2-liter engine: (1st) 3.29:1; (2nd) 1.89:1; (3rd) 1.21:1; (4th) 0.88:1; (Rev) 3.14:1. TorqueFlite three-speed automatic standard on Gran Fury, optional on others. Gran Fury gear ratios: (1st) 2.74:1; (2nd) 1.54:1; (3rd) 1.00:1; (Rev) 2.22:1. Horizon/TC3/Reliant ratios: (1st) 2.69:1; (2nd) 1.55:1; (3rd) 1.00:1; (Rev) 2.10:1. Standard final drive ratio: (Horizon/TC3) 3.37:1 w/4spd; (Horizon/TC3 Miser) 2.69:1 w/4spd; (Horizon/TC3 w/2.2-liter four) 3.13:1 w/4spd, 2.78:1 w/auto.; (Reliant) 2.69:1 w/4spd, 2.78:1 w/auto.; (Gran Fury six) 2.94:1. Steering: (Horizon/TC3/Reliant) rack and pinion; (Gran Fury) recirculating ball. Suspension: (Horizon/TC3) Iso-Strut independent coil front w/anti-sway bar, semi-independent trailing arm coil rear w/integral anti-sway; (TC3 Turismo) sport susp., same as TC3 with rear anti-sway bar; (Reliant) Iso-Strut front, flex-beam rear axle w/trailing links and coil springs; (Gran Fury) front torsion bars and anti-sway bar, rear leaf springs. Brakes: Front disc, rear drum. Ignition: Electronic. Body construction: Unibody. Fuel tank: 13 gal. exc. (Gran Fury) 18 gal.

DRIVETRAIN OPTIONS: Engines: 2.2-liter four: Horizon/TC3 ($112). 2.6-liter four: Reliant ($171). 318 cu. in., 2Bbl. V-8: Gran Fury ($70). 318 cu. in., 4Bbl. V-8: G. Fury ($70). Transmission: TorqueFlite: Horizon/TC3/Reliant ($396). Power Accessories: Power steering: Horizon/TC3 ($190); Reliant ($195). Power brakes: Horizon/TC3/Reliant ($93). Suspension: H.D. susp.: Reliant/G. Fury ($26). Sport susp.: TC3 ($52). Other: Performance exhaust system: TC3 Turismo ($31). 430-amp battery: Horizon/TC3 ($26). 500-amp battery: Reliant/G. Fury ($43). Engine block heater: Horizon/TC3 ($18). Max. cooling ($141). California emission system ($65). High-altitude emission system (NC).

HORIZON/TC3 CONVENIENCE/APPEARANCE OPTIONS: Option Packages: Sport appearance pkg.: TC3 Cust ($138). Bright exterior accent group: Cust ($85-$121). Two-tone paint pkg.: Cust ($113-$186). Light group ($74). Comfort/Convenience: Air cond. ($612). Rear defroster, electric ($120). Automatic speed control ($155). Tinted glass: 4dr. ($82). Rallye instrument cluster: Cust ($127). Electric clock w/trip odometer ($48). Intermittent wipers ($47). Rear wiper/washer: 4dr. ($117). Mirrors: Dual remote chrome: 4dr. ($47). Dual sport remote: TC3 ($55). Lighted vanity ($50). Entertainment: AM radio: Miser ($78). AM/FM stereo radio ($106-$184); w/8track player ($192-$270); w/cassette ($242- $320). Radio upgrade ($15-$27). Exterior: Removable glass sunroof: TC3 ($275). Rear spoiler: TC3 Cust ($68). Black vinyl bodyside molding: 4dr. ($45). Bumper guards: Cust 4dr. ($56). Front nerf strips: Cust 4dr. ($25). Rear nerf strips: Cust ($25). Bodyside/deck tape stripe: Cust 4dr. ($39). Luggage rack: 4dr. ($93). Undercoating ($39). Lower body protective coating ($39). Interior: Console, shift lever: Cust ($41). Cloth/vinyl bucket seats: Miser ($27). Vinyl bucket seats (NC) exc. Miser. Tonneau cover: TC3 ($64). Cargo area carpet w/sound insulation: TC3 Cust ($56). Wheels and Tires: Luxury wheel covers (NC). Cast aluminum 14 in. wheels: TC3 ($231). 13 in. Rallye wheels: Cust/Euro 4dr. ($45). 14 in. Rallye wheels: TC3 (NC). P175/75R13 WSW ($58). P175/75R13 SBR WSW ($134). P195/60R14 SBR BSW: TC3 Cust ($173). P195/60R14 SBR RWL: TC3 Cust ($257); Turismo ($84). Conventional spare tire ($51).

RELIANT CONVENIENCE/APPEARANCE OPTIONS: Option Packages: Cabriolet roof pkg.: Cust/SE 2dr. ($696). Light pkg. ($89-$98). Comfort/Convenience: Air cond. ($676). Rear defroster ($125). Automatic speed control ($155). Power seat ($197). Power front windows ($165). Power door locks ($106-$152). Power decklid/liftgate release ($32). Tinted glass ($88). Steering wheel: Luxury ($50); Sport ($50-$90); Leather-wrapped ($50- 90); Tilt ($95). Digital clock ($61). Intermitent wipers ($47). Liftgate wiper/washer: wag ($117). Horns and Mirrors: Dual horns ($12). Remote left mirror ($22). Dual remote mirrors ($64-$86). Lighted vanity mirror, right ($50). Entertainment: AM radio: base ($78). AM/FM stereo radio ($106-$184); w/8track player ($192-$270); w/cassette ($242- $320); w/CB ($364-$442). Dual front speakers ($27). Premium speakers ($126). Delete AM radio ($56 credit). Exterior: Removable glass sunroof ($275). Full vinyl roof: 4dr. ($157). Padded landau roof: 2dr. ($157). Door edge protectors ($15-$25). Sill moldings ($23). Bumper guards, front or rear ($28). Bodyside tape stripe ($48) exc. SE wag (NC). Luggage rack ($106). Special sound insulation ($87). Undercoating ($39). Vinyl lower body protection ($39). Interior: Console: Cust/SE ($100). Vinyl bench seat: base (NC). Cloth/vinyl bench seat: base ($31). Vinyl reclining bucket seats: Cust ($132-$151); SE (NC). Cloth reclining bucket seats: Cust ($249-$270); SE ($98). Color-keyed mats: front ($25); rear ($20). Color-keyed seatbelts ($28). Tonneau cover: wag ($64). Trunk dress-up ($51). Wheels and Tires: Deluxe 13 in. wheel covers ($52). Luxury 14 in. wheel covers ($41-$93). 14 in. wire wheel covers ($257- $309). Rallye wheels, 13 or 14 in. ($41-$93). Cast aluminum 14 in. wheels ($357-$409). P175/75R13 GBR wide WSW ($58). P185/70R13 SBR wide WSW ($194). P185/70R14 GBR wide WSW ($207). Conventional spare tire ($50).

GRAN FURY CONVENIENCE/APPEARANCE OPTIONS: Option Packages: Basic group ($1143). Light pkg. ($139). Protection group ($119). Comfort/Convenience: Air cond. ($731). Rear defroster, electric ($125). Auto. speed control ($155). Power windows ($235). Power door locks ($152). Power decklid release ($32). Illuminated entry system ($72). Leather-wrapped steering wheel ($50). Tilt steering wheel ($95). Digital clock ($61). Intermittent wipers ($47). Mirrors: Remote driver's ($22). Dual remote chrome ($65). Lighted vanity ($58). Entertainment: AM/FM stereo radio ($106); w/ 8track tape player ($192); w/CB ($364). Search-tune AM/FM stereo ($239). Electronic-tuning AM/FM stereo w/cassette ($455). Dual front speakers ($28). Premium speakers ($126). Power antenna ($55). Radio delete ($56 credit). Exterior: Power glass sunroof ($982). Full vinyl roof ($158). Vinyl bodyside moldings ($46). Upper door frame moldings ($41). Bodyside/deck/hood stripe ($109). Body sound insulation ($30). Undercoating ($39). Interior: Vinyl bench seat ($58). Trunk dress-up ($51). Wheels and Tires: Premium wheel covers ($93). Wire wheel covers ($257). Forged aluminum wheels ($364). P205/75R15 SBR WSW ($116). Conventional spare ($51).

HISTORY: Introduced: October 14, 1981. Model year production: Chrysler reported a total of 232,386 passenger cars shipped. Calendar year production: 241,181. Calendar year sales by U.S. dealers: 251,628. Model year sales by U.S. dealers: 255,892 (not incl. 40,431 imported Colts and 12,607 Sapporos).

Historical Footnotes: Chrysler/Plymouth sales for the model year fell 9 percent; but since other automakers fared even worse, the Division gained a larger market share. Plymouth scored considerably worse, however, with each line except the rebodied rear-drive Gran Fury posting a sharp sales decline. Gran Fury sales almost doubled. Reliant remained the Division's best seller by far, taking one-third of CP sales even with a lagging total this year. TC3 coupes were now marketed separately from the Horizon sedan. At mid-year, a Rampage car/pickup based on the TC3/024 design went on the market.

1983 PLYMOUTH

Chrysler's Trans-4 2.2-liter four-cylinder engine added 10 horsepower this year, with compression jacked up to 9.0:1. Standard on Reliant and optional on Horizon/Turismo, the 2.2 engine had reworked manifolds and cylinder head, and recalibrated fuel/spark control. A new (97 cu. in.) 1.6-liter four, built by Peugeot, replaced the former 105 cu. in. (1.7-liter) four as base Horizon/Turismo powerplant after the start of the model year. A five-speed manual transaxle became optional on Horizon, Turismo and Reliant. Little appearance change was evident on Plymouth models.

1983 Horizon four-door hatchback (CM)

HORIZON — SERIES M — FOUR — Base and Custom Horizons were the two choices for 1983, as the low-budget Miser faded away. The Euro-Sedan disappeared as well. Taillamps, though similar in shape to 1983, showed horizontal lens ribbing and larger backup lenses. Otherwise, appearance changed little. After the model year began, a new 1.6-liter four, built by Peugeot, gradually began to replace the former Volkswagen-based 1.7-liter powerplant. A four-speed manual transaxle was standard again, but this year a new five-speed (overdrive) unit became available. Actually, it was the same old four-speed with an extra gear hooked up. The five-speed was offered with either the base 1.7 or optional 2.2-liter four. Horizons had standard power brakes and low-back reclining padded bucket seats. A restyled woodtone-finished instrument panel held a quartz clock and trip odometer. Standard equipment on the base model included bumper rub strips, lighter, quartz clock, locking glovebox, dual horns, black body moldings, black remote-control driver's mirror, day/night mirror, trip odometer, and intermittent wipers. Custom added the woodtone instrument panel, chrome driver's mirror, deluxe wheel covers, and bright moldings for backlight, partial belt, liftgate, bodyside, sill and upper door frame.

1983 Turismo 2.2 coupe (CM)

TURISMO — SERIES M — FOUR — The Horizon-based coupe changed its name from TC3 to Turismo this year, and the Miser disappeared. Otherwise, nothing drastic happened. Two models were offered: the base Turismo with 1.7-liter (later 1.6-liter) four, and the Turismo 2.2 with a high-performance, 100-horsepower version of the 2.2-liter engine. Actually, that powerplant didn't produce so much more power than the standard optional 2.2, which rose from 84 to 94 horsepower this year with a compression boost. Optional this year was a five-speed manual transaxle, to replace the basic four-speed. Standard power brakes were improved. Standard equipment included halogen headlamps, tachometer, trip odometer, maintenance-free battery, and cloth/vinyl sport high-back bucket seats with dual recliners. Also standard: tinted glass, front bumper rub strip, cigarette lighter, clock, dual horns, padded instrument panel with woodtone applique, power liftgate release, left remote (black) mirror, bodyside and hatchback stripes, intermittent wipers, and a four-spoke steering wheel. In addition to the high-output engine, Turismo 2.2 added an AM radio, sport suspension, 14 in. Rallye wheels, simulated hood scoop, and dual remote-control sport mirrors. Turismo 2.2 also included a performance exhaust system and unique tape graphics that included a wide bodyside stripe that dipped down at the front, along with a rear liftgate spoiler, front storage and shift lever console, and low- profile SBR tires. Chrysler claimed that a Turismo "leaves more expensive sport cars in the dust," while the most economical version warranted an EPA mileage estimate of 32 MPG (50 highway) with the base engine and four-speed.

RELIANT — SERIES P — FOUR — Model selection dwindled slightly, leaving only the station wagon in Reliant's Custom series, but retaining the base and SE editions as before. Choices included base and Special Edition two- or four-doors, and Custom or Special Edition wagons. The base overhead-cam, 2.2-liter four- cylinder engine gained 10 horsepower, now producing 94 at 5200 R.P.M., partly as a result of a rise in compression ratio to 9.0:1. That engine used an electronic feedback two- barrel carburetor. As before, one engine option was offered: the Mitsubishi-built 2.6-liter MCA-Jet Silent Shaft four. This year, a five-speed manual transaxle was available, to replace the standard four-speed. Wide-ratio TorqueFlite automatic also remained on

1983 Reliant station wagon (CM)

the option list, with high-ratio first and second gears. Chrysler called Reliant the "highest mileage, six-passenger front-wheel drive car in America," with an EPA estimate of 29 MPG in the city and 41 on the highway. Power brakes now were standard, as was a maintenance- free battery. A "Pass-Flasher" signal was added to the multi- function steering column lever. The fuel filler cap had a new plastic tether strap. Redesigned door latches were quieter. New ram-air features went into the heat/vent system, which added a dash vent. Optional air conditioning now offered bi-level operation through upper and lower outlets. Bodies featured a pentastar on the deck lid, along with 'Plymouth' and 'Reliant' letters on opposite sides. Vertical red reflectors stood at the rear of quarter panels. Full- width taillamps included square backup lamps flanking the license plate. Reliants had standard halogen headlamps and a stand-up pentastar hood ornament. The grille contained five bright horizontal bars and a center vertical bar. Inside was a color-keyed instrument panel with rosewood woodtone touches, and deluxe two-spoke steering wheel. Standard upholstery consisted of an all-vinyl bench seat in blue, red, or beige. Optional: Madison (blue or red) or Kingsley (beige) cloth bench seat with vinyl door trim panels. Special Edition models (and Custom wagon) had an all-cloth bench seat with center armrest in silver (except wagon), blue, red, or beige. Optional at no cost was a saddle vinyl bench seat in the same colors. Optional at extra cost: all-cloth back bucket seats with dual recliners, also in the same colors. Body colors were: Formal Black, Nightwatch Blue, Pearl White, Silver crystal coat, Beige crystal coat, Crimson Red, Sable Brown, Charcoal Gray metallic, or Glacier Blue crystal coat. Also one two-tone combination: Charcoal Gray metallic/Silver crystal coat. All models carried bodyside moldings with vinyl inserts; bright drip rail moldings; bright windshield, quarter window and backlight moldings. Special Editions added rear door glass louvers, bright belt and decklid moldings, upper door frame moldings, bright taillamp accents, black paint graphics for the bright grille, bright front/rear rub strips with vinyl inserts, and Special Edition plaque on rear roof pillar. Optional at no cost was an all-cloth split back seat with center armrest. Custom and SE had a standard AM radio. SE wagons had woodgrain bodyside and liftgate appliques with woodgrain surround moldings. Standard tires were P175/75R13 glass-belted radials.

1983 Gran Fury sedan (CM)

GRAN FURY — SERIES B — SIX/V-8— Apart from four new body colors, not much was different on the last rear-drive Plymouth. As before, only one four- door sedan model was offered. Base engine once again was the 225 cu. in. (3.7-liter) Slant Six with three-speed TorqueFlite automatic; optional, the 318 cu. in. (5.2-liter) V-8. Standard equipment included tinted glass, halogen headlamps, power steering and brakes, AM radio, cloth/vinyl bench seats with folding center armrest, and color-keyed seatbelts. Also standard: front bumper guards, front/rear bumper rub strips, dual horns, courtesy lights, day/night mirror, driver's outside mirror, wheel opening and belt moldings, drip rail and sill moldings, two-spoke steering wheel, two-speed wipers, and a trip odometer. Tires were P195/75R15 glass-belted radials, with deluxe wheel covers and a compact spare. A total of 8,400 police packages were installed on Gran Fury, which remained popular with fleet buyers and families.

I.D. DATA: Plymouth again had a 17-symbol Vehicle Identification Number (VIN) on the upper left corner of the instrument panel, visible through the windshield. Coding is similar to 1982. This year's engine codes (symbol eight) are: 'A' L497 2Bbl.; 'B' L4105 2Bbl.; 'C' L4135 2Bbl.; 'G' L4156 2Bbl.; 'H' L6-225 1Bbl.; 'P' V8318 2Bbl. Model year code (symbol ten) changed to 'D' 1983. Symbol eleven is Assembly Plant: 'A' Detroit; 'D' Belvidere, IL; 'F' Newark, DE; 'G' or 'X' St. Louis; 'R' Windsor, Ontario. Engine number locations are the same as 1981-82.

HORIZON (FOUR)

Model Number	Body/Style Number	Body Type & Seating	Factory Price	Shipping Weight	Production Total
ME	44	4-dr. Hatch-5P	5841	2165	35,796
MH	44	4-dr. Cust Hatch-5P	6071	2195	10,675

TURISMO (FOUR)

Model Number	Body/Style Number	Body Type & Seating	Factory Price	Shipping Weight	Production Total
MH	24	2-dr. Hatch-5P	6379	2170	22,527

361

TURISMO 2.2 (FOUR)

MP	24	2-dr. Hatch-5P	7303	2330	9,538

RELIANT (FOUR)

PL	21	2-dr. Sedan-6P	6577	2300	16,109
PL	41	4-dr. Sedan-6P	6718	2300	69,112

RELIANT CUSTOM (FOUR)

PH	45	4-dr. Sta Wag-6P	7636	2410	38,264

RELIANT SPECIAL EDITION (FOUR)

PH	21	2-dr. Sedan-6P	7260	2310	5,852
PH	41	4-dr. Sedan-6P	7417	2340	13,434
PP	45	4-dr. Sta Wag-6P	8186	2465	3,791

GRAN FURY SALON (SIX/V-8)

BL	41	4-dr. Sedan-6P	8248/8473	3320/3455	15,739

FACTORY PRICE AND WEIGHT NOTE: Gran Fury price and weight to left of slash is for six-cylinder, to right for V-8. **MODEL NUMBER NOTE:** Some sources identify models using he new VIN data to indicate Car Line, Price Class and Body Style. Example: base Reliant four-door (PL41) has the equivalent number P26, which translates to Reliant line, Low price class, and four-door sedan body. See I.D. Data section for breakdown.

ENGINE DATA: BASE FOUR (late Horizon, Turismo): Inline, overhead-cam four-cylinder. Cast iron block; aluminum head. Displacement: 97.3 cu. in. (1.6 liters). Bore & stroke: 3.17 x 3.07 in. Compression ratio: 8.8:1. Brake horsepower: 62 at 4800 R.P.M. Torque: 86 lbs.-ft. at 3200 R.P.M. Five main bearings. Solid valve lifters. Carburetor: 2Bbl. VIN Code: A. BASE FOUR (early Horizon, Turismo): Inline, overhead-cam four-cylinder. Cast iron block; aluminum head. Displacement: 104.7 cu. in. (1.7 liters). Bore & stroke: 3.13 x 3.40 in. Compression ratio: 8.2:1. Brake horsepower: 63 at 4800 R.P.M. Torque: 83 lbs.-ft. at 2400 R.P.M. Five main bearings. Solid valve lifters. Carburetor: 2Bbl. Holley 6520. VIN Code: B. BASE FOUR (Reliant, Turismo 2.2); OPTIONAL (Horizon, Turismo): Inline, overhead-cam four-cylinder. Cast iron block; aluminum head. Displacement: 135 cu. in. (2.2 liters). Bore & stroke: 3.44 x 3.62 in. Compression ratio: 9.0:1. Brake horsepower: 94 at 5200 R.P.M. (Turismo 2.2, 100 at 5200 R.P.M.). Torque: 117 lbs.-ft. at 3200 R.P.M. (Turismo 2.2, 122 at 3200 R.P.M.). Five main bearings. Hydraulic valve lifters. Carburetor: 2Bbl. Holley 6520. VIN Code: C. OPTIONAL FOUR (Reliant): Inline, overhead-cam four-cylinder. Cast iron block; aluminum head. Displacement: 156 cu. in. (2.6 liters). Bore & stroke: 3.59 x 3.86 in. Compression ratio: 8.2:1. Brake horsepower: 93 at 4500 R.P.M. Torque: 132 lbs.-ft. at 2500 R.P.M. Five main bearings. Solid valve lifters. Carburetor: 2Bbl. Mikuni. VIN Code: G. BASE SIX (Gran Fury): Inline, overhead-valve six. Cast iron block and head. Displacement: 225 cu. in. (3.7 liters). Bore & stroke: 3.40 x 4.12 in. Compression ratio: 8.4:1. Brake horsepower: 90 at 3600 R.P.M. Torque: 165 lbs.-ft. at 1600 R.P.M. Four main bearings. Hydraulic valve lifters. Carburetor: 1Bbl. Holley 6145. VIN Code: H. OPTIONAL V-8 (Gran Fury): 90-degree, overhead valve V-8. Cast iron block and head. Displacement: 318 cu. in. (5.2 liters). Bore & stroke: 3.91 x 3.31 in. Compression ratio: 8.5:1. Brake horsepower: 130 at 4000 R.P.M. Torque: 230 lbs.-ft. at 1600 R.P.M. Five main bearings. Hydraulic valve lifters. Carburetor: 2Bbl. Carter BBD. VIN Code: P.

CHASSIS DATA: Wheelbase: (Horizon) 99.1 in.; (Turismo) 96.6 in.; (Reliant) 100.1 in.; (Gran Fury) 112.7 in. Overall Length: (Horizon) 164.8 in.; (Turismo) 173.3 in.; (Reliant) 176.0 in.; (Reliant wag) 176.2 in.; (Gran Fury) 205.7 in. Height: (Horizon) 53.1 in.; (Turismo) 50.8 in.; (Reliant 2dr.) 52.3 in.; (Reliant 4-dr.) 52.7 in.; (Reliant wag) 52.4 in.; (Gran Fury) 55.3 in. Width: (Horizon) 65.8 in.; (Turismo) 66.7 in.; (Reliant) 68.6 in.; (G. Fury) 74.2 in. Front Tread: (Horiz/Tur) 56.1 in.; (Reliant) 57.6 in.; (G. Fury) 60.0 in. Rear Tread: (Horiz/Tur) 55.6 in.; (Reliant) 57.0 in.; (G. Fury) 59.5 in. Standard Tires: (Horiz/Tur/Reliant) P175/75R13 GBR; (Turismo 2.2) P195/60R14 SBR RWL; (Gran Fury) P195/75R15.

TECHNICAL: Transmission: Four-speed manual (floor shift) standard on Horizon/Turismo w/1.7-liter engine: (1st) 3.45:1; (2nd) 1.94:1; (3rd) 1.29:1; (4th) 0.97:1; (Rev) 3.17:1. Four-speed manual (floor shift) standard on Reliant and Horizon/Turismo w/1.6- or 2.2-liter engine: (1st) 3.29:1; (2nd) 1.89:1; (3rd) 1.21:1; (4th) 0.88:1; (Rev) 3.14:1. Five-speed manual optional on Horizon/Turismo: (1st) 3.29:1; (2nd) 1.89:1; (3rd) 1.21:1; (4th) 0.88:1; (5th) 0.72:1; (Rev) 3.14:1. TorqueFlite three-speed automatic standard on Gran Fury and Reliant w/2.6-liter engine, optional on others. Gran Fury gear ratios: (1st) 2.74:1; (2nd) 1.54:1; (3rd) 1.00:1; (Rev) 2.22:1. Horizon/Turismo/Reliant ratios: (1st) 2.69:1; (2nd) 1.55:1; (3rd) 1.00:1; (Rev) 2.10:1. Standard final drive ratio: (Horizon/Turismo) 2.69:1 w/4spd, 2.59:1 w/auto.; (Horizon/Turismo w/2.2-liter four) 2.20:1 w/5spd, 2.78:1 w/auto.; (Reliant) 2.69:1 w/4spd, 2.20:1 w/5spd, 2.78:1 w/auto.; (Gran Fury) 2.94:1. Steering: (Horizon/Turismo/Reliant) rack and pinion; (Gran Fury) recirculating ball. Suspension: (Horizon/Turismo) Iso-Strut independent coil front w/anti-sway bar, semi-independent trailing arm coil rear w/available anti-sway bar; (Reliant) Iso-Strut front with integral linkless antisway bar, flex-arm beam rear axle w/trailing links and coil springs; (Gran Fury) front transverse torsion bars and anti-sway bar, semi-elliptic rear leaf springs. Brakes: Front disc, rear drum. Ignition: Electronic. Body construction: Unibody. Fuel tank: 13 gal. exc. (Gran Fury) 18 gal.

DRIVETRAIN OPTIONS: Engines: 2.2-liter four: Horizon/Turismo ($134). 2.6-liter four: Reliant ($259). 318 cu. in., 2Bbl. V-8: Gran Fury ($225). Transmission/Differential: Five-speed trans.: Horizon/Turismo/Reliant ($75). TorqueFlite: Horiz/Tur/Reliant ($439). Performance axle ratio: Horiz/Tur/Reliant ($22). Power Accessories: Power steering: Horiz/Tur/Reliant ($214). Suspension: H.D. susp.: Horizon 4dr. ($34); Reliant/G. Fury ($26). Other: 500-amp battery: Reliant/G. Fury ($43). Max. cooling: Horizon/Turismo/Reliant ($141). California emission system ($75). High-altitude emission system (NC).

HORIZON/TURISMO CONVENIENCE/APPEARANCE OPTIONS: Option Packages: Same selection and prices as equivalent Dodge Omni and Charger models; see Dodge listing.

RELIANT CONVENIENCE/APPEARANCE OPTIONS: Same selection and prices as Dodge Aries; see Dodge listing.

GRAN FURY CONVENIENCE/APPEARANCE OPTIONS: Option Packages: Basic group ($1308). Light pkg. ($147). Protection group ($132). Comfort/Convenience: Air conditioning, semi-auto ($787). Rear defroster, electric ($138). Automatic speed control ($174). Power windows ($255). Power door locks ($159). Power decklid release ($40). Illuminated entry system ($75). Leather- wrapped steering wheel ($53). Tilt steering wheel ($99). Digital clock ($64). Intermittent wipers ($52). Mirrors: Remote driver's ($23). Dual remote, chrome ($67). Lighted vanity, right ($61). Entertainment: AM/FM stereo radio ($109). Electronic-tuning AM/FM stereo ($154-$263); w/cassette ($293-$402). Dual front speakers ($28). Premium speakers ($126). Power antenna ($60). Radio delete ($56 credit). Exterior Trim: Power glass sunroof ($1041). Full vinyl roof ($172). Vinyl bodyside moldings ($57). Upper door frame moldings ($44). Bodyside/deck/hood stripe ($109). Body sound insulation ($43). Undercoating ($41). Interior: Vinyl bench seat ($60). Trunk dress-up ($54). Wheels and Tires: Premium wheel covers ($94). Wire wheel covers ($257). P205/75R15 SBR WSW ($116). Conventional spare ($63).

HISTORY: Introduced: October 1, 1982. Model year production: Chrysler reported a total of 240,837 passenger cars shipped. Calendar year production: 310,748. Calendar year sales by U.S. dealers: 265,608. Model year sales by U.S. dealers: 265,564 (not incl. 44,534 captive imports).

Historical Footnotes: Horizon and Reliant sales enjoyed a modest rise in the 1983 model year, while the rear-drive Gran Fury slipped a bit. On the import scene, Champ switched to the Colt name at the start of the 1983 model year, but sales continued slow. In fact, no imports did Chrysler-Plymouth much good in sales.

1984 PLYMOUTH

After a long history under Chrysler product hoods, the old familiar Slant Six engine was gone. Gran Fury now came only with the 318 cu. in. V-8. Reliant's optional 2.6-four, built by Mitsubishi, gained 8 horsepower. "Match it. If you can" was this year's catalog slogan. The Turismo coupe got a significant restyle, while Horizon and Reliant added a new grille design.

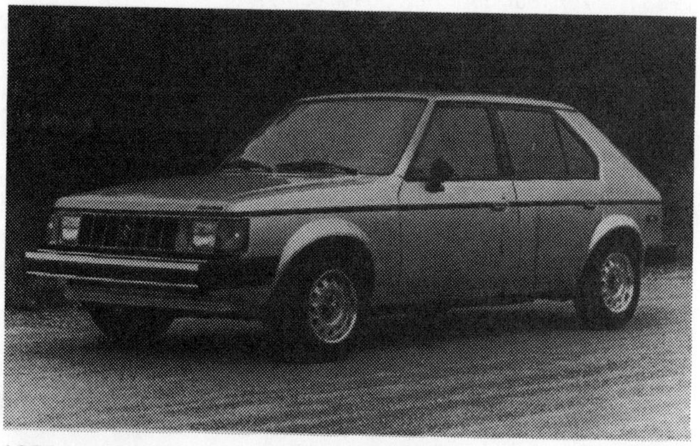

1984 Horizon four-door hatchback (CM)

HORIZON — SERIES M — FOUR — Described as "an American Value Classic," Plymouth's subcompact sedan gained an altered front-end look this year. Horizon's new grille consisted of a bright surrounding frame that contained six narrow bright vertical bars, with center pentastar emblem, all over a horizontal-pattern black background. New single rectangular recessed halogen headlamps and amber wraparound park/signal lamps were similar to 1983, with 'Plymouth' block lettering again above the left headlamp. Bodies were treated to chip-resistant lower bodyside urethane primer. The base model's Euro treatment included blackout bodyside and liftgate moldings, black windshield and back window moldings, black belt moldings and upper door frames, and black driver's remote mirror. Among its standard equipment, Horizon had a 335-amp maintenance-free battery. A new instrument panel held three round gauges, and a trip odometer. All-weather steel-belted radial tires rode 13 in. argent steel wheels with bright black hub covers, wheel nuts and trim rings. Bright bumpers held black rub strips and long end caps. Inside were new cloth/vinyl contoured low-back bucket seats with adjustable head restraints and recliners, a four-spoke sport steering wheel with center pad, passenger vanity mirror, and folding rear shelf security panel. The standard 1.6-liter engine and four-speed transaxle was rated 34 MPG (49 highway) in EPA mileage estimates. As before, a 2.2-liter four was available, and either a five-speed manual or three- speed automatic transaxle. The high-output 2.2-liter, introduced in 1983 on Dodge's Shelby Charger, became optional on Horizon/Turismo this year. Horizon SE (which replaced the former Custom line) carried a new digital AM radio with electronic/manual tuning and digital clock, sport cloth/vinyl high-back bucket seats with integral headrests and recliners, carpeted cargo area trim panels, remote driver's chrome mirror, and SBR narrow whitewalls with new deluxe wheel covers. SE also included bright liftgate window, upper door frame, sill, and belt moldings; and bright/black bodyside and liftgate moldings. Body colors were: Spice Brown or Charcoal Gray metallic; Beige, Glacier Blue or Radiant Silver crystal coat; Nightwatch Blue; Graphic Red; White and Black. Garnet Red pearl coat cost extra, and SE could have a choice of three two-tones. Options included electronic-tuning stereo systems, cruise control, and a rear wiper/washer.

TURISMO — SERIES M — FOUR — Up front, Turismo's most noticeable appearance change was a switch from single headlamps to quad rectangular units, in a new soft front-end design. The grille was similar to 1983, though: just two wide slots (separated by a single horizontal bar) in the sloping body-color panel. Below the new integral bumper rub strip was a single, much larger slot, flanked by recessed parking/signal lamps. Along the bodysides ran new wide soft-touch protective moldings. Not only was a different quarter-window applique used, but the large far- rear triangular window of previous coupe models was gone. This year's design held only two side windows, with a horizontally-ribbed trim panel stretching from the quarter window back to the liftgate. Wide wraparound taillamps with horizontally-ribbed lenses had square backup lenses toward the center, near the license plate opening. New deluxe wheel covers highlighted the 13 in. steel-belted radial tires. This was the first significant restyle since the coupe's introduction in 1979. Standard equipment included the Peugeot-built

1984 Turismo 2.2 two-door hatchback (CM)

1.6-liter four-cylinder engine, four-speed manual transaxle, power brakes, tinted glass, a maintenance-free battery, power liftgate release, and driver's black remote mirror. Cloth/vinyl low-back bucket seats came in a choice of red, blue, beige or charcoal/silver or brown/saddle two-tone. Solid body colors were the same as Horizon, and Turismo could have a choice of four two-tones. Turismo 2.2 featured the high-output 2.2-liter engine and new close-ratio five-speed transaxle, along with a performance exhaust sytem, new rear spoiler, sport suspension, dual remote sport (black) mirrors, and new 14 in. Rallye wheels with low-profile SBR raised-black-letter tires. Large 'Turismo 2.2' tape graphics went near the base of each door, while the hood no longer held a simulated scoop. Turismo 2.2 came only in two-tone paint treatments, different from the standard model; but the secondary color was applied only along the lower edge of the body, making the two-tone less obvious. A new Rallye instrument cluster held a tachometer, trip odometer, voltmeter, temp, fuel and oil pressure gauges. An electronic-tuning AM radio with digital clock was standard. Cloth/vinyl low-back reclining bucket seats were standard, with high-back buckets available. Among the options was Ultimate Sound stereo with a cassette player, four speakers, and Dolby noise reduction. Turismos used an Iso-Strut front suspension with integral linkless anti-sway bar. At the rear was a beam axle and trailing arm system with coil springs, track bar, and torsion-tube anti-roll control. Turismo 2.2 added a rear anti-sway bar. Chrysler reported that 8,060 Duster packages were installed, though that option wasn't announced at introduction time.

1984 Reliant coupe (CM)

RELIANT — SERIES P — FOUR — Plymouth's six-model compact lineup was the same as 1983: base two-door or four-door sedan, Custom wagon, and SE two- or four-door sedan and wagon. Base engine remained the 2.2-liter Trans4. Optional again was the Mitsubishi-built 2.6-liter, which added horsepower this year with a compression boost and recalibrated spark/carburetion. Brakes had a dual proportioning valve. Both a five-speed manual transaxle and three-speed TorqueFlite were available. This year's restyled grille consisted of two horizontal and one vertical thin bright bars, surrounded by a heavier upper and side molding, with pentastar emblem in the middle. Clear vertical rectangular parking lamps stood between the grille and recessed single rectangular headlamps, with wraparound amber marker lenses at the outside. Color-keyed front/rear bumper strips were new. So were wide taillamps with horizontally-ribbed lenses, which didn't quite reach the quarter panel tips. Backup lenses sat toward the center, alongside the license plate opening. Wagons had new wraparound taillamps. Reliant's Iso-Strut front suspension with integral linkless anti-sway bar was reworked. Rear suspension was a beam axle and trailing arm design with track bar and torsion tube anti-roll control. The gas tank grew to 14 gallons this year. All radios had electronic tuning and a built-in digital clock. A new instrument cluster held analog gauges and a trip odometer. Standard equipment included a maintenance-free battery, halogen headlamps, new locking glovebox, vinyl bench seats, deluxe wheel covers, power brakes, two-speed wipers, P175/80R13 SBR tires, and bumper rub strips. SE carried a Special Edition plaque on the rear roof pillar. Standard SE fittings included twin vertical quarter-window (or back door window) louvers, plus bright moldings for decklid, backlight, windshield, upper door frames, belt, and taillamps. Reliant SE cloth-trim vinyl bench seats had a center armrest. Also inside was a new woodtone (upper/lower) instrument panel, as opposed to the base Reliant's upper woodtone treatment only. An AM radio was standard on SE, and on the Custom wagon. Body colors were: Crimson Red, Garnet Red or Mink Brown pearl coat, Beige or Glacier Blue crystal coat, Nightwatch Blue, Black, Charcoal or Radiant Silver crystal coat, or White. Two two-tones were available on four-door models.

GRAN FURY — SERIES B — V-8 — Apart from the loss of the six-cylinder powerplant, the Mbodied Gran Fury changed little. The 318 cu. in. (5.2- liter) V-8, optional for several years, now became standard. Gran Fury now rode larger (P205/75R15) steel-belted radial whitewall tires. The standard AM radio had digital readouts and a built-in digital clock. Other standard equipment included power brakes and steering, front bumper guards, carpeting, cigarette lighter, tinted glass, halogen headlamps, dual horns, courtesy lights, day/night mirror, and a cloth/vinyl bench seat with center armrest. Gran Fury displayed moldings for the drip rail, windshield, belt, wheel openings, and sill. Options included a full vinyl roof, power glass sunroof, power windows and door locks, and wire wheel covers. Available this year was a 60/40 cloth-upholstered front seat with center rear armrest. A total of 6,661 police packages were installed on Gran Fury models, 6,516 of which were reported as being for police use.

I.D. DATA: Plymouth again had a 17-symbol Vehicle Identification Number (VIN) on the upper left corner of the instrument panel, visible through the windshield. Coding was similar to 1983. Model year code changed to 'E' for 1984. Two engine codes were dropped ('B' for L4105 and 'H' for L6225) and one was added: 'F' H.O. L4135 2Bbl. Code 'R' for Windsor assembly plant was dropped. Engine number locations are the same as 1981-83.

HORIZON (FOUR)

Model Number	Body/Style Number	Body Type & Seating	Factory Price	Shipping Weight	Production Total
ME	44	4-dr. Hatch-5P	6138	2095	62,903
MH	44	4-dr. SE Hatch-5P	6456	2160	15,661

TURISMO (FOUR)

MH	24	2-dr. Hatch-5P	6868	2120	38,835

TURISMO 2.2 (FOUR)

MP	24	2-dr. Hatch-5P	7662	2300	10,881

RELIANT (FOUR)

PL	21	2-dr. Sedan-6P	7235	2335	14,533
PL	41	4-dr. Sedan-6P	7347	2340	72,595

RELIANT CUSTOM (FOUR)

PH	45	4-dr. Sta Wag-6P	8134	2430	39,207

RELIANT SE (FOUR)

PH	21	2-dr. Sedan-6P	7861	2345	5,287
PH	41	4-dr. Sedan-6P	7987	2375	16,223
PP	45	4-dr. Sta Wag-6P	8593	2480	4,338

1984 Gran Fury four-door sedan (CM)

GRAN FURY SALON (V-8)

BL	41	4-dr. Sedan-6P	9655	3470	14,516

Gran Fury Production Note: Of total production, 6,516 were for police use.

MODEL NUMBER NOTE: Some sources identify models using the VIN data to indicate Car Line, Price Class and Body Style. Example: base Reliant four-door (PL41) has the equivalent number P26, which translates to Reliant line, Low price class, and four-door sedan body. See I.D. Data section for breakdown.

ENGINE DATA: BASE FOUR (Horizon, Turismo): Inline, overhead-cam four-cylinder. Cast iron block; aluminum head. Displacement: 97.3 cu. in. (1.6 liters). Bore & stroke: 3.17 x 3.07 in. Compression ratio: 8.8:1. Brake horsepower: 64 at 4800 R.P.M. Torque: 87 lbs.-ft. at 2800 R.P.M. Five main bearings. Solid valve lifters. Carburetor: 2Bbl. Holley 6520. VIN Code: A. BASE FOUR (Reliant, Turismo 2.2); OPTIONAL (Horizon, Turismo): Inline, overhead-cam four-cylinder. Cast iron block; aluminum head. Displacement: 135 cu. in. (2.2 liters). Bore & stroke: 3.44 x 3.62 in. Compression ratio: 9.0:1. Brake horsepower: 96 at 5200 R.P.M. (Turismo 2.2, 101 at 5200 R.P.M.). Torque: 119 lbs.-ft. at 3200 R.P.M. (Turismo 2.2, 124 at 3200 R.P.M.). Five main bearings. Hydraulic valve lifters. Carburetor: 2Bbl. Holley 6520. VIN Code: C. OPTIONAL FOUR (Turismo, Turismo): High-performance version of 135 cu. in. four above, with fuel injection Horsepower: 110 at 5200 R.P.M. Torque: 129 lbs.- ft. at 3600 R.P.M. VIN Code: F. OPTIONAL FOUR (Reliant): Inline, overhead-cam four-cylinder. Cast iron block; aluminum head. Displacement: 156 cu. in. (2.6 liters). Bore & stroke: 3.59 x 3.86 in. Compression ratio: 8.7:1. Brake horsepower: 101 at 4800 R.P.M. Torque: 140 lbs.-ft. at 2800 R.P.M. Five main bearings. Solid valve lifters. Carburetor: 2Bbl. Mikuni. VIN Code: G. BASE V-8 (Gran Fury): 90-degree, overhead valve V-8. Cast iron block and head. Displacement: 318 cu. in. (5.2 liters). Bore & stroke: 3.91 x 3.31 in. Compression ratio: 8.7:1. Brake horsepower: 130 at 4000 R.P.M. Torque: 235 lbs.-ft. at 1600 R.P.M. Five main bearings. Hydraulic valve lifters. Carburetor: 2Bbl. Carter BBD. VIN Code: P. POLICE V-8 (Gran Fury): Same as 318 cu. in. V-8 above, with 4Bbl. carburetor Compression ratio: 8.4:1. Horsepower: 165 at 4400 R.P.M. Torque: 240 lbs.-ft. at 1600 R.P.M.

CHASSIS DATA: Wheelbase: (Horizon) 99.1 in.; (Turismo) 96.6 in.; (Reliant) 100.3 in.; (Gran Fury) 112.7 in. Overall Length: (Horizon) 164.8 in.; (Turismo) 174.8 in.; (Reliant) 176.1 in.; (Reliant wag) 176.2 in.; (Gran Fury) 205.7 in. Height: (Horizon) 53.1 in.; (Turismo) 50.8 in.; (Reliant 2dr.) 52.3 in.; (Reliant 4-dr.) 52.7 in.; (Reliant wag) 52.4 in.; (Gran Fury) 55.3 in. Width: (Horizon) 65.8 in.; (Reliant) 68.6 in.; (Gran Fury) 74.2 in. Front Tread: (Horizon/Turismo) 56.1 in.; (Reliant) 57.6 in.; (Gran Fury) 60.0 in. Rear Tread: (Horizon/Turismo) 55.6 in.; (Reliant) 57.0 in.; (Gran Fury) 59.5 in. Standard Tires: (Horizon/Turismo) P165/80R13 SBR; (Turismo 2.2) P195/60R14 SBR RBL; (Reliant) P175/80R13 SBR BSW; (Gran Fury) P205/75R15.

TECHNICAL: Transmission: Four-speed manual (floor shift) standard on Reliant and Horizon/Turismo w/1.6- or 2.2-liter engine: (1st) 3.29:1; (2nd) 1.89:1; (3rd) 1.21:1; (4th) 0.88:1; (Rev) 3.14:1. Five-speed manual optional on Horizon/Turismo/Reliant: (1st) 3.29:1; (2nd) 2.08:1; (3rd) 1.45:1; (4th) 1.04:1; (5th) 0.72:1; (Rev) 3.14:1. TorqueFlite three-speed automatic standard on Gran Fury and required on Reliant w/2.6-liter engine, optional on others. Gran Fury gear ratios: (1st) 2.74:1; (2nd) 1.54:1; (3rd) 1.00:1; (Rev) 2.22:1. Horizon/Turismo/Reliant ratios: (1st) 2.69:1; (2nd) 1.55:1; (3rd) 1.00:1; (Rev) 2.10:1. Standard final drive ratio: (Horizon/Turismo) 2.69:1 w/4spd; (Horizon/Turismo w/2.2-liter four) 2.20:1 w/5spd, 2.78:1 w/auto.; (Horizon/Turismo w/H.O. 2.2-liter) 2.57:1 w/5spd, 3.02:1 w/auto.; (Reliant) 2.69:1 w/4spd, 2.20:1 w/5spd, 2.78:1 w/auto., 3.02:1 w/2.6-liter; (Gran Fury) 2.26:1. Steering/Suspension/Brakes/Body: same as 1983. Fuel Tank: (Horizon/Turismo) 13 gal.; (Reliant) 14 gal.; (Gran Fury) 18 gal.

DRIVETRAIN OPTIONS: Engines: 2.2-liter four: Horizon/Turismo ($134). High-performance 2.2-liter: Horizon/Turismo ($256) exc. Turismo 2.2 ($122). 2.6-liter four: Reliant ($271). Transmission/Differential: Five-speed trans.: Horizon/Turismo/Reliant ($75). TorqueFlite: Horiz/Tur/Reliant ($439). Performance axle ratio: Horiz/Tur/Reliant ($22). Power Accessories: Power steering: Horiz/Tur/Reliant ($219). Suspension: H.D. susp.: Horizon 4dr. ($36); Reliant wag, G. Fury ($26). Other: 500-amp battery: Reliant/G. Fury ($44). Max. cooling: Horiz/Tur/Reliant ($141). California emission system ($99).

HORIZON/TURISMO CONVENIENCE/APPEARANCE OPTIONS: Option Packages: Same selection and prices as equivalent Dodge Omni and Charger models (but without GLH package); see Dodge listing.

RELIANT CONVENIENCE/APPEARANCE OPTIONS: Same selection and prices as equivalent Dodge Aries models; see Dodge listing.

GRAN FURY CONVENIENCE/APPEARANCE OPTIONS: Option Packages: Basic group ($1351). Light pkg. ($153). Protection group ($133). Comfort/Convenience: Air conditioning, semi-auto ($792). Rear defroster, electric ($143). Automatic speed control ($179). Power windows ($260). Power door locks ($175). Power decklid release ($40). Illuminated entry system ($75). Leather-wrapped steering wheel ($60). Tilt steering wheel ($110). Intermittent wipers ($53). Mirrors: Remote driver's ($24). Dual remote, chrome ($67). Lighted vanity, right ($58). Electronic-Tuning Radios: AM/FM stereo ($125). Seek/scan AM/FM stereo ($125-250); w/cassette ($264-$389). Premium speakers ($126). Power antenna ($60). Radio delete ($39 credit). Exterior: Power glass sunroof ($1041). Full vinyl roof ($185). Vinyl bodyside moldings ($57). Upper door frame moldings ($46). Bodyside/deck/hood stripe ($109). Body sound insulation ($66). Undercoating ($43). Interior: Vinyl split-back bench seat ($60). Trunk dress-up ($57). Wheels/Tires: Premium wheel covers ($96). Wire wheel covers ($263). Conventional spare ($93).

HISTORY: Introduced: October 2, 1983. Model year production: Chrysler reported a total of 294,979 passenger cars shipped. Calendar year production: 378,242. Calendar year sales by U.S. dealers: 289,244. Model year sales by U.S. dealers: 277,171 (not incl. 46,477 captive imports).

Historical Footnotes: Horizon sales rose 49.1 percent for the model year; Turismo, 24.5 percent. Reliant fared less well, as sales dropped nearly 9 percent. Like other Chrysler products, Plymouths came with a 5/50 (five-year, 50,000-mile) powertrain and outer panel rust-through warranty that went into effect after the basic 12-month/12,000-mile warranty expired. As for Plymouth's captive imports, an optional turbo engine was added to Colt, a new Colt Vista appeared, and Sapporo was replaced by Conquest (based on Mitsubishi's Starion).

1985 PLYMOUTH

New to Plymouth was Chrysler's turbocharged 2.2-liter four, now offered as an option on the new Caravelle (which was actually the previous year's Chrysler E Class under another name). Instead of a new slogan for the full-line factory sales catalog, Plymouth just added a set of parentheses to the 1984 version, advising customers to "Match them. (If You Can!)" Also promoted was the 5/50 Protection Plan. Plymouths used more galvanized metal, to help prevent rusting. In addition to urethane lower body coating, all bodies got a final clear crystal coat over the acrylic paint. A selection of discount option packages could reduce the total price paid for extra equipment. All Plymouths had new high-output alternators. Manual-shift models had a new shift indicator light. This year's body colors (not available on every model) were: Black, Nightwatch Blue, Graphic Red, Cream, Gold Dust, Radiant Silver, Crimson Red, Spice, Ice Blue, and White crystal coat; plus Gunmetal Blue, Mink Brown, Garnet Red or Charcoal pearl coat. Five two-tone combinations also were offered: four on Horizon and/or Turismo, and two on Caravelle.

HORIZON — SERIES M — FOUR — Three body colors were new, but Horizon looked just about the same this year, with its bright vertical grille bars over a black background and center pentastar. "An American value with European flair" was Chrysler's way of describing the subcompact base sedan, promoted for its Euro-styling. For the most part, all that meant was a set of black moldings rather than the bright-and-black ones mounted on the step-up SE model. A new shift indicator light came with manual-transaxle models. Tinted glass became standard, but the former

1985 Horizon four-door hatchback (CM)

dual-note horn changed back to single. Standard equipment included power brakes, 1.6-liter four-cylinder engine, four-speed manual transaxle, bumper rub strips, lighter, tethered gas cap, tinted glass, locking glovebox, black remote-control driver's mirror, day/night mirror, and intermittent wipers. As before, the 2.2-liter Trans4 engine was available, along with a five-speed gearbox or three-speed TorqueFlite. Cloth/vinyl low-back bucket seats were standard on the base model; high-back buckets on the SE. Other SE extras included an electronic-tuning AM radio with built-in digital clock, remote-control chrome driver's mirror, and whitewall tires. New options included an AM stereo (and FM stereo) radio, and high-back bucket seats with dual recliners. Neither the luggage rack nor the heavy-duty suspension, formerly optional, were offered this year. One interior trim color was new.

1985 Turismo Duster two-door hatchback (CM)

TURISMO — SERIES M — FOUR — Plymouth's subcompact coupe carried on with the same overall appearance as in 1984, when it lost the old triangular back quarter windows and switched to quad headlamps. Turismo's grille consisted of two wide slots, one above the other in the body-color panel, with amber parking lamps below the bumper rub strip. Wide ribbed wraparound taillamps held backup lenses near their inner ends. Base engine, as before, was the Peugeot-built 1.6-liter four with four-speed manual transaxle. Cloth/vinyl low-back front bucket seats with dual recliners were standard. All Turismos had gauges in a Rallye cluster, while manual-shift models (except the Turismo 2.2) added a new shift indicator light. Standard equipment included a power liftgate release, tinted glass, halogen headlamps, driver's remote mirror, power brakes, and intermittent wipers. A new Ultimate Sound radio was available. Turismo 2.2, billed as "a serious driving machine," came with the High-Output 110-horsepower 2.2-liter engine and five-speed close-ratio manual gearbox. This year's version added an air dam, front fender extensions and sill spoilers. Also standard: a sport suspension including rear anti-sway bar, performance exhaust, and 14 in. Rallye wheels that held P195/60R14 raised-letter tires. An electronic-tuning AM radio with digital clock and dual black aereo remote mirrors were standard too. Available for the base Turismo was a Duster package, with a few sporty-look features but no powertrain changes. The package included a rear spoiler, bodyside and liftgate tape stripes, high-back cloth/vinyl bucket seats, 'Duster' and 'Plymouth' decals on front fenders and liftgate, and 13 in. Rallye wheels. A total of 27,444 Duster packages were installed. Chrysler's 2.2-liter four was available for the base Turismo, along with five-speed manual gearing or three-speed TorqueFlite.

1985 Reliant four-door station wagon (CM)

RELIANT — SERIES P — FOUR — Eight restyled models in three price classes made up this year's lineup, two more than in 1984. Modified body styling included more rounded corners. The rear deck was slightly higher, while the nose looked a bit longer. Reliant wore an all-new grille: a simple symmetrical crosshatch pattern within a bright frame that tapered inward at the base. In the grille's center was a pentastar emblem. Housings for the single rectangular headlamps tapered to match the grille edges. Outboard were amber wraparound parking/signal lamp lenses with two thin horizontal

divider strips. Their housings curved a bit at the lower outside corners. Though similar to the 1984 version, with backup lenses adjacent to the license plate opening, this year's taillamps grew larger and wrapped around the quarter panels, angled a bit at the front. Marker lenses moved down into the bodyside moldings. Reliants had a standard 2.2-liter Trans4 engine and four-speed manual transaxle, power brakes, dual-path Iso-Strut front suspension, rack-and-pinion steering, two-spoke steering wheel, vinyl bench seats and door trim panels, and inside hood release. A new padded-top instrument panel held a set of gauges, including a trip odometer and new fuel-economy shift indicator light (with manual transaxle only). Instrument panels showed more black trim than before. A new flat-face climate control panel eliminated protruding buttons. Door panels held new map pockets. Stepping up, Reliant SE added intermittent wipers, a cloth bench seat with fold-down center armrest, electronic-tuning AM radio with built-in digital clock, woodtone lower instrument panel bezel, passenger vanity mirror, and black upper door frames. LE added a passenger vanity mirror with map/reading light, cloth/vinyl bench seat with adjustable head restraints and fold-down center armrest, woodtone upper/lower instrument panel bezels, dual horns, trunk light, and black remote left mirror. The LE station wagon had a standard tonneau cover. SE and LE also carried black/bright belt, C-pillar, and drip rail moldings. Two-doors had quarter-window louvers. Optional were the Mitsubishi-built 2.6-liter four, five-speed manual transaxle, and TorqueFlite. New options included an electronic-tuning radios with AM stereo, heavy-duty suspension with gas-filled shocks and struts, and full-length console (with bucket seats). Reliant's body colors were: Black, Ice Blue, Nightwatch Blue, Cream, Gold Dust, Radiant Silver, Crimson Red or White crystal coat; Garnet Red, Gunmetal Blue or Mink Brown pearl coat.

1985 Caravelle SE four-door sedan (CM)

CARAVELLE — SERIES J — FOUR — New to Plymouth but not to the Chrysler product line was a new six-passenger, front-drive four-door sedan, related to the Kcar Reliant. Riding a longer 103.3 in. wheelbase, Caravelle measured 185.7 in. overall. Base engine was the fuel-injected 2.2-liter OHC Trans4, with two options available: the Mitsubishi-built 2.6-liter, or Chrysler's own 146-horsepower turbocharged 2.2-liter four. Chrysler's was the only domestic turbo engine that used a water-cooled bearing housing. A simple crosshatch-patterned, slanted grille peaked forward at the center and aligned with the quad rectangular headlamps. Each pair of headlamps was separated by a narrow strip of the body-color panel. Small rectangular parking lamps went down below the narrow protective bumper strip, which ran back to the front wheel opening to contain marker lenses. The bumper strip also peaked forward at its center, to match the grille shape. Below it was a single wide slot, roughly grille width. Caravelle's bodyside featured a sculptured look, with twin creases: one just above the door handles, the other in line with bumper rub strips. The hood also held two creases, which ran forward to meet the grille. A stand-up pentastar hood ornament was standard. Described as "tastefully subtle," the wide taillamp lenses each were divided into six side-by-side sections, the inner one containing a backup lens and the outer red one wrapping around the quarter panel. Each unit also held two bright horizontal divider strips. On the decklid were 'Plymouth' and 'Caravelle' block letters, along with a center pentastar badge. The recessed license plate housing aligned with the taillamps. Bumper strips extended forward to the wheel opening and contained rear marker lenses to match the front lenses. Ample standard equipment included a Graphic Message Center with warning lights, power rack-and-pinion steering, power brakes, three-speed TorqueFlite, intermittent wipers, halogen headlamps, twin mirrors (left one remote-controlled) and AM radio with built-in clock. Also standard: wheel covers, P185/70R14 steel-belted radial whitewall tires, remote decklid and fuel filler door releases, and warning chimes. Among the options: an 11-message Electronic Voice Alert system, Ultimate Sound stereo, cast aluminum wheels, and wire wheel covers. The six-window design held six passengers on standard cloth/vinyl bench seats with a fold-down center armrest up front. An optional 50/50 front seat had dual center armrests and recliners, as well as center consolettes and seatback pockets. A two-spoke steeering wheel (both spokes aimed downward) was standard, as was a woodtone instrument panel. Only one price level was offered at first: the premium SE.

1985 Gran Fury four-door sedan (CM)

GRAN FURY — SERIES B — V-8 — With new roller lifters and a compression boost, Gran Fury's standard two-barrel carbureted 318 cu. in. V-8 gained 10 horsepower this year. Otherwise, not much was new on Plymouth's full-size rear-drive four-door sedan, which continued to appeal mainly to fleet buyers. 'Plymouth' block letters were inset across the grille header. The grille itself had a very "busy" look, with crosshatching within each of eight side-by-side vertical segments. The crosshatch pattern continued in a series of squarish segments that extended outward beneath the quad rectangular headlamps. Those segments contained the parking lenses and met similarly-patterned

amber side marker lenses at the fender tips. Backup lenses were inset into the inner ends of Gran Fury's wide wraparound taillamps. 'Gran Fury' script stood on front fenders, at the cowl. Bright moldings around wheel openings were standard, as was a cloth/vinyl front bench seat with folding center armrest. Other standards: tinted glass, power brakes and steering, front bumper guards, open-frame pentastar hood ornament, halogen headlamps, P205/75R15 steel-belted radial whitewalls, and electronic-tuning AM radio with digital clock. Sole engine was the 318 cu. in. (5.2-liter) V-8 with three-speed TorqueFlite. New this year was a standard 400-amp maintenance-free, low-profile battery. Newly optional: an Ultimate Sound AM stereo/FM stereo radio with cassette player and graphic equalizer. Color-keyed vinyl bodyside moldings also were available. So was a 60/40 velour bench seat. As usual, a high-performance Police V-8 and heavy-duty suspension could be ordered. A total of 7,152 Gran Fury sedans had the AHB police package.

I.D. DATA: Plymouth again had a 17-symbol Vehicle Identification Number (VIN) on the upper left corner of the instrument panel, visible through the windshield. Coding was similar to 1984. The first digit indicates Country: '1' U.S.A. The second symbol is Make: 'P' Plymouth. Third is Vehicle Type: '3' passenger car. The next symbol ('B') indicates manual seatbelts. Symbol five is Car Line: 'M' Horizon; 'P' Reliant; 'J' Caravelle; 'B' Gran Fury. Symbol six is Series (price class): '1' Economy; '2' Low; '3' Medium; '4' High; '5' Premium. Symbol seven is Body Style: '1' 2-dr. sedan; '4' 2-dr. hatchback; '6' 4-dr. sedan; '8' 4-dr. hatchback; '9' 4-dr. wagon. Eighth is the Engine Code: 'A' L497 2Bbl.; 'C' L4135 2Bbl.; 'D' L4135 FI; 'E' Turbo L4135 FI; 'F' H.O. L4135 2Bbl.; 'G' L4156 2Bbl.; 'P' V8318 2Bbl. Next comes a check digit. Symbol ten indicates Model Year: 'F' 1985. Symbol eleven is Assembly Plant: 'A' Detroit; 'D' Belvidere, IL; 'F' Newark, DE; 'G' or 'X' St. Louis. The last six digits make up the sequential serial number, starting with 100001. Engine numbers and Body Code Plates are in the same locations as 1981-84.

HORIZON (FOUR)

Model Number	Body/Style Number	Body Type & Seating	Factory Price	Shipping Weight	Production Total
LME	44	4-dr. Hatch-5P	5999	2095	71,846
LMH	44	4-dr. SE Hatch-5P	6342	2120	16,165

TURISMO (FOUR)

LMH	24	2-dr. Hatch-5P	6584	2160	44,377

TURISMO 2.2 (FOUR)

LMP	24	2-dr. Hatch-5P	7515	2300	7,785

RELIANT (FOUR)

KPL	21	2-dr. Sedan-6P	6924	2335	11,317
KPL	41	4-dr. Sedan-6P	7039	2340	46,972

RELIANT SE (FOUR)

KPM	21	2-dr. Sedan-6P	7321	2345	9,530
KPM	41	4-dr. Sedan-6P	7439	2375	27,231
KPH	45	4-dr. Sta Wag-6P	7909	2480	27,489

RELIANT LE (FOUR)

KPH	21	2-dr. Sedan-6P	7659	2345	4,110
KPH	41	4-dr. Sedan-6P	7792	2375	7,072
KPP	45	4-dr. Sta Wag-6P	8378	2480	4,017

CARAVELLE SE (FOUR)

EJH	41	4-dr. Sedan-6P	9007	N/A	39,971

GRAN FURY SALON (V-8)

MBL	41	4-dr. Sedan-6P	9658	3470	19,102

MODEL NUMBER NOTE: Some sources identify models using the VIN data to indicate Car Line, Price Class and Body Style. Example: base Reliant four-door (KPL41) has the equivalent number P26, which translates to Reliant line, Low price class, and four-door sedan body. See I.D. Data section for breakdown.

ENGINE DATA: BASE FOUR (Horizon, Turismo): Inline, overhead-cam four-cylinder. Cast iron block; aluminum head. Displacement: 97.3 cu. in. (1.6 liters). Bore & stroke: 3.17 x 3.07 in. Compression ratio: 8.8:1. Brake horsepower: 64 at 4800 R.P.M. Torque: 87 lbs.-ft. at 2800 R.P.M. Five main bearings. Solid valve lifters. Carburetor: 2Bbl. Holley 6520. VIN Code: A. **BASE FOUR** (Reliant); **OPTIONAL** (Horizon, Turismo): Inline, overhead-cam four-cylinder. Cast iron block; aluminum head. Displacement: 135 cu. in. (2.2 liters). Bore & stroke: 3.44 x 3.62 in. Compression ratio: 9.0:1. Brake horsepower: 96 at 5200 R.P.M. Torque: 119 lbs.-ft. at 3200 R.P.M. Five main bearings. Hydraulic valve lifters. Carburetor: 2Bbl. Holley 6520. VIN Code: C. **BASE FOUR** (Caravelle): Same as 135 cu. in. four above, but with electronic fuel injection. Horsepower: 99 at 5600 R.P.M. Torque: 121 lbs.-ft. at 3200 R.P.M. VIN Code: D. **BASE FOUR** (Turismo 2.2): High-output version of 135 cu. in. four, with fuel injection Compression: 9.6:1. Horsepower: 110 at 5600 R.P.M. Torque: 129 lbs.-ft. at 3600 R.P.M. VIN Code: F. **TURBO FOUR; OPTIONAL** (Caravelle): Same as 135 cu. in. four abouve, with EFI and turbocharger Compression: 8.1:1. Horsepower: 146 at 5200 R.P.M. Torque: 168 lbs.-ft. at 3200 R.P.M. VIN Code: E. **OPTIONAL FOUR** (Reliant, Caravelle): Inline, overhead-cam four-cylinder. Cast iron block; aluminum head. Displacement: 156 cu. in. (2.6 liters). Bore & stroke: 3.59 x 3.86 in. Compression ratio: 8.7:1. Brake horsepower: 101 at 4800 R.P.M. Torque: 140 lbs.-ft. at 2800 R.P.M. Five main bearings. Solid valve lifters. Carburetor: 2Bbl. Mikuni. VIN Code: G. **BASE V-8** (Gran Fury): 90-degree, overhead valve V-8. Cast iron block and head. Displacement: 318 cu. in. (5.2 liters). Bore & stroke: 3.91 x 3.31 in. Compression ratio: 9.0:1. Brake

horsepower: 140 at 3600 R.P.M. Torque: 265 lbs.-ft. at 1600 R.P.M. Five main bearings. Hydraulic valve lifters. Carburetor: 2Bbl. Holley 6280. VIN Code: P. POLICE V-8 (Gran Fury): Same as 318 cu. in. V-8 above, with 4Bbl. carburetor Compression ratio: 8.0:1. Horsepower: 175 at 4000 R.P.M. Torque: 250 lbs.-ft. at 3200 R.P.M.

CHASSIS DATA: Wheelbase: (Horizon) 99.1 in.; (Turismo) 96.5 in.; (Reliant) 100.3 in.; (Caravelle) 103.3 in.; (Gran Fury) 112.7 in. Overall Length: (Horizon) 162.1 in.; (Turismo) 174.8 in.; (Reliant) 178.6 in.; (Reliant wag) 179.0 in.; (Caravelle) 185.7 in.; (Gran Fury) 205.7 in. Height: (Horizon) 53.0 in.; (Turismo) 50.7 in.; (Reliant 2dr.) 52.7 in.; (Reliant 4-dr.) 52.9 in.; (Reliant wag) 53.2 in.; (Caravelle) 53.1 in.; (Gran Fury) 55.3 in. Width: (Horizon) 66.2 in.; (Turismo) 65.9 in.; (Reliant) 68.0 in.; (Caravelle) 68.4 in.; (Gran Fury) 74.2 in. Front Tread: (Horizon/Turismo) 56.1 in.; (Reliant/Caravelle) 57.6 in.; (Gran Fury) 60.0 in. Rear Tread: (Horizon/Turismo) 55.7 in.; (Reliant/Caravelle) 57.2 in.; (Gran Fury) 59.5 in. Standard Tires: (Horizon/Turismo) P165/80R13 SBR BSW exc. SE, WSW; (Turismo 2.2) P195/60R14 SBR RBL; (Reliant) P175/80R13 SBR BSW; (Caravelle) P185/70R14 SBR WSW; (Gran Fury) P205/75R15 SBR WSW.

TECHNICAL: Transmission: Four-speed manual (floor shift) standard on Reliant and Horizon/Turismo w/1.6- or 2.2-liter engine: (1st) 3.29:1; (2nd) 1.89:1; (3rd) 1.21:1; (4th) 0.88:1; (Rev) 3.14:1. Five-speed manual optional on Horizon/Turismo, standard on 2.2-liter: (1st) 3.29:1; (2nd) 2.08:1; (3rd) 1.45:1; (4th) 1.04:1; (5th) 0.72:1; (Rev) 3.14:1. TorqueFlite three-speed automatic standard on Gran Fury and Caravelle, required on Reliant w/2.6-liter engine, optional on others. Gran Fury gear ratios: (1st) 2.74:1; (2nd) 1.54:1; (3rd) 1.00:1; (Rev) 2.22:1. Front-drive ratios: (1st) 2.69:1; (2nd) 1.55:1; (3rd) 1.00:1; (Rev) 2.10:1. Standard final drive ratio: (Horizon/Turismo) 2.69:1 w/4spd; (Horizon w/2.2-liter four) 2.20:1 w/5spd, 2.78:1 w/auto.; (Turismo w/2.2-liter) 2.20:1 w/5spd, 3.02:1 w/auto.; (Turismo w/H.O. 2.2-liter) 2.78:1 w/5spd; (Reliant) 2.69:1 w/4spd, 2.20:1 w/5spd, 2.78:1 w/auto., (Reliant w/2.6-liter or wagon) 3.02:1 w/auto.; (Caravelle) 3.02:1; (Gran Fury) 2.26:1. Steering: (Horizon/Turismo/Reliant/Caravelle) rack and pinion; (Gran Fury) recirculating ball. Suspension: (Horizon/Turismo) Iso-Strut independent coil front w/anti-sway bar, semi-independent trailing arm coil rear; (Reliant) Dual path Iso-Strut front w/linkless anti- sway bar, rear axle w/trailing flex arm and track bar; (Caravelle) Iso-Strut front w/linkless anti-sway bar, beam rear axle w/trailing arms and coil springs; (Gran Fury) front transverse torsion bars and anti-sway bar, semi-elliptic rear leaf springs. Brakes: Front disc, rear drum. Ignition: Electronic. Body construction: Unibody. Fuel tank: (Horizon/Turismo) 13 gal.; (Reliant/Caravelle) 14 gal.; (Gran Fury) 18 gal.

DRIVETRAIN OPTIONS: Engines: 2.2-liter four: Horizon/Turismo ($134); Turismo 2.2 (NC). Turbo 2.2-liter four: Caravelle ($610). 2.6-liter four: Reliant/Caravelle ($271). Transmission/Differential: Five-speed trans.: Horizon/Turismo/Reliant ($75). TorqueFlite: Horiz/Tur/Reliant ($439). Performance axle ratio: Horiz/Tur/Reliant ($22). Power Accessories: Power steering: Horizon/Turismo/Reliant ($219). Suspension: H.D. susp.: Reliant ($58); G. Fury ($26). Euro handling susp.: Caravelle ($57). Other: 500-amp battery: Reliant/Caravelle/G. Fury ($44). Max. cooling: Horizon/Turismo/Reliant ($141). California emission system ($99). High-altitude emissions (NC).

HORIZON/TURISMO CONVENIENCE/APPEARANCE OPTIONS: Option Packages: Duster pkg.: Turismo ($96-$115). Sun/Sound/Shade pkg.: Turismo/2.2 ($512). Auto. trans. discount pkg. ($765-$886). 2.2-liter engine and five-speed discount pkg. ($295-$408). Light group ($55-$84). Protection group ($88-$189). Note: Other Horizon/Turismo options similar to equivalent Dodge Omni/Charger models; see Dodge listing.

RELIANT CONVENIENCE/APPEARANCE OPTIONS: Same selection and prices as equivalent Dodge Aries models; see Dodge listing.

CARAVELLE CONVENIENCE/APPEARANCE OPTIONS: Option Packages: Popular equipment discount pkg. ($609). Protection pkg. ($81). Comfort/Convenience: Air cond. ($757). Rear defroster ($148). Auto. speed control ($179). Power windows ($270). Power door locks ($180). Power seat ($225). Illuminated entry system ($75). Tinted glass ($115). Electronic voice alert ($66). Leather-wrapped steering wheel ($50). Tilt steering wheel ($115). Lighting and Mirrors: Cornering lamps ($60). Dual power remote-control mirrors ($86). Lighted vanity mirror ($58). Electronic-tuning Radios w/digital clock: AM/FM stereo ($125). Seek/scan AM/FM stereo w/cassette ($299-$424). Ultimate sound stereo w/cassette ($509-$634). Premium speakers ($126). Radio delete ($56 credit). Exterior: Two-tone paint: cpe/sed ($187). Pearl coat paint ($40). Vinyl bodyside moldings ($55). Door edge protectors ($25). Bumper guards ($56). Undercoating ($43). Interior: Vinyl bench seat ($31). Cloth 50/50 bench seat ($304). Color-keyed mats ($45). Trunk dress-up ($51). Wheels and Tires: Wire wheel covers, locking ($272). Cast aluminum wheels ($370). Conventional spare tire ($83).

GRAN FURY CONVENIENCE/APPEARANCE OPTIONS: Option Packages: Equipment pkg.: Popular ($537). Salon luxury pkg. ($536). Light pkg. ($158). Protection group ($133). Comfort/Convenience: Air conditioning, semi-auto ($812). Rear defroster, electric ($148). Automatic speed control ($179). Power windows ($270). Power door locks ($180). Power decklid release ($40). Illuminated entry system ($75). Tilt steering wheel ($115). Intermittent wipers ($53). Mirrors: Remote driver's ($24). Dual remote chrome ($67). Electronic-Tuning Radios w/digital clock: AM/FM stereo ($125). Seek/scan AM/FM stereo w/cassette ($264-$389). Ultimate sound AM stereo/FM stereo w/cassette ($474-$599). Radio delete ($56 credit). Exterior: Full vinyl roof ($185). Pearl coat paint ($40). Vinyl bodyside moldings ($57). Upper door frame moldings ($46). Body sound insulation ($66). Undercoating ($43). Interior: Vinyl split-back bench seat ($60). Cloth/vinyl 60/40 seat ($312). Trunk dress-up ($56). Wheels/Tires: Premium turbine wheel covers ($96). Conventional spare ($93).

HISTORY: Introduced: October 2, 1984. Model year production: Chrysler reported a total of 336,984 passenger cars shipped. Calendar year production (U.S.): 369,486. Calendar year sales by U.S. dealers: 329,731. Model year sales by U.S. dealers: 333,100 (not incl. 46,015 imports).

Historical Footnotes: Prices on most models were cut as the model year opened, though they rose again later on, passing the 1984 levels. Horizon's price reduction was intended to make the car more competitive with Escort and Chevette. The Caravelle name, found on a domestic Plymouth model for the first time, had been used on a bigger rear-drive model in Canada. Gran Fury sales rose 32 percent for the model year, reaching 18,734. Horizon/Turismo sold well also, up by some 17 percent. Reliant (and its twin Dodge Aries) remained Chrysler's best sellers.

1986 PLYMOUTH

A new 153 cu. in. (2.5-liter) engine replaced the Mitsubishi 2.6-liter as optional equipment in the front-drive Reliant and Caravelle. The fuel-injected, overhead cam design, with 9.0:1 compression, was rated 100 horsepower at 4800 R.P.M. Derived from the 2.2-liter, it had a longer stroke. Twin nodular iron balance shafts counter-rotated at twice crankshaft speed to improve the engine's smoothness. Only the Horizon/Turismo fours (1.6- and 2.2-liter) clung to carburetion. New single-point injection with a low- pressure fuel regulator and speed-compensating feature went into all the others. Its Electronic Control Unit not only adjusted the air/fuel mixture and spark timing, but kept a record of engine operations to spot malfunctions. A new air cleaner housing on 2.2- and 2.5-liter fours was easier to remove, and their cylinder heads were modified to speed up combustion and improve idling. A new four-cylinder labyrinth distributor was smaller and had fewer parts. All models had a new (required) center high-mounted stop lamp. Four-way adjustable head restraints became available on Caravelle. All front-drive models could have "precision-feel" power steering, which had been introduced in 1985.

1986 Horizon four-door hatchback (CM)

HORIZON — SERIES M — FOUR — Little changed in Plymouth's five-passenger subcompact sedan, which again came in two models: blackout-trimmed base Horizon and bright-trimmed SE. The base model included 13 in. wheels with bright trim rings and P165/80R13 steel-belted radial tires, tinted glass, locking glovebox, convenience lights, power brakes, halogen headlamps, fold-down rear seat, and security shelf panel. Horizon SE added high-back cloth/vinyl bucket seats, an AM radio with digital clock, and whitewall tires. Standard engine, as before, was the 1.6- liter Peugeot four with four-speed manual transaxle. Optional: Chrysler's carbureted 2.2-liter with five-speed or TorqueFlite automatic.

1986 Turismo Duster two-door hatchback (CM)

TURISMO — SERIES M — FOUR — This was mainly a carryover year for Plymouth's two-door hatchback coupe. Base engine was again the Peugeot-built 1.6- liter four, hooked to a four-speed manual transaxle. Optional: Chrysler's carbureted 2.2-liter four, five-speed manual transaxle, and three-speed TorqueFlite. Standard equipment included power brakes, bucket seats up front, inside hood and power hatch releases, locking glovebox, day/night mirror, remote-control driver's mirror, soft wide bodyside moldings, two-speed intermittent wipers, maintenance-free battery, tinted glass, and halogen headlamps. Base Turismos carried P165/80R13 steel-belted radial tires. Performance-minded buyers again could choose the Turismo 2.2, with high-output 2.2-liter engine and close-ratio five- speed, as well as a 2.78:1 drive ratio and sport suspension. Its body sported sill extensions, a front air dam and fender extensions, along with paint and tape graphics and name decals. Standard 195/60R14 SBR raised-black-letter tires rode Rallye wheels. Equipment included dual remote mirrors, an AM radio with digital clock, heavy-duty radiator, and performance exhaust. For dress-up only, the Duster package contained Rallye instrumentation, 13 in. rallye wheels with bright trim rings and liftgate striping, 'Duster' and 'Plymouth' decals, and high-back reclining cloth/vinyl bucket seats with increased lateral support. A total of 16,987 Duster packages were installed.

RELIANT K — SERIES P — FOUR — Appearance of the popular Reliant, near twin to Dodge's Aries, didn't change much this year. The crosshatch-patterned grille sat in a tapered-side frame, with center pentastar emblem. Housings for the single recessed rectangular headlamps were angled to follow the grille shape. Outboard were large wraparound amber parking lights. At the rear, large wraparound taillamps had lenses with wide horizontal ribs, with backup lenses alongside the recessed license plate opening. The decklid displayed 'Plymouth' block letters on the driver's side, 'Reliant K' on the right, and a pentastar in the middle. Two-door, four-door and station wagon bodies were offered again, in SE and top-level LE trim; as well as a base two-door and four-door. Standard equipment grew this year. Base Reliants had P175/80R13 SBR

1986 Reliant K four-door sedan (CM)

tires on 13 in. wheels with hubcaps; SE added wheel covers with 16 squarish holes around the rim. Standard equipment on the base Reliant included a maintenance-free battery, power brakes, lighter, halogen headlamps with bright bezels, vinyl bench seat, trip odometer, and two-speed wipers. SE added a trunk light, glovebox and map/reading light, intermittent wipers, cloth/vinyl bench seat with center armrest, remote black driver's mirror, and AM radio with digital clock. Also included: a passenger vanity mirror with map light, black upper door frames and quarter-window trim, and wide black bodyside moldings with argent stripe and bright insert. An optional SE Popular Equipment Discount package included tinted glass, power steering, TorqueFlite, and dual remote mirrors. Top-rung LE Reliants included an AM stereo/FM stereo radio with built-in digital clock, map/reading light, special sound insulation, 14 in. sport wheel covers with a pattern of four-rib segments radiating outward in six directions, and cloth/vinyl front bench seat with center armrest. The LE wagon had power steering and dual remote-control black mirrors; its bodyside/liftgate woodtone applique could be deleted for credit. Base engine was the fuel-injected 2.2-liter four, now coupled to a five-speed close-ratio manual overdrive transaxle (formerly four-speed). SE and LE models could have the new 2.5-liter four with twin balance shafts, as well as TorqueFlite automatic. Underneath was a dual-path Iso-Strut front suspension. Reliant K body colors were: Black, Light Cream, Radiant Silver, White, Gold Dust, Gunmetal Blue or Golden Bronze pearl coat, Ice Blue, and Garnet Red or Dark Cordovan pearl coat.

1986 Caravelle SE Turbo four-door sedan (CM)

CARAVELLE — SERIES J — FOUR — For its second year in the Plymouth lineup, the spacious six-passenger sedan got a number of exterior and interior revisions. A new, less-equipped base model joined the original SE. The new vertically-oriented grille with center pentastar emblem had a crosshatch pattern, divided into six sections by five slightly wider vertical bars. Horizontal parking lamps set into the bumper. Wraparound side marker lenses stood outboard of recessed quad rectangular headlamps with new bezels. Also new this year: a soft bumper fascia, decklid panels and body moldings, and accent tape stripes. This year's taillamps had subtle horizontal ribbing, with a more curved look at the ends that wrapped around the quarter panels. Base engine was the fuel-injected 2.2-liter four; optional, either the new 2.5-liter or the turbocharged 2.2-liter. Standard equipment included power steering and brakes, digital clock, tethered gas cap, remote fuel filler door release, tinted glass, halogen headlamps, dual-note horn, twin outside mirrors, and P185/70R14 steel-belted radial whitewall tires. SE added a remote decklid release, remote-controlled dual outside mirrors, upper body tape stripes, and intermittent wipers. Base Caravelles had bench seats, while new individually-adjustable cloth/vinyl 50/50 front seats went into SE. Seats had armrests, recliners and seatback pockets. An AM stereo/FM stereo radio with digital clock became standard on SE; AM radio only on the base Caravelle.

GRAN FURY — SERIES B — V-8 — Traditional in style and powered again by the old familiar 318 cu. in. V-8 with two-barrel carburetor, Gran Fury managed to stick around in the lineup because of its popularity with fleet buyers and large families. The six-passenger Salon sedan had TorqueFlite automatic transmission as well as power brakes and steering. Also standard: front bumper guards, tethered gas cap, tinted glass, halogen headlamps, a hood ornament, wheel opening moldings, AM radio with built-in digital clock, and P205/75R15 steel-belted radial whitewalls. An optional Salon Luxury package included wire wheel covers, illuminated entry system, leather-wrapped steering wheel, and lighted passenger vanity mirror. The Popular Equipment Discount Package included an electric rear window defroster, tilt steering, dual remote chrome mirrors, and AM stereo/FM stereo radio with digital clock. As before, a high-performance engine with four-barrel carburetor and heavy-duty equipment was available only to law enforcement agencies. A total of 5,133 police packages were installed on Gran Fury sedans. Gran Fury was a near twin to Dodge's Diplomat.

I.D. DATA: Plymouth again had a 17-symbol Vehicle Identification Number (VIN) on the upper left corner of the instrument panel, visible through the windshield. Coding was similar to 1984. The first digit indicates Country: '1' U.S.A. The second symbol is Make: 'P' Plymouth. Third is Vehicle Type: '3' passenger car. The next symbol ('B') indicates manual seatbelts. Symbol five is Car Line: 'M' Horizon; 'P' Reliant; 'J' Caravelle; 'B' Gran Fury. Symbol six is Series (price class): '1' Economy; '2' Low; '3' Medium; '4' High; '5' Premium. Symbol seven is Body Style: '1' 2-dr. sedan; '4'

2-dr. hatchback; '6' 4-dr. sedan; '8' 4-dr. hatchback; '9' 4-dr. wagon. Eighth is the Engine Code: 'A' L497 2Bbl.; 'C' L4135 2Bbl.; 'D' L4135 FI; 'E' Turbo L4135 FI; '8' H.O. L4135 2Bbl.; 'K' L4153 FI; 'P' V8318 2Bbl. Next comes a check digit. Symbol ten indicates Model Year: 'G' 1986. Symbol eleven is Assembly Plant: 'A' Detroit; 'D' Belvidere, IL; 'F' Newark, DE; 'G' or 'X' St. Louis. The last six digits make up the sequential serial number, starting with 100001. Engine numbers and Body Code Plates are in the same locations as 1981-85.

HORIZON (FOUR)

Model Number	Body/Style Number	Body Type & Seating	Factory Price	Shipping Weight	Production Total
LME	44	4-dr. Hatch-5P	6209	2105	76,458
LMH	44	4-dr. SE Hatch-5P	6558	2125	8,050

TURISMO (FOUR)

LMH	24	2-dr. Hatch-5P	6787	2170	41,899

TURISMO 2.2 (FOUR)

LMP	24	2-dr. Hatch-5P	7732	2300	4,488

RELIANT (FOUR)

KPL	21	2-dr. Sedan-6P	7184	2380	2,573
KPL	41	4-dr. Sedan-6P	7301	2390	26,220

RELIANT SE (FOUR)

KPM	21	2-dr. Sedan-6P	7639	2400	10,707
KPM	41	4-dr. Sedan-6P	7759	2415	47,827
KPM	45	4-dr. Sta Wag-6P	8186	2470	22,154

RELIANT LE (FOUR)

KPH	21	2-dr. Sedan-6P	8087	2440	2,482
KPH	41	4-dr. Sedan-6P	8207	2460	5,941
KPH	45	4-dr. Sta Wag-6P	8936	2560	5,101

CARAVELLE (FOUR)

EJM	41	4-dr. Sedan-6P	9241	2535	18,968
EJH	41	4-dr. SE Sedan-6P	9810	2540	15,654

GRAN FURY SALON (V-8)

MBL	41	4-dr. Sedan-6P	10086	3470	14,761

MODEL NUMBER NOTE: Some sources identify models using the VIN data to indicate Car Line, Price Class, and Body Style. Example: base Reliant four-door (KPL41) has the equivalent number P26, which translates to Reliant line, Low price class, and four-door sedan body. See I.D. Data section for breakdown.

ENGINE DATA: BASE FOUR (Horizon, Turismo): Inline, overhead-cam four-cylinder. Cast iron block; aluminum head. Displacement: 97.3 cu. in. (1.6 liters). Bore & stroke: 3.17 x 3.07 in. Compression ratio: 8.8:1. Brake horsepower: 64 at 4800 R.P.M. Torque: 87 lbs.-ft. at 2800 R.P.M. Five main bearings. Solid valve lifters. Carburetor: 2Bbl. Holley 6520. VIN Code: A. OPTIONAL FOUR (Horizon, Turismo): Inline, overhead-cam four-cylinder. Cast iron block; aluminum head. Displacement: 135 cu. in. (2.2 liters). Bore & stroke: 3.44 x 3.62 in. Compression ratio: 9.5:1. Brake horsepower: 96 at 5200 R.P.M. Torque: 119 lbs.-ft. at 3200 R.P.M. Five main bearings. Hydraulic valve lifters. Carburetor: 2Bbl. Holley 6520. VIN Code: C. BASE FOUR (Reliant, Caravelle): Same as 135 cu. in. four above, but with electronic fuel injection Compression 9.5:1. Horsepower: 97 at 5200 R.P.M. Torque: 122 lbs.-ft. at 3200 R.P.M. VIN Code: D. BASE FOUR (Turismo 2.2): High-output carbureted version of 135 cu. in. four. Compression: 9.6:1. Horsepower: 110 at 5600 R.P.M. Torque: 129 lbs.-ft. at 3600 R.P.M. VIN Code: 8. TURBO FOUR; OPTIONAL (Caravelle): Same as 135 cu. in. four above, with EFI and turbocharger Compression: 8.1:1. Horsepower: 146 at 5200 R.P.M. Torque: 170 lbs.-ft. at 3600 R.P.M. VIN Code: E. OPTIONAL FOUR (Reliant, Caravelle): Inline, overhead-cam four-cylinder. Cast iron block; aluminum head. Displacement: 153 cu. in. (2.5 liters). Bore & stroke: 3.44 x 4.09 in. Compression ratio: 9.0:1. Brake horsepower: 100 at 4800 R.P.M. Torque: 136 lbs.-ft. at 2800 R.P.M. Five main bearings. Electronic fuel injection. VIN Code: K. BASE V-8 (Gran Fury): 90-degree, overhead valve V-8. Cast iron block and head. Displacement: 318 cu. in. (5.2 liters). Bore & stroke: 3.91 x 3.31 in. Compression ratio: 9.0:1. Brake horsepower: 140 at 3600 R.P.M. Torque: 265 lbs.-ft. at 1600 R.P.M. Five main bearings. Hydraulic valve lifters. Carburetor: 2Bbl. Holley 6280. VIN Code: P. POLICE V-8 (Gran Fury): Same as 318 cu. in. V-8 above, with Rochester 4Bbl. carburetor Compression ratio: 8.0:1. Horsepower: 175 at 4000 R.P.M. Torque: 250 lbs.-ft. at 3200 R.P.M.

CHASSIS DATA: Wheelbase: (Horizon) 99.1 in.; (Turismo) 96.5 in.; (Reliant) 100.3 in.; (Reliant wag) 100.4 in.; (Caravelle) 103.3 in.; (Gran Fury) 112.6 in. Overall Length: (Horizon) 163.2 in.; (Turismo) 174.8 in.; (Reliant) 178.6 in.; (Reliant wag) 178.5 in.; (Caravelle) 185.2 in.; (Gran Fury) 204.6 in. Height: (Horizon) 53.0 in.; (Turismo) 50.7 in.; (Reliant 2dr.) 52.5 in.; (Reliant wag) 53.2 in.; (Caravelle) 53.1 in.; (Gran Fury) 55.1 in. Width: (Horizon) 63.8 in.; (Turismo) 65.9 in.; (Reliant/Caravelle) 68.0 in.; (Gran Fury) 72.4 in. Front Tread: (Horizon/Turismo) 56.1 in.; (Reliant/Caravelle) 57.6 in.; (Gran Fury) 60.5 in. Rear Tread: (Horizon/Turismo) 55.7 in.; (Reliant/Caravelle) 57.2 in.; (Gran Fury) 60.0 in. Standard Tires: (Horizon/Turismo) P165/80R13 SBR BSW exc. SE, WSW; (Turismo 2.2) P195/60R14 SBR RBL; (Reliant) P175/80R13 SBR BSW; (Reliant LE, Caravelle) P185/70R14 SBR; (Gran Fury) P205/75R15 SBR WSW.

TECHNICAL: Transmission: Four-speed manual (floor shift) standard on Horizon/Turismo w/1.6-liter engine. Five-speed manual standard on Reliant and Turismo 2.2. TorqueFlite three-speed automatic standard on Caravelle and Gran Fury, optional on others. Gran Fury gear ratios: (1st) 2.74:1; (2nd) 1.54:1; (3rd) 1.00:1; (Rev) 2.22:1. Front-drive ratios: (1st) 2.69:1; (2nd) 1.55:1; (3rd) 1.00:1; (Rev) 2.10:1. Standard final drive ratio: (Horizon/Turismo) 2.69:1 w/4spd; (Horizon/Turismo w/2.2-liter four) 2.20:1 w/5spd, 2.78:1 w/auto.; (Turismo 2.2) 2.78:1 w/5spd; (Reliant) 2.20:1 w/5spd, 2.78:1 w/auto., (Reliant w/2.5-liter) 3.02:1 w/auto.; (Caravelle) 3.02:1; (Gran Fury) 2.26:1. Steering/Brakes/Body: same as 1985. Suspension: (Horizon/Turismo) Iso-Strut independent coil front w/anti-sway bar, semi-independent trailing arm coil rear; (Reliant) Dual-path Iso-Strut front w/linkless anti-sway bar, beam rear axle w/trailing arms and coil springs; (Caravelle) Iso-Strut front w/linkless anti-sway bar, beam rear axle w/trailing arms and anti-sway bar; (Gran Fury) front transverse torsion bars and anti-sway bar, semi-elliptic rear leaf springs. Fuel tank: (Horizon/Turismo) 13 gal.; (Reliant/Caravelle) 14 gal.; (Gran Fury) 18 gal.

DRIVETRAIN OPTIONS: Engines: 2.2-liter four: Horizon/Turismo ($138); Turismo 2.2 (NC). Turbo 2.2-liter four: Caravelle ($628). 2.5-liter four: Reliant/Caravelle ($279). Transmission/Differential: Five-speed trans.: Horizon/Turismo ($77). TorqueFlite: Horizon/Turismo/Reliant ($478). Performance (3.02:1) axle ratio: Horiz/Tur/Reliant ($23). Power Accessories: Power steering: Horizon/Turismo/Reliant ($226). Suspension: H.D. susp.: Reliant ($60); G. Fury ($27). Euro handling susp.: Caravelle ($58). Other: 500-amp battery: Caravelle/G. Fury ($45). Max. cooling: Horizon/Turismo ($145). California emission system ($102).

HORIZON/TURISMO CONVENIENCE/APPEARANCE OPTIONS: Option Packages: Duster pkg.: Turismo ($99-$125). Sun/Sound/Shade pkg.: Turismo 2.2 ($562). Auto. trans. discount pkg. ($808-$933). 2.2-liter engine and five-speed discount pkg. ($304-$420). Light group ($57-$86). Protection group ($90-$194). Note: Individual Horizon/Turismo options are the same as those offered on equivalent Dodge Omni/Charger models; see Dodge listing.

RELIANT CONVENIENCE/APPEARANCE OPTIONS: Same selection and prices as equivalent Dodge Aries models; see Dodge listing. Reliant SE could get sport wheel covers rather than the deluxe wheel covers offered on Aries, for the same price ($49).

CARAVELLE CONVENIENCE/APPEARANCE OPTIONS: Option Packages: Popular equipment discount pkg. ($515-$689). Luxury equipment pkg.: SE ($960). Deluxe convenience pkg. ($302). Power convenience pkg. ($463). Light pkg. ($139). Comfort/Convenience: Air cond. ($780). Rear defroster ($152). Power seat: SE ($232). Intermittent wipers: base ($55). Mirrors: Left remote (right manual): base ($25). Electronic-tuning Radios w/digital clock: AM stereo/FM stereo: base ($149). Seek/scan AM stereo/FM stereo w/cassette ($287-$436). Ultimate sound stereo w/cassette ($503-$652). Exterior: Pearl coat paint ($41). Bodyside moldings ($57). Bumper guards ($58). Undercoating ($44). Interior: Color-keyed mats ($46). Trunk dress-up ($53). Wheels/Tires: Wire wheel covers, locking ($231-$280). Conventional spare tire ($85).

GRAN FURY CONVENIENCE/APPEARANCE OPTIONS: Option Packages: Popular equipment pkg. ($588). Salon luxury pkg. ($561). Light pkg. ($132). Protection group ($137). Comfort/Convenience: Air conditioning, semi-auto ($836). Rear defroster, electric ($152). Automatic speed control ($184). Power windows ($278). Power door locks ($185). Power decklid release ($41). Tilt steering wheel ($118). Intermittent wipers ($55). Mirrors: Remote driver's ($25). Dual remote chrome ($69). Electronic-Tuning Radios w/digital clock: AM stereo/FM stereo ($149). Seek/scan AM stereo/FM stereo w/cassette ($251-$400). Ultimate sound AM stereo/FM stereo w/cassette ($467-$616). Radio delete ($56 credit). Exterior: Full vinyl roof ($191). Pearl coat paint ($41). Vinyl bodyside moldings ($59). Upper door frame moldings ($47). Body sound insulation ($68). Undercoating ($44). Interior: Vinyl split-back bench seat ($62). Cloth/vinyl 60/40 split bench seat ($321). Trunk dress-up ($58). Wheels/Tires: Premium wheel covers ($99). Conventional spare ($96).

HISTORY: Introduced: October 1, 1985. Model year production: Chrysler reported a total of 303,283 passenger cars shipped. Calendar year production: 422,619 (incl. 36,856 early '87 Sundance models). Calendar year sales by U.S. dealers: 362,798. Model year sales by U.S. dealers: 335,079 (not incl. 69,402 imports).

Historical Footnotes: Horizon sales grew as a result of the "America" advertising campaign, introduced in spring 1986. The subcompact became Chrysler-Plymouth's No. 3 best seller. Gran Fury sold well too, though it was subject to a gas guzzler penalty from the government. The carbureted V-8 just couldn't manage the 26 MPG requirement, it seemed, especially since no overdrive automatic transmission was offered. The new Plymouth Sundance was expected to begin production in spring 1986 as a 1987 model.

Performance and Pontiac almost seemed synonymous back in the 1960s. As the company reached its Golden Anniversary year in 1976, that performance had become somewhat subdued. But, it wasn't forgotten. The Trans Am still carried a 400 cu. in. V-8 as standard and could hold a big 455 V-8. Engine sizes diminished the next year, to a maximum of 403 cu. in. but, Pontiac usually managed to put something extra into its Firebird lineup. Already, though, powerplants were beginning the shrinkage that would hit every domestic automaker. Bodies would get similar treatment starting in '77.

1976 Astre Formal Window coupe (P)

A new Sunbird subcompact arrived in 1976 to join the less sporty Astre. That pair and several other models could get a five-speed gearbox. In addition to downsizing of full-size models, 1977 brought the end of the inline six as a Pontiac engine; only vee-type sixes would be used through the next decade and beyond. As in other GM divi-

1976 Ventura SJ Cordova Landau coupe (P)

1978 Ventura LJ four-door sedan

sions, the variety of engines available (built by more than one manufacturer) produced considerable confusion in the late 1970s. A 350 cu. in. V-8, for instance, might come from any of three GM factories. At mid-year 1977 a new Phoenix compact arrived, ready to take over Ventura's spot as the only compact with a four-cylinder engine. Collectors, though, would be far more interested in a limited-production model that appeared at the same time: the Can Am edition of the LeMans coupe. Only 1,377 of those were built. Pontiac's new "Iron Duke" four would find its way under plenty of GM hoods — even some on cars outside the GM fold.

1979 Firebird Trans Am Silver Anniversary coupe (P)

Grand Am returned in 1978, sporting a soft rubber front-end panel. Pontiac's mid-size cars were downsized, as sales hit record levels. Next year, a new "crossflow" cylinder head went into four-cylinder powerplants and Trans Ams had the option of four-wheel power disc brakes. For added looks, Grand Prix models could get a set of real wire wheels — a choice not offered on Pontiacs since the 1930s.

1980 Phoenix LJ hatchback sedan (JG)

As the 1980s began, the whole auto industry was suffering economic woes. Pontiac was no exception. High hopes were placed on the new front-drive "efficiency-sized" Phoenix, which was Pontiac's version of the soon-to-be-notorious X-car. No engines larger than 350 cu. in. were available and a new 265 cu. in. (4.3-liter) V-8 highlighted the continuing trend toward smaller powerplants. Fours and V-6s soon would become the norm, through V-8s remained available in a number of models. Diesel power went under Pontiac hoods as an option for the first time in 1980. Not many enthusiasts are likely to seek those examples out, but an electronic-control (E/C) 301 cu. in. (4.9-liter) V-8, used by performance models, may

prove more tempting. More desirable yet: the turbo-charged 301 V-8 offered in Trans Am.

1981 Grand LeMans Safari wagon (P)

The popular Grand Prix was restyled for 1981. Later that year came another Chevrolet clone, the little T1000, based on Chevette. Sales may have been weak, but that didn't keep Pontiac (or other companies) from jacking up prices mightily during these years, as serious inflation plagued the national economy.

1982 Firebird Trans Am coupe (OCW)

Firebird's aging design needed attention, so wind-tunnel testing helped to produce an aero-restyled 'bird for 1982. It was still a rear-drive car, but with a more contemporary look. Front-wheel-drive was the trend, though, and Pontiac concurred by offering new J2000 and 6000 models. The latter featured a wedge profile that soon would become standard in "sporty" sedans. The Catalina name-plate was retired, but Bonneville returned in G-body form, kin to Grand Prix. Bowing in another way to the changing automotive scene, the "Iron Duke" four added fuel injection.

"World class" was the way Pontiac described the 6000 STE performance-oriented sedan introduced for 1983 with a standard V-6 engine. Most domestic automakers seemed eager to emulate the European sedans, in styling as well as performance and handling. Firebirds adopted a five-speed manual gearbox and a convertible arrived bearing the 2000 badge. Not since 1975 had Pontiac offered a ragtop. Parisienne was the name given to a new full-size, rear-drive sedan/wagon. Even with the rise of

four and V-6 power, Pontiacs had more V-8s this year than in 1982.

1984 Fiero MS4 coupe (P)

After several years in retirement, the Sunbird name returned in 1984 on the former 2000 series, which added a turbocharger option. Even more significant was the arrival of the two-seater Fiero, wearing a plastic body over a "space frame/chassis." Fiero sold briskly at first, but sagged somewhat later, never quite meeting the company's hopes. Total sales rose impressively this year, after four depressed seasons. At the corporate level, Pontiac joined Chevrolet and GM of Canada to become the new C-P-C group.

Pontiac's stated goal was to develop cars that were "performance-oriented" and "fun to drive," appealing to entry-level, younger buyers. Joining Fiero in 1985 was the "driver-oriented" Grand Am. It was created to attract the "new values" motorist (to use two more automotive buzz-words of the mid-1980s). Furthering that goal in 1986 was a new Grand Am SE and Sunbird GT. Later, a Fiero GT fastback bowed. Collectors in search of a memorable model could instead turn to Grand Prix, especially to the limited-production Grand Prix 2+2. Since only 200 were built and sold only in the South, they're likely to remain among the rarest modern-day Pontiacs.

1985 Parisienne Brougham sedan (AA)

Collectors tend to think in terms of Trans Am and Grand Prix models. A sensible choice, since that pair has been popular all along and likely to remain so. A turbo V-8 Trans Am or one with cross-flow fuel injection might be a bit more mechanically troublesome than a high-output car-bureted edition, but is still worth hanging onto. Tucked here and there among the other Pontiac models, though, are a few with slightly less obvious attractions, but smaller price tags. If you can't snag a '77 Can Am, '86 Grand Prix 2+2 or full-performance Trans Am, there's always an S/E or Formula Firebird or an ordinary LeMans with a good selection of appearance options.

1976 PONTIAC

A sporty new subcompact (Sunbird) entered Pontiac's 1976 lineup, while major changes hit the personal-luxury Grand Prix. Many models had smaller engines than before, including a 260 cu. in. V-8 under LeMans hoods and a 350 for the new Grand Prix. A new five-speed manual transmission (overdrive fifth gear), intended to boost gas mileage, was offered as an option on Astre and Sunbird, and on the LeMans Sport Coupe and the Ventura with 260 V-8. Also to improve economy, cars with air conditioning got a lower idle speed when the unit was not operating. Most models got lower axle ratios (especially the 2.41: final drive ratio). All Pontiacs now had a catalytic converter (except Astre/Sunbird with the single-barrel 140 four), which had been introduced a year earlier. A Radial Tuned Suspension (RTS) was standard on LeMans, Firebird, Grand Prix and full-size models; optional on Astre, Sunbird and Ventura. Most Pontiacs could also get a new Rally RTS Handling package that included a rear stabilizer bar. Bumpers and brakes were revised this year to meet new federal standards. Firebirds used a urethane foam bumper system, Astres a leaf spring and rubber-block energy absorbers; other models had a hydraulic energy absorber.

1976 Astre coupe (P)

ASTRE — SERIES 2H — FOUR — Pontiac's subcompact came in two-door coupe or hatchback form, or as a Safari two-door station wagon. Round headlamps sat in squarish recessed housings. A recessed two-section crosshatch (eggcrate) grille held rather large, inset parking/signal lights. On the body-color grille divider (a Pontiac "trademark") was the typical vee-shaped emblem. Below the bumper was a wide air intake slot. Two new interior trim packages were available. The luxury version included doeskin seats, luxury door trim, upgraded sound insulation and thick, cut-pile carpeting. Standard equipment included a 140 cu. in. (2.3-liter) four-cylinder engine with one-barrel carburetor, three-speed manual gearbox (floor shift), front bucket seats, heater/defroster, A78 x 13 blackwall tires, inside hood release, and window and roof drip moldings. A new five-speed manual gearbox became optional. Astre's GT option was offered on both hatchback and wagon, included a two-barrel version of the 140 four, four-speed gearbox, BR78 x 13 SBR tires, and rally gauge cluster.

SUNBIRD — SERIES 2H — FOUR — New for 1976, the sporty subcompact Sunbird rode a 97 inch wheelbase. Base engine was a 140 cu. in. (2.3-liter) four, with new 231 cu. in. (3.8-liter) V-6 from Buick optional. Sunbird's standard interior included bucket seats in cloth and Morrokide. Both rectangular quad headlamps and the twin crosshatch grille inserts were recessed between the customary Pontiac divider with vee-shaped emblem. Standard equipment included a three-speed floor-shift manual transmission, heater/defroster, front bucket seats, carpeting, custom wheel covers, window and roof drip moldings, wheel opening moldings, and A78 x 13 blackwall tires. A luxury appointment group was optional. So was a new five-speed manual transmission.

1976 Ventura SJ Cordova Landau coupe (P)

VENTURA — SERIES 2X — SIX/V-8 — Compact in size, Ventura came in base and SJ trim, in three body styles: two-door coupe or hatchback, and four-door sedan. Ventura rode a 111 inch wheelbase and carried a standard 250 cu. in. inline six-cylinder engine. Two V-8s were optional: 260 or 350 cu. in. displacement. A new five- speed manual gearbox became optional on models with the 260 cu. in. V-8 engine. Options included cruise control and a landau coupe roof. An appearance group including special body striping and black window frames was offered on two-door models. Single round

headlamps were mounted in squarish housings. On each side of a peaked divider bar were crosshatch grille inserts arranged in three rows (with two horizontal divider bars). Park/signal lamps stood behind bars at the outer ends of the grille. Ventura's standard equipment included the 250 cu. in. six with three-speed manual (floor lever) transmission, heater/defroster, E78 x 14 blackwall tires, windshield and back window moldings, and carpeting. Hatchbacks and sedans also had roof drip moldings. Hatchbacks included a fold-down back seat. Ventura SJ added custom finned wheel covers, dual horns, courtesy lamps, rocker panel and wheel opening moldings, window moldings, and full-width front seats.

1976 Formula Firebird coupe (P)

FIREBIRD — SERIES 2F — SIX/V-8 — Four models made up the famed Firebird lineup: base, Esprit, and performance-minded Formula and Trans Am. Each featured body-colored urethane bumpers at both ends this year. Base powerplant was the 250 cu. in. inline six, but Trans Am could go as high as a 455 cu. in. V-8. New options this year included a canopy top, new appearance package (Formula only), and fuel economy indicator. Trans Am came in five body colors: Cameo White, Firethorn Red, Sterling Silver, Carousel Red, and Goldenrod Yellow. Firebird's typical twin-section grille with mesh pattern sat in a sloping front panel. Single square headlamps were recessed. Park/signal lamps stood at tne ends of a wide opening below the bumper strip. Standard Firebird/Esprit equipment included the 250 cu. in. six with three-speed manual gearbox, dual horns, FR78 x 15 blackwall SBR tires, power steering, and radial-tuned suspension. Espirt included sport mirrors (driver's side rreote-controlled) and deluxe wheel covers. Formula had a 350 cu. in. two-barrel V-8, either four-speed manual or Turbo Hydra-matic, the sport mirrors, and a full-length console. Trans Am included an air dam, rear decklid spoiler, shaker hood, Rally II wheels with trim rings, rally gauges, GR70 x 15 tires, and the 400 cu. in. four-barrel V-8.

1976 Grand LeMans coupe (P)

LE MANS — SERIES 2A — SIX/V-8 — Quad rectangular headlamps gave LeMans a new front-end appearance. Base and Grand LeMans came in two-door hardtop coupe and four-door hardtop sedan form, while the LeMans Sport Coupe was (obviously) coupe only. Two-doors had a formal-look rear quarter window, while the Sport Coupe's window was louvered. Park/signal lamps were at outer ends of a single bumper slot, next to the bumper guards. The LeMans grille consisted of thin vertical bars, arranged in sections per side of the peaked divider bar (which displayed a Pontiac mblem). Two four-door (two-seat) wagons were availabe: LeMans Safari and Grand LeMans Safari. Both could also have an optional rear-facing third seat. Grand LeMans had a wide variety of interior possibilities: standard notchback full- width seat (cloth and vinyl); optional 60/40 seating (cloth, vinyl or velour); and bucket seats (perforated vinyl, corduroy, velour or leather). LeMans standard equipment included the 250 cu. in. six with three-speed manual shift, radial-tuned suspension, FR78 x 15 SBR tires, rocker panel moldings, and dual horns. Wagons had a 400 cu. in. two-barrel V-8, Turbo Hydra-matic, power brakes, and HR78 x 15 tires. Grand LeMans models had either a five-speed manual gearbox or Turbo Hydra-matic, along with deluxe wheel covers and an electric clock. Both Grand LeMans and the Sport Coupe had wheel opening moldings, and either full-width seating or bucket seats. A new five-speed manual transmission was available on the LeMans Sport Coupe.

GRAND PRIX — SERIES 2G — V-8 — Front-end appearance of Pontiac's personal-luxury coupe was the same as Bonneville (above), with the same sharp hood creases that came to a point at the front, and the same new wrapover-fin grille. New base engine was the 350 cu. in. (5.7-liter) V-8. Grand Prix got a new full-width front seat with fold-down center armrest. Standard Grand Prix equipment included the 350 cu. in. V-8 with two-barrel carburetor, Turbo Hydra-matic, power brakes and steering, GR78 x 15 blackwall SBR tires, radial- tuned suspension, clock, heaeter/defroster, full-width seats with center armrest, window and hold moldings, rocker panel and wheel opening moldings, and roof drip moldings. Grand Prix SJ added the 400 cu. in. 4Bbl. V-8, bucket seats (with console), special wheel covers, and courtesy lights. A

371

1976 Grand Prix LJ 50th Anniversary T-top coupe (P)

limited-edition Golden Anniversary model featured special paint and striping, removable roof panels, and a commemorative stand-up hood ornament. An LJ luxury appointments group included velour bucket seats, thick cut- pile carpeting, and two-tone body color.

CATALINA — SERIES 2B — V-8 — Pontiac's lowest-priced full-size model was similar in appearance to Bonneville (below), but had five thick horizontal bars across its grille. A Custom option, however, gave it the same new front-end look as Bonneville. Standard equipment included a 400 cu. in. two-barrel V-8, Turbo Hydra- matic, power brakes and steering, HR78 x 15 blackwall SBR tires, radial-tuned suspension, and heater/defroster.

1976 Bonneville Brougham sedan (P)

BONNEVILLE — SERIES 2B — V-8 — Base and Brougham models were available in the top full- size line. Bonneville Brougham was the newest model, offered in two-door hardtop coupe or four-door hardtop sedan form. All models (including Grand Safari wagon) featured a new front-end look with quad rectangular headlamps. A new wranover "waterfall" grille looked like a set of many "fins" on each side of the divider bar, which held Pontiac's emblem. Headlamps were separated from the fender-tip wraparound park/signal lights. Wraparound taillamps had upper and lower sections. Four-door wagons came with two seats, but a forward-facing third seat was available. Standard equipment for the base Bonneville was similar to Catalina, but included a formal roof and deluxe wheel covers. Bonneville Brougham included a four-barrel 400 cu. in. V-8, driver's remote mirror, accent paint stripes, power windows, and electric clock. Wagons came with a 455 cu. in. V-8 engine and LR78 x 15 tires.

I.D. DATA: The 13-symbol Vehicle Identification Number (VIN) was located on the upper left surface of the instrument panel, visible through the windshield. The first digit is '2', indicating Pontiac division. The second symbol is a letter indicating series: 'C' Astre; 'M' Sunbird; 'Y' Ventura; 'Z' Ventura SJ; 'D' LeMans; 'F' LeMans Sport Coupe; 'G' Grand LeMans; 'S' Firebird; 'T' Firebird Esprit; 'U' Firebird Formula; 'W' Firebird Trans Am; 'L' Catalina; 'P' Bonneville; 'R' Bonneville Brougham; 'J' Grand Prix; 'K' Grand Prix SJ. Next come two digits that denote body type: '11' 2dr. pillar coupe; '17' 2dr. hatchback coupe; '27' 2dr. thin-pillar coupe; '37' 2dr. HT coupe; '47' 2dr. HT coupe; '57' 2dr. HT coupe; '77' 2dr. hatchback coupe; '87' 2dr. HT coupe; '29' 4dr. HT sedan; '49' 4dr. HT sedan; '69' 4dr. thin-pillar 4 window sedan; '15' 2dr. station wagon; '35' 4dr. 2seat wagon; '45' 4dr. 3seat wagon. The fifth symbol is a letter indicating engine code: 'A' L4140 1Bbl.; 'B' L4140 2Bbl.; 'C' V6231 2Bbl.; 'D' L6250 1Bbl.; 'F' V8260 2Bbl.; 'H' or 'M' J8350 2Bbl.; 'E' or 'J' J8350 4Bbl. 'R' V8400 2Bbl.; 'S' V8400 4Bbl. 'W' V8455 4Bbl. The sixth symbol denotes model year ('6' 1976). Next is a plant code: 'A' Lakewood, Georgia; 'C' Southgate, Calif.; 'G' Framingham, Mass.; 'L' Van Nuys, Calif.; 'N' Norwood, Ohio; 'P' Pontiac, Mich.; 'T' Tarrytown, NY; 'U' Lordstown, Ohio; 'W' Willow Run, Mich.; 'X' Fairfax, Kansas; '1' Oshawa, Ontario; '2' Ste. Therese, Quebec. The final six digits are the sequential serial number, which began with 100,001.

ASTRE (FOUR)

Model Number	Body/Style Number	Body Type & Seating	Factory Price	Shipping Weight	Production Total
2H	C11	2-dr. Cpe-4P	3064	2439	18,143
2H	C77	2-dr. Hatch Cpe-4P	3179	2505	19,116
2H	C15	2-dr. Safari Wag-4P	3306	2545	13,125

SUNBIRD (FOUR//V-6

2H	M27	2-dr. Cpe-4P	3431/3607	2653/--	52,031

VENTURA (SIX/V-8)

2X	Y27	2-dr. Cpe-5P	3326/3416	3234/3393	28,473
2X	Y17	2-dr. Hatch Cpe-5P	3503/3593	3348/3507	6,428
2X	Y69	4-dr. Sed-5P	3361/3451	3271/3430	27,773

VENTURA SJ (SIX/V-8)

2X	Z27	2-dr. Cpe-5P	3612/3702	3290/3449	4,815
2X	Z17	2-dr. Hatch Cpe-5P	3775/3865	3380/3539	1,823
2X	Z69	4-dr. Sed-5P	3637/3727	3326/3485	4,804

FIREBIRD (SIX/V-8)

2F	S87	2-dr. HT Cpe-4P	3906/4046	3383/3563	21,209

FIREBIRD ESPRIT (SIX/V-8)

2F	T87	2-dr. HT Cpe-4P	4162/4302	3431/3611	22,252

FIREBIRD FORMULA (V-8)

2F	U87	2-dr. HT Cpe-4P	4566	3625	20,613

1976 Firebird Trans Am Special Edition (P)

FIREBIRD TRANS AM (V-8)

2F	W87	2-dr. HT Cpe-4P	4987	3640	46,701

LE MANS (SIX/V-8)

2A	D37	2-dr. HT Cpe-6P	3768/3908	3651/3826	21,130
2A	D29	4-dt. HT Sed-6P	3813/3953	3760/3935	22,199

LE MANS SAFARI (V-8)

2A	D35	4-dr. 2S Wag-6P	4687	4336	Note 1
2A	D45	4-dr. 3S Wag-9P	4820	4374	Note 1

LE MANS SPORT COUPE (SIX/V-8)

2A	F37	2-dr. HT Cpe-6P	3916/4056	3668/3843	15,582

GRAND LE MANS (SIX/V-8)

2A	G37	2-dr. HT Cpe-6P	4330/4470	3747/3922	14,757
2A	G29	4-dr. HT Sed-6P	4433/4573	3860/4035	8,411

1976 Grand LeMans Safari wagon (CP)

GRAND LE MANS SAFARI (V-8)

2A	G35	4-dr. 2S Wag-6P	4928	4389	Note 1
2A	G45	4-dr. 3S Wag-9P	5061	4427	Note 1

Note 1: A total of 8,249 two-seat and 5,901 three-seat LeMans Safari wagons were produced (base and Grand).

GRAND PRIX (V-8)

2G	J57	2-dr. HT Cpe-5P	4798	4048	110,814

GRAND PRIX SJ (V-8)

2G	K57	2-dr. HT Cpe-5P	5223	4052	88,232

GRAND PRIX LJ (V-8)

2G	N/A	2-dr. HT Cpe-5P	N/A	N/A	29,045

Note: LJ was actually a $625 option package for Grand Prix.

CATALINA (V-8)

2B	L57	2-dr. HT Cpe-6P	4844	4256	15,262
2B	L69	4-dr. Sed-6P	4767	4276	47,235

CATALINA SAFARI (V-8)

2B	L35	4-dr. 2S Wag-6P	5324	4944	4,735
2B	L45	4-dr. 3S Wag-9P	5473	5000	5,513

BONNEVILLE (V-8)

2B	P47	2-dr. HT Cpe-6P	5246	4308	9,189
2B	P49	4-dr. HT Sed-6P	5312	4460	14,942

BONNEVILLE BROUGHAM (V-8)

2B	R47	2-dr. HT Cpe-6P	5734	4341	10,466
2B	R49	4-dr. HT Sed-6P	5906	4514	20,236

GRAND SAFARI (V-8)

2B	P35	4-dr. 2S Wag-6P	5746	5035	3,462
2B	P45	4-dr. 3S Wag-9P	5895	5091	6,176

FACTORY PRICE AND WEIGHT NOTE: For Ventura, LeMans and Firebird, prices and weights to left of slash are for six-cylinder, to right for V-8 engine.

ENGINE DATA: BASE FOUR (Astre, Sunbird): Inline. Overhead cam. Four-cylinder. Aluminum block and cast iron head. Displacement: 140 cu. in. (2.3 liters). Bore & stroke: 3.50 x 3.63 in. Compression ratio: 7.9:1. Brake horsepower: 70 at 4400 R.P.M. Torque: 107 lbs.-ft. at 2400 R.P.M. Five main bearings. Hydraulic valve lifters. Carburetor: 1Bbl. Rochester. VIN Code: A. OPTIONAL FOUR (Astre, Sunbird): Same as 140 cu. in. four above, except Horsepower: 84 at 4400 R.P.M. Torque: 113 lbs.-ft. at 3200 R.P.M. Carb: 2Bbl. Holley 366829. VIN Code: B. OPTIONAL V-6 (Sunbird): 90-degree, overhead-valve V-6. Cast iron block and head. Displacement: 231 cu. in. (3.8 liters). Bore & stroke: 3.80 x 3.40 in. Compression ratio: 8.0:1. Brake horsepower: 105 at 3400 R.P.M. Torque: 185 lbs.-ft. at 2000 R.P.M. Four main bearings. Hydraulic valve lifters. Carburetor: 2Bbl. Rochester. VIN Code: C. BASE SIX (Ventura, Firebird, LeMans): Inline. Overhead valve. Six-cylinder. Cast iron block and head. Displacement: 250 cu. in. (4.1 liters). Bore & stroke: 3.87 x 3.53 in. Compression ratio: 8.3:1. Brake horsepower: 110 at 3600 R.P.M. Torque: 185 lbs.-ft. at 1200 R.P.M. Seven main bearings. Hydraulic valve lifters. Carburetor: 1Bbl. Rochester. VIN Code: D. OPTIONAL V-8 (Ventura, LeMans): 90-degree, overhead valve V-8. Cast iron block and head. Displacement: 260 cu. in. (4.3 liters). Bore & stroke: 3.50 x 3.39 in. Compression ratio: 7.5:1. Brake horsepower: 110 at 3400 R.P.M. Torque: 205 lbs.-ft. at 1600 R.P.M. Five main bearings. Hydraulic valve lifters. Carburetor: 2Bbl. Rochester. VIN Code: F. BASE V-8 (Grand Prix, Firebird Formula); OPTIONAL (Firebird, LeMans): 90-degree, overhead valve V-8. Cast iron block and head. Displacement: 350 cu. in. (5.7 liters). Bore & stroke: 3.88 x 3.75 in. Compression ratio: 7.6:1. Brake horsepower: 160 at 4000 R.P.M. Torque: 280 lbs.-ft. at 2000 R.P.M. Five main bearings. Hydraulic valve lifters. Carburetor: 2Bbl. Rochester. VIN Code: H or M. OPTIONAL V-8 (Ventura): 90-degree, overhead valve V-8. Cast iron block and head. Displacement: 350 cu. in. (5.7 liters). Bore & stroke: 3.80 x 3.85 in. Compression ratio: 8.0:1. Brake horsepower: 140 at 3200 R.P.M. Torque: 280 lbs.-ft. at 1600 R.P.M. Five main bearings. Hydraulic valve lifters. Carburetor: 2Bbl. Rochester. OPTIONAL V-8 (Ventura): Same as 350 cu. in. V-8 above, with Rochester four-barrel carburetor Horsepower: 155 at 3400 R.P.M. Torque: 280 lbs.- ft. at 1800 R.P.M. BASE V-8 (Catalina, Bonneville, LeMans Safari wagon); OPTIONAL (LeMans, Grand Prix): 90-degree, overhead valve V-8. Cast iron block and head. Displacement: 400 cu. in. (6.6 liters). Bore & stroke: 4.12 x 3.75 in. Compression ratio: 7.6:1. Brake horsepower: 170 at 4000 R.P.M. Torque: 310 lbs.-ft. at 1600 R.P.M. Five main bearings. Hydraulic valve lifters. Carburetor: 2Bbl. Rochester. VIN Code: R. BASE V-8 (Trans Am, Bonneville Brougham, Grand Prix SJ); OPTIONAL V-8 (LeMans, Firebird, Grand Prix, Catalina, Bonneville): Same as 400 cu. in. V-8 above, except Horsepower: 185 at 3600 R.P.M. Torque: 310 lbs.-ft. at 1600 R.P.M. Carburetor: 4Bbl. Rochester. VIN Code: S. BASE V-8 (Catalina and Grand Safari wagons); OPTIONAL V-8 (LeMans, Firebird, Grand Prix, Catalina, Bonneville): 90-degree, overhead valve V-8. Cast iron block and head. Displacement: 455 cu. in. (7.5 liters). Bore & stroke: 4.15 x 4.21 in. Compression ratio: 7.6:1. Brake horsepower: 200 at 3500 R.P.M. Torque: 330 lbs.-ft. at 2000 R.P.M. Five main bearings. Hydraulic valve lifters. Carburetor: 4Bbl. Rochester. VIN Code: W.

CHASSIS DATA: Wheelbase: (Astre/Sunbird) 97.0 in.; (Ventura) 111.1 in.; (Firebird) 108.1 in.; (LeMans 2dr.) 112.0 in.; (LeM 4dr.) 116.0 in.; (Grand Prix) 116.0 in.; (Catalina cpe/sed) 123.4 in.; (Catalina wag) 127.0 in.; (Bonneville) 123.4 in. Overall Length: (Astre) 177.6 in.; (Sunbird) 177.8 in.; (Ventura) 199.6 in.; (Firebird) 196.8 in.; (LeMans 2dr.) 208.0 in.; (LeM 4dr.) 212.0 in.; (LeM wag) 215.4 in.; (G.P.) 212.7 in.; (Catalina cpe/sed, Bonn.) 226.0 in.; (Catalina wag) 231.3 in. Height: (Astre hatch) 50.0 in.; (Astre notch/wag) 51.8 in.; (Sunbird) 49.8 in.; (Ventura 2dr.) 52.3 in.; (Ventura 4dr.) 53.2 in.; (Firebird) 49.1 in.; (LeM 2dr.) 52.7 in.; (LeM 4dr.) 53.5 in.; (LeM wag) 55.3 in.; (Esprit/Formula) 49.4 in.; (Trans Am) 49.6 in.; (G.P.) 52.6 in.; (Catalina cpe) 53.5 in.; (Catalina sed, Bonn.) 54.2 in.; (Catalina wag) 57.8 in. Width: (Astre/Sunbird) 65.4 in.; (Ventura) 72.4 in.; (Firebird) 73.0 in.; (LeM) 77.4 in.; (G.P.) 77.8 in.; (Catalina cpe/sed, Bonn.) 79.6 in.; (Catalina wag) 79.4 in. Front Tread: (Astre/Sunbird) 55.2 in.; (Ventura) 61.8 in.; (Firebird) 60.9 in.; (Firebird Formula) 61.3 in.; (Trans Am) 61.2 in.; (LeM) 61.6 in.; (G.P.) 61.6 in.; (Catalina/Bonn.) 63.9 in. Rear Tread: (Astre/Sunbird) 54.1 in.; (Ventura) 59.6 in.; (Firebird) 60.0 in.; (Firebird Formula) 60.4 in.; (LeM) 61.1 in.; (Trans Am) 60.3 in.; (G.P.) 61.1 in.; (Catalina/Bonn.) 64.0 in. Standard Tires: (Astre) A78 x 13; (Sunbird) A78 x 13 exc. V-6, B78 x 13; (Ventura) E78 x 14; (Firebird) FR78 x 15; (Firebird Formula) N/A; (Trans Am) GR70 x 15; (LeMans) FR78 x 15 exc. wagon, HR78 x 15; (G.P.) GR78 x 15; (Catalina) HR78 x 15 exc. wagon, LR78 x 15; (Bonn.) HR78 x 15.

TECHNICAL: Transmission: Three-speed manual transmission standard on Astre, Sunbird, Ventura, LeMans and Firebird six (floor lever except Ventura/LeMans). Gear ratios: (1st) 3.11:1; (2nd) 1.84:1; (3rd) 1.00:1; (Rev) 3.22:1. Optional four-speed manual shift on Astre/Sunbird four-cylinder: (1st) 3.75:1; (2nd) 2.16:1; (3rd) 1.38:1; (4th) 1.00:1; (Rev) 3.82:1. Optional four-speed on Astre/Sunbird six: (1st) 3.11:1; (2nd) 2.20:1; (3rd) 1.47:1; (4th) 1.00:1; (Rev) 3.11:1. Four-speed manual shift on Firebird V-8: (1st) 2.43:1; (2nd) 1.61:1; (3rd) 1.23:1; (4th) 1.00:1; (Rev) 2.35:1. Three-speed Turbo Hydra-matic standard on Grand Prix, Catalina and Bonneville; optional on others. Astre/Sunbird automatic gear ratios: (1st) 2.52:1; (2nd) 1.52:1; (3rd) 1.00:1; (Rev) 1.94:1. Ventura/LeMans/Firebird (V8350 or smaller) THM gear ratios: (1st) 2.52:1; (2nd) 1.52:1; (3rd) 1.00:1; (Rev) 1.92:1. LeMans/Grand Prix/Bonn./Catalina (and Firebird V8400/455) THM gear ratios: (1st) 2.48:1; (2nd) 1.48:1; (3rd) 1.00:1; (Rev) 2.08:1. Standard final drive ratio: (Astre) 2.92:1 w/3spd, 2.93:1 w/4spd, 2.92 :1 w/auto.; (Sunbird) 2.92:1 w/3spd, 2.93:1 w/4spd, 2.92:1 w/auto., 3.42:1 w/87 H.P. four, 2.56:1 w/V-6; (Ventura six) 2.73:1 w/3spd, 2.73:1 or 3.08:1 w/auto.; (Ventura V-8) 2.56:1; (Firebird six) 2.73:1; (Firebird V-8) 2.41:1; (LeMans) 2.73:1 w/3spd, 2.73:1 or 3.08:1 w/auto.; (LeMans V8260) 3.08:1 w/3spd, 2.73:1 w/auto.; (LeMans V8350/400) 2.41:1; (LeMans V8400 wagon) 2.56:1; (Trans Am) 3.08:1 w/4spd, 3.23:1 w/V8455; (Grand Prix) 2.41:1; (Catalina) 2.41:1 exc. wagon, 2.56:1; (Bonneville) 2.56:1. Steering: Recirculating ball. Front Suspension: (Astre) coil springs and control arms; (Firebird/LeMans) coil springs w/lower trailing links and anti-sway bar; (others) coil springs and anti-sway bar. Rear Suspension: (Astre/Sunbird) rigid axle with coil springs, lower trailing radius arms and upper torque arms; (Ventura/Firebird) semi-elliptic leaf springs with anti-sway bar; (LeMans/Bonneville/Grand Prix) rigid axle with coil springs, lower trailing radius arms, upper torque arms and anti-sway bar; Brakes: Front disc, rear drum. Ignition: Electronic. Body construction: (Astre/Sunbird) unit; (Ventura) unit w/front frame section; (Firebird) unit w/separate partial frame; (others) separate body and frame. Fuel tank: (Astre) 16 gal.; (Sunbird) 18.5 gal.; (Ventura) 20.5 gal.; (Firebird) 20.2 gal.; (LeMans) 21.8 gal.; (Grand Prix) 25 gal.; (Catalina) 25.8 gal. exc. wagon, 22 gal.; (Bonn.) 25.8 gal.

DRIVETRAIN OPTIONS: Engines: 140 cu. in. 2Bbl. four: Astre/Sunbird ($56). 231 cu. in. V-6: Sunbird ($176). 260 cu. in. 2Bbl. V-8: Ventura/LeMans ($90). 350 cu. in. 2Bbl. V-8: Ventura/LeMans/Firebird ($140). 350 cu. in. 4Bbl. V-8: Ventura/LeMans/Firebird ($195); Firebird Formula ($55); Grand Prix ($55). 400 cu. in. 2Bbl. V-8: LeMans ($203); Grand Prix ($63). 400 cu. in. 4Bbl. V-8: LeMans/Firebird ($258); LeM wagon ($55); Firebird Formula ($118); Catalina/Bonn. ($73); Grand Prix ($118). 455 cu. in. V-8: LeMans ($321); LeM wagon ($118); Catalina/Bonn. ($137); Bonn. brghm ($64); Grand Prix ($181); Grand Prix SJ ($63). Performance pkg. (455 V-8): Trans Am ($125). Transmission/Differential: Three-speed floor shift: Ventura ($29). Four-speed manual trans.: Astre/Sunbird ($60). Close- ratio four-speed: Firebird ($242). Five-speed manual trans.: Astre/Sunbird ($244); Ventura ($262); LeMans spt cpe ($262); Firebird ($262); Formula/Trans Am (NC). Turbo Hydra-matic: Astre ($244); Ventura/LeMans ($262); Grand LeMans (NC). M40 Turbo Hydra-matic: LeM ($286); Grand LeM ($24); LeM wagon (NC). Safe-T-Track differential: Astre/Sunbird ($48); Ventura/LeM/Firebird ($51); Catalina/Bonn. ($55); Grand Prix ($54). Performance axle: Astre/Sunbird ($12). Brakes/Steering: Power brakes: Astre/Sunbird ($55); Ventura/LeM/Firebird ($58). Power steering: Astre/Sunbird ($120); Ventura/LeM ($136). Suspension: Radial-tuned susp.: Astre ($130-$162). Rally RTS handling pkg.: Astre ($12); Sunbird ($24); Ventura ($40); LeM ($57-$101); Grand Prix ($66-$89). Firm ride pkg.: Ventura/LeM ($10); Catalina/Bonn. ($10). Super lift shock absorbers: LeM ($46); Catalina/Bonn. ($47); Grand Prix ($46). Automatic level control: Catalina/Bonn. ($46-$93). Other: H.D. radiator: Astre/Sunbird ($28); Ventura ($18). Super-cooling radiator: LeM/Firebird/Grand Prix ($27-$49); Catalina/Bonn. ($27-$50). H.D. battery ($15-$17). H.D. alternator: LeM/Firebird ($42); Catalina/Bonn. ($43); Grand Prix ($42). Engine block heater ($11-$12). Medium trailer group: LeMans ($97-$119); Catalina/Bonn. ($98-$121); Grand Prix ($97-$119). Heavy trailer group ($109-$165). California emissions ($50).

OPTION PACKAGES: Astre GT pkg.: hatch/Safari ($426-$465). Astre luxury appointment group: hatch/Safari ($104). Astre custom exterior ($59-$88). Sunbird luxury appointment group ($139). Sunbird luxury trim group ($126). Ventura special appearance group: 2dr. ($70-$92). LeMans custom trim group: sedan ($88). Firebird custom trim group ($81). Firebird Formula appearance pkg. ($100). Catalina custom group ($201-$228). Grand Prix LJ luxury appointments group ($336-$680). Grand Prix SJ golden anniversary pkg. ($550).

MAJOR CONVENIENCE/APPEARANCE OPTIONS: Air conditioning ($424-$512). Automatic air conditioning: LeMans ($513); Grand Prix ($542); Catalina/Bonneville ($549). Cruise control ($73); N/A on Sunbird/Astre. Power seat: LeM/Cat./Bonn./G.P. ($124-$126). Power windows ($99-$159); N/A on Sunbird/Astre. Cornering lamps: Catalina/Bonn./Grand Prix ($41). Power sunroof: LeMans/Grand Prix ($370). Removable sunroof: Sunbird ($149). Landau top: LeMans ($109); Grand Prix ($119). Padded landau top: Ventura ($150); Grand Prix/LeMans ($174); Catalina/Bonn. ($222). Cordova top w/formal quarter windows: Sunbird ($132). Cordova top: LeMans ($109); Grand Prix ($119); Catalina/Bonneville ($125-$150). Rear-facing third seat: Safari ($149). Woodgrain siding: Safari wagons ($154-$156).

HISTORY: Introduced: September 25, 1975. Model year production: 748,842. Calendar year production (U.S.): 784,630. Calendar year sales by U.S. dealers: 753,093. Model year sales by U.S. dealers: 700,931.

Historical Footnotes: This was Pontiac's Golden Anniversary year, marking the 50th anniversary of the introduction of the Oakland. Production rose for the model year, and sales jumped even more. Only the subcompact Astre found fewer customers in 1976 than the prior year.

1977 PONTIAC

This year brought a switch from the old inline six to V-6 powerplants as base engines, as well as downsizing of full-size models. This move, it was claimed, would produced a "new generation of full-size cars." In keeping with the coming reduction of engine displacements, the 455 cu. in. V-8 was dropped. Three different 350 V-8s were used, from three different manufacturers. Highlight of the season may have been the introduction of the Can Am Limited Edition LeMans, which appeared at the Greater Los Angeles Auto Show in January 1977. A new Formula package, based on the sporty Firebird model, was offered this year on Astre and Sunbird models. Two all-new Pontiac engines were available: the "Iron Duke" 151 cu. in. (2.5-liter) four, and a 301 cu. in. (5.0- liter) V-8. Both had the same bore and stroke dimensions: 4.00 x 3.00 inches. The four produced 90 horsepower at 4400 R.P.M.; the V-8, 135 at 3800. Weighing just 452 pounds, the 301 was said to be one of the lightest domestic V-8 engines on the market.

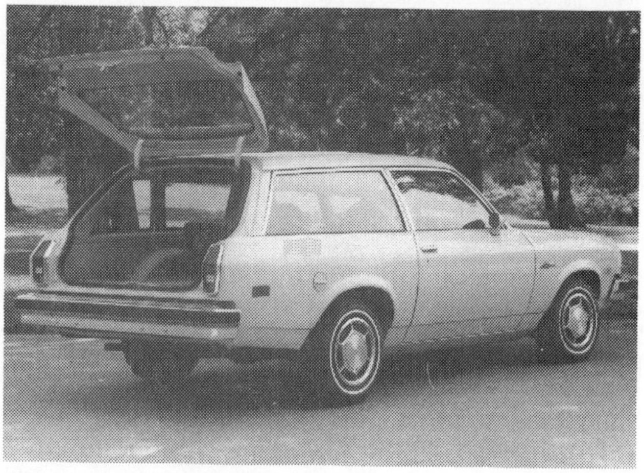

1977 Astre Safari wagon (P)

ASTRE — SERIES 2H — FOUR — Once again, the subcompact Astre came in coupe, hatchback coupe, and two-door Safari wagon form. This year it had a fresh front-end look with new grille, as well as revised interior trim. Astre's front end held single round headlamps in round recessed housings. On each side of the body-color vee-shaped center panel (with Pontiac vee-shaped emblem) were four holes in a single row, that formed the grille. The outer "holes" were actually the park/signal lights, while the others contained a set of thin vertical strips. New Astre options included 13 inch cast aluminum wheels. A luxury trim group included luxury seating, custom door trim with map pockets, rear ashtrays and other extras, available in hatchback and Safari models. Base engine for the coupe was the 140 cu. in. (2.3-liter) four, but hatchback and Safari models carried the new "Iron Duke" 151 cu. in. (2.5- liter) four and standard four-speed manual. A five-speed gearbox was optional, along with three-speed Turbo Hydra- matic.

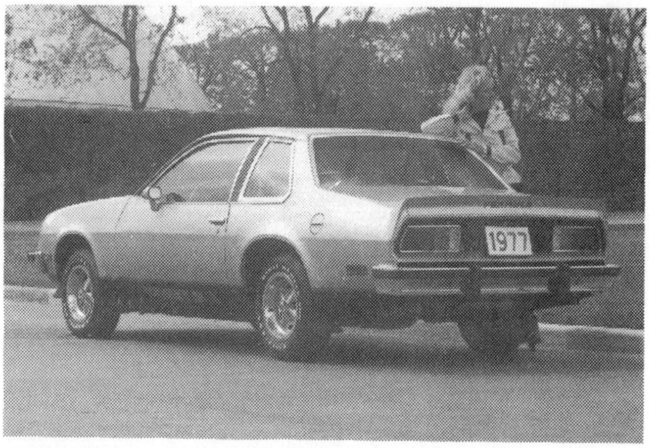

1977 Formula Sunbird coupe (P)

SUNBIRD — SERIES 2H — FOUR/V-6 — Like most other Pontiacs this year, Sunbird had a new grille and front end appearance. Quad rectangular headlamps stood alongside a recessed grille that consisted of roundish lements, similar to Firebird's. Base engine was the new 151 cu. in. (2.5-liter) four, with 231 cu. in. (3.8-liter) V-6 available. Also optional: cast aluminum wheels. A new Sunbird Sport-Hatch (hatchback) version appeared, with special paint and striping, to join the original two-door coupe.

VENTURA — SERIES 2X — FOUR/V-6/V-8 — Ventura featured a new grille design, as well as a posher interior with Grand Prix-style dash. Base and SJ models came in coupe, hatchback and sedan models. Base engine was the 231 cu. in. (3.8-liter) V-6, with a 301 or 350 cu. in. V-8 available. Three-speed column shift was standard; four-speed manual optional with V-8 power; a five-speed with the available four-cylinder engine. Ventura's grille had a wide body-color center panel (with

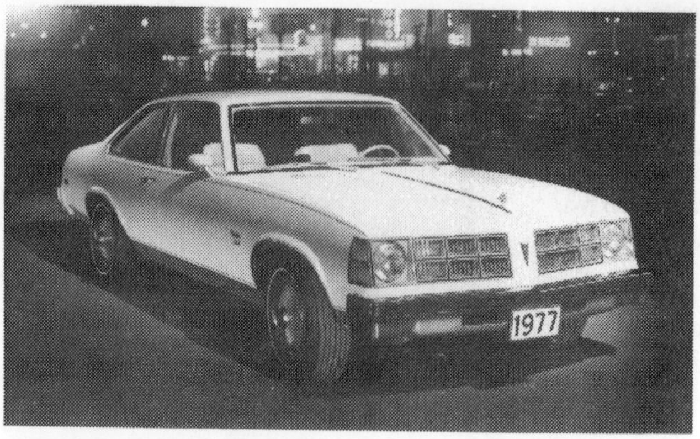

1977 Ventura SJ coupe (P)

customary Pontiac emblem) to split the twin sections. Each section contained six rectangular holes (two rows), each of which had an internal vertical-theme pattern. Single round rectangular headlamps met two-section marker lenses on the fender sides. Front bumpers held two small slots. Parking/signal lamps were behind the outer grille sections.

PHOENIX — SERIES 2X — FOUR/V-6/V-8 — Phoenix was a late arrival to the Pontiac lineup; see 1978 listing for data.

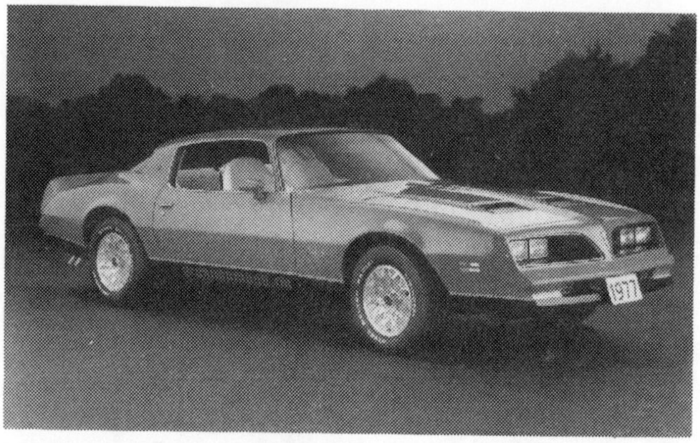

1977 Formula Firebird coupe (P)

FIREBIRD — SERIES 2F — V-6/V-8 — New front-end styling for the Firebird coupe featured quad rectangular headlamps and an "aggressive" grille. Four models were offered: base, Esprit, and performance Formula and Trans Am. Formula's new hood held simulated air scoops; at its rear was a spoiler. Wheelbase was 108 inches, and engine choices ranged from a 231 cu. in. (3.8-liter) V-6 to the 403 cu. in. (6.6-liter) V-8. Firebird's new grille was deeply recessed, directly in line with the quad rectangular headlamps. Its simple pattern consisted of a series of roundish (hexagonal) holes, resembling fencing more than a customary grille. A 'Pontiac' nameplate went on the driver's side of the grille. Crossbar- trimmed amber park/signal lamps were also recessed, but into the outer ends of twin air intake slots below the bumper strip. The center front panel protruded forward to a slight point and contained the usual Pontiac emblem, but its sides were much more sharply angled than the prior version. Esprit could have a new blue Sky Bird appearance package, with blue velour seating, two-tone blue body, and lue cast aluminum wheels. Firebird Formula came with a new 301 cu. in. (5.0-liter) two-barrel V-8. Its body displayed blacked-out trim, dual hood scoope, and large 'Formula' graphics on the lower door. Trans Am had a new shaker came with a standard 400 or 403 cu. in. V-8, but could also get an optional 'T/A 6.6' powerplant.

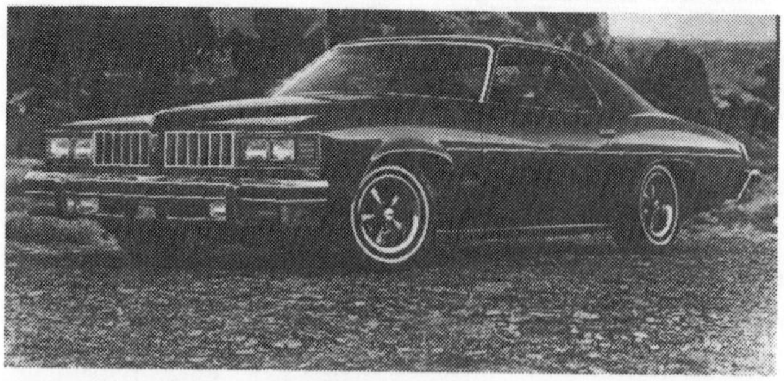

1977 LeMans Sport Coupe (CP)

LE MANS — SERIES 2A — V-6/V-8 — The mid-size LeMans had a new front end appearance and revised engine selection. Base engine was the 231 cu. in. (3.8-liter) V-6, except for Safari wagons which had a standard 350 cu. in. (5.7-liter) V-8. The 6.6-liter V-8 was available on all models. New LeMans options included 15 inch cast aluminum wheels, wire wheel covers, and new-styled deluxe wheel covers. Grand LeMans could get a new AM/FM radio with digital clock. A LeMans GT option (for Sport Coupe) included distinctive two-tone paint, bold striping, Rally RTS handling package, and body-color Rally II wheels. Base LeMans models had quad rectangular headlamps alongside a grille made up only of heavy vertical bars, forming six sections on each side of a protruding center divider. That divider formed a point that carried forward from

the prominent hood creases, and contained the triangular Pontiac emblem at the tip. Headlamp frames continued outward to surround wraparound single-section marker lenses. Park/signal lights were at the outer ends of twin bumper slots. Grand LeMans had a similar front-end look, but its grille sections included a horizontal divider, forming a 5 x 2 pattern of square holes on each side. Each of those 20 holes contained a smaller square. One of the more notable Pontiacs of the decade was the Can Am, a performance version of the LeMans Sport Coupe. Only 1,377 were produced. Can Am included the performance T/A 400 cu. in. (6.6-liter) V-8 (403 V-8 in California) along with body-colored Rally II wheels, a blacked-out grille assembly, and GR70 x 15 SBR tires. Can Am was promoted as a "fun car" along with Trans Am, offered only in Cameo White body color. Equipment included Turbo Hydra-matic, power brakes, variable-ratio power steering, front and rear stabilizer bars, body-color Rally II wheels, front/rear protective rubber bumper strips, and body- color dual sport mirrors (driver's side remote-controlled). A Grand Prix instrument panel assembly included a rally gauge cluster and clock. A Rally RTS handling package was standard. Appearance features included tri-tone colored accent tape striping on hood, front fenders, doors and sport mirrors; black lower bodyside with accent stripe; black rocker panel moldings; full-width rear deck spoiler with tri-tone accent stripe (front and rear); tri-tone 'CAN AM' identification on ront end, front fender and rear deck; blacked-out windshield, backlight, door window and belt moldings; and custom 'CAN AM' interior identification. The Trans Am-style "shaker" hood scoop had tri-tone 'T/A 6.6' identification and accent stripes. Early Can Am models also included a selection of options: SafTTrack rear axle, white-letter GR70 x 15 tires, custom sport steering wheels, Soft Ray tinted glass, dual horns, front/rear floor mats, and custom color-keyed seatbelts. Other available options included air conditioning, radio, and choice of white, black or firethorn interior trim color (or firethorn/white) in notchback, full-width or bucket seats.

1977 Grand Prix SJ coupe (P)

GRAND PRIX — SERIES 2G — V-8 — Three personal-luxury models were offered this year: base, sporty SJ, and luxury LJ. Base and LJ models had a standard 350 cu. in. (5.7-liter) V-8, while SJ came with a 6.6-liter V-8 (optional in the others). New Grand Prix options included CB radios and a digital AM/FM stereo information center and clock. This year's grille was no longer a wrapover style: only five vertical sections of bold elements on each side of the divider. The grille pattern repeated in two sections below the bumper. Quad rectangular headlamps were now separated by clear park/signal lights, forming three separate units on each side. Very narrow amber vertical marker lenses stood to the rear of front fender tips. Both hood and decklid showed sharp creases. Standard equipment included power brakes and steering, GR78 x 15 blackwall steel-belted radial tires, three-speed automatic transmission, heater/defroster, wheel opening and rocker panel moldings, window and roof drip moldings, and a clock. LJ added velour seat upholstery, a remote-controlled driver's mirror, and deluxe wheel covers. SJ had a 6.6-liter V-8 engine, GR70 x 15 tires, Rally II wheels with trim rings, accent striping, bucket seats with console, Rally RTS handling package, and rally gauges.

1977 Catalina sedan (P)

CATALINA — SERIES 2B — V-8 — Though reduced in outside dimensions, and weighing considerably less than before, both Catalina and Bonneville offered more head and rear leg room. The new design featured less door glass curvature, as well as a higher roofline. Full-size models rode a 116 inch wheelbase. Front ends held quad rectangular headlamps. Mechanical features included a Freedom battery and engine/air conditioning electrical diagnostic connector. Catalinas had a new brushed-knit cloth interior. Catalina's horizontal-theme grille had a slightly vee- shape center vertical segment (with Pontiac 'vee' emblem). It was part of a bold frame containing three horizontal bars (upper lower and center), which stood ahead of a set of horizontal ribs, forming four sections in all (two on each side). Parking/signal lights were below the bumper rub strip, while two-section marker lenses wrapped around the front fender, following the line of the quad rectangular headlamps. Bumper slots were in the bumper, just inside the bumper guards. Base engine was a 231 cu. in. (3.8-liter) V-6; optional, either a 350 cu. in. or 403 cu. in. V-8. Safari (and Grand Safari) wagons had a new three-way tailgate, two lockable storage areas and a 350 cu. in. V-8, and available rear- facing third seat. All full-size coupes and sedans could have a CB radio option. Standard equipment included automatic transmission, power brakes and steering, FR78 x 15 blackwall glass-belted radial tires, heater/defroster, and moldings at roof drip, window, wheel openings and rocker panels.

1977 Bonneville coupe (P)

BONNEVILLE — SERIES 2B — V-8 — Offered in coupe and sedan form, the new Bonneville had a flush eggcrate-style grille pattern on each side of the central 'vee' segment (with Pontiac emblem). Left and right grille segments formed a 4 x 4 pattern, with each segment containing internal crosshatching (a pattern within a pattern). The grille pattern repeated in two bumper slots, just inside the bumper guards. Framing for the quad rectangular headlamps continued outward to enclose four- section marker lenses. Park/signal lights were in the bumper. Interior choices were Lombardy velour cloth or Morrokide. Base engine was the 350 cu. in. (5.7-liter) four-barrel V-8, with 6.6-liter V-8 available. Brougham included a luxury interior package, and could have Valencia striped cloth trim. Standard Bonneville equipment was similar to Catalina's, but included rear fender skirts, deluxe wheel covers, and luxury steering wheel. Brougham added a Cordova top, driver's remote mirror, 60/40 seat with center armrest, power windows, and custom interior trim. Wagons had HR78 x 15 tires and a three-way tailgate with power back window.

I.D. DATA: Pontiac's 13-symbol Vehicle Identification Number (VIN) was located on the upper left surface of the instrument panel, visible through the windshield. The first digit is '2', indicating Pontiac division. The second symbol is a letter indicating series: 'C' Astre; 'M' Sunbird; 'X' Phoenix; 'Y' Ventura; 'Z' Ventura SJ; 'D' LeMans; 'F' LeMans Sport Coupe; 'G' Grand LeMans; 'S' Firebird; 'T' Firebird Esprit; 'U' Firebird Formula; 'W' Firebird Trans Am; 'L' Catalina; 'N' Bonneville; 'Q' Bonneville Brougham; 'J' Grand Prix; 'K' Grand Prix LJ; 'H' Grand Prix SJ. Next come two digits that denote body type: '07' 2dr. hatchback coupe; '11' 2dr. pillar coupe; '17' 2dr. hatchback coupe; '27' 2dr. sport coupe; '37' 2dr. HT coupe; '57' 2dr. HT coupe; '77' 2dr. hatchback coupe; '87' 2dr. HT coupe; '29' 4dr. HT sedan; '69' 4dr. thin-pillar 4 window sedan; '15' 2dr. station wagon; '35' 4dr. 2seat wagon. The fifth symbol is a letter indicating engine code: 'B' L4140 2Bbl.; 'V' L4151 2Bbl.; 'C' V6231 2Bbl.; 'Y' V8301 2Bbl.; 'U' V8305 4Bbl.; 'P' V8350 4Bbl. (L76); 'R' V8350 (L34); 'L' V8350 4Bbl. (LM1); 'Z' V8400 4Bbl.; 'K' V8403 4Bbl. The sixth symbol denotes model year ('7' 1977). Next is a plant code: 'A' Lakewood, Georgia; 'L' Van Nuys, Calif.; 'N' Norwood, Ohio; 'P' Pontiac, Mich.; 'T' Tarrytown, NY; 'U' Lordstown, Ohio; 'W' Willow Run, Mich.; 'X' Fairfax, Kansas; '1' Oshawa, Ontario; '2' Ste. Therese, Quebec. The final six digits are the sequential serial number, starting with 100,001 (except Astre/Sunbird, 500,001).

ASTRE (FOUR)

Model Number	Body/Style Number	Body Type & Seating	Factory Price	Shipping Weight	Production Total
2H	C11	2-dr. Cpe-4P	3304	2480	10,327
2H	C77	2-dr. Hatch Cpe-4P	3429	2573	12,120
2H	C15	2-dr. Safari Wag-4P	3594	2608	10,341

SUNBIRD (FOUR/V-6)

2H	M27	2-dr. Cpe-4P	3659/3779	2662/ --	41,708
2H	M07	2-dr. Hatch Cpe-4P	3784/3904	2693/ --	13,690

VENTURA (V-6/V-8)

2X	Y27	2-dr. Cpe-5P	3596/3661	3127/3212	26,675
2X	Y17	2-dr. Hatch Cpe-5P	3791/3856	3249/3334	4,015
2X	Y69	4-dr. Sed-5P	3650/3715	3167/3252	27,089

VENTURA SJ (V-6/V-8)

2X	Z27	2-dr. Cpe-5P	3945/4010	3206/3291	3,418
2X	Z17	2-dr. Hatch Cpe-5P	4124/4189	3293/3378	1,100
2X	Z69	4-dr. Sed-5P	3972/4037	3236/3321	4,339

PHOENIX (V-6/V-8)

2X	X27	2-dr. Cpe-	4075/4075	3227/3339	10,489
2X	X69	4-dr. Sed-	4122/4122	3275/3387	13,639

Ventura/Phoenix Engine Note: A four-cylinder engine was available for $120 credit.

FIREBIRD (V-6/V-8)

2F	S87	2-dr. HT Cpe-4P	4269/4334	3264/3349	30,642

FIREBIRD ESPRIT (V-6/V-8)

2F	T87	2-dr. HT Cpe-4P	4550/4615	3312/3397	34,548

FIREBIRD FORMULA (V-8)

2F	U87	2-dr. HT Cpe-4P	4976	3411	21,801

FIREBIRD TRANS AM (V-8)

2F	W87	2-dr. HT Cpe-4P	5456	3526	68,745

LE MANS (V-6/V-8)

2A	D37	2-dr. HT Cpe-6P	4045/4110	3550/3635	16,038
2A	D29	4-dt. HT Sed-6P	4093/4158	3638/3723	23,060

LE MANS SAFARI (V-8)

2A	D35	4-dr. 2S Wag-6P	4877	4135	10,081

LE MANS SPORT COUPE (V-6/V-8)

2A	F37	2-dr. HT Cpe-6P	4204/4269	3558/3643	12,277

LE MANS CAN AM (V-8)

2A	N/A	2-dr. HT Cpe-6P	N/A	N/A	1,377

1977 Grand LeMans coupe (P)

GRAND LE MANS (V-6/V-8)

2A	G37	2-dr. HT Cpe-6P	4602/4667	3587/3672	7,581
2A	G29	4-dr. HT Sed-6P	4730/4795	3740/3825	5,584

GRAND LE MANS SAFARI (V-8)

2A	G35	4-dr. 2S Wag-6P	5132	4179	5,393

GRAND PRIX (V-8)

2G	J57	2-dr. HT Cpe-6P	5108	3804	168,247

GRAND PRIX LJ (V-8)

2G	K57	2-dr. HT Cpe-6P	5471	3815	66,741

GRAND PRIX SJ (V-8)

2G	H57	2-dr. HT Cpe-6P	5742	3976	53,442

CATALINA (V-6/V-8)

2B	L37	2-dr. HT Cpe-6P	5052/5118	3473/3570	14,752
2B	L69	4-dr. Sed-6P	5049/5115	3501/3598	46,926

CATALINA SAFARI (V-8)

2B	L35	4-dr. 2S Wag-6P	5491	4024	13,058

BONNEVILLE (V-8)

2B	N37	2-dr. HT Cpe-6P	5410	3579	37,817
2B	N69	4-dr. Sed-6P	5456	3616	13,697

BONNEVILLE BROUGHAM (V-8)

2B	Q37	2-dr. HT Cpe-6P	5896	3617	15,901
2B	Q69	4-dr. Sed-6P	5991	3680	47,465

1977 Bonneville Grand Safari wagon (CP)

GRAND SAFARI (V-8)

2B	N35	4-dr. 2S Wag-6P	5771	4066	18,304

Safari Note: A third seat was available in all LeMans and Catalina/Bonneville Safari wagon models.

FACTORY PRICE AND WEIGHT NOTE: For Ventura, LeMans and Firebird, prices and weights to left of slash are for V-6, to right for V-8 engine except Sunbird, four and V-6.

ENGINE DATA: BASE FOUR (Astre coupe); OPTIONAL (Sunbird): Inline. Overhead cam. Four-cylinder. Aluminum block. Displacement: 140 cu. in. (2.3 liters). Bore & stroke: 3.50 x 3.63 in. Compression ratio: 8.0:1. Brake horsepower: 84 at 4400 R.P.M. Torque: 117 lbs.-ft. at 2400 R.P.M. Five main bearings. Hydraulic valve lifters. Carburetor: 2Bbl. VIN Code: B. BASE FOUR (Astre hatch/wagon, Sunbird); OPTIONAL (Astre coupe, Ventura): Inline. Overhead valve. Four-cylinder. Cast iron block and head. Displacement: 151 cu. in. (2.5 liters). Bore & stroke: 4.00 x 3.00 in. Compression ratio: 8.3:1. Brake horsepower: 90 at 4400 R.P.M. Torque: 128 lbs.-ft. at 2400 R.P.M. Five main bearings. Hydraulic valve lifters. Carburetor: 2Bbl. Holley 5210C. VIN Code: V. BASE V-6 (Ventura, Firebire, LeMans, Catalina); OPTIONAL (Sunbird): 90-degree, overhead-valve V-6. Cast iron block and head. Displacement: 231 cu. in. (3.8 liters). Bore & stroke: 3.80 x 3.40 in. Compression ratio: 8.0:1. Brake horsepower: 105 at 3200 R.P.M. Torque: 185 lbs.-ft. at 2000 R.P.M. Four main bearings. Hydraulic valve lifters. Carburetor: 2Bbl. Rochester 2GC. VIN Code: C. BASE V-8 (Firebird Formula, Bonneville, Grand Prix); OPTIONAL (Ventura, Firebird, LeMans, Catalina): 90-degree, overhead valve V-8. Cast iron block and head. Displacement: 301 cu. in. (5.0 liters). Bore & stroke: 4.00 x 3.00 in. Compression ratio: 8.2:1. Brake horsepower: 135 at 3800 R.P.M. Torque: 235-245 lbs.-ft. at 2000 R.P.M. (full-size, 250 at 1600). Five main bearings. Hydraulic valve lifters. Carburetor: 2Bbl. VIN Code: Y. OPTIONAL V-8 (Ventura, Firebird): 90-degree, overhead valve V-8. Cast iron block and head. Displacement: 305 cu. in. (5.0 liters). Bore & stroke: 3.74 x 3.48 in. Compression ratio: 8.5:1. Brake horsepower: 145 at 3800 R.P.M. Torque: 245 lbs.-ft. at 2400 R.P.M. Five main bearings. Hydraulic valve lifters. Carburetor: 2Bbl. Rochester 2GC. VIN Code: U. OPTIONAL V-8 (Firebird, LeMans, Catalina, Bonneville, Grand Prix): 90-degree, overhead valve V-8. Cast iron block and head. Displacement: 350 cu. in. (5.7 liters). Bore & stroke: 3.88 x 3.75 in. Compression ratio: 7.6:1. Brake horsepower: 170 at 000 R.P.M. Torque: 280 lbs.-ft. at 1800 R.P.M. Five main bearings. Hydraulic valve lifters. Carburetor: 4Bbl. Rochester M4MC. VIN Code: P. ALTERNATE V-8 (Firebird, LeMans, Catalina, Bonneville, Grand Prix): 90-degree, overhead valve V-8. Cast iron block and head. Displacement: 350 cu. in. (5.7 liters). Bore & stroke: 4.00 x 3.48 in. Compression ratio: 8.5:1. Brake horsepower: 170 at 3800 R.P.M. Torque: 270 lbs.-ft. at 2400 R.P.M. Five main bearings. Hydraulic valve lifters. Carburetor: 4Bbl. Rochester M4MC. Chevrolet-built. VIN Code: L. ALTERNATE V-8 (Firebird, LeMans, Catalina, Bonneville, Grand Prix): 90-degree, overhead valve V-8. Cast iron block and head. Displacement: 350 cu. in. (5.7 liters). Bore & stroke: 4.06 x 3.38 in. Compression ratio: 8.0:1. Brake horsepower: 170 at 3800 R.P.M. Torque: 275 lbs.-ft. at 2000 R.P.M. Five main bearings. Hydraulic valve lifters. Carburetor: 4Bbl. Rochester M4MC. Oldsmobile-built. VIN Code: R. BASE V-8 (Grand Prix SJ); OPTIONAL (Firebird, LeMans, Catalina, Bonneville, Grand Prix): 90-degree, overhead valve V-8. Cast iron block and head. Displacement: 400 cu. in. (6.6 liters). Bore & stroke: 4.12 x 3.75 in. Compression ratio: 7.6:1. Brake horsepower: 180 at 3600 R.P.M. Torque: 325 lbs.-ft. at 1600 R.P.M. Five main bearings. Hydraulic valve lifters. Carburetor: 4Bbl. Rochester M4MC. VIN Code: Z. BASE V-8 (Firebird Trans Am): Same as 400 cu. in. V-8 above, but Compression ratio: 8.0:1. Horsepower: 200 at 3600 R.P.M. Torque: 325 lbs.-ft. at 2400 R.P.M. ALTERNATE V-8 (Firebird, LeMans, Catalina, Bonneville, Grand Prix): 90-degree, overhead valve V-8. Cast iron block and head. Displacement: 403 cu. in. (6.6 liters). Bore & stroke: 4.35 x 3.38 in. Compression ratio: 8.0:1. Brake horsepower: 185 at 3600 R.P.M. Torque: 320 lbs.-ft. at 2200 R.P.M. Five main bearings. Hydraulic valve lifters. Carburetor: 4Bbl. Rochester M4MC. VIN Code: K.

CHASSIS DATA: Wheelbase: (Astre/Sunbird) 97.0 in.; (Ventura) 111.1 in.; (Firebird) 108.1 in.; (LeMans 2dr.) 112.0 in.; (Grand Prix) 116.0 in.; (Catalina/Bonn.) 115.9 in. Overall Length: (Astre) 177.6 in.; (Sunbird) 177.8 in.; (Ventura) 199.6 in.; (Firebird) 196.8 in.; (LeMans 2dr.) 208.0 in.; (LeM 4dr.) 212.0 in.; (LeM wag) 215.4 in.; (G.P.) 212.7 in.; (Catalina/Bonn.) 213.8 in.; (Catalina wag) 214.7 in. Height: (Astre hatch) 50.0 in.; (Astre notch/wag) 51.8 in.; (Sunbird) 49.8 in.; (Ventura 2dr.) 52.3 in.; (Ventura 4dr.) 53.2 in.; (Firebird) 49.1 in.; (Esprit/Formula) 49.4 in.; (Trans Am) 49.6 in.; (LeM 2dr.) 52.7 in.; (LeM 4dr.) 53.5 in.; (LeM wag) 55.3 in.; (G.P.) 52.6 in.; (Catalina/Bonn.) 53.9 in.; (Catalina/Bonn. wag) 58.2 in.; (Cat. wag) 57.3 in. Width: (Astre/Sunbird) 65.4 in.; (Ventura) 72.4 in.; (Firebird) 73.0 in.; (LeM) 77.4 in.; (G.P.) 77.8 in.; (Cat./Bonn.) 75.4 in. Front Tread: (Astre/Sunbird) 55.2 in.; (Ventura) 61.2 in.; (Ventura SJ) 61.8 in.; (Firebird) 60.9 in.; (Firebird Formula) 61.3 in.; (Trans Am) 61.2 in.; (LeM) 61.6 in.; (G.P.) 61.6 in.; (Cat./Bonn.) 61.7 in. Rear Tread: (Astre/Sunbird) 54.1 in.; (Ventura) 59.0 in.; (Firebird) 60.0 in.; (Firebird Formula) 60.4 in.; (Trans Am) 60.3 in.; (LeM) 61.1 in.; (G.P.) 61.1 in.; (Cat./Bonn.) 60.7 in. Standard Tires: (Astre) A78 x 13 exc. wagon, BR78 x 13; (Sunbird) A78 x 13; (Ventura) E78 x 14; (Firebird) FR78 x 15; (Trans Am) GR70 x 15; (LeMans) FR78 x 15 exc. wagon, HR78 x 15; (Grand Prix) N/A; (Grand Prix SJ) GR70 x 15; (Cat.) FR78 x 15 exc. wagon, HR78 x 15; (Bonn.) FR78 x 15.

TECHNICAL: Transmission: Three-speed manual transmission standard on Ventura, LeMans and Firebird. Four-speed manual standard on Astre/Sunbird and Firebird Formula; optional on Firebird and Ventura V-8. Five-speed manual optional on Astre/Sunbird and Ventura four-cylinder. Three-speed Turbo Hydra-matic standard on other models, optional on all. Standard final drive ratio: (Astre cpe) 3.42:1; (Astre hatch/wag) 2.73:1; (Sunbird) 2.73:1 w/four, 2.56:1 w/V-6; (Ventura) 3.42:1 w/four,

3.08:1 w/V-6, 3.23:1 w/V-8; (Firebird) 3.08:1 w/four, 3.23:1 w/V8301, 2.41:1 w/V8350; (Trans Am) 3.23:1 or 3.42:1; (LeMans) 3.08:1 w/V-6, 2.56:1 w/V8301, 2.41:1 w/V8350/400, 2.56:1 w/V8403; (Grand Prix) 2.56:1 w/V8301, 2.41:1 w/V8350/400/403, (Catalina) 2.73:1 w/V-6; (Bonneville) 2.41:1; (Safari) 2.56:1. Steering: Recirculating ball. Front Suspension: (Astre) coil springs and control arms; (Firebird/LeMans) coil springs w/lower trailing links and anti-sway bar; (others) coil springs and anti-sway bar. Rear Suspension: (Astre/Sunbird) rigid axle with coil springs, lower trailing radius arms and upper torque arms; (Ventura/Firebird) semi-elliptic leaf springs with anti-sway bar; (LeMans/Bonneville/Grand Prix) rigid axle with coil springs, lower trailing radius arms, upper torque arms and anti-sway bar. Brakes: Front disc, rear drum. Ignition: Electronic. Body construction: (Astre/Sunbird) unit; (Ventura) unit w/front frame section; (Firebird) unit w/separate partial frame; (others) separate body and frame. Fuel Tank: (Astre) 16 gal.; (Sunbird) 18.5 gal.; (Ventura) 20.5 gal.; (Firebird) 20.2 gal.; (LeMans) 21.8 gal. exc. wagon, 22 gal.; (Grand Prix) 25 gal.; (Catalina/Bonn.) 20 gal. exc. wagon, 22.5 gal.

DRIVETRAIN OPTIONS: Engines: 140 cu. in. 2Bbl. four: Astre ($20); Ventura cpe/sed ($120 credit). 231 cu. in. V-6: Sunbird ($120). 301 cu. in. V-8: Ventura/Firebird/LeM ($65); Catalina ($66). 305 cu. in. 2Bbl. V-8: Ventura ($65). 350 cu. in. 4Bbl. V-8: Ventura/LeMans/Firebird ($155); LeMans Safari ($90); Firebird Formula ($90); Grand Prix ($90). 400 cu. in. 4Bbl. V-8: LeMans ($220); LeM wagon ($155); Firebird Formula ($155-$205); Trans Am ($50); Catalina ($223); Bonn. ($157); Grand Prix ($155). 403 cu. in. 4Bbl. V-8: LeMans ($220); LeM wagon ($155); Firebird Formula ($155); Catalina ($223); Bonn. ($157); Grand Prix ($155). Transmission/Differential: M15 three-speed manual trans.: LeM ($282). Three-speed floor shift: Ventura ($31). Four-speed manual floor shift trans.: Ventura w/V8301 ($257). Four-speed manual trans.: Firebird ($257). Five-speed manual trans.: Astre/Sunbird ($248); Ventura four ($282). Turbo Hydra-matic: Astre/Sunbird/Ventura/Firebird ($248); LeMans (N/A). Safe-T-Track differential: Astre/Sunbird ($50); Ventura/LeM/Firebird ($54); Catalina/Bonn./G.P. ($58). Brakes/Steering: Power brakes: Astre/Sunbird ($58); Ventura/LeM/Firebird ($61). Power steering: Astre/Sunbird ($129); Ventura/LeM ($146). Suspension: Rally RTS handling pkg.: Astre ($55-$215); Sunbird ($44-$215); Ventura ($44); Firebird ($46-$116); LeM ($36- $158); Cat. ($130-$156); Bonn. ($93-$111); Grand Prix ($34- $102). Firm ride pkg. ($11) except Astre/Sunbird. Superlift shock absorbers: LeM/G.P. ($49); Catalina/Bonn. ($50). Automatic level control: Catalina/Bonn. ($52-$102). Other: H.D. radiator: Astre/Sunbird ($30); Ventura ($27-$55). Super-cooling radiator ($27-$55) except Astre/Sunbird. H.D. battery ($18-$18). Maintenance-free battery ($31). H.D. alternator: LeM/Firebird ($45); Catalina/Bonn. ($46); Grand Prix ($45). Engine block heater ($12-$13). Class I trailer group: LeM/G.P. ($109-$133); Bonn./Cat. ($110-$135). Medium trailer group: LeMans/G.P. ($127-$151); Catalina/Bonn. ($128- $153). Heavy trailer group: Bonn./Cat. ($139-$199). California emissions ($70). High-altitude option ($22).

OPTION PACKAGES: Astre Formula appearance group ($447-$558). Astre special appearance pkg.: w/Formula ($34). Astre luxury appointment group: hatch/Safari ($147). Astre custom exterior ($63-$94). Astre custom interior ($141-$183). Sunbird Formula appearance group ($436-$543). Sunbird special appearance group ($82). Sunbird luxury appointment group ($147). Sunbird luxury trim group ($144). LeMans GT: spt cpe ($446-$463). LeMans custom trim group: sedan/wag ($92-$208). Firebird "Skybird" appearance pkg.: Esprit ($325-$342). Trans Am special edition ($556-$1143). Firebird custom trim group ($27-$118). Firebird Formula appearance pkg. ($127). Catalina special appearance group ($140). Bonneville special appearance group ($135). Sarafi custom trim group ($167-$286).

MAJOR CONVENIENCE/APPEARANCE OPTIONS: Air conditioning ($442-$540). Automatic air conditioning: LeMans/Grand Prix ($539-$552); Catalina/Bonneville ($579). Cruise control ($80-$84); N/A on Sunbird/Astre. Power seat: LeM/Cat./Bonn./G.P. ($137-$139). Power windows ($108-$151); N/A on Sunbird/Astre. Cornering lamps: Catalina/Bonn./Grand Prix ($44). Power glass sunroof: LeMans/Grand Prix ($625); Catalina/Bonn. ($898). Power steel sunroof: LeMans/Grand Prix ($394); Catalina/Bonn. ($735). Glass sunroof: Firebird ($587). Padded landau top: Grand Prix/LeMans ($180). Cordova vinyl top: Sunbird ($83-$144); Ventura ($93); LeMans ($111); Grand Prix ($121); Catalina/Bonneville ($135-$140). Canopy top: Firebird ($105). Landau vinyl top: Sunbird ($144); Ventura ($162); LeMans ($111); Grand Prix ($121). Canopy vinyl top: LeMans ($151); Catalina/Bonneville ($107-$112). Formal landau vinyl top: Catalina/Bonneville ($277-$282). Rear spoiler: Astre/Sunbird ($45); Firebird ($51).

HISTORY: Introduced: September 30, 1976. Model year production: 911,050. Calendar year production (U.S.): 875,958. Calendar year sales by U.S. dealers: 808.467. Model year sales by U.S. dealers: 811,904.

Historical Footnotes: Sales rose considerably for the 1977 model year, paving the way for another increase the next time around. The downsized full-size models sold better than their bigger predecessors. A.C. Mair was Pontiac's General Manager at this time.

1978 PONTIAC

Both Astre and Ventura faded away. Following the downsizing of full-size models for 1977, the mid-size Lemans, Grand LeMans and personal-luxury Grand Prix received similar treatment this year. Returning this season was the Grand Am nameplate.

1978 Sunbird coupe (JAG)

SUNBIRD — SERIES 2H — FOUR/V-6 — Basic appearance of Pontiac's remaining subcompact was similar to 1977 with staggered, recessed quad rectangular headlamps at the ends of each front-end opening. This year's narrow grilles consisted of all vertical bars on each side of the tapered, body-color divider (with Pontiac emblem). 'Sunbird' script was on the cowl, below the bodyside molding. Bright taillamps frames had two horizontal separator ribs. Backup lights sat at inner ends and amber lenses in the center of each unit. Base engine was the 151 cu. in. (2.5-liter) four with four-speed manual. Equipment includes A78 x 13 tires (B78 x 13 on wagons), heater/defroster, and bucket seats. Sport coupe and hatchback models included bright grille and drip moldings and custom wheel covers.

1978 Phoenix LJ coupe (CP)

PHOENIX — SERIES 2X — FOUR/V-6/V-8 — Ventura was gone, but the compact came in two-door coupe, four-door sedan and hatchback coupe form. A wide center divider at the front held 'Pontiac' lettering below a Pontiac emblem. Grille framing extended to the single recessed rectangular headlamps and tall clear/marker side markers. The grille consisted of four vertical dividers, forming five sections on each side, with subdued vertical bars in each portion. A large Phoenix emblem was low on the cowl. Flush-mount taillamps in bright frames had two divider ribs. Backup lights were in the center of each lens set. Base engine was the 231 cu. in. (3.8-liter) V-6 with three-speed manual shift. Equipment included E78 x 14 blackwall tires, hubcaps, lighter, heater/defroster, and an instrument cluster similar to Grand Prix. LJ added a stand-up hood ornament, wheel opening and rocker panel moldings, and deluxe wheel covers.

1978 Firebird Trans Am coupe

FIREBIRD — SERIES 2F — V-6/V-8 — Appearance of the sporty Firebird was similar to 1977, with rectangular quad headlamps and a dark grille. Wide three-row taillamps had backup lights at the inner ends, close to the license plate. Taillamp ribs filled most of the ack panel. Base engine was the 231 cu. in. (3.8-liter) V-6 with three-speed shift. Formula had a 305 cu. in. (5.0-liter) V-8, while Trans Am carried a 400 cu. in. four-barrel V-8. Equipment included Endura bumpers, hubcaps, dual horns, FR78 x 15 SBR tires, bucket seats, and heater/defroster. Esprit added wheel covers, sport mirrors, bright hood and wheel opening moldings, and custom pedal trim. Trans Am included a front air dam, black grille, rear spoiler, sport mirrors, rear wheel air deflectors, Rally II wheels, "shaker" hood and air cleaner, and rally instrument panel with tachometer. Formula and Trans Am had power brakes. Automatic transmission was standard on Formula and Trans Am, but Formula could have a four-speed manual at no extra cost.

1978 LeMans Safari wagon (CP)

LE MANS — SERIES 2A — V-6/V-8 — The downsized mid-size Pontiacs were 8-17 inches shorter and 530 to 925 pounds lighter than before, boosting fuel economy without loss of interior space. LeMans and Grand LeMans came in two-door coupe and four-door sedan body styles, along with a four-door Safari wagon. Body features included soft, body-colored front/rear bumpers on coupes and sedans. Single rectangular headlamps were used. The headlamp dimmer was now column-mounted. An AM/FM stereo radio with cassette player was available. Options included power vent rear windows (for sedans). Base engine was the 231 cu. in. (3.8-liter) V-6; optional, a 305 cu. in. (5.0-liter) V-8. A wide body-color divider with emblem separated the grille into the customary twin sections. Each 3 x 3 crosshatch grille section stood

over subdued vertical bars. Wraparound amber side marker lenses were split into three sections. Two small air slots were below the bumper strip. Wraparound taillamps had two horizontal dividers and stretched full-width to the recessed license plate. Standard equipment included a three-speed manual floor shift, wheel opening moldings, P185/75R14 FBR blackwall tires, hubcaps, and a heater/defroster. Grand LeMans added a hood ornament and moldings, lower bodyside moldings, and black rocker panel moldings.

GRAND AM — SERIES 2A — V-8 — A single series, coupe and sedan, made up the Grand Am lineup, which featured a soft front-end panel and two-tone paint. Standard equipment included 205/70R14 steel-belted radial tires and Rally RTS suspension. Base engine was the 301 cu. in. (4.9-liter) V-8; optional, a four-barrel version of the same powerplant. Four body-color vertical strips separated each grille section in the sloping front panel into five segments. The protruding body-color center divider held a Pontiac emblem. Recessed single rectangular headlamps stood above clear park/signal lamps, with the same framework wrapping to clear/amber side marker lenses. 'Grand Am' nameplates went on the forward end of front fenders. At the rear were horizontally-ribbed wraparound taillamps. Grand Am standard equipment was similar to LeMans but included an automatic transmission (with four-speed manual optional), power brakes/steering, two-tone paint, and P205/70R14 blackwall SBR tires.

1978 Grand Prix SJ coupe

GRAND PRIX — SERIES 2G — V-6/V-8 — Three Grand Prix models were offered again this year: base, sporty SJ, and luxury LJ. All three now rode a 108 inch wheelbase, measuring 201.2 inches in length (nearly 17 inches shorter than their predecessors). Weights were cut by 600 to 750 pounds. The base Grand Prix had a notchback front seat with either vinyl or cloth upholstery. Grand Prix LJ came with a loose-pillow style cloth notchback front seat. Optional on SJ and LJ: leather upholstery in Viscount design. Base engine was the 231 cu. in. (3.8-liter) V-6, but LJ had a 301 cu. in. (4.9-liter) two-barrel V-8 and LJ a four-barrel 301. Equipment also included a three-speed manual gearbox, wide rocker panel moldings, wheel opening moldings, clock, and P195/75R14 SBR blackwall tires. SJ added P205/70R14 tires, a 301 cu. in. four-barrel V-8, power brakes and steering, automatic transmission, and vinyl front bucket seats. LJ had wide rocker panel moldings with extensions, a two-tone 301 V-8, automatic, power brakes/steering, body-color mirrors, and deluxe wheel covers. The new-size Grand Prix displayed a rather tall grille in a bright, heavy frame with four vertical bars on each side of the bright center bar, which held no emblem. A tall hood ornament had 'GP' letters at the base. Clear park/signal lamps stood between each pair of quad headlamps, as in 1977. 'Grand Prix' script went above the left headlamp. All told, the grille (and the whole front end) showed a more upright, squared-off look than before. Hood creases were far less prominent, meeting the grille ends rather than coming to a point at the center. Large squarish taillamps contained five horizontal divider ribs. The license plate was mounted in the decklid.

CATALINA — SERIES 2B — V-6/V-8 — Styling of both full-size models was similar to 1977, when the pair was downsized. Catalina's revised grille consisted of five horizontal strips over subdued vertical strips. Small clear park/signal lamps were in the bumper. Alongside the quad rectangular headlamps were two-section amber wraparound marker lenses. The bright grille divider held no emblem. 'Catalina' lettering went on the cowl, 'Pontiac' over the driver's side headlamps. Wraparound taillamps had two horizontal ribs, with backup lights at the inner ends. The recessed license plate was on a level with the taillamps. Catalina's base engine was the Buick-built 231 cu. in. (3.8-liter) V-6, with 301, 350 and 400/403 cu. in. V-8 available. Equipment included automatic transmission, power brakes/steering, FR78 x 15 radial tires, front/rear bumper strips, and heater/defroster.

1978 Bonneville Brougham sedan

BONNEVILLE — SERIES 2B — V-8 — Like Catalina, the full-size Bonneville was similar to 1977, but had a revised grille. This one had four vertical divider bars on each side of the bright center divider (with emblem), instead of the former eggcrate design. Wraparound marker lenses were in the same frames as headlamps, extending to four-section amber side marker lenses. 'Pontiac' lettering went over the left headlamp again. The hood ornament was an octagon within an octagon. As before, small clear park/signal lamps were bumper-mounted. 'Bonneville' lettering went on the lower cowl. Wraparound taillamps were new. Standard equipment was similar to Catalina, but a two-barrel 301 V-8 was standard, along with fender skirts and wheel covers. Brougham added a 60/40 front seat, clock, and power windows.

I.D. DATA: Pontiac's 13-symbol Vehicle Identification Number (VIN) was located on the upper left surface of the instrument panel, visible through the windshield. The first digit is '2', indicating Pontiac division. The second symbol is a letter indicating series: 'E' Sunbird; 'M' Sunbird; 'Y' Phoenix; 'Z' Phoenix LJ; 'D' LeMans; 'F' Grand LeMans; 'G' Grand Am; 'S' Firebird; 'T' Firebird Esprit; 'U' Firebird Formula; 'W' Firebird Trans Am; 'L' Catalina; 'N' Bonneville; 'Q' Bonneville Brougham; 'J' Grand Prix; 'K' Grand Prix LJ; 'H' Grand Prix SJ. Next come two digits that denote body type: '07' 2dr. hatchback coupe; '17' 2dr. hatchback coupe; '27' 2dr. coupe; '37' 2dr. coupe; '87' 2dr. HT coupe; '19' 4dr. 6window sedan; '69' 4dr. 4 window sedan; '15' 2dr. station wagon; '35' 4dr. 2seat wagon. The fifth symbol is a letter indicating engine code: 'V' L4151 2Bbl.; 'A' V6231 2Bbl.; 'Y' V8301 2Bbl.; 'W' V8301 4Bbl.; 'U' V8305 2Bbl.; 'X' V8350 4Bbl.; 'L' V8350 4Bbl. (L34); 'L' V8350 4Bbl. (LM1); 'Z' V8400 4Bbl. The sixth symbol denotes model year ('8' 1978). Next is a plant code: 'A' Lakewood, Georgia; 'B' Baltimore; 'L' Van Nuys, Calif.; 'N' Norwood, Ohio; 'P' Pontiac, Mich.; 'T' Tarrytown, NY; 'U' Lordstown, Ohio; 'W' Willow Run, Mich.; 'X' Fairfax, Kansas; '1' Oshawa, Ontario; '2' Ste. Therese, Quebec. The final six digits are the sequential serial number.

1978 Formula Sunbird Sport hatchback coupe

SUNBIRD (FOUR/V-6)

Model Number	Body/Style Number	Body Type & Seating	Factory Price	Shipping Weight	Production Total
2H	E27	2-dr. Cpe-4P	3540/3710	2662/--	20,413
2H	M07	2-dr. Hatch Cpe-4P	3912/4082	2694/--	25,380
2H	M27	2-dr. Spt Cpe-4P	3773/3943	2662/--	32,572
2H	M15	2-dr. Sta Wag-4P	3741/3911	2610/--	8,424

PHOENIX (V-6/V-8)

2X	Y27	2-dr. Cpe-6P	3872/4022	3119/3215	26,143
2X	Y69	4-dr. Sed-6P	3947/4097	3169/3265	32,529
2X	Y17	2-dr. Hatch-6P	4068/4218	3202/3298	3,252

PHOENIX LJ (V-6/V-8)

2X	Z27	2-dr. Cpe-6P	4357/4507	3228/3324	6,210
2X	Z69	4-dr. Sed-6P	4432/4582	3277/3373	8,393

Phoenix Engine Note: A four-cylinder engine was available for $170 credit.

FIREBIRD (V-6/V-8)

2F	S87	2-dr. HT Cpe-4P	4545/4695	3254/3377	32,672

FIREBIRD ESPRIT (V-6/V-8)

2F	T87	2-dr. HT Cpe-4P	4842/4992	3285/3408	36,926

FIREBIRD FORMULA (V-8)

2F	U87	2-dr. HT Cpe-4P	5448	3452	24,346

1978 Firebird Trans Am Gold Special Edition T-top (CP)

FIREBIRD TRANS AM (V-8)

2F	W87	2-dr. HT Cpe-4P	5799	3511	93,341

LE MANS (V-6/V-8)

2A	D27	2-dr. HT Cpe-6P	4405/4555	3038/3159	20,581
2A	D19	4-dt. HT Sed-6P	4480/4630	3047/3168	22,728

LE MANS SAFARI (V-6/V-8)

2A	D35	4-dr. 2S Wag-6P	4937/5086	3225/3372	15,714

1978 Grand LeMans coupe

GRAND LE MANS (V-6/V-8)

2A	F27	2-dr. HT Cpe-6P	4777/4927	3070/3190	18,433
2A	F19	4-dr. HT Sed-6P	4881/5031	3098/3218	21,252

GRAND LE MANS SAFARI (V-6/V-8)

2A	F35	4-dr. 2S Wag-6P	5265/5415	3242/3389	11,125

GRAND AM (V-8)

2A	G27	2-dr. Cpe-6P	5464	3209	7,767
2A	G19	4-dr. Sed-6P	5568	3239	2,841

GRAND PRIX (V-6/V-8)

2G	J37	2-dr. Cpe-6P	4800/5030	3101/3224	127,253

GRAND PRIX LJ (V-8)

2G	K37	2-dr. Cpe-6P	5815	3216	65,122

GRAND PRIX SJ (V-8)

2G	H37	2-dr. Cpe-6P	6088	3229	36,069

CATALINA (V-6/V-8)

2B	L37	2-dr. Cpe-6P	5375/5525	3438/3559	9,224
2B	L69	4-dr. Sed-6P	5410/5560	3470/3591	39,707

CATALINA SAFARI (V-8)

2B	L35	4-dr. 2S Wag-6P	5924	3976	12,819

BONNEVILLE (V-8)

2B	N37	2-dr. Cpe-6P	5831	3581	22,510
2B	N69	4-dr. Sed-6P	5931	3637	48,647

BONNEVILLE BROUGHAM (V-8)

2B	Q37	2-dr. Cpe-6P	6577	3611	36,192
2B	Q69	4-dr. Sed-6P	6677	3667	17,948

GRAND SAFARI (V-8)

2B	N35	4-dr. 2S Wag-6P	6227	4002	13,847

FACTORY PRICE AND WEIGHT NOTE: Prices and weights to left of slash are for V-6, to right for V-8 engine except Sunbird, four and V-6.

ENGINE DATA: BASE FOUR (Sunbird); OPTIONAL (Phoenix): Inline. Overhead valve. Four-cylinder. Cast iron block and head. Displacement: 151 cu. in. (2.3 liters). Bore & stroke: 4.00 x 3.00 in. Compression ratio: 8.3:1. Brake horsepower: 85 at 4400 R.P.M. Torque: 123 lbs.-ft. at 2800 R.P.M. Five main bearings. Hydraulic valve lifters. Carburetor: 2Bbl. Holley 5210C. VIN Code: V. BASE V-6 (Phoenix, Firebird, LeMans, Catalina, Grand Prix); OPTIONAL (Sunbird): 90-degree, overhead-valve V-6. Cast iron block and head. Displacement: 231 cu. in. (3.8 liters). Bore & stroke: 3.80 x 3.40 in. Compression ratio: 8.0:1. Brake horsepower: 105 at 3200-3400 R.P.M. Torque: 185 lbs.-ft. at 2000 R.P.M. Four main bearings. Hydraulic valve lifters. Carburetor: 2bbl. Rochester 2GC. VIN Code: A. BASE V-8 (Grand Am, Bonneville, Grand Prix LJ); OPTIONAL (Grand Prix, Catalina): 90-degree, overhead-valve V-8. Cast iron block and head. Displacement: 301 cu. in. (5.0 liters). Bore & stroke: 4.00 x 3.00 in. Compression ratio: 8.2:1. Brake horsepower: 140 at 3600 R.P.M. Torque: 235 lbs.-ft. at 2000 R.P.M. Five main bearings. Hydraulic valve lifters. Carburetor: 2Bbl. Rochester M2MC. VIN Code: Y. BASE V-8 (Grand Prix SJ); OPTIONAL (Grand Am, Grand Prix): Same as 301 cu. in. V-8 above, with 4Bbl. carburetor (Rochester M4MC) Horsepower: 150 at 4000 R.P.M. Torque: 239 lbs.-ft. at 2000 R.P.M. VIN Code: W. BASE V-8 (Firebird Formula); OPTIONAL (Phoenix, Firebird, LeMans, Grand Prix SJ/LJ): 90-degree, overhead valve V-8. Cast iron block and head. Displacement: 305 cu. in. (5.0 liters). Bore & stroke: 3.74 x 3.48 in. Compression ratio: 8.4:1. Brake horsepower: 145 at 3800 R.P.M. Torque: 245 lbs.-ft. at 2400 R.P.M. Five main bearings. Hydraulic valve lifters. Carburetor: 2Bbl. Rochester 2GC. VIN Code: U. OPTIONAL V-8 (Firebird, Catalina, Bonneville): 90-degree, overhead valve V-8. Cast iron block and head. Displacement: 350 cu. in. (5.7 liters). Bore & stroke: 3.80 x 3.85 in. Compression ratio: 8.0:1. Brake horsepower: 155 at 3400 R.P.M. Torque: 280 lbs.-ft. at 1800 R.P.M. Five main bearings. Hydraulic valve lifters. Carburetor: 4Bbl. Rochester M4MC. Buick-built. VIN Code: X. ALTERNATE V-8 (Firebird, Catalina, Bonneville): 90-degree, overhead valve V-8. Cast iron block and head. Displacement: 350 cu. in. (5.7 liters). Bore & stroke: 4.00 x 3.48 in. Compression ratio: 8.2:1. Brake horsepower: 170 at 3800 R.P.M. Torque: 270 lbs.-ft. at 2400 R.P.M. Five main bearings. Hydraulic valve lifters. Carburetor: 4Bbl. Rochester M4MC. Chevrolet-built. VIN Code: L. ALTERNATE V-8 (Firebird, Catalina, Bonneville): 90-degree, overhead valve V-8. Cast iron block and head. Displacement: 350 cu. in. (5.7 liters). Bore & stroke: 4.06 x 3.38 in. Compression ratio: 7.9:1. Brake horsepower: 170 at 3800 R.P.M. Torque: 275 lbs.-ft. at 2000 R.P.M. Five main bearings. Hydraulic valve lifters. Carburetor: 4Bbl. Rochester M4MC. Oldsmobile-built. VIN Code: R. BASE V-8 (Trans Am); OPTIONAL (Firebird Formula, Catalina, Bonneville): 90-degree, overhead valve V-8. Cast iron block and head. Displacement: 400 cu. in. (6.6 liters). Bore & stroke: 4.12 x 3.75 in. Compression ratio: 7.7:1. Brake horsepower: 180 at 3600 R.P.M. Torque: 325 lbs.-ft. at 1600 R.P.M. Five main bearings. Hydraulic valve lifters. Carburetor: 4Bbl. Rochester M4MC. VIN Code: Z. OPTIONAL T/A V-8 (Firebird Formula/Trans Am): Same as 400 cu. in. V-8 above, but Compression ratio: 8.1:1. Horsepower: 220 at 4000 R.P.M. Torque: 320 lbs.-ft. at 2800 R.P.M. NOTE: A 403 cu. in. V-8 was used in California models.

CHASSIS DATA: Wheelbase: (Sunbird) 97.0 in.; (Phoenix) 111.1 in.; (Firebird) 108.1 in.; (LeMans) 108.1 in.; (Grand Prix) 108.1 in.; (Catalina/Bonn.) 115.9 in. Overall Length: (Sunbird) 177.8 in.; (Sunbird hatch) 178.3 in.; (Sunbird wag) 177.6 in.; (Phoenix) 203.4 in.; (Firebird) 196.8 in.; (LeMans cpe) 199.2 in.; (LeM sed) 198.5 in.; (LeM wag) 197.8 in.; (G.P.) 201.2 in.; (Catalina/Bonn.) 214.3 in.; (Safari wag) 215.1 in. Height: (Sunbird) 49.6 in.; (Sunbird hatch) 49.9 in.; (Sunbird wag) 51.8 in.; (Phoenix) 52.3 in.; (Firebird) 49.3 in.; (Formula/Trans Am) 49.5 in.; (LeM cpe) 53.5 in.; (LeM sed) 54.4 in.; (LeM wag) 54.8 in.; (G.P.) 53.3 in.; (Catalina/Bonn. cpe) 53.9 in.; (Catalina/Bonn. sed) 54.5 in.; (Safari wag) 57.3 in. Width: (Sunbird) 65.4 in.; (Phoenix) 73.2 in.; (Firebird) 3.4 in.; (LeM) 72.4 in.; (LeM wag) 72.6 in.; (G.P.) 72.8 in.; (Cat./Bonn.) 78.0 in.; (Safari wag) 80.0 in. Front Tread: (Sunbird) 55.2 in. exc. hatch, 54.7 in.; (Phoenix) 61.8 in.; (Firebird) 60.9 in.; (Firebird Formula) 61.3 in.; (Trans Am) 61.2 in.; (LeM) 58.5 in.; (G.P.) 58.5 in.; (Cat./Bonn.) 61.7 in.; (Safari) 62.1 in. Rear Tread: (Sunbird) 54.1 in. exc. hatch, 53.6 in.; (Phoenix) 59.6 in.; (Firebird) 60.0 in.; (Firebird Formula) 60.4 in.; (Trans Am) 60.3 in.; (LeM) 57.8 in.; (G.P.) 57.8 in.; (Cat./Bonn.) 60.7 in.; (Safari) 64.1 in. Standard Tires: (Sunbird) A78 x 13 exc. wagon, B78 x 13; (Phoenix) E78 x 14; (Firebird) FR78 x 15; (Trans Am) GR70 x 15; (LeMans) P185/75R14; (Grand Am) P205/70R14; (Grand Prix) P195/75R14; (Cat./Bonn.) FR78 x 15.

TECHNICAL: Transmission: Three-speed manual transmission standard on Phoenix, LeMans, Firebird, and base Grand Prix (floor lever standard on LeMans, optional on Phoenix. Four-speed manual standard on Sunbird, optional on Firebird, Phoenix and Grand Am. Five-speed manual optional on Sunbird. Three-speed Turbo Hydra-matic standard on other models, optional on all. Standard final drive ratio: Gear ratios not available. Steering: Recirculating ball. Front Suspension: (Firebird/LeMans) coil springs w/lower trailing links and anti-sway bar; (others) coil springs and anti-sway bar. Rear Suspension: (Sunbird) rigid axle with coil springs, lower trailing radius arms and upper torque arms and anti-sway bar. Brakes: Front disc, rear drum. Ignition: Electronic. Body construction: (Sunbird) unit; (Firebird) unit w/separate partial frame; (others) separate body and frame. Fuel tank: (Sunbird) 18.5 gal. exc. wagon, 16 gal.; (Phoenix) 21 gal.; (Firebird) 21 gal.; (LeMans) 17.5 gal. exc. wagon, 18.3 gal.; (Grand Am) 15 gal.; (Grand Prix) 15 gal.; (Catalina/Bonn.) 21 gal. exc. wagon, 22 gal.

DRIVETRAIN OPTIONS: Engines: 140 cu. in. 2Bbl. four: Phoenix ($170 credit). 231 cu. in. V-6: Sunbird ($170). 301 cu. in., 2Bbl. V-8: Catalina/Grand Prix ($150). 301 cu. in., 4Bbl. V-8: Grand Prix ($200); Grand Prix LJ ($50); Grand Am ($50). 305 cu. in., 2Bbl. V-8: Phoenix/Firebird/LeM/G.P. ($150). 350 cu. in., 4Bbl. V-8: Phoenix/Firebird/Catalina ($265); LeMans Safari ($265); Firebird Formula ($115); Bonneville ($115). 400 cu. in., 4Bbl. V-8: Catalina ($330); Bonn. ($330). T/A 400 4Bbl. V-8: Formula ($280); Trans Am ($75). 403 cu. in., 4Bbl. V-8: Firebird Formula ($205); Catalina ($330); Bonn. ($180). Transmission/Differential: Three-speed floor shift: Phoenix ($33). Four-speed manual floor shift trans.: Phoenix w/V8305 ($125); Firebird/LeM ($125); Formula ($182 credit). Five- speed manual trans.: Sunbird ($175). Turbo Hydra-matic: Sunbird ($270); Phoenix/Firebird/LeM/Grand Prix ($307); Formula/Trans Am (NC). Saf-T-Track differential: Sunbird ($56); LeM/Firebird/G.P. ($60); Catalina/Bonn. ($64). Brakes/Steering: Power brakes: Sunbird (N/A); Phoenix/LeM/Firebird/G.P. ($69). Power steering: Sunbird ($134); Phoenix/LeM/G.P. ($152). Suspension: Rally RTS handling pkg.: Sunbird ($2-$230); Phoenix ($172-$217); LeM ($42-$179); Cat. ($140-$169); Bonn. ($102-$120); Grand Prix ($67-$120). Firm ride pkg. ($12) except Sunbird. Superlift shock absorbers: LeM/G.P. ($52); Catalina/Bonn. ($53). Automatic level control: LeM/G.P./Catalina/Bonn. ($63-$116). Other: H.D. radiator: Sunbird ($32); Phoenix ($31-$56). Super-cooling radiator ($31-$57) except Sunbird. H.D. battery ($17-$20). H.D. alternator: Sunbird/Phoenix/Firebird ($31); Catalina/Bonn. ($18-$49). Engine block heater ($13- $14). Class I trailer group: Bonn./Cat. ($117-$143). Medium trailer group: LeMans/G.P. ($116-$141). Heavy trailer group: Bonn./Cat. ($117-$178). California emissions ($75-$100). High-altitude option ($33).

OPTION PACKAGES: Sunbird Formula group ($448-$621). Sunbird appearance group: cpe ($87). Phoenix cpe/sed appearance pkg. ($73). Firebird "Skybird" appearance pkg.: Esprit ($426-$461). Trans Am special edition ($1259). Firebird custom trim group ($35- $154). Firebird Formula appearance pkg. ($137). Firebird Trans Am special performance pkg. ($249-$324). LeMans Safari security pkg. ($35-$40). LeMans exterior paint appearance ($159). LeMans custom exterior (40-$75). LeMans custom trim group ($134-$247). Full-size exterior paint pkg. ($159). Safari custom trim group ($205-$370). Grand Prix exterior appearance ($119-$165).

MAJOR CONVENIENCE/APPEARANCE OPTIONS: Air conditioning ($470-$581). Automatic air conditioning: LeMans/Grand Prix ($584); Catalina/Bonneville ($626). Cruise control ($90-$95); N/A on Sunbird. Power seat: LeM/Cat./Bonn./G.P. ($151). Power windows ($118-$190); N/A on Sunbird. Cornering lamps: Catalina/Bonn./Grand Prix ($47). Power glass sunroof: LeMans/Grand Prix ($699); Catalina/Bonn. ($895). Power steel sunroof: LeMans/Grand Prix ($499); Catalina/Bonn. ($695). Glass sunroof: Sunbird ($172). Hatch roof: Firebird/Grand Prix ($625). Full vinyl cordova top: Phoenix ($97); LeMans ($116); Grand Prix ($121); Catalina/Bonneville ($142). Padded landau top: Grand Prix/LeMans ($239); Catalina/Bonn. ($294). Landau cordova top: Sunbird ($153); Phoenix ($179). Canopy top: Firebird ($111). Rear-facing third seat: Safari ($175).

HISTORY: Introduced: October 6, 1977. Model year production: 900,380. Calendar year production (U.S.): 867,008. Calendar year sales by U.S. dealers: 896,980. Model year sales by U.S. dealers: 871,391.

Historical Footnotes: Model year sales set a new record in 1978, beating the 1968 total. Contributing to the rise were strong sales of Trans Am and the shrunken mid-size models, but Sunbird also showed an increase.

1979 PONTIAC

This was not a year of startling change, except for some shifts in engine availabilty. No surprise there, as the late 1970s were years of considerable revision (and confusion) in powerplant choices. California models had their own engine possibilities, as did cars sold for high altitude operation. Full-size models got a new front and rear appearance as well as new interior trim, and Firebird received a dramatically different look. Wire wheels became optional on Grand Prix. Formula and Trans Am Firebirds could get four-wheel power disc brakes.

1979 Formula Sunbird hatchback coupe

SUNBIRD — SERIES 2H — FOUR/V-6 — Appearance of the subcompact Pontiac was similar to 1978, but the small twin grilles now contained horizontal strips (formerly vertical). Equipment was similar to 1978, with standard 151 cu. in. (2.5-liter) four and optional 231 cu. in. V-6 or 305 cu.in. V-8. A four-speed manual gearbox was standard. Tires were A78 x 13 except B78 x 13 with V-6 engines. Sport Coupe and Sport Hatch models added custom wheel covers, rocker panel and wheel opening moldings, and custom vinyl bucket seats.

1979 Phoenix LJ coupe (CP)

PHOENIX — SERIES 2X — V-6/V-8 — Each side of this year's Phoenix grille contained five side-by-side sections, with subdued vertical bars in each one and clear park/signal lamps in outer ends. Otherwise, appearance was similar to 1978. The compact Phoenix came in five models: base coupe, hatchback and sedan, and LJ coupe and sedan. New two-tone paint was offered in four color combinations. Base engine was the 231 cu. in. (3.8-liter) V-6, with 305 cu. in. two-barrel V-8 optional. A

350 cu. in. V-8 was offered for California and high-altitude models. The four-cylinder credit option was no longer available. Phoenix could get a light-duty trailer-towing package that handled units up to one ton.

1979 Formula Firebird coupe (JG)

FIREBIRD — SERIES 2F — V-6/V-8 — Front ends of the new Firebirds were far different from predecessors. Quad rectangular headlamps now stood in separate recessed housings, in a sharply sloped center panel that had a peak and an emblembut no grille. Instead, horizontally-ribbed lower grilles went into twin slots below the bumper area, with clear park/signal lamps at outer ends. At the rear was a full-width horizontally-ribbed panel. Base Firebird equipment included Buick's 231 cu. in. (3.8-liter) V-6, three-speed manual shift, power steering, and FR78 x 15 steel-belted radials. Esprit added wheel covers, sport mirrors (driver's remote), and extra body moldings. Formula had a 301 cu. in. V-8, automatic transmission, power brakes, black-accented grille, non- functional twin hood scoop, Rally II wheels with trim rings, console, and P225/70R15 blackwall SBR tires. Trans Am had a 403 cu. in. four-barrel V-8, four-speed manual transmission, power brakes, air dam, rear spoiler, "shaker" hood, and chrome side-splitter tailpipe extensions.

1979 LeMans coupe (JG)

LE MANS — SERIES 2A — V-6/V-8 — Styling of the mid-size LeMans was similar to before, but the grille contained more holes, now displaying a 6 x 4 pattern. Amber side marker lenses now were split into four sections rather than three. Base engine was the 231 cu. in. (3.8-liter) V-6, with three-speed manual shift. Equipment included body-color bumpers with rub strips, P185/75R14 glass-belted radial tires, hubcaps,

1979 Grand LeMans sedan (P)

and wheel opening moldings. Grand LeMans added a hood ornament and windsplit molding, lower bodyside moldings, brushed aluminum center pillar, and door panel pull straps. Engine options included a 301 cu. in. V-8 (two- or four-barrel carb), and 305 cu. in. four-barrel V-8. Safari wagons had a 5.0-liter V-8 as standard, and could also have a 350 V-8.

1979 Grand Am coupe (P)

GRAND AM — SERIES 2A — V-8 — Except for amber park/signal and marker lenses, appearance of the Grand Am changed little this year. Equipment was similar to LeMans, but with power steering, two-tone body color, blackout taillamps, P205/70R14 steel- belted radials, and Rally RTS handling package.

1979 Grand Prix LJ coupe (P)

GRAND PRIX — SERIES 2G — V-6/V-8 — Horizontal and vertical bars now made up the Grand Prix grille, forming a 3 x 7 pattern of wide holes on each side of a narrow (for Pontiac) center divider. Amber park/signal lenses went between each pair of rectangular quad headlamps.

1979 Catalina coupe (P)

CATALINA — SERIES 2B — V-6/V-8 — Both Catalina and Bonneville gained a front/rear restyle this year. Coupe and sedan models were offered again, along with a Catalina Safari wagon. Changes included a new grille, park/signal lamps, taillamps and side marker lamps. Wagons kept their former taillamp design. Though similar to before, the new front end held a horizontal-theme grille made up of four rows (formerl six). Amber wraparound front marker lenses were split into four sections instead of two. As before, small clear park/signal lamps were bumper-mounted. Rectangular quad headlamps continued. Base engine was the 231 cu. in. (3.8-liter) V-6. A 350 cu. in. four-barrel V-8 was available for high-altitude models. A 301 cu. in. (4.9-liter) two- barrel V-8 (350 four-barrel in California); and a 403 V-8 was available in high-altitude regions. Both light and heavy-duty trailering packages were optional. New "Cloud Dillon" cloth seat trim was used. Full-size options included wire wheel covers, power windows and door locks, power six-way 60/40 split front seats, air conditioning, AM/FM stereo, a padded Landau Cordova top, and cushion tilt steering wheel.

BONNEVILLE — SERIES 2B — V-8 — Like Catalina, Bonneville and Bonneville Brougham got a design change including new grille, park/signal lamps, taillamps and side markers. All models had new deluxe wheel covers. For the first time, coupes could have optional cloth bucket seats with a console. Bonneville's base engine was a 301 cu. in. (4.9-liter) two-barrel V-8; or 350 four-barrel for California/high-altitude models. Grand Safari got a name change to, simply, Bonneville Safari. A third seat was vailable again. This year's seat trim was Chamonix cloth (Dante cloth on Brougham, which used a new pillow-style design). Bonneville's grille elements were whole vertical rectangles, not just single vertical bars as in 1978. Five of them appeared on each side

1979 Bonneville Brougham sedan (P)

of the center divider. Instead of four-section amber side marker lenses, this year's were two- section. Pontiac's 13-symbol Vehicle Identification Number (VIN) was located on the upper left surface of the instrument panel, visible through the windshield. The first digit is '2', indicating Pontiac division. The second symbol is a letter indicating series: 'E' Sunbird; 'M' Sunbird Sport; 'Y' Phoenix; 'Z' Phoenix LJ; 'D' LeMans; 'F' Grand LeMans; 'G' Grand Am; 'S' Firebird; 'T' Firebird Esprit; 'U' Firebird Formula; 'W' Firebird Trans Am; 'L' Catalina; 'N' Bonneville; 'Q' Bonneville Brougham; 'J' Grand Prix; 'K' Grand Prix LJ; 'H' Grand Prix SJ. Next come two digits that denote body type: '07' 2dr. hatchback coupe; '17' 2dr. hatchback coupe; '27' 2dr. coupe; '37' 2dr. coupe; '87' 2dr. HT coupe; '19' 4dr. 6window sedan; '69' 4dr. 4 window sedan; '15' 2dr. station wagon; '35' 4dr. 2seat wagon. The fifth symbol is a letter indicating engine code: 'V' L4151 2Bbl.; 'A' V6231 2Bbl.; 'Y' V8301 2Bbl.; 'W' V8301 4Bbl.; 'G' V8305 2Bbl.; 'H' V8305 4Bbl.; 'X' V8350 4Bbl. (L37); 'R' V8350 4Bbl. (L34); 'L' V8350 4Bbl. (LM1); 'Z' V8400 4Bbl.; 'K' V8403 4Bbl. The sixth symbol denotes model year ('9' 1979). Next is a plant code: 'A' Lakewood, Georgia; 'B' Baltimore; 'L' Van Nuys, Calif.; 'N' Norwood, Ohio; 'P' Pontiac, Mich.; 'T' Tarrytown, NY; 'U' Lordstown, Ohio; 'W' Willow Run, Mich.; 'X' Fairfax, Kansas; '1' Oshawa, Ontario; '2' Ste. Therese, Quebec. The final six digits are the sequential serial number.

1979 Sunbird Astre Safari wagon (JG)

SUNBIRD (FOUR/V-6)

Model Number	Body/Style Number	Body Type & Seating	Factory Price	Shipping Weight	Production Total
2H	E27	2-dr. Cpe-4P	3781/3981	2593/--	40,560
2H	M07	2-dr. Hatch Cpe-4P	4064/4264	2642/--	24,221
2H	M27	2-dr. Spt Cpe-4P	3964/4164	2593/--	30,087
2H	M15	2-dr. Sta Wag-4P	4138/4338	2651/--	2,902

PHOENIX (V-6/V-8)

2X	Y27	2-dr. Cpe-6P	4089/4284	3127/3345	9,233
2X	Y69	4-dr. Sed-6P	4189/4384	3177/3395	10,565
2X	Y17	2-dr. Hatch-6P	4239/4434	3210/3428	923

1979 Phoenix LJ sedan (P)

PHOENIX LJ (V-6/V-8)

2X	Z27	2-dr. Cpe-6P	4589/4784	3236/3454	1,826
2X	Z69	4-dr. Sed-6P	4689/4884	3285/3503	2,353

FIREBIRD (V-6/V-8)					
2F	S87	2-dr. HT Cpe-4P	4825/5020	3257/3330	38,642

FIREBIRD ESPRIT (V-6/V-8)					
2F	T87	2-dr. HT Cpe-4P	5193/5388	3287/3360	30,853

FIREBIRD FORMULA (V-8)					
2F	U87	2-dr. HT Cpe-4P	6018	3460	24,851

1979 Firebird Trans Am T-top coupe (P)

FIREBIRD TRANS AM (V-8)					
2F	W87	2-dr. HT Cpe-4P	6299	3551	117,108

FIREBIRD TRANS AM LIMITED EDITION (V-8)					
2F	X87	2-dr. HT Cpe-4P	10620	3551	N/A

LE MANS (V-6/V-8)					
2A	D27	2-dr. Cpe-6P	4608/4803	3036/3115	14,197
2A	D19	4-dt. Sed-6P	4708/4903	3042/3121	26,958

LE MANS SAFARI (V-6/V-8)					
2A	D35	4-dr. 2S Wag-6P	5216/5411	3200/3328	27,517

GRAND LE MANS (V-6/V-8)					
2A	F27	2-dr. Cpe-6P	4868/5063	3058/3137	13,020
2A	F19	4-dr. Sed-6P	4993/5188	3087/3166	28,577

1979 Grand LeMans Safari wagon (JG)

GRAND LE MANS SAFARI (V-6/V-8)					
2A	F35	4-dr. 2S Wag-6P	5560/5755	3234/3362	20,783

GRAND AM (V-6/V-8)					
2A	G27	2-dr. Cpe-6P	5084/5279	3080/3159	4,021
2A	G19	4-dr. Sed-6P	5209/5404	3084/3163	1,865

1979 Grand Prix SJ coupe (JG)

GRAND PRIX (V-6/V-8)					
2G	J37	2-dr. Cpe-6P	5113/5308	3126/3205	124,815

GRAND PRIX LJ (V-8)					
2G	K37	2-dr. Cpe-5P	6192	3285	61,175

GRAND PRIX SJ (V-8)					
2G	H37	2-dr. Cpe-5P	6438	3349	24,060

CATALINA (V-6/V-8)					
2B	L37	2-dr. Cpe-6P	5690/5885	3476/3593	5,410
2B	L69	4-dr. Sed-6P	5746/5941	3508/3625	28,121

CATALINA SAFARI (V-8)					
2B	L35	4-dr. 2S Wag-6P	6273	3997	13,353

BONNEVILLE (V-8)					
2B	N37	2-dr. Cpe-6P	6205	3616	34,127
2B	N69	4-dr. Sed-6P	6330	3672	71,906

BONNEVILLE BROUGHAM (V-8)					
2B	Q37	2-dr. Cpe-6P	6960	3659	39,094
2B	Q69	4-dr. Sed-6P	7149	3726	17,364

BONNEVILLE SAFARI (V-8)					
2B	N35	4-dr. 2S Wag-6P	6632	4022	16,925

FACTORY PRICE AND WEIGHT NOTE: Prices and weights to left of slash are for V-6, to right for V-8 engine except Sunbird, four and V-6.

ENGINE DATA: BASE FOUR (Sunbird): Inline. Overhead valve. Four-cylinder. Cast iron block and head. Displacement: 151 cu. in. (2.5 liters). Bore & stroke: 4.00 x 3.00 in. Compression ratio: 8.2:1. Brake horsepower: 85 at 4400 R.P.M. Torque: 123 lbs.-ft. at 2800 R.P.M. Five main bearings. Hydraulic valve lifters. Carburetor: 2Bbl. Rochester 2SE. VIN Code: V. BASE V-6 (Phoenix, Firebird, LeMans, Catalina, Grand Prix); OPTIONAL (Sunbird): 90-degree, overhead-valve V-6. Cast iron block and head. Displacement: 231 cu. in. (3.8 liters). Bore & stroke: 3.80 x 3.40 in. Compression ratio: 8.0:1. Brake horsepower: 105 at 3200-3400 R.P.M. Torque: 185 lbs.-ft. at 2000 R.P.M. Four main bearings. Hydraulic valve lifters. Carburetor: 2Bbl. Rochester M2ME. Buick-built. VIN Code: A. BASE V-8 (Bonneville, Grand Prix LJ, Safari); OPTIONAL (Firebird, LeMans, Grand Prix, Catalina): 90-degree, overhead valve V-8. Cast iron block and head. Displacement: 301 cu. in. (5.0 liters). Bore & stroke: 4.00 x 3.04 in. Compression ratio: 8.1:1. Brake horsepower: 140 at 3600 R.P.M. Torque: 235 lbs.-ft. at 2000 R.P.M. Five main bearings. Hydraulic valve lifters. Carburetor: 2Bbl. Rochester M2MC. VIN Code: Y. BASE V-8 (Firebird Formula, Grand Prix SJ); OPTIONAL (Firebird, Trans Am, LeMans, Grand Am, Bonneville, Catalina, Grand Prix): Same as 301 cu. in. V-8 above, with 4Bbl. carburetor (Rochester M4MC) Horsepower: 150 at 4000 R.P.M. Torque: 240 lbs.-ft. at 2000 R.P.M. VIN Code: W. OPTIONAL V-8 (Sunbird, Phoenix): 90-degree, overhead valve V-8. Cast iron block and head. Displacement: 305 cu. in. (5.0 liters). Bore & stroke: 3.74 x 3.48 in. Compression ratio: 8.4:1. Brake horsepower: 145 at 3800 R.P.M. Torque: 245 lbs.-ft. at 2400 R.P.M. Five main bearings. Hydraulic valve lifters. Carburetor: 2Bbl. Rochester 2GC. VIN Code: U. ALTERNATE V-8 (Sunbird, Phoenix, Firebird): Same as 305 cu. in. V-8 above, but Horsepower: 133 at 4000 R.P.M. Torque: 244 lbs.-ft. at 2000 R.P.M. OPTIONAL V-8 (LeMans): Same as 305 cu. in. V-8 above, but with four-barrel carburetor Horsepower: 150 at 4000 R.P.M. Torque: 225 lbs.-ft. at 2400 R.P.M. VIN Code: H. OPTIONAL V-8 (Phoenix, Firebird, Catalina, Bonneville, LeMans Safari): 90-degree, overhead valve V-8. Cast iron block and head. Displacement: 350 cu. in. (5.7 liters). Bore & stroke: 4.00 x 3.48 in. Compression ratio: 8.2:1. Brake horsepower: 160 at 3800 R.P.M. Torque: 260 lbs.-ft. at 2400 R.P.M. Five main bearings. Hydraulic valve lifters. Carburetor: 4Bbl. Rochester M4MC. Chevrolet-built. VIN Code: L. ALTERNATE V-8 (Phoenix, Firebird, Catalina, Bonneville, LeMans Safari): Same as 350 cu. in. V-8 above, but Bore & stroke: 3.80 x 3.85 in. Compression ratio: 8.0:1. Brake horsepower: 155 at 3400 R.P.M. Torque: 280 lbs.-ft. at 1800 R.P.M. Buick-built. VIN Code: X. ALTERNATE V-8 (Phoenix, Firebird, Catalina, Bonneville, LeMans Safari): Same as 350 cu. in. V-8 above, but Bore & stroke: 4.06 x 3.38 in. Compression ratio: 7.9:1. Brake horsepower: 160 at 3600 R.P.M. Torque: 270 lbs.-ft. at 2000 R.P.M. Oldsmobile- built. VIN Code: R. OPTIONAL V-8 (Firebird Formula, Trans Am): 90-degree, overhead valve V-8. Cast iron block and head. Displacement: 400 cu. in. (6.6 liters). Bore & stroke: 4.12 x 3.75 in. Compression ratio: 8.1:1. Brake horsepower: 220 at 4000 R.P.M. Torque: 320 lbs.-ft. at 2800 R.P.M. Five main bearings. Hydraulic valve lifters. Carburetor: 4Bbl. Rochester M4MC. VIN Code: Z. BASE V-8 (Trans Am); OPTIONAL (Firebird Formula): 90-degree, overhead valve V-8. Cast iron block and head. Displacement: 403 cu. in. (6.6 liters). Bore & stroke: 4.35 x 3.38 in. Compression ratio: 7.9:1. Brake horsepower: 185 at 3600 R.P.M. Torque: 320 lbs.-ft. at 2000 R.P.M. Five main bearings. Hydraulic valve lifters. Carburetor: 4Bbl. Rochester M4MC. Oldsmobile-built. VIN Code: K.

CHASSIS DATA: Wheelbase: (Sunbird) 97.0 in.; (Phoenix) 111.1 in.; (Firebird) 108.2 in.; (LeMans) 108.1 in.; (Grand Prix) 108.1 in.; (Catalina/Bonn.) 116.0 in. Overall Length: (Sunbird) 179.2 in.; (Sunbird wag) 178.0 in.; (Phoenix) 203.4 in.; (Firebird) 196.8 in.; (LeMans) 198.5 in.; (LeM wag) 197.8 in.; (G.P.) 201.2 in.; (Catalina/Bonn.) 214.3 in.; (Safari wag) 215.1 in. Height: (Sunbird) 49.6 in.; (Sunbird wag) 51.8 in.; (Phoenix cpe) 52.3 in.; (Phoenix sed) 53.2 in.; (Firebird) 49.3 in.; (LeM cpe) 53.5 in.; (LeM sed) 54.4 in.; (LeM wag) 54.8 in.; (G.P.) 53.3 in.; (Catalina/Bonn. cpe) 53.9 in.; (Catalina/Bonn. sed) 54.5 in.; (Safari wag) 57.3 in. Width: (Sunbird) 65.4 in.; (Phoenix) 72.4 in.; (Firebird) 73.0 in.; (LeM) 72.4 in.; (LeM wag) 72.6 in.; (G.P.) 72.7 in.; (Cat./Bonn.) 76.4 in.; (Safari wag) 79.9 in. Front Tread: (Sunbird) 55.3 in.; (Phoenix) 61.9 in.; (Firebird) 61.3 in.; (LeM) 58.5 in.; (G.P.) 58.5 in.; (Cat./Bonn.) 61.7 in.;

(Safari) 62.0 in. Rear Tread: (Sunbird) 54.1 in.; (Phoenix) 59.6 in.; (Firebird) 60.0 in.; (LeM) 57.8 in.; (G.P.) 57.8 in.; (Cat./Bonn.) 60.7 in.; (Safari) 64.1 in. Standard Tires: (Sunbird) A78 x 13; (Phoenix) E78 x 14; (Firebird) FR78 x 15; (Firebird Formula/Trans Am) P225/70R15; (LeMans) P185/75R14; (Grand Am) P205/70R14; (Grand Prix) P195/75R14; (Cat./Bonn.) FR78 x 15.

TECHNICAL: Transmission: Three-speed manual transmission standard on Phoenix, LeMans, Firebird, and base Grand Prix. Four-speed manual standard on Sunbird, optional on Firebird, Phoenix and LeMans. Five-speed manual optional on Sunbird. Three-speed Turbo Hydra-matic standard on other models, optional on all. Standard final drive ratio: (Sunbird) 2.73:1 w/four and 4spd, 2.93:1 w/V-6 and 4spd; (Phoenix) 3.08:1 w/4spd, 2.56:1 w/V-6 and auto., 2.41:1 w/V-8 and auto.; (Firebird V-6) 3.08:1 w/3spd; (Firebird V8302) 2.41:1, 3.08:1 or 2.73:1; (Firebird V8350) 3.08:1 (Firebird V8400) 3.23:1 (Firebird V8403) 2.41:1; (LeMans V-6) 2.73:1 w/3spd, 2.93:1 w/4spd, 2.41:1 or 3.23:1 w/auto.; (LeMans V-8) 2.41:1, 2.29:1 or 2.73:1; (Grand Prix) 2.93:1 w/V-6, 2.14:1 or 2.29:1 w/V-8; (Catalina/Bonneville) 2.73:1 w/V-6, 2.29:1 or 2.56:1 w/V8301, 2.41:1 w/V8350; (Safari) 2.56:1 or 2.73:1. Steering: Recirculating ball. Front Suspension: (Sunbird) coil springs and control arms; (Firebird/LeMans) coil springs w/lower trailing links and anti-sway bar; (others) coil springs and anti-sway bar. Rear Suspension: (Sunbird) rigid axle with coil springs, lower trailing radius arms and upper torque arms; (Phoenix) rigid axle w/semi-elliptic leaf springs; (Firebird) semi-elliptic leaf springs w/anti-sway bar; (LeMans/Bonneville/Grand Prix) rigid axle with coil springs, lower trailing radius arms and upper torque arms. Brakes: Front disc, rear drum; four-wheel disc brakes available on Firebird Formula and Trans Am. Ignition: Electronic. Body construction: (Sunbird) unit; (Firebird) unit w/separate partial frame; (others) separate body and frame. Fuel tank: (Sunbird) 18.5 gal. exc. wagon, 16 gal.; (Phoenix) 21 gal.; (Firebird) 21 gal.; (LeMans) 18.1 gal. exc. wagon, 18.2 gal.; (Grand Prix) 18.1 gal.; (Catalina/Bonn.) 21 gal.

DRIVETRAIN OPTIONS: Engines: 231 cu. in. V-6: Sunbird ($200); Grand Prix LJ ($195 credit). 301 cu. in., 2Bbl. V-8: Firebird/LeMans/Catalina/Grand Prix ($195). 301 cu. in., 4Bbl. V-8: Firebird ($280); Firebird Formula ($85); Trans Am ($165 credit); LeMans/Grand Prix/Catalina ($255); Grand Prix LJ ($60); Bonneville ($60). 305 cu. in., 2Bbl. V-8: Sunbird ($395); Phoenix/Firebird ($195). 305 cu. in., 4Bbl. V-8: LeMans/Grand Prix ($255); Grand Prix LJ ($60). 350 cu. in., 4Bbl. V-8: Phoenix/Firebird/Catalina ($320); LeMans Safari ($320); Firebird Formula ($125); Bonneville ($125). T/A 400 cu. in., 4Bbl. V-8: Formula ($340); Trans Am ($90). 403 cu. in., 4Bbl. V-8: Firebird Formula ($250); Catalina ($195). Transmission/Differential: Four-speed manual floor shift trans.: Phoenix w/V8305 ($135); Firebird/LeM/G.P. ($135); Grand Prix LJ/SJ ($200 credit). Five-speed manual trans.: Sunbird ($175). Turbo Hydra-matic: Sunbird ($295); Phoenix/Firebird/LeM/Grand Prix ($335); Trans Am (NC). Limited-slip differential: Sunbird ($59); LeM/Firebird/G.P. ($63); Catalina/Bonn. ($67). Brakes/Steering: Power brakes: Sunbird ($71); Phoenix/LeM/Firebird/G.P. ($76). Power four-wheel disc brakes: Firebird Formula/Trans Am ($150). Power steering: Sunbird ($146); Phoenix/LeM/G.P. ($163). Suspension: Rally RTS handling pkg.: Sunbird ($38-$120); Phoenix ($182-$230); LeM ($44-$189); Cat. ($150-$180); Bonn. ($109-$128); Grand Prix ($72-$128). Firm ride pkg. ($13) except Sunbird. Superlift shock absorbers: LeM/G.P. ($54); Catalina/Bonn. ($55). Automatic level control: LeM/G.P./Catalina/Bonn. ($66-$121). Other: H.D. radiator: Sunbird ($33); Phoenix ($32-$59). H.D. cooling: Sunbird ($26-$59). Super-cooling radiator ($32-$60) except Sunbird/Phoenix. H.D. battery ($18-$21). H.D. alternator: Sunbird/Phoenix/Firebird/LeM/G.P. ($32); Catalina/Bonn. ($23-$55). Engine block heater ($14-$15). Light trailer group: Bonn./Cat. ($122-$150). Medium trailer group: LeMans/G.P. ($121-$148). Heavy trailer group: Bonn./Cat. ($122-$187). California emissions ($83-$150). High-altitude option ($35).

OPTION PACKAGES: Sunbird Formula group ($415-$591). Sunbird sport hatch graphics pkg. ($73). Sunbird appearance group: cpe ($91). Phoenix custom exterior ($91-$97). Phoenix exterior appearance pkg. ($166). Phoenix appearance pkg. ($76). Firebird "Red Bird" appearance pkg.: Esprit ($449-$491). Trans Am special edition ($674); w/hatch roof ($1329). Firebird appearance pkg. ($92). Firebird Formula Trans Am special performance pkg. ($250-$434). LeMans Safari security pkg. ($37-$42). LeMans luxury group ($148-$348). LeMans exterior paint appearance ($166). LeMans custom exterior ($46-$98). LeMans custom trim group ($145-$259). Full-size exterior paint pkg. ($166). Grand Prix exterior appearance ($124-$172). Grand Prix appearance pkg. ($197-$264).

MAJOR CONVENIENCE/APPEARANCE OPTIONS: Air conditioning ($496-$605). Automatic air conditioning: LeMans/Grand Prix ($653); Catalina/Bonneville ($688). Cruise control ($103-$108); N/A on Sunbird. Power seat: LeM/Cat./Bonn./G.P. ($163-$166). Power windows ($126-$205); N/A on Sunbird. Cornering lamps: Catalina/Bonn./Grand Prix ($49). Power glass sunroof: LeMans/Grand Prix ($729); Catalina/Bonn. ($925). Power steel sunroof: LeMans/Grand Prix ($925); Catalina/Bonn. ($725). Removable glass sunroof: Sunbird ($180). Hatch roof: Firebird/Grand Prix ($655). Full vinyl cordova top: Phoenix ($99); LeMans ($116); Catalina/Bonneville ($145). Padded landau top: Grand Prix/LeMans ($239); Catalina/Bonn. ($298). Landau top: Sunbird ($156); Phoenix ($190). Canopy top: Firebird ($116). Rear-facing third seat: Safari ($183). Wire wheels: Grand Prix ($425-$499).

HISTORY: Introduced: September 28, 1978. Model year production: 907,412. Calendar year production (U.S.): 713,475. Calendar year sales by U.S. dealers: 781,042. Model year sales by U.S. dealers: 828,603 (incl. 42,852 early 1980 front-drive Phoenix models).

Historical Footnotes: At the end of 1979, Robert C. Stempel (later to become head of General Motors) was named Pontiac's general manager. Sales slipped a bit for the model year, with only Sunbird and LeMans showing a slight increase. Sunbird's "Iron Duke" four-cylinder engine switched to a cross-flow cylinder head, and would soon become the standard powerplant for many GM models, especially transverse-mounted in the new front-drive Xcars. An alternate version was supplied for rear-drive installations.

1980 PONTIAC

A new front-wheel-drive Phoenix, close kin to the Chevrolet Citation Xcar and powered by a four or V-6, was the major news of the year. The 400/403 cu. in. V-8 were out. Biggest powerplant was now the 350 cu. in. V-8, and that only on a few models (used more on California Pontiacs, actually). Two new V-8 powerplants appeared: a 265 cu. in. (4.3-liter) two-barrel, and diesel 350 cu. in. (5.7-liter), which came from Oldsmobile. An electronic-control (E/C) 301 cu. in. (4.9-liter) V-8 went under performance-model hoods. Also on the engine front, a turbocharged 301 V-8 became available on Trans Am; and Chevrolet's V6229 served as an equivalent to the Buick 231 V-6. As for appearance, full-size models gained a major restyle.

SUNBIRD — SERIES 2H — FOUR/V-6 — Only coupe, sport coupe and sport hatch models were available, as the Safari wagon was dropped. Sunbird had a new eggcrate-pattern grille, and new park/signal lamps. New seating came in five colors. Standard bucket seats now had smooth headrests. Luxury interior trim was now

1980 Sunbird Sport hatchback coupe (AA)

Ramrod striped velour. Options included new sport accent striping. Base engine was the crossflow 151 cu. in. (2.5-liter) four, with four-speed manual gearbox. Optional: a 231 cu. in. (3.8-liter) V-6 and automatic transmission. The formerly optional 305 cu. in. V-8 had been dropped in mid-1979. The optional five-speed gearbox dropped out this year. An additional hatchback model (E07) was added later in the season.

1980 Phoenix SJ coupe (AA)

PHOENIX — SERIES 2X — FOUR/V-6 — The new front-wheel-drive compact debuted in April 1979, and entered its first full model year with minimal change. A two-door coupe and five-door (actually four-door) hatchback sedan were offered. Base drivetrain was Pontiac's 151 cu. in. (2.5-liter) four, transverse mounted, with four-speed manual overdrive transaxle and floor lever. Optional: Chevrolet's 173 cu. in. (2.8-liter) V-6 and automatic shift. Front suspension used MacPherson struts; at the rear was a trailing axle with coil springs and track bar. Each of the twin grille sections consisted of large (3 x 3 pattern) holes over tight crosshatching. Clear vertical parking/signal lamps stood between the grille and single rectangular headlamps. Horizontal taillamps each had two horizontal and two vertical trim strips, with backup lights toward the center, next to the license plate. Body-colored bumpers had bright strips. Standard equipment included P185/80R13 glass-belted radial blackwall tires, hubcaps with Pontiac crest, and AM radio. Phoenix LJ added a stand-up hood ornament, bright wide rocker panel moldings, wheel covers, accent striping, and sport mirrors. An SJ option package included black grilles and headlamp bezels, Phoenix bird emblem on center pillar, vinyl bucket seats, P205 tires on Rally wheels, Rally RTS suspension, and accent color on lower body and bumpers. New stripe colors were made available for the full year, and base seating carried a different fabric. The sporty SJ option had new two-tone color combinations. A brushed aluminum Bpillar applique for the hatchback sedan was first available alone, later only as part of a custom exterior group. Accent paint stripes were first standard, then became optional.

1980 Firebird Esprit "Yellow Bird" T-top coupe (CP)

FIREBIRD — SERIES 2F — V-6/V-8 — Appearance changes were minimal, but Firebird got a sharply altered engine selection this year. Base engine for base and Esprit models remained the 231 cu. in. (3.8-liter) V-6; optional, the new 265 cu. in. (4.3-liter) V-8 and the 301 cu. in. (4.9-liter) four-barrel. Trans Ams now carried the E/C 301 cu. in. four-barrel V-8, which was optional on Formula models. Both Trans Am and Formula could also get a new turbocharged 301 four-barrel. As in other models, California cars had a modified selection, including a 305 cu. in. V-8 standard in Trans Am and Formula. Base and Esprit Firebirds still had standard three-speed manual shift, while Formula and Trans Am carried automatics. All California 'birds were automatic-equipped. Dual exhausts came in a lighter-weight design this year. Turbo models included a unique hood with special bird decal. Turbo graphics went on the hood and decklid spoiler. Another bird decal was available for non-turbo Trans Ams. A new "Yellow Bird" option package with gold accent striping replaced the former Redbird. Trans Am could again get a black-painted Special Edition package, either with or without a hatch roof. New Trans Am graphics colors included bronze/burgundy and a revised red/gold combination. New seating came in five colors. Dark blue was a new interior color. New optional electronic-tuning stereo radios came with a four-speaker system. Tungsten halogen headlamps remained available.

1980 Grand LeMans sedan (P)

LE MANS — SERIES 2A — V-6/V-8 — Design changes for LeMans and Grand LeMans included new grilles, park/signal lamps, front side marker lamps, and taillamps (for coupe/sedan). Two new interior colors were available: blue and maroon. LeMans door panels had new simulated welt and stitch lines centered between bright mylar moldings. Grand LeMans door panels had wide mylar moldings. All models had standard power brakes. Safari wagons could have a double two-tone paint treatment at no extra cost, instead of the standard simulated woodgraining. That woodgrain came in a new red elm pattern this year. New options included electronic-tuning stereo radios and extended-range speakers. Each grille section consisted of horizontal bars, with clear park/signal lamps behind the outer ends. The wide center panel held a Pontiac emblem above 'Pontiac' block lettering. Wraparound clear/amber marker lenses had four horizontal trim ribs. Single rectangular headlamps were used. Base coupe/sedan engine was now Chevrolet's 229 cu. in. (3.8-liter) V-6 with three-speed manual gearbox, whereas other Pontiacs used Buick's 231 V-6. Options included the new 265 cu. in. (4.3-liter) V-8 and Turbo Hydra-matic, as well as a 301 cu. in. (4.9-liter) four-barrel V-8. California models could have a 305 V-8.

1980 Grand Am coupe (AA)

GRAND AM — SERIES 2A — V-8 — Grand Am now came in coupe form only, carrying the 301 u. in. E/C engine (as in Trans Am) with automatic transmission. California Grand Ams had a 305 V-8 instead. In addition to a new soft-fascia front end, Grand Am added ample standard equipment in an attempt to attain a performance image. The list included bucket seats (with console), sport mirrors, Rally IV wheels, and custom sport steering wheel. A new silver upper body accent stripe was standard, and Rally RTS suspension had larger front/rear stabilizer bars. All Grand Am bodies had a new Ontario Grey lower accent color. Each of the twin grille sections was divided into three sections, with thin body-color separators between, and each held horizontal strips. A wide peaked center divider held a Pontiac vee-shaped emblem that extended from the hood crease. Front bumpers held two air slots. Single rectangular headlamps stood directly above clear park/signal lamps.

1980 Grand Prix SJ coupe (AA)

GRAND PRIX — SERIES 2G — V-6/V-8 — Three Grand Prix models were offered again: base, luxury LJ, and sporty SJ. Standard engine was again the 231 cu. in. (3.8-liter) V-6, except for SJ, which carried the new 301 cu. in. (4.9-liter) E/C four-barrel V-8. Base and LJ models could have the new 265 cu. in. (4.3-liter) V-8. California SJ models had a 305 V-8 with four-barrel, which was also optional on base/LJ. Manual gearboxes were no longer available. Every Grand Prix had automatic transmission as well as power brakes and steering. Appearance changes included a new grille and grille bumper inserts, with a larger look than before. The all- bright grille

contained vertical bars on each side of a fairly narrow bright divider. Between each pair of rectangular headlamps were clear park/signal lamps. Taillamp housings, lenses and bezels were new this year. 'GP' lettering was sonic-welded to the center of each lens. Grand Prix LJ and SJ had new tapered wheel opening moldings, and revised multiple accent striping. The optional double two- tone paint treatment also was revised. Inside were new cloth door trim panels. Base models had a pull strap above dual bright/black moldings; SJ/LJ, a drop handle. New cloth seats went into base models, whereas LJ had the same seating as base models with luxury trim option. Newly optional: electronic-tuning stereo radios and extended-range speakers. Halogen headlamps also were offered.

1980 Catalina (AA)

CATALINA/BONNEVILLE — SERIES 2B — V-6/V-8 — Full-size Pontiacs (Catalina, Bonneville and Bonneville Brougham) all featured new front-end sheetmetal as part of their first significant restyle since the 1977 debut in downsized form. Weights were cut about 100 pounds, aerodynamics improved, engine sizes reduced. The new design displayed a lower profile and more aero-look front, with new roof, sail panels, doors, and quarter panels. Lengthening both the front and rear overhang produced a longer overall look, even though dimensions did not change much. The hood was lowered and decklid raised. Air dams and baffles were added to the body. Coupes had a more formal roofline, while four-door sedans had a restyled upper window area. A compact spare added luggage space. Decklids and taillamp housings were new this year. Catalina used narrow taillamps, while Bonneville's were full-width wraparound with two horizontal trim strips. For a change, Catalina and Bonneville shared similar front-end appearance. Both had a bold, all-bright vertical- theme grille (with pattern extended below the bumper). It consisted of four vertical bars on each side of the bright divider, which held a Pontiac emblem. The flush bumper design included plastic inner fender skirts. Tungsten-halogen headlamps, which first appeared in mid-year 1979, continued as an option. Headlamp bezels wrapped around the front fenders. Cornering lamps had body-colored bezels and were mounted higher on the fender this year, rather than in the lower bodyside molding. New park/signal lamps were set between the headlamps (similar to the 1979 Grand Prix arrangement). Front side markers had new amber lenses and two horizontal ribs. Coupes and sedans had new two-tone paint treatments and accent striping. Safari wagons again carried simulated woodgrain side paneling, but in a "planked" red elm design. Bonneville Safaris could have ordinary two-tone paint instead of the woodgrain. Bonnevilles had new full-length bodyside moldings as well as a new Bpillar applique. New landau padded roofs also were offered. Catalina upholstery was Dover II knit cloth, whereas Bonnevilles had new Patrician striped velour cloth. Brougham seating was Prima cloth knit, which had a longer nap than the former Dante cloth. New Embassy leather was optional on Broughams. To improve ride and durability, the front suspension held new ball joints and a rebushed front stabilizer bar. Wheel covers now had openings for improved brake/bearing cooling. New tire sizes took higher pressures. A new side frame jack was included. New options included electronic- tuning signal-seeking digital AM/FM stereo radios, extended- range speakers, and power outside mirrors. Base engine this year for both Catalina and Bonneville was the 231 cu. in. (3.8-liter) V-6. Bonneville Brougham carried the new 265 cu. in. (4.3-liter) V-8, which was optional on other models. Wagons had a 301 cu. in. (4.9- liter) four-barrel V-8. The Oldsmobile-built diesel was available for Bonneville Brougham and Safari wagons only. Pontiac's 13-symbol Vehicle Identification Number (VIN) was located on the upper left surface of the instrument panel, visible through the windshield. The first digit is '2', indicating Pontiac division. The second symbol is a letter indicating series: 'E' Sunbird; 'M' Sunbird Sport; 'Y' Phoenix; 'Z' Phoenix LJ; 'D' LeMans; 'F' Grand LeMans; 'G' Grand Am; 'S' Firebird; 'T' Firebird Esprit; 'V' Firebird Formula; 'W' Firebird Trans Am; 'L' Catalina; 'N' Bonneville; 'R' Bonneville Brougham; 'J' Grand Prix; 'K' Grand Prix LJ; 'H' Grand Prix SJ. Next come two digits that denote body type: '07' 2dr. hatchback coupe; '27' 2dr. coupe; '37' 2dr. coupe; '87' 2dr. plain-back coupe; '19' 4dr. 6window sedan; '68' 4dr. 6window hatchback; '69' 4dr. 4 window sedan; '35' 4dr. 2seat wagon. The fifth symbol is a letter indicating engine code: 'V' or '5' L4151 2Bbl.; '7' V6173 2Bbl.; 'A' V6231 2Bbl.; 'S' V8265 2Bbl.; 'W' V8301 4Bbl.; 'T' Turbo V8301 4Bbl.; 'H' V8305 4Bbl.; 'R' V8350 4Bbl.; 'N' diesel V8350. The sixth symbol denotes model year ('A' 1980). Next is a plant code: 'B' Baltimore; 'L' Van Nuys, Calif.; 'N' Norwood, Ohio; 'P' Pontiac, Mich.; 'T' Tarrytown, NY; '7' Lordstown, Ohio; 'X' Fairfax, Kansas; '6' Oklahoma City; '1' Oshawa, Ontario; '2' Ste. Therese, Quebec. The final six digits are the sequential serial number.

SUNBIRD (FOUR/V-6)

Model Number	Body/Style Number	Body Type & Seating	Factory Price	Shipping Weight	Production Total
2H	E27	2-dr. Cpe-4P	4371/4596	2603/--	105,847
2H	M07	2-dr. Hatch Cpe-4P	4731/4956	2657/--	52,952
2H	M27	2-dr. Spt Cpe-4P	4620/4845	2609/--	29,180
2H	E07	2-dr. Hatch-4P	4808/5033	2651/--	Note 1

Note 1: Production included in hatchback coupe figure above.

PHOENIX (FOUR/V-6)

2X	Y37	2-dr. Cpe-5P	5067/5292	2496/2535	49,485
2X	Y68	5-dr. Hatch-5P	5251/5476	2539/2578	72,875

PHOENIX LJ (FOUR/V-6)

2X	Z37	2-dr. Cpe-5P	5520/5745	2531/2570	23,674
2X	Z68	5-dr. Hatch-5P	5704/5929	2591/2630	32,257

FIREBIRD (V-6/V-8)

2F	S87	2-dr. HT Cpe-4P	5604/5784	3269/3342	29,811

FIREBIRD ESPRIT (V-6/V-8)

2F	T87	2-dr. HT Cpe-4P	5967/6147	3304/3377	17,277

1980 Formula Firebird coupe (CP)

FIREBIRD FORMULA (V-8)

2F	V87	2-dr. HT Cpe-4P	6955	3410	9,356

1980 Firebird Turbo Trans Am Indy Pace Car (IMSC)

FIREBIRD TRANS AM (V-8)

2F	W87	2-dr. HT Cpe-4P	7179	3429	50,896

LE MANS (V-6/V-8)

2A	D27	2-dr. Cpe-6P	5274/5454	3024/3104	9,110
2A	D19	4-dr. Sed-6P	5377/5557	3040/3120	20,485

LE MANS SAFARI (V-6/V-8)

2A	D35	4-dr. 2S Wag-6P	5861/6041	3232/3359	12,912

GRAND LE MANS (V-6/V-8)

2A	F27	2-dr. Cpe-6P	5560/5740	3050/3130	6,477
2A	F19	4-dr. Sed-6P	5728/5908	3089/3169	18,561

GRAND LE MANS SAFARI (V-6/V-8)

2A	F35	4-dr. 2S Wag-6P	6274/6454	3265/3392	14,832

GRAND AM (V-8)

2A	G27	2-dr. Cpe-6P	7299	3299	1,647

GRAND PRIX (V-6/V-8)

2G	J37	2-dr. Cpe-6P	6219/6399	3139/3263	72,659

GRAND PRIX LJ (V-6/V-8)

2G	K37	2-dr. Cpe-6P	6598/6778	3279/3406	34,968

GRAND PRIX SJ (V-8)

2G	H37	2-dr. Cpe-6P	7296	3291	7,087

CATALINA (V-6/V-8)

2B	L37	2-dr. Cpe-6P	6341/6521	3394/3503	3,319
2B	L69	4-dr. Sed-6P	6397/6577	3419/3528	10,408

CATALINA SAFARI (V-8)

2B	L35	4-dr. 2S Wag-6P	7044	3929	2,931

BONNEVILLE (V-6/V-8)

2B	N37	2-dr. Cpe-6P	6667/6847	3431/3540	16,771
2B	N69	4-dr. Sed-6P	6792/6972	3478/3587	26,112

1980 Bonneville Brougham sedan (AA)

BONNEVILLE BROUGHAM (V-8)

2B	R37	2-dr. Cpe-6P	7696	3571	12,374
2B	R69	4-dr. Sed-6P	7885	3639	21,249

BONNEVILLE SAFARI (V-8)

2B	N35	4-dr. 2S Wag-6P	7625	3949	5,309

FACTORY PRICE AND WEIGHT NOTE: Prices and weights to left of slash are for V-6, to right for V-8 engine except Sunbird/Phoenix, four and V-6.

ENGINE DATA: BASE FOUR (Sunbird, Phoenix): Inline. Overhead valve. Four-cylinder. Cast iron block and head. Displacement: 151 cu. in. (2.5 liters). Bore & stroke: 4.00 x 3.00 in. Compression ratio: 8.2:1. Brake horsepower: 86 at 4000 R.P.M. (Phoenix, 90 at 4000). Torque: 128 lbs.-ft. at 2400 R.P.M. (Phoenix, 134 at 2400). Five main bearings. Hydraulic valve lifters. Carburetor: 2Bbl. Rochester 2SE. VIN Code: V or 5. OPTIONAL V-6 (Phoenix): 60-degree, overhead valve six-cylinder. Cast iron block and aluminum head. Displacement: 173 cu. in. (2.8 liters). bore & stroke: 3.50 x 3.00 in. Compression ratio: 8.5:1. Brake horsepower: 115 at 4800 R.P.M. Torque: 150 lbs.-ft. at 2000 R.P.M. Four main bearings. Hydraulic valve lifters. Carburetor: 2Bbl. Rochester 2SE. VIN Code: 7. BASE V-6 (LeMans): 90-degree, overhead-valve V-6. Cast iron block and head. Displacement: 229 cu. in. (3.8 liters). Bore & stroke: 3.74 x 3.48 in. Compression ratio: 8.6:1. Brake horsepower: 115 at 4000 R.P.M. Torque: 175 lbs.-ft. at 2000 R.P.M. Four main bearings. Hydraulic valve lifters. Carburetor: 2Bbl. Rochester M2ME. Chevrolet-built. VIN Code: K BASE V-6 (Firebird, Grand Prix, Catalina, Bonneville); OPTIONAL (Sunbird): 90-degree, overhead-valve V-6. Cast iron block and head. Displacement: 231 cu. in. (3.8 liters). Bore & stroke: 3.80 x 3.40 in. Compression ratio: 8.0:1. Brake horsepower: 110 at 3800 R.P.M. (Sunbird, 115 at 3800). Torque: 190 lbs.-ft. at 1600 R.P.M. (Sunbird, 188 at 2000). Four main bearings. Hydraulic valve lifters. Carburetor: 2Bbl. Rochester 2SE. Buick-built. VIN Code: A. OPTIONAL V-8. (Firebird, LeMans, Grand Prix, Catalina, Bonneville): 90-degree, overhead valve V-8. Cast iron block and head. Displacement: 265 cu. in. (4.3 liters). Bore & stroke: 3.75 x 3.00 in. Compression ratio: 8.3:1. Brake horsepower: 120 at 3600 R.P.M. Torque: 210 lbs.-ft. at 1600 R.P.M. Five main bearings. Hydraulic valve lifters. Carburetor:2Bbl. VIN Code: S. BASE V-8 (Firebird Formula/Trans Am); OPTIONAL (Firebird, LeMans, Grand Prix, Catalina, Bonneville): 90-degree, overhead valve V-8. Cast iron block and head. Displacement: 301 cu. in. (5.0 liters). Bore & stroke: 4.00 x 3.00 in. Compression ratio: 8.1:1. Brake horsepower: 140 at 4000 R.P.M. Torque: 240 lbs.-ft. at 1800 R.P.M. Five main bearings. Hydraulic valve lifters. Carburetor: 4Bbl. Rochester. VIN Code: W. OPTIONAL E/C V-8 (Firebird Formula, Trans Am, Grand Am, Grand Prix SJ); Same as 301 cu. in V-8 above, but horsepower: 155 at 4400 R.P.M. Torque: 240 lbs.-ft. at 2200 R.P.M. TURBOCHARGED V-8 (Firebird Formula, Trans Am): Same as 301 cu. in V-8 above, with turbocharger. Compression ratio: 7.6:1. Horsepower: 210 at 4000 R.P.M. Torque: 345 lbs.-ft. at 2000 R.P.M. VIN Code: T. NOTE: A 305 cu. in four-barrel V-8 was available in California Pontiacs (Firebird, LeMans, Grand Am, Grand Prix): Displacement: 305 cu. in (5.0 liters). Bore & stroke: 3.74 x 3.48 in. Compression ratio: 8.4:1. Brake horsepower: 150 at 3800 R.P.M. Torque: 230 lbs.-ft. at 2400 R.P.M. Five main bearings. Hydraulic valve lifters. VIN Code: H. OPTIONAL V-8 (Safari and California full-size models): 90-degree, overhead valve V-8. Cast iron block and head. Displacement: 350 cu. in (5.7 liters). Bore & stroke: 4.06 x 3.39 in. Compression ratio: 8.0:1. Brake horsepower: 160 at 3600 R.P.M. Torque: 270 lbs.-ft. at 2000 R.P.M. Hydraulic valve

lifters. Carburetor: 4Bbl. Rochester E4MC. Oldsmobile-built. VIN Code: R. DIESEL V-8 (Catalina, Bonneville, Safari): 90-degree, overhead valve V-8. Cast iron block and head. Displacement: 350 cu. in. (5.7 liters). Bore & stroke: 4.06 x 3.39 in. Compression ratio: 22.5:1. Brake horsepower: 105 at 3200 R.P.M. Torque: 205 lbs.-ft. at 1600 R.P.M. Five main bearings. Hydraulic valve lifters. Fuel injection. Oldsmobile-built. VIN Code: N.

CHASSIS DATA: Wheelbase: (Sunbird) 97.0 in.; (Phoenix) 104.9 in.; (Firebird) 108.2 in.; (LeMans) 108.1 in.; (Grand Prix) 108.1 in.; (Catalina/Bonn.) 116.0 in. Overall Length: (Sunbird) 179.2 in.; (Phoenix cpe) 182.1 in.; (Phoenix hatch) 179.3 in.; (Firebird) 196.8 in.; (LeMans) 198.6 in.; (LeM wag) 197.8 in.; (G.P.) 201.4 in.; (Catalina/Bonn.) 214.0 in.; (Safari wag) 216.7 in. Height: (Sunbird) 49.6 in.; (Sunbird hatch) 49.9 in.; (Phoenix cpe) 53.5 in.; (Phoenix sed) 53.4 in.; (Firebird) 49.3 in.; (LeM cpe) 53.5 in.; (LeM sed) 54.4 in.; (LeM wag) 54.8 in.; (G.P.) 53.3 in.; (Catalina/Bonn. cpe) 54.7 in.; (Catalina/Bonn. sed) 55.2 in.; (Safari wag) 57.1 in. Width: (Sunbird) 65.4 in.; (Phoenix) 69.1 in.; (Firebird) 73.0 in.; (LeM) 72.4 in.; (LeM wag) 72.6 in.; (G.P.) 72.7 in.; (Cat./Bonn.) 76.4 in.; (Safari wag) 79.9 in. Front Tread: (Sunbird) 55.3 in.; (Phoenix) 58.7 in.; (Firebird) 61.3 in.; (LeM) 58.5 in.; (G.P.) 58.5 in.; (Cat./Bonn.) 61.7 in.; (Safari) 62.1 in. Rear Tread: (Sunbird) 54.1 in.; (Phoenix) 57.0 in.; (Firebird) 60.0 in.; (LeM) 57.8 in. exc. wagon, 58.0 in.; (G.P.) 57.8 in.; (Cat./Bonn.) 60.7 in.; (Safari) 64.1 in. Standard Tires: (Sunbird) A78 x 13 exc. V-6, B78 x 13; (Phoenix) P185/80R13 GBR; (Firebird) P205/75R15 SBR; (Firebird Formula/Trans Am) P225/70R15 SBR; (LeMans) P185/75R14 GBR exc. wagon, P195/75R14 GBR; (Grand Am) P205/70R14 SBR; (Grand Prix) P195/75R14 SBR; (Cat./Bonn.) P205/75R15 SBR; (Safari) P225/75R15.

TECHNICAL: Transmission: Three-speed manual transmission standard on base Firebird and LeMans. Four-speed manual standard on Sunbird and Phoenix. Three-speed Turbo Hydra-matic standard on other models, optional on all. Standard final drive ratio: (Sunbird) 2.73:1 or 2.93:1 w/four, 2.93:1 w/V-6 and 4spd, 2.56:1 w/V-6 and auto.; (Phoenix) 2.71:1 w/4spd, 2.53:1 w/four and auto., 2.84:1 w/V-6 and auto.; (Firebird V-6) 3.08:1 w/3spd, 2.56:1 w/auto.; (Firebird V-8) 2.41:1; (Firebird Trans Am/Formula) 2.41:1 except 3.08:1 w/turbo or E/C V-8; (LeMans V-6) 2.73:1 w/3spd, 2.41:1 w/auto.; (LeMans V-8) 2.29:1 or 2.14:1; (LeMans Safari) 2.73:1 w/V-6, 2.41:1 w/V8265, 2.29:1 w/V8301; (Grand Am) 2.93:1; (Grand Prix) 2.41:1 w/V-6, 2.29:1 w/V8265, 2.14:1 w/V8301; (Grand Prix SJ) 2.93:1; (Catalina/Bonneville) 3.23:1 w/V-6, 2.56:1 w/V8265, 2.41:1 w/V8301 or diesel; (Safari) 2.56:1 w/V8301, 2.73:1 w/V8350 or diesel. Steering: (Phoenix) rack and pinion; (others) recirculating ball. Front Suspension: (Sunbird) coil springs and control arms; (Phoenix) MacPherson struts w/lower control arms and anti-sway bar; (Firebird/LeMans) coil springs w/lower trailing links and anti-sway bar; (others) coil springs and anti-sway bar. Rear Suspension: (Sunbird) rigid axle with coil springs, lower trailing radius arms and upper torque arms; (Phoenix) single-beam trailing axle w/track bar and coil springs; (Firebird) semi-elliptic leaf springs with anti-sway bar; (LeMans/Bonneville/Grand Prix) rigid axle with coil springs, lower trailing radius arms and upper torque arms. Brakes: Front disc, rear drum. Ignition: Electronic. Body construction: (Sunbird/Phoenix) unit; (Firebird) unit w/separate partial frame; (others) separate body and frame. Fuel tank: (Sunbird) 18.5 gal.; (Phoenix) 14 gal.; (Firebird) 21 gal.; (LeMans) 18.1 gal. exc. wagon, 18.2 gal.; (Grand Prix) 18.1 gal.; (Catalina/Bonn.) 25 gal.; (Safari) 22 gal.

DRIVETRAIN OPTIONS: Engines: 173 cu. in. V-6: Phoenix ($225). 231 cu. in. V-6: Sunbird ($225). 265 cu. in., 2Bbl. V-8: Firebird ($150); LeMans/Grand Prix/Catalina/Bonneville ($180). 301 cu. in., 4Bbl. V-8: Firebird ($325); Trans Am ($180 credit); LeMans/Grand Prix/Catalina/Bonneville ($295); Bonn. Brghm ($115). E/C 301 cu. in., 4Bbl. V-8: Firebird Formula ($150). Turbo 301 cu. in. V-8: Firebird Formula ($530); Trans Am ($350). 305 cu. in., 4Bbl. V-8: LeMans/Grand Prix ($295); Firebird ($295); Grand Prix SJ ($150 credit); Grand Am ($150 credit). 350 cu. in., 4Bbl. V-8: Catalina/Bonneville ($425); Bonneville Brougham ($245); Safari ($130). Diesel 350 cu. in. V-8: Bonn. Brghm ($915); Safari ($860). Transmission/Differential: Turbo Hydra-matic: Sunbird ($320); Phoenix ($337); Firebird/LeM ($358). Limited-slip differential: Sunbird ($64); LeM/Firebird/G.P. ($68); Catalina/Bonn. ($73). Brakes/Steering: Power brakes: Sunbird/Phoenix ($76); Firebird ($81). Power four-wheel disc brakes: Firebird Formula/Trans Am ($162). Power steering: Sunbird ($158); Phoenix/G.P. ($164); LeM ($174). Suspension: Rally RTS handling pkg.: Sunbird ($44-$227); Phoenix ($52-$219); LeM ($142-$228); Grand Am ($64); Cat./Bonn. ($45); Grand Prix ($143-$157). Firm ride pkg. ($14) except Sunbird. Superlift shock absorbers: Phoenix ($55); Catalina/Bonn. ($60). Automatic level control: Catalina/Bonn. ($72-$132). Other: H.D. radiator: Sunbird ($36); Phoenix ($35-$60). H.D. cooling: Sunbird ($28-$64). Super-cooling radiator: Firebird ($35-$64); Cat./Bonn. ($35-$65). H.D. battery ($19-$23) exc. diesel ($46). H.D. alternator: Sunbird ($10-$34); Phoenix ($10-$43); Firebird ($15-$51); LeM/G.P./Cat./Bonn. ($15-$51). Engine block heater ($16). Light trailer group: Phoenix ($35-$74). Medium trailer group: LeMans/G.P. ($132-$161); Cat./Bonn. ($133-$163). California emissions ($250) exc. diesel ($83).

OPTION PACKAGES: Sunbird Formula group ($496-$674). Sunbird sport hatch graphics pkg. ($55). Phoenix custom exterior ($79-$123). Phoenix luxury trim pkg. ($209-$324). Phoenix SJ option ($460-$502). Firebird "Yellow Bird" appearance pkg.: Esprit ($505-$550). Trans Am Special Edition ($748); w/hatch roof ($1443). Firebird Formula appearance pkg. ($100). Firebird Formula/Trans Am special performance pkg. ($281-$481). LeMans Safari security pkg. ($40-$45). LeMans luxury trim group ($161-$271). LeMans two-paint appearance ($180). LeMans custom exterior ($51-$107). LeMans custom trim group ($131-$305). Full-size exterior appearance pkg. ($180). Grand Prix two-tone paint appearance ($134-$186); double two-tone ($213-$288). Full-size custom trim group. ($181-$435).

MAJOR CONVENIENCE/APPEARANCE OPTIONS: Air conditioning ($531-$647). Automatic air conditioning: LeMans/Grand Prix ($700); Catalina/Bonneville ($738). Cruise control ($105-$118); N/A on Sunbird. Power seat ($165-$179); N/A on Sunbird. Power windows ($132-$221); N/A on Sunbird. Cornering lamps: Catalina/Bonn./Grand Prix ($53). Power glass sunroof: LeMans/Grand Prix ($773); Catalina/Bonn. ($981). Power steel sunroof: LeMans/Grand Prix ($561); Catalina/Bonn. ($770). Removable glass sunroof: Sunbird ($193); Phoenix ($240). Hatch roof: Firebird/Grand Prix ($695). Full vinyl cordova top: LeMans ($124); Catalina/Bonneville ($155). Padded landau top: Phoenix ($179); Grand Prix/LeMans ($239); Catalina/Bonn. ($248). Landau top: Sunbird ($165). Rear-facing third seat: Safari ($199). Wire wheels: Grand Prix ($460-$540).

HISTORY: Introduced: October 11, 1979 except Phoenix, April 19, 1979. Model year production: 770,821. Calendar year production (U.S.): 556,413. Calendar year sales by U.S. dealers: 614,897. Model year sales by U.S. dealers: 638,656 (not incl. 42,852 early 1980 front-drive Phoenix models counted in 1979 total).

Historical Footnotes: Production fell considerably for the 1980 model year. Unlike many models facing their final year in the lineup, Sunbird had a strong sales year. This was a bad time throughout the industry. Still, sagged sales caused Pontiac to slip back into fourth place among the GM divisions, after ranking No. 3 for three years. Even if Pontiac couldn't sell impressive numbers of cars, it supplied plenty of engines to the other GM divisions. William E. Hoglund became general manager, after a brief turn by Robert Stempel. A white limited-edition Turbo Trans Am served as Indy Pace Car.

1981 PONTIAC

Whopping price rises greeted Pontiac customers as the 1981 model year began. Highlights included a notable change in Grand Prix appearance and a new formal look for LeMans sedans. Pontiac also adopted a Chevette clone, dubbed T1000. All models now included a lightweight Freedom II battery, and all gas engines had a Computer Command Control (CCC) system to control the air/fuel mixture. Optional cruise control, available on all models, added a "resume" feature that allowed return to former speed setting by touching the switch. All except T1000 and Firebird could have new puncture-sealing tires.

1981 T-1000 five-door hatchback sedan (P)

T1000 — SERIES 2T — FOUR — Pontiac finally offered an equivalent to Chevrolet's subcompact rear-drive Chevette, with the same 1.6-liter four-cylinder engine. It debuted at the Chicago Auto Show in February 1981, as a mid-year addition. See 1982 listing for details.

1981 Phoenix SJ coupe (P)

PHOENIX — SERIES 2X — V-6/V-8 — Base and LJ models made up the Phoenix lineup again, in two-door coupe or five-door hatchback body styles. Base engine was the 151 cu. in. (2.5-liter) four with four-speed manual transaxle. An SJ option package included black body trim and solid color paint. SJ versions could also get an appearance package with two-tone paint, striping, and bold SJ Phoenix door graphics. Newly optional for the SJ coupe: a decklid spoiler and front air dam. This year's grille was dominated by vertical bars. A new multi-function turn signal lever controlled a pulse windshield wiper. New optional wide bodyside moldings came in all colors. Automatic transmissions could get a floor lever. Phoenix standard equipment included P185/80R13 fiberglass-belted tires, argent hubcaps with Pontiac crest, compact spare tire, body-color bumpers with bright strips, front bench seat, and AM radio. Hatchbacks had bright rocker panel and wheel opening moldings. LJ added a stand-up hood ornament and windsplit molding, bright wide rocker panel moldings, wheel covers, notchback front seat with center armrest, dual horns, and bright window moldings.

1981 Formula Firebird coupe (P)

FIREBIRD — SERIES 2F — V-6/V-8 — Appearance was the same as 1980, but Firebird's engine selection was modified a bit this year. Formula now carried a standard 265 cu. in. (4.3-liter) V-8, which was optional on the base and Esprit. Trans Am again had a 301 cu. in. (4.9- liter) four-barrel V-8 with Electronic Spark Control. Both Trans Am and Formula could have a turbocharged 301 V-8. The turbo was now available in California. As in 1980, a four- speed manual gearbox was available for Formula and Trans Am with the four-barrel 305 cu. in. (5.0-liter) V-8. Standard power brakes now included a low-drag front caliper. A new two-color bird decal for the hood, and reflective bird decal for Trans Am's gas filler door, became available. Base Firebird standard equipment included the 231 cu. in. (3.8-liter) V-6 and three-speed manual shift (floor lever with console), power brakes/steering, P205/75R15 SBR blackwall tires, blackout grille with argent accents, hubcaps with Pontiac crest, and rosewood-grain instrument panel applique. Esprit added an automatic transmission, wheel covers, wheel opening moldings, wide rocker panel moldings, and body-color sport mirrors (left remote). Formula had a 265 cu. in. (4.3-liter) two-barrel V-8 and automatic, P225/70R15 tires, (simulated) twin hood air scoop, body-color mirrors, rear deck spoiler, and Rally II wheels with trim rings. Trans Am included the 301 V-8 and automatic, P225/70R15 tires, black-accent grille and headlamp bezels, wheel-opening air deflectors, side-split tailpipe extensions, engine-turned dash trim plate, rally gauges (with tachometer), Shaker hood, and Rally II wheels.

1981 Catalina sedan (CP)

CATALINA/BONNEVILLE — SERIES 2B — V-6/V-8 — Pontiac's full-size lineup again included Catalina, Bonneville, and Bonneville Brougham. Front-end appearance was similar to 1980, but the new grille had a tight crosshatch pattern repeated in twin bumper slots. Park/signal lamps were between the headlamps. Bonneville also had new taillamps, and the Catalina sedan added new side window moldings. Base engine was the 231 cu. in. (3.8-liter) V-6, hooked to automatic transmisison with locking torque converter clutch. Models with the optional 307 cu. in. (5.0- liter) V-8 required the new four-speed automatic transmission with overdrive top gear. Wagons had the 307 V-8 and four- speed automatic as standard. All full-size models could also have a 350 cu. in. (5.7-liter) diesel V-8. Full-size standard equipment included power brakes and steering, P205/75R15 blackwalls, stand-up hood ornament and windsplit molding, bumper rub strips, rocker panel moldings, and rear bumper guards. Catalina coupes/sedans had vinyl seat upholstery. Bonneville added fender skirts, deluxe wheel covers, notchback front seat, and hood edge molding. Bonneville Brougham included 60/40 notchback front seating, a remote driver's mirror, clock, and power windows. Safari wagons had P225/75R15 tires, three-way tailgate, power tailgate window, driver's remote (passenger manual) outside mirrors, and simulated woodgrain paneling or (on Bonneville) two-tone paint.

1981 LeMans coupe (CP)

LE MANS — SERIES 2A — V-6/V-8 — LeMans displayed a lower and more horizontal front-end look that included a revised front fascia panel and grille. The twin eggcrate-style grilles (4 x 3 pattern), on each side of a tapered center panel with Pontiac emblem, contained new park/signal lamps at their outer ends. Rectangular quad headlamps were new, and wraparound marker lenses had two horizontal trim ribs. Wide wraparound taillamps had one horizontal trim strip and a series of vertical strips, forming squares, with backup lenses at the center adjoining the license plate. Sedans added a new formal roof. A fully padded vinyl top was optional. Base engine was the 231 cu. in. (3.8-liter) V-6 with three-speed manual shift (automatic in station wagons, and in California). Automatic transmissions had a torque converter clutch. New standard equipment included power steering, a compact spare tire, and side-lift frame jack. Custom finned wheel covers were a new option. Standard equipment included P185/75R14 fiberglass-belted blackwall tires, power brakes and steering, wheel opening moldings, body-color bumpers with bright rub strips, and hubcaps with Pontiac crest. Coupes had black/bright pillar moldings. Grand LeMans added a hood ornament and windsplit molding, window and lower bodyside moldings, black rocker panel moldings, and folding front center armrest.

I.D. DATA: Pontiac had a new 17-symbol Vehicle Identification Number (VIN) this year, located on the upper left surface of the instrument panel, visible through the windshield. The first three symbols ('1G2') indicate Pontiac division. Symbol four is restraint system ('A' manual seatbelts). Symbol five is car line/series: 'M' T1000; 'Y' Phoenix; 'Z' Phoenix LJ; 'D' LeMans; 'F' Grand LeMans; 'S' Firebird; 'T' Firebird Esprit; 'V' Firebird Formula; 'W' Firebird Trans Am; 'X' Firebird Trans Am Turbo Special Edition; 'J' Grand Prix; 'K' Grand Prix LJ; 'P' Grand Prix Brougham; 'L' Catalina; 'N' Bonneville; 'R' Bonneville Brougham. In sixth and seventh position are two digits that denote body type: '07' 2-dr. hatchback coupe; '27' 2-dr. coupe; '37' 2-dr. hardtop coupe; '87' 2-dr. hardtop coupe; '19' 4-dr. 6window sedan; '68' 5-dr. hatchback sedan; '69' 4-dr. 4 window sedan; '35' 4-dr. station wagon. Symbol eight is a letter indicating engine code: '5' L4151 2Bbl.; 'X' V6173 2Bbl.; 'A' V6231 2Bbl.; 'S' V8265 2Bbl.; 'W' V8301 4Bbl.; 'T' Turbo V8301 4Bbl.; 'H' V8305 2Bbl.; 'Y' V8307 4Bbl.; 'N' diesel V8350. Next is a check digit. The tenth symbol denotes model year ('B' 1981). Symbol eleven is a plant code: 'B' Baltimore; 'L' Van Nuys, Calif.; 'N' Norwood, Ohio; 'P' Pontiac, Mich.; 'T' Tarrytown, NY; '7' Lordstown, Ohio; 'X' Fairfax, Kansas; '6' Oklahoma City; '1' Oshawa, Ontario; '2' Ste. Therese, Quebec. The final six digits are the sequential serial number.

1981 Grand Prix Brougham coupe (P)

GRAND PRIX — SERIES 2G — V-6/V-8 — All new body sheetmetal found its way onto Pontiac's personal-luxury coupe. Grand Prix's new aerodynamic wedge profile featured a low front end and raised deck, improving drag coefficient by some 20 percent. Base and LJ models were offered, along with a new top-rung Brougham instead of the former SJ. Though similar in shape to the 1980 version, the new grille was wider, since parking/lamps were no longer between the rectangular headlamps. The pattern of the horizontal-strip grille extended below the bumper strip, into two large slots. Small parking/signal lamps were mounted in the bumper strip. Base engine was the 231 cu. in. (3.8-liter) V-6 with automatic and lock-up torque converter clutch. Optional: a 265 cu. in. (4.3-liter) V-8 or 350 cu. in. diesel. New tires used higher pressure to cut rolling resistance. Standard equipment included power brakes/steering, P195/75R14 blackwall tires, bright-accented bumper strips, stand-up hood ornament, hubcaps with crest, rocker panel and wheel opening moldings, and notchback seat with center armrest. LJ included wide rocker panel moldings (with extensions), dual body-color sport mirrors (driver's remote), and wide wheel opening moldings. Brougham added a long list of equipment, including opera lamps, padded landau vinyl roof with formal back window, new finned wheel covers, power windows, and 60/40 front seat.

Model Number	Body/Style Number	Body Type & Seating	Factory Price	Shipping Weight	Production Total
T1000 (FOUR)					
2T	M08	3-dr. Hatch-4P	5358	2058	26,415
2T	M68	5-dr. Hatch-4P	5504	2122	43,779
PHOENIX (FOUR/V-6)					
2X	Y37	2-dr. Cpe-5P	6307/6432	2450/2555	31,829
2X	Y68	5-dr. Hatch-5P	6498/6623	2497/2552	62,693
PHOENIX LJ (FOUR/V-6)					
2X	Z37	2-dr. Cpe-5P	6778/6903	2492/2547	11,975
2X	Z68	5-dr. Hatch-5P	6969/7094	2552/2607	21,372
FIREBIRD (V-6/V-8)					
2F	S87	2-dr. HT Cpe-4P	6901/6951	3275/3350	20,541
FIREBIRD ESPRIT (V-6/V-8)					
2F	T87	2-dr. HT Cpe-4P	7645/7695	3312/3387	10,938
FIREBIRD FORMULA (V-6/V-8)					
2F	V87	2-dr. HT Cpe-4P	7854/7904	3397/3472	5,927

1981 "Bandit" Trans Am T-top coupe (CP)

FIREBIRD TRANS AM (V-8)

| 2F | W87 | 2-dr. HT Cpe-4P | 8322 | 3419 | 33,493 |
| 2F | X87 | 2-dr. Turbo SE-4P | 12257 | N/A | Note 1 |

Note 1: Production included in basic Trans Am total.

LE MANS (V-6/V-8)

2A	D27	2-dr. Cpe-6P	6689/6739	3035/3151	2,578
2A	D69	4-dr. Sed-6P	6797/6847	3052/3168	22,186
2A	D69/Y83	4-dr. LJ Sed-6P	7100/ --	N/A	Note 2

Note 2: Production included in basic sedan total.

LE MANS SAFARI (V-6/V-8)

| 2A | D35 | 4-dr. 2S Wag-6P | 7316/7366 | 3240/3386 | 13,358 |

GRAND LE MANS (V-6/V-8)

| 2A | F27 | 2-dr. Cpe-6P | 6976/7026 | 3063/3179 | 1,819 |
| 2A | F69 | 4-dr. Sed-6P | 7153/7203 | 3108/3224 | 25,241 |

GRAND LE MANS SAFARI (V-6/V-8)

| 2A | F35 | 4-dr. 2S Wag-6P | 7726/7776 | 3279/3425 | 16,683 |

GRAND PRIX (V-6/V-8)

| 2G | J37 | 2-dr. HT Cpe-6P | 7424/7474 | 3166/3287 | 74,786 |

GRAND PRIX LJ (V-6/V-8)

| 2G | K37 | 2-dr. HT Cpe-6P | 7803/7853 | 3195/3316 | 46,842 |

GRAND PRIX BROUGHAM (V-6/V-8)

| 2G | P37 | 2-dr. HT Cpe-6P | 8936/8986 | 3231/3342 | 26,083 |

CATALINA (V-6/V-8)

| 2B | L37 | 2-dr. Cpe-6P | 7367/7417 | 3421/3540 | 1,074 |
| 2B | L69 | 4-dr. Sed-6P | 7471/7521 | 3429/3548 | 6,456 |

CATALINA SAFARI (V-8)

| 2B | L35 | 4-dr. 2S Wag-6P | 8666 | 3924 | 2,912 |

BONNEVILLE (V-6/V-8)

| 2B | N37 | 2-dr. Cpe-6P | 7649/7699 | 3443/3562 | 14,940 |
| 2B | N69 | 4-dr. Sed-6P | 7776/7826 | 3461/3580 | 32,056 |

1981 Bonneville Brougham coupe (P)

BONNEVILLE BROUGHAM (V-6/V-8)

| 2B | R37 | 2-dr. Cpe-6P | 8580/8630 | 3443/3562 | 14,317 |
| 2B | R69 | 4-dr. Sed-6P | 8768/8818 | 3461/3580 | 23,395 |

BONNEVILLE SAFARI (V-8)

| 2B | N35 | 4-dr. 2S Wag-6P | 9205 | 3949 | 6,855 |

FACTORY PRICE AND WEIGHT NOTE: Prices and weights to left of slash are for V-6, to right for V-8 engine except Phoenix, four and V-6.

ENGINE DATA: BASE FOUR (T1000): Inline. Overhead cam. Four-cylinder. Cast iron block and head. Displacement: 97 cu. in. (1.6 liters). Bore & stroke: 3.23 x 2.98 in. Compression ratio: 8.6:1. Brake horsepower: 70 at 5200 R.P.M. Torque: 82 lbs.-ft. at 2400 R.P.M. Five main bearings. Hydraulic valve lifters. Carburetor: 2Bbl. Holley 5210C. VIN Code: 9. BASE FOUR (Phoenix): Inline. Overhead valve. Four-cylinder. Cast iron block and head. Displacement: 151 cu. in. (2.5 liters). Bore & stroke: 4.00 x 3.00 in. Compression ratio: 8.2:1. Brake horsepower: 84 at 4000 R.P.M. Torque: 125 lbs.-ft. at 2400 R.P.M. Five main bearings. Hydraulic valve lifters. Carburetor: 2Bbl. Rochester 2SE. VIN Code: 5. OPTIONAL V-6 (Phoenix): 60-degree, overhead valve six-cylinder. Cast iron block and aluminum head. Displacement: 173 cu. in. (2.8 liters). Bore & stroke: 3.50 x 3.00 in. Compression ratio: 8.5:1. Brake horsepower: 110 at 4800 R.P.M. Torque: 145 lbs.-ft. at 2400 R.P.M. Four main bearings. Hydraulic valve lifters. Carburetor: 2Bbl. Rochester. Chevrolet-built. VIN Code: X. BASE V-6 (Firebird, LeMans, Grand Prix, Catalina, Bonneville): 90-degree, overhead-valve V-6. Cast iron block and head. Displacement: 231 cu. in. (3.8 liters). Bore & stroke: 3.80 x 3.40 in. Compression ratio: 8.0:1. Brake horsepower: 110 at 3800 R.P.M. Torque: 190 lbs.-ft. at 1600 R.P.M. Four main bearings. Hydraulic valve lifters. Carburetor: 2Bbl. Rochester M2ME. Buick-built. VIN Code: A. BASE V-8 (Firebird Formula); OPTIONAL (Firebird, LeMans, Grand Prix, Catalina, Bonneville): 90-degree, overhead valve V-8. Cast iron block and head. Displacement: 265 cu. in. (4.3 liters). Bore & stroke: 3.75 x 3.00 in. Compression ratio: 8.3:1. Brake horsepower: 120 at 4000 R.P.M. Torque: 205 lbs.-ft. at 2000 R.P.M. Five main bearings. Hydraulic valve lifters. Carburetor: 2Bbl. Rochester E2ME. VIN Code: S. BASE V-8 (Safari); OPTIONAL (Firebird, Catalina, Bonneville, LeMans Safari): 90-degree, overhead valve V-8. Cast iron block and head. Displacement: 301 cu. in. (5.0 liters). Bore & stroke: 4.00 x 3.00 in. Compression ratio: 8.1:1. Brake horsepower: 135 at 3600 R.P.M. Torque: 235 lbs.-ft. at 1600 R.P.M. Five main earings. Hydraulic valve lifters. Carburetor: 4Bbl. VIN Code: W. BASE V-8 (Firebird Trans Am); OPTIONAL (Firebird): Same as 301 cu. in. V-8 above, but Horsepower: 150 at 4000 R.P.M. Torque: 245 lbs.-ft. at 2000 R.P.M. TURBOCHARGED V-8 (Firebird Formula, Trans Am): Same as 301 cu. in. V-8 above, with turbocharger Compression ratio: 7.5:1. Horsepower: 200 at 4000 R.P.M. Torque: 340 lbs.-ft. at 2000 R.P.M. VIN Code: T. OPTIONAL V-8 (Firebird Formula/Trans Am): 90-degree, overhead valve V-8. Cast iron block and head. Displacement: 305 cu. in. (5.0 liters). Bore & stroke: 3.74 x 3.48 in. Compression ratio: 8.4:1. Brake horsepower: 145 at 3800 R.P.M. Torque: 240 lbs.-ft. at 2400 R.P.M. Five main bearings. Hydraulic valve lifters. Carburetor: 4Bbl. Rochester E4ME. Chevrolet-built. VIN Code: H. BASE V-8 (Safari); OPTIONAL (Catalina, Bonneville): 90-degree, overhead valve V-8. Cast iron block and head. Displacement: 307 cu. in. (5.0 liters). Bore & stroke: 3.80 x 3.38 in. Compression ratio: 8.0:1. Brake horsepower: 145 at 3800 R.P.M. Torque: 240 lbs.-ft. at 2400 R.P.M. Hydraulic valve lifters. Carburetor: 4Bbl. Rochester E4ME. Oldsmobile-built. VIN Code: Y. DIESEL V-8 (Grand Prix, Catalina, Bonneville, Safari): 90-degree, overhead valve V-8. Cast iron block and head. Displacement: 350 cu. in. (5.7 liters). Bore & stroke: 4.06 x 3.39 in. Compression ratio: 22.5:1. Brake horsepower: 105 at 3200 R.P.M. Torque: 205 lbs.-ft. at 1600 R.P.M. Five main bearings. Hydraulic valve lifters. Fuel injection. Oldsmobile-built. VIN Code: N.

CHASSIS DATA: Wheelbase: (Phoenix) 104.9 in.; (Firebird) 108.2 in.; (LeMans) 108.1 in.; (Grand Prix) 108.1 in.; (Catalina/Bonn.) 116.0 in. Overall Length: (Phoenix cpe) 182.1 in.; (Phoenix hatch) 179.3 in.; (Firebird) 196.1 in.; (LeMans) 198.6 in.; (LeM wag) 197.8 in.; (G.P.) 201.4 in.; (Catalina/Bonn.) 214.0 in.; (Safari wag) 216.7 in. Height: (Phoenix cpe) 53.5 in.; (Phoenix sed) 53.4 in.; (Firebird) 49.3 in.; (LeM) 53.5 in.; (LeM wag) 54.4 in.; (G.P.) 54.7 in.; (Catalina/Bonn. cpe) 56.0 in.; (Catalina/Bonn. sed) 56.7 in.; (Safari wag) 57.1 in. Width: (Phoenix) 69.1 in.; (Firebird) 73.0 in.; (LeM) 72.4 in.; (LeM wag) 71.9 in.; (G.P.) 72.7 in.; (Cat./Bonn.) 75.4 in.; (Safari wag) 75.8 in. Front Tread: (Phoenix) 58.7 in.; (Firebird) 61.3 in.; (LeM) 58.5 in.; (G.P.) 58.5 in.; (Cat./Bonn.) 61.7 in.; (Safari) 62.1 in. Rear Tread: (Phoenix) 57.0 in.; (Firebird) 60.0 in.; (LeM) 57.8 in. exc. wagon, 58.0 in.; (G.P.) 57.8 in.; (Cat./Bonn.) 60.7 in.; (Safari) 64.1 in. Standard Tires: (Phoenix) P185/80R13 GBR; (Firebird) P205/75R15 SBR; (Firebird Formula/Trans Am) P225/70R15 SBR; (LeMans) P185/75R14 GBR exc. wagon, P195/75R14 GBR; (Grand Prix) P195/75R14 GBR; (Cat./Bonn.) P205/75R15 SBR; (Safari) P225/75R15 SBR.

TECHNICAL: Transmission: Three-speed manual transmission standard on base Firebird and LeMans. Four-speed manual standard on T1000 and Phoenix. Three-speed Turbo Hydra-matic standard on other models. Four-speed overdrive automatic available on full-size models (standard on Safari). Standard final drive ratio: (Phoenix) 2.69:1 w/4spd, 2.53:1 w/four and auto., 2.84:1 w/V-6 and auto. 2.96:1 or 3.33:1 w/H.O. V-6; (Firebird V-6) 3.08:1 w/3spd, 2.56:1 w/auto.; (Firebird V8265) 2.41:1; (Firebird V8301) 2.56:1; (Firebird Trans Am/Formula) 2.41:1 w/V8265, 2.56:1 w/V8301, 3.08:1 w/turbo or 305 V-8; (LeMans V-6) 2.73:1 w/3spd, 2.41:1 w/auto.; (LeMans V-8) 2.29:1; (LeMans Safari) 2.73:1 w/V-6, 2.41:1 w/V8265, 2.29:1 w/V8301; (Grand Prix) 2.41:1 w/V-6, 2.29:1 w/V8265, 2.14:1 w/V8301; (Catalina/Bonneville) 2.73:1 w/V-6, 2.41:1 w/V-8 exc. 3.08:1 w/V8301 and 4spd auto.; (Safari) 3.08:1 w/V8301, 2.73:1 w/diesel. Steering: (Phoenix) rack and pinion; (others) recirculating ball. Front Suspension: (Phoenix) MacPherson struts w/lower control arms and anti-sway bar; (Firebird/LeMans) coil springs w/lower trailing links

and anti-sway bar; (others) coil springs and anti-sway bar. Rear Suspension: (Phoenix) single-beam trailing axle w/track bar and coil springs; (Firebird) semi-elliptic leaf springs with anti-sway bar; (LeMans/Bonneville/Grand Prix) rigid axle with coil springs, lower trailing radius arms and upper torque arms. Brakes: Front disc, rear drum. Ignition: Electronic. Body construction: (Phoenix) unit; (Firebird) unit w/separate partial frame; (others) separate body and frame. Fuel Tank: (Phoenix) 14 gal.; (Firebird) 21 gal.; (LeMans) 18.1 gal. exc. wagon, 18.2 gal.; (Grand Prix) 18.1 gal.; (Catalina/Bonn.) 25 gal.; (Safari) 22 gal. NOTE: Dimensions and technical details for T1000, added at mid-year, not available; see 1982 listing for data.

DRIVETRAIN OPTIONS: Engines: 173 cu. in. V-6: Phoenix ($125). 265 cu. in., 2Bbl. V-8: Firebird/LeMans/Grand Prix/Catalina/Bonneville ($50). 301 cu. in., 4Bbl. V-8: Safari ($50). E/C 301 cu. in., 4Bbl. V-8: Firebird ($215). Turbo 301 cu. in. V-8: Firebird Formula ($652); Trans Am ($437). 305 cu. in., 4Bbl. V-8: Firebird Formula ($75); Trans Am ($140 credit). 307 cu. in., 4Bbl. V-8: Catalina/Bonneville ($50). Diesel 350 cu. in. V-8: Grand Prix/Catalina/Bonn. Brghm ($695). Transmission/Differential: Turbo Hydra-matic: Phoenix/Firebird/LeMans ($349). Overdrive automatic trans.: Catalina/Bonneville cpe/sed ($153). Limited-slip differential: Firebird/LeM/G.P./Catalina/Bonn. ($67). Brakes/Steering: Power brakes: Phoenix ($79). Power four- wheel disc brakes: Firebird ($158). Power steering: Phoenix ($168). Suspension: Rally RTS handling pkg.: Phoenix ($173-$245) except w/SJ option ($1-$73); Cat./Bonn. ($44). Rally handling susp.: LeM ($202-$241). Superlift shock absorbers: Phoenix/Catalina/Bonn. ($57). H.D. springs: Phoenix/LeM/G.P./Cat./Bonn. ($14-$15). Automatic level control: Catalina/Bonn. ($85-$142). Other: H.D. radiator: Phoenix ($38-$63). H.D. cooling: LeM ($34); Cat./Bonn. ($34-$63). Super-cooling radiator: Firebird ($34-$63); Cat./Bonn. ($34-$63). H.D. battery ($22) exc. diesel ($44). H.D. alternator: Phoenix ($10-$43); Firebird ($51); LeM/G.P./Cat./Bonn. ($15-$51). Engine block heater ($16). Light trailer group: Phoenix ($120-$135); LeM/Cat./Bonn. ($129-$158); G.P. ($139-$158). Medium trailer group: Cat./Bonn. ($129-$158). California emissions ($46) exc. diesel ($182).

OPTION PACKAGES: Phoenix custom exterior ($85-$130). Phoenix apperance pkg. ($187). Phoenix SJ appearance pkg. ($118). Phoenix luxury trim pkg. ($223-$344). Phoenix SJ option ($404-$449). Trans Am Special Edition ($735); w/hatch roof ($1430). Firebird Formula appearance pkg. ($200). Firebird Formula/Trans Am special performance pkg. ($350-$546). Firebird custom trim ($45-$164). LeMans Safari security pkg. ($40). LeMans luxury trim group ($160-$270). LeMans appearance pkg. ($180). LeMans custom exterior ($44-$100). LeMans custom trim group ($130- $303). Grand Prix appearance ($184). Full-size appearance pkg. ($177). Full-size custom trim group ($176-$398).

MAJOR CONVENIENCE/APPEARANCE OPTIONS: Air conditioning ($560-$625). Automatic air conditioning: LeMans/Grand Prix ($677); Catalina/Bonneville ($708); Safari ($83). Cruise control ($132-$135). Power seat ($173). Power windows ($140-$211). Cornering lamps: Catalina/Bonn./Grand Prix ($51-$52). Power glass sunroof: LeMans/Grand Prix ($773); Catalina/Bonn. ($981). Power steel sunroof: LeMans/Grand Prix ($561); Catalina/Bonn. ($704). Hatch roof: Firebird/Grand Prix ($663-$889). Full vinyl cordova top: LeMans ($115); Catalina/Bonneville ($142). Padded landau cordova top: Phoenix ($178); LeMans ($192); Grand Prix/Bonn. ($222). Rear-facing third seat: Safari ($194).

HISTORY: Introduced: September 25, 1980. Model year production: 600,543. Calendar year production (U.S.): 519,292. Calendar year sales by U.S. dealers: 552,384. Model year sales by U.S. dealers: 601,218 (incl. 34,424 early 1982 J2000 models).

Historical Footnotes: Production fell for the model year, for the second year in a row. Sales slipped too, but not by as much. Firebird dropped sharply, though part of that loss may have been due to expectations of a fully restyled version for 1982. Only Grand Prix showed a sales rise. Pontiac's CAFE figure for 1981 was just over 23 MPG (with 22 the required standard). William E. Hoglund was the division's new general manager. In addition to sales of Pontiac's "Iron Duke" four-cylinder engine to other GM divisions, it even found its way under AMC hoods. Early in the year, Pontiac abandoned production of V-8 powerplants, after building them since 1955.

1982 PONTIAC

A new, aerodynamically restyled Firebird was 1982's foremost news from Pontiac. Also new this year: front- wheel-drive J2000 and 6000 models. The old Catalina and Bonneville were gone, but a revised Bonneville G entered the lineup.

1982 T1000 hatchback coupe (P)

T1000 — SERIES 2T — FOUR — Differing little from Chevrolet's Chevette, the T1000 contained the smallest four-cylinder engine ever in a Pontiac: just 98 cu. in. (1.6 liter). A five-speed manual transmission was available this year on the three-door hatchback version of Pontiac's smallest car. A new dark argent grille with widely separated vertical bars (and wide center bar with emblem) highlighted the front end, which had single rectangular headlamps in black bezels. Small park/signal lamps were bumper-mounted. Bumpers held black rubber end caps. Taillamps were wraparound style. Standard reclining bucket seats were upholstered in vinyl, with Pompey cloth optional. T1000's suspension was returned. Standard equipment included the 1.6-liter OHC four- cylinder engine, four-speed manual transmission, front/rear bumper guards

and rub strips, AM radio, P155/80R13 glass- belted blackwall tires, wide black/bright bodyside moldings, argent styled steel wheels, wide vinyl-clad black rocker panel moldings, and black-finish window frames. Three-doors had swingout rear quarter windows.

1982 J2000 LE coupe (JG)

J2000 — SERIES 2J — FOUR — Introduced as an early 1982 model, the five-passenger subcompact J2000's front-drive chassis rode a 101.2 inch wheelbase. Two-door coupe, three-door hatchback, four-door sedan and four-door wagon bodies were available in base form. The sporty SE came only as a hatchback, while the luxury LE appeared as a coupe or sedan. Each model had standard reclining front bucket seats. Hatchbacks and wagons had full-folding back seats, while SE had a split folding rear seat. An S model was added later. A sharply sloped front panel formed a tapered body-color center divider with emblem, between twin recessed grilles. Quad rectangular headlamps were used. Park/signal lamps were below the bumper strip. A full-width air slot between the parking lamps displayed an eggcrate pattern similar to that of the upper grilles. Wide wraparound taillamps sat in a full-width panel with horizontal ribbing, with backup lenses in the center of each unit. Small rear lenses could be seen in the bumper area. The rear license plate was bumper- mounted. Base J2000 engine was a transverse-mounted 112 cu. in. (1.8-liter) four with two-barrel carburetor, hooked to a four-speed manual transaxle. The engine's fast-burn combustion chamber had a centrally-positioned spark plug with high turbulence, with 9.0:1 compression. The electronic control module had built-in diagnostics. Front suspension was MacPherson struts; in back, a double-crank trailing-twist rear axle. Variable-rate coil springs helped balance the front and rear suspension. Standard equipment included power brakes, locking fuel filler door, body-color bumpers with rub strips, swing-out rear quarter windows (coupe/hatchback), AM radio with digital clock, Rally wheels, P175/80R13 fiberglass-belted tires, and reclining front bucket seats. Hatchbacks and LE had wide bodyside moldings and rocker panel moldings. SE added Viscount trim, a gauge set and driver's remote mirror.

1982 Phoenix First Level sedan (P)

PHOENIX — SERIES 2X — FOUR/V-6 — Fuel injection was added to the base Phoenix 151 cu. in. (2.5-liter) four this year. A new SJ coupe or hatchback carried as standard a high-output 173 cu. in. (2.8-liter) V-6. A lower-powered version of the V-6 was optional in other Phoenix models, as was three-speed automatic to replace the standard four-speed manual shift. SJ included standard power steering and brakes, cast aluminum wheels, Rally RTS suspension, black grille and moldings, and SJ graphics package. The Phoenix steering gear moved to the engine cradle this year, for better isolation. Styling was similar to 1981.

1982 Firebird SE coupe (P)

FIREBIRD — SERIES 2F — FOUR/V-6/V-8 — Instead of the previous four models, the revised Firebird came in three variations: base, luxury S/E, and Trans Am. Each one had its own suspension and tire setup. Base engine was now a fuel-injected 151 cu. in. (2.5-liter) four, hooked to four-speed manual gearbox. S/E carried a standard 173 cu. in. (2.8-liter) two-barrel V-6, also with four-speed, while Trans Am had a 305 cu. in. (5.0-liter) four-barrel V-8 with the four-speed. Trans Am could also step up to a dual throttle-body (crossfire) fuel injection V-8 with fresh-air hood induction. A low nose now held hidden halogen headlamps, electrically controlled. Park/signal lamps sat in squat slots inboard of the headlamps, barely visible with headlamp doors shut. The twin air slots contained horizontal bars. At the rear was a large, contoured, frameless all-glass hatch. Taillamps were in a full-width back panel. Reclining front bucket seats were standard. A new Formula steering wheel had an energy-absorbing hub. A WS6 suspension (optional on S/E and Trans Am) included P215/65R15 SBR tires on 7 inch aluminum wheels, larger stabilizer bars, four-wheel disc brakes, positraction rear axle, and tuned springs/shocks/bushings. Standard Firebird equipment included P195/75R14 glass-belted blackwall tires, hubcaps, black-finished grille, front air dam, power brakes and steering, front stabilizer bar, side window defoggers, and black-finished instrument panel. S/E added full-width black taillamps, body-color bodyside moldings, lower accent paint (with striping), turbo cast aluminum wheels, P205/70R14 steel-belted blackwalls, and rear stabilizer bar. Trans Am included bird decals on hood and sail panel, front fender air extractors, front/rear wheel opening flares, and aero wing decklid spoiler.

1982 6000 LE sedan (OCW)

6000 — SERIES 2A — FOUR/V-6 — Based on the Xcar design, the contemporary-styled 6000 carried five passengers and was designed with "internationally competitive" ride/handling characteristics. Base and LE models came in two-door coupe or four-door sedan body styles. Standard powerplant was a fuel-injected 151 cu. in. (2.5-liter) four with three-speed automatic transmission. Vertical bars made up each side of the split grille. Recessed quad headlamps were used, with parking/signal lamps down in the bumper strip. Wraparound taillamps had horizontal trim ribs. Backup lights adjoined the license plate opening. Standard 6000 equipment included automatic transmission, power brakes/steering, black rocker panel moldings, front air dam, black driver's mirror, wheel opening and roof drip moldings, P185/80R13 blackwall GBR tires, hubcaps, AM radio, side window defoggers, and day/night mirror. LE added deluxe wheel covers, lower door edge moldings, a locking gas filler door, overhead assist straps, and black-finished rocker panel area.

1982 Grand Prix coupe (Richard Petty/STP race car)

GRAND PRIX — SERIES 2G — V-6 — Restyled a year before, Grand Prix continued its aero wedge shape with low front end and higher deck. Appearance was similar to before, but with a tight pattern of vertical bars (formerly horizontal) in the twin grilles. The grille pattern repeated in two tall bumper slots. Small park/signal lamps went into the bumper strip, which crossed the grille just below its up/down midpoint. "Grand Prix' script decorated the left grille. Base engine was the 231 cu. in. (3.8-liter) V-6 from Buick, with automatic transmission (which had a lock-up torque converter clutch). A 252 cu. in. (4.1-liter) V-6 cost just $95 more. No gasoline V-8 was available, but a V-8 diesel cost $924. Four trim levels were available, including two new ones for the Brougham. The base Brougham was trimmed as in 1981, including a notchback loose-pillow 60/40 seat. A new Brougham Landau option included opera lamps, a formal back window, padded landau roof, power windows, and Tampico carpeting. Base, LJ and Brougham models were offered.

BONNEVILLE G — SERIES 2G — V-6/V-8 — This new Bonneville, still rear-drive, was smaller and more fuel-efficient than its predecessor, riding a 108.1 inch wheelbase. Base and Brougham trim levels were available on the formal-roof four-door sedan. A single station wagon model also was offered. Base engine was a 231 cu. in. (3.8-liter) V-6 with three-speed automatic transmission. Optional: either a 252 cu. in. (4.1-liter) V-6, or the 350 diesel V-8. A relatively narrow center divider (with emblem) separated the twin grilles, each made up of vertical bars. Quad rectangular headlamps stood directly above wide park/signal lamps. Two-row wraparound taillamps had a checkerboard look. Standard Bonneville equipment included power brakes and

1982 Bonneville G station wagon (JG)

steering, P195/75R14 blackwall GBR tires, body-color bumpers, front bumper guards, wide rocker panels (with extensions), roof drip moldings, a stand-up hood ornament (with windsplit), wheel opening moldings, wheel covers, and electric clock. Brougham added opera lamps, simulated teak instrument panel trim, and 60/40 front seat with fold-down armrest,

I.D. DATA: Pontiac's 17-symbol Vehicle Identification Number (VIN) was on the upper left surface of the instrument panel, visible through the windshield. The first three symbols ('1G2') indicate Pontiac division. Symbol four is restraint system ('A' manual seatbelts). Symbol five is car line/series: 'L' T1000; 'B' J2000; 'E' J2000 S; 'C' J2000 LE; 'D' J2000 SE; 'Y' Phoenix; 'Z' Phoenix LJ; 'T' Phoenix SJ; 'F' 6000; 'G' 6000 LE; 'S' Firebird; 'X' Firebird S/E; 'W' Firebird Trans Am; 'J' Grand Prix; 'K' Grand Prix LJ; 'P' Grand Prix Brougham; 'N' Bonneville G; 'R' Bonneville G Brougham. In sixth and seventh position are two digits that denote body type: '08' 3dr. hatchback coupe; '27' 2dr. coupe; '37' 2dr. coupe; '77' 3dr. hatchback; '87' 2dr. coupe; '19' 4dr. 6window sedan; '68' 5dr. hatchback sedan; '69' 4dr. 4 window sedan; '35' 4dr. station wagon. Symbol eight is a letter indicating engine code: 'C' L497 2Bbl.; 'O' L4109 2Bbl.; 'G' L4112 2Bbl.; 'R' or '2' L4151 FI; 'X' or '1' V6173 2Bbl.; 'Z' H.O. V6173 2Bbl.;'A' V6231 2Bbl.; '4' V6252 4Bbl.; 'T' diesel V6262; 'H' V8305 4Bbl.; '7' V8305 FI; 'N' diesel V8350. Next is a check digit. The tenth symbol denotes model year ('C' 1982). Symbol eleven is a plant code: 'A' Lakewood, GA; 'G' Framingham, MA; 'K' Leeds, MO; 'L' Van Nuys, CA; 'N' Norwood, Ohio; 'P' Pontiac, Mich.; 'T' Tarrytown, NY; 'Y' Wilmington, DE; '7' Lordstown, Ohio; '6' Oklahoma City; '1' Oshawa, Ontario. The final six digits are the sequential serial number.

T1000 (FOUR)

Model Number	Body/Style Number	Body Type & Seating	Factory Price	Shipping Weight	Production Total
2T	L08	3-dr. Hatch-4P	5752	2034	21,053
2T	L68	5-dr. Hatch-4P	5945	2098	23,416

J2000 (FOUR)

2J	B27	2-dr. Cpe-5P	6999	2295	15,865
2J	B77	3-dr. Hatch-5P	7275	2353	21,219
2J	B69	4-dr. Sedan-5P	7203	2347	29,920
2J	B35	4-dr. Sta Wag-5P	7448	2418	16,014

J2000 S (FOUR)

2J	E27	2-dr. Cpe-5P	6734	N/A	2,722
2J	E69	4-dr. Sedan-5P	6902	N/A	2,760
2J	E35	4-dr. Sta Wag-5P	7208	N/A	1,245

J2000 LE (FOUR)

2J	C27	2-dr. Cpe-5P	7372	2300	6,313
2J	C69	4-dr. Sedan-5P	7548	2352	14,268

J2000 SE (FOUR)

2J	D77	3-dr. Hatch-5P	7654	2358	8,533

Price Note: J2000 prices rose $50-$93 shortly after introduction.

PHOENIX (FOUR/V-6)

2X	Y37	2-dr. Cpe-5P	6964/7182	2386/2450	12,282
2X	Y68	5-dr. Hatch-5P	7172/7390	2476/2540	24,026

PHOENIX LJ (FOUR/V-6)

2X	Z37	2-dr. Cpe-5P	7449/7687	2386/2450	4,436
2X	Z68	5-dr. Hatch-5P	7658/7876	2476/2540	7,161

Phoenix Price Note: V-6 price includes the required power brakes.

1982 Phoenix SJ coupe (JG)

PHOENIX SJ (V-6)

2X	T37	2-dr. Cpe-5P	8723	2450	994
2X	T68	5-dr. Hatch-5P	8884	2540	268

FIREBIRD (FOUR/V-6)

2F	S87	2-dr. Cpe-4P	7996/8121	N/A	41,683

Engine Note: A 305 cu. in. V-8 cost $170 more than the V-6 on base Firebird.

FIREBIRD S/E (V-6/V-8)

2F	X87	2-dr. Cpe-4P	9624/9819	N/A	21,719

1982 Firebird Trans Am coupe (OCW)

FIREBIRD TRANS AM (V-8)

2F	W87	2-dr. Cpe-4P	9658	N/A	52,960

6000 (FOUR/V-6)

2A	F27	2-dr. Cpe-5P	8729/8854	N/A	6,505
2A	F19	4-dr. Sed-5P	8890/9015	N/A	17,751
2A	G27	2-dr. LE Cpe-5P	9097/9222	N/A	7,025
2A	G19	4-dr. LE Sed-5P	9258/9383	N/A	26,253

GRAND PRIX (V-6)

2G	J37	2-dr. HT Cpe-6P	8333	3276	37,672

GRAND PRIX LJ (V-6)

2G	K37	2-dr. HT Cpe-6P	8788	3276	29,726

GRAND PRIX BROUGHAM (V-6)

2G	P37	2-dr. HT Cpe-6P	9209	3276	12,969

BONNEVILLE G (V-6/V-8)

2G	N69	4-dr. Sed-6P	8527/8622	3203/ --	44,378
2G	N35	4-dr. Sta Wag-6P	8414/8789	3380/ --	16,100

BONNEVILLE G BROUGHAM (V-6/V-8)

2G	R69	4-dr. Sed-6P	8985/9080	3213/ --	20,035

FACTORY PRICE AND WEIGHT NOTE: Prices and weights to left of slash are for V-6, to right for V-8 engine except Phoenix/Firebird/6000, four and V-6.

ENGINE DATA: BASE FOUR (T1000): Inline. Overhead cam. Four-cylinder. Cast iron block and head. Displacement: 97 cu. in. (1.6 liters). Bore & stroke: 3.23 x 2.98 in. Compression ratio: 9.2:1. Brake horsepower: 62 at 5200 R.P.M. Torque: 82 lbs.-ft. at 2400 R.P.M. Five main bearings. Hydraulic valve lifters. Carburetor: 2Bbl. Holley 6510C. VIN Code: C. BASE FOUR (J2000): Inline. Overhead valve. Four-cylinder. Cast iron block and head. Displacement: 112 cu. in. (1.8 liters). Bore & stroke: 3.50 x 2.91 in. Compression ratio: 9.0:1. Brake horsepower: 88 at 5100 R.P.M. Torque: 100 lbs.-ft. at 2800 R.P.M. Five main bearings. Hydraulic valve lifters. Carburetor: 2Bbl. Rochester E2SE. VIN Code: G. OPTIONAL FOUR (J2000): Inline. Overhead cam. Four-cylinder. Cast iron block and aluminum head. Displacement: 109 cu. in. (1.8 liters). Bore & stroke: 3.34 x 3.13 in. Compression ratio: 9.0:1. Brake horsepower: 82 at 5200 R.P.M. Torque: 96 lbs.-ft. at 2800 R.P.M. Five main bearings. Hydraulic valve lifters. Carburetor: 2Bbl. Rochester. VIN Code: O. BASE FOUR (Phoenix, Firebird, 6000): Inline. Overhead valve. Four-cylinder. Cast iron block and head. Displacement: 151 cu. in. (2.5 liters). Bore & stroke: 4.00 x 3.00 in. Compression ratio: 8.2:1. Brake horsepower: 90 at 4000 R.P.M. Torque: 134 lbs.-ft. at 2400 R.P.M. Five main bearings. Throttle-body fuel injection. VIN Code: R or 2. OPTIONAL V-6 (Phoenix, Firebird, 6000): 60-degree, overhead valve six-cylinder. Cast iron block and aluminum head. Displacement: 173 cu. in. (2.8 liters). Bore & stroke: 3.50 x 3.00 in. Compression ratio: 8.5:1. Brake horsepower: 112 at 4800 R.P.M. (Firebird, 105 at 4800). Torque: 145 lbs.-ft. at 2400 R.P.M. (Firebird, 142 at 2400). Four main bearings. Hydraulic valve lifters. Carburetor: 2Bbl. Rochester E2SE. VIN Code: X or 1. OPTIONAL V-6 (Phoenix SJ): High-output version of 173 cu. in. V-6 above Compression ratio: 8.9:1. Horsepower: 130 at 5400 R.P.M. Torque: 145 lbs.-ft. at 2400 R.P.M. VIN Code: Z. BASE V-6 (Grand Prix, Bonneville): 90-degree, overhead-valve V-6. Cast iron block and head. Displacement: 231 cu. in. (3.8 liters). Bore & stroke: 3.80 x 3.40 in. Compression ratio: 8.0:1. Brake horsepower: 110 at 3800 R.P.M. Torque: 190 lbs.-ft. at 1600 R.P.M. Four main bearings. Hydraulic valve lifters. Carburetor: 2Bbl. Rochester E2ME. Buick-built. VIN Code: A. OPTIONAL V-6 (Grand Prix): 90-degree, overhead-valve V-6. Cast iron block and head. Displacement: 252 cu. in. (4.1 liters). Bore & stroke: 3.96 x 3.40 in. Compression ratio: 8.0:1. Brake horsepower: 125 at 4000 R.P.M. Torque: 205 lbs.-ft. at 2000 R.P.M. Four main bearings. Hydraulic valve lifters. Carburetor: 2Bbl. Buick- built. VIN Code: 4. DIESEL V-6 (6000, Bonneville): 90-degree, overhead valve V-6. Cast iron block and head. Displacement: 262 cu. in. (4.3 liters). Bore & stroke: 4.06 x 3.38 in. Compression ratio: 21.6:1. Brake horsepower: 85 at 3600 R.P.M. Torque: 165 lbs.-ft. at 1600 R.P.M. Four main bearings. Hydraulic valve lifters. Fuel injection. VIN Code: T. BASE V-8 (Firebird Trans Am); OPTIONAL (Firebird): 90-degree, overhead valve V-8. Cast iron block and head. Displacement: 305 cu. in. (5.0 liters). Bore & stroke: 3.74 x 3.48 in. Compression ratio: 8.6:1. Brake horsepower: 145 at 4000 R.P.M. Torque: 240 lbs.-ft. at 2400 R.P.M. Five main bearings. Hydraulic valve lifters. Carburetor: 4Bbl. Rochester E4ME. Chevrolet-built. VIN Code: H. OPTIONAL V-8 (Trans Am): Same as 305 cu. in. V-8 above, with throttle-body fuel injection Compression ratio: 9.5:1. Horsepower: 165 at 4200 R.P.M. Torque: 240 lbs.-ft. at 2400 R.P.M. VIN Code: 7. DIESEL V-8 (Grand Prix Bonneville): 90-degree, overhead valve V-8. Cast iron block and head. Displacement: 350 cu. in. (5.7 liters). Bore & stroke: 4.06 x 3.39 in. Compression ratio: 21.6:1. Brake horsepower: 105 at 3200 R.P.M. Torque: 205 lbs.-ft. at 1600 R.P.M. Five main bearings. Hydraulic valve lifters. Fuel injection. Oldsmobile-built. VIN Code: N.

CHASSIS DATA: Wheelbase: (T1000 3dr.) 94.3 in.; (T1000 5dr.) 97.3 in.; (J2000) 101.2 in.; (Phoenix) 104.9 in.; (Firebird) 101.0 in.; (6000) 104.8 in.; (Grand Prix) 108.1 in.; (Bonn.) 108.1 in. Overall Length: (T1000 3dr.) 161.9 in.; (T1000 5dr.) 164.9 in.; (J2000 cpe) 169.4 in.; (J2000 sed) 171.4 in.; (J2000 wag) 175.3 in.; (Phoenix cpe) 182.1 in.; (Phoenix hatch) 179.3 in.; (Firebird) 189.8 in.; (6000) 188.7 in.; (G.P.) 201.9 in.; (Bonn. wag) 197.8 in. Height: (T1000) 52.9 in.; (J2000 cpe) 51.3 in.; (J2000 sed/wag) 53.3 in.; (Phoenix cpe) 53.5 in.; (Phoenix sed) 53.4 in.; (Firebird) 49.8 in.; (6000) 53.3 in.; (G.P.) 54.7 in.; (Bonn.) 55.8 in.; (Bonn. wag) 56.1 in. Width: (T1000) 61.8 in.; (J2000) 64.9 in.; (Phoenix cpe) 69.1 in.; (Phoenix sed) 69.6 in.; (Firebird) 72.0 in.; (6000) 67.7 in.; (G.P.) 72.1 in.; (Bonn.) 71.3 in.; (Bonn. wag) 72.6 in. Front Tread: (T1000) 51.2 in.; (J2000) 55.4 in.; (Phoenix) 58.7 in.; (Firebird) 60.7 in.; (6000) 58.7 in.; (G.P.) 58.5 in.; (Bonn.) 58.5 in. Rear Tread: (T1000) 51.2 in.; (J2000) 55.1 in.; (Phoenix) 57.0 in.; (Firebird) 60.6 in.; (6000) 56.9 in.; (G.P.) 57.8 in.; (Bonn.) 57.8 in.; (Bonn. wag) 58.0 in. Standard Tires: (T1000) P155/80R13 GBR BSW; (J2000) P175/80R13 GBR BSW; (Phoenix) P185/80R13 GBR BSW; (Firebird) P195/75R14 GBR BSW; (Firebird S/E, Trans Am) P205/70R14 SBR BSW; (6000) P185/80R13 GBR BSW; (Grand Prix) P195/75R14 SBR BSW; (Bonn.) P195/75R14 GBR BSW.

TECHNICAL: Transmission: Four-speed manual standard on T1000, J2000, Phoenix and Firebird (base and S/E). Three-speed Turbo Hydra-matic standard on other models, optional on all. Standard final drive ratio: (T1000) 3.36:1 w/109 four, 3.32:1 w/112 four; (Phoenix) 3.32:1 except 3.65:1 w/H.O. V-6; (Firebird) 3.23:1 w/V-6, 3.23:1 w/V-8; (6000) 2.39:1 w/four, 2.53:1 w/V-6; (Grand Prix) 2.41:1 w/V-6, 2.29:1 w/V-8; (Bonneville) 2.73:1 w/V-6, 2.41:1 w/V-8. Steering: (T1000/J2000/Phoenix/6000) rack and pinion; (others) recirculating ball. Front Suspension: (J2000/Phoenix) MacPherson struts w/lower control arms and anti-sway bar; (Firebird) modified MacPherson struts w/coil springs between lower control arm and Xmember; (6000) MacPherson struts w/coil springs; (others) coil springs and anti-sway bar. Rear Suspension: (T1000) rigid axle w/longitudinal trailing radium arms, transverse bar, coil springs and anti-sway bar; (J2000) rigid axle w/coil springs; (Phoenix) single-beam trailing axle w/track bar and coil springs; (Firebird) torque arm/track bar w/coil springs, and anti-sway bar on S/E and Trans Am; (6000) trailing arm and beam w/coil springs and anti-sway bar; (Bonneville/Grand Prix) rigid axle with coil springs, lower trailing radius arms and upper torque arms. Brakes: Front disc, rear drum. Ignition: Electronic. Body construction: (T1000/J2000/Phoenix/Firebird/6000) unit; (others) separate body and frame. Fuel Tank: (T1000) 12.5 gal.; (J2000) 14 gal.; (Phoenix) 14 gal.; (Firebird) 16 gal.; (6000) 15.7 gal.; (Grand Prix) 18.2 gal.; (Bonneville) 20.6 gal.

DRIVETRAIN OPTIONS: Engines: 151 cu. in. four: Firebird S/E ($125 credit). 173 cu. in. V-6: Phoenix/Firebird/6000 ($125). 252 cu. in., 4Bbl. V-6: Grand Prix, Bonneville ($95). Diesel 262 cu. in. V-6: 6000 ($824). 305 cu. in., 4Bbl. V-8: Grand Prix, Bonn. ($295); Firebird S/E ($170-195). Dual EFI engine pkg.: Trans Am ($899). Diesel 350 cu. in. V-8: Grand Prix/Bonn. ($924). Transmission/Differential: Five-speed manual trans.: T1000 ($196). Turbo Hydra-matic: T1000 ($380); J2000 ($370); Phoenix/Firebird ($396); Trans Am ($72). Limited-slip differential: Firebird/Bonn. ($76). Brakes/Steering: Power brakes: T1000/Phoenix ($93). Power four-wheel disc brakes: Firebird ($255) but (NC) w/performance pkg. Power steering: T1000 ($190); J2000 ($180); Phoenix ($195). Suspension: Electronic susp.: 6000 ($165). Rally RTS handling pkg.: J2000 ($46); Phoenix V-6 ($317) except SJ ($88). Superlift shock absorbers: Phoenix/6000/Bonn. ($64). H.D. springs: Phoenix/6000/G.P./Bonn. ($16). Other: H.D. radiator: T1000 ($40-70); J2000 ($37-$67); Phoenix ($72); Firebird ($40). H.D. cooling: 6000/G.P./Bonn. ($40). H.D. battery ($22-$25) exc. diesel ($52). H.D. alternator: J2000 ($25); Phoenix ($16-$51); Firebird ($15- $51); G.P./Bonn. ($51). Engine block heater ($17-$18). California emissions ($65) exc. diesel ($205).

OPTION PACKAGES: J2000 custom exterior group ($79). J2000 hatchback custom trim group ($195). Phoenix two-tone apperance pkg. ($148-$176). Phoenix luxury trim pkg. ($208-$356). Firebird Trans Am Recaro option ($2486-$2968). Firebird S/E and Trans Am special performance pkg. ($387-$417). Firebird custom exterior ($73-$134). Firebird luxury trim ($299-$844). Grand Prix Brougham Landau pkg. ($810). Grand Prix appearance ($205). Bonneville two-tone paint appearance ($205). Bonneville wagon custom trim group ($211). Lamp groups: ($37- $45) except Bonneville ($21-$51).

MAJOR CONVENIENCE/APPEARANCE OPTIONS: Air conditioning ($595-$675). Cruise control ($145-$165); N/A on 1000. Power seat ($183-$197); N/A on 1000. Power windows ($152-$235); N/A on 1000. Cornering lamps: Bonn./G.P. ($58). Power glass sunroof: Grand Prix ($875). Removable glass sunroof: J2000/Phoenix/6000 ($261-$275). Hatch roof: Firebird/Grand Prix ($790-$826). Full vinyl cordova top: Bonneville ($140). Padded landau cordova top: Phoenix ($195); Bonn./G.P. ($220). Woodgrain paneling: Bonn. wagon ($288).

HISTORY: Introduced: September 24, 1981 except J2000, May 1981; T1000/Phoenix, December 12, 1981; and Firebird/6000, January 14, 1982. Model year production: 547,271. Calendar year production (U.S.): 411,324. Calendar year sales by U.S. dealers: 483,149. Model year sales by U.S. dealers: 461,845 (not incl. 34,424 early 1982 J2000 models counted in 1981 total).

Historical Footnotes: Production fell again for the model year. Sales slipped even further. Several Pontiacs (6000 and some Phoenix models) reached EPA estimates of 40 MPG (highway), while T1000 managed 42, and the new J2000 series 43 on the highway. The new Firebird design had received extensive wind-tunnel testing.

1983 PONTIAC

Introduced this year was a "world class" performance- oriented 6000 STE sedan. Firebirds added a five-speed manual gearbox, and the 2000 series of J-bodied subcompacts got a fuel-injected standard engine and five-speed manual shift. On a minor note, the 'T' disappeared from T1000 and 'J' from 2000 models. Far more noteworthy was the arrival of a 2000 (Sunbird) convertible, the first ragtop Pontiac since 1975. Returning this year was a full-size sedan and wagon, under the Parisienne name.

1983 Pontiac 1000 hatchback coupe (P)

1000 — SERIES 2T — FOUR — Body changes included more use of black accents, intended to give a sporty international feel to Pontiac's smallest model. Powertrain was again the overhead-cam 1.6- liter four with four-speed manual transmission. The standard AM radio could be deleted (for credit). Standard equipment also included reclining front bucket seats. Joining this year's option list: sport striping, a custom trim group, and black luggage rack. A diesel was announced, but failed to materialize.

1983 Pontiac 2000 sedan (P)

2000 — SERIES 2J — FOUR — Base powertrain for the 2000 series was now a fuel-injected, overhead-cam 1.8-liter four, hooked to five-speed manual transaxle. Coupe, sedan, hatchback and station wagon bodies were offered. Appearance was similar to 1982, with the twin grilles now consisting of several horizontal bars. Recessed quad headlamps stood alongside the small grille inserts. At the center of the front-end panel was a wide, tapered divider with emblem. Small park/signal lamps were below the bumper strip. Standard equipment included power brakes, bumper rub strips, console, side window defogger, fully reclining bucket seats, red instrument lighting, woodgrain dash, wide bodyside moldings, and P175/80R13 glass-belted radial tires on Rally wheels. LE's revised equipment list added an AM radio, bright rocker panel and wheel opening moldings, and cushion steering wheel. SE rode P195/70R13 tires on

finned turbo cast aluminum wheels and included a rear spoiler, power steering, two-tone paint, and handling package. The new convertible had power windows, foglamps, and tinted glass. Lear Siegler adjustable front bucket seats were now available for the LE sedan or SE hatchback.

1983 Phoenix SJ coupe (P)

PHOENIX — SERIES 2X — FOUR/V-6 — Restyling was intended to give Phoenix more of a "Pontiac" look. This year's grille consisted of all horizontal bars. Otherwise, appearance was similar to 1982. A two-door coupe and four-door hatchback sedan came in base, LJ, or sporty SJ trim. A fuel-injected 151 cu. in. (2.5- liter) four with four-speed manual transaxle was standard, with 173 cu. in. (2.8-liter) V-6 and automatic optional. SJ included a high-output 2.8 V-6 and a performance handling package with Goodyear Eagle GT SBR tires on 6inch cast aluminum turbo wheels. A different package with 13inch wheels was available for other models. Standard equipment included an AM radio, vinyl front bench seat, P185/80R13 glass-belted radials on Rally wheels, and color-keyed bumpers with black/bright rub strips. LJ added a notchback front seat, narrow rocker panel moldings, black bodyside moldings, and charcoal wheel opening moldings. SJ included power brakes and steering, tachometer, handling suspension, wide black rocker panel moldings, bucket front seats, and P195/70R14 SBr tires on sport aluminum wheels.

1983 Firebird Trans Am coupe (P)

FIREBIRD — SERIES 2F — FOUR/V-6/V-8 — Major changes to Firebird were in the powertrain, as styling was similar to the 1982 redesign. Both four- and five-speed manual gearboxes were available this year, along with a four-speed automatic. S/E got a high-output version of the 173 cu. in. (2.8-liter) V-6, along with the five-speed. Base models again carried a standard fuel-injected 151 cu. in. (2.5-liter) four with four-speed manual shift. S/E had new cloth seats and a split-folding back seat (also available in the custom trim package). New Lear Siegler articulated front bucket seats became optional. Trans Am again carried a standard 5.0-liter V-8, but with the new five-speed and a 3.73: axle ratio. Standard equipment included power brakes/steering, reclining front bucket seats, and P195/75R14 glass-belted radial tires. S/E added P205/70R14 SBR tires on turbo cast aluminum wheels, a handling suspension, five-speed gearbox, sport mirrors, color-keyed bodyside moldings, and lower accent paint with striping. Trans Am had a rear spoiler and wheel opening flares.

1983 Pontiac 6000 coupe (P)

6000 — SERIES 2A — FOUR/V-6 — The new 6000 STE was created to appeal to buyers who craved Euro-style ride and handling. Offered in a choice of five subtle two-tone combinations, its distinctive body featured six front lights (including center foglamps), wide bodyside moldings, and wraparound neutral-density dual-lens taillamps. The inline lighting trio left little room for a grille on each side of the divider: just narrow black horizontal strips. Small park/signal lamps were in the bumper strip. A Driver Information Center displayed warnings and reminders for service. Orthopedically-designed front bucket seats were fully adjustable. An electronic-tuning seek/scan stereo radio with graphic equalizer and clock was standard. Also standard: automatic air conditioning and power mirrors, windows and door locks. Powertrain consisted of a high-output 173 cu. in. (2.8-liter) V-6 hooked to three-speed automatic transaxle. Hitting the ground were Goodyear Eagle GT steel- belted radial tires on 14 inch aluminum wheels. Electronic ride control, with an on-board air compressor adjusting pressure to the shock absorbers, was standard. The compressor could also be used to inflate a tire. Turning to the regular 6000 series, a coupe and sedan were offered in base and LE trim, each with a standard 151 cu. in. (2.5-liter) four and three-speed automatic. Options included a 2.8-liter gas V-6 and 4.3 diesel V-6. Joining the option list was a Y99 high- performance rally suspension package. LE models had a 45/45 seat, with recliner optional. Base/LE twin grilles again consisted of vertical bars. Standard 6000 equipment included an AM radio, rear stabilizer bar, power brakes/steering, black mirrors, black front air dam, black rocker panel moldings, vinyl notchback front seats, and P185/80R13 glass-belted tires on Rally wheels. LE added a black pillar applique, quartz digital clock, and map pockets. 6000 STE rode P195/70R14 tires and had power windows, speed control, tinted glass, air conditioning, AM/FM stereo with cassette player and equalizer, two-tone paint, foglamps, and much more on its basic equipment list.

1983 Grand Prix Brougham coupe (P)

GRAND PRIX — SERIES 2G — V-6/V-8 — Pontiac's personal-luxury coupes were said to get a more modern look this year, but little change was evident beyond a slightly revised grille pattern. Base engine was again the Buick-built 231 cu. in. (3.8-liter) V-6, with three-speed automatic. This year a V-8 option returned: a four-barrel 5.0-liter edition. The 350 cu. in. diesel V-8 also was available. Standard equipment included power steering and brakes.

1983 Bonneville Brougham sedan (P)

BONNEVILLE — SERIES 2G — V-6/V-8 — Mid-size sedans had the same engine selections as Grand Prix, and looked similar to 1982. Standard equipment included Buick's 231 cu. in. (3.8-liter) V-6 with automatic transmission, power brakes/steering, wide rocker panel moldings with extensions, wheel opening moldings, P195/75R14 tires, bumper guards and rub strips, electric clock, and day/night mirror. Brougham added cloth 60/40 notchback seating, opera lamps, and a bright pillar applique.

PARISIENNE — SERIES 2B — V-6/V-8 — The full-size, rear-wheel-drive Parisienne had a conventional front end appearance with quad rectangular headlamps and vertical-bar twin grilles. Two sedans and a station wagon were offered. Standard equipment included the 3.8-liter V-6 engine and three-speed automatic, power brakes/steering, P205/75R15 SBR blackwall tires, narrow bright rocker panel and wheel opening moldings, color-keyed bodyside moldings, cloth 50/50 seating, bumper rub strips, and deluxe wheel covers. Brougham added luxury cloth 60/40 seating (with passenger recliner). Wagons rode P225/75R15 tires and had the 5.0-liter V-8 engine and four-speed overdrive automatic.

I.D. DATA: Pontiac's 17-symbol Vehicle Identification Number (VIN) was on the upper left surface of the instrument panel, visible through the windshield. The first three symbols ('1G2') indicate Pontiac division. Symbol four is restraint system ('A' manual seatbelts). Symbol five is car line/series: 'L' 1000; 'B' 2000; 'C' 2000 LE; 'D' 2000 SE; 'Y' Phoenix; 'Z' Phoenix LJ; 'T' Phoenix SJ; 'F' 6000; 'G' 6000 LE; 'H' 6000 STE; 'S' Firebird; 'X' Firebird S/E; 'W' Firebird Trans Am; 'J' Grand Prix; 'K' Grand Prix LJ; 'P' Grand Prix Brougham; 'N' Bonneville; 'R' Bonneville Brougham; 'L' Parisienne; 'T' Parisienne Brougham. In sixth and seventh position are two digits that denote body type: '08' 3dr. hatchback coupe; '27' 2dr. coupe; '37' 2dr. coupe; '77' 3dr. hatchback; '87' 2dr. coupe; '19' 4dr. 6window sedan; '68' 5dr. hatchback sedan; '69' 4dr. 4 window sedan; '35' 4dr. station wagon. Symbol eight is a letter indicating engine code: 'C' L498 2Bbl.; 'O' L4109 FI; 'P' L4122 FI; 'R' or '2' L4151 FI; 'X' or '1' V6173 2Bbl.; 'Z' H.O. V6173 2Bbl.;'A' V6231 2Bbl.; 'T' diesel V6262; 'H' V8305 4Bbl.; '7' V8305 FI; 'N' diesel V8350. Next is a check digit. The tenth symbol denotes model year ('D' 1983). Symbol eleven is a plant code: 'A' Lakewood, GA; 'B' Baltimore, MD; 'G' Framingham, MA; 'L' Van Nuys, CA; 'N' Norwood, Ohio; 'T' Tarrytown, NY; 'Y' Wilmington, DE; '7' Lordstown, Ohio; '1' Oshawa, Ontario; '2' St. Therese, Quebec. The final six digits are the sequential serial number.

1000 (FOUR)

Model Number	Body/Style Number	Body Type & Seating	Factory Price	Shipping Weight	Production Total
2T	L08	3-dr. Hatch-4P	5582	2081	13,171
2T	L68	5-dr. Hatch-4P	5785	2130	12,806

2000 (FOUR)

2J	B27	2-dr. Cpe-5P	6499	2353	22,063
2J	B77	3-dr. Hatch-5P	6809	2413	7,331
2J	B69	4-dr. Sedan-5P	6621	2412	24,833
2J	B35	4-dr. Sta Wag-5P	6926	2487	10,214

1983 Pontiac 2000 Sunbird convertible (P)

2000 LE (FOUR)

2J	C27	2-dr. Cpe-5P	7020	2385	2,690
2J	C69	4-dr. Sedan-5P	7194	2436	6,957
2J	C35	4-dr. Sta Wag-5P	7497	2517	1,780
2J	N/A	2-dr. Conv.-5P	N/A	N/A	626

2000 SE (FOUR)

2J	D77	3-dr. Hatch-5P	8393	2470	1,835

PHOENIX (FOUR/V-6)

2X	Y37	2-dr. Cpe-5P	6942/7192	2485/2549	7,205
2X	Y68	5-dr. Hatch-5P	7087/7337	2542/2606	13,377

PHOENIX LJ (FOUR/V-6)

2X	Z37	2-dr. Cpe-5P	7489/7739	2526/2590	2,251
2X	Z68	5-dr. Hatch-5P	7698/7948	2574/2638	3,635

PHOENIX SJ (V-6)

2X	T37	2-dr. Cpe-5P	8861	2581	853
2X	T68	5-dr. Hatch-5P	8948	2642	172

FIREBIRD (FOUR/V-6)

2F	S87	2-dr. Cpe-4P	8399/8549	2866/2948	32,020

Engine Note: A 305 cu. in. V-8 cost $200-$225 more than the V-6 on base Firebird.

FIREBIRD S/E (V-6/V-8)

2F	X87	2-dr. Cpe-4P	10322/10397	2965/3145	10,934

FIREBIRD TRANS AM (V-8)

2F	W87	2-dr. Cpe-4P	10396	3107	31,930

6000 (FOUR/V-6)

2A	F27	2-dr. Cpe-5P	8399/8549	2693/2741	3,524
2A	F19	4-dr. Sed-5P	8569/8719	2736/2779	20,267
2A	G27	2-dr. LE Cpe-5P	8837/8987	2711/2754	4,278
2A	G19	4-dr. LE Sed-5P	8984/9134	2750/2793	33,676

1983 Pontiac 6000 STE sedan (P)

6000 STE (V-6)

2A	H19	4-dr. Sed-5P	13572	2823	6,719

GRAND PRIX (V-6/V-8)

2G	J37	2-dr. Cpe-6P	8698/8923	N/A	41,511

GRAND PRIX LJ (V-6/V-8)

2G	K37	2-dr. Cpe-6P	9166/9391	N/A	33,785

GRAND PRIX BROUGHAM (V-6/V-8)

2G	P37	2-dr. Cpe-6P	9781/10006	N/A	10,502

BONNEVILLE (V-6/V-8)

2G	N69	4-dr. Sed-6P	8899/9124	3214/3290	47,003
2G	N35	4-dr. Sta Wag-6P	9112/9337	3275/3351	17,551

BONNEVILLE BROUGHAM (V-6/V-8)

2G	R69	4-dr. Sed-6P	9399/9624	3210/3286	19,335

PARISIENNE (V-6/V-8)

2B	L69	4-dr. Sed-6P	9609/9889	N/A	9,279
2B	L35	4-dr. Sta Wag-6P	--/9927	N/A	3,027

PARISIENNE BROUGHAM (V-6/V-8)

2B	T69	4-dr. Sed-6P	9879/10159	N/A	5,139

FACTORY PRICE AND WEIGHT NOTE: Prices and weights to left of slash are for V-6, to right for V-8 engine except Phoenix/Firebird/6000, four and V-6

ENGINE DATA: BASE FOUR (1000): Inline. Overhead cam. Four-cylinder. Cast iron block and head. Displacement: 98 cu. in. (1.6 liters). Bore & stroke: 3.23 x 2.98 in. Compression ratio: 9.0:1. Brake horsepower: 65 at 5200 R.P.M. Torque: 80 lbs.-ft. at 3200 R.P.M. Five main bearings. Hydraulic valve lifters. Carburetor: 2Bbl. VIN Code: C. BASE FOUR (2000): Inline. Overhead cam. Four-cylinder. Cast iron block and aluminum head. Displacement: 109 cu. in. (1.8 liters). Bore & stroke: 3.34 x 3.13 in. Compression ratio: 9.0:1. Brake horsepower: 84 at 5200 R.P.M. Torque: 102 lbs.-ft. at 2800 R.P.M. Five main bearings. Hydraulic valve lifters. Electronic fuel injection. VIN Code: O. OPTIONAL FOUR (2000): Inline. Overhead cam. Four-cylinder. Cast iron block and head. Displacement: 122 cu. in. (2.0 liters). Bore & stroke: 3.50 x 3.15 in. Compression ratio: 9.3:1. Brake horsepower: 88 at 4600 R.P.M. Torque: 110 lbs.-ft. at 2400 R.P.M. Five main bearings. Hydraulic valve lifters. Electronic fuel injection. VIN Code: P. BASE FOUR (Phoenix, Firebird, 6000): Inline. Overhead valve. Four-cylinder. Cast iron block and head. Displacement: 151 cu. in. (2.5 liters). Bore & stroke: 4.00 x 3.00 in. Compression ratio: 8.2:1. Brake horsepower: 90-94 at 4000 R.P.M. Torque: 132-135 lbs.-ft. at 2800 R.P.M. Five main bearings. Hydraulic valve lifters. Throttle-body fuel injection. VIN Code: R or 2. OPTIONAL V-6 (Phoenix, Firebird, 6000): 60-degree. overhead valve six-cylinder. Cast iron block and aluminum head. Displacement: 173 cu. in. (2.8 liters). Bore & stroke: 3.50 x 3.00 in. Compression ratio: 8.5:1. Brake horsepower: 112 at 4800 R.P.M. (Firebird, 107 at 4800). Torque: 145 lbs.-ft. at 2400 R.P.M. (Firebird, 145 at 2100). Four main bearings. Hydraulic valve lifters. Carburetor: 2Bbl. Rochester E2SE. VIN Code: X or 1. BASE V-6 (Phoenix SJ, Firebird S/E, 6000 STE): High-output version of 173 cu. in. V-6 above Compression ratio: 8.9:1. Horsepower: 130-135 at 5400 R.P.M. (Firebird, 125 H.P.) Torque: 145 lbs.-ft. at 2400 R.P.M. VIN Code: Z. BASE V-6 (Grand Prix, Bonneville, Parisienne): 90-degree, overhead-valve V-6. Cast iron block and head. Displacement: 231 cu. in. (3.8 liters). Bore & stroke: 3.80 x 3.40 in. Compression ratio: 8.0:1. Brake horsepower: 110 at 3800 R.P.M. Torque: 190 lbs.-ft. at 1600 R.P.M. Four main bearings. Hydraulic valve lifters. Carburetor: 2Bbl. Rochester E2ME. Buick-built. VIN Code: A. DIESEL V-6 (6000): 90-degree, overhead valve V-6. Cast iron block and head. Displacement: 260 cu. in. (4.3 liters). Bore & stroke: 4.06 x 3.38 in. Compression ratio: 21.6:1. Brake horsepower: 85 at 3600 R.P.M. Torque: 165 lbs.-ft. at 1600 R.P.M. Five main bearings. Hydraulic valve lifters. Fuel injection. VIN Code: T. BASE V-8 (Firebird Trans

Am); OPTIONAL (Firebird, Grand Prix, Bonneville): 90-degree, overhead valve V-8. Cast iron block and head. Displacement: 305 cu. in. (5.0 liters). Bore & stroke: 3.74 x 3.48 in. Compression ratio: 8.6:1. Brake horsepower: 150 at 4000 R.P.M. Torque: 240 lbs.-ft. at 2400 R.P.M. Five main bearings. Hydraulic valve lifters. Carburetor: 4Bbl. Rochester E4ME. Chevrolet-built. VIN Code: H. OPTIONAL V-8 (Trans Am): Same as 305 cu. in. V-8 above, with crossfire fuel injection Compression ratio: 9.5:1. Horsepower: 175 at 4200 R.P.M. Torque: 250 lbs.-ft. at 2800 R.P.M. VIN Code: 7. DIESEL V-8 (Grand Prix, Bonneville): 90-degree, overhead valve V-8. Cast iron block and head. Displacement: 350 cu. in. (5.7 liters). Bore & stroke: 4.06 x 3.39 in. Compression ratio: 21.6:1. Brake horsepower: 105 at 3200 R.P.M. Torque: 200 lbs.-ft. at 1600 R.P.M. Five main bearings. Hydraulic valve lifters. Fuel injection. Oldsmobile-built. VIN Code: N.

CHASSIS DATA: Wheelbase: (1000 3dr.) 94.3 in.; (1000 5dr.) 97.3 in.; (2000) 101.2 in.; (Phoenix) 104.9 in.; (Firebird) 101.0 in.; (6000) 104.8 in.; (Grand Prix) 108.1 in.; (Bonn.) 108.1 in. Overall Length: (1000 3dr.) 161.9 in.; (1000 5dr.) 164.9 in.; (2000 cpe) 173.6 in.; (2000 sed/wag) 175.9 in.; (Phoenix cpe) 182.1 in.; (Phoenix hatch) 183.1 in.; (Firebird) 189.8 in.; (6000) 188.7 in.; (G.P.) 201.9 in.; (Bonn.) 198.6 in.; (Bonn. wag) 197.8 in. Height: (1000) 52.9 in.; (2000 cpe) 53.5 in.; (2000 hatch) 51.9 in.; (2000 sed/wag) 54.8 in.; (Phoenix cpe) 53.5 in.; (Phoenix sed) 53.4 in.; (Firebird) 49.8 in.; (6000) 54.8 in.; (G.P.) 54.7 in.; (Bonn.) 55.8 in.; (Bonn. wag) 56.1 in. Width: (1000) 61.8 in.; (2000) 68.6 in.; (Phoenix cpe) 69.1 in.; (Phoenix sed) 69.6 in.; (Firebird) 72.0 in.; (6000) 68.2 in.; (G.P.) 72.1 in.; (Bonn.) 71.3 in.; (Bonn. wag) 72.6 in. Front Tread: (1000) 51.2 in.; (2000) 55.5 in.; (Phoenix) 58.7 in.; (Firebird) 60.7 in.; (6000) 58.7 in.; (G.P.) 58.5 in.; (Bonn.) 58.5 in. Rear Tread: (1000) 51.2 in.; (2000) 55.1 in.; (Phoenix) 57.0 in.; (Firebird) 61.6 in.; (6000) 57.0 in.; (G.P.) 57.8 in.; (Bonn.) 57.8 in. Standard Tires: (1000) P155/80R13 GBR BSW; (2000) P175/80R13 GBR BSW; (2000 SE) P195/70R13; (Phoenix) P185/80R13 GBR BSW; (Phoenix SJ) P195/70R14 SBR; (Firebird) P195/75R14 GBR BSW; (Firebird S/E, Trans Am) P205/70R14 SBR BSW; (6000) P185/80R13 GBR BSW; (6000 STE) P195/70R14 SBR; (Grand Prix) P195/75R14 SBR BSW; (Bonn.) P195/75R14 GBR BSW.

TECHNICAL: Transmission: Four-speed manual standard on 1000, Phoenix and base Firebird. Five-speed manual standard on 2000 and Firebird S/E. Three-speed Turbo Hydra-matic standard on other models, optional on all. Standard final drive ratio: (1000) 3.36:1 w/5spd; (2000) 3.83:1 w/5spd, 3.91:1 w/4spd, 3.18:1 w/auto.; (Phoenix) 3.32:1 except 3.06:1 w/H.O. V-6; (Firebird) 3.42:1 w/4spd, 3.73:1 w/V-6 and 5spd, 3.23:1 w/V-8 and 5spd, 3.08:1 w/3spd auto., 3.23:1 or 2.93:1 w/4spd auto.; (6000) 2.39:1 except 3.33:1 w/H.O. V-6; (Grand Prix/Bonneville) 2.73:1 w/V-6, 2.73:1 w/V-8. Steering: (1000/2000/Phoenix/6000) rack and pinion; (others) recirculating ball. Front Suspension: (2000/Phoenix/6000) MacPherson struts w/lower control arms and anti-sway bar; (Firebird) modified MacPherson struts w/coil springs between lower control arm and Xmember; (others) coil springs and anti-sway bar. Rear Suspension: (1000) four-link rigid axle w/torque tube and Panhard rod; (2000) beam axle w/coil springs and trailing arms; (Phoenix) single-beam trailing axle w/track bar and coil springs; (Firebird) torque arm/track bar w/coil springs and anti-sway bar; (6000) trailing arms and beam axle w/coil springs and integral anti-sway bar; (Bonneville/Grand Prix) four-link rigid axle with coil springs, lower trailing radius arms and upper torque arms. Brakes: Front disc, rear drum. Ignition: Electronic. Body construction: (1000/2000/Phoenix/Firebird/6000) unit; (others) separate body and frame. Fuel Tank: (1000) 12.5 gal.; (2000) 14 gal.; (Phoenix) 14.6 gal.; (Firebird) 16 gal.; (6000) 15.7 gal.; (Grand Prix/Bonneville) 17.5 gal.

DRIVETRAIN OPTIONS: Engines: 2.0-liter four: 2000 ($50 credit). 151 cu. in. four: Firebird S/E ($300 credit). 173 cu. in. V-6: Phoenix/Firebird/6000 ($150). Diesel 262 cu. in. V-6: 6000 ($599). 305 cu. in., 4Bbl. V-8: Firebird ($350-$375); Firebird S/E ($50-$75); Grand Prix/Bonneville ($225). Crossfire EFI 305 cu. in. V-8: Trans Am ($858). Diesel 350 cu. in. V-8: Grand Prix/Bonn. ($799). Transmission/Differential: Four-speed manual trans.: 2000 ($75 credit). Five-speed manual trans.: 1000 ($75); Firebird ($125). Three-speed automatic trans.: 1000 ($395); 2000 ($320); Phoenix ($425); Firebird S/E ($195). Four- speed automatic trans.: Firebird ($525); S/E and Trans Am ($295). Limited-slip differential: Firebird/G.P./Bonn. ($95). Brakes/Steering: Power brakes: 1000 ($95); Phoenix ($100). Power four-wheel disc brakes: Firebird ($274) but (NC) w/performance pkg. Power steering: 1000/2000 ($199); Phoenix ($210). Suspension: Electronic susp.: 6000 ($165). Rally handling pkg.: 2000 ($48); Phoenix/6000/Firebird/G.P. ($50). Superlift shock absorbers: 6000/G.P./Bonn. ($64). Other: H.D. radiator: 1000/2000 ($40-$70). H.D. cooling ($40- $70). H.D. battery ($25) exc. diesel ($50). H.D. alternator ($25-$51). Engine block heater ($18). California emissions ($75) exc. diesel ($215).

OPTION PACKAGES: 1000 custom trim ($151). 2000 custom exterior group ($56-$86). 2000 custom trim group ($249-$299). 2000 security pkg. ($19). Phoenix upper exterior group ($98-$108); lower ($56). Firebird Trans Am Recaro option ($3160-$3610). Firebird S/E and Trans Am special performance pkg. ($408). Firebird custom exterior ($51-$112). 6000 rally pkg. ($618). 6000 custom exterior ($56). Grand Prix Brougham Landau pkg. ($549). Bonneville wagon custom trim group ($376). Lamp groups ($34- $46) except Bonneville ($22-$52) and 2000 LE ($88).

MAJOR CONVENIENCE/APPEARANCE OPTIONS: Air conditioning ($625-$725). Cruise control ($170). Power seat ($210-$420); N/A on 1000. Power windows ($180-$255); N/A on 1000. Cornering lamps: Bonn./G.P. ($68). Power glass sunroof: Grand Prix ($895). Removable glass sunroof: 2000/Phoenix/6000 ($295). Hatch roof: Firebird/Grand Prix ($825-$861). Full vinyl cordova top: Bonneville ($155). Padded top: Phoenix ($215); Bonn./G.P. ($240). Louvered rear sunshields: 2000 ($199); Firebird ($210). Two-tone paint: 2000 ($101); Phoenix ($105-$135); G.P./Bonn. ($205). Lear Siegler bucket seats: 2000 ($400); Firebird ($400-$1294). Woodgrain paneling: Bonn. wagon ($283).

HISTORY: Introduced: September 23, 1982 except Firebird, November 18, 1982. Model year production: 462,279. Calendar year production (U.S.): 414,842. Calendar year sales by U.S. dealers: 553,135. Model year sales by U.S. dealers: 513,239.

Historical Footnotes: Production fell for the fourth year in a row. The 6000 series posted a notable sales gain, partly due to the new 6000 STE. Pontiac was trying to boost its performance image at this time, with the debut of a high-output V-8 for Trans Am as well as the Euro-styled 6000 STE. Big (relatively) V-8s were popular with many buyers, but they didn't help Pontiac to meet CAFE fuel economy standards. Nevertheless, over one-fourth of engines in 1983 were V-8s, as opposed to less than 16 percent a year earlier.

1984 PONTIAC

Series 2000 got a name change, adding the Sunbird label. Totally new this year was the two-seater plastic-bodied Fiero. In addition, Pontiac offered a turbocharged engine for the 2000 Sunbird, a high-tech 6000 STE, and a high-output carbureted V-8 for Trans Am.

1984 2000 Sunbird convertible (P)

1984 Fiero Indy Pace Car Replica (P)

FIERO — SERIES 2P — FOUR — Displaying little trim apart from a tiny shield emblem ahead of the front hood, Fiero was described as a "revolutionary two-seat, mid-engine sports car," the first such model built in America. The sleek (if somewhat stubby) wedge shape with compact front area offered a drag coefficient of 0.377. Glass surfaces were nearly flush with the body. Headlamps were hidden. Flush-mounted at the rear were black, full-width, neutral-density reflex taillamps. If trim was absent, black accents were not. "Enduraflex" body panel skins were corrosion-resistant. SMC panels went on horizontal portions (hood, roof, decklid, upper rear quarter panel). Reinforced reaction injection molded (RRIM) urethane panels with higher resistance to dents were used in vulnerable spots, including front fenders and doors. Fiero used a space frame of high-strength steel, described as similar to a racing car's roll cage. Rear-wheel drive, Fiero rode a 93.4 inch wheelbase and carried a 92-horsepower, 151 cu. in. (2.5-liter) four- cylinder engine. Three models were available: coupe with four-speed transmission, 2.42:1 axle ratio and 13 inch tires; sport coupe with 4.10:1 axle ratio; and an SE with special WS6 performance handling package and standard rear deck luggage rack. Inside the cockpit was a free-standing instrument cluster with electric speedometer, trip odometer, gas gauge, voltmeter and temperature gauge. Lights warned of door or engine compartment lid ajar, upshift indicator, seatbelts not affixed, oil pressure, and need to check engine. A column- mounted lever controlled turn signals, dimmer, wiper/washer, and (optional) cruise control. Fiero standard equipment included a four-speed manual transmission, P185/80R13 blackwall SBR tires, retractable halogen headlamps, driver's remote mirror, bodyside moldings, rub strips, full-length console, tachometer, map pocket, reclining bucket seats, and four-spoke steering wheel. SE had P215/80R13 tires and a padded Formula steering wheel.

transmission, dual sport mirrors (driver's remote), power windows, special moldings, AM radio, tinted glass, power brakes and steering, and rear-seat entrance lamps. Styling was similar to 1983, but lower air slots were narrower, without the former eggcrate pattern. Clear foglamps replaced the usual small inset grilles on S/E and LE, giving them the look of 6000 STE. Standard equipment included a five-speed gearbox, Rally wheels, reclining front bucket seats, power brakes, P175/80R13 glass-belted tires, bumper rub strips, digital clock, console, and side window defogers. LE added an AM radio, Formula three-spoke steering wheel, cloth bucket seats, bright rocker panel moldings, and foglamps. SE included a tachometer, power steering, leather-wrapped steering wheel, turbo cast aluminum wheels, two-tone paint, black rocker panel moldings, P205/60R14 tires, and handling package. Convertibles had power steering, tachometer, power windows, power top, tinted glass, bright rocker moldings, and sport mirrors (driver's remote).

1984 Phoenix hatchback sedan (P)

PHOENIX — SERIES 2X — FOUR/V-6 — For its final season, the Xbodied Phoenix compact came in the same body styles and trim levels and changed little. Base engine was Pontiac's own 151 cu. in. (2.5-liter) four with fuel injection, hooked to four-speed manual transaxle. Optional: a high-output 173 cu. in. (2.8-liter) V-6, along with the Y99 handling suspension. Standard equipment included an AM radio, vinyl bench seating, P185/80R13 tires, color-keyed bumpers, and halogen headlamps. LE added cloth notchback seating, a three-spoke Formula steering wheel, custom wheel covers, narrow rocker panel moldings, wide black vinyl bodyside moldings, and charcoal wheel opening moldings. SE included power brakes and steering, a leather-wrapped steering wheel, tachometer, P195/70R14 tires on sport aluminum wheels, wide black rocker panel moldings, graphics, and cloth reclining front bucket seats.

1984 1000 Hatchback sedan (P)

1000 — SERIES 2T — FOUR — As before, the Chevette clone came in three- and five- door hatchback form. A new sport package included a black spoiler, sport striping, black sport mirrors, special handling components, and formula steering wheel. Base 1000 engine was the 98 cu. in. (1.6-liter) overhead-cam four, with four-speed manual gearbox. Five-speed manual shift was optional, as was three-speed automatic. Standard equipment included an AM radio, front air dam, clock, mini console, black/bright grille, argent styled steel Rally wheels, reclining front bucket seats, black rocker panel moldings, black bumper guards and rub strips, and locking glovebox.

2000 SUNBIRD — SERIES 2J — FOUR — Biggest news for Sunbird was a turbocharged 1.8-liter overhead-cam engine, standard on S/E and optional in base and LE models (except wagons). Pontiac claimed the turbo could hit 60 MPH in 9 seconds with standard four-speed manual gearbox. Along with the turbo four came a WS6 performance handling package, P205/60R14 Goodyear Eagle GT steel-belted radial tires on new turbo wheels, tachometer, boost gauge, and power steering. Introduced in 1983, the LE convertible included a power top, five-speed manual

1984 Firebird Trans Am T-top coupe (P)

FIREBIRD — SERIES 2F — FOUR/V-6/V-8 — Trans Am got a performance boost with a high-output four-barrel version of the 305 cu. in. (5.0-liter) V-8. That powerplant, first offered as an option late in the 1983 model year, replaced the former crossfire fuel-injected V-8. It was rated 190 horsepower at 4800 R.P.M., and produced 240 lbs.-ft. of torque. This year's Trans Am came with a standard five-speed manual gearbox and 3.73:1 axle ratio, ready to deliver 060 times in the 7.2 second neighborhood (and quarter miles claimed in the low 15s). Four-cylinder engines in the base Firebird also got a boost with a swirl port combustion chamber, 9.0:1 compression ratio, and cooler spark plugs. Firebird S/E again came with a standard 173 cu. in. (2.8-liter) high-output V-6. New S/E features included a color-coordinated, leather-wrapped steering wheel, shift lever and parking brake handle. As before, could have the four-cylinder engine or 305 V-8 instead of its standard V-6. Trans Am could get an optional aero package, in 15 color combinations, including new front/rear fascia, bigger air dam, door and rocker panel extensions, and wide lower body graphics. Also available: a Recaro package with gold strobe graphics and gold deep-dish turbo wheels. Appearance was similar to 1983. Base Firebird equipment included a 151 cu. in. (2.5-liter) four with

four-speed manual shift, power brakes/steering, P195/75R14 tires on Rally sport wheels, tinted liftback glass, and vinyl reclining front bucket seats. S/E included front and rear stabilizer bars, the high-output 2.8-liter V-6, five-speed gearbox, handling suspension, tachometer, leather map pocket, cloth seat upholstery, lower accent paint (with striping), sport mirrors, color-keyed bodyside moldings, and P205/70R14 tires on turbo cast aluminum wheels. Trans Am included the 305 V-8 with five-speed, black aero turbo cast aluminum wheels, rear wheel opening flares, rear spoiler, and front fender air extractors.

1984 6000 LE wagon (P)

6000 — SERIES 2A — FOUR/V-6 — Aero restyling highlighted this year's mid-size 6000 series, headed by the performance-oriented 6000 STE, which added an electronic instrument panel with digital speedometer and analog tachometer. A new bar-chart display showed fuel level, temperature and voltage. STE also included a programmable Driver's Information Center that monitored car systems. Electronics also controlled the ride, and the stereo radio (which had a five-band graphic equalizer). No other Pontiac offered this radio. At the suspension, an air compressor automatically provided pressure to the shocks to maintain optimum height and increase the spring rate as the car's load changed. As before, 6000 STE had a minimal option list: just a choice of six two-tone colors, suede leather interior, and removable sunroof. A high-output 173 cu. in. (2.8-liter) V-6 rated 130 horsepower provided the power to a three-speed automatic transaxle. Four-wheel disc brakes were new this year. A station wagon joined the basic 6000 coupe/sedan lineup. Base engine was a 151 cu. in. (2.5-liter) four with fuel injection, hooked to three-speed automatic transaxle. Optional again: a 173 cu. in. (2.8-liter) V-6 or diesel V-6. Wider wraparound taillamps now reached to the backup lenses alongside the license plate. Grille inserts now had a pattern made up of both vertical and horizontal bars. Standard 6000 equipment included power brakes and steering, AM radio, black rocker panel moldings, black bumper rub strips, mini bumper guards, vinyl notchback front seating, P185/75R14 tires on Rally wheels, bodyside moldings with black vinyl insert, and wheel opening moldings. LE added a black pillar applique, cloth upholstery, locking fuel filler door, and map pockets. 6000 STE included the high-output V-6, power windows, AM/FM stereo radio with cassette, black wide bodyside and rocker panel moldings, two-tone paint, air conditioning, four-wheel power disc brakes, tinted glass, electronic ride control, and reclining 45/45 front seating with cloth upholstery and dual six-way adjustment with lumbar support. 6000 STE tires were P195/70R14 blackwalls.

1984 Grand Prix coupe (P)

GRAND PRIX — SERIES 2G — V-6/V-8 — The rear-drive, six-passenger personal-luxury Pontiac again came in three models: base, LE and Brougham. Appearance was similar to 1983, with many vertical bars in the side-by-side twin grilles. Standard equipment included the 231 cu. in. (3.8-liter) V-6, three-speed automatic, power brakes/steering, P195/75R14 SBR tires, cushioned steering wheel, formal rear quarter windows, narrow rocker panel moldings, wheel opening moldings, chrome lower bumpers, black bumper guards, clock, and woodgrain dash. LE added wide rocker panel moldings with extensions, a four-spoke sport steering wheel, color-keyed sport mirrors, and wide windowsill and hood edge moldings. Brougham included power windows, 55/45 seating, and teakwood grain instrument panel.

1984 Bonneville LJ sedan (P)

BONNEVILLE — SERIES 2G — V-6/V-8 — The station wagon was dropped from the Bonneville line this year, but an LE model joined the base and Brougham four-door sedans. Base engine was the 231 cu. in. (3.8-liter) V-6 with three-speed automatic; optional, a 305 cu. in. (5.0-liter) gas V-8 or 350 diesel, with either three- or four-speed automatic. Appearance was similar to 1983. Standard equipment included the 231 cu. in. V-6, three-speed automatic, power brakes/steering, wide rocker panel moldings with extensions, P195/75R14 tires, clock, bumper guards and rub strips, and wheel opening moldings. Brougham added 55/45 cloth seating, opera lamps, and padded vinyl Cordova top.

PARISIENNE — SERIES 2B — V-6/V-8 — Pontiac's full-size rear-drive sedan held six passengers in the traditional style. Also available: a four-door station wagon and Brougham sedan. All models rode a 116-inch wheelbase. Appearance was similar to 1983. Each of the twin grilles contained six vertical bars, with added vertical bars within each segment. Large park/signal lamps were in the bumper, with quad rectangular headlamps above. Wraparound amber side markers extended outward from the headlamp framework. Buick's 231 cu. in. (3.8-liter) V-6 was the base powerplant, with three-speed automatic transmission. Wagons carried the 305 cu. in. (5.0-liter) V-8 and four-speed overdrive automatic; that combination was optional on sedans. All models could also get the Oldsmobile 350 V-8 diesel. Standard equipment included power brakes/steering, cloth 50/50 seating, narrow bright rocker panel moldings, color-keyed bodyside moldings, two-tone paint, bumper rub strips, quartz clock, P205/75R15 tires, and bright wheel opening moldings. Brougham had cloth 55/45 seating with passenger recliner.

I.D. DATA: Pontiac's 17-symbol Vehicle Identification Number (VIN) was on the upper left surface of the instrument panel, visible through the windshield. The first three symbols ('1G2') indicate Pontiac division. Symbol four is restraint system ('A' manual seatbelts). Symbol five is car line/series: 'E' Fiero; 'M' Fiero Sport; 'F' Fiero SE; 'L' T1000; 'B' 2000 Sunbird; 'C' 2000 Sunbird LE; 'D' 2000 Sunbird SE; 'Y' Phoenix; 'Z' Phoenix LE; 'T' Phoenix SJ; 'F' 6000; 'G' 6000 LE; 'H' 6000 STE; 'S' Firebird; 'X' Firebird S/E; 'W' Firebird Trans Am; 'J' Grand Prix; 'K' Grand Prix LE; 'P' Grand Prix Brougham; 'N' Bonneville; 'R' Bonneville Brougham; 'S' Bonneville LE; 'L' Parisienne; 'T' Parisienne Brougham. In sixth and seventh position are two digits that denote body type: '08' 3dr. hatchback coupe; '27' 2dr. coupe; '37' 2dr. coupe; '77' 3dr. hatchback; '87' 2dr. coupe; '19' 4dr. 6window sedan; '68' 5dr. hatchback sedan; '69' 4dr. 4 window sedan; '35' 4dr. station wagon. Symbol eight is an engine code: 'C' L498 2Bbl.; 'O' L4109 FI; 'J' turbo L4109 FI; 'P' L4122 FI; 'R' or '2' L4151 FI; 'X' or '1' V6173 2Bbl.; 'Z' H.O. V6173 2Bbl.;'A' V6231 2Bbl.; 'T' diesel V6262; 'H' V8305 4Bbl.; 'G' H.O. V8305; 'N' diesel V8350. Next is a check digit. The tenth symbol denotes model year ('E' 1984). Symbol eleven is a plant code: 'B' Baltimore; 'L' Van Nuys, CA; 'N' Norwood, Ohio; 'P' Pontiac, MI; 'T' Tarrytown, NY; 'X' Fairfax, Kansas; 'Y' Wilmington, DE; '7' Lordstown, Ohio; '1' Oshawa, Ontario; '2' St. Therese, Quebec. The final six digits are the sequential serial number.

FIERO (FOUR)

Model Number	Body/Style Number	Body Type & Seating	Factory Price	Shipping Weight	Production Total
2P	E37	2-dr. Cpe-2P	7999	2458	7,099
2P	M37	2-dr. Spt Cpe-2P	8499	2458	62,070
2P	F37	2-dr. SE Cpe-2P	9599	2458	67,671

1000 (FOUR)

2T	L08	3-dr. Hatch-4P	5621	2081	19,628
2T	L68	5-dr. Hatch-4P	5824	2130	17,118

2000 SUNBIRD (FOUR)

2J	B27	2-dr. Cpe-5P	6675	2353	53,070
2J	B77	3-dr. Hatch-5P	6995	2413	12,245
2J	B69	4-dr. Sedan-5P	6799	2412	59,312
2J	B35	4-dr. Sta Wag-5P	7115	2487	15,143

2000 SUNBIRD LE (FOUR)

2J	C27	2-dr. Cpe-5P	7333	2385	5,189
2J	C69	4-dr. Sedan-5P	7499	2436	11,183
2J	C35	4-dr. Sta Wag-5P	7019	2517	2,011
2J	N/A	2-dr. Conv.-4P	11749	2449	5,458

2000 SUNBIRD SE (FOUR)

2J	D27	2-dr. Cpe-5P	9019	N/A	2,141
2J	D77	3-dr. Hatch-5P	9489	N/A	2,165
2J	D69	4-dr. Sedan-5P	9185	N/A	1,373

PHOENIX (FOUR/V-6)

2X	Y37	2-dr. Cpe-5P	7090/7440	2485/2549	7,461
2X	Y68	5-dr. Hatch-5P	7165/7515	2542/2606	11,545

PHOENIX LE (FOUR/V-6)

2X	Z37	2-dr. Cpe-5P	7683/8033	2526/2590	1,357
2X	Z68	5-dr. Hatch-5P	7816/8166	2574/2638	1,783

Price Note: Phoenix V-6 prices include $100 for the required power brakes.

PHOENIX SJ (V-6)

2X	T37	2-dr. Cpe-5P	9071	2581	701

FIREBIRD (FOUR/V-6)

2F	S87	2-dr. Cpe-4P	8349/8724	2866/2948	62,621

Engine Note: A 305 cu. in. V-8 cost $300 more than the V-6 on base Firebird.

FIREBIRD S/E (V-6/V-8)

2F	X87	2-dr. Cpe-4P	10649/10849	2965/3145	10,309

FIREBIRD TRANS AM (V-8)

2F	W87	2-dr. Cpe-4P	10699	3107	55,374

6000 (FOUR/V-6)

2A	F27	2-dr. Cpe-5P	8699/8949	2693/2741	4,171
2A	F19	4-dr. Sed-5P	8873/9123	2736/2779	35,202
2A	F35	4-dr. Sta Wag-5P	9221/9471	2911/ --	8,423
2A	G27	2-dr. LE Cpe-5P	9142/9392	2711/2754	4,731
2A	G19	4-dr. LE Sed-5P	9292/9542	2750/2793	41,218
2A	G35	4-dr. LE Wag-5P	9612/9862	2919/ --	9,211

6000 STE (V-6)

2A	H19	4-dr. Sed-5P	14437	2823	19,236

GRAND PRIX (V-6/V-8)

2G	J37	2-dr. Cpe-6P	9145/9520	N/A	36,893

GRAND PRIX LE (V-6/V-8)

2G	K37	2-dr. Cpe-6P	9624/9999	3207	31,037

GRAND PRIX BROUGHAM (V-6/V-8)

2G	P37	2-dr. Cpe-6P	10299/10674	3217	9,514

BONNEVILLE (V-6/V-8)

2G	N69	4-dr. Sed-6P	9131/9506	3214/3290	40,908
2G	S69	4-dr. LE Sed-6P	9358/9733	3275/3351	17,451

BONNEVILLE BROUGHAM (V-6/V-8)

2G	R69	4-dr. Sed-6P	9835/10210	3210/3286	15,030

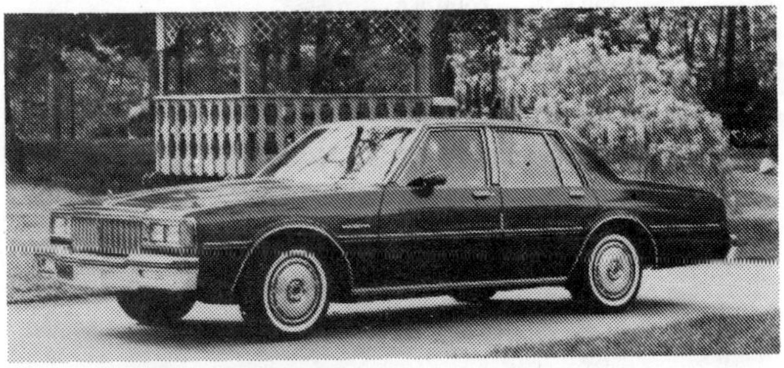

1984 Parisienne sedan (P)

PARISIENNE (V-6/V-8)

2B	L69	4-dr. Sed-6P	9881/10431	N/A	18,713
2B	L35	4-dr. Sta Wag-6P	-- /10394	3948	16,599

PARISIENNE BROUGHAM (V-6/V-8)

2B	T69	4-dr. Sed-6P	10281/10831	N/A	25,212

FACTORY PRICE AND WEIGHT NOTE: Prices and weights to left of slash are for V-6, to right for V-8 engine except Phoenix/Firebird/6000, four and V-6.

ENGINE DATA: BASE FOUR (1000): Inline. Overhead cam. Four-cylinder. Cast iron block and head. Displacement: 98 cu. in. (1.6 liters). Bore & stroke: 3.23 x 2.98 in. Compression ratio: 9.0:1. Brake horsepower: 65 at 5200 R.P.M. Torque: 80 lbs.-ft. at 3200 R.P.M. Five main bearings. Hydraulic valve lifters. Carburetor: 2Bbl. VIN Code: C. BASE FOUR (2000): Inline. Overhead cam. Four-cylinder. Cast iron block and aluminum head. Displacement: 109 cu. in. (1.8 liters). Bore & stroke: 3.34 x 3.13 in. Compression ratio: 9.0:1. Brake horsepower: 84 at 5200 R.P.M. Torque: 102 lbs.-ft. at 2800 R.P.M. Five main bearings. Hydraulic valve lifters. Electronic fuel injection. VIN Code: 0. OPTIONAL TURBO FOUR (2000): Same as 109 cu. in. four above, with port fuel injection and turbocharger Compression ratio: 8.0:1. Horsepower: 150 at 5600 R.P.M. Torque: 150 lbs.-ft. at 2800 R.P.M. VIN Code: J. OPTIONAL FOUR (2000): Inline. Overhead valve. Four-cylinder. Cast iron block and head. Displacement: 122 cu. in. (2.0 liters). Bore & stroke: 3.50 x 3.15 in. Compression ratio: 9.3:1. Brake horsepower: 88 at 4800 R.P.M. Torque: 110 lbs.-ft. at 2400 R.P.M. Five main bearings. Hydraulic valve lifters. Electronic fuel injection. VIN Code: P. BASE FOUR (Fiero, Phoenix, Firebird, 6000): Inline. Overhead valve. Four-cylinder. Cast iron block and head. Displacement: 151 cu. in. (2.5 liters). Bore & stroke: 4.00 x 3.00 in. Compression ratio: 9.0:1. Brake horsepower: 92 at 4000-4400 R.P.M. Torque: 132-134 lbs.-ft. at 2800 R.P.M. Five main bearings. Hydraulic valve lifters. Throttle-body fuel injection. VIN Code: R or 2. OPTIONAL V-6 (Phoenix, Firebird, 6000): 60-degree, overhead valve six-cylinder. Cast iron block and aluminum head. Displacement: 173 cu. in. (2.8 liters). Bore & stroke: 3.50 x 3.00 in. Compression ratio: 8.5:1. Brake horsepower: 112 at 4800 R.P.M. (Firebird, 107 at 4800). Torque: 145 lbs.-ft. at 2100 R.P.M. Four main bearings. Hydraulic valve lifters. Carburetor: 2Bbl. Rochester E2SE. VIN Code: X or 1. BASE V-6 (Phoenix SJ, Firebird S/E, 6000 STE): High-output version of 173 cu. in. V-6 above Compression ratio: 8.9:1. Horsepower: 130 at 5400 R.P.M. (Firebird, 125 H.P.) Torque: 145 lbs.-ft. at 2400 R.P.M. VIN Code: Z. BASE V-6 (Grand Prix, Bonneville, Parisienne): 90-degree, overhead-valve V-6. Cast iron block and head. Displacement: 231 cu. in. (3.8 liters). Bore & stroke: 3.80 x 3.40 in. Compression ratio: 8.0:1. Brake horsepower: 110 at 3800 R.P.M. Torque: 190 lbs.-ft. at 1600 R.P.M. Four main bearings. Hydraulic valve lifters. Carburetor: 2Bbl. Rochester E2ME. Buick-built. VIN Code: A. DIESEL V-6 (6000): 90-degree, overhead valve V-6. Cast iron block and head. Displacement: 260 cu. in. (4.3 liters). Bore & stroke: 4.06 x 3.38 in. Compression ratio: 21.6:1. Brake horsepower: 85 at 3600 R.P.M. Torque: 165 lbs.-ft. at 1600 R.P.M. Four main bearings. Hydraulic valve lifters. Fuel injection. VIN Code: T. BASE V-8 (Firebird Trans Am); OPTIONAL (Firebird, Grand Prix, Bonneville): 90-degree, overhead valve V-8. Cast iron block and head. Displacement: 305 cu. in. (5.0 liters). Bore & stroke: 3.74 x 3.48 in. Compression ratio: 8.6:1. Brake horsepower: 150 at 4000 R.P.M. Torque: 240 lbs.-ft. at 2400 R.P.M. Five main bearings. Hydraulic valve lifters. Carburetor: 4Bbl. Rochester E4ME. Chevrolet-built. VIN Code: H. OPTIONAL V-8 (Trans Am): High-output version of 305 cu. in. V-8 Compression ratio: 9.5:1. Horsepower: 190 at 4800 R.P.M. Torque: 240 lbs.-ft. at 3200 R.P.M. DIESEL V-8 (Grand Prix, Bonneville, Parisienne): 90-degree, overhead valve V-8. Cast iron block and head. Displacement: 350 cu. in. (5.7 liters). Bore & stroke: 4.06 x 3.39 in. Compression ratio: 22.5:1. Brake horsepower: 105 at 3200 R.P.M. Torque: 200 lbs.-ft. at 1600 R.P.M. Five main bearings. Hydraulic valve lifters. Fuel injection. Oldsmobile-built. VIN Code: N.

CHASSIS DATA: Wheelbase: (Fiero) 93.4 in.; (1000 3dr.) 94.3 in.; (1000 5dr.) 97.3 in.; (2000) 101.2 in.; (Phoenix) 104.9 in.; (Firebird) 101.0 in.; (6000) 104.9 in.; (Grand Prix) 108.1 in.; (Bonn.) 108.1 in.; (Parisienne) 115.9 in. Overall Length: (Fiero) 160.7 in.; (1000 3dr.) 161.9 in.; (1000 5dr.) 164.7 in.; (2000) 173.7 in.; (2000 wag) 175.8 in.; (Phoenix) 183.0 in.; (Firebird) 189.9 in.; (6000) 188.1 in.; (6000 wag) 191.2 in.; (G.P.) 201.9 in.; (Bonn.) 198.5 in.; (Parisienne) 212.0 in.; (Parisienne wag) 215.0 in. Height: (Fiero) 46.9 in.; (1000) 52.8 in.; (2000 cpe) 51.9 in.; (2000 conv.) 52.7 in.; (2000 sed) 53.8 in.; (2000 wag) 54.1 in.; (Phoenix) 53.7 in.; (Firebird) 49.7 in.; (6000) 53.3-53.8 in.; (G.P.) 54.7 in.; (Bonn.) 55.8 in.; (Parisienne sed) 56.4 in.; (Parisienne wag) 58.1 in. Width: (Fiero) 68.9 in.; (1000) 61.8 in.; (2000 cpe/conv.) 65.9 in.; (2000 hatch) 66.6 in.; (2000 sed/wag) 66.2 in.; (Phoenix cpe) 69.0-69.1 in.; (Firebird) 72.0 in.; (6000) 72.0 in.; (G.P.) 72.3 in.; (Bonn.) 71.6 in.; (Parisienne) 75.2 in. exc. wagon, 79.3 in. Front Tread: (Fiero) 57.8 in.; (1000) 51.2 in.; (2000) 55.4 in.; (Phoenix) 58.7 in.; (Firebird) 60.7 in.; (6000) 58.7 in.; (G.P.) 58.5 in.; (Bonn.) 58.5 in.; (Parisienne) 61.7 in.; (Parisienne wag) 62.2 in. Rear Tread: (Fiero) 58.7 in.; (1000) 51.2 in.; (2000) 55.2 in.; (Phoenix) 57.0 in.; (Firebird) 61.6 in.; (6000) 57.0 in.; (G.P.) 57.8 in.; (Bonn.) 57.8 in.; (Parisienne) 60.7 in.; (Parisienne wag) 64.1 in. Standard Tires: (Fiero) P185/80R13; (1000) P155/80R13; (2000) P175/80R13 GBR BSW; (2000 SE/conv.) P195/70R13 SBR; (Phoenix) P185/80R13 GBR; (Phoenix SE) P195/70R14; (Firebird) P195/75R14; (Firebird Trans Am) P205/70R14 SBR BSW; (6000) P185/75R14 SBR; (6000 STE) P195/70R14 SBR; (Grand Prix) P195/75R14 SBR; (Bonn.) P195/75R14 SBR.; (Parisienne sed) P205/75R15 SBR; (Parisienne wag) P225/75R15 SBR.

TECHNICAL: Transmission: Four-speed manual standard on Fiero, 1000, Phoenix and base Firebird. Five-speed manual standard on 2000 and Firebird S/E, optional on 1000. Three-speed Turbo Hydra- matic standard on other models, optional on all. Four-speed overdrive automatic available on Firebird, 6000, Grand Prix, Bonneville and Parisienne. Standard final drive ratio: (Fiero) 4.10:1 w/4spd, 3.18:1 w/auto.; (1000) 3.36:1; (2000) 2.55:1 w/5spd, 2.96:1 or 3.32:1 w/4spd, 3.33:1 or 3.43:1 w/auto.; (Phoenix four) 2.42:1 w/4spd, 2.39:1 w/auto.; (Phoenix V-6) 2.69:1 w/4spd, 2.84:1 w/auto.; (Phoenix H.O. V-6) 2.96:1 w/4spd, 3.33:1 w/auto.; (Firebird) 3.42:1 w/4spd, 3.73:1 w/four and 5spd or auto., 3.42:1 or 3.23:1 w/V-6, 3.73:1 w/H.O. V-6, 3.73:1 or 3.23:1 w/V-8; (Firebird H.O. V-8) 3.23:1 w/5spd, 3.42:1 w/auto.; (6000) 2.39:1 w/four, 2.84:1 or 3.06:1 w/V-6, 3.33:1 w/H.O. V-6; (Grand Prix/Bonneville) 2.41:1 w/V-6, 2.29:1 or 2.73:1 w/V-8; (Parisienne) 2.73:1. Steering: (Fiero/1000/2000/Phoenix/6000) rack and pinion; (others) recirculating ball. Front Suspension: (2000/Phoenix/6000) MacPherson struts w/lower control arms and anti-sway bar; (Firebird) modified MacPherson struts w/coil springs between lower control arm and Xmember; (others) coil springs and anti-sway bar. Rear Suspension: (Fiero) MacPherson struts w/lower control arms; (1000) four-link rigid axle w/torque tube and Panhard rod; (2000) beam axle w/coil springs and trailing arms; (Phoenix) single-beam trailing axle w/track bar and coil springs; (Firebird) torque arm/track bar w/coil springs and anti-sway bar; (6000) trailing arms and beam axle w/coil springs and integral anti-sway bar; (Bonneville/Grand Prix/Parisienne) four-link rigid axle with coil springs, lower trailing radius arms and upper torque arms. Brakes: Front disc, rear drum except 6000 STE, four-wheel disc. Ignition: Electronic. Body construction: (Fiero/1000/2000/Phoenix/Firebird/6000) unit; (others) separate body and frame. Fuel Tank: (Fiero) 10.2 gal.; (1000) 12.5 gal.; (2000) 13.6 gal.; (Phoenix) 14.6 gal.; (Firebird) 15.9 gal.; (6000) 15.7 gal.; (Grand Prix/Bonneville) 18.1 gal.; (Parisienne sed) 25 gal.; (Parisienne wag) 22 gal.

DRIVETRAIN OPTIONS: Engines: Turbo 1.8-liter four: 2000 ($1309-$1546). 2.0-liter four: 2000 ($50 credit). 151 cu. in. four: Firebird S/E ($350 credit). 173 cu. in. V-6: Phoenix/Firebird/6000 ($250). H.O. 173 cu. in. V-6: Phoenix ($400). Diesel 262 cu. in. V-6: 6000 ($575). 305 cu. in., 4Bbl. V-8: Firebird ($550); Firebird S/E ($220); Grand Prix/Bonneville/Parisienne ($375). H.O. 305 cu. in. V-8: Trans Am ($530). Diesel 350 cu. in. V-8: Grand Prix/Bonn./Parisienne ($801). Transmission/Differential: Four-speed manual trans.: 2000 ($75 credit). Five-speed manual trans.: 1000 ($75); Firebird ($125). Three-speed automatic trans.: 1000 ($395); 2000 ($320-$395); Phoenix/Firebird ($425). Four-speed automatic trans.: Firebird ($525); S/E and Trans Am ($295); 6000/Grand Prix/Bonneville/Parisienne ($175). Limited-slip differential: Firebird/G.P./Bonn./Parisienne ($95). Brakes/Steering: Power brakes: 1000 ($95); Phoenix ($100). Power four-wheel disc brakes: Firebird ($179) but (NC) w/performance pkg. Power steering: 1000/2000 ($204); Phoenix ($215). Suspension: Electronic susp.: 6000 ($165). Rally tuned susp.: 2000 ($48); Phoenix/6000/Firebird/G.P. ($50); Parisienne ($49). Superlift shock absorbers: 6000/G.P./Bonn./Parisienne ($64). H.D. springs: Bonn. ($16). Other: H.D. cooling ($40-$70). H.D. battery ($25-$26) exc. diesel ($52). H.D. alternator ($25-$51). Engine block heater ($18-$19). California emissions ($99).

OPTION PACKAGES: Fiero special performance pkg. ($459). 1000 sport/handling pkg. ($464). 1000 custom trim ($167). 2000 custom exterior group ($86). 2000 custom trim group ($308-$358). 2000 security pkg. ($19). Phoenix upper exterior group ($98-$108); lower ($56). Firebird Trans Am Recaro option ($3061-$3160). Firebird S/E and Trans Am special performance pkg. ($134- $408). Firebird aero exterior appearance pkg. ($199). Firebird black appearance pkg. ($123-$152). Firebird custom exterior ($51-$112). 6000 rally pkg. ($341-$449). 6000 custom exterior ($56). 6000 wagon security pkg. ($44). Grand Prix Brougham Landau pkg. ($469). Lamp groups ($30-$47) except 6000 LE ($79-$88).

MAJOR CONVENIENCE/APPEARANCE OPTIONS: Air conditioning ($630-$730). Cruise control ($175). Power seat ($210-$430); N/A on 1000/Fiero. Power windows ($185- $260); N/A on 1000. Cornering lamps: Bonn./G.P. ($68); Parisienne ($55). Power glass sunroof: 2000 ($300); Grand Prix ($895). Removable glass sunroof: Fiero/2000/Phoenix/6000 ($300). Hatch roof: Firebird/Grand Prix ($825-$861). Full vinyl cordova top: Bonneville ($160). Padded cordova landau top: Phoenix ($220); G.P. ($245). Sport landau top: 6000 ($735-$773). Padded top: Bonn. ($245). Parisienne ($185). Louvered rear sunshields: 2000 ($199); Firebird ($210). Two- tone paint: 2000 ($101-$151); Phoenix ($105-$135); Firebird ($205-$291); G.P./Bonn. ($205). Lear Siegler bucket seats: 2000 ($400); Firebird ($400-$759); leather ($945-$1304). Third seat: 6000 wagon ($215). Woodgrain paneling: 6000/LE wagon ($250-$325); Parisienne wagon ($387).

HISTORY: Introduced: September 22, 1983. Model year production: 827,576. Calendar year production (U.S.): 491,370. Calendar year sales by U.S. dealers: 704,684. Model year sales by U.S. dealers: 707,007.

Historical Footnotes: After four bad years, Pontiac enjoyed a gigantic leap upward in production for model year 1984. Sales, too, rose markedly. Sunbird and 6000 sales showed the greatest gains, along with the big Parisienne. The new Fiero delivered a claimed 12.5 second time to 60 MPH with the standard four- speed manual gearbox, as well as EPA mileage estimates of 27 (city) and 47 (highway). With 4.10:1 axle, acceleration time dropped by one second. Pontiac became part of the new GM CPC group, and J. Michael Losh took over as the division's general manager.

1985 PONTIAC

Grand Am was the big name for 1985: a new "driver- oriented" sports coupe. It joined a set of recently- introduced models intended to expand Pontiac's performance image beyond the long-lived Trans Am. That list included the plastic-bodied Fiero, turbo-powered Sunbird, and European- influenced 6000 STE.

1985 Fiero GT coupe (P)

FIERO — SERIES 2P — FOUR — A new GT model joined the original trio this year, carrying a 173 cu. in. (2.8-liter) V-6 engine with multi-port fuel injection. The new V-6 was optional in sport and SE coupes. The GT's appearance stemmed from the 1984 Fiero Indy 500 Pace Car, including new "Enduraflex" front/rear fascia, rocker panel extensions, and (optional) decklid spoiler. A WS6 performance suspension and P215/60R14 Eagle GT tires (on turbo wheels) were available. The standard 151 cu. in. (2.5- liter) four came with a new Isuzu five-manual gearbox. V-6 models had a four-speed. Either one could get three-speed automatic. Otherwise, appearance was similar to 1984.

1985 Pontiac 1000 hatchback sedan (P)

1000 — SERIES 2T — FOUR — At the entry-level end of the Pontiac scale, both three- and five-door models could now have the optional five-speed manual gearbox. Base engine remained the 1.6-liter overhead- cam four, with four-speed manual. Seven new body colors were available, and four new interior colors. Appearance was similar to 1984.

1985 Sunbird LE Turbo convertible (P)

SUNBIRD — SERIES 2J — FOUR — Turbo power was available under Sunbird hoods in the form of a 150-horsepower version of the 1.8-liter OHC four- cylinder engine. That powerplant had multi-port fuel injection, and delivered 150 lbs.-ft. of torque. The turbo option was available on both base and LE models (but not the wagon). It included P205/60R14 SBR tires on turbo wheels, WS6 suspension, tachometer and turbo boost gauge, power steering, new hood louvers, and special turbo identification. Other models had a non-turbo edition of the 1.8 engine. Two-door notchback and hatchback coupes were offered, along with a sedan, four-door station wagon, and convertible. Appearance changed little from 1984. Standard equipment included a non-turbo 1.8-liter four, five-speed manual transmission, reclining front bucket seats, remote hatch/trunk release, and console. LE added an AM radio and wheel trim rings. Convertibles had power steering, power windows and tinted glass. Sunbird SE included the turbocharged engine and four-speed manual transaxle, as well as power steering and sport mirrors.

1985 Grand Am LE coupe (P)

GRAND AM — SERIES 2N — FOUR/V-6 — Ranked as a "sports specialty coupe," Grand Am (like many other mid-1980s domestic models) was targeted at youthful, upscale buyers who demanded good handling and performance, and might otherwise turn to imports. The five- passenger coupe came in base and LE trim. Standard engine was the fuel-injected "Tech IV" 151 cu. in. (2.5-liter) four, with five-speed manual gearbox. A 125 horsepower, 181 cu. in. (3.0-liter) V-6 with multi-port fuel injection and automatic transmission also was available. So was a Y99 rally suspension package to enhance the basic model's handling characteristics. Grand Am sported sculptured lines with smooth body curves, with Pontiac's traditional (yet modern) split grille up front. A tapered hood sloped back to a flush-fit, steeply raked windshield. Inside were reclining front bucket seats, a console, instrument panel pods close to the steering wheel, and analog speedometer and gas gauge. Full analog gauges and electronic instruments were both optional. So was a six- function Driver Information Center. Optional hi-tech turbo cast aluminum wheels and 215/60R14 Goodyear Eagle GT tires were said to give the car an "aggressive wide track stance."

1985 Firebird Trans Am T-top coupe (P)

FIREBIRD — SERIES 2F — FOUR/V-6/V-8 — According to Firebird's chief designer, John Schinella, the famed coupe became "more of a thoroughbred in 1985" with a "more aggressive" image and dramatic restyling. Also new was a V-8 powerplant with tuned-port fuel injection, intended to deliver a 0-60 MPH time in the 8.1 second neighborhood. Optional in Trans Am, the 205 horsepower V-8 produced 270 lbs.-ft. of torque. Engine choices also included the base 151 cu. in. (2.5-liter) four, fuel-injected 173 cu. in. (2.8- liter) V-6, standard 5.0-liter V-8, and 190-horsepower high- output V-8. Firebird's standard ride/handling package now included all of the components of the former Y99 option (except tires). An improved Y99 package included 15 inch wheels. Basic appearance was similar to 1984. But Trans Am displayed new aero-tuned rocker and quarter panel extensions, a new hood with twin louvers near the front, and built-in foglamps where the big air slots otherwise would be. Diamond spoke wheels were a new option this year.

1985 6000 STE sedan (AA)

6000 — SERIES 2A — FOUR/V-6 — A new 173 cu. in. (2.8-liter) V-6 engine with multi-port fuel injection was available in the 6000 series, and standard in the performance-minded 6000 STE. Base engine was a 151 cu. in. (2.5-liter) "Tech IV" four; optional, a carbureted 2.8 V-6 or 4.3-liter diesel V-6. STE got a front/rear restyle, as well as a few body changes evident from the side. A new front fascia included a wide bumper rub strip. At the rear were full-width, neutral- density taillamps. Wider bodyside moldings were used. Standard again was an electronic instrument panel with Driver Information Center, but color was added to the cluster. In addition to coupe and sedan bodies, the 6000 again offered a station wagon with woodgrain side paneling (and optional rear-facing third seat). Grille shape was similar to 1984, but with a wider center divider bar and horizontal bars in each insert. 6000 STE again had a long standard equipment list, which included power four-wheel disc brakes, power windows, rally- tuned electronic ride control, AM/FM stereo with cassette, 45/45 cloth upholstery with six-way adjustment and lumbar support, speed control, foglamps, dual exhausts, electronic air conditioning, and two-tone paint.

1985 Grand Prix Brougham coupe (AA)

GRAND PRIX — SERIES 2G — V-6/V-8 — A new vertical-bar grille was evident at Grand Prix's front end, and new taillamps at the rear. Nine new paint colors were available, making an even dozen. A Delco 2000 AM radio was standard. Base engine remained the 231 cu. in. (3.8-liter) V-6 with three-speed automatic. Optional: the 5.0-liter V-8 with either three- or four-speed automatic. Standard equipment included formal rear quarter windows, power steering/brakes, narrow rocker panel moldings, wheel opening moldings, chrome lower bumpers, mini black bumper guards, bright-accented bumper rub strips, clock, and P195/75R14 steel-belted radials. LE added wide rocker panel moldings with extensions, color-keyed sport mirrors, and wide windowsill and hood edge moldings. Brougham added 55/45 notchback seating, power windows, and door courtesy lights.

1985 Bonneville Brougham sedan (P)

BONNEVILLE — SERIES 2G — V-6/V-8 — Three trim levels made up the Bonneville line: base, LE, and elegant Brougham. All had a standard 231 cu. in. (3.8- liter) V-6 with three-speed automatic. And all could get an optional 5.0-liter V-8 with either three- or four-speed automatic. A dozen body colors were available, including nine new ones. An electronic-tuning sound system was available for the first time. Standard equipment included power brakes and steering, bumper guards and rub strips, wide rocker panel moldings with extensions, wheel opening moldings, cloth notchback seating, clock, and P195/75R14 steel-belted radial blackwall tires. LE added belt reveal moldings, a pillar applique, and sport steering wheel. Brougham included 55/45 notchback seats with cloth upholstery, lower door courtesy lights, and opera lamps.

PARISIENNE — SERIES 2B — V-6/V-8 — Rear-drive was very much alive at Pontiac in the form of the last remaining full-size models, which displayed a fresh look this year. Though similar overall to the 1984 edition, this year's sedan quarter panels, decklid and taillamps came from the 1981 Bonneville rather than Chevrolet Caprice (as had been the case). The new look included a revised bumper and rub strips, and

1985 Parisienne sedan (JG)

fender skirts with moldings. Extra-wide lower bodyside moldings and color-keyed bodyside moldings were new. A new windsplit hood molding became standard. Broughams included opera lamps. The four-door sedan came in base and Brougham trim. The Safari wagon carried eight passengers. A new notchback seat was standard, with "loose pillow" style; 45/55 seating available. A fuel- injected 262 cu. in. (4.3-liter) V-6 was now the base powerplant, with three-speed automatic. Wagons had a standard 5.0-liter V-8 (optional on sedan), and both could get the 350 cu. in. diesel for the last time.

I.D. DATA: Pontiac's 17-symbol Vehicle Identification Number (VIN) was on the upper left surface of the instrument panel, visible through the windshield. The first three symbols ('1G2') indicate Pontiac division. Symbol four is restraint system ('A' manual seatbelts). Symbol five is car line/series: 'E' Fiero; 'M' Fiero Sport; 'F' Fiero SE; 'G' Fiero GT; 'L' T1000; 'B' Sunbird; 'C' Sunbird LE; 'D' Sunbird SE; 'E' Grand Am; 'V' Grand Am LE; 'F' 6000; 'G' 6000 LE; 'H' 6000 STE; 'S' Firebird; 'X' Firebird SE; 'W' Firebird Trans Am; 'J' Grand Prix; 'K' Grand Prix LE; 'P' Grand Prix Brougham; 'N' Bonneville; 'R' Bonneville Brougham; 'S' Bonneville LE; 'L' Parisienne; 'T' Parisienne Brougham. In sixth and seventh position are two digits that denote body type: '08' 3dr. hatchback coupe; '27' 2dr. coupe; '37' 2dr. coupe; '77' 3dr. hatchback; '87' 2dr. coupe; '67' 2dr. conv. coupe; '19' 4dr. 6window sedan; '68' 5dr. hatchback sedan; '69' 4dr. 4 window sedan; '35' 4dr. station wagon. Symbol eight is an engine code: 'C' L498 2Bbl.; 'O' L4109 FI; 'J' turbo L4109 FI; 'P' L4122 FI; 'U' or '2' L4151 FI; 'X' or '5' V6173 2Bbl.; '5', '9' or 'W' V6173 FI; 'L' V6181 FI; 'A' V6231 2Bbl.; '7' V6262 FI; 'T' diesel V6262; 'H' V8305 4Bbl.; 'G' H.O. V8305 FI; 'F' V8305 FI; 'N' diesel V8350. Next is a check digit. The tenth symbol denotes model year ('F' 1985). Symbol eleven is a plant code: 'A' Lakewood, GA; 'L' Van Nuys, CA; 'N' Norwood, Ohio; 'P' Pontiac, MI; 'T' Tarrytown, NY; 'X' Fairfax, Kansas; 'M' Lansing, MI; '7' Lordstown, Ohio; '1' Oshawa, Ontario; '2' St. Therese, Quebec. The final six digits are the sequential serial number.

FIERO (FOUR)

Model Number	Body/Style Number	Body Type & Seating	Factory Price	Shipping Weight	Production Total
2P	E37	2-dr. Cpe-2P	8495	2454	5,280
2P	M37	2-dr. Spt Cpe-2P	8995	2500	23,823
2P	F37	2-dr. SE Cpe-2P	9995	2525	24,734
2P	G37	2-dr. GT Cpe-2P	11795	N/A	22,534

1000 (FOUR)

2T	L08	3-dr. Hatch-4P	5445	2081	8,647
2T	L68	5-dr. Hatch-4P	5695	2130	8,216

SUNBIRD (FOUR)

2J	B27	2-dr. Cpe-5P	6875	2353	39,721
2J	B77	3-dr. Hatch-5P	7215	2413	5,235
2J	B69	4-dr. Sedan-5P	6995	2412	44,553
2J	B35	4-dr. Sta Wag-5P	7335	2487	7,371

SUNBIRD LE (FOUR)

2J	C27	2-dr. Cpe-5P	7555	2385	3,424
2J	C69	4-dr. Sedan-5P	7725	2436	6,287
2J	C35	4-dr. Sta Wag-5P	8055	2517	1,036
2J	C67	2-dr. Conv.-4P	12035	N/A	2,114

SUNBIRD SE (FOUR)

2J	D27	2-dr. Cpe-5P	9295	2360	965
2J	D77	3-dr. Hatch-5P	9765	2435	535
2J	D69	4-dr. Sedan-5P	9455	2416	658

GRAND AM (FOUR/V-6)

2N	E27	2-dr. Cpe-5P	7995/8480	2419/--	40,273

GRAND AM LE (FOUR/V-6)

2N	V27	2-dr. Cpe-5P	8485/8970	2447/--	42,269

FIREBIRD (FOUR/V-6)

2F	S87	2-dr. Cpe-4P	8763/9013	2866/2948	46,644

Engine Note: A 305 cu. in. V-8 cost $300 more than the V-6 on base Firebird.

FIREBIRD SE (V-6/V-8)

2F	X87	2-dr. Cpe-4P	11063/11263	2965/3145	5,208

FIREBIRD TRANS AM (V-8)

2F	W87	2-dr. Cpe-4P	11113	3107	44,028

6000 (FOUR/V-6)

2A	F27	2-dr. Cpe-5P	8899/9159	2698/2741	4,493
2A	F19	4-dr. Sed-5P	9079/9339	2736/2779	54,424
2A	F35	4-dr. Sta Wag-5P	9435/9695	2815/ --	8,491
2A	G27	2-dr. LE Cpe-5P	9385/9645	2711/2754	3,777
2A	G19	4-dr. LE Sed-5P	9539/9799	2750/2793	54,284
2A	G35	4-dr. LE Wag-5P	9869/10129	2832/ --	8,025

6000 STE (V-6)

2A	H19	4-dr. Sed-5P	14829	2823	22,728

GRAND PRIX (V-6/V-8)

2G	J37	2-dr. Cpe-6P	9569/9959	3148/ --	30,365

GRAND PRIX LE (V-6/V-8)

2G	K37	2-dr. Cpe-6P	10049/10439	3168/ --	21,195

GRAND PRIX BROUGHAM (V-6/V-8)

2G	P37	2-dr. Cpe-6P	10749/11139	3186/ --	8,223

BONNEVILLE (V-6/V-8)

2G	N69	4-dr. Sed-6P	9549/9939	3214/3290	34,466
2G	S69	4-dr. LE Sed-6P	9789/10179	3275/3351	10,503

BONNEVILLE BROUGHAM (V-6/V-8)

2G	R69	4-dr. Sed-6P	10280/10669	3210/3286	8,425

PARISIENNE (V-6/V-8)

2B	L69	4-dr. Sed-6P	10395/10635	3350/ --	25,638
2B	L35	4-dr. Sta Wag-8P	-- /10495	3944	17,638

PARISIENNE BROUGHAM (V-6/V-8)

2B	T69	4-dr. Sed-6P	11125/11365	3378/ --	38,831

FACTORY PRICE AND WEIGHT NOTE: Prices and weights to left of slash are for V-6, to right for V-8 engine except Firebird/Grand Am/6000, four and V-6.

ENGINE DATA: BASE FOUR (1000): Inline. Overhead cam. Four-cylinder. Cast iron block and head. Displacement: 98 cu. in. (1.6 liters). Bore & stroke: 3.23 x 2.98 in. Compression ratio: 9.0:1. Brake horsepower: 65 at 5200 R.P.M. Torque: 80 lbs.-ft. at 3200 R.P.M. Five main bearings. Hydraulic valve lifters. Carburetor: 2Bbl. VIN Code: C. BASE FOUR (Sunbird): Inline. Overhead cam. Four-cylinder. Cast iron block and aluminum head. Displacement: 109 cu. in. (1.8 liters). Bore & stroke: 3.34 x 3.13 in. Compression ratio: 9.0:1. Brake horsepower: 82 at 5200 R.P.M. Torque: 102 lbs.-ft. at 2800 R.P.M. Five main bearings. Hydraulic valve lifters. Electronic fuel injection. VIN Code: 0. OPTIONAL TURBO FOUR (Sunbird): Same as 109 cu. in. four above, with port fuel injection and turbocharger Compression ratio: 8.0:1. Horsepower: 150 at 5600 R.P.M. Torque: 150 lbs.-ft. at 2800 R.P.M. VIN Code: J. OPTIONAL FOUR (Sunbird): Inline. Overhead valve. Four-cylinder. Cast iron block and head. Displacement: 122 cu. in. (2.0 liters). Bore & stroke: 3.50 x 3.15 in. Compression ratio: 9.3:1. Brake horsepower: 88 at 4800 R.P.M. Torque: 110 lbs.-ft. at 2400 R.P.M. Five main bearings. Hydraulic valve lifters. Electronic fuel injection. VIN Code: P. BASE FOUR (Fiero, Grand Am, Firebird, 6000): Inline. Overhead valve. Four-cylinder. Cast iron block and head. Displacement: 151 cu. in. (2.5 liters). Bore & stroke: 4.00 x 3.00 in. Compression ratio: 9.0:1. Brake horsepower: 92 at 4400 R.P.M. (Firebird, 88 at 4400). Torque: 132-134 lbs.-ft. at 2800 R.P.M. Five main bearings. Hydraulic valve lifters. Throttle-body fuel injection. VIN Code: U or 2. OPTIONAL V-6 (6000): 60-degree, overhead valve six-cylinder. Cast iron block and aluminum head. Displacement: 173 cu. in. (2.8 liters). Bore & stroke: 3.50 x 3.00 in. Compression ratio: 8.5:1. Brake horsepower: 112 at 4800 R.P.M. Torque: 145 lbs.-ft. at 2100 R.P.M. Four main bearings. Hydraulic valve lifters. Carburetor: 2Bbl. VIN Code: X. BASE V-6 (Firebird SE, 6000 STE); OPTIONAL (Fiero, Firebird): Fuel-injected version of 173 cu. in. V-6 above Compression ratio: 8.9:1. Horsepower: 130 at 4800 R.P.M. (Firebird, 135 at 5100). Torque: 160-165 lbs.-ft. at 3600 R.P.M. VIN Code: 5, 9 or W. OPTIONAL V-6 (Grand Am): 90-degree, overhead-valve V-6. Cast iron block and head. Displacement: 181 cu. in. (3.0 liters). Bore & stroke: 3.80 x 2.70 in. Compression ratio: 9.0:1. Brake horsepower: 125 at 4900 R.P.M. Torque: 154 lbs.-ft. at 2400 R.P.M. Four main bearings. Hydraulic valve lifters. Fuel injection. VIN Code: L. BASE V-6 (Grand Prix, Bonneville): 90-degree, overhead-valve V-6. Cast iron block and head. Displacement: 231 cu. in. (3.8 liters). Bore & stroke: 3.80 x 3.40 in. Compression ratio: 8.0:1. Brake horsepower: 110 at 3800 R.P.M. Torque: 190 lbs.-ft. at 1600 R.P.M. Four main bearings. Hydraulic valve lifters. Carburetor: 2Bbl. Rochester E2ME. Buick-built. VIN Code: A. BASE V-6 (Parisienne): 90-degree, overhead-valve V-6. Cast iron block and head. Displacement: 262 cu. in. (4.3 liters). Bore & stroke: 4.00 x 3.48 in. Compression ratio: N/A. Brake horsepower: 130 at 3600 R.P.M. Torque: 210 lbs.-ft. at 2000 R.P.M. Four main bearings. Hydraulic valve lifters. Throttle-body fuel injection. VIN Code: 7. DIESEL V-6 (6000): 90-degree, overhead valve V-6. Cast iron block and head. Displacement: 260 cu. in. (4.3 liters). Bore & stroke: 4.06 x 3.38 in. Compression ratio: 21.6:1. Brake horsepower: 85 at 3600 R.P.M. Torque: 165 lbs.-ft. at 1600 R.P.M. Four main bearings. Hydraulic valve lifters. Fuel injection. VIN Code: T. BASE V-8 (Firebird Trans Am); OPTIONAL (Firebird, Grand Prix, Bonneville, Parisienne): 90-degree, overhead valve V-8. Cast iron block and head. Displacement: 305 cu. in. (5.0 liters). Bore & stroke: 3.74 x 3.48 in. Compression ratio: 9.5:1. Brake horsepower: 165 at 4200 R.P.M. Torque: 250 lbs.-ft. at 2400 R.P.M. Five main bearings. Hydraulic valve lifters. Carburetor: 4Bbl. Chevrolet-built. VIN Code: H. OPTIONAL V-8 (Trans Am): High-output version of 305 cu. in. V-8 Compression ratio: 9.5:1. Horsepower: 190 at 4800 R.P.M. Torque: 240 lbs.-ft. at 3200 R.P.M. VIN Code: G. OPTIONAL V-8 (Trans Am): Fuel-injected version of 305 cu. in. V-8 Horsepower: 205 at 4400 R.P.M. Torque: 275 lbs.-ft. at 3200 R.P.M. VIN Code: F. DIESEL V-8 (Parisienne): 90-degree, overhead valve V-8. Cast iron block and head. Displacement: 350 cu. in. (5.7 liters). Bore & stroke: 4.06 x 3.39 in. Compression ratio: 22.5:1. Brake horsepower: 105 at 3200 R.P.M. Torque: 200 lbs.-ft. at 1600 R.P.M. Five main bearings. Hydraulic valve lifters. Fuel injection. Oldsmobile-built. VIN Code: N.

CHASSIS DATA: Wheelbase: (Fiero) 93.4 in.; (1000 3dr.) 94.3 in.; (1000 5dr.) 97.3 in.; (Sunbird) 101.2 in.; (Grand Am) 103.4 in.; (Firebird) 101.0 in.; (6000) 104.8 in.; (Grand Prix) 108.1 in.; (Bonn.) 108.1 in.; (Parisienne) 116.0 in. Overall Length: (Fiero) 160.7 in.; (1000 3dr.) 161.9 in.; (1000 5dr.) 164.9 in.; (Sunbird) 175.4 in.; (Sunbird wag) 176.5 in.; (Grand Am) 177.5 in.; (Firebird) 189.9 in.; (6000) 188.8 in.; (6000 wag) 191.2 in.; (G.P.) 201.9 in.; (Bonn.) 200.2 in.; (Parisienne) 212.4 in.; (Parisienne wag) 215.1 in. Height: (Fiero) 46.9 in.; (1000) 52.8-52.9 in.; (Sunbird cpe) 51.9 in.; (Sunbird conv.) 52.7 in.; (Sunbird sed) 53.8 in.; (Sunbird wag) 54.1 in.; (Grand Am) 52.5 in.; (Firebird) 49.7 in.; (6000) 53.3-53.8 in.; (G.P.) 54.7 in.; (Bonn.) 55.8 in.; (Parisienne sed) 56.4 in.; (Parisienne wag) 58.1 in. Width: (Fiero) 68.9 in.; (1000) 61.8 in.; (Sunbird cpe/conv.) 65.9 in.; (Sunbird hatch) 66.6 in.; (Sunbird sed/wag) 66.2 in.; (Grand Am) 67.3 in.; (Firebird) 72.4 in.; (6000) 67.7- 67.8 in.; (G.P.) 72.3 in.; (Bonn.) 71.6 in.; (Parisienne) 76.4 in. exc. wagon, 79.3 in. Front Tread: (Fiero) 57.8 in.; (1000) 51.2 in.; (Sunbird) 55.4 in.; (Grand Am) 55.6 in.; (Firebird) 60.7 in.; (6000) 58.7 in.; (G.P.) 58.5 in.; (Bonn.) 58.5 in.; (Parisienne) 61.8 in.; (Parisienne wag) 62.2 in. Rear Tread: (Fiero) 58.7 in.; (1000) 51.2 in.; (Sunbird) 55.2 in.; (Grand Am) 55.1 in.; (Firebird) 61.6 in.; (6000) 56.9 in.; (G.P.) 57.8 in.; (Bonn.) 57.8 in.; (Parisienne) 60.8 in.; (Parisienne wag) 64.1 in. Standard Tires: (Fiero) P185/80R13; (1000) P155/80R13 GBR BSW; (Sunbird) P175/80R13 SBR BSW; (Grand Am) P185/80R13 SBR BSW; (Firebird) P195/75R14 SBR BSW; (Firebird SE) P205/70R14 SBR BSW; (6000) P185/75R14 SBR; (6000 STE) P195/70R14 SBR; (Grand Prix) P195/75R14 SBR; (Bonn.) P195/75R14 SBR; (Parisienne sed) P205/75R15 SBR; (Parisienne wag) P225/75R15 SBR.

TECHNICAL: Transmission: Four-speed manual standard on Fiero, 1000, and base Firebird. Five-speed manual standard on Sunbird, Firebird and Grand Am, optional on 1000. Three-speed Turbo Hydra-matic standard on other models. Four-speed overdrive automatic available on Firebird, 6000, Grand Prix, Bonneville and Parisienne. Standard final drive ratio: (Fiero) N/A; (1000) 3.36:1; (Sunbird) 2.55:1 w/5spd, 2.96:1 or 3.32:1 w/4spd, 3.33:1 or 3.43:1 w/auto.; (Grand Am) 2.48:1 w/5spd, 2.84:1 w/auto.; (Firebird) 3.42:1 w/4spd, 3.73:1 w/four and 5spd or auto., 3.42:1 w/V-6, 3.27:1 w/V-8; (Trans Am) 3.27:1 except 3.70:1 w/H.O. V-8 and 3.27:1 w/FI V-8; (6000) 2.39:1 w/four, 2.84:1 or 3.06:1 w/V-6; (6000 STE) 3.18:1; (Grand Prix/Bonneville) 2.41:1; (Parisienne) 2.56:1; (Parisienne wagon) 2.73:1. Steering: (Fiero/1000/Sunbird/Phoenix/6000) rack and pinion; (others) recirculating ball. Front Suspension: (Sunbird/Phoenix/6000) MacPherson struts w/lower control arms and anti-sway bar; (Grand Am) MacPherson struts and anti-sway bar; (Firebird) modified MacPherson struts w/coil springs between lower control arm and Xmember; (others) coil springs and anti-sway bar. Rear Suspension: (Fiero) MacPherson struts w/lower control arms; (1000) four-link rigid axle w/torque tube and Panhard rod; (Sunbird) beam axle w/coil springs and trailing arms; (Grand Am) semi-independent beam axle w/trailing arms and coil springs; (Firebird) torque arm/track bar w/coil springs and anti-sway bar; (6000) trailing arms and beam axle w/coil springs and integral anti-sway bar; (Bonneville/Grand Prix/Parisienne) four-link rigid axle with coil springs, lower trailing radius arms and upper torque arms. Brakes: Front disc, rear drum except 6000 STE, four-wheel disc. Ignition: Electronic. Body construction: (Fiero/1000/Sunbird/Phoenix/Firebird/6000) unit; (others) separate body and frame. Fuel Tank: (Fiero) 10.2 gal.; (1000) 12.2 gal.; (Sunbird) 13.6 gal.; (Grand Am) 13.6 gal.; (Firebird) 15.9 gal.; (6000) 15.7 gal.; (Grand Prix/Bonneville) 18.1 gal.; (Parisienne sed) 25 gal.; (Parisienne wag) 22 gal.

DRIVETRAIN OPTIONS: Engines: Turbo 1.8-liter four: Sunbird ($1248-$1486); std. on SE. 173 cu. in., 2Bbl. V-6: 6000 ($260). 173 cu. in., FI V-6: Fiero ($595); Firebird ($350); 6000 ($435). 181 cu. in. V-6: Grand Am ($560). Diesel 262 cu. in. V-6: 6000 ($335). 305 cu. in., 4Bbl. V-8: Firebird ($650); Firebird SE ($300); Grand Prix/Bonneville ($390); Parisienne ($240). H.O. 305 cu. in. V-8, 4Bbl. or FI: Trans Am ($695). Diesel 350 cu. in. V-8: Parisienne sed ($341); Parisienne wagon ($101). Transmission/Differential: Four-speed manual trans.: Fiero SE ($50 credit); Sunbird ($75 credit). Five-speed manual trans.: 1000 ($75). Three-speed automatic trans.: Fiero ($425-$475); Fiero GT ($750); 1000 ($395); Sunbird ($350-$425); Grand Am ($425). Four-speed automatic trans.: Firebird ($325); 6000/Grand Prix/Bonneville/Parisienne ($175). Limited-slip differential: Firebird/G.P./Bonn./Parisienne ($95-$100). Brakes/Steering: Power brakes: 1000 ($94). Power four-wheel disc brakes: Firebird ($179) but (NC) w/performance pkg. Power steering: 1000 ($204); Sunbird ($215). Suspension: Electronic susp.: 6000 ($165). Rally tuned susp.: Firebird ($30); Sunbird/Grand Am/6000/Firebird/G.P. ($50); Parisienne ($49). Superlift shock absorbers: 6000/G.P./Bonn./Parisienne ($64). H.D. springs: Parisienne ($16). Other. H.D. cooling ($40-$70). H.D. battery ($25-$26) exc. iesel ($52). H.D. alternator ($25-$51). Engine block heater ($18-$19). California emissions ($99).

OPTION PACKAGES: Fiero special performance pkg. ($174-$491). 1000 sport/handling pkg. ($464). 1000 custom trim ($167). Sunbird custom exterior group ($86). Sunbird custom trim group ($308- $358). Sunbird security pkg. ($19). Firebird Trans Am special performance pkg. ($664). Firebird black appearance pkg. ($123-$152). Firebird custom exterior ($51-$112). Firebird luxury interior trim ($349-$359). 6000 sport landau coupe ($665-$703). 6000 rally pkg. ($441-$479). 6000 custom exterior ($56). 6000 wagon security pkg. ($44). Grand Prix Brougham Landau pkg. ($469). Lamp groups ($21-$47) except 6000 LE ($79-$88).

MAJOR CONVENIENCE/APPEARANCE OPTIONS: Air conditioning ($630-$730). Cruise control ($175). Power seat ($215-$488); N/A on 1000/Fiero. Power windows ($185- $260); N/A on 1000. Cornering lamps: Bonn./G.P. ($68); Parisienne ($55). Power glass sunroof: Parisienne ($1195). Removable glass sunroof: Fiero/Sunbird/Grand Am/6000 ($300- $310). Hatch roof: Firebird/Grand Prix ($825-$875). Full vinyl roof: Bonneville ($160). Padded cordova landau roof: G.P. ($245). Aero wing spoiler: Trans Am ($199). Padded full vinyl roof: Bonn. ($245); Parisienne ($185). Louvered rear sunshields: Sunbird ($199); Firebird ($210). Two-tone paint: Sunbird ($101-$151); Firebird/6000 ($205); G.P./Bonn. ($205- $291); Parisienne sed ($205). Lear Siegler bucket seats: Sunbird ($400); Firebird ($400-$759); leather ($945-$1304). Recaro bucket seats: Firebird ($636-$995). Woodgrain paneling: Parisienne wagon ($345).

HISTORY: Introduced: October 2, 1984 except Sunbird/Firebird, November 8, 1984; 1000, November 11, 1984; and Fiero, January 10, 1985. Model year production: 735,161. Calendar year production (U.S.): 684,901. Calendar year sales by U.S. dealers: 796,795. Model year sales by U.S. dealers: 785,643.

Historical Footnotes: First built only in Canada, the 6000 series expanded production to the Tarrytown, New York plant for 1985. Sales rose moderately for the model year, with 6000 and Parisienne posting impressive increases. Small cars weren't doing as well. Fiero sales continued relatively good, if beneath expectations. The 6000 was Pontiac's best seller. Well over half of Pontiacs now carried fuel-injected engines.

1986 PONTIAC

"Driver-oriented" models continued to get ample attention with the introduction of an SE variant for Grand Am and a Sunbird GT. All Pontiacs now had the required high-mount center stop lamp. Most appealing to collectors would be the limited-production Grand Prix 22 coupe.

1986 Fiero GT coupe (P)

FIERO — SERIES 2P — FOUR/V-6 — Three models made up the two-seater coupe line: base, Sport, and SE. A black-accented aero package gave SE its own styling cues. Its standard 151 cu. in. (2.5-liter) fuel- injected "Tech IV" four, with dual-trumpet exhaust, coupled with a five-speed manual transaxle (from Isuzu). Optional again: a 173 cu. in. (2.8-liter) V-6 with multi-port fuel injection. SE came with a standard Rally Tuned suspension, including 14 inch cast aluminum wheels. Four-cylinder SE models had P195/70R14 tires; V-6, P215/60R14. Standard reclining bucket seats wore Pallex cloth. Optional leather/suede/cloth trim replaced the former fleece/suede. Standard tires for base and Sport Coupe models were P185/75R14, with new tri-tech wheel covers (aluminum wheels optional). New sail-panel stereo speakers replaced the former headrest units. Body colors included black, silver, red, white and gold. Overall appearance was similar to 1985, but the smooth-surfaced front end now held a single center air slot, with separate openings for parking/signal lamps. A fastback GT model was announced for late arrival.

1986 Pontiac 1000 hatchback sedan (P)

1000 — SERIES 2T — FOUR — For its final year, the subcompact 1000 again came in two body styles: three- and five-door hatchback. Standard engine was again the 1.6-liter OHC four, with four-speed manual shift. A five-speed and automatic were optional. An optional sport handling package included a heavier front stabilizer bar and a rear stabilizer bar, as well as cast aluminum wheels, dual mirrors, and sport body striping. Also optional: a new four-spoke steering wheel. Standard equipment included a Delco AM radio, front mini-console, reclining front seats, and folding full-width back seat.

1986 Sunbird GT hatchback coupe (P)

SUNBIRD — SERIES 2J — FOUR — Most notable of Sunbird's changes was the new GT level, offered on coupe, hatchback, convertible and sedan bodies. A station wagon remained available at the base level, and the SE lineup included a convertible. Aimed at enthusiasts, the GT included a sloped front fascia with partly hidden quad halogen headlamps, and a rear spoiler. GT equipment included narrow black bodyside moldings and dual sport mirrors. Two-door GT models also had wheel flares, turbo aluminum wheels, and P215/60R14 Eagle GT tires. A turbocharged version of the 1.8-liter engine, rated 150 horsepower delivered a claimed 8.5 second 060 time. GT also included a performance handling package and power steering. Inside was a backlid round-dial instrument cluster that included a turbo boost gauge and tachometer, and an electric speedometer. A rally console extension included a thumbwheel mileage/event reminder. The four-spoke rally urethane steering wheel had horn bars on each side of the hub. Leather wrapping was optional. Genor cloth upholstery was standard. Base and SE models were still around, but LE became an option package for base sedans and wagons rather than a model on its own. Sedans and wagons got a blackout taillamp treatment to replace the former bright framing. SE models had a revised taillamp design, wide bodyside moldings, foglamps (making six front lights in all), and blackout trim on belt moldings, drip rails, and door handles. All models had a backlit instrument cluster, with standard temp gauge. The base four-cylinder 1.8 liter engine developed 84 horsepower, but the former 2.0-liter option was no longer available.

1986 Grand Am SE coupe (P)

GRAND AM — SERIES 2N — FOUR/V-6 — A sporty four-door joined the original Grand Am coupe, along with a "sophisticated" SE series aimed at enthusiasts. SE, said its design studio head, offered a "boldly aggressive appearance." The approach was similar to that used for the 6000 STE. This edition had an aero ground-effects package that included a low front bumper air dam, side skirts, and deep rear extension, as well as flush composite headlamps and built-in foglamps. SE also had a unique monochrome paint treatment, with grille, emblems and cast aluminum wheels color-coordinated to the body. At the rear were neutral- density taillamps. Standard engine was a 181 cu. in. (3.0- liter) V-6 with multi-port fuel injection, hooked to three-speed automatic. The Y99 rally tuned suspension included thick front/rear stabilizer bars and P215/60R14 Eagle GT tires. SE interiors contained tone-on-tone Pallex seat trim, color-coordinated with the body color. Standard equipment included a four-way (manual-control) driver's bucket seat; leather-wrapped steering wheel, parking brake handle and gearshift knob; header-mount reading lamp; rear roof courtesy lamp; visor vanity mirror; and seek/scan AM/FM stereo. Options included a six-speaker sound system, tilt steering, and cruise control. Appearance of the "ordinary" base and LE Grand Am changed little this year, except for new high-gloss black moldings on LE models. Base engine was the "Tech IV" 151 cu. in. (2.5-liter) four with fuel injection, and five-speed manual transaxle. New Flame Red was one of the dozen available body colors. Turbo cast aluminum wheels were optional again. Base/LE models could also get the 3.0-liter V-6, with three-speed automatic.

1986 Firebird coupe (P)

FIREBIRD — SERIES 2F — FOUR/V-6/V-8 — New taillamps and center filler panel gave the base Firebird a modified look, different from the upscale models. New lower body accent paint with sports striping became standard. Also standard: dual sport mirrors and rear spoiler. The optional hood bird graphic decal also changed in appearance. All models had a power pull-down hatch, with electric remote release optional; and all carried 15-inch tires. New options included a programmable,

1986 Firebird Trans Am T-top coupe (P)

electrically- controlled day/night mirror. All base and SE models with V-6 or V-8 now had the optional Rally Tuned suspension with P215/65R15 tires on 7- inch Rally II wheels. New lightweight pistons went into the base "Tech IV" 151 cu. in. (2.5-liter) four, which drove a standard five-speed manual gearbox. SE carried a standard 173 cu. in. (2.8-liter) V-6 with multi-port fuel injection. Both base and SE models could have a 5.0-liter four-barrel V-8 with either five-speed or automatic. Trans Am had a standard 155-horsepower version of the 5.0-liter V-8, and an option of tuned-port fuel injection that delivered 190 horsepower. Five-speed manual shift was standard, and four-speed overdrive automatic required with the TPI engine. The standard Y99 Rally Tuned suspension came with P215/60R15 tires on 7-inch cast aluminum wheels. Trans Am's WS6 suspension package included four-wheel disc brakes, a limited-slip differential, larger front/rear stabilizer bars, and P245/50VR16 Gatorback tires. A new backlit instrument cluster included an electric speedometer, which read up to 140 MPH reading when equipped with the TPI V-8.

1986 6000 STE wagon (P)

6000 — SERIES 2A — FOUR/V-6 — Most notable of the improvements in the 6000 line was standard anti-lock braking, introduced during the model year on 6000 STE as part of its standard four-wheel power disc brake system. Radio controls moved to the steering wheel this year (duplicated on the dash). 6000 STE had a revised grille (lacking the traditional Pontiac split design), along with aerodynamic flush halogen headlamps and foglamps. Standard STE engine was a 173 cu. in. (2.8-liter) V-6 with multi-port fuel injection, delivering 130 horsepower. The standard three-speed automatic transmission now connected with a 3.18:1 final drive ratio. An electronic instrument cluster remained standard, with new vacuum fluorescent unit. A new pod held controls for power windows, door locks and mirrors. As before, 6000 STE had an almost nonexistent options list: just a six-way power driver/passenger seat with recliners, sunroof, and suede interior trim. Base and LE models had a standard 151 cu. in. (2.5-liter) four with three-speed automatic. Options included both carbureted and fuel-injected versions of the 2.8 V-6. Four- speed overdrive automatic was available for V-6 models.

1986 Grand Prix 2+2 Aerodynamic Coupe (P)

GRAND PRIX — SERIES 2G — V-6/V-8 — As before, three series were available on the rear- drive personal-luxury coupe: base, LE and Brougham. Standard engine was Buick's 231 cu. in. (3.8-liter) V-6, with three- speed automatic. A 5.0-liter V-8 with four-speed overdrive automatic was optional. Taillamps and bezels were slightly revised. Three-section taillamps had a 'GP' octagon in the center lens. Though similar to 1985, this year's grille had fewer vertical bars. Interiors had a notchback seat with center armrest. A new optional visor vanity mirror came with dual-intensity lamps. Onlyl 200 examples of the 22 coupe were built, all of them sold by dealers in southeastern states. The 22 was a streeet version of the NASCAR racer, driven by Richard Petty in the 1986-87 season. Under the hood was a 165-horsepower version of the 305 cu. in. V-8, producing 245 lbs.-ft. of torque. Selling price was $18,214, but dealers quickly marked the few units available up around $22,000. Claimed quarter-mile time was 17.6 second, with a speed of 80 MPH. The 22 had a gray body with twin-shade red striping on the lower panels. A 'Pontiac 22' nameplate went in red/gray on black went on the left of the black honeycomb grille. 'Pontiac 22' lettering also went on the door, and 'Pontiac Grand Prix' identification on the deck. The 22 option was RPO code Y97.

1986 Bonneville Brougham sedan (P)

402

BONNEVILLE — SERIES 2G — V-6/V-8 — Appearance was similar to 1985. The six-passenger mid- size sedan came in base, LE and Brougham trim, in a dozen body colors. Base engine was the 231 cu. in. (3.8-liter) V-6 with three-speed automatic. Optional: a 5.0-liter V-8 with four-speed overdrive automatic. Standard equipment included power brakes and steering, AM radio, notchback front seat with fold-down center armrest, and custom wheel covers. LE added a four-spoke sport steering wheel, pillar applique, and belt reveal moldings. Brougham added a 55/45 front seat, cushion steering wheel, and door courtesy lamps.

1986 Parisienne Brougham sedan (P)

PARISIENNE — SERIES 2B — V-6/V-8 — Once again, the full-size rear-drive Pontiacs came in base or Brougham trim as a four-door sedan, or as an eight- passenger station wagon. New fine-textured velour cloth trim went into Brougham sedans. Turbo-finned cast aluminum wheels were optional on sedans. Optional instruments now included a voltmeter instead of a fuel economy gauge. Base engine was a 4.3-liter fuel-injected V-6, with three-speed automatic. Wagons carried a 5.0-liter V-8 and four-speed automatic.

I.D. DATA: Pontiac's 17-symbol Vehicle Identification Number (VIN) was on the upper left surface of the instrument panel, visible through the windshield. The first three symbols ('1G2') indicate Pontiac division. Symbol four is restraint system ('A' manual seatbelts). Symbol five is car line/series: 'E' Fiero; 'M' Fiero Sport; 'F' Fiero SE; 'G' Fiero GT; 'L' T1000; 'B' Sunbird; 'U' Sunbird GT; 'D' Sunbird SE; 'E' Grand Am; 'V' Grand Am LE; 'W' Grand Am SE; 'F' 6000; 'G' 6000 LE; 'E' 6000 SE; 'H' 6000 STE; 'S' Firebird; 'X' Firebird SE; 'W' Firebird Trans Am; 'J' Grand Prix; 'K' Grand Prix LE; 'P' Grand Prix Brougham; 'N' Bonneville; 'R' Bonneville Brougham; 'S' Bonneville LE; 'L' Parisienne; 'T' Parisienne Brougham. In sixth and seventh position are two digits that denote body type: '08' 3dr. hatchback coupe; '27' 2dr. coupe; '37' 2dr. coupe; '77' 3dr. hatchback; '87' 2dr. coupe; '97' 2dr. coupe; '67' 2dr. conv. coupe; '19' 4dr. 6window sedan; '68' 5dr. hatchback sedan; '69' 4dr. 4 window sedan; '35' 4dr. station wagon. Symbol eight is an engine code: 'C' L498 2Bbl.; 'O' L4109 FI; 'J' turbo L4109 FI; 'R' or 'U' L4151 FI; 'X' V6173 2Bbl.; 'S', 'W' or '9' V6173 FI; 'L' V6181 FI; 'A' V6231 2Bbl.; 'Z' V6262 FI; 'H' V8305 4Bbl.; 'G' H.O. V8305; 'F' V8305 FI. Next is a check digit. The tenth symbol denotes model year ('G' 1986). Symbol eleven is a plant code: 'A' Lakewood, GA; 'L' Van Nuys, CA; 'N' Norwood, Ohio; 'P' Pontiac, MI; 'T' Tarrytown, NY; 'X' Fairfax, Kansas; 'M' Lansing, MI; '7' Lordstown, Ohio; '1' Oshawa, Ontario; '2' St. Therese, Quebec. The final six digits are the sequential serial number.

FIERO (FOUR/V-6)

Model Number	Body/Style Number	Body Type & Seating	Factory Price	Shipping Weight	Production Total
2P	E37	2-dr. Cpe-2P	8949/ --	2480	9,143
2P	M37	2-dr. Spt Cpe-2P	9449/ --	2493	24,866
2P	F37	2-dr. SE Cpe-2P	10595/11240	7499	32,305
2P	G97	2-dr. GT Cpe-2P	-- /12875	N/A	17,660

1000 (FOUR)

2T	L08	3-dr. Hatch-4P	5749	2059	12,266
2T	L68	5-dr. Hatch-4P	5969	2118	9,423

SUNBIRD (FOUR)

2J	B69	4-dr. Sedan-5P	7495	2336	60,080
2J	B35	4-dr. Sta Wag-5P	7879	2397	7,445

SUNBIRD SE (FOUR)

2J	D27	2-dr. Cpe-5P	7469	2285	37,526
2J	D77	3-dr. Hatch-5P	7829	2330	3,822
2J	D67	2-dr. Conv.-4P	12779	2464	1,598

1986 Sunbird Turbo GT hatchback coupe (P)

SUNBIRD GT (FOUR)

2J	U27	2-dr. Cpe-5P	9459	2396	18,118
2J	U77	3-dr. Hatch-5P	9819	2419	2,442
2J	U69	4-dr. Sedan-5P	9499	2398	2,802
2J	U67	2-dr. Conv.-4P	14399	2573	1,268

GRAND AM (FOUR/V-6)

2N	E27	2-dr. Cpe-5P	8549/9624	2423/ --	69,545
2N	E69	4-dr. Sedan-5P	8749/9824	2496/ --	49,166

GRAND AM LE (FOUR/V-6)

2N	V27	2-dr. Cpe-5P	9079/10154	2458/ --	48,530
2N	V69	4-dr. Sedan-5P	9279/10354	2521/ --	31,790

1986 Grand Am SE sedan (P)

GRAND AM SE (V-6)

2N	W27	2-dr. Cpe-5P	11499	2605	15,506
2N	W69	4-dr. Sedan-5P	11749	2683	8,957

FIREBIRD (FOUR/V-6)

2F	S87	2-dr. Cpe-4P	9279/9629	2789/ --	59,334

Engine Note: A 305 cu. in. V-8 cost $400 more than the V-6 on base Firebird.

FIREBIRD SE (V-6/V-8)

2F	X87	2-dr. Cpe-4P	11995/12395	2909/ --	2,259

FIREBIRD TRANS AM (V-8)

2F	W87	2-dr. Cpe-4P	12395	3132	48,870

6000 (FOUR/V-6)

2A	F27	2-dr. Cpe-6P	9549/10159	2668/ --	4,739
2A	F19	4-dr. Sed-6P	9729/10339	2713/ --	81,531
2A	F35	4-dr. Sta Wag-6P	10095/10705	2849/ --	10,094
2A	G27	2-dr. LE Cpe-6P	10049/10659	2687/ --	4,803
2A	G19	4-dr. LE Sed-6P	10195/10805	2731/ --	67,697
2A	G35	4-dr. LE Wag-6P	10579/11189	2867/ --	7,556
2A	E19	4-dr. SE Sed-6P	-- /11179	N/A	7,348
2A	E35	4-dr. SE Wag-6P	-- /11825	N/A	1,308

6000 STE (V-6)

2A	H19	4-dr. Sed-5P	15949	3039	26,299

GRAND PRIX (V-6/V-8)

2G	J37	2-dr. Cpe-6P	10259/10974	3161/--	21,668
2G	N/A	2-dr. 2+2 Cpe-5P	-- /18214	N/A	200

GRAND PRIX LE (V-6/V-8)

2G	K37	2-dr. Cpe-6P	10795/11510	3178/ --	13,918

GRAND PRIX BROUGHAM (V-6/V-8)

2G	P37	2-dr. Cpe-6P	11579/12294	3201/ --	4,798

BONNEVILLE (V-6/V-8)

2G	N69	4-dr. Sed-6P	10249/10964	3143/ --	27,801
2G	S69	4-dr. LE Sed-6P	10529/11244	3152/ --	7,179

BONNEVILLE BROUGHAM (V-6/V-8)

2G	R69	4-dr. Sed-6P	11079/11794	3172/ --	5,941

PARISIENNE (V-6/V-8)

2B	L69	4-dr. Sed-6P	11169/11734	3427/ --	27,078
2B	L35	4-dr. Sta Wag-8P	-- /11779	-- /3985	14,464

PARISIENNE BROUGHAM (V-6/V-8)

2B	T69	4-dr. Sed-6P	11949/12514	3456/ --	43,540

FACTORY PRICE AND WEIGHT NOTE: Prices and weights to left of slash are for V-6, to right for V-8 engine except Fiero/Firebird/Grand Am/6000, four and V-8. Most prices of optional V-6 (or V-8) include an extra $175 for the cost of the required four-speed overdrive automatic transmission.

ENGINE DATA: BASE FOUR (1000): Inline. Overhead cam. Four-cylinder. Cast iron block and head. Displacement: 98 cu. in. (1.6 liters). Bore & stroke: 3.23 x 2.98 in. Compression ratio: 9.0:1. Brake horsepower: 65 at 5200 R.P.M. Torque: 80 lbs.-ft. at 3200 R.P.M. Five main bearings. Hydraulic valve lifters. Carburetor: 2Bbl. VIN Code: C. BASE FOUR (Sunbird): Inline. Overhead cam. Four-cylinder. Cast iron block and aluminum head. Displacement: 109 cu. in. (1.8 liters). Bore & stroke: 3.34 x 3.13 in. Compression ratio: 8.8:1. Brake horsepower: 84 at 5200 R.P.M. Torque: 98 lbs.-ft. at 2800 R.P.M. Five main bearings. Hydraulic valve lifters. Electronic fuel injection. VIN Code: O. OPTIONAL TURBO FOUR (Sunbird): Same as 109 cu. in. four above, with multi-port fuel injection and turbocharger Compression ratio: 8.0:1. Horsepower: 150 at 5600 R.P.M. Torque: 150 lbs.-ft. at 2800 R.P.M. VIN Code: J. BASE FOUR (Fiero, Grand Am, Firebird, 6000): Inline. Overhead valve. Four-cylinder. Cast iron block and head. Displacement: 151 cu. in. (2.5 liters). Bore & stroke: 4.00 x 3.00 in. Compression ratio: 9.0:1. Brake horsepower: 92 at 4400 R.P.M. (Firebird, 88 at 4400). Torque: 132-134 lbs.-ft. at 2800 R.P.M. Five main bearings. Hydraulic valve lifters. Throttle-body fuel injection. VIN Code: R or U. OPTIONAL V-6 (6000): 60-degree, overhead valve six-cylinder. Cast iron block and aluminum head. Displacement: 173 cu. in. (2.8 liters). Bore & stroke: 3.50 x 3.00 in. Compression ratio: 8.50:1. Brake horsepower: 112 at 4800 R.P.M. Torque: 145 lbs.-ft. at 2100 R.P.M. Four main bearings. Hydraulic valve lifters. Carburetor: 2Bbl. VIN Code: X. BASE V-6 (Firebird SE, 6000 STE); OPTIONAL (Fiero, Firebird): Fuel-injected version of 173 cu. in. V-6 above Compression ratio: 8.9:1. Horsepower: 125 at 4800 R.P.M. (Fiero, 140 at 5200; Firebird, 135 at 5100) Torque: 155-175 lbs.-ft. at 3600 R.P.M. VIN Code: S, W or 9. BASE V-6 (Grand Am SE); OPTIONAL (Grand Am): 90-degree, overhead-valve V-6. Cast iron block and head. Displacement: 181 cu. in. (3.0 liters). Bore & stroke: 3.80 x 2.70 in. Compression ratio: 9.0:1. Brake horsepower: 125 at 4900 R.P.M. Torque: 150 lbs.-ft. at 2400 R.P.M. Four main bearings. Hydraulic valve lifters. Multi-port fuel injection. VIN Code: L. BASE V-6 (Grand Prix, Bonneville): 90-degree, overhead-valve V-6. Cast iron block and head. Displacement: 231 cu. in. (3.8 liters). Bore & stroke: 3.80 x 3.40 in. Compression ratio: 8.0:1. Brake horsepower: 110 at 3800 R.P.M. Torque: 190 lbs.-ft. at 1600 R.P.M. Four main bearings. Hydraulic valve lifters. Carburetor: 2Bbl. Buick- built. VIN Code: A. BASE V-6 (Parisienne): 90-degree, overhead-valve V-6. Cast iron block and head. Displacement: 262 cu. in. (4.3 liters). Bore & stroke: 4.00 x 3.48 in. Compression ratio: N/A. Brake horsepower: 130 at 3600 R.P.M. Torque: 210 lbs.-ft. at 2000 R.P.M. Four main bearings. Hydraulic valve lifters. Throttle-body fuel injection. VIN Code: Z. BASE V-8 (Firebird Trans Am, Parisienne wagon); OPTIONAL (Firebird, Grand Prix, Bonneville, Parisienne): 90-degree, overhead valve V-8. Cast iron block and head. Displacement: 305 cu. in. (5.0 liters). Bore & stroke: 3.74 x 3.48 in. Compression ratio: 9.5:1. Brake horsepower: 150 at 4200 R.P.M. (Trans Am, 155 at 4000; Parisienne, 165 at 4200). Torque: 235-245 lbs.-ft. at 2000-2400 R.P.M. Five main bearings. Hydraulic valve lifters. Carburetor: 4Bbl. Chevrolet-built. VIN Code: H. OPTIONAL V-8 (Trans Am): High-output version of 305 cu. in. V-8 Compression ratio: 9.5:1. Horsepower: 190 at 4800 R.P.M. Torque: 240 lbs.-ft. at 3200 R.P.M. VIN Code: G. OPTIONAL V-8 (Trans Am): Fuel-injected version of 305 cu. in. V-8 Horsepower: 205 at 4000 R.P.M. Torque: 270 lbs.-ft. at 3200 R.P.M. VIN Code: F.

CHASSIS DATA: Wheelbase: (Fiero) 93.4 in.; (1000 3dr.) 94.3 in.; (1000 5dr.) 97.3 in.; (Sunbird) 101.2 in.; (Grand Am) 103.4 in.; (Firebird) 101.0 in.; (6000) 104.9 in.; (Grand Prix) 108.1 in.; (Bonn.) 108.1 in.; (Parisienne) 116.0 in. Overall Length: (Fiero) 160.7 in.; (1000 3dr.) 161.9 in.; (1000 5dr.) 164.9 in.; (Sunbird) 175.4 in.; (Sunbird wag) 176.5 in.; (Grand Am) 177.5 in.; (Firebird) 188.1 in.; (6000) 188.8 in.; (6000 wag) 193.2 in.; (G.P.) 201.9 in.; (Bonn.) 200.2 in.; (Parisienne) 212.3 in.; (Parisienne wag) 215.1 in. Height: (Fiero) 46.9 in.; (1000) 52.8-52.9 in.; (Sunbird cpe) 51.9 in.; (Sunbird conv.) 52.7 in.; (Sunbird sed) 53.8 in.; (Sunbird wag) 54.1 in.; (Grand Am) 52.5 in.; (Firebird) 50.0 in.; (6000 cpe) 53.3 in.; (6000 sed) 53.7 in.; (6000 wag) 54.1 in.; (G.P.) 54.7 in.; (Bonn.) 55.8 in.; (Parisienne sed) 56.6 in.; (Parisienne wag) 57.4 in. Width: (Fiero) 68.9 in.; (1000) 61.8 in.; (Sunbird cpe/conv.) 65.9 in.; (Sunbird hatch) 66.6 in.; (Sunbird sed/wag) 66.2 in.; (Grand Am) 66.5 in.; (Firebird) 72.4 in.; (6000) 72.0 in.; (G.P.) 72.3 in.; (Bonn.) 71.6 in.; (Parisienne) 75.3 in. exc. wagon; 79.3 in. Front Tread: (Fiero) 57.8 in.; (1000) 51.2 in.; (Sunbird) 55.4 in.; (Grand Am) 55.5 in.; (Firebird) 60.7 in.; (6000) 58.7 in.; (G.P.) 58.5 in.; (Parisienne) 61.8 in.; (Parisienne wag) 62.2 in. Rear Tread: (Fiero) 58.7 in.; (1000) 51.2 in.; (Sunbird) 55.2 in.; (Grand Am) 55.2 in.; (Firebird) 61.6 in.; (6000) 57.0 in.; (G.P.) 57.8 in.; (Bonn.) 57.8 in.; (Parisienne) 60.7 in.; (Parisienne wag) 64.1 in. Standard Tires: (Fiero) P185/75R14 SBR BSW; (Fiero SE) P195/70R14; (1000) P155/80R13 GBR BSW; (Sunbird) P175/80R13 SBR BSW; (Grand Am) P185/80R13 SBR BSW; (Firebird) P215/65R15 SBR BSW; (6000) P185/75R14 SBR; (6000 STE) P195/70R14 SBR; (Grand Prix) P195/75R14 SBR BSW; (Bonn.) P195/75R14 SBR; (Parisienne sed) P205/75R15 SBR; (Parisienne wag) P225/75R15 SBR.

TECHNICAL: Transmission: Four-speed manual standard on Fiero V-6 and 1000. Five-speed manual standard on Fiero four, Sunbird, Firebird and Grand Am; optional on 1000. Three-speed Turbo Hydra-matic standard on other models. Four-speed overdrive automatic available on Firebird, 6000, Grand Prix, and Bonneville; standard on Parisienne. Standard final drive ratio: (Fiero) 2.48:1 w/5spd, 3.18:1 w/auto.; (Fiero V-6) 2.96:1 w/4spd, 3.06:1 w/auto.; (1000) 3.36:1 w/5spd, 3.43:1 w/auto.; (Sunbird) 2.55:1 w/5spd, 3.43:1 w/auto.; (Sunbird turbo 2.96:1 w/5spd, 3.33:1 w/auto.; (Grand Am) 2.48:1 w/5spd, 2.84:1 w/auto.; (Firebird) 3.73:1 or 3.70:1 w/four, 3.42:1 w/V-6, 2.77:1 w/V-8; (Trans Am) 3.27:1 except 3.70:1 w/H.O. V-8; (6000) 2.39:1 w/four, 2.84:1 w/auto.; (6000 STE) 3.18:1; (Grand Prix/Bonneville) 2.41:1; (Parisienne) 2.56:1; (Parisienne wagon) 2.73:1. Steering/Suspension/Brakes/Body: same as 1985, except anti- lock braking on 6000 STE. Fuel Tank: (Fiero) 10.2 gal.; (1000) 12.2 gal.; (Sunbird) 13.6 gal.; (Grand Am) 13.6 gal.; (Firebird) 15.5 gal.; (6000) 15.7 gal.; (Grand Prix/Bonneville) 18.1 gal.; (Parisienne sed) 25 gal.; (Parisienne wag) 22 gal.

DRIVETRAIN OPTIONS: Engines: Turbo 1.8-liter four: Sunbird ($1511) except SE conv. ($1296; std. on GT. 173 cu. in., 2Bbl. V-6: 6000 ($435). 173 cu. in., FI V-6: Fiero ($645); Firebird ($350); 6000 ($560). 181 cu. in. V-6: Grand Am ($610). 262 cu. in. V-6: Grand Prix ($150). 305 cu. in., 4Bbl. V-8: Firebird ($750); Firebird SE ($400); Grand Prix/Bonneville ($540); Parisienne ($390). H.O. 305 cu. in. V-8, 4Bbl. or FI: Trans Am ($695). Transmission/Differential: Four-speed manual trans.: Fiero SE ($50 credit); Sunbird ($75 credit). Five-speed manual trans.: 1000 ($75); Sunbird GT ($75). Three-speed automatic trans.: Fiero ($465); Fiero GT ($515); 1000 ($425); Sunbird ($390- $465); Grand Am ($465). Four-speed automatic trans.: Firebird ($465); 6000/Grand Prix/Bonneville/Parisienne ($175). Limited-slip differential: Firebird/G.P./Bonn./Parisienne ($100). Brakes/Steering: Power brakes: 1000 ($100). Power four-wheel disc brakes: Firebird ($179) but (NC) w/performance pkg. Power steering: 1000/Sunbird ($215). Suspension: Rally tuned susp.: Fiero/Sunbird/Grand Am/6000/G.P./Parisienne ($50). Superlift shock absorbers: 6000/G.P./Bonn./Parisienne ($64). H.D. springs: Parisienne ($16). Other: H.D. cooling ($40-$70). H.D. battery ($26). H.D. alternator ($25-$51). Engine block heater ($18-$19). California emissions ($99).

OPTION PACKAGES: 1000 sport/handling pkg. ($358). 1000 custom trim ($151). Sunbird custom exterior group ($86). Sunbird custom trim group ($244-$493). Sunbird security pkg. ($19). Firebird Trans Am special performance pkg. ($664). Firebird luxury interior trim ($349-$359). 6000 custom exterior ($56). Grand Prix Brougham Landau pkg. ($469). Lamp groups ($21-$47).

MAJOR CONVENIENCE/APPEARANCE OPTIONS: Air conditioning ($645-$750). Cruise control ($175); N/A on 1000. Power seat ($215-$225); N/A on 1000/Fiero. Dual eight- way power seats: 6000 STE ($508). Power windows ($195-$285); N/A on 1000. Cornering lamps: Bonn./G.P. ($68); Parisienne ($55). Power glass sunroof: Parisienne ($1230). Removable glass sunroof: Fiero/Sunbird/Grand Am/6000 ($310). Hatch roof: Firebird/Grand Prix ($850-$886). Full vinyl roof: Bonneville ($160). Padded landau roof: G.P. ($245-$322). Padded full vinyl roof: Bonn. ($245); Parisienne ($185). Rear spoiler: Fiero ($269); Firebird SE ($70). Louvered rear sunshields: Sunbird ($199); Firebird ($210); Trans Am ($95).. Two-tone paint: Sunbird ($101-$151); Grand Am ($101); Firebird/6000 ($205); G.P./Bonn. ($205); Parisienne sed ($205). Recaro bucket seats: Firebird ($636-$995).

HISTORY: Introduced: October 3, 1985 except Grand Am, August 28, 1985 and Fiero, January 3, 1986. Model year production: 952,943. Calendar year production (U.S.): 775,247. Calendar year sales by U.S. dealers: 841,441. Model year sales by U.S. dealers: 840,137.

Historical Footnotes: Pontiac's anti-lock braking (ABS), like that of other GM divisions, came from the Teves organization in West Germany. The division's market share rose by one percent in model year 1986, as a result of moderately increased sales. Even with V-6 power available, Fiero sales continued below the anticipated level, and fell this year (though over 71,000 did find customers). Grand Am, on the other hand, wasn't so far from doubling its 1985 sales total. Pontiac's version of the Nbody design attracted considerably more buyers than the equivalents from Buick and Oldsmobile. Firebird sales slipped a bit, but the Trans Am remained popular. Grand Prix and Bonneville declined rather sharply. Poor sales of the subcompact 1000 prompted its discontinuance for 1987, when a new front-drive Bonneville would appear. Pontiac was also planning to introduced a Korean import under the LeMans name for 1987.

ALTERNATIVE CARS

The information that you will find in the 'Alternative Cars' section of *The Standard Catalog of American Cars 1976-1986* covers lesser known American made cars. In the majority of cases, these are models actually built inside the borders of the United States. However, a handful of makes built by Americans in other countries — primarily for the U.S. market — are discussed.

1976 Mohs Ostentatienne Opera Sedan

Types of cars covered range from $100,000-plus exotics to Volkswagen based kits which, in some cases, originally sold for below $5,000. The cars are listed by model name, rather than the name of the manufacturer. We decided to go this route because collectors attending shows and auctions tend to relate to these cars by the name on the radiator or body badge, rather than the factory door.

Circa 1976 Alfa Romeo race car

For some of these cars, rather extensive amounts of information were readily available — specifications down to bore and stroke and gas tank capacity. In other cases, little more than a sales brochure listing minimal technical data could be found. Therefore, some listings will be quite short, while others are lengthy and include specifications.

For some marques that entered series production — such as Excalibur — the entries are broken out by model year and the photos are arranged accordingly. In other cases, a single entry covers a range of years. As you can imagine, when a photo is presented, most of the data

1978 Excalibur Series III SS roadster

relates to the history of the company in the same year as shown in the photo. For example, if you see a picture of a 1979 Auburn boattail replica, the information most likely applies to the 1979 model year only.

1983 Duntov Turbo Vette

At the rear of the Alternative Cars section, there are two pages of late listings. These photos and accompanying information arrived at Krause Publications after the pages in this book had been pasted up, but we thought you'd want to have the extra models included in this initial attempt to 'catalog' America's late-model alternatives to Detroit-built vehicles.

1983 Stutz Blackhawk VII coupe

Naturally, the process of cataloging is an ongoing one and we fully expect this section to expand and improve over the years. We invite all automotive enthusiasts, students of history or those involved in the alternative car industries to help us gather additional facts, specifications and photos for such purposes. Contributions can be send to: Krause Publications, 700 E. State St., Iola, WI 54990.

A

Circa 1976 Alfa Romeo race car

ALFA ROMEO — Antique and Classic Cars, Inc., of Buffalo, N.Y. marketed this early fiberglass bodied kit car. It is a copy of a 1931 Alfa Romeo two-man race car. The kit sold for $895 in 1976. It is designed for the Volkswagen chassis and drivetrain. Assembly time required was advertised as 70 hours. No special mechanical skills were needed to build the kit the manufacturer claimed.

1980 Allison TD replica roadster

ALLISON MG-TD — Allison Replicars, Ltd., of Port Orange, Fla., had been producing this car seven years by 1980. The company's literature promised a flawless, wave-free fiberglass body, original TD side curtains, door locks and hinges and hand-rolled pleated upholstery. Specifications that matched the original TD exactly included height (52.9 in.), width (58.6 in.), overall length (144 in.) and height from ground to top of radiator (38 in.). However, at 1,550 lbs., the Allison kit was 55 lbs. lighter than the authentic item, despite its ½ in. longer (94.5 in.) wheelbase. It used the 96.6 cid Volkswagen ohv six giving 72 hp at 4400 RPM. The Allison TD came with Michelin XZX steel-belted radial tires and optional real wire wheels with splined knock-off hubs. The windshield was exactly like the original and folded down, but the floorpan was of modern fiberglass. Allison promised 39-41 mpg driving economy.

1980 American Turbo T-top coupe

AMERICAN TURBO — This vehicle represented an extensive modification of the Chevrolet Corvette done by American Custom Industries, Inc., a company which maintained its world headquarters in Sylvania, Ohio. The Coachworks Division specialized in building special edition American Turbo, GT and Sports Wagon editions of the Corvette. The company also had a Fiberglass Division that produced bolt-on aftermarket body panels for Corvettes. R. Schuller was its president and M. Lavine was vice-president. The firm had some 40 employees and later opened a European branch in Spain. A stock Corvette engine was maintained, using the 350 cid version with 8.5:1 compression ratio in 1980. Also kept was the factory's rear wheel drive set up, gear box (optional Turbo-Hydramatic) and eight-inch wide tires of size HR60x15 in front and LR60x15 in rear. The Corvette ladder frame chassis with crossmembers was used, plus front and rear independent suspension. Disc brakes with an 11.75 in. diameter and internal radial fins were also standard on the $32,000 American Turbo. It had a 98 in. wheelbase, 61 in. front track; 62 in. rear track and overall length of 3,320 lbs. Delco-Remy's "High-Energy" ignition system was used and retractable headlamps were featured. The rear axle had a 3.360:1 ratio. Other features included Deluxe upholstery; LED read-out gauge cluster and front and rear remote radar detectors, which owners needed when approaching the claimed top speed of 130 mph. Some 40 cars were produced in 1981, perhaps a typical year's business. Later, in 1983, the company marketed the same basic car under the name Duntov Turbo Convertible (although it was still actually a T-top coupe) using a 240 hp version of the 350 cid Chevy V-8. By that time, the price had increased to $38,500 for the base version and $55,000 for a Phase III edition (with a 500 hp engine and 148 mph top speed). Of course, cruise control, electric windows and doors, air conditioning, P-radial tires, modular wheels and a wood interior trim package had been added to the standard equipment list.

1980 Auburn dual cowl Phaeton

1981 Auburn boattail speedster

AUBURN BOATTAIL — Auburn Cord Duesenberg Motor Co., of Los Angeles, Calif., sold two- and four-passenger Auburn boattail speedster replicas patterned after the original 1934-1935 Classic. Ford 351, 400 or 429 cid V-8s were available in the tubular steel X-frame chassis. The car has a 132 inch wheelbase and 211 in. length and weighs about 4,200 lbs. Factory air conditioning, power steering, a tilt steering wheel, power brakes, tinted glass, racing type exhaust manifolds were standard equipment. Brass or gold plating was optional at extra cost. The fully-assembled replicar was base priced at $27,500 in 1981.

1980 Auburn 886 boattail speedster

AUBURN 886 — Classic Cars of London, Ontario (Canada) produced a complete ready-to-drive replica of the 1935 Auburn Model 851 speedster. The Auburn 886 has a fiberglass body and came with 302 cid Ford or 305 cid Chevrolet V-8 engines. Select Shift automatic transmission is standard. The car has a 127 in. wheelbase, 191 in. overall length and weighs in at 3,200 lbs.

AUBURN SPEEDSTER — V-8 — Glenn Pray's Auburn replica (listed below) had been around for a decade, but wasn't alone. This version was turned out by a separate company in Buffalo, New York. Like Pray's, it had a fiberglass body, but with a smaller Ford V-8 engine (351 cu. in.). SelectShift CruiseOMatic was standard. The company was purchased in 1973 by F.P. Pro, president of Glassic (listed separately), and production transferred to Florida.

I.D. DATA: Not available.

AUBURN SPEEDSTER (V-8)

Model Number	Body/Style Number	Body Type & Seating	Factory Price	Shipping Weight	Production Total
N/A	N/A	2-dr. Roadster-2P	18000	N/A	N/A

ENGINE DATA: BASE V-8: 90-degree, overhead valve V-8. Cast iron block and head. Displacement: 351 cu. in. (5.8 liters). Bore & stroke: 4.00 x 3.50. Compression ratio: 9.0:1. Brake horsepower: 240 at 4600 R.P.M. Torque: 353 lbs.-ft. at 2600 R.P.M. Five main bearings. Hydraulic valve lifters. Carburetor: 2Bbl. Ford-built.

CHASSIS DATA: Wheelbase: N/A. Overall Length: N/A. Height: N/A. Width: N/A. Front Tread: 63.3 in. Rear Tread: 64.3 in. Standard Tires: 8.20 x 15.

TECHNICAL: Transmission: Three-speed Select-Shift Cruise-O-Matic standard, with limited-slip differential. Standard final drive ratio: N/A. Steering: N/A. Suspension: Front coil springs w/lower trailing arms and anti-sway bar; rigid rear axle w/lower trailing radium arms, upper torque arms, transverse linkage bar and coil springs. Brakes: Drum (11 in. dia.). Body construction: Fiberglass body on separate box-type ladder frame. Fuel Tank: N/A.

OPTIONS: Air conditioning.

MANUFACTURER: Auburn Motor Car Corp., Palm Beach, Florida. Founded in 1973, after purchase of Auburn Speedsters Company from Daniel Lauricella of Buffalo, New York. Company president was F.P. Pro. (also president of Glassic). Production continued after 1976 under the name Replicars.

AUBURN SPEEDSTER — V-8 — Glenn Pray, who produced the first 1937 Cord replicas in 1964, started turning out Auburns in 1967, powered by large-block Ford V-8 engines on a modified Ford Galaxie chassis. Production at his Oklahoma plant continued through the 1970s. In addition to the authentically-styled Model 866 speedster, Pray offered a Model 874 dual-cowl phaeton that followed the speedster's lines but had never existed in the 1930s. Bodies were fiberglass, thus lighter in weight than the original.

I.D. DATA: Not available.

AUBURN SPEEDSTER (V-8)

Model Number	Body/Style Number	Body Type & Seating	Factory Price	Shipping Weight	Production Total
866	N/A	2-dr. Roadster-2P	24900	3200	Note 1

AUBURN PHAETON (V-8)

874	N/A	4-dr. Phaeton-4P	60000	4100	Note 1

Note 1: Total production was 12 cars in 1977, 14 cars in 1978, and 15 cars in 1979; further data not available.

PRICE NOTE: Prices and specifications shown are for 1978 models.

ENGINE DATA: BASE V-8: 90-degree, overhead valve V-8. Cast iron block and head. Displacement: 460 cu. in. (7.5 liters). Bore & stroke: 4.36 x 3.85 in. Compression ratio: 8.0:1. Brake horsepower: 208 at 4000 R.P.M. Torque: 356 lbs.-ft. at 2000 R.P.M. Five main earings. Hydraulic valve lifters. Carburetor: 4Bbl. Motorcraft 9510. Built by Ford (Lincoln).

CHASSIS DATA: Wheelbase: (spdstr) 127 in.; (phaeton) 140 in. Overall Length: (spdstr) 191 in.; (phaeton) 204 in. Height: 58 in. Front Tread: 63 in. Rear Tread: 65 in. Standard Tires: JR78 x 15.

TECHNICAL: Transmission: Three-speed SelectShift automatic standard. Gear ratios: (1st) 2.46:1; (2nd) 1.46:1; (3rd) 1.00:1; (Rev) 2.18:1. Standard final drive ratio: 2.75:1. Steering: Recirculating ball. Suspension: Front coil springs w/lower trailing arms and anti-sway bar; rigid rear axle w/lower trailing radium arms, upper torque arms, transverse linkage bar and coil springs. Brakes: Front disc, rear drum. Body construction: Fiberglass body on separate box-type ladder frame. Fuel Tank: (spdstr) 18 gal.; (phaeton) 25 gal.

OPTIONS: Wire wheels. Speedster could also have air conditioning. and a tonneau cover, which were standard on the phaeton.

MANUFACTURER: Auburn-Cord-Duesenberg Co., Broken Arrow, Oklahoma. G.A. Pray, president.

AUBURN SPEEDSTER/PHAETON — V-12 AND V-8 — Elegant Motors was another producer of Auburn replicas, mainly in kit form, offered first with a Jaguar V-12 engine, later with a Corvette V-8. A factory flyer admitted that its reproduction was not an exact-scale replica, but boasted a large selection of authentic features.

I.D. DATA: Not available.

AUBURN SPEEDSTER (V-8)

Model Number	Body/Style Number	Body Type & Seating	Factory Price	Shipping Weight	Production Total
856	N/A	2-dr. Roadster-2P	37000	3000	Note 1

AUBURN PHAETON (V-8)

898	N/A	4-dr. Phaeton-4P	50000	N/A	Note 1

Note 1: Total production was 160 cars in 1981 and 140 in 1982; other data N/A.

PRICE NOTE: Prices and specifications shown are for 1977 models.

ENGINE DATA: BASE V-12 (1977-80): 60-degree, overhead-cam V-12. Aluminum block and head. Displacement: 326 cu. in. (5.3 liters). Bore & stroke: 3.54 x 2.76 in. Brake horsepower: 288 at 5750 R.P.M. Torque: 295 lb.-ft. at 3500 R.P.M. Seven main bearings. Lucas Bosch EFI. Jaguar-built. BASE V-8 (1981-84): 90-degree, overhead valve V-8. Cast iron block and head. Displacement: 350 cu. in. (5.7 liters). Bore & stroke: 4.00 x 3.00 in. Compression ratio: 8.9:1. Brake horsepower: 230 at 5200 R.P.M. Torque: 275 lbs.-ft. at 3600 R.P.M. Five main bearings. Hydraulic valve lifters. Carburetor: 4Bbl. Rochester. Built by Chevrolet.

CHASSIS DATA: Wheelbase: 128 in. Overall Length: 203.9 in. Height: 57.1 in. Standard Tires: P205/70VR15 (later P225/70R15).

TECHNICAL: Transmission: Four-speed manual standard. Gear ratios (early models): (1st) 3.24:1; (2nd) 1.90:1; (3rd) 1.39:1; (4th) 1.00:1; (Rev) 3.43:1. Standard final drive ratio: 3.07:1. Steering: Recirculating ball. Suspension: Front coil springs w/anti-sway bar; independent rear w/transverse leaf spring. Brakes: Front disc, rear drum (later all-disc). Body construction: Fiberglass body on separate box-type ladder frame. Fuel Tank: 20 gal. (later 24).

OPTIONS: Dual exhausts. Supercharger. Air conditioning. Power windows. Leather upholstery. Tonneau cover.

MANUFACTURER: Elegant Motors Inc., Indianapolis, Indiana. Established 1971; production began in 1974.

AUBURN SPEEDSTER — V-8 — Of the several companies that produced Auburn speedster replicas, California Custom Coachworks ranked among the best, according to many observers. Production of an 876 Speedster began in 1976, mainly in kit form; a phaeton in 1978. By 1979, the company's focus had shifted to fully assembled cars rather than kits.

I.D. DATA: Not available.

AUBURN SPEEDSTER (V-8)

Model Number	Body/Style Number	Body Type & Seating	Factory Price	Shipping Weight	Production Total
876	N/A	2-dr. Roadster-2P	37500	3200	N/A

ENGINE DATA: BASE V-8: 90-degree, overhead valve V-8. Cast iron block and head. Displacement: 400 cu. in. (6.6 liters). Brake horsepower: 159 at 3400 R.P.M. Five main bearings. Hydraulic valve lifters. Carburetor: 2Bbl. Built by Ford.

CHASSIS DATA: Wheelbase: 127 in. Overall Length: 191 in. Height: 58 in. Front Tread: 63 in. Rear Tread: 65 in.

TECHNICAL: Transmission: Three-speed automatic standard. Standard final drive ratio: N/A. Steering: N/A. Suspension: N/A. Brakes: N/A. Body construction: Fiberglass body on separate frame.

OPTIONS: N/A.

MANUFACTURER: California Custom Coach, Pasadena, California.

1982 Aurora Cobra roadster

AURORA COBRA — A high output 302 cid Ford V-8 powers the Aurora MKII, a replica of the legendary Shelby Cobra race car. It utilizes a Jaguar suspension and rear differential. Aurora Cars Ltd., a Canadian firm located in Richmond Hill, Ontario, said it hoped to sell 100 units of the $36,000 replicar.

1976 Avanti II coupe

1976 AVANTI II

AVANTI II — MODEL RQ-B — V-8 — The original Studebaker-based Avanti (which means 'forward' in Italian) had been conceived in 1962 by Sherwood Egbert, then president of Studebaker. Design was supervised by the renowned Raymond Loewy, heading a team of three that supposedly finished the job in two weeks. Press reports at the time called Avanti the "best looking thing on wheels." When Studebaker ceased production in South Bend, Indiana in 1964, the end of Avanti seemed certain. While the company moved briefly into Canada before expiring completely, production there included only ordinary passenger models. Both the Avanti and GT Hawk were abandoned. Long-time Studebaker-Packard dealers Nathaniel (Nate) Altman and Leo Newman came to the rescue, after trying to interest other automakers in taking over Avanti production. They bought part of the vacated Studebaker factory and all the dies, parts and rights to the Avanti. After forming Avanti Motor Corp. in 1965, they began production on a limited basis, using Chevrolet Corvette drivetrains. Fortunately for admirers of the body lines, they retained the original design with little modification, apart from a slight upward tilting of the front end to accommodate the different engine size. The fiberglass body was supplied by Molded Fiber-Glass of Ashtabula, Ohio (which also made the Corvette body). Though running changes have been the practice throughout Avanti's history, the basic design has continued with surprisingly little alteration. Changes have been made to improve the car's ride, handling and performance, as well as to comply with safety standards. Although there have been, and continue to be, Avanti dealers, many purchasers picked up their cars at South Bend, where they could also get a tour of the facility. Original Avantis were collectible from the beginning, even while Studebaker Corp. was still in operation. The same has

been true of the Avanti II. Partly because of the timeless design, partly as a result of the limited numbers produced, few cars have consistently held their value as well. That fact is hardly ignored in advertising for the current models. The 1976 version, like each of its predecessors, was little changed in appearance—difficult to distinguish from the original. The price, however, was up to $12,195 (from $9945 a year earlier). Single round headlamps sat in recessed rectangular housings. An 'Avanti II' nameplate was on the front panel, and on the decklid. Narrow vertical marker lenses stood at the very tip of front fenders. Below the thin front bumper was an air intake. Inside features included Stewart-Warner gauges and recessed rocker-type safety switches. Standard equipment included Turbo Hydra-matic, collapsible steering post, heavy-duty adjustable shocks, F78 whitewalls, and a 400 cu. in. Corvette engine with dual exhausts. A hand-crafted tool pouch went in the trunk. Inside were a padded roll bar, electric clock, vanity tray, console, vacuum gauge, 160 MPH speedometer, tachometer, and command center high-back bucket seats. Other features included hydraulic front bumper guards and a locking gas filler door. Avanti's reinforced fiberglass body sat on a heavy-duty Xmember steel frame (actually derived from the 1962 Studebaker Wagonaire). The rear axle held radius rods, and both front and rear had stabilizer bars. Up front were power disc brakes; in back, new duo-servo self-adjusting rear brakes, and a booster with proportioning valve. Production methods differed completely from all other domestics. Avantis were "produced with careful, handcraft methods with a cadre of genuine automobile mechanics assigned total responsibility for each automobile." The body itself had 117 fiberglass parts. Assembly and finishing took 2-3 months. Every car was water-tested (the only car manufacturer to do so) and got a 150-250 mile road test. Acrylic lacquer paint could be ordered in any automotive color. Earlier buyers could have chosen the famous Hurst four-speed stick shift instead of automatic, but that option (while still mentioned in literature) had been dropped in 1974. Interiors came in 400 upholstery choices—and the company would even agree to install a completely different fabric, supplied by the customer. Though not quite sports-car caliber in terms of handling, Avanti was no slouch at performance, able to manage a 0-60 time of around 8 seconds. Rather loud exhausts had been an Avanti trademark from the beginning, a result of low-restriction mufflers.

I.D. DATA: Not available.

AVANTI II (V-8)

Model Number	Body/Style Number	Body Type & Seating	Factory Price	Shipping Weight	Production Total
RQ-B	N/A	2-dr. HT Spt Cpe-4P	12195	3250	175

ENGINE DATA: BASE V-8: 90-degree, overhead valve V-8. Cast iron block and head. Displacement: 400 cu. in. (6.6 liters). Bore & stroke: 4.13 x 3.75 in. Compression ratio: 8.5:1. Brake horsepower: 175 at 3600 R.P.M. Torque: 305 lbs.-ft. at 2000 R.P.M. Five main bearings. Hydraulic valve lifters. Carburetor: 4Bbl. Rochester. Chevrolet-built.

CHASSIS DATA: Wheelbase: 109 in. Overall Length: 197.5 in. Height: 54.0 in. Width: 70.4 in. Front Tread: 57.4 in. Rear Tread: 56.6 in. Wheel Size: 5.5 or 6 in. x 15. Standard Tires: F78 x 15.

TECHNICAL: Transmission: Three-speed Turbo Hydra-matic standard. Gear ratios: (1st) 2.48:1; (2nd) 1.48:1; (3rd) 1.00:1; (Rev) 2.00:1. Standard final drive ratio: 3.31:1. Steering: Worm and roller. Suspension: Front coil springs, control arms and anti-sway bar; rigid rear axle w/upper torque arms, semi-elliptic leaf springs and anti-sway bar. Brakes: Front disc, rear drum. Body construction: Fiberglass body on box-type ladder frame. Fuel Tank: 19 gal.

OPTIONS: Twin traction limited-slip differential ($100). Power steering ($100). Air conditioning ($425). Cruise control ($125). Electric door locks ($100). Electric windows ($100). Electric trunk release ($50). Tilt steering ($100). Rear window electric deicer ($100). Lucas fog or driving lights ($60). Right side mirror ($15). Left remote-control mirror ($25). Blaupunkt AM/FM stereo with four speakers ($250). Blaupunkt Berlin ultra super signal-seeking radio w/cassette and automatic antenna ($1200). Stereo 8track player ($150). Stereo cassette player ($200). Rear electric antenna ($25). Automatic electric antenna ($75). Electric sunroof ($695). Electric moonroof ($995). Door and fender protectors ($25). Luggage rack ($100). Sound deadener ($40). Sun band in windshield ($25). Tinted side windows ($25). Decorator fabric or custom vinyl interior ($100). Contemporary imported fabrics ($300). Suede and leather interiors ($900). Luxury shag and plush "home" carpeting ($100). Removable front or rear seat center armrest ($25-$50). Genuine wood veneer dash and console panels ($250). Luxury trunk carpet ($50). Magnum 500 chrome wheels with bullet hubs ($300). Borrani wire wheels with knockoff hubs ($1450). Whitewall radial tires ($250). Boat trailer hitch ($100).

MANUFACTURER: Avanti Motor Corp., South Bend, Indiana. CEO and president, N.D. (Nate) Altman. Established 1965. 95 workers.

1977 AVANTI II

AVANTI II — MODEL RQ-B — V-8 — As usual, little change in appearance was evident this year. Under the hood, however, the former 400 cu. in. V-8 dropped away, replaced by a 350 cu. in. V-8 engine (again from Chevrolet).

I.D. DATA: Not available.

AVANTI II (V-8)

Model Number	Body/Style Number	Body Type & Seating	Factory Price	Shipping Weight	Production Total
RQ-B	N/A	2-dr. HT Spt Cpe-4P	13195	3250	180

ENGINE DATA: BASE V-8: 90-degree, overhead valve V-8. Cast iron block and head. Displacement: 350 cu. in. (5.7 liters). Bore & stroke: 4.00 x 3.48 in. Compression ratio: 8.2:1. Brake horsepower: 180 at 4000 R.P.M. Torque: 270 lbs.-ft. at 2400 R.P.M. Five main bearings. Hydraulic valve lifters. Carburetor: 4Bbl. Rochester 17056220. Dual exhausts. Chevrolet-built.

CHASSIS DATA: same as 1976.

TECHNICAL: same as 1976.

MAJOR OPTIONS: Air conditioning. Power sunroof. Tinted glass. Cruise control. Power steering. Tilt steering wheel. Power windows. Leather upholstery. Foglamps. Magnum 500 chrome wheels. Borrani wire wheels. Rear window deicer. Note: Additional options similar to 1976.

MANUFACTURER: Avanti Motor Corp., South Bend, Indiana.

1978 AVANTI II

AVANTI II — MODEL RQ-B — V-8 — Standard equipment now included air conditioning, tinted glass, and a back window deicer. Otherwise, appearance and equipment changed little.

I.D. DATA: Not available.

AVANTI II (V-8)

Model Number	Body/Style Number	Body Type & Seating	Factory Price	Shipping Weight	Production Total
RQ-B	N/A	2-dr. HT Spt Cpe-4P	15970	3250	190

ENGINE DATA: BASE V-8: 90-degree, overhead valve V-8. Cast iron block and head. Displacement: 350 cu. in. (5.7 liters). Bore & stroke: 4.00 x 3.48 in. Compression ratio: 8.2:1. Brake horsepower: 180 at 4000 R.P.M. Torque: 270 lbs.-ft. at 2400 R.P.M. Five main bearings. Hydraulic valve lifters. Carburetor: 4Bbl. Rochester 17058202. Dual exhausts. Chevrolet-built.

CHASSIS DATA: Wheelbase: 109 in. Overall Length: 197.8 in. Height: 54.4 in. Width: 70.4 in. Front Tread: 57.4 in. Rear Tread: 56.6 in. Wheel Size: 6 in. x 15 in. Standard Tires: F78 x 15.

TECHNICAL: Transmission: Three-speed Turbo Hydra-matic standard. Gear ratios: (1st) 2.52:1; (2nd) 1.52:1; (3rd) 1.00:1; (Rev) 1.94:1. Standard final drive ratio: 3.07:1. Steering: Cam and lever. Suspension: Front coil springs, control arms and anti-sway bar; rigid rear axle w/upper torque arms, semi-elliptic leaf springs and anti-sway bar. Brakes: Front disc, rear drum. Body construction: Fiberglass body on box-type ladder frame. Fuel Tank: 19 gal.

MAJOR OPTIONS: Power sunroof ($695). Cruise control ($125). Power windows ($100). Power door locks ($100). Stereo 8-track ($150). Stereo cassette player ($200). Suede and leather upholstery ($800). Reclining front seats ($100). Foglamps. Luggage rack ($100). Borrani wire wheels ($1450). Premium radial WSW tires ($250).

Note: Additional options similar to 1976.

MANUFACTURER: Avanti Motor Corp., South Bend, Indiana.

1979 AVANTI II

AVANTI II — MODEL RQ-B — V-8 — Once again, Avanti appearance and equipment changed little. Sole engine was again Chevrolet's 350 cu. in. V-8 with dual exhausts and Turbo Hydra-matic. Standard equipment included power brakes and steering, tilt steering wheel, air conditioning, windshield sun band, tinted side windows, Blaupunkt AM/FM stereo with four speakers, rear window electric de-icer, radial glass-belted whitewalls, and rear electric AM/FM/CB antenna. Interiors came in decorator fabric or custom vinyl. Acrylic lacquer paint could be in any automotive color. Adjustable heavy-duty shocks were standard, along with front and rear anti-sway bars. The dash held a 160 MPH speedometer and tachometer; in the trunk, a handcrafted tool pouch.

I.D. DATA: Not available.

AVANTI II (V-8)

Model Number	Body/Style Number	Body Type & Seating	Factory Price	Shipping Weight	Production Total
RQ-B	N/A	2-dr. HT Spt Cpe-4P	17670	3570	195

ENGINE DATA: BASE V-8: 90-degree, overhead valve V-8. Cast iron block and head. Displacement: 350 cu. in. (5.7 liters). Bore & stroke: 4.00 x 3.48 in. Compression ratio: 8.2:1. Brake horsepower: 185 at 4000 R.P.M. Torque: 280 lbs.-ft. at 2400 R.P.M. Five main bearings. Hydraulic valve lifters. Carburetor: 4Bbl. Rochester 17059202. Dual exhausts. Chevrolet-built.

CHASSIS DATA: Wheelbase: 109 in. Overall Length: 197.8 in. Height: 54.4 in. Width: 70.4 in. Front Tread: 57.4 in. Rear Tread: 56.6 in. Wheel Size: 8 in. x 15 in. Standard Tires: P225/70R15.

TECHNICAL: Transmission: Three-speed Turbo Hydra-matic standard. Gear ratios: (1st) 2.52:1; (2nd) 1.52:1; (3rd) 1.00:1; (Rev) 1.93:1. Standard final drive ratio: 3.55:1. Steering: Cam and lever. Suspension: Front coil springs, control arms and anti-sway bar; rigid rear axle w/radius rods, semi-elliptic leaf springs and anti-sway bar. Brakes: Front disc, rear drum. Body construction: Fiberglass body on box-type ladder frame. Fuel Tank: 19 gal.

OPTIONS: Cruise control ($125). Electric moonroof ($995). Electric sunroof ($695). Electric windows ($150). Electric door locks ($125). Electric trunk release ($50). Intermittent wipers ($50). AM/FM stereo with 8-track ($100); w/cassette ($150); with CB ($200). Truck mount CB ($350). Cibie fog or driving lamps ($70). Fixed right mirror ($15). Luggage rack, trunk- mount ($100). Reclining seat, driver's or passenger's ($100 each). Two front Recaro seats ($1100). Suede and leather interiors ($1000). Wood veneer dash and console panels ($250). Trunk mat ($50). Removable wire wheel covers ($200). Wire wheels ($1450). Magnum 500 wheels ($350). Steel belted radial whitewalls ($350). Boat trailer hitch ($50).

MANUFACTURER: Avanti Motor Corp., South Bend, Indiana.

1980 AVANTI II

AVANTI II — MODEL RQ-B — V-8 — Appearance of the Studebaker-derived Avanti changed little this year. Standard equipment included air conditioning, power brakes and steering, tilt steering, AM/FM stereo, rear window de-icer, tinted glass, tilt steering wheel, and built-in headrests. Automatic transmission and power windows also were standard. The AM/FM/CB radio came with a retractable antenna.

I.D. DATA: Not available.

AVANTI II (V-8)

Model Number	Body/Style Number	Body Type & Seating	Factory Price	Shipping Weight	Production Total
RQ-B	N/A	2-dr. HT Spt Cpe-4P	18995	3570	190

ENGINE DATA: BASE V-8: 90-degree, overhead valve V-8. Cast iron block and head. Displacement: 350 cu. in. (5.7 liters). Bore & stroke: 4.00 x 3.48 in. Compression ratio: 8.2:1. Brake horsepower: 190 at 4400 R.P.M. Torque: 280 lbs.-ft. at 2400 R.P.M. Five main bearings. Hydraulic valve lifters. Carburetor: 4Bbl. Rochester 17059207. Dual exhausts. Chevrolet-built.

CHASSIS DATA: same as 1979.

TECHNICAL: Transmission: Three-speed Turbo Hydra-matic 400 standard. Gear ratios: (1st) 2.48:1; (2nd) 1.48:1; (3rd) 1.00:1; (Rev) 2.07:1. Standard final drive ratio: 3.07:1. Steering: Cam and lever. Suspension: Front coil springs, control arms and anti-sway bar. Brakes: Front disc, rear drum. Body construction: Fiberglass body on box-type ladder frame. Fuel Tank: 19 gal.

MAJOR OPTIONS: Cruise control ($150). Electric moonroof ($995). Electric sunroof. Foglamps. Electric windows ($150). Power door locks ($125). Luggage rack ($100). Recaro front seats ($1100). Suede and leather interiors ($1200). Reclining front seats ($100 each). Wood veneer dash and console panels. Wire wheels. Magnum 500 wheels ($350).

Note: Complete option list N/A; similar to 1979.

MANUFACTURER: Avanti Motor Corp., South Bend, Indiana.

1981 Avanti II coupe

1981 AVANTI II

AVANTI II — V-8 — As usual, the 1981 Avanti differed little from the 1980 version. Under the hood, though, was a significant change: a shift from the 350 cu. in. V-8 to a 305 V-8 (again from Chevrolet). Standard equipment included air conditioning, heated rear window, tinted glass, AM/FM/CB stereo radio, tilt steering wheel, power brakes and steering, limited-slip differential, and built-in headrests.

I.D. DATA: Not available.

AVANTI II (V-8)

Model Number	Body/Style Number	Body Type & Seating	Factory Price	Shipping Weight	Production Total
RQ-B	N/A	2-dr. HT Spt Cpe-4P	20495	3570	200

ENGINE DATA: BASE V-8: 90-degree, overhead valve V-8. Cast iron block and head. Displacement: 305 cu. in. (5.7 liters). Bore & stroke: 3.74 x 3.48 in. Compression ratio: 8.6:1. Brake horsepower: 155 at 4000 R.P.M. Torque: 240 lbs.-ft. at 1600 R.P.M. Five main bearings. Hydraulic valve lifters. Carburetor: 4Bbl. Rochester. Chevrolet-built.

CHASSIS DATA: Same as 1979-80.

TECHNICAL: Transmission: Three-speed Turbo Hydra-matic 350 standard. Gear ratios: (1st) 2.52:1; (2nd) 1.52:1; (3rd) 1.00:1; (Rev) 1.93:1. Standard final drive ratio: 2.72:1. Steering: Cam and lever. Suspension: Front coil springs, control arms and anti-sway bar; rigid rear axle w/upper torque arms, semi-elliptic leaf springs and anti-sway bar. Brakes: Front disc, rear drum. Body construction: Fiberglass body on box-type ladder frame. Fuel Tank: 19 gal.

MAJOR OPTIONS: Cruise control ($150). Electric moonroof ($995). Electric windows. Electric door locks ($125). Foglamps. Luggage rack ($100). Recaro front seats ($1100). Suede and leather interiors ($1200). Reclining front seats. Wood veneer dash and console panels. Wire wheels ($1160). Magnum 500 wheels ($350).

Note: Complete option list N/A; similar to 1979.

MANUFACTURER: Avanti Motor Corp., South Bend, Indiana.

1982 AVANTI

AVANTI — V-8 — Appearance and equipment changed little, but the Avanti company took on new ownership, headed by Stephen H. Blake. Avanti's catalog described it as an "American-made car, unique in the world." Each one required 14 weeks of work. Fiberglass bodies mounted a reinforced steel perimeter frame and received 16 coats of hand-sanded primer and acrylic lacquer. Four weeks were needed for final prep and testing, with at least 150 miles of road testing. An almost unlimited choice of body color and interior trims was offered. Standard front buckets could be replaced by optional Recaro orthopedically-engineered bucket seats. Unlike most car interiors, optional leather didn't only go on seat surfaces; about 300 square feet was used. Dashboards and consoles could be silver brushed aluminum finish, simulated walnut grain, or one of three genuine wood veneers. Avanti's 305 cu. in. V-8 now came with four-speed (overdrive) Turbo Hydra-matic. Standard equipment included power brakes and steering, air conditioning, AM/FM stereo with cassette, rear window deicer, tinted glass, tilt steering wheel, and limited-slip differential.

I.D. DATA: Not available.

AVANTI (V-8)

Model Number	Body/Style Number	Body Type & Seating	Factory Price	Shipping Weight	Production Total
N/A	N/A	2-dr. Spt Cpe-4P	22995	3570	200

ENGINE DATA: same as 1981.

CHASSIS DATA: same as 1979-81.

TECHNICAL: Transmission: Four-speed overdrive Turbo Hydra-matic 2004R standard. Gear ratios: (1st) 2.74:1; (2nd) 1.52:1; (3rd) 1.00:1; (overdrive 4th) 0.76:1; (Rev) 2.07:1. Standard final drive ratio: 3.08:1. Steering: Cam and lever. Suspension: Front coil springs, control arms and anti-sway bar; rigid rear axle w/upper torque arms, semi-elliptic leaf springs and anti-sway bar. Brakes: Front disc, rear drum. Body construction: Fiberglass body on box-type ladder frame. Fuel Tank: 19 gal.

MAJOR OPTIONS: Cruise control. Electric moonroof. Electric windows. Foglamps. Recaro front seats. Leather interior. Reclining front seats. Wood veneer dash and console panels. Wire wheels. Magnum 500 wheels.

Note: Complete option list N/A; similar to 1979.

MANUFACTURER: Avanti Motor Corp. (new ownership), South Bend, Indiana. Stephen Blake, president and CEO.

Historical Footnotes: This version of Avanti Motor Corp. was formed in 1982 by real-estate developer Stephen H. Blake, a Washington DC real-estate developer and Avanti enthusiast, who bought the company from founders Newman and Altman for about $5 million. Among other changes, Blake wanted to reduce the number of man-hours required per car, currently 800, by having workers do more than one job. This was possible because Avanti had always been a non-union plant, paying its employees well under the prevailing UAW wage. Blake also wanted to produce a convertible Avanti, using a design by Richard Straman; and offer a manual transmission. The 'II' designation disappeared from Avantis under Blake's stewardship.

1983 Avanti II coupe

1983 AVANTI

AVANTI — V-8 — Little changed in Avanti appearance or equipment for 1983. Standard equipment again included air conditioning, heated rear window, tinted glass, tilt steering wheel, limited-slip differential, and built-in headrest.

I.D. DATA: Not available.

AVANTI (V-8)

Model Number	Body/Style Number	Body Type & Seating	Factory Price	Shipping Weight	Production Total
N/A	N/A	2-dr. Spt Cpe-4P	24995	3690	N/A

ENGINE DATA: same as 1981-82.

CHASSIS DATA: same as 1979-82.

TECHNICAL: same as 1982.

MAJOR OPTIONS: Cruise control. Electric moonroof. Electric windows. Electric door locks. Foglamps. Recaro front seats. Leather interior. Reclining front seats. Wood veneer dash and console panels. Wire wheels. Magnum 500 wheels.

Note: Complete option list N/A; similar to 1979.

MANUFACTURER: Avanti Motor Corp., South Bend, Indiana.

Historical Footnotes: A special Avanti with tube frame and racing V-8 engine participated in the 24 Hours of Daytona race in spring 1983.

1984 AVANTI

AVANTI — V-8 — Prices and horsepower took a giant leap upward this year. Dimensions also changed a bit: shorter length and narrower wheels. Standard equipment included the 305 cu. in. V-8, four-speed Turbo Hydra-matic, power brakes and steering, air conditioning, rear window deicer, AM/FM stereo with cassette, radar detector, power windows, power mirrors, cruise control, central locking, tinted glass, tilt steering wheel, limited-slip differential, and built-in headrest.

I.D. DATA: Not available.

AVANTI (V-8)

Model Number	Body/Style Number	Body Type & Seating	Factory Price	Shipping Weight	Production Total
N/A	N/A	2-dr. Spt Cpe-4P	31860	3680	287

ENGINE DATA: BASE V-8: 90-degree, overhead valve V-8. Cast iron block and head. Displacement: 305 cu. in. (5.7 liters). Bore & stroke: 3.73 x 3.48 in. Compression ratio: 9.5:1. Brake horsepower: 190 at 4800 R.P.M. Torque: 240 lbs.-ft. at 3200 R.P.M. Five main bearings. Hydraulic valve lifters. Carburetor: 4Bbl. Rochester. Chevrolet-built.

CHASSIS DATA: Wheelbase: 109 in. Overall Length: 193.1 in. Height: 54.4 in. Width: 70.4 in. Front Tread: 57.4 in. Rear Tread: 56.6 in. Wheel Size: 7 in. x 15 in. Standard Tires: P205/75R15 (P215/60R15 front and P245/60R15 rear available).

TECHNICAL: Transmission: Four-speed overdrive Turbo Hydra-matic standard. Gear ratios: (1st) 3.06:1; (2nd) 1.62:1; (3rd) 1.00:1; (overdrive 4th) 0.67:1; (Rev) 2.07:1. Standard final drive ratio: 2.87:1. Steering: Cam and lever. Suspension: Front coil springs, control arms and anti-sway bar. Brakes: Front disc, rear drum. Body construction: Fiberglass body on box-type ladder frame. Fuel Tank: 19 gal.

MAJOR OPTIONS: Touring pkg.: Goodyear Eagle GT tires on Western wheels ($1635). Cruise control. Electric sunroof ($1395). Electric windows. Electric door locks. Foglamps. Recaro front seats. Leather interior ($1495). Reclining front seats. Wood veneer dash and console panels. Wire wheels. Magnum 500 wheels.

Note: Complete option list N/A.

MANUFACTURER: Avanti Motor Corp., South Bend, Indiana.

1985 AVANTI

AVANTI — V-8 — Appearance and equipment of the Touring Coupe changed little this year, though its price took another giant jump. More significant was the announcement of a new Avanti GT, carrying on the original's styling but with some major changes. The design was by Herb Adams, with a goal of cutting weight and lowering the car's center of gravity. The old recirculating ball steering was replaced by rack-and-pinion; disc/drum brakes by all discs. An independent rear suspension was used. A steel backbone replaced the Touring Coupe's heavy Xmember frame. The result: a car 4 inches lower than before. Since the body sat lower on the chassis, fender flares were required.

I.D. DATA: Not available.

AVANTI (V-8)

Model Number	Body/Style Number	Body Type & Seating	Factory Price	Shipping Weight	Production Total
N/A	N/A	2-dr. Tour Cpe-4P	37995	3680	N/A
N/A	N/A	2-dr. GT Spt Cpe-4P	37995	N/A	N/A

ENGINE DATA: BASE V-8: 90-degree, overhead valve V-8. Cast iron block and head. Displacement: 305 cu. in. (5.7 liters). Bore & stroke: 3.73 x 3.48 in. Compression ratio: 9.5:1. Brake horsepower: 190 at 4000 R.P.M. (GT, 205 at 4800 R.P.M.). Torque: 240 lbs.-ft. at 1600 R.P.M. (GT, 250 at 3200). Five main bearings. Hydraulic valve lifters. Carburetor: 4Bbl. Rochester. Chevrolet-built.

CHASSIS DATA: Wheelbase: 109 in. Overall Length: 193.1 in. Height: 54.4 in. (GT, 48 in.). Width: 70.4 in. Front Tread: 57.4 in. (GT, 62.5 in.). Rear Tread: 56.6 in. (GT, 62.5 in.). Wheel Size: 7 in. x 15 in. (GT, 8 x 16 in.). Standard Tires: P205/75R15 (GT, 245/50VR16).

TECHNICAL: Transmission: Four-speed overdrive Turbo Hydra-matic standard. Gear ratios: (1st) 3.06:1; (2nd) 1.63:1; (3rd) 1.00:1; (overdrive 4th) 0.70:1; (Rev) 2.07:1. Five-speed manual available on GT. Standard final drive ratio: 2.87:1 (GT, 3.31:1). Steering: Recirculating ball (GT, rack-and-pinion). Suspension: Front coil springs, control arms and anti-sway bar; rigid rear axle w/upper torque arms, semi-elliptic leaf springs and anti-sway bar. (GT, unequal-length Aarms w/coil springs, Koni shocks and anti-sway bar, front and rear). Brakes: Front disc, rear drum (GT, 10.5 in. discs). Body construction: Fiberglass body on box-type ladder frame (GT, steel backbone frame). Fuel Tank: 19 gal.

MAJOR OPTIONS: Cruise control. Electric moonroof. Electric windows. Electric door locks. Foglamps. Recaro front seats. Leather upholstery. Reclining front seats. Wood veneer dash and console panels. Wire wheels. Magnum 500 wheels. P215/60R15 tires. P245/60R15 tires.

Note: Complete option list N/A.

MANUFACTURER: Avanti Motor Corp., South Bend, Indiana.

Historical Footnotes: Bankruptcy proceedings in 1985 meant there were no 1986 Avantis. Avanti filed for protection from creditors on June 27, 1985. Stephen Blake, president and CEO from 1982 on, resigned in February 1986. Eight bids were made on the company before its assets and rights were purchased on April 30, 1986 for about $700,000 by Michael E. Kelly, who then formed the New Avanti Motor Corp. Kelly had grown up in South Bend. Avantis were produced again for 1987 (introduced in September 1986). Then, with Kelly at the helm, Avanti moved to Youngstown, Ohio in late 1987, effectively severing its long connection with South Bend. Over 11,000 workers applied for the 165 jobs expected at Youngstown. Avanti continued as a non-union company, paying workers an average of $7.10 an hour in 1986, and a similar amount after the Ohio move (compared to $13 an hour at a nearby GM plant). Organizing efforts by the UAW prompted claims that the company could not survive paying union wages. Avanti soon offered a convertible model and a longer Luxury Sport Coupe, as well as a manual gearbox. In 1988, Avanti also bought rights to import the Puma sports car from Brazil.

B

1982 Barrington pheaton

BARRINGTON — The Barrington is a "1929 Mercedes" kit car sold under the Barrington name by a firm called Prestige Classics. Ads identified the Wayzata, Minn. company as a branch of a telemarketing firm. Prestige Classic brochures indicated the firm built some of its own kits and also marketed those produced by other manufacturers. The Barrington was promoted strictly as a Ford Pinto based kit, although both the four- and six-cylinder Pinto engines could be accomodated in the package. It came in nine colors. Features include chrome side exhausts, leather hood strap, velour or leather upholstery and wire basket wheels.

1983 Barrister roadster

BARRISTER — A Corvette is used as the basis for the Barrister, a $59,950 exotic car built by Barrister Kustom Koach Ltd. The North Hollywood, Calif. firm offered the fiberglass bodied two-passenger convertible with leather trimmed seats, suede upper dashboard section, hand-etched side windows and Italian marble inserts. It utilizes a Chevrolet 350 cid V-8 engine.

1981 BCW 52 roadster

BCW 52 — An exact, full-size reproduction of the 1952 MG TD, the BCW 52 roadster was marketed by British Coachworks Ltd., of Arnold, Pa. Its 1981 components package price was $6,495 for a rear-engined, VW-based version. Components to make a front engine ''T Series'' version were marketed for $7,995 that same year. Both share a 94.5 in. wheelbase and 147 in. overall length. The front engine configuration uses Chevette or Pontiac T1000 components and weighs some 1,900 lbs. versus about 1,575 lbs. for the VW-based kits.

1981 Berlina coupe

1982 Berlina coupe SF

1983 Berlina coupe SF

1983 Berlina Turbo coupe

BERLINA — Berlina Motor Car Sales of Knoxville, Tenn., offered the Berlina coupe. Byron R. Cooper, of Cooper's Corvette Center, was involved in marketing of the fiberglass exoticar designed by Phillips. The company secured a 13,000 sq. ft. facility in Knoxville for assembly of its cars.

1981 Blakely Bearcat roadster

BLAKELY — Blakely AutoWorks Ltd. was founded by D. Blakely in 1972. The firm was based in Princeton, Wis. and had 36 employees in 1979. It produced the Bantam kit car (1972); Bearcat (1973) and Bearcat S (1976) turning out as many as 126 cars in its 1977 model year. Pinto-based, the 1980 Bearcat S was $9,250.

1982 Bradford Limited Edition roadster

BRADFORD — Marketed by Bradford Motorcars, of Dania, Fla., this is a neo-classic roadster featuring hand-finished glove leather seats, convertible top with headliner, optional hardtop, leather boot, hand carved vent windows and a hand-finished imported wood dashboard. A five-year powertrain warranty was originally provided.

1979 Bradley Baron roadster

BRADLEY BARON — The Bradley Baron convertible is built by Bradley Automotive of Plymouth, Minn. Inspired by the 1929 Mercedes-Benz, it utilizes a VW chassis and engine. The body is made of reinforced fiberglass. Standard equipment includes a windshield, retractable cloth top, chrome headlamps, carpeting, rolled and pleated simulated leather upholstery, bumpers and full instrumentation.

1981 Bradley Baron electric roadster

BRADLEY BARON ELECTRIC — Bradley Automotive, of Plymouth, Minn., became interested in electric powered cars and added an electric powered version of the Bradley Baron to its line. It is a kit car patterned loosely after the looks of a 1929 Mercedes. The electric elements required for quiet, energy efficient driving come from General Electric Co.'s EVSO branch in Virginia.

1980 Bradley GT Limited Edition gullwing coupe

412

BRADLEY GT — The Bradley GT is a sports car kit produced by Bradley Automotive, of Plymouth, Minn. It features a gull-wing fiberglass body and recessed headlamps. The Volkswagen engine and chassis (1969 or later recommended) is employed.

1980 Bradley GTII Collector Series gullwing coupe

BRADLEY GT II GULL-WING — The Bradley GT II gull-wing coupe, from Bradley Automotive, of Plymouth, Minn., features a fiberglass body designed for the VW chassis and engine. High-compression gas pistons operate the doors automatically. Improvements over the standard GT include front and rear bumpers and a distinctive louvered hood.

1980 Bradley GTElectric gullwing coupe

BRADLEY GTElectric — General Electric Co.'s *Load Currents* newsletter announced the development of an electric powered Bradley GT II sports car in Feb. 1980. GE's Electric Vehicle Systems Operation (EVSO) branch in Charlottesville, Va. built the first of these cars using a kit furnished by Bradley Automotive. Its Tracer I electric propulsion system incorporates the EV-1 SCR controller and traction motor by General Electric. It has a top speed in excess of 75 mph and accelerates from 0-30 mph in eight seconds. In 1980, a driving range of 85 miles was promoted and operating cost was said to be about a penny per mile. General Electric said this model would become part of the Bradley line, which then included MG and '57 T-bird replicas.

1980 Bradley MGT roadster

BRADLEY MGT — Bradley Automotive, Inc., of Plymouth, Minn., introduced its MGT convertible in 1980. It is a kit car patterned after the 1952 MGTD and utilizing the Volkswagen engine/chassis so popular with kit car makers.

1981 Bradley MGT electric roadster

BRADLEY MGT Electric — As part of the 1980 Chrysler bailout bill, Se. James A. McClure (R-Idaho) added an amendment that provided incentives for electric vehicle development. Bradley Automotive, of Plymouth, Minn., was quick to react and soon released and electric power option for its MGT replica kit.

Circa 1977 Bugatti roadster

BUGATTI — One of the first kit car makers was Antique and Classic Cars, Inc., which was located in the Brisbane Building in Buffalo, N.Y. The firm also had a showroom in Clarance, N.Y. In 1976, its Bugatti kit retailed for just $795. All of the company's early kits utilized the Volkswagen chassis and could be assembled in 70 hours.

1980 Bugatti roadster

BUGATTI Type 35B — Classic Motor Carriages, Inc., of Hallendale, Fla. produces this Bugatti kit car. It comes in red, bright yellow, white, green or blue. It is based on the 1927 Bugatti Type 35B roadster and utilizes a Volkswagen chassis. Whellbase is 94.5 in. with a 154 in. overall length. The stock 1600 cc. Volkswagen engine provides 9.9 seconds zero-to-sixty performance and 26-35 mpg.

1981 Burley hot rod Beetle sedan

BURLEY "HOT ROD" BEETLE — Burley Design, of Mendon, Utah, decided to improve the Volkswagen Beetle by adding fat tires and a replica 1932 Ford grille. Along with numerous other modifications, this creates an odd-looking vehicle that seems like a cross between a hot rod and a dune buggy with a Germanic flair.

C

1985 "Cabriolet" rumbleseat convertible

('34) CABRIOLET — Golden Age Auto Corp., of Albion, Mich., planned to make 44 of its luxurious "'34 Cabriolets" by the end of 1985. The company also announced that no more than 550 of the cars, replicas of the 1934 Ford rumbleseat convertible, would be manufactured in any one year. Production startup was announced on June 3, 1985. Nelson R. "Skip" Turner — a former Ford Motor Co. engineer — was behind the $30,000-$35,000 replica. It was to be marketed through Ford and Lincoln-Mercury dealers. The design is a near exact copy of the original, based on a Ford Ranger suspension/drivetrain, with a small V-6 as the standard power plant and a larger V-6 optional. Specifications include a 112 in. wheelbase, 186 in. length, 67.5 in. width and 65 in. height. A cellular phone was one of just four options available.

1983 Ceres three-wheel coupe

CERES — The Ceres, built by Creative Cars, Inc., of Rockford, Ill. is a three-wheeled, two-passenger car with a steel reinforced fiberglass body. A mid-mounted three-cylinder Daihatsu one-liter engine drives the rear wheels through a two-speed automatic transmission. The manufacturer claimed a top speed of over 90 mph and highway mileage of 62 mpg. Introductory price was $13,875.

1976 Checker Marathon limousine

1976 CHECKER

MARATHON — SERIES A-12 — SIX/V-8 — Founded in 1922 by Morris Markin, a Russian immigrant, Checker soon established itself as a builder of durable vehicles that stood aside from the whims of change. The company prevailed in its rivalry with John Hertz of Yellow Taxi through the Chicago gangland days. The familiar "slab-sided" Checker body, introduced as the A8 taxicab in 1956, was first offered to private passenger-car buyers in late 1959 as the Superba. Changes were minimal through the next decade-and-a-half: not much more than 5 MPH bumpers, a switch from round to square turn signal lenses, catalytic converters (starting in 1975), and federally-mandated reflectors. First offered with Continental engines, Checker switched to Chevrolet powerplants (inline six and V-8) in 1965. The station wagon body style was dropped in 1975, leaving only four-door sedans. Built for rugged use, Checkers featured a double-channel X-frame with five X-members, as well as reinforced body center posts. That kind of construction meant a heavyweight car, with the lightest model approaching three tons. Rear floors were virtually flat, rooflines high to allow great headroom. Body parts (bolt-on fenders, grillework, side panels) could be replaced in minimum time. Front and rear bumpers were interchangeable. The standard Model A12, on 120 inch wheelbase, came with a 250 cu. in. inline six-cylinder engine. The long-wheelbase A12E carried a standard 350 cu. in. V-8, which was also optional on the smaller model. (Model A11 and A11E designations were for taxicabs.) Most engine parts were readily accessible. Complete data on the 1976 model are not available, but similar to the '77; see next listing for standard equipment and appearance details.

I.D. DATA: Not available.

MARATHON (SIX)

Model Number	Body/Style Number	Body Type & Seating	Factory Price	Shipping Weight	Production Total
A-12	N/A	4-dr. Sedan-6P	5749	3775	Note 1

MARATHON (V-8)

Model Number	Body/Style Number	Body Type & Seating	Factory Price	Shipping Weight	Production Total
A-12	N/A	4-dr. Sedan-6P	N/A	3839	Note 1
A-12E	N/A	4-dr. DeL Sed-6P	6736	4137	Note 1

Note 1: A total of 4,790 Checkers (private and taxi) were built in 1976.

ENGINE DATA: BASE SIX (Standard model): Inline, overhead valve six-cylinder. Cast iron block and head. Displacement: 250 cu. in. (4.1 liters). Bore & stroke: 3.88 x 3.53 in. Compression ratio: 8.2:1. Brake horsepower: 105 at 3800 R.P.M. Torque: 186 lbs.-ft. at 1200 R.P.M. Seven main bearings. Hydraulic valve lifters. Carburetor: 1Bbl. Rochester 17056014. Chevrolet-built. BASE V-8 (Deluxe model): 90-degree, overhead valve V-8. Cast iron block and head. Displacement: 350 cu. in. (5.7 liters). Bore & stroke: 4.00 x 3.48 in. Compression ratio: 8.2:1. Brake horsepower: 145 at 3800 R.P.M. Torque: 250 lbs.-ft. at 2200 R.P.M. Five main bearings. Hydraulic valve lifters. Carburetor: 2Bbl. Rochester 17056114. Chevrolet-built.

CHASSIS DATA: Wheelbase: 120 in. (DeLuxe, 129 in.). Overall Length: 204.8 in. (DeLuxe, 213.8 in.). Height: 62.8 in. Width: 76 in. Front Tread: 64.5 in. Rear Tread: 63.3 in. Wheel size: 6 x 15 in. Standard Tires: G78 x 15.

TECHNICAL: Transmission: Turbo Hydra-matic 400 three-speed automatic standard. Gear ratios: (1st) 2.48:1; (2nd) 1.48:1; (3rd) 1.00:1; (Rev) 2.07:1. Standard final drive ratio: 3.31:1. Steering: Recirculating ball. Suspension: Front coil springs with control arms and anti-sway bar; rigid rear axle with semi-elliptic leaf springs. Brakes: Front disc (11.75 in. dia.), rear drum. Ignition: Delco-Remy HEI. Body construction: Separate body and box-type ladder frame. Fuel Tank: 21.6 gal.

MAJOR OPTIONS: Limited-slip differential. Air conditioning. Auxiliary rear seats. HR78 x 15 tires. Note: Other options similar to 1977; see next listing.

MANUFACTURER: Checker Motors Corp., Kalamazoo, Michigan. Established 1922. David R. Markin, chairman/president. 600 workers.

HISTORY: Calendar year sales: 4,681 (mainly taxis).

1977 CHECKER

MARATHON — SERIES A-12 — SIX/V-8 — "Being practical is never out of style." That was the strongest selling point for Checker in the 1970s. As the factory brochure proclaimed, "It's functional. It's spacious. It's sensible....A tribute to the common sense of its owner." Only a small fraction of those owners were private, however: typically at least 90 percent of Checkers were destined for taxi use. Base engine for the short-wheelbase Model A12 was again Chevrolet's 250 cu. in. inline six, but the A12E switched from a 350 V-8 to a 305. The 350 remained optional, however, in both models. A Turbo Hydra-matic 400 transmission was standard. So were power steering and brakes. Checkers had coil spring front suspension and five-leaf semi-elliptic rear

springs. Checkers had a winged emblem at the front of the hood and quad round headlamps, with amber parking lamps just below. 'Marathon' script stood on the cowl. Round amber marking lamps were on front fenders. The wide, bright grille kept the same look year after year. Vertical-style taillamps each consisted of two round lenses, one above the other. Standard equipment included G78 x 15 bias-belt L/RB blackwall tires; two-speed electric wiper/washers; heater/defroster; front side vent windows; rubber fender shields; door-ajar warning light; four seats of lap belts; two sets of shoulder harnesses and lap belt combination; rear door pull handles; inside day/night mirror; padded instrument panel; and dual padded sunvisors. Directional signals included a lane-change feature. The step-on parking brake had a warning light. Body paint was DuPont acrylic enamel in 94 color choices. Chair-high seats came with vinyl upholstery in a wide variety of colors. Square forward-facing auxiliary seats were optional in Model A12E, for nine-passenger capacity. Also optional: covered rear quarter windows.

I.D. DATA: Not available.

MARATHON (SIX)

Model Number	Body/Style Number	Body Type & Seating	Factory Price	Shipping Weight	Production Total
A-12	N/A	4-dr. Sedan-6P	N/A	3775	Note 1

MARATHON (V-8)

Model Number	Body/Style Number	Body Type & Seating	Factory Price	Shipping Weight	Production Total
A-12	N/A	4-dr. Sedan-6P	N/A	N/A	Note 1
A-12E	N/A	4-dr. DeL Sed-6P	N/A	4137	Note 1

Note 1: A total of 5,377 Checkers were built in the model year; all but 337 were taxicabs.

ENGINE DATA: BASE SIX (Standard model): Inline, overhead valve six-cylinder. Cast iron block and head. Displacement: 250 cu. in. (4.1 liters). Bore & stroke: 3.88 x 3.53 in. Compression ratio: 8.3:1. Brake horsepower: 110 at 3800 R.P.M. Torque: 195 lbs.-ft. at 1600 R.P.M. Seven main bearings. Hydraulic valve lifters. Carburetor: 1Bbl. Rochester 17057014. Chevrolet-built. BASE V-8 (Deluxe model): 90-degree, overhead valve V-8. Cast iron block and head. Displacement: 305 cu. in. (5.0 liters). Bore & stroke: 3.74 x 3.48 in. Compression ratio: 8.5:1. Brake horsepower: 145 at 3800 R.P.M. Torque: 245 lbs.-ft. at 2400 R.P.M. Five main bearings. Hydraulic valve lifters. Carburetor: 2Bbl. Rochester 17057108. Chevrolet-built. OPTIONAL V-8 (both models): 90-degree, overhead valve V-8. Cast iron block and head. Displacement: 350 cu. in. (5.7 liters). Bore & stroke: 4.00 x 3.48 in. Compression ratio: 8.5:1. Brake horsepower: 170 at 3800 R.P.M. Torque: 270 lbs.-ft. at 2400 R.P.M. Five main bearings. Hydraulic valve lifters. Carburetor: 4Bbl. Rochester 17057202. Chevrolet-built.

CHASSIS DATA: same as 1976.

TECHNICAL: same as 1976.

OPTIONS: 305 two-barrel or 350 four-barrel V-8. Trac-Lok rear axle. Trunk-mounted battery and shield. Six-leaf rear springs. Heavier shocks. Transmission oil cooler. Heavy-duty coolant. Air conditioning. Power rear door locks. Tinted glass. Auxiliary under-seat heater. Rear defogger. Spotlight. AM or AM/FM radio. Two-way radio antenna. Undercoating. Auxiliary seats. Front armrests. Driver's card case. Life-GuardR partition. Full wheel covers. Whitewalls. HR78 x 15 Firestone 500 SBR tires. Roof lamp. Taxi lettering details.

MANUFACTURER: Checker Motors Corp., Kalamazoo, Michigan. David R. Markin, chairman/president.

HISTORY: Calendar year sales: 4,568 (mainly taxis).

Historical Footnotes: Checker also made a 15-passenger limousine called the Aerobus 15.

1978 CHECKER

MARATHON — SERIES A-12 — SIX/V-8 — Checkers changed little in appearance or equipment, except that a 90-horsepower inline six was used in California models.

I.D. DATA: Not available.

MARATHON (SIX)

Model Number	Body/Style Number	Body Type & Seating	Factory Price	Shipping Weight	Production Total
A-12	N/A	4-dr. Sedan-6P	6419	3765	Note 1

MARATHON (V-8)

Model Number	Body/Style Number	Body Type & Seating	Factory Price	Shipping Weight	Production Total
A-12	N/A	4-dr. Sedan-6P	N/A	3862	Note 1
A-12E	N/A	4-dr. DeL Sed-6P	7472	4062	Note 1

Note 1: A total of 5,503 Checkers were built in model year 1978 (only 307 for private sale).

ENGINE DATA: BASE SIX (Standard model): Inline, overhead valve six-cylinder. Cast iron block and head. Displacement: 250 cu. in. (4.1 liters). Bore & stroke: 3.88 x 3.53 in. Compression ratio: 8.1:1. Brake horsepower: 110 at 3800 R.P.M. Torque: 190 lbs.-ft. at 1600 R.P.M. Seven main bearings. Hydraulic valve lifters. Carburetor: 1Bbl. Rochester 17058020. Chevrolet-built. BASE V-8 (Deluxe model); OPTIONAL (Standard model): 90-degree, overhead valve V-8. Cast iron block and head. Displacement: 305 cu. in. (5.0 liters). Bore & stroke: 3.74 x 3.48 in. Compression ratio: 8.4:1. Brake horsepower: 145 at 3800 R.P.M. Torque: 245 lbs.-ft. at 2400 R.P.M. Five main bearings. Hydraulic valve lifters. Carburetor: 2Bbl. Rochester 17058108B. Chevrolet-built. OPTIONAL V-8 (both models): 90-degree, overhead valve V-8. Cast iron block and head. Displacement: 350 cu. in. (5.7 liters). Bore & stroke: 4.00 x 3.48 in. Compression ratio: 8.2:1. Brake horsepower: 160 at 3800 R.P.M. Torque: 260 lbs.-ft. at 2400 R.P.M. Five main bearings. Hydraulic valve lifters. Carburetor: 4Bbl. Rochester 17058504A. Chevrolet-built.

CHASSIS DATA: same as 1976-77.

TECHNICAL: Transmission: Turbo Hydra-matic 400 three-speed automatic standard. Gear ratios: (1st) 2.48:1; (2nd) 1.48:1; (3rd) 1.00:1; (Rev) 2.07:1. Standard final drive 3.07:1 w/six, 2.72:1 w/V-8. Steering: Recirculating ball. Suspension: Front coil springs with control arms and anti- sway bar; rigid rear axle with semi-elliptic leaf springs. Brakes: Front disc (11.75 in. dia.), rear drum. Ignition: Delco-Remy HEI. Body construction: Separate body and box-type ladder frame. Fuel Tank: 21.6 gal.

OPTIONS: 305 cu. in. V-8 engine ($179). 350 cu. in. V-8 ($322) exc. ($145) for A12E. Trac-Lok differential ($71). Front air conditioning ($474). Dual air cond. ($855). Rear defogger ($46). Aux. heater ($83). Auxiliary rear seats ($75); deluxe ($257). Power rear door locks ($75); all doors ($138). AM radio ($99); AM/FM ($165). Vinyl roof ($194) Tinted glass. Heavy-duty shocks. HR78 x 15 Firestone 500 tires.

Note: Complete option list not available, but similar to 1979; see next listing.

MANUFACTURER: Checker Motors Corp., Kalamazoo, Michigan. David Markin, chairman/president.

1979 CHECKER

MARATHON — SERIES A-12 — SIX/V-8 — Appearance and equipment changed little, as usual. Standard equipment included the Chevrolet 250 cu. in. six- cyilnder engine; dual master cylinder brake system with power front disc brakes; power steering; three-speed automatic; two-speed electric wiper/washers; 63-amp generator; 80-amp battery; rear door pull handles; full wheel covers; rubber fender shields; and day/night mirror. P215/75 blackwalls rode 15 in. wheels, replacing the former G78 x 15 size. The Marathon DeLuxe A12E, on 129 in. wheelbase, had a 305 V-8 and vinyl roof, and required P225 radial tires.

I.D. DATA: Not available.

MARATHON (SIX)

Model Number	Body/Style Number	Body Type & Seating	Factory Price	Shipping Weight	Production Total
A-12	N/A	4-dr. Sedan-6P	7314	3740	Note 1

MARATHON (V-8)

Model Number	Body/Style Number	Body Type & Seating	Factory Price	Shipping Weight	Production Total
A-12	N/A	4-dr. Sedan-6P	7515	3862	Note 1
A-12E	N/A	4-dr. DeL Sed-6P	8389	3999	Note 1

Note 1: A total of 5,231 Checkers were built in the model year (all except 270 were taxicabs).

ENGINE DATA: same as 1978.

CHASSIS DATA: Wheelbase: 120 in. (DeLuxe, 129 in.). Overall Length: 204.8 in. (DeLuxe, 213.8 in.). Height: 62.8 in. Width: 78 in. Front Tread: 64.5 in. Rear Tread: 63.3 in. Wheel size: 6 x 15 in. Standard Tires: P215/75R15 Firestone 721 blackwall SBR.

TECHNICAL: same as 1978.

OPTIONS: 305 cu. in. V-8 engine ($201). 350 cu. in. V-8, required in Calif. ($322) exc. on A12E ($121). Aux. transmission oil cooler ($92). Trac-Lok axle ($78.50). Firm ride shocks ($14). Skid bar ($6.50). 145 lb. rear springs ($29.50). Rear helper springs ($38). Optional cooling ($58). Front air cond. ($520). Dual air cond. ($921). Auxiliary floor heater ($89.50). Rear defogger ($50). Four electric door locks ($141); left one standard. AM radio ($101.50). AM/FM ($171). Rear speaker ($43.50). Vinyl roof: A12 ($209). Two-tone paint ($46). Metallic paint ($197). Elimination of quarter window ($131.50); vinyl roof required on A12. Chrome fender shields ($48). California pkg. for six ($276). Aux. rear seats ($84); deluxe ($292). Front carpet ($45). Additional ashtrays ($10 each). P215 whitewall tires ($50). P225 blackwalls ($63). P225 whitewalls ($113).

MANUFACTURER: Checker Motors Corp., Kalamazoo, Michigan. David Markin, chairman/president. 1000 workers.

1980 CHECKER

MARATHON — SERIES A-12 — V-6/V-8 — Checkers came with new, smaller engines this year. A 229 cu. in. V-6 replaced the former inline six as base engine in Model A12, while a 267 cu. in. V-8 replaced the 305. The 305 engine remained available in California (rated 155 horsepower), but the 350 cu. in. V-8 was gone. Also available was a new diesel powerplant. Standard equipment included three-speed Turbo Hydra-matic transmission, heater/defroster, P215/75R15 tires, two- speed wiper/washers, power front disc brakes, power steering, safety day/night mirror, and front side vent windows. Rear carpeting, rubber fender shields, rear door pull handles, full wheel covers, and rear-mounted battery with shield also were standard. Long-wheelbase Model A-12E came with the 267 cu. in. V-8 engine and vinyl roof, and required P225/75R15 tires. Fenders and grille were bolt-on type; front and rear bumpers interchangeable.

I.D. DATA: Not available.

MARATHON (V-6)

Model Number	Body/Style Number	Body Type & Seating	Factory Price	Shipping Weight	Production Total
A-12	N/A	4-dr. Sedan-6P	8118	3680	Note 1

MARATHON (V-8)

Model Number	Body/Style Number	Body Type & Seating	Factory Price	Shipping Weight	Production Total
A-12	N/A	4-dr. Sedan-6P	N/A	N/A	Note 1
A-12E	N/A	4-dr. DeL Sed-6P	9192	3999	Note 1

Note 1: A total of 2,574 Checkers were built in the model year. Price Note: Diesel-engine models cost $10,473 and $11,310, respectively. As usual, taxi models were cheaper ($7597 for A11 and $8321 for A11E).

ENGINE DATA: BASE V-6 (Standard model): 90-degree, overhead valve V-6. Cast iron block and head. Displacement: 229 cu. in. (3.8 liters). Bore & stroke: 3.74 x 3.48 in. Compression ratio: 8.6:1. Brake horsepower: 115 at 4000 R.P.M. Torque: 175 lbs.-ft. at 2000 R.P.M. Four main bearings. Hydraulic valve lifters. Carburetor: 2Bbl. Rochester 1780130. BASE V-8 (Deluxe model); OPTIONAL (Standard model): 90-degree, overhead valve V-8. Cast iron block and head. Displacement: 267 cu. in. (4.4 liters). Bore & stroke: 3.50 x 3.48 in. Compression ratio: 8.3:1. Brake horsepower: 120 at 3600 R.P.M. Torque: 215 lbs.-ft. at 2000 R.P.M. Five main bearings. Hydraulic valve lifters. Carburetor: 2Bbl. Rochester 17080138. OPTIONAL V-8 (both models): 90-degree, overhead valve V-8. Cast iron block and head. Displacement: 305 cu. in. (5.0 liters). Bore & stroke: 3.74 x 3.48 in. Compression ratio: 8.6:1. Brake horsepower: 155 at 4000 R.P.M. Torque: 230 lbs.-ft. at 2400 R.P.M. Five main bearings. Hydraulic valve lifters. Carburetor: 2Bbl. OPTIONAL DIESEL V-8 (both models): 90-degree, overhead valve V-8. Cast iron block and head. Displacement: 350 cu. in. (5.7 liters). Bore & stroke: 4.06 x 3.39 in. Compression ratio: 22.5:1. Brake horsepower: 125 at 3600 R.P.M. Torque: 225 lbs.-ft. at 1600 R.P.M. Five main bearings. Hydraulic valve lifters. Fuel injection.

CHASSIS DATA: Wheelbase: 120 in. (DeLuxe, 129 in.). Overall Length: 204.8 in. (DeLuxe, 213.8 in.). Height: 62.8 in. Width: 76 in. Front Tread: 64.5 in. Rear Tread: 63.3 in. Wheel size: 6 x 15 in. Standard Tires: P215/75R15 exc. (A12E) P225/75R15.

TECHNICAL: Transmission: Turbo Hydra-matic 400 three-speed automatic standard. Gear ratios: (1st) 2.48:1; (2nd) 1.48:1; (3rd) 1.00:1; (Rev) 2.07:1. Standard final drive ratio: 2.72:1. Steering: Recirculating ball. Suspension: Front coil springs with control arms and anti- sway bar; rigid rear axle with semi-elliptic leaf springs. Brakes: Front disc (11.86 in. dia.), rear drum. Ignition: Delco-Remy HEI. Body construction: Separate body and box-type ladder frame. Fuel Tank: 21.6 gal.

OPTIONS: 267 cu. in. V-8 engine ($237). 305 cu. in. V-8; required in Calif. ($214) exc. on A12E ($677). 105-amp alternator ($217). Trac-Lok axle ($86). Aux. transmission oil cooler ($97). Firm ride shocks ($14.50). Skid bar ($12). 145-lb. rear springs ($29.50). Rear helper springs ($38). Optional cooling ($58). Front air cond. ($579). Dual air cond. ($1007). Auxiliary floor heater ($97.50). Rear defogger ($53.50). Four electric door locks ($171). Rear electric door locks only ($92). Tinted glass ($68.50); windshield ($25). Left-hand spotlight ($68). Right mirror ($11). AM radio ($114). AM/FM radio ($192). Rear speaker ($46). Vinyl roof ($230). Two-tone paint ($55). Metallic paint ($230). Elimination of quarter window ($131.50); vinyl roof required on A12. Chrome fender shields ($55.50). Aux. rear seats ($98.50); deluxe ($329). Front carpet ($48.50). Additional ashtrays ($11 each). P215 whitewall tires ($75.50). P225 blackwalls ($75.50). P225 whitewalls ($115).

MANUFACTURER: Checker Motors Corp., Kalamazoo, Michigan. David Markin, chairman/president.

1981 Checker Marathon four-door taxicab

1981 CHECKER

MARATHON — SERIES A-12 — V-6/V-8 — Appearance and equipment were similar to 1980. Prices jumped considerably this year, as they had in 1980.

I.D. DATA: Not available.

MARATHON (V-6)

Model Number	Body/Style Number	Body Type & Seating	Factory Price	Shipping Weight	Production Total
A-12	N/A	4-dr. Sedan-6P	9632	3680	Note 1

MARATHON (V-8)

Model Number	Body/Style Number	Body Type & Seating	Factory Price	Shipping Weight	Production Total
A-12	N/A	4-dr. Sedan-6P	9869	N/A	Note 1
A-12E	N/A	4-dr. DeL Sed-6P	10706	3999	Note 1

Note 1: A total of 2,950 Checkers were produced in the model year (private and taxi).

ENGINE DATA: BASE V-6 (Standard model): 90-degree, overhead valve V-8. Cast iron block and head. Displacement: 229 cu. in. (3.8 liters). Bore & stroke: 3.73 x 3.48 in. Compression ratio: 8.6:1. Brake horsepower: 110 at 4200 R.P.M. Torque: 170 lbs.-ft. at 2000 R.P.M. Four main bearings. Hydraulic valve lifters. Carburetor: 2Bbl. Rochester 1780130. BASE V-8 (Deluxe model); OPTIONAL (Standard model): 90-degree, overhead valve V-8. Cast iron block and head. Displacement: 267 cu. in. (4.4 liters). Bore & stroke: 3.50 x 3.48 in. Compression ratio: 8.3:1. Brake horsepower: 115 at 4000 R.P.M. Torque: 200 lbs.-ft. at 2400 R.P.M. Five main bearings. Hydraulic valve lifters. Carburetor: 2Bbl. Rochester 17080138. OPTIONAL V-8 (both models): 90-degree, overhead valve V-8. Cast iron block and head. Displacement: 305 cu. in. (5.0 liters). Bore & stroke: 3.74 x 3.48 in. Compression ratio: 8.6:1. Brake horsepower: 150 at 3800 R.P.M. Torque: 240 lbs.-ft. at 2400 R.P.M. Five main bearings. Hydraulic valve lifters. Carburetor: 2Bbl. Rochester 17080502. OPTIONAL DIESEL V-8 (both models): 90-degree, overhead valve V-8. Cast iron block and head. Displacement: 350 cu. in. (5.7 liters). Bore & stroke: 4.06 x 3.38 in. Compression ratio: 22.5:1. Brake horsepower: 105 at 3200 R.P.M. Torque: 200 lbs.-ft. at 1600 R.P.M. Five main bearings. Hydraulic valve lifters. Fuel injection.

CHASSIS DATA: same as 1980.

TECHNICAL: same as 1980.

MAJOR OPTIONS: 267 cu. in. V-8 engine ($237). 305 cu. in. V-8 ($343); required in Calif. ($914). Front air cond. ($711). Dual air cond. ($1211). Rear defogger ($62). Four electric door locks ($198); rear only ($104). AM radio ($145); AM/FM ($231). Vinyl roof ($269).

Note: Complete option list not available, but similar to 1980.

MANUFACTURER: Checker Motors Corp., Kalamazoo, Michigan. David Markin, chairman/president.

1982 Checker Marathon four-door taxicab

1982 CHECKER

MARATHON — SERIES A-12 — V-6/V-8 — Appearance and equipment were similar to 1980-81. Once again, prices jumped sharply.

I.D. DATA: Not available.

MARATHON (V-6)

Model Number	Body/Style Number	Body Type & Seating	Factory Price	Shipping Weight	Production Total
A-12	N/A	4-dr. Sedan-6P	10950	3680	Note 1

MARATHON (V-8)

| A-12 | N/A | 4-dr. Sedan-6P | 11187 | N/A | Note 1 |
| A-12E | N/A | 4-dr. DeL Sed-6P | 12025 | 3839 | Note 1 |

Note 1: A total of 2,000 Checkers were produced in this final model year (private and taxis).

ENGINE DATA: BASE V-6 (Standard model): 90-degree, overhead valve V-8. Cast iron block and head. Displacement: 229 cu. in. (3.8 liters). Bore & stroke: 3.73 x 3.48 in. Compression ratio: 8.6:1. Brake horsepower: 110 at 4200 R.P.M. Torque: 170 lbs.-ft. at 2000 R.P.M. Four main bearings. Hydraulic valve lifters. Carburetor: 2Bbl. Rochester 1780130. BASE V-8 (Deluxe model): 90-degree, overhead valve V-8. Cast iron block and head. Displacement: 267 cu. in. (4.4 liters). Bore & stroke: 3.50 x 3.48 in. Compression ratio: 8.3:1. Brake horsepower: 115 at 4000 R.P.M. Torque: 205 lbs.-ft. at 2400 R.P.M. Five main bearings. Hydraulic valve lifters. Carburetor: 2Bbl. Rochester 17080138. OPTIONAL DIESEL V-8 (both models): 90-degree, overhead valve V-8. Cast iron block and head. Displacement: 350 cu. in. (5.7 liters). Bore & stroke: 4.06 x 3.38 in. Compression ratio: 22.5:1. Brake horsepower: 105 at 3200 R.P.M. Torque: 200 lbs.-ft. at 1600 R.P.M. Five main bearings. Hydraulic valve lifters. Fuel Injection.

CHASSIS DATA: Wheelbase: 120 in. (DeLuxe, 129 in.). Overall Length: 201.6 in. (DeLuxe, 210.6 in.). Height: 62.8 in. Width: 78 in. Front Tread: 64.5 in. Rear Tread: 63.3 in. Wheel size: 6 x 15 in. Standard Tires: P215/75R15 exc. (A12E) P225/75R15.

TECHNICAL: same as 1980-81.

OPTIONS: 267 cu. in. V-8 engine ($237). Propane 229 cu. in. V-6 ($275). Tilt steering ($127). Front air cond. ($750). Dual air cond. ($1315). Rear defogger ($68). Floor heater ($132). Four electric door locks ($211); rear only ($119). AM radio ($152). Vinyl roof ($290). Oval opera windows ($342). Aux. rear seats: A12 ($121). Deluxe aux. rear seats: A12E ($415).

Note: Complete option list N/A; similar to 1980 listing.

Historical Footnotes: A completely different kind of Checker was anticipated for 1983. Thoughts about a replacement for the antiquated, three-decades-old design stretched back a dozen years. There had been a Ghia-designed prototype in 1970. A proposal from a Michigan design/engineering company had been rejected in 1975. Ed Cole, who'd joined Checker after retiring as GM president in the mid-1970s, naturally envisioned a further connection with General Motors, the long-time supplier of Checker's drivetrains. Some thought was given to making the new Checker a stretched version of GM's Xbody, but obstacles shunted aside that prospect. It would definitely be front-drive, in any case. *Motor Trend* reported that the next choice was a GM mid-size chassis, with special independent rear suspension (dubbed "Marsh Mellow") developed by Jerry Marsh of Firestone. Amid speculation that three wheelbases would be offered on that platform, the company instead went out of business. After six decades of production, the final Checker automobile was built on July 12, 1982.

MANUFACTURER: Checker Motors Corp., Kalamazoo, Michigan. David Markin, chairman/president.

1976 Citicar commuter vehicle

CITICAR — ELECTRIC — At least in terms of the number built, CitiCar was the most successful of the 1970s electric cars. Appearance was typical of the small electrics: a boxy wedge shape with sharp, flat slope that stretched backward from the front bumper (with windshield at that same sloping angle). The two-door body was made of Cycolac plastic, over an aluminum-tubing roll-cage frame. Headlamps were the stand-up type. Two passengers fit inside. Over 2,000 examples of CitiCar I were in use by the time series II was issued for 1978. Actually, it was aimed mainly at the U.S. Department of Energy. A full hatchback was standard. CitiCar II had a new solid state control system with infinite speed, and a 6 H.P. motor instead of the original 3.5 H.P. The price rose to $3396.

I.D. DATA: Not available.

CITICAR (ELECTRIC)

Model Number	Body/Style Number	Body Type & Seating	Factory Price	Production Weight	Total
I	N/A	2-dr. Cpe-2P	2738	1250	Note 1

Note 1: A total of 424 CitiCars were produced in 1976.

CHASSIS DATA: Wheelbase: 63 in. Overall Length: 95 in. Height: 59.5 in. Width: 55 in. Front Tread: 43 in. Rear Tread: 44 in. Standard Tires: 4.80 x 12.

TECHNICAL: Motor: 48-volt (3.5 or 6 horsepower) GE series-wound, with electro-mechanical regulator; 4100 R.P.M. max. Three-speed voltage switching. Automatic direct gear drive. Batteries: Eight 6-volt lead-acid. Built-in charger. Separate 12-volt battery for accessories. Suspension: Independent front, rigid rear axle. Body: Plastic, on aluminum frame. Brakes: 7 in. drum.

RATINGS: Range: to 50 miles; up to 100 miles per day with intermittent charging. Top Speed: 38 MPH (44 MPH with later model). Acceleration: 0-30 MPH in 13.9 seconds.

OPTIONS: List not available.

Historical Footnotes: Developed by Robert Beaumont, CitiCar was considered the first mass-produced electric car. At first, Sebring-Vanguard sold as many CitiCars as they could build. A total of 608 were produced in 1974 (its first year); 1,193 in 1975. So 1976 showed a sharp drop. Some automotive writers who tested the CitiCar gave moderately favorable reviews, though *Consumer Reports* gave both CitiCar and the similar Elcar a Not Acceptable rating for major safety and operating problems. One major flaw was the brakes, which were quite small even for a lightweight car. Production continued as the similar Comuta-Car (listed below).

MANUFACTURER: Sebring-Vanguard Inc., Columbia, Maryland and Sebring, Florida.

1982 Classic Speedster cabriolet

CLASSIC SPEEDSTER — By 1982, Classic Motor Carriages, a Florida kit car maker, listed a Miami address in its brochures. In addition to Bugatti, Bugatti Custom and Gazelle kit cars, the firm began offering two versions of a replica Porsche Speedster. The Classic Speedster version is a Porsche 356A lookalike intended for a Volkswagen chassis. It has an 82¾ in. wheelbase, 154 in. overall height and weight of 1,585 lbs. Zero-to-sixty performance of 9.5 seconds was advertised.

1982 Classic Speedster C cabriolet

CLASSIC SPEEDSTER C — The Classic Speedster C was a kit car advertised as a racing version of the same manufacturer's Classic Speedster. A brochure said the low-slung, fiberglass bodied replica "brings back Sebring, Laguna Seca and Watkins Glen." Any 12-volt Volkswagen Beetle or Super Beetle running gear is the basis for this vehicle.

1978 Clenet Series I convertible

1976-79 CLENET

CLENET — SERIES I — V-8 — Though styled in the image of 1930s luxury cars such as Mercedes and Jaguar, the "neoclassic" Clenet was not a true replica. Built on a Continental Mark V chassis with 120 inch wheelbase, it carried a stock Continental drivetrain: 351 cu. in. V-8 engine, three-speed automatic transmission, and front disc brakes. Because stock parts were used, the cars could be serviced at Lincoln dealers. Not an original, ground-up design, Clenet's steel body was modified from a production car (surprisingly, the MG Midget, which prompted some scoffing from critics). Only the cockpit (doors and windshield) and trunk came from an MG, but that choice kept Clenet's interior space closer to MG-size than to luxury dimensions. Construction of each car required about 1,600 man-hours. Long, sweeping front fenders flowed smoothly into short running boards, which met wide rear fenders. The extremely long, side-opening hood had a large number of short vertical louvers. Old-style round, separately-mounted headlamps were used. The grille was "classic" upright style. Large driving lights sat close together, just above the split front bumper. Long air horns actually worked, but the four exhaust pipes coming out of the hood side did not. An outside spare tire at the rear was flanked by a split rear bumper. Wire wheels came from the Mark V. Running boards held wood rub strips, and decklid held wooden rub strips. Each car's production number was displayed on a silver door plaque. Interior touches included a hand-rubbed black walnut dashboard (said to come from ancient trees), Connolly leather upholstery, and leather-padded steering wheel. Carpeting was Wilton lamb's wool, from Britain. Standard equipment included adjustable reclining seatbacks, tinted glass, cruise control, adjustable steering column, tonneau cover, and air conditioning. The roadster body carried just two people.

I.D. DATA: Not available.

CLENET (V-8)

Model Number	Body/Style Number	Body Type & Seating	Factory Price	Production Weight	Total
I	N/A	2-dr. Rdstr.-2P	65000	3908	Note 1
II	N/A	2-dr. Conv.-4P	N/A	3774	Note 2

Note 1: Total production in 1977 was 65 units; in 1979, 125 units. **Note 2:** Four-passenger (Series II) model was first announced in October 1978; see next listing for details.

PRICE/SPECIFICATION NOTE: Prices and specifications shown are for 1979 models.

ENGINE DATA: BASE V-8: 90-degree, overhead-valve V-8. Cast iron block and head. Displacement: 351 cu. in. (5.7 liters). Bore & stroke: 4.00 x 3.50 in. Compression ratio: 8.0:1. Brake horsepower: 135 at 3400 R.P.M. Torque: N/A. Five main bearings. Hydraulic valve lifters. Carburetor: 2Bbl. Ford/Motorcraft 2150. Ford-built (Lincoln).

CHASSIS DATA: Wheelbase: (rdstr) 120.4 in.; (conv.) 136 in. Overall Length: (rdstr) 192 in.; (conv.) 221 in. Height: (rdstr) 73.5 in.; (conv.) 62.5 in. Width: (rdstr) 73.6 in.; (conv.) 73 in. Front Tread: (rdstr) 62.9 in.; (conv.) 62.2 in. Rear Tread: (rdstr) 62.6 in.; (conv.) 62 in. Wheel size: 7 x 15 in. Standard Tires: LR78 x 15.

TECHNICAL: Transmission: Three-speed automatic transmission standard. Gear ratios: (1st) 2.40:1; (2nd) 1.47:1; (3rd) 1.00:1; (Rev) 2.00:1. Standard final drive ratio: (rdstr) 2.75:1; (conv.) 3.08:1. Steering: Recirculating ball. Suspension: Front coil springs w/lower trailing links and anti-sway bar; rigid rear axle w/lower trailing radius arms, upper oblique torque arms and coil springs. Brakes: Front disc, rear drum. Ignition: Electronic. Body construction: Separate body on perimeter frame. Fuel Tank: 21 gal.

OPTIONS: Limited-slip differential (3.00:1 ratio). Rear anti-sway bar. 235/60VR15 tires. Bilstein shock absorbers. Metallic paint. Hardtop.

MANUFACTURER: Clenet Coachworks, Santa Barbara (Goleta), California. Established 1976. Alain J.M. Clenet, president. 85 workers.

Historical Footnotes: Company founder and designer Alain Clenet, who arrived in the U.S. from France in 1965, was the son of a major French Ford dealer. As a teenager, he had been trained in design, engineering and fine arts. Clenet worked as a stylist at AMC, then as a consultant, before starting his own company to produce limited-production vehicles. Before long, he was considered a leader in the "neoclassic" car revival. The cars grew especially popular in California. Initial price was $27,500, but that rose to $39,500 by mid-1977, and $67,500 by the end of the car's run. The car was shown at the Los Angeles Auto Expo in April 1976, attracting plenty of attention—and orders. In time, people even tried to pay bribes to get their names on the waiting list. The company's gross zoomed from just $150,000 in 1976 to $3.7 million in 1978.

1980 Clenet Series II convertible

1980-81 CLENET

CLENET CABRIOLET — SERIES II — V-8 — Appearance of the four-passenger Clenet, introduced in August 1979, was similar to the two-passenger roadster, including the rear-mounted outside spare tire. Four big, bright exposed (simulated) exhaust pipes poked out each side of the long, razor-edge hood. The grille was Rolls-Royce style, slightly peaked forward. Large round, screened clear parking lamps were flanked by smaller round lamps. A plaque displayed the car's production number, along with the manufacturer's name. The windshield was curved. Roll-down quarter windows had etched glass. 'CLENET' lettering was low on the rear quarter. Running boards held wood strips. Front bucket seats were standard. The engine was a Ford-built 302 cu. in. V-8 instead of the previous 351.

1981 Clenet Series II phaeton

I.D. DATA: Not available.

CLENET SERIES II (V-8)

Model Number	Body/Style Number	Body Type & Seating	Factory Price	Production Weight	Total
II	N/A	2-dr. Conv.-4P	67500	4050	Note 1

Note 1: Production in 1980 was 125 units.

Price Note: Price shown is for 1980; factory price rose to $83,500 in 1981.

ENGINE DATA: BASE V-8: 90-degree, overhead-valve V-8. Cast iron block and head. Displacement: 302 cu. in. (5.0 liters). Bore & stroke: 4.00 x 3.00 in. Compression ratio: 8.4:1. Brake horsepower: 130 at 3600 R.P.M. Torque: 230 lbs.-ft. at 1600 R.P.M. Five main bearings. Hydraulic valve lifters. Carburetor: Variable- venturi Ford 7200. Ford-built (Mercury Marquis).

CHASSIS DATA: Wheelbase: 136 in. Overall Length: 224 in. Height: 62.5 in. Width: 74 in. Front Tread: 62.2 in. Rear Tread: 62 in. Wheel size: 5.5 x 14 in. Standard Tires: P205/75R14 BSW.

TECHNICAL: Transmission: SelectShift three-speed automatic standard. Gear ratios: (1st) 2.46:1; (2nd) 1.46:1; (3rd) 1.00:1; (Rev) 2.20:1. Standard final drive ratio: 2.26:1. Steering: Recirculating ball. Suspension: Front coil springs w/unequal length Aarms and anti-sway bar; rigid rear axle w/four links and coil springs. Brakes: Front disc, rear drum. Ignition: Electronic. Body construction: Separate body on perimeter frame. Fuel Tank: 19 gal.

OPTIONS: Not available.

MANUFACTURER: Clenet Coachworks, Santa Barbara (Goleta), California. Alain J.M. Clenet, president. 150 workers.

Historical Footnotes: After the first announcement of the four-passenger Series II, in 1978, the production limit of 500 cars was said to have been spoken for within 30 days. Alain Clenet now told reporters he wanted to be a "manufacturer" rather than a "coachbuilder." With that goal in mind, a modern Euro-styled four-door sedan was among the company's future plans. A dealer network was now in place.

1982 Clenet Series II phaeton

1982-84 CLENET

CLENET SERIES III ASHA — V-8 — A revised roadster, though similar in appearance to prior Clenets, rode a different (124 inch) wheelbase with unibody construction.

I.D. DATA: Not available.

CLENET SERIES III ASHA (V-8)

Model Number	Body/Style Number	Body Type & Seating	Factory Price	Production Weight	Total
III	N/A	2-dr. Rdstr-2P	75000	3740	N/A

Price Note: Price shown is for 1982.

ENGINE DATA: BASE V-8: 90-degree, overhead-valve V-8. Cast iron block and head. Displacement: 302 cu. in. (5.0 liters). Bore & stroke: 4.00 x 3.00 in. Compression ratio: 8.0:1. Brake horsepower: N/A. Torque: N/A. Five main bearings. Hydraulic valve lifters. Carburetor: 2Bbl. Motorcraft. Ford-built (Lincoln-Mercury).

CHASSIS DATA: Wheelbase: 124 in. Overall Length: 204.5 in. Height: 54 in. Width: 74 in. Front Tread: 62.2 in. Rear Tread: 62 in. Standard Tires: P235/75R15.

TECHNICAL: Transmission: SelectShift three-speed automatic standard. Standard final drive ratio: 3.42:1. Steering: Recirculating ball. Suspension: Front coil springs w/unequal length Aarms and anti-sway bar; rigid rear axle w/four links and coil springs. Brakes: Front disc, rear drum. Ignition: Electronic. Fuel Tank: 19 gal.

OPTIONS: Not available.

MANUFACTURER: Clenet Coachworks, Santa Barbara (Goleta), California. Alain J.M. Clenet, president.

1985 CLENET

CLENET SERIES III ASHA — V-8 — Appearance and equipment were similar to 1982-84. Leather upholstery and power seats were among the car's standard fittings.

I.D. DATA: Not available.

CLENET SERIES III ASHA (V-8)

Model Number	Body/Style Number	Body Type & Seating	Factory Price	Production Weight	Total
III	N/A	2-dr. Rdstr-2P	74000	3600	N/A

ENGINE DATA: BASE V-8: 90-degree, overhead-valve V-8. Cast iron block and head. Displacement: 302 cu. in. (5.0 liters). Bore & stroke: 4.00 x 3.00 in. Compression ratio: 8.3:1. Brake horsepower: 165 at 3800 R.P.M. Torque: 245 lbs.-ft. at 2000 R.P.M. Five main bearings. Hydraulic valve lifters. Fuel injection. Ford-built.

CHASSIS DATA: Wheelbase: 124 in. Overall Length: 204.5 in. Height: 53.6 in. Width: 71 in. Front Tread: 62 in. Rear Tread: 62 in. Standard Tires: N/A.

TECHNICAL: Transmission: Four-speed overdrive automatic standard. Gear ratios: (1st) 2.40:1; (2nd) 1.47:1; (3rd) 1.00:1; (4th) 0.67:1; (Rev) 2.00:1. Standard final drive ratio: 3.42:1. Steering: Recirculating ball. Suspension: Front coil springs w/lower arms and anti-sway bar; rigid rear axle w/trailing links and coil springs. Brakes: Front disc, rear drum. Ignition: Electronic. Fuel Tank: 22.7 gal.

OPTIONS: Hardtop.

MANUFACTURER: Clenet Coachworks, Santa Barbara (Goleta), California. Alain Clenet, president.

1986 Clenet convertible

1986 CLENET

CLENET — SERIES III ASHA — V-8 — By 1986, Clenet offered three models: the Series III ASHA roadster and a hardtop version, as well as the four-passenger Series II Cabriolet. The all-steel unibodied cars carried Lincoln-Mercury V-8 engines, and were available in a numbered limited edition of 500. Each hand-built model required about 1,200 man-hours. Features included walnut dash facing, Danish teak wood accents, leather upholstery, etched vent panes, and a backlit crystal ashtray. Standard equipment included power steering and brakes, tilt steering, automatic temperature control, automatic parking brake release, wire rims with stainless spokes, cruise control, English wool carpeting, power seats, and electric hood and trunk releases.

I.D. DATA: Not available.

CLENET SERIES III ASHA (V-8)

Model Number	Body/Style Number	Body Type & Seating	Factory Price	Production Weight	Total
III	N/A	2-dr. Rdstr-2P	82500	5750	N/A
III	N/A	2-dr. HT-2P	78500	N/A	N/A

CLENET SERIES II CABRIOLET (V-8)

II	N/A	2-dr. Cabr.-4P	98000	4090	N/A

ENGINE DATA: BASE V-8: 90-degree, overhead-valve V-8. Cast iron block and head. Displacement: 302 cu. in. (5.0 liters). Bore & stroke: 4.00 x 3.00 in. Compression ratio: 8.0:1. Brake horsepower: N/A. Torque: N/A. Five main bearings. Hydraulic valve lifters. Motorcraft "fuel-injected" 2Bbl. feedback carburetor. Ford-built.

CHASSIS DATA: Wheelbase: (III) 124 in.; (II) 136 in. Overall Length: (III) 204.5 in.; (II) 224 in. Height: (III) 54 in.; (II) 62.5 in. Width: 74 in. Front Tread: 62.2 in. Rear Tread: 62 in. Standard Tires: (III) P235/75R15.

TECHNICAL: Transmission: Four-speed overdrive automatic standard. Standard final drive ratio: (III) 3.42:1; (II) 3.08:1. Steering: Recirculating ball. Suspension: Front coil springs w/anti-sway bar (Silent Strut system); rigid rear axle w/four links and coil springs. Brakes: Front disc, rear drum. Ignition: Electronic. Fuel Tank: (III) 19 gal.

OPTIONS: Hardtop.

MANUFACTURER: Clenet Coachworks, Carpinteria, California. Alfred DiMora, president.

Historical Footnotes: *Automotive Age* called Clenet "America's Rolls-Royce."

COMUTA-CAR — ELECTRIC — Serving as a successor to the CitiCar, the Florida-built Comuta-Car had a dealership network in place by 1979. Unlike many electrics that were conversions of an existing model, this one was built from the ground up as an electric car. An impact-resistant Cycolac ABS body went atop a rectangular aluminum chassis with tubular aluminum body support. Eight 6volt batteries were used; batteries were expected to last 12,000-18,000 miles. The charging system could be supplemented by the use of solar panels. A Comuta-Van also was produced. Standard equipment included a heater/defroster, tinted glass hatchback, custom rally stripes, and steel-belted Michelin ZX radial tires.

I.D. DATA: Not available.

COMUTA-CAR (ELECTRIC)

Model Number	Body/Style Number	Body Type & Seating	Factory Price	Production Weight	Total
111-DW	N/A	2-dr. Cpe-2P	4995	1475	N/A

NOTE: Prices and all specifications are for 1980 model.

CHASSIS DATA: Wheelbase: 63 in. Overall Length: 117 in. Height: 58 in. Width: 55 in. Front Tread: 43 in. Rear Tread: 44 in. Standard Tires: 125 x 12 radial.

TECHNICAL: Motor: Series-wound DC 6 H.P. Batteries: Eight 6-volt. Built-in charger. Suspension: Leaf springs, front and rear.

RATINGS: Range: up to 50 miles (30-40 in city). Cruising Speed: 38 MPH. Acceleration: 0-35 MPH in 19 seconds.

OPTIONS: AM radio ($89.50). AM/FM radio ($150). Tinted windshield ($50). Radial spare tire and Comuta-Car jack ($85). Right-hand mirror ($12).

MANUFACTURER: Commuter Vehicles Inc. (subsidiary of General Engines Co.), Sebring, Florida.

Historical Footnotes: A letter from Comuta-Car's national sales manager said they expected to have production falling behind demand at this time, due to the current energy situation. Already, however, interest in electric-powered vehicles was beginning to fade away—all the more so as gasoline prices stabilized and no crisis seemed imminent.

1981 Contemporary Classics 427 Cobra SC427 roadster

CONTEMPORARY COBRA — By 1981, Contemporary Classics Motor Car Co., of Mount Vernon, N.Y., had produced over 80 Cobra replica units. The firm's product was available in component form or fully-assembled. A variety of options were offered to customers, including 289 cid and 427 cid engine configurations.

1981 Cord 815SE convertible

CORD 815SE — The front-wheel drive 815SE, by Southeastern Replicars, Inc., was a replica of the 812 Cord using a 350 cid Chevrolet V-8, automatic transmission and torsion bar front suspension. The gas powered version retailed for $49,950 in 1980. A diesel version was optional and sold for $57,950 that year. Specifications included a 125 in. wheelbase, 196 in. overall length and 3,700 lb. curb weight. The body was fiberglass over a steel tube frame. Dave Samuels was founder of the Largo, Fla. company. Buck Dunivens handled West Coast sales in Laguna Beach, Calif.

1980 Custom Bugatti roadster

CUSTOM BUGATTI — Produced by Classic Motor Carriages, of Hallendale, Fla., the Custom Bugatti kit is a replica of the Type 55 Bugatti competition roadster designed for a Volkswagen chassis. It has a 94.5 in. wheelbase, 166 in. overall length and weight of 1,550 lbs.

D

1980 Daytona MIGI roadster

DAYTONA MIGI — For many years, LaVerne Martincic had encouraged her husband to make a reproduction of the MG-Td. In November, 1974, the first molds for such a car were produced. The company's fiberglass replica of the British sports car came on the market the following February. This kit car uses a Volkswagen chassis and 1600 cc. engine. It has a 94.5 in. wheelbase and weighs about 1,375 lbs. In 1980, the body kit sold for $2,095, with two-tone finish costing $100 extra. A complete package, including accessiries, was available from the Holly Hill, Fla. company for $4,750 the same year. A detailed assembly manual was provided.

1980 Daytona Moya roadster

DAYTONA MOYA — Joe Martincic, chief engineer at Daytona Automotive Fiberglass (DAF) wanted to capture the essence of Jaguars, Bugattis and Morgans in his Moya roadster. It had a fiberglass body reinforced with steel tubing and designed to fit a Volkswagen Beetle chassis. Assembly of the 147 in. long replicar required about 100 hours. A comprehensive accessories package and choice of 10 colors was offered. Velvet, velour or vinyl interiors, also in 10 colors, were offered, too. The firm had its headquarters in Holly Hill, Fla.

1983 De Courville roadster

De COURVILLE — N. de Courville started his San Jose, Calif. company as the de Courville Group, Inc. It then became an independent replicar-making firm producing a vehicle called the DeCourville roadster around 1982-1983. The company called its factory the Gatsby Works and later used that name on a replicar. The De Courville roadster carried a $65,500 price tag, so it was no kit car, even though neo-classic styling was featured. It was more of an "exoticar" aimed at the upscale end of the market. The roadster body was fashioned of steel and had two individual, leather-upholstered bucket seats. The car was big, with a 118.3 in. wheelbase and 181.5 in. overall length. It tipped the scales at 3,400 lbs. and had a 39.4 ft. turn circle. The powerplant was a 302 cid Ford V-8 producing 139 nhp at 3600 rpm. A Ford automatic transmission was used, too. This gave the car a hefty top speed of about 110 mph, even though 26 mpg driving economy was promised. Other features included front disc/rear drum brakes, recirculating ball steering (four turns lock-to-lock) and a 12 volt electrical system. A strange feature of the car was quad headlamps, mounted in old-fashioned looking chrome plated buckets.

1981 Delorean DMC gullwing coupe

DELOREAN — SERIES DMC-12 — V-6 — A sleek, sophisticated sports/luxury car with stainless steel-clad plastic body, the controversial DeLorean was conceived as one man's personal expression of the ultimate in elite automobiles. Initial conceptions evolved around 1974, followed by a series of complicated financial maneuvers to raise capital and establish production capability. The basic design came from the Italian stylist Giorgio Giugario in 1974. Appearance features included a slim front treatment, gull-wing doors, fastback roof and kammback tail. Former Pontiac engineer Bill Collins developed the unique chassis, which used an overhead-cam Renault V-6 engine, mounted at the rear; independent front and rear suspension; and a full- length backbone frame that bolted directly to the body. Power was transmitted via a Renault transaxle. Coachwork was fiberglass-reinforced plastic, clad in stainless steel. Other design highlights included quad rectangular quartz headlamps, integral front spoiler, turbine wheels, five-speed manual transmission, and Bosch fuel injection. Automatic transmission was optional. Interior appointments were rich and lavish, including such features as glove leather upholstery. The original, projected list price was set at $25,000. Top speed was 130 MPH, and the car drew attention wherever it was seen. A five-year, 50,000-mile warranty (backed by an independent insurance company) was provided with each DeLorean sold. Standard equipment included counterbalanced gull-wing doors, leather seats and trim, air conditioning, power windows, adjustable steering wheel, multi-speaker stereo system, electric door mirrors, tinted glass, and an electric locking system.

I.D. DATA: Serial number range was SCED-T26-T8-BD000500 to SCED-T26-T8-DD02014.

1981 DELOREAN (V-6)

Model Number	Body/Style Number	Body Type & Seating	Factory Price	Production Weight	Total
DMC-12	N/A	2-dr. Spt Cpe-2P	26175	2700	Note 1

1982 DELOREAN (V-6)

Model Number	Body/Style Number	Body Type & Seating	Factory Price	Production Weight	Total
DMC-12	N/A	2-dr. Spt Cpe-2P	29825	3100	Note 1

Note 1: Approximately 4,000 DeLoreans were shipped to the United States during two years of production.

ENGINE DATA: BASE V-6: 90-degree, dual overhead-camshaft V-6. Aluminum block and heads. Displacement: 174 cu. in. (2.85 liters). Bore & stroke: 3.58 x 2.87 in. Compression ratio: 8.8:1. Brake horsepower: 130 at 5500 R.P.M. Torque: 166 lbs.-ft. at 3000 R.P.M. Four main bearings. Hydraulic valve lifters. Bosch K- Jetronic mechanical fuel injection.

CHASSIS DATA: Wheelbase: 95 in. Overall Length: 168 in. Height: 46 in. Width: 73 in. Front Tread: 65.4 in. Rear Tread: 62.7 in. Wheel size: (front) 6 x 14 in.; (rear) 8 x 15 in. Standard Tires: Goodyear NCT SBR (front) 195/60HR14; (rear) 235/60HR15.

Note: Revised dimensions were announced for the 1982 model.

TECHNICAL: Transmission: Fully synchronized five-speed manual standard. Gear ratios: (1st) 3.36:1; (2nd) 2.06:1; (3rd) 1.38:1; (4th) 1.06:1; (5th) 0.82:1; (Rev) 3.18:1. Three-speed automatic transmission optional. Standard final drive ratio: 3.44:1. Steering: Rack-and-pinion. Suspension: (front) unequal-length upper/lower control arms with coil springs and anti-sway bar; (rear) independent with diagonal trailing radius arms, upper/low links and coil springs. Brakes: Power vented disc (front) 10 in.; (rear) 10.5 in. Body construction: Stainless steel-clad plastic. Ignition: Bosch electronic. Fuel Tank: 16 gal.

OPTIONS: Not available.

MANUFACTURER: DeLorean Motor Co., New York City. John Z. DeLorean, chairman. Factory in Northern Ireland.

HISTORICAL FOOTNOTES: From the beginning, through the car's stab at popularity and into the company's abrupt decline, attention was focused at least as much on the man as the machine. John Zachary DeLorean, raised in New York City, was the son of a Detroit autoworker. He attended Lawrence Institute of Technology and received a degree in mechanical engineering. In 1952, DeLorean earned his masters degree in automotive engineering from the Chrysler Institute. That same year, he left Chrysler to work as Packard's head of research and development. In 1956, he began a brilliant career with General Motors, starting in Pontiac's advanced engineering department. DeLorean played major roles in creating the innovative 1961 Tempest, the first Pontiac GTO, and the Tempest OHC-Six engine. DeLorean went on to become general manager of Pontiac and brought such cars as the Firebird, the first Trans Am and the 1969 Grand Prix into existence. In 1969, he became general manager of Chevrolet and turned to development of the Vega subcompact. In 1972, he was promoted to vice-president in charge of GM's domestic car and truck group (at $600,000 a year).

Always somewhat of a rebel and maverick, DeLorean left GM in 1973 and soon set out to build his own company and car. Early in 1974, he formed the John Z. DeLorean Corporation to establish a financial base. Next, the DeLorean Motor Car Company was formed as a subsidiary. DeLorean attracted millions of dollars from investors, including comedian Johnny Carson (who purchased 250,000 shares). The search for a factory location took DeLorean to Western Europe, Puerto Rice and, finally in 1978, to Northern Ireland. Here, the British Government offered to provide loans and tax breaks, in hopes of generating jobs for unemployed people living in an impoverished section of West Belfast. A non-operable mockup of the DMC-12 was produced by Ital Design studios in July 1975. The first running prototype appeared in October 1976, powered by a 2.8-liter Citroen Four (which proved unacceptable). Soon thereafter, the production 2.8-liter OHC Six (used successfully in Peugeots, Renaults and Volvos) was adopted. Delivery of production models was promised for June 1979, and the press gave ample publicity to the car. Not until April 1981, however, did production become a reality. Most of the 345 U.S. dealers had no cars to sell until July of that year. Sticker price for the 1981 version rose a bit above the $25,000 projection and, by 1982, climbed close to $30,000. Shipments to the U.S. neared 4,000 cars. Criticism began quickly, for a number of design and performance points. Sales were slow, and dealer asking prices soon fell to about $18,500 for 1981 models, $21,900 for 1982s. The latter incorporated a number of significant detail improvements. Sluggish sales also multiplied the firm's financial problems, as a tangled web of fancy corporate footwork eventually came to light. During winter 1982, the British House of Commons became concerned about protecting its $138 million investment. Shortly thereafter, investigation focused on misdealings and the company was placed in receivership. A search for a takeover buyer proved unsuccessful. On October 18, 1982 the British Government would close the business since, according to the Receiver's Office, in addition to its own debt, over $70 million was owed to other creditors. Hours later, on October 19, John DeLorean was arrested by U.S. Justice Department and F.B.I. officers at a Los Angeles airport, charged with nine counts of racketeering and drug trafficking. According to the Justice Department, the 57-year-old automaker—in an effort to salvage his foundering company—had become involved in a scheme to import 220 pounds of cocaine. The *New York Times* reported that DeLorean would have earned a $60 million profit from that deal. After release on $10 million bond, DeLorean was arraigned on November 8, 1982. He pleaded not guilty, with his attorneys reporting they would seek dismissal on grounds that the wide publicity surrounding the case was attributable to misconduct by government officials. He was eventually found innocent of the drug charges. After a four-year series of court actions, in December 1986 DeLorean also was acquitted of criminal fraud charges, but agreed to pay creditors $9.4 million (far less than the $80 million claim made by the British government). Moderate collector demand for DeLoreans began early on. One car sold for $31,000 at auction when it was only months old, in November 1981. The car's early problems cannot be overlooked, however. They include electrical system failures, creaking of fiberglass body panels (under the stainless steel outer skin), loose-fitting control knobs and buttons, and a body that's nearly impossible to keep clean. Although the company claimed a 0-60 MPH acceleration time of 8.5 seconds, and 130 MPH top speed, others have declared DeLorean's performance "sluggish" and "uninspiring." Those two terms never did apply to the car's creator.

1984 DiNapoli five-passenger touring

DINAPOLI — The stunning looking Dinapoli is an exotic car that saw very low production. Only about seven of these five-passenger tourings were made. They were conceived as the ultimate in Italian auto body styling and hand-craftsmanship. Features include a specially balanced Corvette engine and powertrain; power steering; power brakes; power windows; interior with Connolly leather Recaro seats and English wool trim; genuine teakwood dashboard; Blaupunkt stereo with headrest speakers; lit vanity mirror and many more first-class accoutrements.

1979 Doval Shadow B convertible

DOVAL SHADOW "B" — The Doval Shadow was introduced as "The Classic of the '80s," although the car in the company's sales brochure wore 1979 license plates. It features a handbuilt aluminum body. Power comes from a 351 cid Ford V-8. The luxury convertible has a 118 in. wheelbase, 74 in. width and overall length of 200 in. Alan Hager and Don Hart designed the car, manufactured by Doval Coach Ltd., of East Haven, Conn. Standard equipment includes a Connolly leather interior, Wilton carpets, air conditioning, chrome wire wheels and an AM/FM stereo tape deck.

1976 Duesenberg SSJ roadster

1976-77 DUESENBERG

DUESENBERG SSJ — V-8 — The original Duesenberg was a hard act to follow—and to recreate decades later. A California company began production of a replica of the short-wheelbase 1936 SSJ roadster in 1970, first powered by a supercharged Chrysler V-8 engine. By 1974, the blower disappeared, replaced by a 440 cu. in. Chrysler powerplant. A modified Dodge truck chassis was used, holding an aluminum body styled like the original. Initial price had been $14,500, but that hit the half-a-hundred mark by 1976. All cars built by special order (2-3 a month). As in the original, big exhaust pipes came out the side of the hood, and the car held a rear-mounted spare tire.

I.D. DATA: Not available.

DUESENBERG SSJ (V-8)

Model Number	Body/Style Number	Body Type & Seating	Factory Price	Shipping Weight	Production Total
SSJ	N/A	2-dr. Rdstr-2P	50000	3600	Note 1

Note 1: A total of 25 cars were reported to have been produced in 1976, and 15 in 1977.

ENGINE DATA: BASE V-8: 90-degree, overhead valve V-8. Cast iron block and head. Displacement: 440 cu. in. (7.2 liters). Bore & stroke: 4.32 x 3.75 in. Compression ratio: 8.2:1. Brake horsepower: 215 at 4000 R.P.M. Torque: 330 lbs.-ft. at 3200 R.P.M. Five main bearings. Hydraulic valve lifters. Carburetor: 4Bbl. Carter TQ-9009S. Chrysler-built.

CHASSIS DATA: Wheelbase: 128 in. Overall Length: 166.5 in. Height: 60 in. Width: 78.5 in. Front Tread: 63.3 in. Rear Tread: 64.6 in. Standard Tires: 7.00/7.50 x 18.

TECHNICAL: Transmission: TorqueFlite three-speed automatic standard. Gear ratios: (1st) 2.45:1; (2nd) 1.45:1; (3rd) 1.00:1; (Rev) 2.20:1. Standard final drive ratio: 3.54:1. Steering: Recirculating ball. Suspension: Rigid front and rear axles w/semi-elliptic leaf springs; friction front shock absorbers, hydraulic rear. Brakes: Front and rear drum (12.5 in. drum dia.). Body construction: Separate body and channel ladder frame. Fuel Tank: 21 gal.

OPTIONS: Air conditioning.

MANUFACTURER: Duesenberg Corp., Inglewood, California. E.W. Rose, director. Production began in 1970; company reorganized in 1972. Production of a phaeton model was in the planning stage, but did not appear.

Appearance and equipment were similar to 1976-77, but the factory price rose 20 percent. 1979 would be the final year for this Duesenberg replicar (though other companies also produced Duesie replicas). Standard equipment included wire wheels and a tonneau cover.

I.D. DATA: Not available.

DUESENBERG SSJ (V-8)

Model Number	Body/Style Number	Body Type & Seating	Factory Price	Shipping Weight	Production Total
SSJ	N/A	2-dr. Rdstr-2P	60000	3600	N/A

ENGINE DATA: same as 1976-77.

CHASSIS DATA: same as 1976-77.

TECHNICAL: same as 1976-77.

OPTIONS: Air conditioning.

MANUFACTURER: Duesenberg Corp., Inglewood, California. E.W. Rose, director.

1979 Duesenberg II Model J boattail speedster

1980 Duesenberg II Model J speedster

1981 Duesenberg II Royalton Phaeton

1982 Duesenberg II Torpedo Speedster

1982 Duesenberg II roadster

1984 Duesenberg II Murphy roadster

421

DUESENBERG II — V-8 — Another attempt to revive the Duesenberg name was made in the late 1970s by a Wisconsin firm. Described as "a masterpiece of classic elegance," this replica of the one-off 1933 SJ Speedster carried a Lincoln 460 cu. in. V-8 engine and automatic transmission. A quartet of rakishly angled (if ineffectual) stainless steel exhaust pipes pushed out each side of the hood. The body was steel-reinforced fiberglass. Features included full-size Duesenberg headlamps, original-style chromed steel radiator shell and ornamentation, twin bugle horns, and engine-turned dash. Standard equipment included leather upholstery, power brakes and steering, air conditioning, cruise control, power windows, six-way power seats, AM/FM with 8track, and disappearing convertible top.

I.D. DATA: Not available.

DUESENBERG II (V-8)

Model Number	Body/Style Number	Body Type & Seating	Factory Price	Shipping Weight	Production Total
II	N/A	2-dr. Rdstr-2P	N/A	N/A	N/A

ENGINE DATA: BASE V-8: 90-degree, overhead valve V-8. Cast iron block and head. Displacement: 460 cu. in. Ford-built.

CHASSIS DATA: Wheelbase: 153.5 in. Overall Length: 224 in.

TECHNICAL: Transmission: Three-speed automatic standard. Standard final drive ratio: N/A. Steering: N/A. Suspension: Twin Ibeam front, leaf spring rear. Brakes: N/A.

OPTIONS: Wire wheels.

MANUFACTURER: Elite Heritage Motors Corp., Elroy, Wisconsin.

DUESENBERG TOWN SEDAN — V-8

Harlan and Kenneth Duesenberg, grandnephews of Fred and August (the original Duesenberg brothers) wanted to produce a car that would carry their name into the modern age. This wasn't the first "modern" car to carry on the Duesenberg mystique (and name). Mike Rollins of Detroit built a prototype roadster on a Packard chassis in 1959, with Duesenberg engine but modern styling. Fred 'Fritz' Duesenberg, son of one of the company's founders, displayed another prototype in 1966, designed by Virgil Exner and built in Italy by Ghia. Powerplant was a modified Chrysler V-8. To get started with their own version, Harlan and Kenneth connected with Robert Peterson of Lehman-Peterson Co. (maker of hearses, ambulances and stretch limos) to form Duesenberg Brothers, Inc. The design chosen and built into a prototype was, surprisingly, not a streamlined design at all, but a rather boxy-looking, slab-sided affair. Formal and expensive looking it was, with heavy rear-quarter pillars, but hardly an eye-catcher. Oh, it had some Duesenberg touches, like a twin-section "bow-tie" bumper that looked something like an upper lip. But this hardly appeared to mark the "Renaissance of 'The World's Finest Motor Car'" that the nephews promised. A Cadillac frame was stretched to 133 in. wheelbase. Up front was a formal-looking, Continental-style vertical-bar grille. Quad vertically-stacked headlamps were used. Standard equipment included a Cadillac 425 cu. in. V-8 with Bendix electronic fuel injection, power steering, disc brakes, wool carpets, mahogany instrumental panel, and wire wheels. After two years of announcements, only a single prototype had been built by 1979. Undaunted, the nephews were also planning a "Renaissance" model with two turbochargers, producing 650 horsepower.

I.D. DATA: Not available.

DUESENBERG (V-8)

Model Number	Body/Style Number	Body Type & Seating	Factory Price	Production Weight	Total
N/A	N/A	4-dr. Twn Sed-5P	100000	4540	1

ENGINE DATA: BASE V-8: 90-degree, overhead-valve V-8. Cast iron block and head. Displacement: 425 cu. in. (7.0 liters). Bore & stroke: 4.08 x 4.06 in. Compression ratio: 8.2:1. Brake horsepower: 195 at 3800 R.P.M. Torque: 320 lbs.-ft. at 2400 R.P.M. Five main bearings. Hydraulic valve lifters. Electronic fuel injection. Cadillac-built.

CHASSIS DATA: Wheelbase: 133 in. Overall Length: 233 in. Height: 57.4 in. Width: 79 in. Front Tread: 61.7 in. Rear Tread: 60.7 in. Wheel size: 6 x 15 in. Standard Tires: GR78 x 15.

TECHNICAL: Transmission: Turbo Hydra-matic 400 three-speed automatic transmission standard. Gear ratios: (1st) 2.48:1; (2nd) 1.48:1; (3rd) 1.00:1; (Rev) 2.07:1. Standard final drive ratio: 3.08:1. Steering: Recirculating ball. Suspension: Front coil springs w/unequal-length Aarms and anti-sway bar; rigid rear axle w/four trailing arms, coil springs and automatic level control. Brakes: Disc. Ignition: Delco-Remy HEI. Body construction: Separate body on ladder-type frame. Fuel Tank: N/A.

PROPOSED OPTION: Twin turbochargers.

MANUFACTURER: Duesenberg Brothers, Mundelein, Illinois.

E

1976 ELCAR

2000 WAGONETTE — ELECTRIC Designed by Zagato in Italy, the two-door, four-passenger Elcar looked like a miniature van. Because of the short (59 inch) wheelbase and stubby shape, it looked unusually tall. Viewed from the side, the door took up almost the entire profile. A steel frame held a reinforced fiberglass body. The chassis had independent front and rear wheels, with rigid rear axle. Power source was a 48-volt, 6 H.P. motor run from a dozen 12-volt batteries. With a 35-40 MPH top speed, it was built for urban use and could be recharged in any 110-volt outlet, in 78 hours. To alleviate logical customer fears, the company claimed that by resting for 20-30 minutes, the batteries would recharge themselves to go a few more miles.

CINDERELLA — ELECTRIC — The company's alternate electric model was something completely different: a "Victorian" style two-passenger carriage with tiller steering, which looked like an early automobile. It had large-diameter wire wheels and steel coach lamps. The 24-volt motor ran on four 6-volt batteries.

I.D. DATA: Not available.

ELCAR (ELECTRIC)

Model Number	Body/Style Number	Body Type & Seating	Factory Price	Production Weight	Total
2000 Wagonette 2-dr. Cpe-4P 4000			1500	N/A	
Cinderella 2-dr. Rdst. 2-P N/A			600	N/A	

CHASSIS DATA: Wheelbase: (Wagonette) 59 in. Overall Length: (Wagon) 100 in.; (Cind.) 85 in. Height: (Wagon) 64 in.; (Cind.) 54 in. but 66 in. w/top raised. Width: (Wagon) 53 in.; (Cind.) 50 in. Standard Tires: (Wagon) 145 SR x 10; (Cind.) 2.75 x 18.

TECHNICAL: Motor: (Wagon) 48-volt, 6 horsepower; (Cind.) 24-volt, 2 H.P.

Batteries: (Wagon) Twelve 12-volt (100 ampere-hour) connected in series-parallel; (Cind.) Four 6-volt (200 amp-hour). Brakes: (Wagon) hydraulic; (Cind.) hydraulic at rear only.

RATINGS: Range: (Wagon) 40 miles max.; (Cind.) 40-50 miles. Top Speed: (Wagon) 35-40 MPH; (Cind.) 18-20 MPH.

OPTIONS: List not available.

MANUFACTURER: Illinois Electric Car Corp., Northlake, Illinois.

Historical Footnotes: Elcar and CitiCar were the only two electric cars to have sold in appreciable numbers by 1976. In a survey of users, however, *Popular Mechanics* magazine found that only 5 percent of the respondents were Elcar owners while 95 percent had a CitiCar.

ELECTRA KING — PFS SERIES — ELECTRIC — Production of two-passenger (and four-passenger) Electra King models began as early as 1961. The company called its product "The King of Electric Cars." Early versions had open sides and a surrey-style top, with rear-facing second seat. The first ones were three-wheelers; a four-wheel model was added in 1967. Full-height doors began in 1972, eliminating the former plastic side curtains. As of 1974-75, Electra Kings came with three or four wheels, a tiller or steering wheel, and either foot or hand controls. The reinforced fiberglass "coupe" bodies had what appeared to be an unusually tall passenger compartment, because of the car's short length. A variety of body and motor sizes were offered.

I.D. DATA: Not available.

ELECTRA KING (ELECTRIC)

Model Number	Body/Style Number	Body Type & Seating	Factory Price	Production Weight	Total
PFS	N/A	2-dr. Cpe-2P	N/A	Note 1	N/A
PFS	N/A	2-dr. Cpe-4P	N/A	Note 1	N/A

Note 1: Three-wheelers weighed about 990 pounds, four-wheelers 1,090 pounds.

MODEL NOTE: A variety of models in the PFS series were available, with three- or four-wheel drive and various motor horsepowers. Model numbers took the form PFS 123, PFS 125, etc.

CHASSIS DATA: Wheelbase: 65 in. Overall Length: 101 in. Height: 60. Width: 45 in.

TECHNICAL: Motor: GE 36-volt series-wound (1 to 3.5 horsepower). Batteries: Six 6-volt (170-190 ampere-hour); weight 56 lbs. Drive: Chain, to one rear wheel. Body: Fiberglass reinforced, on aluminum frame.

RATINGS: Range: 22-56 miles max. depending on motor size. Top Speed: 16-32 MPH; varies with motor size.

OPTIONS: List not available.

MANUFACTURER: B & Z Electric Car Co., Long Beach, California.

1979 Elegant Collector Series 852 Auburn speedster

1980 Elegant Collector Series 852 Auburn speedster

ELEGANT 852 AUBURN SPEEDSTER — Del Amy's Elegant Motors, of Indianapolis, Ind., entered the replicar/kit car market in the early 1970s. The "Collectors Series" 852 Auburn Speedster was sold as a fully-assembled fiberglass replica of the original Classic made in Auburn, Ind. Limited production of 300 units was scheduled. Though specifications vary with model year, the company's 1981 brochure listed a 127 in. wheelbase, 202 in. overall length and 3,200 lb. weight. Power comes from a supercharged V-8 engine. Tire size was 7.00 x 15.

1984 Elegant 856 Auburn speedster

ELEGANT 856 AUBURN SPEEDSTER — *Motor Trend* rated Elegant Motor's 856 Speedster "The best of the Auburn replicas" in 1981. This vehicle — priced at $40,000 that year — was a copy of the original 856 Auburn boattail speedster. It features a fuel-injected 288 hp Jaguar V-12 engine, four-speed manual gear box, box type ladder frame with crossmembers, coil spring front suspension and independent rear suspension. The 856 Auburn has a 128 in. wheelbase, 203.94 in. overall length 57.09 in height and weight of approximately 3,000 lbs.

ELEGANT 898 AUBURN REPLICA — Elegant Motors also produced an upscale version of its Auburn replica that came in two trim levels: 898 Phaeton or 898 Elegante. They were priced at $50,000 and $60,000, respectively, in 1981. Specifications are basically the same as for the firm's 856 Auburn Speedster.

1984 Elegant CH gullwing coupe

ELEGANT CH GULL-WING COUPE — Elegant Motors, of Indianapolis, Ind., produced this quality replica of Bill Thomas' 1963-1966 Cheetah competition coupe. It uses a cage-braced fiberglass body shell and Corvette engine/transmission/chassis. Series 1 Lightning (90 in. wheelbase); Series 2 Super Matchless (98 in. wheelbase) and Series 3 (streamlined extended convertible) versions were offered, as well as Sprint and Persian kits. Prices ranged from $10,995-15,995 for modular packages and $35,000-$45,000 for built-up cars.

1984 Elegant 820 SC Cord phaeton

ELEGANT 820 SC CORD PHAETON — Produced and marketed exclusively by Elegant Motors of Indianapolis, Ind., the 820 SC Phaeton is a replica of the original Cord classic. Features including a continental spare tire and various types of chassis configurations were available for front and rear wheel drive models.

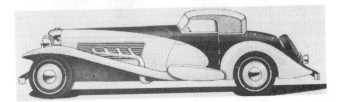

1984 Elegant LeGrande LE Sportster

ELEGANT LE GRANDE SPORTSTER — Another replica from Elegant Motors, of Indianapolis, is the LeGrande SE Sportster. It was introduced in the fall of 1983. The design of this neo-classic was inspired by the famous Greta Garbo Duesenberg, which sold for a record price last year.

1984 Elegant 427 Sports Roadster

ELEGANT 427 SPORTS ROADSTER — The 427 Sports Roadster marketed by Elegant Motors is a replica of the AC Cobra. It has been offered in various "assemblies" ranging from the $25,000 Warrior to the $60,000 Attack Series Three. Wheelbases of 90 in. or 98 in. were optional. Small-block or big-block Ford and General Motors V-8s were listed in a 1984 brochure. Corvette or Jaguar suspensions were optional. Finished cars weighed 2,000 to 2,500 lbs. Competition and Warrior kit versions were also available to home builders. In 1983, the price range for the kits was $4,995-$5,995.

1983 Elite Laser JX2 roadster

ELITE LASER J2X — Elite Enterprises, of Cokata, Minn., sold this kit car replica of a Cad-Allard. The complete package retailed for $4,995. Factory options ranged from a 14 in. wood steering wheel ($139) to a universal frame and crossmember option with a $795 price tag. Leather upholstery could be ordered upon a special price quote. Volkswagen running gear was easily adopted to the standard J2X custom universal frame. However, the kit could also be built up for a four-cylinder, V-6 or V-8 chassis/front engine layout.

1978 Elite Laser 917 gullwing coupe

ELITE LASER 917 — This kit car is marketed by Elite Enterprises of Cokata, Minn. The company was formed in 1968. Design of the Laser 917 is inspired by the famous Porsche 917 race car. It mounts on a Volkswagen Beetle, Ghia or Type III chassis. A wide range of accessories was available. The complete sports car kit sold for $5,495 in 1983. Values for this car are sometimes listed in *NADA Official Used Car Guides* under Volkswagen. It has a 94.5 in. wheelbase; 43 in. height; 173¾ in. overall length and its manufacturer claims a top speed of over 100 mph.

423

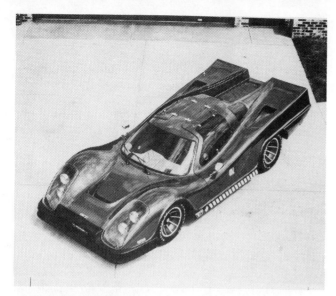

1983 Elite Laser 917 gullwing coupe

1980 ERA 427SC Cobra roadster

1983 ERA AC Cobra roadster

ERA 427 SC COBRA — Era Replica Automobiles, of New Britain, Conn., has produced its 427 SC Cobra as an unassembled, fully engineered production car. A price of $14,800 for the standard assembly was advertised in 1980. A fiberglass body on rectangular steel tube chassis forms the basis of the front engine/ rear drive sports car. It comes with a Ford small-block V-8 or big-block V-8 and a choice of C-6 automatic or four-speed manual transmissions. The car's wheelbase is 90 in., while overall length measures 156 in.

1976 EXCALIBUR

EXCALIBUR — SERIES III — V-8 — The Excalibur name goes back as far as 1952, when industrial designer Brooks Stevens produced an aluminum- bodied two-passenger sports car dubbed Excalibur I, on a Henry J chassis. Actual Excalibur history, however, began in 1965, with the production of Excalibur II. Stevens, who was connected with Studebaker during its final years at South Bend, Indiana, wanted to produce a modern car in the image of a sports classic of the past. The result, based roughly on the 1928-29 Mercedes SSK, rode a Studebaker convertible chassis. Stevens's original intention to use Studebaker power was sidetracked by the abandonment of Stude production, so a Corvette engine went under the Excalibur's hood instead. Styling changed little over the next decade, though powerplants moved from the original Corvette 327 cu. in. V-8 to the big 454 in 1972. Production reached a peak in 1974-75, when 144 and 150 cars (respectively) came out of the Wisconsin factory. Series III had been introduced in 1975. Excalibur bodies were hand-layed-up fiberglass. Bumpers, exhaust system and body hardware were handcrafted, of either stainless steel or aluminum. Three exhaust pipes protruded out each side of the hood. Fenders held dual sidemount tires. Four external air horns were standard. Headlamps and parking lamps were separately mounted. 'Excalibur' lettering was on the right side of the radiator-style grille, which displayed a very tight crosshatch pattern. Up top was a round see-thru "radiator cap" hood ornament. Excaliburs featured real wire wheels,

low-cut doors, low windshields, and authentic convertible tops with side curtains. Front/rear bucket seats were leather-upholstered. Standard equipment included a 454 cu. in. Chevrolet V-8 engine and Corvette suspension, all-weather removable hardtop, tonneau cover, air conditioning, heater, tilt/telescoping steering wheel, limited-slip differential, and leather upholstery.

I.D. DATA: Not available.

EXCALIBUR (V-8)

Model Number	Body/Style Number	Body Type & Seating	Factory Price	Shipping Weight	Production Total
III	N/A	2-dr. Roadster-2P	20000	4350	Note 1
III	N/A	2-dr. Phaeton-4P	20000	4350	Note 1

Note 1: Total production in 1976 was 250 units.

ENGINE DATA: BASE V-8: 90-degree, overhead valve V-8. Cast iron block and head. Displacement: 454 cu. in. (7.4 liters). Bore & stroke: 4.25 x 4.00 in. Compression ratio: 7.9:1. Brake horsepower: 215 at 4000 R.P.M. Torque: 350 lbs.-ft. at 2400 R.P.M. Five main bearings. Hydraulic valve lifters. Carburetor: 4Bbl. Rochester 7045200. Chevrolet-built.

CHASSIS DATA: Wheelbase: 112 in. Overall Length: 175 in. Height: 58 in. Width: 72 in. Front Tread: 62.5 in. Rear Tread: 62.5 in. Wheel size: 7.5 x 15 in. Standard Tires: GR78 x 15.

TECHNICAL: Transmission: Turbo-Hydramatic 400 three-speed automatic transmission standard. Gear ratios: (1st) 2.48:1; (2nd) 1.48:1; (3rd) 1.00:1; (Rev) 2.08:1. Standard final drive ratio: 2.73:1. Steering: Recirculating ball. Suspension: Front coil springs, control arms and anti-sway bar; independent rear with semi-axle as upper pivoting arm, angular strut rod as lower arm, transverse semi-elliptic leaf springs, trailing radius arms, anti-sway bar, and adjustable shocks. Brakes: Four-wheel disc. Ignition: Delco-Remy HEI. Body construction: Separate body and box-type ladder frame. Fuel Tank: 25 gal.

OPTIONS: Not available.

MANUFACTURER: Name changed from SS Automobile Inc. to Excalibur Automobile Corp., Milwaukee, Wisconsin. David B. Stevens, president; A.K. Stevens, chairman; William C. Stevens, general manager. 50 employees. Established in 1964.

Historical Footnotes: Hollywood types were among the first to "discover" the Excalibur and turn it into a status symbol. Excalibur has a longer production history than any of the rival "neoclassic" models such as Clenet and Sceptre.

1977 EXCALIBUR

EXCALIBUR — SERIES III — V-8 — Appearance and equipment were similar to 1976.

I.D. DATA: Not available.

EXCALIBUR (V-8)

Model Number	Body/Style Number	Body Type & Seating	Factory Price	Shipping Weight	Production Total
III	N/A	2-dr. Roadster-2P	23000	4350	Note 1
III	N/A	2-dr. Phaeton-4P	23000	4350	Note 1

Note 1: Total production in 1977 was 250 units.

ENGINE DATA: same as 1976.

CHASSIS DATA: same as 1976.

TECHNICAL: same as 1976.

OPTIONS: Not available.

MANUFACTURER: Excalibur Automobile Corp., Milwaukee, Wisconsin. David B. Stevens, president.

1978 EXCALIBUR

EXCALIBUR — SERIES III — V-8 — Appearance and equipment were similar to 1976-77.

I.D. DATA: Not available.

EXCALIBUR (V-8)

Model Number	Body/Style Number	Body Type & Seating	Factory Price	Shipping Weight	Production Total
III	N/A	2-dr. Roadster-2P	25200	4350	Note 1
III	N/A	2-dr. Phaeton-4P	25200	4350	Note 1

Note 1: Total production in 1978 was 295 units.

ENGINE DATA: same as 1976-77.

CHASSIS DATA: same as 1976-77.

TECHNICAL: same as 1976-77.

OPTIONS: Not available.

MANUFACTURER: Excalibur Automobile Corp., Milwaukee, Wisconsin. David B. Stevens, president.

1979 EXCALIBUR

EXCALIBUR — SERIES III — V-8 — Appearance and equipment were similar to 1976-78. Excaliburs had only one option: 60-spoke chrome wire wheels, priced at $1500. When Corvettes ceased to come with a 454 cu. in. V-8 engine, Excalibur turned to Chevrolet truck engines of that displacment. Corvette's independent front and rear suspension was used.

I.D. DATA: Not available.

EXCALIBUR (V-8)

Model Number	Body/Style Number	Body Type & Seating	Factory Price	Shipping Weight	Production Total
III	N/A	2-dr. Roadster-2P	27600	4350	Note 1
III	N/A	2-dr. Phaeton-4P	27600	4350	Note 1

Note 1: Total production in 1979 was 295 units.

ENGINE DATA: same as 1976-78.

CHASSIS DATA: same as 1976-78.

TECHNICAL: same as 1976-78.

OPTIONS: 60-spoke chrome wire wheels ($1500).

MANUFACTURER: Excalibur Automobile Corp., Milwaukee, Wisconsin. David B. Stevens, president. 90 workers.

1980 Excalibur Series IV roadster

1980 EXCALIBUR

EXCALIBUR — SERIES III — V-8 — Appearance and equipment were similar to 1976-79.

I.D. DATA: Not available.

EXCALIBUR (V-8)

Model Number	Body/Style Number	Body Type & Seating	Factory Price	Shipping Weight	Production Total
III	N/A	2-dr. Roadster-2P	28800	4350	Note 1
III	N/A	2-dr. Phaeton-4P	28800	4350	Note 1

Note 1: Total production in 1979 was 95 units (a substantial drop from the usual 250 units or more).

ENGINE DATA: same as 1976-79.

CHASSIS DATA: same as 1976-79.

TECHNICAL: same as 1976-79.

OPTIONS: Not available.

MANUFACTURER: Excalibur Automobile Corp., Milwaukee, Wisconsin. David B. Stevens, president.

1981 Excalibur Series IV phaeton

1981 EXCALIBUR

EXCALIBUR — SERIES IV — V-8 — The new Series IV Excalibur came only in phaeton form, with a whopping price increase over the previous edition. Powerplant shrunk from the former 454 cu. in. V-8 down to 305 cu. in. size, again supplied by Chevrolet. Styling was similar to before. However, the car itself grew in every dimension: now 125 in. wheelbase (formerly 112) and 207 in. long (formerly 175). Even the gas tank grew, from 25 to 33 gallon capacity. Series IV was styled after the 1937-38 Mercedes 500/540K (but, as in previous versions, not a true replica).

I.D. DATA: Not available.

EXCALIBUR (V-8)

Model Number	Body/Style Number	Body Type & Seating	Factory Price	Shipping Weight	Production Total
IV	N/A	2-dr. Phaeton-4P	43500	4400	235

ENGINE DATA: BASE V-8: 90-degree, overhead valve V-8. Cast iron block and head. Displacement: 305 cu. in. (5.0 liters). Bore & stroke: 3.74 x 3.48 in. Compression ratio: 8.0:1. Brake horsepower: 155 at 4000 R.P.M. Torque: 230 lbs.-ft. at 2400 R.P.M. Five main bearings. Hydraulic valve lifters. Carburetor: 4Bbl. Rochester. Chevrolet-built.

CHASSIS DATA: Wheelbase: 125 in. Overall Length: 207 in. Height: 59 in. Width: 75 in. Front Tread: 63 in. Rear Tread: 63 in. Wheel size: 7.5 x 15 in. Standard Tires: GR78 x 15.

TECHNICAL: Transmission: Turbo-Hydramatic 400 three-speed automatic transmission standard. Gear ratios: (1st) 2.48:1; (2nd) 1.48:1; (3rd) 1.00:1; (Rev) 2.08:1. Standard final drive ratio: 2.73:1. Steering: Recirculating ball. Suspension: Front coil springs, control arms and anti-sway bar; independent rear with semi-axle as upper pivoting arm, angular strut rod as lower arm, transverse semi-elliptic leaf springs, trailing radius arms, anti-sway bar, and adjustable shocks. Brakes: Four-wheel disc. Ignition: Delco-Remy HEI. Body construction: Separate body and box-type ladder frame. Fuel Tank: 33 gal.

OPTIONS: Removable hardtop.

MANUFACTURER: Excalibur Automobile Corp., Milwaukee, Wisconsin. David B. Stevens, president. 125 workers.

1982 Excalibur Series IV roadster

1982 EXCALIBUR

EXCALIBUR — SERIES IV — V-8 — A roadster returned to the Excalibur selection, in the larger size introduced for 1981. Standard equipment included four-wheel power disc brakes, variable-ratio power steering, dual electric air horns, center driving light, and dual interior-controlled spotlights. The suspension was independent on all four wheels. Also standard: Blaupunkt AM/FM stereo radio with casssette player; cruise control; leather seats; power windows; and 305 cu. in. V-8 engine with Turbo Hydra-matic.

I.D. DATA: Not available.

EXCALIBUR (V-8)

Model Number	Body/Style Number	Body Type & Seating	Factory Price	Shipping Weight	Production Total
IV	N/A	2-dr. Roadster-4P	49700	4400	Note 1
IV	N/A	2-dr. Phaeton-4P	49700	4400	Note 1

Note 1: Total production in 1982 was 212 units.

ENGINE DATA: BASE V-8: 90-degree, overhead valve V-8. Cast iron block and head. Displacement: 305 cu. in. (5.0 liters). Bore & stroke: 3.74 x 3.48 in. Compression ratio: 8.6:1. Brake horsepower: 155 at 4000 R.P.M. Torque: 225 lbs.-ft. at 2400 R.P.M. Five main bearings. Hydraulic valve lifters. Carburetor: 4Bbl. Rochester. Chevrolet-built.

CHASSIS DATA: Wheelbase: 125 in. Overall Length: 207 in. Height: 59 in. Width: 75 in. Front Tread: 63 in. Rear Tread: 63 in. Wheel size: 7.5 x 15 in. Standard Tires: GR78 x 15, or P235/75R15 Goodyear.

TECHNICAL: Transmission: Turbo-Hydramatic 400 three-speed automatic transmission standard. Gear ratios: (1st) 2.48:1; (2nd) 1.48:1; (3rd) 1.00:1; (Rev) 2.08:1. Standard final drive ratio: 2.72:1 Positraction. Steering: Recirculating ball. Suspension: Front coil springs, A arms and anti-sway bar; independent rear with semi-axle as upper pivoting arm, angular strut rod as lower arm, transverse semi-elliptic leaf springs, trailing radius arms, anti-sway bar, and adjustable shocks. Brakes: Four-wheel disc. Ignition: Delco-Remy HEI. Body construction: Separate body and box-type ladder frame. Fuel Tank: 30 gal.

OPTIONS: Removable hardtop.

MANUFACTURER: Excalibur Automobile Corp., Milwaukee, Wis.

1983 Excalibur Series IV roadster

1983 EXCALIBUR

EXCALIBUR — SERIES IV — V-8 — Appearance and equipment were similar to 1981-82. Excalibur's roadster, which now cost more than a phaeton, was a 22 configuration with rumble seat.

I.D. DATA: Not available.

EXCALIBUR (V-8)

Model Number	Body/Style Number	Body Type & Seating	Factory Price	Shipping Weight	Production Total
IV	N/A	2-dr. Roadster-4P	57500	4400	N/A
IV	N/A	2-dr. Phaeton-4P	52500	4400	N/A

1983 Excalibur Series IV pheaton

ENGINE DATA: same as 1982.

CHASSIS DATA: same as 1982.

TECHNICAL: same as 1982.

OPTIONS: Not available.

MANUFACTURER: Excalibur Automobile Corp., Milwaukee, Wisconsin. David B. Stevens, president.

1984 Excalibur Signature 20th Anniversary phaeton

1984 EXCALIBUR

EXCALIBUR — SERIES IV — V-8 — Appearance and equipment were similar to 1981-83, though Excalibur's gas tank returned to 25-gallon capacity. Four-speed overdrive Turbo Hydra-matic replaced the former three-speed version.

I.D. DATA: Not available.

426

1984 Excalibur Signature 20th Anniversary roadster

EXCALIBUR (V-8)

Model Number	Body/Style Number	Body Type & Seating	Factory Price	Shipping Weight	Production Total
IV	N/A	2-dr. Roadster-4P	59000	4400	N/A
IV	N/A	2-dr. Phaeton-4P	56500	4400	N/A

ENGINE DATA: BASE V-8: 90-degree, overhead valve V-8. Cast iron block and head. Displacement: 305 cu. in. (5.0 liters). Bore & stroke: 3.74 x 3.48 in. Compression ratio: 8.5:1. Brake horsepower: 155 at 4000 R.P.M. Torque: 230 lbs.-ft. at 2400 R.P.M. Five main bearings. Hydraulic valve lifters. Carburetor: 4Bbl. Rochester. Chevrolet-built.

CHASSIS DATA: Wheelbase: 125 in. Overall Length: 207 in. Height: 59 in. Width: 75 in. Front Tread: 63 in. Rear Tread: 63 in. Wheel size: 8 x 15 in. Standard Tires: P235/75R15.

TECHNICAL: Transmission: Turbo-Hydramatic 700R4 four-speed automatic transmission standard. Gear ratios: (1st) 3.06:1; (2nd) 1.62:1; (3rd) 1.00:1; (4th) 0.70:1; (Rev) 2.09:1. Standard final drive ratio: 3.07:1. Steering: Recirculating ball. Suspension: Front coil springs, control arms and anti-sway bar; independent rear with semi-axle as upper pivoting arm, angular strut rod as lower arm, transverse semi-elliptic leaf springs, trailing radius arms, anti-sway bar, and adjustable shocks. Brakes: Four-wheel disc. Ignition: Delco-Remy HEI. Body construction: Separate body and box-type ladder frame. Fuel Tank: 25 gal.

OPTIONS: Not available.

MANUFACTURER: Excalibur Automobile Corp., Milwaukee, Wisconsin. David B. Stevens, president.

1985 EXCALIBUR

EXCALIBUR — SIGNATURE SERIES — V-8 — Another new series greeted Excalibur buyers, though basic appearance and structure were similar to previous editions. Sole engine was again the Chevrolet 305 cu. in. V-8 with four-speed automatic transmission.

I.D. DATA: Not available.

EXCALIBUR (V-8)

Model Number	Body/Style Number	Body Type & Seating	Factory Price	Shipping Weight	Production Total
N/A	N/A	2-dr. Roadster-4P	62000	4400	N/A
N/A	N/A	2-dr. Phaeton-4P	59500	4400	N/A

ENGINE DATA: same as 1984.

CHASSIS DATA: same as 1984.

TECHNICAL: Transmission: Turbo-Hydramatic 700R4 four-speed automatic transmission standard. Gear ratios: (1st) 3.06:1; (2nd) 1.62:1; (3rd) 1.00:1; (4th) 0.70:1; (Rev) 2.09:1. Standard final drive ratio: 3.73:1. Steering: Recirculating ball. Suspension: Front coil springs, control arms and anti-sway bar; independent rear with semi-axle as upper pivoting arm, angular strut rod as lower arm, transverse semi-elliptic leaf springs, and trailing radius arms. Brakes: Four-wheel disc. Ignition: Delco-Remy HEI. Body construction: Separate body and box-type ladder frame. Fuel Tank: 25 gal.

OPTIONS: Not available.

MANUFACTURER: Excalibur Automobile Corp., Milwaukee, Wisconsin. David B. Stevens, president.

1986 Excalibur Series IV Royale phaeton

RECENT EXCALIBUR HISTORY: Specifications and prices were announced for the 1986 Excalibur, including a new Royale and Limited series. However, the financially troubled company, owned by the Stevens family, went into bankruptcy, filing Chapter 11 in mid-1986. Late that year, The Acquisition Company bought the assets for $2.3 million, and Henry A. Warner became president. The new company would build a sedan and limousine in addition to open models. Production resumed in December 1986, with the 1987 models.

F

1985 FiberFab MG roadster

FIBERFAB MG — Fiberfab International, of Minneapolis, Minn., markets an MG replica kit manufactured in Miami, Fla. It is patterned after the 1952 MG-TD and uses Ford, Chevrolet or Volkswagen running gear. Specifications include a 94 in. wheelbase, 146 in. overall length and 52 in. height with top raised. Power comes from four-cylinder engines and P165/15 tires are used.

1985 Fiberfab 1929 Replica phaeton

FIBERFAB 1929 MERCEDES — Fiberfab's 1929 Mercedes replica is manufactured in Miami, Fla. and sold by Fiberfab International, of Minneapolis. A Chevette, 1974-1980 Ford Pinto, 1974-1978 Mustang II, 1974-1980 Mercury Bobcat or Volkswagen chassis can be employed in construction, depending on what donor cars an owner has available and whether front or rear wheel drive is preferred. The front-engined kit cars feature a 98 in. wheelbase, 47 in. height (with top) and 156 in. overall length. Rear-engined versions feature a 94.5 in. wheelbase. Fuel economy of over 26 mpg is advertised.

1982 '57 Bird convertible

FIFTY-SEVEN ('57) BIRD — In 1982, Prestige Classics marketed the '57 Bird, a replica of the last Ford two-seat Thunderbird. It came with its own box steel frame with mounts for the Ford 2000 cc. or 2300 cc. V-6s or 289/302 cid V-8s. A soft top and continental kit were among available options. Prestige Classics offered manufacturer, marketing and customer services from its Wayzata, Minn. headquarters.

1976 Frazer Nash roadster

FRAZER NASH — Introduced in 1976, the Frazer Nash kit car was the third in a series produced by an industry pioneer, Antique and Classic Cars, Inc. The Buffalo, N.Y. firm released this new kit at a price of $1,295. It was a copy of the 1934 British racing sports car designed to fit the Volkswagen platform. Assembly took approximately 70 hours and required no special skills.

G

1983 Grasshopper commuter vehicle

GASHOPPER — Appropriately named the gashopper, this 200 lb. three-wheel car was made by the Bolt-on Parts company of Miami, Fla. It was said to deliver up to 100 mpg fuel economy. A monoque body is featured. The Gashopper also had independent suspension, a two-speed transmission, tiller steering and a nearly $2,000 price tag. It was said to have a top speed of 30 mph.

1982 Gatsby cabriolet

GATSBY — Gatsby Productions of San Jose, Calif., described its product as a "component car." Basic kits started at $3,000. The Gatsby uses GM or Ford LTD running gear. Ads described the basic model as the "cabriolet." The Gatsby body is made of solid steel. Fenders are constructed of hand-laid fiberglass.

1980 Gazelle phaeton

GAZELLE — Classic Motor Carriages, Inc., of Hallandale, Fla. sells the Gazelle kit car, a loose replica of the 1929 Mercedes SSK. Designed to fit either the Ford Pinto or Volkswagen Beetle chassis, it has a 94½ in. wheelbase, 156 in. length and weight of 1,550-1,950 lbs. depending upon which chassis is used. The body style is that of an all-weather phaeton.

1976 Glassic Romulous roadster

1976 GLASSIC/ROMULUS

GLASSIC — **V-8** — One of the early replicars, Glassic was a recreation of the Model A Ford. Production began in 1966, under the direction of Jack Faircloth. The fiberglass-bodied roadster, built on an International-Harvester Scout chassis, was later joined by a phaeton. The company was bought in 1972 by Fred Pro, who switched to an updated version of Ford's 302 cu. in. V-8, hooked to three-speed SelectShift Cruise-O-Matic. Little changed this year.

ROMULUS — **V-8** — A totally different replicar had been added for 1975: a reproduction of the classic 1935 Auburn Speedster. Standard equipment included leather upholstery, power windows, air conditioning, and vinyl top. Engine was the same as that used for the Model A replica.

I.D. DATA: Not available.

GLASSIC (V-8)

Model Number	Body/Style Number	Body Type & Seating	Factory Price	Shipping Weight	Production Total
N/A	N/A	2-dr. Rdstr-2P	9990	2485	N/A
N/A	N/A	2-dr. Phaeton-2P	9990	N/A	N/A

ROMULUS (V-8)

N/A	N/A	2-dr. Rdstr-2P	19000	3200	N/A

ENGINE DATA: BASE V-8: 90-degree, overhead valve V-8. Cast iron block and head. Displacement: 302 cu. in. (5.0 liters). Bore & stroke: 4.00 x 3.00 in. Compression ratio: 8.5:1. Brake horsepower: 138 at 4000 R.P.M. Torque: 230 lbs.-ft. at 2600 R.P.M. Five main bearings. Hydraulic valve lifters. Carburetor: 2Bbl. Rawsonville 9510 (D3GF-BB). Ford-built.

CHASSIS DATA: Wheelbase: (Glassic) 102 in.; (Romulus) 127 in. Overall Length: (Glassic) 153 in.; (Romulus) 205 in. Height: (Glassic) 60 in.; (Romulus) 57 in. Width: (Glassic) 65 in.; (Romulus) 76 in. Front Tread: (Glassic) 54 in.; (Romulus) 64 in. Rear Tread: (Glassic) 56.5 in.; (Romulus) 65.5 in. Wheel size: (Glassic) 5.5 x 14 in.; (Romulus) 5.5 x 15 in. Standard Tires: (Glassic) E78 x 14; (Romulus) H78 x 15.

TECHNICAL: Transmission: Three-speed SelectShift Cruise-O-Matic standard. Gear ratios: (1st) 2.40:1; (2nd) 1.47:1; (3rd) 1.00:1; (Rev) 2.00:1. Standard final drive ratio: 3.25:1. Steering: Recirculating ball. Suspension: Rigid front and rear axles with semi-elliptic leaf springs. Brakes: Front/rear drum. Body construction: Separate body and frame. Fuel Tank: (Glassic) 12.6 gal.; (Romulus) 18 gal.

OPTIONS: Air conditioning (Glassic).

MANUFACTURER: Glassic Motor Car Co., Palm Beach, Florida. Factory in Boynton Beach, Florida had about 125 workers. Fred P. Pro was company president. Glassic Industries had been founded in 1968, then changed hands in 1972 to become Glassic Motor Car. Production continued later under the name Replicars. (See Auburn listings for other Auburn speedster replicas.)

1979 Greenwood Turbo

GREENWOOD TURBO—The Greenwood Turbo was a modified Corvette custom converted into an ultra-high-performance car by American Custom Shop, Inc. The first Turbo Corvettes were made in 1975. R. Schuller was president of the 30 employee firm, which was headquartered in Sylvania, Ohio. The 1979 Greenwood Turbo used the 350 cid Corvette engine with 4 x 3.48 in. bore and stroke and linked to Turbo-Hydra-Matic transmission. A top speed of 130 mph was claimed. The 1979 price for this model was $28,000. The body style was that of a T-top coupe modified with wheel flares, a rear air foil, power bulge hood and special louvered body panels. The same basic car was marked in later years as the American Turbo and the Duntov turbo.

1981 Gullwing 300 SL coupe

GULL-WING 300 SL — Car, Inc. of Lansing, Ill., introduced its replica of the Mercedes 300 SL on April 28, 1981. The company promised a limited run of 1,480 copies would be built over five years. The hand-laid fiberglass body sits on a tubular steel frame. Under the hood is a Chrysler slant six linked to a MoPar automatic transmission. Michelin red stripe 185x15 tires and Tru-Spoke wire wheels were standard. It has a 94.5 in. wheelbase, 177.95 in. overall length and advertised top speed of 109 mph with 30 mpg fuel economy.

1981 Hawkeye T-bird hardtop

HAWKEYE T-BIRD — Hawkeye Motor Classics Limited, of Waverly, Iowa, marketed a fiberglass replica of the 1957 Ford Thunderbird in 1981. It resembles the original down to its removable hardtop with port hole windows.

I

1979 Intermeccanica Speedster

INTERMECCANICA — A replica of the classic mid-'50s Porsche Speedster was manufactured by Automobili Intermeccanica of Santa Ana, Calif. A.E.T. Baumgartner, president of the firm, designed his $6,985 replicar to fit the Volkswagen chassis. The VW 1600 engine was used, of course. The chassis featured a box section perimeter frame, twin swinging longitudinal trailing arms, tranverse laminated torsion bars, antiroll bar, telescopic shocks and transverse rear torsion bars. The speedster had an 82.7 in. wheelbase. The fiberglass body seated two passengers and a tonneau cover was included as standard equipment. Options included a turbocharger. Automobilia Intermeccanica claimed a top speed of 110 mph and 33.6 mpg driving economy.

J

1983 Johnson convertible

JOHNSON RUMBLESEAT ROADSTER — This exoticar combined classic styling features with a Cadillac V-8 and running gear. The resulting vehicle was described as "a driving machine of superior power and character." This model was introduced by Johnson Motor Cars Limited, of Ft. Lauderdale, Fla.

K

1981 Kanzler coupe

KANZLER COUPE — Designed by Ernest Kanzler, this exoticar was produced by J. Alan Rowland's Newport Coachworks in Santa Ana, Calif. It features a sculptural fiberglass front and rear molded around an all-steel Mercury Cougar body and mounted on a stretched and reinforced Cougar chassis. Power comes from a 351 cid Lincoln V-8 hooked to a three-speed Select-Shift automatic transmission. It has a 120.4 in. wheelbase, 207 in. overall length and weighs 3,600 lbs. Priced at $60,000 in 1979, the Kanzler was introduced April 2, 1979 at Auto Expo in New York City. Production of 250 copies was anticipated.

1980 Kellmark GT coupe

KELLMARK GT — Kellmark Corp., of Okemos, Mich., produced GT and GTS models as kits or factory assembled cars. The sleek fiberglass body is mounted on the firm's own tubular reinforced chassis. Engine options range from a 1.6 liter Volkswagen engine to a 2.0 liter Porsche powerplant and a 180 hp V-6. In 1980, the modular unit Mark II provided the body at $7,200. Some $3,146 worth of options could be ordered to add to the regular standard equipment list, which was fairly extensive.

1980 Kellmark GTS coupe

KELLMARK GTS — A $1,000 option for the Kellmark GT was the GTS package including silver metallic paint, leather interior and a deluxe padded dash with blacked-out finish. Like the base model, this car could be purchased already assembled or as a kit designed to fit a '69 or newer Volkswagen chassis. David B. Niles was president of the New Kellmark Corp.

L

1980 LaCrosse convertible

LaCROSSE — A.E. Baumgartner was president of Automobili Intermeccanica, in Santa Ana, Calif., a company that had 45 employees and produced 325 cars in 1978, a typical year. The LaCrosse was a four-seat roadster selling for $44,900. Features included Connally leather upholstery, Wilton carpeting, air conditioning, electric windows and a 351 cid Ford V-8. It had a 132 in. wheelbase, 210 in. overall length and weighed 4,200 lbs. Top speed was 106 mph.

429

1980 Lafer MG replica roadster

LAFER MP — Lafer Auto Sales of North Hollywood, Calif., marketed this replica of the 1952 MG-TD designed by furniture designer Percival Lafer. It has a reinforced ployester monoblock body designed for a Volkswagen chassis. The kit was/is manufactured in Brazil. A 1600 cc. Volkswagen engine is employed. In 1981, the deluxe version sold for $13,900 fully equipped and finished.

1982 Lance phaeton

LANCE — The Lance was a kit car by Piper's. It was sold by Motorcar Classics of North Hollywood, Calif. It could be assembled around a wide selection of powertrains including four-cylinder and six-cylinder Pinto, Mustang II V-8 (302 cid) or Volkswagen engines. It is another kit patterned after the 1929 Mercedes SS roadster. Slam door locks, a coupe top, luggage rack, exhaust stacks and horns are all among standard equipment.

1980 Lindberg Mercedes roadster

LINDBERG — The Lindberg roadster was a replica of a 1934 Mercedes powered by a diesel engine. Lindberg Engineering, Inc. was headquartered in Tollhouse, Calif. Among the firm's product line is an Auburn boattail speedster and an unusual replica of the Bugatti Royale Berline de Voyage.

1983 Lyon Mark V roadster

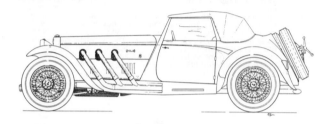
1983 Lyon Mark VII drophead coupe

LYON — Russ Lyon was president of Lyon Motor Works, Inc., a Ramona, Calif. company that built two exotic sports type cars. The Mark V roadster uses a blown Jaguar 3.8 liter doch six-cylinder engine in a box-tubular frame. It sold for $135,000. The 108 in. wheelbase, aluminum bodied Lyon can do 0-60 mph in 4.8 seconds and 130 mph, according to original manufacturer's literature. It measures 162 in. long and 46 in. high and weighs 2,445 lbs. The Lyon Mark VI drophead coupe, a second model on a 117 in. wheelbase, came with the same engine or a Jaguar V-12 for $8,000 extra. It was base priced at $142,500. Both models carried a three-year warranty.

M

1981 Manta Gran Turismo coupe

MANTA — Manta Cars, of Santa Ana, Calif., produced a hand-built, fiberglass-bodied high-performance sports car called the Manta Gran Turismo coupe. It is 160 in. long, but only 39 in. high. Power comes from either a Ford V-6 or Chevy/Ford small-block V-8 linked to a General Motors four-speed transaxle. Full independent suspension and disc/drum brakes are features. A truss-type square tube frame incorporates an enclosed fuel cell and built-in roll bar. Five standard and three optional colors were available.

1981 Manta Montage Grand Touring

MANTA MONTAGE — The Montage is a fiberglass-bodied, mid-engined sports car manufactured by Manta Cars, of Santa Ana, Calif. It has a German designed and engineered chassis resembling that of a European sports racer, although it is very economical and usable on U.S. highways. An air-cooled Volkswagen powerplant was standard equipment. Porsche, Corvair, Mazda and Buick V-6 engines were optional. The 170 in. long car has a top speed of over 100 mph and gives up to 35 mpg.

1981 Merlin Edition convertible

MERLIN EDITION — The Merlin Edition was announced by Magic Marketing and Distributing Co. in 1981. It is a fully-engineered convertible conversion that features European GT styling combined with outstanding fuel economy. Many options, from a Nardi steering wheel to custom wheels were available. Production of only 250 copies was scheduled.

1981 MG-TF replica roadster

MG-TF — Classic Car Reproductions, of Milwaukee, Wis., advertised its product as the "world's first MG-TF replica" back in 1981. Two years of design and development went into the car, which was actually produced by Daytona Automotive Fiberglass. It was available with Honda, Volkswagen or four-cylinder Ford engines.

1982 Mercedes Benz 500K roadster

M-B 500K — This replicar was built by The Classic Factory, of Pomona, Calif. In 1982, the price for a completed car was $55,000, while the basic body component kit sold for $14,995 the same year. A 302 cid Ford V-8 and automatic transmission are used. Completed vehicles carried a 24 month/24,000 mile warranty.

1980 Minimark Classic roadster

MINI MARK — The Mini Mark is designed for people who want a car with the classic car look, but practical driving capabilities. Bremen Sport Equipment Co., of Bremen, Ind., produced the heavy, fiberglass construction body. It fits the VW platform and drivetrain. Air conditioning and a convertible top were available. Alvin D. Hildenbrand was president of the company in 1980. The firm also produced the Sebring, a European styled GT sports car that sold as a kit for $995 or fully-built for $12,500.

1982 Mondrea Sports Roadster

MONDREA — Mondrea is the name of a kit car with the styling of a 1950s Ferrari roadster. Builders seeking economy could select the KS500 components package for use with a Volkswagen chassis and drivetrain. Those seeking performance could order the KS501 package with a custom built frame that accomodates V-6 or V-8 engines. Kendrick Industries of Wheat Ridge, Colo., was the manufacturer of the hand-laid fiberglass body.

1978 Monocoque Box

1979 Monocoque Box

MONOCOQUE BOX — Although there are several strange looking cars included in this catalog, this creation rates as one of the most unusual. It was a product of Monocoque Engineering, a Costa Mesa, Calif. firm first established in 1968 as Design Co. Its president, D.E. Hanebrink, apparently changed the name of the company in 1970. The Monocoque Box sold for the hefty price of $8,800 in 1978. It had a reinforced plastic body

with two seats and one front opening door. It was mounted on a box-type perimeter frame with crossmembers. Both front and rear independent suspensions were used, the front being of wishbone design with swinging semi-axles and the rear using coil springs with telescopic dampers. For power, a four-cylinder Honda 1600 cc. engine was employed and linked to a five-speed gear box. Steering was rack-and-pinion. The "Box" featured a 77 inch wheelbase, 124 inch overall length and weighed only about 1,000 lbs. Ground clearance was a hefty 10 inches. A 68 inch track was featured front and rear. Disc brakes were fitted and the electrical system was 12 volts with a 35 amp alternator, Mitsubishi distributor and four headlamps. The car — if it could be described as that — actually looked like a rectangular box on wheels with a large slanted windshield up front. Below the windshield, two square headlamps were mounted on each side of the body in rectangular protuberances, with the license plate receptacle in the center. There were large windows on either side of the cockpit and cycle fenders attached to the bodysides. The rear of the Box featured four large horizontal louvers. Optional equipment available included aluminum wheels, amphibious drive gear, an air/oil suspension system and an oversized fuel tank. Monocoque Engineering claimed a top speed of 75 mph for its 1978 model and 47 mpg fuel economy. In 1979, the price of the Monocoque Box took a huge jump. It now sold for $18,000. However, there were some changes in specifications. The most obvious was a higher advertised top speed — 125 mph — even though the same Honda power plant was being used. (The company also promoted a 14 second time for the standing-start ¼-mile). In addition, the aluminum wheels, previously an option, were now standard equipment and wore fat HR70 x 15 tires.

1980 Moselle convertible

MOSELLE — The Moselle convertible was inspired by the 1928 Mercedes Benz SS. Leather upholstery, air conditioning, automatic transmission and a four-cylinder Ford engine were on its long list of standard equipment. It has a 137 in. wheelbase, 210 in. overall length and weight of 2,600 lbs. Moselle Coach Works, Inc., of Tarzana, Calif., produced the $29,750 list price exoticar.

1976 Mohs Ostentatienne coupe

1976-78 MOHS

OSTENTATIENNE OPERA — V-8 — While maverick inventor Bruce Baldwin Mohs may not be entitled to mention in this catalog by virtue of his car's production total, he does deserve recognition for making a strong stab at a narrow portion of the market. Mohs built the prototype of his Ostentatienne Opera Sedan in 1967, and it attracted quite a bit of attention—especially from celebrities visiting the Madison, Wisconsin area. They might even be picked up from the airport in the Ostentatienne prototype. Through the next decade, Mr. Mohs had a standing offer to build one for any interested parties. Unfortunately, few real prospects arrived at the factory's doorstep. Few cars have ever been so aptly named, as the Mohs was nothing if not ostentatious and unorthodox. Packed with intriguing features, it was also designed with safety uppermost. Each bodyside held a full-length steel rail to protect against broadside collision, making installation of conventional doors impossible. The answer? Use just a single door, at the rear, hinged to the roof. Rather than opening outward, it swung upward (similar to a liftback). Bucket seats would swing when the car turned, to keep passengers secure. Cantilever roof beams held roll bars. An unusually long standard equipment list held such items as sealed beam taillamps and a refrigerator. Standard equipment also included velvet upholstery, a walnut-grain dashboard with 24K gold inlay, water-cooled automatic transmission, and huge nitrogen-filled tires. Base engine was an International Harvester 304 cu. in. V-8, but buyers (if any) could have a massive 549 cu. in. V-8 instead. The car sat on a modified truck chassis.

I.D. DATA: Not available.

OSTENTATIENNE OPERA (V-8)

Model Number	Body/Style Number	Body Type & Seating	Factory Price	Shipping Weight	Production Total
A	N/A	1-dr. Sedan-4P	19600	5740	Note 1

432

Note 1: Various sources have estimated Mohs production at a maximum of 3-4 vehicles per year (included the Safarikar, which had ceased production by 1976). However, a news report in the late 1970s stated that only the prototype Ostentatienne (built in 1967) had actually been produced, and none sold. Even if no Ostentatiennes were built after 1975, the car remained "officially" available until the late 1970s.

ENGINE DATA: BASE V-8: Overhead valve V-8. Cast iron block and head. Displacement: 304 cu. in. (5.0 liters). Bore & stroke: 3.87 x 3.22 in. Compression ratio: 8.2:1. Brake horsepower: 193 at 4400 R.P.M. Torque: 272 lbs.-ft. at 2800 R.P.M. Five main bearings. Hydraulic valve lifters. Carburetor: 2Bbl. Holley. Built by International Harvester. OPTIONAL V-8: Overhead valve V-8. Cast iron block and head. Displacement: 549 cu. in. (9.0 liters). Bore & stroke: 4.50 x 4.31 in. Compression ratio: N/A. Brake horsepower: 250 at 4400 R.P.M. Torque: N/A. Five main bearings. Hydraulic valve lifters. Built by International Harvester.

CHASSIS DATA: Wheelbase: 119 in. Overall Length: 246 in. Height: 69 in. Width: 90 in. Front Tread: 74 in. Rear Tread: 74 in. Standard Tires: 7.50 x 20.

TECHNICAL: Transmission: Borg-Warner three-speed automatic standard. Standard final drive ratio: 3.11:1. Steering: Recirculating ball. Suspension: Longitudinal front torsion bars; rigid rear axle w/semi-elliptic leaf springs. Brakes: Drum. Body construction: Separate body and frame. Fuel Tank: 17 gal.

OPTIONS: N/A.

MANUFACTURER: Mohs Seaplane Corp., Madison, Wisconsin.

Historical Footnotes: Sales were far from unheard of at the Mohs operation. A handful of Safarikars (a dual cowl phaeton with retractable metal top), introduced in 1971, managed to find buyers. Mohs also produced a variety of other vehicles, from tiny motor scooters to seaplanes, with sales topping 1,300 by 1971. Though the Ostentatienne may have lacked buyers, it transported a number of celebrities at one time or another, including Johnny Carson, Lawrence Welk and Tom Jones. According to a flyer issued on the 25th anniversary (1973) of Mohs in business, his cars had been featured in *Time* and *Fortune* magazines in the late 1960s, and appeared in productions by Alfred Hitchcock and John Forsythe.

P

1983 Packard convertible

PACKARD — The $59,995 Packard Sport Convertible is a product of Bayliff Coach Corp., a company based in Lima, Ohio. The firm offered two Packard coupes, a sedan and a "Carribbean" convertible, as well as a line of limousines priced from $69,995 to $94,995. The cars are based on Buick Riviera and Cadillac Fleetwood mechanicals.

1982 PC-MG-TD-52 roadster

PC-MG-TD-52 — Prestige Classics, of Wayzata, Minn., called its version of the T series MG replicar kit the PC-MG-TD-52, which seems to tell the whole story.

1982 PC Speedster cabriolet

PC SPEEDSTER — The Volkswagen frame and air-cooled four-cylinder engine are the basis for this 1955 Porsche Speedster replica from Prestige Classics. The Wayzata, Minn. company advertised that the car's steel frame was an integral part of the body. The doors came pre-hung to close tolerances. Seats were pre-upholstered. Door latches came installed and the fiberglass body was pre-drilled for all hardware. It was sold as a kit or turn-key component car.

1983 Piper Rogue

PIPER ROGUE — W.H. Piper established the Piper Automobile Co. in 1982. It was based in Salina, Kansas and had 18 employees. The company's product was a "classically" styled four-seater roadster with a price tag of $24,500 in turn-key form. Standard features included individual bucket seats and a tonneau cover, while wire wheels were optional at extra-cost. The Rogue sat on a 95.67 in. wheelbase and stretched 150 in. end-to-end. It was 65 inches wide and cleared the ground by six inches. Front track was 56.69 in., while rear track was an even 57 inches. The 1,990 lb. car sat an a platform type chassis with front subframe. A McPherson strut front suspension, with wishbones, coil springs and telescopic shocks was used. At the rear was a rigid rear axle mounted with coil springs and telescopic shocks, plus lower trailing radius arms, upper oblique torque arms and a transverse linkage bar. Steering was rack-and-pinion requiring 4.08 turns lock-to-lock. Disc brakes were used up front, drumsa at the rear. The engine employed was a 302 cid Ford Granda V-8 with 8.4:1 compression and a two-barrel downdraft carburetor. It developed 134 hp at 3600 RPM and 245 lbs.-ft. of torque at 1600 RPM. The Rogue's electrical system featured a 12-volt 36 amp-hour battery, 60 amp alternator, Ford Motorcraft distributor and twin headlamps mounted in chrome-plated buckets on the clamshell style front fenders. The transmission employed was Ford's C-4 automatic featuring an hydraulic torque converter and planetary gears with three ratios. Manual gear selection was possible with this automatic, too. A hypoid, bevel-gear rear axle was employed with 3.08:1 gearing. DR78 x 14 whitewall tires were mounted on six inch wide wheel rims.

1981 Puma Project utility vehicle

PROJECT PUMA

PUMA — This fiberglass kit car resembled a cross between a dune buggy and a jeep. It was finished in bright orange.

R

1981 Reminiscent Motors Golden Eagle Roadster

REMINISCENT GOLDEN EAGLE — The Golden Eagle is a replica of the 1932 Chevrolet roadster produced by Reminiscent Motors, Inc., of Michigan. A newer version of this or a similar Chevrolet replicar is being manufactured, today, by Experi — Metal & Plastics, Co., of Warren, Mich.

1980 Replicars roadster

REPLICARS—President J.W. Faircloth established Replicars, Inc. in 1975. The company's head office was in West Palm Beach. Fla. The firm had 32 employees and produced 134 cars in a typical year (1977). In 1978, the product line consisted of three models: Pheaton ($15,950); Roadster ($16,450) and Hardtop ($18,450). They had fiberglass bodies patterned after the appearance of a Model A Ford. Under the hood was a 302 cid Ford V-8 developing 135 hp. It was attached to Ford's Select-Shift automatic transmission. This combination provided a top speed of about 106 mph. The cars shared a 102 in. wheelbase, front and rear tracks of 65.5 in., a height of 54.5 in. and weighed about 2,500 lbs. Standard equipment included individual bucket seats, tinted glass, air conditioning and wire wheels. Metallic paint finish was optional. Technical features included rack-and-pinion steering, front disc breaks, 12-volt electricals and transistorized ignition system. Size E78 x 14 tires were mounted on five inch wide wheel rims. Fuel economy of 15 mpg was about tops for these V-8 powered Ford replicars.

S

1983 Saxon Classic Roadster

SAXON — Classic Roadsters, Ltd. built the Saxon. G. Rutherford, president, established the Fargo, N.D. firm in 1979. C.P. Rutherford was director of marketing. The company built 105 cars in 1981. By 1983, 36 people were employed there. The Saxon was a fiberglass-bodied copy of a classic Austin-Healey and sold for $17,999 in 1983. It had a 94 in. wheelbase, a height of 52 in. a 58 in. front track and 59 in. rear track and measured 155 in. from bumper-to-bumper. A four-cylinder Ford engine was employed. It had 140 cid, a 9.1:1 compression ratio and a two-barrel Holley carburetor. Output was 86 hp at 4600 RPM. A top speed of 120 mph was claimed. Other technical features included a four-speed gearbox, coil spring suspension with rear rigid axle, racl-and-pinion steering and front disc/rear drum brakes. The finished car weighed some 1,980 lbs. Factory options included automatic transmission, air conditioning, wire wheels, leather upholstery, removable hardtop and roll-up windows.

1980 Sceptre 6.6 convertible

1979-80 SCEPTRE

SCEPTRE 6.6S — V-8 — Of all the "neoclassic" models produced in the 1970s, many observers ranked Sceptre with the best of the lot. Vaguely resembling certain European roadsters of the 1930s, it was a tasteful and streamlined design—modern but based on the Art Deco era. Designed by Tom McBurney and Ray Kinney, it had a long hood an1 abbreviated trunk, with a traditional small cockpit area and separate fenders. Edge of the fiberglass body were smooth and rounded, pleasing to the eye, starting with the gracefully sloped nose and vertical-bar grille. As in nearly all such models, huge non-working exhaust pipes ran out the hood sides (and through the running boards). Few observers were likely to guess that the main body structure (like Clenet's) came from an MG Midget. Nor were they likely to spot components that originated on a Lotus, Pantera or Firebird; or the replicas of early Lincoln mirrors and Packard taillamps. Sceptre rode a modifed Cougar chassis (118 in. wheelbase) with extra bracing, and carried a stock Cougar 400 cu. in. V-8 with three-speed automatic transmission. To allow for the long, narrow hood and improve weight distribution, the engine was lowered 4 inches and moved 2 feet rearward from its standard position. For added safety, a frame made up of 2 x 3 inch rectangular steel surrounded the passenger compartment. A 19.5-gallon racing fuel cell replaced the standard tank. Tru-Spoke wire wheels held Firestone GR70 x 15 tires. Sceptres could be serviced at Lincoln-Mercury dealers. A simulated spare tire was visible in the trunk lid. Interiors held Connolly leather, a Brazilian walnut veneer dashboard, and leather-padded Nardi steering wheel. Standard equipment included a Clarion four-speaker AM/FM stereo with cassette, air conditioning, three windshield wipers, and cruise control. Bodies received 25 coats of lacquer.

I.D. DATA: Not available.

SCEPTRE 6.6S (V-8)

Model Number	Body/Style Number	Body Type & Seating	Factory Price	Production Weight	Total
6.6S	N/A	2-dr. Rdstr-2P	50000	3045	Note 1

Note 1: Production figures not available, but was to be limited to 500 cars. An estimated 250-300 were sold in 1979.

ENGINE DATA: BASE V-8: 90-degree, overhead-valve V-8. Cast iron block and head. Displacement: 400 cu. in. (6.6 liters). Bore & stroke: 4.00 x 4.00 in. Compression ratio: 8.0:1. Brake horsepower: 168 at 4000 R.P.M. Torque: N/A. Five main bearings. Hydraulic valve lifters. Carburetor: 4Bbl. Ford. Built by Ford.

CHASSIS DATA: Wheelbase: 118.4 in. Overall Length: 188.5 in. Height: 54 in. Width: 74.5 in. Front Tread: 65 in. Rear Tread: 65 in. Wheel size: 6 x 15 in. Standard Tires: GR70 x 15.

TECHNICAL: Transmission: SelectShift three-speed automatic standard. Gear ratios: (1st) 2.46:1; (2nd) 1.46:1; (3rd) 1.00:1; (Rev) 2.18:1. Standard final drive ratio: 3.00:1. Steering: Recirculating ball. Suspension: Front coil springs w/anti-sway bar and four shocks; rigid rear axle w/trailing radius arms, upper oblique torque arms, coil springs and four shocks. Brakes: Front disc, rear drum. Ignition: Electronic. Body construction: Separate body on modified torque box ladder frame. Fuel Tank: 19.5 gal.

OPTIONS: Hardtop. Tonneau cover. Halogen headlamps. Mouton lambswool overlay.

MANUFACTURER: Sceptre Motor Car Co., Santa Barbara (Goleta Valley), California. M. Broggie, president. 30 workers.

434

1980 Shay Model A roadster

SHAY MODEL A — In early 1979, Model A and Model T Motor Car Reproduction, Co., introduced the limited edition Shay Reproduction Model A Roadster. Harry Shay designed this fiberglass-bodied copy of the famous Ford. It used a Pinto drivetrain. The company was formed in 1978 and operated an engineering and pilot production plant in Wixom, Mich. and another factory in Battle Creek. Corporate headquarters were in Detroit's Renaissance Center. Ten thousand copies of the fully-assembled replica were announced sold to Ford and Lincoln-Mercury dealers, in advance, in a July, 1980 press release.

1980 Shay '55 Bird

SHAY '55 BIRD — The '55 Thunderbird replica designed and engineered by Harry Shay was introduced in December, 1979. The reproduction commemorated the Silver Anniversary of the Classic T-bird. It was supposed to be marketed through participating Ford and Lincoln-Mercury dealers. After the '55 Bird was released, the Detroit manufacturer had plans to sell reproductions of the '65 Mustang, Model A pickup, '32 Ford B (street rod), '40 Linocln and Model T.

1979 Silver Volt electric luxury sedan

SILVER VOLT — The Silver Volt is a luxury market, electric-powered sedan designed by Harry Lauve. In 1979, the Electric Auto Corp., of Troy, Mich., advertised it would be showing the car at the National Automobile Dealers Association (NADA) convention in Las Vegas. The purpose was to attract prospective distributors.

1981 Southeastern Replicars Auburn boattail speedster

SOUTHEASTERN AUBURN — Dave Samuel's Southeastern Replicars, Inc. claimed to be the largest producer of Auburn replicars in 1981. A four-passenger Phaeton and 2+2 Phaeton Speedster were sold by the Largo, Fla. firm at $37,000 and $39,000 respectively. There was also a $35,000 two-passenger Speedster. Two-passenger models ride a 127 in. wheelbase, while the four-passenger jobs are 10 in. longer. A 350 cid Chevrolet V-8 and Turbo-Hydramatic transmission are features. Interiors are trimmed in genuine leather with Wilton carpets.

1980 Splinter station wagon

SPLINTER STATION WAGON — Splinter Auto Works, Inc., of Plymouth, Ind. built two models for the replica market. One is a "woodie" station wagon and the other is a similar "woodie" pickup truck. King P. Aitken III was president of the firm. The Splinter features a tubular steel chassis and body made of fine quality fiberglass and durable hardwoods. The Chevette chassis is used, giving a 94.5 in. wheelbase, 12 ft. 3 in. length, 1,785 lb. net weight and 1,600 cc. engine.

1981 Spyder roadster

SPYDER — Classic Motors International, Inc., of Mishawaka, Ind., marketed the Spyder, a reproduction of the classic 1955 Porsche Speedster. The hand-laid fiberglass body took five to six weeks to build. A steel chassis is used. Powertrain options included either 356 or 912 Porsche engines with four-speed Type 1 transaxle. Zero-to-sixty performance of 5.8 seconds with a top speed of 140 mph was advertised in 1981. Three built-up models were available: Spyder S ($22,950); Spyder Cabriolet ($25,760) and Spyder Carrera ($32,717). Curtis J. Paluzzi was general manager of the firm in 1981.

1976 SQUIRE

SQUIRE SS 100 — SIX — Inspired by late '30s Jaguar SS 100 (first car to carry the Jaguar name), the Squire had a steel-reinforced fiberglass body, made in Italy by Carrozzeria Ramponi. Powerplant was a modified Ford 250 cu. in. inline six, hooked to a four-speed manual gearbox. Standard equipment included wire wheels, a tonneau cover, and spare tire cover.

I.D. DATA: Not available.

SQUIRE SS 100 (SIX)

Model Number	Body/Style Number	Body Type & Seating	Factory Price	Shipping Weight	Production Total
SS100	N/A	2-dr. Rdstr-2P	N/A	2200	N/A

ENGINE DATA: BASE SIX: Inline, overhead valve six-cylinder. Cast iron block and head. Displacement: 250 cu. in. (4.1 liters). Bore & stroke: 3.68 x 3.91 in. Compression ratio: N/A. Brake horsepower: 170 at 4500 R.P.M. Torque: N/A. Seven main bearings. Hydraulic valve lifters. Carburetor: 2Bbl. Autolite. Built by Ford.

CHASSIS DATA: Wheelbase: 104.5 in. Overall Length: 150 in. Height: 44 in. Width: 61 in. Front Tread: 59 in. Rear Tread: 59 in. Wheel size: 6 x 15 in. Standard Tires: 205 x 15 Pirelli SBR.

TECHNICAL: Transmission: Four-speed manual transmission (floor shift) standard. Gear ratios: (1st) 2.20:1; (2nd) 1.66:1; (3rd) 1.31:1; (4th) 1.00:1; (Rev) 2.20:1. Standard final drive ratio: 3.25:1. Steering: Recirculating ball. Suspension: Front torsion bars, control arms, coil springs and anti-sway bar; rigid rear axle with semi-elliptic leaf springs and torsion bars. Brakes: Front/rear drum. Body construction: Separate body and ladder-type frame. Fuel Tank: 22 gal.

OPTIONS: Cruise-O-Matic transmission. Air conditioning.

MANUFACTURER: Auto Sport Importers, Inc., Philadelphia, PA.

1978 SS-100 roadster

SS-100 — By 1978, Antique & Classic Automotive, Inc., one of the pioneer kit car companies, had switched to fancier advertising and fancier products. The company, originally based in a Buffalo, N.Y. office building, also moved to Sonwill Industrial Park in the same city. Its latest kit was the SS-100 roadster, a copy of the 1937 Swallow Sidecar (Jaguar) SS-100. Its features include flowing wings, a folding windscreen and chromed 12 in. headlamps.

1976 Stutz Blackhawk coupe

1976 STUTZ

BLACKHAWK VI — V-8 — Although a Stutz Bearcat replica had been produced in 1969, this one, starting a year later, was completely different: a modernistic design, similar in appearance to the Duesenberg II. The Blackhawk coupe used a Pontiac Grand Prix chassis, and the engine was a modified big-block Pontiac hooked to Turbo Hydra-matic. In 1972, the engine grew to 455 cu. in. and a Limousine on a Cadillac Fleetwood Brougham chassis was added (but dropped by 1974). Virgil Exner, one-time styling chief at Chrysler, created the bizarre, eye-catching design. According to the sales brochure, it "embodies the same uncompromising standards that characterized the original Stutz—and some of the same classic features." Steel bodies (not fiberglass) were hand crafted in Torino, Italy by Carrozzeria de Modena. Each one took three months. A huge external exhaust pipe (simulated) ran out of a hole in the lower cowl, then along the bottom of the rocker panel toward the rear. Single round headlamps, almost free- standing style, were flanked by round free-standing (truly separate) parking/signal lamps at the front of fendertip depressions. The headlamps were similar to those on the Exner-designed early 1960s Imperial. A rather narrow radiator grille was peaked to a slight "vee" at the top and protruded well forward of the headlamps, setting at the front of a long, tapering hood. It had a Stutz 'S' emblem at the top, and a crosshatch pattern divided into two side-by-side sections. Three strong, bright horizontal bars over the lower portion of the grille met the bumper on either side. A sweeping bodyside molding sloped down from the very top of the front fender tip, toward the rear wheel opening, up and over, then back down to the very tip of the rear quarter panel. The two-door body had no quarter windows. Two-tone paint schemes were split at those sweeping bodyside moldings. An exposed simulated tire mount was available, or the buyer could get a traditional tonneau back end which consisted of a bulge over what would be the ordinary decklid. Taillamps with the exposed-tire were round, with smaller round circles inside. For the traditional style back end, large horizontal taillamps on each side were built into the top of the bumper. Each one had a horizontal divider (also part of the bumper). Stutz interiors held European leather, fur carpeting, matched burled English walnut, and 24K gold moldings. Bodies were covered with the most costly lacquer that could be found. Tires were 17-inch Firestone LXX. Standard equipment included air conditioning, limited-slip differential, adjustable steering wheel, tinted glass, power windows, power seats, power sunroof, leather upholstery, back window deicer, and built-in headrests.

I.D. DATA: Not available.

BLACKHAWK VI (V-8)

Model Number	Body/Style Number	Body Type & Seating	Factory Price	Shipping Weight	Production Total
VI	N/A	2-dr. Coupe-5P	47500	N/A	55

ENGINE DATA: BASE V-8: 90-degree, overhead valve V-8. Cast iron block and head. Displacement: 455 cu. in. (7.5 liters). Bore & stroke: 4.15 x 4.21 in. Compression ratio: 10.5:1. Brake horsepower: 431. Torque: N/A. Five main bearings. Hydraulic valve lifters. Dual exhausts. Carburetor: 4Bbl. Built by Pontiac.

CHASSIS DATA: Wheelbase: 116 in. Overall Length: 227 in. Height: 54 in. Width: 79 in. Front Tread: 61.9 in. Rear Tread: 61.1 in. Standard Tires: GR78 x 15.

TECHNICAL: Transmission: Turbo Hydra-matic three-speed transmission standard. Gear ratios: (1st) 2.48:1; (2nd) 1.48:1; (3rd) 1.00:1; (Rev) 2.08:1. Standard final drive ratio: N/A. Steering: Recirculating ball. Suspension: Front coil springs, control arms and anti-sway bar; rigid rear axle with lower trailing radius arms, upper oblique torque arms and coil springs. Brakes: Disc. Body construction: Separate body and perimeter box frame. Fuel Tank: N/A.

OPTIONS: Not available.

MANUFACTURER: Stutz Motor Car of America, Inc., New York City. James D. O'Donnell, president.

Historical Footnotes: The baroque modern Stutz soon became a favorite of celebrities and movie stars, including Tommy Smothers and Phyllis Diller. Elvis Presley owned four.

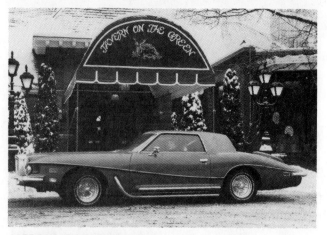

1977 Stutz Blackhawk coupe

1977 STUTZ

BLACKHAWK VI — V-8 — Appearance and equipment were similar to 1976.

I.D. DATA: Not available.

BLACKHAWK VI (V-8)

Model Number	Body/Style Number	Body Type & Seating	Factory Price	Shipping Weight	Production Total
VI	N/A	2-dr. Coupe-5P	50000	N/A	50

ENGINE DATA: same as 1976.

CHASSIS DATA: same as 1976.

TECHNICAL: same as 1976.

OPTIONS: Not available.

MANUFACTURER: Stutz Motor Car of America, Inc., New York City. J.D. O'Donnell, president.

1978 STUTZ

BLACKHAWK VI — V-8 — Appearance and equipment were similar to 1976-77, but the Stutz price rose considerably, from $50,000 to $64,500. The engine, again supplied by Pontiac, shrunk from 455 to 403 cu. in., and down to a far more modest 185 horsepower. Brakes were now front disc and rear drum.

I.D. DATA: Not available.

BLACKHAWK VI (V-8)

Model Number	Body/Style Number	Body Type & Seating	Factory Price	Shipping Weight	Production Total
VI	N/A	2-dr. Coupe-5P	64500	4450	50

ENGINE DATA: BASE V-8: 90-degree, overhead valve V-8. Cast iron block and head. Displacement: 403 cu. in. (6.6 liters). Bore & stroke: 4.35 x 3.38 in. Compression ratio: 7.9:1. Brake horsepower: 185 at 3600 R.P.M. Torque: 320 lbs.-ft. at 2000 R.P.M. Five main bearings. Hydraulic valve lifters. Dual exhausts. Carburetor: 4Bbl. Built by Pontiac.

CHASSIS DATA: Wheelbase: 116 in. Overall Length: 227 in. Height: 54 in. Width: 79 in. Front Tread: 61.6 in. Rear Tread: 61.1 in. Standard Tires: GR78 x 15.

TECHNICAL: Transmission: Turbo Hydra-matic three-speed transmission standard. Standard final drive ratio: N/A. Steering: Recirculating ball. Suspension: Front coil springs, control arms and anti-sway bar; rigid rear axle with lower trailing radius arms, upper oblique torque arms and coil springs. Brakes: Front disc, rear drum. Body construction: Separate body and perimeter box frame. Fuel Tank: 25 gal.

OPTIONS: Air conditioning. Tinted glass. Power sunroof. Power windows. Power seats. Leather upholstery.

MANUFACTURER: Stutz Motor Car of America, Inc., New York City. J.D. O'Donnell, president.

1979 STUTZ

BLACKHAWK VI — V-8 — BEARCAT — V-8 — IV PORTE — V-8 — Two models joined the Stutz lineup for 1979: a IV Porte four-door sedan, and a Bearcat convertible coupe. The latter's price entered the six-figure range ($107,000). Otherwise, appearance and equipment were similar to 1976-78.

I.D. DATA: Not available.

BLACKHAWK VI (V-8)

Model Number	Body/Style Number	Body Type & Seating	Factory Price	Shipping Weight	Production Total
VI	N/A	2-dr. Coupe-5P	69500	4450	Note 1

BEARCAT (V-8)

N/A	N/A	2-dr. Conv.-5P	107000	4550	Note 1

IV PORTE (V-8)

IV	N/A	4-dr. Sedan-6P	69500	4500	Note 1

Note 1: Total Stutz production was 60 units.

ENGINE DATA: same as 1978.

CHASSIS DATA: Wheelbase: 116 in. Overall Length: 227 in. exc. sedan, 224 in. Height: 54 in. Width: 79 in. Front Tread: 61.6 in. Rear Tread: 61.1 in. Standard Tires: N/A.

TECHNICAL: same as 1978.

OPTIONS: same as 1978.

MANUFACTURER: Stutz Motor Car of America, Inc., New York City. J.D. O'Donnell, president.

1980 Stutz Blackhawk VI coupe

1980 STUTZ

BLACKHAWK VI — V-8 — BEARCAT — V-8 — IV PORTE — V-8 — ROYALE LIMOUSINE — V-8 — A new Royale limousine was added, with a larger (425 cu. in.) V-8 engine. The Porte sedan switched to a smaller (350 cu. in.) V-8. The new limousine could even be ordered with throne seating for two—raised hydraulically above the roofline, presumably so its owner could be viewed by his inferiors. As though the convertible wasn't expensive enough when introduced a year earlier, it rose this time to $129,000. But that was nothing compared to the limo, which carried a price tag of $235,000. Otherwise, appearance and equipment were similar to 1979.

I.D. DATA: Not available.

BLACKHAWK VI (V-8)

Model Number	Body/Style Number	Body Type & Seating	Factory Price	Shipping Weight	Production Total
VI	N/A	2-dr. Coupe-6P	69500	4450	Note 1

1980 Stutz Bearcat convertible

BEARCAT (V-8)

N/A	N/A	2-dr. Conv.-6P	129000	4550	Note 1

1980 Stutz IV Porte sedan

IV PORTE (V-8)

Model Number	Body/Style Number	Body Type & Seating	Factory Price	Shipping Weight	Production Total
IV	N/A	4-dr. Sedan-6P	74765	4500	Note 1

1980 Stutz Royale limousine

ROYALE (V-8)

N/A	N/A	4-dr. Limo-7P	235000	N/A	Note 1

Note 1: Total Stutz production was 60 units.

ENGINE DATA: BASE V-8 (Porte sedan): 90-degree, overhead valve V-8. Cast iron block and head. Displacement: 350 cu. in. (5.7 liters). Bore & stroke: 4.08 x 3.38 in. Compression ratio: 7.9:1. Brake horsepower: 160 at 3600 R.P.M. Torque: 220 lbs.-ft. at 2000 R.P.M. Five main bearings. Hydraulic valve lifters. Carburetor: 4Bbl. Rochester M4MC. BASE V-8 (Blackhawk, Bearcat): 90-degree, overhead valve V-8. Cast iron block and head. Displacement: 403 cu. in. (6.6 liters). Bore & stroke: 4.35 x 3.38 in. Compression ratio: 7.9:1. Brake horsepower: 185 at 3600 R.P.M. Torque: 320 lbs.-ft. at 2000 R.P.M. Five main bearings. Hydraulic valve lifters. Carburetor: 4Bbl. Built by Pontiac. BASE V-8 (Royale limo): 90-degree, overhead valve V-8. Cast iron block and head. Displacement: 425 cu. in. (7.0 liters). Bore & stroke: 4.08 x 4.06 in. Compression ratio: 8.2:1. Brake horsepower: 180 at 4000 R.P.M. Torque: 320 lbs.-ft. at 2000 R.P.M. Five main bearings. Hydraulic valve lifters. Carburetor: 4Bbl. Rochester M4ME.

CHASSIS DATA: Wheelbase: 116 in. exc. limo, 171.9 in. Overall Length: 227 in. exc. sedan, 224 in.; limo, 295.3 in. Height: 54 in. exc. limo, 56 in. Width: 79 in. exc. limo, 80 in. Front Tread: 61.6 in. exc. sedan/limo, 61.7 in. Rear Tread: 61.1 in. exc. sedan/limo, 60.7 in. Standard Tires: N/A.

TECHNICAL: Transmission: Turbo Hydra-matic three-speed transmission standard. Gear ratios: (1st) 2.52:1; (2nd) 1.52:1; (3rd) 1.00:1; (Rev) 1.93:1. THM 400 standard on Royale: (1st) 2.48:1; (2nd) 1.48:1; (3rd) 1.00:1; (Rev) 2.07:1. Standard final drive ratio: N/A. Steering: Recirculating ball. Suspension: Front coil springs, control arms and anti-sway bar; rigid rear axle with lower trailing radius arms, upper oblique torque arms and coil springs (exc. limo); adjustable shocks. Brakes: Front disc, rear drum. Body construction: Separate body and perimeter box frame. Fuel Tank: 25 gal. exc. sedan/limo, 20.6 gal.

OPTIONS: (Blackhawk/Bearcat): Air conditioning. Tinted glass. Power sunroof. Power windows. Power seats. Leather upholstery. (Porte sedan): On-board computer. (Royale limo): Throne seat w/hydraulic lift. Power sunroof. Shorter wheelbase.

MANUFACTURER: Stutz Motor Car of America, Inc., New York City. J.D. O'Donnell, president.

1981 STUTZ

BLACKHAWK VII — V-8 — BEARCAT — V-8 — IV PORTE — V-8 — ROYALE LIMOUSINE — V-8 — A Blackhawk VII replaced the VI, but appearance and equipment were similar to 1980. The 403 cu. in. engine was dropped, making a 350 standard in all models except the limousine.

I.D. DATA: Not available.

BLACKHAWK VII (V-8)

Model Number	Body/Style Number	Body Type & Seating	Factory Price	Shipping Weight	Production Total
VII	N/A	2-dr. Coupe-6P	79500	4450	Note 1

BEARCAT (V-8)

N/A	N/A	2-dr. Conv.-6P	129500	4550	Note 1

IV PORTE (V-8)

IV	N/A	4-dr. Sedan-6P	79500	4500	Note 1

ROYALE (V-8)

N/A	N/A	4-dr. Limo-7P	275000	N/A	Note 1

Note 1: Total Stutz production was 45 units.

ENGINE DATA: BASE V-8 (Blackhawk, Bearcat, Porte): 90-degree, overhead valve V-8. Cast iron block and head. Displacement: 350 cu. in. (5.7 liters). Bore & stroke: 4.06 x 3.38 in. Compression ratio: 7.9:1. Brake horsepower: 160 at 3600 R.P.M. Torque: 270 lbs.-ft. at 2000 R.P.M. Five main bearings. Hydraulic valve lifters. Carburetor: 4Bbl. Rochester M4MC. BASE V-8 (Royale limo): 90-degree, overhead valve V-8. Cast iron block and head. Displacement: 425 cu. in. (7.0 liters). Bore & stroke: 4.08 x 4.06 in. Compression ratio: 8.2:1. Brake horsepower: 180 at 4000 R.P.M. Torque: 320 lbs.-ft. at 2000 R.P.M. Five main bearings. Hydraulic valve lifters. Carburetor: 4Bbl. Rochester M4ME.

CHASSIS DATA: same as 1980.

TECHNICAL: Transmission: Turbo Hydra-matic 350 three-speed transmission standard. Gear ratios: (1st) 2.52:1; (2nd) 1.52:1; (3rd) 1.00:1; (Rev) 1.93:1. THM 400 standard on Royale: (1st) 2.48:1; (2nd) 1.48:1; (3rd) 1.00:1; (Rev) 2.07:1. Standard final drive ratio: N/A. Steering: Recirculating ball. Suspension: Front coil springs, control arms and anti-sway bar; rigid rear axle with lower trailing radius arms, upper torque arms, coil springs and anti-sway bar (exc. limo); adjustable shocks. Brakes: Front disc, rear drum. Body construction: Separate body and perimeter box frame. Fuel Tank: 25 gal. exc. sedan, 20.6 gal.

OPTIONS: (Blackhawk/Bearcat/Porte) Power sunroof. (Royale limo) Throne seat w/hydraulic lift. Power sunroof. Shorter wheelbase.

MANUFACTURER: Stutz Motor Car of America, Inc., New York City. J.D. O'Donnell, president.

1982 STUTZ

BLACKHAWK VII — V-8 — BEARCAT — V-8 — IV PORTE — V-8 — ROYALE LIMOUSINE — V-8 — Appearance and equipment were similar to 1980-81.

I.D. DATA: Not available.

BLACKHAWK VII (V-8)

Model Number	Body/Style Number	Body Type & Seating	Factory Price	Shipping Weight	Production Total
VII	N/A	2-dr. Coupe-6P	84500	4450	Note 1

BEARCAT (V-8)

N/A	N/A	2-dr. Conv.-6P	129500	4550	Note 1

IV PORTE (V-8)

IV	N/A	4-dr. Sedan-6P	84500	4500	Note 1

ROYALE (V-8)

N/A	N/A	4-dr. Limo-7P	285000	N/A	Note 1

Note 1: Total Stutz production was 50 units.

ENGINE DATA: same as 1981.

CHASSIS DATA: same as 1980-81.

TECHNICAL: Transmission: Turbo Hydra-matic 350 three-speed transmission standard. Gear ratios: (1st) 2.52:1; (2nd) 1.52:1; (3rd) 1.00:1; (Rev) 1.93:1. THM 400 standard on Royale: (1st) 2.48:1; (2nd) 1.48:1; (3rd) 1.00:1; (Rev) 2.07:1. Standard final drive ratio: N/A. Steering: Recirculating ball. Suspension: Front coil springs, control arms and anti-sway bar; rigid rear axle with lower trailing radius arms, upper torque arms, coil springs and anti-sway bar (exc. limo); automatic/adjustable shocks. Brakes: Front disc, rear drum. Body construction: Separate body and perimeter box frame. Fuel Tank: 25 gal. exc. sedan, 20.6 gal.

OPTIONS: same as 1981.

MANUFACTURER: Stutz Motor Car of America, Inc., New York City. J.D. O'Donnell, president.

1984 Stutz Blackhawk convertible

1983-84 STUTZ

BLACKHAWK VII — V-8 — BEARCAT — V-8 — VICTORIA — V-8 — ROYALE LIMOUSINE — V-8 — Appearance and equipment were similar to 1980-82. A longer Victoria model replaced the Porte sedan—and carried a much higher price tag. Prices remained the same for 1984.

I.D. DATA: Not available.

BLACKHAWK VII (V-8)

Model Number	Body/Style Number	Body Type & Seating	Factory Price	Shipping Weight	Production Total
VII	N/A	2-dr. Coupe-6P	84500	4450	N/A

BEARCAT (V-8)

N/A	N/A	2-dr. Conv.-6P	129500	4550	N/A

VICTORIA (V-8)

N/A	N/A	4-dr. Sedan-6P	125000	4500	N/A

ROYALE (V-8)

N/A	N/A	4-dr. Limo-7P	285000	N/A	N/A	

ENGINE DATA: same as 1981-82.

CHASSIS DATA: Wheelbase: 116 in. exc. Victoria, 126 in.; limo, 171.9 in. Overall Length: 227 in. exc. Victoria, 234 in.; limo, 295.3 in. Height: 54 in. exc. limo, 56 in. Width: 79 in. exc. limo, 80 in. Front Tread: 61.6 in. exc. sedan/limo, 61.7 in. Rear Tread: 61.1 in. exc. sedan/limo, 60.7 in. Standard Tires: N/A.

TECHNICAL: same as 1982.

OPTIONS: (Blackhawk/Bearcat/Victoria) Power sunroof. (Royale limo) Throne seat w/hydraulic lift. Power sunroof. Shorter wheelbase.

MANUFACTURER: Stutz Motor Car of America, Inc., New York City. J.D. O'Donnell, president.

1985 STUTZ

BLACKHAWK VII — V-8 — BEARCAT — V-8 — VICTORIA — V-8 — ROYALE LIMOUSINE — V-8 — Appearance and equipment were similar to 1980-84. Bearcat and Victoria prices were cut substantially this year.

I.D. DATA: Not available.

BLACKHAWK VII (V-8)

Model Number	Body/Style Number	Body Type & Seating	Factory Price	Shipping Weight	Production Total
VII	N/A	2-dr. Coupe-6P	84500	4450	N/A

BEARCAT (V-8)

N/A	N/A	2-dr. Conv.-6P	109500	4550	N/A

VICTORIA (V-8)

N/A	N/A	4-dr. Sedan-6P	99500	4500	N/A

ROYALE (V-8)

N/A	N/A	4-dr. Limo-7P	285000	N/A	N/A

ENGINE DATA: same as 1981-84.

CHASSIS DATA: same as 1983-84.

TECHNICAL: same as 1982-84.

OPTIONS: same as 1983-84.

MANUFACTURER: Stutz Motor Car of America, Inc., New York City. J.D. O'Donnell, president.

T

1981 TF 1800 Victor roadster

TF-1800 — Victor Replicat of America was a Division of Southern Coachworks, Inc. Brian Metcalfe was president of the Rochester, N.Y. firm. The company sold a replica based on the 1955 MG-TF. It is unique among products of this type in that it uses MGB drivetrain and suspension components in conjunction with state-of-the-art frame- and body-making techniques. The TF-1800 could be purchased as a kit for $7,495 or as a complete vehicle for $16,500.

1981 Thoroughbred 540K cabriolet

THOROUGHBRED 540K — Thoroughbred Motor Cars, Inc. was located in Redmond, Wash. The Thoroughbred 540K was said to be inspired by the Classic Mercedes 500K series. It came as a kit complete with its own chassis to receive the suspension and steering gear from a Ford Mustang II, Mercury Bobcat or Ford Pinto. Engine/transmission choices were Ford/Chevrolet V-6, straight six or small-block V-8 and synchromesh or automatic. A deluxe kit retailed for $8,995 in 1981. Factory options totaling $430 were available. Specifications include a 120 in. wheelbase, 67 in. width, 180 in. overall length and approximate weight of 2,600 lbs.

1986 Thoroughbred 300 SCR roadster

THOROUGHBRED 300 SLR — This classic was inspired by the Mercedes 300 SLR and hand-crafted by Sterling Coachworks, of Bellevue, Wash.. It features professional craftsmanship and a 325 hp Chevrolet V-8, plus leather interior, spoke wheel rims and a wooden steering wheel. The price was approximately $34,950.

1982 Tiffany Classic coupe

TIFFANY — Classic Motor Carriages of Miami, Fla., marketed this car as the Classic Tiffany, but it is better known to enthusiasts by its last name alone. It is a fiberglass-bodied coupe with sidemounted spare tires. The same manufacturer also produces kit cars and has a showroom in Hallandale, Fla. Its products are also displayed in many airports.

1981 Tiger two-seat Sports Roadster

TIGER — The Tiger is a two-seat sports car combining modern roadability with the styling of yesteryear. Thoroughbred Cars, Inc., of Redmond, Wash., sold it in kit form or as a completed vehicle. The car uses a Volkswagen transaxle/engine assembly in conjunction with its own steel racing type chassis. It has a 100 in. wheelbase. The fiberglass body measures 13 ft. 4 in. long. A front engine version uses either the Pinto or Mustang II suspension. A deluxe kit sold for $8,000, not including cost of the ''donor'' car.

1981 Timmis Ford V-8 roadster

TIMMIS-FORD V-8 — Most people consider Canadian vehicles ''American cars'' and most Ford lovers consider this Canadian replica to be the finest ever made. Andrew J. Timmis, of Victoria, B.C., built 10 cars in 1979 and more after the spring of 1981. All are exact copies of the 1934 Ford rumbleseat roadster using 1934 engines specially built at the Ford remanufacturing plant, as well as brand new Ford parts from the late 1940s to mid-1950s. The steel-bodied replica sold for $30,000 here, in 1981. Production of the model started way back in 1968.

1980 Tomorrow's Classic Corvette replica roadster

1980 Tomorrow's Classic Auburn phaeton

TOMORROW'S CLASSIC — J.T. Richey established a replicar-making firm in Hattiesburg, Miss. Two models were offered. The company's $14,500 Corvette Replica looked like the original classic. It had a fiberglass body and a 231 cid/110 hp V-6 as standard equipment. Turbo-Hydramatic transmission was featured. The Corvette copycat rode a 102 in. wheelbase and stretched 167 in. end-to-end. It tipped the scales at 3,200 lbs. An integral chassis with separate partial front box frame was used. Front suspension was independent with wishbones, coil springs, anti-roll bar and telescopic shocks. A rigid axle, coil springs, anti-roll bar and telescopic shocks were used on the rear. An option was a 302 cid V-8 with a four-barrel carburetor and 155 hp. The same company also marketed a $35,000 Auburn boattail speedster replicar using the 155 hp 305 cid V-8 as base equipment. It had a 132 in. wheelbase, 204 in. overall length and weight of 3,500 lbs.

1980 Total Replica Ford 'B' phaeton

TOTAL FORD 'B' — Total Performance, Inc. was a Wallingford, Conn. firm that produced a rarther interesting replica of the very popular 1932 Ford Model B phaeton. The company was established in 1971 and producing about 40 cars per year by 1978. At that point, it employed 20 people. M.V. Lauria was president and G.C. Gallicchio was vice-president. The car was also known as the ''Hi Boy'' and carried a $15,500 price tag. It had a fiberglass body mounted on a 106 in. wheelbase box-perimeter chassis, with Turbo-Hydramatic transmission attachment. The power plant was the 350 cid/250 hp Chevrolet V-8 with a Holley 450 four-barrel carburetor. This gave the 2,850 car a top speed of about 100 mph. It was 68 in. wide and 64.5 in. high and stretched 186 inches bumper-to-bumper. Standard equipment included a rumble seat, front bench seat, chrome windshield frame, tinted glass, heater, luggage rack with matching chrome bumpers, wire wheels and a sunshine roof

1976-78 TRANSFORMER I

TRANSFORMER I — ELECTRIC — Unlike most electric vehicles, which were tiny and boxy, the Transformer I looked like a mid-size American car. That was no surprise, since its body was that of a GM mid-size Abody coupe, differing mainly in a solid panel at the front (replacing the ordinary grille) and a decklid hump. Wheelbase was 112 inches, length 212—immensely larger than a typical electric. Transformer I was, in the words of a company brochure, ''the world's first luxury electric passenger car....Tomorrow's car of today.'' At least it was the first large, luxury electric in nearly half a century. Prices reached the luxury level, too, in the Cadillac and Mercedes neighborhood. Target market was ''the aficionado who appreciates a unique vehicle combined with superb engineering.'' Robert R. Aronson developed the car over a nine-year period, using a 180-volt tri-polar lead-cobalt battery system of his own creation. The battery system weighed about 2,900 pounds, which sounds like a lot but was actually considerably less than an equivalent lead-acid battery setup, which would also demand longer recharge times. With the trunk compartment totally full of batteries, the car weighed 5,850 pounds. Batteries could be quick-charged to 80 percent of full power in about 45 minutes, plugging into one of the company's proposed charging stations. The on-board slow charger could plug into any 110- or 220-volt outlet. Long-distance motorists could tow a trailer-mounted generator, which gave an 1,100-mile range in any 24hour period. The Transformer I was intended not only for urban driving, but for highway use, with a top speed of 60 MPH or more. It could cruise at 50-55 MPH, and had a range of 30-100 miles before recharging of some kind was needed. Acceleration of 0-30 MPH in 8 seconds wouldn't set any records, but was a lot swifter than most electrics. Replacing the customary grille was a solid, protruding front panel, with 'Transformer I' script on the passenger side and another script on the driver's side. On the quarter panel was a little script that said 'Electric.' A very large trunk bulge suggested the fact that all the space was occupied by batteries. A 'Transformer I Electric' nameplate went on that bulge, which extended upward from the decklid. 'Transformer I' script was also on the cowl, along with 'Electric' script at the front of front fenders, above the side marker lenses. In sum, plenty of clues to show this was an electric vehicle. Inside were an operating voltage meter, and a fuel consumption (in amps) meter. Standard equipment included power brakes and steering, automatic transmission, power windows, power skyroof, six-way power seats, tilt steering wheel, tinted glass, and AM/FM stereo. Leather upholstery was standard. Obviously, everything was battery- powered. Battery life was estimated at 50,000 miles, and replacements cost about $1500.

I.D. DATA: Not available.

TRANSFORMER I (ELECTRIC)

Model Number	Body/Style Number	Body Type & Seating	Factory Price	Production Weight	Total
I	N/A	2-dr. Cpe-5P	Note 1	5850	N/A

Note 1: Factory price was about $30,000.

CHASSIS DATA: Wheelbase: 112 in. Overall Length: 212.3 in. Height: N/A. Width: 76.6 in. Front Tread: 61.5 in. Rear Tread: 60.7 in. Standard Tires: N/A.

TECHNICAL: Motor: 32 horsepower; 1800 R.P.M. Batteries: 180-volt tri-polar lead-cobalt battery system. Charging Time: 45 minutes for 80 percent charge; 8 hours with on-board charger.

RATINGS: Range: 100 miles max. Top Speed: 60-70 MPH. Cruising Speed: 50-55 MPH. Acceleration: 0-30 MPH in 8 seconds.

OPTIONS: List not available.

MANUFACTURER: Electric Fuel Propulsion Corp. (E.F.P.), Troy, Michigan. Robert R. Aronson, founder/president.

Historical Footnotes: Production began in July 1975. The company expected to produce 250 in 1976 and 500 the next year. Orders were in hand for at least 100 cars by mid-1975 (especially from electrical utility companies, as well as a dozen from Avis to be used as rentals). In a 1976 sales letter, company vice- president Donald K. Cooper delcared that ''We feel we've built a real thoroughbred.'' They were willing to either sell or lease the car. A licensing agreement gave rights to E.F.P. patents/technology to Electric Auto Corporation, which developed Electric Limousine and Silver Volt models.

1983 Trihawk roadster

TRIHAWK — The Trihawk was a three-wheeler built by Hawk Vehicles of Dana Point, Calif. Power comes from a 1.3 liter horizontally-opposed Citroen air-cooled engine that drives the front wheels via a five-speed transaxle. The fiberglass-bodied Trihawk features a 98 in. wheelbase and 1,380 lb. shipping weight. A convertible top and side curtains are standard equipment.

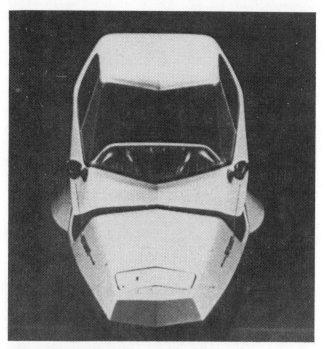

1980 Trimuter three-wheel commuter vehicle

TRI-MUTER — The Trimuter G was produced by Quincy-Lynn Enterprises, Inc., a firm based in Phoenix, Ariz. It was a three-wheeled coupe with fiberglass body, one clamshell door and a 16 hp Briggs & Stratton engine priced at $4,995. LED instrumentation and an electric power team were optional. The car featured an 88 in. wheelbase, 900 lb. shipping weight and promised 60 mpg economy.

U

1983 Urba Centurian coupe

URBA CENTURIAN — The Urba Centurian was one of the cars displayed at the International Kit Car and Replica Show held in July 1983 at Ceasars Palace in Las Vegas. It was made by Quincy-Lynn Enterprises, of Phoenix, Ariz. Power comes from a Kubota three-cylinder engine. It was claimed the car did up to 65 mph and gave fuel economy of 128 mpg at an average 35 mph. It has an 83 in. wheelbase and 156 in. overall length.

1981 Valiente convertible

VALIENTE — York Coachworks, Inc., of Olney, Ill., introduced the Valiente automobile in Dec. 1980. Darrell York and Ken W. Maines were principals in the firm, which received an automobile manufacturing company charter from the state of Illinois. Features of the marque include Connelly leather upholstered Recaro bucket seats, hand-picked walnut trim and a Lincoln-Continental V-8.

V

1979 Veep utility truck

VEEP — The Veep was a jeep-like kit car by Hadley Engineering, of Costa Mesa, Calif. The body was described as an original jeep body modified for easy Veep application including a cut and fully reinforced rear engine compartment with floor relief for Volkswagen pedals and special floor plate for a Volkswagen shift lever. A box section frame with X member bracing was supplied. It included front and rear suspension clamps. Other options included a roll bar, top assembly, bucket seat kit and street legal light kit.

1982 Vokaro Sports Roadster

VOKARO — The Vokaro was a fiberglass bodied sports car available in kit form for only $1,195 in 1982. Vopard Enterprises, of Sunisun City, Calif. distributed this component vehicle.

W

1979 Weitz X-600 sports car

WEITZ X-600 — This was fashion designer John Weitz's "dream car." It was a sports car featuring an all-aluminum body by Mallalieu Cars Ltd., of Great Britain. The design had interflowing character lines and was made to go with an American engine, drive gear and suspension. It was scheduled to debute in late fall of 1979, with a hardtop, hatchback and wagon to follow. Weitz is an international licensed amateur race driver.

1981 West Coast Cobra roadster

WEST COAST — This was one of numerous AC/Cobra replicas. It was apparently produced/marketed by a firm located on the West Coast.

X

1983 X-Gas coupe

X-GAS — James G. Sawyer, president of a company called Ronal Research Corp., of Fraser, Mich., was the guiding light behind this experimental fuel efficient vehicle. Leslie Viland, of Detroit Testing Laboratory tested the car to 172 mpg. It had a 14 hp, one-cylinder diesel power plant.

1981 XK1 three-wheel coupe

XK-1 — The three-wheel XK-1 commuter vehicle was produced by Kobel Enterprises, of San Antonio, Texas. It had a top speed of 55 mph. Fuel economy of 50 mpg was claimed by its maker. The body kit came as a preassembled unit with hinged canopy, bulkheads and interior panels bonded in place. Other features include integral wheel wells, air inlets for engine cooling and a standard rear louver. Parts from the Honda Civic and Toyota Celica were used in its construction. In most states, the XK-1 could be registered as a motorcycle for additional cost savings.

1982 XK120 roadster

XK-120 — American Custom and Component Cars, of Boise, Idaho, sold the XK-120. It came as an easy-to-assemble kit car designed by Auto Design, of San Jose, Calif. It bolted to the Pinto/Mustang II/Mercury Bobcat chassis and came in standard kit form, partly completed form or fully finished. Features included steel spring seats custom made for the XK-120, plus a padded dash with VDO instrumentation. A Toyota truck-based version was available, too, but the maker recommended the easier-to-build Ford conversion.

1982 XK140 Jaguar roadster

XK-140 JAG — Prestige Classics, of Wayzata, Minn., marketed this kit version of the 1952 Jaguar. Its body bolted directly to a special factory built frame that accomodated a front-mounted Pinto engine. The body came in six prime gelcoat colors. Rear wheel skirts were a regular feature. Prestige Classics was a division of Tele-Marketing Business Specialties, Inc. The company made some kits of its own and also sold other firms' products.

441

Z

1983 Zimmer Golden Spirit coupe

1985 Golden Zimmer coupe

1986 Zimmer Classic coupe

ZIMMER — Zimmer Motor Cars Corporation, of Pompano Beach, Florida began selling the Zimmer Golden Spirit in 1980. Called by some a neo-classic, the Golden Spirit combines styling reminiscent of the classic era with the service ease and dependability of a modern Ford Motor Corporation chassis and drivetrain.

The Golden Spirit begins as a Ford Mustang which, while retaining the basic sheet metal of the passenger compartment, is stretched and extensively modified into a finished product which is intended to evoke the grace and elegance of a period often referred to as "the golden era of the automobile."

If the appearance of the Zimmer brings back memories of an earlier time, the mechanical aspects of the vehicle are in sharp contrast. Power assists, air conditioning, sophisticated sound systems and virtually all of the amenities typical of a modern, luxury automobile are available to the Golden Spirit buyer.

INDY PACE CARS

1976: Buick T-top coupe V-6 engine (IMSC)

1977: Oldsmobile T-top coupe (IMSC)

1978: Chevrolet Limited Edition Corvette T-top coupe (IMSC)

1979: Ford Mustang II T-top coupe (IMSC)

445

1980: Pontiac Turbo-Trans Am T-top coupe (IMSC)

1981: Buick T-top coupe

1982: Chevrolet Camaro Z-28 T-top hatchback coupe (IMSC)

1983: Buick Riviera convertible (IMSC)

1984: Pontiac Fiero Sport Coupe (IMSC)

1985: Oldsmobile convertible (IMSC)

1986: Chevrolet Corvette Limited Edition roadster (IMSC)

COLLECTOR CLUB LIST

General Interest

Antique Automobile Club of Amer.
501 W. Governor Rd.
Hershey, PA 17033

Canadian Street Rod Assoc.
604 River Rd. S.
Peterborough, Ont. K9J 1E7
Canada

The Classic Car Club Of America
O'Hare Lake Office Plaza
2300 E. Devon Ave., Suite 126
Des Plains, IL 60018

Contemporary Hist. Vehicle
Assoc.
P.O. Box 40
Antioch, TN 37013

Historical Automobile Society of
Canada
820 York Road, RR2
Guelph, Ontario, N1H 6H8 Canada

Horseless Carriage Club of Amer.
PO Box 1050
Temple City, CA 91780

Milestone Car Society
P.O. Box 50850
Indianapolis, IN 46250

National Street Rod Assoc.
4030 Park Ave.
Memphis, TN 38111

Veteran Motor Car Club
18840 Pearl Road
PO Box 36788
Strongsville, OH 44136

Single Marque Clubs

Abarth Registry
1298 Birch Street
Uniondale, NY 11553

Alfa Romeo Owners Club
2304 San Pasqual Valley Rd.
Escondido, CA 92027

Allard Models
The Allard Owners Club
1 Dalmeny Avenue
London N7 OLD England

The Allard Register
8 Paget Close
Horsham
West Sussex RH13 6HD England

Alvis Owners Club
The Hill House
Rushock, Nr Droitwich
Worcester, England

American Motors Models
(Also see Nash & Hudson)
AMC Rambler Club
2645 Ashton Rd
Cleveland Heights, OH 44118

Nat'l American Motors Drivers &
Racers Ass'n.
923 Plainfield Road
Countryside, IL 60525

American Motors Owners Assoc.
1615 Purvis Ave.
Janesville, WI 53545

Marlin Owners Club
RD 5 Box 187
Coatesville, PA 19320

Classic AMX Club Int'l
7963 Depew St.
Arvada, CO 80003

Amilcar Registry
The Vinery
Wanborough Manor
Nr Gutldford CU3 2JR England

Amphicar
14330 Iseli Road
Santa Fe Springs, CA 90670

Amphibious Auto Club of Amer.
3281 Elk Court
Yorktown Heights, NY 10598

Armstrong-Siddeley Owners Club
15 Plantation Drive, West End
South Cave, Brough
N. Humberside HU15 2JD
England

Aston Martin Owners Club
USA Center
195 Mt. Paran Road NW
Atlanta, GA 30327

Auburn-Cord-Duesenberg Club
RD 6, Box 4183
Rome, NY 13440

Audi Int'l Motor Car Club
318 Harvard St., Suite 10
Brookline, MA 02146

Austin Models
Austin 10 Drivers Club Ltd.
3 Estcourt Drive, Widmer End
High Wycombe
Bucks HP15 6AH England

Austin Counties Car Club
Swallowfield Farm
Church Road
Mannings Heath
Horsham RH13 6JE
Sussex, United Kingdom

American Austin Bantam Club
2409 E. 38
Des Moines, IA 50317

Mini Owners
100 Prince St.
Fairfield, CT 06430

Mini Registry
876 Turk Hill Rd.
Fairport, NY 14450

N.A. Mini-Moke Register
PO Box 9110
So. Lake Tahoe, CA 95731

Austin-Healey Models
Austin-Healey Club of America
603 E. Euclid Avenue
Arlington Heights, IL 60004

Austin-Healey Club
Box 6197-R
San Jose, CA 95150

Austin-Healey Sports & Touring
P.O. Box 360
N. Baldwin, NY 11510

NA Auto Union Register
1023 Los Trancos Road
Portola Valley, CA 94025

Avanti Owners Ass'n Int'l
PO Box 296
Westminster, CO 80090

Bentley Models
Bentley Drivers Club
2139 Torry Pines Road
La Jolia, CA 92037

Bentley Drivers Club, Ltd.
W.O. Bentley Memorial Bldg.
16 Chearsley Road
Long Crendon
Aylesbury, Bucks HP18 9AW
England

Berkeley Exchange
46 Elm Street
North Andover, MA 01845

BMW Models
BMW Car Club of America
345 Harvard St.
Cambridge, MA 02138

BMW 700 Register
15931 Carrara St.
Hacienda Heights, CA 91745

BMW Vintage Club of Amer., Inc.
148 Linden St.
Wellesley, MA 02181

BMW Car Club of Canada
PO Box 232, Station K
Toronto, Ontario, M4P 2G5 Canada

BMW 507 Club USA
Hilltown Pike
Hilltown, PA 18927

Borgward Models
Borgward Owners Club
77 New Hampshire Ave.
Bay Shore, LI, NY 11706

Borgward Owners Club-West
644 N. Santa Cruz Ave
Los Gatos, CA 95030

Bour-Davis Car Club
PO Box 3304
Shreveport, LA 71133

Bricklin Int'l Owners Club
20 Bradford St.
New Providence, NJ 07974

American Bugatti Club
2366 Huntington Dr.
San Marino, CA 91108

Buick Models
Buick Club of America
P.O. Box 898
Garden Grove, CA 92642

Buick Compact Club of America
Rt. 1 Box 39B
Marion, TX 78124

McLaughlin-Buick Club of Canada
333 Centennial Road
West Hill, Ont., M1C 2A4 Canada

1932 Buick Registry
3000 Warren Rd
Indiana, PA 15701

1966-67 Riviera Directory
Box 825
Dearborn, MI 48121

Buick GS Club of America
1213 Gornto Road
Valdosta, GA 31602

Riviera Owners Assoc.
PO Box 26344
Lakewood, CO 80226

Cadillac Models
Cadillac-LaSalle Club
3340 Poplar Dr.
Warren, MI 48091

Cadillac Club International
Box One
Palm Springs, CA 92263

Cadillac Convertible Owners of
Amer.
P.O. Box 920
Thiells, N.Y. 10984

Brougham Owners Assoc.
1957-60 Eldorado Broughams
829 W. Wesley St.
Atlanta, GA 30327

Cartercar Club
10208 Aviary Drive
San Diego, CA 92131

Checker Car Club of Amer.
469 Tremaine Ave.
Kenmore, NY 14217

Cheetah Registry
956 Calle Primavera
San Dimas, CA 91773

Chevrolet (Corvette, Corvair &
Camaro)
Early Four Cylinder Chev Club
PO Box 62
San Leandro, CA 94557

National Chevelle Owners Assoc.
P.O. Box 5014
Greensboro, NC 27435

National Nomad Club
4691 Mariposa Dr.
Englewood, Co 80
110

Classic Chevy Club Int'l
(1955-1957 cars)
P.O. Box 17188
Orlando, FL 32860

Tri-Chevy Assoc
431 Caldwell
Chicago Hts. IL 60411

1955-57 Chevy Owners Assoc.
157 Coram-Mt. Sanai Rd.
Coram, NY 11727

Vintage Chevrolet Club of Amer.
P.O. Box 5387
Orange, CA 92667

Inliners Int'l
(Chev & GMC inline racing
engines)
840 Tornell Ave.
Turlock, CA 95380

National Impala Assoc.
PO Box 968
Spearfish, SD 57783

Late Great Chevy Club
(1958-1964 cars)
P.O. Box 17824
Orlando, FL 32860

National 409 Chevy Club
2510 E. 14th St.
Long Beach, CA 90804

Corvair Society of Amer.
2506 Gross Point Road
Evanston, IL 60201

National Corvette Owners Assoc.
900 S. Washington St.
Falls Church, VA 22046

National Corvette Restorers
Society
6291 Day Road
Cincinnati, OH 45247

National Council of Corvette
Clubs
P.O. Box 325
Troy, OH 45373

Corvette Club of America
PO Box 30223
Washington, D.C. 20814

Int'l Registry of Early Corvettes
PO Box 666
Corvallis, OR 97339

National Nostalgic Nova
(1962-1979 Chevy Nova)
PO Box 2344
York, PA 17405

Camaro Owners of Amer.
701 N. Keyser Ave.
Box 961
Scranton, PA 18501

U.S. Camaro Club
PO Box 24489
ffffffdfdf Huber Heights, OH
45424

Cosworth Vega Owners Assoc.
P.O. Box 910
22032 Trailway Lane
El Toro, CA 92630

The Chevy Association
Box 172
Elwood, IL 60421

The 1965-66 Full Size Chevy
126 Charles Road
Southampton, PA 18966

International Camaro Club, Inc.
2001 Pittston Ave.
Scranton, PA 18505

Chrysler (DeSoto, Dodge, Plymouth)
Airflow Club of Amer.
2029 Minoru Drive
Altadena, CA 91001

Barracuda Owners Club
167 Clarence
Torrington, CT 06790

Chrysler Products Owners
3511 Madison Place
Hyattsville, MD 20782

Chrysler 300 Club Int'l
19 Donegal Court
Ann Arbor, MI 48104

Chrysler 300 Club, Inc.
1120 Stonewood Ct.
Gladstone, OR 97027

Slant 6 Club of America
PO Box 4414
Salem, OR 97302

Daytona-Superbird Club
13717 W. Green Meadow Dr.
New Berlin, WI 53151

T/A AAR Special Interest Auto
Club
PO Box 30022
Columbus, OH 43230

Nat'l DeSoto Club
412 Cumnock Road
Inverness, IL 60067

DeSoto Club of America
105 E. 96th
Kansas City, MO 64114

Spirit of Adventure
PO Box 611
Hudson, WI 54016

Dodge Brothers Club
4 Willow St.
Milford, NH 03055

Dodge Wayfarer Registry
10905 Ft. Washington Road £102
Ft. Washington, MD 20744

Imperial Owners Club
P.O. Box 991
Scranton, PA 18503

Mo-Par Trans Am. Assoc.
525 Nashua Rd.
Liberty, MO 64068

Mopar Muscle Club
P.O. Box 368R
Lockport, IL 60441

National Chrysler Products Club
2119 Duncan Avenue
Allison Park, PA 15101

National Hemi Owners Assoc.
137 North View Road
Blanchester, OH 45107

Plymouth Barracuda/Cuda
Owners Club
16 Brentwood Drive
Peabody, MA 01960

Plymouth 4 & 6 Cyl.
203 Main St. E.
Cavalier, ND 58220

Scat Pack Club
P.O. Box 2303
Dearborn, MI 48123

Town & Country Owners Registry
406 W. 34th St.
Kansas City, MO 64111

Walter P. Chrysler Club
Box 4705
No. Hollywood, CA 91607

Chrysler Products Slant 6 Club
14 Fairview Place
New Rochelle, NY 10805

Chrysler Classic Car Club
445 E. Hudson
Toledo, OH 43608

Citroen
Citroen Car Club
PO Box 743
Hollywood, CA 90028

Citroen Quarterly Car Club
263 North St.
Boston, MA 02113

Citroen 2CV Club USA
PO Box 743
Hollywood, CA 90028

Crosley Automobile Club
1633 Aldoro Drive
Waukesha, WI 53186

DAF Club
19 Middleton Road
Greenport, NY 11944

Daimler
Daimler & Lanchester Owners
Club
57 Northcote Road
London, SW11 1NP England

Daimler & Lanchester Owners
Club of NA
78 William St.
Streetsville, Ont. L5M 1J3 Canada

Datsun
Datsun Owners Assoc.
12966 Crowley St
Arleta, CA 91331

Z Club of America
550 Lexington Ave.
Clifton, NJ 07011

United 510 Owners
960 San Antonio Ave.
Palo Alto, CA 94303

Davis Three-Wheeler Club of Am.
3033 Crestline Road
Bakersfield, CA 93306

Delahaye Club
3419 E. Denny Way
Seattle, WA 98122

DeLorean
DeLorean Club Int'l
Box 23040
Seattle, WA 98102

DeLorean Owners Assoc.
10568 Ashton Ave.
Los Angeles, CA 90024

Devin Register
Box 18
Nyack, NY 10960

DeSoto Club of Amer.
105 E. 96th
Kansas City, MO 64114

Durant Family Register
2700 Timber Lane
Green Bay, WI 54303-5899

Edsel Models
Edsel Owners Club, Inc.
3632 London Lane
Ft. Worth, TX 75766

International Edsel Club
P.O. Box 86
Polo, IL 61064

Edsel Restorers Group
30715 Nine Mile Road
Farmington Hills, MI 48024

Erskine Register
441 E. St. Clair
Almont, MI 48003

Facel Vega Owners Club
1650 E. 104th Street
Los Angeles, CA 90002

Ferrari
Ferrari Owners Club
1708 Seabright Ave.
Long Beach, CA 90813

Ferrari Club of America
Box 1129
Homewood, IL 60430

Ferrari Data Bank
PO Box 425, Rt. 3
Jasper, FL 32052

Fiat
Fiat Club of America, Inc.
Box 192
Somerville, MA 02143-0192

Fiat 600/600D Exchange Club
5220 Brittany Drive South
Apt. 1406
St. Petersburg, FL 33715

Topolino Register of North Amer.
3301 Shetland Road
Beavercreek, OH 45385

The Other Dino
167 Mandalay
Kalamazoo, MI 49009

Fiat Multipla Newsletter
8562 Hayshed Lane
Columbia, MD 21045

Ford Models
Early Ford V-8 Club of Amer.
P.O. Box 2122
San Leandro, CA 94577

Fabulous Fifties Ford Club
P.O. Box 286
Riverside, CA 92502

Ford Galaxie Club of America
1014 Chestnut St.,
P.O. Box 2206
Bremerton, WA 98310

Fairlane Club of America
819 Milwaukee Street
Denver, CO 80206

Ford-Mercury Club of Amer.
P.O. Box 3551
Hayward, CA 94540

Ford-Mercury Restorers Club
P.O. Box 2133
Dearborn, MI 48123

The Falcon Club of Amer.
629 N. Hospital Drive
Jacksonville, AR 72076

Special Interest Fords of the '50s
23018 Berry Pine Drive
Spring, TX 77373

Crown Victoria Assoc.
Rt. 5
Bryan, OH 43506

International Ford Retractable
Club
P.O. Box 92
Jerseyville, IL 62052

1954 Ford Club of Amer.
2314 Wakeforest Court
Arlington, TX 76012

Model T Ford Club of Amer.
Box 7400
Burbank, CA 91510-7400

Model T Ford Club Int'l
PO Box 438315
Chicago, IL 60643-8315

Model T Ford Register
14 Breck Farm Lane
Taverham, Norwich
England

Model A Ford Club of America
PO Box 250 S. Cypress
La Habra, CA 90631

Model A Drivers Inc.
1804 DeGrand St.
Green Bay, WI 54304

Model A Restorers Club
24822 Michigan Ave.
Dearborn, MI 48121

Model A Cabriolet Club
PO Box 515
Porter, TX 77365

1930-31 Ford A Deluxe Phaeton
Club
PO Box 20847
Castro Valley, CA 94546

The Mustang Club of Amer.
P.O. Box 447
Lithonia, GA 30058

Mustang Owners Club
2829 Cagua Dr. N.E.
Albuquerque, NM 87110

'71 429 Mustang Registry
PO Box 1472
Fair Oaks, CA 95628

Ranchero Club of America
1339 Beverly Rd.
Port Vue, PA 15133

Nifty Fifties Ford Club
P.O. Box 142
Macedonia, OH 44056

Classic T-Bird Club Int'l
PO Box 4148
Santa Fe Springs, CA 90670-1148

Vintage T-Bird Club of Amer.
P.O. Box 2250
Dearborn, MI 48123

Thunderbirds of America
Box 2766
Cedar Rapids, IA 52406

Meteor Car Club
General Delivery
Bowmanville
Ontario, Canada L1C 3K1

Mustang & Classic Ford Club
P.O. Box 963
North Attleboro, MA 02761

Performance Ford Club of Amer.
P.O. Box 32
Asheville, OH 43103

Ford Sidevalve Owners Club
8103 Prince George Dr.
Ft. Washington, MD 20744

Associated Fords of the '50s
PO Box 66161
Portland, OR 97226

H.W. Franklin Club
Cazenovia College
Cazenovia, NY 13035

Glas Owners Club
717 Spring Valley Pkwy.
Elko, NV 89801

Graham Owners Club
5262 NW Westgate Rd.
Silverdale, WA 98383

Hispano-Suiza Society
PO Box 688
Hayward, CA 94543

Honda
Honda Car Club
Box 4383
North Hollywood, CA 91607

Honda Car Int'l
Box 242
Deptford, NJ 08096

Honda 600 Car Club
PO Box 4383
N. Hollywood, CA 91607

Hudson-Essex-Terraplane Club
100 E. Cross St.
Ypsilanti, MI 48197

Hupmobile Club Inc.
6820 Burma Road
Folsom, CA 95630

Impulse Int'l Auto Club
Box 2327
San Anselmo, CA 94960

Iso & Bizzarrini Owners Club
Box 717
Menlo Park, CA 94026

Isotta Fraschini Owners Assoc.
35 Ligonier Drive, NE
North Fort Myers, FL 33903

Jaguar Models
Jaguar Club of No. Amer.
600 Whilow Tree Rd.
Leonia, NJ 07605

Classic Jaguar Assoc.
Rt. 2, Box 43
Templeton, CA 93465

Classic Jaguar Assoc.
2860 W. Victoria Drive
Alpine, CA 92001

Assoc. of Jensen Owners
Box 1091
Syracuse, NY 13202

Jewett Owners Club
24005 Clawiter Road
Hayward, CA 94545

Jordan Register
58 Bradford Blvd.
Yonkers, NY 10710

Kaiser-Frazer Owners Club
PO Box Y
East Stroudsburg, PA 18301

King Midget & Eshelman Registry
50 Oakwood Drive
Ringwood, NJ o7456

Kissel Kar Klub
147 N. Rural St.
PO Box 305
Hartford, WI 53027

Knight-Overland Registry
2765 Joel Place, NE
Atlanta, GA 30360

Kurtis Kraft Register
Drawer 220
Oneonta, NY 13820

Lagonda Club
68 Savill Road
Lindfield, Haywards Heath
Susses RH16 2NN England

Lamborghini Models
Lamborghini Owners Club
PO Box 7214
St. Petersburg, FL 33734

Nuova Lamborghini Club
4 Sol Brae Way
Orinda, CA 94563

Lancia
Lancia Motor Club, Ltd.
"The Old Shire House"
Aylton, Ledbury
Herefordshire HR8 2QE England

American Lancia Club
2100 E. Ohio Street
Pittsburgh, PA 15212

Lincoln Models
Lincoln Owner's Club
821 West Chicago St.
Algonquin, IL 60102

Lincoln-Zephyr Owners Club
2107 Steimruck Road
Elizabethtown, PA 17022

Continental MKII Owners Ass'n
17230 Oldenberg Road
Apple Valley, CA 92307

Road Race Lincoln Register
461 Woodland Drive
Wis. Rapids, WI 54494

Lincoln-Cont. Owners Club
P.O. Box 549
Nogales, AZ 85621

Linc. Cosmopolitan Union
2914 Gulford
Royal Oak, MI 48073

Lincoln Cosmopolitan Owners
Registry
266 Scofield Drive
Moraga, CA 94556

Lotus
Club Elite
23999 Box Canyon Road
Canoga Park, CA 91304

Lotus Ltd.
Box L
College Park, MD 20740

Marmon (Roosevelt) Club
PO Box 8031
Canton, OH 44711

Maserati
Maserati Owners Club of NA
Box 6554
Orange, CA 92667

Maserati Club Int'l (DBA M.I.E.)
Box 772
Mercer Island, WA 98040

Maxwell Registry
RD 4, Box 8
Lingonier, PA 15658

Mazda
Mazda RX-7 Club
1774 S. Alvira
Los Angeles, CA 90035

RX-7 Club of America
4020 Palos Verdes Dr., N
Suite 108
Rolling Hills Estates, CA 90274

MG Models
No. Amer. MGA Register
412 Whitree Lane
Chesterfield, MO 63017

MG Car Club Ltd.
67 Wide Bargate, Boston
Lincolnshire, PE21 6LE England

New England MG T Register
Drawer 220
Oneonta, NY 13820

Classic MG Club
1307 Ridgecrest Rd.
Orlando, FL 32806

Amer. MGB Assoc.
P.O. Box 11401
Chicago, IL 60611

MG Car Club Ltd.
600 Wilow Tree Rd.
Leonia, NJ 07605

MG Enthusiasts
P.O. Box 86
Locust Valley, NY 11560

MG Octagon Car Club
36 Queensville Avenue
Stafford ST17 4LS, England

Mercer Associates
842 E. Avenue
Bay Head, NJ 08742

Mercury Models
The Mercury Club
702 Center Street
McKeesport, PA 15132

Cougar Club of America
18660 River Cliff Dr.
Fairview Park, OH 44126

Mid-Century Mercury Car Club
5707 35th Ave.
Kenosha, WI 53142

Comet Enthusiasts Group
2520 Homewood Place
White Bear Lake, MN 55110

Cougar Eliminator Union
2914 Gulford
Royal Oak, MI 48073

Mercedes-Benz
Mercedes-Benz Club of Amer.
P.O. Box 9985
Colorado Springs, CO 80932

Mercedes Gull Wing Group
2229 Via Cerritos
Pablos Verdes Estates, CA 90274

Mercedes 190SL Group
3 Westpark Court
Ferndale, MD 21061

Metz Owners Club Register
216 Central Avenue
W. Caldwell, NJ 07006

Micro Car Club
5220 Brittany Drive S.
No. 1302
St. Petersburg, FL 33715

Micro/Minicar Club
Box 3248
Long Beach, CA 90803

Morgan
Morgan Owners Register
88 Barre Drive
Lancaster, PA 17601

Morgan 3-Wheeler Club
PO Box 99
Ringoes, NJ 08551

Morgan Sports Car Club
22 Montpellier Spa Road
Cheltenham, Glouchestershire,
GL50 1UL England

Morgan 3/4 Group, Ltd.
1 Farm Road
Ardsley, NY 10502

Morris Models
Morris Minor Registry
2311 30th Ave.
San Francisco, CA 94116

Morris Register
20 Chestnut Ave.
Gosfield, Near Halstead
Essex CO9 1TD England

Bullnose Morris Club
123 Lakeside Close
Hough Green
Widnes, Cheshire, England

Nash (& Metro. Also see AMC)
Nash Car Club of Amer.
Rt 1, Box 253
Clinton, IA 52732

Nash-Healey Car Club
530 Edgewood Ave.
Trafford, PA 15085

Metropolitan Club
Box 2951 New River Stage
Phoenix, AZ 85029

Metro Owners Club of NA
839 W. Race Street
Somerset, PA 15301

Nash Metropolitan Club
2244 Cross St.
LaCanada, CA 91011

Metropolitan Owners Club
49 Carleton
Westbury, NY 11590

NSU Enthusiasts USA
PO Box 1281
Farmington, NM 87401

Oldsmobile Models
Hurst/Olds Club of Amer.
3623 Burchfield
Lansing, MI 48901

Oldsmobile Performance
45 Rochelle Ave.
Rochelle Park, NY 07662

Oldsmobile Club of America
P.O. Box 16216
Lansing, MI 48901

Curved Dash Olds Club
3455 Florida Ave. No.
Minneapolis, MN 55427

National Antique Oldsmobile Club
PO Box 483
Elmont, NY 11003

National 442 Owners Club
PO Box 594
Kirkland, WA 98083

Opel Models
North American Opel GT
PO Box 373
New Lenox, IL 60451

Opel USA
PO Box 203
64 Eaton Road
Tolland, CT 06084

Opel Motorsport Club
14176 Ft. Apache Court
Victorville, CA 92342

Packard Models
Packards Int'l Motor Car Club
302 French St.
Santa Ana, CA 92701

The Packard Club
Packard Auto Clasics, Inc
P.O. Box 2808
Oakland, CA 94618

The Packard Caribbean Roster
P.O. Box 765
Huntington Beach, CA 92648

Packard Truck Organization
RD 1, Box 256
York Springs, PA 17372

Packard V-8 Roster, '55-'56
84 Hoy Ave.
Fords, NJ 08863

Pantara
Pantara International
5540 Farralone Ave.
Woodland Hills, CA 91367

Pantara Owners Club of America
1532 Nelson Street
W. Covina, CA 91732

Peerless GT Register of Amer.
PO Box 673
Rockville, MD 20851

Peugeot 403 Convertible
4, rue Mugnier
Maisons-Laffitte
78600 France

Pierce-Arrow Society
135 Edgerton St.
Rochester, NY 14607

Pontiac Models
Pontiac Oakland Club Int'l
P.O. Box 4789
Culver City, CA 90230

Classic G.T.O. Club
P.O. Box 392
Dallas, TX 75221

G.T.O. Ass'n of Amer.
1634 Briarson
Saginaw, MI 48604

Oakland-Pontiac Enthusiasts
Organ.
1083 Woodlow Street
Pontiac, MI 48054

Trans Am Club
P.O. Box 917
Champaign, IL 61820

Trans Am Club of America
P.O. Box 33085
North Royalton, OH 44133

Trans Am Club U.S.A.
Box99
Medford, MA 02153

Judge GTO International
114 Prince George Drive
Hampton, VA 23669

Worldwide Fiero Club
176 Edgebrook Rd.
Trenton, NJ 08691

Fiero Owners Club of America
1941 E. Edinger Ave.
Santa Ana, CA 92705

Porsche Models
Porsche Club of Amer.
161 Oscaleta Rd.
Ridgefield, CT 06877

Porsche Owners
Box 2791
Fullerton, CA 92633

356 Registry
10552 Margate Terr.
Cincinnati, OH 45241

Porsche 914 Owners Assoc.
555 S. Palm Canyon 110A
Suite 165
Palm Springs, CA 92264

Powell Sports Wagon Registry
Box 416
Cavalier, ND 58220

Railton Owners Club
"Fairmiles" Barnes Hall Road
Burncross, Sheffield, England

Renault
United Renault Club of Amer.
Box 2277
Cypress, CA 90730

Dauphine Club of NA
PO Box 423
Cazenovia, NY 13035

Renault Club of America
Box 8568
Rockville, MD 20856-8568

REO Club of America
7971 Vernon Rd., Rt. 4
Clay, NY 13041

Rickenbacker Car Club of Amer.
82 S. Ellicott St.
Williamsville, NY 14221

Riley Motor Club USA, Inc.
PO Box 4162
Anaheim, CA 92803

Rolls-Royce
Rolls Royce Owners Club Inc.
P.O. Box 2001
Mechanicsburg, PA 17055

Phantom III Tech. Soc.
PO Box 25
Mechanicsburg, PA 17055

Saab
Saab Clubs of NA
60 Charles Street
S. Meriden, CT 06460

Saab Sonett Registry
2345 Franklin Ave. E
Seattle, WA 98102

Sabra Registry
7040 N. Navajo Ave.
Milwaukee, WI 53217

Shelby Model
Shelby Owners of America, Inc.
RR 4, Box 179A
Great Bend, KS 67530

Shelby Dodge Automobile Club
P.O. Box 759
West Redding, CT 06896

Shelby American Auto Club
22 Olmstead Rd.
West Redding, CT 06896

Siata/Fiat 8V Register
Box 2111
Ranchos Palos Verdes, CA 90274

No. Amer. Singer Owners Club
6176 Caleta
Goleta, CA 93117

Stevens-Duryea Assoc.
3565 Newhaven Road
Pasadena, CA 91107

Stephens Owners Registry
401 Brokker Road
Brandon, FL 33511

Studebaker Models
Erkine Register
441 E. St. Clair
Almont, MI 48003

Antique Studebaker Club
4476 Matilija Avenue
Sherman Oaks, CA 91423

Studebaker Drivers Club
PO Box 901696
Dallas, TX 75390

Avanti Owners Association Int'l.
PO Box 296
Westminster, CO 80030

Subaru 360 Drivers Club
4934 East Timrod Street
Tucson, AZ 85711

Sunbeam
Sunbeam Alpine Club
1752 Oswald Place
Santa Clara, CA 95051

Sunbeam Car Club
43 Terrace Avenue
Ossining, NY 10562

Tatra Owners Register
Box 118
E. Norwich, NY 11732

Toyota
Toyota Celica Supra Club
904 Silver Spur Road
Ste. 182-N
Rolling Hills Estates, CA 90274

Toyota Sports 800 Club
224 Debby Drive
Palm Springs, CA 92262

Triumph Models
Triumph Travelers Sports Car
Club
Box 60314
Sunnyvale, CA 94088-0314

Vintage Triumph Register
PO Box 36477
Grosse Point, MI 48236

Triumph Register of Amer.
5650 Brook Road NW
Lancaster, OH 43130

Tucker Club of Amer.
982 Doerner Rd.
Roseburg, OR 97470

TVR Car Club
4450 S. Park Ave.
Apt. 1609
Chevy Chase, MD 20815

Volkswagen
VW Club of America
PO Box 154
North Aurora, IL 60542-0154

Vintage VW Club of America
Eastern Region
818 Main Street
Portage, PA 15946

Vintage VW Club of America
Western Region
PO Box 4097
Santa Barbara, CA 93140

SOTO (Transports)
PO Box 17234
Irvine, CA 92713

Karmann-Ghia Registry
5705 Gordon Drive
Harrisburg, PA 17112

GTI Club Int'l
731 Pacific, Suite 71
San Luis Obispo, CA 93401

Volvo Models
Volvo Club of America
P.O. Box 710
Durham, NH 03824-0710

Volvo Sports America 1800
1203 W. Cheltenham Ave.
Melrose Park, PA 19126

White Owners Registry
1624 Perkins Drive
Arcadia, CA 91006

Wills
The Wills Club
1604 James Road
Wantagh, NY 11793

Wills St. Claire Club
721 Jenkinson St.
Port Huron, MI 48060

Willys Models
Willys Overland Jeepster Club
Box 12042
El Paso, TX 79912

Midstates Jeepster Assoc.
7025 Lorraine Terrace
Stickney, IL 60402

The Willys Club
719 Lehigh Street
Bowmanstown, PA 18030

Willys Overland Knight Registry
1325 New Jersey Ave.
Lorain, OH 44052

Willys-8 Registry
1415 Baker Street
Penticton, BC Canada
V2A 6B7

Willys Aero (Registry Only)
220 N. Brighton St.
Burbank, CA 91506-2302

Woodill Wildfire Registry
826 Villa Ridge Road
Falls Church, VA 22046

Related Organizations

Automobile License Plate Collectors Assoc.
PO Box 712
Weston, WV 26452

Automobile Objects d'art Club
252 N. 7th Street
Allentown, PA 18102

British Motorcar Club
BIR-106
Rocky Hill, CT 06067

Canadian Street Rod Assoc.
604 River Road South
Peterborough, Ont. Canada K9J 1E7

Electric Auto Assoc.
1249 Lane Street
Belmont, CA 94002

Fordson Tractor Club
250 Robinson Road
Cave Junction, OR 97532

Hubcap Collectors Club Int'l
Box 54
Buckley, MI 49620

Key Chain Collectors Club
888 8th Ave.
New York, NY 10019

Kustom Kemps of America
2548 Glacier Dr.
Wichita, KS 67215

Madison Ave. Sports Car Driving
& Chowder Society
30 Sumner Road
Greenwich, CT 06830

Micro/Minicar Club
Box 3248
Long Beach, CA 90803

Military Vehicle Coll. Club
PO Box 33697
Thornton, CO 80233

Mullins Owners Club
1427 W. Idaho Ave.
St. Paul, MN 55108

Pace Car Society
1490 Overhill Road
Golden, CO 80401

Pioneer Machinery Club
RR 4
LeMars, IA 51031

Police Car Collectors
PO Box 112256
Tacoma, WA 98411-2256

Registry of Italian Oddities
3205 Valley Vista Road
Walnut Creek, CA 94598

Sedan Deliveries of Calif.
PO Box 1265
Vista, CA 92083

Society of Automotive Historians
Automotive History Collection
Detroit Public Library
5201 Woodward Ave.
Detroit, MI 48202

Steam Auto Club of Amer.
1227 W. Voorhees St.
Danville, IL 61832

U.S.A. Convertible Club
PO Box 8240
Cincinnati, OH 45208

Vintage Automobile of Quebec
C.P. 367
Succ. C
Montreal, Quebec H2L 4K3
Canada

Fire Truck Models
S.P.A.A.M.F.A.A.
P.O. Box 2005
Eastwood Sta.
Syracuse, NY 13220-2005

Ahrens-Fox Fire Buffs Assoc.
365 Neiffer Road
Schwenksville, PA 19473

Union Historical Fire Society
1307 N. 19th St.
Allentown, PA 18103

Motorcycle Clubs
Antique Motorcycle Club, Inc.
3431 W. 10th
Wichita, KS 67203

AJS/Matchless Owners Club of
England, NA Section
PO Box 317
Yardley, PA 19067

Vintage BMW Motorcycle
Owners, Ltd.
PO Box 67
Exeter, NH 03833

Vincent Motorcycle Club, NE
551 W. Walnut St.
Lancaster, PA 17603

Cushman Club of Amer.
1116 Rosedale
Ponca City, OK 74604

Vincent Owners Club
6204 Wissachickon Ave.
Philadelphia, PA 19144

Vintage Motor Bike Club
P.O. Box 123
Carolina, RI 02812

Vintage Japanese Motorcycle
612 Hoge Bldg.
Seattle, WA 98104

Bus & Professional Vehicles
International Bus Collectors
c/o Redden Archives
18 Lambert Ave.
Lynn, MA 01902

Motor Bus Society
P.O. Box 7058
West Trenton, NJ 08628

Bus History Association
2350 Dundas St. West, Apt 2413
Toronto, Ontario, Canada M6P
4B1

Emergency Vehicle Collectors
Club
118 Highway 101 W.
Port Angeles, WA 98362

Professional Car Society
PO Box 09636
Columbus, OH 43209

Racing Organizations
Sports Car Club of America
6750 S. Emporia Street
Suite 400
Englewood, CO 80112

Vintage Sports Car Drivers
Assoc.
Box C, 15 W. Burton Pl.
Chicago, IL 60610

Williams Grove Old Timers
1 Speedway Dr.
Mechanicsburg, PA 17055

Nat'l Assoc. of Auto Racing Mem-
orabilia Collectors
214 Meadow Street
Naugatuck, CT 06770

Antique Auto Racing Soc.
Rt 1 Box 172
Ixonia, WI 53036

Nat'l Auto Racing Hist. Soc.
1488 W. Clifton
Lakewood, OH 44107

Vintage American Race Cars
4626 Paradise Road
Seville, OH 44273

Vintage Sports Car Club of
America
170 Wetherhall Road
Garden City, NY 11530

Atlantic Coast Old Timers Auto
Racing Club
PO Box 3067
Alexandria, VA 22302

New England Antique Racers,
Inc.
PO Box 18354
East Hartford, CT 06118

Midwest Auto Racing Club
PO Box 2
Flossmoor, IL 60422

Vintage Auto Racing Assoc. of
Canada
RR 3
King, Ontario L0G 1K0
Canada

Toys and Models
Ertl Collector's Club
Dept. 776A
Hwys 136 & 20
Dyersville, IA 52040

Matchbox Collectors Club
PO Box 119
WoodRidge, NJ 07075

Model Car Collectors Ass'n
5113 Sugar Loaf Dr.
Roanoke, VA 24018

Station Wagons
National Woodie Club
283 Nazareth Pike
Bethlehem, PA 18017

Truck Clubs
Amer. Truck Hist. Society
Saunders Building
PO Box 59200
Birmingham, AL 35259

Antique Truck Club of Amer.
PO Box 291
Hershey, PA 17033

Light Commercial Vehicle Ass'n
Rt 14, Box 468
Jonesboro, TN 37659

Int'l Harvester Restorers Club
PO Box 2281
Elkhart, IN 46516

Graham Bros. Truck & Bus Club
9894 Fairtree Drive
Stongsville, OH 44136

Diamond T Register
PO Box 1657
St. Cloud, MN 56302

Nat'l Panel Del'y Club
4002½ Hermitage Rd.
Richmond, VA 23227

Motor Truck, Bus & Fire Engine
Club
330 N. Edwards Ave.
Syracuse, NY 13206

Vintage White Truck Assoc.
629 Terminal Way £21
Costa Mesa, CA 92627

Ultra Van
1199 Dunsyre Dr.
Lafayette, CA 94549

REGIONS/LOCAL

ALABAMA

Gadsden Antique Auto Club
113 Buckingham Pl.
Gadsden, AL 35901

Old South Antique Auto Club
Rt. 9, Box 72B
Eight Mile, AL 36613

ARKANSAS

Arkansas Antique Car Club
610 S. 12th St.
Paragould, AR 72450

Arkansas Traveler Antique Auto Club
7521 Gable Dr.
Little Rock, AR 72205

Bootheel Antique Car Club
562 N. 7th St.
Piggott, AR 72454

Dixie Car Club of Benton, Ark.
PO Box 1255
Benton, AR 72015

Foothills of the Ozarks Antique Car Club
Rt. 1, Box 212
Rogers, AR 72756

Fort Smith Antique Automobile Club
3301 S. 95th
Fort Smith, AR 72903

Mid-America Old Time Automobile
Association
Museum of Automobiles
Rt. 3, Petit Jean Mountain
Morrilton, AR 72110

Razorback Antique Auto Club
Rt. 1, Box 796
Heber Springs, AR 72543

Valley Antique Automobile Club
704 Ave. 2, NE
Atkins, AR 72823

Vintage and Classic Cars of Hot Springs
907 Prospect
Hot Springs, AR 71901

ARIZONA

Arizona Edsel Club
8324 E. Via Dorado
Scottsdale, AZ 85258

Arizona MG T Roadrunners
PO Box 246
Tempe, AZ 85281

Cactus Corvair Club
PO Box 11471
Phoenix, AZ 85061

Contemporary Historical Vehicle
Association
Southern Arizona Region
3464 S. Manitoba
Tucson, AZ 85730

Early Ford V-8 Club
Phoenix Chapter
1502 W. 1st Pl.
Mesa, AZ 85201

Ford Falcon Club of Arizona
10209 N. 64th St.
Scottsdale, AZ 85253

Packards International
Arizona Region
3008 E. Cheery Lynn Rd.
Phoenix, AZ 85016

The Ranchero Torino Club of Arizona
800 N. 4th Ave.
Tucson, AZ 85705

CALIFORNIA

American Truck Historical Society
Central California Chapter
6412 East Keyes Rd.
Turlock, CA 95380

Antique Automobile Club of America
Redwood Empire Region
PO Box 3901
Santa Rosa, CA 95402

Arcane Auto Society
875 Folsom St.
San Francisco, CA 94107

Association of Calif. Car Clubs
827 Fourth St. #208
Santa Monica, CA 90403

Austin-Healey Club
Pacific Centre,   PO Box 6197
San Jose, CA 95150

Avanti Owner Ass'n. Int'l.
San Diego Chapter
7840 Michelle Dr.
La Mesa, CA 92041

Avanti Owners Ass'n. Int'l.
Southern California Chapter
3211 Wendy
Los Alamitos, CA 90720

California Assoc. of Tiger Owners
4508 El Reposo Dr.
Eagle Rock, CA 90065

California Capri Club
422 Bradrick
San Leandro, CA 94578

California MGT Register
4911 Winnetka Ave.
Woodland Hills, CA 91364

California Vehicle Foundation
5240 Fruitridge Rd.
Sacramento, CA 95820

Central Calif. MoPar Association
PO Box 5659
Stockton, CA 95205

Central Cast Triumphs
718 "D" W. Victoria
Santa Barbara, CA 93101

Classic Car Club of America
Southern California Region
1232 Highland Ave.
Glendale, CA 91202

Contemporary Historical Vehicle
Association
Costal Valleys Region
P.O. Box 2194
Canoga Park, CA 91306

Contemporary Historical Vehicle
Association
Redwood Region
3253 La Canada Rd.
Lafayette, CA 94549

Contemporary Historical Vehicle
Association
Southern California Region
PO Box 254
Fullerton, CA 92632

Contemporary Historical Vehicle
Association
Verdrego Vintage Vehicles Region
PO Box 8036
La Cresenta, CA 91214

Corsa West of Los Angeles
PO Box 5023
Mission Hills, CA 91345

DeLorean Owners Association
10568 Ashton Ave.
Los Angeles, CA 90024

Desert Tin of Southern California
PO Box 329
Sunnymead, CA 92388

Earl C. Anthony Inc. Packard Motor Car
Club
PO Box 24973
Los Angeles, CA 90024

Early Ford V-8 Club
San Diego Region
Box 715
La Mesa, CA 92041

Falcon Club of Los Angeles
PO Box 5694
Elmonte, CA 91734

Ford Falcon Club of San Diego
PO Box 33306
San Diego, CA 92103

Ford-Mercury Club of America
Cable Car Chapter
22588 7th St.
Hayward, CA 94541

Ford-Mercury Club of America
Mid-Atlantic Chapter
3616 Woodburn Rd.
Annandale, CA 22003

Ford-Mercury Club of America
San Fernando Valley Chapter
22706 Catley St.
Canogo Park, CA 91367

Ford-Mercury Club of America
San Gabriel Valley Chapter
PO Box 943
Baldwin Park, CA 91706

Horseless Carriage Club of Southern
California
4527 Yosemite Way
Los Angeles, CA 90065

Hudson-Essex-Terraplane Club
California Inlnand Chapter
15808 Glazebrook Dr.
La Mirada, CA 90638

Hudson-Essex-Terraplane Club
Northern California Chapter
PO Box 2454
Berkeley, CA 94702

Kaiser-Frazer Owners Club International
Southern California Region
3248 Washington Place
La Crescenta, CA 91214

Last of the Thirties Club
PO Box I
Manteca, CA 95336

Long Beach Model T Club
PO Box 7112
Long Beach, CA 90807

Lowrds of Fresno/Clovis
1330 N. Jackson
Fresno, CA 93703

Mustang Club of Southern California
Chino, CA 91710

Mustang Owners Club of California
PO Box 8261
Van Neys, CA 91409

Nash Club of America
Southern California Region
2428 Level St.
Anaheim, CA 92804

Northern California Chrysler Products Club
11271 Fardon Ave.
Los Altos, CA 94022

Northern California Falcon Club
6501 Halifax St.
Citrus Heights, CA 95621

Northern Calif. Kit Car Club
60 Rider Court
Walnut Creek, CA 94595

Northern California Packards
P.O. Box 7763
Fremont, CA 94537

North Valley Unique Car Club
988 Ellene Ave.
Chico, CA 95926

The 57 Oldsmobile Chapter
151 Riviera Ct.
Chula Vista, CA 92011

Orange County Model T Ford Club Inc.
1922 S. Anaheim Blvd.
Anaheim, CA 92805

Pacific Austin Bantam Club
12304 Lambert Avenue
El Monte, CA 91732

Pontiac Oakland Club International
Southern California Region
1307 Santanella Terrace
Corona del Mar, CA 92625

Renault Club of Southern California
1516 East Santa Ana St.
Anaheim, CA 92805

Sacramento Valley Citroen Club
3348 Ardenridge Dr.
Sacramento, CA 95825

San Diego MG Club
P.O. Box 112111
San Diego, CA 92111

South Bay AMX Club
1980 Kingman Ave.
San Jose, CA 95128

Southern California Willys Overland
Jeepsters Club
5935 Harvey Way
Lakewood, CA 90713

Special Ts
PO Box 1778
Golita, CA 93116

Studebaker Drivers Club
Beach Cities Chapter
17th St. at Newport Freeway
Santa Ana, CA

Studebaker Drivers Club
Orange County Beach Cities Chapter
PO Box 1536
Newport Beach, CA 92663

Triumph Travelers SCC
1658 Meadowlark
Sunnyvale, CA 94007

Vintage Chevrolet Club of America
Foothill Region
1751 E. Alosta Ave.
Glendora, CA 91740

Vintage Chevrolet Club of America
Sacramento Valley Region
8780 Golden Spur Dr.
Roseville, CA 95678

West Coast Kustoms
PO Box 329
Sunnymead, CA 92388

Western States Corvette Council
2321 Falling Water Court
Santa Clara, CA 95054

Willys Aero Survival Count
3248 Washington Pl.
La Cresenta, CA 91214

COLORADO

Alfa Club of Colorado
11253 E. 6th. Pl.
Aurora, CO 80010

Am. MGB Assoc. & Rocky Mtn. MGT
Register
1218 Steele
Denver, CO 80206

Classic Chevys of Colorado
6621 Fielding Cr.
Colorado Springs, CO 80911

Classic GTO Association of Denver
6883 Wyman Way
Westminster, CO 80030

Coloradans
2000 W. 92nd Ave., #275
Federal Heights, CO 80221

Colorado Association of Tiger Owners
7939-2 York
Denver, CO 80229

Colorado Camaro Club
1164 Regina Lane
Northglenn, CO 80233

Colorado Classic Thunderbird Club
15 Flower St.
Lakewood, CO 80226

Colorado Continental Convertible Club
695 Dudley St.
Lakewood, CO 80226

Colorado Street Rod Association
12416 Bellaire
Thornton, CO 80241

Denver Coupe & Sedan
2755 W. 12th Ave. Pl.
Broomfield, CO 80020

Denver Mustang Club
5704 W. Leewood Dr.
Littleton, CO 80123

High Plains Nash
1974 S. Huron
Denver, CO 80223

Lotus-Colorado
7673 Beverly Blvd.
Castle Rock, CO 80104

Mile High Buick
47355 Galapaco
Englewood, CO 80110

Mile High Nomads
6208 W. 92nd Pl.
Westminster, CO 80030

Mile High Skyliners
750 S. Brianwood Dr.
Lakewood, CO 80226

Model A Denver
1082 S. Harrison
Denver, CO 80209

Model A Ford Club
Pikes Peak Chapter
PO Box 1929
Colorado Springs, CO 80901

Pikes Peak Corvair
205 N. El Paso St.
Colorado Springs, CO 80903

Porsche Club of America
Rocky Mountain Region
10 Brookside Dr.
Littleton, CO 80121

Rocky Mountain Classic Chevys
P.O. Box 1125
Idaho Springs, CO 80452

Rocky Mountain CORSA
9753 W. Verginia Dr.
Lakewood, CO 80226

Rocky Mountain Isetta Club
6516 Constellation Dr.
Fort Collins, CO 80525

Rocky Mountain Jaguar Club
1575 W. Byers Pl.
Denver, CO 80223

Rocky Mountain Military Vehicle
4675 Teller St.
Wheatridge, CO 80033

Rocky Mountain Packard
2920 Ward Ct.
Denver, CO 80033

Rocky Mountain Thunderbird Club
2860 S. Kenton Ct.
Aurora, CO 80014

Rocky Mountain 1958-'66 Thunderbird
Club
451 E. 58th Avenue, No. 1185
Denver, CO 80216

Rocky Mt. UN-Club
1204 S. Uvalda
Aurora, CO 80012

Studebaker Drivers Club
Studebaker Conestoga
320 W. 80th Ave.
Denver, CO 80221

Thunderbirds of Colorado Limited
10442 Brewer Dr.
Northglenn, CO 80234

Veteran Motor Car Club of America
Loveland Chapter
2112 Champa St.
Loveland, CO 80537

Veteran Motor Car Club of America
Arkansas Valley Chapter
439 Westwood Lane
Pueblo, CO 81005

Veteran Motor Car Club of America
Royal Gorge Chapter
1411 Walnut
Canon City, CO 81212

Ye Old Auto Club
14706 E. 134th Pl
Brighton, CO 80601

Yesteryears Classics
9800 Lunceford Lane
Northglenn, CO 80221

CONNECTICUT

Connecticut Custom Kemps
165 Buckingham Ave.
Milford, CT 06460

Connecticut Valley Willys Overland
Jeepster Club
15 Conrad Drive
W. Hartford, CT 06107

The Eastern Packard Club
P.O. Box 153
Fairfield, CT 06430

Historical Automobile Club
Litchfield Hills
31 Morningside Dr.
Torrington, CT 06790

New England Antique Racers Inc.
PO Box 18354
East Hartford, CT 06118

New England Street Rodders Inc.
75 Tolland Turnpike
Manchester, CT 06040

FLORIDA

Antique Automobile Club of America
Florida West Coast Region
2871 County Rd. 70
Palm Harbor, FL 33563

Antique Auto Club of Cape Canaveral
PO Box 1611
Cocoa, FL 32922

Central Florida Camaro Club
PO Box 20321
Orlando, FL 32814

Contemporary Historical Vehicle
Association
Sunshine Region
2552 58th Ave. N
St. Petersburg, FL 33714

Ford Lincoln Mercury Club of Florida
P.O. Box 13514
Tampa, FL 33681

Gold Coast T-Bird Club
1675 NW 43rd St.
Oakland Park, FL 33309

Mercury Club of South Florida
4132 SW 22nd St.
Fort Lauderdale, FL 33317

Miami Corvette Association
249 Lafayette Drive
Miami Springs, FL 33166

Orlando Area Studebaker Club
PO Box 698
Altamone Springs, FL 32714

Panama City Classic and Antique Car
Association
P.O. Box 1962
Panama City, FL 32401

Pin-Mar Antique Club
PO Box 1235
Pinellas Park, FL 33565

Road Knights of South Florida
4132 SW 22nd St.
Fort Lauderdale, FL 33317

South Florida Corvairs
PO Box 895
Fort Lauderdale, FL 33302

Studebaker Drivers Club
Central Florida Chapter
916 Toddsmill Trace
Tarpon Springs, FL 33589

Studebaker Drivers Club
Orlando Area Chapter
PO Box 802
Fern Park, FL 32730

GEORGIA

Buick Club of America
Dixie Chapter
2141 Ithica Dr.
Marietta, GA 30067

Chrysler 300 Club
Mid-South Chapter
Rt. 1, Box 119
Pendergrass, GA 30567

Corvair Atlanta
599 Inglewood Drive
Smyrna, GA 30080

ILLINOIS

American Motors Car Club
Heart of Illinois Chapter
RR1, Box 50
Brimfield, IL 61517

Antique Automobile Club of America
Mississippi Valley Region
2047 32nd St.
Rock Island, IL 61201

Automobile Collectors Club of the Greater
Belleville (Ill.) Area
105 Van Rue Dr.
Belleville, IL 62221

Capri Club of Chicago
7158 W. Armitage
Chicago, IL 60635

Central Illinois Vintage Car Club
PO Box 986
Decatur, IL 62523

Chicagoland Thunderbirds
1041 Rand
Villa Park, IL 60181

CORSA
Chicagoland Corvair Enthusiasts
519 E. Forest Ave.
West Chicago, IL 60185

Greater Chicago Classic Chevy Club
111 Dato Ct.
Streamwood, IL 60107

Illinois Valley Olds Chapter
18650 South 76th Avenue
Tenley Park, IL 60477

John Bearce Ford Mustang Club
662 Knoll Crest Dr.
Peoria, IL 61614

Kane Kounty Kar Klub
302 Richards St.
Geneva, IL 60134

Late Great Chevy Club
Northern Illinois Chapter
800 Hayes Ct.
Harvard, IL 60033

Lincoln Land Kustoms
15817 N. Regency Pl.
Chillicothe, IL 61523

McLean County Antique Auto Club
1340 E. Empire
Bloomington, IL 61701

Midwest Antique Classic Motorcycle Club
721 S. Julian St.
Naperville, IL 60540

Mississippi Valley Historic Auto Club
1108 N. 5th St.
Quincy, IL 62301

Model A Restorers Club
Illinois Region
4001 N. Denley
Schiller Park, IL 60176

Model A Restorers Club Inc.
Calumet Region
8817 S. Moody Ave.
Oak Lawn, IL 60453

Mustang Club of America
Southern Illinois Region
Alton, IL

Northern Illinois Late Great Chevys
800 Hayes Court
Harvard, IL 60033

Old Town Escorts Ltd. Model Car Club
1933 N. Sedgwick St.
Chicago, IL 60614

Pontiac Oakland Club International
Illinois Chapter
904 W. Parker Dr.
Schaumburg, IL 80194

Prairie Capital Corvair Association
PO Box 954
Springfield, IL 62705

Quad Cities Cruisers
1411-31st St.
Rock Island, IL 61201

Rock River Restorers
PO Box 872
Rock Falls, IL 61071

Rods of Lincoln Land
2440 Nan St.
Aurora, IL 60504

Rustic Auto Club
RR 4
Pontiac, IL 61764

Vintage Chevrolet Club of America
Great Lakes Region
1258 Balmoral Ave.
Calumet City, IL 60409

Walter P. Chrysler Club
Northern Illinois Region
327 Highland Ave.
Elmhurst, IL 60126

Windy City Z Club
1419 Adams Street
Lake in the Hills, IL 60102

INDIANA

Antique & Classic Auto Club
4400 S. 9th St.
Terre Haute, IN 47802

Early Birds of Hoosierland Inc.
507 Howard Ct.
Fairmont, IN 46928

Elkhart Vintage Auto Club
P.O. Box 489
Elkhart, IN 46415

Falcons Over Indiana
Rt. 4, Box 116
Alexandria, IN 46001

Hoosier Convertible Club
3434 E. 136th St.
Carmel, IN 46032

Indiana Leadsleds
5408 Winding Way
Muncie, IN 47302

Indiana Street Rod Association
7046 Forest Park Dr.
Indianapolis, IN 46217

Lincoln Continental Owners Club
Hoosier Region
6416 Dean Rd.
Indianapolis, IN 46220

Michiana Antique Auto Club Inc.
910 State St.
LaPorte, IN 46350

Old Fort Model A Region
P.O. Box 13586
Fort Wayne, IN 46869

Owners & Enthusiasts of '55, '56 & '57
Thunderbirds
609 East 6th St.
Alexandria, IN 46001

Packards International
Indiana Region
613 W. Orchard Lane
Greenwood, IN 46142

IOWA

Iowa Street Rodders Association
Box 6086
East Des Moines Station
Des Moines, IA 50309

Midstates Jeepster Association
3175 Kaufman Ave.
Dubuque, IA 52001

Northeast Iowa Classic Chevy Club Inc.
PO Box 1206
Waterloo, IA 50704

Northern Iowa Association for the
Preservation & Restoration of Antique
Cars   (N.I.A.P.R.A.)
1998 10th Ave. N.
Fort Dodge, IA 50501

North Iowa Vintage Auto Club
RR 1
Mason City, IA 50401

Quad Cities Antique Ford Club
1705 Prairie Vista Circle
Bettendorf, IA 52722

Street Sweepers
2418 Wilkes Ave.
Davenport, IA 52804

The Wanderers
712 14th Ave.
Coralville, IA 52241

KANSAS

Contemporary Historial Vehicle Association
Sunflower Region
1312 E. 15th St.
Lawrence, KS 66044

Fundamentals
3102 Palisade
Wichita, KS 67217

Kontinental Kustoms Kar Klub
2061 S. Palisade
Wichita, KS 67213

Midwest MGA Club
11731 W. 101st Street
Overland Park, KS 66214

Mo-Kan T-Bird Club
10505 Mohawk Lane
Leawood, KS 66206

Nifty-Fifties Classic Chevy Club
RR1, Box 19
Wakeeney, KS 67672

KENTUCKY

Ancient Age City Street Rods
2453 Eastway Dr.
Lexington, KY 40503

Obsolete Iron Rod & Custom Club
4059 Richland Ave.
Louisville, KY 40207

River City Street Rods
7507 Mallard Drive
Pleasure Ridge Park, KY 40258

LOUISIANA

Ark-La-Tex Antique & Classic Car Assoc.
P.O. Box 3353
Shreveport, LA 71103

GTO Association of America
Cabri' D Acadienne (Louisiana) Chapter
105 Cajun Street
Broussard, LA 70518

Cenla Old Car Club
P.O. Box 402
Alexandria, LA 71301

Florida Parishes Vintage Car Club of
Louisiana Inc.
P.O. Box 38
Ponchatoula, LA 70454

Mid-South Region Old Car Club
907 N. 35th St.
West Monroe, LA 71201

The Old Car Club of Baton Rouge
3221 McConnell Dr.
Baton Rouge, LA 70809

Ruston Antique Car Club of LA
Rt. 3, Box 194B
Ruston, LA 71270

MAINE

Kruise Knights
PO Box 66
Kittery Pointe, ME 04905

MARYLAND

Antique Automobile Club of America
Eastern Shore Region
Box 144, 300 Corporation Rd.
Sharptown, MD 21861

Antique Club of Greater Baltimore
208 Brightside Ave.
Pikesville, MD 21208

Convertible Owners Club of Greater
Baltimore
11311 Woodland Dr.
Timonium, MD 21093

Free State Kustoms
2205 Cedar Lane
Edgewood, MD 21040

Group Corvair
4008 Bedford Pl.
Suitland, MD 20746

GTO Association of America
The Royal GTOS (MD/VA/DC) Chapters
441 Henryton S
Laural, MD 20707

Southern Maryland Antique Auto Club
PO Box 264
White Plains, MD 20695

Washington Volvo Club
Bethesda, MD 20816

MASSACHUSETTS

Antique Chevrolet Club
13 Sears St.
Burlington, MA 01803

Antique Truck Club of New England
280 W. First Street
S. Boston, MA 02127

Bay State Antique Auto Club
Box 491
Norwood, MA 02062

Buick Club of America
Minute Man Chapter
125 Strasser Ave.
Westwood, MA 02090

Colonial Convair Club
40 Woodcrest Rd.
Boxford, MA 01921

Connecticut Valley Corvair
PO Box 35
Woronco, MA 01097

Connecticut Valley Willys Overland
Jeepster Club
20 Colonial Ave.
Springfield, MA 01109

The Fall River Antique Auto Club
1751 Rodman St.
Fall River, MA 02721

Hudson-Essex-Terraplane Club
New England Chapter
12 Albert Rd.
Peabody, MA 01960

Massachusetts Antique Fire Apparatus
Association
PO Box 3332
Peabody, MA 01960

Massachusetts Street Rod Association
10 Mohawk Dr.
Tewksbury, MA 01876

Model A Restorers Club of MA
Gilmore Hall
138 and Carver St.
Raynham, MA

Mustang & Classic Ford Club of
New England
P.O. Box 963
North Attleboro, MA 02761

New England Military Vehicles Collectors
Club
PO Box 907
Salem, MA 01970

New England Packards
PO Box 5002
Billerica, MA 01821

North-East Chevy/GMC Trucking Club
PO Box 155
Millers Falls, MA 10349

Northshore Old Car Club
111 Boston St.
North Andover, MA 01845

Plymouth County Auto Club
PO Box 124
N. Plymouth, MA 02360

MICHIGAN

Classic Car Club of America
Michigan Region
13332 Winchester
Huntington Woods, MI 48070

CORSA
Detroit Area Chapter
267 Arizona
Rochester, MI 48063

Detroit Triumph Sportscar Club
13201 Common Rd.
Warren, MI 48093

Grand Rapids Antique Car Club
PO Box 1523
Grand Rapids, MI 49501

Horseless Carriage Clug of America
Grand Rapids Region
Grand Rapids Public Museum
54 Jefferson Ave. S. E.
Grand Rapids, MI

International Antique Auto Club
905 McCandless St.
Sault Ste. Marie, MI 49783

Kalamazoo Antique Auto Restorers Club
7383 N. 12
Kalamazoo, MI 49009

Lo-Lifes
37111 Foxchase
Farmington Hills, MI

Michigan License Plate Collectors
Association
2902 E. Pierson Road
Flint, MI 48506

Outcast Wheels of Michigan
2118 Audley N.E.
Grand Rapids, MI 49505

Southwestern Michigan Car Collectors
1734 Smyers Dr.
Benton Harbor, MI 49022

Veteran Motor Car Club of America
Great Lakes Region
5601 Hatchery Rd.
Drayton Plains, MI 48020

Wanderers of Western Michigan
5041 Butternut Dr.
Holland, MI 49423

West Michigan Street Rod Association
PO Box 4
Muskegon, MI 49443

MINNESOTA

Antique Automobile Club of America
Central Chapter
8207 Clinton Ave. S.
Bloomington, MN 55420

Auto Restorers Club
PO Box 138
Eagle Lake, MN

Buick Club of America
Gopher State Chapter
PO Box 8964
Minneapolis, MN 55408

Chevy's Best
7527 Chicago Ave.
Richfield, MN 55423

Cruisin Customs Car Club
2540 E. 17th Ave.
N. St. Paul, MN 55109

The Early Ford V-8 Club of America
Twin Cities Regional Group
PO Box 20236
Minneapolis, MN 55420

Ford-Mercury Club of America
North Land Late Eight
1097 W. Iowa Ave.
St. Paul, MN 55117

GTO Association of America
Land of Lake GTOs (Minnesota)
1630 E. Sandhurst Drive
Maplewood, MN 55109

IMCA Oldtimers
10113 West 34th St.
Minnetonka, MN 55343

Kustom Kemps of Minnesota
5532 Vernon Ave. So.
Edina, MN 55436

Minnesota Packards
Packard Club Region
Box 19119, Diamond Lake Station
Minneapolis, MN 55419

Minnesota Street Rod Association
4045 Hodgson Rd, Apt. 123
Shoreview, MN 55112

Model A Restorers Club
Twin Cities Model A Chapter
2712 Murray Ave. NE
Minneapolis, MN 55418

North Suburban Auto Enthusiasts
13064 Talor St. NE
Blaine, MN 55434

Old Style Auto Club
PO Box 464
Houston, MN 55943

Pontiac-Oakland Club International
Tomahawk Chapter
2325 NE Taft St.
Minneapolis, MN 55418

Red River Wheelers
PO Box 332
Crookston, MN 56716

St. Cloud Antique Auto Club
St. Cloud, MN 56302

Stephen Auto Club
RR1, Box 103
Stephen, MN 56757

Studebaker Drivers Club
Minn. Region (includes North Star & North
Land Wheels)
PO Box 1004
Duluth, MN 55810

'T' Totalers of Minnesota
Model T Ford Club International
5319 Minnehaha Ave. So.
Minneapolis, MN 55417

Valley Vintage
Rt. 1, Box 48
Hawley, MN 56549

Vintage Car Club
922 Lincoln Ave, East
Alexandria, MN 56308

Vintage Chevrolet Club of America
Viking Region
Rt. 1, Box 75A
Buffalo, MN 55313

MISSISSIPPI

Antique Automobile & Engine Club of
Mississippi
Gulf Hills Inn
Ocean Springs, MS 39564

Antique Vehicle Club of Mississippi
Box 347
Flora, MS 39071

Bear Creek Collector's Car Club
Box 773
Belmont, MS 38827

Cadillac Club
507 E. Walnut
Ripley, MS 38663

Mid-America Old Time Auto Association
323 Enchanted Dr.
Vicksburg, MS 39180

Mississippi Antique Car Club
604 Racove Dr.
Tupelo, MS 38801

Mississippi Model A Ford Restorers Club
1601 Twin Oak Dr.
Clinton, MS 39056

Oxford Antique Motorcar Association
1413 So. 10th St.
Oxford, MS 38655

Pine Belt Antique Automobile Club Inc.
200 Robin Dr.
Petal, MS 39465 (Hattiesburg)

Studebaker Drivers Club
Central Mississippi Chapter
1313 Crawford
Vicksburg, MS 39180

Vintage Wheels
1517 57th Court
Meridian, MS 39301

MISSOURI

Ford-Mercury Club of America
Gateway Chapter
PO Box 6641
St. Louis, MO 63125

GTO Association of America
Gateway GTO Association (MK/IL)
2161 Yale Apt. 3
St. Louis, MO 63143

Horseless Carriage Club of Missouri Inc.
226 Henry Ave.
Manchester, MO 63011

KC Kustoms
416 Pine
Cameron, MO 64429

Knight Owls Kustoms
2311 N. Benton
Springfield, MO 65803

Kustom Kemps of St. Louis
10007 Killoren
St. Louis, MO 63123

Lowdowners
2066 N. Albertha
Springfield, MO 65803

Lowdowners
Rt. 3, Box 252
Strafford, MO 65757

Metro Antique Auto Club
5308 Phelps Rd.
Kansas City, MO 64136

Midwest MGA Club
816 Wyandotte
Kansas City, MO 64105

Mississippi Valley Packards
602 S. Franklin
Farmington, MO 63640

Ozark Antique Auto Club
214 Jackson Road
Republic, MO 65738

Rod-Tiques
P.O. Box 1942
Independence, MO 64055

Strollers
916 E. Fairview
Carthage, MO 64836

Studebaker Drivers Club
Missouri/Illinois "Gateway" Chapter
701 Kehrs Mill Rd.
Baldwin, MO 63011

MONTANA

Garden City Rods & Customs
Box 2251
Missoula, MT 59806

Glacier Street Rod Assoc.
600 Morning View Dr.
Kalispell, MT 59901

Treasure State Classics
1119 Toucan
Helena, MT 59601

NEBRASKA

Classic Thunderbird Club of Omaha
1802 S. 76th Ave.
Omaha, NE 68124

Custom Classics
PO Box 4418
Omaha, NE 68104

Goldenrod Antique Car Club
1605 Avenue C
Cozad, NE 69130

Meadowlark Model A Club Inc.
PO Box 6011
Omaha, NE 68106

Midwest Street Rod Association
PO Box 3705
Omaha, NE 68103

Mustang Car Club of Omaha
1835 N. 49 Ave.
Omaha, NE 68104

Nebraskaland Model T and Antique Car
Club
2221 S. 37th
Lincoln, NE 685

Nebraskaland Thunderbird Club Inc.
7922 Himebaugh Ave.
Omaha, NE 68134

Studebaker Drivers Club
Buffalo Bill Chapter
223 Reid
North Platte, NE 69101

Vintage Chevrolet Club of America
Eastern Neb./Western Iowa
2555 S. 125 Ave.
Omaha, NE 68144

Vintage Chevrolet Club of America
Tower of the Plains Region
Box 552
Milford, NE 68405

NEW HAMPSHIRE

Kustom Kings of New Hampshire
Watson Rd.
Exeter, NH 03833

New England Sonett Club
PO Box 4362
Manchester, NH 03108

NEW JERSEY

Bayshore Corvair Association
PO Box 815
Jackson, NJ 08527

Buick Club of America
Jersey Shore Buick
2425 Cedar St.
Manasquan, NJ 08736

Central Jersey Mustang Club
P.O. Box 354
Pennington, NJ 08534

Garden State Classic T-Bird Club
965 Swenlin Dr.
Vineland, NJ 08360
Jersey Late Greats '58-'64 Chevys
PO Box 1294
Hightstown, NJ 08520

Kustom Knights
84 Alberta Dr.
Saddle Brook, NJ 07662

The Lagonda Club
10 Crestwood Trail, Lake Mohawk
Sparta, NJ 07871

Model A Ford Club Inc.
Delaware Valley
c/o no. 8 Jade Lane
Cherry Hill, NJ 08002

New Jersey Renegades
2046 Lentz Ave.
Union, NJ 07083

North Jersey Thunderbird Association
8 Stag Trail
Fairfield, NJ 07006

Packards East
84 Hoy Ave.
Fords, N.J. 08863

Restored Rusty Relics
189 Marcotte Lane
Bergenfield, NJ 07621

Studebaker Drivers Club
Garden State Chapter
181 Villa Place
Rahway, NJ 07065

Triumph Association
North New Jersey Chapter
15 Northwood Ave., Apt. A-8
Summit, NJ 07901

Vintage Chevrolet Club of America
Historic New Jersey Region
52 Colson Ave.
Trenton, NJ 08610

Vintage Triumph Register
Detroit Triumph SCC
13201 Common
Warren, NJ

NEW YORK

Albany Rods & Kustoms
153 Stonington Hill Rd.
Voorhesville, NY 12186

Antique Automobile Club of America
Lake Erie Region
Pin Oak Dr.
Williamville, NY 14221

Antique Automobile Club of America
Staten Island Region
Box 244 GPO
Staten Island, NY 10314

Automobilists of the Upper Hudson Valley
Apt. A-13 Village One Apt.
587 Bdwy
Menands, NY 12204

Contemporary Historical Vehicle
Association
Big Apple Region
73-17 68 Rd.
Middle Village, NY 11379

Crosley Auto Club Inc.
3323 Eaton Rd.
Williamson, NY 14589

Early Ford V-8 Club
Long Island Regional Club
23 Fairview Ave.
Valley Stream, NY 11581

Hudson Valley Classic Chevy Club
Richard M. Warner
22 Pellbridge Dr.
Hopewell Junction, NY 12533

H.W. Franklin Club
Cazenovia College
Cazenovia, NY 13035

Long Island Chevy Owners Association
19 Twin Lane N.
Wantagh, NY 11793

Long Island Ford-Mercury Club
P.O. Box 336
Ronkonkoma, NY 11779

Lost Angels
116 McNaughton Ave.
Cheektowaga, NY 14225

The New England "T" Register, LTS.
Drawer 220
Oneonta, NY 13820

Oldsmobile Performance
45 Rochelle Ave.
Rochelle Park, NY 07662

Thunderbird Owners of New York
127 Ocean Ct.
Massapequa, NY 11758

Vintage Chevrolet Club of America
Long Island Region
27 Ashwood Ct.
East Northport, NY 11731

V-8 Club
Scoby Hill Rd.
Springville, NY 14141

NORTH CAROLINA

Austin-Healey Club
Triad Area
PO Box 5640
Winston, Salem, NC 27113

Carolina Mountain Rods & Classics
PO Box 1644
Hendersonville, NC 28739

OHIO

Antique Automobile Club of America
Central Chapter of Ohio Region
8166 Brownsville Road S.E.
Glenford, OH 43739

Buckeye Motorcar Association
PO Box 128
Newark, OH 43055

Buick Club of America
Central Ohio Chapter
90 E. Cherry St.
Sunbury, OH 43074

Car Coddlers of Ohio Inc.
PO Box 2094
Sandusky, OH 44870

Central Ohio Buick Club
115 Glenmont Ave.
Columbus, OH 43214

Citroen Car Club of Ohio
38570 Butcher Rd.
Leetonia, OH 44431

Friends of the Crawford Auto-Aviation
Museum
PO Box 751
Willoughby, OH 44094

The Great Lakes Roadster Club
PO Box 302
Bath, OH 44210

Jaquar Club of Ohio
2874 Chadbourne Road
Shaker Heights, OH 44120

Kustom Kemps of Ohio
Rt. 1, Box 326
Dover, OH 44622

Lancaster Old Car Club
PO Box 322
Lancaster, OH 43130

Mahoning Valley Olde Car Club Inc.
623 N. Hartford Ave.
Youngstown, OH 44509

Massillon Area Car Club
7981 Windward Terrace Circle NW
Massillon, OH 44646

Miami Valley Kruzers
514½ W. Greene St.
Piqua, OH 45356

Ohio Chrysler Products Antique Auto Club
5198 Harmony Lane
Willoughby, OH 44094

Packards International
Midwest Region
365 St. Leger Ave.
Akron, OH 44305

Penn-Ohio Model A Ford Club
139 East Main Street
Shelby, OH 44875

Street Survivors Car Club
745 County Line Road
Hopewell, OH 43746

Tri-State F-100 (53-56)
128 West 72nd Street
Cincinnati, OH 45016

United States Camaro Club
P.O. Box 24489
Huber Heights, OH 45424

Valley Street Rodders
PO Box 1000
Millfield, OH 45761

Vintage Vettes of Cincy
5868 H. Highwood
Fairfield, OH 45014

Y-City Custom Car Association
2090 Shady Ln.
Zanesville, OH 43701

OKLAHOMA

C.A.R.S. Unlimted of Western Oklahoma
PO Box 2845
Elk City, OK 73648

Freeloaders
PO Box 1055
Poteau, OK 74953

GTO Association of America
Goats of Northeastern Oklahoma Chapter
1200 W. Austin Pl.
Broken Arrow, OK 97106

OREGON

Classic AMX Club of Eugene
PO Box 8162
Coburg, OR 97401

Ford-Mercury Club of America
Santian Chapter
2932 Hill SE
Albany, OR 97321

Ford-Mercury Club of America
Sunset Chapter
PO Box 254
Banks, OR 97106

Goat Herd GTO Club of Oregon
P.O. Box 23924
Portland, OR 97223

Northwest Opel Club
6490 SE Hale
Milwaukee, OR 97222

Pacific NW Convertible Club
P.O. Box 16511
Portland, OR 97216

Till-A-Wheels Multi-Marque
PO Box 461
Tillamook, OR 97141

PENNSYLVANIA

Antique Automobile Club of America
Pottstown Region
951 N. 12th St.
Reading, PA 19604

Buick Club of America
Free Spirit Chapter
2100 W. Market St.
Pottsville, PA 17901

Buick Club of America
National Pike Chapter
385 Leonard Ave.
Washington, PA 15301

1953-54 Buick Skylark Registry
737 St. Claire Ave.
Erie, PA 16505

Central PA Corvair Club
1751 Chesley Road
York, PA 17403

Chester County PA Antique Car Club
814 Spruce Ave.
West Chester, PA 19380

Fairlane Club of America
721 Drexel Ave.
Drexel Hill, PA 19026

GTO Assocociation of America
Northeastern GTOs
98 Regent St.
Wilkes-Barre, PA 18702

Lambda Car Club
1944 South St.
Philadelphia, PA 19146

Lehigh Valley Model "A" Club
PO Box 9031
Bethlehem, PA 18018-9031

Mercedes-Benz Club of Northeast Pa.
229 Cedar Street
Allentown, PA 18102

The Mercury Club
702 Center St.
McKeesport, PA 15132

Model A Restorers Club
Delaware Valley Region
4215 Howell St.
Phil., PA 19135

Mustang Club of America
First Pennsylvania Mustang Club Chapter
610 Fitch Rd.
Hatboro, PA 19040

National Chrysler Products Club
Presque Isle Tri-State Region
5661 Buffalo Rd.
Erie, PA 16510

Northeast Hemi Owners Association
681 Black Road
Bryn Mawr, PA 19010

Pharaohs
622 Horning St.
Pittsburgh, PA 15227

Pontiac Owners Club International
Keystone Chapter
9 Top-of-the-Oaks
Chadds Ford, PA 19317

Quaker City Citroen Car Club
307 Summit Ave.
Fort Washington, PA 19034

The Ranchero Club
1339 Beverly Road
Port Vue, PA 15133

Tigers East/Alpines East
PO Box 1260
Kulpsville, PA 19443

Society for the Appreciation and
Preservation of Antique Motorized Fire
Apparatus in America
Union Historical Fire Society Chapter
1307 N. 19th
Allentown, PA 18104

Studebaker Drivers Club
Keystone Region
Rd. 1357
Bethel, PA 19507

Willys Club
509 W. Germantown Pike
Norristown, PA 19403

The Worthington Register
1918/1938 T, A & B Tractors
Rd. 2, Box 44
Mertztown, PA 19539

RHODE ISLAND

Cadillac-LaSalle Club Inc.
New England Region
160 Edgewood Blvd.
Providence, RI 02905

Mustang Car Club of New England
Box 1554
Woonsocket, RI 02895

Rhode Island Vintage Wheels
12 Austin St.
Wakefield, RI 02879

SOUTH CAROLINA

Camaros of Columbia
39 East Fern Ct.
Columbia, SC 29210

SOUTH DAKOTA

Dakota Territories Model A Club
PO Box 1204
Sioux Fall, SD 57101

Horseless Carriage Club of America
Sioux Falls Region
4300 S. Briarwood Ave.
Sioux Falls, SD 57103

TENNESSEE

Forked Deer Antique Car Club
2511 E. Count St.
Dyersburg, TN 38024

Magnolia Antique Car Club
Rt. 2, Box 139
Michie, TN 38357

Memphis Old Time Car Club
1749 Graceland Cove
Memphis, TN 38116

Nifty Fifties Cruisin Club
5000 New Haven Ave.
Memphis, TN 38117

Tennessee Valley Automobile Club
PO Box 116
Paris, TN 38242

West Tennessee Antique Car Club
44 Grassland Dr.
Jackson, TN 38301

TEXAS

Amarillo Antique Car Club
203 E. Hastings
Amarillo, TX 79108

Antique Automobile Club of America
Golden Triangle Chapter
98 Orgain
Beaumont, TX 77707

Antique Automobile Club of America
Texas Region
1431 Ridgeview St.
Mesquite, TX 75149

Austin Area Street Machines Association
Rt. 2, Box 51-A
Manor, TX 78653

Austin-Healey Club of America
South Texas Region
1800 San Pedro
San Antonio, TX 78212

Corvette Owners Association of South
Texas
Rt. 1, Box 119-B
4080 Menger Road
Wetmore, TX 78163

'50s Customs of Houston
6101 Pinemont Bldg. Q
Houston, TX 77092

Early Ford V-8 Club of America
Southern Texas Regional Group
4438 Newport Woods
San Antonio, TX 78249

Early Ford V-8 Club of America
Golden Spread Region
Box 1782
Amarillo, TX 79105

El Rey De La Tierra Mojada
5757 Alpha Road, #201
Dallas, TX 75240

Ford-Mercury Club of America
Longhorn Late Eight
10905 Scotsmeadow
Dallas, TX 75218

GTO Association of America
Lone Star GTO Club Chapter
1105 Floradale Drive
Austin, TX 78753

Kustom Krusiers of Texomaland
607 N. Second
Honey Grove, TX 75446

Lone Star Edsel Club
2209 B. Chasewych
Austin, TX 78745

Lubbock Mustang Club
5421 88th St.
Lubbock, TX 79424

Model T Ford Club of America
Dallas-Fort Worth Chapter Inc.
4606 Princeton
Garland, TX 75042

Piney Wood As
PO Box 7855
The Woodlands, TX 77387

Porsche Club of America
Long Horn Region Inc.
4426 Newport Woods
San Antonio, TX 78249

North San Antonio Street Machines
120 Wagon Trail
San Antonio, TX 78231

Packards International
Texas Region
359 Sussex
San Antonio, TX 78221

Pontiac-Oakland International
South Central Texas Chapter
3023 Clearfield
San Antonio, TX 78230

San Antonio Classic Thunderbird Club
607 Jackson Keller
San Antonio, TX 78216

San Antonio Mustang Club
12118 Ridge Spur
San Antonio, TX 78247

San Antonio Street Rods
3901 S. Presa
San Antonio, TX 78210

South Texas Four Wheelers
7350 Nickle
San Antonio, TX 78249

South Texas Triumphs
6710 Country Breeze
San Antonio, TX 78240

Texas Corvette Association
1806 Oak Mountain
San Antonio, TX 78232

UTAH

Ford-Mercury Club of America
Rocky Mountain Chapter
2926 Banbury Rd.
Salt Lake City, UT 84121

Kustoms of Utah
91 E. 400 S.
Centerville, UT 84014

VIRGINIA

Antique Automobile Club of America
Tidewater Region
5500 Elizabeth Ave.
Norfolk, VA 23502

Antique Automobile Club of America
Tri-Country Region
Rt. 1, Box 91
Linville, VA 22834

GTO Association of America
Greater Tidewater Owners Society (GTOS)
3632 Starlighter Drive
Virginia Beach, VA 23452

Model A Ford Cabriolet Club
6406 Glenbard Road
Burke, VA 22015

Mustang Club of America
National Capital Region
9397 Shouse Drive
Vienna, VA 22180

Old Dominion Packard Club
901 Dirk Drive
Richmond, VA 23227

VERMONT

Vermont Automobile Enthusiasts
Milton, VT 05468

WASHINGTON

Buick Club of America
Puget Sound Chapter
13003 3rd Ave.
Everett, WA 98204

Cascade V-8 Club
PO Box 3811
Federal Way, WA 98063

Early Ford V-8 Club of America
Cascade Regional Group
PO Box 3811
Federal Way, WA 98003

Ethyl Forever Car Club
PO Box 2262
Seattle, WA 98111

Ford-Mercury Club of America
Spokane Chapter
N. 11711 Hemlock St.
Spokane, WA 99218

Henry's Haulers
Ford F100 Truck Club of Western
Washington
1315 Hollis Terrace
Bremerton, WA 98310

National 442 Owners Club
PO Box 594
Kirkland, WA 98033

Northwest Classic Chevy Club
15010 NE 9th Pl.
Bellevue, WA 98007

Old Dominion Packard Club
Box 533, Fair Street
Bethany, WA 26032

WISCONSIN

Antique Automobile Club of America
Blackhawk Region
RR 3, Rockalve #196
Janesville, WI 53545

Badger Antique Auto Club
PO Box 763
Poynette, WI 53955

Badger Street Machines
723 Topeka Dr.
Lake Mills, WI 53551

Bay Area Rod and Customs
P.O. Box 453
Ashland, WI 54806

Beldenville Old Car Club
Route 1, Box 215
Ellsworth, WI 54011

Buick Club of America
Cream City Chapter
2503 East Whittaker Ave.
St. Francis, WI 53207

Cars Unlimited of Milwaukee
PO Box 18197
Milwaukee, WI 53218

Central Wis. Auto Collectors
PO Box 2132
Oshkosh, WI 54903

Central Wis. Rods & Customs
864 Oak Ridge Ln.
Stevens Point, WI 54481

Classic Car Club of America
Wisconsin Region
9345 N. Waverly Dr.
Bayside, WI 53217

Classic Car Restorers Society
1170 Aspen Dr.
Burlington, WI 53105

CORSA
Capital City Corvair Club
4217 Barby Lane
Madison, WI 53704

Fondy Vintage Auto Club
PO Box 131
Fond du Lac, WI 54935

Great Lakes Caminos
PO Box 13701
Milwaukee, WI 53213

Hudson-Essex-Terraplane
Chicago/Milwaukee Chapter
9059 N. 60th St.
Brown Deer, WI 53223

Mercedes-Benz Club of America
Green Bay Chapter
612 Sunrise Ln.
Green Bay, WI 54301

Milwaukee Corvair Club
2523 E. Armour Av.
Milwaukee, WI 53207

Mishicot Racing Team Car Club
Box 158
Mishicot, WI 54228

North Central Classics & Customs Auto
Club
N4056 Oriole Dr.
Medford, WI 54451

North East Wisconsin Corvair Club
1270 Morgan Ave.
Oshkosh, WI 54901

Oldsmobile Club of Wisconsin
PO Box 435
Sturtevant, WI 53177

Old Time Auto Club
Rt. 6, Box 615
Waupaca, WI 54981

Original GTO Club
PO Box 18438
Milwaukee, WI 53218

Pontiac-Oakland Club International
Badger State Chapter
1119 S. 117th St.
West Allis, WI 53214

River City Street Rods
PO Box 434
Eau Claire, WI 54702

R & D Motor Club Ltd.
PO Box 129
Hales Corners, WI 53130

Show-N-Go Ltd. Car Club
525 Pine St.
Hartford, WI 53027

Stevens Point Old Car Club
1556 Elk St., PO Box 346
Stevens Point, WI 54481

Studebaker Drivers Club
Badger State Chapter
5399 Old Town Hall Rd.
Eau Claire, WI 54701

Studebaker Drivers Club
Northland Wheels Chapter
2218 John Ave.
Superior, WI 54880

Studebaker Drivers Club
Wisconsin Region
217 Farnham St.,   PO Box 772
Marshall, WI 53559

Trans-Am Club of America
Southeast Wisconsin Chapter
PO Box 07084
Milwaukee, WI 53207

Tri-County Antique Auto Club
Rt. 1, Box 39
Unity, WI 54488

Waukesha Olde Car Club
P.O. Box 144
Waukesha, WI 53187

48 & Under Car Club
708 Water St.
Sauk City, WI 53583

Waukesha Olde Car Club
PO Box 144
Waukesha, WI 53187

Wisconsin Edsel Club
1729A S. 24th Street
Milwaukee, WI 53204

Wizards of Rods
5 Madden St.
Mauston, WI 53948

WYOMING

Sweetwater County Street Rods
605 Juniper
Green River, WY 82935

FOREIGN

Antique & Classic Car Club of Canada
12 Clinton Ct.
Brampton, Ontario
L6Z 1Z6 Canada

Classic GTO Club of Ontario (Canada)
GTOAA Chapter
149 Victoria Drive
Uxbridge, Ontario
Canada, L0C 1K0

MUSEUMS IN AMERICA

ALABAMA

The Vintage Motor Museum
850 Government
Mobile, AL 36602

ALASKA

Alaska Historical & Transportation
Museum
Box 920
Palmer, AL 99645

ARIZONA

Hall of Fame Museum
6101 E. Van Buren
Phoenix, AZ 85008

ARKANSAS

The Museum of Automobiles
Petit Jean Mountain
Morrilton, AK 72110

CALIFORNIA

Concours Motorcars
619 E. Fourth St.
Santa Ana, CA 92703

Firehouse Museum
1972 Columbia Street
San Diego, CA 92117

Los Angeles Museum of
Natural History - Exposition Park
900 Exposition Blvd.
Los Angeles, CA 90007

Merle Norman Classic Beauty Collection
15180 Bledsoe Street
San Sylmar, CA 91342

Movieland Wax Museum
P.O. Box 5130
7711 Beach Boulevard
Buena Park, CA 90602

Millers Horse & Buggy Ranch
9425 Yosemite Blvd.
Modesto, CA 95351

National Maritime Museum
Hyde Street Pier
San Francisco, CA 94100

Metropolitan Historical Collection
5330 Laurel Canyon Boulevard
North Hollywood, CA 91607

Wagons to Wings Museum
15060 Foothill Road
Morgan Hill, CA 95037

Toyota Museum
1901 South Western Avenue
Torrance, CA 90509

Blackhawk Auto Collection
1975 San Ramon Valley Boulevard
San Ramon, CA 94583

COLORADO

Dougherty Museum Collection
8382 1075h Street
Longmont, CO 80501

Forney Transportation Museum
1416 Platte
Denver, CO 80200

Front Wheel Drive Auto Museum
250 North Main Street
Brighton, CO 80601

Ghost Town
Corner of Highway 24 West & 21st Street
Colorado Springs, CO 80907

CONNECTICUT

Hartford Automobile Club
815 Farmington Avenue
West Hartford, CT 06119

Museum of Connecticut History
231 Capitol Avenue
Hartford, CT 06115

DELAWARE

Delaware Agricultural Museum
866 North Dupont Highway
Dover, DE 19901

Memours Mansion & Gardens
P.O. Box 109
Rockland Road
Wilmington, DE 19899

DISTRICT OF COLUMBIA

Smithsonian Institution
14th & Constitution
Washington, D.C. 20560

FLORIDA

Bellm Cars & Music of Yesterday
5500 North Tamiami Trail
Sarasota, FL 33577

Elliott Museum
Hutchinson Island
Stuart, FL 33494

Silver Springs Antique Car Collection
State Road 40
Ocala, FL 32670

The Birthplace of Speed Museum
160 East Franada Boulevard
Ormond Beach, FL 32074

GEORGIA

Antique Auto & Music Museum
Stone Mountain Memorial Park
Sonte Mountain, GA 30088

IDAHO

Grant's Antique Cars & Museum
5603 Franklin Road
Boise, ID 83705

Idaho State Historical Society
Transportation Museum
Boise, ID 83705

Vintage Wheel Museum
218 Cedar Street
Sandpoint, ID 83864

ILLINOIS

Gasoline Alley
c/o Hitchin-Post Inn
1765 N. Milwaukee
Libertyville, IL 60048

Fagan's Antique & Classic Automobile
Museum
162nd Street & Clairmont Avenue
Markham, IL 60426

Grant Hills Antique Auto Museum
U.S. Highway 20
Galena, IL 61036

Hartung's Automotive Museum
3623 West Lake Street
Glenview, IL 60025

Lazarus Motor Museum
Box 368
211 Walnut St.
Forreston, IL 61030

Martin's Antique Automobile Museum
R.R. 1
Route 16
Metamora, IL 61548

Museum of Science & Industry
57th & Lakeshore Drive
Chicago, IL 60637

The Time Was Village Museum
U.S. Highway 51-52
Mendota, IL 61342

Volo Antique Auto Museum & Village
Route 120
Volo, IL 60073

Quinsippi Auto Museum
All America City Park
Quincy, IL 62301

INDIANA

Auburn - Cord - Duesenberg Museum
1600 South Wayne Street
Auburn, IN 46706

Early Wheels Museum
817 Wabash Avenue
Terre Haute, IN 47801

Elwood Haynes Museum
1915 South Webster Street
Kokomo, IN 46902

Indianapolis Motor Speedway & Hall of
Fame Museum
4790 West 16th Street
Speedway, IN 46224

Museum of Transportation &
Communication
P.O. Box 83
Forest Park
Noblesville, IN 46060

Plew's Indy 500 Museum, Inc.
9648 West Morris Street
Indianapolis, IN 46231

Bill Goodwin Museum
757 South Harrison St.
Frankfort, IN 46041

Studebaker National Museum
TWO LOCATIONS:
520 S. Lafayette St.

120 South St. Joseph St.
South Bend, IN 46600

IOWA

Auto Museum
Sioux Center, IA 51250

Don Jensen Museum
411 4th Ave.
N. Humbolt, IA 50548

464

Iowa State Historical Museum
East 12th & Grand Avenue
Des Moines, IA 50319

Van Horn's Truck Museum
Highway 65
Mason City, IA 50401

KANSAS

Kansas State Historical Society Museum
120 West Tenth Street
Topeka, KS 66612

Van Arnsdale Antique
Highway 50
Macksville, KS 67557

LOUISIANA

Cars of Yesteryear Museum
P.O. Box 15080
12137 Airline Highway
Baton Rouge, LA 70801

Firefighters Museum
427 Laurel St.
Baton Rouge, LA 70801

MAINE

Boothbay Auto Museum
Box 123
Route 27
Boothbay, ME 04537

The Owls Head Transportation Museum
Box 277
Knox County Airport
Owls Head, ME 04854

Stanley Museum
PO Box 280
Kingfield, ME 04947

Wells Auto Museum
Route 1
Wells, ME 04090

MARYLAND

Fire Museum of Maryland
1301 York Road
Lutherville, MD 21093

U.S. Army Ordnance Museum
Aberdeen Proving Ground, MD 21005

MASSACHUSETTS

Heritage Plantation Auto Museum
Grove & Pine Streets
Sandwich, MA 02563

Sturbridge Auto Museum
P.O. Box 486
Sturbridge, MA 01566

Museum of Transportation
Larz Anderson Park
15 Newton St.
Brookline, MA 02146

MICHIGAN

Alfred P. Sloan Museum
1221 E. Kearsley Street
Flint, MI 48500

Automotive Hall of Fame, Inc.
P.O. Box 1742
Northwood Institute
Midland, MI 48640

Detroit Historical Museum
5401 Woodward
Detroit, MI 48202

Gilmore/CCCA Car Museum
6865 Hickory Road
Hickory Corners, MI 49060

Henry Ford Museum & Greenfield Village
P.O. Box 1970
20900 Oakwood Boulevard
Dearborn, MI 48120

Poll Museum of Transportation
353 East Sixth Street
Holland, MI 49423

R.E. Olds Museum
240 Museum Drive
Lansing, MI 48933

Domino's Rearview Mirror
3815 Plaza Drive
Ann Arbor, MI 48108

Pontiac Museum
c/o John Sawruk
One Pontiac Plaza
Pontiac, MI 48053

MINNESOTA

Roaring 20's Auto Museum
Highway 55
Brooten, MN 56316

MISSISSIPPI

Frank's Museum and Antiques
Highway 45 South
Booneville, MS 38829

MISSOURI

Kelsey's Antique Auto Museum
Camden, MO 65020

Memoryville, U.S.A.
Autos of Yesteryear
Route 63 North
Rolla, MO 65401

National Museum of Transportation
3015 Barrett Station Road
St. Louis, MO 63122

Ozark Auto Show & Museum
West Highway 76
Branson, MO 65616

Patee House Museum
Box 1022
12th & Penn Streets
St. Joseph, MO 64503

Turpen Enterprises
Classic & Antique Cars
1206 West Highway 76
Branson, MO 65616

MONTANA

Dudley Garage
Stonewall Hall
Virginia City, MT 59755

Oscar's Dreamland
Route 9
Billings, MT 59102

Polson - Flathead Historical Museum
704 Main Street
Polson, MT 59860

Towe Antique Ford Collection
P.O. Box 748
1106 Main Street
Deer Lodge, MT 59722

World Museum of Mining &
Hellroarin' Gulch
West Park Street
Butte, MT 59701

NEBRASKA

Chevyland, U.S.A.
Route 2
Elm Creek, NE 68836

Hastings Museum
1330 North Burlington
Hastings, NE 68901

Sawyer's Sandhill Museum
Highway 20
Valentine, NE 69201

Stuhr Museum of the Prairie Pioneer
3133 West Highway 34
Grand Island, NE 68801

Harold Warp Pioneer Village
P.O. Box 68
Minden, NE 68959

NEVADA

Harrah's Automobile Collection
P.O. Box 104
Glendale Road
Reno, NV 89504

Imperial Palace Auto Collection
3535 Las Vegas Blvd.
Las Vegas, NV 89109

NEW HAMPSHIRE

Crossroads of America Museum
Box 436
Route 302 & Trudeau Road
Bethleham, NH 03579

The Grand Manor
Routes 16 & 302
Glen, NH 03838

NEW JERSEY

Space Farms
Route 519
Beemerville, NJ

NEW MEXICO

Antique Auto Barn
National Parks Highway 16 - 180
Carlsbad, NM 88220

NEW YORK

American Museum of Fire Fighting
Harry Howard Avenue
Hudson, NY 12534

Bridgewater Auto Museum
Box 152
US Route 20
Bridgewater, NY 13313

Collector Cars Inc.
56 West Merrick Rd.
Freeport, NY 11520

Himes Museum of Motor Racing Nostalgia
15 O'Neil Avenue
Bay Shore, NY 11706

Watkins Glen Racing Museum and
National Motor Racing Hall of Fame
110 North Franklin Street
Watkins Glen, NY 14891

Old Rhinebeck Aerodrome
Stone Church Road off Route 9
Rhinebeck, NY 12572

William F. Badgley Historical Museum
Schoharie, NY 12157

Wilson Historical Museum
Route 425
Wilson, NY 14172

NORTH CAROLINA

Estes-Winn-Blomberg Antique Car Museum
Ashville, NC 28804

N.C. Transportation Museum
Spencer Shops Historic Site
P.O. Box 165
Spencer, NC 28159

Rearview Mirror Museum
300 East Baltic Ave.
Nags Head, NC 27959

NORTH DAKOTA

Bonanzaville USA
I-94 and U.S. 10
P.O. Box 719
West Fargo, ND 58078

OHIO

Allen County Museum
620 West Market Street
Lima, OH 45801

Canton Classic Car Museum
555 Market Avenue South
Canton, OH 44702

Carillion Park
Patterson & Carillion Boulevard
Dayton, OH 45409

Frederick C. Crawford
Auto-Aviation Museum
10825 East Boulevard
Cleveland, OH 44106

Goodyear World of Rubber
1144 East Market Street
Akron, OH 44316

Scio Pottery Museum
Box 565
Intersection of Ohio Routes 151 & 646
Scio, OH 43988

OKLAHOMA

Antiques, Inc.
P.O. Box 1997
2215 West Shawnee
Muskogee, OK 74401

Museum of Spcial Interest Cars
Shawnee, OK 74801

Oklahoma State Firefighters Museum
2716 NE 50th Street
Oklahoma City, OK 73105

OREGON

Tillmook County Pioneer Museum
2106 2nd Street
Tillamook, OR 97141

PENNSYLVANIA

Gast Classic Motorcars
Route 986
R.D. 2, Box 1G
Strasburg, PA 17579

Alan Dent Antique Car Museum
Box 254
Lightstreet, PA 17839

Boyertown Museum of Historic Vehicles
P.O. Box 30
Reading Avenue & Warwick Street
Boyertown, PA 19512

Colonial Flying Corps. Museum
Box 17
Newark Road
Toughkenamon, PA 19374

Pollock Auto Showcase I
70 South Franklin Street
Pottstown, PA 19464

Station Square Trans. Museum
450 The Landmarks Bldg.
One Station Square
Pittsburgh, PA 15219

Swigart Museum
Museum Park
Huntingdon, PA 16652

William Penn Memorial Museum
P.O. Box 1026
Third & North Streets
Harrisburg, PA 17120

Harley-Davidson Museum
York, PA

RHODE ISLAND

Newport Automobile Museum
One Casino Terrace
Newport, RI 02840

SOUTH CAROLINA

NMPA Stock Car Hall of Fame
Joe Weatherly Museum
P.O. Box 500
Highway 34
Darlington, SC 29532

SOUTH DAKOTA

Autos of Yesteryear Museum
Alcester, SD 57001

Horseless Carriage Museum
Highway 16 - Mt. Rushmore Rd. - Box 2933
Rapid City, SD 57701

Ledbetter's Auto Museum
U.S. 16 West
Custer, SD 57730

Old West Museum
P.O. Box 275
Highway I-90, Exit 260
Chamberlain, SD 57325

Pioneer Auto Museum
Junction of I-90 & US Highway 16 & 83
Murdo, SD 57559

TENNESSEE

Old Car Museum
Hwy 51 S.
Union City, TN 38261

Car Collector Hall of Fame
1534 Demon Breun Street
Nashville, TN 37203

Dixie Gunworks, Inc.
P.O. Box 130
Gunpowder Lane
Union City, TN 38261

Smoky Mountain Car Museum
Box 1385
Pigeon Forge, TN 37863-1385

Reed's 1950 Antique Car Museum
Route 2 - Lost Sea Pike
Sweetwater, TN 37874

TEXAS

Central Texas Museum of Automotive History
Highway 304
Rosanky, TX 78953

Classic Car Showcase & Wax Museum
Box 543
Star Route
Keerville, TX 78028

McAllen Hudson Museum
3100 Colbath Road
McAllen, TX 78501

Panhandle-Plains Historical Museum
P.O. Box 967, W.T. Station
U.S. Highway 87 on 4th Avenue
Canyon, TX 79016

Pate Museum of Transportation
P.O. Box 711
U.S. Highway 377
Ft. Worth, TX 76101

San Antonio Museum of Transportation
Hemis Fair Plaza - P.O. 2601
San Antonio, TX 78205

Second Armored Division Museum
Fort Hood
Killeen, TX 76541

The Fire Museum of Texas
702 Safari Parkway
Grand Prairie, TX 75050

Galveston Automobile Museum
1309 Tremont Street
Galveston, TX 77550

Vidas Vintage Vehicles
I-45 North
Spring, TX 77380

UTAH

Bonneville Speedway Museum
P.O. Box 39
Wendover, UT 84083

Kimball-Browning Car Museum
25th Street & Wall Avenue
Ogden, UT 84401

VERMONT

Bennington Museum
Bennington, VT 05201

Westminster MG Car Museum
c/o Gerard Goquen
P.O. Box 37 South St.
Walpole, NH 03608

VIRGINIA

Historic Car & Carriage Caravan
Box 748
Luray Caverns
Luray, VA 28835

Roanoke Transportation Museum
802 Wiley Drive S.W:
Roanoke, VA 24015

Glade Mountain Museum
Route 1 Box 73
Atkins, VA 24311

Pettits Museum of Motoring Memories
P.O. Box 445
Louisa, VA 23093

Roaring Twenties Antique Car Museum
State Rt 230
Hood, VA 22723

Edgar Rohr Collection Museum
Box 71
9203 N. West
Manassas, VA 22110

WASHINGTON

Lynden Pioneer Museum
Third & Front Streets
Lynden, WA 98264

Museum of History & Industry
2161 East Hamlin Street
Seattle, WA 98112

WISCONSIN

Brooks Stevens Automotive Museum
10325 North Port Washington Road
Mequon, WI 53092

David Uihlein Antique Racing Car Museum
236 Hamilton Road
Turn Halle
Cedarburg, WI 53012

Dells Auto Museum
Wisconsin Dells, WI 53965

Four Wheel Drive Museum
Entrance of Walter A. Olen Park
Foot of East 11th Street
Clintonville, WI 54929

Midway Auto Museum
P.O. Box 183
Route 2
Birnamwood, WI 54414

Zunker's Antique
3722 MacArthur Drive
Manitowoc, WI 54220

CANADA

Firefighters' Museum
451 Main St.
Yarmouth, Nova Scotia
Tel. (902) 742-5525

Reynolds Museum
4118 - 57 St.
Wetaskiwin, Alberta, Canada T9A 2B6

Canadian Automotive Museum
99 Simcoe St. South
Oshawa, Canada, Ontario L1H 4G-

Classic Car Museum
813 Douglas St.
Victoria, B.C., Canada V8W 2B9

National Museum of Science & Technology
1867 St. Laurent Blvd.
Ottawa, Ontario, Canada K1A 0M8

HOW TO USE THE COLLECTOR CAR VALUE GUIDE

On the following pages is a **COLLECTOR CAR VALUE GUIDE**. The value of an old car is a "ballpark" estimate at best. The estimates contained here are based upon national and regional data compiled by the editors of *Old Cars Weekly* and *Old Cars Price Guide*. These data include actual bids and prices at collector car auctions and sales, classified and display advertising of such vehicles, verified reports of private sales and input from experts.

Value estimates are listed for cars in six different states of condition. These conditions (1-6) are illustrated and explained in the **VEHICLE CONDITION SCALE** on the page next following. Values are for complete vehicles; not parts cars, except as noted. Modified-car values are not included, but can be estimated by figuring the cost of restoring to original condition and adjusting the figures shown here.

Appearing below is a section of chart taken from the **COLLECTOR CAR VALUE GUIDE** to illustrate the following elements:

A. MAKE The make of car, or marque name, appears in large, boldface type at the beginning of each value section.

B. DESCRIPTION The extreme left-hand column indicates vehicle year, model name, body type, engine configuration and, in some cases, wheelbase.

C. CONDITION CODE The six columns to the right are headed by the numbers one through six (1-6) which correspond to the conditions described in the **VEHICLE CONDITION SCALE** on the following page.

D. VALUE. The value estimates, in dollars, appear below their respective condition code headings and across from the vehicle descriptions.

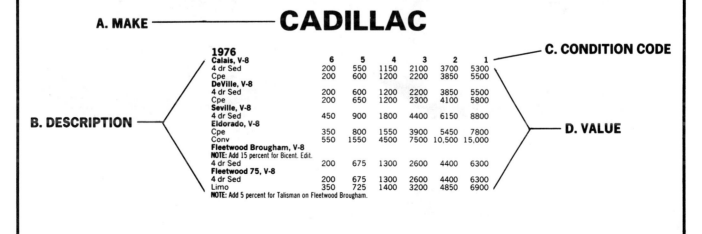

A. MAKE ——————— CADILLAC

C. CONDITION CODE

B. DESCRIPTION

D. VALUE

1976	6	5	4	3	2	1
Calais, V-8						
4 dr Sed	200	550	1150	2100	3700	5300
Cpe	200	600	1200	2200	3850	5500
DeVille, V-8						
4 dr Sed	200	600	1200	2200	3850	5500
Cpe	200	650	1200	2300	4100	5800
Seville, V-8						
4 dr Sed	450	900	1800	4400	6150	8800
Eldorado, V-8						
Cpe	350	800	1550	3900	5450	7800
Conv	550	1550	4500	7500	10,500	15,000
Fleetwood Brougham, V-8						
NOTE: Add 15 percent for Bicent. Edit.						
4 dr Sed	200	675	1300	2600	4400	6300
Fleetwood 75, V-8						
4 dr Sed	200	675	1300	2600	4400	6300
Limo	350	725	1400	3200	4850	6900
NOTE: Add 5 percent for Talisman on Fleetwood Brougham.						

VEHICLE CONDITION SCALE

Excellent

1) EXCELLENT: Restored to current maximum professional standards of quality in every area, or perfect original with components operating and appearing as new. A 95-plus point show car that is not driven.

Fine

2) FINE: Well-restored, or a combination of superior restoration and excellent original. Also, an *extremely* well-maintained original showing very minimal wear.

Very Good

3) VERY GOOD: Completely operable original or "older restoration" showing wear. Also, a good amateur restoration, all presentable and serviceable inside and out. Plus, combinations of well-done restoration and good operable components or a partially restored car with all parts necessary to complete and/or valuable NOS parts.

Good

4) GOOD: A driveable vehicle needing no or only minor work to be functional. Also, a deteriorated restoration or a very poor amateur restoration. All components may need restoration to be "excellent," but the car is mostly useable "as is."

Restorable

5) RESTORABLE: Needs *complete* restoration of body, chassis and interior. May or may not be running, but isn't weathered, wrecked or stripped to the point of being useful only for parts.

Parts Car

6) PARTS CAR: May or may not be running, but is weathered, wrecked and/or stripped to the point of being useful primarily for parts.

COLLECTOR CAR VALUE GUIDE

AMC

1976	6	5	4	3	2	1
Gremlin, V-8						
2 dr Sed	125	250	750	1150	2450	3500
Cus 2 dr Sed	150	300	900	1250	2650	3800
Hornet, V-8						
4 dr Sed	125	200	600	1100	2200	3100
2 dr Sed	100	175	525	1050	2100	3000
2 dr Hatch	125	200	600	1100	2250	3200
4 dr Sptabt	125	200	600	1100	2300	3300
Pacer, 6-cyl.						
2 dr Sed	125	250	750	1150	2450	3500
Matador, V-8						
4 dr Sed	100	175	525	1050	2100	3000
Cpe	125	200	600	1100	2250	3200
Sta Wag	125	200	600	1100	2200	3100

NOTE: Deduct 5 percent for 6 cylinder.

1977	6	5	4	3	2	1
Gremlin, V-8						
2 dr Sed	150	300	900	1250	2600	3700
Cus 2 dr Sed	150	300	900	1250	2650	3800
Hornet, V-8						
4 dr Sed	125	200	600	1100	2250	3200
2 dr Sed	125	200	600	1100	2200	3100
2 dr Hatch	125	200	600	1100	2300	3300
Sta Wag	125	250	750	1150	2400	3400
Pacer, 6-cyl.						
2 dr Sed	125	250	750	1150	2500	3600
Sta Wag	150	300	900	1250	2600	3700
Matador, V-8						
4 dr Sed	125	200	600	1100	2200	3100
Cpe	125	200	600	1100	2300	3300
Sta Wag	125	200	600	1100	2250	3200

NOTE: Deduct 5 percent for 6 cylinder.
Add 10 percent for AMX package.

1978	6	5	4	3	2	1
Gremlin						
2 dr Sed	125	250	750	1150	2400	3400
Cus 2 dr Sed	125	250	750	1150	2450	3500
Concord						
4 dr Sed	100	175	525	1050	2050	2900
2 dr Sed	100	175	525	1050	1950	2800
2 dr Hatch	100	175	525	1050	2100	3000
Sta Wag	125	200	600	1100	2200	3100
Pacer						
2 dr Hatch	125	200	600	1100	2300	3300
Sta Wag	125	250	750	1150	2400	3400
AMX						
2 dr Hatch	125	250	750	1150	2500	3600
Matador						
4 dr Sed	100	175	525	1050	1950	2800
Cpe	100	175	525	1050	2100	3000
Sta Wag	100	175	525	1050	2050	2900

1979	6	5	4	3	2	1
Spirit, 6-cyl.						
2 dr Hatch	125	250	750	1150	2450	3500
2 dr Sed	125	250	750	1150	2400	3400
Spirit DL, 6-cyl.						
2 dr Hatch	125	250	750	1150	2500	3600
2 dr Sed	125	250	750	1150	2450	3500
Spirit Limited, 6-cyl.						
2 dr Hatch	150	300	900	1250	2600	3700
2 dr Sed	125	250	750	1150	2500	3600

NOTE: Deduct 5 percent for 4-cyl.

Concord, V-8	6	5	4	3	2	1
4 dr Sed	125	200	600	1100	2200	3100
2 dr Sed	100	175	525	1050	2100	3000
2 dr Hatch	125	200	600	1100	2250	3200
4 dr Sta Wag	125	200	600	1100	2250	3200
Concord DL, V-8						
4 dr Sed	125	200	600	1100	2250	3200
2 dr Sed	125	200	600	1100	2200	3100
2 dr Hatch	125	200	600	1100	2300	3300
4 dr Sta Wag	125	200	600	1100	2300	3300
Concord Limited, V-8						
4 dr Sed	125	200	600	1100	2300	3300
2 dr Sed	125	200	600	1100	2250	3200
4 dr Sta Wag	125	250	750	1150	2400	3400

NOTE: Deduct 5 percent for 6-cyl.

Pacer DL, V-8	6	5	4	3	2	1
2 dr Hatch	125	250	750	1150	2400	3400
2 dr Sta Wag	125	250	750	1150	2450	3500
Pacer Limited, V-8						
2 dr Hatch	125	250	750	1150	2450	3500
2 dr Sta Wag	125	250	750	1150	2500	3600

NOTE: Deduct 5 percent for 6-cyl.

AMX, V-8	6	5	4	3	2	1
2 dr Hatch	150	300	900	1250	2600	3700

NOTE: Deduct 7 percent for 6-cyl.

1980	6	5	4	3	2	1
Spirit, 6-cyl.						
2 dr Hatch	150	350	950	1350	2800	4000
2 dr Cpe	150	300	900	1350	2700	3900
2 dr Hatch DL	150	350	950	1450	2900	4100
2 dr Cpe DL	150	350	950	1350	2800	4000
2 dr Hatch Limited	150	400	1000	1550	3050	4300
2 dr Cpe Limited	150	350	950	1450	3000	4200

NOTE: Deduct 10 percent for 4-cyl.

Concord, 6-cyl.	6	5	4	3	2	1
4 dr Sed	125	250	750	1150	2500	3600
2 dr Cpe	125	250	750	1150	2450	3500
4 dr Sta Wag	150	300	900	1250	2600	3700
4 dr Sed DL	150	300	900	1250	2600	3700
2 dr Cpe DL	125	250	750	1150	2500	3600
4 dr Sta Wag DL	150	300	900	1250	2650	3800
4 dr Sed Limited	150	300	900	1350	2700	3900
2 dr Cpe Limited	150	300	900	1250	2650	3800
4 dr Sta Wag Limited	150	300	900	1350	2700	3900
Pacer, 6-cyl.						
2 dr Hatch DL	125	250	750	1150	2500	3600
2 dr Sta Wag DL	150	300	900	1250	2600	3700
2 dr Hatch Limited	150	300	900	1250	2650	3800
2 dr Sta Wag Limited	150	300	900	1350	2700	3900
AMX, 6-cyl.						
2 dr Hatch	150	350	950	1450	3000	4200
Eagle 4WD, 6-cyl.						
4 dr Sed	200	500	1100	1900	3500	5000
2 dr Cpe	200	500	1100	1850	3350	4900
4 dr Sta Wag	200	550	1150	2000	3600	5200
4 dr Sed Limited	200	550	1150	2000	3600	5200
2 dr Cpe Limited	200	500	1100	1950	3600	5100
4 dr Sta Wag Limited	200	550	1150	2100	3700	5300

1981	6	5	4	3	2	1
Spirit, 4-cyl.						
2 dr Hatch	150	300	900	1250	2600	3700
2 dr Cpe	125	250	750	1150	2500	3600
2 dr Hatch DL	150	300	900	1350	2700	3900
2 dr Cpe DL	150	300	900	1250	2650	3800
Spirit, 6-cyl.						
2 dr Hatch	150	350	950	1450	2900	4100
2 dr Cpe	150	350	950	1350	2800	4000
2 dr Hatch DL	150	400	1000	1550	3050	4300
2 dr Cpe DL	150	350	950	1450	3000	4200
Concord, 6-cyl.						
4 dr Sed	150	300	900	1250	2600	3700
2 dr Cpe	125	250	750	1150	2500	3600
4 dr Sta Wag	150	300	900	1250	2650	3800
4 dr Sed DL	150	300	900	1250	2650	3800
2 dr Cpe DL	150	300	900	1250	2600	3700
4 dr Sta Wag DL	150	300	900	1350	2700	3900
4 dr Sed Limited	150	300	900	1350	2700	3900
2 dr Cpe Limited	150	300	900	1250	2650	3800
4 dr Sta Wag Limited	150	350	950	1350	2800	4000

NOTE: Deduct 12 percent for 4-cyl.

Eagle 50 4WD, 4-cyl.	6	5	4	3	2	1
2 dr Hatch SX4	150	450	1050	1800	3300	4800
2 dr Hatchback	150	450	1050	1750	3250	4700
2 dr Hatch SX4 DL	200	500	1100	1900	3500	5000
2 dr Hatchback DL	200	500	1100	1850	3350	4900
Eagle 50 4WD, 6-cyl.						
2 dr Hatch SX4	200	550	1150	2000	3600	5200
2 dr Hatchback	200	500	1100	1950	3600	5100
2 dr Hatch SX4 DL	200	550	1150	2100	3800	5400
2 dr Hatchback DL	200	550	1150	2100	3700	5300

1982	6	5	4	3	2	1
Spirit, 6-cyl.						
2 dr Hatch	150	350	950	1450	3000	4200
2 dr Cpe	150	350	950	1450	2900	4100
2 dr Hatch DL	150	400	1000	1600	3100	4400
2 dr Cpe DL	150	400	1000	1550	3050	4300

NOTE: Deduct 10 percent for 4-cyl.

Concord, 6-cyl.	6	5	4	3	2	1
4 dr Sed	150	300	900	1250	2650	3800
2 dr Cpe	150	300	900	1250	2600	3700
4 dr Sta Wag	150	300	900	1350	2700	3900
4 dr Sed DL	150	300	900	1350	2700	3900
2 dr Cpe DL	150	300	900	1250	2650	3800
4 dr Sta Wag DL	150	350	950	1350	2800	4000
4 dr Sed Limited	150	350	950	1350	2800	4000
2 dr Cpe Limited	150	300	900	1350	2700	3900
4 dr Sta Wag Limited	150	350	950	1450	2900	4100

NOTE: Deduct 12 percent for 4-cyl.

Eagle 50 4WD, 4-cyl.	6	5	4	3	2	1
2 dr Hatch SX4	200	500	1100	1850	3350	4900
2 dr Hatchback	150	500	1050	1800	3300	4800
2 dr Hatch SX4 DL	200	500	1100	1950	3600	5100
2 dr Hatchback DL	200	500	1100	1900	3500	5000
Eagle 50 4WD, 6-cyl.						
2 dr Hatch SX4	200	550	1150	2100	3700	5300
2 dr Hatchback	200	550	1150	2000	3600	5200
2 dr Hatch SX4 DL	200	600	1200	2200	3850	5500
2 dr Hatchback DL	200	550	1150	2100	3800	5400
Eagle 30 4WD, 4-cyl.						
4 dr Sed	150	450	1050	1750	3250	4700
2 dr Cpe	150	450	1050	1700	3200	4600
4 dr Sta Wag	150	450	1050	1800	3300	4800
4 dr Sed Limited	150	450	1050	1800	3300	4800
2 dr Cpe Limited	150	450	1050	1750	3250	4700
4 dr Sta Wag Limited	200	500	1100	1900	3500	5000
Eagle 30 4WD, 6-cyl.						
4 dr Sed	200	500	1100	1950	3600	5100
2 dr Cpe	200	500	1100	1900	3500	5000
4 dr Sta Wag	200	550	1150	2100	3700	5300
4 dr Sed Limited	200	550	1150	2100	3700	5300
2 dr Cpe Limited	200	550	1150	2000	3600	5200
4 dr Sta Wag Limited	200	600	1200	2200	3850	5500

1983	6	5	4	3	2	1
Spirit, 6-cyl.						
2 dr Hatch DL	150	400	1000	1550	3050	4300
2 dr Hatch GT	150	400	1000	1600	3100	4400

Concord, 6-cyl.	6	5	4	3	2	1
4 dr Sed	150	300	900	1350	2700	3900
4 dr Sta Wag	150	350	950	1350	2800	4000
4 dr Sed DL	150	350	950	1350	2800	4000
4 dr Sta Wag DL	150	350	950	1450	2900	4100
4 dr Sta Wag Limited	150	400	1000	1550	3050	4300
Alliance, 4-cyl.						
2 dr Sed	125	250	750	1150	2500	3600
4 dr Sed L	150	300	900	1250	2600	3700
2 dr Sed L	150	300	900	1250	2600	3700
4 dr Sed DL	150	300	900	1250	2650	3800
2 dr Sed DL	150	300	900	1250	2650	3800
4 dr Sed Limited	150	300	900	1350	2700	3900
Eagle 50 4WD, 4-cyl.						
2 dr Hatch SX4	200	500	1100	1900	3500	5000
2 dr Hatch SX4 DL	200	550	1150	2000	3600	5200
Eagle 50 4WD, 6-cyl.						
2 dr Hatch SX4	200	550	1150	2100	3800	5400
2 dr Hatch SX4 DL	200	600	1200	2200	3900	5600
Eagle 30 4WD, 4-cyl.						
4 dr Sed	150	450	1050	1800	3300	4800
4 dr Sta Wag	200	500	1100	1900	3500	5000
4 dr Sta Wag Limited	200	550	1150	2000	3600	5200
Eagle 30 4WD, 6-cyl.						
4 dr Sed	200	550	1150	2000	3600	5200
4 dr Sta Wag	200	550	1150	2100	3800	5400
4 dr Sta Wag Limited	200	600	1200	2200	3900	5600

BUICK

1976

Skyhawk, V-6	6	5	4	3	2	1
2 dr Hatch	125	250	750	1150	2400	3400
Skylark S, V-8						
Cpe	125	250	750	1150	2500	3600
Skylark, V-8						
4 dr Sed	125	250	750	1150	2500	3600
Cpe	150	300	900	1250	2600	3700
2 dr Hatch	150	300	900	1250	2650	3800
Skylark SR, V-8						
4 dr Sed	150	300	900	1250	2600	3700
Cpe	150	300	900	1250	2650	3800
2 dr Hatch	150	300	900	1350	2700	3900
Century Special, V-6						
2 dr	125	250	750	1150	2450	3500
Century, V-8						
4 dr	150	350	950	1350	2800	4000
2 dr	150	300	900	1250	2600	3700
Century Custom, V-8						
4 dr	150	300	900	1250	2600	3700
2 dr	150	300	900	1250	2650	3800
2S Sta Wag	125	250	750	1150	2500	3600
3S Sta Wag	150	300	900	1250	2600	3700
Regal, V-8						
4 dr	150	300	900	1250	2600	3700
2 dr	150	300	900	1250	2650	3800
LeSabre, V-6						
4 dr Sed	125	200	600	1100	2250	3200
4 dr HdTp	125	250	750	1150	2450	3500
Cpe	125	250	750	1150	2500	3600
LeSabre Custom, V-8						
4 dr	125	250	750	1150	2500	3600
4 dr HdTp	150	300	900	1250	2600	3700
Cpe	150	300	900	1250	2650	3800
Estate, V-8						
2S Sta Wag	125	250	750	1150	2400	3400
3S Sta Wag	125	250	750	1150	2450	3500
Electra 225, V-8						
4 dr HdTp	150	300	900	1250	2650	3800
Cpe	150	300	900	1350	2700	3900
Electra 225 Custom, V-8						
4 dr HdTp	150	350	950	1350	2800	4000
Cpe	150	350	950	1450	3000	4200
Riviera, V-8						
2 dr Spt Cpe	150	400	1000	1650	3150	4500

NOTE: Deduct 5 percent for 6 cylinder.

1977

Skyhawk, V-6						
2 dr Hatch	100	150	450	1000	1750	2500
Skylark S, V-8						
Cpe	100	150	450	1000	1900	2700
Skylark, V-8						
4 dr Sed	100	150	450	1000	1900	2700
Cpe	100	175	525	1050	1950	2800
2 dr Hatch	100	175	525	1050	2050	2900
Skylark SR, V-8						
4 dr Sed	100	175	525	1050	1950	2800
Cpe	100	175	525	1050	2050	2900
2 dr Hatch	100	175	525	1050	2100	3000
Century, V-8						
4 dr Sed	125	250	750	1150	2450	3500
Cpe	125	250	750	1150	2500	3600
Century Custom, V-8						
4 dr Sed	125	250	750	1150	2500	3600
Cpe	150	300	900	1250	2600	3700
2S Sta Wag	125	250	750	1150	2400	3400
3S Sta Wag	125	250	750	1150	2450	3500
Regal, V-8						
4 dr Sed	150	300	900	1250	2650	3800
Cpe	150	300	900	1350	2700	3900
LeSabre, V-8						
4 dr Sed	125	250	750	1150	2500	3600
Cpe	150	300	900	1250	2600	3700
LeSabre Custom, V-8						
4 dr Sed	150	300	900	1250	2600	3700
Cpe	150	300	900	1250	2650	3800
Spt Cpe	150	300	900	1350	2700	3900
Electra 225, V-8						
4 dr Sed	150	300	900	1350	2700	3900
Cpe	150	350	950	1350	2800	4000
Electra 225 Limited, V-8						
4 dr Sed	150	350	950	1450	2900	4100
Cpe	150	400	1000	1550	3050	4300
Riviera, V-8						
Cpe	150	400	1000	1600	3100	4400

NOTE: Deduct 5 percent for V-6.

1978

Skyhawk	6	5	4	3	2	1
2 dr 'S' Hatch	125	200	600	1100	2250	3200
2 dr Hatch	125	250	750	1150	2400	3400
Skylark						
'S' Cpe	125	200	600	1100	2300	3300
4 dr Sed	125	250	750	1150	2400	3400
Cpe	125	250	750	1150	2400	3400
2 dr Hatch	125	250	750	1150	2450	3500
Skylark Custom						
4 dr Sed	125	250	750	1150	2400	3400
Cpe	125	250	750	1150	2450	3500
2 dr Hatch	125	250	750	1150	2500	3600
Century Special						
4 dr Sed	125	250	750	1150	2450	3500
Cpe	125	250	750	1150	2500	3600
Sta Wag	125	250	750	1150	2400	3400
Century Custom						
4 dr Sed	125	250	750	1150	2500	3600
Cpe	150	300	900	1250	2600	3700
Sta Wag	125	250	750	1150	2450	3500
Century Sport						
Cpe	150	300	900	1350	2700	3900
Century Limited						
4 dr Sed	150	300	900	1250	2650	3800
Cpe	150	300	900	1350	2700	3900
Regal						
Cpe	150	300	900	1250	2600	3700
Spt Cpe	150	300	900	1250	2650	3800
Regal Limited						
Cpe	150	350	950	1350	2800	4000
LeSabre						
4 dr Sed	150	300	900	1250	2600	3700
Cpe	150	300	900	1250	2650	3800
Spt Turbo Cpe	150	350	950	1450	2900	4100
LeSabre Custom						
4 dr Sed	150	300	900	1250	2650	3800
Cpe	150	300	900	1350	2700	3900
Estate Wagon						
Sta Wag	150	300	900	1250	2600	3700
Electra 225						
4 dr Sed	150	300	900	1350	2700	3900
Cpe	150	350	950	1450	3000	4200
Electra Limited						
4 dr Sed	150	350	950	1350	2800	4000
Cpe	150	400	1000	1650	3150	4500
Electra Park Avenue						
4 dr Sed	150	350	950	1450	3000	4200
Cpe	150	450	1050	1800	3300	4800
Riviera						
Cpe	200	600	1200	2200	3850	5500

1979

Skyhawk, V-6						
2 dr Hatch	125	250	750	1150	2450	3500
2 dr 'S' Hatch	125	250	750	1150	2400	3400
Skylark 'S', V-8						
'S' Cpe	125	200	600	1100	2300	3300
Skylark, V-8						
4 dr Sed	125	250	750	1150	2450	3500
Cpe	125	250	750	1150	2450	3500
Hatch	125	250	750	1150	2500	3600
Skylark Custom, V-8						
4 dr Sed	125	250	750	1150	2500	3600
Cpe	125	250	750	1150	2500	3600

NOTE: Deduct 5 percent for 6 cyl.

Century Special, V-8						
4 dr Sed	125	250	750	1150	2500	3600
Cpe	125	250	750	1150	2450	3500
Sta Wag	125	250	750	1150	2500	3600
Century Custom, V-8						
4 dr Sed	150	300	900	1250	2600	3700
Cpe	125	250	750	1150	2500	3600
Sta Wag	150	300	900	1250	2600	3700
Century Sport, V-8						
Cpe	150	350	950	1350	2800	4000
Century Limited, V-8						
4 dr Sed	150	300	900	1350	2700	3900

NOTE: Deduct 7 percent for 6-cyl.

Regal, V-6						
Cpe	150	300	900	1350	2700	3900
Regal Sport Turbo, V-6						
Cpe	150	400	1000	1600	3100	4400
Regal, V-8						
Cpe	150	350	950	1350	2800	4000
Regal Limited, V-8 & V-6						
V-6 Cpe	150	300	900	1350	2700	3900
V-8 Cpe	150	350	950	1450	3000	4200
LeSabre, V-8						
4 dr Sed	150	300	900	1350	2700	3900
Cpe	150	300	900	1250	2650	3800
LeSabre Limited, V-8						
4 dr Sed	150	350	950	1350	2800	4000
Cpe	150	300	900	1350	2700	3900

NOTE: Deduct 7 percent for V-6.

LeSabre Sport Turbo, V-6						
Cpe	150	400	1000	1650	3150	4500
LeSabre Estate Wagon						
Sta Wag	150	350	950	1350	2800	4000
Electra 225, V-8						
4 dr Sed	150	350	950	1450	2900	4100
Cpe	150	400	1000	1550	3050	4300
Electra Limited, V-8						
4 dr Sed	150	400	1000	1550	3050	4300
Cpe	150	450	1050	1700	3200	4600
Electra Park Avenue, V-8						
4 dr Sed	150	450	1050	1700	3200	4600
Cpe	200	500	1100	1850	3350	4900
Riviera, V-8						
Cpe 'S'	200	600	1200	2300	4000	5700

NOTE: Deduct 10 percent for V-6.

1980

Skyhawk, V-6						
2 dr Hatch S	150	300	900	1250	2600	3700
2 dr Hatch	150	300	900	1250	2650	3800
Skylark, V-6						
4 dr Sed	150	300	900	1250	2650	3800
2 dr Cpe	150	300	900	1350	2700	3900
4 dr Sed Limited	150	300	900	1350	2700	3900

	6	5	4	3	2	1
2 dr Cpe Limited	150	350	950	1350	2800	4000
4 dr Sed Spt	150	350	950	1450	2900	4100
2 dr Cpe Spt	150	350	950	1450	3000	4200
NOTE: Deduct 10 percent for 4-cyl.						
Century, V-8						
4 dr Sed	125	250	750	1150	2500	3600
2 dr Cpe	150	300	900	1250	2650	3800
4 dr Sta Wag Est	150	300	900	1250	2600	3700
2 dr Cpe Spt	150	300	900	1350	2700	3900
NOTE: Deduct 12 percent for V-6.						
Regal, V-8						
2 dr Cpe	150	300	900	1350	2700	3900
2 dr Cpe Limited	150	350	950	1350	2800	4000
NOTE: Deduct 12 percent for V-6.						
Regal Turbo, V-6						
2 dr Cpe	200	600	1200	2200	3850	5500
LeSabre, V-8						
4 dr Sed	150	350	950	1450	2900	4100
2 dr Cpe	150	350	950	1450	3000	4200
4 dr Sed Limited	150	400	1000	1550	3050	4300
2 dr Cpe Limited	150	400	1000	1600	3100	4400
4 dr Sta Wag Est	150	400	1000	1550	3050	4300
LeSabre Turbo, V-6						
2 dr Cpe Spt	200	500	1100	1850	3350	4900
Electra, V-8						
4 dr Sed Limited	150	450	1050	1700	3200	4600
2 dr Cpe Limited	150	450	1050	1750	3250	4700
4 dr Sed Park Ave	150	450	1050	1750	3250	4700
2 dr Cpe Park Ave	150	450	1050	1800	3300	4800
4 dr Sta Wag Est	200	500	1100	1850	3350	4900
Riviera S Turbo, V-6						
2 dr Cpe	200	675	1300	2500	4350	6200
Riviera, V-8						
2 dr Cpe	350	725	1400	3000	4700	6700

1981

	6	5	4	3	2	1
Skylark, V-6						
4 dr Sed	150	300	900	1350	2700	3900
2 dr Cpe	150	350	950	1350	2800	4000
4 dr Sed Limited	150	350	950	1350	2800	4000
2 dr Cpe Limited	150	350	950	1450	2900	4100
4 dr Sed Sport	150	350	950	1450	3000	4200
2 dr Cpe Sport	150	400	1000	1550	3050	4300
NOTE: Deduct 10 percent for 4-cyl.						
Century, V-8						
4 dr Sed	150	300	900	1250	2600	3700
4 dr Sta Wag	150	300	900	1250	2650	3800
4 dr Sed Limited	150	300	900	1250	2650	3800
4 dr Sta Wag Est	150	300	900	1350	2700	3900
NOTE: Deduct 12 percent for V-6.						
Regal, V-8						
2 dr Cpe	150	300	900	1350	2700	3900
2 dr Cpe Limited	150	350	950	1350	2800	4000
NOTE: Deduct 12 percent for V-6.						
Regal Turbo, V-6						
2 dr Cpe Sport	200	600	1200	2200	3900	5600
LeSabre, V-8						
4 dr Sed	150	350	950	1450	3000	4200
2 dr Cpe	150	400	1000	1550	3050	4300
4 dr Sed Limited	150	400	1000	1550	3050	4300
2 dr Cpe Limited	150	400	1000	1600	3100	4400
4 dr Sta Wag Est	150	400	1000	1650	3150	4500
NOTE: Deduct 12 percent for V-6 except Estate Wag.						
Electra, V-8						
4 dr Sed Limited	150	400	1000	1600	3100	4400
2 dr Cpe Limited	150	400	1000	1650	3150	4500
4 dr Sed Park Ave	150	450	1050	1700	3200	4600
2 dr Cpe Park Ave	150	450	1050	1750	3250	4700
4 dr Sta Wag Est	150	450	1050	1750	3250	4700
NOTE: Deduct 15 percent for V-6 except Estate Wag.						
Riviera, V-8						
2 dr Cpe	350	725	1400	3100	4800	6800
Riviera, V-6						
2 dr Cpe	200	650	1250	2400	4200	6000
2 dr Cpe Turbo T Type	200	675	1300	2600	4400	6300

1982

	6	5	4	3	2	1
Skyhawk, 4-cyl.						
4 dr Sed Cus	150	300	900	1250	2650	3800
2 dr Cpe Cus	150	300	900	1350	2700	3900
4 dr Sed Limited	150	300	900	1350	2700	3900
2 dr Cpe Limited	150	350	950	1350	2800	4000
Skylark, V-6						
4 dr Sed	150	350	950	1350	2800	4000
2 dr Cpe	150	350	950	1450	2900	4100
4 dr Sed Limited	150	350	950	1450	3000	4200
2 dr Cpe Limited	150	400	1000	1550	3050	4300
4 dr Sed Sport	150	400	1000	1600	3100	4400
2 dr Cpe Sport	150	400	1000	1650	3150	4500
NOTE: Deduct 10 percent for 4-cyl.						
Regal, V-6						
4 dr Sed	150	400	1000	1600	3100	4400
2 dr Cpe	150	400	1000	1650	3150	4500
2 dr Cpe Turbo	200	600	1200	2200	3850	5500
4 dr Sed Limited	150	450	1050	1750	3250	4700
2 dr Cpe Limited	150	450	1050	1800	3300	4800
4 dr Sta Wag	150	450	1050	1800	3300	4800
Century, V-6						
4 dr Sed Cus	150	450	1050	1700	3200	4600
2 dr Cpe Cus	150	450	1050	1750	3250	4700
4 dr Sed Limited	200	500	1100	1850	3350	4900
2 dr Cpe Limited	200	500	1100	1900	3500	5000
NOTE: Deduct 10 percent for 4-cyl.						
LeSabre, V-8						
4 dr Sed Cus	150	450	1050	1800	3300	4800
2 dr Cpe Cus	200	500	1100	1850	3350	4900
4 dr Sed Limited	200	500	1100	1850	3350	4900
2 dr Cpe Limited	200	500	1100	1900	3500	5000
4 dr Sta Wag Est	200	500	1100	1900	3500	5000
NOTE: Deduct 12 percent for V-6 except Estate Wag.						
Electra, V-8						
4 dr Sed Limited	200	500	1100	1850	3350	4900
2 dr Cpe Limited	200	500	1100	1950	3600	5100
4 dr Sed Park Ave	200	550	1150	2000	3600	5200
2 dr Cpe Park Ave	200	550	1150	2100	3800	5400
4 dr Sta Wag Est	200	550	1150	2100	3800	5400
NOTE: Deduct 15 percent for V-6 except Estate Wag.						
Riviera, V-6						
2 dr Cpe	350	700	1350	2800	4550	6500
2 dr Cpe T Type	350	725	1400	3100	4800	6800
2 dr Conv	650	2000	5100	8500	11,900	17,000
Riviera, V-8						
2 dr Cpe	350	750	1450	3300	4900	7000
2 dr Conv	650	2300	5400	9000	12,600	18,000

1983

	6	5	4	3	2	1
Skyhawk, 4-cyl.						
4 dr Sed Cus	150	300	900	1350	2700	3900
2 dr Cpe Cus	150	350	950	1350	2800	4000
4 dr Sta Wag Cus	150	350	950	1350	2800	4000
4 dr Sed Limited	150	350	950	1450	3000	4200
2 dr Cpe Limited	150	400	1000	1550	3050	4300
4 dr Sta Wag Limited	150	400	1000	1550	3050	4300
2 dr Cpe T Type	200	500	1100	1850	3350	4900
Skylark, V-6						
4 dr Sed Cus	150	350	950	1450	2900	4100
2 dr Cpe Cus	150	350	950	1450	3000	4200
4 dr Sed Limited	150	350	950	1450	3000	4200
2 dr Cpe Limited	150	400	1000	1550	3050	4300
2 dr Cpe T Type	200	500	1100	1950	3600	5100
NOTE: Deduct 10 percent for 4-cyl. except T Type.						
Century, V-6						
4 dr Sed Cus	150	350	950	1450	3000	4200
2 dr Cpe Cus	150	400	1000	1550	3050	4300
4 dr Sed Limited	150	400	1000	1550	3050	4300
2 dr Cpe Limited	150	400	1000	1600	3100	4400
4 dr Sed T Type	200	500	1100	1900	3500	5000
2 dr Cpe T Type	200	600	1200	2200	3850	5500
NOTE: Deduct 12 percent for 4-cyl. except T Type.						
Regal, V-6						
4 dr Sed	150	400	1000	1550	3050	4300
2 dr Cpe	150	400	1000	1600	3100	4400
4 dr Sed Limited	150	400	1000	1650	3150	4500
2 dr Cpe Limited	150	450	1050	1700	3200	4600
4 dr Sed T Type	200	650	1200	2300	4100	5800
2 dr Cpe T Type	200	675	1300	2500	4350	6200
4 dr Sta Wag	150	450	1050	1750	3250	4700
LeSabre, V-8						
4 dr Sed Cus	200	500	1100	1900	3500	5000
2 dr Cpe Cus	200	500	1100	1950	3600	5100
4 dr Sed Limited	200	550	1150	2000	3600	5200
2 dr Cpe Limited	200	550	1150	2100	3700	5300
4 dr Sta Wag	200	550	1150	2100	3700	5300
NOTE: Deduct 12 percent for V-6 except Estate.						
Electra, V-8						
4 dr Sed Limited	200	550	1150	2000	3600	5200
2 dr Cpe Limited	200	550	1150	2100	3700	5300
4 dr Sed Park Ave	200	550	1150	2100	3800	5400
2 dr Cpe Park Ave	200	600	1200	2200	3850	5500
4 dr Sta Wag Est	200	600	1200	2200	3850	5500
NOTE: Deduct 15 percent for V-6.						
Riviera, V-6						
2 dr Cpe	350	700	1350	2800	4550	6500
2 dr Conv	650	2000	5100	8500	11,900	17,000
2 dr T Type	350	775	1500	3750	5250	7500
Riviera, V-8						
2 dr Cpe	350	750	1450	3300	4900	7000
2 dr Conv	650	2300	5400	9000	12,600	18,000

CADILLAC

1976

	6	5	4	3	2	1
Calais, V-8						
4 dr Sed	200	550	1150	2100	3700	5300
Cpe	200	600	1200	2200	3850	5500
DeVille, V-8						
4 dr Sed	200	600	1200	2200	3850	5500
Cpe	200	650	1200	2300	4100	5800
Seville, V-8						
4 dr Sed	450	900	1800	4400	6150	8800
Eldorado, V-8						
Cpe	350	800	1550	3900	5450	7800
Conv	550	1550	4500	7500	10,500	15,000
Fleetwood Brougham, V-8						
NOTE: Add 15 percent for Bicent. Edit.						
4 dr Sed	200	675	1300	2600	4400	6300
Fleetwood 75, V-8						
4 dr Sed	200	675	1300	2600	4400	6300
Limo	350	725	1400	3200	4850	6900
NOTE: Add 5 percent for Talisman on Fleetwood Brougham.						

1977

	6	5	4	3	2	1
DeVille, V-8						
4 dr Sed	200	600	1200	2200	3850	5500
Cpe	200	650	1250	2400	4200	6000
Seville, V-8						
4 dr Sed	350	700	1350	2800	4550	6500
Eldorado, V-8						
Cpe	350	775	1500	3750	5250	7500
Fleetwood Brougham, V-8						
4 dr Sed	350	700	1350	2800	4550	6500
Fleetwood 75, V-8						
4 dr Sed	350	725	1400	3000	4700	6700
Limo	350	725	1400	3200	4850	6900
NOTE: Add 10 percent for Biarritz.						

1978

	6	5	4	3	2	1
Seville						
4 dr Sed	350	700	1350	2900	4600	6600
DeVille						
4 dr Sed	150	450	1050	1700	3200	4600
Cpe	150	450	1050	1750	3250	4700
Eldorado						
Cpe	350	825	1600	4000	5600	8000
Fleetwood Brougham						
4 dr Sed	200	550	1150	2000	3600	5200
Fleetwood Limo						
4 dr	350	725	1400	3000	4700	6700
4 dr Formal	350	725	1400	3200	4850	6900
NOTE: Add 10 percent for Biarritz.						

1979

	6	5	4	3	2	1
Seville, V-8						
4 dr Sed	350	750	1450	3300	4900	7000

DeVille, V-8	6	5	4	3	2	1
4 dr Sed	200	550	1150	2000	3600	5200
Cpe	200	600	1200	2200	3850	5500
Eldorado, V-8						
Cpe	350	750	1450	3300	4900	7000
Fleetwood Brougham, V-8						
4 dr Sed	200	600	1200	2200	3850	5500
Fleetwood Limo						
4 dr Sed	350	725	1400	3000	4700	6700
4 dr Formal Sed	350	725	1400	3200	4850	6900

NOTES: Deduct 12 percent for diesel.
Add 10 percent for Biarritz.

1980

Seville, V-8	6	5	4	3	2	1
4 dr Sed	350	700	1350	2700	4500	6400
DeVille, V-8						
4 dr Sed	200	550	1150	2100	3800	5400
2 dr Cpe	200	600	1200	2200	3850	5500
Eldorado, V-8						
2 dr Cpe	350	775	1500	3750	5250	7500
Fleetwood Brougham, V-8						
4 dr Sed	200	650	1250	2400	4150	5900
2 dr Cpe	200	650	1250	2400	4200	6000
Fleetwood, V-8						
4 dr Limo	350	725	1400	3200	4850	6900
4 dr Formal	350	750	1450	3400	5000	7100

1981

Seville, V-8						
4 dr Sed	350	700	1350	2800	4550	6500
DeVille, V-8						
4 dr Sed	200	600	1200	2200	3850	5500
2 dr Cpe	200	600	1200	2200	3900	5600
Eldorado, V-8						
2 dr Cpe	350	825	1600	4000	5600	8000
Fleetwood Brougham, V-8						
4 dr Sed	200	650	1250	2400	4200	6000
2 dr Cpe	200	675	1300	2500	4300	6100
Fleetwood, V-8						
4 dr Limo	350	750	1450	3300	4900	7000
4 dr Formal	350	750	1450	3500	5050	7200

1982

Cimarron, 4-cyl.						
4 dr Sed	200	550	1150	2000	3600	5200
Seville, V-8						
4 dr Sed	350	700	1350	2900	4600	6600
DeVille, V-8						
4 dr Sed	200	600	1200	2300	4000	5700
2 dr Cpe	200	650	1200	2300	4100	5800
Eldorado, V-8						
2 dr Cpe	350	875	1700	4250	5900	8500
Fleetwood Brougham, V-8						
4 dr Sed	200	675	1300	2500	4350	6200
2 dr Cpe	200	675	1300	2600	4400	6300
Fleetwood, V-8						
4 dr Limo	350	750	1450	3500	5050	7200
4 dr Formal	350	775	1500	3700	5200	7400

1983

Cimarron, 4-cyl.						
4 dr Sed	200	600	1200	2200	3850	5500
Seville, V-8						
4 dr Sed	350	725	1400	3000	4700	6700
DeVille, V-8						
4 dr Sed	200	650	1250	2400	4150	5900
2 dr Cpe	200	650	1250	2400	4200	6000
Eldorado, V-8						
2 dr Cpe	450	900	1900	4500	6300	9000
Fleetwood Brougham, V-8						
4 dr Sed	350	700	1350	2700	4500	6400
2 dr Cpe	350	700	1350	2800	4550	6500
Fleetwood, V-8						
4 dr Limo	350	775	1500	3700	5200	7400
4 dr Formal	350	800	1550	3800	5300	7600

CHEVROLET

1976

Chevette, 4-cyl.	6	5	4	3	2	1
2 dr Scooter	125	200	600	1100	2250	3200
2 dr Hatch	125	250	750	1150	2400	3400
Vega, 4-cyl.						
2 dr	100	175	525	1050	2100	3000
2 dr Hatch	125	200	600	1100	2200	3100
Cosworth Hatch	350	825	1600	4000	5600	8000
Sta Wag	125	200	600	1100	2250	3200
Est Sta Wag	125	200	600	1100	2300	3300
Nova, V-8						
Cpe	125	250	750	1150	2400	3400
2 dr Hatch	125	250	750	1150	2450	3500
4 dr Sed	125	200	600	1100	2300	3300
Nova Concours, V-8						
Cpe	125	250	750	1150	2450	3500
2 dr Hatch	125	250	750	1150	2500	3600
4 dr Sed	125	250	750	1150	2400	3400
Monza, 4-cyl.						
Twn Cpe	125	250	750	1150	2400	3400
2 dr Hatch	125	250	750	1150	2400	3400
Malibu, V-8						
2 dr	125	250	750	1150	2450	3500
4 dr Sed	125	250	750	1150	2400	3400
2S Sta Wag ES	100	175	525	1050	2050	2900
3S Sta Wag ES	125	200	600	1100	2200	3100
Malibu Classic, V-8						
2 dr	150	350	950	1350	2800	4000
Landau Cpe	150	350	950	1450	3000	4200
4 dr Sed	125	250	750	1150	2450	3500
Laguna Type S-3, V-8						
Cpe	150	400	1000	1650	3150	4500
Monte Carlo, V-8						
Cpe	200	500	1100	1900	3500	5000
Landau Cpe	200	600	1200	2200	3850	5500
Impala, V-8						
4 dr Sed	125	200	600	1100	2300	3300
4 dr Spt Sed	125	250	750	1150	2400	3400
Cus Cpe	150	350	950	1350	2800	4000

	6	5	4	3	2	1
2S Sta Wag	125	250	750	1150	2400	3400
3S Sta Wag	125	250	750	1150	2450	3500
Caprice Classic, V-8						
4 dr Sed	125	250	750	1150	2450	3500
4 dr Spt Sed	125	250	750	1150	2500	3600
Cpe	150	350	950	1450	3000	4200
Landau Cpe	150	400	1000	1650	3150	4500
2S Sta Wag	125	250	750	1150	2450	3500
3S Sta Wag	125	250	750	1150	2500	3600
Camaro						
Cpe	200	650	1250	2400	4200	6000
Cpe LT	350	750	1450	3300	4900	7000

1977

Chevette, 4-cyl.						
2 dr Hatch	100	175	525	1050	2050	2900
Vega, 4-cyl.						
Spt Cpe	100	150	450	1000	1800	2600
2 dr Hatch	100	150	450	1000	1900	2700
Sta Wag	100	175	525	1050	1950	2800
Est Wag	100	175	525	1050	2050	2900
Nova, V-8						
Cpe	125	250	750	1150	2450	3500
2 dr Hatch	125	250	750	1150	2500	3600
4 dr Sed	125	250	750	1150	2400	3400
Nova Concours, V-8						
Cpe	125	250	750	1150	2500	3600
2 dr Hatch	150	300	900	1250	2600	3700
4 dr Sed	125	250	750	1150	2450	3500
Monza, 4-cyl.						
Twn Cpe	125	250	750	1150	2450	3500
2 dr Hatch	125	250	750	1150	2450	3500
Malibu, V-8						
Cpe	125	250	750	1150	2400	3400
4 dr Sed	125	250	750	1150	2450	3500
2S Sta Wag	125	200	600	1100	2200	3100
3S Sta Wag	125	200	600	1100	2250	3200
Malibu Classic, V-8						
Cpe	125	250	750	1150	2450	3500
Landau Cpe	150	350	950	1350	2800	4000
4 dr Sed	125	250	750	1150	2500	3600
2S Sta Wag	125	200	600	1100	2300	3300
3S Sta Wag	125	250	750	1150	2400	3400
Monte Carlo, V-8						
Cpe	200	500	1100	1900	3500	5000
Landau Cpe	200	600	1200	2200	3850	5500
Impala, V-8						
Cpe	150	350	950	1350	2800	4000
4 dr Sed	125	250	750	1150	2450	3500
2S Sta Wag	125	250	750	1150	2450	3500
3S Sta Wag	125	250	750	1150	2500	3600
Caprice Classic, V-8						
Cpe	150	350	950	1450	3000	4200
4 dr Sed	150	300	900	1250	2600	3700
2S Sta Wag	125	250	750	1150	2500	3600
3S Sta Wag	150	300	900	1250	2600	3700
Camaro						
Spt Cpe	350	750	1450	3300	4900	7000
Spt Cpe LT	350	775	1500	3750	5250	7500
Spt Cpe Z28	350	825	1600	4000	5600	8000

1978

Chevette						
2 dr Scooter	100	175	525	1050	1950	2800
2 dr Hatch	100	175	525	1050	1950	2800
4 dr Hatch	100	175	525	1050	2050	2900
Nova						
Cpe	125	250	750	1150	2400	3400
2 dr Hatch	125	250	750	1150	2400	3400
4 dr Sed	125	200	600	1100	2300	3300
Nova Custom						
Cpe	125	250	750	1150	2450	3500
4 dr Sed	125	250	750	1150	2400	3400
Monza						
Cpe 2 plus 2	125	250	750	1150	2500	3600
'S' Cpe	125	250	750	1150	2450	3500
Cpe	125	250	750	1150	2400	3400
Sta Wag	125	200	600	1100	2200	3100
Est Wag	125	200	600	1100	2250	3200
Spt Cpe 2 plus 2	150	350	950	1350	2800	4000
Spt Cpe	150	300	900	1250	2650	3800
Malibu						
Spt Cpe	125	250	750	1150	2500	3600
4 dr Sed	125	250	750	1150	2450	3500
Sta Wag	125	250	750	1150	2450	3500
Malibu Classic						
Spt Cpe	150	300	900	1250	2600	3700
4 dr Sed	125	250	750	1150	2500	3600
Sta Wag	125	250	750	1150	2500	3600
Monte Carlo						
Cpe	150	450	1050	1750	3250	4700
Impala						
Cpe	150	350	950	1350	2800	4000
4 dr Sed	150	300	900	1250	2600	3700
Sta Wag	150	300	900	1250	2600	3700
Caprice Classic						
Cpe	150	400	1000	1550	3050	4300
4 dr Sed	150	350	950	1350	2800	4000
Sta Wag	150	350	950	1350	2800	4000
Camaro						
Cpe	200	650	1250	2400	4200	6000
LT Cpe	350	700	1350	2800	4550	6500
Z-28 Cpe	350	750	1450	3300	4900	7000

1979

Chevette, 4-cyl.						
4 dr Hatch	100	175	525	1050	2050	2900
2 dr Hatch	100	175	525	1050	2050	2900
2 dr Scooter	100	175	525	1050	1950	2800
Nova, V-8						
4 dr Sed	125	250	750	1150	2400	3400
2 dr Sed	125	200	600	1100	2300	3300
2 dr Hatch	125	250	750	1150	2450	3500
Nova Custom, V-8						
4 dr Sed	125	250	750	1150	2450	3500
2 dr Sed	125	250	750	1150	2400	3400

NOTE: Deduct 5 percent for 6-cyl.

Monza, 4-cyl.						
2 dr 2 plus 2 Hatch	150	300	900	1250	2600	3700
2 dr	125	250	750	1150	2500	3600
Sta Wag	125	200	600	1100	2250	3200
2 dr Spt 2 plus 2 Hatch	150	300	900	1250	2650	3800

Malibu, V-8	6	5	4	3	2	1
4 dr Sed	125	250	750	1150	2500	3600
Spt Cpe	150	300	900	1250	2650	3800
Sta Wag	150	300	900	1250	2600	3700
Malibu Classic, V-8						
4 dr Sed	150	300	900	1250	2600	3700
Spt Cpe	150	300	900	1350	2700	3900
Landau Cpe	150	350	950	1350	2800	4000
Sta Wag	150	300	900	1250	2650	3800
NOTE: Deduct 5 percent for 6-cyl.						
Monte Carlo, V-8						
Spt Cpe	200	500	1100	1900	3500	5000
Landau Cpe	200	600	1200	2200	3850	5500
NOTE: Deduct 10 percent for 6-cyl.						
Impala, V-8						
4 dr Sed	150	300	900	1250	2650	3800
2 dr Sed	150	300	900	1250	2600	3700
Landau Cpe	150	300	900	1350	2700	3900
2S Sta Wag	150	300	900	1250	2600	3700
3S Sta Wag	150	300	900	1250	2650	3800
Caprice Classic, V-8						
4 dr Sed	150	350	950	1350	2800	4000
2 dr Sed	150	350	950	1450	2900	4100
Landau Cpe	150	350	950	1450	3000	4200
2S Sta Wag	150	350	950	1450	2900	4100
3S Sta Wag	150	350	950	1450	3000	4200
NOTE: Deduct 15 percent for 6-cyl.						
Camaro, V-8						
Spt Cpe	200	650	1200	2300	4100	5800
Rally Cpe	350	700	1350	2700	4500	6400
Berlinetta Cpe	350	700	1350	2900	4600	6600
Z-28 Cpe	350	725	1400	3200	4850	6900
NOTE: Deduct 20 percent for 6-cyl.						

1980

Chevette, 4-cyl.						
2 dr Hatch Scooter	125	200	600	1100	2250	3200
2 dr Hatch	125	200	600	1100	2300	3300
4 dr Hatch	125	250	750	1150	2400	3400
Citation, 6-cyl.						
4 dr Hatch	125	250	750	1150	2450	3500
2 dr Hatch	125	250	750	1150	2400	3400
2 dr Cpe	125	250	750	1150	2500	3600
2 dr Cpe Clb	150	300	900	1250	2600	3700
NOTE: Deduct 10 percent for 4-cyl.						
Monza, 4-cyl.						
2 dr Hatch 2 plus 2	125	250	750	1150	2400	3400
2 dr Hatch Spt 2 plus 2	125	250	750	1150	2500	3600
2 dr Cpe	125	250	750	1150	2450	3500
NOTE: Add 10 percent for V-6.						
Malibu, V-8						
4 dr Sed	125	250	750	1150	2500	3600
2 dr Cpe Spt	150	300	900	1250	2650	3800
4 dr Sta Wag	150	300	900	1250	2600	3700
NOTE: Deduct 10 percent for V-6.						
Malibu Classic, V-8						
4 dr Sed	150	300	900	1250	2600	3700
2 dr Cpe Spt	150	300	900	1350	2700	3900
2 dr Cpe Lan	150	350	950	1350	2800	4000
4 dr Sta Wag	150	300	900	1250	2650	3800
NOTE: Deduct 10 percent for 6-cyl.						
Camaro, 6-cyl.						
2 dr Cpe Spt	200	675	1300	2500	4300	6100
2 dr Cpe RS	200	675	1300	2600	4400	6300
2 dr Cpe Berlinetta	350	700	1350	2700	4500	6400
Camaro, V-8						
2 dr Cpe Spt	350	700	1350	2800	4550	6500
2 dr Cpe RS	350	725	1400	3000	4700	6700
2 dr Cpe Berlinetta	350	725	1400	3100	4800	6800
2 dr Cpe Z28	350	750	1450	3300	4900	7000
Monte Carlo, 6-cyl.						
2 dr Cpe Spt	200	550	1150	2100	3800	5400
2 dr Cpe Lan	200	600	1200	2200	3850	5500
Monte Carlo, V-8						
2 dr Cpe Spt	200	650	1200	2300	4100	5800
2 dr Cpe Lan	200	650	1250	2400	4150	5900
Impala, V-8						
4 dr Sed	150	300	900	1350	2700	3900
2 dr Cpe	150	350	950	1350	2800	4000
4 dr Sta Wag 2S	150	350	950	1350	2800	4000
4 dr Sta Wag 3S	150	350	950	1450	2900	4100
NOTE: Deduct 12 percent for 6-cyl. sedan and coupe only.						
Caprice Classic, V-8						
4 dr Sed	150	350	950	1350	2800	4000
2 dr Cpe	150	350	950	1450	3000	4200
2 dr Cpe Lan	150	400	1000	1600	3100	4400
4 dr Sta Wag 2S	150	350	950	1450	2900	4100
4 dr Sta Wag 3S	150	350	950	1450	3000	4200

1981

Chevette, 4-cyl.						
2 dr Hatch Scooter	125	200	600	1100	2300	3300
2 dr Hatch	125	250	750	1150	2400	3400
4 dr Hatch	125	250	750	1150	2450	3500
Citation, 6-cyl.						
4 dr Hatch	125	250	750	1150	2500	3600
2 dr Hatch	125	250	750	1150	2450	3500
NOTE: Deduct 10 percent for 4-cyl.						
Malibu, V-8						
4 dr Sed Spt	150	300	900	1250	2600	3700
2 dr Cpe Spt	150	300	900	1250	2650	3800
4 dr Sta Wag	150	300	900	1250	2650	3800
NOTE: Deduct 10 percent for 6-cyl.						
Malibu Classic, V-8						
4 dr Sed Spt	150	300	900	1250	2650	3800
2 dr Cpe Spt	150	300	900	1350	2700	3900
2 dr Cpe Lan	150	350	950	1350	2800	4000
4 dr Sta Wag	150	300	900	1350	2700	3900
Camaro, 6-cyl.						
2 dr Cpe Spt	200	675	1300	2500	4350	6200
2 dr Cpe Berlinetta	350	700	1350	2700	4500	6400
Camaro, V-8						
2 dr Cpe Spt	350	700	1350	2900	4600	6600
2 dr Cpe Berlinetta	350	725	1400	3100	4800	6800
2 dr Cpe Z28	350	750	1450	3500	5050	7200
Monte Carlo, 6-cyl.						
2 dr Cpe Spt	200	600	1200	2200	3850	5500
2 dr Cpe Lan	200	600	1200	2200	3900	5600
Monte Carlo, V-8						
2 dr Cpe Spt	200	650	1250	2400	4150	5900
2 dr Cpe Lan	200	650	1250	2400	4200	6000
Impala, V-8	6	5	4	3	2	1
4 dr Sed	150	350	950	1350	2800	4000
2 dr Cpe	150	350	950	1450	2900	4100
4 dr Sta Wag 2S	150	350	950	1450	2900	4100
4 dr Sta Wag 3S	150	350	950	1450	3000	4200
NOTE: Deduct 12 percent for 6-cyl. on sedan and coupe only.						
Caprice Classic, V-8						
4 dr Sed	150	350	950	1450	3000	4200
2 dr Cpe	150	400	1000	1550	3050	4300
2 dr Cpe Lan	150	400	1000	1650	3150	4500
4 dr Sta Wag 2S	150	400	1000	1550	3050	4300
4 dr Sta Wag 3S	150	400	1000	1600	3100	4400
NOTE: Deduct 15 percent for 6-cyl. coupe and sedan only.						

1982

Chevette, 4-cyl.						
2 dr Hatch Scooter	125	250	750	1150	2400	3400
4 dr Hatch Scooter	125	250	750	1150	2450	3500
2 dr Hatch	125	250	750	1150	2450	3500
4 dr Hatch	125	250	750	1150	2500	3600
Cavalier, 4-cyl.						
4 dr Sed Cadet	150	300	900	1250	2600	3700
2 dr Cpe Cadet	150	300	900	1250	2650	3800
4 dr Sta Wag Cadet	150	300	900	1250	2650	3800
4 dr Sed	150	300	900	1250	2650	3800
2 dr Cpe	150	300	900	1350	2700	3900
2 dr Hatch	150	300	900	1350	2700	3900
4 dr Sta Wag	150	350	950	1350	2800	4000
4 dr Sed CL	150	350	950	1350	2800	4000
2 dr Cpe CL	150	350	950	1450	2900	4100
2 dr Hatch CL	150	350	950	1450	3000	4200
4 dr Sta Wag CL	150	350	950	1450	3000	4200
Citation, 6-cyl.						
4 dr Hatch	150	300	900	1250	2650	3800
2 dr Hatch	150	300	900	1250	2600	3700
2 dr Cpe	150	300	900	1250	2650	3800
NOTE: Deduct 10 percent for 4-cyl.						
Malibu, V-8						
4 dr Sed	150	350	950	1450	2900	4100
4 dr Sta Wag	150	350	950	1450	3000	4200
NOTE: Deduct 10 percent for 6-cyl.						
Celebrity, 6-cyl.						
4 dr Sed	150	350	950	1450	3000	4200
2 dr Cpe	150	400	1000	1550	3050	4300
NOTE: Deduct 10 percent for 6-cyl.						
Camaro, 6-cyl.						
2 dr Cpe Spt	200	675	1300	2600	4400	6300
2 dr Cpe Berlinetta	350	700	1350	2800	4550	6500
Camaro, V-8						
2 dr Cpe Spt	350	725	1400	3000	4700	6700
2 dr Cpe Berlinetta	350	725	1400	3200	4850	6900
2 dr Cpe Z28	350	775	1500	3700	5200	7400
Monte Carlo, 6-cyl.						
2 dr Cpe Spt	200	600	1200	2300	4000	5700
Monte Carlo, V-8						
2 dr Cpe Spt	200	675	1300	2500	4300	6100
Impala, V-8						
4 dr Sed	150	400	1000	1600	3100	4400
4 dr Sta Wag 2S	150	400	1000	1600	3100	4400
4 dr Sta Wag 3S	150	400	1000	1650	3150	4500
NOTE: Deduct 12 percent for 6-cyl. on sedan only.						
Caprice Classic, V-8						
4 dr Sed	150	450	1050	1700	3200	4600
2 dr Spt Cpe	150	450	1050	1750	3250	4700
4 dr Sta Wag 3S	150	450	1050	1750	3250	4700
NOTE: Deduct 15 percent for 6-cyl. coupe and sedan only.						

1983

Chevette, 4-cyl.						
2 dr Hatch Scooter	125	250	750	1150	2450	3500
4 dr Hatch Scooter	125	250	750	1150	2500	3600
2 dr Hatch	125	250	750	1150	2500	3600
4 dr Hatch	150	300	900	1250	2600	3700
Cavalier, 4-cyl.						
4 dr Sed	150	300	900	1350	2700	3900
2 dr Cpe	150	350	950	1350	2800	4000
4 dr Sta Wag	150	350	950	1350	2800	4000
4 dr Sed CS	150	350	950	1350	2800	4000
2 dr Cpe CS	150	350	950	1450	2900	4100
2 dr Hatch CS	150	350	950	1450	3000	4200
4 dr Sta Wag CS	150	350	950	1450	3000	4200
Citation, 6-cyl.						
4 dr Hatch	150	300	900	1350	2700	3900
2 dr Hatch	150	300	900	1250	2650	3800
2 dr Cpe	150	300	900	1350	2700	3900
NOTE: Deduct 10 percent for 4-cyl.						
Malibu, V-8						
4 dr Sed	150	350	950	1450	3000	4200
4 dr Sta Wag	150	400	1000	1550	3050	4300
NOTE: Deduct 10 percent for 6-cyl.						
Celebrity, V-6						
4 dr Sed	150	400	1000	1550	3050	4300
2 dr Cpe	150	400	1000	1600	3100	4400
NOTE: Deduct 10 percent for 4-cyl.						
Camaro, 6-cyl.						
2 dr Cpe Spt	350	700	1350	2700	4500	6400
2 dr Cpe Berlinetta	350	700	1350	2900	4600	6600
Camaro, V-8						
2 dr Cpe Spt	350	725	1400	3100	4800	6800
2 dr Cpe Berlinetta	350	750	1450	3300	4900	7000
2 dr Cpe Z28	350	775	1500	3750	5250	7500
Monte Carlo, 6-cyl.						
2 dr Cpe Spt	200	650	1200	2300	4100	5800
Monte Carlo, V-8						
2 dr Cpe Spt	200	675	1300	2500	4350	6200
Impala, V-8						
4 dr Sed	150	400	1000	1650	3150	4500
NOTE: Deduct 12 percent for 6-cyl.						
Caprice Classic, V-8						
4 dr Sed	150	450	1050	1750	3250	4700
4 dr Sta Wag	150	450	1050	1750	3250	4700
NOTE: Deduct 15 percent for 6-cyl.						

CORVETTE

1976	6	5	4	3	2	1
Cpe	800	3900	7800	13,000	18,200	26,000
1977						
Cpe	800	4050	8100	13,500	18,900	27,000

1978	6	5	4	3	2	1
Cpe	800	4200	8400	14,000	19,600	28,000

Note: Add 10 percent for pace car or anniversary model.
Add 20 percent for L82 engine option.

1979						
Spt Cpe	800	4050	8100	13,500	18,900	27,000

NOTE: Add 20 percent for L82 engine option.

1980						
Cpe	800	3600	7200	12,000	16,800	24,000

1981						
Cpe	800	3750	7500	12,500	17,500	25,000

1982						
Cpe	800	3750	7500	12,500	17,500	25,000
Hatch	800	3900	7800	13,000	18,200	26,000

CHRYSLER

1976

Cordoba, V-8	6	5	4	3	2	1
2 dr HdTp	200	500	1100	1900	3500	5000
Newport, V-8						
4 dr Sed	125	250	750	1150	2450	3500
2 dr HdTp	150	300	900	1350	2700	3900
4 dr HdTp	150	300	900	1250	2600	3700
Newport Custom, V-8						
4 dr Sed	125	250	750	1150	2500	3600
2 dr HdTp	150	350	950	1350	2800	4000
4 dr HdTp	150	300	900	1250	2650	3800
Town & Country, V-8						
2S Sta Wag	125	250	750	1150	2500	3600
3S Sta Wag	150	300	900	1250	2600	3700
New Yorker Brougham, V-8						
2 dr HdTp	150	350	950	1450	3000	4200
4 dr HdTp	150	300	900	1250	2650	3800

1977

LeBaron, V-8						
4 dr Sed	150	300	900	1250	2650	3800
Cpe	150	350	950	1350	2800	4000
LeBaron Medallion, V-8						
4 dr Sed	150	350	950	1350	2800	4000
Cpe	150	350	950	1450	3000	4200
Cordoba, V-8						
2 dr HdTp	200	500	1100	1900	3500	5000
Newport, V-8						
4 dr Sed	125	250	750	1150	2500	3600
2 dr HdTp	150	350	950	1350	2800	4000
4 dr HdTp	150	300	900	1250	2650	3800
Town & Country, V-8						
2S Sta Wag	150	300	900	1250	2600	3700
3S Sta Wag	150	300	900	1250	2650	3800
New Yorker Brougham, V-8						
2 dr HdTp	150	400	1000	1650	3150	4500
4 dr HdTp	150	300	900	1350	2700	3900

1978

LeBaron						
4 dr 'S' Sed	125	250	750	1150	2400	3400
'S' Cpe	125	250	750	1150	2450	3500
4 dr Sed	125	250	750	1150	2450	3500
Cpe	125	250	750	1150	2500	3600
Town & Country						
Sta Wag	125	250	750	1150	2450	3500
LeBaron Medallion						
4 dr Sed	125	250	750	1150	2500	3600
Cpe	150	300	900	1250	2600	3700
Cordoba						
Cpe	200	500	1100	1900	3500	5000
Newport						
4 dr	150	300	900	1250	2600	3700
2 dr	150	300	900	1250	2650	3800
New Yorker Brougham						
4 dr	150	300	900	1350	2700	3900
2 dr	150	350	950	1350	2800	4000

1979

LeBaron, V-8						
4 dr Sed	125	250	750	1150	2450	3500
Cpe	125	250	750	1150	2500	3600
LeBaron Salon, V-8						
4 dr Sed	125	250	750	1150	2500	3600
Cpe	150	300	900	1250	2600	3700
LeBaron Medallion, V-8						
4 dr Sed	150	300	900	1250	2650	3800
Cpe	150	300	900	1350	2700	3900
LeBaron Town & Country						
Sta Wag	150	300	900	1250	2650	3800

NOTE: Deduct 5 percent for 6-cyl.

Cordoba, V-8						
Cpe	200	500	1100	1850	3350	4900

NOTE: Add 20 percent for 300 option.

Newport, V-8						
4 dr Sed	150	300	900	1350	2700	3900

NOTE: Deduct 7 percent for 6-cyl.

New Yorker, V-8						
4 dr Sed	150	350	950	1450	2900	4100

1980

LeBaron, V-8						
4 dr Sed Spl 6-cyl	125	250	750	1150	2450	3500
4 dr Sed	125	250	750	1150	2500	3600
2 dr Cpe	150	300	900	1250	2650	3800
4 dr Sta Wag	150	300	900	1350	2700	3900
4 dr Sed Salon	150	300	900	1250	2600	3700
2 dr Cpe Salon	150	300	900	1250	2650	3800
4 dr Sta Wag T&C	150	350	950	1350	2800	4000
4 dr Sed Medallion	150	300	900	1350	2700	3900
2 dr Cpe Medallion	150	350	950	1350	2800	4000
Cordoba, V-8						
2 dr Cpe Specialty	200	650	1250	2400	4200	6000
2 dr Cpe Spl Crown	350	700	1350	2800	4550	6500
2 dr Cpe Spl LS	200	650	1250	2400	4150	5900

NOTE: Deduct 12 percent for 6-cyl.

Newport, V-8						
4 dr Sed	150	400	1000	1550	3050	4300

New Yorker, V-8	6	5	4	3	2	1
4 dr Sed	150	400	1000	1650	3150	4500

1981

LeBaron, V-8						
4 dr Sed Spl	150	300	900	1250	2600	3700
2 dr Cpe Spl	150	300	900	1250	2650	3800
4 dr Sta Wag	150	350	950	1350	2800	4000
4 dr Sed Salon	150	300	900	1350	2700	3900
2 dr Cpe Salon	150	350	950	1350	2800	4000
4 dr Sta Wag T&C	150	350	950	1450	2900	4100
4 dr Sed Medallion	150	350	950	1350	2800	4000
2 dr Cpe Medallion	150	350	950	1450	2900	4100

NOTE: Deduct 12 percent for 6-cyl.

Cordoba, V-8						
2 dr Cpe Specialty LS	200	650	1250	2400	4200	6000
2 dr Cpe Specialty	200	675	1300	2500	4300	6100

NOTE: Deduct 12 percent for 6-cyl.

Newport, V-8						
4 dr Sed	150	400	1000	1600	3100	4400

NOTE: Deduct 10 percent for 6-cyl.

New Yorker, V-8						
4 dr Sed	150	450	1050	1700	3200	4600
Imperial, V-8						
2 dr Cpe	200	650	1250	2400	4200	6000

1982

LeBaron, 4-cyl.						
4 dr Sed	150	350	950	1350	2800	4000
2 dr Cpe Specialty	150	350	950	1350	2800	4000
2 dr Conv	200	550	1150	2100	3800	5400
4 dr Sed Medallion	150	350	950	1450	2900	4100
2 dr Cpe Specialty Medallion	150	350	950	1450	2900	4100
2 dr Conv Medallion	200	600	1200	2200	3850	5500
4 dr Sta Wag T&C	150	400	1000	1600	3100	4400
Cordoba, V-8						
2 dr Cpe Specialty LS	200	675	1300	2500	4300	6100
2 dr Cpe Specialty	200	675	1300	2500	4350	6200

NOTE: Deduct 12 percent for 6-cyl.

New Yorker, V-8						
4 dr Sed	150	450	1050	1750	3250	4700

NOTE: Deduct 11 percent for 6-cyl.

Imperial, V-8						
2 dr Cpe Luxury	200	650	1250	2400	4200	6000

1983

LeBaron, 4-cyl.						
4 dr Sed	150	350	950	1450	2900	4100
2 dr Cpe	150	350	950	1450	2900	4100
4 dr Limo	200	500	1100	1850	3350	4900
4 dr Sta Wag T&C	150	400	1000	1650	3150	4500
2 dr Conv	200	600	1200	2200	3850	5500
E Class, 4-cyl.						
4 dr Sed	150	400	1000	1650	3150	4500
Cordoba, V-8						
2 dr Cpe	200	675	1300	2600	4400	6300

NOTE: Deduct 12 percent for 6-cyl.

New Yorker, 4-cyl.						
4 dr Sed	150	450	1050	1800	3300	4800
New Yorker Fifth Avenue, V-8						
4 dr Sed	200	500	1100	1850	3350	4900
4 dr Sed Luxury	200	500	1100	1900	3500	5000

NOTE: Deduct 12 percent for 6-cyl.

Imperial, V-8						
2 dr Cpe	200	650	1250	2400	4200	6000

DODGE

1976

Colt, 4-cyl.	6	5	4	3	2	1
4 dr Sed	125	200	600	1100	2200	3100
Cpe	125	200	600	1100	2250	3200
2 dr Carousel HdTp	125	250	750	1150	2450	3500
Sta Wag	125	200	600	1100	2250	3200
2 dr HdTp GT	125	250	750	1150	2400	3400
Dart Sport, 6-cyl.						
Spt Cpe	125	250	750	1150	2400	3400
Dart Swinger Special, 6-cyl.						
2 dr HdTp	125	250	750	1150	2450	3500
Dart, 6-cyl.						
4 dr Sed	125	200	600	1100	2300	3300
Swinger	125	250	750	1150	2400	3400
2 dr HdTp	125	250	750	1150	2500	3600
Aspen, V-8						
4 dr Sed	125	250	750	1150	2400	3400
Spt Cpe	125	250	750	1150	2500	3600
Sta Wag	125	250	750	1150	2450	3500
Aspen Custom, V-8						
4 dr Sed	125	250	750	1150	2450	3500
Spt Cpe	150	300	900	1250	2600	3700
Aspen Special Edition, V-8						
4 dr Sed	125	250	750	1150	2500	3600
Spt Cpe	150	300	900	1250	2650	3800
Sta Wag	150	300	900	1250	2600	3700
Coronet, V-8						
4 dr Sed	125	250	750	1150	2400	3400
2S Sta Wag	125	200	600	1100	2300	3300
3S Sta Wag	125	250	750	1150	2400	3400
Coronet Brougham, V-8						
4 dr Sed	125	250	750	1150	2450	3500
Crestwood, V-8						
2S Sta Wag	125	250	750	1150	2400	3400
3S Sta Wag	125	250	750	1150	2450	3500
Charger, V-8						
2 dr HdTp	150	450	1050	1750	3250	4700
2 dr HdTp Spt	150	450	1050	1800	3300	4800
Charger Special Edition, V-8						
2 dr HdTp	200	500	1100	1850	3350	4900
Monaco, V-8						
4 dr Sed	150	300	900	1350	2700	3900
Sta Wag	150	300	900	1250	2600	3700
Royal Monaco, V-8						
4 dr Sed	150	350	950	1350	2800	4000
2 dr HdTp	150	350	950	1450	3000	4200
2S Sta Wag	150	350	950	1350	2800	4000
3S Sta Wag	150	350	950	1450	2900	4100
Royal Monaco Brougham, V-8						
4 dr Sed	125	250	750	1150	2500	3600
2 dr HdTp	150	350	950	1450	3000	4200
Sta Wag	150	350	950	1450	2900	4100

1977

	6	5	4	3	2	1
Colt, 4-cyl.						
4 dr Sed	125	200	600	1100	2250	3200
Cpe	125	200	600	1100	2300	3300
Cus Cpe	125	250	750	1150	2400	3400
2 dr Carousel HdTp	125	250	750	1150	2500	3600
Sta Wag	125	200	600	1100	2300	3300
2 dr HdTp GT	125	250	750	1150	2450	3500
Aspen, V-8						
4 dr Sed	125	250	750	1150	2450	3500
Spt Cpe	150	300	900	1250	2600	3700
Sta Wag	125	250	750	1150	2400	3400
Aspen Custom, V-8						
4 dr Sed	125	250	750	1150	2500	3600
Spt Cpe	150	300	900	1250	2650	3800
Aspen Special Edition, V-8						
4 dr Sed	150	300	900	1250	2600	3700
Spt Cpe	150	350	950	1350	2800	4000
Sta Wag	150	300	900	1250	2650	3800
Monaco, V-8						
4 dr Sed	125	250	750	1150	2450	3500
2 dr HdTp	150	300	900	1250	2650	3800
2S Sta Wag	125	250	750	1150	2400	3400
3S Sta Wag	125	250	750	1150	2450	3500
Monaco Brougham, V-8						
4 dr Sed	150	300	900	1250	2600	3700
2 dr HdTp	150	350	950	1350	2800	4000
Monaco Crestwood, V-8						
2S Sta Wag	125	250	750	1150	2400	3400
3S Sta Wag	125	250	750	1150	2450	3500
Charger Special Edition, V-8						
2 dr HdTp	200	500	1100	1950	3600	5100
Diplomat, V-8						
4 dr Sed	150	350	950	1450	3000	4200
Cpe	150	400	1000	1600	3100	4400
Diplomat Medallion, V-8						
4 dr Sed	150	400	1000	1600	3100	4400
Cpe	150	450	1050	1700	3200	4600
Royal Monaco, V-8						
4 dr Sed	150	400	1000	1550	3050	4300
2 dr HdTp	150	400	1000	1650	3150	4500
Sta Wag	150	400	1000	1600	3100	4400
Royal Monaco Brougham, V-8						
4 dr Sed	150	300	900	1250	2600	3700
2 dr HdTp	150	400	1000	1550	3050	4300
2S Sta Wag	150	350	950	1450	2900	4100
3S Sta Wag	150	350	950	1450	3000	4200

1978

	6	5	4	3	2	1
Omni						
4 dr Hatch	125	200	600	1100	2300	3300
Colt						
4 dr Sed	125	200	600	1100	2250	3200
Cpe	125	200	600	1100	2300	3300
Cus Cpe	125	250	750	1150	2400	3400
Sta Wag	125	200	600	1100	2250	3200
Aspen						
4 dr Sed	125	250	750	1150	2450	3500
Cpe	125	250	750	1150	2500	3600
Sta Wag	125	250	750	1150	2450	3500
Monaco						
4 dr Sed	125	250	750	1150	2500	3600
2 dr	150	300	900	1250	2600	3700
3S Sta Wag	150	300	900	1250	2600	3700
2S Sta Wag	125	250	750	1150	2500	3600
Monaco Brougham						
4 dr Sed	150	300	900	1250	2600	3700
2 dr	150	300	900	1250	2650	3800
3S Sta Wag	150	300	900	1250	2650	3800
2S Sta Wag	150	300	900	1250	2600	3700
Charger SE						
2 dr	200	550	1150	2000	3600	5200
Magnum XE						
Cpe	200	550	1150	2100	3700	5300
Challenger						
Cpe	200	600	1200	2200	3900	5600
Diplomat						
4 dr 'S' Sed	150	300	900	1350	2700	3900
'S' Cpe	150	350	950	1350	2800	4000
4 dr Sed	150	350	950	1350	2800	4000
Cpe	150	350	950	1450	2900	4100
Sta Wag	150	350	950	1350	2800	4000
Diplomat Medallion						
4 dr Sed	150	350	950	1450	2900	4100
Cpe	150	350	950	1450	3000	4200

1979

	6	5	4	3	2	1
Omni, 4-cyl.						
4 dr Hatch	125	200	600	1100	2250	3200
2 dr Hatch	125	200	600	1100	2300	3300
Colt, 4-cyl.						
2 dr Hatch	125	200	600	1100	2200	3100
2 dr Cus Hatch	125	200	600	1100	2250	3200
Cpe	125	200	600	1100	2300	3300
4 dr Sed	125	200	600	1100	2250	3200
Sta Wag	125	200	600	1100	2300	3300
Aspen, V-8						
4 dr Sed	125	250	750	1150	2500	3600
Cpe	150	300	900	1250	2600	3700
Sta Wag	125	250	750	1150	2500	3600
NOTE: Deduct 5 percent for 6-cyl.						
Magnum XE, V-8						
2 dr	200	600	1200	2200	3850	5500
Challenger, 4-cyl.						
Cpe	200	600	1200	2300	4000	5700
Diplomat, V-8						
4 dr Sed	150	300	900	1350	2700	3900
Cpe	150	350	950	1350	2800	4000
Diplomat Salon, V-8						
4 dr Sed	150	350	950	1350	2800	4000
Cpe	150	350	950	1450	2900	4100
Sta Wag	150	350	950	1350	2800	4000
Diplomat Medallion, V-8						
4 dr Sed	150	350	950	1450	3000	4200
Cpe	150	400	1000	1550	3050	4300
NOTE: Deduct 5 percent for 6-cyl.						
St. Regis, V-8						
4 dr Sed	150	400	1000	1600	3100	4400
NOTE: Deduct 5 percent for 6-cyl.						

1980

	6	5	4	3	2	1
Omni, 4-cyl.						
4 dr Hatch	125	250	750	1150	2450	3500
2 dr Hatch 2 plus 2 024	150	300	900	1350	2700	3900
Colt, 4-cyl.						
2 dr Hatch	125	250	750	1150	2400	3400
2 dr Hatch Cus	125	250	750	1150	2450	3500
4 dr Sta Wag	125	250	750	1150	2500	3600
Aspen, 6-cyl.						
4 dr Sed Spl	150	300	900	1250	2650	3800
2 dr Cpe Spl	150	300	900	1350	2700	3900
Aspen, V-8						
4 dr Sed	150	350	950	1350	2800	4000
2 dr Cpe	150	350	950	1450	2900	4100
4 dr Sta Wag	150	350	950	1450	2900	4100
NOTE: Deduct 10 percent for 6-cyl.						
Challenger						
2 dr Cpe	150	450	1050	1700	3200	4600
Diplomat, V-8						
4 dr Sed	125	250	750	1150	2450	3500
2 dr Cpe	125	250	750	1150	2500	3600
4 dr Sta Wag	150	300	900	1250	2650	3800
4 dr Sed Salon	125	250	750	1150	2500	3600
2 dr Cpe Salon	150	300	900	1250	2600	3700
4 dr Sta Wag Salon	150	300	900	1350	2700	3900
4 dr Sed Medallion	150	300	900	1250	2600	3700
2 dr Cpe Medallion	150	300	900	1250	2650	3800
NOTE: Deduct 10 percent for 6-cyl.						
Mirada, V-8						
2 dr Cpe Specialty S	200	650	1250	2400	4150	5900
2 dr Cpe Specialty	200	675	1300	2500	4300	6100
NOTE: Deduct 12 percent for 6-cyl.						
St. Regis, V-8						
4 dr Sed	150	350	950	1450	2900	4100
NOTE: Deduct 12 percent for 6-cyl.						

1981

	6	5	4	3	2	1
Omni, 4-cyl.						
4 dr Hatch Miser	125	250	750	1150	2500	3600
2 dr Hatch 024 Miser	150	300	900	1350	2700	3900
4 dr Hatch	150	300	900	1250	2650	3800
2 dr Hatch 024	150	350	950	1450	2900	4100
Colt, 4-cyl.						
2 dr Hatch	125	250	750	1150	2450	3500
2 dr Hatch DeL	125	250	750	1150	2500	3600
2 dr Hatch Cus	150	300	900	1250	2600	3700
Aries, 4-cyl.						
4 dr Sed	125	250	750	1150	2500	3600
2 dr Sed	150	300	900	1250	2600	3700
4 dr Sed Cus	150	300	900	1250	2600	3700
2 dr Sed Cus	150	300	900	1250	2650	3800
4 dr Sta Wag Cus	150	350	950	1350	2800	4000
4 dr Sed SE	150	300	900	1350	2700	3900
2 dr Sed SE	150	350	950	1350	2800	4000
4 dr Sta Wag SE	150	350	950	1450	3000	4200
Challenger, 4-cyl.						
2 dr Cpe	150	400	1000	1650	3150	4500
Diplomat, V-8						
4 dr Sed Spt	125	250	750	1150	2500	3600
2 dr Cpe Spt	150	300	900	1250	2600	3700
4 dr Sed Salon	150	300	900	1250	2600	3700
2 dr Cpe Salon	150	300	900	1250	2650	3800
4 dr Sed Medallion	150	300	900	1350	2700	3900
2 dr Cpe Medallion	150	350	950	1350	2800	4000
4 dr Sta Wag	150	350	950	1450	2900	4100
NOTE: Deduct 10 percent for 6-cyl.						
Mirada, V-8						
2 dr Cpe	200	650	1250	2400	4200	6000
NOTE: Deduct 12 percent for 6-cyl.						
St. Regis, V-8						
4 dr Sed	150	350	950	1450	3000	4200
NOTE: Deduct 12 percent for 6-cyl.						

1982

	6	5	4	3	2	1
Colt, 4-cyl.						
2 dr Hatch	150	300	900	1250	2600	3700
4 dr Hatch	150	300	900	1250	2650	3800
2 dr Hatch DeL	150	300	900	1350	2700	3900
2 dr Hatch Cus	150	350	950	1350	2800	4000
4 dr Hatch Cus	150	300	900	1350	2700	3900
Omni, 4-cyl.						
4 dr Hatch Miser	150	300	900	1250	2600	3700
2 dr Hatch 024 Miser	150	350	950	1350	2800	4000
4 dr Hatch Cus	150	300	900	1250	2650	3800
2 dr Hatch 024 Cus	150	350	950	1450	3000	4200
4 dr Hatch Euro	150	400	1000	1550	3050	4300
2 dr Hatch 024 Charger	150	400	1000	1650	3150	4500
Aries, 4-cyl.						
4 dr Sed	150	300	900	1250	2650	3800
2 dr Cpe	150	350	950	1350	2800	4000
4 dr Sed Cus	150	350	950	1350	2800	4000
2 dr Cpe Cus	150	350	950	1450	2900	4100
4 dr Sta Wag Cus	150	350	950	1450	3000	4200
4 dr Sed SE	150	300	900	1350	2700	3900
2 dr Cpe SE	150	350	950	1450	3000	4200
4 dr Sta Wag SE	150	400	1000	1600	3100	4400
400, 4-cyl.						
2 dr Cpe Specialty	150	350	950	1350	2800	4000
4 dr Sed	150	350	950	1450	2900	4100
2 dr Cpe Specialty LS	150	350	950	1450	3000	4200
4 dr Sed LS	150	400	1000	1550	3050	4300
2 dr Conv	200	550	1150	2100	3700	5300
Challenger, 4-cyl.						
2 dr Cpe	150	450	1050	1750	3250	4700
Diplomat, V-8						
4 dr Sed	150	350	950	1450	2900	4100
4 dr Sed Medallion	150	400	1000	1550	3050	4300
NOTE: Deduct 10 percent for 6-cyl.						
Mirada, V-8						
2 dr Cpe Specialty	200	675	1300	2500	4300	6100
NOTE: Deduct 12 percent for 6-cyl.						

1983

	6	5	4	3	2	1
Colt, 4-cyl.						
4 dr Hatch	150	300	900	1250	2650	3800
2 dr Hatch	150	300	900	1350	2700	3900
2 dr Hatch DeL	150	350	950	1350	2800	4000
4 dr Hatch Cus	150	300	900	1350	2700	3900
2 dr Hatch Cus	150	350	950	1450	3000	4200
Omni, 4-cyl.						
4 dr Hatch	150	350	950	1350	2800	4000
4 dr Hatch Cus	150	400	1000	1550	3050	4300

Charger, 4-cyl.	6	5	4	3	2	1
2 dr Hatch	150	400	1000	1600	3100	4400
2 dr Hatch 2 plus 2	150	450	1050	1700	3200	4600
2 dr Hatch Shelby	200	600	1200	2200	3850	5500
Aries, 4-cyl.						
4 dr Sed	150	300	900	1350	2700	3900
2 dr Sed	150	300	900	1250	2650	3800
4 dr Sta Wag Cus	150	400	1000	1550	3050	4300
4 dr Sed SE	150	350	950	1350	2800	4000
2 dr Sed SE	150	300	900	1350	2700	3900
4 dr Sta Wag SE	150	400	1000	1650	3150	4500
Challenger, 4-cyl.						
2 dr Cpe	150	450	1050	1800	3300	4800
400, 4-cyl.						
4 dr Sed	150	350	950	1450	3000	4200
2 dr Cpe	150	350	950	1450	2900	4100
2 dr Conv	200	550	1150	2100	3800	5400
600, 4-cyl.						
4 dr Sed	150	400	1000	1600	3100	4400
4 dr Sed ES	150	450	1050	1700	3200	4600
Diplomat, V-8						
4 dr Sed	150	350	950	1450	3000	4200
4 dr Sed Medallion	150	400	1000	1600	3100	4400
NOTE: Deduct 10 percent for 6-cyl.						
Mirada, V-8						
2 dr Cpe Specialty	200	675	1300	2500	4350	6200
NOTE: Deduct 12 percent for 6-cyl.						

FORD

1976

Pinto, 4-cyl.	6	5	4	3	2	1
2 dr Sed	125	250	750	1150	2450	3500
2 dr Rbt	125	250	750	1150	2500	3600
Sta Wag	150	300	900	1250	2600	3700
Squire Wag	150	300	900	1250	2650	3800
NOTE: Add 10 percent for V-6.						
Maverick, V-8						
4 dr Sed	125	250	750	1150	2400	3400
2 dr Sed	125	200	600	1100	2300	3300
NOTE: Deduct 5 percent for 6-cyl.						
Torino, V-8						
4 dr Sed	125	250	750	1150	2450	3500
2 dr HdTp	125	250	750	1150	2500	3600
Gran Torino, V-8						
4 dr Sed	125	250	750	1150	2500	3600
2 dr HdTp	150	300	900	1250	2600	3700
Gran Torino Brougham, V-8						
4 dr Sed	150	300	900	1250	2600	3700
2 dr HdTp	150	300	900	1250	2650	3800
Station Wagons, V-8						
2S Torino	125	250	750	1150	2450	3500
2S Gran Torino	125	250	750	1150	2500	3600
2S Gran Torino Squire	150	300	900	1250	2600	3700
Granada, V-8						
4 dr Sed	125	200	600	1100	2250	3200
2 dr Sed	125	200	600	1100	2300	3300
Granada Ghia, V-8						
4 dr Sed	125	200	600	1100	2300	3300
2 dr Sed	125	250	750	1150	2400	3400
Elite, V-8						
2 dr HdTp	150	300	900	1250	2600	3700
Custom, V-8						
4 dr Sed	125	250	750	1150	2400	3400
LTD, V-8						
4 dr Sed	125	250	750	1150	2500	3600
2 dr Sed	150	300	900	1250	2650	3800
LTD Brougham V-8						
4 dr Sed	150	300	900	1250	2650	3800
2 dr Sed	150	350	950	1350	2800	4000
LTD Landau, V-8						
4 dr Sed	150	350	950	1350	2800	4000
2 dr Sed	150	350	950	1450	3000	4200
Station Wagons, V-8						
Ranch Wag	125	250	750	1150	2500	3600
LTD Wag	150	300	900	1250	2650	3800
Ctry Squire Wag	150	350	950	1350	2800	4000
Thunderbird						
2 dr HdTp	150	450	1050	1800	3300	4800

1977

Pinto, 4-cyl.						
2 dr Sed	125	250	750	1150	2500	3600
2 dr Rbt	150	300	900	1250	2600	3700
Sta Wag	150	300	900	1250	2650	3800
Squire Wag	150	300	900	1350	2700	3900
NOTE: Add 5 percent for V-6.						
Maverick, V-8						
4 dr Sed	125	250	750	1150	2450	3500
2 dr Sed	125	250	750	1150	2400	3400
NOTE: Deduct 5 percent for 6-cyl.						
Granada, V-8						
4 dr Sed	125	200	600	1100	2250	3200
2 dr Sed	125	200	600	1100	2300	3300
Granada Ghia, V-8						
4 dr Sed	125	250	750	1150	2400	3400
2 dr Sed	125	250	750	1150	2450	3500
LTD II "S", V-8						
4 dr Sed	125	200	600	1100	2300	3300
2 dr Sed	125	250	750	1150	2400	3400
LTD II, V-8						
4 dr Sed	125	250	750	1150	2400	3400
2 dr Sed	125	250	750	1150	2450	3500
LTD II Brougham, V-8						
4 dr Sed	125	250	750	1150	2500	3600
2 dr Sed	150	300	900	1250	2600	3700
Station Wagons, V-8						
2S LTD II	125	250	750	1150	2450	3500
3S LTD II	125	250	750	1150	2500	3600
3S LTD II Squire	150	300	900	1250	2650	3800
LTD, V-8						
4 dr Sed	150	300	900	1250	2600	3700
2 dr Sed	150	300	900	1250	2650	3800
LTD Landau, V-8						
4 dr Sed	150	300	900	1350	2700	3900
2 dr Sed	150	350	950	1350	2800	4000

Station Wagons, V-8	6	5	4	3	2	1
2S LTD	150	300	900	1250	2650	3800
3S LTD	150	300	900	1350	2700	3900
3S Ctry Squire	150	350	950	1350	2800	4000
Thunderbird						
2 dr	150	450	1050	1700	3200	4600
2 dr Landau	150	450	1050	1750	3250	4700

1978

Fiesta						
Hatch	100	175	525	1050	1950	2800
Pinto						
2 dr	100	175	525	1050	2050	2900
3 dr Rbt	125	250	750	1150	2500	3600
Sta Wag	150	300	900	1250	2600	3700
Fairmont						
4 dr Sed	125	200	600	1100	2200	3100
2 dr Sed	100	175	525	1050	2100	3000
Cpe Futura	125	250	750	1150	2450	3500
Sta Wag	125	200	600	1100	2250	3200
Granada						
4 dr Sed	125	200	600	1100	2250	3200
2 dr Sed	125	200	600	1100	2200	3100
LTD II 'S'						
4 dr	125	200	600	1100	2200	3100
2 dr	100	175	525	1050	2100	3000
LTD II						
4 dr	125	200	600	1100	2250	3200
2 dr	125	200	600	1100	2200	3100
LTD II Brougham						
4 dr	125	200	600	1100	2300	3300
2 dr	125	200	600	1100	2250	3200
LTD						
4 dr	125	250	750	1150	2500	3600
2 dr	150	300	900	1250	2600	3700
2S Sta Wag	125	250	750	1150	2450	3500
LTD Landau						
4 dr	150	300	900	1250	2650	3800
2 dr	150	300	900	1350	2700	3900
Thunderbird						
2 dr	200	500	1100	1900	3500	5000
2 dr Town Landau	200	650	1250	2400	4200	6000
2 dr Diamond Jubilee	350	750	1450	3300	4900	7000

1979

Fiesta, 4-cyl.						
3 dr Hatch	100	175	525	1050	2050	2900
Pinto, V-6						
2 dr Sed	125	200	600	1100	2200	3100
Rbt	125	250	750	1150	2500	3600
Sta Wag	125	250	750	1150	2500	3600
Squire Wag	150	300	900	1250	2600	3700
NOTE: Deduct 5 percent for 4-cyl.						
Fairmont, 6-cyl.						
4 dr Sed	125	200	600	1100	2250	3200
2 dr Sed	125	200	600	1100	2200	3100
Cpe	125	250	750	1150	2500	3600
Sta Wag	125	200	600	1100	2300	3300
Squire Wag	125	250	750	1150	2400	3400
NOTE: Deduct 5 percent for 4-cyl. Add 5 percent for V-8.						
Granada, V-8						
4 dr Sed	125	200	600	1100	2300	3300
2 dr Sed	125	200	600	1100	2250	3200
NOTE: Deduct 5 percent for 6-cyl.						
LTD II, V-8						
4 dr Sed	125	200	600	1100	2250	3200
2 dr Sed	125	200	600	1100	2200	3100
LTD II Brougham, V-8						
4 dr Sed	125	200	600	1100	2300	3300
2 dr Sed	125	200	600	1100	2250	3200
LTD, V-8						
4 dr Sed	125	250	750	1150	2500	3600
2 dr Sed	125	250	750	1150	2400	3400
2S Sta Wag	125	250	750	1150	2450	3500
3S Sta Wag	125	250	750	1150	2500	3600
2S Squire Wag	150	300	900	1250	2600	3700
3S Squire Wag	150	300	900	1250	2650	3800
LTD Landau						
4 dr Sed	150	300	900	1250	2650	3800
2 dr Sed	125	250	750	1150	2500	3600
Thunderbird, V-8						
2 dr	150	400	1000	1650	3150	4500
2 dr Landau	150	450	1050	1750	3250	4700
2 dr Heritage	200	500	1100	1900	3500	5000

1980

Fiesta, 4-cyl.						
2 dr Hatch	125	200	600	1100	2200	3100
Pinto, 4-cyl.						
2 dr Cpe Pony	125	200	600	1100	2250	3200
2 dr Sta Wag Pony	125	250	750	1150	2400	3400
2 dr Cpe	125	200	600	1100	2300	3300
2 dr Hatch	125	250	750	1150	2400	3400
2 dr Sta Wag	125	250	750	1150	2450	3500
2 dr Sta Wag Squire	125	250	750	1150	2500	3600
Fairmont, 6-cyl.						
4 dr Sed	125	250	750	1150	2400	3400
2 dr Sed	125	200	600	1100	2300	3300
4 dr Sed Futura	125	250	750	1150	2500	3600
2 dr Cpe Futura	150	350	950	1450	2900	4100
4 dr Sta Wag	150	300	900	1250	2650	3800
NOTES: Deduct 10 percent for 4-cyl. Add 12 percent for V-8.						
Granada, V-8						
4 dr Sed	150	300	900	1350	2700	3900
2 dr Sed	150	300	900	1250	2650	3800
4 dr Sed Ghia	150	350	950	1450	2900	4100
2 dr Sed Ghia	150	350	950	1350	2800	4000
4 dr Sed ESS	150	350	950	1450	3000	4200
2 dr Sed ESS	150	350	950	1450	2900	4100
NOTE: Deduct 10 percent for 6-cyl.						
LTD, V-8						
4 dr Sed S	150	350	950	1450	3000	4200
4 dr Sta Wag S 3S	150	400	1000	1600	3100	4400
4 dr Sta Wag S 2S	150	400	1000	1550	3050	4300
4 dr Sed	150	400	1000	1550	3050	4300
2 dr Sed	150	350	950	1450	3000	4200
4 dr Sta Wag 3S	150	400	1000	1650	3150	4500
4 dr Sta Wag 2S	150	400	1000	1600	3100	4400
4 dr Sta Wag CS 3S	150	450	1050	1750	3250	4700
4 dr Sta Wag CS 2S	150	450	1050	1700	3200	4600

LTD Crown Victoria, V-8	6	5	4	3	2	1
4 dr Sed	150	450	1050	1700	3200	4600
2 dr Sed	150	400	1000	1650	3150	4500
Thunderbird, V-8						
2 dr Cpe	200	600	1200	2200	3850	5500
2 dr Cpe Twn Lan	200	650	1200	2300	4100	5800
2 dr Cpe Silver Anniv	200	650	1250	2400	4200	6000

1981

Escort, 4-cyl.	6	5	4	3	2	1
2 dr Hatch	125	200	600	1100	2250	3200
4 dr Hatch	125	200	600	1100	2300	3300
2 dr Hatch L	125	200	600	1100	2300	3300
4 dr Hatch L	125	250	750	1150	2400	3400
2 dr Hatch GL	125	250	750	1150	2400	3400
4 dr Hatch GL	125	250	750	1150	2450	3500
2 dr Hatch GLX	125	250	750	1150	2450	3500
4 dr Hatch GLX	125	250	750	1150	2500	3600
2 dr Hatch SS	125	250	750	1150	2500	3600
4 dr Hatch SS	150	300	900	1250	2600	3700
Fairmont, 6-cyl.						
2 dr Sed S	125	250	750	1150	2400	3400
4 dr Sed	125	250	750	1150	2450	3500
2 dr Sed	125	250	750	1150	2450	3500
4 dr Futura	125	250	750	1150	2500	3600
2 dr Cpe Futura	150	350	950	1450	3000	4200
4 dr Sta Wag	150	300	900	1350	2700	3900
4 dr Sta Wag Futura	150	350	950	1350	2800	4000

NOTES: Deduct 10 percent for 4-cyl.
Add 12 percent for V-8.

Granada, 6-cyl.	6	5	4	3	2	1
4 dr Sed L	150	300	900	1250	2650	3800
2 dr Sed L	150	300	900	1250	2600	3700
4 dr Sed GL	150	300	900	1350	2700	3900
2 dr Sed GL	150	300	900	1250	2650	3800
4 dr Sed GLX	150	350	950	1350	2800	4000
2 dr Sed GLX	150	300	900	1350	2700	3900

NOTES: Deduct 10 percent for 4-cyl.
Add 12 percent for V-8.

LTD, V-8	6	5	4	3	2	1
4 dr Sed S	150	400	1000	1550	3050	4300
4 dr Sta Wag S 3S	150	400	1000	1650	3150	4500
4 dr Sta Wag S 2S	150	400	1000	1600	3100	4400
4 dr Sed	150	400	1000	1600	3100	4400
2 dr Sed	150	400	1000	1550	3050	4300
4 dr Sta Wag 3S	150	450	1050	1700	3200	4600
4 dr Sta Wag 2S	150	400	1000	1650	3150	4500
4 dr Sta Wag CS 3S	150	450	1050	1800	3300	4800
4 dr Sta Wag CS 2S	150	450	1050	1750	3250	4700
LTD Crown Victoria, V-8						
4 dr Sed	150	450	1050	1800	3300	4800
2 dr Sed	150	450	1050	1750	3250	4700
Thunderbird, V-8						
2 dr Cpe	200	600	1200	2200	3900	5600
2 dr Cpe Twn Lan	200	650	1200	2300	4100	5800
2 dr Cpe Heritage	200	650	1250	2400	4150	5900

NOTE: Deduct 15 percent for 6-cyl.

1982

Escort, 4-cyl.	6	5	4	3	2	1
2 dr Hatch	125	200	600	1100	2300	3300
4 dr Hatch	125	250	750	1150	2400	3400
2 dr Hatch L	125	250	750	1150	2400	3400
4 dr Hatch L	125	250	750	1150	2450	3500
4 dr Sta Wag L	125	250	750	1150	2500	3600
2 dr Hatch GL	125	250	750	1150	2450	3500
4 dr Hatch GL	125	250	750	1150	2500	3600
4 dr Sta Wag GL	150	300	900	1250	2600	3700
2 dr Hatch GLX	125	250	750	1150	2500	3600
4 dr Hatch GLX	150	300	900	1250	2600	3700
4 dr Sta Wag GLX	150	300	900	1250	2650	3800
2 dr Hatch GT	150	300	900	1350	2700	3900
EXP, 4-cyl.						
2 dr Cpe	150	400	1000	1650	3150	4500
Fairmont Futura, 4-cyl.						
4 dr Sed	100	175	525	1050	2100	3000
2 dr Sed	100	175	525	1050	2050	2900
2 dr Cpe Futura	125	200	600	1100	2300	3300
Fairmont Futura, 6-cyl.						
4 dr Sed	150	300	900	1250	2600	3700
2 dr Cpe Futura	150	400	1000	1550	3050	4300
Granada, 6-cyl.						
4 dr Sed L	150	300	900	1350	2700	3900
2 dr Sed L	150	300	900	1250	2650	3800
4 dr Sed GL	150	350	950	1350	2800	4000
2 dr Sed GL	150	300	900	1350	2700	3900
4 dr Sed GLX	150	350	950	1450	2900	4100
2 dr Sed GLX	150	350	950	1350	2800	4000

NOTE: Deduct 10 percent for 4-cyl.

Granada Wagon, 6-cyl.	6	5	4	3	2	1
4 dr Sta Wag L	150	350	950	1450	3000	4200
4 dr Sta Wag GL	150	400	1000	1550	3050	4300
LTD, V-8						
4 dr Sed S	150	400	1000	1600	3100	4400
4 dr Sed S	150	400	1000	1650	3150	4500
2 dr Sed	150	400	1000	1600	3100	4400
LTD Crown Victoria, V-8						
4 dr Sed	200	500	1100	1850	3350	4900
2 dr Sed	150	450	1050	1800	3300	4800
LTD Station Wagon, V-8						
4 dr Sta Wag S 2S	150	400	1000	1650	3150	4500
4 dr Sta Wag S 3S	150	450	1050	1700	3200	4600
4 dr Sta Wag 2S	150	450	1050	1700	3200	4600
4 dr Sta Wag 3S	150	450	1050	1750	3250	4700
4 dr Sta Wag CS 2S	150	450	1050	1800	3300	4800
4 dr Sta Wag CS 3S	200	500	1100	1850	3350	4900
Thunderbird, V-8						
2 dr Cpe	200	650	1200	2300	4100	5800
2 dr Cpe Twn Lan	200	650	1250	2400	4200	6000
2 dr Cpe Heritage	200	675	1300	2500	4350	6200

NOTE: Deduct 15 percent for V-6.

1983

Escort, 4-cyl.	6	5	4	3	2	1
2 dr Hatch L	125	250	750	1150	2400	3400
4 dr Hatch L	125	250	750	1150	2450	3500
4 dr Sta Wag L	125	250	750	1150	2500	3600
2 dr Hatch GL	125	250	750	1150	2450	3500
4 dr Hatch GL	125	250	750	1150	2500	3600
4 dr Sta Wag GL	150	300	900	1250	2600	3700
2 dr Hatch GLX	125	250	750	1150	2500	3600
4 dr Hatch GLX	150	300	900	1250	2600	3700

	6	5	4	3	2	1
4 dr Sta Wag GLX	150	300	900	1250	2650	3800
2 dr Hatch GT	150	300	900	1250	2600	3700
EXP, 4-cyl.						
2 dr Cpe	150	400	1000	1650	3150	4500
Fairmont Futura, 4-cyl.						
4 dr Sed S	125	250	750	1150	2400	3400
2 dr Sed S	125	200	600	1100	2300	3300
4 dr Sed	125	250	750	1150	2450	3500
2 dr Sed	125	250	750	1150	2400	3400
2 dr Cpe	150	300	900	1250	2650	3800
Fairmont Futura, 6-cyl.						
4 dr Sed	150	300	900	1250	2600	3700
2 dr Sed	125	250	750	1150	2500	3600
2 dr Cpe	150	400	1000	1550	3050	4300
LTD, 4-cyl.						
4 dr Sed	150	350	950	1450	2900	4100
4 dr Sed Brgm	150	400	1000	1550	3050	4300
LTD, 6-cyl.						
4 dr Sed	150	350	950	1450	3000	4200
4 dr Sed Brgm	150	400	1000	1600	3100	4400
4 dr Sta Wag	150	450	1050	1700	3200	4600
LTD Crown Victoria, V-8						
4 dr Sed	200	500	1100	1900	3500	5000
2 dr Sed	200	500	1100	1850	3350	4900
4 dr Sta Wag 2S	200	500	1100	1950	3600	5100
4 dr Sta Wag 3S	200	550	1150	2000	3600	5200
Thunderbird, 4-cyl. Turbo						
2 dr Cpe	350	750	1450	3300	4900	7000
Thunderbird, V-8						
2 dr Cpe	350	775	1500	3750	5250	7500
2 dr Cpe Heritage	350	800	1550	3900	5450	7800

NOTE: Deduct 15 percent for V-6.

MUSTANG

1976

Mustang II, V-6	6	5	4	3	2	1
2 dr	150	300	900	1350	2700	3900
3 dr 2 plus 2	150	350	950	1450	2900	4100
2 dr Ghia	150	400	1000	1550	3050	4300

NOTE: Deduct 10 percent for 4-cyl.
Add 20 percent for V-8.
Add 15 percent for Cobra II.

Mach I, V-6	6	5	4	3	2	1
3 dr	200	500	1100	1900	3500	5000

1977

Mustang II, V-6	6	5	4	3	2	1
2 dr	150	350	950	1350	2800	4000
3 dr 2 plus 2	150	350	950	1450	3000	4200
2 dr Ghia	150	400	1000	1600	3100	4400

NOTE: Deduct 10 percent for 4-cyl.
Add 15 percent for Corba II option.
Add 20 percent for V-8.

Mach I, V-6	6	5	4	3	2	1
2 dr	200	500	1100	1900	3500	5000

1978

Mustang II	6	5	4	3	2	1
Cpe	150	350	950	1450	2900	4100
3 dr 2 plus 2	150	400	1000	1550	3050	4300
Cpe Ghia	150	400	1000	1600	3100	4400
Mach I, V-6						
Cpe	200	500	1100	1900	3500	5000

NOTE: Add 20 percent for V-8.
Add 15 percent for Cobra II option.
Add 30 percent for King Cobra option.

1979

Mustang, V-6	6	5	4	3	2	1
2 dr Sed	150	350	950	1450	3000	4200
3 dr Sed	150	400	1000	1550	3050	4300
2 dr Ghia Sed	150	400	1000	1650	3150	4500
3 dr Ghia Sed	150	450	1050	1700	3200	4600

1980

Mustang, 6-cyl.	6	5	4	3	2	1
2 dr Cpe	150	400	1000	1550	3050	4300
2 dr Hatch	150	400	1000	1600	3100	4400
2 dr Cpe Ghia	150	450	1050	1700	3200	4600
2 dr Hatch Ghia	150	450	1050	1750	3250	4700

NOTES: Deduct 11 percent for 4-cyl.
Add 15 percent for V-8.

1981

Mustang, 6-cyl.	6	5	4	3	2	1
2 dr Cpe S	150	400	1000	1600	3100	4400
2 dr Cpe	150	450	1050	1700	3200	4600
2 dr Hatch	150	450	1050	1750	3250	4700
2 dr Cpe Ghia	150	450	1050	1750	3250	4700
2 dr Hatch Ghia	150	450	1050	1800	3300	4800

NOTES: Deduct 11 percent for 4-cyl.
Add 15 percent for V-8.

1982

Mustang, 4-cyl.	6	5	4	3	2	1
2 dr Cpe L	150	350	950	1350	2800	4000
2 dr Cpe GL	150	350	950	1450	2900	4100
2 dr Hatch GL	150	350	950	1450	3000	4200
2 dr Cpe GLX	150	400	1000	1600	3100	4400
2 dr Hatch GLX	150	400	1000	1650	3150	4500
Mustang, 6-cyl.						
2 dr Cpe L	150	400	1000	1600	3100	4400
2 dr Cpe GL	150	400	1000	1650	3150	4500
2 dr Hatch GL	150	450	1050	1700	3200	4600
2 dr Cpe GLX	150	450	1050	1800	3300	4800
2 dr Hatch GLX	200	500	1100	1850	3350	4900
Mustang, V-8						
2 dr Hatch GT	200	550	1150	2000	3600	5200

1983

Mustang, 4-cyl.	6	5	4	3	2	1
2 dr Cpe L	150	350	950	1450	2900	4100
2 dr Cpe GL	150	350	950	1450	3000	4200
2 dr Hatch GL	150	400	1000	1600	3100	4400
2 dr Cpe GLX	150	400	1000	1650	3150	4500
2 dr Hatch GLX	150	450	1050	1700	3200	4600

Mustang, 6-cyl.	6	5	4	3	2	1
2 dr Cpe GL	150	450	1050	1700	3200	4600
2 dr Hatch GL	150	450	1050	1750	3250	4700
2 dr Cpe GLX	200	500	1100	1850	3350	4900
2 dr Hatch GLX	200	500	1100	1900	3500	5000
2 dr Conv GLX	200	650	1250	2400	4200	6000
Mustang, V-8						
2 dr Hatch GT	350	700	1350	2800	4550	6500
2 dr Conv GT	350	775	1500	3750	5250	7500

LINCOLN

1976
Continental, V-8	6	5	4	3	2	1
4 dr Sed	350	700	1350	2900	4600	6600
Cpe	350	725	1400	3100	4800	6800
Mark IV, V-8						
Cpe	350	875	1700	4250	5900	8500

1977
Versailles, V-8						
4 dr Sed	350	850	1650	4100	5700	8200
Continental, V-8						
4 dr Sed	350	725	1400	3100	4800	6800
Cpe	350	750	1450	3300	4900	7000
Mark V, V-8						
Cpe	350	875	1700	4250	5900	8500

1978
Versailles						
4 dr Sed	200	650	1250	2400	4200	6000
Continental						
4 dr Sed	150	450	1050	1750	3250	4700
Cpe	200	500	1100	1850	3350	4900
Mark V						
Cpe	350	725	1400	3000	4700	6700

NOTE: Add 10 percent for diamond jubilee.
Add 5 percent for Collector Series.
Add 5 percent for Designer Series.

1979
Versailles, V-8						
4 dr Sed	200	650	1250	2400	4200	6000
Continental, V-8						
4 dr Sed	200	500	1100	1900	3500	5000
Cpe	200	550	1150	2000	3600	5200
Mark V, V-8						
Cpe	350	725	1400	3000	4700	6700

NOTE: Add 5 percent for Collector Series.

1980
Versailles, V-8						
4 dr Sed	200	675	1300	2500	4300	6100
Continental, V-8						
4 dr Sed	200	650	1250	2400	4200	6000
2 dr Cpe	200	675	1300	2500	4350	6200
Mark VI, V-8						
4 dr Sed	350	750	1450	3300	4900	7000
2 dr Cpe	350	750	1450	3500	5050	7200

1981
Town Car, V-8						
4 dr Sed	200	650	1200	2300	4100	5800
2 dr Cpe	200	650	1250	2400	4150	5900
Mark VI						
4 dr Sed	200	600	1200	2300	4000	5700
2 dr Cpe	200	650	1200	2300	4100	5800

1982
Town Car, V-8						
4 dr Sed	350	700	1350	2800	4550	6500
Mark VI, V-8						
4 dr Sed	200	675	1300	2500	4300	6100
2 dr Cpe	200	675	1300	2500	4350	6200
Continental, V-8						
4 dr Sed	450	900	1900	4500	6300	9000

1983
Town Car, V-8						
4 dr Sed	350	725	1400	3100	4800	6800
Mark VI, V-8						
4 dr Sed	200	675	1300	2500	4300	6100
2 dr Cpe	200	675	1300	2500	4350	6200
Continental, V-8						
4 dr Sed	450	900	1900	4500	6300	9000

MERCURY

1976
Bobcat, 4-cyl.	6	5	4	3	2	1
3 dr	125	250	750	1150	2500	3600
Sta Wag	150	300	900	1250	2600	3700
Comet, V-8						
4 dr Sed	125	250	750	1150	2450	3500
2 dr Sed	125	250	750	1150	2400	3400
Monarch, V-8						
4 dr Sed	125	200	600	1100	2300	3300
2 dr Sed	125	250	750	1150	2400	3400
Monarch Ghia, V-8						
4 dr Sed	125	250	750	1150	2450	3500
2 dr Sed	125	250	750	1150	2500	3600
Monarch Grand Ghia, V-8						
4 dr Sed	150	300	900	1350	2700	3900
Montego, V-8						
4 dr Sed	125	250	750	1150	2500	3600
Cpe	150	300	900	1250	2600	3700
Montego MX, V-8						
4 dr Sed	150	300	900	1250	2650	3800
Cpe	150	300	900	1350	2700	3900
Montego Brougham, V-8						
4 dr Sed	150	350	950	1350	2800	4000
Cpe	150	350	950	1450	2900	4100
Station Wagons, V-8						
Montego MX	150	300	900	1250	2600	3700
Montego Vill	150	300	900	1250	2650	3800
Cougar XR7, V-8						
2 dr HdTp	150	300	900	1250	2650	3800

Marquis, V-8	6	5	4	3	2	1
4 dr Sed	125	250	750	1150	2500	3600
Cpe	150	300	900	1250	2600	3700
Marquis Brougham, V-8						
4 dr Sed	150	300	900	1250	2650	3800
Cpe	150	300	900	1350	2700	3900
Grand Marquis, V-8						
4 dr Sed	150	350	950	1350	2800	4000
Cpe	150	350	950	1450	2900	4100
Station Wagons, V-8						
Marquis	150	300	900	1250	2650	3800
Col Pk	150	300	900	1350	2700	3900

1977
Bobcat, 4-cyl.						
3 dr	150	300	900	1250	2600	3700
Sta Wag	150	300	900	1250	2650	3800
Vill Wag	150	300	900	1350	2700	3900

NOTE: Add 5 percent for V-6.

Comet, V-8						
4 dr Sed	125	250	750	1150	2500	3600
2 dr Sed	150	300	900	1250	2600	3700
Monarch, V-8						
4 dr Sed	125	250	750	1150	2400	3400
2 dr Sed	125	250	750	1150	2450	3500
Monarch Ghia, V-8						
4 dr Sed	125	250	750	1150	2500	3600
2 dr Sed	150	300	900	1250	2600	3700
Cougar, V-8						
4 dr Sed	150	300	900	1250	2650	3800
2 dr Sed	150	300	900	1350	2700	3900
Cougar Brougham, V-8						
4 dr Sed	150	300	900	1350	2700	3900
2 dr Sed	150	350	950	1350	2800	4000
Cougar XR7, V-8						
2 dr	150	350	950	1450	3000	4200
Station Wagons, V-8						
Cougar	150	300	900	1250	2650	3800
Vill	150	300	900	1350	2700	3900
Marquis, V-8						
4 dr Sed	150	300	900	1350	2700	3900
2 dr Sed	150	350	950	1350	2800	4000
Marquis Brougham, V-8						
4 dr Sed	150	300	900	1350	2700	3900
2 dr Sed	150	350	950	1350	2800	4000
Grand Marquis, V-8						
4 dr HdTp	150	350	950	1450	2900	4100
2 dr HdTp	150	350	950	1450	3000	4200
Station Wagons, V-8						
2S Marquis	150	300	900	1350	2700	3900
3S Marquis	150	350	950	1350	2800	4000

1978
Bobcat						
3 dr Rbt	125	250	750	1150	2500	3600
Sta Wag	150	300	900	1250	2600	3700
Zephyr						
4 dr Sed	125	200	600	1100	2300	3300
2 dr Sed	125	200	600	1100	2250	3200
Cpe	125	250	750	1150	2450	3500
Sta Wag	125	250	750	1150	2400	3400
Monarch						
4 dr Sed	125	200	600	1100	2300	3300
2 dr Sed	125	250	750	1150	2400	3400
Cougar						
4 dr	125	250	750	1150	2450	3500
2 dr	125	250	750	1150	2500	3600
Cougar XR7						
2 dr	150	350	950	1450	2900	4100
Marquis						
4 dr	150	300	900	1250	2650	3800
2 dr	150	300	900	1350	2700	3900
Sta Wag	150	300	900	1250	2650	3800
Marquis Brougham						
4 dr	150	300	900	1350	2700	3900
2 dr	150	350	950	1350	2800	4000
Grand Marquis						
4 dr	150	350	950	1450	2900	4100
2 dr	150	350	950	1450	3000	4200

1979
Bobcat, 4-cyl.						
3 dr Rbt	150	300	900	1250	2600	3700
Wag	125	250	750	1150	2500	3600
Villager Wag	150	300	900	1250	2600	3700
Capri, 4-cyl.						
Cpe	150	300	900	1250	2650	3800
Ghia Cpe	150	350	950	1350	2800	4000

NOTES: Add 5 percent for 6-cyl.
Add 8 percent for V-8.

Zephyr, 6-cyl.						
4 dr Sed	125	250	750	1150	2400	3400
Cpe	125	250	750	1150	2500	3600
Spt Cpe	150	300	900	1250	2650	3800
Sta Wag	125	250	750	1150	2450	3500

NOTE: Add 5 percent for V-8.

Monarch, V-8						
4 dr Sed	125	250	750	1150	2400	3400
Cpe	125	250	750	1150	2500	3600

NOTE: Deduct 5 percent for 6-cyl.

Cougar, V-8						
4 dr Sed	125	250	750	1150	2500	3600
2 dr	150	300	900	1250	2600	3700
2 dr XR7	150	350	950	1450	2900	4100
Marquis, V-8						
4 dr	150	300	900	1250	2650	3800
2 dr	150	300	900	1350	2700	3900
Marquis Brougham, V-8						
4 dr	150	300	900	1350	2700	3900
2 dr	150	350	950	1350	2800	4000
Grand Marquis, V-8						
4 dr	150	350	950	1350	2900	4000
2 dr	150	350	950	1450	2900	4100
Station Wagons, V-8						
3S Marquis	150	300	900	1250	2650	3800
3S Colony Park	150	350	950	1350	2800	4000

1980
Bobcat, 4-cyl.						
2 dr Hatch	125	250	750	1150	2450	3500
2 dr Sta Wag	125	250	750	1150	2500	3600
2 dr Sta Wag Villager	150	300	900	1250	2650	3800

	6	5	4	3	2	1
Capri, 6-cyl.						
2 dr Hatch	150	450	1050	1750	3250	4700
2 dr Hatch Ghia	200	500	1100	1900	3500	5000
NOTE: Deduct 10 percent for 4-cyl.						
Zephyr, 6-cyl.						
4 dr Sed	125	250	750	1150	2450	3500
2 dr Sed	125	250	750	1150	2400	3400
2 dr Cpe Z-7	150	350	950	1450	3000	4200
4 dr Sta Wag	150	300	900	1350	2700	3900
NOTE: Deduct 10 percent for 4-cyl.						
Monarch, V-8						
4 dr Sed	150	350	950	1450	3000	4200
2 dr Cpe	150	350	950	1450	2900	4100
NOTE: Deduct 10 percent for 4-cyl.						
Cougar XR7, V-8						
2 dr Cpe	200	650	1200	2300	4100	5800
Marquis, V-8						
4 dr Sed	150	400	1000	1600	3100	4400
2 dr Sed	150	400	1000	1550	3050	4300
Marquis Brougham, V-8						
4 dr Sed	150	450	1050	1700	3200	4600
2 dr Sed	150	400	1000	1650	3150	4500
Grand Marquis, V-8						
4 dr Sed	150	450	1050	1750	3250	4700
2 dr Sed	150	450	1050	1700	3200	4600
4 dr Sta Wag 2S	150	450	1050	1750	3250	4700
4 dr Sta Wag 3S	150	450	1050	1800	3300	4800
4 dr Sta Wag CP 2S	200	500	1100	1850	3350	4900
4 dr Sta Wag CP 3S	200	500	1100	1900	3500	5000
1981						
Lynx, 4-cyl.						
2 dr Hatch	125	200	600	1100	2300	3300
2 dr Hatch L	125	250	750	1150	2400	3400
4 dr Hatch L	125	250	750	1150	2450	3500
2 dr Hatch GL	125	250	750	1150	2450	3500
4 dr Hatch GL	125	250	750	1150	2500	3600
2 dr Hatch GS	125	250	750	1150	2500	3600
4 dr Hatch GS	150	300	900	1250	2600	3700
2 dr Hatch RS	150	300	900	1250	2600	3700
4 dr Hatch RS	150	300	900	1250	2650	3800
2 dr Hatch LS	150	300	900	1250	2650	3800
Zephyr, 6-cyl.						
4 dr Sed S	125	250	750	1150	2450	3500
4 dr Sed	125	250	750	1150	2500	3600
2 dr Sed	125	250	750	1150	2450	3500
2 dr Cpe Z-7	150	400	1000	1550	3050	4300
4 dr Sta Wag	150	350	950	1350	2800	4000
NOTE: Deduct 10 percent for 4-cyl.						
Capri, 6-cyl.						
2 dr Hatch	200	500	1100	1900	3500	5000
2 dr Hatch GS	200	550	1150	2000	3600	5200
NOTE: Deduct 10 percent for 4-cyl.						
Cougar, 6-cyl.						
4 dr Sed	150	350	950	1450	3000	4200
2 dr Sed	150	350	950	1450	2900	4100
NOTE: Deduct 10 percent for 4-cyl.						
Cougar XR7, V-8						
2 dr Cpe	200	650	1250	2400	4150	5900
NOTE: Deduct 12 percent for 6-cyl.						
Marquis, V-8						
4 dr Sed	150	400	1000	1600	3100	4400
Marquis Brougham, V-8						
4 dr Sed	150	450	1050	1700	3200	4600
2 dr Sed	150	400	1000	1650	3150	4500
Grand Marquis, V-8						
4 dr Sed	150	450	1050	1800	3300	4800
2 dr Sed	150	450	1050	1750	3250	4700
4 dr Sta Wag 2S	150	450	1050	1800	3300	4800
4 dr Sta Wag 3S	200	500	1100	1850	3350	4900
4 dr Sta Wag CP 2S	200	500	1100	1900	3500	5000
4 dr Sta Wag CP 3S	200	500	1100	1950	3600	5100
1982						
Lynx, 4-cyl.						
2 dr Hatch	125	250	750	1150	2400	3400
4 dr Hatch	125	250	750	1150	2450	3500
2 dr Hatch L	125	250	750	1150	2450	3500
4 dr Hatch L	125	250	750	1150	2500	3600
4 dr Sta Wag L	150	300	900	1250	2600	3700
2 dr Hatch GL	125	250	750	1150	2500	3600
4 dr Hatch GL	150	300	900	1250	2600	3700
4 dr Sta Wag GL	150	300	900	1250	2650	3800
2 dr Hatch GS	150	300	900	1250	2600	3700
4 dr Hatch GS	150	300	900	1250	2650	3800
4 dr Sta Wag GS	150	300	900	1350	2700	3900
2 dr Hatch LS	150	300	900	1250	2650	3800
4 dr Hatch LS	150	300	900	1350	2700	3900
4 dr Sta Wag LS	150	350	950	1350	2800	4000
2 dr Hatch RS	150	300	900	1350	2700	3900
LN7, 4-cyl.						
2 dr Hatch	150	450	1050	1700	3200	4600
Zephyr, 6-cyl.						
4 dr Sed	150	300	900	1250	2600	3700
2 dr Cpe Z-7	150	400	1000	1550	3050	4300
4 dr Sed GS	150	300	900	1250	2650	3800
2 dr Cpe Z-7 GS	150	400	1000	1650	3150	4500
Capri, 4-cyl.						
2 dr Hatch	150	450	1050	1750	3250	4700
2 dr Hatch L	150	450	1050	1800	3300	4800
2 dr Hatch GS	200	500	1100	1900	3500	5000
Capri, 6-cyl.						
2 dr Hatch L	200	550	1150	2100	3700	5300
2 dr Hatch GS	200	600	1200	2200	3850	5500
Capri, V-8						
2 dr Hatch RS	200	600	1200	2200	3900	5600
Cougar, 6-cyl.						
4 dr Sed GS	150	350	950	1350	2800	4000
2 dr Sed GS	150	300	900	1350	2700	3900
4 dr Sta Wag GS	150	350	950	1450	3000	4200
4 dr Sed LS	150	350	950	1450	2900	4100
2 dr Sed LS	150	350	950	1350	2800	4000
Cougar XR7, V-8						
2 dr Cpe	200	650	1250	2400	4200	6000
2 dr Cpe LS	200	675	1300	2500	4350	6200
NOTE: Deduct 10 percent for 6-cyl.						
Marquis, V-8						
4 dr Sed	150	400	1000	1650	3150	4500
Marquis Brougham, V-8						
4 dr Sed	150	450	1050	1750	3250	4700
2 dr Cpe	150	450	1050	1700	3200	4600
Grand Marquis, V-8						
4 dr Sed	200	500	1100	1850	3350	4900
2 dr Cpe	150	450	1050	1800	3300	4800
4 dr Sta Wag 2S	200	500	1100	1850	3350	4900
4 dr Sta Wag 3S	200	500	1100	1900	3500	5000
4 dr Sta Wag CP 2S	200	500	1100	1950	3600	5100
4 dr Sta Wag CP 3S	200	550	1150	2000	3600	5200
1983						
Lynx, 4-cyl.						
2 dr Hatch L	125	250	750	1150	2500	3600
4 dr Hatch L	150	300	900	1250	2600	3700
4 dr Sta Wag L	150	300	900	1250	2650	3800
2 dr Hatch GS	150	300	900	1250	2600	3700
4 dr Hatch GS	150	300	900	1250	2650	3800
4 dr Sta Wag GS	150	300	900	1350	2700	3900
2 dr Hatch LS	150	300	900	1250	2650	3800
4 dr Hatch LS	150	300	900	1350	2700	3900
4 dr Sta Wag LS	150	350	950	1350	2800	4000
2 dr Hatch RS	150	300	900	1350	2700	3900
4 dr Hatch LTS	150	350	950	1350	2800	4000
LN7, 4-cyl.						
2 dr Hatch	150	450	1050	1750	3250	4700
2 dr Hatch Sport	150	450	1050	1800	3300	4800
2 dr Hatch Grand Sport	200	500	1100	1900	3500	5000
2 dr Hatch RS	200	550	1150	2000	3600	5200
Zephyr, V-6						
4 dr Sed	150	300	900	1250	2650	3800
2 dr Cpe Z-7	150	400	1000	1600	3100	4400
4 dr Sed GS	150	300	900	1350	2700	3900
2 dr Cpe Z-7 GS	150	450	1050	1700	3200	4600
NOTE: Deduct 10 percent for 4-cyl.						
Capri, 4-cyl.						
2 dr Hatch	150	450	1050	1800	3300	4800
2 dr Hatch H-L	200	500	1100	1850	3350	4900
2 dr Hatch GS	200	500	1100	1950	3600	5100
Capri, 6-cyl.						
2 dr Hatch L	200	550	1150	2100	3800	5400
2 dr Hatch GS	200	600	1200	2200	3900	5600
Capri, V-8						
2 dr Hatch RS	200	650	1200	2300	4100	5800
Cougar, V-8						
2 dr Cpe	350	750	1450	3300	4900	7000
2 dr Cpe LS	350	750	1450	3500	5050	7200
NOTE: Deduct 15 percent for V-6.						
Marquis, 4-cyl.						
4 dr Sed	150	350	950	1450	3000	4200
4 dr Brougham	150	400	1000	1600	3100	4400
Marquis, 6-cyl.						
4 dr Sed	150	400	1000	1600	3100	4400
4 dr Sta Wag	150	450	1050	1750	3250	4700
4 dr Sed Brgm	150	450	1050	1800	3300	4800
4 dr Sta Wag Brgm	200	500	1100	1900	3500	5000
Grand Marquis, V-8						
4 dr Sed	200	550	1150	2000	3600	5200
2 dr Cpe	200	500	1100	1950	3600	5100
4 dr Sed LS	200	550	1150	2100	3800	5400
2 dr Cpe LS	200	550	1150	2100	3700	5300
4 dr Sta Wag 2S	200	600	1200	2200	3850	5500
4 dr Sta Wag 3S	200	600	1200	2200	3900	5600

OLDSMOBILE

	6	5	4	3	2	1
1976						
Starfire, V-6						
Spt Cpe	125	200	600	1100	2300	3300
Spt Cpe SX	125	250	750	1150	2400	3400
NOTE: Add 5 percent for V-8.						
Omega F-85, V-8						
Cpe	125	200	600	1100	2200	3100
Omega, V-8						
4 dr Sed	125	200	600	1100	2250	3200
Cpe	125	200	600	1100	2300	3300
Hatch	125	250	750	1150	2400	3400
Omega Brougham V-8						
4 dr Sed	125	200	600	1100	2300	3300
Cpe	125	250	750	1150	2400	3400
Hatch	125	250	750	1150	2450	3500
Cutlass "S", V-8						
4 dr Sed	125	200	600	1100	2200	3100
Cpe	125	200	600	1100	2250	3200
Cutlass Supreme, V-8						
4 dr Sed	125	200	600	1100	2250	3200
Cpe	125	200	600	1100	2300	3300
Cutlass Salon, V-8						
4 dr Sed	125	250	750	1150	2400	3400
Cpe	125	250	750	1150	2450	3500
Cutlass Supreme Brougham, V-8						
Cpe	125	250	750	1150	2500	3600
Station Wagons, V-8						
2S Cruiser	125	200	600	1100	2300	3300
3S Cruiser	125	250	750	1150	2400	3400
2S Vista Cruiser	125	250	750	1150	2400	3400
3S Vista Cruiser	125	250	750	1150	2450	3500
Delta 88, V-8						
4 dr Sed	125	250	750	1150	2400	3400
2 dr Sed	125	250	750	1150	2450	3500
Delta 88 Royle, V-8						
4 dr Sed	125	250	750	1150	2500	3600
2 dr Sed	150	300	900	1250	2600	3700
Station Wagons, V-8						
2S Cus Cruiser	125	250	750	1150	2400	3400
3S Cus Cruiser	125	250	750	1150	2450	3500
Ninety-Eight, V-8						
4 dr Lux Sed	150	300	900	1250	2650	3800
Lux Cpe	150	300	900	1350	2700	3900
4 dr Regency Sed	150	300	900	1350	2700	3900
Regency Cpe	150	350	950	1350	2800	4000
Toronado, V-8						
Cus Cpe	200	600	1200	2200	3850	5500
Brgm Cpe	200	650	1250	2400	4200	6000
NOTE: Deduct 5 percent for V-6.						
1977						
Starfire, V-6						
Spt Cpe	100	175	525	1050	2050	2900
Spt Cpe SX	125	200	600	1100	2200	3100
NOTE: Add 5 percent for V-8.						

	6	5	4	3	2	1
Omega F85, V-8						
Cpe	100	150	450	1000	1900	2700
Omega, V-8						
4 dr Sed	125	250	750	1150	2400	3400
Cpe	125	250	750	1150	2450	3500
2 dr Hatch	125	250	750	1150	2500	3600
Omega Brougham, V-8						
4 dr Sed	125	250	750	1150	2450	3500
Cpe	125	250	750	1150	2500	3600
2 dr Hatch	150	300	900	1250	2600	3700
NOTE: Deduct 5 percent for V-6.						
Cutlass - "S", V-8						
4 dr Sed	125	200	600	1100	2250	3200
2 dr Sed	125	200	600	1100	2300	3300
Cutlass Supreme, V-8						
4 dr Sed	125	250	750	1150	2400	3400
2 dr Sed	125	250	750	1150	2450	3500
Cutlass Salon, V-8						
2 dr	125	250	750	1150	2450	3500
Cutlass Supreme Brougham, V-8						
4 dr Sed	125	250	750	1150	2500	3600
2 dr Sed	150	300	900	1250	2650	3800
Station Wagons, V-8						
3S Cruiser	125	250	750	1150	2450	3500
Delta 88, V-8						
4 dr Sed	125	250	750	1150	2450	3500
Cpe	125	250	750	1150	2500	3600
Delta 88 Royale, V-8						
4 dr Sed	150	300	900	1250	2600	3700
Cpe	150	300	900	1250	2650	3800
Station Wagons, V-8						
2S Cus Cruiser	125	250	750	1150	2500	3600
3S Cus Cruiser	150	300	900	1250	2600	3700
Ninety Eight, V-8						
4 dr Lux Sed	150	300	900	1350	2700	3900
Lux Cpe	150	350	950	1350	2800	4000
4 dr Regency Sed	150	350	950	1350	2800	4000
Regency Cpe	150	350	950	1450	2900	4100
Toronado, V-8						
Cpe	200	500	1100	1900	3500	5000
NOTE: Add 20 percent for XSR model. Deduct 5 percent for V-6.						

1978

	6	5	4	3	2	1
Starfire						
Cpe	100	175	525	1050	2100	3000
Cpe SX	125	200	600	1100	2250	3200
Omega						
4 dr Sed	125	250	750	1150	2450	3500
Cpe	125	250	750	1150	2500	3600
2 dr Hatch	150	300	900	1250	2600	3700
Omega Brougham						
4 dr Sed	125	250	750	1150	2500	3600
Cpe	150	300	900	1250	2600	3700
Cutlass Salon						
4 dr Sed	125	200	600	1100	2300	3300
Cpe	125	250	750	1150	2400	3400
Cutlass Salon Brougham						
4 dr Sed	125	250	750	1150	2400	3400
Cpe	125	250	750	1150	2450	3500
Cutlass Supreme						
Cpe	125	250	750	1150	2500	3600
Cutlass Calais						
Cpe	150	300	900	1250	2600	3700
Cutlass Supreme Brougham						
Cpe	150	300	900	1250	2650	3800
Cutlass Cruiser						
2S Sta Wag	125	250	750	1150	2450	3500
Delta 88						
4 dr Sed	125	250	750	1150	2500	3600
Cpe	150	300	900	1250	2600	3700
Delta 88 Royale						
4 dr Sed	150	300	900	1250	2600	3700
Cpe	150	300	900	1250	2650	3800
Custom Cruiser						
Sta Wag	125	250	750	1150	2500	3600
Ninety Eight						
4 dr Lux Sed	150	300	900	1350	2700	3900
Lux Cpe	150	350	950	1350	2800	4000
4 dr Regency Sed	150	350	950	1350	2800	4000
Regency Cpe	150	350	950	1450	2900	4100
Toronado Brougham						
Cpe	200	500	1100	1900	3500	5000
NOTE: Add 20 percent for SXR.						

1979

	6	5	4	3	2	1
Starfire, 4-cyl.						
Spt Cpe	125	200	600	1100	2200	3100
Spt Cpe SX	125	200	600	1100	2250	3200
Omega, V-8						
Sed	125	250	750	1150	2500	3600
Cpe	150	300	900	1250	2600	3700
Hatch	150	300	900	1250	2650	3800
Omega Brougham, V-8						
Sed	150	300	900	1250	2600	3700
Cpe	150	300	900	1250	2650	3800
Cutlass Salon, V-8						
Sed	125	250	750	1150	2400	3400
Cpe	125	250	750	1150	2450	3500
Cutlass Salon Brougham, V-8						
Sed	125	250	750	1150	2450	3500
Cpe	125	250	750	1150	2500	3600
Cutlass Supreme, V-8						
Cpe	150	300	900	1250	2600	3700
Cutlass Calais, V-8						
Cpe	150	300	900	1250	2650	3800
Cutlass Supreme Brougham, V-8						
Cpe	150	300	900	1350	2700	3900
Cutlass Cruiser, V-8						
Sta Wag	125	250	750	1150	2500	3600
Cutlass Cruiser Brougham, V-8						
Sta Wag	150	300	900	1250	2600	3700
Delta 88, V-8						
Sed	150	300	900	1250	2650	3800
Cpe	150	300	900	1350	2700	3900
Delta 88 Royale, V-8						
Sed	150	300	900	1350	2700	3900
Cpe	150	350	950	1350	2800	4000
Custom Cruiser, V-8						
2S Sta Wag	150	300	900	1350	2700	3900
3S Sta Wag	150	350	950	1350	2800	4000
Ninety Eight						
Lux Sed	150	350	950	1450	2900	4100
Lux Cpe	150	350	950	1450	3000	4200
Regency Sed	150	400	1000	1550	3050	4300
Regency Cpe	150	400	1000	1600	3100	4400
Toronado						
Cpe	200	500	1100	1850	3350	4900
NOTE: Deduct 5 percent for V-6. Deduct 10 percent for diesel.						

1980

	6	5	4	3	2	1
Starfire, 4-cyl.						
2 dr Cpe	150	300	900	1250	2650	3800
2 dr Cpe SX	150	300	900	1350	2700	3900
Omega, V-6						
4 dr Sed	150	300	900	1250	2650	3800
2 dr Cpe	150	300	900	1350	2700	3900
NOTE: Deduct 10 percent for 4-cyl.						
Omega Brougham, V-6						
4 dr Sed	150	300	900	1350	2700	3900
2 dr Cpe	150	350	950	1350	2800	4000
NOTE: Deduct 10 percent for 4-cyl.						
Cutlass, V-8						
4 dr Sed	125	250	750	1150	2500	3600
NOTE: Deduct 12 percent for V-6.						
Cutlass Salon, V-8						
2 dr Cpe	150	300	900	1350	2700	3900
NOTE: Deduct 12 percent for V-6.						
Cutlass Salon Brougham, V-8						
2 dr Cpe	150	350	950	1350	2800	4000
NOTE: Deduct 12 percent for V-6.						
Cutlass Supreme, V-8						
2 dr Cpe	150	350	950	1450	2900	4100
NOTE: Deduct 12 percent for V-6.						
Cutlass LS, V-8						
4 dr Sed	150	300	900	1250	2600	3700
NOTE: Deduct 12 percent for V-6.						
Cutlass Calais, V-8						
2 dr Cpe	150	350	950	1450	3000	4200
NOTE: Deduct 12 percent for V-6.						
Cutlass Brougham, V-8						
4 dr Sed	150	300	900	1250	2650	3800
2 dr Cpe Supreme	150	350	950	1450	3000	4200
NOTE: Deduct 12 percent for V-6.						
Cutlass Cruiser, V-8						
4 dr Sta Wag	150	300	900	1350	2700	3900
4 dr Sta Wag Brgm	150	350	950	1350	2800	4000
NOTE: Deduct 12 percent for V-6.						
Delta 88, V-8						
4 dr Sed	150	350	950	1450	2900	4100
2 dr Cpe	150	350	950	1450	3000	4200
NOTE: Deduct 12 percent for V-6.						
Delta 88 Royale, V-8						
4 dr Sed	150	350	950	1450	3000	4200
2 dr Cpe	150	400	1000	1550	3050	4300
NOTE: Deduct 12 percent for V-6.						
Delta 88 Royale Brougham, V-8						
4 dr Sed	150	400	1000	1600	3100	4400
2 dr Cpe	150	400	1000	1650	3150	4500
NOTE: Deduct 12 percent for V-6.						
Custom Cruiser, V-8						
4 dr Sta Wag 2S	150	400	1000	1550	3050	4300
4 dr Sta Wag 3S	150	400	1000	1600	3100	4400
Ninety Eight, V-8						
4 dr Sed Lux	150	450	1050	1700	3200	4600
4 dr Sed Regency	200	500	1100	1850	3350	4900
2 dr Cpe Regency	200	500	1100	1950	3600	5100
Toronado Brougham, V-8						
2 dr Cpe	350	700	1350	2700	4500	6400

1981

	6	5	4	3	2	1
Omega, V-6						
4 dr Sed	150	300	900	1350	2700	3900
2 dr Cpe	150	350	950	1350	2800	4000
NOTE: Deduct 10 percent for 4-cyl.						
Omega Brougham, V-6						
4 dr Sed	150	350	950	1350	2800	4000
2 dr Cpe	150	350	950	1450	2900	4100
NOTE: Deduct 10 percent for 4-cyl.						
Cutlass, V-8						
4 dr Sed	150	300	900	1250	2600	3700
NOTE: Deduct 12 percent for V-6.						
Cutlass Supreme, V-8						
2 dr Cpe	150	350	950	1450	3000	4200
NOTE: Deduct 12 percent for V-6.						
Cutlass LS, V-8						
4 dr Sed	150	300	900	1250	2650	3800
NOTE: Deduct 12 percent for V-6.						
Cutlass Calais, V-8						
2 dr Cpe	150	400	1000	1600	3100	4400
NOTE: Deduct 12 percent for V-6.						
Cutlass Supreme Brougham, V-8						
2 dr Cpe	150	400	1000	1550	3050	4300
NOTE: Deduct 12 percent for V-6.						
Cutlass Brougham, V-8						
4 dr Sed	150	300	900	1350	2700	3900
NOTE: Deduct 12 percent for V-6.						
Cutlass Cruiser, V-8						
4 dr Sta Wag	150	300	900	1350	2700	3900
4 dr Sta Wag Brgm	150	350	950	1350	2800	4000
NOTE: Deduct 12 percent for V-6.						
Delta 88, V-8						
4 dr Sed	150	350	950	1450	3000	4200
2 dr Cpe	150	400	1000	1550	3050	4300
NOTE: Deduct 12 percent for V-6.						
Delta 88 Royale, V-8						
4 dr Sed	150	400	1000	1550	3050	4300
2 dr Cpe	150	400	1000	1600	3100	4400
NOTE: Deduct 12 percent for V-6.						
Delta 88 Royale Brougham, V-8						
4 dr Sed	150	400	1000	1650	3150	4500
2 dr Cpe	150	450	1050	1700	3200	4600
Custom Cruiser, V-8						
4 dr Sta Wag 2S	150	400	1000	1600	3100	4400
4 dr Sta Wag 3S	150	400	1000	1650	3150	4500
Ninety Eight, V-8						
4 dr Sed Lux	150	450	1050	1750	3250	4700
4 dr Sed Regency	150	450	1050	1800	3300	4800
2 dr Cpe Regency	200	500	1100	1850	3350	4900
NOTE: Deduct 12 percent for V-6.						

Toronado Brougham, V-8	6	5	4	3	2	1
2 dr Cpe	350	725	1400	3000	4700	6700

NOTE: Deduct 12 percent for V-6.

1982

Firenza, 4-cyl.
4 dr Sed	150	300	900	1350	2700	3900
2 dr Cpe S	150	300	900	1350	2700	3900
4 dr Sed LX	150	350	950	1350	2800	4000
2 dr Cpe SX	150	350	950	1450	2900	4100

Omega, V-6
4 dr Sed	150	350	950	1350	2800	4000
2 dr Cpe	150	350	950	1450	2900	4100

NOTE: Deduct 10 percent for 4-cyl.

Omega Brougham, V-6
4 dr Sed	150	350	950	1450	2900	4100
2 dr Cpe	150	350	950	1450	3000	4200

NOTE: Deduct 10 percent for 4-cyl.

Cutlass Supreme, V-8
4 dr Sed	150	400	1000	1650	3150	4500
2 dr Cpe	150	450	1050	1700	3200	4600

NOTE: Deduct 12 percent for V-6.

Cutlass Supreme Brougham, V-8
4 dr Sed	150	450	1050	1700	3200	4600
2 dr Cpe	150	450	1050	1750	3250	4700

NOTE: Deduct 12 percent for V-6.

Cutlass Calais, V-8
2 dr Cpe	150	450	1050	1800	3300	4800

NOTE: Deduct 12 percent for V-6.

Cutlass Cruiser, V-8
4 dr Sta Wag	150	450	1050	1750	3250	4700

Cutlass Ciera, V-6
4 dr Sed	150	400	1000	1650	3150	4500
2 dr Cpe	150	450	1050	1700	3200	4600

NOTE: Deduct 10 percent for 4-cyl.

Cutlass Ciera LS, V-6
4 dr Sed	150	450	1050	1700	3200	4600
2 dr Cpe	150	450	1050	1750	3250	4700

NOTE: Deduct 10 percent for 4-cyl.

Cutlass Ciera Brougham, V-6
4 dr Sed	150	450	1050	1750	3250	4700
2 dr Cpe	150	450	1050	1800	3300	4800

NOTE: Deduct 10 percent for 4-cyl.

Delta 88, V-8
4 dr Sed	150	400	1000	1650	3150	4500

NOTE: Deduct 12 percent for V-6.

Delta 88 Royale, V-8
4 dr Sed	150	450	1050	1800	3300	4800
2 dr Cpe	200	500	1100	1850	3350	4900

NOTE: Deduct 12 percent for V-6.

Delta 88 Royale Brougham, V-8
4 dr Sed	200	500	1100	1850	3350	4900
2 dr Cpe	200	500	1100	1900	3500	5000

NOTE: Deduct 12 percent for V-6.

Custom Cruiser, V-8
4 dr Sta Wag	200	500	1100	1850	3350	4900

Ninety Eight Regency, V-8
4 dr Sed	200	500	1100	1950	3600	5100
2 dr Cpe	200	550	1150	2000	3600	5200
4 dr Sed Brgm	200	550	1150	2000	3600	5200

NOTE: Deduct 12 percent for V-6.

Toronado Brougham, V-8
2 dr Cpe	350	725	1400	3100	4800	6800

NOTE: Deduct 12 percent for V-6.

1983

Firenza, 4-cyl.
4 dr Sed	150	350	950	1350	2800	4000
2 dr Cpe S	150	350	950	1350	2800	4000
4 dr Sed LX	150	350	950	1450	2900	4100
2 dr Cpe SX	150	350	950	1450	3000	4200
4 dr Sta Wag	150	350	950	1450	3000	4200
4 dr Sta Wag LX	150	400	1000	1550	3050	4300

Omega, V-6
4 dr Sed	150	350	950	1450	2900	4100
2 dr Cpe	150	350	950	1450	3000	4200

NOTE: Deduct 10 percent for 4-cyl.

Omega Brougham, V-6
4 dr Sed	150	350	950	1450	3000	4200
2 dr Cpe	150	400	1000	1550	3050	4300

NOTE: Deduct 10 percent for 4-cyl.

Cutlass Supreme, V-8
4 dr Sed	150	450	1050	1700	3200	4600
2 dr Cpe	150	450	1050	1750	3250	4700

NOTE: Deduct 12 percent for V-6.

Cutlass Supreme Brougham, V-8
4 dr Sed	150	450	1050	1750	3250	4700
2 dr Cpe	150	450	1050	1800	3300	4800

NOTE: Deduct 12 percent for V-6.

Cutlass Calais, V-8
2 dr Cpe	200	500	1100	1850	3350	4900

NOTE: Deduct 12 percent for V-6.

Cutlass Cruiser, V-8
4 dr Sta Wag	150	450	1050	1800	3300	4800

NOTE: Deduct 12 percent for V-6.

Cutlass Ciera, V-6
4 dr Sed	150	450	1050	1700	3200	4600
2 dr Cpe	150	450	1050	1750	3250	4700

NOTE: Deduct 10 percent for 4-cyl.

Cutlass Ciera Brougham, V-6
4 dr Sed	150	450	1050	1750	3250	4700
2 dr Cpe	150	450	1050	1800	3300	4800

NOTE: Deduct 10 percent for 4-cyl.

Delta 88, V-8
4 dr Sed	150	450	1050	1800	3300	4800

NOTE: Deduct 12 percent for V-6.

Delta 88 Royale, V-8
4 dr Sed	200	500	1100	1850	3350	4900
2 dr Cpe	200	500	1100	1900	3500	5000

NOTE: Deduct 12 percent for V-6.

Delta 88 Royale Brougham, V-8
4 dr Sed	200	500	1100	1950	3600	5100
2 dr Cpe	200	550	1150	2000	3600	5200

NOTE: Deduct 12 percent for V-6.

Custom Cruiser, V-8
4 dr Sta Wag	200	500	1100	1950	3600	5100

Ninety Eight Regency, V-8
4 dr Sed	200	550	1150	2100	3700	5300
2 dr Cpe	200	600	1200	2200	3850	5500
4 dr Sed Brgm	200	550	1150	2100	3800	5400

NOTE: Deduct 13 percent for V-6.

Toronado Brougham, V-8	6	5	4	3	2	1
2 dr Cpe	350	725	1400	3200	4850	6900

NOTE: Deduct 13 percent for V-6.

PLYMOUTH

1976

Arrow, 4-cyl.
	6	5	4	3	2	1
Hatch	125	200	600	1100	2300	3300
GT Hatch	125	250	750	1150	2400	3400

Valiant, 6-cyl.
Duster Spt Cpe	125	250	750	1150	2400	3400
4 dr Sed Valiant	125	200	600	1100	2250	3200
2 dr HdTp Scamp Spec	125	200	600	1100	2300	3300
2 dr HdTp Scamp	125	250	750	1150	2450	3500

Volare, V-8
4 dr Sed	150	300	900	1250	2600	3700
Spt Cpe	150	350	950	1450	2900	4100
Sta Wag	150	300	900	1250	2650	3800

Volare Custom, V-8
4 dr Sed	150	300	900	1250	2650	3800
Spt Cpe	150	350	950	1450	3000	4200

Volare Premier, V-8
4 dr Sed	150	300	900	1350	2700	3900
Spt Cpe	150	400	1000	1600	3100	4400
Sta Wag	150	350	950	1350	2800	4000

Fury, V-8
4 dr Sed	125	200	600	1100	2300	3300
2 dr HdTp	150	350	950	1450	2900	4100
4 dr Sed Salon	125	250	750	1150	2400	3400
2 dr HdTp Spt	150	400	1000	1550	3050	4300
2S Suburban	125	250	750	1150	2400	3400
3S Suburban	125	250	750	1150	2450	3500
2S Spt Suburban	125	250	750	1150	2500	3600
3S Spt Suburban	150	300	900	1250	2650	3800

Gran Fury, V-8
4 dr Sed	125	250	750	1150	2400	3400

Gran Fury Custom, V-8
4 dr Sed	125	250	750	1150	2450	3500
2 dr HdTp	150	300	900	1250	2650	3800

Gran Fury Brougham, V-8
4 dr Sed	125	250	750	1150	2450	3500
2 dr HdTp	150	350	950	1450	2900	4100
2S Gran Fury Sta Wag	150	300	900	1250	2650	3800
3S Gran Fury Sta Wag	150	350	950	1350	2800	4000

1977

Arrow, 4-cyl.
Hatch	125	200	600	1100	2300	3300
GS Hatch	125	250	750	1150	2400	3400
GT Hatch	125	250	750	1150	2450	3500

Volare, V-8
4 dr Sed	125	200	600	1100	2300	3300
Spt Cpe	125	250	750	1150	2450	3500
Sta Wag	125	250	750	1150	2400	3400

Volare Custom, V-8
4 dr Sed	125	250	750	1150	2400	3400
Spt Cpe	125	250	750	1150	2500	3600

Volare Premier, V-8
4 dr Sed	125	250	750	1150	2450	3500
Spt Cpe	150	300	900	1250	2600	3700
Sta Wag	125	250	750	1150	2500	3600

Fury, V-8
4 dr Spt Sed	125	250	750	1150	2400	3400
2 dr Spt HdTp	150	350	950	1450	3000	4200
3S 4 dr Sub	125	200	600	1100	2250	3200
3S 4 dr Spt Sub	125	200	600	1100	2300	3300

Gran Fury, V-8
4 dr Sed	125	250	750	1150	2450	3500
2 dr HdTp	150	350	950	1350	2800	4000

Gran Fury Brougham, V-8
4 dr Sed	125	250	750	1150	2500	3600
2 dr HdTp	150	350	950	1450	3000	4200

Station Wagons, V-8
2S Gran Fury	125	250	750	1150	2400	3400
3S Gran Fury Spt	125	250	750	1150	2500	3600

1978

Horizon
4 dr Hatch	125	250	750	1150	2400	3400

Arrow
2 dr Hatch	125	250	750	1150	2450	3500
2 dr GS Hatch	125	250	750	1150	2500	3600
2 dr GT Hatch	150	300	900	1250	2600	3700

Volare
4 dr Sed	125	250	750	1150	2500	3600
Spt Cpe	150	300	900	1250	2650	3800
Sta Wag	150	300	900	1250	2600	3700

Sapporo
Cpe	150	300	900	1250	2650	3800

Fury
4 dr Sed	125	250	750	1150	2500	3600
2 dr	150	300	900	1250	2600	3700
4 dr Salon	150	300	900	1250	2600	3700
2 dr Spt	150	300	900	1250	2650	3800

Station Wagons
3S Fury Sub	150	300	900	1250	2600	3700
2S Fury Sub	125	250	750	1150	2500	3600
3S Spt Fury Sub	150	300	900	1250	2650	3800
2S Spt Fury Sub	150	300	900	1250	2600	3700

1979

Champ, 4-cyl.
2 dr Hatch	125	250	750	1150	2400	3400
2 dr Cus Hatch	125	250	750	1150	2450	3500

Horizon, 4-cyl.
4 dr Hatch	125	250	750	1150	2450	3500
TC 3 Hatch	150	300	900	1250	2600	3700

Arrow, 4-cyl.
2 dr Hatch	125	250	750	1150	2500	3600
2 dr GS Hatch	150	300	900	1250	2600	3700
2 dr GT Hatch	150	300	900	1250	2650	3800

Volare, V-8
Sed	150	300	900	1250	2650	3800
Spt Cpe	150	350	950	1350	2800	4000
Sta Wag	150	300	900	1350	2700	3900

Sapporo, 4-cyl.
Cpe	150	300	900	1350	2700	3900

1980

Champ, 4-cyl.	6	5	4	3	2	1
2 dr Hatch	125	200	600	1100	2300	3300
Custom 2 dr Hatch	125	250	750	1150	2400	3400
Horizon, 4-cyl.						
4 dr Hatch	125	250	750	1150	2400	3400
2 dr Hatch 2 plus 2 TC3	150	300	900	1250	2650	3800
Arrow, 4-cyl.						
2 dr Hatch	150	400	1000	1650	3150	4500
Fire Arrow, 4-cyl.						
2 dr Hatch	150	450	1050	1700	3200	4600
Volare, V-8						
4 dr Sed	125	250	750	1150	2400	3400
2 dr Cpe	125	250	750	1150	2450	3500
4 dr Sta Wag	150	300	900	1250	2600	3700
NOTE: Deduct 10 percent for 6-cyl.						
Sapporo, 4-cyl.						
2 dr Cpe	150	300	900	1350	2700	3900
Gran Fury, V-8						
4 dr Sed	150	300	900	1250	2650	3800
NOTE: Deduct 10 percent for 6-cyl.						
Gran Fury Salon, V-8						
4 dr Sed	150	350	950	1350	2800	4000
NOTE: Deduct 10 percent for 6-cyl.						

1981

Champ, 4-cyl.						
2 dr Hatch	125	250	750	1150	2400	3400
DeL 2 dr Hatch	125	250	750	1150	2450	3500
Cus 2 dr Hatch	125	250	750	1150	2500	3600
Horizon, 4-cyl.						
Miser 4 dr Hatch	125	250	750	1150	2450	3500
Miser 4 dr Hatch TC3	150	300	900	1250	2650	3800
4 dr Hatch	150	300	900	1250	2600	3700
2 dr Hatch TC3	150	350	950	1350	2800	4000
Reliant, 4-cyl.						
4 dr Sed	125	250	750	1150	2400	3400
2 dr Cpe	125	250	750	1150	2450	3500
Reliant Custom, 4-cyl.						
4 dr Sed	125	250	750	1150	2450	3500
2 dr Cpe	125	250	750	1150	2500	3600
4 dr Sta Wag	150	300	900	1250	2650	3800
Reliant SE, 4-cyl.						
4 dr Sed	125	250	750	1150	2500	3600
2 dr Cpe	150	300	900	1250	2600	3700
4 dr Sta Wag	150	300	900	1350	2700	3900
Sapporo, 4-cyl.						
2 dr HdTp	150	350	950	1350	2800	4000
Gran Fury, V-8						
4 dr Sed	150	350	950	1450	2900	4100
NOTE: Deduct 10 percent for 6-cyl.						

1982

Champ, 4-cyl.						
4 dr Hatch	125	250	750	1150	2400	3400
2 dr Hatch	125	250	750	1150	2450	3500
DeL 2 dr Hatch	125	250	750	1150	2500	3600
Cus 4 dr Hatch	125	250	750	1150	2500	3600
Cus 2 dr Hatch	150	300	900	1250	2600	3700
Horizon, 4-cyl.						
Miser 4 dr Hatch	125	250	750	1150	2500	3600
Miser 2 dr Hatch TC3	150	300	900	1350	2700	3900
Cus 4 dr Hatch	150	300	900	1250	2600	3700
Cus 2 dr Hatch	150	300	900	1250	2650	3800
E Type 4 dr Hatch	150	300	900	1350	2700	3900
Turismo, 4-cyl.						
2 dr Hatch TC3	150	400	1000	1650	3150	4500
Reliant, 4-cyl.						
4 dr Sed	125	250	750	1150	2500	3600
2 dr Cpe	150	300	900	1250	2600	3700
Reliant Custom, 4-cyl.						
4 dr Sed	150	300	900	1250	2600	3700
2 dr Cpe	150	300	900	1250	2650	3800
4 dr Sta Wag	150	300	900	1350	2700	3900
Reliant SE, 4-cyl.						
4 dr Sed	150	300	900	1250	2650	3800
2 dr Cpe	150	300	900	1350	2700	3900
4 dr Sta Wag	150	350	950	1350	2800	4000
Sapporo						
2 dr HdTp	150	450	1050	1750	3250	4700
Gran Fury, V-8						
4 dr Sed	150	350	950	1350	2800	4000
NOTE: Deduct 10 percent for 6-cyl.						

1983

Colt, 4-cyl.						
4 dr Hatch	150	300	900	1250	2600	3700
2 dr Hatch	150	300	900	1250	2650	3800
DeL 4 dr Hatch	150	300	900	1350	2700	3900
Cus 4 dr Hatch	150	350	950	1350	2800	4000
Cus 2 dr Hatch	150	350	950	1450	2900	4100
Horizon, 4-cyl.						
4 dr Hatch	150	300	900	1250	2650	3800
Cus 4 dr Hatch	150	300	900	1350	2700	3900
Turismo, 4-cyl.						
2 dr Hatch	150	400	1000	1650	3150	4500
2 dr Hatch 2 plus 2	150	450	1050	1800	3300	4800
Reliant, 4-cyl.						
4 dr Sed	150	300	900	1250	2600	3700
2 dr Cpe	150	300	900	1250	2650	3800
4 dr Sta Wag	150	350	950	1350	2800	4000
Reliant SE, 4-cyl.						
4 dr Sed	150	300	900	1250	2650	3800
2 dr Cpe	150	300	900	1350	2700	3900
4 dr Sta Wag	150	350	950	1450	2900	4100
Sapporo, 4-cyl.						
2 dr HdTp	150	450	1050	1800	3300	4800
Gran Fury, V-8						
4 dr Sed	150	350	950	1450	2900	4100
NOTE: Deduct 10 percent for 6-cyl.						

PONTIAC

1976

Astre, 4-cyl.	6	5	4	3	2	1
Cpe	125	200	600	1100	2200	3100
Hatch	125	200	600	1100	2250	3200
Sta Wag	125	200	600	1100	2300	3300

Sunbird, 4-cyl.	6	5	4	3	2	1
Cpe	150	400	1000	1550	3050	4300
Ventura, V-8						
4 dr Sed	150	350	950	1450	2900	4100
Cpe	150	350	950	1450	3000	4200
Hatch	150	400	1000	1550	3050	4300
Ventura SJ, V-8						
4 dr Sed	150	350	950	1450	3000	4200
Cpe	150	400	1000	1550	3050	4300
Hatch	150	400	1000	1600	3100	4400
LeMans, V-8						
4 dr Sed	150	400	1000	1550	3050	4300
Cpe	150	400	1000	1600	3100	4400
2S Safari Wag	150	350	950	1450	3000	4200
3S Safari Wag	150	400	1000	1550	3050	4300
LeMans Sport Cpe, V-8						
Cpe	150	450	1050	1750	3250	4700
Grand LeMans, V-8						
4 dr Sed	150	400	1000	1600	3100	4400
2 dr Sed	150	400	1000	1650	3150	4500
2S Safari Wag	150	400	1000	1550	3050	4300
3S Safari Wag	150	400	1000	1600	3100	4400
Catalina, V-8						
4 dr Sed	150	350	950	1450	3000	4200
Cpe	150	400	1000	1550	3050	4300
2S Safari Wag	150	450	1050	1700	3200	4600
3S Safari Wag	150	350	950	1450	3000	4200
Bonneville, V-8						
4 dr Sed	150	400	1000	1600	3100	4400
Cpe	150	400	1000	1650	3150	4500
Bonneville Brougham, V-8						
4 dr Sed	150	450	1050	1700	3200	4600
Cpe	150	450	1050	1800	3300	4800
Grand Safari, V-8						
2S Sta Wag	150	400	1000	1550	3050	4300
3S Sta Wag	150	400	1000	1600	3100	4400
Grand Prix, V-8						
Cpe	200	500	1100	1900	3500	5000
Cpe SJ	200	550	1150	2000	3600	5200
Cpe LJ	200	600	1200	2300	4000	5700
NOTE: Add 10 percent for T tops & Anniversary model.						
Firebird, V-8						
Cpe	200	600	1200	2300	4000	5700
Esprit Cpe	200	650	1250	2400	4200	6000
Formula Cpe	200	675	1300	2500	4350	6200
Trans Am Cpe	350	700	1350	2700	4500	6400

1977

Astre, 4-cyl.						
Cpe	100	175	525	1050	1950	2800
Hatch	100	175	525	1050	2050	2900
Sta Wag	100	175	525	1050	2100	3000
Sunbird, 4-cyl.						
Cpe	150	350	950	1350	2800	4000
Hatch	150	350	950	1450	2900	4100
Phoenix, V-8						
4 dr Sed	150	300	900	1350	2700	3900
Cpe	150	350	950	1350	2800	4000
Ventura, V-8						
4 dr Sed	150	300	900	1350	2700	3900
Cpe	150	350	950	1350	2800	4000
Hatch	150	350	950	1450	2900	4100
Ventura SJ, V-8						
4 dr Sed	150	350	950	1350	2800	4000
Cpe	150	350	950	1450	2900	4100
Hatch	150	350	950	1450	3000	4200
LeMans, V-8						
4 dr Sed	150	350	950	1350	2800	4000
Cpe	150	350	950	1450	2900	4100
2S Sta Wag	150	300	900	1350	2700	3900
3S Sta Wag	150	350	950	1350	2800	4000
LeMans Sport Cpe, V-8						
NOTE: Add 20 percent for Can Am option.						
Cpe	150	400	1000	1600	3100	4400
Grand LeMans, V-8						
4 dr Sed	150	350	950	1450	2900	4100
Cpe	150	350	950	1450	3000	4200
2S Sta Wag	150	350	950	1350	2800	4000
3S Sta Wag	150	350	950	1450	2900	4100
Catalina, V-8						
4 dr Sed	150	300	900	1350	2700	3900
Cpe	150	350	950	1350	2800	4000
2S Safari Wag	150	300	900	1250	2650	3800
3S Safari Wag	150	300	900	1350	2700	3900
Bonneville, V-8						
4 dr Sed	150	350	950	1450	2900	4100
Cpe	150	350	950	1450	3000	4200
Bonneville Brougham, V-8						
4 dr Sed	150	400	1000	1550	3050	4300
Cpe	150	400	1000	1650	3150	4500
Grand Safari						
2S Sta Wag	150	350	950	1450	3000	4200
3S Sta Wag	150	400	1000	1550	3050	4300
Grand Prix, V-8						
Cpe	150	450	1050	1750	3250	4700
Cpe LJ	200	500	1100	1900	3500	5000
Cpe SJ	200	650	1250	2400	4200	6000
Firebird, V-8						
Cpe	200	650	1200	2300	4100	5800
Esprit Cpe	200	650	1250	2400	4200	6000
Formula Cpe	200	675	1300	2600	4400	6300
Trans Am Cpe	350	700	1350	2800	4550	6500

1978

Sunbird						
Cpe	100	175	525	1050	2050	2900
Spt Cpe	100	175	525	1050	2100	3000
Spt Hatch	125	200	600	1100	2200	3100
Spt Wag	100	175	525	1050	2100	3000
Phoenix						
4 dr Sed	100	175	525	1050	2100	3000
Cpe	125	200	600	1100	2300	3300
Hatch	125	200	600	1100	2200	3100
Phoenix LJ						
4 dr Sed	125	200	600	1100	2200	3100
Cpe	125	250	750	1150	2450	3500
LeMans						
4 dr Sed	150	350	950	1350	2800	4000
Cpe	150	350	950	1450	3000	4200
2S Sta Wag	150	350	950	1350	2800	4000

	6	5	4	3	2	1
Grand LeMans						
4 dr Sed	150	350	950	1450	2900	4100
Cpe	150	400	1000	1550	3050	4300
2S Sta Wag	150	350	950	1450	2900	4100
Grand Am						
4 dr Sed	150	350	950	1450	3000	4200
Cpe	150	400	1000	1650	3150	4500
Catalina						
4 dr Sed	150	350	950	1350	2800	4000
Cpe	150	350	950	1450	2900	4100
2S Sta Wag	150	350	950	1450	3000	4200
Bonneville						
4 dr Sed	150	400	1000	1550	3050	4300
Cpe	150	400	1000	1650	3150	4500
2S Sta Wag	150	400	1000	1650	3150	4500
Bonneville Brougham						
4 dr Sed	150	400	1000	1650	3150	4500
Cpe	150	450	1050	1750	3250	4700
Grand Prix						
Cpe	200	500	1100	1850	3350	4900
Cpe LJ	200	500	1100	1900	3500	5000
Cpe SJ	200	550	1150	2000	3600	5200
Firebird, V-8, 108" wb						
Cpe	200	650	1250	2400	4200	6000
Esprit Cpe	200	675	1300	2500	4350	6200
Formula Cpe	350	700	1350	2800	4550	6500
Trans Am Cpe	350	725	1400	3000	4700	6700

1979
Sunbird	6	5	4	3	2	1
Cpe	100	175	525	1050	2100	3000
Spt Cpe	125	200	600	1100	2200	3100
Hatch	125	200	600	1100	2200	3100
Sta Wag	125	200	600	1100	2250	3200
Phoenix						
Sed	125	200	600	1100	2200	3100
Cpe	125	200	600	1100	2300	3300
Hatch	125	200	600	1100	2250	3200
Phoenix LJ						
Sed	125	200	600	1100	2250	3200
Cpe	125	250	750	1150	2400	3400
LeMans						
Sed	150	350	950	1450	2900	4100
Cpe	150	400	1000	1550	3050	4300
Sta Wag	150	350	950	1450	2900	4100
Grand LeMans						
Sed	150	350	950	1450	3000	4200
Cpe	150	400	1000	1650	3150	4500
Sta Wag	150	350	950	1450	3000	4200
Grand Am						
Sed	150	400	1000	1650	3150	4500
Cpe	150	450	1050	1750	3250	4700
Catalina						
Sed	150	350	950	1450	2900	4100
Cpe	150	350	950	1450	3000	4200
Sta Wag	150	350	950	1450	2900	4100
Bonneville						
Sed	150	400	1000	1600	3100	4400
Cpe	150	400	1000	1650	3150	4500
Sta Wag	150	400	1000	1600	3100	4400
Bonneville Brougham						
Sed	150	450	1050	1700	3200	4600
Cpe	150	450	1050	1800	3300	4800
Grand Prix						
Cpe	200	500	1100	1900	3500	5000
LJ Cpe	200	550	1150	2000	3600	5200
SJ Cpe	200	550	1150	2100	3800	5400
Firebird, V-8, 108" wb						
Cpe	200	675	1300	2500	4350	6200
Esprit Cpe	350	700	1350	2700	4500	6400
Formula Cpe	350	700	1350	2900	4600	6600
Trans Am Cpe	350	725	1400	3100	4800	6800

1980
Sunbird, V-6	6	5	4	3	2	1
2 dr Cpe	125	250	750	1150	2450	3500
2 dr Hatch	125	250	750	1150	2500	3600
2 dr Spt Cpe	125	250	750	1150	2500	3600
2 dr Cpe Hatch	150	300	900	1250	2600	3700
NOTE: Deduct 10 percent for 4-cyl.						
Phoenix, V-6						
2 dr Cpe	150	300	900	1250	2600	3700
4 dr Sed Hatch	125	250	750	1150	2500	3600
NOTE: Deduct 10 percent for 4-cyl.						
Phoenix LJ, V-6						
2 dr Cpe	150	300	900	1250	2650	3800
4 dr Sed Hatch	150	300	900	1250	2600	3700
NOTE: Deduct 10 percent for 4-cyl.						
LeMans, V-8						
4 dr Sed	150	300	900	1250	2600	3700
2 dr Cpe	150	300	900	1350	2700	3900
4 dr Sta Wag	150	300	900	1250	2650	3800
NOTE: Deduct 10 percent for V-6.						
Grand LeMans, V-8						
4 dr Sed	150	300	900	1250	2650	3800
2 dr Cpe	150	350	950	1350	2800	4000
4 dr Sta Wag	150	300	900	1350	2700	3900
NOTE: Deduct 10 percent for V-6.						
Grand Am, V-8						
2 dr Cpe	150	350	950	1450	2900	4100
Firebird, V-8						
2 dr Cpe	350	700	1350	2900	4600	6600
2 dr Cpe Esprit	350	725	1400	3000	4700	6700
2 dr Cpe Formula	350	725	1400	3100	4800	6800
2 dr Cpe Trans Am	350	750	1450	3300	4900	7000
NOTE: Deduct 15 percent for V-6.						
Catalina, V-8						
4 dr Sed	150	300	900	1250	2650	3800
2 dr Cpe	150	300	900	1350	2700	3900
4 dr Sta Wag 2S	150	300	900	1350	2700	3900
4 dr Sta Wag 3S	150	350	950	1350	2800	4000
NOTE: Deduct 10 percent for V-6.						
Bonneville, V-8						
4 dr Sed	150	300	900	1350	2700	3900
2 dr Cpe	150	350	950	1350	2800	4000
4 dr Sta Wag 2S	150	350	950	1350	2800	4000
4 dr Sta Wag 3S	150	350	950	1450	2900	4100
NOTE: Deduct 10 percent for V-6.						
Bonneville Brougham, V-8						
4 dr Sed	150	350	950	1450	2900	4100
2 dr Cpe	150	400	1000	1550	3050	4300
NOTE: Deduct 10 percent for V-6.						

Grand Prix, V-8	6	5	4	3	2	1
2 dr Cpe	200	600	1200	2300	4000	5700
2 dr Cpe LJ	200	650	1200	2300	4100	5800
2 dr Cpe SJ	200	650	1250	2400	4150	5900
NOTE: Deduct 10 percent for V-6.						

1981
T1000, 4-cyl.						
2 dr Sed Hatch	125	250	750	1150	2450	3500
4 dr Sed Hatch	125	250	750	1150	2500	3600
Phoenix, V-6						
2 dr Cpe	150	300	900	1250	2600	3700
4 dr Sed Hatch	125	250	750	1150	2500	3600
NOTE: Deduct 10 percent for 4-cyl.						
Phoenix LJ, V-6						
2 dr Cpe	150	300	900	1250	2650	3800
4 dr Sed Hatch	150	300	900	1250	2600	3700
NOTE: Deduct 10 percent for 4-cyl.						
LeMans, V-8						
4 dr Sed	150	300	900	1350	2700	3900
4 dr Sed LJ	150	350	950	1350	2800	4000
2 dr Cpe	150	350	950	1350	2800	4000
4 dr Sta Wag	150	350	950	1350	2800	4000
NOTE: Deduct 10 percent for V-6.						
Grand LeMans, V-8						
4 dr Sed	150	450	1050	1700	3200	4600
2 dr Cpe	150	350	950	1450	3000	4200
4 dr Sta Wag	150	350	950	1450	3000	4200
NOTE: Deduct 10 percent for V-6.						
Firebird, V-8						
2 dr Cpe	350	725	1400	3000	4700	6700
2 dr Cpe Esprit	350	725	1400	3100	4800	6800
2 dr Cpe Formula	350	725	1400	3200	4850	6900
2 dr Cpe Trans Am	350	750	1450	3500	5050	7200
2 dr Cpe Trans Am SE	350	775	1500	3750	5250	7500
NOTE: Deduct 15 percent for V-6.						
Catalina, V-8						
4 dr Sed	150	350	950	1450	3000	4200
2 dr Cpe	150	400	1000	1550	3050	4300
4 dr Sta Wag 2S	150	400	1000	1550	3050	4300
4 dr Sta Wag 3S	150	400	1000	1600	3100	4400
NOTE: Deduct 10 percent for V-6.						
Bonneville, V-8						
4 dr Sed	150	400	1000	1550	3050	4300
2 dr Cpe	150	400	1000	1600	3100	4400
4 dr Sta Wag 2S	150	400	1000	1600	3100	4400
4 dr Sta Wag 3S	150	400	1000	1650	3150	4500
NOTE: Deduct 10 percent for V-6.						
Bonneville Brougham, V-8						
4 dr Sed	150	400	1000	1650	3150	4500
2 dr Cpe	150	450	1050	1700	3200	4600
Grand Prix, V-8						
2 dr Cpe	200	650	1200	2300	4100	5800
2 dr Cpe LJ	200	650	1250	2400	4150	5900
2 dr Cpe Brgm	200	650	1250	2400	4200	6000
NOTE: Deduct 10 percent for V-6.						

1982
T1000, 4-cyl.						
4 dr Sed Hatch	150	300	900	1250	2600	3700
2 dr Cpe Hatch	125	250	750	1150	2500	3600
J2000 S, 4-cyl.						
4 dr Sed	150	300	900	1350	2700	3900
2 dr Cpe	150	350	950	1350	2800	4000
4 dr Sta Wag	150	350	950	1350	2800	4000
J2000, 4-cyl.						
4 dr Sed	150	350	950	1350	2800	4000
2 dr Cpe	150	350	950	1450	2900	4100
2 dr Cpe Hatch	150	350	950	1450	3000	4200
4 dr Sta Wag	150	350	950	1450	3000	4200
J2000 LE, 4-cyl.						
4 dr Sed	150	350	950	1450	2900	4100
2 dr Cpe	150	350	950	1450	3000	4200
J2000 SE, 4-cyl.						
2 dr Cpe Hatch	150	400	1000	1600	3100	4400
Phoenix, V-6						
4 dr Sed Hatch	150	300	900	1250	2650	3800
2 dr Cpe	150	300	900	1350	2700	3900
NOTE: Deduct 10 percent for 4-cyl.						
Phoenix LJ, V-6						
4 dr Sed Hatch	150	300	900	1350	2700	3900
2 dr Cpe	150	350	950	1350	2800	4000
NOTE: Deduct 10 percent for 4-cyl.						
Phoenix SJ, V-6						
4 dr Sed Hatch	150	350	950	1350	2800	4000
2 dr Cpe	150	350	950	1450	2900	4100
6000, V-6						
4 dr Sed	150	350	950	1450	3000	4200
2 dr Cpe	150	400	1000	1550	3050	4300
NOTE: Deduct 10 percent for 4-cyl.						
6000 LE, V-6						
4 dr Sed	150	400	1000	1550	3050	4300
2 dr Cpe	150	400	1000	1600	3100	4400
NOTE: Deduct 10 percent for 4-cyl.						
Firebird, V-8						
2 dr Cpe	350	725	1400	3100	4800	6800
2 dr Cpe SE	350	750	1450	3400	5000	7100
2 dr Cpe Trans Am	350	775	1500	3750	5250	7500
NOTE: Deduct 15 percent for V-6.						
Bonneville, V-6						
4 dr Sed	150	400	1000	1650	3150	4500
4 dr Sta Wag	150	400	1000	1650	3150	4500
Bonneville Brougham						
4 dr Sed	150	450	1050	1750	3250	4700
Grand Prix, V-6						
2 dr Cpe	200	650	1250	2400	4150	5900
2 dr Cpe LJ	200	675	1300	2500	4300	6100
2 dr Cpe Brgm	200	675	1300	2500	4350	6200

1983
1000, 4-cyl.						
4 dr Sed Hatch	150	300	900	1250	2650	3800
2 dr Cpe	150	300	900	1250	2600	3700
2000, 4-cyl.						
4 dr Sed	150	350	950	1350	2800	4000
2 dr Cpe	150	350	950	1450	2900	4100
2 dr Cpe Hatch	150	350	950	1450	3000	4200
4 dr Sta Wag	150	350	950	1450	3000	4200
2000 LE, 4-cyl.						
4 dr Sed	150	350	950	1450	3000	4200
2 dr Cpe	150	400	1000	1550	3050	4300
4 dr Sta Wag	150	400	1000	1550	3050	4300

2000 SE, 4-cyl.	6	5	4	3	2	1
2 dr Cpe Hatch	150	400	1000	1600	3100	4400
Sunbird, 4-cyl.						
2 dr Conv	350	875	1700	4250	5900	8500
Phoenix, V-6						
4 dr Sed Hatch	150	300	900	1350	2700	3900
2 dr Cpe	150	350	950	1350	2800	4000
NOTE: Deduct 10 percent for 4-cyl.						
Phoenix LJ, V-6						
4 dr Sed Hatch	150	350	950	1350	2800	4000
2 dr Cpe	150	350	950	1450	2900	4100
NOTE: Deduct 10 percent for 4-cyl.						
Phoenix SJ, V-6						
4 dr Sed Hatch	150	350	950	1450	2900	4100
2 dr Cpe	150	350	950	1450	3000	4200
6000, V-6						
4 dr Sed	150	400	1000	1550	3050	4300
2 dr Cpe	150	400	1000	1600	3100	4400
NOTE: Deduct 10 percent for 4-cyl.						

6000 LE, V-6	6	5	4	3	2	1
4 dr Sed	150	400	1000	1600	3100	4400
2 dr Cpe	150	400	1000	1650	3150	4500
NOTE: Deduct 10 percent for 4-cyl.						
6000 STE, V-6						
4 dr Sed	150	450	1050	1750	3250	4700
Firebird, V-8						
2 dr Cpe	350	725	1400	3200	4850	6900
2 dr Cpe SE	350	750	1450	3500	5050	7200
2 dr Cpe Trans Am	350	800	1550	3800	5300	7600
NOTE: Deduct 15 percent for V-6.						
Bonneville, V-8						
4 dr Sed	150	450	1050	1800	3300	4800
4 dr Brgm	200	500	1100	1850	3350	4900
4 dr Sta Wag	200	500	1100	1850	3350	4900
NOTE: Deduct 10 percent for V-6.						
Grand Prix, V-8						
2 dr Cpe	200	650	1250	2400	4200	6000
2 dr Cpe LJ	200	675	1300	2500	4350	6200
2 dr Cpe Brgm	200	675	1300	2600	4400	6300